C000244332

The Oxford Dictionary and Usage Guide

to the English Language

The Oxford Dictionary and Usage Guide
to the English Language

BCA

LONDON NEW YORK SYDNEY TORONTO

This edition published 1995 by BCA
by arrangement with Oxford University Press

CN 9038

Typeset by Pure Tech Corporation, Pondicherry, India
and Latimer Trend Ltd., Plymouth
Printed in Great Britain
on acid-free paper by
Clays (plc), Bungay, Suffolk

Contents

Guide to English Usage

Dictionary

Editorial Staff

Usage Guide

Editor	E. S. C. Weiner
Assistant Editors	Andrew Delahunty
	Janet Whitcut

Dictionary

Editor	Maurice Waite
Assistant Editor	Andrew Hodgson
Contributing Editors	Anna Howes
	Louise Jones
	Bernadette Paton
	Anne St John-Hall
Keyboarders	Anne Whear
	Pam Marjara
	Kay Pepler
Schools English Consultant	Elaine Ashmore-Short

Guide to English Usage

Introduction

The *Guide to English Usage* aims to give guidance in as clear, concise, and systematic a manner as possible on matters of pronunciation, spelling, meaning, and grammar about which there is controversy or uncertainty. It has five special features:

1. *Layout.* In the *Guide* the subject of usage is divided into four fields: *word formation, pronunciation, vocabulary*, and *grammar*. Each field is covered by a separate section of the book, and each of the four sections has its own alphabetical arrangement of entries. Each entry is headed by its title in **bold type**. All the words that share a particular kind of spelling, sound, or construction can therefore be treated together. This makes for both economy and comprehensiveness of treatment.

2. *Explanation.* The explanations given in each entry are intended to be simple and straightforward, even where the subject is inevitably slightly complicated. They take into account the approaches developed by modern linguistic analysis, but employ the traditional terms of grammar as much as possible. (A glossary of all grammatical terms used in this book will be found on pp. 1–5 ff.) Technical symbols and abbreviations, and the phonetic alphabet, are not used at all.

3. *Exemplification.* Wherever appropriate, example sentences are given to illustrate the point being discussed. The majority of these are real examples, many drawn from the works of some of the best twentieth-century writers. Even informal or substandard usage has been illustrated in this way, taken, for example, from speeches in novels.

4. *Recommendation.* Recommendations are clearly set out. The blob • is used to state a warning, restriction, or prohibition. The square □ is used, particularly in section I, where a recommendation is given alongside acceptable alternatives. The emphasis of the recommendations is on the degree of acceptability in standard English, rather than on a dogmatic distinction of right and wrong. Much that is condemned as 'bad English' is better regarded as appropriate in informal contexts but inappropriate in formal ones. The appropriateness of usage to context is indicated by the fairly rough categories 'formal' and 'informal', 'standard', 'regional', and 'non-standard', 'jocular', and so on. Some of the ways in which American usage differs from British are pointed out.

5. *Reference.* Ease of access is a priority of the *Guide*. Its four-part division means that (roughly speaking) only a quarter of the total range of pages need be looked through in order to find a particular entry. But this should rarely be necessary, since there is an index in which every subject and every word and affix covered by the *Guide* can be found. Within each section there are many cross-references to other entries; these are indicated by **bold type** and followed by the page number if necessary.

In addition to the four main sections described at 1 above, the *Guide* has two *appendices*: I is an outline of the principles of punctuation; and II lists some of the clichés and overworked diction most widely disliked at present.

Grammatical terms used in this book

Where an example is partly in italics and partly in roman type, it is the words in roman that exemplify the term being defined.

absolute used independently of its customary grammatical relationship or construction, e.g. Weather permitting, *I will come*.

acronym a word formed from the initial letters of other words, e.g. *NATO*.

active applied to a verb whose subject is also the source of the action of the verb, e.g. *We* saw *him*; opposite of **passive**.

adjective a word that names an attribute, used to describe a noun or pronoun, e.g. small *child*, *it is* small.

adverb a word that modifies an adjective, verb, or another adverb, expressing a relation of place, time, circumstance, manner, cause, degree, etc., e.g. *gently*, *accordingly*, *now*, *here*, *why*.

agent noun a noun denoting the doer of an action, e.g. *builder*.

agent suffix a suffix added to a verb to form an agent noun, e.g. *-er*.

agree to have the same grammatical number, gender, case, or person as another word.

analogy the formation of a word, derivative, or construction in imitation of an existing word or pattern.

animate denoting a living being.

antecedent a noun or phrase to which a relative pronoun refers back.

antepenultimate last but two.

antonym a word of contrary meaning to another.

apposition the placing of a word, especially a noun, syntactically parallel to another, e.g. *William the Conqueror*.

article *a/an* (**indefinite** article) or *the* (**definite** article).

attributive designating a noun, adjective, or phrase expressing an attribute, characteristically preceding the word it qualifies, e.g. *old* in *the old dog*; opposite of **predicative**.

auxiliary verb a verb used in forming tenses, moods, and voices of other verbs.

case the form (**subjective, objective,** or **possessive**) of a noun or pronoun, expressing relation to some other word.

clause a distinct part of a sentence including a **subject** (sometimes by implication) and **predicate**.

collective noun a singular noun denoting many individuals; see page 77.

collocation an expression consisting of two (or more) words frequently juxtaposed, especially adjective + noun, e.g. *derisory offer*, *heavy drinker*.

comparative the form of an adjective or adverb expressing a higher degree of a quality, e.g. *braver*, *worse*.

comparison the differentiation of the **comparative** and **superlative** degrees from the positive (basic) form of an adjective or adverb.

complement a word or words necessary to complete a grammatical construction: the complement of a clause, e.g. *John is* (a) thoughtful (man), *Solitude makes John* thoughtful; of an adjective, e.g. *John is glad* of your help; of a preposition, e.g. *I thought of* John.

compound preposition a preposition made up of more than one word, e.g. *with regard to*.

concord agreement between words in gender, number, or person, e.g. *the girl who* is *here*, *you who* are *alive*, Those *men* work.

conditional designating (1) a clause which expresses a condition, or (2) a mood of the verb used in the consequential clause of a conditional sentence, e.g. (1) *If he had come*, (2) *I* should have seen *him*.

consonant (1) a speech sound in which breath is at least partly obstructed, combining with a **vowel** to form a syllable; (2) a letter usually used to represent (1); e.g. *ewe* is written with vowel + consonant + vowel, but is pronounced as consonant (y) + vowel (oo).

coordination the linking of two or more parts of a compound sentence that are equal in importance, e.g. *He sang and she played the piano*.

correlative coordination coordination by means of pairs of corresponding words regularly used together, e.g. *either . . or*.

countable designating a noun that refers in the singular to one and in the plural to more than one, and can be qualified by *a*, *one*, *every*, etc. and *many*, *two*, *three*, etc.; opposite of **mass (noun)**.

diminutive denoting a word referring to a small, liked, or despised member of the class denoted by the corresponding root word, e.g. *ringlet*, *Johnny*, *princeling*.

diphthong: see **digraph,** p. 56.

direct object the **object** that expresses the primary object of the action of the verb, e.g. *He sent* a present *to his son*.

disyllabic having two syllables.

double passive: see p. 79 f.

elide to omit by **elision**.

elision the omission of a vowel or syllable in pronouncing, e.g. *let's*.

ellipsis the omission from a sentence of words needed to complete a construction or sense.

elliptical involving **ellipsis**.

feminine the gender to which words referring to female beings usually belong.

finite designating (part of) a verb limited by person and number, e.g. *I* am, *He* comes.

formal designating the type of English used publicly for some serious purpose, either in writing or in public speeches.

future the tense of a verb referring to an event yet to happen: **simple future,** e.g. *I shall go*; **future in the past,** referring to an event that was yet to happen at a time prior to the time of speaking, e.g. *He said he* would go.

gerund the part of the verb which can be used like a noun, ending in *-ing*, e.g. *What is the use of my* scolding *him?*

govern (said of a verb or preposition) to have (a noun or pronoun, or a case) dependent on it.

group possessive: see p. 81.

hard designating a letter, chiefly *c* or *g*, that indicates a guttural sound, as in *cot* or *got*.

***if*-clause** a clause introduced by *if*.

imperative the mood of a verb expressing command, e.g. Come *here*!

inanimate opposite of **animate.**

indirect object the person or thing affected by the action of the verb but not primarily acted upon, e.g. *I gave* him *the book*.

infinitive the basic form of a verb that does not indicate a particular tense or number or person; the ***to*-infinitive**, used with preceding *to*, e.g. *I want* to know; the **bare infinitive,** without preceding *to*, e.g. *Help me* pack.

inflection a part of a word, usually a suffix, that expresses grammatical relationship, such as number, person, tense, etc.; also used to refer to the process by which this part is added.

informal designating the type of English used in private conversation, personal letters, and popular public communication.

intransitive designating a verb that does not take a direct object, e.g. *I must* think.

intrusive *r*: see p. 34.

linking *r*: see p. 34.

living designating a **prefix** or **suffix** that can be freely used to form new compounds.

loanword a word adopted by one language from another.

main clause the principal clause of a sentence.

masculine the gender to which words referring to male beings usually belong.

mass noun (or **uncountable noun**) a noun that refers to something regarded as grammatically indivisible, treated only as singular, and never qualified by *those, many, two, three,* etc.; opposite of **countable** noun.

modal relating to the **mood** of a verb; used to express mood.

mood form of a verb serving to indicate whether it is to express fact, command, permission, wish, etc.

monosyllabic having one syllable.

nominal designating a phrase or clause that is used like a noun, e.g. What you need *is a drink.*

nonce-word a word coined for one occasion.

non-finite designating (a part of) a verb not limited by person and number, e.g. the infinitive, gerund, or participle.

non-restrictive: see p. 89 f.

noun a word used to denote a person, place, or thing.

noun phrase a phrase functioning within the sentence as a noun, e.g. The one over there *is mine.*

object a noun or its equivalent governed by an active transitive verb, e.g. *I will take* that one.

objective the case of a pronoun typically used when the pronoun is the object of a verb or governed by a preposition, e.g. *me, him.*

paradigm the complete pattern of inflection of a noun, verb, etc.

participle the part of a verb used like an adjective but retaining some verbal qualities (tense and government of an object) and also used to form compound verb forms: the **present participle** ends in *-ing,* the **past participle** of regular verbs in *-ed,* e.g. *While* doing *her work she had* kept *the baby* amused.

passive designating a form of the verb by which the verbal action is attributed to the person or thing to whom it is actually directed (i.e. the logical object is the grammatical subject), e.g. *He* was seen *by us*; opposite of **active**.

past a tense expressing past action or state, e.g. *I* arrived *yesterday.*

past perfect a tense expressing action already completed prior to the time being spoken or written about, e.g. *I* had arrived *by then.*

pejorative disparaging, depreciatory.

penultimate last but one.

perfect a tense denoting completed action or action viewed in relation to the present; e.g. *I* have finished *now*; **perfect infinitive,** e.g. *He seems* to have finished *now.*

periphrasis a roundabout way of expressing something.

person one of the three classes of personal pronouns or verb-forms, denoting the person speaking (**first person**), the person spoken to (**second person**), and the person or thing spoken about (**third person**).

phrasal verb an expression consisting of a verb and an adverb (and preposition), e.g. *break down, look forward to.*

phrase a group of words without a predicate, functioning like an adjective, adverb, or noun.

plural denoting more than one.

polysyllabic having more than one syllable.

possessive the case of a noun or a pronoun indicating possession, e.g. *John's*; **possessive pronoun,** e.g. *my, his*.

predicate the part of a clause consisting of what is said of the subject, including verb + complement or object.

predicative designating (especially) an adjective that forms part or the whole of the predicate, e.g. *The dog is* old.

prefix a verbal element placed at the beginning of a word to qualify its meaning, e.g. *ex-, non-*.

preposition a word governing a noun or pronoun, expressing the relation of the latter to other words, e.g. *seated* at *the table*.

prepositional phrase a phrase consisting of a preposition and its complement, e.g. *I am surprised* at your reaction.

present a tense expressing action now going on or habitually performed in past and future, e.g. *He* commutes *daily*.

pronoun a word used instead of a noun to designate (without naming) a person or thing already known or indefinite, e.g. *I, you, he*, etc., *anyone, something*, etc.

proper name a name used to designate an individual person, animal, town, ship, etc.

qualify (of an adjective or adverb) to attribute some quality to (a noun or adjective/verb).

reflexive implying the subject's action on himself, herself, or itself; **reflexive pronoun**, e.g. *myself, yourself*, etc.

relative: see p. 89 f.

restrictive: see p. 89.

semi-vowel a sound intermediate between vowel and consonant, e.g. the sound of *y* and *w*.

sentence adverb an adverb that qualifies or comments on the whole sentence, not one of the elements in it, e.g. Unfortunately, *he missed his train*.

simple future: see **future**.

singular denoting a single person or thing.

soft designating a letter, chiefly *c* or *g*, that indicates a sibilant sound, as in *city* or *germ*.

split infinitive: see p. 91 f.

stem the essential part of a word to which inflections and other suffixes are added, e.g. *un*limit*ed*.

stress the especially heavy vocal emphasis falling on one (the **stressed**) syllable of a word more than on the others.

subject the element in a clause (usually a noun or its equivalent) about which something is predicated (the latter is the **predicate**).

subjective the case of a pronoun typically used when the pronoun is the subject of a clause.

subjunctive the mood of a verb denoting what is imagined, wished, or possible, e.g. *I insist that it* be *finished*.

subordinate clause a clause dependent on the main clause and functioning like a noun, adjective, or adverb within the sentence, e.g. *He said* that you had gone.

substitute verb the verb *do* used in place of another verb, e.g. '*He likes chocolate*.' 'Does *he*?'

suffix a verbal element added at the end of a word to form a derivative, e.g. *-ation, -ing, -itis, -ize*.

superlative the form of an adjective or adverb expressing the highest or a very high degree of a quality, e.g. *bravest, worst*.

synonym a word that means exactly or nearly the same as another.

transitive designating a verb that takes a direct object, e.g. *I* said *nothing*.

uncountable noun: see **mass noun**.

unreal condition (especially in a **conditional** sentence) a condition which will not be or has not been fulfilled.

unstressed designating a word, syllable, or vowel not having **stress**.

variant a form of a word etc. that differs in spelling or pronunciation from another (often the main or usual) form.

verb a part of speech that predicates.

vowel (1) an open speech sound made without audible friction and capable of forming a syllable with or without a consonant; (2) a letter usually used to represent (1), e.g. *a*, *e*, *i*, *o*, *u*.

***wh*-question word** a convenient term for the interrogative and relative words, most beginning with *wh*: *what*, *when*, *where*, *whether*, *which*, *who*, *whom*, *whose*, *why*, *how*.

Abbreviations

Amer.	American
COD	*The Concise Oxford Dictionary* (edn. 8, Oxford, 1990)
Hart's Rules	*Hart's Rules for Compositors and Readers* (edn. 39, Oxford, 1983)
MEU	H. W. Fowler, *A Dictionary of Modern English Usage* (edn. 2, revised by Sir Ernest Gowers, Oxford, 1965)
OED	*The Oxford English Dictionary* (edn. 2, Oxford, 1989)
OWD	*The Oxford Writers' Dictionary* (Oxford, 1990)
TLS	*The Times Literary Supplement*

Word formation

This section deals with the forms of single words and word elements as regards spelling, including that of inflected and compounded forms and of those formed by adding prefixes and suffixes; little space has been given to meaning or use. There is some treatment of words requiring hyphens or capitals, but for a further discussion the reader is referred to the *Oxford Writers' Dictionary* and *Hart's Rules*. Some notes are added where the conventions of American spelling differ.

Where there is widespread variation in spelling, the spelling recommended is that preferred (as its 'house style') by Oxford University Press.

abbreviations

It is usual to indicate an abbreviation by placing a point (full stop) after it, e.g.

H. G. Wells, five miles S. (= south), *p. 7* (= page 7).

However, no point is used:

1. With a sequence of capitals alone, e.g. *BBC*, *AD* (and not with acronyms, e.g. *Aslef*, *Naafi*).

2. With the numerical abbreviations *1st*, *2nd*, etc.

3. With *C*, *F* (of temperature), chemical symbols, and measures of length, weight, time, etc., e.g. *cm*, *ft*, *cwt*, *lb*, *kg*.

4. After *Dr*, *Revd*, *Mr*, *Mrs*, *Ms*, *Mme*, *Mlle*, *St*, *Hants*, *Northants*, *p* (= penny or pence).

5. In colloquial abbreviations, e.g. *co-op*, *vac*.

-able and *-ible*

Adjectives ending in *-able* generally owe their form to the Latin termination *-abilis* or the Old French *-able* (or both), and those in *-ible* to the Latin *-ibilis*. The suffix *-able* is also added to words of 'distinctly French or English origin' (*OED*, s.v. *-ble*), and as a living element to English roots. Nouns in *-ability*, *-ibility* undergo the same changes.

A. Words ending in *-able*. The following alterations are made to the stem:

1. Silent final *-e* is dropped (see p. 10 f.).

Exceptions: words whose stem ends in *-ce*, *-ee*, *-ge*, and:

blameable	*nameable*
dyeable	*rateable*
giveable (but *forgivable*)	*ropeable*
hireable	*saleable*
holeable	*shareable*
likeable	*sizeable*
liveable	*tameable*
	unshakeable

● Amer. spelling tends to omit *-e-* in the words above.

2. Final *-y* becomes *-i-* (see p. 22).

Exception: *flyable*.

3. A final consonant may be doubled (see p. 10 f.).

Exceptions:

inferable	*referable*
preferable (but *conferrable*)	*transferable*

4. Most verbs of more than two syllables ending in *-ate* drop this ending before *-able*, e.g. *alienable*, *calculable*, etc. Verbs of two syllables ending in *-ate* form adjectives in *-able* regularly, e.g. *creatable*, *debatable*, etc.

B. Words ending in *-ible*. These are fewer, since *-ible* is not a living suffix (i.e. it cannot be freely used to form new words). Below is a list of the commonest. Almost all form their negative in *in-*, *il-*, etc.; the exceptions are indicated by (*un*).

accessible	*comprehensible*
adducible	*contemptible*
admissible	*convertible*
audible	*corrigible*
avertible	*corruptible*
collapsible	*credible*
combustible	*defensible*
compatible	*destructible*

digestible
dirigible
discernible
divisible
edible
eligible
exhaustible
expressible
extensible
fallible
(un)feasible
flexible
forcible
fusible
gullible
horrible
indelible
(un)intelligible
irascible
legible
negligible
ostensible
perceptible
perfectible
permissible
persuasible
plausible
possible
reducible
reprehensible
repressible
reproducible
resistible
responsible
reversible
risible
sensible
(un)susceptible
tangible
terrible
vincible
visible

ae and oe

In words derived from Latin and Greek, these are now always written as separate letters, not as the ligatures *ae, oe*, e.g. *aeon, gynaecology*; *amoeba, Oedipus*. The simple *e* is preferable in several words once commonly spelt with *ae, oe*, especially *medieval* and *ecology, ecumenical*.

• In Amer. spelling, *e* replaces *ae, oe* in many words, e.g. *gynecology, diarrhea.*

American spelling

Differences between Amer. and British spelling are mentioned at the following places: ***-able* and *-ible*** (p. 7); ***ae* and *oe*** (p. 8); ***-ce* or *-se*** (p. 9); **doubling of final consonant** (p. 10); **dropping of silent *-e*** (p. 11); **hyphens** (p. 14); ***l* and *ll*** (p. 15); ***-oul-*** (p. 16); ***-our* or *-or*** (p. 16); **past of verbs, formation of** (p. 16 f.); ***-re* or *-er*** (p. 20); ***-yse* or *-yze*** (p. 21).

See also **difficult and confusable spellings** (pp. 22 ff.) *passim*.

ante- and anti-

ante- (from Latin) = 'before'; *anti-* (from Greek) = 'against, opposite to'. Note especially *antechamber* and *antitype*.

-ant or -ent

-ant is the noun ending, *-ent* the adjective ending in:

dependant	*dependent*
descendant	*descendent*
pendant	*pendent*
propellant	*propellent*

independent is both adjective and noun; *dependence, independence* are the abstract nouns.

The following are correct spellings:

ascendant, -ncy	*relevant, -nce*
attendant, -nce	*repellent, -nce, -ncy*
contribuent	*superintendent, -ncy*
expellent	*tendency*
impellent	*transcendent, -nce*
intendant, -ncy	

a or an

A. Before *h*.

1. Where *h* is pronounced, use *a*, e.g. *a harvest, hero, hope.*
2. Where *h* is silent, use *an*, e.g. *an heir, honour, honorarium.*
3. Where *h* is pronounced but the first syllable is unstressed, use *a*, e.g. *a hotel.*

• The older usage, e.g. *an hotel*, is now almost obsolete.

B. Before capital letter abbreviations, follow the pronunciation.

1. Where the abbreviation is pronounced as letter-names, e.g.

a B road   *a UN resolution*

but

an A road   *an MP*

2. Where the abbreviation is pronounced as a word, e.g.

a RADA student   *a SABENA airline typist*

but

an AIDS conference   *an OPEC minister*

But where the abbreviation would in speech be pronounced as a word, use *a* or *an* as appropriate, e.g. *a MS* 'a manuscript'.

-ative or -ive

Correct are:

(*a*) *authoritative* *exploitative* *interpretative* *qualitative* *quantitative*
(*b*) *absorptive* *assertive* *preventive* *supportive*

The forms *interpretive* (which has a special computing meaning) and *preventative* also occur.

by- prefix

One word: *bygone, byline, byname, bypass, bypath, byplay, byroad, bystander, byway, byword*; the others (e.g. *by-election, by-product*) are hyphened.

● *Bye* (noun) in sport, *bye-bye* (= good-bye) take final *-e*.

c and ck

Words ending in *-c* interpose *k* before *-ed*, *-er*, *-ing*, *-y*, e.g.:

colicky *frolicked, -ing* *mimicked, -ing* *panicky* *picnicked, -er, -ing* *plastic-macked* *tarmacked, -ing* *trafficked, -ing*

Exceptions: *arced, -ing, zinced, zincify, zincing.*

Before *-ism*, *-ist*, *-ity*, and *-ize* *c* remains and is pronounced soft, e.g. *physicist, italicize.*

capital or small initials

There are four classes of word that especially give trouble.

A. Compass points. Use capitals:

1. When abbreviated, e.g. *NNE for north-north-east.*
2. When denoting a region, e.g. *unemployment in the North.*
3. When part of a geographical name with recognized status, e.g. *Northern Ireland, East Africa, Western Australia.*
4. In bridge.

Otherwise use small initials, e.g. *a south-easter.*

B. Parties, denominations, and organizations.

'The general rule is: capitalization makes a word more specific and limited in its reference: contrast a Christian scientist (man of science) and a Christian Scientist (member of the Church of Christ Scientist).' (*Hart's Rules*, pp. 10–11.)

So, for example, *Conservative, Democratic* (names of parties); *Roman Catholic, Congregational*; but *conservative, democratic* (as normal adjectives), *catholic sympathies, congregational singing.*

C. Words derived from proper names.

When connection with the proper name is indirect or allusive, use a small initial letter, e.g.

jersey, platonic (*love*), *pasteurize.*

When the connection of a derived adjective or verb with a proper name is felt to be alive, use a capital, e.g.

Platonic (*philosophy*), *Anglicize.*

● Adjectives of nationality usually retain the capital even when used in transferred senses, e.g. *Dutch courage, Turkish delight.* The chief exceptions are *arabic* (*numeral*), *roman* (*numeral, type*).

D. Proprietary names.

The name of a product or process, if registered as a trade mark, is a proprietary name, and should be given a capital initial, e.g. *Araldite, Coca-Cola, Marmite, Xerox.*

-cede or -ceed

Exceed, proceed, succeed; the other similar verbs have *-cede*, e.g. *concede, intercede, precede, recede.* Note also *supersede.*

-ce or -se

Advice, device, licence, and *practice* are nouns; the related verbs are spelt with *-se*: *advise, devise, license, practise.* Similarly *prophecy* (noun), *prophesy* (verb).

● Amer. spelling favours *license, practise* for both noun and verb; but the nouns *defence, offence, pretence* are spelt with *c* in Britain, *s* in America.

co- prefix

Most words with this prefix have no hyphen. Those that are usually spelt with a hyphen are:

1. A few words with *o* following, e.g. *co-op, co-opt* (but *cooperate, uncooperative, coordinate*).

2. Words in which the hyphen preserves correct syllabication, so aiding recognition, e.g. *co-respondent* (distinguished from *correspondent*).

3. Words in which *co-* is a living prefix meaning 'fellow-', e.g. *co-author, co-star*.

doubling of final consonant

1. Before certain suffixes beginning with a vowel, the final consonant of the stem word is doubled:

(*a*) if the preceding vowel is written with a single letter (or single letter preceded by *qu*) and

(*b*) if that vowel bears the main stress (hence all monosyllables are included).

So *bed, bedding* but *head, heading*; *occúr, occúrred* but *óffer, óffered*; *befít, befítted* but *bénefit, bénefited*.

Suffixes which cause this doubling include:

(*a*) The verb inflections *-ed, -ing*, e.g.

begged, begging *revved, revving*
bussed, bussing *trekked, trekking*

(*b*) The suffixes *-able, -age, -en, -er, -ery, -est, -ish, -y*, e.g.

clubbable *waggery*
tonnage *saddest*
sadden *priggish*
trapper *shrubby*

2. Words of more than one syllable, not stressed on the last syllable, do not double the final consonant, unless it is *l*, when a suffix beginning with a vowel is added, e.g.

biased *gossipy* *turbaned*
blossoming *lettered* *wainscoted*
faceted *pilotage* *wickedest*
focusing *targeted* *womanish*

Exception: *worship* makes *worshipped, -ing*.

Note that some other words in which the final syllable has a full vowel (not obscure *e* or *i*) also double this consonant, e.g.

format *horsewhip* *leap-frog*
handicap *humbug* *sandbag*
hobnob *kidnap* *zigzag*

● Amer. sometimes *kidnaped, kidnaping, worshiped, worshiping*.

3. Consonants that are never doubled are *c, h, w, x, y*.

4. When endings beginning with a vowel are added, *l* is *always* doubled after a single vowel wherever the stress falls, e.g.

controllable *jeweller*
flannelled *panelling*

Note also *woollen, woolly*.

Exceptions: *parallel* makes *paralleled, -ing*; *devil* makes *devilish*.

● In Amer. spelling *l* obeys the same rules as the other consonants (except *c, h, w, x, y*), e.g. *traveler*, but *pally*.

Note also Amer. *woolen* (but *woolly*).

5. A silent final consonant is not doubled. Endings are added as if the consonant were pronounced, e.g.

crocheted, -ing *rendezvouses* (third person singular)
pince-nezed
précised *rendezvousing*

dropping of silent -e

A. When a suffix beginning with a vowel (including *-y*) is added to a word ending in silent *-e* (including *e* following another vowel), the *-e* is dropped; e.g.

braver, bravery, bravest *hoed*
dyed, dyer *issued*
freer, freest *manoeuvred*

adorable *imaginable*
analysable *manoeuvrable*
bribable *usable*

cleavage *dotage*

centring *housing*
gluing *queuing*

whitish *mousy*

Exceptions:

(*a*) Words ending in *-ce* and *-ge* retain the *e* to indicate the softness of the consonant, e.g. *bridgeable*.

(*b*) In a number of *-able* adjectives, *e* is retained. See list on p. 7.
(*c*) The few *-able* adjectives formed on verbs ending in consonant + *-le*; e.g. *handleable.*
(*d*) *acreage, mileage.*
(*e*) *ee, oe,* and *ye* remain, e.g.

agreeing	*dyeing*	*hoeing*
canoeing	*eyeing*	*shoeing*

(*f*) *blueing, cueing.*
(*g*) *routeing, singeing, swingeing* are distinguished from *routing* 'putting to flight', *singing,* and *swinging.*
(*h*) *moreish, ogreish.*
(*i*) See ***-y* or *-ey* adjectives,** p. 21f. Both *stagy* and *stagey* are acceptable.
For change of *i* to *y, dying, lying,* etc., see p. 15.

B. When a suffix beginning with a consonant is added to a word ending in silent *-e*, the *-e* is retained, e.g.

abridgement	*houseful*
acknowledgement	*judgement* (*judgment* often in legal works)
awesome	
definitely	*whiteness*

Exceptions: *argument, awful, duly, eerily, eeriness, fledgling, truly, wholly.*

● In Amer. spelling *e* is dropped after *dg* and before a suffix beginning with a consonant, e.g. *abridgment, judgment.*

C. Final silent *-e* is often omitted in Amer. spelling, and so is final silent *-ue* in the endings *-gogue, -logue,* e.g.

ax	*adz*	*program*
analog	*epilog*	*pedagog*

-efy or *-ify*

The chief words with *-efy* (*-efied, -efication,* etc.) are:

liquefy	*rubefy*	*tumefy*
putrefy	*stupefy*	
rarefy	*torrefy*	

All the others have *-ify* etc. See also ***-ified* or *-yfied,*** p. 14.

-ei- or *-ie-*

The rule '*i* before *e* except after *c*' holds good for nearly all words in which the vowel-sound is *ee*, as *Aries, hygienic, yield,* but *ceiling, deceit, receive.*
Exceptions: *prima facie, specie, species, superficies.*

The following words which are, or can be, pronounced with the *ee*-sound have *ei*:

caffeine	*heinous*	*protein*
casein	*inveigle*	*seise*
codeine	*Madeira*	*seize*
counterfeit	*neither*	*seizure*
deceive	*peripeteia*	*weir*
either	*plebeian*	*weird*

Note also *forfeit, surfeit,* and many proper names, e.g. *Keith, Leith, Neil, Reid, Sheila.*

en- or *in-*

The following pairs of words can give trouble:

encrust (verb)	*incrustation*
engrain (verb) to dye in the raw state	*ingrain* (adjective) dyed in the yarn
	ingrained deeply rooted
enquire ask	*inquire* undertake a formal investigation
enquiry question	*inquiry* official investigation
ensure make sure	*insure* take out insurance (against risk: note *assurance* of life)

Although *enquire, enquiry* and *inquire, inquiry* are used almost interchangeably by many people, they are usually used as above.

-er and *-est*

These suffixes of comparison may require:
1. Doubling of final consonant (see p. 10f.).
2. Dropping of silent *-e* (see p. 10f.).
3. Change of *y* to *i* (see p. 22).

-erous or *-rous*

The ending *-erous* is normal in adjectives related to nouns ending in *-er*, e.g. *murderous, thunderous.* But:

ambidextrous	*meandrous*
cumbrous	*monstrous*
disastrous	*wondrous*
leprous	

final vowels before suffixes

A. For treatment of final *-e* and *-y* before suffixes see **dropping of silent *-e*,** p. 10f., and ***y* to *i*,** p. 22.

B. For treatment of final *-o* before *-s* (suffix), see **plural formation,** p. 18 and ***-s* suffix,** p. 20.

C. In nearly all other cases, the final vowels *-a*, *-i*, *-o*, and *-u* are unaffected by suffixes and do not affect them:

skier	*vetoer*
cameras	*(he) rumbas*
corgis	*(she) skis*
emus	*taxis*
echoing	*skiing*
radioing	*taxiing*
baaed	*radioed*
concertinaed	*subpoenaed*
echoed	*taxied*
mascaraed	*tiaraed*
mustachioed	

The *-ed* spelling is preferable for this last group, but an *-'d* spelling is often acceptable, especially after the letter *a*, e.g. *rumba'd*. This spelling is preferable in *idea'd* (having ideas) and *ski'd* (from *ski*, contrasting with *skied* from *sky*).

D. Final *-é* in words taken from French is retained before all suffixes; the *e* of *-ed* is dropped after it, e.g.

appliquéd	*chasséing*
attachés	*communiqués*
cafés	*émigrés*
canapés	*soufflés*

for- and *fore-*

Note especially:

forbear refrain	*forebear* ancestor
forgather	*foreclose*
forgo abstain from	*forego* precede

f to *v*

Certain nouns that end in *f* or *f* followed by silent *e* change this *f* to *v* in some derivatives. In some cases, there is variation or uncertainty:

beef: plural *beeves* oxen, *beefs* kinds of beef.

calf (young animal): *calfish* calflike; *calves-foot jelly*.

calf (of leg): (*enormously*) *calved* having (enormous) calves.

corf (basket): plural *corves*.

dwarf: plural *dwarfs*. ● *Dwarves* is increasingly found.

elf: *elfish* and *elvish* are both acceptable; *elfin* but *elven* (in fantasy writings).

handkerchief: plural *handkerchiefs*.

hoof: plural usually *hooves*; the historic form *hoofs* is also common; adjective *hoofed* or *hooved*.

knife: verb *knife*.

leaf: *leaved* having leaves (*broad-leaved* etc.) but *leafed* as past of *leaf* (*through a book* etc.).

life: *lifelong* lasting a lifetime; *livelong* (*day* etc., poetic: the *i* is short); the plural of *still life* is *still lifes*.

oaf: plural *oafs*.

roof: plural *roofs*. ● *Rooves* is commonly heard and sometimes written, but the written use should be avoided.

scarf (garment): plural *scarves*; *scarfed* wearing a scarf.

scarf (joint): plural and verb keep *f*.

sheaf: plural *sheaves*; verb *sheaf* or *sheave*; *sheaved* made into a sheaf.

shelf: plural *shelves*; *shelvy* having sandbanks.

staff: plural *staffs* but archaic and musical *staves*.

turf: plural *turfs* or *turves*; verb *turf*; *turfy*.

wharf: plural *wharves* or *wharfs*.

wolf: *wolfish* of a wolf.

-ful suffix

The adjectival suffix *-ful* may require the following changes in spelling:

1. Change of *y* to *i* (see p. 22).
2. Simplification of *-ll* (see ***l* and *ll*,** p. 15).

hyphens

A. Hyphens are used to connect words that are more closely linked to each other than to the surrounding syntax. Unfortunately their use is not consistent. Some pairs or groups of words are written as a single word (e.g. *motorway*, *railwayman*), others, despite their equally close bond, as separate words (e.g. *motor cycle, pay slip*); very similar pairs may be found with a hyphen (e.g. *motor-cyclist, pay-bed*). There are no hard and fast rules that will predict whether a group of words should be written as one, with a hyphen, or separately. For individual items, consult the most recent edition of *COD*.

1. Groups consisting of attributive noun + noun are probably the most unpredictable. Such a group generally remains written as separate words until it is recognized as a lexical item with a special meaning, when it may receive a hyphen. Eventually it may be written as one word, but this usually happens when the two nouns are monosyllabic and there is no clash between the final letter of the first and the first letter of the second.

   This generalization is, however, a very weak guide to what happens in practice. Compare, for example, *coal tar, coal-sack, coalfield; oil well, oil-painting, oilfield*.

2. Nouns derived from phrasal verbs, consisting of verb + adverb, are slightly more predictable. They are either hyphened or written as one, e.g. *play-off, set-back, turn-out; feedback, layout, turnover*. Phrases consisting of *-er* + adverb are usually hyphened, e.g. *runner-up*; those consisting of *-ing* + adverb are usually left as two words, e.g. *Your coming back surprised me*, unless they have become a unit with a special meaning, e.g. *Gave him a going-over*.

3. Various collocations which are not otherwise hyphened are given hyphens before a noun, e.g.

   (*a*) adjective + noun: *a common-sense argument* (but *This is common sense*), *an open-air restaurant* (but *eating in the open air*).

   (*b*) preposition + noun: *an out-of-date aircraft* (but *This is out of date*), *an in-depth interview* (but *interviewing him in depth*).

   (*c*) participle + adverb: *a longed-for departure* (but *the departure greatly longed for*).

   (*d*) other syntactic groups used attributively, e.g. *An all-but-unbearable mixture* (Lynne Reid Banks).

4. Collocations of adverb + adjective (or participle) are usually written as two words, e.g. *a less interesting topic, an amazingly good performance,* but may very occasionally take a hyphen to avoid misunderstanding, e.g. *Sir Edgar, who had heard one or two more-sophisticated rumours* (Angus Wilson) (this does not mean 'one or two additional sophisticated rumours').

   See also **well,** p. 72.

5. When two words that form a close collocation but are not normally joined by a hyphen enter into combination with another word that requires a hyphen, it may be necessary to join them with a hyphen as well to avoid an awkward or even absurd result, e.g. *natural gas* needs no hyphen in *natural gas pipeline,* but *natural-gas-producer* may be preferred to the ambiguous *natural gas-producer*. Occasionally a real distinction in meaning may be indicated, e.g. *The non-German-speakers at the conference used interpreters* versus *The non-German speakers at the conference were all Austrians.*

6. A group of words forming a syntactic unit normally has hyphens, e.g. *court-martial* (verb), *happy-go-lucky* (adjective), *good-for-nothing, stick-in-the-mud, ne'er-do-well* (nouns).

7. A hyphen is used to indicate a common second element in all but the last word of a list, e.g. *two-, three-, or fourfold.*

B. With most prefixes and suffixes it is normal to write the whole compound as a single word; the use of the hyphen is exceptional, and the writing of prefix or suffix and stem as two words virtually unknown.

The hyphen is used in the following cases:

1. After a number of prefixes that can be freely used to form new compounds:

   ex- (= formerly), e.g. *ex-President*; *neo-* (denoting a revived movement), e.g. *neo-Nazism*; *non-*, e.g. *non-stick*;

pro- (= in favour of), e.g. *pro-marketeer*; *self-*, e.g. *self-destructive*.

Exceptions: *Neoplatonism* (*-ic*, etc.); *selfsame*, *unselfconscious*.

2. After a number of prefixes to aid recognition of the second element, e.g. *anti-g*, or to distinguish the compound from another word identically spelt, e.g. *un-ionized* (as against *unionized*); see also ***co-* prefix, *re-* prefix**.
3. Between a prefix ending with a vowel and a stem beginning with the same vowel, e.g. *de-escalate*, *pre-empt*; see also ***co-* prefix, *re-* prefix**.
4. Between a prefix and a stem beginning with a capital letter, e.g. *anti-Darwinian*, *hyper-Calvinism*, *Pre-Raphaelite*.
5. With some living suffixes forming specially coined compounds, e.g. *Mickey Mouse-like*; or still regarded to some extent as full words, such as *-wise* (= as regards ——), e.g. *Weather-wise we have had a good summer*.
6. In irregularly formed compounds, e.g. *unget-at-able*.
7. With the suffix *-like* after a stem ending in *-l*, e.g. *eel-like*, and when attached to a word of two or more syllables, e.g. *cabbage-like*; with the suffix *-less* after a stem ending in double *-l*, e.g. *bell-less*, *will-lessness*.

Note. In Amer. spelling there is a greater tendency than in British spelling to write compounds as one word, rather than hyphened, e.g. *nonplaying*, *nonprofit*, *roundhouse*, *runback*.

-ified or -yfied

-ified is usual, whatever the stem of the preceding element, e.g.

citified	*gentrified*
countrified	*sissified*
Frenchified	*yuppified*

But *ladyfied*.

in- or un-

There is no comprehensive set of rules, but the following guidelines are offered. Note that *in-* takes the form of *il-*, *im-*, or *ir-* before initial *l*, *m*, or *r*.

1. *in-* properly belongs to words derived from Latin, whereas *un-* combines with any English word. Hence

(*a*) *un-* may be expected to spread to words originally having *in-*. This has happened when the *in-* word has developed a sense more specific than merely the negative of the stem word:

unapt	*inept*
unartistic	*inartistic*
unhuman	*inhuman*
unmaterial	*immaterial*
unmoral	*immoral*
unreligious	*irreligious*
unsolvable	*insoluble*

(*b*) It is always possible to coin a nonce-word with *un-*:

A small bullied-looking woman with unabundant brown hair (Kingsley Amis)

2. Adjectives and participles ending in *-ed* and *-ing* rarely accept *in-*.

Exception: *inexperienced*.

3. *in-* seems to be preferred before *ad-*, *co-* (*col-*, *com-*, *con-*, *cor-*), *de-*, *di*(*s*)-, *ex-*, *per-*. Important exceptions are:

unadventurous	*undeniable*
uncommunicative	*undesirable*
unconditional	*undetectable*
unconscionable	*unexceptionable*
unconscious	*unexceptional*
uncooperative	*unpersuasive*
undemonstrative	

4. *un-* is preferred before *em-*, *en-*, *im-*, *in-*, *inte*(*r*)-.

5. Adjectives ending in *-able* usually take *in-* if the stem preceding the suffix *-able* is not, by itself, an English word:

palpable, stem *palp-*, negative *im-*

Exceptions: *unamenable*, *unamiable*, *unconscionable*.

They usually take *un-* if the stem is a short English word:

unbridgeable *unreadable*

Exceptions: *incurable*, *immovable*, *impassable* (that cannot be traversed: but *impassible* = unfeeling).

But no generalization covers those with a longer English stem:

illimitable *undeniable*
invariable *unmistakable*

Note: Rule 2 overrides rule 3 (e.g. *uncomplaining*, *undisputed*, *unperturbed*) and rule 3 overrides rule 5 (*unconscionable*).

i to *y*

When the suffix *-ing* is added to words (chiefly verbs) that end in *-ie*, *e* is dropped (see **dropping of silent** ***-e***, p. 10), and *i* becomes *y*, e.g.

dying *tying*

Exceptions: *hie*, *sortie*, make *hieing*, *sortieing*. Both *stymieing* and *stymying* are acceptable.

-ize and *-ise*

-ize should be preferred to *-ise* as a verbal ending where both are in use, according to Oxford University Press house style, and is also usual in North America. Both spellings are common in the UK.

1. The choice arises only where the ending is pronounced *eyes*, not where it is *ice*, *iss*, or *eez*.

So: *precise*, *promise*, *chemise*, *expertise*.

2. The choice applies only to the verbal suffix with the sense 'make into, treat with, or act in the way of (the stem word)'.

Hence are eliminated

(*a*) nouns in *-ise*:

compromise *franchise*
demise *merchandise*
disguise *revise*
enterprise *surmise*
exercise *surprise*

(*b*) verbs corresponding to a noun which has *-is-* as a part of the stem, or identical with a noun in *-ise*:

advertise *arise*
advise *chastise*
apprise *circumcise*
enfranchise *incise*
excise *premise*
improvise *prise* (*open*)
comprise *supervise*
despise *televise*
devise

3. Most *-ize* verbs are formed on familiar English stems, e.g. *authorize*, *symbolize*; or with a slight alteration to the stem, e.g. *agonize*, *sterilize*. A few have no such immediate stem: *aggrandize* (cf. *aggrandizement*), *baptize* (cf. *baptism*), *catechize* (cf. *catechism*), *recognize* (cf. *recognition*); and *capsize*.

l and *ll*

Whether to write a single or double *l* can be a problem:

1. Where a suffix is added to single final *l*: see **doubling of final consonants**, p. 10 f.

2. *l* is single when it is the last letter of the following verbs:

annul *enrol* *fulfil*
appal *enthral* *impel*
distil *extol* *instil*

These double the *l* before a vowel (see p. 10 f.), but not before *-ment*:

enrolment *distillation* *enthralling*

● In Amer. spelling *l* is usually double here except in *annul*(*ment*), *extol*.

3. Final *-ll* usually becomes *l* before a consonant, e.g.

almighty, *almost*, etc. *skilful*
chilblain *thraldom*
dully *wilful*

Exception: Before *-ness*, *-ll* remains in *dullness*, *fullness*.

● In Amer. spelling *ll* is usual in *skillful*, *thralldom*, *willful*.

-ly

The suffix *-ly* forms adjectives and adverbs, e.g. *earth*, *earthly*; *sad*, *sadly*. One of the following spelling changes may be required:

1. If the word ends in double *ll*, add only *-y*, e.g. *fully*, *shrilly*.

2. If the word ends in consonant + *le*, change *e* to *y*, e.g. *ably*, *singly*, *subtly*, *supply*, *terribly*.

3. If the word ends in consonant + *y*, change *y* to *i* and add *-ly*, e.g. *drily*, *happily*.

Exceptions: *shyly*, *slyly*, *spryly*, *wryly*.

4. Unstressed *ey* changes to *i*, e.g. *matily*.

5. If the word ends in *-ic*, add *-ally*, e.g. *basically*, *scientifically*.

Exceptions: *politicly* (from *politic*, distinguished from *politically*, from *political*), *publicly*.

6. Final *-e* is dropped before *-ly* in *duly*, *eerily*, *truly*, *wholly*.

7. Final *-y* changes to *i* before *-ly* in *daily*, *gaily*.

-ness

It may require the change of *y* to *i*: see p. 22.

-or and -er

They both mean 'person or thing that performs (a verb)'. But:

1. *-er* is the living suffix, forming most agent nouns; but *-or* is common with words of Latin origin, e.g.

chopper, *producer*, *avenger*, *qualifier*, *organizer*; *counsellor*, *carburettor*, *conqueror*.

2. *-or* follows *-at-* to form *-ator*, e.g. *duplicator*, *incubator*.

Exception: *debater*.

Note: nouns such as *idolater* do not contain the agent suffix.

3. Both suffixes are very common after *-s-*, *-ss-*, and *-t-* (apart from *-at-*). So *supervisor*, *prospector*, but *adviser*, *perfecter*. Only rough guidelines can be given: *-tor* usually follows *-c*, unstressed *i*, and *u*, e.g. *actor*, *compositor*; *-ter* usually follows *f*, *gh*, *l*, *r*, and *s*, e.g. *drifter*, *fighter*.

4. A functional distinction is made between *-or* and *-er* in the following:

accepter one who accepts	*acceptor* (in scientific use)
caster one who casts, casting machine	*castor* beaver; plant giving oil; sugar (sprinkler); wheel
censer for incense	*censor* official
resister one who resists	*resistor* electrical device
sailer ship of specified power	*sailor* seaman

5. A number of words have *-er* in normal use but *-or* in Law:

abetter	*mortgager*
accepter	*settler*
granter	*vender*

-oul-

In *mould*, *moulder*, *moult*, *smoulder*, Amer. spelling favours *o* alone instead of *ou*.

-our or -or

1. In agent nouns, only *-or* occurs as the ending (cf. ***-or* and *-er***), e.g. *actor*, *counsellor*.

Exception: *saviour*.

2. In abstract nouns, *-our* is usual, e.g. *colour*, *favour*, *humour*. Only the following end in *-or*:

error	*pallor*	*terror*
horror	*squalor*	*torpor*
languor	*stupor*	*tremor*
liquor		

● In Amer. English *-or* is usual here except in *glamour*.

3. Nouns in *-our* change this to *-or* before the suffixes *-ation*, *-iferous*, *-ific*, *-ize*, and *-ous*, e.g.

coloration, *humorous*, *soporific*, *vaporize*.

Exception: *colourize*.

But *-our* keeps the *u* before other suffixes, e.g.

armourer, *behaviourism*, *colourful*, *favourite*, *honourable*.

Exceptions: *humorist*, *rigorist*.

past of verbs, formation of

A. Regular verbs add *-ed* for the past tense and past participle, and may make the following spelling changes:

1. Doubling of final consonant (see p. 10).
2. Dropping of silent *-e* (see p. 10 f.).
3. Change of *y* to *i* (see p. 22).

Note *laid*, *paid*, and *said* from *lay*, *pay*, and *say*.

B. A number of verbs vary between *-ed* and *-t* (and in some cases a different vowel-sound in the stem):

burned, burnt	*learned, learnt*
dreamed, dreamt	*smelled, smelt*
kneeled, knelt	*spelled, spelt*
leaned, leant	*spilled, spilt*
leaped, leapt	*spoiled, spoilt*

The *-t* form is usual in Received Pronunciation* and should be written by those who pronounce it. The regular form is usual in Amer. English.

Bereave is regular when the reference is to the loss of relatives by death; *bereft* is used for loss of possessions.

Cleave is a rare word with two opposite meanings: (i) = stick; *A man . . shall cleave unto his wife* (Genesis 2: 24) (regular). (ii) = split. The past tense *clave* is archaic; *clove*, *cleft*, and regular *cleaved* are all permissible, but *cleaved* is usual in scientific and technical contexts. The past participle varies in certain fixed expressions, *cloven-footed*, *cloven hoof*, *cleft palate*, *cleft stick*; *cleaved* is probably best used elsewhere.

C. A number of verbs vary in the past participle only between the regular form and one ending in *-(e)n*:

hew, mow, saw, sew, shear, show, sow, strew, swell.

In most of these the latter form is to be preferred; in British English it is obligatory when the participle is used as an attributive adjective. So *new-mown hay*, *a sawn-off* (Amer. *sawed-off*) *shotgun*, *shorn* (not *sheared*) *of one's strength*, *a swollen gland*; *swollen* or *swelled head* (= conceit) is a colloquial exception.

D. The past tense has *-a-*, the past participle *-u-*, in

begin	*shrink*	*stink*
drink	*sing*	*swim*
ring	*sink*	

* See p. 55.

● It is an error to use *begun*, *drunk*, etc. for the past tense.

E. The following verbs can cause difficulty:

abide (*by*) makes *abided*
alight makes *alighted*
bet: *betted* is increasingly common beside *bet*
bid (make a bid): *bid*
bid (command; say (goodnight etc.)): *bid* is usual (*bade*, *bidden* are archaic)
broadcast unchanged in past tense and past participle
chide: *chided* is now usual (older *chid*)
forecast unchanged in past tense and past participle
hang: *hanged* for capital punishment; otherwise *hung*
highlight makes *highlighted*
knit: *knitted* is usual, but *knit* metaphorical
light makes *lit* but *lighted* attributively (*a lighted match*)
quit makes *quit*, but *quitted* is also occasionally found
reeve (nautical) makes *rove*
rid unchanged in past tense and past participle
speed makes *sped*, but *speeded* in the senses 'cause to go at (a certain) speed' and 'travel at illegal speed'
spit makes *spat* ● Amer. *spit*
spotlight makes *spotlighted*
stave: (to dent) *staved* or *stove*; (to ward off) *staved*
sweat makes *sweated* ● Amer. *sweat*
thrive: *thrived* is increasingly common beside *throve*, *thriven*

plural formation

Most nouns simply add *-s*, e.g. *cats*, *dogs*, *horses*, *cameras*.

A. The regular plural suffix *-s* is preceded by *-e-*:

1. After sibilant consonants, i.e. after

ch: e.g. *benches*, *coaches*, *matches* (but not *lochs*, *stomachs* where the *ch* has a different sound)
s: e.g. *buses*, *gases*, *pluses*, *yeses* (single *s* is not doubled)
sh: e.g. *ashes*, *bushes*

ss: e.g. *grasses, successes*
x: e.g. *boxes, sphinxes*
z: e.g. *buzzes, waltzes* (*fezzes, quizzes* have double *z*)

Proper names follow the same rule, e.g. *the Joneses, the Rogerses, the two Charleses.*

2. After *-y* (not preceded by a vowel), which changes to *i*, e.g. *ladies, soliloquies, spies*.

Exceptions: proper names, e.g. *the Willoughbys, the three Marys*; also *lay-bys, standbys, zlotys* (Polish currency).

3. After *-o* in certain words:

bravoes (= ruffians; *bravos* = shouts of 'bravo!')	*mementoes*
	mosquitoes
	mottoes
buffaloes	*Negroes*
calicoes	*noes*
cargoes	*peccadilloes*
dingoes	*porticoes*
dominoes	*potatoes*
echoes	*salvoes*
embargoes	*stuccoes*
goes	*tomatoes*
grottoes	*tornadoes*
haloes	*torpedoes*
heroes	*vetoes*
innuendoes	*volcanoes*
mangoes	

The forms *grottos, innuendos, mangos, mementos, porticos, salvos* also occur. Words not in the above list add only *-s*.

It is helpful to remember that *-e-* is never inserted:

(*a*) when the *o* follows another vowel, e.g. *cuckoos, ratios*.
(*b*) when the word is an abbreviation, e.g. *hippos, kilos*.
(*c*) with proper names, e.g. *Lotharios, Figaros, the Munros*.

4. With words which change final *f* to *v* (see p. 12f.).

B. Plural of compound nouns.

1. Compounds made up of a noun followed by an adjective, prepositional phrase, or adverb attach *-s* to the noun, e.g.

(*a*) *courts martial* *heirs presumptive*
But *brigadier-generals, lieutenant-colonels, sergeant-majors.*
(*b*) *sons-in-law* *tugs of war*
(*c*) *hangers-on* *passers-by*

Note: Informally, type (*a*) often pluralize the second word.

2. Compounds which contain no (apparent) noun add *-s* at the end. So also do nouns formed from phrasal verbs and compounds ending in *-ful*, e.g.

(*a*) *forget-me-nots* *will-o'-the-wisps*
(*b*) *pullovers* *set-ups*
(*c*) *handfuls* *spoonfuls*

3. Compounds containing *man* or *woman* make both elements plural, e.g.

menservants *women doctors*

C. The plural of these nouns in *-s* is unchanged:

biceps	*means*	*species*
congeries	*mews*	*superficies*
forceps	*series*	*thrips*
innings		

The following are mass nouns, not plurals: *bona fides* (= 'good faith'), *kudos*

● The singulars *bona-fide* (as a noun; there is an adjective *bona-fide*), *congery, kudo*, sometimes seen, are erroneous.

D. Plural of nouns of foreign origin. The foreign patterns are given below, with the words that normally follow them. Elsewhere, it is recommended to use the regular *-s* plural, even though some words accept either plural.

1. *-a* (Latin and Greek) becomes *-ae*:

alga	*lamina*	*nebula*
alumna	*larva*	*papilla*

Note: *formula* has *-ae* in mathematical and scientific use.

2. *-eau, -eu* (French) add *-x*:

beau	*château*	*plateau*
bureau	*milieu*	*tableau*

But *beaus, bureaus, milieus, plateaus* are also acceptable.

3. *-ex, -ix* (Latin) become *-ices*:

appendix	*cortex*	*matrix*
codex	*helix*	*radix*

Note: *index, vortex* have *-ices* in mathematical and scientific use, and *appendixes* is common for the internal organ.

4. *-is* (Greek and Latin) becomes *-es* (pronounced *eez*):

amanuensis *hypothesis*
analysis *metamorphosis*
antithesis *oasis*
axis *parenthesis*
basis *synopsis*
crisis *thesis*
ellipsis

5. *-o* (Italian) becomes *-i*:

concerto grosso (*concerti grossi*)
graffito *ripieno*
maestro *virtuoso*

But *maestros*, *ripienos*, *virtuosos* are also acceptable, and *solo*, *soprano* may have *-i* in technical contexts.

6. *-on* (Greek) becomes *-a*:

criterion *parhelion* *phenomenon*

Note: The plural of *automaton* is in *-a* when used collectively.

7. *-s* (French) is unchanged in the plural:

chamois *corps* *fracas*
chassis *faux pas* *patois*

Also (not a noun in French): *rendezvous*.

8. *-um* (Latin) becomes *-a*:

addendum *effluvium*
bacterium *emporium*
candelabrum *epithalamium*
compendium *erratum*
corrigendum *maximum*
cranium *minimum*
crematorium *quantum*
curriculum *scholium*
datum *spectrum*
desideratum *speculum*
dictum *stratum*

The forms *compendiums*, *emporiums*, *epithalamiums* are acceptable variants.

Note: *medium* in scientific use, and in the sense 'means of communication' has plural in *-a*; the collective plural of *memorandum* 'things to be noted' is in *-a*; *rostrum* and *vacuum* have *-a* in technical use.

9. *-us* (Latin) becomes *-i*:

alumnus *bronchus* *calculus*
bacillus *cactus* *fungus*
gladiolus *nucleus* *stimulus*
locus *radius* *terminus*
narcissus

Note: *focus* has plural in *-i* in scientific use; genius has plural *genii* when used to mean 'guardian spirit'; *corpus*, *genus*, *opus* become *corpora*, *genera*, *opera* (or, to avoid confusion, *opuses*).

• The following are plural; they should normally not be construed as singulars (see also in section III):

bacteria *graffiti* *phenomena*
candelabra *insignia* *regalia*
criteria *media* *strata*
data

E. There is no need to use an apostrophe before *-s*:

1. After figures: *the 1890s*.
2. After abbreviations: *KOs*, *MPs*, *SOSs*.

But it is needed in: *dot the i's and cross the t's*, *do's and don'ts*.

possessive case

To form the possessive:

1. Add *-'s* to singulars, and to plurals not ending in *-s*, e.g.

Bill's book *his master's voice*
children's *Father Christmas's*
a fortnight's holiday

2. Add an apostrophe to *-s* plurals, e.g.

the Johnsons' dog *the octopuses' tentacles*
two weeks' holiday

French names ending in silent *s* or *x* add *-'s*, e.g. *Dumas's* (= Dumah's), *Crémieux's*.

Names ending in *-es* pronounced *iz* take only an apostrophe, e.g. *Bridges'*, *Moses'*.

Polysyllables not accented on the last or second last syllable can take the apostrophe alone, e.g. *Nicholas'* or *Nicholas's*.

It is the custom in classical works to use the apostrophe alone for ancient classical names ending in *-s*, e.g. *Ceres'*, *Mars'*.

Jesus' 'is an accepted liturgical archaism' (*Hart's Rules*, p. 31). But in non-liturgical use, *Jesus's* is acceptable.

Before the word *sake*, be guided by the pronunciation, e.g.

for goodness' sake	but	*for God's sake*
		for Charles's sake

After *-x* and *-z*, use *-'s*, e.g. *Ajax's*, *Berlioz's*.

3. In *I'm going to the butcher's, to Brown's, to Susan's*, etc. the apostrophe signals an ellipsis of 'shop', 'business', or 'establishment'. But many businesses use the title *Browns*, *Greens*, etc., without an apostrophe (e.g. *Debenhams*, *Barclays Bank*). No apostrophe is necessary in a Debenhams store or in *go to the cleaners*.

4. The apostrophe must not be used:

(*a*) with the plural non-possessive *-s*: notices such as *TEA'S* are often seen, but are wrong.

(*b*) in the possessive pronouns *hers*, *its*, *ours*, *theirs*, *yours*; the possessive of *who* is *whose*.

- *it's* = *it is* or *it has*; *who's* = *who is* or *who has*.

- There are no words *her's*, *our's*, *their's*, *your's*.

-re or -er

The principal words in which the ending *-re* (with the unstressed *er* sound—there are others with the sound *ruh*, e.g. *macabre*, or *ray*, e.g. *padre*) is found are:

accoutre	*metre* (note *meter* the measuring device)
**acre*	
amphitheatre	
**cadre*	*mitre*
calibre	*nitre*
centre	*ochre*
**euchre*	**ogre*
fibre	*philtre*
goitre	*reconnoitre*
litre	*sabre*
louvre	*sceptre*
**lucre*	*sepulchre*
lustre	*sombre*
manoeuvre	*spectre*
**massacre*	*theatre*
meagre	*titre*
**mediocre*	**wiseacre*

- All but those marked * are spelt with *-er* in Amer. English.

re- prefix

This prefix is followed by a hyphen:

1. Before another *e*, e.g. *re-echo, re-entry*.

2. So as to distinguish the compound so formed from the more familiar identically spelt word written solid, e.g.

re-cover (put new cover on): *recover*
re-form (form again): *reform*
re-sign (sign again): *resign*

silent final consonants

French words with silent final consonants give difficulty over plurals, possessives, and verbal inflections. See pp. 18 f, 10.

-s suffix

A. As the inflection of the plural of nouns: see **plural formation**.

B. As the inflection of the third person singular present indicative of verbs, it requires the insertion of *-e-*:

1. After sibilants (*ch*, *s*, *sh*, *x*, *z*), e.g. *catches*, *tosses*, *pushes*, *fixes*, *buzzes*; note that single *s* and *z* are subject to doubling of final consonant (see p. 10 f.), e.g. *nonplusses*, *quizzes*, *whizzes*.
2. After *y*, which may become *i* (see p. 22), e.g. *cries*, *copies*.
3. After *o*: *echo*, *go*, *torpedo*, *veto*, like the corresponding nouns, insert *-e-* before *-s*; *crescendo*, *radio*, *solo*, *zero* should have *-s* alone, but there is variation.

-xion or -ction

Complexion, *crucifixion*, *effluxion*, *fluxion* all have *-x-*; *connection*, *deflection*, *inflection*, *reflection* all have *-ct-*; both *genuflection* and *genuflexion* occur.

-y, -ey, or -ie nouns

The diminutive or pet form of nouns can be spelt *-y*, *-ey*, or *-ie*. Most nouns which end in the sound of *-y* are so spelt, e.g.

aunty *baby* *nappy*

The following are the main diminutives spelt with *-ey* (*-ey* nouns of other kinds are excluded from the list):

goosey	*matey*
housey-housey	*nursey*
Limey	*Sawney*
lovey-dovey	*slavey*

The following list contains the diminutives in *-ie*, and many similar nouns. Most Scottish diminutives are spelt with *-ie*, e.g. *corbie, kiltie*.

beanie	*goalie*
birdie	*junkie*
bookie	*Kewpie* (doll)
brownie	*laddie*
budgie	*lassie*
caddie (golf; *tea caddy*)	*mealie* (maize; *mealy* adjective)
chappie	*Mountie*
charlie	*movie*
clippie	*nightie*
cookie	*oldie*
coolie	*pinkie* (little finger)
dearie	*pixie*
doggie (noun; *doggy* adjective)	*quickie*
	rookie
genie (spirit; plural *genii*)	*sheltie*
	softie
Geordie	*Tin Lizzie*
gillie	*walkie-talkie*
girlie	*zombie*

Note: *bogie* (undercarriage), *bogey* (golf score, ghost).

-y or -ey adjectives

When *-y* is added to a word to form an adjective, the following changes in spelling occur:

1. Doubling of final consonant (see p. 10 f.).

2. Dropping of silent *-e* (see p. 10).

Exceptions:

(*a*) After *u*:

bluey	*gluey*
cliquey	*tissuey*

(*b*) Where the retention of *-e* helps to clarify the sense:

cagey	*dicey*	*pacey*
cakey	*dikey*	*pricey*
chocolatey	*matey*	*smiley*
cottagey	*orangey*	*villagey*

Note also *holey* (distinguished from *holy*); *phoney*.

3. Insertion of *-e-* when *-y* is also the final letter of the stem:

clayey	*sprayey*
skyey	*wheyey*

Also in *gooey*.

4. Adjectives ending in unstressed *-ey* (2 (*a*) and (*b*) and 3 above) change this *-ey* to *-i-* before the comparative and superlative suffixes *-er* and *-est* and the adverbial suffix *-ly*, e.g.

cagey: cagily	*gooey: gooier*
cliquey: cliquier	*matey: matily*
dicey: dicier	*pricey: pricier*

Before *-ness* there is variation, e.g.

cagey: cageyness, caginess	*wheyey: wheyiness*
matey: mateyness, matiness	

y or i

There is often uncertainty about whether *y* or *i* should be written in the following words:

Write *i* in:	Write *y* in:
cider	*dyke*
cipher	*gypsy*
Libya	*lyke-wake*
lich-gate	*lynch law*
linchpin	*pygmy*
sibyl (classical)	*style* (manner)
siphon	*stylus*
siren	*stymie*
stile (in fence)	*Sybil* (frequently as Christian name)
timpani (drums)	*syllabub*
tiro	*sylvan*
witch hazel	*syrup*
	tyke
	tympanum (ear-drum)
	tyre (of wheel)
	wych-elm

-yse or -yze

This verbal ending (e.g. in *analyse, paralyse*) should not be written with *z* (though *z* is normally used in such words in America).

y to *i*

A. Words that end in *-y* after a vowel retain the *-y* before certain suffixes.

So *enjoyable, conveyed, gayer, donkeys, buys, joyful, coyly*.

Exceptions: *daily, gaily,* and adjectives ending in unstressed *-ey* (see p. 21).

B. If the *-y* follows a consonant (or silent *u* after *g* or *q*), it changes to *-i-* before:

1. *-able*, e.g. *deniable*. (But *flyable*).
2. *-ed*, e.g. *carried*.
3. *-er, -est*, e.g. *carrier, driest*.

Exceptions: *fryer, shyer* (one that shies), *skyer* (in cricket). Both *flyer* and *flier* occur, as do *drier* (one that dries) and *dryer*.

4. *-es*, e.g. *ladies, carries*. (But see p. 18.)
5. *-ful* (adjectives), e.g. *beautiful*. (*Bellyful* is not an adjective.)
6. *-less* (adjectives), e.g. *merciless, remediless*.

Exceptions: some rare compounds, e.g. *countryless*.

7. *-ly* (adverbs), e.g. *drily, happily, plaguily*.

Exceptions: *shyly, slyly, spryly, wryly*.

8. *-ment* (nouns), e.g. *embodiment, merriment*.
9. *-ness* (nouns), e.g. *happiness, cliquiness*.

Exceptions: *dryness, flyness, shyness, slyness, spryness, wryness*; *busyness* (distinguished from *business*).

DIFFICULT AND CONFUSABLE SPELLINGS
(not covered earlier)

The list below contains words (i) which occasion difficulty in spelling; (ii) of which various spellings exist; or (iii) which need to be distinguished from other words spelt similarly. In each case the recommended form is given, and in some cases is followed by the mark □ and the rejected variant. Misspellings, and spellings which are essentially American, are preceded by the mark ●. Where the rejected variant is widely separated alphabetically from the recommended form, the former is preceded by the mark □ and followed by 'use' and the recommended form.

accommodation
adaptor
adviser
□ *aerie*: use *eyrie*
ait □ not *eyot*
align, alignment ● not *aline, alinement*
allege
alleluia □ not *alleluya*
almanac (*almanack* only in some titles)
aluminium ● Amer. *aluminum*
ambiance (term in art)
ambience surroundings
amok □ not *amuck*
ancillary ● not *ancilliary*
annex (verb)
annexe (noun)
any one (of a number)
anyone anybody
any time
any way any manner
anyway at all events
apophthegm ● Amer. *apothegm*
apostasy
archaeology
artefact □ not *artifact*
aubrietia □ not *aubretia*
aught anything □ not *ought*
autarchy despotism
autarky self-sufficiency
auxiliary
aye yes □ not *ay*
aye always
bail out obtain release □ not *bale out*
bale out from aircraft □ not *bail out*
balk (verb)
balmy like balm
barbecue ● not *barbeque*
barmy (informal) mad
baulk timber
behove ● Amer. *behoove*
bivouac (noun and verb)
bivouacked, bivouacking
blond (of man)
blonde (of woman)
born: *be born* (of child)

borne: carried or given birth to
brand-new
brier □ not *briar*
bur clinging seed □ not *burr*
burr rough edge, drill, rock, accent, etc. □ not *bur*
caftan □ not *kaftan*
calendar almanac
calender press
caliph
calligraphy
calliper □ not *caliper*
callous (adjective)
callus (noun)
camellia shrub
canvas (noun) cloth
canvas (verb) cover with canvas (past canvassed)
canvass (verb)
carcass □ not *carcase*
caviar □ not *caviare*
chameleon
chancellor
chaperon □ not *chaperone*
Charollais
cheque (bank)
chequer (noun) pattern (verb) variegate; ● Amer. *checker*
chilli pepper
chivvy, chivvied
choosy
chord (music; geometry)
chukker (polo)
clarinettist ● Amer. *clarinetist*
coco palm
cocoa chocolate
coconut
colander strainer
commit(ment)
committee
comparative
complement make complete
compliment praise
conjuror
connection
conscientious
consensus
cord string, flex, spinal or vocal *cord*, rib of cloth
cornelian □ not *carnelian*
corslet armour, underwear □ not *corselet*
cosy ● Amer. *cozy*
council assembly
councillor member of council
counsel advice, barrister
counsellor adviser
court martial (noun)
court-martial (verb)
crape black fabric
crêpe thin fabric; rubber; pancake
crevasse large fissure in ice
crevice small fissure
crosier □ not *crozier*
crumby covered in crumbs
crummy (informal) dirty, inferior
curb restrain, restraint
curtsy □ not *curtsey*
□ *czar*: use *tsar*
dare say ● not *daresay*
debonair
descendant
desiccated
□ *despatch*: use *dispatch*
devest (only Law: general use *divest*)
dinghy boat
dingy grimy
disc ● Amer. *disk*
discreet judicious
discrete separate
disk (in computing)
dispatch □ not *despatch*
dissect
dissociate □ not *disassociate*
disyllable
doily □ not *doyley*
douse quench □ not *dowse*
dowse use divining rod
draft military party, money order, sketch
draftsman (documents)
draught act of drawing, act of drinking, vessel's depth, current of air ● Amer. *draft*
draughtsman one who draws plans; piece in game of draughts
ecology
ecstasy
ecumenical
educationist □ not *educationalist*
□ *eikon*: use *icon*
elegiac ● not *elegaic*
embarrassment
embed □ not *imbed*
employee (masculine and feminine; no accent)
enclose
enclosure (but *Inclosure Acts*)
encyclopedia □ not *encyclopaedia*
envelop (verb)

envelope (noun)
erupt break out
espresso □ not *expresso*
ethereal □ not *etherial*
everlasting
every one (of a number)
everyone everybody
exalt raise, praise
expatriate ● not *expatriot*
exult rejoice
□ *eyot*: use *ait*
eyrie □ not *aerie*
faecal
faeces
fascia □ not *facia*
fee'd (*a fee'd lawyer*) □ not *feed*
feldspar □ not *felspar*
ferrule cap on stick
ferule cane
fetid □ not *foetid*
florescence flowering
flotation □ not *floatation*
flu □ not *'flu*
fluorescence light radiation
foetal, foetus □ Amer. and medicine, *fetal, fetus*
fogy □ not *fogey*
forbade □ not *forbad*
forestall
for ever for always
forever continually
forty
fount (typeface) ● Amer. *font*
furore ● Amer. *furor*
fusilier
fusillade
gaol (official use) □ Amer. *jail* (both forms used in Brit. English)
gaoler (as for *gaol*)
gauge measure
gazump ● not *gazoomph*, etc.
gibe jeer □ not *jibe*
gild make gold
□ *gild* association: use *guild*
glycerine
gormandize eat greedily
gormless
gourmand glutton
gram □ not *gramme*
grandad
granddaughter
grayling (fish, butterfly)
grey ● Amer. *gray*
griffin fabulous creature □ not *gryphon*
griffon vulture, dog
grisly terrible
grizzly grey-haired; bear
groin (anatomy; architecture)
groyne breakwater
guerrilla
guild association
gybe (nautical) ● Amer. *jibe*
haemo- (prefix = 'blood')
haemorrhage
haemorrhoids
hallelujah
harass
hark
harum-scarum
hearken
hiccup □ not *hiccough*
Hindu
homoeopathy
homogeneous all the same
homogenous having common descent
honorific
□ *hooping cough*: use *whooping cough*
horsy □ not *horsey*
hummus chick-pea spread
humous of humus
humus rich soil
hurrah, hurray ● not *hoorah, hooray*
hypocrisy
hypocrite
icon
idiosyncrasy
idyll
ignoramus plural *ignoramuses*
□ *imbed*: use *embed*
impostor
inadvisable
□ *inclose, inclosure*: use *en-*
inoculate
input, inputting
in so far
insomuch
inure
investor
irrupt enter violently
its of it
it's it is, it has
jail (see *gaol*)
jailor (see *gaol*)
jam pack tightly; conserve
jamb door-post
□ *jibe*: use *gibe, gybe*
● Amer. also = accord with
□ *kaftan*: use *caftan*

kerb pavement ● Amer. *curb*
ketchup
□ *khalif*: use *caliph*
kilogram
kilometre
Koran □ not *Qur'an*
labyrinth
lachrymal of tears
lachrymose tearful
lacquer
lacrimal (in science)
lacrimate, -ation, -atory (in science)
ledger account book
leger line (in music)
liaison
licence (noun)
license (verb)
licensee
□ *licorice*: use *liquorice*
lightening making light
lightning (with thunder)
linage number of lines
lineage ancestry
lineament feature
liniment embrocation
liqueur flavoured alcoholic liquor
liquor
liquorice □ not *licorice*
□ *litchi*: use *lychee*
literature
littérateur
littoral
loath(some) (adjectives)
loathe (verb)
lodestar
lodestone □ not *loadstone*
longevity
longitude ● not *longtitude*
lour frown □ not *lower*
lychee □ not *litchi*
Mac (prefix) spelling depends on the custom of the one bearing the name; in alphabetical arrangement, treat as Mac however spelt
mac (informal) mackintosh
mackintosh □ not *macintosh*
maharaja
maharanee
□ *Mahomet*: use *Muhammad*
mandolin
manikin dwarf, anatomical model
manila hemp, paper
manilla African bracelet
mannequin (live) model
manoeuvrable ● Amer. *maneuverable*
mantel(piece)
mantle cloak
marijuana □ not *marihuana*
marquis
marshal (noun and verb)
marten weasel
martial of war (*martial law*)
martin bird
matins □ not *mattins*
matt lustreless □ not *mat*
medieval ● not *mediaeval*
mendacity lying
mendicity being a beggar
millenary thousandth anniversary
millennium thousand years
milli- (prefix = one-thousandth)
millipede □ not *millepede*
milometer ● not *mileometer*
miniature
minuscule ● not *miniscule*
missis (slang) □ not *missus*
misspell
mistle thrush □ not *missel*
mizen (nautical)
mnemonic
moneyed
moneys □ not *monies*
mongoose (plural *mongooses*)
moustache ● Amer. *mustache*
mouth (verb) ● not *mouthe*
mucous (adjective)
mucus (noun)
Muhammad
Muslim ● not *Moslem*
naive, naivety □ not *naïve, naïvety, naïveté*
naught nothing
negligée □ not *negligee, négligé*
negligible
nerve-racking ● not *-wracking*
net not subject to deduction □ not *nett*
nonplussed
nonsuch unrivalled person or thing □ not *nonesuch*
no one nobody
nought the figure zero
numskull □ not *numbskull*
O used to form a vocative (*O Caesar*)
occurrence
● *of*: not to be written instead of *have* in, e.g., *'Did you go?' 'I would have, if it hadn't rained.'*
omelette □ not *omelet*

on to ● not *onto*
orangeade
orang-utan □ not *orang-outang*
outcast person cast out
outcaste casteless Hindu
oyez! □ not *oyes!*
paediatric
palaeo- (prefix = ancient)
palate roof of mouth
palette artist's board
pallet mattress, machine part, platform for loads
panda animal
pander pimp; to gratify
panellist ● Amer. *panelist*
paraffin
parallel, paralleled, paralleling
partisan □ not *partizan*
pastel (crayon)
pastille
pawpaw (fruit) □ not *papaw*
pedal (use) foot lever
peddle sell as pedlar
pederast
pedigreed
pedlar vendor of small wares ● Amer. *peddler*
Pekingese dog, inhabitant of Peking □ not *Pekinese*
peninsula (noun)
peninsular (adjective)
pennant (nautical) piece of rigging, flag
pennon (military) long narrow flag
peony
phone (informal) telephone □ not *'phone*
pi pious
pidgin simplified language
pie jumbled type
pigeon bird; *not one's pigeon* not one's affair
piggyback □ not *pickaback*
pilau □ not *pilaff, pilaw*
pimento aromatic spice
pimiento sweet pepper
plane (informal) aeroplane □ not *'plane*
plebeian
plenitude ● not *plentitude*
plimsoll □ not *plimsole*
plough ● Amer. *plow*
pommel knob, saddle-bow
pore (*over* e.g. a map)
practice (noun)
practise (verb)
precede come before
précised
predominant(ly) ● not *predominate(ly)*
premise say as introduction
premises foregoing matters, building
premiss (in logic) proposition
principal chief
principle truth, moral basis
prise force open
privilege
Privy Council
Privy Counsellor
proceed go on, continue
program (in computing) ● Amer. in all senses
programme (general use)
promoter
pukka
pummel pound with fists
pupillage □ not *pupilage*
putt (in golf)
pyjamas ● Amer. *pajamas*
quadraphony, quadraphonic □ not quadro- ● not *quadri-*
quatercentenary ● not *quarter-*
questionnaire
□ *Qur'an*: use *Koran*
rabbet groove in woodwork (also *rebate*)
racket (for ball games) □ not *racquet*
rackets game
racoon □ not *raccoon*
radical (chemistry)
radicle (botany)
raja □ not *rajah*
rarity
raze □ not *rase*
recompense
Renaissance ● not *Renascence*
renege □ not *renegue*
repairable (of material)
reparable (of loss)
restaurateur
reverend (deserving reverence; title of clergy)
reverent (showing reverence)
review survey, report
revue musical entertainment
rhyme ● not *rime*
riband (sport, heraldry)
ribbon
rigor (medical) shivering-fit
rigour severity ● Amer. *rigor*
rill stream
rille (on moon)

rime frost
role □ not *rôle*
Romania
rule the roost □ not *roast*
rumba □ not *rhumba*
saccharin (noun)
saccharine (adjective)
salutary beneficial
salutatory welcoming
sanatorium ● Amer. *sanitarium*
satire literary work
satiric(al) of satire
satyr woodland deity
satyric of satyrs
scallop □ not *scollop*
scallywag ● Amer. *scalawag*
sceptic ● Amer. *skeptic*
scrimmage tussle ● also term in Amer. football
scrummage (Rugby)
sear to scorch, wither(ed)
secrecy
selvage
separate
sere of gunlock; in ecology
sergeant (military, police)
serjeant (law)
sestet (in a sonnet)
□ *sett* (noun): use *set*
sextet (in music, etc.)
Shakespearian □ not *Shakespearean*
shanty hut, song
sharif Muslim leader □ not *sherif*
sheath (noun)
sheathe (verb)
sheikh
□ *sherif*: use *sharif*
sheriff county officer
Shia (branch of Islam)
show ● not *shew*
sibylline
Sinhalese □ not *Singhalese*
smart alec □ not *aleck*
smooth (adjective and verb) ● not *smoothe*
sobriquet □ not *soubriquet*
solemness
some time (come and see me some time)
sometime former, formerly
spinal cord □ not *chord*
spirituel having refinement of mind
sprightly ● not *spritely*
spurt □ not *spirt*
squirearchy □ not *squirarchy*
stanch (verb) stop a flow □ not *staunch*
State (capital S for the political unit)
stationary at rest
stationery paper, etc.
staunch loyal □ not *stanch*
step-parent
stoep (South Africa) veranda
storey division of building ● Amer. *story*
storeyed having storeys
storied celebrated in story
stoup for holy water, etc. □ not *stoop*
straight without curve
strait narrow
strait-jacket
sty for pigs; on eyelid ● not *stye*
subtlety
subtly ● not *subtlely*
sulphur ● Amer. *sulfur*
summons command to appear (plural summonses)
summons (verb inflected *summonsed*)
supersede ● not *supercede*
swap □ not *swop*
swat hit sharply
swot study hard
sycamore (member of maple genus)
synthesist, synthesize ● not *synthet-*
teasel (plant)
tee-hee (laugh)
teetotalism
teetotaller ● Amer. *teetotaler*
tell (archaeology)
template □ not *templet*
tenet principle
thank you ● not *thankyou*
thank-you (noun), *thank-you letter*
threshold
tic contraction of muscles
tick-tack semaphore □ not *tic-tac*
titbit ● Amer. *tidbit*
titillate excite
titivate □ not *tittivate*
today
tomorrow
tonight
tonsillar, tonsillitis
toupee
Trades Union Congress
trade union □ not *trades union*
traipse trudge □ not *trapes*
tranquillity, tranquillize
transferable
transonic □ not *transsonic*
transsexual □ not *transexual*
transship(ment) □ not *tranship(ment)*

trolley
troop (soldiers)
trooper member of troop
troupe (performers)
trouper member of troupe
tsar □ not *czar*
T-shirt
Turco- (combining form of Turkish)
tympanum ear-drum
tyre ● Amer. *tire*
'un (informal for *one*)
under way ● not *under weigh* or *underway*
valance curtain, drapery
valence (in chemistry)
veld □ not *veldt*
vendor
veranda □ not *verandah*
vermilion
vice tool ● Amer. *vise*
villain evil-doer
villein serf
visor □ not *vizor*
vocal cord □ not *chord*
wagon □ not *waggon*
waiver forgoing of right
wastable
waver be unsteady
weird
whiskey (Irish, Amer.)
whisky (Scotch)
Whit Monday, Sunday
whiz □ not *whizz*
whooping cough
who's who is, who has
whose of whom
wisteria □ not *wistaria*
withhold
woebegone
woeful ● not *woful*
wrath anger
wreath (noun)
wreathe (verb)
wroth angry
yoghurt □ not *yogurt*

Pronunciation

This section is in two parts: A, general points of pronunciation, and B, a list of preferred pronunciations.

The recommending of any one pronunciation naturally implies the existence of a standard. There are many varieties of spoken English, but the treatment here is based upon British Received Pronunciation (RP), the neutral national standard used in broadcasting and taught to foreigners.

A. GENERAL POINTS OF PRONUNCIATION

It is impossible to lay down hard and fast rules here, since pronunciation is continually changing, and at any time there is bound to be considerable variation. Uncertainty about pronunciation also arises from the irregularity of English spelling.

The entries are arranged in alphabetical order of individual letters, or sequences of letters, that repeatedly cause difficulty. There are also three other kinds of entry, which deal with (*a*) American pronunciation, (*b*) the reduction of common words in rapid speech, and (*c*) patterns of stress.

a

1. There is variation in the pronunciation of *a* between the sound heard in *calm*, *father* and that heard in *cat*, *fan*, in

(*a*) the suffix *-graph* (in *photograph*, *telegraph*, etc.), where the sound of *calm* is preferred except where *-ic* is added (e.g. in *photographic*) where only the *a* of *cat* is used.

(*b*) the prefix *trans-* (as in *transfer*, *translate*, etc.), where either kind of *a* is acceptable.

2. The word endings *-ada*, *-ade*, and *-ado* occasion difficulty.

(*a*) In *-ada* words, *a* is as in *calm*, e.g. *armada*, *cicada*.

(*b*) In most *-ade* words, *a* is as in *made*, e.g. *barricade*.
Exceptions: *a* as in *calm* in

aubade *façade* *promenade*
ballade *gambade* *roulade*
charade *pomade* *saccade*

and in loan-words from French, e.g. *oeillade*.

(*c*) In most *-ado* words, *a* is as in *calm*, e.g. *bravado*.
Exceptions: *a* as in *made* in *bastinado*, *tornado*.

3. *a* in *-alia* is like *a* in *alien*, e.g. in *marginalia*.

4. *a* before *ls* and *lt* in many words is pronounced either like *aw* in *bawl* or *o* in *doll*, e.g. in

alter *palsy* *waltz*

The same variation occurs with *au* in *assault*, *fault*, *somersault*, *vault*.

Note: in several words *a* before *ls* and *lt* can only be pronounced like *a* in *sally*, e.g.

Alsatian *contralto* *peristalsis*
alto *Malthusian* *saltation*

5. The *a* in *-ata*, *-atum*, and *-atus* is usually pronounced as in *mate*, e.g. in *apparatus*. Exceptions: *cantata*, *cassata*, *chipolata*, *desideratum* (plural *desiderata*), *erratum* (plural *errata*), *serenata*, *sonata*, *toccata* with *a* as in *calm*; *stratum*, *stratus* with the *a* of *mate* or *calm*.

-age

The standard pronunciation of the following words of French origin ending in *-age* is with stress on the first syllable, *a* as in *calm*, and *g* as in *regime*.

arbitrage *dressage* *mirage*
barrage *fuselage* *persiflage*
camouflage *garage* *sabotage*
collage *massage*

Note that *montage* is stressed on the second syllable.

● The pronunciation of *-age* as in *cabbage* is non-standard in all of these words except for *arbitrage*. Amer. pronunciation stresses the final syllable in some of them.

□ It is acceptable to use the sound of *g* as in *large* in several of these, particularly *garage*.

American pronunciation

Where the American pronunciation of individual forms and words significantly differs from the British, this is indicated as part of the individual entries in this Section. Among the many constant features of 'General American'* pronunciation, such as the pronunciation of *r* wherever it occurs in the spelling (see ***r***, p. 34), perhaps the most relevant here is a matter of stress. In words of four syllables and over, in which the main stress falls on the first or second syllable, there is a strong secondary stress on the last syllable but one, the vowel of which is fully enunciated, e.g. *cóntemplàtive, térritòry*.

-arily

In a few five-syllable adverbs ending with *-arily*, there is a tendency to stress the *a* for ease of pronunciation. Some in common use are:

arbitrarily	*ordinarily*
momentarily	*temporarily*
necessarily	*voluntarily*

Rapid colloquial speech, probably under the influence of Amer. English (see **American pronunciation**, above), has adopted a pronunciation with the *a* sounding like *e* in *verily*, which it would be pedantic to censure.

The case of the word *primarily* is different. It contains only four syllables, which can be reduced to the easily pronounced spoken form prim'rily.

● There is therefore no need to pronounce the word with stress on the second syllable. Pronunciations like pri-*merr*-ily or pri-*marr*-ily are not acceptable in careful speech.

* 'A form of U.S. speech without marked dialectal or regional characteristics' (*OED*).

-ed

1. In the following adjectives the ending *-ed* is pronounced as a separate syllable:

accursed	*naked*	*wicked*
cragged	*rugged*	*wretched*
deuced	*sacred*	

Note: *accursed* and *deuced* can also be pronounced as one syllable.

2. The following words have different meanings according to whether *-ed* is pronounced as a separate syllable or not. In most cases the former pronunciation indicates an adjective (as with the list under 1 above), the latter part of a verb.

	(*a*) *-ed* as separate syllable	(*b*) *-ed* pronounced *'d*
aged	= very old (*he is very aged, an aged man*)	= having the age of (one etc.) (*a boy aged three*); past of *to age* (*he has aged greatly*)
beloved	used before noun (*beloved brethren*); = beloved person (*my beloved is mine*)	used as predicate (*he was beloved by all*)
blessed	= fortunate, holy, sacred (*blessed are the meek, the blessed saints*)	part of *to bless*; sometimes also in senses listed in left-hand column
crabbed	= cross-grained, hard to follow, etc.	past of *to crab*
crooked	= not straight, dishonest	= having transverse handle (*crooked stick*); past of *to crook*

cursed		
	before noun = damnable	past of *to curse*
dogged		
	= tenacious	past of *to dog*
jagged		
	= indented	past of *to jag*
learned		
	= erudite	past of *to learn* (usually *learnt*)
ragged		
	= rough, torn, etc.	past of *to rag*

-edly, -edness

When the further suffixes *-ly* and *-ness* are added to adjectives ending in *-ed*, an uncertainty arises about whether to pronounce this *-ed-* as a separate syllable. Such can be divided into three kinds.

1. Those in which *-ed* is already a separate syllable (*a*) because it is preceded by *d* or *t* or (*b*) because the adjective is one of those discussed in the entry for ***-ed*** above; e.g. *belated*, *wicked*. When either *-ly* or *-ness* are added, *-ed-* remains a separate syllable, e.g. (i) *belatedly*, *wickedly*; (ii) *belatedness*, *wickedness*.

2. Those in which the syllable preceding *-ed* is unstressed, i.e. if *-(e)d* is removed the word ends in an unstressed syllable, e.g. *embarrassed*, *self-centred*. When either *-ly* or *-ness* are added, *-ed-* remains non-syllabic (i.e. it sounds like 'd), e.g.

(i) *abandonedly* *embarrassedly* *self-centredly* *variedly*

(ii) *self-centredness* (= -center'dness) *studiedness*

3. Those in which the syllable preceding *-ed* is stressed, i.e. if *-(e)d* is removed the word ends in a stressed syllable, or is a monosyllable, e.g. *assured*, *fixed*.

● (i) When *-ly* is added *-ed* becomes an extra syllable, e.g.

advisedly *allegedly* *assuredly* *deservedly* *fixedly* *markedly* professedly *unfeignedly*

Exceptions:

There are a few exceptions to this rule, e.g. *subduedly*, *tiredly* (*-ed* is not a separate syllable). Some words show variation, e.g. *depressedly*, *shamefacedly*.

● Note that some adverbs formed on adjectives in *-ed* sound awkward whether *-ed-* is pronounced as a separate syllable or not. Because of this, some authorities discourage the formation of words like *boredly*, *discouragedly*.

(ii) When *-ness* is added, there is greater variation. In *COD -ed-* is an extra syllable in only the following:

concernedness *deservedness* *fixedness* *markedness* *mixedness* *preparedness* *unashamedness*

while *informedness* has this pronunciation as an alternative.

Many other words are not specially marked, and it has probably become increasingly rare for *-ed-* to be separately sounded.

□ It is acceptable *not* to make *-ed-* a separate syllable in words of this type.

-ein(e)

The ending *-ein*(*e*) (originally two syllables) is now usually pronounced like *-ene* in *polythene* in

caffeine *codeine* *casein* *protein*

Note: *casein* can also be pronounced with *-ein* disyllabic.

-eity

The traditional pronunciation of *e* in this termination is as in *me*, e.g. in

contemporaneity *homogeneity* *deity* *simultaneity* *heterogeneity* *spontaneity*

There is increasingly a tendency to substitute the sound of *e* in *café*, *suede*, although some speakers pronounce the first two syllables of *deity* like *deer*, and so with the other words. The same variation is found in the sequence *-ei-* in the words *deism, deist, reify, reification* (but not *theism, theist*).

-eur

This termination, occurring in words originally taken from French, in which it is the agent suffix, normally carries the stress and sounds like *er* in *deter, refer*, e.g. in:

agent provocateur	*masseur*
coiffeur	*raconteur*
connoisseur (con-a-*ser*)	*restaurateur*
	saboteur
entrepreneur	*secateurs*

Stress is on the first syllable usually in

amateur (and *amateurish*: *am*-a-ter-ish)
chauffeur

Stress can also be on the second syllable in *chauffeur*.

Feminine nouns can be formed from some of these by the substitution of *-se* for *-r*: the resulting termination is pronounced like *urze* in *furze*, e.g. *coiffeuse, masseuse, saboteuse*.

liqueur is pronounced li-*cure* (Amer. li-*cur*).

g

A. In certain less familiar words there is often uncertainty as to whether *g* preceding *e, i*, and (especially) *y* is pronounced hard as in *get* or soft as in *gem*.

1. The prefix *gyn(o)-* meaning 'woman' now always has a hard *g*, as in *gynaecology, gynoecium*.

2. The element *-gyn-* with the same meaning, occurring inside the word, usually has a soft *g*, as in *androgynous, misogynist*.

3. The elements *gyr-* (from a root meaning 'ring') and *-gitis* (in names of diseases) always have a soft *g*, as in

gyrate	*gyro (-scope, -compass*, etc.)
gyre (poetic, = gyrate, gyration)	*laryngitis*

4. The following, among many other words, have a hard *g*:

gibbous	*gill* (fish's organ)
gig (all senses)	*gingham*

● *g* should be hard in *analogous*.

5. The following have a soft *g*:

gibber	*gypsophila*
gibe	*gypsum*
gill (measure)	*gyrfalcon*
gillyflower	*longevity*
giro (payment system)	*panegyric*
gybe	

6. The following can vary, but usually have a hard *g*:

demagogic, -y *pedagogic, -y*

7. The following can vary, but usually have a soft *g*:

gibberish *hegemony*

B. See ***-age***, p. 29.

-gm

g is silent in the sequence *gm* at the end of the word:

diaphragm *phlegm*

But the *g* is pronounced between vowels:

enigma *phlegmatic*

h

1. Initial *h* is silent in *heir, honest, honour, hour*, and their derivatives; also in *honorarium*. It is sounded in *habitué*.
2. Initial *h* used commonly to be silent if the first syllable was unstressed, as in *habitual, hereditary, historic, hotel*. This pronunciation is now old-fashioned. (See also ***a* or *an***, p. 8.)

-ies

The ending *-ies* is usually pronounced as one syllable (like *ies* in *diesel*) in:

caries	*rabies*
congeries	*scabies*
facies	

● The reduction of this ending to a sound like the ending of *armies, babies*, etc., should be avoided in careful speech.

Exceptions: *series* and *species* can have either pronunciation.

-ile

The ending *-ile* is normally pronounced like *isle*, e.g. in

docile *missile* *sterile*

● The usual Amer. pronunciation in most words of this kind is with the sound of *il* in *daffodil* or *pencil*.

The pronunciation is like *eel* in:

automobile *-mobile* (suffix)
imbecile

-ile forms two syllables in *campanile* (rhyming with *Ely*), *cantabile* (pronounced can-*tah*-bi-ly), and *sal volatile* (rhyming with *philately*).

ng

There is a distinction between *ng* representing a single sound and *ng* representing a compound consisting of this sound followed by the sound of hard *g*.

1. The single sound is the only one to occur at the end of a word, e.g. in *song*, *writing*.

2. The single sound also occurs in the middle of words, but usually in compounds of a word ending in *-ng* + a suffix, e.g.

bringing *kingly* *stringy*
hanged *longish* *wrongful*

3. The compound sound, *ng* + *g*, is otherwise normal in the middle of words, e.g. in *hungry*, *language*, and also, as an exception to rule 2, in *longer*, *-est*, *prolongation*, *stronger*, *-est*, *younger*, *-est*.

● 4. It is non-standard:

(*a*) To pronounce *bringing*, *writing*, etc. as bringin, writin.
(*b*) To use *n* for *ng* in *length*, *strength*. (The pronunciation lenkth, strenkth is acceptable.)
(*c*) To use *nk* for *ng* in *anything*, *everything*, *nothing*, *something*.
(*d*) To use *ng* + *g* in all cases of *ng*, i.e. in words covered by rules 1 and 2 as well as 3. This pronunciation is, however, normal in certain regional forms of English.

o

1. In many words the *u*-sound as in *butter* is spelt with *o*, e.g. *come*. There is an increasing tendency to pronounce a few such words with the sound of *o* in *body*.

(*a*) More usually with the *u*-sound:

accomplice *constable* *mongrel*
accomplish *frontier*

(*b*) More usually with the *o*-sound:

combat *dromedary* *pomegranate*
comrade *hovel* *pommel* (noun)
conduit *hover* *sojourn*

2. Before *ff*, *ft*, *ss*, *st*, and *th*, in certain words, there was formerly a variety of RP in which *o* was pronounced like *aw* in *law*, so that *off*, *often*, etc. sounded like *orf*, *orphan*, etc.

● This pronunciation is now non-standard.

3. Before double *ll*, *o* has the long sound (as in *pole*) in some words, and the short sound (as in *Polly*) in others.

(*a*) With the long sound:

boll *roll* *toll*
droll *scroll* *troll*
knoll *stroll* *wholly*
poll (vote, head) *swollen*

(*b*) With the short sound:
doll, *loll*, *moll*, *poll* (parrot), and most words in which another syllable follows, e.g. *collar*, *holly*, *pollen*, etc.

4. Before *lt*, *o* is pronounced long, e.g. *bolt*, *revolt*.

● The substitution of short *o* in these words is non-standard.

5. Before *lv*, *o* is pronounced short, e.g.

absolve *involve* *revolver*
dissolve *resolve* *solve*

● The substitution of long *o* in these words is non-standard.

ough

Although most words with *ough* are familiar, difficulties may arise with the following:

brougham	(a kind of carriage) *broo*-am or broom
chough	(bird) chuff
clough	(ravine) cluff
hough	(animal's joint), same as, and sounds like, *hock*
slough	(swamp) rhymes with *plough*
slough	(snake's skin) sluff
sough	(sound) rhymes with *plough* (also *tough*)

phth

This sequence should sound like *fth* (in *fifth, twelfth*), e.g. in *diphtheria, diphthong, monophthong, naphtha, ophthalmic.*

● It is non-standard to pronounce these as if written *dip-theria* etc.

Initially, as in the words *phthisical, phthisis,* the *ph* can be silent; it is also usually silent in *apophthegm.*

pn-, ps-, pt-

In these sequences at the beginning of words, it is normal not to pronounce the *p-*. The exception is *psi* representing the name of a Greek letter, used, e.g., as a symbol.

r

1. When *r* is the last letter of a word or precedes 'silent' final *e,* it is normally silent in RP, e.g. in *four, here, runner.*

But when another word, beginning with a vowel sound, follows in the same sentence, it is normal to pronounce the final *r,* e.g. in *four hours, here it is, runner-up.*

This is called the 'linking *r*'.

● It is standard to use linking *r* and unnatural to try to avoid it.

2. A closely connected feature of the spoken language is what is called 'intrusive *r*'. This occurs when an *r*-sound is introduced where there is no letter *r* in the spelling:

(*a*) after a word such as *villa,* ending with the obscure *a*-sound:

*a villa-*r *in Italy*

Here it is acceptable in rapid, informal speech.

(*b*) after the sounds of *ah* and *aw,* and the *eu* of *milieu,* both between words and before endings:

*The Shah-*r *of Iran*	a milieu-r in which . . .
*law-*r *and order*	draw-r-*ing room*

● The use of intrusive *r* here is very widely unacceptable. Indeed, it should not be used anywhere in formal speech.

3. There is a tendency in certain words to drop *r* if it is closely followed (or in a few cases, preceded) by another *r* at the beginning of an unstressed syllable, e.g. in

deteriorate pronounced deteriate
February pronounced Febuary
honorary pronounced honary (prefer hon'rary)
itinerary pronounced itinery
library pronounced lib'ry
secretary pronounced seketry or seketerry
temporary pronounced tempary (prefer temp'rary)

● This should be avoided, especially in formal speech.

reduced forms

In rapid speech, many shorter grammatical words, being lightly stressed, tend to be reduced either by the obscuring of their vowels or the loss of a consonant or both. They may even be attached to one another or to more prominent words. Similarly, some such words are in rapid speech omitted altogether, while longer but common words are shortened by the elision of unstressed syllables. Typical examples are:

gonna, wanna	= going to, want to
kinda, sorta	= kind of, sort of
gimme, lemme	= give me, let me
'snot	= it's not
innit, wannit	= isn't it, wasn't it
doncher, dunno	= don't you, I don't know

what's he say, where d'you find it, we done it, what you want it for?

'spect or *I'xpect* = I expect
(I) spose = I suppose
cos, course, on'y, praps, probly = because, of course, only, perhaps, probably

• Most of these reduced forms (with the possible exception of *innit, wannit*) are natural in informal RP, but should be avoided in formal contexts.

s, sh, z, and *zh*

In certain kinds of word, where the spelling is *ci, si,* or *ti,* or where it is *s* before long *u*, there is variation between two or more of the four sounds which may be represented as:

s as in *sun*
sh as in *ship*
z as in *zone*
zh representing the sound of *s* in *leisure* or *g* in *regime*

1. There is variation between *s* and *sh* in words such as:

appreciate *negotiate*
associate *omniscient*
glacial *sociology*

This variation does not occur in all words with a similar structure: only *s* is used in *glaciation, pronunciation* (= -see-*ay*-shon), and only *sh* in *partiality* (par-shee-*al*-ity). Only *sh* occurs in *initial, racial, sociable, spatial, special,* etc.

2. There is variation between *s* and *sh* in *sensual, sexual, issue, tissue,* and between *z* and *zh* in *casual, casuist, visual.*

3. There is variation between *sh* and *zh* in *aversion, equation, immersion, version.*

□ Either variant is acceptable in each of these kinds of word, although in all of them *sh* is the traditional pronunciation.

4. In the names of some countries and regions ending in *-sia,* and in the adjectives derived from them, there is variation between *sh* and *zh,* and in some cases *z(i)* and *s(i)* as well. So:

Asian = *A*-shan or *A*-zhan
Asiatic = A-shi-*at*-ic or A-zhi-*at*-ic or A-zi-*at*-ic or A-si-*at*-ic
Australasian = Austral-*a*-zhan or -shan
Indonesian = Indo-*nee*-shan or -zhan or -zi-an or -si-an
Persian = *Per*-shan or *Per*-zhan

• The pronunciation with *sh* is the most widely acceptable. The pronunciation with *zh* is also generally acceptable.

5. There is variation between *zh* and *z(i)* in *artesian (well), Cartesian, Caucasian,* and *Friesian.*

□ Either variant is acceptable.

stress

1. The position of the stress accent is the key to the pronunciation of many English polysyllabic words, since unstressed vowels are subject to reduction in length, obscuration of quality, and, quite often, complete elision. Compare the sound of the stressed vowel in the words on the left with that of the same vowel, unstressed, in the words on the right:

a:	humánity	húman
	monárchic	mónarch
	practicálity	práctically (-ic'ly)
	secretárial	sécretary (-t'ry)
e:	presént (verb)	présent (noun)
	protést	protestátion
	mystérious	mýstery (= myst'ry)
i:	satírical	sátirist
	combíne	combinátion
	anxíety	ánxious (= anksh'ous)
o:	ecónomy	ecónomic
	oppóse	ópposite
	históric	hístory (= hist'ry)
u:	luxúrious	lúxury
	indústrial	índustry

Many of the most hotly disputed questions of pronunciation centre on the placing of the stress.

2. It is impossible to formulate rules accounting for the position of the stress in every English word, but two very general observations can be made.

(*a*) Although the stress can fall on any syllable, more than three unstressed syllables cannot easily be uttered in sequence. Hence, for example, five-syllable words with stress on the first or last syllable are rare. Very often in polysyllabic words at least one syllable bears a secondary stress, e.g. *cáterpìllar, còntrovèrtibílity*.

(*b*) Some patterns of stress are clearly associated with spelling or with grammatical function (or, especially, with variation of grammatical function in a single word). For example, almost all words ending in *-ic* and *-ical* are stressed on the syllable immediately preceding the suffix. There is only a handful of exceptions: *Arabic, arithmetic* (noun), *arsenic, catholic, choleric, heretic, lunatic, politic(s), rhetoric.*

Some general tendencies will now be described, and related to the existing canons of acceptability.

3. *Two-syllable words*

There is a fixed, although not invariable, pattern, by which nouns and adjectives are stressed on the first syllable, and verbs on the second, e.g.

accent *import* *torment*
conflict *present* *transfer*
fragment *suspect*

nouns: *climate* verbs: *create*
mandate *dictate*

This pattern has recently exercised an influence over several other words not originally conforming to it. The words

ally *defect* *rampage*
combine *intern*

were all originally stressed on the second syllable; but as nouns, they are all usually stressed on the first. Exactly the same tendency has affected

dispute *research*
recess *romance*

but in these words, the stressing of the noun on the first syllable is rejected in good usage. The following nouns and adjectives (not corresponding to identically spelt verbs) show the same transference of stress: *adept, adult, chagrin, supine.*

In the verbs *combat, contact, harass,* and *traverse,* a tendency towards stress on the second syllable is discernible, but the new stress has been fully accepted only in the word *traverse.*

4. *Three-syllable words*

Of the three possible stress patterns in three-syllable words, that with stress on the first syllable is the best established.

(*a*) Words with stress on the final syllable are rare. In some, a stress on the first syllable is acceptable in RP, e.g. artisan, *commandant, confidant, partisan, promenade*; in others it is not, e.g. *cigarette, magazine.*

(*b*) Many words originally having stress on the second syllable now commonly have stress on the first, e.g.

abdomen *obdurate* *remonstrate*
albumen *precedent* (noun) *secretive*
composite *subsidence*

In some other words the pronunciation with stress on the first syllable has not been accepted as standard, e.g. in

Byzantine *contribute*
clandestine *distribute*

(*c*) There is a tendency in a few words to move the stress from the first to the second syllable. It is generally resisted in standard usage, e.g. in

combatant *exquisite* *stigmata*
deficit *patina*

all of which have stress on the first syllable. But it has prevailed in *aggrandize, chastisement, conversant, doctrinal, environs, pariah, urinal.*

5. *Four-syllable words*

Broadly speaking, it has been traditional in RP to favour stress on the first syllable of these, so that the shift to the second syllable has been strongly resisted in:

applicable *demonstrable*
aristocrat *illustrative*
capitalist *intricacy*
contumacy *lamentable*

With the words *controversy*, *formidable*, and *kilometre* in particular, a pronunciation with stress on the second syllable arouses strong disapproval on the part of many people.

In many words one of the two middle unstressed syllables is elided:

adversary	*participle*
comparable	*preferable*
migratory	*primarily*
momentary	*promissory*
necessary	*voluntary*

However, many words have been, or are being, adapted to the antepenultimate stress pattern, e.g.

centenary	*miscellany*
despicable	*nomenclature*
explicable	*pejorative*
hospitable	*peremptory*
metallurgy	*transferable*

Because antepenultimate stress has been accepted in most of these words, it is difficult to reject it elsewhere. Analogy is the obvious argument in some cases, i.e. the analogy of *capital*, *demonstrate*, *illustrate*, *intricate*, etc. for the words related to them, but this cannot be used everywhere.

6. *Five-syllable words*
Five-syllable words originally stressed on the first syllable have been affected by the difficulty of uttering more than three unstressed syllables in sequence (see 2(*a*) above). The stress has been shifted to the second syllable in *laboratory*, *obligatory*, whereas in *veterinary* the fourth syllable is elided, and usually the second as well. For *arbitrarily*, *momentarily*, etc., see ***-arily***, p. 30.

t

1. In rapid speech, *t* is often dropped from the sequence *cts*, so that *acts*, *ducts*, *pacts* sound like *axe*, *ducks*, *packs*.

● This should be avoided in careful speech.

2. The sounding of *t* in *often* is a spelling pronunciation: the traditional form in RP rhymes with *soften*.

th

1. Monosyllabic nouns ending in *-th* after a vowel sound (or vowel + *r*) form the plural by adding *-s* in the usual way, but the resulting sequence *ths* may be voiceless as in *myths*, or voiced as in *mouths*.

(*a*) The following are like *myth*:

berth	*fourth*	*moth*
birth	*girth*	*sleuth*
breath	*growth*	*sloth*
death	*hearth*	*smith*
faith	*heath*	*wraith*

(*b*) The following are like *mouth*:

oath	*sheath*	*wreath*
path	*truth*	*youth*

bath, *cloth*, *lath*, *swath* vary, but are now commonly like *myth*.

2. Note that final *th* is like *th* in *bathe*, *father* in:

bequeath	*booth*
betroth	*mouth* (verb)

booth can also be pronounced to rhyme with *tooth*.

u

The sound of long *u*, as in *cube*, *cubic*, *cue*, *use* is also spelt *eu*, *ew*, and *ui*, as in *feud*, *few*, *pursuit*. It is properly a compound of two sounds, the semi-vowel *y* followed by the long vowel elsewhere written *oo*. Hence the word *you* (= y + oo) sounds like the name of the letter *U*, *ewe*, and *yew*.

After some consonants the *y* is lost, leaving only the *oo*-sound.

1. After *ch*, *j*, *r*, the sound of *sh*, and *l* following a consonant. So *brewed*, *chews*, *chute*, *Jules*, *rude*, sound like *brood*, *choose*, *shoot*, *joules*, *rood*, and *blew*, *glue*, etc. sound as if they were spelt *bloo*, *gloo*, etc.

2. In a stressed syllable after *l* not following a consonant. *COD* gives only the *oo* pronunciation in many words, e.g. *lubricate*, *lucid*, *ludicrous*, etc., and either pronunciation for others, e.g. *lunar*, *Lutheran*, *allude*, *voluminous*, and (with secondary stress) *absolute*, *interlude*. However, *lewd* and *lieu* are given only the *yoo* pronunciation.

□ In all syllables of these kinds, the *oo*-sound is probably the predominant type, but either is acceptable.

● In *unstressed* syllables, however, the *yoo*-sound is the only one possible, e.g. in

deluge	*soluble*	*value*
prelude	*valuable*	*volume*

Contrast *solute* (= *sol*-yoot) with *salute* (= sa-*loot*).

3. After *s*, there is variation. Most people now use *oo* in *Susan* and *Sue*, and where another vowel follows, as in *sewer* and *suicide*, but *yoo* in *pseudo-*, *assume*, and *pursue*.

In an unstressed syllable, the *y*-sound is kept:

capsule *consular* *peninsula*

□ Apart from in *Susan* and *Sue*, and in an unstressed syllable, either pronunciation is acceptable.

4. After *d*, *n*, and *t*, the loss of the *y*-sound is non-standard, e.g. in *due*, *new*, *tune*.

Note: In Amer. English loss of the *y*-sound is normal after these consonants and *l* and *s*.

● The tendency to make *t* and *d* preceding this sound in stressed syllables sound like *ch* and *j*, e.g. *Tuesday*, *duel* as if *Choosday*, *jewel*, should be avoided in careful speech. In unstressed syllables (e.g. in *picture*, *procedure*) it is normal.

ul

After *b*, *f*, and *p*, the sequence *ul* sounds like *ool* in *wool* in some words, e.g. in *bull*, *pull*, and like *ull* in *hull* in others, e.g. in *bulk*, *pulp*. In a few words there is uncertainty or variation.

(*a*) Normally with *u* as in *hull*:

Bulgarian	*effulgent*	*pullulate*
catapult	*fulminate*	*pulmonary*
ebullient	*fulvous*	*pulverize*

(*b*) Normally with *u* as in *bull*:

bulwark *fulmar* *fulsome*

(*c*) With variation: *fulcrum*.

urr

In Standard English the stressed vowel of *furry* and *occurring* is like that of *stirring*, not that of *hurry* and *occurrence*.

● The two sounds are identical in normal Amer. English.

wh

In some regions *wh* is preceded or accompanied by an *h*-sound.

□ This pronunciation is not standard in RP, but is acceptable to most RP-speakers.

B. PREFERRED PRONUNCIATIONS

The entries in this list are of three kinds. Some are words, mainly unusual ones, that have only one current pronunciation, which cannot be deduced with certainty from the spelling. Others have one pronunciation, which is slurred in rapid speech; these reduced forms are noted, with a warning against using them in careful speech. The third and largest group is of words with two or more current pronunciations. Both (or all) are given, with notes as to their acceptability.

The approach throughout is fairly flexible.

Where American pronunciations differ significantly, they are noted in brackets, or sometimes stand alone after the recommended one, implying that the use of the American form is incorrect in British speech.

The symbol ● is used to warn against forms especially to be avoided.

abdomen: stress on 1st syllable in general use; on 2nd in the speech of many members of the medical profession.

accomplice, accomplish: the pronunciation with 2nd syllable as *come* rather than as in *comma* is now predominant.

acoustic: 2nd syllable as *coo*, not *cow*.

acumen: stress on 1st syllable; the traditional pronunciation has stress on 2nd syllable.

adept (adjective): stress on 1st or 2nd syllable; (noun) on 1st syllable.

adult (adjective and noun): stress on 1st syllable.

adversary: stress on 1st syllable.

aficionado: a-fiss-eon-*ah*-do.

ague: two syllables.

albumen: stress on 1st syllable.

ally (noun): stress on 1st syllable; (verb) on 1st or 2nd syllable; **allied** preceding a noun is stressed on 1st syllable.

analogous: *g* as in *log*; not a-*na*-lo-jus.

Antarctic: ● do not drop the first *c*.

anti- (prefix): rhymes with *shanty*, not, as often Amer., *ant eye*.

apache (Indian): rhymes with *patchy*; (street ruffian) rhymes with *cash*.

apartheid: 3rd syllable like *hate*. ● Not *apart-ite* or *apart-hide*.

apophthegm: *a*-po-them.

apparatus: 3rd syllable like *rate*; not appar-*ah*-tus.

applicable: stress either on 1st syllable or on 2nd.

apposite: 3rd syllable like that of *opposite*.

arbitrarily: stress properly on 1st syllable, informally on 3rd.

Arctic: ● do not drop the first *c*.

Argentine: 3rd syllable as in *turpentine*.

argot: rhymes with *cargo*.

aristocrat: stress on 1st syllable. ● Not (except Amer.) a-*rist*-ocrat.

artisan: stress originally on 3rd syllable; Amer. pronunciation with stress on 1st syllable is now common in Britain.

aspirant: stress either on 1st syllable or on 2nd.

asthma: *ass*-ma is the familiar pronunciation; to sound the *th* is pedantic (Amer. *az*-ma).

ate: rhymes with *bet* or *bate* (also the Amer. pronunciation).

audacious: *au* as in *audience*, not as in *gaucho*.

auld lang syne: 3rd word like *sign*, not *zine*.

auxiliary: awg-*zil*-yer-ri.

azure: now usually *az*-yoor.

banal: 2nd syllable like that of *canal* or *morale* (Amer. rhymes with *anal*).

basalt: 1st *a* as in *gas*, 2nd as in *salt*; stress on either.

bathos: *a* as in *paper*.

bestial: 1st syllable like *best* not *beast*.

blackguard: *blagg*-ard.

bolero (dance): stress on 2nd syllable; (jacket) stress on 1st.

booth: rhymes with *smooth* or *tooth*.

bouquet: first syllable as *book*, not as *beau*.

Bourbon (dynasty): 1st syllable as *bourgeois*; (US whisky) as *bur*.

breeches: rhymes with *pitches*.

brochure: stress on 1st syllable.

brusque: should be Anglicized: broosk or brusk.

bureau: stress on 1st syllable.

burgh (in Scotland): sounds like *borough*.

Byzantine: stress on 2nd syllable (Amer. *biz*-en-teen).

cadaver: 2nd syllable as in *waver*, *average*, or *lava*.
cadaverous: 2nd syllable like 1st of *average*.
cadre: rhymes with *harder*.
caliph: rhymes with *bailiff*, or 1st syllable as in *pal*.
camellia: rhymes with *Amelia*.
canine: 1st syllable as *can* or *cane*.
canton (subdivision): 2nd syllable as 1st of *tonic*; (military, also in **cantonment**) 2nd syllable as that of *cartoon*.
capitalist: stress on 1st syllable.
Caribbean: stress on 3rd syllable more usual, but on 2nd is also acceptable.
carillon: rhymes with *trillion* (Amer. *carry*-lon).
caryatid: stress on 2nd *a*.
catacomb: 3rd syllable as *comb*, or rhyming with *tomb*.
catechumen: stress on 3rd syllable (catty-*cue*-men).
centenary: sen-*tee*-nary (Amer. *sen*-tenary).
cento: *c* as in *cent*, not *cello*.
centrifugal, centripetal: stress originally on 2nd syllable, but now usually on 3rd.
certification: stress on 1st and 4th syllables, not 2nd and 4th.
cervical: stress either on 1st syllable (with last two syllables as in *vertical*) or on 2nd (rhyming with *cycle*) (Amer. only the first pronunciation).
chaff: rhymes with *staff*.
chagrin: stress on 1st syllable; 2nd as *grin* (Amer. stress on 2nd syllable).
chamois (antelope): *sham*-wah; (leather) shammy.
chastisement: stress on 1st or 2nd syllable.
chimera: *ch* = k, not sh.
chiropodist: strictly *ch* = k, but as sh is common.
choleric: 1st two syllables like *collar*.
chutzpa: 1st syllable rhymes with p*uts*; the initial sound should properly be pronounced like the *ch* in *loch*.
cigarette: stress on 3rd syllable (Amer. on 1st).
clandestine: stress on 2nd syllable.
clangour: rhymes with *anger*.
clientele: kleeon-*tell*.
clique: rhymes with *leak*, not *lick*.
coccyx: *cc* = ks.
colander: 1st syllable as *cull*.
combat (verb), **combatant, -ive:** stress on 1st syllable (Amer. on 2nd).
combine (noun): stress on 1st syllable.
commandant: stress on 3rd syllable, or now often on 1st.
communal: stress on 1st syllable.
commune (noun): stress on 1st syllable.
comparable: stress on 1st syllable, not on 2nd.
compensatory: the older (and Amer.) pronunciation has stress on 2nd syllable, but stress on 3rd is now common.
compilation: 2nd syllable as *pill*.
composite: stress on 1st syllable; 3rd as that of *opposite* (Amer. stress on 2nd syllable).
conch: originally = *conk*; now often with *ch* as in *lunch*.
conduit: last three letters formerly like those of *circuit*, but now usually *con*-dew-it.
confidant(e): stress on 1st or on last syllable, which rhymes with *ant*.
congener: stress on 1st or 2nd syllable; *o* as *con*; *g* as in *gin*.
congeries: con-*jeer*-eez or con-*jeer*-y-eez.
congratulatory: stress on 2nd or 4th syllable.
conjugal: stress on 1st syllable.
consuetude: stress on 1st syllable; *sue* like *swi* in *swift*.
consummate (adjective): stress on 2nd syllable; (verb) on 1st syllable, 3rd syllable as *mate*.
contact (noun): stress on 1st syllable; (verb) stress on 1st or 2nd.
contemplative: stress on 2nd syllable.
contrarily (on the contrary): stress on 1st syllable; (perversely) stress on 2nd syllable.
contribute: stress on 2nd syllable. ● The pronunciation with stress on 1st syllable is not accepted as standard.
controversy: stress on 1st syllable. ● The now common pronunciation with stress on 2nd is strongly disapproved by many users of RP.
contumacy: stress on 1st syllable (Amer. on 2nd).
contumely: three syllables with stress on the 1st.

conversant: now usually stressed on 2nd syllable.
courier: *ou* as in *could*.
courteous: 1st syllable like *curt*.
courtesan: 1st syllable like *court*.
courtesy: 1st syllable like *curt*.
covert: 1st syllable like that of *cover*. ● The pronunciation *co*-vert is chiefly Amer.
cul-de-sac: 1st syllable may rhyme with *dull* or *full*.
culinary: *cul-* now usually as in *culprit*; formerly as in *peculiar*.
cyclical: 1st syllable like *cycle*, though *sick* is also common.
dais: originally one syllable; now only with two.
data: 1st syllable as *date*. ● Does not rhyme with *sonata*.
decade: stress on 1st syllable. ● The pronunciation with stress on 2nd syllable is not accepted as standard.
defect (noun): stress on 1st syllable is now usual.
deficit: stress on 1st syllable.
deify, deity: properly with *e* as in *me*; pronunciation with *e* as in *suede*, *fête* is increasingly common.
delirious: 2nd syllable as 1st of *lyrical*, not *Leary*.
demesne: 2nd syllable sounds like *main*.
demonstrable: stress now usually on the 2nd syllable.
deprivation: 1st two syllables like those of *deprecation*.
derisive, derisory: 2nd syllable like *rice*.
despicable: stress on 1st syllable; informally on 2nd.
desuetude: as for **consuetude**.
desultory: stress on 1st syllable.
deteriorate: ● do not drop 4th syllable, i.e. not deteri-ate.
detour: *dee*-tour not *day*-tour (Amer. de-*tour*).
deus ex machina: *day*-us ex *mak*-ina, not ma-*shee*-na.
dilemma: 1st syllable like *dill* or, now commonly, like *die*.
dinghy: either ding-gy or rhyming with *stringy*.
diphtheria, diphthong: *ph* = f not p.
disciplinary: the older (and Amer.) pronunciation has stress on 1st syllable, but it is now usually on the 3rd.
disputable: stress on 2nd syllable.
dispute (noun): stress on 2nd syllable, not on 1st.
dissect: 1st syllable as *Diss*. ● Does not rhyme with *bisect*.
distribute: stress on 2nd syllable. ● The pronunciation with stress on the 1st is considered incorrect by some people.
doctrinal: stress now usually on the 2nd syllable (with *i* as in *mine*).
dolorous, dolour: 1st syllable like *doll* (Amer. like *dole*).
dour: rhymes with *poor* not *power*.
dubiety: last three syllables like those of *anxiety*.
ducat: 1st syllable like *duck*.
dynastic, dynasty: 1st syllable like *din* (Amer. like *dine*).
ebullient: *u* as in *dull*, not as in *bull*.
economic: *e* as in *extra* or as in *equal*: both are current.
Edwardian: 2nd syllable as *ward*.
e'er (poetry, = *ever*): sounds like *air*.
efficacy: stress on 1st syllable, not 2nd.
ego: 1st syllable as that of *eager*.
egocentric, egoism, etc.: 1st syllable like *egg* (Amer. usually as **ego**).
either: *ei* as in **height** or *seize* (Amer. only the second).
elixir: rhymes with *licks ear*.
enclave: *en-* as in *end*, *a* as in *slave*.
entirety: now usually entire-ety; formerly entire-ty.
envelope: *en-* as in *end*; the pronunciation as in *on* is widespread but disliked by many RP speakers.
environs: rhymes with *sirens*.
epoxy: stress on 2nd syllable.
equerry: stress properly on 2nd syllable, but commonly on 1st.
espionage: now usually with *-age* as in *camouflage*.
et cetera: etsetera. ● Not eksetera.
explicable: stress originally on 1st syllable, now usually on 2nd.
exquisite: stress originally on 1st syllable, now usually on 2nd.
extraordinary: 1st *a* is silent.
fakir: sounds like *fake*-ear.
falcon: *a* as in *talk*, not as in *alcove*.
fascia: rhymes with *Alsatia*; in medicine, often like *fashion*.
fascism, fascist: 1st syllable like that of *fashion*.

February: ● do not drop the 1st *r*: *feb*-roor-y, not *feb*-yoor-y or *feb*-wa-ry or *feb*-yoo-erry (Amer. *feb*-roo-erry).
fetid, fetish: *e* as in *fetter*.
fifth: in careful speech, do not drop the 2nd *f*.
finance: stress on 1st syllable (only with *i* as in *fine*) or on 2nd (with *i* as in *fin* or *fine*).
flaccid: *cc* as in *accident*, or rhyming with *acid*.
forbade: 2nd syllable like *bad*.
formidable: stress on 1st syllable; informally, on 2nd.
forte (one's strong point): originally (and Amer.) like *fort*, but now usually like the musical term *forte*.
foyer: *foy*-ay or, less commonly, *fwah*-yay (Amer. *foy*-er).
fracas (singular): *frack*-ah, (plural) *frack*-ahz (Amer. *frake*-us).
fulminate: *u* as in *dull*.
fulsome: *u* formerly as in *dull*, now always as in *full*.
furore: three syllables (Amer. **furor** with two).
Gaelic: 1st syllable as *gale*.
gala: 1st *a* as in *calm*. ● The former pronunciation with *a* as in *gale* is still used in the North and US.
gallant: stress on 1st syllable; (polite to women) stress on 1st or 2nd.
garage: stress on 1st syllable, *age* as in *camouflage* (or rhyming with *large*). ● Pronunciation to rhyme with *carriage* is disapproved of by many RP speakers.
garrulity: stress on 2nd syllable, which sounds like *rule*.
garrulous: stress on 1st syllable.
gaseous: 1st syllable like *gas*.
genuine: *ine* as in *engine*.
genus: *e* as in *genius*; **genera** (plural) has *e* as in *general*.
gibber, gibberish: with *g* as in *gin*.
glacial: 1st *a* as in *glade*.
golf: *o* as in *got*. ● The pronunciation goff is old-fashioned.
gone: *o* as in *on*. ● The pronunciation gawn is non-standard.
government: ● In careful speech, do not drop the 1st *n* (or the whole 2nd syllable).
gratis: *a* as in *grate*; but grahtis and grattis are common.
greasy: *s* may be as in *cease* or *easy*.
grievous: ● does not rhyme with *previous*.
guacamole: gwark-er-*mole*-i.
gunwale: gunn'l.
half-past: ● In careful speech, avoid saying hah past or hoff posst.
hara-kiri: ● not harry-carry.
harass(ment): stress on 1st syllable. ● The pronunciation with stress on the 2nd is considered incorrect by some people.
have: in rapid speech, the weakly stressed *have* sounds like weakly stressed *of*. When stress is restored to it, it should become *have*, as in '*You couldn't 've done it*', '*I could* have' (not '*I could* of').
hectare: 2nd syllable like *tare* or, less commonly, *tar*.
hegemony: stress on 2nd syllable, *g* as in *get* or (as also Amer.) as in *gem*.
Hegira: stress on 1st syllable, which is like *hedge*.
heinous: *ei* as in *rein*. ● The pronunciation rhyming with *Venus* is disliked by many RP speakers; that rhyming with *genius* is erroneous.
homo- (prefix = same): *o* now usually as in *hoe*.
homoeopath: 1st two syllables rhyme with *Romeo*.
homogeneous: last three syllables sound like *genius*.
honorarium: *h* silent, *a* as in *rare*.
hospitable: stress on 1st or 2nd syllable.
hotel: *h* to be pronounced.
housewifery: stress on 1st syllable, *i* as in *whiff*.
hovel, hover: *o* as in *hot*. ● Pronunciation with *o* as in *love* is now only Amer.
idyll, idyllic: *i* as in *idiot*.
illustrative: stress on 1st syllable (Amer. on 2nd).
imbroglio: *g* is silent; rhymes with *folio*.
impious: stress on 1st syllable; on 2nd in **impiety**.
importune: stress on 3rd syllable or (some speakers) on 2nd.
inchoate: stress on 1st syllable.
indict: *c* is silent; rhymes with *incite*.
indisputable: stress on 3rd syllable.
inexplicable: stress usually on 3rd syllable.
infamous: stress on 1st syllable.

inherent: 1st *e* as in *here* or *error*.
intaglio: *g* is silent, *a* as in *pal* or *pass*.
integral: stress on 1st syllable. ● The pronunciation with stress on the 2nd is considered incorrect by some people. The pronunciation *int*-re-gal is erroneous.
intern (verb): stress on 2nd syllable; (noun, Amer.) on 1st.
internecine: stress on 3rd syllable, last syllables like *knee sign*.
interstice: stress on 2nd syllable.
intestinal: the traditional pronunciation has stress on 2nd syllable, 3rd like *tin*; now commonly with stress on 3rd, pronounced *tine*.
intricacy: stress on 1st syllable.
invalid (sick person): stress on 1st syllable, 2nd *i* as in *lid* or *machine*; (verb) stress on 1st syllable, 2nd *i* as in *machine*; (not valid) stress on 2nd syllable.
inveigle: 2nd syllable as in *vague* or rhyming with *beagle*.
inventory: like *infantry* with *v* instead of *f*.
irrefragable: stress on 2nd syllable.
irreparable: stress on 2nd syllable.
irrevocable: stress on 2nd syllable.
issue: *ss* as in *mission*; but rhyming with *miss you* is common.
isthmus: in careful speech, do not drop the *th*.
January: *jan*-yoor-y (Amer. *jan*-yooerry).
jejune: stress on 2nd syllable.
jewellery: jewel-ry. ● Not jool-ery.
joule (unit): rhymes with *fool*.
jubilee: stress on 1st syllable. ● Not 3rd.
jugular: 1st syllable like *jug*: formerly as in *conjugal*.
junta: pronounce as written. ● Hoonta, an attempt to reproduce the Spanish, is the standard Amer. pronunciation.
karaoke: 1st two syllables properly like those of *caramel*, but (to avoid the awkward hiatus) often like *carry*.
kilometre: stress on 1st syllable. ● The pronunciation with stress on the 2nd is considered incorrect by many people.
knoll: *o* as in *no*.
laboratory: stress on 2nd syllable. ● The former pronunciation, with stress on 1st, is now chiefly Amer. (with *ory* as in *Tory*).
lamentable: stress on 1st syllable.
languor: as for **clangour**.
lasso: stress on 2nd syllable, *o* as in *do*.
lather: rhymes with *rather* or *gather*.
leeward (in general use): *lee*-ward; (nautical) like *lured*.
leisure: rhymes with *pleasure* (Amer. with *seizure*).
length: *ng* as in *long*. ● Not lenth.
levee (reception): like *levy*; (Amer., embankment) may be stressed on 2nd.
library: in careful speech avoid dropping the 2nd syllable (li-bry).
lichen: sounds like *liken*.
lieutenant: 1st syllable like *left* (Amer. like *loot*).
liquorice: licker-iss.
longevity: *ng* as in *lunge*.
longitude: *ng* as in *lunge* or as in *linger*. ● Not *longtitude*.
lour: rhymes with *hour*.
lugubrious: loo-*goo*-brious.
machete: *ch* as in *machine* or *attach*; rhymes with *Betty*.
machination: *ch* as in *mechanical*, but pronunciation as in *machine* is increasingly common.
machismo, macho: *ch* as in *attach*, not as in *mechanical*.
magazine: stress on 3rd syllable (Amer. has stress on 1st).
mandatory: stress on 1st syllable.
margarine: *g* as in *Margery*.
marital: stress on 1st syllable.
massage: stress on 1st syllable (Amer. on 2nd).
matrix: *a* as in *mate*; **matrices** the same, with stress on 1st.
medicine: two syllables (med-sin). ● The pronunciation with three syllables is normal in Scotland and the US, but is disapproved of by many users of RP.
mediocre: 1st syllable like *mead*.
metallurgy, -ist: stress on 2nd syllable. ● The older pronunciation with stress on 1st is now chiefly Amer.
metamorphosis: stress on 3rd syllable.
metope: two syllables.
midwifery: stress on 1st syllable, *i* as in *whiff*.
mien: sounds like *mean*.

migraine: 1st syllable like *me* (Amer. like *my*).
migratory: stress on 1st syllable.
millenary: stress on 2nd syllable, which is like *Len*.
miscellany: stress on 2nd syllable (Amer. on 1st).
mischievous: stress on 1st syllable. ● Not rhyming with *previous*.
misericord: stress on 2nd syllable.
mnemonic: stress on 2nd syllable, 1st like *nimble* not *Newman*.
mocha: like *mocker* (Amer. rhyming with *coca*).
momentary, -ily: stress on 1st syllable.
mullah: *u* as in *dull*.
municipal: stress on 2nd syllable.
nadir: *nay*-dear.
naive: nah-*Eve* or nigh-*Eve*.
naivety: has three syllables.
nascent: *a* as in *fascinate*.
necessarily: in formal speech, has stress on 1st syllable; informally stressed on 3rd (e.g. *not necessarily!*).
neither: as for **either**.
nephew: formerly with *ph* like *v*, but now usually *neff*-you.
nicety: has three syllables.
niche: nitch or neesh.
nomenclature: stress on 2nd syllable. The pronunciation with stress on 1st and 3rd syllables is now chiefly Amer.
nonchalant: stress on 1st syllable, *ch* as in *machine*.
nuclear: *newk*-lee-er. ● Not as if spelt *nucular*.
nucleic: stress on 2nd syllable, which has *e* as in *equal*.
obdurate: stress on 1st syllable.
obeisance: 2nd syllable like *base*.
obligatory: stress on 2nd syllable.
obscenity: *e* as in *scent*.
occurrence: 2nd syllable like the 1st in *current*.
oche (darts): rhymes with *hockey*.
o'er (poetry, = over): now usually rhyming with *goer*.
of: see **have**.
often: the traditional pronunciation has a silent *t*, as in *soften*; the sounding of the *t* is sometimes heard.
ominous: 1st syllable as that of *omelette*.
ophthalmic: *ph* = f not p.
opus: *o* as in *open*.
ormolu: *orm*-o-loo with weak 2nd *o* as in *Caroline*.
p (abbreviation for *penny*, *pence*): in formal context, say *penny* (after 1) or *pence*. ● 'Pee' is informal only.
pace (with all due respect to): like *pacey*.
paella: usually pie-*ell*-a rather than pah-*ell*-a.
panegyric: stress on 3rd syllable, *g* as in *gin*, *y* as in *lyric*.
paprika: stress on 1st syllable (Amer. on 2nd).
pariah: the older pronunciation rhymes with *carrier*; the pronunciation rhyming with *Isaiah* is now common (and normal Amer.).
participle: stress on 1st syllable; 1st *i* may be dropped. ● The stressing of 2nd syllable is not yet standard.
particularly: in careful speech, avoid saying particuly.
partisan: as **artisan**.
pasty (pie): *a* now usually as in *lass*.
patent: 1st syllable like *pate*. ● Some have 1st syllable like *pat* in *Patent Office*, *letters patent*.
pathos: as for **bathos**.
patina: stress on 1st syllable.
patriarch: 1st *a* as in *paper*.
patriot(ic): *a* as in *pat* or *paper*.
patron, patroness: *a* as in *paper*.
patronage, patronize: *a* as in *pat*.
pejorative: stress on 2nd syllable. ● The older pronunciation, with stress on 1st syllable, is now rare.
peremptory: stress on 2nd syllable (Amer. on 1st).
perhaps: in careful speech, two syllables with *h*, not *r*, sounded; informally praps.
pharmacopoeia: stress on *oe*; *-poeia* rhymes with *idea*.
philharmonic: 2nd *h* is traditionally silent.
phthisis: *ph* is silent.
pianist: stress on 1st *i*, *ia* as in *Ian*.
piano (instrument): *a* as in *man*; (= softly) *a* as in *calm*.
piazza: *zz* = ts.
pistachio: *a* as in *calm*, *ch* as in *machine*.
plaid, plait: rhyme with *lad*, *flat*.
plastic: now rhymes with *fantastic*, rather than with the *a* of *calm*.

plenty: ● *plenny* is non-standard.
pogrom: stress on the 1st syllable.
pomegranate: *pommy*-gran-it is now usual, rather than *pom*-gran-it.
porpoise: *oise* like *ose* in *purpose*.
posthumous: *h* is silent.
pot-pourri: stress on 2nd syllable (Amer. on 3rd), *pot-* like *Poe*.
precedence, precedent, precedented: stress on 1st syllable, which sounds like *press*; but on 2nd for *precedent* (adjective).
predilection: ● not as if spelt predeliction.
preferable: stress on 1st syllable.
premise (verb): stress on 2nd syllable, rhyming with *surmise*.
prestige: stress on 2nd syllable, *i* and *g* as in *regime*.
prestigious: rhymes with *religious*.
prima facie: *pry*-ma *fay*-shee.
primarily: stress on 1st syllable. ● The pronunciation with stress on the 2nd, used by some Americans, is disapproved of by many users of RP.
primer (school-book): *i* as in *prime*. ● The older pronunciation with *i* as in *prim* survives in New Zealand.
privacy: *i* as in *privet* or *private*; the latter is the older pronunciation.
probably: in careful speech, three syllables; informally often probbly.
proboscis: pro-*boss*-iss.
process (noun): *o* as in *probe*. ● An older pronunciation with *o* as in *profit* is now only Amer.
process (verb, to treat): like the noun; (to walk in procession) stress on 2nd syllable.
promissory: stress on 1st syllable.
pronunciation: 2nd syllable like *nun*. ● Not pro-*noun*-ciation.
prosody: 1st syllable like that of *prospect*.
protean: stress originally on 1st syllable, now commonly on 2nd.
protégé: 1st syllable like *protestant* (Amer. like *protest*).
proven: *o* as in *prove*, but pronunciation like *woven* is widespread.
proviso: 2nd syllable as that of *revise*.
puissance (show-jumping): pronounced with approximation to French, *pui* = pwi, *a* nasalized; (in poetry) may be *pwiss*-ance or *pew*-iss-ance, depending on scansion.
pursuivant: *Percy*-vant.
pyramidal: stress on 2nd syllable.
quaff: rhymes with *scoff*.
quagmire: *a* originally as in *wag*, now usually as in *quad*.
qualm: rhymes with *calm*; to rhyme with *shawm* is now rare.
quandary: stress on 1st syllable.
quasi: the vowels are like those in *wayside*.
quatercentenary: *kwatt*-er-, not *quarter-*.
questionnaire: 1st two syllables like *question*.
rabid: 1st syllable like that of *rabbit*.
rabies: 2nd syllable like *bees*, not like *babies*.
rampage (verb): stress on 2nd syllable; (noun) on 1st or 2nd.
rapport: stress on 2nd syllable, which sounds like *pore* (Amer. like *port*).
ratiocinate: 1st two syllables like *ratty*, stress on 3rd.
rationale: *ale* as in *morale*.
really: rhymes with *ideally*, *clearly*, not with *freely*.
recess (noun and verb): stress on 2nd syllable.
recognize: ● do not drop the *g*.
recondite: stress on 1st or 2nd syllable.
recuperate: 2nd syllable like the 1st of *Cupid*.
referable: stress on 2nd syllable.
remediable, -al: stress on 2nd syllable, *e* as in *medium*.
remonstrate: stress on 1st syllable.
Renaissance: stress on 2nd syllable, *ai* as in *plaice*.
renege: rhymes with *league* or *plague*. ● *g* as in *get*.
reportage: *age* as in *camouflage*, but with stress.
research (noun): stress on 2nd syllable. ● The Amer. pronunciation with stress on the 1st is now quite widespread in Britain, but is considered incorrect by some people.
respite: stress on 1st syllable, 2nd like *spite* (Amer. like *spit*).
restaurant: pronunciation with final *t* silent and second *a* nasalized is preferred by many, but that with *ant* = ont is now more common.
revanchism: *anch* as in *ranch*.
ribald: 1st syllable like *rib*.

risible: rhymes with *visible*.
risqué: *riss*-kay or riss-*kay*.
romance: stress on 2nd syllable. ● Pronunciation with stress on 1st syllable, usually in sense 'love affair, love story', is considered incorrect by some people.
Romany: 1st syllable as that of *romp* or *rope*.
rotatory: stress on 1st or 2nd syllable.
rowan: *ow* as in *low* or *cow*.
rowlock: rhymes with *Pollock*.
sacrilegious: now always rhymes with *religious*.
sahib: sounds like *Saab*.
salsify: *sal*-si-fee.
salve (noun, ointment; verb, soothe): properly rhymes with *halve*, but now usually with *valve* (Amer. with *have*).
salve (save ship): rhymes with *valve*.
satiety: as for **dubiety**.
Saudi: rhymes with *rowdy*, not *bawdy*.
scabies: as for **rabies**.
scabrous: *a* as in *skate* (Amer. as in *scab*).
scallop: rhymes with *wallop* or (Amer.) with *gallop*.
scarify (make an incision): rhymes with *clarify*. ● Not to be confused with slang *scarify* (terrify) pronounced *scare*-ify.
scenario: *sc* as in *scene*, *ario* as in *impresario* (Amer. with *a* as in *Mary*).
schedule: *sch* as in *Schubert* (Amer. as in *school*).
schism: properly, *ch* is silent (siz'm); but skiz'm is often heard.
schist (rock): *sch* as in *Schubert*.
schizo-: skitso.
scilicet: 1st syllable like that of *silent* or *silly*.
scone: traditionally rhymes with *on*.
second (to support): stress on 1st syllable; (to transfer) on 2nd.
secretary: *sek*-re-try. ● Not *sek*-e-try or *sek*-e-terry or (Amer.) *sek*-re-terry.
secretive: stress on 1st syllable.
segue: *seg*-way.
seise, seisin: *ei* as in *seize*.
seismic: 1st syllable like *size*.
seraglio: *g* silent, *a* as in *ask*.
shaman: 1st syllable like *sham*, not *shame*.
sheikh: sounds like *shake* (Amer. like *chic*).
simultaneous: *i* as in *simple* (Amer. as in *Simon*).
sinecure: properly, *i* as in *sign*, but *i* as in *sin* is common.
Sinhalese: sin-(h)al-*ese*.
Sioux: soo.
sisal: 1st syllable like the 2nd of *precise*.
sixth: in careful speech, avoid the pronunciation sikth.
slalom: *a* as in *spa*.
slaver (dribble): *a* as in *have*.
sleight: sounds like *slight*.
sloth: rhymes with *both*.
slough (bog): rhymes with *bough*; (to cast a skin) with *tough*.
sobriquet: 1st syllable like that of *sober*.
sojourn: 1st *o* as in *sob* (Amer. as in *sober*).
solder: *o* as in *sob* (Amer. pronunciation is sodder or sawder).
solecism: *o* as in *sob*.
solenoid: stress on 1st syllable, *o* as in *sober* or as in *sob*.
sonorous: stress on 1st syllable, 1st *o* as in *sob*.
soporific: 1st *o* now usually as in *sob*.
sough (rushing sound): rhymes with *plough*.
sovereignty: *sov*'renty. ● Not sov-*rain*-ity.
Soviet: *o* as in *sober* or *sob*.
species: *ci* as in *precious*. ● Not *spee*-seez.
spinet: may be stressed on either syllable.
spontaneity: as for **deify, deity**.
stalwart: 1st syllable like *stall*.
status: 1st syllable like *stay*. ● Not *statt*-us.
stigmata: stress on 1st syllable. ● Not with *ata* as in *sonata*.
strafe: rhymes with *staff*.
stratosphere: *a* as in *Stratford*.
stratum, strata: *a* of 1st syllable like 1st *a* of *sonata*.
strength: *ng* as in *strong*. ● Not *strenth*.
suave, suavity: *a* as 1st *a* in *lava*.
subsidence: stress originally on 2nd syllable with *i* as in *side*; now often with stress on 1st and *i* as in *sit*.
substantial: 1st *a* as in *ant*, not *aunt*.
substantive (in grammar): stress on 1st syllable; (separate, permanent) on 2nd.
suffragan: *g* as in *get*.
suit: now usually with *oo*, though *yoo* is common.
supererogatory: stress on 4th syllable.
superficies: super-*fish*-(i-)eez.

supine (adjective)**:** stress on 1st syllable (Amer. on 2nd).
suppose: ● in careful speech, has two syllables.
surety: now usually *sure*-et-y; originally *sure*-ty.
surveillance: ● do not drop the *l*; = sur-*vey*-lance.
suzerain: *u* as in *Susan.*
swath: *a* as in *water* or to rhyme with *cloth.*
syndrome: two syllables (formerly three).
Taoiseach: *tee*-sh'kh, the last sound pronounced like *ch* in *loch.*
taxidermist: stress on 1st syllable.
temporarily: stress on 1st syllable: *temp*-ra-rily. ● Not tempo-*rar*-ily.
Tibetan: 2nd syllable like *bet*, not *beat.*
tirade: tie-*raid.*
tissue: as for **issue**.
tonne: sounds like *ton.* ● To avoid misunderstanding, *metric* can be prefixed; but in most spoken contexts the slight difference between the weights will not matter.
tortoise: as for **porpoise**.
tourniquet: 3rd syllable like *croquet* (Amer. turn-a-*kit*).
towards: the form with two syllables is now the most common; some speakers say tords.
trachea: stress on *e* (Amer. on 1st *a*, pronounced as in *trade*).
trait: 2nd *t* is silent (in Amer. pronunciation, it is sounded).
trajectory: stress on 1st syllable or (and Amer.) on 2nd.
transferable: stress on 2nd syllable.
transition: tran-*zish*-on. ● tran-*sizh*-on is now rare.
transparent: last two syllables like *apparent* or *parent.*
trauma, traumatic: *au* as in *cause* (Amer. as in *gaucho*).
traverse (noun)**:** stress on 1st syllable; (verb) on 2nd syllable.
trefoil: stress on 1st syllable, *e* as in *even* or as in *ever.*
triumvir: 1st two syllables like those of *triumphant.*
troth: rhymes with *both* (Amer. with *cloth*).
trow: traditionally rhymes with *know.*
truculent: 1st *u* as in *truck*; formerly as in *true.*
turquoise: *tur*-kwoyz or *tur*-kwahz.
ululate: *yool*-yoo-late.
umbilical: stress on 2nd syllable.
unprecedented: 2nd syllable like *press.*
untoward: the older pronunciation rhymed with *lowered*, but the pronunciation with stress on the 3rd syllable is now usual.
Uranus: stress on 1st or 2nd syllable.
urinal: stress on 1st or 2nd syllable.
usual: in careful speech, avoid complete loss of *u* (*yoo*-zh'l).
uvula: *yoo*-vyoo-la.
uxorious: 1st *u* as *Uxbridge.*
vacuum: now frequently two, not three, syllables (*vak*-yoom).
vagary: now stressed on 1st, rather than 2nd, syllable.
vagina, vaginal: stress on 2nd syllable, *i* as in *china.*
valance: rhymes with *balance.*
valence, -cy (chemistry)**:** *a* as in *ale.*
valet: those who employ them sound the *t.*
valeting: rhymes with **balloting**.
Valkyrie: stress on 1st syllable.
vase: *a* as in *dance* (Amer. rhymes with *face* or *phase*).
veld: sounds like *felt.*
venison: *ven*-i-z'n or *ven*-i-s'n are usual.
veterinary: stress on 1st syllable, with reduction (*vet*-rin-ry). ● Not *vet*-nary or (Amer.) *vet*-rin-ery.
vice (in *vice versa*)**:** rhymes with *spicy.*
vicegerent: three syllables, 2nd *e* as in *errant.*
victualler, victuals: sound like *vitt*-ell-er, vittles.
viola (instrument)**:** stress on 2nd syllable, *i* as in *Fiona*; (flower) stress on 1st syllable, *i* as in *vie.*
vitamin: *i* as in *hit* (Amer. as in *vital*).
viz. (= videlicet)**:** in speech, it is customary to say *namely.*
voluntarily: stress on 1st syllable.
waistcoat: the older pronunciation was *wess*-kot (with 2nd syllable like *mascot*); but now usually as spelt.
walnut, walrus: ● do not drop the *l.*
werewolf: 1st syllable like *weir* or *wear.*
whoop (cry of excitement)**:** = woop; (cough) = hoop; both rhyme with *loop.*
wrath: rhymes with *cloth* (Amer. with *hath*).
wroth: as for **troth**.

yoghurt: *yogg*-urt (Amer. *yoh*-gurt).

zoology: in careful speech, best pronounced with 1st *o* as in *zone.* ● The common pronunciation zoo-*ol*-ogy is considered incorrect by some people.

Vocabulary

This section is concerned with problems of meaning, construction, derivation, and diction. The main aim is to recommend the meaning or construction most appropriate for formal writing or speaking, but some attention is paid to informal and American usage.

aboriginal (noun) should be used in formal contexts as the singular of *aborigines*. However, when referring to the aboriginal inhabitants of Australia, *Aborigine* and *Aborigines* (with capitals) are now preferred.

account, to reckon, consider, is not followed by *as*, e.g. *Account him wise*.

affect, to have an influence on, e.g. *Hugh was immensely affected by the way Randall had put it* (Iris Murdoch).
● Do not confuse with *effect* to accomplish, e.g. *Effect changes*. ● There is a noun *effect* 'result, property', e.g. *to good effect, personal effects*; but no noun *affect* except in the specialized language of Psychology.

affinity *between* or *with*, not *to* or *for*, e.g. *Ann felt an affinity with them* (Iris Murdoch); *Points of affinity between Stephen and Bloom* (Anthony Burgess).

afflict: see **inflict**.

aftermath can be used of any after-effects, e.g. *The aftermath of war*. It is pedantic to object to the sense 'unpleasant consequences' on the ground of derivation.

agenda (from a Latin plural) is usually a singular noun (with plural *agendas*), e.g. *It's a short agenda, by the way* (Edward Hyams). But it is occasionally found as a plural meaning 'things to be done' (singular *agendum*).

aggravate (1) To make worse. (2) To annoy, exasperate.
● Sense (2) is regarded by some people as incorrect, but is common informally. The participial adjective *aggravating* is often used in sense (2) by good writers, e.g. *He had pronounced and aggravating views* (Graham Greene).

ain't (= are not, is not, have not, has not) is not used in Standard English except in representations of dialect speech, or humorously. *Aren't* (= are not) is also a recognized colloquialism for *am not* in *aren't I*.

alibi, a claim that when an alleged act took place one was elsewhere.
● The sense 'an excuse' is unacceptable to some people, e.g. *Low spirits make you seem complaining . . I have an alibi because I'm going to have a baby* (L. P. Hartley).

all of (= the whole of, every one of) is usual before pronouns, e.g. *And so say all of us*, or often paralleling *none of* etc. before nouns, e.g. *Marshall Stone has all of the problems but none of the attributes of a star* (Frederic Raphael). Otherwise *all* + noun is normal, e.g. *All the King's men*.
● The general use of *all of* before nouns is Amer. only.

all right. This phrase is popularly thought of as a unit, e.g. *an all-right bloke*, but the expression remains largely an informal one.
● *Alright* remains non-standard, even where the standard spelling is cumbersome, as in: *I just wanted to make sure it was all all right* (Iris Murdoch).

allude means 'refer indirectly'; an *allusion* is 'an indirect reference', e.g. *He would allude to her . . but never mention her by name* (E. M. Forster).
● The words are not mere synonyms for *refer, reference*.

alternative (adjective and noun). The use of *alternative* with reference to more than two options, though sometimes criticized, is acceptable, e.g. *Many alternative methods*. ● Do not confuse with *alternate* happening or following in turns, e.g. *Alternate joy and misery*. The use of *alternate* for *alternative* is, however, acceptable in Amer. English:

Liaison and Reserve watched alternate exits in buildings (Norman Mailer).

altogether. ● Beware of using *altogether* (meaning 'in total') when *all together* (meaning 'all at once, all in one place') is meant, e.g. *They went up all together to the hotel and sat down to tea* (John Galsworthy). But *altogether* is correct in *There's too much going on altogether at the moment* (Evelyn Waugh).

amend, to alter to something better, e.g. *If you consider my expression inadequate I am willing to amend it* (G. B. Shaw); noun *amendment*.

● Do not confuse with *emend* to remove errors from (something written), e.g. *An instance of how the dictionary may be emended or censored* (Frederic Raphael); noun *emendation*. An *emendation* will almost always be an *amendment*, but the converse is not true.

analogous means 'similar in certain respects'. It is not a mere synonym for *similar*.

anticipate (1) To be aware of (something) in advance and take suitable action, to deal with (a thing) or perform (an action) in advance, e.g. *His power to .. anticipate every change of volume and tempo* (C. Day Lewis); *I shall anticipate any such opposition by tendering my resignation now* (Angus Wilson); *She had anticipated execution by suicide* (Robert Graves).

(2) To forestall (another person), e.g. *I'm sorry—do go on. I did not mean to anticipate you* (John le Carré).

(3) To expect, regard as probable (an event), e.g. *Serious writers .. anticipated that the detective story might supersede traditional fiction; Left-wing socialists really anticipated a Fascist dictatorship* (A. J. P. Taylor).

● Sense (3) is well established in informal use, but is regarded as incorrect by many people. Use *expect* in formal contexts. In any case, *anticipate* cannot be followed, as *expect* can, by the infinitive (*I expect to see him* or *him to come*) or a personal object (*I expect him today*) and cannot mean 'expect as one's due' (*I expect good behaviour from pupils*).

antithetical means 'contrasted, opposite', not merely 'opposed'.

appraise, to estimate the value or quality of, e.g. *I appraised her skills*.

● Do not confuse with *apprise*, to inform, e.g. *Apprised, sir, of my daughter's sudden flight . ., I followed her at once* (Oscar Wilde).

approve (1) (Followed by direct object) authorize, e.g. *The naval plan was approved by the war council* (A. J. P. Taylor).

(2) (With *of*) consider good, e.g. *All the books approved of by young persons of cultivated taste* (C. P. Snow).

● *Approve* should not be used in sense (2) with a direct object, as (wrongly) in *Laziness, rudeness, and untidiness are not approved in this establishment* (correctly, *approved of*).

apt, followed by the *to*-infinitive, carries no implication that the state or action expressed by the verb is undesirable from the point of view of its grammatical subject (though it often is from that of the writer), e.g. *In weather like this he is apt to bowl at the batsman's head* (Robert Graves). It indicates that the subject has a habitual tendency, e.g. *Time was apt to become confusing* (Muriel Spark). Compare **liable**, which, however, is not complementary to *apt to*, but overlaps with it; *apt to*, followed by a verb with undesirable overtones, = 'habitually or customarily liable to'.

Arab is now the usual term for 'native of Arabia' or an Arabic-speaking country, not *Arabian*.

aren't: see **ain't**.

Argentine, Argentinian can be both noun (= a native of Argentina) and adjective (= belonging to Argentina).

● Only the former is used in *Argentine Republic*. It rhymes with *turpentine*.

artiste, a professional public performer of either sex.

as (1) = *that*, *which*, or *who* (relative) is now non-standard except after *same*, *such*, e.g. *Such countries as France*; but not *I know somebody who knows this kid as went blind* (Alan Sillitoe, representing regional speech).

(2) = *that* (conjunction), introducing a

noun clause, is now non-standard, e.g. in *I don't know as you'll like it*.

as from is used in formal dating to mean 'on and after' (a date), e.g. *As from 15 October*. *As of*, originally Amer., has the same meaning and use. ● *As of now*, *yesterday*, and the like, are informal only.

Asian (1) *Asian* is to be preferred when used of persons to *Asiatic*, which is now widely considered derogatory. *Asiatic* is acceptable in e.g. *Asiatic cholera*.
(2) In Britain an *Asian* is also a person who comes from (or whose parents come from) the Indian subcontinent.

aside from: Amer., = apart from, except for.

as if, as though (1) Followed by the past tense when the verb refers to an unreal possibility, e.g. *It's not as though he lived like a Milord* (Evelyn Waugh).
(2) Followed by the present tense when the statement is true, or might be true, e.g. *I suppose you get on pretty well with your parents. You look as though you do* (Kingsley Amis).

attention. *Someone called it to my attention* (Alison Lurie) represents an illogical reversal of the idiom; *someone called* (or *drew*) *my attention to it* or *someone brought it to my attention* would be better in formal contexts.

author (verb) is a rarely required synonym for *write*; *co-author*, however, is acceptable as a verb.

avenge: one avenges an injured person or oneself *on* (occasionally *against*) an offender, or a wrong *on* an offender; the noun is *vengeance* (*on*), and the idea is usually of justifiable retribution, as distinct from **revenge**.

avert, to ward off (a danger), e.g. *Many disastrous sequels to depression might be averted if the victims received support* (William Styron).
● Do not confuse with *escape*, as this writer has done: *On a couple of occasions he only narrowly averted being arrested*.

aware is normally followed by an *of*-phrase or a *that*-clause, but can also be preceded by an adverb in the sense 'aware of, appreciative of (the subject indicated by the adverb)', a chiefly Amer. use, e.g. *The most technically aware* (W. S. Graham).
● In popular usage *aware* is sometimes used alone in the sense 'well-informed', e.g. *a very aware person*. This use should be avoided in formal contexts.

bacteria is the plural of *bacterium*, not a singular noun.

baluster, a short, fat pillar, especially in a balustrade; *banister*, an upright supporting a stair handrail (usually plural).

beg the question, to assume the truth of what is to be proved, e.g. *That pompous question-begging word 'Evolution'* (H. G. Wells). ● It does not mean (1) to avoid giving a straight answer; or (2) to invite the obvious question (that . .).

behalf: *on behalf of X* (= in X's interest, as X's representative) should not be confused with *on the part of X* (= done by X); *behalf* cannot replace *part* in *His death was due to panic on his part*.

benign (in Medicine) has *malignant* as its antonym.

beside (preposition) is used of spatial relationships, or in figurative adaptations of these, e.g. *Beside oneself with joy*; *Quite beside the point*; *besides* = in addition to, other than, e.g. *Eros includes other things besides sexual activity* (C. S. Lewis).

between. There is no objection to the use of *between* to express relations, actions, etc. involving more than two parties; *among* should not be substituted in, e.g., *Cordial relations between Britain, Greece, and Turkey*.
See also **choose between**.

bi- (prefix). *Biannual* = appearing (etc.) twice a year; *biennial* = recurring (etc.) every two years. *Bimonthly*, *biweekly*, and *biyearly* mean either 'twice' or 'every two', and are therefore best avoided.
● Use *twice a month* or *semi-monthly*, *twice a week* or *semi-weekly*, and *twice a year* in the first sense, and *every two months*, *fortnightly* or *every two weeks*, and *every two years* in the second sense.

billion, etc. (1) Traditional British usage has a *billion* = a million million (1,000,000,000,000 = 10^{12}), a *trillion* = a $million^3$ (10^{18}), and a *quadrillion* = a $million^4$ (10^{24}).
(2) The US usage makes each 'step' from *million* to *quadrillion*, and beyond, a power of 1,000; i.e. *million* = 1000^2, *billion* = 1000^3, *trillion* = 1000^4, *quadrillion* = 1000^5.
(3) For the quantity 'thousand million' (1000^3 = 10^9), many people now use the American *billion*. Most British national newspapers have officially adopted it too.
● In general contexts it is probably safer to use *thousand million* (X,000 m.). But where the sense is vague, e.g. *A billion miles away*, *Billions of stars*, the exact value is immaterial. Note that American *trillion* (10^{12}) = traditional British *billion*.

but = 'except', followed by a pronoun: see p. 77.

candelabra is strictly speaking the plural of *candelabrum* and is best kept so in written English.
● *Candelabra* (singular), *candelabras* (plural) are often found in informal use.

censure, to criticize harshly and unfavourably. ● Do not confuse with *censor* to suppress (the whole or parts of books, plays, etc.).

centre about, (a)round, meaning (figuratively) 'to revolve around, have as its main centre' is criticized by many authorities, though used by good writers, e.g. *A rather restless, cultureless life, centring round tinned food,* Picture Post, *the radio and the internal combustion engine* (George Orwell). It can be avoided by using *to be centred in* or *on.*

century. Strictly, since the first century ran from the year 1 to the year 100, the first year of a given century should be that ending in the digits 01, and the last year of the preceding century should be the year before.
● In popular usage, understandably, the reference of these terms has been moved back, so that the twenty-first century will be regarded as running from 2000 to 2099. Beware of ambiguity here.

character. ● Avoid using adjective + *character* to replace an abstract noun, e.g. write *the antiquity of the fabric*, not *the ancient character of the fabric.*

charisma (1) Properly, a theological word (plural *charismata*) designating any of the gifts of the Holy Spirit. (2) In general use, the capacity to inspire followers with devotion and enthusiasm. The adjective is *charismatic.*

choose between: this construction, and *choice between,* are normally followed by *and* in written English but sometimes by *or*, e.g. *The poorest girl alive may not be able to choose between being Queen of England or Principal of Newnham; but she can choose between ragpicking and flowerselling* (G. B. Shaw).

chronic is used of a disease that is long-lasting, though perhaps intermittent (the opposite is *acute*); it is used similarly of other conditions, e.g. *The commodities of which there is a chronic shortage* (George Orwell). ● The sense 'objectionable, bad, severe' is very informal.

cohort properly means:
(1) an ancient Roman military unit, equal to 1/10 of a legion; (2) a band of warriors; (3) a group of persons banded together in common cause; (4) a group of persons with a common statistical characteristic.
● The sense 'companion, ally', though quite common, especially in Amer. English, is much criticized and should be avoided.

comparable is followed by *with* in sense (1) of **compare** and by *to* in sense (2). The latter is much the more usual use, e.g. *The little wooden crib-figures .. were by no means comparable to the mass-produced figures* (Muriel Spark).

compare. In formal use, the following distinctions of sense are made: (1) 'Make a comparison of x with y', followed by *with*, e.g. *You've got to compare method with method, and ideal with ideal* (John le Carré).
(2) 'Say to be similar to, liken to', followed by *to*, e.g. *To call a bishop a*

mitred fool and compare him to a mouse (G. B. Shaw).
(3) Intransitively, = 'to stand comparison', followed by *with*, e.g. *The American hipsters' writings cannot begin to compare with the work of . . Celine and Genet* (Norman Mailer).

• *Compare with* is loosely used in sense (2), e.g. *How can you compare the Brigadier with my father?* (John Osborne). Conversely, in the separate clause *(as) compared with* or *to x*, *to* occurs as well as *with*, e.g. *Compared to Sarajevo, Belfast was paradise.*

comparison is usually followed by *with*, especially in *by* or *in comparison with.* It is followed by *to* when the sense is 'the action of likening (to)', e.g. *The comparison of philosophy to a yelping she-dog.*

complaisant, disposed to comply with others' wishes; noun *complaisance.*
• Do not confuse with *complacent* self-satisfied (noun *complacency*).

compose can mean 'constitute, make up' with the constituents as subject and the whole as object, e.g. *The tribes which composed the German nation.* In the passive, the whole is subject and the constituents object, e.g. *The German nation was composed of tribes.*

comprise. The proper constructions with *comprise* are the converse of those used with **compose**. (1) In the active, meaning 'consist of', with the whole as subject and the constituents as object, e.g. *The faculty comprises the following six departments.*

• In sense (1), *comprise* differs from *consist* in not being followed by *of.* Unlike *include*, *comprise* indicates a comprehensive statement of constituents.
(2) In the passive, meaning 'be embraced *in*', with the constituents as subject and the whole as object, e.g. *Fifty American dollars comprised in a single note* (Graham Greene).

• *Comprise* is often used as a synonym of **compose**, e.g. *The twenty-odd children who now comprise the school* (Miss Read). This is commonly regarded as incorrect, and is worse in the passive, since *comprise* is not followed by *of*; write *The faculty is composed* (not *comprised*) *of six departments.*

condole, to express sympathy, is always followed by *with*, e.g. *Many . . had come . . to condole with them about their brother* (*Revised English Bible*).
• Do not confuse with *console* 'to comfort', followed by direct object.

conduce, to lead or contribute (to a result), is always followed by *to*; similarly *conducive* (adjective); e.g. *The enterprise . . conduced to cut-price jobs* (J. I. M. Stewart).

conform may be followed by *to* or *with*, e.g. *The United Nations . . conformed to Anglo-American plans* (A. J. P. Taylor); *Having himself no . . tastes he relied upon whatever conformed with those of his companion* (John le Carré).

congeries, a collection of things massed together, is a singular noun, unchanged in the plural. • The form *congery*, formed in the misapprehension that *congeries* is plural only, is incorrect.

connote, denote. *Connote* means 'to imply in addition to the primary meaning, to imply as a consequence or condition', e.g. *To exploit all the connotations that lie latent in a word* (Anthony Burgess). *Denote* means 'to be the sign of, indicate, signify', e.g. *A proper name . . denotes a person* (Stephen Ullman).

• The two terms are kept rigidly distinct in Logic, but in popular usage *connote* frequently verges on the sense of *denote. Denote* cannot be used in the senses of *connote*, e.g. in *His silence does not connote hesitation* (Iris Murdoch).

consequent, following as a result, adverb *consequently*, e.g. *Two engaged in a common pursuit do not consequently share personal identity* (Muriel Spark). These are nearly always to be used rather than *consequential* 'following indirectly' and *consequentially*, which are more specialized.

consist: *consist of* = be made up of; *consist in* = have as its essence, e.g. *All enjoyment consists in undetected sinning* (G. B. Shaw).

continual, frequently recurring; *continuous*, uninterrupted; similarly the adverbs; e.g. *He was continually sending . . military advice* (Robert Graves); *There was a continuous rattle from the one-armed bandits* (Graham Greene).

continuance, continuation. The former relates mainly to the sense of *continue* 'to be still in existence', the latter to the sense 'to resume', e.g. *The great question of our continuance after death* (J. S. Huxley); *As if contemplating a continuation of her assault* (William Trevor).

cousin (1) The children of brothers or sisters are *first cousins* to each other. (2) The children of first cousins are *second cousins* to each other. (3) The child of one's first cousin, or the first cousin of one's parent, is one's *first cousin once removed*. (4) The grandchild of one's first cousin, or the first cousin of one's grandparent, is one's *first cousin twice removed*; and so on. (5) *Cousin-german* = first cousin.

credible, believable. ● Do not confuse with *credulous*, gullible, as e.g. in *Even if one is credible* (correctly *credulous*) *enough to believe in their ability*.

crescendo, used figuratively, means 'a progressive increase in force or effect'. Do not use it for *climax*, e.g. in *The storm reached a crescendo* (correctly *a climax*) *at midnight*.

criteria is the plural of *criterion*, not a singular noun.

crucial, decisive, critical, e.g. *His medical studies were not merely an episode in the development of his persona but crucial to it* (Frederic Raphael).
● The weakened sense 'important' is informal only.

data (1) In scientific, philosophical, and general use, usually treated as plural, e.g. *The optical data are incomplete* (*Nature*); the singular is *datum*.
(2) In computing and allied fields it is treated as a mass noun (i.e. a collective item), and used with words like *this*, *that*, and *much*, and with singular verbs; it is sometimes so treated in general use. ● Some people object to use (2), though it is more common than use (1). ● *Data* cannot be preceded by *a*, *every*, *each*, *either*, *neither*, and cannot be given a plural form *datas*.

decidedly, decisively. *Decidedly*, undoubtedly, e.g. *The bungalow had a decidedly English appearance* (Muriel Spark). *Decisively* (1) conclusively, e.g. *The definition of 'capital' itself depends decisively on the level of technology employed* (E. F. Schumacher); (2) unhesitatingly, e.g. *The young lady . . decisively objected to him* (G. B. Shaw).

decimate (originally) to kill or destroy one in every ten of; (now usually) to destroy a large proportion of, e.g. *All my parents' friends, my friends' brothers were getting killed. Our circle was decimated* (Rosamond Lehmann).
● *Decimate* does not mean 'defeat utterly'.

decline (verb: to refuse) has no derived noun; we have to make do with *refusal* if *declining* cannot be used.

definitive, decisive, unconditional, final; (of an edition) authoritative; e.g. *The Gold Cup flat handicap, the official and definitive result of which he had read in the Evening Telegraph* (James Joyce).
● Do not use instead of *definite* (= distinct, precise). A *definite no* is a firm refusal. A *definitive no* is an authoritative decision that something is not the case.

delusion, illusion. A general distinction can be drawn, though it is not absolute. *Delusion* denotes a false belief held tenaciously, arising mainly from the internal workings of the mind; e.g. *He's been sent here for delusions. His most serious delusion is that he's a murderer* (Robert Graves).
Illusion denotes a false impression derived either from the external world, e.g. *optical illusion*, or from faulty thinking, e.g. *I still imagine I could live in Rome, but it may be an illusion* (Iris Murdoch). It is in this second sense that *illusion* is almost equivalent to *delusion*; cf. *I have no delusions that knock-outs are likely* (Frederic Raphael). *Delusion* carries the sense of *being deluded* (by oneself or another), whereas no verb is implied in *illusion*; on the other hand, one can be said to be *disillusioned*, whereas *delusion* forms no such derivative.

demean (1) *Demean oneself* = behave (usually with adverbial expression), e.g. *He demeaned himself well.* This is now rare. (2) *Demean* (*someone* or *something*) = lower in status, especially with *oneself*, e.g. *Nor must you think that you demean yourself by treading the boards* (W. Somerset Maugham).

denote: see **connote**.

depend, to be controlled or determined by (a condition or cause), is followed by *on* or *upon*.

● The use of *it depends* followed, without *on* or *upon*, by an interrogative clause, is informal only, e.g. *It depends how you tackle the problem.*

depreciate, deprecate. *Depreciate* (1) to make or become lower in value; (2) to belittle, disparage, e.g. *To defend our record we seem forced to depreciate the Africans* (*Listener*); *To become a little more forthcoming and less self-depreciating* (Richard Adams).

Deprecate (1) (with a plan, purpose, etc. as the object) to deplore, e.g. *I deprecate this extreme course, because it is good neither for my pocket nor for their own souls* (G. B. Shaw). (2) (with a person as the object) to express disapproval of, disparage, e.g. *Anyone who has reprinted his reviews is in no position to deprecate our reprinter* (Christopher Ricks).

● Sense (2) of *deprecate* tends to take on the sense of *depreciate* (2), especially in conjunction with *self*. This use is frequently found in good writers, e.g. *A humorous self-deprecation about one's own advancing senility* (Aldous Huxley). It is, however, widely regarded as incorrect.

derisive = scoffing; *derisory* = (1) scoffing, (2) so small or unimportant as to be ridiculous (now the more usual sense), e.g. *The £40 . . you'll pay for any of the current sets is derisory compared with the £16.50 charged . . 39 years ago* (*Independent*).

dialect (form of speech) forms *dialectal* as its adjective; *dialectic* (form of reasoning) can be adjective as well as noun, or can have *dialectical* as its adjective.

dice is the normal singular as well as the plural; the old singular, *die*, is found only in *the die is cast, straight* (or *true*) *as a die*, and in mathematical contexts.

dichotomy in non-technical use means 'differentiation into two contrasting categories' and is frequently followed by *between*, e.g. *An absolute dichotomy between science on the one hand and faith on the other.*

● It does not mean *dilemma* or *ambivalence.*

die (noun): see **dice**.

different can be followed by *from, to*, or *than.*

(1) *Different from* is the most favoured by good writers, and is acceptable in all contexts, e.g. *It is also an 'important' book, in a sense different from the sense in which that word is generally used* (George Orwell).

(2) *Different to* is common informally. It sometimes sounds more natural than *different from*, e.g. when yoked with *similar* and followed by a phrase introduced by *to*: *His looks are neither especially similar nor markedly different to those of his twin brother.*

(3) *Different than* is established in Amer. English, but is not uncommon in British use, e.g. *Both came from a different world than the housing estate outside London* (Doris Lessing). *Different than* usefully avoids the repetition and the relative construction required after *different from* in sentences like *I was a very different man in 1935 from what I was in 1916* (Joyce Cary). This could be recast as *I was a very different man in 1935 than I was in 1916* or *than in 1916.* Compare *The American theatre, which is suffering from a different malaise than ours,* which is greatly preferable to *suffering from a different malaise from that which ours is suffering from.*

Uses (2) and (3) are long established, and are especially common when *different* is part of an adverbial clause (e.g. *in a different way*) or when the adverb *differently* is used, e.g. *Things were constructed very differently now than in former times* (Trollope); *Puts one in a different position to your own father* (John Osborne).

differential, a technical term in Mathematics, an abbreviation for *differential gear*, or a difference in wage between groups of workers. ● It is not a synonym for *difference*.

digraph = two letters standing for a single sound, e.g. *ea* in *head, gh* in *cough*; *ligature* = a typographical symbol consisting of two letters joined together, e.g. ﬁ, ﬂ, æ, œ. The term *diphthong* is best restricted to the sense 'a union of two vowels pronounced in one syllable', e.g. *i* in *find, ei* in *rein*, and *eau* in *bureau*.

dilemma (1) A choice between two (or more) undesirable alternatives, e.g. *The dilemma of cutting public services or increasing taxes* (*The Times*). (2) More loosely, a perplexing situation involving choice, e.g. *The dilemma of the 1960s about whether nice girls should sleep with men* (Alan Watkins). ● It is not merely a synonym for *problem*.

diphthong: see **digraph**.

direct is used as an adverb meaning: (1) straight, e.g. *Another door led direct to the house* (Evelyn Waugh); (2) without intermediaries, e.g. *I appeal now, over your head, . . direct to the august oracle* (G. B. Shaw).

directly is used in most of the main senses of the adjective, e.g. *Why don't you deal directly with the wholesalers?* (G. B. Shaw); *The wind is blowing directly on shore*; *directly opposite, opposed*.

● It is not usually used to mean 'straight', since it can also mean 'without delay', e.g. *Just a night in London—I'll be back directly* (Iris Murdoch).

discomfit, to thwart, disconcert; similarly *discomfiture*. ● Do not confuse with *discomfort* (now rare as a verb, = make uneasy).

disinterest, lack of interest, indifference, e.g. *Buried the world under a heavy snowfall of disinterest* (Christopher Fry).

● The use of *disinterest* in this sense may be objected to on the same grounds as sense (2) of **disinterested**; but the word is rarely used in any other sense.

disinterested (1) Impartial, unbiased, e.g. *Thanks to his scientific mind he understood—a proof of disinterested intelligence which had pleased her* (Virginia Woolf). The noun is *disinterestedness*. (2) Uninterested, indifferent, e.g. *It is not that we are disinterested in these subjects, but that we are better qualified to talk about our own interests* (*The Times*). The noun is **disinterest**.

● Sense (2) is common, but is widely regarded as incorrect and is avoided by careful writers, who prefer *uninterested*.

disposal is the noun from *dispose of* (get off one's hands, deal with); *disposition* is from *dispose* (arrange, incline).

distinctive, characteristic, e.g. *A light, entirely distinctive smell* (Susan Hill).

● Do not confuse with *distinct*, separate, individual, definite, e.g. *Trying to put into words an impression that was not distinct in my own mind* (W. Somerset Maugham).

drunk, drunken. In older and literary usage, the predicative and attributive forms respectively; now usually meaning respectively 'intoxicated' and 'fond of drinking', e.g. *They were lazy, irresponsible, and drunken; but today they were not drunk. Drunken* also means 'exhibiting drunkenness', e.g. *a drunken brawl.*

due to (1) That ought to be given to, e.g. *The respect due to the boss's nephew* (Vladimir Nabokov). (2) To be ascribed to, e.g. *Half the diseases of modern civilization are due to starvation of the affections in the young* (G. B. Shaw). *Due* is here an adjective, which needs to be attached to a noun as complement (see example above), or as part of a verbless adjective clause, e.g. *A few days' temporary absence of mind due to sunstroke* (Muriel Spark). (3) = *owing to*. Good writers now not uncommonly use *due to* as a compound preposition, where no noun is involved, e.g. *It . . didn't begin until twenty past due to a hitch* (William Trevor).

● This third use of *due to* is widely regarded as unacceptable. It can often be avoided by the addition of the verb *to be* and *that*, e.g. It is *due to your provident care* that .. *improvements are being made* (*Revised English Bible*).

effect: see **affect**.

e.g., i.e.: *E.g.* (short for Latin *exempli gratia*) = for example: *Many countries of Asia, e.g. India, Indonesia, and Malaysia. I.e.* (short for Latin *id est*) = that is: *It was natural that the largest nation (i.e. India) should take the lead.*

egoism, -ist(ic), egotism, -ist(ic). *Egoism* denotes self-interest (often contrasted with *altruism*), e.g. *Egoistic instincts concerned with self-preservation or the good of the Ego* (Gilbert Murray). *Egotism* is the practice of talking or thinking excessively about oneself, self-centredness, e.g. *He is petty, selfish, vain, egotistical; he is spoilt; he is a tyrant* (Virginia Woolf).

● In practice the senses tend to overlap, e.g. *Human loves don't last, .. they are far too egoistic* (Iris Murdoch); *A complete egotist in all his dealings with women* (Joyce Cary).

egregious, flagrant, outrageous; used mainly with words like *ass, folly, waste*, e.g. *Wark tenderly forgives her most egregious clerical errors* (Martin Amis). It does not mean simply 'offending, errant' as in *If sanctuary officers spot a particularly egregious diver they will direct him to the surface.*

either (adjective and pronoun). (1) One or other of the two, e.g. *Simple explanations are for simple minds. I've no use for either* (Joe Orton). (2) Each of the two, e.g. *Every few kilometres on either side of the road, there were .. guard-posts* (Graham Greene).

● *Either* is frequently used in sense (2), with reference to a thing that comes naturally in a pair, e.g. *end, hand, side*. This use is sometimes ignorantly condemned but is commonly found in good writers of all periods.

elder (adjective) the earlier-born (of two related or indicated persons), e.g. *The first and elder wife .. returned .. to Jericho* (Muriel Spark); *He is my elder by ten years. Eldest* first-born or oldest surviving (member of family etc.).

elusive (rather than *elusory*) is the usual adjective related to *elude*; *illusory* (rather than *illusive*) is that related to *illusion*.

enjoin: one can enjoin an action, etc., *on* someone, or enjoin someone *to* do something; e.g. *To .. enjoin celibacy on its .. clergy* and *That enables and enjoins the citizen to earn his own living* (G. B. Shaw). In legal writing, *to enjoin* (a person) *from* (doing something) is also found.

enormity (1) Great wickedness (of something), e.g. *Hugh was made entirely speechless .. by the enormity of the proposal* (Iris Murdoch); a serious offence, e.g. *To pass sentence on Wingfield for his enormities* (David Garnett). (2) Enormousness. ● Sense (2) is common, but is regarded by many people as incorrect.

enthuse, to show or fill with enthusiasm, is chiefly informal.

● **equally as** (+ adjective) should not be used for *equally*, e.g. in *How to apply it was equally as important*, or for *as*, e.g. *The Government are equally as guilty as the Opposition.*

event: *in the event of* is followed by a noun or gerund, e.g. *In the event of the earl's death, the title will lapse.*

● *In the event that*, used for *if*, is avoided by good writers; it is even less acceptable with *that* omitted, e.g. *In the event the car overturns.*

ever. When placed after a *wh*-question word, *ever* should be written separately, e.g. *Where ever have you been?, when ever is he coming?, who ever would have thought it?, why ever did you do it?, how ever shall I escape?* When used with a relative pronoun or adverb to give it force, *ever* is written as one word with it, e.g. *Wherever you go I'll follow*; *whenever he washes up he breaks something*; *there's a reward for whoever* (not *whomever*) *finds it*; *whatever else you do, don't get lost*; *however it's done, it's difficult.*

evidence, evince. *Evidence* (verb), to attest, e.g. *There was an innate refinement .. about Gerty which was* *unmistakably evidenced in her delicate hands* (James Joyce).

Evince, to show that one has (a quality), e.g. *Highly evolved sentiments and needs (sometimes said to be distinctively human, though birds and animals . . evince them)* (G. B. Shaw).

● *Evince* should not be confused with *evoke* to call up (a response, a feeling, etc.), e.g. *A timely and generous act which evoked a fresh outburst of emotion* (James Joyce).

exceedingly, extremely; *excessively*, beyond measure, immoderately.

excepting (preposition) is only used after *not* and *always*.

exceptionable, to which exception may be taken; *unexceptionable* with which no fault may be found, e.g. *The opposite claim would seem to him unexceptionable even if he disagreed with it* (George Orwell).

● Do not confuse with *(un)exceptional*, that is (not) unusual or outstanding.

excess. *In excess of.* ● Prefer *more than*, e.g. in *The Data Centre, which processes in excess of 1200 jobs per week*.

expect (1) in the sense 'suppose, think' is informal; (2) see **anticipate**.

explicit, express. *Explicit*, leaving nothing implied, e.g. *I had been too tactful, . . too vague . . But I now saw that I ought to have been more explicit* (Iris Murdoch); *express*, definite, unmistakable in import, e.g. *Idolatry fulsome enough to irritate Jonson into an express disavowal of it* (G. B. Shaw).

exposure (to) should not be used for *experience (of)*, e.g. in *Candidates who have had exposure to North American markets*.

express (adjective): see **explicit**.

facility in the sense 'ease in doing something', e.g. *I knew that I had a facility with words* (George Orwell), should not be confused with a similar sense of *faculty*, viz. 'specific ability', e.g. *Hess . . had that odd faculty, peculiar to lunatics, of falling into strained positions* (Rebecca West).

factious: see **fractious**.

factitious, not natural; artificial; e.g. *Factitious value. Fictitious*, simulated; imaginary, e.g. *Rumours of false accounting and fictitious loans* (*The Economist*).

farther, farthest: though originally interchangeable with *further, furthest*, these words are now only used where the sense of 'distance' is involved, e.g. *The farther mysteries of the cosmos* (J. I. M. Stewart). ● Even in this sense many people prefer *further, furthest*.

feasible, capable of being done, e.g. *Young people believing that niceness and innocence are politically as well as morally feasible* (J. I. M. Stewart).

● It is sometimes used for 'possible' or 'probable', but whichever of these is appropriate should be used instead.

fewer: see **less**.

fictitious: see **factitious**.

flammable, easily set on fire; preferable as a warning of danger to *inflammable*, which may be mistaken for a negative. The real negatives are *non-flammable* and *non-inflammable*.

flaunt, to display ostentatiously, e.g. *He's unemployed by the way, so don't flaunt your fabulous wealth in front of him* (Joseph O'Connor).

● Do not confuse with *flout* 'to disobey openly and scornfully', e.g. *His deliberate flouting of one still supposedly iron rule* (Frederic Raphael): *flout* should have been used by the public figure reported as having said *Those wanting to flaunt the policy would recognize that public opinion was not behind them*.

following, consequent on, is used in two ways. (1) Properly, as an adjective, dependent on a preceding noun, e.g. *During demonstrations following the hanging of two British soldiers*. (2) By extension, as a quasi-preposition, e.g. *The prologue was written by the company following an incident witnessed by them*.

● Many people regard use (2) as erroneous (cf. **due to** (3)). It can also give rise to ambiguity, e.g. *Police arrested a man following the hunt*. In any case, *following* should not be used merely for *after* (e.g. *Following supper they went to bed*).

for . The subject of a clause of which the verb is the *to-* infinitive is normally preceded by *for*, e.g. *For him to stay elsewhere is unthinkable*. But if the clause is a direct object, *for* is omitted: hence *I could not bear for him to stay elsewhere* is non-standard.

forbid can be followed by a personal object and a *to*-infinitive, e.g. *My means forbade me to indulge in such delightful fantasies* (Lawrence Durrell) or by an *-ing* form (see p. 83 f.), e.g. *Politeness . . forbade my doubting them* (Dickens). ● Do not use with *from* as in *She has an injunction forbidding him from calling her on the telephone*.

forensic (1) of or used in courts of law, e.g. *forensic science*; (2) of or involving forensic science, e.g. *forensic examination*. ● Sense (2) is often deplored, but is widespread.

former (latter). When referring to the first (last) of three or more, *the first* (*the last*) should be used, not *the former* (*the latter*).

fortuitous means 'happening by chance', e.g. *His presence is not fortuitous. He has a role to play* (André Brink).

● It does not mean either 'fortunate' or 'timely', as (incorrectly) in *He could not believe it. It was too fortuitous to be chance*.

fractious, unruly; peevish. ● Do not confuse with *factious* 'given to, or proceeding from, faction', e.g. *A divisive past and a fractious* (correctly, *factious*) *present*.

fruition, fulfilment, especially in *be brought to, come to, grow to, reach,* etc. *fruition*, once stigmatized, is now standard.

fulsome is a pejorative term, applied to *flattery, praise, affection,* etc., and means 'cloying, disgusting by excess', e.g. *They listened to fulsome speeches* (Beryl Bainbridge). ● *Fulsome* is not now regarded as a synonym of *copious*, its original meaning.

further, furthest: see **farther, farthest**.

geriatric means 'pertaining to the health and welfare of the elderly'; it is very informal (and may be offensive) to use it for *old* or *outdated*, or as a noun meaning 'old, outdated, or senile person'.

gourmand, glutton; *gourmet*, connoisseur of good food.

graffiti is the plural of *graffito*. The use of *graffiti* as a singular or mass noun is regarded as incorrect by some people but is common, e.g. in *Graffiti is an eyesore*.

half. The use of *half* to mean *half-past* is indigenous to Britain and has been remarked on since the 1930s, e.g. *We'd easily get the half-five bus* (William Trevor); it remains non-standard.

hardly. (1) *Hardly* is not used with negative constructions.

● Expressions like *I couldn't hardly tell what he meant* (substitute *I could hardly tell . .*) are non-standard.

(2) *Hardly* and *scarcely* are followed by *when* or *before*, not *than*, e.g. *Hardly had Grimes left the house when a tall young man . . presented himself at the front door* (Evelyn Waugh).

heir apparent, one whose right of inheritance cannot be superseded by the birth of another heir; as opposed to an *heir presumptive*, whose right can be so superseded.

● *Heir apparent* does not mean 'seeming heir'.

help. *More than*, or *as little as, one can help* are illogical but established idioms, e.g. *They will not respect more than they can help treaties extracted from them under duress* (Winston Churchill).

hoi polloi can be preceded by *the*, even though *hoi* is the Greek *the*, e.g. *The screens with which working archaeologists baffle the* hoi polloi (Frederic Raphael).

● **homogenous** is a frequent error for *homogeneous*. A word *homogenous* exists, but only as a technical term in biology. *Homogeneous* means 'of the same kind, uniform', e.g. *The style throughout was homogeneous but the authors' names were multiform* (Evelyn Waugh).

hopefully, thankfully. These adverbs are used in two ways: (1) As adverbs of manner = 'in a hopeful/thankful way', e.g. *I moved to the East Coast, and in 1938 hopefully built another boat* (Arthur Ransome); *When it thankfully*

dawned on her that the travel agency . . would be open (Muriel Spark). (2) As sentence adverbs, conveying the speaker's comment on the statement, e.g. *Hopefully they will be available in the autumn* (*Guardian*); *The editor, thankfully, has left them as they were written* (TLS).
● Use (2) is very common but regarded by many people as unacceptable. The main reason is that other commenting sentence adverbs, such as *regrettably*, can be converted to the form *it is regrettable that* —, but these are to be resolved as *it is to be hoped that*— and *one is thankful that* —. (The same objection could be, but is not, made to *happily* and *unhappily* which mean *one is (un)happy* not *it is (un)happy that* —, e.g. in *Unhappily children do hurt flies* (Jean Rhys).) A further objection is that ambiguity can arise from the interplay of senses (1) and (2), e.g. *Any decision to trust Egypt . . and move forward hopefully toward peace . . in the Middle East* (*Guardian Weekly*). It is recommended that sense (2) should be restricted to informal contexts.

how ever: see **ever**.

i.e.: see **e.g., i.e**.

if in certain constructions (usually linking two adjectives or adverbs) can be ambiguous, e.g. *A great play, if not the greatest, by this author*. ● It is best to paraphrase such sentences as, e.g., either *A great play, though not the greatest by this author* or *A great play, perhaps* (or *very nearly*) *the greatest by this author*.

ignorant is better followed by *of* than by *about*, e.g. *The residents are . . ignorant of their rights* (*Independent*).

ilk. *Of that ilk* is a Scots term, meaning 'of the same place or name', e.g. *Wemyss of that ilk* = Wemyss of Wemyss. ● By a misunderstanding *ilk* has come to mean 'sort, lot' (usually pejorative), e.g. *Joan Baez and other vocalists of that ilk* (David Lodge). This should be avoided in formal English.

ill used predicatively = 'unwell'; *sick* used predicatively = 'about to vomit, in the act of vomiting', e.g. *I felt sick*; *I was violently sick*; used attributively = 'unwell', e.g. *a sick man*, except in collocations like *sick bay, sick leave*. ● It is non-standard to use *ill* for 'in the act of vomiting' or *sick* predicatively for 'unwell' (though the latter is standard Amer.), except in *off sick* 'away on sick leave'.

illusion: see **delusion**.

illusory: see **elusive**.

impact, used figuratively, is best confined to contexts of someone or something striking another, e.g. *The most dynamic colour combination if used too often loses its impact*. It is weakened if used as a mere synonym for *effect* or *influence*.

impedance, the resistance of an electric circuit to alternating current. ● Do not confuse with *impediment*, a hindrance, a defect (in speech etc.), e.g. *A serious impediment to his marriage* (Evelyn Waugh).

imply, infer. *Imply* (1) to involve the truth or existence of; (2) to express indirectly, insinuate, hint at. *Infer* to reach (an opinion), deduce, from facts and reasoning, e.g. *She left it to my intelligence to infer her meaning. I inferred it all right* (W. Somerset Maugham). ● *Infer* should not be used for sense (2) of *imply*, as in *I have inferred once, and I repeat, that Limehouse is the most overrated excitement in London* (H. V. Morton).

imprimatur, official licence to print. ● Do not confuse with *imprint*, the name of the publisher/printer, place of publication/printing, etc., on the verso of the title-page or at the end of a book.

inapt, inept. *Inapt* = 'not apt', 'unsuitable'; *inept* = (1) unskilful, e.g. *Foxtrots and quicksteps, at which he had been so inept* (David Lodge); (2) inappropriate, e.g. *ineptly dressed*; (3) absurd, silly.

inchoate means 'just begun, underdeveloped', e.g. *Trying to give his work a finished look—and all the time . . the stuff's fatally inchoate* (John Wain). ● It does not mean *chaotic* or *incoherent*.

include: see **comprise** (1).

infer: see **imply**.

inflammable: see **flammable**.

inflict, afflict. One *inflicts* something *on* someone or *afflicts* someone *with* something. ● Do not use *inflict with* where *afflict with* is meant, e.g. in *The miners are still out, and industry is inflicted* (correctly, *afflicted*) *with a kind of creeping paralysis.*

ingenious, clever at inventing, etc.; noun *ingenuity*; *ingenuous* open, frank, innocent; noun *ingenuousness.*

insignia is, in origin, a plural noun, e.g. *Fourteen different airline insignia* (David Lodge); its singular, rarely encountered, is *insigne.* ● Use as a countable noun is non-standard, e.g. in *The insignias that immune system cells use to tell friend from foe.*

intense, existing in a high degree, e.g. *The intense evening sunshine* (Iris Murdoch); *intensive* employing much effort, concentrated, e.g. *Intensive care.*

interface (noun) (1) A surface forming a common boundary, e.g. *The interfaces between solid and solid, solid and liquid.* (2) A piece of equipment in which interaction occurs between two systems, processes, etc., e.g. *Modular interfaces to adapt the general-purpose computer to the equipment.* (3) A point of interaction between two systems, organizations, or disciplines, e.g. *The interface between physics and music* (*Nature*).

● Sense (3) is deplored by many people, since it is often overused for *meeting-point, liaison, link,* etc., e.g. *The need for the interface of lecturer and student will diminish.*

interface (verb), to connect with (another piece of equipment) by an interface, e.g. *Using the Kontron image analyser interfaced to the computer* (*Brain*).

● *Interface* is nowadays regrettably overused as a synonym for *interact* (*with*), as, e.g., in *The ideal candidate will have the ability to interface effectively with other departments.*

internment, confinement (from verb *intern*).

● Do not confuse with *interment,* burial (from verb *inter*).

invite (noun = 'invitation') remains informal only.

ironic, ironical, ironically. The noun *irony* can mean (1) a way of speaking in which the intended meaning (for those with insight) is the opposite to, or very different from, that expressed by the words used; or (2) an ill-timed or perverse outcome.

The adjectives *ironic, ironical,* and the adverb *ironically* are commonly used in sense (1) of *irony*, e.g. *Ironical silent apology for the absence of naked women and tanks of gin from the amenities* (Kingsley Amis). They are also frequently found in sense (2), e.g. *The fact that after all she had been faithful to me was ironic* (Graham Greene). ● Some people object to this use, especially when *ironic* or *ironically* introduces a trivial oddity, e.g. *It was ironic that he thought himself locked out when the key was in his pocket all the time.*

kind of, sort of (1) *A kind of, a sort of* should not be followed by *a* before the noun, e.g. *a kind of shock,* not *a kind of a shock.* (2) *Kind of, sort of,* etc., followed by a plural noun, are often qualified by plural words like *these, those,* or followed by a plural verb, e.g. *They would be on those sort of terms* (Anthony Powell). This is widely regarded as incorrect except in informal use: substitute *that* (etc.) *kind* (or *sort*) *of* or *of that kind* (or *sort*), e.g. *this kind of car is unpopular* or *cars of this kind are unpopular.* (3) *Kind of, sort of* used adverbially, e.g. *I kind of expected it,* are informal only.

kudos is a mass noun like *glory* or *fame.*

● It is not a plural noun and there is no singular *kudo.*

latter: see **former**.

laudable, praiseworthy; *laudatory,* expressing praise.

lay (verb), past *laid,* = 'put down, arrange', etc. is only transitive, e.g. *Lay her on the bed*; *They laid her on the bed.* ● To use *lay* for 'lie', e.g. *She wants to lay down*; *She was laying on the bed,* is non-standard, even though fairly common in speech. Cf. **lie**.

leading question, in Law, is a question that prompts the desired answer, e.g. *The solicitor . . at once asked me some* *leading questions . . I had to try to be both forthcoming and discreet* (C. P. Snow).

● It does not mean a 'principal (or loaded or searching) question'.

learn with a person as the object, = 'teach', is non-standard, or occasionally jocular as in *I'll learn you*.

less (adjective) is the comparative of (*a*) *little*, and, like the latter, is used with mass nouns, e.g. *I owe him little duty and less love* (Shakespeare); *fewer* is the comparative of (*a*) *few*, and both are used with plurals, e.g. *Few people have their houses broken into; and fewer still have them burnt* (G. B. Shaw).

● *Less* is quite often used informally as the comparative of *few*, e.g. *Our copiers have less parts inside them so there's less to go wrong* (*Office Magazine*). This is regarded as incorrect in formal English.

● *Less* should not be used as the comparative of *small* (or some similar adjective such as *low*), e.g. *a lower price* not *a less price*.

lesser, not so great as the other or the rest e.g. *The lesser celandine*. ● *Lesser* should not be used for 'not so big' or 'not so large': its opposition to *greater* is essential. It cannot replace *smaller* in *A smaller prize will probably be offered*.

lest is very formal; it is followed by *should* or (in exalted style) the subjunctive, e.g. *Lest the eye wander aimlessly, a Doric temple stood by the water's edge* (Evelyn Waugh); *Lest some too sudden gesture or burst of emotion should turn the petals brown* (Patrick White).

let, to allow (followed by the bare infinitive) is rare in the passive: the effect is usually unidiomatic, e.g. *Halfdan's two sons . . are let owe their lives to a trick* (Gwyn Jones).

liable (1) can be followed by *to* + a noun or noun phrase in the sense 'subject to, likely to suffer from', or by an infinitive; (2) carries the implication that what is expressed is undesirable, e.g. *Receiving in the bedroom is liable to get a woman talked about* (Tom Stoppard); (3) can indicate either the mere possibility, or the habituality, of what is expressed by the verb, e.g. *The kind of point that one is always liable to miss* (George Orwell).

● The sense 'likely to' is American, e.g. *Boston is liable to be the ultimate place for holding the convention*.

Contrast **apt**.

lie (verb) past *lay*, *lain*, = 'recline', 'be situated', is only intransitive, e.g. *Lie down on the bed*; *The ship lay at anchor until yesterday*; *Her left arm, on which she had lain all night, was numb*. Although correct, *lain* can sound somewhat stilted, and *been lying* is often preferred.

● To use *lie* for 'lay', e.g. *Lie her on the bed*, is non-standard. The past *lay* and participle *lain* are quite often wrongly used for *laid* out of over-correctness, e.g. *He had lain this peer's honour in the dust*. Cf. **lay**.

ligature: see **digraph**.

like, indicating resemblance between two things: (1) It is normally used as an adjective followed by a noun, noun phrase, or pronoun (in the objective case), e.g. *There can't be many fellows about with brains like yours* (P. G. Wodehouse); *He loathes people like you and me* (not *. . and I*). It can be used to mean 'such as', e.g. *Good writers like Dickens*.

● In formal contexts some people prefer *such as* to be used if more than one example is mentioned, e.g. *He dealt in types, such as the rich bitch, the honest whore, the socializing snob* (*London Magazine*).

(2) It is often used as a conjunction with a dependent clause, e.g. *Everything went wrong . . like it does in dreams* (Iris Murdoch), or with an adverbial phrase, e.g. *It was as if I saw myself. Like in a looking-glass* (Jean Rhys). ● Although this use of *like* as a conjunction is not uncommon in formal writing, it is best avoided, except informally. Use *as*, e.g. *Do you mean to murder me as you murdered the Egyptian?* (*Revised English Bible*), or recast the sentence, e.g. *A costume like those that the others wore*.

(3) It is often informally used to mean 'as if', e.g. *You wake like someone hit you on the head* (T. S. Eliot). • This use is very informal.

likely (adverb), in the sense 'probably', must be preceded by *more, most, quite*, or *very*, e.g. *Its inhabitants . . very likely do make that claim for it* (George Orwell).

• The use without the qualifying adverb is standard only in Amer. English, e.g. *They'll likely turn ugly* (Eugene O'Neill).

linguist means 'one whose subject is linguistics' as well as 'one skilled in the use of languages'; there is no other suitable term (*linguistician* exists but is not commonly used).

literally. In very informal speech, *literally* is used as an intensifying adverb without meaning apart from its emotive force.

• This use should be avoided in writing or formal speech, since it almost invariably involves absurdity, e.g. *The dwarfs mentioned here are literally within a stone's throw of the Milky Way* (*New Scientist*).

loan (verb) has some justification in financial contexts, e.g. *The gas industry is . . loaning money to Government* (*Observer*). It should not be used merely as a variant for *lend*.

locate can mean 'discover the exact position of', e.g. *She had located and could usefully excavate her Saharan highland emporium* (Margaret Drabble); it should not be used to mean merely 'find'.

lot. *A lot of*, though somewhat informal, is acceptable in serious writing; *lots of* is not.

luncheon is formal; *lunch* should normally be used, except in fixed expressions like *luncheon voucher*.

luxuriant, profuse in growth, prolific, e.g. *His hair . . does not seem to have been luxuriant even in its best days* (G. B. Shaw). • Do not confuse with *luxurious* (the adjective from *luxury*), e.g. *The food, which had always been good, was now luxurious* (C. P. Snow).

majority can mean 'the greater number of a countable set', and is then followed by the plural, e.g. *The majority of the plays produced were failures* (G. B. Shaw).

• *Great* (or *huge, vast*, etc.) can precede *majority* in this sense, e.g. *The first thing you gather from the vast majority of the speakers* (C. S. Lewis); but not *greater, greatest*. • *Majority* is not used to mean 'the greater part of a quantity', e.g. *I was doing most of the cooking* (not *the majority of the cooking*).

malignant: see **benign**.

masterful, domineering, e.g. *People might say she was tyrannical, domineering, masterful* (Virginia Woolf).

• Do not confuse with *masterly*, very skilful, e.g. *A masterly piece of work*.

maximize, to make as great as possible.

• It should not be used for 'to make as good, easy, etc. as possible' or 'to make the most of' as in *To maximize customer service*; *To maximize this situation*.

means (1) Money resources: a plural noun, e.g. *You might find out from Larry . . what his means are* (G. B. Shaw).

(2) That by which a result is brought about. It may be used either as a singular or as a plural, e.g. (singular) *The press was, at this time, the only means . . of influencing opinion* (A. J. P. Taylor); (plural) *All the time-honoured means of meeting the opposite sex* (Frederic Raphael).

• Beware of mixing singular and plural, as in *The right to resist by every* (singular) *means that are* (plural) *consonant with the law of God*.

media, agency, means (of communication etc.), is a plural noun, e.g. *The communication media inflate language because they dare not be honest* (Anthony Burgess). Its singular is *medium* (rare except in *mass medium*).

• Although *media* is commonly treated as a singular noun, this use should be avoided, as should the plural form *medias*. *Medium* (in Spiritualism) forms its plural in *-s*.

militate: see **mitigate**.

minimize, to reduce to, or estimate at, the minimum, e.g. *Each side was inclined* *to minimize its own losses in battle.* ● It does not mean *lessen* and therefore cannot be qualified by adverbs like *greatly*.

minority. *Large, vast,* etc. *minority* can mean either 'almost half', or 'a number who are very much the minority': although it usually means the former, it is best to avoid the ambiguity.

mitigate, alleviate, moderate (usually transitive), e.g. *Its heat mitigated by the strong sea-wind* (Anthony Burgess).
● Do not confuse with *militate* (intransitive) *against*, to have effect against, e.g. *The very fact that Leamas was a professional could militate against his interests* (John le Carré).

momentum, impetus. ● Do not confuse with *moment* 'importance', e.g. *An error of some moment* (not *momentum*).

more than one is followed by a singular verb and is referred back to by singular pronouns, e.g. *More than one popular dancing man inquired anxiously at his bank* (Evelyn Waugh).

motif, motive. *Motif* (1) theme in an artistic work, (2) decorative pattern, (3) ornament sewn on a garment. *Motive*, what induces a person to act in a particular way. *Motive* might have been a better choice in the following: *Fear of failure is a strong motif in men's lives.*

motivate, to be the motive of (a person, an action), e.g. *A . . tax grab motivated by the politics of envy* (*Daily Express*). ● It does not mean 'justify', e.g. (wrongly) in *The publisher motivates the slim size of these volumes by claiming it makes them more likely to be read.*

mutual (1) Felt, done, etc., by each to(wards) the other, e.g. *mutual affection.* (2) Standing in a (specified) relation to each other, e.g. *mutual beneficiaries.* This sense is now rare. (3) Shared, e.g. *a mutual friend.* ● Sense (3) is acceptable in a small number of collocations, such as that indicated, in which *common* might be ambiguous; cf. *They had already formed a small island of mutual Englishness* (Muriel Spark): *common Englishness* might imply vulgarity. Otherwise *common* is preferable, e.g. in *By common* (rather than *mutual*) *agreement they finished the card-game at nine.*

naturalist, expert in natural history; *naturist*, nudist.

nature. ● Avoid using adjective + *nature* as a periphrasis for an abstract noun, e.g. write *The dangerousness of the spot*, not *The dangerous nature of the spot.*

need (*this needs changing* etc.): see **want**.

neighbourhood. *In the neighbourhood of* is an unnecessarily cumbersome periphrasis for *round about, approximately.*

neither (adverb). ● It is non-standard to use it instead of *either* to strengthen a preceding negative, e.g. *There were no books either* (not *neither*).

non-flammable: see **flammable**.

normalcy is chiefly Amer. ● Prefer *normality.*

not only: see **only** (4).

no way (1) (Initially, followed by inversion of verb and subject) = 'not at all, by no means', e.g. *No way will you stop prices . . going up again* (James Callaghan). ● Informal only. (2) = 'certainly not', e.g. *'Did you go up in the elevator?' 'No way.'* ● Chiefly Amer.; informal only.

number. *A number* (*of*) takes the plural, *the number* (*of*) the singular, e.g. *A number of people around us were unashamedly staring* (Bruce Arnold); *The number of accidents has decreased.*

obligate (verb) is in Britain only used in Law. ● There is no gain in using it (as often in Amer. usage) for *oblige.*

oblivious, in the sense 'unaware of', may be followed by *of* or *to*, e.g. *'When the summer comes,' said Lord Marchmain, oblivious of the deep corn . . outside his windows* (Evelyn Waugh); *Rose seemed oblivious to individuals* (Angus Wilson). ● This sense is now fully established in the language.

obscene ● Avoid using it as a general term of disapproval, e.g. *TV's claim to 'show it like it is' in 1990 appears as obscene as it did in the Falklands War.*

of used for *have*: see **of,** p. 25, and **have,** p. 42.

off of used for the preposition *off*, e.g. *Picked him off of the floor*, is non-standard.

one (pronoun) (1) = 'any person, people in general' has *one*, *one's*, and *oneself* as objective, possessive, and reflexive forms. ● These forms should point back to a previous use of *one*, e.g. *One always did, in foreign parts, become friendly with one's fellow-countrymen more quickly than one did at home* (Muriel Spark). *One* should not be mixed with *he* (*him*, *his*, etc.) (acceptable Amer. usage) or *we*, *you*, etc.
(2) = single thing or person, following *any*, *every*, and *some*; the resulting phrase is written as two words and is distinct from *anyone*, *everyone*, *someone*, e.g. *Any one* (*of these*) *will do*.

ongoing has a valid use meaning 'that is happening and will continue', e.g. *The refugee problem in our time is an ongoing problem* (Robert Kee). ● The vague or tautologous use of *ongoing* should be avoided, as in the cliché *ongoing situation*.

only (1) In spoken English, it is usual to place *only* between subject and verb, e.g. *He only saw Bill yesterday*: intonation shows whether *only* limits *he*, *saw*, *Bill*, or *yesterday*.
(2) It is an established idiom that, in a sentence containing *only* + verb + another item, in the absence of special intonation, *only* is understood as limiting that other item. *I only want some water* is the natural way of saying *I want only some water*. If there is more than one item following the verb, *only* often limits the item nearest the end of the sentence, e.g. *A type of mind that can only accept ideas if they are put in the language he would use himself* (Doris Lessing) (= only if . .); but not always, e.g. *The captain was a thin unapproachable man .. who only appeared once at table* (Graham Greene) (= only once).
(3) Despite the idiom described under (2), there are often sentences in which confusion can arise. If this is likely, *only* should be placed before the item which it limits, e.g. *The coalminer is second in importance only to the man who ploughs the soil* (George Orwell).
(4) *Not only* should not be placed in the position before the verb. This is a fairly common slip, e.g. *Katherine's marriage not only kept her away, but at least two of Mr. March's cousins* (C. P. Snow); *kept not only her* would be better. If placing it before the verb is inevitable, the verb should be repeated after *but* (*also*), e.g. *It not only brings the coal out but brings the roof down as well* (George Orwell).

ordinance (1) authoritative decree; (2) religious rite. ● Do not confuse with *ordnance*, (1) mounted guns, (2) government service dealing with military stores and materials. Note also *Ordnance Survey*.

orient, orientate. They are virtually synonymous. In general use, *orientate* seems to predominate, but either is acceptable.

other than can be used where *other* is an adjective or pronoun, e.g. *He was no other than the rightful lord*; *The acts of any person other than myself*. ● *Other* cannot be treated as an adverb: *otherwise* should be used instead, e.g. in *cannot react other than angrily*.

out used as a preposition instead of *out of*, e.g. *looked out the window*, is non-standard.

outside of (1) = 'apart from' is informal only, e.g. *The need of some big belief outside of art* (Roger Fry, in a letter).
(2) = beyond the limits of, e.g. *The most important such facility outside of Japan* (*Gramophone*). ● In sense (2) *outside* alone is preferable.

outstanding. ● Do not use in the sense 'remaining undetermined, unpaid, etc.' where ambiguity with the sense 'eminent, striking' can arise, e.g. *In a moment we'll give you the other outstanding results* (in a sports commentary).

overly, excessively, too, is still regarded as an Americanism, e.g. *overly cautious*.
● Use *excessively*, *too*, or *over-* instead; for *not overly*, *not very* or *none too* make satisfactory replacements.

overseas (adjective and adverb) is now more usual than *oversea*.

owing to, unlike **due to,** has for long been established as a compound preposition meaning 'because of', e.g. *My rooms became uninhabitable, owing to a burst gas-pipe* (C. P. Snow). ● *Owing to the fact that* should be avoided: use a conjunction like *because.*

pace means 'despite (someone)'s opinion', e.g. *Our civilization,* pace *Chesterton, is founded on coal* (George Orwell).
● It does not mean 'according to (someone)' or 'notwithstanding (something)'.

parameter. (1) (In technical use) a quantity constant in the case considered, but varying in different cases.
(2) A (measurable) defining characteristic, e.g. *The three major parameters of colour—brightness, hue, and saturation.*
(3) (Loosely) a limit or boundary, e.g. *Within the parameters of the parole system* (*The Times*); an aspect or feature, e.g. *The main parameters of the problem.* ● Use (3) is a popular dilution of the word's meaning, probably influenced (at least in the first quotation) by *perimeter*; it should be avoided.

parricide refers to the killing of a near relative, especially of a parent; *patricide* only to the killing of one's father.

part (on the part of): see **behalf**.

partially, partly. Apart from the (rare) use of *partially* to mean 'in a partial or biased way', these two words are largely interchangeable; but *partly . . partly* is more usual than *partially . . partially*, e.g. *Partly in verse and partly in prose.*

peer, as in *to have no peer*, means 'equal', not 'superior'.

pence is sometimes informally used as a singular, *one pence.* ● Normally *penny* should be used in the singular.

perquisite (informal abbreviation *perk*) extra profit attached to employment, e.g. *The dead man's clothes are the perquisites of the layer-out* (Lawrence Durrell). ● Do not confuse with *prerequisite* 'something required as a precondition', e.g. *Her mere comforting presence . . was already a prerequisite to peaceful sleep* (Lynne Reid Banks).

persistency is limited in sense to 'perseverance', e.g. *They made repeated requests for compensation, but an official apology was the only reward for their persistency*; *persistence* is sometimes used in that sense, e.g. *Phil Davies' try . . was just reward for the flanker's persistence* (*Independent on Sunday*), but more often for 'continued existence', e.g. *The persistence of this primitive custom.*

perspicuous, easily understood; expressing things clearly; similarly *perspicuity*; e.g. *There is nothing more desirable in composition than perspicuity* (Southey).
● Do not confuse with *perspicacious*, having insight, and *perspicacity*, e.g. *Her perspicacity at having guessed his passion* (Vita Sackville-West).

***petit bourgeois*, petty bourgeois.** The meaning is the same. If the former is used, the correct French inflections should be added: *petits bourgeois* (plural), *petite(s) bourgeoise(s)* (feminine (plural)); also *petite bourgeoisie.*

phenomena is the plural of *phenomenon.*
● It cannot be used as a singular and cannot form a plural *phenomenas.*

picaresque (of a style of fiction) dealing with the episodic adventures of rogues.
● It does not mean 'transitory' or 'roaming'.

pivotal, crucial, decisive, e.g. *The pardon of Richard Nixon was pivotal to those who made up their minds at the last minute.* ● Do not use it merely to mean *vital.*

plaid, shawl-like garment; *tartan,* woollen cloth with distinctive pattern; the pattern itself.

● **plus** (conjunction), = 'and in addition', is not generally acceptable in Standard English, e.g. *They arrived late, plus they were hungry.*

polity, a form of civil government, e.g. *A republican polity*; a state. ● It does not mean *policy* or *politics.*

portentous can mean: (1) Like a portent, ominous, e.g. *Fiery-eyed with a sense of portentous utterance* (Muriel Spark).

(2) Prodigious. (3) Solemn, pompous, e.g. *A portentous commentary on Holy Scripture* (Lord Hailsham).
• Sense (3) is sometimes criticized, but is an established, slightly jocular use.
• The form *portentious* (due to the influence of *pretentious*) is erroneous.

post, pre. Their use as full words (not prefixes) should be avoided, e.g. in *Post the Geneva meeting of Opec* (*Daily Telegraph*); *Pre my being in office* (Henry Kissinger).

practicable, practical. When applied to things, *practicable* means 'able to be done', e.g. (with the negative *impracticable*), *Schemes which look very fine on paper, but which, as we well know, are impracticable* (C. S. Lewis); *practical* 'suited to the conditions', e.g. *Having considered the problem, he came up with several practical suggestions.*

pre: see **post, pre.**

precipitous, like a precipice, e.g. *A precipitous marble staircase* (Evelyn Waugh). • Do not confuse with *precipitate*, hasty, rash, e.g. *Precipitate departure.*

predicate (verb) (1) (Followed by *of*) to assert as a property of, e.g. *That easy Bohemianism—conventionally predicated of the 'artistic' temperament* (J. I. M. Stewart). (2) (Followed by *on*) to found or base (a statement etc.) on.
• Sense (2) tends to sound pretentious. Use *found*, or *base, on.*

pre-empt (1) To acquire in advance, e.g. *Contributions pre-empt a slice of incomes which would otherwise be available for saving* (Enoch Powell). (2) To preclude, forestall, e.g. *The Nazi régime by its own grotesque vileness pre-empted fictional effort* (Listener).
• Sense (2) is better expressed by *preclude* or *forestall.* • *Pre-empt* is not a synonym for *prevent.*

prefer. The rejected alternative is introduced by *to*, e.g. *People preferred darkness to light* (*Revised English Bible*). But when the rejected alternative is an infinitive, it is preceded by *rather than* (not *than* alone), e.g. *I'd prefer to be stung to death rather than to wake up . . with half of me shot away* (John Osborne). • *Prefer . . over* is chiefly Amer.

preferable to means 'more desirable than' and is therefore intensified by *far*, *greatly*, or *much*, not *more.*

preference. The alternatives are introduced by *for* and *over*, e.g. *The preference for a single word over a phrase or clause* (Anthony Burgess); but *in preference* is followed by *to.*

prejudice (1) = bias, is followed by *against* or *in favour of*; (2) = detriment, is followed by *to*; (3) = injury, is followed by *of* (in the phrase *to the prejudice of*).

prepared: *to be prepared to,* to be willing to, has been criticized, but is now established usage, e.g. *One should kill oneself, which, of course, I was not prepared to do* (Cyril Connolly).

prerequisite: see **perquisite.**

prescribe, to lay down as a rule to be followed; *proscribe*, to forbid by law.

presently (1) Soon, e.g. *Presently we left the table and sat in the garden-room* (Evelyn Waugh). (2) Now, e.g. *The praise presently being heaped upon him* (*The Economist*). • Sense (2) (long current in Amer. English) is regarded as incorrect by some people but is widely used and often sounds more natural than *at present.*

prestigious (1) Characterized by magic, deceptive, e.g. *The prestigious balancing act which he was constantly obliged to perform* (TLS): now rare. (2) Having prestige, e.g. *A career in pure science is still more socially prestigious . . than one in engineering* (*The Times*): a fully acceptable sense.

prevaricate, to speak or act evasively or misleadingly; *procrastinate*, to postpone action.

prevent is followed by *from* + the gerund, or by the possessive case + the gerund, e.g. *prevent me from going* or *prevent my going.* • *Prevent me going* is informal only.

• **pre-war** as an adverb, in, e.g., *Some time pre-war there was a large contract out for tender* (*Daily Telegraph*): prefer *before the war.*

pristine (1) Ancient, original. (2) Unspoilt, e.g. *Pristine snow reflects about 90 per cent of incident sunlight* (Fred Hoyle).
• *Pristine* does not mean 'spotless', 'pure', or 'fresh'.

procrastinate: see **prevaricate**.

prone (followed by *to*) is used like **liable**, but usually with a personal subject, e.g. *My literary temperament rendering me especially prone to 'all that kind of poisonous nonsense'* (Cyril Connolly).

proportion means 'a comparative part'; it is not a mere *part*.

proscribe: see **prescribe**.

protagonist, the leading character in a story or incident.

● In Greek drama there was only one protagonist, but this is no reason to debar the use of the word in the plural, e.g. *We .. sometimes mistook a mere supernumerary in a fine dress for one of the protagonists* (C. S. Lewis).

● Do not confuse with *proponent*: the word contains the Greek prefix *prot-* 'first', not the prefix *pro-* 'in favour of', and does not mean 'champion, advocate'.

protest (verb, transitive) to affirm solemnly, e.g. *He protested his innocence.* ● The sense 'object to', e.g. in *The residents have protested the sale,* is Amer. only.

proven. It is not the standard past participle of *prove* in British English (it is standard Scots and Amer.); it is, however, common attributively in expressions such as *of proven ability*.

provenance, origin, place of origin, is used in Britain; the form *provenience* is its usual Amer. equivalent.

prudent, careful, circumspect, e.g. *What is the difference in matrimonial affairs, between the mercenary and the prudent move?* (Jane Austen); *prudential,* involving or marked by prudence, e.g. *prudential motives*.

pry, to prise (open etc.): chiefly Amer., but occasionally in British literary use. The normal sense is 'peer' or 'inquire'.

quadrillion: see **billion**.

question: (1) *No question that* (or *but*), no doubt that, e.g. *There can be no question that the burning of Joan of Arc must have been a most instructive and interesting experiment* (G. B. Shaw).
(2) *No question of*, no possibility of, e.g. *There can be no question of tabulating successes and failures* (C. S. Lewis). See also **beg the question, leading question**.

quote (noun = quotation) is informal only (except in Printing and Commerce).

● **re** (in the matter of, referring to) is better avoided and should not be used for 'about, concerning'.

reason. *The reason* (*why*) . . *is* . . should be followed by *that*, not *because*.

recoup (1) (transitive) to reimburse, e.g. *Dixon felt he could recoup himself a little for the expensiveness of the drinks* (Kingsley Amis); also *to recoup one's losses*; (2) (intransitive) to make good one's loss, e.g. *I had . . so many debts that if I didn't return to England to recoup, we might have to run for it* (Chaim Bermant).

● This word is not synonymous with *recuperate*.

recuperate (1) (intransitive) to recover from ill-health, financial loss, etc., e.g. *I've got a good mind .. to put all my winnings on red and give him a chance to recuperate* (Graham Greene); (2) (transitive) to recover (health, a loss, material). In sense (2) *recover* is preferable.

redolent, smelling *of* something, e.g. *Corley's breath redolent of rotten cornjuice* (James Joyce); also 'strongly suggestive of', e.g. *The missive most redolent of money and sex* (Martin Amis).

referendum. ● The plural *referendums* is preferable to *referenda*.

refute, to disprove (a statement etc.), e.g. *The case against most of them must have been so easily refuted that they could hardly rank as suspects* (Rebecca West); to prove (a person) to be in error, e.g. *German scholars whose function is to be refuted in a footnote* (Frederic Raphael). ● *Refute* does not mean 'deny' or 'repudiate' (an allegation etc.).

regalia is a plural noun, meaning 'emblems of royalty or of an order'. It has no singular in ordinary English.

region: *in the region of*, an unwieldy periphrasis for *round about, approximately*, is better avoided.

register office is the official term for *registry office*.

regretfully, in a regretful manner; *regrettably*, it is to be regretted (that).
● *Regretfully* should not be used where *regrettably* is intended: *The investigators, who must regretfully remain anonymous* (TLS), reads as a guess at the investigators' feelings instead of an expression of the writer's opinion, which was what was intended. Compare **hopefully** (2).

renege (intransitive), to fail to fulfil an undertaking, is usually constructed with *on*, e.g. *It . . reneged on Britain's commitment to the East African Asians* (*The Times*).

replace: see **substitute**.

resource is often confused with *recourse* and *resort*. *Resource* means (1) a reserve upon which one can draw (often used in the plural); (2) an expedient to which one can turn in difficulty; (3) mental capabilities for amusing oneself etc.; (4) ability to deal with a crisis, e.g. *A man of infinite resource*. *Recourse* means the action of turning to a possible source of help, e.g. *have recourse to, without recourse to*. *Resort* means (1) the action of turning to a possible source of help (= *recourse*); frequently in the phrase *in the last resort*, as a last expedient; (2) a thing to which one can turn in difficulty.

responsible for (1) Liable to be called to account for, e.g. *I'm not responsible for what uncle Percy does* (E. M. Forster).
(2) Obliged to take care of, e.g. *The Prime Minister was directly responsible for the security service* (Harold Wilson).
(3) Being the cause of, e.g. *A war-criminal responsible for so many unidentified deaths* (Graham Greene).
● Beware of using senses (1) or (2) where sense (3) can be understood, e.g. *Now, as Secretary for Trade, he is directly responsible for pollution* (*The Times*).

restive (1) Unmanageable, rejecting control, obstinate, e.g. *The I.L.P. . . had been increasingly restive during the second Labour government, and now . . voluntarily disaffiliated from the Labour party* (A. J. P. Taylor).
(2) Restless, fidgety, e.g. *The audiences were . . apt to be restive and noisy at the back* (J. B. Priestley). ● Sense (2) is objected to by some, but is quite commonly used by good writers.

revenge: one revenges oneself or a wrong (*on* an offender); one is revenged (*for* a wrong): the noun is *revenge* (*on*), and the idea is usually of retaliation. Cf. **avenge**.

reverend, deserving reverence; *reverent*, showing reverence.
(*The*) *Revd*, plural *Revds*, is the abbreviation of *Reverend* as a clergy title and should be used in preference to *Rev.*

reversal is the noun corresponding to the verb *reverse*; *reversion* is the noun corresponding to the verb *revert*.

same. ● It is non-standard to use *same as* for 'in the same way as', e.g. *But I shouldn't be able to serve them personally, same as I do now* (L. P. Hartley).

sanction (verb) to give approval to, to authorize. ● It does not mean 'impose sanctions on'.

sc. (short for Latin *scilicet* = to wit) introduces (1) a word to be supplied, e.g. *He asserted that he had met him* (*sc. the defendant*), or (2) a word to be substituted to render an expression intelligible, e.g. '*I wouldn't of* (*sc. have*) *done' was her answer*.

scabrous (1) Rough, scaly. (2) Risqué, indecent, e.g. *Silly and scabrous titters about Greek pederasty* (C. S. Lewis).
● *Scabrous* does not mean 'scathing, scurrilous'.

scarcely: see **hardly**.

scarify, to loosen or scratch the surface of.
● The verb *scarify* (pronounced scare-ify) 'scare, terrify' is informal only.

scenario (1) An outline of the plot of a play. (2) A detailed film script. (3) A postulated (usually future) sequence of events, e.g. *Several of the computer 'scenarios' include a catastrophic and sudden collapse of population* (*Observer*).
● Sense (3) is valid when a detailed narrative of events that might happen is denoted. The word should not be used loosely for *scene, situation, circumstance*, etc.

scilicet: see **sc.**

Scottish is now the usual adjective; *Scotch* is restricted to certain fixed expressions, e.g. *Scotch broth, egg, whisky*; *Scots* is used mainly for Scottish English, in the names of regiments, and in *Scotsman, Scotswoman* (*Scotchman, -woman* are old-fashioned). For the inhabitants of Scotland, the plural noun *Scots* is normal.

seasonable, suitable for the time or season, opportune; *unseasonable* occurring at the wrong time or season, e.g. *You are apt to be pressed to drink a glass of vinegary port at an unseasonable hour* (Somerset Maugham). ● Do not confuse with *seasonal*, occurring at a particular season, e.g. *There is a certain seasonal tendency to think better of the Government . . in spring* (*The Economist*).

senior, superior are followed by *to*. They contain the idea of 'more' and so cannot be constructed with *more . . than*, e.g. *There are several officers senior*, or *superior in rank, to him*, not *. . more senior*, or *more superior in rank, than him*.

sensibility, sensitiveness of feeling, e.g. *The man's moving fingers . . showed no sign of acute sensibility* (Graham Greene). ● *Sensibility* does not mean 'possession of good sense'.

sensual, fleshly; indulging oneself with physical pleasures, showing that one does this, e.g. *His sensual eye took in her slim feminine figure* (Angus Wilson); *sensuous*, appealing to the senses (without the pejorative implications of *sensual*), e.g. *I got up and ran about the . . meadow in my bare feet. I remember the sensuous pleasure of it* (C. Day Lewis); *sensory*, of sensation or the senses, e.g. *sensory experience*.

serendipity, the faculty of making pleasant discoveries by accident; the adjective is *serendipitous*. ● *Serendipitous* does not mean merely 'fortunate'.

sic (Latin for *thus*) is placed in brackets after a word to show that the word is quoted exactly as in the original, e.g. *Daisy Ashford's novel* The Young Visiters (*sic*).

sick: see **ill**.

similar should be followed by *to*, not *as*. The following is non-standard: *Wolverton Seconds showed similar form as their seniors in their two home games*.

● **sit, stand.** The use of the past participles *sat, stood* with the verb *to be*, meaning *to be sitting, standing*, is non-standard, e.g. *I'd be sat there falling asleep* (Kingsley Amis).

situation. A useful noun for 'state of affairs' which may validly be preceded by a defining adjective, e.g. *the financial, industrial, military situation*. ● The substitution of an attributive noun for an adjective before *situation* is often tautologous (e.g. *a crisis situation, people in work situations*: *crises* and *work* are themselves *situations*). The placing of an attributive phrase before *situation* should be avoided, e.g. *The deep space situation, a balance-of-terror situation*. ● Avoid the cliché **ongoing** *situation*.

sled is Amer. for *sledge*; *sleigh* is a sledge for passengers that is drawn by horses (or reindeer).

so meaning 'therefore' may be preceded by *and* but need not be; e.g. *I had received no word from Martha all day, so I was drawn back to the casino* (Graham Greene).

so-called (1) has long been used in the sense 'called by this term, but not entitled to it'; (2) is now often used without implication of incorrectness, especially in Science.

sort of: see **kind of**.

specialty, except for its use in Law, is an equivalent of *speciality* restricted to North America.

spectate, to be a spectator, is informal only.

● *Watch* is usually an adequate substitute, e.g. in *A spectating, as opposed to a reading, audience* (*Listener*).

strata is the plural of *stratum*. ● It is incorrect to treat it as a singular noun, e.g. in *This strata*.

style. (1) Adjective + *-style* used to qualify a noun, e.g. *European-style clothing*, is acceptable.

(2) Adjective or noun + *-style*, forming an adverb, is somewhat informal,

e.g. *A revolution, British-style* (A. J. P. Taylor).

substantial, of real value; of solid material; having much property; in essentials; e.g. *substantial damages*; *a substantial house, yeoman*; *substantial agreement*. ● It is not merely a synonym of *large*.

substantive (adjective) is mainly technical; e.g. *substantive rank*, in the services, is permanent, not acting.

substitute (verb) to put (someone or something) in place of another: with *for*; e.g. *Substituted it for the broken one*.

● The sense 'replace (someone or something) *by* or *with* another' is incorrect, or at best highly informal, e.g. in *Having substituted her hat with a steel safety helmet, she toured the site* (better, *Having replaced her hat with* . . or *Having substituted a steel safety helmet for* . .).

such as: see **like**.

superior: see **senior**.

suppositious, hypothetical, e.g. *We might take a small cottage . . our suppositious cottage* (James Joyce); *supposititious*, fraudulently substituted, e.g. *Russia . . is the supposititious child of necessity in the household of theory* (H. G. Wells).

synchronize (transitive), to make simultaneous. ● It is not a synonym for *combine* or *coordinate*.

than: see **different**, **other than**, **prefer**, **senior**.

thankfully: see **hopefully**.

the (article). When a name like *The Times* or *The Hague* is used attributively, *The* is dropped, e.g. *A* Times *correspondent*, *Last year's Hague conference*. If *the* precedes the name in such a construction, it is not part of the name, and is therefore not given a capital initial (or italics), e.g. *A report from the* Times *correspondent*.

the (adverb) with a comparative means 'thereby', e.g. *What student is the better for mastering these distinctions?* This combination can enter into such expressions as *The more the merrier*. It cannot be used with *than*. Avoid putting *any the more*, *none the less* for *any more*, *no less*, e.g. in *The intellectual release had been no less* (not *none the less*) *marked than the physical*.

then may precede a noun as a neat alternative to *at that time*, e.g. *the then Prime Minister*. ● It should not be placed before the noun if it would sound equally well in its usual position, e.g. *Harold Macmillan was the then Prime Minister* could equally well be . . *was then the Prime Minister*. Rather than *The then existing constitution* write *The constitution then existing*.

there- adverbs, e.g. *therein, thereon, thereof*, etc., are mostly very formal and should be avoided in ordinary writing (apart from certain idiomatic adverbs, e.g. *thereabouts, thereby, thereupon*); e.g. *We did not question this reasoning, and there lay our mistake* (Evelyn Waugh): a lesser writer might have written *therein*.

through, up to and including, e.g. *Friday through Tuesday*, though useful, is Amer. only.

too followed by an adjective used attributively should be confined to special effects, e.g. *A small too-pretty house* (Graham Greene). ● In normal prose it is a clumsy construction, e.g. *The crash came during a too-tight loop*.

tooth-comb and *fine tooth-comb* are now established expressions whose illogicality it is pedantic to object to.

tortuous, torturous. Do not confuse: *tortuous* means (1) twisting, e.g. *A tortuous route*; (2) devious, e.g. *A tortuous mind*. *Torturous* means 'involving torture, excruciating'.

transcendent, surpassing others (e.g. *Of transcendent importance*), (of God) above and distinct from the universe; *transcendental*, visionary, beyond experience, etc. (Other more technical senses of each word are ignored here.)

transpire (figuratively): (1) To leak out, come to be known, e.g. *What had transpired concerning that father was not so reassuring* (John Galsworthy). (2) To occur, happen, e.g. *What transpired between them is unknown* (David Cecil). ● Sense (2) is regarded by many people as unacceptable, especially if the idea of something emerging from ignorance is absent: it should therefore not be used in sentences like *A storm transpired*.

trillion: see **billion**.

triumphal, of or celebrating a triumph, e.g. *A triumphal arch*; *triumphant*, victorious, exultant.

try (verb) in writing normally followed by the *to*-infinitive: *try and* + bare infinitive is informal. This latter construction is uncommon in negative contexts (except in the imperative, e.g. *Don't try and jump*), in the third person singular, and in the past tense.

turbid (1) muddy, thick; (2) confused, disordered. *Turgid* (1) swollen; (2) (of language) inflated, pompous.

underlay (verb) (past *underlaid*) to lay something under, e.g. *Underlaid the tiles with felt*; *underlie* (past tense *underlay*, past participle *underlain*) to lie under; to be the basis of; to exist beneath the surface of, e.g. *The arrogance that underlay their cool good manners* (Doris Lessing).

unequivocal, not ambiguous, unmistakable, e.g. *His refusal .. was unequivocal. 'Not in a million years' was the expression he used* (P. G. Wodehouse); similarly *unequivocally* adverb.

● The forms *unequivocable*, *-ably* are erroneous.

unexceptionable, -al: see **exceptionable**.

unique: (1) Being the only one of its kind, e.g. *This vase is considered unique*: in this sense *unique* cannot be qualified by adverbs like *most, so, thoroughly*, etc. (2) Unusual, remarkable, singular, e.g. *The most unique man I ever met*. ● Sense (2) is regarded by many people as incorrect. Substitute a suitable synonym.

unlike (adverb) may govern a noun, noun phrase, or pronoun, just as *like* may, e.g. *A sarcasm unlike ordinary sarcasm* (V. S. Pritchett). ● It may not govern a clause or adverbial phrase, e.g. *He was unlike he had ever been*; *Unlike in countries of lesser economic importance*.

● **various** cannot be followed by *of* (as, for example, *several* can), as (wrongly) in *Various of the Commonwealth representatives*.

venal, able to be bribed, influenced by bribery; *venial*, pardonable.

vengeance: see **avenge**.

verbal (1) of or in words; (2) of a verb; (3) spoken rather than written. ● Some people prefer *oral* for sense (3). However, *verbal* is the usual term in many idioms, such as *verbal communication, contract, evidence*.

verge (verb) in *verge on, upon*, to border on, e.g. *Verging on the ridiculous*, is in origin a different word from *verge* in *verge to, towards* to incline towards, approach, e.g. *Industrial disputes always verged towards violence* (A. J. P. Taylor). Both are acceptable.

vermin is usually treated as plural, e.g. *A lot of parasites, vermin who feed on God's love and charity* (Joyce Cary).

via (1) By way of (a place), e.g. *To London via Reading*. (2) Through the agency of, e.g. *They had sent a photo of Tina as a baby to the .. mother via a social worker* (*Independent*). ● Sense (2) is informal.

waive to refrain from insisting on, to dispense with, e.g. *To waive the formalities*. ● Do not confuse this with *wave*, chiefly with *aside, away*, as (wrongly) in *But the Earl simply waived the subject away with his hand* (Trollope).

want, need. ● The two legitimate constructions exemplified by *Your hair needs* or *wants cutting* and *We want* or *need this changed* are not correctly to be combined into *We want* or *need this changing*.

well is joined by a hyphen to a following participle before a noun, e.g. *A well-worn argument*. Predicatively a hyphen is not necessary unless the combination is to be distinguished in meaning from the two words written separately, e.g. *He is well-spoken* but *The words were well spoken*.

what ever, when ever, where ever: see **ever**.

whence meaning 'from where' need not be preceded by *from*.

who ever: see **ever**.

whoever, any one who, no matter who: use *whoever* for the objective case as well as the subjective, rather than the rather stilted *whomever*, e.g. *Whoever he painted now was transfigured into that image on the canvas* (Kathleen Jones). • Beware of introducing the objective *whomever* incorrectly, as in *A black mark for whomever it was that ordered the verges to be shorn* (*Daily Telegraph*).

-wise (suffix) added to nouns (1) forming adverbs of manner, is very well established in fixed expressions like *clockwise*; (2) forming viewpoint adverbs (meaning 'as regards —'), e.g. *moneywise*. • (2) should be restricted to informal contexts. • Adverbs of type (2) are formed on nouns only: hence sentences like *The ratepayers would have to shoulder an extra burden financial-wise* are incorrect (substitute . . *burden finance-wise* or *financial burden*).

• **without** = 'unless' is non-standard, e.g. *Do not leave without you tell me.*

womankind is better than *womenkind* (cf. *mankind*).

worth while is usually written as two words predicatively, but as one attributively, e.g. *He thought it worth while*, or *a worthwhile undertaking, to publish the method*.

write with personal object, e.g. *I will write you about it*, is not acceptable British English (but is good Amer. English).

Grammar

This section deals with specific problems of grammar; it makes no attempt at a systematic exposition of English syntax.

Wherever possible, the headings chosen for the entries are the words or grammatical endings which actually cause problems (e.g. *as*, *may* or *might*, *-ing*). But inevitably many entries have had to be given abstract labels (e.g. *double passive*, *subjunctive*). To compensate for this, a number of cross-references are included. The aim throughout is to tackle a particular problem immediately and to give a recommendation as soon as the problem has been identified.

adverbial relative clauses

A relative clause, expressing time, manner, or place, can follow a noun governed by a preposition (*on the day* in the example below):

> *The town was shelled by heavy guns on the day* that we departed (Edmund Blunden)

It is possible for the relative clause to begin with the same preposition and *which*, e.g.

> *On the day* on which the books were opened *three hundred thousand pounds were subscribed* (Lord Macaulay)

But it is a perfectly acceptable idiom to use a relative clause introduced by *that*, or often omitting *that*, without repeating the preposition, especially after the nouns *day*, *morning*, *night*, *time*, *year*, etc., *manner*, *sense*, *way* (see p. 95), *place*, e.g.

> *Envy in the consuming sense* that certain persons display *the trait* (Anthony Powell)
> *If he would take it in the sense* she meant it (L. P. Hartley)

adverbs without *-ly*

Most adverbs consist of an adjective + the ending *-ly*, e.g. *badly*, *differently*. For the changes in spelling that the addition of *-ly* may require, see p. 15 f. Normally the use of the ordinary adjective as an adverb, without *-ly*, is non-standard, e.g.

> *I was sent for* special
> *The Americans speak* different *from us*

There are, however, a number of words which are both adjective and adverb and cannot add the adverbial ending *-ly*, e.g.

alone	*fast*	*low*
enough	*little*	*much*
far	*long*	*still*

Some other adjectives can be used as adverbs both with and without *-ly*. The two forms have different meanings, e.g.

deep	*high*	*near*
hard	*late*	

The forms without *-ly* are the adverbs more closely similar in meaning to the adjectives, as the following examples illustrate:

deep: *He read deep into the night*
hard: *They hit me hard in the chest*
He lost his hard-earned money
high: *It soared high above us*
Don't fix your hopes too high
late: *I will stay up late to finish it*
A drawing dated as late as 1960
near: *As near as makes no difference*
Near-famine conditions

The forms with *-ly* have meanings more remote from those of the adjectives:

deeply is chiefly figurative, e.g. *Deeply in love*
hardly = 'scarcely', e.g. *He hardly earned his money*
highly is chiefly figurative, e.g. *Highly amusing*
lately = 'recently', e.g. *I have been very tired lately*
nearly = 'almost', e.g. *We are nearly there*

• The forms with and without *-ly* should not be confused.

See also ***-lily* adverbs**.

article, omission of

To omit, or not to omit, *a* (*an*) and *the*?

Omission of the definite or indefinite article before a noun or noun phrase in apposition to a name is a journalistic device, e.g.

> *Clarissa, American business woman, comes to England* (*Radio Times*)
> *Nansen, hero and humanitarian, moves among them* (*The Times*)

It is more natural to write *an American business woman, the hero and humanitarian.*

Similarly, when the name follows the noun or noun phrase, the effect is of journalistic style, e.g.

> *Best-selling novelist Barbara Cartland*
> *Unemployed labourer William Smith*

Preferably write: *The best-selling novelist, An unemployed labourer* (with a comma before and after the name which follows).

After *as* it is possible to omit *a* or *the*, e.g.

> *As manipulator of words, the author reminded me of X. Y.*

It is preferable not to omit these words, however.

as, case following

In the following sentences, the pronoun is in the subjective case, because it would be the subject if a verb were supplied:

> *I am, my lord, as well deriv'd as* he (Shakespeare) (in full, *as he is*)
> *Widmerpool . . might not have heard the motif so often as* I (Anthony Powell) (in full, *as I had*)

Informal usage permits the objective case, e.g. *You are just as intelligent as* him.

Formal English uses the objective case only when the pronoun would be the object if a verb were supplied:

> *I thought you preferred John to Mary, but I see that you like her just as much as* him (= *as much as you like him*)

In real usage, sentences like this are not very natural. It is more usual for the verb to be included.

as if, as though

For the tense following these see p. 51.

auxiliary verbs

There are sixteen auxiliary verbs in English, three primary auxiliaries (used in the compounding of ordinary verbs) and thirteen modal auxiliaries (used to express mood, and, to some extent, tense).

Primary: *be, do, have*

Modal:	*can*	*ought* (*to*)
	could	*shall*
	dare	*should*
	may	*used* (*to*)
	might	*will*
	must	*would*
	need	

Auxiliaries differ from regular verbs in the following ways:

(1) They can precede the negative *not*, instead of taking the *do not* construction, e.g. *I cannot* but *I do not know*;
(2) They can precede the subject in questions, instead of taking *do*, e.g. *Can you hear* but *Do you know*.

The modal auxiliaries additionally differ from regular verbs in the following ways:

(3) They do not add *-s* for the third person present, and do not form a past tense in *-ed*; e.g. *He must go*; *he must have seen it*.
(4) They are usually followed by the bare infinitive; e.g. *He will go, he can go* (not 'to go' as with other verbs, e.g. *He intends to go, he is able to go*).

Use of auxiliaries

In reported speech and some other *that*-clauses *can, may, shall*, and *will* become *could, might, should*, and *would* for the past tense:

> *He said that he* could *do it straight away*
> *I told you that I* might *arrive unexpectedly*
> *I knew that when I grew up I* should *be a writer* (George Orwell)

Did you think that the money you brought would *be enough?*

In clauses of this kind, the auxiliaries *must, need*, and *ought* can also be used for the past tense:

This business . . meant that I must *go to London* (Evelyn Waugh)
To go to church had made her feel she need *not reproach herself for impropriety* (V. S. Pritchett)
She was quite aware that she ought *not to quarter Freddy there* (G. B. Shaw)

Note that this use is restricted to *that*-clauses. It would not be permissible to use *must, need*, or *ought* for the past tense in a main sentence; one could not say: *Yesterday I must go*.

Further discussion of the use of auxiliary verbs will be found under **can and *may*, *dare, have, need, ought, shall* and *will*, *should* and *would, used to, were* or *was***.

but, case following

The personal pronoun following *but* (= 'except') should be in the case it would have if a verb were supplied.

I walked through the mud . . Who but I? (Kipling)
Our uneducated brethren who have, under God, no defence but us (C. S. Lewis)

In the Kipling example *I* is used because it would be the subject of *I walked*. In the Lewis example *us* is used because it would be the object of *who have* (i.e. 'who have *us*').

can and may

The auxiliary verbs *can* and *may* are both used to express permission, but *may* is more formal and polite:

May I offer you a spot? . . I can recommend the Scotch
Can I have a word with you? . . In private. Get lost, young Jane (both examples from P. G. Wodehouse)

collective nouns

Collective nouns are singular words that denote many individuals, e.g.

audience	*family*	*orchestra*
board (of directors etc.)	*fleet*	*parliament*
	gang	*squad*
	government	*staff*
class	*group*	*team*
club	*herd*	*tribe*
committee	*jury*	*union* (i.e. trade union)
company	*majority*	
congregation	*nation*	
crowd		

the bourgeoisie	*the nobility*
the Cabinet	*the public*
the élite	*the upper class*
the intelligentsia	*the working class*

It is normal for collective nouns to be followed by singular verbs and pronouns:

The Government is *determined to beat inflation, as* it has *promised*
Their family is *huge:* it consists *of five boys and three girls*
The bourgeoisie is *despised for not being proletarian* (C. S. Lewis)

The singular verb and pronouns are preferable unless the collective clearly refers to separate individuals, e.g.

The Cabinet has made its *decision*, but
The Cabinet are *resuming* their *places around the table*
The Brigade of Guards is *on parade*, but
The Brigade of Guards are *above average height*

The singular should always be used if the collective noun is qualified by a singular word like *this, that, every*, etc.:

This family is *divided*
Every team has *its chance to win*

If a relative clause follows, it must be *which* + singular verb or *who* + plural verb, e.g.

It was not the intelligentsia . . which was *gathered there* (John Galsworthy)
The working party who *had been preparing the decorations* (Evelyn Waugh)

● Do not mix singular and plural, as (wrongly) in

The congregation were *now dispersing*. It *tended to form knots and groups*

comparison of adjectives and adverbs

Whether to use *-er, -est* or *more, most*.

The two ways are:

(*a*) The addition of the suffixes *-er* and *-est* (for spelling changes that may be required see p. 10 f.). Monosyllabic adjectives and adverbs almost always require these suffixes, e.g. *big* (*bigger, biggest*), *soon* (*sooner, soonest*), and so do many of two syllables, e.g. *narrow* (*narrower, narrowest*), *silly* (*sillier, silliest*).

(*b*) The placing of *more* and *most* before the adjective or adverb. These are used with adjectives of three syllables or more (e.g. *difficult, memorable*), participles (e.g. *bored, boring*), many adjectives of two syllables (e.g. *afraid, widespread*), adjectives containing any suffix except *-ly* or *-y* (e.g. *awful, childish, harmless, static*), and adverbs ending in *-ly* (e.g. *highly, slowly*).

Adjectives with two syllables vary in this matter.

There are many which never take the suffixes, e.g.

antique devoid steadfast

There are also many adjectives which are acceptable with either, e.g.

clever extreme polite
common pleasant solemn

The choice is largely a matter of style.

Even monosyllabic adjectives can sometimes take *more* and *most*:

(i) When two adjectives are compared with each other, e.g.
More dead than alive
More good than bad
More well-known than popular
This is standard (we would not say 'better than bad').

(ii) Occasionally, for stylistic reasons, e.g.
This was never more true than at present

(iii) Thoughtlessly, e.g.
Facts that should be more well known
The most well-dressed man in town
Wimbledon will be yet more hot tomorrow

● These are not acceptable: substitute *better known, best-dressed*, and *hotter*.

comparisons

Comparisons between two persons or things require the comparative (*-er* or *more*) in constructions like the following:

I cannot tell which of the two is the elder (not *eldest*)
Which of the two is more likely to win? (not *most likely*)
Of the two teams, they are the slower-moving (not *slowest-moving*)

The superlative is of course used for more than two.

compound subject

A subject consisting of two singular nouns or noun phrases joined by *and* normally takes a plural verb:

My son and daughter are *twins*
Where to go and what to see were *my main concern*

If one half of the subject is *I* or *you*, and the other is a noun or *he, she*, or *it*, or if the subject is *you and I*, the verb must be plural.

He and I are *good friends*
Do *my sister and I look alike?*
You and your mother have *similar talents*
You and I are *hardly acquainted*

But if the compound represents a single item, it takes a singular verb:

The bread and butter was *scattered on the floor* (W. Somerset Maugham)
The Stars and Stripes was *flying at half-mast*

And similarly if the two parts of the subject refer to a single individual:

My son and heir is *safe!*

See also ***neither . . nor*** and **subjects joined by (*either* . .) *or*.**

coordination

The linking of two main clauses by a comma alone, though sometimes said to be incorrect, is on occasion used by good writers. It should be regarded as acceptable if used sparingly.

The peasants possess no harrows, they merely plough the soil several times over (George Orwell)

Charles carried a mackintosh over his arm, he was stooping a little (C. P. Snow)

correlative conjunctions

The correct placing of the pairs

both . . and	*neither . . nor*
either . . or	*not only . . but (also)*

A sentence containing any of these pairs must be so constructed that the part introduced by the first member of the pair 'matches' the part introduced by the second member.

The rule is that if one covers up the two correlative words and all between them, the sentence should remain grammatical.

The following sentence illustrates this rule:

Candidates will have a background in either commercial electronics or *university research*

Because *in* precedes *either*, it need not be repeated after *or*. If it had followed *either*, it would have had to be inserted after *or* as well.

In the following example the preposition *of* comes after *either* and must therefore be repeated after *or*:

He did not wish to pay the price either *of peace* or *of war* (George Orwell)

This conforms with the rule stated above.

It is, however, not uncommon for the conjunctions to be placed so that the two halves are not quite parallel, even in the writings of careful authors, e.g.

I end neither *with a death* nor *a marriage* (W. Somerset Maugham)

Here, *with* belongs to both halves and needs to be repeated after *nor*.

This is a fairly trivial slip that rarely causes difficulty (except in the case of *not only*: see p. 65).

● A more serious error is the placing of the first correlative conjunction too late, so that words belonging only to the first half are carried over to the second, e.g.

The other Exocet was either destroyed or blew up (BBC News)

This should be carefully avoided.

dangling participles: see participles

dare

The verb *to dare* can be used either like a regular verb or like an auxiliary.

As an ordinary verb it forms such parts as:

I dare	*I do not dare*	*do I dare?*
he dares	*he did not dare*	*does he dare?*
he dared	*I have dared*	*did he dare?*

As an auxiliary verb it forms:

I dare not	*he dared not*
he dare not	*dared he?*
dare he?	

The first use, as an ordinary verb, is always acceptably followed by the *to*-infinitive, e.g.

I knew what I would find if I dared to look (Jean Rhys)

But many of the forms can also be followed by the bare infinitive. This sometimes sounds more natural:

Don't you dare put that light on (Shelagh Delaney)

The second use requires the bare infinitive, e.g.

How dare he keep secrets from me? (G. B. Shaw)

double passive

The construction whereby a passive infinitive directly follows a passive verb is correctly used in the following:

The prisoners were ordered to be shot

The rule is that if the subject and the first passive verb can be changed into the active, leaving the passive infinitive intact, the sentence is correctly formed. The example above (if a subject, say *he*, is supplied) can be changed back to:

He ordered the prisoners *to be shot*

An active infinitive could equally well be part of the sentence, e.g.

The prisoners were ordered to march

The examples below violate the rule because both verbs have to be made active in order to form a grammatical sentence:

The order was attempted to be carried out (active: *He attempted to carry out the order*)

A new definition was sought to be inserted in the Bill

(active: *He sought to insert a new definition in the Bill*)

This 'double passive' construction is unacceptable.

The passive of the verbs *to fear* and *to say* can be followed by either an active or a passive infinitive, e.g.

(i) *The passengers are feared* to have drowned

The escaped prisoner is said to be very dangerous

or

(ii) *The passengers are feared* to have been killed

The escaped prisoner is said to have been sighted

The construction at (ii) is entirely acceptable. Both constructions occur with other verbs of saying (e.g. *to allege, to assert, to imply*):

Morris demonstrated that Mr Elton was obviously implied to be impotent (David Lodge)

either . . or: see **subjects joined by (*either . .*) *or*.**

either (pronoun)

Either is a singular pronoun and requires a singular verb:

Enormous evils, either of which depends *on somebody else's voice* (Louis MacNeice)

In the following example the plural verb accords with the notional meaning 'both parents were not'.

It was improbable that either of our parents were *giving thought to the matter* (J. I. M. Stewart)

This is quite common, but should be avoided in formal prose.

gender of indefinite expressions

It is often uncertain what personal pronoun should be used to refer back to the following pronouns and adjectives:

any	*no* (+ noun)
anybody	*nobody*
anyone	*none*
each	*no one*
every (+ noun)	*some* (+ noun)
everybody	*somebody*
everyone	*someone*

and also to refer back to (*a*) *person*, used indefinitely, or a male and a female noun linked by (*either . .*) *or* or *neither . . nor*, e.g.

Has anybody eaten his/their *lunch yet?*

An angry person may vent his/their *feelings on* his/their *family*

Neither John nor Mary has a home of their/his or her *own*

If it is known that the individuals referred to are all of the same sex, there is no difficulty; use *he* or *she* as appropriate:

Everyone in the women's movement has had her *own experience of sexual discrimination*

If, however, the sex of those referred to is mixed or unknown, the difficulty arises that English has no singular pronoun to denote common gender.

The grammarians' recommendation has traditionally been that *he* (*him, himself, his*) should be used:

Everyone took his *place in a half-circle about the fire* (Malcolm Bradbury)

(The context shows that the company was mixed.)

The long street in which nobody knows his *neighbour* (G. B. Shaw)

Each person should give as he *has decided for* himself (*Revised English Bible*)

Popular usage, however, has for at least five centuries favoured the plural pronoun *they* (*them, themselves, their*):

It's the sort of thing any of us would dislike, wouldn't they? (C. P. Snow)

Delavacquerie allowed everyone to examine the proofs as long as they *wished* (Anthony Powell)

This is entirely acceptable in informal speech. It is becoming increasingly common, to avoid the perhaps inequitable use of *he* to include both sexes, but is not yet fully accepted in more formal contexts.

One can avoid the difficulty by writing *he or she*:

Nobody has room in his or her *life for more than one such relationship at a time* (G. B. Shaw)

But this grows unwieldy with repetition:

If I ever wished to disconcert anyone, all I had to do was to ask him (or her) *how many friends* he/she *had* (Frederic Raphael)

• The form *themself* is sometimes used as a singular pronoun: *I think somebody should immediately address themself to this problem* (Alice Thomas Ellis)

This use is not generally regarded as acceptable.

group possessive

The group possessive is the construction by which the ending *-'s* is added to the last word of a noun phrase, e.g.

The king of Spain's daughter
John and Mary's baby
Somebody else's umbrella
A quarter of an hour's drive

Expressions like these are natural and acceptable.

Informal language, however, extends the construction to longer and more loosely connected phrases, often with ludicrous effect.

The people in the house opposite's geraniums
The woman I told you about on the phone yesterday's name is Thompson
The man who called last week's umbrella is still in the hall

• Expressions of this sort should not be used in serious prose. Substitute:

The geraniums of the people in the house opposite
The name of the woman I told you about on the phone yesterday is Thompson
The umbrella of the man who called last week is still in the hall

have

1. The verb *to have*, in some of its uses, can form its interrogative and negative either with or without the verb *to do*, e.g. *Do you have/have you?, You don't have/you haven't.*

In sentences like those below, *have* is a verb of event, meaning 'experience'. The interrogative and negative are always formed with *do*:

Do you *ever* have *nightmares?*
We did not have *an easy time getting here*

In the next pair of sentences, *have* is a verb of state, meaning 'possess'. When used in this sense, the interrogative and negative can be formed without *do*:

What have you *in common with the child of five whose photograph your mother keeps?* (George Orwell)
The truth was that he hadn't *the answer* (Joyce Cary)

In more informal language, the verb *got* is added, e.g. *What have you got, He hadn't got the answer*. This is not usually suitable for formal usage and is not usual in American English.

It was formerly usual to distinguish the sense 'experience' from the sense 'possess' by using *do* for the first but not for the second (but only in the present tense). Hence *I don't have indigestion* (as a rule) was kept distinct from *I haven't (got) indigestion* (at the moment). The use of the *do*-construction when the meaning was 'possess' was an Americanism, but it is now generally acceptable.

• However, the use of *do* as a substitute verb for *have*, common informally, is not acceptable in formal prose:

I had stronger feelings than she did (substitute *than she had*)

2. *Have* is often wrongly inserted after *I'd* in sentences like:

If I'd have *known she'd be here I don't suppose I'd have come* (Character in play by John Osborne)

This is common, and hardly noticed, in speech, but should not occur in formal writing. The correct construction is:

If I'd known *she'd be here* . .

he who, she who

He who and *she who* are correctly used when *he* and *she* are the subject of the main clause, and *who* is the subject of the relative clause:

He who *hesitates is lost*
She who *was a star in the old play may find herself a super in the new* (C. S. Lewis)

In these examples *he* and *she* are the subjects of *is lost* and *may find* respectively; *who* is the subject of *hesitates* and *was*.

He who and *she who* should change to *him who* and *her who* if the personal pronouns are not the subject of the main clause:

The distinction between the man who gives with conviction and him (not *he*) *who is simply buying a title*

Similarly *who* becomes *whom*—if it is not the subject of its clause:

I sought him whom *my soul loveth* (Authorized Version)

See also ***who* and *whom* (interrogative and relative pronouns)**.

-ics, nouns in

Nouns ending in *-ics* are sometimes treated as singular and sometimes as plural. Examples are:

economics	*linguistics*	*physics*
electronics	*mathematics*	*politics*
ethics	*metaphysics*	*statistics*

When used strictly as the name of a discipline they are treated as singular:

Psychometrics is *unable to investigate the nature of intelligence* (*Guardian*)
The quest for a hermeneutics (TLS)

So also when the complement is singular:

Pure mathematics is *a non-inductive . . science* (Gilbert Ryle)

When they mean a manifestation of qualities, often accompanied by a possessive, they are treated as plural:

His politics were *a mixture of fear, greed and envy* (Joyce Cary)
The acoustics in this hall are *dreadful*
Their tactics were *cowardly*

So also when they denote activities or behaviour:

acrobatics	*dramatics*	*heroics*
athletics	*gymnastics*	*hysterics*

e.g. *The mental gymnastics required* are *beyond me.*

These words usually remain plural even with a singular complement:

The acrobatics are *just the social side* (Tom Stoppard)

infinitive, present or perfect

The perfect infinitive is correctly used when it refers to an earlier time than that referred to by the verb on which it depends, e.g.

If it were real life and not a play, that is the part it would be best to have acted (C. S. Lewis)
Someone seems to have been making *a beast of himself here* (Evelyn Waugh)

In the above examples, the infinitives *to have acted* and *to have been making* relate to actions earlier in time than the verbs *would be best* and *seems.*

Only if both verbs refer to the past, and the infinitive to an earlier past, should a perfect infinitive follow a past or perfect verb, e.g.

When discussing sales with him yesterday, I should have liked to have seen *the figures beforehand*

In this example *I should have liked* denotes the speaker's feelings during the discussion and *to have seen* denotes an action imagined as occurring before the discussion.

If the state or action denoted by the infinitive occurred at the same time as the other verb, then the present infinitive should be used:

She would have liked to see *what was on the television* (Kingsley Amis)

The 'double past' is often accidentally used informally, e.g.

I should have liked to have gone *to the party*

A literary example is:

Mr. McGregor threw down the sack .. in a way that would have been extremely painful to the Flopsy Bunnies, if they had happened to have been *inside it* (Beatrix Potter)

This should be avoided.

-ing (gerund and participle)

1. The *-ing* form of a verb can in some contexts be used in either of two constructions:

(i) as a gerund (verbal noun) with a possessive noun or pronoun, e.g.

In the event of Randall's not going (Iris Murdoch)

She did not like his being *High Church* (L. P. Hartley)

(ii) as a participle with a noun or objective pronoun, e.g.

What further need would there have been to speak of another priest arising? (*New English Bible*)

Dixon did not like him doing *that* (Kingsley Amis)

The choice arises only when the accompanying word is a proper or personal noun (e.g. *John, father, teacher*) or a personal pronoun.

In formal usage, prefer the possessive construction wherever it is possible and natural:

To whom, without its being *ordered, the waiter immediately brought a plate of eggs and bacon* (Evelyn Waugh)

The danger of Joyce's turning *them into epigrams* (Anthony Burgess)

But it is certainly not wrong to use the non-possessive construction if it sounds more natural, as in the *New English Bible* quotation above. Moreover, there is sometimes a nuance of meaning. *She did not like his being High Church* suggests merely that she did not like the fact that he was High Church, whereas *Dixon did not like him doing that* suggests an element of repugnance to the person as well as to his action.

When using most non-personal nouns (e.g. *luggage, permission*), groups of nouns (e.g. *father and mother*), non-personal pronouns (e.g. *something*), and groups of pronouns (e.g. *some of them*), the possessive would not sound idiomatic at all. Examples are:

Travellers in Italy could depend on their luggage *not* being *stolen* (G. B. Shaw)

His lines were cited .. without his permission having *been asked* (*The Times*)

Due to her father and mother being *married* (Compton Mackenzie)

The air of something *unusual* having *happened* (Arthur Conan Doyle)

He had no objection to some of them listening (Arnold Bennett)

When the word preceding the *-ing* form is a regular plural noun ending in *-s*, there is no spoken distinction between the two forms. It is unnecessary to write an apostrophe:

If she knew about her daughters *attending the party* (Anthony Powell)

2. There is also variation between the two uses of the *-ing* form after nouns like *difficulty, point, trouble,* and *use.*

Formal English requires the gerundial use, the gerund being introduced by *in* (or *of* after *use*):

There was .. no difficulty in finding *parking space* (David Lodge)

Informal usage permits the placing of the *-ing* form immediately after the noun, forming a participial construction, e.g.

The chairman had difficulty concealing *his irritation*

• This is not acceptable in formal usage.

I or *me*, *we* or *us*, etc.

There is often confusion about which case to use here.

1. When the personal pronoun stands alone, as when it forms the answer to a question, formal usage requires it to have the case it would have if the verb were supplied:

Who killed Cock Robin?—I (in full, *I killed him*)

Which of you did he approach?—Me (in full, *he approached me*)

Informal usage permits the objective case in both kinds of sentence, but this is not acceptable in formal style. However, the subjective case often sounds stilted. It is then best to provide a verb, e.g.

Who likes cooking?—I do
Who can cook?—I can

2. When a personal pronoun follows *it is, it was, it may be*, etc., it should have the subjective case in formal usage:

We are given no clue as to what it must have felt like to be he (C. S. Lewis)

Informal usage favours the objective case:

I thought it might have been him *at the door*
Don't tell me it's them *again!*

• This is not acceptable in formal usage.

When *who* or *whom* follows, the subjective case is obligatory in formal usage and quite usual informally:

It was she *who winched up that infernal machine* (Joseph Conrad)

The informal use of the objective case often sounds substandard:

It was her *who would get the blood off* (Character in work by Patrick White)

(For agreement between the personal pronoun antecedent and the verb in *It is I who* etc., see ***I who, you who*, etc.**)

In constructions which have the form *I am* + noun or noun phrase + *who*, the verb following *who* is always in the third person (singular or plural):

I am the sort of person who likes *peace and quiet*

I should or *I would*

There is often uncertainty whether to use *should* or *would* with *I* and *we* before verbs such as *like* or *think* and before *rather* and *sooner*.

1. *Should* is correct before verbs of liking, e.g. *be glad, be inclined, care, like*, and *prefer*:

Would you like a beer?—I should prefer *a cup of coffee, if you don't mind*

The very occasions on which we should *most like to write a slashing review* (C. S. Lewis)

2. *Should* is correct with verbs such as *imagine, say*, and *think*:

I should imagine *that you are right*
I should say *so*
I shouldn't *have* thought *it was difficult*

3. *Would* is correct before the adverbs *rather* and *sooner*, e.g.

I would *truly* rather *be in the middle of this than sitting in that church in a tight collar* (Susan Hill)

Would is always correct with *you, he, she, it*, and *they*.

See also ***should* and *would***.

I who, you who, etc.

The verb following *I, you, he*, etc. + *who* should agree with the pronoun:

I, who have *no savings to speak of, had to pay for the work*

This remains so even with *me, him*, etc.:

They made me, who have *no savings at all, pay for the work* (not *who has*)

When *it is* etc. precedes *I who* etc., the same rule applies:

It's I who have *done it*
It could have been we who were *mistaken*

Informal usage sometimes permits the third person to be used (especially when the verb *to be* follows *who*):

You who's *supposed to be so practical!*

• This is not acceptable in formal usage.

-lily adverbs

When the suffix *-ly* is added to an adjective which already ends in *-ly*, the resulting adverb tends to sound odd, e.g. *friendlily*.

Adverbs of this kind are divided into three groups:

(i) Those formed from adjectives in which the final *-ly* is not a suffix, e.g. *holily, jollily, sillily*. These are the least objectionable and are quite often used.

(ii) Those of three syllables formed from adjectives in which the final *-ly* is itself a suffix, e.g. *friendlily*, *ghastlily*, *lovelily*, *statelily*, *uglily*. These are occasionally found.

(iii) Those of four (or more) syllables formed from adjectives in which the final *-ly* is itself a suffix, e.g. *heavenlily*, *scholarlily*. Such words are deservedly rare.

The adverbs of groups (ii) and (iii) should be avoided if possible, by using the adjective with a noun like *manner* or *way*, e.g. *In a scholarly manner*.

A few adjectives in *-ly* can be used adverbially to qualify other adjectives, e.g. *beastly cold*, *ghastly pale*.

may or might

There is sometimes confusion about whether to write *He may have* or *He might have*.

1. If at the time of speaking or writing the truth of the event is still unknown, then either *may* or *might* is acceptable:

As they all wore so many different clothes of identically the same kind . ., there may *have been several more or several less* (Evelyn Waugh)

For all we knew we were both bastards, although of course there might *have been a ceremony* (Graham Greene)

2. If the event did not in fact occur, use *might*:

If that had come ten days ago my whole life might *have been different* (Evelyn Waugh)

It might *have been better if the Russian Revolution had never taken place* (*The Times*)

● It is a common error to use *may* instead of *might* here:

If he (President Galtieri) *had not invaded, then eventually the islands* may *have fallen into their lap*

Schoenberg may *never have gone atonal but for the break-up of his marriage*

(*Might* should be substituted for *may* in each of the above.)

measurement, nouns of

There is some uncertainty about when to use the singular form, and when the plural, of nouns of measurement.

1. These nouns remain singular when compounded with a numeral and used attributively before another noun:

A six-foot *wall*	*A five*-pound *note*
A three-mile *walk*	*A 1,000*-megaton *bomb*
A ten-hectare *field*	*A three*-litre *bottle*

2. *Foot* remains in the singular form in expressions such as:

I am six foot   *She is five foot two*

But *feet* is used where an adjective, or the word *inches*, follows, e.g.

I am six feet tall   *She is five feet three inches*

Stone and *hundredweight* remain singular, e.g.

I weigh eleven stone   Three hundredweight of coal

Metric measurements always take the plural form when not used attributively:

This measures three metres by two metres

Informally, some other nouns of measurement are used in the singular form in plural expressions, e.g.

That will be two pound fifty, please

● This is non-standard.

See also **quantity, nouns of**.

need

The verb *to need*, when followed by an infinitive, can be used either like an ordinary verb or like an auxiliary.

1. *Need* is used like an ordinary verb, and followed by the *to*-infinitive, in the present tense when the sentence is neither negative nor interrogative, in the past tense always, and in all compound tenses (e.g. the future and perfect):

One needs friends, one needs to *be a friend* (Susan Hill)

One did not need to *be a clairvoyant to see that war .. was coming* (George Orwell)

2. *Need* can be used like an auxiliary verb in the present tense in negative and interrogative sentences. This means that:

(*a*) The third person singular does not add *-s*:

He need not come

(*b*) For the interrogative, *need I* (*you* etc.) replaces *do I need*:

Need I *add that she is my bitterest enemy?* (G. B. Shaw)

(*c*) The bare infinitive follows instead of the *to*-infinitive:

Company that keeps them smaller than they need be (*Bookseller*) (This is negative in sense, for it implies *They need not be as small as this*)

This auxiliary verb use is optional, not obligatory. The regular constructions are equally correct:

He does not need to ..
Do I need to add ..
Smaller than they need to be ..

It is important, however, to avoid mixing the two kinds of construction, as in the two following examples:

One needs not be *told that* (etc.)
What proved vexing, it needs be *said, was* (etc.)

neither .. nor

Two singular subjects linked by *neither .. nor* can be constructed with either a singular or a plural verb. Strictly and logically a singular verb is required:

Neither he nor his wife has *arrived*
There is *neither a book nor a picture in the house*

Informal usage permits the plural:

Neither painting nor fighting feed *men* (Ruskin)

When one subject is plural and the other singular, the verb should be plural and the plural subject placed nearer to it:

Neither the teacher nor the pupils understand *the problem*

When one subject is *I* or *you* and the other is a third person pronoun or a noun, or when one is *I* and the other *you*, the verb can agree with the nearer subject. However, this may sound odd, e.g.

Neither my son nor I am *good at figures*

One can recast the sentence, but this can spoil the effect. It is often better to use the plural:

Neither Isabel nor I are *timid people* (H. G. Wells)

This is not illogical if *neither .. nor* is regarded as the negative of *both .. and*.

neither (pronoun)

Neither is singular, and strictly requires a singular verb:

Neither of us likes *to be told what to do*

Informal usage permits a plural verb and complement:

Neither of us are good players

Although this is widely regarded as incorrect, it has been an established construction for three or four centuries:

Neither were great inventors (Dryden)

One should prefer the singular unless it leads to awkwardness, as when neither *he* nor *she* is appropriate:

John and Mary will have to walk. Neither of them have *brought* their *cars*

none (pronoun)

The pronoun *none* can be followed either by singular verb and singular pronouns, or by plural ones. Either is acceptable.

Singular: *None of them* was *allowed to forget for a moment* (Anthony Powell)
Plural: *None of the fountains ever* play (Evelyn Waugh)

ought

Oughtn't or *didn't ought?*

The standard negative of *ought* is *ought not* or *oughtn't*:

A look from Claudia showed me I ought not *to have begun it* (V. S. Pritchett)

Being an auxiliary verb, *ought* does not require the verb *do*. It is non-standard to form the negative with *do* (*didn't ought*):

I hope that none here will say I did anything I didn't ought. (Character in work by Michael Innes)

When the negative is used in a 'question tag', it should be formed according to the rule above:

You ought to be pleased, oughtn't you? (not *didn't you?*)

In the same way *do* should not be substituted for *ought*, e.g.

Ought he to go?—Yes, he ought (not *he did*)

You ought not to be pleased, ought *you?* (not *did you?*)

participles

A participle used in place of a verb in a subordinate clause must have an explicit subject to qualify. If no subject precedes it, the participle is understood to qualify the subject of the main sentence. In the following sentences the participles *running* and *propped* qualify the subjects *she* and *we*:

Running *to catch a bus, she just missed it* (Anthony Powell)

We both lay there, propped *on our elbows* (Lynne Reid Banks)

It is a frequent error to begin a sentence with a participial clause, and to continue it with a subject to which the participle is not related:

Driving *along the road*, the church *appeared on our left*
(*We*, not *the church*, is the subject of *driving*)

Having been relieved *of his portfolio in 1976*, the scheme *was left to his successor at the Ministry to complete*
(*He*, or a proper name, is the subject of *having been relieved*)

Participles that appear to be attached to the wrong subject are sometimes known as dangling (or unattached or hanging) participles.

Such sentences must be recast:

Driving along the road, we saw *the church* appear *on our left*

As we were *driving along the road, the church appeared on our left*

Jones *having been relieved of his portfolio in 1976, the scheme was left to his successor at the Ministry to complete*

When the participial clause includes a subject it should not be separated by a comma from the participle:

Bernadette being her niece, *she feels responsible for the girl's moral welfare* (David Lodge) (Not: *Bernadette, being her niece, she* . .)

But if the participle qualifies the subject of the main sentence, its clause is either marked off by a pair of commas or not marked off at all:

The man, hoping to escape, *jumped on to a bus*

A man carrying a parcel *jumped on to the bus*

The rule that a participle must have an explicit subject does not apply to participial clauses whose subject is indefinite (= 'one' or 'people'). In these the clause comments on the content of the sentence:

Judging *from his appearance, he has had a night out*

Roughly speaking, *this is how it went*

The participial clauses here are equivalent to 'If one judges . .', 'If one speaks . .'. Expressions of this kind are entirely acceptable.

See also **unattached phrases**.

preposition at end

It is a natural feature of the English language that many sentences and clauses end with a preposition, and the alleged rule that forbids this should be disregarded.

The preposition *cannot* be moved to an earlier place in many sentences, e.g.

What did you do that for?

What a mess this room is in!

The bed had not been slept in

Where there is a choice, it is very often a matter of style. The preposition has been placed before the relative pronoun in:

The present is the only time in which *any duty can be done* (C. S. Lewis)

But it stands near the end in:

Harold's Philistine outlook, which she had acquiesced in *for ten years* (L. P. Hartley)

But notice that some prepositions cannot come at the end:

An annual sum, in return for *which she agreed to give me house room* (William Trevor)

During *which week will the festival be held?*

One would not write *Which she agreed to give me house room* in return for, and *Which week will the festival be held* during?

One should be guided by what sounds natural. There is no need to alter the position of the preposition merely in deference to the alleged rule.

quantity, nouns of

The numerals *hundred, thousand, million, billion, trillion*, and the words *dozen* and *score* are sometimes used in the singular and sometimes in the plural.

1. They always have the singular form if they are qualified by a preceding word, whether it is singular (e.g. *a, one*) or plural (e.g. *many, several, two, three*, etc.), and whether or not they are used attributively before a noun or with nothing following:

A hundred days
Three hundred will be enough
I will take two dozen
Two dozen eggs

● The use of the plural form here is incorrect:

The population is now three millions (correctly *three million*)

Although they are singular, they always take plural verbs:

There were *about a dozen of them approaching* (Anthony Powell)

2. They take the plural form when they denote indefinite quantities. Usually they are followed by *of* or stand alone:

Are there any errors?—Yes, hundreds
He has dozens of friends
Many thousands of people are homeless

See also **measurement, nouns of**.

reflexive pronouns

These normally refer back to the subject of the clause or sentence in which they occur, e.g.

I *congratulated* myself *on outwitting everyone else*

Can't you *do anything for* yourself?

Sometimes it is permissible to use a reflexive pronoun to refer to someone who is not the subject, e.g.

It was their success, both with myself *and others, that confirmed* me *in what has since been my career* (Evelyn Waugh)

You *have the feeling that all their adventures have happened to* yourself (George Orwell)

To have written *me* and *you* respectively in these sentences would not have been grammatically incorrect.

A reflexive pronoun is often used after such words as

as	*but*	*like*
as for	*except*	*than*

e.g. *For those who*, like himself, *felt it indelicate to raise an umbrella in the presence of death* (Iris Murdoch)

It can be a very useful way to avoid the difficult choice between *I, he, she*, etc. (which often sound stilted) and *me, him, her*, etc. (which are grammatically incorrect) after the words *as, but*, and *than*, e.g.

None of them was more surprised than myself *that I'd spoken* (Lynne Reid Banks)

Here *than I* would be strictly correct, while *than me* would be informal.

Naturally a reflexive pronoun cannot be used in the ways outlined above if confusion would result. One would not write:

John was as surprised as himself *that he had been appointed*

but would substitute the person's name, or *he himself was*, for *himself*, or recast the sentence.

relative clauses

A relative clause is a clause introduced by a relative pronoun and used to qualify a preceding noun or pronoun (called its antecedent), e.g. *The visitor* (antecedent) *whom* (relative pronoun) *you were expecting* (remainder of relative clause) *has arrived*; *He* who hesitates *is lost*.

Exceptionally, there are nominal relative clauses in which the antecedent and relative pronoun are combined in one *wh*-pronoun, e.g. What you need *is a drink*: see ***what* (relative pronoun)**.

Relative clauses can be either restrictive or non-restrictive. A restrictive relative clause identifies the antecedent, e.g. *A suitcase* which has lost its handle *is useless*. Here the antecedent *suitcase* is defined by the clause.

A non-restrictive relative clause merely adds further information, e.g. *He carried the suitcase*, which had lost its handle, *on one shoulder*.

Notice that no commas are used to mark off a restrictive relative clause, but when a non-restrictive relative clause comes in the middle of the sentence, it is marked off by a comma at each end.

There are two kinds of relative pronouns:

(i) The *wh*-type: *who*, *whom*, *whose*, *which*, and, in nominal relative clauses only, *what*.
(ii) The pronoun *that* (which can be omitted in some circumstances: see ***that* (relative pronoun), omission of**).

When one relative clause is followed by another, the second relative pronoun

(*a*) may or may not be preceded by a conjunction; and
(*b*) may or may not be omitted.

(*a*) A conjunction is not required if the second relative clause qualifies an antecedent inside the first relative clause:

I found a firm which *had some components* for which *they had no use*

Here *for which .. use* qualifies *components* which is part of the relative clause qualifying *firm*. *And* or *but* should not be inserted before *for which*.

But if both clauses qualify the same antecedent, a conjunction is required:

Help me with these shelves which I have to take home but *which will not fit in my car*

(*b*) The second relative pronoun can be omitted if (i) it qualifies the same antecedent as the first, and (ii) it plays the same part in its clause as the first (i.e. subject or object):

George, who *takes infinite pains and* (who) *never cuts corners, is our most dependable worker*

Here both *who*'s qualify *George*, and are the subjects of their clauses, so the second can be omitted.

But if the second relative pronoun plays a different part in its clause, it cannot be omitted:

George, whom *everybody likes but* who *rarely goes to a party, is shy*

Here *whom* is the object, *who* is the subject, in their clauses, so *who* must be kept.

See also **preposition at end, *that* (relative pronoun), omission of, *what* (relative pronoun), *which* or *that* (relative pronouns), *who* and *whom* (interrogative and relative pronouns), *who* or *which* (relative pronouns), *whose* or *of which* in relative clauses, *who/whom* or *that* (relative pronouns)**.

shall and will

'The horror of that moment', the King went on, 'I shall never, never *forget!' 'You will, though,' the Queen said, 'if you don't make a memorandum of it.'* (Lewis Carroll)

The traditional rule in standard British English is:

1. In the first person, singular and plural.

(*a*) *I shall, we shall* express the simple future, e.g.

I am not a manual worker and please God I never shall *be one* (George Orwell)

In the following pages we shall *see good words .. losing their edge* (C. S. Lewis)

(*b*) *I will, we will* express intention or promises on the part of the speaker, e.g.

I will *take you to see her tomorrow morning* (P. G. Wodehouse)

I will *no longer accept responsibility for the fruitless loss of life* (Susan Hill)

2. For the second and third persons, singular and plural, the rule is exactly the converse.

(*a*) *You, he, she, it*, or *they will* express the simple future, e.g.

Will *it disturb you if I keep the lamp on for a bit?* (Susan Hill)

Seraphina will *last much longer than a car*. (Graham Greene)

(*b*) *You, he, she, it*, or *they shall* express intention or promises made by the speaker, e.g.

One day you shall *know my full story* (Evelyn Waugh)

The two uses of *will*, and one of those of *shall*, are well illustrated by:

'I will *follow you to the ends of the earth,' replied Susan, passionately. 'It* will *not be necessary,' said George. 'I am only going down to the coal-cellar. I* shall *spend the next half-hour or so there.'* (P. G. Wodehouse)

In informal usage *I will* and *we will* are quite often used for the simple future, e.g.

I will *be a different person when I live in England* (Character in work by Jean Rhys)

More often the distinction is covered up by using *'ll*, e.g.

I don't quite know when I'll *get the time to write again* (Susan Hill)

• The use of *will* for *shall* in the first person, though common, is not regarded as fully acceptable in formal usage.

should and would

When used for (*a*) the future in the past or (*b*) the conditional,

should goes with *I* and *we*

would goes with *you, he, she, it*, and *they*

(*a*) The future in the past.

First person:

Julia and I, who had left . ., thinking we should *not return* (Evelyn Waugh)

The person's imagined statement or thought at the time was:

We shall *not return*

with *shall*, not *will* (see ***shall* and *will***).

Second and third persons:

He was there. Later, he would *not be there* (Susan Hill)

The person's statement or thought at the time was

He will *not be there*

(*b*) The conditional.

First person:

I should *view with the strongest disapproval any proposal to abolish manhood suffrage* (C. S. Lewis)

Second and third persons:

If you took 3 ft off the average car, you would *have another six million feet of road space* (*The Times*)

In informal usage, *I would* and *we would* are very common in both kinds of sentence:

I wondered whether I would *have to wear a black suit*

I would *have been content, I would never have repeated it* (Both examples from Graham Greene)

The use of *would* with the first person is understandable, because *should* (in all persons) has a number of uses, including 'ought to'; sometimes the context does not make it clear whether I should do means 'it would be the case that I did' or 'I ought to do', e.g.

I wondered whether, when I was cross-examined, I should *admit that I knew the defendant*

• This use of *I would* and *we would* is not, however, regarded as fully acceptable in formal language.

See also ***I should* or *I would***.

singular or plural

1. When subject and complement are different in number (i.e. one is singular, the other plural), the verb normally agrees with the subject, e.g.

(Plural subject)

Ships are *his chief interest*

Liqueur chocolates are *our speciality* (Singular subject)

What we need is *customers*
Our speciality is *liqueur chocolates*

2. A plural subject used as a name counts as singular, e.g.

Sons and Lovers has *always been one of Lawrence's most popular novels*

3. A singular phrase that happens to end with a plural word should nevertheless be followed by a singular verb, e.g.

One in six has (not *have*) *this problem*

4. A problem often arises when such words as *average*, *maximum*, *minimum*, and *total* are used like this:

An average of 27,000 quotations has (or *have*) *been sent in each year*
A total of 335 British cases of AIDS has (or *have*) *been reported*

Strictly speaking the verb should agree with the singular noun, but in practice it is often made to agree with the nearest (and in the above examples, plural) noun. This often seems more natural.

5. If the subject of a relative clause is the same as the antecedent, the verb in the relative clause agrees in number with the antecedent, e.g.

It is the children *who* are *the first consideration* (E. M. Forster)

If the relative clause follows *one of the* + a plural noun, either *one* or the noun may be the antecedent. If *one* is the antecedent the verb should be singular, e.g.

One of the most dependable of the older girls, who was *made responsible* (Flora Thompson)

If the plural noun is the antecedent the verb should be plural, e.g.

He is one of the few businessmen who like *journalists* (i.e. 'one of the few journalist-liking businessmen')

● The singular is often used by mistake, e.g. in

The theory of black holes . . may perhaps be considered as one of the aspects of general-relativistic physics which is *better understood* (*Nature*)

where the sense must be 'one of the better-understood aspects'.

See also **collective nouns, compound subject, *-ics*, nouns in, quantity, nouns of, *-s* plural or singular, *what* (relative pronoun).**

split infinitive

This means the separation of *to* from the infinitive by one or more intervening words, e.g. *He used* to continually refer *to the subject*. In this *continually* splits *to refer* into two parts.

It is often said that an infinitive should never be split, but this is too rigid a rule; rather, avoid splitting unless the avoidance leads to clumsiness or ambiguity.

1. Good writers usually avoid splitting the infinitive by placing the adverb before the infinitive:

One meets people who have learned actually to prefer *the tinned fruit to the fresh* (C. S. Lewis)

He did not want positively to suggest *that she was dominant* (Iris Murdoch)

On the other hand, it is quite natural in speech, and permissible in writing, to say:

What could it be like to actually live *in France?*

To really let *the fact that these mothers were mothers sink in*
(Both examples from Kingsley Amis)

2. Avoidance of ambiguity.

When an adverb closely qualifies the infinitive verb it may often be better to split the infinitive. The following example is ambiguous in writing, though in speech stress would make the meaning clear:

It fails completely to carry conviction

Either it means 'It totally fails . .', in which case *completely* should precede *fails*, or it means 'It fails to carry complete conviction', in which case that should be written, or the infinitive should be split.

3. Avoidance of clumsiness.

It took more than an excited elderly man . . socially to discompose *him . .* (Anthony Powell)

In this example *socially* belongs closely with *discompose*: it is not 'to discompose in a social way' but 'to cause social discomposure'. In such cases, it may be better either to split the infinitive or to recast the sentence than to separate the adverb from the verb.

4. Unavoidable split infinitive.

There are certain adverbial constructions which must immediately precede the verb and therefore split the infinitive, e.g. *more than*:

> *Enough new ships are delivered* to more than make up *for the old ones being retired*

And a writer may have sound stylistic reasons for allowing a parenthetic expression to split an infinitive:

> *It would be an act of gratuitous folly* to, as he had put it to Mildred, make *trouble for himself* (Iris Murdoch)

-s plural or singular

Some nouns that end in *-s* are treated as singulars, taking singular verbs and pronouns.

1. *news*
2. Diseases:

diabetes	*rabies*
measles	*rickets*
mumps	*shingles*

Measles and *rickets* can also be treated as ordinary plurals.

3. Games:

billiards	*dominoes*	*ninepins*
bowls	*draughts*	*skittles*

4. Countries:

the Bahamas	*the Philippines*
the Netherlands	*the United States*

These are treated as singular when considered as a political unit, or when the complement is singular, e.g.

> *The Philippines* is *a predominantly agricultural country*
>
> *The United States* has *withdrawn its ambassador*

The Bahamas and *the Philippines* are also the geographical names of groups of islands, and in this use can be treated as plurals, e.g.

> *The Bahamas* were *settled by British subjects*

Flanders and *Wales* are always singular. So are the city names *Athens*, *Brussels*, *Naples*, etc.

See also *-ics*, **nouns in.**

subjects joined by (*either . .*) or

When two singular subjects are joined by *or* or *either .. or*, the strict rule is that they require a singular verb and singular pronouns:

> *Either Peter or John* has *had* his *breakfast already*
>
> *A traffic warden or a policeman* is *always on the watch*

However, 'at all times there has been a tendency to use the plural with two or more singular subjects when their mutual exclusion is not emphasized' (*OED*), e.g.

> *On which rage or wantonness vented* themselves (George Eliot)

When one subject is plural, it is best to put the verb in the plural, and place the plural subject nearer to the verb:

> *Either the child or the parents* are *to blame*

When personal pronouns are involved, the verb is usually made to agree with the nearer of the two subjects:

> *Either he or I* am *going to win*
>
> *Either he or you* have *got to give in*
>
> *Either you or your teacher* has *made a mistake*

This form of expression very often sounds awkward:

> Am *I or he going to win?*

It is usually best to recast the sentence by adding another verb:

> *Am I going to win, or is he?*
>
> *Either he has got to give in, or you have*

subjunctive

The present subjunctive form is identical with the indicative, except in the third person singular, which does not end in *-s*. The past subjunctive is indentical with the indicative throughout. In the verb *to be*, however, the present subjunctive is *be*, whereas the present tense is *am*, *are*, or *is*. For the past subjunctive of *to be* (*were*) see ***were* or *was*.**

The subjunctive is familiar in a number of fixed expressions which cause no problems:

Be *that as it may*	*Heaven* help *us*
Come *what may*	*Long* live *the Queen*
God bless *you*	*So* be *it*
God save *the Queen*	Suffice *it to say that*

There are two other uses of the subjunctive that may cause difficulty, but they are entirely optional apart from the past subjunctive *were*.

1. In *that*-clauses after words expressing command, hope, intention, wish, etc. Typical introducing words are

demand that	*proposal that*
insist that	*suggest that*
be insistent that	*suggestion that*

Typical examples are:

He had been insisting that they keep *the night of the twenty-second free* (C. P. Snow)

Joseph was insistent that his wishes be *carried out* (W. Somerset Maugham)

Your suggestion that I fly *out* (David Lodge)

Until recently this use of the subjunctive was restricted to very formal language, where it is still usual, e.g.

The Lord Chancellor put the motion that the House go *into Committee*

It is, however, a usual American idiom, and is now quite acceptable in British English, but *should* or *may* or (especially in informal use) the ordinary indicative, depending on the context, will do equally well:

Your demand that he should *pay the money back surprised him*

I insist that the boy goes *to school this minute*

● Beware of constructions in which the sense hangs on a fine distinction between subjunctive and indicative, e.g.

The most important thing for Argentina is that Britain recognize *her sovereignty over the Falklands*

The implication is that Britain does not recognize it. A change of *recognize* to *recognizes* would drastically reverse this implication. The use of *should recognize* would render the sense unmistakable.

2. In certain clauses introduced by *though* and *if*, the subjunctive can be used to express reserve about an action or state, e.g.

Though he be *the devil himself he shall do as I say*

The University is a place where a poor man, if he be *virtuous, may live a life of dignity and simplicity* (A. C. Benson)

This is very formal. It should not be used in ordinary prose, where sometimes the indicative and sometimes an auxiliary such as *may* are entirely acceptable, e.g.

Though he may be *an expert, he should listen to advice*

If this is *the case, then I am in error*

than, case following

In the following sentences, the pronoun is in the subjective case, because it would be the subject if a verb were supplied:

You are two stone heavier than I (G. B. Shaw) (= *than I am*)

We pay more rent than they (= *than they do*)

In the sentence below, the objective case is used, because the pronoun would be the object if there were a verb:

Jones treated his wife badly. I think that he liked his dog better than her (= *than he liked her*)

Informal English permits the objective case everywhere, e.g.

You do it very well. Much better than me

The preferred formal alternative, with the subjective, often sounds stilted. When this is so, it can be avoided by supplying the verb:

We pay more rent than they do

The pronoun *whom* is always used after *than*, rather than *who*:

Professor Smith, than whom *there is scarcely anyone better qualified to judge, believes it to be pre-Roman*

that (conjunction), omission of

1. The conjunction *that* introducing a noun clause and used after verbs of saying, thinking, knowing, etc., can often be omitted in informal usage:

I told him (that) *he was wrong*
Are you sure (that) *this is the place?*

Generally speaking, the omission of *that* is inappropriate in formal prose.

That should never be omitted if other parts of the sentence (apart from the indirect object) intervene:

I told him, as I have told everyone, that *he was wrong*
Are you sure in your own mind that *this is the place?*

The omission of *that* makes it difficult, in written prose, to follow the sense.

2. When *that* is part of the correlative pairs of conjunctions *so . . that* and *such . . that*, or of the compound conjunctions *so that, now that*, it can be omitted in informal usage.

• It should not be omitted in formal style:

He walked so fast (or *at such a speed*) that *I could not keep up*
I'll move my car so that *you can park in the drive*
Are you lonely now that *your children have left home?*

that (relative pronoun), omission of

The relative pronoun *that* can often be omitted, but in formal contexts the omission is best limited to short clauses which stand next to their antecedents:

None of the cars (that) *I saw had been damaged*
Nothing (that) *I could say made any difference*

That cannot be omitted when it is the subject of the relative clause, e.g.

Nothing that *occurred to me made any difference*
None of the cars that *were under cover had been damaged*

See also **adverbial relative clauses** and ***way*, relative clause following**.

there is or *there are*

In a sentence introduced by *there* + part of *to be*, the latter agrees in number with whatever follows:

There was *a great deal to be said for this scheme*
There are *many advantages in doing it this way*

In very informal language *there is* or *there was* is often heard before a plural:

There's two coloured-glass windows in the chapel (Character in work by Evelyn Waugh)

• This is non-standard.

to

The preposition *to* can stand at the end of a clause or sentence as a substitute for an omitted *to*-infinitive, e.g.

He had tried not to think about Emma . ., but of course it was impossible not to (Iris Murdoch)

This is standard usage.

unattached participles: see **participles**.

unattached phrases

An adjectival or adverbial phrase, introducing a sentence, must qualify the subject of the sentence, e.g.

While not entirely in agreement with the plan, *he had no serious objections to it*
After two days on a life-raft, *the survivors were rescued by helicopter*

It is a common error to begin a sentence with a phrase of this kind, and then to continue it with a quite different subject, e.g.

After six hours without food in a plane on the perimeter at Heathrow, *the flight was cancelled*

The phrase *After . . Heathrow* anticipates a subject like *the passengers*. Such a sentence should either have a new beginning, e.g.

After the passengers had spent *six hours* . .

or a new main clause, e.g.

After six hours . . *Heathrow*, the passengers learnt that *the flight had been cancelled*

used to

The negative and interrogative of *used to* can be formed in two ways:

(i) Negative: *used not to*
Interrogative: *used X to?*

Examples:

Used you to beat your mother? (G. B. Shaw)

You used not to have a moustache, used you? (Evelyn Waugh)

(ii) Negative: *did not use to, didn't use to*
Interrogative: *did X use to?*

Examples:

She didn't use to find sex revolting (John Braine)

Did you use to be a flirt? (Eleanor Farjeon)

□ Either form is acceptable. On the whole *used you to, used he to*, etc. tend to sound rather stilted and over-formal.

• The correct spellings of the negative forms are:

usedn't to and *didn't use to*

way, relative clause following

(*The*) *way* can be followed by a relative clause with or without *that*. There is no need to include the preposition *in*:

It may have been the way he smiled (Jean Rhys)

She couldn't give a dinner party the way the young lad's mother could (William Trevor)

were or was

There is often confusion about whether to use *were* or *was* in the first or third person singular.

Formal usage requires *were*

1. In conditional sentences where the condition is 'unreal', e.g.

It would probably be more marked if the subject were *more dangerous* (George Orwell)

(The 'subject' is not very 'dangerous' in fact)

If anyone were *to try to save me, I would refuse* (Jean Rhys)

(The condition is regarded as unlikely)

2. Following *as if* and *as though*, e.g.

He wore it with an air of melancholy, as though it were *court mourning* (Evelyn Waugh)

(For a permissible exception see p. 51)

3. In *that*-clauses after *to wish*, e.g.

He wishes he were *travelling with you* (Angus Wilson)

4. In the fixed expressions *As it were, If I were you*

Notice that in all these constructions the clause with *were* refers to something unreal.

Were may also be used in dependent questions, e.g.

Hilliard wondered whether Barton were *not right after all* (Susan Hill)

□ This is not obligatory even in very formal prose. *Was* is acceptable instead.

we (with phrase following)

Expressions consisting of *we* or *us* followed by a qualifying word or phrase are often misused with the wrong case.

If the expression is the subject, *we* should be used:

(Correct) *Not always laughing as heartily as* we English *are supposed to do* (J. B. Priestley)

(Incorrect) *We all make mistakes, even* us anarchists (Character in work by Alison Lurie)

If the expression is the object or the complement of a preposition, *us* should be used:

(Correct) *Had shut down all their Dutch ports against* us English (Kipling)

(Incorrect) *The Manchester Guardian has said some nice things about* we in the North-East

what (relative pronoun)

What can be used as a relative pronoun only when introducing nominal relative clauses, e.g.

> *So much of* what you tell me *is strange, different from* what I was led to expect (Jean Rhys)

Here *what* is equivalent to *that which* or *the thing(s) which*.

• *What* qualifies an antecedent only in non-standard speech, e.g.

> *The young gentleman* what's *arranged everything* (Character in work by Evelyn Waugh)

A *what*-clause used as the subject of a sentence almost always takes a singular verb, even if there is a plural complement, e.g.

> *What interests him* is *less events* .. *than the reverberations they set up* (Frederic Raphael)

Very occasionally the form of the sentence may render the plural more natural, e.g.

> *What once were great houses* are *now petty offices*

which or *that* (relative pronouns)

There is a degree of uncertainty about whether to use *which* or *that* with a non-personal antecedent (for personal antecedents see ***who/whom* or *that***). The general rule is that *which* is used in relative clauses to which the reader's attention is to be drawn, while *that* is used in clauses which do not need special emphasis.

Which is almost always used in non-restrictive clauses, i.e. those that add further information. Example:

> *The men are getting rum issue*, which they deserve (Susan Hill)

• The use of *that* in non-restrictive clauses should be avoided, although it is sometimes employed by good writers to suggest a tone of familiarity, e.g.

> *Getting out of Alec's battered old car* that *looked as if it had been in collision with many rocks, Harold had a feeling of relief* (L. P. Hartley)

It should not, however, be used in ordinary prose.

Both *which* and *that* can be used in restrictive (i.e. identifying) relative clauses. Some guidelines follow:

1. *Which* preferred.

(*a*) Clauses which add significant information often sound better with *which*, e.g.

> *Not nearly enough for the social position* which *they had to keep up* (D. H. Lawrence)

(*b*) Clauses which are separated from their antecedent, especially by another noun, sound better with *which*, e.g.

> *Larry told her the story of the young airman* which *I narrated at the beginning of this book* (W. Somerset Maugham)

(*c*) *Which* after a preposition is often a better choice than *that* with the preposition at the end of the sentence (see also **preposition at end**), e.g.

> *I'm telling you about a dream* in which *ordinary things are marvellous* (William Trevor)
>
> (*A dream that ordinary things are marvellous in* would not sound natural)

2. *That* preferred.

In clauses that do not fall into the above categories *that* can usually be used. There is no reason to reject *that* if

(*a*) the antecedent is impersonal,
(*b*) the clause is restrictive,
(*c*) preposition precedes the relative pronoun, and
(*d*) the sentence does not sound strained or excessively colloquial.

Example:

> *I read the letters, none of them very revealing,* that *littered his writing table* (Evelyn Waugh)

Here, *which* would be acceptable, but is not necessary.

When the antecedent is an indefinite pronoun (e.g. *anything, everything*) or contains a superlative adjective qualifying the impersonal antecedent (e.g. *the biggest car*) English idiom tends to prefer *that* to *which*:

Is there nothing small that *the children could buy you for Christmas?*
This is the most expensive hat that *you could have bought*

Note that *that* can sometimes be used when one is not sure whether to use *who* or *which*:

This was the creature, neither child nor woman, that *drove me through the dusk that summer evening* (Evelyn Waugh)

who and *whom* (interrogative and relative pronouns)

1. Formal usage restricts the use of *who* to the subject of the clause only, e.g.

I who'*d never read anything before but the newspaper* (W. Somerset Maugham)

When the pronoun is the object or the complement of a preposition, *whom* must be used:

Why are we being served by a man whom *neither of us likes?* (William Trevor)
The real question is food (or freedom) for whom (C. S. Lewis)

• The use of *who* as object or prepositional complement is acceptable only informally, e.g.

Who *are you looking for?*
The person who *I'm looking for is rather elusive*

See also ***than*, case following**.

2. *Whom* for *who*.

Whom is sometimes mistakenly used for *who* because the writer believes it to be the object, or the complement of a preposition.

(*a*) For the interrogative pronoun, the case of *who/whom* is determined by its role in the interrogative clause:

He never had any doubt about who *was the real credit to the family* (J. I. M. Stewart)

Who here is the subject of *was*. One should not be confused by *about*, which governs the whole clause, not *who* alone.

The error is seen in:

Whom *among our poets . . could be called one of the interior decorators of the 1950s?*
(Read *Who* . . because it is the subject of *be called*)

Whom is correct in:

He knew whom *it was from* (L. P. Hartley)
(Here *whom* is governed by *from*)

(*b*) For the relative pronoun, when followed by a parenthetic clause such as *they say, he thinks*, etc., the case of the pronoun *who/whom* is determined by the part it plays in the relative clause if the parenthetic statement is omitted:

Sheikh Yamani, who they say *is the richest man in the Middle East*
(Not *whom they say* since *who* is the subject of *is*, not the object of *say*)

But *whom* is correct in:

Sheikh Yamani, whom they believe to be *the richest man in the Middle East*
Here *they believe* could not be removed leaving the sentence intact. *Whom* is its object: the simple clause would be *They believe* him to be *the richest man*.

See also ***I who, you who,* etc**.

who or *which* (relative pronouns)

A *wh*-pronoun introducing a relative clause must be *who* (*whom*) if the antecedent is personal, e.g.

Suzanne was a woman who *had no notion of reticence* (W. Somerset Maugham)

But it must be *which* if the antecedent is non-personal, e.g.

There was a suppressed tension about her which *made me nervous* (Lynne Reid Banks)

If the relative clause is non-restrictive, i.e. it adds new information, the *wh*-type of pronoun *must* be used (as above).

If the relative clause is restrictive, i.e. identifying, one can use either the appropriate *wh*-pronoun (as above), or the non-variable pronoun *that*. See ***which* or *that* (relative pronouns)** and ***who/whom* or *that* (relative pronouns)**.

whose or *of which* in relative clauses

The relative pronoun *whose* can be used as the possessive of *which* as well as of *who*. The rule sometimes enunciated that *of which* must always be used after a non-personal antecedent should be ignored, as it is by good writers, e.g.

The little book whose *yellowish pages she knew* (Virginia Woolf)

In some sentences, *of which* would be almost impossible, e.g.

The lawns about whose *closeness of cut his father worried the gardener daily* (Susan Hill)

There is, of course, no rule prohibiting *of which* if it sounds natural, e.g.

A little town the name of which *I have forgotten* (W. Somerset Maugham)

Whose can only be used as the non-personal possessive in *relative* clauses. Interrogative *whose* refers only to persons, as in *Whose book is this?*

who/whom or *that* (relative pronouns)

In formal usage, *who/whom* is always acceptable as the relative pronoun referring to a person. (See ***who* and *whom* (interrogative and relative pronouns)**.)

In non-restrictive relative clauses, i.e. those which add new information, *who/whom* is obligatory, e.g.

It was not like Coulter, who *was a cheerful man* (Susan Hill)

In restrictive (i.e. identifying) relative clauses, *who/whom* is usually quite acceptable:

The masters who *taught me Divinity told me that biblical texts were highly untrustworthy* (Evelyn Waugh)

It is generally felt that the relative pronoun *that* is slightly depreciatory if applied to a person. Hence it tends to be avoided in formal usage.

However, if

(i) the relative pronoun is the object, and
(ii) the personality of the antecedent is suppressed

that may well be appropriate, e.g.

They looked now just like the GIs that *one saw in Viet Nam* (David Lodge)

Informally *that* is acceptable with any personal antecedent, e.g.

Honey, it's me that *should apologize* (David Lodge)

● This should be avoided in formal style.

you and I or *you and me*

When a personal pronoun is linked by *and* or *or* to a noun or another pronoun, the rule is exactly as it would be for the pronoun standing alone.

1. If the two words linked by *and* or *or* constitute the subject, the pronoun should be in the subjective case, e.g.

Only she *and her mother cared for the old house*
Who could go?—Either you or he

The use of the objective case is quite common, but it is non-standard, e.g. (examples from the speech of characters in novels)

That's how we look at it, me *and Martha* (Kingsley Amis)
Either Mary had to leave or me (David Lodge)

2. If the two words linked by *and* or *or* constitute the object of the verb, or the complement of a preposition, the objective case must be used:

The afternoon would suit her *and John better*

● Although the use of the subjective case is very common informally, it remains non-standard, e.g.

It was this that set Charles and I *talking of old times*
Between you and I

This last expression is very commonly heard. *Between you and me* should always be substituted.

Appendix I
Principles of punctuation

apostrophe

1. Used to indicate the possessive case: see p. 19 f.

2. Used to mark an omission, e.g. *e'er*, *we'll*, *he's*, *'69*.

• Sometimes written, but unnecessary, in a number of curtailed words, e.g. *bus*, *cello* (not *'bus*, etc.). See also p. 19 f.

brackets

See: 1. **parentheses**.
  2. **square brackets**.

colon

1. Links two grammatically complete clauses, but marks a step forward to main theme, to effect, to conclusion, e.g. *To commit sin is to break God's law: sin, in fact, is lawlessness*.

2. Introduces a list of items (a dash should not be added), e.g. *The following were present: J. Smith, J. Brown, M. Jones*.

It is used after such expressions as *for example*, *namely*, *the following*, *to resume*, *to sum up*.

3. Introduces, formally and emphatically, speech or a quotation, e.g. *I told them: 'Do not in any circumstances open this door.'*

comma

1. Used between adjectives which each qualify a noun in the same way, e.g. *A cautious, eloquent man*.

But when adjectives qualify the noun in different ways, or when one adjective qualifies another, no comma is used, e.g. *A distinguished foreign author*, *a bright red tie*.

2. Separates items (including the last) in a list of more than two, e.g. *Potatoes, peas, and carrots*; *Potatoes, peas, or carrots*; *Potatoes, peas, etc.*; *He has shares in Guinness, Tate and Lyle, and Marks and Spencer*.

• But *A black and white TV set*.

3. Separates coordinated main clauses, e.g. *Cars will turn here, and coaches will go straight on*. But not when they are closely linked, e.g. *Do as I tell you and you'll never regret it*.

4. Marks the beginning and end of a parenthesis, e.g. *I am sure, however, that it will not happen*; *Fred, who is bald, complained of the cold*.

• Not with restrictive relative clauses, e.g. *Men who are bald should wear hats*.

5. Follows a participial or verbless clause, a salutation, or a vocative, e.g. *Having had breakfast, I went for a walk*; *The sermon over, the congregation filed out*; *Ladies and gentlemen, I give you a toast*.

• Not *The sermon, being over*, (etc.).

• No comma in expressions like *My son John*.

6. Separates a phrase or subordinate clause from the main clause so as to avoid misunderstanding, e.g. *He did not go to church, because he was playing golf*; *In 1982, 1918 seemed a long time ago*.

• A comma should not separate a phrasal subject from its predicate, or a verb from an object that is a clause: *A car with such a high-powered engine, should not let you down* and *They believed, that nothing could go wrong* are both incorrect.

7. Introduces direct speech, e.g. *They answered, 'Here we are.'*

8. Follows *Dear Sir*, *Dear John*, etc., in letters, and *Yours sincerely*, etc.

• No comma is needed between month and year in dates, e.g. *In December 1992* or between number and road in addresses, e.g. *12 Acacia Avenue*.

dash

1. The *en rule* is distinct (in print) from the **hyphen** (see p. 12 f.) and joins items wherever movement or opposition, rather than cooperation or unity, is felt; it resembles *to* or *versus*, e.g. *The 1914–18 war; current–voltage characteristic; The London–Horsham–Brighton route; The Fischer–Spassky match; The Marxist–Trotskyite split.*

● Note *The Marxist-Leninist position; The Franco-Prussian war* with hyphens.

It is also used for joint authors, e.g. *The Lloyd–Jones hypothesis* (two men), but *The Lloyd-Jones hypothesis* (one double-barrelled name).

2. The *em rule* (the familiar dash) marks an interruption in a sentence. A pair of them can enclose a parenthesis or a statement interrupted by an interlocutor; e.g. *He was not—you may disagree with me, Henry—much of an artist; 'I didn't—' 'Speak up, boy!' '—hear anything.'* It can be used informally to replace the colon (use 1).

exclamation mark

Used after an exclamatory word, phrase, or sentence. It usually counts as the concluding full stop. It may also be used within square brackets, after a quotation, to express the editor's amusement, dissent, or surprise.

full stop

1. Used at the end of all sentences which are not questions or exclamations. The next word should normally begin with a capital letter.

2. Used after **abbreviations**: see p. 7. If the abbreviation ends the sentence, the point serves as the closing full stop, e.g. *She kept dogs, cats, birds, etc.* but *She kept pets* (*dogs, cats, birds, etc.*).

3. When a sentence concludes with a quotation which itself ends with a full stop, question mark, or exclamation mark, no further full stop is needed, e.g. *He cried, 'Be off!'* But if the quotation is short, and the introducing sentence has much greater weight, the full stop follows the quotation mark, e.g. *Over the entrance to the temple at Delphi were written the words 'Know thyself'.*

4. A sequence of three full stops marks an omission; a fourth is added if this ends a sentence, e.g. *One critic wrote 'A guidebook ... that I would not want to be without.... It has been my constant companion.'*

hyphen: see p. 12 f.

parentheses

Enclose:

1. Interpolations by the writer himself, e.g. *Mr. X* (*as I shall call him*) *now spoke.*
2. An authority, explanation, reference, or translation.
3. In the report of a speech, interruptions by the audience.
4. Reference letters or figures, e.g. (1), (*a*).
5. Optional words, e.g. *There are many* (*apparent*) *difficulties.*

period: see **full stop**.

question mark

1. Follows every question which expects a separate answer. The next word should begin with a capital letter.

● Not used after indirect questions, e.g. *He asked me why I was there.*

2. May be placed before a word, etc., whose accuracy is doubted, e.g. *T. Tallis ?1505–85.*

quotation marks

1. Single quotation marks are used for a first quotation; double for a quotation within this; single again for a further quotation inside that.

2. The closing quotation mark should come before all punctuation marks unless these form part of the quotation itself, e.g. *Did Nelson really say 'Kiss me, Hardy'?* but *Then she asked, 'What is your name?'* (see also **full stop,** 3).

The comma at the end of a quotation, when words such as *he said* follow, is kept inside the quotation, e.g. *'That is nonsense,' he iid*. The commas on either side of *he iid*, etc., when these words interrupt the uotation, should be outside the quotation iarks, e.g. *'That', he said, 'is nonsense.'* ut the first comma goes inside the quota-on marks if it would be part of the utter-nce even if there were no interruption, g. *'That, my dear fellow,' he said, 'is non-ense'.*

. Quotation marks are used when citing tles of articles in magazines, chapters of ooks, poems, and songs.

Not for titles of books of the Bible; nor or any passage that is not a verbatim uotation.

'itles of books and magazines are usually rinted in italic.

semicolon

Separates clauses of similar importance that are too closely linked to require a full stop, e.g. *To err is human; to forgive, divine.* It is often used as a stronger division in a sentence that already includes commas, e.g. *He came out of the house, which lay back from the road, and saw her at the end of the path; but instead of continuing towards her, he hid until she had gone.*

square brackets

Enclose comments, corrections, explanations, interpolations, notes, or translations, which have been added by subsequent editors, e.g. *My right honourable friend* [*John Brown*] *is mistaken.*

Appendix II
Clichés and modish and inflated diction

A cliché is an outworn phrase. One cannot avoid using some clichés: they are too common, and are often useful. In writing serious prose, however, one should choose one's own words if they express the idea more precisely. 'Modish and inflated diction' refers to currently fashionable words and phrases. Some of these are scientific or technical in origin, others may be the creation of the media; but what they have in common is their popularity. It would be difficult to ban them completely, but they should be used with restraint. Some examples follow, of both cliché and modish diction.

at the end of the day
at this moment (or *point*) *in time*
-awareness (e.g. *brand-awareness*)
back burner (*on the* ——)
ball game (*a different*, etc., ——)
basically (as a filler)
bottom line
by and large (sometimes used with no meaning)
-centred (e.g. *discovery-centred*)
conspicuous by one's absence
constructive (used tautologously, e.g. *A constructive suggestion*)
definitely
-deprivation (e.g. *status-deprivation*)
dialogue
dimension (= feature, factor)
-directed (e.g. *task-directed*)
-driven (e.g. *consumer-driven*)
environment
escalate (= increase, intensify)
-friendly (e.g. *consumer-friendly*)
grind to a halt (= end, stop)
if you like (explanatory tag)
integrate, integrated
in terms of
in the order of (= about)
in this day and age
-ize (suffix, forming vogue words, e.g. *normalize, permanentize, prioritize, respectabilize*)
leave severely alone
life-style
low profile (*keep, or maintain, a* ——)
massive (= huge)
matrix
methodology (= method)
name of the game, the
-oriented (e.g. *marketing-oriented*)
overkill
persona (= character)
proposition
quantum jump/leap
real (especially in *very real*)
-related (e.g. *church-related*)
simplistic (= oversimplified)
syndrome
take on board (= accept, grasp)
totality of, the
track-record (= record)
until such time as
utilize (= use)
valid
viability
vibrant
you know (as a filler)
you name it

See also the entries in Section III for:

antithetical	*exposure*
author	*feasible*
aware	*following*
character	*hopefully*
crucial	*impact*
decimate	*interface*
dichotomy	*ironic*
differential	*literally*
dilemma	*locate*
event (in the event that)	*maximize*
	nature
excess (in excess of)	*neighbourhood* (in the neighbourhood of)

no way
obligate
obscene
ongoing
overly
parameter
pivotal
predicate
pre-empt
pristine
proportion
region (in the *region of*)
scenario
situation
substantial

Index

Words and phrases are entered in strict alphabetical order, ignoring spaces between two or more words forming a compound or phrase (hence *as for* follows *ascendant* and *court martial* follows *courtesy*).

An asterisk is placed in front of forms or spellings that are not recommended; reference to the page(s) indicated will show the reason for this ruling in each case.

Individual words, parts of words, and phrases discussed in this book are given in *italics*, to distinguish them from subjects, which are in roman type.

Dictionary

Features of the dictionary

Headwords

(words given their own entries) are in bold type:

abandon /əˈbænd(ə)n/ ● *verb* desert ...

or in bold italic type if they are borrowed from another language and are usually printed in italics:

autobahn

Variant spellings are shown:

almanac ... (also **almanack**)

Words that are different but are spelt the same way (homographs) are printed with raised numbers:

abode[1]
abode[2]

Variant American spellings are labelled *US*:

anaemia ... (*US* **anemia**)

Pronunciations

are given in the International Phonetic Alphabet. See p. 155 for an explanation.

Parts of speech

are shown in italic:

abhor ... *verb*
abhorrence ... *noun*

If a word is used as more than one part of speech, each comes after a ● :

abandon ... ● *noun* ... ● *verb* ...

For explanations of parts of speech, see the panels at the dictionary entries for *noun*, *verb*, etc.

Inflections

Irregular and difficult forms are given for:

nouns:

ability ... (*plural* **-ies**)
sheep ... (*plural* same)
tomato ... (*plural* **-es**)

(Irregular plurals are not given for compounds such as *footman* and *schoolchild*.)

verbs:

abate ... (**-ting**)
abut ... (**-tt-**) [indicating **abutted**, **abutting**]
ring ... (*past tense* **rang**; *past participle* **rung**)

adjectives:

good ... (**better**, **best**)
narrow ... (**-er**, **-est**)
able ... (**-r**, **-st**)

adverbs:

well ... (**better**, **best**)

Definitions

Round brackets are used for

a optional words, e.g. at

back ... *verb* (cause to) go backwards

(because *back* can mean either 'go backwards' or 'cause to go backwards')

b typical objects of verbs:

bank ... *verb* deposit (money) at bank

c typical subjects of verbs:

break ... *verb* (of waves) curl over and foam

d typical nouns qualified by an adjective:

catchy ... (of tune) easily remembered

Subject labels

are sometimes used to help define a word:

sharp ... *Music* above true pitch

Register labels

are used if a word is slang, colloquial, or formal:

ace ... *adjective slang* excellent

Coarse slang means that a word, although widely used, is still unacceptable to many people.

Offensive means that a word is offensive to members of a particular ethnic, religious, or other group.

Phrases

are entered under their main word:

company ... **in company with**

A comma in a phrase indicates alternatives:

in, to excess

means that *in excess* and *to excess* are both phrases.

Compounds

are entered under their main word or element (usually the first):

air ... **air speed** ... **airstrip**

unless they need entries of their own:

broad
broadcast
broadside

A comma in a compound indicates alternatives:

block capitals, letters

means that *block capitals* and *block letters* are both compounds.

Derivatives

are put at the end of the entry for the word they are derived from:

rob ... **robber** *noun*

unless they need defining:

drive ...
driver *noun* person who drives; golf club for driving from tee.

Cross-references

are printed in small capitals:

anatto = ANNATTO.
arose *past* of ARISE.

Definitions will be found at the entries referred to.

Note on proprietary terms

This dictionary includes some words which are, or are asserted to be, proprietary names or trade marks. Their inclusion does not imply that they have acquired for legal purposes a non-proprietary or general significance, nor is any other judgement implied concerning their legal status. In cases where the editor has some evidence that a word is used as a proprietary name or trade mark this is indicated by the label *proprietary term*, but no judgement concerning the legal status of such words is made or implied thereby.

Pronunciation symbols

Consonants

b	*b*ut
d	*d*og
f	*f*ew
g	*g*et
h	*h*e
j	*y*es
k	*c*at
l	*l*eg
m	*m*an
n	*n*o
p	*p*en
r	*r*ed
s	*s*it
t	*t*op
v	*v*oice
w	*w*e
z	*z*oo
ʃ	*sh*e
ʒ	vi*s*ion
θ	*th*in
ð	*th*is
ŋ	ri*ng*
x	lo*ch*
tʃ	*ch*ip
dʒ	*j*ar

Vowels

æ	c*a*t
ɑː	*ar*m
e	b*e*d
ɜː	h*er*
ɪ	s*i*t
iː	s*ee*
ɒ	h*o*t
ɔː	s*aw*
ʌ	r*u*n
ʊ	p*u*t
uː	t*oo*
ə	*a*go
aɪ	m*y*
aʊ	h*ow*
eɪ	d*ay*
əʊ	n*o*
eə	h*air*
ɪə	n*ear*
ɔɪ	b*oy*
ʊə	p*oor*
aɪə	f*ire*
aʊə	s*our*

(ə) signifies the indeterminate sound in gard*e*n, carn*a*l, and rhyth*m*.

The mark ˜ indicates a nasalized sound, as in the following vowels that are not natural in English:

æ̃ (*in*génue)
ɑ̃ (él*an*)
ɔ̃ (b*on* voyage)

The main or primary stress of a word is shown by ˈ before the relevant syllable.

Aa

A *abbreviation* ampere(s). □ **A-bomb** atomic bomb; **A level** advanced level in GCE exam.

a /ə, eɪ/ *adjective* (called the indefinite article) (also **an** /æn, ən/ before vowel sound) one, some, any; per.

AA *abbreviation* Automobile Association; Alcoholics Anonymous; anti-aircraft.

aardvark /ˈɑːdvɑːk/ *noun* mammal with tubular snout and long tongue.

aback /əˈbæk/ *adverb* □ **taken aback** disconcerted, surprised.

abacus /ˈæbəkəs/ *noun* (*plural* **-es**) frame with wires along which beads are slid for calculating.

abaft /əˈbɑːft/ *Nautical* ● *adverb* in or towards stern of ship. ● *preposition* nearer stern than.

abandon /əˈbænd(ə)n/ ● *verb* desert; give up (hope etc.). ● *noun* freedom from inhibitions. □ **abandonment** *noun*.

abandoned *adjective* deserted; unrestrained.

abase /əˈbeɪs/ *verb* (**-sing**) humiliate; degrade. □ **abasement** *noun*.

abashed /əˈbæʃt/ *adjective* embarrassed; disconcerted.

abate /əˈbeɪt/ *verb* (**-ting**) make or become less strong etc. □ **abatement** *noun*.

abattoir /ˈæbətwɑː/ *noun* slaughterhouse.

abbess /ˈæbɪs/ *noun* female head of abbey of nuns.

abbey /ˈæbɪ/ *noun* (*plural* **-s**) (building occupied by) community of monks or nuns.

abbot /ˈæbət/ *noun* head of community of monks.

abbreviate /əˈbriːvɪeɪt/ *verb* shorten. □ **abbreviation** *noun*.

ABC /eɪbiːˈsiː/ *noun* alphabet; rudiments of subject; alphabetical guide.

abdicate /ˈæbdɪkeɪt/ *verb* renounce or resign from (throne etc.). □ **abdication** *noun*.

abdomen /ˈæbdəmən/ *noun* belly; rear part of insect etc. □ **abdominal** /æbˈdɒmɪn(ə)l/ *adjective*.

abduct /əbˈdʌkt/ *verb* carry off illegally, kidnap. □ **abduction** *noun*; **abductor** *noun*.

aberrant /æˈberənt/ *adjective* showing aberration.

aberration /æbəˈreɪʃ(ə)n/ *noun* deviation from normal type or accepted standard; distortion.

abet /əˈbet/ *verb* encourage (offender), assist (offence). □ **abetter**, *Law* **abettor** *noun*.

abeyance /əˈbeɪəns/ *noun* (usually after *in*, *into*) temporary disuse; suspension.

abhor /əbˈhɔː/ *verb* (**-rr-**) detest; regard with disgust.

abhorrence /əbˈhɒrəns/ *noun* disgust, detestation.

abhorrent *adjective* (often + *to*) disgusting.

abide /əˈbaɪd/ *verb* (**-ding**, *past & past participle* **abode** /əˈbəʊd/ or **abided**) tolerate; (+ *by*) act in accordance with (rule); keep (promise).

abiding /əˈbaɪdɪŋ/ *adjective* enduring, permanent.

ability /əˈbɪlɪtɪ/ *noun* (*plural* **-ies**) (often + *to do*) capacity, power; cleverness, talent.

abject /ˈæbdʒekt/ *adjective* miserable; degraded; despicable. □ **abjection** /-ˈdʒek-/ *noun*.

abjure /əbˈdʒʊə/ *verb* renounce on oath. □ **abjuration** /-dʒʊˈreɪ-/ *noun*.

ablaze /əˈbleɪz/ *adjective & adverb* on fire; glittering; excited.

able /ˈeɪb(ə)l/ *adjective* (**-r**, **-st**) (+ *to do*) having power; talented. □ **able-bodied** healthy, fit. □ **ably** *adverb*.

ablution /əˈbluːʃ(ə)n/ *noun* (usually in *plural*) ceremonial washing of hands etc.; *colloquial* washing onself.

abnegate /ˈæbnɪgeɪt/ *verb* (**-ting**) give up, renounce. □ **abnegation** *noun*.

abnormal /æbˈnɔːm(ə)l/ *adjective* exceptional; deviating from the norm. □ **abnormality** /-ˈmæl-/ *noun*; **abnormally** *adverb*.

aboard /əˈbɔːd/ *adverb & preposition* on or into (ship, aircraft, etc.).

abode[1] /əˈbəʊd/ *noun* dwelling place.

abode[2] *past & past participle* of ABIDE.

abolish /əˈbɒlɪʃ/ *verb* end existence of. □ **abolition** /æbəˈlɪʃ(ə)n/ *noun*; **abolitionist** /æbəˈlɪʃənɪst/ *noun*.

abominable /əˈbɒmɪnəb(ə)l/ *adjective* detestable, loathsome; *colloquial* very unpleasant. □ **Abominable Snowman** yeti. □ **abominably** *adverb*.

abominate /əˈbɒmɪneɪt/ *verb* (**-ting**) detest, loathe. □ **abomination** *noun*.

aboriginal /æbəˈrɪdʒɪn(ə)l/ ● *adjective* indigenous; (usually **Aboriginal**) of the Australian Aborigines. ● *noun* aboriginal inhabitant, esp. (usually **Aboriginal**) of Australia.

aborigines /æbəˈrɪdʒɪnɪz/ *plural noun* aboriginal inhabitants, esp. (usually **Aborigines**) of Australia.

■ **Usage** It is best to refer to one *Aboriginal* but several *Aborigines*, although *Aboriginals* is also acceptable.

abort /əˈbɔːt/ *verb* miscarry; effect abortion of; (cause to) end before completion.

abortion /əˈbɔːʃ(ə)n/ *noun* natural or (esp.) induced expulsion of foetus before it can survive; stunted or misshapen creature. □ **abortionist** *noun*.

abortive /əˈbɔːtɪv/ *adjective* fruitless, unsuccessful.

abound /əˈbaʊnd/ *verb* be plentiful; (+ *in*, *with*) be rich in, teem with.

about /əˈbaʊt/ ● *preposition* on subject of; relating to, in relation to; at a time near to; around (in); surrounding; here and there in. ● *adverb* approximately; nearby; in every direction; on the move, in action; all around. □ **about-face**, **-turn** turn made so as to face opposite direction, change of policy etc.; **be about to do** be on the point of doing.

above /əˈbʌv/ ● *preposition* over, on top of, higher than; more than; higher in rank, importance, etc. than; too great or good for; beyond reach of. ● *adverb* at or to higher point, overhead; earlier on page or in book. □ **above all** more than anything else; **above-board** without concealment.

abracadabra /æbrəkəˈdæbrə/ *interjection* supposedly magic word.

abrade /əˈbreɪd/ *verb* (**-ding**) scrape or wear away by rubbing.

abrasion /əˈbreɪʒ(ə)n/ *noun* rubbing or scraping away; resulting damaged area.

abrasive /əˈbreɪsɪv/ ● *adjective* capable of rubbing or grinding down; harsh or hurtful in manner. ● *noun* abrasive substance.

abreast /əˈbrest/ *adverb* side by side and facing same way; (+ *of*) up to date with.

abridge /əˈbrɪdʒ/ *verb* (**-ging**) shorten (a book etc.). □ **abridgement** *noun*.

abroad /əˈbrɔːd/ *adverb* in or to foreign country; widely; in circulation.

abrogate /ˈæbrəgeɪt/ *verb* (**-ting**) repeal, abolish (law etc.). □ **abrogation** *noun.*

abrupt /əˈbrʌpt/ *adjective* sudden, hasty; curt; steep. □ **abruptly** *adverb*; **abruptness** *noun.*

abscess /ˈæbsɪs/ *noun* (*plural* **-es**) swelling containing pus.

abscond /əbˈskɒnd/ *verb* flee, esp. to avoid arrest; escape.

abseil /ˈæbseɪl/ ● *verb* descend (building etc.) by using doubled rope fixed at higher point. ● *noun* such a descent.

absence /ˈæbsəns/ *noun* being away; duration of this; (+ *of*) lack. □ **absence of mind** inattentiveness.

absent ● *adjective* /ˈæbsənt/ not present or existing; lacking; inattentive. ● *verb* /əbˈsent/ (**absent oneself**) go or stay away. □ **absently** *adverb.*

absentee /æbsənˈtiː/ *noun* person not present.

absenteeism /æbsənˈtiːɪz(ə)m/ *noun* absenting oneself from work, school, etc.

absent-minded *adjective* forgetful, inattentive. □ **absent-mindedly** *adverb*; **absent-mindedness** *noun.*

absinthe /ˈæbsɪnθ/ *noun* wormwood-based, aniseed-flavoured liqueur.

absolute /ˈæbsəluːt/ *adjective* complete, utter; unconditional; despotic; not relative; (of adjective or transitive verb) without expressed noun or object; (of decree etc.) final. □ **absolute majority** one over all rivals combined; **absolute temperature** one measured from absolute zero; **absolute zero** lowest possible temperature (−273.15°C or 0°K).

absolutely *adverb* completely; in an absolute sense; *colloquial* quite so, yes.

absolution /æbsəˈluːʃ(ə)n/ *noun* formal forgiveness of sins.

absolutism /ˈæbsəluːtɪz(ə)m/ *noun* absolute government. □ **absolutist** *noun.*

absolve /əbˈzɒlv/ *verb* (**-ving**) (often + *from, of*) free from blame or obligation.

absorb /əbˈsɔːb/ *verb* incorporate; assimilate; take in (heat etc.); deal with easily, reduce intensity of; (often as **absorbing** *adjective*) engross attention of; consume (resources).

absorbent /əbˈsɔːbənt/ ● *adjective* tending to absorb. ● *noun* absorbent substance.

absorption /əbˈsɔːpʃ(ə)n/ *noun* absorbing, being absorbed. □ **absorptive** *adjective.*

abstain /əbˈsteɪn/ *verb* (usually + *from*) refrain (from indulging); decline to vote.

abstemious /əbˈstiːmɪəs/ *adjective* moderate or ascetic, esp. in eating and drinking. □ **abstemiously** *adverb.*

abstention /əbˈstenʃ(ə)n/ *noun* abstaining, esp. from voting.

abstinence /ˈæbstɪnəns/ *noun* abstaining, esp. from food or alcohol. □ **abstinent** *adjective.*

abstract ● *adjective* /ˈæbstrækt/ of or existing in theory rather than practice, not concrete; (of art etc.) not representational. ● *verb* /əbˈstrækt/ (often + *from*) remove; summarize. ● *noun* /ˈæbstrækt/ summary; abstract idea, work of art, etc.

abstracted *adjective* inattentive. □ **abstractedly** *adverb.*

abstraction /əbˈstrækʃ(ə)n/ *noun* abstracting; abstract idea; abstract qualities in art; absent-mindedness.

abstruse /əbˈstruːs/ *adjective* hard to understand; profound.

absurd /əbˈsɜːd/ *adjective* wildly inappropriate; ridiculous. □ **absurdity** *noun* (*plural* **-ies**); **absurdly** *adverb.*

ABTA /ˈæbtə/ *abbreviation* Association of British Travel Agents.

abundance /əˈbʌnd(ə)ns/ *noun* plenty; more than enough; wealth.

abundant *adjective* plentiful; (+ *in*) rich. □ **abundantly** *adverb.*

abuse ● *verb* /əˈbjuːz/ (**-sing**) use improperly; misuse; maltreat; insult verbally. ● *noun* /əˈbjuːs/ misuse; insulting language; corrupt practice. □ **abuser** /əˈbjuːzə/ *noun.*

abusive /əˈbjuːsɪv/ *adjective* insulting, offensive. □ **abusively** *adverb.*

abut /əˈbʌt/ *verb* (**-tt-**) (+ *on*) border on; (+ *on, against*) touch or lean on.

abysmal /əˈbɪzm(ə)l/ *adjective* very bad; dire. □ **abysmally** *adverb.*

abyss /əˈbɪs/ *noun* deep chasm.

AC *abbreviation* alternating current.

a/c *abbreviation* account.

acacia /əˈkeɪʃə/ *noun* tree with yellow or white flowers.

academia /ækəˈdiːmɪə/ *noun* the world of scholars.

academic /ækəˈdemɪk/ ● *adjective* scholarly; of learning; of no practical relevance. ● *noun* teacher or scholar in university etc. □ **academically** *adverb.*

academician /əkædəˈmɪʃ(ə)n/ *noun* member of Academy.

academy /əˈkædəmɪ/ *noun* (*plural* **-ies**) place of specialized training; (**Academy**) society of distinguished scholars, artists, scientists, etc.; *Scottish* secondary school.

acanthus /əˈkænθəs/ *noun* (*plural* **-es**) spring herbaceous plant with spiny leaves.

ACAS /ˈeɪkæs/ *abbreviation* Advisory, Conciliation, and Arbitration Service.

accede /əkˈsiːd/ *verb* (**-ding**) (+ *to*) take office, esp. as monarch; assent to.

accelerate /əkˈseləreɪt/ *verb* (**-ting**) increase speed (of); (cause to) happen earlier. □ **acceleration** *noun.*

accelerator *noun* device for increasing speed, esp. pedal in vehicle; *Physics* apparatus for imparting high speeds to charged particles.

accent ● *noun* /ˈæksənt/ style of pronunciation of region or social group (see panel); emphasis; prominence given to syllable by stress or pitch; mark on letter indicating pronunciation (see panel). ● *verb* /ækˈsent/ emphasize; write or print accents on.

accentuate /əkˈsentʃʊeɪt/ *verb* (**-ting**) emphasize, make prominent. □ **accentuation** *noun.*

accept /əkˈsept/ *verb* willingly receive; answer (invitation etc.) affirmatively; regard favourably; receive as valid or suitable. □ **acceptance** *noun.*

acceptable *adjective* worth accepting; tolerable. □ **acceptability** *noun*; **acceptably** *adverb.*

access /ˈækses/ ● *noun* way of approach or entry; right or opportunity to reach, use, or visit. ● *verb* gain access to (data) in computer.

accessible /əkˈsesɪb(ə)l/ *adjective* reachable or obtainable; easy to understand. □ **accessibility** *noun.*

accession /əkˈseʃ(ə)n/ *noun* taking office, esp. as monarch; thing added.

accessory /əkˈsesərɪ/ *noun* (*plural* **-ies**) additional or extra thing; (usually in *plural*) small attachment or item of dress; (often + *to*) person who abets in or is privy to illegal act.

accident /ˈæksɪd(ə)nt/ *noun* unintentional unfortunate esp. harmful event; event without apparent cause; unexpected event. □ **accident-prone** clumsy; **by accident** unintentionally.

accidental /æksɪˈdent(ə)l/ ● *adjective* happening or done by chance or accident. ● *noun Music* sharp, flat, or natural indicating momentary departure of note from key signature. □ **accidentally** *adverb*.

acclaim /əˈkleɪm/ ● *verb* welcome or applaud enthusiastically. ● *noun* applause; welcome; public praise. □ **acclamation** /æklə-/ *noun*.

acclimatize /əˈklaɪmətaɪz/ *verb* (also **-ise**) (**-zing** or **-sing**) adapt to new climate or conditions. □ **acclimatization** *noun*.

accolade /ˈækəleɪd/ *noun* praise given; touch made with sword at conferring of knighthood.

accommodate /əˈkɒmədeɪt/ *verb* (**-ting**) provide lodging or room for; adapt, harmonize, reconcile; do favour to; (+ *with*) supply.

■ **Usage** *Accommodate*, *accommodation*, etc. are spelt with two *ms*, not one.

accommodating *adjective* obliging.

accommodation *noun* lodgings; adjustment, adaptation; convenient arrangement. □ **accommodation address** postal address used instead of permanent one.

accompaniment /əˈkʌmpənɪmənt/ *noun* instrumental or orchestral support for solo instrument, voice, or group; accompanying thing.

accompany /əˈkʌmpənɪ/ *verb* (**-ies**, **-ied**) go with, attend; (usually in *passive*; + *with*, *by*) be done or found with; *Music* play accompaniment for. □ **accompanist** *noun Music*.

accomplice /əˈkʌmplɪs/ *noun* partner in crime.

accomplish /əˈkʌmplɪʃ/ *verb* succeed in doing; achieve, complete.

accomplished *adjective* clever, skilled.

accomplishment *noun* completion (of task etc.); acquired esp. social skill; thing achieved.

accord /əˈkɔːd/ ● *verb* (often + *with*) be consistent or in harmony; grant, give. ● *noun* agreement; consent. □ **of one's own accord** on one's own initiative.

accordance *noun* □ **in accordance with** in conformity to.

according *adverb* (+ *to*) as stated by; (+ *to*, *as*) in proportion to or as.

accordingly *adverb* as circumstances suggest or require; consequently.

accordion /əˈkɔːdɪən/ *noun* musical reed instrument with concertina-like bellows, keys, and buttons.

accost /əˈkɒst/ *verb* approach and speak boldly to.

account /əˈkaʊnt/ ● *noun* narration, description; arrangement at bank etc. for depositing and withdrawing money etc.; statement of financial transactions with balance; importance; behalf. ● *verb* consider as. □ **account for** explain, answer for, kill, destroy; **on account** to be paid for later, in part payment; **on account of** because of; **on no account** under no circumstances; **take account of**, **take into account** consider.

accountable *adjective* responsible, required to account for one's conduct; explicable. □ **accountability** *noun*.

accountant *noun* professional keeper or verifier of financial accounts. □ **accountancy** *noun*; **accounting** *noun*.

accoutrements /əˈkuːtrəmənts/ *plural noun* equipment, trappings.

accredit /əˈkredɪt/ *verb* (**-t-**) (+ *to*) attribute; (+ *with*) credit; (usually + *to*, *at*) send (ambassador etc.) with credentials.

accredited *adjective* officially recognized; generally accepted.

accretion /əˈkriːʃ(ə)n/ *noun* growth by accumulation or organic enlargement; the resulting whole; matter so added.

accrue /əˈkruː/ *verb* (**-ues**, **-ued**, **-uing**) (often + *to*) come as natural increase or advantage, esp. financial.

accumulate /əˈkjuːmjʊleɪt/ *verb* (**-ting**) acquire increasing number or quantity of; amass, collect; grow numerous; increase. □ **accumulation** *noun*; **accumulative** /-lətɪv/ *adjective*.

accumulator *noun* rechargeable electric cell; bet placed on sequence of events, with winnings and stake from each placed on next.

accurate /ˈækjʊrət/ *adjective* precise; conforming exactly with truth etc. □ **accuracy** *noun*; **accurately** *adverb*.

accursed /əˈkɜːsɪd/ *adjective* under a curse; *colloquial* detestable, annoying.

accusative /əˈkjuːzətɪv/ *Grammar* ● *noun* case expressing object of action. ● *adjective* of or in accusative.

accuse /əˈkjuːz/ *verb* (**-sing**) (often + *of*) charge with fault or crime; blame. □ **accusation** /æk-/ *noun*; **accusatory** *adjective*.

accustom /əˈkʌstəm/ *verb* (+ *to*) make used to.

accustomed *adjective* (usually + *to*) used (to a thing); customary.

ace ● *noun* playing card with single spot; person who excels in some activity; *Tennis* unreturnable service.

Accent

1 A person's accent is the way he or she pronounces words, and people from different regions and different groups in society have different accents. For instance, most people in northern England say *path* with a 'short' *a*, while most people in southern England say it with a 'long' *a*, and in America and Canada the *r* in *far* and *port* is generally pronounced, while in south-eastern England, for example, it is not. Everyone speaks with an accent, although some accents may be regarded as having more prestige, such as 'Received Pronunciation' (RP) in the UK.

2 An accent on a letter is a mark added to it to alter the sound it stands for. In French, for example, there are

´ (acute), as in *état* — ¨ (diaeresis), as in *Noël*
` (grave), as in *mère* — ¸ (cedilla), as in *français*
ˆ (circumflex), as in *guêpe*

and German has

¨ (umlaut), as in *München*.

There are no accents on native English words, but many words borrowed from other languages still have them, such as *blasé* and *façade*.

● *adjective slang* excellent. □ **within an ace of** on the verge of.

acerbic /əˈsɜːbɪk/ *adjective* harsh and sharp, esp. in speech or manner. □ **acerbity** *noun* (*plural* **-ies**).

acetate /ˈæsɪteɪt/ *noun* compound of acetic acid, esp. the cellulose ester; fabric made from this.

acetic /əˈsiːtɪk/ *adjective* of or like vinegar. □ **acetic acid** clear liquid acid in vinegar.

acetone /ˈæsɪtəʊn/ *noun* colourless volatile solvent of organic compounds.

acetylene /əˈsetɪliːn/ *noun* inflammable hydrocarbon gas, used esp. in welding.

ache /eɪk/ ● *noun* continuous dull pain; mental distress. ● *verb* (**aching**) suffer from or be the source of an ache.

achieve /əˈtʃiːv/ *verb* (**-ving**) reach or attain by effort; accomplish (task etc.); be successful. □ **achiever** *noun*; **achievement** *noun*.

Achilles /əˈkɪliːz/ *noun* □ **Achilles heel** vulnerable point; **Achilles tendon** tendon attaching calf muscles to heel.

achromatic /ækrəʊˈmætɪk/ *adjective* transmitting light without separating it into colours; free from colour. □ **achromatically** *adverb*.

achy /ˈeɪkɪ/ *adjective* (**-ier, -iest**) suffering from aches.

acid /ˈæsɪd/ ● *noun Chemistry* substance that neutralizes alkalis, turns litmus red, and usually contains hydrogen and is sour; *slang* drug LSD. ● *adjective* having properties of acid; sour; biting, sharp. □ **acid drop** sharp-tasting boiled sweet; **acid house** synthesized music with simple beat, associated with hallucinogenic drugs; **acid rain** rain containing acid formed from industrial waste in atmosphere; **acid test** severe or conclusive test. □ **acidic** /əˈsɪd-/ *adjective*; **acidify** /əˈsɪd-/ *verb* (**-ies, -ied**); **acidity** /-ˈsɪd-/ *noun*.

acidulous /əˈsɪdjʊləs/ *adjective* somewhat acid.

acknowledge /əkˈnɒlɪdʒ/ *verb* (**-ging**) recognize, accept truth of; confirm receipt of (letter etc.); show that one has noticed; express gratitude for.

acknowledgement *noun* (also **acknowledgment**) acknowledging; thing given or done in gratitude; letter etc. confirming receipt; (usually in *plural*) author's thanks, prefacing book.

acme /ˈækmɪ/ *noun* highest point.

acne /ˈæknɪ/ *noun* skin condition with red pimples.

acolyte /ˈækəlaɪt/ *noun* assistant, esp. of priest.

aconite /ˈækənaɪt/ *noun* any of various poisonous plants, esp. monkshood; drug made from these.

acorn /ˈeɪkɔːn/ *noun* fruit of oak.

acoustic /əˈkuːstɪk/ *adjective* of sound or sense of hearing; (of musical instrument etc.) without electrical amplification. □ **acoustically** *adverb*.

acoustics *plural noun* properties (of a room etc.) in transmitting sound; (treated as *singular*) science of sound.

acquaint /əˈkweɪnt/ *verb* (+ *with*) make aware of or familiar with. □ **be acquainted with** know.

acquaintance *noun* being acquainted; person one knows slightly. □ **acquaintanceship** *noun*.

acquiesce /ækwɪˈes/ *verb* (**-cing**) agree, esp. tacitly. □ **acquiescence** *noun*; **acquiescent** *adjective*.

acquire /əˈkwaɪə/ *verb* (**-ring**) gain possession of. □ **acquired immune deficiency syndrome** = AIDS; **acquired taste** liking developed by experience.

acquirement *noun* thing acquired or attained.

acquisition /ækwɪˈzɪʃ(ə)n/ *noun* (esp. useful) thing acquired; acquiring, being acquired.

acquisitive /əˈkwɪzɪtɪv/ *adjective* keen to acquire things.

acquit /əˈkwɪt/ *verb* (**-tt-**) (often + *of*) declare not guilty; (**acquit oneself**) behave, perform, (+ *of*) discharge (duty etc.). □ **acquittal** *noun*.

acre /ˈeɪkə/ *noun* measure of land, 4840 sq. yards, 0.405 ha.

acreage /ˈeɪkərɪdʒ/ *noun* number of acres.

acrid /ˈækrɪd/ *adjective* bitterly pungent. □ **acridity** /-ˈkrɪd-/ *noun*.

acrimonious /ækrɪˈməʊnɪəs/ *adjective* bitter in manner or temper. □ **acrimony** /ˈækrɪmənɪ/ *noun*.

acrobat /ˈækrəbæt/ *noun* performer of acrobatics. □ **acrobatic** /-ˈbæt-/ *adjective*.

acrobatics /ækrəˈbætɪks/ *plural noun* gymnastic feats.

acronym /ˈækrənɪm/ *noun* word formed from initial letters of other words (e.g. *laser*, *NATO*).

acropolis /əˈkrɒpəlɪs/ *noun* citadel of ancient Greek city.

across /əˈkrɒs/ ● *preposition* to or on other side of; from one side to another side of. ● *adverb* to or on other side; from one side to another. □ **across the board** applying to all.

acrostic /əˈkrɒstɪk/ *noun* poem etc. in which first (or first and last) letters of lines form word(s).

acrylic /əˈkrɪlɪk/ ● *adjective* made from acrylic acid. ● *noun* acrylic fibre, fabric, or paint.

acrylic acid *noun* a pungent liquid organic acid.

act ● *noun* thing done, deed; process of doing; item of entertainment; pretence; main division of play; decree of legislative body. ● *verb* behave; perform actions or functions; (often + *on*) have effect; perform in play etc.; pretend; play part of. □ **act for** be (legal) representative of; **act up** *colloquial* misbehave, give trouble.

acting *adjective* serving temporarily as.

actinism /ˈæktɪnɪz(ə)m/ *noun* property of short-wave radiation that produces chemical changes, as in photography.

action /ˈækʃ(ə)n/ *noun* process of doing or acting; forcefulness, energy; exertion of energy or influence; deed, act; (**the action**) series of events in story, play, etc., *slang* exciting activity; battle; mechanism of instrument; style of movement; lawsuit. □ **action-packed** full of action or excitement; **action replay** playback of part of television broadcast; **out of action** not functioning.

actionable *adjective* providing grounds for legal action.

activate /ˈæktɪveɪt/ *verb* (**-ting**) make active or radioactive. □ **activation** *noun*.

active /ˈæktɪv/ ● *adjective* marked by action; energetic, diligent; working, operative; *Grammar* (of verb) of which subject performs action (e.g. *saw* in *he saw a film*). ● *noun Grammar* active form or voice. □ **active service** military service in wartime. □ **actively** *adverb*.

activism *noun* policy of vigorous action, esp. for a political cause. □ **activist** *noun*.

activity /ækˈtɪvɪtɪ/ *noun* (*plural* **-ies**) being active; busy or energetic action; (often in *plural*) occupation, pursuit.

actor /ˈæktə/ *noun* person who acts in play, film, etc.

actress /ˈæktrɪs/ *noun* female actor.

actual /ˈæktʃʊəl/ *adjective* existing, real; current. □ **actuality** /-ˈæl-/ *noun* (*plural* **-ies**).

actually *adverb* in fact, really.

actuary /ˈæktʃʊərɪ/ *noun* (*plural* **-ies**) statistician, esp. one calculating insurance risks and premiums. □ **actuarial** /-ˈeər-/ *adjective*.

actuate /ˈæktʃʊeɪt/ *verb* (**-ting**) cause to move, function, act.

acuity /əˈkjuːɪtɪ/ *noun* acuteness.

acumen /ˈækjʊmen/ *noun* keen insight or discernment.

acupuncture /ˈækju:pʌŋktʃə/ *noun* medical treatment using needles in parts of the body. □ **acupuncturist** *noun*.

acute /əˈkju:t/ *adjective* (**-r**, **-st**) keen, penetrating; shrewd; (of disease) coming quickly to crisis; (of angle) less than 90°. □ **acute** (**accent**) mark (´) over letter indicating pronunciation. □ **acutely** *adverb*.

AD *abbreviation* of the Christian era (*Anno Domini*).

ad *noun colloquial* advertisement.

adage /ˈædɪdʒ/ *noun* proverb, maxim.

adagio /əˈdɑ:ʒɪəʊ/ *Music* ● *adverb & adjective* in slow time. ● *noun* (*plural* **-s**) adagio passage.

adamant /ˈædəmənt/ *adjective* stubbornly resolute. □ **adamantly** *adverb*.

Adam's apple /ˈædəmz/ *noun* cartilaginous projection at front of neck.

adapt /əˈdæpt/ *verb* (+ *to*) fit, adjust; (+ *to*, *for*) make suitable, modify; (usually + *to*) adjust to new conditions. □ **adaptable** *adjective*; **adaptation** /æd-/ *noun*.

adaptor *noun* device for making equipment compatible; *Electricity* device for connecting several electrical plugs to one socket.

add *verb* join as increase or supplement; unite (numbers) to get their total; say further. □ **add up** find total of; (+ *to*) amount to.

addendum /əˈdendəm/ *noun* (*plural* **-da**) thing to be added; material added at end of book.

adder /ˈædə/ *noun* small venomous snake.

addict /ˈædɪkt/ *noun* person addicted, esp. to drug; *colloquial* devotee.

addicted /əˈdɪktɪd/ *adjective* (usually + *to*) dependent on a drug as a habit; devoted to an interest. □ **addiction** *noun*.

addictive /əˈdɪktɪv/ *adjective* causing addiction.

addition /əˈdɪʃ(ə)n/ *noun* adding; person or thing added. □ **in addition** (often + *to*) also, as well.

additional *adjective* added, extra. □ **additionally** *adverb*.

additive /ˈædɪtɪv/ *noun* substance added, esp. to colour, flavour, or preserve food.

addle /ˈæd(ə)l/ *verb* (**-ling**) muddle, confuse; (usually as **addled** *adjective*) (of egg) become rotten.

address /əˈdres/ ● *noun* place where person lives or organization is situated; particulars of this, esp. for postal purposes; speech delivered to an audience. ● *verb* write postal directions on; direct (remarks etc.); speak or write to; direct one's attention to.

addressee /ædreˈsi:/ *noun* person to whom letter etc. is addressed.

adduce /əˈdju:s/ *verb* (**-cing**) cite as proof or instance. □ **adducible** *adjective*.

adenoids /ˈædɪnɔɪds/ *plural noun* enlarged lymphatic tissue between nose and throat, often hindering breathing. □ **adenoidal** /-ˈnɔɪ-/ *adjective*.

adept ● *adjective* /əˈdept, ˈædept/ (+ *at*, *in*) skilful. ● *noun* /ˈædept/ adept person.

adequate /ˈædɪkwət/ *adjective* sufficient, satisfactory. □ **adequacy** *noun*; **adequately** *adverb*.

adhere /ədˈhɪə/ *verb* (**-ring**) (usually + *to*) stick fast; behave according to (rule etc.); give allegiance.

adherent ● *noun* supporter. ● *adjective* adhering. □ **adherence** *noun*.

adhesion /ədˈhi:ʒ(ə)n/ *noun* adhering.

adhesive /ədˈhi:sɪv/ ● *adjective* sticky, causing adhesion. ● *noun* adhesive substance.

ad hoc /æd ˈhɒk/ *adverb & adjective* for one particular occasion or use.

adieu /əˈdju:/ *interjection* goodbye.

ad infinitum /æd ɪnfɪˈnaɪtəm/ *adverb* without limit; for ever.

adipose /ˈædɪpəʊz/ *adjective* of fat, fatty. □ **adiposity** /-ˈpɒs-/ *noun*.

adjacent /əˈdʒeɪs(ə)nt/ *adjective* lying near; adjoining. □ **adjacency** *noun*.

adjective /ˈædʒɪktɪv/ *noun* word indicating quality of noun or pronoun (see panel). □ **adjectival** /-ˈtaɪv-/ *adjective*.

adjoin /əˈdʒɔɪn/ *verb* be next to and joined with.

adjourn /əˈdʒɜ:n/ *verb* postpone, break off; (+ *to*) transfer to (another place). □ **adjournment** *noun*.

adjudge /əˈdʒʌdʒ/ *verb* (**-ging**) pronounce judgement on; pronounce or award judicially. □ **adjudg(e)ment** *noun*.

adjudicate /əˈdʒu:dɪkeɪt/ *verb* (**-ting**) act as judge; adjudge. □ **adjudication** *noun*; **adjudicator** *noun*.

adjunct /ˈædʒʌŋkt/ *noun* (+ *to*, *of*) subordinate or incidental thing.

adjure /əˈdʒʊə/ *verb* (**-ring**) (usually + *to do*) beg or command. □ **adjuration** *noun*.

Adjective

An adjective is a word that describes a noun or pronoun, e.g.

red, clever, German, depressed, battered, sticky, shining

Most can be used either before a noun, e.g.

the red *house* — *a* clever *woman*

or after a verb like *be*, *seem*, or *call*, e.g.

The house is red. — *I wouldn't call him* lazy.
She seems very clever.

Some can be used only before a noun, e.g.

the chief *reason* (one cannot say **the reason is chief*)

Some can be used only after a verb, e.g.

The ship is still afloat. (one cannot say **an afloat ship*)

A few can be used only immediately after a noun, e.g.

the president elect (one cannot say either **an elect president* or **The president is elect*)

adjust /ə'dʒʌst/ *verb* order, position; regulate; arrange; (usually + *to*) adapt; harmonize. □ **adjustable** *adjective*; **adjustment** *noun*.

adjutant /'ædʒʊt(ə)nt/ *noun* army officer assisting superior in administrative duties.

ad lib /æd 'lɪb/ ● *verb* (**-bb-**) improvise. ● *adjective* improvised. ● *adverb* to any desired extent.

Adm. *abbreviation* Admiral.

administer /əd'mɪnɪstə/ *verb* manage (affairs); formally deliver, dispense.

administration /ədmɪnɪ'streɪʃ(ə)n/ *noun* administering, esp. public affairs; government in power.

administrative /əd'mɪnɪstrətɪv/ *adjective* of the management of affairs.

administrator /əd'mɪnɪstreɪtə/ *noun* manager of business, public affairs, or person's estate.

admirable /'ædmərəb(ə)l/ *adjective* deserving admiration; excellent. □ **admirably** *adverb*.

admiral /'ædmər(ə)l/ *noun* commander-in-chief of navy; high-ranking naval officer, commander.

Admiralty *noun* (*plural* **-ies**) (in full **Admiralty Board**) *historical* committee superintending Royal Navy.

admire /əd'maɪə/ *verb* regard with approval, respect, or satisfaction; express admiration of. □ **admiration** /ædmə'reɪ-/ *noun*; **admirer** *noun*; **admiring** *adjective*; **admiringly** *adverb*.

admissible /əd'mɪsɪb(ə)l/ *adjective* worth accepting or considering; allowable. □ **admissibility** *noun*.

admission /əd'mɪʃ(ə)n/ *noun* acknowledgement (of error etc.); (right of) entering; entrance charge.

admit /əd'mɪt/ *verb* (**-tt-**) (often + *to be, that*) acknowledge, recognize as true; (+ *to*) confess to; let in; accommodate; take (patient) into hospital; (+ *of*) allow as possible.

admittance *noun* admitting or being admitted, usually to a place.

admittedly *adverb* as must be admitted.

admixture /æd'mɪkstʃə/ *noun* thing added, esp. minor ingredient; adding of this.

admonish /əd'mɒnɪʃ/ *verb* reprove; urge; (+ *of*) warn. □ **admonishment** *noun*; **admonition** /ædmə'nɪ-/ *noun*; **admonitory** *adjective*.

ad nauseam /æd 'nɔ:zɪæm/ *adverb* to a sickening extent.

ado /ə'du:/ *noun* fuss; trouble.

adobe /ə'dəʊbɪ/ *noun* sun-dried brick.

adolescent /ædə'lesənt/ ● *adjective* between childhood and adulthood. ● *noun* adolescent person. □ **adolescence** *noun*.

adopt /ə'dɒpt/ *verb* legally take (child) as one's own; take over (another's idea etc.); choose; accept responsibility for; approve (report etc.). □ **adoption** *noun*.

adoptive *adjective* because of adoption.

adorable /ə'dɔ:rəb(ə)l/ *adjective* deserving adoration; *colloquial* delightful, charming.

adore /ə'dɔ:/ *verb* (**-ring**) love intensely; worship; *colloquial* like very much. □ **adoration** /ædə'reɪ-/ *noun*; **adorer** *noun*.

adorn /ə'dɔ:n/ *verb* add beauty to, decorate. □ **adornment** *noun*.

adrenal /ə'dri:n(ə)l/ ● *adjective* of adrenal glands. ● *noun* (in full **adrenal gland**) either of two ductless glands above the kidneys.

adrenalin /ə'drenəlɪn/ *noun* stimulative hormone secreted by adrenal glands.

adrift /ə'drɪft/ *adverb & adjective* drifting; *colloquial* unfastened, out of order.

adroit /ə'drɔɪt/ *adjective* dexterous, skilful.

adsorb /əd'sɔ:b/ *verb* attract and hold thin layer of (gas or liquid) on its surface. □ **adsorbent** *adjective & noun*; **adsorption** *noun*.

adulation /ædjʊ'leɪʃ(ə)n/ *noun* obsequious flattery.

adult /'ædʌlt/ ● *adjective* grown-up, mature; of or for adults. ● *noun* adult person. □ **adulthood** *noun*.

adulterate /ə'dʌltəreɪt/ *verb* (**-ting**) debase (esp. food) by adding other substances. □ **adulteration** *noun*.

adultery /ə'dʌltərɪ/ *noun* voluntary sexual intercourse of married person other than with spouse. □ **adulterer**, **adulteress** *noun*; **adulterous** *adjective*.

adumbrate /'ædʌmbreɪt/ *verb* (**-ting**) indicate faintly or in outline; foreshadow. □ **adumbration** *noun*.

advance /əd'vɑ:ns/ ● *verb* (**-cing**) move or put forward; progress; pay or lend beforehand; promote; present (idea etc.). ● *noun* going forward; progress; prepayment, loan; payment beforehand; (in *plural*) amorous approaches; rise in price. ● *adjective* done etc. beforehand. □ **advance on** approach threateningly; **in advance** ahead, beforehand.

advanced *adjective* well ahead; socially progressive. □ **advanced level** high level GCE exam.

advancement *noun* promotion of person, cause, etc.

advantage /əd'vɑ:ntɪdʒ/ ● *noun* beneficial feature; benefit, profit; (often + *over*) superiority; *Tennis* next point after deuce. ● *verb* (**-ging**) benefit, favour. □ **take advantage of** make good use of; exploit. □ **advantageous** /ædvən'teɪdʒəs/ *adjective*.

Advent /'ædvent/ *noun* season before Christmas; coming of Christ; (**advent**) arrival.

Adventist *noun* member of sect believing in imminent second coming of Christ.

adventure /əd'ventʃə/ ● *noun* unusual and exciting experience; enterprise. ● *verb* (**-ring**) dare, venture. □ **adventure playground** one with climbing frames etc.

adventurer *noun* (*feminine* **adventuress**) person who seeks adventure esp. for personal gain or pleasure; financial speculator.

adventurous *adjective* venturesome, enterprising.

adverb /'ædvɜ:b/ *noun* word indicating manner, degree, circumstance, etc. used to modify verb, adjective, or other adverb (see panel). □ **adverbial** /əd'vɜ:-/ *adjective*.

adversary /'ædvəsərɪ/ *noun* (*plural* **-ies**) enemy; opponent. □ **adversarial** /-'seə-/ *adjective*.

adverse /'ædvɜ:s/ *adjective* unfavourable; harmful. □ **adversely** *adverb*.

adversity /əd'vɜ:sɪtɪ/ *noun* misfortune.

advert /'ædvɜ:t/ *noun colloquial* advertisement.

advertise /'ædvətaɪz/ *verb* (**-sing**) promote publicly to increase sales; make generally known; seek to sell, fill (vacancy), or (+ *for*) buy or employ by notice in newspaper etc.

advertisement /əd'vɜ:tɪsmənt/ *noun* public announcement advertising something; advertising.

advice /əd'vaɪs/ *noun* recommendation on how to act; information; notice of transaction.

advisable /əd'vaɪzəb(ə)l/ *adjective* to be recommended; expedient. □ **advisability** *noun*.

advise /əd'vaɪz/ *verb* (**-sing**) give advice (to); recommend; (usually + *of, that*) inform.

advisedly /əd'vaɪzɪdlɪ/ *adverb* deliberately.

adviser *noun* person who advises, esp. officially.

advisory /əd'vaɪzərɪ/ *adjective* giving advice.

advocaat /ædvə'kɑ:t/ *noun* liqueur of eggs, sugar, and brandy.

advocacy /'ædvəkəsɪ/ *noun* support or argument for cause etc.

advocate ● *noun* /'ædvəkət/ (+ *of*) person who speaks in favour; person who pleads for another, esp. in law court. ● *verb* /ˈædvəkeɪt/ (**-ting**) recommend by argument.

adze /ædz/ *noun* (*US* **adz**) axe with arched blade at right angles to handle.

aegis /ˈiːdʒɪs/ *noun* protection; support.

aeolian harp /iːˈəʊlɪən/ *noun* (*US* **eolian harp**) stringed instrument sounding when wind passes through it.

aeon /ˈiːɒn/ *noun* (also **eon**) long or indefinite period; an age.

aerate /ˈeəreɪt/ *verb* (**-ting**) charge with carbon dioxide; expose to air. □ **aeration** *noun*.

aerial /ˈeərɪəl/ ● *noun* device for transmitting or receiving radio signals. ● *adjective* from the air; existing in the air; like air.

aero- *combining form* air; aircraft.

aerobatics /eərəˈbætɪks/ *plural noun* feats of spectacular flying of aircraft; (treated as *singular*) performance of these.

aerobics /eəˈrəʊbɪks/ *plural noun* vigorous exercises designed to increase oxygen intake. □ **aerobic** *adjective*.

aerodrome /ˈeərədrəʊm/ *noun* small airport or airfield.

aerodynamics /eərəʊdaɪˈnæmɪks/ *plural noun* (usually treated as *singular*) dynamics of solid bodies moving through air. □ **aerodynamic** *adjective*.

aerofoil /ˈeərəfɔɪl/ *noun* structure with curved surfaces (e.g. aircraft wing), designed to give lift in flight.

aeronautics /eərəʊˈnɔːtɪks/ *plural noun* (usually treated as *singular*) science or practice of motion in the air. □ **aeronautical** *adjective*.

aeroplane /ˈeərəpleɪn/ *noun* powered heavier-than-air aircraft with wings.

aerosol /ˈeərəsɒl/ *noun* pressurized container releasing substance as fine spray.

aerospace /ˈeərəʊspeɪs/ *noun* earth's atmosphere and outer space; aviation in this.

aesthete /ˈiːsθiːt/ *noun* person who appreciates beauty.

aesthetic /iːsˈθetɪk/ *adjective* of or sensitive to beauty; tasteful. □ **aesthetically** *adverb*; **aestheticism** /-sɪz(ə)m/ *noun*.

aetiology /iːtɪˈɒlədʒɪ/ *noun* (*US* **etiology**) study of causation or of causes of disease. □ **aetiological** /-əˈlɒdʒ-/ *adjective*.

afar /əˈfɑː/ *adverb* at or to a distance.

affable /ˈæfəb(ə)l/ *adjective* friendly; courteous. □ **affability** *noun*; **affably** *adverb*.

affair /əˈfeə/ *noun* matter, concern; love affair; *colloquial* thing, event; (in *plural*) business.

affect /əˈfekt/ *verb* produce effect on; (of disease etc.) attack; move emotionally; use for effect; pretend to feel; (+ *to do*) pretend.

■ **Usage** *Affect* is often confused with *effect*, which means 'to bring about'.

affectation /æfekˈteɪʃ(ə)n/ *noun* artificial manner; pretentious display.

affected *adjective* pretended; full of affectation.

affection /əˈfekʃ(ə)n/ *noun* goodwill, fond feeling; disease.

affectionate /əˈfekʃənət/ *adjective* loving. □ **affectionately** *adverb*.

affidavit /æfɪˈdeɪvɪt/ *noun* written statement on oath.

affiliate /əˈfɪlɪeɪt/ *verb* (**-ting**) (+ *to*, *with*) attach to, connect to, or adopt as member or branch.

affiliation *noun* affiliating, being affiliated. □ **affiliation order** legal order compelling supposed father to support illegitimate child.

affinity /əˈfɪnɪtɪ/ *noun* (*plural* **-ies**) attraction; relationship; resemblance; *Chemistry* tendency of substances to combine with others.

affirm /əˈfɜːm/ *verb* state as fact; make solemn declaration in place of oath. □ **affirmation** /æfəˈmeɪʃ(ə)n/ *noun*.

affirmative /əˈfɜːmətɪv/ ● *adjective* affirming, expressing approval. ● *noun* affirmative statement.

affix ● *verb* /əˈfɪks/ attach, fasten; add in writing. ● *noun* /ˈæfɪks/ addition; prefix, suffix.

afflict /əˈflɪkt/ *verb* distress physically or mentally.

affliction *noun* distress, suffering; cause of this.

Adverb

An adverb is used:

1 with a verb, to say:

- **a** how something happens, e.g. *He walks* quickly.
- **b** where something happens, e.g. *I live* here.
- **c** when something happens, e.g. *They visited us* yesterday.
- **d** how often something happens, e.g. *We* usually *have coffee*.

2 to strengthen or weaken the meaning of:

- **a** a verb, e.g. *He* really *meant it. I* almost *fell asleep*.
- **b** an adjective, e.g. *She is* very *clever. This is a* slightly *better result*.
- **c** another adverb, e.g. *It comes off* terribly *easily. The boys* nearly *always get home late*.

3 to add to the meaning of a whole sentence, e.g.

He is probably *our best player*. Luckily, *no one was hurt*.

In writing or in formal speech, it is **incorrect** to use an adjective instead of an adverb. For example, use

Do it properly. and not **Do it* proper.

but note that many words are both an adjective and an adverb, e.g.

adjective	*adverb*
a fast *horse*	*He ran* fast.
a long *time*	*Have you been here* long?

affluent /'æfluənt/ *adjective* rich. □ **affluence** *noun.*

afford /ə'fɔːd/ *verb* (after *can, be able to*) have enough money, time, etc., for; be able to spare (time etc.); (+ *to do*) be in a position; provide.

afforest /ə'fɒrɪst/ *verb* convert into forest; plant with trees. □ **afforestation** *noun.*

affray /ə'freɪ/ *noun* breach of peace by fighting or rioting in public.

affront /ə'frʌnt/ ● *noun* open insult. ● *verb* insult openly; embarrass.

Afghan /'æfgæn/ ● *noun* native, national, or language of Afghanistan. ● *adjective* of Afghanistan. □ **Afghan hound** tall dog with long silky hair.

afield /ə'fiːld/ *adverb* to or at a distance.

aflame /ə'fleɪm/ *adverb & adjective* in flames; very excited.

afloat /ə'fləʊt/ *adverb & adjective* floating; at sea; out of debt.

afoot /ə'fʊt/ *adverb & adjective* in operation; progressing.

afore /ə'fɔː/ *preposition & adverb archaic* before.

afore- *combining form* previously.

aforethought *adjective* (after noun) premeditated.

a fortiori /eɪ fɔːtɪ'ɔːraɪ/ *adverb & adjective* with stronger reason. [Latin]

afraid /ə'freɪd/ *adjective* alarmed, frightened. □ **be afraid** *colloquial* politely regret.

afresh /ə'freʃ/ *adverb* anew; with fresh start.

African /'æfrɪkən/ ● *noun* native of Africa; person of African descent. ● *adjective* of Africa.

Afrikaans /æfrɪ'kɑːns/ *noun* language derived from Dutch, used in S. Africa.

Afrikaner /æfrɪ'kɑːnə/ *noun* Afrikaans-speaking white person in S. Africa.

Afro /'æfrəʊ/ ● *adjective* (of hair) tightly-curled and bushy. ● *noun* (*plural* **-s**) Afro hairstyle.

Afro- *combining form* African.

aft /ɑːft/ *adverb* at or towards stern or tail.

after /'ɑːftə/ ● *preposition* following in time; in view of; despite; behind; in pursuit or quest of; about, concerning; in allusion to or imitation of. ● *conjunction* later than. ● *adverb* later; behind. ● *adjective* later. □ **after all** in spite of everything; **afterbirth** placenta etc. discharged after childbirth; **aftercare** attention after leaving hospital etc.; **after-effect** delayed effect of accident etc.; **afterlife** life after death; **afters** *colloquial* sweet dessert; **aftershave** lotion applied to face after shaving; **afterthought** thing thought of or added later.

aftermath /'ɑːftəmæθ/ *noun* consequences.

afternoon /ɑːftə'nuːn/ *noun* time between midday and evening.

afterwards /'ɑːftəwədz/ *adverb* later, subsequently.

again /ə'gen/ *adverb* another time; as previously; in addition; on the other hand. □ **again and again** repeatedly.

against /ə'genst/ *preposition* in opposition to; into collision or in contact with; to the disadvantage of; in contrast to; in anticipation of; as compensating factor to; in return for.

agape /ə'geɪp/ *adjective* gaping.

agate /'ægət/ *noun* usually hard streaked chalcedony.

agave /ə'geɪvɪ/ *noun* spiny-leaved plant.

age ● *noun* length of past life or existence; *colloquial* (often in *plural*) a long time; historical period; old age. ● *verb* (**ageing**) (cause to) show signs of age; grow old; mature. □ **come of age** reach legal adult status; **under age** not old enough.

aged *adjective* /eɪdʒd/ of the age of; /'eɪdʒɪd/ old.

ageism /'eɪdʒɪz(ə)m/ *noun* prejudice or discrimination on grounds of age.

ageless /'eɪdʒlɪs/ *adjective* never growing or appearing old.

agency /'eɪdʒənsɪ/ *noun* (*plural* **-ies**) business or premises of agent; action; intervention.

agenda /ə'dʒendə/ *noun* (*plural* **-s**) list of items to be considered at meeting; things to be done.

agent /'eɪdʒ(ə)nt/ *noun* person acting for another in business etc.; person or thing producing effect.

agent provocateur /ɑːʒɑ̃ prəvɒkə'tɜː/ *noun* (*plural* ***agents provocateurs*** same pronunciation) person tempting suspected offenders to self-incriminating action. [French]

agglomerate /ə'glɒmərеɪt/ *verb* (**-ting**) collect into mass. □ **agglomeration** *noun.*

agglutinate /ə'gluːtɪneɪt/ *verb* (**-ting**) stick as with glue. □ **agglutination** *noun*; **agglutinative** /-nətɪv/ *adjective.*

aggrandize /ə'grændaɪz/ *verb* (also **-ise**) (**-zing** or **-sing**) increase power, rank, or wealth of; make seem greater. □ **aggrandizement** /-dɪz-/ *noun.*

aggravate /'ægrəveɪt/ *verb* (**-ting**) increase seriousness of; *colloquial* annoy. □ **aggravation** *noun.*

■ **Usage** The use of *aggravate* to mean 'annoy' is considered incorrect by some people, but it is common in informal use.

aggregate ● *noun* /'ægrɪgət/ sum total; crushed stone etc. used in making concrete. ● *adjective* /'ægrɪgət/ collective, total. ● *verb* /'ægrɪgeɪt/ collect together, unite; *colloquial* amount to. □ **aggregation** *noun.*

aggression /ə'greʃ(ə)n/ *noun* unprovoked attack; hostile act or feeling. □ **aggressor** *noun.*

aggressive /ə'gresɪv/ *adjective* given to aggression; forceful, self-assertive. □ **aggressively** *adverb.*

aggrieved /ə'griːvd/ *adjective* having grievance.

aggro /'ægrəʊ/ *noun slang* aggression; difficulty.

aghast /ə'gɑːst/ *adjective* amazed and horrified.

agile /'ædʒaɪl/ *adjective* quick-moving; nimble. □ **agility** /ə'dʒɪlɪtɪ/ *noun.*

agitate /'ædʒɪteɪt/ *verb* (**-ting**) disturb, excite; (often + *for, against*) campaign, esp. politically; shake briskly. □ **agitation** *noun*; **agitator** *noun.*

AGM *abbreviation* annual general meeting.

agnail /'ægneɪl/ *noun* torn skin at root of fingernail; resulting soreness.

agnostic /æg'nɒstɪk/ ● *noun* person who believes that existence of God is not provable. ● *adjective* of agnosticism. □ **agnosticism** /-sɪz(ə)m/ *noun.*

ago /ə'gəʊ/ *adverb* in the past.

agog /ə'gɒg/ *adjective* eager, expectant.

agonize /'ægənaɪz/ *verb* (also **-ise**) (**-zing** or **-sing**) undergo mental anguish; (cause to) suffer agony; (as **agonized** *adjective*) expressing agony.

agony /'ægənɪ/ *noun* (*plural* **-ies**) extreme physical or mental suffering; severe struggle. □ **agony aunt** *colloquial* writer answering letters in **agony column** *colloquial*, section of magazine etc. offering personal advice.

agoraphobia /ægərə'fəʊbɪə/ *noun* extreme fear of open spaces. □ **agoraphobic** *adjective.*

agrarian /ə'greərɪən/ ● *adjective* of land or its cultivation. ● *noun* advocate of redistribution of land.

agree /ə'griː/ *verb* (**-ees, -eed,**) (often + *with*) hold similar opinion, be or become in harmony, suit, be compatible; (+ *to do*) consent; reach agreement about.

agreeable *adjective* pleasing; willing to agree. □ **agreeably** *adverb.*

agreement *noun* act or state of agreeing; arrangement, contract.

agriculture /'ægrɪkʌltʃə/ *noun* cultivation of the soil and rearing of animals. □ **agricultural** /-'kʌl-/ *adjective*; **agriculturalist** /-'kʌl-/ *noun*.

agronomy /ə'grɒnəmɪ/ *noun* science of soil management and crop production. □ **agronomist** *noun*.

aground /ə'graʊnd/ *adjective & adverb* on(to) bottom of shallow water.

ague /'eɪgju:/ *noun* shivering fit; *historical* malarial fever.

ah /ɑ:/ *interjection expressing surprise, pleasure, or realization.*

aha /ɑ:'hɑ:/ *interjection expressing surprise, triumph, mockery, etc.*

ahead /ə'hed/ *adverb* in advance, in front; (often + *on*) in the lead (on points etc.).

ahoy /ə'hɔɪ/ *interjection Nautical* call used in hailing.

AI *abbreviation* artificial insemination; artificial intelligence.

aid ● *noun* help; person or thing that helps. ● *verb* help; promote (recovery etc.). □ **in aid of** in support of, *colloquial* for purpose of.

aide /eɪd/ *noun* aide-de-camp; assistant.

aide-de-camp /eɪd də 'kɑ̃/ *noun* (*plural* **aides-** same pronunciation) officer assisting senior officer.

Aids *noun* (also **AIDS**) acquired immune deficiency syndrome.

ail *verb* be ill or in poor condition.

aileron /'eɪlərɒn/ *noun* hinged flap on aircraft wing.

ailment *noun* illness, esp. minor one.

aim ● *verb* intend, try; (usually + *at*) direct, point; take aim. ● *noun* purpose, object; directing of weapon etc. at object. □ **take aim** direct weapon etc. at object.

aimless *adjective* purposeless. □ **aimlessly** *adverb*.

ain't /eɪnt/ *colloquial* am not, is not, are not; has not, have not.

■ **Usage** The use of *ain't* is incorrect in standard English.

air ● *noun* mixture chiefly of oxygen and nitrogen surrounding earth; open space; earth's atmosphere, often as place where aircraft operate; appearance, manner; (in *plural*) affected manner; tune. ● *verb* expose (room, clothes, etc.) to air, ventilate; express and discuss publicly. □ **airbase** base for military aircraft; **air-bed** inflatable mattress; **airborne** transported by air, (of aircraft) in the air; **airbrick** brick perforated for ventilation; **Air Commodore** RAF officer next above Group Captain; **air-conditioned** *adjective* equipped with **air-conditioning**, regulation of humidity and temperature in building, apparatus for this; **airfield** area with runway(s) for aircraft; **air force** branch of armed forces fighting in the air; **airgun** gun using compressed air to fire pellets; **air hostess** stewardess in aircraft; **air letter** sheet of paper forming airmail letter; **airlift** *noun* emergency transport of supplies etc. by air, *verb* transport thus; **airline** public air transport company; **airliner** large passenger aircraft; **airlock** stoppage of flow by air bubble in pipe etc., compartment giving access to pressurized chamber; **airmail** system of transporting mail by air, mail carried thus; **airman** pilot or member of aircraft crew; **Air (Chief, Vice-) Marshal** high ranks in RAF; **airplane** *US* aeroplane; **airport** airfield with facilities for passengers and cargo; **air raid** attack by aircraft; **air rifle** rifle using compressed air to fire pellets; **airs and graces** affected manner; **airship** powered aircraft lighter than air; **airsick** nauseous from air travel; **airspace** air above a country; **air speed** aircraft's speed relative to air; **airstrip** strip of ground for take-off and landing of aircraft; **air terminal** building with transport to and from airport; **air traffic controller** official who controls air traffic by radio; **airway** recognized route of aircraft, passage for air into lungs; **airwoman** woman pilot or member of aircraft crew; **by air** by or in aircraft; **on the air** being broadcast.

aircraft *noun* (*plural* same) aeroplane, helicopter. □ **aircraft carrier** warship that carries and acts as base for aircraft; **aircraftman**, **aircraftwoman** lowest rank in RAF.

Airedale /'eədeɪl/ *noun* terrier of large rough-coated breed.

airless *adjective* stuffy; still, calm.

airtight *adjective* impermeable to air.

airworthy *adjective* (of aircraft) fit to fly. □ **airworthiness** *noun*.

airy *adjective* (**-ier**, **-iest**) well-ventilated; flippant; light as air. □ **airy-fairy** *colloquial* unrealistic, impractical.

aisle /aɪl/ *noun* side part of church divided by pillars from nave; passage between rows of pews, seats, etc.

aitchbone /'eɪtʃbəʊn/ *noun* rump bone of animal; cut of beef over this.

ajar /ə'dʒɑ:/ *adverb & adjective* (of door etc.) slightly open.

Akela /ɑ:'keɪlə/ *noun* adult leader of Cub Scouts.

akimbo /ə'kɪmbəʊ/ *adverb* (of arms) with hands on hips and elbows out.

akin /ə'kɪn/ *adjective* related; similar.

alabaster /'æləbɑ:stə/ ● *noun* translucent usually white form of gypsum. ● *adjective* of alabaster; white, smooth.

à la carte /æ lɑ: 'kɑ:t/ *adverb & adjective* with individually priced dishes.

alacrity /ə'lækrɪtɪ/ *noun* briskness; readiness.

à la mode /æ lɑ: 'məʊd/ *adverb & adjective* in fashion; fashionable.

alarm /ə'lɑ:m/ ● *noun* warning of danger etc.; warning sound or device; alarm clock; apprehension. ● *verb* frighten, disturb; warn. □ **alarm clock** clock that rings at set time. □ **alarming** *adjective*.

alarmist /ə'lɑ:mɪst/ *noun* person spreading unnecessary alarm.

alas /ə'læs/ *interjection expressing grief or regret.*

alb *noun* long white vestment worn by Christian priests.

albatross /'ælbətrɒs/ *noun* long-winged seabird related to petrel; *Golf* score of 3 strokes under par for hole.

albeit /ɔ:l'bi:ɪt/ *conjunction* although.

albino /æl'bi:nəʊ/ *noun* (*plural* **-s**) person or animal lacking pigment in skin, hair, and eyes. □ **albinism** /'ælbɪnɪz(ə)m/ *noun*.

album /'ælbəm/ *noun* book for displaying photographs etc.; long-playing gramophone record; set of these.

albumen /'ælbjʊmɪn/ *noun* egg white.

albumin /'ælbjʊmɪn/ *noun* water-soluble protein found in egg white, milk, blood, etc.

alchemy /'ælkəmɪ/ *noun* medieval chemistry, esp. seeking to turn base metals into gold. □ **alchemist** *noun*.

alcohol /'ælkəhɒl/ *noun* colourless volatile liquid, esp. as intoxicant present in wine, beer, spirits, etc. and as a solvent, fuel, etc.; liquor containing this; other compound of this type.

alcoholic /ælkə'hɒlɪk/ ● *adjective* of, like, containing, or caused by alcohol. ● *noun* person suffering from alcoholism.

alcoholism /'ælkəhɒlɪz(ə)m/ *noun* condition resulting from addiction to alcohol.

alcove /'ælkəʊv/ *noun* recess in wall of room, garden, etc.

alder /ˈɔːldə/ *noun* tree related to birch.

alderman /ˈɔːldəmən/ *noun esp. historical* civic dignitary next in rank to mayor.

ale *noun* beer.

alert /əˈlɜːt/ ● *adjective* watchful. ● *noun* alarm; state or period of special vigilance. ● *verb* (often + *to*) warn.

alfalfa /ælˈfælfə/ *noun* clover-like plant used for fodder.

alfresco /ælˈfreskəʊ/ *adjective & adverb* in the open air.

alga /ˈælgə/ *noun* (*plural* **-gae** /-dʒiː/) (usually in *plural*) non-flowering stemless water plant.

algebra /ˈældʒɪbrə/ *noun* branch of mathematics using letters to represent numbers. □ **algebraic** /-ˈbreɪɪk/ *adjective*.

Algol /ˈælgɒl/ *noun* high-level computer-programming language.

algorithm /ˈælgərɪð(ə)m/ *noun* process or rules for (esp. computer) calculation etc.

alias /ˈeɪlɪəs/ ● *adverb* also known as. ● *noun* assumed name.

alibi /ˈælɪbaɪ/ *noun* (*plural* **-s**) proof that one was elsewhere; excuse.

■ **Usage** The use of *alibi* to mean 'an excuse' is considered incorrect by some people.

alien /ˈeɪlɪən/ ● *adjective* (often + *to*) unfamiliar, repugnant; foreign; of beings from another world. ● *noun* non-naturalized foreigner; a being from another world.

alienate /ˈeɪlɪəneɪt/ *verb* (**-ting**) estrange; transfer ownership of. □ **alienation** *noun*.

alight[1] /əˈlaɪt/ *adjective* on fire; lit up.

alight[2] /əˈlaɪt/ *verb* (often + *from*) get down or off; come to earth, settle.

align /əˈlaɪn/ *verb* place in or bring into line; (usually + *with*) ally (oneself etc.). □ **alignment** *noun*.

alike /əˈlaɪk/ ● *adjective* similar, like. ● *adverb* in similar way.

alimentary /ælɪˈmentərɪ/ *adjective* concerning nutrition; nourishing. □ **alimentary canal** channel through which food passes during digestion.

alimony /ˈælɪmənɪ/ *noun* money payable to a divorced or separated spouse.

alive /əˈlaɪv/ *adjective* living; lively, active; (usually + *to*) alert to; (usually + *with*) swarming with.

alkali /ˈælkəlaɪ/ *noun* (*plural* **-s**) substance that neutralizes acids, turns litmus blue, and forms caustic solutions in water. □ **alkaline** *adjective*; **alkalinity** /-ˈlɪn-/ *noun*.

alkaloid /ˈælkəlɔɪd/ *noun* plant-based compound often used as drug, e.g. morphine, quinine.

all /ɔːl/ ● *adjective* whole amount, number, or extent of. ● *noun* all people or things concerned; (+ *of*) the whole of. ● *adverb* entirely, quite. □ **all along** from the beginning; **all but** very nearly; **all for** *colloquial* strongly in favour of; **all-clear** signal that danger or difficulty is over; **all fours** hands and knees; **all in** exhausted; **all-in** inclusive of all; **all in all** everything considered; **all out** (**all-out** before noun) involving all one's strength etc.; **all over** completely finished, in or on all parts of one's body; **all-purpose** having many uses; **all right** satisfactory, safe and sound, in good condition, satisfactorily, I consent; **all-right** (before noun) *colloquial* acceptable; **all round** in all respects, for each person; **all-round** (of person) versatile; **all-rounder** versatile person; **All Saints' Day** 1 Nov.; **all the same** nevertheless; **all there** *colloquial* mentally alert or normal; **all together** all at once, all in one place; **at all** (with negative or in questions) in any way, to any extent; **in all** in total, altogether.

■ **Usage** See note at ALTOGETHER.

Allah /ˈælə/ *noun: Muslim name of* God.

allay /əˈleɪ/ *verb* lessen; alleviate.

allege /əˈledʒ/ *verb* declare, esp. without proof. □ **allegation** /ælɪˈgeɪʃ(ə)n/ *noun*; **allegedly** /əˈledʒɪdlɪ/ *adverb*.

allegiance /əˈliːdʒ(ə)ns/ *noun* loyalty; duty of subject.

allegory /ˈælɪgərɪ/ *noun* (*plural* **-ies**) story with moral represented symbolically. □ **allegorical** /-ˈgɒr-/ *adjective*; **allegorize** *verb* (also **-ise**) (**-zing** or **-sing**).

allegretto /ælɪˈgretəʊ/ *Music* ● *adverb & adjective* in fairly brisk tempo. ● *noun* (*plural* **-s**) allegretto movement or passage.

allegro /əˈlegrəʊ/ *Music* ● *adverb & adjective* in lively tempo. ● *noun* (*plural* **-s**) allegro movement or passage.

alleluia /ælɪˈluːjə/ (also **hallelujah** /hæl-/) ● *interjection* God be praised. ● *noun* (*plural* **-s**) song of praise to God.

allergic /əˈlɜːdʒɪk/ *adjective* (+ *to*) having allergy to, *colloquial* having strong dislike for; caused by allergy.

allergy /ˈælədʒɪ/ *noun* (*plural* **-ies**) reaction to certain substances.

alleviate /əˈliːvɪeɪt/ *verb* (**-ting**) make (pain etc.) less severe. □ **alleviation** *noun*.

alley /ˈælɪ/ *noun* (*plural* **-s**) narrow street or passage; enclosure for skittles, bowling, etc.

alliance /əˈlaɪəns/ *noun* formal union or association of states, political parties, etc. or of families by marriage.

allied /ˈælaɪd/ *adjective* connected or related; (also **Allied**) associated in an alliance.

alligator /ˈælɪgeɪtə/ *noun* large reptile of crocodile family.

alliteration /əlɪtəˈreɪʃ(ə)n/ *noun* recurrence of same initial letter or sound in adjacent or nearby words, as in *The fair breeze blew, the white foam flew, the furrow followed free*. □ **alliterate** /-ˈlɪt-/ *verb*; **alliterative** /əˈlɪtərətɪv/ *adjective*.

allocate /ˈæləkeɪt/ *verb* (**-ting**) (usually + *to*) assign. □ **allocation** *noun*.

allot /əˈlɒt/ *verb* (**-tt-**) apportion or distribute to (person).

allotment /əˈlɒtmənt/ *noun* small plot of land rented for cultivation; share; allotting.

allow /əˈlaʊ/ *verb* (often + *to do*) permit; assign fixed sum to; (usually + *for*) provide or set aside for a purpose. □ **allow for** take into consideration.

allowance *noun* amount or sum allowed, esp. regularly; deduction, discount. □ **make allowances** (often + *for*) judge leniently.

alloy /ˈælɔɪ/ ● *noun* mixture of metals; inferior metal mixed esp. with gold or silver. ● *verb* mix (metals); /əˈlɔɪ/ debase by admixture; spoil (pleasure).

allspice /ˈɔːlspaɪs/ *noun* spice made from berry of pimento plant; this berry.

allude /əˈluːd/ *verb* (**-ding**) (+ *to*) make allusion to.

allure /əˈljʊə/ ● *verb* (**-ring**) attract, charm, entice. ● *noun* attractiveness, charm. □ **allurement** *noun*.

allusion /əˈluːʒ(ə)n/ *noun* (often + *to*) passing or indirect reference. □ **allusive** /-sɪv/ *adjective*.

alluvium /əˈluːvɪəm/ *noun* (*plural* **-via**) deposit left by flood, esp. in river valley. □ **alluvial** *adjective*.

ally ● *noun* /ˈælaɪ/ (*plural* **-ies**) state or person formally cooperating or united with another, esp. in war. ● *verb* (also /əˈlaɪ/) (**-ies, -ied**) (often **ally oneself with**) combine in alliance (with).

Alma Mater /ælmə ˈmɑːtə/ *noun* one's university, school, or college.

almanac /ˈɔːlmənæk/ *noun* (also **almanack**) calendar, usually with astronomical data.

almighty /ɔːlˈmaɪtɪ/ ● *adjective* infinitely powerful; very great. ● *noun* (**the Almighty**) God.

almond /ˈɑːmənd/ *noun* kernel of nutlike fruit related to plum; tree bearing this.

almoner /ˈɑːmənə/ *noun* social worker attached to hospital.

almost /ˈɔːlməʊst/ *adverb* all but, very nearly.

alms /ɑːmz/ *plural noun historical* donation of money or food to the poor. ▫ **almshouse** charitable institution for the poor.

aloe /ˈæləʊ/ *noun* plant with toothed fleshy leaves; (in *plural*) strong laxative from aloe juice. ▫ **aloe vera** /ˈvɪərə/ variety yielding substance used in cosmetics, this substance.

aloft /əˈlɒft/ *adjective & adverb* high up, overhead.

alone /əˈləʊn/ ● *adjective* without company or help; lonely. ● *adverb* only, exclusively.

along /əˈlɒŋ/ ● *preposition* beside or through (part of) the length of. ● *adverb* onward, into more advanced state; with oneself or others; beside or through (part of) thing's length. ▫ **alongside** at or close to side (of); **along with** in addition to.

aloof /əˈluːf/ ● *adjective* unconcerned, unsympathetic. ● *adverb* away, apart.

aloud /əˈlaʊd/ *adverb* audibly.

alp *noun* high mountain, esp. (**the Alps**) those in Switzerland and adjacent countries.

alpaca /ælˈpækə/ *noun* S. American llama-like animal; its long wool; fabric made from this.

alpha /ˈælfə/ *noun* first letter of Greek alphabet (Α, α). ▫ **alpha and omega** beginning and end; **alpha particle** helium nucleus emitted by radioactive substance.

alphabet /ˈælfəbet/ *noun* set of letters or signs used in a language. ▫ **alphabetical** /-ˈbet-/ *adjective*.

alphanumeric /ælfənjuːˈmerɪk/ *adjective* containing both letters and numbers.

alpine /ˈælpaɪn/ ● *adjective* of high mountains or (**Alpine**) the Alps. ● *noun* plant suited to mountain regions; = rock plant.

already /ɔːlˈredɪ/ *adverb* before the time in question; as early as this.

alright *adverb* = ALL RIGHT.

■ **Usage** Although *alright* is widely used, it is not correct in standard English.

Alsatian /ælˈseɪʃ(ə)n/ *noun* large dog of a breed of wolfhound.

also /ˈɔːlsəʊ/ *adverb* in addition, besides. ▫ **also-ran** loser in race, undistinguished person.

altar /ˈɔːltə/ *noun* flat table or block for offerings to deity; Communion table.

alter /ˈɔːltə/ *verb* change in character, shape, etc. ▫ **alteration** *noun*.

altercation /ɔːltəˈkeɪʃ(ə)n/ *noun* dispute, wrangle.

alternate ● *adjective* /ɔːlˈtɜːnət/ (with noun in *plural*) every other; (of things of two kinds) alternating. ● *verb* /ˈɔːltəneɪt/ (**-ting**) (often + *with*) arrange or occur by turns; (+ *between*) go repeatedly from one to another. ▫ **alternating current** electric current regularly reversing direction. ▫ **alternately** *adverb*; **alternation** *noun*.

■ **Usage** See note at ALTERNATIVE.

alternative /ɔːlˈtɜːnətɪv/ ● *adjective* available as another choice; unconventional. ● *noun* any of two or more possibilities; choice. ▫ **alternatively** *adverb*.

■ **Usage** The adjective *alternative* is often confused with *alternate*, which is correctly used in 'there will be a dance on alternate Saturdays'.

alternator /ˈɔːltəneɪtə/ *noun* dynamo generating alternating current.

although /ɔːlˈðəʊ/ *conjunction* though.

altimeter /ˈæltɪmiːtə/ *noun* instrument measuring altitude.

altitude /ˈæltɪtjuːd/ *noun* height, esp. of object above sea level or horizon.

alto /ˈæltəʊ/ ● *noun* (*plural* **-s**) = CONTRALTO; highest adult male singing voice; singer with this. ● *adjective* having range of alto.

altogether /ɔːltəˈgeðə/ *adverb* totally; on the whole; in total.

■ **Usage** Note that *altogether* means 'in total', as in *six rooms altogether*, whereas *all together* means 'all at once' or 'all in one place' as in *six rooms all together*.

altruism /ˈæltruːɪz(ə)m/ *noun* unselfishness as principle of action. ▫ **altruist** *noun*; **altruistic** /-ˈɪs-/ *adjective*.

alumina /əˈluːmɪnə/ *noun* aluminium oxide; emery.

aluminium /æljʊˈmɪnɪəm/ *noun* (*US* **aluminum** /əˈluːmɪnəm/) a light silvery metallic element.

alumnus /əˈlʌmnəs/ *noun* (*plural* **-ni** /-naɪ/) former pupil or student.

always /ˈɔːlweɪz/ *adverb* at all times; whatever the circumstances; repeatedly.

Alzheimer's disease /ˈæltshaɪməz/ *noun* brain disorder causing senility.

AM *abbreviation* amplitude modulation.

am *1st singular present of* BE.

a.m. *abbreviation* before noon (*ante meridiem*).

amalgam /əˈmælgəm/ *noun* mixture, blend; alloy of any metal with mercury.

amalgamate /əˈmælgəmeɪt/ *verb* (**-ting**) mix; unite. ▫ **amalgamation** *noun*.

amanuensis /əmænjuːˈensɪs/ *noun* (*plural* **-enses** /-siːz/) assistant, esp. writing from dictation.

amaranth /ˈæmərænθ/ *noun* plant with green, red, or purple flowers; imaginary unfading flower. ▫ **amaranthine** /-ˈrænθaɪn/ *adjective*.

amaryllis /æməˈrɪlɪs/ *noun* plant with lily-like flowers.

amass /əˈmæs/ *verb* heap together, accumulate.

amateur /ˈæmətə/ *noun* person engaging in pursuit as pastime not profession; person with limited skill. ▫ **amateurish** *adjective*; **amateurism** *noun*.

amatory /ˈæmətərɪ/ *adjective* of sexual love.

amaze /əˈmeɪz/ *verb* (**-zing**) fill with surprise or wonder. ▫ **amazement** *noun*; **amazing** *adjective*.

Amazon /ˈæməzən/ *noun* one of a mythical race of female warriors; (**amazon**) strong or athletic woman. ▫ **Amazonian** /-ˈzəʊ-/ *adjective*.

ambassador /æmˈbæsədə/ *noun* diplomat living abroad as representative of his or her country; promoter. ▫ **ambassadorial** /-ˈdɔː-/ *adjective*.

amber /ˈæmbə/ ● *noun* yellow translucent fossil resin; colour of this. ● *adjective* of or like amber.

ambergris /ˈæmbəgrɪs/ *noun* waxlike substance from sperm whale, used in perfumes.

ambidextrous /æmbɪˈdekstrəs/ *adjective* able to use either hand equally well.

ambience /ˈæmbɪəns/ *noun* surroundings, atmosphere.

ambient /ˈæmbɪənt/ *adjective* surrounding.

ambiguous /æmˈbɪgjʊəs/ *adjective* having a double meaning; difficult to classify. ▫ **ambiguity** /-ˈgjuː-/ *noun* (*plural* **-ies**).

ambit /ˈæmbɪt/ *noun* scope, bounds.

ambition /æmˈbɪʃ(ə)n/ *noun* determination to succeed; object of this.

ambitious *adjective* full of ambition.

ambivalent /æm'bɪvələnt/ *adjective* having mixed feelings towards person or thing. □ **ambivalence** *noun*.

amble /'æmb(ə)l/ ● *verb* (**-ling**) walk at leisurely pace. ● *noun* leisurely pace.

ambrosia /æm'brəʊzɪə/ *noun* food of the gods in classical mythology; delicious food etc.

ambulance /'æmbjʊləns/ *noun* vehicle for taking patients to hospital; mobile army hospital.

ambulatory /'æmbjʊlətərɪ/ *adjective* of or for walking.

ambuscade /æmbəs'keɪd/ *noun & verb* (**-ding**) ambush.

ambush /'æmbʊʃ/ ● *noun* surprise attack by people hiding; hiding place for this. ● *verb* attack from ambush; waylay.

ameliorate /ə'mi:lɪəreɪt/ *verb* (**-ting**) make or become better. □ **amelioration** *noun*; **ameliorative** /-rətɪv/ *adjective*.

amen /ɑ:'men/ *interjection* (esp. at end of prayer) so be it.

amenable /ə'mi:nəb(ə)l/ *adjective* responsive, docile; (often + *to*) answerable (to law etc.).

amend /ə'mend/ *verb* correct error in; make minor alterations in.

amendment *noun* minor alteration or addition in document etc.

amends *noun* □ **make amends** (often + *for*) give compensation.

amenity /ə'mi:nɪtɪ/ *noun* (*plural* **-ies**) pleasant or useful feature or facility; pleasantness (of a place etc.).

American /ə'merɪkən/ ● *adjective* of America, esp. the US. ● *noun* native, citizen, or inhabitant of America, esp. the US; English as spoken in the US. □ **Americanize** *verb* (also **-ise**) (**-zing** or **-sing**).

Americanism *noun* word etc. of US origin or usage.

amethyst /'æməθɪst/ *noun* purple or violet semi-precious stone.

amiable /'eɪmɪəb(ə)l/ *adjective* friendly and pleasant, likeable. □ **amiability** *noun*; **amiably** *adverb*.

amicable /'æmɪkəb(ə)l/ *adjective* friendly. □ **amicably** *adverb*.

amid /ə'mɪd/ *preposition* in the middle of.

amidships /ə'mɪdʃɪps/ *adverb* in(to) the middle of a ship.

amidst /ə'mɪdst/ = AMID.

amino acid /ə'mi:nəʊ/ *noun* organic acid found in proteins.

amir = EMIR.

amiss /ə'mɪs/ ● *adjective* out of order, wrong. ● *adverb* wrong(ly), inappropriately. □ **take amiss** be offended by.

amity /'æmɪtɪ/ *noun* friendship.

ammeter /'æmɪtə/ *noun* instrument for measuring electric current.

ammo /'æməʊ/ *noun slang* ammunition.

ammonia /ə'məʊnɪə/ *noun* pungent strongly alkaline gas; solution of this in water.

ammonite /'æmənaɪt/ *noun* coil-shaped fossil shell.

ammunition /æmjʊ'nɪʃ(ə)n/ *noun* bullets, shells, grenades, etc.; information usable in argument.

amnesia /æm'ni:zɪə/ *noun* loss of memory. □ **amnesiac** *adjective & noun*.

amnesty /'æmnɪstɪ/ *noun* (*plural* **-ies**) general pardon, esp. for political offences.

amniocentesis /æmnɪəʊsen'ti:sɪs/ *noun* (*plural* **-teses** /-si:z/) sampling of amniotic fluid to detect foetal abnormality.

amniotic fluid /æmnɪ'ɒtɪk/ *noun* fluid surrounding embryo.

amoeba /ə'mi:bə/ *noun* (*plural* **-s**) microscopic single-celled organism living in water.

amok /ə'mɒk/ *adverb* □ **run amok**, **amuck** /ə'mʌk/ run wild.

among /ə'mʌŋ/ *preposition* (also **amongst**) surrounded by; included in or in the category of; from the joint resources of; between.

amoral /eɪ'mɒr(ə)l/ *adjective* beyond morality; without moral principles.

amorous /'æmərəs/ *adjective* showing or feeling sexual love.

amorphous /ə'mɔ:fəs/ *adjective* of no definite shape; vague; non-crystalline.

amount /ə'maʊnt/ ● *noun* total number, size, value, extent, etc. ● *verb* (+ *to*) be equivalent in number, size, etc. to.

amour /ə'mʊə/ *noun* (esp. secret) love affair.

amp *noun* ampere; *colloquial* amplifier.

ampere /'æmpeə/ *noun* SI unit of electric current.

ampersand /'æmpəsænd/ *noun* the sign '&' (= *and*).

amphetamine /æm'fetəmi:n/ *noun* synthetic stimulant drug.

amphibian /æm'fɪbɪən/ *noun* amphibious animal or vehicle.

amphibious /æm'fɪbɪəs/ *adjective* living or operating on land and in water; involving military forces landed from the sea.

amphitheatre /'æmfɪθɪətə/ *noun* round open building with tiers of seats surrounding central space.

amphora /'æmfərə/ *noun* (*plural* **-rae** /-ri:/) Greek or Roman two-handled jar.

ample /'æmp(ə)l/ *adjective* (**-r**, **-st**) plentiful, extensive; more than enough. □ **amply** *adverb*.

amplifier /'æmplɪfaɪə/ *noun* device for amplifying sounds or electrical signals.

amplify /'æmplɪfaɪ/ *verb* (**-ies**, **-ied**) increase strength of (sound or electrical signal); add details to (story etc.). □ **amplification** *noun*.

amplitude /'æmplɪtju:d/ *noun* spaciousness; maximum departure from average of oscillation, alternating current, etc. □ **amplitude modulation** modulation of a wave by variation of its amplitude.

ampoule /'æmpu:l/ *noun* small sealed capsule holding solution for injection.

amputate /'æmpjʊteɪt/ *verb* (**-ting**) cut off surgically (limb etc.). □ **amputation** *noun*; **amputee** /-'ti:/ *noun*.

amuck = AMOK.

amulet /'æmjʊlɪt/ *noun* charm worn against evil.

amuse /ə'mju:z/ *verb* (**-sing**) cause to laugh or smile; interest, occupy. □ **amusing** *adjective*.

amusement *noun* being amused; thing that amuses, esp. device for entertainment at fairground etc. □ **amusement arcade** indoor area with slot machines etc.

an see A.

anabolic steroid /ænə'bɒlɪk/ *noun* synthetic steroid hormone used to build muscle.

anachronism /ə'nækrənɪz(ə)m/ *noun* attribution of custom, event, etc. to wrong period; thing thus attributed; out-of-date person or thing. □ **anachronistic** /-'nɪs-/ *adjective*.

anaconda /ænə'kɒndə/ *noun* large S. American constrictor.

anaemia /ə'ni:mɪə/ *noun* (*US* **anemia**) deficiency of red blood cells or their haemoglobin, causing pallor and listlessness. □ **anaemic** *adjective*.

anaesthesia /ænɪs'θi:zɪə/ *noun* (*US* **anes-**) artificially induced insensibility to pain.

anaesthetic /ænɪs'θetɪk/ (*US* **anes-**) ● *noun* drug, gas, etc., producing anaesthesia. ● *adjective* producing anaesthesia.

anaesthetist /ə'ni:sθətɪst/ *noun* (*US* **anes-**) person who administers anaesthetics.
anaesthetize /ə'ni:sθətaɪz/ *verb* (also **-ise**; *US* also **anes-**) (**-zing** or **-sing**) administer anaesthetic to.
anagram /'ænəgræm/ *noun* word or phrase formed by transposing letters of another.
anal /'eɪn(ə)l/ *adjective* of the anus.
analgesia /ænəl'dʒi:zɪə/ *noun* absence or relief of pain.
analgesic /ænəl'dʒi:sɪk/ ● *noun* pain-killing drug. ● *adjective* pain-killing.
analogous /ə'næləgəs/ *adjective* (usually + *to*) partially similar or parallel.
analogue /'ænəlɒg/ (*US* **analog**) ● *noun* analogous thing. ● *adjective* (of computer (usually **analog**), watch, etc.) using physical variables (e.g. voltage, position of hands) to represent numbers.
analogy /ə'nælədʒɪ/ *noun* (*plural* **-ies**) correspondence, similarity; reasoning from parallel cases.
analyse /'ænəlaɪz/ *verb* (**-sing**) (*US* **analyze**; **-zing**) perform analysis on.
analysis /ə'nælɪsɪs/ *noun* (*plural* **-lyses** /-si:z/) detailed examination; *Chemistry* determination of constituent parts; psychoanalysis.
analyst /'ænəlɪst/ *noun* person who analyses.
analytical /ænə'lɪtɪkəl/ *adjective* (also **analytic**) of or using analysis.
analyze *US* = ANALYSE.
anarchism /'ænəkɪz(ə)m/ *noun* belief that government and law should be abolished. □ **anarchist** *noun*; **anarchistic** /-'kɪstɪk/ *adjective*.
anarchy /'ænəkɪ/ *noun* disorder, esp. political. □ **anarchic** /ə'nɑ:kɪk/ *adjective*.
anathema /ə'næθəmə/ *noun* (*plural* **-s**) detested thing; Church's curse.
anatomy /ə'nætəmɪ/ *noun* (*plural* **-ies**) (science of) animal or plant structure. □ **anatomical** /ænə'tɒmɪk(ə)l/ *adjective*; **anatomist** *noun*.
anatto = ANNATTO.
ANC *abbreviation* African National Congress.
ancestor /'ænsestə/ *noun* person, animal, or plant from which another has descended or evolved; prototype.
ancestral /æn'sestr(ə)l/ *adjective* inherited from ancestors.
ancestry /'ænsestrɪ/ *noun* (*plural* **-ies**) lineage; ancestors collectively.
anchor /'æŋkə/ ● *noun* metal device used to moor ship to sea-bottom. ● *verb* secure with anchor; fix firmly; cast anchor. □ **anchorman** coordinator, esp. compère in broadcast.
anchorage /'æŋkərɪdʒ/ *noun* place for anchoring; lying at anchor.
anchorite /'æŋkəraɪt/ *noun* hermit, recluse.
anchovy /'æntʃəvɪ/ *noun* (*plural* **-ies**) small strong-flavoured fish of herring family.
ancien régime /ɑ̃sjæ re'ʒi:m/ *noun* superseded regime, esp. that of pre-Revolutionary France. [French]
ancient /'eɪnʃ(ə)nt/ *adjective* of times long past; very old.
ancillary /æn'sɪlərɪ/ ● *adjective* subsidiary, auxiliary; (esp. of health workers) providing essential support. ● *noun* (*plural* **-ies**) auxiliary; ancillary worker.
and *conjunction connecting words, clauses, or sentences.*
andante /æn'dæntɪ/ *Music* ● *adverb & adjective* in moderately slow time. ● *noun* andante movement or passage.
androgynous /æn'drɒdʒɪnəs/ *adjective* hermaphrodite.
android /'ændrɔɪd/ *noun* robot with human appearance.
anecdote /'ænɪkdəʊt/ *noun* short, esp. true, story. □ **anecdotal** /-'dəʊt(ə)l/ *adjective*.
anemia *US* = ANAEMIA.
anemic *US* = ANAEMIC.
anemometer /ænɪ'mɒmɪtə/ *noun* instrument for measuring wind force.
anemone /ə'nemənɪ/ *noun* plant related to buttercup.
aneroid barometer /'ænərɔɪd/ *noun* barometer that measures air pressure by registering its action on lid of box containing vacuum.
anesthesia etc. *US* = ANAESTHESIA etc.
aneurysm /'ænjʊrɪz(ə)m/ *noun* (also **aneurism**) excessive enlargement of artery.
anew /ə'nju:/ *adverb* again; in different way.
angel /'eɪndʒ(ə)l/ *noun* attendant or messenger of God usually represented as human with wings; kind or virtuous person. □ **angel cake** light sponge cake; **angelfish** small fish with winglike fins. □ **angelic** /æn'dʒelɪk/ *adjective*; **angelically** *adverb*.
angelica /æn'dʒelɪkə/ *noun* aromatic plant; its candied stalks.
angelus /'ændʒɪləs/ *noun* RC prayers said at morning, noon, and sunset; bell rung for this.
anger /'æŋgə/ ● *noun* extreme displeasure. ● *verb* make angry.
angina /æn'dʒaɪnə/ *noun* (in full **angina pectoris**) chest pain brought on by exertion, owing to poor blood supply to heart.
angle[1] /'æŋg(ə)l/ ● *noun* space between two meeting lines or surfaces, esp. as measured in degrees; corner; point of view. ● *verb* (**-ling**) move or place obliquely; present (information) in biased way.
angle[2] /'æŋg(ə)l/ *verb* (**-ling**) fish with line and hook; (+ *for*) seek objective indirectly. □ **angler** *noun*.
Anglican /'æŋglɪkən/ ● *adjective* of Church of England. ● *noun* member of Anglican Church. □ **Anglicanism** *noun*.
Anglicism /'æŋglɪsɪz(ə)m/ *noun* English expression or custom.
Anglicize /'æŋglɪsaɪz/ *verb* (also **-ise**) (**-zing** or **-sing**) make English in character etc.
Anglo- *combining form* English or British (and).
Anglo-Catholic /æŋgləʊ'kæθəlɪk/ ● *adjective* of High Church Anglican group emphasizing its Catholic tradition. ● *noun* member of this group.
Anglo-Indian /æŋgləʊ'ɪndɪən/ ● *adjective* of England and India; of British descent but Indian residence. ● *noun* Anglo-Indian person.
Anglophile /'æŋgləʊfaɪl/ *noun* admirer of England or the English.
Anglo-Saxon /æŋgləʊ'sæks(ə)n/ ● *adjective* of English Saxons before Norman Conquest; of English descent. ● *noun* Anglo-Saxon person or language; *colloquial* plain (esp. crude) English.
angora /æŋ'gɔ:rə/ *noun* fabric made from hair of angora goat or rabbit. □ **angora cat**, **goat**, **rabbit** long-haired varieties.
angostura /æŋgə'stjʊərə/ *noun* aromatic bitter bark of S. American tree.
angry /'æŋgrɪ/ *adjective* (**-ier**, **-iest**) feeling or showing anger; (of wound etc.) inflamed, painful. □ **angrily** *adverb*.
angst /æŋst/ *noun* anxiety, neurotic fear; guilt.
angstrom /'æŋstrəm/ *noun* unit of wavelength measurement.
anguish /'æŋgwɪʃ/ *noun* severe mental or physical pain. □ **anguished** *adjective*.
angular /'æŋgjʊlə/ *adjective* having sharp corners or (of person) features; (of distance) measured by angle. □ **angularity** /-'lær-/ *noun*.

aniline /'ænɪli:n/ *noun* colourless oily liquid used in dyes, drugs, and plastics.

animadvert /ænɪmæd'vɜ:t/ *verb* (+ *on*) *literary* criticize, censure. □ **animadversion** *noun*.

animal /'ænɪm(ə)l/ ● *noun* living organism, esp. other than man, having sensation and usually ability to move; brutish person. ● *adjective* of or like animal; carnal.

animality /ænɪ'mælɪtɪ/ *noun* the animal world; animal behaviour.

animate ● *adjective* /'ænɪmət/ having life; lively. ● *verb* /'ænɪmeɪt/ (**-ting**) enliven; give life to.

animated /'ænɪmeɪtɪd/ *adjective* lively; living; (of film) using animation.

animation /ænɪ'meɪʃ(ə)n/ *noun* liveliness; being alive; technique of film-making by photographing sequence of drawings or positions of puppets etc. to create illusion of movement.

animator /'ænɪmeɪtə/ *noun* artist who prepares animated films.

animism /'ænɪmɪz(ə)m/ *noun* belief that inanimate objects and natural phenomena have souls. □ **animist** *noun*; **animistic** /-'mɪs-/ *adjective*.

animosity /ænɪ'mɒsɪtɪ/ *noun* (*plural* **-ies**) hostility.

animus /'ænɪməs/ *noun* hostility, ill feeling.

anion /'ænaɪən/ *noun* negatively charged ion.

anise /'ænɪs/ *noun* plant with aromatic seeds.

aniseed /'ænɪsi:d/ *noun* seed of anise.

ankle /'æŋk(ə)l/ *noun* joint connecting foot with leg.

anklet /'æŋklɪt/ *noun* ornament worn round ankle.

ankylosis /æŋkɪ'ləʊsɪs/ *noun* stiffening of joint by fusing of bones.

annals /'æn(ə)lz/ *plural noun* narrative of events year by year; historical records. □ **annalist** *noun*.

annatto /ə'nætəʊ/ *noun* (also **anatto**) orange-red food colouring made from tropical fruit.

anneal /ə'ni:l/ *verb* heat (metal, glass) and cool slowly, esp. to toughen.

annelid /'ænəlɪd/ *noun* segmented worm, e.g. earthworm.

annex /æ'neks/ *verb* (often + *to*) add as subordinate part; take possession of. □ **annexation** *noun*.

annexe /'æneks/ *noun* supplementary building.

annihilate /ə'naɪəleɪt/ *verb* (**-ting**) destroy utterly. □ **annihilation** *noun*.

anniversary /ænɪ'vɜ:sərɪ/ *noun* (*plural* **-ies**) yearly return of date of event; celebration of this.

Anno Domini /ænəʊ 'dɒmɪnaɪ/ see AD.

annotate /'ænəteɪt/ *verb* (**-ting**) add explanatory notes to. □ **annotation** *noun*.

announce /ə'naʊns/ *verb* (**-cing**) make publicly known; make known the approach of. □ **announcement** *noun*.

announcer *noun* person who announces, esp. in broadcasting.

annoy /ə'nɔɪ/ *verb* (often in *passive* + *at, with*) anger or distress slightly; harass. □ **annoyance** *noun*.

annual /'ænjʊəl/ ● *adjective* reckoned by the year; recurring yearly. ● *noun* book etc. published yearly; plant living only one year. □ **annually** *adverb*.

annuity /ə'nju:ɪtɪ/ *noun* (*plural* **-ies**) yearly grant or allowance; investment yielding fixed annual sum for stated period.

annul /ə'nʌl/ *verb* (**-ll-**) declare invalid; cancel, abolish. □ **annulment** *noun*.

annular /'ænjʊlə/ *adjective* ring-shaped.

annulate /'ænjʊlət/ *adjective* marked with or formed of rings.

annunciation /ənʌnsɪ'eɪʃ(ə)n/ *noun* announcement, esp. (**Annunciation**) that made by the angel Gabriel to Mary.

anode /'ænəʊd/ *noun* positive electrode.

anodize /'ænədaɪz/ *verb* (also **-ise**) (**-zing** or **-sing**) coat (metal) with protective layer by electrolysis.

anodyne /'ænədaɪn/ ● *adjective* pain-relieving; soothing. ● *noun* anodyne drug etc.

anoint /ə'nɔɪnt/ *verb* apply oil or ointment to, esp. ritually.

anomalous /ə'nɒmələs/ *adjective* irregular, abnormal.

anomaly /ə'nɒməlɪ/ *noun* (*plural* **-ies**) anomalous thing.

anon /ə'nɒn/ *adverb archaic* soon.

anon. *abbreviation* anonymous.

anonymous /ə'nɒnɪməs/ *adjective* of unknown name or authorship; featureless. □ **anonymity** /ænə'nɪm-/ *noun*.

anorak /'ænəræk/ *noun* waterproof usually hooded jacket.

anorexia /ænə'reksɪə/ *noun* lack of appetite, esp. (in full **anorexia nervosa** /nɜ:'vəʊsə/) obsessive desire to lose weight by refusing to eat. □ **anorexic** *adjective & noun*.

another /ə'nʌðə/ ● *adjective* an additional or different. ● *pronoun* an additional or different person or thing.

answer /'ɑ:nsə/ ● *noun* something said or done in reaction to a question, statement, or circumstance; solution to a problem. ● *verb* make an answer or response (to); suit; (+ *to, for*) be responsible to or for; (+ *to*) correspond to (esp. description). □ **answer back** answer insolently; **answering machine**, **answerphone** tape recorder which answers telephone calls and takes messages.

answerable *adjective* (usually + *to, for*) responsible; that can be answered.

ant *noun* small usually wingless insect living in complex social group. **anteater** mammal feeding on ants; **anthill** moundlike ants' nest.

antacid /æn'tæsɪd/ *noun & adjective* preventive or corrective of acidity.

antagonism /æn'tægənɪz(ə)m/ *noun* active hostility.

antagonist /æn'tægənɪst/ *noun* opponent. □ **antagonistic** /-'nɪs-/ *adjective*.

antagonize /æn'tægənaɪz/ *verb* (also **-ise**) (**-zing** or **-sing**) provoke.

Antarctic /æn'tɑ:ktɪk/ ● *adjective* of south polar region. ● *noun* this region.

ante /'æntɪ/ *noun* stake put up by poker player before receiving cards; amount payable in advance.

ante- /'æntɪ/ *prefix* before.

antecedent /æntɪ'si:d(ə)nt/ ● *noun* preceding thing or circumstance; *Grammar* word, phrase, etc., to which another word refers; (in *plural*) person's ancestors. ● *adjective* previous.

antechamber /'æntɪtʃeɪmbə/ *noun* ante-room.

antedate /æntɪ'deɪt/ *verb* (**-ting**) precede in time; give earlier than true date to.

antediluvian /æntɪdɪ'lu:vɪən/ *adjective* before the Flood; *colloquial* very old.

antelope /'æntɪləʊp/ *noun* (*plural* same or **-s**) swift deerlike animal.

antenatal /æntɪ'neɪtəl/ *adjective* before birth; of pregnancy.

antenna /æn'tenə/ *noun* (*plural* **-tennae** /-ni:/) each of pair of feelers on head of insect or crustacean; (*plural* **-s**) aerial.

anterior /æn'tɪərɪə/ *adjective* nearer the front; (often + *to*) prior.

ante-room /'æntɪru:m/ *noun* small room leading to main one.

anthem /ˈænθəm/ *noun* choral composition for church use; song of praise, esp. for nation.

anther /ˈænθə/ *noun* part of stamen containing pollen.

anthology /ænˈθɒlədʒɪ/ *noun* (*plural* **-ies**) collection of poems, essays, stories, etc.

anthracite /ˈænθrəsaɪt/ *noun* hard kind of coal.

anthrax /ˈænθræks/ *noun* disease of sheep and cattle transmissible to humans.

anthropocentric /ænθrəpəʊˈsentrɪk/ *adjective* regarding humankind as centre of existence.

anthropoid /ˈænθrəpɔɪd/ ● *adjective* human in form. ● *noun* anthropoid ape.

anthropology /ænθrəˈpɒlədʒɪ/ *noun* study of humankind, esp. societies and customs. □ **anthropological** /-pəˈlɒdʒ-/ *adjective*; **anthropologist** *noun*.

anthropomorphism /ænθrəpəˈmɔːfɪz(ə)m/ *noun* attributing of human characteristics to god, animal, or thing. □ **anthropomorphic** *adjective*; **anthropomorphize** *verb* (also **-ise**) (**-zing** or **-sing**).

anthropomorphous /ænθrəpəˈmɔːfəs/ *adjective* human in form.

anti- /ˈæntɪ/ *prefix* opposed to; preventing; opposite of; unconventional.

anti-abortion /-əˈbɔːʃ(ə)n/ *adjective* opposing abortion. □ **anti-abortionist** *noun*.

anti-aircraft /-ˈeəkrɑːft/ *adjective* for defence against enemy aircraft.

antibiotic /-baɪˈɒtɪk/ ● *noun* substance that can inhibit or destroy bacteria etc. ● *adjective* functioning as antibiotic.

antibody /ˈæntɪbɒdɪ/ *noun* (*plural* **-ies**) blood protein produced in reaction to antigens.

antic /ˈæntɪk/ *noun* (usually in *plural*) foolish behaviour.

anticipate /ænˈtɪsɪpeɪt/ *verb* (**-ting**) deal with or use before proper time; expect; forestall. □ **anticipation** *noun*; **anticipatory** *adjective*.

anticlimax /-ˈklaɪmæks/ *noun* disappointing conclusion to something significant.

anticlockwise /-ˈklɒkwaɪz/ ● *adverb* in opposite direction to hands of clock. ● *adjective* moving anticlockwise.

anticyclone /-ˈsaɪkləʊn/ *noun* system of winds rotating outwards from area of high pressure, producing fine weather.

antidepressant /-dɪˈpres(ə)nt/ ● *noun* drug etc. alleviating depression. ● *adjective* alleviating depression.

antidote /ˈæntɪdəʊt/ *noun* medicine used to counteract poison.

antifreeze /ˈæntɪfriːz/ *noun* substance added to water (esp. in vehicle's radiator) to lower its freezing point.

antigen /ˈæntɪdʒ(ə)n/ *noun* foreign substance causing body to produce antibodies.

anti-hero /ˈæntɪhɪərəʊ/ *noun* (*plural* **-es**) central character in story, lacking conventional heroic qualities.

antihistamine /-ˈhɪstəmiːn/ *noun* drug that counteracts effect of histamine, used esp. to treat allergies.

anti-lock /ˈæntɪlɒk/ *adjective* (of brakes) not locking when applied suddenly.

antimony /ˈæntɪmənɪ/ *noun* brittle silvery metallic element.

anti-nuclear /-ˈnjuːklɪə/ *adjective* opposed to development of nuclear weapons or power.

antipathy /ænˈtɪpəθɪ/ *noun* (*plural* **-ies**) (often + *to*, *for*, *between*) strong aversion or dislike. □ **antipathetic** /-ˈθet-/ *adjective*.

antiperspirant /-ˈpɜːspərənt/ *noun* substance inhibiting perspiration.

antiphon /ˈæntɪf(ə)n/ *noun* hymn sung alternately by two groups. □ **antiphonal** /-ˈtɪf-/ *adjective*.

antipodes /ænˈtɪpədiːz/ *plural noun* places diametrically opposite each other on the earth, esp. (also **Antipodes**) Australasia in relation to Europe. □ **antipodean** /-ˈdiːən/ *adjective & noun*.

antiquarian /æntɪˈkweərɪən/ ● *adjective* of or dealing in rare books. ● *noun* antiquary.

antiquary /ˈæntɪkwərɪ/ *noun* (*plural* **-ies**) student or collector of antiques etc.

antiquated /ˈæntɪkweɪtɪd/ *adjective* old-fashioned.

antique /ænˈtiːk/ ● *noun* old valuable object, esp. piece of furniture etc. ● *adjective* of or existing since old times; old-fashioned.

antiquity /ænˈtɪkwətɪ/ *noun* (*plural* **-ies**) ancient times, esp. before Middle Ages; (in *plural*) great age; remains from ancient times.

antirrhinum /æntɪˈraɪnəm/ *noun* snapdragon.

anti-Semitic /-sɪˈmɪtɪk/ *adjective* prejudiced against Jews. □ **anti-Semite** /-ˈsiːmaɪt/ *noun*; **anti-Semitism** /-ˈsem-/ *noun*.

antiseptic /-ˈseptɪk/ ● *adjective* counteracting sepsis by destroying germs. ● *noun* antiseptic substance.

antisocial /-ˈsəʊʃ(ə)l/ *adjective* not sociable; opposed or harmful to society.

■ **Usage** It is a mistake to use *antisocial* instead of *unsocial* in the phrase *unsocial hours*.

antistatic /-ˈstætɪk/ *adjective* counteracting effect of static electricity.

antithesis /ænˈtɪθəsɪs/ *noun* (*plural* **-theses** /-siːz/) (often + *of*, *to*) direct opposite; contrast; rhetorical use of strongly contrasted words. □ **antithetical** /-ˈθet-/ *adjective*.

antitoxin /-ˈtɒksɪn/ *noun* antibody counteracting toxin. □ **antitoxic** *adjective*.

antitrades /-ˈtreɪdz/ *plural noun* winds blowing above and in opposite direction to trade winds.

antiviral /-ˈvaɪər(ə)l/ *adjective* effective against viruses.

antler /ˈæntlə/ *noun* branched horn of deer.

antonym /ˈæntənɪm/ *noun* word opposite in meaning to another, e.g. *wet* is an antonym of *dry*.

anus /ˈeɪnəs/ *noun* (*plural* **-es**) excretory opening at end of alimentary canal.

anvil /ˈænvɪl/ *noun* iron block on which metals are worked.

anxiety /æŋˈzaɪətɪ/ *noun* (*plural* **-ies**) troubled state of mind; worry; eagerness.

anxious /ˈæŋkʃəs/ *adjective* mentally troubled; marked by anxiety; (+ *to do*) uneasily wanting. □ **anxiously** *adverb*.

any /ˈenɪ/ ● *adjective* one or some, no matter which. ● *pronoun* any one; any number or amount. ● *adverb* at all. □ **anybody** *pronoun* any person, *noun* an important person; **anyhow** anyway, at random; **anyone** anybody; **anything** any thing, a thing of any kind; **anyway** in any way, in any case; **anywhere** (in or to) any place.

AOB *abbreviation* any other business.

aorta /eɪˈɔːtə/ *noun* (*plural* **-s**) main artery carrying blood from heart.

apace /əˈpeɪs/ *adverb literary* swiftly.

apart /əˈpɑːt/ *adverb* separately; into pieces; at or to a distance.

apartheid /əˈpɑːteɪt/ *noun* racial segregation, esp. in S. Africa.

apartment /əˈpɑːtmənt/ *noun* (*US* or esp. for holidays) flat; (usually in *plural*) room.

apathy /ˈæpəθɪ/ *noun* lack of interest, indifference. □ **apathetic** /-ˈθet-/ *adjective*.

apatosaurus /əpætə'sɔːrəs/ *noun* (*plural* **-ruses**) large long-necked plant-eating dinosaur.

ape ● *noun* tailless monkey; imitator. ● *verb* (**-ping**) imitate.

aperient /ə'pɪərɪənt/ *adjective & noun* laxative.

aperitif /əperɪ'tiːf/ *noun* alcoholic drink before meal.

aperture /'æpətʃə/ *noun* opening or gap, esp. variable one letting light into camera.

apex /'eɪpeks/ *noun* (*plural* **-es**) highest point; tip.

aphasia /ə'feɪzɪə/ *noun* loss of verbal understanding or expression.

aphelion /ə'fiːlɪən/ *noun* (*plural* **-lia**) point of orbit farthest from sun.

aphid /'eɪfɪd/ *noun* insect infesting plants.

aphis /'eɪfɪs/ *noun* (*plural* **aphides** /-diːz/) aphid.

aphorism /'æfərɪz(ə)m/ *noun* short wise saying. □ **aphoristic** /-'rɪs-/ *adjective*.

aphrodisiac /æfrə'dɪzɪæk/ ● *adjective* arousing sexual desire. ● *noun* aphrodisiac substance.

apiary /'eɪpɪərɪ/ *noun* (*plural* **-ies**) place where bees are kept. □ **apiarist** *noun*.

apiculture /'eɪpɪkʌltʃə/ *noun* bee-keeping.

apiece /ə'piːs/ *adverb* for each one.

aplomb /ə'plɒm/ *noun* self-assurance.

apocalypse /ə'pɒkəlɪps/ *noun* destructive event; revelation, esp. about the end of the world. □ **apocalyptic** /-'lɪp-/ *adjective*.

Apocrypha /ə'pɒkrɪfə/ *plural noun* Old Testament books not in Hebrew Bible; (**apocrypha**) writings etc. not considered genuine. □ **apocryphal** *adjective*.

apogee /'æpədʒiː/ *noun* highest point; point farthest from earth in orbit of moon etc.

apolitical /eɪpə'lɪtɪk(ə)l/ *adjective* not interested or involved in politics.

apologetic /əpɒlə'dʒetɪk/ *adjective* expressing regret. □ **apologetically** *adverb*.

apologia /æpə'ləudʒə/ *noun* formal defence of conduct or opinions.

apologist /ə'pɒlədʒɪst/ *noun* person who defends by argument.

apologize /ə'pɒlədʒaɪz/ *verb* (also **-ise**) (**-zing** or **-sing**) make apology.

apology /ə'pɒlədʒɪ/ *noun* (*plural* **-ies**) regretful acknowledgement of offence or failure; explanation.

apophthegm /'æpəθem/ *noun* short wise saying.

apoplexy /'æpəpleksɪ/ *noun* sudden paralysis caused by blockage or rupture of brain artery. □ **apoplectic** /-'plek-/ *adjective*.

apostasy /ə'pɒstəsɪ/ *noun* (*plural* **-ies**) abandonment of belief, faith, etc.

apostate /ə'pɒsteɪt/ *noun* person who renounces belief. □ **apostatize** /-tət-/ *verb* (also **-ise**) (**-zing** or **-sing**).

a posteriori /eɪ pɒsterɪ'ɔːraɪ/ *adjective & adverb* from effects to causes.

Apostle /ə'pɒs(ə)l/ *noun* any of twelve men sent by Christ to preach gospel; (**apostle**) leader of reform.

apostolic /æpəs'tɒlɪk/ *adjective* of Apostles; of the Pope.

apostrophe /ə'pɒstrəfɪ/ *noun* punctuation mark (') indicating possession or marking omission of letter(s) or number(s) (see panel).

apostrophize *verb* (also **-ise**) (**-zing** or **-sing**) address (esp. absent person or thing).

apothecary /ə'pɒθəkərɪ/ *noun* (*plural* **-ies**) *archaic* pharmacist.

Apostrophe '

This is used:

1 to indicate possession:

with a singular noun:

a boy's book; a week's work; the boss's salary.

with a plural already ending with *s*:

a girls' school; two weeks' newspapers; the bosses' salaries.

with a plural not already ending with *s*:

the children's books; women's liberation.

with a singular name:

Bill's book; John's coat; Barnabas' (or *Barnabas's*) *book; Nicholas'* (or *Nicholas's*) *coat.*

with a name ending in *-es* that is pronounced /-ɪz/:

Bridges' poems; Moses' mother

and before the word *sake*:

for God's sake; for goodness' sake; for Nicholas' sake

but it is often omitted in a business name:

Barclays Bank.

2 to mark an omission of one or more letters or numbers:

he's (*he is* or *he has*)
can't (*cannot*)
won't (*will not*)
the summer of '68 (*1968*)
haven't (*have not*)
we'll (*we shall*)
o'clock (*of the clock*)

3 when letters or numbers are referred to in plural form:

mind your p's and q's; find all the number 7's.

but it is unnecessary in, e.g.

MPs; the 1940s.

apotheosis /əpɒθɪˈəʊsɪs/ *noun* (*plural* **-oses** /-siːz/) deification; glorification or sublime example (of thing).

appal /əˈpɔːl/ *verb* (**-ll-**) dismay; horrify.

apparatus /æpəˈreɪtəs/ *noun* equipment for scientific or other work.

apparel /əˈpær(ə)l/ *noun formal* clothing. □ **apparelled** *adjective*.

apparent /əˈpærənt/ *adjective* obvious; seeming. □ **apparently** *adverb*.

apparition /æpəˈrɪʃ(ə)n/ *noun* thing that appears, esp. of startling kind; ghost.

appeal /əˈpiːl/ ● *verb* make earnest or formal request; (usually + *to*) be attractive; (+ *to*) resort to for support; (often + *to*) apply to higher court for revision of judicial decision; *Cricket* ask umpire to declare batsman out. ● *noun* appealing; request for aid; attractiveness.

appear /əˈpɪə/ *verb* become or be visible; seem; present oneself; be published.

appearance *noun* appearing; outward form; (in *plural*) outward show of prosperity, virtue, etc.

appease /əˈpiːz/ *verb* (**-sing**) make calm or quiet, esp. conciliate (aggressor) with concessions; satisfy (appetite etc.). □ **appeasement** *noun*.

appellant /əˈpelənt/ *noun* person who appeals to higher court.

appellation /æpəˈleɪʃ(ə)n/ *noun formal* name, title.

append /əˈpend/ *verb* (usually + *to*) attach, affix; add.

appendage /əˈpendɪdʒ/ *noun* thing attached; addition.

appendectomy /æpenˈdektəmɪ/ *noun* (also **appendicectomy** /əpendɪˈsektəmɪ/) (*plural* **-ies**) surgical removal of appendix.

appendicitis /əpendɪˈsaɪtɪs/ *noun* inflammation of appendix.

appendix /əˈpendɪks/ *noun* (*plural* **-dices** /-siːz/) tubular sac attached to large intestine; addition to book etc.

appertain /æpəˈteɪn/ *verb* (+ *to*) belong, relate to.

appetite /ˈæpɪtaɪt/ *noun* (usually + *for*) desire (esp. for food); inclination, desire.

appetizer /ˈæpɪtaɪzə/ *noun* (also **-iser**) thing eaten or drunk to stimulate appetite.

appetizing /ˈæpɪtaɪzɪŋ/ *adjective* (also **-ising**) (esp. of food) stimulating appetite.

applaud /əˈplɔːd/ *verb* express approval (of), esp. by clapping; commend.

applause /əˈplɔːz/ *noun* warm approval, esp. clapping.

apple /ˈæp(ə)l/ *noun* roundish firm fruit. □ **apple of one's eye** cherished person or thing; **apple-pie bed** bed with sheets folded so that one cannot stretch out one's legs; **apple-pie order** extreme neatness.

appliance /əˈplaɪəns/ *noun* device etc. for specific task.

applicable /ˈæplɪkəb(ə)l/ *adjective* (often + *to*) that may be applied. □ **applicability** *noun*.

applicant /ˈæplɪkənt/ *noun* person who applies for job etc.

application /æplɪˈkeɪʃ(ə)n/ *noun* formal request; applying; thing applied; diligence; relevance; use.

applicator /ˈæplɪkeɪtə/ *noun* device for applying ointment etc.

appliqué /æˈpliːkeɪ/ ● *noun* work in which cut-out fabric is fixed on to other fabric. ● *verb* (**-qués**, **-quéd**, **-quéing**) decorate with appliqué.

apply /əˈplaɪ/ *verb* (**-ies**, **-ied**) (often + *for*, *to*, *to do*) make formal request; (often + *to*) be relevant; make use of; (often + *to*) put or spread (on); (**apply oneself**; often + *to*) devote oneself.

appoint /əˈpɔɪnt/ *verb* assign job or office to; (often + *for*) fix (time etc.); (as **appointed** *adjective*) equipped, furnished.

appointment *noun* appointing, being appointed; arrangement for meeting; job available; (in *plural*) equipment, fittings.

apportion /əˈpɔːʃ(ə)n/ *verb* (often + *to*) share out. □ **apportionment** *noun*.

apposite /ˈæpəzɪt/ *adjective* (often + *to*) well expressed, appropriate.

apposition /æpəˈzɪʃ(ə)n/ *noun* juxtaposition, esp. of syntactically parallel words etc. (e.g. *my friend Sue*).

appraise /əˈpreɪz/ *verb* (**-sing**) estimate value or quality of. □ **appraisal** *noun*.

appreciable /əˈpriːʃəb(ə)l/ *adjective* significant; considerable.

appreciate /əˈpriːʃɪeɪt/ *verb* (**-ting**) (highly) value; be grateful for; understand, recognize; rise in value. □ **appreciation** *noun*; **appreciative** /-ʃətɪv/ *adjective*.

apprehend /æprɪˈhend/ *verb* arrest; understand.

apprehension /æprɪˈhenʃ(ə)n/ *noun* fearful anticipation; arrest; understanding.

apprehensive /æprɪˈhensɪv/ *adjective* uneasy, fearful. □ **apprehensively** *adverb*.

apprentice /əˈprentɪs/ ● *noun* person learning trade by working for agreed period. ● *verb* (usually + *to*) engage as apprentice. □ **apprenticeship** *noun*.

apprise /əˈpraɪz/ *verb* (**-sing**) (usually + *of*) inform.

approach /əˈprəʊtʃ/ ● *verb* come nearer (to) in space or time; be similar to; approximate to; set about; make tentative proposal to. ● *noun* act or means of approaching; approximation; technique; part of aircraft's flight before landing.

approachable /əˈprəʊtʃəb(ə)l/ *adjective* friendly; able to be approached.

approbation /æprəˈbeɪʃ(ə)n/ *noun* approval, consent.

appropriate ● *adjective* /əˈprəʊprɪət/ suitable, proper. ● *verb* (**-ting**) /əˈprəʊprɪeɪt/ take possession of; devote (money etc.) to special purpose. □ **appropriately** *adverb*; **appropriation** *noun*.

approval /əˈpruːv(ə)l/ *noun* approving; consent. □ **on approval** returnable if not satisfactory.

approve /əˈpruːv/ *verb* (**-ving**) sanction; (often + *of*) regard with favour.

approx. *abbreviation* approximate(ly).

approximate ● *adjective* /əˈprɒksɪmət/ fairly correct; near to the actual. ● *verb* /əˈprɒksɪmeɪt/ (**-ting**) (often + *to*) be or make near. □ **approximately** *adverb*; **approximation** *noun*.

appurtenances /əˈpɜːtɪnənsɪz/ *plural noun* accessories; belongings.

APR *abbreviation* annual(ized) percentage rate.

Apr. *abbreviation* April.

après-ski /æpreɪˈskiː/ ● *noun* activities after a day's skiing. ● *adjective* suitable for these. [French]

apricot /ˈeɪprɪkɒt/ ● *noun* small orange-yellow peach-like fruit; its colour. ● *adjective* orange-yellow.

April /ˈeɪpr(ə)l/ *noun* fourth month of year. □ **April Fool** victim of hoax on 1 Apr.

a priori /eɪ praɪˈɔːraɪ/ ● *adjective* from cause to effect; not derived from experience; assumed without investigation. ● *adverb* deductively; as far as one knows.

apron /ˈeɪprən/ *noun* garment protecting front of clothes; area on airfield for manoeuvring or loading; part of stage in front of curtain.

apropos /æprəˈpəʊ/ ● *adjective* appropriate; *colloquial* (often + *of*) in respect of. ● *adverb* appropriately; incidentally.

apse /æps/ *noun* arched or domed recess esp. at end of church.

apsis /ˈæpsɪs/ *noun* (*plural* **apsides** /-diːz/) aphelion or perihelion of planet, apogee or perigee of moon.

apt *adjective* suitable, appropriate; (+ *to do*) having a tendency; quick to learn.

aptitude /ˈæptɪtjuːd/ *noun* talent; ability, esp. specified.

aqualung /ˈækwəlʌŋ/ *noun* portable underwater breathing-apparatus.

aquamarine /ækwəməˈriːn/ ● *noun* bluish-green beryl; its colour. ● *adjective* bluish-green.

aquaplane /ˈækwəpleɪn/ ● *noun* board for riding on water, pulled by speedboat. ● *verb* (**-ning**) ride on this; (of vehicle) glide uncontrollably on wet surface.

aquarelle /ækwəˈrel/ *noun* painting in transparent water-colours.

aquarium /əˈkweərɪəm/ *noun* (*plural* **-s**) tank for keeping fish etc.

Aquarius /əˈkweərɪəs/ *noun* eleventh sign of zodiac.

aquatic /əˈkwætɪk/ *adjective* growing or living in water; done in or on water.

aquatint /ˈækwətɪnt/ *noun* etched print like water-colour.

aqueduct /ˈækwɪdʌkt/ *noun* water channel, esp. raised structure across valley.

aqueous /ˈeɪkwɪəs/ *adjective* of or like water.

aquiline /ˈækwɪlaɪn/ *adjective* of or like an eagle; (of nose) curved.

Arab /ˈærəb/ ● *noun* member of Semitic people inhabiting originally Saudi Arabia, now Middle East generally; horse of breed originally native to Arabia. ● *adjective* of Arabia or Arabs.

arabesque /ærəˈbesk/ *noun* decoration with intertwined leaves, scrollwork, etc.; ballet posture with one leg extended horizontally backwards.

Arabian /əˈreɪbɪən/ ● *adjective* of Arabia. ● *noun* Arab.

Arabic /ˈærəbɪk/ ● *noun* language of Arabs. ● *adjective* of Arabs or their language. □ **arabic numerals** 1, 2, 3, etc.

arable /ˈærəb(ə)l/ *adjective* fit for growing crops.

arachnid /əˈræknɪd/ *noun* creature of class comprising spiders, scorpions, etc.

Aramaic /ærəˈmeɪɪk/ ● *noun* language of Syria at time of Christ. ● *adjective* of or in Aramaic.

arbiter /ˈɑːbɪtə/ *noun* arbitrator; person influential in specific field.

arbitrary /ˈɑːbɪtrərɪ/ *adjective* random; capricious, despotic. □ **arbitrarily** *adverb*.

arbitrate /ˈɑːbɪtreɪt/ *verb* (**-ting**) settle dispute between others. □ **arbitration** *noun*; **arbitrator** *noun*.

arboreal /ɑːˈbɔːrɪəl/ *adjective* of or living in trees.

arboretum /ɑːbəˈriːtəm/ *noun* (*plural* **-ta**) tree-garden.

arboriculture /ˈɑːbərɪkʌltʃə/ *noun* cultivation of trees and shrubs.

arbour /ˈɑːbə/ *noun* (*US* **arbor**) shady garden alcove enclosed by trees etc.

arc *noun* part of circumference of circle or other curve; luminous discharge between two electrodes. □ **arc lamp** one using electric arc; **arc welding** using electric arc to melt metals to be welded.

arcade /ɑːˈkeɪd/ *noun* covered walk, esp. lined with shops; series of arches supporting or along wall.

Arcadian /ɑːˈkeɪdɪən/ *adjective* ideally rustic.

arcane /ɑːˈkeɪn/ *adjective* mysterious, secret.

arch[1] ● *noun* curved structure supporting bridge, floor, etc. as opening or ornament. ● *verb* form arch; provide with or form into arch.

arch[2] *adjective* self-consciously or affectedly playful.

archaeology /ɑːkɪˈɒlədʒɪ/ *noun* (*US* **archeology**) study of ancient cultures, esp. by excavation of physical remains. □ **archaeological** /-əˈlɒdʒ-/ *adjective*; **archaeologist** *noun*.

archaic /ɑːˈkeɪɪk/ *adjective* antiquated; (of word) no longer in ordinary use; of early period in culture.

archaism /ˈɑːkeɪɪz(ə)m/ *noun* archaic word etc.; use of the archaic. **archaistic** /-ˈɪst-/ *adjective*.

archangel /ˈɑːkeɪndʒ(ə)l/ *noun* angel of highest rank.

archbishop /ɑːtʃˈbɪʃəp/ *noun* chief bishop.

archbishopric *noun* office or diocese of archbishop.

archdeacon /ɑːtʃˈdiːkən/ *noun* church dignitary next below bishop. □ **archdeaconry** *noun* (*plural* **-ies**).

archdiocese /ɑːtʃˈdaɪəsɪs/ *noun* archbishop's diocese. □ **archdiocesan** /-daɪˈɒsɪs(ə)n/ *adjective*.

arch-enemy /ɑːtʃˈenəmɪ/ *noun* (*plural* **-ies**) chief enemy.

archeology *US* = ARCHAEOLOGY.

archer /ˈɑːtʃə/ *noun* person who shoots with bow and arrows.

archery /ˈɑːtʃərɪ/ *noun* shooting with bow and arrows.

archetype /ˈɑːkɪtaɪp/ *noun* original model, typical specimen. □ **archetypal** /-ˈtaɪp-/ *adjective*.

archipelago /ɑːkɪˈpeləgəʊ/ *noun* (*plural* **-s**) group of islands; sea with many islands.

architect /ˈɑːkɪtekt/ *noun* designer of buildings etc.; (+ *of*) person who brings about specified thing.

architectonic /ɑːkɪtekˈtɒnɪk/ *adjective* of architecture.

architecture /ˈɑːkɪtektʃə/ *noun* design and construction of buildings; style of building. □ **architectural** /-ˈtek-/ *adjective*.

architrave /ˈɑːkɪtreɪv/ *noun* moulded frame round doorway or window; main beam laid across tops of classical columns.

archive /ˈɑːkaɪv/ *noun* (usually in *plural*) collection of documents or records; place where these are kept.

archivist /ˈɑːkɪvɪst/ *noun* keeper of archives.

archway /ˈɑːtʃweɪ/ *noun* arched entrance or passage.

Arctic /ˈɑːktɪk/ ● *adjective* of north polar region; (**arctic**) very cold. ● *noun* Arctic region.

ardent /ˈɑːd(ə)nt/ *adjective* eager, fervent, passionate; burning. □ **ardently** *adverb*.

ardour /ˈɑːdə/ *noun* zeal, enthusiasm.

arduous /ˈɑːdjʊəs/ *adjective* hard to accomplish; strenuous.

are see BE.

area /ˈeərɪə/ *noun* extent or measure of surface; region; space set aside for a purpose; scope, range; space in front of house basement.

arena /əˈriːnə/ *noun* centre of amphitheatre; scene of conflict; sphere of action.

aren't /ɑːnt/ are not; (in questions) am not.

arête /æˈreɪt/ *noun* sharp mountain ridge.

argon /ˈɑːgɒn/ *noun* inert gaseous element.

argot /ˈɑːgəʊ/ *noun* jargon of group or class.

argue /ˈɑːgjuː/ *verb* (**-ues**, **-ued**, **-uing**) exchange views, esp. heatedly; (often + *that*) maintain by reasoning; (+ *for*, *against*) reason. □ **arguable** *adjective*; **arguably** *adverb*.

argument /ˈɑːgjʊmənt/ *noun* (esp. heated) exchange of views; reason given; reasoning; summary of book etc. □ **argumentation** /-men-/ *noun*.

argumentative /ɑːgjʊˈmentətɪv/ *adjective* fond of arguing.

argy-bargy /ɑːdʒɪˈbɑːdʒɪ/ *noun jocular* dispute, wrangle.

aria /ˈɑːrɪə/ *noun* song for one voice in opera, oratorio, etc.

arid /ˈærɪd/ *noun* dry, parched. □ **aridity** /əˈrɪd-/ *noun*.

Aries /ˈeəriːz/ *noun* first sign of zodiac.

aright /ə'raɪt/ *adverb* rightly.

arise /ə'raɪz/ *verb* (**-sing**; *past* **arose** /ə'rəʊz/; *past participle* **arisen** /ə'rɪz(ə)n/) originate; (usually + *from, out of*) result; emerge; rise.

aristocracy /ærɪs'tɒkrəsɪ/ *noun* (*plural* **-ies**) ruling class, nobility.

aristocrat /'ærɪstəkræt/ *noun* member of aristocracy.

aristocratic /ærɪstə'krætɪk/ *adjective* of the aristocracy; grand, distinguished.

arithmetic ● *noun* /ə'rɪθmətɪk/ science of numbers; computation, use of numbers. ● *adjective* /ærɪθ'metɪk/ (also **arithmetical**) of arithmetic.

ark *noun* ship in which Noah escaped the Flood. □ **Ark of the Covenant** wooden chest containing tables of Jewish law.

arm[1] *noun* upper limb of human body; sleeve; raised side part of chair; branch; armlike thing. □ **armchair** chair with arms, theoretical rather than active; **arm in arm** with arms linked; **armpit** hollow under arm at shoulder; **at arm's length** at a distance; **with open arms** cordially. □ **armful** *noun*.

arm[2] ● *noun* (usually in *plural*) weapon; branch of military forces; (in *plural*) heraldic devices. ● *verb* equip with arms; equip oneself with arms; make (bomb) ready. □ **up in arms** (usually + *against, about*) actively resisting.

armada /ɑ:'mɑ:də/ *noun* fleet of warships.

armadillo /ɑ:mə'dɪləʊ/ *noun* (*plural* **-s**) S. American burrowing mammal with plated body.

Armageddon /ɑ:mə'ged(ə)n/ *noun* huge battle at end of world.

armament /'ɑ:məmənt/ *noun* military weapon etc.; equipping for war.

armature /'ɑ:mətʃə/ *noun* rotating coil or coils of dynamo or electric motor; iron bar placed across poles of magnet; framework on which sculpture is moulded.

armistice /'ɑ:mɪstɪs/ *noun* truce.

armlet /'ɑ:mlɪt/ *noun* band worn round arm.

armorial /ɑ:'mɔ:rɪəl/ *adjective* of heraldic arms.

armour /'ɑ:mə/ *noun* protective covering formerly worn in fighting; metal plates etc. protecting ship, car, tank, etc.; armoured vehicles. □ **armoured** *adjective*.

armourer *noun* maker of arms or armour; official in charge of arms.

armoury /'ɑ:mərɪ/ *noun* (*plural* **-ies**) arsenal.

army /'ɑ:mɪ/ *noun* (*plural* **-ies**) organized armed land force; vast number; organized body.

arnica /'ɑ:nɪkə/ *noun* plant with yellow flowers; medicine made from it.

aroma /ə'rəʊmə/ *noun* pleasing smell; subtle quality. □ **aromatic** /ærə'mætɪk/ *adjective*.

aromatherapy *noun* use of plant extracts and oils in massage. □ **aromatherapist** *noun*.

arose *past* of ARISE.

around /ə'raʊnd/ ● *adverb* on every side; all round; *colloquial* in existence, near at hand. ● *preposition* on or along the circuit of; on every side of; here and there in or near; about.

arouse /ə'raʊz/ *verb* (**-sing**) induce (esp. emotion); awake from sleep; stir into activity; stimulate sexually. □ **arousal** *noun*.

arpeggio /ɑ:'pedʒɪəʊ/ *noun* (*plural* **-s**) notes of chord played in rapid succession.

arrack /'ærək/ *noun* alcoholic spirit made esp. from rice.

arraign /ə'reɪn/ *verb* indict, accuse; find fault with. □ **arraignment** *noun*.

arrange /ə'reɪndʒ/ *verb* (**-ging**) put in order; plan or provide for; (+ *to do, for*) take measures; (+ *with* person) agree about procedure for; *Music* adapt (piece). □ **arrangement** *noun*.

arrant /'ærənt/ *adjective* downright, utter.

arras /'ærəs/ *noun* tapestry wall-hanging.

array /ə'reɪ/ ● *noun* imposing series; ordered arrangement, esp. of troops. ● *verb* deck, adorn; set in order; marshal (forces).

arrears /ə'rɪəz/ *plural noun* outstanding debt; what remains undone. □ **in arrears** behindhand, esp. in payment.

arrest /ə'rest/ ● *verb* lawfully seize; stop; catch attention of. ● *noun* arresting, being arrested; stoppage.

arrival /ə'raɪv(ə)l/ *noun* arriving; person or thing arriving.

arrive /ə'raɪv/ *verb* (**-ving**) come to destination; (+ *at*) reach (conclusion); *colloquial* become successful, be born.

arrogant /'ærəgənt/ *adjective* aggressively assertive or presumptuous. □ **arrogance** *noun*; **arrogantly** *adverb*.

arrogate /'ærəgeɪt/ *verb* (**-ting**) claim without right. □ **arrogation** *noun*.

arrow /'ærəʊ/ *noun* pointed missile shot from bow; representation of this, esp. to show direction. □ **arrowhead** pointed tip of arrow.

arrowroot /'ærəʊru:t/ *noun* nutritious starch.

arsenal /'ɑ:sən(ə)l/ *noun* place where weapons and ammunition are made or stored.

arsenic /'ɑ:sənɪk/ *noun* brittle semi-metallic element; its highly poisonous trioxide.

arson /'ɑ:sən/ *noun* crime of deliberately setting property on fire. □ **arsonist** *noun*.

art *noun* human creative skill, its application; branch of creative activity concerned with imitative and imaginative designs, sounds, or ideas, e.g. painting, music, writing; creative activity resulting in visual representation; thing in which skill can be exercised; (in *plural*) certain branches of learning (esp. languages, literature, history, etc.) as distinct from sciences; knack; cunning. □ **art nouveau** /ɑ: nu:'vəʊ/ art style of late 19th c., with flowing lines.

artefact /'ɑ:tɪfækt/ *noun* (also **artifact**) man-made object.

arterial /ɑ:'tɪərɪəl/ *adjective* of or like artery. □ **arterial road** important main road.

arteriosclerosis /ɑ:tɪərɪəʊsklɪə'rəʊsɪs/ *noun* hardening and thickening of artery walls.

artery /'ɑ:tərɪ/ *noun* (*plural* **-ies**) blood vessel carrying blood from heart; main road or railway line.

artesian well /ɑ:'ti:zɪən/ well in which water rises by natural pressure through vertically drilled hole.

artful /'ɑ:tfʊl/ *adjective* sly, crafty. □ **artfully** *adverb*.

arthritis /ɑ:'θraɪtɪs/ *noun* inflammation of joint. □ **arthritic** /-'θrɪt-/ *adjective & noun*.

arthropod /'ɑ:θrəpɒd/ *noun* animal with segmented body and jointed limbs, e.g. insect, spider, crustacean.

artichoke /'ɑ:tɪtʃəʊk/ *noun* plant allied to thistle; its partly edible flower; Jerusalem artichoke.

article /'ɑ:tɪk(ə)l/ ● *noun* item or thing; short piece of non-fiction in newspaper etc.; clause of agreement etc.; = DEFINITE ARTICLE, INDEFINITE ARTICLE. ● *verb* employ under contract as trainee.

articular /ɑ:'tɪkjʊlə/ *adjective* of joints.

articulate ● *adjective* /ɑ:'tɪkjʊlət/ fluent and clear in speech; (of speech) in which separate sounds and words are clear; having joints. ● *verb* /ɑ:'tɪkjʊleɪt/ (**-ting**) speak distinctly; express clearly; connect with joints. □ **articulated lorry** one with sections connected by flexible joint. □ **articulately** *adverb*; **articulation** *noun*.

artifact = ARTEFACT.

artifice /ˈɑːtɪfɪs/ *noun* trick; cunning; skill.

artificer /ɑːˈtɪfɪsə/ *noun* craftsman.

artificial /ɑːtɪˈfɪʃ(ə)l/ *adjective* not natural; imitating nature; insincere. □ **artificial insemination** non-sexual injection of semen into uterus; **artificial intelligence** (use of) computers replacing human intelligence; **artificial respiration** manual or mechanical stimulation of breathing. □ **artificiality** /-ʃɪˈæl-/ *noun*; **artificially** *adverb*.

artillery /ɑːˈtɪlərɪ/ *noun* large guns used in fighting on land; branch of army using these. □ **artilleryman** *noun*.

artisan /ɑːtɪˈzæn/ *noun* skilled worker or craftsman.

artist /ˈɑːtɪst/ *noun* person who practises any art, esp. painting; artiste. □ **artistic** *adjective*; **artistically** *adverb*; **artistry** *noun*.

artiste /ɑːˈtiːst/ *noun* professional singer, dancer, etc.

artless *adjective* guileless, ingenuous; natural; clumsy. □ **artlessly** *adverb*.

arty *adjective* (**-ier**, **-iest**) pretentiously or affectedly artistic.

arum /ˈeərəm/ *noun* plant with arrow-shaped leaves.

Aryan /ˈeərɪən/ ● *noun* speaker of any Indo-European language. ● *adjective* of Aryans.

as /æz, əz/ ● *adverb* to the same extent. ● *conjunction* in the same way that; while, when; since, seeing that; although. ● *preposition* in the capacity or form of. □ **as ... as ...** to the same extent that ... is, does, etc.

asafoetida /æsəˈfetɪdə/ *noun* (*US* **asafetida**) resinous pungent gum.

asbestos /æsˈbestɒs/ *noun* fibrous silicate mineral; heat-resistant or insulating substance made from this.

ascend /əˈsend/ *verb* slope upwards; go or come up, climb.

ascendancy *noun* (often + *over*) dominant control.

ascendant *adjective* rising. □ **in the ascendant** gaining or having power or authority.

ascension /əˈsenʃ(ə)n/ *noun* ascent, esp. (**Ascension**) of Christ into heaven.

ascent /əˈsent/ *noun* ascending, rising; upward path or slope.

ascertain /æsəˈteɪn/ *verb* find out for certain. □ **ascertainment** *noun*.

ascetic /əˈsetɪk/ ● *adjective* severely abstinent; self-denying. ● *noun* ascetic person. □ **asceticism** /-tɪs-/ *noun*.

ascorbic acid /əˈskɔːbɪk/ *noun* vitamin C.

ascribe /əˈskraɪb/ *verb* (**-bing**) (usually + *to*) attribute; regard as belonging. □ **ascription** /-ˈskrɪp-/ *noun*.

asepsis /eɪˈsepsɪs/ *noun* absence of sepsis or harmful bacteria; aseptic method in surgery. □ **aseptic** *adjective*.

asexual /eɪˈseksjʊəl/ *adjective* without sex or sexuality; (of reproduction) not involving fusion of gametes. □ **asexually** *adverb*.

ash[1] *noun* (often in *plural*) powdery residue left after burning; (in *plural*) human remains after cremation; (**the Ashes**) trophy in cricket between England and Australia. □ **ashcan** *US* dustbin; **ashtray** receptacle for tobacco ash; **Ash Wednesday** first day of Lent.

ash[2] *noun* tree with silver-grey bark; its wood.

ashamed /əˈʃeɪmd/ *adjective* embarrassed by shame; (+ *to do*) reluctant owing to shame.

ashen /ˈæʃ(ə)n/ *adjective* grey, pale.

ashore /əˈʃɔː/ *adverb* to or on shore.

ashram /ˈæʃræm/ *noun* religious retreat for Hindus.

Asian /ˈeɪʃ(ə)n/ ● *adjective* of Asia. ● *noun* native of Asia; person of Asian descent.

aside /əˈsaɪd/ ● *adverb* to or on one side; away, apart. ● *noun* words spoken aside, esp. by actor to audience.

asinine /ˈæsɪnaɪn/ *adjective* asslike; stupid.

ask /ɑːsk/ *verb* call for answer to or about; seek to obtain from another person; invite; (+ *for*) seek to obtain or meet. □ **ask after** inquire about (esp. person).

askance /əˈskæns/ *adverb* sideways. □ **look askance at** regard suspiciously.

askew /əˈskjuː/ ● *adverb* crookedly. ● *adjective* oblique; awry.

aslant /əˈslɑːnt/ ● *adverb* at a slant. ● *preposition* obliquely across.

asleep /əˈsliːp/ ● *adjective* sleeping; *colloquial* inattentive; (of limb) numb. ● *adverb* into state of sleep.

asp *noun* small venomous snake.

asparagus /əsˈpærəgəs/ *noun* plant of lily family; its edible shoots.

aspect /ˈæspekt/ *noun* feature, viewpoint, etc. to be considered; appearance, look; side facing specified direction.

aspen /ˈæspən/ *noun* poplar with fluttering leaves.

asperity /æsˈperɪtɪ/ *noun* sharpness of temper or tone; roughness.

aspersion /əsˈpɜːʃ(ə)n/ *noun* □ **cast aspersions on** defame.

asphalt /ˈæsfælt/ ● *noun* bituminous pitch; mixture of this with gravel etc. for surfacing roads etc. ● *verb* surface with asphalt.

asphodel /ˈæsfədel/ *noun* kind of lily.

asphyxia /æsˈfɪksɪə/ *noun* lack of oxygen in blood; suffocation.

asphyxiate /əsˈfɪksɪeɪt/ *verb* (**-ting**) suffocate. □ **asphyxiation** *noun*.

aspic /ˈæspɪk/ *noun* clear savoury jelly.

aspidistra /æspɪˈdɪstrə/ *noun* house plant with broad tapering leaves.

aspirant /ˈæspɪrənt/ ● *adjective* aspiring. ● *noun* person who aspires.

aspirate ● *noun* /ˈæspərət/ sound of *h*; consonant blended with this. ● *verb* /ˈæspəreɪt/ (**-ting**) pronounce with *h*; draw (fluid) by suction from cavity.

aspiration /æspəˈreɪʃ(ə)n/ *noun* ambition, desire; aspirating.

aspire /əˈspaɪə/ *verb* (**-ring**) (usually + *to*, *after*, *to do*) have ambition or strong desire.

aspirin /ˈæsprɪn/ *noun* (*plural* same or **-s**) white powder used to reduce pain and fever; tablet of this.

ass *noun* 4-legged animal with long ears, related to horse; donkey; stupid person.

assail /əˈseɪl/ *verb* attack physically or verbally. □ **assailant** *noun*.

assassin /əˈsæsɪn/ *noun* killer, esp. of political or religious leader.

assassinate /əˈsæsɪneɪt/ *verb* (**-ting**) kill for political or religious motives. □ **assassination** *noun*.

assault /əˈsɔːlt/ ● *noun* violent physical or verbal attack; *Law* threat or display of violence against person. ● *verb* make assault on. □ **assault and battery** *Law* threatening act resulting in physical harm to person.

assay /əˈseɪ/ ● *noun* test of metal or ore for ingredients and quality. ● *verb* make assay of.

assegai /ˈæsɪgaɪ/ *noun* light iron-tipped S. African spear.

assemblage /əˈsemblɪdʒ/ *noun* assembled group.

assemble /əˈsemb(ə)l/ *verb* (**-ling**) fit together parts of; fit (parts) together; bring or come together.

assembly /ə'semblɪ/ *noun* (*plural* **-ies**) assembling; assembled group, esp. as parliament etc.; fitting together of parts. ▫ **assembly line** machinery arranged so that product can be progressively assembled.

assent /ə'sent/ ● *noun* consent, approval. ● *verb* (usually + *to*) agree, consent.

assert /ə'sɜːt/ *verb* declare; enforce claim to; (**assert oneself**) insist on one's rights.

assertion /ə'sɜːʃ(ə)n/ *noun* declaration; forthright statement.

assertive *adjective* asserting oneself; forthright, positive. ▫ **assertively** *adverb*; **assertiveness** *noun*.

assess /ə'ses/ *verb* estimate size or quality of; estimate value of (property etc.) for taxation. ▫ **assessment** *noun*.

assessor *noun* person who assesses taxes etc.; judge's technical adviser in court.

asset /'æset/ *noun* useful or valuable person or thing; (usually in *plural*) property and possessions.

assiduous /ə'sɪdjʊəs/ *adjective* persevering, hard-working. ▫ **assiduity** /æsɪ'djuːɪtɪ/ *noun*; **assiduously** *adverb*.

assign /ə'saɪn/ *verb* allot; appoint; fix (time, place, etc.); (+ *to*) ascribe to, *Law* transfer formally to.

assignation /æsɪg'neɪʃ(ə)n/ *noun* appointment, esp. made by lovers; assigning, being assigned.

assignee /əsaɪ'niː/ *noun Law* person to whom property or right is assigned.

assignment /ə'saɪnmənt/ *noun* task or mission; assigning, being assigned.

assimilate /ə'sɪmɪleɪt/ *verb* (**-ting**) absorb or be absorbed into system; (usually + *to*) make like. ▫ **assimilable** *adjective*; **assimilation** *noun*; **assimilative** /-lətɪv/ *adjective*.

assist /ə'sɪst/ *verb* (often + *in*) help. ▫ **assistance** *noun*.

assistant *noun* helper; subordinate worker; = SHOP ASSISTANT.

assizes /ə'saɪzɪz/ *plural noun historical* court periodically administering civil and criminal law.

Assoc. *abbreviation* Association.

associate ● *verb* /ə'səʊʃɪeɪt/ (**-ting**) connect mentally; join, combine; (usually + *with*) have frequent dealings. ● *noun* /ə'səʊʃɪət/ partner, colleague; friend, companion. ● *adjective* /ə'səʊʃɪət/ joined, allied.

association /əsəʊsɪ'eɪʃ(ə)n/ *noun* group organized for joint purpose; associating, being associated; connection of ideas. ▫ **association football** kind played with round ball which may be handled only by goalkeeper.

assonance /'æsənəns/ *noun* partial resemblance of sound between syllables, as in *run-up*, or *wary* and *barely*. ▫ **assonant** *adjective*.

assorted /ə'sɔːtɪd/ *adjective* of various sorts, mixed.

assortment /ə'sɔːtmənt/ *noun* diverse group or mixture.

assuage /ə'sweɪdʒ/ *verb* (**-ging**) soothe; appease.

assume /ə'sjuːm/ *verb* (**-ming**) take to be true; undertake; simulate; take on (aspect, attribute, etc.).

assumption /ə'sʌmpʃ(ə)n/ *noun* assuming; thing assumed; (**Assumption**) reception of Virgin Mary bodily into heaven.

assurance *noun* declaration; insurance, esp. of life; certainty; self-confidence.

assure /ə'ʃʊə/ *verb* (**-ring**) (often + *of*) convince; tell (person) confidently; ensure, guarantee (result etc.); insure (esp. life).

assuredly /ə'ʃʊərɪdlɪ/ *adverb* certainly.

aster /'æstə/ *noun* plant with bright daisy-like flowers.

asterisk /'æstərɪsk/ *noun* symbol (*) used to indicate omission etc.

astern /ə'stɜːn/ *adverb* in or to rear of ship or aircraft; backwards.

asteroid /'æstərɔɪd/ *noun* any of numerous small planets between orbits of Mars and Jupiter.

asthma /'æsmə/ *noun* condition marked by difficulty in breathing. ▫ **asthmatic** /-'mæt-/ *adjective & noun*.

astigmatism /ə'stɪgmətɪz(ə)m/ *noun* eye or lens defect resulting in distorted images. ▫ **astigmatic** /æstɪg'mætɪk/ *adjective*.

astir /ə'stɜː/ *adverb & adjective* in motion; out of bed.

astonish /ə'stɒnɪʃ/ *verb* amaze, surprise. ▫ **astonishment** *noun*.

astound /ə'staʊnd/ *verb* astonish greatly.

astrakhan /æstrə'kæn/ *noun* dark curly fleece of Astrakhan lamb; cloth imitating this.

astral /'æstr(ə)l/ *adjective* of stars; starry.

astray /ə'streɪ/ *adverb & adjective* away from right way. ▫ **go astray** be lost.

astride /ə'straɪd/ ● *adverb* (often + *of*) with one leg on each side. ● *preposition* astride of.

astringent /ə'strɪndʒənt/ ● *adjective* contracting body tissue, esp. to check bleeding; austere, severe. ● *noun* astringent substance. ▫ **astringency** *noun*.

astrolabe /'æstrəleɪb/ *noun* instrument for measuring altitude of stars etc.

astrology /ə'strɒlədʒɪ/ *noun* study of supposed planetary influence on human affairs. ▫ **astrologer** *noun*; **astrological** /æstrə'lɒdʒ-/ *adjective*.

astronaut /'æstrənɔːt/ *noun* space traveller.

astronautics /æstrə'nɔːtɪks/ *plural noun* (treated as *singular*) science of space travel. ▫ **astronautical** *adjective*.

astronomical /æstrə'nɒmɪk(ə)l/ *adjective* (also **astronomic**) of astronomy; vast. ▫ **astronomically** *adverb*.

astronomy /ə'strɒnəmɪ/ *noun* science of celestial bodies. ▫ **astronomer** *noun*.

astrophysics /æstrəʊ'fɪzɪks/ *plural noun* (treated as *singular*) study of physics and chemistry of celestial bodies. ▫ **astrophysical** *adjective*; **astrophysicist** *noun*.

astute /ə'stjuːt/ *adjective* shrewd. ▫ **astutely** *adverb*; **astuteness** *noun*.

asunder /ə'sʌndə/ *adverb literary* apart.

asylum /ə'saɪləm/ *noun* sanctuary; = POLITICAL ASYLUM; *historical* mental institution.

asymmetry /eɪ'sɪmətrɪ/ *noun* lack of symmetry. ▫ **asymmetric(al)** /-'met-/ *adjective*.

at /æt, ət/ *preposition expressing position, point in time or on scale, engagement in activity, value or rate, or motion or aim towards*.

atavism /'ætəvɪz(ə)m/ *noun* resemblance to remote ancestors; reversion to earlier type. ▫ **atavistic** /-'vɪs-/ *adjective*.

ate *past* of EAT.

atelier /ə'telɪeɪ/ *noun* workshop; artist's studio.

atheism /'eɪθɪɪz(ə)m/ *noun* belief that no God exists. ▫ **atheist** *noun*; **atheistic** /-'ɪst-/ *adjective*.

atherosclerosis /æθərəʊsklə'rəʊsɪs/ *noun* formation of fatty deposits in the arteries.

athlete /'æθliːt/ *noun* person who engages in athletics, exercises, etc. ▫ **athlete's foot** fungal foot disease.

athletic /æθ'letɪk/ *adjective* of athletes or athletics; physically strong or agile. ▫ **athletically** *adverb*; **athleticism** *noun*.

athletics *plural noun* (usually treated as *singular*) physical exercises, esp. track and field events.

atlas /'ætləs/ *noun* book of maps.

atmosphere /ˈætməsfɪə/ *noun* gases enveloping earth, other planet, etc.; tone, mood, etc., of place, book, etc.; unit of pressure. □ **atmospheric** /-ˈfer-/ *adjective.*

atmospherics /ætməsˈferɪks/ *plural noun* electrical disturbance in atmosphere; interference with telecommunications caused by this.

atoll /ˈætɒl/ *noun* ring-shaped coral reef enclosing lagoon.

atom /ˈætəm/ *noun* smallest particle of chemical element that can take part in chemical reaction; this as source of nuclear energy; minute portion or thing. □ **atom bomb** bomb in which energy is released by nuclear fission.

atomic /əˈtɒmɪk/ *adjective* of atoms; of or using atomic energy or atom bombs. □ **atomic bomb** atom bomb; **atomic energy** nuclear energy; **atomic number** number of protons in nucleus of atom; **atomic weight** ratio of mass of one atom of element to 1/12 mass of atom of carbon-12.

atomize /ˈætəmaɪz/ *verb* (also **-ise**) (**-zing** or **-sing**) reduce to atoms or fine spray.

atomizer *noun* (also **-iser**) aerosol.

atonal /eɪˈtəʊn(ə)l/ *adjective Music* not written in any key. □ **atonality** /-ˈnæl-/ *noun.*

atone /əˈtəʊn/ *verb* (**-ning**) (usually + *for*) make amends. □ **atonement** *noun.*

atrium /ˈeɪtrɪəm/ *noun* (*plural* **-s** or **atria**) either of upper cavities of heart.

atrocious /əˈtrəʊʃəs/ *adjective* very bad; wicked. □ **atrociously** *adverb.*

atrocity /əˈtrɒsɪtɪ/ *noun* (*plural* **-ies**) wicked or cruel act.

atrophy /ˈætrəfɪ/ ● *noun* wasting away, esp. through disuse. ● *verb* (**-ies, -ied**) suffer atrophy; cause atrophy in.

atropine /ˈætrəpiːn/ *noun* poisonous alkaloid in deadly nightshade.

attach /əˈtætʃ/ *verb* fasten, affix, join; (in *passive*; + *to*) be very fond of; (+ *to*) attribute or be attributable to.

attaché /əˈtæʃeɪ/ *noun* specialist member of ambassador's staff. □ **attaché case** small rectangular document case.

attachment *noun* thing attached, esp. for particular purpose; affection, devotion; attaching, being attached.

attack /əˈtæk/ ● *verb* try to hurt or deflect using force; criticize adversely; act harmfully on; *Sport* try to score against; vigorously apply oneself to. ● *noun* act of attacking; sudden onset of illness. □ **attacker** *noun.*

attain /əˈteɪn/ *verb* gain, accomplish; reach; (+ *to*) arrive at (goal etc.).

attainment *noun* attaining; (often in *plural*) skill, achievement.

attar /ˈætɑː/ *noun* perfume made from rose-petals.

attempt /əˈtempt/ ● *verb* try; try to accomplish or conquer. ● *noun* (often + *at*, *on*) attempting; endeavour.

attend /əˈtend/ *verb* be present at; go regularly to; (often + *to*) apply mind or oneself; (+ *to*) deal with; accompany, wait on. □ **attender** *noun.*

attendance *noun* attending; number of people present.

attendant ● *noun* person attending, esp. to provide service. ● *adjective* accompanying; (often + *on*) waiting.

attention /əˈtenʃ(ə)n/ *noun* act or faculty of applying one's mind, notice; consideration, care; *Military* erect attitude of readiness; (in *plural*) courtesies.

attentive /əˈtentɪv/ *adjective* (+ *to*) paying attention. □ **attentively** *adverb.*

attenuate /əˈtenjʊeɪt/ *verb* (**-ting**) make thin; reduce in force or value. □ **attenuation** *noun.*

attest /əˈtest/ *verb* certify validity of; (+ *to*) bear witness to. □ **attestation** /æt-/ *noun.*

attic /ˈætɪk/ *noun* room or space immediately under roof of house.

attire /əˈtaɪə/ *noun* clothes, esp. formal.

attired *adjective* dressed, esp. formally.

attitude /ˈætɪtjuːd/ *noun* opinion, way of thinking; (often + *to*) behaviour reflecting this; bodily posture.

attitudinize /ætɪˈtjuːdɪnaɪz/ *verb* (also **-ise**) (**-zing** or **-sing**) adopt attitudes.

attorney /əˈtɜːnɪ/ *noun* person, esp. lawyer, appointed to act for another in business or legal matters; *US* qualified lawyer. □ **Attorney-General** chief legal officer of government.

attract /əˈtrækt/ *verb* (of magnet etc.) draw to itself or oneself; arouse interest or admiration in.

attraction /əˈtrækʃ(ə)n/ *noun* attracting, being attracted; attractive quality; person or thing that attracts.

attractive /əˈtræktɪv/ *adjective* attracting esp. interest or admiration; pleasing. □ **attractively** *noun.*

attribute ● *verb* /əˈtrɪbjuːt/ (**-ting**) (usually + *to*) regard as belonging to or as written, said, or caused by, etc. ● *noun* /ˈætrɪbjuːt/ quality ascribed to person or thing; characteristic quality; object frequently associated with person, office, or status. □ **attributable** /əˈtrɪbjʊtəb(ə)l/ *adjective*; **attribution** /ætrɪˈbjuːʃ(ə)n/ *noun.*

attributive /əˈtrɪbjʊtɪv/ *adjective* expressing an attribute; (of adjective or noun) preceding word it describes.

attrition /əˈtrɪʃ(ə)n/ *noun* gradual wearing down; friction, abrasion.

attune /əˈtjuːn/ *verb* (**-ning**) (usually + *to*) adjust; *Music* tune.

atypical /eɪˈtɪpɪk(ə)l/ *adjective* not typical. □ **atypically** *adverb.*

aubergine /ˈəʊbəʒiːn/ *noun* (plant with) oval usually purple fruit used as vegetable.

aubrietia /ɔːˈbriːʃə/ *noun* (also **aubretia**) dwarf perennial rock plant.

auburn /ˈɔːbən/ *adjective* (usually of hair) reddish-brown.

auction /ˈɔːkʃ(ə)n/ ● *noun* sale in which each article is sold to highest bidder. ● *verb* sell by auction.

auctioneer /ɔːkʃəˈnɪə/ *noun* person who conducts auctions.

audacious /ɔːˈdeɪʃəs/ *adjective* daring, bold; impudent. □ **audacity** /-ˈdæs-/ *noun.*

audible /ˈɔːdɪb(ə)l/ *adjective* that can be heard. □ **audibility** *noun*; **audibly** *adverb.*

audience /ˈɔːdɪəns/ *noun* group of listeners or spectators; group of people reached by any spoken or written message; formal interview.

audio /ˈɔːdɪəʊ/ *noun* (reproduction of) sound. □ **audiotape** magnetic tape for recording sound; **audio typist** person who types from tape recording; **audio-visual** using both sight and sound.

audit /ˈɔːdɪt/ ● *noun* official scrutiny of accounts. ● *verb* (**-t-**) conduct audit of. □ **auditor** *noun.*

audition /ɔːˈdɪʃ(ə)n/ ● *noun* test of performer's ability. ● *verb* assess or be assessed at audition.

auditorium /ɔːdɪˈtɔːrɪəm/ *noun* (*plural* **-s**) part of theatre etc. for audience.

auditory /ˈɔːdɪtərɪ/ *adjective* of hearing.

au fait /əʊ ˈfeɪ/ *adjective* (usually + *with*) conversant.

Aug. *abbreviation* August.

auger /ˈɔːgə/ *noun* tool with screw point for boring holes in wood.

aught /ɔːt/ *noun archaic* anything.

augment /ɔːgˈment/ *verb* make greater, increase. □ **augmentation** *noun*.

augur /ˈɔːgə/ *verb* portend; serve as omen.

augury /ˈɔːgjʊrɪ/ *noun* (*plural* **-ies**) omen; interpretation of omens.

August /ˈɔːgəst/ *noun* eighth month of year.

august /ɔːˈgʌst/ *adjective* venerable, imposing.

auk /ɔːk/ *noun* black and white seabird with small wings.

aunt /ɑːnt/ *noun* parent's sister; uncle's wife. □ **Aunt Sally** game in which sticks or balls are thrown at dummy, target of general abuse.

aunty /ˈɑːntɪ/ *noun* (also **auntie**) (*plural* **-ies**) *colloquial* aunt.

au pair /əʊ ˈpeə/ *noun* young foreign woman who helps with housework in return for room and board.

aura /ˈɔːrə/ *noun* distinctive atmosphere; subtle emanation.

aural /ˈɔːr(ə)l/ *adjective* of ear or hearing. □ **aurally** *adverb*.

aureole /ˈɔːrɪəʊl/ *noun* (also **aureola** /ɔːˈriːələ/) halo.

au revoir /əʊ rəˈvwɑː/ *interjection & noun* goodbye (until we meet again). [French]

auricle /ˈɔːrɪk(ə)l/ *noun* external ear of animal; atrium of heart.

auriferous /ɔːˈrɪfərəs/ *adjective* yielding gold.

aurora /ɔːˈrɔːrə/ *noun* (*plural* **-s** or **-rae** /-riː/) streamers of light above northern (**aurora borealis** /bɒrɪˈeɪlɪs/) or southern (**aurora australis** /ɔːˈstreɪlɪs/) polar region.

auscultation /ɔːskəlˈteɪʃ(ə)n/ *noun* listening to sound of heart etc. to help diagnosis.

auspice /ˈɔːspɪs/ *noun* omen; (in *plural*) patronage.

auspicious /ɔːˈspɪʃəs/ *adjective* promising; favourable.

Aussie /ˈɒzɪ/ *noun & adjective slang* Australian.

austere /ɔːˈstɪə/ *adjective* (**-r**, **-st**) severely simple; stern; morally strict. □ **austerity** /-ˈter-/ *noun*.

austral /ˈɔːstr(ə)l/ *adjective* southern.

Australasian /ɒstrəˈleɪʒ(ə)n/ *adjective* of Australia and SW Pacific islands.

Australian /ɒˈstreɪlɪən/ ● *adjective* of Australia. ● *noun* native or national of Australia.

autarchy /ˈɔːtɑːkɪ/ *noun* absolute rule.

autarky /ˈɔːtɑːkɪ/ *noun* self-sufficiency.

authentic /ɔːˈθentɪk/ *adjective* of undisputed origin, genuine; trustworthy. □ **authentically** *adverb*; **authenticity** /-ˈtɪs-/ *noun*.

authenticate /ɔːˈθentɪkeɪt/ *verb* (**-ting**) establish as true, genuine, or valid. □ **authentication** *noun*.

author /ˈɔːθə/ *noun* (*feminine* **authoress** /ˈɔːθrɪs/) writer of book etc.; originator. □ **authorship** *noun*.

authoritarian /ɔːθɒrɪˈteərɪən/ ● *adjective* favouring strict obedience to authority. ● *noun* authoritarian person.

authoritative /ɔːˈθɒrɪtətɪv/ *adjective* reliable, esp. having authority.

authority /ɔːˈθɒrɪtɪ/ *noun* (*plural* **-ies**) power or right to enforce obedience; (esp. in *plural*) body having this; delegated power; influence based on recognized knowledge or expertise; expert.

authorize /ˈɔːθəraɪz/ *verb* (also **-ise**) (**-zing** or **-sing**) (+ *to do*) give authority to (person); sanction officially. □ **Authorized Version** English translation (1611) of Bible. □ **authorization** *noun*.

autism /ˈɔːtɪz(ə)m/ *noun* condition characterized by self-absorption and withdrawal. □ **autistic** /-ˈtɪs-/ *adjective*.

auto- *combining form* self; one's own; of or by oneself or itself.

autobahn /ˈɔːtəʊbɑːn/ *noun* German, Austrian, or Swiss motorway. [German]

autobiography /ɔːtəʊbaɪˈɒgrəfɪ/ *noun* (*plural* **-ies**) story of one's own life. □ **autobiographer** *noun*; **autobiographical** /-əˈgræf-/ *adjective*.

autocracy /ɔːˈtɒkrəsɪ/ *noun* (*plural* **-ies**) absolute rule by one person.

autocrat /ˈɔːtəkræt/ *noun* absolute ruler. □ **autocratic** /-ˈkræt-/ *adjective*; **autocratically** /-ˈkræt-/ *adverb*.

autocross /ˈɔːtəʊkrɒs/ *noun* motor racing across country or on unmade roads.

autograph /ˈɔːtəgrɑːf/ ● *noun* signature, esp. of celebrity. ● *verb* write on or sign in one's own handwriting.

automate /ˈɔːtəmeɪt/ *verb* (**-ting**) convert to or operate by automation.

automatic /ɔːtəˈmætɪk/ ● *adjective* working by itself, without direct human involvement; done spontaneously; following inevitably; (of firearm) that can be loaded and fired continuously; (of vehicle or its transmission) using gears that change automatically. ● *noun* automatic firearm, vehicle, etc. □ **automatically** *adverb*.

automation *noun* use of automatic equipment in place of manual labour.

automaton /ɔːˈtɒmət(ə)n/ *noun* (*plural* **-mata** or **-s**) machine controlled automatically.

automobile /ˈɔːtəməbiːl/ *noun US* motor car.

automotive /ɔːtəˈməʊtɪv/ *adjective* of motor vehicles.

autonomous /ɔːˈtɒnəməs/ *adjective* self-governing; free to act independently. □ **autonomy** *noun*.

autopsy /ˈɔːtɒpsɪ/ *noun* (*plural* **-ies**) post-mortem.

auto-suggestion /ɔːtəʊsəˈdʒestʃ(ə)n/ *noun* hypnotic or subconscious suggestion made to oneself.

autumn /ˈɔːtəm/ *noun* season between summer and winter. □ **autumnal** /ɔːˈtʌmn(ə)l/ *adjective*.

auxiliary /ɔːgˈzɪljərɪ/ ● *adjective* giving help; additional, subsidiary. ● *noun* (*plural* **-ies**) auxiliary person or thing; (in *plural*) foreign or allied troops in service of nation at war; auxiliary verb. □ **auxiliary verb** one used with another verb to form tenses etc. (see panel).

avail /əˈveɪl/ ● *verb* (often + *to*) be of use; help; (**avail oneself of**) use, profit by. ● *noun* use, profit.

available *adjective* at one's disposal; (of person) free, able to be contacted. □ **availability** *noun*.

avalanche /ˈævəlɑːntʃ/ *noun* mass of snow and ice rapidly sliding down mountain; sudden abundance.

avant-garde /ævɑ̃ˈgɑːd/ ● *noun* innovators, esp. in the arts. ● *adjective* new, pioneering.

avarice /ˈævərɪs/ *noun* greed for wealth. □ **avaricious** /-ˈrɪʃ-/ *adjective*.

avatar /ˈævətɑː/ *noun Hindu Mythology* descent of god to earth in bodily form.

avenge /əˈvendʒ/ *verb* (**-ging**) inflict retribution on behalf of; exact retribution for.

avenue /ˈævənjuː/ *noun* road or path, usually tree-lined; way of approach.

aver /əˈvɜː/ *verb* (**-rr-**) *formal* assert, affirm.

average /ˈævərɪdʒ/ ● *noun* usual amount, extent, or rate; number obtained by dividing sum of given numbers by how many there are. ● *adjective* usual, ordinary; mediocre; constituting average. ● *verb* (**-ging**) amount on average to; do on average; estimate average of. □ **average out (at)** result in average (of); **on average** as an average rate etc.

averse /əˈvɜːs/ *adjective* (usually + *to*) opposed, disinclined.

aversion /əˈvɜːʃ(ə)n/ *noun* (usually + *to*, *for*) dislike, unwillingness; object of this.

avert /əˈvɜːt/ *verb* prevent; (often + *from*) turn away.

aviary /ˈeɪvɪərɪ/ *noun* (*plural* **-ies**) large cage or building for keeping birds.

aviation /eɪvɪˈeɪʃ(ə)n/ *noun* the flying of aircraft.

aviator /ˈeɪvɪeɪtə/ *noun* person who flies aircraft.

avid /ˈævɪd/ *adjective* eager; greedy. □ **avidity** /-ˈvɪd-/ *noun*; **avidly** *adverb*.

avocado /ævəˈkɑːdəʊ/ *noun* (*plural* **-s**) (in full *avocado pear*) dark green pear-shaped fruit with creamy flesh.

avocet /ˈævəset/ *noun* wading bird with long upturned bill.

avoid /əˈvɔɪd/ *verb* keep away or refrain from; escape; evade. □ **avoidable** *adjective*; **avoidance** *noun*.

avoirdupois /ævədəˈpɔɪz/ *noun* system of weights based on pound of 16 ounces.

avow /əˈvaʊ/ *verb formal* declare; confess. □ **avowal** *noun*; **avowedly** /əˈvaʊɪdlɪ/ *adverb*.

avuncular /əˈvʌŋkjʊlə/ *adjective* of or like an uncle.

await /əˈweɪt/ *verb* wait for; be in store for.

awake /əˈweɪk/ ● *verb* (**-king**; *past* **awoke**; *past participle* **awoken**) (also **awaken**) rouse from sleep; cease to sleep; (often + *to*) become alert, aware, or active. ● *adjective* not asleep; alert.

award /əˈwɔːd/ ● *verb* give or order to be given as payment, penalty, or prize. ● *noun* thing awarded; judicial decision.

aware /əˈweə/ *adjective* (often + *of*, *that*) conscious, having knowledge. □ **awareness** *noun*.

awash /əˈwɒʃ/ *adjective* at surface of and just covered by water; (+ *with*) abounding.

away ● *adverb* to or at distance; into non-existence; constantly, persistently. ● *adjective* (of match etc.) played on opponent's ground.

awe /ɔː/ ● *noun* reverential fear or wonder. ● *verb* (**awing**) inspire with awe. □ **awe-inspiring** awesome, magnificent.

aweigh /əˈweɪ/ *adjective* (of anchor) just lifted from sea bottom.

awesome *adjective* inspiring awe.

awful /ˈɔːfʊl/ *adjective colloquial* very bad; very great; *poetical* inspiring awe.

awfully *adverb colloquial* badly; very.

awhile /əˈwaɪl/ *adverb* for a short time.

awkward /ˈɔːkwəd/ *adjective* difficult to use; clumsy; embarrassing, embarrassed; hard to deal with.

awl /ɔːl/ *noun* small tool for pricking holes, esp. in leather.

awning /ˈɔːnɪŋ/ *noun* fabric roof, shelter.

awoke *past of* AWAKE.

awoken *past participle of* AWAKE.

AWOL /ˈeɪwɒl/ *abbreviation colloquial* absent without leave.

awry /əˈraɪ/ ● *adverb* crookedly; amiss. ● *adjective* crooked; unsound.

axe /æks/ ● *noun* (*US* **ax**) chopping-tool with heavy blade; (**the axe**) dismissal (of employees), abandonment of project etc. ● *verb* (**axing**) cut (staff, services, etc.); abandon (project).

axial /ˈæksɪəl/ *adjective* of, forming, or placed round axis.

axiom /ˈæksɪəm/ *noun* established principle; self-evident truth. □ **axiomatic** /-ˈmæt-/ *adjective*.

axis /ˈæksɪs/ *noun* (*plural* **axes** /-siːz/) imaginary line about which object rotates; line dividing regular figure symmetrically; reference line for measurement of coordinates etc.

axle /ˈæks(ə)l/ *noun* spindle on which wheel turns or is fixed.

ayatollah /aɪəˈtɒlə/ *noun* religious leader in Iran.

aye /aɪ/ ● *adverb archaic or dialect* yes. ● *noun* affirmative answer or vote.

azalea /əˈzeɪlɪə/ *noun* kind of rhododendron.

azimuth /ˈæzɪməθ/ *noun* angular distance between point below star etc. and north or south. □ **azimuthal** *adjective*.

azure /ˈæʒə/ *adjective & noun* sky-blue.

Auxiliary verb

An auxiliary verb is used in front of another verb to alter its meaning. Mainly, it expresses:

1 when something happens, by forming a tense of the main verb, e.g. *I* shall *go. He* was *going*.

2 permission, obligation, or ability to do something, e.g. *They* may *go. You* must *go. I* can't *go*.

3 the likelihood of something happening, e.g. *I* might *go. She* would *go if she could*.

The principal auxiliary verbs are:

be	*have*	*must*	*will*
can	*let*	*ought*	*would*
could	*may*	*shall*	
do	*might*	*should*	

Bb

B *abbreviation* black (pencil lead).
b. *abbreviation* born.
BA *abbreviation* Bachelor of Arts.
baa /bɑː/ *noun & verb* (**baas**, **baaed** or **baa'd**) bleat.
babble /'bæb(ə)l/ ● *verb* (**-ling**) talk, chatter, or say incoherently or excessively; (of stream) murmur; repeat foolishly. ● *noun* babbling; murmur of water etc.
babe *noun* baby.
babel /'beɪb(ə)l/ *noun* confused noise, esp. of voices.
baboon /bə'buːn/ *noun* large kind of monkey.
baby /'beɪbɪ/ *noun* (*plural* **-ies**) very young child; childish person; youngest member of family etc.; very young animal; small specimen. □ **baby boom** *colloquial* temporary increase in birth rate; **baby grand** small grand piano.
babysit *verb* (**-tt-**; *past & past participle* **-sat**) look after child while parents are out. □ **babysitter** *noun*.
baccarat /'bækərɑː/ *noun* gambling card game.
bachelor /'bætʃələ/ *noun* unmarried man; person with a university first degree.
bacillus /bə'sɪləs/ *noun* (*plural* **bacilli** /-laɪ/) rod-shaped bacterium. □ **bacillary** *adjective*.
back ● *noun* rear surface of human body from shoulders to hips; upper surface of animal's body; spine; reverse or more distant part; part of garment covering back; defensive player in football etc. ● *adverb* to rear; away from front; in(to) the past or an earlier or normal position or condition; in return; at a distance. ● *verb* help with money or moral support; (often + *up*) (cause to) go backwards; bet on; provide with or serve as back, support, or backing to; *Music* accompany. ● *adjective* situated to rear; past, not current; reversed. □ **backache** ache in back; **backbencher** MP without senior office; **backbiting** malicious talk; **back boiler** one behind domestic fire etc.; **backbone** spine, main support, firmness of character; **backchat** *colloquial* verbal insolence; **backcloth** painted cloth at back of stage; **backdate** make retrospectively valid, put earlier date to; **back door** secret or ingenious means; **back down** withdraw from confrontation; **backdrop** backcloth; **backfire** (of engine or vehicle) undergo premature explosion in cylinder or exhaust pipe, (of plan etc.) have opposite of intended effect; **backhand** *Tennis etc.* (stroke) made with hand across body; **backhanded** indirect, ambiguous; **backhander** *slang* bribe; **backlash** violent, usually hostile, reaction; **backlog** arrears (of work etc.); **back number** old issue of magazine etc.; **back out** (often + *of*) withdraw; **backpack** rucksack; **back-pedal** reverse previous action or opinion; **back room** place where (esp. secret) work goes on; **back seat** less prominent or important position; **backside** *colloquial* buttocks; **backslide** return to bad ways; **backstage** behind the scenes; **backstreet** *noun* side-street, alley, *adjective* illicit, illegal; **backstroke** stroke made by swimmer lying on back; **back to front** with back and front reversed; **backtrack** retrace one's steps, reverse one's policy or opinion; **back up** give (esp. moral) support to, *Computing* make backup of; **backup** support, *Computing* (making of) spare copy of data; **backwash** receding waves, repercussions; **backwater** peaceful, secluded, or dull place, stagnant water fed from stream; **backwoods** remote uncleared forest land.
backgammon /'bækgæmən/ *noun* board game with pieces moved according to throw of dice.
background /'bækgraʊnd/ *noun* back part of scene etc.; inconspicuous position; person's education, social circumstances, etc.; explanatory information etc.
backing *noun* help or support; material used for thing's back or support; musical accompaniment.
backward *adjective* directed backwards; slow in learning; shy.
backwards *adverb* away from one's front; back foremost; in reverse of usual way; into worse state; into past; back towards starting point □ **bend over backwards** *colloquial* make every effort.
bacon /'beɪkən/ *noun* cured meat from back and sides of pig.
bacteriology /bæktɪərɪ'ɒlədʒɪ/ *noun* study of bacteria.
bacterium /bæk'tɪərɪəm/ *noun* (*plural* **-ria**) single-celled micro-organism. □ **bacterial** *adjective*.

■ **Usage** It is a mistake to use the plural form *bacteria* when only one bacterium is meant.

bad *adjective* (**worse**, **worst**) inadequate, defective; unpleasant; harmful; decayed; ill, injured; regretful, guilty; serious, severe; wicked; naughty; incorrect, not valid. □ **bad debt** debt that is not recoverable; **bad-tempered** irritable.
bade *archaic past* of BID.
badge *noun* small flat emblem worn as sign of office, membership, etc. or bearing slogan etc.
badger /'bædʒə/ ● *noun* nocturnal burrowing mammal with black and white striped head. ● *verb* pester.
badinage /'bædɪnɑːʒ/ *noun* banter. [French]
badly *adverb* (**worse**, **worst**) in bad manner; severely; very much.
badminton /'bædmɪnt(ə)n/ *noun* game played with rackets and shuttlecock.
baffle /'bæf(ə)l/ ● *verb* perplex; frustrate. ● *noun* device that hinders flow of fluid or sound. □ **bafflement** *noun*.
bag ● *noun* soft open-topped receptacle; piece of luggage; (in *plural*; usually + *of*) *colloquial* large amount; animal's sac; amount of game shot by one person. ● *verb* secure, take possession of; bulge, hang loosely; put in bag; shoot (game).
bagatelle /bægə'tel/ *noun* game in which small balls are struck into holes on inclined board; mere trifle.
bagel /'beɪg(ə)l/ *noun* ring-shaped bread roll.
baggage /'bægɪdʒ/ *noun* luggage; portable equipment of army.
baggy *adjective* (**-ier, -iest**) hanging loosely.
bagpipes /'bægpaɪps/ *plural noun* musical instrument with windbag for pumping air through reeded pipes.
baguette /bæ'get/ *noun* long thin French loaf.
bail[1] ● *noun* security given for released prisoner's return for trial; person(s) pledging this. ● *verb* (usually + *out*) give bail for and secure release of (prisoner).
bail[2] *noun Cricket* either of two crosspieces resting on stumps.
bail[3] *verb* (also **bale**) (usually + *out*) scoop (water) out of (boat etc.). □ **bail out** = BALE OUT.
bailey /'beɪlɪ/ *noun* (*plural* **-s**) outer wall of castle; court enclosed by this.

bailiff /ˈbeɪlɪf/ *noun* sheriff's officer who executes writs, performs distraints, etc.; landlord's agent or steward.

bailiwick /ˈbeɪlɪwɪk/ *noun* district of bailiff.

bairn /beən/ *noun Scottish & Northern English* child.

bait ● *noun* food to entice prey; allurement. ● *verb* torment (chained animal); harass (person); put bait on or in (fish-hook, trap, etc.).

baize /beɪz/ *noun* usually green felted woollen fabric used for coverings etc.

bake *verb* (**-king**) cook or become cooked by dry heat esp. in oven; *colloquial* be very hot; harden by heat. □ **baking powder** mixture used as raising agent.

Bakelite /ˈbeɪkəlaɪt/ *noun proprietary term* kind of plastic.

baker /ˈbeɪkə/ *noun* professional bread-maker. □ **baker's dozen** thirteen.

bakery /ˈbeɪkərɪ/ *noun* (*plural* **-ies**) place where bread is made or sold.

baksheesh /ˈbækʃiːʃ/ *noun* gratuity, tip.

Balaclava /bæləˈklɑːvə/ *noun* (in full **Balaclava helmet**) woollen covering for head and neck.

balalaika /bæləˈlaɪkə/ *noun* Russian triangular-bodied guitar-like musical instrument.

balance /ˈbæləns/ ● *noun* even distribution of weight or amount, stability of body or mind; weighing apparatus; counteracting weight or force; regulating device in clock etc.; decisive weight or amount; difference between credits and debits; remainder. ● *verb* (**-cing**) bring or come into or keep in equilibrium; offset, compare; equal, neutralize; (usually as **balanced** *adjective*) make well-proportioned and harmonious; equalize debits and credits of account, have debits and credits equal. □ **balance of payments** difference between payments into and out of a country; **balance of power** position in which no country etc. predominates, power held by small group when larger groups are of (almost) equal strength; **balance of trade** difference between exports and imports; **balance sheet** statement giving balance of account; **on balance** all things considered.

balcony /ˈbælkənɪ/ *noun* (*plural* **-ies**) outside balustraded or railed platform with access from upper floor; upper tier of seats in theatre etc.

bald /bɔːld/ *adjective* lacking some or all hair on scalp; without fur, feathers, etc.; with surface worn away; direct. □ **baldly** *adverb*; **baldness** *noun*.

balderdash /ˈbɔːldədæʃ/ *noun* nonsense.

balding /ˈbɔːldɪŋ/ *adjective* becoming bald.

bale[1] ● *noun* bundle of merchandise or hay. ● *verb* (**-ling**) make up into bales. □ **bale out** (also **bail out**) make emergency parachute jump from aircraft.

bale[2] = BAIL[3].

baleful /ˈbeɪlfʊl/ *adjective* menacing; destructive; malignant.

balk = BAULK.

ball[1] /bɔːl/ *noun* spherical object or mass; usually spherical object used in game; rounded part of foot or hand at base of big toe or thumb; cannon ball; delivery or pass of ball in game. □ **ball-bearing** bearing using ring of small balls between its two parts, one such ball; **ballcock** valve operated by floating ball that controls level of water in cistern; **ball game** *US* baseball game, *colloquial* affair or matter; **ballpoint** (**pen**) pen with tiny ball as writing point.

ball[2] /bɔːl/ *noun* formal social gathering for dancing; *slang* enjoyable time.

ballad /ˈbæləd/ *noun* poem or song narrating popular story; slow sentimental song. □ **balladry** *noun*.

ballast /ˈbæləst/ ● *noun* heavy material stabilizing ship, controlling height of balloon, etc.; coarse stone etc. as bed of road or railway. ● *verb* provide with ballast.

ballerina /bæləˈriːnə/ *noun* female ballet dancer.

ballet /ˈbæleɪ/ *noun* dramatic or representational style of dancing to music; piece or performance of ballet. □ **ballet dancer** dancer of ballet. □ **balletic** /bəˈletɪk/ *adjective*.

ballistic /bəˈlɪstɪk/ *adjective* of projectiles. □ **ballistic missile** one that is powered and guided but falls by gravity.

ballistics *plural noun* (usually treated as *singular*) science of projectiles and firearms.

balloon /bəˈluːn/ ● *noun* small inflatable rubber toy or decoration; large inflatable flying bag, esp. one with basket below for passengers; outline containing words or thoughts in strip cartoon. ● *verb* (cause to) swell out like balloon. □ **balloonist** *noun*.

ballot /ˈbælət/ ● *noun* voting in writing and usually secret; votes recorded in ballot. ● *verb* (**-t-**) hold ballot; vote by ballot; take ballot of (voters). □ **ballot box** container for **ballot papers**, slips for marking votes.

ballroom /ˈbɔːlrʊm/ *noun* large room for dancing. □ **ballroom dancing** formal social dancing for couples.

bally /ˈbælɪ/ *adjective & adverb slang mild form of* BLOODY.

ballyhoo /bælɪˈhuː/ *noun* loud noise, fuss; noisy publicity.

balm /bɑːm/ *noun* aromatic ointment; fragrant oil or resin exuded from some trees; thing that heals or soothes; aromatic herb.

balmy /ˈbɑːmɪ/ *adjective* (**-ier**, **-iest**) fragrant, mild, soothing; *slang* crazy.

balsa /ˈbɔːlsə/ *noun* lightweight tropical American wood used for making models.

balsam /ˈbɔːlsəm/ *noun* balm from trees; ointment; tree yielding balsam; any of several flowering plants.

baluster /ˈbæləstə/ *noun* short pillar supporting rail.

balustrade /bæləˈstreɪd/ *noun* railing supported by balusters, esp. on balcony.

bamboo /bæmˈbuː/ *noun* tropical giant woody grass; its hollow stem.

bamboozle /bæmˈbuːz(ə)l/ *verb* (**-ling**) *colloquial* cheat; mystify.

ban ● *verb* (**-nn-**) prohibit, esp. formally. ● *noun* formal prohibition.

banal /bəˈnɑːl/ *adjective* commonplace, trite. □ **banality** /-ˈnæl-/ *noun* (*plural* **-ies**).

banana /bəˈnɑːnə/ *noun* long curved yellow tropical fruit; treelike plant bearing it.

band ● *noun* flat strip or loop of thin material; stripe; group of musicians; organized group of criminals etc.; range of values, esp. frequencies or wavelengths. ● *verb* (usually + *together*) unite; put band on; mark with stripes. □ **bandbox** hatbox; **bandmaster** conductor of band; **bandsman** player in band; **bandstand** outdoor platform for musicians.

bandage /ˈbændɪdʒ/ ● *noun* strip of material for binding wound etc. ● *verb* (**-ging**) bind with bandage.

bandanna /bænˈdænə/ *noun* large patterned handkerchief.

bandeau /ˈbændəʊ/ *noun* (*plural* **-x** /-z/) narrow headband.

bandit /ˈbændɪt/ *noun* robber, esp. of travellers. □ **banditry** *noun*.

bandolier /bændəˈlɪə/ *noun* (also **bandoleer**) shoulder belt with loops or pockets for cartridges.

bandwagon *noun* □ **climb**, **jump on the bandwagon** join popular or successful cause.

bandy[1] /ˈbændɪ/ *adjective* (**-ier**, **-iest**) (of legs) curved wide apart at knees. □ **bandy-legged** *adjective*.

bandy[2] /ˈbændɪ/ *verb* (**-ies**, **-ied**) (often + *about*) pass (story etc.) to and fro, discuss disparagingly; (often + *with*) exchange (blows, insults, etc.).

bane *noun* cause of ruin or trouble.

bang ● *noun* loud short sound; sharp blow. ● *verb* strike or shut noisily; (cause to) make bang. ● *adverb* with bang; *colloquial* exactly. □ **bang on** *colloquial* exactly right.

banger *noun* firework making bang; *slang* sausage, noisy old car.

bangle /ˈbæŋg(ə)l/ *noun* rigid bracelet or anklet.

banian = BANYAN.

banish /ˈbænɪʃ/ *verb* condemn to exile; dismiss from one's mind. □ **banishment** *noun*.

banister /ˈbænɪstə/ *noun* (also **bannister**) (usually in *plural*) uprights and handrail beside staircase.

banjo /ˈbændʒəʊ/ *noun* (*plural* **-s** or **-es**) round-bodied guitar-like musical instrument. □ **banjoist** *noun*.

bank[1] ● *noun* sloping ground on each side of river; raised shelf of ground, esp. in sea; mass of cloud etc. ● *verb* (often + *up*) heap or rise into banks; pack (fire) tightly for slow burning; (cause to) travel round curve with one side higher than the other.

bank[2] ● *noun* establishment, usually a public company, where money is deposited, withdrawn, and borrowed; pool of money in gambling game; storage place. ● *verb* deposit (money) at bank; (often + *at*, *with*) keep money (at bank). □ **bank card** cheque card; **bank holiday** public holiday when banks are closed; **banknote** piece of paper money; **bank on** *colloquial* rely on.

bank[3] *noun* row (of lights, switches, organ keys, etc.).

banker *noun* owner or manager of bank; keeper of bank in gambling game. □ **banker's card** cheque card.

bankrupt /ˈbæŋkrʌpt/ ● *adjective* insolvent; (often + *of*) drained (of emotion etc.). ● *noun* insolvent person. ● *verb* make bankrupt. □ **bankruptcy** *noun* (*plural* **-ies**).

banner /ˈbænə/ *noun* large portable cloth sign bearing slogan or design; flag.

bannister = BANISTER.

bannock /ˈbænək/ *noun Scottish & Northern English* round flat loaf, usually unleavened.

banns *plural noun* announcement of intended marriage read in church.

banquet /ˈbæŋkwɪt/ ● *noun* sumptuous esp. formal dinner. ● *verb* (**-t-**) give banquet for; attend banquet.

banquette /bæŋˈket/ *noun* upholstered bench along wall.

banshee /bænˈʃiː/ *noun* female spirit whose wail warns of death in a house.

bantam /ˈbæntəm/ *noun* kind of small domestic fowl; small but aggressive person. □ **bantamweight** boxing weight (51–54 kg).

banter /ˈbæntə/ ● *noun* good-humoured teasing. ● *verb* tease; exchange banter.

banyan /ˈbænjən/ *noun* (also **banian**) Indian fig tree with self-rooting branches.

baobab /ˈbeɪəʊbæb/ *noun* African tree with massive trunk and edible fruit.

bap *noun* soft flattish bread roll.

baptism /ˈbæptɪz(ə)m/ *noun* symbolic admission to Christian Church, with immersing in or sprinkling with water and usually name-giving. □ **baptismal** /-ˈtɪz-/ *adjective*.

Baptist /ˈbæptɪst/ *noun* member of Church practising adult baptism by immersion.

baptize /bæpˈtaɪz/ *verb* (also **-ise**) (**-zing** or **-sing**) administer baptism to; give name to.

bar[1] ● *noun* long piece of rigid material, esp. used to confine or obstruct; (often + *of*) oblong piece (of chocolate, soap, etc.); band of colour or light; counter for serving alcoholic drinks etc., room or building containing it; counter for particular service; barrier; prisoner's enclosure in law court; section of music between vertical lines; heating element of electric fire; strip below clasp of medal as extra distinction; (**the Bar**) barristers, their profession. ● *verb* (**-rr-**) fasten with bar; (usually + *in*, *out*) keep in or out; obstruct, prevent; (usually + *from*) exclude. ● *preposition* except. □ **bar code** machine-readable striped code on packaging etc.; **barmaid**, **barman**, **bartender** woman, man, person serving in pub etc.

bar[2] *noun* unit of atmospheric pressure.

barathea /bærəˈθiːə/ *noun* fine wool cloth.

barb ● *noun* backward-facing point on arrow, fish-hook, etc.; hurtful remark. ● *verb* fit with barb. □ **barbed wire** wire with spikes, used for fences.

barbarian /bɑːˈbeərɪən/ ● *noun* uncultured or primitive person. ● *adjective* uncultured; primitive.

barbaric /bɑːˈbærɪk/ *adjective* uncultured; cruel; primitive.

barbarism /ˈbɑːbərɪz(ə)m/ *noun* barbaric state or act; non-standard word or expression.

barbarity /bɑːˈbærɪtɪ/ *noun* (*plural* **-ies**) savage cruelty; barbaric act.

barbarous /ˈbɑːbərəs/ *adjective* uncultured; cruel.

barbecue /ˈbɑːbɪkjuː/ ● *noun* meal cooked over charcoal etc. out of doors; party for this; grill etc. used for this. ● *verb* (**-cues**, **-cued**, **-cuing**) cook on barbecue.

barber /ˈbɑːbə/ *noun* person who cuts men's hair.

barbican /ˈbɑːbɪkən/ *noun* outer defence, esp. double tower over gate or bridge.

barbiturate /bɑːˈbɪtjʊrət/ *noun* sedative derived from **barbituric acid** /bɑːbɪˈtjʊərɪk/, an organic acid.

bard *noun* poet; *historical* Celtic minstrel; prizewinner at Eisteddfod. □ **bardic** *adjective*.

bare /beə/ ● *adjective* unclothed, uncovered; leafless; unadorned, plain; scanty, just sufficient. ● *verb* (**-ring**) uncover, reveal. □ **bareback** without saddle; **barefaced** shameless, impudent; **barefoot** with bare feet; **bareheaded** without hat.

barely *adverb* scarcely; scantily.

bargain /ˈbɑːgɪn/ ● *noun* agreement on terms of sale etc.; cheap thing. ● *verb* discuss terms of sale etc. □ **bargain for** be prepared for; **into the bargain** moreover.

barge /bɑːdʒ/ ● *noun* large flat-bottomed cargo boat on canal or river; long ornamental pleasure boat. ● *verb* (**-ging**) (+ *into*) collide with. □ **barge in** interrupt.

bargee /bɑːˈdʒiː/ *noun* person in charge of barge.

baritone /ˈbærɪtəʊn/ *noun* adult male singing voice between tenor and bass; singer with this.

barium /ˈbeərɪəm/ *noun* white metallic element. □ **barium meal** mixture swallowed to reveal digestive tract on X-ray.

bark[1] ● *noun* sharp explosive cry of dog etc. ● *verb* give a bark; speak or utter sharply or brusquely.

bark[2] ● *noun* tough outer layer of tree. ● *verb* graze (shin etc.); strip bark from.

barker *noun* tout at auction or sideshow.

barley /ˈbɑːlɪ/ *noun* cereal used as food and in spirits; (also **barleycorn**) its grain. □ **barley sugar** hard sweet made from sugar; **barley water** drink made from boiled barley.

barm *noun* froth on fermenting malt liquor.

bar mitzvah /bɑː ˈmɪtsvə/ *noun* religious initiation of Jewish boy at 13.

barmy /ˈbɑːmɪ/ *adjective* (**-ier**, **-iest**) *slang* crazy.

barn *noun* building for storing grain etc. □ **barn dance** social gathering for country dancing; **barn owl** kind of owl frequenting barns.

barnacle /ˈbɑːnək(ə)l/ *noun* small shellfish clinging to rocks, ships' bottoms, etc. ☐ **barnacle goose** kind of Arctic goose.
barney /ˈbɑːnɪ/ *noun* (*plural* **-s**) *colloquial* noisy quarrel.
barometer /bəˈrɒmɪtə/ *noun* instrument measuring atmospheric pressure. ☐ **barometric** /bærəˈmetrɪk/ *adjective*.
baron /ˈbærən/ *noun* member of lowest order of British or foreign nobility; powerful businessman etc. ☐ **baronial** /bəˈrəʊnɪəl/ *adjective*.
baroness /ˈbærənɪs/ *noun* woman holding rank of baron; baron's wife or widow.
baronet /ˈbærənɪt/ *noun* member of lowest British hereditary titled order. ☐ **baronetcy** *noun* (*plural* **-ies**).
barony /ˈbærənɪ/ *noun* (*plural* **-ies**) rank or domain of baron.
baroque /bəˈrɒk/ ● *adjective* (esp. of 17th- & 18th-c. European architecture and music) ornate and extravagant in style. ● *noun* baroque style.
barque /bɑːk/ *noun* kind of sailing ship.
barrack[1] /ˈbærək/ *noun* (usually in *plural*, often treated as *singular*) housing for soldiers; large bleak building.
barrack[2] /ˈbærək/ *verb* shout or jeer (at).
barracuda /bærəˈkuːdə/ *noun* (*plural* same or **-s**) large voracious tropical sea fish.
barrage /ˈbærɑːʒ/ *noun* concentrated artillery bombardment; rapid succession of questions etc.; artificial barrier in river etc.
barrel /ˈbær(ə)l/ ● *noun* cylindrical usually convex container; contents or capacity of this; tube forming part of thing, esp. gun or pen. ● *verb* (**-ll-**; *US* **-l-**) put in barrels. ☐ **barrel organ** musical instrument with rotating pin-studded cylinder.
barren /ˈbærən/ *adjective* (**-er, -est**) unable to bear young; unable to produce fruit or vegetation; unprofitable; dull. ☐ **barrenness** *noun*.
barricade /bærɪˈkeɪd/ ● *noun* barrier, esp. improvised. ● *verb* (**-ding**) block or defend with this.
barrier /ˈbærɪə/ *noun* fence etc. barring advance or access; obstacle to communication etc. ☐ **barrier cream** protective skin cream; **barrier reef** coral reef separated from land by channel.
barrister /ˈbærɪstə/ *noun* advocate practising in higher courts.
barrow[1] /ˈbærəʊ/ *noun* two-wheeled handcart; wheelbarrow.
barrow[2] /ˈbærəʊ/ *noun* ancient grave mound.
Bart. *abbreviation* Baronet.
barter /ˈbɑːtə/ ● *verb* exchange goods, rights, etc., without using money. ● *noun* trade by bartering.
basal /ˈbeɪs(ə)l/ *adjective* of, at, or forming base.
basalt /ˈbæsɔːlt/ *noun* dark volcanic rock. ☐ **basaltic** /bəˈsɔːltɪk/ *adjective*.
base[1] ● *noun* what a thing rests or depends on, foundation; principle; starting point; headquarters; main ingredient; number in terms of which other numbers are expressed; substance combining with acid to form salt. ● *verb* (**-sing**) (usually + *on*, *upon*) found, establish; station. ☐ **base rate** interest rate set by Bank of England and used as basis for other banks' rates.
base[2] *adjective* cowardly; despicable; menial; (of coin) alloyed; (of metal) low in value.
baseball *noun* game played esp. in US with bat and ball and circuit of 4 bases.
baseless *adjective* unfounded, groundless.
basement /ˈbeɪsmənt/ *noun* floor below ground level.
bases *plural* of BASE[1], BASIS.
bash ● *verb* strike bluntly or heavily; (often + *up*) *colloquial* attack violently. ● *noun* heavy blow; *slang* attempt, party.
bashful /ˈbæʃfʊl/ *adjective* shy; diffident.
BASIC /ˈbeɪsɪk/ *noun* computer programming language using familiar English words.
basic /ˈbeɪsɪk/ ● *adjective* serving as base; fundamental; simplest, lowest in level. ● *noun* (usually in *plural*) fundamental fact or principle. ☐ **basically** *adverb*.
basil /ˈbæz(ə)l/ *noun* aromatic herb.
basilica /bəˈzɪlɪkə/ *noun* ancient Roman hall with apse and colonnades; similar church.
basilisk /ˈbæzɪlɪsk/ *noun* mythical reptile with lethal breath and look; American crested lizard.
basin /ˈbeɪs(ə)n/ *noun* round vessel for liquids or preparing food in; washbasin; hollow depression; sheltered mooring area; round valley; area drained by river.
basis /ˈbeɪsɪs/ *noun* (*plural* **bases** /-siːz/) foundation; main ingredient or principle; starting point for discussion etc.
bask /bɑːsk/ *verb* relax in warmth and light; (+ *in*) revel in.
basket /ˈbɑːskɪt/ *noun* container made of woven canes, wire, etc.; amount held by this. ☐ **basketball** team game in which goals are scored by putting ball through high nets; **basketry**, **basketwork** art of weaving cane etc., work so produced.
bas-relief /ˈbæsrɪliːf/ *noun* carving or sculpture projecting slightly from background.
bass[1] /beɪs/ ● *noun* lowest adult male voice; singer with this; *colloquial* double bass, bass guitar; low-frequency sound of radio, record player, etc. ● *adjective* lowest in pitch; deep-sounding. ☐ **bass guitar** electric guitar playing low notes. ☐ **bassist** *noun*.
bass[2] /bæs/ *noun* (*plural* same or **-es**) common perch; other fish of perch family.
basset /ˈbæsɪt/ *noun* (in full **basset-hound**) short-legged hunting dog.
bassoon /bəˈsuːn/ *noun* bass instrument of oboe family. ☐ **bassoonist** *noun*.
bast /bæst/ *noun* fibre from inner bark of tree, esp. lime.
bastard /ˈbɑːstəd/ *often offensive* ● *noun* person born of parents not married to each other; *slang* person regarded with dislike or pity, difficult or awkward thing. ● *adjective* illegitimate by birth; hybrid. ☐ **bastardy** *noun*.
bastardize /ˈbɑːstədaɪz/ *verb* (also **-ise**) (**-zing** or **-sing**) corrupt, debase; declare illegitimate.
baste[1] /beɪst/ *verb* (**-ting**) moisten (roasting meat etc.) with fat etc.; beat, thrash.
baste[2] /beɪst/ *verb* (**-ting**) sew with long loose stitches, tack.
bastinado /bæstɪˈneɪdəʊ/ ● *noun* caning on soles of feet. ● *verb* (**-es, -ed**) punish with this.
bastion /ˈbæstɪən/ *noun* projecting part of fortification; thing regarded as protection.
bat[1] ● *noun* implement with handle for hitting ball in games; turn at using this; batsman. ● *verb* (**-tt-**) use bat; hit (as) with bat; take one's turn at batting. ☐ **batsman** person who bats, esp. at cricket.
bat[2] *noun* mouselike nocturnal flying mammal. ☐ **bats** *slang* crazy.
bat[3] *verb* (**-tt-**) ☐ **not bat an eyelid** *colloquial* show no reaction.
batch ● *noun* group, collection, set; loaves baked at one time. ● *verb* arrange in batches.
bated /ˈbeɪtɪd/ *adjective* ☐ **with bated breath** anxiously.
Bath /bɑːθ/ *noun* ☐ **Bath bun** round spiced bun with currants; **Bath chair** invalid's wheelchair.
bath /bɑːθ/ ● *noun* (*plural* **-s** /bɑːðz/) container for sitting in and washing the body; its contents; act of

washing in it; (usually in *plural*) building for swimming or bathing. ● *verb* wash in bath. □ **bath cube** cube of **bath salts**, substance for scenting and softening bath water; **bathroom** room with bath, *US* room with lavatory.

bathe /beɪð/ ● *verb* (**-thing**) immerse oneself in water etc., esp. to swim or wash; immerse in or treat with liquid; (of sunlight etc.) envelop. ● *noun* swim. □ **bathing costume** garment worn for swimming.

bathos /ˈbeɪθɒs/ *noun* lapse from sublime to trivial; anticlimax. □ **bathetic** /bəˈθetɪk/ *adjective*.

bathyscaphe /ˈbæθɪskæf/, **bathysphere** /-sfɪə/ *nouns* vessel for deep-sea diving.

batik /bəˈtiːk/ *noun* method of dyeing textiles by waxing parts to be left uncoloured.

batiste /bæˈtiːst/ *noun* fine cotton or linen fabric.

batman /ˈbætmən/ *noun* army officer's servant.

baton /ˈbæt(ə)n/ *noun* thin stick for conducting orchestra etc.; short stick carried in relay race; stick carried by drum major; staff of office.

batrachian /bəˈtreɪkɪən/ ● *noun* amphibian that discards gills and tail, esp. frog or toad. ● *adjective* of batrachians.

battalion /bəˈtæljən/ *noun* army unit usually of 300–1000 men.

batten[1] /ˈbæt(ə)n/ ● *noun* long narrow piece of squared timber; strip for securing tarpaulin over ship's hatchway. ● *verb* strengthen or (often + *down*) fasten with battens.

batten[2] /ˈbæt(ə)n/ *verb* (often + *on*) thrive at the expense of.

batter /ˈbætə/ ● *verb* strike hard and repeatedly; (esp. as **battered** *adjective*) subject to long-term violence. ● *noun* mixture of flour and eggs beaten up with liquid for cooking. □ **battering ram** *historical* swinging beam for breaching walls.

battery /ˈbætərɪ/ *noun* (*plural* **-ies**) portable container of cell or cells for supplying electricity; series of cages etc. for poultry or cattle; set of connected or similar instruments etc.; emplacement for heavy guns; *Law* physical violence inflicted on person.

battle /ˈbæt(ə)l/ ● *noun* prolonged fight, esp. between armed forces; contest. ● *verb* (**-ling**) (often + *with*, *for*) struggle. □ **battleaxe** medieval weapon, *colloquial* domineering middle-aged woman; **battle-cruiser** *historical* heavy-gunned ship of higher speed and lighter armour than battleship; **battledress** soldier's everyday uniform; **battlefield** scene of battle; **battleship** most heavily armed and armoured warship.

battlement /ˈbæt(ə)lmənt/ *noun* (usually in *plural*) parapet with gaps at intervals at top of wall.

batty /ˈbætɪ/ *adjective* (**-ier**, **-iest**) *slang* crazy.

batwing *adjective* (esp. of sleeve) shaped like a bat's wing.

bauble /ˈbɔːb(ə)l/ *noun* showy trinket.

baulk /bɔːlk/ (also **balk**) ● *verb* (often + *at*) jib, hesitate; thwart, hinder, disappoint. ● *noun* hindrance; stumbling block.

bauxite /ˈbɔːksaɪt/ *noun* claylike mineral, chief source of aluminium.

bawdy /ˈbɔːdɪ/ ● *adjective* (**-ier**, **-iest**) humorously indecent. ● *noun* bawdy talk or writing. □ **bawdy house** brothel.

bawl *verb* shout or weep noisily. □ **bawl out** *colloquial* reprimand severely.

bay[1] *noun* broad curving inlet of sea.

bay[2] *noun* laurel with deep green leaves; (in *plural*) victor's or poet's bay wreath, fame. □ **bay leaf** leaf of bay tree, used for flavouring.

bay[3] *noun* recess; alcove in wall; compartment; allotted area. □ **bay window** window projecting from line of wall.

bay[4] ● *adjective* reddish-brown (esp. of horse). ● *noun* bay horse.

bay[5] ● *verb* bark loudly. ● *noun* bark of large dog, esp. chorus of pursuing hounds. □ **at bay** unable to escape; **keep at bay** ward off.

bayonet /ˈbeɪənet/ ● *noun* stabbing-blade attachable to rifle. ● *verb* (**-t-**) stab with bayonet. □ **bayonet fitting** connecting-part engaged by pushing and twisting.

bazaar /bəˈzɑː/ *noun* oriental market; sale of goods, esp. for charity.

bazooka /bəˈzuːkə/ *noun* anti-tank rocket launcher.

BBC *abbreviation* British Broadcasting Corporation.

BC *abbreviation* before Christ; British Columbia.

BCG *abbreviation* Bacillus Calmette-Guérin, an anti-tuberculosis vaccine.

be /biː/ ● *verb* (*present singular 1st* **am**, *2nd* **are** /ɑː/, *3rd* **is** /ɪz/, *plural* **are** /ɑː/; *past singular 1st* **was** /wɒz/, *2nd* **were** /wɜː/, *3rd* **was** /wɒz/, *plural* **were** /wɜː/; *present participle* **being**; *past participle* **been**) exist, live; occur; remain, continue; have specified identity, state, or quality. ● *auxiliary verb with past participle to form passive, with present participle to form continuous tenses, with infinitive to express duty, intention, possibility, etc.* □ **be-all and end-all** *colloquial* whole being, essence.

beach ● *noun* sandy or pebbly shore of sea, lake, etc. ● *verb* run or haul (boat etc.) on shore. □ **beachcomber** person who searches beaches for articles of value; **beachhead** fortified position set up on beach by landing forces.

beacon /ˈbiːkən/ *noun* signal-fire on hill or pole; signal; signal-station; Belisha beacon.

bead ● *noun* small ball of glass, stone, etc. pierced for threading with others; drop of liquid; small knob in front sight of gun. ● *verb* adorn with bead(s) or beading.

beading *noun* moulding like series of beads.

beadle /ˈbiːd(ə)l/ *noun* ceremonial officer of church, college, etc.

beady *adjective* (**-ier**, **-iest**) (of eyes) small and bright. □ **beady-eyed** with beady eyes, observant.

beagle /ˈbiːg(ə)l/ *noun* small hound used for hunting hares.

beak *noun* bird's horny projecting jaws; *slang* hooked nose; *historical* prow of warship; spout.

beaker /ˈbiːkə/ *noun* tall cup for drinking; lipped glass vessel for scientific experiments.

beam ● *noun* long piece of squared timber or metal used in house-building etc.; ray of light or radiation; bright smile; series of radio or radar signals as guide to ship or aircraft; crossbar of balance; (in *plural*) horizontal cross-timbers of ship. ● *verb* emit (light, radio waves, etc.); shine; smile radiantly. □ **off beam** *colloquial* mistaken.

bean *noun* climbing plant with kidney-shaped seeds in long pods; seed of this or of coffee or other plant. □ **beanbag** small bag filled with dried beans and used as ball, large bag filled with polystyrene pieces and used as seat; **bean sprout** sprout of bean seed as food; **full of beans** *colloquial* lively, exuberant; **not a bean** *slang* no money.

beano /ˈbiːnəʊ/ *noun* (*plural* **-s**) *slang* party, celebration.

bear[1] /beə/ *verb* (*past* **bore**; *past participle* **borne** or **born**) carry; show; produce, yield (fruit); give birth to; sustain; endure, tolerate.

bear[2] /beə/ *noun* heavy thick-furred mammal; rough surly person; person who sells shares for future delivery in hope of buying them more cheaply before then. □ **beargarden** noisy or rowdy scene; **bear-hug** powerful embrace; **bearskin** guardsman's tall furry cap.

bearable *adjective* endurable.

beard /bɪəd/ ● *noun* facial hair on chin etc.; part on animal (esp. goat) resembling beard. ● *verb* oppose, defy. □ **bearded** *adjective.*

bearer *noun* carrier of message, cheque, etc.; carrier of coffin, equipment, etc.

bearing *noun* outward behaviour, posture; (usually + *on*, *upon*) relation, relevance; part of machine supporting rotating part; direction relative to fixed point; (in *plural*) relative position; heraldic device or design.

beast *noun* animal, esp. wild mammal; brutal person; *colloquial* disliked person or thing.

beastly *adjective* (**-ier**, **-iest**) like a beast; *colloquial* unpleasant.

beat ● *verb* (*past* **beat**; *past participle* **beaten**) strike repeatedly or persistently; inflict blows on; overcome, surpass; exhaust, perplex; (often + *up*) whisk (eggs etc.) vigorously; (often + *out*) shape (metal etc.) by blows; pulsate; mark (time of music) with baton, foot, etc.; move or cause (wings) to move up and down. ● *noun* main accent in music or verse; strongly marked rhythm of popular music etc.; stroke on drum; movement of conductor's baton; throbbing; police officer's appointed course; one's habitual round. ● *adjective slang* exhausted, tired out. □ **beat about the bush** not come to the point; **beat down** cause (seller) to lower price by bargaining, (of sun, rain, etc.) shine or fall relentlessly; **beat it** *slang* go away; **beat up** beat with punches and kicks; **beat-up** *colloquial* dilapidated.

beater *noun* whisk; implement for beating carpet; person who rouses game at a shoot.

beatific /bi:əˈtɪfɪk/ *adjective* making blessed; *colloquial* blissful.

beatify /bi:ˈætɪfaɪ/ *verb* (**-ies**, **-ied**) *RC Church* declare to be blessed as first step to canonization; make happy. □ **beatification** *noun.*

beatitude /bi:ˈætɪtju:d/ *noun* blessedness; (in *plural*) blessings in Matthew 5: 3–11.

beau /bəʊ/ *noun* (*plural* **-x** /-z/) boyfriend; dandy.

Beaufort scale /ˈbəʊfət/ *noun* scale of wind speeds.

Beaujolais /ˈbəʊʒəleɪ/ *noun* red or white wine from Beaujolais district of France.

beauteous /ˈbju:tɪəs/ *adjective poetical* beautiful.

beautician /bju:ˈtɪʃ(ə)n/ *noun* specialist in beauty treatment.

beautiful /ˈbju:tɪfʊl/ *adjective* having beauty; *colloquial* excellent. □ **beautifully** *adverb.*

beautify /ˈbju:tɪfaɪ/ *verb* (**-ies**, **-ied**) make beautiful, adorn. □ **beautification** *noun.*

beauty /ˈbju:tɪ/ *noun* (*plural* **-ies**) combination of qualities that delights the sight or other senses or the mind; person or thing having this. □ **beauty queen** woman judged most beautiful in contest; **beauty parlour**, **salon** establishment for cosmetic treatment; **beauty spot** beautiful locality.

beaver ● *noun* large amphibious broad-tailed rodent; its fur; hat of this; (**Beaver**) member of most junior branch of Scout Association. ● *verb colloquial* (usually + *away*) work hard.

becalm /bɪˈkɑ:m/ *verb* deprive (ship etc.) of wind.

became *past* of BECOME.

because /bɪˈkɒz/ *conjunction* for the reason that. □ **because of** by reason of.

beck[1] *noun* brook, mountain stream.

beck[2] *noun* □ **at (person's) beck and call** subject to his or her constant orders.

beckon /ˈbekən/ *verb* (often + *to*) summon by gesture; entice.

become /bɪˈkʌm/ *verb* (**-ming**; *past* **became**; *past participle* **become**) come to be, begin to be; suit, look well on. □ **become of** happen to.

becquerel /ˈbekərel/ *noun* SI unit of radioactivity.

bed ● *noun* place to sleep or rest, esp. piece of furniture for sleeping on; garden plot for plants; bottom of sea, river, etc.; flat base on which thing rests; stratum. ● *verb* (**-dd-**) (usually + *down*) put or go to bed; plant in bed; fix firmly; *colloquial* have sexual intercourse with. □ **bedclothes** sheets, blankets, etc.; **bedpan** pan for use as toilet by invalid in bed; **bedridden** confined to bed by infirmity; **bedrock** solid rock under alluvial deposits etc., basic principles; **bedroom** room for sleeping in; **bedsitting room**, **bedsitter** combined bedroom and sitting-room; **bedsore** sore developed by lying in bed; **bedspread** cloth for covering bed; **bedstead** framework of bed; **bedtime** hour for going to bed.

bedaub /bɪˈdɔ:b/ *verb* smear with paint etc.

bedding *noun* mattress and bedclothes; litter for cattle etc. □ **bedding plant** annual flowering plant put in garden bed.

bedeck /bɪˈdek/ *verb* adorn, decorate.

bedevil /bɪˈdev(ə)l/ *verb* (**-ll-**; *US* **-l-**) torment, confuse, trouble. □ **bedevilment** *noun.*

bedlam /ˈbedləm/ *noun* scene of confusion or uproar.

Bedouin /ˈbedʊɪn/ *noun* (*plural* same) nomadic Arab of the desert.

bedraggled /bɪˈdræg(ə)ld/ *adjective* dishevelled, untidy.

bee *noun* 4-winged stinging insect, collecting nectar and pollen and producing wax and honey; busy worker; meeting for combined work or amusement. □ **beehive** hive; **beeline** straight line between two places; **beeswax** wax secreted by bees for honeycomb.

Beeb *noun* (**the Beeb**) *colloquial* the BBC.

beech *noun* smooth-barked glossy-leaved tree; its wood. □ **beechmast** fruit of beech.

beef ● *noun* meat of ox, bull, or cow; (*plural* **beeves** or *US* **-s**) beef animal; (*plural* **-s**) *slang* protest. ● *verb slang* complain. □ **beefburger** hamburger; **beefeater** warder in Tower of London; **beefsteak** thick slice of beef for grilling or frying; **beef tea** stewed beef extract for invalids; **beef tomato** large tomato.

beefy *adjective* (**-ier**, **-iest**) like beef; solid, muscular.

been *past participle* of BE.

beep ● *noun* short high-pitched sound. ● *verb* emit beep.

beer /bɪə/ *noun* alcoholic liquor made from fermented malt etc. flavoured esp. with hops. □ **beer garden** garden where beer is sold and drunk; **beer mat** small mat for beer glass.

beery *adjective* (**-ier**, **-iest**) showing influence of beer; like beer.

beeswing /ˈbi:zwɪŋ/ *noun* filmy crust on old port wine etc.

beet *noun* plant with succulent root used for salads etc. and sugar-making (see BEETROOT, SUGAR BEET).

beetle[1] /ˈbi:t(ə)l/ ● *noun* insect with hard protective outer wings. ● *verb* (**-ling**) *colloquial* (+ *about*, *off*, etc.) hurry, scurry.

beetle[2] /ˈbi:t(ə)l/ ● *adjective* projecting, shaggy, scowling. ● *verb* (usually as **beetling** *adjective*) overhang.

beetle[3] /ˈbi:t(ə)l/ *noun* heavy-headed tool for ramming, crushing, etc.

beetroot *noun* beet with dark red root used as vegetable.

befall /bɪˈfɔ:l/ *verb* (*past* **befell**; *past participle* **befallen**) *poetical* happen; happen to.

befit /bɪˈfɪt/ *verb* (**-tt-**) be appropriate for.
befog /bɪˈfɒg/ *verb* (**-gg-**) obscure; envelop in fog.
before /bɪˈfɔː/ ● *conjunction* sooner than; rather than. ● *preposition* earlier than; in front of, ahead of; in presence of. ● *adverb* ahead, in front; previously, already; in the past.
beforehand *adverb* in anticipation, in readiness, before time.
befriend /bɪˈfrend/ *verb* act as friend to; help.
befuddle /bɪˈfʌd(ə)l/ *verb* (**-ling**) make drunk; confuse.
beg *verb* (**-gg-**) ask for as gift; ask earnestly, entreat; live by begging; ask formally. □ **beg the question** assume truth of thing to be proved; **go begging** be unwanted.

■ **Usage** The expression *beg the question* is often used incorrectly to mean 'to invite the obvious question (that ...)'.

began *past* of BEGIN.
begat *archaic past* of BEGET.
beget /bɪˈget/ *verb* (**-tt-**; *past* **begot**, *archaic* **begat**; *past participle* **begotten**) *literary* be the father of; give rise to.
beggar /ˈbegə/ ● *noun* person who begs or lives by begging; *colloquial* person. ● *verb* make poor; be too extraordinary for (belief, description, etc.).
beggarly *adjective* mean; poor, needy.
begin /bɪˈgɪn/ *verb* (**-nn-**; *past* **began**; *past participle* **begun**) perform first part of; come into being; (often + *to do*) start, take first step, (usually in negative) *colloquial* show any likelihood, be sufficient.
beginner *noun* learner.
beginning *noun* time at which thing begins; source, origin; first part.
begone /bɪˈgɒn/ *interjection poetical* go away at once!
begonia /bɪˈgəʊnɪə/ *noun* plant with ornamental foliage and bright flowers.
begot *past* of BEGET.
begotten *past participle* of BEGET.
begrudge /bɪˈgrʌdʒ/ *verb* (**-ging**) grudge; feel or show resentment at or envy of; be dissatisfied at.
beguile /bɪˈgaɪl/ *verb* (**-ling**) charm, divert; delude, cheat. □ **beguilement** *noun*.
beguine /bɪˈgiːn/ *noun* W. Indian dance.
begum /ˈbeɪgəm/ *noun* (in India, Pakistan, and Bangladesh) Muslim woman of high rank; (**Begum**) *title of married Muslim woman*.
begun *past participle* of BEGIN.
behalf /bɪˈhɑːf/ *noun* □ **on behalf of, on (person's) behalf** in the interests of, as representative of.
behave /bɪˈheɪv/ *verb* (**-ving**) react or act in specified way; (often **behave oneself**) conduct oneself properly; work well (or in specified way).
behaviour /bɪˈheɪvjə/ *noun* (*US* **behavior**) manners, conduct, way of behaving. □ **behavioural** *adjective*.
behaviourism *noun* (*US* **behaviorism**) study of human actions by analysis of stimulus and response. □ **behaviourist** *noun*.
behead /bɪˈhed/ *verb* cut head from (person); execute thus.
beheld *past & past participle* of BEHOLD.
behest /bɪˈhest/ *noun literary* command, request.
behind /bɪˈhaɪnd/ ● *preposition* in or to rear of; hidden by, on farther side of; in past in relation to; inferior to; in support of. ● *adverb* in or to rear; on far side; remaining after others' departure; (usually + *with*) in arrears. ● *noun colloquial* buttocks. □ **behindhand** in arrears, behind time, too late; **behind time** unpunctual; **behind the times** old-fashioned, antiquated.
behold /bɪˈhəʊld/ *verb* (*past & past participle* **beheld**) *literary* look at; take notice, observe.
beholden /bɪˈhəʊld(ə)n/ *adjective* (usually + *to*) under obligation.
behove /bɪˈhəʊv/ *verb* (**-ving**) *formal* be incumbent on; befit.
beige /beɪʒ/ ● *noun* pale sandy fawn colour. ● *adjective* of this colour.
being /ˈbiːɪŋ/ *noun* existence; constitution, nature; existing person etc.
belabour /bɪˈleɪbə/ *verb* (*US* **belabor**) attack physically or verbally.
belated /bɪˈleɪtɪd/ *adjective* coming (too) late. □ **belatedly** *adverb*.
bel canto /bel ˈkæntəʊ/ *noun* singing marked by full rich tone.
belch ● *verb* emit wind from stomach through mouth; (of volcano, gun, etc.) emit (fire, smoke, etc.). ● *noun* act of belching.
beleaguer /bɪˈliːgə/ *verb* besiege; vex; harass.
belfry /ˈbelfrɪ/ *noun* (*plural* **-ies**) bell tower; space for bells in church tower.
belie /bɪˈlaɪ/ *verb* (**belying**) give false impression of; fail to confirm, fulfil, or justify.
belief /bɪˈliːf/ *noun* act of believing; what one believes; trust, confidence; acceptance as true.
believe /bɪˈliːv/ *verb* (**-ving**) accept as true; think; (+ *in*) have faith or confidence in; trust word of; have religious faith. □ **believable** *adjective*; **believer** *noun*.
Belisha beacon /bəˈliːʃə/ *noun* flashing orange ball on striped post, marking pedestrian crossing.
belittle /bɪˈlɪt(ə)l/ *verb* (**-ling**) disparage. □ **belittlement** *noun*.
bell *noun* hollow esp. cup-shaped metal body emitting musical sound when struck; sound of bell; bell-shaped thing. □ **bell-bottomed** (of trousers) widening below knee; **bell pull** cord pulled to sound bell; **bell push** button pressed to ring electric bell; **give (person) a bell** *colloquial* telephone him or her.
belladonna /beləˈdɒnə/ *noun* deadly nightshade; drug obtained from this.
belle /bel/ *noun* handsome woman; reigning beauty.
belles-lettres /bel ˈletr/ *plural noun* (also treated as *singular*) writings or studies of purely literary kind.
bellicose /ˈbelɪkəʊs/ *adjective* eager to fight.
belligerent /bɪˈlɪdʒərənt/ ● *adjective* engaged in war; given to constant fighting; pugnacious. ● *noun* belligerent person or nation. □ **belligerence** *noun*.
bellow /ˈbeləʊ/ ● *verb* emit deep loud roar. ● *noun* bellowing sound.
bellows /ˈbeləʊz/ *plural noun* (also treated as *singular*) device for driving air into fire, organ, etc.; expandable part of camera etc.
belly /ˈbelɪ/ ● *noun* (*plural* **-ies**) cavity of body containing stomach, bowels, etc.; stomach; front of body from waist to groin; underside of animal; cavity or bulging part of anything. ● *verb* (**-ies**, **-ied**) swell out. □ **bellyache** *noun colloquial* stomach pain, *verb slang* complain noisily or persistently; **belly button** *colloquial* navel; **belly dance** dance by woman (**belly dancer**) with voluptuous movements of belly; **belly laugh** loud unrestrained laugh.
bellyful *noun* enough to eat; *colloquial* more than one can tolerate.
belong /bɪˈlɒŋ/ *verb* (+ *to*) be property of, assigned to, or member of; fit socially; be rightly placed or classified.
belongings *plural noun* possessions, luggage.
beloved /bɪˈlʌvɪd/ ● *adjective* loved. ● *noun* beloved person.

below /bɪˈləʊ/ ● *preposition* under; lower than; less than; of lower rank or importance etc. than; unworthy of. ● *adverb* at or to lower point or level; further on in book etc.

belt ● *noun* strip of leather etc. worn round waist or across chest; continuous band in machinery; distinct strip of colour etc.; zone, district. ● *verb* put belt round; *slang* thrash; *slang* move rapidly. □ **below the belt** unfair(ly); **belt out** *slang* sing or play (music) loudly; **belt up** *slang* be quiet, *colloquial* put on seat belt; **tighten one's belt** economize; **under one's belt** securely acquired.

bemoan /bɪˈməʊn/ *verb* lament, complain about.

bemuse /bɪˈmjuːz/ *verb* (**-sing**) make (person) confused.

bench *noun* long seat of wood or stone; carpenter's or laboratory table; magistrate's or judge's seat; lawcourt. □ **benchmark** surveyor's mark at point in line of levels; standard, point of reference.

bend ● *verb* (*past & past participle* **bent** except in *bended knee*) force into curve or angle; be altered in this way; incline from vertical; bow, stoop; interpret or modify (rule) to suit oneself; (force to) submit. ● *noun* bending, curve; bent part of thing; (**the bends**) *colloquial* symptoms due to too rapid decompression under water. □ **round the bend** *colloquial* crazy, insane.

bender *noun slang* wild drinking spree.

beneath /bɪˈniːθ/ ● *preposition* below, under; unworthy of. ● *adverb* below, underneath.

Benedictine /benɪˈdɪktɪn/ ● *noun* monk or nun of Order of St Benedict; /-tiːn/ *proprietary term* kind of liqueur. ● *adjective* of St Benedict or his order.

benediction /benɪˈdɪkʃ(ə)n/ *noun* utterance of blessing. □ **benedictory** *adjective*.

benefaction /benɪˈfækʃ(ə)n/ *noun* charitable gift; doing good.

benefactor /ˈbenɪfæktə/ *noun* (*feminine* **benefactress**) person who has given financial or other help.

benefice /ˈbenɪfɪs/ *noun* living from a church office.

beneficent /bɪˈnefɪsənt/ *adjective* doing good; actively kind. □ **beneficence** *noun*.

beneficial /benɪˈfɪʃ(ə)l/ *adjective* advantageous. □ **beneficially** *adverb*.

beneficiary /benɪˈfɪʃərɪ/ *noun* (*plural* **-ies**) receiver of benefits; holder of church living.

benefit /ˈbenɪfɪt/ ● *noun* advantage, profit; payment made under insurance or social security; performance or game etc. of which proceeds go to particular player or charity. ● *verb* (**-t-**; *US* **-tt-**) do good to; receive benefit. □ **benefit of the doubt** assumption of innocence rather than guilt.

benevolent /bɪˈnevələnt/ *adjective* wishing to do good; charitable; kind and helpful. □ **benevolence** *noun*.

Bengali /beŋˈgɔːlɪ/ ● *noun* (*plural* **-s**) native or language of Bengal. ● *adjective* of Bengal.

benighted /bɪˈnaɪtɪd/ *adjective* intellectually or morally ignorant.

benign /bɪˈnaɪn/ *adjective* kindly, gentle; favourable; salutary; *Medicine* mild, not malignant. □ **benignity** /bɪˈnɪgnɪtɪ/ *noun*.

benignant /bɪˈnɪgnənt/ *adjective* kindly; beneficial. □ **benignancy** *noun*.

bent ● *past & past participle* of BEND. ● *adjective* curved or having angle; *slang* dishonest, illicit; (+ *on*) set on doing or having. ● *noun* inclination, bias; (+ *for*) talent for.

benumb /bɪˈnʌm/ *verb* make numb; deaden; paralyse.

benzene /ˈbenziːn/ *noun* chemical got from coal tar and used as solvent.

benzine /ˈbenziːn/ *noun* spirit obtained from petroleum and used as cleaning agent.

benzoin /ˈbenzəʊɪn/ *noun* fragrant resin of E. Asian tree. □ **benzoic** /-ˈzəʊɪk/ *adjective*.

bequeath /bɪˈkwiːð/ *verb* leave by will; transmit to posterity.

bequest /bɪˈkwest/ *noun* bequeathing; thing bequeathed.

berate /bɪˈreɪt/ *verb* (**-ting**) scold.

bereave /bɪˈriːv/ *verb* (**-ving**) (esp. as **bereaved** *adjective*) (often + *of*) deprive of relative, friend, etc., esp. by death. □ **bereavement** *noun*.

bereft /bɪˈreft/ *adjective* (+ *of*) deprived of.

beret /ˈbereɪ/ *noun* round flat brimless cap of felt etc.

berg *noun* iceberg.

bergamot /ˈbɜːgəmɒt/ *noun* perfume from fruit of a dwarf orange tree; an aromatic herb.

beriberi /berɪˈberɪ/ *noun* nervous disease caused by deficiency of vitamin B'.

Bermuda shorts /bəˈmjuːdə/ *plural noun* close-fitting knee-length shorts.

berry /ˈberɪ/ *noun* (*plural* **-ies**) any small round juicy stoneless fruit.

berserk /bəˈzɜːk/ *adjective* (esp. after *go*) wild, frenzied.

berth ● *noun* sleeping place; ship's place at wharf; sea-room; *colloquial* situation, appointment. ● *verb* moor (ship) in berth; provide sleeping berth for.

beryl /ˈberɪl/ *noun* transparent (esp. green) precious stone; mineral species including this and emerald.

beryllium /bəˈrɪlɪəm/ *noun* hard white metallic element.

beseech /bɪˈsiːtʃ/ *verb* (*past & past participle* **besought** /-ˈsɔːt/ or **beseeched**) entreat; ask earnestly for.

beset /bɪˈset/ *verb* (**-tt-**; *past & past participle* **beset**) attack or harass persistently.

beside /bɪˈsaɪd/ *preposition* at side of, close to; compared with; irrelevant to. □ **beside oneself** frantic with anger or worry etc.

besides ● *preposition* in addition to; apart from. ● *adverb* also, as well.

besiege /bɪˈsiːdʒ/ *verb* (**-ging**) lay siege to; crowd round eagerly; assail with requests.

besmirch /bɪˈsmɜːtʃ/ *verb* soil, dishonour.

besom /ˈbiːz(ə)m/ *noun* broom made of twigs.

besotted /bɪˈsɒtɪd/ *adjective* infatuated; stupefied.

besought *past & past participle* of BESEECH.

bespatter /bɪˈspætə/ *verb* spatter all over; defame.

bespeak /bɪˈspiːk/ *verb* (*past* **bespoke**; *past participle* **bespoken**) engage beforehand; order (goods); be evidence of.

bespectacled /bɪˈspektək(ə)ld/ *adjective* wearing spectacles.

bespoke /bɪˈspəʊk/ *adjective* made to order.

best ● *adjective* (*superlative* of GOOD) most excellent. ● *adverb* (*superlative* of WELL[1]) in the best way; to greatest degree. ● *noun* that which is best. ● *verb colloquial* defeat, outwit. □ **best man** bridegroom's chief attendant at wedding; **best-seller** book with large sale, author of such book; **do one's best** do all one can.

bestial /ˈbestɪəl/ *adjective* brutish; of or like beasts. □ **bestiality** /-ˈæl-/ *noun*.

bestiary /ˈbestɪərɪ/ *noun* (*plural* **-ies**) medieval treatise on beasts.

bestir /bɪˈstɜː/ *verb* (**-rr-**) (**bestir oneself**) exert or rouse oneself.

bestow /bɪˈstəʊ/ *verb* (+ *on*, *upon*) confer as gift. □ **bestowal** *noun*.

bestrew /bɪˈstruː/ *verb* (*past participle* **bestrewed** or **bestrewn**) strew; lie scattered over.

bestride /bɪ'straɪd/ *verb* (**-ding**; *past* **bestrode**; *past participle* **bestridden**) sit astride on; stand astride over.

bet ● *verb* (**-tt-**; *past & past participle* **bet** or **betted**) risk one's money etc. against another's on result of event. ● *noun* such arrangement; sum of money bet.

beta /'bi:tə/ *noun* second letter of Greek alphabet (B, β). ▫ **beta-blocker** drug used to prevent unwanted stimulation of the heart in angina etc.; **beta particle** fast-moving electron emitted by radioactive substance.

betake /bɪ'teɪk/ *verb* (**-king**; *past* **betook**; *past participle* **betaken**) (**betake oneself**) go.

betatron /'bi:tətrɒn/ *noun* apparatus for accelerating electrons.

betel /'bi:t(ə)l/ *noun* leaf chewed with betel-nut. ▫ **betel-nut** seed of tropical palm.

bête noire /beɪt 'nwɑ:/ *noun* (*plural* ***bêtes noires*** same pronunciation) particularly disliked person or thing. [French]

bethink /bɪ'θɪŋk/ *verb* (*past & past participle* **bethought** /-'θɔ:t/) (**bethink oneself**) *formal* reflect, stop to think; be reminded.

betide /bɪ'taɪd/ *verb* ▫ **woe betide** (**person**) misfortune will befall him or her.

betimes /bɪ'taɪmz/ *adverb literary* in good time, early.

betoken /bɪ'təʊkən/ *verb* be sign of.

betook *past* of BETAKE.

betray /bɪ'treɪ/ *verb* be disloyal to (a person, one's country, etc.); give up or reveal treacherously; reveal involuntarily; be evidence of. ▫ **betrayal** *noun*.

betroth /bɪ'trəʊð/ *verb* (usually as **betrothed** *adjective*) bind with promise to marry. ▫ **betrothal** *noun*.

better /'betə/ ● *adjective* (*comparative* of GOOD) more excellent; partly or fully recovered from illness. ● *adverb* (*comparative* of WELL[1]) in better manner; to greater degree. ● *noun* better thing or person. ● *verb* improve (upon); surpass. ▫ **better off** in better (esp. financial) situation; **get the better of** defeat, outwit.

betterment *noun* improvement.

between /bɪ'twi:n/ ● *preposition* in or into space or interval; separating; shared by; to and from; taking one or other of. ● *adverb* (also **in between**) between two or more points, between two extremes.

bevel /'bev(ə)l/ ● *noun* slope from horizontal or vertical in carpentry etc.; sloping edge or surface; tool for marking angles. ● *verb* (**-ll-**; *US* **-l-**) impart bevel to, slant.

beverage /'bevərɪdʒ/ *noun formal* drink.

bevvy /'bevɪ/ *slang* ● *noun* (*plural* **-ies**) ● *verb* (**-ies, -ied**) drink.

bevy /'bevɪ/ *noun* (*plural* **-ies**) company, flock.

bewail /bɪ'weɪl/ *verb* wail over; mourn for.

beware /bɪ'weə/ *verb* (only in *imperative* or *infinitive*) take heed; (+ *of*) be cautious of.

bewilder /bɪ'wɪldə/ *verb* perplex, confuse. ▫ **bewilderment** *noun*.

bewitch /bɪ'wɪtʃ/ *verb* enchant, greatly delight; cast spell on.

beyond /bɪ'jɒnd/ ● *preposition* at or to further side of; outside the range or understanding of; more than. ● *adverb* at or to further side, further on. ● *noun* (**the beyond**) life after death. ▫ **back of beyond** very remote place.

bezel /'bez(ə)l/ *noun* sloped edge of chisel etc.; oblique face of cut gem; groove holding watch-glass or gem.

bezique /bɪ'zi:k/ *noun* card game for two.

biannual /baɪ'ænjʊəl/ *adjective* occurring etc. twice a year.

bias /'baɪəs/ ● *noun* predisposition, prejudice; distortion of statistical results; edge cut obliquely across weave of fabric; *Sport* bowl's curved course due to its lopsided form. ● *verb* (**-s-** or **-ss-**) give bias to; prejudice; (as **biased** *adjective*) influenced (usually unfairly). ▫ **bias binding** strip of fabric cut obliquely and used to bind edges.

biathlon /baɪ'æθlən/ *noun* athletic contest in skiing and shooting. ▫ **biathlete** *noun*.

bib *noun* cloth put under child's chin while eating; upper part of apron etc.

Bible /'baɪb(ə)l/ *noun* Christian scriptures; (**bible**) copy of these; (**bible**) *colloquial* any authoritative book. ▫ **biblical** /'bɪb-/ *adjective*.

bibliography /bɪblɪ'ɒgrəfɪ/ *noun* (*plural* **-ies**) list of books of any author, subject, etc.; history of books, their editions, etc. ▫ **bibliographer** *noun*; **bibliographical** /-ə'græf-/ *adjective*.

bibliophile /'bɪblɪəfaɪl/ *noun* collector of books, book-lover.

bibulous /'bɪbjʊləs/ *adjective* fond of or addicted to alcoholic drink.

bicameral /baɪ'kæmər(ə)l/ *adjective* having two legislative chambers.

bicarb /'baɪkɑ:b/ *noun colloquial* bicarbonate of soda.

bicarbonate /baɪ'kɑ:bənɪt/ *noun* any acid salt of carbonic acid; (in full **bicarbonate of soda**) compound used in cooking and as antacid.

bicentenary /baɪsen'ti:nərɪ/ *noun* (*plural* **-ies**) 200th anniversary.

bicentennial /baɪsen'tenɪəl/ ● *noun* bicentenary. ● *adjective* recurring every 200 years.

biceps /'baɪseps/ *noun* (*plural* same) muscle with double head or attachment, esp. that at front of upper arm.

bicker /'bɪkə/ *verb* quarrel, wrangle pettily.

bicuspid /baɪ'kʌspɪd/ ● *adjective* having two cusps. ● *noun* bicuspid premolar tooth.

bicycle /'baɪsɪk(ə)l/ ● *noun* two-wheeled pedal-driven vehicle. ● *verb* (**-ling**) ride bicycle.

bid ● *verb* (**-dd-**; *past* **bid**, *archaic* **bade** /bæd, beɪd/; *past participle* **bid**, *archaic* **bidden**) make offer; make bid; command, invite; *literary* utter (greeting, farewell) to; *Cards* state before play number of tricks intended. ● *noun* act of bidding; amount bid; *colloquial* attempt, effort.

biddable *adjective* obedient, docile.

bidding *noun* command, invitation.

bide *verb* (**-ding**) *archaic or dialect* stay, remain. ▫ **bide one's time** wait for good opportunity.

bidet /'bi:deɪ/ *noun* low basin that one can sit astride to wash crotch area.

biennial /baɪ'enɪəl/ ● *adjective* lasting 2 years; recurring every 2 years. ● *noun* plant that flowers, fruits, and dies in second year.

bier /bɪə/ *noun* movable stand on which coffin or corpse rests.

biff *slang* ● *noun* smart blow. ● *verb* strike.

bifid /'baɪfɪd/ *adjective* divided by cleft into two parts.

bifocal /baɪ'fəʊk(ə)l/ ● *adjective* (of spectacle lenses) with two parts of different focal lengths. ● *noun* (in *plural*) bifocal spectacles.

bifurcate /'baɪfəkeɪt/ *verb* (**-ting**) divide into two branches; fork. ▫ **bifurcation** *noun*.

big ● *adjective* (**-gg-**) large; important; grown-up; boastful; *colloquial* ambitious, generous; (usually + *with*) advanced in pregnancy. ● *adverb colloquial* in big manner; with great effect, impressively. ▫ **Big Apple** *US slang* New York City; **Big Brother** seemingly benevolent dictator; **big business** large-scale commerce; **big end** end of connecting rod in engine, encircling crank-pin; **big-head** *colloquial* conceited person; **big-headed** conceited; **big-hearted** generous; **big shot** *colloquial* important person; **big time** *slang* highest rank among entertainers; **big top** main tent at circus;

bigwig *colloquial* important person; **in a big way** *colloquial* with great enthusiasm. □ **biggish** *adjective*.

bigamy /ˈbɪgəmɪ/ *noun* (*plural* **-ies**) crime of making second marriage while first is still valid. □ **bigamist** *noun*; **bigamous** *adjective*.

bight /baɪt/ *noun* recess of coast, bay; loop of rope.

bigot /ˈbɪgət/ *noun* obstinate and intolerant adherent of creed or view. □ **bigoted** *adjective*; **bigotry** *noun*.

bijou /ˈbiːʒuː/ ● *noun* (*plural* **-x** same pronunciation) jewel, trinket. ● *adjective* (**bijou**) small and elegant. [French]

bike *colloquial* ● *noun* bicycle; motorcycle. ● *verb* (**-king**) ride a bike. □ **biker** *noun*.

bikini /bɪˈkiːnɪ/ *noun* (*plural* **-s**) woman's brief two-piece bathing suit.

bilateral /baɪˈlætər(ə)l/ *adjective* of, on, or with two sides; between two parties. □ **bilaterally** *adverb*.

bilberry /ˈbɪlbərɪ/ *noun* (*plural* **-ies**) N. European heathland shrub; its small dark blue edible berry.

bile *noun* bitter fluid secreted by liver to aid digestion; bad temper, peevishness.

bilge /bɪldʒ/ *noun* nearly flat part of ship's bottom; (in full **bilge-water**) foul water in bilge; *slang* nonsense, rubbish.

bilharzia /bɪlˈhɑːtsɪə/ *noun* disease caused by tropical parasitic flatworm.

biliary /ˈbɪlɪərɪ/ *adjective* of bile.

bilingual /baɪˈlɪŋgw(ə)l/ *adjective* of, in, or speaking two languages.

bilious /ˈbɪlɪəs/ *adjective* affected by disorder of the bile; bad-tempered.

bilk *verb slang* evade payment of, cheat.

bill[1] ● *noun* statement of charges for goods, work done, etc.; draft of proposed law; poster; programme of entertainment; *US* banknote. ● *verb* send statement of charges to; announce, put in programme; (+ *as*) advertise as. □ **bill of exchange** written order to pay sum on given date; **bill of fare** menu; **billposter**, **billsticker** person who pastes up advertisements on hoardings etc.

bill[2] ● *noun* beak (of bird); narrow promontory. ● *verb* (of doves etc.) stroke bill with bill. □ **bill and coo** exchange caresses.

bill[3] *noun historical* weapon with hook-shaped blade.

billabong /ˈbɪləbɒŋ/ *noun Australian* branch of river forming backwater.

billboard *noun* large outdoor board for advertisements.

billet[1] /ˈbɪlɪt/ ● *noun* place where soldier etc. is lodged; *colloquial* appointment, job. ● *verb* (**-t-**) quarter (soldiers etc.).

billet[2] /ˈbɪlɪt/ *noun* thick piece of firewood; small metal bar.

billet-doux /bɪlɪˈduː/ *noun* (*plural* **billets-doux** /-ˈduːz/) love letter.

billhook *noun* concave-edged pruning-instrument.

billiards /ˈbɪljədz/ *noun* game played with cues and 3 balls on cloth-covered table. □ **billiard ball**, **room**, **table**, etc., ones used for billiards.

billion /ˈbɪljən/ *noun* (*plural* same) thousand million; million million; (**billions**) *colloquial* very large number. □ **billionth** *adjective & noun*.

billow /ˈbɪləʊ/ ● *noun* wave; any large mass. ● *verb* rise or move in billows. □ **billowy** *adjective*.

billy[1] /ˈbɪlɪ/ *noun* (*plural* **-ies**) (in full **billycan**) *Australian* tin or enamel outdoor cooking pot.

billy[2] /ˈbɪlɪ/ *noun* (*plural* **-ies**) (in full **billy goat**) male goat.

bin *noun* large receptacle for rubbish or storage. □ **binliner** bag for lining rubbish bin; **binman** *colloquial* dustman.

binary /ˈbaɪnərɪ/ *adjective* of two parts, dual; of system using digits 0 and 1 to code information.

bind /baɪnd/ ● *verb* (*past & past participle* **bound** /baʊnd/) tie or fasten tightly; restrain; (cause to) cohere; compel, impose duty on; edge with braid etc.; fasten (pages of book) into cover. ● *noun colloquial* nuisance; restriction.

binder *noun* cover for loose papers; substance that binds things together; *historical* sheaf-binding machine; bookbinder.

bindery *noun* (*plural* **-ies**) bookbinder's workshop.

binding ● *noun* book cover; braid etc. for edging. ● *adjective* obligatory.

bindweed *noun* convolvulus.

binge /bɪndʒ/ *slang* ● *noun* bout of excessive eating, drinking, etc.; spree. ● *verb* (**-ging**) indulge in binge.

bingo /ˈbɪŋgəʊ/ *noun* gambling game in which each player marks off numbers on card as they are called.

binnacle /ˈbɪnək(ə)l/ *noun* case for ship's compass.

binocular /baɪˈnɒkjʊlə/ *adjective* for both eyes.

binoculars /bɪˈnɒkjʊləz/ *plural noun* instrument with lens for each eye, for viewing distant objects.

binomial /baɪˈnəʊmɪəl/ ● *noun* algebraic expression of sum or difference of two terms. ● *adjective* consisting of two terms.

bio- *combining form* biological; life.

biochemistry /baɪəʊˈkemɪstrɪ/ *noun* chemistry of living organisms. □ **biochemical** *adjective*; **biochemist** *noun*.

biodegradable /baɪəʊdɪˈgreɪdəb(ə)l/ *adjective* able to be decomposed by bacteria or other living organisms.

biography /baɪˈɒgrəfɪ/ *noun* (*plural* **-ies**) written life of person. □ **biographer** *noun*; **biographical** /-əˈgræf-/ *adjective*.

biological /baɪəˈlɒdʒɪk(ə)l/ *adjective* of biology; of living organisms. □ **biological warfare** use of bacteria etc. to spread disease among enemy. □ **biologically** *adverb*.

biology /baɪˈɒlədʒɪ/ *noun* study of living organisms. □ **biologist** *noun*.

bionic /baɪˈɒnɪk/ *adjective* having electronically operated body parts.

biorhythm /ˈbaɪəʊrɪð(ə)m/ *noun* biological cycle thought to affect person's physical or mental state.

biosphere /ˈbaɪəʊsfɪə/ *noun* earth's crust and atmosphere containing life.

bipartite /baɪˈpɑːtaɪt/ *adjective* of two parts; involving two parties.

biped /ˈbaɪped/ ● *noun* two-footed animal. ● *adjective* two-footed.

biplane /ˈbaɪpleɪn/ *noun* aeroplane with two pairs of wings, one above the other.

birch ● *noun* tree with thin peeling bark; bundle of birch twigs used for flogging. ● *verb* flog with birch.

bird *noun* feathered vertebrate with two wings and two feet; *slang* young woman. □ **a bird in the hand** something secured or certain; **birdlime** sticky stuff spread to catch birds; **bird of passage** migratory bird, person who travels habitually; **bird of prey** one hunting animals for food; **birdseed** seeds as food for caged birds; **bird's-eye view** general view from above; **birds of a feather** similar people; **bird table** platform on which food for wild birds is placed.

birdie /ˈbɜːdɪ/ *noun colloquial* little bird; *Golf* hole played in one under par.

biretta /bɪˈretə/ *noun* square cap of RC priest.

Biro /ˈbaɪərəʊ/ *noun* (*plural* **-s**) *proprietary term* kind of ballpoint pen.

birth *noun* emergence of young from mother's body; origin, beginning; ancestry; inherited position. □ **birth control** prevention of undesired pregnancy;

birthday anniversary of birth; **birthmark** unusual mark on body from birth; **birth rate** number of live births per thousand of population per year; **birthright** rights belonging to one by birth; **give birth to** produce (young).

biscuit /ˈbɪskɪt/ *noun* thin unleavened cake, usually crisp and sweet; fired unglazed pottery; light brown colour.

bisect /baɪˈsekt/ *verb* divide into two (usually equal) parts. □ **bisection** *noun*; **bisector** *noun*.

bisexual /baɪˈsekʃʊəl/ ● *adjective* feeling or involving sexual attraction to members of both sexes; hermaphrodite. ● *noun* bisexual person. □ **bisexuality** /-ˈæl-/ *noun*.

bishop /ˈbɪʃəp/ *noun* senior clergyman usually in charge of diocese; mitre-shaped chess piece.

bishopric /ˈbɪʃəprɪk/ *noun* office or diocese of bishop.

bismuth /ˈbɪzməθ/ *noun* reddish-white metallic element; compound of it used medicinally.

bison /ˈbaɪs(ə)n/ *noun* (*plural* same) wild ox.

bisque[1] /biːsk/ *noun* rich soup.

bisque[2] /bɪsk/ *noun* advantage of one free point or stroke in certain games.

bisque[3] /bɪsk/ *noun* fired unglazed pottery.

bistre /ˈbɪstə/ *noun* brown pigment made from soot.

bistro /ˈbiːstrəʊ/ *noun* (*plural* **-s**) small informal restaurant.

bit[1] *noun* small piece or amount; short time or distance; mouthpiece of bridle; cutting part of tool etc. □ **bit by bit** gradually.

bit[2] *past* of BITE.

bit[3] *noun Computing* unit of information expressed as choice between two possibilities.

bitch /bɪtʃ/ ● *noun* female dog, fox, or wolf; *offensive slang* spiteful woman. ● *verb colloquial* speak spitefully; grumble.

bitchy *adjective slang* spiteful. □ **bitchily** *adverb*; **bitchiness** *noun*.

bite ● *verb* (**-ting**; *past* **bit**; *past participle* **bitten**) nip or cut into or off with teeth; sting; penetrate, grip; accept bait; be harsh in effect, esp. intentionally. ● *noun* act of biting; wound so made; small amount to eat; pungency; incisiveness.

bitter /ˈbɪtə/ ● *adjective* having sharp pungent taste, not sweet; showing or feeling resentment; harsh, virulent; piercingly cold. ● *noun* bitter beer, strongly flavoured with hops; (in *plural*) liquor with bitter flavour, esp. of wormwood. □ **bitterly** *adverb*; **bitterness** *noun*.

bittern /ˈbɪt(ə)n/ *noun* wading bird of heron family.

bitty *adjective* (**-ier**, **-iest**) made up of bits.

bitumen /ˈbɪtjʊmɪn/ *noun* tarlike mixture of hydrocarbons derived from petroleum. □ **bituminous** /bɪˈtjuːmɪnəs/ *adjective*.

bivalve /ˈbaɪvælv/ ● *noun* aquatic mollusc with hinged double shell. ● *adjective* with such a shell.

bivouac /ˈbɪvʊæk/ ● *noun* temporary encampment without tents. ● *verb* (**-ck-**) make, or camp in, bivouac.

bizarre /bɪˈzɑː/ *adjective* strange in appearance or effect; grotesque.

blab *verb* (**-bb-**) talk or tell foolishly or indiscreetly.

black ● *adjective* colourless from absence or complete absorption of light; very dark-coloured; of human group with dark skin, esp. African; heavily overcast; angry, gloomy; sinister, wicked; declared untouchable by workers in dispute. ● *noun* black colour, paint, clothes, etc.; (player using) darker pieces in chess etc.; (of tea or coffee) without milk; member of dark-skinned race, esp. African. ● *verb* make black; declare (goods etc.) 'black'. □ **black and blue** badly bruised; **black and white** not in colour, comprising only opposite extremes, (after *in*) in print; **black art** black magic; **blackball** exclude from club, society, etc.; **black beetle** common cockroach; **black belt** (holder of) highest grade of proficiency in judo, karate, etc.; **black box** flight recorder; **black comedy** comedy presenting tragedy in comic terms; **black eye** bruised skin round eye; **blackfly** kind of aphid; **Black Forest gateau** chocolate sponge with cherries and whipped cream; **blackhead** black-topped pimple; **black hole** region of space from which matter and radiation cannot escape; **black ice** thin hard transparent ice; **blacklead** graphite; **blackleg** *derogatory* person refusing to join strike etc.; **black magic** magic supposed to invoke evil spirits; **Black Maria** *slang* police van; **black market** illicit traffic in rationed, prohibited, or scarce commodities; **Black Mass** travesty of Mass in worship of Satan; **black out** effect blackout on, undergo blackout; **blackout** temporary loss of consciousness or memory; loss of electric power, radio reception, etc.; compulsory darkness as precaution against air raids; **black pudding** sausage of blood, suet, etc.; **Black Rod** chief usher of House of Lords; **black sheep** disreputable member; **blackshirt** *historical* Fascist; **black spot** place of danger or trouble; **blackthorn** thorny shrub bearing white flowers and sloes; **black tie** man's formal evening dress; **black velvet** mixture of stout and champagne; **black widow** venomous spider of which female devours male; **in the black** in credit or surplus.

blackberry *noun* (*plural* **-ies**) dark edible fruit of bramble.

blackbird *noun* European songbird.

blackboard *noun* board for chalking on in classroom etc.

blackcurrant *noun* small black fruit; shrub on which it grows.

blacken *verb* make or become black; slander.

blackguard /ˈblægɑːd/ *noun* villain, scoundrel. □ **blackguardly** *adjective*.

blacking *noun* black polish for boots and shoes.

blacklist ● *noun* list of people etc. in disfavour. ● *verb* put on blacklist.

blackmail ● *noun* extortion of payment in return for silence; use of threats or pressure. ● *verb* extort money from (person) thus. □ **blackmailer** *noun*.

blacksmith *noun* smith working in iron.

bladder /ˈblædə/ *noun* sac in humans and other animals, esp. that holding urine.

blade *noun* cutting part of knife etc.; flat part of oar, spade, propeller, etc.; flat narrow leaf of grass and cereals; flat bone in shoulder.

blame ● *verb* (**-ming**) assign fault or responsibility to; (+ *on*) assign responsibility for (error etc.) to. ● *noun* responsibility for bad result; blaming, attributing of responsibility. □ **blameworthy** deserving blame. □ **blameless** *adjective*.

blanch /blɑːntʃ/ *verb* make or grow pale; peel (almonds etc.) by scalding; immerse briefly in boiling water; whiten (plant) by depriving it of light.

blancmange /bləˈmɒndʒ/ *noun* sweet opaque jelly of flavoured cornflour and milk.

bland *adjective* mild; insipid, tasteless; gentle, suave. □ **blandly** *adverb*.

blandishment /ˈblændɪʃmənt/ *noun* (usually in *plural*) flattering attention; cajolery.

blank ● *adjective* not written or printed on; (of form etc.) not filled in; (of space) empty; without interest, result, or expression. ● *noun* space to be filled up in form etc.; blank cartridge; empty surface; dash written in place of word. □ **blank cartridge** one without bullet; **blank cheque** one with amount left for payee to fill in; **blank verse** unrhymed verse, esp. iambic pentameters. □ **blankly** *adverb*.

blanket /ˈblæŋkɪt/ ● *noun* large esp. woollen sheet as bed-covering etc.; thick covering layer. ● *adjective* general, covering all cases or classes. ● *verb* (**-t-**) cover (as) with blanket. □ **blanket stitch** stitch used to finish edges of blanket etc.

blare ● *verb* (**-ring**) sound or utter loudly; make sound of trumpet. ● *noun* blaring sound.

blarney /ˈblɑːnɪ/ ● *noun* cajoling talk, flattery. ● *verb* (**-eys**, **-eyed**) flatter, use blarney.

blasé /ˈblɑːzeɪ/ *adjective* bored or indifferent, esp. through familiarity.

blaspheme /blæsˈfiːm/ *verb* (**-ming**) treat religious name or subject irreverently; talk irreverently about.

blasphemy /ˈblæsfəmɪ/ *noun* (*plural* **-ies**) (instance of) blaspheming. □ **blasphemous** *adjective*.

blast /blɑːst/ ● *noun* strong gust; explosion; destructive wave of air from this; loud note from wind instrument, car horn, whistle, etc.; *colloquial* severe reprimand. ● *verb* blow up with explosive; blight; (cause to) make explosive sound. ● *interjection* damn. □ **blast furnace** one for smelting with compressed hot air driven in; **blast off** (of rocket) take off from launching site; **blast-off** *noun*.

blasted *colloquial* ● *adjective* annoying. ● *adverb* extremely.

blatant /ˈbleɪt(ə)nt/ *adjective* flagrant, unashamed. □ **blatantly** *adverb*.

blather /ˈblæðə/ ● *noun* (also **blether** /ˈbleðə/) foolish talk. ● *verb* talk foolishly.

blaze[1] ● *noun* bright flame or fire; violent outburst of passion; bright display or light. ● *verb* (**-zing**) burn or shine brightly or fiercely; burn with excitement etc. □ **blaze away** shoot continuously.

blaze[2] ● *noun* white mark on face of horse or chipped in bark of tree. ● *verb* (**-zing**) mark (tree, path) with blaze(s).

blazer *noun* jacket without matching trousers, esp. lightweight and part of uniform.

blazon /ˈbleɪz(ə)n/ *verb* proclaim; describe or paint (coat of arms). □ **blazonry** *noun*.

bleach ● *verb* whiten in sunlight or by chemical process. ● *noun* bleaching substance or process.

bleak *adjective* exposed, windswept; dreary, grim.

bleary /ˈblɪərɪ/ *adjective* (**-ier**, **-iest**) dim-sighted, blurred. □ **bleary-eyed** having dim sight.

bleat ● *verb* utter cry of sheep, goat, etc.; speak plaintively. ● *noun* bleating cry.

bleed *verb* (*past & past participle* **bled**) emit blood; draw blood from; *colloquial* extort money from.

bleep ● *noun* intermittent high-pitched sound. ● *verb* make bleep; summon by bleep.

bleeper *noun* small electronic device alerting person to message by bleeping.

blemish /ˈblemɪʃ/ ● *noun* flaw, defect, stain. ● *verb* spoil, mark, stain.

blench *verb* flinch, quail.

blend ● *verb* mix (various sorts) into required sort; become one; mingle intimately. ● *noun* mixture.

blender *noun* machine for liquidizing or chopping food.

blenny /ˈblenɪ/ *noun* (*plural* **-ies**) spiny-finned sea fish.

bless *verb* ask God to look favourably on; consecrate; glorify (God); thank; make happy.

blessed /ˈblesɪd/ *adjective* holy; *euphemistic* cursed; *RC Church* beatified.

blessing *noun* invocation of divine favour; grace said at meals; benefit, advantage.

blether = BLATHER.

blew *past of* BLOW[1].

blight /blaɪt/ ● *noun* disease of plants caused esp. by insects; such insect; harmful or destructive force. ● *verb* affect with blight; destroy; spoil.

blighter *noun colloquial* annoying person.

blimey /ˈblaɪmɪ/ *interjection slang: expressing surprise.*

blimp *noun* small non-rigid airship; (also (**Colonel**) **Blimp**) reactionary person.

blind /blaɪnd/ ● *adjective* without sight; without adequate foresight, discernment, or information; (often + *to*) unwilling or unable to appreciate (a factor); not governed by purpose; reckless; concealed; closed at one end. ● *verb* deprive of sight or judgement; deceive. ● *noun* screen for window; thing used to hide truth; obstruction to sight or light. ● *adverb* blindly. □ **blind date** *colloquial* date between two people who have not met before; **blind man's buff** game in which blindfold player tries to catch others; **blind spot** spot on retina insensitive to light, area where vision or judgement fails; **blindworm** slow-worm. □ **blindly** *adverb*; **blindness** *noun*.

blindfold ● *verb* cover eyes of (person) with tied cloth etc. ● *noun* cloth etc. so used. ● *adjective & adverb* with eyes covered; without due care.

blink ● *verb* shut and open eyes quickly; (often + *back*) prevent (tears) by blinking; shine unsteadily, flicker. ● *noun* act of blinking; momentary gleam. □ **blink at** ignore, shirk; **on the blink** *slang* (of machine etc.) out of order.

blinker ● *noun* (usually in *plural*) either of screens on bridle preventing horse from seeing sideways. ● *verb* obscure with blinkers; (as **blinkered** *adjective*) prejudiced, narrow-minded.

blinking *adjective & adverb slang: expressing mild annoyance.*

blip *noun* minor deviation or error; quick popping sound; small image on radar screen.

bliss *noun* perfect joy; being in heaven. □ **blissful** *adjective*; **blissfully** *adverb*.

blister /ˈblɪstə/ ● *noun* small bubble on skin filled with watery fluid; any swelling resembling this. ● *verb* become covered with blisters; raise blister on.

blithe /blaɪð/ *adjective* cheerful, happy; carefree, casual. □ **blithely** *adverb*.

blithering /ˈblɪðərɪŋ/ *adjective colloquial* utter, hopeless; contemptible.

blitz /blɪts/ *colloquial* ● *noun* intensive (esp. aerial) attack. ● *verb* inflict blitz on.

blizzard /ˈblɪzəd/ *noun* severe snowstorm.

bloat *verb* inflate, swell.

bloater *noun* herring cured by salting and smoking.

blob *noun* small drop or spot.

bloc *noun* group of governments etc. sharing some common purpose.

block ● *noun* solid piece of hard material; large building, esp. when subdivided; group of buildings surrounded by streets; obstruction; large quantity as a unit; piece of wood or metal engraved for printing. ● *verb* obstruct; restrict use of; stop (cricket ball) with bat. □ **blockbuster** *slang* very successful film, book, etc.; **blockhead** stupid person; **block capitals**, **letters** separate capital letters; **block out** shut out (light, noise, view, etc.); **block up** shut in, fill (window etc.) in; **block vote** vote proportional in size to number of people voter represents; **mental block** mental inability due to subconscious factors.

blockade /blɒˈkeɪd/ ● *noun* surrounding or blocking of place by enemy. ● *verb* (**-ding**) subject to blockade.

blockage *noun* obstruction.

bloke *noun slang* man, fellow.

blond (of woman, usually **blonde**) ● *adjective* light-coloured, fair-haired. ● *noun* blond person.

blood /blʌd/ ● *noun* fluid, usually red, circulating in arteries and veins of animals; killing, bloodshed; passion, temperament; race, descent; relationship. ● *verb* give first taste of blood to (hound); initiate (person). □ **blood bank** store of blood for transfusion; **bloodbath** massacre; **blood count** number of corpuscles in blood; **blood-curdling** horrifying; **blood donor** giver of blood for transfusion; **blood group** any of types of human blood; **bloodhound** large keen-scented dog used for tracking; **blood-letting** surgical removal of blood; **blood orange** red-fleshed orange; **blood poisoning** diseased condition due to bacteria in blood; **blood pressure** pressure of blood in arteries; **blood relation** one related by birth; **bloodshed** killing; **bloodshot** (of eyeball) inflamed; **blood sport** one involving killing of animals; **bloodstream** circulating blood; **bloodsucker** leech, extortioner; **bloodthirsty** eager for bloodshed; **blood vessel** vein, artery, or capillary carrying blood.

bloodless *adjective* without blood or bloodshed; unemotional; pale.

bloody ● *adjective* (**-ier**, **-iest**) of or like blood; running or stained with blood; involving bloodshed, cruel; *coarse slang* annoying, very great. ● *adverb coarse slang* extremely. ● *verb* (**-ies**, **-ied**) stain with blood. □ **bloody-minded** *colloquial* deliberately uncooperative.

bloom /blu:m/ ● *noun* flower; flowering state; prime; freshness; fine powder on fruit etc. ● *verb* bear flowers; be in flower; flourish.

bloomer[1] *noun slang* blunder.

bloomer[2] *noun* long loaf with diagonal marks.

bloomers *plural noun colloquial* woman's long loose knickers.

blooming ● *adjective* flourishing, healthy; *slang* annoying, very great. ● *adverb slang* extremely.

blossom /'blɒsəm/ ● *noun* flower; mass of flowers on tree. ● *verb* open into flower; flourish.

blot ● *noun* spot of ink etc.; disgraceful act; blemish. ● *verb* (**-tt-**) make blot on; stain; dry with blotting paper. □ **blot out** obliterate, obscure; **blotting paper** absorbent paper for drying wet ink.

blotch *noun* inflamed patch on skin; irregular patch of colour. □ **blotchy** *adjective* (**-ier**, **-iest**).

blotter *noun* device holding blotting paper.

blouse /blaʊz/ *noun* woman's shirtlike garment; type of military jacket.

blow[1] /bləʊ/ ● *verb* (*past* **blew** /blu:/; *past participle* **blown**) send directed air-current esp. from mouth; drive or be driven by blowing; move as wind does; sound (wind instrument); (*past participle* **blowed**) *slang* curse, confound; clear (nose) by forceful breath; pant; make or shape by blowing; break or burst suddenly; (cause to) break electric circuit; *slang* squander. ● *noun* blowing; short spell in fresh air. □ **blow-dry** arrange (hair) while using hand-held dryer; **blowfly** bluebottle; **blow in** send inwards by explosion, *colloquial* arrive unexpectedly; **blowlamp** device with flame for plumbing, burning off paint, etc.; **blow out** extinguish by blowing, send outwards by explosion; **blow-out** *colloquial* burst tyre, *slang* large meal; **blow over** fade away; **blowpipe** tube for blowing through, esp. one from which dart or arrow is projected; **blowtorch** *US* blowlamp; **blow up** explode, *colloquial* rebuke strongly, inflate, *colloquial* enlarge (photograph); **blow-up** *colloquial* enlargement of photograph.

blow[2] /bləʊ/ *noun* hard stroke with hand or weapon; disaster, shock.

blower /'bləʊə/ *noun* device for blowing; *colloquial* telephone.

blowy /'bləʊɪ/ *adjective* (**-ier**, **-iest**) windy.

blowzy /'blaʊzɪ/ *adjective* (**-ier**, **-iest**) coarse-looking, red-faced; dishevelled.

blub *verb* (**-bb-**) *slang* sob.

blubber /'blʌbə/ ● *noun* whale fat. ● *verb* sob noisily. □ **blubbery** *adjective*.

bludgeon /'blʌdʒ(ə)n/ ● *noun* heavy club. ● *verb* beat with bludgeon; coerce.

blue /blu:/ ● *adjective* (**-r**, **-st**) coloured like clear sky; sad, depressed; pornographic. ● *noun* blue colour, paint, clothes, etc.; person who represents Oxford or Cambridge University at sport; (in *plural*) type of melancholy music of American black origin, (**the blues**) depression. ● *verb* (**blues**, **blued**, **bluing** or **blueing**) *slang* squander. □ **blue baby** one with congenital heart defect; **bluebell** woodland plant with bell-shaped blue flowers; **blueberry** small edible blue or blackish fruit of various plants; **blue blood** noble birth; **bluebottle** large buzzing fly; **blue cheese** cheese with veins of blue mould; **blue-collar** manual, industrial; **blue-eyed boy** *colloquial* favourite; **bluegrass** type of country and western music; **Blue Peter** blue flag with central white square hoisted before sailing; **blueprint** photographic print of building plans etc. in white on blue paper, detailed plan; **bluestocking** *usually derogatory* intellectual woman; **blue tit** small blue and yellow bird; **blue whale** rorqual (largest known living mammal).

bluff[1] ● *verb* pretend to have strength, knowledge, etc. ● *noun* bluffing.

bluff[2] ● *adjective* blunt, frank, hearty; with steep or vertical broad front. ● *noun* bluff headland.

blunder /'blʌndə/ ● *noun* serious or foolish mistake. ● *verb* make blunder; move about clumsily.

blunderbuss /'blʌndəbʌs/ *noun historical* short large-bored gun.

blunt ● *adjective* without sharp edge or point; plain-spoken. ● *verb* make blunt. □ **bluntly** *adverb*; **bluntness** *noun*.

blur ● *verb* (**-rr-**) make or become less distinct; smear. ● *noun* indistinct object, sound, memory, etc.

blurb *noun* promotional description, esp. of book.

blurt *verb* (usually + *out*) utter abruptly or tactlessly.

blush ● *verb* be or become red (as) with shame or embarrassment; be ashamed. ● *noun* blushing; pink tinge.

blusher *noun* coloured cosmetic for cheeks.

bluster /'blʌstə/ ● *verb* behave pompously; storm boisterously. ● *noun* noisy pompous talk, empty threats. □ **blustery** *adjective*.

BMA *abbreviation* British Medical Association.

BMX *noun* organized bicycle racing on dirt track; bicycle used for this.

BO *abbreviation colloquial* body odour.

boa /'bəʊə/ *noun* large snake that kills its prey by crushing it; long stole of fur or feathers. □ **boa constrictor** species of boa.

boar *noun* male wild pig; uncastrated male pig.

board ● *noun* thin piece of sawn timber; material resembling this; slab of wood etc., e.g. ironing board, notice board; thick stiff card; provision of meals; directors of company; committee; (**the boards**) stage. ● *verb* go on board (ship etc.); receive, or provide with, meals and usually lodging; (usually + *up*) cover with boards. □ **board game** game played on a board; **boarding house** unlicensed house providing board and lodging; **boarding school** one in which pupils live in term-time; **boardroom** room where board of directors meets; **on board** on or into ship, train, aircraft, etc.

boarder *noun* person who boards, esp. at boarding school.

boast ● *verb* declare one's achievements etc. with excessive pride; have (desirable thing). ● *noun* boasting; thing one is proud of. □ **boastful** *adjective*.

boat ● *noun* small vessel propelled by oars, sails, or engine; ship; long low jug for sauce etc. ● *verb* go in boat, esp. for pleasure. □ **boat-hook** long pole with hook for moving boats; **boathouse** shed at water's edge for boats; **boatman** person who hires out or provides transport by boats; **boat people** refugees travelling by sea; **boat-train** train scheduled to connect with ship.

boater *noun* flat straw hat with straight brim.

boatswain /ˈbəʊs(ə)n/ *noun* (also **bosun**) ship's officer in charge of equipment and crew.

bob[1] ● *verb* (**-bb-**) move up and down; rebound; cut (hair) in bob; curtsy. ● *noun* bobbing movement; curtsy; hairstyle with hair hanging evenly above shoulders; weight on pendulum etc. □ **bobtail** docked tail, horse or dog with this.

bob[2] *noun* (*plural* same) *historical slang* shilling (= 5p).

bobbin /ˈbɒbɪn/ *noun* spool or reel for thread etc.

bobble /ˈbɒb(ə)l/ *noun* small woolly ball on hat etc.

bobby /ˈbɒbɪ/ *noun* (*plural* **-ies**) *colloquial* police officer.

bobsled *noun US* bobsleigh.

bobsleigh *noun* racing sledge steered and braked mechanically.

bod *noun colloquial* person.

bode *verb* (**-ding**) □ **bode well, ill** be good or bad sign.

bodge /bɒdʒ/ = BOTCH.

bodice /ˈbɒdɪs/ *noun* part of woman's dress above waist.

bodily /ˈbɒdɪlɪ/ ● *adjective* of the body. ● *adverb* as a whole (body); in person.

bodkin /ˈbɒdkɪn/ *noun* blunt thick needle for drawing tape etc. through hem.

body /ˈbɒdɪ/ *noun* (*plural* **-ies**) physical structure of person or animal, alive or dead; person's or animal's trunk; main part; group of people regarded as unit; quantity, mass; piece of matter; *colloquial* person; full or substantial quality of flavour etc.; body stocking. □ **body-building** exercises to enlarge and strengthen muscles; **bodyguard** escort or personal guard; **body politic** state, nation; **body shop** workshop where bodywork is repaired; **body stocking** woman's undergarment covering trunk; **bodywork** outer shell of vehicle.

Boer /bɔː/ *noun* S. African of Dutch descent.

boffin /ˈbɒfɪn/ *noun colloquial* research scientist.

bog *noun* (area of) wet spongy ground; *slang* lavatory. □ **bogged down** unable to move or make progress. □ **boggy** *adjective* (**-ier, -iest**).

bogey[1] /ˈbəʊgɪ/ *noun* (*plural* **-s**) *Golf* score of one more than par for hole; (formerly) par.

bogey[2] /ˈbəʊgɪ/ *noun* (also **bogy**) (*plural* **-eys** or **-ies**) evil or mischievous spirit; awkward thing.

boggle /ˈbɒg(ə)l/ *verb* (**-ling**) *colloquial* be startled or baffled.

bogie /ˈbəʊgɪ/ *noun* wheeled undercarriage below locomotive etc.

bogus /ˈbəʊgəs/ *adjective* sham, spurious.

bogy = BOGEY[2].

Bohemian /bəʊˈhiːmɪən/ ● *noun* native of Bohemia; (also **bohemian**) socially unconventional person, esp. artist or writer. ● *adjective* of Bohemia; (also **bohemian**) socially unconventional. □ **bohemianism** *noun*.

boil[1] ● *verb* (of liquid or its vessel) bubble up with heat, reach temperature at which liquid turns to vapour; bring to boiling point; subject to heat of boiling water, cook thus; be agitated like boiling water. ● *noun* boiling; boiling point. □ **boiling (hot)** *colloquial* very hot; **boiling point** temperature at which a liquid boils; **boil over** spill over in boiling.

boil[2] *noun* inflamed pus-filled swelling under skin.

boiler *noun* apparatus for heating hot-water supply; tank for heating water or turning it into steam; vessel for boiling things in. □ **boiler suit** protective garment combining trousers and shirt.

boisterous /ˈbɔɪstərəs/ *adjective* noisily cheerful; violent, rough.

bold /bəʊld/ *adjective* confident; adventurous; courageous; impudent; distinct, vivid. □ **boldly** *adverb*; **boldness** *noun*.

bole *noun* trunk of tree.

bolero *noun* (*plural* **-s**) /bəˈleərəʊ/ Spanish dance; /ˈbɒlərəʊ/ woman's short jacket without fastenings.

boll /bəʊl/ *noun* round seed vessel of cotton, flax, etc.

bollard /ˈbɒlɑːd/ *noun* short thick post in street etc.; post on ship or quay for securing ropes to.

boloney /bəˈləʊnɪ/ *noun slang* nonsense.

bolshie /ˈbɒlʃɪ/ *adjective* (**-r, -st**) (also **Bolshie**) *slang* rebellious, uncooperative.

bolster /ˈbəʊlstə/ ● *noun* long cylindrical pillow. ● *verb* (usually + *up*) encourage, support, prop up.

bolt[1] /bəʊlt/ ● *noun* door-fastening of metal bar and socket; headed metal pin secured with rivet or nut; discharge of lightning; bolting. ● *verb* fasten with bolt; (+ *in, out*) keep in or out by bolting door; dart off, run away; (of horse) escape from control; gulp down unchewed; run to seed. □ **bolt-hole** means of escape; **bolt upright** erect.

bolt[2] /bəʊlt/ *verb* (also **boult**) sift.

bomb /bɒm/ ● *noun* container filled with explosive, incendiary material, etc., designed to explode and cause damage; (**the bomb**) the atomic bomb; *slang* large amount of money. ● *verb* attack with bombs; drop bombs on; *colloquial* travel fast. □ **bombshell** great surprise or disappointment.

bombard /bɒmˈbɑːd/ *verb* attack with heavy guns etc.; question or abuse persistently; subject to stream of high-speed particles. □ **bombardment** *noun*.

bombardier /bɒmbəˈdɪə/ *noun* artillery NCO below sergeant; *US* airman who releases bombs from aircraft.

bombast /ˈbɒmbæst/ *noun* pompous or extravagant language. □ **bombastic** /-ˈbæs-/ *adjective*.

Bombay duck /ˈbɒmbeɪ/ *noun* dried fish eaten as relish, esp. with curry.

bomber *noun* aircraft equipped for bombing; person who throws or plants bomb. □ **bomber jacket** one gathered at waist and cuffs.

bona fide /bəʊnə ˈfaɪdɪ/ *adjective & adverb* in good faith, genuine(ly).

bonanza /bəˈnænzə/ *noun* source of great wealth; large output, esp. from mine.

bon-bon *noun* sweet.

bond ● *noun* thing or force that unites or (usually in *plural*) restrains; binding agreement; certificate issued by government or company promising to repay money at fixed rate of interest; adhesiveness; document binding person to pay or repay money; linkage of atoms in molecule. ● *verb* bind or connect together; put in bond. □ **bond paper** high-quality writing paper; **in bond** stored by Customs until duty is paid.

bondage /ˈbɒndɪdʒ/ *noun* slavery; subjection to constraint.

bondsman /ˈbɒndzmən/ *noun* serf, slave.

bone ● *noun* any of separate parts of vertebrate skeleton; (in *plural*) skeleton, esp. as remains; substance of which bones consist. ● *verb* (**-ning**) remove bones from. ◻ **bone china** fine semi-translucent earthenware; **bone dry** completely dry; **bone idle** completely idle; **bone marrow** fatty substance in cavity of bones; **bonemeal** crushed bone as fertilizer; **boneshaker** jolting vehicle.

bonfire *noun* open-air fire.

bongo /'bɒŋgəʊ/ *noun* (*plural* **-s** or **-es**) either of pair of small drums played with fingers.

bonhomie /bɒnɒ'mi:/ *noun* geniality.

bonkers /'bɒŋkəz/ *adjective slang* crazy.

bonnet /'bɒnɪt/ *noun* woman's or child's hat tied under chin; Scotsman's floppy beret; hinged cover over engine of vehicle.

bonny /'bɒnɪ/ *adjective* (**-ier**, **-iest**) *esp. Scottish & Northern English* healthy-looking, attractive.

bonsai /'bɒnsaɪ/ *noun* (*plural* same) dwarfed tree or shrub; art of growing these.

bonus /'bəʊnəs/ *noun* extra benefit or payment.

bon voyage /bɔ̃ vwɑ:'jɑ:ʒ/ *interjection* have a good trip. [French]

bony /'bəʊnɪ/ *adjective* (**-ier**, **-iest**) thin with prominent bones; having many bones; of or like bone.

boo ● *interjection expressing disapproval or contempt; sound intended to surprise*. ● *noun* utterance of 'boo'. ● *verb* (**boos**, **booed**) utter boos (at).

boob ● *noun colloquial* silly mistake; *slang* woman's breast. ● *verb colloquial* make mistake.

booby /'bu:bɪ/ *noun* (*plural* **-ies**) silly or awkward person. ◻ **booby prize** prize for coming last; **booby trap** practical joke in form of trap, disguised bomb etc. triggered by unknowing victim.

book /bʊk/ ● *noun* written or printed work with pages bound along one side; work intended for publication; bound set of tickets, stamps, matches, cheques, etc.; (in *plural*) set of records or accounts; main division of literary work or Bible; telephone directory; *colloquial* magazine; libretto; record of bets made. ● *verb* reserve (seat etc.) in advance; engage (entertainer etc.); take personal details of (offender); enter in book or list. ◻ **bookcase** cabinet of shelves for books; **bookend** prop to keep books upright; **bookkeeper** person who keeps accounts; **bookmaker** professional taker of bets; **bookmark** thing for marking place in book; **bookplate** decorative personalized label in book; **book token** voucher exchangeable for books; **bookworm** *colloquial* devoted reader, larva that eats through books.

bookie /'bʊkɪ/ *noun colloquial* bookmaker.

bookish *adjective* fond of reading; getting knowledge mainly from books.

booklet /'bʊklɪt/ *noun* small usually paper-covered book.

boom[1] /bu:m/ ● *noun* deep resonant sound. ● *verb* make or speak with boom.

boom[2] /bu:m/ ● *noun* period of economic prosperity or activity. ● *verb* be suddenly prosperous.

boom[3] /bu:m/ *noun* pivoted spar to which sail is attached; long pole carrying camera, microphone, etc.; barrier across harbour etc.

boomerang /'bu:məræŋ/ ● *noun* flat V-shaped Australian hardwood missile returning to thrower. ● *verb* (of plan) backfire.

boon[1] /bu:n/ *noun* advantage; blessing.

boon[2] /bu:n/ *adjective* intimate, favourite.

boor /bʊə/ *noun* ill-mannered person. ◻ **boorish** *adjective*.

boost /bu:st/ *colloquial* ● *verb* promote, encourage; increase, assist; push from below. ● *noun* boosting.

booster *noun* device for increasing power or voltage; auxiliary engine or rocket for initial speed; dose renewing effect of earlier one.

boot /bu:t/ ● *noun* outer foot-covering reaching above ankle; luggage compartment of car; *colloquial* firm kick, dismissal. ● *verb* kick; (often + *out*) eject forcefully; (usually + *up*) make (computer) ready.

bootee /bu:'ti:/ *noun* baby's soft shoe.

booth /bu:ð/ *noun* temporary structure used esp. as market stall; enclosure for telephoning, voting, etc.

bootleg /'bu:tleg/ ● *adjective* smuggled, illicit. ● *verb* (**-gg-**) illicitly make or deal in. ◻ **bootlegger** *noun*.

bootstrap /'bu:tstræp/ *noun* ◻ **pull oneself up by one's bootstraps** better oneself by one's unaided effort.

booty /'bu:tɪ/ *noun* loot, spoils; *colloquial* prize.

booze *colloquial* ● *noun* alcoholic drink. ● *verb* (**-zing**) drink alcohol, esp. excessively. ◻ **boozy** *adjective* (**-ier**, **-iest**).

boozer *noun colloquial* habitual drinker; public house.

bop *colloquial* ● *noun* spell of dancing, esp. to pop music; *colloquial* hit, blow. ● *verb* (**-pp-**) dance, esp. to pop music; *colloquial* hit.

boracic /bə'ræsɪk/ *adjective* of borax. ◻ **boracic acid** boric acid.

borage /'bɒrɪdʒ/ *noun* plant with leaves used as flavouring.

borax /'bɔ:ræks/ *noun* salt of boric acid used as antiseptic.

border /'bɔ:də/ ● *noun* edge, boundary, or part near it; line or region separating countries; distinct edging, esp. ornamental strip; long narrow flower-bed. ● *verb* put or be border to; adjoin. ◻ **borderline** *noun* line marking boundary or dividing two conditions, *adjective* on borderline.

bore[1] ● *verb* (**-ring**) make (hole), esp. with revolving tool; make hole in. ● *noun* hollow of firearm barrel or cylinder; diameter of this; deep hole made to find water etc.

bore[2] ● *noun* tiresome or dull person or thing. ● *verb* (**-ring**) weary by tedious talk or dullness. ◻ **bored** *adjective*; **boring** *adjective*.

bore[3] *noun* very high tidal wave rushing up estuary.

bore[4] *past of* BEAR[1].

boredom *noun* being bored (BORE[2]).

boric acid /'bɔ:rɪk/ *noun* acid used as antiseptic.

born *adjective* existing as a result of birth; being (specified thing) by nature; (usually + *to do*) destined.

borne *past participle of* BEAR[1].

boron /'bɔ:rɒn/ *noun* non-metallic element.

borough /'bʌrə/ *noun* administrative area, esp. of Greater London; *historical* town with municipal corporation.

borrow /'bɒrəʊ/ *verb* get temporary use of (something to be returned); use another's (invention, idea, etc.). ◻ **borrower** *noun*.

Borstal /'bɔ:st(ə)l/ *noun historical* residential institution for youth custody.

bosom /'bʊz(ə)m/ *noun* person's breasts; *colloquial* each of woman's breasts; enclosure formed by breast and arms; emotional centre. ◻ **bosom friend** intimate friend.

boss[1] *colloquial* ● *noun* employer, manager, or supervisor. ● *verb* (usually + *about, around*) give orders to.

boss[2] *noun* round knob or stud.

boss-eyed *adjective colloquial* cross-eyed; crooked.

bossy *adjective* (**-ier**, **-iest**) *colloquial* domineering. ◻ **bossiness** *noun*.

bosun = BOATSWAIN.

botany /ˈbɒtənɪ/ *noun* study of plants. □ **botanic(al)** /bəˈtæn-/ *adjective*; **botanist** *noun*.

botch ● *verb* bungle; patch clumsily. ● *noun* bungled or spoilt work.

both /bəʊθ/ ● *adjective & pronoun* the two (not only one). ● *adverb* with equal truth in two cases.

bother /ˈbɒðə/ ● *verb* trouble, worry; take trouble. ● *noun* person or thing that bothers; nuisance; trouble, worry. ● *interjection of irritation.* □ **bothersome** /-səm/ *adjective*.

bottle /ˈbɒt(ə)l/ ● *noun* container, esp. glass or plastic, for storing liquid; liquid in bottle; *slang* courage. ● *verb* (**-ling**) put into bottles; preserve (fruit etc.) in jars; (+ *up*) restrain (feelings etc.). □ **bottle bank** place for depositing bottles for recycling; **bottle green** dark green; **bottleneck** narrow congested area esp. on road etc., thing that impedes; **bottle party** one to which guests bring bottles of drink.

bottom /ˈbɒtəm/ ● *noun* lowest point or part; buttocks; less honourable end of table, class, etc.; ground under water; basis; essential character. ● *adjective* lowest, last. ● *verb* find extent of; touch bottom (of); (usually + *out*) reach its lowest level. □ **bottom line** *colloquial* underlying truth, ultimate criterion.

bottomless *adjective* without bottom; inexhaustible.

botulism /ˈbɒtjʊlɪz(ə)m/ *noun* poisoning caused by bacillus in badly preserved food.

boudoir /ˈbu:dwɑ:/ *noun* woman's private room.

bougainvillaea /bu:gənˈvɪlɪə/ *noun* tropical plant with large coloured bracts.

bough /baʊ/ *noun* branch of tree.

bought *past & past participle* of BUY.

bouillon /ˈbu:jɒn/ *noun* clear broth.

boulder /ˈbəʊldə/ *noun* large smooth rock.

boulevard /ˈbu:ləvɑ:d/ *noun* broad tree-lined street.

boult = BOLT[2].

bounce /baʊns/ ● *verb* (**-cing**) (cause to) rebound; *slang* (of cheque) be returned to payee by bank when there are no funds to meet it; rush boisterously. ● *noun* rebound; *colloquial* swagger, self-confidence; *colloquial* liveliness. □ **bouncy** *adjective* (**-ier, -iest**).

bouncer *noun slang* doorman ejecting troublemakers from nightclub etc.

bouncing *adjective* big and healthy.

bound[1] /baʊnd/ ● *verb* spring, leap; (of ball etc.) bounce. ● *noun* springy leap; bounce.

bound[2] /baʊnd/ ● *noun* (usually in *plural*) limitation, restriction; border, boundary. ● *verb* limit; be boundary of. □ **out of bounds** outside permitted area.

bound[3] /baʊnd/ *adjective* (usually + *for*) starting or having started.

bound[4] /baʊnd/ *past & past participle* of BIND. □ **bound to** certain to; **bound up with** closely associated with.

boundary /ˈbaʊndərɪ/ *noun* (*plural* **-ies**) line marking limits; *Cricket* hit crossing limit of field, runs scored for this.

boundless *adjective* unlimited.

bounteous /ˈbaʊntɪəs/ *adjective poetical* bountiful.

bountiful /ˈbaʊntɪfʊl/ *adjective* generous; ample.

bounty /ˈbaʊntɪ/ *noun* (*plural* **-ies**) generosity; official reward; gift.

bouquet /bu:ˈkeɪ/ *noun* bunch of flowers; scent of wine; compliment. □ **bouquet garni** (/ˈgɑ:nɪ/) bunch or bag of herbs for flavouring.

bourbon /ˈbɜ:bən/ *noun US* whisky from maize and rye.

bourgeois /ˈbʊəʒwɑ:/ *often derogatory* ● *adjective* conventionally middle-class; materialist; capitalist. ● *noun* (*plural* same) bourgeois person.

bourgeoisie /bʊəʒwɑ:ˈzi:/ *noun* bourgeois class.

bourn /bɔ:n/ *noun* stream.

bourse /bʊəs/ *noun* money market, esp. (**Bourse**) Stock Exchange in Paris.

bout *noun* spell of work etc.; fit of illness; wrestling or boxing match.

boutique /bu:ˈti:k/ *noun* small shop selling fashionable clothes etc.

bouzouki /bu:ˈzu:kɪ/ *noun* (*plural* **-s**) form of Greek mandolin.

bovine /ˈbəʊvaɪn/ *adjective* of cattle; dull, stupid.

bow[1] /bəʊ/ ● *noun* weapon for shooting arrows; rod with horsehair stretched from end to end for playing violin etc.; knot with two loops, ribbon etc. so tied; shallow curve or bend. ● *verb* use bow on (violin etc.). □ **bow-legged** having bandy legs; **bow tie** necktie in form of bow; **bow window** curved bay window.

bow[2] /baʊ/ ● *verb* incline head or body, esp. in greeting or acknowledgement; submit; incline (head etc.). ● *noun* bowing.

bow[3] /baʊ/ *noun* (often in *plural*) front end of boat or ship; rower nearest bow.

bowdlerize /ˈbaʊdləraɪz/ *verb* (also **-ise**) (**-zing** or **-sing**) expurgate. □ **bowdlerization** *noun*.

bowel /ˈbaʊəl/ *noun* (often in *plural*) intestine; (in *plural*) innermost parts.

bower /ˈbaʊə/ *noun* arbour; summer house. □ **bowerbird** Australasian bird, the male of which constructs elaborate runs.

bowie knife /ˈbəʊɪ/ *noun* long hunting knife.

bowl[1] /bəʊl/ *noun* dish, esp. for food or liquid; hollow part of tobacco pipe, spoon, etc.

bowl[2] /bəʊl/ ● *noun* hard heavy ball made with bias to run in curve; (in *plural*; usually treated as *singular*) game with these on grass. ● *verb* roll (ball etc.); play bowls; *Cricket* deliver ball, (often + *out*) put (batsman) out by knocking off bails with bowled ball; (often + *along*) go along rapidly. □ **bowling alley** long enclosure for skittles or tenpin bowling; **bowling green** lawn for playing bowls.

bowler[1] /ˈbəʊlə/ *noun Cricket etc.* player who bowls.

bowler[2] /ˈbəʊlə/ *noun* hard round felt hat.

bowsprit /ˈbəʊsprɪt/ *noun* spar running forward from ship's bow.

box[1] ● *noun* container, usually flat-sided and firm; amount contained in this; compartment in theatre, law court, etc.; telephone box; facility at newspaper office for replies to advertisement; (**the box**) *colloquial* television; enclosed area or space. ● *verb* put in or provide with box. □ **box girder** hollow girder with square cross-section; **box junction** yellow-striped road area which vehicle may enter only if exit is clear; **box office** ticket office at theatre etc.; **box pleat** two parallel pleats forming raised band.

box[2] ● *verb* fight with fists as sport; slap (person's ears). ● *noun* slap on ear.

box[3] *noun* evergreen shrub with small dark green leaves; its wood.

boxer *noun* person who boxes; short-haired dog with puglike face. □ **boxer shorts** man's loose underpants.

boxing *noun* fighting with fists, esp. as sport. □ **boxing glove** padded glove worn in this.

Boxing Day *noun* first weekday after Christmas Day.

boy ● *noun* male child, young man; son; male servant. ● *interjection expressing pleasure, surprise, etc.* □ **boyfriend** person's regular male companion; **boy scout** Scout. □ **boyhood** *noun*; **boyish** *adjective*.

boycott /ˈbɔɪkɒt/ ● *verb* refuse social or commercial relations with; refuse to handle (goods). ● *noun* such refusal.

bra /brɑː/ *noun* woman's undergarment supporting breasts.

brace ● *noun* device that clamps or fastens tightly; timber etc. strengthening framework; (in *plural*) straps supporting trousers from shoulders; wire device for straightening teeth; (*plural* same) pair. ● *verb* (**-cing**) make steady by supporting; fasten tightly; (esp. as **bracing** *adjective*) invigorate; (often **brace oneself**) prepare for difficulty, shock, etc.

bracelet /ˈbreɪslɪt/ *noun* ornamental band or chain worn on wrist or arm; *slang* handcuff.

brachiosaurus /brækiəˈsɔːrəs/ *noun* (*plural* **-ruses**) huge long-necked plant-eating dinosaur.

bracken /ˈbrækən/ *noun* large coarse fern; mass of these.

bracket /ˈbrækɪt/ ● *noun* support projecting from vertical surface; shelf fixed to wall with this; punctuation mark used in pairs—( ), [ ]—enclosing words or figures (see panel); group classified as similar or falling between limits. ● *verb* (**-t-**) enclose in brackets; group in same category

brackish /ˈbrækɪʃ/ *adjective* (of water) slightly salty.

bract *noun* leaflike part of plant growing before flower.

brad *noun* thin flat nail.

bradawl /ˈbrædɔːl/ *noun* small boring-tool.

brae /breɪ/ *noun Scottish* hillside.

brag ● *verb* (**-gg-**) talk boastfully. ● *noun* card game like poker; boastful statement or talk.

braggart /ˈbrægət/ *noun* boastful person.

Brahma /ˈbrɑːmə/ *noun* Hindu Creator; supreme Hindu reality.

Brahman /ˈbrɑːmən/ *noun* (*plural* **-s**) (also **Brahmin**) member of Hindu priestly caste.

braid ● *noun* woven band as edging or trimming; *US* plait of hair. ● *verb US* plait; trim with braid.

Braille /breɪl/ *noun* system of writing and printing for the blind, with patterns of raised dots.

brain ● *noun* organ of soft nervous tissue in vertebrate's skull; centre of sensation or thought; (often in *plural*) intelligence, *colloquial* intelligent person. ● *verb* dash out brains of. □ **brainchild** *colloquial* person's clever idea or invention; **brain drain** *colloquial* emigration of skilled people; **brainstorm** mental disturbance; **brainstorming** pooling of spontaneous ideas about problem etc.; **brains trust** group of experts answering questions, usually impromptu; **brainwash** implant ideas or esp. ideology into (person) by repetition etc.; **brainwave** *colloquial* bright idea.

brainy *adjective* (**-ier**, **-iest**) intellectually clever.

braise /breɪz/ *verb* (**-sing**) stew slowly in closed container with little liquid.

brake ● *noun* device for stopping or slowing wheel or vehicle; thing that impedes. ● *verb* (**-king**) apply brake; slow or stop with brake.

bramble /ˈbræmb(ə)l/ *noun* wild thorny shrub, esp. blackberry.

bran *noun* husks separated from flour.

branch /brɑːntʃ/ ● *noun* limb or bough of tree; lateral extension or subdivision of river, railway, family, etc.; local office of business. ● *verb* (often + *off*) divide, diverge. □ **branch out** extend one's field of interest.

brand ● *noun* particular make of goods; trade mark, label, etc.; (usually + *of*) characteristic kind; identifying mark made with hot iron, iron stamp for this; piece of burning or charred wood; stigma; *poetical* torch. ● *verb* mark with hot iron; stigmatize; assign trade mark etc. to; impress unforgettably. □ **brand new** completely new.

brandish /ˈbrændɪʃ/ *verb* wave or flourish.

brandy /ˈbrændɪ/ *noun* (*plural* **-ies**) strong spirit distilled from wine or fermented fruit juice. □ **brandy snap** crisp rolled gingerbread wafer.

brash *adjective* vulgarly assertive; impudent. □ **brashly** *adverb*; **brashness** *noun*.

brass /brɑːs/ ● *noun* yellow alloy of copper and zinc; brass objects; brass wind instruments; *slang* money; brass memorial tablet; *colloquial* effrontery. ● *adjective* made of brass. □ **brass band** band of brass instruments; **brass rubbing** reproducing of design from engraved brass on paper by rubbing with heelball, impression obtained thus; **brass tacks** *slang* essential details.

brasserie /ˈbræsərɪ/ *noun* restaurant, originally one serving beer with food.

brassica /ˈbræsɪkə/ *noun* plant of cabbage family.

brassière /ˈbræzɪə/ *noun* bra.

brassy /ˈbrɑːsɪ/ *adjective* (**-ier**, **-iest**) of or like brass; impudent; vulgarly showy; loud and blaring.

brat *noun usually derogatory* child.

bravado /brəˈvɑːdəʊ/ *noun* show of boldness.

Brackets ( ) [ ]

Round brackets, also called parentheses, are used mainly to enclose:

1 explanations and extra information or comment, e.g.

Zimbabwe (formerly Rhodesia)
He is (as he always was) a rebel.
This is done using integrated circuits (see page 38).

2 in this dictionary, optional words or parts of words, e.g.

crossword (puzzle) **king-size(d)**

and the type of word which can be used with the word being defined, e.g.

low ... (of opinion) unfavourable
can ... preserve (food etc.) in can

Square brackets are used mainly to enclose:

1 words added by someone other than the original writer or speaker, e.g.
Then the man said, 'He [the police officer] can't prove I did it.'

2 various special types of information, such as stage directions, e.g.
HEDLEY: Goodbye! [Exit].

brave ● *adjective* (**-r**, **-st**) able to face and endure danger or pain; *formal* splendid, spectacular. ● *verb* (**-ving**) face bravely or defiantly. ● *noun* N. American Indian warrior. □ **bravely** *adverb*; **bravery** *noun*.

bravo /brɑːˈvəʊ/ *interjection & noun* (*plural* **-s**) *cry of approval.*

bravura /brəˈvjʊərə/ *noun* brilliance of execution; music requiring brilliant technique.

brawl ● *noun* noisy quarrel or fight. ● *verb* engage in brawl; (of stream) flow noisily.

brawn *noun* muscular strength; muscle, lean flesh; jellied meat made esp. from pig's head. □ **brawny** *adjective* (**-ier**, **-iest**).

bray ● *noun* cry of donkey; harsh sound. ● *verb* make a bray; utter harshly.

braze *verb* (**-zing**) solder with alloy of brass.

brazen /ˈbreɪz(ə)n/ ● *adjective* shameless; of or like brass. ● *verb* (+ *out*) face or undergo defiantly. □ **brazenly** *adverb*.

brazier /ˈbreɪzɪə/ *noun* pan or stand for holding burning coals.

Brazil nut /brəˈzɪl/ *noun* large 3-sided S. American nut.

breach /briːtʃ/ ● *noun* breaking or neglect of rule, duty, promise, etc.; breaking off of relations, quarrel; gap. ● *verb* break through; make gap in; break (law etc.).

bread /bred/ *noun* baked dough of flour usually leavened with yeast; necessary food; *slang* money. □ **breadcrumb** small fragment of bread, esp. (in *plural*) for use in cooking; **breadline** subsistence level; **breadwinner** person whose work supports a family.

breadth /bredθ/ *noun* broadness, distance from side to side; freedom from mental limitations or prejudices.

break /breɪk/ ● *verb* (*past* **broke**; *past participle* **broken** /ˈbrəʊk(ə)n/) separate into pieces under blow or strain; shatter; make or become inoperative; break bone in (limb etc.); interrupt, pause; fail to observe or keep; make or become weak, destroy; weaken effect of (fall, blow, etc.); tame, subdue; surpass (record); reveal or be revealed; come, produce, change, etc., with suddenness or violence; (of waves) curl over and foam; (of voice) change in quality at manhood or with emotion; escape, emerge from. ● *noun* breaking; point where thing is broken; gap; pause in work etc.; sudden dash; a chance; *Cricket* deflection of ball on bouncing; points scored in one sequence at billiards etc. □ **break away** make or become free or separate; **break down** fail or collapse, demolish, analyse; **breakdown** mechanical failure, loss of (esp. mental) health, collapse, analysis; **break even** make neither profit nor loss; **break in** intrude forcibly esp. as thief, interrupt, accustom to habit; **breakneck** (of speed) dangerously fast; **break off** detach by breaking, bring to an end, cease talking etc.; **break open** open forcibly; **break out** escape by force, begin suddenly, (+ *in*) become covered in (rash etc.); **breakthrough** major advance in knowledge etc.; **break up** break into pieces, disband, part; **breakup** disintegration, collapse; **breakwater** barrier breaking force of waves; **break wind** release gas from anus.

breakable *adjective* easily broken.

breakage *noun* broken thing; breaking.

breaker *noun* heavy breaking wave.

breakfast /ˈbrekfəst/ ● *noun* first meal of day. ● *verb* have breakfast.

bream *noun* (*plural* same) yellowish freshwater fish; similar sea fish.

breast /brest/ ● *noun* either of two milk-secreting organs on woman's chest; chest; part of garment covering this; seat of emotions. ● *verb* contend with; reach top of (hill). □ **breastbone** bone connecting ribs in front; **breastfeed** feed (baby) from breast; **breastplate** armour covering chest; **breaststroke** stroke made while swimming on breast by extending arms forward and sweeping them back.

breath /breθ/ *noun* air drawn into or expelled from lungs; one respiration; breath as perceived by senses; slight movement of air. □ **breathtaking** astounding, awe-inspiring; **breath test** test with Breathalyser.

breathalyse *verb* give breath test to.

Breathalyser /ˈbreθəlaɪzə/ *noun proprietary term* instrument for measuring alcohol in breath.

breathe /briːð/ *verb* (**-thing**) take air into lungs and send it out again; live; utter or sound, esp. quietly; pause; send out or take in (as) with breathed air. □ **breathing-space** time to recover, pause.

breather /ˈbriːðə/ *noun* short rest period.

breathless /ˈbreθlɪs/ *adjective* panting, out of breath; still, windless. □ **breathlessly** *adverb*.

bred *past & past participle* of BREED.

breech /briːtʃ/ *noun* back part of gun or gun barrel; (in *plural*) short trousers fastened below knee. □ **breech birth** birth in which buttocks emerge first.

breed ● *verb* (*past & past participle* **bred**) produce offspring; propagate; raise (animals); yield, result in; arise, spread; train, bring up; create (fissile material) by nuclear reaction. ● *noun* stock of animals within species; race, lineage; sort, kind. □ **breeder reactor** nuclear reactor creating surplus fissile material. □ **breeder** *noun*.

breeding *noun* raising of offspring; social behaviour; ancestry.

breeze[1] ● *noun* gentle wind. ● *verb* (**-zing**) (+ *in*, *out*, *along*, etc.) *colloquial* saunter casually.

breeze[2] *noun* small cinders. **breeze-block** lightweight building block made from breeze.

breezy *adjective* (**-ier**, **-iest**) slightly windy.

Bren *noun* lightweight quick-firing machine-gun.

brent *noun* small migratory goose.

brethren see BROTHER.

Breton /ˈbret(ə)n/ ● *noun* native or language of Brittany. ● *adjective* of Brittany.

breve /briːv/ *noun Music* note equal to two semibreves; mark (˘) indicating short or unstressed vowel.

breviary /ˈbriːvɪərɪ/ *noun* (*plural* **-ies**) book containing RC daily office.

brevity /ˈbrevɪtɪ/ *noun* conciseness, shortness.

brew ● *verb* make (beer etc.) by infusion, boiling, and fermenting; make (tea etc.) by infusion; undergo these processes; be forming. ● *noun* amount brewed; liquor brewed. □ **brewer** *noun*.

brewery /ˈbruːərɪ/ *noun* (*plural* **-ies**) factory for brewing beer etc.

briar[1,2] = BRIER[1,2].

bribe ● *verb* (**-bing**) persuade to act improperly by gift of money etc. ● *noun* money or services offered in bribing. □ **bribery** *noun*.

bric-a-brac /ˈbrɪkəbræk/ *noun* cheap ornaments, trinkets, etc.

brick ● *noun* small rectangular block of baked clay, used in building; toy building block; brick-shaped thing; *slang* generous or loyal person. ● *verb* (+ *in*, *up*) close or block with brickwork. ● *adjective* made of bricks. □ **brickbat** piece of brick, esp. as missile, insult; **bricklayer** person who builds with bricks; **brickwork** building or work in brick.

bridal /ˈbraɪd(ə)l/ *adjective* of bride or wedding.

bride *noun* woman on her wedding day and shortly before and after it. **bridegroom** man on his wedding day and shortly before and after it; **bridesmaid** woman or girl attending bride at wedding.

bridge[1] ● *noun* structure providing way over road, railway, river, etc.; thing joining or connecting; superstructure from which ship is directed; upper bony part of nose; prop under strings of violin etc.; bridgework. ● *verb* (**-ging**) be or make bridge over. □ **bridgehead** position held on enemy's side of river etc.; **bridgework** dental structure covering gap and joined to teeth on either side; **bridging loan** loan to cover interval between buying one house and selling another.

bridge[2] *noun* card games derived from whist.

bridle /ˈbraɪd(ə)l/ ● *noun* headgear for controlling horse etc.; restraining thing. ● *verb* (**-ling**) put bridle on, control, curb; express resentment, esp. by throwing up head and drawing in chin. □ **bridle path** rough path for riders or walkers.

Brie /briː/ *noun* flat round soft creamy French cheese.

brief /briːf/ ● *adjective* of short duration; concise; scanty. ● *noun* (in *plural*) short pants; summary of case for guidance of barrister; instructions for a task. ● *verb* instruct (barrister) by brief; inform or instruct in advance. □ **in brief** to sum up. □ **briefly** *adverb*.

briefcase /ˈbriːfkeɪs/ *noun* flat document case.

brier[1] /braɪə/ *noun* (also **briar**) wild-rose bush.

brier[2] /braɪə/ *noun* (also **briar**) white heath of S. Europe; tobacco pipe made from its root.

brig[1] *noun* two-masted square-rigged ship.

brig[2] *noun Scottish & Northern English* bridge.

brigade /brɪˈgeɪd/ *noun* military unit forming part of division; organized band of workers etc.

brigadier /brɪgəˈdɪə/ *noun* army officer next below major-general.

brigand /ˈbrɪgənd/ *noun* member of robber gang.

bright /braɪt/ *adjective* emitting or reflecting much light, shining; vivid; clever; cheerful. □ **brighten** *verb*; **brightly** *adverb*; **brightness** *noun*.

brill[1] *noun* (*plural* same) flatfish resembling turbot.

brill[2] *adjective colloquial* excellent.

brilliant /ˈbrɪlɪənt/ ● *adjective* bright, sparkling; highly talented; showy; *colloquial* excellent. ● *noun* diamond of finest quality. □ **brilliance** *noun*; **brilliantly** *adverb*.

brilliantine /ˈbrɪljəntiːn/ *noun* cosmetic for making hair glossy.

brim ● *noun* edge of vessel; projecting edge of hat. ● *verb* (**-mm-**) fill or be full to brim.

brimstone /ˈbrɪmstəʊn/ *noun archaic* sulphur.

brindled /ˈbrɪnd(ə)ld/ *adjective* brown with streaks of other colour.

brine *noun* salt water; sea water.

bring *verb* (*past & past participle* **brought** /brɔːt/) come with, carry, convey; cause, result in; be sold for; submit (criminal charge); initiate (legal action). □ **bring about** cause to happen; **bring down** cause to fall; **bring forward** move to earlier time, transfer from previous page or account, draw attention to; **bring in** introduce, produce as profit; **bring off** succeed in; **bring on** cause to happen, appear or progress; **bring out** emphasize, publish; **bring round** restore to consciousness, win over; **bring up** raise and educate, vomit, draw attention to.

brink *noun* edge of precipice etc.; furthest point before danger, discovery, etc. □ **brinkmanship** policy of pursuing dangerous course to brink of catastrophe.

briny /ˈbraɪnɪ/ ● *adjective* (**-ier, -iest**) of brine or sea, salt. ● *noun* (**the briny**) *slang* the sea.

briquette /brɪˈket/ *noun* block of compressed coal dust as fuel.

brisk *adjective* active, lively, quick. □ **briskly** *adverb*.

brisket /ˈbrɪskɪt/ *noun* animal's breast, esp. as joint of meat.

brisling /ˈbrɪzlɪŋ/ *noun* (*plural* same or **-s**) small herring or sprat.

bristle /ˈbrɪs(ə)l/ ● *noun* short stiff hair, esp. one used in brushes etc. ● *verb* (**-ling**) (of hair etc.) stand up; cause to bristle; show irritation; (usually + *with*) be covered (with) or abundant (in). □ **bristly** *adjective*.

British /ˈbrɪtɪʃ/ ● *adjective* of Britain. ● *plural noun* (**the British**) the British people. □ **British Summer Time** = SUMMER TIME.

Briton /ˈbrɪt(ə)n/ *noun* inhabitant of S. Britain before Roman conquest; native of Great Britain.

brittle /ˈbrɪt(ə)l/ *adjective* apt to break, fragile.

broach /brəʊtʃ/ *verb* raise for discussion; pierce (cask) to draw liquor; open and start using.

broad /brɔːd/ ● *adjective* large across, extensive; of specified breadth; full, clear; explicit; general; tolerant; coarse; (of accent) marked, strong. ● *noun* broad part; *US slang* woman; (**the Broads**) large areas of water in E. Anglia. □ **broad bean** bean with large flat seeds, one such seed; **broadloom** (carpet) woven in broad width; **broad-minded** tolerant, liberal; **broadsheet** large-sized newspaper. □ **broaden** *verb*; **broadly** *adverb*.

broadcast ● *verb* (*past & past participle* **-cast**) transmit by radio or television; take part in such transmission; scatter (seed) etc.; disseminate widely. ● *noun* radio or television programme or transmission. □ **broadcaster** *noun*; **broadcasting** *noun*.

broadside *noun* vigorous verbal attack; firing of all guns on one side of ship. □ **broadside on** sideways on.

brocade /brəˈkeɪd/ *noun* fabric woven with raised pattern.

broccoli /ˈbrɒkəlɪ/ *noun* brassica with greenish flower heads.

brochure /ˈbrəʊʃə/ *noun* booklet, pamphlet, esp. containing descriptive information.

broderie anglaise /brəʊdərɪ ɑ̃ˈgleɪz/ *noun* open embroidery on usually white cotton or linen.

brogue /brəʊg/ *noun* strong shoe with ornamental perforations; rough shoe of untanned leather; marked local, esp. Irish, accent.

broil *verb* grill (meat); make or be very hot.

broiler *noun* young chicken for broiling.

broke ● *past* of BREAK. ● *adjective colloquial* having no money, bankrupt.

broken /ˈbrəʊkən/ ● *past participle* of BREAK. ● *adjective* that has been broken; reduced to despair; (of language) spoken imperfectly; interrupted. □ **broken-hearted** crushed by grief; **broken home** family disrupted by divorce or separation.

broker *noun* middleman, agent; stockbroker. □ **broking** *noun*.

brokerage *noun* broker's fee or commission.

brolly /ˈbrɒlɪ/ *noun* (*plural* **-ies**) *colloquial* umbrella.

bromide /ˈbrəʊmaɪd/ *noun* binary compound of bromine, esp. one used as sedative; trite remark.

bromine /ˈbrəʊmiːn/ *noun* poisonous liquid non-metallic element with choking smell.

bronchial /ˈbrɒŋkɪəl/ *adjective* of two main divisions of windpipe or smaller tubes into which they divide.

bronchitis /brɒŋˈkaɪtɪs/ *noun* inflammation of bronchial mucous membrane.

bronco /ˈbrɒŋkəʊ/ *noun* (*plural* **-s**) wild or half-tamed horse of western US.

brontosaurus /brɒntəˈsɔːrəs/ *noun* (*plural* **-ruses**) = APATOSAURUS.

bronze /brɒnz/ ● *noun* brown alloy of copper and tin; its colour; work of art or medal in it. ● *adjective* made of or coloured like bronze. ● *verb* (**-zing**) make or grow brown; tan. □ **Bronze Age** period when tools were of bronze; **bronze medal** medal given usually as third prize.

brooch /brəʊtʃ/ *noun* ornamental hinged pin.

brood /ˈbruːd/ ● *noun* bird's or other animal's young produced at one hatch or birth; *colloquial* children of a family. ● *verb* worry or ponder, esp. resentfully; (of hen) sit on eggs.

broody *adjective* (**-ier**, **-iest**) (of hen) wanting to brood; sullenly thoughtful; *colloquial* (of woman) wanting pregnancy.

brook[1] /brʊk/ *noun* small stream.

brook[2] /brʊk/ *verb* tolerate; allow.

broom /bruːm/ *noun* long-handled brush for sweeping; chiefly yellow-flowered shrub. □ **broomstick** broom-handle.

Bros. *abbreviation* Brothers.

broth /brɒθ/ *noun* thin meat or fish soup.

brothel /ˈbrɒθ(ə)l/ *noun* premises for prostitution.

brother /ˈbrʌðə/ *noun* man or boy in relation to his siblings; close man friend; (*plural* also **brethren** /ˈbreðrɪn/) member of male religious order; (*plural* also **brethren**) fellow Christian etc.; fellow human being. □ **brother-in-law** (*plural* **brothers-in-law**) wife's or husband's brother, sister's husband. □ **brotherly** *adjective*.

brotherhood *noun* relationship (as) between brothers; (members of) association for mutual help etc.

brought *past & past participle* of BRING.

brow /braʊ/ *noun* forehead; (usually in *plural*) eyebrow; summit of hill; edge of cliff etc.

browbeat *verb* (*past* **-beat**, *past participle* **-beaten**) intimidate, bully.

brown /braʊn/ ● *adjective* of colour of dark wood or rich soil; dark-skinned; tanned. ● *noun* brown colour, paint, clothes, etc. ● *verb* make or become brown. □ **brown bread** bread made of wholemeal or wheatmeal flour; **browned off** *colloquial* bored, fed up; **Brown Owl** adult leader of Brownies; **brown rice** unpolished rice; **brown sugar** partially refined sugar. **brownish** *adjective*.

Brownie /ˈbraʊnɪ/ *noun* junior Guide; (**brownie**) small square of chocolate cake with nuts; (**brownie**) benevolent elf.

browse /braʊz/ ● *verb* (**-sing**) read or look around desultorily; feed on leaves and young shoots. ● *noun* browsing; twigs, shoots, etc. as fodder.

bruise /bruːz/ ● *noun* discoloration of skin caused by blow or pressure; similar damage on fruit etc. ● *verb* (**-sing**) inflict bruise on; be susceptible to bruises.

bruiser *noun colloquial* tough brutal person.

bruit /bruːt/ *verb* (often + *abroad*, *about*) spread (report or rumour).

brunch *noun* combination of breakfast and lunch.

brunette /bruːˈnet/ *noun* woman with dark hair.

brunt *noun* chief impact of attack etc.

brush ● *noun* cleaning or hairdressing or painting implement of bristles etc. set in holder; application of brush; short esp. unpleasant encounter; fox's tail; carbon or metal piece serving as electrical contact. ● *verb* use brush on; touch lightly, graze in passing. □ **brush off** dismiss abruptly; **brush-off** dismissal, rebuff; **brush up** clean up or smarten, revise (subject, skill); **brushwood** undergrowth, thicket, cut or broken twigs etc.; **brushwork** painter's way of using brush.

brusque /brʊsk/ *adjective* abrupt, offhand. □ **brusquely** *adverb*; **brusqueness** *noun*.

Brussels sprout /ˈbrʌs(ə)lz/ *noun* brassica with small cabbage-like buds on stem; such bud.

brutal /ˈbruːt(ə)l/ *adjective* savagely cruel; mercilessly frank. □ **brutality** /-ˈtæl-/ *noun* (*plural* **-ies**); **brutalize** *verb* (also **-ise**) (**-zing**, **-sing**).

brute /bruːt/ ● *noun* cruel person; *colloquial* unpleasant person; animal other than man. ● *adjective* unthinking; cruel, stupid. □ **brutish** *adjective*.

bryony /ˈbraɪənɪ/ *noun* (*plural* **-ies**) climbing hedge plant.

B.Sc. *abbreviation* Bachelor of Science.

BST *abbreviation* British Summer Time.

Bt. *abbreviation* Baronet.

bubble /ˈbʌb(ə)l/ ● *noun* thin sphere of liquid enclosing air or gas; air-filled cavity in glass etc.; transparent domed cavity. ● *verb* (**-ling**) send up or rise in bubbles; make sound of boiling. □ **bubble and squeak** cooked potatoes and cabbage fried together; **bubble bath** additive to make bathwater bubbly; **bubblegum** chewing gum that can be blown into bubbles.

bubbly ● *adjective* (**-ier**, **-iest**) full of bubbles; exuberant. ● *noun colloquial* champagne.

bubonic /bjuːˈbɒnɪk/ *adjective* (of plague) marked by swellings esp. in groin and armpits.

buccaneer /bʌkəˈnɪə/ *noun* pirate; adventurer. □ **buccaneering** *adjective & noun*.

buck[1] ● *noun* male deer, hare, or rabbit. ● *verb* (of horse) jump vertically with back arched, throw (rider) thus; (usually + *up*) *colloquial* cheer up, hurry up. □ **buckshot** coarse shot for gun; **buck-tooth** projecting upper tooth.

buck[2] *noun US & Australian slang* dollar.

buck[3] *noun slang* small object placed before dealer at poker. □ **pass the buck** *colloquial* shift responsibility.

bucket /ˈbʌkɪt/ ● *noun* usually round open container with handle, for carrying or holding water etc.; amount contained in this; (in *plural*) *colloquial* large quantities; compartment or scoop in waterwheel, dredger, or grain elevator. ● *verb* (**-t-**) *colloquial* (often + *down*) (esp. of rain) pour heavily; (often + *along*) move jerkily or bumpily. □ **bucket seat** one with rounded back, to fit one person; **bucket shop** agency dealing in cheap airline tickets, unregistered broking agency.

buckle /ˈbʌk(ə)l/ ● *noun* clasp with usually hinged pin for securing strap or belt etc. ● *verb* (**-ling**) fasten with buckle; (cause to) crumple under pressure. □ **buckle down** make determined effort.

buckram /ˈbʌkrəm/ *noun* coarse linen etc. stiffened with paste etc.

buckshee /bʌkˈʃiː/ *adjective & adverb slang* free of charge.

buckwheat *noun* seed of plant related to rhubarb.

bucolic /bjuːˈkɒlɪk/ *adjective* of shepherds, rustic, pastoral.

bud ● *noun* projection from which branch, leaf, or flower develops; flower or leaf not fully open; asexual growth separating from organism as new animal. ● *verb* (**-dd-**) form buds; begin to grow or develop; graft bud of (plant) on another plant.

Buddhism /ˈbʊdɪz(ə)m/ *noun* Asian religion founded by Gautama Buddha. □ **Buddhist** *adjective & noun*.

buddleia /ˈbʌdlɪə/ *noun* shrub with flowers attractive to butterflies.

buddy /ˈbʌdɪ/ *noun* (*plural* **-ies**) *colloquial* friend; mate.

budge *verb* (**-ging**) move in slightest degree; (+ *up*) move to make room for another person.

budgerigar /bʌdʒərɪˈgɑː/ *noun* small parrot often kept as pet.

budget /ˈbʌdʒɪt/ ● *noun* amount of money needed or available; (**the Budget**) annual estimate of country's revenue and expenditure; similar estimate for person or group. ● *verb* (**-t-**) (often + *for*) allow or arrange for in budget. ◻ **budgetary** *adjective*.

budgie /ˈbʌdʒɪ/ *noun colloquial* budgerigar.

buff ● *adjective* of yellowish beige colour. ● *noun* this colour; *colloquial* enthusiast; velvety dull yellow leather. ● *verb* polish; make (leather) velvety. ◻ **in the buff** *colloquial* naked.

buffalo /ˈbʌfələʊ/ *noun* (*plural* same or **-es**) any of various kinds of ox; American bison.

buffer[1] *noun* apparatus for deadening impact esp. of railway vehicles. ◻ **buffer state** minor one between two larger ones, regarded as reducing friction.

buffer[2] *noun slang* old or incompetent fellow.

buffet[1] /ˈbʊfeɪ/ *noun* room or counter where refreshments are sold; self-service meal of several dishes set out at once; (also /ˈbʌfɪt/) sideboard. ◻ **buffet car** railway coach in which refreshments are served.

buffet[2] /ˈbʌfɪt/ ● *verb* (**-t-**) strike repeatedly. ● *noun* blow with hand; shock.

buffoon /bəˈfuːn/ *noun* silly or ludicrous person; jester. ◻ **buffoonery** *noun*.

bug ● *noun* small insect; concealed microphone; *colloquial* error in computer program etc.; *slang* virus, infection; *slang* enthusiasm, obsession. ● *verb* (**-gg-**) conceal microphone in; *slang* annoy.

bugbear *noun* cause of annoyance; object of baseless fear.

buggy /ˈbʌgɪ/ *noun* (*plural* **-ies**) small sturdy motor vehicle; lightweight pushchair; light horse-drawn vehicle for one or two people.

bugle /ˈbjuːg(ə)l/ ● *noun* brass instrument like small trumpet. ● *verb* (**-ling**) sound bugle. ◻ **bugler** *noun*.

build /bɪld/ ● *verb* (*past & past participle* **built** /bɪlt/) construct or cause to be constructed; develop or establish. ● *noun* physical proportions; style of construction. ◻ **build in** incorporate; **build up** increase in size or strength, praise, gradually establish or be established; **build-up** favourable description in advance, gradual approach to climax, accumulation.

builder *noun* contractor who builds houses etc.

building *noun* house or other structure with roof and walls. ◻ **building society** financial organization (not public company) that pays interest on savings accounts, lends money esp. for mortgages, etc.

built /bɪlt/ *past & past participle* of BUILD. ◻ **built-in** integral; **built-up** covered with buildings.

bulb *noun* rounded base of stem of some plants; light bulb; bulb-shaped thing or part.

bulbous /ˈbʌlbəs/ *adjective* bulb-shaped; bulging.

bulge ● *noun* irregular swelling; *colloquial* temporary increase. ● *verb* (**-ging**) swell outwards. ◻ **bulgy** *adjective*.

bulimia /bjʊˈlɪmɪə/ *noun* (in full **bulimia nervosa** /nɜːˈvəʊsə/) disorder in which overeating alternates with self-induced vomiting, fasting, etc.

bulk ● *noun* size, magnitude, esp. when great; (**the bulk**) the greater part; large quantity. ● *verb* seem (in size or importance); make thicker. ◻ **bulk buying** buying in quantity at discount; **bulkhead** upright partition in ship, aircraft, etc.

bulky /ˈbʌlkɪ/ *adjective* (**-ier, -iest**) large, unwieldy.

bull[1] /bʊl/ *noun* uncastrated male ox; male whale or elephant etc.; bull's-eye of target; person who buys shares in hope of selling at higher price later. ◻ **bulldog** short-haired heavy-jowled sturdy dog, tenacious and courageous person; **Bulldog clip** strong sprung clip for papers etc.; **bulldoze** clear with bulldozer, *colloquial* intimidate, *colloquial* make (one's way) forcibly; **bulldozer** powerful tractor with broad upright blade for clearing ground; **bullfight** public baiting, and usually killing, of bulls; **bullfinch** pink and black finch; **bullfrog** large American frog with booming croak; **bullring** arena for bullfight; **bull's-eye** centre of target, hard minty sweet; **bull terrier** cross between bulldog and terrier. ◻ **bullish** *adjective*.

bull[2] /bʊl/ *noun* papal edict.

bull[3] /bʊl/ *noun slang* nonsense; *slang* unnecessary routine tasks; absurdly illogical statement.

bullet /ˈbʊlɪt/ *noun* small pointed missile fired from revolver etc. ◻ **bulletproof** resistant to bullets.

bulletin /ˈbʊlɪtɪn/ *noun* short official statement; short broadcast news report.

bullion /ˈbʊlɪən/ *noun* gold or silver in lump or valued by weight.

bullock /ˈbʊlək/ *noun* castrated bull.

bully[1] /ˈbʊlɪ/ ● *noun* (*plural* **-ies**) person coercing others by fear. ● *verb* (**-ies, -ied**) persecute or oppress by force or threats. ● *interjection* (+ *for*) very good.

bully[2] /ˈbʊlɪ/ (in full **bully off**) ● *noun* (*plural* **-ies**) putting ball into play in hockey. ● *verb* (**-ies, -ied**) start play thus.

bully[3] /ˈbʊlɪ/ *noun* (in full **bully beef**) corned beef.

bulrush /ˈbʊlrʌʃ/ *noun* tall rush; *Biblical* papyrus.

bulwark /ˈbʊlwək/ *noun* defensive wall, esp. of earth; person or principle that protects; (usually in *plural*) ship's side above deck.

bum[1] *noun slang* buttocks. ◻ **bumbag** small pouch worn round waist.

bum[2] *US slang* ● *noun* loafer, dissolute person. ● *verb* (**-mm-**) (often + *around*) loaf, wander around; cadge. ● *adjective* of poor quality.

bumble /ˈbʌmb(ə)l/ *verb* (**-ling**) (+ *on*) speak ramblingly; be inept; blunder. ◻ **bumble-bee** large bee with loud hum.

bump ● *noun* dull-sounding blow or collision; swelling caused by it; uneven patch on road etc.; prominence on skull, thought to indicate mental faculty. ● *verb* come or strike with bump against; hurt thus; (usually + *along*) move along with jolts. ◻ **bump into** *colloquial* meet by chance; **bump off** *slang* murder; **bump up** *colloquial* increase. ◻ **bumpy** *adjective* (**-ier, -iest**).

bumper ● *noun* horizontal bar on motor vehicle to reduce damage in collisions; *Cricket* ball rising high after pitching; brim-full glass. ● *adjective* unusually large or abundant.

bumpkin /ˈbʌmpkɪn/ *noun* rustic or awkward person.

bumptious /ˈbʌmpʃəs/ *adjective* self-assertive, conceited.

bun *noun* small sweet cake or bread roll often with dried fruit; small coil of hair at back of head.

bunch ● *noun* cluster of things growing or fastened together; lot; *colloquial* gang, group. ● *verb* arrange in bunch(es); gather in folds; come, cling, or crowd together.

bundle /ˈbʌnd(ə)l/ ● *noun* collection of things tied or fastened together; set of nerve fibres etc.; *slang* large amount of money. ● *verb* (**-ling**) (usually + *up*) tie in bundle; (usually + *into*) throw or move carelessly; (usually + *out, off, away*, etc.) send away hurriedly.

bung ● *noun* stopper, esp. for cask. ● *verb* stop with bung; *slang* throw. ◻ **bunged up** blocked up.

bungalow /ˈbʌŋgələʊ/ *noun* one-storeyed house.

bungee /ˈbʌndʒɪ/ *noun* elasticated cord. ◻ **bungee jumping** sport of jumping from great height while secured by bungee.

bungle /ˈbʌŋg(ə)l/ ● *verb* (**-ling**) mismanage, fail to accomplish; work awkwardly. ● *noun* bungled work or attempt.

bunion /ˈbʌnjən/ *noun* swelling on foot, esp. on side of big toe.

bunk[1] *noun* shelflike bed against wall. ◻ **bunk bed** each of two or more bunks one above the other.

bunk[2] *slang* ◻ **do a bunk** run away.

bunk[3] *noun slang* nonsense, humbug.

bunker *noun* container for fuel; reinforced underground shelter; sandy hollow in golf course.

bunkum /ˈbʌŋkəm/ *noun* nonsense, humbug.

bunny /ˈbʌnɪ/ *noun* (*plural* **-ies**) *childish name for* rabbit.

Bunsen burner /ˈbʌns(ə)n/ *noun* small adjustable gas burner used in laboratory.

bunting[1] /ˈbʌntɪŋ/ *noun* small bird related to finches.

bunting[2] /ˈbʌntɪŋ/ *noun* flags and other decorations; loosely woven fabric for these.

buoy /bɔɪ/ ● *noun* anchored float as navigational mark etc.; lifebuoy. ● *verb* (usually + *up*) keep afloat, encourage; (often + *out*) mark with buoy(s).

buoyant /ˈbɔɪənt/ *adjective* apt to float; resilient; exuberant. ◻ **buoyancy** *noun*.

bur *noun* (also **burr**) clinging seed vessel or flower head, plant producing burs; clinging person.

burble /ˈbɜːb(ə)l/ *verb* (**-ling**) talk ramblingly; make bubbling sound.

burden /ˈbɜːd(ə)n/ ● *noun* thing carried, load; oppressive duty, expense, emotion, etc.; refrain of song; theme. ● *verb* load, encumber, oppress. ◻ **burden of proof** obligation to prove one's case. ◻ **burdensome** *adjective*.

burdock /ˈbɜːdɒk/ *noun* plant with prickly flowers and docklike leaves.

bureau /ˈbjʊərəʊ/ *noun* (*plural* **-s** or **-x** /-z/) writing desk with drawers; *US* chest of drawers; office or department for specific business; government department.

bureaucracy /bjʊəˈrɒkrəsɪ/ *noun* (*plural* **-ies**) government by central administration; government officials esp. regarded as oppressive and inflexible; conduct typical of these.

bureaucrat /ˈbjʊərəkræt/ *noun* official in bureaucracy. ◻ **bureaucratic** /-ˈkrætɪk/ *adjective*.

burgeon /ˈbɜːdʒ(ə)n/ *verb* grow rapidly, flourish.

burger /ˈbɜːgə/ *noun colloquial* hamburger.

burgher /ˈbɜːgə/ *noun* citizen, esp. of foreign town.

burglar /ˈbɜːglə/ *noun* person who commits burglary.

burglary *noun* (*plural* **-ies**) illegal entry into building to commit theft or other crime.

burgle /ˈbɜːg(ə)l/ *verb* (**-ling**) commit burglary (on).

burgundy /ˈbɜːgəndɪ/ *noun* (*plural* **-ies**) red or white wine produced in Burgundy; dark red colour.

burial /ˈberɪəl/ *noun* burying, esp. of corpse; funeral.

burlesque /bɜːˈlesk/ ● *noun* comic imitation, parody; *US* variety show, esp. with striptease. ● *adjective* of or using burlesque. ● *verb* (**-ques**, **-qued**, **-quing**) parody.

burly /ˈbɜːlɪ/ *adjective* (**-ier**, **-iest**) large and sturdy.

burn[1] ● *verb* (*past & past participle* **burnt** or **burned**) (cause to) be consumed by fire; blaze or glow with fire; (cause to) be injured or damaged by fire, sun, or great heat; use or be used as fuel; produce (hole etc.) by fire or heat; char in working; brand; give or feel sensation or pain (as) of heat. ● *noun* sore or mark made by burning. ◻ **burn out** be reduced to nothing by burning, (cause to) fail by burning, (usually **burn oneself out**) suffer exhaustion; **burnt offering** sacrifice offered by burning.

burn[2] *noun Scottish* brook.

burner *noun* part of lamp or cooker etc. that emits flame.

burnish /ˈbɜːnɪʃ/ *verb* polish by rubbing.

burnt *past & past participle of* BURN[1].

burp *verb & noun colloquial* belch.

burr[1] *noun* whirring sound; rough sounding of *r*; rough edge on metal etc.

burr[2] = BUR.

burrow /ˈbʌrəʊ/ ● *noun* hole dug by animal as dwelling. ● *verb* make burrow; make by digging; (+ *into*) investigate or search.

bursar /ˈbɜːsə/ *noun* treasurer of college etc.; holder of bursary.

bursary /ˈbɜːsərɪ/ *noun* (*plural* **-ies**) grant, esp. scholarship.

burst ● *verb* (*past & past participle* **burst**) fly violently apart or give way suddenly, explode; rush, move, speak, be spoken, etc. suddenly or violently. ● *noun* bursting, explosion, outbreak; spurt.

burton /ˈbɜːt(ə)n/ *noun* ◻ **go for a burton** *slang* be lost, destroyed, or killed.

bury /ˈberɪ/ *verb* (**-ies**, **-ied**) place (corpse) in ground, tomb, or sea; put underground, hide in earth; consign to obscurity; (**bury oneself** or in *passive*) involve (oneself) deeply. ◻ **bury the hatchet** cease to quarrel.

bus ● *noun* (*plural* **buses**, *US* **busses**) large public passenger vehicle usually plying on fixed route. ● *verb* (**buses** or **busses**, **bussed**, **bussing**) go by bus; *US* transport by bus (esp. to aid racial integration). ◻ **busman's holiday** leisure spent in same occupation as working hours; **bus shelter** shelter for people waiting for bus; **bus station** centre where buses depart and arrive; **bus stop** regular stopping place of bus.

busby /ˈbʌzbɪ/ *noun* (*plural* **-ies**) tall fur cap worn by hussars etc.

bush[1] /bʊʃ/ *noun* shrub, clump of shrubs; clump of hair or fur; *Australian etc.* uncultivated land, woodland. ◻ **bush-baby** small African lemur; **Bushman** member or language of a S. African aboriginal people; **bushman** dweller or traveller in Australian bush; **bush telegraph** rapid informal spreading of information etc.

bush[2] /bʊʃ/ *noun* metal lining of axle-hole etc.; electrically insulating sleeve.

bushel /ˈbʊʃ(ə)l/ *noun* measure of capacity for corn, fruit, etc. (8 gallons, 36.4 litres).

bushy *adjective* (**-ier**, **-iest**) growing thickly or like bush; having many bushes.

business /ˈbɪznɪs/ *noun* one's occupation or profession; one's own concern, task, duty; serious work; (difficult or unpleasant) matter or affair; thing(s) needing dealing with; buying and selling, trade; commercial firm. ◻ **businesslike** practical, systematic; **businessman**, **businesswoman** person engaged in trade or commerce.

busk *verb* perform esp. music in street etc. for tips. ◻ **busker** *noun*.

bust[1] *noun* human chest, esp. of woman; sculpture of head, shoulders, and chest.

bust[2] *colloquial* ● *verb* (*past & past participle* **bust** or **busted**) burst, break; raid, search; arrest. ● *adjective* burst, broken; bankrupt. ◻ **bust-up** quarrel, violent split or separation.

bustard /bˈʌstəd/ *noun* large swift-running bird.

bustle[1] /ˈbʌs(ə)l/ ● *verb* (**-ling**) (often + *about*) move busily and energetically; make (person) hurry; (as **bustling** *adjective*) active, lively. ● *noun* excited activity.

bustle[2] /ˈbʌs(ə)l/ *noun historical* padding worn under skirt to puff it out behind.

busy /ˈbɪzɪ/ ● *adjective* (**-ier**, **-iest**) occupied or engaged in work etc.; full of activity; fussy. ● *verb* (**-ies**, **-ied**) occupy, keep busy. ◻ **busybody** meddlesome person; **busy Lizzie** house plant with usually red, pink, or white flowers. □ **busily** *adverb*.

but ● *conjunction* however; on the other hand; otherwise than. ● *preposition* except, apart from. ● *adverb* only. □ **but for** without the help or hindrance etc. of; **but then** however.

butane /ˈbjuːteɪn/ *noun* hydrocarbon used in liquefied form as fuel.

butch /bʊtʃ/ *adjective slang* masculine, tough-looking.

butcher /ˈbʊtʃə/ ● *noun* person who sells meat; slaughterer of animals for food; brutal murderer. ● *verb* slaughter or cut up (animal); kill wantonly or cruelly; *colloquial* ruin through incompetence. □ **butchery** *noun* (*plural* **-ies**).

butler /ˈbʌtlə/ *noun* chief manservant of household.

butt[1] ● *verb* push with head; (cause to) meet end to end. ● *noun* push or blow with head or horns. □ **butt in** interrupt, meddle.

butt[2] *noun* (often + *of*) object of ridicule etc.; mound behind target; (in *plural*) shooting range.

butt[3] *noun* thicker end, esp. of tool or weapon; stub of cigarette etc.

butt[4] *noun* cask.

butter /ˈbʌtə/ ● *noun* yellow fatty substance made from cream, used as spread and in cooking; substance of similar texture. ● *verb* spread, cook, etc., with butter. □ **butter-bean** dried large flat white kind; **buttercup** plant with yellow flowers; **butterfingers** *colloquial* person likely to drop things; **buttermilk** liquid left after butter-making; **butter muslin** thin loosely woven cloth; **butterscotch** sweet made of butter and sugar; **butter up** *colloquial* flatter.

butterfly /ˈbʌtəflaɪ/ *noun* (*plural* **-ies**) insect with 4 often showy wings; (in *plural*) nervous sensation in stomach. □ **butterfly nut** kind of wing-nut; **butterfly stroke** method of swimming with both arms lifted at same time.

buttery[1] *adjective* like or containing butter.

buttery[2] *noun* (*plural* **-ies**) food store or snack-bar, esp. in college.

buttock /ˈbʌtək/ *noun* either protuberance on lower rear part of human trunk; corresponding part of animal.

button /ˈbʌt(ə)n/ ● *noun* disc or knob sewn to garment etc. as fastening or for ornament; knob etc. pressed to operate electronic equipment. ● *verb* (often + *up*) fasten with buttons. □ **button mushroom** small unopened mushroom.

buttonhole ● *noun* slit in cloth for button; flower(s) worn in lapel buttonhole. ● *verb* (**-ling**) *colloquial* accost and detain (reluctant listener).

buttress /ˈbʌtrɪs/ ● *noun* support built against wall etc. ● *verb* support or strengthen.

buxom /ˈbʌksəm/ *adjective* plump and rosy, large and shapely.

buy /baɪ/ ● *verb* (**buys**, **buying**; *past & past participle* **bought** /bɔːt/) obtain in exchange for money etc.; procure by bribery, bribe; get by sacrifice etc.; *slang* accept, believe. ● *noun colloquial* purchase. □ **buy out** pay (a person) for ownership, an interest, etc.; **buyout** purchase of controlling share in company; **buy up** buy as much as possible of.

buyer *noun* person who buys, esp. stock for large shop. □ **buyer's market** time when goods are plentiful and cheap.

buzz ● *noun* hum of bee etc.; sound of buzzer; low murmur; hurried activity; *slang* telephone call; *slang* thrill. ● *verb* hum; summon with buzzer; (often + *about*) move busily; be filled with activity or excitement. □ **buzzword** *colloquial* fashionable technical word, catchword.

buzzard /ˈbʌzəd/ *noun* large bird of hawk family.

buzzer *noun* electrical buzzing device as signal.

by /baɪ/ ● *preposition* near, beside, along; through action, agency, or means of; not later than; past; via; during; to extent of; according to. ● *adverb* near; aside, in reserve; past. □ **by and by** before long; **by-election** parliamentary election between general elections; **by-product** substance etc. produced incidentally in making of something else; **byroad** minor road; **by the by**, **by the way** incidentally; **byway** byroad or secluded path; **byword** person or thing as notable example, proverb.

bye[1] /baɪ/ *noun Cricket* run made from ball that passes batsman without being hit; (in tournament) position of competitor left without opponent in round.

bye[2] /baɪ/ *interjection* (also **bye-bye**) *colloquial* goodbye.

bygone *adjective* past, departed. □ **let bygones be bygones** forgive and forget past quarrels.

by-law *noun* regulation made by local authority etc.

byline *noun* line in newspaper etc. naming writer of article etc.

bypass ● *noun* main road round town or its centre. ● *verb* avoid.

byre /baɪə/ *noun* cowshed.

bystander *noun* person present but not taking part.

byte /baɪt/ *noun Computing* group of 8 binary digits, often representing one character.

Byzantine /bɪˈzæntaɪn/ *adjective* of Byzantium or E. Roman Empire; of architectural etc. style developed in Eastern Empire; complicated, underhand.

Cc

C[1] *noun* (also **c**) (Roman numeral) 100.
C[2] *abbreviation* Celsius; centigrade.
c.[1] *abbreviation* century; cent(s).
c.[2] *abbreviation circa.*
ca. *abbreviation circa.*
CAA *abbreviation* Civil Aviation Authority.
cab *noun* taxi; driver's compartment in lorry, train, crane, etc.
cabal /kə'bæl/ *noun* secret intrigue; political clique.
cabaret /'kæbəreɪ/ *noun* entertainment in restaurant etc.
cabbage /'kæbɪdʒ/ *noun* vegetable with green or purple leaves forming a round head; *colloquial* dull or inactive person. □ **cabbage white** kind of white butterfly.
cabby /'kæbɪ/ *noun* (*plural* **-ies**) *colloquial* taxi driver.
caber /'keɪbə/ *noun* tree trunk tossed as sport in Scotland.
cabin /'kæbɪn/ *noun* small shelter or house, esp. of wood; room or compartment in aircraft, ship, etc. □ **cabin boy** boy steward on ship; **cabin cruiser** large motor boat with accommodation.
cabinet /'kæbɪnɪt/ *noun* cupboard or case for storing or displaying things; casing of radio, television, etc.; (**Cabinet**) group of senior ministers in government. □ **cabinetmaker** skilled joiner.
cable /'keɪb(ə)l/ ● *noun* encased group of insulated wires for transmitting electricity etc.; thick rope of wire or hemp; cablegram. ● *verb* (**-ling**) send (message) or inform (person) by cable. □ **cable car** small cabin on loop of cable for carrying passengers up and down mountain etc.; **cablegram** message sent by undersea cable etc.; **cable stitch** knitting stitch resembling twisted rope; **cable television** transmission of television programmes by cable to subscribers.
caboodle /kə'bu:d(ə)l/ *noun*. □ **the whole caboodle** *slang* the whole lot.
caboose /kə'bu:s/ *noun* kitchen on ship's deck; *US* guard's van on train.
cabriolet /kæbrɪəʊ'leɪ/ *noun* car with folding top.
cacao /kə'kaʊ/ *noun* (*plural* **-s**) seed from which cocoa and chocolate are made; tree bearing it.
cache /kæʃ/ ● *noun* hiding place for treasure, supplies, etc.; things so hidden. ● *verb* (**-ching**) place in cache.
cachet /'kæʃeɪ/ *noun* prestige; distinguishing mark or seal; flat capsule for medicine.
cack-handed /kæk'hændɪd/ *adjective colloquial* clumsy, left-handed.
cackle /'kæk(ə)l/ ● *noun* clucking of hen; raucous laugh; noisy chatter. ● *verb* (**-ling**) emit cackle; chatter noisily.
cacophony /kə'kɒfənɪ/ *noun* (*plural* **-ies**) harsh discordant sound. □ **cacophonous** *adjective*.
cactus /'kæktəs/ *noun* (*plural* **-ti** /-taɪ/ or **-tuses**) plant with thick fleshy stem and usually spines but no leaves.
CAD *abbreviation* computer-aided design.
cad *noun* man who behaves dishonourably. □ **caddish** *adjective*.
cadaver /kə'dævə/ *noun* corpse. □ **cadaverous** *adjective*.
caddie /'kædɪ/ (also **caddy**) ● *noun* (*plural* **-ies**) golfer's attendant carrying clubs etc. ● *verb* (**caddying**) act as caddie.
caddis /'kædɪs/ *noun* □ **caddis-fly** small nocturnal insect living near water; **caddis-worm** larva of caddis-fly.
caddy[1] /'kædɪ/ *noun* (*plural* **-ies**) small container for tea.
caddy[2] = CADDIE.
cadence /'keɪd(ə)ns/ *noun* rhythm; fall in pitch of voice; tonal inflection; close of musical phrase.
cadenza /kə'denzə/ *noun Music* virtuoso passage for soloist during concerto.
cadet /kə'det/ *noun* young trainee in armed services or police force.
cadge *verb* (**-ging**) *colloquial* get or seek by begging.
cadi /'kɑ:dɪ/ *noun* (*plural* **-s**) judge in Muslim country.
cadmium /'kædmɪəm/ *noun* soft bluish-white metallic element.
cadre /'kɑ:də/ *noun* basic unit, esp. of servicemen; group of esp. Communist activists.
caecum /'si:kəm/ *noun* (*US* **cecum**) (*plural* **-ca**) pouch between small and large intestines.
Caerphilly /keə'fɪlɪ/ *noun* kind of mild pale cheese.
Caesarean /sɪ'zeərɪən/ (*US* **Cesarean**, **Cesarian**) ● *adjective* (of birth) effected by Caesarean section. ● *noun* (in full **Caesarean section**) delivery of child by cutting into mother's abdomen.
caesura /sɪ'zjʊərə/ *noun* (*plural* **-s**) pause in line of verse.
café /'kæfeɪ/ *noun* coffee house, restaurant.
cafeteria /kæfɪ'tɪərɪə/ *noun* self-service restaurant.
cafetière /kæfə'tjeə/ *noun* coffee pot with plunger for pressing grounds to bottom.
caffeine /'kæfi:n/ *noun* alkaloid stimulant in tea leaves and coffee beans.
caftan /'kæftæn/ *noun* (also **kaftan**) long tunic worn by men in Near East; long loose dress.
cage ● *noun* structure of bars or wires, esp. for confining animals; open framework, esp. lift in mine etc. ● *verb* (**-ging**) confine in cage.
cagey /'keɪdʒɪ/ *adjective* (**-ier, -iest**) *colloquial* cautious and non-committal. □ **cagily** *adverb*.
cagoule /kə'gu:l/ *noun* light hooded windproof jacket.
cahoots /kə'hu:ts/ *plural noun* □ **in cahoots** *slang* in collusion.
caiman = CAYMAN.
cairn /keən/ *noun* mound of stones. □ **cairn terrier** small shaggy short-legged terrier.
cairngorm /'keəngɔ:m/ *noun* yellow or wine-coloured semiprecious stone.
caisson /'keɪs(ə)n/ *noun* watertight chamber for underwater construction work.
cajole /kə'dʒəʊl/ *verb* (**-ling**) persuade by flattery, deceit, etc. □ **cajolery** *noun*.
cake ● *noun* mixture of flour, butter, eggs, sugar, etc. baked in oven; flattish compact mass. ● *verb* (**-king**) form into compact mass; (usually + *with*) cover (with sticky mass).
calabash /'kæləbæʃ/ *noun* tropical American tree bearing gourds; bowl or pipe made from gourd.
calabrese /'kæləbri:s, kælə'breɪsɪ/ *noun* variety of broccoli.

calamine /ˈkæləmaɪn/ *noun* powdered zinc carbonate and ferric oxide used in skin lotion.

calamity /kəˈlæmɪtɪ/ *noun* (*plural* **-ies**) disaster. □ **calamitous** *adjective*.

calcareous /kælˈkeərɪəs/ *adjective* of or containing calcium carbonate.

calceolaria /kælsɪəˈleərɪə/ *noun* plant with slipper-shaped flowers.

calcify /ˈkælsɪfaɪ/ *verb* (**-ies, -ied**) harden by deposit of calcium salts. □ **calcification** *noun*.

calcine /ˈkælsaɪn/ *verb* (**-ning**) decompose or be decomposed by roasting or burning. □ **calcination** /-sɪn-/ *noun*.

calcium /ˈkælsɪəm/ *noun* soft grey metallic element.

calculate /ˈkælkjʊleɪt/ *verb* (**-ting**) ascertain or forecast by exact reckoning; plan deliberately. □ **calculable** *adjective*; **calculation** *noun*.

calculated *adjective* done with awareness of likely consequences; (+ *to do*) designed.

calculating *adjective* scheming, mercenary.

calculator *noun* device (esp. small electronic one) used for making calculations.

calculus /ˈkælkjʊləs/ *noun* (*plural* **-luses** or **-li** /-laɪ/) *Mathematics* particular method of calculation; stone in body.

Caledonian /kælɪˈdəʊnɪən/ *literary* ● *adjective* of Scotland. ● *noun* Scot.

calendar /ˈkælɪndə/ *noun* system fixing year's beginning, length, and subdivision; chart etc. showing such subdivisions; list of special dates or events. □ **calendar year** period from 1 Jan. to 31 Dec. inclusive.

calends /ˈkælendz/ *plural noun* (also **kalends**) first of month in ancient Roman calendar.

calf[1] /kɑːf/ *noun* (*plural* **calves** /kɑːvz/) young cow, bull, elephant, whale, etc.; calf leather. □ **calf-love** romantic adolescent love.

calf[2] /kɑːf/ *noun* (*plural* **calves** /kɑːvz/) fleshy hind part of human leg below knee.

calibrate /ˈkælɪbreɪt/ *verb* (**-ting**) mark (gauge) with scale of readings; correlate readings of (instrument) with standard; find calibre of (gun). □ **calibration** *noun*.

calibre /ˈkælɪbə/ *noun* (*US* **caliber**) internal diameter of gun or tube; diameter of bullet or shell; strength or quality of character; ability; importance.

calico /ˈkælɪkəʊ/ ● *noun* (*plural* **-es** or *US* **-s**) cotton cloth, esp. white or unbleached; *US* printed cotton cloth. ● *adjective* of calico; *US* multicoloured.

caliper = CALLIPER.

caliph /ˈkeɪlɪf/ *noun historical* chief Muslim civil and religious ruler.

calk *US* = CAULK.

call /kɔːl/ ● *verb* (often + *out*) cry, shout, speak loudly; emit characteristic sound; communicate with by radio or telephone; summon; make brief visit; order to take place; name, describe, or regard as; rouse from sleep; (+ *for*) demand. ● *noun* shout; bird's cry; brief visit; telephone conversation; summons; need, demand. □ **call box** telephone box; **call-girl** prostitute accepting appointments by telephone; **call in** withdraw from circulation, seek advice or services of; **call off** cancel, order (pursuer) to desist; **call the shots**, **tune** *colloquial* be in control; **call up** *verb* telephone, recall, summon (esp. to do military service); **call-up** *noun* summons to do military service. □ **caller** *noun*.

calligraphy /kəˈlɪgrəfɪ/ *noun* beautiful handwriting; art of this. □ **calligrapher** *noun*; **calligraphic** /kælɪˈgræfɪk/ *adjective*.

calling *noun* profession, occupation; vocation.

calliper /ˈkælɪpə/ *noun* (also **caliper**) metal splint to support leg; (in *plural*) compasses for measuring diameters.

callisthenics /kælɪsˈθenɪks/ *plural noun* exercises for fitness and grace. □ **callisthenic** *adjective*.

callosity /kəˈlɒsɪtɪ/ *noun* (*plural* **-ies**) callus.

callous /ˈkæləs/ *adjective* unfeeling, unsympathetic; (also **calloused**) (of skin) hardened. □ **callously** *adverb*; **callousness** *noun*.

callow /ˈkæləʊ/ *adjective* inexperienced, immature.

callus /ˈkæləs/ *noun* (*plural* **calluses**) area of hard thick skin.

calm /kɑːm/ ● *adjective* tranquil, windless; not agitated. ● *noun* calm condition or period. ● *verb* (often + *down*) make or become calm. □ **calmly** *adverb*; **calmness** *noun*.

calomel /ˈkæləmel/ *noun* compound of mercury used as laxative.

Calor gas /ˈkælə/ *noun proprietary term* liquefied butane under pressure in containers for domestic use.

calorie /ˈkælərɪ/ *noun* unit of heat, amount required to raise temperature of one gram (**small calorie**) or one kilogram (**large calorie**) of water by 1°C.

calorific /kæləˈrɪfɪk/ *adjective* producing heat.

calumny /ˈkæləmnɪ/ *noun* (*plural* **-ies**) slander; malicious misrepresentation. □ **calumnious** /kəˈlʌm-/ *adjective*.

calvados /ˈkælvədɒs/ *noun* apple brandy.

calve /kɑːv/ *verb* (**-ving**) give birth to (calf).

calves *plural* of CALF[1,2].

Calvinism /ˈkælvɪnɪz(ə)m/ *noun* Calvin's theology, stressing predestination. □ **Calvinist** *noun & adjective*; **Calvinistic** /-ˈnɪs-/ *adjective*.

calx *noun* (*plural* **calces** /ˈkælsiːz/) powdery residue left after heating of ore or mineral.

calypso /kəˈlɪpsəʊ/ *noun* (*plural* **-s**) W. Indian song with improvised usually topical words.

calyx /ˈkeɪlɪks/ *noun* (*plural* **calyces** /-lɪsiːz/ or **-es**) leaves forming protective case of flower in bud.

cam *noun* projection on wheel etc., shaped to convert circular into reciprocal or variable motion.

camaraderie /kæməˈrɑːdərɪ/ *noun* friendly comradeship.

camber /ˈkæmbə/ ● *noun* convex surface of road, deck, etc. ● *verb* construct with camber.

cambric /ˈkæmbrɪk/ *noun* fine linen or cotton cloth.

camcorder /ˈkæmkɔːdə/ *noun* combined portable video camera and recorder.

came *past* of COME.

camel /ˈkæm(ə)l/ *noun* long-legged ruminant with one hump (**Arabian camel**) or two humps (**Bactrian camel**); fawn colour.

camellia /kəˈmiːlɪə/ *noun* evergreen flowering shrub.

Camembert /ˈkæməmbeə/ *noun* kind of soft creamy cheese.

cameo /ˈkæmɪəʊ/ *noun* (*plural* **-s**) small piece of hard stone carved in relief; short literary sketch or acted scene; small part in play or film.

camera /ˈkæmrə/ *noun* apparatus for taking photographs or for making motion film or television pictures. □ **cameraman** operator of film or television camera; **in camera** in private.

camiknickers /ˈkæmɪnɪkəz/ *plural noun* woman's knickers and vest combined.

camisole /ˈkæmɪsəʊl/ *noun* woman's under-bodice.

camomile /ˈkæməmaɪl/ *noun* (also **chamomile**) aromatic herb with flowers used to make tea.

camouflage /ˈkæməflɑːʒ/ ● *noun* disguising of soldiers, tanks, etc., so that they blend into background; such disguise; animal's natural blending colouring. ● *verb* (**-ging**) hide by camouflage.

camp[1] ● *noun* place where troops are lodged or trained; temporary accommodation of tents, huts, etc., for detainees, holiday-makers, etc.; fortified site; party supporters regarded collectively. ● *verb* set up or live in camp. □ **camp bed** portable folding bed; **camp follower** civilian worker in military camp, disciple; **campsite** place for camping.

camp[2] *colloquial* ● *adjective* affected, theatrically exaggerated; effeminate; homosexual. ● *noun* camp manner. ● *verb* behave or do in camp way.

campaign /kæm'peɪn/ ● *noun* organized course of action, esp. to gain publicity; series of military operations. ● *verb* take part in campaign. □ **campaigner** *noun*.

campanile /kæmpə'ni:lɪ/ *noun* bell tower, usually free-standing.

campanology /kæmpə'nɒlədʒɪ/ *noun* study of bells; bell-ringing. □ **campanologist** *noun*.

campanula /kæm'pænjʊlə/ *noun* plant with bell-shaped flowers.

camper *noun* person who camps; motor vehicle with beds.

camphor /'kæmfə/ *noun* pungent crystalline substance used in medicine and formerly mothballs.

camphorate *verb* (**-ting**) impregnate with camphor.

campion /'kæmpɪən/ *noun* wild plant with usually pink or white notched flowers.

campus /'kæmpəs/ *noun* (*plural* **-es**) grounds of university or college.

camshaft *noun* shaft carrying cam(s).

can[1] *auxiliary verb* (*3rd singular present* **can**; *past* **could** /kʊd/) be able to; have the potential to; be permitted to.

can[2] ● *noun* metal vessel for liquid; sealed tin container for preservation of food or drink; (in *plural*) *slang* headphones; (**the can**) *slang* prison, *US* lavatory. ● *verb* (**-nn-**) preserve (food etc.) in can. □ **canned music** pre-recorded music; **carry the can** bear responsibility; **in the can** *colloquial* completed.

canal /kə'næl/ *noun* artificial inland waterway; tubular duct in plant or animal.

canalize /'kænəlaɪz/ *verb* (also **-ise**) (**-zing** or **-sing**) convert (river) into canal; provide (area) with canal(s); channel. □ **canalization** *noun*.

canapé /'kænəpeɪ/ *noun* small piece of bread or pastry with savoury topping.

canard /'kænɑ:d/ *noun* unfounded rumour.

canary /kə'neərɪ/ *noun* (*plural* **-ies**) small songbird with yellow feathers.

canasta /kə'næstə/ *noun* card games resembling rummy.

cancan /'kænkæn/ *noun* high-kicking dance.

cancel /'kæns(ə)l/ *verb* (**-ll-**; *US* **-l-**) revoke, discontinue (arrangement); delete; mark (ticket, stamp, etc.) to invalidate it; annul; (often + *out*) neutralize, counterbalance; *Mathematics* strike out (equal factor) on each side of equation etc. □ **cancellation** *noun*.

cancer /'kænsə/ *noun* malignant tumour, disease caused by this; corruption; (**Cancer**) fourth sign of zodiac. □ **cancerous** *adjective*.

candela /kæn'di:lə/ *noun* SI unit of luminous intensity.

candelabrum /kændɪ'lɑ:brəm/ *noun* (also **-bra**) (*plural* **-bra**, *US* **-brums**, **-bras**) large branched candlestick or lampholder.

candid /'kændɪd/ *adjective* frank; (of photograph) taken informally, usually without subject's knowledge. □ **candidly** *adverb*.

candidate /'kændɪdət/ *noun* person nominated for, seeking, or likely to gain, office, position, award, etc.; person entered for exam. □ **candidacy** *noun*; **candidature** *noun*.

candle /'kænd(ə)l/ *noun* (usually cylindrical) block of wax or tallow enclosing wick which gives light when burning. □ **candlelight** light from candle(s); **candlelit** lit by candle(s); **candlestick** holder for candle(s); **candlewick** thick soft yarn, tufted material made from this.

candour /'kændə/ *noun* (*US* **candor**) frankness.

candy /'kændɪ/ ● *noun* (*plural* **-ies**) (in full **sugar-candy**) sugar crystallized by repeated boiling and evaporation; *US* sweets, a sweet. ● *verb* (**-ies**, **-ied**) (usually as **candied** *adjective*) preserve (fruit etc.) in candy. □ **candyfloss** fluffy mass of spun sugar; **candy stripe** alternate white and esp. pink stripes.

candytuft /'kændɪtʌft/ *noun* plant with white, pink, or purple flowers in tufts.

cane ● *noun* hollow jointed stem of giant reed or grass, or solid stem of slender palm, used for wickerwork or as walking stick, plant support, instrument of punishment, etc.; sugar cane. ● *verb* (**-ning**) beat with cane; weave cane into (chair etc.).

canine /'keɪnaɪn/ ● *adjective* of a dog or dogs. ● *noun* dog; (in full **canine tooth**) tooth between incisors and molars.

canister /'kænɪstə/ *noun* small usually metal box for tea etc.; cylinder of shot, tear gas, etc.

canker /'kæŋkə/ ● *noun* disease of trees and plants; ulcerous ear disease of animals; corrupting influence. ● *verb* infect with canker; corrupt. □ **cankerous** *adjective*.

cannabis /'kænəbɪs/ *noun* hemp plant; parts of it used as narcotic.

cannelloni /kænə'ləʊnɪ/ *plural noun* tubes of pasta stuffed with savoury mixture.

cannibal /'kænɪb(ə)l/ *noun* person or animal that eats its own species. □ **cannibalism** *noun*; **cannibalistic** /-'lɪs-/ *adjective*.

cannibalize /'kænɪbəlaɪz/ *verb* (also **-ise**) (**-zing** or **-sing**) use (machine etc.) as source of spare parts.

cannon /'kænən/ ● *noun* automatic aircraft gun firing shells; *historical* (*plural* usually same) large gun; hitting of two balls successively by player's ball in billiards. ● *verb* (usually + *against*, *into*) collide. □ **cannon ball** *historical* large ball fired by cannon.

cannot /'kænɒt/ can not.

canny /'kænɪ/ *adjective* (**-ier**, **-iest**) shrewd; thrifty.

canoe /kə'nu:/ ● *noun* light narrow boat, usually paddled. ● *verb* (**-noes**, **-noed**, **-noeing**) travel in canoe. □ **canoeist** *noun*.

canon /'kænən/ *noun* general law, rule, principle, or criterion; church decree; member of cathedral chapter; set of (esp. sacred) writings accepted as genuine; part of RC Mass containing words of consecration; *Music* piece with different parts taking up same theme successively. □ **canon law** ecclesiastical law.

canonical /kə'nɒnɪk(ə)l/ ● *adjective* according to canon law; included in canon of Scripture; authoritative, accepted; of (member of) cathedral chapter. ● *noun* (in *plural*) canonical dress of clergy.

canonize /'kænənaɪz/ *verb* (also **-ise**) (**-zing** or **-sing**) declare officially to be saint. □ **canonization** *noun*.

canopy /'kænəpɪ/ ● *noun* (*plural* **-ies**) suspended covering over throne, bed, etc.; sky; overhanging shelter; rooflike projection. ● *verb* (**-ies**, **-ied**) supply or be canopy to.

cant[1] ● *noun* insincere pious or moral talk; language peculiar to class, profession, etc.; jargon. ● *verb* use cant.

cant[2] ● *noun* slanting surface, bevel; oblique push or jerk; tilted position. ● *verb* push or pitch out of level.

can't /kɑ:nt/ can not.

cantabile /kæn'tɑːbɪleɪ/ *Music* ● *adverb & adjective* in smooth flowing style. ● *noun* cantabile passage or movement.

cantaloupe /'kæntəluːp/ *noun* (also **cantaloup**) small round ribbed melon.

cantankerous /kæn'tæŋkərəs/ *adjective* bad-tempered, quarrelsome. ▫ **cantankerously** *adverb*; **cantankerousness** *noun*.

cantata /kæn'tɑːtə/ *noun* composition for vocal soloists and usually chorus and orchestra.

canteen /kæn'tiːn/ *noun* restaurant for employees in office, factory, etc.; shop for provisions in barracks or camp; case of cutlery; soldier's or camper's water-flask.

canter /'kæntə/ ● *noun* horse's pace between trot and gallop. ● *verb* (cause to) go at a canter.

canticle /'kæntɪk(ə)l/ *noun* song or chant with biblical text.

cantilever /'kæntɪliːvə/ *noun* bracket, beam, etc. projecting from wall to support balcony etc.; beam or girder fixed at one end only. ▫ **cantilever bridge** bridge made of cantilevers projecting from piers and connected by girders. ▫ **cantilevered** *adjective*.

canto /'kæntəʊ/ *noun* (*plural* **-s**) division of long poem.

canton ● *noun* /'kæntɒn/ subdivision of country, esp. Switzerland. ● *verb* /kæn'tuːn/ put (troops) into quarters.

cantonment /kæn'tuːnmənt/ *noun* lodgings of troops.

cantor /'kæntɔː/ *noun* church choir leader; precentor in synagogue.

canvas /'kænvəs/ *noun* strong coarse cloth used for sails and tents etc. and for oil painting; a painting on canvas.

canvass /'kænvəs/ ● *verb* solicit votes (from), ascertain opinions of; seek custom from; propose (idea etc.). ● *noun* canvassing. ▫ **canvasser** *noun*.

canyon /'kænjən/ *noun* deep gorge.

CAP *abbreviation* Common Agricultural Policy (of EC).

cap ● *noun* soft brimless hat, often with peak; head-covering of nurse etc.; cap as sign of membership of sports team; academic mortarboard; cover resembling cap, or designed to close, seal, or protect something; contraceptive diaphragm; percussion cap; dental crown. ● *verb* (**-pp-**) put cap on; cover top or end of; limit; award sports cap to; form top of; surpass.

capable /'keɪpəb(ə)l/ *adjective* competent, able; (+ *of*) having ability, fitness, etc. for. ▫ **capability** *noun* (*plural* **-ies**); **capably** *adverb*.

capacious /kə'peɪʃəs/ *adjective* roomy. ▫ **capaciousness** *noun*.

capacitance /kə'pæsɪt(ə)ns/ *noun* ability to store electric charge.

capacitor /kə'pæsɪtə/ *noun* type of device for storing electric charge.

capacity /kə'pæsɪtɪ/ ● *noun* (*plural* **-ies**) power to contain, receive, experience, or produce; maximum amount that can be contained etc.; mental power; position or function. ● *adjective* fully occupying available space etc.

caparison /kə'pærɪs(ə)n/ *literary* ● *noun* horse's trappings; finery. ● *verb* adorn.

cape[1] *noun* short cloak.

cape[2] *noun* headland, promontory; (**the Cape**) Cape of Good Hope.

caper[1] /'keɪpə/ ● *verb* jump playfully. ● *noun* playful leap; prank; *slang* illicit activity.

caper[2] /'keɪpə/ *noun* bramble-like shrub; (in *plural*) its pickled buds.

capercaillie /kæpə'keɪlɪ/ *noun* (also **capercailzie** /-'keɪlzɪ/) large European grouse.

capillarity /kæpɪ'lærɪtɪ/ *noun* rise or depression of liquid in narrow tube.

capillary /kə'pɪlərɪ/ ● *adjective* of hair; of narrow diameter. ● *noun* (*plural* **-ies**) capillary tube or blood vessel. ▫ **capillary action** capillarity.

capital /'kæpɪt(ə)l/ ● *noun* chief town or city of a country or region; money etc. with which company starts in business; accumulated wealth; capital letter; head of column or pillar. ● *adjective* involving punishment by death; most important; *colloquial* excellent. ▫ **capital gain** profit from sale of investments or property; **capital goods** machinery, plant, etc.; **capital letter** large kind, used to begin sentence or name; **capital transfer tax** *historical* tax levied on transfer of capital by gift or bequest etc.

capitalism *noun* economic and political system dependent on private capital and profit-making.

capitalist ● *noun* person using or possessing capital; advocate of capitalism. ● *adjective* of or favouring capitalism. ▫ **capitalistic** /-'lɪs-/ *adjective*.

capitalize *verb* (also **-ise**) (**-zing** or **-sing**) convert into or provide with capital; write (letter of alphabet) as capital, begin (word) with capital letter; (+ *on*) use to one's advantage. ▫ **capitalization** *noun*.

capitulate /kə'pɪtjʊleɪt/ *verb* (**-ting**) surrender. ▫ **capitulation** *noun*.

capon /'keɪpən/ *noun* castrated cock.

cappuccino /kæpʊ'tʃiːnəʊ/ *noun* (*plural* **-s**) frothy milky coffee.

caprice /kə'priːs/ *noun* whim; lively or fanciful work of music etc.

capricious /kə'prɪʃəs/ *adjective* subject to whims, unpredictable. ▫ **capriciously** *adverb*; **capriciousness** *noun*.

Capricorn /'kæprɪkɔːn/ *noun* tenth sign of zodiac.

capsicum /'kæpsɪkəm/ *noun* plant with edible fruits; red, green, or yellow fruit of this.

capsize /kæp'saɪz/ *verb* (**-zing**) (of boat) be overturned; overturn (boat).

capstan /'kæpst(ə)n/ *noun* thick revolving cylinder for winding cable etc.; revolving spindle controlling speed of tape on tape recorder. ▫ **capstan lathe** lathe with revolving tool holder.

capsule /'kæpsjuːl/ *noun* small soluble case enclosing medicine; detachable compartment of spacecraft or nose-cone of rocket; enclosing membrane; dry fruit releasing seeds when ripe.

Capt. *abbreviation* Captain.

captain /'kæptɪn/ ● *noun* chief, leader; leader of team; commander of ship; pilot of civil aircraft; army officer next above lieutenant. ● *verb* be captain of. ▫ **captaincy** *noun* (*plural* **-ies**).

caption /'kæpʃ(ə)n/ ● *noun* wording appended to illustration or cartoon; wording on cinema or television screen; heading of chapter, article etc. ● *verb* provide with caption.

captious /'kæpʃəs/ *adjective* fault-finding.

captivate /'kæptɪveɪt/ *verb* (**-ting**) fascinate, charm. ▫ **captivation** *noun*.

captive /'kæptɪv/ ● *noun* confined or imprisoned person or animal. ● *adjective* taken prisoner; confined; unable to escape. ▫ **captivity** /-'tɪv-/ *noun*.

captor /'kæptə/ *noun* person who captures.

capture /'kæptʃə/ ● *verb* (**-ring**) take prisoner; seize; portray in permanent form; record on film or for use in computer. ● *noun* act of capturing; thing or person captured.

Capuchin /'kæpjʊtʃɪn/ *noun* friar of branch of Franciscans; (**capuchin**) monkey with hair like black hood.

car *noun* motor vehicle for driver and small number of passengers; railway carriage of specified type; *US* any railway carriage or van. □ **car bomb** terrorist bomb placed in or under parked car; **car boot sale** sale of goods from (tables stocked from) boots of cars; **car park** area for parking cars; **car phone** radio-telephone for use in car etc.; **carport** roofed open-sided shelter for car; **carsick** nauseous through car travel.

caracul = KARAKUL.

carafe /kəˈræf/ *noun* glass container for water or wine.

caramel /ˈkærəmel/ *noun* burnt sugar or syrup; kind of soft toffee. □ **caramelize** *verb*.

carapace /ˈkærəpeɪs/ *noun* upper shell of tortoise or crustacean.

carat /ˈkærət/ *noun* unit of weight for precious stones; measure of purity of gold.

caravan /ˈkærəvæn/ *noun* vehicle equipped for living in and usually towed by car; people travelling together, esp. across desert. □ **caravanner** *noun*.

caravanserai /kærəˈvænsəraɪ/ *noun* Eastern inn with central courtyard.

caravel /ˈkærəvel/ *noun historical* small light fast ship.

caraway /ˈkærəweɪ/ *noun* plant with small aromatic fruit (**caraway seed**) used in cakes etc.

carbide /ˈkɑːbaɪd/ *noun* binary compound of carbon.

carbine /ˈkɑːbaɪn/ *noun* kind of short rifle.

carbohydrate /kɑːbəˈhaɪdreɪt/ *noun* energy-producing compound of carbon, hydrogen, and oxygen.

carbolic /kɑːˈbɒlɪk/ *noun* (in full **carbolic acid**) kind of disinfectant and antiseptic. □ **carbolic soap** soap containing this.

carbon /ˈkɑːbən/ *noun* non-metallic element occurring as diamond, graphite, and charcoal, and in all organic compounds; carbon copy, carbon paper. □ **carbon copy** copy made with carbon paper; **carbon dating** determination of age of object from decay of carbon-14; **carbon dioxide** gas found in atmosphere and formed by respiration; **carbon fibre** thin filament of carbon used as strengthening material; **carbon-14** radioactive carbon isotope of mass 14; **carbon monoxide** poisonous gas formed by burning carbon incompletely; **carbon paper** thin carbon-coated paper for making copies; **carbon tax** tax on fuels producing greenhouse gases; **carbon-12** stable isotope of carbon used as a standard.

carbonate /ˈkɑːbəneɪt/ ● *noun* salt of carbonic acid. ● *verb* (**-ting**) fill with carbon dioxide.

carbonic /kɑːˈbɒnɪk/ *adjective* containing carbon. □ **carbonic acid** weak acid formed from carbon dioxide in water.

carboniferous /kɑːbəˈnɪfərəs/ *adjective* producing coal.

carbonize /ˈkɑːbənaɪz/ *verb* (also **-ise**) (**-zing** or **-sing**) reduce to charcoal or coke; convert to carbon; coat with carbon. □ **carbonization** *noun*.

carborundum /kɑːbəˈrʌndəm/ *noun* compound of carbon and silicon used esp. as abrasive.

carboy /ˈkɑːbɔɪ/ *noun* large globular glass bottle.

carbuncle /ˈkɑːbʌŋk(ə)l/ *noun* severe skin abscess; bright red jewel.

carburettor /kɑːbəˈretə/ *noun* apparatus mixing air with petrol vapour in internal-combustion engine.

carcass /ˈkɑːkəs/ *noun* (also **carcase**) dead body of animal or bird or (*colloquial*) person; framework; worthless remains.

carcinogen /kɑːˈsɪnədʒ(ə)n/ *noun* substance producing cancer. □ **carcinogenic** /-ˈdʒen-/ *adjective*.

card[1] *noun* thick stiff paper or thin pasteboard; piece of this for writing or printing on, esp. to send greetings, to identify person, or to record information; small rectangular piece of plastic used to obtain credit etc.; playing card; (in *plural*) card-playing; (in *plural*) *colloquial* employee's tax etc. documents; programme of events at race meeting etc.; *colloquial* eccentric person. □ **cardcarrying** registered as member (esp. of political party); **card index** index with separate card for each item; **cardphone** public telephone operated by card instead of money; **cardsharp** swindler at card games; **card vote** block vote.

card[2] ● *noun* wire brush etc. for raising nap on cloth etc. ● *verb* brush with card.

cardamom /ˈkɑːdəməm/ *noun* seeds of SE Asian aromatic plant used as spice.

cardboard *noun* pasteboard or stiff paper.

cardiac /ˈkɑːdɪæk/ *adjective* of the heart.

cardigan /ˈkɑːdɪgən/ *noun* knitted jacket.

cardinal /ˈkɑːdɪn(ə)l/ ● *adjective* chief, fundamental; deep scarlet. ● *noun* one of leading RC dignitaries who elect Pope. □ **cardinal number** number representing quantity (1, 2, 3, etc.); compare ORDINAL.

cardiogram /ˈkɑːdɪəʊgræm/ *noun* record of heart movements.

cardiograph /ˈkɑːdɪəʊgrɑːf/ *noun* instrument recording heart movements. □ **cardiographer** /-ˈɒgrəfə/ *noun*; **cardiography** /-ˈɒgrəfɪ/ *noun*.

cardiology /kɑːdɪˈɒlədʒɪ/ *noun* branch of medicine concerned with heart. □ **cardiologist** *noun*.

cardiovascular /kɑːdɪəʊˈvæskjʊlə/ *adjective* of heart and blood vessels.

care /keə/ ● *noun* (cause of) anxiety or concern; serious attention; caution; protection, charge; task. ● *verb* (**-ring**) (usually + *about*, *for*, *whether*) feel concern or interest or affection. □ **in care** (of child) under local authority supervision; **take care** be careful, (+ *to do*) not fail or neglect; **take care of** look after, deal with, dispose of.

careen /kəˈriːn/ *verb* turn (ship) on side for repair; move or swerve wildly.

career /kəˈrɪə/ ● *noun* professional etc. course through life; profession or occupation; swift course. ● *adjective* pursuing or wishing to pursue a career; working permanently in specified profession. ● *verb* move or swerve wildly.

careerist *noun* person predominantly concerned with personal advancement.

carefree *adjective* light-hearted, joyous.

careful *adjective* painstaking; cautious; taking care, not neglecting. □ **carefully** *adverb*; **carefulness** *noun*.

careless *adjective* lacking care or attention; unthinking, insensitive; light-hearted. □ **carelessly** *adverb*; **carelessness** *noun*.

carer *noun* person who cares for sick or elderly person, esp. at home.

caress /kəˈres/ ● *verb* touch lovingly. ● *noun* loving touch.

caret /ˈkærət/ *noun* mark indicating insertion in text.

caretaker ● *noun* person in charge of maintenance of building. ● *adjective* taking temporary control.

careworn *adjective* showing effects of prolonged anxiety.

cargo /ˈkɑːgəʊ/ *noun* (*plural* **-es** or **-s**) goods carried by ship or aircraft.

Caribbean /kærəˈbiːən/ *adjective* of the West Indies.

caribou /ˈkærɪbuː/ *noun* (*plural* same) N. American reindeer.

caricature /ˈkærɪkətʃʊə/ ● *noun* grotesque usually comically exaggerated representation. ● *verb* (**-ring**) make or give caricature of. □ **caricaturist** *noun*.

caries /ˈkeəriːz/ *noun* (*plural* same) decay of tooth or bone.

carillon /kəˈrɪljən/ *noun* set of bells sounded from keyboard or mechanically; tune played on this.

Carmelite /'kɑːməlaɪt/ ● *noun* friar of Order of Our Lady of Mount Carmel; nun of similar order. ● *adjective* of Carmelites.

carminative /'kɑːmɪnətɪv/ ● *adjective* relieving flatulence. ● *noun* carminative drug.

carmine /'kɑːmaɪn/ ● *adjective* of vivid crimson colour. ● *noun* this colour; pigment from cochineal.

carnage /'kɑːnɪdʒ/ *noun* great slaughter.

carnal /'kɑːn(ə)l/ *adjective* worldly; sensual; sexual. □ **carnality** *noun*.

carnation /kɑː'neɪʃ(ə)n/ ● *noun* clove-scented pink; rosy-pink colour. ● *adjective* rosy-pink.

carnelian = CORNELIAN.

carnival /'kɑːnɪv(ə)l/ *noun* festivities or festival, esp. preceding Lent; merrymaking.

carnivore /'kɑːnɪvɔː/ *noun* animal or plant that feeds on flesh. □ **carnivorous** /-'nɪvərəs-/ *adjective*.

carob /'kærəb/ *noun* seed pod of Mediterranean tree used as chocolate substitute.

carol /'kær(ə)l/ ● *noun* joyous song, esp. Christmas hymn. ● *verb* (**-ll-**; *US* **-l-**) sing carols; sing joyfully.

carotene /'kærətiːn/ *noun* orange-coloured pigment in carrots etc.

carotid /kə'rɒtɪd/ ● *noun* each of two main arteries carrying blood to head. ● *adjective* of these arteries.

carouse /kə'raʊz/ ● *verb* (**-sing**) have lively drinking party. ● *noun* such party. □ **carousal** *noun*; **carouser** *noun*.

carp[1] *noun* (*plural* same) freshwater fish often bred for food.

carp[2] *verb* find fault, complain. □ **carper** *noun*.

carpal /'kɑːp(ə)l/ ● *adjective* of the wrist-bones. ● *noun* wrist-bone.

carpel /'kɑːp(ə)l/ *noun* female reproductive organ of flower.

carpenter /'kɑːpɪntə/ ● *noun* person skilled in woodwork. ● *verb* do woodwork; make by woodwork. □ **carpentry** *noun*.

carpet /'kɑːpɪt/ ● *noun* thick fabric for covering floors etc.; piece of this; thing resembling this. ● *verb* (**-t-**) cover (as) with carpet; *colloquial* rebuke. □ **carpet-bag** travelling bag originally made of carpet-like material; **carpet-bagger** *colloquial* political candidate etc. without local connections; **carpet slipper** soft slipper; **carpet sweeper** implement for sweeping carpets.

carpeting *noun* material for carpets; carpets collectively.

carpus /'kɑːpəs/ *noun* (*plural* **-pi** /-paɪ/) group of small bones forming wrist.

carrageen /'kærəgiːn/ *noun* edible red seaweed.

carriage /'kærɪdʒ/ *noun* railway passenger vehicle; wheeled horse-drawn passenger vehicle; conveying of goods; cost of this; bearing, deportment; part of machine that carries other parts; gun carriage. □ **carriage clock** portable clock with handle; **carriageway** part of road used by vehicles.

carrier /'kærɪə/ *noun* person or thing that carries; transport or freight company; carrier bag; framework on bicycle for carrying luggage or passenger; person or animal that may transmit disease without suffering from it; aircraft carrier. □ **carrier bag** plastic or paper bag with handles; **carrier pigeon** pigeon trained to carry messages; **carrier wave** high-frequency electromagnetic wave used to convey signal.

carrion /'kærɪən/ *noun* dead flesh; filth. □ **carrion crow** crow feeding on carrion.

carrot /'kærət/ *noun* plant with edible tapering orange root; this root; incentive. □ **carroty** *adjective*.

carry /'kærɪ/ *verb* (**-ies**, **-ied**) support or hold up, esp. while moving; have with one; convey; (often + *to*) take (process etc.) to specified point; involve; transfer (figure) to column of higher value; hold in specified way; (of newspaper etc.) publish; (of radio or television station) broadcast; keep (goods) in stock; (of sound) be audible at a distance; win victory or acceptance for; win acceptance from; capture. □ **carry away** remove, inspire, deprive of self-control; **carrycot** portable cot for baby; **carry forward** transfer (figure) to new page or account; **carry it off** do well under difficulties; **carry off** remove (esp. by force), win, (esp. of disease) kill; **carry on** continue, *colloquial* behave excitedly, (often + *with*) *colloquial* flirt; **carry-on** *colloquial* fuss; **carry out** put into practice; **carry-out** take-away; **carry over** carry forward, postpone; **carry through** complete, bring safely out of difficulties.

cart ● *noun* open usually horse-drawn vehicle for carrying loads; light vehicle for pulling by hand. ● *verb* carry in cart; *slang* carry with difficulty. □ **cart horse** horse of heavy build; **cartwheel** wheel of cart, sideways somersault with arms and legs extended.

carte blanche /kɑːt 'blɑ̃ʃ/ *noun* full discretionary power.

cartel /kɑː'tel/ *noun* union of suppliers etc. set up to control prices.

Cartesian coordinates /kɑː'tiːzɪən/ *plural noun* system of locating point by its distance from two perpendicular axes.

Carthusian /kɑː'θjuːzɪən/ ● *noun* monk of contemplative order founded by St Bruno. ● *adjective* of this order.

cartilage /'kɑːtɪlɪdʒ/ *noun* firm flexible connective tissue in vertebrates. □ **cartilaginous** /-'lædʒ-/ *adjective*.

cartography /kɑː'tɒgrəfɪ/ *noun* map-drawing. □ **cartographer** *noun*; **cartographic** /-tə'græf-/ *adjective*.

carton /'kɑːt(ə)n/ *noun* light esp. cardboard container.

cartoon /kɑː'tuːn/ *noun* humorous esp. topical drawing in newspaper etc.; sequence of drawings telling story; such sequence animated on film; full-size preliminary design for work of art. □ **cartoonist** *noun*.

cartouche /kɑː'tuːʃ/ *noun* scroll-like ornament; oval enclosing name and title of pharaoh.

cartridge /'kɑːtrɪdʒ/ *noun* case containing explosive charge or bullet; sealed container of film etc.; component carrying stylus on record player; ink-container for insertion in pen. □ **cartridge-belt** belt with pockets or loops for cartridges; **cartridge paper** thick paper for drawing etc.

carve *verb* (**-ving**) make or shape by cutting; cut pattern etc. in; (+ *into*) form pattern etc. from; cut (meat) into slices. □ **carve out** take from larger whole; **carve up** subdivide, drive aggressively into path of (another vehicle). □ **carver** *noun*.

carvery *noun* (*plural* **-ies**) restaurant etc. with joints displayed for carving.

carving *noun* carved object, esp. as work of art. □ **carving knife** knife for carving meat.

cascade /kæs'keɪd/ ● *noun* waterfall, esp. one in series. ● *verb* (**-ding**) fall in or like cascade.

case[1] /keɪs/ *noun* instance of something occurring; hypothetical or actual situation; person's illness, circumstances, etc. as regarded by doctor, social worker, etc.; such a person; crime etc. investigated by detective or police; suit at law; sum of arguments on one side; (valid) set of arguments; *Grammar* relation of word to others in sentence, form of word expressing this. □ **case law** law as established by decided cases; **casework** social work concerned with individual's background; **in any case** whatever the truth or possible outcome is; **in case** in the event that, lest, in provision against a possibility; **in case of** in the event of; **is (not) the case** is (not) so.

case[2] /keɪs/ ● *noun* container or cover enclosing something. ● *verb* (**-sing**) enclose in case; (+ *with*) surround with; *slang* inspect closely, esp. for criminal purpose. □ **case-harden** harden surface of (esp. steel), make callous.

casein /'keɪsɪɪn/ *noun* main protein in milk and cheese.

casement /'keɪsmənt/ *noun* (part of) window hinged to open like door.

cash ● *noun* money in coins or notes; full payment at time of purchase. ● *verb* give or obtain cash for. □ **cash and carry** (esp. wholesaling) system of cash payment for goods removed by buyer, store where this operates; **cashcard** plastic card for use in cash dispenser; **cash crop** crop produced for sale; **cash desk** counter etc. where goods are paid for; **cash dispenser** automatic machine for withdrawal of cash; **cash flow** movement of money into and out of a business; **cash in** obtain cash for, (usually + *on*) *colloquial* profit (from); **cash register** till recording sales, totalling receipts, etc.; **cash up** count day's takings.

cashew /'kæʃu:/ *noun* evergreen tree bearing kidney-shaped edible nut; this nut.

cashier[1] /kæ'ʃɪə/ *noun* person dealing with cash transactions in bank etc.

cashier[2] /kæ'ʃɪə/ *verb* dismiss from service.

cashmere /kæʃ'mɪə/ *noun* fine soft (material of) wool, esp. of Kashmir goat.

casing *noun* enclosing material or cover.

casino /kə'si:nəʊ/ *noun* (*plural* **-s**) public room etc. for gambling.

cask /kɑ:sk/ *noun* barrel, esp. for alcoholic liquor.

casket /'kɑ:skɪt/ *noun* small box for holding valuables; *US* coffin.

cassava /kə'sɑ:və/ *noun* plant with starchy roots; starch or flour from these.

casserole /'kæsərəʊl/ ● *noun* covered dish for cooking food in oven; food cooked in this. ● *verb* (**-ling**) cook in casserole.

cassette /kə'set/ *noun* sealed case containing magnetic tape, film, etc., ready for insertion in tape recorder, camera, etc.

cassia /'kæsɪə/ *noun* tree whose leaves and pod yield senna.

cassis /kæ'sɪ:s/ *noun* blackcurrant flavouring for drinks etc.

cassock /'kæsək/ *noun* long usually black or red clerical garment.

cassowary /'kæsəweərɪ/ *noun* (*plural* **-ies**) large flightless Australian bird.

cast /kɑ:st/ ● *verb* (*past & past participle* **cast**) throw; direct, cause to fall; express (doubts etc.); let down (anchor etc.); shed or lose; register (vote); shape (molten metal etc.) in mould; make (product) thus; (usually + *as*) assign (actor) to role; allocate roles in (play, film, etc.); (+ *in*, *into*) arrange (facts etc.) in specified form. ● *noun* throwing of missile, dice, fishing line, etc.; thing made in mould; moulded mass of solidified material; actors in play etc.; form, type, or quality; tinge of colour; slight squint; worm-cast. □ **cast about, around** search; **cast aside** abandon; **casting vote** deciding vote when votes on two sides are equal; **cast iron** hard but brittle iron alloy; **cast-iron** of cast iron, very strong, unchallengeable; **cast off** abandon, finish piece of knitting; **cast-off** abandoned or discarded (thing, esp. garment); **cast on** make first row of piece of knitting.

castanet /kæstə'net/ *noun* (usually in *plural*) each of pair of hand-held wooden or ivory shells clicked together in time with esp. Spanish dancing.

castaway /'kɑ:stəweɪ/ ● *noun* shipwrecked person. ● *adjective* shipwrecked.

caste /kɑ:st/ *noun* any of Hindu hereditary classes whose members have no social contact with other classes; exclusive social class.

castellated /'kæstəleɪtɪd/ *adjective* built with battlements. □ **castellation** *noun*.

caster = CASTOR.

castigate /'kæstɪgeɪt/ *verb* (**-ting**) rebuke; punish. □ **castigation** *noun*.

castle /'kɑ:s(ə)l/ ● *noun* large fortified residential building; *Chess* rook. ● *verb* (**-ling**) *Chess* make combined move of king and rook.

castor /'kɑ:stə/ *noun* (also **caster**) small swivelled wheel enabling heavy furniture to be moved; container perforated for sprinkling sugar etc. □ **castor sugar** finely granulated white sugar.

castor oil *noun* vegetable oil used as laxative and lubricant.

castrate /kæs'treɪt/ *verb* (**-ting**) remove testicles of. □ **castration** *noun*.

casual /'kæʒʊəl/ ● *adjective* chance; not regular or permanent; unconcerned, careless; (of clothes etc.) informal. ● *noun* casual worker; (usually in *plural*) casual clothes or shoes. □ **casually** *adverb*.

casualty /'kæʒʊəltɪ/ *noun* (*plural* **-ies**) person killed or injured in war or accident; thing lost or destroyed; casualty department; accident. □ **casualty department** part of hospital for treatment of casualties.

casuist /'kæʒʊɪst/ *noun* person who resolves cases of conscience etc., esp. cleverly but falsely; sophist, quibbler. □ **casuistic** *adjective*; **casuistry** /-'ɪs-/ *noun*.

cat *noun* small furry domestic quadruped; wild animal of same family; *colloquial* malicious or spiteful woman; cat-o'-nine-tails. □ **cat burglar** burglar who enters by climbing to upper storey; **catcall** (make) shrill whistle of disapproval; **catfish** fish with whisker-like filaments round mouth; **cat flap** small flap allowing cat passage through outer door; **catnap** (have) short sleep; **cat-o'-nine-tails** *historical* whip with nine knotted cords; **cat's cradle** child's game with string; **cat's-eye** *proprietary term* reflector stud set into road; **cat's-paw** person used as tool by another; **catsuit** close-fitting garment with trouser legs, covering whole body; **catwalk** narrow walkway; **rain cats and dogs** rain hard.

catachresis /kætə'kri:sɪs/ *noun* (*plural* **-chreses** /-si:z/) incorrect use of words. □ **catachrestic** /-'kres-/ *adjective*.

cataclysm /'kætəklɪz(ə)m/ *noun* violent upheaval. □ **cataclysmic** /-'klɪz-/ *adjective*.

catacomb /'kætəku:m/ *noun* (often in *plural*) underground cemetery.

catafalque /'kætəfælk/ *noun* decorated bier, esp. for state funeral etc.

Catalan /'kætəlæn/ ● *noun* native or language of Catalonia in Spain. ● *adjective* of Catalonia.

catalepsy /'kætəlepsɪ/ *noun* trance or seizure with rigidity of body. □ **cataleptic** /-'lep-/ *adjective & noun*.

catalogue /'kætəlɒg/ (*US* **catalog**) ● *noun* complete or extensive list, usually in alphabetical or other systematic order. ● *verb* (**-logues, -logued, -loguing**; *US* **-logs, -loged, -loging**) make catalogue of; enter in catalogue.

catalysis /kə'tælɪsɪs/ *noun* (*plural* **-lyses** /-si:z/) acceleration of chemical reaction by catalyst. □ **catalyse** *verb* (**-sing**) (*US* **-lyze**; **-zing**).

catalyst /ˈkætəlɪst/ *noun* substance speeding chemical reaction without itself permanently changing; person or thing that precipitates change.

catalytic /kætəˈlɪtɪk/ *adjective* involving or causing catalysis. □ **catalytic converter** device in vehicle for converting pollutant gases into less harmful ones.

catamaran /kætəməˈræn/ *noun* boat or raft with two parallel hulls.

catapult /ˈkætəpʌlt/ ● *noun* forked stick with elastic for shooting stones; *historical* military machine for hurling stones etc.; device for launching glider etc. ● *verb* launch with catapult; fling forcibly; leap or be hurled forcibly.

cataract /ˈkætərækt/ *noun* waterfall, downpour; progressive opacity of eye lens.

catarrh /kəˈtɑː/ *noun* inflammation of mucous membrane, air-passages, etc; mucus in nose caused by this. □ **catarrhal** *adjective*.

catastrophe /kəˈtæstrəfɪ/ *noun* great usually sudden disaster; denouement of drama. □ **catastrophic** /kætəˈstrɒf-/ *adjective*; **catastrophically** /kætəˈstrɒf-/ *adverb*.

catch /kætʃ/ ● *verb* (*past & past participle* **caught** /kɔːt/) capture in trap, hands, etc.; detect or surprise; intercept and hold (moving thing) in hand etc.; *Cricket* dismiss (batsman) by catching ball before it hits ground; contract (disease) by infection etc.; reach in time and board (train etc.); apprehend; check or be checked; become entangled; (of artist etc.) reproduce faithfully; reach or overtake. ● *noun* act of catching; *Cricket* chance or act of catching ball; amount of thing caught; thing or person caught or worth catching; question etc. intended to deceive etc.; unexpected difficulty or disadvantage; device for fastening door etc.; musical round. □ **catch fire** begin to burn; **catch on** *colloquial* become popular, understand what is meant; **catch out** detect in mistake etc., *Cricket* catch; **catchpenny** intended merely to sell quickly; **catchphrase** phrase in frequent use; **catch up** (often + *with*) reach (person etc. ahead), make up arrears, involve, fasten; **catchword** phrase or word in frequent use, word so placed as to draw attention.

catching *adjective* infectious.

catchment area *noun* area served by school, hospital, etc.; area from which rainfall flows into river etc.

catchy *adjective* (**-ier**, **-iest**) (of tune) easily remembered, attractive.

catechism /ˈkætɪkɪz(ə)m/ *noun* (book containing) principles of a religion in form of questions and answers; series of questions.

catechize /ˈkætɪkaɪz/ *verb* (also **-ise**) (**-zing** or **-sing**) instruct by question and answer. □ **catechist** *noun*.

catechumen /kætɪˈkjuːmən/ *noun* person being instructed before baptism.

categorical /kætɪˈgɒrɪk(ə)l/ *adjective* unconditional, absolute, explicit. □ **categorically** *adverb*.

categorize /ˈkætɪgəraɪz/ *verb* (also **-ise**) (**-zing** or **-sing**) place in category. □ **categorization** *noun*.

category /ˈkætɪgərɪ/ *noun* (*plural* **-ies**) class or division (of things, ideas, etc.).

cater /ˈkeɪtə/ *verb* supply food; (+ *for*) provide what is required for. □ **caterer** *noun*.

caterpillar /ˈkætəpɪlə/ *noun* larva of butterfly or moth; (**Caterpillar**) (in full **Caterpillar track**) *proprietary term* articulated steel band passing round wheels of vehicle for travel on rough ground.

caterwaul /ˈkætəwɔːl/ *verb* howl like cat.

catgut *noun* thread made from intestines of sheep etc. used for strings of musical instruments etc.

catharsis /kəˈθɑːsɪs/ *noun* (*plural* **catharses** /-siːz/) emotional release; emptying of bowels.

cathartic /kəˈθɑːtɪk/ ● *adjective* effecting catharsis. ● *noun* laxative.

cathedral /kəˈθiːdr(ə)l/ *noun* principal church of diocese.

Catherine wheel /ˈkæθrɪn/ *noun* rotating firework.

catheter /ˈkæθɪtə/ *noun* tube inserted into body cavity to introduce or drain fluid.

cathode /ˈkæθəʊd/ *noun* negative electrode of cell; positive terminal of battery. □ **cathode ray** beam of electrons from cathode of vacuum tube; **cathode ray tube** vacuum tube in which cathode rays produce luminous image on fluorescent screen.

catholic /ˈkæθlɪk/ ● *adjective* universal; broad-minded; all-embracing; (**Catholic**) Roman Catholic; (**Catholic**) including all Christians or all of Western Church. ● *noun* (**Catholic**) Roman Catholic. □ **Catholicism** /kəˈθɒlɪs-/ *noun*; **catholicity** /-əˈlɪs-/ *noun*.

cation /ˈkætaɪən/ *noun* positively charged ion. □ **cationic** /-ˈɒnɪk/ *adjective*.

catkin /ˈkætkɪn/ *noun* spike of usually hanging flowers of willow, hazel, etc.

catmint *noun* pungent plant attractive to cats.

catnip *noun* catmint.

cattery *noun* (*plural* **-ies**) place where cats are boarded.

cattle /ˈkæt(ə)l/ *plural noun* large ruminants, bred esp. for milk or meat. □ **cattle grid** grid over ditch, allowing vehicles to pass over but not livestock.

catty *adjective* (**-ier**, **-iest**) spiteful. □ **cattily** *adverb*; **cattiness** *noun*.

Caucasian /kɔːˈkeɪʒ(ə)n/ ● *adjective* of the white or light-skinned race. ● *noun* Caucasian person.

caucus /ˈkɔːkəs/ *noun* (*plural* **-es**) *US* meeting of party members to decide policy; *often derogatory* (meeting of) group within larger organization.

caudal /ˈkɔːd(ə)l/ *adjective* of, like, or at tail.

caudate /ˈkɔːdeɪt/ *adjective* tailed.

caught *past & past participle* of CATCH.

caul /kɔːl/ *noun* membrane enclosing foetus; part of this sometimes found on child's head at birth.

cauldron /ˈkɔːldrən/ *noun* large vessel for boiling things in.

cauliflower /ˈkɒlɪflaʊə/ *noun* cabbage with large white flower head.

caulk /kɔːk/ *verb* (*US* **calk**) stop up (ship's seams); make watertight.

causal /ˈkɔːz(ə)l/ *adjective* relating to cause (and effect). □ **causality** /-ˈzæl-/ *noun*.

causation /kɔːˈzeɪʃ(ə)n/ *noun* causing, causality.

cause /kɔːz/ ● *noun* thing producing effect; reason or motive; justification; principle, belief, or purpose; matter to be settled, or case offered, at law. ● *verb* (**-sing**) be cause of; produce; (+ *to do*) make.

cause célèbre /kɔːz seˈlebr/ *noun* (*plural* ***causes célèbres*** same pronunciation) lawsuit that excites much interest. [French]

causeway /ˈkɔːzweɪ/ *noun* raised road across low ground or water; raised path by road.

caustic /ˈkɔːstɪk/ ● *adjective* corrosive, burning; sarcastic, biting. ● *noun* caustic substance. □ **caustic soda** sodium hydroxide. □ **causticity** /-ˈtɪs-/ *noun*.

cauterize /ˈkɔːtəraɪz/ *verb* (also **-ise**) (**-zing** or **-sing**) burn (tissue), esp. to stop bleeding.

caution /ˈkɔːʃ(ə)n/ ● *noun* attention to safety; warning; *colloquial* amusing or surprising person or thing. ● *verb* warn, admonish.

cautionary *adjective* warning.

cautious /ˈkɔːʃəs/ *adjective* having or showing caution. □ **cautiously** *adverb*; **cautiousness** *noun*.

cavalcade /kævəlˈkeɪd/ *noun* procession of riders, cars, etc.

cavalier /kævəˈlɪə/ ● *noun* courtly gentleman; *archaic* horseman; (**Cavalier**) *historical* supporter of Charles I in English Civil War. ● *adjective* offhand, supercilious, curt.
cavalry /ˈkævəlrɪ/ *noun* (*plural* **-ies**) (usually treated as *plural*) soldiers on horseback or in armoured vehicles.
cave ● *noun* large hollow in side of cliff, hill, etc., or underground. ● *verb* (**-ving**) explore caves. □ **cave in** (cause to) subside or collapse, yield, submit.
caveat /ˈkævɪæt/ *noun* warning, proviso.
cavern /ˈkæv(ə)n/ *noun* cave, esp. large or dark one.
cavernous *adjective* full of caverns; huge or deep as cavern.
caviar /ˈkævɪɑ:/ *noun* (also **caviar**) pickled sturgeon-roe.
cavil /ˈkævɪl/ ● *verb* (**-ll-**; *US* **-l-**) (usually + *at*, *about*) make petty objections. ● *noun* petty objection.
cavity /ˈkævɪtɪ/ *noun* (*plural* **-ies**) hollow within solid body; decayed part of tooth. □ **cavity wall** two walls separated by narrow space.
cavort /kəˈvɔ:t/ *verb* caper.
caw ● *noun* cry of rook etc. ● *verb* utter this cry.
cayenne /keɪˈen/ *noun* (in full **cayenne pepper**) powdered red pepper.
cayman /ˈkeɪmən/ *noun* (also **caiman**) (*plural* **-s**) S. American alligator-like reptile.
CB *abbreviation* citizens' band; Commander of the Order of the Bath.
CBE *abbreviation* Commander of the Order of the British Empire.
CBI *abbreviation* Confederation of British Industry.
cc *abbreviation* cubic centimetre(s).
CD *abbreviation* compact disc; *Corps Diplomatique*.
CD-ROM *abbreviation* compact disc read-only memory.
cease /si:s/ *formal verb* (**-sing**) stop; bring or come to an end. □ **cease-fire** (order for) truce; **without cease** unending.
ceaseless *adjective* without end. □ **ceaselessly** *adverb*.
cedar /ˈsi:də/ *noun* evergreen conifer; its durable fragrant wood.
cede /si:d/ *verb* (**-ding**) *formal* give up one's rights to or possession of.
cedilla /sɪˈdɪlə/ *noun* mark (̧) under *c* (in French, to show it is pronounced /s/, not /k/).
ceilidh /ˈkeɪlɪ/ *noun* informal gathering for music, dancing, etc.
ceiling /ˈsi:lɪŋ/ *noun* upper interior surface of room; upper limit; maximum altitude of aircraft.
celandine /ˈseləndaɪn/ *noun* yellow-flowered plant.
celebrant /ˈselɪbrənt/ *noun* person performing rite, esp. priest at Eucharist.
celebrate /ˈselɪbreɪt/ *verb* (**-ting**) mark with or engage in festivities; perform (rite or ceremony); praise publicly. □ **celebration** *noun*; **celebratory** /-ˈbreɪt-/ *adjective*.
celebrity /sɪˈlebrɪtɪ/ *noun* (*plural* **-ies**) well-known person; fame.
celeriac /sɪˈlerɪæk/ *noun* variety of celery.
celery /ˈselərɪ/ *noun* plant of which stalks are used as vegetable.
celesta /sɪˈlestə/ *noun* keyboard instrument with steel plates struck with hammers.
celestial /sɪˈlestɪəl/ *adjective* of sky or heavenly bodies; heavenly, divinely good.
celibate /ˈselɪbət/ ● *adjective* unmarried, or abstaining from sexual relations, often for religious reasons. ● *noun* celibate person. □ **celibacy** *noun*.
cell /sel/ *noun* small room, esp. in prison or monastery; small compartment, e.g. in honeycomb; small active political group; unit of structure of organic matter; enclosed cavity in organism etc.; vessel containing electrodes for current-generation or electrolysis. □ **cellphone** portable radio-telephone.
cellar /ˈselə/ *noun* underground storage room; stock of wine in cellar.
cello /ˈtʃeləʊ/ *noun* (*plural* **-s**) bass instrument of violin family, held between legs of seated player. □ **cellist** *noun*.
Cellophane /ˈseləfeɪn/ *noun proprietary term* thin transparent wrapping material.
cellular /ˈseljʊlə/ *adjective* consisting of cells; of open texture, porous. □ **cellularity** /-ˈlær-/ *noun*.
cellulite /ˈseljʊlaɪt/ *noun* lumpy fat, esp. on women's hips and thighs.
celluloid /ˈseljʊlɔɪd/ *noun* plastic made from camphor and cellulose nitrate; cinema film.
cellulose /ˈseljʊləʊs/ *noun* carbohydrate forming plant-cell walls; paint or lacquer consisting of cellulose acetate or nitrate in solution.
Celsius /ˈselsɪəs/ *adjective* of scale of temperature on which water freezes at 0° and boils at 100°.
Celt /kelt/ *noun* (also **Kelt**) member of an ethnic group including inhabitants of Ireland, Wales, Scotland, Cornwall, and Brittany.
Celtic /ˈkeltɪk/ ● *adjective* of the Celts. ● *noun* group of Celtic languages.
cement /sɪˈment/ ● *noun* substance made from lime and clay, mixed with water, sand, etc. to form mortar or concrete; adhesive. ● *verb* unite firmly, strengthen; apply cement to.
cemetery /ˈsemɪtrɪ/ *noun* (*plural* **-ies**) burial ground, esp. one not in churchyard.
cenotaph /ˈsenətɑ:f/ *noun* tomblike monument to person(s) whose remains are elsewhere.
Cenozoic /si:nəˈzəʊɪk/ ● *adjective* of most recent geological era, marked by evolution of mammals etc. ● *noun* this era.
censer /ˈsensə/ *noun* incense-burning vessel.
censor /ˈsensə/ ● *noun* official with power to suppress or expurgate books, films, news, etc., on grounds of obscenity, threat to security, etc. ● *verb* act as censor of; make deletions or changes in. □ **censorial** /-ˈsɔ:r-/ *adjective*; **censorship** *noun*.

■ **Usage** As a verb, *censor* is often confused with *censure*, which means 'to criticize harshly'.

censorious /senˈsɔ:rɪəs/ *adjective* severely critical.
censure /ˈsenʃə/ ● *verb* (**-ring**) criticize harshly; reprove. ● *noun* hostile criticism; disapproval.
census /ˈsensəs/ *noun* (*plural* **-suses**) official count of population etc.
cent /sent/ *noun* one-hundredth of dollar or other decimal unit of currency.
cent. *abbreviation* century.
centaur /ˈsentɔ:/ *noun* creature in Greek mythololgy with head, arms, and trunk of man joined to body and legs of horse.
centenarian /sentɪˈneərɪən/ ● *noun* person 100 or more years old. ● *adjective* 100 or more years old.
centenary /senˈti:nərɪ/ ● *noun* (*plural* **-ies**) (celebration of) 100th anniversary. ● *adjective* of a centenary; recurring every 100 years.
centennial /senˈtenɪəl/ ● *adjective* lasting 100 years; recurring every 100 years. ● *noun US* centenary.
centi- *combining form* one-hundredth.
centigrade /ˈsentɪgreɪd/ *adjective* Celsius.

■ **Usage** *Celsius* is the better term to use in technical contexts.

centilitre /ˈsentɪli:tə/ *noun* (*US* **centiliter**) one-hundredth of litre (0.018 pint).
centime /ˈsɑ̃ti:m/ *noun* one-hundredth of franc.

centimetre /ˈsentɪmiːtə/ *noun* (*US* **centimeter**) one-hundredth of metre (0.394 in.).

centipede /ˈsentɪpiːd/ *noun* arthropod with wormlike body and many legs.

central /ˈsentr(ə)l/ *adjective* of, forming, at, or from centre; essential, principal. □ **central bank** national bank issuing currency etc.; **central heating** heating of building from central source; **central processor**, **central processing unit** computer's main operating part. □ **centrality** *noun*; **centrally** *adverb*.

centralize *verb* (also **-ise**) (**-zing** or **-sing**) concentrate (administration etc.) at single centre; subject (state etc.) to this system. □ **centralization** *noun*.

centre /ˈsentə/ (*US* **center**) ● *noun* middle point; pivot; place or buildings forming a central point or main area for an activity; point of concentration or dispersion; political party holding moderate opinions; filling in chocolate etc. ● *verb* (**-ring**) (+ *in*, *on*, *round*) have as main centre; place in centre. □ **centrefold** centre spread that folds out, esp. with nude photographs; **centre forward**, **back** *Football etc.* middle player in forward or half-back line; **centre of gravity** point at which the mass of an object effectively acts; **centrepiece** ornament for middle of table, main item; **centre spread** two facing middle pages of magazine etc.

centrifugal /sentrɪˈfjuːg(ə)l/ *adjective* moving or tending to move from centre. □ **centrifugal force** apparent force acting outwards on body revolving round centre. □ **centrifugally** *adverb*.

centrifuge /ˈsentrɪfjuːdʒ/ *noun* rapidly rotating machine for separating e.g. cream from milk.

centripetal /senˈtrɪpɪt(ə)l/ *adjective* moving or tending to move towards centre. □ **centripetally** *adverb*.

centrist /ˈsentrɪst/ *noun often derogatory* person holding moderate views. □ **centrism** *noun*.

cents. *abbreviation* centuries.

centurion /senˈtjʊərɪən/ *noun* commander of century in ancient Roman army.

century /ˈsentʃərɪ/ *noun* (*plural* **-ies**) 100 years; *Cricket* score of 100 runs by one batsman; company in ancient Roman army.

■ **Usage** Strictly speaking, because the 1st century ran from the year 1 to the year 100, the first year of a century ends in 1. However, a century is commonly regarded as starting with a year ending in 00, the 20th century thus running from 1900 to 1999.

cephalic /səˈfælɪk/ *adjective* of or in head.

cephalopod /ˈsefələpɒd/ *noun* mollusc with tentacles on head, e.g. octopus.

ceramic /sɪˈræmɪk/ ● *adjective* made of esp. baked clay; of ceramics. ● *noun* ceramic article.

ceramics *plural noun* ceramic products collectively; (usually treated as *singular*) ceramic art.

cereal /ˈsɪərɪəl/ ● *noun* edible grain; breakfast food made from cereal. ● *adjective* of edible grain.

cerebellum /serɪˈbeləm/ *noun* (*plural* **-s** or **-bella**) part of brain at back of skull.

cerebral /ˈserɪbr(ə)l/ *adjective* of brain; intellectual. □ **cerebral palsy** paralysis resulting from brain damage before or at birth.

cerebration /serɪˈbreɪʃ(ə)n/ *noun* working of brain.

cerebrospinal /serɪbrəʊˈspaɪn(ə)l/ *adjective* of brain and spine.

cerebrum /ˈserɪbrəm/ *noun* (*plural* **-bra**) principal part of brain, at front of skull.

ceremonial /serɪˈməʊnɪəl/ ● *adjective* of or with ceremony, formal. ● *noun* system of rites or ceremonies.

ceremonious /serɪˈməʊnɪəs/ *adjective* fond of or characterized by ceremony, formal. □ **ceremoniously** *adverb*.

ceremony /ˈserɪmənɪ/ *noun* (*plural* **-ies**) formal procedure; formalities, esp. ritualistic; excessively polite behaviour. □ **stand on ceremony** insist on formality.

cerise /səˈriːz/ *noun & adjective* light clear red.

cert /sɜːt/ *noun* (esp. **dead cert**) *slang* a certainty.

certain /ˈsɜːt(ə)n/ *adjective* convinced; indisputable; (often + *to do*) sure, destined; reliable; particular but not specified; some.

certainly *adverb* undoubtedly; (in answer) yes.

certainty *noun* (*plural* **-ies**) undoubted fact; absolute conviction; reliable thing or person.

certificate ● *noun* /səˈtɪfɪkət/ document formally attesting fact. ● *verb* /səˈtɪfɪkeɪt/ (**-ting**) (esp. as **certificated** *adjective*) provide with certificate; license or attest by certificate. □ **certification** /sɜː-/ *noun*.

certify /ˈsɜːtɪfaɪ/ *verb* (**-ies**, **-ied**) attest (to); declare by certificate; officially declare insane. □ **certifiable** *adjective*.

certitude /ˈsɜːtɪtjuːd/ *noun* feeling certain.

cerulean /səˈruːlɪən/ *adjective* sky-blue.

cervical /səˈvaɪk(ə)l/ *adjective* of cervix or neck. □ **cervical smear** specimen from neck of womb for examination.

cervix /ˈsɜːvɪks/ *noun* (*plural* **cervices** /-siːz/) necklike structure, esp. neck of womb; neck.

Cesarean (also **Cesarian**) *US* = CAESAREAN.

cessation /seˈseɪʃ(ə)n/ *noun* ceasing.

cession /ˈseʃ(ə)n/ *noun* ceding; territory ceded.

cesspit /ˈsespɪt/ *noun* pit for liquid waste or sewage.

cesspool /ˈsespuːl/ *noun* cesspit.

cetacean /sɪˈteɪʃ(ə)n/ ● *noun* member of order of marine mammals including whales. ● *adjective* of cetaceans.

cf. *abbreviation* compare (Latin *confer*).

CFC *abbreviation* chlorofluorocarbon (compound used as refrigerant, aerosol propellant, etc.).

cg *abbreviation* centigram(s).

CH *abbreviation* Companion of Honour.

Chablis /ˈʃæbliː/ *noun* (*plural* same /-liːz/) dry white wine from Chablis in France.

chaconne /ʃəˈkɒn/ *noun* musical variations over ground bass; dance to this.

chafe /tʃeɪf/ ● *verb* (**-fing**) make or become sore or damaged by rubbing; irritate; show irritation, fret; rub (esp. skin) to warm. ● *noun* sore caused by rubbing.

chaff /tʃɑːf/ ● *noun* separated grain-husks; chopped hay or straw; good-humoured teasing; worthless stuff. ● *verb* tease, banter.

chaffinch /ˈtʃæfɪntʃ/ *noun* a common European finch.

chafing dish /ˈtʃeɪfɪŋ/ *noun* vessel in which food is cooked or kept warm at table.

chagrin /ˈʃægrɪn/ ● *noun* acute vexation or disappointment. ● *verb* affect with this.

chain ● *noun* connected series of links, thing resembling this; (in *plural*) fetters, restraining force; sequence, series, or set; unit of length (66 ft). ● *verb* (often + *up*) secure with chain. □ **chain gang** *historical* convicts chained together at work etc.; **chain mail** armour made from interlaced rings; **chain reaction** reaction forming products which themselves cause further reactions, series of events each due to previous one; **chainsaw** motor-driven saw with teeth on loop of chain; **chain-smoke** smoke continuously, esp. by lighting next cigarette etc. from previous one; **chain store** one of series of shops owned by one firm.

chair ● *noun* seat usually with back for one person; (office of) chairperson; professorship; *US* electric chair. ● *verb* be chairperson of (meeting); carry aloft in triumph. □ **chairlift** series of chairs on loop of cable for carrying passengers up and down mountain etc.; **chairman**, **chairperson**, **chairwoman** person who presides over meeting, board, or committee.

chaise /ʃeɪz/ *noun* horse-drawn usually open carriage for one or two people.

chaise longue /ʃeɪz 'lɒŋ/ *noun* (*plural* **chaise longues** or **chaises longues** /'lɒŋ(z)/) sofa with one arm rest.

chalcedony /kæl'sedənɪ/ *noun* (*plural* **-ies**) type of quartz.

chalet /'ʃæleɪ/ *noun* Swiss hut or cottage; similar house; small cabin in holiday camp etc.

chalice /'tʃælɪs/ *noun* goblet; Eucharistic cup.

chalk /tʃɔːk/ ● *noun* white soft limestone; (piece of) similar, sometimes coloured, substance for writing or drawing. ● *verb* rub, mark, draw, or write with chalk. □ **chalky** *adjective* (**-ier**, **-iest**).

challenge /'tʃælɪndʒ/ ● *noun* call to take part in contest etc. or to prove or justify something; demanding or difficult task; call to respond. ● *verb* (**-ging**) issue challenge to; dispute; (as **challenging** *adjective*) stimulatingly difficult. □ **challenger** *noun*.

chamber /'tʃeɪmbə/ *noun* hall used by legislative or judicial body; body that meets in it, esp. a house of a parliament; (in *plural*) set of rooms for barrister(s), esp. in Inns of Court; (in *plural*) judge's room for hearing cases not needing to be taken in court; *archaic* room, esp. bedroom; cavity or compartment in body, machinery, etc. (esp. part of gun that contains charge). □ **chambermaid** woman who cleans hotel bedrooms; **chamber music** music for small group of instruments; **Chamber of Commerce** association to promote local commercial interests; **chamber pot** vessel for urine etc., used in bedroom.

chamberlain /'tʃeɪmbəlɪn/ *noun* officer managing royal or noble household; treasurer of corporation etc.

chameleon /kə'miːlɪən/ *noun* lizard able to change colour for camouflage.

chamfer /'tʃæmfə/ ● *verb* bevel symmetrically. ● *noun* bevelled surface.

chamois /'ʃæmwɑː/ *noun* (*plural* same /-wɑːz/) small mountain antelope; /'ʃæmɪ/ (piece of) soft leather from sheep, goats, etc.

chamomile = CAMOMILE.

champ[1] ● *verb* munch or bite noisily. ● *noun* chewing noise. □ **champ at the bit** show impatience.

champ[2] *noun slang* champion.

champagne /ʃæm'peɪn/ *noun* white sparkling wine from Champagne in France.

champion /'tʃæmpɪən/ ● *noun* person or thing that has defeated all rivals; person who fights for cause or another person. ● *verb* support cause of, defend. ● *adjective colloquial* splendid.

championship *noun* (often in *plural*) contest to decide champion in sport etc.; position of champion.

chance /tʃɑːns/ ● *noun* possibility; (often in *plural*) probability; unplanned occurrence; fate. ● *adjective* fortuitous. ● *verb* (**-cing**) *colloquial* risk; happen. □ **chance on** happen to find.

chancel /'tʃɑːns(ə)l/ *noun* part of church near altar.

chancellery /'tʃɑːnsələrɪ/ *noun* (*plural* **-ies**) chancellor's department, staff, or residence; *US* office attached to embassy.

chancellor /'tʃɑːnsələ/ *noun* state or legal official; head of government in some European countries; nonresident honorary head of university; (in full **Lord Chancellor**) highest officer of the Crown, presiding in House of Lords; (in full **Chancellor of the Exchequer**) UK finance minister.

Chancery /'tʃɑːnsərɪ/ *noun* Lord Chancellor's division of High Court of Justice.

chancy /'tʃɑːnsɪ/ *adjective* (**-ier**, **-iest**) uncertain; risky.

chandelier /ʃændə'lɪə/ *noun* branched hanging support for lights.

chandler /'tʃɑːndlə/ *noun* dealer in oil, candles, soap, paint, etc.

change /tʃeɪndʒ/ ● *noun* making or becoming different; low-value money in small coins; money returned as balance of that given in payment; new experience; substitution of one thing or person for another; one of different orders in which bells can be rung. ● *verb* (**-ging**) undergo, show, or subject to change; take or use another instead of; interchange; give or get money in exchange for; put fresh clothes or coverings on; (often + *with*) exchange. □ **change hands** be passed to different owner. □ **changeful** *adjective*; **changeless** *adjective*.

changeable *adjective* inconstant; able to change or be changed.

changeling *noun* child believed to be substitute for another.

channel /'tʃæn(ə)l/ ● *noun* piece of water connecting two seas; (**the Channel**) the English Channel; medium of communication, agency; band of frequencies used for radio and television transmission; course in which thing moves; hollow bed of water; navigable part of waterway; passage for liquid; lengthwise strip on recording tape etc. ● *verb* (**-ll-**; *US* **-l-**) guide, direct; form channel(s) in.

chant /tʃɑːnt/ ● *noun* spoken singsong phrase; melody for reciting unmetrical texts; song. ● *verb* talk or repeat monotonously; sing or intone (psalm etc.).

chanter *noun* melody-pipe of bagpipes.

chantry /'tʃɑːntrɪ/ *noun* (*plural* **-ies**) endowment for singing of masses; priests, chapel, etc., so endowed.

chaos /'keɪɒs/ *noun* utter confusion; formless matter supposed to have existed before universe's creation. □ **chaotic** /keɪ'ɒtɪk/ *adjective*.

chap[1] *noun colloquial* man, boy.

chap[2] ● *verb* (**-pp-**) (esp. of skin) develop cracks or soreness; (of wind etc.) cause this. ● *noun* (usually in *plural*) crack in skin etc.

chaparral /ʃæpə'ræl/ *noun US* dense tangled brushwood.

chapatti /tʃə'pɑːtɪ/ *noun* (also **chupatty**) (*plural* **chapattis** or **chupatties**) flat thin cake of unleavened bread.

chapel /'tʃæp(ə)l/ *noun* place for private worship in cathedral or church, with its own altar; place of worship attached to private house, institution, etc.; place or service of worship for Nonconformists; branch of printers' or journalists' trade union at a workplace.

chaperon /'ʃæpərəʊn/ ● *noun* person, esp. older woman, in charge of young unmarried woman on certain social occasions. ● *verb* act as chaperon to.

chaplain /'tʃæplɪn/ *noun* member of clergy attached to private chapel, institution, ship, regiment, etc. □ **chaplaincy** *noun* (*plural* **-ies**).

chaplet /'tʃæplɪt/ *noun* wreath or circlet for head; string of beads, short rosary.

chapter /'tʃæptə/ *noun* division of book; period of time; canons of cathedral etc.; meeting of these.

char[1] *verb* (**-rr-**) blacken with fire, scorch; burn to charcoal.

char[2] *colloquial* ● *noun* charwoman. ● *verb* (**-rr-**) work as charwoman. □ **charlady**, **charwoman** one employed to do housework.

char[3] *noun slang* tea.

char[4] *noun* (*plural* same) a kind of trout.

charabanc /ˈʃærəbæŋ/ *noun* early form of motor coach.

character /ˈkærɪktə/ *noun* distinguishing qualities or characteristics; moral strength; reputation; person in novel, play, etc.; *colloquial* (esp. eccentric) person; letter, symbol; testimonial.

characteristic /kærɪktəˈrɪstɪk/ ● *adjective* typical, distinctive. ● *noun* characteristic feature or quality. □ **characteristically** *adverb*.

characterize *verb* (also **-ise**) (**-zing** or **-sing**) describe character of; (+ *as*) describe as; be characteristic of. □ **characterization** *noun*.

charade /ʃəˈrɑːd/ *noun* (usually in *plural*, treated as *singular*) game of guessing word(s) from acted clues; absurd pretence.

charcoal *noun* black residue of partly burnt wood etc.

charge ● *verb* (**-ging**) ask (amount) as price; ask (person) for amount as price; (+ *to*, *up to*) debit cost of to; (often + *with*) accuse (of offence); (+ *to do*) instruct or urge to do; (+ *with*) entrust with; make rushing attack (on); (often + *up*) give electric charge to, store energy in; (often + *with*) load, fill. ● *noun* price, financial liability; accusation; task; custody; person or thing entrusted; (signal for) impetuous attack, esp. in battle; appropriate amount of material to be put in mechanism at one time, esp. explosive in gun; cause of electrical phenomena in matter. □ **charge card** credit card, esp. used at particular shop; **in charge** having command. □ **chargeable** *adjective*.

chargé d'affaires /ʃɑːʒeɪ dæˈfeə/ *noun* (*plural* **chargés d'affaires** same pronunciation) ambassador's deputy; envoy to minor country.

charger *noun* cavalry horse; apparatus for charging battery.

chariot /ˈtʃærɪət/ *noun historical* two-wheeled horse-drawn vehicle used in ancient warfare and racing.

charioteer /tʃærɪəˈtɪə/ *noun* chariot driver.

charisma /kəˈrɪzmə/ *noun* power to inspire or attract others; divinely conferred power or talent. □ **charismatic** /kærɪzˈmætɪk/ *adjective*.

charitable /ˈtʃærɪtəb(ə)l/ *adjective* generous to those in need; of or connected with a charity; lenient in judging others. □ **charitably** *adverb*.

charity /ˈtʃærɪtɪ/ *noun* (*plural* **-ies**) giving voluntarily to those in need; organization for helping those in need; love of fellow men; lenience in judging others.

charlatan /ˈʃɑːlət(ə)n/ *noun* person falsely claiming knowledge or skill. □ **charlatanism** *noun*.

charlotte /ˈʃɑːlɒt/ *noun* pudding of stewed fruit under bread etc.

charm ● *noun* power of delighting, attracting, or influencing; trinket on bracelet etc.; object, act, or word(s) supposedly having magic power. ● *verb* delight, captivate; influence or protect (as) by magic; obtain or gain by charm. □ **charmer** *noun*.

charming *adjective* delightful. □ **charmingly** *adverb*.

charnel house /ˈtʃɑːn(ə)l/ *noun* place containing corpses or bones.

chart ● *noun* map esp. for sea or air navigation or showing weather conditions etc.; sheet of information in form of tables or diagrams; (usually in *plural*) *colloquial* list of currently best-selling pop records. ● *verb* make chart of.

charter ● *noun* written grant of rights, esp. by sovereign or legislature; written description of organization's functions etc. ● *verb* grant charter to; hire (aircraft etc.). □ **charter flight** flight by chartered aircraft.

chartered *adjective* qualified as member of professional body that has royal charter.

Chartism *noun* working-class reform movement of 1837–48. □ **Chartist** *noun*.

chartreuse /ʃɑːˈtrɜːz/ *noun* green or yellow brandy liqueur.

chary /ˈtʃeərɪ/ *adjective* (**-ier**, **-iest**) cautious; sparing.

chase[1] /tʃeɪs/ ● *verb* (**-sing**) pursue; (+ *from*, *out of*, *to*, etc.) drive; hurry; (usually + *up*) *colloquial* pursue (thing overdue); *colloquial* try to attain; court persistently. ● *noun* pursuit; unenclosed hunting-land.

chase[2] /tʃeɪs/ *verb* (**-sing**) emboss or engrave (metal).

chaser *noun* horse for steeplechasing; *colloquial* drink taken after another of different kind.

chasm /ˈkæz(ə)m/ *noun* deep cleft in earth, rock, etc.; wide difference in opinion etc.

chassis /ˈʃæsɪ/ *noun* (*plural* same /-sɪz/) base frame of vehicle; frame for (radio etc.) components.

chaste /tʃeɪst/ *adjective* abstaining from extramarital or from all sexual intercourse; pure, virtuous; unadorned. □ **chastely** *adverb*; **chasteness** *noun*.

chasten /ˈtʃeɪs(ə)n/ *verb* (esp. as **chastening**, **chastened** *adjectives*) restrain; punish.

chastise /tʃæsˈtaɪz/ *verb* (**-sing**) rebuke severely; punish, beat. □ **chastisement** *noun*.

chastity /ˈtʃæstɪtɪ/ *noun* being chaste.

chasuble /ˈtʃæzjʊb(ə)l/ *noun* sleeveless outer vestment worn by celebrant of Eucharist.

chat ● *verb* (**-tt-**) talk in light familiar way. ● *noun* informal talk. □ **chatline** telephone service setting up conversations between groups of people on separate lines; **chat show** television or radio broadcast with informal celebrity interviews; **chat up** *colloquial* chat to, esp. flirtatiously.

chateau /ˈʃætəʊ/ *noun* (*plural* **-x** /-z/) large French country house.

chatelaine /ˈʃætəleɪn/ *noun* mistress of large house; *historical* appendage to woman's belt for carrying keys etc.

chattel /ˈtʃæt(ə)l/ *noun* (usually in *plural*) movable possession.

chatter /ˈtʃætə/ ● *verb* talk fast, incessantly, or foolishly. ● *noun* such talk.

chatty *adjective* (**-ier**, **-iest**) fond of or resembling chat.

chauffeur /ˈʃəʊfə/ *noun* person employed to drive car. ● *verb* drive (car or person).

chauvinism /ˈʃəʊvɪnɪz(ə)m/ *noun* exaggerated or aggressive patriotism; excessive or prejudiced support or loyalty for something. □ **chauvinist** *noun*; **chauvinistic** /-ˈnɪs-/ *adjective*.

cheap *adjective* low in price; charging low prices; of low quality or worth; easily got. □ **cheaply** *adverb*; **cheapness** *noun*.

cheapen *verb* make or become cheap; degrade.

cheapskate *noun esp. US colloquial* stingy person.

cheat ● *verb* (often + *into*, *out of*) deceive; (+ *of*) deprive of; gain unfair advantage. ● *noun* person who cheats; deception. □ **cheat on** *colloquial* be sexually unfaithful to.

check ● *verb* test, examine, verify; stop or slow motion of; *colloquial* rebuke; threaten opponent's king at chess; *US* agree on comparison; *US* deposit (luggage etc.). ● *noun* test for accuracy, quality, etc.; stopping or slowing of motion; rebuff; restraint; pattern of small squares; fabric so patterned; (also as *interjection*) exposure of chess king to attack; *US* restaurant bill; *US* cheque; *US* token of identification for left luggage etc.; *US* counter used in card games. □ **check in** register at hotel, airport, etc.; **check-in** act or place of checking in; **check out** leave hotel etc. with due formalities; **checkout** act of checking out, pay-desk in supermarket etc.; **check-up** thorough (esp. medical) examination.

checked *adjective* having a check pattern.

checker = CHEQUER.
checkmate ● *noun* (also as *interjection*) check at chess from which king cannot escape. ● *verb* (**-ting**) put into checkmate; frustrate.
Cheddar /ˈtʃedə/ *noun* kind of firm smooth cheese.
cheek ● *noun* side of face below eye; impertinence, impertinent speech; *slang* buttock. ● *verb* be impertinent to.
cheeky *adjective* (**-ier**, **-iest**) impertinent. □ **cheekily** *adverb*; **cheekiness** *noun*.
cheep ● *noun* shrill feeble note of young bird. ● *verb* make such cry.
cheer ● *noun* shout of encouragement or applause; mood, disposition; (as **cheers** *interjection*) *colloquial: expressing good wishes or thanks.* ● *verb* applaud; (usually + *on*) urge with shouts; shout for joy; gladden, comfort. □ **cheer up** make or become less sad.
cheerful *adjective* in good spirits; bright, pleasant. □ **cheerfully** *adverb*; **cheerfulness** *noun*.
cheerless *adjective* gloomy, dreary.
cheery *adjective* (**-ier**, **-iest**) cheerful. □ **cheerily** *adverb*.
cheese /tʃi:z/ *noun* food made from milk curds; cake of this with rind; thick conserve of fruit. □ **cheeseburger** hamburger with cheese in or on it; **cheesecake** tart filled with sweetened curds, *slang* sexually stimulating display of women; **cheesecloth** thin loosely woven cloth; **cheesed** *slang* (often + *off*) bored, fed up; **cheese-paring** stingy; **cheese plant** climbing plant with holey leaves. □ **cheesy** *adjective*.
cheetah /ˈtʃi:tə/ *noun* swift-running spotted feline resembling leopard.
chef /ʃef/ *noun* (esp. chief) cook in restaurant etc.
Chelsea /ˈtʃelsɪ/ *noun* □ **Chelsea bun** kind of spiral-shaped currant bun; **Chelsea pensioner** inmate of Chelsea Royal Hospital for old or disabled soldiers.
chemical /ˈkemɪk(ə)l/ ● *adjective* of, made by, or employing chemistry. ● *noun* substance obtained or used in chemistry. □ **chemical warfare** warfare using poison gas and other chemicals. □ **chemically** *adverb*.
chemise /ʃəˈmi:z/ *noun historical* woman's loose-fitting undergarment or dress.
chemist /ˈkemɪst/ *noun* dealer in medicinal drugs etc.; expert in chemistry.
chemistry /ˈkemɪstrɪ/ *noun* (*plural* **-ies**) science of elements and their laws of combination and change; *colloquial* sexual attraction.
chenille /ʃəˈni:l/ *noun* tufted velvety yarn; fabric made of this.
cheque /tʃek/ *noun* written order to bank to pay sum of money; printed form for this. □ **chequebook** book of forms for writing cheques; **cheque card** card issued by bank to guarantee honouring of cheques up to stated amount.
chequer /ˈtʃekə/ (also **checker**) ● *noun* (often in *plural*) pattern of squares often alternately coloured; (in *plural*; usually **checkers**) *US* game of draughts. ● *verb* mark with chequers; variegate, break uniformity of; (as **chequered** *adjective*) with varied fortunes.
cherish /ˈtʃerɪʃ/ *verb* tend lovingly; hold dear; cling to.
cheroot /ʃəˈru:t/ *noun* cigar with both ends open.
cherry /ˈtʃerɪ/ ● *noun* (*plural* **-ies**) small stone fruit, tree bearing it, wood of this; light red. ● *adjective* of light red colour.
cherub /ˈtʃerəb/ *noun* representation of winged child; beautiful child; (*plural* **-im**) angelic being. □ **cherubic** /tʃɪˈru:bɪk/ *adjective*.
chervil /ˈtʃɜ:vɪl/ *noun* herb with aniseed flavour.
chess *noun* game for two players with 16 **chessmen** each, on chequered **chessboard** of 64 squares.
chest *noun* large strong box; part of body enclosed by ribs, front surface of body from neck to bottom of ribs; small cabinet for medicines etc. □ **chest of drawers** piece of furniture with set of drawers in frame.
chesterfield /ˈtʃestəfi:ld/ *noun* sofa with arms and back of same height.
chestnut /ˈtʃesnʌt/ ● *noun* glossy hard brown edible nut; tree bearing it; horse chestnut; reddish-brown horse; *colloquial* stale joke etc.; reddish-brown. ● *adjective* reddish-brown.
chesty *adjective* (**-ier**, **-iest**) *colloquial* inclined to or symptomatic of chest disease. □ **chestily** *adverb*; **chestiness** *noun*.
cheval glass /ʃəˈvæl/ *noun* tall mirror pivoting in upright frame.
chevalier /ʃevəˈlɪə/ *noun* member of certain orders of knighthood etc.
chevron /ˈʃevrən/ *noun* V-shaped line or stripe.
chew ● *verb* work (food etc.) between teeth. ● *noun* act of chewing; chewy sweet. □ **chewing gum** flavoured gum for chewing; **chew on** work continuously between teeth, think about; **chew over** discuss, think about.
chewy *adjective* (**-ier**, **-iest**) requiring or suitable for chewing.
chez /ʃeɪ/ *preposition* at the home of. [French]
Chianti /kɪˈæntɪ/ *noun* (*plural* **-s**) red wine from Chianti in Italy.
chiaroscuro /kɪɑ:rəˈskʊərəʊ/ *noun* treatment of light and shade in painting; use of contrast in literature etc.
chic /ʃi:k/ ● *adjective* (**chic-er**, **chic-est**) stylish, elegant. ● *noun* stylishness, elegance.
chicane /ʃɪˈkeɪn/ ● *noun* artificial barrier or obstacle on motor-racing course; chicanery. ● *verb* (**-ning**) *archaic* use chicanery; (usually + *into, out of*, etc.) cheat (person).
chicanery /ʃɪˈkeɪnərɪ/ *noun* (*plural* **-ies**) clever but misleading talk; trickery, deception.
chick *noun* young bird; *slang* young woman.
chicken /ˈtʃɪkɪn/ ● *noun* domestic fowl; its flesh as food; young domestic fowl; youthful person. ● *adjective colloquial* cowardly. ● *verb* (+ *out*) *colloquial* withdraw through cowardice. □ **chicken feed** food for poultry, *colloquial* insignificant amount esp. of money; **chickenpox** infectious disease with rash of small blisters; **chicken wire** light wire netting.
chickpea *noun* pealike seed used as vegetable.
chickweed *noun* a small weed.
chicle /ˈtʃɪk(ə)l/ *noun* juice of tropical tree, used in chewing gum.
chicory /ˈtʃɪkərɪ/ *noun* (*plural* **-ies**) salad plant; its root, roasted and ground and used with or instead of coffee; endive.
chide *verb* (**-ding**; *past* **chided** or **chid**; *past participle* **chided** or **chidden**) *archaic* scold, rebuke.
chief /tʃi:f/ ● *noun* leader, ruler; head of tribe, clan, etc.; head of department etc. ● *adjective* first in position, importance, or influence; prominent, leading.
chiefly *adverb* above all; mainly but not exclusively.
chieftain /ˈtʃi:ft(ə)n/ *noun* leader of tribe, clan, etc. □ **chieftaincy** *noun* (*plural* **-ies**).
chiffchaff /ˈtʃɪftʃæf/ *noun* small European warbler.
chiffon /ˈʃɪfɒn/ *noun* diaphanous silky fabric.
chignon /ˈʃi:njɔ̃/ *noun* coil of hair at back of head.
chihuahua /tʃɪˈwɑ:wə/ *noun* tiny smooth-coated dog.
chilblain /ˈtʃɪlbleɪn/ *noun* itching swelling on hand, foot, etc., caused by exposure to cold.

child /tʃaɪld/ *noun* (*plural* **children** /ˈtʃɪldrən/) young human being; one's son or daughter; (+ *of*) descendant, follower, or product of. □ **child benefit** regular state payment to parents of child up to certain age; **childbirth** giving birth to child; **child's play** easy task. □ **childless** *adjective*.
childhood *noun* state or period of being a child.
childish *adjective* of or like child; immature, silly. □ **childishly** *adverb*; **childishness** *noun*.
childlike *adjective* innocent, frank, etc., like child.
chili = CHILLI.
chill ● *noun* cold sensation; feverish cold; unpleasant coldness (of air etc.); depressing influence. ● *verb* make or become cold; depress, horrify; preserve (food or drink) by cooling. ● *adjective literary* chilly.
chilli /ˈtʃɪlɪ/ *noun* (also **chili**) (*plural* **-es**) hot-tasting dried red capsicum pod. □ **chilli con carne** /kɒn ˈkɑːnɪ/ chilli-flavoured mince and beans.
chilly *adjective* (**-ier**, **-iest**) rather cold; sensitive to cold; unfriendly, unemotional.
chime ● *noun* set of attuned bells; sounds made by this. ● *verb* (**-ming**) (of bells) ring; show (time) by chiming; (usually + *together*, *with*) be in agreement. □ **chime in** interject remark, join in harmoniously.
chimera /kaɪˈmɪərə/ *noun* monster in Greek mythology with lion's head, goat's body, and serpent's tail; bogey; wild impossible scheme or fancy. □ **chimerical** /-ˈmerɪk(ə)l/ *adjective*.
chimney /ˈtʃɪmnɪ/ *noun* (*plural* **-s**) channel conducting smoke etc. away from fire etc.; part of this above roof; glass tube protecting lamp-flame. □ **chimney breast** projecting wall round chimney; **chimney pot** pipe at top of chimney; **chimney sweep** person who clears chimneys of soot.
chimp *noun colloquial* chimpanzee.
chimpanzee /tʃɪmpənˈziː/ *noun* manlike African ape.
chin *noun* front of lower jaw. □ **chinless wonder** ineffectual person; **chinwag** *noun & verb slang* chat.
china /ˈtʃaɪnə/ ● *noun* fine white or translucent ceramic ware; things made of this. ● *adjective* made of china. □ **china clay** kaolin.
chinchilla /tʃɪnˈtʃɪlə/ *noun* S. American rodent; its soft grey fur; breed of cat or rabbit.
chine ● *noun* backbone; joint of meat containing this; ridge. ● *verb* (**-ning**) cut (meat) through backbone.
Chinese /tʃaɪˈniːz/ ● *adjective* of China. ● *noun* Chinese language; (*plural* same) native or national of China, person of Chinese descent. □ **Chinese lantern** collapsible paper lantern, plant with inflated orange-red calyx; **Chinese leaf** lettuce-like cabbage.
chink[1] *noun* narrow opening.
chink[2] ● *verb* (cause to) make sound of glasses or coins striking together. ● *noun* this sound.
chintz *noun* printed multicoloured usually glazed cotton cloth.
chip ● *noun* small piece cut or broken off; place where piece has been broken off; strip of potato usually fried; *US* potato crisp; counter used as money in some games; microchip. ● *verb* (**-pp-**) (often + *off*) cut or break (piece) from hard material; (often + *at*, *away at*) cut pieces off (hard material); be apt to break at edge; (usually as **chipped** *adjective*) make (potato) into chips. □ **chipboard** board made of compressed wood chips.
chipmunk /ˈtʃɪpmʌŋk/ *noun* N. American striped ground squirrel.
chipolata /tʃɪpəˈlɑːtə/ *noun* small thin sausage.
Chippendale /ˈtʃɪpəndeɪl/ *adjective* of an 18th-c. elegant style of furniture.
chiropody /kɪˈrɒpədɪ/ *noun* treatment of feet and their ailments. □ **chiropodist** *noun*.
chiropractic /kaɪərəʊˈpræktɪk/ *noun* treatment of disease by manipulation of spinal column. □ **chiropractor** /ˈkaɪə-/ *noun*.
chirp ● *verb* (of small bird etc.) utter short thin sharp note; speak merrily. ● *noun* chirping sound.
chirpy *adjective* (**-ier**, **-iest**) *colloquial* cheerful. □ **chirpily** *adverb*.
chirrup /ˈtʃɪrəp/ ● *verb* (**-p-**) chirp, esp. repeatedly. ● *noun* chirruping sound.
chisel /ˈtʃɪz(ə)l/ ● *noun* tool with bevelled blade for shaping wood, stone, or metal. ● *verb* (**-ll-**; *US* **-l-**) cut or shape with chisel; (as **chiselled** *adjective*) (of features) clear-cut; *slang* defraud.
chit[1] *noun derogatory or jocular* young small woman; young child.
chit[2] *noun* written note.
chit-chat *noun colloquial* light conversation, gossip.
chivalry /ˈʃɪvəlrɪ/ *noun* medieval knightly system; honour and courtesy, esp. to the weak. □ **chivalrous** *adjective*; **chivalrously** *adverb*.
chive *noun* herb related to onion.
chivvy /ˈtʃɪvɪ/ *verb* (**-ies**, **-ied**) urge persistently, nag.
chloral /ˈklɔːr(ə)l/ *noun* compound used in making DDT, sedatives, etc.
chloride /ˈklɔːraɪd/ *noun* compound of chlorine and another element or group.
chlorinate /ˈklɔːrɪneɪt/ *verb* (**-ting**) impregnate or treat with chlorine. □ **chlorination** *noun*.
chlorine /ˈklɔːriːn/ *noun* poisonous gas used for bleaching and disinfecting.
chlorofluorocarbon see CFC.
chloroform /ˈklɒrəfɔːm/ ● *noun* colourless volatile liquid formerly used as general anaesthetic. ● *verb* render unconscious with this.
chlorophyll /ˈklɒrəfɪl/ *noun* green pigment in most plants.
choc *noun colloquial* chocolate. □ **choc ice** bar of ice cream covered with chocolate.
chock ● *noun* block of wood, wedge. ● *verb* make fast with chock(s). □ **chock-a-block** (often + *with*) crammed together, full; **chock-full** (often + *of*) crammed full.
chocolate /ˈtʃɒklət/ ● *noun* food made as paste, powder, or solid block from ground cacao seeds; sweet made of or covered with this; drink containing chocolate; dark brown. ● *adjective* made from chocolate; dark brown.
choice ● *noun* act of choosing; thing or person chosen; range to choose from; power to choose. ● *adjective* of superior quality.
choir /kwaɪə/ *noun* regular group of singers; chancel in large church. □ **choirboy**, **choirgirl** boy or girl singer in church choir.
choke ● *verb* (**-king**) stop breathing of (person or animal); suffer such stoppage; block up; (as **choked** *adjective*) speechless from emotion, disgusted, disappointed. ● *noun* valve in carburettor controlling inflow of air; device for smoothing variations of alternating electric current.
choker *noun* close-fitting necklace.
choler /ˈkɒlə/ *noun historical* bile; *archaic* anger, irascibility.
cholera /ˈkɒlərə/ *noun* infectious often fatal bacterial disease of small intestine.
choleric /ˈkɒlərɪk/ *adjective* easily angered.
cholesterol /kəˈlestərɒl/ *noun* sterol present in human tissues including the blood.
choose /tʃuːz/ *verb* (**-sing**; *past* **chose** /tʃəʊz/; *past participle* **chosen**) select out of greater number; (usually + *between*, *from*) take one or another; (usually + *to do*) decide.

choosy /ˈtʃuːzɪ/ *adjective* (**-ier**, **-iest**) *colloquial* fussy; hard to please.

chop[1] ● *verb* (**-pp-**) (usually + *off*, *down*, etc.) cut with axe etc.; (often + *up*) cut into small pieces; strike (ball) with heavy edgewise blow. ● *noun* cutting blow; thick slice of meat usually including rib; (**the chop**) *slang* dismissal from job, killing, being killed.

chop[2] *noun* (usually in *plural*) jaw.

chop[3] *verb* (**-pp-**) ▫ **chop and change** vacillate.

chopper *noun* large-bladed short axe; cleaver; *colloquial* helicopter.

choppy *adjective* (**-ier**, **-iest**) (of sea etc.) fairly rough.

chopstick /ˈtʃɒpstɪk/ *noun* each of pair of sticks held in one hand as eating utensils by Chinese, Japanese, etc.

chop suey /tʃɒpˈsuːɪ/ *noun* (*plural* **-s**) Chinese-style dish of meat fried with vegetables.

choral /ˈkɔːr(ə)l/ *adjective* of, for, or sung by choir or chorus.

chorale /kəˈrɑːl/ *noun* simple stately hymn tune; choir.

chord[1] /kɔːd/ *noun* combination of notes sounded together.

chord[2] /kɔːd/ *noun* straight line joining ends of arc; string of harp etc.

chore *noun* tedious or routine task, esp. domestic.

choreography /kɒrɪˈɒɡrəfɪ/ *noun* design or arrangement of ballet etc. ▫ **choreograph** /ˈkɒrɪəɡrɑːf/ *verb*; **choreographer** *noun*; **choreographic** /-əˈɡræf-/ *adjective*.

chorister /ˈkɒrɪstə/ *noun* member of choir, esp. choirboy.

chortle /ˈtʃɔːt(ə)l/ ● *noun* gleeful chuckle. ● *verb* (**-ling**) chuckle gleefully.

chorus /ˈkɔːrəs/ ● *noun* (*plural* **-es**) group of singers, choir; music for choir; refrain of song; simultaneous utterance; group of singers and dancers performing together; group of performers commenting on action in ancient Greek play, any of its utterances. ● *verb* (**-s-**) utter simultaneously.

chose *past* of CHOOSE.

chosen *past participle* of CHOOSE.

chough /tʃʌf/ *noun* red-legged crow.

choux pastry /ʃuː/ *noun* very light pastry made with eggs.

chow *noun slang* food; Chinese breed of dog.

chow mein /tʃaʊ ˈmeɪn/ *noun* Chinese-style dish of fried noodles usually with shredded meat and vegetables.

christen /ˈkrɪs(ə)n/ *verb* baptize; name. ▫ **christening** *noun*.

Christendom /ˈkrɪsəndəm/ *noun* Christians worldwide.

Christian /ˈkrɪstʃ(ə)n/ ● *adjective* of Christ's teaching; believing in or following Christian religion; charitable, kind. ● *noun* adherent of Christianity. ▫ **Christian era** era counted from Christ's birth; **Christian name** forename, esp. given at christening; **Christian Science** system of belief including power of healing by prayer alone; **Christian Scientist** adherent of this.

Christianity /krɪstɪˈænɪtɪ/ *noun* Christian religion, quality, or character.

Christmas /ˈkrɪsməs/ *noun* (period around) festival of Christ's birth celebrated on 25 Dec. ▫ **Christmas box** present or tip given at Christmas; **Christmas Day** 25 Dec.; **Christmas Eve** 24 Dec.; **Christmas pudding** rich boiled pudding with dried fruit; **Christmas rose** white-flowered hellebore flowering in winter; **Christmas tree** evergreen tree decorated at Christmas. ▫ **Christmassy** *adjective*.

chromatic /krəˈmætɪk/ *adjective* of colour, in colours; *Music* of or having notes not belonging to prevailing key. ▫ **chromatic scale** scale that proceeds by semitones. ▫ **chromatically** *adverb*.

chrome /krəʊm/ *noun* chromium; yellow pigment got from a compound of chromium.

chromium /ˈkrəʊmɪəm/ *noun* metallic element used as shiny decorative or protective coating.

chromosome /ˈkrəʊməsəʊm/ *noun Biology* threadlike structure occurring in pairs in cell nucleus, carrying genes.

chronic /ˈkrɒnɪk/ *adjective* (of disease) long-lasting; (of patient) having chronic illness; *colloquial* bad, intense, severe. ▫ **chronically** *adverb*.

chronicle /ˈkrɒnɪk(ə)l/ ● *noun* record of events in order of occurrence. ● *verb* (**-ling**) record (events) thus.

chronological /krɒnəˈlɒdʒɪk(ə)l/ *adjective* according to order of occurrence. ▫ **chronologically** *adverb*.

chronology /krəˈnɒlədʒɪ/ *noun* (*plural* **-ies**) science of computing dates; (document displaying) arrangement of events etc. according to date.

chronometer /krəˈnɒmɪtə/ *noun* time-measuring instrument, esp. one used in navigation.

chrysalis /ˈkrɪsəlɪs/ *noun* (*plural* **-lises**) pupa of butterfly or moth; case enclosing it.

chrysanthemum /krɪˈsænθəməm/ *noun* garden plant flowering in autumn.

chub *noun* (*plural* same) thick-bodied river fish.

chubby *adjective* (**-ier**, **-iest**) plump, round.

chuck[1] ● *verb colloquial* fling or throw carelessly; (often + *in*, *up*) give up; touch playfully, esp. under chin. ● *noun* act of chucking; (**the chuck**) *slang* dismissal. ▫ **chuck out** *colloquial* expel, discard.

chuck[2] ● *noun* cut of beef from neck to ribs; device for holding workpiece or bit. ● *verb* fix in chuck.

chuckle /ˈtʃʌk(ə)l/ ● *verb* (**-ling**) laugh quietly or inwardly. ● *noun* quiet or suppressed laugh.

chuff *verb* (of engine etc.) work with regular sharp puffing sound.

chuffed *adjective slang* delighted.

chug *verb* (**-gg-**) make intermittent explosive sound; move with this.

chukker /ˈtʃʌkə/ *noun* period of play in polo.

chum *noun colloquial* close friend. ▫ **chum up** (**-mm-**) (often + *with*) become close friend (of). ▫ **chummy** *adjective* (**-ier**, **-iest**).

chump *noun colloquial* foolish person; thick end of loin of lamb or mutton; lump of wood.

chunk *noun* lump cut or broken off.

chunky *adjective* (**-ier**, **-iest**) consisting of or resembling chunks; small and sturdy.

chunter /ˈtʃʌntə/ *verb colloquial* mutter, grumble.

chupatty = CHAPATTI.

church *noun* building for public Christian worship; public worship; (**Church**) Christians collectively, clerical profession, organized Christian society. ▫ **churchgoer** person attending church regularly; **churchman** member of clergy or Church; **churchwarden** elected lay representative of Anglican parish; **churchyard** enclosed ground round church, esp. used for burials.

churl *noun* bad-mannered, surly, or stingy person. ▫ **churlish** *adjective*.

churn ● *noun* large milk can; butter-making machine. ● *verb* agitate (milk etc.) in churn; make (butter) in churn; (usually + *up*) upset, agitate. ▫ **churn out** produce in large quantities.

chute[1] /ʃuːt/ *noun* slide for taking things to lower level.

chute[2] /ʃuːt/ *noun colloquial* parachute.

chutney /'tʃʌtnɪ/ *noun* (*plural* **-s**) relish made of fruits, vinegar, spices, etc.

chyle /kaɪl/ *noun* milky fluid into which chyme is converted.

chyme /kaɪm/ *noun* pulp formed from partly-digested food.

CIA *abbreviation* (in *US*) Central Intelligence Agency.

ciabatta /tʃə'bɑːtə/ *noun* Italian bread made with olive oil.

ciao /tʃaʊ/ *interjection colloquial* goodbye; hello.

cicada /sɪ'kɑːdə/ *noun* winged chirping insect.

cicatrice /'sɪkətrɪs/ *noun* scar of healed wound.

cicely /'sɪsəlɪ/ *noun* (*plural* **-ies**) flowering plant related to parsley and chervil.

CID *abbreviation* Criminal Investigation Department.

cider /'saɪdə/ *noun* drink of fermented apple juice.

cigar /sɪ'gɑː/ *noun* roll of tobacco leaves for smoking.

cigarette /sɪgə'ret/ *noun* finely-cut tobacco rolled in paper for smoking.

cilium /'sɪlɪəm/ *noun* (*plural* **cilia**) hairlike structure on animal cells; eyelash. ◻ **ciliary** *adjective*.

cinch /sɪntʃ/ *noun colloquial* certainty; easy task.

cinchona /sɪŋ'kəʊnə/ *noun* S. American evergreen tree; (drug from) its bark which contains quinine.

cincture /'sɪŋktʃə/ *noun literary* girdle, belt, or border.

cinder /'sɪndə/ *noun* residue of coal etc. after burning.

Cinderella /sɪndə'relə/ *noun* person or thing of unrecognized merit.

cine- /sɪnɪ/ *combining form* cinematographic.

cinema /'sɪnɪmɑː/ *noun* theatre where films are shown; films collectively; art or industry of producing films. ◻ **cinematic** /-'mæt-/ *adjective*.

cinematography /sɪnɪmə'tɒgrəfɪ/ *noun* art of making films. ◻ **cinematographer** *noun*; **cinematographic** /-mætə'græfɪk/ *adjective*.

cineraria /sɪnə'reərɪə/ *noun* plant with bright flowers and downy leaves.

cinnabar /'sɪnəbɑː/ *noun* red mercuric sulphide; vermilion.

cinnamon /'sɪnəmən/ *noun* aromatic spice from bark of SE Asian tree; this tree; yellowish-brown.

cinquefoil /'sɪŋkfɔɪl/ *noun* plant with compound leaf of 5 leaflets.

Cinque Port /sɪŋk/ *noun* any of (originally 5) ports in SE England with ancient privileges.

cipher /'saɪfə/ (also **cypher**) ● *noun* secret or disguised writing, key to this; arithmetical symbol 0; person or thing of no importance. ● *verb* write in cipher.

circa /'sɜːkə/ *preposition* (usually before date) about. [Latin]

circle /'sɜːk(ə)l/ ● *noun* perfectly round plane figure; roundish enclosure or structure; curved upper tier of seats in theatre etc.; circular route; set or restricted group; people grouped round centre of interest. ● *verb* (**-ling**) (often + *round, about*) move in or form circle.

circlet /'sɜːklɪt/ *noun* small circle; circular band, esp. as ornament.

circuit /'sɜːkɪt/ *noun* line, course, or distance enclosing an area; path of electric current, apparatus through which current passes; judge's itinerary through district, such a district; chain of theatres, cinemas, etc. under single management; motor-racing track; sphere of operation; sequence of sporting events.

circuitous /sɜː'kjuːɪtəs/ *adjective* indirect, roundabout.

circuitry /'sɜːkɪtrɪ/ *noun* (*plural* **-ies**) system of electric circuits.

circular /'sɜːkjʊlə/ ● *adjective* having form of or moving in circle; (of reasoning) using point to be proved as argument for its own truth; (of letter etc.) distributed to several people. ● *noun* circular letter etc. ◻ **circular saw** power saw with rotating toothed disc. ◻ **circularity** /-'lærɪtɪ/ *noun*.

circularize *verb* (also **-ise**) (**-zing** or **-sing**) send circular to.

circulate /'sɜːkjʊleɪt/ *verb* (**-ting**) be or put in circulation; send circulars to; mingle among guests etc.

circulation *noun* movement from and back to starting point, esp. that of blood from and to heart; transmission, distribution; number of copies sold. ◻ **circulatory** *adjective*.

circumcise /'sɜːkəmsaɪz/ *verb* (**-sing**) cut off foreskin or clitoris of. ◻ **circumcision** /-'sɪʒ(ə)n/ *noun*.

circumference /sə'kʌmfərəns/ *noun* line enclosing circle; distance round.

circumflex /'sɜːkəmfleks/ *noun* (in full **circumflex accent**) mark (ˆ) over vowel indicating pronunciation.

circumlocution /sɜːkəmlə'kjuːʃ(ə)n/ *noun* roundabout expression; evasive speech; verbosity. ◻ **circumlocutory** /-'lɒkjʊt-/ *adjective*.

circumnavigate /sɜːkəm'nævɪgeɪt/ *verb* (**-ting**) sail round. ◻ **circumnavigation** *noun*.

circumscribe /'sɜːkəmskraɪb/ *verb* (**-bing**) enclose or outline; lay down limits of; confine, restrict. ◻ **circumscription** /-'skrɪpʃ(ə)n/ *noun*.

circumspect /'sɜːkəmspekt/ *adjective* cautious, taking everything into account. ◻ **circumspection** /-'spekʃ(ə)n/ *noun*; **circumspectly** *adverb*.

circumstance /'sɜːkəmst(ə)ns/ *noun* fact, occurrence, or condition, esp. (in *plural*) connected with or affecting an event etc.; (in *plural*) financial condition; ceremony, fuss.

circumstantial /sɜːkəm'stænʃ(ə)l/ *adjective* (of account, story) detailed; (of evidence) tending to establish a conclusion by reasonable inference.

circumvent /sɜːkəm'vent/ *verb* evade, outwit.

circus /'sɜːkəs/ *noun* (*plural* **-es**) travelling show of performing acrobats, clowns, animals, etc.; *colloquial* scene of lively action, group of people in common activity; open space in town, where several streets converge; *historical* arena for sports and games.

cirrhosis /sɪ'rəʊsɪs/ *noun* chronic liver disease.

cirrus /'sɪrəs/ *noun* (*plural* **cirri** /-raɪ/) white wispy cloud.

cissy = SISSY.

Cistercian /sɪs'tɜːʃ(ə)n/ ● *noun* monk or nun of strict Benedictine order. ● *adjective* of the Cistercians.

cistern /'sɪst(ə)n/ *noun* tank for storing water; underground reservoir.

citadel /'sɪtəd(ə)l/ *noun* fortress protecting or dominating city.

citation /saɪ'teɪʃ(ə)n/ *noun* citing or passage cited; description of reasons for award.

cite *verb* (**-ting**) mention as example; quote (book etc.) in support; mention in military dispatches; summon to law court.

citizen /'sɪtɪz(ə)n/ *noun* native or national of state; inhabitant of a city. ◻ **citizen's band** system of local intercommunication by radio. ◻ **citizenship** *noun*.

citrate /'sɪtreɪt/ *noun* salt of citric acid.

citric /'sɪtrɪk/ *adjective* ◻ **citric acid** sharp-tasting acid in citrus fruits.

citron /'sɪtrən/ *noun* tree bearing large lemon-like fruits; this fruit.

citronella /sɪtrə'nelə/ *noun* a fragrant oil; grass from S. Asia yielding it.

citrus /ˈsɪtrəs/ *noun* (*plural* **-es**) tree of group including orange, lemon, and grapefruit; (in full **citrus fruit**) fruit of such tree.

city /ˈsɪtɪ/ *noun* (*plural* **-ies**) large town; town created city by charter and containing cathedral; (**the City**) part of London governed by Lord Mayor and Corporation, business quarter of this, commercial circles.

civet /ˈsɪvɪt/ *noun* (in full **civet cat**) catlike animal of Central Africa; strong musky perfume got from this.

civic /ˈsɪvɪk/ *adjective* of city or citizenship.

civics *plural noun* (usually treated as *singular*) study of civic rights and duties.

civil /ˈsɪv(ə)l/ *adjective* of or belonging to citizens; non-military; polite, obliging; *Law* concerning private rights and not criminal offences. □ **civil defence** organization for protecting civilians in wartime; **civil engineer** person who designs or maintains roads, bridges, etc.; **civil list** annual allowance by Parliament for royal family's household expenses; **civil marriage** one solemnized without religious ceremony; **civil servant** member of civil service; **civil service** all non-military and non-judicial branches of state administration; **civil war** one between citizens of same country.

civilian /sɪˈvɪlɪən/ ● *noun* person not in armed forces. ● *adjective* of or for civilians.

civility /sɪˈvɪlɪtɪ/ *noun* (*plural* **-ies**) politeness; act of politeness.

civilization *noun* (also **-sation**) advanced stage of social development; peoples regarded as having achieved, or been instrumental in evolving, this.

civilize /ˈsɪvɪlaɪz/ *verb* (also **-ise**) (**-zing** or **-sing**) bring out of barbarism; enlighten, refine.

cl *abbreviation* centilitre(s).

clack ● *verb* make sharp sound as of boards struck together. ● *noun* such sound.

clad *adjective* clothed; provided with cladding.

cladding *noun* protective covering or coating.

claim ● *verb* assert; demand as one's due; represent oneself as having; (+ *to do*) profess. ● *noun* demand; (+ *to*, *on*) right or title; assertion; thing claimed.

claimant *noun* person making claim, esp. in lawsuit or for state benefit.

clairvoyance /kleəˈvɔɪəns/ *noun* supposed faculty of perceiving the future or the unseen. □ **clairvoyant** *noun & adjective*.

clam ● *noun* edible bivalve mollusc. ● *verb* (**-mm-**) (+ *up*) *colloquial* refuse to talk.

clamber /ˈklæmbə/ *verb* climb using hands or with difficulty.

clammy /ˈklæmɪ/ *adjective* (**-ier**, **-iest**) damp and sticky.

clamour /ˈklæmə/ (*US* **clamor**) ● *noun* shouting, confused noise; protest, demand. ● *verb* make clamour, shout. □ **clamorous** *adjective*.

clamp[1] ● *noun* device, esp. brace or band of iron etc., for strengthening or holding things together; device for immobilizing illegally parked vehicles. ● *verb* strengthen or fasten with clamp; immobilize with clamp. □ **clamp down** (usually + *on*) become stricter (about).

clamp[2] *noun* heap of earth and straw over harvested potatoes etc.

clan *noun* group of families with common ancestor, esp. in Scotland; family holding together; group with common interest. □ **clannish** *adjective*; **clansman**, **clanswoman** *noun*.

clandestine /klænˈdestɪn/ *adjective* surreptitious, secret.

clang ● *noun* loud resonant metallic sound. ● *verb* (cause to) make clang.

clangour /ˈklæŋgə/ *noun* (*US* **clangor**) continued clanging. □ **clangorous** *adjective*.

clank ● *noun* sound as of metal on metal. ● *verb* (cause to) make clank.

clap ● *verb* (**-pp-**) strike palms of hands together, esp. as applause; put or place quickly or with determination; (+ *on*) give friendly slap on. ● *noun* act of clapping; explosive noise, esp. of thunder; slap. □ **clap eyes on** *colloquial* see.

clapper *noun* tongue or striker of bell. □ **clapperboard** device in film-making for making sharp noise to synchronize picture and sound.

claptrap *noun* insincere or pretentious talk; nonsense.

claque /klæk/ *noun* people hired to applaud.

claret /ˈklærət/ *noun* red Bordeaux wine.

clarify /ˈklærɪfaɪ/ *verb* (**-ies**, **-ied**) make or become clear; free from impurities; make transparent. □ **clarification** *noun*.

clarinet /klærɪˈnet/ *noun* woodwind instrument with single reed. □ **clarinettist** *noun*.

clarion /ˈklærɪən/ *noun* rousing sound; *historical* war-trumpet.

clarity /ˈklærɪtɪ/ *noun* clearness.

clash ● *noun* loud jarring sound as of metal objects struck together; collision; conflict; discord of colours etc. ● *verb* (cause to) make clash; coincide awkwardly; (often + *with*) be discordant or at variance.

clasp /klɑːsp/ ● *noun* device with interlocking parts for fastening; embrace, handshake; bar on medal-ribbon. ● *verb* fasten (as) with clasp; grasp, embrace. □ **clasp-knife** large folding knife.

class /klɑːs/ ● *noun* any set of people or things grouped together or differentiated from others; division or order of society; *colloquial* high quality; set of students taught together; their time of meeting; their course of instruction. ● *verb* place in a class. □ **classmate** person in same class at school; **classroom** room where class of students is taught. □ **classless** *adjective*.

classic /ˈklæsɪk/ ● *adjective* first-class; of lasting importance; typical; of ancient Greek or Latin culture etc.; (of style) simple and harmonious; famous because long-established. ● *noun* classic writer, artist, work, or example; (in *plural*) study of ancient Greek and Latin.

classical *adjective* of ancient Greek or Latin literature etc.; (of language) having form used by standard authors; (of music) serious or conventional.

classicism /ˈklæsɪsɪz(ə)m/ *noun* following of classic style; classical scholarship. □ **classicist** *noun*.

classify /ˈklæsɪfaɪ/ *verb* (**-ies**, **-ied**) arrange in classes; class; designate as officially secret. □ **classification** *noun*.

classy /ˈklɑːsɪ/ *adjective* (**-ier**, **-iest**) *colloquial* superior. □ **classiness** *noun*.

clatter /ˈklætə/ ● *noun* sound as of hard objects struck together. ● *verb* (cause to) make clatter.

clause /klɔːz/ *noun* group of words including finite verb (see panel); single statement in treaty, law, contract, etc.

claustrophobia /klɔːstrəˈfəʊbɪə/ *noun* abnormal fear of confined places. □ **claustrophobic** *adjective*.

clavichord /ˈklævɪkɔːd/ *noun* small keyboard instrument with very soft tone.

clavicle /ˈklævɪk(ə)l/ *noun* collar-bone.

claw ● *noun* pointed nail on animal's foot; foot armed with claws; pincers of shellfish; device for grappling, holding, etc. ● *verb* scratch, maul, or pull with claws or fingernails.

clay *noun* stiff sticky earth, used for bricks, pottery, etc. □ **clay pigeon** breakable disc thrown into air as target for shooting. □ **clayey** *adjective*.

claymore /ˈkleɪmɔː/ *noun historical* Scottish two-edged broad-bladed sword.

clean ● *adjective* free from dirt; clear; pristine; not obscene or indecent; attentive to cleanliness; clear-cut; without record of crime etc.; fair. ● *adverb* completely; simply; in a clean way. ● *verb* make or become clean. ● *noun* process of cleaning. □ **clean-cut** sharply outlined, (of person) clean and tidy; **clean out** clean thoroughly, *slang* empty or deprive (esp. of money); **clean-shaven** without beard or moustache; **clean up** make tidy or clean, *slang* acquire as or make profit. □ **cleaner** *noun*; **cleanness** *noun*.

cleanly[1] *adverb* in a clean way.

cleanly[2] /ˈklenlɪ/ *adjective* (**-ier**, **-iest**) habitually clean; attentive to cleanness and hygiene. □ **cleanliness** *noun*.

cleanse /klenz/ *verb* (**-sing**) make clean or pure. □ **cleanser** *noun*.

clear ● *adjective* free from dirt or contamination; not clouded; transparent; readily perceived or understood; able to discern readily; convinced; (of conscience) guiltless; unobstructed; net; complete; (often + *of*) free, unhampered. ● *adverb* clearly; completely; apart. ● *verb* make or become clear; (often + *of*) free from obstruction etc.; (often + *of*) show (person) to be innocent; approve (person etc.) for special duty, access, etc.; pass through (customs); pass over or by without touching; make (sum) as net gain; pass (cheque) through clearing house. □ **clear-cut** sharply defined; **clear off** *colloquial* go away; **clear out** empty, remove, *colloquial* go away; **clear-out** tidying by emptying and sorting; **clear up** tidy, solve; **clearway** road where vehicles may not stop. □ **clearly** *adverb*; **clearness** *noun*.

clearance *noun* removal of obstructions etc.; space allowed for passing of two objects; special authorization; clearing for special duty, of cheque, etc.; clearing out.

clearing *noun* treeless area in forest. □ **clearing bank** member of clearing house; **clearing house** bankers' institution where cheques etc. are exchanged, agency for collecting and distributing information etc.

cleat *noun* device for fastening ropes to projection on gangway, sole, etc. to provide grip.

cleavage *noun* hollow between woman's breasts; division; line along which rocks etc. split.

cleave[1] *verb* (**-ving**; *past* **clove** /kləʊv/, **cleft**, or **cleaved**; *past participle* **cloven**, **cleft**, or **cleaved**) *literary* break or come apart; make one's way through.

cleave[2] *verb* (**-ving**) (+ *to*) *literary* adhere.

cleaver *noun* butcher's heavy chopping tool.

clef *noun Music* symbol at start of staff showing pitch of notes on it.

cleft[1] *adjective* split, partly divided. □ **cleft palate** congenital split in roof of mouth.

cleft[2] *noun* split, fissure.

clematis /ˈklemətɪs/ *noun* climbing flowering plant.

clement /ˈklemənt/ *adjective* mild; merciful. □ **clemency** *noun*.

clementine /ˈklementiːn/ *noun* small tangerine-like fruit.

clench ● *verb* close tightly; grasp firmly. ● *noun* clenching action; clenched state.

clergy /ˈklɜːdʒɪ/ *noun* (*plural* **-ies**) (usually treated as *plural*) those ordained for religious duties.

clergyman /ˈklɜːdʒɪmən/ *noun* member of clergy.

cleric /ˈklerɪk/ *noun* member of clergy.

clerical *adjective* of clergy or clergymen; of or done by clerks.

clerihew /ˈklerɪhjuː/ *noun* witty or comic 4-line biographical verse.

clerk /klɑːk/ ● *noun* person employed to keep records, accounts, etc.; secretary or agent of local council, court, etc.; lay officer of church. ● *verb* work as clerk.

clever /ˈklevə/ *adjective* (**-er**, **-est**) skilful, talented, quick to understand and learn; adroit; ingenious. □ **cleverly** *adverb*; **cleverness** *noun*.

cliché /ˈkliːʃeɪ/ *noun* hackneyed phrase or opinion.

clichéd *adjective* hackneyed, full of clichés.

click ● *noun* slight sharp sound. ● *verb* (cause to) make click; *colloquial* become clear, understood, or popular; (+ *with*) become friendly with.

client /ˈklaɪənt/ *noun* person using services of lawyer or other professional person; customer.

clientele /kliːɒnˈtel/ *noun* clients collectively; customers.

cliff *noun* steep rock face, esp. on coast. □ **cliff-hanger** story etc. with strong element of suspense.

climacteric /klaɪˈmæktərɪk/ *noun* period of life when fertility and sexual activity are in decline.

climate /ˈklaɪmɪt/ *noun* prevailing weather conditions of an area; region with particular weather conditions; prevailing trend of opinion etc. □ **climatic** /-ˈmæt-/ *adjective*; **climatically** /-ˈmæt-/ *adverb*.

climax /ˈklaɪmæks/ ● *noun* event or point of greatest intensity or interest, culmination. ● *verb colloquial* reach or bring to a climax. □ **climactic** *adjective*.

climb /klaɪm/ ● *verb* (often + *up*) ascend, mount, go up; (of plant) grow up wall etc. by clinging etc.; rise, esp. in social rank. ● *noun* action of climbing; hill etc. (to be) climbed. □ **climber** *noun*.

clime *noun literary* region; climate.

clinch ● *verb* confirm or settle conclusively; (of boxers) become too closely engaged; secure (nail or rivet) by driving point sideways when through. ● *noun* clinching, resulting state; *colloquial* embrace.

cling *verb* (*past & past participle* **clung**) (often + *to*) adhere; (+ *to*) be emotionally dependent on or unwilling to give up; (often + *to*) maintain grasp. □ **cling film** thin transparent plastic covering for food. □ **clingy** *adjective* (**-ier**, **-iest**).

Clause

A clause is a group of words that includes a finite verb. If it makes complete sense by itself, it is known as a main clause, e.g.

The sun came out.

Otherwise, although it makes some sense, it must be attached to a main clause; this is known as a subordinate clause, e.g.

when the sun came out
(as in *When the sun came out, we went outside.*)

clinic /ˈklɪnɪk/ *noun* private or specialized hospital; place or occasion for giving medical treatment or specialist advice; teaching of medicine at hospital bedside.

clinical *adjective* of or for the treatment of patients; objective, coldly detached; (of room etc.) bare, functional. ▫ **clinically** *adverb*.

clink[1] ● *noun* sharp ringing sound. ● *verb* (cause to) make clink.

clink[2] *noun slang* prison.

clinker /ˈklɪŋkə/ *noun* mass of slag or lava; stony residue from burnt coal.

clinker-built *adjective* (of boat) with external planks overlapping downwards.

clip[1] ● *noun* device for holding things together; piece of jewellery fastened by clip; set of attached cartridges for firearm. ● *verb* (**-pp-**) fix with clip. ▫ **clipboard** board with spring clip for holding papers etc.

clip[2] ● *verb* (**-pp-**) cut with shears or scissors; cut hair or wool of; *colloquial* hit sharply; omit (letter) from word; omit parts of (words uttered); punch hole in (ticket) to show it has been used; cut from newspaper etc. ● *noun* clipping; *colloquial* sharp blow; extract from motion picture; yield of wool.

clipper *noun* (usually in *plural*) instrument for clipping; *historical* fast sailing ship.

clipping *noun* piece clipped, esp. from newspaper.

clique /kli:k/ *noun* exclusive group of people. ▫ **cliquey** *adjective* (**cliquier**, **cliquiest**); **cliquish** *adjective*.

clitoris /ˈklɪtərɪs/ *noun* small erectile part of female genitals.

Cllr. *abbreviation* Councillor.

cloak ● *noun* loose usually sleeveless outdoor garment; covering. ● *verb* cover with cloak; conceal, disguise. ▫ **cloakroom** room for outdoor clothes or luggage, *euphemistic* lavatory.

clobber[1] /ˈklɒbə/ *verb slang* hit (repeatedly); defeat; criticize severely.

clobber[2] /ˈklɒbə/ *noun slang* clothing, belongings.

cloche /klɒʃ/ *noun* small translucent cover for outdoor plants; woman's close-fitting bell-shaped hat.

clock[1] ● *noun* instrument measuring and showing time; measuring device resembling this; *colloquial* speedometer, taximeter, or stopwatch; seed-head of dandelion. ● *verb colloquial* (often + *up*) attain or register (distance etc.); time (race etc.) by stopwatch. ▫ **clock in** (or **on**), or **out** (or **off**) register time of arrival, or departure, by automatic clock; **clockwise** (moving) in same direction as hands of clock; **clockwork** mechanism with coiled springs etc. on clock principle; **like clockwork** with mechanical precision.

clock[2] *noun* ornamental pattern on side of stocking or sock.

clod *noun* lump of earth or clay.

clog ● *noun* wooden-soled shoe. ● *verb* (**-gg-**) (often + *up*) (cause to) become obstructed, choke; impede.

cloister /ˈklɔɪstə/ ● *noun* covered walk esp. in college or ecclesiastical building; monastic life; seclusion. ● *verb* seclude.

clone ● *noun* group of organisms produced asexually from one ancestor; one such organism; *colloquial* person or thing regarded as identical to another. ● *verb* (**-ning**) propagate as clone.

close[1] /kləʊs/ ● *adjective* (often + *to*) at short distance or interval; having strong or immediate relation; (almost) in contact; dense, compact; nearly equal; rigorous; concentrated; stifling; shut; secret; niggardly. ● *adverb* at short distance or interval. ● *noun* street closed at one end; precinct of cathedral. ▫ **close harmony** singing of parts within an octave; **close-knit** tightly interlocked, closely united; **close season** season when killing of game etc. is illegal; **close shave** *colloquial* narrow escape; **close-up** photograph etc. taken at short range. ▫ **closely** *adverb*; **closeness** *noun*.

close[2] /kləʊz/ ● *verb* (**-sing**) shut; block up; bring or come to an end; end day's business; bring or come closer or into contact; make (electric circuit) continuous. ● *noun* conclusion, end. ▫ **closed-circuit** (of television) transmitted by wires to restricted number of receivers; **closed shop** business etc. where employees must belong to specified trade union.

closet /ˈklɒzɪt/ ● *noun* small room; cupboard; water-closet. ● *adjective* secret. ● *verb* (**-t-**) shut away, esp. in private consultation etc.

closure /ˈkləʊʒə/ *noun* closing, closed state; procedure for ending debate.

clot ● *noun* thick lump formed from liquid, esp. blood; *colloquial* foolish person. ● *verb* (**-tt-**) form into clots.

cloth /klɒθ/ *noun* woven or felted material; piece of this; (**the cloth**) the clergy.

clothe /ˈkləʊð/ *verb* (**-thing**; *past & past participle* **clothed** or **clad**) put clothes on; provide with clothes; cover as with clothes.

clothes /kləʊðz/ *plural noun* things worn to cover body and limbs; bedclothes. ▫ **clothes-horse** frame for airing washed clothes.

clothier /ˈkləʊðɪə/ *noun* dealer in men's clothes.

clothing /ˈkləʊðɪŋ/ *noun* clothes.

cloud /klaʊd/ ● *noun* visible mass of condensed watery vapour floating in air; mass of smoke or dust; (+ *of*) great number of (birds, insects, etc.) moving together; state of gloom, trouble, or suspicion. ● *verb* cover or darken with cloud(s); (often + *over*, *up*) become overcast or gloomy; make unclear. ▫ **cloudburst** sudden violent rainstorm. ▫ **cloudless** *adjective*.

cloudy *adjective* (**-ier**, **-iest**) covered with clouds; not transparent, unclear. ▫ **cloudiness** *noun*.

clout /klaʊt/ ● *noun* heavy blow; *colloquial* influence, power of effective action; piece of cloth or clothing. ● *verb* hit hard.

clove[1] /kləʊv/ *noun* dried bud of tropical tree, used as spice.

clove[2] /kləʊv/ *noun* segment of compound bulb, esp. of garlic.

clove[3] *past* of CLEAVE[1].

clove hitch *noun* knot for fastening rope round pole etc.

cloven /ˈkləʊv(ə)n/ *adjective* split. ▫ **cloven hoof, foot** divided hoof, as of oxen, sheep, etc., or the Devil.

clover /ˈkləʊvə/ *noun* kind of trefoil used as fodder. ▫ **in clover** in ease and luxury.

clown /klaʊn/ ● *noun* comic entertainer, esp. in circus; foolish or playful person. ● *verb* (often + *about*, *around*) behave like clown.

cloy *verb* satiate or sicken by sweetness, richness, etc.

club ● *noun* heavy stick used as weapon; stick with head, used in golf; association of people for social, sporting, etc. purposes; premises of this; playing card of suit marked with black trefoils; (in *plural*) this suit. ● *verb* (**-bb-**) strike (as) with club; (+ *together*) combine, esp. to make up sum of money. ▫ **club foot** congenitally deformed foot; **clubhouse** premises of club; **clubland** area with many nightclubs; **clubroot** disease of cabbages etc.; **club sandwich** sandwich with 2 layers of filling and 3 slices of bread or toast.

cluck ● *noun* chattering cry of hen. ● *verb* emit cluck(s).

clue ● *noun* guiding or suggestive fact; piece of evidence used in detection of crime; word(s) used to indicate word(s) for insertion in crossword. ● *verb* (**clues**, **clued**, **cluing** or **clueing**) provide clue to. □ **clue in**, **up** *slang* inform.

clump ● *noun* (+ *of*) cluster, esp. of trees. ● *verb* form clump; heap or plant together; tread heavily.

clumsy /ˈklʌmzɪ/ *adjective* (**-ier**, **-iest**) awkward in movement or shape; difficult to handle or use; tactless. □ **clumsily** *adverb*; **clumsiness** *noun*.

clung *past & past participle* of CLING.

cluster /ˈklʌstə/ ● *noun* close group or bunch of similar people or things. ● *verb* be in or form into cluster(s); (+ *round*, *around*) gather round.

clutch[1] ● *verb* seize eagerly; grasp tightly; (+ *at*) snatch at. ● *noun* tight or (in *plural*) cruel grasp; (in vehicle) device for connecting engine to transmission, pedal operating this. □ **clutch bag** handbag without handles.

clutch[2] *noun* set of eggs; brood of chickens.

clutter /ˈklʌtə/ ● *noun* crowded untidy collection of things. ● *verb* (often + *up*, *with*) crowd untidily, fill with clutter.

cm *abbreviation* centimetre(s).

Cmdr. *abbreviation* Commander.

CND *abbreviation* Campaign for Nuclear Disarmament.

CO *abbreviation* Commanding Officer.

Co. *abbreviation* company; county.

c/o *abbreviation* care of.

coach ● *noun* single-decker bus usually for longer journeys; railway carriage; closed horse-drawn carriage; sports trainer or private tutor. ● *verb* train or teach. □ **coachload** group of tourists etc. travelling by coach; **coachman** driver of horse-drawn carriage; **coachwork** bodywork of road or rail vehicle.

coagulate /kəʊˈægjʊleɪt/ *verb* (**-ting**) change from liquid to semi-solid; clot, curdle. □ **coagulant** *noun*; **coagulation** *noun*.

coal *noun* hard black mineral used as fuel etc.; piece of this. □ **coalface** exposed surface of coal in mine; **coalfield** area yielding coal; **coal gas** mixed gases formerly extracted from coal and used for heating, cooking, etc.; **coal mine** place where coal is dug; **coal miner** worker in coal mine; **coal scuttle** container for coal for domestic fire; **coal tar** tar extracted from coal; **coal tit** small bird with greyish plumage.

coalesce /kəʊəˈles/ *verb* (**-cing**) come together and form a whole. □ **coalescence** *noun*; **coalescent** *adjective*.

coalition /kəʊəˈlɪʃ(ə)n/ *noun* temporary alliance, esp. of political parties; fusion into one whole.

coaming /ˈkəʊmɪŋ/ *noun* raised border round ship's hatches etc.

coarse /kɔːs/ *adjective* rough or loose in texture; of large particles; lacking refinement; crude, obscene. □ **coarse fish** freshwater fish other than salmon and trout. □ **coarsely** *adverb*; **coarsen** *verb*; **coarseness** *noun*.

coast ● *noun* border of land near sea; seashore. ● *verb* ride or move (usually downhill) without use of power; make progress without exertion; sail along coast. □ **coastguard** (member of) group of people employed to keep watch on coasts, prevent smuggling, etc.; **coastline** line of seashore, esp. with regard to its shape. □ **coastal** *adjective*.

coaster *noun* ship that sails along coast; tray or mat for bottle or glass.

coat ● *noun* sleeved outer garment, overcoat, jacket; animal's fur or hair; layer of paint etc. ● *verb* (usually + *with*, *in*) cover with coat or layer; form covering on. □ **coat of arms** heraldic bearings or shield; **coat-hanger** shaped piece of wood etc. for hanging clothes on.

coating *noun* layer of paint etc.; cloth for coats.

coax *verb* persuade gradually or by flattery; (+ *out of*) obtain (thing) from (person) thus; manipulate gently.

coaxial /kəʊˈæksɪəl/ *adjective* having common axis; (of electric cable etc.) transmitting by means of two concentric conductors separated by insulator.

cob *noun* roundish lump; domed loaf; corn cob; large hazelnut; sturdy short-legged riding-horse; male swan.

cobalt /ˈkəʊbɔːlt/ *noun* silvery-white metallic element; (colour of) deep blue pigment made from it.

cobber /ˈkɒbə/ *noun Australian & NZ colloquial* companion, friend.

cobble[1] /ˈkɒb(ə)l/ ● *noun* (in full **cobblestone**) rounded stone used for paving. ● *verb* (**-ling**) pave with cobbles.

cobble[2] /ˈkɒb(ə)l/ *verb* (**-ling**) mend or patch (esp. shoes); (often + *together*) assemble roughly.

cobbler *noun* mender of shoes; (in *plural*) *slang* nonsense.

COBOL /ˈkəʊbɒl/ *noun* computer language for use in business operations.

cobra /ˈkəʊbrə/ *noun* venomous hooded snake.

cobweb /ˈkɒbweb/ *noun* spider's network or thread. □ **cobwebby** *adjective*.

coca /ˈkəʊkə/ *noun* S. American shrub; its leaves chewed as stimulant.

cocaine /kəʊˈkeɪn/ *noun* drug from coca, used as local anaesthetic and as stimulant.

coccyx /ˈkɒksɪks/ *noun* (*plural* **coccyges** /-dʒiːz/) bone at base of spinal column.

cochineal /kɒtʃɪˈniːl/ *noun* scarlet dye; insects whose dried bodies yield this.

cock[1] ● *noun* male bird, esp. domestic fowl; *slang* (as form of address) friend, fellow; *slang* nonsense; firing lever in gun released by trigger; tap or valve controlling flow. ● *verb* raise or make upright; turn or move (eye or ear) attentively or knowingly; set (hat etc.) aslant; raise cock of (gun). □ **cock-a-hoop** exultant; **cock-a-leekie** Scottish soup of boiled fowl with leeks; **cockcrow** dawn; **cock-eyed** *colloquial* crooked, askew, absurd.

cock[2] *noun* conical heap of hay or straw.

cockade /kɒˈkeɪd/ *noun* rosette etc. worn in hat.

cockatoo /kɒkəˈtuː/ *noun* crested parrot.

cockchafer /ˈkɒktʃeɪfə/ *noun* large pale brown beetle.

cocker /ˈkɒkə/ *noun* (in full **cocker spaniel**) small spaniel.

cockerel /ˈkɒkər(ə)l/ *noun* young cock.

cockle /ˈkɒk(ə)l/ *noun* edible bivalve shellfish; its shell; (in full **cockleshell**) small shallow boat; pucker or wrinkle. □ **cockles of the heart** innermost feelings.

cockney /ˈkɒknɪ/ ● *noun* (*plural* **-s**) native of London, esp. East End; cockney dialect. ● *adjective* of cockneys.

cockpit *noun* place for pilot etc. in aircraft or spacecraft or for driver in racing car; arena of war etc.

cockroach /ˈkɒkrəʊtʃ/ *noun* dark brown insect infesting esp. kitchens.

cockscomb /ˈkɒkskəʊm/ *noun* cock's crest.

cocksure /kɒkˈʃɔː/ *adjective* arrogantly confident.

cocktail /ˈkɒkteɪl/ *noun* drink of spirits, fruit juices, etc.; appetizer containing shellfish etc.; any hybrid mixture. □ **cocktail stick** small pointed stick.

cocky *adjective* (**-ier**, **-iest**) *colloquial* conceited, arrogant. □ **cockiness** *noun*.

coco /ˈkəʊkəʊ/ *noun* (*plural* **-s**) coconut palm.

cocoa /ˈkəʊkəʊ/ *noun* powder of crushed cacao seeds; drink made from this.

coconut /ˈkəʊkənʌt/ *noun* large brown seed of coco, with edible white lining enclosing milky juice. □ **coconut matting** matting made from fibre of coconut husks; **coconut shy** fairground sideshow where balls are thrown to dislodge coconuts.

cocoon /kəˈku:n/ ● *noun* silky case spun by larva to protect it as pupa; protective covering. ● *verb* wrap (as) in cocoon.

cocotte /kəˈkɒt/ *noun* small fireproof dish for cooking and serving food.

COD *abbreviation* cash (*US* collect) on delivery.

cod[1] *noun* (also **codfish**) (*plural* same) large sea fish. □ **cod liver oil** medicinal oil rich in vitamins.

cod[2] *noun & verb* (**-dd-**) *slang* hoax, parody.

coda /ˈkəʊdə/ *noun* final passage of piece of music.

coddle /ˈkɒd(ə)l/ *verb* (**-ling**) treat as an invalid, pamper; cook in water just below boiling point. □ **coddler** *noun*.

code ● *noun* system of signals or of symbols etc. used for secrecy, brevity, or computer processing of information; systematic set of laws etc.; standard of moral behaviour. ● *verb* (**-ding**) put into code.

codeine /ˈkəʊdi:n/ *noun* alkaloid derived from morphine, used as pain-killer.

codex /ˈkəʊdeks/ *noun* (*plural* **codices** /ˈkəʊdɪsi:z/) manuscript volume esp. of ancient texts.

codger /ˈkɒdʒə/ *noun* (usually in **old codger**) *colloquial* (strange) person.

codicil /ˈkəʊdɪsɪl/ *noun* addition to will.

codify /ˈkəʊdɪfaɪ/ *verb* (**-ies**, **-ied**) arrange (laws etc.) into code. □ **codification** *noun*.

codling[1] /ˈkɒdlɪŋ/ *noun* (also **codlin**) variety of apple; moth whose larva feeds on apples.

codling[2] *noun* (*plural* same) small cod.

co-education /kəʊedju:ˈkeɪʃ(ə)n/ *noun* education of both sexes together. □ **co-educational** *adjective*.

coefficient /kəʊɪˈfɪʃ(ə)nt/ *noun Mathematics* quantity or expression placed before and multiplying another; *Physics* multiplier or factor by which a property is measured.

coeliac disease /ˈsi:lɪæk/ *noun* intestinal disease whose symptoms include adverse reaction to gluten.

coequal /kəʊˈi:kw(ə)l/ *adjective & noun* equal.

coerce /kəʊˈɜ:s/ *verb* (**-cing**) persuade or restrain by force. □ **coercion** /-ˈɜ:ʃ(ə)n/ *noun*; **coercive** *adjective*.

coeval /kəʊˈi:v(ə)l/ *formal* ● *adjective* of the same age; contemporary. ● *noun* coeval person or thing.

coexist /kəʊɪgˈzɪst/ *verb* (often + *with*) exist together, esp. in mutual tolerance. □ **coexistence** *noun*; **coexistent** *adjective*.

coextensive /kəʊɪkˈstensɪv/ *adjective* extending over same space or time.

C. of E. *abbreviation* Church of England.

coffee /ˈkɒfɪ/ *noun* drink made from roasted and ground seeds of tropical shrub; cup of this; the shrub; the seeds; pale brown. □ **coffee bar** café selling coffee and light refreshments from bar; **coffee bean** seed of coffee; **coffee mill** small machine for grinding coffee beans; **coffee morning** morning gathering, esp. for charity, at which coffee is served; **coffee shop** small restaurant, esp. in hotel or store; **coffee table** small low table; **coffee-table book** large illustrated book.

coffer /ˈkɒfə/ *noun* large box for valuables; (in *plural*) funds, treasury; sunken panel in ceiling etc.

coffin /ˈkɒfɪn/ *noun* box in which corpse is buried or cremated.

cog *noun* each of series of projections on wheel etc. transferring motion by engaging with another series.

cogent /ˈkəʊdʒ(ə)nt/ *adjective* (of argument etc.) convincing, compelling. □ **cogency** *noun*; **cogently** *adverb*.

cogitate /ˈkɒdʒɪteɪt/ *verb* (**-ting**) ponder, meditate. □ **cogitation** *noun*.

cognac /ˈkɒnjæk/ *noun* French brandy.

cognate /ˈkɒgneɪt/ ● *adjective* descended from same ancestor or root. ● *noun* cognate person or word.

cognition /kɒgˈnɪʃ(ə)n/ *noun* knowing, perceiving, or conceiving, as distinct from emotion and volition. □ **cognitive** /ˈkɒg-/ *adjective*.

cognizance /ˈkɒgnɪz(ə)ns/ *noun formal* knowledge or awareness.

cognizant /ˈkɒgnɪz(ə)nt/ *adjective formal* (+ *of*) having knowledge or being aware of.

cognomen /kɒgˈnəʊmen/ *noun* nickname; *Roman History* surname.

cohabit /kəʊˈhæbɪt/ *verb* (**-t-**) live together as husband and wife. □ **cohabitation** *noun*.

cohere /kəʊˈhɪə/ *verb* (**-ring**) stick together; (of reasoning) be logical or consistent.

coherent *adjective* intelligible; consistent, easily understood. □ **coherence** *noun*; **coherently** *adverb*.

cohesion /kəʊˈhi:ʒ(ə)n/ *noun* sticking together; tendency to cohere. □ **cohesive** /-sɪv/ *adjective*.

cohort /ˈkəʊhɔ:t/ *noun* one-tenth of Roman legion; people banded together.

coif /kɔɪf/ *noun historical* close-fitting cap.

coiffeur /kwa:ˈfɜ:/ *noun* (*feminine* **coiffeuse** /-ˈfɜ:z/) hairdresser.

coiffure /kwa:ˈfjʊə/ *noun* hairstyle.

coil ● *verb* arrange or be arranged in concentric rings; move sinuously. ● *noun* coiled arrangement (of rope, electrical conductor, etc.); single turn of something coiled; flexible contraceptive device in womb.

coin ● *noun* stamped disc of metal as official money; metal money. ● *verb* make (coins) by stamping; invent (word, phrase). □ **coin box** telephone operated by coins.

coinage *noun* coining; system of coins in use; invention of word, invented word.

coincide /kəʊɪnˈsaɪd/ *verb* (**-ding**) occur at same time; (often + *with*) agree or be identical.

coincidence /kəʊˈɪnsɪd(ə)ns/ *noun* remarkable concurrence of events etc., apparently by chance. □ **coincident** *adjective*.

coincidental /kəʊɪnsɪˈdent(ə)l/ *adjective* in the nature of or resulting from coincidence. □ **coincidentally** *adverb*.

coir /ˈkɔɪə/ *noun* coconut fibre used for ropes, matting, etc.

coition /kəʊˈɪʃ(ə)n/ *noun* coitus.

coitus /ˈkəʊɪtəs/ *noun* sexual intercourse. □ **coital** *adjective*.

coke[1] ● *noun* solid left after gases have been extracted from coal. ● *verb* (**-king**) convert (coal) into coke.

coke[2] *noun slang* cocaine.

Col. *abbreviation* Colonel.

col *noun* depression in summit-line of mountain chain.

cola /ˈkəʊlə/ *noun* W. African tree with seeds containing caffeine; carbonated drink flavoured with these.

colander /ˈkʌləndə/ *noun* perforated vessel used as strainer in cookery.

cold /kəʊld/ ● *adjective* of or at low temperature; not heated; having lost heat; feeling cold; (of colour) suggesting cold; *colloquial* unconscious; lacking ardour or friendliness; dispiriting; (of hunting-scent) grown faint. ● *noun* prevalence of low temperature; cold weather; infection of nose or throat. ● *adverb* unrehearsed. □ **cold-blooded** having body temperature varying with that of environment, callous; **cold call** marketing call on person not previously interested in product; **cold cream** cleansing ointment; **cold feet** fear, reluctance; **cold fusion** nuclear fusion at room temperature; **cold shoulder** unfriendly treatment; **cold turkey** *slang* abrupt withdrawal from addictive drugs; **cold war** hostility between nations without actual fighting; **in cold blood** without emotion; **throw cold water on** discourage. □ **coldly** *adverb*; **coldness** *noun*.

coleslaw /ˈkəʊlslɔː/ *noun* salad of sliced raw cabbage etc.

coley /ˈkəʊlɪ/ *noun* (*plural* **-s**) any of several edible fish, esp. rock-salmon.

colic /ˈkɒlɪk/ *noun* spasmodic abdominal pain. □ **colicky** *adjective*.

colitis /kəˈlaɪtɪs/ *noun* inflammation of colon.

collaborate /kəˈlæbəreɪt/ *verb* (**-ting**) (often + *with*) work jointly. □ **collaboration** *noun*; **collaborative** /-rətɪv/ *adjective*; **collaborator** *noun*.

collage /ˈkɒlɑːʒ/ *noun* picture made by gluing pieces of paper etc. on to backing.

collapse /kəˈlæps/ ● *noun* falling down of structure; sudden failure of plan etc.; physical or mental breakdown. ● *verb* (**-sing**) (cause to) undergo collapse; *colloquial* relax completely after effort. □ **collapsible** *adjective*.

collar /ˈkɒlə/ ● *noun* neckband, upright or turned over, of coat, shirt, dress, etc.; leather band round animal's neck; band, ring, or pipe in machinery. ● *verb* capture, seize, appropriate; *colloquial* accost. □ **collar-bone** bone joining breastbone and shoulder blade.

collate /kəˈleɪt/ *verb* (**-ting**) collect and put in order. □ **collator** *noun*.

collateral /kəˈlætər(ə)l/ ● *noun* security pledged as guarantee for repayment of loan. ● *adjective* side by side; additional but subordinate; descended from same ancestor but by different line. □ **collaterally** *adverb*.

collation *noun* collating; light meal.

colleague /ˈkɒliːg/ *noun* fellow worker, esp. in profession or business.

collect[1] /kəˈlekt/ ● *verb* bring or come together; assemble, accumulate; seek and acquire (books, stamps, etc.); obtain (contributions, taxes, etc.) from people; call for, fetch; concentrate (one's thoughts etc.); (as **collected** *adjective*) not perturbed or distracted. ● *adjective & adverb US* (of telephone call, parcel, etc.) to be paid for by recipient.

collect[2] /ˈkɒlekt/ *noun* short prayer of Anglican or RC Church.

collectable /kəˈlektɪb(ə)l/ *adjective* worth collecting.

collection /kəˈlekʃ(ə)n/ *noun* collecting, being collected; things collected; money collected, esp. at church service etc.

collective /kəˈlektɪv/ ● *adjective* of or relating to group or society as a whole; joint; shared. ● *noun* cooperative enterprise; its members. □ **collective bargaining** negotiation of wages etc. by organized group of employees; **collective noun** singular noun denoting group of individuals. □ **collectively** *adverb*; **collectivize** *verb* (also **-ise**) (**-zing** or **-sing**).

collectivism *noun* theory or practice of collective ownership of land and means of production. □ **collectivist** *noun & adjective*.

collector *noun* person collecting things of interest; person collecting taxes, rents, etc.

colleen /ˈkɒliːn/ *noun Irish* girl.

college /ˈkɒlɪdʒ/ *noun* establishment for further, higher, or professional education; teachers and students in a college; school; organized group of people with shared functions and privileges.

collegiate /kəˈliːdʒɪət/ *adjective* of or constituted as college, corporate; (of university) consisting of different colleges.

collide /kəˈlaɪd/ *verb* (**-ding**) (often + *with*) come into collision or conflict.

collie /ˈkɒlɪ/ *noun* sheepdog originally of Scottish breed.

collier /ˈkɒlɪə/ *noun* coal miner; coal ship, member of its crew.

colliery /ˈkɒlɪərɪ/ *noun* (*plural* **-ies**) coal mine and its buildings.

collision /kəˈlɪʒ(ə)n/ *noun* violent impact of moving body against another or fixed object; clashing of interests etc.

collocate /ˈkɒləkeɪt/ *verb* (**-ting**) place (word etc.) next to another. □ **collocation** *noun*.

colloid /ˈkɒlɔɪd/ *noun* substance consisting of minute particles; mixture, esp. viscous solution, of this and another substance. □ **colloidal** *adjective*.

colloquial /kəˈləʊkwɪəl/ *adjective* of ordinary or familiar conversation, informal. □ **colloquially** *adverb*.

colloquialism /kəˈləʊkwɪəlɪz(ə)m/ *noun* colloquial word or phrase.

colloquy /ˈkɒləkwɪ/ *noun* (*plural* **-quies**) *literary* talk, dialogue.

collude /kəˈluːd/ *verb* (**-ding**) conspire. □ **collusion** /-ʒ(ə)n/ *noun*; **collusive** /-sɪv/ *adjective*.

collywobbles /ˈkɒlɪwɒb(ə)lz/ *plural noun colloquial* ache or rumbling in stomach; apprehensive feeling.

cologne /kəˈləʊn/ *noun* eau-de-Cologne or similar toilet water.

colon[1] /ˈkəʊlən/ *noun* punctuation mark (:) used between main clauses or before list or quotation (see panel).

colon[2] /ˈkəʊlən/ *noun* lower and greater part of large intestine.

colonel /ˈkɜːn(ə)l/ *noun* army officer commanding regiment, next in rank below brigadier. □ **colonelcy** *noun* (*plural* **-ies**).

colonial /kəˈləʊnɪəl/ ● *adjective* of a colony or colonies; of colonialism. ● *noun* inhabitant of colony.

colonialism *noun* policy of having colonies.

colonist /ˈkɒlənɪst/ *noun* settler in or inhabitant of colony.

colonize /ˈkɒlənaɪz/ *verb* (also **-ise**) (**-zing** or **-sing**) establish colony in; join colony. □ **colonization** *noun*.

colonnade /kɒləˈneɪd/ *noun* row of columns, esp. supporting roof. □ **colonnaded** *adjective*.

colony /ˈkɒlənɪ/ *noun* (*plural* **-ies**) settlement or settlers in new territory remaining subject to mother country; people of one nationality, occupation, etc. forming community in town etc.; group of animals that live close together.

colophon /ˈkɒləf(ə)n/ *noun* tailpiece in book.

color etc. *US* = COLOUR etc.

Colorado beetle /kɒləˈrɑːdəʊ/ *noun* small beetle destructive to potato.

coloration /kʌləˈreɪʃ(ə)n/ *noun* (also **colouration**) colouring, arrangement of colours.

coloratura /kɒlərəˈtʊərə/ *noun* elaborate passages in vocal music; singer of these, esp. soprano.

colossal /kəˈlɒs(ə)l/ *adjective* huge; *colloquial* splendid. □ **colossally** *adverb*.

colossus /kəˈlɒsəs/ *noun* (*plural* **-ssi** /-saɪ/ or **-ssuses**) statue much bigger than life size; gigantic or remarkable person etc.

colour /ˈkʌlə/ (*US* **color**) ● *noun* one, or any mixture, of the constituents into which light is separated in rainbow etc.; use of all colours as in photography; colouring substance, esp. paint; skin pigmentation, esp. when dark; ruddiness of face; appearance or aspect; (in *plural*) flag of regiment or ship etc.; coloured ribbon, rosette, etc. worn as symbol of school, club, political party, etc. ● *verb* give colour to; paint, stain, dye; blush; influence. □ **colour-blind** unable to distinguish certain colours; **colour-blindness** *noun*; **colour scheme** arrangement of colours; **colour supplement** magazine with colour printing, sold with newspaper.

coloured (*US* **colored**) ● *adjective* having colour; wholly or partly of non-white descent; *South African* of mixed white and non-white descent. ● *noun* coloured person.

colourful *adjective* (*US* **colorful**) full of colour or interest. □ **colourfully** *adverb*.

colouring *noun* (*US* **coloring**) appearance as regards colour, esp. facial complexion; application of colour; substance giving colour.

colourless *adjective* (*US* **colorless**) without colour, lacking interest.

colt /kəʊlt/ *noun* young male horse; *Sport* inexperienced player.

colter *US* = COULTER.

coltsfoot *noun* (*plural* **-s**) yellow wild flower with large leaves.

columbine /ˈkɒləmbaɪn/ *noun* garden plant with purple-blue flowers.

column /ˈkɒləm/ *noun* pillar, usually round, with base and capital; column-shaped thing; series of numbers, one under the other; vertical division of printed page; part of newspaper regularly devoted to particular subject or written by one writer; long, narrow arrangement of advancing troops, vehicles, etc.

columnist /ˈkɒləmnɪst/ *noun* journalist contributing regularly to newspaper etc.

coma /ˈkəʊmə/ *noun* (*plural* **-s**) prolonged deep unconsciousness.

comatose /ˈkəʊmətəʊs/ *adjective* in coma; sleepy.

comb /kəʊm/ ● *noun* toothed strip of rigid material for arranging hair; thing like comb, esp. for dressing wool etc.; red fleshy crest of fowl, esp. cock etc.; honeycomb. ● *verb* draw comb through (hair), dress (wool etc.) with comb; *colloquial* search (place) thoroughly.

combat /ˈkɒmbæt/ ● *noun* struggle, fight. ● *verb* (**-t-**) do battle (with); strive against, oppose.

combatant /ˈkɒmbət(ə)nt/ ● *noun* fighter. ● *adjective* fighting.

combative /ˈkɒmbətɪv/ *adjective* pugnacious.

combe = COOMB.

combination /kɒmbɪˈneɪʃ(ə)n/ *noun* combining, being combined; combined state; combined set of things or people; motorcycle with side-car; sequence of numbers etc. used to open **combination lock**.

combine ● *verb* /kəmˈbaɪn/ (**-ning**) join together; unite; form into chemical compound. ● *noun* /ˈkɒmbaɪn/ combination of esp. businesses. □ **combine harvester** /ˈkɒmbaɪn/ combined reaping and threshing machine.

combustible /kəmˈbʌstɪb(ə)l/ ● *adjective* capable of or used for burning. ● *noun* combustible substance. □ **combustibility** *noun*.

combustion /kəmˈbʌstʃ(ə)n/ *noun* burning; development of light and heat from combination of substance with oxygen.

come /kʌm/ *verb* (**-ming**; *past* **came**; *past participle* **come**) move or be brought towards or reach a place, time, situation, or result; be available; occur; become; traverse; *colloquial* behave like. □ **come about** happen; **come across** meet or find by chance, give specified impression, *colloquial* be effective or understood; **come again** *colloquial* what did you say?; **come along** make progress, hurry up; **come apart** disintegrate; **come at** attack; **comeback** return to success, *slang* retort or retaliation; **come back (to)** recur to memory (of); **come by** obtain; **come clean** *colloquial* confess; **comedown** loss of status; **come down** lose position, be handed down, be reduced; **come forward** offer oneself for task etc.; **come in** become fashionable or seasonable, prove to be; **come in for** receive; **come into** inherit; **come off** succeed, occur, fare; **come off it** *colloquial expression of disbelief*; **come on** make progress; **come out** emerge, become known, be published, go on strike, (of photograph or its subject) be (re)produced clearly, (of stain) be removed; **come out with** declare, disclose; **come over** come some distance to visit, (of feeling) affect, appear or sound in specifed way; **come round** pay informal visit, recover consciousness, be converted to another's opinion; **come through** survive; **come to** recover consciousness, amount to; **come up** arise, be mentioned or discussed, attain position; **come up with** produce (idea etc.); **come up against** be faced with; **come upon** meet or find by chance.

comedian /kəˈmiːdɪən/ *noun* humorous performer; actor in comedy; *slang* buffoon.

comedienne /kəmiːdɪˈen/ *noun* female comedian.

comedy /ˈkɒmədɪ/ *noun* (*plural* **-ies**) play or film of amusing character; humorous kind of drama etc.; humour; amusing aspects. □ **comedic** /kəˈmiːdɪk/ *adjective*.

comely /ˈkʌmlɪ/ *adjective* (**-ier**, **-iest**) *literary* handsome, good-looking. □ **comeliness** *noun*.

comestibles /kəˈmestɪb(ə)lz/ *plural noun formal* things to eat.

Colon :

This is used:

1 between two main clauses of which the second explains, enlarges on, or follows from the first, e.g.

It was not easy: to begin with I had to find the right house.

2 to introduce a list of items (a dash should not be added), and after expressions such as *namely, for example, to resume, to sum up,* and *the following,* e.g.

You will need: a tent, a sleeping bag, cooking equipment, and a rucksack.

3 before a quotation, e.g.

The poem begins: 'Earth has not anything to show more fair'.

comet /'kɒmɪt/ *noun* hazy object with 'tail' moving in path round sun.

comeuppance /kʌm'ʌpəns/ *noun colloquial* deserved punishment.

comfort /'kʌmf(ə)t/ ● *noun* physical or mental well-being; consolation; person or thing bringing consolation; (usually in *plural*) things that make life comfortable. ● *verb* console. ◻ **comfortless** *adjective*.

comfortable /'kʌmfətəb(ə)l/ *adjective* giving ease; at ease; having adequate standard of living; appreciable. ◻ **comfortably** *adverb*.

comforter /'kʌmfətə/ *noun* person who comforts; baby's dummy; *archaic* woollen scarf.

comfrey /'kʌmfrɪ/ *noun* tall plant with bell-like flowers.

comfy /'kʌmfɪ/ *adjective* **(-ier, -iest)** *colloquial* comfortable.

comic /'kɒmɪk/ ● *adjective* of or like comedy; funny. ● *noun* comedian; periodical in form of comic strips. ◻ **comic strip** sequence of drawings telling comic story. ◻ **comical** *adjective*; **comically** *adverb*.

comma /'kɒmə/ *noun* punctuation mark (,) indicating pause or break between parts of sentence (see panel).

command /kə'mɑːnd/ ● *verb* give formal order to; have authority or control over; have at one's disposal; deserve and get; look down over, dominate. ● *noun* order, instruction; holding of authority, esp. in armed forces; mastery; troops or district under commander. ◻ **command module** control compartment in spacecraft; **command performance** one given at royal request.

commandant /'kɒməndænt/ *noun* commanding officer, esp. of military academy.

commandeer /kɒmən'dɪə/ *verb* seize (esp. goods) for military use; take possession of without permission.

commander *noun* person who commands, esp. naval officer next below captain. ◻ **commander-in-chief** (*plural* **commanders-in-chief**) supreme commander, esp. of nation's forces.

Comma ,

The comma marks a slight break between words, phrases, etc. In particular, it is used:

1 to separate items in a list, e.g.

red, white, and blue or *red, white and blue*
We bought some shoes, socks, gloves, and handkerchiefs.
potatoes, peas, or carrots or *potatoes, peas or carrots*

2 to separate adjectives that describe something in the same way, e.g.

It is a hot, dry, dusty place.

but not if they describe it in different ways, e.g.

a distinguished foreign author

or if one adjective adds to or alters the meaning of another, e.g.

a bright red tie.

3 to separate main clauses, e.g.

Cars will park here, and coaches will turn left.

4 to separate a name or word used to address someone, e.g.

David, I'm here.
Well, Mr Jones, we meet again.
Have you seen this, my friend?

5 to separate a phrase, e.g.

Having had lunch, we went back to work.

especially in order to clarify meaning, e.g.

In the valley below, the village looked very small.

6 after words that introduce direct speech, or after direct speech where there is no question mark or exclamation mark, e.g.

They answered, 'Here we are.'
'Here we are,' they answered.

7 after *Dear Sir, Dear Sarah,* etc., and *Yours faithfully, Yours sincerely,* etc. in letters.

8 to separate a word, phrase, or clause that is secondary or adds information or a comment, e.g.

I am sure, however, that it will not happen.
Fred, who is bald, complained of the cold.

but not with a relative clause (one usually beginning with *who, which,* or *that*) that restricts the meaning of the noun it follows, e.g.

Men who are bald should wear hats.

No comma is needed between a month and a year in dates, e.g.

in December 1993

or between a number and a road in addresses, e.g.

17 Devonshire Avenue

commanding *adjective* impressive; giving wide view; substantial.

commandment *noun* divine command.

commando /kəˈmɑːndəʊ/ *noun* (*plural* **-s**) unit of shock troops; member of this.

commemorate /kəˈmeməreɪt/ *verb* (**-ting**) preserve in memory by celebration or ceremony; be memorial of. ◻ **commemoration** *noun*; **commemorative** /-rətɪv/ *adjective*.

commence /kəˈmens/ *verb* (**-cing**) *formal* begin. ◻ **commencement** *noun*.

commend /kəˈmend/ *verb* praise; recommend; entrust. ◻ **commendation** /kɒm-/ *noun*.

commendable *adjective* praiseworthy. ◻ **commendably** *adverb*.

commensurable /kəˈmenʃərəb(ə)l/ *adjective* (often + *with*, *to*) measurable by same standard; (+ *to*) proportionate to. ◻ **commensurability** *noun*.

commensurate /kəˈmenʃərət/ *adjective* (usually + *with*) extending over same space or time; (often + *to*, *with*) proportionate.

comment /ˈkɒment/ ● *noun* brief critical or explanatory note or remark; opinion; commenting. ● *verb* (often + *on*, *that*) make comment(s). ◻ **no comment** *colloquial* I decline to answer your question.

commentary /ˈkɒməntərɪ/ *noun* (*plural* **-ies**) broadcast description of event happening; series of comments on book or performance etc.

commentate /ˈkɒmənteɪt/ *verb* (**-ting**) act as commentator.

commentator *noun* writer or speaker of commentary.

commerce /ˈkɒmɜːs/ *noun* buying and selling; trading.

commercial /kəˈmɜːʃ(ə)l/ ● *adjective* of, in, or for commerce; done or run primarily for financial profit; (of broadcasting) financed by advertising. ● *noun* television or radio advertisement. ◻ **commercial broadcasting** broadcasting financed by advertising; **commercial traveller** firm's representative visiting shops etc. to get orders. ◻ **commercially** *adverb*.

commercialize *verb* (also **-ise**) (**-zing** or **-sing**) exploit or spoil for profit; make commercial. ◻ **commercialization** *noun*.

Commie /ˈkɒmɪ/ *noun slang derogatory* Communist.

commingle /kəˈmɪŋg(ə)l/ *verb* (**-ling**) *literary* mix, unite.

commiserate /kəˈmɪzəreɪt/ *verb* (**-ting**) (usually + *with*) have or express sympathy. ◻ **commiseration** *noun*.

commissar /ˈkɒmɪsɑː/ *noun historical* head of government department in USSR.

commissariat /kɒmɪˈseərɪət/ *noun* department responsible for supply of food etc. for army; food supplied.

commissary /ˈkɒmɪsərɪ/ *noun* (*plural* **-ies**) deputy, delegate.

commission /kəˈmɪʃ(ə)n/ ● *noun* authority to perform task; person(s) given such authority; order for specially produced thing; warrant conferring officer rank in armed forces; rank so conferred; pay or percentage received by agent; committing. ● *verb* empower, give authority to; give (artist etc.) order for work; order (work) to be written etc.; give (officer) command of ship; prepare (ship) for active service; bring (machine etc.) into operation. ◻ **in** or **out of commission** ready or not ready for active service.

commissionaire /kəmɪʃəˈneə/ *noun* uniformed door attendant.

commissioner *noun* person commissioned to perform specific task; member of government commission; representative of government in district etc.

commit /kəˈmɪt/ *verb* (**-tt-**) do or make (crime, blunder, etc.); (usually + *to*) entrust, consign; send (person) to prison; pledge or bind (esp. oneself) to policy or course of action; (as **committed** *adjective*) (often + *to*) dedicated, obliged.

commitment *noun* engagement, obligation; committing, being committed; dedication, committing oneself.

committal *noun* act of committing esp. to prison, grave, etc.

committee /kəˈmɪtɪ/ *noun* group of people appointed for special function by (and usually out of) larger body.

commode /kəˈməʊd/ *noun* chamber pot in chair or box with cover; chest of drawers.

commodious /kəˈməʊdɪəs/ *adjective* roomy.

commodity /kəˈmɒdɪtɪ/ *noun* (*plural* **-ies**) article of trade.

commodore /ˈkɒmədɔː/ *noun* naval officer next above captain; commander of squadron or other division of fleet; president of yacht club.

common /ˈkɒmən/ ● *adjective* (**-er**, **-est**) occurring often; ordinary, of the most familiar kind; shared by all; belonging to the whole community; *derogatory* inferior, vulgar; *Grammar* (of gender) referring to individuals of either sex. ● *noun* piece of open public land. ◻ **common ground** point or argument accepted by both sides; **common law** unwritten law based on custom and precedent; **common-law husband, wife** partner recognized by common law without formal marriage; **Common Market** European Community; **common or garden** *colloquial* ordinary; **common room** room for social use of students or teachers at college etc.; **common sense** good practical sense; **common time** *Music* 4 crotchets in a bar; **in common** shared, in joint use.

commonalty /ˈkɒmənəltɪ/ *noun* (*plural* **-ies**) general community, common people.

commoner *noun* person below rank of peer.

commonly *adverb* usually, frequently.

commonplace /ˈkɒmənpleɪs/ ● *adjective* lacking originality; ordinary. ● *noun* event, topic, etc. that is ordinary or usual; trite remark.

commons /ˈkɒmənz/ *plural noun* the common people; (**the Commons**) House of Commons.

commonwealth /ˈkɒmənwelθ/ *noun* independent state or community; (**the Commonwealth**) association of UK with states previously part of British Empire; republican government of Britain 1649–60.

commotion /kəˈməʊʃ(ə)n/ *noun* noisy disturbance.

communal /ˈkɒmjʊn(ə)l/ *adjective* shared between members of group or community; (of conflict etc.) between communities. ◻ **communally** *adverb*.

commune[1] /ˈkɒmjuːn/ *noun* group of people sharing accommodation and goods; small administrative district in France etc.

commune[2] /kəˈmjuːn/ *verb* (**-ning**) (usually + *with*) speak intimately; feel in close touch.

communicant /kəˈmjuːnɪkənt/ *noun* receiver of Holy Communion.

communicate /kəˈmjuːnɪkeɪt/ *verb* (**-ting**) impart, transmit (news, feelings, disease, ideas, etc.); (often + *with*) have social dealings. ◻ **communicator** *noun*.

communication *noun* communicating, being communicated; letter, message, etc.; connection or means of access; social dealings; (in *plural*) science and practice of transmitting information.

□ **communication cord** cord or chain pulled to stop train in emergency; **communication(s) satellite** artificial satellite used to relay telephone calls, TV, radio, etc.

communicative /kə'mju:nɪkətɪv/ *adjective* ready to talk and impart information.

communion /kə'mju:niən/ *noun* sharing, esp. of thoughts, interests, etc.; fellowship; group of Christians of same denomination; (**Holy Communion**) Eucharist.

communiqué /kə'mju:nɪkeɪ/ *noun* official communication, esp. news report.

communism /'kɒmjʊnɪz(ə)m/ *noun* social system based on public ownership of most property; political theory advocating this; (usually **Communism**) form of socialist society in Cuba, China, etc. □ **communist, Communist** *noun & adjective*; **communistic** /-'nɪstɪk/ *adjective*.

community /kə'mju:nɪtɪ/ (*plural* **-ies**) *noun* group of people living in one place or having same religion, ethnic origin, profession, etc.; commune; joint ownership. □ **community centre** place providing social facilities for neighbourhood; **community charge** *historical* tax levied locally on every adult; **community home** institution housing young offenders; **community singing** singing by large group; **community spirit** feeling of belonging to community.

commute /kə'mju:t/ *verb* (**-ting**) travel some distance to and from work; (usually + *to*) change (punishment) to one less severe.

commuter *noun* person who commutes to and from work.

compact[1] ● *adjective* /kəm'pækt/ closely packed together; economically designed; concise; (of person) small but well-proportioned. ● *verb* /kəm'pækt/ make compact. ● *noun* /'kɒmpækt/ small flat case for face powder etc. □ **compact disc** disc from which digital information or sound is reproduced by reflection of laser light. □ **compactly** *adverb*; **compactness** *noun*.

compact[2] /'kɒmpækt/ *noun* agreement, contract.

companion /kəm'pænjən/ *noun* person who accompanies or associates with another; person paid to live with another; handbook, reference book; thing that matches another; (**Companion**) member of some orders of knighthood. □ **companionway** staircase from ship's deck to cabins etc.

companionable *adjective* sociable, friendly. □ **companionably** *adverb*.

companionship *noun* friendship; being together.

company /'kʌmpənɪ/ *noun* (*plural* **-ies**) number of people assembled; guest(s); commercial business; actors etc. working together; subdivision of infantry battalion. □ **in company with** together with; **part company** (often + *with*) separate; **ship's company** entire crew.

comparable /'kɒmpərəb(ə)l/ *adjective* (often + *with, to*) able to be compared. □ **comparability** *noun*; **comparably** *adverb*.

■ **Usage** *Comparable* is often pronounced /kəm'pærəb(ə)l/ (with the stress on the *-par-*), but this is considered incorrect by some people.

---

comparative /kəm'pærətɪv/ ● *adjective* perceptible or estimated by comparison; relative; of or involving comparison; *Grammar* (of adjective or adverb) expressing higher degree of a quality. ● *noun Grammar* comparative expression or word. □ **comparatively** *adverb*.

compare /kəm'peə/ ● *verb* (**-ring**) (usually + *to*) express similarities in; (often + *to, with*) estimate similarity of; (often + *with*) bear comparison. ● *noun* comparison. □ **compare notes** exchange ideas or opinions.

comparison /kəm'pærɪs(ə)n/ *noun* comparing; example of similarity; (in full **degrees of comparison**) *Grammar* positive, comparative, and superlative forms of adjectives and adverbs. □ **bear comparison** (often + *with*) be able to be compared favourably.

compartment /kəm'pɑ:tmənt/ *noun* space partitioned off within larger space.

compass /'kʌmpəs/ *noun* instrument showing direction of magnetic north and bearings from it; (usually in *plural*) V-shaped hinged instrument for drawing circles and taking measurements; scope, range.

compassion /kəm'pæʃ(ə)n/ *noun* pity.

compassionate /kəm'pæʃənət/ *adjective* showing compassion; sympathetic. □ **compassionate leave** leave granted on grounds of bereavement etc. □ **compassionately** *adverb*.

compatible /kəm'pætɪb(ə)l/ *adjective* (often + *with*) able to coexist; (of equipment) able to be used in combination. □ **compatibility** *noun*.

compatriot /kəm'pætrɪət/ *noun* person from one's own country.

compel /kəm'pel/ *verb* (**-ll-**) force, constrain; arouse irresistibly; (as **compelling** *adjective*) arousing strong interest.

compendious /kəm'pendɪəs/ *adjective* comprehensive but brief.

compendium /kəm'pendɪəm/ *noun* (*plural* **-s** or **-dia**) abridgement, summary; collection of table games etc.

compensate /'kɒmpenseɪt/ *verb* (**-ting**) recompense, make amends; counterbalance.

compensation *noun* compensating, being compensated; money etc. given as recompense. □ **compensatory** /-'seɪt-/ *adjective*.

compère /'kɒmpeə/ ● *noun* person introducing variety show. ● *verb* (**-ring**) act as compère (to).

compete /kəm'pi:t/ *verb* (**-ting**) take part in contest etc., (often + *with* or *against* person, *for* thing) strive.

competence /'kɒmpɪt(ə)ns/ *noun* being competent; ability.

competent *adjective* adequately qualified or capable; effective. □ **competently** *adverb*.

competition /kɒmpə'tɪʃ(ə)n/ *noun* (often + *for*) competing; event in which people compete; other people competing; opposition.

competitive /kəm'petɪtɪv/ *adjective* of or involving competition; (of prices etc.) comparing well with those of rivals; having strong urge to win. □ **competitiveness** *noun*.

competitor /kəm'petɪtə/ *noun* person who competes; rival, esp. in business.

compile /kəm'paɪl/ *verb* (**-ling**) collect and arrange (material) into list, book, etc. □ **compilation** /kɒmpɪ'leɪʃ(ə)n/ *noun*.

complacent /kəm'pleɪs(ə)nt/ *adjective* smugly self-satisfied or contented. □ **complacency** *noun*.

complain /kəm'pleɪn/ *verb* express dissatisfaction; (+ *of*) say that one is suffering from (an ailment), state grievance concerning. □ **complainant** *noun*.

complaint *noun* complaining; grievance, cause of dissatisfaction; formal protest; ailment.

complaisant /kəm'pleɪz(ə)nt/ *adjective formal* deferential; willing to please; acquiescent. □ **complaisance** *noun*.

complement ● *noun* /'kɒmplɪmənt/ thing that completes; full number; word(s) added to verb to complete predicate of sentence; amount by which angle is less than 90°. ● *verb* /-ment/ complete; form complement to. ▫ **complementary** /-'men-/ *adjective*.

complete /kəm'pli:t/ ● *adjective* having all its parts; finished, total. ● *verb* (**-ting**) finish; make complete; fill in (form etc.). ▫ **completely** *adverb*; **completeness** *noun*; **completion** *noun*.

complex /'kɒmpleks/ ● *noun* buildings, rooms, etc. made up of related parts; group of usually repressed feelings or thoughts causing abnormal behaviour or mental state. ● *adjective* complicated; consisting of related parts. ▫ **complexity** /kəm'pleks-/ *noun* (*plural* **-ies**).

complexion /kəm'plekʃ(ə)n/ *noun* natural colour, texture, and appearance of skin, esp. of face; aspect.

compliance /kəm'plaɪəns/ *noun* obedience to request, command, etc.; capacity to yield.

compliant *adjective* obedient; yielding. ▫ **compliantly** *adverb*.

complicate /'kɒmplɪkeɪt/ *verb* (**-ting**) make difficult or complex; (as **complicated** *adjective*) complex, intricate.

complication *noun* involved or confused condition; complicating circumstance; difficulty; (often in *plural*) disease or condition arising out of another.

complicity /kəm'plɪsɪtɪ/ *noun* partnership in wrongdoing.

compliment ● *noun* /'kɒmplɪmənt/ polite expression of praise; (in *plural*) formal greetings accompanying gift etc. ● *verb* /-ment/ (often + *on*) congratulate; praise.

complimentary /kɒmplɪ'mentərɪ/ *adjective* expressing compliment; given free of charge.

comply /kəm'plaɪ/ *verb* (**-ies**, **-ied**) (often + *with*) act in accordance (with request or command).

component /kəm'pəʊnənt/ ● *adjective* being part of larger whole. ● *noun* component part.

comport /kəm'pɔ:t/ *verb* (**comport oneself**) *literary* conduct oneself; behave. ▫ **comportment** *noun*.

compose /kəmpəʊz/ *verb* (**-sing**) create in music or writing; make up, constitute; arrange artistically; set up (type); arrange in type; (as **composed** *adjective*) calm, self-possessed.

composer *noun* person who composes esp. music.

composite /'kɒmpəzɪt/ ● *adjective* made up of parts; (of plant) having head of many flowers forming one bloom. ● *noun* composite thing or plant.

composition /kɒmpə'zɪʃ(ə)n/ *noun* act of putting together; thing composed; school essay; arrangement of parts of picture etc.; constitution of substance; compound artificial substance.

compositor /kəm'pɒzɪtə/ *noun* person who sets up type for printing.

compost /'kɒmpɒst/ *noun* mixture of decayed organic matter used as fertilizer.

composure /kəm'pəʊʒə/ *noun* calm manner.

compote /'kɒmpəʊt/ *noun* fruit in syrup.

compound[1] /'kɒmpaʊnd/ ● *noun* mixture of two or more things; word made up of two or more existing words; substance formed from two or more elements chemically united. ● *adjective* made up of two or more ingredients or parts; combined, collective. ● *verb* /kəm'paʊnd/ mix or combine; increase (difficulties etc.); make up (whole); settle (matter) by mutual agreement. ▫ **compound fracture** one complicated by wound; **compound interest** interest paid on capital and accumulated interest.

compound[2] /'kɒmpaʊnd/ *noun* enclosure, fenced-in space.

comprehend /kɒmprɪ'hend/ *verb* understand; include.

comprehensible *adjective* that can be understood.

comprehension *noun* understanding; text set as test of understanding; inclusion.

comprehensive ● *adjective* including all or nearly all; (of motor insurance) providing protection against most risks. ● *noun* (in full **comprehensive school**) secondary school for children of all abilities. ▫ **comprehensively** *adverb*.

compress ● *verb* /kəm'pres/ squeeze together, bring into smaller space or shorter time. ● *noun* /'kɒmpres/ pad pressed on part of body to relieve inflammation, stop bleeding, etc. ▫ **compressible** *adjective*.

compression /kəm'preʃ(ə)n/ *noun* compressing; reduction in volume of fuel mixture in internal-combustion engine before ignition.

compressor *noun* machine for compressing air or other gas.

comprise /kəm'praɪz/ *verb* (**-sing**) include; consist of.

■ **Usage** It is a mistake to use *comprise* to mean 'to compose or make up'.

compromise /'kɒmprəmaɪz/ ● *noun* agreement reached by mutual concession; (often + *between*) intermediate state between conflicting opinions etc. ● *verb* (**-sing**) settle dispute by compromise; modify one's opinions, demands, etc.; bring into disrepute or danger by indiscretion.

comptroller /kən'trəʊlə/ *noun* controller.

compulsion /kəm'pʌlʃ(ə)n/ *noun* compelling, being compelled; irresistible urge.

compulsive *adjective* compelling; resulting or acting (as if) from compulsion; irresistible. ▫ **compulsively** *adverb*.

compulsory *adjective* required by law or rule. ▫ **compulsorily** *adverb*.

compunction /kəm'pʌŋkʃ(ə)n/ *noun* guilty feeling; slight regret.

compute /kəm'pju:t/ *verb* (**-ting**) calculate; use computer. ▫ **computation** /kɒm-/ *noun*.

computer *noun* electronic device for storing and processing data, making calculations, or controlling machinery. ▫ **computer-literate** able to use computers; **computer science** study of computers; **computer virus** code maliciously introduced into program to destroy data etc.

computerize /kəm'pju:təraɪz/ *verb* (also **-ise**) (**-zing** or **-sing**) equip with or store, perform, or produce by computer. ▫ **computerization** *noun*.

comrade /'kɒmreɪd/ *noun* companion in some activity; fellow socialist or Communist. ▫ **comradeship** *noun*.

con[1] *slang* ● *noun* confidence trick. ● *verb* (**-nn-**) swindle, deceive.

con[2] *noun* (usually in *plural*) reason against.

con[3] *verb* (*US* **conn**) (**-nn-**) direct steering of (ship).

concatenation /kɒnkætɪ'neɪʃ(ə)n/ *noun* series of linked things or events.

concave /kɒn'keɪv/ *adjective* curved like interior of circle or sphere. ▫ **concavity** /-'kæv-/ *noun*.

conceal /kən'si:l/ *verb* hide; keep secret. ▫ **concealment** *noun*.

concede /kən'si:d/ *verb* (**-ding**) admit to be true; admit defeat in; grant.

conceit /kən'si:t/ *noun* personal vanity; *literary* far-fetched comparison.

conceited *adjective* vain. ▫ **conceitedly** *adverb*.

conceive /kən'si:v/ *verb* (**-ving**) become pregnant (with); (often + *of*) imagine; (usually in *passive*) formulate (plan etc.). ▫ **conceivable** *adjective*; **conceivably** *adverb*.

concentrate /'kɒnsəntreɪt/ ● *verb* (**-ting**) (often + *on*) focus one's attention; bring together to one point;

increase strength of (liquid etc.) by removing water etc.; (as **concentrated** *adjective*) strong. ● *noun* concentrated solution.

concentration *noun* concentrating, being concentrated; weight of substance in given amount of mixture; mental attention. □ **concentration camp** place for detention of political prisoners etc.

concentric /kən'sentrɪk/ *adjective* having common centre. □ **concentrically** *adverb*.

concept /'kɒnsept/ *noun* general notion; abstract idea.

conception /kən'sepʃ(ə)n/ *noun* conceiving, being conceived; idea; understanding.

conceptual /kən'septjʊəl/ *adjective* of mental concepts. □ **conceptually** *adverb*.

conceptualize *verb* (also **-ise**) (**-zing** or **-sing**) form concept or idea of. □ **conceptualization** *noun*.

concern /kən'sɜ:n/ ● *verb* be relevant or important to; relate to, be about; worry, affect; (**concern oneself**; often + *with, about, in*) interest or involve oneself. ● *noun* anxiety, worry; matter of interest or importance to one; firm, business.

concerned *adjective* involved, interested; anxious, troubled.

concerning *preposition* about, regarding.

concert /'kɒnsət/ *noun* musical performance; agreement.

concerted /kən'sɜ:tɪd/ *adjective* jointly planned.

concertina /kɒnsə'ti:nə/ ● *noun* portable musical instrument like accordion but smaller. ● *verb* (**-nas, -naed** /-nəd/ or **-na'd, -naing**) compress or collapse in folds like those of concertina.

concerto /kən'tʃeətəʊ/ *noun* (*plural* **-tos** or **-ti** /-tɪ/) composition for solo instrument(s) and orchestra.

concession /kən'seʃ(ə)n/ *noun* conceding, thing conceded; reduction in price for certain category of people; right to use land, sell goods, etc. □ **concessionary** *adjective*.

conch /kɒntʃ/ *noun* large spiral shell of various marine gastropod molluscs; such gastropod.

conchology /kɒŋ'kɒlədʒɪ/ *noun* study of shells.

conciliate /kən'sɪlɪeɪt/ *verb* (**-ting**) make calm; pacify; reconcile. □ **conciliation** *noun*; **conciliator** *noun*; **conciliatory** *adjective*.

concise /kən'saɪs/ *adjective* brief but comprehensive. □ **concisely** *adverb*; **conciseness** *noun*; **concision** *noun*.

conclave /'kɒnkleɪv/ *noun* private meeting; assembly or meeting-place of cardinals for election of pope.

conclude /kən'klu:d/ *verb* (**-ding**) bring or come to end; (often + *from, that*) infer; settle (treaty etc.).

conclusion /kən'klu:ʒ(ə)n/ *noun* ending; judgement reached by reasoning; summing-up; settling of peace etc. □ **in conclusion** lastly.

conclusive /kən'klu:sɪv/ *adjective* decisive, convincing. □ **conclusively** *adverb*.

concoct /kən'kɒkt/ *verb* make by mixing ingredients; invent (story, lie, etc.). □ **concoction** *noun*.

concomitant /kən'kɒmɪt(ə)nt/ ● *adjective* (often + *with*) accompanying. ● *noun* accompanying thing. □ **concomitance** *noun*.

concord /'kɒŋkɔ:d/ *noun* agreement, harmony. □ **concordant** /kən'kɔ: d(ə)nt/ *adjective*.

concordance /kən'kɔ:d(ə)ns/ *noun* agreement; index of words used in book or by author.

concordat /kən'kɔ:dæt/ *noun* agreement, esp. between Church and state.

concourse /'kɒŋkɔ:s/ *noun* crowd; large open area in railway station etc.

concrete /'kɒŋkri:t/ ● *adjective* existing in material form, real; definite. ● *noun* mixture of gravel, sand, cement, and water used for building. ● *verb* (**-ting**) cover with or embed in concrete.

concretion /kən'kri:ʃ(ə)n/ *noun* hard solid mass; forming of this by coalescence.

concubine /'kɒŋkjʊbaɪn/ *noun literary* mistress; (among polygamous peoples) secondary wife.

concupiscence /kən'kju:pɪs(ə)ns/ *noun formal* lust. □ **concupiscent** *adjective*.

concur /kən'kɜ:/ *verb* (**-rr-**) (often + *with*) agree; coincide.

concurrent /kən'kʌrənt/ *adjective* (often + *with*) existing or in operation at the same time. □ **concurrence** *noun*; **concurrently** *adverb*.

concuss /kən'kʌs/ *verb* subject to concussion.

concussion /kən'kʌʃ(ə)n/ *noun* temporary unconsciousness or incapacity due to head injury; violent shaking.

condemn /kən'dem/ *verb* express strong disapproval of; (usually + *to*) sentence (to punishment), doom (to something unpleasant); pronounce unfit for use. □ **condemnation** /kɒndem'neɪʃ(ə)n/ *noun*.

condensation /kɒnden'seɪʃ(ə)n/ *noun* condensing, being condensed; condensed liquid; abridgement.

condense /kən'dens/ *verb* (**-sing**) make denser or more concise; reduce or be reduced from gas to liquid.

condescend /kɒndɪ'send/ *verb* (+ *to do*) graciously consent to do a thing while showing one's superiority; (+ *to*) pretend to be on equal terms with (inferior); (as **condescending** *adjective*) patronizing. □ **condescendingly** *adverb*; **condescension** *noun*.

condiment /'kɒndɪmənt/ *noun* seasoning or relish for food.

condition /kən'dɪʃ(ə)n/ ● *noun* stipulation; thing on fulfilment of which something else depends; state of being or fitness of person or thing; ailment; (in *plural*) circumstances. ● *verb* bring into desired state; accustom; determine; be essential to.

conditional *adjective* (often + *on*) dependent, not absolute; *Grammar* (of clause, mood, etc.) expressing condition. □ **conditionally** *adverb*.

condole /kən'dəʊl/ *verb* (**-ling**) (+ *with*) express sympathy with (person) over loss etc.

■ **Usage** *Condole* is commonly confused with *console*, which means 'to comfort'.

condolence *noun* (often in *plural*) expression of sympathy.

condom /'kɒndɒm/ *noun* contraceptive sheath.

condominium /kɒndə'mɪnɪəm/ *noun* joint rule or sovereignty; *US* building containing individually owned flats.

condone /kən'dəʊn/ *verb* (**-ning**) forgive, overlook.

condor /'kɒndɔ:/ *noun* large S. American vulture.

conducive /kən'dju:sɪv/ *adjective* (often + *to*) contributing or helping (towards someting).

conduct ● *noun* /'kɒndʌkt/ behaviour; manner of conducting business, war, etc. ● *verb* /kən'dʌkt/ lead, guide; control, manage; be conductor of (orchestra etc.); transmit by conduction; (**conduct oneself**) behave.

conduction /kən'dʌkʃ(ə)n/ *noun* transmission of heat, electricity, etc.

conductive /kən'dʌktɪv/ *adjective* transmitting heat, electricity, etc. □ **conductivity** /kɒndʌk'tɪv-/ *noun*.

conductor *noun* director of orchestra etc.; (*feminine* **conductress**) person who collects fares on bus etc.; conductive thing.

conduit /'kɒndɪt/ *noun* channel or pipe for conveying liquid or protecting insulated cable.

cone *noun* solid figure with usually circular base and tapering to a point; cone-shaped object; dry fruit of pine or fir; ice cream cornet.

coney = CONY.

confab /'kɒnfæb/ *noun colloquial* confabulation.

confabulate /kən'fæbjʊleɪt/ *verb* (**-ting**) talk together. □ **confabulation** *noun*.

confection /kən'fekʃ(ə)n/ *noun* sweet dish or delicacy.

confectioner *noun* dealer in sweets or pastries etc. □ **confectionery** *noun*.

confederacy /kən'fedərəsɪ/ *noun* (*plural* **-ies**) alliance or league, esp. of confederate states.

confederate /kən'fedərət/ ● *adjective esp. Politics* allied. ● *noun* ally; accomplice. ● *verb* /-reɪt/ (**-ting**) (often + *with*) bring or come into alliance. □ **Confederate States** those which seceded from US in 1860–1.

confederation /kənfedə'reɪʃ(ə)n/ *noun* union or alliance, esp. of states.

confer /kən'fɜː/ *verb* (**-rr-**) (often + *on, upon*) grant, bestow; (often + *with*) meet for discussion.

conference /'kɒnfər(ə)ns/ *noun* consultation; meeting for discussion.

conferment /kən'fɜːmənt/ *noun* conferring (of honour etc.).

confess /kən'fes/ *verb* acknowledge, admit; declare one's sins, esp. to priest; (of priest) hear confession of.

confessedly /kən'fesɪdlɪ/ *adverb* by one's own or general admission.

confession /kən'feʃ(ə)n/ *noun* act of confessing; thing confessed; statement of principles etc.

confessional ● *noun* enclosed place where priest hears confession. ● *adjective* of confession.

confessor *noun* priest who hears confession.

confetti /kən'fetɪ/ *noun* small bits of coloured paper thrown by wedding guests at bride and groom.

confidant /'kɒnfɪdænt/ *noun* (*feminine* **confidante** same pronunciation) person trusted with knowledge of one's private affairs.

confide /kən'faɪd/ *verb* (**-ding**) (usually + *to*) tell (secret) or entrust (task). □ **confide in** talk confidentially to.

confidence /'kɒnfɪd(ə)ns/ *noun* firm trust; feeling of certainty; self-reliance; boldness; something told as a secret. □ **confidence trick** swindle in which victim is persuaded to trust swindler; **confidence trickster** person using confidence tricks; **in confidence** as a secret; **in (person's) confidence** trusted with his or her secrets.

confident *adjective* feeling or showing confidence. □ **confidently** *adverb*.

confidential /kɒnfɪ'denʃ(ə)l/ *adjective* spoken or written in confidence; entrusted with secrets; confiding. □ **confidentiality** /-ʃɪ'æl-/ *noun*; **confidentially** *adjective*.

configuration /kənfɪgjʊ'reɪʃ(ə)n/ *noun* manner of arrangement; shape; outline. □ **configure** /-'fɪgə/ *verb*.

confine ● *verb* /kən'faɪn/ (**-ning**) keep or restrict within certain limits; imprison. ● *noun* /'kɒnfaɪn/ (usually in *plural*) boundary. □ **be confined** be in childbirth.

confinement /kən'faɪnmənt/ *noun* confining, being confined; childbirth.

confirm /kən'fɜːm/ *verb* provide support for truth or correctness of; establish more firmly; formally make definite; administer confirmation to.

confirmation /kɒnfə'meɪʃ(ə)n/ *noun* confirming circumstance or statement; rite confirming baptized person as member of Christian Church.

confirmed *adjective* firmly settled in habit or condition.

confiscate /'kɒnfɪskeɪt/ *verb* (**-ting**) take or seize by authority. □ **confiscation** *noun*.

conflagration /kɒnflə'greɪʃ(ə)n/ *noun* large destructive fire.

conflate /kən'fleɪt/ *verb* (**-ting**) fuse together, blend. □ **conflation** *noun*.

conflict ● *noun* /'kɒnflɪkt/ struggle, fight; opposition; (often + *of*) clashing of opposed interests etc. ● *verb* /kən'flɪkt/ clash, be incompatible.

confluent /'kɒnflʊənt/ ● *adjective* merging into one. ● *noun* stream joining another. □ **confluence** *noun*.

conform /kən'fɔːm/ *verb* comply with rules or general custom; (+ *to, with*) be in accordance with.

conformable *adjective* (often + *to*) similar; (often + *with*) consistent.

conformation /kɒnfɔː'meɪʃ(ə)n/ *noun* thing's structure or shape.

conformist ● *noun* person who conforms to established practice. ● *adjective* conventional. □ **conformism** *noun*.

conformity *noun* conforming with established practice; suitability.

confound /kən'faʊnd/ ● *verb* baffle; confuse; *archaic* defeat. □ **confound (person, thing)!** *interjection expressing annoyance*.

confounded *adjective colloquial* damned.

confront /kən'frʌnt/ *verb* meet or stand facing, esp. in hostility or defiance; (of problem etc.) present itself to; (+ *with*) bring face to face with. □ **confrontation** /kɒn-/ *noun*; **confrontational** /kɒn-/ *adjective*.

confuse /kən'fjuːz/ *verb* (**-sing**) bewilder; mix up; make obscure; (often as **confused** *adjective*) throw into disorder. □ **confusing** *adjective*; **confusion** *noun*.

confute /kən'fjuːt/ *verb* (**-ting**) prove to be false or wrong. □ **confutation** /kɒn-/ *noun*.

conga /'kɒŋgə/ *noun* Latin American dance, usually performed in single file; tall narrow drum beaten with hands.

congeal /kən'dʒiːl/ *verb* make or become semi-solid by cooling; (of blood) coagulate.

congenial /kən'dʒiːnɪəl/ *adjective* having sympathetic nature, similar interests, etc.; (often + *to*) suited or agreeable. □ **congeniality** /-'æl-/ *noun*; **congenially** *adverb*.

congenital /kən'dʒenɪt(ə)l/ *adjective* existing or as such from birth. □ **congenitally** *adverb*.

conger /'kɒŋgə/ *noun* large sea eel.

congest /kən'dʒest/ *verb* (esp. as **congested** *adjective*) affect with congestion.

congestion *noun* abnormal accumulation or obstruction, esp. of traffic etc. or of mucus in nose etc.

conglomerate /kən'glɒmərət/ ● *adjective* gathered into rounded mass. ● *noun* heterogeneous mass; business etc. corporation of merged firms. ● *verb* /-reɪt/ (**-ting**) collect into coherent mass. □ **conglomeration** *noun*.

congratulate /kən'grætʃʊleɪt/ *verb* (**-ting**) (often + *on*) express pleasure at happiness, excellence, or good fortune of (person). □ **congratulatory** /-lətərɪ/ *adjective*.

congratulation *noun* congratulating, (usually in *plural*) expression of this.

congregate /'kɒŋgrɪgeɪt/ *verb* (**-ting**) collect or gather in crowd.

congregation *noun* assembly of people, esp. for religious worship; group of people regularly attending particular church etc.

congregational *adjective* of a congregation; (**Congregational**) of or adhering to Congregationalism.

Congregationalism *noun* system in which individual churches are self-governing. □ **Congregationalist** *noun*.

congress /'kɒŋgres/ *noun* formal meeting of delegates for discussion; (**Congress**) national legislative body of US etc. □ **congressman**, **congresswoman** member of US Congress. □ **congressional** /kən'greʃ-/ *adjective*.

congruent /'kɒŋgrʊənt/ *adjective* (often + *with*) suitable, agreeing; *Geometry* (of figures) coinciding exactly when superimposed. □ **congruence** *noun*.

conic /'kɒnɪk/ *adjective* of a cone.

conical *adjective* cone-shaped.

conifer /'kɒnɪfə/ *noun* cone-bearing tree. □ **coniferous** /kə'nɪfərəs/ *adjective*.

conjectural /kən'dʒektʃər(ə)l/ *adjective* involving conjecture.

conjecture /kən'dʒektʃə/ ● *noun* formation of opinion on incomplete information, guess. ● *verb* (**-ring**) guess.

conjoin /kən'dʒɔɪn/ *verb formal* join, combine.

conjoint /kən'dʒɔɪnt/ *adjective formal* associated, conjoined.

conjugal /'kɒndʒʊg(ə)l/ *adjective* of marriage; between husband and wife.

conjugate ● *verb* /'kɒndʒʊgeɪt/ (**-ting**) give the different forms of (verb); unite, become fused. ● *adjective* /-gət/ joined together.

conjugation *noun Grammar* system of verbal inflection.

conjunct /kən'dʒʌŋkt/ *adjective* joined; combined; associated.

conjunction *noun* joining, connection; word used to connect sentences, clauses, or words (see panel); combination of events or circumstances. □ **conjunctive** *adjective*.

conjunctiva /kɒndʒʌŋk'taɪvə/ *noun* (*plural* **-s**) mucous membrane covering front of eye and inside of eyelid.

conjunctivitis /kəndʒʌŋktɪ'vaɪtɪs/ *noun* inflammation of conjunctiva.

conjure /'kʌndʒə/ *verb* (**-ring**) perform seemingly magical tricks, esp. by movement of hands. □ **conjure up** produce as if by magic, evoke.

conjuror *noun* (also **conjurer**) performer of conjuring tricks.

conk[1] *verb colloquial* (usually + *out*) break down; become exhausted; faint; fall asleep.

conk[2] *slang* ● *noun* (punch on) nose or head. ● *verb* hit on nose or head.

conker /'kɒŋkə/ *noun* horse chestnut fruit; (in *plural*) children's game played with conkers on strings.

con man *noun* confidence trickster.

connect /kə'nekt/ *verb* (often + *to*, *with*) join, be joined; associate mentally or practically; (+ *with*) (of train etc.) arrive in time for passengers to transfer to another; put into communication by telephone; (usually in *passive*; + *with*) unite or associate with (others) in relationship etc. □ **connecting rod** rod between piston and crankpin etc. in engine. □ **connector** *noun*.

connection *noun* (also **connexion**) connecting, being connected; point at which things are connected; association of ideas; link, esp. by telephone; (often in *plural*) (esp. influential) relative or associate; connecting train etc.

connective *adjective* connecting. □ **connective tissue** body tissue forming tendons and ligaments, supporting organs, etc.

conning tower /'kɒnɪŋ/ *noun* raised structure of submarine containing periscope; wheelhouse of warship.

connive /kə'naɪv/ *verb* (**-ving**) (+ *at*) tacitly consent to (wrongdoing); conspire. □ **connivance** *noun*.

connoisseur /kɒnə'sɜː/ *noun* (often + *of*, *in*) person with good taste and judgement.

connote /kə'nəʊt/ *verb* (**-ting**) imply in addition to literal meaning; mean. □ **connotation** /kɒnə-/ *noun*; **connotative** /'kɒnəteɪtɪv/ *adjective*.

connubial /kə'nju:bɪəl/ *adjective* conjugal.

conquer /'kɒŋkə/ *verb* overcome, defeat; be victorious; subjugate. □ **conqueror** *noun*.

conquest /'kɒŋkwest/ *noun* conquering; something won; person whose affections have been won.

consanguineous /kɒnsæŋ'gwɪnɪəs/ *adjective* descended from same ancestor; akin. □ **consanguinity** *noun*.

conscience /'kɒnʃ(ə)ns/ *noun* moral sense of right and wrong, esp. as affecting behaviour. □ **conscience money** money paid to relieve conscience, esp. in respect of evaded payment etc.; **conscience-stricken** made uneasy by bad conscience.

conscientious /kɒnʃɪ'enʃəs/ *adjective* diligent and scrupulous. □ **conscientious objector** person who refuses to do military service on grounds of conscience. □ **conscientiously** *adverb*; **conscientiousness** *noun*.

conscious /'kɒnʃəs/ *adjective* awake and aware of one's surroundings etc.; (usually + *of*, *that*) aware, knowing; intentional. □ **consciously** *adverb*; **consciousness** *noun*.

conscript ● *verb* /kən'skrɪpt/ summon for compulsory state (esp. military) service. ● *noun* /'kɒnskrɪpt/ conscripted person. □ **conscription** *noun*.

Conjunction

A conjunction is used to join parts of sentences which usually, but not always, contain their own verbs, e.g.

He found it difficult but *I helped him.*
They made lunch for Alice and *Mary.*
I waited until *you came.*

The most common conjunctions are:

after	*for*	*since*	*unless*
although	*if*	*so*	*until*
and	*in order that*	*so that*	*when*
as	*like*	*than*	*where*
because	*now*	*that*	*whether*
before	*once*	*though*	*while*
but	*or*	*till*	

consecrate /'kɒnsɪkreɪt/ *verb* (**-ting**) make or declare sacred; dedicate formally to religious purpose; (+ *to*) devote to (a purpose). ▫ **consecration** *noun*.

consecutive /kən'sekjʊtɪv/ *adjective* following continuously; in unbroken or logical order. ▫ **consecutively** *adverb*.

consensus /kən'sensəs/ *noun* (often + *of*) general agreement or opinion.

consent /kən'sent/ ● *verb* (often + *to*) express willingness, give permission; agree. ● *noun* agreement; permission.

consequence /'kɒnsɪkwəns/ *noun* result of what has gone before; importance.

consequent /'kɒnsɪkwənt/ *adjective* that results; (often + *on*, *upon*) following as consequence. ▫ **consequently** *adverb*.

consequential /kɒnsɪ'kwenʃ(ə)l/ *adjective* resulting, esp. indirectly; important.

conservancy /kən'sɜːvənsɪ/ *noun* (*plural* **-ies**) body controlling river, port, etc. or concerned with conservation; official environmental conservation.

conservation /kɒnsə'veɪʃ(ə)n/ *noun* preservation, esp. of natural environment. ▫ **conservationist** *noun*.

conservative /kən'sɜːvətɪv/ ● *adjective* averse to rapid change; (of estimate) purposely low; (usually **Conservative**) of Conservative Party. ● *noun* conservative person; (usually **Conservative**) member or supporter of Conservative Party. ▫ **Conservative Party** political party promoting free enterprise. ▫ **conservatism** *noun*.

conservatoire /kən'sɜːvətwɑː/ *noun* (usually European) school of music or other arts.

conservatory /kən'sɜːvətərɪ/ *noun* (*plural* **-ies**) greenhouse for tender plants; esp. *US* conservatoire.

conserve ● *verb* /kən'sɜːv/ (**-ving**) preserve, keep from harm or damage. ● *noun* /'kɒnsɜːv/ fruit etc. preserved in sugar; fruit jam, esp. fresh.

consider /kən'sɪdə/ *verb* contemplate; deliberate thoughtfully; make allowance for, take into account; (+ *that*) have the opinion that; show consideration for; regard as; (as **considered** *adjective*) (esp. of an opinion) formed after careful thought.

considerable *adjective* a lot of; notable, important. ▫ **considerably** *adverb*.

considerate /kən'sɪdərət/ *adjective* giving thought to feelings or rights of others. ▫ **considerately** *adverb*.

consideration /kənsɪdə'reɪʃ(ə)n/ *noun* careful thought; being considerate; fact or thing taken into account; compensation, payment. ▫ **take into consideration** make allowance for.

considering *preposition* in view of.

consign /kən'saɪn/ *verb* (often + *to*) commit, deliver; send (goods etc.). ▫ **consignee** /kənsaɪ'niː/ *noun*; **consignor** *noun*.

consignment *noun* consigning, goods consigned.

consist /kən'sɪst/ *verb* (+ *of*) be composed of; (+ *in*, *of*) have its essential features in.

consistency *noun* (*plural* **-ies**) degree of density or firmness, esp. of thick liquids; being consistent.

consistent *adjective* constant to same principles; (usually + *with*) compatible. ▫ **consistently** *adverb*.

consistory *noun* (*plural* **-ies**) *RC Church* council of cardinals.

consolation /kɒnsə'leɪʃ(ə)n/ *noun* alleviation of grief or disappointment; consoling person or thing. ▫ **consolation prize** one given to competitor just failing to win main prize. ▫ **consolatory** /kən'sɒl-/ *adjective*.

console[1] /kən'səʊl/ *verb* (**-ling**) bring consolation to.

■ **Usage** *Console* is often confused with *condole*. To condole with someone is to express sympathy with them.

console[2] /'kɒnsəʊl/ *noun* panel for switches, controls, etc.; cabinet for television etc.; cabinet with keys and stops of organ; bracket supporting shelf etc.

consolidate /kən'sɒlɪdeɪt/ *verb* (**-ting**) make or become strong or secure; combine (territories, companies, debts, etc.) into one whole. ▫ **consolidation** *noun*.

consommé /kən'sɒmeɪ/ *noun* clear meat soup.

consonance /'kɒnsənəns/ *noun* agreement, harmony.

consonant ● *noun* speech sound that forms syllable only in combination with vowel; letter(s) representing this. ● *adjective* (+ *with*, *to*) consistent with; in agreement or harmony. ▫ **consonantal** /-'næn-/ *adjective*.

consort[1] ● *noun* /'kɒnsɔːt/ wife or husband, esp. of royalty. ● *verb* /kən'sɔːt/ (usually + *with*, *together*) keep company; harmonize.

consort[2] /'kɒnsɔːt/ *noun Music* group of players or instruments.

consortium /kən'sɔːtɪəm/ *noun* (*plural* **-tia** or **-s**) association, esp. of several business companies.

conspicuous /kən'spɪkjʊəs/ *adjective* clearly visible; attracting attention. ▫ **conspicuously** *adverb*.

conspiracy /kən'spɪrəsɪ/ *noun* (*plural* **-ies**) act of conspiring; plot.

conspirator /kən'spɪrətə/ *noun* person who takes part in conspiracy. ▫ **conspiratorial** /-'tɔː-/ *adjective*.

conspire /kən'spaɪə/ *verb* (**-ring**) combine secretly for unlawful or harmful purpose; (of events) seemingly work together.

constable /'kʌnstəb(ə)l/ *noun* (also **police constable**) police officer of lowest rank; governor of royal castle. ▫ **Chief Constable** head of police force of county etc.

constabulary /kən'stæbjʊlərɪ/ *noun* (*plural* **-ies**) police force.

constancy /'kɒnstənsɪ/ *noun* dependability; faithfulness.

constant ● *adjective* continuous; frequently occurring; having constancy. ● *noun Mathematics & Physics* unvarying quantity. ▫ **constantly** *adverb*.

constellation /kɒnstə'leɪʃ(ə)n/ *noun* group of fixed stars.

consternation /kɒnstə'neɪʃ(ə)n/ *noun* amazement, dismay.

constipate /'kɒnstɪpeɪt/ *verb* (**-ting**) (esp. as **constipated** *adjective*) affect with constipation.

constipation *noun* difficulty in emptying bowels.

constituency /kən'stɪtjʊənsɪ/ *noun* (*plural* **-ies**) body electing representative; area represented.

constituent /kən'stɪtjʊənt/ ● *adjective* making part of whole; appointing, electing. ● *noun* member of constituency; component part.

constitute /'kɒnstɪtjuːt/ *verb* (**-ting**) be essence or components of; amount to; establish.

constitution /kɒnstɪ'tjuːʃ(ə)n/ *noun* composition; set of principles by which state etc. is governed; person's inherent state of health, strength, etc.

constitutional ● *adjective* of or in line with the constitution; inherent. ● *noun* walk taken as exercise. ▫ **constitutionally** *adverb*.

constitutive /'kɒnstɪtjuːtɪv/ *adjective* able to form or appoint; constituent.

constrain /kən'streɪn/ *verb* compel; confine; (as **constrained** *adjective*) forced, embarrassed.

constraint *noun* compulsion; restriction; self-control.

constrict /kən'strɪkt/ *verb* make narrow or tight; compress. □ **constriction** *noun*; **constrictive** *adjective*.

constrictor *noun* snake that kills by compressing; muscle that contracts a part.

construct ● *verb* /kən'strʌkt/ fit together, build; *Geometry* draw. ● *noun* /'kɒnstrʌkt/ thing constructed, esp. by the mind. □ **constructor** /kən'strʌktə/ *noun*.

construction /kən'strʌkʃ(ə)n/ *noun* constructing; thing constructed; syntactical arrangement; interpretation. □ **constructional** *adjective*.

constructive /kən'strʌktɪv/ *adjective* positive, helpful. □ **constructively** *adverb*.

construe /kən'stru:/ *verb* (**-strues**, **-strued**, **struing**) interpret; (often + *with*) combine (words) grammatically; translate literally.

consubstantiation /kɒnsəbstænʃɪ'eɪʃ(ə)n/ *noun* presence of Christ's body and blood together with bread and wine in Eucharist.

consul /'kɒns(ə)l/ *noun* official appointed by state to protect its interests and citizens in foreign city; *historical* either of two annually-elected magistrates in ancient Rome. □ **consular** /-sjʊlə/ *adjective*.

consulate /'kɒnsjʊlət/ *noun* offices or position of consul.

consult /kən'sʌlt/ *verb* seek information or advice from; (often + *with*) refer to; take into consideration.

consultant /kən'sʌlt(ə)nt/ *noun* person who gives professional advice; senior medical specialist. □ **consultancy** *noun*.

consultation /kɒnsəl'teɪʃ(ə)n/ *noun* (meeting for) consulting.

consultative /kən'sʌltətɪv/ *adjective* of or for consultation.

consume /kən'sju:m/ *verb* (**-ming**) eat or drink; use up; destroy. □ **consumable** *adjective*.

consumer *noun* user of product or service. □ **consumer goods** goods for consumers, not for producing other goods.

consumerism *noun* protection or promotion of consumers' interests; *often derogatory* continual increase in consumption. □ **consumerist** *adjective*.

consummate ● *verb* /'kɒnsəmeɪt/ (**-ting**) complete (esp. marriage by sexual intercourse). ● *adjective* /kən'sʌmɪt/ complete, perfect; fully skilled. □ **consummation** /kɒnsə-/ *noun*.

consumption /kən'sʌmpʃ(ə)n/ *noun* consuming, being consumed; purchase and use of goods etc.; *archaic* tuberculosis of lungs.

consumptive /kən'sʌmptɪv/ *archaic* ● *adjective* suffering or tending to suffer from tuberculosis. ● *noun* consumptive person.

cont. *abbreviation* continued.

contact /'kɒntækt/ ● *noun* condition or state of touching, meeting, or communicating; person who is, or may be, contacted for information etc.; person likely to carry contagious disease through being near infected person; connection for passage of electric current. ● *verb* get in touch with. □ **contact lens** small lens placed on eyeball to correct vision.

contagion /kən'teɪdʒ(ə)n/ *noun* spreading of disease by contact; moral corruption. □ **contagious** *adjective*.

contain /kən'teɪn/ *verb* hold or be capable of holding within itself; include; comprise; prevent from moving or extending; control, restrain.

container *noun* box etc. for holding things; large metal box for transporting goods.

containment /kən'teɪnmənt/ *noun* action or policy of preventing expansion of hostile country or influence.

contaminate /kən'tæmɪneɪt/ *verb* (**-ting**) pollute; infect. □ **contaminant** *noun*; **contamination** *noun*.

contemplate /'kɒntəmpleɪt/ *verb* (**-ting**) survey with eyes or mind; regard as possible; intend. □ **contemplation** *noun*.

contemplative /kən'templətɪv/ *adjective* of or given to (esp. religious) contemplation.

contemporaneous /kəntempə'reɪnɪəs/ *adjective* (usually + *with*) existing or occurring at same time.

contemporary /kən'tempərərɪ/ ● *adjective* belonging to same time; of same age; modern in style or design. ● *noun* (*plural* **-ies**) contemporary person or thing.

contempt /kən'tempt/ *noun* feeling that person or thing deserves scorn or reproach; condition of being held in contempt; (in full **contempt of court**) disobedience to or disrespect for court of law. □ **contemptible** *adjective*.

contemptuous *adjective* feeling or showing contempt. □ **contemptuously** *adverb*.

contend /kən'tend/ *verb* compete; (usually + *with*) argue; (+ *that*) maintain that. □ **contender** *noun*.

content[1] /kən'tent/ ● *adjective* satisfied; (+ *to do*) willing. ● *verb* make content; satisfy. ● *noun* contented state; satisfaction. □ **contented** *adjective*; **contentment** *noun*.

content[2] /'kɒntent/ *noun* (usually in *plural*) what is contained, esp. in vessel, house, or book; amount contained; substance of book etc. as opposed to form; capacity, volume.

contention /kən'tenʃ(ə)n/ *noun* dispute, rivalry; point contended for in argument.

contentious /kən'tenʃəs/ *adjective* quarrelsome; likely to cause argument.

contest ● *noun* /'kɒntest/ contending; a competition. ● *verb* /kən'test/ dispute; contend or compete for; compete in.

contestant /kən'test(ə)nt/ *noun* person taking part in contest.

context /'kɒntekst/ *noun* what precedes and follows word or passage; relevant circumstances. □ **contextual** /kən'tekstjʊəl/ *adjective*.

contiguous /kən'tɪgjʊəs/ *adjective* (usually + *with*, *to*) touching; in contact.

continent[1] /'kɒntɪnənt/ *noun* any of the earth's main continuous bodies of land; (**the Continent**) the mainland of Europe.

continent[2] /'kɒntɪnənt/ *adjective* able to control bowels and bladder; exercising esp. sexual self-restraint. □ **continence** *noun*.

continental /kɒntɪ'nent(ə)l/ *adjective* of or characteristic of a continent or (**Continental**) the Continent. □ **continental breakfast** light breakfast of coffee, rolls, etc.; **continental quilt** duvet; **continental shelf** shallow seabed bordering continent.

contingency /kən'tɪndʒənsɪ/ *noun* (*plural* **-ies**) event that may or may not occur; something dependent on another uncertain event.

contingent ● *adjective* (usually + *on*, *upon*) conditional, dependent; that may or may not occur; fortuitous. ● *noun* group (of troops, ships, etc.) forming part of larger group; people sharing interest, origin, etc.

continual /kən'tɪnjʊəl/ *adjective* frequently recurring; always happening. □ **continually** *adverb*.

continuance /kən'tɪnjʊəns/ *noun* continuing in existence or operation; duration.

continuation /kəntɪnjʊ'eɪʃ(ə)n/ *noun* continuing, being continued; thing that continues something else.

continue /kən'tɪnju:/ *verb* (**-ues**, **-ued**, **-uing**) maintain; resume; prolong; remain.

continuity /kɒntɪ'nju:ɪtɪ/ *noun* (*plural* **-ies**) being continuous; logical sequence; detailed scenario of film; linkage of broadcast items.

continuo /kən'tɪnjʊəʊ/ *noun* (*plural* **-s**) *Music* bass accompaniment played usually on keyboard instrument.

continuous /kən'tɪnjʊəs/ *adjective* connected without break; uninterrupted. ▫ **continuously** *adverb*.

continuum /kən'tɪnjʊəm/ *noun* (*plural* **-nua**) thing with continuous structure.

contort /kən'tɔːt/ *verb* twist or force out of normal shape. ▫ **contortion** *noun*.

contortionist *noun* entertainer who adopts contorted postures.

contour /'kɒntʊə/ *noun* outline; (in full **contour line**) line on map joining points at same altitude.

contraband /'kɒntrəbænd/ ● *noun* smuggled goods. ● *adjective* forbidden to be imported or exported.

contraception /kɒntrə'sepʃ(ə)n/ *noun* use of contraceptives.

contraceptive /kɒntrə'septɪv/ ● *adjective* preventing pregnancy. ● *noun* contraceptive device or drug.

contract ● *noun* /'kɒntrækt/ written or spoken agreement, esp. one enforceable by law; document recording it. ● *verb* /kən'trækt/ make or become smaller; (usually + *with*) make contract; (often + *out*) arrange (work) to be done by contract; become affected by (a disease); incur (debt); draw together; shorten. ▫ **contract bridge** type of bridge in which only tricks bid and won count towards game; **contract in** (or **out**) elect (not) to enter scheme etc.

contraction /kən'trækʃ(ə)n/ *noun* contracting; shortening of uterine muscles during childbirth; shrinking; diminution; shortened word.

contractor /kən'træktə/ *noun* person who undertakes contract, esp. in building, engineering, etc.

contractual /kən'træktjʊəl/ *adjective* of or in the nature of a contract.

contradict /kɒntrə'dɪkt/ *verb* deny; oppose verbally; be at variance with. ▫ **contradiction** *noun*; **contradictory** *adjective*.

contradistinction /kɒntrədɪs'tɪŋkʃ(ə)n/ *noun* distinction made by contrasting.

contraflow /'kɒntrəfləʊ/ *noun* transfer of traffic from usual half of road to lane(s) of other half.

contralto /kən'træltəʊ/ *noun* (*plural* **-s**) lowest female singing voice; singer with this voice.

contraption /kən'træpʃ(ə)n/ *noun* machine or device, esp. strange one.

contrapuntal /kɒntrə'pʌnt(ə)l/ *adjective Music* of or in counterpoint.

contrariwise /kən'treərɪwaɪz/ *adverb* on the other hand; in the opposite way.

contrary /'kɒntrərɪ/ ● *adjective* (usually + *to*) opposed in nature, tendency, or direction; /kən'treərɪ/ perverse, self-willed. ● *noun* (**the contrary**) the opposite. ● *adverb* (+ *to*) in opposition. ▫ **on the contrary** the opposite is true.

contrast ● *noun* /'kɒntrɑːst/ comparison showing differences; difference so revealed; (often + *to*) thing or person having different qualities; degree of difference between tones in photograph or television picture. ● *verb* /kən'trɑːst/ (often + *with*) compare to reveal contrast; show contrast.

contravene /kɒntrə'viːn/ *verb* (**-ning**) infringe; conflict with. ▫ **contravention** /-'ven-/ *noun*.

contretemps /'kɒntrətɑ̃/ *noun* (*plural* same /-tɑ̃z/) unlucky accident; unfortunate occurrence.

contribute /kən'trɪbjuːt/ *verb* (**-ting**) (often + *to*) give jointly with others to common purpose; supply (article etc.) for publication with others; (+ *to*) help to bring about. ▫ **contribution** /kɒntrɪ'bjuːʃ(ə)n/ *noun*; **contributor** *noun*; **contributory** *adjective*.

■ **Usage** *Contribute* is often pronounced /'kɒntrɪbjuːt/ (with the stress on the *con-*), but this is considered incorrect by some people.

contrite /kən'traɪt/ *adjective* penitent, feeling guilt. ▫ **contrition** /-'trɪʃ-/ *noun*.

contrivance *noun* something contrived, esp. device or plan; act of contriving.

contrive /kən'traɪv/ *verb* (**-ving**) devise, plan; (often + *to do*) manage.

contrived *adjective* artificial, forced.

control /kən'trəʊl/ ● *noun* power of directing or restraining; self-restraint; means of restraining or regulating; (usually in *plural*) device to operate machine, vehicle, etc.; place where something is controlled or verified; standard of comparison for checking results of experiment. ● *verb* (**-ll-**) have control of; regulate; hold in check; verify. ▫ **in control** (often + *of*) in charge; **out of control** no longer manageable.

controller *noun* person or thing that controls; person controlling expenditure.

controversial /kɒntrə'vɜːʃ(ə)l/ *adjective* causing or subject to controversy.

controversy /'kɒntrəvɜːsɪ/ *noun* (*plural* **-ies**) dispute, argument.

■ **Usage** *Controversy* is often pronounced /kən'trɒvəsɪ/ (with the stress on the *-trov-*), but this is considered incorrect by some people.

controvert /kɒntrə'vɜːt/ *verb* dispute, deny.

contuse /kən'tjuːz/ *verb* (**-sing**) bruise. ▫ **contusion** *noun*.

conundrum /kə'nʌndrəm/ *noun* riddle; hard question.

conurbation /kɒnɜː'beɪʃ(ə)n/ *noun* group of towns united by expansion.

convalesce /kɒnvə'les/ *verb* (**-cing**) recover health after illness.

convalescent /kɒnvə'les(ə)nt/ ● *adjective* recovering from illness. ● *noun* convalescent person. ▫ **convalescence** *noun*.

convection /kən'vekʃ(ə)n/ *noun* heat transfer by upward movement of heated medium.

convector /kən'vektə/ *noun* heating appliance that circulates warm air by convection.

convene /kən'viːn/ *verb* (**-ning**) summon; assemble. ▫ **convener**, **convenor** *noun*.

convenience /kən'viːnɪəns/ *noun* state of being convenient; suitability; advantage; useful thing; public lavatory. ▫ **convenience food** food needing little preparation.

convenient *adjective* serving one's comfort or interests; suitable; available or occurring at suitable time or place; well situated. ▫ **conveniently** *adverb*.

convent /'kɒnv(ə)nt/ *noun* religious community, esp. of nuns; its house.

convention /kən'venʃ(ə)n/ *noun* general agreement on social behaviour etc. by implicit consent of majority; customary practice; assembly, conference; agreement, treaty.

conventional *adjective* depending on or according with convention; bound by social conventions; not spontaneous or sincere; (of weapons etc.) non-nuclear. ▫ **conventionally** *adverb*.

converge /kən'vɜːdʒ/ *verb* (**-ging**) come together or towards same point; (+ *on*, *upon*) approach from different directions. ▫ **convergence** *noun*; **convergent** *adjective*.

conversant /kən'vɜːs(ə)nt/ *adjective* (+ *with*) well acquainted with.

conversation /kɒnvə'seɪʃ(ə)n/ *noun* informal spoken communication; instance of this.

conversational *adjective* of or in conversation; colloquial. □ **conversationally** *adverb.*

conversationalist *noun* person fond of or good at conversation.

converse[1] /kən'vɜ:s/ *verb* (**-sing**) (often + *with*) talk.

converse[2] /'kɒnvɜ:s/ ● *adjective* opposite, contrary, reversed. ● *noun* converse statement or proposition. □ **conversely** *adverb.*

conversion /kən'vɜ:ʃ(ə)n/ *noun* converting, being converted; converted (part of) building.

convert ● *verb* /kən'vɜ:t/ (usually + *into*) change; cause (person) to change belief etc.; change (money etc.) into different form or currency etc.; alter (building) for new purpose; *Rugby* kick goal after (try). ● *noun* /'kɒnvɜ:t/ person converted, esp. to religious faith.

convertible /kən'vɜ:tɪb(ə)l/ ● *adjective* able to be converted. ● *noun* car with folding or detachable roof.

convex /'kɒnveks/ *adjective* curved like outside of sphere or circle.

convey /kən'veɪ/ *verb* transport, carry; communicate (meaning etc.); transfer by legal process; transmit (sound etc.).

conveyance *noun* conveying, being conveyed; vehicle; legal transfer of property, document effecting this.

conveyancing *noun* branch of law dealing with transfer of property. □ **conveyancer** *noun.*

conveyor *noun* person or thing that conveys. □ **conveyor belt** endless moving belt conveying articles in factory etc.

convict ● *verb* /kən'vɪkt/ (often + *of*) prove or declare guilty. ● *noun* /'kɒnvɪkt/ *esp. historical* sentenced criminal.

conviction /kən'vɪkʃ(ə)n/ *noun* convicting, being convicted; being convinced; firm belief.

convince /kən'vɪns/ *verb* (**-cing**) firmly persuade. □ **convincing** *adjective*; **convincingly** *adverb.*

convivial /kən'vɪvɪəl/ *adjective* fond of company; sociable, lively. □ **conviviality** /-'æl-/ *noun.*

convocation /kɒnvə'keɪʃ(ə)n/ *noun* convoking; large formal gathering.

convoke /kən'vəʊk/ *verb* (**-king**) call together; summon to assemble.

convoluted /kɒnvə'lu:tɪd/ *adjective* coiled, twisted; complex.

convolution /kɒnvə'lu:ʃ(ə)n/ *noun* coiling; coil, twist; complexity.

convolvulus /kən'vɒlvjʊləs/ *noun* (*plural* **-es**) twining plant, esp. bindweed.

convoy /'kɒnvɔɪ/ *noun* group of ships, vehicles, etc. travelling together. □ **in convoy** as a group.

convulse /kən'vʌls/ *verb* (**-sing**) affect with convulsions.

convulsion *noun* (usually in *plural*) violent irregular motion of limbs or body caused by involuntary contraction of muscles; violent disturbance; (in *plural*) uncontrollable laughter. □ **convulsive** *adjective*; **convulsively** *adverb.*

cony /'kəʊnɪ/ *noun* (*plural* **-ies**) (also **coney**) rabbit; its fur.

coo ● *noun* soft murmuring sound as of doves. ● *verb* (**coos**, **cooed**) emit coo.

cooee /'ku:i:/ *interjection used to attract attention.*

cook /kʊk/ ● *verb* prepare (food) by heating; undergo cooking; *colloquial* falsify (accounts etc.). ● *noun* person who cooks. □ **cookbook** *US* cookery book; **cooking apple** one suitable for eating cooked.

cooker *noun* appliance or vessel for cooking food; fruit (esp. apple) suitable for cooking.

cookery *noun* art of cooking. □ **cookery book** book containing recipes.

cookie /'kʊkɪ/ *noun US* sweet biscuit.

cool /ku:l/ ● *adjective* of or at fairly low temperature; suggesting or achieving coolness; calm; lacking enthusiasm; unfriendly; *slang esp. US* marvellous. ● *noun* coolness; cool place; *slang* composure. ● *verb* (often + *down*, *off*) make or become cool. □ **coolly** /'ku:llɪ/ *adverb*; **coolness** *noun.*

coolant *noun* cooling agent, esp. fluid.

cooler *noun* vessel in which thing is cooled; *slang* prison cell.

coomb /ku:m/ *noun* (also **combe**) valley on side of hill; short valley running up from coast.

coon /ku:n/ *noun US* racoon.

coop /ku:p/ ● *noun* cage for keeping poultry. ● *verb* (often + *up*, *in*) confine.

co-op /'kəʊɒp/ *noun colloquial* cooperative society or shop.

cooper *noun* maker or repairer of casks and barrels.

cooperate /kəʊ'ɒpəreɪt/ *verb* (also **co-operate**) (**-ting**) (often + *with*) work or act together. □ **cooperation** *noun.*

cooperative /kəʊ'ɒpərətɪv/ (also **co-operative**) ● *adjective* willing to cooperate; (of business etc.) jointly owned and run by members, with profits shared. ● *noun* cooperative society or enterprise.

co-opt /kəʊ'ɒpt/ *verb* appoint to committee etc. by invitation of existing members. □ **co-option** *noun*; **co-optive** *adjective.*

coordinate (also **co-ordinate**) ● *verb* /kəʊ'ɔ:dɪneɪt/ (**-ting**) cause to work together efficiently; work or act together effectively. ● *adjective* /-nət/ equal in status. ● *noun* /-nət/ *Mathematics* each of set of quantities used to fix position of point, line, or plane; (in *plural*) matching items of clothing. □ **coordination** *noun*; **coordinator** *noun.*

coot /ku:t/ *noun* black waterfowl with white horny plate on head; *colloquial* stupid person.

cop *slang* ● *noun* police officer; capture. ● *verb* (**-pp-**) catch. □ **cop-out** cowardly evasion; **not much cop** of little value or use.

copal /'kəʊp(ə)l/ *noun* kind of resin used for varnish.

copartner /kəʊ'pɑ:tnə/ *noun* partner, associate. □ **copartnership** *noun.*

cope[1] *verb* (**-ping**) deal effectively or contend; (often + *with*) manage.

cope[2] *noun* priest's long cloaklike vestment.

copeck /'kəʊpek/ *noun* (also **kopek**, **kopeck**) hundredth of rouble.

copier /'kɒpɪə/ *noun* machine that copies (esp. documents).

copilot /'kəʊpaɪlət/ *noun* second pilot in aircraft.

coping /'kəʊpɪŋ/ *noun* top (usually sloping) course of masonry in wall. □ **coping stone** stone used in coping.

copious /'kəʊpɪəs/ *adjective* abundant; producing much. □ **copiously** *adverb.*

copper[1] /'kɒpə/ ● *noun* red-brown metal; bronze coin; large metal vessel for boiling laundry. ● *adjective* made of or coloured like copper. □ **copperplate** copper plate for engraving or etching, print taken from it, ornate sloping handwriting.

copper[2] /'kɒpə/ *noun slang* police officer.

coppice /'kɒpɪs/ *noun* area of undergrowth and small trees.

copulate /'kɒpjʊleɪt/ *verb* (**-ting**) (often + *with*) (esp. of animals) have sexual intercourse. □ **copulation** *noun.*

copy /'kɒpɪ/ ● *noun* (*plural* **-ies**) thing made to look like another; specimen of book etc.; material to be printed, esp. regarded as good etc. reading matter.

● *verb* (**-ies**, **-ied**) make copy of; imitate. □ **copy-typist** typist working from document or recording; **copywriter** writer of copy, esp. for advertisements.

copyist /ˈkɒpɪɪst/ *noun* person who makes copies.

copyright ● *noun* exclusive right to print, publish, perform, etc., material. ● *adjective* protected by copyright. ● *verb* secure copyright for (material).

coquette /kəˈket/ *noun* woman who flirts. □ **coquettish** *adjective*; **coquetry** /ˈkɒkɪtrɪ/ *noun* (*plural* **-ies**).

coracle /ˈkɒrək(ə)l/ *noun* small boat of wickerwork covered with waterproof material.

coral /ˈkɒr(ə)l/ ● *noun* hard substance built up by marine polyps. ● *adjective* of (red or pink colour of) coral. □ **coral island**, **reef** one formed by growth of coral.

cor anglais /kɔːr ˈɒŋgleɪ/ *noun* (*plural* **cors anglais** /kɔːz/) woodwind instrument like oboe but lower in pitch.

corbel /ˈkɔːb(ə)l/ *noun* stone or timber projection from wall, acting as supporting bracket.

cord ● *noun* thick string; piece of this; similar structure in body; ribbed cloth, esp. corduroy; (in *plural*) corduroy trousers; electric flex. ● *verb* secure with cords.

cordial /ˈkɔːdɪəl/ ● *adjective* heartfelt; friendly. ● *noun* fruit-flavoured drink. □ **cordiality** /-ˈæl-/ *noun*; **cordially** *adverb*.

cordite /ˈkɔːdaɪt/ *noun* smokeless explosive.

cordless *adjective* (of handheld electric device) battery-powered.

cordon /ˈkɔːd(ə)n/ ● *noun* line or circle of police etc.; ornamental cord or braid; fruit tree trained to grow as single stem. ● *verb* (often + *off*) enclose or separate with cordon of police etc.

cordon bleu /kɔːdɒn ˈblɜː/ *adjective* (of cooking) first-class.

corduroy /ˈkɔːdərɔɪ/ *noun* fabric with velvety ribs.

core ● *noun* horny central part of certain fruits, containing seeds; centre or most important part; part of nuclear reactor containing fissile material; inner strand of electric cable; piece of soft iron forming centre of magnet etc. ● *verb* (**-ring**) remove core from.

co-respondent /kəʊrɪˈspɒnd(ə)nt/ *noun* person cited in divorce case as having committed adultery with respondent.

corgi /ˈkɔːgɪ/ *noun* (*plural* **-s**) short-legged breed of dog.

coriander /kɒrɪˈændə/ *noun* aromatic plant; its seed, used as flavouring.

cork ● *noun* thick light bark of S. European oak; bottle-stopper made of cork etc. ● *verb* (often + *up*) stop, confine; restrain (feelings etc.).

corkage *noun* charge made by restaurant etc. for serving customer's own wine etc.

corked *adjective* (of wine) spoilt by defective cork.

corkscrew ● *noun* spiral steel device for extracting corks from bottles. ● *verb* move spirally.

corm *noun* swollen underground stem in certain plants, e.g. crocus.

cormorant /ˈkɔːmərənt/ *noun* diving seabird with black plumage.

corn[1] *noun* cereal before or after harvesting, esp. chief crop of a region; grain or seed of cereal plant; *colloquial* something corny. □ **corn cob** cylindrical centre of maize ear; **corncrake** ground-nesting bird with harsh cry; **corn dolly** plaited straw figure; **cornflakes** breakfast cereal of toasted maize flakes; **cornflour** fine-ground maize flour; **cornflower** blue-flowered plant originally growing in cornfields; **corn on the cob** maize eaten from the corn cob.

corn[2] *noun* small tender hard area of skin, esp. on toe.

cornea /ˈkɔːnɪə/ *noun* transparent circular part of front of eyeball.

corned *adjective* preserved in salt or brine.

cornelian /kɔːˈniːlɪən/ *noun* (also **carnelian** /kɑː-/) dull red variety of chalcedony.

corner /ˈkɔːnə/ ● *noun* place where converging sides, edges, streets, etc. meet; recess formed by meeting of two internal sides of room, box, etc.; difficult or inescapable position; remote or secluded place; action or result of buying whole available stock of a commodity; *Football & Hockey* free kick or hit from corner of pitch. ● *verb* force into difficult or inescapable position; buy whole available stock of (commodity); dominate (market) in this way; go round corner. □ **cornerstone** stone in projecting angle of wall, indispensable part or basis.

cornet /ˈkɔːnɪt/ *noun* brass instrument resembling trumpet; conical wafer for holding ice cream.

cornice /ˈkɔːnɪs/ *noun* ornamental moulding, esp. along top of internal wall.

Cornish /ˈkɔːnɪʃ/ ● *adjective* of Cornwall. ● *noun* Celtic language of Cornwall. □ **Cornish pasty** pastry envelope containing meat and vegetables.

cornucopia /kɔːnjʊˈkəʊpɪə/ *noun* horn overflowing with flowers, fruit, etc., as symbol of plenty.

corny *adjective* (**-ier**, **-iest**) *colloquial* banal; feebly humorous; sentimental.

corolla /kəˈrɒlə/ *noun* whorl of petals forming inner envelope of flower.

corollary /kəˈrɒlərɪ/ *noun* (*plural* **-ies**) proposition that follows from one proved; (often + *of*) natural consequence.

corona /kəˈrəʊnə/ *noun* (*plural* **-nae** /-niː/) halo round sun or moon, esp. that seen in total eclipse of sun.

coronary /ˈkɒrənərɪ/ *noun* (*plural* **-ies**) coronary thrombosis. □ **coronary artery** artery supplying blood to heart; **coronary thrombosis** blockage of coronary artery by blood clot.

coronation /kɒrəˈneɪʃ(ə)n/ *noun* ceremony of crowning sovereign.

coroner /ˈkɒrənə/ *noun* official holding inquest on deaths thought to be violent or accidental.

coronet /ˈkɒrənɪt/ *noun* small crown.

corpora *plural* of CORPUS.

corporal[1] /ˈkɔːpr(ə)l/ *noun* army or air-force NCO next below sergeant.

corporal[2] /ˈkɔːpər(ə)l/ *adjective* of human body. □ **corporal punishment** physical punishment.

corporate /ˈkɔːpərət/ *adjective* of, being, or belonging to a corporation or group.

corporation /kɔːpəˈreɪʃ(ə)n/ *noun* group of people authorized to act as individual, esp. in business; civic authorities.

corporative /ˈkɔːpərətɪv/ *adjective* of corporation; governed by or organized in corporations.

corporeal /kɔːˈpɔːrɪəl/ *adjective* bodily, physical, material.

corps /kɔː/ *noun* (*plural* same /kɔːz/) military unit with particular function; organized group of people.

corpse /kɔːps/ *noun* dead body.

corpulent /ˈkɔːpjʊlənt/ *adjective* fleshy, bulky. □ **corpulence** *noun*.

corpus /ˈkɔːpəs/ *noun* (*plural* **-pora** /-pərə/) body or collection of writings, texts, etc.

corpuscle /ˈkɔːpʌs(ə)l/ *noun* minute body or cell in organism, esp. (in *plural*) red or white cells in blood of vertebrates. □ **corpuscular** /-ˈpʌskjʊlə/ *adjective*.

corral /kəˈrɑːl/ ● *noun US* pen for horses, cattle, etc.; enclosure for capturing wild animals. ● *verb* (**-ll-**) put or keep in corral.

correct /kəˈrekt/ ● *adjective* true, accurate; proper, in accordance with taste, standards, etc. ● *verb* set right; mark errors in; admonish; counteract. □ **correctly** *adverb*; **correctness** *noun*.

correction *noun* correcting, being corrected; thing substituted for what is wrong.

correctitude /kəˈrektɪtjuːd/ *noun* consciously correct behaviour.

corrective ● *adjective* serving to correct or counteract. ● *noun* corrective measure or thing.

correlate /ˈkɒrəleɪt/ ● *verb* **(-ting)** (usually + *with*, *to*) have or bring into mutual relation. ● *noun* either of two related or complementary things. □ **correlation** *noun*.

correlative /kəˈrelətɪv/ ● *adjective* (often + *with*, *to*) having a mutual relation; (of words) corresponding and regularly used together. ● *noun* correlative thing or word.

correspond /kɒrɪˈspɒnd/ *verb* (usually + *to*) be similar or equivalent; (usually + *to*, *with*) agree; (usually + *with*) exchange letters.

correspondence *noun* agreement or similarity; (exchange of) letters. □ **correspondence course** course of study conducted by post.

correspondent *noun* person who writes letter(s); person employed to write or report for newspaper or broadcasting.

corridor /ˈkɒrɪdɔː/ *noun* passage giving access into rooms; passage in train giving access into compartments; strip of territory of one state running through that of another; route for aircraft over foreign country.

corrigendum /kɒrɪˈdʒendəm/ *noun* (*plural* **-da**) error to be corrected.

corrigible /ˈkɒrɪdʒɪb(ə)l/ *adjective* able to be corrected.

corroborate /kəˈrɒbəreɪt/ *verb* **(-ting)** give support to, confirm. □ **corroboration** *noun*; **corroborative** /-rətɪv/ *adjective*; **corroboratory** /-rət(ə)rɪ/ *adjective*.

corrode /kəˈrəʊd/ *verb* **(-ding)** wear away, esp. by chemical action; destroy gradually; decay.

corrosion /kəˈrəʊʒ(ə)n/ *noun* corroding, being corroded; corroded area. □ **corrosive** /-sɪv/ *adjective & noun*.

corrugate /ˈkɒrəgeɪt/ *verb* **(-ting)** (esp. as **corrugated** *adjective*) bend into wavy ridges. □ **corrugation** *noun*.

corrupt /kəˈrʌpt/ ● *adjective* influenced by or using bribery; immoral, wicked. ● *verb* make or become corrupt. □ **corruptible** *adjective*; **corruption** *noun*; **corruptly** *adverb*.

corsage /kɔːˈsɑːʒ/ *noun* small bouquet worn by woman.

corsair /kɔːˈseə/ *noun* pirate ship; pirate.

corset /ˈkɔːsɪt/ *noun* tight-fitting supporting undergarment worn esp. by women. □ **corsetry** *noun*.

cortège /kɔːˈteɪʒ/ *noun* procession, esp. for funeral.

cortex /ˈkɔːteks/ *noun* (*plural* **-tices** /-tɪsiːz/) outer part of organ, esp. brain. □ **cortical** *adjective*.

cortisone /ˈkɔːtɪzəʊn/ *noun* hormone used in treating inflammation and allergy.

corvette /kɔːˈvet/ *noun* small naval escort-vessel.

cos[1] /kɒs/ *noun* crisp long-leaved lettuce.

cos[2] /kɒz/ *abbreviation* cosine.

cosh *colloquial* ● *noun* heavy blunt weapon. ● *verb* hit with cosh.

cosine /ˈkəʊsaɪn/ *noun* ratio of side adjacent to acute angle (in right-angled triangle) to hypotenuse.

cosmetic /kɒzˈmetɪk/ ● *adjective* beautifying, enhancing; superficially improving; (of surgery etc.) restoring or enhancing normal appearance. ● *noun* cosmetic preparation. □ **cosmetically** *adverb*.

cosmic /ˈkɒzmɪk/ *adjective* of the cosmos; of or for space travel. □ **cosmic rays** high-energy radiations from outer space.

cosmogony /kɒzˈmɒgənɪ/ *noun* (*plural* **-ies**) (theory about) origin of universe.

cosmology /kɒzˈmɒlədʒɪ/ *noun* science or theory of universe. □ **cosmological** /-məˈlɒdʒ-/ *adjective*; **cosmologist** *noun*.

cosmonaut /ˈkɒzmənɔːt/ *noun* Russian astronaut.

cosmopolitan /kɒzməˈpɒlɪt(ə)n/ ● *adjective* of or knowing all parts of world; free from national limitations. ● *noun* cosmopolitan person. □ **cosmopolitanism** *noun*.

cosmos /ˈkɒzmɒs/ *noun* universe as a well-ordered whole.

Cossack /ˈkɒsæk/ *noun* member of S. Russian people famous as horsemen.

cosset /ˈkɒsɪt/ *verb* **(-t-)** pamper.

cost ● *verb* (*past & past participle* **cost**) have as price; involve as loss or sacrifice; (*past & past participle* **costed**) fix or estimate cost of. ● *noun* price; loss, sacrifice; (in *plural*) legal expenses. □ **cost-effective** effective in relation to cost; **cost of living** cost of basic necessities of life; **cost price** price paid for thing by person who later sells it.

costal /ˈkɒst(ə)l/ *adjective* of ribs.

costermonger /ˈkɒstəmʌŋgə/ *noun* person who sells fruit etc. from barrow.

costive /ˈkɒstɪv/ *adjective* constipated.

costly *adjective* **(-ier, -iest)** costing much, expensive. □ **costliness** *noun*.

costume /ˈkɒstjuːm/ ● *noun* style of dress, esp. of particular place or period; set of clothes; clothing for particular activity; actor's clothes for part. ● *verb* provide with costume. □ **costume jewellery** artificial jewellery.

costumier /kɒsˈtjuːmɪə/ *noun* person who deals in or makes costumes.

cosy /ˈkəʊzɪ/ (*US* **cozy**) ● *adjective* **(-ier, -iest)** snug, comfortable. ● *noun* (*plural* **-ies**) cover to keep teapot etc. hot. □ **cosily** *adverb*; **cosiness** *noun*.

cot *noun* small high-sided bed for child etc.; small light bed. □ **cot death** unexplained death of sleeping baby.

cote *noun* shelter for birds or animals.

coterie /ˈkəʊtərɪ/ *noun* exclusive group of people sharing interests.

cotoneaster /kətəʊnɪˈæstə/ *noun* shrub bearing red or orange berries.

cottage /ˈkɒtɪdʒ/ *noun* small house, esp. in the country. □ **cottage cheese** soft white lumpy cheese; **cottage industry** small business carried on at home; **cottage pie** shepherd's pie.

cottager *noun* person who lives in cottage.

cotter /ˈkɒtə/ *noun* (also **cotter pin**) wedge or pin for securing machine part such as bicycle pedal crank.

cotton /ˈkɒt(ə)n/ *noun* soft white fibrous substance covering seeds of certain plants; such a plant; thread or cloth from this. □ **cotton on** (often + *to*) *colloquial* begin to understand; **cotton wool** wadding originally made from raw cotton.

cotyledon /kɒtɪˈliːd(ə)n/ *noun* first leaf produced by plant embryo.

couch[1] /kaʊtʃ/ ● *noun* upholstered piece of furniture for several people; sofa. ● *verb* (+ *in*) express in (language of specified kind). □ **couch potato** *US slang* person who likes lazing at home.

couch[2] /kuːtʃ/ *noun* (in full **couch grass**) kind of grass with long creeping roots.

couchette /kuːˈʃet/ *noun* railway carriage with seats convertible into sleeping berths; berth in this.

cougar /ˈkuːgə/ *noun US* puma.

cough /kɒf/ ● *verb* expel air from lungs with sudden sharp sound. ● *noun* (sound of) coughing; condition of respiratory organs causing coughing. □ **cough mixture** medicine to relieve cough; **cough up** eject with coughs, *slang* give (money, information, etc.) reluctantly.

could *past* of CAN[1].

couldn't /ˈkʊd(ə)nt/ could not.

coulomb /ˈku:lɒm/ *noun* SI unit of electrical charge.

coulter /ˈkəʊltə/ *noun* (*US* **colter**) vertical blade in front of ploughshare.

council /ˈkaʊns(ə)l/ *noun* (meeting of) advisory, deliberative, or administrative body; local administrative body of county, city, town, etc. □ **council flat, house** one owned and let by local council; **council tax** local tax based on value of property and number of residents.

councillor *noun* member of (esp. local) council.

counsel /ˈkaʊns(ə)l/ ● *noun* advice, esp. formal; consultation; (*plural* same) legal adviser, esp. barrister; group of these. ● *verb* (**-ll-**; *US* **-l-**) advise, esp. on personal problems. □ **counsellor** (*US* **counselor**) *noun*.

count[1] ● *verb* find number of, esp. by assigning successive numerals; repeat numbers in order; (+ *in*) include or be included in reckoning; consider to be. ● *noun* counting, reckoning; total; *Law* each charge in an indictment. □ **countdown** counting numbers backwards to zero, esp. before launching rocket etc.; **count on** rely on; **count out** exclude, disregard.

count[2] *noun* foreign noble corresponding to earl.

countenance /ˈkaʊntɪnəns/ ● *noun* face or its expression; composure; moral support. ● *verb* (**-cing**) support, approve.

counter[1] *noun* flat-topped fitment in shop etc. across which business is conducted; small disc used for playing or scoring in board games, cards, etc.; device for counting things.

counter[2] ● *verb* oppose, contradict; meet by countermove. ● *adverb* in opposite direction. ● *adjective* opposite. ● *noun* parry, countermove.

counteract /kaʊntəˈrækt/ *verb* neutralize or hinder by contrary action. □ **counteraction** *noun*.

counter-attack *verb & noun* attack in reply to enemy's attack.

counterbalance ● *noun* weight or influence balancing another. ● *verb* (**-cing**) act as counterbalance to.

counter-clockwise *adverb & adjective US* anticlockwise.

counter-espionage *noun* action taken against enemy spying.

counterfeit /ˈkaʊntəfɪt/ ● *adjective* imitation; forged; not genuine. ● *noun* forgery, imitation. ● *verb* imitate fraudulently; forge.

counterfoil *noun* part of cheque, receipt, etc. retained as record.

counter-intelligence *noun* counter-espionage.

countermand /kaʊntəˈmɑ:nd/ *verb* revoke, recall by contrary order.

countermeasure *noun* action taken to counteract danger, threat, etc.

countermove *noun* move or action in opposition to another.

counterpane *noun* bedspread.

counterpart *noun* person or thing equivalent or complementary to another; duplicate.

counterpoint *noun* harmonious combination of melodies in music; melody combined with another; contrasting argument, plot, literary theme, etc.

counterpoise ● *noun* counterbalance; state of equilibrium. ● *verb* (**-sing**) counterbalance.

counter-productive *adjective* having opposite of desired effect.

counter-revolution *noun* revolution opposing former one or reversing its results.

countersign ● *verb* add confirming signature to. ● *noun* password spoken to person on guard.

countersink *verb* (*past & past participle* **-sunk**) shape (screw-hole) so that screw-head lies level with surface; provide (screw) with countersunk hole.

counter-tenor *noun* male alto singing voice; singer with this.

countervailing /ˈkaʊntəveɪlɪŋ/ *adjective* (of influence etc.) counterbalancing.

counterweight *noun* counterbalancing weight.

countess /ˈkaʊntɪs/ *noun* earl's or count's wife or widow; woman with rank of earl or count.

countless *adjective* too many to count.

countrified /ˈkʌntrɪfaɪd/ *adjective* rustic.

country /ˈkʌntrɪ/ *noun* (*plural* **-ies**) nation's territory, state; land of person's birth or citizenship; rural districts, as opposed to towns; region with regard to its aspect, associations, etc.; national population, esp. as voters. □ **country and western** type of folk music originated by southern US whites; **country dance** traditional dance; **countryman, countrywoman** person of one's own country or district; person living in rural area; **countryside** rural areas.

county /ˈkaʊntɪ/ *noun* (*plural* **-ies**) territorial division of country, forming chief unit of local administration; *US* political and administrative division of State; people, esp. gentry, of county. □ **county council** elected governing body of county; **county court** law court for civil cases; **county town** administrative capital of county.

coup /ku:/ *noun* (*plural* **-s** /ku:z/) successful stroke or move; *coup d'état*.

coup de grâce /ku: də ˈgrɑ:s/ *noun* finishing stroke. [French]

coup d'état /ku: deɪˈtɑ:/ *noun* (*plural* ***coups d'état*** same pronunciation) sudden overthrow of government, esp. by force. [French]

coupé /ˈku:peɪ/ *noun* (*US* **coupe** /ku:p/) two-door car with hard roof and sloping back.

couple /ˈkʌp(ə)l/ ● *noun* (about) two; two people who are married or in a sexual relationship; pair of partners in a dance etc. ● *verb* (**-ling**) link, fasten, or associate together; copulate.

couplet /ˈkʌplɪt/ *noun* two successive lines of rhyming verse.

coupling /ˈkʌplɪŋ/ *noun* link connecting railway carriages or parts of machinery.

coupon /ˈku:pɒn/ *noun* ticket or form entitling holder to something.

courage /ˈkʌrɪdʒ/ *noun* ability to disregard fear; bravery. □ **courageous** /kəˈreɪdʒəs/ *adjective*; **courageously** *adverb*.

courgette /kʊəˈʒet/ *noun* small vegetable marrow.

courier /ˈkʊrɪə/ *noun* person employed to guide and assist group of tourists; special messenger.

course /kɔ:s/ ● *noun* onward movement or progression; direction taken; line of conduct; series of lectures, lessons, etc.; each successive part of meal; golf course, race-course, etc.; sequence of medical treatment etc.; continuous line of masonry or bricks at one level of building; channel in which water flows. ● *verb* (**-sing**) use hounds to hunt (esp. hares); move or flow freely. □ **in the course of** during; **of course** naturally, as expected, admittedly.

court /kɔ:t/ ● *noun* number of houses enclosing a yard; courtyard; rectangular area for a game; (in full **court of law**) judicial body hearing legal cases; courtroom; sovereign's establishment and retinue. ● *verb* pay amorous attention to, seek to win favour of; try to win (fame etc.); unwisely invite. □ **court card** playing card that is king, queen, or jack; **court house** building in which judicial court is held, *US* county administrative offices; **court martial** (*plural* **courts martial**) judicial court of military officers; **court-martial** (**-ll-**; *US* **-l-**) try by court martial; **courtroom** room in which court of law sits; **court shoe** woman's light shoe with low-cut upper; **courtyard** space enclosed by walls or buildings.

courteous /ˈkɜːtɪəs/ *adjective* polite, considerate. □ **courteously** *adverb*; **courteousness** *noun*.

courtesan /kɔːtɪˈzæn/ *noun* prostitute, esp. one with wealthy or upper-class clients.

courtesy /ˈkɜːtəsɪ/ *noun* (*plural* **-ies**) courteous behaviour or act. □ **by courtesy of** with formal permission of; **courtesy light** light in car switched on when door is opened.

courtier /ˈkɔːtɪə/ *noun* person who attends sovereign's court.

courtly *adjective* (**-ier**, **-iest**) dignified; refined in manners. □ **courtliness** *noun*.

courtship *noun* courting, wooing.

couscous /ˈkuːskuːs/ *noun* N. African dish of cracked wheat steamed over broth.

cousin /ˈkʌz(ə)n/ *noun* (also **first cousin**) child of one's uncle or aunt.

couture /kuːˈtjʊə/ *noun* design and making of fashionable garments.

couturier /kuːˈtjʊərɪeɪ/ *noun* fashion designer.

cove /kəʊv/ *noun* small bay or inlet; sheltered recess.

coven /ˈkʌv(ə)n/ *noun* assembly of witches.

covenant /ˈkʌvənənt/ ● *noun* agreement; *Law* sealed contract. ● *verb* agree, esp. by legal covenant.

Coventry /ˈkɒvəntrɪ/ *noun* □ **send to Coventry** refuse to associate with or speak to.

cover /ˈkʌvə/ ● *verb* (often + *with*) protect or conceal with cloth, lid, etc.; extend over; protect, clothe; include; (of sum) be large enough to meet (expense); protect by insurance; report on for newspaper, television, etc.; travel (specified distance); aim gun etc. at; protect by aiming gun. ● *noun* thing that covers, esp. lid, wrapper, etc.; shelter, protection; funds to meet liability or contingent loss; place-setting at table. □ **cover charge** service charge per person in restaurant; **cover note** temporary certificate of insurance; **cover up** *verb* cover completely, conceal; **cover-up** *noun* concealing of facts; **take cover** find shelter.

coverage *noun* area or amount covered; reporting of events in newspaper etc.

covering letter *noun* explanatory letter with other documents.

coverlet /ˈkʌvəlɪt/ *noun* bedspread.

covert /ˈkʌvət/ ● *adjective* secret, disguised. ● *noun* shelter, esp. thicket hiding game. □ **covertly** *adverb*.

covet /ˈkʌvɪt/ *verb* (**-t-**) desire greatly (esp. thing belonging to another person). □ **covetous** *adjective*.

covey /ˈkʌvɪ/ *noun* (*plural* **-s**) brood of partridges; family, set.

coving /ˈkəʊvɪŋ/ *noun* curved surface at junction of wall and ceiling.

cow[1] /kaʊ/ *noun* fully-grown female of esp. domestic bovine animal; female of elephant, rhinoceros, whale, seal, etc. □ **cowboy**, **cowgirl** person who tends cattle, esp. in western US, *colloquial* unscrupulous or incompetent business person; **cowherd** person who tends cattle; **cowhide** (leather made from) cow's hide; **cow-pat** round flat piece of cow-dung; **cowpox** disease of cows, source of smallpox vaccine.

cow[2] /kaʊ/ *verb* intimidate.

coward /ˈkaʊəd/ *noun* person easily frightened. □ **cowardly** *adjective*.

cowardice /ˈkaʊədɪs/ *noun* lack of bravery.

cower /ˈkaʊə/ *verb* crouch or shrink back in fear.

cowl /kaʊl/ *noun* (hood of) monk's cloak; (also **cowling**) hood-shaped covering of chimney or shaft. □ **cowl neck** wide loose roll neck on garment.

cowrie /ˈkaʊrɪ/ *noun* tropical mollusc with bright shell; its shell as money in parts of Asia etc.

cowslip /ˈkaʊslɪp/ *noun* yellow-flowered primula growing in pastures etc.

cox ● *noun* coxswain. ● *verb* act as cox (of).

coxcomb /ˈkɒkskəʊm/ *noun* conceited showy person.

coxswain /ˈkɒks(ə)n/ *noun* person who steers esp. rowing boat.

coy *adjective* affectedly shy; irritatingly reticent. □ **coyly** *adverb*.

coyote /kɔɪˈəʊtɪ/ *noun* (*plural* same or **-s**) N. American wild dog.

coypu /ˈkɔɪpuː/ *noun* (*plural* **-s**) amphibious rodent like small beaver, originally from S. America.

cozen /ˈkʌz(ə)n/ *verb literary* cheat, defraud; beguile.

cozy *US* = COSY.

crab ● *noun* shellfish with 10 legs; this as food; (in full **crab-louse**) (often in *plural*) parasite infesting human body. ● *verb* (**-bb-**) *colloquial* criticize, grumble; spoil. □ **catch a crab** (in rowing) get oar jammed under water, miss water; **crab-apple** wild apple tree, its sour fruit.

crabbed /kræbɪd/ *adjective* crabby; (of handwriting) ill-formed, illegible.

crabby *adjective* (**-ier**, **-iest**) morose, irritable. □ **crabbily** *adverb*.

crack ● *noun* sudden sharp noise; sharp blow; narrow opening; break or split; *colloquial* joke, malicious remark; sudden change in vocal pitch; *slang* crystalline cocaine. ● *verb* (cause to) make crack; suffer crack or partial break; (of voice) change pitch sharply; tell (joke); open (bottle of wine etc.); break into (safe); find solution to (problem); give way, yield; hit sharply; (as **cracked** *adjective*) crazy, (of wheat) coarsely broken. □ **crack-brained** crazy; **crackdown** *colloquial* severe measures (esp. against lawbreakers); **crack down on** *colloquial* take severe measures against; **crack of dawn** daybreak; **crackpot** *colloquial* eccentric or impractical person; **crack up** *colloquial* collapse under strain.

cracker *noun* small paper cylinder containing paper hat, joke, etc., exploding with crack when ends are pulled; explosive firework; thin crisp savoury biscuit.

crackers *adjective slang* crazy.

crackle /ˈkræk(ə)l/ ● *verb* (**-ling**) make repeated light cracking sound. ● *noun* such a sound. □ **crackly** *adjective*.

crackling *noun* crisp skin of roast pork.

cracknel /ˈkrækn(ə)l/ *noun* light crisp biscuit.

cradle /ˈkreɪd(ə)l/ ● *noun* baby's bed, esp. on rockers; place regarded as origin of something; supporting framework or structure. ● *verb* (**-ling**) contain or shelter as in cradle.

craft /krɑːft/ *noun* special skill or technique; occupation needing this; (*plural* same) boat, vessel, aircraft, or spacecraft; cunning.

craftsman /ˈkrɑːftsmən/ *noun* (*feminine* **-woman**) person who practises a craft. □ **craftsmanship** *noun*.

crafty *adjective* (**-ier**, **-iest**) cunning, artful. □ **craftily** *adverb*.

crag *noun* steep rugged rock.

craggy *adjective* (**-ier**, **-iest**) rugged; rough-textured.

cram *verb* (**-mm-**) fill to bursting; (often + *in*, *into*) force; study or teach intensively for exam.

crammer *noun* institution that crams pupils for exam.

cramp ● *noun* painful involuntary contraction of muscles. ● *verb* affect with cramp; restrict, confine.

cramped *adjective* (of space) small; (of handwriting) small and with the letters close together.

crampon /'kræmpɒn/ *noun* spiked iron plate fixed to boot for climbing on ice.

cranberry /'krænbərɪ/ *noun* (*plural* **-ies**) (shrub bearing) small red acid berry.

crane ● *noun* machine with projecting arm for moving heavy weights; large long-legged wading bird. ● *verb* (**-ning**) stretch (one's neck) in order to see something. □ **crane-fly** two-winged long-legged fly; **cranesbill** kind of wild geranium.

cranium /'kreɪnɪəm/ *noun* (*plural* **-s** or **-nia**) bones enclosing brain, skull. □ **cranial** *adjective*.

crank ● *noun* part of axle or shaft bent at right angles for converting rotary into reciprocal motion or vice versa; eccentric person. ● *verb* turn with crank. □ **crankpin** pin attaching connecting rod to crank; **crankshaft** shaft driven by crank; **crank up** start (engine) by turning crank.

cranky *adjective* (**-ier**, **-iest**) eccentric; shaky; *esp. US* crotchety.

cranny /'krænɪ/ *noun* (*plural* **-ies**) chink, crevice.

crape *noun* crêpe, usually of black silk, formerly used for mourning.

craps *plural noun* (also **crap game**) *US* gambling game played with dice.

crapulent /'kræpjʊlənt/ *adjective* suffering the effects of drunkenness. □ **crapulence** *noun*; **crapulous** *adjective*.

crash ● *verb* (cause to) make loud smashing noise; (often + *into*) (cause to) collide or fall violently; fail, esp. financially; *colloquial* gatecrash; (of computer, system, etc.) fail suddenly; (often + *out*) *slang* fall asleep, sleep. ● *noun* sudden violent noise; violent fall or impact, esp. of vehicle; ruin, esp. financial; sudden collapse, esp. of computer, system, etc. ● *adjective* done rapidly or urgently. □ **crash barrier** barrier to prevent car leaving road; **crash-dive** *verb* (of submarine) dive hastily and steeply, (of aircraft) dive and crash, *noun* such a dive; **crash-helmet** helmet worn to protect head; **crash-land** land or cause (aircraft etc.) to land with crash; **crash landing** instance of crash-landing.

crass *adjective* grossly stupid; insensitive. □ **crassly** *adverb*; **crassness** *noun*.

crate ● *noun* slatted wooden case; *slang* old aircraft, car, etc. ● *verb* (**-ting**) pack in crate.

crater /'kreɪtə/ *noun* mouth of volcano; bowl-shaped cavity, esp. hollow on surface of moon etc.

cravat /krə'væt/ *noun* man's scarf worn inside open-necked shirt.

crave *verb* (**-ving**) (often + *for*) long or beg for.

craven /'kreɪv(ə)n/ *adjective* cowardly, abject.

craving *noun* strong desire, longing.

craw *noun* crop of bird or insect.

crawfish *noun* (*plural* same) large spiny sea-lobster.

crawl ● *verb* move slowly, esp. on hands and knees or with body close to ground; *colloquial* behave obsequiously; (often + *with*) be filled with moving people or things; (esp. of skin) creep. ● *noun* crawling motion; slow rate of motion; fast swimming stroke.

crayfish /'kreɪfɪʃ/ *noun* (*plural* same) lobster-like freshwater crustacean; crawfish.

crayon /'kreɪən/ ● *noun* stick or pencil of coloured wax, chalk, etc. ● *verb* draw or colour with crayons.

craze ● *verb* (**-zing**) (usually as **crazed** *adjective*) make insane; produce fine surface cracks on, develop such cracks. ● *noun* usually temporary enthusiasm; object of this.

crazy *adjective* (**-ier**, **-iest**) insane, mad; foolish; (usually + *about*) *colloquial* extremely enthusiastic. □ **crazy paving** paving made of irregular pieces. □ **crazily** *adverb*.

creak ● *noun* harsh scraping or squeaking sound. ● *verb* emit creak; move stiffly. □ **creaky** *adjective* (**-ier**, **-iest**).

cream ● *noun* fatty part of milk; its yellowish-white colour; food or drink like or made with cream; cream-like cosmetic etc.; (usually + *the*) best part or pick of something. ● *verb* take cream from; make creamy; form cream or scum. ● *adjective* yellowish-white. □ **cream cheese** soft rich cheese made of cream and unskimmed milk; **cream cracker** crisp unsweetened biscuit; **cream off** remove best part of; **cream of tartar** purified tartar, used in medicine, baking powder, etc.; **cream tea** afternoon tea with scones, jam, and cream. □ **creamy** *adjective* (**-ier**, **-iest**).

creamer *noun* cream substitute for coffee; jug for cream.

creamery *noun* (*plural* **-ies**) factory producing dairy products; dairy.

crease /kri:s/ ● *noun* line made by folding or crushing; *Cricket* line defining position of bowler or batsman. ● *verb* (**-sing**) make creases in, develop creases.

create /kri:'eɪt/ *verb* (**-ting**) bring into existence; originate; invest with rank; *slang* make fuss.

creation /kri:'eɪʃ(ə)n/ *noun* creating, being created; (usually **the Creation**) God's creating of the universe; (usually **Creation**) all created things; product of imaginative work.

creative /kri:'eɪtɪv/ *adjective* inventive, imaginative. □ **creatively** *adverb*; **creativity** /-'tɪv-/ *noun*.

creator /kri:'eɪtə/ *noun* person who creates; (**the Creator**) God.

creature /'kri:tʃə/ *noun* living being, esp. animal; person, esp. one in subservient position; anything created.

crèche /kreʃ/ *noun* day nursery.

credence /'kri:d(ə)ns/ *noun* belief.

credentials /krɪ'denʃ(ə)lz/ *plural noun* documents attesting to person's education, character, etc.

credible /'kredɪb(ə)l/ *adjective* believable; worthy of belief. □ **credibility** *noun*.

■ **Usage** *Credible* is sometimes confused with *credulous*, which means 'gullible'.

---

credit /'kredɪt/ ● *noun* belief, trust; good reputation; person's financial standing; power to obtain goods before payment; acknowledgement of payment by entry in account, sum entered; acknowledgement of merit or (usually in *plural*) of contributor's services to film, book, etc.; grade above pass in exam; educational course counting towards degree. ● *verb* (**-t-**) believe; (usually + *to*, *with*) enter on credit side of account. □ **credit card** card authorizing purchase of goods on credit; **credit (person) with** ascribe to him or her; **credit rating** estimate of person's suitability for commercial credit; **creditworthy** suitable to receive credit; **on credit** with arrangement to pay later; **to one's credit** in one's favour.

creditable *adjective* praiseworthy. □ **creditably** *adverb*.

creditor *noun* person to whom debt is owing.

credo /'kri:dəʊ/ *noun* (*plural* **-s**) creed.

credulous /'kredjʊləs/ *adjective* too ready to believe; gullible. □ **credulity** /krɪ'dju:-/ *noun*.

■ **Usage** *Credulous* is sometimes confused with *credible*, which means 'believable'.

---

creed *noun* set of beliefs; system of beliefs; (often **the Creed**) formal summary of Christian doctrine.

creek *noun* inlet on sea-coast; arm of river; stream.

creel *noun* fisherman's wicker basket.

creep ● *verb* (*past & past participle* **crept**) crawl; move stealthily, timidly, or slowly; (of plant) grow along ground or up wall etc.; advance or develop gradually; (of flesh) shudder with horror etc. ● *noun* act of creeping; (**the creeps**) *colloquial* feeling of revulsion or fear; *slang* unpleasant person; gradual change in shape of metal under stress.

creeper *noun* creeping or climbing plant.

creepy *adjective* (**-ier, -iest**) *colloquial* feeling or causing horror or fear. □ **creepy-crawly** (*plural* **-crawlies**) small crawling insect etc. □ **creepily** *adverb*.

cremate /krɪ'meɪt/ *verb* (**-ting**) burn (corpse) to ashes. □ **cremation** *noun*.

crematorium /kremə'tɔ:rɪəm/ *noun* (*plural* **-ria** or **-s**) place where corpses are cremated.

crenellated /'krenəleɪtɪd/ *adjective* having battlements. □ **crenellation** *noun*.

Creole /'kri:əʊl/ ● *noun* descendant of European settlers in W. Indies or Central or S. America, or of French settlers in southern US; person of mixed European and black descent; language formed from a European and African language. ● *adjective* of Creoles; (usually **creole**) of Creole origin etc.

creosote /'kri:əsəʊt/ ● *noun* oily wood-preservative distilled from coal tar. ● *verb* (**-ting**) treat with creosote.

crêpe /kreɪp/ *noun* fine crinkled fabric; thin pancake with savoury or sweet filling; wrinkled sheet rubber used for shoe-soles etc. □ **crêpe de Chine** /də 'ʃi:n/ fine silk crêpe; **crêpe paper** thin crinkled paper.

crept *past & past participle of* CREEP.

crepuscular /krɪ'pʌskjʊlə/ *adjective* of twilight; (of animal) active etc. at twilight.

crescendo /krɪ'ʃendəʊ/ *Music* ● *noun* (*plural* **-s**) gradual increase in loudness. ● *adjective & adverb* increasing in loudness.

■ **Usage** *Crescendo* is sometimes wrongly used to mean a climax rather than the progress towards it.

crescent /'kres(ə)nt/ ● *noun* sickle shape, as of waxing or waning moon; thing with this shape, esp. curved street. ● *adjective* crescent-shaped.

cress *noun* plant with pungent edible leaves.

crest ● *noun* comb or tuft on animal's head; plume of helmet; top of mountain, wave, etc.; *Heraldry* device above shield or on writing paper etc. ● *verb* reach crest of; crown; serve as crest to; form crest. □ **crestfallen** dejected. □ **crested** *adjective*.

cretaceous /krɪ'teɪʃəs/ *adjective* chalky.

cretin /'kretɪn/ *noun* person with deformity and mental retardation caused by thyroid deficiency; *colloquial* stupid person. □ **cretinism** *noun*; **cretinous** *adjective*.

cretonne /kre'tɒn/ *noun* heavy cotton usually floral upholstery fabric.

crevasse /krə'væs/ *noun* deep open crack in glacier.

crevice /'krevɪs/ *noun* narrow opening or fissure, esp. in rock.

crew[1] /kru:/ ● *noun* group of people working together, esp. manning ship, aircraft, spacecraft, etc.; these, other than the officers. ● *verb* supply or act as crew (member) for; act as crew. □ **crew cut** close-cropped hairstyle; **crew neck** round close-fitting neckline.

crew[2] *archaic past of* CROW.

crewel /'kru:əl/ *noun* thin worsted yarn for embroidery.

crib ● *noun* baby's small bed or cot; model of Nativity with manger; *colloquial* plagiarism; translation; *colloquial* cribbage. ● *verb* (**-bb-**) copy unfairly; confine in small space.

cribbage /'krɪbɪdʒ/ *noun* a card game.

crick ● *noun* sudden painful stiffness, esp. in neck. ● *verb* cause crick in.

cricket[1] /'krɪkɪt/ *noun* team game, played on grass pitch, in which ball is bowled at wicket defended with bat by player of other team. □ **not cricket** *colloquial* unfair behaviour. □ **cricketer** *noun*.

cricket[2] /'krɪkɪt/ *noun* jumping chirping insect.

cried *past & past participle of* CRY.

crier /'kraɪə/ *noun* (also **cryer**) official making public announcements in law court or street.

crikey /'kraɪkɪ/ *interjection slang: expressing astonishment.*

crime *noun* act punishable by law; such acts collectively; evil act; *colloquial* shameful act.

criminal /'krɪmɪn(ə)l/ ● *noun* person guilty of crime. ● *adjective* of, involving, or concerning crime; *colloquial* deplorable. □ **criminality** /-'næl-/ *noun*; **criminally** *adverb*.

criminology /krɪmɪ'nɒlədʒɪ/ *noun* study of crime. □ **criminologist** *noun*.

crimp *verb* press into small folds or waves; corrugate.

Crimplene /'krɪmpli:n/ *noun proprietary term* synthetic crease-resistant fabric.

crimson /'krɪmz(ə)n/ *adjective & noun* rich deep red.

cringe *verb* (**-ging**) cower; (often + *to*) behave obsequiously.

crinkle /'krɪŋk(ə)l/ ● *noun* wrinkle, crease. ● *verb* (**-ling**) form crinkles (in). □ **crinkly** *adjective*.

crinoline /'krɪnəlɪn/ *noun* hooped petticoat.

cripple /'krɪp(ə)l/ ● *noun* lame person. ● *verb* (**-ling**) lame, disable; damage seriously.

crisis /'kraɪsɪs/ *noun* (*plural* **crises** /-si:z/) time of acute danger or difficulty; decisive moment.

crisp ● *adjective* hard but brittle; bracing; brisk, decisive; clear-cut; crackling; curly. ● *noun* (in full **potato crisp**) very thin fried slice of potato. ● *verb* make or become crisp. □ **crispbread** thin crisp biscuit. □ **crisply** *adverb*; **crispness** *noun*.

crispy *adjective* (**-ier, -iest**) crisp.

criss-cross ● *noun* pattern of crossing lines. ● *adjective* crossing; in crossing lines. ● *adverb* crosswise. ● *verb* intersect repeatedly; mark with criss-cross lines.

criterion /kraɪ'tɪərɪən/ *noun* (*plural* **-ria**) principle or standard of judgement.

■ **Usage** It is a mistake to use the plural form *criteria* when only one criterion is meant.

critic /'krɪtɪk/ *noun* person who criticizes; reviewer of literary, artistic, etc. works.

critical *adjective* fault-finding; expressing criticism; providing textual criticism; of the nature of a crisis, decisive; marking transition from one state to another. □ **critically** *adverb*.

criticism /'krɪtɪsɪz(ə)m/ *noun* finding fault, censure; work of critic; critical article, remark, etc.

criticize /'krɪtɪsaɪz/ *verb* (also **-ise**) (**-zing** or **-sing**) find fault with; discuss critically.

critique /krɪ'ti:k/ *noun* critical analysis.

croak ● *noun* deep hoarse sound, esp. of frog. ● *verb* utter or speak with croak; *slang* die. □ **croaky** *adjective* (**-ier**, **-iest**); **croakily** *adverb*.

Croat /'krəʊæt/ (also **Croatian** /krəʊ'eɪʃ(ə)n/) ● *noun* native of Croatia; person of Croatian descent; Slavonic dialect of Croats. ● *adjective* of Croats or their dialect.

crochet /ˈkrəʊʃeɪ/ ● *noun* needlework of hooked yarn producing lacy patterned fabric. ● *verb* (**crocheted** /-ʃeɪd/; **crocheting** /-ʃeɪɪŋ/) make by crochet.

crock[1] *noun colloquial* old or worn-out person or vehicle.

crock[2] *noun* earthenware jar; broken piece of this.

crockery *noun* earthenware or china dishes, plates, etc.

crocodile /ˈkrɒkədaɪl/ *noun* large amphibious reptile; *colloquial* line of school children etc. walking in pairs. □ **crocodile tears** insincere grief.

crocus /ˈkrəʊkəs/ *noun* (*plural* **-es**) small plant with corm and yellow, purple, or white flowers.

croft ● *noun* small piece of arable land; small rented farm in Scotland or N. England. ● *verb* farm croft.

crofter *noun* person who farms croft.

Crohn's disease /krəʊnz/ *noun* inflammatory disease of alimentary tract.

croissant /ˈkrwʌsɑ̃/ *noun* rich crescent-shaped roll.

cromlech /ˈkrɒmlek/ *noun* dolmen; prehistoric stone circle.

crone *noun* withered old woman.

crony /ˈkrəʊnɪ/ *noun* (*plural* **-ies**) friend; companion.

crook /krʊk/ ● *noun* hooked staff of shepherd or bishop; bend, curve; *colloquial* swindler, criminal. ● *verb* bend, curve.

crooked /ˈkrʊkɪd/ *adjective* (**-er**, **-est**) not straight, bent; *colloquial* dishonest. □ **crookedly** *adverb*; **crookedness** *noun*.

croon /kru:n/ ● *verb* hum or sing in low voice. ● *noun* such singing. □ **crooner** *noun*.

crop ● *noun* produce of any cultivated plant or of land; group or amount produced at one time; handle of whip; very short haircut; pouch in bird's gullet where food is prepared for digestion. ● *verb* (**-pp-**) cut off; bite off, eat down; cut (hair) short; raise crop on (land); bear crop. □ **crop circle** circle of crops inexplicably flattened; **crop up** occur unexpectedly.

cropper *noun slang* □ **come a cropper** fall heavily, fail badly.

croquet /ˈkrəʊkeɪ/ ● *noun* lawn game with hoops, wooden balls, and mallets; croqueting. ● *verb* (**croqueted** /-keɪd/; **croqueting** /-keɪɪŋ/) drive away (opponent's ball) by striking one's own ball placed in contact with it.

croquette /krəˈket/ *noun* fried breaded ball of meat, potato, etc.

crosier /ˈkrəʊzɪə/ *noun* (also **crozier**) bishop's ceremonial hooked staff.

cross ● *noun* upright stake with transverse bar, used in antiquity for crucifixion; representation of this as emblem of Christianity; cross-shaped thing or mark, esp. two short intersecting lines (+ or ×); cross-shaped military etc. decoration; intermixture of breeds, hybrid; (+ *between*) mixture of two things; trial, affliction. ● *verb* (often + *over*) go across; place crosswise; draw line(s) across; make sign of cross on or over; meet and pass; thwart; (cause to) interbreed; cross-fertilize (plants). ● *adjective* (often + *with*) peevish, angry; transverse; reaching from side to side; intersecting; reciprocal. □ **at cross purposes** misunderstanding each other; **crossbar** horizontal bar, esp. between uprights; **cross-bench** bench in House of Lords for non-party members; **crossbones** see SKULL AND CROSSBONES; **crossbow** bow fixed across wooden stock with mechanism working string; **cross-breed** (produce) hybrid animal or plant; **cross-check** check by alternative method; **cross-country** across fields etc., not following roads, *noun* such a race; **cross-examine** question (esp. opposing witness in law court); **cross-examination** such questioning; **cross-eyed** having one or both eyes turned inwards; **cross-fertilize** fertilize (animal or plant) from another of same species; **crossfire** firing of guns in two crossing directions; **cross-grained** (of wood) with grain running irregularly, (of person) perverse or intractable; **cross-hatch** shade with crossing parallel lines; **cross-legged** (sitting) with legs folded across each other; **cross off**, **out** cancel, expunge; **crossover** point or process of crossing; **crosspatch** *colloquial* bad-tempered person; **cross-ply** (of tyre) having crosswise layers of cords; **cross-question** cross-examine, quiz; **cross-reference** reference to another passage in same book; **crossroad** (usually in *plural*) intersection of roads; **cross-section** drawing etc. of thing as if cut through, representative sample; **cross stitch** cross-shaped stitch; **crosswise** intersecting, diagonally; **crossword** (**puzzle**) puzzle in which words crossing each other vertically and horizontally have to be filled in from clues; **on the cross** diagonally. □ **crossly** *adverb*; **crossness** *noun*.

crossing *noun* place where things (esp. roads) meet; place for crossing street; journey across water.

crotch *noun* fork, esp. between legs (of person, trousers, etc.).

crotchet /ˈkrɒtʃɪt/ *noun Music* black-headed note with stem, equal to quarter of semibreve and usually one beat.

crotchety *adjective* peevish.

crouch ● *verb* stand, squat, etc. with legs bent close to body. ● *noun* this position.

croup[1] /kru:p/ *noun* laryngitis in children, with sharp cough.

croup[2] /kru:p/ *noun* rump, esp. of horse.

croupier /ˈkru:pɪə/ *noun* person in charge of gaming table.

croûton /ˈkru:tɒn/ *noun* small piece of fried or toasted bread served esp. with soup.

crow /krəʊ/ ● *noun* any of various kinds of large black-plumaged bird; cry of cock or baby. ● *verb* (*past* **crowed** or *archaic* **crew** /kru:/) (of cock) utter loud cry; (of baby) utter happy sounds; exult. □ **crow's-foot** wrinkle at outer corner of eye; **crow's-nest** shelter for look-out man at ship's masthead.

crowbar *noun* iron bar used as lever.

crowd /kraʊd/ ● *noun* large gathering of people; *colloquial* particular set of people. ● *verb* (cause to) collect in crowd; (+ *with*) cram with; (+ *into*, *through*, etc.) force way into, through, etc.; *colloquial* come aggressively close to. □ **crowd out** exclude by crowding.

crown /kraʊn/ ● *noun* monarch's jewelled headdress; (**the Crown**) monarch as head of state, his or her authority; wreath for head as emblem of victory; top part of head, hat, etc.; visible part of tooth, artificial replacement for this; coin worth 5 shillings or 25 pence. ● *verb* put crown on; make king or queen; (often as **crowning** *adjective*) be consummation, reward, or finishing touch to; *slang* hit on head. □ **Crown colony** British colony controlled by the Crown; **Crown Court** court of criminal jurisdiction in England and Wales; **crown jewels** sovereign's regalia; **crown prince** male heir to throne; **crown princess** wife of crown prince, female heir to throne.

crozier = CROSIER.

CRT *abbreviation* cathode ray tube.

cruces *plural* of CRUX.

crucial /ˈkru:ʃ(ə)l/ *adjective* decisive, critical; very important; *slang* excellent. □ **crucially** *adverb*.

crucible /ˈkru:sɪb(ə)l/ *noun* melting pot for metals.

cruciferous /kru:ˈsɪfərəs/ *adjective* with 4 equal petals arranged crosswise.

crucifix /ˈkru:sɪfɪks/ *noun* image of Christ on Cross.

crucifixion /kru:sɪ'fɪkʃ(ə)n/ *noun* crucifying, esp. of Christ.
cruciform /'kru:sɪfɔ:m/ *adjective* cross-shaped.
crucify /'kru:sɪfaɪ/ *verb* (**-ies**, **-ied**) put to death by fastening to cross; persecute, torment.
crude ● *adjective* in natural or raw state; lacking finish, unpolished; rude, blunt; indecent. ● *noun* natural mineral oil. □ **crudely** *adverb*; **crudeness** *noun*; **crudity** *noun*.
crudités /kru:dɪ'teɪ/ *plural noun* hors d'oeuvre of mixed raw vegetables. [French]
cruel /'kru:əl/ *adjective* (**-ll-** or **-l-**) causing pain or suffering, esp. deliberately; harsh, severe. □ **cruelly** *adverb*; **cruelty** *noun* (*plural* **-ies**).
cruet /'kru:ɪt/ *noun* set of small salt, pepper, etc. containers for use at table.
cruise /kru:z/ ● *verb* (**-sing**) sail about, esp. travel by sea for pleasure, calling at ports; travel at relaxed or economical speed; achieve objective with ease. ● *noun* cruising voyage. □ **cruise missile** one able to fly low and guide itself.
cruiser *noun* high-speed warship; cabin cruiser. □ **cruiserweight** light heavyweight.
crumb /krʌm/ ● *noun* small fragment esp. of bread; soft inner part of loaf; (**crumbs** *interjection*) *slang: expressing dismay*. ● *verb* coat with breadcrumbs; crumble (bread). □ **crumby** *adjective*.
crumble /'krʌmb(ə)l/ ● *verb* (**-ling**) break or fall into fragments, disintegrate. ● *noun* dish of cooked fruit with crumbly topping. □ **crumbly** *adjective* (**-ier**, **-iest**).
crumhorn = KRUMMHORN.
crummy /'krʌmɪ/ *adjective* (**-ier**, **-iest**) *slang* squalid, inferior.
crumpet /'krʌmpɪt/ *noun* flat soft yeasty cake eaten toasted.
crumple /'krʌmp(ə)l/ *verb* (**-ling**) (often + *up*) crush or become crushed into creases; give way, collapse.
crunch ● *verb* crush noisily with teeth; make or emit crunch. ● *noun* crunching sound; *colloquial* decisive event. □ **crunchy** *adjective* (**-ier**, **-iest**).
crupper /'krʌpə/ *noun* strap looped under horse's tail to hold harness back.
crusade /kru:'seɪd/ ● *noun historical* medieval Christian military expedition to recover Holy Land from Muslims; vigorous campaign for cause. ● *verb* (**-ding**) take part in crusade. □ **crusader** *noun*.
cruse /kru:z/ *noun archaic* earthenware jar.
crush ● *verb* compress violently so as to break, bruise, etc.; crease, crumple; defeat or subdue completely. ● *noun* act of crushing; crowded mass of people; drink made from juice of crushed fruit; (usually + *on*) *colloquial* infatuation.
crust ● *noun* hard outer part of bread etc.; pastry covering pie; rocky outer part of the earth; deposit, esp. on sides of wine bottle. ● *verb* cover with, form into, or become covered with crust.
crustacean /krʌ'steɪʃ(ə)n/ ● *noun* hard-shelled usually aquatic animals, e.g. crab or lobster. ● *adjective* of crustaceans.
crusty *adjective* (**-ier**, **-iest**) having a crisp crust; irritable, curt.
crutch *noun* support for lame person, usually with cross-piece fitting under armpit; support; crotch.
crux *noun* (*plural* **-es** or **cruces** /'kru:si:z/) decisive point at issue.
cry /kraɪ/ ● *verb* (**cries**, **cried**) (often + *out*) make loud or shrill sound, esp. to express pain, grief, joy, etc.; weep; (often + *out*) utter loudly, exclaim; (+ *for*) appeal for. ● *noun* (*plural* **cries**) loud shout of grief, fear, joy, etc.; loud excited utterance; urgent appeal; fit of weeping; call of animal. □ **cry-baby** person who weeps frequently; **cry down** disparage; **cry off** withdraw from undertaking; **cry out for** need badly; **cry wolf** see WOLF; **a far cry** a long way.
cryer = CRIER.
crying *adjective* (of injustice etc.) flagrant, demanding redress.
cryogenics /kraɪəʊ'dʒenɪks/ *noun* branch of physics dealing with very low temperatures. □ **cryogenic** *adjective*.
crypt /krɪpt/ *noun* vault, esp. below church, usually used as burial place.
cryptic *adjective* obscure in meaning; secret, mysterious. □ **cryptically** *adverb*.
cryptogam /'krɪptəgæm/ *noun* plant with no true flowers or seeds, e.g. fern or fungus. □ **cryptogamic** /-'gæm-/ *adjective*.
cryptogram /'krɪptəgræm/ *noun* text written in cipher.
crystal /'krɪst(ə)l/ ● *noun* (piece of) transparent colourless mineral; (articles of) highly transparent glass; substance solidified in definite geometrical form. ● *adjective* of or as clear as crystal. □ **crystal ball** glass globe supposedly used in foretelling the future.
crystalline /'krɪstəlaɪn/ *adjective* of or as clear as crystal.
crystallize /'krɪstəlaɪz/ *verb* (also **-ise**) (**-zing** or **-sing**) form into crystals; make or become definite; preserve or be preserved in sugar. □ **crystallization** *noun*.
CS gas *noun* tear gas used to control riots.
cu. *abbreviation* cubic.
cub ● *noun* young of fox, bear, lion, etc.; **Cub** (**Scout**) junior Scout; *colloquial* young newspaper reporter. ● *verb* give birth to (cubs).
cubby-hole /'kʌbɪhəʊl/ *noun* very small room; snug space.
cube /kju:b/ ● *noun* solid contained by 6 equal squares; cube-shaped block; product of a number multiplied by its square. ● *verb* (**-bing**) find cube of; cut into small cubes. □ **cube root** number which produces given number when cubed.
cubic /'kju:bɪk/ *adjective* of 3 dimensions; involving cube of a quantity. □ **cubic metre** etc., volume of cube whose edge is one metre etc. □ **cubical** *adjective*.
cubicle /'kju:bɪk(ə)l/ *noun* small screened space, esp. sleeping compartment.
cubism /'kju:bɪz(ə)m/ *noun* art style in which objects are represented geometrically. □ **cubist** *adjective & noun*.
cubit /'kju:bɪt/ *noun* ancient measure of length, approximately length of forearm.
cuboid /'kju:bɔɪd/ ● *adjective* like a cube; cube-shaped. ● *noun* solid with 6 rectangular faces.
cuckold /'kʌkəʊld/ ● *noun* husband of adulteress. ● *verb* make cuckold of.
cuckoo /'kʊku:/ ● *noun* bird with characteristic cry and laying eggs in nests of small birds. ● *adjective slang* crazy. □ **cuckoo clock** clock with figure of cuckoo emerging to make call on the hour; **cuckoo-pint** wild arum; **cuckoo-spit** froth exuded by larvae of certain insects.
cucumber /'kju:kʌmbə/ *noun* long green fleshy fruit used in salads.
cud *noun* half-digested food chewed by ruminant.
cuddle /'kʌd(ə)l/ ● *verb* (**-ling**) hug; lie close and snug; nestle. ● *noun* prolonged hug.
cuddly *adjective* (**-ier**, **-iest**) soft and yielding.
cudgel /'kʌdʒ(ə)l/ ● *noun* thick stick used as weapon. ● *verb* (**-ll-**; *US* **-l-**) beat with cudgel.
cue[1] /kju:/ ● *noun* last words of actor's speech as signal for another to begin; signal, hint. ● *verb* (**cues**,

cued, **cueing** or **cuing**) give cue to. □ **cue in** insert cue for; **on cue** at correct moment.

cue[2] /kju:/ ● *noun* long rod for striking ball in billiards etc. ● *verb* (**cues**, **cued**, **cueing** or **cuing**) strike with cue. □ **cue ball** ball to be struck with cue.

cuff[1] *noun* end part of sleeve; trouser turn-up; (in *plural*) *colloquial* handcuffs. □ **cuff link** either of pair of fasteners for shirt cuffs; **off the cuff** extempore, without preparation.

cuff[2] ● *verb* strike with open hand. ● *noun* such a blow.

cuisine /kwɪ'zi:n/ *noun* style of cooking.

cul-de-sac /'kʌldəsæk/ *noun* (*plural* **culs-de-sac** same pronunciation, or **cul-de-sacs** /-sæks/) road etc. closed at one end.

culinary /'kʌlɪnərɪ/ *adjective* of or for cooking.

cull ● *verb* select, gather; pick (flowers); select and kill (surplus animals). ● *noun* culling; animal(s) culled.

culminate /'kʌlmɪneɪt/ *verb* (**-ting**) (usually + *in*) reach highest or final point. □ **culmination** *noun*.

culottes /kju:'lɒts/ *plural noun* woman's trousers cut like skirt.

culpable /'kʌlpəb(ə)l/ *adjective* deserving blame. □ **culpability** *noun*.

culprit /'kʌlprɪt/ *noun* guilty person.

cult *noun* religious system, sect, etc.; devotion or homage to person or thing.

cultivar /'kʌltɪvɑ:/ *noun* plant variety produced by cultivation.

cultivate /'kʌltɪveɪt/ *verb* (**-ting**) prepare and use (soil) for crops; raise (plant etc.); (often as **cultivated** *adjective*) improve (manners etc.); nurture (friendship etc.). □ **cultivation** *noun*.

cultivator *noun* agricultural implement for breaking up ground etc.

culture /'kʌltʃə/ ● *noun* intellectual and artistic achievement or expression; refined appreciation of arts etc.; customs and civilization of a particular time or people; improvement by mental or physical training; cultivation of plants, rearing of bees etc.; quantity of bacteria grown for study. ● *verb* (**-ring**) grow (bacteria) for study. □ **culture shock** disorientation felt by person subjected to unfamiliar way of life. □ **cultural** *adjective*.

cultured *adjective* having refined tastes etc. □ **cultured pearl** one formed by oyster after insertion of foreign body into its shell.

culvert /'kʌlvət/ *noun* underground channel carrying water under road etc.

cumbersome /'kʌmbəsəm/ *adjective* (also **cumbrous** /'kʌmbrəs/) inconveniently bulky, unwieldy.

cumin /'kʌmɪn/ *noun* (also **cummin**) plant with aromatic seeds; these as flavouring.

cummerbund /'kʌməbʌnd/ *noun* waist sash.

cumulative /'kju:mjʊlətɪv/ *adjective* increasing in force etc. by successive additions. □ **cumulatively** *adverb*.

cumulus /'kju:mjʊləs/ *noun* (*plural* **-li** /-laɪ/) cloud formation of heaped-up rounded masses.

cuneiform /'kju:nɪfɔ:m/ ● *noun* writing made up of wedge shapes. ● *adjective* of or using cuneiform.

cunning /'kʌnɪŋ/ ● *adjective* (**-er**, **-est**) deceitful, crafty; ingenious. ● *noun* ingenuity; craft. □ **cunningly** *adverb*.

cup ● *noun* small bowl-shaped drinking vessel; cupful; cup-shaped thing; flavoured usually chilled wine, cider, etc.; cup-shaped trophy as prize. ● *verb* (**-pp-**) make cup-shaped; hold as in cup. □ **Cup Final** final match in (esp. football) competition; **cup-tie** match in such competition. □ **cupful** *noun*.

■ **Usage** A *cupful* is a measure, and so *three cupfuls* is a quantity of something; *three cups full* means the actual cups and their contents, as in *He brought us three cups full of water.*

cupboard /'kʌbəd/ *noun* recess or piece of furniture with door and usually shelves.

Cupid /'kju:pɪd/ *noun* Roman god of love, pictured as winged boy with bow.

cupidity /kju:'pɪdɪtɪ/ *noun* greed, avarice.

cupola /'kju:pələ/ *noun* small dome; revolving gun-turret on ship or in fort.

cuppa /'kʌpə/ *noun colloquial* cup of (tea).

cur *noun* mangy bad-tempered dog; contemptible person.

curable /'kjʊərəb(ə)l/ *adjective* able to be cured.

curaçao /'kjʊərəsəʊ/ *noun* (*plural* **-s**) orange-flavoured liqueur.

curacy /'kjʊərəsɪ/ *noun* (*plural* **-ies**) curate's office or position.

curare /kjʊə'rɑ:rɪ/ *noun* vegetable poison used on arrows by S. American Indians.

curate /'kjʊərət/ *noun* assistant to parish priest. □ **curate's egg** thing good in parts.

curative /'kjʊərətɪv/ ● *adjective* tending to cure. ● *noun* curative agent.

curator /kjʊə'reɪtə/ *noun* custodian of museum etc.

curb ● *noun* check, restraint; (bit with) chain etc. passing under horse's lower jaw; kerb. ● *verb* restrain; put curb on.

curd *noun* (often in *plural*) coagulated acidic milk product, made into cheese or eaten as food.

curdle /'kɜ:d(ə)l/ *verb* (**-ling**) coagulate. □ **make one's blood curdle** horrify one.

cure /kjʊə/ ● *verb* (often + *of*) restore to health, relieve; eliminate (evil etc.); preserve (meat etc.) by salting etc. ● *noun* restoration to health; thing that cures; course of treatment.

curé /'kjʊəreɪ/ *noun* parish priest in France etc. [French]

curette /kjʊə'ret/ ● *noun* surgeon's scraping-instrument. ● *verb* (**-tting**) scrape with this. □ **curettage** *noun*.

curfew /'kɜ:fju:/ *noun* signal or time after which people must remain indoors.

curie /'kjʊərɪ/ *noun* unit of radioactivity.

curio /'kjʊərɪəʊ/ *noun* (*plural* **-s**) rare or unusual object.

curiosity /kjʊərɪ'ɒsɪtɪ/ *noun* (*plural* **-ies**) desire to know; inquisitiveness; rare or strange thing.

curious /'kjʊərɪəs/ *adjective* eager to learn; inquisitive; strange, surprising. □ **curiously** *adverb*.

curl ● *verb* (often + *up*) bend or coil into spiral; move in curve; (of upper lip) be raised in contempt; play curling. ● *noun* curled lock of hair; anything spiral or curved inwards. □ **curly** *adjective* (**-ier**, **-iest**).

curler *noun* pin, roller, etc. for curling hair.

curlew /'kɜ:lju:/ *noun* long-billed wading bird with musical cry.

curling *noun* game like bowls played on ice with round flat stones.

curmudgeon /kə'mʌdʒ(ə)n/ *noun* bad-tempered or miserly person. □ **curmudgeonly** *adjective*.

currant /'kʌrənt/ *noun* small seedless dried grape; (fruit of) any of various shrubs producing red, black, or white berries.

currency /'kʌrənsɪ/ *noun* (*plural* **-ies**) money in use in a country; being current; prevalence (of ideas etc.).

current ● *adjective* belonging to present time; happening now; in general circulation or use. ● *noun* body of moving water, air, etc., passing through still water etc.; movement of electrically charged particles; general tendency or course. □ **current account** bank account that may be drawn on by cheque without notice. □ **currently** *adverb*.

curriculum /kəˈrɪkjʊləm/ *noun* (*plural* **-la**) course of study. □ **curriculum vitae** /ˈviːtaɪ/ brief account of one's education, career, etc.

curry[1] /ˈkʌrɪ/ ● *noun* (*plural* **-ies**) meat, vegetables, etc. cooked in spicy sauce, usually served with rice. ● *verb* (**-ies**, **-ied**) make into or flavour like curry. □ **curry powder** mixture of spices for making curry.

curry[2] /ˈkʌrɪ/ *verb* (**-ies**, **-ied**) groom (horse etc.) with curry-comb; dress (leather). □ **curry-comb** metal device for grooming horses etc.; **curry favour** ingratiate oneself.

curse /kɜːs/ ● *noun* invocation of destruction or punishment; violent or profane exclamation; thing causing evil. ● *verb* (**-sing**) utter curse against; (usually in *passive*; + *with*) afflict with; swear. □ **cursed** /ˈkɜːsɪd/ *adjective*.

cursive /ˈkɜːsɪv/ ● *adjective* (of writing) having joined characters. ● *noun* cursive writing.

cursor /ˈkɜːsə/ *noun* indicator on VDU screen showing particular position in displayed matter.

cursory /ˈkɜːsərɪ/ *adjective* hasty, hurried. □ **cursorily** *adverb*.

curt *adjective* noticeably or rudely brief. □ **curtly** *adverb*; **curtness** *noun*.

curtail /kɜːˈteɪl/ *verb* cut short, reduce. □ **curtailment** *noun*.

curtain /ˈkɜːt(ə)n/ ● *noun* piece of cloth etc. hung up as screen, esp. at window; rise or fall of stage curtain; curtain-call; (in *plural*) *slang* the end. ● *verb* provide or (+ *off*) shut off with curtains. □ **curtain-call** audience's applause summoning actors to take bow; **curtain-raiser** short opening play etc., preliminary event.

curtsy /ˈkɜːtsɪ/ (also **curtsey**) ● *noun* (*plural* **-ies** or **-eys**) woman's or girl's acknowledgement or greeting made by bending knees. ● *verb* (**-ies**, **-ied** or **-eys**, **-eyed**) make curtsy.

curvaceous /kɜːˈveɪʃəs/ *adjective colloquial* (esp. of woman) shapely.

curvature /ˈkɜːvətʃə/ *noun* curving; curved form; deviation of curve from plane.

curve ● *noun* line or surface of which no part is straight; curved line on graph. ● *verb* (**-ving**) bend or shape so as to form curve. □ **curvy** *adjective* (**-ier**, **-iest**).

curvet /kɜːˈvet/ ● *noun* horse's frisky leap. ● *verb* (**-tt-** or **-t-**) perform curvet.

curvilinear /kɜːvɪˈlɪnɪə/ *adjective* contained by or consisting of curved lines.

cushion /ˈkʊʃ(ə)n/ ● *noun* bag stuffed with soft material for sitting on etc.; protection against shock; padded rim of billiard table; air supporting hovercraft. ● *verb* provide or protect with cushions; mitigate effects of.

cushy /ˈkʊʃɪ/ *adjective* (**-ier**, **-iest**) *colloquial* (of job etc.) easy, pleasant.

cusp *noun* point at which two curves meet, e.g. horn of crescent moon.

cuss *colloquial* ● *noun* curse; awkward person. ● *verb* curse.

cussed /ˈkʌsɪd/ *adjective colloquial* awkward, stubborn.

custard /ˈkʌstəd/ *noun* pudding or sweet sauce of eggs or flavoured cornflour and milk.

custodian /kʌsˈtəʊdɪən/ *noun* guardian, keeper.

custody /ˈkʌstədɪ/ *noun* guardianship; imprisonment. □ **custodial** /-ˈstəʊ-/ *adjective*.

custom /ˈkʌstəm/ *noun* usual behaviour; established usage; business dealings, customers; (in *plural*; also treated as *singular*) duty on imports, government department or (part of) building at port etc. dealing with this. □ **custom house** customs office at frontier etc.; **custom-built**, **-made** made to customer's order.

customary /ˈkʌstəmərɪ/ *adjective* in accordance with custom; usual. □ **customarily** *adverb*.

customer *noun* person who buys goods or services; *colloquial* person of specified (esp. awkward) kind.

customize *verb* (also **-ise**) (**-zing** or **-sing**) make or modify to order; personalize.

cut ● *verb* (**-tt-**; *past & past participle* **cut**) divide, wound, or penetrate with edged instrument; detach, trim, etc. by cutting; (+ *loose*, *open*, etc.) loosen by cutting; (esp. as **cutting** *adjective*) cause pain to; reduce (prices, wages, services, etc.); make by cutting or removing material; cross, intersect; divide (pack of cards); edit (film), stop cameras; end acquaintance or ignore presence of; *US* deliberately miss (class etc.); chop (ball); switch off (engine etc.); (+ *across*, *through*, etc.) pass through as shorter route. ● *noun* act of cutting; division or wound made by cutting; stroke with knife, sword, whip, etc.; reduction (in price, wages, services, etc.); cessation (of power supply etc.); removal of part of play, film, etc.; *slang* commission, share of profits, etc.; style in which hair, clothing, etc. is cut; particular piece of meat; cutting of ball; deliberate ignoring of person. □ **a cut above** noticeably superior to; **cut and dried** completely decided, inflexible; **cut back** reduce (expenditure), prune; **cut-back** reduction in expenditure; **cut both ways** serve both sides; **cut corners** do task perfunctorily; **cut glass** glass with patterns cut on it; **cut in** interrupt, pull in too closely in front of another vehicle; **cut one's losses** abandon an unprofitable scheme; **cut no ice** *slang* have no influence; **cut off** *verb* remove by cutting, bring to abrupt end, interrupt, disconnect, *adjective* isolated; **cut out** shape by cutting, (cause to) cease functioning, stop doing or using; **cut-out** device for automatic disconnection; **cutthroat** *noun* murderer, *adjective* murderous, (of competition) intense and merciless; **cutthroat razor** one with long unguarded blade set in handle; **cut a tooth** have it appear through gum; **cut up** cut in pieces, (usually in *passive*) greatly distress; **cut up rough** show resentment.

cutaneous /kjuːˈteɪnɪəs/ *adjective* of the skin.

cute /kjuːt/ *adjective colloquial esp. US* attractive, sweet; clever, ingenious. □ **cutely** *adverb*; **cuteness** *noun*.

cuticle /ˈkjuːtɪk(ə)l/ *noun* skin at base of fingernail or toenail.

cutlass /ˈkʌtləs/ *noun historical* short broad-bladed curved sword.

cutlery /ˈkʌtlərɪ/ *noun* knives, forks, and spoons for use at table.

cutlet /ˈkʌtlɪt/ *noun* neck-chop of mutton or lamb; small piece of veal etc. for frying; flat cake of minced meat etc.

cutter *noun* person or thing that cuts; (in *plural*) cutting tool; small fast sailing ship; small boat carried by large ship.

cutting ● *noun* piece cut from newspaper etc.; piece cut from plant for replanting; excavated channel in hillside etc. for railway or road. ● *adjective* that cuts; hurtful. □ **cuttingly** *adverb*.

cuttlefish /ˈkʌt(ə)lfɪʃ/ *noun* (*plural* same or **-es**) 10-armed sea mollusc ejecting black fluid when pursued.

cutwater *noun* forward edge of ship's prow; wedge-shaped projection from pier of bridge.

C.V. *abbreviation* (also **CV**) curriculum vitae.

cwm /kuːm/ *noun* (in Wales) coomb.

cwt *abbreviation* hundredweight.

cyanide /'saɪənaɪd/ *noun* highly poisonous substance used in extraction of gold and silver.

cyanosis /saɪə'nəʊsɪs/ *noun* bluish skin due to oxygen-deficient blood.

cybernetics /saɪbə'netɪks/ *plural noun* (usually treated as *singular*) science of control systems and communications in animals and machines. □ **cybernetic** *adjective*.

cyclamen /'sɪkləmən/ *noun* plant with pink, red, or white flowers with backward-turned petals.

cycle /'saɪk(ə)l/ ● *noun* recurrent round or period (of events, phenomena, etc.); series of related poems etc.; bicycle, tricycle, etc. ● *verb* (**-ling**) ride bicycle etc.; move in cycles. □ **cycle lane** part of road reserved for bicycles; **cycle track**, **cycleway** path for bicycles.

cyclic /'saɪklɪk/ *adjective* (also **cyclical** /'sɪklɪk(ə)l/) recurring in cycles; belonging to chronological cycle. □ **cyclically** *adverb*.

cyclist /'saɪklɪst/ *noun* rider of bicycle.

cyclone /'saɪkləʊn/ *noun* winds rotating around low-pressure region; violent destructive form of this. □ **cyclonic** /-'klɒn-/ *adjective*.

cyclotron /'saɪklətrɒn/ *noun* apparatus for acceleration of charged atomic particles revolving in magnetic field.

cygnet /'sɪgnɪt/ *noun* young swan.

cylinder /'sɪlɪndə/ *noun* solid or hollow roller-shaped body; container for liquefied gas etc.; piston-chamber in engine. □ **cylindrical** /-'lɪn-/ *adjective*.

cymbal /'sɪmb(ə)l/ *noun* concave disc struck usually with another to make ringing sound.

cynic /'sɪnɪk/ *noun* person with pessimistic view of human nature. □ **cynical** *adjective*; **cynically** *adverb*; **cynicism** /-sɪz(ə)m/ *noun*.

cynosure /'saɪnəzjʊə/ *noun* centre of attention or admiration.

cypher = CIPHER.

cypress /'saɪprəs/ *noun* conifer with dark foliage.

Cypriot /'sɪprɪət/ (also **Cypriote** /-əʊt/) ● *noun* native or national of Cyprus. ● *adjective* of Cyprus.

Cyrillic /sɪ'rɪlɪk/ ● *adjective* of alphabet used esp. for Russian and Bulgarian. ● *noun* this alphabet.

cyst /sɪst/ *noun* sac formed in body, containing liquid matter.

cystic *adjective* of the bladder; like a cyst. □ **cystic fibrosis** hereditary disease usually with respiratory infections.

cystitis /sɪ'staɪtɪs/ *noun* inflammation of the bladder.

czar = TSAR.

czarina = TSARINA.

Czech /tʃek/ ● *noun* native or national of Czech Republic, or *historical* Czechoslovakia; language of Czech people. ● *adjective* of Czechs or their language; of Czech Republic.

Czechoslovak /tʃekə'sləʊvæk/ (also **Czechoslovakian** /-slə'vækɪən/) *historical* ● *noun* native or national of Czechoslovakia. ● *adjective* of Czechoslovaks or Czechoslovakia.

Dd

D *noun* (also **d**) (Roman numeral) 500. □ **D-Day** day of Allied invasion of France (6 June 1944), important or decisive day.

d. *abbreviation* died; (pre-decimal) penny.

dab[1] ● *verb* (**-bb-**) (often + *at*) press briefly and repeatedly with cloth etc.; (+ *on*) apply by dabbing; (often + *at*) aim feeble blow; strike lightly. ● *noun* dabbing; small amount (of paint etc.) dabbed on; light blow.

dab[2] *noun* (*plural* same) kind of marine flatfish.

dabble /ˈdæb(ə)l/ *verb* (**-ling**) (usually + *in, at*) engage (in an activity etc.) superficially; move about in shallow water etc. □ **dabbler** *noun*.

dabchick *noun* little grebe.

dab hand *noun* (usually + *at*) expert.

da capo /dɑː ˈkɑːpəʊ/ *adverb Music* repeat from beginning.

dace *noun* (*plural* same) small freshwater fish.

dacha /ˈdætʃə/ *noun* Russian country cottage.

dachshund /ˈdækshʊnd/ *noun* short-legged long-bodied dog.

dactyl /ˈdæktɪl/ *noun* metrical foot of one long followed by two short syllables. □ **dactylic** /-ˈtɪl-/ *adjective*.

dad *noun colloquial* father.

daddy /ˈdædɪ/ *noun* (*plural* **-ies**) *colloquial* father. □ **daddy-long-legs** crane-fly.

dado /ˈdeɪdəʊ/ *noun* (*plural* **-s**) lower, differently decorated, part of interior wall.

daffodil /ˈdæfədɪl/ *noun* spring bulb with trumpet-shaped yellow flowers.

daft /dɑːft/ *adjective* (**-er**, **-est**) foolish, silly, crazy.

dagger /ˈdægə/ *noun* short knifelike weapon; obelus.

daguerreotype /dəˈgerəʊtaɪp/ *noun* early photograph using silvered plate.

dahlia /ˈdeɪlɪə/ *noun* garden plant with large showy flowers.

Dáil (Eireann) /dɔɪl ˈeɪrən/ *noun* lower house of Parliament in Republic of Ireland.

daily /ˈdeɪlɪ/ ● *adjective* done, produced, or occurring every (week)day. ● *adverb* every day; constantly. ● *noun* (*plural* **-ies**) *colloquial* daily newspaper; cleaning woman.

dainty /ˈdeɪntɪ/ ● *adjective* (**-ier**, **-iest**) delicately pretty or small; choice; fastidious. ● *noun* (*plural* **-ies**) delicacy. □ **daintily** *adverb*; **daintiness** *noun*.

daiquiri /ˈdækərɪ/ *noun* (*plural* **-s**) cocktail of rum, lime juice, etc.

dairy /ˈdeərɪ/ ● *noun* (*plural* **-ies**) place for processing, distributing, or selling milk and milk products. ● *adjective* of, containing, or used for milk and milk products. □ **dairymaid** woman employed in dairy; **dairyman** man looking after cows.

dais /ˈdeɪɪs/ *noun* low platform, esp. at upper end of hall.

daisy /ˈdeɪzɪ/ *noun* (*plural* **-ies**) flowering plant with white radiating petals. □ **daisy chain** string of field daisies threaded together; **daisy wheel** spoked disc bearing printing characters, used in word processors and typewriters.

dale *noun* valley.

dally /ˈdælɪ/ *verb* (**-ies**, **-ied**) delay; waste time; (often + *with*) flirt. □ **dalliance** *noun*.

Dalmatian /dælˈmeɪʃ(ə)n/ *noun* large white dog with dark spots.

dam[1] ● *noun* barrier across river etc., usually forming reservoir or preventing flooding. ● *verb* (**-mm-**) provide or confine with dam; (often + *up*) block up, obstruct.

dam[2] *noun* mother (of animal).

damage /ˈdæmɪdʒ/ ● *noun* harm; injury; (in *plural*) financial compensation for loss or injury; (**the damage**) *slang* cost. ● *verb* (**-ging**) inflict damage on.

damask /ˈdæməsk/ ● *noun* fabric with woven design made visible by reflection of light. ● *adjective* made of damask; velvety pink. □ **damask rose** old sweet-scented rose.

dame *noun* (**Dame**) (title of) woman who has been knighted; comic female pantomime character played by man; *US slang* woman.

damn /dæm/ ● *verb* (often as *interjection*) curse; censure; condemn to hell; (often as **damning** *adjective*) show or prove to be guilty. ● *noun* uttered curse. ● *adjective & adverb* damned. □ **damn all** *slang* nothing.

damnable /ˈdæmnəb(ə)l/ *adjective* hateful; annoying.

damnation /dæmˈneɪʃ(ə)n/ ● *noun* eternal punishment in hell. ● *interjection expressing anger*.

damned /dæmd/ ● *adjective* damnable. ● *adverb* extremely.

damp ● *adjective* slightly wet. ● *noun* slight diffused or condensed moisture. ● *verb* make damp; (often + *down*) discourage, make burn less strongly; *Music* stop vibration of (string etc.). □ **damp course** layer of damp-proof material in wall to keep damp from rising. □ **dampness** *noun*.

dampen *verb* make or become damp; discourage.

damper *noun* device that reduces shock, vibration, or noise; discouraging person or thing; metal plate in flue to control draught.

damsel /ˈdæmz(ə)l/ *noun archaic* young unmarried woman.

damson /ˈdæmz(ə)n/ *noun* small dark purple plum.

dance /dɑːns/ ● *verb* (**-cing**) move rhythmically, usually to music; perform (dance role etc.); jump or bob about. ● *noun* dancing as art; style or form of this; social gathering for dancing; lively motion. □ **dance attendance (on)** serve obsequiously. □ **dancer** *noun*.

dandelion /ˈdændɪlaɪən/ *noun* yellow-flowered wild plant.

dander *noun* □ **get one's dander up** *colloquial* become angry.

dandle /ˈdænd(ə)l/ *verb* (**-ling**) bounce (child) on one's knees etc.

dandruff /ˈdændrʌf/ *noun* flakes of dead skin in hair.

dandy /ˈdændɪ/ ● *noun* (*plural* **-ies**) man excessively devoted to style and fashion. ● *adjective* (**-ier**, **-iest**) *colloquial* splendid. □ **dandy-brush** stiff brush for grooming horses.

Dane *noun* native or national of Denmark; *historical* Viking invader of England.

danger /ˈdeɪndʒə/ *noun* liability or exposure to harm; thing causing harm. □ **danger list** list of those dangerously ill; **danger money** extra payment for dangerous work.

dangerous *adjective* involving or causing danger. □ **dangerously** *adverb*.

dangle /ˈdæŋɡ(ə)l/ *verb* (**-ling**) hang loosely; hold or carry swaying loosely; hold out (temptation etc.).

Danish /ˈdeɪnɪʃ/ ● *adjective* of Denmark. ● *noun* Danish language; (**the Danish**) the Danish people. ▫ **Danish blue** white blue-veined cheese; **Danish pastry** yeast cake with icing, nuts, fruit, etc.

dank *adjective* damp and cold.

daphne /ˈdæfnɪ/ *noun* a flowering shrub.

dapper *adjective* neat and precise, esp. in dress; sprightly.

dapple /ˈdæp(ə)l/ *verb* (**-ling**) mark with spots of colour or shade; mottle. ▫ **dapple-grey** (of horse) grey with darker spots; **dapple grey** such a horse.

Darby and Joan *noun* devoted old married couple. ▫ **Darby and Joan club** social club for pensioners.

dare /deə/ ● *verb* (**-ring**; *3rd singular present* often **dare**) (+ *(to) do*) have the courage or impudence (to); (usually + *to do*) defy, challenge. ● *noun* challenge. ▫ **daredevil** reckless (person); **I dare say** very likely, I grant that.

daring ● *noun* adventurous courage. ● *adjective* bold, prepared to take risks. ▫ **daringly** *adverb*.

dariole /ˈdærɪəʊl/ *noun* dish cooked and served in a small mould.

dark ● *adjective* with little or no light; of deep or sombre colour; (of a person) with dark colouring; gloomy; sinister; angry; secret, mysterious. ● *noun* absence of light or knowledge; unlit place. ▫ **after dark** after nightfall; **Dark Ages** 5th–10th-c., unenlightened period; **dark horse** little-known person who is unexpectedly successful; **darkroom** darkened room for photographic work; **in the dark** without information or light. ▫ **darken** *verb*; **darkly** *adverb*; **darkness** *noun*.

darling /ˈdɑːlɪŋ/ ● *noun* beloved or endearing person or animal. ● *adjective* beloved, lovable; *colloquial* charming.

darn[1] ● *verb* mend by interweaving wool etc. across hole. ● *noun* darned area.

darn[2] *verb, interjection, adjective, & adverb colloquial mild form of* DAMN.

darnel /ˈdɑːn(ə)l/ *noun* grass growing in cereal crops.

dart ● *noun* small pointed missile; (in *plural* treated as *singular*) indoor game of throwing darts at a dartboard; sudden rapid movement; tapering tuck in garment. ● *verb* (often + *out, in, past*, etc.) move, send, or go suddenly or rapidly. ▫ **dartboard** circular target in game of darts.

Darwinian /dɑːˈwɪnɪən/ ● *adjective* of Darwin's theory of evolution. ● *noun* adherent of this. ▫ **Darwinism** /ˈdɑː-/ *noun*; **Darwinist** /ˈdɑː-/ *noun*.

dash ● *verb* rush; strike or fling forcefully so as to shatter; frustrate, dispirit; *colloquial* (as *interjection*) damn. ● *noun* rush, onset; punctuation mark (—) used to indicate break in sense (see panel); longer signal of two in Morse code; slight admixture; (capacity for) impetuous vigour. ▫ **dashboard** instrument panel of vehicle or aircraft; **dash off** write hurriedly.

dashing *adjective* spirited; showy.

dastardly /ˈdæstədlɪ/ *adjective* cowardly, despicable.

data /ˈdeɪtə/ *plural noun* (also treated as *singular*) known facts used for inference or reckoning; quantities or characters operated on by computer. ▫ **data bank** store or source of data; **database** structured set of data held in computer; **data processing** series of operations on data by computer.

■ **Usage** In scientific, philosophical, and general use, *data* is usually considered to mean a number of items and is treated as plural, with *datum* as its singular. In computing and allied subjects (and sometimes in general use), it is treated as singular, as in *Much useful data has been collected*. However, *data* is not singular, and it is wrong to say *a data* or *every data* or to make the plural form *datas*.

date[1] ● *noun* day of month; historical day or year; day, month, and year of writing etc. at head of document etc.; period to which work of art etc. belongs; time when an event takes place; *colloquial* social appointment, esp. with person of opposite sex; *US colloquial* person to be met at this. ● *verb* (**-ting**) mark with date; assign date to; (+ *to*) assign to a particular time, period, etc.; (often + *from, back to*, etc.) have origin at a particular time; expose as or appear old-fashioned; *US colloquial* make date with, go out together as sexual partners. ▫ **date line** line partly along meridian 180° from Greenwich, to the east of which date is a day earlier than to the west; date and place of writing at head of newspaper article etc.; **out of date** (**out-of-date** before noun) old-fashioned, obsolete; **to date** until now; **up to date** (**up-to-date** before noun) fashionable, current.

date[2] *noun* oval stone fruit; (in full **date-palm**) tree bearing this.

dative /ˈdeɪtɪv/ *Grammar* ● *noun* case expressing indirect object or recipient. ● *adjective* of or in the dative.

datum /ˈdeɪtəm/ *singular of* DATA.

daub /dɔːb/ ● *verb* paint or spread (paint etc.) crudely or unskilfully; smear (surface) with paint etc. ● *noun* paint etc. daubed on a surface; crude painting; clay etc. coating wattles to form wall.

daughter /ˈdɔːtə/ *noun* female child in relation to her parents; female descendant or member of family etc. ▫ **daughter-in-law** (*plural* **daughters-in-law**) son's wife.

Dash –

This is used:

1 to mark the beginning and end of an interruption in the structure of a sentence:

My son—where has he gone?—would like to meet you.

2 to show faltering speech in conversation:

Yes—well—I would—only you see—it's not easy.

3 to show other kinds of break in a sentence, where a comma, semicolon, or colon would traditionally be used, e.g.

Come tomorrow—if you can.
The most important thing is this—don't rush the work.

A dash is not used in this way in formal writing.

daunt /dɔːnt/ *verb* discourage, intimidate. □ **daunting** *adjective*.

dauntless *adjective* intrepid, persevering.

dauphin /ˈdɔːfɪn/ *noun historical* eldest son of King of France.

Davenport /ˈdævənpɔːt/ *noun* kind of writing desk; *US* large sofa.

davit /ˈdævɪt/ *noun* small crane on ship for holding lifeboat.

daw *noun* jackdaw.

dawdle /ˈdɔːd(ə)l/ *verb* (**-ling**) walk slowly and idly; waste time, procrastinate.

dawn ● *noun* daybreak; beginning. ● *verb* (of day) begin, grow light; (often + *on, upon*) become evident (to). □ **dawn chorus** birdsong at daybreak.

day *noun* time between sunrise and sunset; 24 hours as a unit of time; daylight; time during which work is normally done; (also *plural*) historical period; (**the day**) present time; period of prosperity. □ **daybreak** first light in morning; **day centre** place for care of elderly or handicapped during day; **daydream** (indulge in) fantasy etc. while awake; **day off** day's holiday; **day release** part-time education for employees; **day return** reduced fare or ticket for a return journey in one day; **day school** school for pupils living at home; **daytime** part of day when there is natural light; **day-to-day** mundane, routine; **day-trip** trip completed in one day.

daylight *noun* light of day; dawn; visible gap between things; (usually in *plural*) *slang* life. □ **daylight robbery** blatantly excessive charge; **daylight saving** longer summer evening daylight, achieved by putting clocks forward.

daze ● *verb* (**-zing**) stupefy, bewilder. ● *noun* dazed state.

dazzle /ˈdæz(ə)l/ ● *verb* (**-ling**) blind or confuse temporarily with sudden bright light; impress or overpower with knowledge, ability, etc. ● *noun* bright confusing light. □ **dazzling** *adjective*.

dB *abbreviation* decibel(s).

DC *abbreviation* direct current; District of Columbia; da capo.

DDT *abbreviation* colourless chlorinated hydrocarbon used as insecticide.

deacon /ˈdiːkən/ *noun* (in episcopal churches) minister below priest; (*feminine* **deaconess** /-ˈnes/) (in Nonconformist churches) lay officer.

deactivate /drˈæktɪveɪt/ *verb* (**-ting**) make inactive or less reactive.

dead /ded/ ● *adjective* no longer alive; numb; *colloquial* extremely tired or unwell; (+ *to*) insensitive to; not effective; extinct; extinguished; inanimate; lacking vigour; not resonant; quiet; not transmitting sounds; out of play; abrupt; complete. ● *adverb* absolutely, completely; *colloquial* very. ● *noun* time of silence or inactivity. □ **dead beat** utterly exhausted; **deadbeat** tramp; **dead duck** useless person or thing; **dead end** closed end of road etc.; **dead-end** having no prospects; **dead heat** race in which competitors tie; **dead letter** law etc. no longer observed; **deadline** time limit; **deadlock** *noun* state of unresolved conflict, *verb* bring or come to a standstill; **dead loss** useless person or thing; **dead man's handle** handle on electric train etc. disconnecting power supply if released; **dead march** funeral march; **dead on** exactly right; **deadpan** lacking expression or emotion; **dead reckoning** estimation of ship's position from log, compass, etc., when visibility is bad; **dead shot** unerring marksman; **dead weight** inert mass, heavy burden; **dead wood** *colloquial* useless person(s) or thing(s).

deaden *verb* deprive of or lose vitality, force, etc.; (+ *to*) make insensitive.

deadly ● *adjective* (**-ier, -iest**) causing fatal injury or serious damage; intense; accurate; deathlike; dreary. ● *adverb* as if dead; extremely. □ **deadly nightshade** plant with poisonous black berries.

deaf /def/ *adjective* wholly or partly unable to hear; (+ *to*) refusing to listen or comply. □ **deaf-aid** hearing aid; **deaf-and-dumb alphabet, language** sign language; **deaf mute** deaf and dumb person. □ **deafness** *noun*.

deafen *verb* (often as **deafening** *adjective*) overpower or make deaf with noise, esp. temporarily. □ **deafeningly** *adverb*.

deal[1] ● *verb* (*past & past participle* **dealt** /delt/) (+ *with*) take measures to resolve, placate, etc., do business or associate with, treat (subject); (often + *by, with*) behave in specified way; (+ *in*) sell; (often + *out, round*) distribute; administer. ● *noun* (usually **a good** or **great deal**) large amount, considerably; business arrangement etc.; specified treatment; dealing of cards, player's turn to deal.

deal[2] *noun* fir or pine timber, esp. as boards.

dealer *noun* trader; player dealing at cards.

dealings *plural noun* conduct or transactions.

dean *noun* head of ecclesiastical chapter; (usually **rural dean**) clergyman supervising parochial clergy; college or university official with disciplinary functions; head of university faculty.

deanery *noun* (*plural* **-ies**) dean's house or position; parishes presided over by rural dean.

dear ● *adjective* beloved; *used before person's name, esp. at beginning of letter*; (+ *to*) precious; expensive. ● *noun* dear person. ● *adverb* at great cost. ● *interjection* (usually **oh dear!** or **dear me!**) *expressing surprise, dismay, etc.* □ **dearly** *adverb*.

dearth /dɜːθ/ *noun* scarcity, lack.

death /deθ/ *noun* dying, end of life; being dead; cause of death; destruction. □ **deathblow** blow etc. causing death, or action, event, etc. ending something; **death-mask** cast of dead person's face; **death penalty** capital punishment; **death rate** yearly deaths per 1000 of population; **death-rattle** gurgling in throat at death; **death row** part of prison for those sentenced to death; **death squad** paramilitary group; **death-trap** unsafe place, vehicle, etc.; **death-warrant** order of execution; **death-watch beetle** beetle that bores into wood and makes ticking sound. □ **deathlike** *adjective*.

deathly ● *adjective* (**-ier, -iest**) like death. ● *adverb* in deathly manner.

deb *noun colloquial* débutante.

débâcle /deɪˈbɑːk(ə)l/ *noun* utter collapse; confused rush.

debar /drˈbɑː/ *verb* (**-rr-**) (+ *from*) exclude. □ **debarment** *noun*.

debase /drˈbeɪs/ *verb* (**-sing**) lower in character, quality, or value; depreciate (coin) by alloying etc. □ **debasement** *noun*.

debatable /drˈbeɪtəb(ə)l/ *adjective* questionable.

debate /drˈbeɪt/ ● *verb* (**-ting**) discuss or dispute, esp. formally; consider, ponder. ● *noun* discussion, esp. formal.

debauch /drˈbɔːtʃ/ ● *verb* corrupt, deprave, debase; (as **debauched** *adjective*) dissolute. ● *noun* bout of debauchery.

debauchee /dɪbɔːˈtʃiː/ *noun* debauched person.

debauchery *noun* excessive sensual indulgence.

debenture /drˈbentʃə/ *noun* company bond providing for payment of interest.

debilitate /drˈbɪlɪteɪt/ *verb* (**-ting**) enfeeble. □ **debilitation** *noun*.

debility *noun* feebleness, esp. of health.

debit /ˈdebɪt/ ● *noun* entry in account recording sum owed. ● *verb* (**-t-**) (+ *against, to*) enter on debit side of account.
debonair /debəˈneə/ *adjective* self-assured; pleasant.
debouch /dɪˈbaʊtʃ/ *verb* come out into open ground; (often + *into*) (of river etc.) merge. □ **debouchment** *noun*.
debrief /diːˈbriːf/ *verb* question (diplomat etc.) about completed mission. □ **debriefing** *noun*.
debris /ˈdebriː/ *noun* scattered fragments; wreckage.
debt /det/ *noun* money etc. owing; obligation; state of owing.
debtor *noun* person owing money etc.
debug /diːˈbʌg/ *verb* (**-gg-**) remove hidden microphones from; remove defects from.
debunk /diːˈbʌŋk/ *verb colloquial* expose as spurious or false.
début /ˈdeɪbjuː/ *noun* first public appearance.
débutante /ˈdebjuːtɑːnt/ *noun* young woman making her social début.
Dec. *abbreviation* December.
deca- *combining form* ten.
decade /ˈdekeɪd/ *noun* 10 years; set or series of 10.
decadence /ˈdekəd(ə)ns/ *noun* moral or cultural decline; immoral behaviour. □ **decadent** *adjective*.
decaffeinated /diːˈkæfmeɪtɪd/ *adjective* with caffeine removed.
decagon /ˈdekəgən/ *noun* plane figure with 10 sides and angles. □ **decagonal** /-ˈkæg-/ *adjective*.
decahedron /dekəˈhiːdrən/ *noun* solid figure with 10 faces. □ **decahedral** *adjective*.
decamp /diːˈkæmp/ *verb* depart suddenly; break up or leave camp.
decant /dɪˈkænt/ *verb* pour off (wine etc.) leaving sediment behind.
decanter *noun* stoppered glass container for decanted wine or spirit.
decapitate /dɪˈkæpɪteɪt/ *verb* (**-ting**) behead. □ **decapitation** *noun*.
decarbonize /diːˈkɑːbənaɪz/ *verb* (also **-ise**) (**-zing** or **-sing**) remove carbon etc. from (engine of car etc.). □ **decarbonization** *noun*.
decathlon /dɪˈkæθlən/ *noun* athletic contest of 10 events. □ **decathlete** *noun*.
decay /dɪˈkeɪ/ ● *verb* (cause to) rot or decompose; decline in quality, power, etc. ● *noun* rotten state; decline.
decease /dɪˈsiːs/ *noun formal esp. Law* death.
deceased *formal* ● *adjective* dead. ● *noun* (**the deceased**) person who has died.
deceit /dɪˈsiːt/ *noun* deception; trick. □ **deceitful** *adjective*.
deceive /dɪˈsiːv/ *verb* (**-ving**) make (person) believe what is false; (**deceive oneself**) persist in mistaken belief; mislead; be unfaithful to.
decelerate /diːˈseləreɪt/ *verb* (**-ting**) (cause to) reduce speed. □ **deceleration** *noun*.
December /dɪˈsembə/ *noun* twelfth month of year.
decency /ˈdiːsənsɪ/ *noun* (*plural* **-ies**) correct, honourable, or modest behaviour; (in *plural*) proprieties, manners.
decennial /dɪˈsenɪəl/ *adjective* lasting 10 years; recurring every 10 years.
decent /ˈdiːs(ə)nt/ *adjective* conforming with standards of decency; not obscene; respectable; acceptable; kind. □ **decently** *adverb*.
decentralize /diːˈsentrəlaɪz/ *verb* (also **-ise**) (**-zing** or **-sing**) transfer (power etc.) from central to local authority. □ **decentralization** *noun*.
deception /dɪˈsepʃ(ə)n/ *noun* deceiving, being deceived; thing that deceives.
deceptive /dɪˈseptɪv/ *adjective* likely to mislead.
deci- *combining form* one-tenth.
decibel /ˈdesɪbel/ *noun* unit used in comparison of sound etc. levels.
decide /dɪˈsaɪd/ *verb* (**-ding**) (usually + *to do, that, on, about*) resolve after consideration; settle (issue etc.); (usually + *between, for, against, in favour of, that*) give judgement.
decided *adjective* definite, unquestionable; positive, resolute. □ **decidedly** *adverb*.
deciduous /dɪˈsɪdjʊəs/ *adjective* (of tree) shedding leaves annually; (of leaves etc.) shed periodically.
decimal /ˈdesɪm(ə)l/ ● *adjective* (of system of numbers, weights, measures, etc.) based on 10; of tenths or 10; proceeding by tens. ● *noun* decimal fraction. □ **decimal fraction** fraction expressed in tenths, hundredths, etc., esp. by units to right of decimal point; **decimal point** dot placed before fraction in decimal fraction.
decimalize *verb* (also **-ise**) (**-zing** or **-sing**) express as decimal; convert to decimal system. □ **decimalization** *noun*.
decimate /ˈdesɪmeɪt/ *verb* (**-ting**) destroy large proportion of. □ **decimation** *noun*.

■ **Usage** *Decimate* should not be used to mean 'defeat utterly'.

decipher /dɪˈsaɪfə/ *verb* convert (coded information) into intelligible language; determine the meaning of. □ **decipherable** *adjective*.
decision /dɪˈsɪʒ(ə)n/ *noun* deciding; resolution after consideration; settlement; resoluteness.
decisive /dɪˈsaɪsɪv/ *adjective* conclusive, settling an issue; quick to decide. □ **decisively** *adverb*; **decisiveness** *noun*.
deck ● *noun* platform in a ship serving as a floor; floor of bus etc.; section for playing discs or tapes etc. in sound system; *US* pack of cards. ● *verb* (often + *out*) decorate. □ **deck-chair** outdoor folding chair.
declaim /dɪˈkleɪm/ *verb* speak, recite, etc. as if addressing audience. □ **declamation** *noun*; **declamatory** /-ˈklæm-/ *adjective*.
declaration /dekləˈreɪʃ(ə)n/ *noun* declaring; emphatic, deliberate, or formal statement.
declare /dɪˈkleə/ *verb* (**-ring**) announce openly or formally; pronounce; (usually + *that*) assert emphatically; acknowledge possession of (dutiable goods, income, etc.); *Cricket* close (innings) voluntarily before team is out; *Cards* name trump suit. □ **declaratory** /-ˈklær-/ *adjective*.
declassify /diːˈklæsɪfaɪ/ *verb* (**-ies**, **-ied**) declare (information etc.) to be no longer secret. □ **declassification** *noun*.
declension /dɪˈklenʃ(ə)n/ *noun Grammar* variation of form of noun etc., to show grammatical case; class of nouns with same inflections; deterioration.
declination /deklɪˈneɪʃ(ə)n/ *noun* downward bend; angular distance north or south of celestial equator; deviation of compass needle from true north.
decline /dɪˈklaɪn/ ● *verb* (**-ning**) deteriorate, lose strength or vigour; decrease; refuse; slope or bend downwards; *Grammar* state case forms of (noun etc.). ● *noun* deterioration.
declivity /dɪˈklɪvɪtɪ/ *noun* (*plural* **-ies**) downward slope.
declutch /diːˈklʌtʃ/ *verb* disengage clutch of motor vehicle.
decode /diːˈkəʊd/ *verb* (**-ding**) decipher. □ **decoder** *noun*.
decoke /diːˈkəʊk/ *verb* (**-king**) *colloquial* decarbonize.
décolletage /deɪkɒlˈtɑːʒ/ *noun* low neckline of woman's dress. [French]

décolleté /deɪ'kɒlteɪ/ *adjective* (also ***décolletée***) having low neckline. [French]

decompose /di:kəm'pəʊz/ *verb* **(-sing)** rot; separate into elements. □ **decomposition** /di:kɒmpə'zɪʃ(ə)n/ *noun*.

decompress /di:kəm'pres/ *verb* subject to decompression.

decompression /di:kəm'preʃ(ə)n/ *noun* release from compression; reduction of pressure on deep-sea diver etc. □ **decompression chamber** enclosed space for decompression.

decongestant /di:kən'dʒest(ə)nt/ *noun* medicine etc. that relieves nasal congestion.

decontaminate /di:kən'tæmɪneɪt/ *verb* **(-ting)** remove contamination from. □ **decontamination** *noun*.

décor /'deɪkɔ:/ *noun* furnishings and decoration of room, stage, etc.

decorate /'dekəreɪt/ *verb* **(-ting)** adorn; paint, wallpaper, etc. (room etc.); give medal or award to.

decoration *noun* decorating; thing that decorates; medal etc.; (in *plural*) flags etc. put up on festive occasion.

decorative /'dekərətɪv/ *adjective* pleasing in appearance. □ **decoratively** *adverb*.

decorator *noun* person who decorates for a living.

decorous /'dekərəs/ *adjective* having or showing decorum. □ **decorously** *adverb*.

decorum /dɪ'kɔ:rəm/ *noun* polite dignified behaviour.

decoy ● *noun* /'di:kɔɪ/ thing or person used as lure; bait, enticement. ● *verb* /dɪ'kɔɪ/ lure by decoy.

decrease ● *verb* /dɪ'kri:s/ **(-sing)** make or become smaller or fewer. ● *noun* /'di:kri:s/ decreasing; amount of this.

decree /dɪ'kri:/ ● *noun* official legal order; legal decision. ● *verb* **(-ees, -eed)** ordain by decree. □ **decree absolute** final order for completion of divorce; **decree nisi** /'naɪsaɪ/ provisional order for divorce.

decrepit /dɪ'krepɪt/ *adjective* weakened by age or infirmity; dilapidated. □ **decrepitude** *noun*.

decry /dɪ'kraɪ/ *verb* **(-ies, -ied)** disparage.

dedicate /'dedɪkeɪt/ *verb* **(-ting)** (often + *to*) devote (oneself) to a purpose etc.; address (book etc.) to friend or patron etc.; devote (building etc.) to saint etc.; (as **dedicated** *adjective*) having single-minded loyalty. □ **dedicatory** *adjective*.

dedication *noun* dedicating; words with which book is dedicated.

deduce /dɪ'dju:s/ *verb* **(-cing)** (often + *from*) infer logically. □ **deducible** *adjective*.

deduct /dɪ'dʌkt/ *verb* (often + *from*) subtract; take away; withhold.

deductible *adjective* that may be deducted esp. from tax or taxable income.

deduction /dɪ'dʌkʃ(ə)n/ *noun* deducting; amount deducted; inference from general to particular.

deductive *adjective* of or reasoning by deduction.

deed *noun* thing done; action; legal document. □ **deed of covenant** agreement to pay regular sum, esp. to charity; **deed poll** deed made by one party only, esp. to change one's name.

deem *verb formal* consider, judge.

deep ● *adjective* extending far down or in; to or at specified depth; low-pitched; intense; profound; (+ *in*) fully absorbed, overwhelmed. ● *adverb* deeply; far down or in. ● *noun* deep state; **(the deep)** *poetical* the sea. □ **deep-freeze** *noun* freezer, *verb* freeze or store in freezer; **deep-fry** fry with fat covering food. □ **deepen** *verb*; **deeply** *adverb*.

deer *noun* (*plural* same) 4-hoofed grazing animal, male usually with antlers. □ **deerstalker** cloth peaked cap with ear-flaps.

deface /dɪ'feɪs/ *verb* **(-cing)** disfigure. □ **defacement** *noun*.

de facto /deɪ 'fæktəʊ/ ● *adjective* existing in fact, whether by right or not. ● *adverb* in fact.

defame /dɪ'feɪm/ *verb* **(-ming)** attack good name of. □ **defamation** /defə'meɪʃ(ə)n/ *noun*; **defamatory** /-'fæm-/ *adjective*.

default /dɪ'fɔ:lt/ ● *noun* failure to act, appear, or pay; option selected by computer program etc. unless given alternative instruction. ● *verb* fail to fulfil obligations. □ **by default** because of lack of an alternative etc. □ **defaulter** *noun*.

defeat /dɪ'fi:t/ ● *verb* overcome in battle, contest, etc.; frustrate, baffle. ● *noun* defeating, being defeated.

defeatism *noun* readiness to accept defeat. □ **defeatist** *noun & adjective*.

defecate /'di:fɪkeɪt/ *verb* **(-ting)** evacuate the bowels. □ **defecation** *noun*.

defect ● *noun* /'di:fekt/ shortcoming; fault. ● *verb* /dɪ'fekt/ desert one's country, cause, etc., for another. □ **defection** *noun*; **defector** *noun*.

defective /dɪ'fektɪv/ *adjective* faulty; imperfect. □ **defectiveness** *noun*.

defence /dɪ'fens/ *noun* (*US* **defense**) (means of) defending; justification; defendant's case or counsel; players in defending position; (in *plural*) fortifications. □ **defenceless** *adjective*.

defend /dɪ'fend/ *verb* (often + *against*, *from*) resist attack made on; protect; uphold by argument; *Law* conduct defence (of); compete to retain (title). □ **defender** *noun*.

defendant *noun* person accused or sued in court of law.

defense *US* = DEFENCE.

defensible /dɪ'fensɪb(ə)l/ *adjective* able to be defended or justified.

defensive /dɪ'fensɪv/ *adjective* done or intended for defence; over-reacting to criticism. □ **on the defensive** expecting criticism, ready to defend. □ **defensively** *adverb*; **defensiveness** *noun*.

defer[1] /dɪ'fɜ:/ *verb* **(-rr-)** postpone. □ **deferment** *noun*.

defer[2] /dɪ'fɜ:/ *verb* **(-rr-)** (+ *to*) yield or make concessions.

deference /'defərəns/ *noun* respectful conduct; compliance with another's wishes. □ **in deference to** out of respect for.

deferential /defə'renʃ(ə)l/ *adjective* respectful. □ **deferentially** *adverb*.

defiance /dɪ'faɪəns/ *noun* open disobedience; bold resistance. □ **defiant** *adjective*; **defiantly** *adverb*.

deficiency /dɪ'fɪʃənsɪ/ *noun* (*plural* **-ies**) being deficient; (usually + *of*) lack or shortage; thing lacking; deficit. □ **deficiency disease** disease caused by lack of essential element in diet.

deficient /dɪ'fɪʃ(ə)nt/ *adjective* (often + *in*) incomplete or insufficient.

deficit /'defɪsɪt/ *noun* amount by which total falls short; excess of liabilities over assets.

defile[1] /dɪ'faɪl/ *verb* **(-ling)** make dirty; pollute; profane. □ **defilement** *noun*.

defile[2] /dɪ'faɪl/ ● *noun* narrow gorge or pass. ● *verb* **(-ling)** march in file.

define /dɪ'faɪn/ *verb* **(-ning)** give meaning of; describe scope of; outline; mark out the boundary of. □ **definable** *adjective*.

definite /'defɪnɪt/ *adjective* certain; clearly defined; precise. □ **definite article** the word (*the* in English) placed before a noun and implying a specific object, person, or idea. □ **definitely** *adverb*.

definition /defɪˈnɪʃ(ə)n/ *noun* defining; statement of meaning of word etc.; distinctness in outline.
definitive /dɪˈfɪnɪtɪv/ *adjective* decisive, unconditional, final; most authoritative.
deflate /dɪˈfleɪt/ *verb* (**-ting**) let air out of (tyre etc.); (cause to) lose confidence; subject (economy) to deflation.
deflation *noun* deflating; reduction of money in circulation to combat inflation. □ **deflationary** *adjective*.
deflect /dɪˈflekt/ *verb* bend or turn aside from purpose or course; (often + *from*) (cause to) deviate. □ **deflection** *noun*.
deflower /diːˈflaʊə/ *verb* deprive of virginity; ravage.
defoliate /diːˈfəʊlɪeɪt/ *verb* (**-ting**) destroy leaves of. □ **defoliant** *noun*; **defoliation** *noun*.
deforest /diːˈfɒrɪst/ *verb* clear of forests. □ **deforestation** *noun*.
deform /dɪˈfɔːm/ *verb* (often as **deformed** *adjective*) make ugly or misshapen, disfigure. □ **deformation** /diː-/ *noun*.
deformity /dɪˈfɔːmɪtɪ/ *noun* (*plural* **-ies**) being deformed; malformation.
defraud /dɪˈfrɔːd/ *verb* (often + *of*) cheat by fraud.
defray /dɪˈfreɪ/ *verb* provide money for (cost). □ **defrayal** *noun*.
defrock /diːˈfrɒk/ *verb* deprive (esp. priest) of office.
defrost /diːˈfrɒst/ *verb* remove frost or ice from; unfreeze; become unfrozen.
deft *adjective* dexterous, skilful. □ **deftly** *adverb*; **deftness** *noun*.
defunct /dɪˈfʌŋkt/ *adjective* no longer existing or in use; dead.
defuse /diːˈfjuːz/ *verb* (**-sing**) remove fuse from (bomb etc.); reduce tension in (crisis etc.).
defy /dɪˈfaɪ/ *verb* (**-ies**, **-ied**) resist openly; present insuperable obstacles to; (+ *to do*) challenge to do or prove something.
degenerate /dɪˈdʒenərət/ ● *adjective* having lost usual or good qualities; immoral. ● *noun* degenerate person etc. ● *verb* /-reɪt/ (**-ting**) become degenerate; get worse. □ **degeneracy** *noun*; **degeneration** *noun*.
degrade /dɪˈgreɪd/ *verb* (**-ding**) (often as **degrading** *adjective*) humiliate; dishonour; reduce to lower rank. □ **degradation** /degrəˈdeɪʃ(ə)n/ *noun*.
degree /dɪˈgriː/ *noun* stage in scale, series, or process; unit of measurement of angle or temperature; extent of burns; academic rank conferred by university etc.
dehumanize /diːˈhjuːmənaɪz/ *verb* (also **-ise**) (**-zing** or **-sing**) remove human qualities from; make impersonal. □ **dehumanization** *noun*.
dehydrate /diːhaɪˈdreɪt/ *verb* (**-ting**) remove water from; make dry; (often as **dehydrated** *adjective*) deprive of fluids, make very thirsty. □ **dehydration** *noun*.
de-ice /diːˈaɪs/ *verb* (**-cing**) remove ice from; prevent formation of ice on. □ **de-icer** *noun*.
deify /ˈdiːɪfaɪ/ *verb* (**-ies**, **-ied**) make god or idol of. □ **deification** *noun*.
deign /deɪn/ *verb* (+ *to do*) condescend.
deism /ˈdiːɪz(ə)m/ *noun* reasoned belief in existence of a god. □ **deist** *noun*; **deistic** /-ˈɪstɪk/ *adjective*.
deity /ˈdeɪɪtɪ/ *noun* (*plural* **-ies**) god or goddess; divine status or nature.
déjà vu /deɪʒɑː ˈvuː/ *noun* illusion of having already experienced present situation. [French]
dejected /dɪˈdʒektɪd/ *adjective* sad, depressed. □ **dejectedly** *adverb*; **dejection** *noun*.
delay /dɪˈleɪ/ ● *verb* postpone; make or be late. ● *noun* delaying, being delayed; time lost by this.
delectable /dɪˈlektəb(ə)l/ *adjective* delightful.
delectation /diːlekˈteɪʃ(ə)n/ *noun* enjoyment.
delegate ● *noun* /ˈdelɪgət/ elected representative sent to conference; member of delegation etc. ● *verb* /ˈdelɪgeɪt/ (**-ting**) (often + *to*) commit (power etc.) to deputy etc.; entrust (task) to another; send or authorize as representative.
delegation /delɪˈgeɪʃ(ə)n/ *noun* group representing others; delegating, being delegated.
delete /dɪˈliːt/ *verb* (**-ting**) strike out (word etc.). □ **deletion** *noun*.
deleterious /delɪˈtɪərɪəs/ *adjective* harmful.
delft *noun* (also **delftware**) type of glazed earthenware.
deli /ˈdelɪ/ *noun* (*plural* **-s**) *colloquial* delicatessen.
deliberate ● *adjective* /dɪˈlɪbərət/ intentional, considered; unhurried. ● *verb* /dɪˈlɪbəreɪt/ (**-ting**) think carefully; discuss. □ **deliberately** *adverb*.
deliberation /dɪlɪbəˈreɪʃ(ə)n/ *noun* careful consideration or slowness.
deliberative /dɪˈlɪbərətɪv/ *adjective* (esp. of assembly etc.) of or for deliberation.
delicacy /ˈdelɪkəsɪ/ *noun* (*plural* **-ies**) being delicate; choice food.
delicate /ˈdelɪkət/ *adjective* fine in texture, quality, etc.; subtle, hard to discern; susceptible, tender; requiring tact. □ **delicately** *adverb*.
delicatessen /delɪkəˈtes(ə)n/ *noun* shop selling esp. exotic cooked meats, cheeses, etc.
delicious /dɪˈlɪʃəs/ *adjective* highly enjoyable esp. to taste or smell. □ **deliciously** *adverb*.
delight /dɪˈlaɪt/ ● *verb* (often as **delighted** *adjective*) please greatly; (+ *in*) take great pleasure in. ● *noun* great pleasure; thing that delights. □ **delightful** *adjective*; **delightfully** *adverb*.
delimit /dɪˈlɪmɪt/ *verb* (**-t-**) fix limits or boundary of. □ **delimitation** *noun*.
delineate /dɪˈlɪnɪeɪt/ *verb* (**-ting**) portray by drawing or in words. □ **delineation** *noun*.
delinquent /dɪˈlɪŋkwənt/ ● *noun* offender. ● *adjective* guilty of misdeed; failing in a duty. □ **delinquency** *noun*.
deliquesce /delɪˈkwes/ *verb* (**-cing**) become liquid; dissolve in moisture from the air. □ **deliquescence** *noun*; **deliquescent** *adjective*.
delirious /dɪˈlɪrɪəs/ *adjective* affected with delirium; wildly excited. □ **deliriously** *adverb*.
delirium /dɪˈlɪrɪəm/ *noun* disordered state of mind, with incoherent speech etc.; wildly excited mood. □ **delirium tremens** /ˈtriːmenz/ psychosis of chronic alcoholism with tremors and hallucinations.
deliver /dɪˈlɪvə/ *verb* convey (letters, goods) to destination; (often + *to*) hand over; (often + *from*) save, rescue, set free; assist in giving birth or at birth of; utter (speech); launch or aim (blow etc.); (in full **deliver the goods**) *colloquial* provide or carry out what is required.
deliverance *noun* rescuing.
delivery /dɪˈlɪvərɪ/ *noun* (*plural* **-ies**) delivering; distribution of letters etc.; thing delivered; childbirth; manner of delivering.
dell *noun* small wooded valley.
delouse /diːˈlaʊs/ *verb* (**-sing**) rid of lice.
delphinium /delˈfɪnɪəm/ *noun* (*plural* **-s**) garden plant with spikes of usually blue flowers.
delta /ˈdeltə/ *noun* triangular alluvial tract at mouth of river; fourth letter of Greek alphabet (Δ, δ); fourth-class mark for work etc. □ **delta wing** triangular swept-back wing of aircraft.
delude /dɪˈluːd/ *verb* (**-ding**) deceive, mislead.
deluge /ˈdeljuːdʒ/ ● *noun* flood; downpour of rain; overwhelming rush. ● *verb* (**-ging**) flood, inundate.
delusion /dɪˈluːʒ(ə)n/ *noun* false belief or hope. □ **delusive** *adjective*; **delusory** *adjective*.

de luxe /də 'lʌks/ *adjective* luxurious; superior; sumptuous.

delve *verb* (**-ving**) (often + *in, into*) research, search deeply; *poetical* dig.

demagogue /'deməgɒg/ *noun* political agitator appealing to emotion. □ **demagogic** /-'gɒgɪk/ *adjective*; **demagogy** /-gɒgɪ/) *noun*.

demand /dɪ'mɑːnd/ ● *noun* insistent and peremptory request; desire for commodity; urgent claim. ● *verb* (often + *of, from, to do, that*) ask for insistently; require; (as **demanding** *adjective*) requiring effort, attention, etc. □ **demand feeding** feeding baby whenever it cries.

demarcation /diːmɑː'keɪʃ(ə)n/ *noun* marking of boundary or limits; trade union practice of restricting job to one union. □ **demarcate** /'diː-/ *verb* (**-ting**).

demean /dɪ'miːn/ *verb* (usually **demean oneself**) lower dignity of.

demeanour /dɪ'miːnə/ *noun* (*US* **demeanor**) bearing; outward behaviour.

demented /dɪ'mentɪd/ *adjective* mad.

dementia /dɪ'menʃə/ *noun* chronic insanity. □ **dementia praecox** /'priːkɒks/ schizophrenia.

demerara /demə'reərə/ *noun* light brown cane sugar.

demerit /diː'merɪt/ *noun* fault, defect.

demesne /dɪ'miːn/ *noun* landed property, estate; possession (of land) as one's own.

demigod /'demɪgɒd/ *noun* partly divine being; *colloquial* godlike person.

demijohn /'demɪdʒɒn/ *noun* large wicker-cased bottle.

demilitarize /diː'mɪlɪtəraɪz/ *verb* (also **-ise**) (**-zing** or **-sing**) remove army etc. from (zone etc.).

demi-monde /'demɪmɒnd/ *noun* class of women of doubtful morality; semi-respectable group. [French]

demise /dɪ'maɪz/ *noun* death; termination.

demisemiquaver /demɪ'semɪkweɪvə/ *noun Music* note equal to half semiquaver.

demist /diː'mɪst/ *verb* clear mist from (windscreen etc.). □ **demister** *noun*.

demo /'deməʊ/ *noun* (*plural* **-s**) *colloquial* demonstration, esp. political.

demobilize /diː'məʊbɪlaɪz/ *verb* (also **-ise**) (**-zing** or **-sing**) disband (troops etc.). □ **demobilization** *noun*.

democracy /dɪ'mɒkrəsɪ/ *noun* (*plural* **-ies**) government by the whole population, usually through elected representatives; state so governed.

democrat /'deməkræt/ *noun* advocate of democracy; (**Democrat**) member of US Democratic Party.

democratic /demə'krætɪk/ *adjective* of, like, or practising democracy; favouring social equality. □ **democratically** *adverb*; **democratize** /dɪ'mɒkrətaɪz/ *verb* (also **-ise**) (**-zing** or **-sing**); **democratization** *noun*.

demography /dɪ'mɒgrəfɪ/ *noun* study of statistics of birth, deaths, disease, etc. □ **demographic** /demə'græfɪk/ *adjective*.

demolish /dɪ'mɒlɪʃ/ *verb* pull down (building); destroy; refute; eat up voraciously. □ **demolition** /demə'lɪʃ(ə)n/ *noun*.

demon /'diːmən/ *noun* devil; evil spirit; forceful or skilful performer. □ **demonic** /dɪ'mɒnɪk/ *adjective*.

demoniac /dɪ'məʊnɪæk/ ● *adjective* frenzied; supposedly possessed by evil spirit; of or like demons. ● *noun* demoniac person. □ **demoniacal** /diːmə'naɪək(ə)l/ *adjective*.

demonology /diːmə'nɒlədʒɪ/ *noun* study of demons.

demonstrable /'demənstrəb(ə)l/ *adjective* able to be shown or proved. □ **demonstrably** *adverb*.

demonstrate /'demənstreɪt/ *verb* (**-ting**) show (feelings etc.); describe and explain by experiment etc.; prove truth or existence of; take part in public demonstration.

demonstration *noun* demonstrating; (+ *of*) show of feeling etc.; political public march, meeting, etc.; proof by logic, argument, etc.

demonstrative /dɪ'mɒnstrətɪv/ *adjective* showing feelings readily; affectionate; *Grammar* indicating person or thing referred to. □ **demonstratively** *adverb*; **demonstrativeness** *noun*.

demonstrator /'demənstreɪtə/ *noun* person making or taking part in demonstration.

demoralize /diː'mɒrəlaɪz/ *verb* (also **-ise**) (**-zing** or **-sing**) destroy morale of. □ **demoralization** *noun*.

demote /diː'məʊt/ *verb* (**-ting**) reduce to lower rank or class. □ **demotion** /-'məʊʃ(ə)n/ *noun*.

demotic /dɪ'mɒtɪk/ ● *noun* colloquial form of a language. ● *adjective* colloquial, vulgar.

demotivate /diː'məʊtɪveɪt/ *verb* (**-ting**) cause to lose motivation. □ **demotivation** *noun*.

demur /dɪ'mɜː/ ● *verb* (**-rr-**) (often + *to, at*) raise objections. ● *noun* (usually in negative) objection, objecting.

demure /dɪ'mjʊə/ *adjective* (**-r, -st**) quiet, modest; coy. □ **demurely** *adverb*.

demystify /diː'mɪstɪfaɪ/ *verb* (**-ies, -ied**) remove mystery from.

den *noun* wild animal's lair; place of crime or vice; small private room.

denarius /dɪ'neərɪəs/ *noun* (*plural* **-rii** /-rɪaɪ/) ancient Roman silver coin.

denationalize /diː'næʃənəlaɪz/ *verb* (also **-ise**) (**-zing** or **-sing**) transfer (industry etc.) from national to private ownership. □ **denationalization** *noun*.

denature /diː'neɪtʃə/ *verb* (**-ring**) change properties of; make (alcohol) unfit for drinking.

dendrology /den'drɒlədʒɪ/ *noun* study of trees. □ **dendrologist** *noun*.

denial /dɪ'naɪəl/ *noun* denying or refusing.

denier /'denjə/ *noun* unit of weight measuring fineness of silk, nylon, etc.

denigrate /'denɪgreɪt/ *verb* (**-ting**) sully reputation of. □ **denigration** *noun*; **denigratory** /-'greɪt-/ *adjective*.

denim /'denɪm/ *noun* twilled cotton fabric; (in *plural*) jeans etc. made of this.

denizen /'denɪz(ə)n/ *noun* (usually + *of*) inhabitant or occupant.

denominate /dɪ'nɒmɪneɪt/ *verb* (**-ting**) give name to, describe as, call.

denomination *noun* Church or religious sect; class of measurement or money; name, esp. for classification. □ **denominational** *adjective*.

denominator *noun* number below line in vulgar fraction; divisor.

denote /dɪ'nəʊt/ *verb* (**-ting**) (often + *that*) be sign of; indicate; be name for, signify. □ **denotation** /diːnə'teɪʃ(ə)n/ *noun*.

denouement /deɪ'nuːmɑ̃/ *noun* final resolution in play, novel, etc.

denounce /dɪ'naʊns/ *verb* (**-cing**) accuse publicly; inform against.

dense /dens/ *adjective* closely compacted; crowded together; stupid. □ **densely** *adverb*; **denseness** *noun*.

density /'densɪtɪ/ *noun* (*plural* **-ies**) denseness; quantity of mass per unit volume; opacity of photographic image.

dent ● *noun* depression in surface; noticeable adverse effect. ● *verb* make dent in.

dental /'dent(ə)l/ *adjective* of teeth or dentistry; (of sound) made with tongue-tip against front teeth. □ **dental floss** thread used to clean between teeth; **dental surgeon** dentist.

dentate /'denteɪt/ *adjective* toothed, notched.
dentifrice /'dentɪfrɪs/ *noun* tooth powder or toothpaste.
dentine /'denti:n/ *noun* hard dense tissue forming most of tooth.
dentist /'dentɪst/ *noun* person qualified to treat, extract, etc., teeth. ◻ **dentistry** *noun.*
denture /'dentʃə/ *noun* (usually in *plural*) removable artificial teeth.
denude /dɪ'nju:d/ *verb* **(-ding)** make naked or bare; (+ *of*) strip of (covering etc.). ◻ **denudation** /di:-/ *noun.*
denunciation /dɪnʌnsɪ'eɪʃ(ə)n/ *noun* denouncing.
deny /dɪ'naɪ/ *verb* **(-ies, -ied)** declare untrue or non-existent; repudiate; (often + *to*) withhold from; (**deny oneself**) be abstinent.
deodorant /di:'əʊdərənt/ *noun* substance applied to body or sprayed into air to conceal smells.
deodorize /di:'əʊdəraɪz/ *verb* (also **-ise**) **(-zing** or **-sing)** remove smell of. ◻ **deodorization** *noun.*
deoxyribonucleic acid /di:ɒksɪraɪbəʊnju:'kleɪɪk/ see DNA.
dep. *abbreviation* departs; deputy.
depart /dɪ'pɑ:t/ *verb* (often + *from*) go away, leave; (usually + *for*) set out; (usually + *from*) deviate. ◻ **depart this life** *formal* die.
departed ● *adjective* bygone. ● *noun* **(the departed)** *euphemistic* dead person or people.
department *noun* separate part of complex whole, esp. branch of administration; division of school etc.; section of large store; area of expertise; French administrative district. ◻ **department store** shop with many departments. ◻ **departmental** /di:pɑ:t'ment(ə)l/ *adjective.*
departure /dɪ'pɑ:tʃə/ *noun* departing; new course of action etc.
depend /dɪ'pend/ *verb* (often + *on, upon*) be controlled or determined by; (+ *on, upon*) need, rely on.
dependable *adjective* reliable. ◻ **dependability** *noun.*
dependant *noun* person supported, esp. financially, by another.
dependence *noun* depending, being dependent; reliance.
dependency *noun* (*plural* **-ies**) country etc. controlled by another; dependence (on drugs etc.).
dependent *adjective* (usually + *on*) depending; unable to do without (esp. drug); maintained at another's cost; (of clause etc.) subordinate to word etc.
depict /dɪ'pɪkt/ *verb* represent in painting etc.; describe. ◻ **depiction** *noun.*
depilate /'depɪleɪt/ *verb* **(-ting)** remove hair from. ◻ **depilation** *noun*; **depilator** *noun.*
depilatory /dɪ'pɪlətərɪ/ ● *adjective* that removes unwanted hair. ● *noun* (*plural* **-ies**) depilatory substance.
deplete /dɪ'pli:t/ *verb* **(-ting)** (esp. as **depleted** *adjective*) reduce in numbers, quantity, etc.; exhaust. ◻ **depletion** *noun.*
deplorable /dɪ'plɔ:rəb(ə)l/ *adjective* exceedingly bad. ◻ **deplorably** *adverb.*
deplore /dɪ'plɔ:/ *verb* **(-ring)** find deplorable; regret.
deploy /dɪ'plɔɪ/ *verb* spread out (troops) into line for action; use (arguments etc.) effectively. ◻ **deployment** *noun.*
deponent /dɪ'pəʊnənt/ *noun* person making deposition under oath.
depopulate /di:'pɒpjʊleɪt/ *verb* **(-ting)** reduce population of. ◻ **depopulation** *noun.*
deport /dɪ'pɔ:t/ *verb* remove forcibly or exile to another country; (**deport oneself**) behave (well, badly, etc.). ◻ **deportation** /di:-/ *noun.*
deportee /di:pɔ:'ti:/ *noun* deported person.
deportment *noun* bearing, demeanour.
depose /dɪ'pəʊz/ *verb* **(-sing)** remove from office; dethrone; (usually + *to, that*) testify on oath.
deposit /dɪ'pɒzɪt/ ● *noun* money in bank account; thing stored for safe keeping; payment as pledge or first instalment; returnable sum paid on hire of item; layer of accumulated matter. ● *verb* **(-t-)** entrust for keeping; pay or leave as deposit; put or lay down. ◻ **deposit account** bank account that pays interest but is not usually immediately accessible.
depositary /dɪ'pɒzɪtərɪ/ *noun* (*plural* **-ies**) person to whom thing is entrusted.
deposition /depə'zɪʃ(ə)n/ *noun* deposing; sworn evidence; giving of this; depositing.
depositor *noun* person who deposits money, property, etc.
depository /dɪ'pɒzɪtərɪ/ *noun* (*plural* **-ies**) storehouse; store (of wisdom etc.); depositary.
depot /'depəʊ/ *noun* military storehouse or headquarters; place where vehicles, e.g. buses, are kept; goods yard.
deprave /dɪ'preɪv/ *verb* **(-ving)** corrupt morally.
depravity /dɪ'prævɪtɪ/ *noun* (*plural* **-ies**) moral corruption; wickedness.
deprecate /'deprɪkeɪt/ *verb* **(-ting)** express disapproval of. ◻ **deprecation** *noun*; **deprecatory** /-'keɪtərɪ/ *adjective.*

■ **Usage** *Deprecate* is often confused with *depreciate.*

depreciate /dɪ'pri:ʃɪeɪt/ *verb* **(-ting)** diminish in value; belittle. ◻ **depreciatory** /-ʃətərɪ/ *adjective.*

■ **Usage** *Depreciate* is often confused with *deprecate.*

depreciation *noun* depreciating; decline in value.
depredation /deprɪ'deɪʃ(ə)n/ *noun* (usually in *plural*) despoiling, ravaging.
depress /dɪ'pres/ *verb* make dispirited; lower; push down; reduce activity of (esp. trade); (as **depressed** *adjective*) suffering from depression. ◻ **depressing** *adjective*; **depressingly** *adverb.*
depressant ● *adjective* reducing activity, esp. of body function. ● *noun* depressant substance.
depression /dɪ'preʃ(ə)n/ *noun* extreme dejection; long slump; lowering of atmospheric pressure; hollow on a surface.
depressive /dɪ'presɪv/ ● *adjective* tending towards depression; tending to depress. ● *noun* chronically depressed person.
deprivation /deprɪ'veɪʃ(ə)n/ *noun* depriving, being deprived.
deprive /dɪ'praɪv/ *verb* **(-ving)** (usually + *of*) prevent from having or enjoying; (as **deprived** *adjective*) lacking what is needed, underprivileged.
Dept. *abbreviation* Department.
depth *noun* deepness; measure of this; wisdom; intensity; (usually in *plural*) deep, lowest, or inmost part, middle (of winter etc.), abyss, depressed state. ◻ **depth-charge** bomb exploding under water; **in depth** thoroughly.
deputation /depjʊ'teɪʃ(ə)n/ *noun* delegation.
depute /dɪ'pju:t/ *verb* **(-ting)** (often + *to*) delegate (task, authority); authorize as representative.
deputize /'depjʊtaɪz/ *verb* (also **-ise**) **(-zing** or **-sing)** (usually + *for*) act as deputy.
deputy /'depjʊtɪ/ *noun* (*plural* **-ies**) person appointed to act for another; parliamentary representative in some countries.
derail /di:'reɪl/ *verb* cause (train etc.) to leave rails. ◻ **derailment** *noun.*
derange /dɪ'reɪndʒ/ *verb* **(-ging)** (usually as **deranged** *adjective*) make insane. ◻ **derangement** *noun.*

Derby /'dɑ:bɪ/ *noun* (*plural* **-ies**) annual horse race at Epsom; similar race or sporting event.

derelict /'derɪlɪkt/ ● *adjective* dilapidated; abandoned. ● *noun* vagrant; abandoned property.

dereliction /derɪ'lɪkʃ(ə)n/ *noun* (usually + *of*) neglect (of duty etc.).

deride /dɪ'raɪd/ *verb* (**-ding**) mock. □ **derision** /-'rɪʒ-/ *noun*.

de rigueur /də rɪ'gɜ:/ *adjective* required by fashion or etiquette.

derisive /dɪ'raɪsɪv/ *adjective* scoffing, ironical. □ **derisively** *adverb*.

derisory /dɪ'raɪsərɪ/ *adjective* (of sum offered etc.) ridiculously small; derisive.

derivation /derɪ'veɪʃ(ə)n/ *noun* deriving, being derived; origin or formation of word; tracing of this.

derivative /dɪ'rɪvətɪv/ ● *adjective* derived, not original. ● *noun* derived word or thing.

derive /dɪ'raɪv/ *verb* (**-ving**) (usually + *from*) get or trace from a source; (+ *from*) arise from; (usually + *from*) assert origin and formation of (word etc.).

dermatitis /dɜ:mə'taɪtɪs/ *noun* inflammation of skin.

dermatology /dɜ:mə'tɒlədʒɪ/ *noun* study of skin diseases. □ **dermatological** /-tə'lɒdʒ-/ *adjective*; **dermatologist** *noun*.

derogatory /dɪ'rɒgətərɪ/ *adjective* disparaging; insulting.

derrick /'derɪk/ *noun* crane; framework over oil well etc. for drilling machinery.

derris /'derɪs/ *noun* insecticide made from powdered root of tropical plant.

derv *noun* diesel fuel for road vehicles.

dervish /'dɜ:vɪʃ/ *noun* member of Muslim fraternity vowed to poverty and austerity.

DES *abbreviation historical* Department of Education and Science.

descale /di:'skeɪl/ *verb* (**-ling**) remove scale from.

descant /'deskænt/ *noun* harmonizing treble melody above basic hymn tune etc.

descend /dɪ'send/ *verb* come, go, or slope down; sink; (usually + *on*) make sudden attack or visit; (+ *to*) stoop (to unworthy act); be passed on by inheritance. □ **be descended from** have as an ancestor.

descendant /dɪ'send(ə)nt/ *noun* person etc. descended from another.

descent /dɪ'sent/ *noun* act or way of descending; downward slope; lineage; decline, fall; sudden attack.

describe /dɪ'skraɪb/ *verb* (**-bing**) state appearance, characteristics, etc. of; (+ *as*) assert to be; draw or move in (curve etc.).

description /dɪ'skrɪpʃ(ə)n/ *noun* describing, being described; sort, kind.

descriptive /dɪ'skrɪptɪv/ *adjective* describing, esp. vividly.

descry /dɪ'skraɪ/ *verb* (**-ies**, **-ied**) catch sight of; discern.

desecrate /'desɪkreɪt/ *verb* (**-ting**) violate sanctity of. □ **desecration** *noun*; **desecrator** *noun*.

desegregate /di:'segrɪgeɪt/ *verb* (**-ting**) abolish racial segregation in. □ **desegregation** *noun*.

deselect /di:sɪ'lekt/ *verb* reject (esp. sitting MP) in favour of another. □ **deselection** *noun*.

desensitize /di:'sensɪtaɪz/ *verb* (also **-ise**) (**-zing** or **-sing**) reduce or destroy sensitivity of. □ **desensitization** *noun*.

desert[1] /dɪ'zɜ:t/ *verb* leave without intending to return; (esp. as **deserted** *adjective*) forsake, abandon; run away from military service. □ **deserter** *noun Military*; **desertion** *noun*.

desert[2] /'dezət/ *noun* dry barren, esp. sandy, tract. □ **desert island** (usually tropical) uninhabited island.

desertification /dɪzɜ:tɪfɪ'keɪʃ(ə)n/ *noun* making or becoming a desert.

deserts /dɪ'zɜ:ts/ *plural noun* deserved reward or punishment.

deserve /dɪ'zɜ:v/ *verb* (**-ving**) (often + *to do*) be worthy of (reward, punishment); (as **deserving** *adjective*) (often + *of*) worthy (esp. of help, praise, etc.). □ **deservedly** /-vɪdlɪ/ *adverb*.

desiccate /'desɪkeɪt/ *verb* (**-ting**) remove moisture from, dry out. □ **desiccation** *noun*.

desideratum /dɪzɪdə'rɑ:təm/ *noun* (*plural* **-ta**) something lacking but desirable.

design /dɪ'zaɪn/ ● *noun* (art of producing) sketch or plan for product; lines or shapes as decoration; layout; established form of product; mental plan; purpose. ● *verb* produce design for; be designer; intend; (as **designing** *adjective*) crafty, scheming. □ **have designs on** plan to take, seduce, etc.

designate ● *verb* /'dezɪgneɪt/ (**-ting**) (often + *as*) appoint to office or function; specify; (often + *as*) describe as. ● *adjective* /'dezɪgnət/ (after noun) appointed but not yet installed.

designation /dezɪg'neɪʃ(ə)n/ *noun* name or title; designating.

designedly /dɪ'zaɪnɪdlɪ/ *adverb* intentionally.

designer ● *noun* person who designs e.g. clothing, machines, theatre sets; draughtsman. ● *adjective* bearing label of famous fashion designer; prestigious. □ **designer drug** synthetic equivalent of illegal drug.

desirable /dɪ'zaɪərəb(ə)l/ *adjective* worth having or doing; sexually attractive. □ **desirability** *noun*.

desire /dɪ'zaɪə/ ● *noun* unsatisfied longing; expression of this; request; thing desired; sexual appetite. ● *verb* (**-ring**) (often + *to do*, *that*) long for; request.

desirous *adjective* (usually + *of*) desiring, wanting; hoping.

desist /dɪ'zɪst/ *verb* (often + *from*) cease.

desk *noun* piece of furniture with writing surface, and often drawers; counter in hotel, bank, etc.; section of newspaper office.

desktop *noun* working surface of desk; computer for use on ordinary desk. □ **desktop publishing** printing with desktop computer and high-quality printer.

desolate ● *adjective* /'desələt/ left alone; uninhabited; dreary, forlorn. ● *verb* /'desəleɪt/ (**-ting**) depopulate; devastate; (esp. as **desolated** *adjective*) make wretched. □ **desolately** /-lətlɪ/ *adverb*; **desolation** *noun*.

despair /dɪ'speə/ ● *noun* loss or absence of hope; cause of this. ● *verb* (often + *of*) lose all hope.

despatch = DISPATCH.

desperado /despə'rɑ:dəʊ/ *noun* (*plural* **-es** or *US* **-s**) desperate or reckless criminal etc.

desperate /'despərət/ *adjective* reckless from despair; violent and lawless; extremely dangerous or serious; (usually + *for*) needing or desiring very much. □ **desperately** *adverb*; **desperation** *noun*.

despicable /'despɪkəb(ə)l, dɪ'spɪk-/ *adjective* contemptible. □ **despicably** *adverb*.

despise /dɪ'spaɪz/ *verb* (**-sing**) regard as inferior or contemptible.

despite /dɪ'spaɪt/ *preposition* in spite of.

despoil /dɪ'spɔɪl/ *verb* (often + *of*) plunder, rob. □ **despoliation** /-spəʊlɪ-/ *noun*.

despondent /dɪ'spɒnd(ə)nt/ *adjective* in low spirits, dejected. □ **despondence** *noun*; **despondency** *noun*; **despondently** *adverb*.

despot /'despɒt/ *noun* absolute ruler; tyrant. □ **despotic** /-'spɒt-/ *adjective*.

despotism /'despətɪz(ə)m/ *noun* rule by despot.

dessert /dɪ'zɜ:t/ *noun* sweet course of a meal. □ **dessertspoon** medium-sized spoon for dessert, (also **dessertspoonful**) amount held by this.

destabilize /di:'steɪbɪlaɪz/ *verb* (also **-ise**) (**-zing** or **-sing**) make unstable; subvert (esp. foreign government). □ **destabilization** *noun*.

destination /destɪ'neɪʃ(ə)n/ *noun* place to which person or thing is going.

destine /'destɪn/ *verb* (**-ning**) (often + *to*, *for*, *to do*) appoint; preordain; intend. □ **be destined to** be fated to.

destiny /'destɪnɪ/ *noun* (*plural* **-ies**) fate; this as power.

destitute /'destɪtju:t/ *adjective* without food or shelter etc.; (usually + *of*) lacking. □ **destitution** /-'tju:-/ *noun*.

destroy /dɪ'strɔɪ/ *verb* pull or break down; kill; make useless; ruin financially; defeat.

destroyer /dɪ'strɔɪə/ *noun* fast medium-sized warship; person or thing that destroys.

destruct /dɪ'strʌkt/ *verb* destroy or be destroyed deliberately. □ **destructible** *adjective*.

destruction *noun* destroying, being destroyed.

destructive *adjective* destroying or tending to destroy; negatively critical.

desuetude /dɪ'sju:ɪtju:d/ *noun formal* state of disuse.

desultory /'dezəltərɪ/ *adjective* constantly turning from one subject to another; unmethodical.

detach /dɪ'tætʃ/ *verb* (often + *from*) unfasten and remove; send (troops) on separate mission; (as **detached** *adjective*) impartial, unemotional, (of house) standing separate. □ **detachable** *adjective*.

detachment *noun* indifference; impartiality; detaching, being detached; troops etc. detached for special duty.

detail /'di:teɪl/ ● *noun* small separate item or particular; these collectively; minor or intricate decoration; small part of picture etc. shown alone; small military detachment. ● *verb* give particulars of, relate in detail; (as **detailed** *adjective*) containing many details, itemized; assign for special duty. □ **in detail** item by item, minutely.

detain /dɪ'teɪn/ *verb* keep waiting, delay; keep in custody. □ **detainment** *noun*.

detainee /di:teɪ'ni:/ *noun* person kept in custody, esp. for political reasons.

detect /dɪ'tekt/ *verb* discover; perceive. □ **detectable** *adjective*; **detection** *noun*; **detector** *noun*.

detective /dɪ'tektɪv/ *noun* person, usually police officer, investigating crime etc.

détente /deɪ'tɑ̃t/ *noun* relaxing of strained international relations. [French]

detention /dɪ'tenʃ(ə)n/ *noun* detaining, being detained. □ **detention centre** short-term prison for young offenders.

deter /dɪ'tɜ:/ *verb* (**-rr-**) (often + *from*) discourage or prevent, esp. through fear.

detergent /dɪ'tɜ:dʒ(ə)nt/ ● *noun* synthetic cleansing agent used with water. ● *adjective* cleansing.

deteriorate /dɪ'tɪərɪəreɪt/ *verb* (**-ting**) become worse. □ **deterioration** *noun*.

determinant /dɪ'tɜ:mɪnənt/ *noun* decisive factor.

determinate /dɪ'tɜ:mɪnət/ *adjective* limited; of definite scope or nature.

determination /dɪtɜ:mɪ'neɪʃ(ə)n/ *noun* resolute purpose; deciding, determining.

determine /dɪ'tɜ:mɪn/ *verb* (**-ning**) find out precisely; settle, decide; (+ *to do*) resolve; be decisive factor in.

determined *adjective* resolute. □ **be determined** (usually + *to do*) be resolved. □ **determinedly** *adverb*.

determinism /dɪ'tɜ:mɪnɪz(ə)m/ *noun* theory that action is determined by forces independent of will. □ **determinist** *noun & adjective*; **deterministic** /-'nɪs-/ *adjective*.

deterrent /dɪ'terənt/ ● *adjective* deterring. ● *noun* thing that deters (esp. nuclear weapon).

detest /dɪ'test/ *verb* hate, loathe. □ **detestation** /di:tes'teɪʃ(ə)n/ *noun*.

detestable /dɪ'testəb(ə)l/ *adjective* hated, loathed.

dethrone /di:'θrəʊn/ *verb* (**-ning**) remove from throne or high regard. □ **dethronement** *noun*.

detonate /'detəneɪt/ *verb* (**-ting**) set off (explosive charge); be set off. □ **detonation** *noun*.

detonator *noun* device for detonating.

detour /'di:tʊə/ *noun* divergence from usual route; roundabout course.

detoxify /di:'tɒksɪfaɪ/ *verb* (**-ies**, **-ied**) remove poison or harmful substances from. □ **detoxification** *noun*.

detract /dɪ'trækt/ *verb* (+ *from*) diminish. □ **detraction** *noun*.

detractor *noun* person who criticizes unfairly.

detriment /'detrɪmənt/ *noun* damage, harm; cause of this. □ **detrimental** /-'men-/ *adjective*.

detritus /dɪ'traɪtəs/ *noun* gravel, rock, etc. produced by erosion; debris.

de trop /də 'trəʊ/ *adjective* superfluous; in the way. [French]

deuce[1] /dju:s/ *noun* two on dice or cards; *Tennis* score of 40 all.

deuce[2] /dju:s/ *noun* (**the deuce**) (in exclamations) the Devil.

deuterium /dju:'tɪərɪəm/ *noun* stable isotope of hydrogen with mass about twice that of the usual isotope.

Deutschmark /'dɔɪtʃmɑ:k/ *noun* chief monetary unit of Germany.

devalue /di:'vælju:/ *verb* (**-ues**, **-ued**, **-uing**) reduce value of, esp. currency relative to others or to gold. □ **devaluation** *noun*.

devastate /'devəsteɪt/ *verb* (**-ting**) lay waste; cause great destruction to; (often as **devastated** *adjective*) overwhelm with shock or grief. □ **devastation** *noun*.

devastating *adjective* crushingly effective; overwhelming; *colloquial* stunningly beautiful. □ **devastatingly** *adverb*.

develop /dɪ'veləp/ *verb* (**-p-**) make or become fuller, bigger, or more elaborate, etc.; bring or come to active, visible, or mature state; begin to exhibit or suffer from; build on (land); convert (land) to new use; treat (photographic film) to make image visible. □ **developing country** poor or primitive country. □ **developer** *noun*.

development *noun* developing, being developed; stage of growth or advancement; newly developed thing, event, etc.; area of developed land, esp. with buildings. □ **developmental** /-'ment(ə)l/ *adjective*.

deviant /'di:vɪənt/ ● *adjective* deviating from normal, esp. sexual, behaviour. ● *noun* deviant person or thing. □ **deviance** *noun*; **deviancy** *noun* (*plural* **-ies**).

deviate /'di:vɪeɪt/ *verb* (**-ting**) (often + *from*) turn aside; diverge. □ **deviation** *noun*.

device /dɪ'vaɪs/ *noun* thing made or adapted for particular purpose; scheme, trick; heraldic design. □ **leave (person) to his** or **her own devices** leave (person) to do as he or she wishes.

devil /ˈdev(ə)l/ ● *noun* (usually **the Devil**) Satan; supreme spirit of evil; personified evil; mischievously clever person. ● *verb* (**-ll-**; *US* **-l-**) (usually as **devilled** *adjective*) cook with hot spices. ◻ **devil-may-care** cheerful and reckless; **devil's advocate** person who tests proposition by arguing against it.

devilish ● *adjective* of or like a devil; mischievous. ● *adverb colloquial* very. ◻ **devilishly** *adverb*.

devilment *noun* mischief; wild spirits.

devilry /ˈdevəlrɪ/ *noun* (*plural* **-ies**) wickedness; reckless mischief; black magic.

devious /ˈdiːvɪəs/ *adjective* not straightforward, underhand; winding, circuitous. ◻ **deviously** *adverb*; **deviousness** *noun*.

devise /dɪˈvaɪz/ *verb* (**-sing**) plan or invent; *Law* leave (real estate) by will.

devoid /dɪˈvɔɪd/ *adjective* (+ *of*) lacking, free from.

devolution /diːvəˈluːʃ(ə)n/ *noun* delegation of power esp. to local or regional administration. ◻ **devolutionist** *noun & adjective*.

devolve /dɪˈvɒlv/ *verb* (**-ving**) (+ *on*, *upon*, etc.) (of duties etc.) pass or be passed to another; (+ *on*, *to*, *upon*) (of property) descend to.

devote /dɪˈvəʊt/ *verb* (**-ting**) (+ *to*) apply or give over to (particular activity etc.).

devoted *adjective* loving, loyal. ◻ **devotedly** *adverb*.

devotee /devəʊˈtiː/ *noun* (usually + *of*) enthusiast, supporter; pious person.

devotion /dɪˈvəʊʃ(ə)n/ *noun* (usually + *to*) great love or loyalty; worship; (in *plural*) prayers. ◻ **devotional** *adjective*.

devour /dɪˈvaʊə/ *verb* eat voraciously; (of fire etc.) engulf, destroy; take in greedily (with eyes or ears).

devout /dɪˈvaʊt/ *adjective* earnestly religious or sincere. ◻ **devoutly** *adverb*; **devoutness** *noun*.

dew *noun* condensed water vapour forming on cool surfaces at night; similar glistening moisture. ◻ **dewberry** fruit like blackberry; **dew-claw** rudimentary inner toe on some dogs; **dewdrop** drop of dew; **dew point** temperature at which dew forms. ◻ **dewy** *adjective* (**-ier**, **-iest**).

Dewey Decimal system /ˈdjuːɪ/ *noun* system of library classification.

dewlap *noun* fold of loose skin hanging from throat esp. in cattle.

dexter /ˈdekstə/ *adjective* on or of the right-hand side (observer's left) of a heraldic shield etc.

dexterous /ˈdekstrəs/ *adjective* (also **dextrous**) skilful at handling. ◻ **dexterity** /-ˈter-/ *noun*; **dexterously** *adverb*.

dhal /dɑːl/ *noun* (also **dal**) kind of split pulse from India; dish made with this.

dharma /ˈdɑːmə/ *noun* right behaviour; Buddhist truth; Hindu moral law.

dhoti /ˈdəʊtɪ/ *noun* (*plural* **-s**) loincloth worn by male Hindus.

dia. *abbreviation* diameter.

diabetes /daɪəˈbiːtiːz/ *noun* disease in which sugar and starch are not properly absorbed by the body.

diabetic /daɪəˈbetɪk/ ● *adjective* of or having diabetes; for diabetics. ● *noun* diabetic person.

diabolical /daɪəˈbɒlɪk(ə)l/ *adjective* (also **diabolic**) of the Devil; inhumanly cruel or wicked; extremely bad. ◻ **diabolically** *adverb*.

diabolism /daɪˈæbəlɪz(ə)m/ *noun* worship of the Devil; sorcery.

diaconate /daɪˈækənət/ *noun* office of deacon; deacons collectively.

diacritic /daɪəˈkrɪtɪk/ *noun* sign (e.g. accent) indicating sound or value of letter.

diacritical *adjective* distinguishing.

diadem /ˈdaɪədem/ *noun* crown.

diaeresis /daɪˈɪərəsɪs/ *noun* (*plural* **-reses** /-siːz/) (*US* **dieresis**) mark (¨) over vowel to show it is sounded separately.

diagnose /daɪəgˈnəʊz/ *verb* (**-sing**) make diagnosis of.

diagnosis /daɪəgˈnəʊsɪs/ *noun* (*plural* **-noses** /-siːz/) identification of disease or fault from symptoms etc.

diagnostic /daɪəgˈnɒstɪk/ ● *adjective* of or assisting diagnosis. ● *noun* symptom.

diagnostics *noun* (treated as *plural*) programs etc. used to identify faults in computing; (treated as *singular*) science of diagnosing disease.

diagonal /daɪˈægən(ə)l/ ● *adjective* crossing a straight-sided figure from corner to corner, oblique. ● *noun* straight line joining two opposite corners. ◻ **diagonally** *adverb*.

diagram /ˈdaɪəgræm/ *noun* outline drawing, plan, etc. of thing or process. ◻ **diagrammatic** /-grəˈmætɪk/ *adjective*.

dial /ˈdaɪəl/ ● *noun* plate with scale and pointer for measuring; numbered disc on telephone for making connection; face of clock or watch; disc on television etc. for selecting channel etc. ● *verb* (**-ll-**; *US* **-l-**) select (telephone number) with dial. ◻ **dialling tone** sound indicating that telephone caller may dial.

dialect /ˈdaɪəlekt/ *noun* regional form of language (see panel).

dialectic /daɪəˈlektɪk/ *noun* process or situation involving contradictions or conflict of opposites and their resolution; = DIALECTICS.

dialectical *adjective* of dialectic. ◻ **dialectical materialism** Marxist theory that historical events arise from conflicting economic (and therefore social) conditions. ◻ **dialectically** *adverb*.

dialectics *noun* (treated as *singular* or *plural*) art of investigating truth by discussion and logic.

dialogue /ˈdaɪəlɒg/ *noun* (*US* **dialog**) conversation, esp. in a play, novel, etc.; discussion between people of different opinions.

dialysis /daɪˈæləsɪs/ *noun* (*plural* **-lyses** /-siːz/) separation of particles in liquid by differences in their ability to pass through membrane; purification of blood by this technique.

diamanté /dɪəˈmɑ̃teɪ/ *adjective* decorated with synthetic diamonds etc.

Dialect

Everyone speaks a particular dialect: that is, a particular type of English distinguished by its vocabulary and its grammar. Different parts of the world and different groups of people speak different dialects: for example, Australians may say *arvo* while others say *afternoon*, and a London Cockney may say *I done it* while most other people say *I did it*. A dialect is not the same thing as an accent, which is the way a person pronounces words.

See also the panel at STANDARD ENGLISH.

diameter /daɪˈæmɪtə/ *noun* straight line passing through centre of circle or sphere to its edges; transverse measurement.

diametrical /daɪəˈmetrɪk(ə)l/ *adjective* (also **diametric**) of or along diameter; (of opposites) absolute. ▫ **diametrically** *adverb*.

diamond /ˈdaɪəmənd/ *noun* transparent very hard precious stone; rhombus; playing card of suit marked with red rhombuses. ▫ **diamond jubilee, wedding** 60th (or 75th) anniversary of reign or wedding.

diapason /daɪəˈpeɪz(ə)n/ *noun* compass of musical instrument or voice; either of two main organ stops.

diaper /ˈdaɪəpə/ *noun US* baby's nappy.

diaphanous /daɪˈæfənəs/ *adjective* (of fabric etc.) light and almost transparent.

diaphragm /ˈdaɪəfræm/ *noun* muscular partititon between thorax and abdomen in mammals; = DUTCH CAP; vibrating disc in microphone, telephone, loudspeaker, etc.; device for varying aperture of camera lens.

diapositive /daɪəˈpɒsɪtɪv/ *noun* positive photographic transparency.

diarist /ˈdaɪərɪst/ *noun* person famous for keeping diary.

diarrhoea /daɪəˈri:ə/ *noun* (*US* **diarrhea**) condition of excessively loose and frequent bowel movements.

diary /ˈdaɪərɪ/ *noun* (*plural* **-ies**) daily record of events etc.; book for this or for noting future engagements.

Diaspora /daɪˈæspərə/ *noun* dispersion of the Jews; the dispersed Jews.

diatonic /daɪəˈtɒnɪk/ *adjective Music* (of scale etc.) involving only notes of prevailing key.

diatribe /ˈdaɪətraɪb/ *noun* forceful verbal criticism.

diazepam /daɪˈæzɪpæm/ *noun* tranquillizing drug.

dibble /ˈdɪb(ə)l/ ● *noun* (also **dibber** /ˈdɪbə/) tool for making small holes for planting. ● *verb* (**-ling**) plant with dibble.

dice ● *noun* (*plural* same) small cube marked on each face with 1–6 spots, used in games or gambling; game played with dice. ● *verb* (**-cing**) gamble, take risks; cut into small cubes.

dicey /ˈdaɪsɪ/ *adjective* (**dicier**, **diciest**) *slang* risky, unreliable.

dichotomy /daɪˈkɒtəmɪ/ *noun* (*plural* **-ies**) division into two.

dichromatic /daɪkrəʊˈmætɪk/ *adjective* of two colours.

dick[1] *noun colloquial* (esp. in **clever dick**) person.

dick[2] *noun slang* detective.

dickens /ˈdɪkɪnz/ *noun* (**the dickens**) (usually after *how, what, why,* etc.) *colloquial* the Devil.

dicky /ˈdɪkɪ/ ● *noun* (*plural* **-ies**) *colloquial* false shirt-front. ● *adjective* (**-ier**, **-iest**) *slang* unsound. ▫ **dicky bow** *colloquial* bow tie.

dicotyledon /daɪkɒtɪˈli:d(ə)n/ *noun* flowering plant with two cotyledons. ▫ **dicotyledonous** *adjective*.

Dictaphone /ˈdɪktəfəʊn/ *noun proprietary term* machine for recording and playing back dictation for typing.

dictate ● *verb* /dɪkˈteɪt/ (**-ting**) say or read aloud (material to be recorded etc.); state authoritatively; order peremptorily. ● *noun* /ˈdɪkt-/ (usually in *plural*) authoritative requirement of conscience etc. ▫ **dictation** *noun*.

dictator *noun* usually unelected absolute ruler; omnipotent or domineering person. ▫ **dictatorship** *noun*.

dictatorial /dɪktəˈtɔ:rɪəl/ *adjective* of or like a dictator; overbearing. ▫ **dictatorially** *adverb*.

diction /ˈdɪkʃ(ə)n/ *noun* manner of enunciation.

dictionary /ˈdɪkʃənərɪ/ *noun* (*plural* **-ies**) book listing (usually alphabetically) and explaining words of a language, or giving corresponding words in another language; similar book of terms for reference.

dictum /ˈdɪktəm/ *noun* (*plural* **dicta** or **-s**) formal expression of opinion; a saying.

did *past* of DO[1]

didactic /dɪˈdæktɪk/ *adjective* meant to instruct; (of person) tediously pedantic. ▫ **didactically** *adverb*; **didacticism** /-sɪz(ə)m/ *noun*.

diddle /ˈdɪd(ə)l/ *verb* (**-ling**) *colloquial* swindle.

didgeridoo /dɪdʒərɪˈdu:/ *noun* long tubular Australian Aboriginal musical instrument.

didn't /ˈdɪd(ə)nt/ did not.

die[1] /daɪ/ *verb* (**dying** /ˈdaɪɪŋ/) cease to live or exist; fade away; (of fire) go out; (+ *on*) cease to live or function while in the presence or charge of (person); (+ *of, from, with*) be exhausted or tormented. ▫ **be dying for, to** desire greatly; **die down** become less loud or strong; **die hard** (of habits etc.) die reluctantly; **die-hard** conservative or stubborn person; **die off** die one after another; **die out** become extinct, cease to exist.

die[2] /daɪ/ *noun* engraved device for stamping coins etc.; (*plural* **dice**) a dice. ▫ **die-casting** process or product of casting from metal moulds.

dielectric /daɪɪˈlektrɪk/ ● *adjective* not conducting electricity. ● *noun* dielectric substance.

dierisis *US* = DIAERISIS.

diesel /ˈdi:z(ə)l/ *noun* (in full **diesel engine**) internal-combustion engine in which heat produced by compression of air in the cylinder ignites the fuel; vehicle driven by or fuel for diesel engine. ▫ **diesel-electric** driven by electric current from diesel-engined generator; **diesel oil** petroleum fraction used in diesel engines.

diet[1] /ˈdaɪət/ ● *noun* habitual food; prescribed food. ● *verb* (**-t-**) keep to special diet, esp. to slim. ▫ **dietary** *adjective*; **dieter** *noun*.

diet[2] /ˈdaɪət/ *noun* legislative assembly; *historical* congress.

dietetic /daɪəˈtetɪk/ *adjective* of diet and nutrition.

dietetics *plural noun* (usually treated as *singular*) study of diet and nutrition.

dietitian /daɪəˈtɪʃ(ə)n/ *noun* (also **dietician**) expert in dietetics.

differ /ˈdɪfə/ *verb* (often + *from*) be unlike or distinguishable; (often + *with*) disagree.

difference /ˈdɪfrəns/ *noun* being different or unlike; degree of this; way in which things differ; remainder after subtraction; disagreement. ▫ **make a** (or **all the**, **no**, etc.) **difference** have significant (or very significant, no, etc.) effect; **with a difference** having new or unusual feature.

different /ˈdɪfrənt/ *adjective* (often + *from, to*) unlike, of another nature; separate, unusual. ▫ **differently** *adverb*.

■ **Usage** It is safer to use *different from*, but *different to* is common in informal use.

---

differential /dɪfəˈrenʃ(ə)l/ ● *adjective* constituting or relating to specific difference; of, exhibiting, or depending on a difference; *Mathematics* relating to infinitesimal differences. ● *noun* difference, esp. between rates of interest or wage-rates. ▫ **differential calculus** method of calculating rates of change, maximum or minimum values, etc.; **differential gear** gear enabling wheels to revolve at different speeds on corners.

differentiate /dɪfəˈrenʃɪeɪt/ *verb* (**-ting**) constitute difference between or in; distinguish; become different. ▫ **differentiation** *noun*.

difficult /ˈdɪfɪk(ə)lt/ *adjective* hard to do, deal with, or understand; troublesome.

difficulty /ˈdɪfɪkəltɪ/ *noun* (*plural* **-ies**) being difficult; difficult thing; hindrance; (often in *plural*) distress, esp. financial.

diffident /ˈdɪfɪd(ə)nt/ *adjective* lacking self-confidence. ☐ **diffidence** *noun*; **diffidently** *adverb*.

diffract /dɪˈfrækt/ *verb* break up (beam of light) into series of dark and light bands or coloured spectra. ☐ **diffraction** *noun*; **diffractive** *adjective*.

diffuse ● *verb* /dɪˈfjuːz/ (**-sing**) spread widely or thinly; intermingle. ● *adjective* /dɪˈfjuːs/ spread out; not concentrated; not concise. ☐ **diffusible** *adjective*; **diffusive** *adjective*; **diffusion** *noun*.

dig ● *verb* (**-gg-**; *past & past participle* **dug**) (often + *up*) break up and turn over (ground etc.); make (hole etc.) by digging; (+ *up, out*) obtain by digging, find, discover; excavate; *slang* like, understand; (+ *in, into*) thrust, prod. ● *noun* piece of digging; thrust, poke; *colloquial* pointed remark; archaeological excavation; (in *plural*) lodgings. ☐ **dig in** *colloquial* begin eating; **dig oneself in** prepare defensive position.

digest ● *verb* /daɪˈdʒest/ assimilate (food, information, etc.). ● *noun* /ˈdaɪdʒest/ periodical synopsis of current news etc.; summary, esp. of laws. ☐ **digestible** *adjective*.

digestion *noun* digesting; capacity to digest food.

digestive ● *adjective* of or aiding digestion. ● *noun* (in full **digestive biscuit**) wholemeal biscuit.

digger /ˈdɪgə/ *noun* person or machine that digs; *colloquial* Australian, New Zealander.

digit /ˈdɪdʒɪt/ *noun* any numeral from 0 to 9; finger or toe.

digital /ˈdɪdʒɪt(ə)l/ *adjective* of digits; (of clock, etc.) giving a reading by displayed digits; (of computer) operating on data represented by digits; (of recording) sound-information represented by digits for more reliable transmission. ☐ **digitally** *adverb*.

digitalis /dɪdʒɪˈteɪlɪs/ *noun* heart stimulant made from foxgloves.

digitize *verb* (also **ise**) (**-zing** or **-sing**) convert (computer data etc.) into digital form.

dignified /ˈdɪgnɪfaɪd/ *adjective* having or showing dignity.

dignify /ˈdɪgnɪfaɪ/ *verb* (**ies**, **-ied**) give dignity to.

dignitary /ˈdɪgnɪtərɪ/ *noun* (*plural* **-ies**) person of high rank or office.

dignity /ˈdɪgnɪtɪ/ *noun* (*plural* **-ies**) composed and serious manner; being worthy of respect; high rank or position.

digraph /ˈdaɪgrɑːf/ *noun* two letters representing one sound, e.g. *sh* in *show*, or *ey* in *key*.

■ **Usage** *Digraph* is sometimes confused with *ligature*, which means 'two or more letters joined'.

digress /daɪˈgres/ *verb* depart from main subject. ☐ **digression** *noun*.

dike = DYKE.

dilapidated /dɪˈlæpɪdeɪtɪd/ *adjective* in disrepair. ☐ **dilapidation** *noun*.

dilate /daɪˈleɪt/ *verb* (**-ting**) widen or expand; speak or write at length. ☐ **dilatation** *noun*; **dilation** *noun*.

dilatory /ˈdɪlətərɪ/ *adjective* given to or causing delay.

dilemma /daɪˈlemə/ *noun* situation in which difficult choice has to be made.

■ **Usage** *Dilemma* is sometimes also used to mean 'a difficult situation or predicament', but this is considered incorrect by some people.

dilettante /dɪlɪˈtæntɪ/ *noun* (*plural* **dilettanti** /-tɪ/ or **-s**) dabbler in a subject. ☐ **dilettantism** *noun*.

diligent /ˈdɪlɪdʒ(ə)nt/ *adjective* hard-working; showing care and effort. ☐ **diligence** *noun*; **diligently** *adverb*.

dill *noun* herb with aromatic leaves and seeds.

dilly-dally /dɪlɪˈdælɪ/ *verb* (**-ies**, **-ied**) *colloquial* dawdle, vacillate.

dilute /daɪˈljuːt/ ● *verb* (**-ting**) reduce strength (of fluid) by adding water etc.; weaken in effect. ● *adjective* diluted. ☐ **dilution** *noun*.

diluvial /daɪˈluːvɪəl/ *adjective* of flood, esp. Flood in Genesis.

dim ● *adjective* (**-mm-**) not bright; faintly luminous or visible; indistinctly perceived or remembered; (of eyes) not seeing clearly; *colloquial* stupid. ● *verb* (**-mm-**) make or become dim. ☐ **dimly** *adverb*; **dimness** *noun*.

dime *noun US* 10-cent coin.

dimension /daɪˈmenʃ(ə)n/ *noun* any measurable extent; (in *plural*) size; aspect. ☐ **dimensional** *adjective*.

diminish /dɪˈmɪnɪʃ/ *verb* make or become smaller or less; (often as **diminished** *adjective*) lessen reputation of (person), humiliate.

diminuendo /dɪmɪnjʊˈendəʊ/ *Music* ● *noun* (*plural* **-s**) gradual decrease in loudness. ● *adverb & adjective* decreasing in loudness.

diminution /dɪmɪˈnjuːʃ(ə)n/ *noun* diminishing.

diminutive /dɪˈmɪnjʊtɪv/ ● *adjective* tiny; (of word or suffix) implying smallness or affection. ● *noun* diminutive word or suffix.

dimmer *noun* (in full **dimmer switch**) device for varying brightness of electric light.

dimple /ˈdɪmp(ə)l/ ● *noun* small hollow, esp. in cheek or chin. ● *verb* (**-ling**) produce dimples (in).

din ● *noun* prolonged loud confused noise. ● *verb* (**-nn-**) (+ *into*) force (information) into person by repetition; make din.

dinar /ˈdiːnɑː/ *noun* chief monetary unit of (former) Yugoslavia and several Middle Eastern and N. African countries.

dine *verb* (**-ning**) eat dinner; (+ *on, upon*) eat for dinner; (esp. in **wine and dine**) entertain with food. ☐ **dining-car** restaurant on train; **dining-room** room in which meals are eaten.

diner *noun* person who dines; small dining-room; dining-car; *US* restaurant.

ding-dong /ˈdɪŋdɒŋ/ *noun* sound of chimes; *colloquial* heated argument.

dinghy /ˈdɪŋgɪ/ *noun* (*plural* **-ies**) small, often inflatable, boat.

dingle /ˈdɪŋg(ə)l/ *noun* deep wooded valley.

dingo /ˈdɪŋgəʊ/ *noun* (*plural* **-es**) wild Australian dog.

dingy /ˈdɪndʒɪ/ *adjective* (**-ier**, **-iest**) drab; dirty-looking. ☐ **dinginess** *noun*.

dinkum /ˈdɪŋkəm/ *adjective & adverb* (in full **fair dinkum**) *Australian & NZ colloquial* genuine(ly), honest(ly).

dinky /ˈdɪŋkɪ/ *adjective* (**-ier**, **-iest**) *colloquial* pretty, small and neat.

dinner /ˈdɪnə/ *noun* main meal, at midday or in the evening. ☐ **dinner-dance** formal dinner followed by dancing; **dinner jacket** man's formal evening jacket; **dinner lady** woman who supervises school dinners; **dinner service** set of matching crockery for dinner.

dinosaur /ˈdaɪnəsɔː/ *noun* extinct usually large reptile.

dint ● *noun* dent. ● *verb* mark with dints. ☐ **by dint of** by force or means of.

diocese /ˈdaɪəsɪs/ *noun* district under bishop's pastoral care. ☐ **diocesan** /daɪˈɒsɪs(ə)n/ *adjective*.

diode /ˈdaɪəʊd/ *noun* semiconductor allowing current in one direction and having two terminals; thermionic valve with two electrodes.

dioxide /daɪˈɒksaɪd/ *noun* oxide with two atoms of oxygen.

Dip. *abbreviation* Diploma.

dip ● *verb* (**-pp-**) put or lower briefly into liquid etc.; immerse; go below a surface or level; decline slightly or briefly; slope or extend downwards; go briefly under water; (+ *into*) look cursorily into (book, subject, etc.); (+ *into*) put (hand etc.) into (container) to take something out, use part of (resources); lower or be lowered, esp. in salute; lower beam of (headlights). ● *noun* dipping, being dipped; liquid for dipping; brief bathe in sea etc.; downward slope or hollow; sauce into which food is dipped. □ **dip-switch** switch for dipping vehicle's headlights.

diphtheria /dɪf'θɪərɪə/ *noun* infectious disease with inflammation of mucous membrane esp. of throat.

diphthong /'dɪfθɒŋ/ *noun* union of two vowels in one syllable.

diplodocus /dɪ'plɒdəkəs/ *noun* (*plural* **-cuses**) huge long-necked plant-eating dinosaur.

diploma /dɪ'pləʊmə/ *noun* certificate of educational qualification; document conferring honour, privilege, etc.

diplomacy /dɪ'pləʊməsɪ/ *noun* management of international relations; tact.

diplomat /'dɪpləmæt/ *noun* member of diplomatic service; tactful person.

diplomatic /dɪplə'mætɪk/ *adjective* of or involved in diplomacy; tactful. □ **diplomatic bag** container for dispatching embassy mail; **diplomatic immunity** exemption of foreign diplomatic staff from arrest, taxation, etc.; **diplomatic service** branch of civil service concerned with representing a country abroad. □ **diplomatically** *adverb*.

diplomatist /dɪ'pləʊmətɪst/ *noun* diplomat.

dipper /'dɪpə/ *noun* diving bird; ladle.

dippy /'dɪpɪ/ *adjective* (**-ier**, **-iest**) *slang* crazy, silly.

dipsomania /dɪpsə'meɪnɪə/ *noun* alcoholism. □ **dipsomaniac** *noun*.

dipstick *noun* rod for measuring depth, esp. of oil in vehicle's engine.

dipterous /'dɪptərəs/ *adjective* two-winged.

diptych /'dɪptɪk/ *noun* painted altarpiece on two hinged panels.

dire *adjective* dreadful; ominous; *colloquial* very bad; urgent.

direct /daɪ'rekt/ ● *adjective* extending or moving in straight line or by shortest route, not crooked or circuitous; straightforward, frank; without intermediaries; complete, greatest possible. ● *adverb* in a direct way; by direct route. ● *verb* control; guide; (+ *to do*, *that*) order; (+ *to*) tell way to (place); address (letter etc.); (+ *at*, *to*, *towards*) point, aim, or turn; supervise acting etc. of (film, play, etc.). □ **direct current** electric current flowing in one direction only; **direct debit** regular debiting of bank account at request of payee; **direct-grant school** school funded by government, not local authority; **direct object** primary object of verbal action (see panel at OBJECT); **direct speech** words actually spoken, not reported (see panel); **direct tax** tax on income, paid directly to government. □ **directness** *noun*.

direction /daɪ'rekʃ(ə)n/ *noun* directing; (usually in *plural*) orders, instructions; point to, from, or along which person or thing moves or looks.

directional *adjective* of or indicating direction; sending or receiving radio or sound waves in one direction only.

directive /daɪ'rektɪv/ *noun* order from an authority.

directly ● *adverb* at once, without delay; presently, shortly; exactly; in a direct way. ● *conjunction colloquial* as soon as.

director *noun* person who directs, esp. for stage etc. or as member of board of company. □ **director-general** chief executive. □ **directorial** /-'tɔː-/ *adjective*; **directorship** *noun*.

directorate /daɪ'rektərət/ *noun* board of directors; office of director.

directory /daɪ'rektərɪ/ *noun* (*plural* **-ies**) book with list of telephone subscribers, inhabitants of town etc., members of profession, etc. □ **directory enquiries** telephone service providing subscriber's number on request.

dirge *noun* lament for the dead; dreary piece of music.

dirham /'dɪrəm/ *noun* monetary unit of Morocco and United Arab Emirates.

dirigible /'dɪrɪdʒɪb(ə)l/ ● *adjective* that can be steered. ● *noun* dirigible balloon or airship.

dirk *noun* short dagger.

dirndl /'dɜːnd(ə)l/ *noun* dress with close-fitting bodice and full skirt; gathered full skirt with tight waistband.

dirt *noun* unclean matter that soils; earth; foul or malicious talk; excrement. □ **dirt cheap** *colloquial* extremely cheap; **dirt track** racing track with surface of earth or cinders etc.

dirty /'dɜːtɪ/ ● *adjective* (**-ier**, **-iest**) soiled, unclean; sordid, obscene; unfair; (of weather) rough; muddy-looking. ● *adverb slang* very; in a dirty or obscene way. ● *verb* (**-ies**, **-ied**) make or become dirty. □ **dirty look** *colloquial* look of disapproval or disgust. □ **dirtiness** *noun*.

Direct Speech

Direct speech is the actual words of a speaker quoted in writing.

1 In a novel etc., speech punctuation is used for direct speech:

- **a** The words spoken are usually put in quotation marks.
- **b** Each new piece of speech begins with a capital letter.
- **c** Each paragraph within one person's piece of speech begins with quotation marks, but only the last paragraph ends with them.

2 In a script (the written words of a play, a film, or a radio or television programme):

- **a** The names of speakers are written in the margin in capital letters.
- **b** Each name is followed by a colon.
- **c** Quotation marks are not needed.
- **d** Any instructions about the way the words are spoken or about the scenery or the actions of the speakers (stage directions) are written in the present tense in brackets or italics.

For example:

CHRISTOPHER: [Looks into box.] There's nothing in here.

disability /dɪsəˈbɪlɪtɪ/ *noun* (*plural* **-ies**) permanent physical or mental incapacity; lack of some capacity, preventing action.

disable /dɪˈseɪb(ə)l/ *verb* (**-ling**) deprive of an ability; (often as **disabled** *adjective*) physically incapacitate. ▫ **disablement** *noun*.

disabuse /dɪsəˈbju:z/ *verb* (**-sing**) (usually + *of*) free from mistaken idea; disillusion.

disadvantage /dɪsədˈvɑ:ntɪdʒ/ ● *noun* unfavourable condition or circumstance; loss; damage. ● *verb* (**-ging**) cause disadvantage to. ▫ **at a disadvantage** in an unfavourable position. ▫ **disadvantageous** /dɪsædvənˈteɪdʒəs/ *adjective*.

disadvantaged *adjective* lacking normal opportunities through poverty, disability, etc.

disaffected /dɪsəˈfektɪd/ *adjective* discontented, alienated (esp. politically). ▫ **disaffection** *noun*.

disagree /dɪsəˈgri:/ *verb* (**-ees, -eed**) (often + *with*) hold different opinion; not correspond; upset. ▫ **disagreement** *noun*.

disagreeable *adjective* unpleasant; bad-tempered. ▫ **disagreeably** *adverb*.

disallow /dɪsəˈlaʊ/ *verb* refuse to allow or accept; prohibit.

disappear /dɪsəˈpɪə/ *verb* cease to be visible or in existence or circulation etc.; go missing. ▫ **disappearance** *noun*.

disappoint /dɪsəˈpɔɪnt/ *verb* fail to fulfil desire or expectation of; frustrate. ▫ **disappointing** *adjective*; **disappointment** *noun*.

disapprobation /dɪsæprəˈbeɪʃ(ə)n/ *noun* disapproval.

disapprove /dɪsəˈpru:v/ *verb* (**-ving**) (usually + *of*) have or express unfavourable opinion. ▫ **disapproval** *noun*.

disarm /dɪˈsɑ:m/ *verb* deprive of weapons; abandon or reduce one's own weapons; (often as **disarming** *adjective*) make less hostile, charm, win over. ▫ **disarmament** *noun*; **disarmingly** *adverb*.

disarrange /dɪsəˈreɪndʒ/ *verb* (**-ging**) put into disorder.

disarray /dɪsəˈreɪ/ *noun* disorder.

disassociate /dɪsəˈsəʊʃɪeɪt/ *verb* (**-ting**) dissociate. ▫ **disassociation** *noun*.

disaster /dɪˈzɑ:stə/ *noun* sudden or great misfortune; *colloquial* complete failure. ▫ **disastrous** *adjective*; **disastrously** *adverb*.

disavow /dɪsəˈvaʊ/ *verb* disclaim knowledge or approval of or responsibility for. ▫ **disavowal** *noun*.

disband /dɪsˈbænd/ *verb* break up, disperse.

disbar /dɪsˈbɑ:/ *verb* (**-rr-**) deprive of status of barrister. ▫ **disbarment** *noun*.

disbelieve /dɪsbɪˈli:v/ *verb* (**-ving**) refuse to believe; not believe; be sceptical. ▫ **disbelief** *noun*; **disbelievingly** *adverb*.

disburse /dɪsˈbɜ:s/ *verb* (**-sing**) pay out (money). ▫ **disbursement** *noun*.

disc *noun* flat thinnish circular object; round flat or apparently flat surface or mark; layer of cartilage between vertebrae; gramophone record; *Computing* = DISK. ▫ **disc brake** one using friction of pads against a disc; **disc jockey** presenter of recorded popular music.

discard /dɪsˈkɑ:d/ *verb* reject as unwanted; remove or put aside.

discern /dɪˈsɜ:n/ *verb* perceive clearly with mind or senses; make out. ▫ **discernible** *adjective*.

discerning *adjective* having good judgement or insight. ▫ **discernment** *noun*.

discharge ● *verb* /dɪsˈtʃɑ:dʒ/ (**-ging**) release, let go; dismiss from office or employment; fire (gun etc.); throw; eject; emit, pour out; pay or perform (debt, duty); relieve (bankrupt) of residual liability; release an electrical charge from; relieve of cargo; unload. ● *noun* /ˈdɪstʃɑ:dʒ/ discharging, being discharged; matter or thing discharged; release of electric charge, esp. with spark.

disciple /dɪˈsaɪp(ə)l/ *noun* follower of a teacher or leader, esp. of Christ.

disciplinarian /dɪsɪplɪˈneərɪən/ *noun* enforcer of or believer in strict discipline.

disciplinary /dɪsɪˈplɪnərɪ/ *adjective* of or enforcing discipline.

discipline /ˈdɪsɪplɪn/ ● *noun* control or order exercised over people or animals; system of rules for this; training or way of life aimed at self-control or conformity; branch of learning; punishment. ● *verb* (**-ning**) punish; control by training in obedience.

disclaim /dɪsˈkleɪm/ *verb* disown, deny; renounce legal claim to.

disclaimer *noun* statement disclaiming something.

disclose /dɪsˈkləʊz/ *verb* (**-sing**) expose, make known, reveal. ▫ **disclosure** *noun*.

disco /ˈdɪskəʊ/ *noun* (*plural* **-s**) *colloquial* discothèque.

discolour /dɪsˈkʌlə/ *verb* (*US* **discolor**) cause to change from its usual colour; stain or become stained. ▫ **discoloration** *noun*.

discomfit /dɪsˈkʌmfɪt/ *verb* (**-t-**) disconcert; baffle; frustrate. ▫ **discomfiture** *noun*.

■ **Usage** *Discomfit* is sometimes confused with *discomfort*.

discomfort /dɪsˈkʌmfət/ *noun* lack of comfort; uneasiness of body or mind.

■ **Usage** As a verb, *discomfort* is sometimes confused with *discomfit*.

discompose /dɪskəmˈpəʊz/ *verb* (**-sing**) disturb composure of. ▫ **discomposure** *noun*.

disconcert /dɪskənˈsɜ:t/ *verb* disturb composure of; fluster.

disconnect /dɪskəˈnekt/ *verb* break connection of or between; put (apparatus) out of action by disconnecting parts. ▫ **disconnection** *noun*.

disconnected *adjective* incoherent and illogical.

disconsolate /dɪsˈkɒnsələt/ *adjective* forlorn, unhappy; disappointed. ▫ **disconsolately** *adverb*.

discontent /dɪskənˈtent/ ● *noun* dissatisfaction; lack of contentment. ● *verb* (esp. as **discontented** *adjective*) make dissatisfied.

discontinue /dɪskənˈtɪnju:/ *verb* (**-ues, -ued, -uing**) (cause to) cease; not go on with (activity).

discontinuous /dɪskənˈtɪnjʊəs/ *adjective* lacking continuity; intermittent. ▫ **discontinuity** /-kɒntɪˈnju:ɪtɪ/ *noun*.

discord /ˈdɪskɔ:d/ *noun* disagreement, strife; harsh noise, clashing sounds; lack of harmony. ▫ **discordant** /-ˈkɔ:dənt/ *adjective*.

discothèque /ˈdɪskətek/ *noun* nightclub etc. where pop records are played for dancing.

discount ● *noun* /ˈdɪskaʊnt/ amount deducted from normal price. ● *verb* /dɪsˈkaʊnt/ disregard as unreliable or unimportant; deduct amount from (price etc.); give or get present value of (investment certificate which has yet to mature). ▫ **at a discount** below nominal or usual price.

discountenance /dɪsˈkaʊntɪnəns/ *verb* (**-cing**) disconcert; refuse to approve of.

discourage /dɪsˈkʌrɪdʒ/ *verb* (**-ging**) reduce confidence or spirits of; dissuade, deter; show disapproval of. ▫ **discouragement** *noun*.

discourse ● *noun* /ˈdɪskɔːs/ conversation; lengthy treatment of theme; lecture, speech. ● *verb* /dɪsˈkɔːs/ (**-sing**) converse; speak or write at length.

discourteous /dɪsˈkɜːtɪəs/ *adjective* rude, uncivil. ▫ **discourteously** *adverb*; **discourtesy** *noun* (*plural* **-ies**).

discover /dɪˈskʌvə/ *verb* find or find out, by effort or chance; be first to find or find out in particular case; find and promote (little-known performer).

discovery *noun* (*plural* **-ies**) discovering, being discovered; person or thing discovered.

discredit /dɪsˈkredɪt/ ● *verb* (**-t-**) cause to be disbelieved; harm good reputation of; refuse to believe. ● *noun* harm to reputation; cause of this; lack of credibility.

discreditable *adjective* bringing discredit, shameful.

discreet /dɪˈskriːt/ *adjective* (**-er**, **-est**) tactful, prudent; cautious in speech or action; unobtrusive. ▫ **discreetly** *adverb*; **discreetness** *noun*.

discrepancy /dɪˈskrepənsɪ/ *noun* (*plural* **-ies**) difference; inconsistency.

discrete /dɪˈskriːt/ *adjective* separate; distinct.

discretion /dɪˈskreʃ(ə)n/ *noun* being discreet; prudence, judgement; freedom or authority to act as one thinks fit. ▫ **discretionary** *adjective*.

discriminate /dɪˈskrɪmɪneɪt/ *verb* (**-ting**) (often + *between*) make or see a distinction; (usually + *against*, *in favour of*) treat badly or well, esp. on the basis of race, gender, etc. ▫ **discriminating** *adjective*; **discrimination** *noun*; **discriminatory** /-nətərɪ/ *adjective*.

discursive /dɪsˈkɜːsɪv/ *adjective* rambling, tending to digress.

discus /ˈdɪskəs/ *noun* (*plural* **-cuses**) heavy disc thrown in athletic events.

discuss /dɪsˈkʌs/ *verb* talk about; talk or write about (subject) in detail. ▫ **discussion** *noun*.

disdain /dɪsˈdeɪn/ ● *noun* scorn, contempt. ● *verb* regard with disdain; refrain or refuse out of disdain. ▫ **disdainful** *adjective*.

disease /dɪˈziːz/ *noun* unhealthy condition of organism or part of organism; (specific) disorder or illness. ▫ **diseased** *adjective*.

disembark /dɪsɪmˈbɑːk/ *verb* put or go ashore; get off aircraft, bus, etc. ▫ **disembarkation** /-embɑː-/ *noun*.

disembarrass /dɪsɪmˈbærəs/ *verb* (usually + *of*) rid or relieve (of a load etc.); free from embarrassment. ▫ **disembarrassment** *noun*.

disembodied /dɪsɪmˈbɒdɪd/ *adjective* (of soul etc.) separated from body or concrete form; without a body.

disembowel /dɪsɪmˈbaʊəl/ *verb* (**-ll-**; *US* **-l-**) remove entrails of. ▫ **disembowelment** *noun*.

disenchant /dɪsɪnˈtʃɑːnt/ *verb* disillusion. ▫ **disenchantment** *noun*.

disencumber /dɪsɪnˈkʌmbə/ *verb* free from encumbrance.

disenfranchise /dɪsɪnˈfræntʃaɪz/ *verb* (**-sing**) deprive of right to vote, of citizen's rights, or of franchise held. ▫ **disenfranchisement** *noun*.

disengage /dɪsɪnˈgeɪdʒ/ *verb* (**-ging**) detach; loosen; release; remove (troops) from battle etc.; become detached; (as **disengaged** *adjective*) at leisure, uncommitted. ▫ **disengagement** *noun*.

disentangle /dɪsɪnˈtæŋg(ə)l/ *verb* (**-ling**) free or become free of tangles or complications. ▫ **disentanglement** *noun*.

disestablish /dɪsɪˈstæblɪʃ/ *verb* deprive (Church) of state support; end the establishment of. ▫ **disestablishment** *noun*.

disfavour /dɪsˈfeɪvə/ *noun* (*US* **disfavor**) dislike; disapproval; being disliked.

disfigure /dɪsˈfɪgə/ *verb* (**-ring**) spoil appearance of. ▫ **disfigurement** *noun*.

disgorge /dɪsˈgɔːdʒ/ *verb* (**-ging**) eject from throat; pour forth (food, fluid, etc.).

disgrace /dɪsˈgreɪs/ ● *noun* shame, ignominy; shameful or very bad person or thing. ● *verb* (**-cing**) bring shame or discredit on; dismiss from position of honour or favour.

disgraceful *adjective* causing disgrace; shameful. ▫ **disgracefully** *adverb*.

disgruntled /dɪsˈgrʌnt(ə)ld/ *adjective* discontented; sulky.

disguise /dɪsˈgaɪz/ ● *verb* (**-sing**) conceal identity of, make unrecognizable; conceal. ● *noun* costume, make-up, etc. used to disguise; action, manner, etc. used to deceive; disguised condition.

disgust /dɪsˈgʌst/ ● *noun* strong aversion; repugnance. ● *verb* cause disgust in. ▫ **disgusting** *adjective*; **disgustingly** *adverb*.

dish ● *noun* shallow flat-bottomed container for food; food served in dish; particular kind of food; (in *plural*) crockery etc. to be washed etc. after a meal; dish-shaped object or cavity; *colloquial* sexually attractive person. ● *verb* make dish-shaped; *colloquial* outmanoeuvre, frustrate. ▫ **dish out** *colloquial* distribute, allocate; **dish up** (prepare to) serve meal.

disharmony /dɪsˈhɑːmənɪ/ *noun* lack of harmony, discord.

dishearten /dɪsˈhɑːt(ə)n/ *verb* cause to lose courage or confidence.

dishevelled /dɪˈʃev(ə)ld/ *adjective* (*US* **disheveled**) ruffled, untidy.

dishonest /dɪˈsɒnɪst/ *adjective* fraudulent; insincere. ▫ **dishonestly** *adverb*; **dishonesty** *noun*.

dishonour /dɪˈsɒnə/ (*US* **dishonor**) ● *noun* loss of honour, disgrace; cause of this. ● *verb* disgrace (person, family, etc.); refuse to pay (cheque etc.).

dishonourable *adjective* (*US* **dishonorable**) causing disgrace; ignominious; unprincipled. ▫ **dishonourably** *adverb*.

dishy *adjective* (**-ier**, **-iest**) *colloquial* sexually attractive.

disillusion /dɪsɪˈluːʒ(ə)n/ ● *verb* free from illusion or mistaken belief, esp. disappointingly. ● *noun* disillusioned state. ▫ **disillusionment** *noun*.

disincentive /dɪsɪnˈsentɪv/ *noun* thing that discourages, esp. from a particular line of action.

disincline /dɪsɪnˈklaɪn/ *verb* (**-ning**) (usually as **disinclined** *adjective*) make unwilling. ▫ **disinclination** /-klɪˈneɪ-/ *noun*.

disinfect /dɪsɪnˈfekt/ *verb* cleanse of infection. ▫ **disinfection** *noun*.

disinfectant ● *noun* substance that destroys germs etc. ● *adjective* disinfecting.

disinformation /dɪsɪnfəˈmeɪʃ(ə)n/ *noun* false information, propaganda.

disingenuous /dɪsɪnˈdʒenjʊəs/ *adjective* insincere; not candid. ▫ **disingenuously** *adverb*; **disingenuousness** *noun*.

disinherit /dɪsɪnˈherɪt/ *verb* (**-t-**) deprive of right to inherit; reject as one's heir. ▫ **disinheritance** *noun*.

disintegrate /dɪˈsɪntɪgreɪt/ *verb* (**-ting**) separate into component parts; break up; *colloquial* break down, esp. mentally. ▫ **disintegration** *noun*.

disinter /dɪsɪnˈtɜː/ *verb* (**-rr-**) dig up (esp. corpse). ▫ **disinterment** *noun*.

disinterested /dɪˈsɪntrɪstɪd/ *adjective* impartial; uninterested. ▫ **disinterest** *noun*; **disinterestedly** *adverb*.

■ **Usage** The use of *disinterested* to mean 'uninterested' is common in informal use but is widely considered incorrect. The use of the noun *disinterest* to mean 'lack of interest' is also objected to, but it is rarely used in any other sense and the alternative *uninterest* is rare.

disjointed /dɪs'dʒɔɪntɪd/ *adjective* disconnected, incoherent.

disjunction /dɪs'dʒʌŋkʃ(ə)n/ *noun* separation.

disjunctive /dɪs'dʒʌŋktɪv/ *adjective* involving separation; (of a conjunction) expressing alternative.

disk *noun* flat circular computer storage device. □ **disk drive** mechanism for rotating disk and reading or writing data from or to it.

dislike /dɪs'laɪk/ ● *verb* (**-king**) have aversion to, not like. ● *noun* feeling of repugnance or not liking; object of this.

dislocate /'dɪsləkeɪt/ *verb* (**-ting**) disturb normal connection of (esp. a joint in the body); disrupt. □ **dislocation** *noun*.

dislodge /dɪs'lɒdʒ/ *verb* (**-ging**) disturb or move. □ **dislodgement** *noun*.

disloyal /dɪs'lɔɪəl/ *adjective* unfaithful; lacking loyalty. □ **disloyalty** *noun*.

dismal /'dɪzm(ə)l/ *adjective* gloomy; miserable; dreary; *colloquial* feeble, inept. □ **dismally** *adverb*.

dismantle /dɪs'mænt(ə)l/ *verb* (**-ling**) pull down, take to pieces; deprive of defences, equipment, etc.

dismay /dɪs'meɪ/ ● *noun* feeling of intense disappointment and discouragement. ● *verb* affect with dismay.

dismember /dɪs'membə/ *verb* remove limbs from; partition (country etc.). □ **dismemberment** *noun*.

dismiss /dɪs'mɪs/ *verb* send away; disband; allow to go; terminate employment of, esp. dishonourably; put out of one's thoughts; *Law* refuse further hearing to; *Cricket* put (batsman, side) out. □ **dismissal** *noun*.

dismissive *adjective* dismissing rudely or casually; disdainful. □ **dismissively** *adverb*.

dismount /dɪs'maʊnt/ *verb* get off or down from cycle or horseback etc.; remove (thing) from mounting.

disobedient /dɪsə'bi:dɪənt/ *adjective* disobeying; rebellious. □ **disobedience** *noun*; **disobediently** *adverb*.

disobey /dɪsə'beɪ/ *verb* fail or refuse to obey.

disoblige /dɪsə'blaɪdʒ/ *verb* (**-ging**) refuse to help or cooperate with (person).

disorder /dɪ'sɔ:də/ *noun* confusion; tumult, riot; bodily or mental ailment. □ **disordered** *adjective*.

disorderly *adjective* untidy; confused; riotous.

disorganize /dɪs'ɔ:gənaɪz/ *verb* (also **-ise**) (**-zing** or **-sing**) throw into confusion or disorder; (as **disorganized** *adjective*) badly organized, untidy. □ **disorganization** *noun*.

disorientate /dɪs'ɔ:rɪənteɪt/ *verb* (also **disorient**) (**-ting**) confuse (person) as to his or her bearings. □ **disorientation** *noun*.

disown /dɪs'əʊn/ *verb* deny or give up any connection with; repudiate.

disparage /dɪ'spærɪdʒ/ *verb* (**-ging**) criticize; belittle. □ **disparagement** *noun*.

disparate /'dɪspərət/ *adjective* essentially different, unrelated.

disparity /dɪ'spærɪtɪ/ *noun* (*plural* **-ies**) inequality, difference; incongruity.

dispassionate /dɪ'spæʃənət/ *adjective* free from emotion; impartial. □ **dispassionately** *adverb*.

dispatch /dɪs'pætʃ/ (also **despatch**) ● *verb* send off; perform (task etc.) promptly; kill; *colloquial* eat (food) quickly. ● *noun* dispatching, being dispatched; official written message, esp. military or political; promptness, efficiency. □ **dispatch box** case for esp. parliamentary documents; **dispatch rider** motorcyclist etc. carrying messages.

dispel /dɪ'spel/ *verb* (**-ll-**) drive away (esp. unwanted ideas or feelings); scatter.

dispensable /dɪ'spensəb(ə)l/ *adjective* that can be dispensed with.

dispensary /dɪ'spensərɪ/ *noun* (*plural* **-ies**) place where medicines etc. are dispensed.

dispensation /dɪspen'seɪʃ(ə)n/ *noun* distributing, dispensing; exemption from penalty, rule, etc.; ordering or management, esp. of world by Providence.

dispense /dɪ'spens/ *verb* (**-sing**) distribute; administer; make up and give out (medicine); (+ *with*) do without, make unnecessary.

dispenser *noun* person who dispenses something; device that dispenses selected amount at a time.

disperse /dɪ'spɜ:s/ *verb* (**-sing**) go or send widely or in different directions, scatter; station at different points; disseminate; separate (light) into coloured constituents. □ **dispersal** *noun*; **dispersion** *noun*.

dispirit /dɪ'spɪrɪt/ *verb* (esp. as **dispiriting, dispirited** *adjectives*) make despondent.

displace /dɪs'pleɪs/ *verb* (**-cing**) move from its place; remove from office; oust, take the place of. □ **displaced person** refugee in war etc. or from persecution.

displacement *noun* displacing, being displaced; amount of fluid displaced by object floating or immersed in it.

display /dɪ'spleɪ/ ● *verb* show; exhibit. ● *noun* displaying; exhibition; ostentation; image shown on a visual display unit etc.

displease /dɪs'pli:z/ *verb* (**-sing**) offend; make angry or upset. □ **displeasure** /-'pleʒə/ *noun*.

disport /dɪ'spɔ:t/ *verb* (also **disport oneself**) frolic, enjoy oneself.

disposable *adjective* that can be disposed of; designed to be discarded after one use.

disposal *noun* disposing of. □ **at one's disposal** available.

dispose /dɪ'spəʊz/ *verb* (**-sing**) (usually + *to, to do*) (usually in *passive*) incline, make willing; (in *passive*) tend; arrange suitably; (as **disposed** *adjective*) having a specified inclination; determine events. □ **dispose of** get rid of, deal with, finish.

disposition /dɪspə'zɪʃ(ə)n/ *noun* natural tendency; temperament; arrangement (of parts etc.).

dispossess /dɪspə'zes/ *verb* (usually + *of*) (esp. as **dispossessed** *adjective*) deprive; oust, dislodge. □ **dispossession** *noun*.

disproof /dɪs'pru:f/ *noun* refutation.

disproportion /dɪsprə'pɔ:ʃ(ə)n/ *noun* lack of proportion.

disproportionate *adjective* out of proportion; relatively too large or too small. □ **disproportionately** *adverb*.

disprove /dɪs'pru:v/ *verb* (**-ving**) prove (theory etc.) false.

disputable *adjective* open to question.

disputant *noun* person in dispute.

disputation /dɪspju:'teɪʃ(ə)n/ *noun* debate, esp. formal; argument, controversy.

disputatious /dɪspju:'teɪʃəs/ *adjective* argumentative.

dispute /dɪ'spju:t/ ● *verb* (**-ting**) hold debate; quarrel; question truth or validity of; contend for; resist. ● *noun* controversy, debate; quarrel; disagreement leading to industrial action.

disqualify /dɪs'kwɒlɪfaɪ/ *verb* (**-ies, -ied**) make or pronounce (competitor, applicant, etc.) unfit or ineligible. □ **disqualification** *noun*.

disquiet /dɪs'kwaɪət/ ● *verb* make anxious. ● *noun* uneasiness, anxiety. □ **disquietude** *noun*.

disquisition /dɪskwɪ'zɪʃ(ə)n/ *noun* discursive treatise or discourse.

disregard /dɪsrɪ'gɑːd/ ● *verb* ignore, treat as unimportant. ● *noun* indifference, neglect.

disrepair /dɪsrɪ'peə/ *noun* bad condition due to lack of repairs.

disreputable /dɪs'repjʊtəb(ə)l/ *adjective* having a bad reputation; not respectable. □ **disreputably** *adverb*.

disrepute /dɪsrɪ'pjuːt/ *noun* lack of good reputation; discredit.

disrespect /dɪsrɪ'spekt/ *noun* lack of respect. □ **disrespectful** *adjective*.

disrobe /dɪs'rəʊb/ *verb* (**-bing**) *literary* undress.

disrupt /dɪs'rʌpt/ *verb* interrupt continuity of; bring disorder to; break (thing) apart. □ **disruption** *noun*; **disruptive** *adjective*.

dissatisfy /dɪ'sætɪsfaɪ/ *verb* (**-ies**, **-ied**) (usually as **dissatisfied** *adjective*; often + *with*) fail to satisfy; make discontented. □ **dissatisfaction** /-'fæk-/ *noun*.

dissect /dɪ'sekt/ *verb* cut in pieces, esp. for examination or post-mortem; analyse or criticize in detail. □ **dissection** *noun*.

■ **Usage** *Dissect* is often wrongly pronounced /daɪ'sekt/ (and sometimes written with only one *s*) because of confusion with *bisect*.

dissemble /dɪ'semb(ə)l/ *verb* (**-ling**) be hypocritical or insincere; conceal or disguise (a feeling, intention, etc.).

disseminate /dɪ'semɪneɪt/ *verb* (**-ting**) scatter about, spread (esp. ideas) widely. □ **dissemination** *noun*.

dissension /dɪ'senʃ(ə)n/ *noun* angry disagreement.

dissent /dɪ'sent/ ● *verb* (often + *from*) disagree, esp. openly; differ, esp. from established or official opinion. ● *noun* such difference; expression of this.

dissenter *noun* person who dissents; (**Dissenter**) Protestant dissenting from Church of England.

dissentient /dɪ'senʃ(ə)nt/ ● *adjective* disagreeing with the established or official view. ● *noun* person who dissents.

dissertation /dɪsə'teɪʃ(ə)n/ *noun* detailed discourse, esp. as submitted for academic degree.

disservice /dɪs'sɜːvɪs/ *noun* harmful action.

dissident /'dɪsɪd(ə)nt/ ● *adjective* disagreeing, esp. with established government. ● *noun* dissident person.

dissimilar /dɪ'sɪmɪlə/ *adjective* not similar. □ **dissimilarity** /-'lærɪtɪ/ *noun* (*plural* **-ies**).

dissimulate /dɪ'sɪmjʊleɪt/ *verb* (**-ting**) dissemble. □ **dissimulation** *noun*.

dissipate /'dɪsɪpeɪt/ *verb* (**-ting**) dispel, disperse; squander; (as **dissipated** *adjective*) dissolute.

dissipation *noun* dissolute way of life; dissipating, being dissipated.

dissociate /dɪ'səʊʃɪeɪt/ *verb* (**-ting**) disconnect or separate; become disconnected; (**dissociate oneself from**) declare oneself unconnected with. □ **dissociation** *noun*.

dissolute /'dɪsəluːt/ *adjective* lax in morals, licentious.

dissolution /dɪsə'luːʃ(ə)n/ *noun* dissolving, being dissolved; dismissal or dispersal of assembly, esp. parliament; breaking up, abolition (of institution); death.

dissolve /dɪ'zɒlv/ *verb* (**-ving**) make or become liquid, esp. by immersion or dispersion in liquid; (cause to) disappear gradually; dismiss (assembly); put an end to, annul; (often + *in*, *into*) be overcome (by tears, laughter, etc.).

dissonant /'dɪsənənt/ *adjective* discordant, harsh-toned; incongruous. □ **dissonance** *noun*.

dissuade /dɪ'sweɪd/ *verb* (**-ding**) (often + *from*) discourage, persuade against. □ **dissuasion** /-'sweɪʒ(ə)n/ *noun*.

distaff /'dɪstɑːf/ *noun* cleft stick holding wool etc. for spinning by hand. □ **distaff side** female branch of family.

distance /'dɪst(ə)ns/ ● *noun* being far off; remoteness; space between two points; distant point; aloofness, reserve; remoter field of vision. ● *verb* (**-cing**) place or cause to seem far off; leave behind in race etc. □ **at a distance** far off; **keep one's distance** remain aloof.

distant *adjective* at specified distance; remote in space, time, relationship, etc.; aloof; abstracted; faint. □ **distantly** *adverb*.

distaste /dɪs'teɪst/ *noun* (usually + *for*) dislike; aversion. □ **distasteful** *adjective*.

distemper[1] /dɪ'stempə/ ● *noun* paint for walls, using glue etc. as base. ● *verb* paint with distemper.

distemper[2] /dɪ'stempə/ *noun* catarrhal disease of dogs etc.

distend /dɪ'stend/ *verb* swell out by pressure from within. □ **distension** /-'sten-/ *noun*.

distich /'dɪstɪk/ *noun* verse couplet.

distil /dɪ'stɪl/ *verb* (*US* **distill**) (**-ll-**) purify or extract essence from (substance) by vaporizing and condensing it and collecting remaining liquid; extract gist of (idea etc.); make (whisky, essence, etc.) by distilling. □ **distillation** *noun*.

distiller *noun* person who distils, esp. alcoholic liquor.

distillery *noun* (*plural* **-ies**) factory etc. for distilling alcoholic liquor.

distinct /dɪ'stɪŋkt/ *adjective* (often + *from*) separate, different in quality or kind; clearly perceptible; definite, decided. □ **distinctly** *adverb*.

distinction /dɪ'stɪŋkʃ(ə)n/ *noun* discriminating, distinguishing; difference between things; thing that differentiates; special consideration or honour; excellence; mark of honour.

distinctive *adjective* distinguishing, characteristic. □ **distinctively** *adverb*; **distinctiveness** *noun*.

distingué /dɪ'stæŋgeɪ/ *adjective* having distinguished air, manners, etc. [French]

distinguish /dɪ'stɪŋgwɪʃ/ *verb* (often + *from*, *between*) see or draw distinctions; characterize; make out by listening or looking etc.; (usually **distinguish oneself**; often + *by*) make prominent. □ **distinguishable** *adjective*.

distinguished *adjective* eminent, famous; dignified.

distort /dɪ'stɔːt/ *verb* pull or twist out of shape; misrepresent (facts etc.); transmit (sound) inaccurately. □ **distortion** *noun*.

distract /dɪ'strækt/ *verb* (often + *from*) draw away attention of; bewilder; (as **distracted** *adjective*) confused, mad, or angry; amuse, esp. to divert from pain etc.

distraction /dɪ'strækʃ(ə)n/ *noun* distracting, being distracted; thing which distracts; amusement, relaxation; mental confusion; frenzy, madness.

distrain /dɪ'streɪn/ *verb* (usually + *upon*) impose distraint (on person, goods, etc.).

distraint /dɪ'streɪnt/ *noun* seizure of goods to enforce payment.

distrait /dɪ'streɪ/ *adjective* inattentive; distraught. [French]

distraught /dɪ'strɔːt/ *adjective* distracted with worry, fear, etc.; very agitated.

distress /dɪ'stres/ ● *noun* suffering caused by pain, grief, anxiety, etc.; poverty; *Law* distraint. ● *verb* cause distress to; make unhappy. □ **distressed** *adjective*; **distressing** *adjective*.

distribute /dɪ'strɪbjuːt/ *verb* (**-ting**) give shares of; deal out; spread about; put at different points; arrange, classify. □ **distribution** /-'bjuː-/ *noun*; **distributive** *adjective*.

■ **Usage** *Distribute* is often pronounced /'dıstrıbju:t/ (with the stress on the *dis-*), but this is considered incorrect by some people.

distributor *noun* agent who supplies goods; device in internal-combustion engine for passing current to each spark plug in turn.

district /'dıstrıkt/ *noun* region; administrative division. □ **district attorney** (in the US) public prosecutor of district; **district nurse** nurse who makes home visits in an area.

distrust /dıs'trʌst/ ● *noun* lack of trust; suspicion. ● *verb* have no confidence in. □ **distrustful** *adjective*.

disturb /dı'stɜ:b/ *verb* break rest or quiet of; worry; disorganize; (as **disturbed** *adjective*) emotionally or mentally unstable.

disturbance *noun* disturbing, being disturbed; tumult, disorder, agitation.

disunion /dıs'ju:nıən/ *noun* separation; lack of union.

disunite /dısju:'naıt/ *verb* (**-ting**) separate; divide. □ **disunity** /-'ju:-/ *noun*.

disuse /dıs'ju:s/ *noun* state of no longer being used.

disused /dıs'ju:zd/ *adjective* no longer in use.

disyllable /daı'sıləb(ə)l/ *noun* word or metrical foot of two syllables. □ **disyllabic** /-'læb-/ *adjective*.

ditch ● *noun* long narrow excavation esp. for drainage or as boundary. ● *verb* make or repair ditches; *slang* abandon, discard.

dither /'dıðə/ ● *verb* hesitate; be indecisive; tremble, quiver. ● *noun colloquial* state of agitation or hesitation. □ **ditherer** *noun*; **dithery** *adjective*.

dithyramb /'dıθıræm/ *noun* ancient Greek wild choral hymn; passionate or inflated poem etc. □ **dithyrambic** /-'ræmbık/ *adjective*.

ditto /'dıtəʊ/ *noun* (*plural* **-s**) the aforesaid, the same (in accounts, lists, etc., or *colloquial* in speech).

ditty /'dıtı/ *noun* (*plural* **-ies**) short simple song.

diuretic /daıjʊ'retık/ ● *adjective* causing increased output of urine. ● *noun* diuretic drug.

diurnal /daı'ɜ:n(ə)l/ *adjective* in or of day; daily; occupying one day.

diva /'di:və/ *noun* (*plural* **-s**) great woman opera singer.

divan /dı'væn/ *noun* low couch or bed without back or ends.

dive ● *verb* (**-ving**) plunge head foremost into water; (of aircraft) descend fast and steeply; (of submarine or diver) submerge; go deeper; (+ *into*) *colloquial* put one's hand into. ● *noun* act of diving; plunge; *colloquial* disreputable nightclub, bar, etc. □ **dive-bomb** bomb (target) from diving aircraft; **diving board** elevated board for diving from.

diver *noun* person who dives, esp. one who works under water; diving bird.

diverge /daı'vɜ:dʒ/ *verb* (**-ging**) (often + *from*) depart from set course; (of opinions etc.) differ; take different courses; spread outward from central point. □ **divergence** *noun*; **divergent** *adjective*.

divers /'daıvɜ:z/ *adjective archaic* various, several.

diverse /daı'vɜ:s/ *adjective* varied.

diversify /daı'vɜ:sıfaı/ *verb* (**-ies**, **-ied**) make diverse; vary; spread (investment) over several enterprises; (often + *into*) expand range of products. □ **diversification** *noun*.

diversion /daı'vɜ:ʃ(ə)n/ *noun* diverting, being diverted; recreation, pastime; alternative route when road is temporarily closed; stratagem for diverting attention. □ **diversionary** *adjective*.

diversity /daı'vɜ:sıtı/ *noun* variety.

divert /daı'vɜ:t/ *verb* turn aside; deflect; distract (attention); (often as **diverting** *adjective*) entertain, amuse.

divest /daı'vest/ *verb* (usually + *of*) unclothe, strip; deprive, rid.

divide /dı'vaıd/ ● *verb* (**-ding**) (often + *in, into*) separate into parts; split or break up; (often + *out*) distribute, deal, share; separate (one thing) from another; classify into parts or groups; cause to disagree; (+ *by*) find how many times number contains another; (+ *into*) be contained exact number of times; (of parliament) vote (by members entering either of two lobbies). ● *noun* dividing line; watershed.

dividend /'dıvıdend/ *noun* share of profits paid to shareholders, football pools winners, etc.; number to be divided.

divider *noun* screen etc. dividing room; (in *plural*) measuring compasses.

divination /dıvı'neıʃ(ə)n/ *noun* supposed foreseeing of the future, using special technique.

divine /dı'vaın/ ● *adjective* (**-r**, **-st**) of, from, or like God or a god; sacred; *colloquial* excellent. ● *verb* (**-ning**) discover by intuition or guessing; foresee; practise divination. ● *noun* theologian. □ **divining-rod** dowser's forked twig. □ **divinely** *adverb*.

diviner *noun* practitioner of divination; dowser.

divinity /dı'vınıtı/ *noun* (*plural* **-ies**) being divine; god; theology.

divisible /dı'vızıb(ə)l/ *adjective* capable of being divided. □ **divisibility** *noun*.

division /dı'vıʒ(ə)n/ *noun* dividing, being divided; dividing one number by another; disagreement; one of parts into which thing is divided; administrative unit, esp. group of army units or of teams in sporting league. □ **divisional** *adjective*.

divisive /dı'vaısıv/ *adjective* causing disagreement. □ **divisively** *adverb*; **divisiveness** *noun*.

divisor /dı'vaızə/ *noun* number by which another is to be divided.

divorce /dı'vɔ:s/ ● *noun* legal dissolution of marriage; separation. ● *verb* (**-cing**) (usually as **divorced** *adjective*) (often + *from*) legally dissolve marriage of; separate by divorce; end marriage with by divorce; separate.

divorcee /dıvɔ:'si:/ *noun* divorced person.

divot /'dıvət/ *noun* piece of turf dislodged by head of golf club.

divulge /daı'vʌldʒ/ *verb* (**-ging**) disclose (secret).

divvy /'dıvı/ *colloquial* ● *noun* (*plural* **-ies**) dividend. ● *verb* (**-ies**, **-ied**) (often + *up*) share out.

Dixie /'dıksı/ *noun* Southern States of US. □ **Dixieland** Dixie, kind of jazz.

dixie /'dıksı/ *noun* large iron cooking pot.

DIY *abbreviation* do-it-yourself.

dizzy /'dızı/ ● *adjective* (**-ier**, **-iest**) giddy; dazed; causing dizziness. ● *verb* (**-ies**, **-ied**) make dizzy; bewilder. □ **dizzily** *adverb*; **dizziness** *noun*.

DJ *abbreviation* disc jockey; dinner jacket.

dl *abbreviation* decilitre(s).

D.Litt. *abbreviation* Doctor of Letters.

DM *abbreviation* Deutschmark.

dm *abbreviation* decimetre(s).

DNA *abbreviation* deoxyribonucleic acid (substance carrying genetic information in chromosomes).

do[1] /du:/ ● *verb* (*3rd singular present* **does** /dʌz/; *past* **did**; *past participle* **done** /dʌn/; *present participle* **doing**) perform, carry out; produce, make; impart; act, proceed; work at; be suitable, satisfy; attend to, deal with; fare; solve; *colloquial* finish; (as **done** *adjective*) finished, completely cooked; *colloquial* exhaust, defeat, kill; *colloquial* cater for; *slang* rob, swindle, prosecute, convict. ● *auxiliary verb used in questions and negative or emphatic statements and commands; as verbal substitute to avoid repetition.* ● *noun* (*plural* **dos** or

do's) *colloquial* elaborate party or other undertaking. □ **do away with** *colloquial* abolish, kill; **do down** *colloquial* swindle, overcome; **do for** be sufficient for, *colloquial* (esp. as **done for** *adjective*) destroy or ruin or kill, *colloquial* do housework for; **do in** *slang* kill, *colloquial* exhaust; **do-it-yourself** (to be) done or made by householder etc.; **do up** fasten, *colloquial* restore, repair, dress up; **do with** (after *could*) would appreciate, would profit by; **do without** forgo, manage without.

do² = DOH.

do. *abbreviation* ditto.

docile /ˈdəʊsaɪl/ *adjective* submissive, easily managed. □ **docility** /-ˈsɪl-/ *noun*.

dock¹ ● *noun* enclosed harbour for loading, unloading, and repair of ships; (usually in *plural*) range of docks with wharves, warehouses, etc. ● *verb* bring or come into dock; join (spacecraft) together in space, be thus joined. □ **dockyard** area with docks and equipment for building and repairing ships.

dock² *noun* enclosure in criminal court for accused.

dock³ *noun* weed with broad leaves.

dock⁴ *verb* cut short (tail); reduce or deduct (money etc.).

docker *noun* person employed to load and unload ships.

docket /ˈdɒkɪt/ ● *noun* document listing goods delivered, jobs done, contents of package, etc. ● *verb* (**-t-**) label with or enter on docket.

doctor /ˈdɒktə/ ● *noun* qualified medical practitioner; holder of doctorate. ● *verb colloquial* tamper with, adulterate; castrate, spay.

doctoral *adjective* of the degree of doctor.

doctorate /ˈdɒktərət/ *noun* highest university degree in any faculty.

doctrinaire /dɒktrɪˈneə/ *adjective* applying theory or doctrine dogmatically.

doctrine /ˈdɒktrɪn/ *noun* what is taught; principle or set of principles of religious or political etc. belief. □ **doctrinal** /-ˈtraɪn(ə)l/ *adjective*.

document ● *noun* /ˈdɒkjʊmənt/ something written etc. that provides record or evidence of events, circumstances, etc. ● *verb* /ˈdɒkjʊment/ prove by or support with documents. □ **documentation** *noun*.

documentary /dɒkjʊˈmentərɪ/ ● *adjective* consisting of documents; factual, based on real events. ● *noun* (*plural* **-ies**) documentary film etc.

dodder /ˈdɒdə/ *verb* tremble, totter, be feeble. □ **dodderer** *noun*; **doddery** *adjective*.

doddle /ˈdɒd(ə)l/ *noun colloquial* easy task.

dodecagon /dəʊˈdekəgən/ *noun* plane figure with 12 sides.

dodecahedron /dəʊdekəˈhiːdrən/ *noun* solid figure with 12 faces.

dodge ● *verb* (**-ging**) move quickly to elude pursuer, blow, etc.; evade by cunning or trickery. ● *noun* quick evasive movement; trick, clever expedient.

dodgem /ˈdɒdʒəm/ *noun* small electrically powered car at funfair, bumped into others in enclosure.

dodgy *adjective* (**-ier**, **-iest**) *colloquial* unreliable, risky.

dodo /ˈdəʊdəʊ/ *noun* (*plural* **-s**) large extinct flightless bird.

DoE *abbreviation* Department of the Environment.

doe *noun* (*plural* same or **-s**) female fallow deer, reindeer, hare, or rabbit.

does *3rd singular present* of DO¹.

doesn't /ˈdʌz(ə)nt/ does not.

doff *verb* take off (hat etc.).

dog ● *noun* 4-legged flesh-eating animal of many breeds akin to wolf etc.; male of this or of fox or wolf; *colloquial* despicable person; (**the dogs**) *colloquial* greyhound racing; mechanical device for gripping. ● *verb* (**-gg-**) follow closely; pursue, track. □ **dogcart** two-wheeled driving-cart with cross seats back to back; **dog-collar** *colloquial* clergyman's stiff collar; **dog days** hottest period of year; **dog-eared** (of book-page etc.) with worn corners; **dog-end** *slang* cigarette-end; **dogfight** fight between aircraft, rough fight; **dogfish** small shark; **doghouse** *US & Australian* kennel (**in the doghouse** *slang* in disgrace); **dog rose** wild hedge-rose; **dogsbody** *colloquial* drudge; **dog-star** Sirius; **dog-tired** tired out.

doge /dəʊdʒ/ *noun historical* chief magistrate of Venice or Genoa.

dogged /ˈdɒgɪd/ *adjective* tenacious. □ **doggedly** *adverb*.

doggerel /ˈdɒgər(ə)l/ *noun* poor or trivial verse.

doggo /ˈdɒgəʊ/ *adverb slang* □ **lie doggo** wait motionless or hidden.

doggy *adjective* of or like dogs; devoted to dogs. □ **doggy bag** bag for restaurant customer to take home leftovers; **doggy-paddle** elementary swimming stroke.

dogma /ˈdɒgmə/ *noun* principle, tenet; doctrinal system.

dogmatic /dɒgˈmætɪk/ *adjective* imposing personal opinions; authoritative, arrogant. □ **dogmatically** *adverb*; **dogmatism** /ˈdɒgmətɪz(ə)m/ *noun*.

doh /dəʊ/ *noun* (also **do**) *Music* first note of scale in tonic sol-fa.

doily /ˈdɔɪlɪ/ *noun* (*plural* **-ies**) small lacy paper mat placed on plate for cakes etc.

doings /ˈduːɪŋz/ *plural noun* actions, exploits; *slang* thing(s) needed.

Dolby /ˈdɒlbɪ/ *noun proprietary term* system used esp. in tape-recording to reduce hiss.

doldrums /ˈdɒldrəmz/ *plural noun* (usually **the doldrums**) low spirits; period of inactivity; equatorial ocean region of calms.

dole ● *noun* unemployment benefit; charitable (esp. niggardly) gift or distribution. ● *verb* (**-ling**) (usually + *out*) distribute sparingly. □ **on the dole** *colloquial* receiving unemployment benefit.

doleful /ˈdəʊlfʊl/ *adjective* mournful; dreary, dismal. □ **dolefully** *adverb*.

doll ● *noun* model of esp. infant human figure as child's toy; *colloquial* attractive young woman; ventriloquist's dummy. ● *verb* (+ *up*) *colloquial* dress smartly.

dollar /ˈdɒlə/ *noun* chief monetary unit in US, Australia, etc.

dollop /ˈdɒləp/ *noun* shapeless lump of food etc.

dolly *noun* (*plural* **-ies**) *child's word for* doll; movable platform for cine-camera etc.

dolman sleeve /ˈdɒlmən/ *noun* loose sleeve cut in one piece with bodice.

dolmen /ˈdɒlmən/ *noun* megalithic tomb with large flat stone laid on upright ones.

dolomite /ˈdɒləmaɪt/ *noun* mineral or rock of calcium magnesium carbonate.

dolphin /ˈdɒlfɪn/ *noun* large porpoise-like sea mammal.

dolt /dəʊlt/ *noun* stupid person. □ **doltish** *adjective*.

Dom *noun: title prefixed to names of some RC dignitaries and Carthusian and Benedictine monks.*

domain /dəˈmeɪn/ *noun* area ruled over; realm; estate etc. under one's control; sphere of authority.

dome ● *noun* rounded vault as roof; dome-shaped thing. ● *verb* (**-ming**) (usually as **domed** *adjective*) cover with or shape as dome.

domestic /dəˈmestɪk/ ● *adjective* of home, household, or family affairs; of one's own country; (of animal) tamed; fond of home life. ● *noun* household servant.

domesticate /də'mestɪkeɪt/ *verb* (**-ting**) tame (animal) to live with humans; accustom to housework etc. ▫ **domestication** *noun*.

domesticity /dɒmə'stɪsɪtɪ/ *noun* being domestic; home life.

domicile /'dɒmɪsaɪl/ ● *noun* dwelling place; place of permanent residence. ● *verb* (**-ling**) (usually as **domiciled** *adjective*) (usually + *at, in*) settle in a place.

domiciliary /dɒmɪ'sɪlɪərɪ/ *adjective formal* (esp. of doctor's etc. visit) to or at person's home.

dominant /'dɒmɪnənt/ ● *adjective* dominating, prevailing. ● *noun Music* 5th note of diatonic scale. ▫ **dominance** *noun*.

dominate /'dɒmɪneɪt/ *verb* (**-ting**) command, control; be most influential or obvious; (of place) overlook. ▫ **domination** *noun*.

domineer /dɒmɪ'nɪə/ *verb* (often as **domineering** *adjective*) behave overbearingly.

Dominican /də'mɪnɪkən/ ● *noun* friar or nun of order founded by St Dominic. ● *adjective* of this order.

dominion /də'mɪnjən/ *noun* sovereignty; realm; domain; *historical* self-governing territory of British Commonwealth.

domino /'dɒmɪnəʊ/ *noun* (*plural* **-es**) any of 28 small oblong pieces marked with 0–6 pips in each half; (in *plural*) game played with these; loose cloak worn with half-mask.

don[1] *noun* university teacher, esp. senior member of college at Oxford or Cambridge; (**Don**) *Spanish title prefixed to man's name.*

don[2] *verb* (**-nn-**) put on (garment).

donate /dəʊ'neɪt/ *verb* (**-ting**) give (money etc.), esp. to charity.

donation *noun* donating, being donated; thing (esp. money) donated.

done /dʌn/ ● *past participle* of DO[1]. ● *adjective* completed; cooked; *colloquial* socially acceptable; (often + *in*) *colloquial* tired out; (esp. as *interjection* in response to offer etc.) accepted. ▫ **be done with** have or be finished with; **done for** *colloquial* in serious trouble.

doner kebab /'dɒnə kɪ'bæb/ *noun* spiced lamb cooked on spit and served in slices, often with pitta bread.

donkey /'dɒŋkɪ/ *noun* (*plural* **-s**) domestic ass; *colloquial* stupid person. ▫ **donkey jacket** thick weatherproof jacket; **donkey's years** *colloquial* very long time; **donkey-work** drudgery.

Donna /'dɒnə/ *noun: title of Italian, Spanish, or Portuguese lady.*

donnish *adjective* like a college don; pedantic.

donor /'dəʊnə/ *noun* person who donates; person who provides blood for transfusion, organ for transplantation, etc.

don't /dəʊnt/ ● *verb* do not. ● *noun* prohibition.

doodle /'du:d(ə)l/ ● *verb* (**-ling**) scribble or draw absent-mindedly. ● *noun* such scribble or drawing.

doom /du:m/ ● *noun* terrible fate or destiny; ruin, death. ● *verb* (usually + *to*) condemn or destine; (esp. as **doomed** *adjective*) consign to ruin, destruction, etc. ▫ **doomsday** day of Last Judgement.

door /dɔ:/ *noun* hinged or sliding barrier closing entrance to building, room, cupboard, etc.; doorway. ▫ **doormat** mat for wiping shoes on, *colloquial* subservient person; **doorstep** step or area immediately outside esp. outer door, *slang* thick slice of bread; **doorstop** device for keeping door open or to keep it from striking wall; **door-to-door** (of selling etc.) done at each house in turn; **doorway** opening filled by door; **out of doors** in(to) open air.

dope ● *noun slang* drug, esp. narcotic; thick liquid used as lubricant etc.; varnish; *slang* stupid person; *slang* information. ● *verb* (**-ping**) give or add drug to; apply dope to.

dopey *adjective* (also **dopy**) (**dopier, dopiest**) *colloquial* half asleep, stupefied; stupid.

doppelganger /'dɒp(ə)lgæŋə/ *noun* (also **doppelgänger** /-geŋə/) apparition or double of living person.

Doppler effect /'dɒplə/ *noun* change in frequency of esp. sound waves when source and observer are moving closer or apart.

dormant /'dɔ:mənt/ *adjective* lying inactive; sleeping; inactive. ▫ **dormancy** *noun*.

dormer /'dɔ:mə/ *noun* (in full **dormer window**) upright window in sloping roof.

dormitory /'dɔ:mɪtərɪ/ *noun* (*plural* **-ies**) sleeping-room with several beds; (in full **dormitory town** etc.) commuter town or suburb.

dormouse /'dɔ:maʊs/ *noun* (*plural* **-mice**) small mouse-like hibernating rodent.

dorsal /'dɔ:s(ə)l/ *adjective* of or on back.

dory /'dɔ:rɪ/ *noun* (*plural* same or **-ies**) edible sea fish.

dosage *noun* size of dose; giving of dose.

dose /dəʊs/ ● *noun* single portion of medicine; amount of radiation received. ● *verb* (**-sing**) give medicine to; (+ *with*) treat with.

doss *verb* (often + *down*) *slang* sleep on makeshift bed or in doss-house. ▫ **doss-house** cheap lodging house. ▫ **dosser** *noun*.

dossier /'dɒsɪeɪ/ *noun* file containing information about person, event, etc.

dot *noun* small spot, esp. as decimal point, part of *i* or *j* etc.; shorter signal of the two in Morse code. ● *verb* (**-tt-**) mark or scatter with dot(s); (often + *about*) scatter like dots; place dot over (letter); partly cover as with dots; *slang* hit. ▫ **dotted line** line of dots for signature etc. on document; **on the dot** exactly on time.

dotage /'dəʊtɪdʒ/ *noun* feeble-minded senility.

dote *verb* (**-ting**) (usually + *on* or as **doting** *adjective*) be excessively fond of.

dotterel /'dɒtər(ə)l/ *noun* small plover.

dotty *adjective* (**-ier, -iest**) *colloquial* eccentric, silly, crazy; (+ *about*) infatuated with.

double /'dʌb(ə)l/ ● *adjective* consisting of two things; multiplied by two; twice as much or many or large etc.; having twice the usual size, quantity, strength, etc.; having some part double; (of flower) with two or more circles of petals; ambiguous; deceitful. ● *adverb* at or to twice the amount; two together. ● *noun* double quantity (of spirits etc.) or thing; twice the amount or quantity; person or thing looking exactly like another; (in *plural*) game between two pairs of players; pair of victories; bet in which winnings and stake from first bet are transferred to second. ● *verb* (**-ling**) make or become double; increase twofold; amount to twice as much as; fold over upon itself; become folded; play (two parts) in same play etc.; (usually + *as*) play twofold role; turn sharply; *Nautical* get round (headland). ▫ **at the double** running; **double agent** spy working for two rival countries etc.; **double-barrelled** (of gun) having two barrels, (of surname) hyphenated; **double-bass** largest instrument of violin family; **double-book** mistakenly reserve (seat, room, etc.) for two people at once; **double-breasted** (of garment) overlapping across body; **double chin** chin with fold of flesh below it; **double cream** thick cream with high fat-content; **double-cross** deceive or betray; **double-dealing** (practising) deceit, esp. in business; **double-decker** bus etc. with two decks, *colloquial* sandwich with two layers of filling; **double Dutch** *colloquial* gibberish; **double eagle** figure of eagle with two heads; **double-edged** presenting both a danger and an advantage; **double figures** numbers from 10 to 99; **double glazing** two layers of glass in window; **double negative** *Grammar* negative statement (incorrectly) containing two negative elements (see note below); **double pneumonia** pneumonia of both lungs; **double standard** rule or principle not impartially applied; **double take** delayed reaction to unexpected element of situation; **double-talk** (usually deliberately) ambiguous or misleading speech.

■ **Usage** Double negatives like *He didn't do nothing* and *I'm never going nowhere like that* are mistakes in standard English because one negative element is redundant. However, two negatives are perfectly acceptable in, for instance, *a not ungenerous sum* (meaning 'quite a generous sum').

double entendre /du:b(ə)l ɑ:n'tɑ:ndrə/ *noun* phrase capable of two meanings, one usually indecent. [French]

doublet /'dʌblɪt/ *noun historical* man's close-fitting jacket; one of pair of similar things.

doubloon /dʌ'blu:n/ *noun historical* Spanish gold coin.

doubt /daʊt/ ● *noun* uncertainty; undecided state of mind; cynicism; uncertain state. ● *verb* feel uncertain or undecided about; hesitate to believe; call in question. □ **in doubt** open to question; **no doubt** certainly, admittedly.

doubtful *adjective* feeling or causing doubt; unreliable. □ **doubtfully** *adverb*.

doubtless *adverb* certainly; probably.

douche /du:ʃ/ ● *noun* jet of liquid applied to part of body for cleansing or medicinal purposes; device for producing this. ● *verb* (**-ching**) treat with douche; use douche.

dough /dəʊ/ *noun* thick paste of flour mixed with liquid for baking; *slang* money. □ **doughnut** (*US* **donut**) small fried cake of sweetened dough. □ **doughy** *adjective* (**-ier**, **-iest**).

doughty /'daʊtɪ/ *adjective* (**-ier**, **-iest**) *archaic* valiant. □ **doughtily** *adverb*.

dour /dʊə/ *adjective* stern, grim, obstinate.

douse /daʊs/ *verb* (also **dowse**) (**-sing**) throw water over; plunge into water; extinguish (light).

dove /dʌv/ *noun* bird with short legs and full breast; advocate of peaceful policies; gentle or innocent person. □ **dovecot(e)** pigeon house.

dovetail ● *noun* mortise-and-tenon joint shaped like dove's spread tail. ● *verb* fit together, combine neatly; join with dovetails.

dowager /'daʊədʒə/ *noun* woman with title or property from her late husband.

dowdy /'daʊdɪ/ *adjective* (**-ier**, **-iest**) (of clothes) unattractively dull; dressed dowdily. □ **dowdily** *adverb*; **dowdiness** *noun*.

dowel /'daʊəl/ *noun* cylindrical peg for holding parts of structure together.

dowelling *noun* rods for cutting into dowels.

dower /'daʊə/ *noun* widow's share for life of husband's estate.

down[1] /daʊn/ ● *adverb* towards or into lower place, esp. to ground; in lower place or position; to or in place regarded as lower, esp. southwards or away from major city or university; in or into low or weaker position or condition; losing by; (of a computer system) out of action; from earlier to later time; in written or recorded form. ● *preposition* downwards along, through, or into; from top to bottom of; along; at lower part of. ● *adjective* directed downwards. ● *verb colloquial* knock or bring etc. down; swallow. ● *noun* reverse of fortune; *colloquial* period of depression. □ **be down to** be the responsibility of, have nothing left but; **down and out** destitute; **down-and-out** destitute person; **downcast** dejected, (of eyes) looking down; **downfall** fall from prosperity or power, cause of this; **downgrade** reduce in rank etc.; **downhearted** despondent; **downhill** *adverb* in descending direction, on a decline, *adjective* sloping down, declining; **down in the mouth** looking unhappy; **down-market** of or to cheaper sector of market; **downpour** heavy fall of rain; **downside** negative aspect, drawback; **downstairs** *adverb* down the stairs, to or on lower floor, *adjective* situated downstairs; **downstream** in direction of flow of stream etc.; **down-to-earth** practical, realistic; **downtown** *US* (of) lower or central part of town or city; **downtrodden** oppressed; **downturn** decline, esp. in economic activity; **down under** *colloquial* in Australia or NZ; **downwind** in direction in which wind is blowing; **down with** *expressing rejection of person or thing*; **have a down on** *colloquial* be hostile to. □ **downward** *adjective & adverb*; **downwards** *adverb*.

down[2] /daʊn/ *noun* baby birds' fluffy covering; bird's under-plumage; fine soft feathers or hairs.

down[3] /daʊn/ *noun* open rolling land; (in *plural*) chalk uplands of S. England etc.

downright ● *adjective* plain, straightforward; utter. ● *adverb* thoroughly.

Down's syndrome *noun* congenital disorder with mental retardation and physical abnormalities.

downy *adjective* (**-ier**, **-iest**) of, like, or covered with down.

dowry /'daʊərɪ/ *noun* (*plural* **-ies**) property brought by bride to her husband.

dowse[1] /daʊz/ *verb* (**-sing**) search for underground water or minerals by holding stick or rod which dips abruptly when over right spot. □ **dowser** *noun*.

dowse[2] = DOUSE.

doxology /dɒk'sɒlədʒɪ/ *noun* (*plural* **-ies**) liturgical hymn etc. of praise to God.

doyen /'dɔɪən/ *noun* (*feminine* **doyenne** /dɔɪ'en/) senior member of group.

doz. *abbreviation* dozen.

doze ● *verb* (**-zing**) sleep lightly, be half asleep. ● *noun* short light sleep. □ **doze off** fall lightly asleep.

dozen /'dʌz(ə)n/ *noun* (*plural* same (after numeral) or **-s**) set of twelve; (**dozens**, usually + *of*) *colloquial* very many.

D.Phil. *abbreviation* Doctor of Philosophy.

Dr *abbreviation* Doctor.

drab *adjective* (**-bb-**) dull, uninteresting; of dull brownish colour. □ **drabness** *noun*.

drachm /dræm/ *noun* weight formerly used by apothecaries, = 1/8 ounce.

drachma /'drækmə/ *noun* (*plural* **-s**) chief monetary unit of Greece.

Draconian /drə'kəʊnɪən/ *adjective* (of laws) harsh, cruel.

draft /drɑ:ft/ ● *noun* preliminary written outline of scheme or version of speech, document, etc.; written order for payment of money by bank; drawing of money on this; detachment from larger group; selection of this; *US* conscription; *US* draught. ● *verb* prepare draft of; select for special duty or purpose; *US* conscript.

draftsman /'drɑ:ftsmən/ *noun* person who drafts documents; person who makes drawings.

drafty *US* = DRAUGHTY.

drag ● *verb* (**-gg-**) pull along with effort; (allow to) trail; (of time etc.) pass tediously or slowly; search bottom of (river etc.) with grapnels, nets, etc. ● *noun* obstruction to progress, retarding force; *colloquial* boring or tiresome task, person, etc.; lure before hounds as substitute for fox; apparatus for dredging; *colloquial* pull at cigarette; *slang* women's clothes worn by men. ▫ **drag out** protract.

draggle /'dræg(ə)l/ *verb* (**-ling**) make dirty and wet by trailing; hang trailing.

dragon /'drægən/ *noun* mythical monster like reptile, usually with wings and able to breathe fire; fierce woman.

dragonfly *noun* (*plural* **-ies**) large long-bodied gauzy-winged insect.

dragoon /drə'gu:n/ ● *noun* cavalryman; fierce fellow. ● *verb* (+ *into*) coerce or bully into.

drain ● *verb* draw off liquid from; draw off (liquid); flow or trickle away; dry or become dry; exhaust; drink to the dregs; empty (glass etc.) by drinking. ● *noun* channel or pipe carrying off liquid, sewage, etc.; constant outflow or expenditure. ▫ **draining board** sloping grooved surface beside sink for draining dishes; **drainpipe** pipe for carrying off water etc.

drainage *noun* draining; system of drains; what is drained off.

drake *noun* male duck.

dram *noun* small drink of spirits etc.; drachm.

drama /'drɑ:mə/ *noun* play for stage or broadcasting; art of writing, acting, or presenting plays; dramatic event or quality.

dramatic /drə'mætɪk/ *adjective* of drama; unexpected and exciting; striking; theatrical. ▫ **dramatically** *adverb.*

dramatics *plural noun* (often treated as *singular*) performance of plays; exaggerated behaviour.

dramatis personae /'dræmətɪs pɜ:'səʊnaɪ/ *plural noun* characters in a play.

dramatist /'dræmətɪst/ *noun* writer of plays.

dramatize /'dræmətaɪz/ *verb* (also **-ise**) (**-zing** or **-sing**) convert into play; make dramatic; behave dramatically. ▫ **dramatization** *noun.*

drank *past of* DRINK.

drape ● *verb* (**-ping**) cover or hang or adorn with cloth etc.; arrange in graceful folds. ● *noun* (in *plural*) *US* curtains.

draper *noun* retailer of textile fabrics.

drapery *noun* (*plural* **-ies**) clothing or hangings arranged in folds; draper's trade or fabrics.

drastic /'dræstɪk/ *adjective* far-reaching in effect; severe. ▫ **drastically** *adverb.*

drat *colloquial* ● *verb* (**-tt-**) (usually as *interjection*) curse. ● *interjection expressing annoyance.*

draught /drɑ:ft/ *noun* (*US* **draft**) current of air indoors; traction; depth of water needed to float ship; drawing of liquor from cask etc.; single act of drinking or inhaling; amount so drunk; (in *plural*) game for two with 12 pieces each, on **draughtboard** (like chessboard). ▫ **draught beer** beer drawn from cask, not bottled.

draughtsman /'drɑ:ftsmən/ *noun* person who makes drawings; piece in game of draughts.

draughty *adjective* (*US* **drafty**) (**-ier**, **-iest**) (of a room etc.) letting in sharp currents of air.

draw ● *verb* (*past* **drew** /dru:/; *past participle* **drawn**) pull or cause to move towards or after one; pull (thing) up, over, or across; attract; pull (curtains) open or shut; take in; (+ *at, on*) inhale from; extract; take from or out; make (line, mark, or outline); make (picture) in this way; represent (thing) in this way; finish (game etc.) with equal scores; proceed to specified position; infer; elicit, evoke; induce; haul up (water) from well; bring out (liquid from tap, wound, etc.); draw lots; obtain by lot; (of tea) infuse; (of chimney, pipe, etc.) promote or allow draught; write out (bill, cheque); search (cover) for game etc.; (as **drawn** *adjective*) looking strained and tense. ● *noun* act of drawing; person or thing that draws custom or attention; drawing of lots, raffle; drawn game etc. ▫ **draw back** withdraw; **drawback** disadvantage; **drawbridge** hinged retractable bridge; **draw in** (of days etc.) become shorter, (of train etc.) arrive at station; **draw out** prolong, induce to talk, (of days etc.) become longer; **drawstring** string or cord threaded through waistband, bag opening, etc.; **draw up** draft (document etc.), bring into order, come to a halt, (**draw oneself up**) make oneself erect.

drawer /'drɔ:ə/ *noun* person who draws; (also /drɔ:/) receptacle sliding in and out of frame (**chest of drawers**) or of table etc.; (in *plural*) knickers, underpants.

drawing *noun* art of representing by line with pencil etc.; picture etc. made thus. ▫ **drawing-board** board on which paper is fixed for drawing on; **drawing-pin** flat-headed pin for fastening paper to a surface.

drawing-room *noun* room in private house for sitting or entertaining in.

drawl ● *verb* speak with drawn-out vowel sounds. ● *noun* drawling utterance or way of speaking.

dray *noun* low cart without sides for heavy loads, esp. beer barrels.

dread /dred/ ● *verb* fear greatly, esp. in advance. ● *noun* great fear or apprehension. ● *adjective* dreaded; *archaic* awe-inspiring.

dreadful *adjective* terrible; *colloquial* very annoying, very bad. ▫ **dreadfully** *adverb.*

dream ● *noun* series of scenes in mind of sleeping person; daydream or fantasy; ideal; aspiration. ● *verb* (*past & past participle* **dreamt** /dremt/ or **dreamed**) experience dream; imagine as in dream; (esp. in negative; + *of, that*) consider possible or acceptable; be inactive or unrealistic. ▫ **dreamer** *noun.*

dreamy *adjective* (**-ier**, **-iest**) given to daydreaming; dreamlike; vague; *colloquial* delightful. ▫ **dreamily** *adverb.*

dreary /'drɪərɪ/ *adjective* (**-ier**, **-iest**) dismal, gloomy, dull. ▫ **drearily** *adverb*; **dreariness** *noun.*

dredge[1] ● *noun* apparatus used to collect oysters etc., or to clear mud etc., from bottom of sea etc. ● *verb* (**-ging**) bring up or clear (mud etc.) with dredge; (+ *up*) bring up (something forgotten); clean with or use dredge.

dredge[2] *verb* (**-ging**) sprinkle with flour etc.

dredger[1] *noun* boat with dredge; dredge.

dredger[2] *noun* container with perforated lid for sprinkling flour etc.

dregs *plural noun* sediment, grounds; worst part.

drench ● *verb* wet thoroughly; force (animal) to take medicine. ● *noun* dose of medicine for animal.

dress ● *verb* put clothes on; have and wear clothes; put on evening dress; arrange or adorn; put dressing on (wound etc.); prepare (poultry, crab, etc.) for cooking or eating; apply manure to. ● *noun* woman's one-piece garment of bodice and skirt; clothing, esp. whole outfit. ▫ **dress circle** first gallery in theatre; **dressmaker** person who makes women's clothes, esp. for a living; **dress rehearsal** (esp. final) rehearsal in costume; **dress up** put on special clothes, make (person, thing) more attractive or interesting.

dressage /'dresɑ:ʒ/ *noun* training of horse in obedience and deportment.

dresser[1] /'dresə/ *noun* tall kitchen sideboard with shelves.

dresser[2] *noun* person who helps actors or actresses to dress for stage.

dressing *noun* putting one's clothes on; sauce, esp. of oil, vinegar, etc., for salads; bandage, ointment, etc. for wound; compost etc. spread over land.

□ **dressing down** *colloquial* scolding; **dressing gown** loose robe worn while one is not fully dressed; **dressing table** table with mirror etc. for use while dressing, applying make-up, etc.

dressy *adjective* (**-ier**, **-iest**) *colloquial* (of clothes or person) smart, elegant.

drew *past of* DRAW.

drey /dreɪ/ *noun* squirrel's nest.

dribble /ˈdrɪb(ə)l/ ● *verb* (**-ling**) allow saliva to flow from the mouth; flow or allow to flow in drops; *Football etc.* move (ball) forward with slight touches of feet etc. ● *noun* act of dribbling; dribbling flow.

driblet /ˈdrɪblɪt/ *noun* small quantity (of liquid etc.).

dribs and drabs *plural noun colloquial* small scattered amounts.

dried *past & past participle of* DRY.

drier[1] *comparative of* DRY.

drier[2] /ˈdraɪə/ *noun* (also **dryer**) machine for drying hair, laundry, etc.

driest *superlative of* DRY.

drift ● *noun* slow movement or variation; this caused by current; intention, meaning, etc. of what is said etc.; mass of snow etc. heaped up by wind; state of inaction; deviation of craft etc. due to current, wind, etc. ● *verb* be carried by or as if by current of air or water; progress casually or aimlessly; (of current) carry; heap or be heaped into drifts. □ **drift-net** net for sea fishing, which is allowed to drift; **driftwood** wood floating on moving water or washed ashore.

drifter *noun* aimless person; fishing boat with drift-net.

drill[1] ● *noun* tool or machine for boring holes; instruction in military exercises; routine procedure in emergency; thorough training, esp. by repetition; *colloquial* recognized procedure. ● *verb* make hole in or through with drill; make (hole) with drill; train or be trained by drill.

drill[2] ● *noun* machine for making furrows, sowing, and covering seed; small furrow for sowing seed in; row of seeds sown by drill. ● *verb* plant in drills.

drill[3] *noun* coarse twilled cotton or linen fabric.

drill[4] *noun* W. African baboon related to mandrill.

drily *adverb* (also **dryly**) in a dry way.

drink ● *verb* (*past* **drank**; *past participle* **drunk**) swallow (liquid); take alcohol, esp. to excess; (of plant etc.) absorb (moisture). ● *noun* liquid for drinking; draught or specified amount of this; alcoholic liquor; glass, portion, etc., of this; (**the drink**) *colloquial* the sea. □ **drink-driver** *colloquial* person driving with excess alcohol in the blood; **drink in** listen eagerly to; **drink to** toast, wish success to; **drink up** drink all or remainder of. □ **drinker** *noun*.

drip ● *verb* (**-pp-**) fall or let fall in drops; (often + *with*) be so wet as to shed drops. ● *noun* liquid falling in drops; drop of liquid; sound of dripping; *colloquial* dull or ineffectual person.

drip-dry ● *verb* dry or leave to dry crease-free when hung up. ● *adjective* able to be drip-dried.

drip-feed ● *verb* feed intravenously in drops. ● *noun* feeding thus; apparatus for doing this.

dripping *noun* fat melted from roasting meat.

drive ● *verb* (**-ving**; *past* **drove** /drəʊv/; *past participle* **driven** /ˈdrɪv(ə)n/) urge forward, esp. forcibly; compel; force into specified state; operate and direct (vehicle etc.); carry or be carried in vehicle; strike golf ball from tee; (of wind etc.) carry along, propel. ● *noun* excursion in vehicle; driveway; street, road; motivation and energy; inner urge; forcible stroke of bat etc.; organized group effort; transmission of power to machinery or wheels of motor vehicle etc.; organized whist, bingo, etc. competition. □ **drive at** seek, intend, mean; **drive-in** (bank, cinema, etc.) used while one sits in one's car; **driveway** private road through garden to house; **driving licence** licence permitting person to drive vehicle; **driving test** official test of competence to drive; **driving wheel** wheel transmitting power of vehicle to ground.

drivel /ˈdrɪv(ə)l/ ● *noun* silly nonsense. ● *verb* (**-ll-**; *US* **-l-**) talk drivel; run at mouth or nose.

driver *noun* person who drives; golf club for driving from tee.

drizzle /ˈdrɪz(ə)l/ ● *noun* very fine rain. ● *verb* (**-ling**) fall in very fine drops.

droll /drəʊl/ *adjective* quaintly amusing, strange, odd. □ **drollery** *noun* (*plural* **-ies**).

dromedary /ˈdrɒmɪdərɪ/ *noun* (*plural* **-ies**) one-humped (esp. Arabian) camel bred for riding.

drone ● *noun* non-working male of honey-bee; idler; deep humming sound; monotonous speaking tone; bass-pipe of bagpipes or its continuous note. ● *verb* (**-ning**) make deep humming sound; speak or utter monotonously.

drool *verb* slobber, dribble; (often + *over*) admire extravagantly.

droop /druːp/ ● *verb* bend or hang down, esp. from fatigue or lack of food, drink, etc.; flag. ● *noun* drooping position; loss of spirit. □ **droopy** *adjective*.

drop ● *noun* globule of liquid that falls, hangs, or adheres to surface; very small amount of liquid; abrupt fall or slope; amount of this; act of dropping; fall in prices, temperature, etc.; drop-shaped thing, esp. pendant or sweet; (in *plural*) liquid medicine swallowed in drops. ● *verb* (**-pp-**) fall, allow to fall; let go; fall, let fall, or shed in drops; sink down from exhaustion or injury; cease, lapse; abandon; *colloquial* cease to associate with or discuss; set down (passenger etc.); utter or be uttered casually; fall or let fall in direction, amount, degree, pitch, etc.; (of person) jump down lightly; let oneself fall; omit; give birth to (lamb); deliver from the air by parachute etc.; *Football* send (ball) or score (goal) by drop-kick. □ **drop back**, **behind** fall back, get left behind; **drop in**, **by** *colloquial* visit casually; **drop-kick** kick at football made by dropping ball and kicking it as it touches ground; **drop off** fall asleep, drop (passenger); **drop out** (often + *of*) *colloquial* cease to participate (in); **drop-out** *colloquial* person who has dropped out of esp. course of study or conventional society; **drop scone** scone made by dropping spoonful of mixture into pan etc.; **drop-shot** tennis shot dropping abruptly after clearing net. □ **droplet** *noun*.

dropper *noun* device for releasing liquid in drops.

droppings *plural noun* dung; thing that falls or has fallen in drops.

dropsy /ˈdrɒpsɪ/ *noun* oedema. □ **dropsical** *adjective*.

dross *noun* rubbish; scum of molten metal; impurities.

drought /draʊt/ *noun* prolonged absence of rain.

drove[1] *past of* DRIVE.

drove[2] /drəʊv/ *noun* moving crowd; (in *plural*) *colloquial* great number; herd or flock moving together.

drover *noun* herder of cattle.

drown /draʊn/ *verb* kill or die by submersion; submerge; flood; drench; deaden (grief etc.) by drinking; (often + *out*) overpower (sound) with louder sound.

drowse /draʊz/ *verb* (**-sing**) be lightly asleep.

drowsy /ˈdraʊzɪ/ *adjective* (**-ier**, **-iest**) very sleepy, almost asleep. □ **drowsily** *adverb*; **drowsiness** *noun*.

drub *verb* (**-bb-**) thrash, beat; defeat thoroughly. □ **drubbing** *noun*.

drudge ● *noun* person who does dull, laborious, or menial work. ● *verb* (**-ging**) work hard or laboriously. □ **drudgery** *noun*.

drug ● *noun* medicinal substance; (esp. addictive) hallucinogen, stimulant, narcotic, etc. ● *verb* (**-gg-**) add drug to (drink, food, etc.); administer drug to; stupefy. ▫ **drugstore** *US* combined chemist's shop and café.

drugget /ˈdrʌgɪt/ *noun* coarse woven fabric used for floor coverings etc.

druggist *noun* pharmacist.

Druid /ˈdru:ɪd/ *noun* ancient Celtic priest; member of a modern Druidic order, esp. the Gorsedd. ▫ **Druidic** /-ˈɪdɪk/ *adjective*; **Druidism** *noun*.

drum ● *noun* hollow esp. cylindrical percussion instrument covered at one or both ends with plastic, skin, etc.; sound of this; cylindrical structure or object; cylinder used for storage etc.; eardrum. ● *verb* (**-mm-**) play drum; beat or tap continuously with fingers etc.; (of bird etc.) make loud noise with wings. ▫ **drumbeat** stroke or sound of stroke on drum; **drum brake** kind in which shoes on vehicle press against drum on wheel; **drum into** drive (facts etc.) into (person) by persistence; **drum machine** electronic device that simulates percussion; **drum major** leader of marching band; **drum majorette** female baton-twirling member of parading group; **drum out** dismiss with ignominy; **drumstick** stick for beating drum, lower leg of fowl for eating; **drum up** summon or get by vigorous effort.

drummer *noun* player of drum.

drunk /drʌŋk/ ● *past participle* of DRINK. ● *adjective* lacking control from drinking alcohol; (often + *with*) overcome with joy, success, power, etc. ● *noun* person who is drunk, esp. habitually.

drunkard /ˈdrʌŋkəd/ *noun* person habitually drunk.

drunken /ˈdrʌŋkən/ *adjective* drunk; caused by or involving drunkenness; often drunk. ▫ **drunkenly** *adverb*; **drunkenness** *noun*.

drupe /dru:p/ *noun* fleshy stone fruit.

dry ● *adjective* (**drier**, **driest**) free from moisture, esp. with moisture having evaporated, drained away, etc; (of eyes) free from tears; (of climate) not rainy; (of river, well, etc.) dried up; (of wine etc.) not sweet; plain, unelaborated; uninteresting; (of sense of humour) ironic, understated; prohibiting sale of alcohol; (of bread) without butter etc.; (of provisions etc.) solid, not liquid; *colloquial* thirsty. ● *verb* (**dries**, **dried**) make or become dry; (usually as **dried** *adjective*) preserve (food) by removing moisture. ▫ **dry-clean** clean (clothes etc.) with solvents without water; **dry-fly** (of fishing) with floating artificial fly; **dry ice** solid carbon dioxide; **dry out** make or become fully dry, treat or be treated for alcoholism; **dry rot** decay in wood not exposed to air, fungi causing this; **dry run** *colloquial* rehearsal; **dry-shod** without wetting one's shoes; **dry up** make or become completely dry, dry dishes. ▫ **dryness** *noun*.

dryad /ˈdraɪæd/ *noun* wood nymph.

dryer = DRIER².

dryly = DRILY.

D.Sc. *abbreviation* Doctor of Science.

DSC, DSM, DSO *abbreviations* Distinguished Service Cross, Medal, Order.

DSS *abbreviation* Department of Social Security (formerly DHSS).

DT *abbreviation* (also **DT's** /di:ˈti:z/) delirium tremens.

DTI *abbreviation* Department of Trade and Industry.

dual /ˈdju:əl/ ● *adjective* in two parts; twofold; double. ● *noun Grammar* dual number or form. ▫ **dual carriageway** road with dividing strip between traffic flowing in opposite directions; **dual control** two linked sets of controls, esp. of vehicle used for teaching driving etc., enabling operation by either of two people. ▫ **duality** /-ˈæl-/ *noun*.

dub¹ *verb* (**-bb-**) make (person) into knight; give name or nickname to.

dub² *verb* (**-bb-**) provide (film etc.) with alternative, esp. translated, soundtrack; add (sound effects, music) to film or broadcast.

dubbin /ˈdʌbɪn/ *noun* (also **dubbing**) grease for softening and waterproofing leather.

dubiety /dju:ˈbaɪətɪ/ *noun literary* doubt.

dubious /ˈdju:bɪəs/ *adjective* doubtful; questionable; unreliable. ▫ **dubiously** *adverb*; **dubiousness** *noun*.

ducal /ˈdju:k(ə)l/ *adjective* of or like duke.

ducat /ˈdʌkət/ *noun* gold coin formerly current in most European countries.

duchess /ˈdʌtʃɪs/ *noun* duke's wife or widow; woman holding rank of duke.

duchy /ˈdʌtʃɪ/ *noun* (*plural* **-ies**) duke's or duchess's territory.

duck ● *noun* (*plural* same or **-s**) swimming bird, esp. domesticated form of mallard or wild duck; female of this; its flesh as food; *Cricket* batsman's score of 0; (also **ducks**) *colloquial* (esp. as form of address) darling. ● *verb* bob down, esp. to avoid being seen or hit; dip head briefly under water; plunge (person) briefly in water. ▫ **duckweed** any of various plants that grow on surface of still water.

duckling *noun* young duck.

duct *noun* channel, tube; tube in body carrying secretions etc.

ductile /ˈdʌktaɪl/ *adjective* (of metal) capable of being drawn into wire; pliable; easily moulded; docile. ▫ **ductility** /-ˈtɪl-/ *noun*.

ductless *adjective* (of gland) secreting directly into bloodstream.

dud *slang* ● *noun* useless or broken thing; counterfeit article; (in *plural*) clothes, rags. ● *adjective* defective, useless.

dude /du:d/ *noun slang* fellow; *US* dandy; *US* city man staying on ranch.

dudgeon /ˈdʌdʒ(ə)n/ *noun* resentment; indignation.

due ● *adjective* owing, payable; merited, appropriate; (often + *to do*) expected or under obligation to do something or arrive at certain time. ● *noun* what one owes or is owed; (usually in *plural*) fee or amount payable. ● *adverb* (of compass point) exactly, directly. ▫ **due to** because of, caused by.

■ **Usage** Many people believe that *due to*, meaning 'because of', should only be used after the verb *to be*, as in *The mistake was due to ignorance*, and not as in *All trains may be delayed due to a signal failure*. Instead, *owing to a signal failure* could be used.

duel /ˈdju:əl/ ● *noun* armed contest between two people, usually to the death; two-sided contest. ● *verb* (**-ll-**; *US* **-l-**) fight duel. ▫ **duellist** *noun*.

duenna /dju:ˈenə/ *noun* older woman acting as chaperon to girls, esp. in Spain.

duet /dju:ˈet/ *noun* musical composition for two performers.

duff ● *noun* boiled pudding. ● *adjective slang* worthless, useless, counterfeit.

duffer /ˈdʌfə/ *noun colloquial* inefficient or stupid person.

duffle /ˈdʌf(ə)l/ *noun* (also **duffel**) coarse woollen cloth. ▫ **duffle bag** cylindrical canvas bag closed by drawstring; **duffle-coat** hooded overcoat of duffle with toggle fastenings.

dug¹ *past & past participle* of DIG.

dug² *noun* udder, teat.

dugong /ˈdu:gɒŋ/ *noun* (*plural* same or **-s**) Asian sea mammal.

dugout *noun* roofed shelter, esp. for troops in trenches; underground shelter; canoe made from tree trunk.

duke /dju:k/ *noun* person holding highest hereditary title of the nobility; sovereign prince ruling duchy or small state. ◻ **dukedom** *noun*.

dulcet /ˈdʌlsɪt/ *adjective* sweet-sounding.

dulcimer /ˈdʌlsɪmə/ *noun* metal-stringed instrument struck with two hand-held hammers.

dull ● *adjective* tedious; not interesting; (of weather) overcast; (of colour, light, sound, etc.) not bright, vivid, or clear; slow-witted; stupid; (of knife-edge etc.) blunt; listless, depressed. ● *verb* make or become dull. ◻ **dullard** *noun*; **dullness** *noun*; **dully** /ˈdʌllɪ/ *adverb*.

duly /ˈdju:lɪ/ *adverb* in due time or manner; rightly, properly.

dumb /dʌm/ *adjective* unable to speak; silent, taciturn; *colloquial* stupid, ignorant. ◻ **dumb-bell** short bar with weight at each end, for muscle-building etc.; **dumbstruck** speechless with surprise.

dumbfound /dʌmˈfaʊnd/ *verb* nonplus; make speechless with surprise.

dumdum /ˈdʌmdʌm/ *noun* (in full **dumdum bullet**) soft-nosed bullet that expands on impact.

dummy /ˈdʌmɪ/ ● *noun* (*plural* **-ies**) model of human figure, esp. as used to display clothes or by ventriloquist or as target; imitation object used to replace real or normal one; baby's rubber teat; *colloquial* stupid person; imaginary player in bridge etc., whose cards are exposed and played by partner. ● *adjective* sham, imitation. ● *verb* (**-ies**, **-ied**) make pretended pass etc. in football. ◻ **dummy run** trial attempt.

dump ● *noun* place for depositing rubbish; *colloquial* unpleasant or dreary place; temporary store of ammunition etc. ● *verb* put down firmly or clumsily; deposit as rubbish; *colloquial* abandon; sell (surplus goods) to foreign market at low price; copy (contents of computer memory etc.) as diagnostic aid or for security.

dumpling /ˈdʌmplɪŋ/ *noun* ball of dough boiled in stew or containing apple etc.

dumps *plural noun* (usually in **down in the dumps**) *colloquial* low spirits.

dumpy /ˈdʌmpɪ/ *adjective* (**-ier**, **-iest**) short and stout.

dun ● *adjective* greyish-brown. ● *noun* dun colour; dun horse.

dunce *noun* person slow at learning.

dunderhead /ˈdʌndəhed/ *noun* stupid person.

dune /dju:n/ *noun* drift of sand etc. formed by wind.

dung ● *noun* excrement of animals; manure. ● *verb* apply dung to (land). ◻ **dunghill** heap of dung or refuse.

dungarees /dʌŋgəˈri:z/ *plural noun* trousers with bib attached.

dungeon /ˈdʌndʒ(ə)n/ *noun* underground prison cell.

dunk *verb* dip food into liquid before eating it.

dunlin /ˈdʌnlɪn/ *noun* red-backed sandpiper.

dunnock /ˈdʌnək/ *noun* hedge sparrow.

duo /ˈdju:əʊ/ *noun* (*plural* **-s**) pair of performers; duet.

duodecimal /dju:əʊˈdesɪm(ə)l/ *adjective* of twelfths or 12; proceeding by twelves.

duodenum /dju:əʊˈdi:nəm/ *noun* (*plural* **-s**) part of small intestine next to stomach. ◻ **duodenal** *adjective*.

duologue /ˈdju:əlɒg/ *noun* dialogue between two people.

dupe /dju:p/ ● *noun* victim of deception. ● *verb* (**-ping**) deceive, trick.

duple /ˈdju:p(ə)l/ *adjective* of two parts. ◻ **duple time** *Music* rhythm with two beats to bar.

duplex /ˈdju:pleks/ ● *noun US* flat on two floors, house subdivided for two families. ● *adjective* having two elements; twofold.

duplicate ● *adjective* /ˈdju:plɪkət/ identical; doubled. ● *noun* /-kət/ identical thing, esp. copy. ● *verb* /-keɪt/ (**-ting**) double; make or be exact copy of; repeat (an action etc.), esp. unnecessarily. ◻ **in duplicate** in two exact copies. ◻ **duplication** *noun*.

duplicator *noun* machine for producing multiple copies of texts.

duplicity /dju:ˈplɪsɪtɪ/ *noun* doubledealing; deceitfulness. ◻ **duplicitous** *adjective*.

durable /ˈdjʊərəb(ə)l/ *adjective* lasting; hard-wearing. ◻ **durability** *noun*.

duration /djʊəˈreɪʃ(ə)n/ *noun* time taken by event. ◻ **for the duration** until end of event, for very long time.

duress /djʊəˈres/ *noun* compulsion, esp. illegal use of force or threats.

Durex /ˈdjʊəreks/ *noun proprietary term* condom.

during /ˈdjʊərɪŋ/ *preposition* throughout; at some point in.

dusk *noun* darker stage of twilight.

dusky *adjective* (**-ier**, **-iest**) shadowy, dim; dark-coloured.

dust ● *noun* finely powdered earth or other material etc.; dead person's remains. ● *verb* wipe the dust from (furniture etc.); sprinkle with powder, sugar, etc. ◻ **dustbin** container for household refuse; **dust bowl** desert made by drought or erosion; **dustcover** dust-sheet, dust-jacket; **dust-jacket** paper cover on hardback book; **dustman** man employed to collect household refuse; **dustpan** pan into which dust is brushed from floor etc.; **dust-sheet** protective cloth over furniture; **dust-up** *colloquial* fight, disturbance.

duster *noun* cloth etc. for dusting furniture etc.

dusty *adjective* (**-ier**, **-iest**) covered with or full of or like dust.

Dutch ● *adjective* of the Netherlands or its people or language. ● *noun* Dutch language; (**the Dutch**) (treated as *plural*) the people of the Netherlands. ◻ **Dutch auction** one in which price is progressively reduced; **Dutch barn** roof on poles over hay etc.; **Dutch cap** dome-shaped contraceptive device fitting over cervix; **Dutch courage** courage induced by alcohol; **Dutchman**, **Dutchwoman** native or national of the Netherlands; **Dutch treat** party, outing, etc. at which people pay for themselves; **go Dutch** share expenses on outing.

dutiable /ˈdju:tɪəb(ə)l/ *adjective* requiring payment of duty.

dutiful /ˈdju:tɪfʊl/ *adjective* doing one's duty; obedient. ◻ **dutifully** *adverb*.

duty /ˈdju:tɪ/ *noun* (*plural* **-ies**) moral or legal obligation; responsibility; tax on certain goods, imports, etc.; job or function arising from a business or office. ◻ **duty-free** (of goods) on which duty is not payable; **on, off duty** working or not working.

duvet /ˈdu:veɪ/ *noun* thick soft quilt used instead of sheets and blankets.

dwarf /dwɔ:f/ ● *noun* (*plural* **-s** or **dwarves** /dwɔ:vz/) person, animal, or plant much below normal size, esp. with normal-sized head and body but short limbs; small mythological being with magical powers. ● *verb* stunt in growth; make look small by contrast.

dwell *verb* (*past & past participle* **dwelt** or **dwelled**) reside, live. ◻ **dwell on** think, write, or speak at length on. ◻ **dweller** *noun*.

dwelling *noun* house, residence.

dwindle /ˈdwɪnd(ə)l/ *verb* (**-ling**) become gradually less or smaller; lose importance.

dye /daɪ/ ● *noun* substance used to change colour of fabric, wood, hair, etc.; colour produced by this. ● *verb* (**dyeing**, **dyed**) colour with dye; dye a specified colour. ◻ **dyer** *noun*.

dying /ˈdaɪɪŋ/ ● *present participle* of DIE[1]. ● *adjective* of, or at the time of, death.

dyke /daɪk/ (also **dike**) ● *noun* embankment built to prevent flooding; low wall. ● *verb* (**-king**) provide or protect with dyke(s).

dynamic /daɪˈnæmɪk/ *adjective* energetic, active; of motive force; of force in operation; of dynamics. □ **dynamically** *adverb*.

dynamics *plural noun* (usually treated as *singular*) mathematical study of motion and forces causing it.

dynamism /ˈdaɪnəmɪz(ə)m/ *noun* energy; dynamic power.

dynamite /ˈdaɪnəmaɪt/ ● *noun* highly explosive mixture containing nitroglycerine. ● *verb* (**-ting**) charge or blow up with this.

dynamo /ˈdaɪnəməʊ/ *noun* (*plural* **-s**) machine converting mechanical into electrical energy; *colloquial* energetic person.

dynast /ˈdɪnəst/ *noun* ruler; member of dynasty.

dynasty /ˈdɪnəstɪ/ *noun* (*plural* **-ies**) line of hereditary rulers. □ **dynastic** /-ˈnæs-/ *adjective*.

dyne *noun Physics* force required to give a mass of one gram an acceleration of one centimetre per second per second.

dysentery /ˈdɪsəntrɪ/ *noun* inflammation of bowels, causing severe diarrhoea.

dysfunction /dɪsˈfʌŋkʃ(ə)n/ *noun* abnormality or impairment of functioning.

dyslexia /dɪsˈleksɪə/ *noun* abnormal difficulty in reading and spelling. □ **dyslectic** /-ˈlektɪk/ *adjective & noun*; **dyslexic** *adjective & noun*.

dyspepsia /dɪsˈpepsɪə/ *noun* indigestion. □ **dyspeptic** *adjective & noun*.

dystrophy /ˈdɪstrəfɪ/ *noun* defective nutrition.

Ee

E *abbreviation* (also **E.**) east(ern). ▫ **E-number** number prefixed by letter E identifying food additive.

each ● *adjective* every one of two or more, regarded separately. ● *pronoun* each person or thing. ▫ **each way** (of bet) backing horse etc. to win or come second or third.

eager /ˈiːɡə/ *adjective* keen, enthusiastic. ▫ **eagerly** *adverb*; **eagerness** *noun*.

eagle /ˈiːɡ(ə)l/ *noun* large bird of prey; *Golf* score of two under par for hole. ▫ **eagle eye** keen sight, watchfulness; **eagle-eyed** *adjective*.

eaglet /ˈiːɡlɪt/ *noun* young eagle.

ear[1] /ɪə/ *noun* organ of hearing, esp. external part; faculty of discriminating sound; attention. ▫ **all ears** listening attentively; **earache** pain in inner ear; **eardrum** membrane of middle ear; **earphone** (usually in *plural*) device worn on ear to listen to recording, radio, etc.; **earplug** device worn in ear as protection from water, noise, etc.; **earring** jewellery worn on ear; **earshot** hearing-range; **ear-trumpet** trumpet-shaped tube formerly used as hearing aid.

ear[2] /ɪə/ *noun* seed-bearing head of cereal plant.

earl /ɜːl/ *noun* British nobleman ranking between marquess and viscount. ▫ **earldom** *noun*.

early /ˈɜːlɪ/ *adjective & adverb* (**-ier**, **-iest**) before due, usual, or expected time; not far on in day or night or in development etc. ▫ **early bird** *colloquial* person who arrives, gets up, etc. early; **early days** too soon to expect results etc.

earmark *verb* set aside for special purpose.

earn /ɜːn/ *verb* obtain as reward for work or merit; bring as income or interest. ▫ **earner** *noun*.

earnest /ˈɜːnɪst/ *adjective* intensely serious. ▫ **in earnest** serious(ly). ▫ **earnestly** *adverb*; **earnestness** *noun*.

earnings /ˈɜːnɪŋz/ *plural noun* money earned.

earth /ɜːθ/ ● *noun* planet we live on (also **Earth**); land and sea as opposed to sky; ground; soil, mould; this world as opposed to heaven or hell; *Electricity* connection to earth as completion of circuit; hole of fox etc. ● *verb Electricity* connect to earth; cover (roots) with earth. ▫ **earthwork** bank of earth in fortification; **earthworm** worm living in earth; **run to earth** find after long search.

earthen *adjective* made of earth or baked clay. ▫ **earthenware** pottery made of fired clay.

earthly *adjective* of earth, terrestrial; *colloquial* (usually with negative) remotely possible. ▫ **not an earthly** *colloquial* no chance or idea whatever.

earthquake *noun* violent shaking of earth's surface.

earthy *adjective* (**-ier**, **-iest**) of or like earth or soil; coarse, crude.

earwig *noun* insect with pincers at rear end.

ease /iːz/ ● *noun* facility, effortlessness; freedom from pain, trouble, or constraint. ● *verb* (**-sing**) relieve from pain etc.; (often + *off*, *up*) become less burdensome or severe; relax, slacken; move or be moved by gentle force.

easel /ˈiːz(ə)l/ *noun* stand for painting, blackboard, etc.

easement *noun Law* right of way over another's property.

easily /ˈiːzɪlɪ/ *adverb* without difficulty; by far; very probably.

east ● *noun* point of horizon where sun rises at equinoxes; corresponding compass point; (usually **the East**) eastern part of world, country, town, etc. ● *adjective* towards, at, near, or facing east; (of wind) from east. ● *adverb* towards, at, or near east; (+ *of*) further east than. ▫ **eastbound** travelling or leading east; **East End** part of London east of City; **east-north-east**, **east-south-east** point midway between east and north-east or south-east. ▫ **eastward** *adjective, adverb, & noun*; **eastwards** *adverb*.

Easter /ˈiːstə/ *noun* festival of Christ's resurrection. ▫ **Easter egg** artificial usually chocolate egg given at Easter; **Easter Saturday** day before Easter, (properly) Saturday after Easter.

easterly /ˈiːstəlɪ/ *adjective & adverb* in eastern position or direction; (of wind) from east.

eastern /ˈiːst(ə)n/ *adjective* of or in east. ▫ **Eastern Church** Orthodox Church. ▫ **easternmost** *adjective*.

easterner *noun* native or inhabitant of east.

easy /ˈiːzɪ/ ● *adjective* (**-ier**, **-iest**) not difficult; free from pain, trouble, or anxiety; relaxed and pleasant; compliant. ● *adverb* with ease, in an effortless or relaxed way. ▫ **easy chair** large comfortable armchair; **easygoing** placid and tolerant; **go easy** (usually + *on*, *with*) be sparing or cautious; **take it easy** proceed gently, relax.

eat *verb* (*past* **ate** /et, eɪt/; *past participle* **eaten**) chew and swallow (food); consume food, have meal; destroy, consume. ▫ **eating apple** one suitable for eating raw; **eat out** have meal away from home, esp. in restaurant; **eat up** eat completely.

eatable ● *adjective* fit to be eaten. ● *noun* (usually in *plural*) food.

eater *noun* person who eats; eating apple.

eau-de-Cologne /əʊdəkəˈləʊn/ *noun* toilet water originally from Cologne.

eaves /iːvz/ *plural noun* underside of projecting roof.

eavesdrop *verb* (**-pp-**) listen to private conversation. ▫ **eavesdropper** *noun*.

ebb ● *noun* outflow of tide. ● *verb* flow back; decline.

ebony /ˈebənɪ/ ● *noun* hard heavy black tropical wood. ● *adjective* made of or black as ebony.

ebullient /ɪˈbʌlɪənt/ *adjective* exuberant. ▫ **ebullience** *noun*; **ebulliently** *adverb*.

EC *abbreviation* European Community; East Central.

eccentric /ɪkˈsentrɪk/ ● *adjective* odd or capricious in behaviour or appearance; not placed centrally, not having axis etc. placed centrally; not concentric; not circular. ● *noun* eccentric person. ▫ **eccentrically** *adverb*; **eccentricity** /eksenˈtrɪs-/ *noun* (*plural* **-ies**).

ecclesiastic /ɪkliːzɪˈæstɪk/ *noun* clergyman.

ecclesiastical *adjective* of the Church or clergy.

ECG *abbreviation* electrocardiogram.

echelon /ˈeʃəlɒn/ *noun* level in organization, society, etc.; wedge-shaped formation of troops, aircraft, etc.

echidna /ɪˈkɪdnə/ *noun* Australian egg-laying spiny mammal.

echo /ˈekəʊ/ ● *noun* (*plural* **-es**) repetition of sound by reflection of sound waves; reflected radio or radar beam; close imitation; circumstance or event reminiscent of earlier one. ● *verb* (**-es**, **-ed**) resound with echo; repeat, imitate; be repeated.

éclair /eɪˈkleə/ *noun* finger-shaped iced cake of choux pastry filled with cream.

éclat /eɪ'klɑː/ *noun* brilliant display; conspicuous success; prestige.
eclectic /ɪ'klektɪk/ ● *adjective* selecting ideas, style, etc. from various sources. ● *noun* eclectic person. □ **eclecticism** /-tɪs-/ *noun*.
eclipse /ɪ'klɪps/ ● *noun* obscuring of light of sun by moon (**solar eclipse**) or of moon by earth (**lunar eclipse**); loss of light or importance. ● *verb* (**-sing**) cause eclipse of; intercept (light); outshine, surpass.
eclogue /'eklɒg/ *noun* short pastoral poem.
ecology /ɪ'kɒlədʒɪ/ *noun* study of relations of organisms to one another and their surroundings. □ **ecological** /iːkə'lɒdʒ-/ *adjective*; **ecologically** /iːkə'lɒdʒ-/ *adverb*; **ecologist** *noun*.
economic /iːkə'nɒmɪk/ *adjective* of economics; profitable; connected with trade and industry. □ **economically** *adverb*.
economical /iːkə'nɒmɪk(ə)l/ *adjective* sparing; avoiding waste. □ **economically** *adverb*.
economics /iːkə'nɒmɪks/ *plural noun* (treated as *singular*) science of production and distribution of wealth; application of this to particular subject. □ **economist** /ɪ'kɒnəmɪst/ *noun*.
economize /ɪ'kɒnəmaɪz/ *verb* (also **-ise**) (**-zing** or **-sing**) make economies; reduce expenditure.
economy /ɪ'kɒnəmɪ/ *noun* (*plural* **-ies**) community's system of wealth creation; frugality, instance of this; sparing use.
ecosystem /'iːkəʊsɪstəm/ *noun* biological community of interacting organisms and their physical environment.
ecru /'eɪkruː/ *noun* light fawn colour.
ecstasy /'ekstəsɪ/ *noun* (*plural* **-ies**) overwhelming joy or rapture; *slang* type of hallucinogenic drug. □ **ecstatic** /ɪk'stætɪk/ *adjective*.
ECT *abbreviation* electroconvulsive therapy.
ectoplasm /'ektəʊplæz(ə)m/ *noun* supposed substance exuding from body of spiritualistic medium during trance.
ecu /'ekjuː/ *noun* (also **Ecu**) (*plural* **-s**) European Currency Unit.
ecumenical /iːkjuː'menɪk(ə)l/ *adjective* of or representing whole Christian world; seeking worldwide Christian unity. □ **ecumenism** /iː'kjuːmən-/ *noun*.
eczema /'eksɪmə/ *noun* kind of inflammation of skin.
ed. *abbreviation* edited by; edition; editor.
Edam /'iːdæm/ *noun* round Dutch cheese with red rind.
eddy /'edɪ/ ● *noun* (*plural* **-ies**) circular movement of water, smoke, etc. ● *verb* (**-ies**, **-ied**) move in eddies.
edelweiss /'eɪd(ə)lvaɪs/ *noun* Alpine plant with woolly white bracts.
edema *US* = OEDEMA.
Eden /'iːd(ə)n/ *noun* (in full **Garden of Eden**) home of Adam and Eve; delightful place or state.
edge ● *noun* boundary-line or margin of area or surface; narrow surface of thin object; meeting-line of surfaces; sharpness; sharpened side of blade; brink of precipice; crest of ridge; effectiveness. ● *verb* (**-ging**) advance gradually or furtively; give or form border to; sharpen. □ **edgeways**, **edgewise** with edge foremost or uppermost; **have the edge on, over** have slight advantage over; **on edge** excited or irritable; **set (person's) teeth on edge** cause unpleasant nervous sensation in.
edging *noun* thing forming edge.
edgy *adjective* (**-ier**, **-iest**) irritable; anxious.
edible /'edɪb(ə)l/ *adjective* fit to be eaten.
edict /'iːdɪkt/ *noun* order proclaimed by authority.
edifice /'edɪfɪs/ *noun* building, esp. imposing one.
edify /'edɪfaɪ/ *verb* (**-ies**, **-ied**) improve morally. □ **edification** *noun*.
edit /'edɪt/ *verb* (**-t-**) prepare for publication or broadcast; be editor of; cut and collate (films etc.) to make unified sequence; reword, modify; (+ *out*) remove (part) from text, recording, etc.
edition /ɪ'dɪʃ(ə)n/ *noun* edited or published form of book etc.; copies of book or newspaper etc. issued at one time; instance of regular broadcast.
editor /'edɪtə/ *noun* person who edits; person who directs writing of newspaper or news programme or section of one; person who selects material for publication. □ **editorship** *noun*.
editorial /edɪ'tɔːrɪəl/ ● *adjective* of editing or an editor. ● *noun* article giving newspaper's views on current topic.
educate /'edjʊkeɪt/ *verb* (**-ting**) train or instruct mentally and morally; provide systematic instruction for. □ **educable** *adjective*; **education** *noun*; **educational** *adjective*; **educator** *noun*.
educationist *noun* (also **educationalist**) expert in educational methods.
Edwardian /ed'wɔːdɪən/ ● *adjective* of or characteristic of reign (1901–10) of Edward VII. ● *noun* person of this period.
EEC *abbreviation* European Economic Community.
EEG *abbreviation* electroencephalogram.
eel *noun* snakelike fish.
eerie /'ɪərɪ/ *adjective* (**-r**, **-st**) strange; weird. □ **eerily** *adverb*.
efface /ɪ'feɪs/ *verb* (**-cing**) rub or wipe out; surpass, eclipse; (**efface oneself**) treat oneself as unimportant. □ **effacement** *noun*.
effect /ɪ'fekt/ ● *noun* result, consequence; efficacy; impression; (in *plural*) possessions; (in *plural*) lighting, sound, etc. giving realism to play etc.; physical phenomenon. ● *verb* bring about.

■ **Usage** As a verb, *effect* should not be confused with *affect*. *He effected an entrance* means 'He got in (somehow)', but *This won't affect me* means 'My life won't be changed by this'.

effective *adjective* operative; impressive; actual; producing intended result. □ **effectively** *adverb*; **effectiveness** *noun*.
effectual /ɪ'fektʃʊəl/ *adjective* producing required effect; valid.
effeminate /ɪ'femɪnət/ *adjective* (of a man) unmanly, womanish. □ **effeminacy** *noun*.
effervesce /efə'ves/ *verb* (**-cing**) give off bubbles of gas. □ **effervescence** *noun*; **effervescent** *adjective*.
effete /ɪ'fiːt/ *adjective* feeble; effeminate.
efficacious /efɪ'keɪʃəs/ *adjective* producing desired effect. □ **efficacy** /'efɪkəsɪ/ *noun*.
efficient /ɪ'fɪʃ(ə)nt/ *adjective* productive with minimum waste of effort; competent, capable. □ **efficiency** *noun*; **efficiently** *adverb*.
effigy /'efɪdʒɪ/ *noun* (*plural* **-ies**) sculpture or model of person.
effloresce /eflɔː'res/ *verb* (**-cing**) burst into flower. □ **efflorescence** *noun*.
effluence /'eflʊəns/ *noun* flowing out (of light, electricity, etc.); what flows out.
effluent /'eflʊənt/ ● *adjective* flowing out. ● *noun* sewage or industrial waste discharged into river etc.; stream flowing from lake etc.
effluvium /ɪ'fluːvɪəm/ *noun* (*plural* **-via**) unpleasant or harmful outflow.
effort /'efət/ *noun* exertion; determined attempt; force exerted; *colloquial* something accomplished. □ **effortless** *adjective*; **effortlessly** *adverb*.
effrontery /ɪ'frʌntərɪ/ *noun* impudence.
effuse /ɪ'fjuːz/ *verb* (**-sing**) pour forth.
effusion /ɪ'fjuːʒ(ə)n/ *noun* outpouring.

effusive /ɪ'fju:sɪv/ *adjective* demonstrative; gushing. □ **effusively** *adverb*; **effusiveness** *noun*.

EFL *abbreviation* English as a foreign language.

Efta /'eftə/ *noun* (also **EFTA**) European Free Trade Association.

e.g. *abbreviation* for example.

egalitarian /ɪgælɪ'teərɪən/ ● *adjective* of or advocating equal rights for all. ● *noun* egalitarian person. □ **egalitarianism** *noun*.

egg[1] *noun* body produced by female of birds, insects, etc., capable of developing into new individual; edible egg of domestic hen; ovum. □ **eggcup** cup for holding boiled egg; **egghead** *colloquial* intellectual; **eggplant** aubergine; **egg white** white or clear part round yolk of egg.

egg[2] *verb* (+ *on*) urge.

eglantine /'egləntaɪn/ *noun* sweet-brier.

ego /'i:gəʊ/ *noun* (*plural* **-s**) the self; part of mind that has sense of individuality; self-esteem.

egocentric /i:gəʊ'sentrɪk/ *adjective* self-centred.

egoism /'i:gəʊɪz(ə)m/ *noun* self-interest as moral basis of behaviour; systematic selfishness; egotism. □ **egoist** *noun*; **egoistic** /-'ɪs-/ *adjective*.

egotism /'i:gətɪz(ə)m/ *noun* self-conceit; selfishness. □ **egotist** *noun*; **egotistic(al)** /-'tɪs-/ *adjective*.

egregious /ɪ'gri:dʒəs/ *adjective* extremely bad; *archaic* remarkable.

egress /'i:gres/ *noun* going out; way out.

egret /'i:grɪt/ *noun* kind of white heron.

Egyptian /ɪ'dʒɪpʃ(ə)n/ ● *adjective* of Egypt. ● *noun* native or national of Egypt; language of ancient Egyptians.

Egyptology /i:dʒɪp'tɒlədʒɪ/ *noun* study of ancient Egypt. □ **Egyptologist** *noun*.

eh /eɪ/ *interjection colloquial: expressing inquiry, surprise, etc.*

eider /'aɪdə/ *noun* northern species of duck. □ **eiderdown** quilt stuffed with soft material, esp. down.

eight /eɪt/ *adjective & noun* one more than seven; 8-oared boat, its crew. □ **eightsome reel** lively Scottish dance for 8 people. □ **eighth** /eɪtθ/ *adjective & noun*.

eighteen /eɪ'ti:n/ *adjective & noun* one more than seventeen. □ **eighteenth** *adjective & noun*.

eighty /'eɪtɪ/ *adjective & noun* (*plural* **-ies**) eight times ten. □ **eightieth** *adjective & noun*.

eisteddfod /aɪ'stedfəd/ *noun* congress of Welsh poets and musicians gathering for musical and literary competition.

either /'aɪðə, 'i:ðə/ ● *adjective & pronoun* one or other of two; each of two. ● *adverb* (with negative) any more than the other. □ **either ... or ...** as one possibility ... and as the other ...

ejaculate /ɪ'dʒækjʊleɪt/ *verb* (**-ting**) emit (semen) in orgasm; exclaim. □ **ejaculation** *noun*.

eject /ɪ'dʒekt/ *verb* throw out, expel; (of pilot etc.) cause oneself to be propelled from aircraft in emergency; emit. □ **ejection** *noun*.

ejector seat *noun* device in aircraft for emergency ejection of pilot etc.

eke *verb* (**eking**) □ **eke out** supplement (income etc.), make (living) or support (existence) with difficulty.

elaborate ● *adjective* /ɪ'læbərət/ minutely worked out; complicated. ● *verb* /ɪ'læbəreɪt/ (**-ting**) work out or explain in detail. □ **elaborately** *adverb*; **elaboration** *noun*.

élan /eɪ'lɑ̃/ *noun* vivacity, dash. [French]

eland /'i:lənd/ *noun* (*plural* same or **-s**) large African antelope.

elapse /ɪ'læps/ *verb* (**-sing**) (of time) pass by.

elastic /ɪ'læstɪk/ ● *adjective* able to resume normal bulk or shape after being stretched or squeezed; springy; flexible. ● *noun* elastic cord or fabric, usually woven with strips of rubber. □ **elastic band** rubber band. □ **elasticity** /i:læ'stɪs-/ *noun*.

elasticated /ɪ'læstɪkeɪtɪd/ *adjective* (of fabric) made elastic by weaving with rubber thread.

elate /ɪ'leɪt/ *verb* (**-ting**) (esp. as **elated** *adjective*) make delighted or proud. □ **elation** *noun*.

elbow /'elbəʊ/ ● *noun* joint between forearm and upper arm; part of sleeve covering elbow; elbow-shaped thing. ● *verb* thrust or jostle (person); make (one's way) thus. □ **elbow-grease** *jocular* vigorous polishing, hard work; **elbow-room** sufficient space to move or work in.

elder[1] /'eldə/ ● *adjective* older; senior. ● *noun* older person; official in early Christian and some modern Churches.

elder[2] /'eldə/ *noun* tree with white flowers and black **elderberries**.

elderly /'eldəlɪ/ *adjective* rather old.

eldest /'eldɪst/ *adjective* first-born; oldest surviving.

eldorado /eldə'rɑ:dəʊ/ *noun* (*plural* **-s**) imaginary land of great wealth.

elect /ɪ'lekt/ ● *verb* choose by voting; choose, decide. ● *adjective* chosen; select, choice; (after noun) chosen but not yet in office.

election /ɪ'lekʃ(ə)n/ *noun* electing, being elected; occasion for this.

electioneer /ɪlekʃə'nɪə/ *verb* take part in election campaign.

elective /ɪ'lektɪv/ *adjective* chosen by or derived from election; entitled to elect; optional.

elector /ɪ'lektə/ *noun* person entitled to vote in election. □ **electoral** *adjective*.

electorate /ɪ'lektərət/ *noun* group of electors.

electric /ɪ'lektrɪk/ *adjective* of, worked by, or charged with electricity; causing or charged with excitement. □ **electric blanket** one heated by internal wires; **electric chair** chair used for electrocution of criminals; **electric eel** eel-like fish able to give electric shock; **electric fire** portable electric heater; **electric shock** effect of sudden discharge of electricity through body of person etc. □ **electrically** *adverb*.

electrical *adjective* of or worked by electricity. □ **electrically** *adverb*.

electrician /ɪlek'trɪʃ(ə)n/ *noun* person who installs or maintains electrical equipment.

electricity /ɪlek'trɪsɪtɪ/ *noun* form of energy present in protons and electrons; science of electricity; supply of electricity.

electrify /ɪ'lektrɪfaɪ/ *verb* (**-ies**, **-ied**) charge with electricity; convert to electric working; startle, excite. □ **electrification** *noun*.

electro- *combining form* of or caused by electricity.

electrocardiogram /ɪlektrəʊ'kɑ:dɪəgræm/ *noun* record of electric currents generated by heartbeat. □ **electrocardiograph** instrument for recording such currents.

electroconvulsive /ɪlektrəʊkən'vʌlsɪv/ *adjective* (of therapy) using convulsive response to electric shocks.

electrocute /ɪ'lektrəkju:t/ *verb* (**-ting**) kill by electric shock. □ **electrocution** /-'kju:ʃ(ə)n/ *noun*.

electrode /ɪ'lektrəʊd/ *noun* conductor through which electricity enters or leaves electrolyte, gas, vacuum, etc.

electroencephalogram /ɪlektrəʊɪn'sefələgræm/ *noun* record of electrical activity of brain. □ **electroencephalograph** instrument for recording such activity.

electrolysis /ɪlek'trɒlɪsɪs/ *noun* chemical decomposition by electric action; breaking up of tumours, hair-roots, etc. thus.

electrolyte /ɪ'lektrəlaɪt/ *noun* solution that can conduct electricity; substance that can dissolve to produce this. □ **electrolytic** /-trəʊ'lɪt-/ *adjective*.

electromagnet /ɪlektrəʊ'mægnɪt/ *noun* soft metal core made into magnet by electric current through coil surrounding it.

electromagnetism /ɪlektrəʊ'mægnɪtɪz(ə)m/ *noun* magnetic forces produced by electricity; study of these.

electron /ɪ'lektrɒn/ *noun* stable elementary particle with charge of negative electricity, found in all atoms and acting as primary carrier of electricity in solids. □ **electron microscope** one with high magnification, using electron beam instead of light.

electronic /ɪlek'trɒnɪk/ *adjective* of electrons or electronics; (of music) produced electronically. □ **electronic mail** messages distributed by a computer system. □ **electronically** *adverb*.

electronics *plural noun* (treated as *singular*) science of movement of electrons in vacuum, gas, semiconductor, etc.

electroplate /ɪ'lektrəʊpleɪt/ ● *verb* (**-ting**) coat with chromium, silver, etc. by electrolysis. ● *noun* electroplated articles.

elegant /'elɪgənt/ *adjective* graceful, tasteful, refined; ingeniously simple. □ **elegance** *noun*; **elegantly** *adverb*.

elegy /'elɪdʒɪ/ *noun* (*plural* **-ies**) sorrowful song or poem, esp. for the dead. □ **elegiac** /-'dʒaɪək/ *adjective*.

element /'elɪmənt/ *noun* component part; substance which cannot be resolved by chemical means into simpler substances; any of **the four elements** (earth, water, air, fire) formerly supposed to make up all matter; wire that gives out heat in electric heater, cooker, etc.; (in *plural*) atmospheric agencies; (in *plural*) rudiments, first principles; (in *plural*) bread and wine of Eucharist. □ **in one's element** in one's preferred situation.

elemental /elɪ'ment(ə)l/ *adjective* of or like the elements or the forces of nature; basic, essential.

elementary /elɪ'mentərɪ/ *adjective* dealing with simplest facts of subject; unanalysable. □ **elementary particle** *Physics* subatomic particle, esp. one not known to consist of simpler ones.

elephant /'elɪf(ə)nt/ *noun* (*plural* same or **-s**) largest living land animal, with trunk and ivory tusks.

elephantiasis /elɪfən'taɪəsɪs/ *noun* skin disease causing gross enlargement of limbs etc.

elephantine /elɪ'fæntaɪn/ *adjective* of elephants; huge; clumsy.

elevate /'elɪveɪt/ *verb* (**-ting**) lift up, raise; exalt in rank etc.; (usually as **elevated** *adjective*) raise morally or intellectually.

elevation *noun* elevating, being elevated; angle above horizontal; height above given level; drawing showing one side of building.

elevator *noun US* lift; movable part of tailplane for changing aircraft's altitude; hoisting machine.

eleven /ɪ'lev(ə)n/ *adjective & noun* one more than ten; team of 11 people in cricket etc. □ **eleventh hour** last possible moment. □ **eleventh** *adjective & noun*.

elevenses /ɪ'levənzɪz/ *noun colloquial* light mid-morning refreshment.

elf *noun* (*plural* **elves** /elvz/) mythological being, esp. small and mischievous one. □ **elfish** *adjective*.

elfin /'elfɪn/ *adjective* of elves; elflike.

elicit /ɪ'lɪsɪt/ *verb* (**-t-**) draw out (facts, response, etc.).

elide /ɪ'laɪd/ *verb* (**-ding**) omit in pronunciation.

eligible /'elɪdʒɪb(ə)l/ *adjective* (often + *for*) fit or entitled to be chosen; desirable or suitable, esp. for marriage. □ **eligibility** *noun*.

eliminate /ɪ'lɪmɪneɪt/ *verb* (**-ting**) remove, get rid of; exclude. □ **elimination** *noun*; **eliminator** *noun*.

elision /ɪ'lɪʒ(ə)n/ *noun* omission of vowel or syllable in pronunciation.

élite /ɪ'li:t/ *noun* select group or class; (**the élite**) the best (of a group).

élitism *noun* advocacy of or reliance on dominance by select group. □ **élitist** *noun & adjective*.

elixir /ɪ'lɪksɪə/ *noun* alchemist's preparation supposedly able to change metal into gold or prolong life indefinitely; aromatic medicine.

Elizabethan /ɪlɪzə'bi:θ(ə)n/ ● *adjective* of time of Elizabeth I or II. ● *noun* person of this time.

elk *noun* (*plural* same or **-s**) large type of deer.

ellipse /ɪ'lɪps/ *noun* regular oval.

ellipsis /ɪ'lɪpsɪs/ *noun* (*plural* **ellipses** /-si:z/) omission of words needed to complete construction or sense.

elliptical /ɪ'lɪptɪk(ə)l/ *adjective* of or like an ellipse; (of language) confusingly concise.

elm *noun* tree with rough serrated leaves; its wood.

elocution /elə'kju:ʃ(ə)n/ *noun* art of clear and expressive speaking.

elongate /'i:lɒŋgeɪt/ *verb* (**-ting**) extend, lengthen. □ **elongation** *noun*.

elope /ɪ'ləʊp/ *verb* (**-ping**) run away to marry secretly. □ **elopement** *noun*.

eloquence /'eləkwəns/ *noun* fluent and effective use of language. □ **eloquent** *adjective*; **eloquently** *adverb*.

else /els/ *adverb* besides; instead; otherwise, if not. □ **elsewhere** in or to some other place.

elucidate /ɪ'lu:sɪdeɪt/ *verb* (**-ting**) throw light on, explain. □ **elucidation** *noun*.

elude /ɪ'lu:d/ *verb* (**-ding**) escape adroitly from; avoid; baffle.

elusive /ɪ'lu:sɪv/ *adjective* difficult to find, catch, or remember; avoiding the point raised. □ **elusiveness** *noun*.

elver /'elvə/ *noun* young eel.

elves *plural* of ELF.

Elysium /ɪ'lɪzɪəm/ *noun Greek Mythology* home of the blessed after death; place of ideal happiness. □ **Elysian** *adjective*.

em *noun Printing* unit of measurement approximately equal to width of M.

emaciate /ɪ'meɪsɪeɪt/ *verb* (**-ting**) (esp. as **emaciated** *adjective*) make thin or feeble. □ **emaciation** *noun*.

emanate /'eməneɪt/ *verb* (**-ting**) (usually + *from*) issue or originate (from source). □ **emanation** *noun*.

emancipate /ɪ'mænsɪpeɪt/ *verb* (**-ting**) free from social, political, or moral restraint. □ **emancipation** *noun*.

emasculate ● *verb* /ɪ'mæskjʊleɪt/ (**-ting**) enfeeble; castrate. ● *adjective* /ɪ'mæskjʊlət/ enfeebled; castrated; effeminate. □ **emasculation** *noun*.

embalm /ɪm'bɑ:m/ *verb* preserve (corpse) from decay; preserve from oblivion; make fragrant.

embankment /ɪm'bæŋkmənt/ *noun* bank constructed to confine water or carry road or railway.

embargo /ɪm'bɑ:gəʊ/ ● *noun* (*plural* **-es**) order forbidding ships to enter or leave port; suspension of commerce or other activity. ● *verb* (**-es**, **-ed**) place under embargo.

embark /ɪm'bɑ:k/ *verb* put or go on board ship; (+ *on*, *in*) begin (enterprise).

embarkation /embɑ:'keɪʃ(ə)n/ *noun* embarking on ship.

embarrass /ɪm'barəs/ *verb* make (person) feel awkward or ashamed; encumber; (as **embarrassed** *adjective*) encumbered with debts. □ **embarrassment** *noun*.

embassy /'embəsɪ/ *noun* (*plural* **-ies**) ambassador's residence or offices; deputation to foreign government.

embattled /ɪm'bæt(ə)ld/ *adjective* prepared or arrayed for battle; fortified with battlements; under heavy attack, in trying circumstances.

embed /ɪm'bed/ *verb* (also **imbed**) (**-dd-**) (esp. as **embedded** *adjective*) fix in surrounding mass.

embellish /ɪm'belɪʃ/ *verb* beautify, adorn; make fictitious additions to. □ **embellishment** *noun*.

ember /'embə/ *noun* (usually in *plural*) small piece of glowing coal etc. in dying fire. □ **ember days** days of fasting and prayer in Christian Church, associated with ordinations.

embezzle /ɪm'bez(ə)l/ *verb* (**-ling**) divert (money) fraudulently to own use. □ **embezzlement** *noun*; **embezzler** *noun*.

embitter /ɪm'bɪtə/ *verb* arouse bitter feelings in. □ **embitterment** *noun*.

emblazon /ɪm'bleɪz(ə)n/ *verb* portray or adorn conspicuously.

emblem /'embləm/ *noun* symbol; (+ *of*) type, embodiment; distinctive badge. □ **emblematic** /-'mæt-/ *adjective*.

embody /ɪm'bɒdɪ/ *verb* (**-ies**, **-ied**) give concrete form to; be expression of; include, comprise. □ **embodiment** *noun*.

embolden /ɪm'bəʊld(ə)n/ *verb* encourage.

embolism /'embəlɪz(ə)m/ *noun* obstruction of artery by blood clot etc.

emboss /ɪm'bɒs/ *verb* carve or decorate with design in relief.

embrace /ɪm'breɪs/ ● *verb* (**-cing**) hold closely in arms; enclose; accept, adopt; include. ● *noun* act of embracing, clasp.

embrasure /ɪm'breɪʒə/ *noun* bevelling of wall at sides of window etc.; opening in parapet for gun.

embrocation /embrə'keɪʃ(ə)n/ *noun* liquid for rubbing on body to relieve muscular pain.

embroider /ɪm'brɔɪdə/ *verb* decorate with needlework; embellish. □ **embroidery** *noun*.

embroil /ɪm'brɔɪl/ *verb* (often + *in*) involve (in conflict or difficulties).

embryo /'embrɪəʊ/ *noun* (*plural* **-s**) unborn or unhatched offspring; thing in rudimentary stage. □ **embryonic** /-'ɒn-/ *adjective*.

emend /ɪ'mend/ *verb* correct, remove errors from (text etc.). □ **emendation** /iː-/ *noun*.

emerald /'emər(ə)ld/ ● *noun* bright green gem; colour of this. ● *adjective* bright green.

emerge /ɪ'mɜːdʒ/ *verb* (**-ging**) come up or out into view or notice. □ **emergence** *noun*; **emergent** *adjective*.

emergency /ɪ'mɜːdʒənsɪ/ *noun* (*plural* **-ies**) sudden state of danger etc., requiring immediate action.

emeritus /ɪ'merɪtəs/ *adjective* retired and holding honorary title.

emery /'emərɪ/ *noun* coarse corundum for polishing metal etc. □ **emery board** emery-coated nail-file.

emetic /ɪ'metɪk/ ● *adjective* that causes vomiting. ● *noun* emetic medicine.

emigrate /'emɪgreɪt/ *verb* (**-ting**) leave own country to settle in another. □ **emigrant** *noun & adjective*; **emigration** *noun*.

émigré /'emɪgreɪ/ *noun* emigrant, esp. political exile.

eminence /'emɪnəns/ *noun* recognized superiority; high ground; (**His**, **Your Eminence**) *title used of or to cardinal*.

eminent /'emɪnənt/ *adjective* distinguished, notable. □ **eminently** *adverb*.

emir /e'mɪə/ *noun* (also **amir** /ə'mɪə/) *title of various Muslim rulers*.

emirate /'emɪrət/ *noun* position, reign, or domain of emir.

emissary /'emɪsərɪ/ *noun* (*plural* **-ies**) person sent on diplomatic mission.

emit /ɪ'mɪt/ *verb* (**-tt-**) give or send out; discharge. □ **emission** /ɪ'mɪʃ(ə)n/ *noun*.

emollient /ɪ'mɒlɪənt/ ● *adjective* softening; soothing. ● *noun* emollient substance.

emolument /ɪ'mɒljʊmənt/ *noun* fee from employment, salary.

emotion /ɪ'məʊʃ(ə)n/ *noun* strong instinctive feeling such as love or fear; emotional intensity or sensibility.

emotional *adjective* of or expressing emotion(s); especially liable to emotion; arousing emotion. □ **emotionalism** *noun*; **emotionally** *adverb*.

■ **Usage** See note at EMOTIVE.

emotive /ɪ'məʊtɪv/ *adjective* of or arousing emotion.

■ **Usage** Although the senses of *emotive* and *emotional* overlap, *emotive* is more common in the sense 'arousing emotion', as in *an emotive issue*, and only *emotional* can mean 'especially liable to emotion', as in *a highly emotional person*.

empanel /ɪm'pæn(ə)l/ *verb* (also **impanel**) (**-ll-**; *US* **-l-**) enter (jury) on panel.

empathize /'empəθaɪz/ *verb* (also **-ise**) (**-zing** or **-sing**) (usually + *with*) exercise empathy.

empathy /'empəθɪ/ *noun* ability to identify with person or object.

emperor /'empərə/ *noun* ruler of empire.

emphasis /'emfəsɪs/ *noun* (*plural* **emphases** /-siːz/) importance attached to something; significant stress on word(s); vigour of expression etc.

emphasize /'emfəsaɪz/ *verb* (also **-ise**) (**-zing** or **-sing**) lay stress on.

emphatic /ɪm'fætɪk/ *adjective* forcibly expressive; (of word) bearing emphasis (e.g. *myself* in *I did it myself*). □ **emphatically** *adverb*.

emphysema /emfɪ'siːmə/ *noun* disease of lungs causing breathlessness.

empire /'empaɪə/ *noun* large group of states under single authority; supreme dominion; large commercial organization etc. owned or directed by one person.

empirical /ɪm'pɪrɪk(ə)l/ *adjective* based on observation or experiment, not on theory. □ **empiricism** /-rɪs-/ *noun*; **empiricist** /-rɪs-/ *noun*.

emplacement /ɪm'pleɪsmənt/ *noun* platform for gun(s); putting in position.

employ /ɪm'plɔɪ/ *verb* use services of (person) in return for payment; use (thing, time, energy, etc.); keep (person) occupied. □ **in the employ of** employed by. □ **employer** *noun*.

employee /emplɔɪ'iː/ *noun* person employed for wages.

employment *noun* employing, being employed; person's trade or profession. □ **employment office** government office finding work for the unemployed.

emporium /em'pɔːrɪəm/ *noun* large shop; centre of commerce.

empower /ɪm'paʊə/ *verb* give power to.

empress /'emprɪs/ *noun* wife or widow of emperor; woman emperor.

empty /'emptɪ/ ● *adjective* (**-ier**, **-iest**) containing nothing; vacant, unoccupied; hollow, insincere; without purpose; *colloquial* hungry; vacuous, foolish.

• *verb* (**-ies**, **-ied**) remove contents of; transfer (contents); become empty; (of river) discharge itself. • *noun* (*plural* **-ies**) *colloquial* emptied bottle etc. ◻ **empty-handed** bringing or taking nothing. ◻ **emptiness** *noun*.

EMS *abbreviation* European Monetary System.

emu /'i:mju:/ *noun* (*plural* **-s**) large flightless Australian bird.

emulate /'emjʊleɪt/ *verb* (**-ting**) try to equal or excel; imitate. ◻ **emulation** *noun*; **emulator** *noun*.

emulsify /ɪ'mʌlsɪfaɪ/ *verb* (**-ies**, **-ied**) make emulsion of. ◻ **emulsifier** *noun*.

emulsion /ɪ'mʌlʃ(ə)n/ *noun* fine dispersion of one liquid in another, esp. as paint, medicine, etc.

en *noun Printing* unit of measurement equal to half em.

enable /ɪ'neɪb(ə)l/ *verb* (**-ling**) (+ *to do*) supply with means or authority; make possible.

enact /ɪ'nækt/ *verb* ordain, decree; make (bill etc.) law; play (part). ◻ **enactment** *noun*.

enamel /ɪ'næm(ə)l/ • *noun* glasslike opaque coating on metal; any hard smooth coating; kind of hard gloss paint; hard coating of teeth. • *verb* (**-ll**; *US* **-l-**) coat with enamel.

enamour /ɪ'næmə/ *verb* (*US* **enamor**) (usually in *passive*; + *of*) inspire with love or delight.

en bloc /ɑ̃ 'blɒk/ *adverb* in a block, all at same time. [French]

encamp /ɪn'kæmp/ *verb* settle in (esp. military) camp. ◻ **encampment** *noun*.

encapsulate /ɪn'kæpsjʊleɪt/ *verb* (**-ting**) enclose (as) in capsule; summarize.

encase /ɪn'keɪs/ *verb* (**-sing**) confine (as) in a case.

encash /ɪn'kæʃ/ *verb* convert into cash. ◻ **encashment** *noun*.

encephalitis /ensefə'laɪtɪs/ *noun* inflammation of brain.

enchant /ɪn'tʃɑ:nt/ *verb* delight; bewitch. ◻ **enchanting** *adjective*; **enchantment** *noun*.

enchanter *noun* (*feminine* **enchantress**) person who enchants, esp. by magic.

encircle /ɪn'sɜ:k(ə)l/ *verb* (**-ling**) surround. ◻ **encirclement** *noun*.

enclave /'enkleɪv/ *noun* part of territory of one state surrounded by that of another; group of people distinct from those surrounding them, esp. ethnically.

enclose /ɪn'kləʊz/ *verb* (**-sing**) surround with wall, fence, etc.; shut in; put in receptacle (esp. in envelope besides letter); (as **enclosed** *adjective*) (of religious community) secluded from outside world.

enclosure /ɪn'kləʊʒə/ *noun* enclosing; enclosed space or area; thing enclosed.

encode /ɪn'kəʊd/ *verb* (**-ding**) put into code.

encomium /ɪn'kəʊmɪəm/ *noun* (*plural* **-s**) formal praise.

encompass /ɪn'kʌmpəs/ *verb* contain, include; surround.

encore /'ɒŋkɔ:/ • *noun* audience's call for repetition of item, or for further item; such item. • *verb* (**-ring**) call for repetition of or by. • *interjection* again.

encounter /ɪn'kaʊntə/ • *verb* meet by chance; meet as adversary. • *noun* meeting by chance or in conflict.

encourage /ɪn'kʌrɪdʒ/ *verb* (**-ging**) give courage to; urge; promote. ◻ **encouragement** *noun*.

encroach /ɪn'krəʊtʃ/ *verb* (usually + *on, upon*) intrude on other's territory etc. ◻ **encroachment** *noun*.

encrust /ɪn'krʌst/ *verb* cover with or form crust; coat with hard casing or deposit.

encumber /ɪn'kʌmbə/ *verb* be burden to; hamper.

encumbrance /ɪn'kʌmbrəns/ *noun* burden; impediment.

encyclical /ɪn'sɪklɪk(ə)l/ *noun* papal letter to all RC bishops.

encyclopedia /ɪnsaɪklə'pi:dɪə/ *noun* (also **-paedia**) book of information on many subjects or on many aspects of one subject.

encyclopedic *adjective* (also **-paedic**) (of knowledge or information) comprehensive.

end • *noun* limit; farthest point; extreme point or part; conclusion; latter part; destruction; death; result; goal, object; remnant. • *verb* bring or come to end. ◻ **endpaper** blank leaf of paper at beginning or end of book; **end-product** final product of manufacture etc.; **end up** be or become eventually, arrive; **in the end** finally; **make ends meet** live within one's income; **no end** *colloquial* to a great extent.

endanger /ɪn'deɪndʒə/ *verb* place in danger. ◻ **endangered species** one in danger of extinction.

endear /ɪn'dɪə/ *verb* (usually + *to*) make dear. ◻ **endearing** *adjective*.

endearment *noun* expression of affection.

endeavour /ɪn'devə/ (*US* **endeavor**) • *verb* try, strive. • *noun* attempt, effort.

endemic /en'demɪk/ *adjective* (often + *to*) regularly found among particular people or in particular area. ◻ **endemically** *adverb*.

ending *noun* end of word or story.

endive /'endaɪv/ *noun* curly-leaved plant used in salads.

endless *adjective* infinite; continual. ◻ **endlessly** *adverb*.

endocrine /'endəʊkraɪn/ *adjective* (of gland) secreting directly into blood.

endogenous /en'dɒdʒɪnəs/ *adjective* growing or originating from within.

endorse /ɪn'dɔ:s/ *verb* (**-sing**) approve; write on (document), esp. sign (cheque); enter details of offence on (driving licence). ◻ **endorsement** *noun*.

endoskeleton /'endəʊskelɪtən/ *noun* internal skeleton.

endow /ɪn'daʊ/ *verb* give permanent income to; (esp. as **endowed** *adjective*) provide with talent or ability.

endowment *noun* endowing; money with which person or thing is endowed. ◻ **endowment mortgage** one in which borrower pays only premiums until policy repays mortgage capital; **endowment policy** life insurance policy paying out on set date or earlier death.

endue /ɪn'dju:/ *verb* (**-dues**, **-dued**, **-duing**) (+ *with*) provide (person) with (quality etc.).

endurance *noun* power of enduring.

endure /ɪn'djʊə/ *verb* (**-ring**) undergo; bear; last.

endways *adverb* with an end facing forwards.

ENE *abbreviation* east-north-east.

enema /'enɪmə/ *noun* injection of liquid etc. into rectum, esp. to expel its contents; liquid used for this.

enemy /'enəmɪ/ • *noun* (*plural* **-ies**) person actively hostile to another; hostile army or nation; member of this; adversary, opponent. • *adjective* of or belonging to enemy.

energetic /enə'dʒetɪk/ *adjective* full of energy. ◻ **energetically** *adverb*.

energize /'enədʒaɪz/ *verb* (also **-ise**) (**-zing** or **-sing**) give energy to.

energy /'enədʒɪ/ *noun* (*plural* **-ies**) force, vigour, activity; ability of matter or radiation to do work.

enervate /'enəveɪt/ *verb* (**-ting**) deprive of vigour. ◻ **enervation** *noun*.

en famille /ɑ̃ fæ'mi:/ *adverb* in or with one's family. [French]

enfant terrible /ɑ̃fɑ̃ te'ri:bl/ *noun* (*plural* ***enfants terribles*** same pronunciation) indiscreet or unruly person. [French]
enfeeble /ɪn'fi:b(ə)l/ *verb* (**-ling**) make feeble. □ **enfeeblement** *noun*.
enfilade /enfɪ'leɪd/ ● *noun* gunfire directed down length of enemy position. ● *verb* (**-ding**) direct enfilade at.
enfold /ɪn'fəʊld/ *verb* wrap; embrace.
enforce /ɪn'fɔ:s/ *verb* (**-cing**) compel observance of; impose. □ **enforceable** *adjective*; **enforcement** *noun*.
enfranchise /ɪn'fræntʃaɪz/ *verb* (**-sing**) give (person) right to vote. □ **enfranchisement** /-tʃɪz-/ *noun*.
engage /ɪn'geɪdʒ/ *verb* (**-ging**) employ, hire; (as **engaged** *adjective*) occupied, busy, having promised to marry; hold (person's attention); cause parts of (gear) to interlock; fit, interlock; bring into battle; come into battle with (enemy); (usually + *in*) take part; (+ *that*, *to do*) undertake. □ **engagement** *noun*.
engender /ɪn'dʒendə/ *verb* give rise to.
engine /'endʒɪn/ *noun* mechanical contrivance of parts working together, esp. as source of power; railway locomotive.
engineer /endʒɪ'nɪə/ ● *noun* person skilled in a branch of engineering; person who makes or is in charge of engines etc.; person who designs and constructs military works; mechanic, technician. ● *verb* contrive, bring about; act as engineer; construct or manage as engineer.
engineering *noun* application of science to design, building, and use of machines etc.
English /'ɪŋglɪʃ/ ● *adjective* of England. ● *noun* language of England, now used in UK, US, and most Commonwealth countries; (**the English**) (treated as *plural*) the people of England. □ **Englishman**, **Englishwoman** native of England.
engraft /ɪn'grɑ:ft/ *verb* (usually + *into*, *on*) graft, implant, incorporate.
engrave /ɪn'greɪv/ *verb* (**-ving**) inscribe or cut (design) on hard surface; inscribe (surface) thus; (often + *on*) impress deeply (on memory etc.). □ **engraver** *noun*.
engraving *noun* print made from engraved plate.
engross /ɪn'grəʊs/ *verb* (usually as **engrossed** *adjective* + *in*) fully occupy.
engulf /ɪn'gʌlf/ *verb* flow over and swamp, overwhelm.
enhance /ɪn'hɑ:ns/ *verb* (**-cing**) intensify; improve. □ **enhancement** *noun*.
enigma /ɪ'nɪgmə/ *noun* puzzling person or thing; riddle. □ **enigmatic** /enɪg'mætɪk/ *adjective*.
enjoin /ɪn'dʒɔɪn/ *verb* command, order.
enjoy /ɪn'dʒɔɪ/ *verb* find pleasure in; (**enjoy oneself**) find pleasure; have use or benefit of; experience. □ **enjoyable** *adjective*; **enjoyably** *adverb*; **enjoyment** *noun*.
enlarge /ɪn'lɑ:dʒ/ *verb* (**-ging**) make or become larger; (often + *on*, *upon*) describe in greater detail; reproduce on larger scale. □ **enlargement** *noun*.
enlarger *noun* apparatus for enlarging photographs.
enlighten /ɪn'laɪt(ə)n/ *verb* inform; (as **enlightened** *adjective*) progressive. □ **enlightenment** *noun*.
enlist /ɪn'lɪst/ *verb* enrol in armed services; secure as means of help or support. □ **enlistment** *noun*.
enliven /ɪn'laɪv(ə)n/ *verb* make lively or cheerful. □ **enlivenment** *noun*.
en masse /ɑ̃ 'mæs/ *adverb* all together. [French]
enmesh /ɪn'meʃ/ *verb* entangle (as) in net.
enmity /'enmɪtɪ/ *noun* (*plural* **-ies**) hostility; state of being an enemy.
ennoble /ɪ'nəʊb(ə)l/ *verb* (**-ling**) make noble. □ **ennoblement** *noun*.
ennui /ɒ'nwi:/ *noun* boredom.
enormity /ɪ'nɔ:mɪtɪ/ *noun* (*plural* **-ies**) great wickedness; monstrous crime; great size.

■ **Usage** Many people believe it is wrong to use *enormity* to mean 'great size'.

enormous /ɪ'nɔ:məs/ *adjective* huge. □ **enormously** *adverb*.
enough /ɪ'nʌf/ ● *adjective* as much or as many as required. ● *noun* sufficient amount or quantity. ● *adverb* to required degree; fairly; very, quite.
enquire /ɪn'kwaɪə/ *verb* (**-ring**) seek information; ask question; inquire.
enquiry *noun* (*plural* **-ies**) asking; inquiry.
enrage /ɪn'reɪdʒ/ *verb* (**-ging**) make furious.
enrapture /ɪn'ræptʃə/ *verb* (**-ring**) delight intensely.
enrich /ɪn'rɪtʃ/ *verb* make rich(er). □ **enrichment** *noun*.
enrol /ɪn'rəʊl/ *verb* (*US* **enroll**) (**-ll-**) (cause to) join society, course, etc.; write name of (person) on list. □ **enrolment** *noun*.
en route /ɑ̃ 'ru:t/ *adverb* on the way. [French]
ensconce /ɪn'skɒns/ *verb* (**-cing**) (usually **ensconce oneself** or in *passive*) settle comfortably.
ensemble /ɒn'sɒmb(ə)l/ *noun* thing viewed as whole; set of clothes worn together; group of performers working together; *Music* passage for ensemble.
enshrine /ɪn'ʃraɪn/ *verb* (**-ning**) enclose in shrine; protect, make inviolable.
ensign /'ensaɪn/ *noun* banner, flag, esp. military or naval flag of nation; standard-bearer; *historical* lowest commissioned infantry officer; *US* lowest commissioned naval officer.
enslave /ɪn'sleɪv/ *verb* (**-ving**) make slave of. □ **enslavement** *noun*.
ensnare /ɪn'sneə/ *verb* (**-ring**) entrap.
ensue /ɪn'sju:/ *verb* (**-sues**, **-sued**, **-suing**) happen later or as a result.
en suite /ɑ̃ 'swi:t/ ● *adverb* forming single unit. ● *adjective* (of bathroom) attached to bedroom; (of bedroom) with bathroom attached.
ensure /ɪn'ʃʊə/ *verb* (**-ring**) make certain or safe.
ENT *abbreviation* ear, nose, and throat.
entail /ɪn'teɪl/ ● *verb* necessitate or involve unavoidably; *Law* bequeath (estate) to specified line of beneficiaries. ● *noun* entailed estate.
entangle /ɪn'tæŋg(ə)l/ *verb* (**-ling**) catch or hold fast in snare etc.; involve in difficulties; complicate. □ **entanglement** *noun*.
entente /ɒn'tɒnt/ *noun* friendly understanding between states. □ **entente cordiale** entente, esp. between Britain and France since 1904.
enter /'entə/ *verb* go or come in or into; come on stage; penetrate; put (name, fact, etc.) into list or record etc.; (usually + *for*) name, or name oneself, as competitor; become member of. □ **enter into** engage in, bind oneself by, form part of, sympathize with; **enter (up)on** begin, begin to deal with, assume possession of.
enteric /en'terɪk/ *adjective* of intestines.
enteritis /entə'raɪtɪs/ *noun* inflammation of intestines.
enterprise /'entəpraɪz/ *noun* bold undertaking; readiness to engage in this; business firm or venture.
enterprising *adjective* showing enterprise.
entertain /entə'teɪn/ *verb* amuse; receive as guest; harbour (feelings); consider (idea). □ **entertainer** *noun*; **entertaining** *adjective*.
entertainment *noun* entertaining; thing that entertains, performance.
enthral /ɪn'θrɔ:l/ *verb* (*US* **enthrall**) (**-ll-**) captivate; please greatly. □ **enthralment** *noun*.

enthrone /ɪn'θrəʊn/ *verb* (**-ning**) place on throne. □ **enthronement** *noun*.
enthuse /ɪn'θju:z/ *verb* (**-sing**) *colloquial* be or make enthusiastic.
enthusiasm /ɪn'θju:zɪæz(ə)m/ *noun* great eagerness or admiration; object of this. □ **enthusiast** *noun*; **enthusiastic** /-'æst-/ *adjective*; **enthusiastically** *adverb*.
entice /ɪn'taɪs/ *verb* (**-cing**) attract by offer of pleasure or reward. □ **enticement** *noun*; **enticing** *adjective*; **enticingly** *adverb*.
entire /ɪn'taɪə/ *adjective* complete; unbroken; absolute; in one piece.
entirely *adverb* wholly.
entirety /ɪn'taɪərətɪ/ *noun* (*plural* **-ies**) completeness; sum total. □ **in its entirety** in its complete form.
entitle /ɪn'taɪt(ə)l/ *verb* (**-ling**) (usually + *to*) give (person) right or claim; give title to. □ **entitlement** *noun*.
entity /'entɪtɪ/ *noun* (*plural* **-ies**) thing with distinct existence; thing's existence.
entomb /ɪn'tu:m/ *verb* place in tomb; serve as tomb for. □ **entombment** *noun*.
entomology /entə'mɒlədʒɪ/ *noun* study of insects. □ **entomological** /-mə'lɒdʒ-/ *adjective*; **entomologist** *noun*.
entourage /'ɒntʊərɑ:ʒ/ *noun* people attending important person.
entr'acte /'ɒntrækt/ *noun* (music or dance performed in) interval in play.
entrails /'entreɪlz/ *plural noun* intestines; inner parts.
entrance[1] /'entrəns/ *noun* place for entering; coming or going in; right of admission.
entrance[2] /ɪn'trɑ:ns/ *verb* (**-cing**) enchant, delight; put into trance.
entrant /'entrənt/ *noun* person who enters exam, profession, etc.
entrap /ɪn'træp/ *verb* (**-pp-**) catch (as) in trap.
entreat /ɪn'tri:t/ *verb* ask earnestly, beg.
entreaty *noun* (*plural* **-ies**) earnest request.
entrecôte /'ɒntrəkəʊt/ *noun* boned steak cut off sirloin.
entrée /'ɒntreɪ/ *noun* main dish of meal; dish served between fish and meat courses; right of admission.
entrench /ɪn'trentʃ/ *verb* establish firmly; (as **entrenched** *adjective*) (of attitude etc.) not easily modified; surround or fortify with trench. □ **entrenchment** *noun*.
entrepreneur /ɒntrəprə'nɜ:/ *noun* person who undertakes commercial venture. □ **entrepreneurial** *adjective*.
entropy /'entrəpɪ/ *noun* measure of disorganization of universe; measure of unavailability of system's thermal energy for conversion into mechanical work.
entrust /ɪn'trʌst/ *verb* (+ *to*) give (person, thing) into care of; (+ *with*) assign responsibility for (person, thing) to.
entry /'entrɪ/ *noun* (*plural* **-ies**) coming or going in; entering, item entered; place of entrance; alley.
entwine /ɪn'twaɪn/ *verb* (**-ning**) twine round, interweave.
enumerate /ɪ'nju:məreɪt/ *verb* (**-ting**) specify (items); count. □ **enumeration** *noun*.
enunciate /ɪ'nʌnsɪeɪt/ *verb* (**-ting**) pronounce (words) clearly; state definitely. □ **enunciation** *noun*.
envelop /ɪn'veləp/ *verb* (**-p-**) wrap up, cover; surround. □ **envelopment** *noun*.
envelope /'envələʊp/ *noun* folded paper cover for letter etc.; wrapper, covering.
enviable /'envɪəb(ə)l/ *adjective* likely to excite envy. □ **enviably** *adverb*.
envious /'envɪəs/ *adjective* feeling or showing envy.
environment /ɪn'vaɪərənmənt/ *noun* surroundings; circumstances affecting person's life. □ **environmental** /-'men-/ *adjective*; **environmentally** /-'men-/ *adverb*.
environmentalist /ɪnvaɪərən'mentəlɪst/ *noun* person concerned with protection of natural environment.
environs /ɪn'vaɪərəns/ *plural noun* district round town etc.
envisage /ɪn'vɪzɪdʒ/ *verb* (**-ging**) visualize, imagine, contemplate.
envoy /'envɔɪ/ *noun* messenger, representative; diplomat ranking below ambassador.
envy /'envɪ/ ● *noun* (*plural* **-ies**) discontent aroused by another's better fortune etc.; object or cause of this. ● *verb* (**-ies**, **-ied**) feel envy of.
enzyme /'enzaɪm/ *noun* protein catalyst of specific biochemical reaction.
eolian harp *US* = AEOLIAN HARP.
eon = AEON.
EP *abbreviation* extended-play (record).
epaulette /'epəlet/ *noun* (*US* **epaulet**) ornamental shoulder-piece, esp. on uniform.
ephedrine /'efədrɪn/ *noun* alkaloid drug used to relieve asthma etc.
ephemera /ɪ'femərə/ *plural noun* things of only short-lived relevance.
ephemeral *adjective* short-lived, transitory.
epic /'epɪk/ ● *noun* long poem narrating adventures of heroic figure etc.; book or film based on this. ● *adjective* like an epic; grand, heroic.
epicene /'epɪsi:n/ *adjective* of or for both sexes; having characteristics of both sexes or of neither sex.
epicentre /'epɪsentə/ *noun* (*US* **epicenter**) point at which earthquake reaches earth's surface.
epicure /'epɪkjʊə/ *noun* person with refined taste in food and drink. □ **epicurism** *noun*.
epicurean /epɪkjʊə'ri:ən/ ● *noun* person fond of pleasure and luxury. ● *adjective* characteristics of an epicurean. □ **epicureanism** *noun*.
epidemic /epɪ'demɪk/ ● *noun* widespread occurrence of particular disease in community at particular time. ● *adjective* in the nature of an epidemic.
epidemiology /epɪdi:mɪ'ɒlədʒɪ/ *noun* study of epidemics and their control.
epidermis /epɪ'dɜ:mɪs/ *noun* outer layer of skin.
epidiascope /epɪ'daɪəskəʊp/ *noun* optical projector giving images of both opaque and transparent objects.
epidural /epɪ'djʊər(ə)l/ ● *adjective* (of anaesthetic) injected close to spinal cord. ● *noun* epidural injection.
epiglottis /epɪ'glɒtɪs/ *noun* flap of cartilage at root of tongue that covers windpipe during swallowing. □ **epiglottal** *adjective*.
epigram /'epɪgræm/ *noun* short poem with witty ending; pointed saying. □ **epigrammatic** /-grə'mæt-/ *adjective*.
epigraph /'epɪgrɑ:f/ *noun* inscription.
epilepsy /'epɪlepsɪ/ *noun* nervous disorder with convulsions and often loss of consciousness. □ **epileptic** /-'lep-/ *adjective* & *noun*.
epilogue /'epɪlɒg/ *noun* short piece ending literary work; short speech at end of play etc.
Epiphany /ɪ'pɪfənɪ/ *noun* (festival on 6 Jan. commemorating) visit of Magi to Christ.
episcopacy /ɪ'pɪskəpəsɪ/ *noun* (*plural* **-ies**) government by bishops; bishops collectively.

episcopal /ɪ'pɪskəp(ə)l/ *adjective* of bishop or bishops; (of church) governed by bishops. □ **Episcopal Church** Anglican Church in Scotland and US.

Episcopalian /ɪpɪskə'peɪlɪən/ ● *adjective* of the Episcopal Church or (**episcopalian**) an episcopal church. ● *noun* member of the Episcopal Church.

episcopate /ɪ'pɪskəpət/ *noun* office or tenure of bishop; bishops collectively.

episode /'epɪsəʊd/ *noun* event as part of sequence; part of serial story; incident in narrative. □ **episodic** /-'sɒd-/ *adjective*.

epistemology /ɪpɪstɪ'mɒlədʒɪ/ *noun* philosophy of knowledge. □ **epistemological** /-ə'lɒdʒ-/ *adjective*.

epistle /ɪ'pɪs(ə)l/ *noun* letter; poem etc. in form of letter.

epistolary /ɪ'pɪstələrɪ/ *adjective* of or in form of letters.

epitaph /'epɪtɑːf/ *noun* words in memory of dead person, esp. on tomb.

epithelium /epɪ'θiːlɪəm/ *noun* (*plural* **-s** or **-lia**) *Biology* tissue forming outer layer of body and lining many hollow structures. □ **epithelial** *adjective*.

epithet /'epɪθet/ *noun* adjective etc. expressing quality or attribute.

epitome /ɪ'pɪtəmɪ/ *noun* person or thing embodying a quality etc.

epitomize *verb* (also **-ise**) (**-zing** or **-sing**) make or be perfect example of (a quality etc.).

EPNS *abbreviation* electroplated nickel silver.

epoch /'iːpɒk/ *noun* period marked by special events; beginning of era. □ **epoch-making** notable, significant.

eponym /'epənɪm/ *noun* word derived from person's name; person whose name is used in this way. □ **eponymous** /ɪ'pɒnɪməs/ *adjective*.

epoxy resin /ɪ'pɒksɪ/ *noun* synthetic thermosetting resin, used esp. as glue.

Epsom salts /'epsəm/ *noun* magnesium sulphate used as purgative.

equable /'ekwəb(ə)l/ *adjective* not varying; moderate; not easily disturbed. □ **equably** *adverb*.

equal /'iːkw(ə)l/ ● *adjective* same in number, size, merit, etc.; evenly matched; having same rights or status. ● *noun* person etc. equal to another. ● *verb* (**-ll-**; *US* **-l-**) be equal to; achieve something equal to. □ **equal opportunity** (often in *plural*) opportunity to compete equally for jobs regardless of race, sex, etc. □ **equally** *adverb*.

■ **Usage** It is a mistake to say *equally as*, as in *She was equally as guilty*. The correct version is *She was equally guilty* or possibly, for example, *She was as guilty as he was*.

equality /ɪ'kwɒlɪtɪ/ *noun* being equal.

equalize *verb* (also **-ise**) (**-zing** or **-sing**) make or become equal; (in games) reach opponent's score. □ **equalization** *noun*.

equalizer *noun* (also **-iser**) equalizing goal etc.

equanimity /ekwə'nɪmɪtɪ/ *noun* composure, calm.

equate /ɪ'kweɪt/ *verb* (**-ting**) (usually + *to*, *with*) regard as equal or equivalent; (+ *with*) be equal or equivalent to.

equation /ɪ'kweɪʒ(ə)n/ *noun* making or being equal; *Mathematics* statement that two expressions are equal; *Chemistry* symbolic representation of reaction.

equator /ɪ'kweɪtə/ *noun* imaginary line round the earth or other body, equidistant from poles.

equatorial /ekwə'tɔːrɪəl/ *adjective* of or near equator.

equerry /'ekwərɪ/ *noun* (*plural* **-ies**) officer attending British royal family.

equestrian /ɪ'kwestrɪən/ *adjective* of horse-riding; on horseback. □ **equestrianism** *noun*.

equiangular /iːkwɪ'æŋgjʊlə/ *adjective* having equal angles.

equidistant /iːkwɪ'dɪst(ə)nt/ *adjective* at equal distances.

equilateral /iːkwɪ'lætər(ə)l/ *adjective* having all sides equal.

equilibrium /iːkwɪ'lɪbrɪəm/ *noun* state of balance; composure.

equine /'ekwaɪn/ *adjective* of or like horse.

equinox /'iːkwɪnɒks/ *noun* time or date at which sun crosses equator and day and night are of equal length.

equip /ɪ'kwɪp/ *verb* (**-pp-**) supply with what is needed.

equipment *noun* necessary tools, clothing, etc.; equipping, being equipped.

equipoise /'ekwɪpɔɪz/ *noun* equilibrium; counterbalancing thing.

equitable /'ekwɪtəb(ə)l/ *adjective* fair, just; *Law* valid in equity. □ **equitably** *adverb*.

equitation /ekwɪ'teɪʃ(ə)n/ *noun* horsemanship; horse-riding.

equity /'ekwɪtɪ/ *noun* (*plural* **-ies**) fairness; principles of justice supplementing law; value of shares issued by company; (in *plural*) stocks and shares not bearing fixed interest.

equivalent /ɪ'kwɪvələnt/ ● *adjective* (often + *to*) equal in value, meaning, etc.; corresponding. ● *noun* equivalent amount etc. □ **equivalence** *noun*.

equivocal /ɪ'kwɪvək(ə)l/ *adjective* of double or doubtful meaning; of uncertain nature; (of person etc.) questionable. □ **equivocally** *adverb*.

equivocate /ɪ'kwɪvəkeɪt/ *verb* (**-ting**) use words ambiguously to conceal truth. □ **equivocation** *noun*.

ER *abbreviation* Queen Elizabeth (*Elizabetha Regina*).

era /'ɪərə/ *noun* system of chronology starting from particular point; historical or other period.

eradicate /ɪ'rædɪkeɪt/ *verb* (**-ting**) root out, destroy. □ **eradication** *noun*.

erase /ɪ'reɪz/ *verb* (**-sing**) rub out; obliterate; remove recording from (magnetic tape etc.).

eraser *noun* piece of rubber etc. for removing esp. pencil marks.

erasure /ɪ'reɪʒə/ *noun* erasing; erased word etc.

ere /eə/ *preposition & conjunction poetical or archaic* before.

erect /ɪ'rekt/ ● *adjective* upright, vertical; (of part of body) enlarged and rigid, esp. from sexual excitement. ● *verb* raise, set upright; build; establish. □ **erection** *noun*.

erectile /ɪ'rektaɪl/ *adjective* that can become erect.

erg *noun* unit of work or energy.

ergo /'ɜːgəʊ/ *adverb* therefore. [Latin]

ergonomics /ɜːgə'nɒmɪks/ *plural noun* (treated as *singular*) study of relationship between people and their working environment. □ **ergonomic** *adjective*.

ergot /'ɜːgət/ *noun* disease of rye etc. caused by fungus.

ERM *abbreviation* Exchange Rate Mechanism.

ermine /'ɜːmɪn/ *noun* (*plural* same or **-s**) stoat, esp. in its white winter fur; this fur.

Ernie /'ɜːnɪ/ *noun* device for drawing prize-winning numbers of Premium Bonds.

erode /ɪ'rəʊd/ *verb* (**-ding**) wear away, gradually destroy. □ **erosion** *noun*; **erosive** *adjective*.

erogenous /ɪ'rɒdʒɪnəs/ *adjective* (of part of body) sexually sensitive.

erotic /ɪ'rɒtɪk/ *adjective* arousing sexual desire or excitement. □ **erotically** *adverb*; **eroticism** /-sɪz-/ *noun*.

erotica *plural noun* erotic literature or art.

err /ɜː/ *verb* be mistaken or incorrect; sin.

errand /'erənd/ *noun* short journey, esp. on another's behalf, to take message etc.; object of journey.

errant /ˈerənt/ *adjective* erring; *literary* travelling in search of adventure.
erratic /ɪˈrætɪk/ *adjective* inconsistent or uncertain in movement or conduct etc. □ **erratically** *adverb*.
erratum /ɪˈrɑːtəm/ *noun* (*plural* **-ta**) error in printing etc.
erroneous /ɪˈrəʊnɪəs/ *adjective* incorrect. □ **erroneously** *adverb*.
error /ˈerə/ *noun* mistake; condition of being morally wrong; degree of inaccuracy in calculation or measurement.
ersatz /ˈeəzæts/ *adjective & noun* substitute; imitation.
erstwhile /ˈɜːstwaɪl/ *adjective* former.
eructation /iːrʌkˈteɪʃ(ə)n/ *noun formal* belching.
erudite /ˈeruːdaɪt/ *adjective* learned. □ **erudition** /-ˈdɪʃ-/ *noun*.
erupt /ɪˈrʌpt/ *verb* break out; (of volcano) shoot out lava etc.; (of rash) appear on skin. □ **eruption** *noun*.
erysipelas /erɪˈsɪpɪləs/ *noun* disease causing deep red inflammation of skin.
escalate /ˈeskəleɪt/ *verb* (**-ting**) increase or develop by stages. □ **escalation** *noun*.
escalator *noun* moving staircase.
escalope /ˈeskəlɒp/ *noun* thin slice of meat, esp. veal.
escapade /ˈeskəpeɪd/ *noun* piece of reckless behaviour.
escape /ɪsˈkeɪp/ ● *verb* (**-ping**) get free; leak; avoid punishment etc.; get free of; elude, avoid. ● *noun* escaping; means of escaping; leakage. □ **escape clause** clause releasing contracting party from obligation in specified circumstances.
escapee /ɪskeɪˈpiː/ *noun* person who has escaped.
escapism *noun* pursuit of distraction and relief from reality. □ **escapist** *adjective & noun*.
escapology /eskəˈpɒlədʒɪ/ *noun* techniques of escaping from confinement, esp. as entertainment. □ **escapologist** *noun*.
escarpment /ɪsˈkɑːpmənt/ *noun* long steep slope at edge of plateau etc.
eschatology /eskəˈtɒlədʒɪ/ *noun* doctrine of death and final destiny. □ **eschatological** /-təˈlɒdʒ-/ *adjective*.
escheat /ɪsˈtʃiːt/ ● *noun* lapse of property to the state etc.; property so lapsing. ● *verb* hand over as escheat, confiscate; revert by escheat.
eschew /ɪsˈtʃuː/ *verb formal* abstain from.
escort ● *noun* /ˈeskɔːt/ person(s) etc. accompanying another for protection or as courtesy; person accompanying another of opposite sex socially. ● *verb* /ɪˈskɔːt/ act as escort to.
escritoire /eskrɪˈtwɑː/ *noun* writing desk with drawers etc.
escutcheon /ɪˈskʌtʃ(ə)n/ *noun* shield bearing coat of arms.
ESE *abbreviation* east-south-east.
Eskimo /ˈeskɪməʊ/ ● *noun* (*plural* same or **-s**) member of people inhabiting N. Canada, Alaska, Greenland, and E. Siberia; their language. ● *adjective* of Eskimos or their language.

■ **Usage** The Eskimos of N. America prefer the name *Inuit*.

ESN *abbreviation* educationally subnormal.
esophagus *US* = OESOPHAGUS.
esoteric /esəˈterɪk, iːsəˈterɪk/ *adjective* intelligible only to those with special knowledge.
ESP *abbreviation* extrasensory perception.
esp. *abbreviation* especially.
espadrille /espəˈdrɪl/ *noun* light canvas shoe with plaited fibre sole.
espalier /ɪˈspælɪə/ *noun* framework for training tree etc.; tree trained on this.
esparto /eˈspɑːtəʊ/ *noun* kind of grass used to make paper.
especial /ɪˈspeʃ(ə)l/ *adjective* special, notable.
especially *adverb* in particular; more than in other cases; particularly.
Esperanto /espəˈræntəʊ/ *noun* artificial universal language.
espionage /ˈespɪənɑːʒ/ *noun* spying or using spies.
esplanade /espləˈneɪd/ *noun* level space, esp. used as public promenade.
espousal /ɪˈspaʊz(ə)l/ *noun* espousing; *archaic* marriage, betrothal.
espouse /ɪˈspaʊz/ *verb* (**-sing**) support (cause); *archaic* marry.
espresso /eˈspresəʊ/ *noun* (*plural* **-s**) coffee made under steam pressure.
esprit de corps /espriː də ˈkɔː/ *noun* devotion to and pride in one's group. [French]
espy /ɪˈspaɪ/ *verb* (**-ies**, **-ied**) catch sight of.
Esq. *abbreviation* Esquire.
esquire /ɪˈskwaɪə/ *noun: title placed after man's name in writing*.
essay ● *noun* /ˈeseɪ/ short piece of writing, esp. on given subject; *formal* attempt. ● *verb* /eˈseɪ/ attempt.
essayist *noun* writer of essays.
essence /ˈes(ə)ns/ *noun* fundamental nature, inherent characteristics; extract obtained by distillation etc.; perfume. □ **in essence** fundamentally.
essential /ɪˈsenʃ(ə)l/ ● *adjective* necessary, indispensable; of or constituting a thing's essence. ● *noun* (esp. in *plural*) indispensable element or thing. □ **essential oil** volatile oil with characteristic odour. □ **essentially** *adverb*.
establish /ɪˈstæblɪʃ/ *verb* set up; settle; (esp. as **established** *adjective*) achieve permanent acceptance for; place beyond dispute. □ **Established Church** Church recognized by state.
establishment *noun* establishing, being established; public institution; place of business; staff, household, etc.; Church system established by law; (**the Establishment**) social group with authority or influence and resisting change.
estate /ɪˈsteɪt/ *noun* landed property; area of homes or businesses planned as a whole; dead person's collective assets and liabilities. □ **estate agent** person whose business is sale and lease of buildings and land on behalf of others; **estate car** car with continuous area for rear passengers and luggage.
esteem /ɪˈstiːm/ ● *verb* (usually in *passive*) think highly of; *formal* consider. ● *noun* high regard.
ester /estə/ *noun* compound formed by replacing the hydrogen of an acid by an organic radical.
estimable /ˈestɪməb(ə)l/ *adjective* worthy of esteem.
estimate ● *noun* /ˈestɪmət/ approximate judgement of cost, value, etc.; approximate price stated in advance for work. ● *verb* /ˈestɪmeɪt/ (**-ting**) form estimate of; (+ *that*) make rough calculation; (+ *at*) put (sum etc.) at by estimating.
estimation /estɪˈmeɪʃ(ə)n/ *noun* estimating; judgement of worth.
estrange /ɪˈstreɪndʒ/ *verb* (**-ging**) (usually in *passive*; often + *from*) alienate, make hostile or indifferent; (as **estranged** *adjective*) no longer living with spouse. □ **estrangement** *noun*.
estrogen *US* = OESTROGEN.
estuary /ˈestjʊərɪ/ *noun* (*plural* **-ies**) tidal mouth of river.
ETA *abbreviation* estimated time of arrival.

et al. *abbreviation* and others (*et alii*).
etc. *abbreviation* et cetera.
et cetera /et 'setrə/ *adverb* (also **etcetera**) and the rest; and so on. **etceteras** *plural noun* the usual extras.
etch *verb* reproduce (picture etc.) by engraving metal plate with acid, esp. to print copies; engrave (plate) thus; practise this craft; (usually + *on, upon*) impress deeply.
etching *noun* print made from etched plate.
eternal /ɪ'tɜ:n(ə)l/ *adjective* existing always; without end or beginning; unchanging; *colloquial* constant, too frequent. ▫ **eternally** *adverb*.
eternity /ɪ'tɜ:nɪtɪ/ *noun* infinite time; endless life after death; (**an eternity**) *colloquial* a very long time.
ethane /'i:θeɪn/ *noun* hydrocarbon gas present in petroleum and natural gas.
ethanol /'eθənɒl/ *noun* alcohol.
ether /'i:θə/ *noun* volatile liquid used as anaesthetic or solvent; clear sky, upper air.
ethereal /ɪ'θɪərɪəl/ *adjective* light, airy; delicate, esp. in appearance; heavenly.
ethic /'eθɪk/ *noun* set of moral principles.
ethical *adjective* relating to morals or ethics; morally correct; (of drug etc.) available only on prescription. ▫ **ethically** *adverb*.
ethics *plural noun* (also treated as *singular*) moral philosophy; (set of) moral principles.
Ethiopian /i:θɪ'əʊpɪən/ ● *noun* native or national of Ethiopia. ● *adjective* of Ethiopia.
ethnic /'eθnɪk/ *adjective* (of social) group having common national or cultural tradition; (of clothes etc.) resembling those of an exotic people; (of person) having specified origin by birth or descent rather than nationality. ▫ **ethnic cleansing** *euphemistic* expulsion or murder of people of ethnic or religious group in certain area. ▫ **ethnically** *adverb*.
ethnology /eθ'nɒlədʒɪ/ *noun* comparative study of peoples. ▫ **ethnological** /-nə'lɒdʒ-/ *adjective*.
ethos /'i:θɒs/ *noun* characteristic spirit of community, people, or system.
ethylene /'eθɪli:n/ *noun* flammable hydrocarbon gas.
etiolate /'i:tɪəleɪt/ *verb* (**-ting**) make pale by excluding light; give sickly colour to. ▫ **etiolation** *noun*.
etiology *US* = AETIOLOGY.
etiquette /'etɪket/ *noun* conventional rules of social behaviour or professional conduct.
étude /eɪ'tju:d/ *noun* musical composition designed to develop player's skill.
etymology /etɪ'mɒlədʒɪ/ *noun* (*plural* **-ies**) origin and sense-development of word; account of these. ▫ **etymological** /-mə'lɒdʒ-/ *adjective*.
eucalyptus /ju:kə'lɪptəs/ *noun* (*plural* **-tuses** or **-ti** /-taɪ/) tall evergreen tree; its oil, used as antiseptic etc.
Eucharist /'ju:kərɪst/ *noun* Christian sacrament in which bread and wine are consecrated and consumed; consecrated elements, esp. bread. ▫ **Eucharistic** /-'rɪs-/ *adjective*.
eugenics /ju:'dʒenɪks/ *plural noun* (also treated as *singular*) improvement of qualities of race by control of inherited characteristics. ▫ **eugenic** *adjective*; **eugenically** *adverb*.
eulogize /'ju:lədʒaɪz/ *verb* (also **-ise**) (**-zing** or **-sing**) extol; praise.
eulogy /'ju:lədʒɪ/ *noun* (*plural* **-ies**) speech or writing in praise or commendation. ▫ **eulogistic** /-'dʒɪs-/ *adjective*.
eunuch /'ju:nək/ *noun* castrated man.
euphemism /'ju:fɪmɪz(ə)m/ *noun* mild expression substituted for blunt one. ▫ **euphemistic** /-'mɪs-/ *adjective*; **euphemistically** /-'mɪs-/ *adverb*.
euphonium /ju:'fəʊnɪəm/ *noun* brass instrument of tuba family.
euphony /'ju:fənɪ/ *noun* pleasantness of sound, esp. in words. ▫ **euphonious** /-'fəʊ-/ *adjective*.
euphoria /ju:'fɔ:rɪə/ *noun* intense sense of well-being and excitement. ▫ **euphoric** /-'fɒr-/ *adjective*.
Eurasian /jʊə'reɪʒ(ə)n/ ● *adjective* of mixed European and Asian parentage; of Europe and Asia. ● *noun* Eurasian person.
eureka /jʊə'ri:kə/ *interjection* I have found it!
Eurodollar /'jʊərəʊdɒlə/ *noun* dollar held in bank in Europe etc.
European /jʊərə'pɪən/ ● *adjective* of, in, or extending over Europe. ● *noun* native or inhabitant of Europe; descendant of one.
Eustachian tube /ju:'steɪʃ(ə)n/ *noun* passage between middle ear and back of throat.
euthanasia /ju:θə'neɪzɪə/ *noun* killing person painlessly, esp. one who has incurable painful disease.
evacuate /ɪ'vækjʊeɪt/ *verb* (**-ting**) remove (people) from place of danger; make empty, clear; withdraw from (place); empty (bowels). ▫ **evacuation** *noun*.
evacuee /ɪvækju:'i:/ *noun* person evacuated.
evade /ɪ'veɪd/ *verb* (**-ding**) escape from, avoid; avoid doing or answering directly; avoid paying (tax) illegally.
evaluate /ɪ'væljʊeɪt/ *verb* (**-ting**) assess, appraise; find or state number or amount of. ▫ **evaluation** *noun*.
evanesce /evə'nes/ *verb* (**-cing**) *literary* fade from sight. ▫ **evanescence** *noun*; **evanescent** *adjective*.
evangelical /i:væn'dʒelɪk(ə)l/ ● *adjective* of or according to gospel teaching; of Protestant groups maintaining doctrine of salvation by faith. ● *noun* member of evangelical group. ▫ **evangelicalism** *noun*.
evangelist /ɪ'vændʒəlɪst/ *noun* writer of one of the 4 Gospels; preacher of gospel. ▫ **evangelism** *noun*; **evangelistic** /-'lɪs-/ *adjective*.
evangelize *verb* (also **-ise**) (**-zing** or **-sing**) preach gospel to. ▫ **evangelization** *noun*.
evaporate /ɪ'væpəreɪt/ *verb* (**-ting**) turn into vapour; (cause to) lose moisture as vapour; (cause to) disappear. ▫ **evaporation** *noun*.
evasion /ɪ'veɪʒ(ə)n/ *noun* evading; evasive answer.
evasive /ɪ'veɪsɪv/ *adjective* seeking to evade.
eve *noun* evening or day before festival etc.; time just before event; *archaic* evening.
even /'i:v(ə)n/ ● *adjective* (**-er, -est**) level, smooth; uniform; equal; equable, calm; divisible by two. ● *adverb* still, yet; (with negative) so much as. ● *verb* (often + *up*) make or become even. ▫ **even if** in spite of the fact that, no matter whether; **even out** become level or regular, spread (thing) over period or among group. ▫ **evenly** *adverb*.
evening /'i:vnɪŋ/ *noun* end part of day, esp. from about 6 p.m. to bedtime. ▫ **evening class** adult education class held in evening; **evening dress** formal clothes for evening wear; **evening star** planet, esp. Venus, conspicuous in west after sunset.
evensong *noun* evening service in Church of England.
event /ɪ'vent/ *noun* thing that happens; fact of thing occurring; item in (esp. sports) programme. ▫ **in any event, at all events** whatever happens; **in the event** as it turns or turned out; **in the event of** if (thing) happens.
eventful *adjective* marked by noteworthy events.
eventual /ɪ'ventʃʊəl/ *adjective* occurring in due course. ▫ **eventually** *adverb*.
eventuality /ɪventʃʊ'ælɪtɪ/ *noun* (*plural* **-ies**) possible event.

ever /'evə/ *adverb* at all times; always; at any time. □ **ever since** throughout period since (then); **ever so** *colloquial* very; **ever such a(n)** *colloquial* a very.

evergreen ● *adjective* retaining green leaves throughout year. ● *noun* evergreen plant.

everlasting *adjective* lasting for ever or a long time; (of flower) retaining shape and colour when dried.

evermore *adverb* for ever; always.

every /'evrɪ/ *adjective* each; all. □ **everybody** every person; **everyday** occurring every day, ordinary; **Everyman** ordinary or typical human being; **every now and again** or **then** occasionally; **everyone** everybody; **every other** each alternate; **everything** all things, the most important thing; **everywhere** in every place.

evict /ɪ'vɪkt/ *verb* expel (tenant) by legal process. □ **eviction** *noun*.

evidence /'evɪd(ə)ns/ ● *noun* (often + *for*, *of*) indication, sign; information given to establish fact etc.; statement etc. admissible in court of law. ● *verb* (**-cing**) be evidence of.

evident *adjective* obvious, manifest.

evidential /evɪ'denʃ(ə)l/ *adjective* of or providing evidence.

evidently *adverb* seemingly; as shown by evidence.

evil /'i:v(ə)l/ ● *adjective* wicked; harmful. ● *noun* evil thing; wickedness. □ **evil eye** gaze believed to cause harm. □ **evilly** *adverb*.

evince /ɪ'vɪns/ *verb* (**-cing**) show, indicate.

eviscerate /ɪ'vɪsəreɪt/ *verb* (**-ting**) disembowel. □ **evisceration** *noun*.

evocative /ɪ'vɒkətɪv/ *adjective* evoking (feelings etc.).

evoke /ɪ'vəʊk/ *verb* (**-king**) call up (feeling etc.). □ **evocation** /evə-/ *noun*.

evolution /i:və'lu:ʃ(ə)n/ *noun* evolving; development of species from earlier forms; unfolding of events etc.; change in disposition of troops or ships. □ **evolutionary** *adjective*.

evolutionist *noun* person who regards evolution as explaining origin of species.

evolve /ɪ'vɒlv/ *verb* (**-ving**) develop gradually and naturally; devise; unfold, open out.

ewe /ju:/ *noun* female sheep.

ewer /'ju:ə/ *noun* water-jug with wide mouth.

ex[1] *preposition* (of goods) sold from (warehouse etc.).

ex[2] *noun colloquial* former husband or wife.

ex- *prefix* formerly.

exacerbate /ek'sæsəbeɪt/ *verb* (**-ting**) make worse; irritate. □ **exacerbation** *noun*.

exact /ɪg'zækt/ ● *adjective* accurate; correct in all details. ● *verb* demand and enforce payment of (fees etc.); demand, insist on. □ **exactness** *noun*.

exaction *noun* exacting, being exacted; illegal or exorbitant demand.

exactitude *noun* exactness.

exactly *adverb* precisely; I agree.

exaggerate /ɪg'zædʒəreɪt/ *verb* (**-ting**) make seem larger or greater than it really is; increase beyond normal or due proportions. □ **exaggeration** *noun*.

exalt /ɪg'zɔ:lt/ *verb* raise in rank, power, etc.; praise, extol; (usually as **exalted** *adjective*) make lofty or noble. □ **exaltation** /eg-/ *noun*.

exam /ɪg'zæm/ *noun* examination, test.

examination /ɪgzæmɪ'neɪʃ(ə)n/ *noun* examining, being examined; detailed inspection; testing of knowledge or ability by questions; formal questioning of witness etc. in court.

examine /ɪg'zæmɪn/ *verb* (**-ning**) inquire into; look closely at; test knowledge or ability of; check health of; question formally. □ **examinee** /-'ni:/ *noun*; **examiner** *noun*.

example /ɪg'zɑ:mp(ə)l/ *noun* thing illustrating general rule; model, pattern; specimen; precedent; warning to others. □ **for example** by way of illustration.

exasperate /ɪg'zɑ:spəreɪt/ *verb* (**-ting**) irritate intensely. □ **exasperation** *noun*.

ex cathedra /eks kə'θi:drə/ *adjective & adverb* with full authority (esp. of papal pronouncement). [Latin]

excavate /'ekskəveɪt/ *verb* (**-ting**) make (hole etc.) by digging; dig out material from (ground); reveal or extract by digging; dig systematically to explore (archaeological site). □ **excavation** *noun*; **excavator** *noun*.

exceed /ɪk'si:d/ *verb* be more or greater than; go beyond, do more than is warranted by; surpass.

exceedingly *adverb* very.

excel /ɪk'sel/ *verb* (**-ll-**) surpass; be pre-eminent.

excellence /'eksələns/ *noun* great merit.

Excellency *noun* (*plural* **-ies**) (**His**, **Her**, **Your Excellency**) *title used of or to ambassador, governor, etc.*

excellent *adjective* extremely good.

except /ɪk'sept/ ● *verb* exclude from general statement etc. ● *preposition* (often + *for*) not including, other than.

excepting *preposition* except.

exception /ɪk'sepʃ(ə)n/ *noun* excepting; thing or case excepted. □ **take exception** (often + *to*) object.

exceptionable *adjective* open to objection.

■ **Usage** *Exceptionable* is sometimes confused with *exceptional*.

exceptional *adjective* forming exception; unusual. □ **exceptionally** *adverb*.

■ **Usage** *Exceptional* is sometimes confused with *exceptionable*.

excerpt ● *noun* /'eksɜ:pt/ short extract from book, film, etc. ● *verb* /ɪk'sɜ:pt/ take excerpts from. □ **excerption** /ɪk'sɜ:pʃ(ə)n/ *noun*.

excess ● *noun* /ɪk'ses/ exceeding; amount by which thing exceeds; intemperance in eating or drinking. ● *adjective* /'ekses/ that exceeds limit or given amount. □ **in, to excess** exceeding proper amount or degree; **in excess of** more than.

excessive /ɪk'sesɪv/ *adjective* too much; too great. □ **excessively** *adverb*.

exchange /ɪks'tʃeɪndʒ/ ● *noun* giving one thing and receiving another in its place; exchanging of money for equivalent, esp. in other currency; centre where telephone connections are made; place where merchants, stockbrokers, etc. transact business; employment office; short conversation. ● *verb* (**-ging**) give or receive in exchange; interchange. □ **exchange rate** price of one currency expressed in another. □ **exchangeable** *adjective*.

exchequer /ɪks'tʃekə/ *noun* former government department in charge of national revenue; royal or national treasury.

excise[1] /'eksaɪz/ *noun* tax levied on goods produced or sold within the country; tax on certain licences.

excise[2] /ɪk'saɪz/ *verb* (**-sing**) cut out or away. □ **excision** /-'sɪʒ-/ *noun*.

excitable *adjective* easily excited. □ **excitability** *noun*.

excite /ɪk'saɪt/ *verb* (**-ting**) move to strong emotion; arouse (feelings etc.); provoke (action etc.); stimulate to activity. □ **excitement** *noun*; **exciting** *adjective*.

exclaim /ɪk'skleɪm/ *verb* cry out suddenly; utter or say thus.

exclamation /eksklə'meɪʃ(ə)n/ *noun* exclaiming; word(s) etc. exclaimed. □ **exclamation mark** punctuation mark (!) indicating exclamation (see panel). □ **exclamatory** /ɪk'sklæmətərɪ/ *adjective*.

exclude /ɪk'sklu:d/ *verb* (**-ding**) shut out, leave out; make impossible, preclude. □ **exclusion** *noun*.

exclusive /ɪk'sklu:sɪv/ ● *adjective* excluding other things; (+ *of*) not including; (of society etc.) tending to exclude outsiders; high-class; not obtainable or published elsewhere. ● *noun* exclusive item of news, film, etc. □ **exclusively** *adverb*; **exclusiveness** *noun*; **exclusivity** /eksklu:'sɪvɪtɪ/ *noun*.

excommunicate /ekskə'mju:nɪkeɪt/ *verb* (**-ting**) deprive (person) of membership and sacraments of Church. □ **excommunication** *noun*.

excoriate /eks'kɔ:rɪeɪt/ *verb* (**-ting**) remove part of skin of by abrasion; remove (skin); censure severely. □ **excoriation** *noun*.

excrement /'ekskrɪmənt/ *noun* faeces.

excrescence /ɪk'skres(ə)ns/ *noun* abnormal or morbid outgrowth. □ **excrescent** *adjective*.

excreta /ɪk'skri:tə/ *plural noun* faeces and urine.

excrete /ɪk'skri:t/ *verb* (**-ting**) (of animal or plant) expel (waste). □ **excretion** *noun*; **excretory** *adjective*.

excruciating /ɪk'skru:ʃɪeɪtɪŋ/ *adjective* acutely painful. □ **excruciatingly** *adverb*.

exculpate /'ekskʌlpeɪt/ *verb* (**-ting**) *formal* free from blame. □ **exculpation** *noun*.

excursion /ɪk'skɜ:ʃ(ə)n/ *noun* journey to place and back, made for pleasure.

excursive /ɪk'skɜ:sɪv/ *adjective literary* digressive.

excuse ● *verb* /ɪk'skju:z/ (**-sing**) try to lessen blame attaching to; serve as reason to judge (person, act) less severely; (often + *from*) grant exemption to; forgive. ● *noun* /ɪk'skju:s/ reason put forward to mitigate or justify offence; apology. □ **be excused** be allowed not to do something or to leave or be absent; **excuse me** *polite request to be allowed to pass, polite apology for interrupting or disagreeing*. □ **excusable** /-'sku:z-/ *adjective*.

ex-directory *adjective* not listed in telephone directory, at subscriber's wish.

execrable /'eksɪkrəb(ə)l/ *adjective* abominable.

execrate /'eksɪkreɪt/ *verb* (**-ting**) express or feel abhorrence for; curse. □ **execration** *noun*.

execute /'eksɪkju:t/ *verb* (**-ting**) carry out, perform; put to death.

execution /eksɪ'kju:ʃ(ə)n/ *noun* carrying out, performance; capital punishment.

executioner *noun* person carrying out death sentence.

executive /ɪg'zekjʊtɪv/ *noun* person or body with managerial or administrative responsibility; branch of government etc. concerned with executing laws, agreements, etc. ● *adjective* concerned with executing laws, agreements, etc. or with administration etc.

executor /ɪg'zekjʊtə/ *noun* (*feminine* **executrix** /-trɪks/) person appointed by testator to carry out terms of will. □ **executorial** /-'tɔ:rɪəl/ *adjective*.

exegesis /eksɪ'dʒi:sɪs/ *noun* explanation, esp. of Scripture. □ **exegetic** /-'dʒetɪk/ *adjective*.

exemplar /ɪg'zemplə/ *noun* model; typical instance.

exemplary *adjective* outstandingly good; serving as example or warning.

exemplify /ɪg'zemplɪfaɪ/ *verb* (**-ies**, **-ied**) give or be example of. □ **exemplification** *noun*.

exempt /ɪg'zempt/ ● *adjective* (often + *from*) free from obligation or liability imposed on others. ● *verb* (+ *from*) make exempt from. □ **exemption** *noun*.

exercise /'eksəsaɪz/ ● *noun* use of muscles etc., esp. for health; task set for physical or other training; use or application of faculties etc.; practice; (often in *plural*) military drill or manoeuvres. ● *verb* (**-sing**) use; perform (function); take exercise; give exercise to; tax powers of; perplex, worry.

exert /ɪg'zɜ:t/ *verb* use; bring to bear; (**exert oneself**) make effort. □ **exertion** *noun*.

exfoliate /eks'fəʊlɪeɪt/ *verb* (**-ting**) come off in scales or layers. □ **exfoliation** *noun*.

ex gratia /eks 'greɪʃə/ ● *adverb* as favour and not under (esp. legal) compulsion. ● *adjective* granted on this basis. [Latin]

exhale /eks'heɪl/ *verb* (**-ling**) breathe out; give off or be given off in vapour. □ **exhalation** /-hə-/ *noun*.

exhaust /ɪg'zɔ:st/ ● *verb* (often as **exhausted** *adjective* or **exhausting** *adjective*) consume, use up; tire out; study or expound completely; empty of contents. ● *noun* waste gases etc. expelled from engine after combustion; pipe or system through which they are expelled. □ **exhaustible** *adjective*; **exhaustion** *noun*.

exhaustive *adjective* complete, comprehensive. □ **exhaustively** *adverb*.

exhibit /ɪg'zɪbɪt/ ● *verb* (**-t-**) show, esp. publicly; display. ● *noun* thing exhibited. □ **exhibitor** *noun*.

exhibition /eksɪ'bɪʃ(ə)n/ *noun* display, public show; exhibiting, being exhibited; scholarship, esp. from funds of college etc.

exhibitioner *noun* student receiving exhibition.

exhibitionism *noun* tendency towards attention-seeking behaviour; compulsion to expose genitals in public. □ **exhibitionist** *noun*.

exhilarate /ɪg'zɪləreɪt/ *verb* (**-ting**) (often as **exhilarating** *adjective* or **exhilarated** *adjective*) enliven, gladden. □ **exhilaration** *noun*.

exhort /ɪg'zɔ:t/ *verb* (often + *to do*) urge strongly or earnestly. □ **exhortation** /eg-/ *noun*; **exhortative** *adjective*; **exhortatory** *adjective*.

exhume /eks'hju:m/ *verb* (**-ming**) dig up. □ **exhumation** *noun*.

exigency /'eksɪdʒənsɪ/ *noun* (*plural* **-ies**) (also **exigence**) urgent need; emergency. □ **exigent** *adjective*.

exiguous /eg'zɪgjʊəs/ *adjective* scanty, small. □ **exiguity** /-'gju:ɪtɪ/ *noun*.

exile /'eksaɪl/ ● *noun* expulsion or long absence from one's country etc.; person in exile. ● *verb* (**-ling**) send into or condemn to exile.

exist /ɪg'zɪst/ *verb* be, have being; occur, be found; live with no pleasure; live.

existence *noun* fact or manner of existing; all that exists. □ **existent** *adjective*.

existential /egzɪ'stenʃ(ə)l/ *adjective* of or relating to existence.

existentialism *noun* philosophical theory emphasizing existence of individual as free and self-determining agent. □ **existentialist** *adjective & noun*.

Exclamation mark !

This is used instead of a full stop at the end of a sentence to show that the speaker or writer is very angry, enthusiastic, insistent, disappointed, hurt, surprised, etc., e.g.

I am not pleased at all!
I just love sweets!
Go away!
I wish I could have gone!
Ow!
He didn't even say goodbye!

exit /'eksɪt/ ● *noun* way out; going out; place where vehicles leave motorway etc.; departure. ● *verb* **(-t-)** make one's exit.

exodus /'eksədəs/ *noun* mass departure; **(Exodus)** that of Israelites from Egypt.

ex officio /eks ə'fɪʃɪəʊ/ *adverb & adjective* by virtue of one's office.

exonerate /ɪg'zɒnəreɪt/ *verb* **(-ting)** free or declare free from blame. □ **exoneration** *noun*.

exorbitant /ɪg'zɔ:bɪt(ə)nt/ *adjective* grossly excessive.

exorcize /'eksɔ:saɪz/ *verb* (also **-ise**) **(-zing** or **-sing)** drive out (evil spirit) by prayers etc.; free (person, place) thus. □ **exorcism** *noun*; **exorcist** *noun*.

exoskeleton /'eksəʊskelɪtən/ *noun* external skeleton.

exotic /ɪg'zɒtɪk/ ● *adjective* introduced from abroad; strange, unusual. ● *noun* exotic plant etc. □ **exotically** *adverb*.

expand /ɪk'spænd/ *verb* increase in size or importance; (often + *on*) give fuller account; become more genial; write out in full; spread out flat. □ **expandable** *adjective*; **expansion** *noun*.

expanse /ɪk'spæns/ *noun* wide area or extent of land, space, etc.

expansionism *noun* advocacy of expansion, esp. of state's territory. □ **expansionist** *noun & adjective*.

expansive *adjective* able or tending to expand; extensive; genial.

expatiate /ɪk'speɪʃɪeɪt/ *verb* **(-ting)** (usually + *on*, *upon*) speak or write at length. □ **expatiation** *noun*.

expatriate ● *adjective* /eks'pætrɪət/ living abroad; exiled. ● *noun* /eks'pætrɪət/ expatriate person. ● *verb* /eks'pætrɪeɪt/ **(-ting)** expel from native country.

expect /ɪk'spekt/ *verb* regard as likely; look for as one's due; *colloquial* suppose. □ **be expecting** *colloquial* be pregnant.

expectant *adjective* expecting; expecting to become; pregnant. □ **expectancy** *noun*; **expectantly** *adverb*.

expectation /ekspek'teɪʃ(ə)n/ *noun* expecting, anticipation; what one expects; probability; (in *plural*) prospects of inheritance.

expectorant /ek'spektərənt/ ● *adjective* causing expectoration. ● *noun* expectorant medicine.

expectorate /ek'spektəreɪt/ *verb* **(-ting)** cough or spit out from chest or lungs; spit. □ **expectoration** *noun*.

expedient /ɪk'spi:dɪənt/ ● *adjective* advantageous; advisable on practical rather than moral grounds. ● *noun* means of achieving an end; resource. □ **expediency** *noun*.

expedite /'ekspɪdaɪt/ *verb* **(-ting)** assist progress of; accomplish quickly.

expedition /ekspɪ'dɪʃ(ə)n/ *noun* journey or voyage for particular purpose; people etc. undertaking this; speed.

expeditionary *adjective* of or used on expedition.

expeditious /ekspɪ'dɪʃəs/ *adjective* acting or done with speed and efficiency.

expel /ɪk'spel/ *verb* **(-ll-)** deprive of membership; force out; eject.

expend /ɪk'spend/ *verb* spend (money, time, etc.); use up.

expendable *adjective* that may be sacrificed or dispensed with.

expenditure /ɪk'spendɪtʃə/ *noun* expending; amount expended.

expense /ɪk'spens/ *noun* cost, charge; (in *plural*) costs incurred in doing job etc., reimbursement of this.

expensive *adjective* costing or charging much. □ **expensively** *adverb*.

experience /ɪk'spɪərɪəns/ ● *noun* personal observation or contact; knowledge or skill based on this; event that affects one. ● *verb* **(-cing)** have experience of; undergo; feel. □ **experiential** /-'en-/ *adjective*.

experienced *adjective* having had much experience; skilful through experience.

experiment /ɪk'sperɪmənt/ ● *noun* procedure adopted to test hypothesis or demonstrate known fact. ● *verb* (also /-ment/) make experiment(s). □ **experimentation** /-men-/ *noun*; **experimenter** *noun*.

experimental /ɪksperɪ'ment(ə)l/ *adjective* based on or done by way of experiment. □ **experimentally** *adverb*.

expert /'ekspɜ:t/ (often + *at*, *in*) ● *adjective* well informed or skilful in a subject. ● *noun* expert person. □ **expertly** *adverb*.

expertise /ekspɜ:'ti:z/ *noun* special skill or knowledge.

expiate /'ekspɪeɪt/ *verb* **(-ting)** pay penalty or make amends for (wrong). □ **expiation** *noun*.

expire /ɪk'spaɪə/ *verb* **(-ring)** come to an end; cease to be valid; die; breathe out. □ **expiration** /ekspɪ-/ *noun*.

expiry *noun* end of validity or duration.

explain /ɪks'pleɪn/ *verb* make intelligible; make known; say by way of explanation; account for. □ **explanation** /eksplə-/ *noun*.

explanatory /ɪk'splænətərɪ/ *adjective* serving to explain.

expletive /ɪk'spli:tɪv/ *noun* swear-word or exclamation.

explicable /ɪk'splɪkəb(ə)l/ *adjective* explainable.

explicit /ɪk'splɪsɪt/ *adjective* expressly stated; stated in detail; definite; outspoken. □ **explicitly** *adverb*; **explicitness** *noun*.

explode /ɪk'spləʊd/ **(-ding)** *verb* expand violently with loud noise; cause (bomb etc.) to do this; give vent suddenly to emotion, esp. anger; (of population etc.) increase suddenly; discredit.

exploit ● *noun* /'eksplɔɪt/ daring feat. ● *verb* /ɪk'splɔɪt/ use or develop for one's own ends; take advantage of (esp. person). □ **exploitation** /eksplɔɪ-/ *noun*; **exploitative** /ɪk'splɔɪt-/ *adjective*.

explore /ɪk'splɔ:/ *verb* **(-ring)** travel through (country etc.) to learn about it; inquire into; examine (part of body), probe (wound). □ **exploration** /eksplə-/ *noun*; **exploratory** /-'splɒr-/ *adjective*; **explorer** *noun*.

explosion /ɪk'spləʊʒ(ə)n/ *noun* exploding; loud noise caused by this; outbreak; sudden increase.

explosive /ɪk'spləʊsɪv/ ● *adjective* tending to explode; likely to cause violent outburst etc. ● *noun* explosive substance.

exponent /ɪk'spəʊnənt/ *noun* person promoting idea etc.; practitioner of activity, profession, etc.; person who explains or interprets; type, representative; *Mathematics* raised number or symbol showing how many of a number are to be multiplied together, e.g. ^{3} in $2^3 = 2 \times 2 \times 2$.

exponential /ekspə'nenʃ(ə)l/ *adjective* (of increase) more and more rapid. □ **exponentially** *adverb*.

export /ɪk'spɔ:t/ ● *verb* sell or send (goods or services) to another country. ● *noun* /'ekspɔ:t/ exporting; exported article or service; (in *plural*) amount exported. □ **exportation** *noun*; **exporter** /ɪk'spɔ:tə/ *noun*.

expose /ɪk'spəʊz/ *verb* **(-sing)** leave unprotected, esp. from weather; (+ *to*) put at risk of, subject to (influence etc.); *Photography* subject (film etc.) to light; reveal, disclose; exhibit, display; **(expose oneself)** display one's genitals indecently in public.

exposé /ek'spəʊzeɪ/ *noun* orderly statement of facts; disclosure of discreditable thing.

exposition /ekspə'zɪʃ(ə)n/ *noun* expounding, explanation; *Music* part of movement in which principal themes are presented; exhibition.

ex post facto /eks pəʊst 'fæktəʊ/ *adjective & adverb* retrospective(ly). [Latin]

expostulate /ɪk'spɒstjʊleɪt/ *verb* (**-ting**) make protest, remonstrate. □ **expostulation** *noun*.

exposure /ɪk'spəʊʒə/ *noun* exposing, being exposed; physical condition resulting from being exposed to elements; *Photography* length of time film etc. is exposed, section of film etc. exposed at one time.

expound /ɪk'spaʊnd/ *verb* set out in detail; explain, interpret.

express /ɪk'spres/ ● *verb* represent by symbols etc. or in language; put into words; squeeze out (juice, milk, etc.); (**express oneself**) communicate what one thinks, feels, or means. ● *adjective* operating at high speed; definitely stated; delivered by specially fast service. ● *adverb* with speed; by express messenger or train. ● *noun* express train etc. □ **expressible** *adjective*.

expression /ɪk'spreʃ(ə)n/ *noun* expressing, being expressed; wording, word, phrase; conveying or depiction of feeling; appearance (of face), intonation (of voice); *Mathematics* collection of symbols expressing quantity. □ **expressionless** *adjective*.

expressionism *noun* style of painting etc. seeking to express emotion rather than depict external world. □ **expressionist** *noun & adjective*.

expressive *adjective* full of expression; (+ *of*) serving to express. □ **expressiveness** *noun*.

expressly *adverb* explicitly.

expropriate /ɪks'prəʊprɪeɪt/ *verb* (**-ting**) take away (property); dispossess. □ **expropriation** *noun*; **expropriator** *noun*.

expulsion /ɪk'spʌlʃ(ə)n/ *noun* expelling, being expelled.

expunge /ɪk'spʌndʒ/ *verb* (**-ging**) erase, remove.

expurgate /'ekspəgeɪt/ *verb* (**-ting**) remove matter considered objectionable from (book etc.); clear away (such matter). □ **expurgation** *noun*; **expurgator** *noun*.

exquisite /'ekskwɪzɪt, ek'skwɪzɪt/ *adjective* extremely beautiful or delicate; acute, keen. □ **exquisitely** *adverb*.

ex-serviceman /eks'sɜːvɪsmən/ *noun* man formerly member of armed forces.

extant /ek'stænt/ *adjective* still existing.

extempore /ɪk'stempərɪ/ *adverb & adjective* without preparation.

extemporize /ɪk'stempəraɪz/ *verb* (also **-ise**) (**-zing** or **-sing**) improvise. □ **extemporization** *noun*.

extend /ɪk'stend/ *verb* lengthen in space or time; lay out at full length; reach or be or make continuous over certain area; (+ *to*) have certain scope; offer or accord (feeling, invitation, etc.); tax powers of. □ **extendible** *adjective*; **extensible** *adjective*.

extension /ɪk'stenʃ(ə)n/ *noun* extending; enlargement, additional part; subsidiary telephone on same line as main one; additional period of time.

extensive /ɪk'stensɪv/ *adjective* large, far-reaching. □ **extensively** *adverb*.

extent /ɪk'stent/ *noun* space covered; width of application, scope.

extenuate /ɪk'stenjʊeɪt/ *verb* (**-ting**) (often as **extenuating** *adjective*) make (guilt etc.) seem less serious by partial excuse. □ **extenuation** *noun*.

exterior /ɪk'stɪərɪə/ ● *adjective* outer; coming from outside. ● *noun* exterior aspect or surface; outward demeanour.

exterminate /ɪk'stɜːmɪneɪt/ *verb* (**-ting**) destroy utterly. □ **extermination** *noun*; **exterminator** *noun*.

external /ɪk'stɜːn(ə)l/ ● *adjective* of or on the outside; coming from outside; relating to a country's foreign affairs; (of medicine) for use on outside of body. ● *noun* (in *plural*) external features or circumstances. □ **externality** /ekstɜː'nælɪtɪ/ *noun*; **externally** *adverb*.

externalize *verb* (also **-ise**) (**-zing** or **-sing**) give or attribute external existence to.

extinct /ɪk'stɪŋkt/ *adjective* no longer existing; no longer burning; (of volcano) that no longer erupts; obsolete.

extinction *noun* making or becoming extinct; extinguishing, being extinguished.

extinguish /ɪk'stɪŋgwɪʃ/ *verb* put out (flame, light, etc.); terminate, destroy; wipe out (debt).

extinguisher *noun* = FIRE EXTINGUISHER.

extirpate /'ekstəpeɪt/ *verb* (**-ting**) destroy; root out. □ **extirpation** *noun*.

extol /ɪk'stəʊl/ *verb* (**-ll-**) praise enthusiastically.

extort /ɪk'stɔːt/ *verb* get by coercion.

extortion *noun* extorting, esp. of money; illegal exaction.

extortionate /ɪk'stɔːʃənət/ *adjective* exorbitant.

extra /'ekstrə/ ● *adjective* additional; more than usual or necessary. ● *adverb* more than usually; additionally. ● *noun* extra thing; thing for which one is charged extra; person playing one of crowd etc. in film; special edition of newspaper; *Cricket* run not scored from hit with bat.

extra- *combining form* outside, beyond scope of.

extract ● *verb* /ɪk'strækt/ take out; obtain against person's will; obtain from earth; copy out, quote; obtain (juice etc.) by pressure, distillation, etc.; derive (pleasure etc.); *Mathematics* find (root of number). ● *noun* /'ekstrækt/ passage from book etc.; preparation containing concentrated constituent of substance.

extraction /ɪk'strækʃ(ə)n/ *noun* extracting; removal of tooth; lineage.

extractor /ɪk'stræktə/ *noun* machine that extracts. □ **extractor fan** one that extracts bad air etc.

extracurricular /ekstrəkə'rɪkjʊlə/ *adjective* outside normal curriculum.

extraditable *adjective* liable to extradition; (of crime) warranting extradition.

extradite /'ekstrədaɪt/ *verb* (**-ting**) hand over (person accused of crime) to state where crime was committed. □ **extradition** /-'dɪʃ-/ *noun*.

extramarital /ekstrə'mærɪt(ə)l/ *adjective* (of sexual relationship) outside marriage.

extramural /ekstrə'mjʊər(ə)l/ *adjective* additional to ordinary teaching or studies.

extraneous /ɪk'streɪnɪəs/ *adjective* of external origin; (often + *to*) separate, irrelevant, unrelated.

extraordinary /ɪk'strɔːdɪnərɪ/ *adjective* unusual, remarkable; unusually great; (of meeting etc.) additional. □ **extraordinarily** *adverb*.

extrapolate /ɪk'stræpəleɪt/ *verb* (**-ting**) estimate (unknown facts or values) from known data. □ **extrapolation** *noun*.

extrasensory /ekstrə'sensərɪ/ *adjective* derived by means other than known senses.

extraterrestrial /ekstrətɪ'restrɪəl/ ● *adjective* outside the earth or its atmosphere. ● *noun* fictional being from outer space.

extravagant /ɪk'strævəgənt/ *adjective* spending (esp. money) excessively; excessive; absurd; costing much. □ **extravagance** *noun*; **extravagantly** *adverb*.

extravaganza /ɪkstrævə'gænzə/ *noun* spectacular theatrical or television production; fanciful composition.

extreme /ɪk'striːm/ ● *adjective* reaching high or highest degree; severe, not moderate; outermost; utmost.

● *noun* either of two things as remote or different as possible; thing at either end; highest degree. ▫ **extreme unction** anointing by priest of dying person. ▫ **extremely** *adverb*.

extremis see IN EXTREMIS.

extremism *noun* advocacy of extreme measures. ▫ **extremist** *adjective & noun*.

extremity /ɪk'stremɪtɪ/ *noun* (*plural* **-ies**) extreme point, end; (in *plural*) hands and feet; condition of extreme adversity.

extricate /'ekstrɪkeɪt/ *verb* (**-ting**) disentangle, release. ▫ **extrication** *noun*.

extrinsic /ek'strɪnsɪk/ *adjective* not inherent or intrinsic; (often + *to*) extraneous. ▫ **extrinsically** *adverb*.

extrovert /'ekstrəvɜ:t/ ● *noun* sociable or unreserved person; person mainly concerned with external things. ● *adjective* typical or having nature of extrovert. ▫ **extroversion** /-'vɜ:-/ *noun*.

extrude /ɪk'stru:d/ *verb* (**-ding**) thrust or squeeze out; shape by forcing through nozzle. ▫ **extrusion** *noun*.

exuberant /ɪg'zju:bərənt/ *adjective* high-spirited, lively; luxuriant, prolific; (of feelings etc.) abounding. ▫ **exuberance** *noun*.

exude /ɪg'zju:d/ *verb* (**-ding**) ooze out; give off; display (emotion) freely. ▫ **exudation** *noun*.

exult /ɪg'zʌlt/ *verb* rejoice. ▫ **exultant** *adjective*; **exultation** /eg-/ *noun*.

eye /aɪ/ ● *noun* organ or faculty of sight; iris of eye; region round eye; gaze; perception; eyelike thing; leaf bud of potato; centre of hurricane; spot, hole, loop. ● *verb* (**eyes**, **eyed**, **eyeing** or **eying**) (often + *up*) observe, watch suspiciously or closely. ▫ **all eyes** watching intently; **eyeball** ball of eye within lids and socket; **eyebath** vessel for applying lotion to eye; **eye-brow** hair growing on ridge over eye; **eye-catching** *colloquial* striking; **eyeglass** lens for defective eye; **eyehole** hole to look through; **eyelash** any of hairs on edge of eyelid; **eyelid** fold of skin that can cover eye; **eyeliner** cosmetic applied as line round eye; **eye-opener** *colloquial* enlightening experience, unexpected revelation; **eyepiece** lens(es) to which eye is applied at end of optical instrument; **eye-shade** device to protect eyes from strong light; **eye-shadow** cosmetic for eyelids; **eyesight** faculty or power of sight; **eyesore** ugly thing; **eye-tooth** canine tooth in upper jaw; **eyewash** lotion for eyes, *slang* nonsense; **eyewitness** person who saw thing happen and can tell of it; **have one's eye on** wish or plan to obtain; **keep an eye on** watch, look after; **see eye to eye** (often + *with*) agree; **set eyes on** see.

eyeful *noun* (*plural* **-s**) *colloquial* good look, visually striking person or thing.

eyelet /'aɪlɪt/ *noun* small hole for passing cord etc. through.

eyrie /'ɪərɪ/ *noun* nest of bird of prey, esp. eagle, built high up.

Ff

F *abbreviation* Fahrenheit.
f *abbreviation* (also **f.**) female; feminine; *Music* forte.
FA *abbreviation* Football Association.
fa = FAH.
fable /ˈfeɪb(ə)l/ *noun* fictional tale, esp. legendary, or moral tale, often with animal characters.
fabled *adjective* celebrated; legendary.
fabric /ˈfæbrɪk/ *noun* woven material; walls, floor, and roof of building; structure.
fabricate /ˈfæbrɪkeɪt/ *verb* (**-ting**) construct, esp. from components; invent (fact), forge (document). □ **fabrication** *noun*.
fabulous /ˈfæbjʊləs/ *adjective colloquial* marvellous; legendary. □ **fabulously** *adverb*.
façade /fəˈsɑːd/ *noun* face or front of building; outward, esp. deceptive, appearance.
face ● *noun* front of head; facial expression; surface; façade of building; side of mountain; dial of clock etc.; functional side of tool, bat, etc.; effrontery; aspect, feature. ● *verb* (**-cing**) look or be positioned towards; be opposite; meet resolutely, confront; put facing on (garment, wall, etc.). □ **face-lift** cosmetic surgery to remove wrinkles etc., improvement in appearance; **face up to** accept bravely; **face value** nominal value, superficial appearance; **lose face** be humiliated; **on the face of it** apparently; **pull a face** distort features; **save face** avoid humiliation.
faceless *adjective* without identity; not identifiable.
facet /ˈfæsɪt/ *noun* aspect; side of cut gem etc.
facetious /fəˈsiːʃəs/ *adjective* intended to be amusing, esp. inappropriately. □ **facetiously** *adverb*; **facetiousness** *noun*.
facia = FASCIA.
facial /ˈfeɪʃ(ə)l/ ● *adjective* of or for the face. ● *noun* beauty treatment for the face. □ **facially** *adverb*.
facile /ˈfæsaɪl/ *adjective* easily achieved but of little value; glib.
facilitate /fəˈsɪlɪteɪt/ *verb* (**-ting**) ease (process etc.). □ **facilitation** *noun*.
facility /fəˈsɪlɪtɪ/ *noun* (*plural* **-ies**) ease, absence of difficulty; dexterity; (esp. in *plural*) opportunity or equipment for doing something.
facing *noun* material over part of garment etc. for contrast or strength; outer covering on wall etc.
facsimile /fækˈsɪmɪlɪ/ *noun* exact copy of writing, picture, etc.
fact *noun* thing known to exist or be true; reality. □ **factsheet** information leaflet; **in fact** in reality, in short; **the facts of life** information on sexual functions etc.
faction /ˈfækʃ(ə)n/ *noun* small dissenting group within larger one, esp. in politics; such dissension. □ **factional** *adjective*.
factious /ˈfækʃəs/ *adjective* of or inclined to faction.
factitious /fækˈtɪʃəs/ *adjective* specially contrived; artificial.
factor /ˈfæktə/ *noun* thing contributing to result; whole number etc. that when multiplied produces given number (e.g. 2, 3, 4, and 6 are the factors of 12).
factorial /fækˈtɔːrɪəl/ *noun* the product of a number and all whole numbers below it.
factory /ˈfæktərɪ/ *noun* (*plural* **-ies**) building(s) for manufacture of goods. □ **factory farming** using intensive or industrial methods of rearing livestock.
factotum /fækˈtəʊtəm/ *noun* (*plural* **-s**) employee doing all kinds of work.
factual /ˈfæktjʊəl/ *adjective* based on or concerned with fact. □ **factually** *adverb*.
faculty /ˈfækəltɪ/ *noun* (*plural* **-ies**) aptitude for particular activity; physical or mental power; group of related university departments; *US* teaching staff of university etc.
fad *noun* craze; peculiar notion.
faddy *adjective* (**-ier**, **-iest**) having petty likes and dislikes.
fade ● *verb* (**-ding**) (cause to) lose colour, light, or sound; slowly diminish; lose freshness or strength. ● *noun* action of fading. □ **fade away** die away, disappear, *colloquial* languish, grow thin.
faeces /ˈfiːsiːz/ *plural noun* (*US* **feces**) waste matter from bowels. □ **faecal** /-k(ə)l/ *adjective*.
fag ● *noun colloquial* tedious task; *slang* cigarette; (at public schools) junior boy who runs errands for a senior. ● *verb* (**-gg-**) (often + *out*) *colloquial* exhaust; act as fag. □ **fag-end** *slang* cigarette-end.
faggot /ˈfægət/ *noun* (*US* **fagot**) baked or fried ball of seasoned chopped liver etc.; bundle of sticks etc.
fah /fɑː/ *noun* (also **fa**) *Music* fourth note of scale in tonic sol-fa.
Fahrenheit /ˈfærənhaɪt/ *adjective* of scale of temperature on which water freezes at 32° and boils at 212°.
faience /ˈfaɪɑ̃s/ *noun* decorated and glazed earthenware and porcelain.
fail ● *verb* not succeed; be or judge to be unsuccessful in (exam etc.); (+ *to do*) be unable, neglect; disappoint; be absent or insufficient; become weaker; cease functioning. ● *noun* failure in exam. □ **fail-safe** reverting to safe condition when faulty; **without fail** for certain, whatever happens.
failed *adjective* unsuccessful; bankrupt.
failing ● *noun* fault; weakness. ● *preposition* in default of.
failure /ˈfeɪljə/ *noun* lack of success; unsuccessful person or thing; non-performance; breaking down, ceasing to function; running short of supply etc.
fain *archaic* ● *adjective* (+ *to do*) willing, obliged. ● *adverb* gladly.
faint ● *adjective* dim, pale; weak, giddy; slight; timid. ● *verb* lose consciousness; become faint. ● *noun* act or state of fainting. □ **faint-hearted** cowardly, timid. □ **faintly** *adverb*; **faintness** *noun*.
fair[1] ● *adjective* just, equitable; blond, not dark; moderate in quality or amount; (of weather) fine; (of wind) favourable; *archaic* beautiful. ● *adverb* in a fair or just manner; exactly, completely. □ **fair and square** exactly, straightforwardly; **fair copy** transcript free from corrections; **fair game** legitimate target or object; **fair play** just treatment or behaviour; **fair-weather friend** friend or ally who deserts in crisis. □ **fairness** *noun*.
fair[2] *noun* stalls, amusements, etc. for public entertainment; periodic market, often with entertainments; trade exhibition. □ **fairground** outdoor site for fair.
Fair Isle *noun* multicoloured knitwear design characteristic of Fair Isle in the Shetlands.
fairly *adverb* in a fair way; moderately; to a noticeable degree.

fairway *noun* navigable channel; mown grass between golf tee and green.

fairy /ˈfeərɪ/ *noun* (*plural* **-ies**) small winged legendary being. ▫ **fairy cake** small iced sponge cake; **fairy godmother** benefactress; **fairyland** home of fairies, enchanted region; **fairy lights** small coloured lights for decoration; **fairy ring** ring of darker grass caused by fungi; **fairy story, tale** tale about fairies, unbelievable story, lie.

fait accompli /feɪt əˈkɒmpliː/ *noun* thing done and past arguing about. [French]

faith /feɪθ/ *noun* trust; religious belief; creed; loyalty, trustworthiness. ▫ **faith-healer** person who practises **faith-healing**, healing dependent on faith rather than treatment.

faithful *adjective* showing faith; (often + *to*) loyal, trustworthy; accurate.

faithfully *adverb* in a faithful way. ▫ **Yours faithfully** *written before signature at end of business letter.*

faithless *adjective* disloyal; without religious faith.

fake ● *noun* thing or person that is not genuine. ● *adjective* counterfeit, not genuine. ● *verb* (**-king**) make fake or imitation of; feign.

fakir /ˈfeɪkɪə/ *noun* Muslim or Hindu religious beggar or ascetic.

falcon /ˈfɔːlkən/ *noun* small hawk trained to hunt.

falconry *noun* breeding and training of hawks.

fall /fɔːl/ ● *verb* (*past* **fell**; *past participle* **fallen**) go or come down freely; descend; (often + *over*) lose balance and come suddenly to ground; slope or hang down; sink lower, decline in power, status, etc.; subside; occur; become; (of face) show dismay etc.; be defeated; die. ● *noun* falling; amount or thing that falls; overthrow; (esp. in *plural*) waterfall; *US* autumn. ▫ **fall back on** have recourse to; **fall behind** be outstripped, be in arrears; **fall down (on)** *colloquial* fail (in); **fall for** be captivated or deceived by; **fall foul of** come into conflict with; **fall guy** *slang* easy victim, scapegoat; **fall in** *Military* take place in parade; **fall in with** meet by chance, agree or coincide with; **falling star** meteor; **fall off** decrease, deteriorate; **fall out** *verb* quarrel, (of hair, teeth, etc.) become detached, result, occur, *Military* come out of formation; **fallout** *noun* radioactive nuclear debris; **fall short of** fail to reach or obtain; **fall through** fail; **fall to** start eating, working, etc.

fallacy /ˈfæləsɪ/ *noun* (*plural* **-ies**) mistaken belief; faulty reasoning; misleading argument. ▫ **fallacious** /fəˈleɪʃəs/ *adjective.*

fallible /ˈfælɪb(ə)l/ *adjective* capable of making mistakes. ▫ **fallibility** *noun.*

Fallopian tube /fəˈləʊpɪən/ *noun* either of two tubes along which ova travel from ovaries to womb.

fallow /ˈfæləʊ/ ● *adjective* (of land) ploughed but left unsown; uncultivated. ● *noun* fallow land.

fallow deer *noun* small deer with white-spotted reddish-brown summer coat.

false /fɔːls/ *adjective* wrong, incorrect; sham, artificial; (+ *to*) deceitful, treacherous, unfaithful; deceptive. ▫ **false alarm** alarm given needlessly; **false pretences** misrepresentations meant to deceive. ▫ **falsely** *adverb*; **falsity** *noun*; **falseness** *noun.*

falsehood *noun* untrue thing; lying, lie.

falsetto /fɔːlˈsetəʊ/ *noun* male voice above normal range.

falsify /ˈfɔːlsɪfaɪ/ *verb* (**-ies, -ied**) fraudulently alter; misrepresent. ▫ **falsification** *noun.*

falter /ˈfɔːltə/ *verb* stumble; go unsteadily; lose courage; speak hesitatingly.

fame *noun* renown, being famous; *archaic* reputation.

famed *adjective* (+ *for*) much spoken of or famous because of.

familial /fəˈmɪlɪəl/ *adjective* of a family or its members.

familiar /fəˈmɪlɪə/ ● *adjective* (often + *to*) well known, often encountered; (+ *with*) knowing (a thing) well; (excessively) informal. ● *noun* intimate friend; supposed attendant of witch etc. ▫ **familiarity** /-ˈær-/ *noun* (*plural* **-ies**); **familiarly** *adverb.*

familiarize /fəˈmɪlɪəraɪz/ *verb* (also **-ise**) (**-zing** or **-sing**) (usually + *with*) make (person etc.) conversant. ▫ **familiarization** *noun.*

family /ˈfæmɪlɪ/ *noun* (*plural* **-ies**) set of relations, esp. parents and children; person's children; household; all the descendants of common ancestor; group of similar things, people, etc.; group of related genera of animals or plants. ▫ **family credit** regular state payment to low-income family; **family planning** birth control; **family tree** genealogical chart.

famine /ˈfæmɪn/ *noun* extreme scarcity, esp. of food.

famish /ˈfæmɪʃ/ *verb* (usually as **famished** *adjective colloquial*) make or become extremely hungry.

famous /ˈfeɪməs/ *adjective* (often + *for*) well-known; celebrated; *colloquial* excellent. ▫ **famously** *adverb.*

fan¹ ● *noun* apparatus, usually with rotating blades, for ventilation etc.; device, semicircular and folding, waved to cool oneself; fan-shaped thing. ● *verb* (**-nn-**) blow air on, (as) with fan; (usually + *out*) spread out like fan. ▫ **fan belt** belt driving fan to cool radiator in vehicle; **fanlight** small, originally semicircular, window over door etc.; **fantail** pigeon with broad tail.

fan² *noun* devotee. ▫ **fan club** (club of) devotees; **fan mail** letters from fans.

fanatic /fəˈnætɪk/ ● *noun* person obsessively devoted to a belief, activity, etc. ● *adjective* excessively enthusiastic. ▫ **fanatical** *adjective*; **fanatically** *adverb*; **fanaticism** /-tɪsɪz(ə)m/ *noun.*

fancier /ˈfænsɪə/ *noun* connoisseur, enthusiast; breeder, esp. of pigeons.

fanciful /ˈfænsɪfʊl/ *adjective* imaginary; indulging in fancies. ▫ **fancifully** *adverb.*

fancy /ˈfænsɪ/ ● *noun* (*plural* **-ies**) inclination, whim; supposition; imagination. ● *adjective* (**-ier, -iest**) extravagant; ornamental. ● *verb* (**-ies, -ied**) (+ *that*) imagine; suppose; *colloquial* find attractive, desire; have unduly high opinion of. ▫ **fancy dress** costume for masquerading; **fancy-free** without (emotional) commitments; **fancy man, woman** woman's or man's lover. ▫ **fancily** *adverb.*

fandango /fænˈdæŋgəʊ/ *noun* (*plural* **-es** or **-s**) lively Spanish dance.

fanfare /ˈfænfeə/ *noun* short showy sounding of trumpets etc.

fang *noun* canine tooth, esp. of dog or wolf; tooth of venomous snake; (prong of) root of tooth.

fantasia /fænˈteɪzɪə/ *noun* free or improvisatory musical etc. composition.

fantasize /ˈfæntəsaɪz/ *verb* (also **-ise**) (**-zing** or **-sing**) daydream; imagine; create fantasy about.

fantastic /fænˈtæstɪk/ *adjective* extravagantly fanciful; grotesque, quaint; *colloquial* excellent, extraordinary. ▫ **fantastically** *adverb.*

fantasy /ˈfæntəsɪ/ *noun* (*plural* **-ies**) imagination, esp. when unrelated to reality; mental image, daydream; fantastic invention or composition.

fanzine /ˈfænziːn/ *noun* magazine for fans of science fiction, a football team, etc.

far (**further, furthest** or **farther, farthest**) ● *adverb* at, to, or by a great distance in space or time; by much. ● *adjective* distant; remote; extreme. ▫ **far and wide** over large area; **far-away** remote, dreamy, distant; **the Far East** countries of E. Asia; **far-fetched** unconvincing, exaggerated, fanciful; **far-flung** widely scattered, remote; **far from** almost the opposite of; **far gone** very ill, drunk, etc.; **far-off** remote; **far-out** *slang* unconventional, excellent; **far-reaching** widely influential or applicable; **far-seeing** showing foresight; **far-sighted** having foresight, *esp. US* long-sighted.

farad /ˈfærəd/ *noun* SI unit of electrical capacitance.

farce /fɑːs/ *noun* comedy with ludicrously improbable plot; absurdly futile proceedings; pretence. □ **farcical** *adjective*.

fare ● *noun* price of journey on public transport; passenger; food. ● *verb* (**-ring**) progress; get on. □ **fare-stage** section of bus route for which fixed fare is charged; stop marking this.

farewell /feəˈwel/ ● *interjection* goodbye. ● *noun* leave-taking.

farina /fəˈriːnə/ *noun* flour of corn, nuts, or starchy roots. □ **farinaceous** /færɪˈneɪʃəs/ *adjective*.

farm ● *noun* land and its buildings used for growing crops, rearing animals, etc.; farmhouse. ● *verb* use (land) thus; be farmer; breed (fish etc.) commercially; (+ *out*) delegate or subcontract (work). □ **farmhand** worker on farm; **farmhouse** house attached to farm; **farmyard** yard adjacent to farmhouse. □ **farming** *noun*.

farmer *noun* owner or manager of farm.

faro /ˈfeərəʊ/ *noun* gambling card-game.

farrago /fəˈrɑːgəʊ/ *noun* (*plural* **-s** or *US* **-es**) medley, hotchpotch.

farrier /ˈfærɪə/ *noun* smith who shoes horses.

farrow /ˈfærəʊ/ ● *verb* give birth to (piglets). ● *noun* litter of pigs.

Farsi /ˈfaːsɪ/ *noun* modern Persian language.

farther = FURTHER.

farthest = FURTHEST.

farthing /ˈfɑːðɪŋ/ *noun historical* coin worth quarter of old penny.

farthingale /ˈfɑːðɪŋgeɪl/ *noun historical* hooped petticoat.

fascia /ˈfeɪʃə/ *noun* (also **facia**) (*plural* **-s**) instrument panel of vehicle; similar panel etc. for operating machinery; long flat surface of wood or stone.

fascicle /ˈfæsɪk(ə)l/ *noun* instalment of book.

fascinate /ˈfæsɪneɪt/ *verb* (**-ting**) (often as **fascinating** *adjective*) capture interest of; attract. □ **fascination** *noun*.

Fascism /ˈfæʃɪz(ə)m/ *noun* extreme right-wing totalitarian nationalist movement in Italy (1922–43); (also **fascism**) any similar movement. □ **Fascist**, **fascist** *noun & adjective*; **Fascistic**, **fascistic** /-ˈʃɪs-/ *adjective*.

fashion /ˈfæʃ(ə)n/ ● *noun* current popular custom or style, esp. in dress; manner of doing something. ● *verb* (often + *into*) form, make. □ **in fashion** fashionable; **out of fashion** not fashionable.

fashionable *adjective* of or conforming to current fashion; of or favoured by high society. □ **fashionably** *adverb*.

fast[1] /fɑːst/ ● *adjective* rapid; capable of or intended for high speed; (of clock) ahead of correct time; firm, fixed, (of colour) not fading; pleasure-seeking. ● *adverb* quickly; firmly; soundly, completely. □ **fastback** car with sloping rear; **fast breeder (reactor)** reactor using neutrons with high kinetic energy; **fast food** restaurant food that is produced quickly; **pull a fast one** *colloquial* try to deceive someone.

fast[2] /fɑːst/ ● *verb* abstain from food. ● *noun* act or period of fasting.

fasten /ˈfɑːs(ə)n/ *verb* make or become fixed or secure; (+ *in*, *up*) shut in, lock securely; (+ *on*) direct (attention) towards; (+ *off*) fix with knot or stitches.

fastener *noun* (also **fastening**) device that fastens.

fastidious /fæˈstɪdɪəs/ *adjective* fussy; easily disgusted, squeamish.

fastness /ˈfɑːstnɪs/ *noun* stronghold.

fat ● *noun* oily substance, esp. in animal bodies; part of meat etc. containing this. ● *adjective* (**-tt-**) plump; containing much fat; thick, substantial. ● *verb* (**-tt-**) (esp. as **fatted** *adjective*) make or become fat. □ **fathead** *colloquial* stupid person; **fat-headed** stupid; **a fat lot** *colloquial* very little. □ **fatless** *adjective*; **fatten** *verb*.

fatal /ˈfeɪt(ə)l/ *adjective* causing or ending in death or ruin. □ **fatally** *adverb*.

fatalism *noun* belief in predetermination; submissive acceptance. □ **fatalist** *noun*; **fatalistic** /-ˈlɪs-/ *adjective*.

fatality /fəˈtælɪtɪ/ *noun* (*plural* **-ies**) death by accident, in war, etc.

fate ● *noun* supposed power predetermining events; destiny; death, destruction. ● *verb* (**-ting**) preordain; (as **fated** *adjective*) doomed, (+ *to do*) preordained.

fateful *adjective* decisive; important; controlled by fate.

father /ˈfɑːðə/ ● *noun* male parent; (usually in *plural*) forefather; originator; early leader; (also **Father**) priest; (**the Father**) God; (in *plural*) elders. ● *verb* be father of; originate. □ **father-in-law** (*plural* **fathers-in-law**) wife's or husband's father; **fatherland** native country. □ **fatherhood** *noun*; **fatherless** *adjective*.

fatherly *adjective* of or like a father.

fathom /ˈfæð(ə)m/ ● *noun* measure of 6ft, esp. in soundings. ● *verb* comprehend; measure depth of (water). □ **fathomable** *adjective*.

fathomless *adjective* too deep to fathom.

fatigue /fəˈtiːg/ ● *noun* extreme tiredness; weakness in metals etc. from repeated stress; non-military army duty, (in *plural*) clothing for this. ● *verb* (**-gues**, **-gued**, **-guing**) cause fatigue in.

fatty ● *adjective* (**-ier**, **-iest**) like or containing fat. ● *noun* (*plural* **-ies**) *colloquial* fat person. □ **fatty acid** type of organic compound.

fatuous /ˈfætjʊəs/ *adjective* vacantly silly; purposeless. □ **fatuity** /fəˈtjuːɪtɪ/ *noun* (*plural* **-ies**); **fatuously** *adverb*; **fatuousness** *noun*.

fatwa /ˈfætwɑː/ *noun* legal ruling by Islamic religious leader.

faucet /ˈfɔːsɪt/ *noun esp. US* tap.

fault /fɔːlt/ ● *noun* defect, imperfection; responsibility for wrongdoing, error, etc.; break in electric circuit; *Tennis etc.* incorrect service; break in rock strata. ● *verb* find fault with. □ **find fault** (often + *with*) criticize or complain (about); **to a fault** excessively. □ **faultless** *adjective*; **faultlessly** *adverb*.

faulty *adjective* (**-ier**, **-iest**) having faults. □ **faultily** *adverb*.

faun /fɔːn/ *noun* Latin rural deity with goat's horns, legs, and tail.

fauna /ˈfɔːnə/ *noun* (*plural* **-s**) animal life of a region or period.

faux pas /fəʊ ˈpɑː/ *noun* (*plural* same /ˈpɑːz/) tactless mistake. [French]

favour /ˈfeɪvə/ (*US* **favor**) ● *noun* kind act; approval, goodwill; partiality; badge, ribbon, etc. as emblem of support. ● *verb* regard or treat with favour; support, facilitate; tend to confirm (idea etc.); (+ *with*) oblige; (as **favoured** *adjective*) having special advantages. □ **in favour** approved of, (+ *of*) in support of or to the advantage of; **out of favour** disapproved of.

favourable *adjective* (*US* **favorable**) well-disposed; approving; promising; helpful, suitable. □ **favourably** *adverb*.

favourite /ˈfeɪvərɪt/ (*US* **favorite**) ● *adjective* preferred to all others. ● *noun* favourite person or thing; competitor thought most likely to win.

favouritism *noun* (*US* **favoritism**) unfair favouring of one person etc.

fawn[1] ● *noun* deer in first year; light yellowish brown. ● *adjective* fawncoloured. ● *verb* give birth to fawn.

fawn[2] *verb* (often + *on*, *upon*) behave servilely; (of dog) show extreme affection.

fax ● *noun* electronic transmission of exact copy of document etc.; such copy; (in full **fax machine**) apparatus used for this. ● *verb* transmit in this way.

faze *verb* (**-zing**) (often as **fazed** *adjective*) *colloquial* disconcert.

FBI *abbreviation* Federal Bureau of Investigation.

FC *abbreviation* Football Club.

FCO *abbreviation* Foreign and Commonwealth Office.

FE *abbreviation* further education.

fealty /ˈfiːəltɪ/ *noun* (*plural* **-ies**) fidelity to feudal lord; allegiance.

fear ● *noun* panic etc. caused by impending danger, pain, etc.; cause of this; alarm, dread. ● *verb* be afraid of; (+ *for*) feel anxiety about; dread; shrink from; revere (God).

fearful *adjective* afraid; terrible, awful; extremely unpleasant. □ **fearfully** *adverb*; **fearfulness** *noun*.

fearless *adjective* not afraid; brave. □ **fearlessly** *adverb*; **fearlessness** *noun*.

fearsome *adjective* frightening. □ **fearsomely** *adverb*.

feasible /ˈfiːzɪb(ə)l/ *adjective* practicable, possible. □ **feasibility** *noun*; **feasibly** *adverb*.

■ **Usage** *Feasible* should not be used to mean 'likely'. *Possible* or *probable* should be used instead.

feast ● *noun* sumptuous meal; religious festival; sensual or mental pleasure. ● *verb* (often + *on*) have feast, eat and drink sumptuously; regale.

feat *noun* remarkable act or achievement.

feather /ˈfeðə/ ● *noun* one of structures forming bird's plumage, with fringed horny shaft; these as material. ● *verb* cover or line with feathers; turn (oar) through air edgeways. □ **feather bed** *noun* bed with feather-stuffed mattress; **feather-bed** *verb* cushion, esp. financially; **feather-brained**, **-headed** silly; **featherweight** amateur boxing weight (54–57 kg). □ **feathery** *adjective*.

feature /ˈfiːtʃə/ ● *noun* characteristic or distinctive part; (usually in *plural*) part of face; specialized article in newspaper etc.; (in full **feature film**) main film in cinema programme. ● *verb* (**-ring**) make or be special feature of; emphasize; take part in. □ **featureless** *adjective*.

Feb. *abbreviation* February.

febrile /ˈfiːbraɪl/ *adjective* of fever.

February /ˈfebrʊərɪ/ *noun* (*plural* **-ies**) second month of year.

fecal *US* = FAECAL.

feces *US* = FAECES.

feckless /ˈfeklɪs/ *adjective* feeble, ineffectual; irresponsible.

fecund /ˈfekənd/ *adjective* fertile. □ **fecundity** /fɪˈkʌndɪtɪ/ *noun*.

fecundate /ˈfekəndeɪt/ *verb* (**-ting**) make fruitful; fertilize. □ **fecundation** *noun*.

fed *past & past participle* of FEED. □ **fed up** (often + *with*) discontented, bored.

federal /ˈfedər(ə)l/ *adjective* of system of government in which self-governing states unite for certain functions; of such a federation; (**Federal**) *US* of Northern States in Civil War. □ **federalism** *noun*; **federalist** *noun*; **federalize** *verb* (also **-ise**) (**-zing** or **-sing**); **federalization** *noun*; **federally** *adverb*.

federate ● *verb* /ˈfedəreɪt/ (**-ting**) unite on federal basis. ● *adjective* /ˈfedərət/ federally organized. □ **federative** /-rətɪv/ *adjective*.

federation /fedəˈreɪʃ(ə)n/ *noun* federal group; act of federating.

fee *noun* payment for professional advice or services; (often in *plural*) payment for admission, membership, licence, education, exam, etc.; money paid for transfer of footballer etc. □ **fee-paying** paying fee(s), (of school) charging fees.

feeble /ˈfiːb(ə)l/ *adjective* (**-r**, **-st**) weak; lacking energy, strength, or effectiveness. □ **feebly** *adverb*.

feed ● *verb* (*past & past participle* **fed**) supply with food; put food in mouth of; eat; graze; keep supplied with; (+ *into*) supply (material) to machine etc.; (often + *on*) nourish, be nourished by. ● *noun* food, esp. for animals or infants; feeding; *colloquial* meal. □ **feedback** information about result of experiment, response, *Electronics* return of part of output signal to input.

feeder *noun* person or thing that feeds in specified way; baby's feeding bottle; bib; tributary; branch road or railway line; electricity main supplying distribution point; feeding apparatus in machine.

feel ● *verb* (*past & past participle* **felt**) examine, search, or perceive by touch; experience; be affected by; (+ *that*) have impression; consider, think; seem; be consciously; (+ *for*, *with*) have sympathy or pity for. ● *noun* feeling; sense of touch; sensation characterizing something. □ **feel like** have wish or inclination for; **feel up to** be ready to face or deal with.

feeler *noun* organ in certain animals for touching, foraging, etc. □ **put out feelers** make tentative proposal.

feeling ● *noun* capacity to feel; sense of touch; physical sensation; emotion; (in *plural*) susceptibilities; sensitivity; notion, opinion. ● *adjective* sensitive; sympathetic. □ **feelingly** *adverb*.

feet *plural* of FOOT.

feign /feɪn/ *verb* simulate; pretend.

feint /feɪnt/ ● *noun* sham attack or diversionary blow; pretence. ● *verb* make a feint. ● *adjective* (of paper etc.) having faintly ruled lines.

feldspar /ˈfeldspɑː/ *noun* (also **felspar** /ˈfelspɑː/) common aluminium silicate.

felicitation /fəlɪsɪˈteɪʃ(ə)n/ *noun* (usually in *plural*) congratulation.

felicitous /fəˈlɪsɪtəs/ *adjective* apt; well-chosen.

felicity /fəˈlɪsɪtɪ/ *noun* (*plural* **-ies**) *formal* great happiness; capacity for apt expression.

feline /ˈfiːlaɪn/ ● *adjective* of cat family; catlike. ● *noun* animal of cat family.

fell[1] *past* of FALL.

fell[2] *verb* cut down (tree); strike down.

fell[3] *noun* hill or stretch of hills in N. England.

fell[4] *adjective* □ **at, in one fell swoop** in a single (originally deadly) action.

fell[5] *noun* animal's hide or skin with hair.

fellow /ˈfeləʊ/ ● *noun* comrade, associate; counterpart, equal; *colloquial* man, boy; incorporated senior member of college; member of learned society. ● *adjective* of same group etc. □ **fellow-feeling** sympathy; **fellow-traveller** person who travels with another, sympathizer with Communist party.

fellowship /ˈfeləʊʃɪp/ *noun* friendly association, companionship; group of associates; position or income of college fellow.

felon /ˈfelən/ *noun* person who has committed felony.

felony /ˈfelənɪ/ *noun* (*plural* **-ies**) serious usually violent crime. □ **felonious** /fɪˈləʊ-/ *adjective*.

felspar = FELDSPAR.

felt[1] ● *noun* fabric of matted and pressed fibres of wool etc. ● *verb* make into or cover with felt; become matted. □ **felt tip** or **pen**, **felt-tip(ped) pen** pen with fibre point.

felt[2] *past & past participle of* FEEL.

female /ˈfiːmeɪl/ ● *adjective* of the sex that can give birth or produce eggs; (of plants) fruit-bearing; of female people, animals, or plants; (of screw, socket, etc.) hollow to receive inserted part. ● *noun* female person, animal, or plant.

feminine /ˈfemɪnɪn/ *adjective* of women; womanly; *Grammar* (of noun) belonging to gender including words for most female people and animals. □ **femininity** /-ˈnɪn-/ *noun*.

feminism /ˈfemɪnɪz(ə)m/ *noun* advocacy of women's rights and sexual equality. □ **feminist** *noun & adjective*.

femme fatale /fæm fæˈtɑːl/ *noun* (*plural* ***femmes fatales*** same pronunciation) dangerously seductive woman. [French]

femur /ˈfiːmə/ *noun* (*plural* **-s** or **femora** /ˈfemərə/) thigh-bone. □ **femoral** /ˈfemər(ə)l/ *adjective*.

fen *noun* low marshy land.

fence ● *noun* barrier or railing enclosing field, garden, etc.; jump for horses; *slang* receiver of stolen goods. ● *verb* (**-cing**) surround (as) with fence; practise sword play; be evasive; deal in (stolen goods). □ **fencer** *noun*.

fencing *noun* fences, material for fences; sword-fighting, esp. as sport.

fend *verb* (+ *off*) ward off; (+ *for*) look after (esp. oneself).

fender *noun* low frame round fireplace; matting etc. to protect side of ship; *US* bumper of vehicle.

fennel /ˈfen(ə)l/ *noun* fragrant plant with edible leaf-stalks and seeds.

fenugreek /ˈfenjuːgriːk/ *noun* leguminous plant with aromatic seeds used for flavouring.

feral /ˈfer(ə)l/ *adjective* wild; (of animal) escaped and living wild.

ferial /ˈfɪerɪəl/ *adjective* (of day) not a church festival or fast.

ferment ● *noun* /ˈfɜːment/ excitement; fermentation; fermenting agent. ● *verb* /fəˈment/ undergo or subject to fermentation; excite.

fermentation /fɜːmenˈteɪʃ(ə)n/ *noun* breakdown of substance by yeasts, bacteria, etc.; excitement.

fern *noun* flowerless plant usually with feathery fronds.

ferocious /fəˈrəʊʃəs/ *adjective* fierce. □ **ferociously** *adverb*; **ferocity** /-ˈrɒs-/ *noun*.

ferret /ˈferɪt/ ● *noun* small polecat used in catching rabbits, rats, etc. ● *verb* (**-t-**) hunt with ferrets; (often + *out*, *about*, etc.) rummage; (+ *out*) search out.

ferric /ˈferɪk/ *adjective* of iron; containing iron in trivalent form.

Ferris wheel /ˈferɪs/ *noun* tall revolving vertical wheel with passenger cars in fairgrounds etc.

ferroconcrete /ferəʊˈkɒŋkriːt/ *noun* reinforced concrete.

ferrous /ˈferəs/ *adjective* containing iron, esp. in divalent form.

ferrule /ˈferuːl/ *noun* ring or cap on end of stick etc.

ferry ● *noun* (*plural* **-ies**) boat etc. for esp. regular transport across water; ferrying place or service. ● *verb* (**-ies**, **-ied**) take or go in ferry; transport from place to place, esp. regularly. □ **ferryman** *noun*.

fertile /ˈfɜːtaɪl/ *adjective* (of soil) abundantly productive; fruitful; (of seed, egg, etc.) capable of growth; inventive; (of animal or plant) able to reproduce. □ **fertility** /-ˈtɪl-/ *noun*.

fertilize /ˈfɜːtɪlaɪz/ *verb* (also **-ise**) (**-zing** or **-sing**) make fertile; cause (egg, female animal, etc.) to develop new individual. □ **fertilization** *noun*.

fertilizer *noun* (also **-iser**) substance added to soil to make it more fertile.

fervent /ˈfɜːv(ə)nt/ *adjective* ardent, intense. □ **fervency** *noun*; **fervently** *adverb*.

fervid /ˈfɜːvɪd/ *adjective* fervent. □ **fervidly** *adverb*.

fervour /ˈfɜːvə/ *noun* (*US* **fervor**) passion, zeal.

fescue /ˈfeskjuː/ *noun* pasture and fodder grass.

fester /ˈfestə/ *verb* make or become septic; cause continuing bitterness; rot; stagnate.

festival /ˈfestɪv(ə)l/ *noun* day or period of celebration; series of cultural events in town etc.

festive /ˈfestɪv/ *adjective* of or characteristic of festival; joyous.

festivity /feˈstɪvɪtɪ/ *noun* (*plural* **-ies**) gaiety, (in *plural*) celebration; party.

festoon /feˈstuːn/ ● *noun* curved hanging chain of flowers, ribbons, etc. ● *verb* (often + *with*) adorn with or form into festoons.

feta /ˈfetə/ *noun* salty white Greek cheese made from ewe's or goat's milk.

fetal *US* = FOETAL.

fetch *verb* go for and bring back; be sold for; draw forth; deal (blow). □ **fetch up** *colloquial* arrive, come to rest.

fetching *adjective* attractive. □ **fetchingly** *adverb*.

fête /feɪt/ ● *noun* outdoor fund-raising event. ● *verb* (**-ting**) honour or entertain lavishly.

fetid /ˈfetɪd/ *adjective* (also **foetid**) stinking.

fetish /ˈfetɪʃ/ *noun* abnormal object of sexual desire; object worshipped by primitive peoples; object of obsessive concern. □ **fetishism** *noun*; **fetishist** *noun*; **fetishistic** /-ˈʃɪs-/ *adjective*.

fetlock /ˈfetlɒk/ *noun* back of horse's leg where tuft of hair grows above hoof.

fetter /ˈfetə/ ● *noun* shackle for ankles; (in *plural*) captivity; restraint. ● *verb* put into fetters, restrict.

fettle /ˈfet(ə)l/ *noun* condition, trim.

fetus *US* = FOETUS.

feud /fjuːd/ ● *noun* prolonged hostility, esp. between families, tribes, etc. ● *verb* conduct feud.

feudal /ˈfjuːd(ə)l/ *adjective* of, like, or according to feudal system; reactionary. □ **feudal system** medieval system in which vassal held land in exchange for allegiance and service to landowner. □ **feudalism** *noun*; **feudalistic** /-ˈlɪs-/ *adjective*.

fever /ˈfiːvə/ ● *noun* abnormally high body temperature; disease characterized by this; nervous agitation. ● *verb* (esp. as **fevered** *adjective*) affect with fever or excitement. □ **fever pitch** state of extreme excitement.

feverfew /ˈfiːvəfjuː/ *noun* aromatic plant, used formerly to reduce fever, now to treat migraine.

feverish *adjective* having symptoms of fever; excited, restless. □ **feverishly** *adverb*.

few ● *adjective* not many. ● *noun* (treated as *plural*) not many; (**a few**) some but not many. □ **a good few** a considerable number (of); **quite a few** *colloquial* a fairly large number (of); **very few** a very small number (of).

fey /feɪ/ *adjective* strange, other-worldly; whimsical.

fez *noun* (*plural* **fezzes**) man's flat-topped conical red cap, worn by some Muslims.

ff *abbreviation Music* fortissimo.

ff. *abbreviation* following pages etc.

fiancé /fɪˈɒnseɪ/ *noun* (*feminine* **-cée** same pronunciation) person one is engaged to.

fiasco /fɪˈæskəʊ/ *noun* (*plural* **-s**) ludicrous or humiliating failure.

fiat /ˈfaɪæt/ *noun* authorization; decree.

fib ● *noun* trivial lie. ● *verb* (**-bb-**) tell fib. □ **fibber** *noun*.

fibre /ˈfaɪbə/ *noun* (*US* **fiber**) thread or filament forming tissue or textile; piece of threadlike glass; substance formed of fibres; moral character; roughage. □ **fibreboard** board made of compressed wood etc. fibres; **fibreglass** fabric made from woven glass fibres, plastic reinforced with glass fibres; **fibre optics** optics using glass fibres, usually to carry signals. □ **fibrous** *adjective*.

fibril /ˈfaɪbrɪl/ *noun* small fibre.

fibroid /ˈfaɪbrɔɪd/ ● *adjective* of, like, or containing fibrous tissue or fibres. ● *noun* benign fibrous tumour, esp. in womb.

fibrosis /faɪˈbrəʊsɪs/ *noun* thickening and scarring of connective tissue.

fibrositis /faɪbrəˈsaɪtɪs/ *noun* rheumatic inflammation of fibrous tissue.

fibula /ˈfɪbjʊlə/ *noun* (*plural* **-lae** /-liː/ or **-s**) bone on outer side of lower leg.

fiche /fiːʃ/ *noun* microfiche.

fickle /ˈfɪk(ə)l/ *adjective* inconstant, changeable. □ **fickleness** *noun*.

fiction /ˈfɪkʃ(ə)n/ *noun* non-factual literature, esp. novels; invented idea, thing, etc.; generally accepted falsehood. □ **fictional** *adjective*.

fictitious /fɪkˈtɪʃəs/ *adjective* imaginary, unreal; not genuine.

fiddle /ˈfɪd(ə)l/ ● *noun colloquial* violin; *colloquial* cheat, fraud; fiddly task. ● *verb* (**-ling**) (often + *with*, *at*) play restlessly; (often + *about*) move aimlessly; (usually + *with*) tamper, tinker; *slang* falsify, swindle, get by cheating; play fiddle. □ **fiddler** *noun*.

fiddling *adjective* petty, trivial; *colloquial* fiddly.

fiddly *adjective* (**-ier**, **-iest**) *colloquial* awkward to do or use.

fidelity /fɪˈdelɪtɪ/ *noun* faithfulness, loyalty; accuracy, precision in sound reproduction.

fidget /ˈfɪdʒɪt/ ● *verb* (**-t-**) move restlessly; be or make uneasy. ● *noun* person who fidgets; (**the fidgets**) restless state or mood. □ **fidgety** *adjective*.

fiduciary /fɪˈdjuːʃərɪ/ ● *adjective* of a trust, trustee, etc.; held or given in trust; (of currency) dependent on public confidence. ● *noun* (*plural* **-ies**) trustee.

fief /fiːf/ *noun* land held under feudal system.

field /fiːld/ ● *noun* area of esp. cultivated enclosed land; area rich in some natural product; competitors; expanse of sea, snow, etc.; battlefield; area of activity or study; *Computing* part of record, representing item of data. ● *verb Cricket etc.* act as fielder(s), stop and return (ball); select (player, candidate, etc.); deal with (questions etc.). □ **field-day** exciting or successful time, military exercise or review; **field events** athletic events other than races; **field glasses** outdoor binoculars; **Field Marshal** army officer of highest rank; **fieldmouse** small long-tailed rodent; **fieldsman** = FIELDER; **field sports** outdoor sports, esp. hunting, shooting, and fishing; **fieldwork** practical surveying, science, sociology, etc. conducted in natural environment; **fieldworker** person doing fieldwork.

fielder *noun Cricket etc.* member (other than bowler) of fielding side.

fieldfare *noun* grey thrush.

fiend /fiːnd/ *noun* evil spirit; wicked or cruel person; mischievous or annoying person; *slang* devotee; difficult or unpleasant thing. □ **fiendish** *adjective*; **fiendishly** *adverb*.

fierce *adjective* (**-r**, **-st**) violently aggressive or frightening; eager; intense. □ **fiercely** *adverb*; **fierceness** *noun*.

fiery /ˈfaɪərɪ/ *adjective* (**-ier**, **-iest**) consisting of or flaming with fire; bright red; burning hot; spirited.

fiesta /fɪˈestə/ *noun* festival, holiday.

FIFA /ˈfiːfə/ *abbreviation* International Football Federation (*Fédération Internationale de Football Association*).

fife /faɪf/ *noun* small shrill flute.

fifteen /fɪfˈtiːn/ *adjective & noun* one more than fourteen; *Rugby* team of fifteen players. □ **fifteenth** *adjective & noun*.

fifth ● *adjective & noun* next after fourth; any of 5 equal parts of thing. □ **fifth column** group working for enemy within country at war.

fifty /ˈfɪftɪ/ *adjective & noun* (*plural* **-ies**) five times ten. □ **fifty-fifty** half and half, equal(ly). □ **fiftieth** *adjective & noun*.

fig *noun* soft fruit with many seeds; tree bearing it. □ **fig leaf** device concealing genitals.

fig. *abbreviation* figure.

fight /faɪt/ ● *verb* (*past & past participle* **fought** /fɔːt/) (often + *against*, *with*) contend with in war, combat, etc.; engage in (battle etc.); (+ *for*) strive to secure or on behalf of; contest (election); strive to overcome; (as **fighting** *adjective*) able and eager or trained to fight. ● *noun* combat; boxing match; battle; struggle; power or inclination to fight. □ **fight back** counter-attack, suppress (tears etc.); **fighting chance** chance of success if effort is made; **fighting fit** extremely fit; **fight off** repel with effort; **fight shy of** avoid; **put up a fight** offer resistance.

fighter *noun* person who fights; aircraft designed for attacking other aircraft.

figment /ˈfɪgmənt/ *noun* imaginary thing.

figurative /ˈfɪgərətɪv/ *adjective* metaphorical; (of art) not abstract, representational. □ **figuratively** *adverb*.

figure /ˈfɪgə/ ● *noun* external form, bodily shape; person of specified kind; representation of human form; image; numerical symbol or number, esp. 0–9; value, amount; (in *plural*) arithmetical calculations; diagram, illustration; dance etc. movement or sequence; (in full **figure of speech**) metaphor, hyperbole, etc. ● *verb* (**-ring**) appear, be mentioned; (usually as **figured** *adjective*) embellish with pattern; calculate; *esp. US colloquial* understand, consider, make sense. □ **figurehead** nominal leader, carved image etc. over ship's prow; **figure on** *esp. US colloquial* count on, expect; **figure out** work out by arithmetic or logic; **figure-skating** skating in prescribed patterns.

figurine /fɪgəˈriːn/ *noun* statuette.

filament /ˈfɪləmənt/ *noun* threadlike strand or fibre; conducting wire or thread in electric bulb.

filbert /ˈfɪlbət/ *noun* (nut of) cultivated hazel.

filch *verb* steal, pilfer.

file[1] ● *noun* folder, box, etc. for holding loose papers; paper kept in this; collection of related computer data; row of people or things one behind another. ● *verb* (**-ling**) place in file or among records; submit (petition for divorce etc.); walk in line. □ **filing cabinet** cabinet with drawers for storing files.

file[2] ● *noun* tool with rough surface for smoothing wood, fingernails, etc. ● *verb* (**-ling**) smooth or shape with file.

filial /ˈfɪlɪəl/ *adjective* of or due from son or daughter.

filibuster /ˈfɪlɪbʌstə/ ● *noun* obstruction of progress in legislative assembly; *esp. US* person who engages in this. ● *verb* act as filibuster.

filigree /ˈfɪlɪgriː/ *noun* fine ornamental work in gold etc. wire; similar delicate work.

filings *plural noun* particles rubbed off by file.

Filipino /fɪlɪˈpiːnəʊ/ ● *noun* (*plural* **-s**) native or national of Philippines. ● *adjective* of Philippines or Filipinos.

fill ● *verb* (often + *with*) make or become full; occupy completely; spread over or through; block up (hole, tooth, etc.); appoint to or hold (office etc.); (as **filling**

adjective) (of food) satisfying. ● *noun* enough to satisfy or fill. □ **fill in** complete (form etc.), fill completely, (often + *for*) act as substitute, *colloquial* inform more fully; **fill out** enlarge or become enlarged, esp. to proper size, fill in (form etc.); **fill up** fill completely, fill petrol tank (of).

filler *noun* material used to fill cavity or increase bulk.

fillet /'fɪlɪt/ ● *noun* boneless piece of fish or meat; (in full **fillet steak**) undercut of sirloin; ribbon etc. binding hair; narrow flat band between mouldings. ● *verb* (**-t-**) remove bones from (fish etc.) or divide into fillets; bind or provide with fillet(s).

filling *noun* material used to fill tooth, sandwich, pie, etc. □ **filling-station** garage selling petrol etc.

fillip /'fɪlɪp/ *noun* stimulus, incentive.

filly /'fɪlɪ/ *noun* (*plural* **-ies**) young female horse.

film ● *noun* thin coating or layer; strip or sheet of plastic etc. coated with light-sensitive emulsion for exposure in camera; story etc. on film; (in *plural*) cinema industry; slight veil, haze, etc. ● *verb* make photographic film of; (often + *over*) cover or become covered (as) with film. □ **film star** well-known film actor or actress. □ **filmy** *adjective* (**-ier**, **-iest**).

filmsetting *noun* typesetting by projecting characters on to photographic film. □ **filmset** *verb*; **filmsetter** *noun*.

Filofax /'faɪləʊfæks/ *noun proprietary term* personal organizer.

filo pastry /'fi:ləʊ/ *noun* pastry in very thin sheets.

filter /'fɪltə/ ● *noun* porous esp. paper device for removing impurities from liquid or gas or making coffee; screen for absorbing or modifying light; device for suppressing unwanted electrical or sound waves; arrangement for filtering traffic. ● *verb* pass through filter; (usually as **filtered** *adjective*) make (coffee) by dripping hot water through ground beans; (+ *through*, *into*, etc.) make way gradually through, into, etc.; (of traffic) be allowed to turn left or right at junction when other traffic is held up. □ **filter tip** (cigarette with) filter for removing some impurities.

filth *noun* disgusting dirt; obscenity.

filthy ● *adjective* (**-ier**, **-iest**) disgustingly dirty; obscene; (of weather) very unpleasant. ● *adverb colloquial* extremely. □ **filthy lucre** dishonourable gain; money.

filtrate /'fɪltreɪt/ ● *verb* (**-ting**) filter. ● *noun* filtered liquid. □ **filtration** *noun*.

fin *noun* organ, esp. of fish, for propelling and steering; similar projection for stabilizing aircraft etc.

finagle /fɪ'neɪg(ə)l/ *verb* (**-ling**) *colloquial* act or obtain dishonestly.

final /'faɪn(ə)l/ ● *adjective* at the end, coming last; conclusive, decisive. ● *noun* last or deciding heat or game; last edition of day's newspaper; (usually in *plural*) exams at end of degree course. □ **finality** /-'næl-/ *noun*; **finally** *adverb*.

finale /fɪ'nɑ:lɪ/ *noun* last movement or section of drama, piece of music, etc.

finalist *noun* competitor in final.

finalize *verb* (also **-ise**) (**-zing** or **-sing**) put in final form; complete. □ **finalization** *noun*.

finance /'faɪnæns/ ● *noun* management of money; monetary support for enterprise; (in *plural*) money resources. ● *verb* (**-cing**) provide capital for. □ **financial** /-'næn-/ *adjective*; **financially** /-'næn-/ *adverb*.

financier /faɪ'nænsɪə/ *noun* capitalist; entrepreneur.

finch *noun* small seed-eating bird.

find /faɪnd/ ● *verb* (*past & past participle* **found**) discover, get by chance or after search; become aware of; obtain, provide; summon up; perceive, experience; consider to be; (often in *passive*) discover to be present; reach; *Law* judge and declare. ● *noun* discovery of treasure etc.; valued thing or person newly discovered. □ **all found** (of wages) with board and lodging provided free; **find out** (often + *about*) discover, detect. □ **finder** *noun*.

finding *noun* (often in *plural*) conclusion reached by inquiry.

fine[1] ● *adjective* of high quality; excellent; good, satisfactory; pure, refined; imposing; bright and clear; small or thin, in small particles; smart, showy; flattering. ● *adverb* finely; very well. □ **fine arts** poetry, music, painting, sculpture, architecture, etc.; **finespun** delicate, too subtle; **fine-tune** make small adjustments to. □ **finely** *adverb*.

fine[2] ● *noun* money paid as penalty. ● *verb* (**-ning**) punish by fine.

finery /'faɪnərɪ/ *noun* showy dress or decoration.

finesse /fɪ'nes/ ● *noun* refinement; subtlety; artfulness; *Cards* attempt to win trick with card that is not the highest held. ● *verb* (**-ssing**) use or manage by finesse; *Cards* make finesse.

finger /'fɪŋgə/ ● *noun* any of terminal projections of hand (usually excluding thumb); part of glove for finger; finger-like object. ● *verb* touch, turn about, or play with fingers. □ **finger-bowl** bowl for rinsing fingers during meal; **finger-dry** dry and style hair by running fingers through it; **fingernail** nail on each finger; **fingerprint** impression made on surface by fingers, used in detecting crime; **finger-stall** protective cover for injured finger; **fingertip** tip of finger.

fingering *noun* manner of using fingers in music; indication of this in score.

finial /'fɪnɪəl/ *noun* ornamental top to gable, canopy, etc.

finicky /'fɪnɪkɪ/ *adjective* (also **finical**, **finicking**) overparticular; fastidious; detailed; fiddly.

finis /'fɪnɪs/ *noun* end, esp. of book.

finish /'fɪnɪʃ/ ● *verb* (often + *off*) bring or come to end or end of; complete; (often + *off*, *up*) complete consuming; treat surface of. ● *noun* last stage, completion; end of race etc.; method etc. of surface treatment.

finite /'faɪnaɪt/ *adjective* limited, not infinite; (of verb) having specific number and person.

Finn *noun* native or national of Finland.

finnan /'fɪnən/ *noun* (in full **finnan haddock**) smoke-cured haddock.

Finnish ● *adjective* of Finland. ● *noun* language of Finland.

fiord /fjɔ:d/ *noun* (also **fjord**) narrow inlet of sea as in Norway.

fir *noun* evergreen conifer with needles growing singly on the stems; its wood. □ **fir-cone** its fruit.

fire ● *noun* state of combustion of substance with oxygen, giving out light and heat; flame, glow; destructive burning; burning fuel in grate etc.; electric or gas heater; firing of guns; fervour, spirit; burning heat. ● *verb* (**-ring**) shoot (gun etc. or missile from it); shoot gun or missile; produce (salute etc.) by shooting; (of gun) be discharged; deliver or utter rapidly; detonate; dismiss (employee); set fire to; supply with fuel; stimulate, enthuse; undergo ignition; bake or dry (pottery, bricks, etc.). □ **fire-alarm** bell etc. warning of fire; **firearm** gun, esp. pistol or rifle; **fire-ball** large meteor, ball of flame; **fire-bomb** incendiary bomb; **firebrand** piece of burning wood, trouble-maker; **fire-break** obstacle preventing spread of fire in forest etc.; **fire-brick** fireproof brick in grate; **fire brigade** group of firefighters; **firedog** support for logs in hearth; **fire door** fire-resistant door; **fire-drill** rehearsal of procedure in case of fire; **fire-engine** vehicle carrying hoses, firefighters, etc.; **fire-escape** emergency staircase etc. for use in fire; **fire extinguisher** apparatus discharging water, foam, etc. to extinguish fire; **firefighter** person who extinguishes fires; **firefly** insect emitting phosphorescent light, e.g. glow-worm; **fire-irons** tongs, poker, and shovel for domestic fire; **fireman** male firefighter, person who tends steam engine or steamship furnace; **fireplace** place in wall for domestic fire; **fire-power** destructive capacity of guns etc.; **fire-practice** fire-drill; **fire-raiser** arsonist; **fireside** area round fireplace; **fire-screen** ornamental screen for fire-place, screen against direct heat of fire; **fire station** headquarters of local fire brigade; **fire-trap** building without fire-escapes etc.; **firework** device producing flashes, bangs, etc. from burning chemicals, (in *plural*) outburst of anger etc.; **on fire** burning, excited; **under fire** being shot at or criticized.

firing *noun* discharge of guns. ▫ **firing line** front line in battle, centre of criticism etc.; **firing squad** soldiers ordered to shoot condemned person.

firm[1] ● *adjective* solid; fixed, steady; resolute; steadfast; (of offer etc.) definite. ● *verb* (often + *up*) make or become firm or secure. ▫ **firmly** *adverb*; **firmness** *noun*.

firm[2] *noun* business concern, its members.

firmament /ˈfɜːməmənt/ *noun* sky regarded as vault.

first ● *adjective* foremost in time, order, or importance. ● *noun* (**the first**) first person or thing; beginning; first occurrence of something notable; first-class degree; first gear; first place in race. ● *adverb* before all or something else; for the first time. ▫ **at first hand** directly from original source; **first aid** emergency medical treatment; **first class** *noun* best category or accommodation, mail given priority, highest division in exam; **first-class** *adjective & adverb* of or by first class, excellent(ly); **first floor** (*US* **second floor**) floor above ground floor; **first-footing** first crossing of threshold in New Year; **firsthand** direct, original; **first mate** (on merchant ship) second in command; **first name** personal or Christian name; **first night** first public performance of play etc.; **first-rate** excellent; **first thing** before anything else, very early. ▫ **firstly** *adverb*.

firth /fɜːθ/ *noun* inlet, estuary.

fiscal /ˈfɪsk(ə)l/ ● *adjective* of public revenue. ● *noun Scottish* procurator fiscal. ▫ **fiscal year** financial year.

fish[1] ● *noun* (*plural* same or **-es**) vertebrate cold-blooded animal living in water; its flesh as food; person of specified kind. ● *verb* try to catch fish (in); (+ *for*) search for; seek indirectly; (+ *up, out*) retrieve with effort. ▫ **fish cake** fried cake of fish and mashed potato; **fish-eye lens** wide-angled lens; **fish farm** place where fish are bred for food; **fish finger** small oblong piece of fish in breadcrumbs; **fish-hook** barbed hook for catching fish; **fish-kettle** oval pan for boiling fish; **fish-knife** knife for eating or serving fish; **fish-meal** ground dried fish as fertilizer etc.; **fishmonger** dealer in fish; **fishnet** open-meshed fabric; **fish-slice** slotted cooking utensil; **fishwife** coarse or noisy woman, woman selling fish.

fish[2] *noun* piece of wood or iron for strengthening mast etc. ▫ **fish-plate** flat plate of iron etc. holding rails together.

fisherman /ˈfɪʃəmən/ *noun* man who catches fish as occupation or sport.

fishery *noun* (*plural* **-ies**) place where fish are caught or reared; industry of fishing or breeding fish.

fishing *noun* occupation or sport of trying to catch fish. ▫ **fishing-rod** tapering rod for fishing.

fishy *adjective* (**-ier**, **-iest**) of or like fish; *slang* dubious, suspect.

fissile /ˈfɪsaɪl/ *adjective* capable of undergoing nuclear fission; tending to split.

fission /ˈfɪʃ(ə)n/ ● *noun* splitting of atomic nucleus; division of cell as mode of reproduction. ● *verb* (cause to) undergo fission.

fissure /ˈfɪʃə/ ● *noun* narrow crack or split. ● *verb* (**-ring**) split.

fist *noun* clenched hand. ▫ **fisticuffs** fighting with the fists. ▫ **fistful** *noun* (*plural* **-s**).

fistula /ˈfɪstjʊlə/ *noun* (*plural* **-s** or **fistulae** /-liː/) abnormal or artificial passage in body. ▫ **fistular** *adjective*; **fistulous** *adjective*.

fit[1] ● *adjective* (**-tt-**) well suited; qualified, competent; in good health or condition; (+ *for*) good enough, right; ready. ● *verb* (**-tt-**) be of right size and shape; find room for; (often + *in, into*) be correctly positioned; (+ *on, together*) fix in place; (+ *with*) supply; befit. ● *noun* way thing fits. ▫ **fit in** (often + *with*) be compatible, accommodate, make room or time for; **fit out, up** equip. ▫ **fitness** *noun*.

fit[2] *noun* sudden esp. epileptic seizure; sudden brief bout or burst.

fitful *adjective* spasmodic, intermittent. ▫ **fitfully** *adverb*.

fitment *noun* (usually in *plural*) fixed item of furniture.

fitted *adjective* made to fit closely; with built-in fittings; built-in.

fitter *noun* mechanic who fits together and adjusts machinery etc.; supervisor of cutting, fitting, etc. of garments.

fitting ● *noun* action of fitting on a garment; (usually in *plural*) fixture, fitment. ● *adjective* proper, befitting. ▫ **fittingly** *adverb*.

five *adjective & noun* one more than four. ▫ **five o'clock shadow** beard growth visible in latter part of day; **five-star** of highest class; **fivestones** jacks played with five pieces of metal etc. and usually no ball.

fiver *noun colloquial* five-pound note.

fives *noun* game in which ball is struck with gloved hand or bat against walls of court.

fix ● *verb* make firm, stable, or permanent; fasten, secure; settle, specify; mend, repair; (+ *on, upon*) direct (eyes etc.) steadily on; attract and hold (attention etc.); identify, locate; *US colloquial* prepare (food, drink); *colloquial* kill, deal with (person); arrange result fraudulently. ● *noun* dilemma, predicament; position determined by bearings etc.; *slang* dose of addictive drug; *colloquial* fraudulently arranged result. ▫ **fix up** arrange, (often + *with*) provide (person). ▫ **fixer** *noun*.

fixate /fɪkˈseɪt/ *verb* (**-ting**) *Psychology* (usually in *passive*, often + *on, upon*) cause to become abnormally attached to person or thing.

fixation /fɪkˈseɪʃ(ə)n/ *noun* fixating, being fixated; obsession.

fixative /ˈfɪksətɪv/ ● *adjective* tending to fix (colours etc.). ● *noun* fixative substance.

fixedly /ˈfɪksɪdlɪ/ *adverb* intently.

fixity *noun* fixed state; stability, permanence.

fixture /ˈfɪkstʃə/ *noun* thing fixed in position; (date fixed for) sporting event; (in *plural*) articles belonging to land or house.

fizz ● *verb* make hissing or spluttering sound; effervesce. ● *noun* fizzing sound; effervescence; *colloquial* effervescent drink. ▫ **fizzy** *adjective* (**-ier**, **-iest**).

fizzle /ˈfɪz(ə)l/ ● *verb* (**-ling**) hiss or splutter feebly. ● *noun* fizzling sound. ▫ **fizzle out** end feebly.

fjord = FIORD.

fl. *abbreviation* fluid; floruit.

flab *noun colloquial* fat, flabbiness.

flabbergast /ˈflæbəgɑːst/ *verb* (esp. as **flabbergasted** *adjective*) *colloquial* astonish; dumbfound.

flabby /'flæbɪ/ *adjective* (**-ier**, **-iest**) (of flesh) limp, not firm; feeble. ▫ **flabbiness** *noun*.

flaccid /'flæksɪd/ *adjective* flabby. ▫ **flaccidity** /-'sɪd-/ *noun*.

flag[1] ● *noun* piece of cloth attached by one edge to pole or rope as country's emblem, standard, or signal. ● *verb* (**-gg-**) grow tired; lag; droop; mark out with flags. ▫ **flag-day** day when charity collects money and gives stickers to contributors; **flag down** signal to stop; **flag-officer** admiral or vice or rear admiral; **flag-pole** flagstaff; **flagship** ship with admiral on board, leading example of thing; **flagstaff** pole on which flag is hung; **flag-waving** *noun* populist agitation, chauvinism, *adjective* chauvinistic.

flag[2] ● *noun* (also **flagstone**) flat paving stone. ● *verb* (**-gg-**) pave with flags.

flag[3] *noun* plant with bladed leaf, esp. iris.

flagellant /'flædʒələnt/ ● *noun* person who flagellates himself, herself, or others. ● *adjective* of flagellation.

flagellate /'flædʒəleɪt/ *verb* (**-ting**) whip or flog, esp. as religious discipline or sexual stimulus. ▫ **flagellation** *noun*.

flageolet /flædʒə'let/ *noun* small flute blown at end.

flagon /'flægən/ *noun* quart bottle or other vessel for wine etc.

flagrant /'fleɪgrənt/ *adjective* blatant; scandalous. ▫ **flagrancy** *noun*; **flagrantly** *adverb*.

flagrante see IN FLAGRANTE DELICTO.

flail ● *verb* (often + *about*) wave or swing wildly; beat (as) with flail. ● *noun* staff with heavy stick swinging from it, used for threshing.

flair *noun* natural talent; style, finesse.

flak *noun* anti-aircraft fire; criticism; abuse.

flake ● *noun* thin light piece of snow etc.; thin broad piece peeled or split off. ● *verb* (**-king**) (often + *away, off*) take or come away in flakes; fall in or sprinkle with flakes. ▫ **flake out** fall asleep or drop from exhaustion, faint.

flaky *adjective* (**-ier**, **-iest**) of, like, or in flakes. ▫ **flaky pastry** lighter version of puff pastry.

flambé /'flɒmbeɪ/ *adjective* (of food) covered with alcohol and set alight briefly.

flamboyant /flæm'bɔɪənt/ *adjective* ostentatious, showy; florid. ▫ **flamboyance** *noun*; **flamboyantly** *adverb*.

flame ● *noun* ignited gas; portion of this; bright light; brilliant orange colour; passion, esp. love; *colloquial* sweetheart. ● *verb* (**-ming**) (often + *out, up*) burn; blaze; (of passion) break out; become angry; shine or glow like flame.

flamenco /flə'meŋkəʊ/ *noun* (*plural* **-s**) Spanish Gypsy guitar music with singing and dancing.

flaming *adjective* emitting flames; very hot; passionate; brightly coloured; *colloquial expressing annoyance*.

flamingo /flə'mɪŋgəʊ/ *noun* (*plural* **-s** or **-es**) tall long-necked wading bird with usually pink plumage.

flammable /'flæməb(ə)l/ *adjective* inflammable.

▪ **Usage** *Flammable* is often used because *inflammable* could be taken to mean 'not flammable'. The negative of *flammable* is *non-flammable*.

flan *noun* pastry case with savoury or sweet filling; sponge base with sweet topping.

flange /flændʒ/ *noun* projecting flat rim, for strengthening etc.

flank ● *noun* side of body between ribs and hip; side of mountain, army, etc. ● *verb* (often as **flanked** *adjective*) be at or move along side of.

flannel /'flæn(ə)l/ ● *noun* woven woollen usually napless fabric; (in *plural*) flannel trousers; face-cloth; *slang* nonsense, flattery. ● *verb* (**-ll-**; *US* **-l-**) *slang* flatter; wash with flannel.

flannelette /flænə'let/ *noun* napped cotton fabric like flannel.

flap ● *verb* (**-pp-**) move or be moved loosely up and down; beat; flutter; *colloquial* be agitated or panicky; *colloquial* (of ears) listen intently. ● *noun* piece of cloth, wood, etc. attached by one side, esp. to cover gap; flapping; *colloquial* agitation; aileron. ▫ **flapjack** sweet oatcake, *esp. US* small pancake.

flapper *noun* person apt to panic; *slang* (in 1920s) young unconventional woman.

flare ● *verb* (**-ring**) blaze with bright unsteady flame; (usually as **flared** *adjective*) widen gradually; burst out, esp. angrily. ● *noun* bright unsteady flame, outburst of this; flame or bright light as signal etc.; gradual widening; (in *plural*) wide-bottomed trousers. ▫ **flare-path** line of lights on runway to guide aircraft; **flare up** *verb* burst into blaze, anger, activity, etc.; **flare-up** *noun* outburst.

flash ● *verb* (cause to) emit brief or sudden light; gleam; send or reflect like sudden flame; burst suddenly into view etc.; move swiftly; send (news etc.) by radio etc.; signal (to) with vehicle lights; show ostentatiously; *slang* indecently expose oneself. ● *noun* sudden bright light or flame; an instant; sudden brief feeling or display; newsflash; *Photography* flashlight. ● *adjective colloquial* gaudy, showy; vulgar. ▫ **flashback** scene set in earlier time than main action; **flash bulb** *Photography* bulb for flashlight; **flash-gun** device operating camera flashlight; **flash in the pan** promising start followed by failure; **flash-lamp** portable flashing electric lamp; **flashlight** *Photography* light giving intense flash, *US* electric torch; **flashpoint** temperature at which vapour from oil etc. will ignite in air, point at which anger is expressed.

flasher *noun slang* man who indecently exposes himself; automatic device for switching lights rapidly on and off.

flashing *noun* (usually metal) strip to prevent water penetration at roof joint etc.

flashy *adjective* (**-ier**, **-iest**) showy; cheaply attractive. ▫ **flashily** *adverb*.

flask /flɑːsk/ *noun* narrow-necked bulbous bottle; hip-flask; vacuum flask.

flat[1] ● *adjective* (**-tt-**) horizontally level; smooth, even; level and shallow; downright; dull; dejected; having lost its effervescence; (of battery) having exhausted its charge; (of tyre etc.) deflated; *Music* below correct or normal pitch, having flats in key signature. ● *adverb* spread out; completely, exactly; flatly. ● *noun* flat part; level esp. marshy ground; *Music* note lowered by semitone, sign (♭) indicating this; flat theatre scenery on frame; punctured tyre; (**the flat**) flat racing, its season. ▫ **flatfish** fish with flattened body, e.g. sole, plaice; **flat foot** foot with flattened arch; **flat-footed** having flat feet, *colloquial* uninspired; **flat out** at top speed, using all one's strength etc.; **flat race** horse race over level ground without jumps; **flat rate** unvarying rate or charge; **flat spin** aircraft's nearly horizontal spin, *colloquial* state of panic; **flatworm** worm with flattened body, e.g. fluke. ▫ **flatly** *adverb*; **flatness** *noun*; **flattish** *adjective*.

flat[2] *noun* set of rooms, usually on one floor, as residence. ▫ **flatmate** person sharing flat. ▫ **flatlet** *noun*.

flatten *verb* make or become flat; *colloquial* humiliate; knock down.

flatter /'flætə/ *verb* compliment unduly; enhance appearance of; (usually **flatter oneself**; usually + *that*) congratulate or delude (oneself etc.).

□ **flatterer** *noun*; **flattering** *adjective*; **flatteringly** *adverb*; **flattery** *noun*.

flatulent /'flætjʊlənt/ *adjective* causing, caused by, or troubled with, intestinal wind; inflated, pretentious. □ **flatulence** *noun*.

flaunt /flɔ:nt/ *verb* display proudly; show off, parade.

■ **Usage** *Flaunt* is often confused with *flout*, which means 'to disobey contemptuously'.

flautist /'flɔ:tɪst/ *noun* flute-player.

flavour /'fleɪvə/ (*US* **flavor**) ● *noun* mixed sensation of smell and taste; distinctive taste, characteristic quality. ● *verb* give flavour to, season. □ **flavour of the month** temporary trend or fashion. □ **flavourless** *adjective*; **flavoursome** *adjective*.

flavouring *noun* (*US* **flavoring**) substance used to flavour food or drink.

flaw ● *noun* imperfection; blemish; crack; invalidating defect. ● *verb* damage; spoil; (as **flawed** *adjective*) morally etc. defective. □ **flawless** *adjective*.

flax *noun* blue-flowered plant grown for its oily seeds (linseed) and for making into linen.

flaxen *adjective* of flax; (of hair) pale yellow.

flay *verb* strip skin or hide off; criticize severely; peel off.

flea *noun* small wingless jumping parasitic insect. □ **flea market** street market selling second-hand goods etc.

fleck ● *noun* small patch of colour or light; speck. ● *verb* mark with flecks.

flection *US* = FLEXION.

fled *past & past participle* of FLEE.

fledgling /'fledʒlɪŋ/ (also **fledgeling**) ● *noun* young bird. ● *adjective* new, inexperienced.

flee *verb* (**flees**; *past & past participle* **fled**) run away (from); leave hurriedly.

fleece ● *noun* woolly coat of sheep etc.; this shorn from sheep; fleecy lining etc. ● *verb* (**-cing**) (often + *of*) strip of money etc., swindle; shear; (as **fleeced** *adjective*) cover as with fleece. □ **fleecy** *adjective* (**-ier, -iest**).

fleet ● *noun* warships under one commander-in-chief; (**the fleet**) navy; vehicles in one company etc. ● *adjective* swift, nimble.

fleeting *adjective* transitory; brief. □ **fleetingly** *adverb*.

Fleming /'flemɪŋ/ *noun* native of medieval Flanders; member of Flemish-speaking people of N. and W. Belgium.

Flemish /'flemɪʃ/ ● *adjective* of Flanders. ● *noun* language of the Flemings.

flesh *noun* soft substance between skin and bones; plumpness, fat; body, esp. as sinful; pulpy substance of fruit etc.; (also **flesh-colour**) yellowish pink colour. □ **flesh and blood** human body, human nature, esp. as fallible, humankind, near relations; **flesh out** make or become substantial; **fleshpots** luxurious living; **flesh-wound** superficial wound; **in the flesh** in person. □ **fleshy** *adjective* (**-ier, -iest**).

fleshly /'fleʃlɪ/ *adjective* worldly; carnal.

fleur-de-lis /flɜ:də'li:/ *noun* (also **fleur-de-lys**) (*plural* **fleurs-** same pronunciation) iris flower; *Heraldry* lily of 3 petals; former royal arms of France.

flew *past* of FLY[1].

flews *plural noun* hanging lips of bloodhound etc.

flex[1] *verb* bend (joint, limb); move (muscle) to bend joint.

flex[2] *noun* flexible insulated cable.

flexible /'fleksɪb(ə)l/ *adjective* able to bend without breaking; pliable; adaptable. □ **flexibility** *noun*; **flexibly** *adverb*.

flexion /'flekʃ(ə)n/ *noun* (*US* **flection**) bending; bent part.

flexitime /'fleksɪtaɪm/ *noun* system of flexible working hours.

flibbertigibbet /flɪbətɪ'dʒɪbɪt/ *noun* gossiping, frivolous, or restless person.

flick ● *noun* light sharp blow; sudden release of bent finger etc. to propel thing; jerk; *colloquial* cinema film, (**the flicks**) the cinema. ● *verb* (often + *away, off*) strike or move with flick. □ **flick-knife** knife with blade that springs out; **flick through** glance at or through by turning over (pages etc.) rapidly.

flicker /'flɪkə/ ● *verb* shine or burn unsteadily; flutter; waver. ● *noun* flickering light or motion; brief feeling (of hope etc.); slightest reaction or degree. □ **flicker out** die away.

flier = FLYER.

flight[1] /flaɪt/ *noun* act or manner of flying; movement, passage, or journey through air or space; timetabled airline journey; flock of birds etc.; (usually + *of*) series of stairs etc.; imaginative excursion; volley; tail of dart. □ **flight bag** small zipped shoulder bag for air travel; **flight-deck** cockpit of large aircraft, deck of aircraft carrier; **flight lieutenant** RAF officer next below squadron leader; **flight path** planned course of aircraft etc.; **flight recorder** device in aircraft recording technical details of flight; **flight sergeant** RAF rank next above sergeant.

flight[2] /flaɪt/ *noun* fleeing; hasty retreat.

flightless *adjective* (of bird etc.) unable to fly.

flighty *adjective* (**-ier, -iest**) frivolous; fickle.

flimsy /'flɪmzɪ/ *adjective* (**-ier, -iest**) insubstantial, rickety; unconvincing; (of clothing) thin. □ **flimsily** *adverb*.

flinch *verb* draw back in fear etc.; shrink; wince.

fling ● *verb* (*past & past participle* **flung**) throw, hurl; rush, esp. angrily; discard rashly. ● *noun* flinging; throw; bout of wild behaviour; whirling Scottish dance.

flint *noun* hard grey stone; piece of this, esp. as tool or weapon; piece of hard alloy used to produce spark. □ **flintlock** old type of gun fired by spark from flint. □ **flinty** *adjective* (**-ier, -iest**).

flip ● *verb* (**-pp-**) toss (coin etc.) so that it spins in air; turn or flick (small object) over; *slang* flip one's lid. ● *noun* act of flipping. ● *adjective* glib; flippant. □ **flip chart** large pad of paper on stand; **flip-flop** sandal with thong between toes; **flip one's lid** *slang* lose selfcontrol, go mad; **flip side** reverse side of gramophone record etc.; **flip through** flick through.

flippant /'flɪpənt/ *adjective* frivolous; disrespectful. □ **flippancy** *noun*; **flippantly** *adverb*.

flipper *noun* limb of turtle, penguin, etc., used in swimming; rubber attachment to foot for underwater swimming.

flirt ● *verb* try to attract sexually but without serious intent; (usually + *with*) superficially engage in, trifle. ● *noun* person who flirts. □ **flirtation** *noun*; **flirtatious** *adjective*; **flirtatiously** *adverb*; **flirtatiousness** *noun*.

flit ● *verb* (**-tt-**) pass lightly or rapidly; make short flights; disappear secretly, esp. to escape creditors. ● *noun* act of flitting.

flitch *noun* side of bacon.

flitter *verb* flit about.

float ● *verb* (cause to) rest or drift on surface of liquid; move or be suspended freely in liquid or gas; launch (company, scheme); offer (stocks, shares, etc.) on stock market; (cause or allow to) have fluctuating exchange rate; circulate or cause (rumour, idea) to circulate. ● *noun* device or structure that floats; electrically powered vehicle or cart; decorated platform or tableau on lorry in procession etc.; supply of loose change, petty cash.

floating *adjective* not settled; variable; not committed. □ **floating rib** lower rib not attached to breastbone.

floaty *adjective* (**-ier**, **-iest**) (of fabric) light and airy.

flocculent /ˈflɒkjʊlənt/ *adjective* like tufts of wool.

flock[1] ● *noun* animals, esp. birds or sheep, as group or unit; large crowd of people; people in care of priest, teacher, etc. ● *verb* (often + *to*, *in*, *out*, *together*) congregate; mass; troop.

flock[2] *noun* shredded wool, cotton, etc. used as stuffing; powdered wool used to make pattern on wallpaper.

floe *noun* sheet of floating ice.

flog *verb* (**-gg-**) beat with whip, stick, etc.; (often + *off*) *slang* sell.

flood /flʌd/ ● *noun* overflowing or influx of water, esp. over land; outburst, outpouring; inflow of tide; (**the Flood**) the flood described in Genesis. ● *verb* overflow; cover or be covered with flood; irrigate; deluge; come in great quantities; overfill (carburettor) with petrol. ◻ **floodgate** gate for admitting or excluding water, (usually in *plural*) last restraint against tear, anger, etc.; **floodlight** (illuminate with) large powerful light; **floodlit** lit thus.

floor /flɔː/ ● *noun* lower surface of room; bottom of sea, cave, etc.; storey; part of legislative chamber where members sit and speak; right to speak in debate; minimum of prices, wages, etc. ● *verb* provide with floor; knock down; baffle; overcome. ◻ **floor manager** stage manager of television production; **floor plan** diagram of rooms etc. on one storey; **floor show** cabaret.

flop ● *verb* (**-pp-**) sway about heavily or loosely; (often + *down*, *on*, *into*) move, fall, sit, etc. awkwardly or suddenly; *slang* collapse, fail; make dull soft thud or splash. ● *noun* flopping motion or sound; *slang* failure. ● *adverb* with a flop.

floppy ● *adjective* (**-ier**, **-iest**) tending to flop; flaccid. ● *noun* (*plural* **-ies**) (in full **floppy disk**) flexible disc for storage of computer data.

flora /ˈflɔːrə/ *noun* (*plural* **-s** or **-rae** /-riː/) plant life of region or period.

floral *adjective* of or decorated with flowers.

floret /ˈflɒrɪt/ *noun* each of small flowers of composite flower head; each stem of head of cauliflower, broccoli, etc.

florid /ˈflɒrɪd/ *adjective* ruddy; ornate; showy.

florin /ˈflɒrɪn/ *noun historical* gold or silver coin, esp. British two-shilling coin.

florist /ˈflɒrɪst/ *noun* person who deals in or grows flowers.

floruit /ˈflɒrʊɪt/ *verb* (of painter, writer, etc.) lived and worked.

floss ● *noun* rough silk of silkworm's cocoon; dental floss. ● *verb* clean (teeth) with dental floss. ◻ **flossy** *adjective* (**-ier**, **-iest**).

flotation /fləʊˈteɪʃ(ə)n/ *noun* launching of commercial enterprise etc.

flotilla /fləˈtɪlə/ *noun* small fleet; fleet of small ships.

flotsam /ˈflɒtsəm/ *noun* floating wreckage. ◻ **flotsam and jetsam** odds and ends, vagrants.

flounce[1] /flaʊns/ ● *verb* (**-cing**) (often + *off*, *out*, etc.) go or move angrily or impatiently. ● *noun* flouncing movement.

flounce[2] /flaʊns/ ● *noun* frill on dress, skirt, etc. ● *verb* (**-cing**) (usually as **flounced** *adjective*) trim with flounces.

flounder[1] /ˈflaʊndə/ *verb* struggle helplessly; do task clumsily.

flounder[2] /ˈflaʊndə/ *noun* (*plural* same) small flatfish.

flour /flaʊə/ ● *noun* meal or powder from ground wheat etc. ● *verb* sprinkle with flour. ◻ **floury** *adjective* (**-ier**, **-iest**).

flourish /ˈflʌrɪʃ/ ● *verb* grow vigorously; thrive, prosper; wave, brandish. ● *noun* showy gesture; ornamental curve in writing; *Music* ornate passage; fanfare.

flout *verb* disobey (law etc.) contemptuously.

■ **Usage** *Flout* is often confused with *flaunt*, which means 'to display proudly or show off'.

flow /fləʊ/ ● *verb* glide along, move smoothly; gush out; circulate; be plentiful or in flood; (often + *from*) result. ● *noun* flowing movement or liquid; stream; rise of tide. ◻ **flow chart**, **diagram**, **sheet** diagram of movement or action in complex activity.

flower /ˈflaʊə/ ● *noun* part of plant from which seed or fruit develops; plant bearing blossom. ● *verb* bloom; reach peak. ◻ **flower-bed** garden bed for flowers; **the flower of** the best of; **flowerpot** pot for growing plant in; **in flower** blooming. ◻ **flowered** *adjective*.

flowery *adjective* florally decorated; (of speech etc.) high-flown; full of flowers.

flowing *adjective* fluent; smoothly continuous; (of hair etc.) unconfined.

flown *past participle* of FLY[1].

flu *noun colloquial* influenza.

fluctuate /ˈflʌktʃʊeɪt/ *verb* (**-ting**) vary, rise and fall. ◻ **fluctuation** *noun*.

flue *noun* smoke duct in chimney; channel for conveying heat.

fluent /ˈfluːənt/ *adjective* expressing oneself easily and naturally, esp. in foreign language. ◻ **fluency** *noun*; **fluently** *adverb*.

fluff ● *noun* soft fur, feathers, fabric particles, etc.; *slang* mistake in performance etc. ● *verb* (often + *up*) shake into or become soft mass; *slang* make mistake in performance etc. ◻ **fluffy** *adjective* (**-ier**, **-iest**).

flugelhorn /ˈfluːg(ə)lhɔːn/ *noun* brass instrument like cornet.

fluid /ˈfluːɪd/ ● *noun* substance, esp. gas or liquid, capable of flowing freely; liquid secretion. ● *adjective* able to flow freely; constantly changing. ◻ **fluid ounce** twentieth or *US* sixteenth of pint. ◻ **fluidity** /-ˈɪdɪtɪ/ *noun*.

fluke[1] /fluːk/ *noun* lucky accident. ◻ **fluky** *adjective* (**-ier**, **-iest**).

fluke[2] /fluːk/ *noun* parasitic flatworm.

flummery /ˈflʌmərɪ/ *noun* (*plural* **-ies**) nonsense; flattery; sweet milk dish.

flummox /ˈflʌməks/ *verb colloquial* bewilder.

flung *past & past participle* of FLING.

flunk *verb US colloquial* fail (esp. exam).

flunkey /ˈflʌŋkɪ/ *noun* (also **flunky**) (*plural* **-eys** or **-ies**) *usually derogatory* footman.

fluorescence /flʊəˈres(ə)ns/ *noun* light radiation from certain substances; property of absorbing invisible light and emitting visible light. ◻ **fluoresce** *verb* (**-scing**); **fluorescent** *adjective*.

fluoridate /ˈflʊərɪdeɪt/ *verb* (**-ting**) add fluoride to (water). ◻ **fluoridation** *noun*.

fluoride /ˈflʊəraɪd/ *noun* compound of fluorine with metal, esp. used to prevent tooth decay.

fluorinate /ˈflʊərɪneɪt/ *verb* (**-ting**) fluoridate; introduce fluorine into (compound). ◻ **fluorination** *noun*.

fluorine /ˈflʊəriːn/ *noun* poisonous pale yellow gaseous element.

flurry /ˈflʌrɪ/ ● *noun* (*plural* **-ies**) gust, squall; burst of activity, excitement, etc. ● *verb* (**-ies**, **-ied**) agitate, confuse.

flush[1] ● *verb* (often as **flushed** *adjective* + *with*) (cause to) glow or blush (with pride etc.); cleanse (drain, lavatory, etc.) by flow of water; (often + *away*, *down*) dispose of thus. ● *noun* glow, blush; rush of water;

cleansing (of lavatory etc.) thus; rush of esp. elation or triumph; freshness, vigour; (also **hot flush**) sudden hot feeling during menopause; feverish redness or temperature etc. ● *adjective* level, in same plane; *colloquial* having plenty of money.

flush[2] *noun* hand of cards all of one suit.

flush[3] *verb* (cause to) fly up suddenly. □ **flush out** reveal, drive out.

fluster /ˈflʌstə/ ● *verb* confuse, make nervous. ● *noun* confused or agitated state.

flute /fluːt/ ● *noun* high-pitched woodwind instrument held sideways; vertical groove in pillar etc. ● *verb* (**-ting**) (often as **fluted** *adjective*) make grooves in; play on flute. □ **fluting** *noun*.

flutter /ˈflʌtə/ ● *verb* flap (wings) in flying or trying to fly; fall quiveringly; wave or flap quickly; move about restlessly; (of pulse etc.) beat feebly or irregularly. ● *noun* fluttering; tremulous excitement; *slang* small bet on horse etc.; abnormally rapid heartbeat; rapid variation of pitch, esp. of recorded sound.

fluvial /ˈfluːvɪəl/ *adjective* of or found in rivers.

flux *noun* flowing, flowing out; discharge; continuous change; substance mixed with metal etc. to assist fusion.

fly[1] /flaɪ/ ● *verb* (**flies**; *past* **flew** /fluː/; *past participle* **flown** /fləʊn/) move or travel through air with wings or in aircraft; control flight of (aircraft); cause to fly or remain aloft; wave; move swiftly; be driven forcefully; flee (from); (+ *at*, *upon*) attack or criticize fiercely. ● *noun* (*plural* **-ies**) (usually in *plural*) flap to cover front fastening on trousers, this fastening; flap at entrance of tent; (in *plural*) space over stage, for scenery and lighting; act of flying. □ **fly-by-night** unreliable; **fly-half** *Rugby* stand-off half; **flyleaf** blank leaf at beginning or end of book; **flyover** bridge carrying road etc. over another; **fly-past** ceremonial flight of aircraft; **fly-post** fix (posters etc.) illegally; **flysheet** canvas cover over tent for extra protection, short tract or circular; **fly-tip** illegally dump (waste); **flywheel** heavy wheel regulating machinery or accumulating power.

fly[2] /flaɪ/ (*plural* **flies**) *noun* two-winged insect; disease caused by flies; (esp. artificial) fly used as bait in fishing. □ **fly-blown** tainted by flies; **flycatcher** bird that catches flies in flight; **fly-fish** *verb* fish with fly; **fly in the ointment** minor irritation or setback; **fly on the wall** unnoticed observer; **fly-paper** sticky treated paper for catching flies; **fly-trap** plant that catches flies; **flyweight** amateur boxing weight (48–51 kg).

fly[3] /flaɪ/ *adjective slang* knowing, clever.

flyer *noun* (also **flier**) airman, airwoman; thing or person that flies in specified way; small handbill.

flying ● *adjective* that flies; hasty. ● *noun* flight. □ **flying boat** boatlike seaplane; **flying buttress** (usually arched) buttress running from upper part of wall to outer support; **flying doctor** doctor who uses aircraft to visit patients; **flying fish** fish gliding through air with winglike fins; **flying fox** fruit-eating bat; **flying officer** RAF officer next below flight lieutenant; **flying saucer** supposed alien spaceship; **flying squad** rapidly mobile police detachment, midwifery unit, etc.; **flying start** start (of race) at full speed, vigorous start.

FM *abbreviation* Field Marshal; frequency modulation.

FO *abbreviation* Flying Officer.

foal ● *noun* young of horse or related animal. ● *verb* give birth to (foal).

foam ● *noun* froth formed in liquid; froth of saliva or sweat; spongy rubber or plastic. ● *verb* emit foam; froth. □ **foam at the mouth** be very angry. □ **foamy** *adjective* (**-ier**, **-iest**).

fob[1] *noun* (attachment to) watch-chain; small pocket for watch etc.

fob[2] *verb* (**-bb-**) □ **fob off** (often + *with*) deceive into accepting something inferior, (often + *on*, *on to*) offload (unwanted thing on person).

focal /ˈfəʊk(ə)l/ *adjective* of or at a focus. □ **focal distance, length** distance between centre of lens etc. and its focus; **focal point** focus, centre of interest or activity.

fo'c's'le = FORECASTLE.

focus /ˈfəʊkəs/ ● *noun* (*plural* **focuses** or **foci** /ˈfəʊsaɪ/) point at which rays etc. meet after reflection or refraction or from which rays etc. seem to come; point at which object must be situated to give clearly defined image; adjustment of eye or lens to produce clear image; state of clear definition; centre of interest or activity. ● *verb* (**-s-** or **-ss-**) bring into focus; adjust focus of (lens, eye); concentrate or be concentrated on; (cause to) converge to focus.

fodder /ˈfɒdə/ *noun* hay, straw, etc. as animal food.

foe *noun* enemy.

foetid = FETID.

foetus /ˈfiːtəs/ *noun* (*US* **fetus**) (*plural* **-tuses**) unborn mammalian offspring, esp. human embryo of 8 weeks or more. □ **foetal** *adjective*.

fog ● *noun* thick cloud of water droplets or smoke suspended at or near earth's surface; thick mist; cloudiness on photographic negative; confused state. ● *verb* (**-gg-**) envelop (as) in fog; perplex. □ **fog-bank** mass of fog at sea; **foghorn** horn warning ships in fog, *colloquial* penetrating voice.

fogey /ˈfəʊgɪ/ *noun* (also **fogy**) (*plural* **-ies** or **-eys**) (esp. **old fogey**) dull old-fashioned person.

foggy *adjective* (**-ier, -iest**) full of fog; of or like fog; vague. □ **not the foggiest** *colloquial* no idea.

foible /ˈfɔɪb(ə)l/ *noun* minor weakness or idiosyncrasy.

foil[1] *verb* frustrate, defeat.

foil[2] *noun* thin sheet of metal; person or thing setting off another to advantage.

foil[3] *noun* blunt fencing sword.

foist *verb* (+ *on*) force (thing, oneself) on to (unwilling person).

fold[1] /fəʊld/ ● *verb* double (flexible thing) over on itself; bend portion of; become or be able to be folded; (+ *away*, *up*) make compact by folding; (often + *up*) *colloquial* collapse, cease to function; enfold; clasp; (+ *in*) mix in gently. ● *noun* folding; line made by folding; hollow among hills.

fold[2] /fəʊld/ *noun* sheepfold; religious group or congregation.

folder *noun* folding cover or holder for loose papers.

foliaceous /fəʊlɪˈeɪʃəs/ *adjective* of or like leaves; laminated.

foliage /ˈfəʊlɪɪdʒ/ *noun* leaves, leafage.

foliar /ˈfəʊlɪə/ *adjective* of leaves. □ **foliar feed** fertilizer supplied to leaves.

foliate ● *adjective* /ˈfəʊlɪət/ leaflike; having leaves. ● *verb* /ˈfəʊlɪeɪt/ (**-ting**) split into thin layers. □ **foliation** *noun*.

folio /ˈfəʊlɪəʊ/ ● *noun* (*plural* **-s**) leaf of paper etc. numbered only on front; sheet of paper folded once; book of such sheets. ● *adjective* (of book) made of folios.

folk /fəʊk/ ● *noun* (*plural* same or **-s**) (treated as *plural*) people in general or of specified class; (in *plural*, usually **folks**) one's relatives; (treated as *singular*) a people or nation; (in full **folk-music**) (treated as *singular*) traditional, esp. working-class, music, or music in style of this. ● *adjective* of popular origin. □ **folklore** traditional beliefs etc., study of these; **folkweave** rough loosely woven fabric.

folksy /ˈfəʊksɪ/ *adjective* (**-ier**, **-iest**) of or like folk art; in deliberately popular style.

follicle /ˈfɒlɪk(ə)l/ *noun* small sac or vesicle, esp. for hair-root. □ **follicular** /fɒˈlɪkjʊlə/ *adjective*.

follow /ˈfɒləʊ/ *verb* go or come after; go along; come next in order or time; practise; understand; take as guide; take interest in; (+ *with*) provide with (sequel etc.); (+ *from*) result from; be necessary inference. □ **follow on** *verb* continue, (of cricket team) bat twice in succession; **follow-on** *noun* instance of this; **follow suit** play card of suit led, conform to another's actions; **follow through** *verb* continue to conclusion, continue movement of stroke after hitting the ball; **follow-through** *noun* instance of this; **follow up** *verb* act or investigate further; **follow-up** *noun* subsequent action.

follower *noun* supporter, devotee; person who follows.

following ● *preposition* after in time; as sequel to. ● *noun* group of supporters. ● *adjective* that follows. □ **the following** what follows, now to be mentioned.

folly /ˈfɒlɪ/ *noun* (*plural* **-ies**) foolishness; foolish act, idea, etc.; building for display only.

foment /fəˈment/ *verb* instigate, stir up (trouble etc.). □ **fomentation** /fəʊmenˈteɪʃ(ə)n/ *noun*.

fond *adjective* (+ *of*) liking; affectionate; doting; foolishly optimistic. □ **fondly** *adverb*; **fondness** *noun*.

fondant /ˈfɒnd(ə)nt/ *noun* soft sugary sweet.

fondle /ˈfɒnd(ə)l/ *verb* (**-ling**) caress.

fondue /ˈfɒndjuː/ *noun* dish of melted cheese.

font[1] *noun* receptacle for baptismal water.

font[2] = FOUNT[2].

fontanelle /fɒntəˈnel/ *noun* (*US* **fontanel**) space in infant's skull, which later closes up.

food /fuːd/ *noun* substance taken in to maintain life and growth; solid food; mental stimulus. □ **food-chain** series of organisms each dependent on next for food; **food poisoning** illness due to bacteria etc. in food; **food processor** machine for chopping and mixing food; **foodstuff** substance used as food.

foodie /ˈfuːdɪ/ *noun colloquial* person who makes a cult of food.

fool[1] ● *noun* unwise or stupid person; *historical* jester, clown. ● *verb* deceive; trick; cheat; joke; tease; (+ *around, about*) play, trifle. □ **act, play the fool** behave in silly way; **foolproof** incapable of misuse or mistake; **fool's paradise** illusory happiness; **make a fool of** make (person) look foolish, trick.

fool[2] *noun* dessert of fruit purée with cream or custard.

foolery *noun* foolish behaviour.

foolhardy *adjective* (**-ier**, **-iest**) foolishly bold; reckless. □ **foolhardily** *adverb*; **foolhardiness** *noun*.

foolish *adjective* lacking good sense or judgement. □ **foolishly** *adverb*; **foolishness** *noun*.

foolscap /ˈfuːlskæp/ *noun* large size of paper, about 330 mm x 200 (or 400) mm.

foot /fʊt/ ● *noun* (*plural* **feet**) part of leg below ankle; lower part or end; (*plural* same or **feet**) linear measure of 12 in. (30.48 cm); metrical unit of verse forming part of line; *historical* infantry. ● *verb* pay (bill); (usually as **foot it**) go on foot. □ **foot-and-mouth** (**disease**) contagious viral disease of cattle etc.; **footfall** sound of footstep; **foot-fault** (in tennis) serving with foot over baseline; **foothill** low hill lying at base of mountain or range; **foothold** secure place for feet in climbing, secure initial position; **footlights** row of floor-level lights along front of stage; **footloose** free to act as one pleases; **footman** liveried servant; **footmark** footprint; **footnote** note at foot of page; **footpath** path for pedestrians only; **footplate** platform for crew in locomotive; **footprint** impression left by foot or shoe; **footsore** having sore feet, esp. from walking; **footstep** (sound of) step taken in walking; **footstool** stool for resting feet on when sitting; **on foot** walking. □ **footless** *adjective*.

footage *noun* a length of TV or cinema film etc.; length in feet.

football *noun* large inflated usually leather ball; team game played with this. □ **football pool**(**s**) organized gambling on results of football matches. □ **footballer** *noun*.

footing *noun* foothold; secure position; operational basis; relative position or status; (often in *plural*) foundations of wall.

footling /ˈfuːtlɪŋ/ *adjective colloquial* trivial, silly.

Footsie /ˈfʊtsɪ/ *noun* FT-SE.

footsie /ˈfʊtsɪ/ *noun colloquial* amorous play with feet.

fop *noun* dandy. □ **foppery** *noun*; **foppish** *adjective*.

for /fə, fɔː/ ● *preposition* in interest, defence, or favour of; appropriate to; regarding; representing; at the price of; as consequence or on account of; in order to get or reach; so as to start promptly at; notwithstanding. ● *conjunction* because, since. □ **be for it** be liable or about to be punished.

forage /ˈfɒrɪdʒ/ ● *noun* food for horses and cattle; searching for food. ● *verb* (**-ging**) (often + *for*) search for food; rummage; collect food from. □ **forage cap** infantry undress cap.

foray /ˈfɒreɪ/ ● *noun* sudden attack, raid. ● *verb* make foray.

forbade (also **forbad**) *past* of FORBID.

forbear[1] /fɔːˈbeə/ *verb* (*past* **forbore**; *past participle* **forborne**) *formal* abstain or refrain from.

forbear[2] = FOREBEAR.

forbearance *noun* patient self-control; tolerance.

forbid /fəˈbɪd/ *verb* (**forbidding**; *past* **forbade** /-bæd/ or **forbad**; *past participle* **forbidden**) (+ *to do*) order not; not allow; refuse entry to. □ **forbidden fruit** thing desired esp. because not allowed.

forbidding *adjective* stern, threatening. □ **forbiddingly** *adverb*.

forbore *past* of FORBEAR[1].

forborne *past participle* of FORBEAR[1].

force ● *noun* strength, power, intense effort; group of soldiers, police, etc.; coercion, compulsion; influence (person etc.) with moral power. ● *verb* (**-cing**) compel, coerce; make way, break into or open by force; drive, propel; (+ *on, upon*) impose or press on (person); cause or produce by effort; strain; artificially hasten maturity of; accelerate. □ **forced landing** emergency landing of aircraft; **forced march** lengthy and vigorous march, esp. by troops; **force-feed** feed (prisoner etc.) against his or her will; **force (person's) hand** make him or her act prematurely or unwillingly.

forceful *adjective* powerful; impressive. □ **forcefully** *adverb*; **forcefulness** *noun*.

force majeure /fɔːs mæˈʒɜː/ *noun* irresistible force; unforeseeable circumstances. [French]

forcemeat /ˈfɔːsmiːt/ *noun* minced seasoned meat for stuffing etc.

forceps /ˈfɔːseps/ *noun* (*plural* same) surgical pincers.

forcible /ˈfɔːsɪb(ə)l/ *adjective* done by or involving force; forceful. □ **forcibly** *adverb*.

ford ● *noun* shallow place where river etc. may be crossed. ● *verb* cross (water) at ford. □ **fordable** *adjective*.

fore ● *adjective* situated in front. ● *noun* front part; bow of ship. ● *interjection* (*in golf*) *warning to person in path of ball.* □ **fore-and-aft** (of sails or rigging) lengthwise, at bow and stern; **to the fore** conspicuous.

forearm[1] /ˈfɔːrɑːm/ *noun* arm from elbow to wrist or fingertips.

forearm[2] /fɔːˈrɑːm/ *verb* arm beforehand, prepare.

forebear /'fɔːbeə/ *noun* (also **forbear**) (usually in *plural*) ancestor.

forebode /fɔː'bəʊd/ *verb* (**-ding**) be advance sign of; portend.

foreboding *noun* expectation of trouble.

forecast ● *verb* (*past & past participle* **-cast** or **-casted**) predict; estimate beforehand. ● *noun* prediction, esp. of weather. □ **forecaster** *noun*.

forecastle /'fəʊks(ə)l/ *noun* (also **fo'c's'le**) forward part of ship, formerly living quarters.

foreclose /fɔː'kləʊz/ *verb* (**-sing**) stop (mortgage) from being redeemable; repossess mortgaged property of (person) when loan is not duly repaid; exclude, prevent. □ **foreclosure** *noun*.

forecourt *noun* part of filling-station with petrol pumps; enclosed space in front of building.

forefather *noun* (usually in *plural*) ancestor.

forefinger *noun* finger next to thumb.

forefoot *noun* front foot of animal.

forefront *noun* leading position; foremost part.

forego = FORGO.

foregoing /fɔː'gəʊɪŋ/ *adjective* preceding; previously mentioned.

foregone conclusion /'fɔːgɒn/ *noun* easily foreseeable result.

foreground *noun* part of view nearest observer.

forehand *Tennis etc.* ● *adjective* (of stroke) played with palm of hand facing forward. ● *noun* forehand stroke.

forehead /'fɒrɪd, 'fɔːhed/ *noun* part of face above eyebrows.

foreign /'fɒrən/ *adjective* of, from, in, or characteristic of country or language other than one's own; dealing with other countries; of another district, society, etc.; (often + *to*) unfamiliar, alien; coming from outside. □ **foreign legion** group of foreign volunteers in (esp. French) army. □ **foreignness** *noun*.

foreigner *noun* person born in or coming from another country.

foreknowledge /fɔː'nɒlɪdʒ/ *noun* knowledge in advance of (an event etc.).

foreleg *noun* animal's front leg.

forelock *noun* lock of hair just above forehead. □ **touch one's forelock** defer to person of higher social rank.

foreman /'fɔːmən/ *noun* (*feminine* **forewoman**) worker supervising others; spokesman of jury.

foremast *noun* mast nearest bow of ship.

foremost ● *adjective* most notable, best; first, front. ● *adverb* most importantly.

forename *noun* first or Christian name.

forensic /fə'rensɪk/ *adjective* of or used in courts of law; of or involving application of science to legal problems.

foreplay *noun* stimulation preceding sexual intercourse.

forerunner *noun* predecessor.

foresail *noun* principal sail on foremast.

foresee /fɔː'siː/ *verb* (*past* **-saw**; *past participle* **-seen**) see or be aware of beforehand. □ **foreseeable** *adjective*.

foreshadow /fɔː'ʃædəʊ/ *verb* be warning or indication of (future event).

foreshore *noun* shore between high and low water marks.

foreshorten /fɔː'ʃɔːt(ə)n/ *verb* portray (object) with apparent shortening due to perspective.

foresight *noun* care or provision for future; foreseeing.

foreskin *noun* fold of skin covering end of penis.

forest /'fɒrɪst/ ● *noun* large area of trees; large number, dense mass. ● *verb* plant with trees; convert into forest.

forestall /fɔː'stɔːl/ *verb* prevent by advance action; deal with beforehand.

forester *noun* manager of forest; expert in forestry; dweller in forest.

forestry *noun* science or management of forests.

foretaste *noun* small preliminary experience of something.

foretell /fɔː'tel/ *verb* (*past & past participle* **-told**) predict, prophesy; indicate approach of.

forethought *noun* care or provision for future; deliberate intention.

forever /fə'revə/ *adverb* always, constantly.

forewarn /fɔː'wɔːn/ *verb* warn beforehand.

foreword *noun* introductory remarks in book, often not by author.

forfeit /'fɔːfɪt/ ● *noun* (thing surrendered as) penalty. ● *adjective* lost or surrendered as penalty. ● *verb* (**-t-**) lose right to, surrender as penalty. □ **forfeiture** *noun*.

forgather /fɔː'gæðə/ *verb* assemble; associate.

forgave *past* of FORGIVE.

forge[1] ● *verb* (**-ging**) make or write in fraudulent imitation; shape by heating and hammering. ● *noun* furnace etc. for melting or refining metal; blacksmith's workshop. □ **forger** *noun*.

forge[2] *verb* (**-ging**) advance gradually. □ **forge ahead** take lead, progress rapidly.

forgery /'fɔːdʒərɪ/ *noun* (*plural* **-ies**) (making of) forged document etc.

forget /fə'get/ *verb* (**forgetting**; *past* **forgot**; *past participle* **forgotten** or *US* **forgot**) lose remembrance of; neglect, overlook; cease to think of; (**forget oneself**) act without dignity. □ **forget-me-not** plant with small blue flowers. □ **forgettable** *adjective*.

forgetful *adjective* apt to forget; (often + *of*) neglectful. □ **forgetfully** *adverb*; **forgetfulness** *noun*.

forgive /fə'gɪv/ *verb* (**-ving**; *past* **forgave**; *past participle* **forgiven**) cease to resent; pardon; remit (debt). □ **forgivable** *adjective*; **forgiveness** *noun*; **forgiving** *adjective*.

forgo /fɔː'gəʊ/ *verb* (also **forego**) (**-goes**; *past* **-went**; *past participle* **-gone**) go without, relinquish.

forgot *past* of FORGET.

forgotten *past participle* of FORGET.

fork ● *noun* pronged item of cutlery; similar large tool for digging etc.; forked part, esp. of bicycle frame; (place of) divergence of road etc. ● *verb* form fork or branch; take one road at fork; dig with fork. □ **fork-lift truck** vehicle with fork for lifting and carrying; **fork out** *slang* pay, esp. reluctantly.

forlorn /fə'lɔːn/ *adjective* sad and abandoned; pitiful. □ **forlorn hope** faint remaining hope or chance. □ **forlornly** *adverb*.

form ● *noun* shape, arrangement of parts, visible aspect; person or animal as visible or tangible; mode in which thing exists or manifests itself; kind, variety; document with blanks to be filled in; class in school; (often as **the form**) customary or correct behaviour or method; set order of words; (of athlete, horse, etc.) condition of health and training; disposition; bench. ● *verb* make, be made; constitute; develop or establish as concept, practice, etc.; (+ *into*) organize; (of troops etc.) bring or move into formation; mould, fashion.

formal /'fɔːm(ə)l/ *adjective* in accordance with rules, convention, or ceremony; (of garden etc.) symmetrical; prim, stiff; perfunctory; drawn up correctly; concerned with outward form. □ **formally** *adverb*.

formaldehyde /fɔː'mældɪhaɪd/ *noun* colourless gas used as preservative and disinfectant.

formalin /'fɔːməlɪn/ *noun* solution of formaldehyde in water.

formalism *noun* strict adherence to external form, esp. in art. □ **formalist** *noun*.

formality /fɔːˈmælɪtɪ/ *noun* (*plural* **-ies**) formal, esp. meaningless, regulation or act; rigid observance of rules or convention.

formalize *verb* (also **-ise**) (**-zing** or **-sing**) give definite (esp. legal) form to; make formal. □ **formalization** *noun*.

format /ˈfɔːmæt/ ● *noun* shape and size (of book etc.); style or manner of procedure etc.; arrangement of computer data etc. ● *verb* (**-tt-**) arrange in format; prepare (storage medium) to receive computer data.

formation /fɔːˈmeɪʃ(ə)n/ *noun* forming; thing formed; particular arrangement (e.g. of troops); rocks or strata with common characteristic.

formative /ˈfɔːmətɪv/ *adjective* serving to form; of formation.

former /ˈfɔːmə/ *adjective* of the past, earlier, previous; (**the former**) the first or first-named of two.

formerly *adverb* in former times; previously.

Formica /fɔːˈmaɪkə/ *noun proprietary term* hard plastic laminate for surfaces.

formic acid /ˈfɔːmɪk/ *noun* colourless irritant volatile acid contained in fluid emitted by ants.

formidable /ˈfɔːmɪdəb(ə)l/ *adjective* inspiring awe, respect, or dread; difficult to deal with. □ **formidably** *adverb*.

■ **Usage** *Formidable* is also pronounced /fəˈmɪdəb(ə)l/ (with the stress on the *-mid-*), but this is considered incorrect by some people.

formless *adjective* without definite or regular form. □ **formlessness** *noun*.

formula /ˈfɔːmjʊlə/ *noun* (*plural* **-s** or **-lae** /-liː/) chemical symbols showing constituents of substance; mathematical rule expressed in symbols; fixed form of words; list of ingredients; classification of racing car, esp. by engine capacity. □ **formulaic** /-ˈleɪɪk/ *adjective*.

formulate /ˈfɔːmjʊleɪt/ *verb* express in formula; express clearly and precisely. □ **formulation** *noun*.

fornicate /ˈfɔːnɪkeɪt/ *verb* (**-ting**) *usually jocular* have extramarital sexual intercourse. □ **fornication** *noun*; **fornicator** *noun*.

forsake /fəˈseɪk/ *verb* (**-king**; *past* **forsook** /-ˈsʊk/; *past participle* **forsaken**) *literary* give up, renounce; desert, abandon.

forswear /fɔːˈsweə/ *verb* (*past* **forswore**; *past participle* **forsworn**) abjure, renounce; (**forswear oneself**) perjure oneself; (as **forsworn** *adjective*) perjured.

forsythia /fɔːˈsaɪθɪə/ *noun* shrub with bright yellow flowers.

fort *noun* fortified building or position. □ **hold the fort** act as temporary substitute.

forte[1] /ˈfɔːteɪ/ *noun* thing in which one excels or specializes.

forte[2] /ˈfɔːteɪ/ *Music* ● *adjective* loud. ● *adverb* loudly. ● *noun* loud playing, singing, or passage.

forth /fɔːθ/ *adverb* forward(s); out; onwards in time. □ **forthcoming** /fɔːθˈkʌmɪŋ/ coming or available soon, produced when wanted, informative, responsive.

forthright *adjective* straightforward, outspoken, decisive.

forthwith /fɔːθˈwɪθ/ *adverb* immediately, without delay.

fortification /fɔːtɪfɪˈkeɪʃ(ə)n/ *noun* fortifying; (usually in *plural*) defensive works.

fortify /ˈfɔːtɪfaɪ/ *verb* (**-ies**, **-ied**) provide with fortifications; strengthen; (usually as **fortified** *adjective*) strengthen (wine etc.) with alcohol, increase nutritive value of (food, esp. with vitamins).

fortissimo /fɔːˈtɪsɪməʊ/ *Music* ● *adjective* very loud. ● *adverb* very loudly. ● *noun* (*plural* **-mos** or **-mi** /-miː/) very loud playing, singing, or passage.

fortitude /ˈfɔːtɪtjuːd/ *noun* courage in pain or adversity.

fortnight /ˈfɔːtnaɪt/ *noun* two weeks.

fortnightly ● *adjective* done, produced, or occurring once a fortnight. ● *adverb* every fortnight. ● *noun* (*plural* **-ies**) fortnightly magazine etc.

Fortran /ˈfɔːtræn/ *noun* (also **FORTRAN**) computer language used esp. for scientific calculations.

fortress /ˈfɔːtrɪs/ *noun* fortified building or town.

fortuitous /fɔːˈtjuːɪtəs/ *adjective* happening by chance. □ **fortuitously** *adverb*; **fortuitousness** *noun*; **fortuity** *noun* (*plural* **-ies**).

fortunate /ˈfɔːtʃənət/ *adjective* lucky, auspicious. □ **fortunately** *adverb*.

fortune /ˈfɔːtʃ(ə)n/ *noun* chance or luck in human affairs; person's destiny; prosperity, wealth; *colloquial* large sum of money. □ **fortune-teller** person claiming to foretell one's destiny.

forty /ˈfɔːtɪ/ *adjective & noun* (*plural* **-ies**) four times ten. □ **forty winks** *colloquial* short sleep. □ **fortieth** *adjective & noun*.

forum /ˈfɔːrəm/ *noun* place of or meeting for public discussion; court, tribunal.

forward /ˈfɔːwəd/ ● *adjective* onward, towards front; bold, precocious, presumptuous; relating to the future; well-advanced. ● *noun* attacking player in football etc. ● *adverb* to front; into prominence; so as to make progress; towards future; forwards. ● *verb* send (letter etc.) on; dispatch; help to advance, promote.

forwards *adverb* in direction one is facing.

forwent *past* of FORGO.

fossil /ˈfɒs(ə)l/ ● *noun* remains or impression of (usually prehistoric) plant or animal hardened in rock; *colloquial* antiquated or unchanging person or thing. ● *adjective* of or like fossil. □ **fossil fuel** natural fuel extracted from ground. □ **fossilize** *verb* (also **-ise**) (**-zing** or **-sing**); **fossilization** *noun*.

foster /ˈfɒstə/ ● *verb* promote growth of; encourage or harbour (feeling); bring up (another's child); assign as foster-child. ● *adjective* related by or concerned with fostering.

fought *past & past participle* of FIGHT.

foul /faʊl/ ● *adjective* offensive, loathsome, stinking; dirty, soiled; *colloquial* awful; noxious; obscene; unfair, against rules; (of weather) rough; entangled. ● *noun* foul blow or play; entanglement. ● *adverb* unfairly. ● *verb* make or become foul; commit foul on (player); (often + *up*) (cause to) become entangled or blocked. □ **foul-mouthed** using obscene or offensive language; **foul play** unfair play, treacherous or violent act, esp. murder. □ **foully** /ˈfaʊllɪ/ *adverb*; **foulness** *noun*.

found[1] *past & past participle* of FIND.

found[2] /faʊnd/ *verb* establish, originate; lay base of; base. □ **founder** *noun*.

found[3] /faʊnd/ *verb* melt and mould (metal), fuse (materials for glass); make thus. □ **founder** *noun*.

foundation /faʊnˈdeɪʃ(ə)n/ *noun* solid ground or base under building; (usually in *plural*) lowest part of building, usually below ground; basis; underlying principle; establishing (esp. endowed institution); base for cosmetics; (in full **foundation garment**) woman's supporting undergarment. □ **foundation-stone** one laid ceremonially at founding of building, basis.

founder /ˈfaʊndə/ *verb* (of ship) fill with water and sink; (of plan) fail; (of horse) stumble, fall lame.

foundling /ˈfaʊndlɪŋ/ *noun* abandoned infant of unknown parentage.

foundry /'faʊndrɪ/ *noun* (*plural* **-ies**) workshop for casting metal.

fount[1] /faʊnt/ *noun poetical* source, spring, fountain.

fount[2] /fɒnt/ *noun* (also **font**) set of printing type of same size and face.

fountain /'faʊntɪn/ *noun* jet(s) of water as ornament or for drinking; spring; (often + *of*) source. □ **fountain-head** source; **fountain pen** pen with reservoir or cartridge for ink.

four /fɔː/ *adjective & noun* one more than three; 4-oared boat, its crew. □ **four-letter word** short obscene word; **four-poster** bed with 4 posts supporting canopy; **four-square** *adjective* solidly based, steady, *adverb* resolutely; **four-stroke** (of internal-combustion engine) having power cycle completed in two up-and-down movements of piston; **four-wheel drive** drive acting on all 4 wheels of vehicle.

fourfold *adjective & adverb* four times as much or many.

foursome *noun* group of 4 people; golf match between two pairs.

fourteen /fɔː'tiːn/ *adjective & noun* one more than thirteen. □ **fourteenth** *adjective & noun*.

fourth /fɔːθ/ *adjective & noun* next after third; any of four equal parts of thing. □ **fourthly** *adverb*.

fowl /faʊl/ *noun* (*plural* same or **-s**) chicken kept for eggs and meat; poultry as food.

fox ● *noun* wild canine animal with red or grey fur and bushy tail; its fur; crafty person. ● *verb* deceive; puzzle. □ **foxglove** tall plant with purple or white flowers; **foxhole** hole in ground as shelter etc. in battle; **foxhound** hound bred to hunt foxes; **fox-hunting** hunting foxes with hounds; **fox-terrier** small short-haired terrier; **foxtrot** ballroom dance with slow and quick steps. □ **foxlike** *adjective*.

foxy *adjective* (**-ier**, **-iest**) foxlike; sly, cunning; reddish-brown. □ **foxily** *adverb*.

foyer /'fɔɪeɪ/ *noun* entrance hall in hotel, theatre, etc.

FPA *abbreviation* Family Planning Association.

Fr. *abbreviation* Father; French.

fr. *abbreviation* franc(s).

fracas /'frækɑː/ *noun* (*plural* same /-kɑːz/) noisy quarrel.

fraction /'frækʃ(ə)n/ *noun* part of whole number; small part, amount, etc.; portion of mixture obtainable by distillation etc. □ **fractional** *adjective*; **fractionally** *adverb*.

fractious /'frækʃəs/ *adjective* irritable, peevish.

fracture /'fræktʃə/ ● *noun* breakage, esp. of bone. ● *verb* (**-ring**) cause fracture in, suffer fracture.

fragile /'frædʒaɪl/ *adjective* easily broken; delicate. □ **fragility** /frə'dʒɪl-/ *noun*.

fragment ● *noun* /'frægmənt/ part broken off; remains or unfinished portion of book etc. ● *verb* /fræg'ment/ break into fragments. □ **fragmental** /-'men-/ *adjective*; **fragmentary** *adjective*; **fragmentation** *noun*.

fragrance /'freɪgrəns/ *noun* sweetness of smell; sweet scent.

fragrant *adjective* sweet-smelling.

frail *adjective* fragile, delicate; morally weak. □ **frailly** /'freɪllɪ/ *adverb*; **frailness** *noun*.

frailty *noun* (*plural* **-ies**) frail quality; weakness, foible.

frame ● *noun* case or border enclosing picture etc.; supporting structure; (in *plural*) structure of spectacles holding lenses; build of person or animal; framework; construction; (in full **frame of mind**) temporary state; single picture on photographic film; (in snooker etc.) triangular structure for positioning balls, round of play; glazed structure to protect plants. ● *verb* (**-ming**) set in frame; serve as frame for; construct, devise; (+ *to*, *into*) adapt, fit; *slang* concoct false charge etc. against; articulate (words). □ **frame-up** *slang* conspiracy to convict innocent person; **framework** essential supporting structure, basic system.

franc *noun* French, Belgian, Swiss, etc. unit of currency.

franchise /'fræntʃaɪz/ ● *noun* right to vote; citizenship; authorization to sell company's goods etc. in particular area; right granted to person or corporation. ● *verb* (**-sing**) grant franchise to.

Franciscan /fræn'sɪskən/ ● *adjective* of (order of) St Francis. ● *noun* Franciscan friar or nun.

franglais /'frɑ̃gleɪ/ *noun* French with many English words and idioms. [French]

Frank *noun* member of Germanic people that conquered Gaul in 6th c. □ **Frankish** *adjective*.

frank ● *adjective* candid, outspoken; undisguised; open. ● *verb* mark (letter etc.) to record payment of postage. ● *noun* franking signature or mark. □ **frankly** *adverb*; **frankness** *noun*.

frankfurter /'fræŋkfɜːtə/ *noun* seasoned smoked sausage.

frankincense /'fræŋkɪnsens/ *noun* aromatic gum resin burnt as incense.

frantic /'fræntɪk/ *adjective* wildly excited; frenzied; hurried, anxious; desperate, violent; *colloquial* extreme. □ **frantically** *adverb*.

fraternal /frə'tɜːn(ə)l/ *adjective* of brothers, brotherly; comradely. □ **fraternally** *adverb*.

fraternity /frə'tɜːnɪtɪ/ *noun* (*plural* **-ies**) religious brotherhood; group with common interests or of same professional class; *US* male students' society; brotherliness.

fraternize /'frætənaɪz/ *verb* (also **-ise**) (**-zing** or **-sing**) (often + *with*) associate, make friends, esp. with enemy etc. □ **fraternization** *noun*.

fratricide /'frætrɪsaɪd/ *noun* killing of one's brother or sister; person who does this. □ **fratricidal** /-'saɪd(ə)l/ *adjective*.

Frau /fraʊ/ *noun* (*plural* **Frauen** /'fraʊən/) *title used of or to married or widowed German-speaking woman.*

fraud /frɔːd/ *noun* criminal deception; dishonest trick; impostor.

fraudulent /'frɔːdjʊlənt/ *adjective* of, involving, or guilty of fraud. □ **fraudulence** *noun*; **fraudulently** *adverb*.

fraught /frɔːt/ *adjective* (+ *with*) filled or attended with (danger etc.); *colloquial* distressing; tense.

Fräulein /'frɔɪlaɪn/ *noun: title used of or to unmarried German-speaking woman.*

fray[1] *verb* wear or become worn; unravel at edge; (esp. as **frayed** *adjective*) (of nerves) become strained.

fray[2] *noun* fight, conflict; brawl.

frazzle /'fræz(ə)l/ *colloquial* ● *noun* worn, exhausted, or shrivelled state. ● *verb* (**-ling**) (usually as **frazzled** *adjective*) wear out; exhaust.

freak ● *noun* monstrosity; abnormal person or thing; *colloquial* unconventional person, fanatic of specified kind. ● *verb* (often + *out*) *colloquial* make or become very angry; (cause to) undergo esp. drug-induced etc. hallucinations or strong emotional experience. □ **freakish** *adjective*; **freaky** *adjective* (**-ier**, **-iest**).

freckle /'frek(ə)l/ ● *noun* light brown spot on skin. ● *verb* (**-ling**) (usually as **freckled** *adjective*) spot or be spotted with freckles. □ **freckly** *adjective* (**-ier**, **-iest**).

free ● *adjective* (**freer** /'friːə/, **freest** /'friːɪst/) not a slave; having personal rights and social and political liberty; autonomous; democratic; unrestricted, not confined; (+ *of*, *from* or *in combination*) exempt from, not containing or subject to; (+ *to do*) permitted, at liberty; costing nothing; available; spontaneous; lavish, unreserved; (of translation) not literal.

● *adverb* freely; without cost. ● *verb* (**frees**, **freed**) make free, liberate; disentangle. ▫ **for free** *colloquial* gratis; **freebooter** pirate; **freeboard** part of ship's side between waterline and deck; **Free Church** Nonconformist Church; **free enterprise** freedom of private business from state control; **free fall** movement under force of gravity only; **free hand** *noun* liberty to act at one's own discretion; **freehand** *adjective* (of drawing) done without ruler, compasses, etc., *adverb* in a freehand way; **free house** pub not controlled by brewery; **freeloader** *slang* sponger; **freeman** holder of freedom of city etc.; **free port** port without customs duties, or open to all traders; **free-range** (of hens etc.) roaming freely, (of eggs) produced by such hens; **free spirit** independent or uninhibited person; **free-standing** not supported by another structure; **freestyle** swimming race in which any stroke may be used, wrestling allowing almost any hold; **freethinker** /-'θɪŋkə/ person who rejects dogma, esp. in religious belief; **free trade** trade without import restrictions etc.; **freeway** *US* motorway; **freewheel** ride bicycle with pedals at rest, act without constraint; **free will** power of acting independently of fate or without coercion.

freebie /'fri:bɪ/ *noun colloquial* thing given free of charge.

freedom *noun* being free; personal or civil liberty; liberty of action; (+ *from*) exemption from; (+ *of*) honorary membership or citizenship of, unrestricted use of (house etc.).

freehold *noun* complete ownership of property for unlimited period; such property. ▫ **freeholder** *noun*.

freelance ● *noun* person working for no fixed employer. ● *verb* work as freelance. ● *adverb* as freelance.

Freemason /'fri:meɪs(ə)n/ *noun* member of fraternity for mutual help with secret rituals. ▫ **Freemasonry** *noun*.

freesia /'fri:zjə/ *noun* fragrant flowering African bulb.

freeze ● *verb* (**-zing**; *past* **froze**; *past participle* **frozen** /'frəʊz(ə)n/) turn into ice or other solid by cold; make or become rigid from cold; be or feel very cold; cover or be covered with ice; refrigerate below freezing point; make or become motionless; (as **frozen** *adjective*) devoid of emotion; make (assets etc.) unrealizable; fix (prices etc.) at certain level; stop (movement in film). ● *noun* period or state of frost; price-fixing etc.; (in full **freeze-frame**) still film-shot. ▫ **freeze-dry** preserve (food) by freezing and then drying in vacuum; **freeze up** *verb* obstruct or be obstructed by ice; **freeze-up** *noun* period of extreme cold; **freezing point** temperature at which liquid freezes.

freezer *noun* refrigerated cabinet for preserving food in frozen state.

freight /freɪt/ *noun* transport of goods; goods transported; charge for transport of goods.

freighter *noun* ship or aircraft for carrying freight.

French ● *adjective* of France or its people or language. ● *noun* French language; (**the French**) (*plural*) the French people. ▫ **French bean** kidney or haricot bean as unripe pods or as ripe seeds; **French bread** long crisp loaf; **French dressing** salad dressing of oil and vinegar; **French fried potatoes**, **French fries** chips; **French horn** coiled brass wind instrument; **French letter** *colloquial* condom; **Frenchman**, **Frenchwoman** native or national of France; **French polish** *noun* shellac polish for wood; **French-polish** *verb*; **French window** glazed door in outside wall.

frenetic /frə'netɪk/ *adjective* frantic, frenzied. ▫ **frenetically** *adverb*.

frenzy /'frenzɪ/ ● *noun* (*plural* **-ies**) wild excitement or fury. ● *verb* (**-ies**, **-ied**) (usually as **frenzied** *adjective*) drive to frenzy. ▫ **frenziedly** *adverb*.

frequency /'fri:kwənsɪ/ *noun* (*plural* **-ies**) commonness of occurrence; frequent occurrence; rate of recurrence (of vibration etc.). ▫ **frequency modulation** *Electronics* modulation by varying carrier-wave frequency.

frequent ● *adjective* /'fri:kwənt/ occurring often or in close succession; habitual. ● *verb* /frɪ'kwent/ go to habitually. ▫ **frequently** /'frɪkwəntlɪ/ *adverb*.

fresco /'freskəʊ/ *noun* (*plural* **-s**) painting in water-colour on fresh plaster.

fresh ● *adjective* newly made or obtained; other, different; new; additional; (+ *from*) lately arrived from; not stale or faded; (of food) not preserved; (of water) not salty; pure; refreshing; (of wind) brisk; *colloquial* cheeky, amorously impudent; inexperienced. ● *adverb* newly, recently. ▫ **freshwater** (of fish etc.) not of the sea. ▫ **freshly** *adverb*; **freshness** *noun*.

freshen *verb* make or become fresh; (+ *up*) wash, tidy oneself, etc.; revive.

fresher *noun colloquial* first-year student at university or (*US*) high school.

freshet /'freʃɪt/ *noun* rush of fresh water into sea; river flood.

freshman /'freʃmən/ *noun* fresher.

fret[1] ● *verb* (**-tt-**) be worried or distressed. ● *noun* worry, vexation. ▫ **fretful** *adjective*; **fretfully** *adverb*.

fret[2] ● *noun* ornamental pattern of straight lines joined usually at right angles. ● *verb* (**-tt-**) adorn with fret etc. ▫ **fretsaw** narrow saw on frame for cutting thin wood in patterns; **fretwork** work done with fretsaw.

fret[3] *noun* bar or ridge on finger-board of guitar etc.

Freudian /'frɔɪdɪən/ ● *adjective* of Freud's theories or method of psychoanalysis. ● *noun* follower of Freud. ▫ **Freudian slip** unintentional verbal error revealing subconscious feelings.

Fri. *abbreviation* Friday.

friable /'fraɪəb(ə)l/ *adjective* easily crumbled. ▫ **friability** *noun*.

friar /'fraɪə/ *noun* member of male non-enclosed religious order. ▫ **friar's balsam** type of inhalant.

friary /'fraɪərɪ/ *noun* (*plural* **-ies**) monastery for friars.

fricassee /'frɪkəseɪ/ ● *noun* pieces of meat in thick sauce. ● *verb* (**fricassees**, **fricasseed**) make fricassee of.

fricative /'frɪkətɪv/ ● *adjective* sounded by friction of breath in narrow opening. ● *noun* such consonant (e.g. *f*, *th*).

friction /'frɪkʃ(ə)n/ *noun* rubbing of one object against another; resistance so encountered; clash of wills, opinions, etc. ▫ **frictional** *adjective*.

Friday /'fraɪdeɪ/ *noun* day of week following Thursday.

fridge *noun colloquial* refrigerator. ▫ **fridge-freezer** combined refrigerator and freezer.

friend /frend/ *noun* supportive and respected associate, esp. one for whom affection is felt; ally; kind person; person already mentioned; (**Friend**) Quaker.

friendly ● *adjective* (**-ier**, **-iest**) outgoing, kindly; (often + *with*) on amicable terms; not hostile; user-friendly. ● *noun* (*plural* **-ies**) friendly match. ▫ **-friendly** not harming, helping; **friendly match** match played for enjoyment rather than competition; **Friendly Society** society for insurance against sickness etc. ▫ **friendliness** *noun*.

friendship *noun* friendly relationship or feeling.

frier = FRYER.

Friesian /'fri:zɪən/ ● *noun* one of breed of black and white dairy cattle. ● *adjective* of Friesians.

frieze /fri:z/ *noun* part of entablature, often filled with sculpture, between architrave and cornice; band of decoration, esp. at top of wall.

frigate /ˈfrɪgɪt/ *noun* naval escort-vessel.

fright /fraɪt/ *noun* (instance of) sudden or extreme fear; grotesque-looking person or thing. □ **take fright** become frightened.

frighten *verb* fill with fright; (+ *away, off, out of, into*) drive by fright. □ **frightening** *adjective*; **frighteningly** *adverb*.

frightful *adjective* dreadful, shocking; ugly; *colloquial* extremely bad; *colloquial* extreme. □ **frightfully** *adverb*.

frigid /ˈfrɪdʒɪd/ *adjective* unfriendly, cold; (of woman) sexually unresponsive; cold. □ **frigidity** /-ˈdʒɪd-/ *noun*.

frill ● *noun* ornamental edging of gathered or pleated material; (in *plural*) unnecessary embellishments. ● *verb* (usually as **frilled** *adjective*) decorate with frill. □ **frilly** *adjective* (**-ier**, **-iest**).

fringe ● *noun* border of tassels or loose threads; front hair cut to hang over forehead; outer limit; unimportant area or part. ● *verb* (**-ging**) adorn with fringe; serve as fringe to. □ **fringe benefit** employee's benefit additional to salary.

frippery /ˈfrɪpərɪ/ *noun* (*plural* **-ies**) showy finery; empty display; (usually in *plural*) knick-knacks.

frisk ● *verb* leap or skip playfully; *slang* search (person). ● *noun* playful leap or skip.

frisky *adjective* (**-ier**, **-iest**) lively, playful.

frisson /ˈfri:sɒn/ *noun* emotional thrill. [French]

fritillary /frɪˈtɪlərɪ/ *noun* (*plural* **-ies**) plant with bell-like flowers; butterfly with red and black chequered wings.

fritter[1] /ˈfrɪtə/ *verb* (usually + *away*) waste triflingly.

fritter[2] /ˈfrɪtə/ *noun* fruit, meat, etc. coated in batter and fried.

frivolous /ˈfrɪvələs/ *adjective* not serious, shallow, silly; trifling. □ **frivolity** /-ˈvɒl-/ *noun* (*plural* **-ies**).

frizz ● *verb* form (hair) into tight curls. ● *noun* frizzed hair or state. □ **frizzy** *adjective* (**-ier**, **-iest**).

frizzle[1] /ˈfrɪz(ə)l/ *verb* (**-ling**) fry or cook with sizzling noise; (often + *up*) burn, shrivel.

frizzle[2] /ˈfrɪz(ə)l/ *verb* (**-ling**) & *noun* frizz.

frock *noun* woman's or girl's dress; monk's or priest's gown. □ **frock-coat** man's long-skirted coat.

frog *noun* tailless leaping amphibian. □ **frog in one's throat** *colloquial* phlegm in throat that hinders speech; **frogman** underwater swimmer equipped with rubber suit and flippers; **frogmarch** hustle forward with arms pinned behind; **frog-spawn** frog's eggs.

frolic /ˈfrɒlɪk/ ● *verb* (**-ck-**) play about merrily. ● *noun* merrymaking.

frolicsome *adjective* playful.

from /frəm/ *preposition expressing separation or origin*.

fromage frais /frɒmɑ:ʒ ˈfreɪ/ *noun* type of soft cheese.

frond *noun* leaflike part of fern or palm.

front /frʌnt/ ● *noun* side or part most prominent or important, or nearer spectator or direction of motion; line of battle; scene of actual fighting; organized political group; demeanour; pretext, bluff; person etc. as cover for subversive or illegal activities; land along edge of sea or lake, esp. in town; forward edge of advancing cold or warm air; auditorium; breast of garment. ● *adjective* of or at front. ● *verb* (+ *on, to, towards*, etc.) have front facing or directed towards; (+ *for*) *slang* act as front for; (usually as **fronted** *adjective* + *with*) provide with or have front; lead (band, organization, etc.). □ **front bench** seats in Parliament for leading members of government and opposition; **front line** foremost part of army or group under attack; **front runner** favourite in race etc.

frontage *noun* front of building; land next to street, water, etc.; extent of front.

frontal *adjective* of or on front; of forehead.

frontier /ˈfrʌntɪə/ *noun* border between countries, district on each side of this; limits of attainment or knowledge in subject; *esp. US historical* border between settled and unsettled country. □ **frontiersman** *noun*.

frontispiece /ˈfrʌntɪspi:s/ *noun* illustration facing title-page of book.

frost ● *noun* frozen dew or vapour; temperature below freezing point. ● *verb* (usually + *over, up*) become covered with frost; cover (as) with frost; (usually as **frosted** *adjective*) roughen surface of (glass) to make opaque. □ **frostbite** injury to body tissue due to freezing; **frostbitten** *adjective*.

frosting *noun* icing for cakes.

frosty *adjective* (**-ier**, **-iest**) cold or covered with frost; unfriendly.

froth ● *noun* foam; idle talk. ● *verb* emit or gather froth. □ **frothy** *adjective* (**-ier**, **-iest**).

frown ● *verb* wrinkle brows, esp. in displeasure or concentration; (+ *at, on*) disapprove of. ● *noun* act of frowning, frowning look.

frowsty /ˈfraʊstɪ/ *adjective* (**-ier**, **-iest**) fusty; stuffy.

frowzy /ˈfraʊzɪ/ *adjective* (also **frowsy**) (**-ier**, **-iest**) fusty; slatternly, dingy.

froze *past* of FREEZE.

frozen *past participle* of FREEZE.

FRS *abbreviation* Fellow of the Royal Society.

fructify /ˈfrʌktɪfaɪ/ *verb* (**-ies**, **-ied**) bear fruit; make fruitful.

fructose /ˈfrʌktəʊz/ *noun* sugar in fruits, honey, etc.

frugal /ˈfru:g(ə)l/ *adjective* sparing; meagre. □ **frugality** /-ˈgæl-/ *noun*; **frugally** *adverb*.

fruit /fru:t/ ● *noun* seed-bearing part of plant or tree; this as food; (usually in *plural*) products, profits, rewards. ● *verb* bear fruit. □ **fruit cake** cake containing dried fruit; **fruit cocktail** diced fruit salad; **fruit machine** gambling machine operated by coins; **fruit salad** dessert of mixed fruit; **fruit sugar** fructose.

fruiterer /ˈfru:tərə/ *noun* dealer in fruit.

fruitful *adjective* productive; successful. □ **fruitfully** *adverb*.

fruition /fru:ˈɪʃ(ə)n/ *noun* realization of aims or hopes.

fruitless *adjective* not bearing fruit; useless, unsuccessful. □ **fruitlessly** *adverb*.

fruity *adjective* (**-ier**, **-iest**) of or resembling fruit; (of voice) deep and rich; *colloquial* slightly indecent.

frump *noun* dowdy woman. □ **frumpish** *adjective*; **frumpy** *adjective* (**-ier**, **-iest**).

frustrate /frʌsˈtreɪt/ *verb* (**-ting**) make (efforts) ineffective; prevent from achieving purpose; (as **frustrated** *adjective*) discontented, unfulfilled. □ **frustrating** *adjective*; **frustratingly** *adverb*; **frustration** *noun*.

fry[1] ● *verb* (**fries**, **fried**) cook in hot fat. ● *noun* fried food, esp. (usually **fries**) chips. □ **frying-pan** shallow long-handled pan for frying; **fry-up** *colloquial* fried bacon, eggs, etc.

fry[2] *plural noun* young or freshly hatched fishes.

fryer *noun* (also **frier**) person who fries; vessel for frying esp. fish.

ft *abbreviation* foot, feet.

FT-SE *abbreviation* Financial Times Stock Exchange (100 share index).

fuchsia /ˈfju:ʃə/ *noun* shrub with drooping flowers.

fuddle /ˈfʌd(ə)l/ ● *verb* (**-ling**) confuse, esp. with alcohol. ● *noun* confusion; intoxication.

fuddy-duddy /ˈfʌdɪdʌdɪ/ *slang* ● *adjective* fussy, old-fashioned. ● *noun* (*plural* **-ies**) such person.

fudge ● *noun* soft toffee-like sweet; faking. ● *verb* (**-ging**) make or do clumsily or dishonestly; fake.

fuel /'fju:əl/ ● *noun* material for burning or as source of heat, power, or nuclear energy; thing that sustains or inflames passion etc. ● *verb* (**-ll-**; *US* **-l-**) supply with fuel; inflame (feeling).

fug *noun colloquial* stuffy atmosphere. □ **fuggy** *adjective* (**-ier**, **-iest**).

fugitive /'fju:dʒɪtɪv/ ● *noun* (often + *from*) person who flees. ● *adjective* fleeing; transient, fleeting.

fugue /fju:g/ *noun* piece of music in which short melody or phrase is introduced by one part and developed by others. □ **fugal** *adjective*.

fulcrum /'fʌlkrəm/ *noun* (*plural* **-s** or **-cra**) point on which lever is supported.

fulfil /fʊl'fɪl/ *verb* (*US* **fulfill**) (**-ll-**) carry out; satisfy; (as **fulfilled** *adjective*) completely happy; (**fulfil oneself**) realize one's potential. □ **fulfilment** *noun*.

full /fʊl/ ● *adjective* holding all it can; replete; abundant; satisfying; (+ *of*) having abundance of, engrossed in; complete, perfect; resonant; plump; ample. ● *adverb* quite, exactly. □ **full back** defensive player near goal in football etc.; **full-blooded** vigorous, sensual, not hybrid; **full-blown** fully developed; **full board** provision of bed and all meals; **full-bodied** rich in quality, tone, etc.; **full frontal** (of nude) fully exposed at front, explicit; **full house** maximum attendance at theatre etc., hand in poker with 3 of a kind and a pair; **full-length** of normal length, not shortened, (of portrait) showing whole figure; **full moon** moon with whole disc illuminated; **full stop** punctuation mark (.) at end of sentence etc. (see panel), complete cessation; **full term** completion of normal pregnancy; **full-time** *adjective* for or during whole of working week, *adverb* on full-time basis. □ **fullness** *noun*.

fully *adverb* completely; at least.

fulmar /'fʊlmə/ *noun* kind of petrel.

fulminate /'fʊlmɪneɪt/ *verb* (**-ting**) criticize loudly and forcibly; explode, flash. □ **fulmination** *noun*.

fulsome /'fʊlsəm/ *adjective* excessive, cloying; insincere. □ **fulsomely** *adverb*.

■ **Usage** *Fulsome* is sometimes wrongly used to mean 'generous', as in *fulsome praise*, or 'generous with praise', as in *a fulsome tribute*.

fumble /'fʌmb(ə)l/ ● *verb* (**-ling**) grope about; handle clumsily or nervously. ● *noun* act of fumbling.

fume ● *noun* (usually in *plural*) exuded smoke, gas, or vapour. ● *verb* (**-ming**) emit fumes; be very angry; subject (oak etc.) to fumes to darken.

fumigate /'fju:mɪgeɪt/ *verb* (**-ting**) disinfect or purify with fumes. □ **fumigation** *noun*; **fumigator** *noun*.

fun *noun* playful amusement; source of this; mockery. □ **funfair** fair consisting of amusements and sideshows; **fun run** *colloquial* sponsored run for charity; **make fun of**, **poke fun at** ridicule.

function /'fʌŋkʃ(ə)n/ ● *noun* proper role etc.; official duty; public or social occasion; *Mathematics* quantity whose value depends on varying values of others. ● *verb* fulfil function; operate.

functional *adjective* of or serving a function; practical rather than attractive. □ **functionally** *adverb*.

functionalism *noun* belief that function should determine design. □ **functionalist** *noun & adjective*.

functionary *noun* (*plural* **-ies**) official.

fund ● *noun* permanently available stock; money set apart for purpose; (in *plural*) money resources. ● *verb* provide with money; make (debt) permanent at fixed interest. □ **fund-raising** raising money for charity etc.; **fund-raiser** *noun*.

fundamental /fʌndə'ment(ə)l/ ● *adjective* of or serving as base or foundation; essential, primary. ● *noun* fundamental principle. □ **fundamentally** *adverb*.

fundamentalism *noun* strict adherence to traditional religious beliefs. □ **fundamentalist** *noun & adjective*.

funeral /'fju:nər(ə)l/ ● *noun* ceremonial burial or cremation of dead. ● *adjective* of or used at funerals. □ **funeral director** undertaker; **funeral parlour** establishment where corpses are prepared for funerals.

funerary /'fju:nərərɪ/ *adjective* of or used at funerals.

funereal /fju:'nɪərɪəl/ *adjective* of or appropriate to funeral; dismal, dark.

Full stop ▪

This is used:

1 at the end of a sentence, e.g.

I am going to the cinema tonight.
The film begins at seven.

The full stop is replaced by a question mark at the end of a question, and by an exclamation mark at the end of an exclamation.

2 after an abbreviation, e.g.

H. G. Wells *p. 19* (=*page 19*) *Sun.* (=*Sunday*)
Ex. 6 (=*Exercise 6*).

Full stops are **not** used with:

- **a** numerical abbreviations, e.g. *1st, 2nd, 15th, 23rd*
- **b** acronyms, e.g. *FIFA, NATO*
- **c** abbreviations that are used as ordinary words, e.g. *con, demo, recap*
- **d** chemical symbols, e.g. Fe, K, H_2O

Full stops are not essential for:

- **a** abbreviations consisting entirely of capitals, e.g. *BBC, AD, BC, PLC*
- **b** *C* (=*Celsius*), *F* (=*Fahrenheit*)
- **c** measures of length, weight, time, etc., except for *in.* (=*inch*), *st.* (=*stone*)
- **d** *Dr, Revd* (but note *Rev.*), *Mr, Mrs, Ms, Mme, Mlle, St* (=*Saint*), *Hants, Northants, p* (=*penny* or *pence*).

fungicide /ˈfʌndʒɪsaɪd/ *noun* substance that kills fungus. □ **fungicidal** /-ˈsaɪd(ə)l/ *adjective*.

fungus /ˈfʌŋgəs/ *noun* (*plural* **-gi** /-gaɪ/ or **-guses**) mushroom, toadstool, or allied plant; spongy morbid growth. □ **fungal** *adjective*; **fungoid** *adjective*; **fungous** *adjective*.

funicular /fjuːˈnɪkjʊlə/ *noun* (in full **funicular railway**) cable railway with ascending and descending cars counterbalanced.

funk *slang* ● *noun* fear, panic. ● *verb* evade through fear.

funky *adjective* (**-ier**, **-iest**) *slang* (esp. of jazz etc.) with heavy rhythm.

funnel /ˈfʌn(ə)l/ ● *noun* tube widening at top, for pouring liquid etc. into small opening; chimney of steam engine or ship. ● *verb* (**-ll-**; *US* **-l-**) (cause to) move (as) through funnel.

funny /ˈfʌnɪ/ *adjective* (**-ier**, **-iest**) amusing, comical; strange. □ **funny bone** part of elbow over which very sensitive nerve passes. □ **funnily** *adverb*.

fur ● *noun* short fine animal hair; hide with fur on it; garment of or lined with this; coating inside kettle etc. ● *verb* (**-rr-**) (esp. as **furred** *adjective*) line or trim with fur; (often + *up*) (of kettle etc.) become coated with fur.

furbelow /ˈfɜːbɪləʊ/ *noun* (in *plural*) showy ornaments.

furbish /ˈfɜːbɪʃ/ *verb* (often + *up*) refurbish.

furcate /ˈfɜːkeɪt/ ● *adjective* forked, branched. ● *verb* (**-ting**) fork, divide. □ **furcation** *noun*.

furious /ˈfjʊərɪəs/ *adjective* very angry, raging, frantic. □ **furiously** *adverb*.

furl *verb* roll up (sail, umbrella); become furled.

furlong /ˈfɜːlɒŋ/ *noun* eighth of mile.

furlough /ˈfɜːləʊ/ *noun* leave of absence.

furnace /ˈfɜːnɪs/ *noun* chamber for intense heating by fire; very hot place.

furnish /ˈfɜːnɪʃ/ *verb* provide with furniture; (often + *with*) supply; (as **furnished** *adjective*) let with furniture. □ **furnishings** *plural noun*.

furniture /ˈfɜːnɪtʃə/ *noun* movable contents of building or room; ship's equipment; accessories, e.g. handles and locks.

furore /fjʊəˈrɔːrɪ/ *noun* (*US* **furor** /ˈfjʊərɔː/) uproar; enthusiasm.

furrier /ˈfʌrɪə/ *noun* dealer in or dresser of furs.

furrow /ˈfʌrəʊ/ ● *noun* narrow trench made by plough; rut; wrinkle. ● *verb* plough; make furrows in.

furry /ˈfɜːrɪ/ *adjective* (**-ier**, **-iest**) like or covered with fur.

further /ˈfɜːðə/ ● *adverb* (also **farther** /ˈfɑːðə/) more distant in space or time; more, to greater extent; in addition. ● *adjective* (also **farther** /ˈfɑːθə/) more distant or advanced; more, additional. ● *verb* promote, favour. □ **further education** education for people above school age; **furthermore** in addition, besides.

furtherance *noun* furthering of scheme etc.

furthest /ˈfɜːðɪst/ (also **farthest** /ˈfɑːðɪst/) ● *adjective* most distant. ● *adverb* to or at the greatest distance.

furtive /ˈfɜːtɪv/ *adjective* sly, stealthy. □ **furtively** *adverb*.

fury /ˈfjʊərɪ/ *noun* (*plural* **-ies**) wild and passionate anger; violence (of storm etc.); (**Fury**) (usually in *plural*) avenging goddess; angry woman.

furze *noun* gorse. □ **furzy** *adjective* (**-ier**, **-iest**).

fuse[1] /fjuːz/ ● *verb* (**-sing**) melt with intense heat; blend by melting; supply with fuse; fail due to melting of fuse; cause fuse(s) of to melt. ● *noun* easily melted wire in circuit, designed to melt when circuit is overloaded.

fuse[2] /fjuːz/ ● *noun* combustible device for igniting bomb etc. ● *verb* (**-sing**) fit fuse to.

fuselage /ˈfjuːzəlɑːʒ/ *noun* body of aircraft.

fusible /ˈfjuːzɪb(ə)l/ *adjective* that can be melted. □ **fusibility** *noun*.

fusilier /fjuːzɪˈlɪə/ *noun* soldier of any of several regiments formerly armed with light muskets.

fusillade /fjuːzɪˈleɪd/ *noun* continuous discharge of firearms or outburst of criticism etc.

fusion /ˈfjuːʒ(ə)n/ *noun* fusing; blending, coalition; nuclear fusion.

fuss ● *noun* excited commotion; bustle; excessive concern about trivial thing; sustained protest. ● *verb* behave with nervous concern; agitate, worry. □ **fusspot** *colloquial* person given to fussing; **make a fuss** complain vigorously; **make a fuss of**, **over** treat affectionately.

fussy *adjective* (**-ier**, **-iest**) inclined to fuss; over-elaborate; fastidious.

fustian /ˈfʌstɪən/ *noun* thick usually dark twilled cotton cloth; bombast.

fusty /ˈfʌstɪ/ *adjective* (**-ier**, **-iest**) musty, stuffy; antiquated.

futile /ˈfjuːtaɪl/ *adjective* useless, ineffectual. □ **futility** /-ˈtɪl-/ *noun*.

futon /ˈfuːtɒn/ *noun* Japanese mattress used as bed; this with frame, convertible into couch.

future /ˈfjuːtʃə/ ● *adjective* about to happen, be, or become; of time to come; *Grammar* (of tense) describing event yet to happen. ● *noun* time to come; future condition or events etc.; prospect of success etc.; *Grammar* future tense; (in *plural*) (on stock exchange) goods etc. sold for future delivery. □ **future perfect** *Grammar* tense giving sense 'will have done'.

futurism *noun* 20th-c. artistic movement celebrating technology etc. □ **futurist** *adjective & noun*.

futuristic /fjuːtʃəˈrɪstɪk/ *adjective* suitable for the future; ultra-modern; of futurism.

futurity /fjuːˈtjʊərɪtɪ/ *noun* (*plural* **-ies**) *literary* future time, events, etc.

fuzz *noun* fluff; fluffy or frizzy hair; (**the fuzz**) *slang* police (officer).

fuzzy /ˈfʌzɪ/ *adjective* (**-ier**, **-iest**) fluffy; blurred, indistinct.

Gg

G □ **G-man** *US colloquial* FBI special agent; **G-string** narrow strip of cloth etc. attached to string round waist for covering genitals.

g *abbreviation* (also **g.**) gram(s).

gab *noun colloquial* talk, chatter.

gabardine /gæbə'di:n/ *noun* a strong twilled cloth; raincoat etc. of this.

gabble /'gæb(ə)l/ ● *verb* (**-ling**) talk or utter unintelligibly or too fast. ● *noun* rapid talk.

gaberdine = GABARDINE.

gable /'geɪb(ə)l/ *noun* triangular part of wall at end of ridged roof. □ **gabled** *adjective*.

gad *verb* (**-dd-**) (+ *about*) go about idly or in search of pleasure. □ **gadabout** person who gads about.

gadfly /'gædflaɪ/ *noun* (*plural* **-ies**) fly that bites cattle.

gadget /'gædʒɪt/ *noun* small mechanical device or tool. □ **gadgetry** *noun*.

Gael /geɪl/ *noun* Scottish or Gaelic-speaking Celt.

Gaelic /'geɪlɪk/ ● *noun* Celtic language of Scots (also /'gælɪk/) or Irish. ● *adjective* of Gaelic or Gaelic-speaking people.

gaff¹ ● *noun* stick with hook for landing fish; barbed fishing-spear. ● *verb* seize (fish) with gaff.

gaff² *noun slang* □ **blow the gaff** let out secret.

gaffe /gæf/ *noun* blunder, tactless mistake.

gaffer /'gæfə/ *noun* old man; *colloquial* foreman, boss; chief electrician in film unit.

gag ● *noun* thing thrust into or tied across mouth to prevent speech etc.; joke or comic scene. ● *verb* (**-gg-**) apply gag to; silence; choke, retch; make jokes.

gaga /'gɑ:gɑ:/ *adjective slang* senile; crazy.

gage¹ *noun* pledge, security; challenge.

gage² *US* = GAUGE.

gaggle /'gæg(ə)l/ *noun* flock (of geese); *colloquial* disorganized group.

gaiety /'geɪətɪ/ *noun* (*US* **gayety**) being gay, mirth; merrymaking; bright appearance.

gaily /'geɪlɪ/ *adverb* in a gay way.

gain ● *verb* obtain, win; acquire, earn; (often + *in*) increase, improve; benefit; (of clock etc.) become fast (by); reach; (often + *on*, *upon*) get closer to (person or thing one is following). ● *noun* increase (of wealth), profit; (in *plural*) money made in trade etc.

gainful /'geɪnfʊl/ *adjective* paid, lucrative. □ **gainfully** *adverb*.

gainsay /geɪn'seɪ/ *verb* deny, contradict.

gait *noun* manner of walking or proceeding.

gaiter /'geɪtə/ *noun* covering of leather etc. for lower leg.

gal. *abbreviation* gallon(s).

gala /'gɑ:lə/ *noun* festive occasion or gathering.

galactic /gə'læktɪk/ *adjective* of galaxy.

galantine /'gælənti:n/ *noun* cold dish of meat boned, spiced, and covered in jelly.

galaxy /'gæləksɪ/ *noun* (*plural* **-ies**) independent system of stars etc. in space; (**the Galaxy**) Milky Way; (+ *of*) gathering of beautiful or famous people.

gale *noun* strong wind; outburst, esp. of laughter.

gall¹ /gɔ:l/ *noun colloquial* impudence; rancour; bile. □ **gall bladder** bodily organ containing bile; **gallstone** small hard mass that forms in gall bladder.

gall² /gɔ:l/ ● *noun* sore made by chafing; (cause of) vexation; place rubbed bare. ● *verb* rub sore; vex, humiliate.

gall³ /gɔ:l/ *noun* growth produced on tree etc. by insect etc.

gallant /'gælənt/ ● *adjective* brave; fine, stately; (/gə'lænt/) attentive to women. ● *noun* (/gə'lænt/) ladies' man. □ **gallantly** *adverb*.

gallantry /'gæləntrɪ/ *noun* (*plural* **-ies**) bravery; courteousness to women; polite act or speech.

galleon /'gælɪən/ *noun historical* (usually Spanish) warship.

galleria /gælə'ri:ə/ *noun* group of small shops, cafés, etc. under one roof.

gallery /'gælərɪ/ *noun* (*plural* **-ies**) room etc. for showing works of art; balcony, esp. in church, hall, etc.; highest balcony in theatre; covered walk, colonnade; passage, corridor.

galley /'gælɪ/ *noun* (*plural* **-s**) *historical* long flat one-decked vessel usually rowed by slaves or criminals; ship's or aircraft's kitchen; (in full **galley proof**) printer's proof before division into pages.

Gallic /'gælɪk/ *adjective* (typically) French; of Gaul or Gauls.

Gallicism /'gælɪsɪz(ə)m/ *noun* French idiom.

gallimimus /gælɪ'maɪməs/ *noun* (*plural* **-muses**) medium-sized dinosaur that ran fast on two legs.

gallinaceous /gælɪ'neɪʃəs/ *adjective* of order of birds including domestic poultry.

gallivant /'gælɪvænt/ *verb colloquial* gad about.

gallon /'gælən/ *noun* measure of capacity (4.546 litres).

gallop /'gæləp/ ● *noun* horse's fastest pace; ride at this pace. ● *verb* (**-p-**) (cause to) go at gallop; talk etc. fast; progress rapidly.

gallows /'gæləʊz/ *plural noun* (usually treated as *singular*) structure for hanging criminals.

Gallup poll /'gæləp/ *noun* kind of opinion poll.

galore /gə'lɔ:/ *adverb* in plenty.

galosh /gə'lɒʃ/ *noun* waterproof overshoe.

galumph /gə'lʌmf/ *verb colloquial* (esp. as **galumphing** *adjective*) move noisily or clumsily.

galvanic /gæl'vænɪk/ *adjective* producing an electric current by chemical action; (of electric current) produced thus; stimulating, full of energy.

galvanize /'gælvənaɪz/ *verb* (also **-ise**) (**-zing** or **-sing**) (often + *into*) rouse by shock; stimulate (as) by electricity; coat (iron, steel) with zinc to protect from rust.

galvanometer /gælvə'nɒmɪtə/ *noun* instrument for measuring electric currents.

gambit /'gæmbɪt/ *noun Chess* opening with sacrifice of pawn etc.; trick, device.

gamble /'gæmb(ə)l/ ● *verb* (**-ling**) play games of chance for money; bet (sum of money); (often + *away*) lose by gambling. ● *noun* risky undertaking; spell of gambling. □ **gambler** *noun*.

gambol /'gæmb(ə)l/ ● *verb* (**-ll-**; *US* **-l-**) jump about playfully. ● *noun* caper.

game¹ ● *noun* form or period of play or sport, esp. competitive one organized with rules; portion of play forming scoring unit; (in *plural*) athletic contests; piece of fun, (in *plural*) tricks; *colloquial* scheme, activity; wild animals or birds etc. hunted for sport or food; their flesh as food. ● *adjective* spirited, eager. ● *verb* (**-ming**) gamble for money. □ **gamekeeper** person employed to breed and protect game; **gamesmanship** art of winning games by psychological means. □ **gamely** *adverb*.

game² *adjective colloquial* (of leg etc.) crippled.
gamete /'gæmi:t/ *noun* mature germ cell uniting with another in sexual reproduction.
gamin /'gæmɪn/ *noun* street urchin; impudent child.
gamine /gæ'mi:n/ *noun* girl gamin; attractively mischievous or boyish girl.
gamma /'gæmə/ *noun* third letter of Greek alphabet (Γ, γ). □ **gamma rays** very short X-rays emitted by radioactive substances.
gammon /'gæmən/ *noun* back end of side of bacon, including leg.
gammy /'gæmɪ/ *adjective* (**-ier**, **-iest**) *slang* (of leg etc.) crippled.
gamut /'gæmət/ *noun* entire range or scope. □ **run the gamut of** experience or perform complete range of.
gamy /'geɪmɪ/ *adjective* (**-ier**, **-iest**) smelling or tasting like high game.
gander /'gændə/ *noun* male goose.
gang ● *noun* set of associates, esp. for criminal purposes; set of workers, slaves, or prisoners. ● *verb colloquial* (+ *up with*) act together with; (+ *up on*) combine against.
ganger /'gæŋə/ *noun* foreman of gang of workers.
gangling /'gæŋglɪŋ/ *adjective* (of person) tall and thin, lanky.
ganglion /'gæŋglɪən/ *noun* (*plural* **ganglia** or **-s**) knot on nerve containing assemblage of nerve cells.
gangly *adjective* (**-ier**, **-iest**) gangling.
gangplank /'gæŋplæŋk/ *noun* plank for walking on to or off boat etc.
gangrene /'gæŋgri:n/ *noun* death of body tissue, usually caused by obstruction of circulation. □ **gangrenous** *adjective*.
gangster /'gæŋstə/ *noun* member of gang of violent criminals.
gangue /gæŋ/ *noun* valueless part of ore deposit.
gangway *noun* passage, esp. between rows of seats; opening in ship's bulwarks; bridge.
gannet /'gænɪt/ *noun* large seabird; *slang* greedy person.
gantry /'gæntrɪ/ *noun* (*plural* **-ies**) structure supporting travelling crane, railway or road signals, rocket-launching equipment, etc.
gaol etc. = JAIL etc.
gap *noun* empty space, interval; deficiency; breach in hedge, wall, etc.; wide divergence.
gape ● *verb* (**-ping**) open mouth wide; be or become wide open; (+ *at*) stare at. ● *noun* open-mouthed stare; opening.
garage /'gærɑ:dʒ/ ● *noun* building for keeping vehicle(s) in; establishment selling petrol etc. or repairing and selling vehicles. ● *verb* (**-ging**) put or keep in garage.
garb ● *noun* clothing, esp. of distinctive kind. ● *verb* dress.
garbage /'gɑ:bɪdʒ/ *noun US* refuse; *colloquial* nonsense.
garble /'gɑ:b(ə)l/ *verb* (**-ling**) (esp. as **garbled** *adjective*) distort or confuse (facts, statements, etc.).
garden /'gɑ:d(ə)n/ ● *noun* piece of ground for growing flowers, fruit, or vegetables, or for recreation; (esp. in *plural*) public pleasure-grounds. ● *verb* cultivate or tend garden. □ **garden centre** place selling plants and garden equipment. □ **gardener** *noun*; **gardening** *noun*.
gardenia /gɑ:'di:nɪə/ *noun* tree or shrub with fragrant flowers.
gargantuan /gɑ:'gæntjʊən/ *adjective* gigantic.
gargle /'gɑ:g(ə)l/ ● *verb* (**-ling**) rinse (throat) with liquid kept in motion by breath. ● *noun* liquid so used.
gargoyle /'gɑ:gɔɪl/ *noun* grotesque carved spout projecting from gutter of building.
garish /'geərɪʃ/ *adjective* obtrusively bright, gaudy. □ **garishly** *adverb*; **garishness** *noun*.
garland /'gɑ:lənd/ ● *noun* wreath of flowers etc. as decoration. ● *verb* adorn or crown with garland(s).
garlic /'gɑ:lɪk/ *noun* plant with pungent bulb used in cookery. □ **garlicky** *adjective colloquial*.
garment /'gɑ:mənt/ *noun* article of dress.
garner /'gɑ:nə/ ● *verb* collect, store. ● *noun* storehouse for corn etc.
garnet /'gɑ:nɪt/ *noun* glassy mineral, esp. red kind used as gem.
garnish /'gɑ:nɪʃ/ ● *verb* decorate (esp. food). ● *noun* decoration, esp. to food.
garret /'gærɪt/ *noun* room, esp. small, cold, etc. immediately under roof.
garrison /'gærɪs(ə)n/ ● *noun* troops stationed in town. ● *verb* (**-n-**) provide with or occupy as garrison.
garrotte /gə'rɒt/ (also **garotte**, *US* **garrote**) ● *verb* (**garrotting**, *US* **garroting**) execute by strangulation, esp. with wire collar. ● *noun* device for this.
garrulous /'gærələs/ *adjective* talkative. □ **garrulity** /gə'ru:lɪtɪ/ *noun*; **garrulousness** *noun*.
garter /'gɑ:tə/ *noun* band to keep sock or stocking up; (**the Garter**) (badge of) highest order of English knighthood. □ **garter stitch** plain knitting stitch.
gas /gæs/ ● *noun* (*plural* **-es**) any airlike substance (i.e. not liquid or solid); such substance (esp. coal gas or natural gas) used as fuel; gas used as anaesthetic; poisonous gas used in war; *US colloquial* petrol; *slang* empty talk, boasting; *slang* amusing thing or person. ● *verb* (**gases**, **gassed**, **gassing**) expose to gas, esp. to kill; *colloquial* talk emptily or boastfully. □ **gasbag** *slang* empty talker; **gas chamber** room filled with poisonous gas to kill people or animals; **gasholder** gasometer; **gas mask** respirator for protection against harmful gases; **gas ring** ring pierced with gas jet(s) for cooking etc.; **gasworks** place where gas is manufactured.
gaseous /'gæsɪəs/ *adjective* of or as gas.
gash ● *noun* long deep cut or wound. ● *verb* make gash in.
gasify /'gæsɪfaɪ/ *verb* (**-ies**, **-ied**) convert into gas. □ **gasification** *noun*.
gasket /'gæskɪt/ *noun* sheet or ring of rubber etc. to seal joint between metal surfaces.
gasoline /'gæsəli:n/ *noun* (also **gasolene**) *US* petrol.
gasometer /gæ'sɒmɪtə/ *noun* large tank from which gas is distributed.
gasp /gɑ:sp/ ● *verb* catch breath with open mouth; utter with gasps. ● *noun* convulsive catching of breath.
gassy /'gæsɪ/ *adjective* (**-ier**, **-iest**) of, like, or full of gas; *colloquial* verbose.
gastric /'gæstrɪk/ *adjective* of stomach. □ **gastric flu** *colloquial* intestinal disorder of unknown cause; **gastric juice** digestive fluid secreted by stomach glands.
gastritis /gæ'straɪtɪs/ *noun* inflammation of stomach.
gastroenteritis /gæstrəʊentə'raɪtɪs/ *noun* inflammation of stomach and intestines.
gastronome /'gæstrənəʊm/ *noun* gourmet. □ **gastronomic** /-'nɒm-/ *adjective*; **gastronomical** /-'nɒm-/ *adjective*; **gastronomically** /-'nɒm-/ *adverb*; **gastronomy** /-'strɒn-/ *noun*.
gastropod /'gæstrəpɒd/ *noun* mollusc that moves using underside of abdomen, e.g. snail.
gate *noun* barrier, usually hinged, used to close opening in wall, fence, etc.; such opening; means of entrance or exit; numbered place of access to aircraft at airport; device regulating passage of water in lock etc.; number of people paying to enter stadium etc.,

money thus taken. □ **gateleg (table)** table with legs in gatelike frame for supporting folding flaps; **gatepost** post at either side of gate; **gateway** opening closed by gate, means of access.

gateau /ˈgætəʊ/ *noun* (*plural* **-s** or **-x** /-z/) large rich elaborate cake.

gatecrash *verb* attend (party etc.) uninvited. □ **gatecrasher** *noun*.

gather /ˈgæðə/ ● *verb* bring or come together; collect (harvest, dust, etc.); infer, deduce; increase (speed); summon up (energy etc.); draw together in folds or wrinkles; (of boil etc.) come to a head. ● *noun* fold or pleat.

gathering *noun* assembly; pus-filled swelling.

GATT /gæt/ *abbreviation* General Agreement on Tariffs and Trade.

gauche /gəʊʃ/ *adjective* socially awkward, tactless. □ **gauchely** *adverb*; **gaucheness** *noun*.

gaucho /ˈgaʊtʃəʊ/ *noun* (*plural* **-s**) cowboy in S. American pampas.

gaudy /ˈgɔːdɪ/ *adjective* (**-ier**, **-iest**) tastelessly showy. □ **gaudily** *adverb*; **gaudiness** *noun*.

gauge /geɪdʒ/ (*US* **gage**) ● *noun* standard measure; instrument for measuring; distance between rails or opposite wheels; capacity, extent; criterion, test. ● *verb* (**-ging**) measure exactly; measure contents of; estimate.

Gaul /gɔːl/ *noun* inhabitant of ancient Gaul. □ **Gaulish** *adjective & noun*.

gaunt /gɔːnt/ *adjective* lean, haggard; grim. □ **gauntness** *noun*.

gauntlet[1] /ˈgɔːntlɪt/ *noun* glove with long loose wrist; *historical* armoured glove.

gauntlet[2] /ˈgɔːntlɪt/ *noun* □ **run the gauntlet** undergo criticism, pass between two rows of people wielding sticks etc., as punishment.

gauze /gɔːz/ *noun* thin transparent fabric; fine mesh of wire etc. □ **gauzy** *adjective* (**-ier**, **-iest**).

gave *past* of GIVE.

gavel /ˈgæv(ə)l/ *noun* auctioneer's, chairman's, or judge's hammer.

gavotte /gəˈvɒt/ *noun* 18th-c. French dance; music for this.

gawk ● *verb colloquial* gawp. ● *noun* awkward or bashful person. □ **gawky** *adjective* (**-ier**, **-iest**).

gawp *verb colloquial* stare stupidly.

gay ● *adjective* light-hearted, cheerful; showy; homosexual; *colloquial* carefree. ● *noun* (esp. male) homosexual.

gayety *US* = GAIETY.

gaze ● *verb* (**-zing**) (+ *at*, *into*, *on*, etc.) look fixedly. ● *noun* intent look.

gazebo /gəˈziːbəʊ/ *noun* (*plural* **-s**) summer house etc. giving view.

gazelle /gəˈzel/ *noun* (*plural* same or **-s**) small graceful antelope.

gazette /gəˈzet/ ● *noun* newspaper; official publication. ● *verb* (**-tting**) publish in official gazette.

gazetteer /gæzɪˈtɪə/ *noun* geographical index.

gazump /gəˈzʌmp/ *verb colloquial* raise price after accepting offer from (buyer); swindle.

gazunder /gəˈzʌndə/ *verb colloquial* lower an offer made to (seller) just before exchange of contracts.

GB *abbreviation* Great Britain.

GBH *abbreviation* grievous bodily harm.

GC *abbreviation* George Cross.

GCE *abbreviation* General Certificate of Education.

GCSE *abbreviation* General Certificate of Secondary Education.

GDR *abbreviation historical* German Democratic Republic.

gear /gɪə/ ● *noun* (often in *plural*) set of toothed wheels working together, esp. those connecting engine to road wheels; particular setting of these; equipment; *colloquial* clothing. ● *verb* (+ *to*) adjust or adapt to; (often + *up*) equip with gears; (+ *up*) make ready. □ **gearbox** (case enclosing) gears of machine or vehicle; **gear lever** lever moved to engage or change gear; **in gear** with gear engaged.

gecko /ˈgekəʊ/ *noun* (*plural* **-s**) tropical house-lizard.

gee /dʒiː/ *interjection expressing surprise etc.*

geese *plural* of GOOSE.

geezer /ˈgiːzə/ *noun slang* man, esp. old one.

Geiger counter /ˈgaɪgə/ *noun* instrument for measuring radioactivity.

geisha /ˈgeɪʃə/ *noun* (*plural* same or **-s**) Japanese professional hostess and entertainer.

gel /dʒel/ ● *noun* semi-solid jelly-like colloid; jelly-like substance for hair. ● *verb* (**-ll-**) form gel; jell.

gelatin /ˈdʒelətɪn/ *noun* (also **gelatine** /-tiːn/) transparent tasteless substance used in cookery, photography, etc. □ **gelatinous** /dʒɪˈlæt-/ *adjective*.

geld /geld/ *verb* castrate.

gelding /ˈgeldɪŋ/ *noun* castrated horse etc.

gelignite /ˈdʒelɪgnaɪt/ *noun* nitroglycerine explosive.

gem /dʒem/ ● *noun* precious stone; thing or person of great beauty or worth. ● *verb* (**-mm-**) adorn (as) with gems.

Gemini /ˈdʒemɪnaɪ/ *noun* third sign of zodiac.

Gen. *abbreviation* General.

gen /dʒen/ *slang* ● *noun* information. ● *verb* (**-nn-**) (+ *up*) gain or give information.

gendarme /ˈʒɒndɑːm/ *noun* police officer in France etc.

gender /ˈdʒendə/ *noun* (grammatical) classification roughly corresponding to the two sexes and sexlessness; one of these classes; person's sex.

gene /dʒiːn/ *noun* unit in chromosome, controlling particular inherited characteristic.

genealogy /dʒiːnɪˈælədʒɪ/ *noun* (*plural* **-ies**) descent traced continuously from ancestor, pedigree; study of pedigrees. □ **genealogical** /-əˈlɒdʒ-/ *adjective*; **genealogically** /-əˈlɒdʒ-/ *adverb*; **genealogist** *noun*.

genera *plural* of GENUS.

general /ˈdʒenər(ə)l/ ● *adjective* including, affecting or applicable to (nearly) all; prevalent, usual; vague; not partial or particular; lacking detail; chief, head. ● *noun* army officer next below Field Marshal; commander of army. □ **general anaesthetic** one affecting whole body; **general election** national election of representatives to parliament; **general practice** work of **general practitioner**, doctor treating cases of all kinds; **general strike** simultaneous strike of workers in all or most trades; **in general** as a rule, usually.

generalissimo /dʒenərəˈlɪsɪməʊ/ *noun* (*plural* **-s**) commander of combined forces.

generality /dʒenəˈrælɪtɪ/ *noun* (*plural* **-ies**) general statement; general applicability; indefiniteness; (+ *of*) majority of.

generalize /ˈdʒenərəlaɪz/ *verb* (also **-ise**) (**-zing** or **-sing**) speak in general or indefinite terms, form general notion(s); reduce to general statement; infer (rule etc.) from particular cases; bring into general use. □ **generalization** *noun*.

generally /ˈdʒenərəlɪ/ *adverb* usually; in most respects; in general sense; in most cases.

generate /ˈdʒenəreɪt/ *verb* (**-ting**) bring into existence, produce.

generation *noun* all people born about same time; stage in family history or in (esp. technological) development; period of about 30 years; production, esp. of electricity; procreation.

generative /ˈdʒenərətɪv/ *adjective* of procreation; productive.

generator *noun* dynamo; apparatus for producing gas, steam, etc.

generic /dʒɪˈnerɪk/ *adjective* characteristic of or relating to class or genus; not specific or special; (of esp. drug) with no brand name. ▫ **generically** *adverb*.

generous /ˈdʒenərəs/ *adjective* giving or given freely; magnanimous; abundant. ▫ **generosity** /-ˈrɒs-/ *noun*; **generously** *adverb*.

genesis /ˈdʒenɪsɪs/ *noun* origin, mode of formation; (**Genesis**) first book of Old Testament.

genetic /dʒɪˈnetɪk/ *adjective* of genetics; of or in origin. ▫ **genetic engineering** manipulation of DNA to modify hereditary features; **genetic fingerprinting** identification of individuals by DNA patterns. ▫ **genetically** *adverb*.

genetics *plural noun* (treated as *singular*) study of heredity and variation among animals and plants. ▫ **geneticist** /-sɪst/ *noun*.

genial /ˈdʒi:nɪəl/ *adjective* sociable, kindly; mild, warm; cheering. ▫ **geniality** /-ˈæl-/ *noun*; **genially** *adverb*.

genie /ˈdʒi:nɪ/ *noun* (*plural* **genii** /-nɪaɪ/) sprite or goblin of Arabian tales.

genital /ˈdʒenɪt(ə)l/ ● *adjective* of animal reproduction or reproductive organs. ● *noun* (in *plural*; also **genitalia**) external reproductive organs.

genitive /ˈdʒenɪtɪv/ *Grammar* ● *noun* case expressing possession, origin, etc., corresponding to *of*, *from*, etc. ● *adjective* of or in this case.

genius /ˈdʒi:nɪəs/ *noun* (*plural* **-es**) exceptional natural ability; person having this; guardian spirit.

genocide /ˈdʒenəsaɪd/ *noun* mass murder, esp. among particular race or nation.

genre /ˈʒɑ̃rə/ *noun* kind or style of art etc.; portrayal of scenes from ordinary life.

gent /dʒent/ *noun colloquial* gentleman; (**the Gents**) *colloquial* men's public lavatory.

genteel /dʒenˈti:l/ *adjective* affectedly refined; upper-class.

gentian /ˈdʒenʃ(ə)n/ *noun* mountain plant with usually blue flowers. ▫ **gentian violet** violet dye used as antiseptic.

Gentile /ˈdʒentaɪl/ ● *adjective* not Jewish; heathen. ● *noun* non-Jewish person.

gentility /dʒenˈtɪlɪtɪ/ *noun* social superiority; genteel habits.

gentle /ˈdʒent(ə)l/ *adjective* (**-r**, **-st**) not rough or severe; mild, kind; well-born; quiet. ▫ **gentleness** *noun*; **gently** *adverb*.

gentlefolk /ˈdʒentəlfəʊk/ *noun* people of good family.

gentleman /ˈdʒentəlmən/ *noun* man; chivalrous well-bred man; man of good social position. ▫ **gentlemanly** *adjective*.

gentlewoman *noun archaic* woman of good birth or breeding.

gentrification /dʒentrɪfɪˈkeɪʃ(ə)n/ *noun* upgrading of working-class urban area by arrival of affluent residents. ▫ **gentrify** *verb* (**-ies**, **-ied**).

gentry /ˈdʒentrɪ/ *plural noun* people next below nobility; *derogatory* people.

genuflect /ˈdʒenju:flekt/ *verb* bend knee, esp. in worship. ▫ **genuflection**, **genuflexion** /-ˈflekʃ(ə)n/ *noun*.

genuine /ˈdʒenju:ɪn/ *adjective* really coming from its reputed source; properly so called; not sham. ▫ **genuinely** *adverb*; **genuineness** *noun*.

genus /ˈdʒi:nəs/ *noun* (*plural* **genera** /ˈdʒenərə/) group of animals or plants with common structural characteristics, usually containing several species; kind, class.

geocentric /dʒi:əˈsentrɪk/ *adjective* considered as viewed from earth's centre; having earth as centre.

geode /ˈdʒi:əʊd/ *noun* cavity lined with crystals; rock containing this.

geodesic /dʒi:əʊˈdi:zɪk/ *adjective* (also **geodetic** /-ˈdet-/) of geodesy. ▫ **geodesic line** shortest possible line on surface between two points.

geodesy /dʒi:ˈɒdɪsɪ/ *noun* study of shape and area of the earth.

geography /dʒɪˈɒgrəfɪ/ *noun* science of earth's physical features, resources, etc.; features of place. ▫ **geographer** *noun*; **geographic(al)** /-əˈgræf-/ *adjective*; **geographically** /-əˈgræf-/ *adverb*.

geology /dʒɪˈɒlədʒɪ/ *noun* science of earth's crust, strata, etc. ▫ **geological** /-əˈlɒdʒ-/ *adjective*; **geologist** *noun*.

geometry /dʒɪˈɒmətrɪ/ *noun* science of properties and relations of lines, surfaces, and solids. ▫ **geometric(al)** /-əˈmet-/ *adjective*; **geometrician** /-ˈtrɪʃ(ə)n/ *noun*.

Geordie /ˈdʒɔ:dɪ/ *noun* native of Tyneside.

georgette /dʒɔ:ˈdʒet/ *noun* kind of fine dress material.

Georgian /ˈdʒɔ:dʒ(ə)n/ *adjective* of time of George I–IV or George V and VI.

geranium /dʒəˈreɪnɪəm/ *noun* (*plural* **-s**) cultivated pelargonium; herb or shrub with fruit shaped like crane's bill.

gerbil /ˈdʒɜ:bɪl/ *noun* mouselike desert rodent with long hind legs.

geriatric /dʒerɪˈætrɪk/ ● *adjective* of geriatrics or old people; *derogatory* old. ● *noun often derogatory* old person.

geriatrics /dʒerɪˈætrɪks/ *plural noun* (usually treated as *singular*) branch of medicine dealing with health and care of old people. ▫ **geriatrician** /-əˈtrɪʃ(ə)n/ *noun*.

germ /dʒɜ:m/ *noun* microbe; portion of organism capable of developing into new one; thing that may develop; rudiment, elementary principle.

German /ˈdʒɜ:mən/ ● *noun* (*plural* **-s**) native, national, or language of Germany. ● *adjective* of Germany. ▫ **German measles** disease like mild measles; **German shepherd (dog)** Alsatian.

german /ˈdʒɜ:mən/ *adjective* (placed after *brother*, *sister*, or *cousin*) having same two parents or grandparents.

germander /dʒɜ:ˈmændə/ *noun* plant of mint family.

germane /dʒɜ:ˈmeɪn/ *adjective* (usually + *to*) relevant.

Germanic /dʒɜ:ˈmænɪk/ ● *adjective* having German characteristics. ● *noun* group of languages including English, German, Dutch, and Scandinavian languages.

germicide /ˈdʒɜ:mɪsaɪd/ *noun* substance that destroys germs. ▫ **germicidal** /-ˈsaɪd(ə)l/ *adjective*.

germinal /ˈdʒɜ:mɪn(ə)l/ *adjective* of germs; in earliest stage of development.

germinate /ˈdʒɜ:mɪneɪt/ *verb* (**-ting**) (cause to) sprout or bud. ▫ **germination** *noun*.

gerontology /dʒerɒnˈtɒlədʒɪ/ *noun* study of old age and ageing.

gerrymander /dʒerɪˈmændə/ *verb* manipulate boundaries of (constituency etc.) to gain unfair electoral advantage.

gerund /ˈdʒerənd/ *noun* verbal noun, in English ending in *-ing*.

Gestapo /geˈstɑ:pəʊ/ *noun historical* Nazi secret police.

gestation /dʒeˈsteɪʃ(ə)n/ *noun* carrying or being carried in womb between conception and birth; this period; development of plan etc. ▫ **gestate** *verb* (**-ting**).

gesticulate /dʒeˈstɪkjʊleɪt/ *verb* (**-ting**) use gestures instead of or with speech. ▫ **gesticulation** *noun*.

gesture /ˈdʒestʃə/ ● *noun* meaningful movement of limb or body; action performed as courtesy or to indicate intention. ● *verb* (**-ring**) gesticulate.

get /get/ *verb* (**getting**; *past* **got**; *past participle* **got** or *US* **gotten**) obtain, earn; fetch, procure; go to reach or catch; prepare (meal); (cause to) reach some state or become; obtain from calculation; contract (disease); contact; have (punishment) inflicted on one; succeed in bringing, placing, etc.; (cause to) succeed in coming or going; *colloquial* understand, annoy, harm, attract; *archaic* beget. □ **get about** go from place to place; **get across** communicate; **get along** (often + *with*) live harmoniously; **get around** = GET ABOUT; **get at** reach, get hold of, *colloquial* imply, *colloquial* nag; **get away** escape; **getaway** *noun*; **get by** *colloquial* cope; **get in** obtain place at college etc., win election; **get off** alight (from), *colloquial* escape with little or no punishment, start, depart, (+ *with*) *colloquial* start sexual relationship with; **get on** make progress, manage, advance, enter (bus etc.), (often + *with*) live harmoniously, (usually as **be getting on**) age; **get out of** avoid, escape; **get over** recover from, surmount; **get round** coax or cajole (person), evade (law etc.), (+ *to*) deal with (task) in due course; **get through** pass (exam etc.), use up (resources), make contact by telephone, (+ *to*) succeed in making (person) understand; **get-together** *colloquial* social assembly; **get up** rise esp. from bed, (of wind etc.) strengthen, organize, stimulate, arrange appearance of; **get-up** *colloquial* style of dress etc.; **have got** possess, (+ *to do*) must.

geyser /ˈgiːzə/ *noun* hot spring; apparatus for heating water.

ghastly /ˈgɑːstlɪ/ *adjective* (**-ier**, **-iest**) horrible, frightful; deathlike, pallid.

ghee /giː/ *noun* Indian clarified butter.

gherkin /ˈgɜːkɪn/ *noun* small cucumber for pickling.

ghetto /ˈgetəʊ/ *noun* (*plural* **-s**) part of city occupied by minority group; *historical* Jews' quarter in city; segregated group or area. □ **ghetto-blaster** large portable radio or cassette player.

ghost /gəʊst/ ● *noun* apparition of dead person etc., disembodied spirit; (+ *of*) semblance; secondary image in defective telescope or television picture. ● *verb* (often + *for*) act as ghost-writer of (book etc.). □ **ghost-writer** writer doing work for which another takes credit. □ **ghostly** *adjective* (**-ier**, **-iest**).

ghoul /guːl/ *noun* person morbidly interested in death etc.; evil spirit; (in Arabic mythology) spirit preying on corpses. □ **ghoulish** *adjective*.

GHQ *abbreviation* General Headquarters.

ghyll = GILL³.

GI /dʒiːˈaɪ/ *noun* soldier in US army.

giant /ˈdʒaɪənt/ ● *noun* mythical being of human form but superhuman size; person, animal, or thing of extraordinary size, ability, etc. ● *adjective* gigantic.

gibber /ˈdʒɪbə/ *verb* chatter inarticulately.

gibberish /ˈdʒɪbərɪʃ/ *noun* unintelligible or meaningless speech or sounds.

gibbet /ˈdʒɪbɪt/ *noun historical* gallows; post with arm from which executed criminal was hung after execution.

gibbon /ˈgɪbən/ *noun* long-armed ape.

gibbous /ˈgɪbəs/ *adjective* convex; (of moon etc.) with bright part greater than semicircle.

gibe /dʒaɪb/ (also **jibe**) ● *verb* (**-bing**) (often + *at*) jeer, mock. ● *noun* jeering remark, taunt.

giblets /ˈdʒɪblɪts/ *plural noun* liver, gizzard, etc. of bird removed and usually cooked separately.

giddy /ˈgɪdɪ/ *adjective* (**-ier**, **-iest**) dizzy, tending to fall or stagger; mentally intoxicated; excitable, flighty; making dizzy. □ **giddiness** *noun*.

gift /gɪft/ *noun* thing given, present; talent; *colloqu* easy task.

gifted *adjective* talented.

gig¹ /gɪg/ *noun* light two-wheeled one-horse carriag light boat on ship; rowing boat, esp. for racing.

gig² /gɪg/ *colloquial* ● *noun* engagement to play musi usually on one occasion. ● *verb* (**-gg-**) perform gig.

giga- /ˈgɪgə/ *combining form* one thousand million.

gigantic /dʒaɪˈgæntɪk/ *adjective* huge, giant-like.

giggle /ˈgɪg(ə)l/ ● *verb* (**-ling**) laugh in half-su pressed spasms. ● *noun* such laugh; *colloquial* amusin person or thing. □ **giggly** *adjective* (**-ier**, **-iest**).

gigolo /ˈdʒɪgələʊ/ *noun* (*plural* **-s**) young man paid b older woman to be escort or lover.

gild¹ /gɪld/ *verb* (*past participle* **gilded** or as *adjective* **gil** cover thinly with gold; tinge with golden colour.

gild² = GUILD.

gill¹ /gɪl/ *noun* (usually in *plural*) respiratory orga of fish etc.; vertical radial plate on underside c mushroom etc.; flesh below person's jaws and ear

gill² /dʒɪl/ *noun* quarter-pint measure.

gill³ /gɪl/ *noun* (also **ghyll**) deep wooded ravine; na row mountain torrent.

gillie /ˈgɪlɪ/ *noun Scottish* man or boy attending hunte or angler.

gillyflower /ˈdʒɪlɪflaʊə/ *noun* clove-scented flowe e.g. wallflower.

gilt¹ /gɪlt/ ● *adjective* overlaid (as) with gold. ● *nou* gilding. □ **gilt-edged** (of securities etc.) having hig degree of reliability.

gilt² /gɪlt/ *noun* young sow.

gimbals /ˈdʒɪmb(ə)lz/ *plural noun* contrivance of ring etc. for keeping things horizontal in ship, aircraf etc.

gimcrack /ˈdʒɪmkræk/ ● *adjective* flimsy, tawdry ● *noun* showy ornament etc.

gimlet /ˈgɪmlɪt/ *noun* small boring-tool.

gimmick /ˈgɪmɪk/ *noun* trick or device, esp. to attrac attention. □ **gimmickry** *noun*; **gimmicky** *adjective*.

gimp /ˈgɪmp/ *noun* twist of silk etc. with cord or wir running through.

gin¹ /dʒɪn/ *noun* spirit distilled from grain or mal and flavoured with juniper berries.

gin² /dʒɪn/ ● *noun* snare, trap; machine separatin cotton from seeds; kind of crane or windlass. ● *ver* (**-nn-**) treat (cotton) in gin; trap.

ginger /ˈdʒɪndʒə/ ● *noun* hot spicy root used in cooking; plant having this root; light reddish-yellow ● *adjective* of ginger colour. ● *verb* flavour with ginger (+ *up*) enliven. □ **ginger ale**, **beer** ginger-flavoure fizzy drinks; **gingerbread** ginger-flavoured treacl cake; **ginger group** group urging party or movemen to stronger action; **ginger-nut** kind of ginger-flavoured biscuit. □ **gingery** *adjective*.

gingerly /ˈdʒɪndʒəlɪ/ ● *adverb* in a careful or cautiou way. ● *adjective* showing extreme care or caution.

gingham /ˈgɪŋəm/ *noun* plain-woven usually checke cotton cloth.

gingivitis /dʒɪndʒɪˈvaɪtɪs/ *noun* inflammation of the gums.

ginkgo /ˈgɪŋkəʊ/ *noun* (*plural* **-s**) tree with fan-shape leaves and yellow flowers.

ginseng /ˈdʒɪnseŋ/ *noun* plant found in E. Asia an N. America; medicinal root of this.

Gipsy = GYPSY.

giraffe /dʒɪˈrɑːf/ *noun* (*plural* same or **-s**) tall 4-legge African animal with long neck.

gird /gɜːd/ (*past & past participle* **girded** or **girt**) encircl or fasten (on) with waistbelt etc. □ **gird (up) one's loins** prepare for action.

girder /ˈgɜːdə/ *noun* iron or steel beam or compound structure used for bridges etc.

girdle[1] /ˈgɜːd(ə)l/ ● *noun* belt or cord worn round waist; corset; thing that surrounds; bony support for limbs. ● *verb* (**-ling**) surround with girdle.

girdle[2] /ˈgɜːd(ə)l/ *noun Scottish & Northern English* = GRIDDLE.

girl /gɜːl/ *noun* female child; *colloquial* young woman; *colloquial* girlfriend; female servant. ▫ **girlfriend** person's regular female companion; **girl guide** Guide; **girl scout** female Scout. ▫ **girlhood** *noun*; **girlish** *adjective*; **girly** *adjective*.

giro /ˈdʒaɪrəʊ/ ● *noun* (*plural* **-s**) system of credit transfer between banks, Post Offices, etc.; cheque or payment by giro. ● *verb* (**-es**, **-ed**) pay by giro.

girt *past & past participle* of GIRD.

girth /gɜːθ/ *noun* distance round a thing; band round body of horse securing saddle.

gist /ˈdʒɪst/ *noun* substance or essence of a matter.

gîte /ʒiːt/ *noun* furnished holiday house in French countryside. [French]

give /gɪv/ ● *verb* (**-ving**; *past* **gave**; *past participle* **given**) transfer possession of freely; provide with; administer; deliver; (often + *for*) make over in exchange or payment; confer; accord; pledge; perform (action etc.); utter, declare; yield to pressure; collapse; yield as product; consign; devote; present, offer (one's hand, arm, etc.); impart, be source of; concede; assume, grant, specify. ● *noun* capacity to comply; elasticity. ▫ **give and take** exchange of talk or ideas, ability to compromise; **give away** transfer as gift, hand over (bride) to bridegroom, betray or expose; **give-away** *colloquial* unintentional disclosure, free or inexpensive thing; **give in** yield, hand in; **give off** emit; **give out** announce, emit, distribute, be exhausted, run short; **give over** *colloquial* desist, hand over, devote; **give up** resign, surrender, part with, renounce hope (of), cease (activity). ▫ **giver** *noun*.

given ● *past participle* of GIVE. ● *adjective* (+ *to*) disposed or prone to; assumed as basis of reasoning etc.; fixed, specified.

gizmo /ˈgɪzməʊ/ *noun* (*plural* **-s**) gadget.

gizzard /ˈgɪzəd/ *noun* bird's second stomach, for grinding food.

glacé /ˈglæseɪ/ *adjective* (of fruit) preserved in sugar; (of cloth etc.) smooth, polished.

glacial /ˈgleɪʃ(ə)l/ *adjective* of ice or glaciers.

glaciated /ˈgleɪsɪeɪtɪd/ *adjective* marked or polished by moving ice; covered with glaciers. ▫ **glaciation** *noun*.

glacier /ˈglæsɪə/ *noun* slowly moving mass of ice on land.

glad *adjective* (**-dd-**) pleased; joyful, cheerful. ▫ **glad rags** *colloquial* best clothes. ▫ **gladden** *verb*; **gladly** *adverb*; **gladness** *noun*.

glade *noun* clear space in forest.

gladiator /ˈglædɪeɪtə/ *noun historical* trained fighter in ancient Roman shows. ▫ **gladiatorial** /-ɪəˈtɔːrɪəl/ *adjective*.

gladiolus /glædɪˈəʊləs/ *noun* (*plural* **-li** /-laɪ/) plant of lily family with bright flower-spikes.

gladsome *adjective poetical* cheerful, joyful.

Gladstone bag /ˈglædst(ə)n/ *noun* kind of light portmanteau.

glair *noun* white of egg; similar or derivative viscous substance.

glamour /ˈglæmə/ *noun* (*US* **glamor**) physical, esp. cosmetic, attractiveness; alluring or exciting beauty or charm. ▫ **glamorize** *verb* (also **-ise**) (**-zing** or **-sing**); **glamorous** *adjective*; **glamorously** *adverb*.

glance /glɑːns/ ● *verb* (**-cing**) (often + *down*, *up*, *over*, etc.) look or refer briefly; (often + *off*) hit at fine angle and bounce off. ● *noun* brief look; flash, gleam; swift oblique stroke in cricket. ▫ **at a glance** immediately on looking.

gland *noun* organ etc. secreting substances for use in body; similar organ in plant.

glanders /ˈglændəz/ *plural noun* contagious horse disease.

glandular /ˈglændjʊlə/ *adjective* of gland(s). ▫ **glandular fever** infectious disease with swelling of lymph glands.

glare /gleə/ ● *verb* (**-ring**) look fiercely; shine oppressively; (esp. as **glaring** *adjective*) be very evident. ● *noun* oppressive light or public attention; fierce look; tawdry brilliance. ▫ **glaringly** *adverb*.

glasnost /ˈglæznɒst/ *noun* (in former USSR) policy of more open government.

glass /glɑːs/ ● *noun* hard, brittle, usually transparent substance made by fusing sand with soda and lime etc.; glass objects collectively; glass drinking vessel, its contents; glazed frame for plants; barometer; covering of watch-face; lens; (in *plural*) spectacles, binoculars; mirror. ● *verb* (usually as **glassed** *adjective*) fit with glass. ▫ **glass-blowing** blowing of semi-molten glass to make glass objects; **glass fibre** glass filaments made into fabric or reinforcing plastic; **glasshouse** greenhouse, *slang* military prison; **glass-paper** paper covered with powdered glass, for smoothing etc.; **glass wool** fine glass fibres for packing and insulation. ▫ **glassful** *noun* (*plural* **-s**).

glassy /ˈglɑːsɪ/ *adjective* (**-ier**, **-iest**) like glass; (of eye etc.) dull, fixed.

glaucoma /glɔːˈkəʊmə/ *noun* eye disease with pressure in eyeball and gradual loss of sight.

glaze ● *verb* (**-zing**) fit with glass or windows; cover (pottery etc.) with vitreous substance or (surface) with smooth shiny coating; (often + *over*) (of eyes) become glassy. ● *noun* substance used for or surface produced by glazing.

glazier /ˈgleɪzɪə/ *noun* person who glazes windows etc.

gleam ● *noun* faint or brief light or show. ● *verb* emit gleam(s).

glean *verb* gather (facts etc.); gather (corn left by reapers). ▫ **gleanings** *plural noun*.

glebe *noun* piece of land yielding revenue to benefice.

glee *noun* mirth, delight; musical composition for several voices. ▫ **gleeful** *adjective*; **gleefully** *adverb*.

glen *noun* narrow valley.

glengarry /glenˈgærɪ/ *noun* (*plural* **-ies**) kind of Highland cap.

glib *adjective* (**-bb-**) speaking or spoken fluently but insincerely. ▫ **glibly** *adverb*; **glibness** *noun*.

glide ● *verb* (**-ding**) move smoothly or continuously; (of aircraft) fly without engine-power; go stealthily. ● *noun* gliding motion.

glider /ˈglaɪdə/ *noun* light aircraft without engine.

glimmer /ˈglɪmə/ ● *verb* shine faintly or intermittently. ● *noun* faint or wavering light; (also **glimmering**) (usually + *of*) small sign.

glimpse /glɪmps/ ● *noun* (often + *of*, *at*) brief view; faint transient appearance. ● *verb* (**-sing**) have brief view of.

glint *verb & noun* flash, glitter.

glissade /glɪˈsɑːd/ ● *noun* controlled slide down snow slope; gliding. ● *verb* (**-ding**) perform glissade.

glissando /glɪˈsændəʊ/ *noun* (*plural* **-di** /-dɪ/ or **-s**) *Music* continuous slide of adjacent notes.

glisten /ˈglɪs(ə)n/ ● *verb* shine like wet or polished surface. ● *noun* glitter.

glitch *noun colloquial* irregularity, malfunction.

glitter /'glɪtə/ ● *verb* shine with brilliant reflected light, sparkle; (often + *with*) be showy. ● *noun* sparkle; showiness; tiny pieces of glittering material.
glitz *noun slang* showy glamour. □ **glitzy** *adjective* (**-ier**, **-iest**).
gloaming /'gləʊmɪŋ/ *noun* twilight.
gloat *verb* (often + *over* etc.) look or ponder with greedy or malicious pleasure.
global /'gləʊb(ə)l/ *adjective* worldwide; all-embracing. □ **global warming** increase in temperature of earth's atmosphere. □ **globally** *adverb*.
globe *noun* spherical object; spherical map of earth; (**the globe**) the earth. □ **globe artichoke** partly edible head of artichoke plant; **globe-trotter** person travelling widely.
globular /'glɒbjʊlə/ *adjective* globe-shaped; composed of globules.
globule /'glɒbju:l/ *noun* small globe, round particle, or drop.
glockenspiel /'glɒkənspi:l/ *noun* musical instrument of bells or metal bars played with hammers.
gloom /glu:m/ *noun* darkness; melancholy, depression.
gloomy /'glu:mɪ/ *adjective* (**-ier**, **-iest**) dark; depressed, depressing.
glorify /'glɔ:rɪfaɪ/ *verb* (**-ies**, **-ied**) make glorious; make seem more splendid than is the case; (as **glorified** *adjective*) treated as more important etc. than it is; extol. □ **glorification** *noun*.
glorious /'glɔ:rɪəs/ *adjective* possessing or conferring glory; *colloquial* splendid, excellent. □ **gloriously** *adverb*.
glory /'glɔ:rɪ/ ● *noun* (*plural* **-ies**) (thing bringing) renown, honourable fame, etc.; adoring praise; resplendent majesty, beauty, etc.; halo of saint. ● *verb* (**-ies**, **-ied**) (often + *in*) take pride.
gloss[1] ● *noun* surface lustre; deceptively attractive appearance; (in full *gloss paint*) paint giving glossy finish. ● *verb* make glossy. □ **gloss over** seek to conceal.
gloss[2] ● *noun* explanatory comment added to text; interpretation. ● *verb* add gloss to.
glossary /'glɒsərɪ/ *noun* (*plural* **-ies**) dictionary of technical or special words, esp. as appendix.
glossy ● *adjective* (**-ier**, **-iest**) smooth and shiny; printed on such paper. ● *noun* (*plural* **-ies**) *colloquial* glossy magazine or photograph.
glottal /'glɒt(ə)l/ *adjective* of the glottis. □ **glottal stop** sound produced by sudden opening or shutting of glottis.
glottis /'glɒtɪs/ *noun* opening at upper end of windpipe between vocal cords.
glove /glʌv/ ● *noun* hand-covering for protection, warmth, etc.; boxing glove. ● *verb* (**-ving**) cover or provide with gloves. □ **glove compartment** recess for small articles in car dashboard; **glove puppet** small puppet fitted on hand.
glow /gləʊ/ ● *verb* emit flameless light and heat; (often + *with*) feel bodily heat or strong emotion; show warm colour; (as **glowing** *adjective*) expressing pride or satisfaction. ● *noun* glowing state, appearance, or feeling. □ **glow-worm** beetle that emits green light.
glower /'glaʊə/ *verb* (often + *at*) scowl.
glucose /'glu:kəʊs/ *noun* kind of sugar found in blood, fruits, etc.
glue ● *noun* substance used as adhesive. ● *verb* (**glues**, **glued**, **gluing** or **glueing**) attach (as) with glue; hold closely. □ **glue ear** blocking of (esp. child's) Eustachian tube; **glue-sniffing** inhalation of fumes from adhesives as intoxicant. □ **gluey** *adjective* (**gluier**, **gluiest**).
glum *adjective* (**-mm-**) dejected, sullen. □ **glumly** *adverb*; **glumness** *noun*.
glut ● *verb* (**-tt-**) feed or indulge to the full, satiate; overstock. ● *noun* excessive supply; surfeit.
gluten /'glu:t(ə)n/ *noun* sticky part of wheat flour.
glutinous /'glu:tɪnəs/ *adjective* sticky, gluelike.
glutton /'glʌt(ə)n/ *noun* excessive eater; (often + *for*) *colloquial* insatiably eager person; voracious animal of weasel family. □ **gluttonous** *adjective*; **gluttonously** *adverb*; **gluttony** *noun*.
glycerine /'glɪsəri:n/ *noun* (also **glycerol**, *US* **glycerin**) colourless sweet viscous liquid used in medicines, explosives, etc.
gm *abbreviation* gram(s).
GMT *abbreviation* Greenwich Mean Time.
gnarled /nɑ:ld/ *adjective* knobbly, twisted, rugged.
gnash /næʃ/ *verb* grind (one's teeth); (of teeth) strike together.
gnat /næt/ *noun* small biting fly.
gnaw /nɔ:/ *verb* (usually + *away* etc.) wear away by biting; (often + *at*, *into*) bite persistently; corrode; torment.
gneiss /naɪs/ *noun* coarse-grained rock of feldspar, quartz, and mica.
gnome /nəʊm/ *noun* dwarf, goblin; (esp. in *plural*) *colloquial* person with sinister influence, esp. financial.
gnomic /'nəʊmɪk/ *adjective* of aphorisms; sententious.
gnomon /'nəʊmɒn/ *noun* rod etc. on sundial, showing time by its shadow.
gnostic /'nɒstɪk/ ● *adjective* of knowledge; having special mystic knowledge. ● *noun* (**Gnostic**) early Christian heretic claiming mystical knowledge. □ **Gnosticism** /-sɪz(ə)m/ *noun*.
GNP *abbreviation* gross national product.
gnu /nu:/ *noun* (*plural* same or **-s**) oxlike antelope.
go[1] ● *verb* (*3rd singular present* **goes** /gəʊz/; *past* **went**; *past participle* **gone** /gɒn/) walk, travel, proceed; participate in (doing something); extend in a certain direction; depart; move, function; make specified movement or sound, *colloquial* say; be, become; elapse, be traversed; (of song etc.) have specified wording etc.; match; be regularly kept, fit; be successful; be sold, (of money) be spent; be relinquished, fail, decline, collapse; be acceptable or accepted; (often + *by*, *with*, *on*, *upon*) be guided by; attend regularly; (+ *to*, *towards*) contribute to; (+ *for*) apply to. ● *noun* (*plural* **goes**) animation; vigorous activity; success; turn, attempt. □ **go-ahead** *adjective* enterprising, *noun* permission to proceed; **go-between** intermediary; **go down** descend, become less, decrease (in price), subside, sink, (of sun) set, deteriorate, cease to function, be recorded, be swallowed, (+ *with*) find acceptance with, *colloquial* leave university, *colloquial* be sent to prison, (+ *with*) become ill with; **go for** go to fetch, prefer, choose, pass or be accounted as, *colloquial* attack, *colloquial* strive to attain; **go-getter** *colloquial* pushily enterprising person; **go in for** compete or engage in; **go-kart**, **-cart** miniature racing car with skeleton body; **go off** explode, deteriorate, fall asleep, begin to dislike; **go off well**, **badly** succeed, fail; **go on** continue, proceed, *colloquial* talk at great length, (+ *at*) *colloquial* nag, use as evidence; **go out** leave room or house, be extinguished, be broadcast, cease to be fashionable, (often + *with*) have romantic or sexual relationship, (usually + *to*) sympathize; **go over** inspect details of, rehearse; **go round** spin, revolve, suffice for all; **go slow** work slowly as industrial protest; **go under** sink, succumb, fail; **go up** rise, increase (in price), be consumed (in flames etc.), explode, *colloquial* enter university; **go without** manage without or forgo

(something); **have a go at** attack, attempt; **on the go** *colloquial* active.

go[2] *noun* Japanese board game.

goad ● *verb* urge with goad; (usually + *on*, *into*) irritate, stimulate. ● *noun* spiked stick for urging cattle; thing that torments or incites.

goal *noun* object of effort; destination; structure into or through which ball is to be driven in certain games; point(s) so won; point where race ends. □ **goalkeeper** player protecting goal; **goalpost** either post supporting crossbar of goal.

goalie *noun colloquial* goalkeeper.

goat *noun* small domesticated mammal with horns and (in male) beard; licentious man; *colloquial* fool. □ **get (person's) goat** *colloquial* irritate him or her.

goatee /gəʊ'tiː/ *noun* small pointed beard.

gob[1] *noun slang* mouth. □ **gobsmacked** *slang* flabbergasted; **gob-stopper** large hard sweet.

gob[2] *slang* ● *noun* clot of slimy matter. ● *verb* (**-bb-**) spit.

gobbet /'gɒbɪt/ *noun* lump of flesh, food, etc.; extract from text set for translation or comment.

gobble[1] /'gɒb(ə)l/ *verb* (**-ling**) eat hurriedly and noisily.

gobble[2] /'gɒb(ə)l/ *verb* (**-ling**) (of turkeycock) make guttural sound; speak thus.

gobbledegook /'gɒbəldɪguːk/ *noun* (also **gobbledeygook**) *colloquial* pompous or unintelligible jargon.

goblet /'gɒblɪt/ *noun* drinking vessel with foot and stem.

goblin /'gɒblɪn/ *noun* mischievous demon.

goby /'gəʊbɪ/ *noun* (*plural* **-ies**) small fish with sucker on underside.

god *noun* superhuman being worshipped as possessing power over nature, human fortunes, etc.; (**God**) creator and ruler of universe; idol; adored person; (**the gods**) (occupants of) gallery in theatre. □ **godchild** person in relation to godparent; **god-daughter** female godchild; **godfather** male godparent; **God-fearing** religious; **God-forsaken** dismal; **godmother** female godparent; **godparent** person who responds on behalf of candidate at baptism; **godsend** unexpected welcome event or acquisition; **godson** male godchild. □ **godlike** *adjective*.

goddess /'gɒdɪs/ *noun* female deity; adored woman.

godhead *noun* divine nature; deity.

godless *adjective* impious, wicked; not believing in God. □ **godlessness** *noun*.

godly /'gɒdlɪ/ *adjective* (**-ier**, **-iest**) pious, devout. □ **godliness** *noun*.

goer /'gəʊə/ *noun* person or thing that goes; *colloquial* lively or sexually promiscuous person. □ **-goer** regular attender.

goggle /'gɒg(ə)l/ ● *verb* (**-ling**) (often + *at*) look with wide-open eyes; (of eyes) be rolled, project; roll (eyes). ● *adjective* (of eyes) protuberant, rolling. ● *noun* (in *plural*) spectacles for protecting eyes. □ **goggle-box** *colloquial* television set.

going /'gəʊɪŋ/ ● *noun* condition of ground as affecting riding etc. ● *adjective* in action; existing, available; current, prevalent. □ **going concern** thriving business; **going-over** (*plural* **goings-over**) *colloquial* inspection or overhaul, *slang* thrashing; **goings-on** strange conduct.

goitre /'gɔɪtə/ *noun* (*US* **goiter**) abnormal enlargement of thyroid gland.

gold /gəʊld/ ● *noun* precious yellow metal; colour of this; coins or articles of gold. ● *adjective* of or coloured like gold. □ **gold-digger** *slang* woman who goes after men for their money; **gold field** area with naturally occurring gold; **goldfinch** brightly coloured songbird; **goldfish** small golden-red Chinese carp; **gold leaf** gold beaten into thin sheet; **gold medal** medal given usually as first prize; **gold plate** vessels of gold, material plated with gold; **gold-plate** plate with gold; **gold-rush** rush to newly discovered gold field; **goldsmith** worker in gold; **gold standard** financial system in which value of money is based on gold.

golden /'gəʊld(ə)n/ *adjective* of gold; coloured or shining like gold; precious, excellent. □ **golden handshake** *colloquial* gratuity as compensation for redundancy or compulsory retirement; **golden jubilee** 50th anniversary of reign; **golden mean** principle of moderation; **golden retriever** retriever with gold-coloured coat; **golden wedding** 50th anniversary of wedding.

golf ● *noun* game in which small hard ball is struck with clubs over ground into series of small holes. ● *verb* play golf. □ **golf ball** ball used in golf, spherical unit carrying type in some electric typewriters; **golf course** area of land on which golf is played; **golf club** club used in golf, (premises of) association for playing golf. □ **golfer** *noun*.

golliwog /'gɒlɪwɒg/ *noun* black-faced soft doll with fuzzy hair.

gonad /'gəʊnæd/ *noun* animal organ producing gametes, e.g. testis or ovary.

gondola /'gɒndələ/ *noun* light Venetian canal-boat; car suspended from airship.

gondolier /gɒndə'lɪə/ *noun* oarsman of gondola.

gone /gɒn/ ● *past participle* of GO[1]. ● *adjective* (of time) past; lost, hopeless, dead; *colloquial* pregnant for specified time.

goner /'gɒnə/ *noun slang* person or thing that is doomed or irrevocably lost.

gong *noun* metal disc giving resonant note when struck; saucer-shaped bell; *slang* medal.

gonorrhoea /gɒnə'riːə/ *noun* (*US* **gonorrhea**) a venereal disease.

goo *noun colloquial* sticky or slimy substance; sickly sentiment. □ **gooey** *adjective* (**gooier**, **gooiest**).

good /gʊd/ ● *adjective* (**better**, **best**) having right qualities, adequate; competent, effective; kind, morally excellent, virtuous; well-behaved; agreeable; considerable; not less than; beneficial; valid. ● *noun* (only in *singular*) good quality or circumstance; (in *plural*) movable property, merchandise. □ **good-for-nothing** worthless (person); **good humour** genial mood; **good-looking** handsome; **good nature** kindly disposition; **goodwill** kindly feeling, established value-enhancing reputation of a business.

goodbye /gʊd'baɪ/ (*US* **goodby**) ● *interjection expressing good wishes at parting*. ● *noun* (*plural* **-byes** or *US* **-bys**) parting, farewell.

goodly /'gʊdlɪ/ *adjective* (**-ier**, **-iest**) handsome; of imposing size etc.

goodness /'gʊdnɪs/ *noun* virtue; excellence; kindness; nutriment.

goody /'gʊdɪ/ ● *noun* (*plural* **-ies**) *colloquial* good person; (usually in *plural*) something good or attractive, esp. to eat. ● *interjection expressing childish delight*. □ **goody-goody** *colloquial* (person who is) smugly or obtrusively virtuous.

goof /guːf/ *slang* ● *noun* foolish or stupid person or mistake. ● *verb* bungle, blunder. □ **goofy** *adjective* (**-ier**, **-iest**).

googly /'guːglɪ/ *noun* (*plural* **-ies**) *Cricket* ball bowled so as to bounce in unexpected direction.

goon /guːn/ *noun slang* stupid person; *esp. US* hired ruffian.

goose /guːs/ *noun* (*plural* **geese** /giːs/) large web-footed bird; female of this; *colloquial* simpleton.

□ **goose-flesh**, **-pimples** (*US* **-bumps**) bristling state of skin due to cold or fright; **goose-step** stiff-legged marching step.

gooseberry /'gʊzbərɪ/ *noun* (*plural* **-ies**) small green usually sour berry; thorny shrub bearing this.

gopher /'gəʊfə/ *noun* American burrowing rodent.

gore[1] *noun* clotted blood.

gore[2] *verb* (**-ring**) pierce with horn, tusk, etc.

gore[3] ● *noun* wedge-shaped piece in garment; triangular or tapering piece in umbrella etc. ● *verb* (**-ring**) shape with gore.

gorge ● *noun* narrow opening between hills; surfeit; contents of stomach. ● *verb* (**-ging**) feed greedily; satiate.

gorgeous /'gɔ:dʒəs/ *adjective* richly coloured; *colloquial* splendid; *colloquial* strikingly beautiful. □ **gorgeously** *adverb*.

gorgon /'gɔ:gən/ *noun* (in Greek mythology) any of 3 snake-haired sisters able to turn people to stone; frightening or repulsive woman.

Gorgonzola /gɔ:gən'zəʊlə/ *noun* rich blue-veined Italian cheese.

gorilla /gə'rɪlə/ *noun* largest anthropoid ape.

gormless /'gɔ:mlɪs/ *adjective colloquial* foolish, lacking sense. □ **gormlessly** *adverb*.

gorse /gɔ:s/ *noun* prickly shrub with yellow flowers.

Gorsedd /'gɔ:seð/ *noun* Druidic order meeting before eisteddfod.

gory /'gɔ:rɪ/ *adjective* (**-ier**, **-iest**) involving bloodshed; bloodstained.

gosh *interjection expressing surprise.*

goshawk /'gɒshɔ:k/ *noun* large short-winged hawk.

gosling /'gɒzlɪŋ/ *noun* young goose.

gospel /'gɒsp(ə)l/ *noun* teaching or revelation of Christ; (**Gospel**) (each of 4 books giving) account of Christ's life in New Testament; portion of this read at church service; thing regarded as absolutely true. □ **gospel music** black American religious singing.

gossamer /'gɒsəmə/ ● *noun* filmy substance of small spiders' webs; delicate filmy material. ● *adjective* light and flimsy as gossamer.

gossip /'gɒsɪp/ ● *noun* unconstrained talk or writing, esp. about people; idle talk; person indulging in gossip. ● *verb* (**-p-**) talk or write gossip. □ **gossip column** regular newspaper column of gossip. □ **gossipy** *adjective*.

got *past & past participle of* GET.

Goth *noun* member of Germanic tribe that invaded Roman Empire in 3rd–5th c.

Gothic *adjective* of Goths; *Architecture* in the pointed-arch style prevalent in W. Europe in 12th–16th c.; (of novel etc.) in a style popular in 18th & 19th c., with supernatural or horrifying events.

gotten *US past participle of* GET.

gouache /gu:'ɑ:ʃ/ *noun* painting with opaque watercolour; pigments used for this.

Gouda /'gaʊdə/ *noun* flat round Dutch cheese.

gouge /gaʊdʒ/ ● *noun* concave-bladed chisel. ● *verb* (**-ging**) cut or (+ *out*) force out (as) with gouge.

goulash /'gu:læʃ/ *noun* stew of meat and vegetables seasoned with paprika.

gourd /gʊəd/ *noun* fleshy fruit of trailing or climbing cucumber-like plant; this plant; dried rind of this fruit used as bottle etc.

gourmand /'gʊəmənd/ *noun* glutton; gourmet.

■ **Usage** The use of *gourmand* to mean a 'gourmet' is considered incorrect by some people.

gourmet /'gʊəmeɪ/ *noun* connoisseur of good food.

gout /gaʊt/ *noun* disease with inflammation of small joints. □ **gouty** *adjective*.

govern /'gʌv(ə)n/ *verb* rule with authority; conduct policy and affairs of; influence or determine; curb, control.

governance *noun* act, manner, or function of governing.

governess /'gʌvənɪs/ *noun* woman employed to teach children in private household.

government *noun* manner or system of governing; group of people governing state. □ **governmental** /-'men-/ *adjective*.

governor *noun* ruler; official governing a province, town, etc.; executive head of each State of US; member of governing body of institution; *slang* one's employer or father; automatic regulator controlling speed of engine etc. □ **Governor-General** representative of Crown in Commonwealth country regarding Queen as head of state. □ **governorship** *noun*.

gown /gaʊn/ *noun* woman's, esp. formal or elegant, long dress; official robe of alderman, judge, cleric, academic, etc.; surgeon's overall.

goy *noun* (*plural* **-im** or **-s**) *Jewish name for* non-Jew.

GP *abbreviation* general practitioner.

GPO *abbreviation* General Post Office.

gr *abbreviation* (also **gr.**) gram(s); grain(s); gross.

grab ● *verb* (**-bb-**) seize suddenly; take greedily; *slang* impress; (+ *at*) snatch at. ● *noun* sudden clutch or attempt to seize; device for clutching.

grace ● *noun* elegance of proportions, manner, or movement; courteous good will; attractive feature; unmerited favour of God; goodwill; delay granted; thanksgiving at meals; (**His**, **Her**, **Your Grace**) *title used of or to duke, duchess, or archbishop.* ● *verb* (**-cing**) (often + *with*) add grace to; bestow honour on. □ **grace note** *Music* note embellishing melody.

graceful *adjective* full of grace or elegance. □ **gracefully** *adverb*.

graceless *adjective* lacking grace or charm.

gracious /'greɪʃəs/ *adjective* kindly, esp. to inferiors; merciful. □ **gracious living** elegant way of life. □ **graciously** *adverb*; **graciousness** *noun*.

gradate /grə'deɪt/ *verb* (**-ting**) (cause to) pass gradually from one shade to another; arrange in steps or grades.

gradation *noun* (usually in *plural*) stage of transition or advance; degree in rank, intensity, etc.; arrangement in grades. □ **gradational** *adjective*.

grade ● *noun* degree in rank, merit, etc.; mark indicating quality of student's work; slope; *US* class in school. ● *verb* (**-ding**) arrange in grades; (+ *up*, *down*, *off*, *into*, etc.) pass between grades; give grade to; reduce to easy gradients. □ **make the grade** succeed.

gradient /'greɪdɪənt/ *noun* sloping road etc.; amount of such slope.

gradual /'grædʒʊəl/ *adjective* happening by degrees; not steep or abrupt. □ **gradually** *adverb*.

graduate ● *noun* /'grædʒʊət/ holder of academic degree. ● *verb* /-eɪt/ (**-ting**) obtain academic degree; (+ *to*) move up to; mark in degrees or portions; arrange in gradations; apportion (tax etc.) according to scale. □ **graduation** *noun*.

graffiti /grə'fi:tɪ/ *plural noun* (*singular* **graffito**) writing or drawing on wall etc.

■ **Usage** *Graffiti* should be used with plural verbs, as in *Graffiti have appeared everywhere.*

graft[1] /grɑ:ft/ ● *noun* shoot or scion planted in slit in another stock; piece of transplanted living tissue; *slang* hard work. ● *verb* (often + *in*, *on*, *together*, etc.) insert (graft); transplant (living tissue); (+ *in*, *on*) insert or fix (thing) permanently to another; *slang* work hard.

graft² /grɑːft/ *colloquial* ● *noun* practices for securing illicit gains in politics or business; such gains. ● *verb* seek or make graft.

Grail *noun* (in full **Holy Grail**) legendary cup or platter used by Christ at Last Supper.

grain ● *noun* fruit or seed of cereal; wheat or allied food-grass; corn; particle of sand, salt, etc.; unit of weight (0.065 g); least possible amount; texture in skin, wood, stone, etc.; arrangement of lines of fibre in wood. ● *verb* paint in imitation of grain of wood; form into grains.

gram *noun* (also **gramme**) metric unit of weight.

grammar /ˈgræmə/ *noun* study or rules of relations between words in (a) language; application of such rules; book on grammar. □ **grammar school** *esp. historical* secondary school with academic curriculum.

grammarian /grəˈmeərɪən/ *noun* expert in grammar.

grammatical /grəˈmætɪk(ə)l/ *adjective* of or according to grammar.

gramophone /ˈgræməfəʊn/ *noun* record player.

grampus /ˈgræmpəs/ *noun* (*plural* **-es**) sea mammal of dolphin family.

gran *noun colloquial* grandmother.

granary /ˈgrænərɪ/ *noun* (*plural* **-ies**) storehouse for grain; region producing much corn.

grand ● *adjective* splendid, imposing; chief, of chief importance; (**Grand**) of highest rank; *colloquial* excellent. ● *noun* grand piano; (*plural* same) (usually in *plural*) *slang* 1,000 dollars or pounds. □ **grand jury** jury to examine validity of accusation before trial; **grand piano** piano with horizontal strings; **grand slam** winning of all of group of matches; **grand total** sum of other totals. □ **grandly** *adverb*; **grandness** *noun*.

grandad *noun* (also **grand-dad**) *colloquial* grandfather.

grandchild *noun* child of one's son or daughter.

granddaughter *noun* one's child's daughter.

grandee /grænˈdiː/ *noun* Spanish or Portuguese noble of highest rank; great personage.

grandeur /ˈgrændʒə/ *noun* majesty, splendour, dignity; high rank, eminence.

grandfather *noun* one's parent's father. □ **grandfather clock** clock in tall wooden case.

grandiloquent /grænˈdɪləkwənt/ *adjective* pompous or inflated in language. □ **grandiloquence** *noun*.

grandiose /ˈgrændɪəʊs/ *adjective* imposing; planned on large scale. □ **grandiosity** /-ˈɒsɪtɪ/ *noun*.

grandma *noun colloquial* grandmother.

grandmother *noun* one's parent's mother.

grandparent *noun* one's parent's parent.

Grand Prix /grɑ̃ ˈpriː/ *noun* any of several international motor-racing events.

grandson *noun* one's child's son.

grandstand *noun* main stand for spectators at racecourse etc.

grange /greɪndʒ/ *noun* country house with farm buildings.

granite /ˈgrænɪt/ *noun* granular crystalline rock of quartz, mica, etc.

granny /ˈgrænɪ/ *noun* (also **grannie**) (*plural* **-ies**) *colloquial* grandmother; (in full **granny knot**) reef-knot crossed wrong way.

grant /grɑːnt/ ● *verb* consent to fulfil; allow to have; give formally, transfer legally; (often + *that*) admit, concede. ● *noun* granting; thing, esp. money, granted. □ **take for granted** assume to be true, cease to appreciate through familiarity. □ **grantor** /grɑːnˈtɔː/ *noun*.

granular /ˈgrænjʊlə/ *adjective* of or like grains or granules.

granulate /ˈgrænjʊleɪt/ *verb* (**-ting**) form into grains; roughen surface of. □ **granulation** *noun*.

granule /ˈgrænjuːl/ *noun* small grain.

grape *noun* usually green or purple berry growing in clusters on vine. □ **grapeshot** *historical* small balls as scattering charge for cannon etc.; **grapevine** vine, means of transmission of rumour.

grapefruit /ˈgreɪpfruːt/ *noun* (*plural* same) large round usually yellow citrus fruit.

graph /grɑːf/ ● *noun* symbolic diagram representing relation between two or more variables. ● *verb* plot on graph.

graphic /ˈgræfɪk/ *adjective* of writing, drawing, etc.; vividly descriptive. □ **graphic arts** visual and technical arts involving design or lettering. □ **graphically** *adverb*.

graphics *plural noun* (usually treated as *singular*) products of graphic arts; use of diagrams in calculation and design.

graphite /ˈgræfaɪt/ *noun* crystalline form of carbon used as lubricant, in pencils, etc.

graphology /grəˈfɒlədʒɪ/ *noun* study of handwriting. □ **graphologist** *noun*.

grapnel /ˈgræpn(ə)l/ *noun* iron-clawed instrument for dragging or grasping; small many-fluked anchor.

grapple /ˈgræp(ə)l/ ● *verb* (**-ling**) (often + *with*) fight at close quarters; (+ *with*) try to manage (problem etc.); grip with hands, come to close quarters with; seize. ● *noun* hold (as) of wrestler; contest at close quarters; clutching-instrument. □ **grappling-iron**, **-hook** grapnel.

grasp /grɑːsp/ ● *verb* clutch at, seize greedily; hold firmly; understand, realize. ● *noun* firm hold, grip; (+ *of*) mastery, mental hold.

grasping *adjective* avaricious.

grass /grɑːs/ ● *noun* (any of several) plants with bladelike leaves eaten by ruminants; pasture land; grass-covered ground; grazing; *slang* marijuana; *slang* informer. ● *verb* cover with turf; *US* pasture; *slang* betray, inform police. □ **grass roots** fundamental level or source, rank and file; **grass snake** small non-poisonous snake; **grass widow**, **widower** person whose husband or wife is temporarily absent. □ **grassy** *adjective* (**-ier**, **-iest**).

grasshopper /ˈgrɑːshɒpə/ *noun* jumping and chirping insect.

grate¹ *verb* (**-ting**) reduce to small particles by rubbing on rough surface; (often + *against*, *on*) rub with, utter with, or make harsh sound, have irritating effect; grind, creak. □ **grater** *noun*.

grate² *noun* (metal) frame holding fuel in fireplace etc.

grateful /ˈgreɪtfʊl/ *adjective* thankful; feeling or showing gratitude. □ **gratefully** *adverb*.

gratify /ˈgrætɪfaɪ/ *verb* (**-ies**, **-ied**) please, delight; indulge. □ **gratification** *noun*.

grating /ˈgreɪtɪŋ/ *noun* framework of parallel or crossed metal bars.

gratis /ˈgrɑːtɪs/ *adverb & adjective* free, without charge.

gratitude /ˈgrætɪtjuːd/ *noun* being thankful.

gratuitous /grəˈtjuːɪtəs/ *adjective* given or done gratis; uncalled-for, motiveless. □ **gratuitously** *adverb*; **gratuitousness** *noun*.

gratuity /grəˈtjuːɪtɪ/ *noun* (*plural* **-ies**) money given for good service.

grave¹ /greɪv/ *noun* hole dug for burial of corpse; mound or monument over this; (**the grave**) death. □ **gravestone** (usually inscribed) stone over grave; **graveyard** burial ground.

grave² /greɪv/ *adjective* weighty, serious; dignified, solemn; threatening. □ **gravely** *adverb*.

grave[3] /greɪv/ *verb* (**-ving**; *past participle* **graven** or **graved**) (+ *in*, *on*) fix indelibly on (memory etc.); *archaic* engrave, carve. □ **graven image** idol.

grave[4] /grɑːv/ *noun* (in full **grave accent**) mark (`) over letter indicating pronunciation.

gravel /ˈgræv(ə)l/ ● *noun* coarse sand and small stones; formation of crystals in bladder. ● *verb* (**-ll-**; *US* **-l-**) lay with gravel.

gravelly /ˈgrævəlɪ/ *adjective* of or like gravel; (of voice) deep and rough-sounding.

gravid /ˈgrævɪd/ *adjective* pregnant.

gravitate /ˈgrævɪteɪt/ *verb* (**-ting**) (+ *to*, *towards*) move, be attracted, or tend by force of gravity to(wards); sink (as) by gravity.

gravitation *noun* attraction between each particle of matter and every other; effect of this, esp. falling of bodies to earth. □ **gravitational** *adjective*.

gravity /ˈgrævɪtɪ/ *noun* force that attracts body to centre of earth etc.; intensity of this; weight; importance, seriousness; solemnity.

gravy /ˈgreɪvɪ/ *noun* (*plural* **-ies**) (sauce made from) juices exuding from meat in and after cooking. □ **gravy-boat** long shallow jug for gravy; **gravy train** *slang* source of easy financial benefit.

gray *US* = GREY.

grayling *noun* (*plural* same) silver-grey freshwater fish.

graze[1] *verb* (**-zing**) feed on growing grass; pasture cattle.

graze[2] ● *verb* (**-zing**) rub or scrape (part of body); (+ *against*, *along*, etc.) touch lightly in passing, move with such contact. ● *noun* abrasion.

grazier /ˈgreɪzɪə/ *noun* person who feeds cattle for market.

grazing *noun* grassland suitable for pasturage.

grease /griːs/ ● *noun* oily or fatty matter, esp. as lubricant; melted fat of dead animal. ● *verb* (**-sing**) smear or lubricate with grease. □ **greasepaint** actor's make-up; **greaseproof** impervious to grease.

greasy /ˈgriːsɪ/ *adjective* (**-ier**, **-iest**) of, like, smeared with, or having too much grease; (of person, manner) unctuous. □ **greasiness** *noun*.

great /greɪt/ ● *adjective* above average in bulk, number, extent, or intensity; important, pre-eminent; imposing, distinguished; of remarkable ability etc.; (+ *at*, *on*) competent, well-informed; *colloquial* very satisfactory. ● *noun* great person or thing. □ **greatcoat** heavy overcoat; **Great Dane** dog of large short-haired breed. □ **greatness** *noun*.

great- /greɪt/ *combining form* (of family relationships) one degree more remote (*great-grandfather*, *great-niece*, etc.).

greatly *adverb* much.

grebe *noun* a diving bird.

Grecian /ˈgriːʃ(ə)n/ *adjective* Greek.

greed *noun* excessive desire, esp. for food or wealth.

greedy /ˈgriːdɪ/ *adjective* (**-ier**, **-iest**) showing greed; (+ *for*, *to do*) eager. □ **greedily** *adverb*.

Greek ● *noun* native, national, or language of Greece. ● *adjective* of Greece.

green ● *adjective* coloured like grass; unripe, unseasoned; not dried, smoked, or tanned; inexperienced; jealous; (also **Green**) concerned with protection of environment, not harmful to environment. ● *noun* green colour, paint, clothes, etc.; piece of grassy public land; grassy area for special purpose; (in *plural*) green vegetables; (also **Green**) supporter of protection of environment. □ **green belt** area of open land for preservation round city; **green card** motorist's international insurance document; **greenfinch** bird with greenish plumage; **green fingers** *colloquial* skill in gardening; **greenfly** green aphid; **greengage** round green plum; **greenhorn** novice; **green light** signal or permission to proceed; **green pound** the agreed value of the pound for payments to agricultural producers in EC; **green-room** room in theatre for actors when off stage; **greensward** grassy turf.

greenery *noun* green foliage.

greengrocer /ˈgriːngrəʊsə/ *noun* retailer of fruit and vegetables. □ **greengrocery** *noun* (*plural* **-ies**).

greenhouse *noun* structure with sides and roof mainly of glass, for rearing plants. □ **greenhouse effect** trapping of sun's warmth in earth's lower atmosphere; **greenhouse gas** gas contributing to greenhouse effect, esp. carbon dioxide.

greet *verb* address on meeting or arrival; receive or acknowledge in specified way; become apparent to (eye, ear, etc.).

greeting *noun* act or words used to greet. □ **greetings card** decorative card carrying goodwill message etc.

gregarious /grɪˈgeərɪəs/ *adjective* fond of company; living in flocks etc. □ **gregariousness** *noun*.

Gregorian calendar /grɪˈgɔːrɪən/ *noun* calendar introduced in 1582 by Pope Gregory XIII.

Gregorian chant /grɪˈgɔːrɪən/ *noun* form of plainsong named after Pope Gregory I.

gremlin /ˈgremlɪn/ *noun colloquial* mischievous sprite said to cause mechanical faults etc.

grenade /grɪˈneɪd/ *noun* small bomb thrown by hand or shot from rifle.

grenadier /grenəˈdɪə/ *noun* (**Grenadier**) member of first regiment of royal household infantry; *historical* soldier armed with grenades.

grew *past* of GROW.

grey /greɪ/ (*US* **gray**) ● *adjective* of colour between black and white; clouded, dull; (of hair) turning white, (of person) having grey hair; anonymous, unidentifiable; undistinguished, boring. ● *noun* grey colour, paint, clothes, etc.; grey horse. ● *verb* make or become grey. □ **grey area** indefinite situation or topic; **Grey Friar** Franciscan friar; **grey matter** darker tissues of brain, *colloquial* intelligence.

greyhound *noun* slender swift dog used in racing.

greylag *noun* European wild goose.

grid *noun* grating; system of numbered squares for map references; network of lines, electric power connections, etc.; pattern of lines marking starting-place on motor-racing track.

griddle /ˈgrɪd(ə)l/ *noun* iron plate placed over heat for baking etc.

gridiron /ˈgrɪdaɪən/ *noun* barred metal frame for broiling or grilling; American football field.

grief /griːf/ *noun* (cause of) intense sorrow. □ **come to grief** meet with disaster.

grievance *noun* real or imagined cause for complaint.

grieve /griːv/ *verb* (**-ving**) (cause to) feel grief.

grievous /ˈgriːvəs/ *adjective* severe; causing grief; injurious; flagrant, heinous. □ **grievously** *adverb*.

griffin /ˈgrɪfɪn/ *noun* (also **gryphon** /-f(ə)n/) mythical creature with eagle's head and wings and lion's body.

griffon /ˈgrɪf(ə)n/ *noun* small coarse-haired terrier-like dog; large vulture; griffin.

grill ● *noun* device on cooker for radiating heat downwards; gridiron; grilled food; (in full **grill room**) restaurant specializing in grills. ● *verb* cook under grill or on gridiron; subject to or experience extreme heat; subject to severe questioning.

grille /grɪl/ *noun* (also **grill**) grating, latticed screen; metal grid protecting vehicle radiator.

grilse /grɪls/ *noun* (*plural* same or **-s**) young salmon that has been to the sea only once.

grim *adjective* (**-mm-**) of stern appearance; harsh, merciless; ghastly, joyless; unpleasant. □ **grimly** *adverb*; **grimness** *noun*.

grimace /ˈgrɪməs/ ● *noun* distortion of face made in disgust etc. or to amuse. ● *verb* (**-cing**) make grimace.

grime ● *noun* deeply ingrained dirt. ● *verb* (**-ming**) blacken, befoul. □ **grimy** *adjective* (**-ier**, **-iest**).

grin ● *verb* (**-nn-**) smile broadly. ● *noun* broad smile.

grind /graɪnd/ ● *verb* (*past & past participle* **ground** /graʊnd/) crush to small particles; sharpen; rub gratingly; (often + *down*) oppress; (often + *away*) work or study hard. ● *noun* grinding; *colloquial* hard dull work. □ **grindstone** thick revolving abrasive disc for grinding, sharpening, etc. □ **grinder** *noun*.

grip ● *verb* (**-pp-**) grasp tightly; take firm hold; compel attention of. ● *noun* firm hold, grasp; way of holding; power of holding attention; intellectual mastery; control of one's behaviour; part of machine that grips; part of weapon etc. that is gripped; hairgrip; travelling bag.

gripe ● *verb* (**-ping**) *colloquial* complain; affect with colic. ● *noun* (usually in *plural*) colic; *colloquial* complaint. □ **Gripe Water** *proprietary term* medicine to relieve colic in babies.

grisly /ˈgrɪzlɪ/ *adjective* (**-ier**, **-iest**) causing horror, disgust, or fear.

grist *noun* corn for grinding. □ **grist to the mill** source of profit or advantage.

gristle /ˈgrɪs(ə)l/ *noun* tough flexible tissue; cartilage. □ **gristly** *adjective*.

grit ● *noun* small particles of sand etc.; coarse sandstone; *colloquial* pluck, endurance. ● *verb* (**-tt-**) spread grit on (icy roads etc.); clench (teeth); make grating sound. □ **gritty** *adjective* (**-ier**, **-iest**).

grits *plural noun* coarse oatmeal; unground husked oats.

grizzle /ˈgrɪz(ə)l/ *verb* (**-ling**) *colloquial* cry fretfully. □ **grizzly** *adjective* (**-ier**, **-iest**).

grizzled *adjective* grey-haired.

grizzly /ˈgrɪzlɪ/ ● *adjective* (**-ier**, **-iest**) grey-haired. ● *noun* (*plural* **-ies**) (in full **grizzly bear**) large fierce N. American bear.

groan ● *verb* make deep sound expressing pain, grief, or disapproval; (usually + *under*, *beneath*, *with*) be loaded or oppressed. ● *noun* sound made in groaning.

groat *noun historical* silver coin worth 4 old pence.

groats *plural noun* hulled or crushed grain, esp. oats.

grocer /ˈgrəʊsə/ *noun* dealer in food and household provisions.

grocery /ˈgrəʊsərɪ/ *noun* (*plural* **-ies**) grocer's trade, shop, or (in *plural*) goods.

grog *noun* drink of spirit (originally rum) and water.

groggy /ˈgrɒgɪ/ *adjective* (**-ier**, **-iest**) incapable, unsteady. □ **groggily** *adverb*.

groin[1] ● *noun* depression between belly and thigh; edge formed by intersecting vaults. ● *verb* build with groins.

groin[2] *US* = GROYNE.

grommet /ˈgrɒmɪt/ *noun* eyelet placed in hole to protect or insulate rope or cable passed through it; tube passed through eardrum to middle ear.

groom /gru:m/ ● *noun* person employed to tend horses; bridegroom. ● *verb* tend (horse); give neat or attractive appearance to; prepare (person) for office or occasion etc.

groove ● *noun* channel, elongated hollow; spiral cut in gramophone record for needle. ● *verb* (**-ving**) make groove(s) in.

groovy /ˈgru:vɪ/ *adjective* (**-ier**, **-iest**) *slang* excellent; of or like a groove.

grope ● *verb* (**-ping**) (usually + *for*) feel about or search blindly; (+ *for*, *after*) search mentally; fondle clumsily for sexual pleasure; feel (one's way). ● *noun* act of groping.

grosgrain /ˈgrəʊgreɪn/ *noun* corded fabric of silk etc.

gross /grəʊs/ ● *adjective* overfed, bloated; coarse, indecent; flagrant; total, not net. ● *verb* produce as gross profit. ● *noun* (*plural* same) 12 dozen. □ **grossly** *adverb*.

grotesque /grəʊˈtesk/ ● *adjective* comically or repulsively distorted; incongruous, absurd. ● *noun* decoration interweaving human and animal features; comically distorted figure or design. □ **grotesquely** *adverb*.

grotto /ˈgrɒtəʊ/ *noun* (*plural* **-es** or **-s**) picturesque cave; structure imitating cave.

grotty /ˈgrɒtɪ/ *adjective* (**-ier**, **-iest**) *slang* unpleasant, dirty, ugly.

grouch /graʊtʃ/ *colloquial* ● *verb* grumble. ● *noun* grumbler; complaint; sulky grumbling mood. □ **grouchy** *adjective* (**-ier**, **-iest**).

ground[1] /graʊnd/ ● *noun* surface of earth; extent of subject; (often in *plural*) foundation, motive; area of special kind; (in *plural*) enclosed land attached to house etc.; area or basis for agreement etc.; surface worked on in painting; (in *plural*) dregs; bottom of sea; floor of room etc. ● *verb* prevent from taking off or flying; run aground, strand; (+ *in*) instruct thoroughly; (often as **grounded** *adjective*) (+ *on*) base cause or principle on. □ **ground control** personnel directing landing etc. of aircraft etc.; **ground cover** low-growing plants; **ground floor** storey at ground level; **ground frost** frost on surface of ground; **groundnut** peanut; **ground-rent** rent for land leased for building; **groundsman** person who maintains sports ground; **ground speed** aircraft's speed relative to ground; **ground swell** heavy sea due to distant or past storm etc.; **groundwork** preliminary or basic work.

ground[2] *past & past participle* of GRIND.

grounding *noun* basic instruction.

groundless *adjective* without motive or foundation.

groundsel /ˈgraʊnds(ə)l/ *noun* yellow-flowered weed.

group /gru:p/ ● *noun* number of people or things near, classed, or working together; number of companies under common ownership; pop group; division of air force. ● *verb* form into group; place in group(s). □ **group captain** RAF officer next below air commodore.

groupie *noun slang* ardent follower of touring pop group(s).

grouse[1] /graʊs/ *noun* (*plural* same) game bird with feathered feet.

grouse[2] /graʊs/ *verb* (**-sing**) & *noun colloquial* grumble.

grout /graʊt/ ● *noun* thin fluid mortar. ● *verb* apply grout to.

grove /grəʊv/ *noun* small wood; group of trees.

grovel /ˈgrɒv(ə)l/ *verb* (**-ll-**; *US* **-l-**) behave obsequiously; lie prone.

grow /grəʊ/ *verb* (*past* **grew**; *past participle* **grown**) increase in size, height, amount, etc.; develop or exist as living plant or natural product; produce by cultivation; become gradually; (+ *on*) become more favoured by; (in *passive*; + *over*) be covered with growth. □ **grown-up** adult; **grow up** mature. □ **grower** *noun*.

growl /ˈgraʊl/ ● *verb* (often + *at*) make low guttural sound, usually of anger; rumble. ● *noun* growling sound; angry murmur.

grown *past participle* of GROW.

growth /grəʊθ/ *noun* process of growing; increase; what has grown or is growing; tumour. □ **growth industry** one that is developing rapidly.

groyne /grɔɪn/ *noun* (*US* **groin**) wall built out into sea to stop beach erosion.
grub ● *noun* larva of insect; *colloquial* food. ● *verb* (**-bb-**) dig superficially; (+ *up*, *out*) extract by digging.
grubby /ˈgrʌbɪ/ *adjective* (**-ier**, **-iest**) dirty.
grudge ● *noun* persistent resentment or ill will. ● *verb* (**-ging**) be unwilling to give or allow, feel resentful about (doing something).
gruel /ˈgrʊəl/ *noun* liquid food of oatmeal etc. boiled in milk or water.
gruelling (*US* **grueling**) *adjective* exhausting, punishing.
gruesome /ˈgru:səm/ *adjective* grisly, disgusting.
gruff *adjective* rough-voiced; surly. ◻ **gruffly** *adverb*.
grumble /ˈgrʌmb(ə)l/ ● *verb* (**-ling**) complain peevishly; rumble. ● *noun* complaint; rumble. ◻ **grumbler** *noun*.
grumpy /ˈgrʌmpɪ/ *adjective* (**-ier**, **-iest**) ill-tempered.
grunt ● *noun* low guttural sound characteristic of pig. ● *verb* utter (with) grunt.
Gruyère /ˈgru:jeə/ *noun* kind of Swiss cheese with holes in.
gryphon = GRIFFIN.
guano /ˈgwɑ:nəʊ/ *noun* (*plural* **-s**) excrement of seabirds, used as manure.
guarantee /gærənˈti:/ ● *noun* formal promise or assurance; guaranty; giver of guaranty or security. ● *verb* (**-tees**, **-teed**) give or serve as guarantee for; promise; secure. ◻ **guarantor** *noun*.
guaranty /ˈgærəntɪ/ *noun* (*plural* **-ies**) written or other undertaking to answer for performance of obligation; thing serving as security.
guard /gɑ:d/ ● *verb* (often + *from*, *against*) defend, protect; keep watch, prevent from escaping; keep in check; (+ *against*) take precautions against. ● *noun* vigilant state; protector; soldiers etc. protecting place or person; official in charge of train; (in *plural*) (usually **Guards**) household troops of monarch; device to prevent injury or accident; defensive posture. ◻ **guardhouse**, **guardroom** building or room for accommodating military guard or for detaining prisoners; **guardsman** soldier in guards or Guards.
guarded *adjective* (of remark etc.) cautious. ◻ **guardedly** *adverb*.
guardian /ˈgɑ:dɪən/ *noun* protector, keeper; person having custody of another, esp. minor. ◻ **guardianship** *noun*.
guava /ˈgwɑ:və/ *noun* edible orange acid fruit; tropical tree bearing this.
gubernatorial /gju:bənəˈtɔ:rɪəl/ *adjective US* of governor.
gudgeon[1] /ˈgʌdʒ(ə)n/ *noun* small freshwater fish.
gudgeon[2] /ˈgʌdʒ(ə)n/ *noun* kind of pivot or pin; tubular part of hinge; socket for rudder.
guelder rose /ˈgeldə/ *noun* shrub with round bunches of white flowers.
Guernsey /ˈgɜ:nzɪ/ *noun* (*plural* **-s**) one of breed of cattle from Guernsey; (**guernsey**) type of thick knitted woollen jersey.
guerrilla /gəˈrɪlə/ *noun* (also **guerilla**) member of one of several independent groups fighting against regular forces.
guess /ges/ ● *verb* estimate without calculation or measurement; conjecture, think likely; conjecture rightly. ● *noun* estimate, conjecture. ◻ **guesswork** guessing.
guest /gest/ *noun* person invited to visit another's house or have meal etc. at another's expense, or lodging at hotel etc. ◻ **guest house** superior boarding house.
guestimate /ˈgestɪmət/ *noun* (also **guesstimate**) estimate based on guesswork and calculation.
guffaw /gʌˈfɔ:/ ● *noun* boisterous laugh. ● *verb* utter guffaw.
guidance /ˈgaɪd(ə)ns/ *noun* advice; guiding.
guide /gaɪd/ ● *noun* person who shows the way; conductor of tours; adviser; directing principle; guidebook; (**Guide**) member of girls' organization similar to Scouts. ● *verb* (**-ding**) act as guide to; lead, direct. ◻ **guidebook** book of information about place etc.; **guided missile** missile under remote control or directed by equipment within itself; **guide-dog** dog trained to lead blind person; **guideline** principle directing action.
Guider /ˈgaɪdə/ *noun* adult leader of Guides.
guild /gɪld/ *noun* (also **gild**) society for mutual aid or with common object; medieval association of craftsmen. ◻ **guildhall** meeting-place of medieval guild, town hall.
guilder /ˈgɪldə/ *noun* monetary unit of Netherlands.
guile /gaɪl/ *noun* sly behaviour; treachery, deceit. ◻ **guileless** *adjective*.
guillemot /ˈgɪlɪmɒt/ *noun* kind of auk.
guillotine /ˈgɪləti:n/ ● *noun* beheading machine; machine for cutting paper; method of shortening debate in parliament by fixing time of vote. ● *verb* (**-ning**) use guillotine on.
guilt /gɪlt/ *noun* fact of having committed offence; (feeling of) culpability.
guiltless *adjective* (often + *of*) innocent.
guilty *adjective* (**-ier**, **-iest**) having, feeling, or causing feeling of guilt. ◻ **guiltily** *adverb*.
guinea /ˈgɪnɪ/ *noun* (*historical* coin worth) £1.05. ◻ **guinea fowl** domestic fowl with white-spotted grey plumage; **guinea pig** domesticated S. American rodent, person used in experiment.
guipure /ˈgi:pjʊə/ *noun* heavy lace of patterned pieces joined by stitches.
guise /gaɪz/ *noun* external, esp. assumed, appearance; pretence.
guitar /gɪˈtɑ:/ *noun* usually 6-stringed musical instrument played with fingers or plectrum. ◻ **guitarist** *noun*.
gulch *noun US* ravine, gully.
gulf *noun* large area of sea with narrow-mouthed inlet; deep hollow, chasm; wide difference of opinion etc. ◻ **Gulf Stream** warm current from Gulf of Mexico to Europe.
gull[1] *noun* long-winged web-footed seabird.
gull[2] *verb* dupe, fool.
gullet /ˈgʌlɪt/ *noun* food-passage from mouth to stomach.
gullible /ˈgʌlɪb(ə)l/ *adjective* easily persuaded or deceived. ◻ **gullibility** *noun*.
gully /ˈgʌlɪ/ *noun* (*plural* **-ies**) water-worn ravine; gutter, drain; *Cricket* fielding position between point and slips.
gulp ● *verb* (often + *down*) swallow hastily or with effort; choke; (+ *down*, *back*) suppress. ● *noun* act of gulping; large mouthful.
gum[1] ● *noun* sticky secretion of some trees and shrubs, used as glue etc.; chewing gum; (also **gumdrop**) hard jelly sweet. ● *verb* (**-mm-**) (usually + *down*, *together*, etc.) fasten with gum; apply gum to. ◻ **gum arabic** gum exuded by some kinds of acacia; **gumboot** rubber boot; **gum tree** tree exuding gum, esp. eucalyptus; **gum up** *colloquial* interfere with, spoil.
gum[2] *noun* (usually in *plural*) firm flesh around roots of teeth. ◻ **gumboil** small abscess on gum.
gummy[1] /ˈgʌmɪ/ *adjective* (**-ier**, **-iest**) sticky; exuding gum.
gummy[2] /ˈgʌmɪ/ *adjective* (**-ier**, **-iest**) toothless.
gumption /ˈgʌmpʃ(ə)n/ *noun colloquial* resourcefulness, enterprise; common sense.

gun ● *noun* metal tube for throwing missiles with explosive propellant; starting pistol; device for discharging grease, electrons, etc., in desired direction; member of shooting party. ● *verb* (**-nn-**) (usually + *down*) shoot with gun; (+ *for*) seek out determinedly to attack or rebuke. □ **gunboat** small warship with heavy guns; **gun carriage** wheeled support for gun; **gun cotton** cotton steeped in acids, used as explosive; **gun dog** dog trained to retrieve game; **gunfire** firing of guns; **gunman** armed lawbreaker; **gun metal** bluish-grey colour, alloy of copper, tin, and usually zinc; **gunpowder** explosive of saltpetre, sulphur, and charcoal; **gunrunner** person selling or bringing guns into country illegally; **gunshot** shot from gun, the range of a gun; **gunslinger** *esp. US* gunman; **gunsmith** maker and repairer of small firearms.

gunge /gʌndz/ *colloquial* ● *noun* sticky substance. ● *verb* (**-ging**) (usually + *up*) clog with gunge. □ **gungy** *adjective*.

gung-ho /gʌŋ'həʊ/ *adjective* (arrogantly) eager.

gunner /'gʌnə/ *noun* artillery soldier; *Nautical* warrant officer in charge of battery, magazine, etc.; airman who operates gun.

gunnery /'gʌnərɪ/ *noun* construction and management, or firing, of large guns.

gunny /'gʌnɪ/ *noun* (*plural* **-ies**) coarse sacking usually of jute fibre; sack made of this.

gunwale /'gʌn(ə)l/ *noun* upper edge of ship's or boat's side.

guppy /'gʌpɪ/ *noun* (*plural* **-ies**) very small brightly coloured tropical freshwater fish.

gurgle /'gɜ:g(ə)l/ ● *verb* (**-ling**) make bubbling sound as of water; utter with such sound. ● *noun* bubbling sound.

gurnard /'gɜ:nəd/ *noun* (*plural* same or **-s**) sea fish with large spiny head.

guru /'gʊru:/ *noun* (*plural* **-s**) Hindu spiritual teacher; influential or revered teacher.

gush ● *verb* flow in sudden or copious stream; speak or behave effusively. ● *noun* sudden or copious stream; effusiveness.

gusher /'gʌʃə/ *noun* oil well emitting unpumped oil; effusive person.

gusset /'gʌsɪt/ *noun* piece let into garment etc. to strengthen or enlarge it.

gust ● *noun* sudden violent rush of wind; burst of rain, smoke, anger, etc. ● *verb* blow in gusts. □ **gusty** *adjective* (**-ier**, **-iest**).

gusto /'gʌstəʊ/ *noun* zest, enjoyment.

gut ● *noun* intestine; (in *plural*) bowels, entrails; (in *plural*) *colloquial* courage and determination; *slang* stomach; (in *plural*) contents, essence; material for violin etc. strings or for fishing line; instinctive, fundamental. ● *verb* (**-tt-**) remove or destroy internal fittings of (buildings); remove guts of. □ **gutless** *adjective*.

gutsy /'gʌtsɪ/ *adjective* (**-ier**, **iest**) *colloquial* courageous; greedy.

gutta-percha /gʌtə'pɜ:tʃə/ *noun* tough plastic substance made from latex.

gutted *adjective slang* bitterly disappointed.

gutter /'gʌtə/ ● *noun* shallow trough below eaves, or channel at side of street, for carrying off rainwater; (**the gutter**) poor or degraded environment; channel, groove. ● *verb* (of candle) burn unsteadily and melt away.

guttering *noun* (material for) gutters.

guttersnipe *noun* street urchin.

guttural /'gʌtər(ə)l/ ● *adjective* throaty, harsh-sounding; (of sound) produced in throat. ● *noun* guttural consonant.

guy[1] /gaɪ/ ● *noun colloquial* man; effigy of Guy Fawkes burnt on 5 Nov. ● *verb* ridicule.

guy[2] /gaɪ/ ● *noun* rope or chain to secure tent or steady crane-load etc. ● *verb* secure with guy(s).

guzzle /'gʌz(ə)l/ *verb* (**-ling**) eat or drink greedily.

gybe /dʒaɪb/ *verb* (*US* **jibe**) (**-bing**) (of fore-and-aft sail or boom) swing across boat, momentarily pointing into wind; cause (sail) to do this; (of boat etc.) change course thus.

gym /dʒɪm/ *noun colloquial* gymnasium; gymnastics. □ **gymslip**, **gym tunic** schoolgirl's sleeveless dress.

gymkhana /dʒɪm'kɑ:nə/ *noun* horse-riding competition.

gymnasium /dʒɪm'neɪzɪəm/ *noun* (*plural* **-siums** or **-sia**) room etc. equipped for gymnastics.

gymnast /'dʒɪmnæst/ *noun* expert in gymnastics.

gymnastic /dʒɪm'næstɪk/ *adjective* of gymnastics. □ **gymnastically** *adverb*.

gymnastics *plural noun* (also treated as *singular*) exercises to develop or demonstrate physical (or mental) agility.

gynaecology /gaɪnɪ'kɒlədʒɪ/ *noun* (*US* **gynecology**) science of physiological functions and diseases of women. □ **gynaecological** /-kə'lɒdʒ-/ *adjective*; **gynaecologist** *noun*.

gypsum /'dʒɪpsəm/ *noun* mineral used esp. to make plaster of Paris.

Gypsy /'dʒɪpsɪ/ *noun* (also **Gipsy**) (*plural* **-ies**) member of nomadic dark-skinned people of Europe.

gyrate /dʒaɪə'reɪt/ *verb* (**-ting**) move in circle or spiral. □ **gyration** *noun*; **gyratory** *adjective*.

gyro /'dʒaɪərəʊ/ *noun* (*plural* **-s**) *colloquial* gyroscope.

gyroscope /'dʒaɪərəskəʊp/ *noun* rotating wheel whose axis is free to turn but maintains fixed direction unless perturbed, esp. used for stabilization.

Hh

H *abbreviation* hard (pencil lead); (water) hydrant; *slang* heroin. □ **H-bomb** hydrogen bomb.

h. *abbreviation* (also **h**) hour(s); (also ***h***) height; hot. □ **h. & c.** hot and cold (water).

ha¹ /hɑː/ (also **hah**) *interjection expressing surprise, triumph, etc.*

ha² *abbreviation* hectare(s).

habeas corpus /heɪbɪəs 'kɔːpəs/ *noun* writ requiring person to be brought before judge etc., esp. to investigate lawfulness of his or her detention.

haberdasher /'hæbədæʃə/ *noun* dealer in dress accessories and sewing goods. □ **haberdashery** *noun* (*plural* **-ies**).

habit /'hæbɪt/ *noun* settled tendency or practice; practice that is hard to give up; mental constitution or attitude; clothes, esp. of religious order.

habitable /'hæbɪtəb(ə)l/ *adjective* suitable for living in. □ **habitability** *noun*.

habitat /'hæbɪtæt/ *noun* natural home of plant or animal.

habitation /hæbɪ'teɪʃ(ə)n/ *noun* inhabiting; house, home.

habitual /hə'bɪtʃʊəl/ *adjective* done as a habit; usual; given to a habit. □ **habitually** *adverb*.

habituate /hə'bɪtʃʊeɪt/ *verb* (**-ting**) (often + *to*) accustom. □ **habituation** *noun*.

habitué /hə'bɪtʃʊeɪ/ *noun* (often + *of*) frequent visitor or resident. [French]

háček /'hætʃek/ *noun* mark used (ˇ) over letter to modify its sound in some languages. [Czech]

hacienda /hæsɪ'endə/ *noun* (in Spanish-speaking countries) plantation etc. with dwelling house.

hack¹ ● *verb* cut or chop roughly; kick shin of; (often + *at*) deal cutting blows; cut (one's way) through; *colloquial* gain unauthorized access to (computer data); *slang* manage, tolerate. ● *noun* kick with toe of boot, wound from this. □ **hacksaw** saw for cutting metal.

hack² ● *noun* horse for ordinary riding; hired horse; person hired to do dull routine work, esp. as writer. ● *adjective* used as hack; commonplace. ● *verb* ride on horseback on road at ordinary pace.

hacker *noun colloquial* computer enthusiast; person who gains unauthorized access to computer network.

hacking *adjective* (of cough) short, dry, and frequent.

hackle /'hæk(ə)l/ *noun* (in *plural*) hairs on animal's neck which rise when it is angry or alarmed; long feather(s) on neck of domestic cock etc.; steel flax-comb. □ **make person's hackles rise** arouse anger or indignation.

hackney /'hæknɪ/ *noun* (*plural* **-s**) horse for ordinary riding. □ **hackney carriage** taxi.

hackneyed /'hæknɪd/ *adjective* overused, trite.

had *past & past participle* of HAVE.

haddock /'hædək/ *noun* (*plural* same) common edible sea fish.

Hades /'heɪdiːz/ *noun* (in Greek mythology) the underworld.

hadj = HAJJ.

hadji = HAJJI.

hadn't /'hæd(ə)nt/ had not.

haematite /'hiːmətaɪt/ *noun* (*US* **hem-**) red or brown iron ore.

haematology /hiːmə'tɒlədʒɪ/ *noun* (*US* **hem-**) study of the blood. □ **haematologist** *noun*.

haemoglobin /hiːmə'gləʊbɪn/ *noun* (*US* **hem-**) oxygen-carrying substance in red blood cells.

haemophilia /hiːmə'fɪlɪə/ *noun* (*US* **hem-**) hereditary tendency to severe bleeding from even a slight injury through failure of blood to clot. □ **haemophiliac** *noun*.

haemorrhage /'hemərɪdʒ/ (*US* **hem-**) ● *noun* profuse bleeding. ● *verb* (**-ging**) suffer haemorrhage.

haemorrhoids /'heməroɪdz/ *plural noun* (*US* **hem-**) swollen veins near anus, piles.

haft /hɑːft/ *noun* handle of knife etc.

hag *noun* ugly old woman; witch. □ **hagridden** afflicted by nightmares or fears.

haggard /'hægəd/ *adjective* looking exhausted and distraught.

haggis /'hægɪs/ *noun* Scottish dish of offal boiled in bag with oatmeal etc.

haggle /'hæg(ə)l/ ● *verb* (**-ling**) (often + *over*, *about*) bargain persistently. ● *noun* haggling.

hagiography /hægɪ'ɒgrəfɪ/ *noun* writing about saints' lives. □ **hagiographer** *noun*.

hah = HA¹.

ha ha /hɑː'hɑː/ *interjection representing laughter*.

ha-ha /'hɑːhɑː/ *noun* ditch with wall in it bounding park or garden.

haiku /'haɪkuː/ *noun* (*plural* same) Japanese 3-line poem of usually 17 syllables.

hail¹ ● *noun* pellets of frozen rain; (+ *of*) barrage, onslaught. ● *verb* (after *it*) hail falls; pour down as or like hail. □ **hailstone** pellet of hail; **hailstorm** period of heavy hail.

hail² ● *verb* signal (taxi etc.) to stop; greet enthusiastically; (+ *from*) originate. ● *interjection archaic or jocular: expressing greeting*. ● *noun* act of hailing.

hair *noun* any or all of fine filaments growing from skin of mammals, esp. of human head; hairlike thing. □ **haircut** (style of) cutting hair; **hairdo** style of or act of styling hair; **hairdresser** person who cuts and styles hair; **hairdressing** *noun*; **hair-drier**, **-dryer** device for drying hair with warm air; **hairgrip** flat hairpin with ends close together; **hairline** edge of person's hair on forehead, very narrow crack or line; **hairnet** piece of netting for confining hair; **hair of the dog** further alcoholic drink taken to cure effects of previous drinking; **hairpiece** false hair augmenting person's natural hair; **hairpin** U-shaped pin for fastening the hair; **hairpin bend** U-shaped bend in road; **hair-raising** terrifying; **hair's breadth** minute distance; **hair shirt** ascetic's or penitent's shirt made of hair; **hair-slide** clip for keeping hair in position; **hair-splitting** quibbling; **hairspray** liquid sprayed on hair to keep it in place; **hairspring** fine spring regulating balance-wheel of watch; **hairstyle** particular way of arranging hair; **hairstylist** *noun*; **hair-trigger** trigger acting on very slight pressure. □ **hairless** *adjective*; **hairy** *adjective* (**-ier**, **-iest**).

hajj /hædʒ/ *noun* (also **hadj**) Islamic pilgrimage to Mecca.

hajji /'hædʒɪ/ *noun* (also **hadji**) (*plural* **-s**) Muslim who has made pilgrimage to Mecca.

haka /'hɑːkə/ *noun NZ* Maori ceremonial war dance; similar dance by sports team before match.

hake *noun* (*plural* same) codlike sea fish.

halal /hɑːˈlɑːl/ *noun* (also **hallal**) meat from animal killed according to Muslim law.

halberd /ˈhælbəd/ *noun historical* combined spear and battleaxe.

halcyon /ˈhælsɪən/ *adjective* calm, peaceful, happy.

hale *adjective* strong and healthy (esp. in **hale and hearty**).

half /hɑːf/ ● *noun* (*plural* **halves** /hɑːvz/) either of two (esp. equal) parts into which a thing is divided; *colloquial* half pint, esp. of beer; *Sport* either of two equal periods of play, half-back; half-price (esp. child's) ticket. ● *adjective* forming a half. ● *adverb* partly. ▫ **half and half** being half one thing and half another; **half-back** player between forwards and full back(s) in football etc.; **half-baked** not thoroughly thought out; **half board** provision of bed, breakfast, and one main meal; **half-brother, -sister** one having only one parent in common; **half-crown** *historical* coin worth 2 shillings and 6 pence (= 12½p); **half-dozen** (about) six; **half-hearted** lacking courage or zeal; **half-heartedly** *adverb*; **half holiday** half day as holiday; **half-hour, half an hour** 30 minutes, point of time 30 minutes after any hour o'clock; **half-hourly** *adjective & adverb*; **half-life** time after which radioactivity etc. is half its original value; **half-mast** position of flag halfway down mast as symbol of mourning; **half measures** unsatisfactory compromise etc.; **half-moon** (shape of) moon with disc half illuminated; **half nelson** see NELSON; **half-term** short holiday halfway through school term; **half-timbered** having walls with timber frame and brick or plaster filling; **half-time** (short break at) mid-point of game or contest; **halftone** photograph representing tones by large or small dots; **half-truth** statement that conveys only part of truth; **half-volley** playing of ball as soon as it bounces off ground; **halfwit** stupid person; **halfwitted** *adjective*.

halfpenny /ˈheɪpnɪ/ *noun* (*plural* **-pennies** or **-pence** /ˈheɪpəns/) *historical* coin worth half penny (withdrawn in 1984).

halfway ● *adverb* at a point midway between two others; to some extent. ● *adjective* situated halfway. ▫ **halfway house** compromise, halfway point, rehabilitation centre, inn etc. between two towns.

halibut /ˈhælɪbət/ *noun* (*plural* same) large flatfish.

halitosis /hælɪˈtəʊsɪs/ *noun* bad breath.

hall /hɔːl/ *noun* entrance area of house; large room or building for meetings, concerts, etc.; large country house or estate; (in full **hall of residence**) residence for students; college dining-room; large public room; *esp. US* corridor. ▫ **hallmark** mark used to show standard of gold, silver, and platinum, distinctive feature; **hallway** entrance hall or corridor.

hallal = HALAL.

hallelujah = ALLELUIA.

hallo = HELLO.

hallow /ˈhæləʊ/ *verb* (usually as **hallowed** *adjective*) make or honour as holy.

Hallowe'en /hæləʊˈiːn/ *noun* eve of All Saints' Day, 31 Oct.

hallucinate /həˈluːsɪneɪt/ *verb* (**-ting**) experience hallucinations.

hallucination *noun* illusion of seeing or hearing something not actually present. ▫ **hallucinatory** /həˈluːsɪnətərɪ/ *adjective*.

hallucinogen /həˈluːsɪnədʒ(ə)n/ *noun* drug causing hallucinations. ▫ **hallucinogenic** /-ˈdʒen-/ *adjective*.

halm = HAULM.

halo /ˈheɪləʊ/ ● *noun* (*plural* **-es**) disc of light shown round head of sacred person; glory associated with idealized person; circle of light round sun or moon etc. ● *verb* (**-es, -ed**) surround with halo.

halogen /ˈhælədʒ(ə)n/ *noun* any of the non-metallic elements (fluorine, chlorine, etc.) which form a salt when combined with a metal.

halon /ˈheɪlɒn/ *noun* gaseous halogen compound used to extinguish fires.

halt[1] /hɔːlt/ ● *noun* stop (usually temporary); minor stopping place on local railway line. ● *verb* (cause to) make a halt.

halt[2] /hɔːlt/ ● *verb* (esp. as **halting** *adjective*) proceed hesitantly. ▫ **haltingly** *adverb*.

halter /ˈhɔːltə/ *noun* rope with headstall for leading or tying up horses etc.; strap passing round back of neck holding dress etc. up, (also **halterneck**) dress etc. held by this.

halva /ˈhælvə/ *noun* confection of sesame flour, honey, etc.

halve /hɑːv/ *verb* (**-ving**) divide into halves; reduce to half.

halves *plural* of HALF.

halyard /ˈhæljəd/ *noun* rope or tackle for raising and lowering sail etc.

ham ● *noun* upper part of pig's leg cured for food; back of thigh; thigh and buttock; *colloquial* inexpert or unsubtle performer or actor; *colloquial* operator of amateur radio station. ● *verb* (**-mm-**) (usually in **ham it up**) *colloquial* overact. ▫ **ham-fisted, -handed** *colloquial* clumsy.

hamburger /ˈhæmbɜːgə/ *noun* cake of minced beef, usually eaten in soft bread roll.

hamlet /ˈhæmlɪt/ *noun* small village, esp. without church.

hammer /ˈhæmə/ ● *noun* tool with heavy metal head at right angles to handle, used for driving nails etc.; similar device, as for exploding charge in gun, striking strings of piano, etc.; auctioneer's mallet; metal ball attached to a wire for throwing as athletic contest. ● *verb* strike or drive (as) with hammer; *colloquial* defeat utterly. ▫ **hammer and tongs** *colloquial* with great energy; **hammerhead** shark with flattened hammer-shaped head; **hammerlock** wrestling hold in which twisted arm is bent behind back; **hammer-toe** toe bent permanently downwards. ▫ **hammering** *noun*.

hammock /ˈhæmək/ *noun* bed of canvas or netting suspended by cords at ends.

hamper[1] /ˈhæmpə/ *noun* large basket, usually with hinged lid and containing food.

hamper[2] /ˈhæmpə/ *verb* obstruct movement of; hinder.

hamster /ˈhæmstə/ *noun* short-tailed mouselike rodent often kept as pet.

hamstring ● *noun* any of 5 tendons at back of human knee; (in quadruped) tendon at back of hock. ● *verb* (*past & past participle* **-strung** or **-stringed**) cripple by cutting hamstrings; impair efficiency of.

hand ● *noun* end part of human arm beyond wrist; similar member of monkey; (often in *plural*) control, disposal, agency; share in action, active support; handlike thing, esp. pointer of clock etc.; right or left side, direction, etc.; skill or style, esp. of writing; person who does or makes something; person etc. as source; manual worker in factory etc.; pledge of marriage; playing cards dealt to player, round or game of cards; *colloquial* round of applause; measure of horse's height, = 4 in. (10.16 cm). ● *verb* (+ *in, to, over, round*, etc.) deliver or transfer (as) with hand. ▫ **at hand** close by; **by hand** by person not machine, not by post; **handbag** small bag carried esp. by woman; **handball** game with ball thrown by hand, *Football* foul touching of ball; **handbell** small bell for ringing by hand; **handbook** short manual or guidebook; **handbrake** brake operated by hand; **handcuff** secure (prisoner) with **handcuffs**, pair of lockable metal rings joined by short chain; **handgun** small firearm held in one hand; **handhold** something for hand to grip; **hand in glove** in collusion; **handmade** made by hand (rather than machine); **hand-me-down** article passed on from another person; **handout** thing given to needy person, information etc. distributed to press etc., notes given out in class; **handover** act of handing over; **hand-over-fist** *colloquial* with rapid progress; **hand-picked** carefully chosen; **handrail** rail along edge of stairs etc.; **hands down** without effort; **handset** part of telephone held in hand; **handshake** clasping of person's hand, esp. as greeting etc.; **hands-on** practical rather than theoretical; **handstand** act of supporting oneself vertically on one's hands; **hand-to-hand** (of fighting) at close quarters; **handwriting** (style of) writing by hand; **take in hand** start doing or dealing with, undertake control or reform of; **to hand** within reach.

handful *noun* (*plural* **-s**) enough to fill the hand; small number or quantity; *colloquial* troublesome person or task.

handicap /ˈhændɪkæp/ ● *noun* physical or mental disability; thing that makes progress difficult; disadvantage imposed on superior competitor to equalize chances; race etc. in which this is imposed. ● *verb* (**-pp-**) impose handicap on; place at disadvantage.

handicapped *adjective* suffering from physical or mental disability.

handicraft /ˈhændɪkrɑːft/ *noun* work requiring manual and artistic skill.

handiwork /ˈhændɪwɜːk/ *noun* work done or thing made by hand, or by particular person.

handkerchief /ˈhæŋkətʃɪf/ *noun* (*plural* **-s** or **-chieves** /-tʃiːvz/) square of cloth used to wipe nose etc.

handle /ˈhænd(ə)l/ ● *noun* part by which thing is held. ● *verb* (**-ling**) touch, feel, operate, etc. with hands; manage, deal with; deal in (goods etc.). □ **handlebar** (usually in *plural*) steering-bar of bicycle etc.

handler *noun* person in charge of trained dog etc.

handsome /ˈhænsəm/ *adjective* (**-r**, **-st**) good-looking; imposing; generous; considerable. □ **handsomely** *adverb*.

handy *adjective* (**-ier**, **-iest**) convenient to handle; ready to hand; clever with hands. □ **handyman** person able to do odd jobs.

hang ● *verb* (*past & past participle* **hung** except as below) (cause to) be supported from above, attach by suspending from top; set up on hinges etc.; place (picture) on wall or in exhibition; attach (wallpaper); (*past & past participle* **hanged**) suspend or be suspended by neck, esp. as capital punishment; let droop; remain or be hung. ● *noun* way thing hangs. □ **get the hang of** *colloquial* get knack of, understand; **hang about**, **around** loiter, not move away; **hangdog** shamefaced; **hang fire** delay acting; **hang-glider** fabric wing on light frame from which pilot is suspended; **hang-gliding** *noun*; **hangman** executioner by hanging; **hangnail** agnail; **hang on** (often + *to*) continue to hold, retain, wait for short time, not ring off during pause in telephoning; **hangover** after-effects of excess of alcohol; **hang up** *verb* hang from hook etc., end telephone conversation; **hang-up** *noun slang* emotional inhibition.

hangar /ˈhæŋə/ *noun* building for housing aircraft etc.

hanger *noun* person or thing that hangs; (in full **coat-hanger**) shaped piece of wood etc. for hanging clothes on. □ **hanger-on** (*plural* **hangers-on**) follower, dependant.

hanging *noun* execution by suspending by neck; (usually in *plural*) drapery for walls etc.

hank *noun* coil of yarn etc.

hanker /ˈhæŋkə/ *verb* (+ *for*, *after*, *to do*) crave, long for. □ **hankering** *noun*.

hanky /ˈhæŋkɪ/ *noun* (also **hankie**) (*plural* **-ies**) *colloquial* handkerchief.

hanky-panky /hæŋkɪˈpæŋkɪ/ *noun slang* misbehaviour; trickery.

Hansard /ˈhænsɑːd/ *noun* verbatim record of parliamentary debates.

hansom /ˈhænsəm/ *noun* (in full **hansom cab**) *historical* two-wheeled horse-drawn cab.

haphazard /hæpˈhæzəd/ *adjective* casual, random. □ **haphazardly** *adverb*.

hapless /ˈhæplɪs/ *adjective* unlucky.

happen /ˈhæpən/ *verb* occur; (+ *to do*) have the (good or bad) fortune; (+ *to*) be fate or experience of; (+ *on*) come by chance on. □ **happening** *noun*.

happy /ˈhæpɪ/ *adjective* (**-ier**, **-iest**) feeling or showing pleasure or contentment; fortunate; apt, pleasing. □ **happy-go-lucky** taking things cheerfully as they happen; **happy hour** time of day when drinks are sold at reduced prices; **happy medium** compromise. □ **happily** *adverb*; **happiness** *noun*.

hara-kiri /hærəˈkɪrɪ/ *noun historical* Japanese suicide by ritual disembowelling.

harangue /həˈræŋ/ ● *noun* lengthy and earnest speech. ● *verb* (**-guing**) make harangue to.

harass /ˈhærəs/ *verb* trouble, annoy; attack repeatedly. □ **harassment** *noun*.

■ **Usage** *Harass* is often pronounced /həˈræs/ (with the stress on the *-rass*), but this is considered incorrect by some people.

harbinger /ˈhɑːbɪndʒə/ *noun* person or thing announcing another's approach, forerunner.

harbour /ˈhɑːbə/ (*US* **harbor**) ● *noun* place of shelter for ships; shelter. ● *verb* give shelter to; entertain (thoughts etc.).

hard ● *adjective* firm, solid; difficult to bear, do, or understand; unfeeling, harsh, severe; strenuous, enthusiastic; *Politics* extreme, radical; (of drinks) strongly alcoholic; (of drug) potent and addictive; (of water) difficult to lather; (of currency etc.) not likely to fall in value; not disputable. ● *adverb* strenuously, severely, intensely. □ **hard and fast** (of rule etc.) strict; **hardback** (book) bound in stiff covers; **hardbitten** *colloquial* tough, cynical; **hardboard** stiff board of compressed wood pulp; **hard-boiled** (of eggs) boiled until yolk and white are solid, (of person) tough, shrewd; **hard cash** coins and banknotes, not cheques etc.; **hard copy** printed material produced by computer; **hardcore** stones, rubble, etc. as foundation; **hard core** central or most enduring part; **hard disk** *Computing* rigid storage disk, esp. fixed in computer; **hard-done-by** unfairly treated; **hard-headed** practical, not sentimental; **hard-hearted** unfeeling; **hard line** firm adherence to policy; **hardliner** *noun*; **hard-nosed** *colloquial* realistic, uncompromising; **hard of hearing** somewhat deaf; **hard-pressed** closely pursued, burdened with urgent business; **hard sell** aggressive salesmanship; **hard shoulder** strip at side of motorway for emergency stops; **hard up** short of money; **hardware** tools, weapons, machinery, etc., mechanical and electronic components of computer; **hardwood** wood of deciduous tree. □ **hardness** *noun*.

harden *verb* make or become hard or unyielding.

hardihood /ˈhɑːdɪhʊd/ *noun* boldness.

hardly *adverb* scarcely; with difficulty.

hardship *noun* severe suffering or privation.

hardy /ˈhɑːdɪ/ *adjective* (**-ier**, **-iest**) robust; capable of endurance; (of plant) able to grow in the open all year. □ **hardiness** *noun*.

hare /heə/ ● *noun* mammal like large rabbit, with long ears, short tail, and long hind legs. ● *verb* (**-ring**) run rapidly. □ **hare-brained** rash, wild.

harebell *noun* plant with pale blue bell-shaped flowers.

harem /ˈhɑːriːm/ *noun* women of Muslim household; their quarters.

haricot /ˈhærɪkəʊ/ *noun* (in full **haricot bean**) French bean with small white seeds; these as vegetable.

hark *verb* (usually in *imperative*) *archaic* listen. □ **hark back** revert to earlier topic.

Harlequin /ˈhɑːlɪkwɪn/ ● *noun* masked pantomime character in diamond-patterned costume. ● *adjective* (**harlequin**) in varied colours.

harlot /ˈhɑːlət/ *noun archaic* prostitute.

harm *noun & verb* damage, hurt.

harmful *adjective* causing or likely to cause harm. □ **harmfully** *adverb*.

harmless *adjective* not able or likely to harm. □ **harmlessly** *adverb*.

harmonic /hɑːˈmɒnɪk/ ● *adjective* of or relating to harmony; harmonious. ● *noun Music* overtone accompanying (and forming a note with) a fundamental at a fixed interval.

harmonica /hɑːˈmɒnɪkə/ *noun* small rectangular instrument played by blowing and sucking air through it.

harmonious /hɑːˈməʊnɪəs/ *adjective* sweet-sounding, tuneful; forming a pleasant or consistent whole; free from dissent. □ **harmoniously** *adverb*.

harmonium /hɑːˈməʊnɪəm/ *noun* keyboard instrument with bellows and metal reeds.

harmonize /ˈhɑːmənaɪz/ *verb* (also **-ise**) (**-zing** or **-sing**) add notes to (melody) to produce harmony; bring into or be in harmony. □ **harmonization** *noun*.

harmony /ˈhɑːmənɪ/ *noun* (*plural* **-ies**) combination of notes to form chords; melodious sound; agreement, concord.

harness /ˈhɑːnɪs/ ● *noun* straps etc. by which horse is fastened to cart etc. and controlled; similar arrangement for fastening thing to person. ● *verb* put harness on; utilize (natural forces), esp. to produce energy.

harp ● *noun* large upright stringed instrument plucked with fingers. ● *verb* (+ *on, on about*) dwell on tediously. □ **harpist** *noun*.

harpoon /hɑːˈpuːn/ ● *noun* spearlike missile for shooting whales etc. ● *verb* spear with harpoon.

harpsichord /ˈhɑːpsɪkɔːd/ *noun* keyboard instrument with strings plucked mechanically. □ **harpsichordist** *noun*.

harpy /ˈhɑːpɪ/ *noun* (*plural* **-ies**) mythological monster with woman's face and bird's wings and claws; grasping unscrupulous person.

harridan /ˈhærɪd(ə)n/ *noun* bad-tempered old woman.

harrier /ˈhærɪə/ *noun* hound used in hunting hares; kind of falcon.

harrow /ˈhærəʊ/ ● *noun* frame with metal teeth or discs for breaking clods of earth. ● *verb* draw harrow over; (usually as **harrowing** *adjective*) distress greatly.

harry /ˈhærɪ/ *verb* (**-ies, -ied**) ravage, despoil; harass.

harsh *adjective* rough to hear, taste, etc.; severe, cruel. □ **harshly** *adverb*; **harshness** *noun*.

hart *noun* (*plural* same or **-s**) male of (esp. red) deer.

hartebeest /ˈhɑːtɪbiːst/ *noun* large African antelope with curved horns.

harum-scarum /heərəmˈskeərəm/ *adjective colloquial* reckless, wild.

harvest /ˈhɑːvɪst/ ● *noun* gathering in of crops etc.; season for this; season's yield; product of any action. ● *verb* reap and gather in.

harvester *noun* reaper, reaping machine.

has *3rd singular present* of HAVE.

hash[1] ● *noun* dish of reheated pieces of cooked meat; mixture, jumble; recycled material. ● *verb* (often + *up*) recycle (old material). □ **make a hash of** *colloquial* make a mess of, bungle.

hash[2] *noun colloquial* hashish.

hashish /ˈhæʃɪʃ/ *noun* narcotic drug got from hemp.

hasn't /ˈhæz(ə)nt/ has not.

hasp /hɑːsp/ *noun* hinged metal clasp passing over staple and secured by padlock.

hassle /ˈhæs(ə)l/ *colloquial* ● *noun* trouble, problem; argument. ● *verb* (**-ling**) harass.

hassock /ˈhæsək/ *noun* kneeling-cushion.

haste /heɪst/ *noun* urgency of movement; hurry. □ **make haste** be quick.

hasten /ˈheɪs(ə)n/ *verb* (cause to) proceed or go quickly.

hasty /ˈheɪstɪ/ *adjective* (**-ier, -iest**) hurried; said, made, or done too quickly. □ **hastily** *adverb*; **hastiness** *noun*.

hat *noun* (esp. outdoor) head-covering. □ **hat trick** *Cricket* taking 3 wickets with successive balls, *Football* scoring of 3 goals in one match by same player, 3 consecutive successes.

hatch[1] *noun* opening in wall between kitchen and dining-room for serving food; opening or door in aircraft etc.; (cover for) hatchway. □ **hatchback** car with rear door hinged at top; **hatchway** opening in ship's deck for lowering cargo.

hatch[2] ● *verb* (often + *out*) emerge from egg; (of egg) produce young animal; incubate; (also + *up*) devise (plot). ● *noun* hatching; brood hatched.

hatch[3] *verb* mark with parallel lines. □ **hatching** *noun*.

hatchet /ˈhætʃɪt/ *noun* light short axe.

hate ● *verb* (**-ting**) dislike intensely. ● *noun* hatred.

hateful *adjective* arousing hatred.

hatred /ˈheɪtrɪd/ *noun* intense dislike; ill will.

hatter *noun* maker or seller of hats.

haughty /ˈhɔːtɪ/ *adjective* (**-ier, -iest**) proud, arrogant. □ **haughtily** *adverb*; **haughtiness** *noun*.

haul /hɔːl/ ● *verb* pull or drag forcibly; transport by lorry, cart, etc. ● *noun* hauling; amount gained or acquired; distance to be traversed.

haulage *noun* (charge for) commercial transport of goods.

haulier /ˈhɔːlɪə/ *noun* person or firm engaged in transport of goods.

haulm /hɔːm/ *noun* (also **halm**) stalk or stem; stalks of beans, peas, potatoes, etc. collectively.

haunch /hɔːntʃ/ *noun* fleshy part of buttock and thigh; leg and loin of deer etc. as food.

haunt /hɔːnt/ ● *verb* (of ghost etc.) visit regularly; frequent (place); linger in mind of. ● *noun* place frequented by person.

haunting *adjective* (of memory, melody, etc.) lingering; poignant, evocative.

haute couture /əʊt kuːˈtjʊə/ *noun* (world of) high fashion.

hauteur /əʊˈtɜː/ *noun* haughtiness.

have /hæv/ ● *verb* (**having**; *3rd singular present* **has** /hæz/; *past & past participle* **had**) *used as auxiliary verb with past participle to form past tenses*; hold in possession or relationship, be provided with; contain as part or quality; experience; (come to) be subjected to a specified state; engage in; tolerate, permit to; give birth to; receive; obtain or know (qualification, language, etc.); *colloquial* get the better of, (usually in *passive*) cheat. ● *noun* (usually in *plural*) *colloquial* wealthy person; *slang* swindle. □ **have on** wear (clothes), have (engagement), *colloquial* hoax; **have-not** (usually in *plural*) person lacking wealth; **have to** be obliged to, must.

haven /ˈheɪv(ə)n/ *noun* refuge; harbour.

haven't /ˈhæv(ə)nt/ have not.

haver /ˈheɪvə/ *verb* hesitate; talk foolishly.

haversack /ˈhævəsæk/ *noun* canvas bag carried on back or over shoulder.

havoc /ˈhævək/ *noun* devastation, confusion.

haw *noun* hawthorn berry.

hawk¹ ● *noun* bird of prey with rounded wings; *Politics* person who advocates aggressive policy. ● *verb* hunt with hawk.

hawk² *verb* carry (goods) about for sale.

hawk³ *verb* clear throat noisily; (+ *up*) bring (phlegm etc.) up thus.

hawker *noun* person who hawks goods.

hawser /ˈhɔːzə/ *noun* thick rope or cable for mooring ship.

hawthorn *noun* thorny shrub with red berries.

hay *noun* grass mown and dried for fodder. ☐ **haycock** conical heap of hay; **hay fever** allergic irritation of nose, throat, etc. caused by pollen, dust, etc.; **haymaking** mowing grass and spreading it to dry; **hayrick**, **haystack** packed pile of hay; **haywire** *colloquial* badly disorganized, out of control.

hazard /ˈhæzəd/ ● *noun* danger, risk; obstacle on golf course. ● *verb* venture on (guess etc.); risk.

hazardous *adjective* risky.

haze *noun* slight mist; mental obscurity, confusion.

hazel /ˈheɪz(ə)l/ *noun* nut-bearing hedgerow shrub; greenish-brown. ☐ **hazelnut** nut of hazel.

hazy *adjective* (**-ier**, **-iest**) misty; vague; confused. ☐ **hazily** *adverb*; **haziness** *noun*.

HB *abbreviation* hard black (pencil lead).

HE *abbreviation* His or Her Excellency; high explosive.

he /hiː/ *pronoun* (as subject of verb) the male person or animal in question; person of unspecified sex. ☐ **he-man** masterful or virile man.

head /hed/ ● *noun* uppermost part of human body, or foremost part of body of animal, containing brain, sense organs, etc.; seat of intellect; thing like head in form or position; top, front, or upper end; person in charge, esp. of school; position of command; individual as unit; side of coin bearing image of head, (in *plural*) this as call when tossing coin; signal-converting device on tape recorder etc.; foam on top of beer etc.; confined body of water or steam, pressure exerted by this; (usually in **come to a head**) climax, crisis. ● *verb* be at front or in charge of; (often + *for*) move or send in specified direction; provide with heading; *Football* strike (ball) with head. ☐ **headache** continuous pain in head, *colloquial* troublesome problem; **headachy** *adjective*; **headband** band worn round head as decoration or to confine hair; **headboard** upright panel at head of bed; **headcount** (counting of) total number of people; **headdress** (esp. ornamental) covering for head; **head-hunting** collecting of enemies' heads as trophies, seeking of staff by approaching people employed elsewhere; **headlamp**, **headlight** (main) light at front of vehicle; **headland** promontory; **headline** heading at top of page, newspaper article, etc., (in *plural*) summary of broadcast news; **headlock** wrestling hold round opponent's head; **headlong** with head foremost, in a rush; **headman** tribal chief; **headmaster**, **headmistress** head teacher; **head-on** (of collision etc.) with front foremost; **headphones** pair of earphones fitting over head; **headquarters** (treated as *singular* or *plural*) organization's administrative centre; **headroom** overhead space; **headset** headphones, often with microphone; **headshrinker** *slang* psychiatrist; **headstall** part of bridle or halter fitting round horse's head; **head start** advantage granted or gained at early stage; **headstone** stone set up at head of grave; **headstrong** self-willed; **head teacher** teacher in charge of school; **headway** progress; **head wind** one blowing from directly in front.

header *noun Football* act of heading ball; *colloquial* headlong dive or plunge.

heading *noun* title at head of page etc.

heady *adjective* (**-ier**, **-iest**) (of liquor etc.) potent; exciting, intoxicating; impetuous; headachy.

heal *verb* (often + *up*) become healthy again; cure; put right (differences). ☐ **healer** *noun*.

health /helθ/ *noun* state of being well in body or mind; mental or physical condition. ☐ **health centre** building containing local medical services; **health food** natural food, thought to promote good health; **health service** public medical service; **health visitor** nurse who visits mothers and babies, the elderly, etc. at home.

healthy *adjective* (**-ier**, **-iest**) having, conducive to, or indicative of, good health. ☐ **healthily** *adverb*; **healthiness** *noun*.

heap ● *noun* disorderly pile; (esp. in *plural*) *colloquial* large number or amount; *slang* dilapidated vehicle. ● *verb* (+ *up*, *together*, etc.) pile or collect in heap; (+ *with*) load copiously with; (+ *on*, *upon*) offer copiously.

hear *verb* (*past & past participle* **heard** /hɜːd/) perceive with ear; listen to; listen judicially to; be informed; (+ *from*) receive message etc. from. ☐ **hearsay** rumour, gossip. ☐ **hearer** *noun*.

hearing *noun* faculty of perceiving sounds; range within which sounds may be heard; opportunity to state one's case; trial of case before court. ☐ **hearing-aid** small sound-amplifier worn by deaf person.

hearse /hɜːs/ *noun* vehicle for carrying coffin.

heart /hɑːt/ *noun* organ in body keeping up circulation of blood by contraction and dilation; region of heart, breast; seat of thought, feeling, or emotion (esp. love); courage; mood; central or innermost part, essence; tender inner part of vegetable etc.; (conventionally) heart-shaped thing; playing card of suit marked with red hearts. ☐ **at heart** in inmost feelings; **by heart** from memory; **have the heart** (usually in negative, + *to do*) be hard-hearted enough; **heartache** mental anguish; **heart attack** sudden heart failure; **heartbeat** pulsation of heart; **heartbreak** overwhelming distress; **heartbreaking** *adjective*; **heartbroken** *adjective*; **heartburn** burning sensation in chest from indigestion; **heartfelt** sincere; **heart-rending** very distressing; **heartsick** despondent; **heartstrings** deepest affections or pity; **heartthrob** *colloquial* object of (esp. immature) romantic feelings; **heart-to-heart** frank (talk); **heart-warming** emotionally moving and encouraging; **take to heart** be much affected by.

hearten *verb* make or become more cheerful. ☐ **heartening** *adjective*.

hearth /hɑːθ/ *noun* floor of fireplace. ☐ **hearthrug** rug laid before fireplace.

heartless *adjective* unfeeling, pitiless. ☐ **heartlessly** *adverb*.

hearty *adjective* (**-ier**, **-iest**) strong, vigorous; (of meal or appetite) large; warm, friendly. ☐ **heartily** *adverb*; **heartiness** *noun*.

heat ● *noun* condition or sensation of being hot; energy arising from motion of molecules; hot weather; warmth of feeling; anger; most intense part or period of activity; preliminary contest, winner(s) of which compete in final. ● *verb* make or become hot; inflame. ▫ **heatproof** able to resist great heat; **heatwave** period of very hot weather; **on heat** (of female animals) sexually receptive.

heated *adjective* angry, impassioned. ▫ **heatedly** *adverb.*

heater *noun* device for heating room, water, etc.

heath /hi:θ/ *noun* flattish tract of uncultivated land with low shrubs; plant growing on heath, esp. heather.

heathen /'hi:ð(ə)n/ ● *noun* person not belonging to predominant religion. ● *adjective* of heathens; having no religion.

heather /'heðə/ *noun* purple-flowered plant of moors and heaths.

heating *noun* equipment used to heat building.

heave ● *verb* (**-ving**; *past & past participle* **heaved** or *esp. Nautical* **hove** /həʊv/) lift, haul, or utter with effort; *colloquial* throw; rise and fall periodically; *Nautical* haul by rope; retch. ● *noun* heaving. ▫ **heave in sight** come into view; **heave to** bring vessel to standstill.

heaven /'hev(ə)n/ *noun* home of God and of blessed after death; place or state of bliss, delightful thing; (**the heavens**) sky as seen from earth. ▫ **heavenly** *adjective.*

heavy /'hevɪ/ ● *adjective* (**-ier**, **-iest**) of great weight, difficult to lift; of great density; abundant; severe, extensive; striking or falling with force; (of machinery etc.) very large of its kind; needing much physical effort; hard to digest; hard to read or understand; (of ground) difficult to travel over; dull, tedious, oppressive; coarse, ungraceful. ● *noun* (*plural* **-ies**) *colloquial* thug (esp. hired); villain. ▫ **heavy-duty** designed to withstand hard use; **heavy-handed** clumsy, oppressive; **heavy hydrogen** deuterium; **heavy industry** that concerned with production of metal and machines etc.; **heavy metal** *colloquial* loud rock music with pounding rhythm; **heavy water** water composed of deuterium and oxygen; **heavyweight** amateur boxing weight (over 81 kg). ▫ **heavily** *adverb*; **heaviness** *noun.*

Hebraic /hi:'breɪɪk/ *adjective* of Hebrew or the Hebrews.

Hebrew /'hi:bru:/ ● *noun* member of a Semitic people in ancient Palestine; their language; modern form of this, used esp. in Israel. ● *adjective* of or in Hebrew; of the Jews.

heckle /'hek(ə)l/ ● *verb* (**-ling**) interrupt or harass (speaker). ● *noun* act of heckling. ▫ **heckler** *noun.*

hectare /'hekteə/ *noun* metric unit of square measure (2.471 acres).

hectic /'hektɪk/ *adjective* busy and confused; excited, feverish. ▫ **hectically** *adverb.*

hecto- /'hektəʊ/ *combining form* one hundred.

hector /'hektə/ *verb* bluster, bully. ▫ **hectoring** *adjective.*

he'd /hi:d/ he had; he would.

hedge ● *noun* fence of bushes or low trees; protection against possible loss. ● *verb* (**-ging**) surround with hedge; (+ *in*) enclose; secure oneself against loss on (bet etc.); avoid committing oneself. ▫ **hedgehog** small spiny insect-eating mammal; **hedge-hop** fly at low altitude; **hedgerow** row of bushes forming hedge; **hedge sparrow** common brown-backed bird.

hedonism /'hi:dənɪz(ə)m/ *noun* (behaviour based on) belief in pleasure as humankind's proper aim. ▫ **hedonist** *noun*; **hedonistic** /-'nɪs-/ *adjective.*

heed ● *verb* attend to; take notice of. ● *noun* care, attention. ▫ **heedless** *adjective*; **heedlessly** *adverb.*

hee-haw /'hi:hɔ:/ *noun & verb* bray.

heel[1] ● *noun* back of foot below ankle; part of sock etc. covering this, or of shoe etc. supporting it; crust end of loaf; *colloquial* scoundrel; (as *interjection*) *command to dog to walk near owner's heel.* ● *verb* fit or renew heel on (shoe); touch ground with heel; (+ *out*) *Rugby* pass ball with heel. ▫ **cool**, **kick one's heels** be kept waiting; **heelball** shoemaker's polishing mixture of wax etc., esp. used in brass rubbing.

heel[2] ● *verb* (often + *over*) (of ship etc.) lean over; cause (ship) to do this. ● *noun* heeling.

hefty /'heftɪ/ *adjective* (**-ier**, **-iest**) (of person) big, strong; (of thing) heavy, powerful.

hegemony /hɪ'gemənɪ/ *noun* leadership.

heifer /'hefə/ *noun* young cow, esp. one that has not had more than one calf.

height /haɪt/ *noun* measurement from base to top; elevation above ground or other level; high point; top; extreme example.

heighten *verb* make or become higher or more intense.

heinous /'heɪnəs/ *adjective* atrocious.

heir /eə/ *noun* (*feminine* **heiress**) person entitled to property or rank as legal successor of former holder. ▫ **heir apparent** one whose claim cannot be superseded by birth of nearer heir; **heirloom** piece of property that has been in family for generations; **heir presumptive** one whose claim may be superseded by birth of nearer heir.

held *past & past participle* of HOLD[1].

helical /'helɪk(ə)l/ *adjective* spiral.

helices *plural* of HELIX.

helicopter /'helɪkɒptə/ *noun* wingless aircraft lifted and propelled by overhead blades revolving horizontally.

heliograph /'hi:lɪəgrɑ:f/ ● *noun* signalling apparatus reflecting flashes of sunlight. ● *verb* send (message) thus.

heliotrope /'hi:lɪətrəʊp/ *noun* plant with fragrant purple flowers.

heliport /'helɪpɔ:t/ *noun* place where helicopters take off and land.

helium /'hi:lɪəm/ *noun* light nonflammable gaseous element.

helix /'hi:lɪks/ *noun* (*plural* **helices** /'hi:lɪsi:z/) spiral or coiled curve.

hell *noun* home of the damned after death; place or state of misery. ▫ **hellish** *adjective*; **hellishly** *adverb.*

he'll /hi:l/ he will; he shall.

hellebore /'helɪbɔ:/ *noun* evergreen plant of kind including Christmas rose.

Hellene /'heli:n/ *noun* Greek. ▫ **Hellenic** /-'len-/ *adjective*; **Hellenism** /-lɪn-/ *noun*; **Hellenist** /-lɪn-/ *noun.*

Hellenistic /helɪ'nɪstɪk/ *adjective* of Greek history, language, and culture of late 4th to late 1st c. BC.

hello /hə'ləʊ/ (also **hallo**, **hullo**) ● *interjection expressing informal greeting or surprise, or calling attention.* ● *noun* (*plural* **-s**) cry of 'hello'.

helm *noun* tiller or wheel for managing rudder. ▫ **at the helm** in control; **helmsman** person who steers ship.

helmet /'helmɪt/ *noun* protective headcover of policeman, motorcyclist, etc.

help ● *verb* provide with means to what is needed or sought, be useful to; (usually in negative) prevent, refrain from. ● *noun* act of helping; person or thing that helps; *colloquial* domestic assistant or assistance; remedy etc.; (**help oneself**) (often + *to*) serve oneself, take without permission. ▫ **helpline** telephone service providing help with problems. ▫ **helper** *noun.*

helpful *adjective* giving help, useful. ▫ **helpfully** *adverb*; **helpfulness** *noun.*

helping *noun* portion of food.

helpless *adjective* lacking help, defenceless; unable to act without help. □ **helplessly** *adverb*; **helplessness** *noun*.

helter-skelter /heltəˈskeltə/ ● *adverb & adjective* in disorderly haste. ● *noun* spiral slide at funfair.

hem[1] ● *noun* border of cloth where edge is turned under and sewn down. ● *verb* (**-mm-**) sew edge thus. □ **hem in** confine, restrict; **hemline** lower edge of skirt etc.; **hemstitch** (make hem with) ornamental stitch.

hem[2] *interjection expressing hesitation or calling attention by slight cough.*

hemisphere /ˈhemɪsfɪə/ *noun* half sphere; half earth, esp. as divided by equator or by line passing through poles; each half of brain. □ **hemispherical** /-ˈsfer-/ *adjective*.

hemlock /ˈhemlɒk/ *noun* poisonous plant with small white flowers; poison made from it.

hemp *noun* (in full **Indian hemp**) Asian herbaceous plant; its fibre used for rope etc.; narcotic drug made from it.

hempen *adjective* made of hemp.

hen *noun* female bird, esp. of domestic fowl. □ **henbane** poisonous hairy plant; **hen-party** *colloquial* party of women only; **henpecked** (of husband) domineered over by his wife.

hence *adverb* from now; for this reason. □ **henceforth**, **henceforward** from this time onwards.

henchman /ˈhentʃmən/ *noun usually derogatory* trusted supporter.

henge *noun* prehistoric circle of wood or stone uprights, as at *Stonehenge*.

henna /ˈhenə/ ● *noun* tropical shrub; reddish dye made from it and used esp. to colour hair. ● *verb* (**hennaed**, **hennaing**) dye with henna.

henry /ˈhenrɪ/ *noun* (*plural* **-s**, **-ies**) SI unit of inductance.

hep = HIP[4].

hepatitis /hepəˈtaɪtɪs/ *noun* inflammation of the liver.

hepta- *combining form* seven.

heptagon /ˈheptəgən/ *noun* plane figure with 7 sides and angles. □ **heptagonal** /-ˈtæg-/ *adjective*.

her ● *pronoun* (as object of verb) the female person or thing in question; *colloquial* she. ● *adjective* of or belonging to her.

herald /ˈher(ə)ld/ ● *noun* messenger; forerunner; official. ● *verb* proclaim approach of; usher in. □ **heraldic** /-ˈræld-/ *adjective*.

heraldry /ˈherəldrɪ/ *noun* (science or art of) armorial bearings.

herb *noun* non-woody seed-bearing plant; plant with leaves, seeds, or flowers used for flavouring, medicine, etc.

herbaceous /hɜːˈbeɪʃəs/ *adjective* of or like herbs. □ **herbaceous border** border in garden etc. containing flowering plants.

herbage *noun* vegetation collectively, esp. pasturage.

herbal ● *adjective* of herbs. ● *noun* book about herbs.

herbalist *noun* dealer in medicinal herbs; writer on herbs.

herbarium /hɜːˈbeərɪəm/ *noun* (*plural* **-ria**) collection of dried plants.

herbicide /ˈhɜːbɪsaɪd/ *noun* poison used to destroy unwanted vegetation.

herbivore /ˈhɜːbɪvɔː/ *noun* plant-eating animal. □ **herbivorous** /-ˈbɪvərəs/ *adjective*.

Herculean /hɜːkjʊˈliːən/ *adjective* having or requiring great strength or effort.

herd ● *noun* number of cattle etc. feeding or travelling together; (**the herd**) *derogatory* large number of people. ● *verb* (cause to) go in herd; tend. □ **herdsman** keeper of herds.

here ● *adverb* in or to this place; *indicating a person or thing*; at this point. ● *noun* this place. □ **hereabout(s)** somewhere near here; **hereafter** (in) future, (in) next world; **hereby** by this means; **herein** *formal* in this place, book, etc.; **hereinafter** *formal* from this point on, below (in document); **hereof** *formal* of this; **hereto** *formal* to this; **heretofore** *formal* formerly; **hereupon** after or in consequence of this; **herewith** with this.

hereditary /hɪˈredɪtərɪ/ *adjective* transmitted genetically from one generation to another; descending by inheritance; holding position by inheritance.

heredity /hɪˈredɪtɪ/ *noun* genetic transmission of physical or mental characteristics; these characteristics; genetic constitution.

heresy /ˈherəsɪ/ *noun* (*plural* **-ies**) *esp. RC Church* religious belief contrary to orthodox doctrine; opinion contrary to what is normally accepted.

heretic /ˈherətɪk/ *noun* believer in heresy. □ **heretical** /hɪˈret-/ *adjective*.

heritable /ˈherɪtəb(ə)l/ *adjective* that can be inherited.

heritage /ˈherɪtɪdʒ/ *noun* what is or may be inherited; inherited circumstances, benefits, etc.; nation's historic buildings, countryside, etc.

hermaphrodite /hɜːˈmæfrədaɪt/ ● *noun* person, animal, or plant with organs of both sexes. ● *adjective* combining both sexes. □ **hermaphroditic** /-ˈdɪt-/ *adjective*.

hermetic /hɜːˈmetɪk/ *adjective* with an airtight seal. □ **hermetically** *adverb*.

hermit /ˈhɜːmɪt/ *noun* person living in solitude. □ **hermit-crab** crab which lives in mollusc's cast-off shell.

hermitage *noun* hermit's dwelling; secluded residence.

hernia /ˈhɜːnɪə/ *noun* protrusion of part of organ through wall of cavity containing it.

hero /ˈhɪərəʊ/ *noun* (*plural* **-es**) person admired for courage, outstanding achievements, etc.; chief male character in play, story, etc. □ **hero-worship** idealization of admired person.

heroic /hɪˈrəʊɪk/ ● *adjective* fit for, or like, a hero; very brave. ● *noun* (in *plural*) over-dramatic talk or behaviour. □ **heroically** *adverb*.

heroin /ˈherəʊɪn/ *noun* sedative addictive drug prepared from morphine.

heroine /ˈherəʊɪn/ *noun* female hero; chief female character in play, story, etc.

heroism /ˈherəʊɪz(ə)m/ *noun* heroic conduct.

heron /ˈherən/ *noun* long-necked long-legged wading bird.

herpes /ˈhɜːpiːz/ *noun* virus disease causing blisters.

Herr /heə/ *noun* (*plural* **Herren** /ˈherən/) *title of German man*.

herring /ˈherɪŋ/ *noun* (*plural* same or **-s**) N. Atlantic edible fish. □ **herring-bone** stitch or weave of small 'V' shapes making zigzag pattern.

hers /hɜːz/ *pronoun* the one(s) belonging to her.

herself /həˈself/ *pronoun: emphatic form of* SHE *or* HER; *reflexive form of* HER.

hertz *noun* (*plural* same) SI unit of frequency (one cycle per second).

he's /hiːz/ he is; he has.

hesitant /ˈhezɪt(ə)nt/ *adjective* hesitating. □ **hesitance** *noun*; **hesitancy** *noun*; **hesitantly** *adverb*.

hesitate /ˈhezɪteɪt/ *verb* (**-ting**) feel or show indecision; pause; (often + *to do*) be reluctant. □ **hesitation** *noun*.

hessian /ˈhesɪən/ *noun* strong coarse hemp or jute sacking.

heterodox /ˈhetərəʊdɒks/ *adjective* not orthodox. ▫ **heterodoxy** *noun*.

heterogeneous /hetərəʊˈdʒiːnɪəs/ *adjective* diverse; varied in content. ▫ **heterogeneity** /-dʒɪˈniːɪtɪ/ *noun*.

heteromorphic /hetərəʊˈmɔːfɪk/ *adjective* (also **heteromorphous** /-ˈmɔːfəs/) *Biology* of dissimilar forms.

heterosexual /hetərəʊˈsekʃʊəl/ ● *adjective* feeling or involving sexual attraction to opposite sex. ● *noun* heterosexual person. ▫ **heterosexuality** /-ˈæl-/ *noun*.

het up *adjective colloquial* overwrought.

heuristic /hjʊəˈrɪstɪk/ *adjective* serving to discover; using trial and error.

hew *verb* (*past participle* **hewn** /hjuːn/ or **hewed**) chop or cut with axe, sword, etc.; cut into shape.

hex ● *verb* practise witchcraft; bewitch. ● *noun* magic spell.

hexa- *combining form* six.

hexagon /ˈheksəgən/ *noun* plane figure with 6 sides and angles. ▫ **hexagonal** /-ˈsæg-/ *adjective*.

hexagram /ˈheksəgræm/ *noun* 6-pointed star formed by two intersecting equilateral triangles.

hexameter /hekˈsæmɪtə/ *noun* verse line of 6 metrical feet.

hey /heɪ/ *interjection calling attention or expressing surprise, inquiry, etc.* ▫ **hey presto!** *conjuror's phrase on completing trick.*

heyday /ˈheɪdeɪ/ *noun* time of greatest success, prime.

HF *abbreviation* high frequency.

HGV *abbreviation* heavy goods vehicle.

HH *abbreviation* Her or His Highness; His Holiness; double-hard (pencil lead).

hi /haɪ/ *interjection calling attention or as greeting.*

hiatus /haɪˈeɪtəs/ *noun* (*plural* **-tuses**) gap in series etc.; break between two vowels coming together but not in same syllable.

hibernate /ˈhaɪbəneɪt/ *verb* (**-ting**) (of animal) spend winter in dormant state. ▫ **hibernation** *noun*.

Hibernian /haɪˈbɜːnɪən/ *archaic poetical* ● *adjective* of Ireland. ● *noun* native of Ireland.

hibiscus /hɪˈbɪskəs/ *noun* (*plural* **-cuses**) cultivated shrub with large brightly coloured flowers.

hiccup /ˈhɪkʌp/ (also **hiccough**) ● *noun* involuntary audible spasm of respiratory organs; temporary or minor stoppage or difficulty. ● *verb* (**-p-**) make hiccup.

hick *noun esp. US colloquial* yokel.

hickory /ˈhɪkərɪ/ *noun* (*plural* **-ies**) N. American tree related to walnut; its wood.

hid *past* of HIDE[1].

hidden *past participle* of HIDE[1]. ▫ **hidden agenda** secret motivation behind policy etc., ulterior motive.

hide[1] ● *verb* (**-ding**; *past* **hid**; *past participle* **hidden** /ˈhɪd(ə)n/) put or keep out of sight; conceal oneself; (usually + *from*) conceal (fact). ● *noun* camouflaged shelter for observing wildlife. ▫ **hide-and-seek** game in which players hide and another searches for them; **hideaway** hiding place, retreat; **hide-out** *colloquial* hiding place.

hide[2] *noun* animal's skin, esp. tanned; *colloquial* human skin. ▫ **hidebound** rigidly conventional.

hideous /ˈhɪdɪəs/ *adjective* repulsive, revolting. ▫ **hideously** *adverb*.

hiding *noun colloquial* thrashing.

hierarchy /ˈhaɪərɑːkɪ/ *noun* (*plural* **-ies**) system of grades of authority ranked one above another. ▫ **hierarchical** /-ˈrɑːk-/ *adjective*.

hieroglyph /ˈhaɪərəglɪf/ *noun* picture representing word or syllable, esp. in ancient Egyptian. ▫ **hieroglyphic** /-ˈglɪf-/ *adjective*; **hieroglyphics** /-ˈglɪf-/ *plural noun*.

hi-fi /ˈhaɪfaɪ/ *colloquial* ● *adjective* of high fidelity. ● *noun* (*plural* **-s**) equipment for such sound reproduction.

higgledy-piggledy /hɪgəldɪˈpɪgəldɪ/ *adverb & adjective* in disorder.

high /haɪ/ ● *adjective* of great or specified upward extent; far above ground or sea level; coming above normal level; of exalted rank or position, of superior quality; extreme, intense; (often + *on*) *colloquial* intoxicated by alcohol or drugs; (of sound) shrill; (of period etc.) at its peak; (of meat etc.) beginning to go bad. ● *noun* high or highest level or number; area of high barometric pressure; *slang* euphoric state, esp. drug-induced. ● *adverb* far up, aloft; in or to high degree; at high price; (of sound) at high pitch. ▫ **high altar** chief altar in church; **highball** *US* drink of spirits and soda etc.; **highbrow** *colloquial* (person) of superior intellect or culture; **high chair** child's chair with long legs and meal-tray; **High Church** section of Church of England emphasizing ritual, priestly authority, and sacraments; **high command** army commander-in-chief and associated staff; **High Commission** embassy from one Commonwealth country to another; **High Court** supreme court of justice for civil cases; **highfalutin(g)** *colloquial* pompous, pretentious; **high fidelity** high-quality sound reproduction; **high-flown** extravagant, bombastic; **high-flyer**, **-flier** person of great potential or ambition; **high frequency** *Radio* 3–30 megahertz; **high-handed** overbearing; **high-handedly** *adverb*; **high-handedness** *noun*; **high heels** woman's shoes with high heels; **high jump** athletic event consisting of jumping over high bar, *colloquial* drastic punishment; **high-level** conducted by people of high rank, (of computer language) close to ordinary language; **high-minded** of firm moral principles; **high-mindedness** *noun*; **high pressure** high degree of activity, atmospheric condition with pressure above average; **high priest** chief priest, head of cult; **high-rise** (of building) having many storeys; **high road** main road; **high school** secondary school; **high sea(s)** seas outside territorial waters; **high-spirited** cheerful; **high street** principal shopping street of town; **high tea** early evening meal of tea and cooked food; **high-tech** employing, requiring, or involved in high technology, imitating its style; **high technology** advanced (esp. electronic) technology; **high tension**, **voltage** electrical potential large enough to injure or damage; **high tide**, water time or level of tide at its peak; **high water mark** level reached at high water.

highland /ˈhaɪlənd/ ● *noun* (usually in *plural*) mountainous country, esp. (**the Highlands**) of N. Scotland. ● *adjective* of highland or Highlands. ▫ **highlander**, **Highlander** *noun*.

highlight ● *noun* moment or detail of vivid interest; bright part of picture; bleached streak in hair. ● *verb* bring into prominence; mark with highlighter.

highlighter *noun* coloured marker pen for emphasizing printed word.

highly *adverb* in high degree, favourably. ▫ **highly-strung** sensitive, nervous.

highness *noun* state of being high; (**His**, **Her**, **Your Highness**) *title of prince, princess, etc.*

highway *noun* public road, main route. ▫ **Highway Code** official handbook for road-users; **highwayman** *historical* (usually mounted) robber of stage-coaches.

hijack /ˈhaɪdʒæk/ ● *verb* seize control of (vehicle, aircraft, etc.), esp. to force it to different destination; steal (goods) in transit. ● *noun* hijacking. ▫ **hijacker** *noun*.

hike ● *noun* long walk, esp. in country for pleasure; rise in prices etc. ● *verb* (**-king**) go on hike. □ **hiker** *noun*.

hilarious /hɪˈleərɪəs/ *adjective* extremely funny; boisterously merry. □ **hilariously** *adverb*; **hilarity** /-ˈlær-/ *noun*.

hill *noun* natural elevation of ground, lower than mountain; heap, mound. □ **hill-billy** *US colloquial often derogatory* person from remote rural area. □ **hilly** *adjective* (**-ier**, **-iest**).

hillock /ˈhɪlək/ *noun* small hill, mound.

hilt *noun* handle of sword, dagger, etc.

him *pronoun* (as object of verb) the male person or animal in question, person of unspecified sex; *colloquial* he.

himself /hɪmˈself/ *pronoun: emphatic form of* HE *or* HIM; *reflexive form of* HIM.

hind[1] /haɪnd/ *adjective* at back. □ **hindquarters** rump and hind legs of quadruped; **hindsight** wisdom after event. □ **hindmost** *adjective*.

hind[2] /haɪnd/ *noun* female (esp. red) deer.

hinder[1] /ˈhɪndə/ *verb* impede; delay.

hinder[2] /ˈhaɪndə/ *adjective* rear, hind.

Hindi /ˈhɪndɪ/ *noun* group of spoken languages in N. India; one of official languages of India, literary form of Hindustani.

hindrance /ˈhɪndrəns/ *noun* obstruction.

Hindu /ˈhɪnduː/ ● *noun* (*plural* **-s**) follower of Hinduism. ● *adjective* of Hindus or Hinduism.

Hinduism /ˈhɪnduːɪz(ə)m/ *noun* main religious and social system of India, including belief in reincarnation and worship of several gods.

Hindustani /hɪndʊˈstɑːnɪ/ *noun* language based on Hindi, used in much of India.

hinge ● *noun* movable joint on which door, lid, etc. swings; principle on which all depends. ● *verb* (**-ging**) (+ *on*) depend on (event etc.); attach or be attached with hinge.

hinny /ˈhɪnɪ/ *noun* (*plural* **-ies**) offspring of female donkey and male horse.

hint ● *noun* indirect suggestion; slight indication; small piece of practical information; faint trace. ● *verb* suggest indirectly. □ **hint at** refer indirectly to.

hinterland /ˈhɪntəlænd/ *noun* district behind that lying along coast etc.

hip[1] *noun* projection of pelvis and upper part of thighbone. □ **hip-flask** small flask for spirits.

hip[2] *noun* fruit of rose.

hip[3] *interjection used to introduce cheer.*

hip[4] *adjective* (also **hep**) (**-pp-**) *slang* trendy, stylish. □ **hip hop**, **hip-hop** subculture combining rap music, graffiti art, and break-dancing.

hippie /ˈhɪpɪ/ *noun* (also **hippy**) (*plural* **-ies**) *colloquial* person (esp. in 1960s) rejecting convention, typically with long hair, jeans, etc.

hippo /ˈhɪpəʊ/ *noun* (*plural* **-s**) *colloquial* hippopotamus.

Hippocratic oath /hɪpəˈkrætɪk/ *noun* statement of ethics of medical profession.

hippodrome /ˈhɪpədrəʊm/ *noun* music-hall, dance hall, etc.; *historical* course for chariot races etc.

hippopotamus /hɪpəˈpɒtəməs/ *noun* (*plural* **-muses** or **-mi** /-maɪ/) large African mammal with short legs and thick skin, living by rivers etc.

hippy = HIPPIE.

hipster[1] /ˈhɪpstə/ ● *adjective* (of garment) hanging from hips rather than waist. ● *noun* (in *plural*) such trousers.

hipster[2] /ˈhɪpstə/ *noun slang* hip person.

hire ● *verb* (**-ring**) obtain use of (thing) or services of (person) for payment. ● *noun* hiring, being hired; payment for this. □ **hire out** grant temporary use of (thing) for payment; **hire purchase** system of purchase by paying in instalments. □ **hirer** *noun*.

hireling /ˈhaɪəlɪŋ/ *noun usually derogatory* person who works for hire.

hirsute /ˈhɜːsjuːt/ *adjective* hairy.

his /hɪz/ ● *adjective* of or belonging to him. ● *pronoun* the one(s) belonging to him.

Hispanic /hɪˈspænɪk/ ● *adjective* of Spain or Spain and Portugal; of Spain and other Spanish-speaking countries. ● *noun* Spanish-speaking person living in US.

hiss /hɪs/ ● *verb* make sharp sibilant sound, as of letter *s*; express disapproval of thus; whisper urgently or angrily. ● *noun* sharp sibilant sound.

histamine /ˈhɪstəmiːn/ *noun* chemical compound in body tissues associated with allergic reactions.

histology /hɪˈstɒlədʒɪ/ *noun* study of tissue structure.

historian /hɪˈstɔːrɪən/ *noun* writer of history; person learned in history.

historic /hɪˈstɒrɪk/ *adjective* famous in history or potentially so; *Grammar* (of tense) used to narrate past events.

historical *adjective* of history; belonging to or dealing with the past; not legendary; studying development over period of time. □ **historically** *adverb*.

historicity /hɪstəˈrɪsɪtɪ/ *noun* historical genuineness or accuracy.

historiography /hɪstɔːrɪˈɒgrəfɪ/ *noun* writing of history; study of this. □ **historiographer** *noun*.

history /ˈhɪstərɪ/ *noun* (*plural* **-ies**) continuous record of (esp. public) events; study of past events; total accumulation of these; (esp. eventful) past or record.

histrionic /hɪstrɪˈɒnɪk/ ● *adjective* (of behaviour) theatrical, dramatic. ● *noun* (in *plural*) insincere and dramatic behaviour designed to impress.

hit ● *verb* (**-tt-**; *past & past participle* **hit**) strike with blow or missile; (of moving body) strike with force; affect adversely; (often + *at*) aim blow; propel (ball etc.) with bat etc.; achieve, reach; *colloquial* encounter, arrive at. ● *noun* blow; shot that hits target; *colloquial* popular success. □ **hit it off** (often + *with*, *together*) get on well; **hit-and-run** (of person) causing damage or injury and leaving immediately, (of accident etc.) caused by such person(s); **hit-or-miss** random.

hitch ● *verb* fasten with loop etc.; move (thing) with jerk; *colloquial* hitchhike; obtain (lift). ● *noun* temporary difficulty, snag; jerk; kind of noose or knot; *colloquial* free ride in vehicle. □ **hitchhike** travel by means of free lifts in passing vehicles; **hitchhiker** *noun*.

hi-tech /ˈhaɪtek/ *adjective* high-tech.

hither /ˈhɪðə/ *adverb formal* to this place. □ **hitherto** up to now.

HIV *abbreviation* human immunodeficiency virus, either of two viruses causing Aids.

hive *noun* beehive. □ **hive off** (**-ving**) separate from larger group.

hives /haɪvz/ *plural noun* skin eruption, esp. nettle-rash.

HM *abbreviation* Her or His Majesty('s).

HMG *abbreviation* Her or His Majesty's Government.

HMI *abbreviation* Her or His Majesty's Inspector (of Schools).

HMS *abbreviation* Her or His Majesty's Ship.

HMSO *abbreviation* Her or His Majesty's Stationery Office.

HNC, HND *abbreviations* Higher National Certificate, Diploma.

ho /həʊ/ *interjection expressing triumph, derision, etc., or calling attention etc.*

hoard /hɔːd/ ● *noun* store (esp. of money or food). ● *verb* amass and store. □ **hoarder** *noun*.

hoarding /ˈhɔːdɪŋ/ *noun* structure erected to carry advertisements; temporary fence round building site etc.

hoar-frost /ˈhɔːfrɒst/ *noun* frozen water vapour on lawns.

hoarse /hɔːs/ *adjective* (of voice) rough, husky; having hoarse voice. □ **hoarsely** *adverb*; **hoarseness** *noun*.

hoary /ˈhɔːrɪ/ *adjective* (**-ier**, **-iest**) white or grey with age; aged; old and trite.

hoax ● *noun* humorous or malicious deception. ● *verb* deceive with hoax.

hob *noun* hotplates etc. on cooker or as separate unit; flat metal shelf at side of fire for heating pans etc. □ **hobnail** heavy-headed nail for boot-sole.

hobble /ˈhɒb(ə)l/ ● *verb* (**-ling**) walk lamely, limp; tie together legs of (horse etc.) to keep it from straying. ● *noun* limping gait; rope etc. used to hobble horse.

hobby /ˈhɒbɪ/ *noun* (*plural* **-ies**) leisure-time activity pursued for pleasure. □ **hobby-horse** stick with horse's head, used as toy, favourite subject or idea.

hobgoblin /ˈhɒbgɒblɪn/ *noun* mischievous imp; bogy.

hobnob /ˈhɒbnɒb/ *verb* (**-bb-**) (usually + *with*) mix socially or informally.

hobo /ˈhəʊbəʊ/ *noun* (*plural* **-es** or **-s**) *US* wandering worker; tramp.

hock[1] *noun* joint of quadruped's hind leg between knee and fetlock.

hock[2] *noun* German white wine.

hock[3] *verb esp. US colloquial* pawn. □ **in hock** in pawn, in debt, in prison.

hockey /ˈhɒkɪ/ *noun* team game played with ball and hooked sticks.

hocus-pocus /həʊkəsˈpəʊkəs/ *noun* trickery.

hod *noun* trough on pole for carrying bricks etc.; portable container for coal.

hodgepodge = HOTCHPOTCH.

hoe ● *noun* long-handled tool for weeding etc. ● *verb* (**hoes**, **hoed**, **hoeing**) weed (crops), loosen (soil), or dig up etc. with hoe.

hog ● *noun* castrated male pig; *colloquial* greedy person. ● *verb* (**-gg-**) *colloquial* take greedily; monopolize. □ **go the whole hog** *colloquial* do thing thoroughly; **hogwash** *colloquial* nonsense.

hogmanay /ˈhɒgmənеɪ/ *noun Scottish* New Year's Eve.

hogshead /ˈhɒgzhed/ *noun* large cask; liquid or dry measure (about 50 gals.).

ho-ho /həʊˈhəʊ/ *interjection representing deep jolly laugh or expressing surprise, triumph, or derision.*

hoick *verb colloquial* (often + *out*) lift or jerk.

hoi polloi /hɔɪ pəˈlɔɪ/ *noun* the masses; ordinary people. [Greek]

hoist ● *verb* raise or haul up; raise with ropes and pulleys etc. ● *noun* act of hoisting; apparatus for hoisting. □ **hoist with one's own petard** caught by one's own trick etc.

hoity-toity /hɔɪtɪˈtɔɪtɪ/ *adjective* haughty.

hokum /ˈhəʊkəm/ *noun esp. US slang* sentimental or unreal material in film etc.; bunkum, rubbish.

hold[1] /həʊld/ ● *verb* (*past & past participle* **held**) keep fast; grasp; keep in particular position; contain, have capacity for; possess, have (property, qualifications, job, etc.); conduct, celebrate; detain; think, believe; not give way; reserve. ● *noun* (+ *on*, *over*) power over; grasp; manner or means of holding. □ **holdall** large soft travelling bag; **hold back** impede, keep for oneself, (often + *from*) refrain; **hold down** repress, *colloquial* be competent enough to keep (job); **hold forth** speak at length or tediously; **hold on** maintain grasp, wait, not ring off; **hold one's tongue** *colloquial* remain silent; **hold out** stretch forth (hand etc.), offer (inducement etc.), maintain resistance, (+ *for*) continue to demand; **hold over** postpone; **hold up** *verb* sustain, display, obstruct, stop and rob by force; **hold-up** *noun* stoppage, delay, robbery by force; **hold with** (usually in negative) *colloquial* approve of.

hold[2] /həʊld/ *noun* cavity in lower part of ship or aircraft for cargo.

holder *noun* device for holding something; possessor of title, shares, etc.; occupant of office etc.

holding *noun* tenure of land; stocks, property, etc. held. □ **holding company** one formed to hold shares of other companies.

hole *noun* empty space in solid body; opening in or through something; burrow; *colloquial* small or gloomy place; *colloquial* awkward situation; (in games) cavity or receptacle for ball, *Golf* section of course from tee to hole. □ **hole up** (**-ling**) *US colloquial* hide oneself. □ **holey** *adjective*.

holiday /ˈhɒlɪdeɪ/ ● *noun* (often in *plural*) extended period of recreation, esp. spent away from home; break from work or school. ● *verb* spend holiday.

holiness /ˈhəʊlɪnɪs/ *noun* being holy or sacred; (**His**, **Your Holiness**) *title of Pope*.

holism /ˈhəʊlɪz(ə)m/ *noun* (also **wholism**) theory that certain wholes are greater than sum of their parts; *Medicine* treating of whole person rather than symptoms of disease. □ **holistic** /-ˈlɪst-/ *adjective*.

hollandaise sauce /hɒlənˈdeɪz/ *noun* creamy sauce of butter, egg yolks, vinegar, etc.

holler /ˈhɒlə/ *verb & noun US colloquial* shout.

hollow /ˈhɒləʊ/ ● *adjective* having cavity; not solid; sunken; echoing; empty; hungry; meaningless; insincere. ● *noun* hollow place; hole; valley. ● *verb* (often + *out*) make hollow, excavate. ● *adverb colloquial* completely.

holly /ˈhɒlɪ/ *noun* (*plural* **-ies**) evergreen prickly-leaved shrub with red berries.

hollyhock /ˈhɒlɪhɒk/ *noun* tall plant with showy flowers.

holm /həʊm/ *noun* (in full **holm-oak**) evergreen oak.

holocaust /ˈhɒləkɔːst/ *noun* wholesale destruction; (**the Holocaust**) mass murder of Jews by Nazis 1939–45.

hologram /ˈhɒləgræm/ *noun* photographic pattern having 3-dimensional effect.

holograph /ˈhɒləgrɑːf/ ● *adjective* wholly in handwriting of person named as author. ● *noun* such document.

holography /həˈlɒgrəfɪ/ *noun* study or production of holograms.

holster /ˈhəʊlstə/ *noun* leather case for pistol or revolver on belt etc.

holy /ˈhəʊlɪ/ *adjective* (**-ier**, **-iest**) morally and spiritually excellent; belonging or devoted to God. □ **Holy Ghost** Holy Spirit; **Holy Land** area between River Jordan and Mediterranean; **holy of holies** inner chamber of Jewish temple, thing regarded as most sacred; **holy orders** those of bishop, priest, and deacon; **Holy Saturday** day before Easter; **Holy See** papacy, papal court; **Holy Spirit** Third Person of Trinity; **Holy Week** week before Easter; **Holy Writ** Bible.

homage /ˈhɒmɪdʒ/ *noun* tribute, expression of reverence.

Homburg /ˈhɒmbɜːg/ *noun* man's felt hat with narrow curled brim and lengthwise dent in crown.

home ● *noun* place where one lives; residence; (esp. good or bad) family circumstances; native land; institution caring for people or animals; place where thing originates, is kept, is most common, etc.; (in games) finishing line in race, goal, home match or win etc. ● *adjective* of or connected with home; carried on or done at home; not foreign; played etc. on team's own ground. ● *adverb* to or at home; to point aimed at. ● *verb* (**-ming**) (of pigeon) return home; (often + *on, in on*) (of missile etc.) be guided to destination. □ **at home** *adjective* in one's house or native land, at ease, well-informed, available to callers; **at-home** *noun* social reception in person's home; **home-brew** beer etc. brewed at home; **Home Counties** those lying round London; **home economics** study of household management; **homeland** native land, any of several areas reserved for black South Africans; **Home Office** British government department concerned with immigration, law and order, etc.; **home rule** self-government; **Home Secretary** minister in charge of Home Office; **homesick** depressed by absence from home; **homesickness** such depression; **homestead** house with outbuildings, farm; **homework** lessons to be done by schoolchild at home. □ **homeless** *adjective*; **homeward** *adjective & adverb*; **homewards** *adverb*.

homely *adjective* (**-ier, -iest**) plain; unpretentious; *US* unattractive; cosy. □ **homeliness** *noun*.

homeopathy etc. *US* = HOMOEOPATHY etc.

Homeric /həʊˈmerɪk/ *adjective* of or in style of the ancient Greek poet Homer; of Bronze Age Greece.

homey *adjective* (**-mier, -miest**) suggesting home; cosy.

homicide /ˈhɒmɪsaɪd/ *noun* killing of person by another; person who kills another. □ **homicidal** /-ˈsaɪd-/ *adjective*.

homily /ˈhɒmɪlɪ/ *noun* (*plural* **-ies**) short sermon; moralizing lecture. □ **homiletic** /-ˈlet-/ *adjective*.

homing *adjective* (of pigeon) trained to fly home; (of device) for guiding to target etc.

hominid /ˈhɒmɪnɪd/ ● *adjective* of mammal family of existing and fossil man. ● *noun* member of this.

hominoid /ˈhɒmɪnɔɪd/ ● *adjective* like a human. ● *noun* animal resembling human.

homoeopathy /həʊmɪˈɒpəθɪ/ *noun* (*US* **homeopathy**) treatment of disease by drugs that in healthy person would produce symptoms of the disease. □ **homoeopath** /ˈhəʊmɪəʊpæθ/ *noun*; **homoeopathic** /-ˈpæθ-/ *adjective*.

homogeneous /hɒməˈdʒiːnɪəs/ *adjective* (having parts) of same kind or nature; uniform. □ **homogeneity** /-dʒɪˈniːɪtɪ/ *noun*; **homogeneously** *adverb*.

■ **Usage** *Homogeneous* is often confused with *homogenous* (and pronounced /həˈmɒdʒənəs/, with the stress on the *-mog-*), but that is a term in biology meaning 'similar owing to common descent'.

homogenize /həˈmɒdʒɪnaɪz/ *verb* (also **-ise**) (**-zing** or **-sing**) make homogeneous; treat (milk) so that cream does not separate.

homologous /həˈmɒləgəs/ *adjective* having same relation, relative position, etc.; corresponding.

homology /həˈmɒlədʒɪ/ *noun* homologous relation, correspondence.

homonym /ˈhɒmənɪm/ *noun* word spelt or pronounced like another but of different meaning.

homophobia /hɒməˈfəʊbɪə/ *noun* hatred or fear of homosexuals. □ **homophobe** /ˈhɒm-/ *noun*; **homophobic** *adjective*.

homophone /ˈhɒməfəʊn/ *noun* word pronounced like another but having different meaning, e.g. *beach, beech*.

Homo sapiens /həʊməʊ ˈsæpɪenz/ *noun* modern humans regarded as a species. [Latin]

homosexual /hɒməˈsekʃʊəl/ ● *adjective* feeling or involving sexual attraction to people of same sex. ● *noun* homosexual person. □ **homosexuality** /-ˈæl-/ *noun*.

Hon. *abbreviation* Honorary; Honourable.

hone ● *noun* whetstone, esp. for razors. ● *verb* (**-ning**) sharpen (as) on hone.

honest /ˈɒnɪst/ ● *adjective* not lying, cheating, or stealing; sincere; fairly earned. ● *adverb colloquial* genuinely, really. □ **honestly** *adverb*.

honesty /ˈɒnɪstɪ/ *noun* being honest, truthfulness; plant with purple or white flowers and flat round pods.

honey /ˈhʌnɪ/ *noun* (*plural* **-s**) sweet sticky yellowish fluid made by bees from nectar; colour of this; sweetness; darling.

honeycomb ● *noun* beeswax structure of hexagonal cells for honey and eggs; pattern arranged hexagonally. ● *verb* fill with cavities; mark with honeycomb pattern.

honeydew *noun* sweet substance excreted by aphids; variety of melon.

honeyed *adjective* sweet, sweet-sounding.

honeymoon ● *noun* holiday of newly married couple; initial period of enthusiasm or goodwill. ● *verb* spend honeymoon.

honeysuckle *noun* climbing shrub with fragrant flowers.

honk ● *noun* sound of car horn; cry of wild goose. ● *verb* (cause to) make honk.

honky-tonk /ˈhɒŋkɪtɒŋk/ *noun colloquial* ragtime piano music.

honor *US* = HONOUR.

honorable *US* = HONOURABLE.

honorarium /ɒnəˈreərɪəm/ *noun* (*plural* **-s** or **-ria**) voluntary payment for professional services.

honorary /ˈɒnərərɪ/ *adjective* conferred as honour; unpaid.

honorific /ɒnəˈrɪfɪk/ *adjective* conferring honour; implying respect.

honour /ˈɒnə/ (*US* **honor**) ● *noun* high respect, public regard; adherence to what is right; nobleness of mind; thing conferred as distinction (esp. official award for bravery or achievement); privilege; (**His, Her, Your Honour**) *title of judge etc.*; person or thing that brings honour; chastity, reputation for this; (in *plural*) specialized degree course or special distinction in exam; (in *plural*) (in card games) 4 or 5 highest-ranking cards; *Golf* right of driving off first. ● *verb* respect highly; confer honour on; accept or pay (bill, cheque) when due. □ **do the honours** perform duties of host etc.

honourable *adjective* (*US* **honorable**) deserving, bringing, or showing honour; (**Honourable**) *courtesy title of MPs, certain officials, and children of certain ranks of the nobility.* □ **honourably** *adverb*.

hooch /huːtʃ/ *noun US colloquial* alcoholic spirits, esp. inferior or illicit.

hood[1] /hʊd/ ● *noun* covering for head and neck, esp. as part of garment; separate hoodlike garment; folding top of car etc.; *US* bonnet of car etc.; protective cover. ● *verb* cover with hood. □ **hooded** *adjective*.

hood[2] /hʊd/ *noun US slang* gangster, gunman.

hoodlum /ˈhuːdləm/ *noun* hooligan; gangster.

hoodoo /ˈhuːduː/ *noun US* bad luck; thing or person that brings this.

hoodwink *verb* deceive, delude.

hoof /huːf/ *noun* (*plural* **-s** or **hooves** /huːvz/) horny part of foot of horse etc. □ **hoof it** *slang* go on foot.

hook /hʊk/ ● *noun* bent piece of metal etc. for catching hold or for hanging things on; curved cutting instrument; hook-shaped thing; hooking stroke; *Boxing* short swinging blow. ● *verb* grasp, secure, fasten, or catch with hook; (in sports) send (ball) in curving or deviating path; *Rugby* secure (ball) in scrum with foot. □ **hook and eye** small hook and loop as fastener; **hook, line, and sinker** completely; **hook-up**

connection, esp. of broadcasting equipment; **hookworm** worm infesting intestines of humans and animals.

hookah /ˈhʊkə/ *noun* tobacco pipe with long tube passing through water to cool smoke.

hooked *adjective* hook-shaped; (often + *on*) *slang* addicted or captivated.

hooker *noun Rugby* player in front row of scrum who tries to hook ball; *slang* prostitute.

hooligan /ˈhuːlɪgən/ *noun* young ruffian. □ **hooliganism** *noun*.

hoop /huːp/ ● *noun* circular band of metal, wood, etc., esp. as part of framework; wooden etc. circle bowled by child or used by circus performer etc.; arch through which balls are hit in croquet. ● *verb* bind with hoop(s). □ **hoop-la** game with rings thrown to encircle prizes.

hoopoe /ˈhuːpuː/ *noun* bird with variegated plumage and fanlike crest.

hooray = HURRAH.

hoot /huːt/ ● *noun* owl's cry; sound of car's horn etc.; shout of derision etc.; *colloquial* (cause of) laughter; (also **two hoots**) *slang* anything, in the slightest. ● *verb* utter hoot(s); greet or drive away with hoots; sound (horn).

hooter *noun* thing that hoots, esp. car's horn or siren; *slang* nose.

Hoover /ˈhuːvə/ ● *noun proprietary term* vacuum cleaner. ● *verb* (**hoover**) clean or (+ *up*) suck up with vacuum cleaner.

hooves *plural* of HOOF.

hop[1] ● *verb* (**-pp-**) (of bird, frog, etc.) spring with all feet at once; (of person) jump on one foot; move or go quickly, leap. ● *noun* hopping movement; *colloquial* dance; short journey, esp. flight. □ **hop in, out** *colloquial* get into or out of car etc.; **hopscotch** child's game of hopping over squares marked on ground.

hop[2] *noun* climbing plant with bitter cones used to flavour beer etc.; (in *plural*) these cones.

hope ● *noun* expectation and desire; person or thing giving cause for hope; what is hoped for. ● *verb* (**-ping**) feel hope; expect and desire.

hopeful *adjective* feeling or inspiring hope, promising.

hopefully *adverb* in a hopeful way; it is to be hoped.

■ **Usage** The use of *hopefully* to mean 'it is to be hoped' is common, but it is considered incorrect by some people.

hopeless *adjective* feeling or admitting no hope; inadequate, incompetent. □ **hopelessly** *adverb*; **hopelessness** *noun*.

hopper *noun* funnel-like device for feeding grain into mill etc.; hopping insect.

horde *noun usually derogatory* large group, gang.

horehound /ˈhɔːhaʊnd/ *noun* herb with aromatic bitter juice.

horizon /həˈraɪz(ə)n/ *noun* line at which earth and sky appear to meet; limit of mental perception, interest, etc.

horizontal /hɒrɪˈzɒnt(ə)l/ ● *adjective* parallel to plane of horizon; level, flat. ● *noun* horizontal line, plane, etc. □ **horizontally** *adverb*.

hormone /ˈhɔːməʊn/ *noun* substance produced by body and transported in tissue fluids to stimulate cells or tissues to growth etc.; similar synthetic substance. □ **hormone replacement therapy** treatment with hormones to relieve menopausal symptoms. □ **hormonal** /-ˈməʊn-/ *adjective*.

horn *noun* hard outgrowth, often curved and pointed, on head of animal; hornlike projection; substance of horns; brass wind instrument; instrument giving warning. □ **hornbeam** tough-wooded hedgerow tree; **hornbill** bird with hornlike excrescence on bill; **horn of plenty** cornucopia; **horn-rimmed** (of spectacles) having rims of horn or similar substance. □ **horned** *adjective*.

hornblende /ˈhɔːnblend/ *noun* dark brown etc. mineral constituent of granite etc.

hornet /ˈhɔːnɪt/ *noun* large species of wasp.

hornpipe *noun* (music for) lively dance associated esp. with sailors.

horny *adjective* (**-ier, -iest**) of or like horn; hard; *slang* sexually excited. □ **horniness** *noun*.

horology /həˈrɒlədʒɪ/ *noun* clockmaking. □ **horological** /hɒrəˈlɒdʒ-/ *adjective*.

horoscope /ˈhɒrəskəʊp/ *noun* prediction of person's future based on position of planets at his or her birth.

horrendous /həˈrendəs/ *adjective* horrifying. □ **horrendously** *adverb*.

horrible /ˈhɒrɪb(ə)l/ *adjective* causing horror; *colloquial* unpleasant. □ **horribly** *adverb*.

horrid /ˈhɒrɪd/ *adjective* horrible; *colloquial* unpleasant.

horrific /həˈrɪfɪk/ *adjective* horrifying. □ **horrifically** *adverb*.

horrify /ˈhɒrɪfaɪ/ *verb* (**-ies**, **-ied**) arouse horror in; shock. □ **horrifying** *adjective*.

horror /ˈhɒrə/ ● *noun* intense loathing or fear; (often + *of*) deep dislike; *colloquial* intense dismay; horrifying thing. ● *adjective* (of films etc.) designed to arouse feelings of horror.

hors d'oeuvre /ɔː ˈdɜːvr/ *noun* appetizer served at start of meal.

horse ● *noun* large 4-legged hoofed mammal with mane, used for riding etc.; adult male horse; vaulting-block; supporting frame. ● *verb* (**-sing**) (+ *around*) fool about. □ **horsebox** closed vehicle for transporting horse(s); **horse brass** brass ornament originally for horse's harness; **horse chestnut** tree with conical clusters of flowers, its dark brown fruit; **horse-drawn** pulled by horse(s); **horsefly** biting insect troublesome to horses; **Horse Guards** cavalry brigade of British household troops; **horsehair** (padding etc. of) hair from mane or tail of horse; **horseman** (skilled) rider on horseback; **horsemanship** skill in riding; **horseplay** boisterous play; **horsepower** (*plural* same) unit of rate of doing work; **horse race** race between horses with riders; **horse racing** sport of racing horses; **horseradish** plant with pungent root used to make sauce; **horse sense** *colloquial* plain common sense; **horseshoe** U-shaped iron shoe for horse, thing of this shape; **horsetail** (plant resembling) horse's tail; **horsewhip** *noun* whip for horse, *verb* beat (person) with this; **horsewoman** (skilled) woman rider on horseback.

horsy *adjective* (**-ier, -iest**) of or like horse; concerned with horses.

horticulture /ˈhɔːtɪkʌltʃə/ *noun* art of gardening. □ **horticultural** /-ˈkʌlt-/ *adjective*; **horticulturist** /-ˈkʌlt-/ *noun*.

hosanna /həʊˈzænə/ *noun & interjection* cry of adoration.

hose /həʊz/ ● *noun* (also **hose-pipe**) flexible tube for conveying liquids; (treated as *plural*) stockings and socks collectively; *historical* breeches. ● *verb* (**-sing**) (often + *down*) water, spray, or drench with hose.

hosier /ˈhəʊzɪə/ *noun* dealer in stockings and socks. □ **hosiery** *noun*.

hospice /ˈhɒspɪs/ *noun* home for (esp. terminally) ill or destitute people; travellers' lodging kept by religious order etc.

hospitable /hɒsˈpɪtəb(ə)l/ *adjective* giving hospitality. □ **hospitably** *adverb*.

hospital /ˈhɒspɪt(ə)l/ *noun* institution providing medical and surgical treatment and nursing for ill and injured people; *historical* hospice.

hospitality /hɒspɪˈtælɪtɪ/ *noun* friendly and generous reception of guests or strangers.

hospitalize /ˈhɒspɪtəlaɪz/ *verb* (also **-ise**) (**-zing** or **-sing**) send or admit to hospital. ◻ **hospitalization** *noun*.

host[1] /həʊst/ *noun* (usually + *of*) large number of people or things.

host[2] /həʊst/ ● *noun* person who entertains another as guest; compère; animal or plant having parasite; recipient of transplanted organ; landlord of inn. ● *verb* be host to (person) or of (event).

host[3] /həʊst/ *noun* (usually **the Host**) bread consecrated in Eucharist.

hostage /ˈhɒstɪdʒ/ *noun* person seized or held as security for fulfilment of a condition.

hostel /ˈhɒst(ə)l/ *noun* house of residence for students etc.; youth hostel.

hostelling *noun* (*US* **hosteling**) practice of staying in youth hostels. ◻ **hosteller** *noun*.

hostelry *noun* (*plural* **-ies**) *archaic* inn.

hostess /ˈhəʊstɪs/ *noun* woman who entertains guests, or customers at nightclub.

hostile /ˈhɒstaɪl/ *adjective* of enemy; (often + *to*) unfriendly, opposed.

hostility /hɒˈstɪlɪtɪ/ *noun* (*plural* **-ies**) being hostile; enmity; warfare; (in *plural*) acts of war.

hot ● *adjective* (**-tt-**) having high temperature, very warm; causing sensation of or feeling heat; pungent; excited; (often + *on*, *for*) eager; (of news) fresh; skilful, formidable; (+ *on*) knowledgeable about; *slang* (of stolen goods) difficult to dispose of. ● *verb* (**-tt-**) (usually + *up*) *colloquial* make or become hot; become more active, exciting, or dangerous. ◻ **hot air** *slang* empty or boastful talk; **hot-air balloon** balloon containing air heated by burners, causing it to rise; **hotbed** (+ *of*) environment conducive to (vice etc.), bed of earth heated by fermenting manure; **hot cross bun** bun marked with cross, eaten on Good Friday; **hot dog** *colloquial* hot sausage in bread roll; **hotfoot** in eager haste; **hothead** impetuous person; **hotheaded** impetuous; **hothouse** heated (mainly glass) building for growing plants, environment conducive to rapid growth; **hotline** direct telephone line; **hotplate** heated metal plate for cooking food or keeping it hot; **hotpot** dish of stewed meat and vegetables; **hot rod** vehicle modified for extra power and speed; **hot seat** *slang* awkward or responsible position, electric chair; **hot water** *colloquial* difficulty, trouble; **hot-water bottle** container filled with hot water to warm bed etc. ◻ **hotly** *adverb*.

hotchpotch /ˈhɒtʃpɒtʃ/ *noun* (also **hodgepodge** /ˈhɒdʒpɒdʒ/) confused mixture, jumble, esp. of ideas.

hotel /həʊˈtel/ *noun* (usually licensed) place providing meals and accommodation for payment.

hotelier /həʊˈtelɪə/ *noun* hotel-keeper.

houmous = HUMMUS.

hound /haʊnd/ ● *noun* dog used in hunting; *colloquial* despicable man. ● *verb* harass or pursue.

hour /aʊə/ *noun* twenty-fourth part of day and night, 60 minutes; time of day, point in time; (in *plural* after numerals in form 18.00, 20.30, etc.) this number of hours and minutes past midnight on the 24-hour clock; period set aside for some purpose; (in *plural*) working or open period; short time; time for action etc.; (**the hour**) each time o'clock of a whole number of hours. ◻ **hourglass** two connected glass bulbs containing sand that takes an hour to pass from upper to lower bulb. ◻ **hourly** *adjective & adverb*.

houri /ˈhʊərɪ/ *noun* (*plural* **-s**) beautiful young woman in Muslim paradise.

house ● *noun* /haʊs/ (*plural* /ˈhaʊzɪz/) building for human habitation; building for special purpose or for keeping animals or goods; (buildings of) religious community; section of boarding school etc.; division of school for games etc.; royal family, dynasty; (premises of) firm or institution; (building for) legislative etc. assembly; audience or performance in theatre etc. ● *verb* /haʊz/ (**-sing**) provide house for; store; enclose or encase (part etc.); fix in socket etc. ◻ **house arrest** detention in one's own house; **houseboat** boat equipped for living in; **housebound** confined to one's house through illness etc.; **housebreaker** burglar; **housebreaking** burglary; **housefly** common fly; **house-husband** man who does wife's traditional duties; **housekeeper** woman managing affairs of house; **housekeeping** management of house, money for this, record-keeping etc.; **houseman** resident junior doctor of hospital; **house-martin** bird which builds nests on house walls etc.; **housemaster**, **housemistress** teacher in charge of house in boarding school; **house music** pop music with synthesized drums and bass and fast beat; **House of Commons** elected chamber of Parliament; **House of Lords** chamber of Parliament that is mainly hereditary; **house plant** one grown indoors; **house-proud** attentive to care etc. of home; **house-trained** (of domestic animal) trained to be clean in house; **house-warming** party celebrating move to new house; **housewife** woman whose chief occupation is managing household; **housewifely** *adjective*; **housework** regular cleaning and cooking etc. in home.

household *noun* occupants of house; house and its affairs. ◻ **household name** well-known name; **household troops** those nominally guarding sovereign; **household word** well-known saying or name.

householder *noun* person who owns or rents house; head of household.

housing /ˈhaʊzɪŋ/ *noun* (provision of) houses; protective casing. ◻ **housing estate** residential area planned as a unit.

hove *past* of HEAVE.

hovel /ˈhɒv(ə)l/ *noun* small miserable dwelling.

hover /ˈhɒvə/ *verb* (of bird etc.) remain in one place in air; (often + *about*, *round*) linger.

hovercraft *noun* (*plural* same) vehicle moving on air-cushion provided by downward blast.

hoverport *noun* terminal for hovercraft.

how /haʊ/ *interrogative & relative adverb* by what means, in what way; in what condition; to what extent. ◻ **however** nevertheless, in whatever way, to whatever extent.

howdah /ˈhaʊdə/ *noun* (usually canopied) seat for riding elephant or camel.

howitzer /ˈhaʊɪtsə/ *noun* short gun firing shells at high elevation.

howl /haʊl/ ● *noun* long doleful cry of dog etc.; prolonged wailing noise; loud cry of pain, rage, derision, or laughter. ● *verb* make howl; weep loudly; utter with howl.

howler *noun colloquial* glaring mistake.

hoy *interjection used to call attention.*

hoyden /ˈhɔɪd(ə)n/ *noun* boisterous girl.

HP *abbreviation* hire purchase; (also **hp**) horsepower.

HQ *abbreviation* headquarters.

hr. *abbreviation* hour.

HRH *abbreviation* Her or His Royal Highness.

HRT *abbreviation* hormone replacement therapy.

HT *abbreviation* high tension.

hub *noun* central part of wheel, rotating on or with axle; centre of interest, activity, etc.

hubble-bubble /ˈhʌb(ə)lbʌb(ə)l/ *noun* simple hookah; confused sound or talk.

hubbub /'hʌbʌb/ *noun* confused noise of talking; disturbance.

hubby /'hʌbɪ/ *noun* (*plural* **-ies**) *colloquial* husband.

hubris /'hju:brɪs/ *noun* arrogant pride, presumption.

huckleberry /'hʌkəlbərɪ/ *noun* (*plural* **-ies**) low N. American shrub; its fruit.

huckster /'hʌkstə/ ● *noun* hawker; aggressive salesman. ● *verb* haggle; hawk (goods).

huddle /'hʌd(ə)l/ ● *verb* (**-ling**) (often + *up*) crowd together; nestle closely; (often + *up*) curl one's body up. ● *noun* confused mass; *colloquial* secret conference.

hue *noun* colour, tint.

hue and cry *noun* loud outcry.

huff ● *noun colloquial* fit of petulance. ● *verb* blow air, steam, etc.; (esp. **huff and puff**) bluster; remove (opponent's man) as forfeit in draughts. □ **huffy** *adjective* (**-ier**, **-iest**).

hug ● *verb* (**-gg-**) squeeze tightly in one's arms, esp. with affection; keep close to, fit tightly around. ● *noun* close clasp.

huge /hju:dʒ/ *adjective* very large or great.

hugely *adverb* extremely, very much.

hugger-mugger /'hʌgəmʌgə/ *adjective & adverb* in secret; in confusion.

Huguenot /'hju:gənəʊ/ *noun historical* French Protestant.

hula /'hu:lə/ *noun* (also **hula-hula**) Polynesian women's dance. □ **hula hoop** large hoop spun round the body.

hulk *noun* body of dismantled ship; *colloquial* large clumsy-looking person or thing.

hulking *adjective colloquial* bulky, clumsy.

hull[1] *noun* body of ship etc.

hull[2] ● *noun* outer covering of fruit. ● *verb* remove hulls of.

hullabaloo /hʌləbə'lu:/ *noun* uproar.

hullo = HELLO.

hum ● *verb* (**-mm-**) make low continuous sound like bee; sing with closed lips; make slight inarticulate sound; *colloquial* be active; *colloquial* smell unpleasantly. ● *noun* humming sound. □ **hummingbird** small tropical bird whose wings hum.

human /'hju:mən/ ● *adjective* of or belonging to species *Homo sapiens*; consisting of human beings; having characteristics of humankind, as being weak, fallible, sympathetic, etc. ● *noun* (*plural* **-s**) human being. □ **human being** man, woman, or child; **human chain** line of people for passing things along etc.; **humankind** human beings collectively; **human rights** those held to belong to all people; **human shield** person(s) placed in line of fire to discourage attack.

humane /hju:'meɪn/ *adjective* benevolent, compassionate; inflicting minimum pain; (of studies) tending to civilize. □ **humanely** *adverb*.

humanism /'hju:mənɪz(ə)m/ *noun* non-religious philosophy based on liberal human values; (often **Humanism**) literary culture, esp. in Renaissance. □ **humanist** *noun*; **humanistic** /-'nɪst-/ *adjective*.

humanitarian /hju:mænɪ'teərɪən/ ● *noun* person who seeks to promote human welfare. ● *adjective* of humanitarians. □ **humanitarianism** *noun*.

humanity /hju:'mænɪtɪ/ *noun* (*plural* **-ies**) human race; human nature; humaneness, benevolence; (usually in *plural*) subjects concerned with human culture.

humanize *verb* (also **-ise**) (**-zing** or **-sing**) make human or humane. □ **humanization** *noun*.

humanly *adverb* within human capabilities; in a human way.

humble /'hʌmb(ə)l/ ● *adjective* (**-r**, **-st**) having or showing low self-esteem; lowly, modest. ● *verb* (**-ling**) make humble; lower rank of. □ **eat humble pie** apologize humbly, accept humiliation. □ **humbly** *adverb*.

humbug /'hʌmbʌg/ ● *noun* deception, hypocrisy; impostor; striped peppermint-flavoured boiled sweet. ● *verb* (**-gg-**) be impostor; hoax.

humdinger /'hʌmdɪŋə/ *noun slang* remarkable person or thing.

humdrum /'hʌmdrʌm/ *adjective* dull, commonplace.

humerus /'hju:mərəs/ *noun* (*plural* **-ri** /-raɪ/) bone of upper arm.

humid /'hju:mɪd/ *adjective* warm and damp.

humidifier /hju:'mɪdɪfaɪə/ *noun* device for keeping atmosphere moist.

humidify /hju:'mɪdɪfaɪ/ *verb* (**-ies**, **-ied**) make (air etc.) humid.

humidity /hju:'mɪdɪtɪ/ *noun* (*plural* **-ies**) dampness; degree of moisture, esp. in atmosphere.

humiliate /hju:'mɪlɪeɪt/ *verb* (**-ting**) injure dignity or self-respect of. □ **humiliating** *adjective*; **humiliation** *noun*.

humility /hju:'mɪlɪtɪ/ *noun* humbleness; meekness.

hummock /'hʌmək/ *noun* hillock, hump.

hummus /'hʊmʊs/ *noun* (also **houmous**) dip of chickpeas, sesame paste, lemon juice, and garlic.

humor *US* = HUMOUR.

humorist /'hju:mərɪst/ *noun* humorous writer, talker, or actor.

humorous /'hju:mərəs/ *adjective* showing humour, comic. □ **humorously** *adverb*.

humour /'hju:mə/ (*US* **humor**) ● *noun* quality of being amusing; expression of humour in literature etc.; (in full **sense of humour**) ability to perceive or express humour; state of mind, mood; each of 4 fluids formerly held to determine physical and mental qualities. ● *verb* gratify or indulge (person, taste, etc.). □ **humourless** *adjective*.

hump ● *noun* rounded lump, esp. on back; rounded raised mass of earth etc.; (**the hump**) *slang* fit of depression or annoyance. ● *verb* (often + *about*) *colloquial* lift or carry with difficulty; make hump-shaped. □ **humpback (whale)** whale with dorsal fin; **humpback bridge** one with steep approach to top; **over the hump** past the most difficult stage.

humph /həmf/ *interjection & noun* inarticulate sound of dissatisfaction etc.

humus /'hju:məs/ *noun* organic constituent of soil formed by decomposition of plants.

hunch ● *verb* bend or arch into a hump. ● *noun* intuitive feeling; hump.

hundred /'hʌndrəd/ *adjective & noun* (*plural* same in first sense) ten times ten; *historical* subdivision of county; (**hundreds**) *colloquial* large number. □ **hundreds and thousands** tiny coloured sweets; **hundredweight** (*plural* same or **-s**) 112 lb (50.80 kg), *US* 100 lb. (45.4 kg) □ **hundredth** *adjective & noun*.

hundredfold *adjective & adverb* a hundred times as much or many.

hung *past & past participle* of HANG. □ **hung-over** suffering from hangover; **hung parliament** parliament in which no party has clear majority.

Hungarian /hʌŋ'geərɪən/ ● *noun* native, national, or language of Hungary. ● *adjective* of Hungary or its people or language.

hunger /'hʌŋgə/ ● *noun* lack of food; discomfort or exhaustion caused by this; (often + *for*, *after*) strong desire. ● *verb* (often + *for*, *after*) crave, desire; feel hunger. □ **hunger strike** refusal of food as protest.

hungry /'hʌŋgrɪ/ *adjective* (**-ier**, **-iest**) feeling, showing, or inducing hunger; craving. □ **hungrily** *adverb*.

hunk *noun* large piece cut off; *colloquial* sexually attractive man.

hunt ● *verb* pursue wild animals for food or sport; (of animal) pursue prey; (+ *after*, *for*) search; (as **hunted** *adjective*) (of look) frightened. ● *noun* hunting; hunting area or society. □ **huntsman** hunter, person in charge of hounds. □ **hunting** *noun*.

hunter *noun* (*feminine* **huntress**) person who hunts; horse ridden for hunting.

hurdle /ˈhɜːd(ə)l/ ● *noun* frame to be jumped over by athlete in race; (in *plural*) hurdle race; obstacle; portable rectangular frame used as temporary fence. ● *verb* (**-ling**) run in hurdle race. □ **hurdler** *noun*.

hurdy-gurdy /hɜːdɪˈgɜːdɪ/ *noun* (*plural* **-ies**) droning musical instrument played by turning handle; *colloquial* barrel organ.

hurl ● *verb* throw violently. ● *noun* violent throw.

hurley /ˈhɜːlɪ/ *noun* (also **hurling**) (stick used in) Irish game resembling hockey.

hurly-burly /hɜːlɪˈbɜːlɪ/ *noun* boisterous activity; commotion.

hurrah /hʊˈrɑː/ (also **hurray** /hʊˈreɪ/) ● *interjection expressing joy or approval*. ● *noun* utterance of 'hurrah'.

hurricane /ˈhʌrɪkən/ *noun* storm with violent wind, esp. W. Indian cyclone. □ **hurricane lamp** lamp with flame protected from wind.

hurry /ˈhʌrɪ/ ● *noun* great haste; eagerness; (with negative or in questions) need for haste. ● *verb* (**-ies**, **-ied**) (cause to) move or act hastily; (as **hurried** *adjective*) hasty, done rapidly. □ **hurriedly** *adverb*.

hurt ● *verb* (*past & past participle* **hurt**) cause pain, injury, or distress to; suffer pain. ● *noun* injury; harm. □ **hurtful** *adjective*; **hurtfully** *adverb*.

hurtle /ˈhɜːt(ə)l/ *verb* (**-ling**) move or hurl rapidly or noisily, come with crash.

husband /ˈhʌzbənd/ ● *noun* married man in relation to his wife. ● *verb* use (resources) economically.

husbandry *noun* farming; management of resources.

hush ● *verb* make, become, or be silent. ● *interjection calling for silence*. ● *noun* silence. □ **hush-hush** *colloquial* highly secret; **hush money** *slang* sum paid to ensure discretion; **hush up** suppress (fact).

husk ● *noun* dry outer covering of fruit or seed. ● *verb* remove husk from.

husky[1] /ˈhʌskɪ/ *adjective* (**-ier**, **-iest**) dry in the throat, hoarse; strong, hefty. □ **huskily** *adverb*.

husky[2] /ˈhʌskɪ/ *noun* (*plural* **-ies**) powerful dog used for pulling sledges.

hussar /hʊˈzɑː/ *noun* light-cavalry soldier.

hussy /ˈhʌsɪ/ *noun* (*plural* **-ies**) pert girl; promiscuous woman.

hustings /ˈhʌstɪŋz/ *noun* election proceedings.

hustle /ˈhʌs(ə)l/ ● *verb* (**-ling**) jostle; (+ *into*, *out of*, etc.) force, hurry; *slang* solicit business. ● *noun* act or instance of hustling. □ **hustler** *noun*.

hut *noun* small simple or crude house or shelter.

hutch *noun* box or cage for rabbits etc.

hyacinth /ˈhaɪəsɪnθ/ *noun* bulbous plant with bell-shaped flowers.

hybrid /ˈhaɪbrɪd/ ● *noun* offspring of two animals or plants of different species etc.; thing of mixed origins. ● *adjective* bred as hybrid; heterogeneous. □ **hybridism** *noun*; **hybridization** *noun*; **hybridize** *verb* (also **-ise**) (**-zing** or **-sing**).

hydra /ˈhaɪdrə/ *noun* freshwater polyp; something hard to destroy.

hydrangea /haɪˈdreɪndʒə/ *noun* shrub with globular clusters of white, blue, or pink flowers.

hydrant /ˈhaɪdrənt/ *noun* outlet for drawing water from main.

hydrate /ˈhaɪdreɪt/ ● *noun* chemical compound of water with another compound etc. ● *verb* (**-ting**) (cause to) combine with water. □ **hydration** *noun*.

hydraulic /haɪˈdrɔːlɪk/ *adjective* (of water etc.) conveyed through pipes etc.; operated by movement of liquid. □ **hydraulically** *adverb*.

hydraulics *plural noun* (usually treated as *singular*) science of conveyance of liquids through pipes etc., esp. as motive power.

hydro /ˈhaɪdrəʊ/ *noun* (*plural* **-s**) *colloquial* hotel etc. originally providing hydropathic treatment; hydroelectric powerplant.

hydro- *combining form* water; combined with hydrogen.

hydrocarbon /haɪdrəʊˈkɑːbən/ *noun* compound of hydrogen and carbon.

hydrocephalus /haɪdrəˈsefələs/ *noun* accumulated fluid in brain, esp. in young children. □ **hydrocephalic** /-sɪˈfælɪk/ *adjective*.

hydrochloric acid /haɪdrəˈklɒrɪk/ *noun* solution of hydrogen chloride in water.

hydrodynamics /haɪdrəʊdaɪˈnæmɪks/ *plural noun* (usually treated as *singular*) science of forces acting on or exerted by liquids.

hydroelectric /haɪdrəʊɪˈlektrɪk/ *adjective* generating electricity by water-power; (of electricity) so generated. □ **hydroelectricity** /-ˈtrɪs-/ *noun*.

hydrofoil /ˈhaɪdrəfɔɪl/ *noun* boat fitted with planes for raising hull out of water at speed; such a plane.

hydrogen /ˈhaɪdrədʒ(ə)n/ *noun* light colourless odourless gas combining with oxygen to form water. □ **hydrogen bomb** immensely powerful bomb utilizing explosive fusion of hydrogen nuclei; **hydrogen peroxide** see PEROXIDE.

hydrogenate /haɪˈdrɒdʒɪneɪt/ *verb* (**-ting**) charge with or cause to combine with hydrogen. □ **hydrogenation** *noun*.

hydrography /haɪˈdrɒgrəfɪ/ *noun* science of surveying and charting seas, lakes, rivers, etc. □ **hydrographer** *noun*; **hydrographic** /-drəˈgræf-/ *adjective*.

hydrology /haɪˈdrɒlədʒɪ/ *noun* science of relationship between water and land.

hydrolyse /ˈhaɪdrəlaɪz/ *verb* (**-sing**) (*US* **-lyze**; **-zing**) decompose by hydrolysis.

hydrolysis /haɪˈdrɒlɪsɪs/ *noun* decomposition by chemical reaction with water.

hydrometer /haɪˈdrɒmɪtə/ *noun* instrument for measuring density of liquids.

hydropathy /haɪˈdrɒpəθɪ/ *noun* (medically unorthodox) treatment of disease by water. □ **hydropathic** /-drəˈpæθ-/ *adjective*.

hydrophobia /haɪdrəˈfəʊbɪə/ *noun* aversion to water, esp. as symptom of rabies in humans; rabies. □ **hydrophobic** *adjective*.

hydroplane /ˈhaɪdrəpleɪn/ *noun* light fast motor boat; finlike device enabling submarine to rise or fall.

hydroponics /haɪdrəˈpɒnɪks/ *noun* growing plants without soil, in sand, water, etc. with added nutrients.

hydrostatic /haɪdrəˈstætɪk/ *adjective* of the equilibrium of liquids and the pressure exerted by liquids at rest.

hydrostatics *plural noun* (usually treated as *singular*) study of hydrostatic properties of liquids.

hydrotherapy /haɪdrəˈθerəpɪ/ *noun* use of water, esp. swimming, in treatment of disease.

hydrous /ˈhaɪdrəs/ *adjective* containing water.

hyena /haɪˈiːnə/ *noun* doglike flesh-eating mammal.

hygiene /ˈhaɪdʒiːn/ *noun* conditions or practices conducive to maintaining health; cleanliness; sanitary science. □ **hygienic** /-ˈdʒiːn-/ *adjective*; **hygienically** /-ˈdʒiːn-/ *adverb*; **hygienist** *noun*.

hygrometer /haɪˈgrɒmɪtə/ *noun* instrument for measuring humidity of air etc.

hygroscopic /haɪgrə'skɒpɪk/ *adjective* tending to absorb moisture from air.

hymen /'haɪmen/ *noun* membrane at opening of vagina, usually broken at first sexual intercourse.

hymenopterous /haɪmə'nɒptərəs/ *adjective* of order of insects with 4 membranous wings, including bees and wasps.

hymn /hɪm/ ● *noun* song of esp. Christian praise. ● *verb* praise or celebrate in hymns.

hymnal /'hɪmn(ə)l/ *noun* book of hymns.

hymnology /hɪm'nɒlədʒɪ/ *noun* composition or study of hymns. □ **hymnologist** *noun.*

hyoscine /'haɪəsi:n/ *noun* alkaloid used to prevent motion sickness etc.

hype /haɪp/ *slang* ● *noun* intensive promotion of product etc. ● *verb* (**-ping**) promote with hype. □ **hyped up** excited.

hyper /'haɪpə/ *adjective slang* hyperactive.

hyper- /'haɪpə/ *prefix* over, above; too.

hyperbola /haɪ'pɜ:bələ/ *noun* (*plural* **-s** or **-lae** /-li:/) curve produced when cone is cut by plane making larger angle with base than side of cone makes. □ **hyperbolic** /-pə'bɒl-/ *adjective.*

hyperbole /haɪ'pɜ:bəlɪ/ *noun* exaggeration, esp. for effect. □ **hyperbolical** /-'bɒl-/ *adjective.*

hyperglycaemia /haɪpəglaɪ'si:mɪə/ *noun* (*US* **hyperglycemia**) excess of glucose in bloodstream.

hypermarket /'haɪpəmɑ:kɪt/ *noun* very large supermarket.

hypermedia /'haɪpəmi:dɪə/ *noun* provision of several media (audio, video, etc.) on one computer system.

hypersensitive /haɪpə'sensɪtɪv/ *adjective* excessively sensitive. □ **hypersensitivity** /-'tɪv-/ *noun.*

hypersonic /haɪpə'sɒnɪk/ *adjective* of speeds more than 5 times that of sound.

hypertension /haɪpə'tenʃ(ə)n/ *noun* abnormally high blood pressure; extreme tension.

hypertext /'haɪpətekst/ *noun* provision of several texts on one computer system.

hyperthermia /haɪpə'θɜ:mɪə/ *noun* abnormally high body-temperature.

hyperthyroidism /haɪpə'θaɪrɔɪdɪz(ə)m/ *noun* overactivity of thyroid gland.

hyperventilation /haɪpəventɪ'leiʃ(ə)n/ *noun* abnormally rapid breathing. □ **hyperventilate** *verb* (**-ting**).

hyphen /'haɪf(ə)n/ ● *noun* punctuation mark (-) used to join or divide words (see panel). ● *verb* hyphenate.

hyphenate /'haɪfəneɪt/ *verb* (**-ting**) join or divide with hyphen. □ **hyphenation** *noun.*

hypnosis /hɪp'nəʊsɪs/ *noun* state like sleep in which subject acts only on external suggestion; artificially induced sleep.

hypnotherapy /hɪpnəʊ'θerəpɪ/ *noun* treatment of mental disorders by hypnosis.

hypnotic /hɪp'nɒtɪk/ ● *adjective* of or causing hypnosis; sleep-inducing. ● *noun* hypnotic drug or influence. □ **hypnotically** *adverb.*

hypnotism /'hɪpnətɪz(ə)m/ *noun* study or practice of hypnosis. □ **hypnotist** *noun.*

hypnotize /'hɪpnətaɪz/ *verb* (also **-ise**) (**-zing** or **-sing**) produce hypnosis in; fascinate.

hypo /'haɪpəʊ/ *noun* sodium thiosulphate, used as photographic fixer.

hypo- /'haɪpəʊ/ *prefix* under; below normal; slightly.

hypochondria /haɪpə'kɒndrɪə/ *noun* abnormal anxiety about one's health.

Hyphen -

This is used:

1 to join two or more words so as to form a compound or single expression, e.g.

mother-in-law, non-stick, dressing-table

This use is growing less common; often you can do without such hyphens:

nonstick, treelike, dressing table

2 to join words in an attributive compound (one put before a noun, like an adjective), e.g.

a well-known man (but *the man is well known*)
an out-of-date list (but *the list is out of date*)

3 to join a prefix etc. to a proper name, e.g.

anti-Darwinian; half-Italian; non-British

4 to make a meaning clear by linking words, e.g.

twenty-odd people/twenty odd people

or by separating a prefix, e.g.

re-cover/recover; re-present/represent; re-sign/resign

5 to separate two identical letters in adjacent parts of a word, e.g.

pre-exist, Ross-shire

6 to represent a common second element in the items of a list, e.g.

two-, three-, or fourfold.

7 to divide a word if there is no room to complete it at the end of the line, e.g.

... *diction-*
ary ...

The hyphen comes at the end of the line, not at the beginning of the next line. In general, words should be divided at the end of a syllable: *dicti-onary* would be quite wrong. In handwriting, typing, and word-processing, it is safest (and often neatest) not to divide words at all.

hypochondriac /haɪpəˈkɒndrɪæk/ ● *noun* person given to hypochondria. ● *adjective* of hypochondria.

hypocrisy /hɪˈpəkrɪsɪ/ *noun* (*plural* **-ies**) simulation of virtue; insincerity.

hypocrite /ˈhɪpəkrɪt/ *noun* person guilty of hypocrisy. □ **hypocritical** /-ˈkrɪt-/ *adjective*; **hypocritically** /-ˈkrɪt-/ *adverb*.

hypodermic /haɪpəˈdɜːmɪk/ ● *adjective* (of drug, syringe, etc.) introduced under the skin. ● *noun* hypodermic injection or syringe.

hypotension /haɪpəʊˈtenʃ(ə)n/ *noun* abnormally low blood pressure.

hypotenuse /haɪˈpɒtənjuːz/ *noun* side opposite right angle of right-angled triangle.

hypothalamus /haɪpəˈθæləməs/ *noun* (*plural* **-mi** /-maɪ/) region of brain controlling body temperature, thirst, hunger, etc.

hypothermia /haɪpəʊˈθɜːmɪə/ *noun* abnormally low body-temperature.

hypothesis /haɪˈpɒθɪsɪs/ *noun* (*plural* **-theses** /-siːz/) supposition made as basis for reasoning etc. □ **hypothesize** *verb* (also **-ise**) (**-zing** or **-sing**).

hypothetical /haɪpəˈθetɪk(ə)l/ *adjective* of or resting on hypothesis. □ **hypothetically** *adverb*.

hypothyroidism /haɪpəʊˈθaɪrɔɪdɪz(ə)m/ *noun* subnormal activity of the thyroid gland.

hypoventilation /haɪpəʊventɪˈleɪʃ(ə)n/ *noun* abnormally slow breathing.

hyssop /ˈhɪsəp/ *noun* small bushy aromatic herb.

hysterectomy /hɪstəˈrektəmɪ/ *noun* (*plural* **-ies**) surgical removal of womb.

hysteria /hɪˈstɪərɪə/ *noun* uncontrollable emotion or excitement; functional disturbance of nervous system.

hysteric /hɪˈsterɪk/ *noun* (in *plural*) fit of hysteria, *colloquial* overwhelming laughter; hysterical person. □ **hysterical** *adjective*; **hysterically** *adverb*.

Hz *abbreviation* hertz.

Ii

I[1] *noun* (also **i**) (Roman numeral) 1.

I[2] /aɪ/ *pronoun used by speaker or writer to refer to himself or herself as subject of verb.*

I[3] *abbreviation* (also **I.**) Island(s); Isle(s).

iambic /aɪ'æmbɪk/ ● *adjective* of or using iambuses. ● *noun* (usually in *plural*) iambic verse.

iambus /aɪ'æmbəs/ *noun* (*plural* **-buses** or **-bi** /-baɪ/) metrical foot of one short followed by one long syllable.

IBA *abbreviation* Independent Broadcasting Authority.

ibex /'aɪbeks/ *noun* (*plural* **-es**) wild mountain goat with large backward-curving ridged horns.

ibid. /'ɪbɪd/ *abbreviation* in same book or passage etc. (*ibidem*).

ibis /'aɪbɪs/ *noun* (*plural* **-es**) stork-like bird with long curved bill.

ice ● *noun* frozen water; portion of ice cream etc. ● *verb* (**icing**) mix with or cool in ice; (often + *over*, *up*) cover or become covered (as) with ice; freeze; cover (a cake etc.) with icing. ◻ **ice age** glacial period; **icebox** compartment in refrigerator for making or storing ice, *US* refrigerator; **ice-breaker** boat designed to break through ice; **icecap** mass of thick ice permanently covering polar region etc.; **ice cream** sweet creamy frozen food; **ice field** extensive sheet of floating ice; **ice hockey** form of hockey played on ice with flat disc instead of ball; **ice lolly** flavoured ice on stick; **ice rink** area of ice for skating etc.; **ice-skate** *noun* boot with blade attached for gliding over ice, *verb* move on ice-skates; **on ice** performed by ice-skaters, *colloquial* in reserve.

iceberg /'aɪsbɜ:g/ *noun* mass of floating ice at sea. ◻ **tip of the iceberg** small perceptible part of something very large or complex.

Icelander /'aɪsləndə/ *noun* native of Iceland.

Icelandic /aɪs'lændɪk/ ● *adjective* of Iceland. ● *noun* language of Iceland.

ichneumon /ɪk'nju:mən/ *noun* (in full **ichneumon fly**) wasplike insect parasitic on other insects; mongoose of N. Africa etc.

ichthyology /ɪkθɪ'ɒlədʒɪ/ *noun* study of fishes. ◻ **ichthyological** /-ə'lɒdʒɪk(ə)l/ *adjective*; **ichthyologist** *noun*.

ichthyosaur /'ɪkθɪəsɔ:/ *noun* large extinct reptile like dolphin.

icicle /'aɪsɪk(ə)l/ *noun* tapering hanging spike of ice, formed from dripping water.

icing *noun* sugar etc. coating for cake etc.; formation of ice on ship or aircraft. ◻ **icing sugar** finely powdered sugar.

icon /'aɪkɒn/ *noun* (also **ikon**) sacred painting, mosaic, etc.; image, statue. ◻ **iconic** /-'kɒn-/ *adjective*.

iconoclast /aɪ'kɒnəklæst/ *noun* person who attacks cherished beliefs; *historical* breaker of religious images. ◻ **iconoclasm** *noun*; **iconoclastic** /-'klæstɪk/ *adjective*.

iconography /aɪkə'nɒgrəfɪ/ *noun* illustration of subject by drawings etc.; study of portraits, esp. of one person, or of artistic images or symbols.

icy /'aɪsɪ/ *adjective* (**-ier**, **-iest**) very cold; covered with or abounding in ice; (of manner) unfriendly.

ID *abbreviation* identification, identity.

I'd /aɪd/ I had; I should; I would.

id *noun Psychology* part of mind comprising instinctive impulses of individual etc.

idea /aɪ'dɪə/ *noun* plan etc. formed by mental effort; mental impression or concept; vague belief or fancy; purpose, intention. ◻ **have no idea** *colloquial* not know at all, be completely incompetent.

ideal /aɪ'di:əl/ ● *adjective* perfect; existing only in idea; visionary. ● *noun* perfect type, thing, principle, etc. as standard for imitation.

idealism *noun* forming or pursuing ideals; representation of things in ideal form; philosophy in which objects are held to be dependent on mind. ◻ **idealist** *noun*; **idealistic** /-'lɪst-/ *adjective*.

idealize *verb* (also **-ise**) (**-zing** or **-sing**) regard or represent as ideal. ◻ **idealization** *noun*.

identical /aɪ'dentɪk(ə)l/ *adjective* (often + *with*) absolutely alike; same; (of twins) developed from single ovum and very similar in appearance. ◻ **identically** *adverb*.

identify /aɪ'dentɪfaɪ/ *verb* (**-ies**, **-ied**) establish identity of; select, discover; (+ *with*) closely associate with; (+ *with*) regard oneself as sharing basic characteristics with; (often + *with*) treat as identical. ◻ **identification** *noun*.

identity /aɪ'dentɪtɪ/ *noun* (*plural* **-ies**) being specified person or thing; individuality; identification or the result of it; absolute sameness.

ideogram /'ɪdɪəgræm/ *noun* (also **ideograph** /-grɑ:f/) symbol representing thing or idea without indicating sounds in its name (e.g. Chinese character, or '=' for 'equals').

ideology /aɪdɪ'ɒlədʒɪ/ *noun* (*plural* **-ies**) scheme of ideas at basis of political etc. theory or system; characteristic thinking of class etc. ◻ **ideological** /-ə'lɒdʒ-/ *adjective*.

idiocy /'ɪdɪəsɪ/ *noun* (*plural* **-ies**) utter foolishness; foolish act; mental condition of idiot.

idiom /'ɪdɪəm/ *noun* phrase etc. established by usage and not immediately comprehensible from the words used; form of expression peculiar to a language; language; characteristic mode of expression. ◻ **idiomatic** /-'mæt-/ *adjective*.

idiosyncrasy /ɪdɪəʊ'sɪŋkrəsɪ/ *noun* (*plural* **-ies**) attitude or form of behaviour peculiar to person. ◻ **idiosyncratic** /-'kræt-/ *adjective*.

idiot /'ɪdɪət/ *noun* stupid person; person too deficient in mind to be capable of rational conduct. ◻ **idiotic** /-'ɒt-/ *adjective*.

idle /'aɪd(ə)l/ ● *adjective* (**-r**, **-st**) lazy, indolent; not in use; unoccupied; useless, purposeless. ● *verb* (**-ling**) be idle; (of engine) run slowly without doing any work; pass (time) in idleness. ◻ **idleness** *noun*; **idler** *noun*; **idly** *adverb*.

idol /'aɪd(ə)l/ *noun* image as object of worship; object of devotion.

idolater /aɪ'dɒlətə/ *noun* worshipper of idols; devout admirer. ◻ **idolatrous** *adjective*; **idolatry** *noun*.

idolize *verb* (also **-ise**) (**-zing** or **-sing**) venerate or love to excess; treat as idol. ◻ **idolization** *noun*.

idyll /'ɪdɪl/ *noun* account of picturesque scene or incident etc.; such scene etc. ◻ **idyllic** /ɪ'dɪlɪk/ *adjective*.

i.e. *abbreviation* that is to say (*id est*).

if *conjunction* on condition or supposition that; *(with past tense) implying that the condition is not fulfilled*; even though; whenever; whether; *expressing wish, request, or (with negative) surprise*. ◻ **if only** even if for no other reason than, I wish that.

igloo /ˈɪɡluː/ *noun* dome-shaped snow house.

igneous /ˈɪɡnɪəs/ *adjective* of fire; (esp. of rocks) produced by volcanic action.

ignite /ɪɡˈnaɪt/ *verb* (**-ting**) set fire to; catch fire; provoke or excite (feelings etc.).

ignition /ɪɡˈnɪʃ(ə)n/ *noun* mechanism for starting combustion in cylinder of motor engine; igniting.

ignoble /ɪɡˈnəʊb(ə)l/ *adjective* (**-r**, **-st**) dishonourable; of low birth or position.

ignominious /ɪɡnəˈmɪnɪəs/ *adjective* humiliating. ◻ **ignominiously** *adverb.*

ignominy /ˈɪɡnəmɪnɪ/ *noun* dishonour, infamy.

ignoramus /ɪɡnəˈreɪməs/ *noun* (*plural* **-muses**) ignorant person.

ignorant /ˈɪɡnərənt/ *adjective* lacking knowledge; (+ *of*) uninformed; *colloquial* uncouth. ◻ **ignorance** *noun.*

ignore /ɪɡˈnɔː/ *verb* (**-ring**) refuse to take notice of.

iguana /ɪɡˈwɑːnə/ *noun* large Central and S. American tree lizard.

iguanodon /ɪɡˈwɑːnədɒn/ *noun* large plant-eating dinosaur.

ikebana /ɪkɪˈbɑːnə/ *noun* Japanese art of flower arrangement.

ikon = ICON.

ilex /ˈaɪleks/ *noun* (*plural* **-es**) plant of genus including holly; holm-oak.

iliac /ˈɪlɪæk/ *adjective* of flank or hip-bone.

ilk *noun colloquial* sort, kind. ◻ **of that ilk** *Scottish* of ancestral estate of same name as family.

I'll /aɪl/ I shall; I will.

ill ● *adjective* in bad health, sick; harmful, unfavourable; hostile, unkind; faulty, deficient. ● *adverb* badly, unfavourably; scarcely. ● *noun* harm; evil. ◻ **ill-advised** unwise; **ill-bred** rude; **ill-favoured** unattractive; **ill-gotten** gained unlawfully or wickedly; **ill health** poor physical condition; **ill-mannered** rude; **ill-natured** churlish; **ill-tempered** morose, irritable; **ill-timed** done or occurring at unsuitable time; **ill-treat**, **-use** treat badly.

illegal /ɪˈliːɡ(ə)l/ *adjective* contrary to law. ◻ **illegality** /-ˈɡæl-/ *noun* (*plural* **-ies**); **illegally** *adverb.*

illegible /ɪˈledʒɪb(ə)l/ *adjective* not legible, unreadable. ◻ **illegibility** *noun*; **illegibly** *adverb.*

illegitimate /ɪlɪˈdʒɪtɪmət/ *adjective* born of parents not married to each other; unlawful; improper; wrongly inferred. ◻ **illegitimacy** *noun.*

illiberal /ɪˈlɪbər(ə)l/ *adjective* narrow-minded; stingy. ◻ **illiberality** /-ˈræl-/ *noun.*

illicit /ɪˈlɪsɪt/ *adjective* unlawful; forbidden. ◻ **illicitly** *adverb.*

illiterate /ɪˈlɪtərət/ ● *adjective* unable to read; uneducated. ● *noun* illiterate person. ◻ **illiteracy** *noun.*

illness *noun* disease; ill health.

illogical /ɪˈlɒdʒɪk(ə)l/ *adjective* devoid of or contrary to logic. ◻ **illogicality** /-ˈkæl-/ *noun* (*plural* **-ies**); **illogically** *adverb.*

illuminate /ɪˈluːmɪneɪt/ *verb* (**-ting**) light up; decorate with lights; decorate (manuscript etc.) with gold, colour, etc.; help to explain (subject etc.); enlighten spiritually or intellectually. ◻ **illuminating** *adjective*; **illumination** *noun.*

illumine /ɪˈljuːmɪn/ *verb* (**-ning**) *literary* light up; enlighten.

illusion /ɪˈluːʒ(ə)n/ *noun* false belief; deceptive appearance. ◻ **be under the illusion** (+ *that*) believe mistakenly. ◻ **illusive** *adjective*; **illusory** *adjective.*

illusionist *noun* conjuror.

illustrate /ˈɪləstreɪt/ *verb* (**-ting**) provide with pictures; make clear, esp. by examples or drawings; serve as example of. ◻ **illustrator** *noun.*

illustration *noun* drawing etc. in book; explanatory example; illustrating.

illustrative /ˈɪləstrətɪv/ *adjective* (often + *of*) explanatory.

illustrious /ɪˈlʌstrɪəs/ *adjective* distinguished, renowned.

I'm /aɪm/ I am.

image /ˈɪmɪdʒ/ ● *noun* representation of object, esp. figure of saint or divinity; reputation or persona of person, company, etc.; appearance as seen in mirror or through lens; idea, conception; simile, metaphor. ● *verb* (**-ging**) make image of; mirror; picture.

imagery /ˈɪmɪdʒərɪ/ *noun* figurative illustration; use of images in literature etc.; images, statuary; mental images collectively.

imaginary /ɪˈmædʒɪnərɪ/ *adjective* existing only in imagination.

imagination /ɪmædʒɪˈneɪʃ(ə)n/ *noun* mental faculty of forming images of objects not present to senses; creative faculty of mind.

imaginative /ɪˈmædʒɪnətɪv/ *adjective* having or showing high degree of imagination. ◻ **imaginatively** *adverb.*

imagine /ɪˈmædʒɪn/ *verb* (**-ning**) form mental image of, conceive; suppose, think.

imago /ɪˈmeɪɡəʊ/ *noun* (*plural* **-s** or **imagines** /ɪˈmædʒɪniːz/) fully developed stage of insect.

imam /ɪˈmɑːm/ *noun* prayer-leader of mosque; *title of some Muslim leaders.*

imbalance /ɪmˈbæləns/ *noun* lack of balance; disproportion.

imbecile /ˈɪmbɪsiːl/ ● *noun colloquial* stupid person; adult with mental age of about 5. ● *adjective* mentally weak, stupid. ◻ **imbecilic** /-ˈsɪlɪk/ *adjective*; **imbecility** /-ˈsɪlɪtɪ/ *noun* (*plural* **-ies**).

imbed = EMBED.

imbibe /ɪmˈbaɪb/ *verb* (**-bing**) drink; drink in; absorb; inhale.

imbroglio /ɪmˈbrəʊlɪəʊ/ *noun* (*plural* **-s**) confused or complicated situation.

imbue /ɪmˈbjuː/ *verb* (**-bues**, **-bued**, **-buing**) (often + *with*) inspire; saturate, dye.

imitate /ˈɪmɪteɪt/ *verb* (**-ting**) follow example of; mimic; make copy of; be like. ◻ **imitable** *adjective*; **imitative** /-tətɪv/ *adjective*; **imitator** *noun.*

imitation *noun* imitating, being imitated; copy; counterfeit.

immaculate /ɪˈmækjʊlət/ *adjective* perfectly clean, spotless; faultless; innocent, sinless. ◻ **immaculately** *adverb*; **immaculateness** *noun.*

immanent /ˈɪmənənt/ *adjective* inherent; (of God) omnipresent. ◻ **immanence** *noun.*

immaterial /ɪməˈtɪərɪəl/ *adjective* unimportant; irrelevant; not material. ◻ **immateriality** /-ˈæl-/ *noun.*

immature /ɪməˈtjʊə/ *adjective* not mature; undeveloped, esp. emotionally. ◻ **immaturity** *noun.*

immeasurable /ɪˈmeʒərəb(ə)l/ *adjective* not measurable, immense. ◻ **immeasurably** *adverb.*

immediate /ɪˈmiːdɪət/ *adjective* occurring at once; direct; nearest; having priority. ◻ **immediacy** *noun*; **immediately** *adverb.*

immemorial /ɪmɪˈmɔːrɪəl/ *adjective* ancient beyond memory.

immense /ɪˈmens/ *adjective* vast, huge. ◻ **immensity** *noun.*

immensely *adverb colloquial* vastly, very much.

immerse /ɪˈmɜːs/ *verb* (**-sing**) (often + *in*) dip, plunge; put under water; (often **immerse oneself** or in *passive*; often + *in*) involve deeply, embed.

immersion /ɪˈmɜːʃ(ə)n/ *noun* immersing, being immersed. ◻ **immersion heater** electric heater designed to be immersed in liquid to be heated.

immigrant /ˈɪmɪɡrənt/ ● *noun* person who immigrates. ● *adjective* immigrating; of immigrants.
immigrate /ˈɪmɪɡreɪt/ *verb* (**-ting**) enter a country to settle permanently. □ **immigration** *noun*.
imminent /ˈɪmɪnənt/ *adjective* soon to happen. □ **imminence** *noun*; **imminently** *adverb*.
immobile /ɪˈməʊbaɪl/ *adjective* motionless; immovable. □ **immobility** *noun*.
immobilize /ɪˈməʊbɪlaɪz/ *verb* (also **-ise**) (**-zing** or **-sing**) prevent from being moved. □ **immobilization** *noun*.
immoderate /ɪˈmɒdərət/ *adjective* excessive. □ **immoderately** *adverb*.
immodest /ɪˈmɒdɪst/ *adjective* conceited; indecent. □ **immodesty** *noun*.
immolate /ˈɪməleɪt/ *verb* (**-ting**) kill as sacrifice. □ **immolation** *noun*.
immoral /ɪˈmɒr(ə)l/ *adjective* opposed to, or not conforming to, (esp. sexual) morality; dissolute. □ **immorality** /ɪməˈrælɪtɪ/ *noun*.
immortal /ɪˈmɔːt(ə)l/ ● *adjective* living for ever; unfading; divine; famous for all time. ● *noun* immortal being, esp. (in *plural*) gods of antiquity. □ **immortality** /-ˈtæl-/ *noun*; **immortalize** *verb* (also **-ise**) (**-zing** or **-sing**).
immovable /ɪˈmuːvəb(ə)l/ *adjective* not movable; unyielding. □ **immovability** *noun*.
immune /ɪˈmjuːn/ *adjective* having immunity; relating to immunity; exempt.
immunity *noun* (*plural* **-ies**) living organism's power of resisting and overcoming infection; (often + *from*) freedom, exemption.
immunize /ˈɪmjuːnaɪz/ *verb* (also **-ise**) (**-zing** or **-sing**) make immune. □ **immunization** *noun*.
immure /ɪˈmjʊə/ *verb* (**-ring**) imprison.
immutable /ɪˈmjuːtəb(ə)l/ *adjective* unchangeable. □ **immutability** *noun*.
imp *noun* mischievous child; little devil.
impact ● *noun* /ˈɪmpækt/ collision, striking; (immediate) effect or influence. ● *verb* /ɪmˈpækt/ drive or wedge together; (as **impacted** *adjective*) (of tooth) wedged between another tooth and jaw. □ **impaction** /ɪmˈpækʃ(ə)n/ *noun*.
impair /ɪmˈpeə/ *verb* damage, weaken. □ **impairment** *noun*.
impala /ɪmˈpɑːlə/ *noun* (*plural* same or **-s**) small African antelope.
impale /ɪmˈpeɪl/ *verb* (**-ling**) transfix on stake. □ **impalement** *noun*.
impalpable /ɪmˈpælpəb(ə)l/ *adjective* not easily grasped; imperceptible to touch.
impart /ɪmˈpɑːt/ *verb* communicate (news etc.); give share of.
impartial /ɪmˈpɑːʃ(ə)l/ *adjective* fair, not partial. □ **impartiality** /-ʃɪˈæl-/ *noun*; **impartially** *adverb*.
impassable /ɪmˈpɑːsəb(ə)l/ *adjective* that cannot be traversed. □ **impassability** *noun*.
impasse /ˈæmpæs/ *noun* deadlock.
impassioned /ɪmˈpæʃ(ə)nd/ *adjective* filled with passion, ardent.
impassive /ɪmˈpæsɪv/ *adjective* not feeling or showing emotion. □ **impassively** *adverb*; **impassivity** /-ˈsɪv-/ *noun*.
impasto /ɪmˈpæstəʊ/ *noun* technique of laying on paint thickly.
impatiens /ɪmˈpeɪʃɪenz/ *noun* any of several plants including busy Lizzie.
impatient /ɪmˈpeɪʃ(ə)nt/ *adjective* not patient; intolerant; restlessly eager. □ **impatience** *noun*; **impatiently** *adverb*.
impeach /ɪmˈpiːtʃ/ *verb* accuse, esp. of treason etc.; call in question; disparage. □ **impeachment** *noun*.
impeccable /ɪmˈpekəb(ə)l/ *adjective* faultless; exemplary. □ **impeccability** *noun*; **impeccably** *adverb*.
impecunious /ɪmpɪˈkjuːnɪəs/ *adjective* having little or no money.
impedance /ɪmˈpiːd(ə)ns/ *noun* total effective resistance of electric circuit etc. to alternating current.
impede /ɪmˈpiːd/ *verb* (**-ding**) obstruct; hinder.
impediment /ɪmˈpedɪmənt/ *noun* hindrance; defect in speech, esp. lisp or stammer.
impedimenta /ɪmpedɪˈmentə/ *plural noun* encumbrances; baggage, esp. of army.
impel /ɪmˈpel/ *verb* (**-ll-**) drive, force; propel.
impend /ɪmˈpend/ *verb* be imminent; hang. □ **impending** *adjective*.
impenetrable /ɪmˈpenɪtrəb(ə)l/ *adjective* not penetrable; inscrutable; inaccessible to influences etc. □ **impenetrability** *noun*.
impenitent /ɪmˈpenɪt(ə)nt/ *adjective* not penitent. □ **impenitence** *noun*.
imperative /ɪmˈperətɪv/ ● *adjective* urgent, obligatory; peremptory; *Grammar* (of mood) expressing command. ● *noun Grammar* imperative mood; command; essential or urgent thing.
imperceptible /ɪmpəˈseptɪb(ə)l/ *adjective* not perceptible; very slight or gradual. □ **imperceptibility** *noun*; **imperceptibly** *adverb*.
imperfect /ɪmˈpɜːfɪkt/ ● *adjective* not perfect; incomplete; faulty; *Grammar* (of past tense) implying action going on but not completed. ● *noun* imperfect tense. □ **imperfectly** *adverb*.
imperfection /ɪmpəˈfekʃ(ə)n/ *noun* imperfectness; fault, blemish.
imperial /ɪmˈpɪərɪəl/ *adjective* of empire or sovereign state ranking with this; of emperor; majestic; (of non-metric weights and measures) used by statute in UK.
imperialism *noun* imperial system of government etc.; *usually derogatory* policy of dominating other nations by acquisition of dependencies or through trade etc. □ **imperialist** *noun & adjective*.
imperil /ɪmˈperɪl/ *verb* (**-ll-**; *US* **-l-**) endanger.
imperious /ɪmˈpɪərɪəs/ *adjective* overbearing, domineering. □ **imperiously** *adverb*.
imperishable /ɪmˈperɪʃəb(ə)l/ *adjective* that cannot perish.
impermanent /ɪmˈpɜːmənənt/ *adjective* not permanent. □ **impermanence** *noun*.
impermeable /ɪmˈpɜːmɪəb(ə)l/ *adjective* not permeable. □ **impermeability** *noun*.
impersonal /ɪmˈpɜːsən(ə)l/ *adjective* having no personality or personal feeling or reference; impartial; unfeeling; *Grammar* (of verb) used esp. with *it* as subject. □ **impersonality** /-ˈnæl-/ *noun*.
impersonate /ɪmˈpɜːsəneɪt/ *verb* (**-ting**) pretend to be, play part of. □ **impersonation** *noun*; **impersonator** *noun*.
impertinent /ɪmˈpɜːtɪnənt/ *adjective* insolent, saucy; irrelevant. □ **impertinence** *noun*; **impertinently** *adverb*.
imperturbable /ɪmpəˈtɜːbəb(ə)l/ *adjective* not excitable; calm. □ **imperturbability** *noun*; **imperturbably** *adverb*.
impervious /ɪmˈpɜːvɪəs/ *adjective* (usually + *to*) impermeable; not responsive.
impetigo /ɪmpɪˈtaɪɡəʊ/ *noun* contagious skin disease.
impetuous /ɪmˈpetjʊəs/ *adjective* acting or done rashly or suddenly; moving violently or fast. □ **impetuosity** /-ˈɒs-/ *noun*; **impetuously** *adverb*.
impetus /ˈɪmpɪtəs/ *noun* moving force; momentum; impulse.
impiety /ɪmˈpaɪətɪ/ *noun* (*plural* **-ies**) lack of piety; act showing this.

impinge /ɪmˈpɪndʒ/ *verb* (**-ging**) (usually + *on*) make impact; (usually + *upon*) encroach.
impious /ˈɪmpɪəs/ *adjective* not pious; wicked.
impish *adjective* of or like imp, mischievous. ▫ **impishly** *adverb*.
implacable /ɪmˈplækəb(ə)l/ *adjective* not appeasable. ▫ **implacability** *noun*; **implacably** *adverb*.
implant ● *verb* /ɪmˈplɑːnt/ insert, fix; instil; plant; (in *passive*) (of fertilized ovum) become attached to wall of womb. ● *noun* /ˈɪmplɑːnt/ thing implanted. ▫ **implantation** *noun*.
implausible /ɪmˈplɔːzɪb(ə)l/ *adjective* not plausible. ▫ **implausibly** *adverb*.
implement ● *noun* /ˈɪmplɪmənt/ tool, utensil. ● *verb* /ˈɪmplɪment/ carry into effect. ▫ **implementation** *noun*.
implicate /ˈɪmplɪkeɪt/ *verb* (**-ting**) (often + *in*) show (person) to be involved (in crime etc.); imply.
implication *noun* thing implied; implying; implicating.
implicit /ɪmˈplɪsɪt/ *adjective* implied though not expressed; unquestioning. ▫ **implicitly** *adverb*.
implode /ɪmˈpləʊd/ *verb* (**-ding**) (cause to) burst inwards. ▫ **implosion** /ɪmˈpləʊʒ(ə)n/ *noun*.
implore /ɪmˈplɔː/ *verb* (**-ring**) beg earnestly.
imply /ɪmˈplaɪ/ *verb* (**-ies**, **-ied**) (often + *that*) insinuate, hint; mean.
impolite /ɪmpəˈlaɪt/ *adjective* uncivil, rude. ▫ **impolitely** *adverb*; **impoliteness** *noun*.
impolitic /ɪmˈpɒlɪtɪk/ *adjective* inexpedient, not advisable. ▫ **impoliticly** *adverb*.
imponderable /ɪmˈpɒndərəb(ə)l/ ● *adjective* that cannot be estimated; very light. ● *noun* (usually in *plural*) imponderable thing. ▫ **imponderability** *noun*; **imponderably** *adverb*.
import ● *verb* /ɪmˈpɔːt/ bring in (esp. foreign goods) from abroad; imply, mean. ● *noun* /ˈɪmpɔːt/ article or (in *plural*) amount imported; importing; meaning, implication; importance. ▫ **importation** *noun*; **importer** /-ˈpɔːtə/ *noun*.
important /ɪmˈpɔːt(ə)nt/ *adjective* (often + *to*) of great consequence; momentous; (of person) having position of authority or rank; pompous. ▫ **importance** *noun*; **importantly** *adverb*.
importunate /ɪmˈpɔːtjʊnət/ *adjective* making persistent or pressing requests. ▫ **importunity** /-ˈtjuːn-/ *noun*.
importune /ɪmpəˈtjuːn/ *verb* (**-ning**) pester (person) with requests; solicit as prostitute.
impose /ɪmˈpəʊz/ *verb* (**-sing**) enforce compliance with; (often + *on*) inflict, lay (tax etc.); (+ *on*, *upon*) take advantage of.
imposing *adjective* impressive, esp. in appearance.
imposition /ɪmpəˈzɪʃ(ə)n/ *noun* imposing, being imposed; unfair demand or burden; tax, duty.
impossible /ɪmˈpɒsɪb(ə)l/ *adjective* not possible; not easy or convenient; *colloquial* outrageous, intolerable. ▫ **impossibility** *noun*; **impossibly** *adverb*.
impost /ˈɪmpəʊst/ *noun* tax, duty.
impostor /ɪmˈpɒstə/ *noun* (also **imposter**) person who assumes false character; swindler.
imposture /ɪmˈpɒstʃə/ *noun* fraudulent deception.
impotent /ˈɪmpət(ə)nt/ *adjective* powerless; (of male) unable to achieve erection of penis or have sexual intercourse. ▫ **impotence** *noun*.
impound /ɪmˈpaʊnd/ *verb* confiscate; shut up in pound.
impoverish /ɪmˈpɒvərɪʃ/ *verb* make poor. ▫ **impoverishment** *noun*.
impracticable /ɪmˈpræktɪkəb(ə)l/ *adjective* impossible in practice. ▫ **impracticability** *noun*; **impracticably** *adverb*.
impractical /ɪmˈpræktɪk(ə)l/ *adjective* not practical; *esp. US* not practicable. ▫ **impracticality** /-ˈkæl-/ *noun*.
imprecation /ɪmprɪˈkeɪʃ(ə)n/ *noun formal* curse.
imprecise /ɪmprɪˈsaɪs/ *adjective* not precise.
impregnable /ɪmˈpregnəb(ə)l/ *adjective* safe against attack. ▫ **impregnability** *noun*.
impregnate /ˈɪmpregneɪt/ *verb* (**-ting**) fill, saturate; make pregnant. ▫ **impregnation** *noun*.
impresario /ɪmprɪˈsɑːrɪəʊ/ *noun* (*plural* **-s**) organizer of public entertainments.
impress ● *verb* /ɪmˈpres/ affect or influence deeply; arouse admiration or respect in; (often + *on*) emphasize; imprint, stamp. ● *noun* /ˈɪmpres/ mark impressed; characteristic quality.
impression /ɪmˈpreʃ(ə)n/ *noun* effect produced on mind; belief; imitation of person or sound, esp. done to entertain; impressing, mark impressed; unaltered reprint of book etc.; issue of book or newspaper etc.; print from type or engraving.
impressionable *adjective* easily influenced.
impressionism *noun* school of painting concerned with conveying effect of natural light on objects; style of music or writing seeking to convey esp. fleeting feelings or experience. ▫ **impressionist** *noun*; **impressionistic** /-ˈnɪs-/ *adjective*.
impressive /ɪmˈpresɪv/ *adjective* arousing respect, approval, or admiration. ▫ **impressively** *adverb*.
imprimatur /ɪmprɪˈmɑːtə/ *noun* licence to print; official approval.
imprint ● *verb* /ɪmˈprɪnt/ (often + *on*) impress firmly, esp. on mind; make impression of (figure etc.) on thing; make impression on with stamp etc. ● *noun* /ˈɪmprɪnt/ impression; printer's or publisher's name in book etc.
imprison /ɪmˈprɪz(ə)n/ *verb* (**-n-**) put into prison; confine. ▫ **imprisonment** *noun*.
improbable /ɪmˈprɒbəb(ə)l/ *adjective* not likely, difficult to believe. ▫ **improbability** *noun*; **improbably** *adverb*.
improbity /ɪmˈprəʊbɪtɪ/ *noun* (*plural* **-ies**) wickedness; dishonesty; wicked or dishonest act.
impromptu /ɪmˈprɒmptjuː/ ● *adverb & adjective* unrehearsed. ● *noun* (*plural* **-s**) impromptu performance or speech; short, usually solo, musical piece, often improvisatory in style.
improper /ɪmˈprɒpə/ *adjective* unseemly, indecent; inaccurate, wrong. ▫ **improperly** *adverb*.
impropriety /ɪmprəˈpraɪətɪ/ *noun* (*plural* **-ies**) indecency; instance of this; incorrectness, unfitness.
improve /ɪmˈpruːv/ *verb* (**-ving**) make or become better; (+ *on*) produce something better than; (as **improving** *adjective*) giving moral benefit. ▫ **improvement** *noun*.
improvident /ɪmˈprɒvɪd(ə)nt/ *adjective* lacking foresight; wasteful. ▫ **improvidence** *noun*; **improvidently** *adverb*.
improvise /ˈɪmprəvaɪz/ *verb* (**-sing**) compose extempore; provide or construct from materials etc. not intended for the purpose. ▫ **improvisation** *noun*; **improvisational** *adjective*; **improvisatory** /-ˈzeɪtərɪ/ *adjective*.
imprudent /ɪmˈpruːd(ə)nt/ *adjective* rash, indiscreet. ▫ **imprudence** *noun*; **imprudently** *adverb*.
impudent /ˈɪmpjʊd(ə)nt/ *adjective* impertinent. ▫ **impudence** *noun*; **impudently** *adverb*.
impugn /ɪmˈpjuːn/ *verb* challenge; call in question.
impulse /ˈɪmpʌls/ *noun* sudden urge; tendency to follow such urges; impelling; impetus.
impulsive /ɪmˈpʌlsɪv/ *adjective* apt to act on impulse; done on impulse; tending to impel. ▫ **impulsively** *adverb*; **impulsiveness** *noun*.

impunity /ɪm'pju:nɪtɪ/ *noun* exemption from punishment or injurious consequences. □ **with impunity** without punishment etc.

impure /ɪm'pjʊə/ *adjective* adulterated; dirty; unchaste.

impurity *noun* (*plural* **-ies**) being impure; impure thing or part.

impute /ɪm'pju:t/ *verb* (**-ting**) (+ *to*) ascribe (fault etc.) to. □ **imputation** *noun*.

in ● *preposition expressing inclusion or position within limits of space, time, circumstance, etc.*; after (specified period of time); with respect to; as proportionate part of; with form or arrangement of; as member of; involved with; within ability of; having the condition of; affected by; having as aim; by means of; meaning; into (with verb of motion or change). ● *adverb expressing position bounded by certain limits, or movement to point enclosed by them*; into room etc.; at home etc.; so as to be enclosed; as part of a publication; in fashion, season, or office; (of player etc.) having turn or right to play; (of transport) at platform etc.; (of season, harvest, ordered goods, etc.) having arrived or been received; (of fire etc.) burning; (of tide) at highest point. ● *adjective* internal, living etc. inside; fashionable; (of joke etc.) confined to small group. □ **in-between** *colloquial* intermediate; **in-house** within an institution, company, etc.; **ins and outs** (often + *of*) details; **in so far as** to the extent that; **in that** because, in so far as; **in-tray** tray for incoming documents etc.; **in with** on good terms with.

in. *abbreviation* inch(es).

inability /ɪnə'bɪlɪtɪ/ *noun* being unable.

inaccessible /ɪnək'sesɪb(ə)l/ *adjective* not accessible; unapproachable. □ **inaccessibility** *noun*.

inaccurate /ɪn'ækjʊrət/ *adjective* not accurate. □ **inaccuracy** *noun* (*plural* **-ies**); **inaccurately** *adverb*.

inaction /ɪn'ækʃ(ə)n/ *noun* absence of action.

inactive /ɪn'æktɪv/ *adjective* not active; not operating. □ **inactivity** /-'tɪv-/ *noun*.

inadequate /ɪn'ædɪkwət/ *adjective* insufficient; incompetent. □ **inadequacy** *noun* (*plural* **-ies**); **inadequately** *adverb*.

inadmissible /ɪnəd'mɪsɪb(ə)l/ *adjective* not allowable. □ **inadmissibility** *noun*; **inadmissibly** *adverb*.

inadvertent /ɪnəd'vɜ:t(ə)nt/ *adjective* unintentional; inattentive. □ **inadvertence** *noun*; **inadvertently** *adverb*.

inadvisable /ɪnəd'vaɪzəb(ə)l/ *adjective* not advisable. □ **inadvisability** *noun*.

inalienable /ɪn'eɪlɪənəb(ə)l/ *adjective* that cannot be transferred to another or taken away.

inane /ɪ'neɪn/ *adjective* silly, senseless; empty. □ **inanity** /-'næn-/ *noun* (*plural* **-ies**).

inanimate /ɪn'ænɪmət/ *adjective* not endowed with animal life; spiritless, dull.

inapplicable /ɪnə'plɪkəb(ə)l/ *adjective* not applicable; irrelevant. □ **inapplicability** *noun*.

inapposite /ɪn'æpəzɪt/ *adjective* not apposite.

inappropriate /ɪnə'prəʊprɪət/ *adjective* not appropriate. □ **inappropriately** *adverb*; **inappropriateness** *noun*.

inapt /ɪn'æpt/ *adjective* not suitable; unskilful. □ **inaptitude** *noun*.

inarticulate /ɪnɑ:'tɪkjʊlət/ *adjective* unable to express oneself clearly; not articulate, indistinct; dumb; not jointed. □ **inarticulately** *adverb*.

inasmuch /ɪnəz'mʌtʃ/ *adverb* (+ *as*) since, because; to the extent that.

inattentive /ɪnə'tentɪv/ *adjective* not paying attention; neglecting to show courtesy. □ **inattention** *noun*; **inattentively** *adverb*.

inaudible /ɪn'ɔ:dɪb(ə)l/ *adjective* that cannot be heard. □ **inaudibly** *adverb*.

inaugural /ɪn'ɔ:gjʊr(ə)l/ ● *adjective* of inauguration. ● *noun* inaugural speech or lecture.

inaugurate /ɪn'ɔ:gjʊreɪt/ *verb* (**-ting**) admit (person) to office; initiate use of or begin with ceremony; begin, introduce. □ **inauguration** *noun*.

inauspicious /ɪnɔ:'spɪʃəs/ *adjective* not of good omen; unlucky.

inborn /'ɪnbɔ:n/ *adjective* existing from birth; innate.

inbred /ɪn'bred/ *adjective* inborn; produced by inbreeding.

inbreeding /ɪn'bri:dɪŋ/ *noun* breeding from closely related animals or people.

Inc. *abbreviation US* Incorporated.

incalculable /ɪn'kælkjʊləb(ə)l/ *adjective* too great for calculation; not calculable beforehand; uncertain. □ **incalculability** *noun*; **incalculably** *adverb*.

incandesce /ɪnkæn'des/ *verb* (**-cing**) (cause to) glow with heat.

incandescent *adjective* glowing with heat, shining; (of artificial light) produced by glowing filament etc. □ **incandescence** *noun*.

incantation /ɪnkæn'teɪʃ(ə)n/ *noun* spell, charm. □ **incantational** *adjective*.

incapable /ɪn'keɪpəb(ə)l/ *adjective* not capable; too honest, kind, etc. to do something; not capable of rational conduct. □ **incapability** *noun*.

incapacitate /ɪnkə'pæsɪteɪt/ *verb* (**-ting**) make incapable or unfit.

incapacity /ɪnkə'pæsɪtɪ/ *noun* inability; legal disqualification.

incarcerate /ɪn'kɑ:səreɪt/ *verb* (**-ting**) imprison. □ **incarceration** *noun*.

incarnate /ɪn'kɑ:nət/ *adjective* in esp. human form.

incarnation /ɪnkɑ:'neɪʃ(ə)n/ *noun* embodiment in flesh; (**the Incarnation**) embodiment of God in Christ; (often + *of*) living type (of a quality etc.).

incautious /ɪn'kɔ:ʃəs/ *adjective* rash. □ **incautiously** *adverb*.

incendiary /ɪn'sendɪərɪ/ ● *adjective* (of bomb) filled with material for causing fires; of arson; guilty of arson; inflammatory. ● *noun* (*plural* **-ies**) incendiary person or bomb.

incense[1] /'ɪnsens/ *noun* gum or spice giving sweet smell when burned; smoke of this, esp. in religious ceremonial.

incense[2] /ɪn'sens/ *verb* (**-sing**) make angry.

incentive /ɪn'sentɪv/ ● *noun* motive, incitement; payment etc. encouraging effort in work. ● *adjective* serving to motivate or incite.

inception /ɪn'sepʃ(ə)n/ *noun* beginning.

incessant /ɪn'ses(ə)nt/ *adjective* unceasing, continual; repeated. □ **incessantly** *adverb*.

incest /'ɪnsest/ *noun* crime of sexual intercourse between people prohibited from marrying because of closeness of their blood relationship.

incestuous /ɪn'sestjʊəs/ *adjective* of or guilty of incest; having relationships restricted to a particular group etc.

inch ● *noun* twelfth of (linear) foot (2.54 cm); this as unit of map-scale (e.g. 1 inch to 1 mile) or as unit of rainfall (= 1 inch depth of water). ● *verb* move gradually. □ **every inch** entirely; **within an inch of one's life** almost to death.

inchoate /ɪn'kəʊeɪt/ *adjective* just begun; undeveloped. □ **inchoation** *noun*.

incidence /'ɪnsɪd(ə)ns/ *noun* range, scope, extent, manner, or rate of occurrence; falling of line, ray, particles, etc. on surface; coming into contact with thing.

incident /ˈɪnsɪd(ə)nt/ ● *noun* event, occurrence; violent episode, civil or military; episode in play, film, etc. ● *adjective* (often + *to*) apt to occur, naturally attaching; (often + *on*, *upon*) (of light etc.) falling.

incidental /ɪnsɪˈdent(ə)l/ *adjective* (often + *to*) minor, supplementary; not essential. □ **incidental music** music played during or between scenes of play, film, etc.

incidentally *adverb* by the way; in an incidental way.

incinerate /ɪnˈsɪnəreɪt/ *verb* (**-ting**) burn to ashes. □ **incineration** *noun*.

incinerator *noun* furnace or device for incineration.

incipient /ɪnˈsɪpɪənt/ *adjective* beginning, in early stage.

incise /ɪnˈsaɪz/ *verb* (**-sing**) make cut in; engrave.

incision /ɪnˈsɪʒ(ə)n/ *noun* cutting, esp. by surgeon; cut.

incisive /ɪnˈsaɪsɪv/ *adjective* sharp; clear and effective.

incisor /ɪnˈsaɪzə/ *noun* cutting-tooth, esp. at front of mouth.

incite /ɪnˈsaɪt/ *verb* (**-ting**) (often + *to*) urge on, stir up. □ **incitement** *noun*.

incivility /ɪnsɪˈvɪlɪtɪ/ *noun* (*plural* **-ies**) rudeness; impolite act.

inclement /ɪnˈklemənt/ *adjective* (of weather) severe, stormy. □ **inclemency** *noun*.

inclination /ɪnklɪˈneɪʃ(ə)n/ *noun* propensity; liking, affection; slope, slant.

incline ● *verb* /ɪnˈklaɪn/ (**-ning**) (usually in *passive*) dispose, influence; have specified tendency; be disposed, tend; (cause to) lean or bend. ● *noun* /ˈɪnklaɪn/ slope.

include /ɪnˈklu:d/ *verb* (**-ding**) comprise, regard or treat as part of whole. □ **inclusion** /-ʒ(ə)n/ *noun*.

inclusive /ɪnˈklu:sɪv/ *adjective* (often + *of*) including; including the limits stated; comprehensive; including all accessory payments. □ **inclusively** *adverb*; **inclusiveness** *noun*.

incognito /ɪnkɒgˈni:təʊ/ ● *adjective & adverb* with one's name or identity concealed. ● *noun* (*plural* **-s**) person who is incognito; pretended identity.

incoherent /ɪnkəʊˈhɪərənt/ *adjective* unintelligible; lacking logic or consistency; not clear. □ **incoherence** *noun*; **incoherently** *adverb*.

incombustible /ɪnkəmˈbʌstɪb(ə)l/ *adjective* that cannot be burnt.

income /ˈɪnkʌm/ *noun* money received, esp. periodically, from work, investments, etc. □ **income tax** tax levied on income.

incoming *adjective* coming in; succeeding another.

incommensurable /ɪnkəˈmenʃərəb(ə)l/ *adjective* (often + *with*) not comparable in size, value, etc.; having no common factor. □ **incommensurability** *noun*.

incommensurate /ɪnkəˈmenʃərət/ *adjective* (often + *with*, *to*) out of proportion; inadequate; incommensurable.

incommode /ɪnkəˈməʊd/ *verb* (**-ding**) *formal* inconvenience; trouble, annoy.

incommodious /ɪnkəˈməʊdɪəs/ *adjective formal* too small for comfort; inconvenient.

incommunicable /ɪnkəˈmju:nɪkəb(ə)l/ *adjective* that cannot be shared or communicated.

incommunicado /ɪnkəmju:nɪˈkɑ:dəʊ/ *adjective* without means of communication, in solitary confinement in prison etc.

incomparable /ɪnˈkɒmpərəb(ə)l/ *adjective* without an equal; matchless. □ **incomparability** *noun*; **incomparably** *adverb*.

incompatible /ɪnkəmˈpætɪb(ə)l/ *adjective* not compatible. □ **incompatibility** *noun*.

incompetent /ɪnˈkɒmpɪt(ə)nt/ *adjective* inept; (often + *to*) lacking the necessary skill, not legally qualified. □ **incompetence** *noun*.

incomplete /ɪnkəmˈpli:t/ *adjective* not complete.

incomprehensible /ɪnkɒmprɪˈhensɪb(ə)l/ *adjective* that cannot be understood.

incomprehension /ɪnkɒmprɪˈhenʃ(ə)n/ *noun* failure to understand.

inconceivable /ɪnkənˈsi:vəb(ə)l/ *adjective* that cannot be imagined. □ **inconceivably** *adverb*.

inconclusive /ɪnkənˈklu:sɪv/ *adjective* (of argument etc.) not convincing or decisive.

incongruous /ɪnˈkɒŋgrʊəs/ *adjective* out of place; absurd; (often + *with*) out of keeping. □ **incongruity** /-ˈgru:ɪtɪ/ *noun* (*plural* **-ies**); **incongruously** *adverb*.

inconsequent /ɪnˈkɒnsɪkwənt/ *adjective* irrelevant; not following logically; disconnected. □ **inconsequence** *noun*.

inconsequential /ɪnkɒnsɪˈkwenʃ(ə)l/ *adjective* unimportant; inconsequent. □ **inconsequentially** *adverb*.

inconsiderable /ɪnkənˈsɪdərəb(ə)l/ *adjective* of small size, value, etc.; not worth considering. □ **inconsiderably** *adverb*.

inconsiderate /ɪnkənˈsɪdərət/ *adjective* not considerate of others; thoughtless. □ **inconsiderately** *adverb*; **inconsiderateness** *noun*.

inconsistent /ɪnkənˈsɪst(ə)nt/ *adjective* not consistent. □ **inconsistency** *noun* (*plural* **-ies**); **inconsistently** *adverb*.

inconsolable /ɪnkənˈsəʊləb(ə)l/ *adjective* that cannot be consoled. □ **inconsolably** *adverb*.

inconspicuous /ɪnkənˈspɪkjʊəs/ *adjective* not conspicuous; not easily noticed. □ **inconspicuously** *adverb*; **inconspicuousness** *noun*.

inconstant /ɪnˈkɒnst(ə)nt/ *adjective* fickle; variable. □ **inconstancy** *noun* (*plural* **-ies**).

incontestable /ɪnkənˈtestəb(ə)l/ *adjective* that cannot be disputed. □ **incontestably** *adverb*.

incontinent /ɪnˈkɒntɪnənt/ *adjective* unable to control bowels or bladder; lacking self-restraint. □ **incontinence** *noun*.

incontrovertible /ɪnkɒntrəˈvɜ:tɪb(ə)l/ *adjective* indisputable. □ **incontrovertibly** *adverb*.

inconvenience /ɪnkənˈvi:nɪəns/ ● *noun* lack of ease or comfort; trouble; cause or instance of this. ● *verb* (**-cing**) cause inconvenience to.

inconvenient *adjective* causing trouble, difficulty, or discomfort; awkward. □ **inconveniently** *adverb*.

incorporate ● *verb* /ɪnˈkɔ:pəreɪt/ (**-ting**) include as part or ingredient; (often + *in*, *with*) unite (in one body); admit as member of company etc.; (esp. as **incorporated** *adjective*) constitute as legal corporation. ● *adjective* /ɪnˈkɔ:pərət/ incorporated. □ **incorporation** *noun*.

incorporeal /ɪnkɔ:ˈpɔ:rɪəl/ *adjective* without substance or material existence. □ **incorporeally** *adverb*.

incorrect /ɪnkəˈrekt/ *adjective* untrue, inaccurate; improper, unsuitable. □ **incorrectly** *adverb*.

incorrigible /ɪnˈkɒrɪdʒɪb(ə)l/ *adjective* that cannot be corrected or improved. □ **incorrigibility** *noun*; **incorrigibly** *adverb*.

incorruptible /ɪnkəˈrʌptɪb(ə)l/ *adjective* that cannot decay or be corrupted. □ **incorruptibility** *noun*; **incorruptibly** *adverb*.

increase ● *verb* /ɪŋˈkri:s/ (**-sing**) become or make greater or more numerous. ● *noun* /ˈɪnkri:s/ growth, enlargement; (of people, animals, or plants) multiplication; increased amount. □ **on the increase** increasing.

increasingly /ɪnˈkri:sɪŋlɪ/ *adverb* more and more.

incredible /ɪn'kredɪb(ə)l/ *adjective* that cannot be believed; *colloquial* surprising, extremely good. □ **incredibility** *noun*; **incredibly** *adverb*.

incredulous /ɪn'kredjʊləs/ *adjective* unwilling to believe; showing disbelief. □ **incredulity** /ɪnkrɪ'dju:lɪtɪ/ *noun*; **incredulously** *adverb*.

increment /'ɪŋkrɪmənt/ *noun* amount of increase; added amount. □ **incremental** /-'ment(ə)l/ *adjective*.

incriminate /ɪn'krɪmɪneɪt/ *verb* (**-ting**) indicate as guilty; charge with crime. □ **incrimination** *noun*; **incriminatory** *adjective*.

incrustation /ɪnkrʌs'teɪʃ(ə)n/ *noun* encrusting, being encrusted; crust, hard coating; deposit on surface.

incubate /'ɪŋkjʊbeɪt/ *verb* (**-ting**) hatch (eggs) by sitting on them or by artificial heat; cause (bacteria etc.) to develop; develop slowly.

incubation *noun* incubating, being incubated; period between infection and appearance of first symptoms.

incubator *noun* apparatus providing warmth for hatching eggs, rearing premature babies, or developing bacteria.

incubus /'ɪŋkjʊbəs/ *noun* (*plural* **-buses** or **-bi** /-baɪ/) demon or male spirit formerly believed to have sexual intercourse with sleeping women; nightmare; oppressive person or thing.

inculcate /'ɪnkʌlkeɪt/ *verb* (**-ting**) (often + *upon, in*) urge, impress persistently. □ **inculcation** *noun*.

incumbency /ɪn'kʌmbənsɪ/ *noun* (*plural* **-ies**) office or tenure of incumbent.

incumbent /ɪn'kʌmbənt/ ● *adjective* lying, pressing; currently holding office. ● *noun* holder of office, esp. benefice. □ **it is incumbent on a person** (+ *to do*) it is a person's duty.

incur /ɪn'kɜ:/ *verb* (**-rr-**) bring on oneself.

incurable /ɪn'kjʊərəb(ə)l/ ● *adjective* that cannot be cured. ● *noun* incurable person. □ **incurability** *noun*; **incurably** *adverb*.

incurious /ɪn'kjʊərɪəs/ *adjective* lacking curiosity.

incursion /ɪn'kɜ:ʃ(ə)n/ *noun* invasion; sudden attack. □ **incursive** *adjective*.

indebted /ɪn'detɪd/ *adjective* (usually + *to*) owing money or gratitude. □ **indebtedness** *noun*.

indecent /ɪn'di:s(ə)nt/ *adjective* offending against decency; unbecoming; unsuitable. □ **indecent assault** sexual attack not involving rape. □ **indecency** *noun*; **indecently** *adverb*.

indecipherable /ɪndɪ'saɪfərəb(ə)l/ *adjective* that cannot be deciphered.

indecision /ɪndɪ'sɪʒ(ə)n/ *noun* inability to decide; hesitation.

indecisive /ɪndɪ'saɪsɪv/ *adjective* not decisive; irresolute; not conclusive. □ **indecisively** *adverb*; **indecisiveness** *noun*.

indecorous /ɪn'dekərəs/ *adjective* improper, undignified; in bad taste. □ **indecorously** *adverb*.

indeed /ɪn'di:d/ ● *adverb* in truth; really; admittedly. ● *interjection expressing irony, incredulity, etc.*

indefatigable /ɪndɪ'fætɪgəb(ə)l/ *adjective* unwearying, unremitting. □ **indefatigably** *adverb*.

indefeasible /ɪndɪ'fi:zɪb(ə)l/ *adjective literary* (esp. of claim, rights, etc.) that cannot be forfeited or annulled.

indefensible /ɪndɪ'fensɪb(ə)l/ *adjective* that cannot be defended. □ **indefensibility** *noun*; **indefensibly** *adverb*.

indefinable /ɪndɪ'faɪnəb(ə)l/ *adjective* that cannot be defined; mysterious. □ **indefinably** *adverb*.

indefinite /ɪn'defɪnɪt/ *adjective* vague, undefined; unlimited; (of adjectives, adverbs, and pronouns) not determining the person etc. referred to. □ **indefinite article** word (*a, an* in English) placed before noun and meaning 'one, some, any'.

indefinitely *adverb* for an unlimited time; in an indefinite manner.

indelible /ɪn'delɪb(ə)l/ *adjective* that cannot be rubbed out; permanent. □ **indelibly** *adverb*.

indelicate /ɪn'delɪkət/ *adjective* coarse, unrefined; tactless. □ **indelicacy** *noun* (*plural* **-ies**); **indelicately** *adverb*.

indemnify /ɪn'demnɪfaɪ/ *verb* (**-ies, -ied**) (often + *against, from*) secure against loss or legal responsibility; (often + *for*) exempt from penalty; compensate. □ **indemnification** *noun*.

indemnity /ɪn'demnɪtɪ/ *noun* (*plural* **-ies**) compensation for damage; sum exacted by victor in war; security against damage or loss; exemption from penalties.

indent ● *verb* /ɪn'dent/ make or impress notches, dents, or recesses in; set back (beginning of line) inwards from margin; draw up (legal document) in duplicate; (often + *for*) make requisition. ● *noun* /'ɪndent/ order (esp. from abroad) for goods; official requisition for stores; indented line; indentation; indenture.

indentation /ɪnden'teɪʃ(ə)n/ *noun* indenting, being indented; notch.

indenture /ɪn'dentʃə/ ● *noun* (usually in *plural*) sealed agreement; formal list, certificate, etc. ● *verb* (**-ring**) *historical* bind by indentures, esp. as apprentice.

independent /ɪndɪ'pend(ə)nt/ ● *adjective* (often + *of*) not depending on authority; self-governing; not depending on another person for one's livelihood or opinions; (of income) making it unnecessary to earn one's livelihood; unwilling to be under obligation to others; not depending on something else for validity etc.; (of institution) not supported by public funds. ● *noun* politician etc. independent of any political party. □ **independence** *noun*; **independently** *adverb*.

indescribable /ɪndɪ'skraɪbəb(ə)l/ *adjective* beyond description; that cannot be described. □ **indescribably** *adverb*.

indestructible /ɪndɪ'strʌktɪb(ə)l/ *adjective* that cannot be destroyed. □ **indestructibility** *noun*; **indestructibly** *adverb*.

indeterminable /ɪndɪ'tɜ:mɪnəb(ə)l/ *adjective* that cannot be ascertained or settled.

indeterminate /ɪndɪ'tɜ:mɪnət/ *adjective* not fixed in extent, character, etc.; vague. □ **indeterminacy** *noun*.

index /'ɪndeks/ ● *noun* (*plural* **-es** or **indices** /'ɪndɪsi:z/) alphabetical list of subjects etc. with references, usually at end of book; card index; measure of prices or wages compared with a previous month, year, etc.; *Mathematics* exponent. ● *verb* furnish (book) with index, enter in index; relate (wages, investment income, etc.) to a price index. □ **index finger** finger next to thumb; **index-linked** related to value of price index.

Indian /'ɪndɪən/ ● *noun* native or national of India; person of Indian descent; (in full **American Indian**) original inhabitant of America. ● *adjective* of India; of the subcontinent comprising India, Pakistan, and Bangladesh; of the original inhabitants of America. □ **Indian corn** maize; **Indian file** single file; **Indian ink** black pigment, ink made from this; **Indian summer** period of calm dry warm weather in late autumn, happy tranquil period late in life.

indiarubber *noun* rubber, esp. for rubbing out pencil marks etc.

indicate /'ɪndɪkeɪt/ *verb* (**-ting**) point out, make known; show; be sign of; require, call for; state briefly; give as reading or measurement; point by hand; use a vehicle's indicator. □ **indication** *noun*.

indicative /ɪn'dɪkətɪv/ ● *adjective* (+ *of*) suggestive, giving indications; *Grammar* (of mood) stating thing as fact. ● *noun Grammar* indicative mood; verb in this mood.

indicator *noun* flashing light on vehicle showing direction in which it is about to turn; person or thing that indicates; device indicating condition of machine etc.; recording instrument; board giving current information.

indices *plural of* INDEX.

indict /ɪn'daɪt/ *verb* accuse formally by legal process.

indictable *adjective* (of an offence) rendering person liable to be indicted; so liable.

indictment *noun* indicting, accusation; document containing this; thing that serves to condemn or censure.

indifference /ɪn'dɪfrəns/ *noun* lack of interest or attention; unimportance.

indifferent *adjective* (+ *to*) showing indifference; neither good nor bad; of poor quality or ability. ▫ **indifferently** *adverb*.

indigenous /ɪn'dɪdʒɪnəs/ *adjective* (often + *to*) native or belonging naturally to a place.

indigent /'ɪndɪdʒ(ə)nt/ *adjective formal* needy, poor. ▫ **indigence** *noun*.

indigestible /ɪndɪ'dʒestɪb(ə)l/ *adjective* difficult or impossible to digest.

indigestion /ɪndɪ'dʒestʃ(ə)n/ *noun* difficulty in digesting food; pain caused by this.

indignant /ɪn'dɪgnənt/ *adjective* feeling or showing indignation. ▫ **indignantly** *adverb*.

indignation /ɪndɪg'neɪʃ(ə)n/ *noun* anger at supposed injustice etc.

indignity /ɪn'dɪgnɪtɪ/ *noun* (*plural* **-ies**) humiliating treatment; insult.

indigo /'ɪndɪgəʊ/ *noun* (*plural* **-s**) deep violet-blue; dye of this colour.

indirect /ɪndaɪ'rekt/ *adjective* not going straight to the point; (of route etc.) not straight. ▫ **indirect object** word or phrase representing person or thing affected by action of verb but not acted on (see panel at OBJECT); **indirect speech** reported speech; **indirect tax** tax on goods and services, not income. ▫ **indirectly** *adverb*.

indiscernible /ɪndɪ'sɜːnɪb(ə)l/ *adjective* that cannot be discerned.

indiscipline /ɪn'dɪsɪplɪn/ *noun* lack of discipline.

indiscreet /ɪndɪ'skriːt/ *adjective* not discreet; injudicious, unwary. ▫ **indiscreetly** *adverb*.

indiscretion /ɪndɪ'skreʃ(ə)n/ *noun* indiscreet conduct or action.

indiscriminate /ɪndɪ'skrɪmɪnət/ *adjective* making no distinctions; done or acting at random. ▫ **indiscriminately** *adverb*.

indispensable /ɪndɪ'spensəb(ə)l/ *adjective* that cannot be dispensed with; necessary. ▫ **indispensably** *adverb*.

indisposed /ɪndɪ'spəʊzd/ *adjective* slightly unwell; averse, unwilling. ▫ **indisposition** /-spə'zɪʃ(ə)n/ *noun*.

indisputable /ɪndɪ'spjuːtəb(ə)l/ *adjective* that cannot be disputed. ▫ **indisputably** *adverb*.

indissoluble /ɪndɪ'sɒljʊb(ə)l/ *adjective* that cannot be dissolved; lasting, stable. ▫ **indissolubly** *adverb*.

indistinct /ɪndɪ'stɪŋkt/ *adjective* not distinct; confused, obscure. ▫ **indistinctly** *adverb*.

indistinguishable /ɪndɪ'stɪŋgwɪʃəb(ə)l/ *adjective* (often + *from*) not distinguishable.

indite /ɪn'daɪt/ *verb* (**-ting**) *formal or jocular* put into words; write (letter etc.).

individual /ɪndɪ'vɪdʒʊəl/ ● *adjective* of, for, or characteristic of single person or thing; having distinct character; designed for use by one person; single; particular. ● *noun* single member of class, group, etc.; single human being; *colloquial* person; distinctive person.

individualism *noun* social theory favouring free action by individuals; being independent or different. ▫ **individualist** *noun*; **individualistic** /-'lɪs-/ *adjective*.

individuality /ɪndɪvɪdʒʊ'ælɪtɪ/ *noun* individual character, esp. when strongly marked; separate existence.

individualize *verb* (also **-ise**) (**-zing** or **-sing**) give individual character to; (esp. as **individualized** *adjective*) personalize.

individually *adverb* one by one; personally; distinctively.

indivisible /ɪndɪ'vɪzɪb(ə)l/ *adjective* not divisible.

indoctrinate /ɪn'dɒktrɪneɪt/ *verb* (**-ting**) teach to accept a particular belief uncritically. ▫ **indoctrination** *noun*.

Indo-European /ɪndəʊjʊərə'pɪən/ ● *adjective* of family of languages spoken over most of Europe and Asia as far as N. India; of hypothetical parent language of this family. ● *noun* Indo-European family of languages; hypothetical parent language of these.

indolent /'ɪndələnt/ *adjective* lazy; averse to exertion. ▫ **indolence** *noun*; **indolently** *adverb*.

indomitable /ɪn'dɒmɪtəb(ə)l/ *adjective* unconquerable; unyielding. ▫ **indomitably** *adverb*.

indoor /'ɪndɔː/ *adjective* done etc. in building or under cover.

indoors /ɪn'dɔːz/ *adverb* in(to) a building.

indubitable /ɪn'djuːbɪtəb(ə)l/ *adjective* that cannot be doubted. ▫ **indubitably** *adverb*.

induce /ɪn'djuːs/ *verb* (**-cing**) prevail on, persuade; bring about; bring on (labour) artificially; bring on labour in (mother); speed up birth of (baby); produce by induction; infer. ▫ **inducible** *adjective*.

inducement *noun* attractive offer; incentive; bribe.

induct /ɪn'dʌkt/ *verb* install into office etc.

inductance *noun* property of electric circuit in which variation in current produces electromotive force.

induction /ɪn'dʌkʃ(ə)n/ *noun* inducting, inducing; act of bringing on (esp. labour) artificially; general inference from particular instances; formal introduction to new job etc.; production of electric or magnetic state by proximity to electric circuit or magnetic field.

inductive /ɪn'dʌktɪv/ *adjective* (of reasoning etc.) based on induction; of electric or magnetic induction.

indulge /ɪn'dʌldʒ/ *verb* (**-ging**) (often + *in*) take one's pleasure freely; yield freely to (desire etc.); gratify by compliance with wishes.

indulgence *noun* indulging; thing indulged in; *RC Church* remission of punishment still due after absolution; privilege granted.

indulgent *adjective* lenient; willing to overlook faults; indulging. ▫ **indulgently** *adverb*.

industrial /ɪn'dʌstrɪəl/ *adjective* of, engaged in, for use in, or serving the needs of, industry; having highly developed industries. ▫ **industrial action** strike or disruptive action by workers as protest; **industrial estate** area of land zoned for factories etc. ▫ **industrially** *adverb*.

industrialism *noun* system in which manufacturing industries predominate.

industrialist *noun* owner or manager in industry.

industrialize *verb* (also **-ise**) (**-zing** or **-sing**) make (nation etc.) industrial. ▫ **industrialization** *noun*.

industrious /ɪn'dʌstrɪəs/ *adjective* hard-working. ▫ **industriously** *adverb*.

industry /ˈɪndəstrɪ/ *noun* (*plural* **-ies**) branch of trade or manufacture; commercial enterprise; trade or manufacture collectively; concerted activity; diligence.

inebriate ● *verb* /ɪˈni:brɪeɪt/ (**-ting**) make drunk; excite. ● *adjective* /ɪˈni:brɪət/ drunken. ● *noun* /ɪˈni:brɪət/ drunkard. □ **inebriation** *noun*.

inedible /ɪnˈedɪb(ə)l/ *adjective* not suitable for eating.

ineducable /ɪnˈedjʊkəb(ə)l/ *adjective* incapable of being educated.

ineffable /ɪnˈefəb(ə)l/ *adjective* too great for description in words; that must not be uttered. □ **ineffability** *noun*; **ineffably** *adverb*.

ineffective /ɪnɪˈfektɪv/ *adjective* not achieving desired effect or results. □ **ineffectively** *adverb*; **ineffectiveness** *noun*.

ineffectual /ɪnɪˈfektʃʊəl/ *adjective* ineffective, feeble. □ **ineffectually** *adverb*.

inefficient /ɪnɪˈfɪʃ(ə)nt/ *adjective* not efficient or fully capable; (of machine etc.) wasteful. □ **inefficiency** *noun*; **inefficiently** *adverb*.

inelegant /ɪnˈelɪgənt/ *adjective* ungraceful, unrefined. □ **inelegance** *noun*; **inelegantly** *adverb*.

ineligible /ɪnˈelɪdʒɪb(ə)l/ *adjective* not eligible or qualified. □ **ineligibility** *noun*.

ineluctable /ɪnɪˈlʌktəb(ə)l/ *adjective* inescapable, unavoidable.

inept /ɪˈnept/ *adjective* unskilful; absurd, silly; out of place. □ **ineptitude** *noun*; **ineptly** *adverb*.

inequality /ɪnɪˈkwɒlɪtɪ/ *noun* (*plural* **-ies**) lack of equality; variability; unevenness.

inequitable /ɪnˈekwɪtəb(ə)l/ *adjective* unfair, unjust.

inequity /ɪnˈekwɪtɪ/ *noun* (*plural* **-ies**) unfairness, injustice.

ineradicable /ɪnɪˈrædɪkəb(ə)l/ *adjective* that cannot be rooted out.

inert /ɪˈnɜ:t/ *adjective* without inherent power of action etc.; chemically inactive; sluggish, slow; lifeless.

inertia /ɪˈnɜ:ʃə/ *noun* property by which matter continues in existing state of rest or motion unless acted on by external force; inertness; tendency to remain unchanged. □ **inertia reel** reel allowing seat belt to unwind freely but locking on impact; **inertia selling** sending of unsolicited goods in hope of making a sale.

inescapable /ɪnɪˈskeɪpəb(ə)l/ *adjective* that cannot be escaped or avoided. □ **inescapably** *adverb*.

inessential /ɪnɪˈsenʃ(ə)l/ ● *adjective* not necessary; dispensable. ● *noun* inessential thing.

inestimable /ɪnˈestɪməb(ə)l/ *adjective* too great etc. to be estimated. □ **inestimably** *adverb*.

inevitable /ɪnˈevɪtəb(ə)l/ *adjective* unavoidable; bound to happen or appear; *colloquial* tiresomely familiar. □ **inevitability** *noun*; **inevitably** *adverb*.

inexact /ɪnɪgˈzækt/ *adjective* not exact. □ **inexactitude** *noun*.

inexcusable /ɪnɪkˈskju:zəb(ə)l/ *adjective* that cannot be justified. □ **inexcusably** *adverb*.

inexhaustible /ɪnɪgˈzɔ:stɪb(ə)l/ *adjective* that cannot be used up.

inexorable /ɪnˈeksərəb(ə)l/ *adjective* relentless. □ **inexorably** *adverb*.

inexpedient /ɪnɪkˈspi:dɪənt/ *adjective* not expedient.

inexpensive /ɪnɪkˈspensɪv/ *adjective* not expensive.

inexperience /ɪnɪkˈspɪərɪəns/ *noun* lack of experience. □ **inexperienced** *adjective*.

inexpert /ɪnˈekspɜ:t/ *adjective* unskilful.

inexpiable /ɪnˈekspɪəb(ə)l/ *adjective* that cannot be expiated.

inexplicable /ɪnɪkˈsplɪkəb(ə)l/ *adjective* that cannot be explained. □ **inexplicably** *adverb*.

inexpressible /ɪnɪkˈspresɪb(ə)l/ *adjective* that cannot be expressed. □ **inexpressibly** *adverb*.

in extremis /ɪn ɪkˈstri:mɪs/ *adjective* at point of death; in great difficulties. [Latin]

inextricable /ɪnɪkˈstrɪkəb(ə)l/ *adjective* that cannot be separated, loosened, or resolved; inescapable. □ **inextricably** *adverb*.

infallible /ɪnˈfælɪb(ə)l/ *adjective* incapable of error; unfailing, sure. □ **infallibility** *noun*; **infallibly** *adverb*.

infamous /ˈɪnfəməs/ *adjective* notoriously vile, evil; abominable. □ **infamously** *adverb*; **infamy** *noun* (*plural* **-ies**).

infant /ˈɪnf(ə)nt/ *noun* child during earliest period of life; thing in early stage of development; *Law* person under 18. □ **infancy** *noun*.

infanta /ɪnˈfæntə/ *noun historical* daughter of Spanish or Portuguese king.

infanticide /ɪnˈfæntɪsaɪd/ *noun* killing of infant, esp. soon after birth; person guilty of this.

infantile /ˈɪnfəntaɪl/ *adjective* of or like infants. □ **infantile paralysis** poliomyelitis.

infantry /ˈɪnfəntrɪ/ *noun* (*plural* **-ies**) (group of) foot-soldiers. □ **infantryman** soldier of infantry regiment.

infatuate /ɪnˈfætjʊeɪt/ *verb* (**-ting**) (usually as **infatuated** *adjective*) inspire with intense fondness. □ **infatuation** *noun*.

infect /ɪnˈfekt/ *verb* affect or contaminate with germ, virus, or disease; imbue, taint.

infection /ɪnˈfekʃ(ə)n/ *noun* infecting, being infected; disease; communication of disease.

infectious *adjective* infecting; transmissible by infection; apt to spread. □ **infectiously** *adverb*.

infelicity /ɪnfɪˈlɪsɪtɪ/ *noun* (*plural* **-ies**) inapt expression; unhappiness. □ **infelicitous** *adjective*.

infer /ɪnˈfɜ:/ *verb* (**-rr-**) deduce, conclude.

■ **Usage** It is a mistake to use *infer* to mean 'imply', as in *Are you inferring that I'm a liar?*

inference /ˈɪnfərəns/ *noun* act of inferring; thing inferred. □ **inferential** /-ˈren(ə)l/ *adjective*.

inferior /ɪnˈfɪərɪə/ ● *adjective* lower in rank etc.; of poor quality; situated below. ● *noun* inferior person.

inferiority /ɪnfɪərɪˈɒrɪtɪ/ *noun* being inferior. □ **inferiority complex** feeling of inadequacy, sometimes marked by compensating aggressive behaviour.

infernal /ɪnˈfɜ:n(ə)l/ *adjective* of hell; hellish; *colloquial* detestable, tiresome. □ **infernally** *adverb*.

inferno /ɪnˈfɜ:nəʊ/ *noun* (*plural* **-s**) raging fire; scene of horror or distress; hell.

infertile /ɪnˈfɜ:taɪl/ *adjective* not fertile. □ **infertility** /-fəˈtɪl-/ *noun*.

infest /ɪnˈfest/ *verb* overrun in large numbers. □ **infestation** *noun*.

infidel /ˈɪnfɪd(ə)l/ ● *noun* disbeliever in esp. the supposed true religion. ● *adjective* of infidels; unbelieving.

infidelity /ɪnfɪˈdelɪtɪ/ *noun* (*plural* **-ies**) being unfaithful.

infighting *noun* conflict or competitiveness in organization; boxing within arm's length.

infiltrate /ˈɪnfɪltreɪt/ *verb* (**-ting**) enter (territory, political party, etc.) gradually and imperceptibly; cause to do this; permeate by filtration; (often + *into*, *through*) introduce (fluid) by filtration. □ **infiltration** *noun*; **infiltrator** *noun*.

infinite /ˈɪnfɪnɪt/ *adjective* boundless; endless; very great or many. □ **infinitely** *adverb*.

infinitesimal /ɪnfɪnɪˈtesɪm(ə)l/ *adjective* infinitely or very small. □ **infinitesimally** *adverb*.

infinitive /ɪn'fɪnɪtɪv/ ● *noun* verb-form expressing verbal notion without particular subject, tense, etc. ● *adjective* having this form.
infinitude /ɪn'fɪnɪtju:d/ *noun literary* infinite number etc.; being infinite.
infinity /ɪn'fɪnɪtɪ/ *noun* (*plural* **-ies**) infinite number or extent; being infinite; boundlessness; infinite distance; *Mathematics* infinite quantity.
infirm /ɪn'fɜ:m/ *adjective* weak.
infirmary /ɪn'fɜ:mərɪ/ *noun* (*plural* **-ies**) hospital; sick-bay in school etc.
infirmity *noun* (*plural* **-ies**) being infirm; particular physical weakness.
in flagrante delicto /ɪn flə'græntɪ dɪ'lɪktəʊ/ *adverb* in act of committing offence. [Latin]
inflame /ɪn'fleɪm/ *verb* (**-ming**) provoke to strong feeling; cause inflammation in; aggravate; make hot; (cause to) catch fire.
inflammable /ɪn'flæməb(ə)l/ *adjective* easily set on fire or excited. □ **inflammability** *noun.*

■ **Usage** Because *inflammable* could be thought to mean 'not easily set on fire', *flammable* is often used instead. The negative of *inflammable* is *non-inflammable.*

inflammation /ɪnflə'meɪʃ(ə)n/ *noun* inflaming; disordered bodily condition marked by heat, swelling, redness, and usually pain.
inflammatory /ɪn'flæmətərɪ/ *adjective* tending to inflame; of inflammation.
inflatable ● *adjective* that can be inflated. ● *noun* inflatable object.
inflate /ɪn'fleɪt/ *verb* (**-ting**) distend with air or gas; (usually + *with*; usually in *passive*) puff up (with pride etc.); resort to inflation of (currency); raise (prices) artificially; (as **inflated** *adjective*) (esp. of language, opinions, etc.) bombastic, exaggerated.
inflation *noun* inflating, being inflated; general rise in prices, increase in supply of money regarded as cause of such rise. □ **inflationary** *adjective.*
inflect /ɪn'flekt/ *verb* change or vary pitch of (voice); modify (word) to express grammatical relation; undergo such modification.
inflection /ɪn'flekʃ(ə)n/ *noun* (also **inflexion**) inflecting, being inflected; inflected form; inflecting suffix etc.; modulation of voice. □ **inflectional** *adjective.*
inflexible /ɪn'fleksɪb(ə)l/ *adjective* unbendable; unbending; unyielding. □ **inflexibility** *noun*; **inflexibly** *adverb.*
inflexion = INFLECTION.
inflict /ɪn'flɪkt/ *verb* deal (blow etc.); impose. □ **infliction** *noun.*
inflight *adjective* occurring or provided during a flight.
inflorescence /ɪnflə'res(ə)ns/ *noun* collective flower head of plant; arrangement of flowers on plant; flowering.
inflow *noun* flowing in; that which flows in.
influence /'ɪnflʊəns/ ● *noun* (usually + *on*) effect a person or thing has on another; (usually + *over*, *with*) ascendancy, moral power; thing or person exercising this. ● *verb* (**-cing**) exert influence on; affect. □ **under the influence** *colloquial* drunk.
influential /ɪnflʊ'enʃ(ə)l/ *adjective* having great influence.
influenza /ɪnflʊ'enzə/ *noun* infectious viral disease with fever, severe aching, and catarrh.
influx /'ɪnflʌks/ *noun* flowing in.
inform /ɪn'fɔ:m/ *verb* tell; (usually + *against*, *on*) give incriminating information about person to authorities.
informal /ɪn'fɔ:m(ə)l/ *adjective* without formality; not formal. □ **informality** /-'mæl-/ *noun* (*plural* **-ies**); **informally** *adverb.*
informant *noun* giver of information.
information /ɪnfə'meɪʃ(ə)n/ *noun* what is told; knowledge; news; formal charge or accusation. □ **information retrieval** tracing of information stored in books, computers, etc.; **information technology** study or use of processes (esp. computers etc.) for storing, retrieving, and sending information.
informative /ɪn'fɔ:mətɪv/ *adjective* giving information, instructive.
informed *adjective* knowing the facts; having some knowledge.
informer *noun* person who informs, esp. against others.
infraction /ɪn'frækʃ(ə)n/ *noun* infringement.
infra dig /ɪnfrə 'dɪg/ *adjective colloquial* beneath one's dignity.
infrared /ɪnfrə'red/ *adjective* of or using radiation just beyond red end of spectrum.
infrastructure /'ɪnfrəstrʌktʃə/ *noun* structural foundations of a society or enterprise; roads, bridges, sewers, etc., regarded as country's economic foundation; permanent installations as basis for military etc. operations.
infrequent /ɪn'fri:kwənt/ *adjective* not frequent. □ **infrequently** *adverb.*
infringe /ɪn'frɪndʒ/ *verb* (**-ging**) break or violate (law, another's rights, etc.); (usually + *on*) encroach, trespass. □ **infringement** *noun.*
infuriate /ɪn'fjʊərɪeɪt/ *verb* (**-ting**) enrage; irritate greatly. □ **infuriating** *adjective.*
infuse /ɪn'fju:z/ *verb* (**-sing**) (usually + *with*) fill (with a quality); steep or be steeped in liquid to extract properties; (usually + *into*) instil (life etc.).
infusible /ɪn'fju:zɪb(ə)l/ *adjective* that cannot be melted. □ **infusibility** *noun.*
infusion /ɪn'fju:ʒ(ə)n/ *noun* infusing; liquid extract so obtained; infused element.
ingenious /ɪn'dʒi:nɪəs/ *adjective* clever at contriving; cleverly contrived. □ **ingeniously** *adverb.*

■ **Usage** *Ingenious* is sometimes confused with *ingenuous.*

ingénue /æʒeɪ'nju:/ *noun* artless young woman, esp. as stage type. [French]
ingenuity /ɪndʒɪ'nju:ɪtɪ/ *noun* inventiveness, cleverness.
ingenuous /ɪn'dʒenjʊəs/ *adjective* artless; frank. □ **ingenuously** *adverb.*

■ **Usage** *Ingenuous* is sometimes confused with *ingenious.*

ingest /ɪn'dʒest/ *verb* take in (food etc.); absorb (knowledge etc.). □ **ingestion** *noun.*
inglenook /'ɪŋgəlnʊk/ *noun* space within opening either side of old-fashioned wide fireplace.
inglorious /ɪn'glɔ:rɪəs/ *adjective* shameful; not famous.
ingoing *adjective* going in.
ingot /'ɪŋgət/ *noun* (usually oblong) mass of cast metal, esp. gold, silver, or steel.
ingrained /ɪn'greɪnd/ *adjective* deeply rooted, inveterate; (of dirt etc.) deeply embedded.
ingratiate /ɪn'greɪʃɪeɪt/ *verb* (**-ting**) (**ingratiate oneself**; usually + *with*) bring oneself into favour. □ **ingratiating** *adjective.*
ingratitude /ɪn'grætɪtju:d/ *noun* lack of due gratitude.
ingredient /ɪn'gri:dɪənt/ *noun* component part in mixture.

ingress /'ɪngres/ *noun* going in; right to go in.

ingrowing *adjective* (of nail) growing into the flesh.

inhabit /ɪn'hæbɪt/ *verb* (**-t-**) dwell in, occupy. □ **inhabitable** *adjective*; **inhabitant** *noun*.

inhalant /ɪn'heɪlənt/ *noun* medicinal substance to be inhaled.

inhale /ɪn'heɪl/ *verb* (**-ling**) breathe in. □ **inhalation** /-hə'leɪʃ(ə)n/ *noun*.

inhaler *noun* device for administering inhalant, esp. to relieve asthma.

inhere /ɪn'hɪə/ *verb* (**-ring**) be inherent.

inherent /ɪn'herənt/ *adjective* (often + *in*) existing in something as essential or permanent attribute. □ **inherently** *adverb*.

inherit /ɪn'herɪt/ *verb* (**-t-**) receive as heir; derive (characteristic) from ancestors; derive or take over (situation) from predecessor. □ **inheritor** *noun*.

inheritance *noun* what is inherited; inheriting.

inhibit /ɪn'hɪbɪt/ *verb* (**-t-**) hinder, restrain, prevent; (as **inhibited** *adjective*) suffering from inhibition; (usually + *from*) prohibit.

inhibition /ɪnhɪ'bɪʃ(ə)n/ *noun* restraint of direct expression of instinct; *colloquial* emotional resistance to thought or action; inhibiting, being inhibited.

inhospitable /ɪnhɒs'pɪtəb(ə)l/ *adjective* not hospitable; affording no shelter.

inhuman /ɪn'hju:mən/ *adjective* brutal, unfeeling, barbarous. □ **inhumanity** /-'mæn-/ *noun* (*plural* **-ies**); **inhumanly** *adverb*.

inhumane /ɪnhju:'meɪn/ *adjective* not humane, callous.

inimical /ɪ'nɪmɪk(ə)l/ *adjective* hostile; harmful.

inimitable /ɪ'nɪmɪtəb(ə)l/ *adjective* that cannot be imitated. □ **inimitably** *adverb*.

iniquity /ɪ'nɪkwɪtɪ/ *noun* (*plural* **-ies**) wickedness; gross injustice. □ **iniquitous** *adjective*.

initial /ɪ'nɪʃ(ə)l/ ● *adjective* of or at beginning. ● *noun* first letter, esp. of person's name. ● *verb* (**-ll-**; *US* **-l-**) mark or sign with one's initials. □ **initially** *adverb*.

initiate ● *verb* /ɪ'nɪʃɪeɪt/ (**-ting**) originate, set going; admit into society, office, etc., esp. with ritual; (+ *into*) instruct in subject. ● *noun* /ɪ'nɪʃɪət/ initiated person. □ **initiation** *noun*; **initiatory** /ɪ'nɪʃjətərɪ/ *adjective*.

initiative /ɪ'nɪʃətɪv/ *noun* ability to initiate, enterprise; first step; (**the initiative**) power or right to begin.

inject /ɪn'dʒekt/ *verb* (usually + *into*) force (medicine etc.) (as) by syringe; administer medicine etc. to (person) by injection; place (quality etc.) where needed in something. □ **injection** *noun*.

injudicious /ɪndʒu:'dɪʃəs/ *adjective* unwise, ill-judged.

injunction /ɪn'dʒʌŋkʃ(ə)n/ *noun* authoritative order; judicial order restraining from specified act or compelling restitution etc.

injure /'ɪndʒə/ *verb* (**-ring**) hurt, harm, impair; do wrong to.

injurious /ɪn'dʒʊərɪəs/ *adjective* hurtful; defamatory; wrongful.

injury /'ɪndʒərɪ/ *noun* (*plural* **-ies**) physical damage, harm; offence to feelings etc.; *esp. Law* wrongful treatment. □ **injury time** extra time at football match etc. to compensate for that lost in dealing with injuries.

injustice /ɪn'dʒʌstɪs/ *noun* unfairness; unjust act.

ink ● *noun* coloured fluid or paste for writing or printing; black liquid ejected by cuttlefish etc. ● *verb* mark, cover, or smear with ink. □ **ink-jet printer** printing machine firing tiny jets of ink at paper; **inkwell** pot for ink, esp. in hole in desk. □ **inky** *adjective* (**-ier, -iest**).

inkling /'ɪŋklɪŋ/ *noun* (often + *of*) hint, slight knowledge or suspicion.

inland ● *adjective* /'ɪnlənd/ remote from sea or border within a country; carried on within country. ● *adverb* /ɪn'lænd/ in or towards interior of country. □ **Inland Revenue** government department assessing and collecting taxes.

in-laws /'ɪnlɔ:z/ *plural noun* relatives by marriage.

inlay ● *verb* /ɪn'leɪ/ (*past & past participle* **inlaid** /ɪn'leɪd/) embed (thing in another); decorate (thing) thus. ● *noun* /'ɪnleɪ/ inlaid material or work; filling shaped to fit tooth-cavity.

inlet /'ɪnlət/ *noun* small arm of sea etc.; piece inserted; way of admission.

inmate /'ɪnmeɪt/ *noun* occupant of house, hospital, prison, etc.

in memoriam /ɪn mɪ'mɔ:rɪæm/ *preposition* in memory of.

inmost /'ɪnməʊst/ *adjective* most inward.

inn *noun* pub, sometimes with accommodation; *historical* house providing lodging etc. for payment, esp. for travellers. □ **innkeeper** keeper of inn; **Inns of Court** 4 legal societies admitting people to English bar.

innards /'ɪnədz/ *plural noun colloquial* entrails.

innate /ɪ'neɪt/ *adjective* inborn; natural. □ **innately** *adverb*.

inner /'ɪnə/ ● *adjective* interior, internal. ● *noun* circle nearest bull's-eye of target. □ **inner city** central area of city, esp. regarded as having social problems; **inner tube** separate inflatable tube in pneumatic tyre. □ **innermost** *adjective*.

innings /'ɪnɪŋz/ *noun* (*plural* same) *esp. Cricket* batsman's or side's turn at batting; term of office etc. when person, party, etc. can achieve something.

innocent /'ɪnəs(ə)nt/ ● *adjective* free from moral wrong; not guilty; guileless; harmless. ● *noun* innocent person, esp. young child. □ **innocence** *noun*; **innocently** *adverb*.

innocuous /ɪ'nɒkjʊəs/ *adjective* harmless.

innovate /'ɪnəveɪt/ *verb* (**-ting**) bring in new ideas etc.; make changes. □ **innovation** *noun*; **innovative** /-vətɪv/ *adjective*; **innovator** *noun*.

innuendo /ɪnjʊ'endəʊ/ *noun* (*plural* **-es** or **-s**) allusive (usually depreciatory or sexually suggestive) remark.

innumerable /ɪ'nju:mərəb(ə)l/ *adjective* countless.

innumerate /ɪ'nju:mərət/ *adjective* not knowing basic mathematics. □ **innumeracy** *noun*.

inoculate /ɪ'nɒkjʊleɪt/ *verb* (**-ting**) treat with vaccine or serum to promote immunity against a disease. □ **inoculation** *noun*.

inoffensive /ɪnə'fensɪv/ *adjective* not objectionable; harmless.

inoperable /ɪ'nɒpərəb(ə)l/ *adjective* that cannot be cured by surgical operation.

inoperative /ɪ'nɒpərətɪv/ *adjective* not working or taking effect.

inopportune /ɪ'nɒpətju:n/ *adjective* not appropriate, esp. as regards time.

inordinate /ɪ'nɔ:dɪnət/ *adjective* excessive. □ **inordinately** *adverb*.

inorganic /ɪnɔ:'gænɪk/ *adjective Chemistry* not organic; without organized physical structure; extraneous.

input /'ɪnpʊt/ ● *noun* what is put in; place of entry of energy, information, etc.; action of putting in or feeding in; contribution of information etc. ● *verb* (**inputting**; *past & past participle* **input** or **inputted**) put in; supply (data, programs, etc.) to computer.

inquest /'ɪŋkwest/ *noun* inquiry held by coroner into cause of death.

inquietude /ɪn'kwaɪɪtju:d/ *noun* uneasiness.

inquire /ɪn'kwaɪə/ *verb* (**-ring**) seek information formally; make inquiry; ask question.

inquiry /ɪn'kwaɪərɪ/ *noun* (*plural* **-ies**) investigation, esp. official; asking; question.
inquisition /ɪnkwɪ'zɪʃ(ə)n/ *noun* investigation; official inquiry; (**the Inquisition**) *RC Church History* ecclesiastical tribunal for suppression of heresy. ▫ **inquisitional** *adjective.*
inquisitive /ɪn'kwɪzɪtɪv/ *adjective* curious, prying; seeking knowledge. ▫ **inquisitively** *adverb*; **inquisitiveness** *noun.*
inquisitor /ɪn'kwɪzɪtə/ *noun* investigator; *historical* officer of Inquisition.
inquisitorial /ɪnkwɪzɪ'tɔ:rɪəl/ *adjective* inquisitor-like; prying.
inroad *noun* (often in *plural*) encroachment; using up of resources etc.; hostile incursion.
inrush *noun* rapid influx.
insalubrious /ɪnsə'lu:brɪəs/ *adjective* (of climate or place) unhealthy.
insane /ɪn'seɪn/ *adjective* mad; *colloquial* extremely foolish. ▫ **insanely** *adverb*; **insanity** /ɪn'sænɪtɪ/ *noun* (*plural* **-ies**).
insanitary /ɪn'sænɪtərɪ/ *adjective* not sanitary.
insatiable /ɪn'seɪʃəb(ə)l/ *adjective* that cannot be satisfied; extremely greedy. ▫ **insatiability** *noun*; **insatiably** *adverb.*
insatiate /ɪn'seɪʃɪət/ *adjective* never satisfied.
inscribe /ɪn'skraɪb/ *verb* (**-bing**) (usually + *in*, *on*) write or carve (words etc.) on surface; mark (surface) with characters; (usually + *to*) write informal dedication in or on (book etc.); enter on list; *Geometry* draw (figure) within another so that some points of their boundaries coincide.
inscription /ɪn'skrɪpʃ(ə)n/ *noun* words inscribed; inscribing.
inscrutable /ɪn'skru:təb(ə)l/ *adjective* mysterious, impenetrable. ▫ **inscrutability** *noun*; **inscrutably** *adverb.*
insect /'ɪnsekt/ *noun* small invertebrate animal with segmented body, 6 legs, and usually wings.
insecticide /ɪn'sektɪsaɪd/ *noun* preparation used for killing insects.
insectivore /ɪn'sektɪvɔ:/ *noun* animal or plant that feeds on insects. ▫ **insectivorous** /-'tɪvərəs/ *adjective.*
insecure /ɪnsɪ'kjʊə/ *adjective* not secure or safe; not feeling safe. ▫ **insecurity** /-'kjʊr-/ *noun.*
inseminate /ɪn'semɪneɪt/ *verb* (**-ting**) introduce semen into; sow (seed etc.). ▫ **insemination** *noun.*
insensate /ɪn'senseɪt/ *adjective* without esp. physical sensibility; stupid.
insensible /ɪn'sensɪb(ə)l/ *adjective* unconscious; unaware; callous; imperceptible. ▫ **insensibility** *noun*; **insensibly** *adverb.*
insensitive /ɪn'sensɪtɪv/ *adjective* not sensitive. ▫ **insensitively** *adverb*; **insensitiveness** *noun*; **insensitivity** /-'tɪv-/ *noun.*
insentient /ɪn'senʃ(ə)nt/ *adjective* inanimate.
inseparable /ɪn'sepərəb(ə)l/ *adjective* that cannot be separated. ▫ **inseparability** *noun*; **inseparably** *adverb.*
insert ● *verb* /ɪn'sɜ:t/ place or put (thing into another). ● *noun* /'ɪnsɜ:t/ thing inserted.
insertion /ɪn'sɜ:ʃ(ə)n/ *noun* inserting; thing inserted.
inset ● *noun* /'ɪnset/ extra piece inserted in book, garment, etc.; small map etc. within border of larger. ● *verb* /ɪn'set/ (**insetting**; *past & past participle* **inset** or **insetted**) put in as inset; decorate with inset.
inshore /ɪn'ʃɔ:/ *adverb & adjective* at sea but close to shore.
inside ● *noun* /ɪn'saɪd/ inner side or part; interior; side of path away from road; (usually in *plural*) *colloquial* stomach and bowels. ● *adjective* /'ɪnsaɪd/ of, on, or in the inside; nearer to centre of games field. ● *adverb* /ɪn'saɪd/ on, in, or to the inside; *slang* in prison. ● *preposition* /ɪn'saɪd/ within, on the inside of; in less than. ▫ **inside out** with inner side turned outwards; **know inside out** know thoroughly.
insider /ɪn'saɪdə/ *noun* person within organization etc.; person privy to secret.
insidious /ɪn'sɪdɪəs/ *adjective* proceeding inconspicuously but harmfully. ▫ **insidiously** *adverb.*
insight *noun* capacity for understanding hidden truths etc.; instance of this.
insignia /ɪn'sɪgnɪə/ *plural noun* badges or marks of office etc.
insignificant /ɪnsɪg'nɪfɪkənt/ *adjective* unimportant; trivial. ▫ **insignificance** *noun.*
insincere /ɪnsɪn'sɪə/ *adjective* not sincere. ▫ **insincerely** *adverb*; **insincerity** /-'ser-/ *noun.*
insinuate /ɪn'sɪnjʊeɪt/ *verb* (**-ting**) hint obliquely; (usually + *into*) introduce subtly or deviously. ▫ **insinuation** *noun.*
insipid /ɪn'sɪpɪd/ *adjective* dull, lifeless; flavourless. ▫ **insipidity** /-'pɪd-/ *noun*; **insipidly** *adverb.*
insist /ɪn'sɪst/ *verb* demand or maintain emphatically. ▫ **insistence** *noun*; **insistent** *adjective*; **insistently** *adverb.*
in situ /ɪn 'sɪtju:/ *adverb* in its original place. [Latin]
insobriety /ɪnsə'braɪətɪ/ *noun* intemperance, esp. in drinking.
insole *noun* removable inner sole for use in shoe.
insolent /'ɪnsələnt/ *adjective* impertinently insulting. ▫ **insolence** *noun*; **insolently** *adverb.*
insoluble /ɪn'sɒljʊb(ə)l/ *adjective* that cannot be solved or dissolved. ▫ **insolubility** *noun*; **insolubly** *adverb.*
insolvent /ɪn'sɒlv(ə)nt/ ● *adjective* unable to pay debts. ● *noun* insolvent debtor. ▫ **insolvency** *noun.*
insomnia /ɪn'sɒmnɪə/ *noun* sleeplessness.
insomniac /ɪn'sɒmnɪæk/ *noun* person suffering from insomnia.
insouciant /ɪn'su:sɪənt/ *adjective* carefree, unconcerned. ▫ **insouciance** *noun.*
inspect /ɪn'spekt/ *verb* look closely at; examine officially. ▫ **inspection** *noun.*
inspector *noun* official employed to inspect or supervise; police officer next above sergeant in rank. ▫ **inspectorate** *noun.*
inspiration /ɪnspə'reɪʃ(ə)n/ *noun* creative force or influence; person etc. stimulating creativity etc.; sudden brilliant idea; divine influence, esp. on writing of Scripture.
inspire /ɪn'spaɪə/ *verb* (**-ring**) stimulate (person) to esp. creative activity; animate; instil thought or feeling into; prompt, give rise to; (as **inspired** *adjective*) characterized by inspiration. ▫ **inspiring** *adjective.*
inspirit /ɪn'spɪrɪt/ *verb* (**-t-**) put life into, animate; encourage.
inst. *abbreviation* instant, of current month.
instability /ɪnstə'bɪlɪtɪ/ *noun* lack of stability.
install /ɪn'stɔ:l/ *verb* place (equipment etc.) in position ready for use; place (person) in office with ceremony. ▫ **installation** /-stə'leɪ-/ *noun.*
instalment *noun* (*US* **installment**) any of several usually equal payments for something; any of several parts, esp. of broadcast or published story.
instance /'ɪnst(ə)ns/ ● *noun* example; particular case. ● *verb* (**-cing**) cite as instance.
instant /'ɪnst(ə)nt/ ● *adjective* occurring immediately; (of food etc.) processed for quick preparation; urgent, pressing; of current month. ● *noun* precise moment; short space of time.
instantaneous /ɪnstən'teɪnɪəs/ *adjective* occurring or done in an instant. ▫ **instantaneously** *adverb.*

instantly *adverb* immediately.

instead /ɪn'sted/ *adverb* (+ *of*) in place of; as substitute or alternative.

instep /'ɪnstep/ *noun* inner arch of foot between toes and ankle; part of shoe etc. fitting this.

instigate /'ɪnstɪgeɪt/ *verb* (**-ting**) bring about by persuasion; incite. □ **instigation** *noun*; **instigator** *noun*.

instil /ɪn'stɪl/ *verb* (*US* **instill**) (**-ll-**) (often + *into*) put (ideas etc. into mind etc.) gradually; put in by drops. □ **instillation** *noun*; **instilment** *noun*.

instinct /'ɪnstɪŋkt/ *noun* inborn pattern of behaviour; innate impulse; intuition. □ **instinctive** /-'stɪŋktɪv/ *adjective*; **instinctively** /-'stɪŋktɪvlɪ/ *adverb*; **instinctual** /-'stɪŋktjʊəl/ *adjective*.

institute /'ɪnstɪtju:t/ ● *noun* organized body for promotion of science, education, etc. ● *verb* (**-ting**) establish; initiate (inquiry etc.); (usually + *to, into*) appoint (person) as cleric in church etc.

institution /ɪnstɪ'tju:ʃ(ə)n/ *noun* (esp. charitable) organization or society; established law or custom; *colloquial* well-known person; instituting, being instituted.

institutional *adjective* of or like an institution; typical of institutions.

institutionalize *verb* (also **-ise**) (**-zing** or **-sing**) (as **institutionalized** *adjective*) made dependent by long period in institution; place or keep in institution; make institutional.

instruct /ɪn'strʌkt/ *verb* teach; (usually + *to do*) direct, command; employ (lawyer); inform. □ **instructor** *noun*.

instruction /ɪn'strʌkʃ(ə)n/ *noun* (often in *plural*) order, direction (as to how thing works etc.); teaching. □ **instructional** *adjective*.

instructive /ɪn'strʌktɪv/ *adjective* tending to instruct; enlightening.

instrument /'ɪnstrəmənt/ *noun* tool, implement; (in full **musical instrument**) contrivance for producing musical sounds; thing used in performing action; person made use of; measuring device, esp. in aircraft; formal (esp. legal) document.

instrumental /ɪnstrə'ment(ə)l/ *adjective* serving as instrument or means; (of music) performed on instruments.

instrumentalist *noun* performer on musical instrument.

instrumentality /ɪnstrəmen'tælɪtɪ/ *noun* agency, means.

instrumentation /ɪnstrəmen'teɪʃ(ə)n/ *noun* provision or use of instruments; arrangement of music for instruments; particular instruments used in piece.

insubordinate /ɪnsə'bɔ:dɪnət/ *adjective* disobedient; unruly. □ **insubordination** *noun*.

insubstantial /ɪnsəb'stænʃ(ə)l/ *adjective* lacking solidity or substance; not real.

insufferable /ɪn'sʌfərəb(ə)l/ *adjective* unbearable; unbearably conceited etc. □ **insufferably** *adverb*.

insufficient /ɪnsə'fɪʃ(ə)nt/ *adjective* not enough, inadequate. □ **insufficiency** *noun*; **insufficiently** *adverb*.

insular /'ɪnsjʊlə/ *adjective* of or like an island; separated, remote; narrow-minded. □ **insularity** /-'lær-/ *noun*.

insulate /'ɪnsjʊleɪt/ *verb* (**-ting**) isolate, esp. by non-conductor of electricity, heat, sound, etc. □ **insulation** *noun*; **insulator** *noun*.

insulin /'ɪnsjʊlɪn/ *noun* hormone regulating the amount of glucose in the blood, the lack of which causes diabetes.

insult ● *verb* /ɪn'sʌlt/ abuse scornfully; offend self-respect etc. of. ● *noun* /'ɪnsʌlt/ insulting remark or action. □ **insulting** *adjective*; **insultingly** *adverb*.

insuperable /ɪn'su:pərəb(ə)l/ *adjective* impossible to surmount; impossible to overcome. □ **insuperability** *noun*; **insuperably** *adverb*.

insupportable /ɪnsə'pɔ:təb(ə)l/ *adjective* unbearable; unjustifiable.

insurance /ɪn'ʃʊərəns/ *noun* procedure or contract securing compensation for loss, damage, injury, or death on payment of premium; sum paid to effect insurance.

insure /ɪn'ʃʊə/ *verb* (**-ring**) (often + *against*) effect insurance with respect to.

insurgent /ɪn'sɜ:dʒ(ə)nt/ ● *adjective* in revolt; rebellious. ● *noun* rebel. □ **insurgence** *noun*.

insurmountable /ɪnsə'maʊntəb(ə)l/ *adjective* insuperable.

insurrection /ɪnsə'rekʃ(ə)n/ *noun* rising in resistance to authority; incipient rebellion. □ **insurrectionist** *noun*.

intact /ɪn'tækt/ *adjective* unimpaired; entire; untouched.

intaglio /ɪn'tɑ:lɪəʊ/ *noun* (*plural* **-s**) gem with incised design; engraved design.

intake *noun* action of taking in; people, things, or quantity taken in; place where water is taken into pipe, or fuel or air into engine.

intangible /ɪn'tændʒɪb(ə)l/ *adjective* that cannot be touched or mentally grasped. □ **intangibility** *noun*; **intangibly** *adverb*.

integer /'ɪntɪdʒə/ *noun* whole number.

integral /'ɪntɪgr(ə)l/ *adjective* of or essential to a whole; complete; of or denoted by an integer.

■ **Usage** *Integral* is often pronounced /ɪn'tegr(ə)l/ (with the stress on the *-teg-*), but this is considered incorrect by some people.

integrate /'ɪntɪgreɪt/ *verb* (**-ting**) combine (parts) into whole; complete by adding parts; bring or come into equal membership of society; desegregate (school etc.), esp. racially. □ **integrated circuit** small piece of material replacing electrical circuit of many components. □ **integration** *noun*.

integrity /ɪn'tegrɪtɪ/ *noun* honesty; wholeness; soundness.

integument /ɪn'tegjʊmənt/ *noun* skin, husk, or other (natural) covering.

intellect /'ɪntəlekt/ *noun* faculty of knowing and reasoning; understanding.

intellectual /ɪntə'lektʃʊəl/ ● *adjective* of, requiring, or using intellect; having highly developed intellect. ● *noun* intellectual person. □ **intellectualize** *verb* (also **-ise**) (**-zing** or **-sing**); **intellectually** *adverb*.

intelligence /ɪn'telɪdʒ(ə)ns/ *noun* intellect; quickness of understanding; collecting of information, esp. secretly for military or political purposes; information so collected; people employed in this. □ **intelligence quotient** number denoting ratio of person's intelligence to the average.

intelligent *adjective* having or showing good intelligence, clever. □ **intelligently** *adverb*.

intelligentsia /ɪntelɪ'dʒentsɪə/ *noun* class of intellectuals regarded as cultured and politically enterprising.

intelligible /ɪn'telɪdʒɪb(ə)l/ *adjective* that can be understood. □ **intelligibility** *noun*; **intelligibly** *adverb*.

intemperate /ɪn'tempərət/ *adjective* immoderate; excessive in consumption of alcohol, or in general indulgence of appetite. □ **intemperance** *noun*.

intend /ɪn'tend/ *verb* have as one's purpose; (usually + *for, as, to do*) design, destine.

intended ● *adjective* done on purpose. ● *noun colloquial* fiancé(e).

intense /ɪn'tens/ *adjective* (**-r**, **-st**) existing in high degree; vehement; violent, forceful; extreme; very emotional. ▫ **intensity** *noun* (*plural* **-ies**); **intensely** *adverb.*

■ **Usage** *Intense* is sometimes confused with *intensive*, and wrongly used to describe a course of study etc.

intensify *verb* (**-ies**, **-ied**) make or become (more) intense. ▫ **intensification** *noun.*

intensive /ɪn'tensɪv/ *adjective* thorough, vigorous; concentrated; of or relating to intensity; increasing production relative to cost. ▫ **-intensive** making much use of; **intensive care** medical treatment with constant supervision of dangerously ill patient. ▫ **intensively** *adverb.*

intent /ɪn'tent/ ● *noun* intention; purpose. ● *adjective* (usually + *on*) resolved, bent; attentively occupied; eager. ▫ **to all intents and purposes** practically. ▫ **intently** *adverb.*

intention /ɪn'tenʃ(ə)n/ *noun* purpose, aim; intending.

intentional *adjective* done on purpose. ▫ **intentionally** *adverb.*

inter /ɪn'tɜː/ *verb* (**-rr-**) bury (corpse etc.).

inter- *combining form* among, between; mutually, reciprocally.

interact /ɪntə'rækt/ *verb* act on each other. ▫ **interaction** *noun.*

interactive *adjective* reciprocally active; (of computer etc.) allowing two-way flow of information between itself and user. ▫ **interactively** *adverb.*

interbreed /ɪntə'briːd/ *verb* (*past & past participle* **-bred**) (cause to) produce hybrid individual.

intercalary /ɪn'tɜːkələrɪ/ *adjective* inserted to harmonize calendar with solar year; having such addition; interpolated.

intercede /ɪntə'siːd/ *verb* (**-ding**) intervene on behalf of another; plead.

intercept /ɪntə'sept/ *verb* seize, catch, stop, etc. in transit; cut off. ▫ **interception** *noun*; **interceptor** *noun.*

intercession /ɪntə'seʃ(ə)n/ *noun* interceding. ▫ **intercessor** *noun.*

interchange ● *verb* /ɪntə'tʃeɪndʒ/ (**-ging**) (of two people) exchange (things) with each other; make exchange of (two things); alternate. ● *noun* /'ɪntətʃeɪndʒ/ reciprocal exchange; alternation; road junction where traffic streams do not cross. ▫ **interchangeable** *adjective.*

inter-city /ɪntə'sɪtɪ/ *adjective* existing or travelling between cities.

intercom /'ɪntəkɒm/ *noun colloquial* system of intercommunication by telephone or radio.

intercommunicate /ɪntəkə'mjuːnɪkeɪt/ *verb* (**-ting**) have communication with each other; (of rooms etc.) open into each other. ▫ **intercommunication** *noun.*

intercommunion /ɪntəkə'mjuːnɪən/ *noun* mutual communion, esp. between religious bodies.

interconnect /ɪntəkə'nekt/ *verb* connect with each other. ▫ **interconnection** *noun.*

intercontinental /ɪntəkɒntɪ'nent(ə)l/ *adjective* connecting or travelling between continents.

intercourse /'ɪntəkɔːs/ *noun* social, international, etc. communication or dealings; sexual intercourse.

interdenominational /ɪntədɪnɒmɪ'neɪʃən(ə)l/ *adjective* of or involving more than one Christian denomination.

interdependent /ɪntədɪ'pend(ə)nt/ *adjective* mutually dependent. ▫ **interdependence** *noun.*

interdict ● *noun* /'ɪntədɪkt/ formal prohibition; *RC Church* sentence debarring person, or esp. place, from ecclesiastical functions and privileges. ● *verb* /ɪntə'dɪkt/ prohibit (action); forbid use of; (usually + *from*) restrain (person). ▫ **interdiction** /-'dɪk-/ *noun*; **interdictory** /-'dɪk-/ *adjective.*

interdisciplinary /ɪntədɪsɪ'plɪnərɪ/ *adjective* of or involving different branches of learning.

interest /'ɪntrəst/ ● *noun* concern, curiosity; quality causing this; subject, hobby, etc., towards which one feels it; advantage; money paid for use of money borrowed etc.; thing in which one has stake or concern; financial stake; legal concern, title, or right. ● *verb* arouse interest of; (usually + *in*) cause to take interest; (as **interested** *adjective*) having private interest, not impartial.

interesting *adjective* causing curiosity; holding the attention. ▫ **interestingly** *adverb.*

interface /'ɪntəfeɪs/ ● *noun* surface forming common boundary of two regions; place where interaction occurs between two systems etc.; apparatus for connecting two pieces of esp. computing equipment so they can be operated jointly. ● *verb* (**-cing**) connect by means of interface; interact.

interfere /ɪntə'fɪə/ *verb* (**-ring**) (often + *with*) meddle; be an obstacle; intervene; (+ *with*) molest sexually.

interference *noun* interfering; fading of received radio signals.

interferon /ɪntə'fɪərɒn/ *noun* protein inhibiting development of virus in cell.

interfuse /ɪntə'fjuːz/ *verb* (**-sing**) mix, blend. ▫ **interfusion** *noun.*

interim /'ɪntərɪm/ ● *noun* intervening time. ● *adjective* provisional, temporary.

interior /ɪn'tɪərɪə/ ● *adjective* inner; inland; internal, domestic. ● *noun* inner part; inside; inland region; home affairs of country; representation of inside of room etc.

interject /ɪntə'dʒekt/ *verb* make (remark etc.) abruptly or parenthetically; interrupt.

interjection /ɪntə'dʒekʃ(ə)n/ *noun* exclamation.

interlace /ɪntə'leɪs/ *verb* (**-cing**) bind intricately together; interweave.

interlard /ɪntə'lɑːd/ *verb* mix (speech etc.) with unusual words or phrases.

interleave /ɪntə'liːv/ *verb* (**-ving**) insert (usually blank) leaves between leaves of (book).

interline /ɪntə'laɪn/ *verb* (**-ning**) put extra layer of material between fabric of (garment) and its lining.

interlink /ɪntə'lɪŋk/ *verb* link together.

interlock /ɪntə'lɒk/ ● *verb* engage with each other by overlapping etc.; lock together. ● *noun* machine-knitted fabric with fine stitches.

interlocutor /ɪntə'lɒkjʊtə/ *noun formal* person who takes part in conversation. ▫ **interlocutory** *adjective.*

interloper /'ɪntələʊpə/ *noun* intruder; person who thrusts himself or herself into others' affairs.

interlude /'ɪntəluːd/ *noun* interval between parts of play etc., performance filling this; contrasting time, event, etc. in middle of something.

intermarry /ɪntə'mærɪ/ *verb* (**-ies**, **-ied**) (+ *with*) (of races, castes, families, etc.) become connected by marriage. ▫ **intermarriage** /-rɪdʒ/ *noun.*

intermediary /ɪntə'miːdɪərɪ/ ● *noun* (*plural* **-ies**) mediator. ● *adjective* acting as mediator; intermediate.

intermediate /ɪntə'miːdɪət/ ● *adjective* coming between in time, place, order, etc. ● *noun* intermediate thing.

interment /ɪn'tɜːmənt/ *noun* burial.

intermezzo /ɪntə'metsəʊ/ *noun* (*plural* **-mezzi** /-sɪ/ or **-s**) *Music* short connecting movement or composition.

interminable /ɪn'tɜːmɪnəb(ə)l/ *adjective* endless; tediously long. □ **interminably** *adverb*.
intermingle /ɪntə'mɪŋg(ə)l/ *verb* **(-ling)** mix together, mingle.
intermission /ɪntə'mɪʃ(ə)n/ *noun* pause, cessation; interval in cinema etc.
intermittent /ɪntə'mɪt(ə)nt/ *adjective* occurring at intervals, not continuous or steady. □ **intermittently** *adverb*.
intermix /ɪntə'mɪks/ *verb* mix together.
intern ● *noun* /'ɪntɜːn/ *US* resident junior doctor in hospital. ● *verb* /ɪn'tɜːn/ confine within prescribed limits. □ **internee** /-'niː/ *noun*; **internment** *noun*.
internal /ɪn'tɜːn(ə)l/ *adjective* of or in the inside of thing; relating to inside of the body; of domestic affairs of country; (of students) attending a university as well as taking its exams; used or applying within an organization; intrinsic; of mind or soul. □ **internal-combustion engine** engine in which motive power comes from explosion of gas or vapour with air in cylinder. □ **internally** *adverb*.
international /ɪntə'næʃən(ə)l/ ● *adjective* existing or carried on between nations; agreed on by many nations. ● *noun* contest (usually in sports) between representatives of different nations; such representative; (**International**) any of 4 successive associations for socialist or Communist action. □ **internationality** /-'næl-/ *noun*; **internationally** *adverb*.
internationalism *noun* advocacy of community of interests among nations. □ **internationalist** *noun*.
internationalize *verb* (also **-ise**) **(-zing** or **-sing)** make international; bring under joint protection etc. of different nations.
internecine /ɪntə'niːsaɪn/ *adjective* mutually destructive.
interpenetrate /ɪntə'penɪtreɪt/ *verb* **(-ting)** penetrate each other; pervade. □ **interpenetration** *noun*.
interpersonal /ɪntə'pɜːsən(ə)l/ *adjective* between people.
interplanetary /ɪntə'plænɪtərɪ/ *adjective* between planets.
interplay /'ɪntəpleɪ/ *noun* reciprocal action.
Interpol /'ɪntəpɒl/ *noun* International Criminal Police Organization.
interpolate /ɪn'tɜːpəleɪt/ *verb* **(-ting)** insert or introduce between other things; make (esp. misleading) insertions in. □ **interpolation** *noun*.
interpose /ɪntə'pəʊz/ *verb* **(-sing)** insert (thing between others); introduce, use, say, etc. as interruption or interference; interrupt; advance (objection etc.) so as to interfere; intervene. □ **interposition** /-pə'zɪʃ(ə)n/ *noun*.
interpret /ɪn'tɜːprɪt/ *verb* **(-t-)** explain the meaning of (esp. words); render, represent; act as interpreter. □ **interpretation** *noun*.
interpreter *noun* person who translates orally.
interracial /ɪntə'reɪʃ(ə)l/ *adjective* between or affecting different races.
interregnum /ɪntə'regnəm/ *noun* (*plural* **-s**) interval with suspension of normal government between successive reigns or regimes; interval, pause.
interrelated /ɪntərɪ'leɪtɪd/ *adjective* related to each other. □ **interrelation** *noun*; **interrelationship** *noun*.
interrogate /ɪn'terəgeɪt/ *verb* **(-ting)** question closely or formally. □ **interrogation** *noun*; **interrogator** *noun*.
interrogative /ɪntə'rɒgətɪv/ ● *adjective* of, like, or used in questions. ● *noun* interrogative word.
interrogatory /ɪntə'rɒgətərɪ/ ● *adjective* questioning. ● *noun* (*plural* **-ies**) set of questions.
interrupt /ɪntə'rʌpt/ *verb* break continuity of (action, speech, etc.); obstruct (view etc.). □ **interruption** *noun*.
intersect /ɪntə'sekt/ *verb* divide by passing or lying across; cross or cut each other.
intersection /ɪntə'sekʃ(ə)n/ *noun* intersecting; place where two roads intersect; point or line common to lines or planes that intersect.
intersperse /ɪntə'spɜːs/ *verb* **(-sing)** (usually + *between, among*) scatter; (+ *with*) vary (thing) by scattering others among it.
interstate /'ɪntəsteɪt/ *adjective* existing etc. between states, esp. of US.
interstellar /ɪntə'stelə/ *adjective* between stars.
interstice /ɪn'tɜːstɪs/ *noun* gap, chink, crevice.
interstitial /ɪntə'stɪʃ(ə)l/ *adjective* forming or in interstices.
intertwine /ɪntə'twaɪn/ *verb* **(-ning)** (often + *with*) twine closely together.
interval /'ɪntəv(ə)l/ *noun* intervening time or space; pause; break; *Music* difference of pitch between two sounds. □ **at intervals** here and there, now and then.
intervene /ɪntə'viːn/ *verb* **(-ning)** occur in meantime; interfere; prevent or modify events; come between people or things; mediate.
intervention /ɪntə'venʃ(ə)n/ *noun* intervening; interference; mediation.
interview /'ɪntəvjuː/ ● *noun* oral examination of applicant; conversation with reporter, for broadcast or publication; meeting of people, esp. for discussion. ● *verb* hold interview with. □ **interviewee** /-vjuː'iː/ *noun*; **interviewer** *noun*.
interweave /ɪntə'wiːv/ *verb* **(-ving**; *past* **-wove**; *past participle* **-woven)** weave together; blend intimately.
intestate /ɪn'testeɪt/ ● *adjective* not having made a will before death. ● *noun* person who has died intestate. □ **intestacy** /-təsɪ/ *noun*.
intestine /ɪn'testɪn/ *noun* (in *singular* or *plural*) lower part of alimentary canal. □ **intestinal** *adjective*.
intimate[1] ● *adjective* /'ɪntɪmət/ closely acquainted; familiar; closely personal; (usually + *with*) having sexual relations; (of knowledge) thorough; close. ● *noun* intimate friend. □ **intimacy** /-məsɪ/ *noun*; **intimately** *adverb*.
intimate[2] /'ɪntɪmeɪt/ *verb* **(-ting)** state or make known; imply. □ **intimation** *noun*.
intimidate /ɪn'tɪmɪdeɪt/ *verb* **(-ting)** frighten, esp. in order to influence conduct. □ **intimidation** *noun*.
into /'ɪntʊ, 'ɪntə/ *preposition expressing motion or direction to point within, direction of attention, or change of state*; after the beginning of; *colloquial* interested in.
intolerable /ɪn'tɒlərəb(ə)l/ *adjective* that cannot be endured. □ **intolerably** *adverb*.
intolerant /ɪn'tɒlərənt/ *adjective* not tolerant. □ **intolerance** *noun*.
intonation /ɪntə'neɪʃ(ə)n/ *noun* modulation of voice, accent; intoning.
intone /ɪn'təʊn/ *verb* **(-ning)** recite with prolonged sounds, esp. in monotone.
in toto /ɪn 'təʊtəʊ/ *adverb* entirely. [Latin]
intoxicant /ɪn'tɒksɪkənt/ ● *adjective* intoxicating. ● *noun* intoxicating substance.
intoxicate /ɪn'tɒksɪkeɪt/ *verb* **(-ting)** make drunk; excite or elate beyond self-control. □ **intoxication** *noun*.
intractable /ɪn'træktəb(ə)l/ *adjective* not easily dealt with; stubborn. □ **intractability** *noun*.
intramural /ɪntrə'mjʊər(ə)l/ *adjective* situated or done within walls of institution etc.

intransigent /ɪn'trænsɪdʒ(ə)nt/ ● *adjective* uncompromising. ● *noun* such person. ▫ **intransigence** *noun*.

intransitive /ɪn'trænsɪtɪv/ *adjective* (of verb) not taking direct object.

intrauterine /ɪntrə'ju:tərам/ *adjective* within the womb.

intravenous /ɪntrə'vi:nəs/ *adjective* in(to) vein(s). ▫ **intravenously** *adverb*.

intrepid /ɪn'trepɪd/ *adjective* fearless; brave.

intricate /'ɪntrɪkət/ *adjective* complicated; perplexingly detailed. ▫ **intricacy** /-kəsɪ/ *noun* (*plural* **-ies**); **intricately** *adverb*.

intrigue ● *verb* /ɪn'tri:g/ (**-gues**, **-gued**, **-guing**) carry on underhand plot; use secret influence; rouse curiosity of. ● *noun* /'ɪntri:g/ underhand plotting or plot; secret arrangement, esp. with romantic associations. ▫ **intriguing** *adjective*; **intriguingly** *adverb*.

intrinsic /ɪn'trɪnzɪk/ *adjective* inherent; essential. ▫ **intrinsically** *adverb*.

intro /'ɪntrəʊ/ *noun* (*plural* **-s**) *colloquial* introduction.

introduce /ɪntrə'dju:s/ *verb* (**-cing**) make (person) known by name to another; announce or present to audience; bring (custom etc.) into use; bring (bill etc.) before Parliament; (+ *to*) initiate (person) in subject; insert; bring in; usher in, bring forward. ▫ **introducible** *adjective*.

introduction /ɪntrə'dʌkʃ(ə)n/ *noun* introducing, being introduced; formal presentation; preliminary matter in book; introductory treatise. ▫ **introductory** *adjective*.

introspection /ɪntrə'spekʃ(ə)n/ *noun* examination of one's own thoughts. ▫ **introspective** *adjective*.

introvert ● *noun* person chiefly concerned with his or her own thoughts; shy thoughtful person. ● *adjective* (also **introverted**) characteristic of an introvert. ▫ **introversion** /-'vɜ:ʃ(ə)n/ *noun*.

intrude /ɪn'tru:d/ *verb* (**-ding**) (+ *on*, *upon*, *into*) come uninvited or unwanted; force on a person. ▫ **intruder** *noun*; **intrusion** /-ʒ(ə)n/ *noun*; **intrusive** /-sɪv/ *adjective*.

intuition /ɪntju:'ɪʃ(ə)n/ *noun* immediate apprehension by mind without reasoning; immediate insight. ▫ **intuit** /ɪn'tju:ɪt/ *verb*; **intuitional** *adjective*.

intuitive /ɪn'tju:ɪtɪv/ *adjective* of, having, or perceived by intuition. ▫ **intuitively** *adverb*; **intuitiveness** *noun*.

Inuit /'ɪnju:ɪt/ ● *noun* (*plural* same or **-s**) N. American Eskimo; language of Inuit. ● *adjective* of Inuit or their language.

inundate /'ɪnʌndeɪt/ *verb* (**-ting**) (often + *with*) flood, overwhelm. ▫ **inundation** *noun*.

inure /ɪ'njʊə/ *verb* (**-ring**) habituate, accustom. ▫ **inurement** *noun*.

invade /ɪn'veɪd/ *verb* (**-ding**) enter (country etc.) with arms to control or subdue it; swarm into; (of disease etc.) attack; encroach on. ▫ **invader** *noun*.

invalid¹ /'ɪnvəlɪd, -li:d/ ● *noun* person enfeebled or disabled by illness or injury. ● *adjective* of or for invalids; sick, disabled. ● *verb* (**-d-**) (often + *out* etc.) remove from active service; disable (person) by illness. ▫ **invalidism** *noun*; **invalidity** /-'lɪd-/ *noun*.

invalid² /ɪn'vælɪd/ *adjective* not valid. ▫ **invalidity** /-və'lɪd-/ *noun*.

invalidate /ɪn'vælɪdeɪt/ *verb* (**-ting**) make invalid. ▫ **invalidation** *noun*.

invaluable /ɪn'væljʊəb(ə)l/ *adjective* beyond price, very valuable.

invariable /ɪn'veərɪəb(ə)l/ *adjective* unchangeable; always the same. ▫ **invariably** *adverb*.

invasion /ɪn'veɪʒ(ə)n/ *noun* invading, being invaded. ▫ **invasive** /-sɪv/ *adjective*.

invective /ɪn'vektɪv/ *noun* violent attack in words.

inveigh /ɪn'veɪ/ *verb* (+ *against*) speak or write with strong hostility against.

inveigle /ɪn'veɪg(ə)l/ *verb* (**-ling**) (+ *into*, *to do*) entice, persuade by guile. ▫ **inveiglement** *noun*.

invent /ɪn'vent/ *verb* create by thought; originate; fabricate. ▫ **inventor** *noun*.

invention /ɪn'venʃ(ə)n/ *noun* inventing, being invented; thing invented; inventiveness.

inventive *adjective* able to invent; imaginative. ▫ **inventively** *adverb*; **inventiveness** *noun*.

inventory /'ɪnvəntərɪ/ ● *noun* (*plural* **-ies**) list of goods etc. ● *verb* (**-ies**, **-ied**) make inventory of; enter in inventory.

inverse /ɪn'vɜ:s/ ● *adjective* inverted in position, order, or relation. ● *noun* inverted state; (often + *of*) direct opposite. ▫ **inverse proportion**, **ratio** relation between two quantities such that one increases in proportion as the other decreases.

inversion /ɪn'vɜ:ʃ(ə)n/ *noun* inverting, esp. reversal of normal order of words.

invert /ɪn'vɜ:t/ *verb* turn upside down; reverse position, order, or relation of. ▫ **inverted commas** quotation marks.

invertebrate /ɪn'vɜ:tɪbrət/ ● *adjective* without backbone. ● *noun* invertebrate animal.

invest /ɪn'vest/ *verb* (often + *in*) apply or use (money) for profit; devote (time etc.) to an enterprise; (+ *in*) buy (something useful or otherwise rewarding); (+ *with*) endue with qualities etc.; (often + *with*, *in*) clothe with insignia of office. ▫ **investor** *noun*.

investigate /ɪn'vestɪgeɪt/ *verb* (**-ting**) inquire into, examine. ▫ **investigation** *noun*; **investigative** /-gətɪv/ *adjective*; **investigator** *noun*.

investiture /ɪn'vestɪtʃə/ *noun* formal investing of person with honours etc.

investment *noun* investing; money invested; property etc. in which money is invested.

inveterate /ɪn'vetərət/ *adjective* (of person) confirmed in (usually undesirable) habit etc.; (of habit etc.) long-established. ▫ **inveteracy** *noun*.

invidious /ɪn'vɪdɪəs/ *adjective* likely to excite ill-will against performer, possessor, etc.

invigilate /ɪn'vɪdʒɪleɪt/ *verb* (**-ting**) supervise examinees. ▫ **invigilation** *noun*; **invigilator** *noun*.

invigorate /ɪn'vɪgəreɪt/ *verb* (**-ting**) give vigour to. ▫ **invigorating** *adjective*.

invincible /ɪn'vɪnsɪb(ə)l/ *adjective* unconquerable. ▫ **invincibility** *noun*; **invincibly** *adverb*.

inviolable /ɪn'vaɪələb(ə)l/ *adjective* not to be violated. ▫ **inviolability** *noun*.

inviolate /ɪn'vaɪələt/ *adjective* not violated; safe (from harm). ▫ **inviolacy** *noun*.

invisible /ɪn'vɪzɪb(ə)l/ *adjective* that cannot be seen. ▫ **invisible exports**, **imports** items for which payment is made by or to another country but which are not goods. ▫ **invisibility** *noun*; **invisibly** *adverb*.

invite ● *verb* /ɪn'vaɪt/ (**-ting**) request courteously to come, to do, etc.; solicit courteously; tend to evoke unintentionally; attract. ● *noun* /'ɪnvaɪt/ *colloquial* invitation. ▫ **invitation** /ɪnvɪ'teɪʃ(ə)n/ *noun*.

inviting *adjective* attractive. ▫ **invitingly** *adverb*.

in vitro /ɪn 'vi:trəʊ/ *adverb* (of biological processes) taking place in test-tube or other laboratory environment. [Latin]

invocation /ɪnvə'keɪʃ(ə)n/ *noun* invoking; calling on, esp. in prayer or for inspiration etc. ▫ **invocatory** /ɪn'vɒkətərɪ/ *adjective*.

invoice /'ɪnvɔɪs/ ● *noun* bill for usually itemized goods etc. ● *verb* (**-cing**) send invoice to; make invoice of.

invoke /ɪnˈvəʊk/ *verb* (**-king**) call on in prayer or as witness; appeal to (law, authority, etc.); summon (spirit) by charms; ask earnestly for (vengeance, justice, etc.).

involuntary /ɪnˈvɒləntərɪ/ *adjective* done etc. without exercise of will; not controlled by will. □ **involuntarily** *adverb*.

involute /ˈɪnvəlu:t/ *adjective* intricate; curled spirally.

involution /ɪnvəˈlu:ʃ(ə)n/ *noun* involving; intricacy; curling inwards, part so curled.

involve /ɪnˈvɒlv/ *verb* (**-ving**) (often + *in*) cause (person, thing) to share experience or effect; imply, make necessary; (often + *in*) implicate (person) in charge, crime, etc.; include or affect in its operation; (as **involved** *adjective*) complicated. □ **involvement** *noun*.

invulnerable /ɪnˈvʌlnərəb(ə)l/ *adjective* that cannot be wounded. □ **invulnerability** *noun*.

inward /ˈɪnwəd/ ● *adjective* directed towards inside; going in; situated within; mental, spiritual. ● *adverb* (also **inwards**) towards inside; in mind or soul.

inwardly *adverb* on the inside; in mind or spirit; not aloud.

inwrought /ɪnˈrɔ:t/ *adjective* (often + *with*) decorated (with pattern); (often + *in*, *on*) (of pattern) wrought (in or on fabric).

iodine /ˈaɪədi:n/ *noun* black solid halogen element forming violet vapour; solution of this used as antiseptic.

IOM *abbreviation* Isle of Man.

ion /ˈaɪən/ *noun* atom or group of atoms that has lost or gained one or more electrons.

ionic /aɪˈɒnɪk/ *adjective* of or using ions.

ionize *verb* (also **-ise**) (**-zing** or **-sing**) convert or be converted into ion(s). □ **ionization** *noun*.

ionosphere /aɪˈɒnəsfɪə/ *noun* ionized region in upper atmosphere. □ **ionospheric** /-ˈsfer-/ *adjective*.

iota /aɪˈəʊtə/ *noun* ninth letter of Greek alphabet (I, ι); (usually with negative) a jot.

IOU /aɪəʊˈju:/ *noun* (*plural* **-s**) signed document acknowledging debt.

IOW *abbreviation* Isle of Wight.

IPA *abbreviation* International Phonetic Alphabet.

ipecacuanha /ɪpɪkækjʊˈɑ:nə/ *noun* root of S. American plant used as emetic etc.

ipso facto /ɪpsəʊ ˈfæktəʊ/ *adverb* by that very fact. [Latin]

IQ *abbreviation* intelligence quotient.

IRA *abbreviation* Irish Republican Army.

Iranian /ɪˈreɪnɪən/ ● *adjective* of Iran (formerly Persia); of group of languages including Persian. ● *noun* native or national of Iran.

Iraqi /ɪˈrɑ:kɪ/ ● *adjective* of Iraq. ● *noun* (*plural* **-s**) native or national of Iraq.

irascible /ɪˈræsɪb(ə)l/ *adjective* irritable; hot-tempered. □ **irascibility** *noun*.

irate /aɪˈreɪt/ *adjective* angry, enraged.

ire /ˈaɪə/ *noun literary* anger.

iridescent /ɪrɪˈdes(ə)nt/ *adjective* showing rainbow-like glowing colours; changing colour with position. □ **iridescence** *noun*.

iris /ˈaɪərɪs/ *noun* circular coloured membrane surrounding pupil of eye; bulbous or tuberous plant with sword-shaped leaves and showy flowers.

Irish /ˈaɪərɪʃ/ ● *adjective* of Ireland. ● *noun* Celtic language of Ireland; (**the Irish**; treated as *plural*) the Irish people. □ **Irish coffee** coffee with dash of whiskey and a little sugar, topped with cream; **Irishman**, **Irishwoman** native of Ireland; **Irish stew** dish of stewed mutton, onions, and potatoes.

irk *verb* irritate, annoy.

irksome *adjective* annoying, tiresome.

iron /ˈaɪən/ ● *noun* common strong grey metallic element; this as symbol of strength or firmness; tool etc. of iron; implement heated to smooth clothes etc.; golf club with iron or steel head; (in *plural*) fetters; (in *plural*) stirrups; (often in *plural*) leg-support to rectify malformations. ● *adjective* of iron; robust; unyielding. ● *verb* smooth (clothes etc.) with heated iron. □ **Iron Age** era characterized by use of iron weapons etc.; **Iron Curtain** *historical* notional barrier to passage of people and information between Soviet bloc and West; **ironing board** narrow folding table etc. for ironing clothes on; **iron lung** rigid case over patient's body for administering prolonged artificial respiration; **ironmonger** dealer in **ironmongery**, household and building hardware; **iron rations** small emergency supply of food; **ironstone** hard iron ore, kind of hard white pottery.

ironic /aɪˈrɒnɪk/ *adjective* (also **ironical**) using or displaying irony. □ **ironically** *adverb*.

irony /ˈaɪrənɪ/ *noun* (*plural* **-ies**) expression of meaning, usually humorous or sarcastic, by use of words normally conveying opposite meaning; apparent perversity of fate or circumstances.

irradiate /ɪˈreɪdɪeɪt/ *verb* (**-ting**) subject to radiation; shine on; throw light on; light up. □ **irradiation** *noun*.

irrational /ɪˈræʃən(ə)l/ *adjective* unreasonable, illogical; not endowed with reason; *Mathematics* not expressible as an ordinary fraction. □ **irrationality** /-ˈnæl-/ *noun*; **irrationally** *adverb*.

irreconcilable /ɪˈrekənsaɪləb(ə)l/ *adjective* implacably hostile; (of ideas etc.) incompatible. □ **irreconcilably** *adverb*.

irrecoverable /ɪrɪˈkʌvərəb(ə)l/ *adjective* that cannot be recovered or remedied.

irredeemable /ɪrɪˈdi:məb(ə)l/ *adjective* that cannot be redeemed, hopeless. □ **irredeemably** *adverb*.

irreducible /ɪrɪˈdju:sɪb(ə)l/ *adjective* not able to be reduced or simplified.

irrefutable /ɪrɪˈfju:təb(ə)l/ *adjective* that cannot be refuted. □ **irrefutably** *adverb*.

irregular /ɪˈregjʊlə/ ● *adjective* not regular; unsymmetrical, uneven; varying in form; not occurring at regular intervals; contrary to rule; (of troops) not in regular army; (of verb, noun, etc.) not inflected according to usual rules. ● *noun* (in *plural*) irregular troops. □ **irregularity** /-ˈlær-/ *noun* (*plural* **-ies**); **irregularly** *adverb*.

irrelevant /ɪˈrelɪv(ə)nt/ *adjective* not relevant. □ **irrelevance** *noun*; **irrelevancy** *noun* (*plural* **-ies**).

irreligious /ɪrɪˈlɪdʒəs/ *adjective* lacking or hostile to religion; irreverent.

irremediable /ɪrɪˈmi:dɪəb(ə)l/ *adjective* that cannot be remedied. □ **irremediably** *adverb*.

irremovable /ɪrɪˈmu:vəb(ə)l/ *adjective* not removable. □ **irremovably** *adverb*.

irreparable /ɪˈrepərəb(ə)l/ *adjective* that cannot be rectified or made good. □ **irreparably** *adverb*.

irreplaceable /ɪrɪˈpleɪsəb(ə)l/ *adjective* that cannot be replaced.

irrepressible /ɪrɪˈpresɪb(ə)l/ *adjective* that cannot be repressed. □ **irrepressibly** *adverb*.

irreproachable /ɪrɪˈprəʊtʃəb(ə)l/ *adjective* faultless, blameless. □ **irreproachably** *adverb*.

irresistible /ɪrɪˈzɪstɪb(ə)l/ *adjective* too strong, convincing, charming, etc. to be resisted. □ **irresistibly** *adverb*.

irresolute /ɪˈrezəlu:t/ *adjective* hesitating; lacking in resolution. □ **irresoluteness** *noun*; **irresolution** /-ˈlu:ʃ(ə)n/ *noun*.

irrespective /ɪrɪˈspektɪv/ *adjective* (+ *of*) not taking into account, regardless of.

irresponsible /ɪrɪ'spɒnsɪb(ə)l/ *adjective* acting or done without due sense of responsibility; not responsible. □ **irresponsibility** *noun*; **irresponsibly** *adverb*.

irretrievable /ɪrɪ'tri:vəb(ə)l/ *adjective* that cannot be retrieved or restored. □ **irretrievably** *adverb*.

irreverent /ɪ'revərənt/ *adjective* lacking in reverence. □ **irreverence** *noun*; **irreverently** *adverb*.

irreversible /ɪrɪ'vɜ:sɪb(ə)l/ *adjective* that cannot be reversed or altered. □ **irreversibly** *adverb*.

irrevocable /ɪ'revəkəb(ə)l/ *adjective* unalterable; gone beyond recall. □ **irrevocably** *adverb*.

irrigate /'ɪrɪgeɪt/ *verb* (**-ting**) water (land) by system of artificial channels; (of stream etc.) supply (land) with water; *Medicine* moisten (wound etc.) with constant flow of liquid. □ **irrigable** *adjective*; **irrigation** *noun*; **irrigator** *noun*.

irritable /'ɪrɪtəb(ə)l/ *adjective* easily annoyed; very sensitive to contact. □ **irritability** *noun*; **irritably** *adverb*.

irritant /'ɪrɪt(ə)nt/ ● *adjective* causing irritation. ● *noun* irritant substance or agent.

irritate /'ɪrɪteɪt/ *verb* (**-ting**) excite to anger, annoy; stimulate discomfort in (part of body). □ **irritating** *adjective*; **irritation** *noun*.

Is. *abbreviation* Island(s); Isle(s).

is *3rd singular present* of BE.

isinglass /'aɪzɪŋglɑ:s/ *noun* kind of gelatin obtained from sturgeon etc.

Islam /'ɪzlɑ:m/ *noun* religion of Muslims, proclaimed by Prophet Muhammad; the Muslim world. □ **Islamic** /-'læm-/ *adjective*.

island /'aɪlənd/ *noun* piece of land surrounded by water; traffic island; detached or isolated thing.

islander *noun* native or inhabitant of island.

isle /aɪl/ *noun literary* (usually small) island.

islet /'aɪlɪt/ *noun* small island.

isn't /'ɪz(ə)nt/ is not.

isobar /'aɪsəbɑ:/ *noun* line on map connecting places with same atmospheric pressure. □ **isobaric** /-'bær-/ *adjective*.

isolate /'aɪsəleɪt/ *verb* (**-ting**) place apart or alone; separate (esp. infectious patient from others); insulate (electrical apparatus), esp. by gap; disconnect. □ **isolation** *noun*.

isolationism *noun* policy of holding aloof from affairs of other countries or groups. □ **isolationist** *noun*.

isomer /'aɪsəmə/ *noun* one of two or more compounds with same molecular formula but different arrangement of atoms. □ **isomeric** /-'mer-/ *adjective*; **isomerism** /aɪ'sɒmərɪz(ə)m/ *noun*.

isosceles /aɪ'sɒsɪli:z/ *adjective* (of triangle) having two sides equal.

isotherm /'aɪsəθɜ:m/ *noun* line on map connecting places with same temperature. □ **isothermal** /-'θɜ:m(ə)l/ *adjective*.

isotope /'aɪsətəʊp/ *noun* any of two or more forms of chemical element with different relative atomic mass and different nuclear but not chemical properties. □ **isotopic** /-'tɒp-/ *adjective*.

Israeli /ɪz'reɪlɪ/ ● *adjective* of modern state of Israel. ● *noun* (*plural* **-s**) native or national of Israel.

issue /'ɪʃu:/ ● *noun* giving out or circulation of shares, notes, stamps, etc.; copies of journal etc. circulated at one time; each of regular series of magazine etc.; outgoing, outflow; point in question, essential subject of dispute; result, outcome; offspring. ● *verb* (**issues**, **issued**, **issuing**) go or come out; give or send out; publish, circulate; supply, (+ *with*) supply with equipment etc.; (+ *from*) be derived, result; (+ *from*) emerge.

isthmus /'ɪsməs/ *noun* (*plural* **-es**) neck of land connecting two larger land masses.

IT *abbreviation* information technology.

it *pronoun* the thing in question; indefinite, undefined, or impersonal subject, action, condition, object, etc.; *substitute for deferred subject or object*; exactly what is needed; perfection; *slang* sexual intercourse, sex appeal. □ **that's it** *colloquial* that is what is required, that is the difficulty, that is the end, enough.

Italian /ɪ'tæljən/ ● *noun* native, national, or language of Italy. ● *adjective* of Italy.

italic /ɪ'tælɪk/ ● *adjective* (of type etc.) of sloping kind; (of handwriting) neat and pointed; (**Italic**) of ancient Italy. ● *noun* (usually in *plural*) italic type.

italicize /ɪ'tælɪsaɪz/ *verb* (also **-ise**) (**-zing** or **-sing**) print in italics.

itch ● *noun* irritation in skin; restless desire; disease with itch. ● *verb* feel irritation or restless desire.

itchy *adjective* (**-ier**, **-iest**) having or causing itch. □ **have itchy feet** *colloquial* be restless, have urge to travel.

it'd /'ɪtəd/ it had; it would.

item /'aɪtəm/ *noun* any one of enumerated things; separate or distinct piece of news etc.

itemize *verb* (also **-ise**) (**-zing** or **-sing**) state by items. □ **itemization** *noun*.

iterate /'ɪtəreɪt/ *verb* (**-ting**) repeat; state repeatedly. □ **iteration** *noun*; **iterative** /-rətɪv/ *adjective*.

itinerant /aɪ'tɪnərənt/ ● *adjective* travelling from place to place. ● *noun* itinerant person.

itinerary /aɪ'tɪnərərɪ/ *noun* (*plural* **-ies**) route; record of travel; guidebook.

it'll /'ɪt(ə)l/ it will; it shall.

its *adjective* of or belonging to it.

it's /ɪts/ it is; it has.

■ **Usage** Because it has an apostrophe, *it's* is easily confused with *its*. Both are correctly used in *Where's the dog?—It's in its kennel, and it's eaten its food* (= *It is in its kennel, and it has eaten its food*.)

itself /ɪt'self/ *pronoun: emphatic & reflexive form of* IT.

ITV *abbreviation* Independent Television.

IUD *abbreviation* intrauterine (contraceptive) device.

I've /aɪv/ I have.

ivory /'aɪvərɪ/ *noun* (*plural* **-ies**) white substance of tusks of elephant etc.; colour of this; (in *plural*) *slang* things made of or resembling ivory, esp. dice, piano keys, or teeth. □ **ivory tower** seclusion from harsh realities of life.

ivy /'aɪvɪ/ *noun* (*plural* **-ies**) climbing evergreen with shiny 5-angled leaves.

Jj

jab ● *verb* (**-bb-**) poke roughly; stab; (+ *into*) thrust (thing) hard or abruptly. ● *noun* abrupt blow or thrust; *colloquial* hypodermic injection.

jabber ● *verb* chatter volubly; utter fast and indistinctly. ● *noun* chatter, gabble.

jabot /'ʒæbəʊ/ *noun* frill on front of shirt or blouse.

jacaranda /dʒækə'rændə/ *noun* tropical American tree with blue flowers or one with hard scented wood.

jacinth /'dʒæsɪnθ/ *noun* reddish-orange zircon used as gem.

jack ● *noun* device for lifting heavy objects, esp. vehicles; lowest-ranking court card; ship's flag, esp. showing nationality; device using single-pronged plug to connect electrical equipment; small white target ball in bowls; (in *plural*) game played with jackstones. ● *verb* (usually + *up*) raise (as) with jack. □ **jackboot** boot reaching above knee; **jack in** *slang* abandon (attempt etc.); **jack-in-the-box** toy figure that springs out of box; **jack of all trades** person with many skills; **jack plug** electrical plug with single prong; **jackstone** metal etc. piece used in tossing games.

jackal /'dʒæk(ə)l/ *noun* African or Asian wild animal of dog family.

jackass *noun* male ass; stupid person.

jackdaw *noun* grey-headed bird of crow family.

jacket /'dʒækɪt/ *noun* short coat with sleeves; covering round boiler etc.; outside wrapper of book; skin of potato. □ **jacket potato** one baked in its skin.

jackknife ● *noun* large clasp-knife. ● *verb* (**-fing**) (of articulated vehicle) fold against itself in accident.

jackpot *noun* large prize, esp. accumulated in game, lottery, etc.

Jacobean /dʒækə'bi:ən/ *adjective* of reign of James I.

Jacobite /'dʒækəbaɪt/ *noun historical* supporter of James II in exile, or of Stuarts.

Jacuzzi /dʒə'ku:zɪ/ *noun* (*plural* **-s**) *proprietary term* large bath with massaging underwater jets.

jade[1] *noun* hard usually green stone for ornaments; green colour of jade.

jade[2] *noun* inferior or worn-out horse.

jaded *adjective* tired out, surfeited.

jag ● *noun* sharp projection of rock etc. ● *verb* (**-gg-**) cut or tear unevenly; make indentations in.

jagged /'dʒægɪd/ *adjective* unevenly cut or torn. □ **jaggedly** *adverb*; **jaggedness** *noun*.

jaguar /'dʒægjʊə/ *noun* large American spotted animal of cat family.

jail /dʒeɪl/ (also **gaol**) ● *noun* place for detention of prisoners; confinement in jail. ● *verb* put in jail. □ **jailbird** prisoner, habitual criminal. □ **jailer** *noun*.

jalap /'dʒæləp/ *noun* purgative drug.

jalopy /dʒə'lɒpɪ/ *noun* (*plural* **-ies**) *colloquial* dilapidated old motor vehicle.

jalousie /'ʒælʊzi:/ *noun* slatted blind or shutter.

jam[1] ● *verb* (**-mm-**) (usually + *into*, *together*, etc.) squeeze or cram into space; become wedged; cause (machinery) to become wedged and so unworkable, become wedged in this way; block (exit, road, etc.) by crowding; (usually + *on*) apply (brakes) suddenly; make (radio transmission) unintelligible with interference. ● *noun* squeeze; stoppage; crowded mass, esp. of traffic; *colloquial* predicament. □ **jam session** (in jazz etc.) improvised ensemble playing.

jam[2] *noun* conserve of boiled fruit and sugar; *colloquial* easy or pleasant thing.

jamb /dʒæm/ *noun* side post or side face of doorway or window frame.

jamboree /dʒæmbə'ri:/ *noun* celebration; large rally of Scouts.

jammy *adjective* (**-ier**, **-iest**) covered with jam; *colloquial* lucky, profitable.

Jan. *abbreviation* January.

jangle /'dʒæŋg(ə)l/ ● *verb* (**-ling**) (cause to) make harsh metallic sound. ● *noun* such sound.

janitor /'dʒænɪtə/ *noun* doorkeeper; caretaker.

January /'dʒænjʊərɪ/ *noun* (*plural* **-ies**) first month of year.

japan /dʒə'pæn/ ● *noun* hard usually black varnish. ● *verb* (**-nn-**) make black and glossy (as) with japan.

Japanese /dʒæpə'ni:z/ ● *noun* (*plural* same) native, national, or language of Japan. ● *adjective* of Japan or its people or language.

jape *noun* practical joke.

japonica /dʒə'pɒnɪkə/ *noun* flowering shrub with red flowers and edible fruits.

jar[1] *noun* container, usually of glass and cylindrical.

jar[2] ● *verb* (**-rr-**) (often + *on*) (of sound, manner, etc.) strike discordantly, grate; (often + *against*, *on*) (cause to) strike (esp. part of body) with vibration or shock; (often + *with*) be at variance. ● *noun* jarring sound, shock, or vibration.

jardinière /ʒɑ:dɪ'njeə/ *noun* ornamental pot or stand for plants.

jargon /'dʒɑ:gən/ *noun* words used by particular group or profession; debased or pretentious language.

jasmine /'dʒæzmɪn/ *noun* shrub with white or yellow flowers.

jasper /'dʒæspə/ *noun* red, yellow, or brown opaque quartz.

jaundice /'dʒɔ:ndɪs/ ● *noun* yellowing of skin caused by liver disease, bile disorder, etc. ● *verb* (as **jaundiced** *adjective*) affected with jaundice; envious, resentful.

jaunt /dʒɔ:nt/ ● *noun* pleasure trip. ● *verb* take a jaunt.

jaunty *adjective* (**-ier**, **-iest**) cheerful and self-confident; sprightly. □ **jauntily** *adverb*; **jauntiness** *noun*.

javelin /'dʒævəlɪn/ *noun* light spear thrown in sport or, formerly, as weapon.

jaw ● *noun* bony structure containing teeth; (in *plural*) mouth, gripping parts of tool etc.; *colloquial* tedious talk. ● *verb slang* speak at tedious length. □ **jawbone** lower jaw in most mammals.

jay *noun* noisy European bird of crow family with vivid plumage. □ **jaywalk** walk across road carelessly or dangerously; **jaywalker** person who does this.

jazz *noun* rhythmic syncopated esp. improvised music of American black origin. □ **and all that jazz** *colloquial* and other related things; **jazz up** enliven.

jazzy *adjective* (**-ier**, **-iest**) of or like jazz; vivid.

jealous /'dʒeləs/ *adjective* resentful of rivalry in love; (often + *of*) envious (of person etc.), protective (of rights etc.). □ **jealously** *adverb*; **jealousy** *noun* (*plural* **-ies**).

jeans /dʒi:nz/ *plural noun* casual esp. denim trousers.

Jeep *noun proprietary term* small sturdy esp. military vehicle with 4-wheel drive.

jeer ● *verb* (often + *at*) scoff, deride. ● *noun* taunt.

Jehovah /dʒə'həʊvə/ *noun* (in Old Testament) God. ▫ **Jehovah's Witness** member of unorthodox Christian sect.

jejune /dʒɪ'dʒu:n/ *adjective* (of ideas, writing, etc.) shallow, naïve, or dry and uninteresting.

jell *verb colloquial* set as jelly; (of ideas etc.) take definite form; cohere.

jellied /'dʒelɪd/ *adjective* (of food etc.) set as or in jelly.

jelly /'dʒelɪ/ *noun* (*plural* **-ies**) (usually fruit-flavoured) semi-transparent dessert set with gelatin; similar preparation as jam or condiment; *slang* gelignite. ▫ **jelly baby** jelly-like babyshaped sweet; **jellyfish** (*plural* same or **-es**) marine animal with jelly-like body and stinging tentacles.

jemmy /'dʒemɪ/ *noun* (*plural* **-ies**) burglar's crowbar.

jeopardize *verb* (also **-ise**) (**-zing** or **-sing**) endanger.

jeopardy /'dʒepədɪ/ *noun* danger, esp. severe.

jerboa /dʒɜ:'bəʊə/ *noun* small jumping desert rodent.

Jeremiah /dʒerɪ'maɪə/ *noun* dismal prophet.

jerk[1] ● *noun* sharp sudden pull, twist, etc.; spasmodic muscular twitch; *slang* fool. ● *verb* move, pull, throw, etc. with jerk. ▫ **jerky** *adjective* (**-ier**, **-iest**); **jerkily** *adverb*; **jerkiness** *noun*.

jerk[2] *verb* cure (beef) by cutting in long slices and drying in the sun.

jerkin /'dʒɜ:kɪn/ *noun* sleeveless jacket.

jeroboam /dʒerə'bəʊəm/ *noun* wine bottle of 4–12 times ordinary size.

jerry-building *noun* building of shoddy houses with bad materials. ▫ **jerry-builder** *noun*; **jerry-built** *adjective*.

jerrycan *noun* kind of petrol- or water-can.

jersey /'dʒɜ:zɪ/ *noun* (*plural* **-s**) knitted usually woollen pullover; knitted fabric; (**Jersey**) dairy cow from Jersey.

Jerusalem artichoke /dʒə'ru:sələm/ *noun* kind of sunflower with edible tubers; this tuber as vegetable.

jest ● *noun* joke; fun; banter; object of derision. ● *verb* joke; fool about. ▫ **in jest** in fun.

jester *noun historical* professional clown at medieval court etc.

Jesuit /'dʒezjʊɪt/ *noun* member of RC Society of Jesus. ▫ **Jesuitical** /-'ɪt-/ *adjective*.

jet[1] ● *noun* stream of water, steam, gas, flame, etc. shot esp. from small opening; spout or nozzle for this purpose; jet engine or plane. ● *verb* (**-tt-**) spurt out in jet(s); *colloquial* send or travel by jet plane. ▫ **jet engine** one using jet propulsion; **jet lag** exhaustion felt after long flight across time zones; **jet plane** one with jet engine; **jet-propelled** having jet propulsion, very fast; **jet propulsion** propulsion by backward ejection of high-speed jet of gas etc.; **jet set** wealthy people who travel widely, esp. for pleasure; **jet-setter** such a person.

jet[2] *noun* hard black lignite, often carved and highly polished. ▫ **jet black** deep glossy black.

jetsam /'dʒetsəm/ *noun* objects washed ashore, esp. jettisoned from ship.

jettison /'dʒetɪs(ə)n/ *verb* throw (cargo, fuel, etc.) from ship or aircraft to lighten it; abandon; get rid of.

jetty /'dʒetɪ/ *noun* (*plural* **-ies**) pier or breakwater protecting or defending harbour etc.; landing-pier.

Jew /dʒu:/ *noun* person of Hebrew descent or whose religion is Judaism.

jewel /'dʒu:əl/ ● *noun* precious stone; this used in watchmaking; jewelled personal ornament; precious person or thing. ● *verb* (**-ll-**; *US* **-l-**) (esp. as **jewelled** *adjective*) adorn or set with jewels.

jeweller *noun* (*US* **jeweler**) maker of or dealer in jewels or jewellery.

jewellery /'dʒu:əlrɪ/ *noun* (also **jewelry**) rings, brooches, necklaces, etc. collectively.

Jewish *adjective* of Jews or Judaism. ▫ **Jewishness** *noun*.

Jewry /'dʒʊərɪ/ *noun* Jews collectively.

Jezebel /'dʒezəbəl/ *noun* shameless or immoral woman.

jib ● *noun* projecting arm of crane; triangular staysail. ● *verb* (**-bb-**) (esp. of horse) stop and refuse to go on; (+ *at*) show aversion to.

jibe[1] = GIBE.

jibe[2] *US* = GYBE.

jiffy /'dʒɪfɪ/ *noun* (*plural* **-ies**) (also **jiff**) *colloquial* short time, moment. ▫ **Jiffy bag** *proprietary term* padded envelope.

jig ● *noun* lively dance; music for this; device that holds piece of work and guides tools operating on it. ● *verb* (**-gg-**) dance jig; (often + *about*) move quickly up and down; fidget.

jigger /'dʒɪgə/ *noun* small glass for measure of spirits.

jiggery-pokery /dʒɪgərɪ'pəʊkərɪ/ *noun colloquial* trickery; swindling.

jiggle /'dʒɪg(ə)l/ ● *verb* (**-ling**) (often + *about*) rock or jerk lightly; fidget. ● *noun* light shake.

jigsaw *noun* (in full **jigsaw puzzle**) picture on board etc. cut into irregular interlocking pieces to be reassembled as pastime; mechanical fine-bladed fret saw.

jihad /dʒɪ'hæd/ *noun* Muslim holy war against unbelievers.

jilt *verb* abruptly rejct or abandon (esp. lover).

jingle /'dʒɪŋg(ə)l/ ● *noun* mixed ringing or clinking noise; repetition of sounds in phrase; short catchy verse in advertising etc. ● *verb* (**-ling**) (cause to) make jingling sound.

jingo /'dʒɪŋgəʊ/ *noun* (*plural* **-es**) blustering patriot. ▫ **jingoism** *noun*; **jingoist** *noun*; **jingoistic** /-'ɪs-/ *adjective*.

jink ● *verb* move elusively; elude by dodging. ● *noun* jinking. ▫ **high jinks** boisterous fun.

jinnee /'dʒɪni:/ *noun* (also **jinn**, **djinn** /dʒɪn/) (*plural* **jinn** or **djinn**) (in Muslim mythology) spirit of supernatural power in human or animal form.

jinx *colloquial* ● *noun* person or thing that seems to bring bad luck. ● *verb* (esp. as **jinxed** *adjective*) subject to bad luck.

jitter /'dʒɪtə/ *colloquial* ● *noun* (**the jitters**) extreme nervousness. ● *verb* be nervous; act nervously. ▫ **jittery** *adjective*.

jive ● *noun* lively dance of 1950s; music for this. ● *verb* (**-ving**) dance to or play jive music. ▫ **jiver** *noun*.

Jnr. *abbreviation* Junior.

job ● *noun* piece of work (to be) done; paid employment; *colloquial* difficult task; *slang* a crime, esp. a robbery. ● *verb* (**-bb-**) do jobs; do piece-work; buy and sell (stocks etc.); deal corruptly with (matter). ▫ **jobcentre** local government office advertising available jobs; **job-hunt** *colloquial* seek employment; **job lot** mixed lot bought at auction etc.

jobber /'dʒɒbə/ *noun* person who jobs; *historical* principal or wholesaler on Stock Exchange.

jobbery *noun* corrupt dealing.

jobless *adjective* unemployed. ▫ **joblessness** *noun*.

job-sharing *noun* sharing of full-time job by two or more people. ▫ **job-share** *noun & verb*.

jockey /'dʒɒkɪ/ ● *noun* rider in horse races. ● *verb* (**-eys**, **-eyed**) cheat, trick. ▫ **jockey for position** manoeuvre for advantage.

jockstrap /'dʒɒkstræp/ *noun* support or protection for male genitals worn esp. in sport.
jocose /dʒə'kəʊs/ *adjective* playful; jocular. □ **jocosely** *adverb*; **jocosity** /-'kɒs-/ *noun* (*plural* **-ies**).
jocular /'dʒɒkjʊlə/ *adjective* fond of joking; humorous. □ **jocularity** /-'lær-/ *noun* (*plural* **-ies**); **jocularly** *adverb*.
jocund /'dʒɒkənd/ *adjective literary* merry, cheerful. □ **jocundity** /dʒə'kʌn-/ *noun* (*plural* **-ies**); **jocundly** *adverb*.
jodhpurs /'dʒɒdpəz/ *plural noun* riding breeches tight below knee.
jog ● *verb* (**-gg-**) run slowly, esp. as exercise; push, jerk; nudge, esp. to alert; stimulate (person's memory). ● *noun* spell of jogging; slow walk or trot; push, jerk; nudge. □ **jogtrot** slow regular trot. □ **jogger** *noun*.
joggle /'dʒɒg(ə)l/ ● *verb* (**-ling**) move in jerks. ● *noun* slight shake.
joie de vivre /ʒwɑː də 'viːvrə/ *noun* exuberance; high spirits. [French]
join ● *verb* (often + *to, together*) put together, fasten, unite; connect (points) by line etc.; become member of (club etc.); take one's place with (person, group, etc.); (+ *in, for*, etc.) take part with (others) in activity etc.; (often + *with, to*) come together, be united; (of river etc.) become connected or continuous with. ● *noun* point, line, or surface of junction. □ **join in** take part in (activity); **join up** enlist for military service.
joiner *noun* maker of furniture and light woodwork. □ **joinery** *noun*.
joint ● *noun* place at which two or more things are joined; device for doing this; point at which two bones fit together; division of animal carcass as meat; *slang* restaurant, bar, etc.; *slang* marijuana cigarette. ● *adjective* held by, done by, or belonging to two or more people etc.; sharing with another. ● *verb* connect by joint(s); divide at joint or into joints. □ **joint stock** capital held jointly.
jointure /'dʒɔɪntʃə/ *noun* estate settled on wife by husband for use after his death.
joist *noun* supporting beam in floor, ceiling, etc.
jojoba /həʊ'həʊbə/ *noun* plant with seeds yielding oil used in cosmetics etc.
joke ● *noun* thing said or done to cause laughter; witticism; ridiculous person or thing. ● *verb* (**-king**) make jokes. □ **jokily** *adverb*; **jokiness** *noun*; **jokingly** *adverb*; **jokey, joky** *adjective*.
joker *noun* person who jokes; playing card used in some games.
jollification /dʒɒlɪfɪ'keɪʃ(ə)n/ *noun* merrymaking.
jolly /'dʒɒlɪ/ ● *adjective* (**-ier, -iest**) cheerful; festive, jovial; *colloquial* pleasant, delightful. ● *adverb colloquial* very. ● *verb* (**-ies, -ied**) (usually + *along*) *colloquial* coax, humour. □ **jollity** *noun* (*plural* **-ies**).
jolt /dʒəʊlt/ ● *verb* shake (esp. in vehicle) with jerk; shock, perturb; move along jerkily. ● *noun* jerk; surprise, shock.
jonquil /'dʒɒŋkwɪl/ *noun* narcissus with white or yellow fragrant flowers.
josh *slang* ● *verb* tease, make fun of. ● *noun* good-natured joke.
joss *noun* Chinese idol. □ **joss-stick** incense stick for burning.
jostle /'dʒɒs(ə)l/ ● *verb* (**-ling**) (often + *against*) knock; elbow; (+ *with*) struggle. ● *noun* jostling.
jot ● *verb* (**-tt-**) (usually + *down*) write briefly or hastily. ● *noun* very small amount.
jotter *noun* small pad or notebook.
joule /dʒuːl/ *noun* SI unit of work and energy.
journal /'dʒɜːn(ə)l/ *noun* newspaper, periodical; daily record of events; diary; account book; part of shaft or axle resting on bearings.
journalese /dʒɜːnə'liːz/ *noun* hackneyed style of writing characteristic of newspapers.
journalism /'dʒɜːnəlɪz(ə)m/ *noun* work of journalist.
journalist /'dʒɜːnəlɪst/ *noun* person writing for or editing newspapers etc. □ **journalistic** /-'lɪs-/ *adjective*.
journey /'dʒɜːnɪ/ ● *noun* (*plural* **-s**) act of going from one place to another; distance travelled, time taken. ● *verb* (**-s, -ed**) make journey, travel. □ **journeyman** qualified mechanic or artisan working for another.
joust /dʒaʊst/ *historical* ● *noun* combat with lances between two mounted knights. ● *verb* engage in joust. □ **jouster** *noun*.
jovial /'dʒəʊvɪəl/ *adjective* merry, convivial, hearty. □ **joviality** /-'æl-/ *noun*; **jovially** *adverb*.
jowl /dʒaʊl/ *noun* jaw, jawbone; cheek; loose skin on throat.
joy *noun* gladness, pleasure; thing causing joy; *colloquial* satisfaction. □ **joyride** *colloquial* (go for) pleasure ride in esp. stolen car; **joystick** control column of aircraft, lever for moving image on VDU screen. □ **joyful** *adjective*; **joyfully** *adverb*; **joyfulness** *noun*; **joyless** *adjective*; **joyous** *adjective*; **joyously** *adverb*.
JP *abbreviation* Justice of the Peace.
Jr. *abbreviation* Junior.
jubilant /'dʒuːbɪlənt/ *adjective* exultant, rejoicing. □ **jubilantly** *adverb*; **jubilation** *noun*.
jubilee /'dʒuːbɪliː/ *noun* anniversary (esp. 25th or 50th); time of rejoicing.
Judaic /dʒuː'deɪɪk/ *adjective* of or characteristic of Jews.
Judaism /'dʒuːdeɪɪz(ə)m/ *noun* religion of Jews.
Judas /'dʒuːdəs/ *noun* traitor.
judder /'dʒʌdə/ ● *verb* shake noisily or violently. ● *noun* juddering.
judge /dʒʌdʒ/ ● *noun* public official appointed to hear and try legal cases; person appointed to decide dispute or contest; person who decides question; person having judgement of specified type. ● *verb* (**-ging**) form opinion (about); estimate; act as judge (of); try legal case; (often + *to do, that*) conclude, consider.
judgement *noun* (also **judgment**) critical faculty, discernment, good sense; opinion; sentence of court of justice; *often jocular* deserved misfortune. □ **Judgement Day** day on which God will judge humankind. □ **judgemental** /-'men-/ *adjective*.
judicature /'dʒuːdɪkətʃə/ *noun* administration of justice; judge's position; judges collectively.
judicial /dʒuː'dɪʃ(ə)l/ *adjective* of, done by, or proper to court of law; of or proper to a judge; having function of judge; impartial. □ **judicially** *adverb*.
judiciary /dʒuː'dɪʃərɪ/ *noun* (*plural* **-ies**) judges collectively.
judicious /dʒuː'dɪʃəs/ *adjective* sensible, prudent. □ **judiciously** *adverb*.
judo /'dʒuːdəʊ/ *noun* sport derived from ju-jitsu.
jug ● *noun* deep vessel for liquids, with handle and lip; contents of this; *slang* prison. ● *verb* (**-gg-**) (usually as **jugged** *adjective*) stew (hare) in casserole. □ **jugful** *noun* (*plural* **-s**).
juggernaut /'dʒʌgənɔːt/ *noun* large heavy lorry; overwhelming force or object.
juggle /'dʒʌg(ə)l/ ● *verb* (**-ling**) (often + *with*) keep several objects in the air at once by throwing and catching; manipulate or rearrange (facts). ● *noun* juggling; fraud. □ **juggler** *noun*.
jugular /'dʒʌgjʊlə/ ● *adjective* of neck or throat. ● *noun* jugular vein. □ **jugular vein** any of large veins in neck carrying blood from head.

juice /dʒu:s/ *noun* liquid part of vegetable, fruit, or meat; animal fluid, esp. secretion; *colloquial* petrol, electricity.

juicy /ˈdʒu:sɪ/ *adjective* (**-ier**, **-iest**) full of juice; *colloquial* interesting, scandalous; *colloquial* profitable. □ **juicily** *adverb*.

ju-jitsu /dʒu:ˈdʒɪtsu:/ *noun* Japanese system of unarmed combat.

ju-ju /ˈdʒu:dʒu:/ *noun* (*plural* **-s**) charm or fetish of some W. African peoples; supernatural power attributed to this.

jujube /ˈdʒu:dʒu:b/ *noun* flavoured jelly-like lozenge.

jukebox /ˈdʒu:kbɒks/ *noun* coin-operated machine playing records or compact discs.

Jul. *abbreviation* July.

julep /ˈdʒu:lep/ *noun* sweet drink, esp. medicated; *US* spirits and water iced and flavoured.

julienne /dʒu:lɪˈen/ ● *noun* vegetables cut into thin strips. ● *adjective* cut into thin strips.

Juliet cap /ˈdʒu:lɪət/ *noun* small close-fitting cap worn by brides etc.

July /dʒu:ˈlaɪ/ *noun* (*plural* **Julys**) seventh month of year.

jumble /ˈdʒʌmb(ə)l/ ● *verb* (**-ling**) (often + *up*) mix; confuse; muddle. ● *noun* confused heap etc.; muddle; articles in jumble sale. □ **jumble sale** sale of second-hand articles, esp. for charity.

jumbo /ˈdʒʌmbəʊ/ *noun* (*plural* **-s**) big animal (esp. elephant), person, or thing. □ **jumbo jet** large airliner for several hundred passengers, esp. Boeing 747.

jump ● *verb* spring from ground etc.; (often + *up*, *from*, *in*, *out*, etc.) rise or move suddenly; jerk from shock or excitement; pass over (obstacle) by jumping; (+ *to*, *at*) reach (conclusion) hastily; (of train etc.) leave (rails); pass (red traffic light); get on or off (train etc.) quickly, esp. illegally; attack (person) unexpectedly. ● *noun* act of jumping; sudden movement caused by shock etc.; abrupt rise in price, status, etc.; obstacle to be jumped, esp. by horse; gap in series etc. □ **jump at** accept eagerly; **jumped-up** *adjective colloquial* upstart; **jump the gun** start prematurely; **jump-jet** vertical take-off jet plane; **jump-lead** cable for carrying current from one battery to another; **jump-off** deciding round in show-jumping; **jump the queue** take unfair precedence; **jump ship** (of seaman) desert; **jump suit** one-piece garment for whole body; **jump to it** *colloquial* act promptly and energetically.

jumper /ˈdʒʌmpə/ *noun* knitted pullover; loose outer jacket worn by sailors; *US* pinafore dress.

jumpy *adjective* (**-ier**, **-iest**) nervous, easily startled. □ **jumpiness** *noun*.

Jun. *abbreviation* June; Junior.

junction /ˈdʒʌŋkʃ(ə)n/ *noun* joining-point; place where railway lines or roads meet. □ **junction box** box containing junction of electric cables etc.

juncture /ˈdʒʌŋktʃə/ *noun* point in time, esp. critical one; joining-point.

June *noun* sixth month of year.

jungle /ˈdʒʌŋg(ə)l/ *noun* land overgrown with tangled vegetation, esp. in tropics; tangled mass; place of bewildering complexity or struggle.

junior /ˈdʒu:nɪə/ ● *adjective* (often + *to*) lower in age, standing, or position; the younger (esp. after name); (of school) for younger pupils. ● *noun* junior person.

juniper /ˈdʒu:nɪpə/ *noun* prickly evergreen shrub or tree with purple berry-like cones.

junk[1] ● *noun* discarded articles, rubbish; anything regarded as of little value; *slang* narcotic drug, esp. heroin. ● *verb* discard as junk. □ **junk food** food which is not nutritious; **junk mail** unsolicited advertising sent by post.

junk[2] *noun* flat-bottomed sailing vessel in China seas.

junket /ˈdʒʌŋkɪt/ ● *noun* pleasure outing; official's tour at public expense; sweetened and flavoured milk curds; feast. ● *verb* (**-t-**) feast, picnic.

junkie /ˈdʒʌŋkɪ/ *noun slang* drug addict.

junta /ˈdʒʌntə/ *noun* (usually military) clique taking power after *coup d'état*.

juridical /dʒʊəˈrɪdɪk(ə)l/ *adjective* of judicial proceedings, relating to the law.

jurisdiction /dʒʊərɪsˈdɪkʃ(ə)n/ *noun* (often + *over*) administration of justice; legal or other authority; extent of this.

jurisprudence /dʒʊərɪsˈpru:d(ə)ns/ *noun* science or philosophy of law.

jurist /ˈdʒʊərɪst/ *noun* expert in law. □ **juristic** /-ˈrɪs-/ *adjective*.

juror /ˈdʒʊərə/ *noun* member of jury.

jury /ˈdʒʊərɪ/ *noun* (*plural* **-ies**) group of people giving verdict in court of justice; judges of competition. □ **jury-box** enclosure in court for jury.

just ● *adjective* morally right, fair; deserved; well-grounded; justified. ● *adverb* exactly; very recently; barely; quite; *colloquial* simply, merely, positively. □ **just now** at this moment, a little time ago. □ **justly** *adverb*.

justice /ˈdʒʌstɪs/ *noun* fairness; authority exercised in maintenance of right; judicial proceedings; magistrate, judge. □ **do justice to** treat fairly, appreciate properly; **Justice of the Peace** lay magistrate.

justify /ˈdʒʌstɪfaɪ/ *verb* (**-ies**, **-ied**) show justice or truth of; (esp. in *passive*) be adequate grounds for, vindicate; *Printing* adjust (line of type) to fill space evenly; (as **justified** *adjective*) just, right. □ **justifiable** *adjective*; **justification** *noun*.

jut ● *verb* (**-tt-**) (often + *out*) protrude. ● *noun* projection.

jute /dʒu:t/ *noun* fibre from bark of E. Indian plant, used for sacking, mats, etc.; plant yielding this.

juvenile /ˈdʒu:vənaɪl/ ● *adjective* youthful; of or for young people; *often derogatory* immature. ● *noun* young person; actor playing juvenile part. □ **juvenile delinquency** offences committed by people below age of legal responsibility; **juvenile delinquent** such offender.

juvenilia /dʒu:vəˈnɪlɪə/ *plural noun* youthful works of author or artist.

juxtapose /dʒʌkstəˈpəʊz/ *verb* (**-sing**) put side by side; (+ *with*) put (thing) beside another. □ **juxtaposition** /-pəˈzɪʃ(ə)n/ *noun*.

K *abbreviation* (also **K.**) kelvin(s); Köchel (list of Mozart's works); (also **k**) 1,000.

k *abbreviation* kilo-; knot(s).

kaftan = CAFTAN.

kaiser /'kaɪzə/ *noun historical* emperor, esp. of Germany or Austria.

kale *noun* variety of cabbage, esp. with wrinkled leaves.

kaleidoscope /kə'laɪdəskəʊp/ *noun* tube containing angled mirrors and pieces of coloured glass producing reflected patterns when shaken; constantly changing scene, group, etc. □ **kaleidoscopic** /-'skɒp-/ *adjective*.

kalends = CALENDS.

kamikaze /kæmɪ'kɑ:zɪ/ ● *noun historical* explosive-laden Japanese aircraft deliberately crashed on to target in 1939–45 war; pilot of this. ● *adjective* reckless, esp. suicidal.

kangaroo /kæŋgə'ru:/ *noun* (*plural* **-s**) Australian marsupial with strong hind legs for jumping. □ **kangaroo court** illegal court held by strikers, mutineers, etc.

kaolin /'keɪəlɪn/ *noun* fine white clay used esp. for porcelain and in medicines.

kapok /'keɪpɒk/ *noun* fine cotton-like material from tropical tree, used to stuff cushions etc.

kaput /kə'pʊt/ *adjective slang* broken, ruined.

karabiner /kærə'bi:nə/ *noun* coupling link used by mountaineers.

karakul /'kærəkʊl/ *noun* (also **caracul**) Asian sheep whose lambs have dark curled fleece; fur of this.

karaoke /kærɪ'əʊkɪ/ *noun* entertainment in nightclubs etc. with customers singing to backing music.

karate /kə'rɑ:tɪ/ *noun* Japanese system of unarmed combat.

karma /'kɑ:mə/ *noun Buddhism & Hinduism* person's actions in one life, believed to decide fate in next; destiny.

kauri /kaʊ'rɪ/ *noun* (*plural* **-s**) coniferous NZ timber tree.

kayak /'kaɪæk/ *noun* Eskimo one-man canoe.

kazoo /kə'zu:/ *noun* toy musical instrument into which player sings wordlessly.

KBE *abbreviation* Knight Commander of the Order of the British Empire.

kea /'ki:ə/ *noun* green and red NZ parrot.

kebab /kɪ'bæb/ *noun* pieces of meat and sometimes vegetables grilled on skewer.

kedge ● *verb* (**-ging**) move (ship) with hawser attached to small anchor. ● *noun* (in full **kedge-anchor**) small anchor for this purpose.

kedgeree /kedʒə'ri:/ *noun* dish of fish, rice, hard-boiled eggs, etc.

keel ● *noun* main lengthwise member of base of ship etc. ● *verb* (often + *over*) (cause to) fall down or over; turn keel upwards. □ **keelhaul** drag (person) under keel as punishment; **on an even keel** steady, balanced.

keen[1] *adjective* enthusiastic, eager; (often + *on*) enthusiastic about, fond of; intellectually acute; (of knife) sharp; (of price) competitive. □ **keenly** *adverb*; **keenness** *noun*.

keen[2] ● *noun* Irish wailing funeral song. ● *verb* (often + *over*, *for*) wail mournfully, esp. at funeral.

keep ● *verb* (*past & past participle* **kept**) have charge of; retain possession of; (+ *for*) retain or reserve (for future); maintain or remain in good or specified condition; restrain; detain; observe or respect (law, secret, etc.); own and look after (animal); clothe, feed, etc. (person); carry on (a business); maintain, guard, protect. ● *noun* maintenance, food; *historical* tower, stronghold. □ **for keeps** *colloquial* permanently; **keep at** (cause to) persist with; **keep away** (often + *from*) avoid, prevent from being near; **keep-fit** regular physical exercises; **keep off** (cause to) stay away from, abstain from, avoid; **keep on** continue, (+ *at*) nag; **keep out** (cause to) stay outside; **keep up** maintain, prevent from going to bed, (often + *with*) not fall behind; **keep up with the Joneses** compete socially with neighbours.

keeper *noun* person who looks after or is in charge of an animal, person, or thing; custodian of museum, forest, etc.; wicket-keeper, goalkeeper; ring holding another on finger.

keeping *noun* custody, charge; (esp. in **in** or **out of keeping with**) agreement, harmony.

keepsake *noun* souvenir, esp. of person.

keg *noun* small barrel. □ **keg beer** beer kept in pressurized metal keg.

kelp *noun* large seaweed suitable for manure.

kelpie /'kelpɪ/ *noun Scottish* malevolent water-spirit; Australian sheepdog.

Kelt = CELT.

kelter = KILTER.

kelvin /'kelvɪn/ *noun* SI unit of temperature.

ken ● *noun* range of knowledge or sight. ● *verb* (**-nn-**; *past & past participle* **kenned** or **kent**) *Scottish & Northern English* recognize, know.

kendo /'kendəʊ/ *noun* Japanese fencing with bamboo swords.

kennel /'ken(ə)l/ ● *noun* small shelter for dog; (in *plural*) breeding or boarding place for dogs. ● *verb* (**-ll-**; *US* **-l-**) put or keep in kennel.

Kenyan /'kenjən/ ● *adjective* of Kenya. ● *noun* native or national of Kenya.

kept *past & past participle* of KEEP.

keratin /'kerətɪn/ *noun* fibrous protein in hair, hooves, claws, etc.

kerb *noun* stone etc. edging to pavement etc. □ **kerb-crawling** *colloquial* driving slowly to pick up prostitute; **kerb drill** rules taught to children about crossing roads.

kerfuffle /kə'fʌf(ə)l/ *noun colloquial* fuss, commotion.

kermes /'kɜ:mɪz/ *noun* female of insect with berry-like appearance that feeds on **kermes oak**, evergreen oak; red dye made from these insects.

kernel /'kɜ:n(ə)l/ *noun* (usually soft) edible centre within hard shell of nut, fruit stone, seed, etc.; central or essential part.

kerosene /'kerəsi:n/ *noun esp. US* fuel oil distilled from petroleum etc.; paraffin oil.

kestrel /'kestr(ə)l/ *noun* small hovering falcon.

ketch *noun* kind of two-masted sailing boat.

ketchup /'ketʃəp/ *noun* (*US* **catsup** /'kætsəp/) spicy sauce made esp. from tomatoes.

kettle /'ket(ə)l/ *noun* vessel for boiling water in. □ **kettledrum** large bowl-shaped drum.

key /ki:/ ● *noun* (*plural* **-s**) instrument for moving bolt of lock, operating switch, etc.; instrument for winding clock etc. or grasping screw, nut, etc.; finger-operated button or lever on typewriter, piano, computer terminal, etc.; explanation, word, or system for understanding list of symbols, code, etc.; *Music* system of related notes based on particular note; roughness of surface helping adhesion of plaster etc. ● *verb* fasten with pin, wedge, bolt, etc.; (often + *in*) enter (data) by means of (computer) keyboard; roughen (surface) to help adhesion of plaster etc. ▫ **keyed up** tense, excited; **keyhole** hole by which key is put into lock; **keynote** prevailing tone or idea, *Music* note on which key is based; **keypad** miniature keyboard etc. for telephone, portable computer, etc.; **keyring** ring for keeping keys on; **keystone** central principle of policy, system, etc., central stone of arch.

keyboard ● *noun* set of keys on typewriter, computer, piano, etc. ● *verb* enter (data) by means of keyboard. ▫ **keyboarder** *noun Computing.*

KG *abbreviation* Knight of the Order of the Garter.

kg *abbreviation* kilogram(s).

KGB *noun historical* secret police of USSR.

khaki /ˈkɑːkɪ/ ● *adjective* dull brownish-yellow. ● *noun* (*plural* **-s**) khaki colour, cloth, or uniform.

khan /kɑːn/ *noun: title of ruler or official in Central Asia.* ▫ **khanate** *noun.*

kHz *abbreviation* kilohertz.

kibbutz /kɪˈbʊts/ *noun* (*plural* **-im** /-iːm/) communal esp. farming settlement in Israel.

kibosh /ˈkaɪbɒʃ/ *noun slang* nonsense. ▫ **put the kibosh on** put an end to.

kick ● *verb* strike, strike out, or propel forcibly with foot or hoof; (often + *at, against*) protest, rebel; *slang* give up (habit); (often + *out*) expel, dismiss; (**kick oneself**, **could kick oneself**) be annoyed with oneself; score (goal) by kicking. ● *noun* kicking action or blow; recoil of gun; *colloquial* temporary enthusiasm, sharp stimulant effect; (often in *plural*) thrill. ▫ **kick about** drift idly, discuss informally; **kickback** recoil, payment esp. for illegal help; **kick the bucket** *slang* die; **kick off** *verb* begin football game, remove (shoes etc.) by kicking, *colloquial* start; **kick-off** *noun* start, esp. of football game; **kick-start(er)** (pedal on) device to start engine of motorcycle etc.; **kick up a fuss** *colloquial* create disturbance, object; **kick upstairs** get rid of by promotion.

kid[1] ● *noun* young goat; leather from this; *colloquial* child. ● *verb* (**-dd-**) (of goat) give birth to kid.

kid[2] *verb* (**-dd-**) *colloquial* deceive, tease. ▫ **no kidding** *slang* that is the truth.

kidnap /ˈkɪdnæp/ *verb* (**-pp-**; *US* **-p-**) carry off (person) illegally, esp. to obtain ransom. ▫ **kidnapper** *noun.*

kidney /ˈkɪdnɪ/ *noun* (*plural* **-s**) either of two organs serving to excrete urine; animal's kidney as food. ▫ **kidney bean** red-skinned kidney-shaped bean; **kidney machine** apparatus able to perform function of damaged kidney; **kidney-shaped** having one side concave and the other convex.

kill ● *verb* deprive of life or vitality; end; (**kill oneself**) *colloquial* overexert oneself, laugh heartily; *colloquial* overwhelm with amusement; switch off; pass (time) while waiting; *Computing* delete; *Sport* stop (ball) dead. ● *noun* (esp. in hunting) act of killing, animal(s) killed. ▫ **killjoy** depressing person; **kill off** destroy completely, bring about death of (fictional character).

killer *noun* person or thing that kills; murderer. ▫ **killer whale** dolphin with prominent dorsal fin.

killing ● *noun* causing death; *colloquial* great financial success. ● *adjective colloquial* very funny; exhausting.

kiln *noun* oven for burning, baking, or drying esp. pottery.

kilo /ˈkiːləʊ/ *noun* (*plural* **-s**) kilogram.

kilo- *combining form* one thousand.

kilobyte /ˈkɪləbaɪt/ *noun Computing* 1,024 bytes as measure of memory size etc.

kilocalorie /ˈkɪləkælərɪ/ *noun* large calorie (see CALORIE).

kilocycle /ˈkɪləsaɪk(ə)l/ *noun historical* kilohertz.

kilogram /ˈkɪləgræm/ *noun* SI unit of mass (2.205 lb).

kilohertz /ˈkɪləhɜːts/ *noun* 1,000 hertz.

kilolitre /ˈkɪləliːtə/ *noun* (*US* **-liter**) 1,000 litres.

kilometre /ˈkɪləmiːtə/ *noun* (*US* **-meter**) 1,000 metres (0.6214 mile).

■ **Usage** *Kilometre* is often pronounced /kɪˈlɒmɪtə/ (with the stress on the *-lom-*), but this is considered incorrect by some people.

kiloton /ˈkɪlətʌn/ *noun* (also **kilotonne**) unit of explosive power equal to that of 1,000 tons of TNT.

kilovolt /ˈkɪləvəʊlt/ *noun* 1,000 volts.

kilowatt /ˈkɪləwɒt/ *noun* 1,000 watts. ▫ **kilowatt-hour** electrical energy equal to 1 kilowatt used for 1 hour.

kilt ● *noun* pleated skirt usually of tartan, traditionally worn by Highland man. ● *verb* tuck up (skirts) round body; (esp. as **kilted** *adjective*) gather in vertical pleats.

kilter /ˈkɪltə/ *noun* (also **kelter** /ˈkeltə/) good working order.

kimono /kɪˈməʊnəʊ/ *noun* (*plural* **-s**) wide-sleeved Japanese robe; similar dressing gown.

kin ● *noun* one's relatives or family. ● *adjective* related.

kind /kaɪnd/ ● *noun* species, natural group of animals, plants, etc.; class, type, variety. ● *adjective* (often + *to*) friendly, benevolent. ▫ **in kind** in same form, (of payment) in goods etc. instead of money.

kindergarten /ˈkɪndəgɑːt(ə)n/ *noun* class or school for young children.

kind-hearted *adjective* of kind disposition. ▫ **kind-heartedly** *adverb*; **kind-heartedness** *noun.*

kindle /ˈkɪnd(ə)l/ *verb* (**-ling**) set on fire, light; inspire; become aroused or animated.

kindling /ˈkɪndlɪŋ/ *noun* small sticks etc. for lighting fires.

kindly /ˈkaɪndlɪ/ ● *adverb* in a kind way; please. ● *adjective* (**-ier**, **-iest**) kind; (of climate etc.) pleasant, mild.

kindred /ˈkɪndrɪd/ ● *adjective* related, allied, similar. ● *noun* blood relationship; one's relations.

kinetic /kɪˈnetɪk/ *adjective* of or due to motion. ▫ **kinetic energy** energy of motion. ▫ **kinetically** *adverb.*

king *noun* (as title usually **King**) male sovereign, esp. hereditary; outstanding man or thing in specified field; largest kind of a thing; chess piece which must be checkmated for a win; crowned piece in draughts; court card depicting king; (**the King**) national anthem when sovereign is male. ▫ **King Charles spaniel** small black and tan kind; **kingcup** marsh marigold; **kingpin** main or large bolt, essential person or thing; **king-size(d)** large. ▫ **kingly** *adjective*; **kingship** *noun.*

kingdom *noun* state or territory ruled by king or queen; spiritual reign of God; domain; division of natural world. ▫ **kingdom come** *colloquial* the next world.

kingfisher *noun* small river bird with brilliant blue plumage, which dives for fish.

kink ● *noun* twist or bend in wire etc.; tight wave in hair; mental peculiarity. ● *verb* (cause to) form kink.

kinky *adjective* (**-ier**, **-iest**) *colloquial* sexually perverted or unconventional; (of clothing) bizarre and sexually provocative. ▫ **kinkily** *adverb.*

kinship *noun* blood relationship; similarity.

kinsman /ˈkɪnzmən/ *noun* (*feminine* **kinswoman**) blood relation.

kiosk /ˈkiːɒsk/ *noun* open-fronted booth selling newspapers, food, etc.; telephone box.

kip *slang* ● *noun* sleep, bed. ● *verb* (**-pp-**) (often + *down*) sleep.

kipper /ˈkɪpə/ ● *noun* fish, esp. herring, split, salted, dried, and usually smoked. ● *verb* treat (herring etc.) this way.

kir /kɪə/ *noun* dry white wine with blackcurrant liqueur.

kirk *noun Scottish & Northern English* church. □ **Kirk-session** lowest court in Church of Scotland.

kirsch /kɪəʃ/ *noun* spirit distilled from cherries.

kismet /ˈkɪzmet/ *noun* destiny.

kiss ● *verb* touch with lips, esp. as sign of love, reverence, etc.; touch lightly. ● *noun* touch of lips; light touch. □ **kiss-curl** small curl of hair on forehead or nape of neck; **kiss of life** mouth-to-mouth resuscitation.

kisser *noun slang* mouth; face.

kissogram *noun* novelty greeting delivered with kiss.

kit ● *noun* equipment, clothing, etc. for particular purpose; specialized, esp. sports, clothing or uniform; set of parts needed to assemble furniture, model, etc. ● *verb* (**-tt-**) supply; (often + *out*) equip with kit. □ **kitbag** usually cylindrical canvas etc. bag for carrying soldier's etc. kit.

kitchen /ˈkɪtʃɪn/ *noun* place where food is cooked; kitchen fitments. □ **kitchen garden** garden for growing fruit and vegetables.

kitchenette /kɪtʃɪˈnet/ *noun* small kitchen or cooking area.

kite *noun* light framework with thin covering flown on long string in wind; soaring bird of prey.

kith /kɪθ/ *noun* □ **kith and kin** friends and relations.

kitsch /kɪtʃ/ *noun* vulgar, pretentious, or worthless art.

kitten /ˈkɪt(ə)n/ ● *noun* young cat, ferret, etc. ● *verb* give birth to (kittens).

kittenish *adjective* playful; flirtatious.

kittiwake /ˈkɪtɪweɪk/ *noun* kind of small seagull.

kitty[1] /ˈkɪtɪ/ *noun* (*plural* **-ies**) joint fund; pool in some card games.

kitty[2] /ˈkɪtɪ/ *noun* (*plural* **-ies**) *childish name for* kitten or cat.

kiwi /ˈkiːwiː/ *noun* flightless NZ bird; (**Kiwi**) *colloquial* New Zealander. □ **kiwi fruit** green-fleshed fruit.

Klaxon /ˈklæks(ə)n/ *noun proprietary term* horn, warning hooter.

Kleenex /ˈkliːneks/ *noun* (*plural* same or **-es**) *proprietary term* disposable paper handkerchief.

kleptomania /kleptəˈmeɪnɪə/ *noun* irresistible urge to steal. □ **kleptomaniac** /-nɪæk/ *adjective & noun.*

km *abbreviation* kilometre(s).

knack /næk/ *noun* acquired faculty of doing something skilfully; habit of action, speech, etc.

knacker /ˈnækə/ ● *noun* buyer of useless horses for slaughter. ● *verb slang* (esp. as **knackered** *adjective*) exhaust, wear out.

knapsack /ˈnæpsæk/ *noun* soldier's or hiker's bag carried on back.

knapweed /ˈnæpwiːd/ *noun* plant with thistle-like flower.

knave /neɪv/ *noun* rogue, scoundrel; jack (in playing cards). □ **knavery** *noun*; **knavish** *adjective.*

knead /niːd/ *verb* work into dough, paste, etc., esp. by hand; make (bread, pottery) thus; massage.

knee /niː/ ● *noun* joint between thigh and lower leg; lap of sitting person; part of garment covering knee. ● *verb* (**knees**, **kneed**, **kneeing**) touch or strike with knee. □ **kneecap** convex bone in front of knee; **knees-up** *colloquial* lively party or gathering.

kneel /niːl/ *verb* (*past & past participle* **knelt**) rest or lower oneself on knee(s).

kneeler *noun* cushion for kneeling on.

knell /nel/ *noun* sound of bell, esp. for death or funeral; event etc. seen as bad omen.

knelt *past & past participle* of KNEEL.

knew *past* of KNOW.

knickerbockers /ˈnɪkəbɒkəz/ *plural noun* loose-fitting breeches gathered in at knee. □ **Knickerbocker Glory** ice cream and fruit in tall glass.

knickers /ˈnɪkəz/ *plural noun* woman's or girl's undergarment for lower torso.

knick-knack /ˈnɪknæk/ *noun* (also **nick-nack**) trinket, small ornament.

knife /naɪf/ ● *noun* (*plural* **knives**) cutting blade or weapon with long sharpened edge fixed in handle; cutting-blade in machine; (**the knife**) *colloquial* surgery. ● *verb* (**-fing**) cut or stab with knife. □ **knife-edge** edge of knife, position of extreme uncertainty; **knife-pleat** overlapping narrow flat pleat.

knight /naɪt/ ● *noun* man awarded non-hereditary title (*Sir*) by sovereign; *historical* man raised to honourable military rank; *historical* lady's champion in tournament etc.; chess piece usually in shape of horse's head. ● *verb* confer knighthood on. □ **knighthood** *noun*; **knightly** *adjective.*

knit /nɪt/ *verb* (**-tt-**; *past & past participle* **knitted** or **knit**) make (garment etc.) by interlocking loops of esp. wool with knitting-needles or knitting machine; make (plain stitch) in knitting; wrinkle (brow); (often + *together*) make or become close, (of broken bone) become joined. □ **knitwear** knitted garments.

knitting *noun* work being knitted. □ **knitting-needle** thin pointed rod used usually in pairs for knitting.

knob /nɒb/ *noun* rounded protuberance, e.g. door handle, radio control, etc.; small lump (of butter, coal, etc.). □ **knobby** *adjective.*

knobbly /ˈnɒblɪ/ *adjective* (**-ier**, **-iest**) hard and lumpy.

knock /nɒk/ ● *verb* strike with audible sharp blow; (often + *at*) strike (door etc.) for admittance; (usually + *in*, *off*, etc.) drive by striking; make (hole) by knocking; (of engine) make thumping etc. noise; *slang* criticize. ● *noun* audible sharp blow; rap, esp. at door. □ **knock about**, **around** treat roughly, wander about aimlessly, (usually + *with*) associate socially; **knock back** *slang* eat or drink, esp. quickly; **knock down** *verb* strike (esp. person) to ground, demolish, (usually + *to*) (at auction) sell to bidder, *colloquial* lower price of; **knock-down** *adjective* (of price) very low; **knock knees** legs curved inward at the knee; **knock-kneed** with knock knees; **knock off** strike off with blow, *colloquial* finish work, do or make rapidly, (often + *from*) deduct (amount) from price, *slang* steal, kill; **knock on the head** put end to (scheme etc.); **knock on wood** *US* touch wood; **knock out** *verb* make unconscious by blow to head, defeat (boxer) by knocking down for count of 10, defeat in knockout competition, *colloquial* tire out; **knock-out** *noun* blow that knocks boxer out, competition in which loser of each match is eliminated, *slang* outstanding person or thing; **knock together** construct hurriedly; **knock up** *verb* make hastily, arouse by knock at door, practise tennis etc. before formal game begins, *US slang* make pregnant; **knock-up** *noun* practice at tennis etc.

knocker *noun* hinged metal device on door for knocking with.

knoll /nəʊl/ *noun* small hill, mound.

knot /nɒt/ ● *noun* intertwining of rope, string, etc. so as to fasten; set method of this; tangle in hair, knitting, etc.; unit of ship's or aircraft's speed equal to one nautical mile per hour; hard mass formed in tree trunk where branch grows out; round cross-grained piece in board caused by this; (usually + *of*) cluster. ● *verb* (**-tt-**) tie in knot; entangle. ▫ **knotgrass** wild plant with creeping stems and pink flowers; **knot-hole** hole in timber where knot has fallen out.

knotty *adjective* (**-ier, -iest**) full of knots; puzzling.

know /nəʊ/ *verb* (*past* **knew** /nju:/; *past participle* **known**) (often + *that, how, what*, etc.) have in the mind, have learnt; be acquainted with; recognize, identify; (often + *from*) be able to distinguish; (as **known** *adjective*) publicly acknowledged. ▫ **in the know** having inside information; **know-how** practical knowledge or skill.

knowing *adjective* cunning; showing knowledge, shrewd.

knowingly *adverb* in a knowing way; consciously, intentionally.

knowledge /ˈnɒlɪdʒ/ *noun* (usually + *of*) awareness, familiarity, person's range of information, understanding (of subject); sum of what is known.

knowledgeable *adjective* (also **knowledgable**) well-informed, intelligent. ▫ **knowledgeably** *adverb*.

known *past participle* of KNOW.

knuckle /ˈnʌk(ə)l/ ● *noun* bone at finger-joint; knee- or ankle-joint of quadruped; this as joint of meat. ● *verb* (**-ling**) strike, rub, etc. with knuckles. ▫ **knuckle down** (often + *to*) apply oneself earnestly; **knuckleduster** metal guard worn over knuckles in fighting, esp. to inflict greater damage; **knuckle under** give in, submit.

KO *abbreviation* knockout.

koala /kəʊˈɑ:lə/ *noun* (also **koala bear**) small Australian bearlike marsupial with thick grey fur.

kohl /kəʊl/ *noun* black powder used as eye make-up, esp. in Eastern countries.

kohlrabi /kəʊlˈrɑ:bɪ/ *noun* (*plural* **-bies**) cabbage with edible turnip-like stem.

kookaburra /ˈkʊkəbʌrə/ *noun* Australian kingfisher with strange laughing cry.

Koran /kɔ:ˈrɑ:n/ *noun* Islamic sacred book.

Korean /kəˈri:ən/ ● *noun* native or national of N. or S. Korea; language of Korea. ● *adjective* of Korea or its people or language.

kosher /ˈkəʊʃə/ ● *adjective* (of food or food-shop) fulfilling requirements of Jewish law; *colloquial* correct, genuine. ● *noun* kosher food or shop.

kowtow /kaʊˈtaʊ/ ● *noun historical* Chinese custom of touching ground with forehead, esp. in submission. ● *verb* (usually + *to*) act obsequiously; perform kowtow.

k.p.h. *abbreviation* kilometres per hour.

kraal /krɑ:l/ *noun South African* village of huts enclosed by fence; enclosure for cattle etc.

kremlin /ˈkremlɪn/ *noun* citadel within Russian town; (**the Kremlin**) that in Moscow, Russian government.

krill *noun* tiny plankton crustaceans eaten by whales etc.

krugerrand /ˈkru:gərænd/ *noun* S. African gold coin.

krummhorn /ˈkrʌmhɔ:n/ *noun* (also **crumhorn**) medieval wind instrument.

krypton /ˈkrɪptɒn/ *noun* gaseous element used in lamps etc.

Kt. *abbreviation* Knight.

kts. *abbreviation* knots.

kudos /ˈkju:dɒs/ *noun colloquial* glory, renown.

kumquat /ˈkʌmkwɒt/ *noun* (also **cumquat**) small orange-like fruit.

kung fu /kʌŋ ˈfu:/ *noun* Chinese form of karate.

kV *abbreviation* kilovolt(s).

kW *abbreviation* kilowatt(s).

kWh *abbreviation* kilowatt-hour(s).

Ll

L[1] *noun* (also **l**) (Roman numeral) 50.

L[2] *abbreviation* Lake. □ **L-plate** sign bearing letter L, attached to vehicle to show that driver is learner.

l *abbreviation* left; line; litre(s).

LA *abbreviation* Los Angeles.

la = LAH.

Lab. *abbreviation* Labour.

lab *noun colloquial* laboratory.

label /'leɪb(ə)l/ ● *noun* piece of paper attached to object to give information about it; classifying phrase etc.; logo, title, or trademark of company. ● *verb* (**-ll-**; *US* **-l-**) attach label to; (usually + *as*) assign to category.

labial /'leɪbɪəl/ ● *adjective* of lips; *Phonetics* pronounced with (closed) lips. ● *noun Phonetics* labial sound.

labium /'leɪbɪəm/ *noun* (*plural* **labia**) each fold of skin of pairs enclosing vulva.

labor etc. *US & Australian* = LABOUR etc.

laboratory /lə'bɒrətərɪ/ *noun* (*plural* **-ies**) place used for scientific experiments and research.

laborious /lə'bɔːrɪəs/ *adjective* needing hard work; (esp. of literary style) showing signs of effort. □ **laboriously** *adverb*.

labour /'leɪbə/ (*US & Australian* **labor**) ● *noun* physical or mental work, exertion; workers, esp. as political force; (**Labour**) the Labour Party; process of giving birth; task. ● *verb* work hard, exert oneself; elaborate needlessly; proceed with difficulty; (as **laboured** *adjective*) done with great effort; (+ *under*) suffer because of. □ **labour camp** prison camp enforcing hard labour; **Labour Exchange** *colloquial or historical* jobcentre; **Labour Party** political party formed to represent workers' interests; **labour-saving** designed to reduce or eliminate work.

labourer *noun* (*US* **laborer**) person doing unskilled paid manual work.

Labrador /'læbrədɔː/ *noun* dog of retriever breed with black or golden coat.

laburnum /lə'bɜːnəm/ *noun* tree with drooping golden flowers and poisonous seeds.

labyrinth /'læbərɪnθ/ *noun* complicated network of passages; intricate or tangled arrangement. □ **labyrinthine** /-'rɪnθaɪn/ *adjective*.

lac *noun* resinous substance from SE Asian insect, used to make varnish and shellac.

lace ● *noun* open patterned fabric or trimming made by twisting, knotting, or looping threads; cord etc. passed through eyelets or hooks for fastening shoes etc. ● *verb* (**-cing**) (usually + *up*) fasten or tighten with lace(s); add spirits to (drink); (+ *through*) pass (shoelace etc.) through. □ **lace-up** shoe fastened with lace.

lacerate /'læsəreɪt/ *verb* (**-ting**) tear (esp. flesh etc.) roughly; wound (feelings etc.). □ **laceration** *noun*.

lachrymal /'lækrɪm(ə)l/ *adjective* (also **lacrimal**) of tears.

lachrymose /'lækrɪməʊs/ *adjective formal* often weeping; tearful.

lack ● *noun* (usually + *of*) deficiency, want. ● *verb* be without or deficient in. □ **lacklustre** (*US* **lackluster**) dull, lacking in vitality etc.

lackadaisical /lækə'deɪzɪk(ə)l/ *adjective* languid; unenthusiastic.

lackey /'lækɪ/ *noun* (*plural* **-s**) servile follower; footman, manservant.

lacking *adjective* undesirably absent; (+ *in*) deficient in.

laconic /lə'kɒnɪk/ *adjective* using few words. □ **laconically** *adverb*.

lacquer /'lækə/ ● *noun* hard shiny shellac or synthetic varnish; substance sprayed on hair to keep it in place. ● *verb* coat with lacquer.

lacrimal = LACHRYMAL.

lacrosse /lə'krɒs/ *noun* hockey-like game played with ball carried in net at end of stick.

lactate /læk'teɪt/ *verb* (**-ting**) (of mammals) secrete milk. □ **lactation** *noun*.

lactic /'læktɪk/ *adjective* of milk.

lactose /'læktəʊs/ *noun* sugar present in milk.

lacuna /lə'kjuːnə/ *noun* (*plural* **-s** or **-nae** /-niː/) missing part, esp. in manuscript; gap.

lacy /'leɪsɪ/ *adjective* (**-ier**, **-iest**) like lace fabric.

lad *noun* boy, youth; *colloquial* man.

ladder /'lædə/ ● *noun* set of horizontal bars fixed at intervals between two uprights for climbing up and down; unravelled stitching in stocking etc.; means of advancement in career etc. ● *verb* cause or develop ladder in (stocking etc.).

lade *verb* (**-ding**; *past participle* **laden**) load (ship); ship (goods); (as **laden** *adjective*) (usually + *with*) loaded, burdened.

la-di-da /lɑːdɪ'dɑː/ *adjective colloquial* pretentious or affected, esp. in manner or speech.

ladle /'leɪd(ə)l/ ● *noun* deep long-handled spoon for serving liquids. ● *verb* (**-ling**) (often + *out*) transfer with ladle.

lady /'leɪdɪ/ *noun* (*plural* **-ies**) woman regarded as having superior status or refined manners; *polite form of address for woman*; *colloquial* wife, girlfriend; (**Lady**) *title used before name of peeresses, peers' female relatives, wives and widows of knights, etc.*; (**Ladies**) women's public lavatory. □ **ladybird** small beetle, usually red with black spots; **Lady chapel** chapel dedicated to Virgin Mary; **Lady Day** Feast of the Annunciation, 25 Mar.; **ladylike** like or appropriate to lady.

Ladyship *noun* □ **Her** or **Your Ladyship** *title used of or to Lady*.

lag[1] ● *verb* (**-gg-**) fall behind; not keep pace. ● *noun* delay.

lag[2] *verb* (**-gg-**) enclose (boiler etc.) with heat-insulating material.

lag[3] *noun slang* habitual convict.

lager /'lɑːgə/ *noun* kind of light beer. □ **lager lout** *colloquial* youth behaving violently through drinking too much.

laggard /'lægəd/ *noun* person lagging behind.

lagging *noun* insulating material for boiler etc.

lagoon /lə'guːn/ *noun* salt-water lake separated from sea by sandbank, reef, etc.

lah *noun* (also **la**) *Music* sixth note of scale in tonic sol-fa.

laid *past & past participle* of LAY[1]. □ **laid-back** relaxed, easy-going.

lain *past participle* of LIE[1].

lair *noun* wild animal's home; person's hiding place.

laird /'leəd/ *noun Scottish* landed proprietor.

laissez-faire /leɪseɪ'feə/ *noun* (also ***laisser-faire***) policy of not interfering. [French]

laity /ˈleɪtɪ/ *noun* lay people, as distinct from clergy.

lake[1] *noun* large body of water surrounded by land. □ **Lake District** region of lakes in Cumbria.

lake[2] *noun* reddish pigment originally made from lac.

lam *verb* (**-mm-**) *slang* hit hard, thrash.

lama /ˈlɑːmə/ *noun* Tibetan or Mongolian Buddhist monk.

lamasery /ˈlɑːməsərɪ/ *noun* (*plural* **-ies**) lama monastery.

lamb /læm/ ● *noun* young sheep; its flesh as food; gentle, innocent, or weak person. ● *verb* (of sheep) give birth.

lambaste /læmˈbeɪst/ *verb* (**-ting**) (also **lambast** /-ˈbæst/) *colloquial* thrash, beat.

lambent /ˈlæmbənt/ *adjective* (of flame etc.) playing on a surface; (of eyes, wit, etc.) gently brilliant. □ **lambency** *noun*.

lambswool *noun* soft fine wool from young sheep.

lame ● *adjective* disabled in foot or leg; (of excuse etc.) unconvincing; (of verse etc.) halting. ● *verb* (**-ming**) make lame, disable. □ **lame duck** helpless person or firm. □ **lamely** *adverb*; **lameness** *noun*.

lamé /ˈlɑːmeɪ/ *noun* fabric with gold or silver thread woven in.

lament /ləˈment/ ● *noun* passionate expression of grief; song etc. of mourning. ● *verb* express or feel grief for or about; utter lament; (as **lamented** *adjective*) recently dead. □ **lamentation** /læmən-/ *noun*.

lamentable /ˈlæməntəb(ə)l/ *adjective* deplorable, regrettable. □ **lamentably** *adverb*.

lamina /ˈlæmɪnə/ *noun* (*plural* **-nae** /-niː/) thin plate or layer. □ **laminar** *adjective*.

laminate ● *verb* /ˈlæmɪneɪt/ (**-ting**) beat or roll into thin plates; overlay with plastic layer etc.; split into layers. ● *noun* /ˈlæmɪnət/ laminated structure, esp. of layers fixed together. □ **lamination** *noun*.

lamp *noun* device for giving light from electricity, gas, oil, etc.; apparatus producing esp. ultraviolet or infrared radiation. □ **lamppost** post supporting street light; **lampshade** usually partial cover for lamp.

lampoon /læmˈpuːn/ ● *noun* satirical attack on person etc. ● *verb* satirize. □ **lampoonist** *noun*.

lamprey /ˈlæmprɪ/ *noun* (*plural* **-s**) eel-like fish with sucker mouth.

Lancastrian /læŋˈkæstrɪən/ ● *noun* native of Lancashire or Lancaster. ● *adjective* of Lancashire or Lancaster; of House of Lancaster in Wars of Roses.

lance /lɑːns/ ● *noun* long spear, esp. one used by horseman. ● *verb* (**-cing**) prick or open with lancet. □ **lance-corporal** army NCO below corporal.

lanceolate /ˈlɑːnsɪələt/ *adjective* shaped like spear-head, tapering to each end.

lancer /ˈlɑːnsə/ *noun historical* soldier of cavalry regiment originally armed with lances; (in *plural*) quadrille.

lancet /ˈlɑːnsɪt/ *noun* small broad two-edged surgical knife with sharp point.

land ● *noun* solid part of earth's surface; ground, soil, expanse of country; nation, state; landed property; (in *plural*) estates. ● *verb* set or go ashore; bring (aircraft) down; alight on ground etc.; bring (fish) to land; (often + *up*) bring to or arrive at certain situation or place; *colloquial* deal (person etc. a blow etc.); (+ *with*) present (person) with (problem etc.); *colloquial* win (prize, appointment, etc.). □ **landfall** approach to land after sea or air journey; **landfill** waste material used to landscape or reclaim land, disposing of waste in this way; **landlady** woman owning rented property or keeping pub, guest-house, etc.; **landlocked** (almost) enclosed by land; **landlord** man owning rented property or keeping pub, guest-house, etc.; **landlubber** person unfamiliar with sea and ships; **landmark** conspicuous object, notable event; **landmine** explosive mine laid in or on ground; **landslide** sliding down of mass of land from cliff or mountain, overwhelming majority in election.

landau /ˈlændɔː/ *noun* (*plural* **-s**) 4-wheeled enclosed carriage with divided top.

landed *adjective* owning or consisting of land.

landing /ˈlændɪŋ/ *noun* platform or passage at top of or part way up stairs. □ **landing-craft** craft used for putting troops and equipment ashore; **landing-gear** undercarriage of aircraft; **landing-stage** platform for disembarking passengers and goods.

landscape /ˈlændskeɪp/ ● *noun* scenery in area of land; picture of it. ● *verb* (**-ping**) improve (piece of land) by **landscape gardening**, laying out of grounds to resemble natural scenery.

lane *noun* narrow road; division of road for one line of traffic; strip of track or water for competitor in race; regular course followed by ship or aircraft.

language /ˈlæŋgwɪdʒ/ *noun* use of words in agreed way as means of human communication; system of words of particular community, country, etc.; faculty of speech; style of expression; system of symbols and rules for computer programs. □ **language laboratory** room with tape recorders etc. for learning foreign language.

languid /ˈlæŋgwɪd/ *adjective* lacking vigour; idle. □ **languidly** *adverb*.

languish /ˈlæŋgwɪʃ/ *verb* lose or lack vitality. □ **languish for** long for; **languish under** live under (depression etc.).

languor /ˈlæŋgə/ *noun* lack of energy; idleness; soft or tender mood or effect. □ **languorous** *adjective*.

lank *adjective* (of grass, hair, etc.) long and limp; thin and tall.

lanky *adjective* (**-ier**, **-iest**) ungracefully thin and long or tall.

lanolin /ˈlænəlɪn/ *noun* fat from sheep's wool used in cosmetics, ointments, etc.

lantern /ˈlænt(ə)n/ *noun* lamp with transparent case protecting flame etc.; glazed structure on top of dome or room; light-chamber of lighthouse. □ **lantern jaws** long thin jaws.

lanyard /ˈlænjəd/ *noun* cord round neck or shoulder for holding knife etc.; *Nautical* short rope.

lap[1] *noun* front of sitting person's body from waist to knees; clothing covering this. □ **lap-dog** small pet dog; **laptop** (microcomputer) suitable for use while travelling.

lap[2] ● *noun* one circuit of racetrack etc.; section of journey etc.; amount of overlap. ● *verb* (**-pp-**) overtake (competitor in race who is a lap behind); (often + *about*, *around*) fold or wrap (garment etc.).

lap[3] ● *verb* (**-pp-**) (esp. of animal) drink by scooping with tongue; (usually + *up*, *down*) drink greedily; (usually + *up*) receive (gossip, praise, etc.) eagerly; (of waves etc.) ripple; make lapping sound against (shore). ● *noun* act or sound of lapping.

lapel /ləˈpel/ *noun* part of coat-front folded back.

lapidary /ˈlæpɪdərɪ/ ● *adjective* concerned with stones; engraved on stone; concise, well-expressed. ● *noun* (*plural* **-ies**) cutter, polisher, or engraver of gems.

lapis lazuli /læpɪs ˈlæzjʊlɪ/ *noun* bright blue gem; its colour.

lapse /læps/ ● *noun* slight error; slip of memory etc.; weak or careless decline into inferior state. ● *verb* (**-sing**) fail to maintain position or standard; (+ *into*) fall back into (inferior or previous state); (of right etc.) become invalid.

lapwing /ˈlæpwɪŋ/ *noun* plover with shrill cry.

larceny /ˈlɑːsənɪ/ *noun* (*plural* **-ies**) theft of personal property. ▫ **larcenous** *adjective*.

larch *noun* deciduous coniferous tree with bright foliage; its wood.

lard ● *noun* pig fat used in cooking etc. ● *verb* insert strips of bacon in (meat etc.) before cooking; (+ *with*) embellish (talk etc.) with (strange terms etc.).

larder *noun* room or cupboard for storing food.

lardy-cake *noun* cake made with lard, currants, etc.

large *adjective* of relatively great size or extent; of larger kind; comprehensive. ▫ **at large** at liberty, as a body or whole; **large as life** in person, esp. prominently. ▫ **largeness** *noun*; **largish** *adjective*.

largely *adverb* to a great extent.

largesse /lɑːˈʒes/ *noun* (also **largess**) money or gifts freely given.

largo /ˈlɑːgəʊ/ *Music* ● *adverb & adjective* in slow time and dignified style. ● *noun* (*plural* **-s**) largo movement or passage.

lariat /ˈlærɪət/ *noun* lasso; rope for tethering animal.

lark[1] *noun* small bird with tuneful song, esp. skylark.

lark[2] *colloquial* ● *noun* frolic; amusing incident; type of activity. ● *verb* (+ *about*) play tricks.

larkspur *noun* plant with spur-shaped calyx.

larva /ˈlɑːvə/ *noun* (*plural* **-vae** /-viː/) insect in stage between egg and pupa. ▫ **larval** *adjective*.

laryngeal /ləˈrɪndʒɪəl/ *adjective* of the larynx.

laryngitis /lærɪnˈdʒaɪtɪs/ *noun* inflammation of larynx.

larynx /ˈlærɪŋks/ *noun* (*plural* **larynges** /ləˈrɪndʒiːz/ or **-xes**) cavity in throat holding vocal cords.

lasagne /ləˈsænjə/ *noun* pasta sheets.

lascivious /ləˈsɪvɪəs/ *adjective* lustful. ▫ **lasciviously** *adverb*.

laser /ˈleɪzə/ *noun* device producing intense beam of special kind of light. ▫ **laser printer** printing machine using laser to produce image.

lash ● *verb* make sudden whiplike movement; beat with whip; (often + *against, down*) (of rain etc.) beat, strike; criticize harshly; rouse, incite; (often + *together, down*) fasten with rope etc. ● *noun* sharp blow with whip etc.; flexible part of whip; eyelash. ▫ **lash out** speak or hit out angrily, *colloquial* spend money extravagantly.

lashings *plural noun colloquial* (often + *of*) plenty.

lass *noun esp. Scottish & Northern English or poetical* girl.

lassitude /ˈlæsɪtjuːd/ *noun* languor; disinclination to exert oneself.

lasso /læˈsuː/ ● *noun* (*plural* **-s** or **-es**) rope with running noose used esp. for catching cattle. ● *verb* (**-es, -ed**) catch with lasso.

last[1] /lɑːst/ ● *adjective* after all others; coming at end; most recent; only remaining. ● *adverb* after all others; on most recent occasion. ● *noun* last, last-mentioned, or most recent person or thing; last mention, sight, etc.; end; death. ▫ **at (long) last** in the end, after much delay; **the last straw** slight addition to task etc. making it unbearable.

last[2] /lɑːst/ *verb* remain unexhausted, adequate, or alive for specified or long time. ▫ **last out** be sufficient for whole of given period.

last[3] /lɑːst/ *noun* shoemaker's model for shaping shoe etc. ▫ **stick to one's last** keep to what one understands.

lasting *adjective* permanent, durable.

lastly *adverb* finally.

lat. *abbreviation* latitude.

latch ● *noun* bar with catch as fastening of gate etc.; spring-lock as fastening of outer door. ● *verb* fasten with latch. ▫ **latchkey** key of outer door; **latch on to** *colloquial* attach oneself to, understand.

late ● *adjective* after due or usual time; far on in day, night, period, etc.; flowering, ripening, etc. towards end of season; no longer alive or having specified status; of recent date. ● *adverb* after due or usual time; far on in time; at or till late hour; at late stage of development; formerly but not now. ▫ **late in the day** at late stage of proceedings etc. ▫ **lateness** *noun*.

lateen sail /ləˈtiːn/ *noun* triangular sail on long yard at angle of 45° to mast.

lately *adverb* not long ago; recently.

latent /ˈleɪt(ə)nt/ *adjective* existing but not developed or manifest; concealed, dormant. ▫ **latency** *noun*.

lateral /ˈlætər(ə)l/ ● *adjective* of, at, towards, or from side(s). ● *noun* lateral shoot or branch. ▫ **lateral thinking** method of solving problems by indirect or illogical methods. ▫ **laterally** *adverb*.

latex /ˈleɪteks/ *noun* milky fluid of esp. rubber tree; synthetic substance like this.

lath /lɑːθ/ *noun* thin flat strip of wood.

lathe /leɪð/ *noun* machine for shaping wood, metal, etc. by rotating article against cutting tools.

lather /ˈlɑːðə/ ● *noun* froth made by agitating soap etc. and water; frothy sweat; state of agitation. ● *verb* (of soap) form lather; cover with lather; *colloquial* thrash.

Latin /ˈlætɪn/ ● *noun* language of ancient Rome. ● *adjective* of or in Latin; of countries or peoples speaking languages developed from Latin; of RC Church. ▫ **Latin America** parts of Central and S. America where Spanish or Portuguese is main language.

Latinate /ˈlætɪneɪt/ *adjective* having character of Latin.

latitude /ˈlætɪtjuːd/ *noun* angular distance N. or S. of equator; (usually in *plural*) regions, climes; freedom from restriction in action or opinion.

latrine /ləˈtriːn/ *noun* communal lavatory, esp. in camp.

latter /ˈlætə/ ● *adjective* second-mentioned of two; nearer the end. ● *noun* (**the latter**) the latter thing or person. ▫ **latter-day** modern, contemporary.

latterly *adverb* recently; in latter part of life or period.

lattice /ˈlætɪs/ *noun* structure of crossed laths or bars with spaces between, used as fence, screen, etc.; arrangement resembling this. ▫ **lattice window** one with small panes set in lead. ▫ **latticed** *adjective*.

Latvian /ˈlætvɪən/ ● *noun* native, national, or language of Latvia. ● *adjective* of Latvia.

laud /lɔːd/ *verb* praise, extol.

laudable *adjective* praiseworthy. ▫ **laudably** *adverb*.

laudanum /ˈlɔːdənəm/ *noun* solution prepared from opium.

laudatory /ˈlɔːdətərɪ/ *adjective* praising.

laugh /lɑːf/ ● *verb* make sounds etc. usual in expressing amusement, scorn, etc.; express by laughing; (+ *at*) make fun of, ridicule. ● *noun* sound or act of laughing; *colloquial* comical person or thing. ▫ **laugh off** shrug off (embarrassment etc.) by joking.

laughable *adjective* amusing; ridiculous. ▫ **laughably** *adverb*.

laughing *noun* laughter. ▫ **laughing gas** nitrous oxide as anaesthetic; **laughing jackass** kookaburra; **laughing stock** object of general derision. ▫ **laughingly** *adverb*.

laughter /ˈlɑːftə/ *noun* act or sound of laughing.

launch[1] /lɔːntʃ/ ● *verb* set (vessel) afloat; hurl or send forth (rocket etc.); start or set in motion (enterprise, person, etc.); formally introduce (new product) with publicity; (+ *into*) make start on; (+ *out*) make start on new enterprise. ● *noun* launching. ◻ **launch pad** platform with structure for launching rockets from.

launch[2] /lɔːntʃ/ *noun* large motor boat.

launder /ˈlɔːndə/ *verb* wash and iron etc. (clothes etc.); *colloquial* transfer (money) to conceal its origin.

launderette /lɔːnˈdret/ *noun* (also **laundrette**) establishment with coin-operated washing machines and driers for public use.

laundress /ˈlɔːndrɪs/ *noun* woman who launders.

laundry /ˈlɔːndrɪ/ *noun* (*plural* **-ies**) place where clothes etc. are laundered; clothes etc. that need to be or have been laundered.

laurel /ˈlɒr(ə)l/ *noun* any of various kinds of shrub with dark green glossy leaves; (in *singular* or *plural*) wreath of bay-leaves as emblem of victory or poetic merit. ◻ **look to one's laurels** beware of losing one's pre-eminence; **rest on one's laurels** stop seeking further success.

lava /ˈlɑːvə/ *noun* matter flowing from volcano and solidifying as it cools.

lavatorial /lævəˈtɔːrɪəl/ *adjective* of or like lavatories; (esp. of humour) relating to excretion.

lavatory /ˈlævətərɪ/ *noun* (*plural* **-ies**) receptacle for urine and faeces, usually with means of disposal; room etc. containing this.

lave *verb* (**-ving**) *literary* wash, bathe; wash against; flow along.

lavender /ˈlævɪndə/ *noun* evergreen fragrant-flowered shrub; its dried flowers used to scent linen; pale purplish colour. ◻ **lavender-water** light perfume.

laver /ˈleɪvə/ *noun* kind of edible seaweed.

lavish /ˈlævɪʃ/ ● *adjective* profuse; abundant; generous. ● *verb* (often + *on*) bestow or spend (money, praise, etc.) abundantly. ◻ **lavishly** *adverb*.

law *noun* rule or set of rules established in a community, demanding or prohibiting certain actions; such rules as social system or branch of study; binding force; (**the law**) legal profession, *colloquial* police; law courts, legal remedy; science or philosophy of law; statement of regularity of natural occurrences. ◻ **law-abiding** obedient to the laws; **law court** court of law; **Law Lord** member of House of Lords qualified to perform its legal work; **lawsuit** bringing of claim etc. before law court; **lay down the law** give dogmatic opinions; **take the law into one's own hands** get one's rights without help of the law.

lawful *adjective* permitted, appointed, or recognized by law; not illegal. ◻ **lawfully** *adverb*; **lawfulness** *noun*.

lawless *adjective* having no laws; disregarding laws. ◻ **lawlessness** *noun*.

lawn[1] *noun* piece of close-mown grass in garden etc. ◻ **lawnmower** machine for cutting lawns; **lawn tennis** tennis played with soft ball on grass or hard court.

lawn[2] *noun* kind of fine linen or cotton.

lawyer /ˈlɔɪə/ *noun* person practising law, esp. solicitor.

lax *adjective* lacking care or precision; not strict. ◻ **laxity** *noun*; **laxly** *adverb*; **laxness** *noun*.

laxative /ˈlæksətɪv/ ● *adjective* helping evacuation of bowels. ● *noun* laxative medicine.

lay[1] ● *verb* (*past & past participle* **laid**) place on surface, esp. horizontally; put or bring into required position or state; make by laying; (of bird) produce (egg); cause to subside or lie flat; (usually + *on*) attribute (blame etc.); make ready (trap, plan); prepare (table) for meal; put fuel ready to light (fire); put down as bet. ● *noun* way, position, or direction in which something lies. ◻ **lay bare** expose, reveal; **lay-by** extra strip beside road where vehicles may park; **lay claim to** claim as one's own; **lay down** relinquish, make (rule), store (wine) in cellar, sacrifice (one's life); **lay in** provide oneself with stock of; **lay into** *colloquial* attack violently with blows or verbally; **lay it on thick** or **with a trowel** *colloquial* flatter, exaggerate grossly; **lay off** discharge (workers) temporarily, *colloquial* desist; **lay on** provide, spread on; **lay out** spread, expose to view, prepare (body) for burial, *colloquial* knock unconscious, expend (money); **layout** way in which land, building, printed matter, etc., is arranged or set out; **lay up** store, save (money), (as **laid up** *adjective*) confined to bed or the house; **lay waste** ravage, destroy.

■ **Usage** It is incorrect in standard English to use *lay* to mean 'lie', as in *She was laying on the floor*.

lay[2] *adjective* not ordained into the clergy; not professionally qualified; of or done by such people. ◻ **layman**, **laywoman** person not in holy orders, one without professional or special knowledge; **lay reader** lay person licensed to conduct some religious services.

lay[3] *noun* short poem meant to be sung; song.

lay[4] *past* of LIE[1].

layer ● *noun* thickness of matter, esp. one of several, covering surface; hen that lays eggs. ● *verb* arrange in layers; propagate (plant) by fastening shoot down to take root.

layette /leɪˈet/ *noun* clothes etc. prepared for newborn child.

lay figure *noun* artist's jointed wooden model of human figure; unrealistic character in novel etc.

laze ● *verb* (**-zing**) spend time idly. ● *noun* spell of lazing.

lazy *adjective* (**-ier**, **-iest**) disinclined to work, doing little work; of or inducing idleness. ◻ **lazybones** *colloquial* lazy person. ◻ **lazily** *adverb*; **laziness** *noun*.

lb *abbreviation* pound(s) weight.

■ **Usage** It is a common mistake to write *lbs* as an abbreviation for *pounds*. *28 lb* is correct.

l.b.w. *abbreviation* leg before wicket.

l.c. *abbreviation* loc. cit.; lower case.

LCD *abbreviation* liquid crystal display.

L/Cpl *abbreviation* Lance-Corporal.

LEA *abbreviation* Local Education Authority.

lea *noun poetical* meadow, field.

leach *verb* make (liquid) percolate through some material; subject (bark, ore, ash, soil) to this; (usually + *away*, *out*) remove (soluble matter) or be removed in this way.

lead[1] /liːd/ ● *verb* (*past & past participle* **led**) conduct, esp. by going in front; direct actions or opinions of; (often + *to*) guide by persuasion; provide access to; pass or spend (life etc.); have first place in; go or be first; play (card) as first player in trick; (+ *to*) result in; (+ *with*) (of newspapers or broadcast) have as main story. ● *noun* guidance, example; leader's place; amount by which competitor is ahead of others; clue; strap etc. for leading dog etc.; *Electricity* conductor carrying current to place of use; chief part in play etc.; *Cards* act or right of playing first. ◻ **lead by the nose** make (someone) do all one wishes them to; **lead-in** introduction, opening; **lead on** entice dishonestly; **lead up the garden path** *colloquial* mislead; **lead up to** form preparation for, direct conversation towards.

lead[2] /led/ ● *noun* heavy soft grey metal; graphite used in pencils; lump of lead used in sounding; blank space between lines of print. ● *verb* cover, frame, or space with lead(s). ◻ **lead-free** (of petrol) without added lead compounds.

leaded /ˈledɪd/ *adjective* (of petrol) with added lead compounds; (of window pane) framed with lead.

leaden /ˈled(ə)n/ *adjective* of or like lead; heavy, slow; lead-coloured.

leader /ˈliːdə/ *noun* person or thing that leads; leading performer in orchestra, quartet, etc.; leading article. □ **leadership** *noun*.

leading /ˈliːdɪŋ/ *adjective* chief, most important. □ **leading aircraftman** one ranking just below NCO in RAF; **leading article** newspaper article giving editorial opinion; **leading light** prominent influential person; **leading note** *Music* seventh note of ascending scale; **leading question** one prompting the answer wanted.

■ **Usage** *Leading question* does not mean a 'principal' or 'loaded' or 'searching' question.

leaf ● *noun* (*plural* **leaves**) flat usually green part of plant growing usually on stem; foliage; single thickness of paper, esp. in book; very thin sheet of metal etc.; hinged part, extra section, or flap of table etc. ● *verb* (of plants etc.) begin to grow leaves; (+ *through*) turn over pages of (book etc.). □ **leaf-mould** soil composed chiefly of decaying leaves. □ **leafage** *noun*; **leafy** *adjective* (**-ier**, **-iest**).

leaflet /ˈliːflɪt/ *noun* sheet of paper, pamphlet, etc., giving information; young leaf.

league[1] /liːg/ ● *noun* people, countries, etc., joining together for particular purpose; group of sports clubs who contend for championship; class of contestants. ● *verb* (**-gues**, **-gued**, **-guing**) (often + *together*) join in league. □ **in league** allied, conspiring; **league table** list in order of success.

league[2] /liːg/ *noun archaic* measure of travelling distance, usually about 3 miles.

leak ● *noun* hole through which liquid etc. passes accidentally in or out; liquid etc. thus passing through; similar escape of electric charge; disclosure of secret information. ● *verb* (let) pass out or in through leak; disclose (secret); (often + *out*) become known. □ **leaky** *adjective* (**-ier**, **-iest**).

leakage *noun* action or result of leaking.

lean[1] ● *verb* (*past & past participle* **leaned** or **leant** /lent/) (often + *across*, *back*, *over*, etc.) be or place in sloping position; (usually + *against*, *on*) rest for support against; (usually + *on*, *upon*) rely, depend; (usually + *to*, *towards*) be inclined or partial. ● *noun* inclination, slope. □ **lean on** *colloquial* put pressure on (person) to act in certain way; **lean-to** building with roof resting against larger building or wall.

lean[2] ● *adjective* (of person etc.) having no superfluous fat; (of meat) containing little fat; meagre. ● *noun* lean part of meat. □ **lean years** time of scarcity. □ **leanness** *noun*.

leaning *noun* tendency or inclination.

leap ● *verb* (*past & past participle* **leaped** or **leapt** /lept/) jump, spring forcefully. ● *noun* forceful jump. □ **by leaps and bounds** with very rapid progress; **leap-frog** game in which player vaults with parted legs over another bending down; **leap year** year with 29 Feb. as extra day.

learn /lɜːn/ *verb* (*past & past participle* **learned** /lɜːnt, lɜːnd/ or **learnt**) get knowledge of or skill in by study, experience, or being taught; commit to memory; (usually + *of*, *about*) be told about, find out.

learned /ˈlɜːnɪd/ *adjective* having much knowledge from studying; showing or requiring learning.

learner *noun* person learning, beginner; (in full **learner driver**) person who is learning to drive but has not yet passed driving test.

learning *noun* knowledge got by study.

lease /liːs/ ● *noun* contract by which owner of land or building allows another to use it for specified time, usually for rent. ● *verb* (**-sing**) grant or take on lease. □ **leasehold** holding of property by lease; **leaseholder** *noun*; **new lease of** (*US* **on**) **life** improved prospect of living, or of use after repair.

leash ● *noun* strap for holding dog(s). ● *verb* put leash on; restrain. □ **straining at the leash** eager to begin.

least ● *adjective* smallest, slightest. ● *noun* least amount. ● *adverb* in the least degree. □ **at least** at any rate; **to say the least** putting the case moderately.

leather /ˈleðə/ ● *noun* material made from skin of animal by tanning etc.; piece of leather for cleaning esp. windows; *slang* cricket ball, football. ● *verb* beat, thrash; cover or polish with leather. □ **leather-jacket** larva of crane-fly.

leatherette /leðəˈret/ *noun* imitation leather.

leathery *adjective* like leather; tough.

leave[1] *verb* (**-ving**; *past & past participle* **left**) go away (from); cause or allow to remain; depart without taking; cease to reside at, belong to, work for, etc.; abandon; (usually + *to*) commit to another person; bequeath; deposit or entrust (object, message, etc.) to be dealt with in one's absence; not consume or deal with. □ **leave off** come to or make an end, stop; **leave out** omit.

leave[2] *noun* permission; (in full **leave of absence**) permission to be absent from duty; period for which this lasts. □ **on leave** absent thus; **take one's leave of** say goodbye to.

leaven /ˈlev(ə)n/ ● *noun* substance used to make dough ferment and rise; transforming influence. ● *verb* ferment (dough) with leaven; permeate, transform.

leavings *plural noun* what is left.

Lebanese /lebəˈniːz/ ● *adjective* of Lebanon. ● *noun* (*plural* same) native or national of Lebanon.

lecher /ˈletʃə/ *noun* lecherous man.

lecherous *adjective* lustful. □ **lecherously** *adverb*; **lechery** *noun*.

lectern /ˈlekt(ə)n/ *noun* stand for holding Bible etc. in church; similar stand for lecturer etc.

lecture /ˈlektʃə/ ● *noun* talk giving information to class etc.; admonition, reprimand. ● *verb* (**-ring**) (often + *on*) deliver lecture(s); admonish, reprimand.

lecturer *noun* person who lectures, esp. as teacher in higher education.

lectureship *noun* university post as lecturer.

led *past & past participle* of LEAD[1].

ledge *noun* narrow shelf or projection from vertical surface.

ledger /ˈledʒə/ *noun* book in which firm's accounts are kept.

lee *noun* shelter given by neighbouring object; side of thing away from the wind. □ **leeway** allowable deviation, drift of ship to leeward.

leech *noun* bloodsucking worm formerly used medicinally for bleeding; person who sponges on others.

leek *noun* vegetable of onion family with long cylindrical white bulb.

leer ● *verb* look slyly, lasciviously, or maliciously. ● *noun* leering look.

leery *adjective* (**-ier**, **-iest**) *slang* knowing, sly; (usually + *of*) wary.

lees /liːz/ *plural noun* sediment of wine etc.; dregs.

leeward /ˈliːwəd, *Nautical* ˈluːəd/ ● *adjective & adverb* on or towards sheltered side. ● *noun* this direction.

left[1] ● *adjective* on or towards west side of person or thing facing north; (also **Left**) *Politics* of the Left. ● *adverb* on or to left side. ● *noun* left part, region, or direction; *Boxing* left hand, blow with this; (often **Left**)

Politics group favouring socialism, radicals collectively. □ **left-hand** on left side; **left-handed** naturally using left hand for writing etc., made by or for left hand, turning to left, (of screw) turned anticlockwise to tighten, awkward, clumsy, (of compliment etc.) ambiguous; **left-handedness** *noun*; **left-hander** left-handed person or blow; **left wing** more radical section of political party, left side of army, football team, etc.; **left-wing** socialist, radical; **left-winger** member of left wing. □ **leftward** *adjective & adverb*; **leftwards** *adverb*.

left² *past & past participle of* LEAVE¹.

leg *noun* each of limbs on which person or animal walks and stands; leg of animal as food; part of garment covering leg; support of chair, table, etc.; section of journey, race, competition, etc.; *Cricket* half of field behind batsman's back. □ **leg before wicket** *Cricket* (of batsman) declared out for illegal obstruction of ball that would have hit wicket; **leg it** (**-gg-**) *colloquial* walk or run hard; **leg warmer** either of pair of tubular knitted garments covering leg from ankle to thigh; **pull** (**person's**) **leg** deceive playfully. □ **legged** *adjective*.

legacy /ˈlegəsɪ/ *noun* (*plural* **-ies**) gift left by will; anything handed down by predecessor.

legal /ˈliːg(ə)l/ *adjective* of, based on, or concerned with law; appointed, required, or permitted by law. □ **legal aid** state help with cost of legal advice; **legal tender** currency that cannot legally be refused in payment of debt. □ **legality** /lɪˈgælɪtɪ/ *noun*; **legally** *adverb*.

legalize /ˈliːgəlaɪz/ *verb* (also **-ise**) (**-zing** or **-sing**) make lawful; bring into harmony with law. □ **legalization** *noun*.

legate /ˈlegət/ *noun* papal ambassador.

legatee /legəˈtiː/ *noun* recipient of legacy.

legation /lɪˈgeɪʃ(ə)n/ *noun* diplomatic minister and his or her staff; this minister's official residence.

legato /lɪˈgɑːtəʊ/ *Music* ● *adverb & adjective* in smooth flowing manner. ● *noun* (*plural* **-s**) legato passage.

legend /ˈledʒ(ə)nd/ *noun* traditional story, myth; *colloquial* famous or remarkable person or event; inscription; explanation on map etc. of symbols used.

legendary *adjective* existing in legend; *colloquial* remarkable, famous.

legerdemain /ledʒədəˈmeɪn/ *noun* sleight of hand; trickery, sophistry.

leger line /ˈledʒə/ *noun Music* short line added for notes above or below range of staff.

legging *noun* (usually in *plural*) close-fitting trousers for women or children; outer covering of leather etc. for lower leg.

leggy *adjective* (**-ier**, **-iest**) long-legged; long-stemmed and weak.

legible /ˈledʒɪb(ə)l/ *adjective* easily read. □ **legibility** *noun*; **legibly** *adverb*.

legion /ˈliːdʒ(ə)n/ ● *noun* division of 3,000–6,000 men in ancient Roman army; other large organized body. ● *adjective* great in number.

legionary ● *adjective* of legions. ● *noun* (*plural* **-ies**) member of legion.

legionnaire /liːdʒəˈneə/ *noun* member of foreign legion. □ **legionnaires' disease** form of bacterial pneumonia.

legislate /ˈledʒɪsleɪt/ *verb* (**-ting**) make laws. □ **legislator** *noun*.

legislation *noun* making laws; laws made.

legislative /ˈledʒɪslətɪv/ *adjective* of or empowered to make legislation.

legislature /ˈledʒɪsleɪtʃə/ *noun* legislative body of a state.

legitimate /lɪˈdʒɪtɪmət/ *adjective* (of child) born of parents married to one another; lawful, proper, regular; logically admissible. □ **legitimacy** *noun*; **legitimately** *adverb*.

legitimize /lɪˈdʒɪtɪmaɪz/ *verb* (also **-ise**) (**-zing** or **-sing**) make legitimate; serve as justification for. □ **legitimization** *noun*.

legume /ˈlegjuːm/ *noun* leguminous plant; edible part of this.

leguminous /lɪˈgjuːmɪnəs/ *adjective* of the family of plants with seeds in pods, e.g. peas and beans.

lei /ˈleɪ/ *noun* Polynesian garland of flowers.

leisure /ˈleʒə/ *noun* free time, time at one's own disposal. □ **at leisure** not occupied, in an unhurried way; **at one's leisure** when one has time; **leisure centre** public building with sports facilities etc.; **leisurewear** informal clothes, esp. sportswear.

leisured *adjective* having ample leisure.

leisurely ● *adjective* relaxed, unhurried. ● *adverb* without hurry.

leitmotif /ˈlaɪtməʊtiːf/ *noun* (also **leitmotiv**) recurring theme in musical etc. composition representing particular person, idea, etc.

lemming /ˈlemɪŋ/ *noun* Arctic rodent reputed to rush, during migration, in large numbers into sea and drown.

lemon /ˈlemən/ *noun* acid yellow citrus fruit; tree bearing it; pale yellow colour. □ **lemon cheese, curd** thick creamy lemon spread. □ **lemony** *adjective*.

lemonade /leməˈneɪd/ *noun* drink made from lemons; synthetic substitute for this, often fizzy.

lemon sole /ˈlemən/ *noun* (*plural* same or **-s**) fish of plaice family.

lemur /ˈliːmə/ *noun* tree-dwelling primate of Madagascar.

lend *verb* (*past & past participle* **lent**) grant temporary use of (thing); allow use of (money) in return for interest; bestow, contribute; (**lend itself to**) be suitable for. □ **lend an ear** listen. □ **lender** *noun*.

length *noun* measurement from end to end; extent in or of time; length of horse, boat, etc. as measure of lead in race; long stretch or extent; degree of thoroughness in action. □ **at length** in detail, after a long time. □ **lengthways** *adverb*; **lengthwise** *adverb & adjective*.

lengthen *verb* make or become longer.

lengthy *adjective* (**-ier**, **-iest**) of unusual length, prolix, tedious.

lenient /ˈliːnɪənt/ *adjective* merciful, not severe, mild. □ **lenience** *noun*; **leniency** *noun*; **leniently** *adverb*.

lens /lenz/ *noun* piece of transparent substance with one or both sides curved, used in spectacles, telescopes, cameras, etc.; combination of lenses used in photography.

Lent *noun* religious period of fasting and penitence from Ash Wednesday to Easter Eve. □ **Lenten** *adjective*.

lent *past & past participle of* LEND.

lentil /ˈlentɪl/ *noun* edible seed of leguminous plant; this plant.

lento /ˈlentəʊ/ *Music* ● *adjective* slow. ● *adverb* slowly. ● *noun* lento movement or passage.

Leo /ˈliːəʊ/ *noun* fifth sign of zodiac.

leonine /ˈliːənaɪn/ *adjective* lionlike; of lions.

leopard /ˈlepəd/ *noun* large animal of cat family with dark-spotted fawn or all black coat, panther.

leotard /ˈliːətɑːd/ *noun* close-fitting one-piece garment worn by dancers etc.

leper /ˈlepə/ *noun* person with leprosy.

leprechaun /ˈleprəkɔːn/ *noun* small mischievous sprite in Irish folklore.

leprosy /'leprəsɪ/ *noun* contagious disease of skin and nerves. ▫ **leprous** *adjective*.

lesbian /'lezbiən/ ● *noun* homosexual woman. ● *adjective* of homosexuality in women. ▫ **lesbianism** *noun*.

lesion /'liːʒ(ə)n/ *noun* damage, injury; change in part of body due to injury or disease.

less ● *adjective* smaller; of smaller quantity; not so much. ● *adverb* to smaller extent, in lower degree. ● *noun* smaller amount, quantity, or number. ● *preposition* minus, deducting.

■ **Usage** The use of *less* to mean 'fewer', as in *There are less people than yesterday*, is incorrect in standard English.

lessee /le'siː/ *noun* (often + *of*) person holding property by lease.

lessen /'les(ə)n/ *verb* diminish.

lesser *adjective* not so great as the other(s).

lesson /'les(ə)n/ *noun* period of teaching; (in *plural*; usually + *in*) systematic instruction; thing learnt by pupil; experience that serves to warn or encourage; passage from Bible read aloud during church service.

lessor /le'sɔː/ *noun* person who lets property by lease.

lest *conjunction* in order that not, for fear that.

let[1] ● *verb* (**-tt-**; *past & past participle* **let**) allow, enable, or cause to; grant use of (rooms, land, etc.) for rent or hire. ● *auxiliary verb in exhortations, commands, assumptions, etc.* ● *noun* act of letting. ▫ **let alone** not to mention; **let be** not interfere with; **let down** *verb* lower, fail to support or satisfy, disappoint; **let-down** *noun* disappointment; **let go** release, lose hold of; **let in** allow to enter, (usually + *for*) involve (person, often oneself) in loss, problem, etc., (usually + *on*) allow (person) to share secret etc.; **let off** fire (gun), cause (steam etc.) to escape, not punish or compel; **let on** *colloquial* reveal secret; **let out** *verb* release, reveal (secret etc.), slacken, put out to rent; **let-out** *noun colloquial* opportunity to escape; **let up** *verb colloquial* become less severe, diminish; **let-up** *noun colloquial* relaxation of effort, diminution.

let[2] *noun* obstruction of ball or player in tennis etc. after which ball must be served again. ▫ **without let or hindrance** unimpeded.

lethal /'liːθ(ə)l/ *adjective* causing or sufficient to cause death. ▫ **lethally** *adverb*.

lethargy /'leθədʒɪ/ *noun* lack of energy; unnatural sleepiness. ▫ **lethargic** /lɪ'θɑːdʒɪk/ *adjective*; **lethargically** /lɪ'θɑːdʒɪkəlɪ/ *adverb*.

letter /'letə/ ● *noun* character representing one or more of sounds used in speech; written or printed communication, usually sent in envelope by post; precise terms of statement; (in *plural*) literature. ● *verb* inscribe letters on; classify with letters. ▫ **letter bomb** terrorist explosive device sent by post; **letter box** box for delivery or posting of letters, slit in door for delivery of letters; **letterhead** printed heading on stationery; **letterpress** printed words in illustrated book, printing from raised type; **to the letter** keeping to every detail.

lettuce /'letɪs/ *noun* plant with crisp leaves used in salad.

leucocyte /'luːkəsaɪt/ *noun* white blood cell.

leukaemia /luː'kiːmɪə/ *noun* (*US* **leukemia**) malignant progressive disease in which too many white blood cells are produced.

Levant /lɪ'vænt/ *noun* (**the Levant**) *archaic* East-Mediterranean region.

Levantine /'levəntaɪn/ ● *adjective* of or trading to the Levant. ● *noun* native or inhabitant of the Levant.

levee /'levɪ/ *noun US* embankment against river floods.

level /'lev(ə)l/ ● *noun* horizontal line or plane; height or value reached; position on real or imaginary scale; social, moral, or intellectual standard; plane of rank or authority; instrument giving line parallel to plane of horizon; level surface, flat country. ● *adjective* flat, not bumpy; horizontal; (often + *with*) on same horizontal plane as something else, having equality with something else; even, uniform, well-balanced. ● *verb* (**-ll-**; *US* **-l-**) make level; raze, completely destroy; (usually + *at*) aim (gun etc.); (usually + *at, against*) direct (accusation etc.). ▫ **do one's level best** *colloquial* do one's utmost; **find one's level** reach right social, intellectual, etc., position; **level crossing** crossing of road and railway etc. at same level; **level-headed** mentally well-balanced, cool; **level pegging** equality of scores etc.; **on the level** *colloquial* truthfully, honestly.

lever /'liːvə/ ● *noun* bar pivoted about fulcrum to transfer force; bar used on pivot to prise or lift; projecting handle used to operate mechanism; means of exerting moral pressure. ● *verb* use lever; lift, move, etc. (as) with lever.

leverage *noun* action or power of lever; means of accomplishing a purpose.

leveret /'levərɪt/ *noun* young hare.

leviathan /lɪ'vaɪəθ(ə)n/ *noun Biblical* sea monster; very large or powerful thing.

Levis /'liːvaɪz/ *plural noun proprietary term* type of (originally blue) denim jeans.

levitate /'levɪteɪt/ *verb* (**-ting**) (cause to) rise and float in air. ▫ **levitation** *noun*.

levity /'levɪtɪ/ *noun* lack of serious thought; frivolity.

levy /'levɪ/ ● *verb* (**-ies**, **-ied**) impose or collect (payment etc.) compulsorily; enrol (troops etc.). ● *noun* (*plural* **-ies**) levying; payment etc. or (in *plural*) troops levied.

lewd /ljuːd/ *adjective* lascivious, indecent.

lexical /'leksɪk(ə)l/ *adjective* of the words of a language; (as) of a lexicon.

lexicography /leksɪ'kɒgrəfɪ/ *noun* compiling of dictionaries. ▫ **lexicographer** *noun*.

lexicon /'leksɪkən/ *noun* dictionary.

Leyden jar /'laɪd(ə)n/ *noun* early kind of capacitor.

LF *abbreviation* low frequency.

liability /laɪə'bɪlɪtɪ/ *noun* (*plural* **-ies**) being liable; troublesome person or thing; handicap; (in *plural*) debts for which one is liable.

liable /'laɪəb(ə)l/ *adjective* legally bound; (+ *to*) subject to; (+ *to do*) under an obligation; (+ *to*) exposed or open to (something undesirable); (+ *for*) answerable for.

■ **Usage** *Liable* is often used to mean 'likely', as in *It is liable to rain*, but this is considered incorrect by some people.

liaise /lɪ'eɪz/ *verb* (**-sing**) (usually + *with, between*) *colloquial* establish cooperation, act as link.

liaison /lɪ'eɪzɒn/ *noun* communication, cooperation; illicit sexual relationship.

liana /lɪ'ɑːnə/ *noun* climbing plant in tropical forests.

liar /'laɪə/ *noun* person who tells lies.

Lib. *abbreviation* Liberal.

lib *noun colloquial* liberation.

libation /laɪ'beɪʃ(ə)n/ *noun* (pouring out of) drink-offering to a god.

libel /'laɪb(ə)l/ ● *noun Law* published false statement damaging to person's reputation, publishing of this; false defamatory statement. ● *verb* (**-ll-**: *US* **-l-**) *Law* publish libel against. ▫ **libellous** *adjective*.

liberal /'lɪbər(ə)l/ ● *adjective* abundant; giving freely; generous; open-minded; not rigorous; (of studies) for general broadening of mind; *Politics* favouring moderate reforms. ● *noun* person of liberal views, esp. (**Liberal**) member of a Liberal Party. □ **Liberal Democrat** member of **Liberal Democrats**, UK political party. □ **liberalism** *noun*; **liberality** /-'ræl-/ *noun*; **liberally** *adverb*.

liberalize *verb* (also **-ise**) (**-zing** or **-sing**) make or become more liberal or less strict. □ **liberalization** *noun*.

liberate /'lɪbəreɪt/ *verb* (**-ting**) (often + *from*) set free; free (country etc.) from aggressor; (as **liberated** *adjective*) (of person etc.) freed from oppressive social conventions. □ **liberation** *noun*; **liberator** *noun*.

libertine /'lɪbəti:n/ *noun* licentious person.

liberty /'lɪbətɪ/ *noun* (*plural* **-ies**) being free, freedom; right or power to do as one pleases; (in *plural*) privileges granted by authority. □ **at liberty** free, (+ *to do*) permitted; **take liberties** (often + *with*) behave in unacceptably familiar way.

libidinous /lɪ'bɪdɪnəs/ *adjective* lustful.

libido /lɪ'bi:dəʊ/ *noun* (*plural* **-s**) psychic impulse or drive, esp. that associated with sex instinct. □ **libidinal** /lɪ'bɪdɪn(ə)l/ *adjective*.

Libra /'li:brə/ *noun* seventh sign of zodiac.

librarian /laɪ'breərɪən/ *noun* person in charge of or assistant in library. □ **librarianship** *noun*.

library /'laɪbrərɪ/ *noun* (*plural* **-ies**) a collection of books, films, records, etc.; room or building etc. where these are kept; series of books issued in similar bindings.

libretto /lɪ'bretəʊ/ *noun* (*plural* **-ti** /-tɪ/ or **-s**) text of opera etc. □ **librettist** *noun*.

lice *plural* of LOUSE.

licence /'laɪs(ə)ns/ *noun* (*US* **license**) official permit to own, use, or do, something, or carry on trade; permission; excessive liberty of action; writer's etc. deliberate deviation from fact.

license /'laɪs(ə)ns/ ● *verb* (**-sing**) grant licence to; authorize use of (premises) for certain purpose. ● *noun US* = LICENCE.

licensee /laɪsən'si:/ *noun* holder of licence, esp. to sell alcoholic liquor.

licentiate /laɪ'senʃɪət/ *noun* holder of certificate of professional competence.

licentious /laɪ'senʃəs/ *adjective* sexually promiscuous.

lichee = LYCHEE.

lichen /'laɪkən/ *noun* plant composed of fungus and alga in association, growing on rocks, trees, etc.

lich-gate /'lɪtʃgeɪt/ *noun* (also **lychgate**) roofed gateway of churchyard.

licit /'lɪsɪt/ *adjective formal* lawful, permitted.

lick ● *verb* pass tongue over; bring into specified condition by licking; (of flame etc.) play lightly over; *colloquial* thrash, defeat. ● *noun* act of licking with tongue; *colloquial* pace, speed; smart blow. □ **lick one's lips, chops** look forward with great pleasure.

licorice = LIQUORICE.

lid *noun* hinged or removable cover, esp. at top of container; eyelid. □ **put the lid on** *colloquial* be the culmination of, put stop to. □ **lidded** *adjective*.

lido /'li:dəʊ/ *noun* (*plural* **-s**) public open-air swimming pool or bathing beach.

lie[1] /laɪ/ ● *verb* (**lying**; *past* **lay**; *past participle* **lain**) be in or assume horizontal position on supporting surface; (of thing) rest on flat surface; remain undisturbed or undiscussed; be kept, remain, or be in specified place etc.; (of abstract things) be in certain relation; be situated or spread out to view etc. ● *noun* way, position, or direction in which something lies. □ **lie in** stay in bed late in morning; **lie-in** *noun*; **lie low** keep quiet or unseen; **lie of the land** state of affairs.

■ **Usage** It is incorrect in standard English to use *lie* to mean 'lay', as in *lie her on the bed*.

lie[2] /laɪ/ ● *noun* intentional false statement; something that deceives. ● *verb* (**lies**, **lied**, **lying**) tell lie(s); (of thing) be deceptive. □ **give the lie to** show the falsity of.

lied /li:d/ *noun* (*plural* **lieder**) German song of Romantic period for voice and piano.

liege /li:dʒ/ *historical* ● *adjective* entitled to receive, or bound to give, feudal service or allegiance. ● *noun* (in full **liege lord**) feudal superior; (usually in *plural*) vassal, subject.

lien /'li:ən/ *noun Law* right to hold another's property till debt on it is paid.

lieu /lju:/ *noun* □ **in lieu** instead; (+ *of*) in place of.

Lieut. *abbreviation* Lieutenant.

lieutenant /lef'tenənt/ *noun* army officer next below captain; naval officer next below lieutenant commander; deputy. □ **lieutenant colonel**, **commander**, **general** officers ranking next below colonel etc. □ **lieutenancy** *noun* (*plural* **-ies**).

life *noun* (*plural* **lives**) capacity for growth, functional activity, and continual change until death; living things and their activity; period during which life lasts; period from birth to present time or from present time to death; duration of thing's existence or ability to function; person's state of existence; living person; business and pleasures of the world; energy, liveliness; biography; *colloquial* imprisonment for life. □ **life assurance** life insurance; **lifebelt** buoyant ring to keep person afloat; **lifeblood** blood as necessary to life, vital factor or influence; **lifeboat** boat for rescues at sea, ship's boat for emergency use; **lifebuoy** buoyant support to keep person afloat; **life cycle** series of changes in life of organism; **lifeguard** expert swimmer employed to rescue bathers from drowning; **Life Guards** regiment of royal household cavalry; **life insurance** insurance which makes payment on death of insured person; **life-jacket** buoyant jacket to keep person afloat; **lifeline** rope etc. used for life-saving, sole means of communication or transport; **life peer** peer whose title lapses on death; **life sentence** imprisonment for life; **life-size(d)** of same size as person or thing represented; **lifestyle** way of life; **life-support machine** respirator; **lifetime** duration of person's life.

lifeless *adjective* dead; unconscious; lacking movement or vitality. □ **lifelessly** *adverb*.

lifelike *adjective* closely resembling life or person or thing represented.

lifer *noun slang* person serving life sentence.

lift ● *verb* (often + *up*, *of*, etc.) raise to higher position, go up, be raised; yield to upward force; give upward direction to (eyes etc.); add interest to; (of fog etc.) rise, disperse; remove (barrier etc.); transport supplies, troops, etc. by air; *colloquial* steal, plagiarize. ● *noun* lifting; ride in another person's vehicle; apparatus for raising and lowering people or things to different floors of building, or for carrying people up or down mountain etc.; transport by air; upward pressure on aerofoil; supporting or elevating influence; elated feeling. □ **lift-off** vertical take-off of spacecraft or rocket.

ligament /'lɪgəmənt/ *noun* band of tough fibrous tissue linking bones.

ligature /'lɪgətʃə/ *noun* tie, bandage; *Music* slur, tie; *Printing* two or more letters joined, e.g. æ.

■ **Usage** *Ligature*, in the *Printing* sense, is sometimes confused with *digraph*, which means 'two letters representing one sound'.

light[1] /laɪt/ ● *noun* electromagnetic radiation that stimulates sight and makes things visible; appearance of brightness; source of light; (often in *plural*) traffic light; flame, spark, or device for igniting; aspect in which thing is regarded; mental or spiritual illumination; vivacity, esp. in person's eyes. ● *verb* (*past* **lit**; *past participle* **lit** or **lighted**) set burning, begin to burn; (often + *up*) give light to; make prominent by light; show (person) way etc. with light; (usually + *up*) (of face or eyes) brighten with pleasure etc. ● *adjective* well-provided with light, not dark; (of colour) pale. □ **bring** or **come to light** reveal or be revealed; **in the light of** taking account of; **light bulb** glass bulb containing metal filament giving light when current is passed through it; **lighthouse** tower with beacon light to warn or guide ships at sea; **lightship** anchored ship with beacon light; **light year** distance light travels in one year.

light[2] /laɪt/ ● *adjective* not heavy; relatively low in weight, amount, density, or intensity; (of railway) suitable for small loads; carrying only light arms; (of food) easy to digest; (of music etc.) intended only as entertainment, not profound; (of sleep or sleeper) easily disturbed; easily done; nimble; cheerful. ● *adverb* lightly; with light load. ● *verb* (*past & past participle* **lit** or **lighted**) (+ *on*, *upon*) come upon or find by chance. □ **light-fingered** given to stealing; **light flyweight** amateur boxing weight (up to 48 kg); **light-headed** giddy, delirious; **light-hearted** cheerful; **light heavyweight** amateur boxing weight (75–81 kg); **light industry** manufacture of small or light articles; **light middleweight** amateur boxing weight (67–71 kg); **lightweight** *adjective* below average weight, of little importance, *noun* lightweight person or thing, amateur boxing weight (57–60kg); **light welterweight** amateur boxing weight (60–63.5 kg). □ **lightly** *adverb*; **lightness** *noun*.

lighten[1] *verb* make or become lighter in weight; reduce weight or load of.

lighten[2] *verb* shed light on, make or grow bright.

lighter[1] *noun* device for lighting cigarettes etc.

lighter[2] *noun* boat for transporting goods between ship and wharf etc.

lightning /ˈlaɪtnɪŋ/ *noun* flash of light produced by electric discharge between clouds or between clouds and ground. □ **lightning-conductor** metal rod or wire fixed to building or mast to divert lightning to earth or sea.

lights *plural noun* lungs of sheep, pigs, etc. as food, esp. for pets.

ligneous /ˈlɪgnɪəs/ *adjective* of the nature of wood.

lignite /ˈlɪgnaɪt/ *noun* brown coal of woody texture.

lignum vitae /lɪgnəm ˈvaɪtɪ/ *noun* a hard-wooded tree.

like[1] ● *adjective* (**more like**, **most like**) similar to another, each other, or original; resembling; such as; characteristic of; in suitable state or mood for. ● *preposition* in manner of, to same degree as. ● *adverb slang* so to speak; *colloquial* probably. ● *conjunction colloquial* as, as if (see note below). ● *noun* counterpart, equal; similar person or thing.

■ **Usage** It is incorrect in standard English to use *like* as a conjunction, as in *Tell it like it is* or *He's spending money like it was going out of fashion*.

like[2] ● *verb* (**-king**) find agreeable or enjoyable; feel attracted by, choose to have, prefer. ● *noun* (in *plural*) things one likes or prefers.

likeable *adjective* (also **likable**) pleasant, easy to like. □ **likeably** *adverb*.

likelihood /ˈlaɪklɪhʊd/ *noun* probability.

likely /ˈlaɪklɪ/ ● *adjective* (**-ier**, **-iest**) probable; such as may well happen or be true; to be expected; promising, apparently suitable. ● *adverb* probably. □ **not likely!** *colloquial* certainly not.

liken *verb* (+ *to*) point out resemblance between (person, thing) and (another).

likeness *noun* (usually + *between*, *to*) resemblance; (+ *of*) semblance, guise; portrait, representation.

likewise *adverb* also, moreover; similarly.

liking *noun* what one likes; one's taste; (+ *for*) fondness, taste, fancy.

lilac /ˈlaɪlək/ ● *noun* shrub with fragrant pinkish-violet or white flowers; pale pinkish-violet colour. ● *adjective* of this colour.

liliaceous /lɪlɪˈeɪʃəs/ *adjective* of the lily family.

lilliputian /lɪlɪˈpjuːʃ(ə)n/ ● *noun* diminutive person or thing. ● *adjective* diminutive.

lilt ● *noun* light springing rhythm; tune with this. ● *verb* (esp. as **lilting** *adjective*) speak etc. with lilt.

lily /ˈlɪlɪ/ *noun* (*plural* **-ies**) tall bulbous plant with large trumpet-shaped flowers; heraldic fleur-de-lis. □ **lily of the valley** plant with fragrant white bell-shaped flowers.

limb[1] /lɪm/ *noun* leg, arm, wing; large branch of tree; branch of cross. □ **out on a limb** isolated.

limb[2] /lɪm/ *noun* specified edge of sun, moon, etc.

limber[1] /ˈlɪmbə/ ● *adjective* lithe, flexible; agile. ● *verb* (usually + *up*) make oneself supple; warm up for athletic etc. activity.

limber[2] /ˈlɪmbə/ ● *noun* detachable front of gun-carriage. ● *verb* attach limber to.

limbo[1] /ˈlɪmbəʊ/ *noun* (*plural* **-s**) supposed abode of souls of unbaptized infants, and of the just who died before Christ; intermediate state or condition of awaiting decision.

limbo[2] /ˈlɪmbəʊ/ *noun* (*plural* **-s**) W. Indian dance in which dancer bends backwards to pass under progressively lowered horizontal bar.

lime[1] ● *noun* white caustic substance got by heating limestone. ● *verb* (**-ming**) treat with lime. □ **limekiln** kiln for heating limestone. □ **limy** *adjective* (**-ier**, **-iest**).

lime[2] *noun* round green acid fruit; tree producing this fruit. □ **lime-green** yellowish-green colour.

lime[3] *noun* (in full **lime tree**) tree with heart-shaped leaves and fragrant creamy blossom.

limelight *noun* intense white light used formerly in theatres; glare of publicity.

limerick /ˈlɪmərɪk/ *noun* humorous 5-line verse.

limestone *noun* rock composed mainly of calcium carbonate.

limit /ˈlɪmɪt/ ● *noun* point, line, or level beyond which something does not or may not extend or pass; greatest or smallest amount permitted. ● *verb* (**-t-**) set or serve as limit to; (+ *to*) restrict to. □ **limitless** *adjective*.

limitation /lɪmɪˈteɪʃ(ə)n/ *noun* limiting, being limited; limit of ability; limiting circumstance.

limn /lɪm/ *verb archaic* paint.

limousine /lɪmʊˈziːn/ *noun* large luxurious car.

limp[1] ● *verb* walk or proceed lamely or awkwardly. ● *noun* lame walk.

limp[2] *adjective* not stiff or firm; without will or energy. □ **limply** *adverb*; **limpness** *noun*.

limpet /ˈlɪmpɪt/ *noun* mollusc with conical shell sticking tightly to rocks.

limpid /ˈlɪmpɪd/ *adjective* clear, transparent. □ **limpidity** /-ˈpɪd-/ *noun*.

linage /ˈlaɪnɪdʒ/ *noun* number of lines in printed or written page etc.; payment by the line.

linchpin /ˈlɪntʃpɪn/ *noun* pin passed through axle-end to keep wheel on; person or thing vital to organization etc.

linctus /ˈlɪŋktəs/ *noun* syrupy medicine, esp. soothing cough mixture.

linden /ˈlɪnd(ə)n/ *noun* = LIME TREE.

line[1] ● *noun* continuous mark made on surface; furrow, wrinkle; use of lines in art; straight or curved track of moving point; outline; limit, boundary; row of persons or things; *US* queue; mark defining area of play or start or finish of race; row of printed or written words; portion of verse written in line; (in *plural*) piece of poetry, words of actor's part; length of cord, rope, etc. serving specified purpose; wire or cable for telephone or telegraph; connection by means of this; single track or branch of railway; regular succession of buses, ships, aircraft, etc., plying between certain places, company conducting this; several generations (of family); stock; manner of procedure, conduct, thought, etc.; channel; department of activity, branch of business; type of product; connected series of military field works, arrangement of soldiers or ships side by side; each of very narrow horizontal sections forming television picture. ● *verb* (**-ning**) mark with lines; position or stand at intervals along. □ **line printer** machine that prints computer output a line at a time; **linesman** umpire's or referee's assistant who decides whether ball has fallen within playing area or not; **line up** *verb* arrange or be arranged in lines, have ready; **line-up** *noun* line of people for inspection, arrangement of team, band, etc.

line[2] *verb* (**-ning**) apply layer of usually different material to cover inside of (garment, box, etc.); serve as lining for; *colloquial* fill (purse etc.).

lineage /ˈlɪnɪɪdʒ/ *noun* lineal descent, ancestry.

lineal /ˈlɪnɪəl/ *adjective* in direct line of descent or ancestry; linear. □ **lineally** *adverb*.

lineament /ˈlɪnɪəmənt/ *noun* (usually in *plural*) distinctive feature or characteristic, esp. of face.

linear /ˈlɪnɪə/ *adjective* of or in lines; long and narrow and of uniform breadth.

linen /ˈlɪnɪn/ ● *noun* cloth woven from flax; articles made or originally made of linen, as sheets, shirts, underwear, etc. ● *adjective* made of linen.

liner[1] *noun* ship or aircraft carrying passengers on regular line.

liner[2] *noun* removable lining.

ling[1] *noun* (*plural* same) long slender marine fish.

ling[2] *noun* kind of heather.

linger /ˈlɪŋgə/ *verb* stay about; (+ *over*, *on*, etc.) dally; be protracted; (often + *on*) die slowly.

lingerie /ˈlæʒərɪ/ *noun* women's underwear and nightclothes.

lingo /ˈlɪŋgəʊ/ *noun* (*plural* **-s** or **-es**) *colloquial* foreign language.

lingual /ˈlɪŋgw(ə)l/ *adjective* of tongue; of speech or languages.

linguist /ˈlɪŋgwɪst/ *noun* person skilled in languages or linguistics.

linguistic /lɪŋˈgwɪstɪk/ *adjective* of language or the study of languages. □ **linguistically** *adverb*.

linguistics *noun* study of language and its structure.

liniment /ˈlɪnɪmənt/ *noun* embrocation.

lining *noun* material used to line surface.

link ● *noun* one loop or ring of chain etc.; one in series; means of connection. ● *verb* (+ *together*, *to*, *with*) connect, join; clasp or intertwine (hands etc.).

linkage *noun* linking or being linked.

links *noun* (treated as *singular* or *plural*) golf course.

Linnaean /lɪˈniːən/ *adjective* of Linnaeus or his system of classifying plants and animals.

linnet /ˈlɪnɪt/ *noun* brown-grey finch.

lino /ˈlaɪnəʊ/ *noun* (*plural* **-s**) linoleum. □ **linocut** design carved in relief on block of linoleum, print made from this.

linoleum /lɪˈnəʊlɪəm/ *noun* canvas-backed material coated with linseed oil, cork, etc.

linseed /ˈlɪnsiːd/ *noun* seed of flax.

lint *noun* linen or cotton with one side made fluffy, used for dressing wounds; fluff.

lintel /ˈlɪnt(ə)l/ *noun* horizontal timber, stone, etc. over door or window.

lion /ˈlaɪən/ *noun* (*feminine* **lioness**) large tawny flesh-eating wild cat of Africa and S. Asia; brave or celebrated person.

lionize *verb* (also **-ise**) (**-zing** or **-sing**) treat as celebrity.

lip *noun* either edge of opening of mouth; edge of cup, vessel, cavity, etc., esp. part shaped for pouring from; *colloquial* impudent talk. □ **lip-read** understand (speech) by observing speaker's lip-movements; **lip-service** insincere expression of support; **lipstick** stick of cosmetic for colouring lips.

liquefy /ˈlɪkwɪfaɪ/ *verb* (**-ies**, **-ied**) make or become liquid. □ **liquefaction** /-ˈfækʃ(ə)n/ *noun*.

liqueur /lɪˈkjʊə/ *noun* any of several strong sweet alcoholic spirits.

liquid /ˈlɪkwɪd/ ● *adjective* having consistency like that of water or oil, flowing freely but of constant volume; having appearance of water; (of sounds) clear, pure; (of assets) easily convertible into cash. ● *noun* liquid substance; *Phonetics* sound of *l* or *r*. □ **liquid crystal** liquid in state approaching that of crystalline solid; **liquid crystal display** visual display in some electronic devices.

liquidate /ˈlɪkwɪdeɪt/ *verb* (**-ting**) wind up affairs of (firm etc.); pay off (debt); wipe out; kill. □ **liquidator** *noun*.

liquidation /lɪkwɪˈdeɪʃ(ə)n/ *noun* liquidating, esp. of firm. □ **go into liquidation** be wound up and have assets apportioned.

liquidity /lɪˈkwɪdɪtɪ/ *noun* (*plural* **-ies**) state of being liquid; having liquid assets.

liquidize *verb* (also **-ise**) (**-zing** or **-sing**) reduce to liquid state.

liquidizer *noun* (also **-iser**) machine for liquidizing foods.

liquor /ˈlɪkə/ *noun* alcoholic (esp. distilled) drink; other liquid, esp. that produced in cooking.

liquorice /ˈlɪkərɪs/ *noun* (also **licorice**) black root extract used as sweet and in medicine; plant from which it is obtained.

lira /ˈlɪərə/ *noun* chief monetary unit of Italy (*plural* **lire** /-rɪ/) and Turkey (*plural* **-s**).

lisle /laɪl/ *noun* fine cotton thread for stockings etc.

lisp ● *noun* speech defect in which *s* is pronounced like *th* in *thick* and *z* like *th* in *this*. ● *verb* speak or utter with lisp.

lissom /ˈlɪsəm/ *adjective* lithe, agile.

list[1] ● *noun* number of items, names, etc. written or printed together as record; (in *plural*) palisades enclosing tournament area. ● *verb* arrange as or enter in list; (as **listed** *adjective*) approved for Stock Exchange dealings, (of a building) of historical importance and officially protected. □ **enter the lists** issue or accept challenge.

list[2] ● *verb* (of ship etc.) lean over to one side. ● *noun* listing position, tilt.

listen /ˈlɪs(ə)n/ *verb* make effort to hear something, attentively hear person speaking; (+ *to*) give attention with ear to, take notice of. □ **listen in** tap telephonic communication, use radio receiving set. □ **listener** *noun*.

listless /ˈlɪstlɪs/ *adjective* lacking energy or enthusiasm. □ **listlessly** *adverb*; **listlessness** *noun*.

lit *past & past participle of* LIGHT[1,2].

litany /ˈlɪtənɪ/ *noun* (*plural* **-ies**) series of supplications to God used in church services; (**the Litany**) that in Book of Common Prayer.

litchi = LYCHEE.

liter *US* = LITRE.

literacy /ˈlɪtərəsɪ/ *noun* ability to read and write.

literal /ˈlɪtər(ə)l/ *adjective* taking words in their basic sense without metaphor etc.; corresponding exactly to original words; prosaic; matter-of-fact. □ **literalism** *noun*; **literally** *adverb*.

literary /ˈlɪtərərɪ/ *adjective* of or concerned with or interested in literature.

literate /ˈlɪtərət/ ● *adjective* able to read and write. ● *noun* literate person.

literati /lɪtəˈrɑːtɪ/ *plural noun* the class of learned people.

literature /ˈlɪtərətʃə/ *noun* written works, esp. those valued for form and style; writings of country or period or on particular subject; *colloquial* printed matter, leaflets, etc.

lithe /laɪð/ *adjective* flexible, supple.

litho /ˈlaɪθəʊ/ *colloquial* ● *noun* lithography. ● *verb* (**-oes**, **-oed**) lithograph.

lithograph /ˈlɪθəgrɑːf/ ● *noun* lithographic print. ● *verb* print by lithography.

lithography /lɪˈθɒgrəfɪ/ *noun* process of printing from plate so treated that ink sticks only to design to be printed. □ **lithographer** *noun*; **lithographic** /lɪθəˈgræfɪk/ *adjective*.

Lithuanian /lɪθjuːˈeɪnɪən/ ● *noun* native, national, or language of Lithuania. ● *adjective* of Lithuania.

litigant /ˈlɪtɪgənt/ ● *noun* party to lawsuit. ● *adjective* engaged in lawsuit.

litigate /ˈlɪtɪgeɪt/ *verb* (**-ting**) go to law; contest (point) at law. □ **litigation** *noun*; **litigator** *noun*.

litigious /lɪˈtɪdʒəs/ *adjective* fond of litigation; contentious.

litmus /ˈlɪtməs/ *noun* dye turned red by acid and blue by alkali.

litre /ˈliːtə/ *noun* (*US* **liter**) metric unit of capacity (1.76 pints).

litter /ˈlɪtə/ ● *noun* refuse, esp. paper, discarded in public place, odds and ends lying about; young animals brought forth at one birth; vehicle containing couch and carried on men's shoulders or by animals; kind of stretcher for sick and wounded; straw etc. as bedding for animals; material for animal's, esp. cat's, indoor toilet. ● *verb* make (place) untidy; give birth to (puppies etc.); provide (horse etc.) with bedding.

little /ˈlɪt(ə)l/ ● *adjective* (**-r**, **-st**; **less** or **lesser**, **least**) small in size, amount, degree, etc.; short in stature; of short distance or duration; (**a little**) certain but small amount of; trivial; only small amount; operating on small scale; humble, ordinary; young, younger. ● *noun* not much, only small amount; short time or distance. ● *adverb* (**less**, **least**) to small extent only; not at all. □ **little by little** by degrees, gradually; **the little people** fairies.

littoral /ˈlɪtər(ə)l/ ● *adjective* of or on the shore. ● *noun* region lying along shore.

liturgy /ˈlɪtədʒɪ/ *noun* (*plural* **-ies**) fixed form of public worship; (**the Liturgy**) the Book of Common Prayer. □ **liturgical** /-ˈtɜːdʒ-/ *adjective*.

live[1] /lɪv/ *verb* (**-ving**) have life; be or remain alive; have one's home; (+ *on*, *off*) subsist or feed on; keep one's position; pass, spend; conduct oneself in specified way; enjoy life to the full. □ **live down** cause (scandal etc.) to be forgotten through blameless behaviour thereafter; **live it up** *colloquial* live exuberantly and extravagantly.

live[2] /laɪv/ ● *adjective* that is alive, living; (of broadcast, performance, etc.) heard or seen while happening or with audience present; of current interest; glowing, burning; (of match, bomb, etc.) not yet kindled or exploded; charged with electricity. ● *adverb* as live performance. □ **livestock** (usually treated as *plural*) animals kept on farm for use or profit; **live wire** spirited person.

liveable /ˈlɪvəb(ə)l/ *adjective* (also **livable**) *colloquial* (usually **liveable-in**) (of house etc.) fit to live in; (of life) worth living; *colloquial* (usually **liveable-with**) (of person) easy to live with.

livelihood /ˈlaɪvlɪhʊd/ *noun* means of living; job, income.

livelong /ˈlɪvlɒŋ/ *adjective* in its entire length.

lively /ˈlaɪvlɪ/ *adjective* (**-ier**, **-iest**) full of life, energetic; (of imagination) vivid; cheerful; *jocular* exciting, dangerous. □ **liveliness** *noun*.

liven /ˈlaɪv(ə)n/ *verb* (often + *up*) make or become lively, cheer up.

liver[1] /ˈlɪvə/ *noun* large glandular organ in abdomen of vertebrates; liver of some animals as food.

liver[2] /ˈlɪvə/ *noun* person who lives in specified way.

liverish /ˈlɪvərɪʃ/ *adjective* suffering from liver disorder; peevish, glum.

liverwort *noun* mosslike plant sometimes lobed like liver.

livery /ˈlɪvərɪ/ *noun* (*plural* **-ies**) distinctive uniform of member of City Company or servant; distinctive guise or marking; distinctive colour scheme for company's vehicles etc. □ **at livery** (of horse) kept for owner at fixed charge; **livery stable** stable where horses are kept at livery or let out for hire.

lives *plural of* LIFE.

livid /ˈlɪvɪd/ *adjective colloquial* furious; of bluish leaden colour.

living /ˈlɪvɪŋ/ ● *noun* being alive; livelihood; position held by clergyman, providing income. ● *adjective* contemporary; now alive; (of likeness) exact; (of language) still in vernacular use. □ **living-room** room for general day use; **living wage** wage on which one can live without privation; **within living memory** within memory of living people.

lizard /ˈlɪzəd/ *noun* reptile with usually long body and tail, 4 legs, and scaly hide.

llama /ˈlɑːmə/ *noun* S. American ruminant kept as beast of burden and for woolly fleece.

Lloyd's /lɔɪdz/ *noun* incorporated society of underwriters in London. □ **Lloyd's Register** annual classified list of all ships.

lo *interjection archaic* look.

loach *noun* (*plural* same or **-es**) small freshwater fish.

load ● *noun* what is (to be) carried; amount usually or actually carried; burden of work, responsibility, care, etc.; (in *plural*; often + *of*) plenty; (**a load of**) a quantity of; amount of power carried by electrical circuit or supplied by generating station. ● *verb* put load on or aboard; place (load) aboard ship or on vehicle etc.; (often + *up*) (of vehicle or person) take load aboard; (often + *with*) burden, strain, overwhelm; put ammunition in (gun), film in (camera), cassette in (tape recorder), program in (computer), etc. □ **load line** Plimsoll line.

loaded *adjective slang* rich, drunk, *US* drugged; (of dice etc.) weighted; (of question or statement) carrying hidden implication.

loadstone = LODESTONE.

loaf[1] *noun* (*plural* **loaves**) unit of baked bread, usually of standard size or shape; other cooked food in loaf shape; *slang* head.

loaf[2] *verb* (often + *about*) spend time idly, hang about.

loam *noun* rich soil of clay, sand, and humus. □ **loamy** *adjective*.

loan ● *noun* thing lent, esp. money; lending, being lent. ● *verb* lend (money, works of art, etc.). □ **on loan** being lent.

loath *adjective* (also **loth**) disinclined, reluctant.

loathe /ləʊð/ *verb* (**-thing**) detest, hate. □ **loathing** *noun*.

loathsome /'ləʊðsəm/ *adjective* arousing hatred or disgust; repulsive.

loaves *plural* of LOAF[1].

lob ● *verb* (**-bb-**) hit or throw (ball etc.) slowly or in high arc. ● *noun* such ball.

lobar /'ləʊbə/ *adjective* of a lobe, esp. of lung.

lobate /'ləʊbeɪt/ *adjective* having lobe(s).

lobby /'lɒbɪ/ ● *noun* (*plural* **-ies**) porch, ante-room, entrance hall, corridor; (in House of Commons) large hall used esp. for interviews between MPs and the public; (also **division lobby**) each of two corridors to which MPs retire to vote; group of lobbyists. ● *verb* (**-ies**, **-ied**) solicit support of (influential person); inform (legislators etc.) in order to influence them. □ **lobby correspondent** journalist who receives unattributable briefings from government.

lobbyist *noun* person who lobbies MP etc.

lobe *noun* lower soft pendulous part of outer ear; similar part of other organs. □ **lobed** *adjective*.

lobelia /lə'bi:lɪə/ *noun* plant with bright, esp. blue, flowers.

lobotomy /lə'bɒtəmɪ/ *noun* (*plural* **-ies**) incision into frontal lobe of brain to relieve mental disorder.

lobster /'lɒbstə/ *noun* marine crustacean with two pincer-like claws; its flesh as food. □ **lobster pot** basket for trapping lobsters.

lobworm *noun* large earthworm used as fishing bait.

local /'ləʊk(ə)l/ ● *adjective* belonging to, existing in, or peculiar to particular place; of the neighbourhood; of or affecting a part and not the whole; (of telephone call) to nearby place and at lower charge. ● *noun* inhabitant of particular place; (often **the local**) *colloquial* local public house. □ **local authority** administrative body in local government; **local colour** touches of detail in story etc. designed to provide realistic background; **local government** system of administration of county, district, parish, etc. by elected representatives of those who live there. □ **locally** *adverb*.

locale /ləʊ'kɑ:l/ *noun* scene or locality of event or occurrence.

locality /ləʊ'kælɪtɪ/ *noun* (*plural* **-ies**) district; thing's site or scene; thing's position.

localize /'ləʊkəlaɪz/ *verb* (also **-ise**) (**-zing** or **-sing**) restrict or assign to particular place; invest with characteristics of place; decentralize.

locate /ləʊ'keɪt/ *verb* (**-ting**) discover exact place of; establish in a place, situate; state locality of.

■ **Usage** In standard English, it is incorrect to use *locate* to mean merely 'find' as in *I can't locate my key*.

location *noun* particular place; locating; natural, not studio, setting for film etc.

loc. cit. *abbreviation* in the passage cited (*loco citato*).

loch /lɒx, lɒk/ *noun* Scottish lake or narrow inlet of the sea.

lock[1] ● *noun* mechanism for fastening door etc. with bolt requiring key of particular shape; section of canal or river confined within sluice-gates for moving boats from one level to another; turning of vehicle's front wheels; interlocked or jammed state; wrestling hold. ● *verb* fasten with lock; (+ *up*) shut (house etc.) thus; (of door etc.) be lockable; (+ *up*, *in*, *into*) enclose (person, thing) by locking; (often + *up*, *away*) store inaccessibly; make or become rigidly fixed; (cause to) jam or catch. □ **lockjaw** form of tetanus in which jaws become rigidly closed; **lock-keeper** keeper of river or canal lock; **lock on to** (of missile etc.) automatically find and then track (target); **lock out** *verb* keep out by locking door, (of employer) subject (employees) to lockout; **lockout** *noun* employer's exclusion of employees from workplace until certain terms are accepted; **locksmith** maker and mender of locks; **lock-up** house or room for temporary detention of prisoners, premises that can be locked up. □ **lockable** *adjective*.

lock[2] *noun* portion of hair that hangs together; (in *plural*) the hair.

locker *noun* (usually lockable) cupboard, esp. for public use.

locket /'lɒkɪt/ *noun* small ornamental case for portrait etc., usually on chain round neck.

locomotion /ləʊkə'məʊʃ(ə)n/ *noun* motion or power of motion from place to place.

locomotive /ləʊkə'məʊtɪv/ ● *noun* engine for pulling trains. ● *adjective* of, having, or bringing about locomotion.

locum tenens /ləʊkəm 'ti:nenz/ *noun* (*plural* **locum tenentes** /tɪ'nenti:z/) (also *colloquial* **locum**) deputy acting esp. for doctor or member of clergy.

locus /'ləʊkəs/ *noun* (*plural* **loci** /-saɪ/) position, place; line or curve etc. made by all points satisfying certain conditions or by defined motion of point, line, or surface.

locust /'ləʊkəst/ *noun* African or Asian grasshopper migrating in swarms and consuming all vegetation.

locution /lə'kju:ʃ(ə)n/ *noun* phrase, word, or idiom; style of speech.

lode *noun* vein of metal ore. □ **lodestar** star used as guide in navigation, esp. pole star; **lodestone**, **loadstone** magnetic oxide of iron, piece of this as magnet.

lodge ● *noun* small house, esp. one for gatekeeper at entrance to park or grounds of large house; porter's room etc.; members or meeting-place of branch of society such as Freemasons; beaver's or otter's lair. ● *verb* (**-ging**) reside, esp. as lodger; provide with sleeping quarters; submit (complaint etc.); become fixed or caught; deposit for security; settle, place.

lodger *noun* person paying for accommodation in another's house.

lodging *noun* temporary accommodation; (in *plural*) room(s) rented for lodging in.

loft ● *noun* attic; room over stable; gallery in church or hall; pigeon house. ● *verb* send (ball etc.) high up.

lofty *adjective* (**-ier**, **-iest**) of imposing height; haughty, aloof; exalted, noble. □ **loftily** *adverb*; **loftiness** *noun*.

log[1] ● *noun* unhewn piece of felled tree; any large rough piece of wood; *historical* floating device for ascertaining ship's speed; record of ship's or aircraft's voyage; any systematic record of experiences etc. ● *verb* (**-gg-**) enter (ship's speed or other transport details) in logbook; enter (data etc.) in regular record; cut into logs. □ **logbook** book containing record or log, vehicle registration document; **log on** or **off**, **log in** or **out** begin or end operations at terminal of esp. multi-access computer.

log[2] *noun* logarithm.

logan /'ləʊgən/ *noun* (in full **logan-stone**) poised heavy stone rocking at a touch.

loganberry /'ləʊgənbərɪ/ *noun* (*plural* **-ies**) dark red fruit, hybrid of blackberry and raspberry.

logarithm /'lɒgərɪð(ə)m/ *noun* an arithmetic exponent used in computation. □ **logarithmic** /-'rɪðmɪk/ *adjective*.

loggerhead /ˈlɒgəhed/ *noun* ◻ **at loggerheads** (often + *with*) disagreeing or disputing.
loggia /ˈləʊdʒə/ *noun* open-sided gallery or arcade.
logging *noun* work of cutting and preparing forest timber.
logic /ˈlɒdʒɪk/ *noun* science of reasoning; chain of reasoning; use of or ability in argument; inexorable force; principles used in designing computer etc. circuits based on these. ◻ **logician** /ləˈdʒɪʃ(ə)n/ *noun*.
logical *adjective* of or according to logic; correctly reasoned, consistent; capable of correct reasoning. ◻ **logicality** /-ˈkæl-/ *noun*; **logically** *adverb*.
logistics /ləˈdʒɪstɪks/ *plural noun* organization of (originally military) services and supplies. ◻ **logistic** *adjective*; **logistical** *adjective*; **logistically** *adverb*.
logo /ˈləʊgəʊ/ *noun* (*plural* **-s**) organization's emblem used in display material.
loin *noun* (in *plural*) side and back of body between ribs and hip-bones; joint of meat from this part of animal. ◻ **loincloth** cloth worn round hips, esp. as sole garment.
loiter /ˈlɔɪtə/ *verb* stand about idly; linger. ◻ **loiter with intent** linger to commit felony.
loll *verb* stand, sit, or recline in lazy attitude; hang loosely.
lollipop /ˈlɒlɪpɒp/ *noun* hard sweet on stick. ◻ **lollipop man, lady** *colloquial* warden using circular sign on pole to stop traffic for children to cross road.
lollop /ˈlɒləp/ *verb* (**-p-**) *colloquial* flop about; move in ungainly bounds.
lolly /ˈlɒlɪ/ *noun* (*plural* **-ies**) *colloquial* lollipop; ice lolly; *slang* money.
lone *adjective* solitary; without companions; isolated; unmarried. ◻ **lone hand** hand played or player playing against the rest at cards, person or action without allies; **lone wolf** loner.
lonely /ˈləʊnlɪ/ *adjective* (**-ier**, **-iest**) without companions; sad because of this; isolated; uninhabited. ◻ **loneliness** *noun*.
loner *noun* person or animal preferring to be alone.
lonesome *adjective esp. US* lonely; causing loneliness.
long[1] ● *adjective* (**longer** /ˈlɒŋgə/, **longest** /ˈlɒŋgɪst/) measuring much from end to end in space or time; (following measurement) in length or duration; consisting of many items; tedious; of elongated shape; reaching far back or forward in time; involving great interval or difference. ● *noun* long interval or period. ● *adverb* (**longer** /ˈlɒŋgə/, **longest** /ˈlɒŋgɪst/) by or for a long time; (following nouns of duration) throughout specified time; (in *comparative*) after implied point of time. ◻ **as, so long as** provided that; **before long** soon; **in the long run** eventually; **longboat** sailing ship's largest boat; **longbow** one drawn by hand and shooting long arrow; **long-distance** travelling or operating between distant places; **long face** dismal expression; **longhand** ordinary handwriting; **long johns** *colloquial* long underpants; **long jump** athletic contest of jumping along ground in one leap; **long-life** (of milk etc.) treated to prolong shelf-life; **long odds** chances with low probability; **long-playing** (of gramophone record) playing for about 20–30 minutes on each side; **long-range** having a long range, relating to period of time far into future; **longshore** existing on or frequenting the shore; **long shot** wild guess or venture; **long sight** ability to see clearly only what is comparatively distant; **long-sighted** having long sight, far-sighted; **long-suffering** bearing provocation patiently; **long-term** of or for long period of time; **long-winded** (of speech or writing) tediously lengthy.
long[2] *verb* (+ *for*, *to do*) have strong wish or desire for. ◻ **longing** *noun & adjective*; **longingly** *adverb*.
long. *abbreviation* longitude.
longevity /lɒnˈdʒevɪtɪ/ *noun formal* long life.
longitude /ˈlɒŋgɪtjuːd/ *noun* angular distance E. or W. of (esp. Greenwich) meridian.
longitudinal /lɒŋgɪˈtjuːdɪn(ə)l/ *adjective* of or in length; running lengthwise; of longitude. ◻ **longitudinally** *adverb*.
longways *adverb* (also **longwise**) in direction parallel with thing's length.
loo *noun colloquial* lavatory.
loofah /ˈluːfə/ *noun* rough bath-sponge made from dried pod of type of gourd.
look /lʊk/ ● *verb* (often + *at*, *down*, *up*, etc.) use or direct one's eyes; examine; make visual or mental search; (+ *at*) consider; (+ *for*) seek; have specified appearance, seem; (+ *into*) investigate; (of thing) face some direction; indicate (emotion) by looks; (+ *to do*) expect. ● *noun* act of looking; gaze, glance; appearance of face, expression; (in *plural*) personal appearance. ◻ **look after** attend to; **look back** (+ *on*, *to*) turn one's thoughts to (something past); **look down (up)on** regard with contempt; **look forward to** await (expected event) eagerly or with specified feelings; **look in** *verb* make short visit; **look-in** *noun colloquial* chance of participation or success; **looking-glass** mirror; **look on** be spectator; **look out** *verb* (often + *for*) be vigilant or prepared; **lookout** *noun* watch, observation-post, person etc. stationed to keep watch, prospect, *colloquial* person's own concern; **look up** search for (esp. information in book), *colloquial* visit (person), improve in prospect; **look up to** respect.
loom[1] /luːm/ *noun* apparatus for weaving.
loom[2] /luːm/ *verb* appear dimly, esp. as vague often threatening shape.
loon /luːn/ *noun* kind of diving bird; *colloquial* crazy person.
loony /ˈluːnɪ/ *slang* ● *noun* (*plural* **-ies**) lunatic. ● *adjective* (**-ier**, **-iest**) crazy.
loop /luːp/ ● *noun* figure produced by curve or doubled thread etc. crossing itself; thing, path, etc. forming this figure; similarly shaped attachment used as fastening; contraceptive coil; endless band of tape or film allowing continuous repetition; repeated sequence of computer operations. ● *verb* form or bend into loop; fasten with loop(s); form loop. ◻ **loop line** railway or telegraph line that diverges from main line and joins it again.
loophole *noun* means of evading rule etc. without infringing it; narrow vertical slit in wall of fort etc.
loopy *adjective* (**-ier**, **-iest**) *slang* crazy.
loose /luːs/ ● *adjective* not tightly held; free from bonds or restraint; not held together; not compact or dense; inexact; morally lax. ● *verb* (**-sing**) free; untie, detach; release; relax (hold etc.). ◻ **at a loose end** unoccupied; **let loose** release; **loose cover** removable cover for armchair etc.; **loose-leaf** (of notebook etc.) with pages that can be removed and replaced; **on the loose** escaped from captivity, enjoying oneself freely. ◻ **loosely** *adverb*.
loosen *verb* make or become loose or looser. ◻ **loosen up** relax.
loot /luːt/ ● *noun* spoil, booty; *slang* money. ● *verb* rob or steal, esp. after rioting etc.; plunder.
lop *verb* (**-pp-**) (often + *off*) cut or remove (part or parts) from whole, esp. branches from tree; prune (tree).
lope ● *verb* (**-ping**) run with long bounding stride. ● *noun* such stride.
lop-eared *adjective* having drooping ears.
lopsided *adjective* unevenly balanced.

loquacious /ləˈkweɪʃəs/ *adjective* talkative. □ **loquacity** /-ˈkwæsɪtɪ/ *noun*.

lord ● *noun* master, ruler; *historical* feudal superior, esp. of manor; peer of realm, person with title *Lord*; (**Lord**) (often **the Lord**) God, Christ; (**Lord**) *title used before name of certain male peers and officials*; (**the Lords**) House of Lords. ● *interjection expressing surprise, dismay, etc.* □ **lord it over** domineer; **Lord Mayor** *title of mayor in some large cities*; **Lord's Day** Sunday; **Lord's Prayer** the Our Father; **Lord's Supper** Eucharist.

lordly *adjective* (**-ier**, **-iest**) haughty, imperious; suitable for a lord.

Lordship *noun* □ **His**, **Your Lordship** *title used of or to man with rank of Lord*.

lore *noun* body of tradition and information on a subject or held by particular group.

lorgnette /lɔːˈnjet/ *noun* pair of eyeglasses or opera-glasses on long handle.

lorn *adjective archaic* desolate, forlorn.

lorry /ˈlɒrɪ/ *noun* (*plural* **-ies**) large vehicle for transporting goods etc.

lose /luːz/ *verb* (**-sing**; *past & past participle* **lost**) be deprived of; cease to have, esp. by negligence; be deprived of (person) by death; become unable to find, follow, or understand; let pass from one's control; be defeated in; get rid of; forfeit (right to something); suffer loss or detriment; cause (person) the loss of; (of clock etc.) become slow; (in *passive*) disappear, perish. □ **be lost without** be dependent on.

loser *noun* person or thing that loses esp. contest; *colloquial* person who regularly fails.

loss *noun* losing, being lost; what is lost; detriment resulting from losing. □ **at a loss** (sold etc.) for less than was paid for it; **be at a loss** be puzzled or uncertain; **loss-leader** item sold at a loss to attract customers.

lost *past & past participle* of LOSE.

lot *noun colloquial* (**a lot**, or **lots**) large number or amount; each of set of objects used to make chance selection; this method of deciding, share or responsibility resulting from it; destiny, fortune, condition; *esp. US* plot, allotment; article or set of articles for sale at auction etc.; group of associated people or things. □ **draw**, **cast lots** decide by lots; **the (whole) lot** total number or quantity.

■ **Usage** *A lot of*, as in *a lot of people*, is fairly informal, though acceptable in serious writing, but *lots of people* is not acceptable.

loth = LOATH.

lotion /ˈləʊʃ(ə)n/ *noun* medical or cosmetic liquid preparation applied externally.

lottery /ˈlɒtərɪ/ *noun* (*plural* **-ies**) means of raising money by selling numbered tickets and giving prizes to holders of numbers drawn at random.

lotto /ˈlɒtəʊ/ *noun* game of chance like bingo.

lotus /ˈləʊtəs/ *noun* legendary plant inducing luxurious langour when eaten; kind of water lily. □ **lotus position** cross-legged position of meditation.

loud ● *adjective* strongly audible; noisy; (of colours etc.) gaudy, obtrusive. ● *adverb* loudly. □ **loudspeaker** apparatus that converts electrical signals into sounds. □ **loudly** *adverb*; **loudness** *noun*.

lough /lɒk, lɒx/ *noun Irish* lake, sea inlet.

lounge ● *verb* (**-ging**) recline comfortably; loll; stand or move idly. ● *noun* place for lounging, esp. sitting-room in house; public room (in hotel etc.); place in airport etc. with seats for waiting passengers; spell of lounging. □ **lounge suit** man's suit for ordinary day wear.

lour /laʊə/ *verb* (also **lower** /laʊə/) frown, look sulle[n]; (of sky etc.) look dark and threatening.

louse /laʊs/ ● *noun* (*plural* **lice**) parasitic insect; (*plu[ral]* **louses**) *slang* contemptible person. ● *verb* (**-sing**) d[e]louse.

lousy /ˈlaʊzɪ/ *adjective* (**-ier**, **-iest**) *colloquial* very ba[d], disgusting, ill; (often + *with*) *colloquial* well supplie[d]; infested with lice.

lout *noun* rough-mannered person. □ **loutish** *adjectiv[e]*.

louvre /ˈluːvə/ *noun* (also **louver**) each of set of ove[r]lapping slats designed to admit air and some ligh[t] and exclude rain; domed structure on roof with sid[e] openings for ventilation etc.

lovable /ˈlʌvəb(ə)l/ *adjective* (also **loveable**) inspirin[g] affection.

lovage /ˈlʌvɪdʒ/ *noun* herb used for flavouring etc.

love /lʌv/ ● *noun* deep affection or fondness; sexua[l] passion; sexual relations; beloved one; sweethear[t]; *colloquial form of address regardless of affection*; *colloqu[ial]* person of whom one is fond; affectionate greeting[s]; (in games) no score, nil. ● *verb* (**-ving**) feel love fo[r]; delight in, admire; *colloquial* like very much. □ **fall i[n] love** (often + *with*) suddenly begin to love; **in lov[e]** (often + *with*) enamoured (of); **love affair** romant[ic] or sexual relationship between two people; **love[-]bird** kind of parakeet; **love-in-a-mist** blue-flowere[d] cultivated plant; **lovelorn** pining from unrequite[d] love; **lovesick** languishing with love; **make lov[e]** (often + *to*) have sexual intercourse (with), pa[y] amorous attention (to).

loveable = LOVABLE.

loveless *adjective* unloving or unloved or both.

lovely *adjective* (**-ier**, **-iest**) *colloquial* pleasing, delightfu[l]; beautiful. □ **loveliness** *noun*.

lover *noun* person in love with another, or havin[g] sexual relations with another; (in *plural*) unmarrie[d] couple in love or having sexual relations; perso[n] who enjoys specified thing.

loving ● *adjective* feeling or showing love, affectionate. ● *noun* affection. □ **loving cup** two-handled drinkin[g] cup passed round at banquets. □ **lovingly** *adverb*.

low[1] /ləʊ/ ● *adjective* not high or tall; not elevated i[n] position; (of sun) near horizon; of humble rank; of small or less than normal amount, extent, o[r] intensity; dejected; lacking vigour; (of sound) no[t] shrill or loud; commonplace; (of opinion) un[]favourable; mean, vulgar. ● *noun* low or lowest leve[l] or number; area of low pressure. ● *adverb* in or t[o] low position; in low tone, at low pitch. □ **lowbrow** *colloquial* not intellectual or cultured; **Low Church** section of Church of England attaching little importance to ritual, priestly authority, and sacraments; **Low Countries** Netherlands, Belgium, and Luxembourg; **low-down** *adjective* mean, dishonourable; *noun colloquial* (**the lowdown**; usually + *on*) relevan[t] information; **lower case** small letters, not capitals; **low frequency** *Radio* 30–300 kilohertz; **low pressure** low degree of activity, atmospheric condition with pressure below average; **Low Sunday** Sunday after Easter; **low tide**, **water** time or level of tide at its ebb; **low water mark** level reached at low water.

low[2] /ləʊ/ ● *noun* sound made by cattle; moo. ● *verb* make this sound.

lower[1] *verb* let or haul down; make or become lower; degrade.

lower[2] = LOUR.

lowland /ˈləʊlənd/ ● *noun* (usually in *plural*) low-lying country. ● *adjective* of or in lowland. □ **lowlander** *noun*.

lowly *adjective* (**-ier**, **-iest**) humble; unpretentious. □ **lowliness** *noun*.

loyal /ˈlɔɪəl/ *adjective* (often + *to*) faithful; steadfast in allegiance etc. □ **loyally** *adverb*; **loyalty** *noun* (*plural* **-ies**).

loyalist *noun* person remaining loyal to legitimate sovereign etc.; (**Loyalist**) supporter of union between Great Britain and Northern Ireland. □ **loyalism** *noun*.

lozenge /ˈlɒzɪndʒ/ *noun* rhombus; small sweet or medicinal tablet to be dissolved in mouth; lozenge-shaped object.

LP *abbreviation* long-playing (record).

LSD *abbreviation* lysergic acid diethylamide, a powerful hallucinogenic drug.

Lt. *abbreviation* Lieutenant; light.

Ltd. *abbreviation* Limited.

lubber /ˈlʌbə/ *noun* clumsy fellow, lout.

lubricant /ˈlu:brɪkənt/ *noun* substance used to reduce friction.

lubricate /ˈlu:brɪkeɪt/ *verb* (**-ting**) apply oil, grease, etc. to; make slippery. □ **lubrication** *noun*.

lubricious /lu:ˈbrɪʃəs/ *adjective* slippery, evasive; lewd. □ **lubricity** *noun*.

lucerne /lu:ˈsɜ:n/ *noun* alfalfa.

lucid /ˈlu:sɪd/ *adjective* expressing or expressed clearly; sane. □ **lucidity** /-ˈsɪd-/ *noun*; **lucidly** *adverb*.

luck *noun* good or bad fortune; circumstances brought by this; success due to chance.

luckless *adjective* unlucky; ending in failure.

lucky *adjective* (**-ier**, **-iest**) having or resulting from good luck; bringing good luck. □ **lucky dip** tub containing articles from which one chooses at random. □ **luckily** *adverb*.

lucrative /ˈlu:krətɪv/ *adjective* profitable. □ **lucratively** *adverb*.

lucre /ˈlu:kə/ *noun derogatory* financial gain.

ludicrous /ˈlu:dɪkrəs/ *adjective* absurd, ridiculous, laughable. □ **ludicrously** *adverb*; **ludicrousness** *noun*.

ludo /ˈlu:dəʊ/ *noun* board game played with dice and counters.

lug ● *verb* (**-gg-**) drag or carry with effort; pull hard. ● *noun* hard or rough pull; *colloquial* ear; projection on object by which it may be carried, fixed in place, etc.

luggage /ˈlʌgɪdʒ/ *noun* suitcases, bags, etc., for traveller's belongings.

lugger /ˈlʌgə/ *noun* small ship with 4-cornered sails (**lugsails**).

lugubrious /lʊˈgu:brɪəs/ *adjective* doleful. □ **lugubriously** *adverb*; **lugubriousness** *noun*.

lukewarm /lu:kˈwɔ:m/ *adjective* moderately warm, tepid; unenthusiastic.

lull ● *verb* soothe, send to sleep; (usually + *into*) deceive (person) into undue confidence; allay (suspicions etc.); (of noise, storm, etc.) lessen, fall quiet. ● *noun* temporary quiet period.

lullaby /ˈlʌləbaɪ/ *noun* (*plural* **-ies**) soothing song to send child to sleep.

lumbago /lʌmˈbeɪgəʊ/ *noun* rheumatic pain in muscles of lower back.

lumbar /ˈlʌmbə/ *adjective* of lower back. □ **lumbar puncture** withdrawal of spinal fluid from lower back for diagnosis.

lumber /ˈlʌmbə/ ● *noun* disused and cumbersome articles; partly prepared timber. ● *verb* (usually + *with*) encumber (person); move in slow clumsy way; cut and prepare forest timber for transporting. □ **lumberjack** person who fells and transports lumber; **lumber-room** room where things in disuse are kept.

lumen /ˈlu:men/ *noun* SI unit of luminous flux.

luminary /ˈlu:mɪnərɪ/ *noun* (*plural* **-ies**) *literary* natural light-giving body; wise person; celebrated member of group.

luminescence /lu:mɪˈnes(ə)ns/ *noun* emission of light without heat. □ **luminescent** *adjective*.

luminous /ˈlu:mɪnəs/ *adjective* shedding light; phosphorescent, visible in darkness. □ **luminosity** /-ˈnɒs-/ *noun*.

lump[1] ● *noun* compact shapeless mass; tumour; swelling, bruise; heavy ungainly person etc. ● *verb* (usually + *together* etc.) class, mass. □ **lump sugar** sugar in small lumps or cubes; **lump sum** sum including number of items or paid down all at once.

lump[2] *verb colloquial* (in contrast with *like*) put up with ungraciously.

lumpish *adjective* heavy, clumsy; stupid.

lumpy *adjective* (**-ier**, **-iest**) full of or covered with lumps. □ **lumpily** *adverb*; **lumpiness** *noun*.

lunacy /ˈlu:nəsɪ/ *noun* (*plural* **-ies**) insanity; great folly.

lunar /ˈlu:nə/ *adjective* of, like, concerned with, or determined by the moon. □ **lunar module** craft for travelling between moon and orbiting spacecraft; **lunar month** period of moon's revolution, (in general use) 4 weeks.

lunate /ˈlu:neɪt/ *adjective* crescent-shaped.

lunatic /ˈlu:nətɪk/ ● *noun* insane person; wildly foolish person. ● *adjective* insane; very reckless or foolish.

lunation /lu:ˈneɪʃ(ə)n/ *noun* interval between new moons, about 29½ days.

lunch ● *noun* midday meal. ● *verb* take lunch; provide lunch for.

luncheon /ˈlʌntʃ(ə)n/ *noun formal* lunch. □ **luncheon voucher** voucher issued to employees and exchangeable for food at restaurant etc.

lung *noun* either of pair of respiratory organs in humans and many other vertebrates.

lunge ● *noun* sudden movement forward; attacking move in fencing. ● *verb* (**-ging**) (usually + *at*) deliver or make lunge.

lupin /ˈlu:pɪn/ *noun* cultivated plant with long tapering spikes of flowers.

lupine /ˈlu:paɪn/ *adjective* of or like wolves.

lupus /ˈlu:pəs/ *noun* inflammatory skin disease.

lurch[1] ● *noun* stagger; sudden unsteady movement or tilt. ● *verb* stagger, move unsteadily.

lurch[2] *noun* □ **leave in the lurch** desert (friend etc.) in difficulties.

lurcher /ˈlɜ:tʃə/ *noun* crossbred dog, usually working dog crossed with greyhound.

lure ● *verb* (**-ring**) (usually + *away*, *into*) entice; recall with lure. ● *noun* thing used to entice, enticing quality (of chase etc.); falconer's apparatus for recalling hawk.

lurid /ˈljʊərɪd/ *adjective* bright and glaring in colour; sensational, shocking; ghastly, wan. □ **luridly** *adverb*.

lurk *verb* linger furtively; lie in ambush; (usually + *in*, *about*, etc.) hide, esp. for sinister purpose; (as **lurking** *adjective*) latent.

luscious /ˈlʌʃəs/ *adjective* richly sweet in taste or smell; voluptuously attractive.

lush[1] *adjective* luxuriant and succulent.

lush[2] *noun slang* alcoholic, drunkard.

lust ● *noun* strong sexual desire; (usually + *for*, *of*) passionate desire for or enjoyment of; sensuous appetite seen as sinful. ● *verb* (usually + *after*, *for*) have strong or excessive (esp. sexual) desire. □ **lustful** *adjective*; **lustfully** *adverb*.

lustre /ˈlʌstə/ *noun* (*US* **luster**) gloss, shining surface; brilliance, splendour; iridescent glaze on pottery and porcelain. □ **lustrous** *adjective*.

lusty *adjective* (**-ier**, **-iest**) healthy and strong; vigorous, lively. □ **lustily** *adverb*.

lute[1] /lu:t/ *noun* guitar-like instrument with long neck and pear-shaped body.
lute[2] /lu:t/ ● *noun* clay or cement for making joints airtight. ● *verb* (**-ting**) apply lute to.
lutenist /'lu:tənɪst/ *noun* lute-player.
Lutheran /'lu:θərən/ ● *noun* follower of Martin Luther; member of Lutheran Church. ● *adjective* of Luther, the doctrines associated with him, or the Protestant Reformation. □ **Lutheranism** *noun*.
lux /lʌks/ *noun* (*plural* same) SI unit of illumination.
luxuriant /lʌg'zjʊərɪənt/ *adjective* growing profusely; exuberant, florid. □ **luxuriance** *noun*; **luxuriantly** *adverb*.

■ **Usage** *Luxuriant* is sometimes confused with *luxurious*.

luxuriate /lʌg'zjʊərɪeɪt/ *verb* (**-ting**) (+ *in*) take self-indulgent delight in, enjoy as luxury.
luxurious /lʌg'zjʊərɪəs/ *adjective* supplied with luxuries; very comfortable; fond of luxury. □ **luxuriously** *adverb*.

■ **Usage** *Luxurious* is sometimes confused with *luxuriant*.

luxury /'lʌkʃərɪ/ ● *noun* (*plural* **-ies**) choice or costly surroundings, possessions, etc.; thing giving comfort or enjoyment but inessential. ● *adjective* comfortable, expensive, etc.
LV *abbreviation* luncheon voucher.
lychee /'laɪtʃɪ/ *noun* (also **litchi**, **lichee**) sweet white juicy brown-skinned fruit; tree bearing this.
lych-gate = LICH-GATE.
Lycra /'laɪkrə/ *noun proprietary term* elastic polyurethane fabric.
lye /laɪ/ *noun* water made alkaline with wood ashes; any alkaline solution for washing.
lying *present participle* of LIE[1,2].
lymph /lɪmf/ *noun* colourless fluid from tissues of body, containing white blood cells; this fluid as vaccine.
lymphatic /lɪm'fætɪk/ *adjective* of, secreting, or carrying lymph; (of person) pale, flabby. □ **lymphatic system** vessels carrying lymph.
lynch /lɪntʃ/ *verb* put (person) to death by mob action without legal trial. □ **lynching** *noun*.
lynx /lɪŋks/ *noun* (*plural* same or **-es**) wild cat with short tail, spotted fur, and proverbially keen sight.
lyre /laɪə/ *noun* ancient U-shaped stringed instrument.
lyric /'lɪrɪk/ ● *adjective* (of poetry) expressing writer's emotion, usually briefly; (of poet) writing in this way; meant or fit to be sung; songlike. ● *noun* lyric poem; (in *plural*) words of song.
lyrical *adjective* lyric; resembling, or using language appropriate to, lyric poetry; *colloquial* highly enthusiastic. □ **lyrically** *adverb*.
lyricism /'lɪrɪsɪz(ə)m/ *noun* quality of being lyrical.
lyricist /'lɪrɪsɪst/ *noun* writer of lyrics.

Mm

M[1] *noun* (also **m**) (Roman numeral) 1,000.

M[2] *abbreviation* (also **M.**) Master; *Monsieur*; motorway; mega-.

m *abbreviation* (also **m.**) male; masculine; married; mile(s); metre(s); million(s); minute(s); milli-.

MA *abbreviation* Master of Arts.

ma /mɑː/ *noun colloquial* mother.

ma'am /mæm/ *noun* madam (esp. used in addressing royal lady).

mac *noun* (also **mack**) *colloquial* mackintosh.

macabre /mə'kɑːbr/ *adjective* gruesome, grim.

macadam /mə'kædəm/ *noun* broken stone as material for road-making; tarmacadam. □ **macadamize** *verb* (also **-ise**) (**-zing** or **-sing**).

macaroni /mækə'rəʊnɪ/ *noun* pasta tubes.

macaroon /mækə'ruːn/ *noun* biscuit made of ground almonds etc.

macaw /mə'kɔː/ *noun* kind of parrot.

mace[1] *noun* staff of office, esp. symbol of Speaker's authority in House of Commons.

mace[2] *noun* dried outer covering of nutmeg as spice.

macédoine /'mæsɪdwɑːn/ *noun* mixture of fruits or vegetables, esp. cut up small.

macerate /'mæsəreɪt/ *verb* (**-ting**) soften by soaking. □ **maceration** *noun*.

machete /mə'ʃetɪ/ *noun* broad heavy knife used in Central America and W. Indies.

machiavellian /mækɪə'velɪən/ *adjective* unscrupulous, cunning.

machination /mækɪ'neɪʃ(ə)n/ *noun* (usually in *plural*) intrigue, plot.

machine /mə'ʃiːn/ ● *noun* apparatus for applying mechanical power, having several interrelated parts; bicycle, motorcycle, etc.; aircraft; computer; controlling system of an organization. ● *verb* (**-ning**) make or operate on with machine. □ **machine-gun** automatic gun that gives continuous fire; **machine-readable** in form that computer can process; **machine tool** mechanically operated tool.

machinery *noun* (*plural* **-ies**) machines; mechanism; organized system; means arranged.

machinist *noun* person who works machine.

machismo /mə'kɪzməʊ/ *noun* being macho; masculine pride.

macho /'mætʃəʊ/ *adjective* aggressively masculine.

macintosh = MACKINTOSH.

mack = MAC.

mackerel /'mækr(ə)l/ *noun* (*plural* same or **-s**) edible sea fish. □ **mackerel sky** sky dappled with rows of small fleecy white clouds.

mackintosh /'mækɪntɒʃ/ *noun* (also **macintosh**) waterproof coat or cloak; cloth waterproofed with rubber.

macramé /mə'krɑːmɪ/ *noun* art of knotting cord or string in patterns; work so made.

macrobiotic /mækrəʊbaɪ'ɒtɪk/ *adjective* of diet intended to prolong life, esp. consisting of wholefoods.

macrocosm /'mækrəʊkɒz(ə)m/ *noun* universe; whole of a complex structure.

mad *adjective* (**-dd-**) insane; frenzied; wildly foolish; infatuated; *colloquial* annoyed. □ **madcap** *adjective* wildly impulsive, *noun* reckless person; **madhouse** *colloquial* confused uproar, *archaic* mental home or hospital; **madman**, **madwoman** mad person. □ **madly** *adverb*; **madness** *noun*.

madam /'mædəm/ *noun polite formal address to woman*; *colloquial* conceited or precocious girl or young woman; woman brothel-keeper.

Madame /mə'dɑːm/ *noun* (*plural* **Mesdames** /meɪ'dɑːm/) *title used of or to French-speaking woman.*

madden *verb* make mad; irritate. □ **maddening** *adjective*.

madder /'mædə/ *noun* herbaceous climbing plant; red dye from its root; synthetic substitute for this dye.

made *past & past participle* of MAKE.

Madeira /mə'dɪərə/ *noun* fortified wine from Madeira; (in full **Madeira cake**) kind of sponge cake.

Mademoiselle /mædəmwə'zel/ *noun* (*plural* **Mesdemoiselles** /meɪdm-/) *title used of or to unmarried French-speaking woman.*

Madonna /mə'dɒnə/ *noun* (**the Madonna**) the Virgin Mary; (**madonna**) picture or statue of her.

madrigal /'mædrɪg(ə)l/ *noun* part-song for several voices, usually unaccompanied.

maelstrom /'meɪlstrəm/ *noun* great whirlpool.

maestro /'maɪstrəʊ/ *noun* (*plural* **maestri** /-strɪ/ or **-s**) eminent musician, esp. teacher or conductor.

Mafia /'mæfɪə/ *noun* organized international group of criminals.

Mafioso /mæfɪ'əʊsəʊ/ *noun* (*plural* **Mafiosi** /-sɪ/) member of the Mafia.

mag *noun colloquial* magazine.

magazine /mægə'ziːn/ *noun* periodical publication containing contributions by various writers; chamber containing cartridges fed automatically to breech of gun; similar device in slide projector etc.; store for explosives, arms, or military provisions.

magenta /mə'dʒentə/ *noun* shade of crimson; aniline dye of this colour.

maggot /'mægət/ *noun* larva, esp. of bluebottle. □ **maggoty** *adjective*.

Magi /'meɪdʒaɪ/ *plural noun* (**the Magi**) the 'wise men from the East' in the Gospel.

magic /'mædʒɪk/ ● *noun* art of influencing events supernaturally; conjuring tricks; inexplicable influence. ● *adjective* of magic. □ **magic lantern** simple form of slide projector.

magical *adjective* of magic; resembling, or produced as if by, magic; wonderful, enchanting. □ **magically** *adverb*.

magician /mə'dʒɪʃ(ə)n/ *noun* person skilled in magic; conjuror.

magisterial /mædʒɪ'stɪərɪəl/ *adjective* imperious; authoritative; of a magistrate.

magistracy /'mædʒɪstrəsɪ/ *noun* (*plural* **-ies**) magisterial office; magistrates.

magistrate /'mædʒɪstreɪt/ *noun* civil officer administering law, esp. one trying minor offences etc.

magnanimous /mæg'nænɪməs/ *adjective* nobly generous, not petty in feelings or conduct. □ **magnanimity** /-nə'nɪm-/ *noun*.

magnate /'mægneɪt/ *noun* person of wealth, authority, etc.

magnesia /mæg'niːʃə/ *noun* magnesium oxide; hydrated magnesium carbonate, used as antacid and laxative.

magnesium /mæg'ni:zɪəm/ *noun* silvery metallic element.

magnet /'mægnɪt/ *noun* piece of iron, steel, etc., having properties of attracting iron and of pointing approximately north when suspended; lodestone; person or thing that attracts.

magnetic /mæg'netɪk/ *adjective* having properties of magnet; produced or acting by magnetism; capable of being attracted by or acquiring properties of magnet; very attractive. □ **magnetic field** area of influence of magnet; **magnetic north** point indicated by north end of compass needle; **magnetic storm** disturbance of earth's magnetic field; **magnetic tape** coated plastic strip for recording sound or pictures.

magnetism /'mægnɪtɪz(ə)m/ *noun* magnetic phenomena; science of these; personal charm.

magnetize /'mægnɪtaɪz/ *verb* (also **-ise**) (**-zing** or **-sing**) make into magnet; attract like magnet. □ **magnetization** *noun.*

magneto /mæg'ni:təʊ/ *noun* (*plural* **-s**) electric generator using permanent magnets (esp. for ignition in internal-combustion engine).

magnificent /mæg'nɪfɪs(ə)nt/ *adjective* splendid; imposing; *colloquial* excellent. □ **magnificence** *noun*; **magnificently** *adverb.*

magnify /'mægnɪfaɪ/ *verb* (**-ies**, **-ied**) make (thing) appear larger than it is, as with lens (**magnifying glass**) etc.; exaggerate; intensify; *archaic* extol. □ **magnification** *noun.*

magnitude /'mægnɪtju:d/ *noun* largeness, size; importance.

magnolia /mæg'nəʊlɪə/ *noun* kind of flowering tree; very pale pinkish colour of its flowers.

magnum /'mægnəm/ *noun* (*plural* **-s**) wine bottle twice normal size.

magpie /'mægpaɪ/ *noun* crow with long tail and black and white plumage; chatterer; indiscriminate collector.

Magyar /'mægjɑ:/ ● *noun* member of the chief ethnic group in Hungary; their language. ● *adjective* of this people.

maharaja /mɑ:hə'rɑ:dʒə/ *noun* (also **maharajah**) *historical title of some Indian princes.*

maharanee /mɑ:hə'rɑ:nɪ/ *noun* (also **maharani**) (*plural* **-s**) *historical* maharaja's wife or widow.

maharishi /mɑ:hə'rɪʃɪ/ *noun* (*plural* **-s**) great Hindu sage.

mahatma /mə'hætmə/ *noun* (in India etc.) revered person.

mah-jong /mɑ:'dʒɒŋ/ *noun* (also **-jongg**) originally Chinese game played with 136 or 144 pieces.

mahogany /mə'hɒgənɪ/ *noun* (*plural* **-ies**) reddish-brown wood used for furniture etc.; colour of this.

mahout /mə'haʊt/ *noun* elephant driver.

maid *noun* female servant; *archaic* girl, young woman. □ **maidservant** female servant.

maiden /'meɪd(ə)n/ ● *noun archaic* girl, young unmarried woman; *Cricket* maiden over. ● *adjective* unmarried; (of voyage, speech by MP, etc.) first. □ **maidenhair** delicate kind of fern; **maiden name** woman's surname before marriage; **maiden over** *Cricket* over in which no runs are scored. □ **maidenly** *adjective.*

mail[1] ● *noun* letters etc. conveyed by post; the post. ● *verb* send by mail. □ **mail order** purchase of goods by post.

mail[2] *noun* armour of metal rings or plates.

maim *verb* cripple, mutilate.

main ● *adjective* chief, principal. ● *noun* principal channel for water, gas, etc., or (usually in *plural*) electricity; (in *plural*) domestic electricity supply as distinct from batteries; *archaic* high seas. □ **in the main** mostly, on the whole; **mainframe** central processing unit of large computer, large computer system; **mainland** continuous extent of land excluding nearby islands etc.; **mainmast** principal mast; **mainsail** lowest sail or sail set on after part of mainmast; **mainspring** principal spring of watch or clock, chief motive power etc.; **mainstay** chief support; **mainstream** prevailing trend of opinion, fashion, etc.

mainly *adverb* mostly; chiefly.

maintain /meɪn'teɪn/ *verb* keep up; keep going; support; assert as true; keep in repair.

maintenance /'meɪntənəns/ *noun* maintaining, being maintained; provision of enough to support life; alimony.

maiolica /mə'jɒlɪkə/ *noun* (also **majolica**) kind of decorated Italian earthenware.

maisonette /meɪzə'net/ *noun* flat on more than one floor; small house.

maize *noun* N. American cereal plant; cobs or grain of this.

Maj. *abbreviation* Major.

majestic /mə'dʒestɪk/ *adjective* stately and dignified; imposing. □ **majestically** *adverb.*

majesty /'mædʒɪstɪ/ *noun* (*plural* **-ies**) stateliness of aspect, language, etc.; sovereign power; (**His**, **Her**, **Your Majesty**) *title used of or to sovereign or sovereign's wife or widow.*

majolica = MAIOLICA.

major /'meɪdʒə/ ● *adjective* greater or relatively great in size etc.; unusually serious or significant; *Music* of or based on scale having semitone next above third and seventh notes; of full legal age. ● *noun* army officer next below lieutenant colonel; person of full legal age; *US* student's main subject or course, student of this. ● *verb* (+ *in*) *US* study or qualify in as a major. □ **major-domo** /-'dəʊməʊ/ (*plural* **-s**) house-steward; **major-general** army officer next below lieutenant general.

majority /mə'dʒɒrɪtɪ/ *noun* (*plural* **-ies**) (usually + *of*) greater number or part; number by which winning vote exceeds next; full legal age.

■ **Usage** *Majority* should strictly be used of a number of people or things, as in *the majority of people*, and not of a quantity of something, as in *the majority of the work.*

make ● *verb* (**-king**; *past & past participle* **made**) construct, frame, create, esp. from parts or other substance; compel; bring about, give rise to; cause to become or seem; write, compose; constitute, amount to; undertake; perform; gain, acquire, obtain as result; prepare for consumption or use; proceed; *colloquial* arrive at or in time for, manage to attend; *colloquial* achieve place in; establish, enact; consider to be, estimate as; secure success or advancement of; accomplish; become; represent as; form in the mind. ● *noun* origin of manufactured goods, brand; way thing is made. □ **make believe** *verb* pretend; **make-believe** *noun* pretence, *adjective* pretended; **make do** (often + *with*) manage (with substitute etc.); **make for** tend to result in, proceed towards; **make good** compensate for, repair, succeed in an undertaking; **make off** depart hastily; **make out** discern, understand, assert, pretend, *colloquial* progress, write out, fill in; **makeshift** (serving as) temporary substitute or device; **make up** *verb* act to overcome (deficiency), complete, (+ *for*) compensate for, be reconciled, put together, prepare, invent (story), apply cosmetics (to); **make-up** *noun* cosmetics, similar preparation used as disguise by actor, person's temperament etc., composition; **makeweight** small quantity added to make full weight; **on the make** *colloquial* intent on gain.

maker *noun* person who makes, esp. (**Maker**) God.

making *noun* (in *plural*) earnings, profit; essential qualities for becoming. □ **be the making of** ensure success of; **in the making** in the course of being made.

malachite /ˈmæləkaɪt/ *noun* green mineral used for ornament.

maladjusted /mæləˈdʒʌstɪd/ *adjective* (of person) unable to cope with demands of social environment. □ **maladjustment** *noun*.

maladminister /mælədˈmɪnɪstə/ *verb* manage badly or improperly. □ **maladministration** *noun*.

maladroit /mæləˈdrɔɪt/ *adjective* bungling, clumsy.

malady /ˈmælədɪ/ *noun* (*plural* **-ies**) ailment, disease.

malaise /məˈleɪz/ *noun* feeling of illness or uneasiness.

malapropism /ˈmæləprɒpɪz(ə)m/ *noun* comical confusion between words.

malaria /məˈleərɪə/ *noun* fever transmitted by mosquitoes. □ **malarial** *adjective*.

Malay /məˈleɪ/ ● *noun* member of a people predominating in Malaysia and Indonesia; their language. ● *adjective* of this people or language.

malcontent /ˈmælkəntent/ ● *noun* discontented person. ● *adjective* discontented.

male ● *adjective* of the sex that can beget offspring by fertilizing; (of plants or flowers) containing stamens but no pistil; (of parts of machinery) designed to enter or fill corresponding hollow part. ● *noun* male person or animal.

malediction /mælɪˈdɪkʃ(ə)n/ *noun* curse. □ **maledictory** *adjective*.

malefactor /ˈmælɪfæktə/ *noun* criminal; evil-doer. □ **malefaction** /-ˈfækʃ(ə)n/ *noun*.

malevolent /məˈlevələnt/ *adjective* wishing evil to others. □ **malevolence** *noun*.

malformation /mælfɔːˈmeɪʃ(ə)n/ *noun* faulty formation. □ **malformed** /-ˈfɔːmd/ *adjective*.

malfunction /mælˈfʌŋkʃ(ə)n/ ● *noun* failure to function normally. ● *verb* function faultily.

malice /ˈmælɪs/ *noun* ill-will; desire to do harm.

malicious /məˈlɪʃəs/ *adjective* given to or arising from malice. □ **maliciously** *adverb*.

malign /məˈlaɪn/ ● *adjective* injurious; malignant; malevolent. ● *verb* speak ill of; slander. □ **malignity** /məˈlɪgnɪtɪ/ *noun*.

malignant /məˈlɪgnənt/ *adjective* (of disease) very virulent; (of tumour) spreading, recurring, cancerous; feeling or showing intense ill-will. □ **malignancy** *noun*.

malinger /məˈlɪŋgə/ *verb* pretend to be ill, esp. to escape duty.

mall /mæl, mɔːl/ *noun* sheltered walk; shopping precinct.

mallard /ˈmælɑːd/ *noun* (*plural* same) kind of wild duck.

malleable /ˈmælɪəb(ə)l/ *adjective* that can be shaped by hammering; pliable. □ **malleability** *noun*.

mallet /ˈmælɪt/ *noun* hammer, usually of wood; implement for striking croquet or polo ball.

mallow /ˈmæləʊ/ *noun* flowering plant with hairy stems and leaves.

malmsey /ˈmɑːmzɪ/ *noun* a strong sweet wine.

malnutrition /mælnjuːˈtrɪʃ(ə)n/ *noun* lack of foods necessary for health.

malodorous /mælˈəʊdərəs/ *adjective* evil-smelling.

malpractice /mælˈpræktɪs/ *noun* improper, negligent, or criminal professional conduct.

malt /mɔːlt/ ● *noun* barley or other grain prepared for brewing etc.; *colloquial* malt whisky. ● *verb* convert (grain) into malt. □ **malted milk** drink made from dried milk and extract of malt; **malt whisky** whisky made from malted barley.

Maltese /mɔːlˈtiːz/ ● *noun* native, national, or language of Malta. ● *adjective* of Malta. □ **Maltese cross** one with equal arms broadened at ends.

maltreat /mælˈtriːt/ *verb* ill-treat. □ **maltreatment** *noun*.

mama /məˈmɑː/ *noun* (also **mamma**) *archaic* mother.

mamba /ˈmæmbə/ *noun* venomous African snake.

mamma = MAMA.

mammal /ˈmæm(ə)l/ *noun* animal of class secreting milk to feed young. □ **mammalian** /-ˈmeɪlɪən/ *adjective*.

mammary /ˈmæmərɪ/ *adjective* of breasts.

Mammon /ˈmæmən/ *noun* wealth regarded as god or evil influence.

mammoth /ˈmæməθ/ ● *noun* large extinct elephant. ● *adjective* huge.

man ● *noun* (*plural* **men**) adult human male; human being, person; the human race; employee, workman; (usually in *plural*) soldier, sailor, etc.; suitable or appropriate person; husband; *colloquial* boyfriend; human being of specified type; piece in chess, draughts, etc. ● *verb* (**-nn-**) supply with person(s) for work or defence. □ **manhole** opening giving person access to sewer, conduit, etc.; **man-hour** work done by one person in one hour; **man in the street** ordinary person; **man-of-war** warship; **manpower** people available for work or military service; **manservant** (*plural* **menservants**) male servant; **mantrap** trap set to catch esp. trespassers.

manacle /ˈmænək(ə)l/ ● *noun* (usually in *plural*) handcuff. ● *verb* (**-ling**) put manacles on.

manage /ˈmænɪdʒ/ *verb* (**-ging**) organize, regulate; succeed in achieving, contrive; succeed with limited resources, cope; succeed in controlling; cope with. □ **managing director** director with executive control or authority. □ **manageable** *adjective*.

management *noun* managing, being managed; administration; people managing a business.

manager *noun* person controlling or administering business etc.; person controlling activities of person, team, etc.; person who manages money etc. in specified way. □ **managerial** /-ˈdʒɪərɪəl/ *adjective*.

manageress /mænɪdʒəˈres/ *noun* woman manager, esp. of shop, hotel, etc.

mañana /mænˈjɑːnə/ *adverb & noun* some time in the future. [Spanish]

manatee /mænəˈtiː/ *noun* large aquatic plant-eating mammal.

Mancunian /mæŋˈkjuːnɪən/ ● *noun* native of Manchester. ● *adjective* of Manchester.

mandarin /ˈmændərɪn/ *noun* (**Mandarin**) official language of China; *historical* Chinese official; influential person, esp. bureaucrat; (in full **mandarin orange**) tangerine.

mandate /ˈmændeɪt/ ● *noun* official command; authority given by electors to government etc.; authority to act for another. ● *verb* (**-ting**) instruct (delegate) how to act or vote.

mandatory /ˈmændətərɪ/ *adjective* compulsory; of or conveying a command.

mandible /ˈmændɪb(ə)l/ *noun* jaw, esp. lower one; either part of bird's beak; either half of crushing organ in mouth-parts of insect etc.

mandolin /mændəˈlɪn/ *noun* kind of lute with paired metal strings plucked with a plectrum.

mandrake /ˈmændreɪk/ *noun* narcotic plant with forked root.

mandrill /ˈmændrɪl/ *noun* large W. African baboon.

mane *noun* long hair on horse's or lion's neck; *colloquial* person's long hair.

manège /mæ'neɪʒ/ *noun* riding-school; movements of trained horse; horsemanship.

maneuver *US* = MANOEUVRE.

manful *adjective* brave, resolute. □ **manfully** *adverb*.

manganese /'mæŋgəni:z/ *noun* grey brittle metallic element; black oxide of this.

mange /meɪndʒ/ *noun* skin disease of dogs etc.

mangel-wurzel /'mæŋg(ə)l wɜ:z(ə)l/ *noun* large beet used as cattle food.

manger /'meɪndʒə/ *noun* eating-trough in stable.

mangle¹ /'mæŋg(ə)l/ *verb* (**-ling**) hack, cut about; mutilate, spoil.

mangle² /'mæŋg(ə)l/ ● *noun* machine with rollers for pressing water out of washed clothes. ● *verb* (**-ling**) put through mangle.

mango /'mæŋgəʊ/ *noun* (*plural* **-es** or **-s**) tropical fruit with yellowish flesh; tree bearing it.

mangold /'mæŋg(ə)ld/ *noun* mangel-wurzel.

mangrove /'mæŋgrəʊv/ *noun* tropical seashore tree with many tangled roots above ground.

mangy /'meɪndʒɪ/ *adjective* (**-ier**, **-iest**) having mange; squalid, shabby.

manhandle *verb* (**-ling**) *colloquial* handle roughly; move by human effort.

manhood *noun* state of being a man; manliness; a man's sexual potency; men of a country.

mania /'meɪnɪə/ *noun* mental illness marked by excitement and violence; (often + *for*) excessive enthusiasm, obsession.

maniac /'meɪnɪæk/ ● *noun colloquial* person behaving wildly; *colloquial* obsessive enthusiast; person suffering from mania. ● *adjective* of or behaving like maniac. □ **maniacal** /mə'naɪək(ə)l/ *adjective*.

manic /'mænɪk/ *adjective* of or affected by mania. □ **manic-depressive** *adjective* relating to mental disorder with alternating periods of elation and depression, *noun* person having such disorder.

manicure /'mænɪkjʊə/ ● *noun* cosmetic treatment of the hands. ● *verb* (**-ring**) give manicure to. □ **manicurist** *noun*.

manifest /'mænɪfest/ ● *adjective* clear to sight or mind; indubitable. ● *verb* make manifest; (**manifest itself**) reveal itself. ● *noun* cargo or passenger list. □ **manifestation** *noun*; **manifestly** *adverb*.

manifesto /mænɪ'festəʊ/ *noun* (*plural* **-s**) declaration of policies.

manifold /'mænɪfəʊld/ ● *adjective* many and various; having various forms, applications, parts, etc. ● *noun* manifold thing; pipe etc. with several outlets.

manikin /'mænɪkɪn/ *noun* little man, dwarf.

Manila /mə'nɪlə/ *noun* strong fibre of Philippine tree; (also **manila**) strong brown paper made of this.

manipulate /mə'nɪpjʊleɪt/ *verb* (**-ting**) handle, esp. with skill; manage to one's own advantage, esp. unfairly. □ **manipulation** *noun*; **manipulator** *noun*.

manipulative /mə'nɪpjʊlətɪv/ *adjective* tending to exploit a situation, person, etc., for one's own ends.

mankind *noun* human species.

manly *adjective* (**-ier**, **-iest**) having qualities associated with or befitting a man. □ **manliness** *noun*.

manna /'mænə/ *noun* food miraculously supplied to Israelites in wilderness.

mannequin /'mænɪkɪn/ *noun* fashion model; dummy for display of clothes.

manner /'mænə/ *noun* way thing is done or happens; (in *plural*) social behaviour; style; (in *plural*) polite behaviour; outward bearing, way of speaking, etc.; kind, sort.

mannered *adjective* behaving in specified way; showing mannerisms.

mannerism *noun* distinctive gesture or feature of style; excessive use of these in art etc.

mannerly *adjective* well-behaved, polite.

mannish *adjective* (of woman) masculine in appearance or manner; characteristic of man as opposed to woman.

manoeuvre /mə'nu:və/ (*US* **maneuver**) ● *noun* planned movement of vehicle or troops; (in *plural*) large-scale exercise of troops etc.; agile or skilful movement; artful plan. ● *verb* (**-ring**) move (thing, esp. vehicle) carefully; perform or cause to perform manoeuvres; manipulate by scheming or adroitness; use artifice. □ **manoeuvrable** *adjective*.

manor /'mænə/ *noun* large country house with lands; *historical* feudal lordship over lands. □ **manorial** /mə'nɔ:rɪəl/ *adjective*.

mansard /'mænsɑ:d/ *noun* roof with 4 sloping sides, each of which becomes steeper halfway down.

manse /mæns/ *noun* (esp. Scottish Presbyterian) minister's house.

mansion /'mænʃ(ə)n/ *noun* large grand house; (in *plural*) block of flats.

manslaughter *noun* unintentional but not accidental unlawful killing of human being.

mantel /'mænt(ə)l/ *noun* mantelpiece, mantelshelf. □ **mantelpiece** structure above and around fireplace, mantelshelf; **mantelshelf** shelf above fireplace.

mantilla /mæn'tɪlə/ *noun* Spanish woman's lace scarf worn over head and shoulders.

mantis /'mæntɪs/ *noun* (*plural* same or **mantises**) kind of predatory insect.

mantle /'mænt(ə)l/ ● *noun* loose sleeveless cloak; covering; fragile tube round gas jet to give incandescent light. ● *verb* (**-ling**) clothe; conceal, envelop.

manual /'mænjʊəl/ ● *adjective* of or done with hands. ● *noun* reference book; organ keyboard played with hands, not feet. □ **manually** *adverb*.

manufacture /mænjʊ'fæktʃə/ ● *noun* making of articles, esp. in factory etc.; branch of industry. ● *verb* (**-ring**) make, esp. on industrial scale; invent, fabricate. □ **manufacturer** *noun*.

manure /mə'njʊə/ ● *noun* fertilizer, esp. dung. ● *verb* (**-ring**) treat with manure.

manuscript /'mænjʊskrɪpt/ ● *noun* book or document written by hand or typed, not printed. ● *adjective* written by hand.

Manx ● *adjective* of Isle of Man. ● *noun* Celtic language of Isle of Man. □ **Manx cat** tailless variety.

many /'menɪ/ ● *adjective* (**more**, **most**) numerous, great in number. ● *noun* (treated as *plural*) many people or things; (**the many**) the majority of people.

Maori /'maʊrɪ/ ● *noun* (*plural* same or **-s**) member of aboriginal NZ race; their language. ● *adjective* of this people.

map ● *noun* flat representation of (part of) earth's surface, or of sky; diagram. ● *verb* (**-pp-**) represent on map. □ **map out** plan in detail.

maple /'meɪp(ə)l/ *noun* kind of tree. □ **maple leaf** emblem of Canada; **maple sugar** sugar got by evaporating sap of some kinds of maple; **maple syrup** syrup got from maple sap or maple sugar.

maquette /mə'ket/ *noun* preliminary model or sketch.

Mar. *abbreviation* March.

mar *verb* (**-rr-**) spoil; disfigure.

marabou /'mærəbu:/ *noun* (*plural* **-s**) large W. African stork; its down as trimming etc.

maraca /mə'rækə/ *noun* clublike bean-filled gourd etc., shaken as percussion instrument.

maraschino /mærə'ski:nəʊ/ *noun* (*plural* **-s**) liqueur made from cherries. ▫ **maraschino cherry** one preserved in maraschino.

marathon /'mærəθ(ə)n/ *noun* long-distance foot race; long-lasting, esp. difficult, undertaking.

maraud /mə'rɔ:d/ *verb* make raid; pillage. ▫ **marauder** *noun*.

marble /'mɑ:b(ə)l/ ● *noun* kind of limestone used in sculpture and architecture; anything of or like marble; small ball of glass etc. as toy; (in *plural*; treated as *singular*) game played with these; (in *plural*) *slang* one's mental faculties; (in *plural*) collection of sculptures. ● *verb* **(-ling)** (esp. as **marbled** *adjective*) give veined or mottled appearance to (esp. paper).

marcasite /'mɑ:kəsaɪt/ *noun* crystalline iron sulphide; crystals of this used in jewellery.

March *noun* third month of year. ▫ **March hare** hare in breeding season.

march[1] ● *verb* walk in military manner or with regular paces; proceed steadily; cause to march or walk. ● *noun* act of marching; uniform military step; long difficult walk; procession as demonstration; progress; piece of music suitable for marching to. ▫ **march past** ceremonial march of troops past saluting point. ▫ **marcher** *noun*.

march[2] *noun historical* boundary (often in *plural*); tract of (often disputed) land between countries etc.

marchioness /mɑ:ʃə'nes/ *noun* marquess's wife or widow; woman holding rank of marquess.

mare /meə/ *noun* female equine animal, esp. horse. ▫ **mare's nest** illusory discovery.

margarine /mɑ:dʒə'ri:n/ *noun* butter substitute made from edible oils etc.

marge /mɑ:dʒ/ *noun colloquial* margarine.

margin /'mɑ:dʒɪn/ *noun* edge or border of surface; plain space round printed page etc.; amount by which thing exceeds, falls short, etc. ▫ **margin of error** allowance for miscalculation or mischance.

marginal *adjective* written in margin; of or at edge; (of constituency) having elected MP with small majority; close to limit, esp. of profitability; insignificant; barely adequate. ▫ **marginally** *adverb*.

marginalize *verb* (also **-ise**) **(-zing** or **-sing)** make or treat as insignificant. ▫ **marginalization** *noun*.

marguerite /mɑ:gə'ri:t/ *noun* ox-eye daisy.

marigold /'mærɪgəʊld/ *noun* plant with golden or bright yellow flowers.

marijuana /mærɪ'hwɑ:nə/ *noun* dried leaves etc. of hemp smoked as drug.

marimba /mə'rɪmbə/ *noun* African and Central American xylophone; orchestral instrument developed from this.

marina /mə'ri:nə/ *noun* harbour for pleasure boats.

marinade /mærɪ'neɪd/ ● *noun* mixture of wine, vinegar, oil, spices, etc., for soaking fish or meat. ● *verb* **(-ding)** soak in marinade.

marinate /'mærɪneɪt/ *verb* **(-ting)** marinade.

marine /mə'ri:n/ ● *adjective* of, found in, or produced by, the sea; of shipping; for use at sea. ● *noun* member of corps trained to fight on land or sea; country's shipping, fleet, or navy.

mariner /'mærɪnə/ *noun* seaman.

marionette /mærɪə'net/ *noun* puppet worked with strings.

marital /'mærɪt(ə)l/ *adjective* of or between husband and wife; of marriage.

maritime /'mærɪtaɪm/ *adjective* connected with the sea or seafaring; living or found near the sea.

marjoram /'mɑ:dʒərəm/ *noun* aromatic herb used in cookery.

mark[1] ● *noun* visible sign left by person or thing; stain, scar, etc; written or printed symbol; number or letter denoting conduct or proficiency; (often + *of*) sign, indication; lasting effect; target, thing aimed at; line etc. serving to indicate position; (followed by numeral) particular design of piece of equipment. ● *verb* make mark on; distinguish with mark; correct and assess (student's work etc.); attach price to; notice, observe; characterize; acknowledge, celebrate; indicate on map etc.; keep close to (opposing player) in games; (in *passive*) have natural marks. ▫ **mark down** reduce price of; **mark off** separate by boundary; **mark out** plan (course), destine, trace out (boundaries etc.); **mark time** march on spot without moving forward, await opportunity to advance; **mark up** *verb* increase price of; **mark-up** *noun* amount added to price by retailer for profit.

mark[2] *noun* Deutschmark.

marked /mɑ:kt/ *adjective* having a visible mark; clearly noticeable. ▫ **markedly** /-kɪdlɪ/ *adverb*.

marker *noun* thing that marks a position; person or thing that marks; pen with broad felt tip; scorer, esp. at billiards.

market /'mɑ:kɪt/ ● *noun* gathering for sale of commodities, livestock, etc.; space for this; (often + *for*) demand for commodity etc.; place or group providing such demand; conditions for buying and selling; stock market. ● *verb* **(-t-)** offer for sale; *archaic* buy or sell goods in market. ▫ **market garden** place where vegetables are grown for market; **market-place** open space for market, commercial world; **market research** surveying of consumers' needs and preferences; **market town** town where market is held; **market value** value as saleable thing; **on the market** offered for sale. ▫ **marketing** *noun*.

marketable *adjective* able or fit to be sold.

marking *noun* (usually in *plural*) identification mark; colouring of fur, feathers, etc.

marksman /'mɑ:ksmən/ *noun* skilled shot, esp. with rifle. ▫ **marksmanship** *noun*.

marl *noun* soil composed of clay and lime, used as fertilizer.

marlinspike /'mɑ:lɪnspaɪk/ *noun* pointed tool used to separate strands of rope or wire.

marmalade /'mɑ:məleɪd/ *noun* preserve of oranges or other citrus fruit.

Marmite /'mɑ:maɪt/ *noun proprietary term* thick brown spread made from yeast and vegetable extract.

marmoreal /mɑ:'mɔ:rɪəl/ *adjective* of or like marble.

marmoset /'mɑ:məzet/ *noun* small bushy-tailed monkey.

marmot /'mɑ:mət/ *noun* burrowing rodent with short bushy tail.

marocain /'mærəkeɪn/ *noun* fabric of ribbed crêpe.

maroon[1] /mə'ru:n/ *adjective & noun* brownish-crimson.

maroon[2] /mə'ru:n/ *verb* put and leave ashore on desolate island or coast; leave stranded.

marquee /mɑ:'ki:/ *noun* large tent.

marquess /'mɑ:kwəs/ *noun* British nobleman ranking between duke and earl.

marquetry /'mɑ:kɪtrɪ/ *noun* inlaid work in wood etc.

marquis /'mɑ:kwɪs/ *noun* (*plural* **-quises**) foreign nobleman ranking between duke and count.

marquise /mɑ:'ki:z/ *noun* marquis's wife or widow; woman holding rank of marquis.

marriage /'mærɪdʒ/ *noun* legal union of man and woman for the purpose of living together; act or ceremony establishing this; particular matrimonial union. ▫ **marriage certificate**, **lines** certificate stating that marriage has taken place; **marriage guidance** counselling of people with marital problems.

marriageable *adjective* free, ready, or fit for marriage.

marrow /ˈmærəʊ/ *noun* large fleshy gourd, cooked as vegetable; bone marrow. □ **marrowbone** bone containing edible marrow; **marrowfat** kind of large pea.

marry /ˈmærɪ/ *verb* (**-ies**, **-ied**) take, join, or give in marriage; enter into marriage; (+ *into*) become member of (family) by marriage; unite intimately.

Marsala /mɑːˈsɑːlə/ *noun* dark sweet fortified wine.

Marseillaise /mɑːseɪˈjeɪz/ *noun* French national anthem.

marsh *noun* low watery ground. □ **marsh gas** methane; **marsh mallow** shrubby herb; **marshmallow** soft sweet made from sugar, albumen, gelatin, etc. □ **marshy** *adjective* (**-ier**, **-iest**).

marshal /ˈmɑːʃ(ə)l/ ● *noun* (**Marshal**) high-ranking officer of state or in armed forces; officer arranging ceremonies, controlling procedure at races, etc. ● *verb* (**-ll-**) arrange in due order; conduct (person) ceremoniously. □ **marshalling yard** yard in which goods trains etc. are assembled.

marsupial /mɑːˈsuːpɪəl/ ● *noun* mammal giving birth to underdeveloped young subsequently carried in pouch. ● *adjective* of or like a marsupial.

mart *noun* trade centre; auction-room; market.

Martello tower /mɑːˈteləʊ/ *noun* small circular coastal fort.

marten /ˈmɑːtɪn/ *noun* weasel-like flesh-eating mammal with valuable fur; its fur.

martial /ˈmɑːʃ(ə)l/ *adjective* of warfare; warlike. □ **martial arts** fighting sports such as judo or karate; **martial law** military government with ordinary law suspended.

Martian /ˈmɑːʃ(ə)n/ ● *adjective* of planet Mars. ● *noun* hypothetical inhabitant of Mars.

martin /ˈmɑːtɪn/ *noun* bird of swallow family.

martinet /mɑːtɪˈnet/ *noun* strict disciplinarian.

Martini /mɑːˈtiːnɪ/ *noun* (*plural* **-s**) *proprietary term* type of vermouth; cocktail of gin and vermouth.

martyr /ˈmɑːtə/ ● *noun* person who undergoes death or suffering for great cause; (+ *to*) *colloquial* constant sufferer from. ● *verb* put to death as martyr; torment. □ **martyrdom** *noun*.

marvel /ˈmɑːv(ə)l/ ● *noun* wonderful thing; (+ *of*) wonderful example of. ● *verb* (**-ll-**; *US* **-l-**) (+ *at*, *that*) feel surprise or wonder.

marvellous /ˈmɑːvələs/ *adjective* (*US* **marvelous**) astonishing; excellent. □ **marvellously** *adverb*.

Marxism /ˈmɑːksɪz(ə)m/ *noun* doctrines of Marx, predicting common ownership of means of production. □ **Marxist** *noun & adjective*.

marzipan /ˈmɑːzɪpæn/ *noun* paste of ground almonds, sugar, etc.

mascara /mæsˈkɑːrə/ *noun* cosmetic for darkening eyelashes.

mascot /ˈmæskɒt/ *noun* person, animal, or thing supposed to bring luck.

masculine /ˈmæskjʊlɪn/ *adjective* of men; manly; *Grammar* belonging to gender including words for most male people and animals. □ **masculinity** /-ˈlɪn-/ *noun*.

maser /ˈmeɪzə/ *noun* device for amplifying or generating microwaves.

mash ● *noun* soft or confused mixture; mixture of boiled bran etc. fed to horses; *colloquial* mashed potatoes. ● *verb* crush (potatoes etc.) to pulp.

mask /mɑːsk/ ● *noun* covering for all or part of face, worn as disguise or for protection, or by surgeon etc. to prevent infection of patient; respirator; likeness of person's face, esp. one made by taking mould from face; disguise. ● *verb* cover with mask; conceal; protect.

masochism /ˈmæsəkɪz(ə)m/ *noun* pleasure in suffering physical or mental pain, esp. as form of sexual perversion. □ **masochist** *noun*; **masochistic** /-ˈkɪs-/ *adjective*.

mason /ˈmeɪs(ə)n/ *noun* person who builds with stone; (**Mason**) Freemason.

Masonic /məˈsɒnɪk/ *adjective* of Freemasons.

masonry /ˈmeɪsənrɪ/ *noun* stonework; mason's work; (**Masonry**) Freemasonry.

masque /mɑːsk/ *noun* musical drama with mime, esp. in 16th & 17th c.

masquerade /mæskəˈreɪd/ ● *noun* false show, pretence; masked ball. ● *verb* (**-ding**) appear in disguise; assume false appearance.

mass¹ ● *noun* cohesive body of matter; dense aggregation; (in *singular* or *plural*; usually + *of*) large number or amount; (usually + *of*) unbroken expanse (of colour etc.); (**the mass**) the majority; (**the masses**) ordinary people; *Physics* quantity of matter body contains. ● *verb* gather into mass; assemble into one body. ● *adjective* of or relating to large numbers of people or things. □ **mass media** means of communication to large numbers of people; **mass production** mechanical production of large quantities of standardized article.

mass² *noun* (often **Mass**) Eucharist, esp. in RC Church; (musical setting of) liturgy used in this.

massacre /ˈmæsəkə/ ● *noun* general slaughter. ● *verb* (**-ring**) make massacre of.

massage /ˈmæsɑːʒ/ ● *noun* kneading and rubbing of muscles etc., usually with hands. ● *verb* (**-ging**) treat thus.

masseur /mæˈsɜː/ *noun* (*feminine* **masseuse** /mæˈsɜːz/) person who gives massage.

massif /ˈmæsiːf/ *noun* mountain heights forming compact group.

massive /ˈmæsɪv/ *adjective* large and heavy or solid; unusually large or severe; substantial. □ **massively** *adverb*.

mast¹ /mɑːst/ *noun* upright to which ship's yards and sails are attached; tall metal structure supporting radio or television aerial; flag-pole.

mast² /mɑːst/ *noun* fruit of beech, oak, etc., esp. as food for pigs.

mastectomy /mæˈstektəmɪ/ *noun* (*plural* **-ies**) surgical removal of a breast.

master /ˈmɑːstə/ ● *noun* person having control or ownership; ship's captain; male teacher; prevailing person; skilled workman; skilled practitioner; holder of university degree above bachelor's; revered teacher; great artist; *Chess etc.* player at international level; thing from which series of copies is made; (**Master**) *title prefixed to name of boy*. ● *adjective* commanding; main, principal; controlling others. ● *verb* overcome, conquer; acquire complete knowledge of. □ **master-key** one opening several different locks; **mastermind** *noun* person with outstanding intellect, *verb* plan and direct (enterprise); **Master of Ceremonies** person introducing speakers at banquet or entertainers at variety show; **masterpiece** outstanding piece of artistry, one's best work; **master-switch** switch controlling electricity etc. supply to entire system.

masterful *adjective* imperious, domineering; very skilful. □ **masterfully** *adverb*.

■ **Usage** *Masterful* is normally used of a person, whereas *masterly* is used of achievements, abilities, etc.

masterly *adjective* very skilful.

■ **Usage** See note at MASTERFUL.

mastery *noun* control, dominance; (often + *of*) comprehensive skill or knowledge.

mastic /ˈmæstɪk/ *noun* gum or resin from certain trees; such tree; waterproof filler and sealant.

masticate /ˈmæstɪkeɪt/ *verb* (**-ting**) chew. □ **mastication** *noun*.

mastiff /ˈmæstɪf/ *noun* large strong kind of dog.

mastodon /ˈmæstədɒn/ *noun* (*plural* same or **-s**) extinct animal resembling elephant.

mastoid /ˈmæstɔɪd/ ● *adjective* shaped like woman's breast. ● *noun* (in full **mastoid process**) conical prominence on temporal bone; (usually in *plural*) *colloquial* inflammation of mastoid.

masturbate /ˈmæstəbeɪt/ *verb* (**-ting**) produce sexual arousal (of) by manual stimulation of genitals. □ **masturbation** *noun*.

mat[1] ● *noun* piece of coarse fabric on floor, esp. for wiping shoes on; piece of material laid on table etc. to protect surface. ● *verb* (**-tt-**) (esp. as **matted** *adjective*) bring or come into thickly tangled state. □ **on the mat** *slang* being reprimanded.

mat[2] = MATT.

matador /ˈmætədɔː/ *noun* bullfighter whose task is to kill bull.

match[1] ● *noun* contest, game; person or thing equal to, exactly resembling, or corresponding to another; marriage; person viewed as marriage prospect. ● *verb* be equal, correspond; be or find match for; (+ *against*, *with*) place in conflict or competition with. □ **matchboard** tongued and grooved board fitting into others; **matchmaker** person who arranges marriages or schemes to bring couples together; **match point** state of game when one side needs only one point to win match; **match up** (often + *with*) fit to form whole, tally; **match up to** be equal to.

match[2] *noun* short thin piece of wood etc., tipped with substance that ignites when rubbed on rough or specially prepared surface. □ **matchbox** box for holding matches; **matchstick** stem of match; **matchwood** wood suitable for matches, minute splinters.

matchless *adjective* incomparable.

mate[1] ● *noun* companion, fellow worker; *colloquial form of address, esp. to another man*; each of a breeding pair, esp. of birds; *colloquial* partner in marriage; subordinate officer on merchant ship; assistant to worker. ● *verb* (**-ting**) come or bring together for breeding.

mate[2] *noun & verb* (**-ting**) checkmate.

material /məˈtɪərɪəl/ ● *noun* that from which thing is made; cloth, fabric; (in *plural*) things needed for activity; person or thing of specified kind or suitable for purpose; (in *singular* or *plural*) information etc. for book etc.; (in *singular* or *plural*) elements. ● *adjective* of matter; not spiritual; of bodily comfort etc.; important, relevant.

materialism *noun* greater interest in material possessions and comfort than in spiritual values; theory that nothing exists but matter. □ **materialist** *noun*; **materialistic** /-ˈlɪs-/ *adjective*.

materialize *verb* (also **-ise**) (**-zing** or **-sing**) become fact, happen; *colloquial* appear, be present; represent in or assume bodily form. □ **materialization** *noun*.

maternal /məˈtɜːn(ə)l/ *adjective* of or like a mother; motherly; related on mother's side.

maternity /məˈtɜːnɪtɪ/ ● *noun* motherhood; motherliness. ● *adjective* for women in pregnancy or childbirth.

matey *adjective* (also **maty**) (**-tier**, **-tiest**) familiar and friendly. □ **matily** *adverb*.

math *noun US colloquial* mathematics.

mathematics /mæθəˈmætɪks/ *plural noun* (also treated as *singular*) science of space, number, and quantity. □ **mathematical** *adjective*; **mathematician** /-məˈtɪʃ(ə)n/ *noun*.

maths *noun colloquial* mathematics.

matinée /ˈmætɪneɪ/ *noun* (*US* **matinee**) theatrical etc. performance in afternoon. □ **matinée coat** baby's short coat.

matins /ˈmætɪnz/ *noun* (also **mattins**) morning prayer.

matriarch /ˈmeɪtrɪɑːk/ *noun* female head of family or tribe. □ **matriarchal** /-ˈɑːk(ə)l/ *adjective*.

matriarchy /ˈmeɪtrɪɑːkɪ/ *noun* (*plural* **-ies**) female-dominated system of society.

matrices *plural* of MATRIX.

matricide /ˈmeɪtrɪsaɪd/ *noun* killing of one's mother; person who does this.

matriculate /məˈtrɪkjʊleɪt/ *verb* (**-ting**) admit (student) to university; be thus admitted. □ **matriculation** *noun*.

matrimony /ˈmætrɪmənɪ/ *noun* marriage. □ **matrimonial** /-ˈməʊnɪəl/ *adjective*.

matrix /ˈmeɪtrɪks/ *noun* (*plural* **matrices** /-siːz/ or **-es**) mould in which thing is cast or shaped; place etc. in which thing is developed; rock in which gems etc. are embedded; *Mathematics* rectangular array of quantities treated as single quantity.

matron /ˈmeɪtrən/ *noun* woman in charge of nursing in hospital; married, esp. staid, woman; woman nurse and housekeeper at school etc.

matronly *adjective* like a matron, esp. portly or staid.

matt *adjective* (also **mat**) dull, not shiny or glossy.

matter /ˈmætə/ ● *noun* physical substance; thing(s), material; (**the matter**; often + *with*) thing that is amiss; content as opposed to form, substance; affair, concern; purulent discharge. ● *verb* (often + *to*) be of importance. □ **a matter of** approximately, amounting to; **matter of course** natural or expected thing; **matter-of-fact** prosaic, unimaginative, unemotional; **no matter** (+ *when*, *how*, etc.) regardless of.

matting *noun* fabric for mats.

mattins = MATINS.

mattock /ˈmætək/ *noun* tool like pickaxe with adze and chisel edge as ends of head.

mattress /ˈmætrɪs/ *noun* fabric case filled with soft or firm material or springs, used on or as bed.

mature /məˈtʃʊə/ ● *adjective* (**-r**, **-st**) fully developed, ripe; adult; careful, considered; (of bill etc.) due for payment. ● *verb* (**-ring**) bring to or reach mature state. □ **maturity** *noun*.

matutinal /mætjuːˈtaɪn(ə)l/ *adjective* of or in morning.

maty = MATEY.

maudlin /ˈmɔːdlɪn/ *adjective* weakly sentimental.

maul /mɔːl/ ● *verb* injure by clawing etc.; handle roughly; damage. ● *noun Rugby* loose scrum; brawl; heavy hammer.

maulstick /ˈmɔːlstɪk/ *noun* stick held to support hand in painting.

maunder /ˈmɔːndə/ *verb* talk ramblingly.

Maundy /ˈmɔːndɪ/ *noun* distribution of **Maundy money**, silver coins minted for English sovereign to give to the poor on **Maundy Thursday**, Thursday before Easter.

mausoleum /mɔːsəˈliːəm/ *noun* magnificent tomb.

mauve /məʊv/ *adjective & noun* pale purple.

maverick /ˈmævərɪk/ *noun* unorthodox or independent-minded person; *US* unbranded calf etc.

maw *noun* stomach of animal.

mawkish /ˈmɔːkɪʃ/ *adjective* feebly sentimental.

maxillary /mækˈsɪlərɪ/ *adjective* of the jaw.

maxim /'mæksɪm/ *noun* general truth or rule of conduct briefly expressed.

maxima *plural* of MAXIMUM.

maximal /'mæksɪm(ə)l/ *adjective* greatest possible in size, duration, etc.

maximize /'mæksɪmaɪz/ *verb* (also **-ise**) (**-zing** or **-sing**) make as large or great as possible. □ **maximization** *noun*.

■ **Usage** *Maximize* should not be used in standard English to mean 'to make as good as possible' or 'to make the most of'.

maximum /'mæksɪməm/ ● *noun* (*plural* **maxima**) highest possible amount, size, etc. ● *adjective* greatest in amount, size, etc.

May *noun* fifth month of year; (**may**) hawthorn, esp. in blossom. □ **May Day** 1 May as Spring festival or as international holiday in honour of workers; **mayfly** insect living briefly in spring as adult; **maypole** decorated pole danced round on May Day; **May queen** girl chosen to preside over May Day festivities.

may *auxiliary verb* (*3rd singular present* **may**; *past* **might** /maɪt/) *expressing possibility, permission, request, wish, etc.* □ **be that as it may** although that is possible.

■ **Usage** Both *can* and *may* are used for asking permission, as in *Can I move?* and *May I move?*, but *may* is better in formal English because *Can I move?* also means 'Am I physically able to move?'

maybe /'meɪbi:/ *adverb* perhaps.

mayday /'meɪdeɪ/ *noun* international radio distress signal.

mayhem /'meɪhem/ *noun* destruction, havoc.

mayonnaise /meɪə'neɪz/ *noun* creamy dressing of oil, egg yolk, vinegar, etc.; dish dressed with this.

mayor /meə/ *noun* head of corporation of city or borough; head of district council with status of borough. □ **mayoral** *adjective*.

mayoralty /'meərəltɪ/ *noun* (*plural* **-ies**) office of mayor; period of this.

mayoress /'meərɪs/ *noun* woman mayor; wife or consort of mayor.

maze *noun* network of paths and hedges designed as puzzle; labyrinth; confused network, mass, etc.

mazurka /mə'zɜ:kə/ *noun* lively Polish dance in triple time; music for this.

MB *abbreviation* Bachelor of Medicine.

MBE *abbreviation* Member of the Order of the British Empire.

MC *abbreviation* Master of Ceremonies; Military Cross.

MCC *abbreviation* Marylebone Cricket Club.

MD *abbreviation* Doctor of Medicine; Managing Director.

me[1] /mi:/ *pronoun used by speaker or writer to refer to himself or herself as object of verb*; *colloquial* I.

■ **Usage** Some people consider it correct to use only *It is I*, but this is very formal or old-fashioned in most situations, and *It is me* is normally quite acceptable. On the other hand, it is not standard English to say *Me and him went* rather than *He and I went*.

me[2] /mi:/ *noun* (also **mi**) *Music* third note of scale in tonic sol-fa.

mead *noun* alcoholic drink of fermented honey and water.

meadow /'medəʊ/ *noun* piece of grassland, esp. used for hay; low ground, esp. near river. □ **meadowsweet** a fragrant flowering plant.

meagre /'mi:gə/ *adjective* (*US* **meager**) scanty in amount or quality.

meal[1] *noun* occasion when food is eaten; the food eaten on one occasion. □ **meal-ticket** *colloquial* source of income.

meal[2] *noun* grain or pulse ground to powder.

mealy *adjective* (**-ier**, **-iest**) of, like, or containing meal. □ **mealy-mouthed** afraid to speak plainly.

mean[1] *verb* (*past & past participle* **meant** /ment/) have as one's purpose, design; intend to convey or indicate; involve, portend; (of word) have as equivalent in same or another language; (+ *to*) be of specified significance to.

mean[2] *adjective* niggardly; not generous; ignoble; of low degree or poor quality; malicious; *US* vicious, aggressive. □ **meanness** *noun*.

mean[3] ● *noun* condition, quality, or course of action equally far from two extremes; term midway between first and last terms of progression; quotient of the sum of several quantities and their number. ● *adjective* (of quantity) equally far from two extremes; calculated as mean.

meander /mɪ'ændə/ ● *verb* wander at random; wind about. ● *noun* (in *plural*) sinuous windings; circuitous journey.

meaning ● *noun* what is meant; significance. ● *adjective* expressive; significant. □ **meaningful** *adjective*; **meaningfully** *adverb*; **meaningless** *adjective*; **meaninglessness** *noun*.

means *plural noun* (often treated as *singular*) action, agent, device, or method producing result; money resources. □ **means test** inquiry into financial resources of applicant for assistance etc.

meantime ● *adverb* meanwhile. ● *noun* intervening period.

meanwhile *adverb* in the intervening time; at the same time.

measles /'mi:z(ə)lz/ *plural noun* (also treated as *singular*) infectious viral disease with red rash.

measly /'mi:zlɪ/ *adjective* (**-ier**, **-iest**) *colloquial* meagre, contemptible.

measure /'meʒə/ ● *noun* size or quantity found by measuring; system or unit of measuring; vessel, rod, tape, etc., for measuring; degree, extent; factor determining evaluation etc.; (usually in *plural*) suitable action; legislative enactment; prescribed extent or amount; poetic metre. ● *verb* (**-ring**) find size, quantity, proportions, etc. of by comparison with known standard; be of specified size; estimate by some criterion; (often + *off*) mark (line etc. of given length); (+ *out*) distribute in measured quantities; (+ *with*, *against*) bring into competition with. □ **measurable** *adjective*; **measurement** *noun*.

measured *adjective* rhythmical; (of language) carefully considered.

measureless *adjective* not measurable; infinite.

meat *noun* animal flesh as food; (often + *of*) chief part.

meaty *adjective* (**-ier**, **-iest**) full of meat; fleshy; of or like meat; substantial, satisfying.

Mecca /'mekə/ *noun* place one aspires to visit.

mechanic /mɪ'kænɪk/ *noun* person skilled in using or repairing machinery.

mechanical *adjective* of, working, or produced by, machines or mechanism; automatic; lacking originality; of mechanics as a science. □ **mechanically** *adverb*.

mechanics /mɪ'kænɪks/ *plural noun* (usually treated as *singular*) branch of applied mathematics dealing with motion; science of machinery; routine technical aspects of thing.

mechanism /'mekənɪz(ə)m/ *noun* structure or parts of machine; system of parts working together; process, method.

mechanize /'mekənaɪz/ *verb* (also **-ise**) (**-zing** or **-sing**) introduce machines in; make mechanical; equip with tanks, armoured cars, etc. □ **mechanization** *noun*.

medal /'med(ə)l/ *noun* commemorative metal disc etc., esp. awarded for military or sporting prowess.

medallion /mɪ'dæljən/ *noun* large medal; thing so shaped, e.g. portrait.

medallist /'medəlɪst/ *noun* (*US* **medalist**) winner of (specified) medal.

meddle /'med(ə)l/ *verb* (**-ling**) (often + *with*, *in*) interfere in others' concerns.

meddlesome *adjective* interfering.

media *plural* of MEDIUM.

■ **Usage** It is a mistake to use *media* with a singular verb, as in *The media is biased*.

mediaeval = MEDIEVAL.

median /'mi:dɪən/ ● *adjective* situated in the middle. ● *noun* straight line from angle of triangle to middle of opposite side; middle value of series.

mediate /'mi:dɪeɪt/ *verb* (**-ting**) act as go-between or peacemaker. □ **mediation** *noun*; **mediator** *noun*.

medical /'medɪk(ə)l/ ● *adjective* of medicine in general or as distinct from surgery. ● *noun colloquial* medical examination. □ **medical certificate** certificate of fitness or unfitness to work etc.; **medical examination** examination to determine person's physical fitness. □ **medically** *adverb*.

medicament /mɪ'dɪkəmənt/ *noun* substance used in curative treatment.

medicate /'medɪkeɪt/ *verb* (**-ting**) treat medically; impregnate with medicinal substance.

medication /medɪ'keɪʃ(ə)n/ *noun* medicinal drug; treatment using drugs.

medicinal /mə'dɪsɪn(ə)l/ *adjective* (of substance) healing.

medicine /'meds(ə)n/ *noun* science or practice of diagnosis, treatment, and prevention of disease, esp. as distinct from surgery; substance, esp. one taken by mouth, used in this. □ **medicine man** witch-doctor.

medieval /medɪ'i:v(ə)l/ *adjective* (also **mediaeval**) of Middle Ages.

mediocre /mi:dɪ'əʊkə/ *adjective* indifferent in quality; second-rate.

mediocrity /mi:dɪ'ɒkrɪtɪ/ *noun* (*plural* **-ies**) being mediocre; mediocre person.

meditate /'medɪteɪt/ *verb* (**-ting**) engage in (esp. religious) contemplation; plan mentally. □ **meditation** *noun*; **meditative** /-tətɪv/ *adjective*.

Mediterranean /medɪtə'reɪnɪən/ *adjective* of the sea between Europe and N. Africa, or the countries bordering on it.

medium /'mi:dɪəm/ ● *noun* (*plural* **media** or **-s**) middle quality, degree, etc. between extremes; environment; means of communication; physical material or form used by artist, composer, etc.; (*plural* **-s**) person claiming to communicate with the dead. ● *adjective* between two qualities etc.; average, moderate. □ **medium-range** (of aircraft, missile, etc.) able to travel medium distance.

medlar /'medlə/ *noun* tree bearing fruit like apple, eaten when decayed; such fruit.

medley /'medlɪ/ *noun* (*plural* **-s**) varied mixture.

medulla /mɪ'dʌlə/ *noun* inner part of certain bodily organs; soft internal tissue of plants. □ **medulla oblongata** /ɒblɒŋ'gɑ:tə/ lowest part of brainstem. □ **medullary** *adjective*.

meek *adjective* humble and submissive or gentle. □ **meekly** *adverb*; **meekness** *noun*.

meerschaum /'mɪəʃəm/ *noun* soft white clay-like substance; tobacco pipe with bowl made from this.

meet[1] ● *verb* (*past & past participle* **met**) encounter or (of two or more people) come together; be present at arrival of (person, train, etc.); come into contact (with); make acquaintance of; deal with (demand etc.); (often + *with*) experience, receive. ● *noun* assembly for a hunt; assembly for athletics.

meet[2] *adjective archaic* fitting, proper.

meeting *noun* coming together; assembly of esp. a society, committee, etc.; race meeting.

mega- *combining form* large; one million; *slang* extremely, very big.

megabyte /'megəbaɪt/ *noun* 2^{20} bytes (approx. 1,000,000) as unit of computer storage.

megalith /'megəlɪθ/ *noun* large stone, esp. prehistoric monument. □ **megalithic** /-'lɪθ-/ *adjective*.

megalomania /megələ'meɪnɪə/ *noun* mental disorder producing delusions of grandeur; passion for grandiose schemes. □ **megalomaniac** *adjective & noun*.

megaphone /'megəfəʊn/ *noun* large funnel-shaped device for amplifying voice.

megaton /'megətʌn/ *noun* unit of explosive power equal to that of 1,000,000 tons of TNT.

meiosis /maɪ'əʊsɪs/ *noun* (*plural* **meioses** /-si:z/) cell division resulting in gametes with half normal chromosome number; ironical understatement.

melamine /'meləmi:n/ *noun* crystalline compound producing resins; plastic made from this.

melancholia /melən'kəʊlɪə/ *noun* depression and anxiety.

melancholy /'melənkəlɪ/ ● *noun* pensive sadness; depression; tendency to this. ● *adjective* sad; depressing. □ **melancholic** /-'kɒl-/ *adjective*.

mêlée /'meleɪ/ *noun* (*US* **melee**) confused fight or scuffle; muddle.

mellifluous /mɪ'lɪfluəs/ *adjective* (of voice etc.) pleasing, musical.

mellow /'meləʊ/ ● *adjective* (of sound, colour, light, or flavour) soft and rich, free from harshness; (of character) gentle; mature; genial. ● *verb* make or become mellow.

melodic /mɪ'lɒdɪk/ *adjective* of melody; melodious.

melodious /mɪ'ləʊdɪəs/ *adjective* of, producing, or having melody; sweet-sounding. □ **melodiously** *adverb*.

melodrama /'melədrɑ:mə/ *noun* sensational play etc. appealing blatantly to emotions; this type of drama. □ **melodramatic** /-drə'mæt-/ *adjective*.

melody /'melədɪ/ *noun* (*plural* **-ies**) arrangement of notes to make distinctive pattern; tune; principal part in harmonized music; tunefulness.

melon /'melən/ *noun* sweet fleshy fruit of various climbers of gourd family.

melt *verb* become liquid or change from solid to liquid by action of heat; dissolve; (as **molten** *adjective*) (esp. of metals etc.) liquefied by heat; soften, be softened; (usually + *into*) merge; (often + *away*) leave unobtrusively. □ **melt down** melt (esp. metal) for reuse, become liquid and lose structure; **melting point** temperature at which solid melts; **melting pot** place for mixing races, theories, etc.

member /'membə/ *noun* person etc. belonging to society, team, group, etc.; (**Member**) person elected to certain assemblies; part of larger structure; part or organ of body, esp. limb.

membership *noun* being a member; number or group of members.

membrane /'membreɪn/ *noun* pliable tissue connecting or lining organs in plants and animals; pliable sheet or skin. □ **membranous** /-brən-/ *adjective*.

memento /mɪ'mentəʊ/ *noun* (*plural* **-es** or **-s**) souvenir of person or event.

memo /ˈmeməʊ/ *noun* (*plural* **-s**) *colloquial* memorandum.
memoir /ˈmemwɑː/ *noun* historical account etc. written from personal knowledge or special sources; (in *plural*) autobiography.
memorable /ˈmemərəb(ə)l/ *adjective* worth remembering; easily remembered. □ **memorably** *adverb*.
memorandum /meməˈrændəm/ *noun* (*plural* **-da** or **-s**) note or record for future use; informal written message, esp. in business etc.
memorial /mɪˈmɔːrɪəl/ ● *noun* object etc. established in memory of person or event. ● *adjective* commemorative.
memoriam see IN MEMORIAM.
memorize /ˈmeməraɪz/ *verb* (also **-ise**) (**-zing** or **-sing**) commit to memory.
memory /ˈmemərɪ/ *noun* (*plural* **-ies**) faculty by which things are recalled to or kept in mind; store of things remembered; remembrance, esp. of person etc.; storage capacity of computer etc.; posthumous reputation.
memsahib /ˈmemsɑːb/ *noun historical* European married woman in India.
men *plural* of MAN.
menace /ˈmenɪs/ ● *noun* threat; dangerous thing or person; *jocular* nuisance. ● *verb* (**-cing**) threaten. □ **menacingly** *adverb*.
ménage /meɪˈnɑːʒ/ *noun* household.
menagerie /mɪˈnædʒərɪ/ *noun* small zoo.
mend ● *verb* restore to good condition; repair; regain health; improve. ● *noun* darn or repair in material etc. □ **on the mend** recovering, esp. in health.
mendacious /menˈdeɪʃəs/ *adjective* lying, untruthful. □ **mendacity** /-ˈdæs-/ *noun* (*plural* **-ies**).
mendicant /ˈmendɪkənt/ ● *adjective* begging; (of friar) living solely on alms. ● *noun* beggar; mendicant friar.
menfolk *plural noun* men, esp. men of family.
menhir /ˈmenhɪə/ *noun* usually prehistoric monument of tall upright stone.
menial /ˈmiːnɪəl/ ● *adjective* (of work) degrading, servile. ● *noun* domestic servant.
meningitis /menɪnˈdʒaɪtɪs/ *noun* (esp. viral) infection and inflammation of membranes enclosing brain and spinal cord.
meniscus /mɪˈnɪskəs/ *noun* (*plural* **menisci** /-saɪ/) curved upper surface of liquid in tube; lens convex on one side and concave on the other.
menopause /ˈmenəpɔːz/ *noun* ceasing of menstruation; period in woman's life when this occurs. □ **menopausal** /-ˈpɔːz(ə)l/ *adjective*.
menses /ˈmensiːz/ *plural noun* flow of menstrual blood etc.
menstrual /ˈmenstrʊəl/ *adjective* of menstruation.
menstruate /ˈmenstrʊeɪt/ *verb* (**-ting**) undergo menstruation.
menstruation *noun* discharge of blood etc. from uterus, usually at monthly intervals.
mensuration /mensjʊəˈreɪʃ(ə)n/ *noun* measuring; measuring of lengths, areas, and volumes.
mental /ˈment(ə)l/ *adjective* of, in, or done by mind; caring for mental patients; *colloquial* insane. □ **mental age** degree of mental development in terms of average age at which such development is attained; **mental deficiency** abnormally low intelligence; **mental patient** sufferer from mental illness. □ **mentally** *adverb*.
mentality /menˈtælɪtɪ/ *noun* (*plural* **-ies**) mental character or disposition.
menthol /ˈmenθɒl/ *noun* mint-tasting organic alcohol found in oil of peppermint etc., used as flavouring and to relieve local pain.
mention /ˈmenʃ(ə)n/ ● *verb* refer to briefly or by name; disclose. ● *noun* reference, esp. by name.
mentor /ˈmentɔː/ *noun* experienced and trusted adviser.
menu /ˈmenjuː/ *noun* (*plural* **-s**) list of dishes available in restaurant etc., or to be served at meal; *Computing* list of options displayed on VDU.
MEP *abbreviation* Member of European Parliament.
mercantile /ˈmɜːkəntaɪl/ *adjective* of trade, trading; commercial. □ **mercantile marine** merchant shipping.
mercenary /ˈmɜːsɪnərɪ/ ● *adjective* primarily concerned with or working for money etc. ● *noun* (*plural* **-ies**) hired soldier in foreign service.
mercer /ˈmɜːsə/ *noun* dealer in textile fabrics.
mercerize /ˈmɜːsəraɪz/ *verb* (also **-ise**) (**-zing** or **-sing**) treat (cotton) with caustic alkali to strengthen and make lustrous.
merchandise /ˈmɜːtʃəndaɪz/ ● *noun* goods for sale. ● *verb* (**-sing**) trade (in); promote (goods, ideas, etc.).
merchant /ˈmɜːtʃ(ə)nt/ *noun* wholesale trader, esp. with foreign countries; *esp. US & Scottish* retail trader. □ **merchant bank** bank dealing in commercial loans and finance; **merchantman** merchant ship; **merchant navy** nation's commercial shipping; **merchant ship** ship carrying merchandise.
merchantable *adjective* saleable.
merciful /ˈmɜːsɪfʊl/ *adjective* showing mercy. □ **mercifulness** *noun*.
mercifully *adverb* in a merciful way; fortunately.
merciless /ˈmɜːsɪləs/ *adjective* showing no mercy. □ **mercilessly** *adverb*.
mercurial /mɜːˈkjʊərɪəl/ *adjective* (of person) volatile; of or containing mercury.
mercury /ˈmɜːkjʊrɪ/ *noun* silvery heavy liquid metal used in barometers, thermometers, etc.; (**Mercury**) planet nearest to the sun. □ **mercuric** /-ˈkjʊər-/ *adjective*; **mercurous** *adjective*.
mercy /ˈmɜːsɪ/ *noun* (*plural* **-ies**) compassion towards defeated enemies or offenders or as quality; act of mercy; thing to be thankful for. □ **at the mercy of** in the power of; **mercy killing** killing done out of pity.
mere[1] /mɪə/ *adjective* (**-st**) being only what is specified. □ **merely** *adverb*.
mere[2] /mɪə/ *noun dialect or poetical* lake.
meretricious /merəˈtrɪʃəs/ *adjective* showily but falsely attractive.
merganser /mɜːˈgænsə/ *noun* (*plural* same or **-s**) a diving duck.
merge *verb* (**-ging**) (often + *with*) combine, join or blend gradually; (+ *in*) (cause to) lose character and identity in (something else).
merger *noun* combining, esp. of two commercial companies etc. into one.
meridian /məˈrɪdɪən/ *noun* circle of constant longitude passing through given place and N. & S. Poles; corresponding line on map etc.
meridional /məˈrɪdɪən(ə)l/ *adjective* of or in the south (esp. of Europe); of a meridian.
meringue /məˈræŋ/ *noun* sugar, whipped egg whites, etc. baked crisp; cake of this.
merino /məˈriːnəʊ/ *noun* (*plural* **-s**) variety of sheep with long fine wool; soft material, originally of merino wool; fine woollen yarn.
merit /ˈmerɪt/ ● *noun* quality of deserving well; excellence, worth; (usually in *plural*) thing that entitles to reward or gratitude. ● *verb* (**-t-**) deserve.
meritocracy /merɪˈtɒkrəsɪ/ *noun* (*plural* **-ies**) government by those selected for merit; group selected in this way.
meritorious /merɪˈtɔːrɪəs/ *adjective* praiseworthy.

merlin /ˈmɜːlɪn/ *noun* kind of small falcon.

mermaid /ˈmɜːmeɪd/ *noun* legendary creature with woman's head and trunk and fish's tail.

merry /ˈmerɪ/ *adjective* (**-ier**, **-iest**) joyous; full of laughter or gaiety; *colloquial* slightly drunk. □ **merry-go-round** fairground ride with revolving model horses, cars, etc.; **merrymaking** festivity. □ **merrily** *adverb*; **merriment** *noun*.

mésalliance /meɪˈzælɪɑ̃s/ *noun* marriage with social inferior. [French]

mescal /ˈmeskæl/ *noun* peyote cactus. □ **mescal buttons** disc-shaped dried tops from mescal, esp. as intoxicant.

mescaline /ˈmeskəlɪn/ *noun* (also **mescalin**) hallucinogenic alkaloid present in mescal buttons.

Mesdames, Mesdemoiselles *plural* of MADAME, MADEMOISELLE.

mesh ● *noun* network structure; each of open spaces in net, sieve, etc.; (in *plural*) network, snare. ● *verb* (often + *with*) (of teeth of wheel) be engaged; be harmonious; catch in net.

mesmerize /ˈmezmərаɪz/ *verb* (also **-ise**) (**-zing** or **-sing**) hypnotize; fascinate. □ **mesmerism** *noun*.

meso- *combining form* middle, intermediate.

mesolithic /mezəʊˈlɪθɪk/ *adjective* of Stone Age between palaeolithic and neolithic periods.

meson /ˈmiːzɒn/ *noun* elementary particle with mass between that of electron and proton.

Mesozoic /mesəʊˈzəʊɪk/ ● *adjective* of geological era marked by development of dinosaurs. ● *noun* this era.

mess ● *noun* dirty or untidy state; state of confusion or trouble; something spilt etc.; disagreeable concoction; soldiers etc. dining together; army dining-hall; meal taken there; domestic animal's excreta; *archaic* portion of liquid or pulpy food. ● *verb* (often + *up*) make mess of, dirty, muddle; *US* (+ *with*) interfere with; take one's meals; *colloquial* defecate. □ **make a mess of** bungle; **mess about**, **around** potter.

message /ˈmesɪdʒ/ *noun* communication sent by one person to another; exalted or spiritual communication.

messenger /ˈmesɪndʒə/ *noun* person who carries message(s).

Messiah /mɪˈsaɪə/ *noun* promised deliverer of Jews; Jesus regarded as this. □ **Messianic** /mesɪˈænɪk/ *adjective*.

Messieurs *plural* of MONSIEUR.

Messrs /ˈmesəz/ *plural* of MR.

messy *adjective* (**-ier**, **-iest**) untidy, dirty; causing or accompanied by a mess; difficult to deal with; awkward. □ **messily** *adverb*.

met *past & past participle* of MEET[1].

metabolism /mɪˈtæbəlɪz(ə)m/ *noun* all chemical processes in living organism producing energy and growth. □ **metabolic** /metəˈbɒlɪk/ *adjective*.

metacarpus /metəˈkɑːpəs/ *noun* (*plural* **-carpi** /-paɪ/) set of bones forming part of hand between wrist and fingers. □ **metacarpal** *adjective*.

metal /ˈmet(ə)l/ ● *noun* any of class of mainly workable elements such as gold, silver, iron, or tin; alloy of any of these; (in *plural*) rails of railway; road-metal. ● *adjective* made of metal. ● *verb* (**-ll-**; *US* **-l-**) make or mend (road) with road-metal; cover or fit with metal.

metallic /mɪˈtælɪk/ *adjective* of or like metal(s); sounding like struck metal.

metallurgy /mɪˈtælədʒɪ/ *noun* science of metals and their application; extraction and purification of metals. □ **metallurgic** /metəˈlɜːdʒɪk/ *adjective*; **metallurgical** /metəˈlɜːdʒɪk(ə)l/ *adjective*; **metallurgist** *noun*.

metamorphic /metəˈmɔːfɪk/ *adjective* of metamorphosis; (of rock) transformed naturally. □ **metamorphism** *noun*.

metamorphose /metəˈmɔːfəʊz/ *verb* (**-sing**) (often + *to*, *into*) change in form or nature.

metamorphosis /metəˈmɔːfəsɪs/ *noun* (*plural* **-phoses** /-siːz/) change of form, esp. from pupa to insect; change of character, conditions, etc.

metaphor /ˈmetəfɔː/ *noun* application of name or description to something to which it is not literally applicable (see panel). □ **metaphoric** /-ˈfɒr-/ *adjective*; **metaphorical** /-ˈfɒr-/ *adjective*; **metaphorically** /-ˈfɒr-/ *adverb*.

metaphysics /metəˈfɪzɪks/ *plural noun* (usually treated as *singular*) philosophy dealing with nature of existence, truth, and knowledge. □ **metaphysical** *adjective*.

metatarsus /metəˈtɑːsəs/ *noun* (*plural* **-tarsi** /-saɪ/) set of bones forming part of foot between ankle and toes. □ **metatarsal** *adjective*.

mete *verb* (**-ting**) (usually + *out*) *literary* apportion, allot.

meteor /ˈmiːtɪə/ *noun* small solid body from outer space becoming incandescent when entering earth's atmosphere.

meteoric /miːtɪˈɒrɪk/ *adjective* rapid; dazzling; of meteors.

meteorite /ˈmiːtɪəraɪt/ *noun* fallen meteor; fragment of rock or metal from outer space.

meteorology /miːtɪəˈrɒlədʒɪ/ *noun* study of atmospheric phenomena, esp. for forecasting weather. □ **meteorological** /-rəˈlɒdʒ-/ *adjective*; **meteorologist** *noun*.

meter[1] /ˈmiːtə/ ● *noun* instrument that measures or records, esp. gas, electricity, etc. used, distance travelled, etc.; parking meter. ● *verb* measure or record by meter.

meter[2] *US* = METRE.

methane /ˈmiːθeɪn/ *noun* colourless odourless inflammable gaseous hydrocarbon, the main constituent of natural gas.

methanol /ˈmeθənɒl/ *noun* colourless inflammable organic liquid, used as solvent.

Metaphor

A metaphor is a figure of speech that goes further than a simile, either by saying that something is something else that it could not normally be called, e.g.

The moon was a ghostly galleon tossed upon cloudy seas.
Stockholm, the Venice of the North

or by suggesting that something appears, sounds, or behaves like something else, e.g.

burning ambition *blindingly obvious*
the long arm of the law

methinks /mɪˈθɪŋks/ *verb* (*past* **methought** /mɪˈθɔːt/) *archaic* it seems to me.
method /ˈmeθəd/ *noun* way of doing something; procedure; orderliness.
methodical /mɪˈθɒdɪk(ə)l/ *adjective* characterized by method or order. ▫ **methodically** *adverb*.
Methodist /ˈmeθədɪst/ ● *noun* member of Protestant denomination originating in 18th-c. Wesleyan evangelistic movement. ● *adjective* of Methodists or Methodism. ▫ **Methodism** *noun*.
methought *past* of METHINKS.
meths *noun colloquial* methylated spirit.
methyl /ˈmeθɪl/ *noun* hydrocarbon radical CH_3. ▫ **methyl alcohol** methanol.
methylate /ˈmeθɪleɪt/ *verb* (**-ting**) mix or impregnate with methanol; introduce methyl group into (molecule).
meticulous /məˈtɪkjʊləs/ *adjective* giving great attention to detail; very careful and precise. ▫ **meticulously** *adverb*.
métier /ˈmetjeɪ/ *noun* one's trade, profession, or field of activity; one's forte. [French]
metonymy /mɪˈtɒnɪmɪ/ *noun* substitution of name of attribute for that of thing meant.
metre /ˈmiːtə/ *noun* (*US* **meter**) SI unit of length (about 39.4 in.); any form of poetic rhythm; basic rhythm of music.
metric /ˈmetrɪk/ *adjective* of or based on the metre. ▫ **metric system** decimal measuring system with metre, litre, and gram or kilogram as units of length, volume, and mass; **metric ton** 1,000 kg.
metrical *adjective* of or composed in metre; of or involving measurement. ▫ **metrically** *adverb*.
metronome /ˈmetrənəʊm/ *noun* device ticking at selected rate to mark musical time.
metropolis /mɪˈtrɒpəlɪs/ *noun* chief city, capital.
metropolitan /metrəˈpɒlɪt(ə)n/ ● *adjective* of metropolis; of mother country as distinct from colonies. ● *noun* bishop with authority over bishops of province.
mettle /ˈmet(ə)l/ *noun* quality or strength of character; spirit, courage. ▫ **mettlesome** *adjective*.
mew[1] ● *noun* cat's cry. ● *verb* utter this sound.
mew[2] *noun* gull, esp. common gull.
mews /mjuːz/ *noun* (treated as *singular*) stabling round yard etc., now used esp. for housing.
mezzanine /ˈmetsəniːn/ *noun* storey between two others (usually ground and first floors).
mezzo /ˈmetsəʊ/ *Music* ● *adverb* moderately. ● *noun* (in full **mezzo-soprano**) (*plural* **-s**) female singing voice between soprano and contralto, singer with this voice. ▫ **mezzo forte** fairly loud(ly); **mezzo piano** fairly soft(ly).
mezzotint /ˈmetsəʊtɪnt/ *noun* method of copper or steel engraving; print so produced.
mf *abbreviation* mezzo forte.
mg *abbreviation* milligram(s).
Mgr. *abbreviation* Manager; *Monseigneur*; Monsignor.
MHz *abbreviation* megahertz.
mi = ME[2].
miaow /mɪˈaʊ/ ● *noun* characteristic cry of cat. ● *verb* make this cry.
miasma /mɪˈæzmə/ *noun* (*plural* **-mata** or **-s**) *archaic* infectious or noxious vapour.
mica /ˈmaɪkə/ *noun* silicate mineral found as glittering scales in granite etc. or crystals separable into thin plates.
mice *plural* of MOUSE.
Michaelmas /ˈmɪkəlməs/ *noun* feast of St Michael, 29 Sept. ▫ **Michaelmas daisy** autumn-flowering aster.
mickey /ˈmɪkɪ/ *noun* (also **micky**) ▫ **take the mickey** (often + *out of*) *slang* tease, mock.
micro /ˈmaɪkrəʊ/ *noun* (*plural* **-s**) *colloquial* microcomputer; microprocessor.
micro- *combining form* small; one-millionth.
microbe /ˈmaɪkrəʊb/ *noun* micro-organism (esp. bacterium) causing disease or fermentation. ▫ **microbial** /-ˈkrəʊb-/ *adjective*.
microbiology /maɪkrəʊbaɪˈɒlədʒɪ/ *noun* study of micro-organisms. ▫ **microbiologist** *noun*.
microchip /ˈmaɪkrəʊtʃɪp/ *noun* small piece of semiconductor used to carry integrated circuits.
microcomputer /ˈmaɪkrəʊkəmpjuːtə/ *noun* small computer with microprocessor as central processor.
microcosm /ˈmaɪkrəkɒz(ə)m/ *noun* (often + *of*) miniature representation, e.g. humankind seen as small-scale model of universe; epitome. ▫ **microcosmic** /-ˈkɒz-/ *adjective*.
microdot /ˈmaɪkrəʊdɒt/ *noun* microphotograph of document etc. reduced to size of dot.
microfiche /ˈmaɪkrəʊfiːʃ/ *noun* small flat piece of film bearing microphotographs of documents etc.
microfilm /ˈmaɪkrəʊfɪlm/ ● *noun* length of film bearing microphotographs of documents etc. ● *verb* photograph on microfilm.
microlight /ˈmaɪkrəʊlaɪt/ *noun* kind of motorized hang-glider.
micrometer /maɪˈkrɒmɪtə/ *noun* gauge for accurate small-scale measurement.
micron /ˈmaɪkrɒn/ *noun* millionth of a metre.
micro-organism /maɪkrəʊˈɔːgənɪz(ə)m/ *noun* microscopic organism.
microphone /ˈmaɪkrəfəʊn/ *noun* instrument for converting sound waves into electrical energy for reconversion into sound.
microphotograph /maɪkrəʊˈfəʊtəgrɑːf/ *noun* photograph reduced to very small size.
microprocessor /maɪkrəʊˈprəʊsesə/ *noun* data processor using integrated circuits contained on microchip(s).
microscope /ˈmaɪkrəskəʊp/ *noun* instrument with lenses for magnifying objects or details invisible to naked eye.
microscopic /maɪkrəˈskɒpɪk/ *adjective* visible only with microscope; extremely small; of the microscope. ▫ **microscopically** *adverb*.
microscopy /maɪˈkrɒskəpɪ/ *noun* use of microscopes.
microsurgery /ˈmaɪkrəʊsɜːdʒərɪ/ *noun* intricate surgery using microscopes.
microwave /ˈmaɪkrəʊweɪv/ ● *noun* electromagnetic wave of length between 1 mm and 30 cm; (in full **microwave oven**) oven using microwaves to cook or heat food quickly. ● *verb* (**-ving**) cook in microwave oven.
micturition /mɪktjʊəˈrɪʃ(ə)n/ *noun formal* urination.
mid- *combining form* middle of. ▫ **midday** middle of day, noon; **mid-life** middle age; **mid-off**, **-on** *Cricket* position of fielder near bowler on off or on side.
midden /ˈmɪd(ə)n/ *noun* dunghill; refuse heap.
middle /ˈmɪd(ə)l/ ● *adjective* at equal distance, time, or number from extremities; central; intermediate in rank, quality, etc.; average. ● *noun* (often + *of*) middle point, position, or part; waist. ▫ **in the middle of** in the process of; **middle age** period between youth and old age; **the Middle Ages** period of European history from *c.* 1000 to 1453; **middle class** *noun* social class between upper and lower, including professional and business workers; **middle-class** *adjective*; **the Middle East** countries from Egypt to Iran inclusive; **middleman** trader

who handles commodity between producer and consumer; **middleweight** amateur boxing weight (71–75 kg).

middling ● *adjective* moderately good. ● *adverb* fairly, moderately.

midge *noun* gnatlike insect.

midget /ˈmɪdʒɪt/ *noun* extremely small person or thing.

midland /ˈmɪdlənd/ ● *noun* (**the Midlands**) inland counties of central England; middle part of country. ● *adjective* of or in midland or Midlands.

midnight *noun* middle of night; 12 o'clock at night. □ **midnight sun** sun visible at midnight during summer in polar regions.

midriff /ˈmɪdrɪf/ *noun* front of body just above waist.

midshipman /ˈmɪdʃɪpmən/ *noun* naval officer ranking next above cadet.

midst *noun* middle. □ **in the midst of** among.

midsummer *noun* period of or near summer solstice, about 21 June. □ **Midsummer Day**, **Midsummer's Day** 24 June.

midwife /ˈmɪdwaɪf/ *noun* (*plural* **-wives**) person trained to assist at childbirth. □ **midwifery** /-wɪfrɪ/ *noun*.

midwinter *noun* period of or near winter solstice, about 22 Dec.

mien /miːn/ *noun literary* person's look or bearing.

might[1] *past* of MAY.

might[2] /maɪt/ *noun* strength, power.

mightn't /ˈmaɪt(ə)nt/ might not.

mighty ● *adjective* (**-ier**, **-iest**) powerful, strong; massive. ● *adverb colloquial* very. □ **mightily** *adverb*.

mignonette /mɪnjəˈnet/ *noun* plant with fragrant grey-green flowers.

migraine /ˈmiːgreɪn/ *noun* recurrent throbbing headache often with nausea and visual disturbance.

migrant /ˈmaɪgrənt/ ● *adjective* migrating. ● *noun* migrant person or animal, esp. bird.

migrate /maɪˈgreɪt/ *verb* (**-ting**) move from one place, esp. one country, to settle in another; (of bird etc.) change habitation seasonally. □ **migration** *noun*; **migratory** /ˈmaɪgrətərɪ/ *adjective*.

mikado /mɪˈkɑːdəʊ/ *noun* (*plural* **-s**) *historical* emperor of Japan.

mike *noun colloquial* microphone.

milch *adjective* (of cow etc.) giving milk.

mild /maɪld/ *adjective* (esp. of person) gentle; not severe or harsh; (of weather) moderately warm; (of flavour) not sharp or strong. □ **mild steel** tough low-carbon steel. □ **mildly** *adverb*; **mildness** *noun*.

mildew /ˈmɪldjuː/ ● *noun* destructive growth of minute fungi on plants, damp paper, leather, etc. ● *verb* taint or be tainted with mildew.

mile *noun* unit of linear measure (1,760 yds, approx. 1.6 km); (in *plural*) *colloquial* great distance or amount; race extending over one mile. □ **milestone** stone beside road to mark distance in miles, significant point (in life, history, etc.).

mileage *noun* number of miles travelled; *colloquial* profit, advantage.

miler *noun colloquial* person or horse specializing in races of one mile.

milfoil /ˈmɪlfɔɪl/ *noun* common yarrow.

milieu /mɪˈljɜː/ *noun* (*plural* **-x** or **-s** /-z/) person's environment or social surroundings.

militant /ˈmɪlɪt(ə)nt/ ● *adjective* combative; aggressively active in support of cause; engaged in warfare. ● *noun* militant person. □ **militancy** *noun*; **militantly** *adverb*.

militarism /ˈmɪlɪtərɪz(ə)m/ *noun* aggressively military policy etc.; military spirit. □ **militarist** *noun*; **militaristic** /-ˈrɪst-/ *adjective*.

military /ˈmɪlɪtərɪ/ ● *adjective* of or characteristic of soldiers or armed forces. ● *noun* (treated as *singular* or *plural*; **the military**) the army.

militate /ˈmɪlɪteɪt/ *verb* (**-ting**) (usually + *against*) have force or effect.

■ **Usage** *Militate* is often confused with *mitigate*, which means 'to make less intense or severe'.

militia /mɪˈlɪʃə/ *noun* military force, esp. one conscripted in emergency. □ **militiaman** *noun*.

milk ● *noun* opaque white fluid secreted by female mammals for nourishing young; milk of cows, goats, etc. as food; milklike liquid of coconut etc. ● *verb* draw milk from (cow etc.); exploit (person, situation). □ **milk chocolate** chocolate made with milk; **milk float** small usually electric vehicle used in delivering milk; **milkmaid** woman who milks cows or works in dairy; **milkman** person who sells or delivers milk; **milk run** routine expedition etc.; **milk shake** drink of whisked milk, flavouring, etc.; **milksop** weak or timid man or youth; **milk tooth** temporary tooth in young mammals.

milky *adjective* (**-ier**, **-iest**) of, like, or mixed with milk; (of gem or liquid) cloudy. □ **Milky Way** luminous band of stars, the Earth's galaxy.

mill ● *noun* building fitted with mechanical device for grinding corn; such device; device for grinding any solid to powder; building fitted with machinery for manufacturing processes etc.; such machinery. ● *verb* grind or treat in mill; (esp. as **milled** *adjective*) produce ribbed edge on (coin); (often + *about*, *round*) move aimlessly. □ **millpond** pond retained by dam for operating mill-wheel; **mill-race** current of water driving mill-wheel; **millstone** each of two circular stones for grinding corn, heavy burden, great responsibility; **mill-wheel** wheel used to drive watermill.

millennium /mɪˈlenɪəm/ *noun* (*plural* **-s** or **millennia**) thousand-year period; (esp. future) period of happiness on earth. □ **millennial** *adjective*.

miller /ˈmɪlə/ *noun* person who owns or works mill, esp. corn-mill; person operating milling machine.

millesimal /mɪˈlesɪm(ə)l/ ● *adjective* thousandth; of, belonging to, or dealing with, thousandth or thousandths. ● *noun* thousandth part.

millet /ˈmɪlɪt/ *noun* cereal plant bearing small nutritious seeds; seed of this.

milli- *combining form* one-thousandth.

millibar /ˈmɪlɪbɑː/ *noun* unit of atmospheric pressure equivalent to 100 pascals.

milligram /ˈmɪlɪgræm/ *noun* (also **-gramme**) one-thousandth of a gram.

millilitre /ˈmɪlɪliːtə/ *noun* (*US* **-liter**) one-thousandth of a litre (0.002 pint).

millimetre /ˈmɪlɪmiːtə/ *noun* (*US* **-meter**) one-thousandth of a metre.

milliner /ˈmɪlɪnə/ *noun* maker or seller of women's hats. □ **millinery** *noun*.

million /ˈmɪljən/ *noun* (*plural* same) one thousand thousand; (**millions**) *colloquial* very large number. □ **millionth** *adjective & noun*.

millionaire /mɪljəˈneə/ *noun* (*feminine* **millionairess**) person possessing over a million pounds, dollars, etc.

millipede /ˈmɪlɪpiːd/ *noun* (also **millepede**) small crawling invertebrate with many legs.

millisecond /ˈmɪlɪsekənd/ *noun* one-thousandth of a second.

milometer /maɪˈlɒmɪtə/ *noun* instrument for measuring number of miles travelled by vehicle.

milt *noun* spleen in mammals; reproductive gland or sperm of male fish.

mime ● *noun* acting without words, using only gestures; performance using mime. ● *verb* (**-ming**) express or represent by mime.

mimeograph /'mɪmɪəgrɑːf/ ● *noun* machine which duplicates from stencil; copy so produced. ● *verb* reproduce in this way.

mimetic /mɪ'metɪk/ *adjective* of or practising imitation or mimicry.

mimic /'mɪmɪk/ ● *verb* (**-ck-**) imitate (person, gesture, etc.), esp. to entertain or ridicule; copy minutely or servilely; resemble closely. ● *noun* person who mimics. □ **mimicry** *noun*.

mimosa /mɪ'məʊzə/ *noun* shrub with globular usually yellow flowers; acacia plant.

Min. *abbreviation* Minister; Ministry.

min. *abbreviation* minute(s); minimum; minim (fluid measure).

minaret /mɪnə'ret/ *noun* tall slender turret next to mosque, used by muezzin.

minatory /'mɪnətərɪ/ *adjective formal* threatening.

mince ● *verb* (**-cing**) cut or grind (meat etc.) finely; (usually as **mincing** *adjective*) walk or speak in affected way. ● *noun* minced meat. □ **mincemeat** mixture of currants, sugar, spices, suet, etc.; **mince pie** (usually small) pie containing mincemeat. □ **mincer** *noun*.

mind /maɪnd/ ● *noun* seat of consciousness, thought, volition, and feeling; attention, concentration; intellect; memory; opinion; sanity. ● *verb* object to; be upset; (often + *out*) heed, take care; look after; concern oneself with. □ **be in two minds** be undecided.

minded *adjective* (usually + *to do*) disposed, inclined. □ **-minded** inclined to think in specified way, or with specified interest.

minder *noun* person employed to look after person or thing; *slang* bodyguard.

mindful *adjective* (often + *of*) taking heed or care.

mindless *adjective* lacking intelligence; brutish; not requiring thought or skill. □ **mindlessly** *adverb*; **mindlessness** *noun*.

mine[1] *pronoun* the one(s) belonging to me.

mine[2] ● *noun* hole dug to extract metal, coal, salt, etc.; abundant source (of information etc.); *military* explosive device placed in ground or water. ● *verb* (**-ning**) obtain (minerals) from mine; (often + *for*) dig in (earth etc.) for ore etc. or to tunnel; lay explosive mines under or in. □ **minefield** area planted with explosive mines; **minesweeper** ship for clearing explosive mines from sea. □ **mining** *noun*.

miner *noun* worker in mine.

mineral /'mɪnər(ə)l/ *noun* inorganic substance; substance obtained by mining; (often in *plural*) artificial mineral water or other carbonated drink. □ **mineral water** water naturally or artificially impregnated with dissolved salts.

mineralogy /mɪnə'rælədʒɪ/ *noun* study of minerals. □ **mineralogical** /-rə'lɒdʒ-/ *adjective*; **mineralogist** *noun*.

minestrone /mɪnɪ'strəʊnɪ/ *noun* soup containing vegetables and pasta, beans, or rice.

mingle /'mɪŋg(ə)l/ *verb* (**-ling**) mix, blend.

mingy /'mɪndʒɪ/ *adjective* (**-ier**, **-iest**) *colloquial* stingy.

mini /'mɪnɪ/ *noun* (*plural* **-s**) *colloquial* miniskirt; (**Mini**) *proprietary term* make of small car.

mini- *combining form* miniature; small of its kind.

miniature /'mɪnɪtʃə/ ● *adjective* much smaller than normal; represented on small scale. ● *noun* miniature object; detailed small-scale portrait. □ **in miniature** on small scale.

miniaturist *noun* painter of miniatures.

miniaturize *verb* (also **-ise**) (**-zing** or **-sing**) produce in smaller version; make small. □ **miniaturization** *noun*.

minibus /'mɪnɪbʌs/ *noun* small bus for about 12 passengers.

minicab /'mɪnɪkæb/ *noun* car used as taxi, hireable only by telephone.

minim /'mɪnɪm/ *noun Music* note equal to two crotchets or half a semibreve; one-sixtieth of fluid drachm.

minimal /'mɪnɪm(ə)l/ *adjective* very minute or slight; being a minimum. □ **minimally** *adverb*.

minimize /'mɪnɪmaɪz/ *verb* (also **-ise**) (**-zing** or **-sing**) reduce to or estimate at minimum; estimate or represent at less than true value etc.

minimum /'mɪnɪməm/ ● *noun* (*plural* **minima**) least possible or attainable amount. ● *adjective* that is a minimum. □ **minimum wage** lowest wage permitted by law or agreement.

minion /'mɪnjən/ *noun derogatory* servile subordinate.

miniskirt /'mɪnɪskɜːt/ *noun* very short skirt.

minister /'mɪnɪstə/ ● *noun* head of government department; member of clergy, esp. in Presbyterian and Nonconformist Churches; diplomat, usually ranking below ambassador. ● *verb* (usually + *to*) help, serve, look after. □ **ministerial** /-'stɪər-/ *adjective*.

ministration /mɪnɪ'streɪʃ(ə)n/ *noun* (usually in *plural*) help, service; ministering, esp. in religious matters.

ministry /'mɪnɪstrɪ/ *noun* (*plural* **-ies**) government department headed by minister; building for this; (**the ministry**) profession of religious minister, ministers of government or religion.

mink *noun* (*plural* same or **-s**) small semi-aquatic stoat-like animal; its fur; coat of this.

minke /'mɪŋkɪ/ *noun* small whale.

minnow /'mɪnəʊ/ *noun* (*plural* same or **-s**) small freshwater carp.

Minoan /mɪ'nəʊən/ ● *adjective* of Cretan Bronze Age civilization. ● *noun* person of this civilization.

minor /'maɪnə/ ● *adjective* lesser or comparatively small in size or importance; *Music* (of scale) having semitone above second, fifth, and seventh notes; (of key) based on minor scale. ● *noun* person under full legal age; *US* student's subsidiary subject or course. ● *verb US* (+ *in*) study (subject) as subsidiary.

minority /maɪ'nɒrɪtɪ/ *noun* (*plural* **-ies**) (often + *of*) smaller number or part, esp. in politics; smaller group of people differing from larger in race, religion, language, etc.; being under full legal age; period of this.

minster /'mɪnstə/ *noun* large or important church; church of monastery.

minstrel /'mɪnstr(ə)l/ *noun* medieval singer or musician; musical entertainer with blacked face.

mint[1] *noun* aromatic herb used in cooking; peppermint; peppermint sweet. □ **minty** *adjective* (**-ier**, **-iest**).

mint[2] ● *noun* (esp. state) establishment where money is coined; *colloquial* vast sum. ● *verb* make (coin); invent (word, phrase, etc.).

minuet /mɪnjʊ'et/ *noun* slow stately dance in triple time; music for this.

minus /'maɪnəs/ ● *preposition* with subtraction of; less than zero; *colloquial* lacking. ● *adjective Mathematics* negative. ● *noun* minus sign; negative quantity; *colloquial* disadvantage. □ **minus sign** symbol (–) indicating subtraction or negative value.

minuscule /'mɪnəskjuːl/ *adjective colloquial* extremely small or unimportant.

minute[1] /'mɪnɪt/ ● *noun* sixtieth part of hour; distance covered in minute; moment; sixtieth part of angular degree; (in *plural*) summary of proceedings

of meeting; official memorandum. ● *verb* (**-ting**) record in minutes; send minutes to. □ **up to the minute** up to date.
minute[2] /maɪ'nju:t/ *adjective* (**-est**) very small; accurate, detailed. □ **minutely** *adverb*.
minutiae /maɪ'nju:ʃɪi:/ *plural noun* very small, precise, or minor details.
minx /mɪŋks/ *noun* pert, sly, or playful girl.
miracle /'mɪrək(ə)l/ *noun* extraordinary, supposedly supernatural, event; remarkable happening. □ **miracle play** medieval play on biblical themes.
miraculous /mɪ'rækjʊləs/ *adjective* being a miracle; supernatural; surprising. □ **miraculously** *adverb*.
mirage /'mɪrɑ:ʒ/ *noun* optical illusion caused by atmospheric conditions, esp. appearance of water in desert; illusory thing.
mire ● *noun* area of swampy ground; mud. ● *verb* (**-ring**) sink in mire; bespatter with mud. □ **miry** *adjective*.
mirror /'mɪrə/ ● *noun* polished surface, usually of coated glass, reflecting image; anything reflecting state of affairs etc. ● *verb* reflect in or as in mirror. □ **mirror image** identical image or reflection with left and right reversed.
mirth *noun* merriment, laughter. □ **mirthful** *adjective*.
misadventure /mɪsəd'ventʃə/ *noun Law* accident without crime or negligence; bad luck.
misalliance /mɪsə'laɪəns/ *noun* unsuitable alliance, esp. marriage.
misanthrope /'mɪsənθrəʊp/ *noun* (also **misanthropist** /mɪ'sænθrəpɪst/) person who hates humankind. □ **misanthropic** /-'θrɒp-/ *adjective*.
misanthropy /mɪ'sænθrəpɪ/ *noun* condition or habits of misanthrope.
misapply /mɪsə'plaɪ/ *verb* (**-ies**, **-ied**) apply (esp. funds) wrongly. □ **misapplication** /-æplɪ'keɪ-/ *noun*.
misapprehend /mɪsæprɪ'hend/ *verb* misunderstand (words, person). □ **misapprehension** *noun*.
misappropriate /mɪsə'prəʊprɪeɪt/ *verb* (**-ting**) take (another's money etc.) for one's own use; embezzle. □ **misappropriation** *noun*.
misbegotten /mɪsbɪ'gɒt(ə)n/ *adjective* illegitimate, bastard; contemptible.
misbehave /mɪsbɪ'heɪv/ *verb* (**-ving**) behave badly. □ **misbehaviour** *noun*.
miscalculate /mɪs'kælkjʊleɪt/ *verb* (**-ting**) calculate wrongly. □ **miscalculation** *noun*.
miscarriage /'mɪskærɪdʒ/ *noun* spontaneous abortion. □ **miscarriage of justice** failure of judicial system.
miscarry /mɪs'kærɪ/ *verb* (**-ies**, **-ied**) (of woman) have miscarriage; (of plan etc.) fail.
miscast /mɪs'kɑ:st/ *verb* (*past & past participle* **-cast**) allot unsuitable part to (actor) or unsuitable actors to (play etc.).
miscegenation /mɪsɪdʒɪ'neɪʃ(ə)n/ *noun* interbreeding of races.
miscellaneous /mɪsə'leɪnɪəs/ *adjective* of mixed composition or character; (+ plural noun) of various kinds. □ **miscellaneously** *adverb*.
miscellany /mɪ'selənɪ/ *noun* (*plural* **-ies**) mixture, medley.
mischance /mɪs'tʃɑ:ns/ *noun* bad luck; instance of this.
mischief /'mɪstʃɪf/ *noun* troublesome, but not malicious, conduct, esp. of children; playfulness; malice; harm, injury. □ **mischievous** /'mɪstʃɪvəs/ *adjective*; **mischievously** /'mɪstʃɪvəslɪ/ *adverb*.
misconceive /mɪskən'si:v/ *verb* (**-ving**) (often + *of*) have wrong idea or conception; (as **misconceived** *adjective*) badly organized etc. □ **misconception** /-'sep-/ *noun*.
misconduct /mɪs'kɒndʌkt/ *noun* improper or unprofessional conduct.
misconstrue /mɪskən'stru:/ *verb* (**-strues**, **-strued**, **-struing**) interpret wrongly. □ **misconstruction** /-'strʌk-/ *noun*.
miscount /mɪs'kaʊnt/ ● *verb* count inaccurately. ● *noun* inaccurate count.
miscreant /'mɪskrɪənt/ *noun* vile wretch, villain.
misdeed /mɪs'di:d/ *noun* evil deed, wrongdoing.
misdemeanour /mɪsdɪ'mi:nə/ *noun* (*US* **misdemeanor**) misdeed; *historical* indictable offence less serious than felony.
misdirect /mɪsdaɪ'rekt/ *verb* direct wrongly. □ **misdirection** *noun*.
miser /'maɪzə/ *noun* person who hoards wealth and lives miserably. □ **miserly** *adjective*.
miserable /'mɪzərəb(ə)l/ *adjective* wretchedly unhappy or uncomfortable; contemptible, mean; causing discomfort. □ **miserably** *adverb*.
misericord /mɪ'zerɪkɔ:d/ *noun* projection under hinged choir stall seat to support person standing.
misery /'mɪzərɪ/ *noun* (*plural* **-ies**) condition or feeling of wretchedness; cause of this; *colloquial* constantly grumbling person.
misfire /mɪs'faɪə/ ● *verb* (**-ring**) (of gun, motor engine, etc.) fail to go off, start, or function smoothly; (of plan etc.) fail to be effective. ● *noun* such failure.
misfit /'mɪsfɪt/ *noun* person unsuited to surroundings, occupation, etc.; garment etc. that does not fit.
misfortune /mɪs'fɔ:tʃ(ə)n/ *noun* bad luck; instance of this.
misgiving *noun* (usually in *plural*) feeling of mistrust or apprehension.
misgovern /mɪs'gʌv(ə)n/ *verb* govern badly. □ **misgovernment** *noun*.
misguided /mɪs'gaɪdɪd/ *adjective* mistaken in thought or action. □ **misguidedly** *adverb*.
mishandle /mɪs'hænd(ə)l/ *verb* (**-ling**) deal with incorrectly or inefficiently; handle roughly.
mishap /'mɪshæp/ *noun* unlucky accident.
mishear /mɪs'hɪə/ *verb* (*past & past participle* **-heard** /-'hɜ:d/) hear incorrectly or imperfectly.
mishmash /'mɪʃmæʃ/ *noun* confused mixture.
misinform /mɪsɪn'fɔ:m/ *verb* give wrong information to, mislead. □ **misinformation** /-fə'm-/ *noun*.
misinterpret /mɪsɪn'tɜ:prɪt/ *verb* (**-t-**) interpret wrongly. □ **misinterpretation** *noun*.
misjudge /mɪs'dʒʌdʒ/ *verb* (**-ging**) judge wrongly. □ **misjudgement** *noun*.
mislay /mɪs'leɪ/ *verb* (*past & past participle* **-laid**) accidentally put (thing) where it cannot readily be found.
mislead /mɪs'li:d/ *verb* (*past & past participle* **-led**) cause to infer what is not true; deceive. □ **misleading** *adjective*.
mismanage /mɪs'mænɪdʒ/ *verb* (**-ging**) manage badly or wrongly. □ **mismanagement** *noun*.
misnomer /mɪs'nəʊmə/ *noun* wrongly used name or term.
misogyny /mɪ'sɒdʒɪnɪ/ *noun* hatred of women. □ **misogynist** *noun*.
misplace /mɪs'pleɪs/ *verb* (**-cing**) put in wrong place; bestow (affections, confidence, etc.) on inappropriate object. □ **misplacement** *noun*.
misprint ● *noun* /'mɪsprɪnt/ printing error. ● *verb* /mɪs'prɪnt/ print wrongly.
mispronounce /mɪsprə'naʊns/ *verb* (**-cing**) pronounce (word etc.) wrongly. □ **mispronunciation** /-nʌnsɪ'eɪ-/ *noun*.
misquote /mɪs'kwəʊt/ *verb* (**-ting**) quote inaccurately. □ **misquotation** *noun*.

misread /mɪs'ri:d/ *verb* (*past & past participle* **-read** /-'red/) read or interpret wrongly.

misrepresent /mɪsreprɪ'zent/ *verb* represent wrongly; give false account of. □ **misrepresentation** *noun*.

misrule /mɪs'ru:l/ ● *noun* bad government. ● *verb* (**-ling**) govern badly.

Miss *noun title of girl or unmarried woman*.

miss ● *verb* fail to hit, reach, meet, find, catch, or perceive; fail to seize (opportunity etc.); regret absence of; avoid; (of engine etc.) misfire. ● *noun* failure. □ **give (thing) a miss** *colloquial* avoid; **miss out** omit.

missal /'mɪs(ə)l/ *noun RC Church* book of texts for Mass; book of prayers.

misshapen /mɪs'ʃeɪpən/ *adjective* deformed, distorted.

missile /'mɪsaɪl/ *noun* object, esp. weapon, suitable for throwing at target or discharging from machine; weapon directed by remote control or automatically.

missing *adjective* not in its place; lost; (of person) not traced but not known to be dead.

mission /'mɪʃ(ə)n/ *noun* task or goal assigned to person or group; journey undertaken as part of this; military or scientific expedition; group of people sent to conduct negotiations or to evangelize; missionary post.

missionary /'mɪʃənərɪ/ ● *adjective* of or concerned with religious missions, esp. abroad. ● *noun* (*plural* **-ies**) person doing missionary work.

missis = MISSUS.

missive /'mɪsɪv/ *noun jocular* letter; official letter.

misspell /mɪs'spel/ *verb* (*past & past participle* **-spelt** or **-spelled**) spell wrongly.

misspend /mɪs'spend/ *verb* (*past & past participle* **-spent**) (esp. as **misspent** *adjective*) spend wrongly or wastefully.

misstate /mɪs'steɪt/ *verb* (**-ting**) state wrongly or inaccurately. □ **misstatement** *noun*.

missus /'mɪsɪz/ *noun* (also **missis**) *colloquial or jocular form of address to woman*; (**the missis**) *colloquial* my or your wife.

mist ● *noun* water vapour in minute drops limiting visibility; condensed vapour obscuring glass etc.; dimness or blurring of sight caused by tears etc. ● *verb* cover or be covered (as) with mist.

mistake /mɪ'steɪk/ ● *noun* incorrect idea or opinion; thing incorrectly done, thought, or judged. ● *verb* (**-king**; *past* **mistook** /-'stʊk/; *past participle* **mistaken**) misunderstand meaning of; (+ *for*) wrongly take (person, thing) for another.

mistaken /mɪ'steɪkən/ *adjective* wrong in opinion or judgement; based on or resulting from error. □ **mistakenly** *adverb*.

mister /'mɪstə/ *noun colloquial or jocular form of address to man*.

mistime /mɪs'taɪm/ *verb* (**-ming**) say or do at wrong time.

mistle thrush /'mɪs(ə)l/ *noun* large thrush that eats mistletoe berries.

mistletoe /'mɪs(ə)ltəʊ/ *noun* parasitic white-berried plant.

mistook *past* of MISTAKE.

mistral /'mɪstr(ə)l/ *noun* cold N or NW wind in S. France.

mistreat /mɪs'tri:t/ *verb* treat badly. □ **mistreatment** *noun*.

mistress /'mɪstrɪs/ *noun* female head of household; woman in authority; female owner of pet; female teacher; woman having illicit sexual relationship with (usually married) man.

mistrial /mɪs'traɪəl/ *noun* trial made invalid by error.

mistrust /mɪs'trʌst/ ● *verb* be suspicious of; feel no confidence in. ● *noun* suspicion; lack of confidence. □ **mistrustful** *adjective*; **mistrustfully** *adverb*.

misty *adjective* (**-ier**, **-iest**) of or covered with mist; dim in outline; obscure. □ **mistily** *adverb*.

misunderstand /mɪsʌndə'stænd/ *verb* (*past & past participle* **-stood** /-'stʊd/) understand incorrectly; misinterpret words or actions of (person). □ **misunderstanding** *noun*.

misuse ● *verb* /mɪs'ju:z/ (**-sing**) use wrongly; ill-treat. ● *noun* /mɪs'ju:s/ wrong or improper use.

mite[1] *noun* small arachnid, esp. of kind found in cheese etc.

mite[2] *noun* small monetary unit; small object or child; modest contribution.

miter *US* = MITRE.

mitigate /'mɪtɪgeɪt/ *verb* (**-ting**) make less intense or severe. □ **mitigation** *noun*.

■ **Usage** *Mitigate* is often confused with *militate*, which means 'to have force or effect'.

---

mitre /'maɪtə/ (*US* **miter**) ● *noun* bishop's or abbot's tall deeply cleft headdress; joint of two pieces of wood at angle of 90°, such that line of junction bisects this angle. ● *verb* (**-ring**) bestow mitre on; join with mitre.

mitt *noun* (also **mitten**) glove with only one compartment for the 4 fingers and another for thumb; glove leaving fingers and thumb-tip bare; *slang* hand; baseball glove.

mix ● *verb* combine or put together (two or more substances or things) so that constituents of each are diffused among those of the other(s); prepare (compound, cocktail, etc.) by combining ingredients; combine (activities etc.); join, be mixed, combine; be compatible; be sociable; (+ *with*) be harmonious with; combine (two or more sound signals) into one. ● *noun* mixing, mixture; proportion of materials in mixture; ingredients prepared commercially for making cake, concrete, etc.

mixed /mɪkst/ *adjective* of diverse qualities or elements; containing people from various backgrounds, of both sexes, etc. □ **mixed marriage** marriage between people of different race or religion; **mixed-up** *colloquial* mentally or emotionally confused, socially ill-adjusted.

mixer *noun* machine for mixing foods etc.; person who manages socially in specified way; (usually soft) drink to be mixed with spirit; device combining separate signals from microphones etc.

mixture /'mɪkstʃə/ *noun* process or result of mixing; combination of ingredients, qualities, etc.

mizen-mast /'mɪz(ə)n/ *noun* mast next aft of main-mast.

ml *abbreviation* millilitre(s); mile(s).

Mlle *abbreviation* (*plural* **-s**) Mademoiselle.

MM *abbreviation* Messieurs; Military Medal.

mm *abbreviation* millimetre(s).

Mme *abbreviation* (*plural* **-s**) Madame.

mnemonic /nɪ'mɒnɪk/ ● *adjective* of or designed to aid memory. ● *noun* mnemonic word, verse, etc. □ **mnemonically** *adverb*.

MO *abbreviation* Medical Officer; money order.

mo /məʊ/ *noun* (*plural* **-s**) *colloquial* moment.

moan ● *noun* low murmur expressing physical or mental suffering or pleasure; *colloquial* complaint. ● *verb* make moan or moans; *colloquial* complain, grumble. □ **moaner** *noun*.

moat *noun* defensive ditch round castle etc., usually filled with water.

mob ● *noun* disorderly crowd; rabble; (**the mob**) *usually derogatory* the populace; *colloquial* gang, group. ● *verb* (**-bb-**) crowd round to attack or admire.

mob-cap *noun historical* woman's indoor cap covering all the hair.

mobile /'məʊbaɪl/ ● *adjective* movable; able to move easily; (of face etc.) readily changing expression; (of shop etc.) accommodated in vehicle to serve various places; (of person) able to change social status. ● *noun* decoration that may be hung so as to turn freely. □ **mobility** /mə'bɪl-/ *noun*.

mobilize /'məʊbɪlaɪz/ *verb* (also **-ise**) (**-zing** or **-sing**) make or become ready for (esp. military) service or action. □ **mobilization** *noun*.

mobster /'mɒbstə/ *noun slang* gangster.

moccasin /'mɒkəsɪn/ *noun* soft flat-soled shoe originally worn by N. American Indians.

mock ● *verb* (often + *at*) ridicule, scoff (at); treat with scorn or contempt; mimic contemptuously. ● *adjective* sham; imitation; as a trial run. □ **mock turtle soup** soup made from calf's head etc.; **mock-up** experimental model of proposed structure etc. □ **mockingly** *adverb*.

mockery *noun* (*plural* **-ies**) derision; counterfeit or absurdly inadequate representation; travesty.

mode *noun* way in which thing is done; prevailing fashion; *Music* any of several types of scale.

model /'mɒd(ə)l/ ● *noun* representation in 3 dimensions of existing person or thing or of proposed structure, esp. on smaller scale; simplified description of system etc.; clay, wax, etc. figure for reproduction in another material; particular design or style, esp. of car; exemplary person or thing; person employed to pose for artist or photographer, or to wear clothes etc. for display; (copy of) garment etc. by well-known designer. ● *adjective* exemplary; ideally perfect. ● *verb* (**-ll-**; *US* **-l-**) fashion or shape (figure) in clay, wax, etc.; (+ *after*, *on*, etc.) form (thing) in imitation of; act or pose as model; (of person acting as model) display (garment).

modem /'məʊdem/ *noun* device for sending and receiving computer data by means of telephone line.

moderate /'mɒdərət/ ● *adjective* avoiding extremes, temperate in conduct or expression; fairly large or good; (of wind) of medium strength; (of prices) fairly low. ● *noun* person of moderate views. ● *verb* /-reɪt/ (**-ting**) make or become less violent, intense, rigorous, etc.; act as moderator of or to. □ **moderately** /-rətlɪ/ *adverb*; **moderation** *noun*.

moderator *noun* arbitrator, mediator; presiding officer; Presbyterian minister presiding over ecclesiastical body.

modern /'mɒd(ə)n/ ● *adjective* of present and recent times; in current fashion, not antiquated. ● *noun* person living in modern times. □ **modernity** /mə'dɜːn-/ *noun*.

modernism *noun* modern ideas or methods, esp. in art. □ **modernist** *noun & adjective*.

modernize *verb* (also **-ise**) (**-zing** or **-sing**) make modern; adapt to modern needs or habits. □ **modernization** *noun*.

modest /'mɒdɪst/ *adjective* having humble or moderate estimate of one's own merits; bashful; decorous; not excessive; unpretentious, not extravagant. □ **modestly** *adverb*; **modesty** *noun*.

modicum /'mɒdɪkəm/ *noun* (+ *of*) small quantity.

modify /'mɒdɪfaɪ/ *verb* (**-ies**, **-ied**) make less severe; make partial changes in. □ **modification** *noun*.

modish /'məʊdɪʃ/ *adjective* fashionable. □ **modishly** *adverb*.

modulate /'mɒdjʊleɪt/ *verb* (**-ting**) regulate, adjust; moderate; adjust or vary tone or pitch of (speaking voice); alter amplitude or frequency of (wave) by using wave of lower frequency to convey signal; *Music* pass from one key to another. □ **modulation** *noun*.

module /'mɒdjuːl/ *noun* standardized part or independent unit in construction, esp. of furniture, building, spacecraft, or electronic system; unit or period of training or education. □ **modular** *adjective*.

modus operandi /məʊdəs ɒpə'rændɪ/ *noun* (*plural* ***modi operandi*** /məʊdɪ/) method of working. [Latin]

modus vivendi /məʊdəs vɪ'vendɪ/ *noun* (*plural* ***modi vivendi*** /məʊdɪ/) way of living or coping; compromise between people agreeing to differ. [Latin]

mog *noun* (also **moggie**) *slang* cat.

mogul /'məʊg(ə)l/ *noun colloquial* important or influential person.

mohair /'məʊheə/ *noun* hair of angora goat; yarn or fabric from this.

Mohammedan = MUHAMMADAN.

moiety /'mɔɪətɪ/ *noun* (*plural* **-ies**) half; each of two parts of thing.

moiré /'mwɑːreɪ/ *adjective* (of silk) watered; (of metal) having clouded appearance.

moist *adjective* slightly wet; damp. □ **moisten** *verb*.

moisture /'mɔɪstʃə/ *noun* water or other liquid diffused as vapour or within solid, or condensed on surface.

moisturize *verb* (also **-ise**) (**-zing** or **-sing**) make less dry (esp. skin by use of cosmetic). □ **moisturizer** *noun*.

molar /'məʊlə/ ● *adjective* (usually of mammal's back teeth) serving to grind. ● *noun* molar tooth.

molasses /mə'læsɪz/ *plural noun* (treated as *singular*) uncrystallized syrup extracted from raw sugar; *US* treacle.

mold *US* = MOULD[1,2,3].

molder *US* = MOULDER.

molding *US* = MOULDING.

moldy *US* = MOULDY.

mole[1] *noun* small burrowing animal with dark velvety fur and very small eyes; *slang* spy established in position of trust in organization. □ **molehill** small mound thrown up by mole in burrowing.

mole[2] *noun* small permanent dark spot on skin.

mole[3] *noun* massive structure as pier, breakwater, or causeway; artificial harbour.

mole[4] *noun* SI unit of amount of substance.

molecule /'mɒlɪkjuːl/ *noun* group of atoms forming smallest fundamental unit of chemical compound. □ **molecular** /mə'lekjʊlə/ *adjective*.

molest /mə'lest/ *verb* annoy or pester (person); attack or interfere with (person), esp. sexually. □ **molestation** *noun*; **molester** *noun*.

moll *noun slang* gangster's female companion; prostitute.

mollify /'mɒlɪfaɪ/ *verb* (**-ies**, **-ied**) soften, appease. □ **mollification** *noun*.

mollusc /'mɒləsk/ *noun* (*US* **mollusk**) invertebrate with soft body and usually hard shell, e.g. snail or oyster.

mollycoddle /'mɒlɪkɒd(ə)l/ *verb* (**-ling**) coddle, pamper.

molt *US* = MOULT.

molten /'məʊlt(ə)n/ *adjective* melted, esp. made liquid by heat.

molto /'mɒltəʊ/ *adverb Music* very.

molybdenum /mə'lɪbdɪnəm/ *noun* silver-white metallic element added to steel to give strength and resistance to corrosion.

moment /'məʊmənt/ *noun* very brief portion of time; exact point of time; importance; product of force and distance from its line of action to a point.

momentary *adjective* lasting only a moment; transitory. □ **momentarily** *adverb*.

momentous /mə'mentəs/ *adjective* very important.

momentum /mə'mentəm/ *noun* (*plural* **-ta**) quantity of motion of moving body, the product of its mass and velocity; impetus gained by movement or initial effort.

Mon. *abbreviation* Monday.

monarch /'mɒnək/ *noun* sovereign with title of king, queen, emperor, empress, or equivalent. □ **monarchic** /mə'nɑ:k-/ *adjective*; **monarchical** /mə'nɑ:k-/ *adjective*.

monarchist *noun* advocate of monarchy.

monarchy *noun* (*plural* **-ies**) government headed by monarch; state with this.

monastery /'mɒnəstrɪ/ *noun* (*plural* **-ies**) residence of community of monks.

monastic /mə'næstɪk/ *adjective* of or like monasteries or monks, nuns, etc. □ **monastically** *adverb*; **monasticism** /-sɪz(ə)m/ *noun*.

Monday /'mʌndeɪ/ *noun* day of week following Sunday.

monetarism /'mʌnɪtərɪz(ə)m/ *noun* control of supply of money as chief method of stabilizing economy. □ **monetarist** *adjective & noun*.

monetary /'mʌnɪtərɪ/ *adjective* of the currency in use; of or consisting of money.

money /'mʌnɪ/ *noun* (*plural* **-s** or **monies**) coins and banknotes as medium of exchange; (in *plural*) sums of money; wealth. □ **moneylender** person lending money at interest; **money market** trade in short-term stocks, loans, etc.; **money order** order for payment of specified sum, issued by bank or Post Office; **money-spinner** thing that brings in a profit.

moneyed /'mʌnɪd/ *adjective* rich.

Mongol /'mɒŋg(ə)l/ ● *adjective* of Asian people now inhabiting Mongolia; resembling this people. ● *noun* Mongolian.

Mongolian /mɒŋ'gəʊlɪən/ ● *noun* native, national, or language of Mongolia. ● *adjective* of or relating to Mongolia or its people or language.

Mongoloid /'mɒŋgəlɔɪd/ ● *adjective* characteristic of Mongolians, esp. in having broad flat yellowish face. ● *noun* Mongoloid person.

mongoose /'mɒŋgu:s/ *noun* (*plural* **-s**) small flesh-eating civet-like mammal.

mongrel /'mʌŋgr(ə)l/ ● *noun* dog of no definable type or breed; any animal or plant resulting from crossing of different breeds or types. ● *adjective* of mixed origin or character.

monies *plural* of MONEY.

monitor /'mɒnɪtə/ ● *noun* person or device for checking; school pupil with disciplinary etc. duties; television set used to select or verify picture being broadcast or to display computer data; person who listens to and reports on foreign broadcasts etc.; detector of radioactive contamination. ● *verb* act as monitor of; maintain regular surveillance over.

monk /mʌŋk/ *noun* member of religious community of men living under vows. □ **monkish** *adjective*.

monkey /'mʌŋkɪ/ ● *noun* (*plural* **-eys**) any of various primates, e.g. baboons, marmosets; mischievous person, esp. child. ● *verb* (**-eys**, **-eyed**) (often + *with*) play mischievous tricks. □ **monkey-nut** peanut; **monkey-puzzle** tree with hanging prickly branches; **monkey wrench** wrench with adjustable jaw.

monkshood /'mʌŋkshʊd/ *noun* poisonous plant with hood-shaped flowers.

mono /'mɒnəʊ/ *colloquial* ● *adjective* monophonic. ● *noun* monophonic reproduction.

mono- *combining form* (usually **mon-** before vowel) one, alone, single.

monochromatic /mɒnəkrə'mætɪk/ *adjective* (of light or other radiation) of single colour or wavelength; containing only one colour.

monochrome /'mɒnəkrəʊm/ ● *noun* photograph or picture in one colour, or in black and white only. ● *adjective* having or using one colour or black and white only.

monocle /'mɒnək(ə)l/ *noun* single eyeglass.

monocular /mə'nɒkjʊlə/ *adjective* with or for one eye.

monody /'mɒnədɪ/ *noun* (*plural* **-ies**) ode sung by one actor in Greek tragedy; poem lamenting person's death.

monogamy /mə'nɒgəmɪ/ *noun* practice or state of being married to one person at a time. □ **monogamous** *adjective*.

monogram /'mɒnəgræm/ *noun* two or more letters, esp. initials, interwoven.

monograph /'mɒnəgrɑ:f/ *noun* treatise on single subject.

monolith /'mɒnəlɪθ/ *noun* single block of stone, esp. shaped into pillar etc.; person or thing like monolith in being massive, immovable, or solidly uniform. □ **monolithic** /-'lɪθ-/ *adjective*.

monologue /'mɒnəlɒg/ *noun* scene in drama in which person speaks alone; dramatic composition for one performer; long speech by one person in conversation etc.

monomania /mɒnə'meɪnɪə/ *noun* obsession by single idea or interest. □ **monomaniac** *noun & adjective*.

monophonic /mɒnə'fɒnɪk/ *adjective* (of sound-reproduction) using only one channel of transmission.

monoplane /'mɒnəpleɪn/ *noun* aeroplane with one set of wings.

monopolist /mə'nɒpəlɪst/ *noun* person who has or advocates monopoly. □ **monopolistic** /-'lɪs-/ *adjective*.

monopolize /mə'nɒpəlaɪz/ *verb* (also **-ise**) (**-zing** or **-sing**) obtain exclusive possession or control of (trade etc.); dominate (conversation) etc. □ **monopolization** *noun*; **monopolizer** *noun*.

monopoly /mə'nɒpəlɪ/ *noun* (*plural* **-ies**) exclusive possession or control of trade in commodity or service; (+ *of*, *US on*) sole possession or control.

monorail /'mɒnəʊreɪl/ *noun* railway with single-rail track.

monosodium glutamate /mɒnəʊ'səʊdɪəm 'glu:təmeɪt/ *noun* sodium salt of glutamic acid used to enhance flavour of food.

monosyllable /'mɒnəsɪləb(ə)l/ *noun* word of one syllable. □ **monosyllabic** /-'læb-/ *adjective*.

monotheism /'mɒnəθi:ɪz(ə)m/ *noun* doctrine that there is only one God. □ **monotheist** *noun*; **monotheistic** /-'ɪst-/ *adjective*.

monotone /'mɒnətəʊn/ *noun* sound continuing or repeated on one note or without change of pitch.

monotonous /mə'nɒtənəs/ *adjective* lacking in variety, tedious through sameness. □ **monotonously** *adverb*; **monotony** *noun*.

monoxide /mə'nɒksaɪd/ *noun* oxide containing one oxygen atom.

Monseigneur /mɒnsen'jɜ:/ *noun* (*plural* ***Messeigneurs*** /mesen'jɜ:/) *title given to eminent French person, esp. prince, cardinal, etc.* [French]

Monsieur /mə'sjɜ:/ *noun* (*plural* **Messieurs** /mes'jɜ:/) *title used of or to French-speaking man.*

Monsignor /mBn'si:njə/ *noun* (*plural* **-nori** /-'njɔ:rɪ/) *title of various RC priests and officials.*

monsoon /mɒn'su:n/ *noun* wind in S. Asia, esp. in Indian Ocean; rainy season accompanying summer monsoon.

monster /'mɒnstə/ ● *noun* imaginary creature, usually large and frightening; inhumanly wicked person; misshapen animal or plant; large, usually ugly, animal or thing. ● *adjective* huge.

monstrance /'mɒnstrəns/ *noun RC Church* vessel in which host is exposed for veneration.

monstrosity /mɒn'strɒsɪtɪ/ *noun* (*plural* **-ies**) huge or outrageous thing.

monstrous /'mɒnstrəs/ *adjective* like a monster; abnormally formed; huge; outrageously wrong; atrocious. ▫ **monstrously** *adverb.*

montage /mɒn'tɑːʒ/ *noun* selection, cutting, and arrangement as consecutive whole, of separate sections of cinema or television film; composite whole made from juxtaposed photographs etc.

month /mʌnθ/ *noun* (in full **calendar month**) each of 12 divisions of year; period of time between same dates in successive calendar months; period of 28 days.

monthly ● *adjective* done, produced, or occurring once every month. ● *adverb* every month. ● *noun* (*plural* **-ies**) monthly periodical.

monument /'mɒnjʊmənt/ *noun* anything enduring that serves to commemorate, esp. structure, building, or memorial stone.

monumental /mɒnjʊ'ment(ə)l/ *adjective* extremely great; stupendous; massive and permanent; of or serving as monument.

moo ● *noun* (*plural* **-s**) characteristic sound of cattle. ● *verb* (**moos**, **mooed**) make this sound.

mooch *verb colloquial* (usually + *about, around*) wander aimlessly; *esp. US* cadge.

mood[1] *noun* state of mind or feeling; fit of bad temper or depression.

mood[2] *noun Grammar* form(s) of verb indicating whether it expresses fact, command, wish, etc.

moody *adjective* (**-ier**, **-iest**) given to changes of mood; gloomy, sullen.

moon ● *noun* natural satellite of the earth, orbiting it monthly, illuminated by and reflecting sun; satellite of any planet. ● *verb* (often + *about, around*) wander aimlessly or listlessly. ▫ **moonbeam** ray of moonlight; **moonlight** *noun* light of moon, *verb colloquial* have other paid occupation, esp. one by night as well as one by day; **moonlit** lit by the moon; **moonshine** foolish or visionary talk, illicit alcohol; **moonshot** launching of spacecraft to moon; **moonstone** feldspar of pearly appearance; **moonstruck** slightly mad.

moony *adjective* (**-ier**, **-iest**) listless; stupidly dreamy.

Moor /mʊə/ *noun* member of a Muslim people of NW Africa. ▫ **Moorish** *adjective.*

moor[1] /mʊə/ *noun* open uncultivated upland, esp. when covered with heather. ▫ **moorhen** small waterfowl; **moorland** large area of moor.

moor[2] /mʊə/ *verb* attach (boat etc.) to fixed object. ▫ **moorage** *noun.*

mooring *noun* (often in *plural*) place where boat etc. is moored; (in *plural*) set of permanent anchors and chains.

moose *noun* (*plural* same) N. American deer; elk.

moot ● *adjective* debatable, undecided. ● *verb* raise (question) for discussion. ● *noun historical* assembly.

mop ● *noun* bundle of yarn or cloth or a sponge on end of stick for cleaning floors etc.; thick mass of hair. ● *verb* (**-pp-**) wipe or clean (as) with mop. ▫ **mop up** wipe with mop, *colloquial* absorb, dispose of, complete occupation of (area etc.) by capturing or killing enemy troops left there.

mope ● *verb* (**-ping**) be depressed or listless. ● *noun* person who mopes. ▫ **mopy** *adjective* (**-ier**, **-iest**).

moped /'məʊped/ *noun* low-powered motorized bicycle.

moquette /mɒ'ket/ *noun* thick pile or looped material used for upholstery etc.

moraine /mə'reɪn/ *noun* area of debris carried down and deposited by glacier.

moral /'mɒr(ə)l/ ● *adjective* concerned with goodness or badness of character or behaviour, or with difference between right and wrong; virtuous in conduct. ● *noun* moral lesson of story etc.; (in *plural*) moral principles or behaviour. ▫ **moral support** psychological rather than physical help. ▫ **morally** *adverb.*

morale /mə'rɑːl/ *noun* confidence, determination, etc. of person or group.

moralist /'mɒrəlɪst/ *noun* person who practises or teaches morality. ▫ **moralistic** /-'lɪs-/ *adjective.*

morality /mə'rælɪtɪ/ *noun* (*plural* **-ies**) degree of conformity to moral principles; moral conduct; science of morals.

moralize /'mɒrəlaɪz/ *verb* (also **-ise**) (**-zing** or **-sing**) (often + *on*) indulge in moral reflection or talk. ▫ **moralization** *noun.*

morass /mə'ræs/ *noun* entanglement; *literary* bog.

moratorium /mɒrə'tɔːrɪəm/ *noun* (*plural* **-s** or **-ria**) (often + *on*) temporary prohibition or suspension (of activity); legal authorization to debtors to postpone payment.

morbid /'mɔːbɪd/ *adjective* (of mind, ideas, etc.) unwholesome; *colloquial* melancholy; of or indicative of disease. ▫ **morbidity** /-'bɪd-/ *noun*; **morbidly** *adverb.*

mordant /'mɔːd(ə)nt/ ● *adjective* (of sarcasm etc.) caustic, biting; smarting; corrosive, cleansing. ● *noun* mordant substance.

more /mɔː/ ● *adjective* greater in quantity or degree; additional. ● *noun* greater quantity, number, or amount. ● *adverb* to greater degree or extent; *forming comparative of adjectives and adverbs.*

morello /mə'reləʊ/ *noun* (*plural* **-s**) sour kind of dark cherry.

moreover /mɔː'rəʊvə/ *adverb* besides, in addition.

mores /'mɔːreɪz/ *plural noun* customs or conventions of community.

morganatic /mɔːgə'nætɪk/ *adjective* (of marriage) between person of high rank and one of lower rank, the latter and the latter's children having no claim to possessions of former.

morgue /mɔːg/ *noun* mortuary; room or file of miscellaneous information kept by newspaper office.

moribund /'mɒrɪbʌnd/ *adjective* at point of death; lacking vitality.

Mormon /'mɔːmən/ *noun* member of Church of Jesus Christ of Latter-Day Saints. ▫ **Mormonism** *noun.*

morn *noun poetical* morning.

morning /'mɔːnɪŋ/ *noun* early part of day till noon or lunchtime. ▫ **morning coat** tailcoat with front cut away; **morning dress** man's morning coat and striped trousers; **morning glory** climbing plant with trumpet-shaped flowers; **morning sickness** nausea felt in morning in pregnancy; **morning star** planet, usually Venus, seen in east before sunrise.

morocco /mə'rɒkəʊ/ *noun* (*plural* **-s**) fine flexible leather of goatskin tanned with sumac.

moron /'mɔːrɒn/ *noun colloquial* very stupid person; adult with mental age of 8–12. ▫ **moronic** /mə'r-/ *adjective.*

morose /mə'rəʊs/ *adjective* sullen, gloomy. ▫ **morosely** *adverb*; **moroseness** *noun.*

morphia /'mɔːfɪə/ *noun* morphine.

morphine /'mɔːfiːn/ *noun* narcotic drug from opium.

morphology /mɔːˈfɒlədʒɪ/ *noun* study of forms of things, esp. of animals and plants and of words and their structure. ▫ **morphological** /-fəˈlɒdʒ-/ *adjective*.

morris dance /ˈmɒrɪs/ *noun* traditional English dance in fancy costume. ▫ **morris dancer** *noun*; **morris dancing** *noun*.

morrow /ˈmɒrəʊ/ *noun* (usually **the morrow**) *literary* following day.

Morse /mɔːs/ *noun* (in full **Morse code**) code in which letters, numbers, etc. are represented by combinations of long and short light or sound signals.

morsel /ˈmɔːs(ə)l/ *noun* mouthful; small piece (esp. of food).

mortal /ˈmɔːt(ə)l/ ● *adjective* subject to or causing death; (of combat) fought to the death; (of enemy) implacable. ● *noun* human being. ▫ **mortal sin** sin depriving soul of salvation. ▫ **mortally** *adverb*.

mortality /mɔːˈtælɪtɪ/ *noun* (*plural* **-ies**) being subject to death; loss of life on large scale; (in full **mortality rate**) death rate.

mortar /ˈmɔːtə/ *noun* mixture of lime or cement, sand, and water, for bonding bricks or stones; short cannon for firing shells at high angles; vessel in which ingredients are pounded with pestle. ▫ **mortarboard** stiff flat square-topped academic cap, flat board for holding mortar.

mortgage /ˈmɔːgɪdʒ/ ● *noun* conveyance of property to creditor as security for debt (usually one incurred by purchase of property); sum of money lent by this. ● *verb* (**-ging**) convey (property) by mortgage.

mortgagee /mɔːgɪˈdʒiː/ *noun* creditor in mortgage.

mortgager /ˈmɔːgɪdʒə/ *noun* (also **mortgagor** /-ˈdʒɔː/) debtor in mortgage.

mortice = MORTISE.

mortician /mɔːˈtɪʃ(ə)n/ *noun US* undertaker.

mortify /ˈmɔːtɪfaɪ/ *verb* (**-ies**, **-ied**) humiliate, wound (person's feelings); bring (body etc.) into subjection by self-denial; (of flesh) be affected by gangrene. ▫ **mortification** *noun*; **mortifying** *adjective*.

mortise /ˈmɔːtɪs/ (also **mortice**) ● *noun* hole in framework to receive end of another part, esp. tenon. ● *verb* (**-sing**) join, esp. by mortise and tenon; cut mortise in. ▫ **mortise lock** lock recessed in frame of door etc.

mortuary /ˈmɔːtjʊərɪ/ ● *noun* (*plural* **-ies**) room or building in which dead bodies are kept until burial or cremation. ● *adjective* of death or burial.

Mosaic /məʊˈzeɪɪk/ *adjective* of Moses.

mosaic /məʊˈzeɪɪk/ *noun* picture or pattern made with small variously coloured pieces of glass, stone, etc.; diversified thing.

moselle /məʊˈzel/ *noun* dry German white wine.

Moslem = MUSLIM.

mosque /mɒsk/ *noun* Muslim place of worship.

mosquito /mɒsˈkiːtəʊ/ *noun* (*plural* **-es**) biting insect, esp. with long proboscis to suck blood. ▫ **mosquito-net** net to keep off mosquitoes.

moss *noun* small flowerless plant growing in dense clusters in bogs and on trees, stones, etc.; *Scottish & Northern English* peatbog. ▫ **mossy** *adjective* (**-ier**, **-iest**).

most /məʊst/ ● *adjective* greatest in quantity or degree; the majority of. ● *noun* greatest quantity or number; the majority. ● *adverb* in highest degree; *forming superlative of adjectives and adverbs*.

mostly *adverb* mainly; usually.

MOT *abbreviation* (in full **MOT test**) compulsory annual test, instituted by Ministry of Transport, of vehicles over specified age.

mot /məʊ/ *noun* (*plural* ***mots*** same pronunciation) (usually ***bon mot*** /bɔ̃/) witty saying. ▫ ***mot juste*** /ˈʒuːst/ most appropriate expression. [French]

mote *noun* speck of dust.

motel /məʊˈtel/ *noun* roadside hotel for motorists.

moth /mɒθ/ *noun* nocturnal insect like butterfly; insect of this type breeding in cloth etc., on which its larva feeds. ▫ **mothball** ball of naphthalene etc. kept with stored clothes to deter moths; **moth-eaten** damaged by moths, time-worn.

mother /ˈmʌðə/ ● *noun* female parent; woman or condition etc. giving rise to something else; (in full **Mother Superior**) head of female religious community. ● *verb* treat as mother does. ▫ **mother country** country in relation to its colonies; **mother-in-law** (*plural* **mothers-in-law**) husband's or wife's mother; **motherland** native country; **mother-of-pearl** iridescent substance forming lining of oyster and other shells; **mother tongue** native language. ▫ **motherhood** *noun*; **motherly** *adjective*.

motif /məʊˈtiːf/ *noun* theme repeated and developed in artistic work; decorative design; ornament sewn separately on garment.

motion /ˈməʊʃ(ə)n/ ● *noun* moving; changing position; gesture; formal proposal put to committee etc.; application to court for order; evacuation of bowels. ● *verb* (often + *to do*) direct (person) by gesture. ▫ **motion picture** *esp. US* cinema film. ▫ **motionless** *adjective*.

motivate /ˈməʊtɪveɪt/ *verb* (**-ting**) supply motive to, be motive of; cause (person) to act in particular way; stimulate interest of (person in activity). ▫ **motivation** *noun*.

motive /ˈməʊtɪv/ ● *noun* what induces person to act; motif. ● *adjective* tending to initiate movement.

motley /ˈmɒtlɪ/ ● *adjective* (**-lier**, **-liest**) diversified in colour; of varied character. ● *noun historical* jester's particoloured costume.

motor /ˈməʊtə/ ● *noun* thing that imparts motion; machine (esp. using electricity or internal combustion) supplying motive power for vehicle or other machine; car. ● *adjective* giving, imparting, or producing motion; driven by motor; of or for motor vehicles. ● *verb* go or convey by motor vehicle. ▫ **motor bike** *colloquial*, **motorcycle** two-wheeled motor vehicle without pedal propulsion; **motor car** car; **motorway** fast road with separate carriageways limited to motor vehicles.

motorcade /ˈməʊtəkeɪd/ *noun* procession of motor vehicles.

motorist *noun* driver of car.

motorize *verb* (also **-ise**) (**-zing** or **-sing**) equip with motor transport; provide with motor.

mottle /ˈmɒt(ə)l/ *verb* (**-ling**) (esp. as **mottled** *adjective*) mark with spots or smears of colour.

motto /ˈmɒtəʊ/ *noun* (*plural* **-es**) maxim adopted as rule of conduct; words accompanying coat of arms; appropriate inscription; joke, maxim, etc. in paper cracker.

mould[1] /məʊld/ (*US* **mold**) ● *noun* hollow container into which substance is poured or pressed to harden into required shape; pudding etc. shaped in mould; form, shape; character, type. ● *verb* shape (as) in mould; give shape to; influence development of.

mould[2] /məʊld/ *noun* (*US* **mold**) furry growth of fungi, esp. in moist warm conditions.

mould[3] /məʊld/ *noun* (*US* **mold**) loose earth; upper soil of cultivated land, esp. when rich in organic matter.

moulder /ˈməʊldə/ *verb* (*US* **molder**) decay to dust; (+ *away*) rot, crumble.

moulding *noun* (*US* **molding**) ornamental strip of plaster etc. applied as architectural feature, esp. in cornice; similar feature in woodwork etc.

mouldy *adjective* (*US* **moldy**) (**-ier**, **-iest**) covered with mould; stale; out of date; *colloquial* dull, miserable.

moult /məʊlt/ (*US* **molt**) ● *verb* shed (feathers, hair, shell, etc.) in renewing plumage, coat, etc. ● *noun* moulting.

mound /maʊnd/ *noun* raised mass of earth, stones, etc.; heap, pile; hillock.

mount[1] ● *verb* ascend; climb on to; get up on (horse etc.); set on horseback; (as **mounted** *adjective*) serving on horseback; (often + *up*) accumulate, increase; set in frame etc., esp. for viewing; organize, arrange (exhibition, attack, etc.). ● *noun* backing etc. on which picture etc. is set for display; horse for riding; setting for gem etc.

mount[2] *noun* (*poetical* except before name) mountain, hill.

mountain /'maʊntɪn/ *noun* large abrupt elevation of ground; large heap or pile; huge quantity; large surplus stock. □ **mountain ash** tree with scarlet berries; **mountain bike** sturdy bicycle with straight handlebars and many gears.

mountaineer /maʊntɪ'nɪə/ ● *noun* person practising mountain climbing. ● *verb* climb mountains as sport. □ **mountaineering** *noun*.

mountainous *adjective* having many mountains; huge.

mountebank /'maʊntɪbæŋk/ *noun* swindler, charlatan.

Mountie /'maʊntɪ/ *noun colloquial* member of Royal Canadian Mounted Police.

mourn /mɔ:n/ *verb* (often + *for, over*) feel or show sorrow or regret; grieve for loss of (dead person etc.).

mourner *noun* person who mourns, esp. at funeral.

mournful *adjective* doleful, sad. □ **mournfully** *adverb*.

mourning *noun* expression of sorrow for dead, esp. by wearing black clothes; such clothes.

mouse /maʊs/ ● *noun* (*plural* **mice**) small rodent; timid or feeble person; *Computing* small device controlling cursor on VDU screen. ● *verb* (also /maʊz/) (**-sing**) (of cat etc.) hunt mice. □ **mouser** *noun*; **mousy** *adjective*.

mousse /mu:s/ *noun* dish of whipped cream, eggs, etc., flavoured with fruit, chocolate, etc., or with meat or fish purée.

moustache /mə'stɑ:ʃ/ *noun* (*US* **mustache**) hair left to grow on upper lip.

mouth ● *noun* /maʊθ/ (*plural* **mouths** /maʊðz/) external opening in head, for taking in food and emitting sound; cavity behind it containing teeth and vocal organs; opening of container, cave, trumpet, volcano, etc.; place where river enters sea. ● *verb* /maʊð/ (**-thing**) say or speak by moving lips silently; utter insincerely or without understanding. □ **mouth-organ** harmonica; **mouthpiece** part of musical instrument, telephone, etc., placed next to lips; **mouthwash** liquid antiseptic etc. for rinsing mouth.

mouthful *noun* (*plural* **-s**) quantity of food etc. that fills the mouth; *colloquial* something difficult to say.

move /mu:v/ ● *verb* (**-ving**) (cause to) change position, posture, home, or place of work; put or keep in motion; rouse, stir; (often + *about, away, off*, etc.) go, proceed; take action; (+ *in*) be socially active in; affect with emotion; (cause to) change attitude; propose as resolution. ● *noun* act or process of moving; change of house, premises, etc.; step taken to secure object; moving of piece in board game. □ **move in with** start to share accommodation with; **move out** leave one's home. □ **movable** *adjective*.

movement *noun* moving, being moved; moving parts of mechanism; group of people with common object; (in *plural*) person's activities and whereabouts; chief division of longer musical work; bowel motion; rise or fall of stock-market prices.

movie /'mu:vɪ/ *noun esp. US colloquial* cinema film.

moving *adjective* emotionally affecting.

mow /məʊ/ *verb* (*past participle* **mowed** or **mown**) cut (grass, hay, etc.) with scythe or machine. □ **mower** *noun*.

MP *abbreviation* Member of Parliament.

mp *abbreviation* mezzo piano.

m.p.g. *abbreviation* miles per gallon.

m.p.h. *abbreviation* miles per hour.

Mr /'mɪstə/ *noun* (*plural* **Messrs**) *title prefixed to name of man or to designation of office etc.*

Mrs /'mɪsɪz/ *noun* (*plural* same) *title of married woman.*

MS *abbreviation* (*plural* **MSS** /em'esɪz/) manuscript; multiple sclerosis.

Ms /mɪz/ *noun title of married or unmarried woman.*

M.Sc. *abbreviation* Master of Science.

Mt. *abbreviation* Mount.

much ● *adjective* existing or occurring in great quantity. ● *noun* great quantity; (usually in negative) noteworthy example. ● *adverb* in great degree; for large part of one's time; often. □ **a bit much** *colloquial* excessive; **much of a muchness** very nearly the same.

mucilage /'mju:sɪlɪdʒ/ *noun* viscous substance obtained from plants; adhesive gum.

muck ● *noun colloquial* dirt, filth; anything disgusting; manure. ● *verb* (usually + *up*) *colloquial* bungle; make dirty; (+ *out*) remove manure from. □ **muck about, around** *colloquial* potter or fool about; **muck in** (often + *with*) *colloquial* share tasks etc.; **muckraking** seeking out and revealing of scandals etc. □ **mucky** *adjective* (**-ier, -iest**).

mucous /'mju:kəs/ *adjective* of or covered with mucus. □ **mucous membrane** mucus-secreting tissue lining body cavities etc.

mucus /'mju:kəs/ *noun* slimy substance secreted by mucous membrane.

mud *noun* soft wet earth. □ **mudguard** curved strip over wheel to protect against mud; **mud-slinging** abuse, slander.

muddle /'mʌd(ə)l/ ● *verb* (**-ling**) (often + *up*) bring into disorder; bewilder; confuse. ● *noun* disorder; confusion. □ **muddle along** progress in haphazard way.

muddy ● *adjective* (**-ier, -iest**) like mud; covered in or full of mud; (of liquid, colour, or sound) not clear; confused. ● *verb* (**-ies, -ied**) make muddy.

muesli /'mju:zlɪ/ *noun* breakfast food of crushed cereals, dried fruit, nuts, etc.

muezzin /mu:'ezɪn/ *noun* Muslim crier who proclaims hours of prayer.

muff[1] *noun* covering, esp. of fur, for keeping hands or ears warm.

muff[2] *verb colloquial* bungle; miss (catch etc.).

muffin /'mʌfɪn/ *noun* light flat round spongy cake, eaten toasted and buttered; *US* similar cake made from batter or dough.

muffle /'mʌf(ə)l/ *verb* (**-ling**) (often + *up*) wrap for warmth or to deaden sound.

muffler *noun* wrap or scarf worn for warmth; thing used to deaden sound.

mufti /'mʌftɪ/ *noun* civilian clothes.

mug[1] ● *noun* drinking vessel, usually cylindrical with handle and no saucer; its contents; gullible person; *slang* face, mouth. ● *verb* (**-gg-**) attack and rob, esp. in public place. □ **mugger** *noun*; **mugging** *noun*.

mug[2] *verb* (**-gg-**) (usually + *up*) *slang* learn (subject) by concentrated study.

muggins /'mʌgɪnz/ *noun* (*plural* same or **mugginses**) *colloquial* gullible person (often meaning oneself).

muggy /'mʌgɪ/ *adjective* (**-ier, -iest**) (of weather etc.) oppressively humid.

Muhammadan /mə'hæməd(ə)n/ *noun & adjective* (also **Mohammedan**) Muslim.

■ **Usage** The term *Muhammadan* is not used by Muslims and is often regarded as offensive.

mulatto /mju:'lætəʊ/ *noun* (*plural* **-s** or **-es**) person of mixed white and black parentage.

mulberry /'mʌlbərɪ/ *noun* (*plural* **-ies**) tree bearing edible purple or white berries; its fruit; dark red, purple.

mulch ● *noun* layer of wet straw, leaves, plastic, etc., put round plant's roots to enrich or insulate soil. ● *verb* treat with mulch.

mule¹ /mju:l/ *noun* offspring of male donkey and female horse or (in general use) vice versa; obstinate person; kind of spinning machine.

mule² /mju:l/ *noun* backless slipper.

muleteer /mju:lə'tɪə/ *noun* mule driver.

mulish *adjective* stubborn.

mull¹ *verb* (often + *over*) ponder.

mull² *verb* heat and spice (wine, beer).

mullah /'mʌlə/ *noun* Muslim learned in theology and sacred law.

mullet /'mʌlɪt/ *noun* (*plural* same) edible sea fish.

mulligatawny /mʌlɪgə'tɔ:nɪ/ *noun* highly seasoned soup originally from India.

mullion /'mʌljən/ *noun* vertical bar between panes in window. □ **mullioned** *adjective*.

multi- *combining form* many.

multicoloured /'mʌltɪkʌləd/ *adjective* of many colours.

multifarious /mʌltɪ'feərɪəs/ *adjective* many and various; of great variety.

multiform /'mʌltɪfɔ:m/ *adjective* having many forms; of many kinds.

multilateral /mʌltɪ'lætər(ə)l/ *adjective* (of agreement etc.) in which 3 or more parties participate; having many sides. □ **multilaterally** *adverb*.

multilingual /mʌltɪ'lɪŋgw(ə)l/ *adjective* in, speaking, or using many languages.

multinational /mʌltɪ'næʃən(ə)l/ ● *adjective* operating in several countries; of several nationalities. ● *noun* multinational company.

multiple /'mʌltɪp(ə)l/ ● *adjective* having several parts, elements, or components; many and various. ● *noun* quantity exactly divisible by another. □ **multiple sclerosis** see SCLEROSIS.

multiplicand /mʌltɪplɪ'kænd/ *noun* quantity to be multiplied.

multiplication /mʌltɪplɪ'keɪʃ(ə)n/ *noun* multiplying.

multiplicity /mʌltɪ'plɪsɪtɪ/ *noun* (*plural* **-ies**) manifold variety; (+ *of*) great number.

multiplier /'mʌltɪplaɪə/ *noun* quantity by which given number is multiplied.

multiply /'mʌltɪplaɪ/ *verb* (**-ies**, **-ied**) obtain from (number) another a specified number of times its value; increase in number, esp. by procreation.

multi-purpose /mʌltɪ'pɜ:pəs/ *adjective* having several purposes.

multiracial /mʌltɪ'reɪʃ(ə)l/ *adjective* of several races.

multitude /'mʌltɪtju:d/ *noun* (often + *of*) great number; large gathering of people; (**the multitude**) the common people. □ **multitudinous** /-'tju:dɪnəs/ *adjective*.

mum¹ *noun colloquial* mother.

mum² *adjective colloquial* silent. □ **mum's the word** say nothing.

mumble /'mʌmb(ə)l/ ● *verb* (**-ling**) speak or utter indistinctly. ● *noun* indistinct utterance.

mumbo-jumbo /mʌmbəʊ'dʒʌmbəʊ/ *noun* (*plural* **-s**) meaningless ritual; meaningless or unnecessarily complicated language; nonsense.

mummer /'mʌmə/ *noun* actor in traditional play or mime.

mummery /'mʌmərɪ/ *noun* (*plural* **-ies**) ridiculous (esp. religious) ceremonial; performance by mummers.

mummify /'mʌmɪfaɪ/ *verb* (**-ies**, **-ied**) preserve (body) as mummy. □ **mummification** *noun*.

mummy¹ /'mʌmɪ/ *noun* (*plural* **-ies**) *colloquial* mother.

mummy² /'mʌmɪ/ *noun* (*plural* **-ies**) dead body preserved by embalming, esp. in ancient Egypt.

mumps *plural noun* (treated as *singular*) infectious disease with swelling of neck and face.

munch *verb* chew steadily.

mundane /mʌn'deɪn/ *adjective* dull, routine; of this world. □ **mundanely** *adverb*.

municipal /mju:'nɪsɪp(ə)l/ *adjective* of municipality or its self-government.

municipality /mju:nɪsɪ'pælɪtɪ/ *noun* (*plural* **-ies**) town or district with local self-government; its governing body.

munificent /mju:'nɪfɪs(ə)nt/ *adjective* (of giver or gift) splendidly generous. □ **munificence** *noun*.

muniment /'mju:nɪmənt/ *noun* (usually in *plural*) document kept as evidence of rights or privileges.

munition /mju:'nɪʃ(ə)n/ *noun* (usually in *plural*) military weapons, ammunition, etc.

mural /'mjʊər(ə)l/ ● *noun* painting executed directly on wall. ● *adjective* of, on, or like wall.

murder /'mɜ:də/ ● *noun* intentional unlawful killing of human being by another; *colloquial* unpleasant or dangerous state of affairs. ● *verb* kill (human being) intentionally and unlawfully; *colloquial* utterly defeat; spoil by bad performance, mispronunciation, etc. □ **murderer**, **murderess** *noun*; **murderous** *adjective*.

murky /'mɜ:kɪ/ (**-ier**, **-iest**) *adjective* dark, gloomy; (of liquid etc.) dirty.

murmur /'mɜ:mə/ ● *noun* subdued continuous sound; softly spoken utterance; subdued expression of discontent. ● *verb* make murmur; utter in low voice.

murrain /'mʌrɪn/ *noun* infectious disease of cattle.

Muscadet /'mʌskədeɪ/ *noun* dry white wine of France from Loire region; variety of grape used for this.

muscat /'mʌskət/ *noun* sweet usually fortified white wine made from musk-flavoured grapes; this grape.

muscatel /mʌskə'tel/ *noun* muscat wine or grape; raisin made from muscat grape.

muscle /'mʌs(ə)l/ ● *noun* fibrous tissue producing movement in or maintaining position of animal body; part of body composed of muscles; strength, power. ● *verb* (**-ling**) (+ *in*, *in on*) *colloquial* force oneself on others. □ **muscle-bound** with muscles stiff and inelastic through excessive exercise; **muscle-man** man with highly developed muscles.

Muscovite /'mʌskəvaɪt/ ● *noun* native or citizen of Moscow. ● *adjective* of Moscow.

muscular /'mʌskjʊlə/ *adjective* of or affecting muscles; having well-developed muscles. □ **muscular dystrophy** hereditary progressive wasting of muscles. □ **muscularity** /-'lær-/ *noun*.

muse¹ /mju:z/ *verb* (**-sing**) (usually + *on*, *upon*) ponder, reflect.

muse² /mju:z/ *noun Greek & Roman Mythology* any of 9 goddesses inspiring poetry, music, etc.; (usually **the muse**) poet's inspiration.

museum /mju:'zi:əm/ *noun* building for storing and exhibiting objects of historical, scientific, or cultural interest. □ **museum piece** object fit for museum, *derogatory* old-fashioned person etc.

mush *noun* soft pulp; feeble sentimentality; *US* maize porridge. □ **mushy** *adjective* (**-ier**, **-iest**).

mushroom /ˈmʌʃrʊm/ ● *noun* edible fungus with stem and domed cap; pinkish-brown colour. ● *verb* appear or develop rapidly. □ **mushroom cloud** mushroom-shaped cloud from nuclear explosion.

music /ˈmjuːzɪk/ *noun* art of combining vocal or instrumental sounds in harmonious or expressive way; sounds so produced; musical composition; written or printed score of this; pleasant sound. □ **music centre** equipment combining radio, record player, tape recorder, etc.; **music-hall** variety entertainment, theatre for this.

musical ● *adjective* of music; (of sounds) melodious, harmonious; fond of or skilled in music; set to or accompanied by music. ● *noun* musical film or play. □ **musicality** /-ˈkæl-/ *noun*; **musically** *adverb*.

musician /mjuːˈzɪʃ(ə)n/ *noun* person skilled in practice of music, esp. professional instrumentalist. □ **musicianship** *noun*.

musicology /mjuːzɪˈkɒlədʒɪ/ *noun* study of history and forms of music. □ **musicological** /-kəˈlɒdʒ-/ *adjective*; **musicologist** *noun*.

musk *noun* substance secreted by male musk deer and used in perfumes; plant which originally had smell of musk. □ **musk deer** small hornless Asian deer; **muskrat** large N. American aquatic rodent with smell like musk, its fur; **musk-rose** rambling rose smelling of musk. □ **musky** *adjective* (**-ier**, **-iest**).

musket /ˈmʌskɪt/ *noun historical* infantryman's (esp. smooth-bored) light gun.

musketeer /mʌskəˈtɪə/ *noun historical* soldier armed with musket.

musketry /ˈmʌskɪtrɪ/ *noun* muskets; soldiers armed with muskets; knowledge of handling small arms.

Muslim /ˈmʊzlɪm/ (also **Moslem** /ˈmɒzləm/) ● *noun* follower of Islamic religion. ● *adjective* of Muslims or their religion.

muslin /ˈmʌzlɪn/ *noun* fine delicately woven cotton fabric.

musquash /ˈmʌskwɒʃ/ *noun* muskrat; its fur.

mussel /ˈmʌs(ə)l/ *noun* edible bivalve mollusc.

must[1] ● *auxiliary verb* (*3rd singular present* **must**; *past* **had to**) be obliged to; be certain to; ought to. ● *noun colloquial* thing that should not be missed.

■ **Usage** The negative *I must not go* means 'I am not allowed to go'. To express a lack of obligation, use *I am not obliged to go*, *I need not go*, or *I haven't got to go*.

must[2] *noun* grape juice before fermentation is complete.

mustache *US* = MOUSTACHE.

mustang /ˈmʌstæŋ/ *noun* small wild horse of Mexico and California.

mustard /ˈmʌstəd/ *noun* plant with yellow flowers; seeds of this crushed into paste and used as spicy condiment. □ **mustard gas** colourless oily liquid whose vapour is powerful irritant.

muster /ˈmʌstə/ ● *verb* collect (originally soldiers); come together; summon (courage etc.). ● *noun* assembly of people for inspection. □ **pass muster** be accepted as adequate.

mustn't /ˈmʌs(ə)nt/ must not.

musty /ˈmʌstɪ/ *adjective* (**-ier**, **-iest**) mouldy, stale; dull, antiquated. □ **mustiness** *noun*.

mutable /ˈmjuːtəb(ə)l/ *adjective literary* liable to change. □ **mutability** *noun*.

mutant /ˈmjuːt(ə)nt/ ● *adjective* resulting from mutation. ● *noun* mutant organism or gene.

mutate /mjuːˈteɪt/ (cause to) undergo mutation.

mutation *noun* change; genetic change which when transmitted to offspring gives rise to heritable variations.

mute /mjuːt/ ● *adjective* silent; refraining from or temporarily bereft of speech; dumb; soundless. ● *noun* dumb person; device for damping sound of musical instrument. ● *verb* (**-ting**) muffle or deaden sound of; (as **muted** *adjective*) (of colours etc.) subdued. □ **mute swan** common white swan. □ **mutely** *adverb*.

mutilate /ˈmjuːtɪleɪt/ *verb* (**-ting**) deprive (person, animal) of limb etc.; destroy usefulness of (limb etc.); excise or damage part of (book etc.). □ **mutilation** *noun*.

mutineer /mjuːtɪˈnɪə/ *noun* person who mutinies.

mutinous /ˈmjuːtɪnəs/ *adjective* rebellious.

mutiny /ˈmjuːtɪnɪ/ ● *noun* (*plural* **-ies**) open revolt, esp. by soldiers or sailors against officers. ● *verb* (**-ies**, **-ied**) engage in mutiny.

mutt *noun slang* stupid person.

mutter /ˈmʌtə/ ● *verb* speak in barely audible manner; (often + *against*, *at*) grumble. ● *noun* muttered words etc.; muttering.

mutton /ˈmʌt(ə)n/ *noun* flesh of sheep as food.

mutual /ˈmjuːtʃʊəl/ *adjective* (of feelings, actions, etc.) experienced or done by each of two or more parties to the other(s); *colloquial* common to two or more people; having same (specified) relationship to each other. □ **mutuality** /-ˈæl-/ *noun*; **mutually** *adverb*.

■ **Usage** The use of *mutual* to mean 'common to two or more people' is considered incorrect by some people, who use *common* instead.

muzzle /ˈmʌz(ə)l/ ● *noun* projecting part of animal's face, including nose and mouth; guard put over animal's nose and mouth; open end of firearm. ● *verb* (**-ling**) put muzzle on; impose silence on.

muzzy /ˈmʌzɪ/ *adjective* (**-ier**, **-iest**) confused, dazed; blurred, indistinct. □ **muzzily** *adverb*.

MW *abbreviation* megawatt(s); medium wave.

my /maɪ/ *adjective* of or belonging to me.

mycology /maɪˈkɒlədʒɪ/ *noun* study of fungi; fungi of particular region.

mynah /ˈmaɪnə/ *noun* (also **myna**) talking bird of starling family.

myopia /maɪˈəʊpɪə/ *noun* short-sightedness; lack of imagination. □ **myopic** /-ˈɒp-/ *adjective*.

myriad /ˈmɪrɪəd/ *literary* ● *noun* indefinitely great number. ● *adjective* innumerable.

myrrh /mɜː/ *noun* gum resin used in perfume, medicine, incense, etc.

myrtle /ˈmɜːt(ə)l/ *noun* evergreen shrub with shiny leaves and white scented flowers.

myself /maɪˈself/ *pronoun: emphatic form of* I[2] *or* ME[1]; *reflexive form of* ME[1].

mysterious /mɪsˈtɪərɪəs/ *adjective* full of or wrapped in mystery. □ **mysteriously** *adverb*.

mystery /ˈmɪstərɪ/ *noun* (*plural* **-ies**) hidden or inexplicable matter; secrecy, obscurity; fictional work dealing with puzzling event, esp. murder; religious truth divinely revealed; (in *plural*) secret ancient religious rites. □ **mystery play** miracle play; **mystery tour** pleasure trip to unspecified destination.

mystic /ˈmɪstɪk/ ● *noun* person who seeks unity with deity through contemplation etc., or believes in spiritual apprehension of truths beyond understanding. □ **mysticism** /-sɪz(ə)m/ *noun*.

mystical *adjective* of mystics or mysticism; of hidden meaning; spiritually symbolic.

mystify /ˈmɪstɪfaɪ/ *verb* (**-ies**, **-ied**) bewilder, confuse. □ **mystification** *noun*.

mystique /mɪsˈtiːk/ *noun* atmosphere of mystery and veneration attending some activity, person, profession, etc.

myth /mɪθ/ *noun* traditional story usually involving supernatural or imaginary people and embodying popular ideas on natural or social phenomena; widely held but false idea; fictitious person, thing, or idea. □ **mythical** *adjective*.

mythology /mɪˈθɒlədʒɪ/ *noun* (*plural* **-ies**) body or study of myths. □ **mythological** /-θəˈlɒdʒ-/ *adjective*; **mythologize** *verb* (also **-ise**) (**-zing** or **-sing**).

myxomatosis /mɪksəməˈtəʊsɪs/ *noun* viral disease of rabbits.

Nn

N *abbreviation* (also **N.**) north(ern).

n *noun* indefinite number.

n. *abbreviation* (also **n**) noun; neuter.

NAAFI /ˈnæfɪ/ *abbreviation* Navy, Army, and Air Force Institutes (canteen for servicemen).

nab *verb* (**-bb-**) *slang* arrest; catch in wrongdoing; grab.

nacre /ˈneɪkə/ *noun* mother-of-pearl from any shelled mollusc. □ **nacreous** /ˈneɪkrɪəs/ *adjective.*

nadir /ˈneɪdɪə/ *noun* point on celestial sphere directly below observer; lowest point; time of despair.

naff *adjective slang* unfashionable; rubbishy.

nag[1] *verb* (**-gg-**) persistently criticize or scold; (often + *at*) find fault or urge, esp. continually; (of pain) be persistent.

nag[2] *noun colloquial* horse.

naiad /ˈnaɪæd/ *noun* water nymph.

nail ● *noun* small metal spike hammered in to fasten things; horny covering on upper surface of tip of human finger or toe. ● *verb* fasten with nail(s); fix or hold tight; secure, catch (person, thing).

naïve /naɪˈiːv/ *adjective* (also **naive**) innocent, unaffected; foolishly credulous. □ **naïvely** *adverb*; **naïvety** *noun.*

naked /ˈneɪkɪd/ *adjective* unclothed, nude; without usual covering; undisguised; (of light, flame, sword, etc.) unprotected. □ **nakedly** *adverb*; **nakedness** *noun.*

namby-pamby /næmbɪˈpæmbɪ/ ● *adjective* insipidly pretty or sentimental; weak. ● *noun* (*plural* **-ies**) namby-pamby person.

name ● *noun* word by which individual person, animal, place, or thing is spoken of etc.; (usually abusive) term used of person; word denoting object or class of objects; reputation, esp. good. ● *verb* (**-ming**) give name to; state name of; mention; specify; cite. □ **name-day** feast-day of saint after whom person is named; **namesake** person or thing having same name as another.

nameless *adjective* having, or showing, no name; left unnamed.

namely *adverb* that is to say; in other words.

nanny /ˈnænɪ/ *noun* (*plural* **-ies**) child's nurse; *colloquial* grandmother; (in full **nanny goat**) female goat.

nano- /ˈnænəʊ/ *combining form* one thousand millionth.

nap[1] ● *noun* short sleep, esp. by day. ● *verb* (**-pp-**) have nap.

nap[2] *noun* raised pile on cloth, esp. velvet.

nap[3] ● *noun* card game; racing tip claimed to be almost a certainty. ● *verb* (**-pp-**) name (horse) as probable winner. □ **go nap** try to take all 5 tricks in nap, risk everything.

napalm /ˈneɪpɑːm/ *noun* thick jellied hydrocarbon mixture used in bombs.

nape *noun* back of neck.

naphtha /ˈnæfθə/ *noun* inflammable hydrocarbon distilled from coal etc.

naphthalene /ˈnæfθəliːn/ *noun* white crystalline substance produced by distilling tar.

napkin /ˈnæpkɪn/ *noun* piece of linen etc. for wiping lips, fingers, etc. at table; baby's nappy.

nappy /ˈnæpɪ/ *noun* (*plural* **-ies**) piece of towelling etc. wrapped round baby to absorb urine and faeces.

narcissism /ˈnɑːsɪsɪz(ə)m/ *noun* excessive or erotic interest in oneself. □ **narcissistic** /-ˈsɪstɪk/ *adjective.*

narcissus /nɑːˈsɪsəs/ *noun* (*plural* **-cissi** /-saɪ/) any of several flowering bulbs, including daffodil.

narcosis /nɑːˈkəʊsɪs/ *noun* unconsciousness; induction of this.

narcotic /nɑːˈkɒtɪk/ ● *adjective* (of substance) inducing drowsiness etc.; (of drug) affecting the mind. ● *noun* narcotic substance or drug.

nark *slang* ● *noun* police informer. ● *verb* annoy.

narrate /nəˈreɪt/ *verb* (**-ting**) give continuous story or account of; provide spoken accompaniment for (film etc.). □ **narration** *noun*; **narrator** *noun.*

narrative /ˈnærətɪv/ ● *noun* ordered account of connected events. ● *adjective* of or by narration.

narrow /ˈnærəʊ/ ● *adjective* (**-er, -est**) of small width; restricted; of limited scope; with little margin; precise, exact; narrow-minded. ● *noun* (usually in *plural*) narrow part of strait, river, pass, etc. ● *verb* become or make narrower; contract; lessen. □ **narrow boat** canal boat; **narrow-minded** rigid or restricted in one's views, intolerant. □ **narrowly** *adverb*; **narrowness** *noun.*

narwhal /ˈnɑːw(ə)l/ *noun* Arctic white whale, male of which has long tusk.

nasal /ˈneɪz(ə)l/ ● *adjective* of nose; (of letter or sound) pronounced with breath passing through nose, e.g. *m, n, ng*; (of voice etc.) having many nasal sounds. ● *noun* nasal letter or sound. □ **nasally** *adverb.*

nascent /ˈnæs(ə)nt/ *adjective* in act of being born; just beginning to be. □ **nascency** /-ənsɪ/ *noun.*

nasturtium /nəˈstɜːʃəm/ *noun* trailing garden plant with edible leaves and bright orange, red, or yellow flowers.

nasty /ˈnɑːstɪ/ ● *adjective* (**-ier, -iest**) unpleasant; difficult to negotiate; (of person or animal) ill-natured, spiteful. ● *noun* (*plural* **-ies**) *colloquial* violent horror film, esp. on video. □ **nastily** *adverb*; **nastiness** *noun.*

Nat. *abbreviation* National(ist); Natural.

natal /ˈneɪt(ə)l/ *adjective* of or from birth.

nation /ˈneɪʃ(ə)n/ *noun* community of people having mainly common descent, history, language, etc., forming state or inhabiting territory. □ **nationwide** extending over whole nation.

national /ˈnæʃən(ə)l/ ● *adjective* of nation; characteristic of particular nation. ● *noun* citizen of specified country. □ **national anthem** song adopted by nation, intended to inspire patriotism; **national grid** network of high-voltage electric power lines between major power stations; **National Insurance** system of compulsory payments from employee and employer to provide state assistance in sickness, retirement, etc.; **national service** *historical* conscripted peacetime military service. □ **nationally** *adverb.*

nationalism *noun* patriotic feeling, principles, etc.; policy of national independence. □ **nationalist** *noun*; **nationalistic** /-ˈlɪs-/ *adjective.*

nationality /næʃəˈnælɪtɪ/ *noun* (*plural* **-ies**) membership of nation; being national; ethnic group within one or more political nations.

nationalize /ˈnæʃənəlaɪz/ *verb* (also **-ise**) (**-zing** or **-sing**) take (industry etc.) into state ownership; make national. □ **nationalization** *noun.*

native /ˈneɪtɪv/ ● *noun* (usually + *of*) person born in specified place; local inhabitant; indigenous animal or plant. ● *adjective* inherent; innate; of one's birth; (usually + *to*) belonging to specified place; born in a place.

nativity /nəˈtɪvɪtɪ/ *noun* (*plural* **-ies**) (esp. **the Nativity**) Christ's birth; birth.

NATO /ˈneɪtəʊ/ *abbreviation* (also **Nato**) North Atlantic Treaty Organization.

natter /ˈnætə/ *colloquial* ● *verb* chatter idly. ● *noun* aimless chatter.

natty /ˈnætɪ/ *adjective* (**-ier**, **-iest**) trim; smart.

natural /ˈnætʃər(ə)l/ ● *adjective* existing in or caused by nature; not surprising; to be expected; unaffected; innate; physically existing; *Music* not flat or sharp. ● *noun colloquial* (usually + *for*) person or thing naturally suitable, adept, etc.; *Music* sign (♮) showing return to natural pitch, natural note. □ **natural gas** gas found in earth's crust; **natural history** study of animals and plants; **natural number** whole number greater than 0; **natural selection** process favouring survival of organisms best adapted to environment.

naturalism *noun* realistic representation in art and literature; philosophy based on nature alone. □ **naturalistic** /-ˈlɪs-/ *adjective*.

naturalist *noun* student of natural history.

naturalize *verb* (also **-ise**) (**-zing** or **-sing**) admit (foreigner) to citizenship; introduce (plant etc.) into another region; adopt (foreign word, custom, etc.). □ **naturalization** *noun*.

naturally *adverb* in a natural way; as might be expected, of course.

nature /ˈneɪtʃə/ *noun* thing's or person's essential qualities or character; physical power causing material phenomena; these phenomena; kind, class.

naturism *noun* nudism. □ **naturist** *noun*.

naught /nɔːt/ *archaic* ● *noun* nothing. ● *adjective* worthless.

naughty /ˈnɔːtɪ/ *adjective* (**-ier**, **-iest**) (esp. of children) disobedient; badly behaved; *colloquial jocular* indecent. □ **naughtily** *adverb*; **naughtiness** *noun*.

nausea /ˈnɔːsɪə/ *noun* inclination to vomit; revulsion.

nauseate /ˈnɔːsɪeɪt/ *verb* (**-ting**) affect with nausea. □ **nauseating** *adjective*.

nauseous /ˈnɔːsɪəs/ *adjective* causing or inclined to vomit; disgusting.

nautical /ˈnɔːtɪk(ə)l/ *adjective* of sailors or navigation. □ **nautical mile** unit of approx. 2,025 yards (1,852 metres).

nautilus /ˈnɔːtɪləs/ *noun* (*plural* **nautiluses** or **nautili** /-laɪ/) kind of mollusc with spiral shell.

naval /ˈneɪv(ə)l/ *adjective* of navy; of ships.

nave[1] *noun* central part of church excluding chancel and side aisles.

nave[2] *noun* hub of wheel.

navel /ˈneɪv(ə)l/ *noun* depression in belly marking site of attachment of umbilical cord. □ **navel orange** one with navel-like formation at top.

navigable /ˈnævɪgəb(ə)l/ *adjective* (of river etc.) suitable for ships; seaworthy; steerable. □ **navigability** *noun*.

navigate /ˈnævɪgeɪt/ *verb* (**-ting**) manage or direct course of (ship, aircraft); sail on (sea, river, etc.); fly through (air); help car-driver etc. by map-reading etc. □ **navigator** *noun*.

navigation *noun* act or process of navigating; art or science of navigating.

navvy /ˈnævɪ/ *noun* (*plural* **-ies**) labourer employed in building roads, canals, etc.

navy /ˈneɪvɪ/ *noun* (*plural* **-ies**) state's warships with their crews, maintenance systems, etc.; (in full **navy blue**) dark blue colour.

nay ● *adverb* or rather; and even; *archaic* no. ● *noun* 'no' vote.

Nazi /ˈnɑːtsɪ/ ● *noun* (*plural* **-s**) *historical* member of German National Socialist party. ● *adjective* of Nazis or Nazism. □ **Nazism** *noun*.

NB *abbreviation* note well (*nota bene*).

NCB *abbreviation historical* National Coal Board.

NCO *abbreviation* non-commissioned officer.

NE *abbreviation* north-east(ern).

Neanderthal /nɪˈændətɑːl/ *adjective* of type of human found in palaeolithic Europe.

neap *noun* (in full **neap tide**) tide with smallest rise and fall.

Neapolitan /nɪəˈpɒlɪt(ə)n/ ● *noun* native of Naples. ● *adjective* of Naples.

near /nɪə/ ● *adverb* (often + *to*) to or at short distance in space or time; closely. ● *preposition* to or at a short distance from in space, time, condition, or resemblance. ● *adjective* close (to); not far in place or time; closely related; (of part of vehicle, animal, or road) on left side; *colloquial* stingy; with little margin. ● *verb* approach, draw near to. □ **the Near East** countries of eastern Mediterranean; **near-sighted** short-sighted.

nearby ● *adjective* near in position. ● *adverb* close.

nearly *adverb* almost; closely. □ **not nearly** nothing like, far from.

neat *adjective* tidy, methodical; elegantly simple; brief and clear; cleverly done; dexterous; (of alcoholic liquor) undiluted. □ **neaten** *verb*; **neatly** *adverb*; **neatness** *noun*.

neath *preposition poetical* beneath.

nebula /ˈnebjʊlə/ *noun* (*plural* **nebulae** /-liː/) cloud of gas and dust seen in night sky, appearing luminous or as dark silhouette. □ **nebular** *adjective*.

nebulous /ˈnebjʊləs/ *adjective* cloudlike; indistinct, vague.

necessary /ˈnesəsərɪ/ ● *adjective* requiring to be done; essential; inevitable. ● *noun* (*plural* **-ies**) (usually in *plural*) any of basic requirements of life. □ **necessarily** *adverb*.

necessitate /nɪˈsesɪteɪt/ *verb* (**-ting**) make necessary (esp. as result).

necessitous /nɪˈsesɪtəs/ *adjective* poor, needy.

necessity /nɪˈsesɪtɪ/ *noun* (*plural* **-ies**) indispensable thing; pressure of circumstances; imperative need; poverty; constraint or compulsion seen as natural law governing human action.

neck ● *noun* part of body connecting head to shoulders; part of garment round neck; narrow part of anything. ● *verb colloquial* kiss and caress amorously. □ **neckline** outline of garment-opening at neck; **necktie** strip of material worn round shirt-collar, knotted at front.

necklace /ˈnekləs/ *noun* string of beads, precious stones, etc. worn round neck; *South African* petrol-soaked tyre placed round victim's neck and lighted.

necromancy /ˈnekrəʊmænsɪ/ *noun* divination by supposed communication with the dead; magic. □ **necromancer** *noun*.

necrophilia /nekrəˈfɪlɪə/ *noun* morbid esp. sexual attraction to corpses.

necropolis /neˈkrɒpəlɪs/ *noun* ancient cemetery.

necrosis /neˈkrəʊsɪs/ *noun* death of tissue. □ **necrotic** /-ˈkrɒt-/ *adjective*.

nectar /ˈnektə/ *noun* sugary substance produced by plants and made into honey by bees; *Mythology* drink of gods.

nectarine /ˈnektərɪn/ *noun* smooth-skinned variety of peach.

NEDC *abbreviation* National Economic Development Council.

née /neɪ/ *adjective* (*US* **nee**) (before married woman's maiden name) born.

need ● *verb* stand in want of; require; (usually + *to do*) be under necessity or obligation. ● *noun* requirement; circumstances requiring action; destitution, poverty; emergency.

needful *adjective* requisite.

needle /ˈniːd(ə)l/ ● *noun* very thin pointed rod with slit ('eye') for thread, used in sewing; knitting-needle; pointer on dial; any small thin pointed instrument, esp. end of hypodermic syringe; obelisk; pointed rock or peak; leaf of fir or pine. ● *verb* **(-ling)** *colloquial* annoy, provoke. ▫ **needlecord** fine-ribbed corduroy fabric; **needlework** sewing or embroidery.

needless *adjective* unnecessary. ▫ **needlessly** *adverb.*

needy *adjective* **(-ier, -iest)** poor, destitute.

ne'er /neə/ *adverb poetical* never. ▫ **ne'er-do-well** good-for-nothing person.

nefarious /nɪˈfeərɪəs/ *adjective* wicked.

negate /nɪˈgeɪt/ *verb* **(-ting)** nullify; deny existence of.

negation *noun* absence or opposite of something positive; act of denying; negative statement; negative or unreal thing.

negative /ˈnegətɪv/ ● *adjective* expressing or implying denial, prohibition, or refusal; lacking positive attributes; opposite to positive; (of quantity) less than zero, to be subtracted; *Electricity* of, containing, or producing, kind of charge carried by electrons. ● *noun* negative statement or word; *Photography* image with black and white reversed or colours replaced by complementary ones. ● *verb* **(-ving)** refuse to accept; veto; disprove; contradict; neutralize. ▫ **negatively** *adverb.*

neglect /nɪˈglekt/ ● *verb* fail to care for or do; (+ *to do*) fail; pay no attention to; disregard. ● *noun* negligence; neglecting, being neglected. ▫ **neglectful** *adjective*; **neglectfully** *adverb.*

negligée /ˈneglɪʒeɪ/ *noun* (also **néglige**) woman's flimsy dressing gown.

negligence /ˈneglɪdʒ(ə)ns/ *noun* lack of proper care or attention; culpable carelessness. ▫ **negligent** *adjective*; **negligently** *adverb.*

negligible /ˈneglɪdʒɪb(ə)l/ *adjective* not worth considering; insignificant.

negotiate /nɪˈgəʊʃɪeɪt/ *verb* **(-ting)** confer in order to reach agreement; obtain (result) by negotiating; deal successfully with (obstacle etc.); convert (cheque etc.) into money. ▫ **negotiable** /-ʃəb-/ *adjective*; **negotiation** *noun*; **negotiator** *noun.*

Negress /ˈniːgrɪs/ *noun* female Negro.

■ **Usage** The term *Negress* is often considered offensive; *black* is usually preferred.

Negro /ˈniːgrəʊ/ ● *noun* (*plural* **-es**) member of dark-skinned (originally) African race; black. ● *adjective* of this race; black.

■ **Usage** The term *Negro* is often considered offensive; *black* is usually preferred.

Negroid /ˈniːgrɔɪd/ ● *adjective* (of physical features etc.) characteristic of black people. ● *noun* black person.

neigh /neɪ/ ● *noun* cry of horse. ● *verb* make a neigh.

neighbour /ˈneɪbə/ (*US* **neighbor**) *noun* person living next door or nearby; fellow human being. ● *verb* border on, adjoin.

neighbourhood *noun* (*US* **neighborhood**) district; vicinity; people of a district.

neighbourly *adjective* (*US* **neighborly**) like good neighbour, friendly, helpful. ▫ **neighbourliness** *noun.*

neither /ˈnaɪðə/ *adjective, pronoun & adverb* not either.

nelson /ˈnels(ə)n/ *noun* wrestling hold in which arm is passed under opponent's arm from behind and hand applied to neck (**half nelson**), or both arms and hands are applied (**full nelson**).

nem. con. *abbreviation* with no one dissenting (*nemine contradicente*). [Latin]

nemesis /ˈneməsɪs/ *noun* justice bringing deserved punishment.

neo- *combining form* new; new form of.

neolithic /niːəˈlɪθɪk/ *adjective* of later Stone Age.

neologism /niːˈɒlədʒɪz(ə)m/ *noun* new word; coining of new words.

neon /ˈniːɒn/ *noun* inert gas giving orange glow when electricity is passed through it.

neophyte /ˈniːəfaɪt/ *noun* new convert; novice of religious order; beginner.

nephew /ˈnefjuː/ *noun* son of one's brother or sister or of one's spouse's brother or sister.

nephritic /nɪˈfrɪtɪk/ *adjective* of or in kidneys.

nephritis /nɪˈfraɪtɪs/ *noun* inflammation of kidneys.

nepotism /ˈnepətɪz(ə)m/ *noun* favouritism to relatives in conferring offices.

nereid /ˈnɪərɪɪd/ *noun* sea nymph.

nerve ● *noun* fibre or bundle of fibres conveying impulses of sensation or motion between brain and other parts of body; coolness in danger; *colloquial* impudence; (in *plural*) nervousness, mental or physical stress. ● *verb* **(-ving)** (usually **nerve oneself**) brace or prepare (oneself). ▫ **nerve-cell** cell transmitting impulses in nerve tissue.

nerveless *adjective* lacking vigour.

nervous *adjective* easily upset, timid, highly strung; anxious; affecting the nerves; (+ *of*) afraid of. ▫ **nervous breakdown** period of mental illness, usually after stress; **nervous system** body's network of nerves. ▫ **nervously** *adverb*; **nervousness** *noun.*

nervy *adjective* **(-ier, -iest)** *colloquial* nervous; easily excited.

nest ● *noun* structure or place where bird lays eggs and shelters young; breeding-place, lair; snug retreat, shelter; brood, swarm; group or set of similar objects. ● *verb* use or build nest; (of objects) fit one inside another. ▫ **nest egg** money saved up as reserve.

nestle /ˈnes(ə)l/ *verb* **(-ling)** settle oneself comfortably; press oneself against another in affection etc.; (+ *in*, *into*, etc.) push (head, shoulders, etc.) affectionately or snugly; lie half hidden or embedded.

nestling /ˈnestlɪŋ/ *noun* bird too young to leave nest.

net[1] ● *noun* open-meshed fabric of cord, rope, etc.; piece of net used esp. to contain, restrain, or delimit, or to catch fish; structure with net used in various games. ● *verb* **(-tt-)** cover, confine, or catch with net; hit (ball) into net, esp. of goal. ▫ **netball** game similar to basketball.

net[2] (also **nett**) ● *adjective* remaining after necessary deductions; (of price) not reducible; (of weight) excluding packaging etc. ● *verb* **(-tt-)** gain or yield (sum) as net profit.

nether /ˈneðə/ *adjective archaic* lower.

nett = NET[2].

netting *noun* meshed fabric of cord or wire.

nettle /ˈnet(ə)l/ ● *noun* plant covered with stinging hairs; plant resembling this. ● *verb* **(-ling)** irritate, provoke. ▫ **nettle-rash** skin eruption like nettle stings.

network ● *noun* arrangement of intersecting horizontal and vertical lines; complex system of railways etc.; people connected by exchange of information etc.; group of broadcasting stations connected for simultaneous broadcast of a programme;

system of interconnected computers. ● *verb* broadcast on network.

neural /ˈnjʊər(ə)l/ *adjective* of nerve or central nervous system.

neuralgia /njʊəˈrældʒə/ *noun* intense pain along a nerve, esp. in face or head. □ **neuralgic** *adjective*.

neuritis /njʊəˈraɪtɪs/ *noun* inflammation of nerve(s).

neuro- /ˈnjʊərəʊ/ *combining form* nerve(s).

neurology /njʊəˈrɒlədʒɪ/ *noun* study of nerve systems. □ **neurological** /-rəˈlɒdʒ-/ *adjective*; **neurologist** *noun*.

neuron /ˈnjʊərɒn/ *noun* (also **neurone** /-rəʊn/) nerve cell.

neurosis /njʊəˈrəʊsɪs/ *noun* (*plural* **-roses** /-siːz/) disturbed behaviour pattern associated with nervous distress.

neurotic /njʊəˈrɒtɪk/ ● *adjective* caused by or relating to neurosis; suffering from neurosis; *colloquial* abnormally sensitive or obsessive. ● *noun* neurotic person.

neuter /ˈnjuːtə/ ● *adjective* neither masculine nor feminine. ● *verb* castrate, spay.

neutral /ˈnjuːtr(ə)l/ ● *adjective* supporting neither of two opposing sides, impartial; vague, indeterminate; (of a gear) in which engine is disconnected from driven parts; (of colours) not strong or positive; *Chemistry* neither acid nor alkaline; *Electricity* neither positive nor negative. ● *noun* neutral state or person. □ **neutrality** /-ˈtræl-/ *noun*.

neutralize *verb* (also **-ise**) (**-zing** or **-sing**) make neutral; make ineffective by opposite force. □ **neutralization** *noun*.

neutrino /njuːˈtriːnəʊ/ *noun* (*plural* **-s**) elementary particle with zero electric charge and probably zero mass.

neutron /ˈnjuːtrɒn/ *noun* elementary particle of about same mass as proton but without electric charge.

never /ˈnevə/ *adverb* at no time, on no occasion; not ever; not at all; *colloquial* surely not. □ **the never-never** *colloquial* hire purchase.

nevermore *adverb* at no future time.

nevertheless /nevəðəˈles/ *adverb* in spite of that; notwithstanding.

new *adjective* of recent origin or arrival; made, discovered, acquired, or experienced for first time; not worn; renewed; reinvigorated; different; unfamiliar. □ **New Age** set of alternative beliefs replacing traditional Western culture; **newborn** recently born; **newcomer** person recently arrived; **newfangled** different from what one is used to; **new moon** moon when first seen as crescent; **New Testament** part of Bible concerned with Christ and his followers; **New World** N. & S. America; **New Year's Day**, **Eve** 1 Jan., 31 Dec.

newel /ˈnjuːəl/ *noun* supporting central post of winding stairs; top or bottom post of stair-rail.

newly *adverb* recently; afresh.

news /njuːz/ *plural noun* (usually treated as *singular*) information about important or interesting recent events, esp. when published or broadcast; (**the news**) broadcast report of news. □ **newsagent** seller of newspapers etc.; **newscast** radio or television broadcast of news reports; **newsletter** informal printed bulletin of club etc.; **newspaper** /ˈnjuːs-/ printed publication of loose folded sheets with news etc.; **newsprint** low-quality paper for printing newspapers; **newsreader** person who reads out broadcast news bulletins; **newsreel** short cinema film of recent events; **news room** room where news is prepared for publication or broadcasting; **newsworthy** topical, worth reporting as news.

newsy *adjective* (**-ier**, **-iest**) *colloquial* full of news.

newt /njuːt/ *noun* small tailed amphibian.

newton /ˈnjuːt(ə)n/ *noun* SI unit of force.

next ● *adjective* (often + *to*) being, placed, or living nearest; nearest in time. ● *adverb* (often + *to*) nearest in place or degree, on first or soonest occasion. ● *noun* next person or thing. ● *preposition colloquial* next to. □ **next door** in next house or room; **next of kin** closest living relative(s).

nexus /ˈneksəs/ *noun* (*plural* same) connected group or series.

NHS *abbreviation* National Health Service.

NI *abbreviation* Northern Ireland; National Insurance.

niacin /ˈnaɪəsɪn/ *noun* nicotinic acid.

nib *noun* pen-point; (in *plural*) crushed coffee or cocoa beans.

nibble /ˈnɪb(ə)l/ ● *verb* (**-ling**) (+ *at*) take small bites at; eat in small amounts; bite gently or playfully. ● *noun* act of nibbling; very small amount of food.

nice *adjective* pleasant, satisfactory; kind, good-natured; fine, (of distinctions) subtle; fastidious. □ **nicely** *adverb*; **niceness** *noun*.

nicety /ˈnaɪsɪtɪ/ *noun* (*plural* **-ies**) subtle distinction or detail; precision. □ **to a nicety** exactly.

niche /niːʃ/ *noun* shallow recess, esp. in wall; comfortable or apt position in life or employment.

nick ● *noun* small cut or notch; *slang* prison, police station; *colloquial* state, condition. ● *verb* make nick(s) in; *slang* steal, arrest, catch. □ **in the nick of time** only just in time.

nickel /ˈnɪk(ə)l/ *noun* silver-white metallic element used esp. in magnetic alloys; *colloquial* US 5-cent coin.

nickname /ˈnɪkneɪm/ ● *noun* familiar or humorous name added to or substituted for real name of person or thing. ● *verb* (**-ming**) give nickname to.

nicotine /ˈnɪkətiːn/ *noun* poisonous alkaloid present in tobacco.

nicotinic acid /nɪkəˈtɪnɪk/ *noun* vitamin of B group.

nictitate /ˈnɪktɪteɪt/ *verb* (**-ting**) blink, wink. □ **nictitation** *noun*.

niece /niːs/ *noun* daughter of one's brother or sister or of one's spouse's brother or sister.

nifty /ˈnɪftɪ/ *adjective* (**-ier**, **-iest**) *colloquial* clever, adroit; smart, stylish.

niggard /ˈnɪɡəd/ *noun* stingy person.

niggardly *adjective* stingy. □ **niggardliness** *noun*.

niggle /ˈnɪɡ(ə)l/ *verb* (**-ling**) fuss over details, find fault in petty way; *colloquial* nag. □ **niggling** *adjective*.

nigh /naɪ/ *adverb & preposition archaic* near.

night /naɪt/ *noun* period of darkness from one day to next; time from sunset to sunrise; nightfall; darkness of night; evening. □ **nightcap** *historical* cap worn in bed, drink before going to bed; **nightclub** club providing entertainment etc. late at night; **nightdress** woman's or child's loose garment worn in bed; **nightfall** end of daylight; **nightjar** nocturnal bird with harsh cry; **night-life** entertainment available at night; **nightmare** terrifying dream or *colloquial* experience; **night safe** safe with access from outer wall of bank for deposit of money when bank is closed; **nightshade** any of various plants with poisonous berries; **nightshirt** long shirt worn in bed.

nightingale /ˈnaɪtɪŋɡeɪl/ *noun* small reddish-brown bird, of which the male sings tunefully, esp. at night.

nightly ● *adjective* happening, done, or existing in the night; recurring every night. ● *adverb* every night.

nihilism /ˈnaɪɪlɪz(ə)m/ *noun* rejection of all religious and moral principles. □ **nihilist** *noun*; **nihilistic** /-ˈlɪs-/ *adjective*.

nil *noun* nothing.

nimble /ˈnɪmb(ə)l/ *adjective* (**-r**, **-st**) quick and light in movement or function; agile. □ **nimbly** *adverb*.

nimbus /ˈnɪmbəs/ *noun* (*plural* **nimbi** /-baɪ/ or **nimbuses**) halo; rain-cloud.

nincompoop /ˈnɪŋkəmpu:p/ *noun* foolish person.

nine *adjective & noun* one more than eight. ◻ **ninepins** (usually treated as *singular*) kind of skittles. ◻ **ninth** /naɪnθ/ *adjective & noun*.

nineteen /naɪnˈti:n/ *adjective & noun* one more than eighteen. ◻ **nineteenth** *adjective & noun*.

ninety /ˈnaɪntɪ/ *adjective & noun* (*plural* **-ies**) nine times ten. ◻ **ninetieth** *adjective & noun*.

ninny /ˈnɪnɪ/ *noun* (*plural* **-ies**) foolish person.

nip[1] ● *verb* (**-pp-**) pinch, squeeze sharply, bite; (often + *off*) remove by pinching etc.; *colloquial* go nimbly. ● *noun* pinch, sharp squeeze, bite; biting cold. ◻ **nip in the bud** suppress or destroy at very beginning.

nip[2] *noun* small quantity of spirits.

nipper *noun* person or thing that nips; claw of crab etc.; *colloquial* young child; (in *plural*) tool with jaws for gripping or cutting.

nipple /ˈnɪp(ə)l/ *noun* small projection in mammals from which in females milk for young is secreted; teat of feeding-bottle; device like nipple in function; nipple-like protuberance.

nippy *adjective* (**-ier**, **-iest**) *colloquial* quick, nimble; chilly.

nirvana /nɪəˈvɑ:nə/ *noun* (in Buddhism) perfect bliss attained by extinction of individuality.

nit *noun* egg or young of louse or other parasitic insect; *slang* stupid person. ◻ **nit-picking** *colloquial* fault-finding in a petty way.

niter *US* = NITRE.

nitrate /ˈnaɪtreɪt/ *noun* salt of nitric acid; potassium or sodium nitrate as fertilizer.

nitre /ˈnaɪtə/ *noun* (*US* **niter**) saltpetre.

nitric acid /ˈnaɪtrɪk/ *noun* colourless corrosive poisonous liquid.

nitrogen /ˈnaɪtrədʒ(ə)n/ *noun* gaseous element forming four-fifths of atmosphere. ◻ **nitrogenous** /-ˈtrɒdʒɪnəs/ *adjective*.

nitroglycerine /naɪtrəʊˈglɪsərɪn/ *noun* (*US* **nitroglycerin**) explosive yellow liquid.

nitrous oxide /ˈnaɪtrəs/ *noun* colourless gas used as anaesthetic.

nitty-gritty /nɪtɪˈgrɪtɪ/ *noun slang* realities or practical details of a matter.

nitwit *noun colloquial* stupid person.

NNE *abbreviation* north-north-east.

NNW *abbreviation* north-north-west.

No = NOH.

No. *abbreviation* number.

no /nəʊ/ ● *adjective* not any; not a; hardly any; *used to forbid thing specified.* ● *adverb* by no amount, not at all. ● *interjection expressing negative reply to question, request, etc.* ● *noun* (*plural* **noes**) utterance of word *no*, denial or refusal; 'no' vote. ◻ **no-ball** unlawfully delivered ball in cricket etc.; **no longer** not now as formerly; **no one** nobody; **no way** *colloquial* it is impossible.

nob[1] *noun slang* person of wealth or high social position.

nob[2] *noun slang* head.

nobble /ˈnɒb(ə)l/ *verb* (**-ling**) *slang* try to influence (e.g. judge); tamper with (racehorse etc.); steal; seize; catch.

nobility /nəʊˈbɪlɪtɪ/ *noun* (*plural* **-ies**) nobleness of character, birth, or rank; class of nobles.

noble /ˈnəʊb(ə)l/ ● *adjective* (**-r**, **-st**) belonging to the aristocracy; of excellent character; magnanimous; of imposing appearance. ● *noun* nobleman; noblewoman. ◻ **nobleman** peer; **noblewoman** peeress. ◻ **nobly** *adverb*.

noblesse oblige /nəʊbles ɒˈbli:ʒ/ *noun* privilege entails responsibility. [French]

nobody /ˈnəʊbədɪ/ ● *pronoun* no person. ● *noun* (*plural* **-ies**) person of no importance.

nocturnal /nɒkˈtɜ:n(ə)l/ *adjective* of or in the night; done or active by night.

nocturne /ˈnɒktɜ:n/ *noun Music* short romantic composition, usually for piano; picture of night scene.

nod ● *verb* (**-dd-**) incline head slightly and briefly; let head droop in drowsiness; be drowsy; show (assent etc.) by nod; (of flowers etc.) bend and sway; make momentary slip or mistake. ● *noun* nodding of head. ◻ **nod off** *colloquial* fall asleep.

noddle /ˈnɒd(ə)l/ *noun colloquial* head.

node *noun* part of plant stem from which leaves emerge; knob on root or branch; natural swelling; intersecting point, esp. of planet's orbit with plane of celestial equator; point or line of least disturbance in vibrating system; point at which curve crosses itself; component in computer network. ◻ **nodal** *adjective*.

nodule /ˈnɒdju:l/ *noun* small rounded lump of anything; small tumour, ganglion, swelling on legume root. ◻ **nodular** *adjective*.

noggin /ˈnɒgɪn/ *noun* small mug; small measure of spirits.

Noh /nəʊ/ *noun* (also **No**) traditional Japanese drama.

noise /nɔɪz/ ● *noun* sound, esp. loud or unpleasant one; confusion of loud sounds. ● *verb* (**-sing**) (usually in *passive*) make public, spread abroad.

noisome /ˈnɔɪsəm/ *adjective literary* harmful, noxious; evil-smelling.

noisy *adjective* (**-ier**, **-iest**) making much noise; full of noise. ◻ **noisily** *adverb*.

nomad /ˈnəʊmæd/ *noun* member of tribe roaming from place to place for pasture; wanderer. ◻ **nomadic** /-ˈmæd-/ *adjective*.

nom de plume /nɒm də ˈplu:m/ *noun* (*plural* ***noms de plume*** same pronunciation) writer's assumed name. [French]

nomenclature /nəʊˈmenklətʃə/ *noun* system of names for things; terminology of a science etc.

nominal /ˈnɒmɪn(ə)l/ *adjective* existing in name only; not real or actual; (of sum of money etc.) very small; of, as, or like noun. ◻ **nominally** *adverb*.

nominate /ˈnɒmɪneɪt/ *verb* (**-ting**) propose (candidate) for election; appoint to office; appoint (date or place). ◻ **nomination** *noun*; **nominator** *noun*.

nominative /ˈnɒmɪnətɪv/ *Grammar* ● *noun* case expressing subject of verb. ● *adjective* of or in this case.

nominee /nɒmɪˈni:/ *noun* person who is nominated.

non- *prefix* not. For words starting with *non-* that are not found below, the root-words should be consulted.

nonagenarian /nəʊnədʒɪˈneərɪən/ *noun* person from 90 to 99 years old.

non-belligerent /nɒnbəˈlɪdʒərənt/ ● *adjective* not engaged in hostilities. ● *noun* non-belligerent state etc.

nonce /nɒns/ *noun* ◻ **for the nonce** for the time being, for the present; **nonce-word** word coined for one occasion.

nonchalant /ˈnɒnʃələnt/ *adjective* calm and casual. ◻ **nonchalance** *noun*; **nonchalantly** *adverb*.

non-combatant /nɒnˈkɒmbət(ə)nt/ *noun* person not fighting in a war, esp. civilian, army chaplain, etc.

non-commissioned /nɒnkəˈmɪʃ(ə)nd/ *adjective* (of officer) not holding commission.

noncommittal /nɒnkəˈmɪt(ə)l/ *adjective* avoiding commitment to definite opinion or course of action.

non-conductor /nɒnkənˈdʌktə/ *noun* substance that does not conduct heat or electricity.

nonconformist /nɒnkənˈfɔ:mɪst/ *noun* person who does not conform to doctrine of established Church, esp. (**Nonconformist**) member of Protestant sect dissenting from Anglican Church; person not conforming to prevailing principle.

nonconformity /nɒnkənfɔːmɪtɪ/ *noun* nonconformists as body; (+ *to*) failure to conform.

non-contributory /nɒnkən'trɪbjʊtərɪ/ *adjective* not involving contributions.

nondescript /'nɒndɪskrɪpt/ ● *adjective* lacking distinctive characteristics, not easily classified. ● *noun* such person or thing.

none /nʌn/ *pronoun* (often + *of*) not any; no person(s). □ **none the** (+ *comparative*), **none too** not in the least.

■ **Usage** The verb following *none* can be singular or plural when it means 'not any of several', e.g. *None of us knows* or *None of us know.*

nonentity /nɒ'nentɪtɪ/ *noun* (*plural* **-ies**) person or thing of no importance; non-existence; non-existent thing.

nonet /nəʊ'net/ *noun* musical composition for 9 performers; the performers; any group of 9.

nonetheless /nʌnðə'les/ *adverb* nevertheless.

non-event /nɒnɪ'vent/ *noun* insignificant event, esp. contrary to hopes or expectations.

non-existent /nɒnɪg'zɪst(ə)nt/ *adjective* not existing. □ **non-existence** *noun*.

non-fiction /nɒn'fɪkʃ(ə)n/ *noun* literary work other than fiction.

non-interference /nɒnɪntə'fɪərəns/ *noun* nonintervention.

non-intervention /nɒnɪntə'venʃ(ə)n/ *noun* policy of not interfering in others' affairs.

nonpareil /nɒnpə'reɪl/ ● *adjective* unrivalled, unique. ● *noun* such person or thing.

non-party /nɒn'pɑːtɪ/ *adjective* independent of political parties.

nonplus /nɒn'plʌs/ *verb* (**-ss-**) completely perplex.

nonsense /'nɒns(ə)ns/ *noun* (often as *interjection*) absurd or meaningless words or ideas; foolish conduct. □ **nonsensical** /-'sen-/ *adjective*.

non sequitur /nɒn 'sekwɪtə/ *noun* conclusion that does not logically follow from the premisses. [Latin]

non-slip /nɒn'slɪp/ *adjective* that does not slip; that prevents slipping.

non-smoker /nɒn'sməʊkə/ *noun* person who does not smoke; train compartment etc. where smoking is forbidden. □ **non-smoking** *adjective*.

non-starter /nɒn'stɑːtə/ *noun colloquial* person or scheme not worth considering.

non-stick /nɒn'stɪk/ *adjective* that does not allow things to stick to it.

non-stop /nɒn'stɒp/ ● *adjective* (of train etc.) not stopping at intermediate stations; done without stopping. ● *adverb* without stopping.

noodle¹ /'nuːd(ə)l/ *noun* strip or ring of pasta.

noodle² /'nuːd(ə)l/ *noun* simpleton.

nook /nʊk/ *noun* corner or recess; secluded place.

noon *noun* 12 o'clock in day, midday. □ **noonday** midday.

noose ● *noun* loop with running knot; snare. ● *verb* (**-sing**) catch with or enclose in noose.

nor *conjunction* and not.

Nordic /'nɔːdɪk/ *adjective* of tall blond Germanic people of Scandinavia.

norm *noun* standard, type; standard amount of work etc.; customary behaviour.

normal /'nɔːm(ə)l/ ● *adjective* conforming to standard; regular, usual, typical; *Geometry* (of line) at right angles. ● *noun* normal value of a temperature etc.; usual state, level, etc. □ **normalcy** *noun esp. US*; **normality** /-'mæl-/ *noun*; **normalize** *verb* (also **-ise**) (**-zing** or **-sing**); **normally** *adverb*.

Norman /'nɔːmən/ ● *noun* (*plural* **-s**) native of medieval Normandy; descendant of people established there in 10th c. ● *adjective* of Normans; of style of medieval architecture found in Britain under Normans.

Norse ● *noun* Norwegian language; Scandinavian language group. ● *adjective* of ancient Scandinavia, esp. Norway. □ **Norseman** *noun*.

north ● *noun* point of horizon 90° anticlockwise from east; corresponding compass point; (usually **the North**) northern part of world, country, town, etc. ● *adjective* towards, at, near, or facing north; (of wind) from north. ● *adverb* towards, at, or near north; (+ *of*) further north than. □ **northbound** travelling or leading north; **north-east**, **-west** point midway between north and east or west; **north-north-east**, **north-north-west** point midway between north and north-east or north-west; **North Star** pole star. □ **northward** *adjective, adverb, & noun*; **northwards** *adverb*.

northerly /'nɔːðəlɪ/ *adjective & adverb* in northern position or direction; (of wind) from north.

northern /'nɔːð(ə)n/ *adjective* of or in the north. □ **northern lights** aurora borealis. □ **northernmost** *adjective*.

northerner *noun* native or inhabitant of north.

Norwegian /nɔː'wiːdʒ(ə)n/ ● *noun* native, national, or language of Norway. ● *adjective* of or relating to Norway.

nose /nəʊz/ ● *noun* organ above mouth, used for smelling and breathing; sense of smell; odour or perfume of wine etc.; projecting part or front end of car, aircraft, etc. ● *verb* (**-sing**) (usually + *about* etc.) search; (often + *out*) perceive smell of, discover by smell; thrust nose against or into; make one's way cautiously forward. □ **nosebag** fodder-bag hung on horse's head; **nosebleed** bleeding from nose; **nose-dive** (make) steep downward plunge.

nosegay *noun* small bunch of flowers.

nosh *slang* ● *verb* eat. ● *noun* food or drink. □ **nosh-up** large meal.

nostalgia /nɒs'tældʒə/ *noun* (often + *for*) yearning for past period; homesickness. □ **nostalgic** *adjective*.

nostril /'nɒstr(ə)l/ *noun* either of two openings in nose.

nostrum /'nɒstrəm/ *noun* quack remedy, patent medicine; pet scheme.

nosy *adjective* (**-ier**, **-iest**) *colloquial* inquisitive, prying.

not *adverb expressing negation, refusal, or denial.* □ **not half** *slang* very much, very, not nearly, *colloquial* not at all; **not quite** almost.

notable /'nəʊtəb(ə)l/ ● *adjective* worthy of note; remarkable; eminent. ● *noun* eminent person. □ **notability** *noun*; **notably** *adverb*.

notary /'nəʊtərɪ/ *noun* (*plural* **-ies**) solicitor etc. who certifies deeds etc. □ **notarial** /-'teər-/ *adjective*.

notation /nəʊ'teɪʃ(ə)n/ *noun* representation of numbers, quantities, musical notes, etc. by symbols; set of such symbols.

notch ● *noun* V-shaped indentation on edge or surface. ● *verb* make notches in; (usually + *up*) score, win, achieve (esp. amount or quantity).

note ● *noun* brief written record as memory aid; short letter; formal diplomatic message; additional explanation in book; banknote; notice, attention; eminence; single musical tone of definite pitch; written sign representing its pitch and duration; quality or tone of speaking. ● *verb* (**-ting**) observe, notice; (often + *down*) record as thing to be remembered; (in *passive*; often + *for*) be well known. □ **notebook** book for making notes in; **notecase** wallet for banknotes; **notelet** small folded card for informal letter; **notepaper** paper for writing letters; **noteworthy** worthy of attention, remarkable.

nothing /ˈnʌθɪŋ/ ● *noun* no thing, not anything; person or thing of no importance; non-existence; no amount; nought. ● *adverb* not at all; in no way.

nothingness *noun* non-existence; worthlessness.

notice /ˈnəʊtɪs/ ● *noun* attention; displayed sheet etc. with announcement; intimation, warning; formal declaration of intention to end agreement or employment at specified time; short published review of new play, book, etc. ● *verb* (**-cing**) (often + *that*, *how*, etc.) perceive, observe. □ **noticeable** *adjective*; **noticeably** *adverb*.

notifiable /ˈnəʊtɪfaɪəb(ə)l/ *adjective* (esp. of disease) that must be notified to authorities.

notify /ˈnəʊtɪfaɪ/ *verb* (**-ies**, **-ied**) (often + *of*, *that*) inform, give notice to (person); make known. □ **notification** *noun*.

notion /ˈnəʊʃ(ə)n/ *noun* concept, idea; opinion; vague understanding; intention.

notional *adjective* hypothetical, imaginary. □ **notionally** *adverb*.

notorious /nəʊˈtɔːrɪəs/ *adjective* well known, esp. unfavourably. □ **notoriety** /-təˈraɪətɪ/ *noun*; **notoriously** *adverb*.

notwithstanding /nɒtwɪðˈstændɪŋ/ ● *preposition* in spite of. ● *adverb* nevertheless.

nougat /ˈnuːgɑː/ *noun* sweet made from nuts, egg white, and sugar or honey.

nought /nɔːt/ *noun* digit 0; cipher; *poetical or archaic* nothing.

noun /naʊn/ *noun* word used to name person or thing (see panel).

nourish /ˈnʌrɪʃ/ *verb* sustain with food; foster, cherish (feeling etc.). □ **nourishing** *adjective*.

nourishment *noun* sustenance, food.

nous /naʊs/ *noun colloquial* common sense.

Nov. *abbreviation* November.

nova /ˈnəʊvə/ *noun* (*plural* **novae** /-viː/ or **-s**) star showing sudden burst of brightness and then subsiding.

novel /ˈnɒv(ə)l/ ● *noun* fictitious prose story of book length. ● *adjective* of new kind or nature.

novelette /nɒvəˈlet/ *noun* short (esp. romantic) novel.

novelist /ˈnɒvəlɪst/ *noun* writer of novels.

novella /nəˈvelə/ *noun* (*plural* **-s**) short novel or narrative story.

novelty /ˈnɒvəltɪ/ *noun* (*plural* **-ies**) newness; new thing or occurrence; small toy etc.

November /nəʊˈvembə/ *noun* eleventh month of year.

novena /nəˈviːnə/ *noun RC Church* special prayers or services on 9 successive days.

novice /ˈnɒvɪs/ *noun* probationary member of religious order; beginner.

noviciate /nəˈvɪʃɪət/ *noun* (also **novitiate**) period of being a novice; religious novice; novices' quarters.

now ● *adverb* at present or mentioned time; immediately; by this time: in the immediate past. ● *conjunction* (often + *that*) because. ● *noun* this time; the present. □ **now and again** or **then** occasionally.

nowadays /ˈnaʊədeɪz/ ● *adverb* at present time or age. ● *noun* the present time.

nowhere /ˈnəʊweə/ ● *adverb* in or to no place. ● *pronoun* no place.

nowt *noun colloquial or dialect* nothing.

noxious /ˈnɒkʃəs/ *adjective* harmful, unwholesome.

nozzle /ˈnɒz(ə)l/ *noun* spout on hose etc.

nr. *abbreviation* near.

NSPCC *abbreviation* National Society for Prevention of Cruelty to Children.

NSW *abbreviation* New South Wales.

NT *abbreviation* New Testament; Northern Territory (of Australia); National Trust.

nuance /ˈnjuːɑ̃s/ *noun* subtle shade of meaning, feeling, colour, etc.

nub *noun* point or gist (of matter or story).

nubile /ˈnjuːbaɪl/ *adjective* (of woman) marriageable, sexually attractive. □ **nubility** *noun*.

nuclear /ˈnjuːklɪə/ *adjective* of, relating to, or constituting a nucleus; using nuclear energy. □ **nuclear energy** energy obtained by nuclear fission or fusion; **nuclear family** couple and their child(ren); **nuclear fission** nuclear reaction in which heavy nucleus splits with release of energy; **nuclear fuel** source of nuclear energy; **nuclear fusion** nuclear reaction in which nuclei of low atomic number fuse with release of energy; **nuclear physics** physics of

Noun

A noun is the name of a person or thing. There are four kinds:

1 common nouns (the words for articles and creatures), e.g.

shoe	in	*The red shoe was left on the shelf.*
box	in	*The large box stood in the corner.*
plant	in	*The plant grew to two metres.*
horse	in	*A horse and rider galloped by.*

2 proper nouns (the names of people, places, ships, institutions, and animals, which always begin with a capital letter), e.g.

Jane	*USS Enterprise*	*Bambi*
London	*Grand Hotel*	

3 abstract nouns (the words for qualities, things we cannot see or touch, and things which have no physical reality), e.g.

truth	*absence*
explanation	*warmth*

4 collective nouns (the words for groups of things), e.g.

committee	*squad*	*the Cabinet*
herd	*swarm*	*the clergy*
majority	*team*	*the public*

atomic nuclei; **nuclear power** power derived from nuclear energy, country that has nuclear weapons.

nucleic acid /nju:'kli:ɪk/ *noun* either of two complex organic molecules (DNA and RNA) present in all living cells.

nucleon /'nju:klɪɒn/ *noun* proton or neutron.

nucleus /'nju:klɪəs/ *noun* (*plural* **nuclei** /-lɪaɪ/) central part or thing round which others collect; kernel; initial part; central core of atom; part of cell containing genetic material.

nude /nju:d/ ● *adjective* naked, unclothed. ● *noun* painting etc. of nude human figure; nude person. □ **in the nude** naked. □ **nudity** *noun.*

nudge ● *verb* (**-ging**) prod gently with elbow to draw attention; push gradually. ● *noun* gentle push.

nudist /'nju:dɪst/ *noun* person who advocates or practises going unclothed. □ **nudism** *noun.*

nugatory /'nju:gətərɪ/ *adjective* futile, trifling; inoperative, not valid.

nugget /'nʌgɪt/ *noun* lump of gold etc., as found in earth; lump of anything.

nuisance /'nju:s(ə)ns/ *noun* person, thing, or circumstance causing annoyance.

null *adjective* (esp. **null and void**) invalid; non-existent; expressionless. □ **nullity** *noun.*

nullify /'nʌlɪfaɪ/ *verb* (**-ies**, **-ied**) neutralize; invalidate. □ **nullification** *noun.*

numb /nʌm/ ● *adjective* deprived of feeling; paralysed. ● *verb* make numb; stupefy, paralyse. □ **numbness** *noun.*

number /'nʌmbə/ ● *noun* arithmetical value representing a quantity; word, symbol, or figure representing this; total count or aggregate; numerical reckoning; quantity, amount; person or thing having place in a series, esp. single issue of magazine, item in programme, etc. ● *verb* include; assign number(s) to; amount to specified number. □ **number one** *colloquial* oneself; **number plate** plate bearing number esp. of motor vehicle.

■ **Usage** The phrase *a number of* is normally used with a plural verb, as in *a number of problems remain.*

numberless *adjective* innumerable.

numeral /'nju:mər(ə)l/ ● *noun* symbol or group of symbols denoting a number. ● *adjective* of or denoting a number.

numerate /'nju:mərət/ *adjective* familiar with basic principles of mathematics. □ **numeracy** *noun.*

numeration /nju:mə'reɪʃ(ə)n/ *noun* process of numbering; calculation.

numerator /'nju:məreɪtə/ *noun* number above line in vulgar fraction.

numerical /nju:'merɪk(ə)l/ *adjective* of or relating to number(s). □ **numerically** *adverb.*

numerology /nju:mə'rɒlədʒɪ/ *noun* study of supposed occult significance of numbers.

numerous /'nju:mərəs/ *adjective* many; consisting of many.

numinous /'nju:mɪnəs/ *adjective* indicating presence of a god; awe-inspiring.

numismatic /nju:mɪz'mætɪk/ *adjective* of or relating to coins or medals.

numismatics *plural noun* (usually treated as *singular*) study of coins and medals. □ **numismatist** /-'mɪzmətɪst/ *noun.*

nun *noun* member of community of women living under religious vows.

nuncio /'nʌnsɪəʊ/ *noun* (*plural* **-s**) papal ambassador.

nunnery *noun* (*plural* **-ies**) religious house of nuns.

nuptial /'nʌpʃ(ə)l/ ● *adjective* of marriage or weddings. ● *noun* (usually in *plural*) wedding.

nurse /nɜ:s/ ● *noun* person trained to care for sick and help doctors or dentists; nursemaid. ● *verb* (**-sing**) work as nurse; attend to (sick person); feed or be fed at breast; hold or treat carefully; foster; harbour. □ **nursing home** private hospital or home.

nursemaid *noun* woman in charge of child(ren).

nursery /'nɜ:sərɪ/ *noun* (*plural* **-ies**) room or place equipped for young children; place where plants are reared for sale. □ **nurseryman** grower of plants for sale; **nursery rhyme** traditional song or rhyme for young children; **nursery school** school for children between ages of 3 and 5.

nurture /'nɜ:tʃə/ ● *noun* bringing up, fostering care; nourishment. ● *verb* (**-ring**) bring up, rear.

nut *noun* fruit consisting of hard shell or pod around edible kernel or seeds; this kernel; small usually hexagonal flat piece of metal with threaded hole through it for screwing on end of bolt to secure it; *slang* head; *slang* crazy person; small lump (of coal etc.). □ **nutcase** *slang* crazy person; **nutcracker** (usually in *plural*) device for cracking nuts; **nuthatch** small bird climbing up and down tree trunks; **nuts** *slang* crazy.

nutmeg /'nʌtmeg/ *noun* hard aromatic seed used as spice etc.; E. Indian tree bearing this.

nutria /'nju:trɪə/ *noun* coypu fur.

nutrient /'nju:trɪənt/ ● *noun* substance providing essential nourishment. ● *adjective* serving as or providing nourishment.

nutriment /'nju:trɪmənt/ *noun* nourishing food.

nutrition /nju:'trɪʃ(ə)n/ *noun* food, nourishment. □ **nutritional** *adjective*; **nutritionist** *noun.*

nutritious /nju:'trɪʃəs/ *adjective* efficient as food.

nutritive /'nju:trɪtɪv/ *adjective* of nutrition; nutritious.

nutshell *noun* hard covering of nut. □ **in a nutshell** in few words.

nutter *noun slang* crazy person.

nutty *adjective* (**-ier**, **-iest**) full of nuts; tasting like nuts; *slang* crazy.

nux vomica /nʌks 'vɒmɪkə/ *noun* E. Indian tree; its seeds, containing strychnine.

nuzzle /'nʌz(ə)l/ *verb* (**-ling**) prod or rub gently with nose; nestle, lie snug.

NW *abbreviation* north-west(ern).

NY *abbreviation US* New York.

nylon /'naɪlɒn/ *noun* strong light synthetic fibre; nylon fabric; (in *plural*) stockings of nylon.

nymph /nɪmf/ *noun* mythological semi-divine female spirit associated with rivers, woods, etc.; immature form of some insects.

nymphomania /nɪmfə'meɪnɪə/ *noun* excessive sexual desire in a woman. □ **nymphomaniac** *noun & adjective.*

NZ *abbreviation* New Zealand.

O[1] □ **O level** *historical* ordinary level in GCE exam.

O[2] /əʊ/ *interjection* = OH; *used before name in exclamation.*

oaf *noun* (*plural* **-s**) awkward lout. □ **oafish** *adjective*; **oafishly** *adverb*; **oafishness** *noun*.

oak *noun* acorn-bearing hardwood tree with lobed leaves; its wood. □ **oak-apple**, **-gall** abnormal growth produced on oak trees by insects.

oakum /ˈəʊkəm/ *noun* loose fibre got by picking old rope to pieces.

OAP *abbreviation* old-age pensioner.

oar /ɔː/ *noun* pole with blade used to propel boat by leverage against water; rower.

oarsman /ˈɔːzmən/ *noun* (*feminine* **-woman**) rower. □ **oarsmanship** *noun*.

oasis /əʊˈeɪsɪs/ *noun* (*plural* **oases** /-siːz/) fertile spot in desert.

oast *noun* hop-drying kiln. □ **oast house** building containing this.

oat *noun* cereal plant grown as food; (in *plural*) grain of this; tall grass resembling this. □ **oatcake** thin oatmeal biscuit; **oatmeal** meal ground from oats, greyish-fawn colour; **sow one's wild oats** indulge in youthful follies before becoming steady. □ **oaten** *adjective*.

oath /əʊθ/ *noun* (*plural* **-s**) /əʊðz/) solemn declaration naming God etc. as witness; curse. □ **on, under oath** having sworn solemn oath.

ob. *abbreviation* died (*obiit*).

obbligato /ɒblɪˈɡɑːtəʊ/ *noun* (*plural* **-s**) *Music* accompaniment forming integral part of a composition.

obdurate /ˈɒbdjʊrət/ *adjective* stubborn; hardened. □ **obduracy** *noun*.

OBE *abbreviation* Officer of the Order of the British Empire.

obedient /əʊˈbiːdɪənt/ *adjective* obeying or ready to obey; submissive to another's will. □ **obedience** *noun*; **obediently** *adverb*.

obeisance /əʊˈbeɪs(ə)ns/ *noun* gesture expressing submission, respect, etc.; homage. □ **obeisant** *adjective*.

obelisk /ˈɒbəlɪsk/ *noun* tapering usually 4-sided stone pillar.

obelus /ˈɒbələs/ *noun* (*plural* **obeli** /-laɪ/) dagger-shaped mark of reference (†).

obese /əʊˈbiːs/ *adjective* very fat. □ **obesity** *noun*.

obey /əʊˈbeɪ/ *verb* carry out command of; do what one is told to do.

obfuscate /ˈɒbfʌskeɪt/ *verb* (**-ting**) obscure, confuse; bewilder. □ **obfuscation** *noun*.

obituary /əˈbɪtjʊərɪ/ ● *noun* (*plural* **-ies**) notice of death(s); brief biography of deceased person. ● *adjective* of or serving as obituary.

object ● *noun* /ˈɒbdʒɪkt/ material thing; person or thing to which action or feeling is directed; thing sought or aimed at; word or phrase representing person or thing affected by action of verb (see panel). ● *verb* /əbˈdʒekt/ (often + *to, against*) express opposition, disapproval, or reluctance; protest. □ **no object** not an important factor. □ **objector** *noun*.

objectify /əbˈdʒektɪfaɪ/ *verb* (**-ies**, **-ied**) present as an object, embody.

objection /əbˈdʒekʃ(ə)n/ *noun* expression of disapproval or opposition; objecting; adverse reason or statement.

objectionable *adjective* unpleasant, offensive; open to objection. □ **objectionably** *adverb*.

objective /əbˈdʒektɪv/ ● *adjective* external to the mind; actually existing; dealing with outward things uncoloured by opinions or feelings; *Grammar* (of case or word) in form appropriate to object. ● *noun* object or purpose; *Grammar* objective case. □ **objectively** *adverb*; **objectivity** /ɒbdʒekˈtɪvɪtɪ/ *noun*.

objet d'art /ɒbʒeɪ ˈdɑː/ *noun* (*plural* ***objets d'art*** same pronunciation) small decorative object. [French]

oblate /ˈɒbleɪt/ *adjective* (of spheroid) flattened at poles.

oblation /əʊˈbleɪʃ(ə)n/ *noun* thing offered to a divine being.

obligate /ˈɒblɪɡeɪt/ *verb* (**-ting**) bind (person) legally or morally.

obligation /ɒblɪˈɡeɪʃ(ə)n/ *noun* compelling power of law, duty, etc.; duty; binding agreement; indebtedness for service or benefit.

Object

There are two types of object:

1 A direct object is a person or thing directly affected by the verb and can usually be found by asking the question 'whom or what?' after the verb, e.g.

The electors chose Mr Smith.
Charles wrote a letter.

2 An indirect object is usually a person or thing receiving something from the subject of the verb, e.g.

He gave me the pen.
(*me* is the indirect object, and *the pen* is the direct object.)
I sent my bank a letter.
(*my bank* is the indirect object, and *a letter* is the direct object.)

Sentences containing an indirect object usually contain a direct object as well, but not always, e.g.
Pay me.

'Object' on its own usually means a direct object.

obligatory /ə'blɪgətərɪ/ *adjective* binding, compulsory. □ **obligatorily** *adverb*.

oblige /ə'blaɪdʒ/ *verb* (**-ging**) compel, require; be binding on; do (person) small favour; (as **obliged** *adjective*) grateful.

obliging *adjective* helpful, accommodating. □ **obligingly** *adverb*.

oblique /ə'bli:k/ ● *adjective* slanting; at an angle; not going straight to the point, indirect; *Grammar* (of case) other than nominative or vocative. ● *noun* oblique stroke. □ **obliquely** *adverb*; **obliqueness** *noun*; **obliquity** /ə'blɪkwɪtɪ/ *noun*.

obliterate /ə'blɪtəreɪt/ *verb* (**-ting**) blot out, leave no clear trace of. □ **obliteration** *noun*.

oblivion /ə'blɪvɪən/ *noun* state of having or being forgotten.

oblivious /ə'blɪvɪəs/ *adjective* unaware or unconscious. □ **obliviously** *adverb*; **obliviousness** *noun*.

oblong /'ɒblɒŋ/ ● *adjective* rectangular with adjacent sides unequal. ● *noun* oblong figure or object.

obloquy /'ɒbləkwɪ/ *noun* abuse, being ill spoken of.

obnoxious /əb'nɒkʃəs/ *adjective* offensive, objectionable. □ **obnoxiously** *adverb*; **obnoxiousness** *noun*.

oboe /'əʊbəʊ/ *noun* double-reeded woodwind instrument. □ **oboist** *noun*.

obscene /əb'si:n/ *adjective* offensively indecent; *colloquial* highly offensive; *Law* (of publication) tending to deprave and corrupt. □ **obscenely** *adverb*; **obscenity** /-'sen-/ *noun* (*plural* **-ies**).

obscure /əb'skjʊə/ ● *adjective* not clearly expressed or easily understood; unexplained; dark, indistinct; hidden, undistinguished. ● *verb* (**-ring**) make obscure or invisible. □ **obscurity** *noun*.

obsequies /'ɒbsɪkwɪz/ *plural noun* funeral.

obsequious /əb'si:kwɪəs/ *adjective* fawning, servile. □ **obsequiously** *adverb*; **obsequiousness** *noun*.

observance /əb'zɜ:v(ə)ns/ *noun* keeping or performance of law, duty, etc.; rite, ceremonial act.

observant *adjective* good at observing. □ **observantly** *adverb*.

observation /ɒbzə'veɪʃ(ə)n/ *noun* observing, being observed; comment, remark; power of perception. □ **observational** *adjective*.

observatory /əb'zɜ:vətərɪ/ *noun* (*plural* **-ies**) building for astronomical or other observation.

observe /əb'zɜ:v/ *verb* (**-ving**) perceive, become aware of; watch; keep (rules etc.); celebrate (rite etc.); remark; take note of scientifically. □ **observable** *adjective*.

observer *noun* person who observes; interested spectator; person attending meeting to note proceedings but without participating.

obsess /əb'ses/ *verb* fill mind of (person) all the time; preoccupy. □ **obsession** *noun*; **obsessional** *adjective*; **obsessive** *adjective*; **obsessively** *adverb*; **obsessiveness** *noun*.

obsidian /əb'sɪdɪən/ *noun* dark glassy rock formed from lava.

obsolescent /ɒbsə'les(ə)nt/ *adjective* becoming obsolete. □ **obsolescence** *noun*.

obsolete /'ɒbsəli:t/ *adjective* no longer used, antiquated.

obstacle /'ɒbstək(ə)l/ *noun* thing obstructing progress.

obstetrics /əb'stetrɪks/ *plural noun* (usually treated as *singular*) branch of medicine or surgery dealing with childbirth. □ **obstetric** *adjective*; **obstetrician** /ɒbstə'trɪʃ(ə)n/ *noun*.

obstinate /'ɒbstɪnət/ *adjective* stubborn, intractable. □ **obstinacy** *noun*; **obstinately** *adverb*.

obstreperous /əb'strepərəs/ *adjective* noisy, unruly. □ **obstreperously** *adverb*; **obstreperousness** *noun*.

obstruct /əb'strʌkt/ *verb* block up; make hard or impossible to pass along or through; retard or prevent progress of.

obstruction /əb'strʌkʃ(ə)n/ *noun* obstructing, being obstructed; thing that obstructs; *Sport* unlawfully obstructing another player.

obstructive *adjective* causing or meant to cause obstruction.

obtain /əb'teɪn/ *verb* acquire; get; have granted to one; be prevalent or established. □ **obtainable** *adjective*.

obtrude /əb'tru:d/ *verb* (**-ding**) (often + *on*, *upon*) thrust (oneself etc.) importunately forward. □ **obtrusion** *noun*.

obtrusive /əb'tru:sɪv/ *adjective* unpleasantly noticeable; obtruding oneself. □ **obtrusively** *adverb*; **obtrusiveness** *noun*.

obtuse /əb'tju:s/ *adjective* dull-witted; (of angle) between 90° and 180°; blunt, not sharp or pointed. □ **obtuseness** *noun*.

obverse /'ɒbvɜ:s/ *noun* counterpart, opposite; side of coin or medal that bears head or principal design; front or top side.

obviate /'ɒbvɪeɪt/ *verb* (**-ting**) get round or do away with (need, inconvenience, etc.).

obvious /'ɒbvɪəs/ *adjective* easily seen, recognized, or understood. □ **obviously** *adverb*; **obviousness** *noun*.

OC *abbreviation* Officer Commanding.

ocarina /ɒkə'ri:nə/ *noun* egg-shaped musical wind instrument.

occasion /ə'keɪʒ(ə)n/ ● *noun* special event or happening; time of this; reason, need; suitable juncture, opportunity. ● *verb* cause, esp. incidentally.

occasional *adjective* happening irregularly and infrequently; made or meant for, acting on, etc. special occasion(s). □ **occasional table** small table for use as required. □ **occasionally** *adverb*.

Occident /'ɒksɪd(ə)nt/ *noun* (**the Occident**) West, esp. Europe and America as distinct from the Orient. □ **occidental** /-'den-/ *adjective*.

occiput /'ɒksɪpʌt/ *noun* back of head. □ **occipital** /-'sɪpɪt-/ *adjective*.

occlude /ə'klu:d/ *verb* (**-ding**) stop up; obstruct; *Chemistry* absorb (gases); (as **occluded** *adjective*) *Meteorology* (of frontal system) formed when cold front overtakes warm front, raising warm air. □ **occlusion** *noun*.

occult /ɒ'kʌlt, 'ɒkʌlt/ *adjective* involving the supernatural, mystical; esoteric. □ **the occult** occult phenomena generally.

occupant /'ɒkjʊpənt/ *noun* person occupying dwelling, office, or position. □ **occupancy** *noun* (*plural* **-ies**).

occupation /ɒkjʊ'peɪʃ(ə)n/ *noun* profession or employment; pastime; occupying or being occupied, esp. by armed forces of another country.

occupational *adjective* of or connected with one's occupation. □ **occupational disease, hazard** one to which a particular occupation renders someone especially liable; **occupational therapy** programme of mental or physical activity to assist recovery from disease or injury.

occupier /'ɒkjʊpaɪə/ *noun* person living in house etc. as owner or tenant.

occupy /'ɒkjʊpaɪ/ *verb* (**-ies**, **-ied**) live in; be tenant of; take up, fill (space, time, or place); take military possession of; place oneself in (building etc.) without authority as protest etc.; hold (office); keep busy.

occur /ə'kɜ:/ *verb* (**-rr-**) take place, happen; be met with or found in some place or conditions; (+ *to*) come into one's mind.

occurrence /ə'kʌrəns/ *noun* happening; incident.

ocean /ˈəʊʃ(ə)n/ *noun* large expanse of sea, esp. one of the 5 named divisions of this, e.g. Atlantic Ocean; (often in *plural*) *colloquial* immense expanse or quantity. ▫ **oceanic** /əʊʃɪˈænɪk/ *adjective*.

oceanography /əʊʃəˈnɒgrəfɪ/ *noun* study of the oceans. ▫ **oceanographer** *noun*.

ocelot /ˈɒsɪlɒt/ *noun* S. American leopard-like cat.

ochre /ˈəʊkə/ *noun* (*US* **ocher**) earth used as pigment; pale brownish-yellow colour. ▫ **ochreous** /ˈəʊkrɪəs/ *adjective*.

o'clock /əˈklɒk/ *adverb* of the clock (used to specify hour).

Oct. *abbreviation* October.

octa- *combining form* (also **oct-** before vowel) eight.

octagon /ˈɒktəgən/ *noun* plane figure with 8 sides and angles. ▫ **octagonal** /-ˈtæg-/ *adjective*.

octahedron /ɒktəˈhiːdrən/ *noun* (*plural* **-s**) solid figure contained by 8 (esp. triangular) plane faces. ▫ **octahedral** *adjective*.

octane /ˈɒkteɪn/ *noun* colourless inflammable hydrocarbon occurring in petrol. ▫ **high-octane** (of fuel used in internal-combustion engines) not detonating rapidly during power stroke; **octane number, rating** figure indicating antiknock properties of fuel.

octave /ˈɒktɪv/ *noun Music* interval of 8 diatonic degrees between two notes, 8 notes occupying this interval, each of two notes at this interval's extremes; 8-line stanza.

octavo /ɒkˈteɪvəʊ/ *noun* (*plural* **-s**) size of book or page with sheets folded into 8 leaves.

octet /ɒkˈtet/ *noun* musical composition for 8 performers; the performers; any group of 8.

octo- *combining form* (also **oct-** before vowel) eight.

October /ɒkˈtəʊbə/ *noun* tenth month of year.

octogenarian /ɒktəʊdʒɪˈneərɪən/ *noun* person from 80 to 89 years old.

octopus /ˈɒktəpəs/ *noun* (*plural* **-puses**) mollusc with 8 suckered tentacles.

ocular /ˈɒkjʊlə/ *adjective* of, for, or by the eyes; visual.

oculist /ˈɒkjʊlɪst/ *noun* specialist in treatment of eyes.

OD /əʊˈdiː/ *slang* ● *noun* drug overdose. ● *verb* (**OD's, OD'd, Od'ing**) take overdose.

odd *adjective* extraordinary, strange; (of job etc.) occasional, casual; not normally considered, unconnected; (of numbers) not divisible by 2; left over, detached from set etc.; (added to weight, sum, etc.) rather more than. ▫ **oddball** *colloquial* eccentric person. ▫ **oddly** *adverb*; **oddness** *noun*.

oddity /ˈɒdɪtɪ/ *noun* (*plural* **-ies**) strange person, thing, or occurrence; peculiar trait; strangeness.

oddment *noun* odd article; something left over.

odds *plural noun* ratio between amounts staked by parties to a bet; chances in favour of or against result; balance of advantage; difference giving an advantage. ▫ **at odds** (often + *with*) in conflict; **odds and ends** remnants, stray articles; **odds-on** state when success is more likely than failure; **over the odds** above general price etc.

ode *noun* lyric poem of exalted style and tone.

odious /ˈəʊdɪəs/ *adjective* hateful, repulsive. ▫ **odiously** *adverb*; **odiousness** *noun*.

odium /ˈəʊdɪəm/ *noun* general dislike or disapproval.

odor *US* = ODOUR.

odoriferous /əʊdəˈrɪfərəs/ *adjective* diffusing (usually pleasant) odours.

odour /ˈəʊdə/ *noun* (*US* **odor**) smell or fragrance; favour or repute. ▫ **odorous** *adjective*; **odourless** *adjective*.

odyssey /ˈɒdɪsɪ/ *noun* (*plural* **-s**) long adventurous journey.

OED *abbreviation* Oxford English Dictionary.

oedema /ɪˈdiːmə/ *noun* (*US* **edema**) excess fluid in body cavities or tissues.

Oedipus complex /ˈiːdɪpəs/ *noun* attraction of child to parent of opposite sex (esp. son to mother). ▫ **Oedipal** *adjective*.

oesophagus /iːˈsɒfəgəs/ *noun* (*US* **esophagus**) (*plural* **-gi** /-dʒaɪ/ or **-guses**) passage from mouth to stomach, gullet.

oestrogen /ˈiːstrədʒ(ə)n/ *noun* (*US* **estrogen**) hormone producing female physical characteristics.

oeuvre /ˈɜːvr/ *noun* works of creative artist considered collectively. [French]

of /ɒv/ *preposition* belonging to, from; concerning; out of; among; relating to; *US* (of time in relation to following hour) to. ▫ **be of** possess, give rise to; **of late** recently; **of old** formerly.

off ● *adverb* away, at or to distance; out of position; loose, separate, gone; so as to be rid of; discontinued, stopped; not available on menu. ● *preposition* from; not on. ● *adjective* further; far; right-hand; *colloquial* annoying; not acceptable; *Cricket* of, in, or into half of field which batsman faces. ● *noun* start of race; *Cricket* the off side. ▫ **off and on** now and then; **offbeat** unconventional, *Music* not coinciding with beat; **off chance** remote possibility; **off colour** unwell, *US* rather indecent; **offhand** without preparation, casual, curt; **off-licence** shop selling alcoholic drink for consumption away from premises; **offline** *Computing adjective* not online, *adverb* with delay between data production and its processing; **off-peak** (of electricity, traffic, etc.) used or for use at times of lesser demand; **offprint** reprint of part of publication; **offshoot** side-shoot or branch, derivative; **offside** (of player in field game) in position where he or she may not play the ball; **off the wall** *slang* crazy, absurd; **off white** white with grey or yellowish tinge.

offal /ˈɒf(ə)l/ *noun* edible organs of animal, esp. heart, liver, etc.; refuse, scraps.

offence /əˈfens/ *noun* (*US* **offense**) illegal act; transgression; upsetting of person's feelings, insult; aggressive action.

offend /əˈfend/ *verb* cause offence to, upset; displease, anger; (often + *against*) do wrong. ▫ **offender** *noun*; **offending** *adjective*.

offense *US* = OFFENCE.

offensive /əˈfensɪv/ ● *adjective* causing offence; insulting; disgusting; aggressive; (of weapon) for attacking. ● *noun* aggressive attitude, action, or campaign. ▫ **offensively** *adverb*; **offensiveness** *noun*.

offer /ˈɒfə/ ● *verb* present for acceptance, refusal, or consideration; (+ *to do*) express readiness, show intention; attempt; present by way of sacrifice. ● *noun* expression of readiness to do or give if desired, or buy or sell; amount offered; proposal, esp. of marriage; bid. ▫ **on offer** for sale at certain (esp. reduced) price.

offering *noun* contribution, gift; thing offered.

offertory /ˈɒfətərɪ/ *noun* (*plural* **-ies**) offering of bread and wine at Eucharist; collection of money at religious service.

office /ˈɒfɪs/ *noun* room or building where administrative or clerical work is done; place for transacting business; department or local branch, esp. for specified purpose; position with duties attached to it; tenure of official position; duty, task, function; (usually in *plural*) piece of kindness, service; authorized form of worship.

officer /ˈɒfɪsə/ *noun* person holding position of authority or trust, esp. one with commission in armed forces; policeman or policewoman; president, treasurer, etc. of society etc.

official /əˈfɪʃ(ə)l/ ● *adjective* of office or its tenure; characteristic of people in office; properly authorized. ● *noun* person holding office or engaged in official duties. □ **official secrets** confidential information involving national security. □ **officialdom** *noun*; **officially** *adverb*.

officialese /əfɪʃəˈliːz/ *noun derogatory* officials' jargon.

officiate /əˈfɪʃɪeɪt/ *verb* (**-ting**) act in official capacity; conduct religious service.

officious /əˈfɪʃəs/ *adjective* domineering; intrusive in correcting etc. □ **officiously** *adverb*; **officiousness** *noun*.

offing /ˈɒfɪŋ/ *noun* □ **in the offing** at hand, ready or likely to happen etc.

offset ● *noun* side-shoot of plant used for propagation; compensation; sloping ledge. ● *verb* (**-setting**; *past & past participle* **-set**) counterbalance, compensate.

offspring *noun* (*plural* same) person's child, children, or descendants; animal's young or descendants.

oft *adverb archaic* often.

often /ˈɒf(ə)n/ *adverb* (**oftener**, **oftenest**) frequently; many times; at short intervals; in many instances.

ogee /ˈəʊdʒiː/ *noun* S-shaped curve or moulding.

ogive /ˈəʊdʒaɪv/ *noun* pointed arch; diagonal rib of vault.

ogle /ˈəʊg(ə)l/ ● *verb* (**-ling**) look lecherously or flirtatiously (at). ● *noun* flirtatious glance.

ogre /ˈəʊgə/ *noun* (*feminine* **ogress** /-grɪs/) man-eating giant. □ **ogreish**, **ogrish** /ˈəʊgərɪʃ/ *adjective*.

oh /əʊ/ *interjection* (also **O**) *expressing surprise, pain, etc.*

ohm /əʊm/ *noun* SI unit of electrical resistance.

OHMS *abbreviation* On Her or His Majesty's Service.

oho /əʊˈhəʊ/ *interjection expressing surprise or exultation.*

OHP *abbreviation* overhead projector.

oil ● *noun* viscous usually inflammable liquid insoluble in water; petroleum. ● *verb* apply oil to, lubricate; treat with oil. □ **oilcake** compressed linseed etc. as cattle food or manure; **oilfield** district yielding mineral oil; **oil paint** paint made by mixing pigment with oil; **oil painting** use of or picture in oil paints; **oil rig** equipment for drilling an oil well; **oilskin** cloth waterproofed with oil, garment or (in *plural*) suit of it; **oil slick** patch of oil, esp. on sea; **oil well** well from which mineral oil is drawn.

oily *adjective* (**-ier**, **-iest**) of, like, covered or soaked with, oil; (of manner) fawning.

ointment /ˈɔɪntmənt/ *noun* smooth greasy healing or cosmetic preparation for skin.

OK /əʊˈkeɪ/ (also **okay**) *colloquial* ● *adjective & adverb* all right. ● *noun* (*plural* **OKs**) approval, sanction. ● *verb* (**OK's**, **OK'd**, **OK'ing**) approve, sanction.

okapi /əʊˈkɑːpɪ/ *noun* (*plural* same or **-s**) African partially striped ruminant mammal.

okay = OK.

okra /ˈəʊkrə/ *noun* tall originally African plant with edible seed pods.

old /əʊld/ *adjective* (**-er**, **-est**) advanced in age; not young or near its beginning; worn, dilapidated, or shabby from age; practised, inveterate; dating from far back; long established; former; *colloquial: used to indicate affection*. □ **old age** later part of normal lifetime; **old-age pension** state retirement pension; **old-age pensioner** person receiving this; **Old Bill** *slang* the police; **old boy** former male pupil of school, *colloquial* elderly man; **old-fashioned** in or according to fashion no longer current, antiquated; **old girl** former female pupil of school, *colloquial* elderly woman; **Old Glory** *US* Stars and Stripes; **old guard** original, past, or conservative members of group; **old hand** experienced or practised person; **old hat** *colloquial* hackneyed; **old maid** *derogatory* elderly unmarried woman, prim and fussy person; **old man** *colloquial* one's father, husband, or employer etc.; **old man's beard** wild clematis; **old master** great painter of former times, painting by such painter; **Old Testament** part of Bible dealing with pre-Christian times; **old wives' tale** unscientific belief; **old woman** *colloquial* one's wife or mother, fussy or timid man; **Old World** Europe, Asia, and Africa. □ **oldish** *adjective*; **oldness** *noun*.

olden *adjective archaic* old, of old.

oldie *noun colloquial* old person or thing.

oleaginous /əʊlɪˈædʒɪnəs/ *adjective* like or producing oil; oily.

oleander /əʊlɪˈændə/ *noun* evergreen flowering Mediterranean shrub.

olfactory /ɒlˈfæktərɪ/ *adjective* of the sense of smell.

oligarch /ˈɒlɪgɑːk/ *noun* member of oligarchy.

oligarchy /ˈɒlɪgɑːkɪ/ *noun* (*plural* **-ies**) government by small group of people; members of such government; state so governed. □ **oligarchic(al)** /-ˈgɑːk-/ *adjective*.

olive /ˈɒlɪv/ ● *noun* oval hard-stoned fruit yielding oil; tree bearing this; dull yellowish green. ● *adjective* olive-green; (of complexion) yellowish-brown. □ **olive branch** gesture of peace or reconciliation.

Olympiad /əˈlɪmpɪæd/ *noun* period of 4 years between Olympic Games; celebration of modern Olympic Games.

Olympian /əˈlɪmpɪən/ *adjective* of Olympus; magnificent, condescending; aloof.

Olympic /əˈlɪmpɪk/ ● *adjective* of the Olympic Games. ● *plural noun* (**the Olympics**) Olympic Games. □ **Olympic Games** ancient Greek athletic festival held every 4 years, or modern international revival of this.

OM *abbreviation* Order of Merit.

ombudsman /ˈɒmbʊdzmən/ *noun* official appointed to investigate complaints against public authorities.

omega /ˈəʊmɪgə/ *noun* last letter of Greek alphabet (Ω, ω); last of series.

omelette /ˈɒmlɪt/ *noun* beaten eggs fried and often folded over filling.

omen /ˈəʊmən/ *noun* event supposedly warning of good or evil; prophetic significance.

ominous /ˈɒmɪnəs/ *adjective* threatening; inauspicious. □ **ominously** *adverb*.

omit /əʊˈmɪt/ *verb* (**-tt-**) leave out; not include; leave undone; (+ *to do*) neglect. □ **omission** /əʊˈmɪʃ(ə)n/ *noun*.

omni- *combining form* all.

omnibus /ˈɒmnɪbəs/ ● *noun formal* bus; volume containing several novels etc. previously published separately. ● *adjective* serving several purposes at once; comprising several items.

omnipotent /ɒmˈnɪpət(ə)nt/ *adjective* all-powerful. □ **omnipotence** *noun*.

omnipresent /ɒmnɪˈprez(ə)nt/ *adjective* present everywhere. □ **omnipresence** *noun*.

omniscient /ɒmˈnɪsɪənt/ *adjective* knowing everything. □ **omniscience** *noun*.

omnivorous /ɒmˈnɪvərəs/ *adjective* feeding on both plant and animal material; *jocular* reading everything that comes one's way. □ **omnivore** /ˈɒmnɪvɔː/ *noun*; **omnivorousness** *noun*.

on ● *preposition* (so as to be) supported by, covering, attached to, etc.; (of time) exactly at; during; close to, in direction of; at, near, concerning, about; added to. ● *adverb* (so as to be) on something; in some direction, forward; in advance; with movement; in operation or activity; *colloquial* willing to participate, approve, bet, etc.; *colloquial* practicable, acceptable; being shown or performed. ● *adjective Cricket* of, in, or into half of field behind batsman's back. ● *noun Cricket* the on side. ▫ **be on about** *colloquial* discuss, esp. tiresomely; **online** directly controlled by or connected to computer; **onscreen** when being filmed; **on to** to a position on.

■ **Usage** See note at ONTO.

ONC *abbreviation* Ordinary National Certificate.

once /wʌns/ ● *adverb* on one occasion only; at some time in past; ever or at all. ● *conjunction* as soon as. ● *noun* one time or occasion. ▫ **at once** immediately, simultaneously; **once-over** *colloquial* rapid inspection.

oncology /ɒŋ'kɒlədʒɪ/ *noun* study of tumours.

oncoming *adjective* approaching from the front.

OND *abbreviation* Ordinary National Diploma.

one /wʌn/ ● *adjective* single and integral in number; only such; without others; identical; forming a unity. ● *noun* lowest cardinal numeral; thing numbered with it; unit, unity; single thing, person, or example; *colloquial* drink. ● *pronoun* any person. ▫ **one-armed bandit** *colloquial* fruit machine with long handle; **one-horse** *colloquial* small, poorly equipped; **one-man** involving or operated by one person only; **one-off** made as the only one, not repeated; **one-sided** unfair, partial; **one-way** allowing movement etc. in one direction only.

oneness *noun* singleness; uniqueness; agreement, sameness.

onerous /'əʊnərəs/ *adjective* burdensome. ▫ **onerousness** *noun*.

oneself *pronoun: emphatic & reflexive form of* ONE. ▫ **be oneself** act in one's natural manner.

ongoing *adjective* continuing, in progress.

onion /'ʌnjən/ *noun* vegetable with edible bulb of pungent smell and flavour.

onlooker *noun* spectator. ▫ **onlooking** *adjective*.

only /'əʊnlɪ/ ● *adverb* solely, merely, exclusively. ● *adjective* existing alone of its or their kind. ● *conjunction colloquial* except that; but then. ▫ **if only** even if for no other reason than, I wish that.

o.n.o. *abbreviation* or near offer.

onomatopoeia /ɒnəmætə'pi:ə/ *noun* formation of word from sound associated with thing named, e.g. *whizz, cuckoo*. ▫ **onomatopoeic** *adjective*.

onset *noun* attack; impetuous beginning.

onslaught /'ɒnslɔ:t/ *noun* fierce attack.

onto *preposition* = ON TO.

■ **Usage** *Onto* is much used but is still not as widely accepted as *into*. It is, however, useful in distinguishing between, e.g., *We drove on to the beach* (i.e. towards it) and *we drove onto the beach* (i.e. into contact with it).

ontology /ɒn'tɒlədʒɪ/ *noun* branch of metaphysics concerned with the nature of being. ▫ **ontological** /-tə'lɒdʒ-/ *adjective*; **ontologically** /-tə'lɒdʒ-/ *adverb*; **ontologist** *noun*.

onus /'əʊnəs/ *noun* (*plural* **onuses**) burden, duty, responsibility.

onward /'ɒnwəd/ ● *adverb* (also **onwards**) advancing; into the future. ● *adjective* forward, advancing.

onyx /'ɒnɪks/ *noun* semiprecious variety of agate with coloured layers.

oodles /'u:d(ə)lz/ *plural noun colloquial* very great amount.

ooh /u:/ *interjection expressing surprised pleasure, pain, excitement, etc.*

oolite /'əʊəlaɪt/ *noun* granular limestone. ▫ **oolitic** /-'lɪt-/ *adjective*.

oomph /ʊmf/ *noun slang* energy, enthusiasm; attractiveness, esp. sex appeal.

ooze[1] ● *verb* (**-zing**) trickle or leak slowly out; (of substance) exude fluid; (often + *with*) give off (a feeling) freely. ● *noun* sluggish flow. ▫ **oozy** *adjective*.

ooze[2] *noun* wet mud. ▫ **oozy** *adjective*.

op *noun colloquial* operation.

op. *abbreviation* opus.

opacity /əʊ'pæsɪtɪ/ *noun* opaqueness.

opal /'əʊp(ə)l/ *noun* semiprecious milk-white or bluish stone with iridescent reflections.

opalescent /əʊpə'les(ə)nt/ *adjective* iridescent. ▫ **opalescence** *noun*.

opaline /'əʊpəlaɪn/ *adjective* opal-like; opalescent.

opaque /əʊ'peɪk/ *adjective* (**-r**, **-st**) not transmitting light; impenetrable to sight; unintelligible; stupid. ▫ **opaquely** *adverb*; **opaqueness** *noun*.

op. cit. *abbreviation* in the work already quoted (*opere citato*).

OPEC /'əʊpek/ *abbreviation* Organization of Petroleum Exporting Countries.

open /'əʊpən/ ● *adjective* not closed, locked, or blocked up; not covered or confined; exposed; (of goal etc.) undefended; undisguised, public; unfolded, spread out; (of fabric) with gaps; frank; open-minded; accessible to visitors or customers; (of meeting, competition, etc.) not restricted; (+ *to*) willing to receive, vulnerable to. ● *verb* make or become open or more open; (+ *into* etc.) give access; establish, set going; start; ceremonially declare open. ● *noun* (**the open**) open air; open competition etc. ▫ **open air** *noun* outdoors; **open-air** *adjective* outdoor; **open day** day when public may visit place normally closed to them; **open-ended** with no limit or restriction; **open-handed** generous; **open-heart surgery** surgery with heart exposed and blood made to bypass it; **open house** hospitality for all visitors; **open letter** one addressed to individual and printed in newspaper etc.; **open-minded** accessible to new ideas, unprejudiced; **open-plan** (of house, office, etc.) having large undivided rooms; **open prison** one with few physical restraints on prisoners; **open question** matter on which different views are legitimate; **open sandwich** one without bread on top; **open sea** expanse of sea away from land. ▫ **openness** *noun*.

opener *noun* device for opening tins or bottles etc.

opening ● *noun* gap, aperture; opportunity; beginning, initial part. ● *adjective* initial, first.

openly *adverb* publicly, frankly.

opera[1] /'ɒpərə/ *noun* musical drama with sung or spoken dialogue. ▫ **opera-glasses** small binoculars for use in theatres etc.; **opera house** theatre for operas.

opera[2] *plural of* OPUS.

operable /'ɒpərəb(ə)l/ *adjective* that can be operated; suitable for treatment by surgical operation.

operate /'ɒpəreɪt/ *verb* (**-ting**) work, control (machine etc.); be in action; perform surgical operation(s); direct military etc. action. ▫ **operating theatre** room for surgical operations.

operatic /ɒpə'rætɪk/ *adjective* of or like opera.

operation *noun* action, working; performance of surgery on a patient; military manoeuvre; financial transaction. ▫ **operational** *adjective*; **operationally** *adverb*.

operative /'ɒpərətɪv/ ● *adjective* in operation; having principal relevance; of or by surgery. ● *noun* worker, artisan.

operator *noun* person operating machine, esp. connecting lines in telephone exchange; person engaging in business.

operetta /ɒpə'retə/ *noun* light opera.

ophidian /əʊ'fɪdiən/ ● *noun* member of suborder of reptiles including snakes. ● *adjective* of this order.

ophthalmia /ɒf'θælmɪə/ *noun* inflammation of eye.

ophthalmic /ɒf'θælmɪk/ *adjective* of or relating to the eye and its diseases. ▫ **ophthalmic optician** one qualified to prescribe as well as dispense spectacles.

ophthalmology /ɒfθæl'mɒlədʒɪ/ *noun* study of the eye. ▫ **ophthalmologist** *noun*.

ophthalmoscope /ɒf'θælməskəʊp/ *noun* instrument for examining the eye.

opiate /'əʊpɪət/ ● *adjective* containing opium; soporific. ● *noun* drug containing opium, usually to ease pain or induce sleep; soothing influence.

opine /əʊ'paɪn/ *verb* (**-ning**) (often + *that*) express or hold as opinion.

opinion /ə'pɪnjən/ *noun* unproven belief; view held as probable; professional advice; estimation. ▫ **opinion poll** assessment of public opinion by questioning representative sample.

opinionated /ə'pɪnjəneɪtɪd/ *adjective* unduly confident in one's opinions.

opium /'əʊpɪəm/ *noun* drug made from juice of certain poppy, used as narcotic or sedative.

opossum /ə'pɒsəm/ *noun* tree-living American marsupial; *Australian & NZ* marsupial resembling this.

opponent /ə'pəʊnənt/ *noun* person who opposes.

opportune /'ɒpətju:n/ *adjective* well-chosen, specially favourable; (of action, event, etc.) well-timed.

opportunism /ɒpə'tju:nɪz(ə)m/ *noun* adaptation of policy to circumstances, esp. regardless of principle. ▫ **opportunist** *noun*; **opportunistic** /-'nɪs-/ *adjective*; **opportunistically** /-'nɪs-/ *adverb*.

opportunity /ɒpə'tju:nɪtɪ/ *noun* (*plural* **-ies**) favourable chance or opening offered by circumstances.

oppose /ə'pəʊz/ *verb* (**-sing**) set oneself against; resist; argue against; (+ *to*) place in opposition or contrast. ▫ **as opposed to** in contrast with. ▫ **opposer** *noun*.

opposite /'ɒpəzɪt/ ● *adjective* facing, on other side; (often + *to, from*) contrary; diametrically different. ● *noun* opposite thing, person, or term. ● *adverb* in opposite position. ● *preposition* opposite to. ▫ **opposite number** person in corresponding position in another group etc.; **the opposite sex** either sex in relation to the other.

opposition /ɒpə'zɪʃ(ə)n/ *noun* antagonism, resistance; being in conflict or disagreement; contrast; group or party of opponents; chief parliamentary party, or group of parties, opposed to party in office; act of placing opposite.

oppress /ə'pres/ *verb* govern tyrannically; treat with gross harshness or injustice; weigh down. ▫ **oppression** *noun*; **oppressor** *noun*.

oppressive *adjective* that oppresses; (of weather) sultry, close. ▫ **oppressively** *adverb*; **oppressiveness** *noun*.

opprobrious /ə'prəʊbrɪəs/ *adjective* (of language) severely scornful; abusive.

opprobrium /ə'prəʊbrɪəm/ *noun* disgrace; cause of this.

opt *verb* (usually + *for*) make choice; decide. ▫ **opt out (of)** choose not to take part etc. (in).

optic /'ɒptɪk/ *adjective* of eye or sight.

optical *adjective* visual; of or according to optics; aiding sight. ▫ **optical fibre** thin glass fibre used to carry light signals; **optical illusion** image which deceives the eye, mental misapprehension caused by this.

optician /ɒp'tɪʃ(ə)n/ *noun* maker, seller, or prescriber of spectacles, contact lenses, etc.

optics *plural noun* (treated as *singular*) science of light and vision.

optimal /'ɒptɪm(ə)l/ *adjective* best, most favourable.

optimism /'ɒptɪmɪz(ə)m/ *noun* inclination to hopefulness and confidence. ▫ **optimist** *noun*; **optimistic** /-'mɪs-/ *adjective*; **optimistically** /-'mɪs-/ *adverb*.

optimize /'ɒptɪmaɪz/ *verb* (also **-ise**) (**-zing** or **-sing**) make best or most effective use of. ▫ **optimization** *noun*.

optimum /'ɒptɪməm/ ● *noun* (*plural* **-ma**) most favourable conditions; best practical solution. ● *adjective* optimal.

option /'ɒpʃ(ə)n/ *noun* choice, choosing; right to choose; right to buy, sell, etc., on specified conditions at specified time. ▫ **keep, leave one's options open** not commit oneself.

optional *adjective* not obligatory. ▫ **optionally** *adverb*.

opulent /'ɒpjʊlənt/ *adjective* wealthy; luxurious; abundant. ▫ **opulence** *noun*.

opus /'əʊpəs/ *noun* (*plural* **opuses** or **opera** /'ɒpərə/) musical composition numbered as one of composer's works; any artistic work.

or *conjunction introducing alternatives*. ▫ **or else** otherwise, *colloquial: expressing threat*.

oracle /'ɒrək(ə)l/ *noun* place at which ancient Greeks etc. consulted gods for advice or prophecy; response received there; person or thing regarded as source of wisdom etc. ▫ **oracular** /ɒ'rækjʊlə/ *adjective*.

oral /'ɔ:r(ə)l/ ● *adjective* spoken, verbal; by word of mouth; done or taken by mouth. ● *noun colloquial* spoken exam. ▫ **orally** *adverb*.

orange /'ɒrɪndʒ/ ● *noun* roundish reddish-yellow citrus fruit; its colour; tree bearing it. ● *adjective* orange-coloured.

orangeade /ɒrɪndʒ'eɪd/ *noun* drink made from or flavoured like oranges, usually fizzy.

orang-utan /ɔ:ræŋu:'tæn/ *noun* (also **orang-outang** /-u:'tæŋ/) large anthropoid ape.

oration /ɔ:'reɪʃ(ə)n/ *noun* formal or ceremonial speech.

orator /'ɒrətə/ *noun* maker of a formal speech; eloquent public speaker.

oratorio /ɒrə'tɔ:rɪəʊ/ *noun* (*plural* **-s**) semi-dramatic musical composition usually on sacred theme.

oratory /'ɒrətərɪ/ *noun* (*plural* **-ies**) art of or skill in public speaking; small private chapel. ▫ **oratorical** /-'tɒr-/ *adjective*.

orb *noun* globe surmounted by cross as part of coronation regalia; sphere, globe; *poetical* celestial body; *poetical* eye.

orbicular /ɔ:'bɪkjʊlə/ *adjective formal* spherical, circular.

orbit /'ɔ:bɪt/ ● *noun* curved course of planet, comet, satellite, etc.; one complete passage round another body; range or sphere of action. ● *verb* (**-t-**) go round in orbit; put into orbit. ▫ **orbiter** *noun*.

orbital *adjective* of orbits; (of road) passing round outside of city.

Orcadian /ɔ:'keɪdɪən/ ● *adjective* of Orkney. ● *noun* native of Orkney.

orchard /'ɔ:tʃəd/ *noun* enclosed piece of land with fruit trees.

orchestra /'ɔ:kɪstrə/ *noun* large group of instrumental performers. ▫ **orchestra pit** part of theatre where orchestra plays. ▫ **orchestral** /ɔ:'kestr(ə)l/ *adjective*.

orchestrate /'ɔ:kɪstreɪt/ *verb* (**-ting**) compose or arrange for orchestral performance; arrange (elements) for desired effect.

orchid /'ɔ:kɪd/ *noun* any of various plants, often with brilliantly coloured or grotesquely shaped flowers.

ordain /ɔ:'deɪn/ *verb* confer holy orders on; decree, order.

ordeal /ɔ:'di:l/ *noun* severe trial; painful or horrific experience.

order /'ɔ:də/ ● *noun* condition in which every part, unit, etc. is in its right place; tidiness; specified sequence; authoritative direction or instruction; state of obedience to law, authority, etc.; direction to supply something, thing(s) (to be) supplied; social class or rank; kind, sort; constitution or nature of the world, society, etc.; *Biology* grouping of animals or plants below class and above family; religious fraternity; grade of Christian ministry; any of 5 classical styles of architecture; company of people distinguished by particular honour, etc., insignia worn by its members; stated form of divine service; system of rules etc. (at meetings etc.). ● *verb* command, prescribe; command or direct (person) to specified destination; direct manufacturer, tradesman, etc. to supply; direct waiter to serve; (often as **ordered** *adjective*) put in order; (of God, fate, etc.) ordain. □ **in** or **out of order** in correct or incorrect sequence; **of** or **in the order of** approximately.

orderly ● *adjective* methodically arranged; tidy; not unruly. ● *noun* (*plural* **-ies**) soldier in attendance on officer; hospital attendant. □ **orderly room** room in barracks for company's business.

ordinal /'ɔ:dɪn(ə)l/ *noun* (in full **ordinal number**) number defining position in a series; compare CARDINAL NUMBER.

ordinance /'ɔ:dɪnəns/ *noun* decree; religious rite.

ordinand /'ɔ:dɪnænd/ *noun* candidate for ordination.

ordinary /'ɔ:dɪnərɪ/ *adjective* normal; not exceptional; commonplace. □ **ordinary level** *historical* lowest in GCE exam; **ordinary seaman** sailor of lowest rank. □ **ordinarily** *adverb*; **ordinariness** *noun*.

ordination /ɔ:dɪ'neɪʃ(ə)n/ *noun* conferring of holy orders; ordaining.

ordnance /'ɔ:dnəns/ *noun* artillery and military supplies; government service dealing with these. □ **Ordnance Survey** government survey of UK producing detailed maps.

ordure /'ɔ:djʊə/ *noun* dung.

ore *noun* naturally occurring mineral yielding metal or other valuable minerals.

oregano /ɒrɪ'gɑ:nəʊ/ *noun* dried wild marjoram as seasoning.

organ /'ɔ:gən/ *noun* musical instrument consisting of pipes that sound when air is forced through them, operated by keys and pedals; similar instrument producing sound electronically; part of body serving some special function; medium of opinion, esp. newspaper. □ **organ-grinder** player of barrel organ.

organdie /'ɔ:gəndɪ/ *noun* fine translucent muslin, usually stiffened.

organic /ɔ:'gænɪk/ *adjective* of or affecting bodily organ(s); (of animals and plants) having organs or organized physical structure; (of food) produced without artificial fertilizers or pesticides; (of chemical compound etc.) containing carbon; organized; inherent, structural. □ **organic chemistry** that of carbon compounds. □ **organically** *adverb*.

organism /'ɔ:gənɪz(ə)m/ *noun* individual animal or plant; living being with interdependent parts; system made up of interdependent parts.

organist *noun* player of organ.

organization /ɔ:gənaɪ'zeɪʃ(ə)n/ *noun* (also **-isation**) organized body, system, or society; organizing, being organized.

organize /'ɔ:gənaɪz/ *verb* (also **-ise**) (**-zing** or **-sing**) give orderly structure to; make arrangements for (person, oneself); initiate, arrange for; (as **organized** *adjective*) make organic or into living tissue. □ **organizer** *noun*.

orgasm /'ɔ:gæz(ə)m/ ● *noun* climax of sexual excitement. ● *verb* have sexual orgasm. □ **orgasmic** /-'gæz-/ *adjective*.

orgy /'ɔ:dʒɪ/ *noun* (*plural* **-ies**) wild party with indiscriminate sexual activity; excessive indulgence in an activity. □ **orgiastic** /-'æs-/ *adjective*.

oriel /'ɔ:rɪəl/ *noun* window projecting from wall at upper level.

orient /'ɔ:rɪənt/ ● *noun* (**the Orient**) the East, countries east of Mediterranean, esp. E. Asia. ● *verb* place or determine position of with aid of compass; find bearings of; (often + *towards*) direct; place (building etc.) to face east; turn eastward or in specified direction.

oriental /ɔ:rɪ'ent(ə)l/ (often **Oriental**) ● *adjective* of the East, esp. E. Asia; of the Orient. ● *noun* native of Orient.

orientate /'ɔ:rɪənteɪt/ *verb* (**-ting**) orient.

orientation *noun* orienting, being oriented; relative position; person's adjustment in relation to circumstances; briefing.

orienteering /ɔ:rɪən'tɪərɪŋ/ *noun* competitive sport of running across rough country with map and compass.

orifice /'ɒrɪfɪs/ *noun* aperture; mouth of cavity.

origami /ɒrɪ'gɑ:mɪ/ *noun* Japanese art of folding paper into decorative shapes.

origan /'ɒrɪgən/ *noun* (also **origanum** /ə'rɪgənəm/) wild marjoram.

origin /'ɒrɪdʒɪn/ *noun* source; starting point; (often in *plural*) parentage.

original /ə'rɪdʒɪn(ə)l/ ● *adjective* existing from the beginning; earliest; innate; not imitative or derived; creative not copied; by artist etc. himself or herself. ● *noun* original pattern, picture, etc. from which another is copied or translated. □ **original sin** innate sinfulness held to be common to all human beings after the Fall. □ **originality** /-'næl-/ *noun*; **originally** *adverb*.

originate /ə'rɪdʒɪneɪt/ *verb* (**-ting**) begin; initiate or give origin to, be origin of. □ **origination** *noun*; **originator** *noun*.

oriole /'ɔ:rɪəʊl/ *noun* kind of bird, esp. **golden oriole** with black and yellow plumage in male.

ormolu /'ɔ:məlu:/ *noun* gilded bronze; gold-coloured alloy; articles made of or decorated with these.

ornament ● *noun* /'ɔ:nəmənt/ thing used to adorn or decorate; decoration; quality or person bringing honour or distinction. ● *verb* /-ment/ adorn, beautify. □ **ornamental** /-'men-/ *adjective*; **ornamentation** /-men-/ *noun*.

ornate /ɔ:'neɪt/ *adjective* elaborately adorned; (of literary style) flowery. □ **ornately** *adverb*.

ornithology /ɔ:nɪ'θɒlədʒɪ/ *noun* study of birds. □ **ornithological** /-θə'lɒdʒ-/ *adjective*; **ornithologist** *noun*.

orotund /'ɒrətʌnd/ *adjective* (of voice) full, round; imposing; (of writing, style, etc.) pompous; pretentious.

orphan /'ɔ:f(ə)n/ ● *noun* child whose parents are dead. ● *verb* bereave of parents.

orphanage *noun* home for orphans.

orrery /'ɒrərɪ/ *noun* (*plural* **-ies**) clockwork model of solar system.

orris root /'ɒrɪs/ *noun* fragrant iris root used in perfumery.

ortho- *combining form* straight, correct.

orthodontics /ɔːθə'dɒntɪks/ *plural noun* (usually treated as *singular*) correction of irregularities in teeth and jaws.

orthodox /'ɔːθədɒks/ *adjective* holding usual or accepted views, esp. on religion, morals, etc.; conventional. ▫ **Orthodox Church** Eastern Church headed by Patriarch of Constantinople, including Churches of Russia, Romania, Greece, etc. ▫ **orthodoxy** *noun*.

orthography /ɔː'θɒgrəfɪ/ *noun* (*plural* **-ies**) spelling, esp. with reference to its correctness. ▫ **orthographic** /-'græf-/ *adjective*.

orthopaedics /ɔːθə'piːdɪks/ *plural noun* (treated as *singular*) (*US* **-pedics**) branch of medicine dealing with correction of diseased or injured bones or muscles. ▫ **orthopaedic** *adjective*; **orthopaedist** *noun*.

OS *abbreviation* old style; Ordinary Seaman; Ordnance Survey; outsize.

Oscar /'ɒskə/ *noun* statuette awarded annually in US for excellence in film acting, directing, etc.

oscillate /'ɒsɪleɪt/ *verb* (**-ting**) (cause to) swing to and fro; vacillate; *Electricity* (of current) undergo high-frequency alternations. ▫ **oscillation** *noun*; **oscillator** *noun*.

oscilloscope /ə'sɪləskəʊp/ *noun* device for viewing oscillations usually on screen of cathode ray tube.

osier /'əʊzɪə/ *noun* willow used in basketwork; shoot of this.

osmosis /ɒz'məʊsɪs/ *noun* passage of solvent through semipermeable partition into another solution; process by which something is acquired by absorption. ▫ **osmotic** /-'mɒt-/ *adjective*.

osprey /'ɒspreɪ/ *noun* (*plural* **-s**) large bird preying on fish.

osseous /'ɒsɪəs/ *adjective* of bone; bony; having bones.

ossify /'ɒsɪfaɪ/ *verb* (**-ies**, **-ied**) turn into bone; harden; make or become rigid or unprogressive. ▫ **ossification** *noun*.

ostensible /ɒ'stensɪb(ə)l/ *adjective* professed; used to conceal real purpose or nature. ▫ **ostensibly** *adverb*.

ostentation /ɒsten'teɪʃ(ə)n/ *noun* pretentious display of wealth; showing off. ▫ **ostentatious** *adjective*.

osteoarthritis /ɒstɪəʊɑː'θraɪtɪs/ *noun* degenerative disease of the joints. ▫ **osteoarthritic** /-'θrɪt-/ *adjective*.

osteopath /'ɒstɪəpæθ/ *noun* person who treats disease by manipulation of bones. ▫ **osteopathy** /-'ɒp-/ *noun*.

osteoporosis /ɒstɪəʊpə'rəʊsɪs/ *noun* brittle bones caused by hormonal change or deficiency of calcium or vitamin D.

ostler /'ɒslə/ *noun historical* stableman at inn.

ostracize /'ɒstrəsaɪz/ *verb* (also **-ise**) (**-zing** or **-sing**) exclude from society, refuse to associate with. ▫ **ostracism** /-sɪz(ə)m/ *noun*.

ostrich /'ɒstrɪtʃ/ *noun* large flightless swift-running African bird; person refusing to acknowledge awkward truth.

OT *abbreviation* Old Testament.

other /'ʌðə/ ● *adjective* further, additional; different; (**the other**) the only remaining. ● *noun* other person or thing. ▫ **the other day**, **week**, etc. a few days etc. ago; **other half** *colloquial* one's wife or husband; **other than** apart from.

otherwise /'ʌðəwaɪz/ ● *adverb* or else; in different circumstances; in other respects; in a different way; as an alternative. ● *adjective* different.

otiose /'əʊtɪəʊs/ *adjective* not required, serving no practical purpose.

OTT *abbreviation colloquial* over-the-top.

otter /'ɒtə/ *noun* furred aquatic fish-eating mammal.

Ottoman /'ɒtəmən/ ● *adjective historical* of Turkish Empire. ● *noun* (*plural* **-s**) Turk of Ottoman period; (**ottoman**) cushioned seat without back or arms, storage-box with padded top.

OU *abbreviation* Open University; Oxford University.

oubliette /uːblɪ'et/ *noun* secret dungeon with trapdoor entrance.

ouch /aʊtʃ/ *interjection expressing sharp or sudden pain.*

ought /ɔːt/ *auxiliary verb expressing duty, rightness, probability, etc.*

oughtn't /'ɔːt(ə)nt/ ought not.

Ouija /'wiːdʒə/ *noun* (in full **Ouija board**) *proprietary term* board marked with letters or signs used with movable pointer to try to obtain messages in seances.

ounce /aʊns/ *noun* unit of weight (1/16 lb, 28.35 g); very small quantity.

our /aʊə/ *adjective* of or belonging to us.

ours /aʊəz/ *pronoun* the one(s) belonging to us.

ourselves /aʊə'selvz/ *pronoun: emphatic form of* WE *or* US; *reflexive form of* US.

ousel = OUZEL.

oust /aʊst/ *verb* drive out of office or power, esp. by seizing place of.

out /aʊt/ ● *adverb* away from or not in place, not at home, office, etc.; into open, sight, notice, etc.; to or at an end; not burning; in error; *colloquial* unconscious; (+ *to do*) determined; (of limb etc.) dislocated. ● *preposition* out of. ● *noun* way of escape. ● *verb* emerge. ▫ **out for** intent on, determined to get; **out of** from inside, not inside, from among, lacking, having no more of, because of.

■ **Usage** The use of *out* as a preposition, as in *He walked out the room*, is not standard English. *Out of* should be used instead.

out- *prefix* so as to surpass; external; out of.

outback *noun Australian* remote inland areas.

outbalance /aʊt'bæləns/ *verb* (**-cing**) outweigh.

outbid /aʊt'bɪd/ *verb* (**-dd-**; *past & past participle* **-bid**) bid higher than.

outboard motor *noun* portable engine attached to outside of boat.

outbreak /'aʊtbreɪk/ *noun* sudden eruption of emotion, war, disease, fire, etc.

outbuilding *noun* shed, barn, etc. detached from main building.

outburst *noun* bursting out, esp. of emotion in vehement words.

outcast ● *noun* person cast out from home and friends. ● *adjective* homeless; rejected.

outclass /aʊt'klɑːs/ *verb* surpass in quality.

outcome *noun* result.

outcrop *noun* rock etc. emerging at surface; noticeable manifestation.

outcry *noun* (*plural* **-ies**) loud public protest.

outdated /aʊt'deɪtɪd/ *adjective* out of date, obsolete.

outdistance /aʊt'dɪst(ə)ns/ *verb* (**-cing**) leave (competitor) behind completely.

outdo /aʊt'duː/ *verb* (**-doing**; *3rd singular present* **-does**; *past* **-did**; *past participle* **-done**) surpass, excel.

outdoor *adjective* done, existing, or used out of doors; fond of the open air.

outdoors /aʊt'dɔːz/ ● *adverb* in(to) the open air. ● *noun* the open air.

outer *adjective* outside, external; farther from centre or inside. ▫ **outer space** universe beyond earth's atmosphere. ▫ **outermost** *adjective*.

outface /aʊt'feɪs/ *verb* (**-cing**) disconcert by staring or by confident manner.

outfall *noun* outlet of river, drain, etc.

outfield *noun* outer part of cricket or baseball pitch. □ **outfielder** *noun*.

outfit *noun* set of equipment or clothes; *colloquial* (organized) group or company.

outfitter *noun* supplier of clothing.

outflank /aʊt'flæŋk/ *verb* get round the flank of (enemy); outmanoeuvre.

outflow *noun* outward flow; what flows out.

outgoing ● *adjective* friendly; retiring from office; going out. ● *noun* (in *plural*) expenditure.

outgrow /aʊt'grəʊ/ *verb* (*past* **-grew**; *past participle* **-grown**) get too big for (clothes etc.); leave behind (childish habit etc.); grow faster or taller than.

outgrowth *noun* offshoot.

outhouse *noun* shed etc., esp. adjoining main house.

outing *noun* pleasure trip.

outlandish /aʊt'lændɪʃ/ *adjective* bizarre, strange. □ **outlandishly** *adverb*; **outlandishness** *noun*.

outlast /aʊt'lɑːst/ *verb* last longer than.

outlaw ● *noun* fugitive from law; *historical* person deprived of protection of law. ● *verb* declare (person) an outlaw; make illegal; proscribe.

outlay *noun* expenditure.

outlet *noun* means of exit; means of expressing feelings; market for goods.

outline ● *noun* rough draft; summary; line(s) enclosing visible object; contour; external boundary; (in *plural*) main features. ● *verb* (**-ning**) draw or describe in outline; mark outline of.

outlive /aʊt'lɪv/ *verb* (**-ving**) live longer than, beyond, or through.

outlook *noun* view, prospect; mental attitude.

outlying *adjective* far from centre; remote.

outmanoeuvre /aʊtmə'nuːvə/ *verb* (**-ring**) (*US* **-maneuver**) outdo by skilful manoeuvring.

outmatch /aʊt'mætʃ/ *verb* be more than a match for.

outmoded /aʊt'məʊdɪd/ *adjective* outdated; out of fashion.

outnumber /aʊt'nʌmbə/ *verb* exceed in number.

outpace /aʊt'peɪs/ *verb* (**-cing**) go faster than; outdo in contest.

outpatient *noun* non-resident hospital patient.

outplacement *noun* help in finding new job after redundancy.

outpost *noun* detachment on guard at some distance from army; outlying settlement etc.

outpouring *noun* (usually in *plural*) copious expression of emotion.

output ● *noun* amount produced (by machine, worker, etc.); electrical power etc. supplied by apparatus; printout, results, etc. from computer; place where energy, information, etc., leaves a system. ● *verb* (**-tt-**; *past & past participle* **-put** or **-putted**) (of computer) supply (results etc.).

outrage ● *noun* forcible violation of others' rights, sentiments, etc.; gross offence or indignity; fierce resentment. ● *verb* (**-ging**) subject to outrage; insult; shock and anger.

outrageous /aʊt'reɪdʒəs/ *adjective* immoderate; shocking; immoral, offensive. □ **outrageously** *adverb*.

outrank /aʊt'ræŋk/ *verb* be superior in rank to.

outré /'uːtreɪ/ *adjective* eccentric, violating decorum. [French]

outrider *noun* motorcyclist or mounted guard riding ahead of car(s) etc.

outrigger *noun* spar or framework projecting from or over side of ship, canoe, etc. to give stability; boat with this.

outright ● *adverb* altogether, entirely; not gradually; without reservation. ● *adjective* downright, complete; undisputed.

outrun /aʊt'rʌn/ *verb* (**-nn-**; *past* **-ran**; *past participle* **-run**) run faster or farther than; go beyond.

outsell /aʊt'sel/ *verb* (*past & past participle* **-sold**) sell more than; be sold in greater quantities than.

outset *noun* □ **at, from the outset** at or from the beginning.

outshine /aʊt'ʃaɪn/ *verb* (**-ning**; *past & past participle* **-shone**) be more brilliant than.

outside ● *noun* /aʊt'saɪd, 'aʊtsaɪd/ external surface, outer part(s); external appearance; position on outer side. ● *adjective* /'aʊtsaɪd/ of, on, or nearer outside; not belonging to particular circle or institution; (of chance etc.) remote; greatest existent or possible. ● *adverb* /aʊt'saɪd/ on or to outside; out of doors; not within or enclosed. ● *preposition* /aʊt'saɪd/ not in; to or at the outside of; external to; beyond limits of. □ **at the outside** (of estimate etc.) at the most; **outside interest** hobby etc. unconnected with one's work.

outsider /aʊt'saɪdə/ *noun* non-member of circle, party, profession, etc.; competitor thought to have little chance.

outsize *adjective* unusually large.

outskirts *plural noun* outer area of town etc.

outsmart /aʊt'smɑːt/ *verb* outwit; be too clever for.

outspoken /aʊt'spəʊkən/ *adjective* saying openly what one thinks; frank. □ **outspokenly** *adverb*; **outspokenness** *noun*.

outspread /aʊt'spred/ *adjective* spread out.

outstanding /aʊt'stændɪŋ/ *adjective* conspicuous, esp. from excellence; still to be dealt with; (of debt) not yet settled. □ **outstandingly** *adverb*.

outstation *noun* remote branch or outpost.

outstay /aʊt'steɪ/ *verb* stay longer than (one's welcome etc.).

outstretched /aʊt'stretʃt/ *adjective* stretched out.

outstrip /aʊt'strɪp/ *verb* (**-pp-**) go faster than; surpass in progress, competition, etc.

out-take *noun* film or tape sequence cut out in editing.

out-tray *noun* tray for outgoing documents.

outvote /aʊt'vəʊt/ *verb* (**-ting**) defeat by majority of votes.

outward /'aʊtwəd/ ● *adjective* directed towards outside; going out; physical; external, apparent. ● *adverb* (also **outwards**) in outward direction, towards outside. □ **outwardly** *adverb*.

outweigh /aʊt'weɪ/ *verb* exceed in weight, value, influence, etc.

outwit /aʊt'wɪt/ *verb* (**-tt-**) be too clever for; overcome by greater ingenuity.

outwith /aʊt'wɪθ/ *preposition Scottish* outside.

outwork *noun* advanced or detached part of fortress etc.; work done off premises of shop, factory, etc. supplying it.

outworn /aʊt'wɔːn/ *adjective* worn out; obsolete.

ouzel /'uːz(ə)l/ *noun* (also **ousel**) small bird of thrush family.

ouzo /'uːzəʊ/ *noun* (*plural* **-s**) Greek aniseed-flavoured alcoholic spirit.

ova *plural* of OVUM.

oval /'əʊv(ə)l/ ● *adjective* shaped like egg, elliptical. ● *noun* elliptical closed curve; thing with oval outline.

ovary /'əʊvərɪ/ *noun* (*plural* **-ies**) either of two ovum-producing organs in female; seed vessel in plant. □ **ovarian** /əʊ'veər-/ *adjective*.

ovation /əʊ'veɪʃ(ə)n/ *noun* enthusiastic applause or reception.

oven /ˈʌv(ə)n/ *noun* enclosed chamber for cooking food in. ▫ **ovenproof** heat-resistant; **oven-ready** (of food) prepared before sale for immediate cooking; **ovenware** dishes for cooking food in oven.

over /ˈəʊvə/ ● *adverb* outward and downward from brink or from erect position; so as to cover whole surface; so as to produce fold or reverse position; above in place or position; from one side, end, etc. to other; from beginning to end with repetition; in excess; settled, finished. ● *preposition* above; out and down from; so as to cover; across; on or to other side, end, etc. of; concerning. ● *noun Cricket* sequence of 6 balls bowled from one end before change is made to other; play during this time. ▫ **over the way** (in street etc.) facing or across from.

over- *prefix* excessively; upper, outer; over; completely.

overact /əʊvəˈrækt/ *verb* act (a role) with exaggeration.

over-active /əʊvəˈræktɪv/ *adjective* too active.

overall ● *adjective* /ˈəʊvərɔːl/ taking everything into account, inclusive, total. ● *adverb* /əʊvərˈɔːl/ including everything; on the whole. ● *noun* /ˈəʊvərɔːl/ protective outer garment; (in *plural*) protective trousers or suit.

overarm *adjective & adverb* with arm raised above shoulder.

overawe /əʊvəˈrɔː/ *verb* (**-wing**) awe into submission.

overbalance /əʊvəˈbæləns/ *verb* (**-cing**) lose balance and fall; cause to do this.

overbearing /əʊvəˈbeərɪŋ/ *adjective* domineering; oppressive.

overblown /əʊvəˈbləʊn/ *adjective* inflated, pretentious; (of flower etc.) past its prime.

overboard *adverb* from ship into water. ▫ **go overboard** *colloquial* show extreme enthusiasm, behave immoderately.

overbook /əʊvəˈbʊk/ *verb* make too many bookings for (aircraft, hotel, etc.).

overcame *past* of OVERCOME.

overcast *adjective* (of sky) covered with cloud; (in sewing) edged with stitching.

overcharge /əʊvəˈtʃɑːdʒ/ *verb* (**-ging**) charge too high a price to; put too much charge into (battery, gun, etc.).

overcoat *noun* warm outdoor coat.

overcome /əʊvəˈkʌm/ *verb* (**-coming**; *past* **-came**; *past participle* **-come**) prevail over, master; be victorious; (usually as **overcome** *adjective*) make faint; (often + *with*) make weak or helpless.

overcrowd /əʊvəˈkraʊd/ *verb* (usually as **overcrowded** *adjective*) cause too many people or things to be in (a place). ▫ **overcrowding** *noun*.

overdevelop /əʊvədɪˈveləp/ *verb* (**-p-**) develop too much.

overdo /əʊvəˈduː/ *verb* (**-doing**; *3rd singular present* **-does**; *past* **-did**; *past participle* **-done**) carry to excess; (as **overdone** *adjective*) overcooked. ▫ **overdo it, things** *colloquial* exhaust oneself.

overdose ● *noun* excessive dose of drug etc. ● *verb* (**-sing**) take overdose.

overdraft *noun* overdrawing of bank account; amount by which account is overdrawn.

overdraw /əʊvəˈdrɔː/ *verb* (*past* **-drew**; *past participle* **-drawn**) draw more from (bank account) than amount in credit; (as **overdrawn** *adjective*) having overdrawn one's account.

overdress /əʊvəˈdres/ *verb* dress ostentatiously or with too much formality.

overdrive *noun* mechanism in vehicle providing gear above top gear for economy at high speeds; state of high activity.

overdue /əʊvəˈdjuː/ *adjective* past the time when due or ready; late, in arrears.

overestimate ● *verb* /əʊvərˈestɪmeɪt/ (**-ting**) form too high an estimate of. ● *noun* /əʊvərˈestɪmət/ too high an estimate. ▫ **overestimation** *noun*.

overexpose /əʊvərɪkˈspəʊz/ *verb* (**-sing**) expose too much to public; expose (film) for too long.

overfish /əʊvəˈfɪʃ/ *verb* deplete (stream etc.) by too much fishing.

overflow ● *verb* /əʊvəˈfləʊ/ flow over; be so full that contents overflow; (of crowd etc.) extend beyond limits or capacity of; flood; (of kindness, harvest, etc.) be very abundant. ● *noun* /ˈəʊvəfləʊ/ what overflows or is superfluous; outlet for excess liquid.

overgrown /əʊvəˈgrəʊn/ *adjective* grown too big; covered with weeds etc. ▫ **overgrowth** *noun*.

overhang ● *verb* /əʊvəˈhæŋ/ (*past & past participle* **-hung**) project or hang over. ● *noun* /ˈəʊvəhæŋ/ fact or amount of overhanging.

overhaul *verb* /əʊvəˈhɔːl/ check over thoroughly and make repairs to if necessary; overtake. ● *noun* /ˈəʊvəhɔːl/ thorough examination, with repairs if necessary.

overhead ● *adverb* /əʊvəˈhed/ above one's head; in sky. ● *adjective* /ˈəʊvəhed/ placed overhead. ● *noun* /ˈəʊvəhed/ (in *plural*) routine administrative and maintenance expenses of a business. ▫ **overhead projector** projector for producing enlarged image of transparency above and behind user.

overhear /əʊvəˈhɪə/ *verb* (*past & past participle* **-heard**) hear as hidden or unintentional listener.

overindulge /əʊvərɪnˈdʌldʒ/ *noun* (**-ging**) indulge to excess.

overjoyed /əʊvəˈdʒɔɪd/ *adjective* filled with great joy.

overkill *noun* excess of capacity to kill or destroy; excess.

overland *adjective & adverb* by land and not sea.

overlap ● *verb* /əʊvəˈlæp/ (**-pp-**) partly cover; cover and extend beyond; partly coincide. ● *noun* /ˈəʊvəlæp/ overlapping; overlapping part or amount.

overlay ● *verb* /əʊvəˈleɪ/ (*past & past participle* **-laid**) lay over; (+ *with*) cover (thing) with (coating etc.). ● *noun* /ˈəʊvəleɪ/ thing laid over another.

overleaf /əʊvəˈliːf/ *adverb* on other side of page of book.

overlie /əʊvəˈlaɪ/ *verb* (**-lying**; *past* **-lay**; *past participle* **-lain**) lie on top of.

overload ● *verb* /əʊvəˈləʊd/ load too heavily (with baggage, work, etc.); put too great a demand on (electrical circuit etc.). ● *noun* /ˈəʊvələʊd/ excessive quantity or demand.

overlook /əʊvəˈlʊk/ *verb* fail to observe; tolerate; have view of from above.

overlord *noun* supreme lord.

overly *adverb* excessively.

overman /əʊvəˈmæn/ *verb* (**-nn-**) provide with too large a crew, staff, etc.

overmuch /əʊvəˈmʌtʃ/ *adverb & adjective* too much.

overnight /əʊvəˈnaɪt/ ● *adverb* for a night; during the night; suddenly. ● *adjective* for use or done etc. overnight; instant.

over-particular /əʊvəpəˈtɪkjʊlə/ *adjective* fussy or excessively particular.

overpass *noun esp. US* bridge by which road or railway line crosses another.

overplay /əʊvəˈpleɪ/ *verb* give undue importance or emphasis to. ▫ **overplay one's hand** act on unduly optimistic estimate of one's chances.

overpower /əʊvəˈpaʊə/ *verb* subdue, reduce to submission; (esp. as **overpowering** *adjective*) be too intense or overwhelming for.

overproduce /əʊvəprə'dju:s/ *verb* (**-cing**) produce in excess of demand or of defined amount. □ **overproduction** *noun*.

overrate /əʊvə'reɪt/ *verb* (**-ting**) assess or value too highly; (as **overrated** *adjective*) not as good as it is said to be.

overreach /əʊvə'ri:tʃ/ *verb* (**overreach oneself**) fail by attempting too much.

overreact /əʊvərɪ'ækt/ *verb* respond more violently etc. than is justified. □ **overreaction** *noun*.

override ● *verb* /əʊvə'raɪd/ (**-ding**; *past* **-rode**; *past participle* **-ridden**) have priority over; intervene and make ineffective; interrupt action of (automatic device). ● *noun* /'əʊvəraɪd/ suspension of automatic function.

overrider *noun* each of pair of projecting pieces on bumper of car.

overrule /əʊvə'ru:l/ *verb* (**-ling**) set aside (decision etc.) by superior authority; reject proposal of (person) in this way.

overrun /əʊvə'rʌn/ *verb* (**-nn-**; *past* **-ran**; *past participle* **-run**) spread over; conquer (territory) by force; exceed time etc. allowed.

overseas ● *adverb* /əʊvə'si:z/ across or beyond sea. ● *adjective* /'əʊvəsi:z/ of places across sea; foreign.

oversee /əʊvə'si:/ *verb* (**-sees**; *past* **-saw**; *past participle* **-seen**) superintend (workers etc.). □ **overseer** *noun*.

over-sensitive /əʊvə'sensɪtɪv/ *adjective* excessively sensitive; easily hurt; quick to react. □ **over-sensitiveness** *noun*; **oversensitivity** /-'tɪv-/ *noun*.

oversew *verb* (*past participle* **-sewn** or **-sewed**) sew (two edges) with stitches lying over them.

oversexed /əʊvə'sekst/ *adjective* having unusually strong sexual desires.

overshadow /əʊvə'ʃædəʊ/ *verb* appear much more prominent or important than; cast into shade.

overshoe *noun* shoe worn over another for protection in wet weather etc.

overshoot /əʊvə'ʃu:t/ *verb* (*past & past participle* **-shot**) pass or send beyond (target or limit); go beyond runway when landing or taking off. □ **overshoot the mark** go beyond what is intended or proper.

oversight *noun* failure to notice; inadvertent omission or mistake; supervision.

oversimplify /əʊvə'sɪmplɪfaɪ/ *verb* (**-ies, -ied**) distort (problem etc.) by putting it in too simple terms. □ **oversimplification** *noun*.

oversleep /əʊvə'sli:p/ *verb* (*past & past participle* **-slept**) sleep beyond intended time of waking.

overspend /əʊvə'spend/ *verb* (*past & past participle* **-spent**) spend beyond one's means.

overspill *noun* what is spilt over or overflows; surplus population leaving one area for another.

overspread /əʊvə'spred/ *verb* (*past & past participle* **-spread**) cover surface of; (as **overspread** *adjective*) (usually + *with*) covered.

overstate /əʊvə'steɪt/ *verb* (**-ting**) state too strongly; exaggerate. □ **overstatement** *noun*.

overstep /əʊvə'step/ *verb* (**-pp-**) pass beyond. □ **overstep the mark** go beyond conventional behaviour.

overstrain /əʊvə'streɪn/ *verb* damage by exertion; stretch too far.

overstrung *adjective* /əʊvə'strʌŋ/ (of person, nerves, etc.) too highly strung; /'əʊvəstrʌŋ/ (of piano) with strings crossing each other obliquely.

oversubscribe /əʊvəsəb'skraɪb/ *verb* (**-bing**) (usually as **oversubscribed** *adjective*) subscribe for more than available amount or number of (offer, shares, places, etc.).

overt /əʊ'vɜ:t/ *adjective* openly done, unconcealed. □ **overtly** *adverb*.

overtake /əʊvə'teɪk/ *verb* (**-king**; *past* **-took**; *past participle* **-taken**) catch up and pass; (of bad luck etc.) come suddenly upon.

overtax /əʊvə'tæks/ *verb* make excessive demands on; tax too highly.

over-the-top *adjective colloquial* excessive.

overthrow ● *verb* /əʊvə'θrəʊ/ (*past* **-threw**; *past participle* **-thrown**) remove forcibly from power; conquer. ● *noun* /'əʊvəθrəʊ/ defeat; downfall.

overtime ● *noun* time worked in addition to regular hours; payment for this. ● *adverb* in addition to regular hours.

overtone *noun Music* any of tones above lowest in harmonic series; subtle extra quality or implication.

overture /'əʊvətjʊə/ *noun* orchestral prelude; (usually in *plural*) opening of negotiations; formal proposal or offer.

overturn /əʊvə'tɜ:n/ *verb* (cause to) fall down or over; upset, overthrow.

overview *noun* general survey.

overweening /əʊvə'wi:nɪŋ/ *adjective* arrogant.

overweight ● *adjective* /əʊvə'weɪt/ above the weight allowed or desirable. ● *noun* /'əʊvəweɪt/ excess weight.

overwhelm /əʊvə'welm/ *verb* overpower with emotion; overcome by force of numbers; bury, submerge utterly.

overwhelming *adjective* too great to resist or overcome; by a great number. □ **overwhelmingly** *adverb*.

overwork /əʊvə'wɜ:k/ ● *verb* (cause to) work too hard; weary or exhaust with work; (esp. as **overworked** *adjective*) make excessive use of. ● *noun* excessive work.

overwrought /əʊvə'rɔ:t/ *adjective* over-excited, nervous, distraught; too elaborate.

oviduct /'əʊvɪdʌkt/ *noun* tube through which ova pass from ovary.

oviform /'əʊvɪfɔ:m/ *adjective* egg-shaped.

ovine /'əʊvaɪn/ *adjective* of or like sheep.

oviparous /əʊ'vɪpərəs/ *adjective* egg-laying.

ovoid /'əʊvɔɪd/ *adjective* (of solid) egg-shaped.

ovulate /'ɒvjʊleɪt/ *verb* (**-ting**) produce ova or ovules, or discharge them from ovary. □ **ovulation** *noun*.

ovule /'ɒvju:l/ *noun* structure containing germ cell in female plant.

ovum /'əʊvəm/ *noun* (*plural* **ova** /'əʊvə/) female egg cell from which young develop after fertilization with male sperm.

ow /aʊ/ *interjection expressing sudden pain.*

owe /əʊ/ *verb* (**owing**) be under obligation to (re)pay or render; (usually + *for*) be in debt; (usually + *to*) be indebted to person, thing, etc. for.

owing /'əʊɪŋ/ *adjective* owed, yet to be paid; (+ *to*) caused by, because of.

owl /aʊl/ *noun* night bird of prey; solemn or wise-looking person. □ **owlish** *adjective*.

owlet /'aʊlɪt/ *noun* small or young owl.

own /əʊn/ ● *adjective* (after *my*, *your*, etc.) belonging to myself, yourself, etc.; not another's. ● *verb* have as property, possess; acknowledge as true or belonging to one. □ **come into one's own** achieve recognition, receive one's due; **hold one's own** maintain one's position, not be defeated; **on one's own** alone, independently, unaided; **own goal** goal scored by mistake against scorer's own side, action etc. having unintended effect of harming person's own interests; **own up** confess.

owner *noun* possessor. □ **owner-occupier** person who owns and occupies house. □ **ownership** *noun*.

ox *noun* (*plural* **oxen**) large usually horned ruminant; castrated male of domestic species of cattle. ▫ **ox-eye daisy** daisy with large white petals and yellow centre; **oxtail** tail of ox, often used in making soup.

oxalic acid /ɒkˈsælɪk/ *noun* intensely sour poisonous acid found in wood sorrel and rhubarb leaves.

oxidation /ɒksɪˈdeɪʃ(ə)n/ *noun* oxidizing, being oxidized.

oxide /ˈɒksaɪd/ *noun* compound of oxygen with another element.

oxidize /ˈɒksɪdaɪz/ *verb* (also **-ise**) (**-zing** or **-sing**) combine with oxygen; rust; cover with coating of oxide. ▫ **oxidization** *noun*.

oxyacetylene /ɒksɪəˈsetɪli:n/ *adjective* of or using mixture of oxygen and acetylene, esp. in cutting or welding metals.

oxygen /ˈɒksɪdʒ(ə)n/ *noun* colourless odourless tasteless gaseous element essential to life and to combustion. ▫ **oxygen tent** enclosure to allow patient to breathe air with increased oxygen content.

oxygenate /ˈɒksɪdʒəneɪt/ *verb* (**-ting**) supply, treat, or mix with oxygen; oxidize.

oyez /əʊˈjes/ *interjection* (also **oyes**) *uttered by public crier or court officer to call for attention.*

oyster /ˈɔɪstə/ ● *noun* bivalve mollusc living on seabed, esp. edible kind. ● *adjective* (in full **oyster-white**) greyish white.

oz *abbreviation* ounce(s).

ozone /ˈəʊzəʊn/ *noun* form of oxygen with pungent odour; *colloquial* invigorating seaside air. ▫ **ozone-friendly** not containing chemicals destructive to ozone layer; **ozone layer** layer of ozone in stratosphere that absorbs most of sun's ultraviolet radiation.

Pp

p *abbreviation* (also **p.**) penny, pence; page; piano (softly). □ **p. & p.** postage and packing.

PA *abbreviation* personal assistant; public address.

pa /pɑː/ *noun colloquial* father.

p.a. *abbreviation* per annum.

pace[1] ● *noun* single step in walking or running; distance covered in this; speed, rate of progression; gait. ● *verb* (**-cing**) walk (over, about), esp. with slow or regular step; set pace for; (+ *out*) measure (distance) by pacing. □ **pacemaker** person who sets pace, natural or electrical device for stimulating heart muscle.

pace[2] /ˈpɑːtʃeɪ/ *preposition* with all due deference to. [Latin]

pachyderm /ˈpækɪdɜːm/ *noun* large thick-skinned mammal, esp. elephant or rhinoceros. □ **pachydermatous** /-ˈdɜːmətəs/ *adjective*.

pacific /pəˈsɪfɪk/ ● *adjective* tending to peace, peaceful; (**Pacific**) of or adjoining the Pacific. ● *noun* (**the Pacific**) ocean between America to the east and Asia to the west.

pacifist /ˈpæsɪfɪst/ *noun* person opposed to war. □ **pacifism** *noun*.

pacify /ˈpæsɪfaɪ/ *verb* (**-ies**, **-ied**) appease (person, anger, etc.); bring (country etc.) to state of peace. □ **pacification** *noun*.

pack ● *noun* collection of things tied or wrapped together for carrying; backpack; set of packaged items; set of playing cards; *usually derogatory* lot, set; group of wild animals or hounds; organized group of Cub Scouts or Brownies; forwards of Rugby team; area of large crowded pieces of floating ice in sea. ● *verb* put together into bundle, box, etc., fill with clothes etc. for transport or storing; cram, crowd together, form into pack; (esp. in *passive*; often + *with*) fill; wrap tightly. □ **packed out** full, crowded; **packhorse** horse for carrying loads; **pack in** *colloquial* stop, give up; **pack it in, up** *colloquial* end or stop it; **pack up** *colloquial* stop working, break down, retire from contest, activity, etc.; **send packing** *colloquial* dismiss summarily.

package ● *noun* parcel; box etc. in which goods are packed; (in full **package deal**) set of proposals or items offered or agreed to as a whole. ● *verb* (**-ging**) make up into or enclose in package. □ **package holiday, tour**, etc., one with fixed inclusive price. □ **packaging** *noun*.

packet /ˈpækɪt/ *noun* small package; *colloquial* large sum of money; *historical* mail-boat.

pact *noun* agreement, treaty.

pad[1] ● *noun* piece of soft stuff used to diminish jarring, raise surface, absorb fluid, etc.; sheets of blank paper fastened together at one edge; fleshy cushion forming sole of foot of some animals; leg-guard in games; flat surface for helicopter take-off or rocket-launching; *slang* lodging. ● *verb* (**-dd-**) provide with pad or padding, stuff; (+ *out*) fill out (book etc.) with superfluous matter.

pad[2] ● *verb* (**-dd-**) walk softly; tramp (along) on foot; travel on foot. ● *noun* sound of soft steady steps.

padding *noun* material used to pad.

paddle[1] /ˈpæd(ə)l/ ● *noun* short oar with broad blade at one or each end; paddle-shaped instrument; fin, flipper; board on paddle-wheel or mill-wheel; action or spell of paddling. ● *verb* (**-ling**) move on water or propel (boat etc.) with paddle(s); row gently. □ **paddle-wheel** wheel for propelling ship, with boards round circumference.

paddle[2] /ˈpæd(ə)l/ ● *verb* (**-ling**) wade about in shallow water. ● *noun* action or spell of paddling.

paddock /ˈpædək/ *noun* small field, esp. for keeping horses in; enclosure where horses or cars are assembled before race.

paddy[1] /ˈpædɪ/ *noun* (*plural* **-ies**) (in full **paddy field**) field where rice is grown; rice before threshing or in the husk.

paddy[2] /ˈpædɪ/ *noun* (*plural* **-ies**) *colloquial* rage, temper.

padlock /ˈpædlɒk/ ● *noun* detachable lock hanging by pivoted hook. ● *verb* secure with padlock.

padre /ˈpɑːdrɪ/ *noun* chaplain in army etc.

paean /ˈpiːən/ *noun* (*US* **pean**) song of praise or triumph.

paediatrics /piːdɪˈætrɪks/ *plural noun* (treated as *singular*) (*US* **pediatrics**) branch of medicine dealing with children's diseases. □ **paediatric** *adjective*; **paediatrician** /-əˈtrɪʃ(ə)n/ *noun*.

paedophile /ˈpiːdəfaɪl/ *noun* (*US* **pedophile**) person feeling sexual attraction towards children.

paella /paɪˈelə/ *noun* Spanish dish of rice, saffron, chicken, seafood, etc.

paeony = PEONY.

pagan /ˈpeɪgən/ ● *noun* heathen, pantheist, etc. ● *adjective* of pagans; heathen; pantheistic. □ **paganism** *noun*.

page[1] ● *noun* leaf of book etc.; each side of this. ● *verb* (**-ging**) number pages of.

page[2] ● *noun* boy or man employed as liveried servant or personal attendant. ● *verb* (**-ging**) call name of (person sought) in public rooms of hotel etc. □ **page-boy** boy attending bride etc., woman's short hairstyle.

pageant /ˈpædʒ(ə)nt/ *noun* spectacular performance, usually illustrative of historical events; any brilliant show.

pageantry *noun* spectacular show or display.

pager *noun* bleeping device calling bearer to telephone etc.

paginate /ˈpædʒɪneɪt/ *verb* (**-ting**) number pages of (book etc.). □ **pagination** *noun*.

pagoda /pəˈgəʊdə/ *noun* temple or sacred tower in China etc.; ornamental imitation of this.

pah *interjection expressing disgust*.

paid *past & past participle* of PAY.

pail *noun* bucket.

pain ● *noun* bodily suffering caused by injury, pressure, illness, etc.; mental suffering; *colloquial* troublesome person or thing. ● *verb* cause pain to. □ **be at** or **take pains** take great care; **in pain** suffering pain; **painkiller** pain-relieving drug.

painful *adjective* causing or (esp. of part of the body) suffering pain; causing trouble or difficulty. □ **painfully** *adverb*.

painless *adjective* not causing pain. □ **painlessly** *adverb*.

painstaking /ˈpeɪnzteɪkɪŋ/ *adjective* careful, industrious, thorough. □ **painstakingly** *adverb*.

paint ● *noun* colouring matter, esp. in liquid form, for applying to surface. ● *verb* cover surface of with paint; portray or make pictures in colours; describe vividly; apply liquid or cosmetic to. □ **paintbox** box holding dry paints for painting pictures; **painted**

lady butterfly with spotted orange-red wings; **paintwork** painted, esp. wooden, surface or area in building etc.

painter[1] *noun* person who paints, esp. as artist or decorator.

painter[2] *noun* rope at bow of boat for tying it up.

painting *noun* process or art of using paint; painted picture.

pair ● *noun* set of two people or things; thing with two joined or corresponding parts; engaged or married or mated couple; two playing cards of same denomination; (either of) two MPs etc. on opposite sides agreeing not to vote on certain occasions. ● *verb* (often + *off*) arrange or unite as pair, in pairs, or in marriage; mate.

Paisley /'peɪzlɪ/ *noun* (*plural* **-s**) pattern of curved feather-shaped figures.

pajamas *US* = PYJAMAS.

Pakistani /pɑːkɪs'tɑːnɪ/ ● *noun* (*plural* **-s**) native or national of Pakistan; person of Pakistani descent. ● *adjective* of Pakistan.

pal *colloquial* ● *noun* friend. ● *verb* (**-ll-**) (+ *up*) make friends.

palace /'pælɪs/ *noun* official residence of sovereign, president, archbishop, or bishop; stately or spacious building.

palaeo- *combining form* (*US* **paleo-**) ancient; prehistoric.

palaeography /pælɪ'ɒgrəfɪ/ *noun* (*US* **paleography**) study of ancient writing and documents.

palaeolithic /pælɪəʊ'lɪθɪk/ *adjective* (*US* **paleolithic**) of earlier Stone Age.

palaeontology /pælɪɒn'tɒlədʒɪ/ *noun* (*US* **paleontology**) study of life in geological past. ◻ **palaeontologist** *noun*.

Palaeozoic /pælɪəʊ'zəʊɪk/ (*US* **Paleozoic**) ● *adjective* of geological era marked by appearance of plants and animals, esp. invertebrates. ● *noun* this era.

palais /'pæleɪ/ *noun colloquial* public dance hall.

palanquin /pælən'kiːn/ *noun* (also **palankeen**) Eastern covered litter for one.

palatable /'pælətəb(ə)l/ *adjective* pleasant to taste; (of idea etc.) acceptable, satisfactory.

palatal /'pælət(ə)l/ ● *adjective* of the palate; (of sound) made with tongue against palate. ● *noun* palatal sound.

palate /'pælət/ *noun* roof of mouth in vertebrates; sense of taste; liking.

palatial /pə'leɪʃ(ə)l/ *adjective* like palace, splendid.

palaver /pə'lɑːvə/ *noun colloquial* tedious fuss and bother.

pale[1] ● *adjective* (of complexion etc.) whitish; faintly coloured; (of colour) faint, (of light) dim. ● *verb* (**-ling**) grow or make pale; (often + *before*, *beside*) seem feeble in comparison (with). ◻ **palely** *adverb*.

pale[2] *noun* pointed piece of wood for fencing etc.; stake; boundary. ◻ **beyond the pale** outside bounds of acceptable behaviour.

paleo- *US* = PALAEO-.

Palestinian /pælɪ'stɪnɪən/ ● *adjective* of Palestine. ● *noun* native or inhabitant of Palestine.

palette /'pælɪt/ *noun* artist's flat tablet for mixing colours on; range of colours used by artist. ◻ **palette-knife** knife with long round-ended flexible blade, esp. for mixing colours or applying or removing paint.

palimony /'pælɪmənɪ/ *noun esp. US colloquial* allowance paid by either of a separated unmarried couple to the other.

palimpsest /'pælɪmpsest/ *noun* writing material used for second time after original writing has been erased.

palindrome /'pælɪndrəʊm/ *noun* word or phrase that reads same backwards as forwards. ◻ **palindromic** /-'drɒm-/ *adjective*.

paling *noun* (in *singular* or *plural*) fence of pales; pale.

palisade /pælɪ'seɪd/ ● *noun* fence of pointed stakes. ● *verb* (**-ding**) enclose or provide with palisade.

pall[1] /pɔːl/ *noun* cloth spread over coffin etc.; ecclesiastical vestment; dark covering. ◻ **pallbearer** person helping to carry or escort coffin at funeral.

pall[2] /pɔːl/ *verb* become uninteresting.

pallet[1] /'pælɪt/ *noun* straw mattress; makeshift bed.

pallet[2] /'pælɪt/ *noun* portable platform for transporting and storing loads.

palliasse /'pælɪæs/ *noun* straw mattress.

palliate /'pælɪeɪt/ *verb* (**-ting**) alleviate without curing; excuse, extenuate. ◻ **palliative** /-ətɪv/ *adjective & noun*.

pallid /'pælɪd/ *adjective* pale, sickly-looking.

pallor /'pælə/ *noun* paleness.

pally *adjective* (**-ier**, **-iest**) *colloquial* friendly.

palm[1] /pɑːm/ *noun* (also **palm tree**) (usually tropical) treelike plant with unbranched stem and crown of large esp. sickle- or fan-shaped leaves; leaf of this as symbol of victory. ◻ **Palm Sunday** Sunday before Easter.

palm[2] /pɑːm/ ● *noun* inner surface of hand between wrist and fingers. ● *verb* conceal in hand. ◻ **palm off** (often + *on*) impose fraudulently (on person).

palmate /'pælmeɪt/ *adjective* shaped like open hand.

palmetto /pæl'metəʊ/ *noun* (*plural* **-s**) small palm tree.

palmist /'pɑːmɪst/ *noun* teller of character or fortune from lines etc. in palm of hand. ◻ **palmistry** *noun*.

palmy /'pɑːmɪ/ *adjective* (**-ier**, **-iest**) of, like, or abounding in palms; flourishing.

palomino /pælə'miːnəʊ/ *noun* (*plural* **-s**) golden or cream-coloured horse with light-coloured mane and tail.

palpable /'pælpəb(ə)l/ *adjective* that can be touched or felt; readily perceived. ◻ **palpably** *adverb*.

palpate /'pælpeɪt/ *verb* (**-ting**) examine (esp. medically) by touch. ◻ **palpation** *noun*.

palpitate /'pælpɪteɪt/ *verb* (**-ting**) pulsate, throb; tremble. ◻ **palpitation** *noun*.

palsy /'pɔːlzɪ/ ● *noun* (*plural* **-ies**) paralysis, esp. with involuntary tremors. ● *verb* (**-ies**, **-ied**) affect with palsy.

paltry /'pɔːltrɪ/ *adjective* (**-ier**, **-iest**) worthless, contemptible, trifling.

pampas /'pæmpəs/ *plural noun* large treeless S. American plains. ◻ **pampas grass** large ornamental grass.

pamper /'pæmpə/ *verb* overindulge.

pamphlet /'pæmflɪt/ *noun* small unbound booklet, esp. controversial treatise.

pamphleteer /pæmflɪ'tɪə/ *noun* writer of (esp. political) pamphlets.

pan[1] ● *noun* flat-bottomed usually metal vessel used in cooking etc.; shallow receptacle or tray; bowl of scales or of lavatory. ● *verb* (**-nn-**) *colloquial* criticize harshly; (+ *off*, *out*) wash (gold-bearing gravel) in pan; search for gold in this way. ◻ **pan out** turn out, work out well or in specified way.

pan[2] ● *verb* (**-nn-**) swing (film-camera) horizontally to give panoramic effect or follow moving object; (of camera) be moved thus. ● *noun* panning movement.

pan- *combining form* all; the whole of (esp. referring to a continent, racial group, religion, etc.).

panacea /pænə'siːə/ *noun* universal remedy.

panache /pə'næʃ/ *noun* assertively flamboyant or confident style.

panama /'pænəmɑː/ *noun* hat of strawlike material with brim and indented crown.

panatella /pænə'telə/ *noun* long thin cigar.

pancake *noun* thin flat cake of fried batter, usually folded or rolled up with filling. ▫ **Pancake Day** Shrove Tuesday (when pancakes are traditionally eaten); **pancake landing** *colloquial* emergency aircraft landing with undercarriage still retracted.

panchromatic /pænkrəʊ'mætɪk/ *adjective* (of film etc.) sensitive to all visible colours of spectrum.

pancreas /'pæŋkrɪəs/ *noun* gland near stomach supplying digestive fluid and insulin. ▫ **pancreatic** /-'æt-/ *adjective*.

panda /'pændə/ *noun* (also **giant panda**) large rare bearlike black and white mammal native to China and Tibet; (also **red panda**) racoon-like Himalayan mammal. ▫ **panda car** police patrol car.

pandemic /pæn'demɪk/ *adjective* (of disease) widespread; universal.

pandemonium /pændɪ'məʊnɪəm/ *noun* uproar; utter confusion; scene of this.

pander /'pændə/ ● *verb* (+ *to*) indulge (person or weakness). ● *noun* procurer, pimp.

pandit = PUNDIT.

pane *noun* single sheet of glass in window or door.

panegyric /pænɪ'dʒɪrɪk/ *noun* eulogy; speech or essay of praise.

panel /'pæn(ə)l/ ● *noun* distinct, usually rectangular, section of surface, esp. of wall, door, or vehicle; group or team of people assembled for discussion, consultation, etc.; strip of material in garment; list of available jurors; jury. ● *verb* (**-ll-**; *US* **-l-**) fit with panels. ▫ **panel game** broadcast quiz etc. played by panel. ▫ **panelling** *noun*.

panellist *noun* (*US* **panelist**) member of panel.

pang *noun* sudden sharp pain or distressing emotion.

pangolin /pæŋ'gəʊlɪn/ *noun* scaly anteater.

panic /'pænɪk/ ● *noun* sudden alarm; infectious fright. ● *verb* (**-ck-**) (often + *into*) affect or be affected with panic. ▫ **panic-stricken**, **-struck** affected with panic. ▫ **panicky** *adjective*.

panicle /'pænɪk(ə)l/ *noun* loose branching cluster of flowers.

panjandrum /pæn'dʒændrəm/ *noun: mock title of great personage*.

pannier /'pænɪə/ *noun* one of pair of baskets or bags etc. carried by beast of burden or on bicycle or motorcycle.

panoply /'pænəplɪ/ *noun* (*plural* **-ies**) complete or splendid array; full armour.

panorama /pænə'rɑːmə/ *noun* unbroken view of surrounding region; picture or photograph containing wide view. ▫ **panoramic** /-'ræm-/ *adjective*.

pansy /'pænzɪ/ *noun* (*plural* **-ies**) garden plant of violet family with richly coloured flowers.

pant ● *verb* breathe with quick breaths; yearn. ● *noun* panting breath.

pantaloons /pæntə'luːnz/ *plural noun* baggy trousers gathered at ankles.

pantechnicon /pæn'teknɪkən/ *noun* large furniture van.

pantheism /'pænθiːɪz(ə)m/ *noun* doctrine that God is everything and everything is God. ▫ **pantheist** *noun*; **pantheistic** /-'ɪs-/ *adjective*.

pantheon /'pænθɪən/ *noun* building with memorials of illustrious dead; deities of a people collectively; temple of all gods.

panther /'pænθə/ *noun* leopard, esp. black; *US* puma.

panties /'pæntɪz/ *plural noun colloquial* short-legged or legless knickers.

pantile /'pæntaɪl/ *noun* curved roof-tile.

pantograph /'pæntəgrɑːf/ *noun* instrument for copying plan etc. on any scale.

pantomime /'pæntəmaɪm/ *noun* dramatic usually Christmas entertainment based on fairy tale; *colloquial* absurd or outrageous behaviour; gestures and facial expressions conveying meaning.

pantry /'pæntrɪ/ *noun* (*plural* **-ies**) room in which provisions, crockery, cutlery, etc. are kept.

pants *plural noun* underpants; knickers; *US* trousers.

pap[1] *noun* soft or semi-liquid food; trivial reading matter.

pap[2] *noun archaic* nipple.

papa /pə'pɑː/ *noun archaic: child's name for* father.

papacy /'peɪpəsɪ/ *noun* (*plural* **-ies**) Pope's office or tenure; papal system.

papal /'peɪp(ə)l/ *adjective* of the Pope or his office.

paparazzo /pæpə'rætsəʊ/ *noun* (*plural* **-zzi** /-tsɪ/) freelance photographer who pursues celebrities to photograph them.

papaya = PAWPAW.

paper /'peɪpə/ ● *noun* substance made in very thin sheets from pulp of wood etc., used for writing, printing, wrapping, etc.; newspaper; (in *plural*) documents; set of exam questions or answers;wallpaper; essay. ● *adjective* not actual, theoretical. ● *verb* decorate (wall etc.) with paper. ▫ **paper-boy, -girl** one who delivers or sells newspapers; **paper-clip** clip of bent wire or plastic for holding sheets of paper together; **paper-knife** blunt knife for opening envelopes etc.; **paper money** banknotes etc.; **paper round** job of regularly delivering newspapers, route for doing this; **paperweight** small heavy object to hold papers down; **paperwork** office record-keeping and administration.

paperback ● *adjective* bound in stiff paper, not boards. ● *noun* paperback book.

papier mâché /pæpɪeɪ 'mæʃeɪ/ *noun* moulded paper pulp used for making models etc.

papilla /pə'pɪlə/ *noun* (*plural* **papillae** /-liː/) small nipple-like protuberance. ▫ **papillary** *adjective*.

papoose /pə'puːs/ *noun* young N. American Indian child.

paprika /'pæprɪkə/ *noun* ripe red pepper; condiment made from this.

papyrus /pə'paɪərəs/ *noun* (*plural* **papyri** /-raɪ/) aquatic plant of N. Africa; ancient writing material made from stem of this; manuscript written on this.

par *noun* average or normal value, degree, condition, etc.; equality, equal footing; *Golf* number of strokes needed by first-class player for hole or course; face value. ▫ **par for the course** *colloquial* what is normal or to be expected.

para /'pærə/ *noun colloquial* paratrooper.

para- *prefix* beside, beyond.

parable /'pærəb(ə)l/ *noun* story used to illustrate moral or spiritual truth.

parabola /pə'ræbələ/ *noun* plane curve formed by intersection of cone with plane parallel to its side. ▫ **parabolic** /pærə'bɒlɪk/ *adjective*.

paracetamol /pærə'siːtəmɒl/ *noun* compound used to relieve pain and reduce fever; tablet of this.

parachute /'pærəʃuːt/ ● *noun* usually umbrella-shaped apparatus allowing person or heavy object to descend safely from a height, esp. from aircraft. ● *verb* (**-ting**) convey or descend by parachute. ▫ **parachutist** *noun*.

parade /pə'reɪd/ ● *noun* public procession; muster of troops etc. for inspection; parade ground; display, ostentation; public square, row of shops. ● *verb* (**-ding**) march ceremonially; assemble for parade; display ostentatiously. ▫ **parade ground** place for muster of troops.

paradigm /ˈpærədaɪm/ *noun* example or pattern, esp. of inflection of word.

paradise /ˈpærədaɪs/ *noun* heaven; place or state of complete bliss; garden of Eden.

paradox /ˈpærədɒks/ *noun* seemingly absurd or self-contradictory though often true statement etc. ◻ **paradoxical** /-ˈdɒks-/ *adjective*; **paradoxically** /-ˈdɒks-/ *adverb*.

paraffin /ˈpærəfɪn/ *noun* inflammable waxy or oily substance got by distillation from petroleum etc., used in liquid form esp. as fuel. ◻ **paraffin wax** solid paraffin.

paragon /ˈpærəgən/ *noun* (often + *of*) model of excellence.

paragraph /ˈpærəgrɑːf/ *noun* distinct passage in book etc. usually marked by indentation of first line; mark of reference (¶); short separate item in newspaper etc.

parakeet /ˈpærəkiːt/ *noun* small usually long-tailed parrot.

parallax /ˈpærəlæks/ *noun* apparent difference in position or direction of object caused by change of observer's position; angular amount of this.

parallel /ˈpærəlel/ ● *adjective* (of lines) continuously equidistant; precisely similar, analogous, or corresponding; (of processes etc.) occurring or performed simultaneously. ● *noun* person or thing analogous to another; comparison; imaginary line on earth's surface or line on map marking degree of latitude. ● *verb* (**-l-**) be parallel or correspond to; represent as similar; compare. ◻ **parallelism** *noun*.

parallelepiped /pærəleləˈpaɪped/ *noun* solid bounded by parallelograms.

parallelogram /pærəˈleləgræm/ *noun* 4-sided rectilinear figure whose opposite sides are parallel.

paralyse /ˈpærəlaɪz/ *verb* (**-sing**) (*US* **-lyze**; **-zing**) affect with paralysis; render powerless, cripple.

paralysis /pəˈrælɪsɪs/ *noun* impairment or loss of esp. motor function of nerves, causing immobility; powerlessness.

paralytic /pærəˈlɪtɪk/ ● *adjective* affected with paralysis; *slang* very drunk. ● *noun* person affected with paralysis.

paramedic /pærəˈmedɪk/ *noun* paramedical worker.

paramedical /pærəˈmedɪk(ə)l/ *adjective* supplementing and supporting medical work.

parameter /pəˈræmɪtə/ *noun Mathematics* quantity constant in case considered, but varying in different cases; (esp. measurable or quantifiable) characteristic or feature; (loosely) boundary, esp. of subject for discussion.

paramilitary /pærəˈmɪlɪtərɪ/ ● *adjective* similarly organized to military forces. ● *noun* (*plural* **-ies**) member of unofficial paramilitary organization.

paramount /ˈpærəmaʊnt/ *adjective* supreme; most important or powerful.

paramour /ˈpærəmʊə/ *noun archaic* illicit lover of married person.

paranoia /pærəˈnɔɪə/ *noun* mental derangement with delusions of grandeur, persecution, etc.; abnormal tendency to suspect and mistrust others. ◻ **paranoiac** *adjective & noun*; **paranoid** /ˈpærənɔɪd/ *adjective & noun*.

paranormal /pærəˈnɔːm(ə)l/ *adjective* beyond the scope of normal scientific investigations etc.

parapet /ˈpærəpɪt/ *noun* low wall at edge of roof, balcony, bridge, etc.; mound along front of trench etc.

paraphernalia /pærəfəˈneɪlɪə/ *plural noun* (also treated as *singular*) personal belongings, miscellaneous accessories, etc.

paraphrase /ˈpærəfreɪz/ ● *noun* restatement of sense of passage etc. in other words. ● *verb* (**-sing**) express meaning of in other words.

paraplegia /pærəˈpliːdʒə/ *noun* paralysis below waist. ◻ **paraplegic** *adjective & noun*.

parapsychology /pærəsaɪˈkɒlədʒɪ/ *noun* study of mental phenomena outside sphere of ordinary psychology.

paraquat /ˈpærəkwɒt/ *noun* quick-acting highly toxic herbicide.

parasite /ˈpærəsaɪt/ *noun* animal or plant living in or on another and feeding on it; person exploiting another or others. ◻ **parasitic** /-ˈsɪt-/ *adjective*; **parasitism** *noun*.

parasol /ˈpærəsɒl/ *noun* light umbrella giving shade from the sun.

paratroops /ˈpærətruːps/ *plural noun* airborne troops landing by parachute. ◻ **paratrooper** *noun*.

paratyphoid /pærəˈtaɪfɔɪd/ *noun* fever resembling typhoid.

parboil /ˈpɑːbɔɪl/ *verb* partly cook by boiling.

parcel /ˈpɑːs(ə)l/ ● *noun* goods etc. packed up in single wrapping; piece of land. ● *verb* (**-ll-**; *US* **-l-**) (+ *up*) wrap into parcel; (+ *out*) divide into portions.

parch *verb* make or become hot and dry; slightly roast.

parchment /ˈpɑːtʃmənt/ *noun* skin, esp. of sheep or goat, prepared for writing etc.; manuscript written on this.

pardon /ˈpɑːd(ə)n/ ● *noun* forgiveness; remission of punishment. ● *verb* forgive; excuse; release from legal consequences of offence etc. ● *interjection* (also **pardon me** or **I beg your pardon**) *formula of apology or disagreement*; *request to repeat something said*. ◻ **pardonable** *adjective*.

pare /peə/ *verb* (**-ring**) trim or reduce by cutting away edge or surface of; (often + *away, down*) whittle away.

parent /ˈpeərənt/ *noun* person who has had or adopted a child; father, mother; source, origin. ◻ **parent company** company of which others are subsidiaries; **parent-teacher association** social and fund-raising organization of school's teachers and parents. ◻ **parental** /pəˈrent(ə)l/ *adjective*; **parenthood** *noun*.

parentage *noun* lineage, descent from or through parents.

parenthesis /pəˈrenθəsɪs/ *noun* (*plural* **-theses** /-siːz/) word, clause, or sentence inserted as explanation etc. into passage independently of grammatical sequence; (in *plural*) round brackets used to mark this; interlude. ◻ **parenthetic** /pærənˈθetɪk/ *adjective*.

par excellence /pɑːr eksəˈlɑ̃s/ *adverb* superior to all others so called. [French]

parfait /ˈpɑːfeɪ/ *noun* rich iced pudding of whipped cream, eggs, etc.; layers of ice cream, meringue, etc., served in tall glass.

pariah /pəˈraɪə/ *noun* social outcast; *historical* member of low or no caste.

parietal /pəˈraɪət(ə)l/ *adjective* of wall of body or any of its cavities. ◻ **parietal bone** either of pair forming part of skull.

paring *noun* strip pared off.

parish /ˈpærɪʃ/ *noun* division of diocese having its own church and clergyman; local government district; inhabitants of parish.

parishioner /pəˈrɪʃənə/ *noun* inhabitant of parish.

parity /ˈpærɪtɪ/ *noun* (*plural* **-ies**) equality; equal status etc.; equivalence; being at par.

park ● *noun* large public garden in town; large enclosed piece of ground attached to country house or laid out or preserved for public use; place where vehicles may be parked; area for specified purpose. ● *verb* place and leave (esp. vehicle) temporarily. □ **parking-lot** *US* outdoor car park; **parking meter** coin-operated meter allocating period of time for which a vehicle may be parked in street; **parking ticket** notice of fine etc. imposed for parking vehicle illegally.

parka /'pɑːkə/ *noun* jacket with hood, as worn by Eskimos, mountaineers, etc.

parkin /'pɑːkɪn/ *noun* oatmeal gingerbread.

parky /'pɑːkɪ/ *adjective* (**-ier**, **-iest**) *colloquial or dialect* chilly.

parlance /'pɑːləns/ *noun* way of speaking.

parley /'pɑːlɪ/ ● *noun* (*plural* **-s**) meeting between representatives of opposed forces to discuss terms. ● *verb* (**-leys**, **-leyed**) (often + *with*) hold parley.

parliament /'pɑːləmənt/ *noun* body consisting of House of Commons and House of Lords and forming (with Sovereign) legislature of UK; similar legislature in other states.

parliamentarian /pɑːləmen'teərɪən/ *noun* member of parliament.

parliamentary /pɑːlə'mentərɪ/ *adjective* of, in, concerned with, or enacted by parliament.

parlour /'pɑːlə/ *noun* (*US* **parlor**) *archaic* sitting-room in private house; *esp. US* shop providing specified goods or services. □ **parlour game** indoor game, esp. word game.

parlous /'pɑːləs/ *adjective archaic* perilous; hard to deal with.

Parmesan /pɑːmɪ'zæn/ *noun* hard Italian cheese usually used grated as flavouring.

parochial /pə'rəʊkɪəl/ *adjective* of a parish; of narrow range, merely local. □ **parochialism** *noun*.

parody /'pærədɪ/ ● *noun* (*plural* **-ies**) humorous exaggerated imitation of author, style, etc.; travesty. ● *verb* (**-ies**, **-ied**) write parody of; mimic humorously. □ **parodist** *noun*.

parole /pə'rəʊl/ ● *noun* temporary or permanent release of prisoner before end of sentence, on promise of good behaviour; such promise. ● *verb* (**-ling**) put (prisoner) on parole.

parotid /pə'rɒtɪd/ ● *adjective* situated near ear. ● *noun* (in full **parotid gland**) salivary gland in front of ear.

paroxysm /'pærəksɪz(ə)m/ *noun* (often + *of*) fit (of pain, rage, coughing, etc.).

parquet /'pɑːkeɪ/ ● *noun* flooring of wooden blocks arranged in a pattern. ● *verb* (**-eted** /-eɪd/, **-eting** /-eɪɪŋ/) floor (room) thus.

parricide /'pærɪsaɪd/ *noun* person who kills his or her parent; such a killing. □ **parricidal** /-'saɪd(ə)l/ *adjective*.

parrot /'pærət/ ● *noun* mainly tropical bird with short hooked bill, of which some species can be taught to repeat words; unintelligent imitator or chatterer. ● *verb* (**-t-**) repeat mechanically. □ **parrot-fashion** (learning or repeating) mechanically, by rote.

parry /'pærɪ/ ● *verb* (**-ies**, **-ied**) ward off, avert. ● *noun* (*plural* **-ies**) act of parrying.

parse /pɑːz/ *verb* (**-sing**) describe (word) or analyse (sentence) in terms of grammar.

parsec /'pɑːsek/ *noun* unit of stellar distance, about 3.25 light years.

parsimony /'pɑːsɪmənɪ/ *noun* carefulness in use of money etc.; meanness. □ **parsimonious** /-'məʊn-/ *adjective*.

parsley /'pɑːslɪ/ *noun* herb used for seasoning and garnishing.

parsnip /'pɑːsnɪp/ *noun* plant with pale yellow tapering root used as vegetable; this root.

parson /'pɑːs(ə)n/ *noun* parish clergyman; *colloquial* any clergyman. □ **parson's nose** fatty flesh at rump of cooked fowl.

parsonage *noun* parson's house.

part ● *noun* some but not all; component, division, portion; share, allotted portion; person's share in an action etc.; assigned character or role; *Music* one of melodies making up harmony of concerted music; side in agreement or dispute; (usually in *plural*) region, direction, way; (in *plural*) abilities. ● *verb* divide into parts; separate; (+ *with*) give up, hand over; make parting in (hair). ● *adverb* partly, in part. □ **on the part of** made or done by; **part and parcel** (usually + *of*) essential part; **part-exchange** *noun* transaction in which article is given as part of payment for more expensive one, *verb* give (article) thus; **part of speech** grammatical class of words (noun, pronoun, adjective, adverb, verb, etc.); **part-song** song for 3 or more voice parts; **part-time** employed for or occupying less than normal working week etc.; **part-timer** part-time worker.

partake /pɑː'teɪk/ *verb* (**-king**; *past* **partook**; *past participle* **partaken**) (+ *of*, *in*) take share of; (+ *of*) eat or drink some of.

parterre /pɑː'teə/ *noun* level garden space filled with flower-beds etc.; *US* pit of theatre.

partial /'pɑːʃ(ə)l/ *adjective* not total or complete; biased, unfair; (+ *to*) having a liking for. □ **partiality** /-ʃɪ'æl-/ *noun*; **partially** *adverb*.

participate /pɑː'tɪsɪpeɪt/ *verb* (**-ting**) (often + *in*) have share or take part. □ **participant** *noun*; **participation** *noun*.

participle /'pɑːtɪsɪp(ə)l/ *noun* word (either **present participle**, e.g. *writing*, or **past participle**, e.g. *written*) formed from verb and used in complex verb-forms or as adjective. □ **participial** /-'sɪp-/ *adjective*.

particle /'pɑːtɪk(ə)l/ *noun* minute portion of matter; smallest possible amount; minor esp. indeclinable part of speech.

particoloured /'pɑːtɪkʌləd/ *adjective* (*US* **-colored**) of more than one colour.

particular /pə'tɪkjʊlə/ ● *adjective* relating to or considered as one as distinct from others; special; scrupulously exact; fastidious. ● *noun* detail, item; (in *plural*) detailed account. □ **in particular** specifically. □ **particularity** /-'lær-/ *noun*.

particularize /pə'tɪkjʊləraɪz/ *verb* (also **-ise**) (**-zing** or **-sing**) name specially or one by one; specify (items). □ **particularization** *noun*.

particularly *adverb* very; specifically; in a fastidious way.

parting *noun* leave-taking; dividing line of combed hair.

partisan /pɑːtɪ'zæn/ ● *noun* strong supporter of party, side, or cause; guerrilla. ● *adjective* of partisans; biased. □ **partisanship** *noun*.

partition /pɑː'tɪʃ(ə)n/ ● *noun* structure dividing a space, esp. light interior wall; division into parts. ● *verb* divide into parts; (+ *off*) separate with partition.

partitive /'pɑːtɪtɪv/ ● *adjective* (of word) denoting part of collective whole. ● *noun* partitive word.

partly *adverb* with respect to a part; to some extent.

partner /'pɑːtnə/ ● *noun* sharer; person associated with others in business; either of pair in marriage etc. or dancing or game. ● *verb* be partner of. □ **partnership** *noun*.

partridge /'pɑːtrɪdʒ/ *noun* (*plural* same or **-s**) kind of game bird.

parturition /pɑːtjʊ'rɪʃ(ə)n/ *noun formal* childbirth.

party /'pɑːtɪ/ *noun* (*plural* **-ies**) social gathering; group of people travelling or working together; political group putting forward candidates in elections and usually organized on national basis; each side in agreement or dispute. □ **party line** set policy of political party etc., shared telephone line; **party wall** wall common to adjoining rooms, buildings, etc.

parvenu /ˈpɑːvənjuː/ *noun* (*plural* **-s**; *feminine* **parvenue**, *plural* **-s**) newly rich social climber; upstart.

pascal /ˈpæsk(ə)l/ *noun* SI unit of pressure; (**Pascal** /pæsˈkɑːl/) computer language designed for training.

paschal /ˈpæsk(ə)l/ *adjective* of Passover; of Easter.

pasha /ˈpɑːʃə/ *noun historical* Turkish officer of high rank.

pasque-flower /ˈpæskflaʊə/ *noun* kind of anemone.

pass[1] /pɑːs/ ● *verb* move onward, proceed; go past; leave on one side or behind; (cause to) be transferred from one person or place to another; surpass; go unremarked or uncensured; move; cause to go; be successful in (exam); allow (bill in Parliament) to proceed; be approved; elapse; happen; spend (time etc.); *Football etc.* kick, hand, or hit (ball etc.) to player of one's own side; (+ *into*, *from*) change; come to an end; be accepted as adequate; discharge from body as or with excreta; utter (judgement etc.). ● *noun* passing, esp. of exam; status of degree without honours; written permission, ticket, or order; *Football etc.* passing of ball; critical position. □ **make a pass at** *colloquial* make sexual advances to; **pass away** die; **passbook** book recording customer's transactions with bank etc.; **passer-by** (*plural* **passers-by**) person who goes past, esp. by chance; **pass for** be accepted as; **passkey** private key to gate etc., master-key; **pass off** fade away, be carried through (in specified way), lightly dismiss, (+ *as*) misrepresent as something false; **pass on** proceed, die, transmit to next person in a series; **pass out** become unconscious, complete military training; **pass over** omit, overlook, make no remark on, die; **pass round** distribute, give to one person after another; **pass up** *colloquial* refuse or neglect (opportunity etc.); **password** prearranged word or phrase to secure recognition, admission, etc.

pass[2] /pɑːs/ *noun* narrow way through mountains.

passable *adjective* adequate, fairly good.

passage /ˈpæsɪdʒ/ *noun* process or means of passing, transit; passageway; right to pass through; journey by sea or air; transition from one state to another; short part of book or piece of music etc.; duct etc. in body.

passageway *noun* narrow way for passing along; corridor.

passé /ˈpæseɪ/ *adjective* (*feminine* **passée**) outmoded; past its prime.

passenger /ˈpæsɪndʒə/ *noun* traveller in or on vehicle (other than driver, pilot, crew, etc.); *colloquial* idle member of team etc.

passerine /ˈpæsəriːn/ ● *noun* bird able to grip branch etc. with claws. ● *adjective* of passerines.

passim /ˈpæsɪm/ *adverb* throughout. [Latin]

passion /ˈpæʃ(ə)n/ *noun* strong emotion; outburst of anger; intense sexual love; strong enthusiasm; object arousing this; (**the Passion**) sufferings of Christ during his last days, Gospel narrative of this or musical setting of it. □ **passion-flower** plant with flower supposed to suggest instruments of Crucifixion; **passion-fruit** edible fruit of some species of passion-flower. □ **passionless** *adjective*.

passionate /ˈpæʃənət/ *adjective* dominated by, easily moved to, or showing passion. □ **passionately** *adverb*.

passive /ˈpæsɪv/ *adjective* acted upon, not acting; submissive; inert; *Grammar* (of verb) of which subject undergoes action (e.g. *was written* in *it was written by me*). □ **passive smoking** involuntary inhalation of others' cigarette smoke. □ **passively** *adverb*; **passivity** /-ˈsɪv-/ *noun*.

Passover /ˈpɑːsəʊvə/ *noun* Jewish spring festival commemorating Exodus from Egypt.

passport /ˈpɑːspɔːt/ *noun* official document showing holder's identity and nationality etc. and authorizing travel abroad.

past /pɑːst/ ● *adjective* gone by; just over; of former time; *Grammar* expressing past action or state. ● *noun* past time or events; person's past life or career; past tense. ● *preposition* beyond. ● *adverb* so as to pass by. □ **past it** *colloquial* old and useless; **past master** expert.

pasta /ˈpæstə/ *noun* dried flour paste in various shapes.

paste /peɪst/ ● *noun* any moist fairly stiff mixture; dough of flour with fat, water, etc.; flour and water or other mixture as adhesive; meat or fish spread; hard glasslike material used for imitation gems. ● *verb* (**-ting**) fasten or coat with paste; *slang* beat, thrash. □ **pasteboard** stiff substance made by pasting together sheets of paper. □ **pasting** *noun*.

pastel /ˈpæst(ə)l/ ● *noun* pale shade of colour; crayon made of dry pigment-paste; drawing in pastel. ● *adjective* of pale shade of colour.

pastern /ˈpæst(ə)n/ *noun* part of horse's foot between fetlock and hoof.

pasteurize /ˈpɑːstʃəraɪz/ *verb* (also **-ise**) (**-zing** or **-sing**) partially sterilize (milk etc.) by heating. □ **pasteurization** *noun*.

pastiche /pæsˈtiːʃ/ *noun* picture or musical composition made up from various sources; literary or other work imitating style of author or period etc.

pastille /ˈpæstɪl/ *noun* small sweet or lozenge.

pastime /ˈpɑːstaɪm/ *noun* recreation; hobby.

pastor /ˈpɑːstə/ *noun* minister, esp. of Nonconformist church.

pastoral /ˈpɑːstər(ə)l/ ● *adjective* of shepherds; of (esp. romanticized) rural life; of pastor. ● *noun* pastoral poem, play, picture, etc; letter from bishop or other pastor to clergy or people.

pastrami /pæˈstrɑːmɪ/ *noun* seasoned smoked beef.

pastry /ˈpeɪstrɪ/ *noun* (*plural* **-ies**) dough of flour, fat, and water; (item of) food made wholly or partly of this.

pasturage *noun* pasture land; pasturing.

pasture /ˈpɑːstʃə/ ● *noun* land covered with grass etc. for grazing animals; herbage for animals. ● *verb* (**-ring**) put (animals) to pasture; graze.

pasty[1] /ˈpæstɪ/ *noun* (*plural* **-ies**) pie of meat etc. wrapped in pastry and baked without dish.

pasty[2] /ˈpeɪstɪ/ *adjective* (**-ier**, **-iest**) pallid.

pat[1] ● *verb* (**-tt-**) strike gently with flat palm or other flat surface, esp. in affection etc. ● *noun* light stroke or tap, esp. with hand in affection etc.; patting sound; small mass, esp. of butter, made (as) by patting.

pat[2] ● *adjective* known thoroughly; apposite, opportune, esp. glibly so. ● *adverb* in a pat way. □ **have off pat** have memorized perfectly.

patch ● *noun* piece put on in mending or as reinforcement; cover protecting injured eye; large or irregular spot on surface; distinct area or period; small plot of ground. ● *verb* mend with patch(es); (often + *up*) piece together; (+ *up*) settle (quarrel etc.), esp. hastily. □ **not a patch on** *colloquial* very much inferior to; **patchwork** stitching together of small pieces of differently coloured cloth to form pattern.

patchy *adjective* (**-ier**, **-iest**) uneven in quality; having patches. □ **patchily** *adverb*.

pate *noun colloquial* head.

pâté /'pæteɪ/ *noun* smooth paste of meat etc. □ ***pâté de foie gras*** /də fwɑ: 'grɑ:/ pâté made from livers of fatted geese.

patella /pə'telə/ *noun* (*plural* **patellae** /-li:/) kneecap.

paten /'pæt(ə)n/ *noun* plate for bread at Eucharist.

patent /'peɪt(ə)nt, 'pæt-/ ● *noun* official document conferring right, title, etc., esp. sole right to make, use, or sell some invention; invention or process so protected. ● *adjective* /'peɪt(ə)nt/ plain, obvious; conferred or protected by patent; (of food, medicine, etc.) proprietary. ● *verb* obtain patent for (invention). □ **patent leather** glossy varnished leather. □ **patently** *adverb.*

patentee /peɪtən'ti:/ *noun* holder of patent.

paterfamilias /peɪtəfə'mɪlɪæs/ *noun* male head of family etc.

paternal /pə'tɜ:n(ə)l/ *adjective* of father, fatherly; related through father.

paternalism *noun* policy of restricting freedom and responsibility by well-meant regulations. □ **paternalistic** /-'lɪs-/ *adjective.*

paternity /pə'tɜ:nɪtɪ/ *noun* fatherhood; one's paternal origin.

paternoster /pætə'nɒstə/ *noun* Lord's Prayer, esp. in Latin.

path /pɑ:θ/ *noun* (*plural* **paths** /pɑ:ðz/ footway, track; line along which person or thing moves. □ **pathway** path, its course.

pathetic /pə'θetɪk/ *adjective* exciting pity, sadness, or contempt. □ **pathetically** *adverb.*

pathogen /'pæθədʒ(ə)n/ *noun* agent causing disease. □ **pathogenic** /-'dʒen-/ *adjective.*

pathological /pæθə'lɒdʒɪk(ə)l/ *adjective* of pathology; of or caused by mental or physical disorder. □ **pathologically** *adverb.*

pathology /pə'θɒlədʒɪ/ *noun* study of disease. □ **pathologist** *noun.*

pathos /'peɪθɒs/ *noun* quality that excites pity or sadness.

patience /'peɪʃ(ə)ns/ *noun* ability to endure delay, hardship, provocation, pain, etc.; perseverance; solo card game.

patient ● *adjective* having or showing patience. ● *noun* person under medical etc. treatment. □ **patiently** *adverb.*

patina /'pætɪnə/ *noun* (*plural* **-s**) film, usually green, on surface of old bronze etc.; gloss produced by age on woodwork etc.

patio /'pætɪəʊ/ *noun* (*plural* **-s**) paved usually roofless area adjoining house; roofless inner courtyard.

patisserie /pə'ti:sərɪ/ *noun* shop where pastries are made and sold; pastries collectively.

patois /'pætwɑ:/ *noun* (*plural* same /-wɑ:z/) regional dialect differing from literary language.

patriarch /'peɪtrɪɑ:k/ *noun* male head of family or tribe; chief bishop in Orthodox and RC Churches; venerable old man. □ **patriarchal** /-'ɑ:k-/ *adjective.*

patriarchate /'peɪtrɪɑ:kət/ *noun* office, see, or residence of patriarch; rank of tribal patriarch.

patriarchy /'peɪtrɪɑ:kɪ/ *noun* (*plural* **-ies**) male-dominated social system, with descent reckoned through male line.

patrician /pə'trɪʃ(ə)n/ ● *noun* person of noble birth, esp. in ancient Rome. ● *adjective* of nobility; aristocratic.

patricide /'pætrɪsaɪd/ *noun* parricide. □ **patricidal** /-'saɪd(ə)l/ *adjective.*

patrimony /'pætrɪmənɪ/ *noun* (*plural* **-ies**) property inherited from father or ancestors; heritage.

patriot /'peɪtrɪət/ *noun* person devoted to and ready to defend his or her country. □ **patriotic** /-'ɒt-/ *adjective*; **patriotism** *noun.*

patrol /pə'trəʊl/ ● *noun* act of walking or travelling round area etc. to protect or supervise it; person(s) or vehicle(s) sent out on patrol; unit of usually 6 in Scout troop or Guide company. ● *verb* (**-ll-**) carry out patrol of; act as patrol. □ **patrol car** car used by police etc. for patrol.

patron /'peɪtrən/ *noun* (*feminine* **patroness**) person who gives financial or other support; customer of shop etc. □ **patron saint** saint regarded as protecting person, place, activity, etc.

patronage /'pætrənɪdʒ/ *noun* patron's or customer's support; right of bestowing or recommending for appointments; condescending manner.

patronize /'pætrənaɪz/ *verb* (also **-ise**) (**-zing** or **-sing**) treat condescendingly; act as patron to; be customer of. □ **patronizing** *adjective.*

patronymic /pætrə'nɪmɪk/ *noun* name derived from that of father or ancestor.

patten /'pæt(ə)n/ *noun historical* wooden sole mounted on iron ring for raising wearer's shoe above mud etc.

patter[1] /'pætə/ ● *noun* sound of quick light taps or steps. ● *verb* (of rain etc.) make this sound.

patter[2] /'pætə/ ● *noun* rapid often glib or deceptive talk. ● *verb* say or talk glibly.

pattern /'pæt(ə)n/ ● *noun* decorative design on surface; regular or logical form, order, etc.; model, design, or instructions from which thing is to be made; excellent example. ● *verb* decorate with pattern; model (thing) on design etc.

patty /'pætɪ/ *noun* (*plural* **-ies**) small pie or pasty.

paucity /'pɔ:sɪtɪ/ *noun* smallness of number or quantity.

paunch /pɔ:ntʃ/ *noun* belly, stomach. □ **paunchy** *adjective.*

pauper /'pɔ:pə/ *noun* very poor person. □ **pauperism** *noun.*

pause /pɔ:z/ ● *noun* temporary stop or silence; *Music* mark denoting lengthening of note or rest. ● *verb* (**-sing**) make a pause; wait.

pavane /pə'vɑ:n/ *noun* (also **pavan** /'pæv(ə)n/) *historical* stately dance; music for this.

pave *verb* (**-ving**) cover (street, floor, etc.) with durable surface. □ **pave the way** (usually + *for*) make preparations. □ **paving** *noun.*

pavement *noun* paved footway at side of road. □ **pavement artist** artist who draws in chalk on pavement for tips.

pavilion /pə'vɪljən/ *noun* building on sports ground for spectators or players; summer house etc. in park; large tent; building or stand at exhibition.

pavlova /pæv'ləʊvə/ *noun* meringue dessert with cream and fruit filling.

paw ● *noun* foot of animal with claws; *colloquial* person's hand. ● *verb* touch with paw; *colloquial* fondle awkwardly or indecently.

pawn[1] *noun* chessman of smallest size and value; person subservient to others' plans.

pawn[2] *verb* deposit (thing) as security for money borrowed; pledge. □ **in pawn** held as security; **pawnbroker** person who lends money at interest on security of personal property; **pawnshop** pawnbroker's place of business.

pawpaw /'pɔ:pɔ:/ *noun* (also **papaya** /pə'paɪə/) pear-shaped mango-like fruit with pulpy orange flesh; tropical tree bearing this.

pay ● *verb* (*past & past participle* **paid**) discharge debt to; give as due; render, bestow (attention etc.); yield adequate return; let out (rope) by slackening it; reward or punish. ● *noun* wages. □ **in the pay of** employed by; **pay-as-you-earn** collection of income tax by deduction at source from wages etc.; **pay-claim** demand for increase in pay; **payday** day on which wages are paid; **pay for** hand over money for, bear cost of, suffer or be punished for; **paying guest** lodger; **payload** part of (esp. aircraft's) load from which revenue is derived; **paymaster** official who pays troops, workmen, etc.; **Paymaster General** Treasury minister responsible for payments; **pay off** pay in full and discharge, *colloquial* yield good results; **pay-off** *slang* payment, climax, end result; **pay phone** coin box telephone; **payroll** list of employees receiving regular pay. ▫ **payee** /peɪ'i:/ *noun*.

payable *adjective* that must or may be paid.

PAYE *abbreviation* pay-as-you-earn.

payment *noun* paying, amount paid; recompense.

payola /peɪ'əʊlə/ *noun esp. US slang* bribe offered for unofficial media promotion of product etc.

PC *abbreviation* Police Constable; personal computer; politically correct; political correctness; Privy Councillor.

p.c. *abbreviation* per cent; postcard.

pd. *abbreviation* paid.

PE *abbreviation* physical education.

pea *noun* climbing plant bearing round edible seeds in pods; one of its seeds; similar plant. ▫ **pea-souper** *colloquial* thick yellowish fog.

peace *noun* quiet, calm; freedom from or cessation of war; civil order. ▫ **peacemaker** person who brings about peace; **peacetime** time when country is not at war.

peaceable *adjective* disposed or tending to peace, peaceful.

peaceful *adjective* characterized by or not infringing peace. ▫ **peacefully** *adverb*; **peacefulness** *noun*.

peach[1] *noun* roundish juicy fruit with downy yellow or rosy skin; tree bearing it; yellowish-pink colour; *colloquial* person or thing of superlative merit. ▫ **peach Melba** dish of ice cream and peaches. ▫ **peachy** *adjective* (**-ier**, **-iest**).

peach[2] *verb colloquial* turn informer; inform.

peacock /'pi:kɒk/ *noun* (*plural* same or **-s**) male peafowl, bird with brilliant plumage and erectile fanlike tail. ▫ **peacock blue** bright lustrous greenish blue of peacock's neck; **peacock butterfly** butterfly with eyelike markings resembling those on peacock's tail.

peafowl /'pi:faʊl/ *noun* kind of pheasant, peacock or peahen.

peahen /'pi:hen/ *noun* female peafowl.

peak[1] ● *noun* pointed top, esp. of mountain; stiff projecting brim at front of cap; highest point of achievement, intensity, etc. ● *verb* reach highest value, quality, etc.

peak[2] *verb* waste away; (as **peaked** *adjective*) pinched-looking.

peaky *adjective* (**-ier**, **-iest**) sickly, puny.

peal ● *noun* loud ringing of bell(s); set of bells; loud repeated sound. ● *verb* (cause to) sound in peal; utter sonorously.

peanut *noun* plant bearing underground pods containing seeds used as food and yielding oil; its seed; (in *plural*) *colloquial* trivial amount, esp. of money. ▫ **peanut butter** paste of ground roasted peanuts.

pear /peə/ *noun* fleshy fruit tapering towards stalk; tree bearing it.

pearl /pɜ:l/ ● *noun* rounded lustrous usually white solid formed in shell of certain oysters and prized as gem; imitation of this; precious thing, finest example. ● *verb poetical* (of moisture) form drops, form drops on; fish for pearls. ▫ **pearl barley** barley rubbed into small rounded grains; **pearl button** button of (real or imitation) mother-of-pearl.

pearly ● *adjective* (**-ier**, **-iest**) resembling a pearl; adorned with pearls. ● *noun* (*plural* **-ies**) pearly king or queen; (in *plural*) pearly king's or queen's clothes. ▫ **Pearly Gates** *colloquial* gates of Heaven; **pearly king**, **queen** London costermonger, or his wife, wearing clothes covered with pearl buttons.

peasant /'pez(ə)nt/ *noun* (in some countries) worker on land, farm labourer; small farmer; *derogatory* lout, boor. ▫ **peasantry** *noun* (*plural* **-ies**).

pease-pudding /pi:z/ *noun* dried peas boiled in cloth.

peat *noun* vegetable matter decomposed by water and partly carbonized; piece of this as fuel. ▫ **peatbog** bog composed of peat. ▫ **peaty** *adjective*.

pebble /'peb(ə)l/ *noun* small stone made smooth by action of water. ▫ **pebble-dash** mortar with pebbles in it as wall-coating. ▫ **pebbly** *adjective*.

pecan /'pi:kən/ *noun* pinkish-brown smooth nut; kind of hickory producing it.

peccadillo /pekə'dɪləʊ/ *noun* (*plural* **-es** or **-s**) trivial offence.

peck[1] ● *verb* strike, pick up, pluck out, or make (hole) with beak; kiss hastily or perfunctorily; *colloquial* (+ *at*) eat (meal) listlessly or fastidiously. ● *noun* stroke with beak; hasty or perfunctory kiss. ▫ **pecking order** social hierarchy.

peck[2] *noun* measure of capacity for dry goods (2 gallons, 9.092 litres).

pecker *noun* ▫ **keep your pecker up** *colloquial* stay cheerful.

peckish *adjective colloquial* hungry.

pectin /'pektɪn/ *noun* soluble gelatinous substance in ripe fruits, causing jam etc. to set.

pectoral /'pektər(ə)l/ ● *adjective* of or for breast or chest. ● *noun* pectoral fin or muscle.

peculiar /pɪ'kju:lɪə/ *adjective* odd; (usually + *to*) belonging exclusively; belonging to the individual; particular, special.

peculiarity /pɪkju:lɪ'ærɪtɪ/ *noun* (*plural* **-ies**) oddity; characteristic; being peculiar.

peculiarly *adverb* more than usually, especially; oddly.

pecuniary /pɪ'kju:nɪərɪ/ *adjective* of or in money.

pedagogue /'pedəgɒg/ *noun archaic or derogatory* schoolmaster.

pedagogy /'pedəgɒdʒɪ/ *noun* science of teaching. ▫ **pedagogic(al)** /-'gɒg-/ *adjective*.

pedal /'ped(ə)l/ ● *noun* lever or key operated by foot, esp. in bicycle, motor vehicle, or some musical instruments. ● *verb* (**-ll-**; *US* **-l-**) work pedals (of); ride bicycle. ● *adjective* /'pi:d(ə)l/ of foot or feet.

pedant /'ped(ə)nt/ *noun derogatory* person who insists on strict adherence to literal meaning or formal rules. ▫ **pedantic** /pɪ'dæntɪk/ *adjective*; **pedantry** *noun*.

peddle /'ped(ə)l/ *verb* (**-ling**) sell as pedlar; advocate; sell (drugs) illegally; engage in selling, esp. as pedlar.

peddler *noun* person who sells drugs illegally; *US* = PEDLAR.

pedestal /'pedɪst(ə)l/ *noun* base of column; block on which something stands.

pedestrian /pɪ'destrɪən/ ● *noun* walker, esp. in town. ● *adjective* prosaic, dull. ▫ **pedestrian crossing** part of road where crossing pedestrians have right of way.

pedicure /'pedɪkjʊə/ *noun* care or treatment of feet, esp. of toenails.

pedigree /'pedɪgri:/ *noun* recorded (esp. distinguished) line of descent of person or animal; genealogical table; *colloquial* thing's history.

pediment /'pedɪmənt/ *noun* triangular part crowning front of building, esp. over portico.

pedlar /ˈpedlə/ *noun* (*US* **peddler**) travelling seller of small wares.

pedometer /pɪˈdɒmɪtə/ *noun* instrument for estimating distance travelled on foot.

pedophile *US* = PAEDOPHILE.

peduncle /pɪˈdʌŋk(ə)l/ *noun* stalk of flower, fruit, or cluster, esp. main stalk bearing solitary flower.

pee *colloquial* ● *verb* (**pees**, **peed**) urinate. ● *noun* urination; urine.

peek *noun & verb* peep, glance.

peel ● *verb* strip rind etc. from; (usually + *off*) take off (skin etc.); become bare of bark, skin, etc.; (often + *off*) flake off. ● *noun* rind or outer coating of fruit, potato, etc.

peeling *noun* (usually in *plural*) piece peeled off.

peep[1] ● *verb* look furtively or through narrow aperture; come cautiously or partly into view; emerge. ● *noun* furtive or peering glance; (usually + *of*) first light of dawn. □ **peep-hole** small hole to peep through; **Peeping Tom** furtive voyeur; **peep-show** exhibition of pictures etc. viewed through lens or peep-hole.

peep[2] ● *verb* cheep, squeak. ● *noun* cheep, squeak; slight sound, utterance, or complaint.

peer[1] *verb* look closely or with difficulty.

peer[2] *noun* (*feminine* **peeress**) duke, marquis, earl, viscount, or baron; equal (esp. in civil standing or rank). □ **peer group** person's associates of same status.

peerage *noun* peers as a class; rank of peer or peeress.

peerless *adjective* unequalled.

peeve *colloquial* ● *verb* (**-ving**) (usually as **peeved** *adjective*) irritate. ● *noun* cause or state of annoyance.

peevish *adjective* querulous, irritable. □ **peevishly** *adverb*.

peewit /ˈpi:wɪt/ *noun* lapwing.

peg ● *noun* wooden, metal, etc. bolt or pin for holding things together, hanging things on, etc.; each of pins used to tighten or loosen strings of violin etc.; forked wooden peg etc. for hanging washing on line; drink, esp. of spirits. ● *verb* (**-gg-**) (usually + *down*, *in*, etc.) fix, mark, or hang out (as) with peg(s); keep (prices etc.) stable. □ **off the peg** (of clothes) ready-made; **peg away** (often + *at*) work persistently; **pegboard** board with holes for pegs; **peg out** *slang* die, mark out boundaries of.

pejorative /pɪˈdʒɒrətɪv/ ● *adjective* derogatory. ● *noun* derogatory word.

peke *noun colloquial* Pekingese.

Pekingese /pi:kɪˈni:z/ *noun* (also **Pekinese**) (*plural* same) dog of small short-legged snub-nosed breed with long silky hair.

pelargonium /peləˈgəʊnɪəm/ *noun* plant with showy flowers; geranium.

pelf *noun* money, wealth.

pelican /ˈpelɪkən/ *noun* large waterfowl with pouch below bill for storing fish. □ **pelican crossing** road crossing-place with traffic lights operated by pedestrians.

pellagra /pəˈlægrə/ *noun* deficiency disease with cracking of skin.

pellet /ˈpelɪt/ *noun* small compressed ball of a substance; pill; small shot.

pellicle /ˈpelɪk(ə)l/ *noun* thin skin; membrane; film.

pell-mell /pelˈmel/ *adverb* headlong; in disorder.

pellucid /pɪˈlu:sɪd/ *adjective* transparent, clear.

pelmet /ˈpelmɪt/ *noun* hanging border concealing curtain-rods etc.

pelt[1] ● *verb* assail with missiles, abuse, etc.; (of rain) come down hard; run at full speed. ● *noun* pelting.

pelt[2] *noun* skin of animal, esp. with hair or fur still on it.

pelvis /ˈpelvɪs/ *noun* lower abdominal cavity in most vertebrates, formed by haunch bones etc. □ **pelvic** *adjective*.

pen[1] ● *noun* implement for writing with ink. ● *verb* (**-nn-**) write. □ **penfriend** friend with whom one communicates by letter only; **penknife** small folding knife; **pen-name** literary pseudonym; **pen-pal** *colloquial* penfriend.

pen[2] ● *noun* small enclosure for cows, sheep, poultry, etc. ● *verb* (**-nn-**) enclose; put or keep in confined space.

pen[3] *noun* female swan.

penal /ˈpi:n(ə)l/ *adjective* of or involving punishment; punishable.

penalize /ˈpi:nəlaɪz/ *verb* (also **-ise**) (**-zing** or **-sing**) subject to penalty or disadvantage; make punishable.

penalty /ˈpenəltɪ/ *noun* (*plural* **-ies**) fine or other punishment; disadvantage, loss, etc., esp. as result of one's own actions; disadvantage imposed in sports for breach of rules etc. □ **penalty area** *Football* area in front of goal within which breach of rules involves award of penalty kick for opposing team; **penalty kick** free kick at goal from close range.

penance /ˈpenəns/ *noun* act of self-punishment, esp. imposed by priest, performed as expression of penitence.

pence *plural* of PENNY.

penchant /ˈpɑ̃ʃɑ̃/ *noun* (+ *for*) inclination or liking for.

pencil /ˈpens(ə)l/ ● *noun* instrument for drawing or writing, esp. of graphite enclosed in wooden cylinder or metal case with tapering end; something used or shaped like this. ● *verb* (**-ll-**; *US* **-l-**) write, draw, or mark with pencil.

pendant /ˈpend(ə)nt/ *noun* ornament hung from necklace etc.

pendent /ˈpend(ə)nt/ *adjective formal* hanging; overhanging; pending.

pending /ˈpendɪŋ/ ● *adjective* awaiting decision or settlement. ● *preposition* until; during.

pendulous /ˈpendjʊləs/ *adjective* hanging down; swinging.

pendulum /ˈpendjʊləm/ *noun* (*plural* **-s**) body suspended so as to be free to swing, esp. regulating movement of clock's works.

penetrate /ˈpenɪtreɪt/ *verb* (**-ting**) make way into or through; pierce; permeate; see into or through; be absorbed by the mind; (as **penetrating** *adjective*) having or suggesting insight, (of voice) easily heard above other sounds, piercing. □ **penetrable** /-trəb(ə)l/ *adjective*; **penetration** *noun*.

penguin /ˈpeŋgwɪn/ *noun* flightless seabird of southern hemisphere.

penicillin /penɪˈsɪlɪn/ *noun* antibiotic obtained from mould.

peninsula /pɪˈnɪnsjʊlə/ *noun* piece of land almost surrounded by water or projecting far into sea etc. □ **peninsular** *adjective*.

penis /ˈpi:nɪs/ *noun* sexual and (in mammals) urinatory organ of male animal.

penitent /ˈpenɪt(ə)nt/ ● *adjective* repentant. ● *noun* penitent person; person doing penance. □ **penitence** *noun*; **penitently** *adverb*.

penitential /penɪˈtenʃ(ə)l/ *adjective* of penitence or penance.

penitentiary /penɪˈtenʃərɪ/ ● *noun* (*plural* **-ies**) *US* prison. ● *adjective* of penance or reformatory treatment.

pennant /ˈpenənt/ *noun* tapering flag, esp. that at masthead of ship in commission.

penniless /ˈpenɪlɪs/ *adjective* destitute.

pennon /'penən/ *noun* long narrow triangular or swallow-tailed flag; long pointed streamer on ship.

penny /'penɪ/ *noun* (*plural* **pence** or, for separate coins only, **pennies**) British coin worth 1/100 of pound, or formerly 1/240 of pound. □ **penny-farthing** early kind of bicycle with large front wheel and small rear one; **penny-pinching** *noun* meanness, *adjective* mean; **a pretty penny** a large sum of money.

pennyroyal /penɪ'rɔɪəl/ *noun* creeping kind of mint.

penology /piː'nɒlədʒɪ/ *noun* study of punishment and prison management.

pension[1] /'penʃ(ə)n/ ● *noun* periodic payment made by government, exemployer, private fund, etc. to person above specified age or to retired, widowed, disabled, etc. person. ● *verb* grant pension to. □ **pension off** dismiss with pension.

pension[2] /pɑ̃'sjɔ̃/ *noun* European, esp. French, boarding house. [French]

pensionable *adjective* entitled or entitling person to pension.

pensioner *noun* recipient of (esp. retirement) pension.

pensive /'pensɪv/ *adjective* deep in thought. □ **pensively** *adverb*.

pent *adjective* (often + *in*, *up*) closely confined; shut in.

penta- *combining form* five.

pentacle /'pentək(ə)l/ *noun* figure used as symbol, esp. in magic, e.g. pentagram.

pentagon /'pentəgən/ *noun* plane figure with 5 sides and angles; (**the Pentagon**) (pentagonal headquarters of) leaders of US defence forces. □ **pentagonal** /-'tæg-/ *adjective*.

pentagram /'pentəgræm/ *noun* 5-pointed star.

pentameter /pen'tæmɪtə/ *noun* line of verse with 5 metrical feet.

Pentateuch /'pentətjuːk/ *noun* first 5 books of Old Testament.

pentathlon /pen'tæθlən/ *noun* athletic contest of 5 events. □ **pentathlete** *noun*.

Pentecost /'pentɪkɒst/ *noun* Whit Sunday; Jewish harvest festival 50 days after second day of Passover.

pentecostal /pentɪ'kɒst(ə)l/ *adjective* (of religious group) emphasizing divine gifts, esp. healing, and often fundamentalist.

penthouse /'penthaʊs/ *noun* flat on roof or top floor of tall building.

penultimate /pɪ'nʌltɪmət/ *adjective & noun* last but one.

penumbra /pɪ'nʌmbrə/ *noun* (*plural* **-s** or **-brae** /-briː/) partly shaded region round shadow of opaque body; partial shadow. □ **penumbral** *adjective*.

penurious /pɪ'njʊərɪəs/ *adjective* poor; stingy.

penury /'penjʊrɪ/ *noun* (*plural* **-ies**) destitution, poverty.

peon /'piːən/ *noun* Spanish-American day-labourer.

peony /'piːənɪ/ *noun* (also **paeony**) (*plural* **-ies**) plant with large globular red, pink, or white flowers.

people /'piːp(ə)l/ ● *plural noun* persons in general; (*singular*) race or nation; (**the people**) ordinary people, esp. as electorate; parents or other relatives; subjects. ● *verb* (**-ling**) (usually + *with*) fill with people; populate; (esp. as **peopled** *adjective*) inhabit.

PEP /pep/ *abbreviation* Personal Equity Plan.

pep *colloquial* ● *noun* vigour, spirit. ● *verb* (**-pp-**) (usually + *up*) fill with vigour. □ **pep pill** one containing stimulant drug; **pep talk** exhortation to greater effort or courage.

pepper /'pepə/ ● *noun* hot aromatic condiment from dried berries of some plants; capsicum plant, its fruit. ● *verb* sprinkle or flavour with pepper; pelt with missiles. □ **pepper-and-salt** of closely mingled dark and light colour; **peppercorn** dried pepper berry, (in full **peppercorn rent**) nominal rent; **pepper-mill** mill for grinding peppercorns by hand.

peppermint *noun* species of mint grown for its strong-flavoured oil; sweet flavoured with this oil; the oil.

pepperoni /pepə'rəʊnɪ/ *noun* sausage seasoned with pepper.

peppery *adjective* of, like, or abounding in pepper; hot-tempered.

pepsin /'pepsɪn/ *noun* enzyme contained in gastric juice.

peptic /'peptɪk/ *adjective* digestive. □ **peptic ulcer** one in stomach or duodenum.

per *preposition* for each; by, by means of, through.

peradventure /pərəd'ventʃə/ *adverb archaic* perhaps.

perambulate /pə'ræmbjʊleɪt/ *verb* (**-ting**) walk through, over, or about. □ **perambulation** *noun*.

perambulator *noun formal* pram.

per annum /pər 'ænəm/ *adverb* for each year.

per capita /pə 'kæpɪtə/ *adverb & adjective* for each person.

perceive /pə'siːv/ *verb* (**-ving**) become aware of by one of senses; apprehend; understand. □ **perceivable** *adjective*.

per cent /pə 'sent/ (*US* **percent**) ● *adverb* in every hundred. ● *noun* percentage; one part in every hundred.

percentage *noun* rate or proportion per cent; proportion.

percentile /pə'sentaɪl/ *noun* each of 99 points at which a range of data is divided to make 100 groups of equal size; each of these groups.

perceptible /pə'septɪb(ə)l/ *adjective* that can be perceived. □ **perceptibility** *noun*; **perceptibly** *adverb*.

perception /pə'sepʃ(ə)n/ *noun* act or faculty of perceiving. □ **perceptual** /-'septʃʊəl/ *adjective*.

perceptive /pə'septɪv/ *adjective* sensitive; discerning; capable of perceiving. □ **perceptively** *adverb*; **perceptiveness** *noun*.

perch[1] ● *noun* bird's resting-place above ground; high place for person or thing to rest on; *historical* measure of length (5½ yds). ● *verb* rest or place on perch.

perch[2] *noun* (*plural* same or **-es**) edible spiny-finned freshwater fish.

perchance /pə'tʃɑːns/ *adverb archaic* maybe.

percipient /pə'sɪpɪənt/ *adjective* perceiving; conscious.

percolate /'pɜːkəleɪt/ *verb* (**-ting**) (often + *through*) filter gradually; (of idea etc.) permeate gradually; prepare (coffee) in percolator. □ **percolation** *noun*.

percolator *noun* apparatus for making coffee by circulating boiling water through ground beans.

percussion /pə'kʌʃ(ə)n/ *noun* playing of music by striking instruments with sticks etc.; such instruments collectively; gentle tapping of body in medical diagnosis; forcible striking of body against another. □ **percussionist** *noun*; **percussive** *adjective*.

perdition /pə'dɪʃ(ə)n/ *noun* damnation.

peregrine /'perɪgrɪn/ *noun* (in full **peregrine falcon**) kind of falcon.

peremptory /pə'remptərɪ/ *adjective* admitting no denial or refusal; imperious. □ **peremptorily** *adverb*.

perennial /pə'renɪəl/ ● *adjective* lasting through the year; (of plant) living several years; lasting long or for ever. ● *noun* perennial plant. □ **perennially** *adverb*.

perestroika /pere'strɔɪkə/ *noun* (in former USSR) reform of economic and political system.

perfect ● *adjective* /'pɜːfɪkt/ complete; faultless; not deficient; very enjoyable; exact, precise; entire, unqualified; *Grammar* (of tense) expressing completed action. ● *verb* /pə'fekt/ make perfect; complete. ● *noun* /'pɜ:fɪkt/ perfect tense. □ **perfect pitch** *Music* ability to recognize pitch of note.

perfection /pə'fekʃ(ə)n/ *noun* being or making perfect; perfect state; perfect person, specimen, etc.

perfectionism *noun* uncompromising pursuit of perfection. □ **perfectionist** *noun*.

perfectly *adverb* quite, completely; in a perfect way.

perfidy /'pɜ:fɪdɪ/ *noun* breach of faith, treachery. □ **perfidious** /-'fɪd-/ *adjective*.

perforate /'pɜ:fəreɪt/ *verb* (**-ting**) pierce, make hole(s) through; make row of small holes in (paper etc.). □ **perforation** *noun*.

perforce /pə'fɔ:s/ *adverb archaic* unavoidably, necessarily.

perform /pə'fɔ:m/ *verb* carry into effect; go through, execute; act, sing, etc., esp. in public; (of animals) do tricks etc. □ **performing arts** drama, music, dance, etc. □ **performer** *noun*.

performance *noun* act, process, or manner of doing or functioning; execution (of duty etc.); performing of or in play etc.; *colloquial* fuss, emotional scene.

perfume /'pɜ:fju:m/ ● *noun* sweet smell; fragrant liquid, esp. for application to the body, scent. ● *verb* (**-ming**) impart perfume to.

perfumer /pə'fju:mə/ *noun* maker or seller of perfumes. □ **perfumery** *noun* (*plural* **-ies**).

perfunctory /pə'fʌŋktərɪ/ *adjective* done merely out of duty; superficial. □ **perfunctorily** *adverb*; **perfunctoriness** *noun*.

pergola /'pɜ:gələ/ *noun* arbour or covered walk arched with climbing plants.

perhaps /pə'hæps/ *adverb* it may be, possibly.

perianth /'periænθ/ *noun* outer part of flower.

perigee /'perɪdʒi:/ *noun* point nearest to earth in orbit of moon etc.

perihelion /perɪ'hi:lɪən/ *noun* (*plural* **-lia**) point nearest to sun in orbit of planet, comet, etc. round it.

peril /'perɪl/ *noun* serious and immediate danger. □ **perilous** *adjective*; **perilously** *adverb*.

perimeter /pə'rɪmɪtə/ *noun* circumference or outline of closed figure; length of this; outer boundary.

period /'pɪərɪəd/ ● *noun* amount of time during which something runs its course; distinct portion of history, life, etc.; occurrence of menstruation, time of this; complete sentence; *esp. US* full stop. ● *adjective* characteristic of past period.

periodic /pɪərɪ'ɒdɪk/ *adjective* appearing or recurring at intervals. □ **periodic table** arrangement of chemical elements by atomic number and chemical properties. □ **periodicity** /-rɪə'dɪsɪtɪ/ *noun*.

periodical ● *noun* magazine etc. published at regular intervals. ● *adjective* periodic. □ **periodically** *adverb*.

peripatetic /perɪpə'tetɪk/ *adjective* (of teacher) working in more than one establishment; going from place to place; itinerant.

peripheral /pə'rɪfər(ə)l/ ● *adjective* of minor importance; of periphery. ● *noun* input, output, or storage device connected to computer.

periphery /pə'rɪfərɪ/ *noun* (*plural* **-ies**) bounding line, esp. of round surface; outer or surrounding area.

periphrasis /pə'rɪfrəsɪs/ *noun* (*plural* **-phrases** /-si:z/) circumlocution, roundabout speech or phrase. □ **periphrastic** /perɪ'fræstɪk/ *adjective*.

periscope /'perɪskəʊp/ *noun* apparatus with tube and mirrors or prisms for viewing objects otherwise out of sight.

perish /'perɪʃ/ *verb* suffer destruction, die; lose natural qualities; (cause to) rot or deteriorate; (in *passive*) suffer from cold.

perishable ● *adjective* subject to speedy decay; liable to perish. ● *noun* perishable thing (esp. food).

perisher *noun slang* annoying person.

perishing *colloquial* ● *adjective* confounded; intensely cold. ● *adverb* confoundedly.

peritoneum /perɪtə'ni:əm/ *noun* (*plural* **-s** or **-nea**) membrane lining abdominal cavity. □ **peritoneal** *adjective*.

peritonitis /perɪtə'naɪtɪs/ *noun* inflammation of peritoneum.

periwig /'perɪwɪg/ *noun historical* wig.

periwinkle[1] /'perɪwɪŋk(ə)l/ *noun* evergreen trailing plant with blue or white flower.

periwinkle[2] /'perɪwɪŋk(ə)l/ *noun* winkle.

perjure /'pɜ:dʒə/ *verb* (**-ring**) (**perjure oneself**) commit perjury; (as **perjured** *adjective*) guilty of perjury. □ **perjurer** *noun*.

perjury /'pɜ:dʒərɪ/ *noun* (*plural* **-ies**) wilful lying while on oath.

perk[1] *verb* □ **perk up** (cause to) recover courage, smarten up, raise (head etc.) briskly.

perk[2] *noun colloquial* perquisite.

perky *adjective* (**-ier**, **-iest**) lively and cheerful.

perm[1] ● *noun* permanent wave. ● *verb* give permanent wave to.

perm[2] *colloquial* ● *noun* permutation. ● *verb* make permutation of.

permafrost /'pɜ:məfrɒst/ *noun* permanently frozen subsoil, as in polar regions.

permanent /'pɜ:mənənt/ *adjective* lasting or intended to last indefinitely. □ **permanent wave** long-lasting artificial wave in hair. □ **permanence** *noun*; **permanently** *adverb*.

permeable /'pɜ:mɪəb(ə)l/ *adjective* capable of being permeated. □ **permeability** *noun*.

permeate /'pɜ:mɪeɪt/ *verb* (**-ting**) penetrate, saturate, pervade; be diffused. □ **permeation** *noun*.

permissible /pə'mɪsɪb(ə)l/ *adjective* allowable. □ **permissibility** *noun*.

permission /pə'mɪʃ(ə)n/ *noun* consent, authorization.

permissive /pə'mɪsɪv/ *adjective* tolerant, liberal; giving permission. □ **permissiveness** *noun*.

permit ● *verb* /pə'mɪt/ (**-tt-**) give consent to; authorize; allow; give opportunity; (+ *of*) allow as possible. ● *noun* /'pɜ:mɪt/ written order giving permission or allowing entry.

permutation /pɜ:mjʊ'teɪʃ(ə)n/ *noun* one of possible ordered arrangements of set of things; combination or selection of specified number of items from larger group.

pernicious /pə'nɪʃəs/ *adjective* destructive, injurious. □ **pernicious anaemia** defective formation of red blood cells through lack of vitamin B.

pernickety /pə'nɪkɪtɪ/ *adjective colloquial* fastidious, over-precise.

peroration /perə'reɪʃ(ə)n/ *noun* concluding part of speech.

peroxide /pə'rɒksaɪd/ ● *noun* (in full **hydrogen peroxide**) colourless liquid used in water solution, esp. to bleach hair; oxide containing maximum proportion of oxygen. ● *verb* (**-ding**) bleach (hair) with peroxide.

perpendicular /pɜ:pən'dɪkjʊlə/ ● *adjective* (usually + *to*) at right angles; upright; very steep; (**Perpendicular**) of or in style of English Gothic architecture of 15th & 16th c. ● *noun* perpendicular line etc. □ **perpendicularity** /-'lærɪtɪ/ *noun*.

perpetrate /'pɜ:pɪtreɪt/ *verb* (**-ting**) commit. □ **perpetration** *noun*; **perpetrator** *noun*.

perpetual /pə'petʃʊəl/ *adjective* lasting for ever or indefinitely; continuous; *colloquial* frequent. □ **perpetually** *adverb*.

perpetuate /pə'petʃʊeɪt/ *verb* (**-ting**) make perpetual; cause to be always remembered. ▫ **perpetuation** *noun*.

perpetuity /pɜːpɪ'tjuːɪtɪ/ *noun* (*plural* **-ies**) perpetual continuance or possession. ▫ **in perpetuity** for ever.

perplex /pə'pleks/ *verb* bewilder, puzzle; complicate, tangle. ▫ **perplexing** *adjective*; **perplexity** *noun*.

per pro. /pɜː 'prəʊ/ *abbreviation* through the agency of (used in signatures) (*per procurantionem*). [Latin].

■ **Usage** The abbreviation *per pro.* (or *p.p.*) is frequently written before the wrong name: "T. Jones, *p.p.* P. Smith" means that P. Smith is signing on behalf of T. Jones.

perquisite /'pɜːkwɪzɪt/ *noun* extra profit additional to main income etc.; customary extra right or privilege.

■ **Usage** *Perquisite* is sometimes confused with *prerequisite*, which means 'a thing required as a precondition'.

perry /'perɪ/ *noun* (*plural* **-ies**) drink made from fermented pear juice.

per se /pɜː 'seɪ/ *adverb* by or in itself, intrinsically. [Latin]

persecute /'pɜːsɪkjuːt/ *verb* (**-ting**) subject to constant hostility and ill-treatment; harass, worry. ▫ **persecution** /-'kjuːʃ(ə)n/ *noun*; **persecutor** *noun*.

persevere /pɜːsɪ'vɪə/ *verb* (**-ring**) continue steadfastly, persist. ▫ **perseverance** *noun*.

Persian /'pɜːʃ(ə)n/ ● *noun* native, national, or language of Persia (now Iran); (in full **Persian cat**) cat with long silky hair. ● *adjective* of Persia (Iran). ▫ **Persian lamb** silky curled fur of young karakul.

persiflage /'pɜːsɪflɑːʒ/ *noun* banter; light raillery.

persimmon /pɜː'sɪmən/ *noun* tropical tree; its edible orange tomato-like fruit.

persist /pə'sɪst/ *verb* (often + *in*) continue to exist or do something in spite of obstacles. ▫ **persistence** *noun*; **persistent** *adjective*; **persistently** *adverb*.

person /'pɜːs(ə)n/ *noun* individual human being; living body of human being; *Grammar* one of 3 classes of pronouns, verb-forms, etc., denoting person etc. speaking, spoken to, or spoken of. ▫ **in person** physically present.

persona /pə'səʊnə/ *noun* (*plural* **-nae** /-niː/) aspect of personality as perceived by others. ▫ ***persona grata*** /'grɑːtə/ (*plural* ***personae gratae*** /-niː, -tiː/) person acceptable to certain others; ***persona non grata*** /nɒn/ (*plural* ***personae non gratae***) person not acceptable.

personable *adjective* pleasing in appearance or demeanour.

personage *noun* person, esp. important one.

personal /'pɜːsən(ə)l/ *adjective* one's own; individual, private; done etc. in person; directed to or concerning individual; referring (esp. in hostile way) to individual's private life; *Grammar* of or denoting one of the 3 persons. ▫ **personal column** part of newspaper devoted to private advertisements and messages; **personal computer** computer designed for use by single individual; **personal equity plan** scheme for taxfree personal investments; **personal organizer** means of keeping track of personal affairs, esp. loose-leaf notebook divided into sections; **personal pronoun** pronoun replacing subject, object, etc., of clause etc.; **personal property** all property except land.

personality /pɜːsə'nælɪtɪ/ *noun* (*plural* **-ies**) distinctive personal character; well-known person; (in *plural*) personal remarks.

personalize *verb* (also **-ise**) (**-zing** or **-sing**) identify as belonging to particular person.

personally *adverb* in person; for one's own part; in a personal way.

personification /pəsɒnɪfɪ'keɪʃ(ə)n/ *noun* type of metaphor in which human qualities are attributed to object, plant, animal, nature, etc., e.g. *Life can play some nasty tricks*.

personify /pə'sɒnɪfaɪ/ *verb* (**-ies**, **-ied**) attribute human characteristics to; symbolize by human figure; (usually as **personified** *adjective*) embody, exemplify typically. ▫ **personification** *noun*.

personnel /pɜːsə'nel/ *noun* staff of an organization; people engaged in particular service, profession, etc. ▫ **personnel department** department of firm etc. dealing with appointment, training, and welfare of employees.

perspective /pə'spektɪv/ ● *noun* art of drawing so as to give effect of solidity and relative position and size; relation as to position and distance, or proportion between visible objects, parts of subject, etc.; mental view of relative importance of things; view, prospect. ● *adjective* of or in perspective. ▫ **in** or **out of perspective** according or not according to rules of perspective, in or not in proportion.

Perspex /'pɜːspeks/ *noun proprietary term* tough light transparent plastic.

perspicacious /pɜːspɪ'keɪʃəs/ *adjective* having mental penetration or discernment. ▫ **perspicacity** /-'kæs-/ *noun*.

perspicuous /pə'spɪkjʊəs/ *adjective* lucid; clearly expressed. ▫ **perspicuity** /-'kjuː-/ *noun*.

perspire /pə'spaɪə/ *verb* (**-ring**) sweat. ▫ **perspiration** /pɜːspɪ'reɪʃ(ə)n/ *noun*.

persuade /pə'sweɪd/ *verb* (**-ding**) cause (person) by argument etc. to believe or do something; convince.

persuasion /pə'sweɪʒ(ə)n/ *noun* persuading; conviction; religious belief or sect.

persuasive /pə'sweɪsɪv/ *adjective* able or tending to persuade. ▫ **persuasively** *adverb*; **persuasiveness** *noun*.

pert *adjective* saucy, impudent; jaunty. ▫ **pertly** *adverb*; **pertness** *noun*.

pertain /pə'teɪn/ *verb* belong, relate.

pertinacious /pɜːtɪ'neɪʃəs/ *adjective* persistent, obstinate. ▫ **pertinacity** /-'næs-/ *noun*.

pertinent /'pɜːtɪnənt/ *adjective* relevant. ▫ **pertinence** *noun*; **pertinency** *noun*.

perturb /pə'tɜːb/ *verb* throw into agitation; disquiet. ▫ **perturbation** *noun*.

peruke /pə'ruːk/ *noun historical* wig.

peruse /pə'ruːz/ *verb* (**-sing**) read; scan. ▫ **perusal** *noun*.

pervade /pə'veɪd/ *verb* (**-ding**) spread through, permeate; be rife among. ▫ **pervasion** *noun*; **pervasive** *adjective*.

perverse /pə'vɜːs/ *adjective* obstinately or wilfully in the wrong; wayward. ▫ **perversely** *adverb*; **perversity** *noun*.

perversion /pə'vɜːʃ(ə)n/ *noun* perverting, being perverted; preference for abnormal form of sexual activity.

pervert ● *verb* /pə'vɜːt/ turn (thing) aside from proper or normal use; lead astray from right behaviour or belief etc.; (as **perverted** *adjective*) showing perversion. ● *noun* /'pɜːvɜːt/ person who is perverted, esp. sexually.

pervious /'pɜːvɪəs/ *adjective* permeable; allowing passage or access.

peseta /pə'seɪtə/ *noun* Spanish monetary unit.

peso /'peɪsəʊ/ *noun* (*plural* **-s**) monetary unit in several Latin American countries.

pessary /'pesərɪ/ *noun* (*plural* **-ies**) device worn in vagina; vaginal suppository.

pessimism /ˈpesɪmɪz(ə)m/ *noun* tendency to take worst view or expect worst outcome. □ **pessimist** *noun*; **pessimistic** /-ˈmɪst-/ *adjective*.

pest *noun* troublesome or destructive person, animal, or thing.

pester /ˈpestə/ *verb* trouble or annoy, esp. with persistent requests.

pesticide /ˈpestɪsaɪd/ *noun* substance for destroying harmful insects etc.

pestilence /ˈpestɪləns/ *noun* fatal epidemic disease, esp. bubonic plague.

pestilent /ˈpestɪlənt/ *adjective* deadly; harmful or morally destructive.

pestilential /pestɪˈlenʃ(ə)l/ *adjective* of pestilence; pestilent.

pestle /ˈpes(ə)l/ *noun* instrument for pounding substances in a mortar.

pet[1] ● *noun* domestic animal kept for pleasure or companionship; favourite. ● *adjective* as, of, or for a pet; favourite; *expressing fondness*. ● *verb* (**-tt-**) fondle, esp. erotically; treat as pet.

pet[2] *noun* fit of ill humour.

petal /ˈpet(ə)l/ *noun* each division of flower corolla.

peter /ˈpiːtə/ *verb* □ **peter out** diminish, come to an end.

petersham /ˈpiːtəʃəm/ *noun* thick ribbed silk ribbon.

petiole /ˈpetɪəʊl/ *noun* leaf-stalk.

petite /pəˈtiːt/ *adjective* (of woman) of small dainty build. [French]

petit four /petɪˈfɔː/ *noun* (*plural* **petits fours** /ˈfɔːz/) very small fancy cake.

petition /pəˈtɪʃ(ə)n/ ● *noun* request, supplication; formal written request, esp. one signed by many people, to authorities etc. ● *verb* make petition to; ask humbly.

petit point /petɪ ˈpwæ/ *noun* embroidery on canvas using small stitches.

petrel /ˈpetr(ə)l/ *noun* seabird, usually flying far from land.

petrify /ˈpetrɪfaɪ/ *verb* (**-ies**, **-ied**) paralyse with terror or astonishment etc.; turn or be turned into stone. □ **petrifaction** /-ˈfækʃ(ə)n/ *noun*.

petrochemical /petrəʊˈkemɪk(ə)l/ *noun* substance obtained from petroleum or natural gas.

petrodollar /ˈpetrəʊdɒlə/ *noun* notional unit of currency earned by petroleum-exporting country.

petrol /ˈpetr(ə)l/ *noun* refined petroleum used as fuel in motor vehicles, aircraft, etc.

petroleum /pɪˈtrəʊlɪəm/ *noun* hydrocarbon oil found in upper strata of earth, refined for use as fuel etc. □ **petroleum jelly** translucent solid mixture of hydrocarbons got from petroleum and used as lubricant etc.

petticoat /ˈpetɪkəʊt/ *noun* woman's or girl's undergarment hanging from waist or shoulders.

pettifogging /ˈpetɪfɒgɪŋ/ *adjective* quibbling; petty; dishonest.

pettish *adjective* fretful, peevish.

petty /ˈpetɪ/ *adjective* (**-ier**, **-iest**) unimportant, trivial; small-minded; minor, inferior. □ **petty cash** money kept for small items of expenditure; **petty officer** naval NCO. □ **pettiness** *noun*.

petulant /ˈpetjʊlənt/ *adjective* peevishly impatient or irritable. □ **petulance** *noun*; **petulantly** *adverb*.

petunia /pɪˈtjuːnɪə/ *noun* cultivated plant with vivid funnel-shaped flowers.

pew *noun* (in church) enclosed compartment or fixed bench with back; *colloquial* seat.

pewter /ˈpjuːtə/ *noun* grey alloy of tin, antimony, and copper; articles made of this.

peyote /peɪˈəʊtɪ/ *noun* a Mexican cactus; hallucinogenic drug prepared from it.

pfennig /ˈfenɪg/ *noun* one-hundredth of Deutschmark.

PG *abbreviation* (of film) classified as suitable for children subject to parental guidance.

pH /piːˈeɪtʃ/ *noun* measure of acidity or alkalinity of a solution.

phagocyte /ˈfægəsaɪt/ *noun* blood corpuscle etc. capable of absorbing foreign matter.

phalanx /ˈfælæŋks/ *noun* (*plural* **phalanxes** or **phalanges** /fəˈlændʒiːz/) group of infantry in close formation; united or organized party or company.

phallus /ˈfæləs/ *noun* (*plural* **phalli** /-laɪ/ or **phalluses**) (esp. erect) penis; image of this. □ **phallic** *adjective*.

phantasm /ˈfæntæz(ə)m/ *noun* illusion; phantom. □ **phantasmal** /-ˈtæzm(ə)l/ *adjective*.

phantasmagoria /fæntæzməˈgɔːrɪə/ *noun* shifting scene of real or imaginary figures. □ **phantasmagoric** /-ˈgɒrɪk/ *adjective*.

phantom /ˈfæntəm/ ● *noun* spectre, apparition; mental illusion. ● *adjective* illusory.

Pharaoh /ˈfeərəʊ/ *noun* ruler of ancient Egypt.

Pharisee /ˈfærɪsiː/ *noun* member of ancient Jewish sect distinguished by strict observance of traditional and written law; self-righteous person; hypocrite. □ **Pharisaic** /-ˈseɪɪk/ *adjective*.

pharmaceutical /fɑːməˈsjuːtɪk(ə)l/ *adjective* of pharmacy; of use or sale of medicinal drugs. □ **pharmaceutics** *noun*.

pharmacist /ˈfɑːməsɪst/ *noun* person qualified to practise pharmacy.

pharmacology /fɑːməˈkɒlədʒɪ/ *noun* study of action of drugs on the body. □ **pharmacological** /-kəˈlɒdʒ-/ *adjective*; **pharmacologist** *noun*.

pharmacopoeia /fɑːməkəˈpiːə/ *noun* book with list of drugs and directions for use; stock of drugs.

pharmacy /ˈfɑːməsɪ/ *noun* (*plural* **-ies**) preparation and dispensing of drugs; pharmacist's shop; dispensary.

pharynx /ˈfærɪŋks/ *noun* (*plural* **pharynges** /-rɪndʒiːz/ or **-xes**) cavity behind mouth and nose. □ **pharyngeal** /færɪnˈdʒiːəl/ *adjective*.

phase /feɪz/ ● *noun* stage of development, process, or recurring sequence; aspect of moon or planet. ● *verb* (**-sing**) carry out by phases. □ **phase in, out** bring gradually into or out of use.

Ph.D. *abbreviation* Doctor of Philosophy.

pheasant /ˈfez(ə)nt/ *noun* long-tailed game bird.

phenomenal /fɪˈnɒmɪn(ə)l/ *adjective* extraordinary, remarkable; of or concerned with phenomena. □ **phenomenally** *adverb*.

phenomenon /fɪˈnɒmɪnən/ *noun* (*plural* **-mena**) observed or apparent object, fact, or occurrence; remarkable person or thing.

■ **Usage** It is a mistake to use the plural form *phenomena* when only one phenomenon is meant.

phew /fjuː/ *interjection expressing disgust, relief, etc.*

phial /ˈfaɪəl/ *noun* small glass bottle.

philander /fɪˈlændə/ *verb* flirt or have casual affairs with women. □ **philanderer** *noun*.

philanthropy /fɪˈlænθrəpɪ/ *noun* love of all humankind; practical benevolence. □ **philanthropic** /-ˈθrɒp-/ *adjective*; **philanthropist** *noun*.

philately /fɪˈlætəlɪ/ *noun* stamp-collecting. □ **philatelist** *noun*.

philharmonic /fɪlhɑːˈmɒnɪk/ *adjective* devoted to music.

philippic /fɪˈlɪpɪk/ *noun* bitter verbal attack.

philistine /ˈfɪlɪstaɪn/ ● *noun* person who is hostile or indifferent to culture. ● *adjective* hostile or indifferent to culture. □ **philistinism** /-stɪn-/ *noun*.

Phillips /ˈfɪlɪps/ *noun proprietary term* □ **Phillips screw, screwdriver** screw with cross-shaped slot, corresponding screwdriver.

philology /fɪˈlɒlədʒɪ/ *noun* study of language. □ **philological** /-ləˈlɒdʒ-/ *adjective*; **philologist** *noun*.

philosopher /fɪˈlɒsəfə/ *noun* expert in or student of philosophy; person who acts philosophically.

philosophical /fɪləˈsɒfɪk(ə)l/ *adjective* (also **philosophic**) of or according to philosophy; calm under adverse circumstances. □ **philosophically** *adverb*.

philosophize /fɪˈlɒsəfaɪz/ *verb* (also **-ise**) (**-zing** or **-sing**) reason like philosopher; theorize.

philosophy /fɪˈlɒsəfɪ/ *noun* (*plural* **-ies**) use of reason and argument in seeking truth and knowledge, esp. of ultimate reality or of general causes and principles; philosophical system; system for conduct of life.

philtre /ˈfɪltə/ *noun* (*US* **philter**) love potion.

phlebitis /flɪˈbaɪtɪs/ *noun* inflammation of vein. □ **phlebitic** /-ˈbɪt-/ *adjective*.

phlegm /flem/ *noun* bronchial mucus ejected by coughing; calmness; sluggishness.

phlegmatic /flegˈmætɪk/ *adjective* calm; sluggish.

phlox /flɒks/ *noun* (*plural* same or **-es**) plant with clusters of white or coloured flowers.

phobia /ˈfəʊbɪə/ *noun* abnormal fear or aversion. □ **phobic** *adjective & noun*.

phoenix /ˈfi:nɪks/ *noun* bird, the only one of its kind, fabled to burn itself and rise from its ashes.

phone *noun & verb* (**-ning**) *colloquial* telephone. □ **phone book** telephone directory; **phonecard** card holding prepaid units for use with cardphone; **phone-in** broadcast programme in which listeners or viewers participate by telephone.

phonetic /fəˈnetɪk/ *adjective* of or representing vocal sounds; (of spelling) corresponding to pronunciation. □ **phonetically** *adverb*.

phonetics *plural noun* (usually treated as *singular*) study or representation of vocal sounds. □ **phonetician** /fəʊnɪˈtɪʃ(ə)n/ *noun*.

phoney /ˈfəʊnɪ/ (also **phony**) *colloquial* ● *adjective* (**-ier**, **-iest**) false, sham, counterfeit. ● *noun* (*plural* **-eys** or **-ies**) phoney person or thing. □ **phoniness** *noun*.

phonic /ˈfɒnɪk/ *adjective* of (vocal) sound.

phonograph /ˈfəʊnəgrɑ:f/ *noun* early form of gramophone.

phonology /fəˈnɒlədʒɪ/ *noun* study of sounds in language. □ **phonological** /fəʊnəˈlɒdʒɪk(ə)l/ *adjective*.

phony = PHONEY.

phosphate /ˈfɒsfeɪt/ *noun* salt of phosphoric acid, esp. used as fertilizer.

phosphorescence /fɒsfəˈres(ə)ns/ *noun* emission of light without combustion or perceptible heat. □ **phosphoresce** *verb* (**-cing**); **phosphorescent** *adjective*.

phosphorus /ˈfɒsfərəs/ *noun* nonmetallic element occurring esp. as waxlike substance appearing luminous in dark. □ **phosphoric** /-ˈfɒrɪk/ *adjective*; **phosphorous** *adjective*.

photo /ˈfəʊtəʊ/ *noun* (*plural* **-s**) photograph. □ **photo finish** close finish of race in which winner is distinguishable only on photograph; **photofit** picture of suspect constructed from composite photographs.

photo- *combining form* light; photography.

photocopier /ˈfəʊtəʊkɒpɪə/ *noun* machine for photocopying documents.

photocopy /ˈfəʊtəʊkɒpɪ/ ● *noun* (*plural* **-ies**) photographic copy of document. ● *verb* (**-ies, -ied**) make photocopy of.

photoelectric /fəʊtəʊɪˈlektrɪk/ *adjective* with or using emission of electrons from substances exposed to light. □ **photoelectric cell** device using this effect to generate current. □ **photoelectricity** /-ˈtrɪsɪtɪ/ *noun*.

photogenic /fəʊtəʊˈdʒenɪk/ *adjective* looking attractive in photographs; producing or emitting light.

photograph /ˈfəʊtəgrɑ:f/ ● *noun* picture formed by chemical action of light on sensitive film. ● *verb* take photograph (of). □ **photographer** /fəˈtɒgrəfə/ *noun*; **photographic** /-ˈgræf-/ *adjective*; **photography** /fəˈtɒgrəfɪ/ *noun*.

photogravure /fəʊtəʊgrəˈvjʊə/ *noun* picture produced from photographic negative transferred to metal plate and etched in; this process.

photojournalism /fəʊtəʊˈdʒɜ:nəlɪz(ə)m/ *noun* reporting of news by photographs in magazines etc.

photolithography /fəʊtəʊlɪˈθɒgrəfɪ/ *noun* lithography using plates made photographically.

photometer /fəʊˈtɒmɪtə/ *noun* instrument for measuring light. □ **photometric** /fəʊtəʊˈmetrɪk/ *adjective*; **photometry** /-ˈtɒmɪtrɪ/ *noun*.

photon /ˈfəʊtɒn/ *noun* quantum of electromagnetic radiation energy.

Photostat /ˈfəʊtəʊstæt/ ● *noun proprietary term* type of photocopier; copy made by it. ● *verb* (**photostat**) (**-tt-**) make Photostat of.

photosynthesis /fəʊtəʊˈsɪnθəsɪs/ *noun* process in which energy of sunlight is used by green plants to form carbohydrates from carbon dioxide and water. □ **photosynthesize** *verb* (also **-ise**) (**-zing** or **-sing**).

phrase /freɪz/ ● *noun* group of words forming conceptual unit but not sentence (see panel); short pithy expression; *Music* short sequence of notes. ● *verb* (**-sing**) express in words; divide (music) into phrases. □ **phrase book** book listing phrases and their foreign equivalents, for use by tourists etc. □ **phrasal** *adjective*

phraseology /freɪzɪˈɒlədʒɪ/ *noun* (*plural* **-ies**) choice or arrangement of words. □ **phraseological** /-zɪəˈlɒdʒ-/ *adjective*.

phrenology /frɪˈnɒlədʒɪ/ *noun historical* study of external form of cranium as supposed indication of mental faculties etc. □ **phrenologist** *noun*.

phut /fʌt/ *adverb colloquial* □ **go phut** collapse, break down.

phylactery /fɪˈlæktərɪ/ *noun* (*plural* **-ies**) small box containing Hebrew texts, worn by Jewish man at prayer.

phylum /ˈfaɪləm/ *noun* (*plural* **phyla**) major division of plant or animal kingdom.

physic /ˈfɪzɪk/ *noun esp. archaic* medicine; medical art or profession.

physical /ˈfɪzɪk(ə)l/ ● *adjective* of the body; of matter; of nature or according to its laws; of physics. ● *noun US* medical examination. □ **physically** *adverb*.

physician /fɪˈzɪʃ(ə)n/ *noun* doctor, esp. specialist in medical diagnosis and treatment.

physics /ˈfɪzɪks/ *plural noun* (usually treated as *singular*) science of properties and interaction of matter and energy. □ **physicist** *noun*.

physiognomy /fɪzɪˈɒnəmɪ/ *noun* (*plural* **-ies**) features or type of face; art of judging character from face etc.

physiology /fɪzɪˈɒlədʒɪ/ *noun* science of functioning of living organisms. □ **physiological** /-əˈlɒdʒ-/ *adjective*; **physiologist** *noun*.

physiotherapy /fɪzɪəʊˈθerəpɪ/ *noun* treatment of injury or disease by exercise, heat, or other physical agencies. □ **physiotherapist** *noun*.

physique /fɪˈzi:k/ *noun* bodily structure and development.

pi /paɪ/ *noun* sixteenth letter of Greek alphabet (Π, π); (as π) symbol of ratio of circumference of circle to diameter (approx. 3.14).

pia mater /paɪə 'meɪtə/ *noun* inner membrane enveloping brain and spinal cord.

pianissimo /pɪə'nɪsɪməʊ/ *Music* ● *adjective* very soft. ● *adverb* very softly. ● *noun* (*plural* **-s** or **-mi** /-mɪ/) very soft playing, singing, or passage.

pianist /'pɪənɪst/ *noun* player of piano.

piano[1] /pɪ'ænəʊ/ *noun* (*plural* **-s**) keyboard instrument with metal strings struck by hammers. ▫ **piano-accordion** accordion with small keyboard like that of piano.

piano[2] /'pjɑ:nəʊ/ *Music* ● *adjective* soft. ● *adverb* softly. ● *noun* (*plural* **-s** or **-ni** /-nɪ/) soft playing, singing, or passage.

pianoforte /pɪænəʊ'fɔ:tɪ/ *noun formal or archaic* = PIANO[1].

piazza /pɪ'ætsə/ *noun* public square or market-place.

pibroch /'pi:brɒk/ *noun* martial or funeral bagpipe music.

picador /'pɪkədɔ:/ *noun* mounted man with lance in bullfight.

picaresque /pɪkə'resk/ *adjective* (of style of fiction) dealing with episodic adventures of rogues.

piccalilli /pɪkə'lɪlɪ/ *noun* (*plural* **-s**) pickle of chopped vegetables, mustard, and spices.

piccolo /'pɪkələʊ/ *noun* (*plural* **-s**) small high-pitched flute.

pick ● *verb* select carefully; pluck, gather (flower, fruit, etc.); probe with fingers or instrument to remove unwanted matter; clear (bone etc.) of scraps of meat etc.; eat (food, meal, etc.) in small bits. ● *noun* picking, selection; (usually + *of*) best; pickaxe; *colloquial* plectrum; instrument for picking. ▫ **pick a lock** open lock with instrument other than proper key, esp. with criminal intent; **pick on** nag at, find fault with, select; **pickpocket** person who steals from pockets; **pick up** take hold of and lift, acquire casually, learn routinely, stop for and take with one, make acquaintance of casually, recover, improve, arrest, detect, manage to receive (broadcast signal etc.), accept responsibility of paying (bill etc.), resume; **pick-up** person met casually, small open truck, part of record player carrying stylus, device on electric guitar etc. that converts string vibrations into electrical signals, act of picking up; **pick-your-own** (of fruit and vegetables) dug or picked by customer at farm etc.

pickaxe /'pɪkæks/ *noun* (*US* **pickax**) tool with sharp-pointed iron cross-bar for breaking up ground etc.

picket /'pɪkɪt/ ● *noun* one or more people stationed to dissuade workers from entering workplace during strike etc.; pointed stake driven into ground; small group of troops sent to watch for enemy. ● *verb* (**-t-**) place or act as picket outside; post as military picket; secure with stakes. ▫ **picket line** boundary established by workers on strike, esp. at workplace entrance, which others are asked not to cross.

pickings *plural noun* perquisites, gleanings.

pickle /'pɪk(ə)l/ ● *noun* (often in *plural*) vegetables etc. preserved in vinegar etc.; liquid used for this; *colloquial* plight. ● *verb* (**-ling**) preserve in or treat with pickle; (as **pickled** *adjective*) *slang* drunk.

picky *adjective* (**-ier, -iest**) *colloquial* highly fastidious.

picnic /'pɪknɪk/ ● *noun* outing including outdoor meal; such meal; something pleasantly or easily accomplished. ● *verb* (**-ck-**) eat meal outdoors.

pictograph /'pɪktəgrɑ:f/ *noun* (also **pictogram** /-græm/) pictorial symbol used as form of writing.

pictorial /pɪk'tɔ:rɪəl/ *adjective* of, expressed in, or illustrated with a picture or pictures. ▫ **pictorially** *adverb*.

picture /'pɪktʃə/ ● *noun* painting, drawing, photograph, etc., esp. as work of art; portrait; beautiful object; scene; mental image; cinema film; (**the pictures**) cinema (performance). ● *verb* (**-ring**) imagine; represent in picture; describe graphically. ▫ **picture postcard** postcard with picture on one side; **picture window** large window of one pane of glass.

picturesque /pɪktʃə'resk/ *adjective* striking and pleasant to look at; (of language etc.) strikingly graphic.

piddle /'pɪd(ə)l/ *verb* (**-ling**) *colloquial* urinate; (as **piddling** *adjective*) *colloquial* trivial; work or act in trifling way.

pidgin /'pɪdʒɪn/ *noun* simplified language, esp. used between speakers of different languages.

pie *noun* dish of meat, fruit, etc., encased in or covered with pastry etc. and baked. ▫ **pie chart** diagram representing relative quantities as sectors of circle; **pie-eyed** *slang* drunk.

piebald /'paɪbɔ:ld/ ● *adjective* having irregular patches of two colours, esp. black and white. ● *noun* piebald animal.

piece /pi:s/ ● *noun* distinct portion forming part of or broken off from larger object; coin; picture, literary or musical composition; example, item; chessman, man at draughts, etc. ● *verb* (**-cing**) (usually + *together*) form into a whole; join. ▫ **of a piece** uniform or consistent; **piece-work** work paid for according to amount done.

pièce de résistance /pjes də reɪ'zi:stɑ̃s/ *noun* (*plural* **pièces de résistance** same pronunciation) most important or remarkable item.

piecemeal ● *adverb* piece by piece, part at a time. ● *adjective* gradual; unsystematic.

pied /paɪd/ *adjective* of mixed colours.

Phrase

A phrase is a group of words that has meaning but does not have a subject, verb, or object (unlike a clause or sentence). It can be:

1 a noun phrase, functioning as a noun, e.g.

I went to see my friend Tom.
The only ones they have *are too small.*

2 an adjective phrase, functioning as an adjective, e.g.

I was very pleased indeed.
This one is better than mine.

3 an adverb phrase, functioning as an adverb, e.g.

They drove off in their car.
I was there ten days ago.

pied-à-terre /pjeɪdɑː'teə/ *noun* (*plural* ***pieds-*** same pronunciation) (usually small) flat, house, etc. kept for occasional use. [French]

pier /pɪə/ *noun* structure built out into sea etc. used as promenade and landing-stage or breakwater; support of arch or of span of bridge; pillar; solid part of wall between windows etc. □ **pier-glass** large tall mirror.

pierce /pɪəs/ *verb* (**-cing**) go through or into like spear or needle; make hole in; make (hole etc.).

pierrot /'pɪərəʊ/ *noun* (*feminine* **pierrette** /pɪə'ret/) French white-faced pantomime character with clown's costume; itinerant entertainer so dressed.

pietà /pɪe'tɑː/ *noun* representation of Virgin Mary holding dead body of Christ. [Italian]

pietism /'paɪətɪz(ə)m/ *noun* extreme or affected piety.

piety /'paɪətɪ/ *noun* piousness.

piffle /'pɪf(ə)l/ *colloquial* ● *noun* nonsense. ● *verb* (**-ling**) talk or act feebly.

pig ● *noun* wild or domesticated animal with broad snout and stout bristly body; *colloquial* greedy, dirty, obstinate, or annoying person; oblong mass of smelted iron or other metal. ● *verb* (**-gg-**) *colloquial* eat (food) greedily. □ **pigheaded** obstinate; **pig-iron** crude iron from smelting-furnace; **pig it** *colloquial* live in disorderly fashion; **pig out** *esp. US slang* eat greedily; **pigsty** sty for pigs; **pigtail** plait of hair hanging from back or each side of head.

pigeon /'pɪdʒ(ə)n/ *noun* bird of dove family. □ **pigeon-hole** *noun* each of set of compartments in cabinet etc. for papers etc., *verb* classify mentally, put in pigeon-hole, put aside for future consideration; **pigeon-toed** having toes turned inwards.

piggery *noun* (*plural* **-ies**) pig farm; pigsty.

piggish *adjective* greedy; dirty; mean.

piggy ● *noun* (*plural* **-ies**) *colloquial* little pig. ● *adjective* (**-ier**, **-iest**) like a pig; (of features etc.) like those of a pig. □ **piggyback** (a ride) on shoulders and back of another person; **piggy bank** pig-shaped money box.

piglet /'pɪglɪt/ *noun* young pig.

pigment /'pɪgmənt/ ● *noun* coloured substance used as paint etc., or occurring naturally in plant or animal tissue. ● *verb* colour (as) with natural pigment. □ **pigmentation** *noun*.

pigmy = PYGMY.

pike *noun* (*plural* same or **-s**) large voracious freshwater fish; spear formerly used by infantry. □ **pikestaff** wooden shaft of pike (**plain as a pikestaff** quite obvious).

pilaff = PILAU.

pilaster /pɪ'læstə/ *noun* rectangular column, esp. one fastened into wall.

pilau /pɪ'laʊ/ *noun* (also **pilaff** /pɪ'lɑːf/) Middle Eastern or Indian dish of rice with meat, spices, etc.

pilchard /'pɪltʃəd/ *noun* small sea fish related to herring.

pile[1] ● *noun* heap of things laid on one another; large imposing building; *colloquial* large amount, esp. of money; series of plates of dissimilar metals laid alternately for producing electric current; nuclear reactor; pyre. ● *verb* (**-ling**) heap; (+ *with*) load with; (+ *in*, *into*, *on*, *out of*, etc.) crowd. □ **pile up** accumulate, heap up; **pile-up** *colloquial* collision of several motor vehicles.

pile[2] *noun* heavy beam driven vertically into ground as support for building etc.

pile[3] *noun* soft projecting surface of velvet, carpet, etc.

piles *plural noun colloquial* haemorrhoids.

pilfer /'pɪlfə/ *verb* steal or thieve in petty way.

pilgrim /'pɪlgrɪm/ *noun* person who journeys to sacred place; traveller. □ **Pilgrim Fathers** English Puritans who founded colony in Massachusetts in 1620.

pilgrimage *noun* pilgrim's journey.

pill *noun* ball or flat piece of medicinal substance to be swallowed whole; (usually **the pill**) *colloquial* contraceptive pill. □ **pillbox** small round shallow box for pills, hat shaped like this, *Military* small round concrete shelter, mainly underground.

pillage /'pɪlɪdʒ/ *verb* (**-ging**) & *noun* plunder.

pillar /'pɪlə/ *noun* slender upright structure used as support or ornament; person regarded as mainstay; upright mass. □ **pillar-box** public postbox shaped like pillar.

pillion /'pɪljən/ *noun* seat for passenger behind motorcyclist etc.

pillory /'pɪlərɪ/ ● *noun* (*plural* **-ies**) *historical* frame with holes for head and hands, allowing an offender to be exposed to public ridicule. ● *verb* (**-ies**, **-ied**) expose to ridicule; *historical* set in pillory.

pillow /'pɪləʊ/ ● *noun* cushion as support for head, esp. in bed; pillow-shaped support. ● *verb* rest (as) on pillow. □ **pillowcase**, **pillowslip** washable cover for pillow.

pilot /'paɪlət/ ● *noun* person operating controls of aircraft; person in charge of ships entering or leaving harbour etc.; experimental or preliminary study or undertaking; guide, leader. ● *adjective* experimental, preliminary. ● *verb* (**-t-**) act as pilot to; guide course of. □ **pilot-light** small gas burner kept alight to light another; **pilot officer** lowest commissioned rank in RAF.

pimento /pɪ'mentəʊ/ *noun* (*plural* **-s**) allspice; sweet pepper.

pimiento /pɪmɪ'entəʊ/ *noun* (*plural* **-s**) sweet pepper.

pimp ● *noun* person who lives off earnings of prostitute or brothel. ● *verb* act as pimp, esp. procure clients for prostitute.

pimpernel /'pɪmpənel/ *noun* scarlet pimpernel.

pimple /'pɪmp(ə)l/ *noun* small hard inflamed spot on skin. □ **pimply** *adjective*.

pin ● *noun* small thin pointed piece of metal with head, used as fastening; wooden or metal peg, rivet, etc.; (in *plural*) *colloquial* legs. ● *verb* (**-nn-**) fasten with pin(s); transfix with pin, lance, etc.; (usually + *on*) fix (responsibility, blame, etc.); seize and hold fast. □ **pinball** game in which small metal balls are shot across board and strike obstacles; **pincushion** small pad for holding pins; **pin down** (often + *to*) bind (person etc.) to promise, arrangement, etc., make (person) declare position or intentions; **pin-money** small sum of money, esp. earned by woman; **pinpoint** *noun* very small or sharp thing, *adjective* precise, *verb* locate with precision; **pinprick** petty irritation; **pins and needles** tingling sensation in limb recovering from numbness; **pinstripe** very narrow stripe in cloth; **pin-table** table used in pinball; **pintail** duck or grouse with pointed tail; **pin-tuck** narrow ornamental tuck; **pin-up** picture of attractive or famous person, pinned up on wall etc.; **pinwheel** small Catherine wheel.

pina colada /piːnə kə'lɑːdə/ *noun* cocktail of pineapple juice, rum, and coconut.

pinafore /'pɪnəfɔː/ *noun* apron, esp. with bib; (in full **pinafore dress**) dress without collar or sleeves, worn over blouse or jumper.

pince-nez /'pænsneɪ/ *noun* (*plural* same) pair of eyeglasses with spring that clips on nose.

pincers /'pɪnsəz/ *plural noun* gripping-tool forming pair of jaws; pincershaped claw in crustaceans etc. □ **pincer movement** converging movement by two wings of army against enemy position.

pinch ● *verb* grip tightly, esp. between finger and thumb; constrict painfully; (of cold etc.) affect painfully; *slang* steal, arrest; stint, be niggardly. ● *noun* pinching; (as **pinched** *adjective*) (of features) drawn; amount that can be taken up with fingers and thumb; stress of poverty etc. □ **at a pinch** in an emergency.

pinchbeck /ˈpɪntʃbek/ ● *noun* goldlike copper and zinc alloy used in cheap jewellery etc. ● *adjective* spurious, sham.

pine[1] *noun* evergreen needle-leaved coniferous tree; its wood. □ **pine cone** fruit of pine; **pine nut**, **kernel** edible seed of some pines.

pine[2] *verb* (**-ning**) (often + *away*) waste away with grief, disease, etc.; (usually + *for*) long.

pineal /ˈpɪnɪəl/ *adjective* shaped like pine cone. □ **pineal gland**, **body** conical gland in brain, secreting hormone-like substance.

pineapple /ˈpaɪnæp(ə)l/ *noun* large juicy tropical fruit with yellow flesh and tough skin.

ping ● *noun* abrupt single ringing sound. ● *verb* (cause to) emit ping.

ping-pong *noun colloquial* table tennis.

pinion[1] /ˈpɪnjən/ ● *noun* outer part of bird's wing; *poetical* wing; flight feather. ● *verb* cut off pinion of (wing or bird) to prevent flight; restrain by binding arms to sides.

pinion[2] /ˈpɪnjən/ *noun* small cogwheel engaging with larger.

pink[1] ● *noun* pale red colour; garden plant with clove-scented flowers; (**the pink**) the most perfect condition. ● *adjective* pink-coloured; *colloquial* mildly socialist. □ **in the pink** *colloquial* in very good health. □ **pinkish** *adjective*; **pinkness** *noun*.

pink[2] *verb* pierce slightly; cut scalloped or zigzag edge on. □ **pinking shears** dressmaker's serrated shears for cutting zigzag edge.

pink[3] *verb* (of vehicle engine) emit high-pitched explosive sounds caused by faulty combustion.

pinnace /ˈpɪnɪs/ *noun* ship's small boat.

pinnacle /ˈpɪnək(ə)l/ *noun* culmination, climax; natural peak; small ornamental turret crowning buttress, roof, etc.

pinnate /ˈpɪneɪt/ *adjective* (of compound leaf) with leaflets on each side of leaf-stalk.

pinny /ˈpɪnɪ/ *noun* (*plural* **-ies**) *colloquial* pinafore.

pint /paɪnt/ *noun* measure of capacity (1/8 gal., 0.568 litre); *colloquial* pint of beer. □ **pint-sized** *colloquial* very small.

pinta /ˈpaɪntə/ *noun colloquial* pint of milk.

pintle /ˈpɪnt(ə)l/ *noun* bolt or pin, esp. one on which some other part turns.

Pinyin /pɪnˈjɪn/ *noun* system of romanized spelling for transliterating Chinese.

pioneer /paɪəˈnɪə/ ● *noun* beginner of enterprise etc.; explorer or settler. ● *verb* initiate (enterprise etc.) for others to follow; act as pioneer.

pious /ˈpaɪəs/ *adjective* devout, religious; sanctimonious; dutiful. □ **piously** *adverb*.

pip[1] *noun* seed of apple, pear, orange, etc.

pip[2] *noun* short high-pitched sound.

pip[3] *verb* (**-pp-**) *colloquial* hit with a shot; (also **pip at** or **to the post**) defeat narrowly.

pip[4] *noun* each spot on dominoes, dice, or playing cards; star on army officer's shoulder.

pip[5] *noun* disease of poultry etc.; (esp. **the pip**) *colloquial* (fit of) depression, boredom, or bad temper.

pipe ● *noun* tube of earthenware, metal, etc., esp. for carrying gas, water, etc.; narrow tube with bowl at one end containing tobacco for smoking; quantity of tobacco held by this; wind instrument of single tube; each tube by which sound is produced in organ; (in *plural*) bagpipes; tubular organ etc. in body; high note or song, esp. of bird; boatswain's whistle; measure of capacity for wine (105 gals., 477 litres). ● *verb* (**-ping**) convey (as) through pipes; play on pipe; (esp. as **piped** *adjective*) transmit (recorded music etc.) by wire or cable; utter shrilly; summon, lead, etc. by sound of pipe or whistle; trim with piping; furnish with pipe(s). □ **pipeclay** fine white clay for tobacco pipes or for whitening leather etc.; **pipe-cleaner** piece of flexible tuft-covered wire to clean inside tobacco pipe; **pipe down** *colloquial* be quiet; **pipe-dream** extravagant fancy, impossible wish, etc.; **pipeline** pipe conveying oil etc. across country, channel of supply or communication; **pipe up** begin to play, sing, etc.

piper *noun* person who plays on pipe, esp. bagpipes.

pipette /pɪˈpet/ *noun* slender tube for transferring or measuring small quantities of liquid.

piping *noun* ornamentation of dress, upholstery, etc. by means of cord enclosed in pipelike fold; ornamental cordlike lines of sugar etc. on cake etc.; length or system of pipes. □ **piping hot** (of food, water, etc.) very or suitably hot.

pipit /ˈpɪpɪt/ *noun* small bird resembling lark.

pippin /ˈpɪpɪn/ *noun* apple grown from seed; dessert apple.

piquant /ˈpiːkənt/ *adjective* agreeably pungent, sharp, appetizing, stimulating. □ **piquancy** *noun*.

pique /piːk/ ● *verb* (**piques**, **piqued**, **piquing**) wound pride of; stir (curiosity). ● *noun* resentment; hurt pride.

piquet /pɪˈket/ *noun* card game for two players.

piracy /ˈpaɪrəsɪ/ *noun* (*plural* **-ies**) activity of pirate.

piranha /pɪˈrɑːnə/ *noun* voracious S. American freshwater fish.

pirate /ˈpaɪərət/ ● *noun* seafaring robber attacking ships; ship used by pirate; person who infringes copyright or regulations or encroaches on rights of others etc. ● *verb* (**-ting**) reproduce (book etc.) or trade (goods) without permission. □ **piratical** /-ˈræt-/ *adjective*.

pirouette /pɪrʊˈet/ ● *noun* dancer's spin on one foot or point of toe. ● *verb* (**-tting**) perform pirouette.

piscatorial /pɪskəˈtɔːrɪəl/ *adjective* of fishing.

Pisces /ˈpaɪsiːz/ *noun* twelfth sign of zodiac.

piscina /pɪˈsiːnə/ *noun* (*plural* **-nae** /-niː/ or **-s**) stone basin near altar in church, for draining water after use.

pistachio /pɪsˈtɑːʃɪəʊ/ *noun* (*plural* **-s**) kind of nut with green kernel.

piste /piːst/ *noun* ski run of compacted snow.

pistil /ˈpɪstɪl/ *noun* female organ in flowers. □ **pistillate** *adjective*.

pistol /ˈpɪst(ə)l/ *noun* small firearm.

piston /ˈpɪst(ə)n/ *noun* sliding cylinder fitting closely in tube and moving up and down in it, used in steam or petrol engine to impart motion; sliding valve in trumpet etc. □ **piston rod** rod connecting piston to other parts of machine.

pit[1] ● *noun* large hole in ground; coal mine; covered hole as trap; depression in skin or any surface; orchestra pit; (**the pits**) *slang* worst imaginable place, situation, person, etc.; area to side of track where racing cars are refuelled etc. during race; sunken area in floor of workshop etc. for inspection or repair of underside of vehicle etc. ● *verb* (**-tt-**) (usually + *against*) set (one's wits, strength, etc.) in competition; (usually as **pitted** *adjective*) make pit(s) in; store in pit. □ **pit bull terrier** small American dog noted for ferocity; **pitfall** unsuspected danger or drawback, covered pit as trap; **pit-head** top of shaft of coal mine, area surrounding this; **pit of the stomach** hollow below base of breastbone.

pit² *verb* (**-tt-**) (usually as **pitted** *adjective*) remove stones from (fruit).

pita = PITTA.

pit-a-pat /ˈpɪtəpæt/ (also **pitter-patter** /ˈpɪtəpætə/) ● *adverb* with sound as of light quick steps; falteringly. ● *noun* such sound.

pitch¹ ● *verb* set up (esp. tent, camp, etc.) in chosen position; throw; express in particular style or at particular level; fall heavily; (of ship etc.) plunge in lengthwise direction; set at particular musical pitch. ● *noun* area of play in esp. outdoor game; height, degree, intensity, etc.; gradient, esp. of roof; *Music* degree of highness or lowness of tone; act or process of pitching; *colloquial* salesman's persuasive talk; place, esp. in street or market, where one is stationed; distance between successive points, lines, etc. □ **pitched battle** vigorous argument etc., planned battle between sides in prepared positions; **pitched roof** sloping roof; **pitchfork** *noun* fork with long handle and two prongs for tossing hay etc., *verb* (+ *into*) thrust forcibly or hastily into office, position, etc.; **pitch in** *colloquial* set to work vigorously; **pitch into** *colloquial* attack vigorously.

pitch² ● *noun* dark resinous tarry substance. ● *verb* coat with pitch. □ **pitch-black**, **-dark** intensely dark; **pitch pine** resinous kinds of pine. □ **pitchy** *adjective* (**-ier**, **-iest**).

pitchblende /ˈpɪtʃblend/ *noun* uranium oxide yielding radium.

pitcher¹ /ˈpɪtʃə/ *noun* large jug, ewer.

pitcher² *noun* player who delivers ball in baseball.

piteous /ˈpɪtɪəs/ *adjective* deserving or arousing pity. □ **piteously** *adverb*; **piteousness** *noun*.

pith *noun* spongy tissue in stems of plants or lining rind of orange etc.; chief part; vigour, energy. □ **pith helmet** sun-helmet made from dried pith of plants.

pithy /ˈpɪθɪ/ *adjective* (**-ier**, **-iest**) condensed and forcible, terse. □ **pithily** *adverb*; **pithiness** *noun*.

pitiable /ˈpɪtɪəb(ə)l/ *adjective* deserving or arousing pity or contempt. □ **pitiably** *adverb*.

pitiful /ˈpɪtɪfʊl/ *adjective* arousing pity; contemptible. □ **pitifully** *adverb*.

pitiless /ˈpɪtɪlɪs/ *adjective* showing no pity. □ **pitilessly** *adverb*.

piton /ˈpiːtɒn/ *noun* peg driven in to support climber or rope.

pitta /ˈpɪtə/ *noun* (also **pita**) originally Turkish unleavened bread which can be split and filled.

pittance /ˈpɪt(ə)ns/ *noun* scanty allowance, small amount.

pitter-patter = PIT-A-PAT.

pituitary /pɪˈtjuːɪtərɪ/ *noun* (*plural* **-ies**) (in full **pituitary gland**) small ductless gland at base of brain.

pity /ˈpɪtɪ/ ● *noun* sorrow for another's suffering; cause for regret. ● *verb* (**-ies**, **-ied**) feel pity for. □ **pitying** *adjective*.

pivot /ˈpɪvət/ ● *noun* shaft or pin on which something turns; crucial person or point. ● *verb* (**-t-**) turn (as) on pivot; provide with pivot. □ **pivotal** *adjective*.

pixie /ˈpɪksɪ/ *noun* (also **pixy**) (*plural* **-ies**) fairy-like being.

pizza /ˈpiːtsə/ *noun* flat piece of dough baked with topping of cheese, tomatoes, etc.

pizzeria /piːtsəˈriːə/ *noun* pizza restaurant.

pizzicato /pɪtsɪˈkɑːtəʊ/ *Music* ● *adverb* plucking. ● *adjective* performed thus. ● *noun* (*plural* **-s** or **-ti** /-tɪ/) pizzicato note or passage.

pl. *abbreviation* plural; place; plate.

placable /ˈplækəb(ə)l/ *adjective* easily appeased; mild-tempered. □ **placability** *noun*.

placard /ˈplækɑːd/ ● *noun* large notice for public display. ● *verb* post placards on.

placate /pləˈkeɪt/ *verb* (**-ting**) conciliate, pacify. □ **placatory** *adjective*.

place ● *noun* particular part of space; space or room of or for person etc.; city, town, village, residence, building; rank, station, position; building or spot devoted to specified purpose; office, employment; duties of this. ● *verb* (**-cing**) put or dispose in place; assign rank, order, or class to; give (order for goods etc.) to firm etc.; (in *passive*) be among first 3 (or 4) in race. □ **in place** suitable, in the right position; **in place of** instead of; **out of place** unsuitable, in the wrong position; **place-kick** *Football* kick made with ball placed on ground; **place-mat** small mat on table at person's place; **place setting** set of cutlery etc. for one person to eat with; **take place** happen; **take the place of** be substituted for. □ **placement** *noun*.

placebo /pləˈsiːbəʊ/ *noun* (*plural* **-s**) medicine with no physiological effect prescribed for psychological reasons; dummy pill etc. used in controlled trial.

placenta /pləˈsentə/ *noun* (*plural* **-tae** /-tiː/ or **-s**) organ in uterus of pregnant mammal that nourishes foetus. □ **placental** *adjective*.

placid /ˈplæsɪd/ *adjective* calm, unruffled; not easily disturbed. □ **placidity** /plə ˈsɪdɪtɪ/ *noun*; **placidly** *adverb*.

placket /ˈplækɪt/ *noun* opening or slit in garment, for fastenings or access to pocket.

plagiarize /ˈpleɪdʒəraɪz/ *verb* (also **-ise**) (**-zing** or **-sing**) take and use (another's writings etc.) as one's own. □ **plagiarism** *noun*; **plagiarist** *noun*; **plagiarizer** *noun*.

plague /pleɪg/ ● *noun* deadly contagious disease; (+ *of*) *colloquial* infestation; great trouble or affliction. ● *verb* (**plaguing**) *colloquial* annoy, bother; afflict, hinder; affect with plague.

plaice /pleɪs/ *noun* (*plural* same) marine flatfish.

plaid /plæd/ *noun* chequered or tartan, esp. woollen, cloth; long piece of this as part of Highland costume.

plain ● *adjective* clear, evident; readily understood; simple; not beautiful or distinguished-looking; straightforward in speech; not luxurious. ● *adverb* clearly; simply. ● *noun* level tract of country; ordinary stitch in knitting. □ **plain chocolate** chocolate made without milk; **plain clothes** ordinary clothes as distinct from esp. police uniform; **plain flour** flour with no raising agent; **plain sailing** simple situation or course of action; **plainsong** traditional church music sung in unison in medieval modes and free rhythm; **plain-spoken** frank. □ **plainly** *adverb*.

plaint *noun Law* accusation, charge; *literary* lamentation.

plaintiff /ˈpleɪntɪf/ *noun* person who brings case against another in law court.

plaintive /ˈpleɪntɪv/ *adjective* mournful-sounding. □ **plaintively** *adverb*.

plait /plæt/ ● *noun* length of hair, straw, etc. in 3 or more interlaced strands. ● *verb* form into plait.

plan ● *noun* method or procedure for doing something; drawing exhibiting relative position and size of parts of building etc.; diagram; map. ● *verb* (**-nn-**) arrange beforehand, scheme; make plan of; design; (as **planned** *adjective*) in accordance with plan; make plans. □ **plan on** (often + present participle) *colloquial* aim at, intend. □ **planning** *noun*.

planchette /plɑːnˈʃet/ *noun* small board on castors, with pencil, said to write messages from spirits when person's fingers rest on it.

plane¹ ● *noun* flat surface (not necessarily horizontal); *colloquial* aeroplane; level of attainment etc. ● *adjective* level as or lying in a plane.

plane[2] ● *noun* tool for smoothing surface of wood by paring shavings from it. ● *verb* **(-ning)** smooth or pare with plane.

plane[3] *noun* tall spreading broad-leaved tree.

planet /ˈplænɪt/ *noun* heavenly body orbiting star. □ **planetary** *adjective*.

planetarium /plænɪˈteərɪəm/ *noun* (*plural* **-s** or **-ria**) building in which image of night sky as seen at various times and places is projected; device for such projection.

plangent /ˈplændʒ(ə)nt/ *adjective literary* loudly lamenting; plaintive; reverberating.

plank ● *noun* long flat piece of timber; item of political or other programme. ● *verb* provide or cover with planks; (usually + *down*) *colloquial* put down roughly, deposit (esp. money).

plankton /ˈplæŋkt(ə)n/ *noun* chiefly microscopic organisms drifting in sea or fresh water.

planner *noun* person who plans new town etc.; person who makes plans; list, table, chart, etc. with information helpful in planning.

plant /plɑːnt/ ● *noun* organism capable of living wholly on inorganic substances and lacking power of locomotion; small plant (other than trees and shrubs); equipment for industrial process; *colloquial* thing deliberately placed for discovery, esp. to incriminate another. ● *verb* place (seed etc.) in ground to grow; fix firmly, establish; cause (idea etc.) to be established, esp. in another person's mind; deliver (blow etc.); *colloquial* place (something incriminating) for later discovery.

plantain[1] /ˈplæntɪn/ *noun* herb yielding seed used as food for birds.

plantain[2] /ˈplæntɪn/ *noun* plant related to banana; banana-like fruit of this.

plantation /plɑːnˈteɪʃ(ə)n/ *noun* estate for cultivation of cotton, tobacco, etc.; number of growing plants, esp. trees, planted together; *historical* colony.

planter *noun* owner or manager of plantation; container for house-plants.

plaque /plæk/ *noun* ornamental tablet of metal, porcelain, etc.; deposit on teeth, where bacteria proliferate.

plasma /ˈplæzmə/ *noun* (also **plasm** /ˈplæz(ə)m/) colourless fluid part of blood etc. in which corpuscles etc. float; protoplasm; gas of positive ions and free electrons in about equal numbers. □ **plasmic** *adjective*.

plaster /ˈplɑːstə/ ● *noun* mixture esp. of lime, sand, and water spread on walls etc.; sticking plaster; plaster of Paris. ● *verb* cover with or like plaster; apply, stick, etc. like plaster to; (as **plastered** *adjective*) *slang* drunk. □ **plasterboard** two boards with core of plaster used for walls etc.; **plaster cast** bandage stiffened with plaster of Paris and wrapped round broken limb etc.; **plaster of Paris** fine white gypsum powder for plaster casts etc. □ **plasterer** *noun*.

plastic /ˈplæstɪk/ ● *noun* synthetic resinous substance that can be given any shape; (in full **plastic money**) *colloquial* credit card(s). ● *adjective* made of plastic; capable of being moulded; giving form to clay, wax, etc. □ **plastic arts** those involving modelling; **plastic explosive** putty-like explosive; **plastic surgery** repair or restoration of lost or damaged etc. tissue. □ **plasticity** /-ˈtɪs-/ *noun*; **plasticize** /-saɪz/ *verb* (also **-ise**) **(-zing** or **-sing)**; **plasticky** *adjective*.

Plasticine /ˈplæstəsiːn/ *noun proprietary term* pliant substance used for modelling.

plate ● *noun* shallow usually circular vessel from which food is eaten or served; similar vessel used for collection in church etc.; table utensils of gold, silver, or other metal; objects of plated metal; piece of metal with inscription, for fixing to door etc.; illustration on special paper in book; thin sheet of metal, glass, etc. coated with sensitive film for photography; flat thin sheet of metal etc.; part of denture fitting to mouth and holding teeth; each of several sheets of rock thought to form earth's crust. ● *verb* **(-ting)** cover (other metal) with thin coating of silver, gold, etc.; cover with plates of metal. □ **plate glass** thick fine-quality glass for mirrors, windows, etc.; **platelayer** workman laying and repairing railway lines. □ **plateful** *noun* (*plural* **-s**).

plateau /ˈplætəʊ/ ● *noun* (*plural* **-x** or **-s** /-z/) area of level high ground; state of little variation following an increase. ● *verb* (**plateaus**, **plateaued**, **plateauing**) (often + *out*) reach level or static state after period of increase.

platelet /ˈpleɪtlɪt/ *noun* small disc in blood, involved in clotting.

platen /ˈplæt(ə)n/ *noun* plate in printing press by which paper is pressed against type; corresponding part in typewriter etc.

platform /ˈplætfɔːm/ *noun* raised level surface, esp. one from which speaker addresses audience, or one along side of line at railway station; floor area at entrance to bus etc.; thick sole of shoe; declared policy of political party.

platinum /ˈplætɪnəm/ *noun* white heavy precious metallic element that does not tarnish. □ **platinum blonde** *adjective* silvery-blond, *noun* person with such hair.

platitude /ˈplætɪtjuːd/ *noun* commonplace remark. □ **platitudinous** /-ˈtjuːd-/ *adjective*.

Platonic /pləˈtɒnɪk/ *adjective* of Plato or his philosophy; (**platonic**) (of love or friendship) not sexual.

platoon /pləˈtuːn/ *noun* subdivision of infantry company.

platter /ˈplætə/ *noun* flat plate or dish.

platypus /ˈplætɪpəs/ *noun* (*plural* **-puses**) Australian aquatic egg-laying mammal with ducklike beak.

plaudit /ˈplɔːdɪt/ *noun* (usually in *plural*) round of applause; commendation.

plausible /ˈplɔːzɪb(ə)l/ *adjective* reasonable, probable; (of person) persuasive but deceptive. □ **plausibility** *noun*; **plausibly** *adverb*.

play ● *verb* occupy or amuse oneself pleasantly; (+ *with*) act light-heartedly or flippantly with (feelings etc.); perform on (musical instrument), perform (piece of music etc.); cause (record etc.) to produce sounds; perform (drama, role); (+ *on*) perform (trick or joke etc.) on; *colloquial* cooperate, do what is wanted; take part in (game); have as opponent in game; move (piece) in game, put (card) on table, strike (ball), etc.; move about in lively or unrestrained way; (often + *on*) touch gently; pretend to be; allow (fish) to exhaust itself pulling against line. ● *noun* recreation; amusement; playing of game; dramatic piece for stage etc.; freedom of movement; fitful or light movement; gambling. □ **play along** pretend to cooperate; **play back** play (what has been recorded); **playback** *noun*; **play ball** *colloquial* cooperate; **playbill** poster announcing play etc.; **playboy** pleasure-seeking usually wealthy man; **play by ear** perform (music) without having seen it written down, (also **play it by ear**) *colloquial* proceed gradually according to results; **play one's cards right** *colloquial* make best use of opportunities and advantages; **play down** minimize; **playfellow** playmate; **play the game** behave honourably; **playground** outdoor area for children to play in; **playgroup** group of preschool children who play together under supervision; **playhouse** theatre; **playing card** small usually oblong card used in games, one of set of usually 52 divided into 4 suits; **play it cool** *colloquial* appear relaxed or indifferent; **playmate** child's companion in play; **play-off** extra match played to decide draw or tie; **plaything** toy; **play up** behave mischievously, annoy in this way, cause trouble; **play with fire** take foolish risks; **playwright** dramatist. □ **player** *noun.*

playful *adjective* fond of or inclined to play; done in fun. □ **playfully** *adverb*; **playfulness** *noun.*

plc *abbreviation* (also **PLC**) Public Limited Company.

plea *noun* appeal, entreaty; *Law* formal statement by or on behalf of defendant; excuse.

pleach *verb* entwine or interlace (esp. branches to form a hedge).

plead *verb* (+ *with*) make earnest appeal to; address court as advocate or party; allege as excuse; (+ *guilty, not guilty*) declare oneself to be guilty or not guilty of a charge; make appeal or entreaty.

pleading *noun* (usually in *plural*) formal statement of cause of action or defence.

pleasant /ˈplez(ə)nt/ *adjective* (**-er**, **-est**) agreeable; giving pleasure. □ **pleasantly** *adverb.*

pleasantry *noun* (*plural* **-ies**) joking remark; polite remark.

please /pliːz/ *verb* (**-sing**) be agreeable to; give joy or gratification to; think fit; (in *passive*) be willing, like; *used in polite requests.* □ **pleased** *adjective*; **pleasing** *adjective.*

pleasurable /ˈpleʒərəb(ə)l/ *adjective* causing pleasure. □ **pleasurably** *adverb.*

pleasure /ˈpleʒə/ ● *noun* satisfaction, delight; sensuous enjoyment; source of gratification; will, choice. ● *adjective* done or used for pleasure.

pleat ● *noun* flattened fold in cloth etc. ● *verb* make pleat(s) in.

pleb *noun colloquial* plebeian.

plebeian /plɪˈbiːən/ ● *noun* commoner, esp. in ancient Rome; working-class person (esp. uncultured). ● *adjective* of the common people; uncultured, coarse.

plebiscite /ˈplebɪsaɪt/ *noun* referendum.

plectrum /ˈplektrəm/ *noun* (*plural* **-s** or **-tra**) thin flat piece of plastic etc. for plucking strings of musical instrument.

pledge ● *noun* solemn promise; thing given as security for payment of debt etc.; thing put in pawn; token; drinking of health. ● *verb* (**-ging**) deposit as security, pawn; promise solemnly by pledge; bind by solemn promise; drink to the health of.

Pleiades /ˈplaɪədiːz/ *plural noun* cluster of stars in constellation Taurus.

plenary /ˈpliːnərɪ/ *adjective* (of assembly) to be attended by all members; entire, unqualified.

plenipotentiary /plenɪpəˈtenʃərɪ/ ● *noun* (*plural* **-ies**) person (esp. diplomat) having full authority to act. ● *adjective* having such power.

plenitude /ˈplenɪtjuːd/ *noun literary* fullness; completeness; abundance.

plenteous /ˈplentɪəs/ *adjective literary* plentiful.

plentiful /ˈplentɪfʊl/ *adjective* existing in ample quantity. □ **plentifully** *adverb.*

plenty /ˈplentɪ/ ● *noun* abundance; quite enough. ● *adjective colloquial* plentiful. ● *adverb colloquial* fully.

plenum /ˈpliːnəm/ *noun* full assembly of people or a committee etc.

pleonasm /ˈpliːənæz(ə)m/ *noun* use of more words than are needed. □ **pleonastic** /-ˈnæstɪk/ *adjective.*

plesiosaur /ˈpliːsɪəsɔː/ *noun* large extinct reptile with flippers and long neck.

plethora /ˈpleθərə/ *noun* overabundance.

pleurisy /ˈplʊərəsɪ/ *noun* inflammation of membrane enclosing lungs. □ **pleuritic** /-ˈrɪt-/ *adjective.*

plexus /ˈpleksəs/ *noun* (*plural* same or **plexuses**) network of nerves or blood vessels.

pliable /ˈplaɪəb(ə)l/ *adjective* easily bent or influenced; supple; compliant. □ **pliability** *noun.*

pliant /ˈplaɪənt/ *adjective* pliable. □ **pliancy** *noun.*

pliers /ˈplaɪəz/ *plural noun* pincers with parallel flat surfaces for bending wire etc.

plight[1] /plaɪt/ *noun* unfortunate condition or state.

plight[2] /plaɪt/ *verb archaic* pledge. □ **plight one's troth** promise to marry.

plimsoll /ˈplɪms(ə)l/ *noun* rubber-soled canvas shoe. □ **Plimsoll line, mark** marking on ship's side showing limit of legal submersion under various conditions.

plinth *noun* base supporting column, vase, statue, etc.

plod *verb* (**-dd-**) walk or work laboriously. □ **plodder** *noun.*

plonk[1] ● *verb* set down hurriedly or clumsily; (usually + *down*) set down firmly. ● *noun* heavy thud.

plonk[2] *noun colloquial* cheap or inferior wine.

plop ● *noun* sound as of smooth object dropping into water. ● *verb* (**-pp-**) (cause to) fall with plop. ● *adverb* with a plop.

plot ● *noun* small piece of land; plan or interrelationship of main events of tale, play, etc.; secret plan, conspiracy. ● *verb* (**-tt-**) make chart, diagram, graph, etc. of; hatch secret plans; devise secretly; mark on chart or diagram. □ **plotter** *noun.*

plough /plaʊ/ (*US* **plow**) ● *noun* implement for furrowing and turning up soil; similar instrument for clearing away snow etc. ● *verb* (often + *up*, *out*, etc.) turn up or extract with plough; furrow, make (furrow); (+ *through*) advance laboriously or cut or force way through; *colloquial* fail in exam. □ **plough back** reinvest (profits) in business; **ploughman** user of plough; **ploughman's lunch** meal of bread, cheese, pickles, etc.; **ploughshare** blade of plough.

plover /ˈplʌvə/ *noun* plump-breasted wading bird.

plow *US* = PLOUGH.

ploy *noun* manoeuvre to gain advantage.

pluck ● *verb* pick or pull out or away; strip (bird) of feathers; pull at, twitch; (+ *at*) tug or snatch at; sound (string of musical instrument) with finger or plectrum. ● *noun* courage; twitch; animal's heart, liver, and lungs. □ **pluck up** summon up (one's courage etc.).

plucky *adjective* (**-ier**, **-iest**) brave, spirited.

plug ● *noun* something fitting into hole or filling cavity; device of metal pins etc. for making electrical connection; spark plug; *colloquial* piece of free publicity; cake or stick of tobacco. ● *verb* (**-gg-**) (often + *up*) stop with plug; *slang* shoot; *colloquial* seek to popularize by frequent recommendation. □ **plug away** (often + *at*) *colloquial* work steadily; **plug-hole** hole for plug, esp. in sink or bath; **plug in** *verb* connect electrically by inserting plug into socket; **plug-in** *adjective* designed to be plugged into socket; **pull the plug** *colloquial* flush toilet; (+ *on*) put an end to by withdrawing resources etc.

plum *noun* roundish fleshy stone fruit; tree bearing this; reddish-purple colour; raisin; *colloquial* prized thing. □ **plum pudding** Christmas pudding.

plumage /ˈpluːmɪdʒ/ *noun* bird's feathers.

plumb /plʌm/ ● *noun* lead ball attached to line for testing water's depth or whether wall etc. is vertical. ● *adverb* exactly; vertically; *US slang* quite, utterly. ● *adjective* vertical. ● *verb* provide with plumbing; fit as part of plumbing system; work as plumber; test with plumb; experience (extreme feeling); learn detailed facts about. □ **plumb line** string with plumb attached.

plumber *noun* person who fits and repairs apparatus of water supply, heating, etc.

plumbing *noun* system or apparatus of water supply etc.; plumber's work.

plume /plu:m/ ● *noun* feather, esp. large and showy one; feathery ornament in hat, hair, etc.; feather-like formation, esp. of smoke. ● *verb* **(-ming)** furnish with plume(s); **(plume oneself on, upon)** pride oneself on.

plummet /ˈplʌmɪt/ ● *noun* plumb, plumb line; sounding line. ● *verb* **(-t-)** fall rapidly.

plummy *adjective* **(-ier, -iest)** *colloquial* (of voice) affectedly rich in tone; *colloquial* good, desirable.

plump[1] ● *adjective* having full rounded shape; fleshy. ● *verb* (often + *up, out*) make or become plump. ▫ **plumpness** *noun*.

plump[2] ● *verb* (+ *for*) decide on, choose. ● *noun* abrupt or heavy fall. ● *adverb colloquial* with plump.

plunder /ˈplʌndə/ ● *verb* rob or steal, esp. in war; embezzle. ● *noun* plundering; property plundered.

plunge ● *verb* **(-ging)** (usually + *in, into*) throw forcefully, dive, (cause to) become or enter into impetuously, immerse completely; move suddenly downward; move with a rush; *colloquial* run up gambling debts. ● *noun* plunging, dive; decisive step.

plunger *noun* part of mechanism that works with plunging or thrusting motion; rubber cup on handle for removing blockages by plunging action.

pluperfect /plu:ˈpɜ:fɪkt/ *Grammar* ● *adjective* expressing action completed prior to some past point of time. ● *noun* pluperfect tense.

plural /ˈplʊər(ə)l/ ● *adjective* more than one in number; denoting more than one. ● *noun* plural word, form, or number.

pluralism *noun* form of society in which minority groups retain independent traditions; holding of more than one office at a time. ▫ **pluralist** *noun*; **pluralistic** /-ˈlɪst-/ *adjective*.

plurality /plʊəˈrælɪtɪ/ *noun* (*plural* **-ies**) state of being plural; pluralism; large number; non-absolute majority (of votes etc.).

pluralize *verb* (also **-ise**) **(-zing** or **-sing)** make plural; express as plural.

plus ● *preposition* with addition of; (of temperature) above zero; *colloquial* having gained. ● *adjective* (after number) at least, (after grade) better than; *Mathematics* positive; additional, extra. ● *noun* plus sign; advantage. ▫ **plus sign** symbol (+) indicating addition or positive value.

■ **Usage** The use of *plus* as a conjunction, as in *they arrived late, plus they wanted a meal*, is considered incorrect except in very informal use.

plush ● *noun* cloth of silk, cotton, etc., with long soft pile. ● *adjective* made of plush; *colloquial* plushy.

plushy *adjective* **(-ier, -iest)** *colloquial* stylish, luxurious.

plutocracy /plu:ˈtɒkrəsɪ/ *noun* (*plural* **-ies**) state in which power belongs to rich; wealthy élite. ▫ **plutocrat** /ˈplu:təkræt/ *noun*; **plutocratic** /-təˈkræt-/ *adjective*.

plutonium /plu:ˈtəʊnɪəm/ *noun* radioactive metallic element.

pluvial /ˈplu:vɪəl/ *adjective* of or caused by rain.

ply[1] /plaɪ/ *noun* (*plural* **-ies**) thickness, layer; strand.

ply[2] /plaɪ/ *verb* **(-ies, -ied)** wield; work at; (+ *with*) supply continuously or approach repeatedly with; (often + *between*) (of vehicle etc.) go to and fro.

plywood *noun* strong thin board made by gluing layers of wood with the direction of the grain alternating.

PM *abbreviation* prime minister.

p.m. *abbreviation* after noon (*post meridiem*).

PMS *abbreviation* premenstrual syndrome.

PMT *abbreviation* premenstrual tension.

pneumatic /nju:ˈmætɪk/ *adjective* filled with air or wind; operated by compressed air.

pneumonia /nju:ˈməʊnɪə/ *noun* inflammation of lung(s).

PO *abbreviation* Post Office; postal order; Petty Officer; Pilot Officer.

po *noun* (*plural* **-s**) *colloquial* chamber pot. ▫ **po-faced** solemn-faced, humourless, smug.

poach[1] *verb* cook (egg) without shell in boiling water; cook (fish etc.) by simmering in small amount of liquid. ▫ **poacher** *noun*.

poach[2] *verb* catch (game or fish) illicitly; (often + *on*) trespass, encroach; appropriate (another's ideas, staff, etc.). ▫ **poacher** *noun*.

pock *noun* (also **pock-mark**) small pus-filled spot, esp. in smallpox. ▫ **pock-marked** *adjective*.

pocket /ˈpɒkɪt/ ● *noun* small bag sewn into or on garment for carrying small articles; pouchlike compartment in suitcase, car door, etc.; financial resources; isolated group or area; cavity in earth etc. containing ore; pouch at corner or on side of billiard or snooker table into which balls are driven. ● *adjective* small, esp. small enough for carrying in pocket. ● *verb* **(-t-)** put into pocket; appropriate; submit to (affront etc.); conceal (feelings). ▫ **in** or **out of pocket** having gained or lost in transaction; **pocketbook** notebook, folding case for papers, paper money, etc.; **pocket knife** small folding knife; **pocket money** money for minor expenses, esp. given to child.

pod ● *noun* long seed vessel, esp. of pea or bean. ● *verb* **(-dd-)** form pods; remove (peas etc.) from pods.

podgy /ˈpɒdʒɪ/ *adjective* **(-ier, -iest)** short and fat.

podium /ˈpəʊdɪəm/ *noun* (*plural* **-s** or **podia**) rostrum.

poem /ˈpəʊɪm/ *noun* metrical composition; elevated composition in verse or prose; something with poetic qualities.

poesy /ˈpəʊəzɪ/ *noun archaic* poetry.

poet /ˈpəʊɪt/ *noun* (*feminine* **poetess**) writer of poems. ▫ **Poet Laureate** poet appointed to write poems for state occasions.

poetaster /pəʊɪˈtæstə/ *noun* inferior poet.

poetic /pəʊˈetɪk/ *adjective* (also **poetical**) of or like poetry or poets. ▫ **poetic justice** well-deserved punishment or reward; **poetic licence** departure from truth etc. for effect. ▫ **poetically** *adverb*.

poetry /ˈpəʊɪtrɪ/ *noun* poet's art or work; poems; poetic or tenderly pleasing quality.

pogo /ˈpəʊgəʊ/ *noun* (*plural* **-s**) (also **pogo stick**) stilt-like toy with spring, used to jump about on.

pogrom /ˈpɒgrəm/ *noun* organized massacre (originally of Jews in Russia).

poignant /ˈpɔɪnjənt/ *adjective* painfully sharp, deeply moving; arousing sympathy; pleasantly piquant. ▫ **poignance** *noun*; **poignancy** *noun*; **poignantly** *adverb*.

poinsettia /pɔɪnˈsetɪə/ *noun* plant with large scarlet bracts surrounding small yellowish flowers.

point ● *noun* sharp end, tip; geometric entity with position but no magnitude; particular place; precise moment; very small mark on surface; decimal point; stage or degree in progress or increase; single item or particular; unit of scoring in games etc., or in evaluation etc.; significant thing, thing actually intended or under discussion; sense, purpose, advantage; characteristic; each of 32 directions marked on compass; (usually in *plural*) pair of tapering movable rails to direct train from one line to another; power point; *Cricket* (position of) fielder near batsman on off side; promontory. ● *verb* (usually + *to, at*) direct (finger, weapon, etc.); direct attention; (+ *at*, *towards*) aim or be directed to; (+ *to*) indicate; give force to (words, action); fill joints of (brickwork) with smoothed mortar or cement; (of dog) indicate presence of game by acting as pointer. □ **at** or **on the point of** on the verge of; **point-blank** at close range, directly, flatly; **point-duty** traffic control by police officer; **point of view** position from which thing is viewed, way of considering a matter; **point out** indicate, draw attention to; **point-to-point** steeplechase for hunting horses; **point up** emphasize.

pointed *adjective* having point; (of remark etc.) cutting, emphasized. □ **pointedly** *adverb*.

pointer *noun* indicator on gauge etc.; rod for pointing at features on screen etc.; *colloquial* hint; dog of breed trained to stand rigid looking at game.

pointless *adjective* purposeless, meaningless; ineffective. □ **pointlessly** *adverb*; **pointlessness** *noun*.

poise /pɔɪz/ ● *noun* composure; equilibrium; carriage (of head etc.). ● *verb* (**-sing**) balance, hold suspended or supported; be balanced or suspended.

poised *adjective* self-assured; carrying oneself with dignity; (often + *for*) ready.

poison /ˈpɔɪz(ə)n/ ● *noun* substance that when absorbed by living organism kills or injures it; *colloquial* harmful influence. ● *verb* administer poison to; kill or injure with poison; treat (weapon) with poison; corrupt, pervert; spoil. □ **poison ivy** N. American climbing plant secreting irritant oil from leaves; **poison-pen letter** malicious anonymous letter. □ **poisoner** *noun*; **poisonous** *adjective*.

poke ● *verb* (**-king**) push with (end of) finger, stick, etc.; (+ *out*, *up*, etc.) (be) thrust forward; (+ *at* etc.) make thrusts; (+ *in*) produce (hole etc.) in by poking; stir (fire). ● *noun* poking; thrust, nudge. □ **poke fun at** ridicule.

poker[1] *noun* metal rod for stirring fire.

poker[2] /ˈpəʊkə/ *noun* card game in which players bet on value of their hands. □ **poker-face** impassive countenance assumed by poker player.

poky /ˈpəʊkɪ/ *adjective* (**-ier**, **-iest**) (of room etc.) small and cramped.

polar /ˈpəʊlə/ *adjective* of or near either pole of earth etc.; having magnetic or electric polarity; directly opposite in character. □ **polar bear** large white bear living in Arctic.

polarity /pəˈlærɪtɪ/ *noun* (*plural* **-ies**) tendency of magnet etc. to point to earth's magnetic poles or of body to lie with axis in particular direction; possession of two poles having contrary qualities; possession of two opposite tendencies, opinions, etc.; electrical condition of body (positive or negative).

polarize /ˈpəʊləraɪz/ *verb* (also **-ise**) (**-zing** or **-sing**) restrict vibrations of (light-waves etc.) to one direction; give polarity to; divide into two opposing groups. □ **polarization** *noun*.

Polaroid /ˈpəʊlərɔɪd/ *noun proprietary term* material in thin sheets polarizing light passing through it; camera that produces print immediately after each exposure; (in *plural*) sunglasses with Polaroid lenses.

Pole *noun* native or national of Poland.

pole[1] *noun* long slender rounded piece of wood, metal, etc., esp. as support etc.; *historical* measure of length (5½ yds). □ **pole-vault** jump over high bar with aid of pole held in hands.

pole[2] *noun* each of two points in celestial sphere (in full **north**, **south pole**) about which stars appear to revolve; each end of axis of earth (in full **North**, **South Pole**) or of other body; each of two opposite points on surface of magnet at which magnetic forces are strongest; positive or negative terminal of electric cell, battery, etc.; each of two opposed principles. □ **pole star** star near N. pole of heavens, thing serving as guide.

poleaxe /ˈpəʊlæks/ (*US* **-ax**) ● *noun historical* battleaxe; butcher's axe. ● *verb* (**-xing**) hit or kill with poleaxe; (esp. as **poleaxed** *adjective*) *colloquial* dumbfound, overwhelm.

polecat /ˈpəʊlkæt/ *noun* small dark brown mammal of weasel family.

polemic /pəˈlemɪk/ ● *noun* verbal attack; controversy; (in *plural*) art of controversial discussion. ● *adjective* (also **polemical**) involving dispute, controversial. □ **polemicist** /-sɪst/ *noun*.

police /pəˈliːs/ ● *noun* (treated as *plural*) civil force responsible for maintaining public order; its members; force with similar functions. ● *verb* (**-cing**) control or provide with police; keep in order, control, administer. □ **police dog** dog used in police work; **police force** body of police of country, district, or town; **policeman**, **policewoman**, **police officer** member of police force; **police state** totalitarian state controlled by political police; **police station** office of local police force.

policy[1] /ˈpɒlɪsɪ/ *noun* (*plural* **-ies**) course of action adopted by government, business, etc.; prudent conduct.

policy[2] /ˈpɒlɪsɪ/ *noun* (*plural* **-ies**) (document containing) contract of insurance. □ **policyholder** person or body holding insurance policy.

polio /ˈpəʊlɪəʊ/ *noun* poliomyelitis.

poliomyelitis /pəʊlɪəʊmaɪəˈlaɪtɪs/ *noun* infectious viral disease of grey matter of central nervous system, with temporary or permanent paralysis.

Polish /ˈpəʊlɪʃ/ ● *adjective* of Poland. ● *noun* language of Poland.

polish /ˈpɒlɪʃ/ ● *verb* (often + *up*) make or become smooth or glossy by rubbing; (esp. as **polished** *adjective*) refine, improve. ● *noun* substance used for polishing; smoothness, glossiness; refinement. □ **polish off** finish quickly.

polite /pəˈlaɪt/ *adjective* (**-r**, **-st**) having good manners, courteous; cultivated, refined. □ **politely** *adverb*; **politeness** *noun*.

politic /ˈpɒlɪtɪk/ ● *adjective* judicious, expedient; prudent, sagacious. ● *verb* (**-ck-**) engage in politics.

political /pəˈlɪtɪk(ə)l/ *adjective* of state or its government; of public affairs; of, engaged in, or taking a side in politics; relating to pursuit of power, status, etc. □ **political asylum** state protection for foreign refugee; **political correctness** avoidance of language or action which excludes ethnic or cultural minorities; **political economy** study of economic aspects of government; **political geography** geography dealing with boundaries etc. of states; **political prisoner** person imprisoned for political reasons.

politically *adverb* in a political way. □ **politically correct** exhibiting political correctness.

politician /pɒlɪˈtɪʃ(ə)n/ *noun* person engaged in politics.

politicize /pəˈlɪtɪsaɪz/ *verb* (also **-ise**) (**-zing** or **-sing**) give political character or awareness to.

politics /ˈpɒlɪtɪks/ *plural noun* (treated as *singular* or *plural*) art and science of government; political life, affairs, principles, etc.; activities relating to pursuit of power, status, etc.

polity /ˈpɒlɪtɪ/ *noun* (*plural* **-ies**) form of civil administration; organized society, state.

polka /ˈpɒlkə/ ● *noun* lively dance; music for this. ● *verb* (**-kas, -kaed** /-kəd/ or **-ka'd**, **-kaing** /-kəɪŋ/) dance polka. □ **polka dot** round dot as one of many forming regular pattern on textile fabric etc.

poll /pəʊl/ ● *noun* (often in *plural*) voting; counting of votes; result of voting, number of votes recorded;

questioning of sample of population to estimate trend of public opinion; head. ● *verb* take or receive vote(s) of, vote; record opinion of (person, group); cut off top of (tree etc.) or (esp. as **polled** *adjective*) horns of (cattle). □ **polling booth** cubicle where voter stands to mark ballot paper; **polling station** building used for voting; **poll tax** *historical* tax levied on every adult.

pollack /'pɒlək/ *noun* (also **pollock**) (*plural* same or **-s**) edible marine fish related to cod.

pollard /'pɒləd/ ● *noun* hornless animal; tree polled to produce close head of young branches. ● *verb* make pollard of (tree).

pollen /'pɒlən/ *noun* fertilizing powder discharged from flower's anther. □ **pollen count** index of amount of pollen in air.

pollinate /'pɒlɪneɪt/ *verb* (**-ting**) sprinkle (stigma of flower) with pollen. □ **pollination** *noun*.

pollock = POLLACK.

pollster *noun* person who organizes opinion poll.

pollute /pə'lu:t/ *verb* (**-ting**) contaminate; make impure. □ **pollutant** *noun*; **polluter** *noun*; **pollution** *noun*.

polo /'pəʊləʊ/ *noun* game like hockey played on horseback. □ **polo-neck** (sweater with) high round turned-over collar.

polonaise /pɒlə'neɪz/ *noun* slow processional dance; music for this.

poltergeist /'pɒltəgaɪst/ *noun* noisy mischievous ghost.

poltroon /pɒl'tru:n/ *noun* coward. □ **poltroonery** *noun*.

poly- *combining form* many; polymerized.

polyandry /'pɒlɪændrɪ/ *noun* polygamy in which one woman has more than one husband.

polyanthus /pɒlɪ'ænθəs/ *noun* (*plural* **-thuses**) cultivated primula.

polychromatic /pɒlɪkrəʊ'mætɪk/ *adjective* many-coloured.

polychrome /'pɒlɪkrəʊm/ ● *adjective* in many colours. ● *noun* polychrome work of art.

polyester /pɒlɪ'estə/ *noun* synthetic fibre or resin.

polyethylene /pɒlɪ'eθɪli:n/ *noun* polythene.

polygamy /pə'lɪgəmɪ/ *noun* practice of having more than one wife or husband at once. □ **polygamist** *noun*; **polygamous** *adjective*.

polyglot /'pɒlɪglɒt/ ● *adjective* knowing, using, or written in several languages. ● *noun* polyglot person.

polygon /'pɒlɪgən/ *noun* figure with many sides and angles. □ **polygonal** /pə'lɪg-/ *adjective*.

polyhedron /pɒlɪ'hi:drən/ *noun* (*plural* **-dra**) solid figure with many faces. □ **polyhedral** *adjective*.

polymath /'pɒlɪmæθ/ *noun* person of great or varied learning.

polymer /'pɒlɪmə/ *noun* compound of molecule(s) formed from repeated units of smaller molecules. □ **polymeric** /-'mer-/ *adjective*; **polymerization** *noun*; **polymerize** *verb* (also **-ise**) (**-zing** or **-sing**).

polyp /'pɒlɪp/ *noun* simple organism with tube-shaped body; small growth on mucous membrane.

polyphony /pə'lɪfənɪ/ *noun* (*plural* **-ies**) contrapuntal music. □ **polyphonic** /pɒlɪ'fɒnɪk/ *adjective*.

polypropylene /pɒlɪ'prəʊpɪli:n/ *noun* any of various thermoplastic materials used for films, fibres, or moulding.

polystyrene /pɒlɪ'staɪəri:n/ *noun* kind of hard plastic.

polysyllabic /pɒlɪsɪ'læbɪk/ *adjective* having many syllables; using polysyllables.

polysyllable /'pɒlɪsɪləb(ə)l/ *noun* polysyllabic word.

polytechnic /pɒlɪ'teknɪk/ *noun* college providing courses in esp. vocational subjects up to degree level.

polytheism /'pɒlɪθi:ɪz(ə)m/ *noun* belief in or worship of more than one god. □ **polytheistic** /-'ɪst-/ *adjective*.

polythene /'pɒlɪθi:n/ *noun* a tough light plastic.

polyunsaturated /pɒlɪʌn'sætʃəreɪtɪd/ *adjective* (of fat) containing several double or triple bonds in each molecule and therefore capable of combining with hydrogen and not associated with accumulation of cholesterol.

polyurethane /pɒlɪ'jʊərəθeɪn/ *noun* synthetic resin or plastic used esp. in paints or foam.

polyvinyl chloride /pɒlɪ'vaɪnɪl/ *noun* see PVC.

pomade /pə'mɑ:d/ *noun* scented ointment for hair.

pomander /pə'mændə/ *noun* ball of mixed aromatic substances; container for this.

pomegranate /'pɒmɪgrænɪt/ *noun* tropical tough-rinded many-seeded fruit; tree bearing this.

pommel /'pʌm(ə)l/ *noun* knob of sword hilt; projecting front of saddle.

pomp *noun* splendid display, splendour; specious glory.

pom-pom /'pɒmpɒm/ *noun* automatic quick-firing gun.

pompon /'pɒmpɒn/ *noun* (also **pompom**) decorative tuft or ball on hat, shoe, etc.

pompous /'pɒmpəs/ *adjective* self-important, affectedly grand or solemn. □ **pomposity** /-'pɒs-/ *noun* (*plural* **-ies**); **pompously** *adverb*; **pompousness** *noun*.

ponce *slang* ● *noun* man who lives off prostitute's earnings. ● *verb* (**-cing**) act as ponce. □ **ponce about** move about effeminately.

poncho /'pɒntʃəʊ/ *noun* (*plural* **-s**) cloak of rectangular piece of material with slit in middle for head.

pond *noun* small body of still water.

ponder /'pɒndə/ *verb* think over; muse.

ponderable /'pɒndərəb(ə)l/ *adjective literary* having appreciable weight.

ponderous /'pɒndərəs/ *adjective* heavy and unwieldy; laborious, dull. □ **ponderously** *adverb*; **ponderousness** *noun*.

pong *noun & verb colloquial* stink. □ **pongy** *adjective* (**-ier, -iest**).

poniard /'pɒnjəd/ *noun* dagger.

pontiff /'pɒntɪf/ *noun* Pope.

pontifical /pɒn'tɪfɪk(ə)l/ *adjective* papal; pompously dogmatic.

pontificate ● *verb* /pɒn'tɪfɪkeɪt/ (**-ting**) be pompously dogmatic. ● *noun* /pɒn'tɪfɪkət/ office of bishop or Pope; period of this.

pontoon[1] /pɒn'tu:n/ *noun* card game in which players try to acquire cards with face value totalling 21.

pontoon[2] /pɒn'tu:n/ *noun* flat-bottomed boat; boat etc. as one of supports of temporary bridge.

pony /'pəʊnɪ/ *noun* (*plural* **-ies**) horse of any small breed. □ **pony-tail** hair drawn back, tied, and hanging down behind head; **pony-trekking** travelling across country on ponies for pleasure.

poodle /'pu:d(ə)l/ *noun* dog of breed with thick curling hair.

pooh /pu:/ *interjection expressing contempt or disgust*. □ **pooh-pooh** express contempt for, ridicule.

pool[1] *noun* small body of still water; small shallow body of any liquid; swimming pool; deep place in river.

pool[2] ● *noun* common supply of people, vehicles, etc., for sharing by group; group of people sharing duties etc.; common fund, e.g. of profits or of gamblers' stakes; arrangement between competing parties to fix prices and share business; game like billiards with usually 16 balls; (**the pools**) football pool. ● *verb* put into common fund; share in common.

poop *noun* stern of ship; furthest aft and highest deck.

poor /pʊə/ *adjective* having little money or means; (+ *in*) deficient in; inadequate; inferior; deserving pity; despicable. □ **poor man's** inferior substitute for.

poorly ● *adverb* in poor manner; badly. ● *adjective* unwell.

pop[1] ● *noun* abrupt explosive sound; *colloquial* effervescent drink. ● *verb* (**-pp-**) (cause to) make pop; (+ *in, out, up*, etc.) move, come, or put unexpectedly or suddenly; *slang* pawn. ● *adverb* with the sound pop. □ **popcorn** maize kernels which burst open when heated; **pop-eyed** *colloquial* with eyes bulging or wide open; **popgun** toy gun shooting pellet etc. by compressed air or spring; **popping crease** *Cricket* line in front of and parallel to wicket; **pop-up** involving parts that pop up automatically.

pop[2] *noun colloquial* (in full **pop music**) highly successful commercial music; pop record or song. □ **pop art** art based on modern popular culture and the mass media; **pop culture** commercial culture based on popular taste; **pop group** ensemble playing pop music.

pop[3] *noun esp. US colloquial* father.

popadam = POPPADAM.

pope *noun* (also **Pope**) head of RC Church.

popinjay /ˈpɒpɪndʒeɪ/ *noun* fop, conceited person.

poplar /ˈpɒplə/ *noun* slender tree with straight trunk and often tremulous leaves.

poplin /ˈpɒplɪn/ *noun* closely woven corded fabric.

poppadam /ˈpɒpədəm/ *noun* (also **poppadom**, **popadam**) thin crisp spiced Indian bread.

popper *noun colloquial* press-stud; thing that pops.

poppet /ˈpɒpɪt/ *noun colloquial* (esp. as term of endearment) small or dainty person.

poppy /ˈpɒpɪ/ *noun* (*plural* **-ies**) plant with bright flowers and milky narcotic juice; artificial poppy worn on Remembrance Sunday. □ **Poppy Day** Remembrance Sunday.

poppycock /ˈpɒpɪkɒk/ *noun slang* nonsense.

populace /ˈpɒpjʊləs/ *noun* the common people.

popular /ˈpɒpjʊlə/ *adjective* generally liked or admired; of, for, or prevalent among the general public. □ **popularity** /-ˈlærɪtɪ/ *noun*; **popularize** *verb* (also **-ise**) (**-zing** or **-sing**); **popularly** *adverb*.

populate /ˈpɒpjʊleɪt/ *verb* (**-ting**) form population of; supply with inhabitants.

population /pɒpjʊˈleɪʃ(ə)n/ *noun* inhabitants of town, country, etc.; total number of these.

populous /ˈpɒpjʊləs/ *adjective* thickly inhabited.

porcelain /ˈpɔːsəlɪn/ *noun* fine translucent ceramic; things made of this.

porch *noun* covered entrance to building.

porcine /ˈpɔːsaɪn/ *adjective* of or like pigs.

porcupine /ˈpɔːkjʊpaɪn/ *noun* large rodent with body and tail covered with erectile spines.

pore[1] *noun* minute opening in surface through which fluids may pass.

pore[2] *verb* (**-ring**) (+ *over*) be absorbed in studying (book etc.).

pork *noun* flesh of pig used as food.

porker *noun* pig raised for food.

porn (also **porno**) *colloquial* ● *noun* pornography. ● *adjective* pornographic.

pornography /pɔːˈnɒgrəfɪ/ *noun* explicit presentation of sexual activity in literature, films, etc., to stimulate erotic rather than aesthetic feelings. □ **pornographic** /-nəˈgræf-/ *adjective*.

porous /ˈpɔːrəs/ *adjective* having pores; permeable. □ **porosity** /-ˈrɒs-/ *noun*.

porphyry /ˈpɔːfɪrɪ/ *noun* (*plural* **-ies**) hard rock with feldspar crystals in fine-grained red mass.

porpoise /ˈpɔːpəs/ *noun* sea mammal of whale family.

porridge /ˈpɒrɪdʒ/ *noun* oatmeal or other cereal boiled in water or milk.

porringer /ˈpɒrɪndʒə/ *noun* small soupbowl.

port[1] *noun* harbour; town possessing harbour.

port[2] *noun* strong sweet fortified wine.

port[3] ● *noun* left-hand side of ship or aircraft looking forward. ● *verb* turn (helm) to port.

port[4] *noun* opening in ship's side for entrance, loading, etc.; porthole. □ **porthole** (esp. glazed) aperture in ship's side to admit light.

portable /ˈpɔːtəb(ə)l/ *adjective* easily movable, convenient for carrying; adaptable in altered circumstances. □ **portability** *noun*.

portage /ˈpɔːtɪdʒ/ *noun* carrying of boats or goods between two navigable waters.

Portakabin /ˈpɔːtəkæbɪn/ *noun proprietary term* prefabricated small building.

portal /ˈpɔːt(ə)l/ *noun* doorway, gate.

portcullis /pɔːtˈkʌlɪs/ *noun* strong heavy grating lowered in defence of fortress gateway.

portend /pɔːˈtend/ *verb* foreshadow as an omen; give warning of.

portent /ˈpɔːtent/ *noun* omen, significant sign; marvellous thing.

portentous /pɔːˈtentəs/ *adjective* like or being portent; pompously solemn.

porter[1] /ˈpɔːtə/ *noun* person employed to carry luggage etc.; dark beer brewed from charred or browned malt. □ **porterhouse steak** choice cut of beef.

porter[2] /ˈpɔːtə/ *noun* gatekeeper or doorkeeper, esp. of large building.

porterage *noun* (charge for) hire of porters.

portfolio /pɔːtˈfəʊlɪəʊ/ *noun* (*plural* **-s**) folder for loose sheets of paper, drawings, etc.; samples of artist's work; list of investments held by investor etc.; office of government minister. □ **Minister without Portfolio** government minister not in charge of department.

portico /ˈpɔːtɪkəʊ/ *noun* (*plural* **-es** or **-s**) colonnade; roof supported by columns, usually serving as porch to building.

portion /ˈpɔːʃ(ə)n/ ● *noun* part, share; helping; destiny or lot. ● *verb* divide into portions; (+ *out*) distribute.

Portland /ˈpɔːtlənd/ *noun* □ **Portland cement** cement manufactured from chalk and clay; **Portland stone** a valuable building limestone.

portly /ˈpɔːtlɪ/ *adjective* (**-ier**, **-iest**) corpulent.

portmanteau /pɔːtˈmæntəʊ/ *noun* (*plural* **-s** or **-x** /-z/) case for clothes etc., opening into two equal parts. □ **portmanteau word** word combining sounds and meanings of two others.

portrait /ˈpɔːtrɪt/ *noun* drawing, painting, photograph, etc. of person or animal; description.

portraiture /ˈpɔːtrɪtʃə/ *noun* portraying; description; portrait.

portray /pɔːˈtreɪ/ *verb* make likeness of; describe. □ **portrayal** *noun*.

Portuguese /pɔːtʃʊˈgiːz/ ● *noun* (*plural* same) native, national, or language of Portugal. ● *adjective* of Portugal.

pose /pəʊz/ ● *verb* (**-sing**) assume attitude, esp. for artistic purpose; (+ *as*) pretend to be; behave affectedly for effect; propound (question, problem); arrange in required attitude. ● *noun* attitude of body or mind; affectation, pretence.

poser *noun* poseur; *colloquial* puzzling question or problem.

poseur /pəʊˈzɜː/ *noun* person who behaves affectedly.

posh *colloquial* ● *adjective* smart; upper-class. ● *adverb* in an upper-class way. □ **poshly** *adverb*; **poshness** *noun*.

posit /ˈpɒzɪt/ *verb* (**-t-**) assume as fact, postulate.

position /pəˈzɪʃ(ə)n/ ● *noun* place occupied by person or thing; way thing is placed; proper place; advantage; mental attitude; situation; rank, status; paid employment; strategic location. ● *verb* place in position. ▫ **in a position to** able to. ▫ **positional** *adjective*.

positive /ˈpɒzɪtɪv/ ● *adjective* explicit, definite, unquestionable; convinced, confident, cocksure; absolute, not relative; *Grammar* (of adjective or adverb) expressing simple quality without comparison; constructive; marked by presence and not absence of qualities; favourable; dealing only with matters of fact, practical; *Mathematics* (of quantity) greater than zero; *Electricity* of, containing, or producing kind of charge produced by rubbing glass with silk; *Photography* showing lights and shades or colours as seen in original image. ● *noun* positive adjective, photograph, quantity, etc. ▫ **positive discrimination** making distinctions in favour of groups believed to be underprivileged; **positive vetting** inquiry into background etc. of candidate for post involving national security. ▫ **positively** *adverb*; **positiveness** *noun*.

positivism *noun* philosophical system recognizing only facts and observable phenomena. ▫ **positivist** *noun & adjective*.

positron /ˈpɒzɪtrɒn/ *noun* elementary particle with same mass as but opposite charge to electron.

posse /ˈpɒsɪ/ *noun* strong force or company; group of law-enforcers.

possess /pəˈzes/ *verb* hold as property, own; have; occupy, dominate mind of. ▫ **possessor** *noun*.

possession /pəˈzeʃ(ə)n/ *noun* possessing, being possessed; thing possessed; occupancy; (in *plural*) property; control of ball by player.

possessive /pəˈzesɪv/ ● *adjective* wanting to retain what one possesses; jealous and domineering; *Grammar* indicating possession. ● *noun Grammar* possessive case or word. ▫ **possessiveness** *noun*.

possibility /pɒsɪˈbɪlɪtɪ/ *noun* (*plural* **-ies**) state or fact of being possible; thing that may exist or happen; (usually in *plural*) capability of being used.

possible /ˈpɒsɪb(ə)l/ ● *adjective* capable of existing, happening, being done, etc.; potential. ● *noun* possible candidate, member of team, etc.; highest possible score.

possibly *adverb* perhaps; in accordance with possibility.

possum /ˈpɒsəm/ *noun colloquial* opossum. ▫ **play possum** *colloquial* pretend to be unconscious or unaware.

post[1] /pəʊst/ ● *noun* upright of timber or metal as support in building, to mark boundary, carry notices, etc.; pole etc. marking start or finish of race. ● *verb* (often + *up*) display (notice etc.) in prominent place; advertise by poster or list.

post[2] /pəʊst/ ● *noun* official conveying of parcels, letters, etc.; single collection or delivery of these; letters etc. dispatched; place where letters etc. are collected. ● *verb* put (letter etc.) into post; (esp. as **posted** *adjective*) (often + *up*) supply with information; enter in ledger. ▫ **postbox** public box for posting mail; **postcard** card for posting without envelope; **postcode** group of letters and figures in postal address to assist sorting; **post-haste** with great speed; **postman**, **postwoman** person who collects or delivers post; **postmark** official mark on letters to cancel stamp; **postmaster**, **postmistress** official in charge of post office; **post office** room or building for postal business; **Post Office** public department or corporation providing postal services.

post[3] /pəʊst/ ● *noun* appointed place of soldier etc. on duty; occupying force; fort; paid employment; trading post. ● *verb* place (soldier etc.) at post; appoint to post or command.

post- *prefix* after, behind.

postage *noun* charge for sending letter etc. by post. ▫ **postage stamp** small adhesive label indicating amount of postage paid.

postal *adjective* of or by post. ▫ **postal order** money order issued by Post Office.

postdate /pəʊstˈdeɪt/ *verb* (**-ting**) give later than actual date to; follow in time.

poster *noun* placard in public place; large printed picture. ▫ **poster paint** gummy opaque paint.

poste restante /pəʊst reˈstɑ̃t/ *noun* department in post office where letters are kept till called for.

posterior /pɒˈstɪərɪə/ ● *adjective* later in time or order; at the back. ● *noun* (in *singular* or *plural*) buttocks.

posterity /pɒˈsterɪtɪ/ *noun* later generations; descendants.

postern /ˈpɒst(ə)n/ *noun archaic* back or side entrance.

postgraduate /pəʊstˈgrædjʊət/ ● *noun* person on course of study after taking first degree. ● *adjective* relating to postgraduates.

posthumous /ˈpɒstjʊməs/ *adjective* occurring after death; published after author's death; born after father's death. ▫ **posthumously** *adverb*.

postilion /pɒˈstɪljən/ *noun* (also **postillion**) rider on near horse of team drawing coach etc. without coachman.

post-impressionism /pəʊstɪmˈpreʃənɪz(ə)m/ *noun* art intending to express individual artist's conception of objects represented. ▫ **post-impressionist** *noun & adjective*.

post-industrial /pəʊstɪnˈdʌstrɪəl/ *adjective* of society or economy no longer reliant on heavy industry.

post-mortem /pəʊstˈmɔːtəm/ ● *noun* examination of body made after death; *colloquial* discussion after conclusion (of game etc.). ● *adverb & adjective* after death.

postnatal /pəʊstˈneɪt(ə)l/ *adjective* existing or occurring after birth.

postpone /pəʊstˈpəʊn/ *verb* (**-ning**) cause to take place at later time. ▫ **postponement** *noun*.

postscript /ˈpəʊstskrɪpt/ *noun* addition at end of letter etc. after signature.

postulant /ˈpɒstjʊlənt/ *noun* candidate, esp. for admission to religious order.

postulate ● *verb* /ˈpɒstjʊleɪt/ (**-ting**) (often + *that*) assume or require to be true, take for granted; claim. ● *noun* /ˈpɒstjʊlət/ thing postulated; prerequisite.

posture /ˈpɒstʃə/ ● *noun* relative position of parts, esp. of body; bearing; mental attitude; condition or state (of affairs etc.). ● *verb* (**-ring**) assume posture, esp. for effect; pose (person).

postwar /pəʊstˈwɔː/ *adjective* occurring or existing after a war.

posy /ˈpəʊzɪ/ *noun* (*plural* **-ies**) small bunch of flowers.

pot[1] ● *noun* rounded ceramic, metal, or glass vessel; flowerpot, teapot, etc.; contents of pot; chamber pot; total amount bet in game etc.; (usually in *plural*) *colloquial* large sum; *slang* cup etc. as prize. ● *verb* (**-tt-**) plant in pot; (usually as **potted** *adjective*) preserve (food) in sealed pot; pocket (ball) in billiards etc.; abridge, epitomize; shoot at, hit, or kill (animal). ▫ **go to pot** *colloquial* be ruined; **pot-belly** protuberant belly; **pot-boiler** work of literature etc. done merely to earn money; **pot-herb** herb grown in kitchen garden; **pothole** deep hole in rock, hole in road surface; **potluck** whatever is available; **pot plant** plant grown in flowerpot; **pot roast** piece of braised meat; **pot-roast** braise; **potsherd** broken piece of ceramic material; **pot-shot** random shot. □ **potful** *noun* (*plural* **-s**).

pot[2] *noun slang* marijuana.

potable /ˈpəʊtəb(ə)l/ *adjective* drinkable.

potash /ˈpɒtæʃ/ *noun* any of various compounds of potassium.

potassium /pəˈtæsɪəm/ *noun* soft silver-white metallic element.

potation /pəˈteɪʃ(ə)n/ *noun* a drink; drinking.

potato /pəˈteɪtəʊ/ *noun* (*plural* **-es**) edible plant tuber; plant bearing this. □ **potato crisp** crisp.

poteen /pɒˈtʃiːn/ *noun Irish* illicit distilled spirit.

potent /ˈpəʊt(ə)nt/ *adjective* powerful, strong; cogent; (of male) able to achieve erection of penis or have sexual intercourse. □ **potency** *noun*.

potentate /ˈpəʊtənteɪt/ *noun* monarch, ruler.

potential /pəˈtenʃ(ə)l/ ● *adjective* capable of coming into being; latent. ● *noun* capability for use or development; usable resources; quantity determining energy of mass in gravitational field or of charge in electric field. □ **potentiality** /-ʃɪˈæl-/ *noun*; **potentially** *adverb*.

pother /ˈpɒðə/ *noun literary* din, fuss.

potion /ˈpəʊʃ(ə)n/ *noun* liquid dose of medicine, poison, etc.

pot-pourri /pəʊˈpʊərɪ/ *noun* (*plural* **-s**) scented mixture of dried petals and spices; musical or literary medley.

pottage /ˈpɒtɪdʒ/ *noun archaic* soup, stew.

potter[1] /ˈpɒtə/ *verb* (*US* **putter**) (often + *about*, *around*) work etc. in aimless or desultory manner; go slowly.

potter[2] /ˈpɒtə/ *noun* maker of ceramic vessels.

pottery /ˈpɒtərɪ/ *noun* (*plural* **-ies**) vessels etc. made of baked clay; potter's work or workshop.

potty[1] /ˈpɒtɪ/ *adjective* (**-ier**, **-iest**) *slang* crazy; insignificant. □ **pottiness** *noun*.

potty[2] *noun* (*plural* **-ies**) *colloquial* chamber pot, esp. for child.

pouch ● *noun* small bag, detachable pocket; baggy area of skin under eyes etc.; baglike receptacle in which marsupials carry undeveloped young, other baglike natural structure. ● *verb* put or make into pouch; take possession of.

pouffe /puːf/ *noun* firm cushion as low seat or footstool.

poulterer /ˈpəʊltərə/ *noun* dealer in poultry and usually game.

poultice /ˈpəʊltɪs/ ● *noun* soft usually hot dressing applied to sore or inflamed part of body. ● *verb* (**-cing**) apply poultice to.

poultry /ˈpəʊltrɪ/ *noun* domestic fowls.

pounce ● *verb* (**-cing**) spring, swoop; (often + *on*, *upon*) make sudden attack, seize eagerly. ● *noun* act of pouncing.

pound[1] *noun* unit of weight equal to 16 oz (454 g); (in full **pound sterling**) monetary unit of UK etc.

pound[2] *verb* crush or beat with repeated strokes; (+ *at*, *on*) deliver heavy blows or gunfire to; (+ *along* etc.) walk, run, etc. heavily.

pound[3] *noun* enclosure where stray animals or officially removed vehicles are kept until claimed.

poundage *noun* commission or fee of so much per pound sterling or weight.

-pounder *combining form* thing or person weighing specified number of pounds; gun firing shell weighing specified number of pounds.

pour /pɔː/ *verb* (usually + *down*, *out*, *over*, etc.) (cause to) flow in stream or shower; dispense (drink); rain heavily; (usually + *in*, *out*, etc.) come or go in profusion or in a rush; discharge copiously.

pout ● *verb* push lips forward, esp. as sign of displeasure; (of lips) be pushed forward. ● *noun* pouting expression.

pouter *noun* kind of pigeon able to inflate crop.

poverty /ˈpɒvətɪ/ *noun* being poor, want; (often + *of*, *in*) scarcity, lack; inferiority, poorness. □ **poverty-stricken** very poor; **poverty trap** situation in which increase of income incurs greater loss of state benefits.

POW *abbreviation* prisoner of war.

powder /ˈpaʊdə/ ● *noun* mass of fine dry particles; medicine or cosmetic in this form; gunpowder. ● *verb* apply powder to; (esp. as **powdered** *adjective*) reduce to powder. □ **powder blue** pale blue; **powder-puff** soft pad for applying cosmetic powder to skin; **powder-room** *euphemistic* women's lavatory. □ **powdery** *adjective*.

power /ˈpaʊə/ ● *noun* ability to do or act; mental or bodily faculty; influence, authority; ascendancy; authorization; influential person etc.; state with international influence; vigour, energy; *colloquial* large number or amount; capacity for exerting mechanical force; mechanical or electrical energy; electricity supply; particular source or form of energy; product obtained by multiplying a number by itself a specified number of times; magnifying capacity of lens. ● *verb* supply with mechanical or electrical energy; (+ *up*, *down*) increase or decrease power supplied to (device), switch on or off. □ **power cut** temporary withdrawal or failure of electric power supply; **powerhouse** power station, person or thing of great energy; **power of attorney** authority to act for another in legal and financial matters; **power point** socket for connection of electrical appliance etc. to mains; **power-sharing** coalition government; **power station** building where electric power is generated for distribution.

powerful *adjective* having great power or influence. □ **powerfully** *adverb*; **powerfulness** *noun*.

powerless *adjective* without power; wholly unable. □ **powerlessness** *noun*.

powwow /ˈpaʊwaʊ/ ● *noun* meeting for discussion (originally among N. American Indians). ● *verb* hold powwow.

pox *noun* virus disease leaving pocks; *colloquial* syphilis.

pp *abbreviation* pianissimo.

pp. *abbreviation* pages.

p.p. *abbreviation* (also **pp**) *per pro*.

PPS *abbreviation* Parliamentary Private Secretary; further postscript (*postpostscriptum*).

PR *abbreviation* public relations; proportional representation.

practicable /ˈpræktɪkəb(ə)l/ *adjective* that can be done or used. □ **practicability** *noun*.

practical /ˈpræktɪk(ə)l/ ● *adjective* of or concerned with practice rather than theory; functional; good at making, organizing, or mending things; realistic; that is such in effect, virtual. ● *noun* practical exam. □ **practical joke** trick played on person. □ **practicality** /-ˈkæl-/ *noun* (*plural* **-ies**).

practically *adverb* virtually, almost; in a practical way.

practice /ˈpræktɪs/ *noun* habitual action; repeated exercise to improve skill; action as opposed to theory; doctor's or lawyer's professional business etc.; procedure, esp. of specified kind. □ **in practice** when applied, in reality, skilled from recent practice; **out of practice** lacking former skill.

practise /ˈpræktɪs/ *verb* (**-sing**) (*US* **-tice**; **-cing**) carry out in action; do repeatedly to improve skill; exercise oneself in or on; (as **practised** *adjective*) expert; engage in (profession, religion, etc.).

practitioner /præk'tɪʃənə/ *noun* professional worker, esp. in medicine.
praesidium = PRESIDIUM.
praetorian guard /pri:'tɔ:rɪən/ *noun* bodyguard of ancient Roman emperor etc.
pragmatic /præg'mætɪk/ *adjective* dealing with matters from a practical point of view. □ **pragmatically** *adverb*.
pragmatism /'prægmətɪz(ə)m/ *noun* pragmatic attitude or procedure; *Philosophy* doctrine that evaluates assertions according to their practical consequences. □ **pragmatist** *noun*.
prairie /'preərɪ/ *noun* large treeless tract of grassland, esp. in N. America.
praise /preɪz/ ● *verb* (**-sing**) express warm approval or admiration of; glorify. ● *noun* praising; commendation. □ **praiseworthy** worthy of praise.
praline /'prɑ:li:n/ *noun* sweet made of nuts browned in boiling sugar.
pram *noun* carriage for baby, pushed by person on foot.
prance /prɑ:ns/ ● *verb* (**-cing**) (of horse) spring from hind legs; walk or behave in an elated or arrogant way. ● *noun* prancing; prancing movement.
prank *noun* practical joke.
prat *noun slang* fool.
prate ● *verb* (**-ting**) talk too much; chatter foolishly. ● *noun* idle talk.
prattle /'præt(ə)l/ ● *verb* (**-ling**) talk in childish or inconsequential way. ● *noun* prattling talk.
prawn *noun* edible shellfish like large shrimp.
pray *verb* (often + *for*, *to do*, *that*) say prayers; make devout supplication; entreat.
prayer /preə/ *noun* request or thanksgiving to God or object of worship; formula used in praying; entreaty. □ **prayer book** book of set prayers; **prayer-mat** small carpet on which Muslims kneel when praying; **prayer-shawl** one worn by male Jews when praying.
pre- *prefix* before (in time, place, order, degree, or importance).
preach *verb* deliver (sermon); proclaim (the gospel etc.); give moral advice obtrusively; advocate, inculcate. □ **preacher** *noun*.
preamble /pri:'æmb(ə)l/ *noun* preliminary statement; introductory part of statute, deed, etc.
prearrange /pri:ə'reɪndʒ/ *verb* (**-ging**) arrange beforehand. □ **prearrangement** *noun*.
prebend /'prebənd/ *noun* stipend of canon or member of chapter; portion of land etc. from which this is drawn. □ **prebendal** /prɪ'bend(ə)l/ *adjective*.
prebendary /'prebəndərɪ/ *noun* (*plural* **-ies**) holder of prebend; honorary canon.
Precambrian /pri:'kæmbrɪən/ ● *adjective* of earliest geological era. ● *noun* this era.
precarious /prɪ'keərɪəs/ *adjective* uncertain, dependent on chance; perilous. □ **precariously** *adverb*; **precariousness** *noun*.
precast /pri:'kɑ:st/ *adjective* (of concrete) cast in required shape before positioning.
precaution /prɪ'kɔ:ʃ(ə)n/ *noun* action taken beforehand to avoid risk or ensure good result. □ **precautionary** *adjective*.
precede /prɪ'si:d/ *verb* (**-ding**) come or go before in time, order, importance, etc.; (+ *by*) cause to be preceded by.
precedence /'presɪd(ə)ns/ *noun* priority; right of preceding others. □ **take precedence** (often + *over*, *of*) have priority.
precedent ● *noun* /'presɪd(ə)nt/ previous case taken as guide or justification etc. ● *adjective* /prɪ'si:d(ə)nt/ preceding.
precentor /prɪ'sentə/ *noun* leader of singing or (in synagogue) prayers of congregation.
precept /'pri:sept/ *noun* rule for action or conduct.
preceptor /prɪ'septə/ *noun* teacher, instructor. □ **preceptorial** /pri:sep'tɔ:rɪəl/ *adjective*.
precession /prɪ'seʃ(ə)n/ *noun* slow movement of axis of spinning body around another axis; such change causing equinoxes to occur earlier in each successive sidereal year.
precinct /'pri:sɪŋkt/ *noun* enclosed area, esp. around building; district in town, esp. where traffic is excluded; (in *plural*) environs.
preciosity /preʃɪ'ɒsɪtɪ/ *noun* affected refinement in art.
precious /'preʃəs/ ● *adjective* of great value; much prized; affectedly refined. ● *adverb colloquial* extremely, very.
precipice /'presɪpɪs/ *noun* vertical or steep face of rock, cliff, mountain, etc.
precipitate ● *verb* /prɪ'sɪpɪteɪt/ (**-ting**) hasten occurrence of; (+ *into*) cause to go into (war etc.) hurriedly or violently; throw down headlong; *Chemistry* cause (substance) to be deposited in solid form from solution; *Physics* condense (vapour) into drops. ● *adjective* /prɪ'sɪpɪtət/ headlong; hasty, rash. ● *noun* /prɪ'sɪpɪtət/ solid matter precipitated; moisture condensed from vapour.
precipitation /prɪsɪpɪ'teɪʃ(ə)n/ *noun* precipitating, being precipitated; rash haste; rain, snow, etc., falling to ground.
precipitous /prɪ'sɪpɪtəs/ *adjective* of or like precipice; steep.
précis /'preɪsi:/ ● *noun* (*plural* same /-si:z/) summary, abstract. ● *verb* (**-cises** /-si:z/, **-cised** /-si:d/, **-cising** /-si:ɪŋ/) make précis of.
precise /prɪ'saɪs/ *adjective* accurately worded; definite, exact; punctilious.
precisely *adverb* in a precise way, exactly; quite so.
precision /prɪ'sɪʒ(ə)n/ ● *noun* accuracy. ● *adjective* designed for or produced by precise work.
preclude /prɪ'klu:d/ *verb* (**-ding**) (+ *from*) prevent; make impossible.
precocious /prɪ'kəʊʃəs/ *adjective* prematurely developed in some respect. □ **precociously** *adverb*; **precociousness** *noun*; **precocity** /-'kɒs-/ *noun*.
precognition /pri:kɒg'nɪʃ(ə)n/ *noun* (esp. supernatural) foreknowledge.
preconceive /pri:kən'si:v/ *verb* (**-ving**) form (opinion etc.) beforehand.
preconception /pri:kən'sepʃ(ə)n/ *noun* preconceived idea; prejudice.
precondition /pri:kən'dɪʃ(ə)n/ *noun* condition that must be fulfilled beforehand.
precursor /pri:'kɜ:sə/ *noun* forerunner; person who precedes in office etc.; harbinger.
predate /pri:'deɪt/ *verb* (**-ting**) precede in time.
predator /'predətə/ *noun* predatory animal; exploiter of others.
predatory /'predətərɪ/ *adjective* (of animal) preying naturally on others; plundering or exploiting others.
predecease /pri:dɪ'si:s/ *verb* (**-sing**) die before (another).
predecessor /'pri:dɪsesə/ *noun* previous holder of office or position; ancestor; thing to which another has succeeded.
predestine /pri:'destɪn/ *verb* (**-ning**) determine beforehand; ordain by divine will or as if by fate. □ **predestination** *noun*.
predetermine /pri:dɪ'tɜ:mɪn/ *verb* (**-ning**) decree beforehand; predestine.
predicament /prɪ'dɪkəmənt/ *noun* difficult or unpleasant situation.

predicate ● *verb* /'predɪkeɪt/ (**-ting**) assert (something) about subject of proposition; (+ *on*) base (statement etc.) on. ● *noun* /'predɪkət/ *Grammar & Logic* what is said about subject of sentence or proposition. ▫ **predicable** *adjective*; **predication** *noun*.

predicative /prɪ'dɪkətɪv/ *adjective Grammar* (of adjective or noun) forming part or all of predicate; that predicates.

predict /prɪ'dɪkt/ *verb* forecast; prophesy. ▫ **predictable** *adjective*; **predictably** *adverb*; **prediction** *noun*.

predilection /pri:dɪ'lekʃ(ə)n/ *noun* (often + *for*) preference, special liking.

predispose /pri:dɪs'pəʊz/ *verb* (**-sing**) influence favourably in advance; (+ *to*, *to do*) render liable or inclined beforehand to. ▫ **predisposition** /-pə'zɪʃ(ə)n/ *noun*.

predominate /prɪ'dɒmɪneɪt/ *verb* (**-ting**) (+ *over*) have control over; prevail; preponderate. ▫ **predominance** *noun*; **predominant** *adjective*; **predominantly** *adverb*.

pre-eminent /pri:'emɪnənt/ *adjective* excelling others; outstanding. ▫ **preeminence** *noun*; **pre-eminently** *adverb*.

pre-empt /pri:'empt/ *verb* forestall; obtain by pre-emption.

■ **Usage** *Pre-empt* is sometimes used to mean *prevent*, but this is considered incorrect in standard English.

pre-emption /pri:'empʃ(ə)n/ *noun* purchase or taking of thing before it is offered to others.

pre-emptive /pri:'emptɪv/ *adjective* pre-empting; *Military* intended to prevent attack by disabling enemy.

preen *verb* (of bird) tidy (feathers, itself) with beak; (of person) smarten or admire (oneself, one's hair, clothes, etc.); (often + *on*) pride (oneself).

prefab /'pri:fæb/ *noun colloquial* prefabricated building.

prefabricate /pri:'fæbrɪkeɪt/ *verb* (**-ting**) manufacture sections of (building etc.) prior to assembly on site.

preface /'prefəs/ ● *noun* introduction to book stating subject, scope, etc.; preliminary part of speech. ● *verb* (**-cing**) (often + *with*) introduce or begin (as) with preface; (of event etc.) lead up to (another). ▫ **prefatory** *adjective*.

prefect /'pri:fekt/ *noun* chief administrative officer of district in France etc.; senior pupil in school, authorized to maintain discipline.

prefecture /'pri:fektʃə/ *noun* district under government of prefect; prefect's office or tenure.

prefer /prɪ'fɜ:/ *verb* (**-rr-**) (often + *to*, *to do*) like better; submit (information, accusation, etc.); promote (person).

preferable /'prefərəb(ə)l/ *adjective* to be preferred, more desirable. ▫ **preferably** *adverb*.

preference /'prefərəns/ *noun* preferring, being preferred; thing preferred; favouring of one person etc. before others; prior right.

preferential /prefə'renʃ(ə)l/ *adjective* of, giving, or receiving preference. ▫ **preferentially** *adverb*.

preferment /prɪ'fɜ:mənt/ *noun formal* promotion to higher office.

prefigure /pri:'fɪgə/ *verb* (**-ring**) represent or imagine beforehand.

prefix /'pri:fɪks/ ● *noun* part-word added to beginning of word to alter meaning, e.g. *re-* in *retake*, *ex-* in *ex-president*; title before name. ● *verb* (often + *to*) add as introduction; join (word, element) as prefix.

pregnant /'pregnənt/ *adjective* having child or young developing in womb; significant, suggestive. ▫ **pregnancy** *noun* (*plural* **-ies**).

preheat /pri:'hi:t/ *verb* heat beforehand.

prehensile /pri:'hensaɪl/ *adjective* (of tail, limb, etc.) capable of grasping.

prehistoric /pri:hɪs'tɒrɪk/ *adjective* of period before written records. ▫ **prehistory** /-'hɪstərɪ/ *noun*.

prejudge /pri:'dʒʌdʒ/ *verb* (**-ging**) form premature judgement on (person etc.).

prejudice /'predʒʊdɪs/ ● *noun* preconceived opinion; (+ *against*, *in favour of*) bias; harm (possibly) resulting from action or judgement. ● *verb* (**-cing**) impair validity of; (esp. as **prejudiced** *adjective*) cause (person) to have prejudice. ▫ **prejudicial** /-'dɪʃ-/ *adjective*.

prelacy /'preləsɪ/ *noun* (*plural* **-ies**) church government by prelates; (**the prelacy**) prelates collectively; office or rank of prelate.

prelate /'prelət/ *noun* high ecclesiastical dignitary, e.g. bishop.

preliminary /prɪ'lɪmɪnərɪ/ ● *adjective* introductory, preparatory. ● *noun* (*plural* **-ies**) (usually in *plural*) preliminary action or arrangement; preliminary trial or contest.

prelude /'prelju:d/ ● *noun* (often + *to*) action, event, etc. serving as introduction; introductory part of poem etc.; *Music* introductory piece of suite, short piece of similar type. ● *verb* (**-ding**) serve as prelude to; introduce with prelude.

premarital /pri:'mærɪt(ə)l/ *adjective* occurring etc. before marriage.

premature /'premətʃə/ *adjective* occurring or done before usual or right time; too hasty; (of baby) born 3 or more weeks before expected time. ▫ **prematurely** *adverb*.

premed /pri:'med/ *noun colloquial* premedication.

premedication /pri:medɪ'keɪʃ(ə)n/ *noun* medication in preparation for operation.

premeditate /pri:'medɪteɪt/ *verb* (**-ting**) think out or plan beforehand. ▫ **premeditation** *noun*.

premenstrual /pri:'menstrʊəl/ *adjective* of the time immediately before menstruation.

premier /'premɪə/ ● *noun* prime minister. ● *adjective* first in importance, order, or time. ▫ **premiership** *noun*.

première /'premɪeə/ ● *noun* first performance or showing of play or film. ● *verb* (**-ring**) give première of.

premise /'premɪs/ *noun* premiss; (in *plural*) house or other building with its grounds etc.; (in *plural*) *Law* previously specified houses, lands, or tenements. ▫ **on the premises** in the house etc. concerned.

premiss /'premɪs/ *noun* previous statement from which another is inferred.

premium /'pri:mɪəm/ ● *noun* amount to be paid for contract of insurance; sum added to interest, wages, etc.; reward, prize. ● *adjective* of best quality and highest price. ▫ **at a premium** highly valued, above usual or nominal price; **Premium (Savings) Bond** government security not bearing interest but with periodic prize draw.

premonition /premə'nɪʃ(ə)n/ *noun* forewarning; presentiment. ▫ **premonitory** /prɪ'mɒnɪtərɪ/ *adjective*.

prenatal /pri:'neɪt(ə)l/ *adjective* existing or occurring before birth.

preoccupy /pri:'ɒkjʊpaɪ/ *verb* (**-ies**, **-ied**) dominate mind of; (as **preoccupied** *adjective*) otherwise engrossed. ▫ **preoccupation** *noun*.

preordain /pri:ɔ:'deɪn/ *verb* ordain or determine beforehand.

prep *noun colloquial* homework; time when this is done.

prepack /pri:'pæk/ *verb* (also **prepackage** /-'pækɪdʒ/) pack (goods) before retail.

preparation /prepə'reɪʃ(ə)n/ *noun* preparing, being prepared; (often in *plural*) thing done to make ready; substance specially prepared.

preparatory /prɪ'pærətərɪ/ ● *adjective* (often + *to*) serving to prepare; introductory. ● *adverb* (often + *to*) as a preparation. □ **preparatory school** private primary or (*US*) secondary school.

prepare /prɪ'peə/ *verb* (**-ring**) make or get ready; get oneself ready.

prepay /pri:'peɪ/ *verb* (*past & past participle* **prepaid**) pay (charge) beforehand; pay postage on beforehand. □ **prepayment** *noun*.

preponderate /prɪ'pɒndəreɪt/ *verb* (**-ting**) (often + *over*) be superior in influence, quantity, or number; predominate. □ **preponderance** *noun*; **preponderant** *adjective*.

preposition /prepə'zɪʃ(ə)n/ *noun* word used before noun or pronoun to indicate its relationship to another word (see panel). □ **prepositional** *adjective*.

prepossess /pri:pə'zes/ *verb* (usually in *passive*) take possession of; prejudice, usually favourably; (as **prepossessing** *adjective*) attractive. □ **prepossession** *noun*.

preposterous /prɪ'pɒstərəs/ *adjective* utterly absurd; contrary to nature or reason. □ **preposterously** *adverb*.

prepuce /'pri:pju:s/ *noun* foreskin.

Pre-Raphaelite /pri:'ræfəlaɪt/ ● *noun* member of group of 19th-c. English artists. ● *adjective* of Pre-Raphaelites; (**pre-Raphaelite**) (esp. of woman) of type painted by Pre-Raphaelites.

pre-record /pri:rɪ'kɔ:d/ *verb* record in advance.

prerequisite /pri:'rekwɪzɪt/ ● *adjective* required as precondition. ● *noun* prerequisite thing.

■ **Usage** *Prerequisite* is sometimes confused with *perquisite* which means 'an extra profit, right, or privilege'.

prerogative /prɪ'rɒgətɪv/ *noun* right or privilege exclusive to individual or class.

Pres. *abbreviation* President.

presage /'presɪdʒ/ ● *noun* omen; presentiment. ● *verb* (**-ging**) portend; indicate (future event etc.); foretell, foresee.

presbyopia /prezbɪ'əʊpɪə/ *noun* long-sightedness. □ **presbyopic** *adjective*.

presbyter /'prezbɪtə/ *noun* priest of Episcopal Church; elder of Presbyterian Church.

Presbyterian /prezbɪ'tɪərɪən/ ● *adjective* (of Church, esp. Church of Scotland) governed by elders all of equal rank. ● *noun* member of Presbyterian Church. □ **Presbyterianism** *noun*.

presbytery /'prezbɪtərɪ/ *noun* (*plural* **-ies**) eastern part of chancel; body of presbyters; RC priest's house.

prescient /'presɪənt/ *adjective* having foreknowledge or foresight. □ **prescience** *noun*.

prescribe /prɪ'skraɪb/ *verb* (**-bing**) advise use of (medicine etc.); lay down authoritatively.

■ **Usage** *Prescribe* is sometimes confused with *proscribe*, which means 'forbid'.

prescript /'pri:skrɪpt/ *noun* ordinance, command.

prescription /prɪ'skrɪpʃ(ə)n/ *noun* prescribing; doctor's (usually written) instruction for composition and use of medicine; medicine thus prescribed.

prescriptive /prɪ'skrɪptɪv/ *adjective* prescribing, laying down rules; arising from custom.

presence /'prez(ə)ns/ *noun* being present; place where person is; personal appearance; person or spirit that is present. □ **presence of mind** calmness and quick-wittedness in sudden difficulty etc.

present[1] /'prez(ə)nt/ ● *adjective* being in place in question; now existing, occurring, or being dealt with etc.; *Grammar* expressing present action or state. ● *noun* (**the present**) now; present tense. □ **at present** now; **for the present** just now; **present-day** of this time, modern.

present[2] /prɪ'zent/ *verb* introduce; exhibit; offer or give (thing) to; (+ *with*) provide (person) with; put (play, film, etc.) before public; reveal; deliver (cheque etc.) for payment etc. □ **present arms** hold rifle etc. in saluting position.

present[3] /'prez(ə)nt/ *noun* gift.

presentable /prɪ'zentəb(ə)l/ *adjective* of good appearance; fit to be shown. □ **presentability** *noun*; **presentably** *adverb*.

presentation /prezən'teɪʃ(ə)n/ *noun* presenting, being presented; thing presented; manner or quality of presenting; demonstration of materials etc., lecture.

presenter *noun* person introducing broadcast programme.

presentiment /prɪ'zentɪmənt/ *noun* vague expectation, foreboding.

presently *adverb* before long; *US & Scottish* at present.

preservative /prɪ'zɜ:vətɪv/ ● *noun* substance for preserving food etc. ● *adjective* tending to preserve.

preserve /prɪ'zɜ:v/ ● *verb* (**-ving**) keep safe or free from decay; maintain, retain; treat (food) to prevent decomposition or fermentation; keep (game etc.) undisturbed for private use. ● *noun* (in *singular* or *plural*)

Preposition

A preposition is used in front of a noun or pronoun to form a phrase. It often describes the position of something, e.g. *under the chair*, or the time at which something happens, e.g. *in the evening*.

Prepositions in common use are:

about	*behind*	*into*	*through*
above	*beside*	*like*	*till*
across	*between*	*near*	*to*
after	*by*	*of*	*towards*
against	*down*	*off*	*under*
along	*during*	*on*	*underneath*
among	*except*	*outside*	*until*
around	*for*	*over*	*up*
as	*from*	*past*	*upon*
at	*in*	*round*	*with*
before	*inside*	*since*	*without*

preserved fruit, jam; place where game etc. is preserved; sphere of activity regarded by person as his or hers alone. □ **preservation** /prezə'veɪʃ(ə)n/ *noun*.

preshrunk /priː'ʃrʌŋk/ *adjective* (of fabric etc.) treated so as to shrink during manufacture and not in use.

preside /prɪ'zaɪd/ *verb* (**-ding**) (often + *at*, *over*) be chairperson or president; exercise control or authority.

presidency /'prezɪdənsɪ/ *noun* (*plural* **-ies**) office of president; period of this.

president /'prezɪd(ə)nt/ *noun* head of republic; head of society or council etc., of certain colleges, or (*US*) of university, company, etc.; person in charge of meeting. □ **presidential** /-'den-/ *adjective*.

presidium /prɪ'sɪdɪəm/ *noun* (also **praesidium**) standing committee, esp. in Communist country.

press[1] ● *verb* apply steady force to; flatten, shape, smooth (esp. clothes); (+ *out*, *of*, *from*, etc.) squeeze (juice etc.); embrace, caress firmly; (+ *on*, *against*, etc.) exert pressure on; be urgent, urge; (+ *for*) demand insistently; (+ *up*, *round*, etc.) crowd; (+ *on*, *forward*, etc.) hasten; (+ *on*, *upon*) force (offer etc.) on; manufacture (gramophone record, car part, etc.) using pressure. ● *noun* pressing; device for compressing, flattening, extracting juice, etc.; machine for printing; (**the press**) newspapers; publicity in newspapers; printing house; publishing company; crowding, crowd; pressure of affairs; large usually shelved cupboard. □ **press agent** person employed to manage advertising and press publicity; **press conference** meeting with journalists; **press gallery** gallery for reporters, esp. in legislative assembly; **press release** statement issued to newspapers etc.; **press-stud** small device fastened by pressing to engage two parts; **press-up** exercise in which prone body is raised by pressing down on hands to straighten arms.

press[2] *verb historical* force to serve in army or navy; bring into use as makeshift. □ **press-gang** *noun historical* group of men employed to press men for navy, *verb* force into service.

pressing ● *adjective* urgent; insistent. ● *noun* thing made by pressing, e.g. gramophone record; series of these made at one time; act of pressing. □ **pressingly** *adverb*.

pressure /'preʃə/ ● *noun* exertion of continuous force, force so exerted, amount of this; urgency; affliction, difficulty; constraining or compelling influence. ● *verb* (**-ring**) (often + *into*) apply pressure to, coerce, persuade. □ **pressure-cooker** pan for cooking quickly under high pressure; **pressure group** group formed to influence public policy.

pressurize *verb* (also **-ise**) (**-zing** or **-sing**) (esp. as **pressurized** *adjective*) maintain normal atmospheric pressure in (aircraft cabin etc.) at high altitude; raise to high pressure; pressure (person).

prestidigitator /prestɪ'dɪdʒɪteɪtə/ *noun formal* conjuror. □ **prestidigitation** *noun*.

prestige /pres'tiːʒ/ ● *noun* respect or reputation. ● *adjective* having or conferring prestige. □ **prestigious** /-'stɪdʒəs/ *adjective*.

presto /'prestəʊ/ *Music* ● *adverb & adjective* in quick tempo. ● *noun* (*plural* **-s**) presto movement or passage.

prestressed /priː'strest/ *adjective* (of concrete) strengthened by stretched wires in it.

presumably /prɪ'zjuːməblɪ/ *adverb* as may reasonably be presumed.

presume /prɪ'zjuːm/ *verb* (**-ming**) (often + *that*) suppose to be true, take for granted; (often + *to do*) venture; be presumptuous; (+ *on*, *upon*) make unscrupulous use of.

presumption /prɪ'zʌmpʃ(ə)n/ *noun* arrogance, presumptuous behaviour; taking for granted; thing presumed to be true; ground for presuming.

presumptive /prɪ'zʌmptɪv/ *adjective* giving grounds for presumption.

presumptuous /prɪ'zʌmptʃʊəs/ *adjective* unduly confident, arrogant. □ **presumptuously** *adverb*; **presumptuousness** *noun*.

presuppose /priːsə'pəʊz/ *verb* (**-sing**) assume beforehand; imply. □ **presupposition** /-sʌpə'zɪʃ(ə)n/ *noun*.

pre-tax /priː'tæks/ *adjective* (of income) before deduction of taxes.

pretence /prɪ'tens/ *noun* (*US* **pretense**) pretending, make-believe; pretext; (+ *to*) (esp. false) claim; ostentation.

pretend /prɪ'tend/ ● *verb* claim or assert falsely; imagine in play; (as **pretended** *adjective*) falsely claimed to be; (+ *to*) profess to have. ● *adjective colloquial* pretended.

pretender *noun* person who claims throne, title, etc.

pretense *US* = PRETENCE.

pretension /prɪ'tenʃ(ə)n/ *noun* (often + *to*) assertion of claim; pretentiousness.

pretentious /prɪ'tenʃəs/ *adjective* making excessive claim to merit or importance; ostentatious. □ **pretentiously** *adverb*; **pretentiousness** *noun*.

preternatural /priːtə'nætʃər(ə)l/ *adjective* extraordinary; supernatural.

pretext /'priːtekst/ *noun* ostensible reason; excuse.

pretty /'prɪtɪ/ ● *adjective* (**-ier**, **-iest**) attractive in delicate way; fine, good; considerable. ● *adverb colloquial* fairly, moderately. ● *verb* (**-ies**, **-ied**) (often + *up*) make pretty. □ **pretty-pretty** *colloquial* too pretty. □ **prettify** *verb* (**-ies**, **-ied**); **prettily** *adverb*; **prettiness** *noun*.

pretzel /'prets(ə)l/ *noun* crisp knot-shaped salted biscuit.

prevail /prɪ'veɪl/ *verb* (often + *against*, *over*) be victorious; be the more usual or predominant; exist or occur in general use; (+ *on*, *upon*) persuade.

prevalent /'prevələnt/ *adjective* generally existing or occurring. □ **prevalence** *noun*.

prevaricate /prɪ'værɪkeɪt/ *verb* (**-ting**) speak or act evasively or misleadingly. □ **prevarication** *noun*; **prevaricator** *noun*.

■ **Usage** *Prevaricate* is often confused with *procrastinate*, which means 'to defer action'.

prevent /prɪ'vent/ *verb* (often + *from doing*) stop, hinder. □ **preventable** *adjective* (also **preventible**); **prevention** *noun*.

■ **Usage** The use of *prevent* without 'from' as in *She prevented me going* is informal. An acceptable further alternative is *She prevented my going*.

preventative /prɪ'ventətɪv/ *adjective & noun* preventive.

preventive /prɪ'ventɪv/ ● *adjective* serving to prevent, esp. disease. ● *noun* preventive agent, measure, drug, etc.

preview /'priːvjuː/ ● *noun* showing of film, play, etc. before it is seen by general public. ● *verb* view or show in advance.

previous /'priːvɪəs/ ● *adjective* (often + *to*) coming before in time or order; *colloquial* hasty, premature. ● *adverb* (+ *to*) before. □ **previously** *adverb*.

pre-war /priː'wɔː/ *adjective* existing or occurring before a war.

prey /preɪ/ ● *noun* animal hunted or killed by another for food; (often + *to*) victim. ● *verb* (+ *on*, *upon*) seek or take as prey; exert harmful influence.

price ● *noun* amount of money for which thing is bought or sold; what must be given, done, etc. to obtain thing; odds. ● *verb* (**-cing**) fix or find price of; estimate value of. □ **at a price** at high cost; **price tag** label on item showing its price.

priceless *adjective* invaluable; *colloquial* very amusing or absurd.

pricey *adjective* (**pricier**, **priciest**) *colloquial* expensive.

prick ● *verb* pierce slightly, make small hole in; (+ *off*, *out*) mark with pricks or dots; trouble mentally; tingle. ● *noun* pricking, mark of it; pain caused as by pricking, mental pain. □ **prick out** plant (seedlings etc.) in small holes pricked in earth; **prick up one's ears** (of dog) erect the ears when alert, (of person) become suddenly attentive.

prickle /ˈprɪk(ə)l/ ● *noun* small thorn; hard-pointed spine; prickling sensation. ● *verb* (**-ling**) cause or feel sensation as of prick(s).

prickly *adjective* (**-ier**, **-iest**) having prickles; irritable; tingling. □ **prickly heat** itchy inflammation of skin near sweat glands; **prickly pear** cactus with pear-shaped edible fruit, its fruit. □ **prickliness** *noun*.

pride ● *noun* elation or satisfaction at one's achievements, possessions, etc.; object of this; unduly high opinion of oneself; proper sense of one's own worth, position, etc.; group (of lions etc.). ● *verb* (**-ding**) (**pride oneself on**, **upon**) be proud of. □ **pride of place** most important position; **take (a) pride in** be proud of.

prie-dieu /priːˈdjɜː/ *noun* (*plural* **-x** same pronunciation) kneeling-desk for prayer.

priest /priːst/ *noun* ordained minister of some Christian churches (above deacon and below bishop); (*feminine* **priestess**) official minister of non-Christian religion. □ **priesthood** *noun*; **priestly** *adjective*.

prig *noun* self-righteous or moralistic person. □ **priggish** *adjective*; **priggishness** *noun*.

prim *adjective* (**-mm-**) stiffly formal and precise; prudish. □ **primly** *adverb*; **primness** *noun*.

prima /ˈpriːmə/ *adjective* □ **prima ballerina** chief female dancer in ballet; **prima donna** chief female singer in opera, temperamental person.

primacy /ˈpraɪməsɪ/ *noun* (*plural* **-ies**) pre-eminence; office of primate.

prima facie /praɪmə ˈfeɪʃɪ/ ● *adverb* at first sight. ● *adjective* (of evidence) based on first impression.

primal /ˈpraɪm(ə)l/ *adjective* primitive, primeval; fundamental.

primary /ˈpraɪmərɪ/ ● *adjective* of first importance; fundamental; original. ● *noun* (*plural* **-ies**) primary colour, feather, school, etc.; *US* primary election. □ **primary colour** one not obtained by mixing others; **primary education** education for children under 11; **primary election** *US* election to select candidate(s) for principal election; **primary feather** large flight feather of bird's wing; **primary school** school for primary education. □ **primarily** /ˈpraɪmərɪlɪ, praɪˈmeərɪlɪ/ *adverb*.

primate /ˈpraɪmeɪt/ *noun* member of highest order of mammals, including apes, man, etc.; archbishop.

prime[1] ● *adjective* chief, most important; of highest quality; primary, fundamental; (of number etc.) divisible only by itself and unity. ● *noun* best or most vigorous stage. □ **prime minister** chief minister of government; **prime time** time when television etc. audience is largest.

prime[2] *verb* (**-ming**) prepare (thing) for use; prepare (gun) for firing or (explosive) for detonation; pour liquid into (pump) to start it working; cover (wood, metal, etc.) with primer; equip (person) with information etc.

primer[1] *noun* substance applied to bare wood, metal, etc. before painting.

primer[2] *noun* elementary school-book; introductory book.

primeval /praɪˈmiːv(ə)l/ *adjective* of first age of world; ancient, primitive.

primitive /ˈprɪmɪtɪv/ ● *adjective* at early stage of civilization; crude, simple. ● *noun* untutored painter with naïve style; picture by such painter. □ **primitively** *adverb*; **primitiveness** *noun*.

primogeniture /praɪməʊˈdʒenɪtʃə/ *noun* being first-born; first-born's right to inheritance.

primordial /praɪˈmɔːdɪəl/ *adjective* existing at or from beginning, primeval.

primrose /ˈprɪmrəʊz/ *noun* plant bearing pale yellow spring flower; this flower; pale yellow. □ **primrose path** pursuit of pleasure.

primula /ˈprɪmjʊlə/ *noun* cultivated plant with flowers of various colours.

Primus /ˈpraɪməs/ *noun proprietary term* portable cooking stove burning vaporized oil.

prince *noun* (as title usually **Prince**) male member of royal family other than king; ruler of small state; nobleman of some countries; (often + *of*) the greatest. □ **Prince Consort** husband of reigning queen who is himself a prince.

princely *adjective* (**-ier**, **-iest**) of or worthy of a prince; sumptuous, splendid.

princess /prɪnˈses/ *noun* (as title usually **Princess** /ˈprɪnses/) prince's wife; female member of royal family other than queen.

principal /ˈprɪnsɪp(ə)l/ ● *adjective* first in importance, chief; leading. ● *noun* chief person; head of some institutions; principal actor, singer, etc.; capital sum lent or invested; person for whom another is agent etc. □ **principal boy** (usually actress playing) leading male role in pantomime. □ **principally** *adverb*.

principality /prɪnsɪˈpælɪtɪ/ *noun* (*plural* **-ies**) state ruled by prince; (**the Principality**) Wales.

principle /ˈprɪnsɪp(ə)l/ *noun* fundamental truth or law as basis of reasoning or action; personal code of conduct; fundamental source or element. □ **in principle** in theory; **on principle** from moral motive.

principled *adjective* based on or having (esp. praiseworthy) principles of behaviour.

prink *verb* (usually **prink oneself**; often + *up*) smarten, dress up.

print ● *verb* produce by applying inked type, plates, etc. to paper etc.; express or publish in print; (often + *on*, *with*) impress, stamp; write in letters that are not joined; produce (photograph) from negative; (usually + *out*) produce computer output in printed form; mark (fabric) with design. ● *noun* mark left on surface by pressure; printed lettering, words, or publication (esp. newspaper); engraving; photograph; printed fabric. □ **in print** (of book etc.) available from publisher, in printed form; **out of print** (of book etc.) no longer available from publisher; **printed circuit** electric circuit with thin conducting strips printed on flat sheet; **printing press** machine for printing from type, plates, etc.; **printout** computer output in printed form.

printer *noun* person who prints books etc.; owner of printing business; device that prints esp. computer output.

prior /ˈpraɪə/ ● *adjective* earlier; (often + *to*) coming before in time, order, or importance. ● *adverb* (+ *to*) before. ● *noun* (*feminine* **prioress**) superior of religious house; (in abbey) deputy of abbot.

priority /praɪˈɒrɪtɪ/ *noun* (*plural* **-ies**) thing considered more important than others; precedence in time, rank, etc.; right to do something before other people. □ **prioritize** *verb* (also **-ise**) (**-zing** or **-sing**).

priory /ˈpraɪərɪ/ *noun* (*plural* **-ies**) religious house governed by prior or prioress.

prise /praɪz/ *verb* (also **prize**) (**-sing** or **-zing**) force open or out by leverage.

prism /ˈprɪz(ə)m/ *noun* solid figure whose two ends are equal parallel rectilinear figures, and whose sides are parallelograms; transparent body of this form with refracting surfaces.

prismatic /prɪzˈmætɪk/ *adjective* of, like, or using prism; (of colours) distributed (as if) by transparent prism.

prison /ˈprɪz(ə)n/ *noun* place of captivity, esp. building to which people are consigned while awaiting trial or for punishment.

prisoner /ˈprɪznə/ *noun* person kept in prison; person or thing confined by illness, another's grasp, etc.; (in full **prisoner of war**) person captured in war.

prissy /ˈprɪsɪ/ *adjective* (**-ier**, **-iest**) prim, prudish. ▫ **prissily** *adverb*; **prissiness** *noun*.

pristine /ˈprɪsti:n/ *adjective* in original condition, unspoilt; ancient.

privacy /ˈprɪvəsɪ/ *noun* (right to) being private; freedom from intrusion or publicity.

private /ˈpraɪvət/ ● *adjective* belonging to an individual, personal; confidential, secret; not public; secluded; not holding public office or official position; not supported, managed, or provided by state. ● *noun* private soldier; (in *plural*) *colloquial* genitals. ▫ **in private** privately; **private detective** detective outside police force; **private enterprise** business(es) not under state control; **private eye** *colloquial* private detective; **private means** unearned income from investments etc.; **private member** MP not holding government office; **private parts** *euphemistic* genitals; **private soldier** ordinary soldier, not officer. ▫ **privately** *adverb*.

privateer /praɪvəˈtɪə/ *noun* (commander of) privately owned and government-commissioned warship.

privation /praɪˈveɪʃ(ə)n/ *noun* lack of comforts or necessities.

privatize /ˈpraɪvətaɪz/ *verb* (also **-ise**) (**-zing** or **-sing**) transfer from state to private ownership. ▫ **privatization** *noun*.

privet /ˈprɪvɪt/ *noun* bushy evergreen shrub used for hedges.

privilege /ˈprɪvɪlɪdʒ/ ● *noun* right, advantage, or immunity belonging to person, class, or office; special benefit or honour. ● *verb* (**-ging**) invest with privilege.

privy /ˈprɪvɪ/ ● *adjective* (+ *to*) sharing secret of; *archaic* hidden, secret. ● *noun* (*plural* **-ies**) lavatory. ▫ **Privy Council** group of advisers appointed by sovereign; **Privy Councillor**, **Counsellor** member of this; **privy purse** allowance from public revenue for monarch's private expenses; **privy seal** state seal formerly affixed to minor documents.

prize[1] ● *noun* reward in competition, lottery, etc.; reward given as symbol of victory or superiority; thing (to be) striven for. ● *adjective* to which prize is awarded; excellent of its kind. ● *verb* (**-zing**) value highly. ▫ **prizefight** boxing match for money.

prize[2] *noun* ship or property captured in naval warfare.

prize[3] = PRISE.

PRO *abbreviation* Public Record Office; public relations officer.

pro[1] *noun* (*plural* **-s**) *colloquial* professional.

pro[2] ● *adjective* in favour. ● *noun* (*plural* **-s**) reason in favour. ● *preposition* in favour of. ▫ **pros and cons** reasons for and against.

proactive /prəʊˈæktɪv/ *adjective* (of person, policy, etc.) taking the initiative.

probability *noun* (*plural* **-ies**) being probable; likelihood; (most) probable event; extent to which thing is likely to occur, measured by ratio of favourable cases to all cases possible. ▫ **in all probability** most probably.

probable /ˈprɒbəb(ə)l/ ● *adjective* (often + *that*) that may be expected to happen or prove true; likely. ● *noun* probable candidate, member of team, etc. ▫ **probably** *adverb*.

probate /ˈprəʊbeɪt/ *noun* official proving of will; verified copy of will.

probation /prəˈbeɪʃ(ə)n/ *noun* system of supervising behaviour of offenders as alternative to prison; testing of character and abilities of esp. new employee. ▫ **probation officer** official supervising offenders on probation. ▫ **probationary** *adjective*.

probationer *noun* person on probation.

probe ● *noun* investigation; device for measuring, testing, etc.; blunt-ended surgical instrument for exploring wound etc.; unmanned exploratory spacecraft. ● *verb* (**-bing**) examine closely; explore with probe.

probity /ˈprəʊbɪtɪ/ *noun* uprightness, honesty.

problem /ˈprɒbləm/ ● *noun* doubtful or difficult question; thing hard to understand or deal with. ● *adjective* causing problems.

problematic /prɒbləˈmætɪk/ *adjective* (also **problematical**) attended by difficulty; doubtful, questionable.

proboscis /prəʊˈbɒsɪs/ *noun* (*plural* **-sces**) long flexible trunk or snout, e.g. of elephant; elongated mouth-parts of some insects.

procedure /prəˈsi:dʒə/ *noun* way of conducting business etc. or performing task; set series of actions. ▫ **procedural** *adjective*.

proceed /prəˈsi:d/ *verb* (often + *to*) go forward or on further, make one's way; (often + *with*, *to do*) continue or resume; adopt course of action; go on to say; (+ *against*) start lawsuit against; (often + *from*) originate.

proceeding *noun* action, piece of conduct; (in *plural*) legal action, published report of discussions or conference.

proceeds /ˈprəʊsi:dz/ *plural noun* profits from sale etc.

process[1] /ˈprəʊses/ ● *noun* course of action or proceeding, esp. series of stages in manufacture etc.; progress or course; natural or involuntary course of change; action at law; summons, writ; *Biology* natural appendage or outgrowth of organism. ● *verb* subject to particular process; (as **processed** *adjective*) (of food) treated, esp. to prevent decay.

process[2] /prəˈses/ *verb* walk in procession.

procession /prəˈseʃ(ə)n/ *noun* people etc. advancing in orderly succession, esp. at ceremony, demonstration, or festivity.

processional ● *adjective* of processions; used, carried, or sung in processions. ● *noun* processional hymn (book).

processor /ˈprəʊsesə/ *noun* machine that processes things; central processor; food processor.

proclaim /prəˈkleɪm/ *verb* (often + *that*) announce publicly or officially; declare to be. ▫ **proclamation** /prɒklə-/ *noun*.

proclivity /prəˈklɪvɪtɪ/ *noun* (*plural* **-ies**) natural tendency.

procrastinate /prəʊˈkræstɪneɪt/ *verb* (**-ting**) defer action. ▫ **procrastination** *noun*.

■ **Usage** *Procrastinate* is often confused with *prevaricate*, which means 'to speak or act evasively or misleadingly'.

procreate /ˈprəʊkrɪeɪt/ *verb* (**-ting**) produce (offspring) naturally. □ **procreation** *noun*; **procreative** /-krɪˈeɪ-/ *adjective*.

proctor /ˈprɒktə/ *noun* university disciplinary official. □ **proctorial** /-ˈtɔːrɪəl/ *adjective*.

procuration /prɒkjʊˈreɪʃ(ə)n/ *noun formal* procuring; action of attorney.

procurator /ˈprɒkjʊreɪtə/ *noun* agent or proxy, esp. with power of attorney. □ **procurator fiscal** (in Scotland) local coroner and public prosecutor.

procure /prəˈkjʊə/ *verb* (**-ring**) succeed in getting; bring about; act as procurer. □ **procurement** *noun*.

procurer *noun* (*feminine* **procuress**) person who obtains women for prostitution.

prod ● *verb* (**-dd-**) poke with finger, stick, etc.; stimulate to action. ● *noun* poke, thrust; stimulus to action.

prodigal /ˈprɒdɪg(ə)l/ ● *adjective* wasteful; (+ *of*) lavish of. ● *noun* spendthrift. □ **prodigal son** repentant wastrel. □ **prodigality** /-ˈgæl-/ *noun*.

prodigious /prəˈdɪdʒəs/ *adjective* marvellous; enormous; abnormal.

prodigy /ˈprɒdɪdʒɪ/ *noun* (*plural* **-ies**) exceptionally gifted person, esp. precocious child; marvellous thing; (+ *of*) wonderful example of.

produce ● *verb* /prəˈdjuːs/ (**-cing**) manufacture or prepare; bring forward for inspection etc.; bear, yield, or bring into existence; cause or bring about; *Geometry* extend or continue (line); bring (play etc.) before public. ● *noun* /ˈprɒdjuːs/ what is produced, esp. agricultural products; amount produced; (often + *of*) result.

producer *noun* person who produces goods etc.; person who supervises production of play, film, broadcast, etc.

product /ˈprɒdʌkt/ *noun* thing or substance produced, esp. by manufacture; result; *Mathematics* quantity obtained by multiplying.

production /prəˈdʌkʃ(ə)n/ *noun* producing, being produced; total yield; thing produced, esp. play etc. □ **production line** systematized sequence of operations to produce commodity.

productive /prəˈdʌktɪv/ *adjective* producing, esp. abundantly. □ **productively** *adverb*; **productiveness** *noun*.

productivity /prɒdʌkˈtɪvɪtɪ/ *noun* capacity to produce; effectiveness of industry, workforce, etc.

Prof. *abbreviation* Professor.

profane /prəˈfeɪn/ ● *adjective* irreverent, blasphemous; obscene; not sacred. ● *verb* (**-ning**) treat irreverently; violate, pollute. □ **profanation** /prɒfə-/ *noun*.

profanity /prəˈfænɪtɪ/ *noun* (*plural* **-ies**) blasphemy; swear-word.

profess /prəˈfes/ *verb* claim openly to have; (often + *to do*) pretend, declare; affirm one's faith in or allegiance to.

professed *adjective* self-acknowledged; alleged, ostensible. □ **professedly** /-sɪdlɪ/ *adverb*.

profession /prəˈfeʃ(ə)n/ *noun* occupation or calling, esp. learned or scientific; people in a profession; declaration, avowal.

professional ● *adjective* of, belonging to, or connected with a profession; competent, worthy of professional; engaged in specified activity as paid occupation, or (*derogatory*) fanatically. ● *noun* professional person. □ **professionally** *adverb*.

professionalism *noun* qualities of professionals, esp. competence, skill, etc.

professor /prəˈfesə/ *noun* highest-ranking academic in university department, *US* university teacher; person who professes a religion etc. □ **professorial** /prɒfɪˈsɔːrɪəl/ *adjective*; **professorship** *noun*.

proffer /ˈprɒfə/ *verb* offer.

proficient /prəˈfɪʃ(ə)nt/ *adjective* (often + *in*, *at*) adept, expert. □ **proficiency** *noun*; **proficiently** *adverb*.

profile /ˈprəʊfaɪl/ ● *noun* side view or outline, esp. of human face; short biographical sketch. ● *verb* (**-ling**) represent by profile. □ **keep a low profile** remain inconspicuous.

profit /ˈprɒfɪt/ ● *noun* advantage, benefit; financial gain, excess of returns over outlay. ● *verb* (**-t-**) be beneficial to; obtain advantage. □ **at a profit** with financial gain; **profit margin** profit after deduction of costs.

profitable *adjective* yielding profit; beneficial. □ **profitability** *noun*; **profitably** *adverb*.

profiteer /prɒfɪˈtɪə/ ● *verb* make or seek excessive profits, esp. illegally. ● *noun* person who profiteers.

profiterole /prəˈfɪtərəʊl/ *noun* small hollow cake of choux pastry with filling.

profligate /ˈprɒflɪgət/ ● *adjective* recklessly extravagant; licentious, dissolute. ● *noun* profligate person. □ **profligacy** *noun*; **profligately** *adverb*.

pro forma /prəʊ ˈfɔːmə/ ● *adverb & adjective* for form's sake. ● *noun* (in full **pro forma invoice**) invoice sent in advance of goods supplied.

profound /prəˈfaʊnd/ *adjective* (**-er**, **-est**) having or demanding great knowledge, study, or insight; intense, thorough; deep. □ **profoundly** *adverb*; **profoundness** *noun*; **profundity** /-ˈfʌndɪtɪ/ *noun* (*plural* **-ies**).

profuse /prəˈfjuːs/ *adjective* (often + *in*, *of*) lavish, extravagant, copious. □ **profusely** *adverb*; **profusion** *noun*.

progenitor /prəʊˈdʒenɪtə/ *noun* ancestor; predecessor; original.

progeny /ˈprɒdʒɪnɪ/ *noun* offspring, descendants; outcome, issue.

progesterone /prəʊˈdʒestərəʊn/ *noun* a sex hormone that helps to initiate and maintains pregnancy.

prognosis /prɒgˈnəʊsɪs/ *noun* (*plural* **-noses** /-siːz/) forecast, esp. of course of disease.

prognostic /prɒgˈnɒstɪk/ ● *noun* (often + *of*) advance indication; prediction. ● *adjective* (often + *of*) foretelling, predictive.

prognosticate /prɒgˈnɒstɪkeɪt/ *verb* (**-ting**) (often + *that*) foretell; betoken. □ **prognostication** *noun*.

programme /ˈprəʊgræm/ (*US* **program**) ● *noun* list of events, performers, etc.; radio or television broadcast; plan of events; course or series of studies, lectures, etc.; (usually **program**) series of instructions for computer. ● *verb* (**-mm-**; *US* **-m-**) make programme of; (usually **program**) express (problem) or instruct (computer) by means of program. □ **programmable** *adjective*; **programmer** *noun*.

progress ● *noun* /ˈprəʊgres/ forward movement; advance, development, improvement; *historical* state journey, esp. by royalty. ● *verb* /prəˈgres/ move forward or onward; advance, develop, improve. □ **in progress** developing, going on.

progression /prəˈgreʃ(ə)n/ *noun* progressing; succession, series.

progressive /prəˈgresɪv/ ● *adjective* moving forward; proceeding step by step; cumulative; favouring rapid reform; modern, efficient; (of disease etc.) increasing in severity or extent; (of taxation) increasing with the sum taxed. ● *noun* (also **Progressive**) advocate of progressive policy. □ **progressively** *adverb*.

prohibit /prəˈhɪbɪt/ *verb* (**-t-**) (often + *from*) forbid; prevent.

prohibition /prəʊhɪˈbɪʃ(ə)n/ *noun* forbidding, being forbidden; edict or order that forbids; (usually **Prohibition**) legal ban on manufacture and sale of alcohol. ▫ **prohibitionist** *noun*.

prohibitive /prəˈhɪbɪtɪv/ *adjective* prohibiting; (of prices, taxes, etc.) extremely high. ▫ **prohibitively** *adverb*.

project ● *noun* /ˈprɒdʒekt/ plan, scheme; extensive essay, piece of research, etc. by student(s). ● *verb* /prəˈdʒekt/ protrude, jut out; throw, impel; forecast; plan; cause (light, image, etc.) to fall on surface; cause (voice etc.) to be heard at distance.

projectile /prəˈdʒektaɪl/ ● *noun* object to be fired (esp. by rocket) or hurled. ● *adjective* of or serving as projectile; projecting, impelling.

projection /prəˈdʒekʃ(ə)n/ *noun* projecting, being projected; thing that protrudes; presentation of image(s) etc. on surface; forecast, estimate; mental image viewed as objective reality; transfer of feelings to other people etc.; representation of earth etc. on plane surface.

projectionist *noun* person who operates projector.

projector /prəˈdʒektə/ *noun* apparatus for projecting image or film on screen.

prolactin /prəʊˈlæktɪn/ *noun* hormone that stimulates milk production after childbirth.

prolapse ● *noun* /ˈprəʊlæps/ (also **prolapsus** /-ˈlæpsəs/) slipping forward or downward of part or organ; prolapsed womb, rectum, etc. ● *verb* /prəˈlæps/ (**-sing**) undergo prolapse.

prolate /ˈprəʊleɪt/ *adjective* (of spheroid) lengthened along polar diameter.

prolegomenon /prəʊlɪˈgɒmɪnən/ *noun* (*plural* **-mena**) (usually in *plural*) preface to book etc., esp. discursive or critical.

proletarian /prəʊlɪˈteərɪən/ ● *adjective* of proletariat. ● *noun* member of proletariat.

proletariat /prəʊlɪˈteərɪət/ *noun* working class; *esp. derogatory* lowest class.

proliferate /prəˈlɪfəreɪt/ *verb* (**-ting**) reproduce; produce (cells etc.) rapidly; increase rapidly, multiply. ▫ **proliferation** *noun*.

prolific /prəˈlɪfɪk/ *adjective* producing many offspring or much output; (often + *of*) abundantly productive; copious.

prolix /ˈprəʊlɪks/ *adjective* lengthy; tedious. ▫ **prolixity** /-ˈlɪks-/ *noun*.

prologue /ˈprəʊlɒg/ *noun* introduction to poem, play, etc.; (usually + *to*) introductory event.

prolong /prəˈlɒŋ/ *verb* extend; (as **prolonged** *adjective*) (tediously) lengthy. ▫ **prolongation** /prəʊlɒŋˈgeɪʃ(ə)n/ *noun*.

prom *noun colloquial* promenade; promenade concert.

promenade /prɒməˈnɑːd/ ● *noun* paved public walk, esp. at seaside; leisure walk. ● *verb* (**-ding**) make promenade (through); lead about, esp. for display. ▫ **promenade concert** one at which (part of) audience is not seated; **promenade deck** upper deck on liner.

promenader *noun* person who promenades; regular attender at promenade concerts.

prominent /ˈprɒmɪnənt/ *adjective* jutting out; conspicuous; distinguished. ▫ **prominence** *noun*.

promiscuous /prəˈmɪskjʊəs/ *adjective* having frequent casual sexual relationships; mixed and indiscriminate; *colloquial* casual. ▫ **promiscuously** *adverb*; **promiscuity** /prɒmɪsˈkjuːɪtɪ/ *noun*.

promise /ˈprɒmɪs/ ● *noun* explicit undertaking to do or not to do something; favourable indications. ● *verb* (**-sing**) (usually + *to do, that*) make promise; (often + *to do*) seem likely; *colloquial* assure.

promising *adjective* likely to turn out well; hopeful, full of promise. ▫ **promisingly** *adverb*.

promissory /ˈprɒmɪsərɪ/ *adjective* expressing or implying promise. ▫ **promissory note** signed document containing promise to pay stated sum.

promontory /ˈprɒməntərɪ/ *noun* (*plural* **-ies**) point of high land jutting out into sea etc.; headland.

promote /prəˈməʊt/ *verb* (**-ting**) (often + *to*) advance (person) to higher office or position; help forward, encourage; publicize and sell. ▫ **promotion** *noun*; **promotional** *adjective*.

promoter *noun* person who promotes, esp. sporting event, theatrical production, etc., or formation of joint-stock company.

prompt ● *adjective* acting, made, or done immediately; ready. ● *adverb* punctually. ● *verb* (usually + *to, to do*) incite; supply (actor, speaker) with next words or with suggestion; inspire. ● *noun* prompting; thing said to prompt actor etc.; sign on computer screen inviting input. ▫ **promptitude** *noun*; **promptly** *adverb*; **promptness** *noun*.

prompter *noun* person who prompts actors.

promulgate /ˈprɒməlgeɪt/ *verb* (**-ting**) make known to the public; proclaim. ▫ **promulgation** *noun*.

prone *adjective* lying face downwards; lying flat, prostrate; (usually + *to, to do*) disposed, liable. ▫ **-prone** likely to suffer. ▫ **proneness** *noun*.

prong *noun* spike of fork.

pronominal /prəʊˈnɒmɪn(ə)l/ *adjective* of, concerning, or being a pronoun.

pronoun /ˈprəʊnaʊn/ *noun* word used as substitute for noun or noun phrase usually already mentioned or known (see panel).

pronounce /prəˈnaʊns/ *verb* (**-cing**) utter or speak, esp. in approved manner; utter formally; state (as) one's opinion; (usually + *on, for, against*, etc.) pass judgement. ▫ **pronounceable** *adjective*; **pronouncement** *noun*.

pronounced *adjective* strongly marked.

pronto /ˈprɒntəʊ/ *adverb colloquial* promptly, quickly.

Pronoun

A pronoun is used as a substitute for a noun or a noun phrase, e.g.

He *was upstairs.*	*Did you see* that?
Anything *can happen now.*	It'*s lovely weather.*

Using a pronoun often avoids repetition, e.g.

I found Jim—he *was upstairs.*
(instead of *I found Jim—Jim was upstairs.*)

Where are your keys?—I've got them.
(instead of *Where are your keys?—I've got my keys.*)

pronunciation /prənʌnsɪ'eɪʃ(ə)n/ *noun* pronouncing of word, esp. with reference to standard; act of pronouncing; way of pronouncing words.

proof /pru:f/ ● *noun* fact, evidence, reasoning, or demonstration that proves something; test, trial; standard of strength of distilled alcohol; trial impression of printed matter for correction. ● *adjective* (often + *against*) impervious to penetration, damage, etc. by a specified thing. ● *verb* make proof, esp. against water or bullets. □ **proofread** read and correct (printed proof); **proofreader** person who does this.

prop[1] ● *noun* rigid support; person or thing that supports, comforts, etc. ● *verb* (**-pp-**) (often + *against*, *up*, etc.) support (as) with prop.

prop[2] *noun colloquial* stage property.

prop[3] *noun colloquial* propeller.

propaganda /prɒpə'gændə/ *noun* organized propagation of a doctrine etc.; *usually derogatory* ideas etc. so propagated. □ **propagandist** *noun*.

propagate /'prɒpəgeɪt/ *verb* (**-ting**) breed from parent stock; (often **propagate itself**) (of plant etc.) reproduce itself; disseminate; transmit. □ **propagation** *noun*; **propagator** *noun*.

propane /'prəʊpeɪn/ *noun* gaseous hydrocarbon used as fuel.

propel /prə'pel/ *verb* (**-ll-**) drive or push forward; urge on. □ **propellant** *noun & adjective*.

propeller *noun* revolving shaft with blades, esp. for propelling ship or aircraft.

propensity /prə'pensɪtɪ/ *noun* (*plural* **-ies**) inclination, tendency.

proper /'prɒpə/ *adjective* accurate, correct; suitable, appropriate; decent, respectable; (usually + *to*) belonging, relating; strictly so called, genuine; *colloquial* thorough. □ **proper name**, **noun** name of person, place, etc. □ **properly** *adverb*.

property /'prɒpətɪ/ *noun* (*plural* **-ies**) thing(s) owned; landed estate; quality, characteristic; movable article used on theatre stage or in film.

prophecy /'prɒfɪsɪ/ *noun* (*plural* **-ies**) prophetic utterance; prediction; prophesying.

prophesy /'prɒfɪsaɪ/ *verb* (**-ies**, **-ied**) (usually + *that*, *who*, etc.) foretell; speak as prophet.

prophet /'prɒfɪt/ *noun* (*feminine* **prophetess**) teacher or interpreter of divine will; person who predicts; (**the Prophet**) Muhammad.

prophetic /prə'fetɪk/ *adjective* (often + *of*) containing a prediction, predicting; of prophet.

prophylactic /prɒfɪ'læktɪk/ ● *adjective* tending to prevent disease etc. ● *noun* preventive medicine or action; *esp. US* condom.

prophylaxis /prɒfɪ'læksɪs/ *noun* preventive treatment against disease.

propinquity /prə'pɪŋkwɪtɪ/ *noun* nearness; close kinship; similarity.

propitiate /prə'pɪʃɪeɪt/ *verb* (**-ting**) appease. □ **propitiation** *noun*; **propitiatory** /-ʃətərɪ/ *adjective*.

propitious /prə'pɪʃəs/ *adjective* favourable, auspicious; (often + *for*, *to*) suitable.

proponent /prə'pəʊnənt/ *noun* person advocating proposal etc.

proportion /prə'pɔ:ʃ(ə)n/ ● *noun* comparative part, share; comparative ratio; correct relation between things or parts of thing; (in *plural*) dimensions. ● *verb* (usually + *to*) make proportionate.

proportional *adjective* in correct proportion; comparable. □ **proportional representation** representation of parties in parliament in proportion to votes they receive. □ **proportionally** *adverb*.

proportionate /prə'pɔ:ʃənət/ *adjective* proportional. □ **proportionately** *adverb*.

proposal /prə'pəʊz(ə)l/ *noun* proposing; scheme etc. proposed; offer of marriage.

propose /prə'pəʊz/ *verb* (**-sing**) put forward for consideration; (usually + *to do*) purpose; (usually + *to*) offer marriage; nominate as member of society etc. □ **propose a toast** ask people to drink to health or in honour of person or thing. □ **proposer** *noun*.

proposition /prɒpə'zɪʃ(ə)n/ ● *noun* statement, assertion; scheme proposed, proposal; statement subject to proof or disproof; *colloquial* problem, opponent, prospect, etc.; *Mathematics* formal statement of theorem or problem; likely commercial enterprise, person, etc.; sexual proposal. ● *verb colloquial* put (esp. sexual) proposal to.

propound /prə'paʊnd/ *verb* offer for consideration.

proprietary /prə'praɪətərɪ/ *adjective* of or holding property; of proprietor; held in private ownership; manufactured by one particular firm. □ **proprietary name**, **term** name of product etc. registered as trade mark.

proprietor /prə'praɪətə/ *noun* (*feminine* **proprietress**) owner. □ **proprietorial** /-'tɔ:r-/ *adjective*.

propriety /prə'praɪɪtɪ/ *noun* (*plural* **-ies**) fitness, rightness; correctness of behaviour or morals; (in *plural*) rules of polite behaviour.

propulsion /prə'pʌlʃ(ə)n/ *noun* driving or pushing forward; force causing this. □ **propulsive** /-'pʌlsɪv/ *adjective*.

pro rata /prəʊ 'rɑ:tə/ ● *adjective* proportional. ● *adverb* proportionally. [Latin]

prorogue /prə'rəʊg/ *verb* (**-gues**, **-gued**, **-guing**) discontinue meetings of (parliament etc.) without dissolving (it); be prorogued. □ **prorogation** /prəʊrə-/ *noun*.

prosaic /prə'zeɪɪk/ *adjective* like prose; unromantic; commonplace. □ **prosaically** *adverb*.

proscenium /prə'si:nɪəm/ *noun* (*plural* **-s** or **-nia**) part of theatre stage in front of curtain and enclosing arch.

proscribe /prə'skraɪb/ *verb* (**-bing**) forbid; denounce; outlaw. □ **proscription** /-'skrɪp-/ *noun*; **proscriptive** /-'skrɪp-/ *adjective*.

■ **Usage** *Proscribe* is sometimes confused with *prescribe* which means 'to impose'.

prose /prəʊz/ ● *noun* ordinary language; not in verse; passage of this, esp. for translation; dullness. ● *verb* (**-sing**) talk tediously.

prosecute /'prɒsɪkju:t/ *verb* (**-ting**) institute legal proceedings against; *formal* carry on (trade etc.). □ **prosecutor** *noun*.

prosecution /prɒsɪ'kju:ʃ(ə)n/ *noun* prosecuting, being prosecuted; prosecuting party.

proselyte /'prɒsəlaɪt/ *noun* convert, esp. recent; convert to Jewish faith. □ **proselytism** /-letɪz(ə)m/ *noun*.

proselytize /'prɒsələtaɪz/ *verb* (also **-ise**) (**-zing** or **-sing**) (seek to) convert.

prosody /'prɒsədɪ/ *noun* science of versification. □ **prosodist** *noun*.

prospect ● *noun* /'prɒspekt/ (often in *plural*) expectation; extensive view; mental picture; possible or likely customer etc. ● *verb* /prə'spekt/ (usually + *for*) explore (for gold etc.). □ **prospector** *noun*.

prospective /prəs'pektɪv/ *adjective* some day to be, expected, future.

prospectus /prəs'pektəs/ *noun* (*plural* **-tuses**) pamphlet etc. advertising or describing school, business, etc.

prosper /'prɒspə/ *verb* succeed, thrive.

prosperity /prɒ'sperɪtɪ/ *noun* prosperous state.

prosperous /ˈprɒspərəs/ *adjective* successful, rich, thriving; auspicious. □ **prosperously** *adverb*.

prostate /ˈprɒsteɪt/ *noun* (in full **prostate gland**) gland secreting component of semen. □ **prostatic** /-ˈstæt-/ *adjective*.

prostitute /ˈprɒstɪtju:t/ ● *noun* person who offers sexual intercourse for payment. ● *verb* (**-ting**) make prostitute of; misuse, offer for sale unworthily. □ **prostitution** *noun*.

prostrate ● *adjective* /ˈprɒstreɪt/ lying face downwards, esp. in submission; lying horizontally; overcome, esp. exhausted. ● *verb* /prɒsˈtreɪt/ (**-ting**) lay or throw flat; overcome, make weak. □ **prostration** *noun*.

prosy /ˈprəʊzɪ/ *adjective* (**-ier**, **-iest**) tedious, commonplace, dull.

protagonist /prəˈtægənɪst/ *noun* chief person in drama, story, etc.; supporter of cause.

■ **Usage** The use of *protagonist* to mean 'a supporter of a cause' is considered incorrect by some people.

protean /ˈprəʊtɪən/ *adjective* variable, versatile.

protect /prəˈtekt/ *verb* (often + *from*, *against*) keep (person etc.) safe; shield.

protection /prəˈtekʃ(ə)n/ *noun* protecting, being protected, defence; person etc. that protects; protectionism; *colloquial* immunity from violence etc. by paying gangsters etc.

protectionism *noun* theory or practice of protecting home industries. □ **protectionist** *noun & adjective*.

protective /prəˈtektɪv/ *adjective* protecting; intended for or giving protection. □ **protective custody** detention of person for his or her own protection. □ **protectively** *adverb*; **protectiveness** *noun*.

protector *noun* (*feminine* **protectress**) person or thing that protects; *historical* regent ruling during minority or absence of sovereign. □ **protectorship** *noun*.

protectorate /prəˈtektərət/ *noun* state controlled and protected by another; such protectorship; *historical* office of protector of kingdom or state; period of this.

protégé /ˈprɒtɪʒeɪ/ *noun* (*feminine* **protégée** same pronunciation) person under protection, patronage, etc. of another.

protein /ˈprəʊti:n/ *noun* any of a class of nitrogenous compounds essential in all living organisms.

pro tem /prəʊ ˈtem/ *adjective & adverb colloquial* for the time being (*pro tempore*).

protest ● *noun* /ˈprəʊtest/ expression of dissent or disapproval; legal written refusal to pay or accept bill. ● *verb* /prəˈtest/ (usually + *against*, *at*, *about*, etc.) make protest; affirm (innocence etc.); write or get protest relating to (bill); *US* object to. □ **protester**, **protestor** *noun*.

Protestant /ˈprɒtɪst(ə)nt/ ● *noun* member or adherent of any of Churches separated from RC Church in Reformation. ● *adjective* of Protestant Churches or Protestants. □ **Protestantism** *noun*.

protestation /prɒtɪsˈteɪʃ(ə)n/ *noun* strong affirmation; protest.

proto- *combining form* first.

protocol /ˈprəʊtəkɒl/ ● *noun* official formality and etiquette; draft, esp. of terms of treaty. ● *verb* (**-ll-**) draft or record in protocol.

proton /ˈprəʊtɒn/ *noun* elementary particle with positive electric charge equal to electron's, and occurring in all atomic nuclei.

protoplasm /ˈprəʊtəplæz(ə)m/ *noun* viscous translucent substance comprising living part of cell in organism. □ **protoplasmic** /-ˈplæzmɪk/ *adjective*.

prototype /ˈprəʊtətaɪp/ *noun* original as pattern for copy, improved form, etc.; trial model of vehicle, machine, etc. □ **prototypic** /-ˈtɪp-/ *adjective*; **prototypical** /-ˈtɪp-/ *adjective*.

protozoan /prəʊtəˈzəʊən/ ● *noun* (*plural* **-s**) (also **protozoon** /-ˈzəʊɒn/, *plural* **-zoa** /-ˈzəʊə/) one-celled microscopic organism. ● *adjective* (also **protozoic** /-ˈzəʊɪk/) of protozoa.

protract /prəˈtrækt/ *verb* (often as **protracted** *adjective*) prolong, lengthen. □ **protraction** *noun*.

protractor *noun* instrument for measuring angles, usually in form of graduated semicircle.

protrude /prəˈtru:d/ *verb* (**-ding**) thrust forward; stick out. □ **protrusion** *noun*; **protrusive** *adjective*.

protuberant /prəˈtju:bərənt/ *adjective* bulging out; prominent. □ **protuberance** *noun*.

proud /praʊd/ *adjective* feeling greatly honoured; haughty, arrogant; (often + *of*) feeling or showing (proper) pride; imposing, splendid; (often + *of*) slightly projecting. □ **do** (**person**) **proud** *colloquial* treat with great generosity or honour. □ **proudly** *adverb*.

prove /pru:v/ *verb* (**-ving**; *past participle* **proved** or *esp. US & Scottish* **proven** /ˈpru:v(ə)n/) (often + *that*) demonstrate to be true by evidence or argument; (**prove oneself**) show one's abilities etc.; (usually + *to be*) be found; test accuracy of; establish validity of (will); (of dough) rise. □ **provable** *adjective*.

■ **Usage** The use of *proven* as the past participle is uncommon except in certain expressions, such as *of proven ability*. It is, however, standard in Scots and American English.

provenance /ˈprɒvɪnəns/ *noun* (place of) origin; history.

provender /ˈprɒvɪndə/ *noun* fodder; *jocular* food.

proverb /ˈprɒvɜ:b/ *noun* short pithy saying in general use.

proverbial /prəˈvɜ:bɪəl/ *adjective* notorious; of or referred to in proverbs. □ **proverbially** *adverb*.

provide /prəˈvaɪd/ *verb* (**-ding**) supply; (usually + *for*, *against*) make due preparation; (usually + *for*) take care of person etc. with money, food, etc.; (often + *that*) stipulate. □ **provided**, **providing** (often + *that*) on condition or understanding that.

providence /ˈprɒvɪd(ə)ns/ *noun* protective care of God or nature; (**Providence**) God; foresight, thrift.

provident /ˈprɒvɪd(ə)nt/ *adjective* having or showing foresight, thrifty.

providential /prɒvɪˈdenʃ(ə)l/ *adjective* of or by divine foresight or intervention; opportune, lucky. □ **providentially** *adverb*.

province /ˈprɒvɪns/ *noun* principal administrative division of country etc.; (**the provinces**) whole of country outside capital; sphere of action; branch of learning.

provincial /prəˈvɪnʃ(ə)l/ ● *adjective* of province(s); unsophisticated, uncultured. ● *noun* inhabitant of province(s); unsophisticated or uncultured person. □ **provincialism** *noun*.

provision /prəˈvɪʒ(ə)n/ ● *noun* providing; (in *plural*) food and drink, esp. for expedition; legal or formal stipulation. ● *verb* supply with provisions.

provisional ● *adjective* providing for immediate needs only, temporary; (**Provisional**) of the unofficial wing of the IRA. ● *noun* (**Provisional**) member of unofficial wing of IRA. □ **provisionally** *adverb*.

proviso /prəˈvaɪzəʊ/ *noun* (*plural* **-s**) stipulation; limiting clause. □ **provisory** *adjective*.

provocation /prɒvəˈkeɪʃ(ə)n/ *noun* provoking, being provoked; cause of annoyance.

provocative /prəˈvɒkətɪv/ *adjective* (usually + *of*) tending or intended to provoke anger, lust, etc. □ **provocatively** *adverb*.

provoke /prə'vəʊk/ *verb* (**-king**) (often + *to*, *to do*) rouse, incite; call forth, cause; (usually + *into*) irritate, stimulate; tempt.

provost /'prɒvəst/ *noun* head of some colleges; head of cathedral chapter; /prə'vəʊ/ (in full **provost marshal**) head of military police in camp or on active service.

prow /praʊ/ *noun* bow of ship; pointed or projecting front part.

prowess /'praʊɪs/ *noun* skill, expertise; valour, gallantry.

prowl /praʊl/ ● *verb* (often + *about*, *around*) roam, esp. stealthily in search of prey, plunder, etc. ● *noun* prowling. ▫ **prowler** *noun*.

prox. *abbreviation* proximo.

proximate /'prɒksɪmət/ *adjective* nearest, next before or after.

proximity /prɒk'sɪmɪtɪ/ *noun* nearness.

proximo /'prɒksɪməʊ/ *adjective* of next month.

proxy /'prɒksɪ/ *noun* (*plural* **-ies**) authorization given to deputy; person authorized to deputize; document authorizing person to vote on another's behalf; vote so given.

prude *noun* excessively squeamish or sexually modest person. ▫ **prudery** *noun*; **prudish** *adjective*; **prudishly** *adverb*; **prudishness** *noun*.

prudent /'pru:d(ə)nt/ *adjective* cautious; politic. ▫ **prudence** *noun*; **prudently** *adverb*.

prudential /pru:'denʃ(ə)l/ *adjective* of or showing prudence.

prune[1] *noun* dried plum.

prune[2] *verb* (**-ning**) (often + *down*) trim (tree etc.) by cutting away dead or overgrown parts; (usually + *off*, *away*) remove (branches etc.) thus; reduce (costs etc.); (often + *of*) clear superfluities from; remove (superfluities).

prurient /'prʊərɪənt/ *adjective* having or encouraging unhealthy sexual curiosity. ▫ **prurience** *noun*.

Prussian /'prʌʃ(ə)n/ ● *adjective* of Prussia. ● *noun* native of Prussia. ▫ **Prussian blue** deep blue (pigment).

prussic acid /'prʌsɪk/ *noun* highly poisonous liquid.

pry /praɪ/ *verb* (**pries**, **pried**) (usually + *into* etc.) inquire impertinently, look inquisitively.

PS *abbreviation* postscript.

psalm /sɑ:m/ *noun* (also **Psalm**) sacred song; (**the** (**Book of**) **Psalms**) book of these in Old Testament.

psalmist /'sɑ:mɪst/ *noun* author or composer of psalm(s).

psalmody /'sɑ:mədɪ/ *noun* practice or art of singing psalms.

Psalter /'sɔ:ltə/ *noun* Book of Psalms; (**psalter**) version or copy of this.

psaltery /'sɔ:ltərɪ/ *noun* (*plural* **-ies**) ancient and medieval plucked stringed instrument.

psephology /sɪ'fɒlədʒɪ/ *noun* statistical study of voting etc. ▫ **psephologist** *noun*.

pseudo- *combining form* (also **pseud-** before vowel) false, not genuine; resembling, imitating.

pseudonym /'sju:dənɪm/ *noun* fictitious name, esp. of author.

psoriasis /sə'raɪəsɪs/ *noun* skin disease with red scaly patches.

PSV *abbreviation* public service vehicle.

psych /saɪk/ *verb colloquial* (usually + *up*) prepare mentally; (often + *out*) intimidate; (usually + *out*) analyse (person's motivation etc.).

psyche /'saɪkɪ/ *noun* soul, spirit, mind.

psychedelic /saɪkə'delɪk/ *adjective* expanding the mind's awareness, hallucinatory; vivid in colour, design, etc.

psychiatry /saɪ'kaɪətrɪ/ *noun* study and treatment of mental disease. ▫ **psychiatric** /-kɪ'ætrɪk/ *adjective*; **psychiatrist** *noun*.

psychic /'saɪkɪk/ ● *adjective* (of person) regarded as having paranormal powers, clairvoyant; of the soul or mind. ● *noun* psychic person, medium.

psychical *adjective* concerning psychic phenomena or faculties; of the soul or mind.

psycho- *combining form* of mind or psychology.

psychoanalysis /saɪkəʊə'nælɪsɪs/ *noun* treatment of mental disorders by bringing repressed fears etc. into conscious mind. ▫ **psychoanalyse** /-'ænəl-/ *verb* (**-sing**); **psychoanalyst** /-'ænəl-/ *noun*; **psychoanalytical** /-ænə'lɪt-/ *adjective*.

psychokinesis /saɪkəʊkɪ'ni:sɪs/ *noun* movement of objects by telepathy.

psychological /saɪkə'lɒdʒɪk(ə)l/ *adjective* of the mind; of psychology; *colloquial* imaginary. ▫ **psychological block** inhibition caused by emotion; **psychological moment** best time to achieve purpose; **psychological warfare** campaign to reduce enemy's morale. ▫ **psychologically** *adverb*.

psychology /saɪ'kɒlədʒɪ/ *noun* (*plural* **-ies**) study of human mind; treatise on or theory of this; mental characteristics. ▫ **psychologist** *noun*.

psychopath /'saɪkəpæθ/ *noun* mentally deranged person, esp. with abnormal social behaviour; mentally or emotionally unstable person. ▫ **psychopathic** /-'pæθ-/ *adjective*.

psychosis /saɪ'kəʊsɪs/ *noun* (*plural* **-choses** /-si:z/) severe mental derangement involving loss of contact with reality.

psychosomatic /saɪkəʊsə'mætɪk/ *adjective* (of disease) mental, not physical, in origin; of both mind and body.

psychotherapy /saɪkəʊ'θerəpɪ/ *noun* treatment of mental disorder by psychological means. ▫ **psychotherapist** *noun*.

psychotic /saɪ'kɒtɪk/ ● *adjective* of or suffering from psychosis. ● *noun* psychotic person.

PT *abbreviation* physical training.

pt *abbreviation* part; pint; point; port.

PTA *abbreviation* parent–teacher association.

ptarmigan /'tɑ:mɪgən/ *noun* bird of grouse family.

Pte. *abbreviation* Private (soldier).

pteridophyte /'terɪdəfaɪt/ *noun* flowerless plant.

pterodactyl /terə'dæktɪl/ *noun* large extinct flying reptile.

PTO *abbreviation* please turn over.

ptomaine /'təʊmeɪn/ *noun* any of a group of compounds (some toxic) in putrefying matter.

pub *noun colloquial* public house.

puberty /'pju:bətɪ/ *noun* period of sexual maturing.

pubes[1] /'pju:bi:z/ *noun* (*plural* same) lower part of abdomen.

pubes[2] *plural* of PUBIS.

pubescence /pju:'bes(ə)ns/ *noun* beginning of puberty; soft down on plant or animal. ▫ **pubescent** *adjective*.

pubic /'pju:bɪk/ *adjective* of pubes or pubis.

pubis /'pju:bɪs/ *noun* (*plural* **pubes** /-bi:z/) front portion of hip bone.

public /'pʌblɪk/ ● *adjective* of the people as a whole; open to or shared by all; done or existing openly; of or from government; involved in community affairs. ● *noun* (treated as *singular* or *plural*) (members of) community as a whole; section of community. ▫ **go public** (of company) start selling shares on open market, reveal one's plans; **in public** publicly, openly; **public address system** equipment of loudspeakers etc.; **public convenience** public lavatory; **public figure** famous person; **public house** place selling alcoholic drink for consumption on premises; **public lending right** right of authors to payment when their books are lent by public libraries; **public relations** professional promotion of company, product, etc.; **public school** independent fee-paying school; *US, Australian, Scottish, etc.* non-fee-paying school; **public-spirited** ready to do things for the community; **public transport** buses, trains, etc. available for public use on fixed routes; **public utility** organization supplying water, gas, etc. to community. □ **publicly** *adverb*.

publican /'pʌblɪkən/ *noun* keeper of public house.

publication /pʌblɪ'keɪʃ(ə)n/ *noun* publishing; published book, periodical, etc.

publicist /'pʌblɪsɪst/ *noun* publicity agent, public relations officer.

publicity /pʌb'lɪsɪtɪ/ *noun* (means of attracting) public attention; (material used for) advertising.

publicize /'pʌblɪsaɪz/ *verb* (also **-ise**) (**-zing** or **-sing**) advertise, make publicly known.

publish /'pʌblɪʃ/ *verb* prepare and issue (book, magazine, etc.) for public sale; make generally known; formally announce.

publisher *noun* person or firm that publishes books etc.

puce /pju:s/ *adjective & noun* purplebrown.

puck[1] *noun* rubber disc used in ice hockey.

puck[2] *noun* mischievous sprite. □ **puckish** *adjective*; **puckishly** *adverb*; **puckishness** *noun*.

pucker /'pʌkə/ ● *verb* gather (often + *up*) into wrinkles, folds, or bulges. ● *noun* such wrinkle etc.

pudding /'pʊdɪŋ/ *noun* sweet cooked dish; savoury dish containing flour, suet, etc.; sweet course of meal; kind of sausage.

puddle /'pʌd(ə)l/ *noun* small (dirty) pool; clay made into watertight coating.

pudenda /pju:'dendə/ *plural noun* genitals, esp. of woman.

pudgy /'pʌdʒɪ/ *adjective* (**-ier**, **-iest**) *colloquial* plump, podgy.

puerile /'pjʊəraɪl/ *adjective* childish, immature. □ **puerility** /-'rɪl-/ *noun* (*plural* **-ies**).

puerperal /pju:'ɜ:pər(ə)l/ *adjective* of or due to childbirth.

puff ● *noun* short quick blast of breath or wind; sound (as) of this; vapour or smoke sent out in one blast; light pastry cake; gathered material in dress etc.; unduly enthusiastic review, advertisement, etc. ● *verb* emit puff(s); smoke or move with puffs; (usually in *passive*; often + *out*) *colloquial* put out of breath; pant; (usually + *up*, *out*) inflate; (usually as **puffed up** *adjective*) elate, make boastful; advertise in exaggerated terms. □ **puff-adder** large venomous African viper; **puffball** ball-shaped fungus; **puff pastry** pastry consisting of thin layers.

puffin /'pʌfɪn/ *noun* N. Atlantic and N. Pacific auk with short striped bill.

puffy *adjective* (**-ier**, **-iest**) swollen, puffed out; *colloquial* short-winded.

pug *noun* (in full **pug-dog**) dog of small breed with flat nose. □ **pug-nose** short flat or snub nose.

pugilist /'pju:dʒɪlɪst/ *noun* boxer. □ **pugilism** *noun*; **pugilistic** /-'lɪs-/ *adjective*.

pugnacious /pʌg'neɪʃəs/ *adjective* disposed to fight. □ **pugnaciously** *adverb*; **pugnacity** /-'næs-/ *noun*.

puissance /'pwi:sɑ̃s/ *noun* jumping of large obstacles in showjumping.

puissant /'pwi:sɒnt/ *adjective literary* powerful; mighty.

puke /pju:k/ *verb & noun* (**-king**) *slang* vomit. □ **pukey** *adjective*.

pukka /'pʌkə/ *adjective colloquial* genuine; reliable.

pulchritude /'pʌlkrɪtju:d/ *noun literary* beauty. □ **pulchritudinous** /-'tju:dɪnəs/ *adjective*.

pull /pʊl/ ● *verb* exert force on (thing etc.) to move it to oneself or origin of force; exert pulling force; extract by pulling; damage (muscle etc.) by abnormal strain; proceed with effort; (+ *on*) draw (weapon) against (person); attract; draw (liquor) from barrel etc.; (+ *at*) pluck at; (often + *on*, *at*) inhale or drink deeply, suck. ● *noun* act of pulling; force thus exerted; influence; advantage; attraction; deep draught of liquor; prolonged effort; handle etc. for applying pull; printer's rough proof; suck at cigarette. □ **pull back** retreat; **pull down** demolish; **pull in** arrive to take passengers, move to side of or off road, *colloquial* earn, *colloquial* arrest; **pull-in** roadside café etc.; **pull off** remove, win, manage successfully; **pull oneself together** recover control of oneself; **pull out** take out, depart, withdraw, leave station or stop, move towards off side; **pull-out** removable section of magazine; **pull round**, **through** (cause to) recover from illness; **pull strings** exert (esp. clandestine) influence; **pull together** work in harmony; **pull up** (cause to) stop moving, pull out of ground, reprimand, check oneself.

pullet /'pʊlɪt/ *noun* young hen, esp. less than one year old.

pulley /'pʊlɪ/ *noun* (*plural* **-s**) grooved wheel(s) for cord etc. to run over, mounted in block and used to lift weight etc.; wheel or drum mounted on shaft and turned by belt, used to increase speed or power.

Pullman /'pʊlmən/ *noun* (*plural* **-s**) luxurious railway carriage or motor coach; sleeping car.

pullover *noun* knitted garment put on over the head.

pullulate /'pʌljʊleɪt/ *verb* (**-ting**) sprout; swarm; develop; (+ *with*) abound with. □ **pullulation** *noun*.

pulmonary /'pʌlmənərɪ/ *adjective* of lungs; having (organs like) lungs; affected with or subject to lung disease.

pulp ● *noun* fleshy part of fruit etc.; soft shapeless mass, esp. of materials for papermaking; cheap fiction. ● *verb* reduce to or become pulp. □ **pulpy** *adjective*; **pulpiness** *noun*.

pulpit /'pʊlpɪt/ *noun* raised enclosed platform for preaching from; (**the pulpit**) preachers collectively, preaching.

pulsar /'pʌlsɑ:/ *noun* cosmic source of regular rapid pulses of radiation.

pulsate /pʌl'seɪt/ *verb* (**-ting**) expand and contract rhythmically; throb, vibrate, quiver. □ **pulsation** *noun*.

pulse[1] ● *noun* rhythmical throbbing of arteries; each beat of arteries or heart; throb or thrill of life or emotion; general feeling; single vibration of sound, electromagnetic radiation, etc.; rhythmical (esp. musical) beat. ● *verb* (**-sing**) pulsate.

pulse[2] *noun* (treated as *singular* or *plural*) (plant producing) edible seeds of peas, beans, lentils, etc.

pulverize /'pʌlvəraɪz/ *verb* (also **-ise**) (**-zing** or **-sing**) reduce or crumble to powder or dust; *colloquial* demolish, crush. □ **pulverization** *noun*.

puma /'pju:mə/ *noun* large tawny American feline.

pumice /'pʌmɪs/ *noun* (in full **pumice stone**) light porous lava used as abrasive; piece of this.

pummel /'pʌm(ə)l/ *verb* (**-ll-**; *US* **-l-**) strike repeatedly, esp. with fists.

pump[1] ● *noun* machine or device for raising or moving liquids or gases; act of pumping. ● *verb* (often + *in*, *out*, *up*, etc.) raise, remove, inflate, empty, etc. (as) with pump; work pump; persistently question (person) to elicit information; move vigorously up and down. □ **pump iron** *colloquial* exercise with weights.

pump[2] *noun* plimsoll; light shoe for dancing etc.

pumpernickel /ˈpʌmpənɪk(ə)l/ *noun* wholemeal rye bread.

pumpkin /ˈpʌmpkɪn/ *noun* large yellow or orange fruit used as vegetable; plant bearing it.

pun ● *noun* humorous use of word(s) with two or more meanings, play on words. ● *verb* (**-nn-**) (usually + *on*) make pun(s).

Punch *noun* grotesque humpbacked puppet in *Punch and Judy* shows.

punch[1] ● *verb* strike with fist; make hole in (as) with punch; pierce (hole) thus. ● *noun* blow with fist; *colloquial* vigour, effective force; instrument or machine for piercing holes or impressing design in leather, metal, etc. □ **pull one's punches** avoid using full force; **punchball** stuffed or inflated ball used for practice in punching; **punch-drunk** stupefied (as) with repeated punches; **punchline** words giving point of joke etc.; **punch-up** *colloquial* fist-fight, brawl. □ **puncher** *noun*.

punch[2] *noun* hot or cold mixture of wine or spirit with water, fruit, spices, etc. □ **punch-bowl** bowl for punch; deep round hollow in hill.

punchy *adjective* (**-ier**, **-iest**) vigorous, forceful.

punctilio /pʌŋkˈtɪlɪəʊ/ *noun* (*plural* **-s**) delicate point of ceremony or honour; petty formality.

punctilious /pʌŋkˈtɪlɪəs/ *adjective* attentive to formality or etiquette; precise in behaviour. □ **punctiliously** *adverb*; **punctiliousness** *noun*.

punctual /ˈpʌŋktʃʊəl/ *adjective* observing appointed time; prompt. □ **punctuality** /-ˈæl-/ *noun*; **punctually** *adverb*.

punctuate /ˈpʌŋktʃʊeɪt/ *verb* (**-ting**) insert punctuation marks in; interrupt at intervals.

punctuation *noun* (system of) punctuating. □ **punctuation mark** any of the marks used in writing to separate sentences, phrases, etc.

puncture /ˈpʌŋktʃə/ ● *noun* prick, pricking; hole made by this. ● *verb* (**-ring**) make or suffer puncture (in); deflate.

pundit /ˈpʌndɪt/ *noun* (also **pandit**) learned Hindu; expert.

pungent /ˈpʌndʒ(ə)nt/ *adjective* having sharp or strong taste or smell; biting, caustic. □ **pungency** *noun*.

punish /ˈpʌnɪʃ/ *verb* inflict penalty on (offender) or for (offence); tax, abuse, or treat severely. □ **punishable** *adjective*; **punishment** *noun*.

punitive /ˈpju:nɪtɪv/ *adjective* inflicting or intended to inflict punishment; extremely severe.

punk *noun* (in full **punk rock**) deliberately outrageous style of rock music; (in full **punk rocker**) fan of this; *esp. US* hooligan, lout.

punkah /ˈpʌŋkə/ *noun* large swinging fan on frame worked by cord or electrically.

punnet /ˈpʌnɪt/ *noun* small basket for fruit etc.

punster /ˈpʌnstə/ *noun* maker of puns.

punt[1] ● *noun* square-ended flat-bottomed boat propelled by long pole. ● *verb* travel or carry in punt.

punt[2] ● *verb* kick (football) dropped from hands before it reaches ground. ● *noun* such kick.

punt[3] *verb colloquial* bet, speculate in shares etc.; (in some card games) lay stake against bank.

punt[4] /pʊnt/ *noun* chief monetary unit of Republic of Ireland.

punter *noun colloquial* person who gambles or bets; customer, client.

puny /ˈpju:nɪ/ *adjective* (**-ier**, **-iest**) undersized; feeble.

pup ● *noun* young dog, wolf, rat, seal, etc. ● *verb* (**-pp-**) give birth to (pups).

pupa /ˈpju:pə/ *noun* (*plural* **pupae** /-pi:/) insect in stage between larva and imago.

pupil[1] /ˈpju:pɪl/ *noun* person being taught.

pupil[2] /ˈpju:pɪl/ *noun* opening in centre of iris of eye.

puppet /ˈpʌpɪt/ *noun* small figure moved esp. by strings as entertainment; person controlled by another. □ **puppet state** country apparently independent but actually under control of another power. □ **puppetry** *noun*.

puppy /ˈpʌpɪ/ *noun* (*plural* **-ies**) young dog; conceited young man. □ **puppy fat** temporary fatness of child or adolescent; **puppy love** calf love.

purblind /ˈpɜ:blaɪnd/ *adjective* partly blind, dim-sighted; obtuse, dull. □ **purblindness** *noun*.

purchase /ˈpɜ:tʃəs/ ● *verb* (**-sing**) buy. ● *noun* buying; thing bought; firm hold on thing, leverage; equipment for moving heavy objects. □ **purchaser** *noun*.

purdah /ˈpɜ:də/ *noun* screening of Muslim or Hindu women from strangers.

pure /pjʊə/ *adjective* unmixed, unadulterated; chaste; not morally corrupt; guiltless; sincere; not discordant; (of science) abstract, not applied. □ **pureness** *noun*; **purity** *noun*.

purée /ˈpjʊəreɪ/ ● *noun* smooth pulp of vegetables or fruit etc. ● *verb* (**-ées**, **-éed**) make purée of.

purely *adverb* in a pure way; merely, solely, exclusively.

purgative /ˈpɜ:gətɪv/ ● *adjective* serving to purify; strongly laxative. ● *noun* purgative thing.

purgatory /ˈpɜ:gətərɪ/ ● *noun* (*plural* **-ies**) place or state of spiritual cleansing, esp. after death and before entering heaven; place or state of temporary suffering or expiation. ● *adjective* purifying. □ **purgatorial** /-ˈtɔ:rɪəl/ *adjective*.

purge /pɜ:dʒ/ ● *verb* (**-ging**) (often + *of*, *from*) make physically or spiritually clean; remove by cleansing; rid of unacceptable members; empty (bowels); *Law* atone for (offence). ● *noun* purging; purgative.

purify /ˈpjʊərɪfaɪ/ *verb* (**-ies**, **-ied**) clear of extraneous elements, make pure; (often + *of*, *from*) cleanse. □ **purification** *noun*; **purificatory** /-fɪkeɪtərɪ/ *adjective*.

purist /ˈpjʊərɪst/ *noun* stickler for correctness, esp. in language. □ **purism** *noun*.

puritan /ˈpjʊərɪt(ə)n/ ● *noun* (**Puritan**) *historical* member of English Protestant group regarding Reformation as incomplete; purist member of any party; strict observer of religion or morals. ● *adjective* (**Puritan**) *historical* of Puritans; scrupulous in religion or morals. □ **puritanical** /-ˈtæn-/ *adjective*; **puritanically** /-ˈtæn-/ *adverb*; **puritanism** *noun*.

purl[1] ● *noun* knitting stitch with needle moved in opposite to normal direction; chain of minute loops. ● *verb* knit with purl stitch.

purl[2] *verb* flow with babbling sound.

purler /ˈpɜ:lə/ *noun colloquial* heavy fall.

purlieu /ˈpɜ:lju:/ *noun* (*plural* **-s**) person's limits or usual haunts; *historical* tract on border of forest; (in *plural*) outskirts, outlying region.

purlin /ˈpɜ:lɪn/ *noun* horizontal beam along length of roof.

purloin /pəˈlɔɪn/ *verb formal or jocular* steal, pilfer.

purple /ˈpɜ:p(ə)l/ ● *noun* colour between red and blue; purple robe, esp. of emperor etc.; cardinal's scarlet official dress. ● *adjective* of purple. ● *verb* (**-ling**) make or become purple. □ **purplish** *adjective*.

purport ● *verb* /pəˈpɔ:t/ profess, be intended to seem; (often + *that*) have as its meaning. ● *noun* /ˈpɜ:pɔ:t/ ostensible meaning; tenor of document or statement. □ **purportedly** *adverb*.

purpose /ˈpɜ:pəs/ ● *noun* object to be attained, thing intended; intention to act; resolution, determination. ● *verb* (**-sing**) have as one's purpose, intend. □ **on**

purpose intentionally; **to good, little, no,** etc. **purpose** with good, little, no, etc., effect or result; **to the purpose** relevant, useful.

purposeful *adjective* having or indicating purpose; intentional. □ **purposefully** *adverb*; **purposefulness** *noun*.

purposeless *adjective* having no aim or plan.

purposely *adverb* on purpose.

purposive /ˈpɜːpəsɪv/ *adjective* having, serving, or done with a purpose; purposeful.

purr /pɜː/ ● *verb* make low vibratory sound of cat expressing pleasure; (of machinery etc.) run smoothly and quietly. ● *noun* purring sound.

purse /pɜːs/ ● *noun* small pouch for carrying money in; *US* handbag; funds; sum given as present or prize. ● *verb* (**-sing**) (often + *up*) contract (esp. lips); become wrinkled. □ **hold the purse-strings** have control of expenditure.

purser /ˈpɜːsə/ *noun* ship's officer who keeps accounts, esp. head steward in passenger vessel.

pursuance /pəˈsjuːəns/ *noun* (+ *of*) carrying out or observance (of plan, rules, etc.).

pursuant /pəˈsjuːənt/ *adverb* (+ *to*) in accordance with.

pursue /pəˈsjuː/ *verb* (**-sues, -sued, -suing**) follow with intent to overtake, capture, or harm; proceed along; engage in (study etc.); carry out (plan etc.); seek after; continue to investigate etc.; persistently importune or assail. □ **pursuer** *noun*.

pursuit /pəˈsjuːt/ *noun* pursuing; occupation or activity pursued. □ **in pursuit of** pursuing.

purulent /ˈpjʊərʊlənt/ *adjective* of, containing, or discharging pus. □ **purulence** *noun*.

purvey /pəˈveɪ/ *verb* provide or supply food etc. as one's business. □ **purveyor** *ncun*.

purview /ˈpɜːvjuː/ *noun* scope of document etc.; range of physical or mental vision.

pus /pʌs/ *noun* thick yellowish liquid produced from infected tissue.

push /pʊʃ/ ● *verb* exert force on (thing) to move it away, cause to move thus; exert such force; thrust forward or upward; (cause to) project; make (one's way) forcibly or persistently; exert oneself; (often + *to, into, to do*) urge, impel; (often + *for*) pursue (claim etc.) persistently; promote, advertise; *colloquial* sell (drug) illegally. ● *noun* act of pushing; force thus exerted; vigorous effort; determination; use of influence to advance person. □ **give** or **get the push** *colloquial* dismiss, be dismissed; **push-bike** *colloquial* bicycle; **pushchair** child's folding chair on wheels; **push off** *colloquial* go away; **pushover** *colloquial* opponent or difficulty easily overcome.

pusher *noun colloquial* seller of illegal drugs.

pushing *adjective* pushy; *colloquial* having nearly reached (specified age).

pushy *adjective* (**-ier, -iest**) *colloquial* excessively self-assertive. □ **pushily** *adverb*; **pushiness** *noun*.

pusillanimous /pjuːsɪˈlænɪməs/ *adjective formal* cowardly, timid. □ **pusillanimity** /-ləˈnɪm-/ *noun*.

puss /pʊs/ *noun colloquial* cat; sly or coquettish girl.

pussy /ˈpʊsɪ/ *noun* (*plural* **-ies**) (also **pussy-cat**) *colloquial* cat. □ **pussyfoot** *colloquial* move stealthily, equivocate; **pussy willow** willow with furry catkins.

pustulate /ˈpʌstjʊleɪt/ *verb* (**-ting**) form into pustules.

pustule /ˈpʌstjuːl/ *noun* pimple containing pus. □ **pustular** *adjective*.

put /pʊt/ ● *verb* (**-tt-**; *past & past participle* **put**) move to or cause to be in specified place, position, or state; (often + *on, to*) impose; (+ *for*) substitute (thing) for (another); express in specified way; (+ *at*) estimate; (+ *into*) express or translate in (words etc.); (+ *into*) invest (money) in; (+ *on*) stake (money) on; (+ *to*) submit for attention; hurl (shot etc.) as sport. ● *noun* throw of shot. □ **put about** spread (rumour etc.); **put across** make understood, achieve by deceit; **put away** restore to usual place, lay aside for future, imprison, consume (food or drink); **put back** restore to usual place, change (meeting etc.) to later time, move back hands of (clock or watch); **put by** lay aside for future; **put down** suppress, *colloquial* snub, record in writing, enter on list, (+ *as, for*) account or reckon, (+ *to*) attribute to, kill (old etc. animal), pay as deposit; **put in** submit (claim), (+ *for*) be candidate for (election etc.), spend (time); **put off** postpone, evade (person) with excuse, dissuade, disconcert; **put on** clothe oneself with, cause (light etc.) to operate, make (transport) available, stage (play etc.), advance hands of (clock or watch), feign, increase one's weight by (specified amount); **put out** disconcert, annoy, inconvenience, extinguish; **put over** put across; **put through** complete, connect by telephone; **put together** make from parts, combine (parts) into whole; **put up** *verb* build, raise, lodge (person), engage in (fight etc.), propose, provide (money) as backer, display (notice), offer for sale etc.; **put-up** *adjective* fraudulent; **put upon** (usually in *passive*) *colloquial* unfairly burden or deceive; **put (person) up to** instigate him or her to; **put up with** endure, tolerate.

putative /ˈpjuːtətɪv/ *adjective formal* reputed, supposed.

putrefy /ˈpjuːtrɪfaɪ/ *verb* (**-ies, -ied**) become or make putrid, go bad; fester; become morally corrupt. □ **putrefaction** /-ˈfæk-/ *noun*; **putrefactive** /-ˈfæk-/ *adjective*.

putrescent /pjuːˈtres(ə)nt/ *adjective* rotting. □ **putrescence** *noun*.

putrid /ˈpjuːtrɪd/ *adjective* decomposed, rotten; noxious; corrupt; *slang* contemptible, very unpleasant. □ **putridity** /-ˈtrɪd-/ *noun*.

putsch /pʊtʃ/ *noun* attempt at revolution.

putt /pʌt/ ● *verb* (**-tt-**) strike (golf ball) on putting green. ● *noun* putting stroke. □ **putting green** smooth turf round hole on golf course.

puttee /ˈpʌtɪ/ *noun historical* long strip of cloth wound round leg for protection and support.

putter[1] *noun* golf club used in putting.

putter[2] *US* = POTTER[1].

putty /ˈpʌtɪ/ ● *noun* paste of chalk, linseed oil, etc. for fixing panes of glass etc. ● *verb* (**-ies, -ied**) fix, fill, etc. with putty.

puzzle /ˈpʌz(ə)l/ ● *noun* difficult or confusing problem; problem or toy designed to test ingenuity etc. ● *verb* (**-ling**) perplex, (usually + *over* etc.) be perplexed; (usually as **puzzling** *adjective*) require much mental effort; (+ *out*) solve using ingenuity etc. □ **puzzlement** *noun*.

PVC *abbreviation* polyvinyl chloride, a plastic used for pipes, electrical insulation, etc.

pyaemia /paɪˈiːmɪə/ *noun* (*US* **pyemia**) severe bacterial infection of blood.

pygmy /ˈpɪgmɪ/ (also **pigmy**) ● *noun* (*plural* **-ies**) member of dwarf people of esp. equatorial Africa; very small person, animal, or thing. ● *adjective* very small.

pyjamas /pəˈdʒɑːməz/ *plural noun* (*US* **pajamas**) suit of trousers and top for sleeping in etc.; loose trousers worn in some Asian countries.

pylon /ˈpaɪlən/ *noun* tall structure esp. as support for electric cables.

pyorrhoea /paɪəˈrɪə/ *noun* (*US* **pyorrhea**) gum disease; discharge of pus.

pyramid /ˈpɪrəmɪd/ *noun* monumental (esp. ancient Egyptian) stone structure with square base and sloping sides meeting at apex; solid of this shape with base of 3 or more sides; pyramid-shaped thing. □ **pyramidal** /-ˈræm-/ *adjective*.

pyre /ˈpaɪə/ *noun* pile of combustible material, esp. for burning corpse.

pyrethrum /paɪˈriːθrəm/ *noun* aromatic chrysanthemum; insecticide from its dried flowers.

Pyrex /ˈpaɪəreks/ *noun proprietary term* a hard heat-resistant glass.

pyrites /paɪˈraɪtiːz/ *noun* (in full **iron pyrites**) yellow sulphide of iron.

pyromania /paɪərəʊˈmeɪnɪə/ *noun* obsessive desire to start fires. ◻ **pyromaniac** *noun & adjective.*

pyrotechnics /paɪərəʊˈteknɪks/ *plural noun* art of making fireworks; display of fireworks. ◻ **pyrotechnic** *adjective.*

pyrrhic /ˈpɪrɪk/ *adjective* (of victory) achieved at too great cost.

python /ˈpaɪθ(ə)n/ *noun* large snake that crushes its prey.

pyx /pɪks/ *noun* vessel for consecrated bread of Eucharist.

Qq

Q *abbreviation* (also **Q.**) question.
QC *abbreviation* Queen's Counsel.
QED *abbreviation* which was to be proved (*quod erat demonstrandum*).
QM *abbreviation* Quartermaster.
qr. *abbreviation* quarter(s).
qt *abbreviation* quart(s).
qua /kwɑː, kweɪ/ *conjunction* in the capacity of.
quack[1] ● *noun* harsh sound made by ducks. ● *verb* utter this sound.
quack[2] *noun* unqualified practitioner, esp. of medicine; *slang* any doctor. ▫ **quackery** *noun*.
quad /kwɒd/ *colloquial* ● *noun* quadrangle; quadruplet; quadraphonics. ● *adjective* quadraphonic.
quadrangle /ˈkwɒdræŋg(ə)l/ *noun* 4-sided plane figure, esp. square or rectangle; 4-sided court, esp. in college etc. ▫ **quadrangular** /-ˈræŋgjʊlə/ *adjective*.
quadrant /ˈkwɒdrənt/ *noun* quarter of circle or sphere or of circle's circumference; optical instrument for measuring angle between distant objects.
quadraphonic /kwɒdrəˈfɒnɪk/ *adjective* (of sound reproduction) using 4 transmission channels. ▫ **quadraphonically** *adverb*; **quadraphonics** *plural noun*.
quadrate ● *adjective* /ˈkwɒdrət/ square, rectangular. ● *noun* /ˈkwɒdrət, -dreɪt/ rectangular object. ● *verb* /kwɒˈdreɪt/ (**-ting**) make square.
quadratic /kwɒˈdrætɪk/ *Mathematics* ● *adjective* involving the square (and no higher power) of unknown quantity or variable. ● *noun* quadratic equation.
quadriceps /ˈkwɒdrɪseps/ *noun* 4-headed muscle at front of thigh.
quadrilateral /kwɒdrɪˈlætər(ə)l/ ● *adjective* having 4 sides. ● *noun* 4-sided figure.
quadrille /kwɒˈdrɪl/ *noun* square dance, music for this.
quadruped /ˈkwɒdrʊped/ *noun* 4-footed animal, esp. mammal.
quadruple /ˈkwɒdrʊp(ə)l/ ● *adjective* fourfold; having 4 parts; (of time in music) having 4 beats in bar. ● *noun* fourfold number or amount. ● *verb* /kwəˈdruːp(ə)l/ multiply by 4.
quadruplet /ˈkwɒdrʊplɪt/ *noun* each of 4 children born at one birth.
quadruplicate ● *adjective* /kwɒˈdruːplɪkət/ fourfold; of which 4 copies are made. ● *verb* /-keɪt/ (**-ting**) multiply by 4.
quaff /kwɒf/ *verb literary* drink deeply; drain (cup etc.) in long draughts.
quagmire /ˈkwɒgmaɪə, ˈkwæg-/ *noun* muddy or boggy area; hazardous situation.
quail[1] *noun* (*plural* same or **-s**) small game bird related to partridge.
quail[2] *verb* flinch, show fear.
quaint *adjective* attractively odd or old-fashioned. ▫ **quaintly** *adverb*; **quaintness** *noun*.
quake ● *verb* (**-king**) shake, tremble. ● *noun colloquial* earthquake.
Quaker *noun* member of Society of Friends. ▫ **Quakerism** *noun*.
qualification /kwɒlɪfɪˈkeɪʃ(ə)n/ *noun* accomplishment fitting person for position or purpose; thing that modifies or limits; qualifying, being qualified. ▫ **qualificatory** /ˈkwɒl-/ *adjective*.
qualify /ˈkwɒlɪfaɪ/ *verb* (**-ies**, **-ied**) (often as **qualified** *adjective*) make competent or fit for purpose or position; make legally entitled; (usually + *for*) satisfy conditions; modify, limit; *Grammar* (of word) attribute quality to (esp. noun); moderate, mitigate; (+ *as*) be describable as. ▫ **qualifier** *noun*.
qualitative /ˈkwɒlɪtətɪv/ *adjective* concerned with quality as opposed to quantity. ▫ **qualitatively** *adverb*.
quality /ˈkwɒlɪtɪ/ ● *noun* (*plural* **-ies**) excellence; degree of excellence; attribute, faculty; relative nature or character; timbre. ● *adjective* of high quality.
qualm /kwɑːm/ *noun* misgiving; scruple of conscience; momentary faint or sick feeling.
quandary /ˈkwɒndərɪ/ *noun* (*plural* **-ies**) perplexed state; practical dilemma.
quango /ˈkwæŋgəʊ/ *noun* (*plural* **-s**) semi-public administrative body appointed by government.
quanta *plural* of QUANTUM.
quantify /ˈkwɒntɪfaɪ/ *verb* (**-ies**, **-ied**) determine quantity of; express as quantity. ▫ **quantifiable** *adjective*.
quantitative /ˈkwɒntɪtətɪv/ *adjective* concerned with quantity as opposed to quality; measured or measurable by quantity.
quantity /ˈkwɒntɪtɪ/ *noun* (*plural* **-ies**) property of things that is measurable; size, extent, weight, amount, or number; (in *plural*) large amounts or numbers; length or shortness of vowel sound or syllable; *Mathematics* value, component, etc. that may be expressed in numbers. ▫ **quantity surveyor** person who measures and prices building work.
quantum /ˈkwɒntəm/ *noun* (*plural* **-ta**) discrete amount of energy proportional to frequency of radiation it represents; required or allowed amount. ▫ **quantum mechanics**, **theory** theory assuming that energy exists in discrete units.
quarantine /ˈkwɒrəntiːn/ ● *noun* isolation imposed on person or animal to prevent infection or contagion; period of this. ● *verb* (**-ning**) put in quarantine.
quark[1] /kwɑːk/ *noun Physics* component of elementary particles.
quark[2] /kwɑːk/ *noun* kind of low-fat curd cheese.
quarrel /ˈkwɒr(ə)l/ ● *noun* severe or angry dispute; break in friendly relations; cause of complaint. ● *verb* (**-ll-**; *US* **-l-**) (often + *with*) find fault; dispute; break off friendly relations. ▫ **quarrelsome** *adjective*.
quarry[1] /ˈkwɒrɪ/ ● *noun* (*plural* **-ies**) place from which stone etc. is extracted. ● *verb* (**-ies**, **-ied**) extract (stone etc.) from quarry. ▫ **quarry tile** unglazed floor-tile.
quarry[2] /ˈkwɒrɪ/ *noun* (*plural* **-ies**) intended victim or prey; object of pursuit.
quart /kwɔːt/ *noun* liquid measure equal to quarter of gallon; two pints (1.136 litre).
quarter /ˈkwɔːtə/ ● *noun* each of 4 equal parts; period of 3 months; point of time 15 minutes before or after any hour; 25 US or Canadian cents, coin worth this; part of town, esp. as occupied by particular class; point of compass, region at this; direction, district; source of supply; (in *plural*) lodgings, accommodation of troops etc.; one-fourth of a lunar month; mercy

towards enemy etc. on condition of surrender; grain measure equivalent to 8 bushels, *colloquial* one-fourth of a pound weight. ● *verb* divide into quarters; put (troops etc.) into quarters; provide with lodgings; *Heraldry* place (coats of arms) on 4 quarters of shield. ☐ **quarterback** player in American football who directs attacking play; **quarter day** day on which quarterly payments are due; **quarterdeck** part of ship's upper deck near stern; **quarter-final** *Sport* match or round preceding semifinal; **quarter-hour** period of 15 minutes; **quartermaster** regimental officer in charge of quartering, rations, etc., naval petty officer in charge of steering, signals, etc.

quarterly ● *adjective* produced or occurring once every quarter of year. ● *adverb* once every quarter of year. ● *noun* (*plural* **-ies**) quarterly journal.

quartet /kwɔːˈtet/ *noun* musical composition for 4 performers; the performers; any group of 4.

quarto /ˈkwɔːtəʊ/ *noun* (*plural* **-s**) size of book or page made by folding sheet of standard size twice to form 4 leaves.

quartz /kwɔːts/ ● *noun* silica in various mineral forms. ● *adjective* (of clock or watch) operated by vibrations of electrically driven quartz crystal.

quasar /ˈkweɪzɑː/ *noun* starlike object with large red shift.

quash /kwɒʃ/ *verb* annul; reject as not valid; suppress, crush.

quasi- /ˈkweɪzaɪ/ *combining form* seemingly, not really; almost.

quaternary /kwəˈtɜːnərɪ/ *adjective* having 4 parts.

quatrain /ˈkwɒtreɪn/ *noun* 4-line stanza.

quatrefoil /ˈkætrəfɔɪl/ *noun* leaf consisting of 4 leaflets; design or ornament in this shape.

quaver /ˈkweɪvə/ ● *verb* (esp. of voice or sound) vibrate, shake, tremble; sing or say with quavering voice. ● *noun Music* note half as long as crotchet; trill in singing; tremble in speech. ☐ **quavery** *adjective*.

quay /kiː/ *noun* artificial landing-place for loading and unloading ships. ☐ **quayside** land forming or near quay.

queasy /ˈkwiːzɪ/ *adjective* (**-ier, -iest**) (of person) nauseous; (of stomach) easily upset; (of the conscience etc.) overscrupulous. ☐ **queasily** *adverb*; **queasiness** *noun*.

queen ● *noun* (as title usually **Queen**) female sovereign; (in full **queen consort**) king's wife; woman, country, or thing pre-eminent of its kind; fertile female among bees, ants, etc.; most powerful piece in chess; court card depicting queen; (**the Queen**) national anthem when sovereign is female; *offensive slang* male homosexual. ● *verb* convert (pawn in chess) to queen when it reaches opponent's side of board. ☐ **queen mother** king's widow who is mother of sovereign; **Queen's Bench** division of High Court of Justice; **Queen's Counsel** counsel to the Crown, taking precedence over other barristers; **the Queen's English** English language correctly written or spoken. ☐ **queenly** *adjective* (**-ier, -iest**).

Queensberry Rules /ˈkwiːnzbərɪ/ *plural noun* standard rules, esp. of boxing.

queer ● *adjective* strange, odd, eccentric; suspect, of questionable character; slightly ill, faint; *offensive slang* (esp. of a man) homosexual. ● *noun offensive slang* homosexual. ● *verb slang* spoil, put out of order. ☐ **in Queer Street** *slang* in difficulty, esp. in debt.

quell *verb* suppress, crush.

quench *verb* satisfy (thirst) by drinking; extinguish (fire or light); cool, esp. with water; stifle, suppress.

quern *noun* hand mill for grinding corn.

querulous /ˈkwerʊləs/ *adjective* complaining; peevish. ☐ **querulously** *adverb*.

query /ˈkwɪərɪ/ ● *noun* (*plural* **-ies**) question; question mark. ● *verb* (**-ies, -ied**) ask, inquire; call in question; dispute accuracy of.

quest ● *noun* search, seeking; thing sought, esp. by medieval knight. ● *verb* (often + *about*) go about in search of something.

question /ˈkwestʃ(ə)n/ ● *noun* sentence worded or expressed so as to seek information or answer; doubt or dispute about matter, raising of such doubt etc.; matter to be discussed or decided; problem requiring solution. ● *verb* ask questions of; subject (person) to examination; throw doubt on. ☐ **be just a question of time** be certain to happen sooner or later; **be a question of** be at issue, be a problem; **call in** or **into question** express doubts about; **in question** being discussed or referred to; **out of the question** not worth questioning, impossible; **question mark** punctuation mark (?) indicating question (see panel); **question-master** person presiding over quiz game etc.; **question time** period in Parliament when MPs may question ministers. ☐ **questioner** *noun*; **questioning** *adjective & noun*; **questioningly** *adverb*.

questionable *adjective* doubtful as regards truth, quality, honesty, wisdom, etc.

questionnaire /kwestʃəˈneə/ *noun* list of questions for obtaining information esp. for statistical analysis.

queue /kjuː/ ● *noun* line or sequence of people, vehicles, etc. waiting their turn. ● *verb* (**-s, -d, queuing** or **queueing**) (often + *up*) form or join queue. ☐ **queue-jump** push forward out of turn in queue.

quibble /ˈkwɪb(ə)l/ ● *noun* petty objection, trivial point of criticism; evasion. ● *verb* (**-ling**) use quibbles.

quiche /kiːʃ/ *noun* savoury flan.

quick ● *adjective* taking only a short time; arriving after only a short time, prompt; with only a short interval; lively, alert, intelligent; (of temper) easily roused. ● *adverb* quickly. ● *noun* soft sensitive flesh, esp. below nails or skin; seat of emotion. ☐ **quicklime** unslaked lime; **quicksand** (often in *plural*) area of loose wet sand that sucks in anything placed on it, treacherous situation etc.; **quickset** (of hedge etc.) formed of cuttings, esp. hawthorn; **quicksilver** mercury; **quickstep** fast foxtrot; **quick-tempered** easily angered; **quick-witted** quick to grasp situation, make repartee, etc.; **quick-wittedness** *noun*. ☐ **quickly** *adverb*.

Question mark ?

This is used instead of a full stop at the end of a sentence to show that it is a question, e.g.

Have you seen the film yet?
You didn't lose my purse, did you?

It is **not** used at the end of a reported question, e.g.

I asked you whether you'd seen the film yet.

quicken *verb* make or become quicker, accelerate; give life or vigour to, rouse; (of woman) reach stage in pregnancy when movements of foetus can be felt; (of foetus) begin to show signs of life.

quid[1] *noun slang* (*plural* same) one pound sterling.

quid[2] *noun* lump of tobacco for chewing.

quid pro quo /kwɪd prəʊ 'kwəʊ/ *noun* (*plural* **quid pro quos**) gift, favour, etc. exchanged for another.

quiescent /kwɪ'es(ə)nt/ *adjective* inert, dormant. □ **quiescence** *noun.*

quiet /'kwaɪət/ ● *adjective* with little or no sound or motion; of gentle or peaceful disposition; unobtrusive, not showy; not overt, disguised; undisturbed, uninterrupted; not busy. ● *noun* silence, stillness; undisturbed state, tranquillity. ● *verb* (often + *down*) make or become quiet, calm. □ **be quiet** (esp. in *imperative*) cease talking etc.; **keep quiet** (often + *about*) say nothing; **on the quiet** secretly. □ **quietly** *adverb*; **quietness** *noun.*

quieten *verb* (often + *down*) make or become quiet or calm.

quietism *noun* passive contemplative attitude towards life. □ **quietist** *noun & adjective.*

quietude /'kwaɪɪtju:d/ *noun* state of quiet.

quietus /kwaɪ'i:təs/ *noun* release from life; death, final riddance.

quiff *noun* man's tuft of hair brushed upwards in front.

quill *noun* (in full **quill-feather**) large feather in wing or tail; hollow stem of this; (in full **quill pen**) pen made of quill; (usually in *plural*) porcupine's spine.

quilt ● *noun* bedspread, esp. of quilted material. ● *verb* line bedspread or garment with padding enclosed between layers of fabric by lines of stitching. □ **quilter** *noun*; **quilting** *noun.*

quin *noun colloquial* quintuplet.

quince *noun* (tree bearing) acid pear-shaped fruit used in jams etc.

quincentenary /kwɪnsen'ti:nərɪ/ ● *noun* (*plural* **-ies**) 500th anniversary; celebration of this. ● *adjective* of this anniversary.

quinine /'kwɪni:n/ *noun* bitter drug used as a tonic and to reduce fever.

Quinquagesima /kwɪŋkwə'dʒesɪmə/ *noun* Sunday before Lent.

quinquennial /kwɪŋ'kwenɪəl/ *adjective* lasting 5 years; recurring every 5 years. □ **quinquennially** *adverb.*

quintessence /kwɪn'tes(ə)ns/ *noun* (usually + *of*) purest and most perfect form, manifestation, or embodiment of quality etc.; highly refined extract. □ **quintessential** /-tɪ'sen-/ *adjective*; **quintessentially** /-tɪ'sen-/ *adverb.*

quintet /kwɪn'tet/ *noun* musical composition for 5 performers; the performers; any group of 5.

quintuple /'kwɪntjʊp(ə)l/ ● *adjective* fivefold, having 5 parts. ● *noun* fivefold number or amount. ● *verb* (**-ling**) multiply by 5.

quintuplet /'kwɪntjʊplɪt/ *noun* each of 5 children born at one birth.

quip ● *noun* clever saying, epigram. ● *verb* (**-pp-**) make quips.

quire *noun* 25 sheets of paper.

quirk *noun* peculiar feature; trick of fate. □ **quirky** *adjective* (**-ier, -iest**).

quisling /'kwɪzlɪŋ/ *noun* collaborator with invading enemy.

quit ● *verb* (**-tting**; *past & past participle* **quitted** or **quit**) give up, let go, abandon; *US* cease, stop; leave or depart from. ● *adjective* (+ *of*) rid of.

quitch *noun* couch grass.

quite *adverb* completely, altogether, absolutely; rather, to some extent; (often + *so*) *said to indicate agreement.* □ **quite a**, **quite some** a remarkable; **quite a few** *colloquial* a fairly large number (of); **quite something** *colloquial* a remarkable thing or person.

quits *adjective* on even terms by retaliation or repayment. □ **call it quits** acknowledge that things are now even, agree to stop quarrelling.

quiver[1] /'kwɪvə/ ● *verb* tremble or vibrate with slight rapid motion. ● *noun* quivering motion or sound.

quiver[2] /'kwɪvə/ *noun* case for arrows.

quixotic /kwɪk'sɒtɪk/ *adjective* extravagantly and romantically chivalrous. □ **quixotically** *adverb.*

Quotation marks ' ' " "

Also called inverted commas, these are used:

1 round a direct quotation (closing quotation marks come after any punctuation which is part of the quotation), e.g.

He said, 'That is nonsense.'
'That', he said, 'is nonsense.'
'That, however,' he said, 'is nonsense.'
Did he say, 'That is nonsense'?
He asked, 'Is that nonsense?'

2 round a quoted word or phrase, e.g.

What does 'integrated circuit' mean?

3 round a word or phrase that is not being used in its central sense, e.g.

the 'king' of jazz
He said he had enough 'bread' to buy a car.

4 round the title of a book, song, poem, magazine article, television programme, etc. (but not a book of the Bible), e.g.

'Hard Times' by Charles Dickens

5 as double quotation marks round a quotation within a quotation, e.g.

He asked, 'Do you know what "integrated circuit" means?'

In handwriting, double quotation marks are usual.

quiz ● *noun* (*plural* **quizzes**) test of knowledge, esp. as entertainment; interrogation, examination. ● *verb* examine by questioning.

quizzical /ˈkwɪzɪk(ə)l/ *adjective* mocking, gently amused. □ **quizzically** *adverb*.

quod *noun slang* prison.

quoin /kɔɪn/ *noun* external angle of building; cornerstone; wedge used in printing or gunnery.

quoit /kɔɪt/ *noun* ring thrown to encircle peg; (in *plural*) game using these.

quondam /ˈkwɒndæm/ *adjective* that once was, former.

quorate /ˈkwɔːreɪt/ *adjective* constituting or having quorum.

Quorn /kwɔːn/ *noun proprietary term* vegetable protein food made from fungus.

quorum /ˈkwɔːrəm/ *noun* minimum number of members that must be present to constitute valid meeting.

quota /ˈkwəʊtə/ *noun* share to be contributed to or received from total; number of goods, people, etc. stipulated or permitted.

quotable *adjective* worth quoting.

quotation /kwəʊˈteɪʃ(ə)n/ *noun* passage or remark quoted; quoting, being quoted; contractor's estimate. □ **quotation marks** inverted commas (' ' or " ") used at beginning and end of quotation etc. (see panel).

quote ● *verb* (**-ting**) cite or appeal to as example, authority, etc.; repeat or copy out passage from; (+ *from*) cite (author, book, etc.); (+ *as*) cite (author etc.) as proof, evidence, etc.; (as *interjection*) *used in dictation etc. to indicate opening quotation marks*; (often + *at*) state price of; state (price) for job. ● *noun colloquial* passage quoted; (usually in *plural*) quotation marks.

quoth /kwəʊθ/ *verb* (only in 1st & 3rd persons) *archaic* said.

quotidian /ˈkwɒˈtɪdɪən/ *adjective* occurring or recurring daily; commonplace, trivial.

quotient /ˈkwəʊʃ(ə)nt/ *noun* result of division sum.

q.v. *abbreviation* which see (*quod vide*).

Rr

R *abbreviation* (also **R.**) *Regina*; *Rex*; River; (also ®) registered as trademark. □ **R & D** research and development.

r. *abbreviation* (also **r**) right; radius.

RA *abbreviation* Royal Academy or Academician; Royal Artillery.

rabbet /ˈræbɪt/ ● *noun* step-shaped channel cut along edge or face of wood etc. to receive edge or tongue of another piece. ● *verb* (**-t-**) join with rabbet; make rabbet in.

rabbi /ˈræbaɪ/ *noun* (*plural* **-s**) Jewish religious leader; Jewish scholar or teacher, esp. of the law. □ **rabbinical** /rəˈbɪn-/ *adjective*.

rabbit /ˈræbɪt/ ● *noun* burrowing mammal of hare family; its fur. ● *verb* (**-t-**) hunt rabbits; (often + *on, away*) *colloquial* talk pointlessly; chatter. □ **rabbit punch** blow with edge of hand on back of neck.

rabble /ˈræb(ə)l/ *noun* disorderly crowd, mob; contemptible or inferior set of people. □ **rabble-rouser** person who stirs up rabble, esp. to agitate for social change.

Rabelaisian /ræbəˈleɪzɪən/ *adjective* exuberantly and coarsely humorous.

rabid /ˈræbɪd/ *adjective* affected with rabies, mad; violent, fanatical. □ **rabidity** /rəˈbɪd-/ *noun*.

rabies /ˈreɪbiːz/ *noun* contagious viral disease of esp. dogs; hydrophobia.

RAC *abbreviation* Royal Automobile Club.

raccoon /rəˈkuːn/ *noun* (also **racoon**) (*plural* same or **-s**) N. American mammal with bushy tail; its fur.

race[1] ● *noun* contest of speed or to be first to achieve something; (in *plural*) series of races for horses etc.; strong current in sea or river; channel. ● *verb* (**-cing**) take part in race; have race with; (+ *with*) compete in speed; cause to race; go at full speed; (usually as **racing** *adjective*) follow or take part in horse racing. □ **racecourse** ground for horse racing; **racehorse** one bred or kept for racing; **race meeting** sequence of horse races at one place; **racetrack** racecourse, track for motor racing; **racing car** one built for racing; **racing driver** driver of racing car.

race[2] *noun* each of the major divisions of humankind, each having distinct physical characteristics; group of people, animals, or plants connected by common descent; any great division of living creatures. □ **race relations** relations between members of different races in same country.

raceme /rəˈsiːm/ *noun* flower cluster with flowers attached by short stalks at equal distances along stem.

racial /ˈreɪʃ(ə)l/ *adjective* of or concerning race; on grounds of or connected with difference in race. □ **racially** *adverb*.

racialism *noun* = RACISM. □ **racialist** *noun & adjective*.

racism *noun* (prejudice based on) belief in superiority of particular race; antagonism towards other races. □ **racist** *noun & adjective*.

rack[1] ● *noun* framework, usually with rails, bars, etc., for holding things; cogged or toothed rail or bar engaging with wheel, pinion, etc.; *historical* instrument of torture stretching victim's joints. ● *verb* inflict suffering on; *historical* torture on rack. □ **rack one's brains** make great mental effort; **rack-rent** extortionate rent.

rack[2] *noun* destruction (esp. in **rack and ruin**).

rack[3] *verb* (often + *off*) draw off (wine etc.) from lees.

racket[1] /ˈrækɪt/ *noun* (also **racquet**) bat with round or oval frame strung with catgut, nylon, etc., used in tennis etc.; (in *plural*) game like squash but in larger court.

racket[2] ● *noun* uproar, din; *slang* scheme for obtaining money etc. by dishonest means; dodge; sly game; *colloquial* line of business.

racketeer /rækɪˈtɪə/ *noun* person who operates dishonest business. □ **racketeering** *noun*.

raconteur /rækɒnˈtɜː/ *noun* teller of anecdotes.

racoon = RACCOON.

racy *adjective* (**-ier**, **-iest**) lively and vigorous in style; risqué; of distinctive quality. □ **raciness** *noun*.

rad *noun* unit of absorbed dose of ionizing radiation.

RADA /ˈrɑːdə/ *abbreviation* Royal Academy of Dramatic Art.

radar /ˈreɪdɑː/ *noun* radio system for detecting the direction, range, or presence of objects; apparatus for this. □ **radar trap** device using radar to detect speeding vehicles.

raddled /ˈræd(ə)ld/ *adjective* worn out.

radial /ˈreɪdɪəl/ ● *adjective* of or arranged like rays or radii; having spokes or radiating lines; acting or moving along such lines; (in full **radial-ply**) (of tyre) having fabric layers arranged radially. ● *noun* radial-ply tyre. □ **radially** *adverb*.

radian /ˈreɪdɪən/ *noun* SI unit of plane angle (about 57°).

radiant /ˈreɪdɪənt/ ● *adjective* emitting or issuing in rays; beaming with joy etc.; splendid, dazzling. ● *noun* point or object from which heat or light radiates. □ **radiance** *noun*; **radiantly** *adverb*.

radiate /ˈreɪdɪeɪt/ *verb* (**-ting**) emit rays of light, heat, etc.; be emitted in rays; emit or spread from a centre; transmit or demonstrate.

radiation *noun* radiating; emission of energy as electromagnetic waves; energy thus transmitted, esp. invisibly; (in full **radiation therapy**) treatment of cancer etc. using e.g. X-rays or ultraviolet light. □ **radiation sickness** sickness caused by exposure to radiation such as gamma rays.

radiator *noun* device for heating room etc. by circulation of hot water etc.; engine-cooling device in motor vehicle or aircraft.

radical /ˈrædɪk(ə)l/ ● *adjective* fundamental; far-reaching, thorough; advocating fundamental reform; forming the basis; primary; of the root of a number or plant. ● *noun* person holding radical views; atom or group of atoms forming base of compound and remaining unchanged during reactions; quantity forming or expressed as root of another. □ **radicalism** *noun*; **radically** *adverb*.

radicchio /rəˈdiːkɪəʊ/ *noun* (*plural* **-s**) chicory with purplish leaves.

radicle /ˈrædɪk(ə)l/ *noun* part of seed that develops into root.

radii *plural* of **radius**.

radio /ˈreɪdɪəʊ/ ● *noun* (*plural* **-s**) transmission and reception of messages etc. by electromagnetic waves of radio frequency; apparatus for receiving, broadcasting, or transmitting radio signals; sound broadcasting (station or channel). ● *verb* (**-es**, **-ed**) send (message) by radio; send message to (person) by radio; communicate or broadcast by radio. □ **radio-controlled** controlled from a distance by radio; **radio telephone** one operating by radio; **radio telescope** aerial system for analysing radiation in the radio-frequency range from stars etc.

radioactive *adjective* of or exhibiting radioactivity.

radioactivity *noun* spontaneous disintegration of atomic nuclei, with emission of usually penetrating radiation or particles.

radiocarbon *noun* radioactive isotope of carbon.

radiogram /ˈreɪdɪəʊgræm/ *noun* combined radio and record player; picture obtained by X-rays etc.; telegram sent by radio.

radiograph /ˈreɪdɪəʊgrɑːf/ ● *noun* instrument recording intensity of radiation; picture obtained by X-rays etc. ● *verb* obtain picture of by X-rays, gamma rays, etc. □ **radiographer** /-ˈɒgrəfə/ *noun*; **radiography** /-ˈɒgrəfɪ/ *noun*.

radiology /reɪdɪˈɒlədʒɪ/ *noun esp. Medicine* study of X-rays and other high-energy radiation. □ **radiologist** *noun*.

radiophonic *adjective* of electronically produced sound, esp. music.

radioscopy /reɪdɪˈɒskəpɪ/ *noun* examination by X-rays etc. of objects opaque to light.

radiotherapy *noun* treatment of disease by X-rays or other forms of radiation.

radish /ˈrædɪʃ/ *noun* plant with crisp pungent root; this root, esp. eaten raw.

radium /ˈreɪdɪəm/ *noun* radioactive metallic element.

radius /ˈreɪdɪəs/ *noun* (*plural* **radii** /-dɪaɪ/ or **-es**) straight line from centre to circumference of circle or sphere; distance from a centre; bone of forearm on same side as thumb.

radon /ˈreɪdɒn/ *noun* gaseous radioactive inert element arising from disintegration of radium.

RAF *abbreviation* Royal Air Force.

raffia /ˈræfɪə/ *noun* palm tree native to Madagascar; fibre from its leaves.

raffish /ˈræfɪʃ/ *adjective* disreputable, rakish; tawdry.

raffle /ˈræf(ə)l/ ● *noun* fund-raising lottery with prizes. ● *verb* (**-ling**) (often + *off*) sell by raffle.

raft /rɑːft/ *noun* flat floating structure of wood etc., used for transport.

rafter /ˈrɑːftə/ *noun* any of sloping beams forming framework of roof.

rag[1] *noun* torn, frayed, or worn piece of woven material; remnant; (in *plural*) old or worn clothes; *derogatory* newspaper. □ **rag-bag** miscellaneous collection; **rag doll** stuffed cloth doll; **ragtime** form of highly syncopated early jazz; **the rag trade** *colloquial* the clothing business; **ragwort** yellow-flowered ragged-leaved plant.

rag[2] ● *noun* fund-raising programme of stunts etc. staged by students; prank; rowdy celebration, disorderly scene. ● *verb* (**-gg-**) tease; play rough jokes on; engage in rough play.

ragamuffin /ˈrægəmʌfɪn/ *noun* child in ragged dirty clothes.

rage ● *noun* violent anger; fit of this. ● *verb* (**-ging**) be full of anger; (often + *at, against*) speak furiously; be violent, be at its height; (as **raging** *adjective*) extreme, very painful. □ **all the rage** very popular, fashionable.

ragged /ˈrægɪd/ *adjective* torn; frayed; in ragged clothes; with a broken or jagged outline or surface; lacking finish, smoothness, or uniformity.

raglan /ˈræglən/ *adjective* (of sleeve) running up to neck of garment.

ragout /ræˈguː/ *noun* highly seasoned stew of meat and vegetables.

raid ● *noun* rapid surprise attack by armed forces or thieves; surprise visit by police etc. to arrest suspects or seize illicit goods. ● *verb* make raid on. □ **raider** *noun*.

rail[1] ● *noun* bar used to hang things on or as protection, part of fence, top of banisters, etc.; steel bar(s) making railway track; railway. ● *verb* provide or enclose with rail(s). □ **railcard** pass entitling holder to reduced rail fares.

rail[2] *verb* (often + *at, against*) complain or protest strongly; rant.

rail[3] *noun* marsh wading bird.

railing *noun* (often in *plural*) fence or barrier made of rails.

raillery /ˈreɪlərɪ/ *noun* good-humoured ridicule.

railroad ● *noun esp. US* railway. ● *verb* (often + *into, through*) coerce, rush.

railway /ˈreɪlweɪ/ *noun* track or set of tracks of steel rails on which trains run; organization and people required to work such a system. □ **railwayman** male railway employee.

raiment /ˈreɪmənt/ *noun archaic* clothing.

rain ● *noun* condensed atmospheric moisture falling in drops; fall of these; falling liquid or objects; (**the rains**) rainy season. ● *verb* (after *it*) rain falls, send in large quantities; fall or send down like rain; lavishly bestow. □ **raincoat** waterproof or water-resistant coat; **rainfall** total amount of rain falling within given area in given time; **rainforest** tropical forest with heavy rainfall; **take a rain check on** reserve right to postpone taking up (offer) until convenient.

rainbow /ˈreɪmbəʊ/ ● *noun* arch of colours formed in sky by reflection, refraction, and dispersion of sun's rays in falling rain etc. ● *adjective* many-coloured. □ **rainbow trout** large trout originally of N. America.

rainy *adjective* (**-ier, -iest**) (of weather, day, climate, etc.) in or on which rain is falling or much rain usually falls. □ **rainy day** time of need in the future.

raise /reɪz/ ● *verb* (**-sing**) put or take into higher position; (often + *up*) cause to rise or stand up or be vertical; increase amount, value, or strength of; (often + *up*) build up; levy, collect; cause to be heard or considered; bring up, educate; breed; remove (barrier); rouse. ● *noun Cards* increase in stake or bid; *US* rise in salary. □ **raise Cain, hell, the roof** be very angry, cause an uproar; **raise a laugh** cause others to laugh.

raisin /ˈreɪz(ə)n/ *noun* dried grape.

raison d'être /reɪzɔ̃ ˈdetr/ *noun* (*plural* ***raisons d'être*** same pronunciation) purpose that accounts for, justifies, or originally caused thing's existence. [French]

raj /rɑːdʒ/ *noun* (**the raj**) *historical* British rule in India.

raja /ˈrɑːdʒə/ *noun* (also **rajah**) *historical* Indian king or prince.

rake[1] ● *noun* implement with long handle and toothed crossbar for drawing hay etc. together, smoothing loose soil, etc.; similar implement. ● *verb* (**-king**) collect or gather (as) with rake; ransack, search thoroughly; direct gunfire along (line) from end to end. □ **rake in** *colloquial* amass (profits etc.); **rake-off** *colloquial* commission or share; **rake up** revive (unwelcome) memory of.

rake[2] *noun* dissolute man of fashion.

rake[3] ● *verb* (**-king**) set or be set at sloping angle. ● *noun* raking position or build; amount by which thing rakes.

rakish *adjective* dashing, jaunty; dissolute. □ **rakishly** *adverb*.

rallentando /rælən'tændəʊ/ *Music* ● *adverb & adjective* with gradual decrease of speed. ● *noun* (*plural* **-s** or **-di** /-dɪ/) rallentando passage.

rally /'rælɪ/ ● *verb* (**-ies**, **-ied**) (often + *round*) bring or come together as support or for action; recover after illness etc., revive; (of prices etc.) increase after fall. ● *noun* (*plural* **-ies**) rallying, being rallied; mass meeting; competition for motor vehicles over public roads; extended exchange of strokes in tennis etc. ▫ **rallycross** motor racing across country.

RAM *abbreviation* Royal Academy of Music; random-access memory.

ram ● *noun* uncastrated male sheep; (**the Ram**) zodiacal sign or constellation Aries; falling weight of pile-driving machine; hydraulic water pump. ● *verb* (**-mm-**) force into place; (usually + *down*, *in*, etc.) beat down or drive in by blows; (of ship, vehicle, etc.) strike, crash against. ▫ **ram-raid** crashing vehicle into shop front in order to steal contents; **ram-raider** *noun*.

Ramadan /'ræmədæn/ *noun* ninth month of Muslim year, with strict fasting from sunrise to sunset.

ramble /'ræmb(ə)l/ ● *verb* (**-ling**) walk for pleasure; talk or write incoherently. ● *noun* walk taken for pleasure.

rambler *noun* person who rambles; straggling or spreading rose.

rambling *adjective* wandering; disconnected, incoherent; irregularly arranged; (of plant) straggling, climbing.

RAMC *abbreviation* Royal Army Medical Corps.

ramekin /'ræmɪkɪn/ *noun* small dish for baking and serving individual portion of food.

ramification /ræmɪfɪ'keɪʃ(ə)n/ *noun* (usually in *plural*) consequence; subdivision.

ramify /'ræmɪfaɪ/ *verb* (**-ies**, **-ied**) (cause to) form branches or subdivisions; branch out.

ramp *noun* slope joining two levels of ground, floor, etc.; stairs for entering or leaving aircraft; transverse ridge in road making vehicles slow down.

rampage ● *verb* /ræm'peɪdʒ/ (**-ging**) (often + *about*) rush wildly; rage, storm. ● *noun* /'ræmpeɪdʒ/ wild or violent behaviour. ▫ **on the rampage** rampaging.

rampant /'ræmpənt/ *adjective* unchecked, flourishing excessively; rank, luxuriant; *Heraldry* (of lion etc.) standing on left hind foot with forepaws in air; fanatical. ▫ **rampancy** *noun*.

rampart /'ræmpɑːt/ *noun* defensive broad-topped wall; defence, protection.

ramrod *noun* rod for ramming down charge of muzzle-loading firearm; thing that is very straight or rigid.

ramshackle /'ræmʃæk(ə)l/ *adjective* rickety, tumbledown.

ran *past* of RUN.

ranch /rɑːntʃ/ ● *noun* cattle-breeding establishment, esp. in US & Canada; farm where other animals are bred. ● *verb* farm on ranch. ▫ **rancher** *noun*.

rancid /'rænsɪd/ *adjective* smelling or tasting like rank stale fat. ▫ **rancidity** /-'sɪd-/ *noun*.

rancour /'ræŋkə/ *noun* (*US* **rancor**) inveterate bitterness; malignant hate. ▫ **rancorous** *adjective*.

rand *noun* monetary unit of South Africa.

random /'rændəm/ *adjective* made, done, etc. without method or conscious choice. ▫ **at random** without particular aim; **random-access** (of computer memory) having all parts directly accessible. ▫ **randomly** *adverb*.

randy /'rændɪ/ *adjective* (**-ier**, **-iest**) eager for sexual satisfaction.

ranee /'rɑːnɪ/ *noun* (also **rani**) (*plural* **-s**) *historical* raja's wife or widow.

rang *past* of RING².

range /reɪndʒ/ ● *noun* region between limits of variation, esp. scope of operation; such limits; area relevant to something; distance attainable by gun or projectile, distance between gun etc. and target; row, series, etc., esp. of mountains; area with targets for shooting; fireplace for cooking; area over which a thing is distributed; distance that can be covered by vehicle without refuelling; stretch of open land for grazing or hunting. ● *verb* (**-ging**) reach; extend; vary between limits; (usually in *passive*) line up, arrange; rove, wander; traverse in all directions. ▫ **rangefinder** instrument for determining distance of object.

ranger *noun* keeper of royal or national park, or of forest; (**Ranger**) senior Guide.

rangy /'reɪndʒɪ/ *adjective* (**-ier**, **-iest**) tall and slim.

rani = RANEE.

rank¹ ● *noun* position in hierarchy; grade of advancement; distinct social class, grade of dignity or achievement; high social position; place in scale; row or line; single line of soldiers drawn up abreast; place where taxis wait for customers. ● *verb* have rank or place; classify, give a certain grade to; arrange in rank. ▫ **rank and file** (usually treated as *plural*) ordinary members of organization; **the ranks** common soldiers.

rank² *adjective* luxuriant; coarse; choked with weeds etc.; foul-smelling; loathsome; flagrant; gross, complete.

rankle /'ræŋk(ə)l/ *verb* (**-ling**) cause persistent annoyance or resentment.

ransack /'rænsæk/ *verb* pillage, plunder; thoroughly search.

ransom /'rænsəm/ ● *noun* sum demanded or paid for release of prisoner. ● *verb* buy freedom or restoration of; hold (prisoner) to ransom; release for a ransom. ▫ **hold to ransom** keep (prisoner) and demand ransom, demand concessions from by threats.

rant ● *verb* speak loudly, bombastically, or violently. ● *noun* piece of ranting. ▫ **rant and rave** express anger noisily and forcefully.

ranunculus /rə'nʌŋkjʊləs/ *noun* (*plural* **-luses** or **-li** /-laɪ/) plant of genus including buttercup.

RAOC *abbreviation* Royal Army Ordnance Corps.

rap¹ ● *noun* smart slight blow; sound of this, tap; *slang* blame, punishment; rhythmic monologue recited to music; (in full **rap music**) style of rock music with words recited. ● *verb* (**-pp-**) strike smartly; make sharp tapping sound; criticize adversely; *Music* perform rap. ▫ **take the rap** suffer the consequences. ▫ **rapper** *noun Music*.

rap² *noun* the least bit.

rapacious /rə'peɪʃəs/ *adjective* grasping, extortionate, predatory. ▫ **rapacity** /-'pæs-/ *noun*.

rape¹ ● *noun* act of forcing esp. woman or girl to have sexual intercourse unwillingly; (often + *of*) violation. ● *verb* (**-ping**) commit rape on.

rape² *noun* plant grown as fodder and for oil from its seed.

rapid /'ræpɪd/ ● *adjective* (**-er**, **-est**) quick, swift. ● *noun* (usually in *plural*) steep descent in river bed, with swift current. ▫ **rapid eye movement** jerky movement of eyes during dreaming. ▫ **rapidity** /rə'pɪd-/ *noun*; **rapidly** *adverb*.

rapier /'reɪpɪə/ *noun* light slender sword for thrusting.

rapine /'ræpaɪn/ *noun rhetorical* plundering.

rapist *noun* person who commits rape.

rapport /ræ'pɔː/ *noun* communication or relationship, esp. when useful and harmonious.

rapprochement /ræ'prɒʃmɑ̃/ *noun* resumption of harmonious relations, esp. between states. [French]

rapscallion /ræp'skæljən/ *noun archaic* rascal.
rapt *adjective* absorbed; intent; carried away with feeling or thought.
rapture /'ræptʃə/ *noun* ecstatic delight; (in *plural*) great pleasure or enthusiasm or expression of it. ▫ **rapturous** *adjective*.
rare[1] *adjective* (**-r**, **-st**) seldom done, found, or occurring; uncommon; exceptionally good; of less than usual density. ▫ **rareness** *noun*.
rare[2] *adjective* (**-r**, **-st**) (of meat) underdone.
rarebit *noun* see WELSH RAREBIT.
rarefy /'reərɪfaɪ/ *verb* (**-ies**, **-ied**) (often as **rarefied** *adjective*) make or become less dense or solid; refine, make (idea etc.) subtle. ▫ **rarefaction** /-'fækʃ(ə)n/ *noun*.
rarely *adverb* seldom, not often.
raring /'reərɪŋ/ *adjective colloquial* eager (esp. in **raring to go**).
rarity /'reərətɪ/ *noun* (*plural* **-ies**) rareness; uncommon thing.
rascal /'rɑːsk(ə)l/ *noun* dishonest or mischievous person. ▫ **rascally** *adjective*.
rase = RAZE.
rash[1] *adjective* reckless; hasty, impetuous. ▫ **rashly** *adverb*; **rashness** *noun*.
rash[2] *noun* skin eruption in spots or patches; (usually + *of*) sudden widespread phenomenon.
rasher /'ræʃə/ *noun* thin slice of bacon or ham.
rasp /rɑːsp/ ● *noun* coarse file; grating noise or utterance. ● *verb* scrape roughly or with rasp; make grating sound; say gratingly; grate on.
raspberry /'rɑːzbərɪ/ *noun* (*plural* **-ies**) red fruit like blackberry; shrub bearing this; *colloquial* sound made by blowing through lips, expressing derision or disapproval.
Rastafarian /ræstə'feərɪən/ (also **Rasta** /'ræstə/) ● *noun* member of Jamaican sect regarding Haile Selassie of Ethiopia (d. 1975) as God. ● *adjective* of this sect.
rat ● *noun* large mouselike rodent; *colloquial* unpleasant or treacherous person. ● *verb* (**-tt-**) hunt or kill rats; (also + *on*) inform (on), desert, betray. ▫ **ratbag** *slang* obnoxious person; **rat race** *colloquial* fiercely competitive struggle.
ratable = RATEABLE.
ratatouille /rætə'tuːɪ/ *noun* dish of stewed onions, courgettes, tomatoes, aubergines, and peppers.
ratchet /'rætʃɪt/ *noun* set of teeth on edge of bar or wheel with catch ensuring motion in one direction only; (in full **ratchet-wheel**) wheel with rim so toothed.
rate ● *noun* numerical proportion between two sets of things or as basis of calculating amount or value; charge, cost, or value; measure of this; pace of movement or change; (in *plural*) tax levied by local authorities according to value of buildings and land occupied. ● *verb* (**-ting**) estimate worth or value of; assign value to; consider, regard as; (+ *as*) rank or be considered as; subject to payment of local rate; deserve. ▫ **at any rate** in any case, whatever happens; **at this rate** if this example is typical; **rate-capping** *historical* imposition of upper limit on local authority rates; **ratepayer** person liable to pay rates.
rateable /'reɪtəb(ə)l/ *adjective* (also **ratable** /'reɪtəb(ə)l/) liable to rates. ▫ **rateable value** value at which business etc. is assessed for rates.
rather /'rɑːðə/ *adverb* by preference; (usually + *than*) more truly; as a more likely alternative; more precisely; to some extent; /rɑː'ðɜː/ most emphatically.
ratify /'rætɪfaɪ/ *verb* (**-ies**, **-ied**) confirm or accept by formal consent, signature, etc. ▫ **ratification** *noun*.
rating /'reɪtɪŋ/ *noun* placing in rank or class; estimated standing of person as regards credit etc.; non-commissioned sailor; (usually in *plural*) popularity of a broadcast as determined by estimated size of audience.
ratio /'reɪʃɪəʊ/ *noun* (*plural* **-s**) quantitative relation between similar magnitudes.
ratiocinate /rætɪ'ɒsɪneɪt/ *verb* (**-ting**) *literary* reason, esp. using syllogisms. ▫ **ratiocination** *noun*.
ration /'ræʃ(ə)n/ ● *noun* official allowance of food, clothing, etc., in time of shortage; (usually in *plural*) fixed daily allowance of food. ● *verb* limit (food etc. or people) to fixed ration; (usually + *out*) share (out) in fixed quantities.
rational /'ræʃən(ə)l/ *adjective* of or based on reason; sensible; endowed with reason; rejecting what is unreasonable; *Mathematics* expressible as ratio of whole numbers. ▫ **rationality** /-'næl-/ *noun*; **rationally** *adverb*.
rationale /ræʃə'nɑːl/ *noun* fundamental reason, logical basis.
rationalism *noun* practice of treating reason as basis of belief and knowledge. ▫ **rationalist** *noun & adjective*; **rationalistic** /-'lɪs-/ *adjective*.
rationalize *verb* (also **-ise**) (**-zing** or **-sing**) (often + *away*) offer rational but specious explanation of (behaviour or attitude); make logical and consistent; make (industry etc.) more efficient by reducing waste. ▫ **rationalization** *noun*.
ratline /'rætlɪn/ *noun* (also **ratlin**) (usually in *plural*) any of the small lines fastened across ship's shrouds like ladder rungs.
rattan /rə'tæn/ *noun* palm with long thin many-jointed stems; cane of this.
rattle /'ræt(ə)l/ ● *verb* (**-ling**) (cause to) give out rapid succession of short sharp sounds; cause such sounds by shaking something; move or travel with rattling noise; (usually + *off*) say or recite rapidly; (usually + *on*) talk in lively thoughtless way; *colloquial* disconcert, alarm. ● *noun* rattling sound; device or plaything made to rattle. ▫ **rattlesnake** poisonous American snake with rattling rings on tail. ▫ **rattly** *adjective*.
rattling ● *adjective* that rattles; brisk, vigorous. ● *adverb colloquial* remarkably (good etc.).
raucous /'rɔːkəs/ *adjective* harsh-sounding; hoarse. ▫ **raucously** *adverb*; **raucousness** *noun*.
raunchy /'rɔːntʃɪ/ *adjective* (**-ier**, **-iest**) *colloquial* sexually boisterous.
ravage /'rævɪdʒ/ ● *verb* (**-ging**) devastate, plunder. ● *noun* (usually in *plural*; + *of*) destructive effect.
rave ● *verb* (**-ving**) talk wildly or deliriously; (usually + *about*, *over*) speak with rapturous admiration; *colloquial* enjoy oneself freely. ● *noun colloquial* highly enthusiastic review; (also **rave-up**) lively party.
ravel /'ræv(ə)l/ *verb* (**-ll-**; *US* **-l-**) entangle, become entangled; fray out.
raven /'reɪv(ə)n/ ● *noun* large glossy black crow with hoarse cry. ● *adjective* glossy black.
ravening /'rævənɪŋ/ *adjective* hungrily seeking prey; voracious.
ravenous /'rævənəs/ *adjective* very hungry; voracious; rapacious. ▫ **ravenously** *adverb*.
raver *noun colloquial* uninhibited pleasure-loving person.
ravine /rə'viːn/ *noun* deep narrow gorge.
raving ● *noun* (usually in *plural*) wild or delirious talk. ● *adjective colloquial* utter, absolute. ● *adverb colloquial* utterly, absolutely.
ravioli /rævɪ'əʊlɪ/ *noun* small square pasta envelopes containing meat, spinach, etc.
ravish /'rævɪʃ/ *verb archaic* rape (woman); enrapture.

ravishing *adjective* lovely, beautiful. □ **ravishingly** *adverb*.

raw *adjective* uncooked; in natural state, not processed or manufactured; inexperienced, untrained; stripped of skin; unhealed; sensitive to touch; (of weather) cold and damp; crude. □ **in the raw** in its natural state, naked; **raw-boned** gaunt; **raw deal** unfair treatment; **rawhide** untanned hide, rope or whip of this; **raw material** material from which manufactured goods are made.

Rawlplug /ˈrɔːlplʌg/ *noun proprietary term* cylindrical plug for holding screw in masonry.

ray[1] *noun* single line or narrow beam of light; straight line in which radiation travels; (in *plural*) radiation; trace or beginning of enlightening influence; any of set of radiating lines, parts, or things; marginal part of daisy etc.

ray[2] *noun* large edible marine fish with flat body.

ray[3] *noun* (also **re**) *Music* second note of scale in tonic sol-fa.

rayon /ˈreɪɒn/ *noun* textile fibre or fabric made from cellulose.

raze *verb* (also **rase**) (**-zing** or **-sing**) completely destroy, tear down.

razor /ˈreɪzə/ *noun* instrument for shaving. □ **razorbill** auk with sharp-edged bill; **razor-blade** flat piece of metal with sharp edge, used in safety razor; **razor-edge**, **razor's edge** keen edge, sharp mountain ridge, critical situation, sharp line of division.

razzle /ˈræz(ə)l/ *noun colloquial* spree. □ **razzle-dazzle** excitement, bustle, extravagant publicity.

razzmatazz /ræzməˈtæz/ *noun* (also **razzamatazz** /ræzə-/) *colloquial* glamorous excitement; insincere activity.

RC *abbreviation* Roman Catholic.

Rd. *abbreviation* Road.

RE *abbreviation* Religious Education; Royal Engineers.

re[1] /riː/ *preposition* in the matter of; about, concerning.

re[2] = RAY[3].

re- *prefix attachable to almost any verb or its derivative, meaning*: once more, anew, afresh; back. For words starting with *re-* that are not found below, the root-words should be consulted.

reach ● *verb* (often + *out*) stretch out, extend; (often + *for*) stretch hand etc.; get as far as, get to or attain; make contact with; pass, hand; take with outstretched hand; *Nautical* sail with wind abeam. ● *noun* extent to which hand etc. can be reached out, influence exerted, etc.; act of reaching out; continuous extent, esp. of river or canal. □ **reach-me-down** *colloquial* ready-made garment. □ **reachable** *adjective*.

react /rɪˈækt/ *verb* (often + *to*) respond to stimulus; change or behave differently due to some influence; (often + *with*) undergo chemical reaction (with other substance); (often + *against*) respond with repulsion to; tend in reverse or contrary direction.

reaction /rɪˈækʃ(ə)n/ *noun* reacting; response; bad physical response to drug etc.; occurrence of condition after its opposite; tendency to oppose change or reform; interaction of substances undergoing chemical change.

reactionary ● *adjective* tending to oppose (esp. political) change or reform. ● *noun* (*plural* **-ies**) reactionary person.

reactivate /rɪˈæktɪveɪt/ *verb* (**-ting**) restore to state of activity. □ **reactivation** *noun*.

reactive /rɪˈæktɪv/ *adjective* showing reaction; reacting rather than taking initiative; susceptible to chemical reaction.

reactor *noun* (in full **nuclear reactor**) device in which nuclear chain reaction is used to produce energy.

read ● *verb* (*past & past participle* **read** /red/) reproduce (written or printed words) mentally or (often + *aloud*, *out*, *off*, etc.) vocally; (be able to) convert (written or printed words or other symbols) into intended words or meaning; interpret; (of meter) show (figure); interpret state of (meter); study (subject) at university; (as **read** /red/ *adjective*) versed in subject (esp. literature) by reading; (of computer) copy or transfer (data); hear and understand (over radio); substitute (word etc.) for incorrect one. ● *noun* spell of reading; *colloquial* book etc. as regards readability. □ **take as read** treat (thing) as if it has been agreed.

readable *adjective* able to be read; interesting to read. □ **readability** *noun*.

reader *noun* person who reads; book intended for reading pratice; device for producing image that can be read from microfilm etc.; (also **Reader**) university lecturer of highest grade below professor; publisher's employee who reports on submitted manuscripts; printer's proof-corrector.

readership *noun* readers of a newspaper etc.; (also **Readership**) position of Reader.

readily *adverb* without reluctance; willingly; easily.

readiness *noun* prepared state; willingness; facility; promptness in argument or action.

reading *noun* act of reading; matter to be read; literary knowledge; entertainment at which something is read; figure etc. shown by recording instrument; interpretation or view taken; interpretation made (of music etc.); presentation of bill to legislature.

ready /ˈredɪ/ ● *adjective* (**-ier**, **-iest**) with preparations complete; in fit state; willing; (of income etc.) easily secured; fit for immediate use; prompt, enthusiastic; (+ *to do*) about to; provided beforehand. ● *adverb usually in combination* beforehand; in readiness. ● *noun slang* (**the ready**) ready money; (**readies**) bank notes. ● *verb* (**-ies**, **-ied**) prepare. □ **at the ready** ready for action; **ready-made**, **ready-to-wear** (esp. of clothes) made in standard size, not to measure; **ready money** cash, actual coin; **ready reckoner** book or table listing standard numerical calculations.

reagent /riːˈeɪdʒ(ə)nt/ *noun* substance used to produce chemical reaction.

real ● *adjective* actually existing or occurring; genuine; appraised by purchasing power. ● *adverb Scottish & US colloquial* really, very. □ **real ale** beer regarded as brewed in traditional way; **real estate** property such as land and houses; **real tennis** original form of tennis played on indoor court.

realism *noun* practice of regarding things in their true nature and dealing with them as they are; fidelity to nature in representation. □ **realist** *noun*.

realistic /rɪəˈlɪstɪk/ *adjective* regarding things as they are; based on facts rather than ideals. □ **realistically** *adverb*.

reality /rɪˈælɪtɪ/ *noun* (*plural* **-ies**) what is real or existent or underlies appearances; (+ *of*) real nature of; real existence; being real; likeness to original. □ **in reality** in fact.

realize *verb* (also **-ise**) (**-zing** or **-sing**) (often + *that*) be or become fully aware of; understand clearly; convert into actuality; convert into money; acquire (profit); be sold for. □ **realizable** *adjective*; **realization** *noun*.

really /ˈrɪəlɪ/ *adverb* in fact; very; I assure you; *expression of mild protest or surprise*.

realm /relm/ *noun formal* kingdom; domain.

realty /ˈriːəltɪ/ *noun* real estate.

ream *noun* 500 sheets of paper; (in *plural*) large quantity of writing.

reap *verb* cut (grain etc.) as harvest; receive as consequences of actions. □ **reaper** *noun*.

rear[1] ● *noun* back part of anything; space or position at back. ● *adjective* at the back. □ **bring up the rear** come last; **rear admiral** naval officer below vice admiral. □ **rearmost** *adjective*.

rear[2] *verb* bring up and educate; breed and care for; cultivate; (of horse etc.) raise itself on hind legs; raise, build.

rearguard *noun* troops detached to protect rear, esp. in retreat. □ **rearguard action** engagement undertaken by rearguard, defensive stand or struggle, esp. when losing.

rearm /riːˈɑːm/ *verb* arm again, esp. with improved weapons. □ **rearmament** *noun*.

rearward /ˈrɪəwəd/ ● *noun* rear. ● *adjective* to the rear. ● *adverb* (also **rearwards**) towards the rear.

reason /ˈriːz(ə)n/ ● *noun* motive, cause, or justification; fact adduced or serving as this; intellectual faculty by which conclusions are drawn; sanity; sense, sensible conduct; moderation. ● *verb* form or try to reach conclusions by connected thought; (+ *with*) use argument with person by way of persuasion; (+ *that*) conclude or assert in argument; (+ *out*) think out.

reasonable *adjective* having sound judgement; moderate; ready to listen to reason; sensible; inexpensive; tolerable. □ **reasonableness** *noun*; **reasonably** *adverb*.

reassure /riːəˈʃʊə/ *verb* (**-ring**) restore confidence to; confirm in opinion etc. □ **reassurance** *noun*; **reassuring** *adjective*.

rebate[1] /ˈriːbeɪt/ *noun* partial refund; deduction from sum to be paid, discount.

rebate[2] /ˈriːbeɪt/ *noun & verb* (**-ting**) rabbet.

rebel ● *noun* /ˈreb(ə)l/ person who fights against, resists, or refuses allegiance to, established government; person etc. who resists authority or control. ● *verb* /rɪˈbel/ (**-ll-**) (usually + *against*) act as rebel; feel or show repugnance.

rebellion /rɪˈbeljən/ *noun* open resistance to authority, esp. organized armed resistance to established government.

rebellious /rɪˈbeljəs/ *adjective* disposed to rebel; in rebellion; unmanageable. □ **rebelliously** *adverb*; **rebelliousness** *noun*.

rebound ● *verb* /rɪˈbaʊnd/ spring back after impact; (+ *upon*) have adverse effect on (doer). ● *noun* /ˈriːbaʊnd/ rebounding, recoil; reaction. □ **on the rebound** while still recovering from emotional shock, esp. rejection by lover.

rebuff /rɪˈbʌf/ ● *noun* rejection of person who makes advances, offers help, etc.; snub. ● *verb* give rebuff to.

rebuke /rɪˈbjuːk/ ● *verb* (**-king**) express sharp disapproval to (person) for fault; censure. ● *noun* rebuking, being rebuked.

rebus /ˈriːbəs/ *noun* (*plural* **rebuses**) representation of word (esp. name) by pictures etc. suggesting its parts.

rebut /rɪˈbʌt/ *verb* (**-tt-**) refute, disprove; force back. □ **rebuttal** *noun*.

recalcitrant /rɪˈkælsɪtrənt/ *adjective* obstinately disobedient; objecting to restraint. □ **recalcitrance** *noun*.

recall /rɪˈkɔːl/ ● *verb* summon to return; recollect, remember; bring back to memory; revoke, annul; revive, resuscitate. ● *noun* (also /ˈriːkɔːl/) summons to come back; act of remembering; ability to remember; possibility of recalling.

recant /rɪˈkænt/ *verb* withdraw and renounce (belief or statement) as erroneous or heretical. □ **recantation** /riːkænˈteɪʃ(ə)n/ *noun*.

recap /ˈriːkæp/ *colloquial* ● *verb* (**-pp-**) recapitulate. ● *noun* recapitulation.

recapitulate /riːkəˈpɪtjʊleɪt/ *verb* (**-ting**) summarize, restate briefly. □ **recapitulation** *noun*.

recast /riːˈkɑːst/ ● *verb* (*past & past participle* **recast**) cast again; put into new form; improve arrangement of. ● *noun* recasting; recast form.

recce /ˈrekɪ/ *colloquial* ● *noun* reconnaissance. ● *verb* (**recced**, **recceing**) reconnoitre.

recede /rɪˈsiːd/ *verb* (**-ding**) go or shrink back; be left at an increasing distance; slope backwards; decline in force or value.

receipt /rɪˈsiːt/ ● *noun* receiving, being received; written or printed acknowledgement of payment received; (usually in *plural*) amount of money received. ● *verb* place written or printed receipt on (bill). □ **in receipt of** having received.

receive /rɪˈsiːv/ *verb* (**-ving**) take or accept (thing offered, sent, or given); acquire; have conferred etc. on one; react to (news etc.) in particular way; stand force or weight of; consent to hear or consider; admit, entertain as guest, greet, welcome; be able to hold; convert (broadcast signals) into sound or pictures (as **received** *adjective*) accepted as authoritative or true. □ **Received Pronunciation** standard pronunciation of English in Britain (see panel at ACCENT).

receiver *noun* part of telephone containing earpiece; (in full **official receiver**) person appointed to administer property of bankrupt person etc. or property under litigation; radio or television receiving apparatus; person who receives stolen goods.

receivership *noun* □ **in receivership** being dealt with by receiver.

recent /ˈriːs(ə)nt/ *adjective* not long past, that happened or existed lately; not long established, modern. □ **recently** *adverb*.

receptacle /rɪˈseptək(ə)l/ *noun* object or space used to contain something.

reception /rɪˈsepʃ(ə)n/ *noun* receiving, being received; way in which person or thing is received; social occasion for receiving guests, esp. after wedding; place where visitors register on arriving at hotel, office, etc.; (quality of) receiving of broadcast signals. □ **reception room** room for receiving guests, clients, etc.

receptionist *noun* person employed to receive guests, clients, etc.

receptive /rɪˈseptɪv/ *adjective* able or quick to receive ideas etc. □ **receptively** *adverb*; **receptiveness** *noun*; **receptivity** /riːsepˈtɪv-/ *noun*.

recess /rɪˈses/ ● *noun* space set back in wall; (often in *plural*) remote or secret place; temporary cessation from work, esp. of Parliament. ● *verb* make recess in; place in recess; *US* take recess, adjourn.

recession /rɪˈseʃ(ə)n/ *noun* temporary decline in economic activity or prosperity; receding, withdrawal.

recessive /rɪˈsesɪv/ *adjective* tending to recede; (of inherited characteristic) appearing in offspring only when not masked by inherited dominant characteristic.

recherché /rəˈʃeəʃeɪ/ *adjective* carefully sought out; far-fetched.

recidivist /rɪˈsɪdɪvɪst/ *noun* person who relapses into crime. □ **recidivism** *noun*.

recipe /ˈresɪpɪ/ *noun* statement of ingredients and procedure for preparing dish etc.; (+ *for*) certain means to.

recipient /rɪˈsɪpɪənt/ *noun* person who receives something.

reciprocal /rɪˈsɪprək(ə)l/ ● *adjective* in return; mutual; *Grammar* expressing mutual relation. ● *noun Mathematics* function or expression so related to another that their product is unity. □ **reciprocally** *adverb*.

reciprocate /rɪˈsɪprəkeɪt/ *verb* (**-ting**) requite, return; (+ *with*) give in return; interchange; (of machine part) move backwards and forwards. □ **reciprocation** *noun*.

reciprocity /resɪˈprɒsɪtɪ/ *noun* condition of being reciprocal; mutual action; give and take.

recital /rɪˈsaɪt(ə)l/ *noun* reciting, being recited; concert of classical music by soloist or small group; (+ *of*) detailed account of (facts etc.); narrative.

recitation /resɪˈteɪʃ(ə)n/ *noun* reciting; piece recited.

recitative /resɪtəˈtiːv/ *noun* passage of singing in speech rhythm, esp. in narrative or dialogue section of opera or oratorio.

recite /rɪˈsaɪt/ *verb* (**-ting**) repeat aloud or declaim from memory; enumerate.

reckless /ˈreklɪs/ *adjective* disregarding consequences or danger etc. □ **recklessly** *adverb*; **recklessness** *noun*.

reckon /ˈrekən/ *verb* (often + *that*) think, consider; count or compute by calculation; (+ *on*) rely or base plans on; (+ *with, without*) take (or fail to take) into account.

reckoning *noun* calculating; opinion; settlement of account.

reclaim /rɪˈkleɪm/ *verb* seek return of (one's property etc.); bring (land) under cultivation from sea etc.; win back from vice, error, or waste condition. □ **reclaimable** *adjective*; **reclamation** /rekləˈ-/ *noun*.

recline /rɪˈklaɪn/ *verb* (**-ning**) assume or be in horizontal or leaning position.

recluse /rɪˈkluːs/ *noun* person given to or living in seclusion. □ **reclusive** *adjective*.

recognition /rekəgˈnɪʃ(ə)n/ *noun* recognizing, being recognized.

recognizance /rɪˈkɒgnɪz(ə)ns/ *noun Law* bond by which person undertakes to observe some condition; sum pledged as surety for this.

recognize /ˈrekəgnaɪz/ *verb* (also **-ise**) (**-zing** or **-sing**) identify as already known; realize or discover nature of; (+ *that*) realize or admit; acknowledge existence, validity, character, or claims of; show appreciation of; reward. □ **recognizable** *adjective*.

recoil ● *verb* /rɪˈkɔɪl/ jerk or spring back in horror, disgust, or fear; shrink mentally in this way; rebound; (of gun) be driven backwards by discharge. ● *noun* /ˈriːkɔɪl/ act or sensation of recoiling.

recollect /rekəˈlekt/ *verb* remember; call to mind.

recollection /rekəˈlekʃ(ə)n/ *noun* act or power of recollecting; thing recollected; person's memory, time over which it extends.

recommend /rekəˈmend/ *verb* suggest as fit for purpose or use; advise (course of action etc.); (of qualities etc.) make acceptable or desirable; (+ *to*) commend or entrust. □ **recommendation** *noun*.

recompense /ˈrekəmpens/ ● *verb* (**-sing**) make amends to; compensate; reward or punish. ● *noun* reward; compensation; retribution.

reconcile /ˈrekənsaɪl/ *verb* (**-ling**) make friendly again after estrangement; (usually **reconcile oneself** or in *passive*; + *to*) make resigned to; settle (quarrel etc.); harmonize; make compatible; show compatibility of. □ **reconcilable** /-ˈsaɪl-/ *adjective*; **reconciliation** /-sɪlɪ-/ *noun*.

recondite /ˈrekəndaɪt/ *adjective* abstruse; obscure.

recondition /riːkənˈdɪʃ(ə)n/ *verb* overhaul, renovate, make usable again.

reconnaissance /rɪˈkɒnɪs(ə)ns/ *noun* survey of region to locate enemy or ascertain strategic features; preliminary survey.

reconnoitre /rekəˈnɔɪtə/ *verb* (*US* **reconnoiter**) (**-ring**) make reconnaissance (of).

reconsider /riːkənˈsɪdə/ *verb* consider again, esp. for possible change of decision.

reconstitute /riːˈkɒnstɪtjuːt/ *verb* (**-ting**) reconstruct; reorganize; rehydrate (dried food etc.). □ **reconstitution** /-ˈtjuːʃ(ə)n/ *noun*.

reconstruct /riːkənˈstrʌkt/ *verb* build again; form impression of (past events) by assembling evidence; re-enact (crime); reorganize. □ **reconstruction** *noun*.

record ● *noun* /ˈrekɔːd/ evidence etc. constituting account of occurrence, statement, etc.; document etc. preserving this; (in full **gramophone record**) disc carrying recorded sound in grooves, for reproduction by record player; facts known about person's past, esp. criminal convictions; best performance or most remarkable event of its kind. ● *verb* /rɪˈkɔːd/ put in writing or other permanent form for later reference; convert (sound etc.) into permanent form for later reproduction. □ **have a record** have criminal conviction; **off the record** unofficially, confidentially; **on record** officially recorded, publicly known; **recorded delivery** Post Office service in which dispatch and receipt are recorded; **record player** apparatus for reproducing sounds from gramophone records.

recorder /rɪˈkɔːdə/ *noun* apparatus for recording; woodwind instrument; (also **Recorder**) barrister or solicitor serving as part-time judge.

recording /rɪˈkɔːdɪŋ/ *noun* process of recording sound etc. for later reproduction; material or programme recorded.

recordist /rɪˈkɔːdɪst/ *noun* person who records sound.

recount /rɪˈkaʊnt/ *verb* narrate; tell in detail.

re-count ● *verb* /riːˈkaʊnt/ count again. ● *noun* /ˈriːkaʊnt/ re-counting, esp. of votes.

recoup /rɪˈkuːp/ *verb* recover or regain (loss); compensate or reimburse for loss.

recourse /rɪˈkɔːs/ *noun* resort to possible source of help; person or thing resorted to.

recover /rɪˈkʌvə/ *verb* regain possession, use, or control of; return to health, consciousness, or normal state or position; secure by legal process; make up for; retrieve. □ **recoverable** *adjective*.

re-cover /riːˈkʌvə/ *verb* cover again; provide (chairs etc.) with new cover.

recovery *noun* (*plural* **-ies**) recovering, being recovered.

recreant /ˈrekrɪənt/ *literary* ● *adjective* cowardly. ● *noun* coward.

re-create /riːkrɪˈeɪt/ *verb* (**-ting**) create anew; reproduce. □ **re-creation** *noun*.

recreation /rekrɪˈeɪʃ(ə)n/ *noun* (means of) entertaining oneself; pleasurable activity. □ **recreation ground** public land for sports etc. □ **recreational** *adjective*.

recriminate /rɪˈkrɪmɪneɪt/ *verb* (**-ting**) make mutual or counter accusations. □ **recrimination** *noun*; **recriminatory** *adjective*.

recrudesce /riːkruːˈdes/ *verb* (**-cing**) *formal* (of disease, problem, etc.) break out again. □ **recrudescence** *noun*; **recrudescent** *adjective*.

recruit /rɪˈkruːt/ ● *noun* newly enlisted serviceman or servicewoman; new member of a society etc. ● *verb* enlist (person) as recruit; form (army etc.) by enlisting recruits; replenish, reinvigorate. □ **recruitment** *noun*.

rectal /ˈrekt(ə)l/ *adjective* of or by means of rectum.

rectangle /ˈrektæŋg(ə)l/ *noun* plane figure with 4 straight sides and 4 right angles. ◻ **rectangular** /-ˈtæŋgjʊlə/ *adjective*.

rectify /ˈrektɪfaɪ/ *verb* (**-ies**, **-ied**) adjust or make right; purify, esp. by repeated distillation; convert (alternating current) to direct current. ◻ **rectifiable** *adjective*; **rectification** *noun*.

rectilinear /rektɪˈlɪnɪə/ *adjective* bounded or characterized by straight lines; in or forming straight line.

rectitude /ˈrektɪtjuːd/ *noun* moral uprightness.

recto /ˈrektəʊ/ *noun* (*plural* **-s**) right-hand page of open book; front of printed leaf.

rector /ˈrektə/ *noun* incumbent of C. of E. parish where in former times all tithes passed to incumbent; head priest of church or religious institution; head of university or college. ◻ **rectorship** *noun*.

rectory *noun* (*plural* **-ies**) rector's house.

rectum /ˈrektəm/ *noun* (*plural* **-s**) final section of large intestine.

recumbent /rɪˈkʌmbənt/ *adjective* lying down, reclining.

recuperate /rɪˈkuːpəreɪt/ *verb* (**-ting**) recover from illness, exhaustion, loss, etc.; regain (health, loss, etc.). ◻ **recuperation** *noun*; **recuperative** /-rətɪv/ *adjective*.

recur /rɪˈkɜː/ *verb* (**-rr-**) occur again or repeatedly; (+ *to*) go back to in thought or speech; (as **recurring** *adjective*) (of decimal fraction) with same figure(s) repeated indefinitely.

recurrent /rɪˈkʌrənt/ *adjective* recurring. ◻ **recurrence** *noun*.

recusant /ˈrekjʊz(ə)nt/ *noun* person refusing submission or compliance, esp. (*historical*) one who refused to attend services of the Church of England. ◻ **recusancy** *noun*.

recycle /riːˈsaɪk(ə)l/ *verb* (**-ling**) convert (waste) to reusable material. ◻ **recyclable** *adjective*.

red ● *adjective* (**-dd-**) of colour from that of blood to deep pink or orange; flushed; bloodshot; (of hair) reddish-brown; having to do with bloodshed, burning, violence, or revolution; *colloquial* Communist. ● *noun* red colour, paint, clothes, etc.; *colloquial* Communist. ◻ **in the red** in debt or deficit; **red admiral** butterfly with red bands; **red-blooded** virile, vigorous; **redbrick** (of university) founded in the 19th or early 20th c.; **red card** *Football* card shown by referee to player being sent off; **red carpet** privileged treatment of eminent visitor; **redcoat** *historical* British soldier; **Red Crescent** equivalent of Red Cross in Muslim countries; **Red Cross** international relief organization; **redcurrant** small red edible berry, shrub bearing it; **red flag** symbol of revolution, danger signal; **red-handed** in act of crime; **redhead** person with red hair; **red herring** irrelevant diversion; **red-hot** heated until red, *colloquial* highly exciting or excited, *colloquial* (of news) completely new; **red lead** red oxide of lead as pigment; **red-letter day** joyfully noteworthy or memorable day; **red light** stop signal, warning; **red meat** meat that is red when raw (e.g. beef); **red neck** conservative working-class white in southern US; **red pepper** cayenne pepper, red fruit of capsicum; **red rag** thing that excites rage; **redshank** sandpiper with bright red legs; **red shift** displacement of spectrum to longer wavelengths in light from receding galaxies; **redstart** red-tailed songbird; **red tape** excessive bureaucracy or formality; **redwing** thrush with red underwings; **redwood** tree with red wood. ◻ **reddish** *adjective*; **redness** *noun*.

redden *verb* make or become red; blush.

redeem /rɪˈdiːm/ *verb* recover by expenditure of effort; make single payment to cancel (regular charge etc.); convert (tokens or bonds) into goods or cash; deliver from sin and damnation; (often as **redeeming** *adjective*) make amends or compensate for; save, rescue, reclaim; fulfil (promise). ◻ **redeemable** *adjective*.

redeemer *noun* one who redeems, esp. Christ.

redemption /rɪˈdempʃ(ə)n/ *noun* redeeming, being redeemed.

redeploy /riːdɪˈplɔɪ/ *verb* send (troops, workers, etc.) to new place or task. ◻ **redeployment** *noun*.

rediffusion /riːdɪˈfjuːʒ(ə)n/ *noun* relaying of broadcast programmes, esp. by cable from central receiver.

redolent /ˈredələnt/ *adjective* (+ *of*, *with*) strongly smelling or suggestive of. ◻ **redolence** *noun*.

redouble /riːˈdʌb(ə)l/ *verb* (**-ling**) make or grow greater or more intense or numerous; double again.

redoubt /rɪˈdaʊt/ *noun Military* outwork or fieldwork without flanking defences.

redoubtable /rɪˈdaʊtəb(ə)l/ *adjective* formidable.

redound /rɪˈdaʊnd/ *verb* (+ *to*) make great contribution to (one's advantage etc.); (+ *upon*, *on*) come back or recoil upon.

redress /rɪˈdres/ ● *verb* remedy; put right again. ● *noun* reparation; (+ *of*) redressing.

reduce /rɪˈdjuːs/ *verb* (**-cing**) make or become smaller or less; (+ *to*) bring by force or necessity; convert to another (esp. simpler) form; bring lower in status, rank, or price; lessen one's weight or size; make (sauce etc.) more concentrated by boiling; weaken; impoverish; subdue. ◻ **reduced circumstances** poverty after relative property. ◻ **reducible** *adjective*.

reduction /rɪˈdʌkʃ(ə)n/ *noun* reducing, being reduced; amount by which prices etc. are reduced; smaller copy of picture etc. ◻ **reductive** *adjective*.

redundant /rɪˈdʌnd(ə)nt/ *adjective* superfluous; that can be omitted without loss of significance; no longer needed at work and therefore unemployed. ◻ **redundancy** *noun* (*plural* **-ies**).

reduplicate /rɪˈdjuːplɪkeɪt/ *verb* (**-ting**) make double; repeat. ◻ **reduplication** *noun*.

re-echo /riːˈekəʊ/ *verb* (**-es**, **-ed**) echo repeatedly; resound.

reed *noun* firm-stemmed water or marsh plant; tall straight stalk of this; vibrating part of some wind instruments. ◻ **reedy** *adjective* (**-ier**, **-iest**).

reef[1] *noun* ridge of rock or coral etc. at or near surface of sea; lode of ore, bedrock surrounding this.

reef[2] ● *noun* each of several strips across sail, for taking it in etc. ● *verb* take in reef(s) of (sail). ◻ **reef-knot** symmetrical double knot.

reefer *noun slang* marijuana cigarette; thick double-breasted jacket.

reek ● *verb* (often + *of*) smell unpleasantly; have suspicious associations. ● *noun* foul or stale smell; *esp. Scottish* smoke; vapour, exhalation.

reel ● *noun* cylindrical device on which thread, paper, film, wire, etc. are wound; device for winding and unwinding line as required, esp. in fishing; lively folk or Scottish dance, music for this. ● *verb* wind on reel; (+ *in*, *up*) draw in or up with reel; stand, walk, etc. unsteadily; be shaken physically or mentally; dance reel. ◻ **reel off** recite rapidly and without apparent effort.

re-entrant /riːˈentrənt/ *adjective* (of angle) pointing inwards.

re-entry /riːˈentrɪ/ *noun* (*plural* **-ies**) act of entering again, esp. (of spacecraft etc.) of re-entering earth's atmosphere.

reeve *noun historical* chief magistrate of town or district; official supervising landowner's estate.

ref[1] *noun colloquial* referee.

ref[2] *noun colloquial* reference.

refectory /rɪˈfektərɪ/ *noun* (*plural* **-ies**) dining-room, esp. in monastery or college. □ **refectory table** long narrow table.

refer /rɪˈfɜː/ *verb* (**-rr-**) (usually + *to*) have recourse to (some authority or source of information); send on or direct; make allusion or be relevant. □ **referred pain** pain felt in part of body other than actual source. □ **referable** *adjective*.

referee /refəˈriː/ ● *noun* umpire, esp. in football or boxing; person referred to for decision in dispute etc.; person willing to testify to character of applicant for employment etc. ● *verb* (**-rees, -reed**) act as referee (for).

reference /ˈrefərəns/ *noun* referring to some authority; scope given to such authority; (+ *to*) relation, respect, or allusion to; direction to page, book, etc. for information; written testimonial, person giving it. □ **reference book** book for occasional consultation. □ **referential** /-ˈren-/ *adjective*.

referendum /refəˈrendəm/ *noun* (*plural* **-s** or **-da**) vote on political question open to entire electorate.

referral /rɪˈfɜːr(ə)l/ *noun* referring of person to medical specialist etc.

refill ● *verb* /riːˈfɪl/ fill again. ● *noun* /ˈriːfɪl/ thing that refills; act of refilling. □ **refillable** *adjective*.

refine /rɪˈfaɪn/ *verb* (**-ning**) free from impurities or defects; (esp. as **refined** *adjective*) make or become more elegant or cultured.

refinement *noun* refining, being refined; fineness of feeling or taste; elegance; added development or improvement; subtle reasoning; fine distinction.

refiner *noun* person or firm refining crude oil, metal, sugar, etc.

refinery *noun* (*plural* **-ies**) place where oil etc. is refined.

refit ● *verb* /riːˈfɪt/ (**-tt-**) *esp. Nautical* make or become serviceable again by repairs etc. ● *noun* /ˈriːfɪt/ refitting.

reflate /riːˈfleɪt/ *verb* (**-ting**) cause reflation of (currency, economy, etc.).

reflation *noun* inflation of financial system to restore previous condition after deflation. □ **reflationary** *adjective*.

reflect /rɪˈflekt/ *verb* throw back (light, heat, sound, etc.); (of mirror etc.) show image of, reproduce to eye or mind; correspond in appearance or effect to; bring (credit, discredit, etc.); (usually + *on, upon*) bring discredit; (often + *on, upon*) meditate; (+ *that, how*, etc.) consider.

reflection /rɪˈflekʃ(ə)n/ *noun* reflecting, being reflected; reflected light, heat, colour, or image; reconsideration; (often + *on*) thing bringing discredit; (often + *on, upon*) comment.

reflective *adjective* (of surface) reflecting; (of mental faculties) concerned in reflection or thought; thoughtful. □ **reflectively** *adverb*.

reflector *noun* piece of glass or metal for reflecting light in required direction; telescope etc. using mirror to produce images.

reflex /ˈriːfleks/ ● *adjective* (of action) independent of will; (of angle) larger than 180°. ● *noun* reflex action; sign, secondary manifestation; reflected light or image. □ **reflex camera** camera in which image is reflected by mirror to enable correct focusing.

reflexive /rɪˈfleksɪv/ *Grammar* ● *adjective* (of word or form) referring back to subject (e.g. *myself* in *I hurt myself*); (of verb) having reflexive pronoun as object. ● *noun* reflexive word or form.

reflexology /riːflekˈsɒlədʒɪ/ *noun* massage to areas of soles of feet. □ **reflexologist** *noun*.

reform /rɪˈfɔːm/ ● *verb* make or become better; abolish or cure (abuse etc.). ● *noun* removal of abuses, esp. political; improvement. □ **reformative** *adjective*.

reformation /refəˈmeɪʃ(ə)n/ *noun* reforming or being reformed, esp. radical improvement in political, religious, or social affairs; (**the Reformation**) 16th-c. movement for reform of abuses in Roman Church ending in establishment of Reformed or Protestant Churches.

reformatory /rɪˈfɔːmətərɪ/ ● *noun* (*plural* **-ies**) *US historical* institution for reform of young offenders. ● *adjective* producing reform.

reformer *noun* advocate of reform.

reformism *noun* policy of reform rather than abolition or revolution. □ **reformist** *noun & adjective*.

refract /rɪˈfrækt/ *verb* deflect (light) at certain angle when it enters obliquely from another medium. □ **refraction** *noun*; **refractive** *adjective*.

refractor *noun* refracting medium or lens; telescope using lens to produce image.

refractory /rɪˈfræktərɪ/ *adjective* stubborn, unmanageable, rebellious; resistant to treatment; hard to fuse or work.

refrain[1] /rɪˈfreɪn/ *verb* (+ *from*) avoid doing (action).

refrain[2] /rɪˈfreɪn/ *noun* recurring phrase or lines, esp. at ends of stanzas.

refresh /rɪˈfreʃ/ *verb* give fresh spirit or vigour to; revive (memory). □ **refreshing** *adjective*; **refreshingly** *adverb*.

refresher *noun* something that refreshes, esp. drink; extra fee to counsel in prolonged lawsuit. □ **refresher course** course reviewing or updating previous studies.

refreshment *noun* refreshing, being refreshed; (usually in *plural*) food or drink.

refrigerant /rɪˈfrɪdʒərənt/ ● *noun* substance used for refrigeration. ● *adjective* cooling.

refrigerate /rɪˈfrɪdʒəreɪt/ *verb* (**-ting**) cool or freeze (esp. food). □ **refrigeration** *noun*.

refrigerator *noun* cabinet or room in which food etc. is refrigerated.

refuge /ˈrefjuːdʒ/ *noun* shelter from pursuit, danger, or trouble; person or place offering this.

refugee /refjʊˈdʒiː/ *noun* person taking refuge, esp. in foreign country, from war, persecution, etc.

refulgent /rɪˈfʌldʒ(ə)nt/ *adjective literary* shining, gloriously bright. □ **refulgence** *noun*.

refund ● *verb* /rɪˈfʌnd/ pay back (money etc.); reimburse. ● *noun* /ˈriːfʌnd/ act of refunding; sum refunded. □ **refundable** /rɪˈfʌn-/ *adjective*.

refurbish /riːˈfɜːbɪʃ/ *verb* brighten up, redecorate. □ **refurbishment** *noun*.

refusal /rɪˈfjuːz(ə)l/ *noun* refusing, being refused; (in full **first refusal**) chance of taking thing before it is offered to others.

refuse[1] /rɪˈfjuːz/ *verb* (**-sing**) withhold acceptance of or consent to; (often + *to do*) indicate unwillingness; not grant (request) made by (person); (of horse) be unwilling to jump (fence etc.).

refuse[2] /ˈrefjuːs/ *noun* items rejected as worthless; waste.

refusenik /rɪˈfjuːznɪk/ *noun historical* Soviet Jew refused permission to emigrate to Israel.

refute /rɪˈfjuːt/ *verb* (**-ting**) prove falsity or error of; rebut by argument; deny or contradict (without argument). □ **refutation** /refjʊˈteɪʃ(ə)n/ *noun*.

■ **Usage** The use of *refute* to mean 'deny, contradict' is considered incorrect by some people. *Repudiate* can be used instead.

reg /redʒ/ *noun colloquial* registration mark.

regain /rɪˈgeɪn/ *verb* obtain possession or use of after loss.

regal /ˈriːg(ə)l/ *adjective* of or by monarch(s); magnificent. □ **regality** /rɪˈgæl-/ *noun*; **regally** *adverb*.

regale /rɪˈgeɪl/ *verb* (**-ling**) entertain lavishly with feasting; (+ *with*) entertain with (talk etc.).

regalia /rɪˈgeɪlɪə/ *plural noun* insignia of royalty or an order, mayor, etc.

regard /rɪˈgɑːd/ ● *verb* gaze on; heed, take into account; look upon or think of in specified way. ● *noun* gaze; steady look; attention, care; esteem; (in *plural*) *expression of friendliness in letter etc.* □ **as regards** about, in respect of; **in this regard** on this point; **in, with regard to** in respect of.

regardful *adjective* (+ *of*) mindful of.

regarding *preposition* concerning; in respect of.

regardless ● *adjective* (+ *of*) without regard or consideration for. ● *adverb* without paying attention.

regatta /rɪˈgætə/ *noun* event consisting of rowing or yacht races.

regency /ˈriːdʒənsɪ/ *noun* (*plural* **-ies**) office of regent; commission acting as regent; regent's or regency commission's period of office; (**Regency**) (in UK) 1811–1820.

regenerate ● *verb* /rɪˈdʒenəreɪt/ (**-ting**) bring or come into renewed existence; improve moral condition of; impart new, more vigorous, or spiritually higher life or nature to; regrow or cause (new tissue) to regrow. ● *adjective* /-rət/ spiritually born again, reformed. □ **regeneration** *noun*; **regenerative** /-rətɪv/ *adjective*.

regent /ˈriːdʒ(ə)nt/ ● *noun* person acting as head of state because monarch is absent, ill, or a child. ● *adjective* (after noun) acting as regent.

reggae /ˈregeɪ/ *noun* W. Indian style of music with strongly accented subsidiary beat.

regicide /ˈredʒɪsaɪd/ *noun* person who kills or helps to kill a king; killing of a king.

regime /reɪˈʒiːm/ *noun* (also **régime**) method of government; prevailing system; regimen.

regimen /ˈredʒɪmən/ *noun* prescribed course of exercise, way of life, and diet.

regiment ● *noun* /ˈredʒɪmənt/ permanent unit of army consisting of several companies, troops, or batteries; (usually + *of*) large or formidable array or number. ● *verb* /-ment/ organize in groups or according to system; form into regiment(s). □ **regimentation** /-men-/ *noun*.

regimental /redʒɪˈment(ə)l/ ● *adjective* of a regiment. ● *noun* (in *plural*) military uniform, esp. of particular regiment.

Regina /rɪˈdʒaɪnə/ *noun* (after name) reigning queen; *Law* the Crown. [Latin]

region /ˈriːdʒ(ə)n/ *noun* geographical area or division, having definable boundaries or characteristics; administrative area, esp. in Scotland; part of body; sphere, realm. □ **in the region of** approximately. □ **regional** *adjective*; **regionally** *adverb*.

register /ˈredʒɪstə/ ● *noun* official list; book in which items are recorded for reference; device recording speed, force, etc.; compass of voice or instrument; form of language used in particular circumstances; adjustable plate for regulating draught etc. ● *verb* set down formally, record in writing; enter or cause to be entered in register; send (letter) by registered post; record automatically, indicate; make mental note of; show (emotion etc.) in face etc.; make impression. □ **registered post** postal procedure with special precautions and compensation in case of loss; **register office** state office where civil marriages are conducted and births, marriages, and deaths are recorded.

registrar /redʒɪˈstrɑː/ *noun* official keeping register; chief administrator in university etc.; hospital doctor training as specialist.

registration /redʒɪˈstreɪʃ(ə)n/ *noun* registering, being registered. □ **registration mark**, **number** combination of letters and numbers identifying vehicle.

registry /ˈredʒɪstrɪ/ *noun* (*plural* **-ies**) place where registers or records are kept. □ **registry office** register office (the official name).

Regius professor /ˈriːdʒɪəs/ *noun* holder of university chair founded by sovereign or filled by Crown appointment.

regress ● *verb* /rɪˈgres/ move backwards; return to former stage or state. ● *noun* /ˈriːgres/ act of regressing. □ **regression** /rɪˈgreʃ(ə)n/ *noun*; **regressive** /rɪˈgresɪv/ *adjective*.

regret /rɪˈgret/ ● *verb* (**-tt-**) feel or express sorrow, repentance, or distress over (action or loss); say with sorrow or remorse. ● *noun* sorrow, repentance, or distress over action or loss. □ **regretful** *adjective*; **regretfully** *adverb*.

regrettable *adjective* undesirable, unwelcome; deserving censure. □ **regrettably** *adverb*.

regular /ˈregjʊlə/ ● *adjective* acting, done, or recurring uniformly; habitual, orderly; conforming to rule or principle; symmetrical; conforming to correct procedure etc.; *Grammar* (of verb etc.) following normal type of inflection; *colloquial* absolute, thorough; (of soldier etc.) permanent, professional. ● *noun* regular soldier; *colloquial* regular customer, visitor, etc.; one of regular clergy. □ **regularity** /-ˈlærɪtɪ/ *noun*; **regularize** *verb* (also **-ise**) (**-zing** or **-sing**); **regularly** *adverb*.

regulate /ˈregjʊleɪt/ *verb* (**-ting**) control by rule, subject to restrictions; adapt to requirements; adjust (clock, watch, etc.) to work accurately. □ **regulator** *noun*.

regulation ● *noun* regulating, being regulated; prescribed rule. ● *adjective* in accordance with regulations, of correct pattern etc.

regulo /ˈregjʊləʊ/ *noun* (usually + numeral) number on scale denoting temperature in gas oven.

regurgitate /rɪˈgɜːdʒɪteɪt/ *verb* (**-ting**) bring (swallowed food) up again to mouth; reproduce (information etc.). □ **regurgitation** *noun*.

rehabilitate /riːhəˈbɪlɪteɪt/ *verb* (**-ting**) restore to normal life by training, etc. esp. after imprisonment or illness; restore to former privileges or reputation or to proper condition. □ **rehabilitation** *noun*.

rehash ● *verb* /riːˈhæʃ/ put into new form without significant change or improvement. ● *noun* /ˈriːhæʃ/ material rehashed; rehashing.

rehearsal /rɪˈhɜːs(ə)l/ *noun* trial performance or practice; rehearsing.

rehearse /rɪˈhɜːs/ *verb* (**-sing**) practise before performing in public; recite or say over; give list of, enumerate.

Reich /raɪx/ *noun* former German state, esp. Third Reich (1933–45).

reign /reɪn/ ● *verb* be king or queen; prevail; (as **reigning** *adjective*) currently holding title. ● *noun* sovereignty, rule; sovereign's period of rule.

reimburse /riːɪmˈbɜːs/ *verb* (**-sing**) repay (person); refund. □ **reimbursement** *noun*.

rein /reɪn/ ● *noun* (in *singular* or *plural*) long narrow strap used to guide horse; means of control. ● *verb* (+ *back*, *up*, *in*) pull back or up or hold in (as) with reins; govern, control.

reincarnate ● *verb* /riːɪnˈkɑːneɪt/ (**-ting**) give esp. human form to again. ● *adjective* /-nət/ reincarnated.

reincarnation /riːɪnkɑːˈneɪʃ(ə)n/ *noun* rebirth of soul in new body.

reindeer /'reɪndɪə/ *noun* (*plural* same or **-s**) subarctic deer with large antlers.

reinforce /riːɪn'fɔːs/ *verb* (**-cing**) support or strengthen, esp. with additional personnel or material. ◻ **reinforced concrete** concrete with metal bars etc. embedded in it.

reinforcement *noun* reinforcing, being reinforced; (in *plural*) additional personnel, equipment, etc.

reinstate /riːɪn'steɪt/ *verb* (**-ting**) replace in former position; restore to former privileges. ◻ **reinstatement** *noun*.

reinsure /riːɪn'ʃʊə/ *verb* (**-ring**) insure again (esp. of insurer transferring risk to another insurer). ◻ **reinsurance** *noun*.

reiterate /riː'ɪtəreɪt/ *verb* (**-ting**) say or do again or repeatedly. ◻ **reiteration** *noun*.

reject ● *verb* /rɪ'dʒekt/ put aside or send back as not to be used, done, or complied with; refuse to accept or believe in; rebuff. ● *noun* /'riːdʒekt/ rejected thing or person. ◻ **rejection** /rɪ'dʒek-/ *noun*.

rejoice /rɪ'dʒɔɪs/ *verb* (**-cing**) feel joy, be glad; (+ *in*, *at*) take delight in.

rejoin[1] /riː'dʒɔɪn/ *verb* join again; reunite.

rejoin[2] /rɪ'dʒɔɪn/ *verb* say in answer; retort.

rejoinder /rɪ'dʒɔɪndə/ *noun* reply, retort.

rejuvenate /rɪ'dʒuːvəneɪt/ *verb* (**-ting**) make (as if) young again. ◻ **rejuvenation** *noun*.

relapse /rɪ'læps/ ● *verb* (**-sing**) (usually + *into*) fall back (into worse state after improvement). ● *noun* relapsing, esp. deterioration in patient's condition after partial recovery.

relate /rɪ'leɪt/ *verb* (**-ting**) narrate, recount; (usually + *to*, *with*) connect in thought or meaning; have reference to; (+ *to*) feel connected or sympathetic to.

related *adjective* connected, esp. by blood or marriage.

relation /rɪ'leɪʃ(ə)n/ *noun* connection between people or things; relative; (in *plural*) dealings (with others); narration.

relationship *noun* state of being related; connection, association; *colloquial* emotional association between two people.

relative /'relətɪv/ ● *adjective* in relation or proportion to something else; implying comparison or relation; (+ *to*) having application or reference to; *Grammar* (of word, clause, etc.) referring to expressed or implied antecedent, attached to antecedent by such word. ● *noun* person connected by blood or marriage; species related to another by common origin; relative word, esp. pronoun. ◻ **relative density** ratio between density of substance and that of a standard (usually water or air). ◻ **relatively** *adverb*.

relativity /relə'tɪvɪtɪ/ *noun* relativeness; *Physics* theory based on principle that all motion is relative and that light has constant velocity in a vacuum.

relax /rɪ'læks/ *verb* make or become less stiff, rigid, tense, formal, or strict; reduce (attention, efforts); cease work or effort; (as **relaxed** *adjective*) at ease, unperturbed.

relaxation /riːlæk'seɪʃ(ə)n/ *noun* relaxing; recreation.

relay /'riːleɪ/ ● *noun* fresh set of people etc. to replace tired ones; supply of material similarly used; relay race; device activating electric circuit; device transmitting broadcast; relayed transmission. ● *verb* /also rɪ'leɪ/ receive (esp. broadcast message) and transmit to others. ◻ **relay race** one between teams of which each member in turn covers part of distance.

release /rɪ'liːs/ ● *verb* (**-sing**) (often + *from*) set free, liberate, unfasten; allow to move from fixed position; make (information) public; issue (film etc.) generally. ● *noun* liberation from restriction, duty, or difficulty; handle, catch, etc. that releases part of mechanism; item made available for publication; film, record, etc. that is released; releasing of film etc.

relegate /'relɪgeɪt/ *verb* (**-ting**) consign or dismiss to inferior position; transfer (team) to lower division of league. ◻ **relegation** *noun*.

relent /rɪ'lent/ *verb* relax severity; yield to compassion.

relentless *adjective* unrelenting. ◻ **relentlessly** *adverb*.

relevant /'relɪv(ə)nt/ *adjective* (often + *to*) bearing on or pertinent to matter in hand. ◻ **relevance** *noun*.

reliable /rɪ'laɪəb(ə)l/ *adjective* that may be relied on. ◻ **reliability** *noun*; **reliably** *adverb*.

reliance /rɪ'laɪəns/ *noun* (+ *in*, *on*) trust or confidence in. ◻ **reliant** *adjective*.

relic /'relɪk/ *noun* object interesting because of its age or associations; part of holy person's body or belongings kept as object of reverence; surviving custom, belief, etc. from past age; (in *plural*) dead body or remains of person, what has survived.

relict /'relɪkt/ *noun* object surviving in primitive form.

relief /rɪ'liːf/ *noun* (feeling accompanying) alleviation of or deliverance from pain, distress, etc.; feature etc. that diversifies monotony or relaxes tension; assistance given to people in special need; replacing of person(s) on duty by another or others; person(s) thus bringing relief; thing supplementing another in some service; method of carving, moulding, etc., in which design projects from surface; piece of sculpture etc. in relief; effect of being done in relief given by colour or shading etc.; vividness, distinctness. ◻ **relief map** one showing hills and valleys by shading or colouring etc.

relieve /rɪ'liːv/ *verb* (**-ving**) bring or give relief to; mitigate tedium of; release (person) from duty by acting as or providing substitute; (+ *of*) take (burden or duty) away from; (**relieve oneself**) urinate, defecate. ◻ **relieved** *adjective*.

religion /rɪ'lɪdʒ(ə)n/ *noun* belief in superhuman controlling power, esp. in personal God or gods entitled to obedience; system of faith and worship.

religiosity /rɪlɪdʒɪ'ɒsɪtɪ/ *noun* state of being religious or too religious.

religious /rɪ'lɪdʒəs/ ● *adjective* devoted to religion, devout; of or concerned with religion; of or belonging to monastic order; scrupulous. ● *noun* (*plural* same) person bound by monastic vows. ◻ **religiously** *adverb*.

relinquish /rɪ'lɪŋkwɪʃ/ *verb* give up, let go, resign, surrender. ◻ **relinquishment** *noun*.

reliquary /'relɪkwərɪ/ *noun* (*plural* **-ies**) receptacle for relic(s).

relish /'relɪʃ/ ● *noun* (often + *for*) liking or enjoyment; appetizing flavour, attractive quality; thing eaten with plainer food to add flavour; (+ *of*) distinctive flavour or taste. ● *verb* get pleasure out of, enjoy greatly; anticipate with pleasure.

reluctant /rɪ'lʌkt(ə)nt/ *adjective* (often + *to do*) unwilling, disinclined. ◻ **reluctance** *noun*; **reluctantly** *adverb*.

rely /rɪ'laɪ/ *verb* (**-ies**, **-ied**) (+ *on*, *upon*) depend with confidence on; be dependent on.

REM *abbreviation* rapid eye movement.

remade *past & past participle* of REMAKE.

remain /rɪ'meɪn/ *verb* be left over; stay in same place or condition; be left behind; continue to be.

remainder /rɪ'meɪndə/ ● *noun* residue; remaining people or things; number left after subtraction or division; (any of) copies of book left unsold. ● *verb* dispose of remainder of (book) at reduced prices.

remains /rɪˈmeɪnz/ *plural noun* what remains after other parts have been removed or used; relics of antiquity etc.; dead body.

remake ● *verb* /riːˈmeɪk/ (**-king**; *past & past participle* **remade**) make again or differently. ● *noun* /ˈriːmeɪk/ remade thing, esp. cinema film.

remand /rɪˈmɑːnd/ ● *verb* return (prisoner) to custody, esp. to allow further inquiry. ● *noun* recommittal to custody. □ **on remand** in custody pending trial; **remand centre** institution for remand of accused people.

remark /rɪˈmɑːk/ ● *verb* (often + *that*) say by way of comment; (usually + *on, upon*) make comment; *archaic* take notice of. ● *noun* comment, thing said; noticing.

remarkable *adjective* worth notice; exceptional, striking. □ **remarkably** *adverb*.

REME /ˈriːmiː/ *abbreviation* Royal Electrical and Mechanical Engineers.

remedial /rɪˈmiːdɪəl/ *adjective* affording or intended as a remedy; (of teaching) for slow or disadvantaged pupils.

remedy /ˈremɪdɪ/ ● *noun* (*plural* **-ies**) (often + *for, against*) medicine or treatment; means of removing anything undesirable; redress. ● *verb* (**-ies, -ied**) rectify, make good. □ **remediable** /rɪˈmiːdɪəb(ə)l/ *adjective*.

remember /rɪˈmembə/ *verb* (often + *to do, that*) keep in the memory; not forget; bring back into one's thoughts; acknowledge in making gift etc.; convey greetings from.

remembrance /rɪˈmembrəns/ *noun* remembering, being remembered; recollection; keepsake, souvenir; (in *plural*) greetings conveyed through third person.

remind /rɪˈmaɪnd/ *verb* (usually + *of, to do, that*) cause (person) to remember or think of.

reminder *noun* thing that reminds; (often + *of*) memento.

reminisce /remɪˈnɪs/ *verb* (**-cing**) indulge in reminiscence.

reminiscence /remɪˈnɪs(ə)ns/ *noun* remembering things past; (in *plural*) *literary* account of things remembered.

reminiscent *adjective* (+ *of*) reminding or suggestive of; concerned with reminiscence.

remiss /rɪˈmɪs/ *adjective* careless of duty; negligent.

remission /rɪˈmɪʃ(ə)n/ *noun* reduction of prison sentence for good behaviour; remittance of debt etc.; diminution of force etc.; (often + *of*) forgiveness (of sins etc.).

remit ● *verb* /rɪˈmɪt/ (**-tt-**) refrain from exacting or inflicting (debt, punishment, etc.); abate, slacken; send (esp. money); (+ *to*) refer to some authority, send back to lower court; postpone, defer; pardon (sins etc.). ● *noun* /ˈriːmɪt/ terms of reference of committee etc.; item remitted.

remittance *noun* money sent; sending of money.

remittent *adjective* (of disease etc.) abating at intervals.

remix ● *verb* /riːˈmɪks/ mix again. ● *noun* /ˈriːmɪks/ remixed recording.

remnant /ˈremnənt/ *noun* small remaining quantity; piece of cloth etc. left when greater part has been used or sold.

remold *US* = REMOULD.

remonstrate /ˈremənstreɪt/ *verb* (**-ting**) (+ *with*) make protest; argue forcibly. □ **remonstrance** /rɪˈmɒnstrəns/ *noun*; **remonstration** *noun*.

remorse /rɪˈmɔːs/ *noun* bitter repentance; compunction; mercy.

remorseful *adjective* filled with repentance. □ **remorsefully** *adverb*.

remorseless *adjective* without compassion. □ **remorselessly** *adverb*.

remote /rɪˈməʊt/ *adjective* (**-r, -st**) distant in place or time; secluded; distantly related; slight, faint; aloof, not friendly. □ **remote control** (device for) control of apparatus etc. from a distance. □ **remotely** *adverb*; **remoteness** *noun*.

remould ● *verb* /riːˈməʊld/ (*US* **remold**) mould again, refashion; reconstruct tread of (tyre). ● *noun* /ˈriːməʊld/ remoulded tyre.

removal /rɪˈmuːv(ə)l/ *noun* removing, being removed; transfer of furniture etc. on moving house.

remove /rɪˈmuːv/ ● *verb* (**-ving**) take off or away from place occupied; convey to another place; dismiss; cause to be no longer available; (in *passive*; + *from*) be distant in condition; (as **removed** *adjective*) (esp. of cousins) separated by a specified number of generations. ● *noun* distance, degree of remoteness; stage in gradation; form or division in some schools. □ **removable** *adjective*.

remunerate /rɪˈmjuːnəreɪt/ *verb* (**-ting**) pay for service rendered. □ **remuneration** *noun*; **remunerative** /-rətɪv/ *adjective*.

Renaissance /rɪˈneɪs(ə)ns/ *noun* revival of classical art and literature in 14th–16th c.; period of this; style of art and architecture developed by it; (**renaissance**) any similar revival. □ **Renaissance man** person with many talents.

renal /ˈriːn(ə)l/ *adjective* of kidneys.

renascent /rɪˈnæs(ə)nt/ *adjective* springing up anew; being reborn. □ **renascence** *noun*.

rend *verb* (*past & past participle* **rent**) *archaic* tear or wrench forcibly.

render /ˈrendə/ *verb* cause to be or become; give in return; pay as due; (often + *to*) give (assistance), show (obedience etc.); present, submit; represent, portray; perform; translate; (often + *down*) melt (fat) down; cover (stone or brick) with plaster. □ **rendering** *noun*.

rendezvous /ˈrɒndɪvuː/ ● *noun* (*plural* same /-vuːz/) agreed or regular meeting-place; meeting by arrangement. ● *verb* (**rendezvouses** /-vuːz/; **rendezvoused** /-vuːd/; **rendezvousing** /-vuːɪŋ/) meet at rendezvous.

rendition /renˈdɪʃ(ə)n/ *noun* interpretation or rendering of dramatic or musical piece.

renegade /ˈrenɪgeɪd/ *noun* deserter of party or principles.

renege /rɪˈniːg, rɪˈneɪg/ *verb* (**-ging**) (often + *on*) go back on promise etc.

renew /rɪˈnjuː/ *verb* make new again; restore to original state; replace; repeat; resume after interruption; grant or be granted continuation of (licence etc.). □ **renewable** *adjective*; **renewal** *noun*.

rennet /ˈrenɪt/ *noun* curdled milk from calf's stomach, or artificial preparation, used in making cheese etc.

renounce /rɪˈnaʊns/ *verb* (**-cing**) consent formally to abandon; repudiate; decline further association with.

renovate /ˈrenəveɪt/ *verb* (**-ting**) restore to good condition; repair. □ **renovation** *noun*; **renovator** *noun*.

renown /rɪˈnaʊn/ *noun* fame, high distinction. □ **renowned** *adjective*.

rent[1] ● *noun* periodical payment for use of land or premises; payment for hire of machinery etc. ● *verb* (often + *from*) take, occupy, or use for rent; (often + *out*) let or hire for rent; (often + *at*) be let at specified rate.

rent² *noun* tear in garment etc.; gap, cleft, fissure.
rent³ *past & past participle* of REND.
rental /ˈrent(ə)l/ *noun* amount paid or received as rent; act of renting.
rentier /ˈrɑ̃tɪeɪ/ *noun* person living on income from property or investments. [French]
renunciation /rɪnʌnsɪˈeɪʃ(ə)n/ *noun* renouncing, self-denial, giving up of things.
rep¹ *noun colloquial* representative, esp. commercial traveller.
rep² *noun colloquial* repertory; repertory theatre or company.
repair¹ /rɪˈpeə/ ● *verb* restore to good condition after damage or wear; set right or make amends for. ● *noun* (result of) restoring to sound condition; good or relative condition for working or using. ◻ **repairable** *adjective*; **repairer** *noun*.
repair² /rɪˈpeə/ *verb* (usually + *to*) resort; go.
reparable /ˈrepərəb(ə)l/ *adjective* that can be made good.
reparation /repəˈreɪʃ(ə)n/ *noun* making amends; (esp. in *plural*) compensation.
repartee /repɑːˈtiː/ *noun* (making of) witty retorts.
repast /rɪˈpɑːst/ *noun formal* meal.
repatriate /riːˈpætrɪeɪt/ *verb* (**-ting**) return (person) to native land. ◻ **repatriation** *noun*.
repay /riːˈpeɪ/ *verb* (*past & past participle* **repaid**) pay back (money); make repayment to (person); reward (action etc.). ◻ **repayable** *adjective*; **repayment** *noun*.
repeal /rɪˈpiːl/ ● *verb* annul, revoke. ● *noun* repealing.
repeat /rɪˈpiːt/ ● *verb* say or do over again; recite, report; recur. ● *noun* repeating; thing repeated, esp. broadcast; *Music* passage intended to be repeated. ◻ **repeatable** *adjective*; **repeatedly** *adverb*.
repeater *noun* person or thing that repeats; firearm that fires several shots without reloading; watch that strikes last quarter etc. again when required; device for retransmitting electrical message.
repel /rɪˈpel/ *verb* drive back; ward off; be repulsive or distasteful to; resist mixing with; push away from itself. ◻ **repellent** *adjective & noun*.
repent /rɪˈpent/ *verb* (often + *of*) feel sorrow about one's actions etc.; wish one had not done, resolve not to continue (wrongdoing etc.). ◻ **repentance** *noun*; **repentant** *adjective*.
repercussion /riːpəˈkʌʃ(ə)n/ *noun* indirect effect or reaction following event etc.; recoil after impact.
repertoire /ˈrepətwɑː/ *noun* stock of works that performer etc. knows or is prepared to perform.
repertory /ˈrepətərɪ/ *noun* (*plural* **-ies**) performance of various plays for short periods by one company; repertory theatres collectively; store of information etc.; repertoire. ◻ **repertory company** one performing plays from repertoire; **repertory theatre** one with repertoire of plays.
repetition /repəˈtɪʃ(ə)n/ *noun* repeating, being repeated; thing repeated, copy. ◻ **repetitious** *adjective*; **repetitive** /rɪˈpetətɪv/ *adjective*.
repine /rɪˈpaɪn/ *verb* (**-ning**) (often + *at*, *against*) fret, be discontented.
replace /rɪˈpleɪs/ *verb* (**-cing**) put back in place; take place of, be or provide substitute for; (often + *with*, *by*) fill up place of.
replacement *noun* replacing, being replaced; person or thing that replaces another.
replay ● *verb* /riːˈpleɪ/ play (match, recording, etc.) again. ● *noun* /ˈriːpleɪ/ replaying of match, recorded incident in game, etc.
replenish /rɪˈplenɪʃ/ *verb* (often + *with*) fill up again. ◻ **replenishment** *noun*.
replete /rɪˈpliːt/ *adjective* (often + *with*) well-fed; filled or well-supplied. ◻ **repletion** *noun*.
replica /ˈreplɪkə/ *noun* exact copy, esp. duplicate made by original artist; model, esp. small-scale.
replicate /ˈreplɪkeɪt/ *verb* make replica of. ◻ **replication** *noun*.
reply /rɪˈplaɪ/ ● *verb* (**-ies**, **-ied**) (often + *to*) make an answer, respond; say in answer. ● *noun* (*plural* **-ies**) replying; what is replied.
report /rɪˈpɔːt/ ● *verb* bring back or give account of; tell as news; describe, esp. as eyewitness; make official or formal statement; (often + *to*) bring to attention of authorities, present oneself as arrived; take down, write description of, etc. for publication; (+ *to*) be responsible to. ● *noun* account given or opinion formally expressed after investigation; description, reproduction, or summary of speech, law case, scene, etc., esp. for newspaper publication or broadcast; common talk, rumour; repute; periodical statement on (esp. pupil's) work etc.; sound of gunshot. ◻ **reportedly** *adverb*.
reporter *noun* person employed to report news etc. for media.
repose¹ /rɪˈpəʊz/ ● *noun* rest; sleep; tranquillity. ● *verb* (**-sing**) rest; lie, esp. when dead.
repose² /rɪˈpəʊz/ *verb* (**-sing**) (+ *in*) place (trust etc.) in.
repository /rɪˈpɒzɪtərɪ/ *noun* (*plural* **-ies**) place where things are stored or may be found; receptacle; (often + *of*) book, person, etc. regarded as store of information, recipient of secrets etc.
reprehend /reprɪˈhend/ *verb formal* rebuke, blame.
reprehensible /reprɪˈhensɪb(ə)l/ *adjective* blameworthy.
represent /reprɪˈzent/ *verb* stand for, correspond to; be specimen of; symbolize; present likeness of to mind or senses; (often + *as*, *to be*) describe or depict, declare; (+ *that*) allege; show or play part of; be substitute or deputy for; be elected by as member of legislature etc.
representation /reprɪzenˈteɪʃ(ə)n/ *noun* representing, being represented; thing that represents another.
representational *adjective* (of art) seeking to portray objects etc. realistically.
representative /reprɪˈzentətɪv/ ● *adjective* typical of class; containing typical specimens of all or many classes; (of government etc.) of elected deputies or based on representation. ● *noun* (+ *of*) sample, specimen, or typical embodiment of; agent; commercial traveller; delegate or deputy, esp. in representative assembly.
repress /rɪˈpres/ *verb* keep under; put down; suppress (esp. unwelcome thought). ◻ **repression** *noun*; **repressive** *adjective*.
reprieve /rɪˈpriːv/ ● *verb* (**-ving**) remit or postpone execution of; give respite to. ● *noun* reprieving, being reprieved.
reprimand /ˈreprɪmɑːnd/ ● *noun* official rebuke. ● *verb* rebuke officially.
reprint ● *verb* /riːˈprɪnt/ print again. ● *noun* /ˈriːprɪnt/ reprinting of book etc.; quantity reprinted.
reprisal /rɪˈpraɪz(ə)l/ *noun* act of retaliation.
reprise /rɪˈpriːz/ *noun Music* repeated passage or song etc.
repro /ˈriːprəʊ/ *noun* (*plural* **-s**) *colloquial* reproduction, copy.
reproach /rɪˈprəʊtʃ/ ● *verb* express disapproval to (person) for fault etc. ● *noun* rebuke, censure; (often + *to*) thing that brings discredit.
reproachful *adjective* full of or expressing reproach. ◻ **reproachfully** *adverb*.

reprobate /'reprəbeɪt/ *noun* unprincipled or immoral person.

reproduce /riːprə'djuːs/ *verb* (**-cing**) produce copy or representation of; produce further members of same species by natural means; (**reproduce itself**) produce offspring. □ **reproducible** *adjective*.

reproduction /riːprə'dʌkʃ(ə)n/ ● *noun* reproducing, esp. of further members of same species; copy of work of art. ● *adjective* (of furniture etc.) imitating earlier style. □ **reproductive** *adjective*.

reproof /rɪ'pruːf/ *noun formal* blame; rebuke.

reprove /rɪ'pruːv/ *verb* (**-ving**) *formal* rebuke.

reptile /'reptaɪl/ *noun* cold-blooded scaly animal of class including snakes, lizards, etc.; grovelling or repulsive person. □ **reptilian** /-'tɪl-/ *adjective*.

republic /rɪ'pʌblɪk/ *noun* state in which supreme power is held by the people or their elected representatives.

republican ● *adjective* of or characterizing republic(s); advocating or supporting republican government. ● *noun* supporter or advocate of republican government; (**Republican**) member of political party styled 'Republican'. □ **republicanism** *noun*.

repudiate /rɪ'pjuːdɪeɪt/ *verb* (**-ting**) disown, disavow, deny; refuse to recognize or obey (authority) or discharge (obligation or debt). □ **repudiation** *noun*.

repugnance /rɪ'pʌgnəns/ *noun* aversion, antipathy; inconsistency or incompatibility of ideas etc.

repugnant /rɪ'pʌgn(ə)nt/ *adjective* distasteful; contradictory.

repulse /rɪ'pʌls/ ● *verb* (**-sing**) drive back; rebuff, reject. ● *noun* defeat, rebuff.

repulsion /rɪ'pʌlʃ(ə)n/ *noun* aversion, disgust; *Physics* tendency of bodies to repel each other.

repulsive /rɪ'pʌlsɪv/ *adjective* causing aversion or loathing. □ **repulsively** *adverb*.

reputable /'repjʊtəb(ə)l/ *adjective* of good reputation, respectable.

reputation /repjʊ'teɪʃ(ə)n/ *noun* what is generally said or believed about character of person or thing; credit, respectability.

repute /rɪ'pjuːt/ ● *noun* reputation. ● *verb* (as **reputed** *adjective*) be generally considered. □ **reputedly** *adverb*.

request /rɪ'kwest/ ● *noun* asking for something, thing asked for. ● *verb* ask to be given, allowed, etc.; (+ *to do*) ask (person) to do something; (+ *that*) ask that.

Requiem /'rekwɪəm/ *noun* (also **requiem**) *esp. RC Church* mass for the dead.

require /rɪ'kwaɪə/ *verb* (**-ring**) need; depend on for success etc.; lay down as imperative; command, instruct; demand, insist on. □ **requirement** *noun*.

requisite /'rekwɪzɪt/ ● *adjective* required, necessary. ● *noun* (often + *for*) thing needed.

requisition /rekwɪ'zɪʃ(ə)n/ ● *noun* official order laying claim to use of property or materials; formal written demand. ● *verb* demand use or supply of.

requite /rɪ'kwaɪt/ *verb* (**-ting**) make return for; reward, avenge; (often + *for*) give in return. □ **requital** *noun*.

reredos /'rɪədɒs/ *noun* ornamental screen covering wall above back of altar.

rescind /rɪ'sɪnd/ *verb* abrogate, revoke, cancel. □ **rescission** /-'sɪʒ-/ *noun*.

rescue /'reskjuː/ ● *verb* (**-ues**, **-ued**, **-uing**) (often + *from*) save or set free from danger or harm. ● *noun* rescuing, being rescued. □ **rescuer** *noun*.

research /rɪ'sɜːtʃ, 'riːsɜːtʃ/ ● *noun* systematic investigation of materials, sources, etc. to establish facts. ● *verb* do research into or for. □ **researcher** *noun*.

resemble /rɪ'zemb(ə)l/ *verb* (**-ling**) be like; have similarity to. □ **resemblance** *noun*.

resent /rɪ'zent/ *verb* feel indignation at; be aggrieved by. □ **resentful** *adjective*; **resentfully** *adverb*; **resentment** *noun*.

reservation /rezə'veɪʃ(ə)n/ *noun* reserving, being reserved; thing reserved (e.g. room in hotel); spoken or unspoken limitation or exception; (in full **central reservation**) strip of land between carriageways of road; area reserved for occupation of aboriginal peoples.

reserve /rɪ'zɜːv/ ● *verb* (**-ving**) put aside or keep back for later occasion or special use; order to be retained or allocated for person at particular time; retain, secure. ● *noun* thing reserved for future use; limitation or exception attached to something; self-restraint, reticence; company's profit added to capital; (in *singular* or *plural*) assets kept readily available, troops withheld from action to reinforce or protect others, forces outside regular ones but available in emergency; extra player chosen as possible substitute in team; land reserved for special use, esp. as habitat.

reserved *adjective* reticent, uncommunicative; set apart for particular use.

reservist *noun* member of reserve forces.

reservoir /'rezəvwɑː/ *noun* large natural or artificial lake as source of water supply; receptacle for fluid; supply of facts etc.

reshuffle /riː'ʃʌf(ə)l/ ● *verb* (**-ling**) shuffle again; change posts of (government ministers etc.). ● *noun* reshuffling.

reside /rɪ'zaɪd/ *verb* (**-ding**) have one's home; (+ *in*) (of right etc.) be vested in, (of quality) be present in.

residence /'rezɪd(ə)ns/ *noun* residing; place where one resides; house, esp. large one. □ **in residence** living or working at specified place.

resident /'rezɪd(ə)nt/ ● *noun* (often + *of*) permanent inhabitant; guest staying at hotel. ● *adjective* residing, in residence; living at one's workplace etc.; (+ *in*) located in.

residential /rezɪ'denʃ(ə)l/ *adjective* suitable for or occupied by dwellings; used as residence; connected with residence.

residual /rɪ'zɪdjʊəl/ *adjective* left as residue or residuum.

residuary /rɪ'zɪdjʊərɪ/ *adjective* of the residue of an estate; residual.

residue /'rezɪdjuː/ *noun* remainder, what is left over; what remains of estate when liabilities have been discharged.

residuum /rɪ'zɪdjʊəm/ *noun* (*plural* **-dua**) substance left after combustion or evaporation; residue.

resign /rɪ'zaɪn/ *verb* (often + *from*) give up job, position, etc.; relinquish, surrender; (**resign oneself to**) accept (situation etc.) reluctantly.

resignation /rezɪg'neɪʃ(ə)n/ *noun* resigning, esp. from job or office; reluctant acceptance of the inevitable.

resigned *adjective* (often + *to*) having resigned oneself; resolved to endure; indicative of this. □ **resignedly** /-nɪdlɪ/ *adverb*.

resilient /rɪ'zɪlɪənt/ *adjective* resuming original form after compression etc.; readily recovering from setback. □ **resilience** *noun*.

resin /'rezɪn/ ● *noun* sticky secretion of trees and plants; (in full **synthetic resin**) organic compound made by polymerization etc. and used in plastics. ● *verb* (**-n-**) rub or treat with resin. □ **resinous** *adjective*.

resist /rɪ'zɪst/ *verb* withstand action or effect of; abstain from (pleasure etc.); strive against, oppose; offer opposition. □ **resistible** *adjective*.

resistance /rɪˈzɪst(ə)ns/ *noun* resisting; power to resist; ability to withstand disease; impeding effect exerted by one thing on another; *Physics* property of hindering passage of electric current, heat, etc.; resistor; secret organization resisting regime, esp. in occupied country. ▫ **resistant** *adjective*.

resistor *noun* device having resistance to passage of electric current.

resit ● *verb* /riːˈsɪt/ (**-tt-**; *past & past participle* **resat**) sit (exam) again after failing. ● *noun* /ˈriːsɪt/ resitting of exam; exam for this.

resoluble /rɪˈzɒljʊb(ə)l/ *adjective* resolvable; (+ *into*) analysable into.

resolute /ˈrezəluːt/ *adjective* determined, decided; purposeful. ▫ **resolutely** *adverb*.

resolution /rezəˈluːʃ(ə)n/ *noun* resolute temper or character; thing resolved on; formal expression of opinion of meeting; (+ *of*) solving of question etc.; resolving, being resolved.

resolve /rɪˈzɒlv/ ● *verb* (**-ving**) make up one's mind, decide firmly; cause to do this; solve, settle; (+ *that*) pass resolution by vote; (often + *into*) (cause to) separate into constituent parts, analyse; *Music* convert or be converted into concord. ● *noun* firm mental decision; determination. ▫ **resolved** *adjective*.

resonant /ˈrezənənt/ *adjective* echoing, resounding; continuing to sound; causing reinforcement or prolongation of sound, esp. by vibration. ▫ **resonance** *noun*.

resonate /ˈrezəneɪt/ *verb* (**-ting**) produce or show resonance; resound. ▫ **resonator** *noun*.

resort /rɪˈzɔːt/ ● *noun* place frequented, esp. for holidays etc.; thing to which recourse is had, expedient; (+ *to*) recourse to, use of. ● *verb* (+ *to*) turn to as expedient; (+ *to*) go often or in numbers to. ▫ **in the** or **as a last resort** when all else has failed.

resound /rɪˈzaʊnd/ *verb* (often + *with*) ring, echo; produce echoes, go on sounding, fill place with sound; be much talked of, produce sensation.

resounding *adjective* ringing, echoing; unmistakable, emphatic.

resource /rɪˈzɔːs/ ● *noun* expedient, device; (often in *plural*) means available; stock that can be drawn on; (in *plural*) country's collective wealth, person's inner strength; skill in devising expedients. ● *verb* (**-cing**) provide with resources.

resourceful *adjective* good at devising expedients. ▫ **resourcefully** *adverb*; **resourcefulness** *noun*.

respect /rɪˈspekt/ ● *noun* deferential esteem; (+ *of*, *for*) heed, regard; detail, aspect; reference, relation; (in *plural*) polite greetings. ● *verb* regard with deference or esteem; treat with consideration, spare. ▫ **respectful** *adjective*; **respectfully** *adverb*.

respectable *adjective* of acceptable social standing, decent in appearance or behaviour; reasonably good in condition, appearance, size, etc. ▫ **respectability** *noun*; **respectably** *adverb*.

respecting *preposition* with regard to.

respective /rɪˈspektɪv/ *adjective* of or relating to each of several individually.

respectively *adverb* for each separately or in turn, and in the order mentioned.

respiration /respəˈreɪʃ(ə)n/ *noun* breathing; single breath in or out; plant's absorption of oxygen and emission of carbon dioxide.

respirator /ˈrespəreɪtə/ *noun* apparatus worn over mouth and nose to filter inhaled air; apparatus for maintaining artificial respiration.

respire /rɪˈspaɪə/ *verb* (**-ring**) breathe; inhale and exhale; (of plant) carry out respiration. ▫ **respiratory** /-ˈspɪr-/ *adjective*.

respite /ˈrespaɪt/ *noun* interval of rest or relief; delay permitted before discharge of obligation or suffering of penalty.

resplendent /rɪˈsplend(ə)nt/ *adjective* brilliant, dazzlingly or gloriously bright. ▫ **resplendence** *noun*.

respond /rɪˈspɒnd/ *verb* answer, reply; (often + *to*) act etc. in response.

respondent ● *noun* defendant, esp. in appeal or divorce case. ● *adjective* in position of defendant.

response /rɪˈspɒns/ *noun* answer, reply; action, feeling, etc. caused by stimulus etc.; (often in *plural*) part of liturgy said or sung in answer to priest.

responsibility /rɪspɒnsəˈbɪlɪtɪ/ *noun* (*plural* **-ies**) (often + *for*, *of*) being responsible, authority; person or thing for which one is responsible.

responsible /rɪˈspɒnsəb(ə)l/ *adjective* (often + *to*, *for*) liable to be called to account; morally accountable for actions; of good credit and repute; trustworthy; (often + *for*) being the cause; involving responsibility. ▫ **responsibly** *adverb*.

responsive /rɪˈspɒnsɪv/ *adjective* (often + *to*) responding readily (to some influence); sympathetic; answering; by way of answer. ▫ **responsiveness** *noun*.

rest[1] ● *verb* cease from exertion or action; be still, esp. to recover strength; lie in sleep or death; give relief or repose to; be left without further investigation or discussion; (+ *on*, *upon*, *against*) place, lie, lean, or depend on; (as **rested** *adjective*) refreshed by resting. ● *noun* repose or sleep; resting; prop or support for steadying something; *Music* (sign denoting) interval of silence. ▫ **at rest** not moving, not agitated or troubled; **rest-cure** prolonged rest as medical treatment; **rest home** place where elderly or convalescent people are cared for; **rest room** *esp. US* public lavatory; **set at rest** settle, reassure.

rest[2] ● *noun* (**the rest**) remainder or remaining parts or individuals. ● *verb* remain in specified state; (+ *with*) be left in the charge of. ▫ **for the rest** as regards anything else.

restaurant /ˈrestərɒnt/ *noun* public premises where meals may be bought and eaten.

restaurateur /restərəˈtɜː/ *noun* keeper of restaurant.

restful *adjective* quiet, soothing.

restitution /restɪˈtjuːʃ(ə)n/ *noun* restoring of property etc. to its owner; reparation.

restive /ˈrestɪv/ *adjective* fidgety; intractable, resisting control.

restless *adjective* without rest; uneasy, agitated, fidgeting. ▫ **restlessly** *adverb*; **restlessness** *noun*.

restoration /restəˈreɪʃ(ə)n/ *noun* restoring, being restored; model or drawing representing supposed original form of thing; (**Restoration**) re-establishment of British monarchy in 1660.

restorative /rɪˈstɒrətɪv/ ● *adjective* tending to restore health or strength. ● *noun* restorative food, medicine, etc.

restore /rɪˈstɔː/ *verb* (**-ring**) bring back to original state by rebuilding, repairing, etc.; give back; reinstate; bring back to former place, condition, or use; make restoration of (extinct animal, ruined building, etc.). ▫ **restorer** *noun*.

restrain /rɪˈstreɪn/ *verb* (usually + *from*) check or hold in; keep under control; repress; confine.

restraint /rɪˈstreɪnt/ *noun* restraining, being restrained; restraining agency or influence; self-control, moderation; reserve of manner.

restrict /rɪˈstrɪkt/ *verb* confine, limit; withhold from general disclosure. ▫ **restriction** *noun*.

restrictive /rɪˈstrɪktɪv/ *adjective* restricting. ▫ **restrictive practice** agreement or practice that limits competition or output in industry.

result /rɪ'zʌlt/ ● *noun* consequence; issue; satisfactory outcome; answer etc. got by calculation; (in *plural*) list of scores, winners, etc. in sporting events or exams. ● *verb* (often + *from*) arise as consequence; (+ *in*) end in.

resultant ● *adjective* resulting. ● *noun* force etc. equivalent to two or more acting in different directions at same point.

resume /rɪ'zju:m/ *verb* (**-ming**) begin again; recommence; take again or back. □ **resumption** /-'zʌmp-/ *noun*; **resumptive** /-'zʌmp-/ *adjective*.

résumé /'rezjʊmeɪ/ *noun* summary.

resurgent /rɪ'sɜ:dʒ(ə)nt/ *adjective* rising or arising again. □ **resurgence** *noun*.

resurrect /rezə'rekt/ *verb colloquial* revive practice or memory of; raise or rise from dead.

resurrection /rezə'rekʃ(ə)n/ *noun* rising from the dead; revival from disuse or decay etc.

resuscitate /rɪ'sʌsɪteɪt/ *verb* (**-ting**) revive from unconsciousness or apparent death; revive, restore. □ **resuscitation** *noun*.

retail /'ri:teɪl/ ● *noun* sale of goods to the public in small quantities. ● *adjective & adverb* by retail; at retail price. ● *verb* sell by retail; (often + *at*, *of*) (of goods) be sold by retail; (also /rɪ'teɪl/) recount. □ **retailer** *noun*.

retain /rɪ'teɪn/ *verb* keep possession of, continue to have, use, etc.; keep in mind; keep in place, hold fixed; secure services of (esp. barrister) by preliminary fee.

retainer *noun* fee for securing person's services; faithful servant; reduced rent paid to retain unoccupied accommodation; person or thing that retains.

retake ● *verb* /ri:'teɪk/ (**-king**; *past* **retook**; *past participle* **retaken**) take (photograph, exam, etc.) again; recapture. ● *noun* /'ri:teɪk/ filming, recording, etc. again; taking of exam etc. again.

retaliate /rɪ'tælɪeɪt/ *verb* (**-ting**) repay in kind; attack in return. □ **retaliation** *noun*; **retaliatory** /-'tæljət-/ *adjective*.

retard /rɪ'tɑ:d/ *verb* make slow or late; delay progress or accomplishment of. □ **retardant** *adjective & noun*; **retardation** /ri:-/ *noun*.

retarded *adjective* backward in mental or physical development.

retch *verb* make motion of vomiting.

retention /rɪ'tenʃ(ə)n/ *noun* retaining, being retained.

retentive /rɪ'tentɪv/ *adjective* tending to retain; (of memory) not forgetful.

rethink ● *verb* /ri:'θɪŋk/ (*past & past participle* **rethought** /-'θɔ:t/) consider again, esp. with view to making changes. ● *noun* /'ri:θɪŋk/ rethinking, reassessment.

reticence /'retɪs(ə)ns/ *noun* avoidance of saying all one knows or feels; taciturnity. □ **reticent** *adjective*.

reticulate ● *verb* /rɪ'tɪkjʊleɪt/ (**-ting**) divide or be divided in fact or appearance into network. ● *adjective* /rɪ'tɪkjʊlət/ reticulated. □ **reticulation** *noun*.

retina /'retɪnə/ *noun* (*plural* **-s** or **-nae** /-ni:/) light-sensitive layer at back of eyeball. □ **retinal** *adjective*.

retinue /'retɪnju:/ *noun* group of people attending important person.

retire /rɪ'taɪə/ *verb* (**-ring**) leave office or employment, esp. because of age; cause (employee) to retire; withdraw, retreat, seek seclusion or shelter; go to bed; *Cricket* (of batsman) suspend one's innings. □ **retired** *adjective*.

retirement *noun* retiring; period spent as retired person; seclusion. □ **retirement pension** pension paid by state to retired people above certain age.

retiring *adjective* shy, fond of seclusion.

retort[1] /rɪ'tɔ:t/ ● *noun* incisive, witty, or angry reply. ● *verb* say by way of retort; repay in kind.

retort[2] /rɪ'tɔ:t/ *noun* vessel with long downward-bent neck for distilling liquids; vessel for heating coal to generate gas.

retouch /ri:'tʌtʃ/ *verb* improve (esp. photograph) by minor alterations.

retrace /rɪ'treɪs/ *verb* (**-cing**) go back over (one's steps etc.); trace back to source or beginning.

retract /rɪ'trækt/ *verb* withdraw (statement etc.); draw or be drawn back or in. □ **retractable** *adjective*; **retraction** *noun*.

retractile /rɪ'træktaɪl/ *adjective* retractable.

retread ● *verb* /ri:'tred/ (*past* **retrod**; *past participle* **retrodden**) tread (path etc.) again; (*past & past participle* **retreaded**) put new tread on (tyre). ● *noun* /'ri:tred/ retreaded tyre.

retreat /rɪ'tri:t/ ● *verb* go back, retire; recede. ● *noun* (signal for) act of retreating; withdrawing into privacy; place of seclusion or shelter; period of seclusion for prayer and meditation.

retrench /rɪ'trentʃ/ *verb* cut down expenses; reduce amount of (costs); economize. □ **retrenchment** *noun*.

retrial /ri:'traɪəl/ *noun* retrying of case.

retribution /retrɪ'bju:ʃ(ə)n/ *noun* recompense, usually for evil; vengeance. □ **retributive** /rɪ'trɪb-/ *adjective*.

retrieve /rɪ'tri:v/ *verb* (**-ving**) regain possession of; find again; obtain (information in computer); (of dog) find and bring in (game); (+ *from*) rescue from (bad state etc.); restore to good state; repair, set right. □ **retrievable** *adjective*; **retrieval** *noun*.

retriever *noun* dog of breed used for retrieving game.

retro /'retrəʊ/ *slang* ● *adjective* reviving or harking back to past. ● *noun* (*plural* **retros**) retro fashion or style.

retro- *combining form* backwards, back.

retroactive /retrəʊ'æktɪv/ *adjective* having retrospective effect.

retrod *past* of RETREAD.

retrodden *past participle* of RETREAD.

retrograde /'retrəgreɪd/ ● *adjective* directed backwards; reverting, esp. to inferior state. ● *verb* move backwards; decline, revert.

retrogress /retrə'gres/ *verb* move backwards; deteriorate. □ **retrogression** *noun*; **retrogressive** *adjective*.

retrorocket /'retrəʊrɒkɪt/ *noun* auxiliary rocket for slowing down spacecraft etc.

retrospect /'retrəspekt/ *noun* □ **in retrospect** when looking back.

retrospection /retrə'spekʃ(ə)n/ *noun* looking back into the past.

retrospective /retrə'spektɪv/ ● *adjective* looking back on or dealing with the past; (of statute etc.) applying to the past as well as the future. ● *noun* exhibition etc. showing artist's lifetime development. □ **retrospectively** *adverb*.

retroussé /rə'tru:seɪ/ *adjective* (of nose) turned up at tip.

retroverted /'retrəʊvɜ:tɪd/ *adjective* (of womb) inclining backwards.

retry /ri:'traɪ/ *verb* (**-ies**, **-ied**) try (defendant, law case) again.

retsina /ret'si:nə/ *noun* resin-flavoured Greek white wine.

return /rɪ'tɜ:n/ ● *verb* come or go back; bring, put, or send back; give in response; yield (profit); say in reply; send (ball) back in tennis etc.; state in answer to formal demand; elect as MP etc. ● *noun* coming, going, putting, giving, sending, or paying back; what is returned; (in full **return ticket**) ticket for journey to place and back again; (in *singular* or *plural*) proceeds, profit; coming in of these; formal statement or report; (in full **return match**, **game**) second game between same opponents; (announcement of) person's election as MP etc. □ **by return (of post)** by the next available post in the return direction; **returning officer** official conducting election in constituency etc. and announcing result.

returnee /rɪtɜːˈniː/ *noun* person who returns home, esp. after war service.

reunify /riːˈjuːnɪfaɪ/ *verb* (**-ies**, **-ied**) restore to political unity. □ **reunification** *noun*.

reunion /riːˈjuːnjən/ *noun* reuniting, being reunited; social gathering, esp. of former associates.

reunite /riːjuːˈnaɪt/ *verb* (**-ting**) (cause to) come together again.

reuse ● *verb* /riːˈjuːz/ (**-sing**) use again. ● *noun* /riːˈjuːs/ second or further use. □ **reusable** *adjective*.

Rev. *abbreviation* Reverend.

rev *colloquial* ● *noun* (in *plural*) revolutions of engine per minute. ● *verb* (**-vv-**) (of engine) revolve; (often + *up*) cause (engine) to run quickly.

revalue /riːˈvæljuː/ *verb* (**-ues**, **-ued**, **-uing**) give different, esp. higher, value to (currency etc.). □ **revaluation** *noun*.

revamp /riːˈvæmp/ *verb* renovate, revise; patch up.

Revd *abbreviation* Reverend.

reveal /rɪˈviːl/ *verb* display, show, allow to appear; (often as **revealing** *adjective*) disclose, divulge.

reveille /rɪˈvælɪ/ *noun* military waking-signal.

revel /ˈrev(ə)l/ ● *verb* (**-ll-**; *US* **-l-**) make merry, be riotously festive; (+ *in*) take keen delight in. ● *noun* (in *singular* or *plural*) revelling. □ **reveller** *noun*; **revelry** *noun* (*plural* **-ies**).

revelation /revəˈleɪʃ(ə)n/ *noun* revealing; knowledge supposedly disclosed by divine or supernatural agency; striking disclosure or realization; (**Revelation** or *colloquial* **Revelations**) last book of New Testament.

revenge /rɪˈvendʒ/ ● *noun* (act of) retaliation; desire for this. ● *verb* (**-ging**) avenge; (**revenge oneself** or in *passive*; often + *on, upon*) inflict retaliation.

revengeful *adjective* eager for revenge.

revenue /ˈrevənjuː/ *noun* income, esp. annual income of state; department collecting state revenue.

reverberate /rɪˈvɜːbəreɪt/ *verb* (**-ting**) (of sound, light, or heat) be returned or reflected repeatedly; return (sound etc.) thus; (of event) produce continuing effect. □ **reverberant** *adjective*; **reverberation** *noun*; **reverberative** /-rətɪv/ *adjective*.

revere /rɪˈvɪə/ *verb* (**-ring**) regard with deep and affectionate or religious respect.

reverence /ˈrevərəns/ ● *noun* revering, being revered; deep respect. ● *verb* (**-cing**) treat with reverence.

reverend /ˈrevərənd/ *adjective* (esp. as title of member of clergy) deserving reverence. □ **Reverend Mother** Mother Superior of convent.

reverent /ˈrevərənt/ *adjective* feeling or showing reverence. □ **reverently** *adverb*.

reverential /revəˈrenʃ(ə)l/ *adjective* of the nature of, due to, or characterized by reverence. □ **reverentially** *adverb*.

reverie /ˈrevərɪ/ *noun* fit of musing; daydream.

revers /rɪˈvɪə/ *noun* (*plural* same /-ˈvɪəz/) (material of) turned-back front edge of garment.

reverse /rɪˈvɜːs/ ● *verb* (**-sing**) turn the other way round or up, turn inside out; convert to opposite character or effect; (cause to) travel backwards; make (engine) work in contrary direction; revoke, annul. ● *adjective* backward, upside down; opposite or contrary in character or order, inverted. ● *noun* opposite or contrary; contrary of usual manner; piece of misfortune, disaster; reverse gear or motion; reverse side; side of coin etc. bearing secondary design; verso of printed leaf. □ **reverse the charges** have recipient of telephone call pay for it; **reverse gear** gear used to make vehicle etc. go backwards; **reversing light** light at rear of vehicle showing it is in reverse gear. □ **reversal** *noun*; **reversible** *adjective*.

reversion /rɪˈvɜːʃ(ə)n/ *noun* return to previous state or earlier type; legal right (esp. of original owner) to possess or succeed to property on death of present possessor.

revert /rɪˈvɜːt/ *verb* (+ *to*) return to (former condition, practice, subject, opinion, etc.); return by reversion. □ **revertible** *adjective*.

review /rɪˈvjuː/ ● *noun* general survey or assessment; survey of past; revision, reconsideration; published criticism of book, play, etc.; periodical in which events, books, etc. are reviewed; inspection of troops etc. ● *verb* survey, look back on; reconsider, revise; hold review of (troops etc.); write review of (book etc.). □ **reviewer** *noun*.

revile /rɪˈvaɪl/ *verb* (**-ling**) abuse verbally.

revise /rɪˈvaɪz/ *verb* (**-sing**) examine and improve or amend; reconsider and alter (opinion etc.); go over (work etc.) again, esp. for examination. □ **revisory** *adjective*.

revision /rɪˈvɪʒ(ə)n/ *noun* revising, being revised; revised edition or form.

revisionism *noun often derogatory* revision or modification of orthodoxy, esp. of Marxism. □ **revisionist** *noun & adjective*.

revitalize /riːˈvaɪtəlaɪz/ *verb* (also **-ise**) (**-zing** or **-sing**) imbue with new vitality.

revival /rɪˈvaɪv(ə)l/ *noun* reviving, being revived; new production of old play etc.; (campaign to promote) reawakening of religious fervour.

revivalism *noun* promotion of esp. religious revival. □ **revivalist** *noun & adjective*.

revive /rɪˈvaɪv/ *verb* (**-ving**) come or bring back to consciousness, life, vigour, use, or notice.

revivify /rɪˈvɪvɪfaɪ/ *verb* (**-ies**, **-ied**) restore to life, strength, or activity. □ **revivification** *noun*.

revoke /rɪˈvəʊk/ ● *verb* (**-king**) rescind, withdraw, cancel; *Cards* fail to follow suit though able to. ● *noun* *Cards* revoking. □ **revocable** /ˈrevəkəb(ə)l/ *adjective*; **revocation** /revəˈkeɪʃ(ə)n/ *noun*.

revolt /rɪˈvəʊlt/ ● *verb* rise in rebellion; affect with disgust; (often + *at, against*) feel revulsion. ● *noun* insurrection; sense of disgust; rebellious mood.

revolting *adjective* disgusting, horrible. □ **revoltingly** *adverb*.

revolution /revəˈluːʃ(ə)n/ *noun* forcible overthrow of government or social order; fundamental change; revolving; single completion of orbit or rotation.

revolutionary ● *adjective* involving great change; of political revolution. ● *noun* (*plural* **-ies**) instigator or supporter of political revolution.

revolutionize *verb* (also **-ise**) (**-zing** or **-sing**) change fundamentally.

revolve /rɪˈvɒlv/ *verb* (**-ving**) turn round; rotate; move in orbit; ponder in the mind; (+ *around*) be centred on.

revolver *noun* pistol with revolving chambers enabling user to fire several shots without reloading.

revue /rɪˈvjuː/ *noun* theatrical entertainment of usually comic sketches and songs.

revulsion /rɪˈvʌlʃ(ə)n/ *noun* abhorrence; sudden violent change of feeling.

reward /rɪˈwɔːd/ ● *noun* return or recompense for service or merit; requital for good or evil; sum offered for detection of criminal, recovery of lost property, etc. ● *verb* give or serve as reward to. ▫ **rewarding** *adjective*.

rewind /riːˈwaɪnd/ *verb* (*past & past participle* **rewound** /-ˈwaʊnd/) wind (film, tape, etc.) back.

rewire /riːˈwaɪə/ *verb* (**-ring**) provide with new electrical wiring.

rework /riːˈwɜːk/ *verb* revise, refashion, remake. ▫ **reworking** *noun*.

Rex *noun* (after name) reigning king; *Law* the Crown. [Latin].

rhapsodize /ˈræpsədaɪz/ *verb* (also **-ise**) (**-zing** or **-sing**) speak or write rhapsodies.

rhapsody /ˈræpsədɪ/ *noun* (*plural* **-ies**) enthusiastic or extravagant speech or composition; melodic musical piece often based on folk culture. ▫ **rhapsodic** /-ˈsɒd-/ *adjective*.

rhea /ˈriːə/ *noun* large flightless S. American bird.

rheostat /ˈriːəstæt/ *noun* instrument used to control electric current by varying resistance.

rhesus /ˈriːsəs/ *noun* (in full **rhesus monkey**) small Indian monkey. ▫ **rhesus factor** antigen occurring on red blood cells of most humans and some other primates; **rhesus-positive**, **-negative** having or not having rhesus factor.

rhetoric /ˈretərɪk/ *noun* art of persuasive speaking or writing; language intended to impress, esp. seen as inflated, exaggerated, or meaningless.

rhetorical /rɪˈtɒrɪk(ə)l/ *adjective* expressed artificially or extravagantly; of the nature of rhetoric. ▫ **rhetorical question** question asked not for information but to produce effect. ▫ **rhetorically** *adverb*.

rheumatic /ruːˈmætɪk/ ● *adjective* of, caused by, or suffering from rheumatism. ● *noun* person suffering from rheumatism; (in *plural*, often treated as *singular*) *colloquial* rheumatism. ▫ **rheumatic fever** fever with pain in the joints. ▫ **rheumatically** *adverb*; **rheumaticky** *adjective colloquial*.

rheumatism /ˈruːmətɪz(ə)m/ *noun* disease marked by inflammation and pain in joints etc.

rheumatoid /ˈruːmətɔɪd/ *adjective* having the character of rheumatism. ▫ **rheumatoid arthritis** chronic progressive disease causing inflammation and stiffening of joints.

rhinestone /ˈraɪnstəʊn/ *noun* imitation diamond.

rhino /ˈraɪnəʊ/ *noun* (*plural* same or **-s**) *colloquial* rhinoceros.

rhinoceros /raɪˈnɒsərəs/ *noun* (*plural* same or **-roses**) large thick-skinned animal with usually one horn on nose.

rhizome /ˈraɪzəʊm/ *noun* underground rootlike stem bearing both roots and shoots.

rhododendron /rəʊdəˈdendrən/ *noun* (*plural* **-s** or **-dra**) evergreen shrub with large flowers.

rhomboid /ˈrɒmbɔɪd/ ● *adjective* (also **rhomboidal** /-ˈbɔɪd-/) like a rhombus. ● *noun* quadrilateral of which only opposite sides and angles are equal.

rhombus /ˈrɒmbəs/ *noun* (*plural* **-buses** or **-bi** /-baɪ/) oblique equilateral parallelogram, e.g. diamond on playing card.

rhubarb /ˈruːbɑːb/ *noun* (stalks of) plant with fleshy leaf-stalks cooked and eaten as dessert; *colloquial* indistinct conversation or noise, from repeated use of word 'rhubarb' by stage crowd.

rhyme /raɪm/ ● *noun* identity of sound at ends of words or verse-lines; (in *singular* or *plural*) rhymed verse; use of rhyme; word providing rhyme. ● *verb* (**-ming**) (of words or lines) produce rhyme; (+ *with*) be or use as rhyme; write rhymes; put into rhyme.

rhythm /ˈrɪð(ə)m/ *noun* periodical accent and duration of notes in music; type of structure formed by this; measured flow of words in verse or prose; *Physiology* pattern of successive strong and weak movements; regularly occurring sequence of events. ▫ **rhythm method** contraception by avoiding sexual intercourse near times of ovulation. ▫ **rhythmic** *adjective*; **rhythmical** *adjective*; **rhythmically** *adverb*.

rib ● *noun* each of the curved bones joined to spine and protecting organs of chest; joint of meat from this part of animal; supporting ridge, timber, rod, etc. across surface or through structure; combination of plain and purl stitches producing ribbed design. ● *verb* (**-bb-**) provide or mark (as) with ribs; *colloquial* tease. ▫ **ribcage** wall of bones formed by ribs round chest; **rib-tickler** something amusing. ▫ **ribbed** *adjective*; **ribbing** *noun*.

ribald /ˈrɪb(ə)ld/ *adjective* irreverent, coarsely humorous. ▫ **ribaldry** *noun*.

riband /ˈrɪbənd/ *noun* ribbon.

ribbon /ˈrɪbən/ *noun* narrow strip or band of fabric; material in this form; ribbon worn to indicate some honour, membership of sports team, etc.; long narrow strip; (in *plural*) ragged strips. ▫ **ribbon development** building of houses along main road outwards from town.

riboflavin /raɪbəʊˈfleɪvɪn/ *noun* (also **riboflavine** /-viːn/) vitamin of B complex, found in liver, milk, and eggs.

ribonucleic acid /raɪbəʊnjuːˈkliːɪk/ *noun* substance controlling protein synthesis in cells.

rice *noun* (grains from) swamp grass grown esp. in Asia. ▫ **rice-paper** edible paper made from pith of an oriental tree and used for painting and in cookery.

rich *adjective* having much wealth; splendid, costly; valuable; abundant, ample; (often + *in*, *with*) abounding; fertile; (of food) containing much fat, spice, etc.; mellow, strong and full; highly amusing or ludicrous. ▫ **richness** *noun*.

riches *plural noun* abundant means; valuable possessions.

richly *adverb* in a rich way; fully, thoroughly.

Richter scale /ˈrɪktə/ *noun* scale of 0–10 for representing strength of earthquake.

rick[1] *noun* stack of hay etc.

rick[2] (also **wrick**) ● *noun* slight sprain or strain. ● *verb* slightly strain or sprain.

rickets /ˈrɪkɪts/ *noun* (treated as *singular* or *plural*) children's deficiency disease with softening of the bones.

rickety /ˈrɪkɪtɪ/ *adjective* shaky, insecure; suffering from rickets.

rickshaw /ˈrɪkʃɔː/ *noun* (also **ricksha** /-ʃə/) light two-wheeled hooded vehicle drawn by one or more people.

ricochet /ˈrɪkəʃeɪ/ ● *noun* rebounding of esp. shell or bullet off surface; hit made after this. ● *verb* (**-cheted** /-ʃeɪd/ or **-chetted** /-ʃetɪd/; **-cheting** /-ʃeɪɪŋ/ or **-chetting** /-ʃetɪŋ/) (of projectile) make ricochet.

ricotta /rɪˈkɒtə/ *noun* soft Italian cheese.

rid *verb* (**-dd-**; *past & past participle* **rid**) (+ *of*) make (person, place) free of.

riddance /ˈrɪd(ə)ns/ *noun* ▫ **good riddance** *expression of relief at getting rid of something or someone.*

ridden *past participle* of RIDE.

riddle[1] /ˈrɪd(ə)l/ ● *noun* verbal puzzle or test, often with trick answer; puzzling fact, thing, or person. ● *verb* (**-ling**) speak in riddles.

riddle[2] /ˈrɪd(ə)l/ ● *verb* (**-ling**) (usually + *with*) make many holes in, esp. with gunshot; (in *passive*) fill, permeate; pass through riddle. ● *noun* coarse sieve.

ride ● *verb* (**-ding**; *past* **rode**; *past participle* **ridden** /ˈrɪd(ə)n/) (often + *on*, *in*) travel or be carried on or in (bicycle, vehicle, horse, etc.); be carried or supported by; cross, be conveyed over; float buoyantly; (as **ridden** *adjective*) (+ *by, with*) dominated by or infested with. ● *noun* journey or spell of riding in vehicle, on horse, etc.; path (esp. through woods) for riding on; amusement for riding on at fairground. ▫ **ride up** (of garment) work upwards when worn; **take for a ride** *colloquial* hoax, deceive.

rider *noun* person riding; additional remark following statement, verdict, etc.

ridge *noun* line of junction of two surfaces sloping upwards towards each other; long narrow hilltop; mountain range; any narrow elevation across surface. ▫ **ridge-pole** horizontal pole of long tent; **ridgeway** road along ridge.

ridicule /ˈrɪdɪkjuːl/ ● *noun* derision, mockery. ● *verb* (**-ling**) make fun of; mock; laugh at.

ridiculous /rɪˈdɪkjʊləs/ *adjective* deserving to be laughed at; unreasonable. ▫ **ridiculously** *adverb*; **ridiculousness** *noun*.

riding[1] /ˈraɪdɪŋ/ *noun* sport or pastime of travelling on horseback.

riding[2] /ˈraɪdɪŋ/ *noun historical* former division of Yorkshire.

Riesling /ˈriːzlɪŋ/ *noun* (white wine made from) type of grape.

rife *adjective* widespread; (+ *with*) abounding in.

riff *noun* short repeated phrase in jazz etc.

riffle /ˈrɪf(ə)l/ ● *verb* (**-ling**) (often + *through*) leaf quickly through (pages); shuffle (cards). ● *noun* riffling; *US* patch of ripples in stream etc.

riff-raff /ˈrɪfræf/ *noun* rabble, disreputable people.

rifle[1] /ˈraɪf(ə)l/ ● *noun* gun with long rifled barrel; (in *plural*) troops armed with these. ● *verb* (**-ling**) make spiral grooves in (gun etc.) to make projectile spin. ▫ **rifle range** place for rifle practice.

rifle[2] /ˈraɪf(ə)l/ *verb* (**-ling**) (often + *through*) search and rob; carry off as booty.

rift *noun* crack, split; cleft; disagreement, dispute. ▫ **rift-valley** one formed by subsidence of section of earth's crust.

rig[1] ● *verb* (**-gg-**) provide (ship) with rigging; (often + *out, up*) fit with clothes or equipment; (+ *up*) set up hastily or as makeshift. ● *noun* arrangement of ship's masts, sails, etc.; equipment for special purpose; oil rig; *colloquial* style of dress, uniform. ▫ **rig-out** *colloquial* outfit of clothes. ▫ **rigger** *noun*.

rig[2] ● *verb* (**-gg-**) manage or fix fraudulently. ● *noun* trick, swindle.

rigging *noun* ship's spars, ropes, etc.

right /raɪt/ ● *adjective* just, morally or socially correct; correct, true; preferable, suitable; in good or normal condition; on or towards east side of person or thing facing north; (also **Right**) *Politics* of the Right; (of side of fabric etc.) meant to show; *colloquial* real, complete. ● *noun* what is just; fair treatment; fair claim; legal or moral entitlement; right-hand part, region, or direction; *Boxing* right hand, blow with this; (often **Right**) *Politics* conservatives collectively. ● *verb* (often *reflexive*) restore to proper, straight, or vertical position; correct, avenge; set in order; make reparation for. ● *adverb* straight; *colloquial* immediately; (+ *to, round, through*, etc.) all the way; (+ *off, out*, etc.) completely; quite, very; justly, properly, correctly, truly; on or to right side. ● *interjection colloquial: expressing agreement or consent*. ▫ **by right(s)** if right were done; **in the right** having justice or truth on one's side; **right angle** angle of 90°; **right-hand** on right side; **right-handed** naturally using right hand for writing etc., made by or for right hand, turning to right, (of screw) turning clockwise to tighten; **right-hander** right-handed person or blow; **right-hand man** essential or chief assistant; **Right Honourable** *title of certain high officials, e.g. Privy Counsellors*; **right-minded**, **-thinking** having sound views and principles; **right of way** right to pass over another's ground, path subject to such right, precedence granted to one vehicle over another; **Right Reverend** *title of bishop*, **right wing** more conservative section of political party etc., right side of football etc. team; **right-wing** conservative, reactionary; **right-winger** member of right wing. ▫ **rightward** *adjective & adverb*; **rightwards** *adverb*.

righteous /ˈraɪtʃəs/ *adjective* morally right; virtuous, law-abiding. ▫ **righteously** *adverb*; **righteousness** *noun*.

rightful *adjective* legitimately entitled to (position etc.); that one is entitled to. ▫ **rightfully** *adverb*.

rightly *adverb* justly, correctly, properly, justifiably.

rigid /ˈrɪdʒɪd/ *adjective* not flexible, unbendable; inflexible, harsh. ▫ **rigidity** /-ˈdʒɪd-/ *noun*; **rigidly** *adverb*.

rigmarole /ˈrɪgmərəʊl/ *noun* complicated procedure; rambling tale etc.

rigor *US* = RIGOUR.

rigor mortis /rɪgə ˈmɔːtɪs/ *noun* stiffening of body after death.

rigorous /ˈrɪgərəs/ *adjective* strict, severe; exact, accurate. ▫ **rigorously** *adverb*; **rigorousness** *noun*.

rigour /ˈrɪgə/ *noun* (*US* **rigor**) severity, strictness, harshness; (in *plural*) harsh conditions; strict application or observance etc.

rile *verb* (**-ling**) *colloquial* anger, irritate.

rill *noun* small stream.

rim *noun* edge or border, esp. of something circular; outer ring of wheel, holding tyre; part of spectacle frames around lens. ▫ **rimless** *adjective*; **rimmed** *adjective*.

rime ● *noun* frost; hoar-frost. ● *verb* (**-ming**) cover with rime.

rind /raɪnd/ *noun* tough outer layer or covering of fruit and vegetables, cheese, bacon, etc.

ring[1] ● *noun* circular band, usually of metal, worn on finger; circular band of any material; line or band round cylindrical or circular object; mark or part etc. resembling ring; ring in cross-section of tree representing one year's growth; enclosure for circus, boxing, betting at races, etc.; people or things arranged in circle, such arrangement; combination of traders, politicians, spies, etc. acting together; gas ring; disc or halo round planet, moon, etc. ● *verb* (often + *round, about, in*) encircle; put ring on (bird etc.). ▫ **ring-binder** loose-leaf binder with ring-shaped clasps; **ring-dove** woodpigeon; **ring finger** finger next to little finger, esp. on left hand; **ringleader** instigator in crime or mischief etc.; **ringmaster** director of circus performance; **ring-pull** (of tin) having ring for pulling to break seal; **ring road** bypass encircling town; **ringside** area immediately beside boxing or circus ring etc.; **ringworm** skin infection forming circular inflamed patches.

ring[2] ● *verb* (*past* **rang**; *past participle* **rung**) (often + *out* etc.) give clear resonant sound; make (bell) ring; call by telephone; (usually + *with, to*) (of place) resound, re-echo; (of ears) be filled with sensation of ringing; (+ *in, out*) usher in or out with bell-ringing; give specified impression. ● *noun* ringing sound or tone; act of ringing bell, sound caused by this; *colloquial* telephone call; set of esp. church bells; specified feeling conveyed by words etc.. ▫ **ring back** make return telephone call to; **ring off** end telephone call; **ring up** make telephone call (to), record (amount) on cash register.

ringlet /ˈrɪŋlɪt/ *noun* curly lock of esp. long hair.

rink *noun* area of ice for skating, curling, etc.; enclosed area for roller-skating; building containing either of these; strip of bowling green; team in bowls or curling.

rinse ● *verb* (**-sing**) (often + *through, out*) wash or treat with clean water etc.; wash lightly; put through clean water after washing; (+ *out, away*) remove by rinsing. ● *noun* rinsing; temporary hair tint.

riot /'raɪət/ ● *noun* disturbance of peace by crowd; loud revelry; (+ *of*) lavish display of; *colloquial* very amusing thing or person. ● *verb* make or engage in riot. □ **run riot** throw off all restraint, spread uncontrolled. □ **rioter** *noun*; **riotous** *adjective*.

RIP *abbreviation* may he, she, or they rest in peace (*requiesca(n)t in pace*).

rip ● *verb* (**-pp-**) tear or cut quickly or forcibly away or apart; make (hole etc.) thus; make long tear or cut in; come violently apart, split. ● *noun* long tear or cut; act of ripping. □ **let rip** *colloquial* (allow to) proceed or act without restraint or interference; **ripcord** cord for releasing parachute from its pack; **rip off** *colloquial* swindle, exploit, steal; **rip-off** *noun* □ **ripper** *noun*.

riparian /raɪ'peərɪən/ *adjective* of or on riverbank.

ripe *adjective* ready to be reaped, picked, or eaten; mature; (often + *for*) fit, ready. □ **ripen** *verb*; **ripeness** *noun*.

riposte /rɪ'pɒst/ ● *noun* quick retort; quick return thrust in fencing. ● *verb* (**-ting**) deliver riposte.

ripple /'rɪp(ə)l/ ● *noun* ruffling of water's surface; small wave(s); gentle lively sound, e.g. of laughter or applause; slight variation in strength of current etc.; ice cream with veins of syrup. ● *verb* (**-ling**) (cause to) form or flow in ripples; show or sound like ripples.

rise /raɪz/ ● *verb* (**-sing**; *past* **rose** /rəʊz/; *past participle* **risen** /'rɪz(ə)n/) come or go up; project or swell upwards; appear above horizon; get up from lying, sitting, or kneeling; get out of bed; (of meeting etc.) adjourn; reach higher level; make social progress; (often + *up*) rebel; come to surface; react to provocation; ascend, soar; have origin, begin to flow. ● *noun* rising; upward slope; increase in amount, extent, pitch, etc.; increase in salary; increase in status or power; height of step, incline, etc.; origin. □ **give rise to** cause, induce; **get, take a rise out of** *colloquial* provoke reaction from; **on the rise** on the increase.

riser *noun* person who rises from bed; vertical piece between treads of staircase.

risible /'rɪzɪb(ə)l/ *adjective* laughable, ludicrous.

rising ● *adjective* advancing; approaching specified age; going up. ● *noun* insurrection. □ **rising damp** moisture absorbed from ground into wall.

risk ● *noun* chance of danger, injury, loss, etc.; person or thing causing risk. ● *verb* expose to risk; venture on, take chances of. □ **at risk** exposed to danger; **at one's (own) risk** accepting responsibility for oneself; **at the risk of** with the possibility of (adverse consequences).

risky *adjective* (**-ier**, **-iest**) involving risk; risqué. □ **riskily** *adverb*; **riskiness** *noun*.

risotto /rɪ'zɒteʊ/ *noun* (*plural* **-s**) Italian savoury rice dish cooked in stock.

risqué /'rɪskeɪ/ *adjective* (of story etc.) slightly indecent.

rissole /'rɪsəʊl/ *noun* fried cake of minced meat coated in breadcrumbs.

ritardando /rɪtɑː'dændəʊ/ *adverb, adjective, & noun* (*plural* **-s** or **-di** /-dɪ/) *Music* = RALLENTANDO.

rite *noun* religious or solemn ceremony or observance. □ **rite of passage** (often in *plural*) event marking change or stage in life.

ritual /'rɪtʃʊəl/ ● *noun* prescribed order esp. of religious ceremony; solemn or colourful pageantry etc.; procedure regularly followed. ● *adjective* of or done as ritual or rite. □ **ritually** *adverb*.

ritualism *noun* regular or excessive practice of ritual. □ **ritualist** *noun*; **ritualistic** /-'lɪs-/ *adjective*; **ritualistically** /-'lɪs-/ *adverb*.

rival /'raɪv(ə)l/ ● *noun* person or thing that competes with another or equals another in quality. ● *verb* (**-ll-**; *US* **-l-**) be rival of or comparable to.

rivalry *noun* (*plural* **-ies**) being rivals; competition.

riven /'rɪv(ə)n/ *adjective literary* split, torn.

river /'rɪvə/ *noun* large natural stream of water flowing to sea, lake, etc.; copious flow. □ **riverside** ground along riverbank.

rivet /'rɪvɪt/ ● *noun* nail or bolt for joining metal plates etc. ● *verb* (**-t-**) join or fasten with rivets; fix, make immovable; (+ *on, upon*) direct intently; (esp. as **riveting** *adjective*) engross.

riviera /rɪvɪ'eərə/ *noun* coastal subtropical region, esp. that of SE France and NW Italy.

rivulet /'rɪvjʊlɪt/ *noun* small stream.

RLC *abbreviation* Royal Logistics Corps.

RM *abbreviation* Royal Marines.

rm. *abbreviation* room.

RN *abbreviation* Royal Navy.

RNA *abbreviation* ribonucleic acid.

RNLI *abbreviation* Royal National Lifeboat Institution.

roach *noun* (*plural* same or **-es**) small freshwater fish.

road *noun* way with prepared surface for vehicles, etc.; route; (usually in *plural*) piece of water near shore in which ships can ride at anchor. □ **any road** *dialect* anyway; **in the** or **one's road** *dialect* forming obstruction; **on the road** travelling; **roadbed** foundation of road or railway, *US* part of road for vehicles; **roadblock** barrier on road to detain traffic; **road fund licence** = TAX DISC; **road-hog** *colloquial* reckless or inconsiderate motorist etc.; **roadhouse** inn etc. on main road; **road-metal** broken stone for roadmaking; **roadshow** touring entertainment etc., esp. radio or television series broadcast from changing venue; **roadstead** sea road for ships; **road tax** tax payable on vehicles; **road test** test of vehicle's roadworthiness; **roadway** part of road used by vehicles; **roadworks** construction or repair of roads; **roadworthy** (of vehicle) fit to be used on road; **roadworthiness** *noun*.

roadie *noun colloquial* assistant of touring band etc., responsible for equipment.

roadster *noun* open car without rear seats.

roam *verb* ramble, wander; travel unsystematically over, through, or about.

roan ● *adjective* (esp. of horse) with coat thickly interspersed with hairs of another colour. ● *noun* roan animal.

roar /rɔː/ ● *noun* loud deep hoarse sound as of lion; loud laugh. ● *verb* (often + *out*) utter loudly, or make roar, roaring laugh, etc.; travel in vehicle at high speed. □ **roaring drunk** very drunk and noisy; **roaring forties** stormy ocean tracts between latitudes 40° and 50°S; **roaring success** great success; **roaring twenties** decade of 1920s.

roast ● *verb* cook or be cooked by exposure to open heat or in oven; criticize severely. ● *adjective* roasted. ● *noun* (dish of) roast meat; meat for roasting; process of roasting.

rob *verb* (**-bb-**) (often + *of*) take unlawfully from, esp. by force; deprive of. □ **robber** *noun*; **robbery** *noun* (*plural* **-ies**).

robe ● *noun* long loose garment, esp. (often in *plural*) as indication of rank, office, etc.; *esp. US* dressing gown. ● *verb* (**-bing**) clothe in robe; dress.

robin /ˈrɒbɪn/ *noun* (also **robin redbreast**) small brown red-breasted bird.

Robin Hood *noun* person who steals from rich to give to poor.

robot /ˈrəʊbɒt/ *noun* automaton resembling or functioning like human; automatic mechanical device; machine-like person. □ **robotic** /-ˈbɒt-/ *adjective*; **robotize** *verb* (also **-ise**) (**-zing** or **-sing**).

robotics /rəʊˈbɒtɪks/ *plural noun* (usually treated as *singular*) science or study of robot design and operation.

robust /rəʊˈbʌst/ *adjective* (**-er**, **-est**) strong, esp. in health and physique; (of exercise etc.) vigorous; straightforward; (of statement etc.) bold. □ **robustly** *adverb*; **robustness** *noun*.

roc *noun* gigantic bird of Eastern legend.

rock[1] *noun* solid part of earth's crust; material or projecting mass of this; (**the Rock**) Gibraltar; large detached stone; *US* stone of any size; firm support or protection; hard sweet usually as peppermint-flavoured stick; *slang* precious stone, esp. diamond. □ **on the rocks** *colloquial* short of money, (of marriage) broken down, (of drink) served with ice cubes; **rock-bottom** very lowest (level); **rock-cake** bun with rough surface; **rock crystal** crystallized quartz; **rock face** vertical surface of natural rock; **rock-garden** rockery; **rock plant** plant that grows on or among rocks; **rock-salmon** catfish, dogfish, etc.; **rock salt** common salt as solid mineral.

rock[2] ● *verb* move gently to and fro; set, keep, or be in such motion; (cause to) sway; oscillate; shake, reel. ● *noun* rocking motion; rock and roll, popular music influenced by this. □ **rock and roll**, **rock 'n' roll** popular dance music with heavy beat and blues influence; **rocking-chair** chair on rockers or springs; **rocking-horse** toy horse on rockers or springs.

rocker *noun* device for rocking, esp. curved bar etc. on which something rocks; rocking-chair; rock music devotee, esp. leather-clad motorcyclist.

rockery *noun* (*plural* **-ies**) pile of rough stones with soil between them for growing rock plants on.

rocket /ˈrɒkɪt/ ● *noun* firework or signal propelled to great height after ignition; engine operating on same principle; rocket-propelled missile, spacecraft, etc. ● *verb* (**-t-**) move rapidly upwards or away; bombard with rockets.

rocketry *noun* science or practice of rocket propulsion.

rocky[1] *adjective* (**-ier**, **-iest**) of, like, or full of rocks.

rocky[2] *adjective* (**-ier**, **-iest**) *colloquial* unsteady, tottering.

rococo /rəˈkəʊkəʊ/ ● *adjective* of ornate style of art, music, and literature in 18th-c. Europe. ● *noun* this style.

rod *noun* slender straight round stick or bar; cane for flogging; fishing-rod; *historical* measure of length (5½ yds.).

rode *past* of RIDE.

rodent /ˈrəʊd(ə)nt/ *noun* mammal with strong incisors and no canine teeth (e.g. rat, squirrel, beaver).

rodeo /ˈrəʊdɪəʊ/ *noun* (*plural* **-s**) exhibition of cowboys' skills; round-up of cattle for branding etc.

roe[1] *noun* (also **hard roe**) mass of eggs in female fish; (also **soft roe**) male fish's milt.

roe[2] *noun* (*plural* same or **-s**) (also **roe-deer**) small kind of deer. **roebuck** male roe.

roentgen /ˈrʌntjən/ *noun* (also **röntgen**) unit of exposure to ionizing radiation.

rogation /rəʊˈgeɪʃ(ə)n/ *noun* (usually in *plural*) litany of the saints chanted on the 3 days (**Rogation Days**) before Ascension Day.

roger /ˈrɒdʒə/ *interjection* your message has been received and understood; *slang* I agree.

rogue /rəʊg/ *noun* dishonest or unprincipled person; *jocular* mischievous person; wild fierce animal driven or living apart from herd; inferior or defective specimen. □ **roguery** *noun* (*plural* **-ies**); **roguish** *adjective*.

roister /ˈrɔɪstə/ *verb* (esp. as **roistering** *adjective*) revel noisily, be uproarious. □ **roisterer** *noun*.

role *noun* (also **rôle**) actor's part; person's or thing's function. □ **role model** person on whom others model themselves; **role-playing**, **-play** acting of characters or situations as aid in psychotherapy, teaching, etc.; **role-play** *verb*.

roll /rəʊl/ ● *verb* (cause to) move or go in some direction by turning over and over on axis; make cylindrical or spherical by revolving between two surfaces or over on itself; gather into mass; (often + *along*, *by*, etc.) move or be carried on or as if on wheels; flatten with roller; rotate; sway or rock; proceed unsteadily; undulate, show undulating motion or surface; sound with vibration. ● *noun* rolling motion or gait; undulation; act of rolling; rhythmic rumbling sound; anything forming cylinder by being turned over on itself without folding; small loaf of bread for one person; official list or register. □ **roll-call** calling of list of names to establish presence; **rolled gold** thin coating of gold applied by roller to base metal; **rolled oats** husked and crushed oats; **rolling-mill** machine or factory for rolling metal into shape; **rolling-pin** roller for pastry; **rolling-stock** company's railway or (*US*) road vehicles; **roll-mop** rolled pickled herring fillet; **roll-neck** having high loosely turned-over collar; **roll-on** applied by means of rotating ball; **roll-on roll-off** (of ship etc.) in which vehicles are driven directly on and off; **roll-top desk** desk with flexible cover sliding in curved grooves; **roll-up** hand-rolled cigarette; **strike off the rolls** debar from practising as solicitor.

roller *noun* revolving cylinder for smoothing, flattening, crushing, spreading, etc.; small cylinder on which hair is rolled for setting; long swelling wave. □ **roller bearing** bearing with cylinders instead of balls; **roller coaster** switchback at fair etc.; **roller-skate** *noun* frame with small wheels, strapped to shoes; boot with small wheels underneath; *verb* move on roller-skates; **roller towel** towel with ends joined.

rollicking /ˈrɒlɪkɪŋ/ *adjective* jovial, exuberant.

roly-poly /rəʊlɪˈpəʊlɪ/ ● *noun* (*plural* **-ies**) (also **roly-poly pudding**) pudding of rolled-up suet pastry covered with jam and boiled or baked. ● *adjective* podgy, plump.

ROM *noun Computing* read-only memory.

Roman /ˈrəʊmən/ ● *adjective* of ancient Rome or its territory or people; of medieval or modern Rome; Roman Catholic; (**roman**) (of type) plain and upright, used in ordinary print; (of the alphabet etc.) based on the ancient Roman system with letters A–Z. ● *noun* (*plural* **-s**) citizen of ancient Roman Republic or Empire, or of modern Rome; Roman Catholic; (**roman**) roman type. □ **Roman candle** firework discharging coloured sparks; **Roman Catholic** *adjective* of part of Christian Church acknowledging Pope as its head, *noun* member of this; **Roman Catholicism** *noun*; **Roman Empire** *historical* that established in 27 BC and divided in AD 395; **Roman law** law code of ancient Rome, forming basis of many modern codes; **Roman nose** one with high bridge; **roman numerals** numerals expressed in letters of Roman alphabet. □ **romanize** *verb* (also **-ise**) (**-zing** or **-sing**); **romanization** *noun*.

romance /rəʊˈmæns/ ● *noun* (also /ˈrəʊ-/) idealized, poetic, or unworldly atmosphere or tendency; love affair; (work of) literature concerning romantic love, stirring action, etc.; medieval tale of chivalry; exaggeration, picturesque falsehood. ● *adjective* (**Romance**) (of a language) descended from Latin. ● *verb* (**-cing**) exaggerate, fantasize; woo.

Romanesque /rəʊmə'nesk/ ● *noun* style of European architecture *c.* 900–1200, with massive vaulting and round arches. ● *adjective* of this style.

Romanian /rəʊ'meɪnɪən/ (also **Rumanian** /ru:-/) ● *noun* native, national, or language of Romania. ● *adjective* of Romania or its people or language.

romantic /rəʊ'mæntɪk/ ● *adjective* of, characterized by, or suggestive of romance; imaginative, visionary; (of literature or music etc.) concerned more with emotion than with form; (also **Romantic**) of the 18th–19th-c. romantic movement or style in European arts. ● *noun* romantic person; romanticist. ▫ **romantically** *adverb*.

romanticism /rəʊ'mæntɪsɪz(ə)m/ *noun* (also **Romanticism**) adherence to romantic style in literature, art, etc. ▫ **romanticist**, **Romanticist** *noun*.

romanticize /rəʊ'mæntɪsaɪz/ *verb* (also **-ise**) (**-zing** or **-sing**) make romantic; exaggerate; indulge in romance.

Romany /'rɒmənɪ/ ● *noun* (*plural* **-ies**) Gypsy; language of Gypsies. ● *adjective* of Gypsies or Romany language.

Romeo /'rəʊmɪəʊ/ *noun* (*plural* **-s**) passionate male lover or seducer.

romp ● *verb* play roughly and energetically; (+ *along*, *past*, etc.) *colloquial* proceed without effort. ● *noun* spell of romping. ▫ **romp in**, **home** *colloquial* win easily.

rompers *plural noun* (also **romper suit**) young child's one-piece garment.

rondeau /'rɒndəʊ/ *noun* (*plural* **-x** same pronunciation or /-z/) short poem with two rhymes only, and opening words used as refrains.

rondel /'rɒnd(ə)l/ *noun* rondeau.

rondo /'rɒndəʊ/ *noun* (*plural* **-s**) musical form with recurring leading theme.

röntgen = ROENTGEN.

rood /ru:d/ *noun* crucifix, esp. on rood-screen; quarter-acre. ▫ **rood-screen** carved screen separating nave and chancel.

roof /ru:f/ ● *noun* (*plural* **roofs** /ru:vz/) upper covering of building; top of covered vehicle etc.; top interior surface of oven, cave, mine, etc. ● *verb* (often + *in*, *over*) cover with roof; be roof of. ▫ **roof of the mouth** palate; **roof-rack** framework for luggage on top of vehicle; **rooftop** outer surface of roof, (in *plural*) tops of houses etc.

rook[1] /rʊk/ ● *noun* black bird of crow family nesting in colonies. ● *verb* *colloquial* charge (customer) extortionately; win money at cards etc., esp. by swindling.

rook[2] /rʊk/ *noun* chess piece with battlement-shaped top.

rookery *noun* (*plural* **-ies**) colony of rooks, penguins, or seals.

rookie /'rʊkɪ/ *noun slang* recruit.

room /ru:m/ ● *noun* space for, or occupied by, something; capacity; part of building enclosed by walls; (in *plural*) apartments or lodgings. ● *verb* *US* have room(s), lodge. ▫ **room service** provision of food etc. in hotel bedroom.

roomy *adjective* (**-ier**, **-iest**) having much room, spacious. ▫ **roominess** *noun*.

roost /ru:st/ ● *noun* bird's perch. ● *verb* (of bird) settle for rest or sleep.

rooster *noun* domestic cock.

root[1] /ru:t/ ● *noun* part of plant below ground conveying nourishment from soil; (in *plural*) fibres or branches of this; plant with edible root, such root; (in *plural*) emotional attachment or family ties in a place; embedded part of hair or tooth etc.; basic cause, source; *Mathematics* number which multiplied by itself a given number of times yields a given number, esp. square root; core of a word. ● *verb* (cause to) take root; (esp. as **rooted** *adjective*) fix or establish firmly; pull up by roots. ▫ **root out** find and get rid of; **rootstock** rhizome, plant into which graft is inserted, source from which offshoots have arisen; **take root** begin to draw nourishment from the soil, become established. ▫ **rootless** *adjective*.

root[2] /ru:t/ *verb* (often + *up*) turn up (ground) with snout etc. in search of food; (+ *around*, *in*, etc.) rummage; (+ *out*, *up*) extract by rummaging; (+ *for*) *US slang* encourage by applause or support.

rope ● *noun* stout cord made by twisting together strands of hemp or wire etc.; (+ *of*) string of onions, pearls etc.; (**the rope**) (halter for) execution by hanging. ● *verb* (**-ping**) fasten or catch with rope; (+ *off*, *in*) enclose with rope. ▫ **know**, **learn**, or **show the ropes** know, learn, show how to do a thing properly; **rope into** persuade to take part (in).

ropy *adjective* (also **ropey**) (**-ier**, **-iest**) *colloquial* poor in quality. ▫ **ropiness** *noun*.

Roquefort /'rɒkfɔ:/ *noun proprietary term* soft blue ewe's-milk cheese.

rorqual /'rɔ:kw(ə)l/ *noun* whale with dorsal fin.

rosaceous /rəʊ'zeɪʃəs/ *adjective* of plant family including the rose.

rosary /'rəʊzərɪ/ *noun* (*plural* **-ies**) *RC Church* repeated sequence of prayers; string of beads for keeping count in this.

rose[1] /rəʊz/ ● *noun* prickly shrub bearing fragrant red, pink, yellow, or white flowers; this flower; pinkish-red colour or (usually in *plural*) complexion; rose-shaped design; circular fitting on ceiling from which electric light hangs by cable; spray nozzle of watering-can etc.; (in *plural*) *used to express ease, luck, etc.* ● *adjective* rose-coloured. ▫ **rosebowl** bowl for cut roses, esp. given as prize; **rosebud** bud of rose, pretty girl; **rose-coloured** pinkish-red, cheerful, optimistic; **rose-hip** fruit of rose; **rose-water** perfume made from roses; **rose-window** circular window with roselike tracery; **rosewood** close-grained wood used in making furniture.

rose[2] *past* of RISE.

rosé /'rəʊzeɪ/ *noun* light pink wine. [French]

rosemary /'rəʊzmərɪ/ *noun* evergreen fragrant shrub used as herb.

rosette /rəʊ'zet/ *noun* rose-shaped ornament made of ribbons etc. or carved in stone etc.

rosin /'rɒzɪn/ ● *noun* resin, esp. in solid form. ● *verb* (**-n-**) rub with rosin.

RoSPA /'rɒspə/ *abbreviation* Royal Society for the Prevention of Accidents.

roster /'rɒstə/ ● *noun* list or plan of turns of duty etc. ● *verb* place on roster.

rostrum /'rɒstrəm/ *noun* (*plural* **rostra** or **-s**) platform for public speaking etc.

rosy /'rəʊzɪ/ *adjective* (**-ier**, **-iest**) pink, red; optimistic, hopeful.

rot ● *verb* (**-tt-**) undergo decay by putrefaction; perish, waste away; cause to rot, make rotten. ● *noun* decay, rottenness; *slang* nonsense; decline in standards etc. ● *interjection* *expressing incredulity or ridicule.* ▫ **rot-gut** *slang* cheap harmful alcohol.

rota /'rəʊtə/ *noun* list of duties to be done or people to do them in turn.

rotary /'rəʊtərɪ/ ● *adjective* acting by rotation. ● *noun* (*plural* **-ies**) rotary machine; (**Rotary**; in full **Rotary International**) worldwide charitable society of businessmen.

rotate /rəʊ'teɪt/ *verb* (**-ting**) move round axis or centre, revolve; arrange or take in rotation. ◻ **rotatory** /'rəʊtətərɪ/ *adjective*.

rotation *noun* rotating, being rotated; recurrent series or period; regular succession; growing of different crops in regular order. ◻ **rotational** *adjective*.

rote *noun* (usually in **by rote**) mechanical repetition (in order to memorize).

rotisserie /rəʊ'tɪsərɪ/ *noun* restaurant etc. where meat is roasted; revolving spit for roasting food.

rotor /'rəʊtə/ *noun* rotary part of machine; rotating aerofoil on helicopter.

rotten /'rɒt(ə)n/ *adjective* (**-er**, **-est**) rotting or rotted; fragile from age etc.; morally or politically corrupt; *slang* disagreeable, worthless. ◻ **rotten borough** *historical* (before 1832) English borough electing MP though having very few voters. ◻ **rottenness** *noun*.

rotter *noun slang* objectionable person.

Rottweiler /'rɒtvaɪlə/ *noun* black-and-tan dog noted for ferocity.

rotund /rəʊ'tʌnd/ *adjective* plump, podgy. ◻ **rotundity** *noun*.

rotunda /rəʊ'tʌndə/ *noun* circular building, esp. domed.

rouble /'ru:b(ə)l/ *noun* (also **ruble**) monetary unit of Russia etc.

roué /'ru:eɪ/ *noun* (esp. elderly) debauchee.

rouge /ru:ʒ/ ● *noun* red cosmetic used to colour cheeks. ● *verb* (**-ging**) colour with or apply rouge; blush.

rough /rʌf/ ● *adjective* having uneven surface, not smooth or level; shaggy; coarse, violent; not mild, quiet, or gentle; (of wine) harsh; insensitive; unpleasant, severe; lacking finish etc.; approximate, rudimentary. ● *adverb* in a rough way. ● *noun* (usually **the rough**) hardship; rough ground; hooligan; unfinished or natural state. ● *verb* make rough; (+ *out*, *in*) sketch or plan roughly. ◻ **rough-and-ready** rough or crude but effective, not over-particular; **rough-and-tumble** *adjective* irregular, disorderly, *noun* scuffle; **roughcast** *noun* plaster of lime and gravel, *verb* coat with this; **rough diamond** uncut diamond, rough but honest person; **rough house** *slang* disturbance, rough fight; **rough it** *colloquial* do without basic comforts; **rough justice** treatment that is approximately fair, unfair treatment; **roughneck** *colloquial* worker on oil rig, rough person; **rough up** *slang* attack violently. ◻ **roughen** *verb*; **roughly** *adverb*; **roughness** *noun*.

roughage *noun* fibrous material in food, stimulating intestinal action.

roughshod /'rʌfʃɒd/ ◻ **ride roughshod over** treat arrogantly.

roulade /ru:'la:d/ *noun* filled rolled piece of meat, sponge, etc.; quick succession of notes.

roulette /ru:'let/ *noun* gambling game with ball dropped on revolving numbered wheel.

round /raʊnd/ ● *adjective* shaped like circle, sphere, or cylinder; done with circular motion; (of number etc.) without odd units; entire, continuous, complete; candid; (of voice etc.) sonorous. ● *noun* round object; revolving motion, circular or recurring course, series; route for deliveries, inspection, etc.; drink etc. for each member of group; one bullet, shell, etc.; slice of bread, sandwich made from two slices, joint of beef from haunch; one period of play etc., one stage in competition, playing of all holes in golf course once; song for unaccompanied voices overlapping at intervals; rung of ladder; (+ *of*) circumference or extent of. ● *adverb* with circular motion, with return to starting point or change to opposite position; to, at, or affecting circumference, area, group, etc.; in every direction from a centre; measuring (specified distance) in girth. ● *preposition* so as to encircle or enclose; at or to points on circumference of; with successive visits to; within a radius of; having as central point; so as to pass in curved course, having thus passed. ● *verb* give or take round shape; pass round (corner etc.); (usually + *up*, *down*) express (number) approximately. ◻ **in the round** with all angles or features shown or considered, with audience all round theatre stage; **Roundhead** *historical* member of Parliamentary party in English Civil War; **round off** make complete or less angular; **round on** attack unexpectedly; **round out** provide with more details, finish; **round robin** petition with signatures in circle to conceal order of writing, tournament in which each competitor plays every other; **Round Table** international charitable association; **round table** assembly for discussion, esp. at conference; **round trip** trip to one or more places and back; **round up** gather or bring together; **round-up** rounding-up, summary.

roundabout ● *noun* road junction with traffic passing in one direction round central island; revolving device in children's playground; merry-go-round. ● *adjective* circuitous.

roundel /'raʊnd(ə)l/ *noun* circular mark; small disc, medallion.

roundelay /'raʊndɪleɪ/ *noun* short simple song with refrain.

rounders /'raʊndəz/ *noun* team game in which players hit ball and run through round of bases.

roundly *adverb* bluntly, severely.

rouse /raʊz/ *verb* (**-sing**) (cause to) wake; (often + *up*) make or become active or excited; anger; evoke (feelings). ◻ **rousing** *adjective*.

roustabout /'raʊstəbaʊt/ *noun* labourer on oil rig; unskilled or casual labourer.

rout /raʊt/ ● *noun* disorderly retreat of defeated troops; overthrow, defeat. ● *verb* put to flight, defeat.

route /ru:t/ ● *noun* way taken (esp. regularly) from one place to another. ● *verb* (**-teing**) send etc. by particular route. ◻ **route march** training-march for troops.

routine /ru:'ti:n/ ● *noun* regular course or procedure, unvarying performance of certain acts; set sequence in dance, comedy act, etc.; sequence of instructions to computer. ● *adjective* performed as routine; of customary or standard kind. ◻ **routinely** *adverb*.

roux /ru:/ *noun* (*plural* same) mixture of fat and flour used in sauces etc.

rove /rəʊv/ *verb* (**-ving**) wander without settling, roam; (of eyes) look about.

rover *noun* wanderer.

row[1] /rəʊ/ *noun* line of people or things; line of seats in theatre etc. ◻ **in a row** forming a row, *colloquial* in succession.

row[2] /rəʊ/ ● *verb* propel (boat) with oars; convey thus. ● *noun* spell of rowing; trip in rowing boat. ◻ **rowing boat** (*US* **row-boat**) small boat propelled by oars. ◻ **rower** *noun*.

row[3] /raʊ/ *colloquial* ● *noun* loud noise, commotion; quarrel, dispute; severe reprimand. ● *verb* make or engage in row; reprimand.

rowan /'rəʊən/ *noun* (in full **rowan tree**) mountain ash; (in full **rowan-berry**) its scarlet berry.

rowdy /'raʊdɪ/ ● *adjective* (**-ier**, **-iest**) noisy and disorderly. ● *noun* (*plural* **-ies**) rowdy person. ◻ **rowdily** *adverb*; **rowdiness** *noun*; **rowdyism** *noun*.

rowel /'raʊəl/ *noun* spiked revolving disc at end of spur.

rowlock /'rɒlək/ *noun* device for holding oar in place.

royal /'rɔɪəl/ ● *adjective* of, suited to, or worthy of king or queen; in service or under patronage of king or queen; of family of king or queen; splendid, on great scale. ● *noun colloquial* member of royal family. □ **royal blue** deep vivid blue; **Royal Commission** commission of inquiry appointed by Crown at request of government; **royal flush** straight poker flush headed by ace; **royal jelly** substance secreted by worker bees and fed to future queen bees; **Royal Navy** British navy; **royal 'we'** use of 'we' instead of 'I' by single person. □ **royally** *adverb*.

royalist *noun* supporter of monarchy, *esp. historical* of King's side in English Civil War.

royalty *noun* (*plural* **-ies**) being royal; royal people; member of royal family; percentage of profit from book, public performance, patent, etc. paid to author etc.; royal right (now esp. over minerals) granted by sovereign; payment made by producer of minerals etc. to owner of site etc.

RP *abbreviation* Received Pronunciation.

RPI *abbreviation* retail price index.

rpm *abbreviation* revolutions per minute.

RSA *abbreviation* Royal Society of Arts; Royal Scottish Academy; Royal Scottish Academician.

RSC *abbreviation* Royal Shakespeare Company.

RSM *abbreviation* Regimental Sergeant-Major.

RSPB *abbreviation* Royal Society for the Protection of Birds.

RSPCA *abbreviation* Royal Society for the Prevention of Cruelty to Animals.

RSV *abbreviation* Revised Standard Version (of Bible).

RSVP *abbreviation* please answer (*répondez s'il vous plaît*).

Rt. Hon. *abbreviation* Right Honourable.

Rt Revd *abbreviation* (also **Rt. Rev.**) Right Reverend.

rub ● *verb* (**-bb-**) move hand etc. firmly over surface of; (usually + *against, in, on, over*) apply (hand etc.) thus; polish, clean, abrade, chafe, or make dry, sore, or bare by rubbing; (+ *in, into, through, over*) apply by rubbing; (often + *together, against, on*) move with friction or slide (objects) against each other; get frayed or worn by friction. ● *noun* action or spell of rubbing; impediment or difficulty. □ **rub off** (usually + *on*) be transferred by contact, be transmitted; **rub out** erase with rubber; **rub up the wrong way** irritate.

rubato /ru:'bɑ:təʊ/ *noun Music* (*plural* **-s** or **-ti** /-tɪ/) temporary disregarding of strict tempo.

rubber[1] /'rʌbə/ *noun* elastic substance made from latex of plants or synthetically; piece of this or other substance for erasing pencil marks; (in *plural*) *US* galoshes. □ **rubber band** loop of rubber to hold papers etc.; **rubberneck** *colloquial* (be) inquisitive sightseer; **rubber plant** tropical plant often grown as house-plant, (also **rubber tree**) tree yielding latex; **rubber stamp** device for inking and imprinting on surface, (person giving) mechanical endorsement of actions etc.; **rubber-stamp** approve automatically. □ **rubberize** *verb* (also **-ise**) (**-zing** or **-sing**); **rubbery** *adjective*.

rubber[2] /'rʌbə/ *noun* series of games between same sides or people at whist, bridge, cricket, etc.

rubbish /'rʌbɪʃ/ ● *noun* waste or worthless matter; litter; trash; (often as *interjection*) nonsense. ● *verb colloquial* criticize contemptuously. □ **rubbishy** *adjective*.

rubble /'rʌb(ə)l/ *noun* rough fragments of stone, brick, etc.

rubella /ru:'belə/ *noun formal* German measles.

Rubicon /'ru:bɪkɒn/ *noun* point from which there is no going back.

rubicund /'ru:bɪkʌnd/ *adjective* ruddy, red-faced.

ruble = ROUBLE.

rubric /'ru:brɪk/ *noun* heading or passage in red or special lettering; explanatory words; established custom or rule; direction for conduct of divine service in liturgical book.

ruby /'ru:bɪ/ ● *noun* (*plural* **-ies**) crimson or rose-coloured precious stone; deep red colour. ● *adjective* ruby-coloured. □ **ruby wedding** 40th wedding anniversary.

RUC *abbreviation* Royal Ulster Constabulary.

ruche /ru:ʃ/ *noun* frill or gathering of lace etc. □ **ruched** *adjective*.

ruck[1] *noun* (**the ruck**) main group of competitors not likely to overtake leaders; undistinguished crowd of people or things; *Rugby* loose scrum.

ruck[2] ● *verb* (often + *up*) crease, wrinkle. ● *noun* crease, wrinkle.

rucksack /'rʌksæk/ *noun* bag carried on back, esp. by hikers.

ruckus /'rʌkəs/ *noun esp. US* row, commotion.

ruction /'rʌkʃ(ə)n/ *noun colloquial* disturbance, tumult; (in *plural*) row.

rudder /'rʌdə/ *noun* flat piece hinged to vessel's stern or rear of aeroplane for steering. □ **rudderless** *adjective*.

ruddy /'rʌdɪ/ *adjective* (**-ier, -iest**) freshly or healthily red; reddish; *colloquial* bloody, damnable.

rude *adjective* impolite, offensive; roughly made; primitive, uneducated; abrupt, sudden; *colloquial* indecent, lewd; vigorous, hearty. □ **rudely** *adverb*; **rudeness** *noun*.

rudiment /'ru:dɪmənt/ *noun* (in *plural*) elements or first principles of subject, imperfect beginning of something undeveloped; vestigial or undeveloped part or organ. □ **rudimentary** /-'mentərɪ/ *adjective*.

rue[1] *verb* (**rues, rued, rueing** or **ruing**) repent of; wish undone or non-existent.

rue[2] *noun* evergreen shrub with bitter strong-scented leaves.

rueful *adjective* genuinely or humorously sorrowful. □ **ruefully** *adverb*.

ruff[1] *noun* projecting starched frill worn round neck; projecting or coloured ring of feathers or hair round bird's or animal's neck; domestic pigeon.

ruff[2] ● *verb* trump at cards. ● *noun* trumping.

ruffian /'rʌfɪən/ *noun* violent lawless person.

ruffle /'rʌf(ə)l/ ● *verb* (**-ling**) disturb smoothness or tranquillity of; gather into ruffle; (often + *up*) (of bird) erect (feathers) in anger, display, etc. ● *noun* frill of lace etc.

rufous /'ru:fəs/ *adjective* reddish-brown.

rug *noun* floor-mat; thick woollen wrap or coverlet.

Rugby /'rʌgbɪ/ *noun* (in full **Rugby football**) team game played with oval ball that may be kicked or carried. □ **Rugby League** partly professional Rugby with teams of 13; **Rugby Union** amateur Rugby with teams of 15.

rugged /'rʌgɪd/ *adjective* (esp. of ground) rough, uneven; (of features) furrowed, irregular; harsh; robust. □ **ruggedly** *adverb*; **ruggedness** *noun*.

rugger /'rʌgə/ *noun colloquial* Rugby.

ruin /'ru:ɪn/ ● *noun* wrecked or spoiled state; downfall; loss of property or position; (in *singular* or *plural*) remains of building etc. that has suffered ruin; cause of ruin. ● *verb* bring to ruin; spoil, damage; (esp. as **ruined** *adjective*) reduce to ruins. □ **ruination** *noun*.

ruinous *adjective* bringing ruin; disastrous; dilapidated.

rule ● *noun* compulsory principle governing action; prevailing custom, standard, normal state of things; government, dominion; straight measuring device, ruler; code of discipline of religious order; *Printing* thin line or dash. ● *verb* (**-ling**) dominate; keep under control; (often + *over*) have sovereign control of;

(often + *that*) pronounce authoritatively; make parallel lines across (paper), make (straight line) with ruler etc. ▫ **as a rule** usually; **rule of thumb** rule based on experience or practice, not theory; **rule out** exclude.

ruler *noun* person exercising government or dominion; straight strip of plastic etc. used to draw or measure.

ruling *noun* authoritative pronouncement.

rum[1] *noun* spirit distilled from sugar cane or molasses. ▫ **rum baba** sponge cake soaked in rum syrup.

rum[2] *adjective* (**-mm-**) *colloquial* queer, strange.

Rumanian = ROMANIAN.

rumba /ˈrʌmbə/ *noun* ballroom dance of Cuban origin; music for this.

rumble /ˈrʌmb(ə)l/ ● *verb* (**-ling**) make continuous deep sound as of thunder; (+ *along, by, past,* etc.) (esp. of vehicle) move with such sound; *slang* see through, detect. ● *noun* rumbling sound.

rumbustious /rʌmˈbʌstʃəs/ *adjective colloquial* boisterous, uproarious.

ruminant /ˈru:mɪnənt/ ● *noun* animal that chews the cud. ● *adjective* of ruminants; meditative.

ruminate /ˈru:mɪneɪt/ *verb* (**-ting**) meditate, ponder; chew the cud. ▫ **rumination** *noun*; **ruminative** /-nətɪv/ *adjective*.

rummage /ˈrʌmɪdʒ/ ● *verb* (**-ging**) search, esp. unsystematically; (+ *up, out*) find among other things. ● *noun* rummaging. ▫ **rummage sale** *esp. US* jumble sale.

rummy /ˈrʌmɪ/ *noun* card game played usually with two packs.

rumour /ˈru:mə/ (*US* **rumor**) ● *noun* (often + *of, that*) general talk, assertion, or hearsay of doubtful accuracy. ● *verb* (usually in *passive*) report by way of rumour.

rump *noun* hind part of mammal or bird, esp. buttocks; remnant of parliament etc. ▫ **rump steak** cut of beef from rump.

rumple /ˈrʌmp(ə)l/ *verb* (**-ling**) crease, ruffle.

rumpus /ˈrʌmpəs/ *noun colloquial* row, uproar.

run ● *verb* (**-nn-**; *past* **ran**; *past participle* **run**) go at pace faster than walk; flee; go or travel hurriedly, briefly, etc.; advance smoothly or (as) by rolling or on wheels; (cause to) be in action or operation; be current or operative; (of bus, train, etc.) travel on its route; (of play etc.) be presented; extend, have course or tendency; compete in or enter (horse etc.) in race etc.; (often + *for*) seek election; (cause to) flow or emit liquid; spread rapidly; perform (errand); publish (article etc.); direct (business etc.); own and use (vehicle); smuggle; (of thought, the eye, etc.) pass quickly; (of tights etc.) ladder. ● *noun* running; short excursion; distance travelled; general tendency; regular route; continuous stretch, spell, or course; (often + *on*) high general demand; quantity produced at one time; general or average type or class; point scored in cricket or baseball; (+ *of*) free use of; animal's regular track; enclosure for fowls etc.; range of pasture; ladder in tights etc.; *Music* rapid scale passage. ▫ **give (person) the run-around** deceive, evade; **on the run** fleeing; **runabout** light car or aircraft; **run across** happen to meet; **run after** pursue; **run away** *verb* (often + *from*) flee, abscond; **runaway** *noun* person, animal, vehicle, etc. running away or out of control; **run down** *verb* knock down, reduce numbers of, (of clock etc.) stop, discover after search, *colloquial* disparage; **run-down** *noun* reduction in numbers, detailed analysis, *adjective* dilapidated, decayed, exhausted; **run dry** cease to flow; **run in** *verb* run (vehicle, engine) carefully when new, *colloquial* arrest; **run-in** *noun colloquial* quarrel; **run into** collide with, encounter, reach as many as; **run low, short** become depleted, have too little; **run off** flee, produce (copies) on machine, decide (race) after tie or heats, write or recite fluently; **run-of-the-mill** ordinary, not special; **run on** continue in operation, speak volubly, continue on same line as preceding matter; **run out** come to an end, (+ *of*) exhaust one's stock of, put down wicket of (running batsman); **run out on** *colloquial* desert; **run over** (of vehicle) knock down or crush, overflow, review quickly; **run through** *verb* examine or rehearse briefly, deal successively with, spend money rapidly, pervade, pierce with blade; **run-through** *noun* rehearsal; **run to** have money or ability for, reach (amount etc.), show tendency to; **run up** *verb* accumulate (debt etc.), build or make hurriedly, raise (flag); **run-up** *noun* (often + *to*) preparatory period; **run up against** meet with (difficulty etc.); **runway** specially prepared airfield surface for taking off and landing.

rune *noun* letter of earliest Germanic alphabet; similar character of mysterious or magic significance. ▫ **runic** *adjective*.

rung[1] *noun* step of ladder; strengthening crosspiece of chair etc.

rung[2] *past participle* of RING[2].

runnel /ˈrʌn(ə)l/ *noun* brook; gutter.

runner *noun* racer; creeping rooting plant-stem; groove, rod, etc. for thing to slide along or on; sliding ring on rod etc.; messenger; long narrow ornamental cloth or rug; (in full **runner bean**) kind of climbing bean. ▫ **runner-up** (*plural* **runners-up** or **runner-ups**) competitor taking second place.

running ● *noun* act or manner of running race etc. ● *adjective* continuous; consecutive; done with a run. ▫ **in** or **out of the running** with good or poor chance of success; **running commentary** verbal description of events in progress; **running knot** one that slips along rope etc. to allow tightening; **running mate** *US* vice-presidential candidate, horse setting pace for another; **running repairs** minor or temporary repairs; **running water** flowing water, esp. on tap.

runny *adjective* (**-ier**, **-iest**) tending to run or flow; excessively fluid.

runt *noun* smallest pig etc. of litter; undersized person.

rupee /ru:ˈpi:/ *noun* monetary unit of India, Pakistan, etc.

rupiah /ru:ˈpi:ə/ *noun* monetary unit of Indonesia.

rupture /ˈrʌptʃə/ ● *noun* breaking, breach; breach in relationship; abdominal hernia. ● *verb* (**-ring**) burst (cell, membrane, etc.); sever (connection); affect with or suffer hernia.

rural /ˈrʊər(ə)l/ *adjective* in, of, or suggesting country.

ruse /ru:z/ *noun* stratagem, trick.

rush[1] ● *verb* go, move, flow, or act precipitately or with great speed; move or transport with great haste; perform or deal with hurriedly; force (person) to act hastily; attack or capture by sudden assault. ● *noun* rushing; violent advance or attack; sudden flow; period of great activity; sudden migration of large numbers; (+ *on, for*) strong demand for a commodity; (in *plural*) *colloquial* first uncut prints of film. ● *adjective* done hastily. ▫ **rush hour** time each day when traffic is heaviest.

rush[2] *noun* marsh plant with slender pith-filled stem; its stem esp. used for making basketware etc.

rusk *noun* slice of bread rebaked as light biscuit, esp. for infants.

russet /ˈrʌsɪt/ ● *adjective* reddish-brown. ● *noun* russet colour; rough-skinned russet-coloured apple.

Russian /ˈrʌʃ(ə)n/ ● *noun* native or national of Russia or (loosely) former USSR; person of Russian descent; language of Russia. ● *adjective* of Russia or (loosely) former USSR or its people; of or in Russian.

□ **Russian roulette** firing of revolver held to one's head after spinning cylinder with one chamber loaded; **Russian salad** mixed diced cooked vegetables with mayonnaise.

rust ● *noun* reddish corrosive coating formed on iron etc. by oxidation; plant disease with rust-coloured spots; reddish-brown. ● *verb* affect or be affected with rust; become impaired through disuse. □ **rustproof** not susceptible to corrosion by rust.

rustic /ˈrʌstɪk/ ● *adjective* of or like country people or country life; unsophisticated; of rough workmanship; made of untrimmed branches or rough timber; *Architecture* with roughened surface. ● *noun* country person, peasant. □ **rusticity** /-ˈtɪs-/ *noun*.

rusticate /ˈrʌstɪkeɪt/ *verb* (**-ting**) expel temporarily from university; retire to or live in the country; make rustic. □ **rustication** *noun*.

rustle /ˈrʌs(ə)l/ ● *verb* (**-ling**) (cause to) make sound as of dry blown leaves; steal (cattle or horses). ● *noun* rustling sound. □ **rustle up** *colloquial* produce at short notice. □ **rustler** *noun*.

rusty *adjective* (**-ier**, **-iest**) rusted, affected by rust; stiff with age or disuse; (of knowledge etc.) impaired by neglect; rust-coloured; discoloured by age.

rut[1] ● *noun* deep track made by passage of wheels; fixed (esp. tedious) practice or routine. ● *verb* (**-tt-**) (esp. as **rutted** *adjective*) mark with ruts.

rut[2] ● *noun* periodic sexual excitement of male deer etc. ● *verb* (**-tt-**) be affected with rut.

ruthless /ˈru:θlɪs/ *adjective* having no pity or compassion. □ **ruthlessly** *adverb*; **ruthlessness** *noun*.

RV *abbreviation* Revised Version (of Bible).

rye /raɪ/ *noun* cereal plant; grain of this, used for bread, fodder, etc.; (in full **rye whisky**) whisky distilled from rye.

Ss

S *abbreviation* (also **S.**) Saint; south(ern).

s. *abbreviation* second(s); *historical* shilling(s); son.

SA *abbreviation* Salvation Army; South Africa; South Australia.

sabbath /'sæbəθ/ *noun* religious rest-day kept by Christians on Sunday and Jews on Saturday.

sabbatical /sə'bætɪk(ə)l/ ● *adjective* (of leave) granted at intervals to university teacher for study or travel. ● *noun* period of sabbatical leave.

saber *US* = SABRE.

sable /'seɪb(ə)l/ ● *noun* (*plural* same or **-s**) small dark-furred mammal; its skin or fur. ● *adjective Heraldry* black; *esp. poetical* gloomy.

sabot /'sæbəʊ/ *noun* wooden or wooden-soled shoe.

sabotage /'sæbətɑːʒ/ ● *noun* deliberate destruction or damage, esp. for political purpose. ● *verb* (**-ging**) commit sabotage on; destroy, spoil.

saboteur /sæbə'tɜː/ *noun* person who commits sabotage.

sabre /'seɪbə/ *noun* (*US* **saber**) curved cavalry sword; light fencing-sword. □ **sabre-rattling** display or threat of military force.

sac *noun* membranous bag in animal or plant.

saccharin /'sækərɪn/ *noun* a sugar substitute.

saccharine /'sækəriːn/ *adjective* excessively sentimental or sweet.

sacerdotal /sækə'dəʊt(ə)l/ *adjective* of priests or priestly office.

sachet /'sæʃeɪ/ *noun* small bag or packet containing shampoo, perfumed substances, etc.

sack[1] ● *noun* large strong bag for coal, food, mail, etc.; amount held by sack; (**the sack**) *colloquial* dismissal, *US slang* bed. ● *verb* put in sack(s); *colloquial* dismiss from employment. □ **sackcloth** coarse fabric of flax or hemp.

sack[2] ● *verb* plunder and destroy (town etc.). ● *noun* such sacking.

sack[3] *noun historical* white wine from Spain etc.

sackbut /'sækbʌt/ *noun* early form of trombone.

sacking *noun* sackcloth.

sacral /'seɪkr(ə)l/ *adjective* of sacrum.

sacrament /'sækrəmənt/ *noun* symbolic Christian ceremony, esp. Eucharist; sacred thing. □ **sacramental** /-'men-/ *adjective*.

sacred /'seɪkrɪd/ *adjective* (often + *to*) dedicated to a god, connected with religion; safeguarded or required, esp. by tradition; inviolable. □ **sacred cow** *colloquial* idea or institution unreasonably held to be above criticism.

sacrifice /'sækrɪfaɪs/ ● *noun* voluntary relinquishing of something valued; thing thus relinquished; loss entailed; slaughter of animal or person, or surrender of possession, as offering to deity; animal, person, or thing thus offered. ● *verb* (**-cing**) give up; (+ *to*) devote to; offer or kill (as) sacrifice. □ **sacrificial** /-'fɪʃ-/ *adjective*.

sacrilege /'sækrɪlɪdʒ/ *noun* violation of what is sacred. □ **sacrilegious** /-'lɪdʒəs/ *adjective*.

sacristan /'sækrɪst(ə)n/ *noun* person in charge of sacristy and church contents.

sacristy /'sækrɪstɪ/ *noun* (*plural* **-ies**) room in church for vestments, vessels, etc.

sacrosanct /'sækrəʊsæŋkt/ *adjective* most sacred; inviolable. □ **sacrosanctity** /-'sæŋkt-/ *noun*.

sacrum /'seɪkrəm/ *noun* (*plural* **sacra** or **-s**) triangular bone between hip-bones.

sad *adjective* (**-dd-**) sorrowful; causing sorrow; regrettable; deplorable. □ **sadden** *verb*; **sadly** *adverb*; **sadness** *noun*.

saddle /'sæd(ə)l/ ● *noun* seat of leather etc. fastened on horse etc.; bicycle etc. seat; joint of meat consisting of the two loins; ridge rising to a summit at each end. ● *verb* (**-ling**) put saddle on (horse etc.); (+ *with*) burden with task etc. □ **saddle-bag** each of pair of bags laid across back of horse etc., bag attached behind bicycle etc. saddle.

saddler *noun* maker of or dealer in saddles etc. □ **saddlery** *noun* (*plural* **-ies**).

sadism /'seɪdɪz(ə)m/ *noun colloquial* enjoyment of cruelty to others; sexual perversion characterized by this. □ **sadist** *noun*; **sadistic** /sə'dɪs-/ *adjective*; **sadistically** /sə'dɪs-/ *adverb*.

sadomasochism /seɪdəʊ'mæsəkɪz (ə)m/ *noun* sadism and masochism in one person. □ **sadomasochist** *noun*; **sadomasochistic** /-'kɪs-/ *adjective*.

s.a.e. *abbreviation* stamped addressed envelope.

safari /sə'fɑːrɪ/ *noun* (*plural* **-s**) expedition, esp. in Africa, to observe or hunt animals. □ **safari park** area where wild animals are kept in open for viewing.

safe ● *adjective* free of danger or injury; secure, not risky; reliable, sure; prevented from escaping or doing harm; cautious. ● *noun* strong lockable cupboard for valuables; ventilated cupboard for provisions. □ **safe conduct** immunity from arrest or harm; **safe deposit** building containing strongrooms and safes for hire. □ **safely** *adverb*.

safeguard ● *noun* protecting proviso, circumstance, etc. ● *verb* guard or protect (rights etc.).

safety /'seɪftɪ/ *noun* being safe; freedom from danger. □ **safety-belt** belt or strap preventing injury, esp. seat-belt; **safety-catch** device preventing accidental operation of gun trigger or machinery; **safety curtain** fireproof curtain to divide theatre auditorium from stage; **safety match** match that ignites only on specially prepared surface; **safety net** net placed to catch acrobat etc. in case of fall; **safety pin** pin with guarded point; **safety razor** razor with guard to prevent user cutting skin; **safety-valve** valve relieving excessive pressure of steam, means of harmlessly venting excitement etc.

saffron /'sæfrən/ ● *noun* deep yellow colouring and flavouring from dried crocus stigmas; colour of this. ● *adjective* deep yellow.

sag ● *verb* (**-gg-**) sink or subside; have downward bulge or curve in middle. ● *noun* state or amount of sagging. □ **saggy** *adjective*.

saga /'sɑːgə/ *noun* long heroic story, esp. medieval Icelandic or Norwegian; long family chronicle; long involved story.

sagacious /sə'geɪʃ(ə)s/ *adjective* showing insight or good judgement. □ **sagacity** /-'gæs-/ *noun*.

sage[1] *noun* aromatic herb with dull greyish-green leaves.

sage[2] ● *noun* wise man. ● *adjective* wise, judicious, experienced. □ **sagely** *adverb*.

Sagittarius /sædʒɪ'teərɪəs/ *noun* ninth sign of zodiac.

sago /'seɪgəʊ/ *noun* (*plural* **-s**) starch used in puddings etc.; (in full **sago palm**) any of several tropical trees yielding this.

sahib /sɑ:b/ *noun historical form of address to European men in India.*

said *past & past participle* of SAY.

sail ● *noun* piece of material extended on rigging to catch wind and propel vessel; ship's sails collectively; voyage or excursion in sailing vessel; wind-catching apparatus of windmill. ● *verb* travel on water by use of sails or engine-power; begin voyage; navigate (ship etc.); travel on (sea); glide or move smoothly or with dignity; (often + *through*) *colloquial* succeed easily. ▫ **sailboard** board with mast and sail, used in windsurfing; **sailcloth** material for sails, kind of coarse linen; **sailing boat**, **ship**, etc., vessel moved by sails; **sailplane** kind of glider.

sailor *noun* seaman or mariner, esp. below officer's rank. ▫ **bad**, **good sailor** person very liable or not liable to seasickness.

sainfoin /'sænfɔɪn/ *noun* pink-flowered plant used as fodder.

saint /seɪnt, before a name usually sənt/ ● *noun* holy or canonized person, regarded as deserving special veneration; very virtuous person. ● *verb* (as **sainted** *adjective*) holy, virtuous. ▫ **sainthood** *noun*; **saintlike** *adjective*; **saintliness** *noun*; **saintly** (**-ier**, **-iest**) *adjective*.

sake[1] *noun* ▫ **for the sake of** out of consideration for, in the interest of, in order to please, get, etc.

sake[2] /'sɑ:kɪ/ *noun* Japanese rice wine.

salaam /sə'lɑ:m/ ● *noun* (*chiefly as Muslim greeting*) Peace!; low bow. ● *verb* make salaam.

salacious /sə'leɪʃəs/ *adjective* erotic; lecherous. ▫ **salaciousness** *noun*; **salacity** /-'læs-/ *noun*.

salad /'sæləd/ *noun* cold mixture of usually raw vegetables etc. often with dressing. ▫ **salad cream** creamy salad dressing; **salad days** period of youthful inexperience; **salad dressing** sauce of oil, vinegar, etc. for salads.

salamander /'sæləmændə/ *noun* newtlike amphibian formerly supposed to live in fire; similar mythical creature.

salami /sə'lɑ:mɪ/ *noun* (*plural* **-s**) highly-seasoned sausage, originally Italian.

sal ammoniac /sæl ə'məʊnɪæk/ *noun* ammonium chloride.

salary /'sælərɪ/ ● *noun* (*plural* **-ies**) fixed regular payment by employer to employee. ● *verb* (**-ies**, **-ied**) (usually as **salaried** *adjective*) pay salary to.

sale *noun* exchange of commodity for money etc.; act or instance of selling; amount sold; temporary offering of goods at reduced prices; event at which goods are sold. ▫ **on**, **for sale** offered for purchase; **saleroom** room where auctions are held; **salesman**, **salesperson**, **saleswoman** person employed to sell goods etc.

saleable *adjective* fit or likely to be sold. ▫ **saleability** *noun*.

salesmanship *noun* skill in selling.

salient /'seɪlɪənt/ ● *adjective* prominent, conspicuous; (of angle) pointing outwards. ● *noun* salient angle; outward bulge in military line.

saline /'seɪlaɪn/ ● *adjective* containing or tasting of salt(s); of salt(s). ● *noun* salt lake, spring, etc.; saline solution. ▫ **salinity** /sə'lɪn-/ *noun*.

saliva /sə'laɪvə/ *noun* colourless liquid produced by glands in mouth. ▫ **salivary** *adjective*.

salivate /'sælɪveɪt/ *verb* (**-ting**) secrete saliva, esp. in excess.

sallow[1] /'sæləʊ/ *adjective* (**-er**, **-est**) (esp. of complexion) yellowish.

sallow[2] /'sæləʊ/ *noun* low-growing willow; shoot or wood of this.

sally /'sælɪ/ ● *noun* (*plural* **-ies**) witticism; military rush; excursion. ● *verb* (**-ies**, **-ied**) (usually + *out*, *forth*) set out for walk etc., make sally.

salmon /'sæmən/ ● *noun* (*plural* same) large silver-scaled fish with orange-pink flesh. ● *adjective* orange-pink. ▫ **salmon-pink** orange-pink; **salmon trout** large silver-coloured trout.

salmonella /sælmə'nelə/ *noun* (*plural* **-llae** /-li:/) bacterium causing food poisoning; such food poisoning.

salon /'sælɒn/ *noun* room or establishment of hairdresser, fashion designer, etc.; *historical* meeting of eminent people at fashionable home; reception room of large house.

saloon /sə'lu:n/ *noun* large room or hall on ship, in hotel, etc., or for specified purpose; saloon car; *US* drinking bar; saloon bar. ▫ **saloon bar** more comfortable bar in public house; **saloon car** car with body closed off from luggage area.

salsa /'sælsə/ *noun* dance music of Cuban origin; kind of spicy tomato sauce.

salsify /'sælsɪfɪ/ *noun* (*plural* **-ies**) plant with long fleshy edible root.

salt /sɔ:lt/ ● *noun* (also **common salt**) sodium chloride, esp. mined or evaporated from sea water, and used esp. for seasoning or preserving food; *Chemistry* substance formed in reaction of an acid with a base; piquancy, wit; (in *singular* or *plural*) substance resembling salt in taste, form, etc.; (esp. in *plural*) substance used as laxative; (also **old salt**) experienced sailor. ● *adjective* containing, tasting of, or preserved with salt. ● *verb* cure, preserve, or season with salt; sprinkle salt on (road etc.). ▫ **salt away**, **down** *slang* put (money etc.) by; **salt-cellar** container for salt at table; **salt-mine** mine yielding rock salt; **salt of the earth** finest or most honest people; **salt-pan** vessel, or hollow near sea, used for getting salt by evaporation; **salt-water** of or living in sea; **take with a pinch** or **grain of salt** be sceptical about; **worth one's salt** efficient, capable.

salting *noun* (esp. in *plural*) marsh overflowed by sea.

saltire /'sɔ:ltaɪə/ *noun* X-shaped cross.

saltpetre /sɔ:lt'pi:tə/ *noun* (*US* **saltpeter**) white crystalline salty substance used in preserving meat and in gunpowder.

salty *adjective* (**-ier**, **-iest**) tasting of or containing salt; witty, piquant. ▫ **saltiness** *noun*.

salubrious /sə'lu:brɪəs/ *adjective* health-giving. ▫ **salubrity** *noun*.

saluki /sə'lu:kɪ/ *noun* (*plural* **-s**) dog of tall slender silky-coated breed.

salutary /'sæljʊtərɪ/ *adjective* producing good effect.

salutation /sælju:'teɪʃ(ə)n/ *noun formal* sign or expression of greeting.

salute /sə'lu:t/ ● *noun* gesture of respect, homage, greeting, etc.; *Military etc.* prescribed gesture or use of weapons or flags as sign of respect etc. ● *verb* (**-ting**) make salute (to); greet; commend.

salvage /'sælvɪdʒ/ ● *noun* rescue of property from sea, fire, etc.; saving and utilization of waste materials; property or materials salvaged. ● *verb* (**-ging**) save from wreck etc. ▫ **salvageable** *adjective*.

salvation /sæl'veɪʃ(ə)n/ *noun* saving, being saved; deliverance from sin and damnation; religious conversion; person or thing that saves. ▫ **Salvation Army** worldwide quasi-military Christian charitable organization.

Salvationist *noun* member of Salvation Army.

salve[1] ● *noun* healing ointment; (often + *for*) thing that soothes. ● *verb* (**-ving**) soothe.

salve[2] *verb* (**-ving**) save from wreck, fire, etc. ▫ **salvable** *adjective*.

salver /'sælvə/ *noun* tray for drinks, letters, etc.

salvo /'sælvəʊ/ *noun* (*plural* **-es** or **-s**) simultaneous firing of guns etc.; round of applause.

sal volatile /sæl və'lætɪlɪ/ *noun* solution of ammonium carbonate, used as smelling salts.

SAM *abbreviation* surface-to-air missile.

Samaritan /sə'mærɪt(ə)n/ *noun* (in full **good Samaritan**) charitable or helpful person; member of counselling organization.

samba /'sæmbə/ ● *noun* ballroom dance of Brazilian origin; music for this. ● *verb* (**-bas**, **-baed** or **-ba'd** /-bəd/, **-baing** /-bəɪŋ/) dance samba.

same ● *adjective* identical; unvarying; just mentioned. ● *pronoun* (**the same**) the same person or thing. ● *adverb* (**the same**) in the same manner. □ **all** or **just the same** nevertheless; **at the same time** simultaneously, notwithstanding. □ **sameness** *noun*.

samosa /sə'məʊsə/ *noun* Indian fried triangular pastry containing spiced vegetables or meat.

samovar /'sæməvɑː/ *noun* Russian tea-urn.

Samoyed /'sæməjed/ *noun* member of a northern Siberian people; (also **samoyed**) dog of white Arctic breed.

sampan /'sæmpæn/ *noun* small boat used in Far East.

samphire /'sæmfaɪə/ *noun* cliff plant used in pickles.

sample /'sɑːmp(ə)l/ ● *noun* small representative part or quantity; specimen; typical example. ● *verb* (**-ling**) take samples of; try qualities of; experience briefly.

sampler /'sɑːmplə/ *noun* piece of embroidery worked to show proficiency.

samurai /'sæmʊraɪ/ *noun* (*plural* same) Japanese army officer; *historical* member of Japanese military caste.

sanatorium /sænə'tɔːrɪəm/ *noun* (*plural* **-riums** or **-ria**) residential clinic, esp. for convalescents and the chronically sick; accommodation for sick people in school etc.

sanctify /'sæŋktɪfaɪ/ *verb* (**-ies**, **-ied**) consecrate, treat as holy; purify from sin; sanction. □ **sanctification** *noun*.

sanctimonious /sæŋktɪ'məʊnɪəs/ *adjective* ostentatiously pious. □ **sanctimoniously** *adverb*; **sanctimony** /'sæŋktɪmənɪ/ *noun*.

sanction /'sæŋkʃ(ə)n/ ● *noun* approval by custom or tradition; express permission; confirmation of law etc.; penalty or reward attached to law; moral impetus for obedience to rule; (esp. in *plural*) (esp. economic) action to coerce state to conform to agreement etc. ● *verb* authorize, countenance; make (law etc.) binding.

sanctity /'sæŋktɪtɪ/ *noun* holiness, sacredness; inviolability.

sanctuary /'sæŋktʃʊərɪ/ *noun* (*plural* **-ies**) holy place; place where birds, wild animals, etc. are protected; place of refuge.

sanctum /'sæŋktəm/ *noun* (*plural* **-s**) holy place, esp. in temple or church; *colloquial* person's den.

sand ● *noun* fine grains resulting from erosion of esp. siliceous rocks; (in *plural*) grains of sand, expanse of sand, sandbank. ● *verb* smooth or treat with sandpaper or sand. □ **sandbag** *noun* bag filled with sand, esp. for making temporary defences, *verb* defend or hit with sandbag(s); **sandbank** sand forming shallow place in sea or river; **sandblast** *verb* treat with jet of sand driven by compressed air or steam, *noun* this jet; **sandcastle** model castle of sand on beach; **sand-dune**, **-hill** dune; **sand-martin** bird nesting in sandy banks; **sandpaper** *noun* paper with abrasive coating for smoothing or polishing wood etc., *verb* treat with this; **sandpiper** bird inhabiting wet sandy places; **sandpit** hollow or box containing sand for children to play in; **sandstone** sedimentary rock of compressed sand; **sandstorm** storm with clouds of sand raised by wind.

sandal /'sænd(ə)l/ *noun* shoe with openwork upper or no upper, fastened with straps.

sandal-tree /'sændəltriː/ *noun* tree yielding sandalwood.

sandalwood /'sændəlwʊd/ *noun* scented wood of sandal-tree.

sandwich /'sænwɪdʒ/ ● *noun* two or more slices of bread with filling; layered cake with jam, cream, etc. ● *verb* put (thing, statement, etc.) between two of different kind; squeeze in between others. □ **sandwich-board** each of two advertising boards worn front and back; **sandwich course** course with alternate periods of study and work experience.

sandy *adjective* (**-ier**, **-iest**) containing or covered with sand; (of hair) reddish; sand-coloured.

sane *adjective* of sound mind, not mad; (of opinion etc.) moderate, sensible.

sang *past* of SING.

sang-froid /sɑ̃'frwɑː/ *noun* calmness in danger or difficulty.

sangria /sæŋ'griːə/ *noun* Spanish drink of red wine with fruit etc.

sanguinary /'sæŋgwɪnərɪ/ *adjective* bloody; bloodthirsty.

sanguine /'sæŋgwɪn/ *adjective* optimistic; (of complexion) florid, ruddy.

Sanhedrin /'sænɪdrɪn/ *noun* court of justice and supreme council in ancient Jerusalem.

sanitarium /sænɪ'teərɪəm/ *noun* (*plural* **-s** or **-ria**) *US* sanatorium.

sanitary /'sænɪtərɪ/ *adjective* (of conditions etc.) affecting health; hygienic. □ **sanitary towel** (*US* **sanitary napkin**) absorbent pad used during menstruation. □ **sanitariness** *noun*.

sanitation /sænɪ'teɪʃ(ə)n/ *noun* sanitary conditions; maintenance etc. of these; disposal of sewage, refuse, etc.

sanitize /'sænɪtaɪz/ *verb* (also **-ise**) (**-zing** or **-sing**) make sanitary, disinfect; *colloquial* censor.

sanity /'sænɪtɪ/ *noun* being sane; moderation.

sank *past* of SINK.

Sanskrit /'sænskrɪt/ ● *noun* ancient and sacred language of Hindus in India. ● *adjective* of or in Sanskrit.

Santa Claus /'sæntə klɔːz/ *noun* person said to bring children presents at Christmas.

sap[1] ● *noun* vital juice of plants; vitality; *slang* foolish person. ● *verb* (**-pp-**) drain of sap; weaken. □ **sappy** *adjective* (**-ier**, **-iest**).

sap[2] ● *noun* tunnel or trench for concealed approach to enemy. ● *verb* (**-pp-**) dig saps; undermine.

sapient /'seɪpɪənt/ *adjective literary* wise; aping wisdom. □ **sapience** *noun*.

sapling /'sæplɪŋ/ *noun* young tree.

sapper *noun* digger of saps; private of Royal Engineers.

sapphire /'sæfaɪə/ ● *noun* transparent blue precious stone; its colour. ● *adjective* (also **sapphire blue**) bright blue.

saprophyte /'sæprəfaɪt/ *noun* plant or micro-organism living on dead organic matter.

saraband /'særəbænd/ *noun* slow Spanish dance; music for this.

Saracen /'særəs(ə)n/ *noun* Arab or Muslim of time of Crusades.

sarcasm /'sɑːkæz(ə)m/ *noun* ironically scornful remark(s). □ **sarcastic** /sɑː'kæstɪk/ *adjective*; **sarcastically** /sɑː'kæstɪkəlɪ/ *adverb*.

sarcophagus /sɑː'kɒfəgəs/ *noun* (*plural* **-gi** /-gaɪ/) stone coffin.

sardine /sɑː'diːn/ *noun* (*plural* same or **-s**) young pilchard etc. tinned tightly packed.

sardonic /sɑːˈdɒnɪk/ *adjective* bitterly mocking; cynical. □ **sardonically** *adverb.*

sardonyx /ˈsɑːdənɪks/ *noun* onyx in which white layers alternate with yellow or orange ones.

sargasso /sɑːˈɡæsəʊ/ *noun* (*plural* **-s** or **-es**) seaweed with berry-like airvessels.

sarge *noun slang* sergeant.

sari /ˈsɑːrɪ/ *noun* (*plural* **-s**) length of material draped round body, worn traditionally by Hindu etc. women.

sarky /ˈsɑːkɪ/ *adjective* (**-ier**, **-iest**) *slang* sarcastic.

sarong /səˈrɒŋ/ *noun* garment of long strip of cloth tucked round waist or under armpits.

sarsaparilla /sɑːsəpəˈrɪlə/ *noun* dried roots of esp. smilax used to flavour drinks and medicines and formerly as tonic; plant yielding these.

sarsen /ˈsɑːs(ə)n/ *noun* sandstone boulder carried by ice in glacial period.

sarsenet /ˈsɑːsnɪt/ *noun* soft silk fabric used esp. for linings.

sartorial /sɑːˈtɔːrɪəl/ *adjective* of men's clothes or tailoring. □ **sartorially** *adverb.*

SAS *abbreviation* Special Air Service.

sash[1] *noun* strip or loop of cloth worn over one shoulder or round waist.

sash[2] *noun* frame holding glass in window sliding up and down in grooves.

sass *US colloquial* ● *noun* impudence. ● *verb* be impudent to. □ **sassy** *adjective* (**-ier**, **-iest**).

sassafras /ˈsæsəfræs/ *noun* small N. American tree; medicinal preparation from its leaves or bark.

Sassenach /ˈsæsənæk/ *noun Scottish usually derogatory* English person.

Sat. *abbreviation* Saturday.

sat *past & past participle of* SIT.

Satan /ˈseɪt(ə)n/ *noun* the Devil.

satanic /səˈtænɪk/ *adjective* of or like Satan; hellish, evil.

Satanism *noun* worship of Satan. □ **Satanist** *noun.*

satchel /ˈsætʃ(ə)l/ *noun* small bag, esp. for carrying school-books.

sate *verb* (**-ting**) *formal* gratify fully, surfeit.

sateen /sæˈtiːn/ *noun* glossy cotton fabric like satin.

satellite /ˈsætəlaɪt/ ● *noun* heavenly or artificial body orbiting earth or other planet; (in full **satellite state**) small country controlled by another. ● *adjective* transmitted by satellite; receiving signal from satellite.

satiate /ˈseɪʃɪeɪt/ *verb* (**-ting**) sate. □ **satiation** *noun.*

satiety /səˈtaɪɪtɪ/ *noun formal* being sated.

satin /ˈsætɪn/ ● *noun* silk etc. fabric glossy on one side. ● *adjective* smooth as satin. □ **satinwood** kind of yellow glossy timber. □ **satiny** *adjective.*

satire /ˈsætaɪə/ *noun* ridicule, irony, etc. used to expose folly, vice, etc.; literary work using satire. □ **satirical** /səˈtɪrɪk(ə)l/ *adjective*; **satirically** /səˈtɪrɪkəlɪ/ *adverb.*

satirist /ˈsætərɪst/ *noun* writer of satires; satirical person.

satirize /ˈsætəraɪz/ *verb* (also **-ise**) (**-zing** or **-sing**) attack or describe with satire.

satisfaction /sætɪsˈfækʃ(ə)n/ *noun* satisfying, being satisfied; thing that satisfies; atonement; compensation.

satisfactory /sætɪsˈfæktərɪ/ *adjective* adequate; causing satisfaction. □ **satisfactorily** *adverb.*

satisfy /ˈsætɪsfaɪ/ *verb* (**-ies**, **-ied**) meet expectations or wishes of; be adequate; meet (an appetite or want); rid (person) of an appetite or want; pay; fulfil, comply with; convince.

satsuma /sætˈsuːmə/ *noun* kind of tangerine.

saturate /ˈsætʃəreɪt/ *verb* (**-ting**) fill with moisture; fill to capacity; cause (substance) to absorb, hold, etc. as much as possible of another substance; supply (market) beyond demand; (as **saturated** *adjective*) (of fat) containing the most possible hydrogen atoms.

saturation *noun* saturating, being saturated. □ **saturation point** stage beyond which no more can be absorbed or accepted.

Saturday /ˈsætədeɪ/ *noun* day of week following Friday.

Saturnalia /sætəˈneɪlɪə/ *noun* (*plural* same or **-s**) ancient Roman festival of Saturn; (**saturnalia**) (treated as *singular* or *plural*) scene of wild revelry.

saturnine /ˈsætənaɪn/ *adjective* of gloomy temperament or appearance.

satyr /ˈsætə/ *noun Greek & Roman Mythology* part-human part-animal woodland deity; lecherous man.

sauce /sɔːs/ ● *noun* liquid or viscous accompaniment to food; something that adds piquancy; *colloquial* impudence. ● *verb* (**-cing**) *colloquial* be impudent to. □ **sauce-boat** jug or dish for serving sauce; **saucepan** cooking vessel usually with handle, used on hob.

saucer /ˈsɔːsə/ *noun* shallow circular dish, esp. for standing cup on.

saucy *adjective* (**-ier**, **-iest**) impudent, cheeky. □ **saucily** *adverb*; **sauciness** *noun.*

sauerkraut /ˈsaʊəkraʊt/ *noun* German dish of pickled cabbage.

sauna /ˈsɔːnə/ *noun* period spent in room with steam bath; this room.

saunter /ˈsɔːntə/ ● *verb* stroll. ● *noun* leisurely walk.

saurian /ˈsɔːrɪən/ *adjective* of or like a lizard.

sausage /ˈsɒsɪdʒ/ *noun* seasoned minced meat etc. in edible cylindrical case; sausage-shaped object. □ **sausage meat** minced meat for sausages etc.; **sausage roll** sausage meat in pastry cylinder.

sauté /ˈsəʊteɪ/ ● *adjective* fried quickly in a little fat. ● *noun* food cooked thus. ● *verb* (*past & past participle* **sautéd** or **sautéed**) cook thus.

savage /ˈsævɪdʒ/ ● *adjective* fierce, cruel; wild, primitive. ● *noun derogatory* member of primitive tribe; brutal or barbarous person. ● *verb* (**-ging**) attack and maul; attack verbally. □ **savagely** *adverb*; **savagery** *noun* (*plural* **-ies**).

savannah /səˈvænə/ *noun* (also **savanna**) grassy plain in tropical or subtropical region.

savant /ˈsæv(ə)nt/ *noun* (*feminine* **savante** same pronunciation) learned person.

save[1] ● *verb* (**-ving**) (often + *from*) rescue or preserve from danger or harm; (often + *up*) keep for future use; relieve (person) from spending (money, time, etc.); prevent exposure to (annoyance etc.); prevent need for; rescue spiritually; *Football etc.* avoid losing (match), prevent (goal) from being scored. ● *noun Football etc.* act of saving goal. □ **savable**, **saveable** *adjective*; **saver** *noun.*

save[2] *preposition & conjunction archaic or poetical* except; but.

saveloy /ˈsævəlɔɪ/ *noun* highly seasoned sausage.

saving ● *noun* anything saved; an economy; (usually in *plural*) money saved; act of preserving or rescuing. ● *preposition* except; without offence to. □ **-saving** making economical use of specified thing; **saving grace** redeeming feature.

saviour /ˈseɪvjə/ *noun* (*US* **savior**) person who saves from danger etc.; (**the**, **our Saviour**) Christ.

savoir faire /sævwɑː ˈfeə/ *noun* ability to behave appropriately; tact. [French]

savory[1] /ˈseɪvərɪ/ *noun* aromatic herb used in cookery.

savory[2] *US* = SAVOURY.

savour /ˈseɪvə/ (*US* **savor**) ● *noun* characteristic taste, flavour, etc.; tinge or hint. ● *verb* appreciate, enjoy; (+ *of*) imply, suggest.

savoury /ˈseɪvərɪ/ (*US* **savory**) ● *adjective* with appetizing taste or smell; (of food) salty or piquant, not sweet; pleasant. ● *noun* (*plural* **-ies**) savoury dish.

savoy /səˈvɔɪ/ *noun* rough-leaved winter cabbage.

savvy /ˈsævɪ/ *slang* ● *verb* (**-ies**, **-ied**) know. ● *noun* knowingness, understanding. ● *adjective* (**-ier**, **-iest**) *US* knowing, wise.

saw[1] ● *noun* implement with toothed blade etc. for cutting wood etc. ● *verb* (*past participle* **sawn** or **sawed**) cut or make with saw; use saw; make to-and-fro sawing motion. ▫ **sawdust** fine wood fragments produced in sawing; **sawfish** (*plural* same or **-es**) large sea fish with toothed flat snout; **sawmill** factory for sawing wood into planks; **sawtooth(ed)** serrated.

saw[2] *past* of SEE[1].

saw[3] *noun* proverb, maxim.

sawyer /ˈsɔːjə/ *noun* person who saws timber.

sax *noun colloquial* saxophone.

saxe /sæks/ *noun & adjective* (in full **saxe blue**; as *adjective* often hyphenated) light greyish-blue.

saxifrage /ˈsæksɪfreɪdʒ/ *noun* small-flowered rock-plant.

Saxon /ˈsæks(ə)n/ ● *noun historical* member or language of Germanic people that occupied parts of England in 5th–6th c.; Anglo-Saxon. ● *adjective historical* of the Saxons; Anglo-Saxon.

saxophone /ˈsæksəfəʊn/ *noun* keyed brass reed instrument used esp. in jazz. ▫ **saxophonist** /ˈsɒfən-/ *noun*.

say ● *verb* (*3rd singular present* **says** /sez/; *past & past participle* **said** /sed/) utter, remark; express; state; indicate; (in *passive*; usually + *to do*) be asserted; (+ *to do*) *colloquial* direct, order; convey (information); adduce, plead; decide; take as example or as near enough; (**the said**) *Law or jocular* the previously mentioned. ● *noun* opportunity to express view; share in decision. ▫ **say-so** *colloquial* power of decision, mere assertion.

saying *noun* maxim, proverb, etc.

sc. *abbreviation* scilicet.

scab ● *noun* crust over healing cut, sore, etc.; skin disease; plant disease; *colloquial derogatory* blackleg. ● *verb* (**-bb-**) form scab; *colloquial derogatory* act as blackleg. ▫ **scabby** *adjective* (**-ier**, **-iest**).

scabbard /ˈskæbəd/ *noun historical* sheath of sword etc.

scabies /ˈskeɪbiːz/ *noun* contagious skin disease causing itching.

scabious /ˈskeɪbɪəs/ *noun* plant with pincushion-shaped flowers.

scabrous /ˈskeɪbrəs/ *adjective* rough, scaly; indecent.

scaffold /ˈskæfəʊld/ *noun* scaffolding; *historical* platform for execution of criminal.

scaffolding *noun* temporary structure of poles, planks, etc. for building work; materials for this.

scald /skɔːld/ ● *verb* burn (skin etc.) with hot liquid or vapour; heat (esp. milk) to near boiling point; (usually + *out*) clean with boiling water. ● *noun* burn etc. caused by scalding.

scale[1] ● *noun* each of thin horny plates protecting skin of fish and reptiles; thing resembling this; incrustation inside kettle etc.; tartar on teeth. ● *verb* (**-ling**) remove scale(s) from; form or come off in scales. ▫ **scaly** *adjective* (**-ier**, **-iest**).

scale[2] *noun* (often in *plural*) weighing machine; (also **scale-pan**) pan of weighing-balance. ▫ **tip**, **turn the scales** be decisive factor, (+ *at*) weigh (specified amount).

scale[3] ● *noun* graded classification system; ratio of reduction or enlargement in map, picture, etc.; relative dimensions; *Music* set of notes at fixed intervals, arranged in order of pitch; set of marks on line used in measuring etc., rule determining distances between these, rod on which these are marked. ● *verb* (**-ling**) climb; represent in proportion; reduce to common scale. ▫ **scale down**, **up** make or become smaller or larger in proportion; **to scale** uniformly in proportion.

scalene /ˈskeɪliːn/ *adjective* (of triangle) having unequal sides.

scallion /ˈskæljən/ *noun esp. US* shallot; spring onion.

scallop /ˈskæləp/ ● *noun* edible bivalve with fan-shaped ridged shells; (in full **scallop shell**) one shell of this, esp. used for cooking or serving food on; (in *plural*) ornamental edging of semicircular curves. ● *verb* (**-p-**) ornament with scallops.

scallywag /ˈskælɪwæg/ *noun* scamp, rascal.

scalp ● *noun* skin and hair on head; *historical* this cut off as trophy by N. American Indian. ● *verb historical* take scalp of.

scalpel /ˈskælp(ə)l/ *noun* small surgical knife.

scam *noun US slang* trick, fraud.

scamp *noun colloquial* rascal, rogue.

scamper /ˈskæmpə/ ● *verb* run and skip. ● *noun* act of scampering.

scampi /ˈskæmpɪ/ *plural noun* large prawns.

scan ● *verb* (**-nn-**) look at intently or quickly; (of verse etc.) be metrically correct; examine (surface etc.) for radioactivity etc.; traverse (region) with radar etc. beam; resolve (picture) into elements of light and shade for esp. television transmission; analyse metre of (line etc.); obtain image of (part of body) using scanner. ● *noun* scanning; image obtained by scanning.

scandal /ˈskænd(ə)l/ *noun* disgraceful event; public outrage; malicious gossip. ▫ **scandalmonger** /-mʌŋgə/ person who spreads scandal. ▫ **scandalous** *adjective*; **scandalously** *adverb*.

scandalize *verb* (also **-ise**) (**-zing** or **-sing**) offend morally, shock.

Scandinavian /skændɪˈneɪvɪən/ ● *noun* native or inhabitant, or family of languages, of Scandinavia. ● *adjective* of Scandinavia.

scanner *noun* device for scanning; diagnostic apparatus measuring radiation, ultrasound reflections, etc. from body.

scansion /ˈskænʃ(ə)n/ *noun* metrical scanning of verse.

scant *adjective* barely sufficient; deficient.

scanty *adjective* (**-ier**, **-iest**) of small extent or amount; barely sufficient. ▫ **scantily** *adverb*; **scantiness** *noun*.

scapegoat /ˈskeɪpgəʊt/ *noun* person blamed for others' faults.

scapula /ˈskæpjʊlə/ *noun* (*plural* **-lae** /-liː/ or **-s**) shoulder blade.

scapular /ˈskæpjʊlə/ ● *adjective* of scapula. ● *noun* monastic short cloak.

scar[1] ● *noun* mark left on skin etc. by wound etc.; emotional damage. ● *verb* (**-rr-**) (esp. as **scarred** *adjective*) mark with or form scar(s).

scar[2] *noun* (also **scaur**) steep craggy part of mountainside.

scarab /ˈskærəb/ *noun* kind of beetle; gem cut in form of beetle.

scarce /skeəs/ ● *adjective* in short supply; rare. ● *adverb archaic or literary* scarcely. ▫ **make oneself scarce** *colloquial* keep out of the way, disappear.

scarcely /ˈskeəslɪ/ *adverb* hardly, only just.

scarcity *noun* (*plural* **-ies**) lack or shortage.

scare /skeə/ ● *verb* (**-ring**) frighten; (as **scared** *adjective*) (usually + *of*) frightened; (usually + *away*, *off*, etc.) drive away by frightening. ● *noun* sudden fright or alarm, esp. caused by rumours. □ **scarecrow** human figure used for frightening birds away from crops, *colloquial* badly-dressed or grotesque person; **scaremonger** /-mʌŋgə/ person who spreads scare(s).

scarf[1] *noun* (*plural* **scarves** /skɑ:vz/ or **-s**) piece of material worn round neck or over head for warmth or ornament.

scarf[2] ● *verb* join ends of (timber etc.) by thinning or notching them and bolting them together. ● *noun* (*plural* **-s**) joint made thus.

scarify /'skærɪfaɪ/ *verb* (**-ies**, **-ied**) make slight incisions in; scratch; criticize etc. mercilessly; loosen (soil). □ **scarification** *noun*.

scarlatina /skɑ:lə'ti:nə/ *noun* scarlet fever.

scarlet /'skɑ:lət/ ● *adjective* of brilliant red tinged with orange. ● *noun* scarlet colour, pigment, clothes, etc. □ **scarlet fever** infectious fever with scarlet rash; **scarlet pimpernel** wild plant with small esp. scarlet flowers.

scarp ● *noun* steep slope, esp. inner side of ditch in fortification. ● *verb* make perpendicular or steep.

scarper /'skɑ:pə/ *verb slang* run away, escape.

scarves *plural* of SCARF[1].

scary *adjective* (**-ier**, **-iest**) *colloquial* frightening.

scat ● *noun* wordless jazz singing. ● *verb* (**-tt-**) sing scat.

scathing /'skeɪðɪŋ/ *adjective* witheringly scornful. □ **scathingly** *adverb*.

scatology /skæ'tɒlədʒɪ/ *noun* preoccupation with excrement or obscenity. □ **scatological** /-tə'lɒdʒ-/ *adjective*.

scatter /'skætə/ ● *verb* throw about, strew; cover by scattering; (cause to) flee; (cause to) disperse; (as **scattered** *adjective*) wide apart, sporadic; *Physics* deflect or diffuse (light, particles, etc.). ● *noun* act of scattering; small amount scattered; extent of distribution. □ **scatterbrain** person lacking concentration; **scatterbrained** *adjective*.

scatty /'skætɪ/ *adjective* (**-ier**, **-iest**) *colloquial* lacking concentration. □ **scattily** *adverb*; **scattiness** *noun*.

scavenge /'skævɪndʒ/ *verb* (**-ging**) (usually + *for*) search for and collect (discarded items).

scavenger /'skævɪndʒə/ *noun* person who scavenges; animal etc. feeding on carrion.

SCE *abbreviation* Scottish Certificate of Education.

scenario /sɪ'nɑ:rɪəʊ/ *noun* (*plural* **-s**) synopsis of film, play, etc.; imagined sequence of future events.

■ **Usage** *Scenario* should not be used in standard English to mean 'situation', as in *It was an unpleasant scenario*.

scene /si:n/ *noun* place of actual or fictitious occurrence; incident; public display of emotion, temper, etc.; piece of continuous action in a play, film, book, etc.; piece(s) of scenery for a play; landscape, view; *colloquial* area of interest or activity. □ **behind the scenes** out of view of audience, secret, secretly; **scene-shifter** person who moves scenery in theatre.

scenery /'si:nərɪ/ *noun* features (esp. picturesque) of landscape; backcloths, properties, etc. representing scene in a play etc.

scenic /'si:nɪk/ *adjective* picturesque; of scenery. □ **scenically** *adverb*.

scent /sent/ ● *noun* characteristic, esp. pleasant, smell; liquid perfume; smell left by animal; clues etc. leading to discovery; power of scenting. ● *verb* discern by smell; sense; (esp. as **scented** *adjective*) make fragrant.

scepter *US* = SCEPTRE.

sceptic /'skeptɪk/ *noun* (*US* **skeptic**) sceptical person; person who questions truth of religions, or the possibility of knowledge. □ **scepticism** /-sɪz(ə)m/ *noun*.

sceptical /'skeptɪk(ə)l/ *adjective* (*US* **skeptical**) inclined to doubt accepted opinions; critical; incredulous. □ **sceptically** *adverb*.

sceptre /'septə/ *noun* (*US* **scepter**) staff borne as symbol of sovereignty.

schedule /'ʃedju:l/ ● *noun* timetable; list, esp. of rates or prices. ● *verb* (**-ling**) include in schedule; make schedule of; list (building) for preservation. □ **on schedule** at time appointed; **scheduled flight**, **service**, etc., regular public one.

schema /'ski:mə/ *noun* (*plural* **schemata** or **-s**) synopsis, outline, diagram.

schematic /skɪ'mætɪk/ ● *adjective* of or as scheme or diagram. ● *noun* diagram, esp. of electronic circuit.

schematize /'ski:mətaɪz/ *verb* (also **-ise**) (**-zing** or **-sing**) put in schematic form.

scheme /ski:m/ ● *noun* systematic arrangement; artful plot; outline, syllabus, etc. ● *verb* (**-ming**) plan, esp. secretly or deceitfully. □ **scheming** *adjective*.

scherzo /'skeətsəʊ/ *noun* (*plural* **-s**) *Music* vigorous and lively movement or composition.

schism /'skɪz(ə)m/ *noun* division of esp. religious group into sects etc. □ **schismatic** /-'mæt-/ *adjective & noun*.

schist /ʃɪst/ *noun* layered crystalline rock.

schizo /'skɪtsəʊ/ *colloquial* ● *adjective* schizophrenic. ● *noun* (*plural* **-s**) schizophrenic person.

schizoid /'skɪtsɔɪd/ ● *adjective* tending to schizophrenia. ● *noun* schizoid person.

schizophrenia /skɪtsə'fri:nɪə/ *noun* mental disorder marked by disconnection between thoughts, feelings, and actions. □ **schizophrenic** /-'fren-/ *adjective & noun*.

schmaltz /ʃmɔ:lts/ *noun colloquial* sickly sentimentality. □ **schmaltzy** *adjective* (**-ier**, **-iest**).

schnapps /ʃnæps/ *noun* any of various spirits drunk in N. Europe.

schnitzel /'ʃnɪts(ə)l/ *noun* veal escalope.

scholar /'skɒlə/ *noun* learned person; holder of scholarship; person of specified academic ability. □ **scholarly** *adjective*.

scholarship *noun* learning, erudition; award of money etc. towards education.

scholastic /skə'læstɪk/ *adjective* of schools, education, etc.; academic.

school[1] /sku:l/ ● *noun* educational institution for pupils up to 19 years old or (*US*) at any level; school buildings, pupils, staff, etc; (time given to) teaching; university department or faculty; group of artists, disciples, etc. following or holding similar principles, opinions, etc.; instructive circumstances. ● *verb* send to school; discipline, train, control; (as **schooled** *adjective*) (+ *in*) educated, trained. □ **schoolboy**, **schoolchild**, **schoolgirl** one who attends school; **school-leaver** person who has just left school; **schoolmaster**, **schoolmistress**, **schoolteacher** teacher in school; **schoolroom** room used for lessons, esp. in private house.

school[2] /sku:l/ *noun* shoal of fish, whales, etc.

schooling *noun* education.

schooner /'sku:nə/ *noun* two-masted fore-and-aft rigged ship; large glass, esp. for sherry; *US & Australian* tall beer glass.

schottische /ʃɒ'ti:ʃ/ *noun* kind of slow polka.

sciatic /saɪˈætɪk/ *adjective* of hip or sciatic nerve; of or having sciatica. □ **sciatic nerve** large nerve from pelvis to thigh.

sciatica /saɪˈætɪkə/ *noun* neuralgia of hip and leg.

science /ˈsaɪəns/ *noun* branch of knowledge involving systematized observation, experiment, and induction; knowledge so gained; pursuit or principles of this; skilful technique. □ **science fiction** fiction with scientific theme; **science park** area containing science-based businesses.

scientific /saɪənˈtɪfɪk/ *adjective* following systematic methods of science; systematic, accurate; of or concerned with science.

scientist /ˈsaɪəntɪst/ *noun* student or expert in science.

sci-fi /ˈsaɪfaɪ/ *noun colloquial* science fiction.

scilicet /ˈsaɪlɪset/ *adverb* that is to say.

scimitar /ˈsɪmɪtə/ *noun* curved oriental sword.

scintillate /ˈsɪntɪleɪt/ (**-ting**) (esp. as **scintillating** *adjective*) talk or act cleverly; sparkle, twinkle. □ **scintillation** *noun*.

scion /ˈsaɪən/ *noun* shoot cut for grafting; young member of family.

scissors /ˈsɪzəz/ *plural noun* (also **pair of scissors** *singular*) cutting instrument with pair of pivoted blades.

sclerosis /skləˈrəʊsɪs/ *noun* abnormal hardening of tissue; (in full **multiple sclerosis**) serious progressive disease of nervous system. □ **sclerotic** /-ˈrɒt-/ *adjective*.

scoff[1] ● *verb* (usually + *at*) speak derisively, mock. ● *noun* mocking words, taunt.

scoff[2] *colloquial* ● *verb* eat (food) greedily. ● *noun* food.

scold /skəʊld/ ● *verb* rebuke; find fault noisily. ● *noun archaic* nagging woman.

sconce *noun* wall-bracket holding candlestick or light-fitting.

scone /skɒn, skəʊn/ *noun* small cake of flour etc. baked quickly.

scoop /sku:p/ ● *noun* short-handled deep shovel; long-handled ladle; excavating part of digging machine etc.; device for serving ice cream etc.; quantity taken up by scoop; scooping movement; exclusive news item; large profit made quickly. ● *verb* (usually + *out*) hollow out or (usually + *up*) lift (as) with scoop; forestall (rival newspaper etc.) with scoop; secure (large profit etc.), esp. suddenly.

scoot /sku:t/ *verb* (esp. in *imperative*) *colloquial* shoot along; depart, flee.

scooter *noun* child's toy with footboard on two wheels and long steering-handle; low-powered motorcycle.

scope *noun* range, opportunity; extent of ability, outlook, etc.

scorch ● *verb* burn or discolour surface of with dry heat; become so discoloured etc.; (as **scorching** *adjective*) *colloquial* (of weather) very hot, (of criticism etc.) stringent. ● *noun* mark of scorching. □ **scorched earth policy** policy of destroying everything that might be of use to invading enemy.

scorcher *noun colloquial* extremely hot day.

score *noun* number of points, goals, etc. made by player or side in game etc.; respective scores at end of game; act of gaining esp. goal; (*plural* same or **-s**) (set of) 20; (in *plural*) a great many; reason, motive; *Music* copy of composition with parts arranged one below another; music for film or play; notch, line, etc. made on surface; record of money owing. ● *verb* (**-ring**) win, gain; make (points etc.) in game; keep score; mark with notches etc.; have an advantage; *Music* (often + *for*) orchestrate or arrange (piece of music); *slang* obtain drugs illegally, make sexual conquest. □ **keep (the) score** register points etc. as they are made; **score (points) off** *colloquial* humiliate, esp. verbally; **scoreboard** large board for displaying score in match etc.

scoria /ˈskɔ:rɪə/ *noun* (*plural* **scoriae** /-rɪi:/) (fragments of) cellular lava; slag.

scorn ● *noun* disdain, contempt, derision. ● *verb* hold in contempt; reject or refuse to do as unworthy.

scornful *adjective* (often + *of*) contemptuous. □ **scornfully** *adverb*.

Scorpio /ˈskɔ:pɪəʊ/ *noun* eighth sign of zodiac.

scorpion /ˈskɔ:pɪən/ *noun* lobster-like arachnid with jointed stinging tail.

Scot *noun* native of Scotland.

Scotch ● *adjective* Scottish, Scots. ● *noun* Scottish, Scots; Scotch whisky. □ **Scotch broth** meat soup with pearl barley etc.; **Scotch egg** hard-boiled egg in sausage meat; **Scotch fir** Scots pine; **Scotch mist** thick mist and drizzle; **Scotch terrier** small rough-coated terrier; **Scotch whisky** whisky distilled in Scotland.

■ **Usage** *Scots* or *Scottish* is preferred to *Scotch* in Scotland, except in the compound nouns given above.

scotch *verb* decisively put an end to; *archaic* wound without killing.

scot-free *adverb* unharmed, unpunished.

Scots ● *adjective* Scottish. ● *noun* Scottish; form of English spoken in (esp. Lowlands of) Scotland. □ **Scotsman**, **Scotswoman** Scot; **Scots pine** kind of pine tree.

Scottish ● *adjective* of Scotland or its inhabitants. ● *noun* (**the Scottish**) (treated as *plural*) people of Scotland.

scoundrel /ˈskaʊndr(ə)l/ *noun* unscrupulous villain; rogue.

scour[1] /skaʊə/ ● *verb* rub clean; (usually + *away*, *off*, etc.) clear by rubbing; clear out (pipe etc.) by flushing through. ● *noun* scouring, being scoured. □ **scourer** *noun*.

scour[2] /skaʊə/ *verb* search thoroughly.

scourge /skɜ:dʒ/ ● *noun* person or thing regarded as causing suffering; whip. ● *verb* (**-ging**) whip; punish, oppress.

Scouse /skaʊs/ *colloquial* ● *noun* Liverpool dialect; (also **Scouser**) native of Liverpool. ● *adjective* of Liverpool.

scout /skaʊt/ ● *noun* person sent out to get information or reconnoitre; search for this; talent-scout; (also **Scout**) member of (originally boys') association intended to develop character. ● *verb* (often + *for*) seek information etc.; (often + *about*, *around*) make search; (often + *out*) *colloquial* explore. □ **Scoutmaster** person in charge of group of Scouts. □ **scouting** *noun*.

Scouter *noun* adult leader of Scouts.

scowl /skaʊl/ ● *noun* sullen or bad-tempered look. ● *verb* wear scowl.

scrabble /ˈskræb(ə)l/ ● *verb* (**-ling**) scratch or grope busily about. ● *noun* scrabbling; (**Scrabble**) *proprietary term* game in which players build up words from letter-blocks on board.

scrag ● *noun* (also **scrag-end**) inferior end of neck of mutton; skinny person or animal. ● *verb* (**-gg-**) *slang* strangle, hang; handle roughly, beat up.

scraggy *adjective* (**-ier**, **iest**) thin and bony. □ **scragginess** *noun*.

scram *verb* (**-mm-**) (esp. in *imperative*) *colloquial* go away.

scramble /ˈskræmb(ə)l/ ● *verb* (**-ling**) clamber, crawl, climb, etc.; (+ *for*, *at*) struggle with competitors (for thing or share); mix indiscriminately; cook (eggs) by stirring in heated pan; alter sound frequencies of (broadcast or telephone conversation) so as to make it unintelligible without special receiver; (of fighter aircraft or pilot) take off rapidly. ● *noun* scrambling; difficult climb or walk; (+ *for*) eager struggle or competition; motorcycle race over rough ground; emergency take-off by fighter aircraft.

scrambler *noun* device for scrambling telephone conversations; motorcycle used for scrambles.

scrap[1] ● *noun* small detached piece, fragment; waste material; discarded metal for reprocessing; (with negative) smallest piece or amount; (in *plural*) odds and ends, bits of uneaten food. ● *verb* (**-pp-**) discard as useless. □ **scrapbook** book in which cuttings etc. are kept; **scrap heap** collection of waste material, state of being discarded as useless; **scrapyard** place where (esp. metal) scrap is collected.

scrap[2] *colloquial* ● *noun* fight or rough quarrel. ● *verb* (**-pp-**) have scrap.

scrape ● *verb* (**-ping**) move hard edge across (surface), esp. to smooth or clean; (+ *away*, *off*, etc.) remove by scraping; rub (surface) harshly against another; scratch, damage, or make by scraping; draw or move with sound (as) of scraping; produce such sound from; (often + *along*, *by*, *through*, etc.) move while (almost) touching; narrowly achieve; (often + *by*, *through*) barely manage, pass exam etc. with difficulty; (+ *together*, *up*) provide or amass with difficulty; be economical; make clumsy bow; (+ *back*) draw (hair) tightly back. ● *noun* act or sound of scraping; scraped place, graze; *colloquial* predicament caused by rashness. □ **scraper** *noun*.

scrapie /ˈskreɪpɪ/ *noun* viral disease of sheep.

scrappy *adjective* (**-ier**, **-iest**) consisting of scraps; incomplete.

scratch ● *verb* score or wound superficially, esp. with sharp object; scrape with the nails to relieve itching; make or form by scratching; (+ *out*, *off*, *through*) erase; withdraw from race or competition; (often + *about*, *around*, etc.) scratch ground etc. in search, search haphazardly. ● *noun* mark, wound, or sound made by scratching; act of scratching oneself; *colloquial* trifling wound; starting line for race etc.; position of those receiving no handicap. ● *adjective* collected by chance; collected or made from whatever is available; with no handicap given. □ **from scratch** from the beginning, without help; **up to scratch** up to required standard.

scratchy *adjective* (**-ier**, **-iest**) tending to make scratches or scratching noise; causing itchiness; (of drawing etc.) careless. □ **scratchily** *adverb*; **scratchiness** *noun*.

scrawl ● *verb* write in hurried untidy way. ● *noun* hurried writing; scrawled note. □ **scrawly** *adjective* (**-ier**, **-iest**).

scrawny /ˈskrɔːnɪ/ *adjective* (**-ier**, **-iest**) lean, scraggy.

scream ● *noun* piercing cry (as) of terror or pain; *colloquial* hilarious occurrence or person. ● *verb* emit scream; utter in or with scream; move with scream; laugh uncontrollably; be blatantly obvious.

scree *noun* (in *singular* or *plural*) small loose stones; mountain slope covered with these.

screech ● *noun* harsh scream or squeal. ● *verb* utter with or make screech. □ **screech-owl** barn owl.

screed *noun* long usually tiresome letter or harangue; layer of cement etc. applied to level a surface.

screen ● *noun* fixed or movable upright partition for separating, concealing, or protecting from heat etc.; thing used to conceal or shelter; concealing stratagem; protection thus given; blank surface on which images are projected; (**the screen**) cinema industry, films collectively; windscreen; large sieve; system for detecting disease, ability, attribute, etc. ● *verb* shelter, hide; protect from detection, censure, etc.; (+ *off*) conceal behind screen; show (film etc.); prevent from causing, or protect from, electrical interference; test (person or group) for disease, reliability, loyalty, etc.; sieve. □ **screenplay** film script; **screen printing** printing process with ink forced through areas of sheet of fine mesh; **screen test** audition for film part; **screenwriter** person who writes for cinema.

screw /skruː/ ● *noun* cylinder or cone with spiral ridge running round it outside (**male screw**) or inside (**female screw**); (in full **woodscrew**) metal male screw with slotted head and sharp point; (in full **screw-bolt**) blunt metal male screw on which nut is threaded; straight screw used to exert pressure; (in *singular* or *plural*) instrument of torture acting thus; (in full **screw propeller**) propeller with twisted blades; one turn of screw; (+ *of*) small twisted-up paper (of tobacco etc.); oblique curling motion; *slang* prison warder. ● *verb* fasten or tighten (as) with screw(s); (of ball etc.) swerve; (+ *out*, *of*) extort from; swindle. □ **screwball** *US slang* crazy or eccentric person; **screwdriver** tool for turning screws by putting tool's tip into screw's slot; **screw up** contract, crumple, or contort, summon up (courage etc.), *slang* bungle, spoil, or upset; **screw-up** *slang* bungle.

screwy *adjective* (**-ier**, **-iest**) *slang* mad, eccentric; absurd. □ **screwiness** *noun*.

scribble /ˈskrɪb(ə)l/ ● *verb* (**-ling**) write or draw carelessly or hurriedly; *jocular* be author or writer. ● *noun* scrawl; hasty note etc.

scribe ● *noun* ancient or medieval copyist of manuscripts; pointed instrument for marking wood etc.; *colloquial* writer. ● *verb* (**-bing**) mark with scribe. □ **scribal** *adjective*.

scrim *noun* open-weave fabric for lining, upholstery, etc.

scrimmage /ˈskrɪmɪdʒ/ ● *noun* tussle, brawl. ● *verb* (**-ging**) engage in scrimmage.

scrimp *verb* skimp.

scrip *noun* provisional certificate of money subscribed to company etc.; extra share(s) instead of dividend.

script ● *noun* text of play, film, or broadcast (see panel at DIRECT SPEECH); handwriting; typeface imitating handwriting; alphabet or other system of writing; examinee's written answer(s). ● *verb* write script for (film etc.). □ **scriptwriter** person who writes scripts for films, etc.

scripture /ˈskrɪptʃə/ *noun* sacred writings; (**Scripture**, **the Scriptures**) the Bible. □ **scriptural** *adjective*.

scrivener /ˈskrɪvənə/ *noun historical* copyist, drafter of documents; notary.

scrofula /ˈskrɒfjʊlə/ *noun* disease with glandular swellings. □ **scrofulous** *adjective*.

scroll /skrəʊl/ ● *noun* roll of parchment or paper; book in ancient roll form; ornamental design imitating roll of parchment. ● *verb* (often + *down*, *up*) move (display on VDU screen) to view later or earlier material.

scrotum /ˈskrəʊtəm/ *noun* (*plural* **scrota** or **-s**) pouch of skin enclosing testicles. □ **scrotal** *adjective*.

scrounge /skraʊndʒ/ *verb* (**-ging**) obtain (things) by cadging. □ **on the scrounge** scrounging. □ **scrounger** *noun*.

scrub[1] ● *verb* (**-bb-**) clean by hard rubbing, esp. with hard brush; (often + *up*) (of surgeon etc.) clean and disinfect hands etc. before operating; *colloquial* cancel; pass (gas etc.) through scrubber. ● *noun* scrubbing, being scrubbed.

scrub[2] *noun* brushwood or stunted trees etc.; land covered with this. □ **scrubby** *adjective* (**-ier**, **-iest**).

scrubber *noun slang* promiscuous woman; apparatus for purifying gases etc.
scruff[1] *noun* back of neck.
scruff[2] *noun colloquial* scruffy person.
scruffy /'skrʌfɪ/ *adjective* (**-ier**, **-iest**) *colloquial* shabby, slovenly, untidy. □ **scruffily** *adverb*; **scruffiness** *noun*.
scrum *noun* scrummage; *colloquial* scrimmage. □ **scrum-half** *Rugby* half-back who puts ball into scrum.
scrummage /'skrʌmɪdʒ/ *noun Rugby* massed forwards on each side pushing to gain possession of ball thrown on ground between them.
scrumptious /'skrʌmpʃəs/ *adjective colloquial* delicious.
scrumpy /'skrʌmpɪ/ *noun colloquial* rough cider.
scrunch ● *verb* (usually + *up*) crumple; crunch. ● *noun* crunch.
scruple /'skru:p(ə)l/ ● *noun* (often in *plural*) moral concern; doubt caused by this. ● *verb* (**-ling**) (+ *to do*; usually in negative) hesitate owing to scruples.
scrupulous /'skru:pjʊləs/ *adjective* conscientious, thorough; careful to avoid doing wrong; over-attentive to details. □ **scrupulously** *adverb*.
scrutineer /skru:tɪ'nɪə/ *noun* person who scrutinizes ballot papers.
scrutinize /'skru:tɪnaɪz/ *verb* (also **-ise**) (**-zing** or **-sing**) subject to scrutiny.
scrutiny /'skru:tɪnɪ/ *noun* (*plural* **-ies**) critical gaze; close examination; official examination of ballot papers.
scuba /'sku:bə/ *noun* (*plural* **-s**) aqualung. □ **scuba-diving** swimming underwater using scuba.
scud ● *verb* (**-dd-**) move straight and fast; skim along; *Nautical* run before wind. ● *noun* scudding; vapoury driving clouds or shower.
scuff ● *verb* graze or brush against; mark or wear out (shoes etc.) thus; shuffle or drag feet. ● *noun* mark of scuffing.
scuffle /'skʌf(ə)l/ ● *noun* confused struggle or fight at close quarters. ● *verb* (**-ling**) engage in scuffle.
scull ● *noun* each of pair of small oars; oar used to propel boat from stern; (in *plural*) sculling race. ● *verb* propel with scull(s).
scullery /'skʌlərɪ/ *noun* (*plural* **-ies**) back kitchen; room where dishes are washed etc.
sculpt *verb* sculpture.
sculptor /'skʌlptə/ *noun* (*feminine* **sculptress**) person who sculptures.
sculpture /'skʌlptʃə/ ● *noun* art of making 3-dimensional forms by chiselling, carving, modelling, casting, etc.; work of sculpture. ● *verb* (**-ring**) represent in or adorn with sculpture; practise sculpture. □ **sculptural** *adjective*.
scum ● *noun* layer of dirt etc. at surface of liquid; *derogatory* worst part, person, or group. ● *verb* (**-mm-**) remove scum from; form scum (on). □ **scumbag** *slang* contemptible person. □ **scummy** *adjective* (**-ier**, **-iest**).
scupper[1] /'skʌpə/ *noun* hole in ship's side draining water from deck.
scupper[2] /'skʌpə/ *verb slang* sink (ship, crew); defeat or ruin (plan etc.); kill.
scurf *noun* dandruff. □ **scurfy** *adjective* (**-ier**, **-iest**).
scurrilous /'skʌrɪləs/ *adjective* grossly or obscenely abusive. □ **scurrility** /skə'rɪl-/ *noun* (*plural* **-ies**); **scurrilously** *adverb*; **scurrilousness** *noun*.
scurry /'skʌrɪ/ ● *verb* (**-ies**, **-ied**) run hurriedly, scamper. ● *noun* (*plural* **-ies**) scurrying sound or movement; flurry of rain or snow.
scurvy /'skɜ:vɪ/ ● *noun* disease resulting from deficiency of vitamin C. ● *adjective* (**-ier**, **-iest**) paltry, contemptible. □ **scurvily** *adverb*.
scut *noun* short tail, esp. of hare, rabbit, or deer.
scutter /'skʌtə/ *verb & noun colloquial* scurry.
scuttle[1] /'skʌt(ə)l/ *noun* coal scuttle; part of car body between windscreen and bonnet.
scuttle[2] /'skʌt(ə)l/ ● *verb* (**-ling**) scurry; flee in undignified way. ● *noun* hurried gait; precipitate flight.
scuttle[3] /'skʌt(ə)l/ ● *noun* hole with lid in ship's deck or side. ● *verb* (**-ling**) let water into (ship) to sink it.
scythe /saɪð/ ● *noun* mowing and reaping implement with long handle and curved blade. ● *verb* (**-thing**) cut with scythe.
SDLP *abbreviation* (in N. Ireland) Social Democratic and Labour Party.
SDP *abbreviation* (in UK) Social Democratic Party.
SE *abbreviation* south-east(ern).
sea *noun* expanse of salt water covering most of earth; area of this; large inland lake; (motion or state of) waves of sea; (+ *of*) vast quantity or expanse. □ **at sea** in ship on the sea, confused; **sea anchor** bag to reduce drifting of ship; **sea anemone** polyp with petal-like tentacles; **seabed** ocean floor; **seaboard** coastline, coastal area; **sea dog** old sailor; **seafarer** traveller by sea; **seafood** edible marine fish or shellfish; **sea front** part of seaside town facing sea; **seagoing** designed for open sea; **seagull** = GULL[1]; **sea horse** small fish with head like horse's; **seakale** plant with young shoots used as vegetable; **sea legs** ability to keep one's balance at sea; **sea level** mean level of sea's surface, used in reckoning heights of hills etc. and as barometric standard; **sea lion** large, eared seal; **seaman** person whose work is at sea, sailor, sailor below rank of officer; **seaplane** aircraft designed to take off from and land on water; **seaport** town with harbour; **sea salt** salt got by evaporating sea water; **seascape** picture or view of sea; **seashell** shell of salt-water mollusc; **seashore** land next to sea; **seasick** nauseous from motion of ship at sea; **seasickness** *noun*; **seaside** sea-coast, esp. as holiday resort; **sea urchin** small marine animal with spiny shell; **seaweed** plant growing in sea; **seaworthy** fit to put to sea.
seal[1] ● *noun* piece of stamped wax etc. attached to document or to receptacle, envelope, etc. to guarantee authenticity or security; metal stamp etc. used in making seal; substance or device used to close gap etc.; anything regarded as confirmation or guarantee; decorative adhesive stamp. ● *verb* close securely or hermetically; stamp, fasten, or fix with seal; certify as correct with seal; (+ *off*) prevent access to or from; (often + *up*) confine securely; settle, decide. □ **sealing wax** mixture softened by heating and used for seals.
seal[2] ● *noun* fish-eating amphibious marine mammal with flippers. ● *verb* hunt seals.
sealant *noun* material for sealing, esp. to make watertight.
seam ● *noun* line where two edges join, esp. of cloth or boards; fissure between parallel edges; wrinkle; stratum of coal etc. ● *verb* join with seam; (esp. as **seamed** *adjective*) mark or score with seam. □ **seamless** *adjective*.
seamstress /'si:mstrɪs/ *noun* woman who sews.
seamy *adjective* (**-ier**, **-iest**) disreputable, sordid; showing seams. □ **seaminess** *noun*.
seance /'seɪɑ̃s/ *noun* meeting at which spiritualist attempts to contact the dead.
sear /sɪə/ *verb* scorch, cauterize; cause anguish to; brown (meat) quickly.
search /sɜ:tʃ/ ● *verb* examine thoroughly to find something; make investigation; (+ *for*, *out*) look for, seek out; (as **searching** *adjective*) keenly questioning. ● *noun* act of searching; investigation. □ **searchlight** outdoor lamp designed to throw

strong beam of light in any direction, light or beam from this; **search party** group of people conducting organized search; **search warrant** official authorization to enter and search building. □ **searcher** *noun*; **searchingly** *adverb*.

season /'si:z(ə)n/ ● *noun* each of climatic divisions of year; proper or suitable time; time when something is plentiful, active, etc.; (**the season**) (also **high season**) busiest period at resort etc.; *colloquial* season ticket. ● *verb* flavour with salt, herbs, etc.; enhance with wit etc.; moderate; (esp. as **seasoned** *adjective*) make or become suitable by exposure to weather or experience. □ **in season** (of food) available plentifully, (of animal) on heat; **season ticket** one entitling holder to unlimited travel, access, etc. in given period.

seasonable *adjective* suitable to season; opportune.

■ **Usage** *Seasonable* is sometimes confused with *seasonal*.

seasonal *adjective* of, depending on, or varying with seasons.

■ **Usage** *Seasonal* is sometimes confused with *seasonable*.

seasoning *noun* salt, herbs, etc. as flavouring for food.

seat ● *noun* thing made or used for sitting on; buttocks, part of garment covering them; part of chair etc. on which buttocks rest; place for one person in theatre etc.; position as MP, committee member, etc., or right to occupy it; machine's supporting or guiding part; location; country mansion; posture on horse. ● *verb* cause to sit; provide sitting accommodation for; (as **seated** *adjective*) sitting; establish in position. □ **seat belt** belt securing seated person in vehicle or aircraft.

seating *noun* seats collectively; sitting accommodation.

sebaceous /sɪ'beɪʃəs/ *adjective* fatty; secreting oily matter.

Sec. *abbreviation* (also **sec.**) secretary.

sec. *abbreviation* second(s).

sec[1] *noun colloquial* (in phrases) second, moment.

sec[2] *adjective* (of wine) dry.

secateurs /sekə'tɜ:z/ *plural noun* pruning clippers.

secede /sɪ'si:d/ *verb* (**-ding**) withdraw formally from political or religious body.

secession /sɪ'seʃ(ə)n/ *noun* seceding. □ **secessionist** *noun & adjective*.

seclude /sɪ'klu:d/ *verb* (**-ding**) keep (person, place) apart from others; (esp. as **secluded** *adjective*) screen from view.

seclusion /sɪ'klu:ʒ(ə)n/ *noun* secluded state or place.

second[1] /'sekənd/ ● *adjective* next after first; additional; subordinate; inferior; comparable to. ● *noun* runner-up; person or thing coming second; second gear; (in *plural*) inferior goods; *colloquial* second helping or course; assistant to boxer, duellist, etc. ● *verb* formally support (nomination, proposal, etc.). □ **second-best** next after best; **second class** second-best group, category, postal service, or accommodation; **second cousin** child of parent's first cousin; **second fiddle** subordinate position; **second-guess** *colloquial* anticipate by guesswork, criticize with hindsight; **second-hand** (of goods) having had previous owner, (of information etc.) obtained indirectly; **second nature** acquired tendency that has become instinctive; **second-rate** inferior; **second sight** clairvoyance; **second string** alternative course of action etc.; **second thoughts** revised opinion; **second wind** renewed capacity for effort after breathlessness or tiredness. □ **seconder** *noun*.

second[2] /'sekənd/ *noun* SI unit of time (1/60 of minute); 1/60 of minute of angle; *colloquial* very short time.

second[3] /sɪ'kɒnd/ *verb* transfer (person) temporarily to another department etc. □ **secondment** *noun*.

secondary /'sekəndərɪ/ ● *adjective* coming after or next below what is primary; derived from or supplementing what is primary; (of education etc.) following primary. ● *noun* (*plural* **-ies**) secondary thing. □ **secondary colour** result of mixing two primary colours.

secondly *adverb* furthermore; as a second item.

secrecy /'si:krəsɪ/ *noun* being secret; keeping of secrets.

secret /'si:krɪt/ ● *adjective* not (to be) made known or seen; working etc. secretly; liking secrecy. ● *noun* thing (to be) kept secret; mystery; effective but not widely known method. □ **in secret** secretly; **secret agent** spy; **secret police** police operating secretly for political ends; **secret service** government department concerned with espionage. □ **secretly** *adverb*.

secretariat /sekrɪ'teərɪət/ *noun* administrative office or department; its members or premises.

secretary /'sekrɪtərɪ/ *noun* (*plural* **-ies**) employee who deals with correspondence, records, making appointments, etc.; official of society etc. who writes letters, organizes business, etc.; principal assistant of government minister, ambassador, etc. □ **secretary bird** long-legged crested African bird; **Secretary-General** principal administrative officer of organization; **Secretary of State** head of major government department, (in US) foreign minister. □ **secretarial** /-'teərɪəl/ *adjective*.

secrete /sɪ'kri:t/ *verb* (**-ting**) (of cell, organ, etc.) produce and discharge (substance); conceal. □ **secretory** *adjective*.

secretion /sɪ'kri:ʃ(ə)n/ *noun* process or act of secreting; secreted substance.

secretive /'si:krətɪv/ *adjective* inclined to make or keep secrets, uncommunicative. □ **secretively** *adverb*; **secretiveness** *noun*.

sect *noun* group sharing (usually unorthodox) religious etc. doctrines; religious denomination.

sectarian /sek'teərɪən/ ● *adjective* of sect(s); bigoted in following one's sect. ● *noun* member of a sect. □ **sectarianism** *noun*.

section /'sekʃ(ə)n/ ● *noun* each of parts into which something is divisible or divided; part cut off; subdivision; *US* area of land, district of town; surgical separation or cutting; cutting of solid by plane, resulting figure or area of this; thin slice cut off for microscopic examination. ● *verb* arrange in or divide into sections; compulsorily commit to psychiatric hospital.

sectional *adjective* of a social group; partisan; made in sections; local rather than general. □ **sectionally** *adverb*.

sector /'sektə/ *noun* branch of an enterprise, the economy, etc.; *Military* portion of battle area; plane figure enclosed between two radii of circle etc.

secular /'sekjʊlə/ *adjective* not concerned with religion, not sacred; (of clerics) not monastic. □ **secularism** *noun*; **secularization** *noun*; **secularize** *verb* (also **-ise**) (**-zing** or **-sing**).

secure /sɪ'kjʊə/ ● *adjective* untroubled by danger or fear; safe; reliable, stable, fixed. ● *verb* (**-ring**) make secure or safe; fasten or close securely; obtain. □ **securely** *adverb*.

security *noun* (*plural* **-ies**) secure condition or feeling; thing that guards or guarantees; safety against espionage, theft, etc.; organization for ensuring this;

thing deposited as guarantee for undertaking or loan; (often in *plural*) document as evidence of loan, certificate of stock, bonds, etc. □ **security risk** person or thing threatening security.

sedan /sɪ'dæn/ *noun* (in full **sedan chair**) *historical* enclosed chair for one person, usually carried on poles by two; *US* saloon car.

sedate /sɪ'deɪt/ ● *adjective* tranquil, serious. ● *verb* (**-ting**) put under sedation. □ **sedately** *adverb*; **sedateness** *noun*.

sedation *noun* treatment with sedatives.

sedative /'sedətɪv/ ● *noun* calming drug or influence. ● *adjective* calming, soothing.

sedentary /'sedəntərɪ/ *adjective* sitting; (of work etc.) done while sitting; (of person) disinclined to exercise.

sedge *noun* grasslike waterside or marsh plant. □ **sedgy** *adjective*.

sediment /'sedɪmənt/ *noun* dregs; matter deposited on land by water or wind. □ **sedimentary** /-'men-/ *adjective*; **sedimentation** *noun*.

sedition /sɪ'dɪʃ(ə)n/ *noun* conduct or speech inciting to rebellion. □ **seditious** *adjective*.

seduce /sɪ'dju:s/ *verb* (**-cing**) entice into sexual activity or wrongdoing; coax or lead astray. □ **seducer** *noun*.

seduction /sɪ'dʌkʃ(ə)n/ *noun* seducing, being seduced; tempting or attractive thing.

seductive /sɪ'dʌktɪv/ *adjective* alluring, enticing. □ **seductively** *adverb*; **seductiveness** *noun*.

sedulous /'sedjʊləs/ *adjective* persevering, diligent, painstaking. □ **sedulity** /sɪ'dju:-/ *noun*; **sedulously** *adverb*.

see[1] *verb* (**sees**; *past* **saw**; *past participle* **seen**) perceive with the eyes; have or use this power; discern mentally, understand; watch; experience; ascertain; imagine, foresee; look at; meet; visit, be visited by; meet regularly; reflect, get clarification; (+ *in*) find attractive in; escort, conduct; witness (event etc.); ensure. □ **see about** attend to, consider; **see off** be present at departure of, *colloquial* get the better of; **see over** inspect, tour; **see red** *colloquial* become enraged; **see through** not be deceived by, support (person) during difficult time, complete (project); **see-through** translucent; **see to** attend to, repair; **see to it** (+ *that*) ensure.

see[2] *noun* area under (arch)bishop's authority; (arch)bishop's office or jurisdiction.

seed ● *noun* part of plant capable of developing into another such plant; seeds collectively, esp. for sowing; semen; prime cause, beginning; offspring; *Tennis etc.* seeded player. ● *verb* place seed(s) in; sprinkle (as) with seed; sow seeds; produce or drop seed; remove seeds from (fruit etc.); place crystal etc. in (cloud) to produce rain; *Tennis etc.* designate (competitor in knockout tournament) so that strong competitors do not meet each other until later rounds, arrange (order of play) thus. □ **go, run to seed** cease flowering as seed develops, become degenerate, unkempt, etc.; **seed-bed** bed prepared for sowing, place of development; **seed-pearl** very small pearl; **seed-potato** potato kept for planting; **seedsman** dealer in seeds.

seedling *noun* young plant raised from seed.

seedy *adjective* (**-ier**, **-iest**) shabby; *colloquial* unwell; full of seed.

seeing *conjunction* (usually + *that*) considering that, inasmuch as, because.

seek *verb* (*past & past participle* **sought** /sɔ:t/) (often + *for, after*) search, inquire; try or want to obtain or reach; request; endeavour. □ **seek out** search for and find. □ **seeker** *noun*.

seem *verb* (often + *to do*) appear, give the impression.

seeming *adjective* apparent but doubtful. □ **seemingly** *adverb*.

seemly /'si:mlɪ/ *adjective* (**-ier**, **-iest**) in good taste, decorous. □ **seemliness** *noun*.

seen *past participle* of SEE[1].

seep *verb* ooze, percolate.

seepage *noun* act of seeping; quantity that seeps.

seer /sɪə/ *noun* person who sees; prophet, visionary.

seersucker /'sɪəsʌkə/ *noun* thin cotton etc. fabric with puckered surface.

see-saw /'si:sɔ:/ ● *noun* long board supported in middle so that children etc. sitting on ends move alternately up and down; this game; up-and-down or to-and-fro motion, contest, etc. ● *verb* play or move (as) on see-saw; vacillate. ● *adjective & adverb* with up-and-down or to-and-fro motion.

seethe /si:ð/ *verb* (**-thing**) boil, bubble; be very angry, resentful, etc.

segment ● *noun* /'segmənt/ part cut off or separable from other parts; part of circle or sphere cut off by intersecting line or plane. ● *verb* /seg'ment/ divide into segments. □ **segmental** /-'ment-/ *adjective*; **segmentation** *noun*.

segregate /'segrɪgeɪt/ *verb* (**-ting**) put apart, isolate; separate (esp. ethnic group) from the rest of the community. □ **segregation** *noun*; **segregationist** *noun & adjective*.

seigneur /seɪn'jɜ:/ *noun* feudal lord. □ **seigneurial** *adjective*.

seine /seɪn/ ● *noun* large vertical fishing net. ● *verb* (**-ning**) fish with seine.

seismic /'saɪzmɪk/ *adjective* of earthquake(s).

seismograph /'saɪzməgrɑ:f/ *noun* instrument for recording earthquake details. □ **seismographic** /-'græf-/ *adjective*.

seismology /saɪz'mɒlədʒɪ/ *noun* the study of earthquakes. □ **seismological** /-mə'lɒdʒ-/ *adjective*; **seismologist** *noun*.

seize /si:z/ *verb* (**-zing**) (often + *on, upon*) take hold or possession of, esp. forcibly, suddenly, or by legal power; take advantage of; comprehend quickly or clearly; affect suddenly; (also **seise**) (usually + *of*) *Law* put in possession of. □ **seize up** (of mechanism) become jammed, (of part of body etc.) become stiff.

seizure /'si:ʒə/ *noun* seizing, being seized; sudden attack of epilepsy, apoplexy, etc.

seldom /'seldəm/ *adverb* rarely, not often.

select /sɪ'lekt/ ● *verb* choose, esp. with care. ● *adjective* chosen for excellence or suitability; exclusive. □ **select committee** parliamentary committee conducting special inquiry. □ **selector** *noun*.

selection /sɪ'lekʃ(ə)n/ *noun* selecting, being selected; person or thing selected; things from which choice may be made; = NATURAL SELECTION.

selective *adjective* of or using selection; able to select; selecting what is convenient. □ **selectively** *adverb*; **selectivity** /-'tɪv-/ *noun*.

selenium /sɪ'li:nɪəm/ *noun* non-metallic element in some sulphide ores.

self ● *noun* (*plural* **selves**/selvz/) individuality, essence; object of introspection or reflexive action; one's own interests or pleasure, concentration on these.

self- *combining form expressing reflexive action, automatic or independent action, or sameness.* □ **self-addressed** addressed to oneself; **self-adhesive** (of envelope etc.) adhesive, esp. without wetting; **self-aggrandizement** enriching oneself, making oneself powerful; **self-assertive** confident or assertive in promoting oneself, one's claims, etc.; **self-assertion** *noun*; **self-assured** self-confident; **self-catering** providing cooking facilities but no food; **self-centred**

preoccupied with oneself; **self-confessed** openly admitting oneself to be; **self-confident** having confidence in oneself; **self-confidence** *noun*; **self-conscious** nervous, shy, embarrassed; **self-consciously** *adverb*; **self-contained** uncommunicative, complete in itself; **self-control** control of oneself, one's behaviour, etc.; **self-critical** critical of oneself, one's abilities, etc.; **self-defence** defence of oneself, one's reputation, etc.; **self-denial** abstinence, esp. as discipline; **self-deprecating** belittling oneself; **self-destruct** (of device etc.) explode or disintegrate automatically, esp. when preset to do so; **self-determination** nation's right to determine own government etc., free will; **self-effacing** retiring, modest; **self-employed** working as freelance or for one's own business etc.; **self-employment** *noun*; **self-esteem** good opinion of oneself; **self-evident** needing no proof or explanation; **self-explanatory** not needing explanation; **self-financing** not needing subsidy; **self-fulfilling** (of prophecy etc.) assured fulfilment by its utterance; **self-governing** governing itself or oneself; **self-government** *noun*; **self-help** use of one's own abilities etc. to achieve success etc.; **self-image** one's conception of oneself; **self-important** conceited, pompous; **self-importance** *noun*; **self-indulgent** indulging one's own pleasures, feelings, etc., (of work of art etc.) lacking control; **self-indulgence** *noun*; **self-interest** one's own interest or advantage; **self-interested** *adjective*; **self-made** successful or rich by one's own efforts; **self-opinionated** obstinate in one's opinion; **self-pity** pity for oneself; **self-portrait** portrait of oneself by oneself; **self-possessed** unperturbed, cool; **self-possession** *noun*; **self-preservation** keeping oneself safe, instinct for this; **self-raising** (of flour) containing a raising agent; **self-reliance** reliance on one's own abilities etc.; **self-reliant** *adjective*; **self-respect** respect for oneself; **self-restraint** self-control; **self-righteous** smugly sure of one's righteousness; **self-righteously** *adverb*; **self-righteousness** *noun*; **self-rule** selfgovernment; **self-sacrifice** selflessness, self-denial; **self-satisfied** complacent; **self-satisfaction** *noun*; **self-seeking** selfish; **self-service** with customers helping themselves and paying cashier afterwards; **self-starter** electric device for starting engine, ambitious person with initiative; **self-styled** called so by oneself; **self-sufficient** capable of supplying one's own needs; **self-sufficiency** *noun*; **self-willed** obstinately pursuing one's own wishes; **self-worth** self-esteem.

selfish *adjective* concerned chiefly with one's own interests or pleasure; actuated by or appealing to self-interest. ◻ **selfishness** *noun*.

selfless *adjective* unselfish.

selfsame /ˈselfseɪm/ *adjective* (**the selfsame**) the very same, the identical.

sell ● *verb* (*past & past participle* **sold** /səʊld/) exchange or be exchanged for money; stock for sale; (+ *at*, *for*) have specified price; betray or prostitute for money etc.; advertise, publicize; cause to be sold; *colloquial* make (person) enthusiastic about (idea etc.). ● *noun colloquial* manner of selling; deception, disappointment. ◻ **sell-by date** latest recommended date of sale; **sell off** sell at reduced prices; **sell out** sell (all one's stock or shares etc.), betray, be treacherous; **sell-out** commercial success, betrayal; **sell short** disparage, underestimate; **sell up** sell one's business, house, etc.

seller *noun* person who sells; thing that sells well or badly as specified. ◻ **seller's market** time when goods are scarce and expensive.

Sellotape /ˈselәteɪp/ ● *noun proprietary term* adhesive usually transparent cellulose tape. ● *verb* (**sellotape**) (**-ping**) fix with Sellotape.

selvage /ˈselvɪdʒ/ *noun* (also **selvedge**) edge of cloth woven to prevent fraying.

selves *plural* of SELF.

semantic /sɪˈmæntɪk/ *adjective* of meaning in language.

semantics *plural noun* (usually treated as *singular*) branch of linguistics concerned with meaning.

semaphore /ˈseməfɔː/ ● *noun* system of signalling with arms or two flags; railway signalling apparatus with arm(s). ● *verb* (**-ring**) signal or send by semaphore.

semblance /ˈsembləns/ *noun* (+ *of*) appearance, show.

semen /ˈsiːmən/ *noun* reproductive fluid of males.

semester /sɪˈmestə/ *noun* half-year term in universities.

semi /ˈsemɪ/ *noun colloquial* (*plural* **-s**) semi-detached house.

semi- *prefix* half; partly.

semibreve /ˈsemɪbriːv/ *noun Music* note equal to 4 crotchets.

semicircle /ˈsemɪsɜːk(ə)l/ *noun* half of circle or its circumference. ◻ **semicircular** /-ˈsɜːkjʊlə/ *adjective*.

semicolon /semɪˈkəʊlən/ *noun* punctuation mark (;) of intermediate value between comma and full stop (see panel).

semiconductor /semɪkənˈdʌktə/ *noun* substance that is a poor electrical conductor when either pure or cold and a good conductor when either impure or hot.

semi-detached /semɪdɪˈtætʃt/ ● *adjective* (of house) joined to another on one side only. ● *noun* such house.

semifinal /semɪˈfaɪn(ə)l/ *noun Sport* match or round preceding final. ◻ **semifinalist** *noun*.

seminal /ˈsemɪn(ə)l/ *adjective* of seed, semen, or reproduction; germinal; (of idea etc.) providing basis for future development.

Semicolon ;

This is used:

1 between clauses that are too short or too closely related to be made into separate sentences; such clauses are not usually connected by a conjunction, e.g.

To err is human; to forgive, divine.

You could wait for him here; on the other hand I could wait in your place; this would save you valuable time.

2 between items in a list which themselves contain commas, if it is necessary to avoid confusion, e.g.

The party consisted of three teachers, who had already climbed with the leader; seven pupils; and two parents.

seminar /ˈsemɪnɑː/ *noun* small class for discussion etc.; short intensive course of study; specialists' conference.
seminary /ˈsemɪnərɪ/ *noun* (*plural* **-ies**) training college for priests etc. ▫ **seminarist** *noun*.
semipermeable /semɪˈpɜːmɪəb(ə)l/ *adjective* (of membrane etc.) allowing small molecules to pass through.
semiprecious /semɪˈpreʃəs/ *adjective* (of gem) less valuable than a precious stone.
semi-professional /semɪprəˈfeʃən(ə)l/ ● *adjective* (of footballer, musician, etc.) paid for activity but not relying on it for living; of semi-professionals. ● *noun* semi-professional person.
semiquaver /ˈsemɪkweɪvə/ *noun Music* note equal to half a quaver.
semi-skimmed /semɪˈskɪmd/ *adjective* (of milk) with some of cream skimmed off.
Semite /ˈsiːmaɪt/ *noun* member of peoples supposedly descended from Shem, including Jews and Arabs.
Semitic /sɪˈmɪtɪk/ *adjective* of Semites, esp. Jews; of languages of family including Hebrew and Arabic.
semitone /ˈsemɪtəʊn/ *noun* half a tone in musical scale.
semivowel /ˈsemɪvaʊəl/ *noun* sound intermediate between vowel and consonant; letter representing this.
semolina /seməˈliːnə/ *noun* hard round grains of wheat used for puddings etc.; pudding of this.
Semtex /ˈsemteks/ *noun proprietary term* odourless plastic explosive.
SEN *abbreviation* State Enrolled Nurse.
Sen. *abbreviation* Senior; Senator.
senate /ˈsenɪt/ *noun* upper house of legislature in some countries; governing body of some universities or (*US*) colleges; ancient Roman state council.
senator /ˈsenətə/ *noun* member of senate. ▫ **senatorial** /-ˈtɔː-/ *adjective*.
send *verb* (*past & past participle* **sent**) order or cause to go or be conveyed; cause to become; send message etc.; grant, bestow, inflict, cause to be. ▫ **send away for** order (goods) by post; **send down** rusticate or expel from university, send to prison; **send for** summon, order by post; **send off** dispatch, attend departure of; **send-off** party etc. at departure of person; **send off for** send away for; **send on** transmit further or in advance of oneself; **send up** *colloquial* ridicule (by mimicking); **send-up** *noun* ▫ **sender** *noun*.
senescent /sɪˈnes(ə)nt/ *adjective* growing old. ▫ **senescence** *noun*.
seneschal /ˈsenɪʃ(ə)l/ *noun* steward of medieval great house.
senile /ˈsiːnaɪl/ *adjective* of old age; mentally or physically infirm because of old age. ▫ **senile dementia** illness of old people with loss of memory etc. ▫ **senility** /sɪˈnɪl-/ *noun*.
senior /ˈsiːnɪə/ ● *adjective* higher in age or standing; (placed after person's name) senior to relative of same name. ● *noun* senior person; one's elder or superior. ▫ **senior citizen** old-age pensioner. ▫ **seniority** /-ˈɒr-/ *noun*.
senna /ˈsenə/ *noun* cassia; laxative from leaves and pods of this.
señor /senˈjɔː/ *noun* (*plural* **señores** /-rez/) *title used of or to Spanish-speaking man*.
señora /senˈjɔːrə/ *noun title used of or to Spanish-speaking esp. married woman*.
señorita /senjəˈriːtə/ *noun title used of or to young Spanish-speaking esp. unmarried woman*.
sensation /senˈseɪʃ(ə)n/ *noun* feeling in one's body; awareness, impression; intense feeling, esp. in community; cause of this; sense of touch.
sensational *adjective* causing or intended to cause public excitement etc.; wonderful. ▫ **sensationalism** *noun*; **sensationalist** *noun & adjective*; **sensationalize** *verb* (also **-ise**) (**-zing** or **-sing**).
sense ● *noun* any of bodily faculties transmitting sensation; sensitiveness of any of these; ability to perceive; (+ *of*) consciousness; appreciation, instinct; practical wisdom; meaning of word etc.; intelligibility, coherence; prevailing opinion; (in *plural*) sanity, ability to think. ● *verb* (**-sing**) perceive by sense(s); be vaguely aware of; (of machine etc.) detect. ▫ **make sense** be intelligible or practicable; **make sense of** show or find meaning of. ▫ **sense of humour** see HUMOUR.
senseless *adjective* pointless, foolish; unconscious. ▫ **senselessly** *adverb*; **senselessness** *noun*.
sensibility *noun* (*plural* **-ies**) capacity to feel; (exceptional) sensitiveness; (in *plural*) tendency to feel offended etc.

■ **Usage** *Sensibility* should not be used in standard English to mean 'possession of good sense'.

sensible /ˈsensɪb(ə)l/ *adjective* having or showing good sense; perceptible by senses; (of clothing etc.) practical; (+ *of*) aware of. ▫ **sensibly** *adverb*.
sensitive /ˈsensɪtɪv/ *adjective* (often + *to*) acutely affected by external impressions, having sensibility; easily offended or hurt; (often + *to*) responsive to or recording slight changes of condition; *Photography* responding (esp. rapidly) to light; (of topic etc.) requiring tact or secrecy. ▫ **sensitively** *noun*; **sensitiveness** *noun*; **sensitivity** /-ˈtɪv-/ *noun* (*plural* **-ies**).
sensitize /ˈsensɪtaɪz/ *verb* (also **-ise**) (**-zing** or **-sing**) make sensitive. ▫ **sensitization** *noun*.
sensor /ˈsensə/ *noun* device to detect or measure a physical property.
sensory /ˈsensərɪ/ *adjective* of sensation or senses.
sensual /ˈsensjʊəl/ *adjective* of physical, esp. sexual, pleasure; enjoying, giving, or showing this. ▫ **sensuality** /-ˈæl-/ *noun*; **sensually** *adverb*.

■ **Usage** *Sensual* is sometimes confused with *sensuous*.

sensuous /ˈsensjʊəs/ *adjective* of or affecting senses, esp. aesthetically. ▫ **sensuously** *adverb*; **sensuousness** *noun*.

■ **Usage** *Sensuous* is sometimes confused with *sensual*.

sent *past & past participle* of SEND.
sentence /ˈsent(ə)ns/ ● *noun* grammatically complete series of words with (implied) subject and predicate (see panel); punishment allotted to person convicted in criminal trial; declaration of this. ● *verb* (**-cing**) declare sentence of, condemn.
sententious /senˈtenʃəs/ *adjective* pompously moralizing; affectedly formal; using maxims. ▫ **sententiousness** *noun*.
sentient /ˈsenʃ(ə)nt/ *adjective* capable of perception and feeling. ▫ **sentience** *noun*; **sentiently** *adverb*.
sentiment /ˈsentɪmənt/ *noun* mental feeling; (often in *plural*) opinion; emotional or irrational view(s); tendency to be swayed by feeling; mawkish tenderness.
sentimental /sentɪˈment(ə)l/ *adjective* of or showing sentiment; showing or affected by emotion rather than reason. ▫ **sentimentalism** *noun*; **sentimentalist** *noun*; **sentimentality** /-ˈtæl-/ *noun*; **sentimentalize** *verb* (also **-ise**) (**-zing** or **-sing**); **sentimentally** *adverb*.
sentinel /ˈsentɪn(ə)l/ *noun* sentry.

sentry /ˈsentrɪ/ *noun* (*plural* **-ies**) soldier etc. stationed to keep guard. ▫ **sentry-box** cabin to shelter standing sentry.

sepal /ˈsep(ə)l/ *noun* division or leaf of calyx.

separable /ˈsepərəb(ə)l/ *adjective* able to be separated. ▫ **separability** *noun*.

separate ● *adjective* /ˈsepərət/ forming unit by itself, existing apart; disconnected, distinct, individual. ● *noun* /ˈsepərət/ (in *plural*) articles of dress not parts of suits. ● *verb* /ˈsepəreɪt/ (**-ting**) make separate, sever; prevent union or contact of; go different ways; (esp. as **separated** *adjective*) cease to live with spouse; secede; divide or sort into parts or sizes; (often + *out*) extract or remove (ingredient etc.). ▫ **separately** *adverb*; **separateness** *noun*; **separator** *noun*.

■ **Usage** *Separate*, *separation*, etc. are not spelt with an *e* in the middle.

separation /sepəˈreɪʃ(ə)n/ *noun* separating, being separated; arrangement by which couple remain married but live apart.

separatist /ˈsepərətɪst/ *noun* person who favours separation, esp. political independence. ▫ **separatism** *noun*.

sepia /ˈsiːpɪə/ *noun* dark reddish-brown colour or paint; brown tint used in photography.

sepoy /ˈsiːpɔɪ/ *noun historical* Indian soldier under European, esp. British, discipline.

sepsis /ˈsepsɪs/ *noun* septic condition.

Sept. *abbreviation* September.

sept *noun* clan, esp. in Ireland.

September /sepˈtembə/ *noun* ninth month of year.

septet /sepˈtet/ *noun* musical composition for 7 performers; the performers; any group of 7.

septic /ˈseptɪk/ *adjective* contaminated with bacteria, putrefying. ▫ **septic tank** tank in which sewage is disintegrated through bacterial activity.

septicaemia /septɪˈsiːmɪə/ *noun* (*US* **septicemia**) blood poisoning.

septuagenarian /septjʊədʒɪˈneərɪən/ *noun* person between 70 and 79 years old.

Septuagesima /septjʊəˈdʒesɪmə/ *noun* third Sunday before Lent.

Septuagint /ˈseptjʊədʒɪnt/ *noun* ancient Greek version of Old Testament.

septum /ˈseptəm/ *noun* (*plural* **septa**) partition such as that between nostrils.

sepulchral /sɪˈpʌlkr(ə)l/ *adjective* of tomb or burial; funereal, gloomy.

sepulchre /ˈsepəlkə/ (*US* **sepulcher**) ● *noun* tomb, burial cave or vault. ● *verb* (**-ring**) lay in sepulchre.

sequel /ˈsiːkw(ə)l/ *noun* what follows; novel, film, etc. that continues story of earlier one.

sequence /ˈsiːkwəns/ *noun* succession; order of succession; set of things belonging next to one another; unbroken series; episode or incident in film etc.

sequential /sɪˈkwenʃ(ə)l/ *adjective* forming sequence or consequence. ▫ **sequentially** *adverb*.

sequester /sɪˈkwestə/ *verb* (esp. as **sequestered** *adjective*) seclude, isolate; sequestrate.

sequestrate /ˈsiːkwɪstreɪt/ *verb* (**-ting**) confiscate; take temporary possession of (debtor's estate etc.). ▫ **sequestration** *noun*.

sequin /ˈsiːkwɪn/ *noun* circular spangle on dress etc. ▫ **sequined**, **sequinned** *adjective*.

sequoia /sɪˈkwɔɪə/ *noun* extremely tall Californian conifer.

sera *plural* of SERUM.

seraglio /səˈrɑːlɪəʊ/ *noun* (*plural* **-s**) harem; *historical* Turkish palace.

seraph /ˈserəf/ *noun* (*plural* **-im** or **-s**) member of highest of 9 orders of angels. ▫ **seraphic** /səˈræfɪk/ *adjective*.

Serb ● *noun* native of Serbia; person of Serbian descent. ● *adjective* Serbian.

Serbian /ˈsɜːbɪən/ ● *noun* Slavonic dialect of Serbs; Serb. ● *adjective* of Serbs or their dialect.

Serbo-Croat /sɜːbəʊˈkrəʊæt/ (also **Serbo-Croatian** /-krəʊˈeɪʃ(ə)n/) ● *noun* main official language of former Yugoslavia, combining Serbian and Croatian dialects. ● *adjective* of this language.

serenade /serəˈneɪd/ ● *noun* piece of music performed at night, esp. under lover's window; orchestral suite for small ensemble. ● *verb* (**-ding**) perform serenade to.

serendipity /serənˈdɪpɪtɪ/ *noun* faculty of making happy discoveries by accident. ▫ **serendipitous** *adjective*.

serene /sɪˈriːn/ *adjective* (**-r**, **-st**) clear and calm; placid, unperturbed. ▫ **serenely** *adverb*; **serenity** /-ˈren-/ *noun*.

serf *noun historical* labourer not allowed to leave the land on which he worked; oppressed person, drudge. ▫ **serfdom** *noun*.

serge *noun* durable woollen fabric.

sergeant /ˈsɑːdʒ(ə)nt/ *noun* non-commissioned army or RAF officer next below warrant officer; police officer next below inspector. ▫ **sergeant major** warrant officer assisting adjutant of regiment or battalion.

serial /ˈsɪərɪəl/ ● *noun* story published, broadcast, or shown in instalments. ● *adjective* of, in, or forming series. ▫ **serial killer** person who murders repeatedly. ▫ **serially** *adverb*.

serialize *verb* (also **-ise**) (**-zing** or **-sing**) publish or produce in instalments. ▫ **serialization** *noun*.

Sentence

A sentence is the basic unit of language in use and expresses a complete thought. There are three types of sentence, each starting with a capital letter, and each normally ending with a full stop, a question mark, or an exclamation mark:

Statement:	*You're happy.*
Question:	*Is it raining?*
Exclamation:	*I wouldn't have believed it!*

A sentence, especially a statement, often has no punctuation at the end in a public notice, a newspaper headline, or a legal document, e.g.

Government cuts public spending

A sentence normally contains a subject and a verb, but may not, e.g.

What a mess! *Where?* *In the sink.*

series /ˈsɪəriːz/ *noun* (*plural* same) number of similar or related things, events, etc.; succession, row, set; *Broadcasting* set of related but individually complete programmes. □ **in series** in ordered succession, (of set of electrical circuits) arranged so that same current passes through each circuit.

serif /ˈserɪf/ *noun* fine cross-line at extremities of printed letter.

serious /ˈsɪərɪəs/ *adjective* thoughtful, earnest; important, requiring thought; not negligible, dangerous; sincere, in earnest; (of music, literature, etc.) intellectual, not popular. □ **seriously** *adverb*; **seriousness** *noun*.

serjeant /ˈsɑːdʒ(ə)nt/ *noun* (in full **serjeant-at-law**, *plural* **serjeants-at-law**) *historical* barrister of highest rank. □ **serjeant-at-arms** official of court, city, or parliament, with ceremonial duties.

sermon /ˈsɜːmən/ *noun* discourse on religion or morals, esp. delivered in church; admonition, reproof.

sermonize *verb* (also **-ise**) (**-zing** or **-sing**) (often + *to*) moralize.

serous /ˈsɪərəs/ *adjective* of or like serum, watery; (of gland etc.) having serous secretion.

serpent /ˈsɜːpənt/ *noun* snake, esp. large; cunning or treacherous person.

serpentine /ˈsɜːpəntaɪn/ ● *adjective* of or like serpent; coiling, sinuous; cunning, treacherous. ● *noun* soft usually dark green rock, sometimes mottled.

SERPS *abbreviation* State Earnings-Related Pension Scheme.

serrated /səˈreɪtɪd/ *adjective* with sawlike edge. □ **serration** *noun*.

serried /ˈserɪd/ *adjective* (of ranks of soldiers etc.) close together.

serum /ˈsɪərəm/ *noun* (*plural* **sera** or **-s**) liquid separating from clot when blood coagulates, esp. used for inoculation; watery fluid in animal bodies.

servant /ˈsɜːv(ə)nt/ *noun* person employed for domestic work; devoted follower or helper.

serve ● *verb* (**-ving**) do service for; be servant to; carry out duty; (+ *in*) be employed in (esp. armed forces); be useful to or serviceable for; meet needs, perform function; go through due period of (apprenticeship, prison sentence, etc.); go through (specified period) of imprisonment etc.; (often + *up*) present (food) to eat; act as waiter; attend to (customer etc.); (+ *with*) supply with (goods); treat (person) in specified way; *Law* (often + *on*) deliver (writ etc.), (+ *with*) deliver writ etc. to; set (ball) in play at tennis etc.; (of male animal) copulate with (female). ● *noun Tennis etc.* service. □ **serve** (**person**) **right** be his or her deserved misfortune. □ **server** *noun*.

service /ˈsɜːvɪs/ ● *noun* (often in *plural*) work done or doing of work for employer or for community etc.; work done by machine etc.; assistance or benefit given; provision of some public need, e.g. transport or (often in *plural*) water, gas, etc.; employment as servant; state or period of employment; Crown or public department or organization; (in *plural*) the armed forces; ceremony of worship; liturgical form for this; (routine) maintenance and repair of machine etc. after sale; assistance given to customers; serving of food etc., quality of this, nominal charge for this; (in *plural*) motorway service area; set of dishes etc. for serving meal; act of serving in tennis etc., person's turn to serve, game in which one serves. ● *verb* (**-cing**) maintain or repair (car, machine, etc.); provide service for. □ **at** (**person's**) **service** ready to serve him or her; **of service** useful; **service area** area near road supplying petrol, refreshments, etc.; **service charge** additional charge for service in restaurant etc.; **service flat** one in which domestic service etc. is provided; **service industry** one providing services, not goods; **serviceman**, **servicewoman** person in armed services; **service road** one giving access to houses etc. lying back from main road; **service station** establishment selling petrol etc. to motorists.

serviceable *adjective* useful, usable; durable but plain. □ **serviceability** *noun*.

serviette /sɜːvɪˈet/ *noun* table napkin.

servile /ˈsɜːvaɪl/ *adjective* of or like slave(s); fawning, subservient. □ **servility** /-ˈvɪl-/ *noun*.

servitude /ˈsɜːvɪtjuːd/ *noun* slavery, subjection.

servo- /ˈsɜːvəʊ/ *combining form* power-assisted.

sesame /ˈsesəmɪ/ *noun* E. Indian plant with oil-yielding seeds; its seeds.

sesqui- /ˈseskwɪ/ *combining form* one and a half.

sessile /ˈsesaɪl/ *adjective Biology* attached directly by base without stalk or peduncle; fixed, immobile.

session /ˈseʃ(ə)n/ *noun* period devoted to an activity; assembly of parliament, court, etc.; single meeting for this; period during which such meetings are regularly held; academic year. □ **in session** assembled for business, not on vacation. □ **sessional** *adjective*.

set ● *verb* (**-tt-**; *past & past participle* **set**) put, lay, or stand in certain position etc.; apply; fix or place ready; dispose suitably for use, action, or display; adjust hands or mechanism of (clock, trap, etc.); insert (jewel) in ring etc.; lay (table) for meal; style (hair) while damp; (+ *with*) ornament or provide (surface) with; bring into specified state, cause to be; harden, solidify; (of sun, moon, etc.) move towards or below earth's horizon; show (story etc.) as happening in a certain time or place; (+ *to do*) cause (person) to do specified thing; (+ *present participle*) start (person, thing) doing something; present or impose as work to be done, problem to be solved, etc.; exhibit as model etc.; initiate (fashion etc.); establish (record etc.); determine, decide; appoint, establish; put parts of (broken or dislocated bone, limb, etc.) together for healing; provide (song, words) with music; arrange (type) or type for (book etc.); (of tide, current, etc.) have a certain motion or direction; (of face) assume hard expression; (of eyes etc.) become motionless; have a certain tendency; (of blossom) form into fruit; (of dancer) take position facing partner; (of hunting dog) take rigid attitude indicating presence of game. ● *noun* group of linked or similar things or persons; section of society; collection of objects for specified purpose; radio or television receiver; *Tennis etc.* group of games counting as unit towards winning match; *Mathematics* collection of things sharing a property; direction or position in which something sets or is set; slip, shoot, bulb, etc. for planting; setting, stage furniture, etc. for play, film, etc.; setting of sun, hair, etc.; = SETT. ● *adjective* prescribed or determined in advance; unchanging, fixed; prepared for action; (+ *on*, *upon*) determined to get, achieve, etc. □ **set about** begin, take steps towards, *colloquial* attack; **set aside** put to one side, keep for future, disregard or reject; **set back** place further back in space or time, impede or reverse progress of, *colloquial* cost (person) specified amount; **set-back** reversal or arrest of progress; **set down** record in writing, allow to alight; **set forth** begin journey, expound; **set in** begin, become established, insert; **set off** begin journey, detonate (bomb etc.), initiate, stimulate, cause (person) to start laughing etc., adorn, enhance, (+ *against*) use as compensating item against; **set on** (cause or urge to) attack; **set out** begin journey, (+ *to do*) intend, exhibit, arrange; **set piece** formal or elaborate arrangement, esp. in art or literature; **set square** right-angled triangular plate for drawing lines at certain angles; **set to** begin doing something vigorously; **set theory** study or use of sets in mathematics; **set-to** (*plural* **-tos**) *colloquial* fight, argument; **set up** place in position or view, start, establish, equip, prepare, *colloquial* cause (person) to look guilty or foolish; **set-up** arrangement or organization, manner or structure of this, instance of setting person up; **set upon** set on.

sett *noun* (also **set**) badger's burrow, paving-block.

settee /se'ti:/ *noun* sofa.

setter *noun* dog of long-haired breed trained to stand rigid on scenting game.

setting *noun* position or manner in which thing is set; surroundings; period, place, etc. of story, film, etc.; frame etc. for jewel; music to which words are set; cutlery etc. for one person at table; operating level of machine.

settle[1] /'set(ə)l/ *verb* (**-ling**) (often + *down*, *in*) establish or become established in abode or lifestyle; (often + *down*) regain calm after disturbance, adopt regular or secure way of life, (+ *to*) apply oneself to; (cause to) sit down or come to rest; make or become composed etc.; determine, decide, agree on; resolve (dispute etc.); agree to terminate (lawsuit); (+ *for*) accept or agree to; pay (bill); (as **settled** *adjective*) established; colonize; subside, sink. □ **settle up** pay money owed etc.

settle[2] /'set(ə)l/ *noun* high-backed bench, often with box under seat.

settlement *noun* settling, being settled; place occupied by settlers, small village; political etc. agreement; arrangement ending dispute; terms on which property is given to person; deed stating these; amount or property given.

settler *noun* person who settles in newly developed region.

seven /'sev(ə)n/ *adjective & noun* one more than six. □ **seventh** *adjective & noun*.

seventeen /sevən'ti:n/ *adjective & noun* one more than sixteen. □ **seventeenth** *adjective & noun*.

seventy /'sevəntɪ/ *adjective & noun* (*plural* **-ies**) seven times ten. □ **seventieth** *adjective & noun*.

sever /'sevə/ *verb* divide, break, or make separate, esp. by cutting.

several /'sevr(ə)l/ ● *adjective* a few; quite a large number; *formal* separate, respective. ● *pronoun* a few; quite a large number. □ **severally** *adverb*.

severance /'sevr(ə)ns/ *noun* severing; severed state. □ **severance pay** payment to employee on termination of contract.

severe /sɪ'vɪə/ *adjective* rigorous and harsh; not negligible, worrying; forceful; extreme; exacting; unadorned. □ **severely** *adverb*; **severity** /-'ver-/ *noun*.

sew /səʊ/ *verb* (*past participle* **sewn** or **sewed**) fasten, join, etc. with needle and thread or sewing machine. □ **sewing machine** machine for sewing or stitching.

sewage /'su:ɪdʒ/ *noun* waste matter carried in sewers. □ **sewage farm**, **works** place where sewage is treated.

sewer /'su:ə/ *noun* (usually underground) conduit for carrying off drainage water and waste matter.

sewerage /'su:ərɪdʒ/ *noun* system of or drainage by sewers.

sewing /'səʊɪŋ/ *noun* material or work to be sewn.

sewn *past participle* of SEW.

sex ● *noun* group of males or females collectively; fact of belonging to either group; sexual instincts, desires, activity, etc.; *colloquial* sexual intercourse. ● *adjective* of or relating to sex or sexual differences. ● *verb* determine sex of; (as **sexed** *adjective*) having specified sexual appetite. □ **sex appeal** sexual attractiveness; **sex life** person's sexual activity; **sex symbol** person famed for sex appeal.

sexagenarian /seksədʒɪ'neərɪən/ *noun* person between 60 and 69 years old.

Sexagesima /seksə'dʒesɪmə/ *noun* second Sunday before Lent.

sexism *noun* prejudice or discrimination against people (esp. women) because of their sex. □ **sexist** *adjective & noun*.

sexless *adjective* neither male nor female; lacking sexual desire or attractiveness.

sextant /'sekst(ə)nt/ *noun* optical instrument for measuring angle between distant objects, esp. sun and horizon in navigation.

sextet /seks'tet/ *noun* musical composition for 6 performers; the performers; any group of 6.

sexton /'sekst(ə)n/ *noun* person who looks after church and churchyard, often acting as bell-ringer and gravedigger.

sextuple /'sekstju:p(ə)l/ *adjective* sixfold.

sextuplet /'sekstjʊplɪt/ *noun* each of 6 children born at one birth.

sexual /'sekʃʊəl/ *adjective* of sex, the sexes, or relations between them. □ **sexual intercourse** insertion of man's penis into woman's vagina. □ **sexuality** /-'æl-/ *noun*; **sexually** *adverb*.

sexy *adjective* (**-ier**, **-iest**) sexually attractive or provocative; *colloquial* (of project etc.) exciting. □ **sexily** *adverb*; **sexiness** *noun*.

SF *abbreviation* science fiction.

Sgt. *abbreviation* Sergeant.

sh *interjection* hush.

shabby /'ʃæbɪ/ *adjective* (**-ier**, **-iest**) faded and worn, dingy, dilapidated; poorly dressed; contemptible. □ **shabbily** *adverb*; **shabbiness** *noun*.

shack ● *noun* roughly built hut or cabin. ● *verb* (+ *up*) *slang* cohabit.

shackle /'ʃæk(ə)l/ ● *noun* metal loop or link closed by bolt, coupling link; fetter; (usually in *plural*) restraint. ● *verb* (**-ling**) fetter, impede, restrain.

shad *noun* (*plural* same or **-s**) large edible marine fish.

shade ● *noun* comparative darkness caused by shelter from direct light and heat; area so sheltered; darker part of picture etc.; a colour, esp. as darker or lighter than one similar; comparative obscurity; slight amount; lampshade; screen moderating light; (in *plural*) *esp. US colloquial* sunglasses; *literary* ghost; (in *plural*; + *of*) reminder of. ● *verb* (**-ding**) screen from light; cover or moderate light of; darken, esp. with parallel lines to represent shadow etc.; (often + *away*, *off*, *into*) pass or change gradually. □ **shading** *noun*.

shadow /'ʃædəʊ/ ● *noun* shade; patch of shade; dark shape projected by body blocking out light; inseparable attendant or companion; person secretly following another; (with negative) slightest trace; insubstantial remnant; shaded part of picture; gloom, sadness. ● *verb* cast shadow over; secretly follow and watch. □ **shadow-boxing** boxing against imaginary opponent; **Shadow Cabinet**, **Minister**, etc., members of opposition party holding posts parallel to those of government. □ **shadowy** *adjective*.

shady /'ʃeɪdɪ/ *adjective* (**-ier**, **-iest**) giving or situated in shade; disreputable, of doubtful honesty.

shaft /ʃɑ:ft/ *noun* narrow usually vertical space for access to mine or (in building) for lift, ventilation, etc.; (+ *of*) ray of (light), stroke of (lightning); handle of tool etc.; long narrow part supporting, connecting, or driving thicker part(s) etc.; *archaic* arrow, spear, its long slender stem; hurtful or provocative remark;

each of pair of poles between which horse is harnessed to vehicle; central stem of feather; column, esp. between base and capital.

shag ● *noun* coarse tobacco; rough mass of hair; (crested) cormorant. ● *adjective* (of carpet) with long rough pile.

shaggy *adjective* (**-ier**, **-iest**) hairy, rough-haired; tangled. □ **shaggy-dog story** lengthy 'joke' without funny ending. □ **shagginess** *noun*.

shagreen /ʃæ'gri:n/ *noun* kind of untanned granulated leather; sharkskin.

shah /ʃɑ:/ *noun historical* ruler of Iran.

shake ● *verb* (**-king**; *past* **shook** /ʃʊk/; *past participle* **shaken**) move violently or quickly up and down or to and fro; (cause to) tremble or vibrate; agitate, shock, disturb; weaken, impair; *colloquial* shake hands. ● *noun* shaking, being shaken; jerk, shock; (**the shakes**) *colloquial* fit of trembling. □ **shake down** settle or cause to fall by shaking, become comfortably settled or established; **shake hands** (often + *with*) clasp hands, esp. at meeting or parting or as sign of bargain; **shake off** get rid of, evade; **shake up** mix (ingredients) or restore to shape by shaking, disturb or make uncomfortable, rouse from lethargy etc.; **shake-up** upheaval, reorganization.

shaker *noun* person or thing that shakes; container for shaking together ingredients of cocktails etc.

Shakespearian /ʃeɪk'spɪərɪən/ *adjective* (also **Shakespearean**) of Shakespeare.

shako /'ʃækəʊ/ *noun* (*plural* **-s**) cylindrical plumed military peaked cap.

shaky *adjective* (**-ier**, **-iest**) unsteady, trembling; infirm; unreliable. □ **shakily** *adverb*; **shakiness** *noun*.

shale *noun* soft rock that splits easily. □ **shaly** *adjective*.

shall *auxiliary verb* (*3rd singular present* **shall**) *used to form future tenses.*

shallot /ʃə'lɒt/ *noun* onion-like plant with cluster of small bulbs.

shallow /'ʃæləʊ/ ● *adjective* having little depth; superficial, trivial. ● *noun* (often in *plural*) shallow place. □ **shallowness** *noun*.

sham ● *verb* (**-mm-**) feign; pretend (to be). ● *noun* imposture, pretence; bogus or false person or thing. ● *adjective* pretended, counterfeit.

shamble /'ʃæmb(ə)l/ ● *verb* (**-ling**) walk or run awkwardly, dragging feet. ● *noun* shambling gait.

shambles *plural noun* (usually treated as *singular*) *colloquial* mess, muddle; butcher's slaughterhouse; scene of carnage.

shambolic /ʃæm'bɒlɪk/ *adjective colloquial* chaotic, disorganized.

shame ● *noun* humiliation caused by consciousness of guilt or folly; capacity for feeling this; state of disgrace or discredit; person or thing that brings disgrace etc.; wrong or regrettable thing. ● *verb* (**-ming**) bring disgrace on, make ashamed; (+ *into*, *out of*) force by shame into or out of. □ **shamefaced** showing shame, bashful.

shameful *adjective* disgraceful, scandalous. □ **shamefully** *adverb*; **shamefulness** *noun*.

shameless *adjective* having or showing no shame; impudent. □ **shamelessly** *adverb*.

shammy /'ʃæmɪ/ *noun* (*plural* **-ies**) *colloquial* chamois leather.

shampoo /ʃæm'pu:/ ● *noun* liquid for washing hair; similar substance for washing cars, carpets, etc. ● *verb* (**-poos**, **-pooed**) wash with shampoo.

shamrock /'ʃæmrɒk/ *noun* trefoil, as national emblem of Ireland.

shandy /'ʃændɪ/ *noun* (*plural* **-ies**) beer with lemonade or ginger beer.

shanghai /ʃæŋ'haɪ/ *verb* (**-hais**, **-haied**, **-haiing**) *colloquial* trick or force (person) to do something, esp. be sailor.

shank *noun* leg, lower part of leg; shaft or stem, esp. joining tool's handle to its working end.

shan't /ʃɑ:nt/ shall not.

shantung /ʃæn'tʌŋ/ *noun* soft undressed Chinese silk.

shanty[1] /'ʃæntɪ/ *noun* (*plural* **-ies**) hut, cabin. □ **shanty town** area with makeshift housing.

shanty[2] /'ʃæntɪ/ *noun* (*plural* **-ies**) (in full **sea shanty**) sailors' work song.

shape ● *noun* outline; form; specific form or guise; good or specified condition; person or thing seen indistinctly; mould, pattern. ● *verb* (**-ping**) give a certain form to, fashion, create; influence; (usually + *up*) show promise; (+ *to*) make conform to. □ **take shape** assume distinct form, develop.

shapeless *adjective* lacking definite or attractive shape. □ **shapelessness** *noun*.

shapely *adjective* (**-ier**, **-iest**) of pleasing shape, well-proportioned. □ **shapeliness** *noun*.

shard *noun* broken fragment of pottery, glass, etc.

share /ʃeə/ ● *noun* portion of whole given to or taken from person; each of equal parts into which company's capital is divided, entitling owner to proportion of profits. ● *verb* (**-ring**) have or use with another or others; get, have, or give share of; (+ *in*) participate in; (+ *out*) divide and distribute. □ **shareholder** owner of shares in a company; **shareout** division and distribution.

shark *noun* large voracious sea fish; *colloquial* swindler, extortioner. □ **sharkskin** skin of shark, smooth slightly shiny fabric.

sharp ● *adjective* having edge or point able to cut or pierce; tapering to a point or edge; abrupt, steep, angular; well-defined; severe, intense; pungent, acid; shrill, piercing; harsh; acute, sensitive, clever; unscrupulous; vigorous, brisk; *Music* above true pitch, a semitone higher than note named. ● *noun Music* sharp note; sign (♯) indicating this; *colloquial* swindler, cheat. ● *adverb* punctually; suddenly; at a sharp angle; *Music* above true pitch. □ **sharp practice** barely honest dealings; **sharpshooter** skilled marksman; **sharp-witted** keenly perceptive or intelligent. □ **sharpen** *verb*; **sharpener** *noun*; **sharply** *adverb*; **sharpness** *noun*.

sharper *noun* swindler, esp. at cards.

shatter /'ʃætə/ *verb* break suddenly in pieces; severely damage, destroy; (esp. in *passive*) severely upset; (usually as **shattered** *adjective*) *colloquial* exhaust.

shave ● *verb* (**-ving**; *past participle* **shaved** or (as *adjective*) **shaven**) remove (hair, bristles) with razor; remove hair with razor from (leg, head, etc.) or from face of (person); reduce by small amount; pare (wood etc.) to shape it; miss or pass narrowly. ● *noun* shaving, being shaved; narrow miss or escape.

shaver *noun* thing that shaves; electric razor; *colloquial* young lad.

shaving *noun* (esp. in *plural*) thin paring of wood.

shawl *noun* large usually rectangular piece of fabric worn over shoulders etc. or wrapped round baby.

she *pronoun* (as subject of verb) the female person or animal in question.

s/he *pronoun: written representation of* 'he or she'.

sheaf ● *noun* (*plural* **sheaves**) bundle of things laid lengthways together and usually tied, esp. reaped corn or collection of papers. ● *verb* make into sheaves.

shear ● *verb* (*past* **sheared**; *past participle* **shorn** or **sheared**) clip wool off (sheep etc.); remove by cutting; cut with scissors, shears, etc.; strip bare, deprive; (often + *of*) distort, be distorted, or break. ● *noun* strain produced by pressure in structure of substance; (in *plural*) (also **pair of shears** *singular*) scissor-shaped clipping or cutting instrument. □ **shearer** *noun*.

sheath /ʃi:θ/ *noun* (*plural* **-s** /ʃi:ðz/) close-fitting cover, esp. for blade; condom. □ **sheath knife** dagger-like knife carried in sheath.

sheathe /ʃi:ð/ *verb* (**-thing**) put into sheath; encase or protect with sheath.

sheaves *plural* of SHEAF.

shebeen /ʃɪ'bi:n/ *noun esp. Irish* unlicensed drinking place.

shed[1] *noun* one-storeyed building for storage or shelter or as workshop etc.

shed[2] *verb* (**-dd-**; *past & past participle* **shed**) let, or cause to, fall off; take off (clothes); reduce (electrical power load); cause to fall or flow; disperse, diffuse, radiate; get rid of.

she'd /ʃi:d/ she had; she would.

sheen *noun* lustre, brightness.

sheep *noun* (*plural* same) mammal with thick woolly coat, esp. kept for its wool or meat; timid, silly, or easily-led person; (usually in *plural*) member of minister's congregation. □ **sheep-dip** preparation or place for cleansing sheep of vermin etc.; **sheepdog** dog trained to guard and herd sheep, dog of breed suitable for this; **sheepfold** enclosure for sheep; **sheepshank** knot for temporarily shortening rope; **sheepskin** sheep's skin with wool on.

sheepish *adjective* embarrassed or shy; ashamed. □ **sheepishly** *adverb*.

sheer[1] ● *adjective* mere, complete; (of cliff etc.) perpendicular; (of textile) diaphanous. ● *adverb* directly, perpendicularly.

sheer[2] *verb* swerve or change course; (often + *away, off*) turn away, esp. from person that one dislikes or fears.

sheet[1] ● *noun* rectangular piece of cotton etc. as part of bedclothes; broad thin flat piece of paper, metal, etc.; wide expanse of water, ice, flame, etc. ● *verb* cover (as) with sheet; (of rain etc.) fall in sheets. □ **sheet metal** metal rolled or hammered etc. into thin sheets; **sheet music** music published in separate sheets.

sheet[2] *noun* rope at lower corner of sail to control it. □ **sheet anchor** emergency anchor, person or thing depended on as last hope.

sheikh /ʃeɪk/ *noun* chief or head of Arab tribe, family, or village; Muslim leader.

sheila /'ʃi:lə/ *noun Australian & NZ offensive slang* girl, young woman.

shekel /'ʃek(ə)l/ *noun* chief monetary unit of Israel; *historical* weight and coin in ancient Israel etc.; (in *plural*) *colloquial* money.

shelduck /'ʃeldʌk/ *noun* (*plural* same or **-s**; *masculine* **sheldrake**, *plural* same or **-s**) brightly coloured wild duck.

shelf *noun* (*plural* **shelves**) wooden etc. board projecting from wall or forming part of bookcase or cupboard; ledge on cliff face etc.; reef, sandbank. □ **on the shelf** (of woman) considered past marriageable age, put aside; **shelf-life** time for which stored thing remains usable; **shelf-mark** code on book to show its place in library.

shell ● *noun* hard outer case of many molluscs, tortoise, egg, nut-kernel, seed, etc.; explosive artillery projectile; hollow container for fireworks, cartridges, etc.; light racing boat; framework of vehicle etc.; walls of unfinished or gutted building etc. ● *verb* remove shell or pod from; fire shells at. □ **come out of one's shell** become less shy; **shellfish** aquatic mollusc with shell, crustacean; **shell out** *colloquial* pay (money); **shell-shock** nervous breakdown caused by warfare; **shell-shocked** *adjective* □ **shell-like** *adjective*.

she'll /ʃi:l/ she will; she shall.

shellac /ʃə'læk/ ● *noun* resin used for making varnish. ● *verb* (**-ck-**) varnish with shellac.

shelter /'ʃeltə/ ● *noun* protection from danger, bad weather, etc.; place providing this. ● *verb* act or serve as shelter to; shield; take shelter.

shelve *verb* (**-ving**) put aside, esp. temporarily; put on shelf; provide with shelves; (of ground) slope.

shelving *noun* shelves; material for shelves.

shepherd /'ʃepəd/ ● *noun* (*feminine* **shepherdess**) person who tends sheep; pastor. ● *verb* tend (sheep); marshal or guide like sheep. □ **shepherd's pie** minced meat baked with covering of (esp. mashed) potato.

sherbet /'ʃɜ:bət/ *noun* flavoured effervescent powder or drink.

sherd *noun* potsherd.

sheriff /'ʃerɪf/ *noun* (also **High Sheriff**) chief executive officer of Crown in county, administering justice etc.; *US* chief law-enforcing officer of county; (also **sheriff-depute**) *Scottish* chief judge of county or district.

sherry /'ʃerɪ/ *noun* (*plural* **-ies**) fortified wine originally from Spain.

she's /ʃi:z/ she is; she has.

Shetland pony /'ʃetlənd/ *noun* pony of small hardy breed.

shew *archaic* = SHOW.

shiatsu /ʃɪ'ætsu:/ *noun* Japanese therapy involving pressure on specific points of body.

shibboleth /'ʃɪbəleθ/ *noun* long-standing formula, doctrine, phrase, etc. espoused by party or sect.

shied *past & past participle* of SHY[2].

shield /ʃi:ld/ ● *noun* piece of defensive armour held in front of body when fighting; person or thing giving protection; shield-shaped trophy; protective plate or screen in machinery etc.; representation of shield for displaying person's coat of arms. ● *verb* protect, screen.

shier *comparative* of SHY[1].

shiest *superlative* of SHY[1].

shift ● *verb* (cause to) change or move from one position to another; remove, esp. with effort; *slang* hurry; *US* change (gear). ● *noun* shifting; relay of workers; period for which they work; device, expedient, trick; woman's loose straight dress; displacement of spectral line; key on keyboard for switching between lower and upper case etc.; *US* gear lever in motor vehicle. □ **make shift** manage, get along; **shift for oneself** rely on one's own efforts; **shift one's ground** alter stance in argument etc.

shiftless *adjective* lacking resourcefulness; lazy.

shifty *adjective* (**-ier**, **-iest**) *colloquial* evasive, deceitful.

Shiite /'ʃi:aɪt/ ● *noun* member of esp. Iranian branch of Islam opposed to Sunnis. ● *adjective* of this branch.

shillelagh /ʃɪ'leɪlɪ/ *noun* Irish cudgel.

shilling /'ʃɪlɪŋ/ *noun historical* former British coin and monetary unit, worth 1/20 of pound; monetary unit in some other countries.

shilly-shally /'ʃɪlɪʃælɪ/ *verb* (**-ies**, **-ied**) be undecided, vacillate.

shimmer /'ʃɪmə/ ● *verb* shine tremulously or faintly. ● *noun* tremulous or faint light.

shin ● *noun* front of leg below knee; cut of beef from this part. ● *verb* (**-nn-**) (usually + *up, down*) climb quickly using arms and legs. □ **shin-bone** tibia.

shindig /'ʃɪndɪg/ *noun* (also **shindy**) *colloquial* lively noisy party; brawl, disturbance.

shine ● *verb* (**-ning**; *past & past participle* **shone** /ʃɒn/ or **shined**) emit or reflect light, be bright, glow; (of sun, star, etc.) be visible; cause to shine; be brilliant, excel; (*past & past participle* **shined**) polish. ● *noun* light, brightness; polish, lustre. □ **take a shine to** *colloquial* take a liking to.

shiner *noun colloquial* black eye.

shingle[1] /'ʃɪŋg(ə)l/ *noun* small rounded pebbles on seashore. □ **shingly** *adjective*.

shingle[2] /'ʃɪŋg(ə)l/ ● *noun* rectangular wooden tile used on roofs etc.; *archaic* shingled hair. ● *verb* (**-ling**) roof with shingles; *archaic* cut (woman's hair) short and tapering.

shingles /'ʃɪŋg(ə)lz/ *plural noun* (usually treated as *singular*) painful viral infection of nerves with rash, esp. round waist.

Shinto /'ʃɪntəʊ/ *noun* (also **Shintoism**) Japanese religion with worship of ancestors and nature-spirits.

shinty /'ʃɪntɪ/ *noun* (*plural* **-ies**) game resembling hockey; stick or ball for this.

shiny *adjective* (**-ier**, **-iest**) having shine; (of clothing) with nap worn off.

ship ● *noun* large seagoing vessel; *US* aircraft; spaceship. ● *verb* (**-pp-**) transport, esp. in ship; take in (water) over ship's side etc.; lay (oars) at bottom of boat; fix (rudder etc.) in place; embark; be hired to work on ship. □ **shipmate** fellow member of ship's crew; **ship off** send away; **shipshape** trim, neat, tidy; **shipwreck** *noun* destruction of ship by storm or collision etc., ship so destroyed, *verb* (usually in *passive*) cause to suffer this; **shipwright** shipbuilder, ship's carpenter; **shipyard** place where ships are built.

shipment *noun* goods shipped; act of shipping goods etc.

shipper *noun* person or company that ships goods.

shipping *noun* transport of goods etc.; ships collectively.

shire /ʃaɪə/ *noun* county. □ **shire horse** heavy powerful horse.

shirk *verb* avoid (duty, work, etc.). □ **shirker** *noun*.

shirr ● *noun* elasticated gathered threads forming smocking. ● *verb* gather (material) with parallel threads. □ **shirring** *noun*.

shirt *noun* upper-body garment of cotton etc., usually with sleeves and collar. □ **in shirtsleeves** not wearing jacket; **shirt dress**, **shirtwaister** dress with bodice like shirt.

shirty *adjective* (**-ier**, **-iest**) *colloquial* annoyed. □ **shirtily** *adverb*; **shirtiness** *noun*.

shish kebab /ʃɪʃ/ *noun* pieces of meat and vegetables grilled on skewer.

shiver[1] /'ʃɪvə/ ● *verb* tremble with cold, fear, etc. ● *noun* momentary shivering movement; (**the shivers**) attack of shivering. □ **shivery** *adjective*.

shiver[2] /'ʃɪvə/ ● *noun* (esp. in *plural*) small fragment, splinter. ● *verb* break into shivers.

shoal[1] ● *noun* multitude, esp. of fish swimming together. ● *verb* form shoal(s).

shoal[2] ● *noun* area of shallow water; submerged sandbank. ● *verb* (of water) become shallow.

shock[1] ● *noun* violent collision, impact, etc.; sudden and disturbing emotional effect; acute prostration following wound, pain, etc.; electric shock; disturbance in stability of organization etc. ● *verb* horrify, outrage; cause shock; affect with electric or pathological shock. □ **shock absorber** device on vehicle etc. for absorbing shock and vibration; **shockproof** resistant to effects of shock; **shock therapy** electroconvulsive therapy; **shock wave** moving region of high air pressure caused by explosion etc.

shock[2] *noun* unkempt or shaggy mass of hair.

shocker *noun colloquial* shocking person or thing; sensational novel etc.

shocking *adjective* causing shock, scandalous; *colloquial* very bad. □ **shocking pink** vibrant shade of pink. □ **shockingly** *adverb*.

shod *past & past participle* of SHOE.

shoddy /'ʃɒdɪ/ *adjective* (**-ier**, **-iest**) poorly made; counterfeit. □ **shoddily** *adverb*; **shoddiness** *noun*.

shoe /ʃu:/ ● *noun* foot-covering of leather etc., esp. one not reaching above ankle; protective metal rim for horse's hoof; thing like shoe in shape or use. ● *verb* (**shoes**, **shoeing**; *past & past participle* **shod**) fit with shoe(s). □ **-shod** having shoes of specified kind; **shoehorn** curved implement for easing heel into shoe; **shoelace** cord for lacing shoe; **shoestring** shoelace, *colloquial* small esp. inadequate amount of money; **shoe-tree** shaped block for keeping shoe in shape.

shone *past & past participle* of SHINE.

shoo ● *interjection used to frighten animals etc. away.* ● *verb* (**shoos**, **shooed**) utter such sound; (usually + *away*) drive away thus.

shook *past* of SHAKE.

shoot /ʃu:t/ ● *verb* (*past & past participle* **shot**) cause (weapon) to discharge missile; kill or wound with bullet, arrow, etc.; send out or discharge rapidly; come or go swiftly or suddenly; (of plant) put forth buds etc., (of bud etc.) appear; hunt game etc. with gun; film, photograph; *esp. Football* score or take shot at (goal); (often + *up*) *slang* inject (drug). ● *noun* young branch or sucker; hunting party or expedition; land on which game is shot. □ **shooting gallery** place for shooting at targets with rifles etc.; **shooting star** small rapidly moving meteor; **shooting stick** walking stick with foldable seat.

shop ● *noun* place for retail sale of goods or services; act of shopping; place for making or repairing something; *colloquial* place of business etc. ● *verb* (**-pp-**) go to shop(s) to make purchases; *slang* inform against. □ **shop around** look for best bargain; **shop assistant** person serving in shop; **shop-floor** production area in factory etc., workers as distinct from management; **shopkeeper** owner or manager of shop; **shoplift** steal goods while appearing to shop; **shoplifter** *noun*; **shop-soiled** soiled or faded by display in shop; **shop steward** elected representative of workers in factory etc.; **shopwalker** supervisor in large shop; **talk shop** talk about one's occupation. □ **shopper** *noun*.

shopping *noun* purchase of goods; goods bought. □ **shopping centre** area containing many shops.

shore[1] *noun* land adjoining sea, lake, etc.; (usually in *plural*) country. □ **on shore** ashore; **shoreline** line where shore meets water.

shore[2] *verb* (**-ring**) (often + *up*) support (as if) with prop(s) or beam(s).

shorn *past participle* of SHEAR.

short ● *adjective* measuring little from end to end in space or time, or from head to foot; (usually + *of*, *on*) deficient, scanty; concise, brief; curt, uncivil; (of memory) unable to remember distant events; (of vowel or syllable) having the less of two recognized durations; (of pastry) easily crumbled; (of a drink of spirits) undiluted. ● *adverb* before the natural or expected time or place; abruptly; rudely. ● *noun* short circuit; *colloquial* short drink; short film. ● *verb* short-circuit. □ **short back and sides** short simple haircut; **shortbread**, **shortcake** rich crumbly biscuit or cake made of flour, butter, and sugar; **short-change** cheat, esp. by giving insufficient change;

short circuit electric circuit through small resistance, esp. instead of through normal circuit; **short-circuit** cause short circuit in, have short circuit, shorten or avoid by taking short cut; **shortcoming** deficiency, defect; **short cut** path or course shorter than usual or normal; **shortfall** deficit; **shorthand** method of rapid writing using special symbols, abbreviated or symbolic means of expression; **short-handed**, **-staffed** understaffed; **shorthorn** animal of breed of cattle with short horns; **short list** list of candidates from whom final selection will be made; **short-list** put on short list; **short-lived** ephemeral; **short-range** having short range, relating to immediate future; **short shrift** curt or dismissive treatment; **short sight** inability to focus except at close range; **short-tempered** easily angered; **short-term** of or for a short period of time; **short-winded** easily becoming breathless. ▫ **shorten** *verb*.

shortage *noun* (often + *of*) deficiency; lack.

shortening *noun* fat for pastry.

shortly *adverb* (often + *before, after*) soon; curtly.

shorts *plural noun* trousers reaching to knees or higher; *US* underpants.

short-sighted *adjective* having short sight; lacking imagination or foresight. ▫ **short-sightedly** *adverb*; **shortsightedness** *noun*.

shot[1] *noun* firing of gun etc.; attempt to hit by shooting or throwing etc.; single missile for gun etc.; (*plural* same or **-s**) small lead pellet of which several are used for single charge; (treated as *plural*) these collectively; photograph, film sequence; stroke or kick in ball game; *colloquial* attempt, guess; person of specified skill in shooting; heavy metal ball thrown in shot-put; *colloquial* drink of spirits; injection of drug etc. ▫ **shotgun** gun for firing small shot at short range; **shotgun wedding** *colloquial* wedding enforced because of bride's pregnancy; **shot-put** athletic contest in which shot is thrown; **shot-putter** *noun*.

shot[2] ● *past & past participle* of SHOOT. ● *adjective* woven so as to show different colours at different angles.

should /ʃʊd/ *auxiliary verb* (*3rd singular present* **should**) *used in reported speech; expressing obligation, likelihood, or tentative suggestion; used to form conditional clause or (in 1st person) conditional mood.*

shoulder /ˈʃəʊldə/ ● *noun* part of body to which arm, foreleg, or wing is attached; either of two projections below neck; animal's upper foreleg as joint of meat; (also in *plural*) shoulder regarded as supportive, comforting, etc.; strip of land next to road; part of garment covering shoulder. ● *verb* push with shoulder; make one's way thus; take on (burden, responsibility, etc.). ▫ **shoulder blade** either flat bone of upper back; **shoulder-length** (of hair etc.) reaching to shoulders; **shoulder pad** pad in garment to bulk out shoulder; **shoulder strap** strap going over shoulder from front to back of garment, strap suspending bag etc. from shoulder.

shouldn't /ˈʃʊd(ə)nt/ should not.

shout /ʃaʊt/ ● *verb* speak or cry loudly; say or express loudly. ● *noun* loud cry calling attention or expressing joy, defiance, approval, etc. ▫ **shout down** reduce to silence by shouting.

shove /ʃʌv/ ● *verb* (**-ving**) push, esp. vigorously or roughly; *colloquial* put casually. ● *noun* act of shoving. ▫ **shove-halfpenny** form of shovelboard played with coins etc. on table; **shove off** start from shore, mooring, etc. in boat, *slang* depart.

shovel /ˈʃʌv(ə)l/ ● *noun* spadelike scoop used to shift earth or coal etc. ● *verb* (**-ll-**; *US* **-l-**) move (as) with shovel. ▫ **shovelboard** game played esp. on ship's deck by pushing discs over marked surface.

shoveller /ˈʃʌvələ/ *noun* (also **shoveler**) duck with shovel-like beak.

show /ʃəʊ/ ● *verb* (*past participle* **shown** or **showed**) be, or allow or cause to be, seen; manifest; offer for inspection; express (one's feelings); accord, grant (favour, mercy, etc.); (of feelings etc.) be manifest; instruct by example; demonstrate, make understood; exhibit; (often + *in, round*, etc.) conduct, lead; *colloquial* appear, arrive. ● *noun* showing; spectacle, exhibition, display; public entertainment or performance; outward appearance, impression produced; ostentation, mere display; *colloquial* undertaking, business. ▫ **good** (or **bad** or **poor**) **show!** *colloquial* that was well (or badly) done; **showbiz** *colloquial* show business; **show business** *colloquial* the entertainment profession; **showcase** glass case or event etc. for displaying goods or exhibits; **showdown** final test or confrontation; **show house**, **flat** furnished and decorated new house or flat on show to prospective buyers; **showjumping** competitive jumping on horseback; **show off** display to advantage, *colloquial* act pretentiously; **show-off** *colloquial* person who shows off; **show-piece** excellent specimen suitable for display; **showroom** room where goods are displayed for sale; **show trial** judicial trial designed to frighten or impress the public; **show up** make or be visible or conspicuous, expose, humiliate, *colloquial* appear or arrive; **show willing** show willingness to help etc.

shower /ˈʃaʊə/ ● *noun* brief fall of rain, snow, etc.; brisk flurry of bullets, dust, etc.; sudden copious arrival of gifts, honours, etc.; (in full **shower-bath**) bath in which water is sprayed from above. ● *verb* descend, send, or give in shower; take shower-bath; (+ *upon, with*) bestow lavishly. ▫ **showery** *adjective*.

showing *noun* display; quality of performance, achievement, etc.; evidence; putting of case etc.

shown *past participle* of SHOW.

showy *adjective* (**-ier**, **-iest**) gaudy; striking. ▫ **showily** *adverb*; **showiness** *noun*.

shrank *past* of SHRINK.

shrapnel /ˈʃræpn(ə)l/ *noun* fragments of exploded bomb etc.

shred ● *noun* scrap, fragment; least amount. ● *verb* (**-dd-**) tear, cut, etc. to shreds. ▫ **shredder** *noun*.

shrew *noun* small long-snouted mouse-like animal; bad-tempered or scolding woman. ▫ **shrewish** *adjective*.

shrewd *adjective* astute; clever. ▫ **shrewdly** *adverb*; **shrewdness** *noun*.

shriek ● *noun* shrill cry or sound. ● *verb* make a shriek; say in shrill tones.

shrike *noun* bird with strong hooked beak.

shrill ● *adjective* piercing and high-pitched. ● *verb* sound or utter shrilly. ▫ **shrillness** *noun*; **shrilly** *adverb*.

shrimp *noun* (*plural* same or **-s**) small edible crustacean; *colloquial* very small person.

shrine *noun* sacred or revered place; casket or tomb holding relics.

shrink ● *verb* (*past* **shrank**; *past participle* **shrunk** or (esp. as *adjective*) **shrunken**) become or make smaller, esp. by action of moisture, heat, or cold; (usually + *from*) recoil, flinch. ● *noun slang* psychiatrist. ▫ **shrink-wrap** wrap (article) in material that shrinks tightly round it.

shrinkage *noun* process or degree of shrinking; allowance for loss by theft or wastage.

shrivel /ˈʃrɪv(ə)l/ *verb* (**-ll-**; *US* **-l-**) contract into wrinkled or dried-up state.

shroud /ʃraʊd/ ● *noun* wrapping for corpse; something which conceals; rope supporting mast. ● *verb* clothe (corpse) for burial; cover, disguise.

Shrove Tuesday /ʃrəʊv/ *noun* day before Ash Wednesday.

shrub *noun* woody plant smaller than tree and usually branching from near ground. □ **shrubby** *adjective*.

shrubbery *noun* (*plural* **-ies**) area planted with shrubs.

shrug ● *verb* (**-gg-**) draw up (shoulders) momentarily as gesture of indifference, ignorance, etc. ● *noun* shrugging movement.

shrunk (also **shrunken**) *past participle* of SHRINK.

shudder /ˈʃʌdə/ ● *verb* shiver from fear, cold, etc.; feel strong repugnance, fear, etc.; vibrate. ● *noun* act of shuddering.

shuffle /ˈʃʌf(ə)l/ ● *verb* (**-ling**) drag or slide (feet) in walking; mix up or rearrange (esp. cards); be evasive; keep shifting one's position. ● *noun* shuffling action or movement; change of relative positions; shuffling dance. □ **shuffle off** remove, get rid of.

shufti /ˈʃʊftɪ/ *noun* (*plural* **-s**) *colloquial* look, glimpse.

shun *verb* (**-nn-**) avoid, keep clear of.

shunt ● *verb* move (train etc.) to another track; (of train) be shunted; redirect. ● *noun* shunting, being shunted; conductor joining two points in electric circuit for diversion of current; *slang* collision of vehicles.

shush /ʃʊʃ/ *interjection & verb* hush.

shut *verb* (**-tt-**; *past & past participle* **shut**) move (door, window, lid, etc.) into position to block opening; become or be capable of being shut; shut door etc. of; become or make closed for trade; fold or contract (book, hand, telescope); bar access to (place). □ **shut down** close, cease working; **shut-eye** *colloquial* sleep; **shut off** stop flow of (water, gas, etc.), separate; **shut out** exclude, screen from view, prevent; **shut up** close all doors and windows of, imprison, put away in box etc., (esp. in *imperative*) *colloquial* stop talking.

shutter ● *noun* movable hinged cover for window; device for exposing film in camera. ● *verb* provide or close with shutter(s).

shuttle /ˈʃʌt(ə)l/ ● *noun* part of loom which carries weft-thread between threads of warp; thread-carrier for lower thread in sewing machine; train, bus, aircraft, etc. used in shuttle service; space shuttle. ● *verb* (**-ling**) (cause to) move to and fro like shuttle. □ **shuttlecock** cork with ring of feathers, or similar plastic device, struck to and fro in badminton; **shuttle diplomacy** negotiations conducted by mediator travelling between disputing parties; **shuttle service** transport system operating to and fro over short distance.

shy[1] ● *adjective* (**-er**, **-est**) timid and nervous in company; self-conscious; easily startled. ● *verb* (**shies**, **shied**) (usually + *at*) (esp. of horse) start back or aside in fright. ● *noun* sudden startled movement. □ **-shy** showing fear or dislike of. □ **shyly** *adverb*; **shyness** *noun*.

shy[2] ● *verb* (**shies**, **shied**) throw, fling. ● *noun* (*plural* **shies**) throw, fling.

shyster /ˈʃaɪstə/ *noun colloquial* person who acts unscrupulously or unprofessionally.

SI *abbreviation* international system of units of measurement (*Système International*).

si /siː/ *noun Music* te.

Siamese /saɪəˈmiːz/ ● *noun* (*plural* same) native or language of Siam (now Thailand); (in full **Siamese cat**) cat of cream-coloured dark-faced short-haired breed with blue eyes. ● *adjective* of Siam. □ **Siamese twins** twins joined together at birth.

sibilant /ˈsɪbɪlənt/ ● *adjective* hissing, sounded with hiss. ● *noun* sibilant speech sound or letter. □ **sibilance** *noun*.

sibling /ˈsɪblɪŋ/ *noun* each of two or more children having one or both parents in common.

sibyl /ˈsɪbɪl/ *noun* pagan prophetess.

sic *adverb* used or spelt thus (confirming form of quoted words). [Latin]

sick ● *adjective* vomiting, disposed to vomit; *esp. US* ill, unwell; (often + *of*) *colloquial* disgusted, surfeited; *colloquial* (of humour) cruel, morbid, perverted, offensive. ● *noun colloquial* vomit. ● *verb* (esp. + *up*) *colloquial* vomit. □ **sickbay** place for sick people; **sickbed** invalid's bed; **sick leave** leave granted because of illness; **sick pay** pay given during sick leave.

sicken *verb* make or become sick, disgusted, etc.; (often + *for*) show symptoms of illness; (as **sickening** *adjective*) disgusting, *colloquial* very annoying. □ **sickeningly** *adverb*.

sickle /ˈsɪk(ə)l/ *noun* short-handled implement with semicircular blade for reaping, lopping, etc.

sickly *adjective* (**-ier**, **-iest**) liable to be ill, weak; faint, pale; causing sickness; mawkish, weakly sentimental.

sickness *noun* being ill; disease; vomiting, nausea.

side ● *noun* each of inner or outer surfaces of object, esp. as distinct from top and bottom or front and back or ends; right or left part of person's or animal's body; part of object, place, etc. that faces specified direction or that is on observer's right or left; either surface of thing regarded as having two; aspect of question, character, etc.; each of sets of opponents in war, game, etc.; cause represented by this; part or region near edge; *colloquial* television channel; each of lines bounding triangle, rectangle, etc.; position nearer or farther than, or to right or left of, dividing line; line of descent through father or mother; spinning motion given to ball by striking it on side; *slang* swagger, assumption of superiority. ● *adjective* of, on, from, or to side; oblique, indirect; subordinate, subsidiary, not main. ● *verb* (**-ding**) take side in dispute etc.; (+ *with*) be on or join same side as. □ **on the side** as sideline, illicitly, *US* as side dish; **sideboard** table or flat-topped chest with drawers and cupboards for crockery etc.; **sideboards**, **sideburns** short side-whiskers; **side by side** standing close together, esp. for mutual encouragement; **sidecar** passenger car attached to side of motorcycle; **side drum** small double-headed drum; **side effect** secondary (usually undesirable) effect; **sidekick** *colloquial* close associate; **sidelight** light from side, small light at side of front of vehicle etc.; **sideline** work etc. done in addition to one's main activity, (usually in *plural*) line bounding side of sports pitch etc., space just outside these for spectators to sit; **side-saddle** *noun* saddle for woman riding with both legs on same side of horse, *adverb* sitting thus on horse; **sideshow** minor show or stall in exhibition, fair, etc.; **sidesman** assistant churchwarden; **sidestep** *noun* step taken sideways, *verb* avoid, evade; **sidetrack** divert from course, purpose, etc.; **sidewalk** *US* pavement; **side-whiskers** hair left unshaven on cheeks; **take sides** support either of (usually) two opposing sides in argument etc.

sidelong ● *adjective* directed to the side. ● *adverb* to the side.

sidereal /saɪˈdɪərɪəl/ *adjective* of or measured or determined by stars.

sideways *adverb & adjective* to or from a side; with one side facing forward.

siding *noun* short track by side of railway line for shunting etc.

sidle /ˈsaɪd(ə)l/ *verb* (**-ling**) walk timidly or furtively.

siege /siːdʒ/ ● *noun* surrounding and blockading of town, castle, etc. □ **lay siege to** conduct siege of; **raise siege** end it.

siemens /ˈsiːmənz/ *noun* (*plural* same) SI unit of electrical conductance.

sienna /sɪ'enə/ *noun* kind of earth used as pigment; its colour of reddish- or yellowish-brown.

sierra /sɪ'erə/ *noun* long jagged mountain chain, esp. in Spain or Spanish America.

siesta /sɪ'estə/ *noun* afternoon nap or rest in hot countries.

sieve /sɪv/ ● *noun* utensil with network or perforated bottom through which liquids or fine particles can pass. ● *verb* (**-ving**) sift.

sift *verb* separate with or cause to pass through sieve; sprinkle through perforated container; closely examine details of, analyse; (of snow, light, etc.) fall as if from sieve.

sigh /saɪ/ ● *verb* emit long deep audible breath in sadness, weariness, relief, etc.; yearn; express with sighs. ● *noun* act of sighing; sound (like that) made in sighing.

sight /saɪt/ ● *noun* faculty of seeing; seeing, being seen; thing seen; range of vision; (usually in *plural*) notable features of a place; device assisting aim with gun or observation with telescope etc.; aim or observation so gained; *colloquial* unsightly person or thing; *colloquial* great deal. ● *verb* get sight of; observe presence of; aim (gun etc.) with sight. □ **at first sight** on first glimpse or impression; **on, at sight** as soon as person or thing is seen; **sight-read** read (music) at sight; **sight-screen** *Cricket* large white screen placed near boundary in line with wicket to help batsman see ball; **sightseer** person visiting sights of place; **sightseeing** *noun*.

sighted *adjective* not blind. □ **-sighted** having specified vision.

sightless *adjective* blind.

sign /saɪn/ ● *noun* indication of quality, state, future event, etc.; mark, symbol, etc.; motion or gesture used to convey information, order, etc.; signboard; each of the 12 divisions of the zodiac. ● *verb* write one's name on (document etc.) as authorization; write (one's name) thus; communicate by gesture. □ **signboard** board bearing name, symbol, etc. displayed outside shop, inn, etc.; **sign in** sign register on arrival, get (person) admitted by signing register; **sign language** series of signs used esp. by deaf or dumb people for communication; **sign off** end contract, work, etc.; **sign on** register to obtain unemployment benefit; **sign out** sign register on departing; **signpost** *noun* post etc. showing directions of roads, *verb* provide with signpost(s); **sign up** engage (person), enlist in armed forces; **signwriter** person who paints signboards etc.

signal[1] /'sɪgn(ə)l/ ● *noun* sign, esp. prearranged one, conveying information or direction; message of such signs; event which causes immediate activity; *Electricity* transmitted impulses or radio waves; sequence of these; device on railway giving instructions or warnings to train drivers etc. ● *verb* (**-ll-**; *US* **-l-**) make signal(s) (to); (often + *to do*) transmit, announce, or direct by signal(s). □ **signal-box** building from which railway signals are controlled; **signalman** railway signal operator.

signal[2] /'sɪgn(ə)l/ *adjective* remarkable, noteworthy. □ **signally** *adverb*.

signalize *verb* (also **-ise**) (**-zing** or **-sing**) make conspicuous or remarkable; indicate.

signatory /'sɪgnətərɪ/ ● *noun* (*plural* **-ies**) party that has signed an agreement, esp. a treaty. ● *adjective* having signed such an agreement.

signature /'sɪgnətʃə/ *noun* person's name or initials used in signing; act of signing; *Music* key signature, time signature; section of book made from one sheet folded and cut. □ **signature tune** tune used esp. in broadcasting to announce a particular programme, performer, etc.

signet /'sɪgnɪt/ *noun* small seal. □ **signet ring** ring with seal set in it.

significance /sɪg'nɪfɪkəns/ *noun* importance; meaning; being significant; extent to which result deviates from hypothesis such that difference is due to more than errors in sampling.

significant /sɪg'nɪfɪkənt/ *adjective* having or conveying meaning; important. □ **significant figure** *Mathematics* digit conveying information about a number containing it. □ **significantly** *adverb*.

signify /'sɪgnɪfaɪ/ *verb* (**-ies**, **-ied**) be sign or symbol of; represent, mean, denote; make known; be of importance, matter. □ **signification** *noun*.

signor /'si:njɔ:/ *noun* (*plural* **-i** /-'njɔ:ri:/) *title used of or to Italian man.*

signora /si:'njɔ:rə/ *noun title used of or to Italian esp. married woman.*

signorina /si:njə'ri:nə/ *noun title used of or to Italian unmarried woman.*

Sikh /si:k/ *noun* member of Indian monotheistic sect.

silage /'saɪlɪdʒ/ *noun* green fodder stored in silo; storage in silo.

silence /'saɪləns/ ● *noun* absence of sound; abstinence from speech or noise; neglect or omission to mention, write, etc. ● *verb* (**-cing**) make silent, esp. by force or superior argument.

silencer *noun* device for reducing noise made by gun, vehicle's exhaust, etc.

silent /'saɪlənt/ *adjective* not speaking; making or accompanied by little or no sound. □ **silently** *adverb*.

silhouette /sɪlu:'et/ ● *noun* dark outline or shadow in profile against lighter background; contour, outline, profile; portrait in profile showing outline only, usually cut from paper or in black on white. ● *verb* (**-tting**) represent or show in silhouette.

silica /'sɪlɪkə/ *noun* silicon dioxide, occurring as quartz and as main constituent of sand etc. □ **siliceous** /sɪ'lɪʃəs/ *adjective*.

silicate /'sɪlɪkeɪt/ *noun* compound of metal(s), silicon, and oxygen.

silicon /'sɪlɪkən/ *noun* non-metallic element occurring in silica and silicates. □ **silicon chip** silicon microchip.

silicone /'sɪlɪkəʊn/ *noun* any organic compound of silicon with high resistance to cold, heat, water, etc.

silicosis /sɪlɪ'kəʊsɪs/ *noun* lung disease caused by inhaling dust containing silica.

silk *noun* fine strong soft lustrous fibre produced by silkworms; thread or cloth made from this; (in *plural*) cloth or garments of silk; *colloquial* Queen's Counsel. □ **silk-screen printing** screen printing; **silkworm** caterpillar which spins cocoon of silk; **take silk** become Queen's Counsel.

silken *adjective* of or resembling silk; soft, smooth, lustrous.

silky *adjective* (**-ier**, **-iest**) like silk in smoothness, softness, etc.; suave. □ **silkily** *adverb*.

sill *noun* slab of wood, stone, etc. at base of window or doorway.

silly /'sɪlɪ/ ● *adjective* (**-ier**, **-iest**) foolish, imprudent; weak-minded; *Cricket* (of fielder or position) very close to batsman. ● *noun* (*plural* **-ies**) *colloquial* silly person. □ **silliness** *noun*.

silo /'saɪləʊ/ *noun* (*plural* **-s**) pit or airtight structure in which green crops are stored for fodder; tower or pit for storage of grain, cement, etc.; underground storage chamber for guided missile.

silt ● *noun* sediment in channel, harbour, etc. ● *verb* (often + *up*) block or be blocked with silt.

silvan = SYLVAN.

silver /'sɪlvə/ ● *noun* greyish-white lustrous precious metal; coins or articles made of or looking like this;

colour of silver. ● *adjective* of or coloured like silver. ● *verb* coat or plate with silver; provide (mirror-glass) with backing of tin amalgam etc.; make silvery; turn grey or white. □ **silver birch** common birch with silvery white bark; **silverfish** (*plural* same or **-es**) small silvery wingless insect, silver-coloured fish; **silver jubilee** 25th anniversary of reign; **silver medal** medal awarded as second prize; **silver paper** aluminium foil; **silver plate** articles plated with silver; **silver-plated** plated with silver; **silver sand** fine pure kind used in gardening; **silver screen** (usually **the silver screen**) cinema films collectively; **silverside** upper side of round of beef; **silversmith** worker in silver; **silver wedding** 25th anniversary of wedding.

silvery *adjective* like silver in colour or appearance; having clear soft ringing sound.

simian /ˈsɪmɪən/ ● *adjective* of anthropoid apes; resembling ape, monkey. ● *noun* ape or monkey.

similar /ˈsɪmɪlə/ *adjective* like, alike; (often + *to*) having resemblance. □ **similarity** /-ˈlær-/ *noun* (*plural* **-ies**); **similarly** *adverb*.

simile /ˈsɪmɪlɪ/ *noun* esp. poetical comparison of two things using *like* or *as* (see panel).

similitude /sɪˈmɪlɪtjuːd/ *noun* guise, appearance; comparison or its expression.

simmer /ˈsɪmə/ ● *verb* be or keep just below boiling point; be in state of suppressed anger or laughter. ● *noun* simmering state. □ **simmer down** become less agitated.

simnel cake /ˈsɪmn(ə)l/ *noun* rich fruit cake, usually with almond paste.

simony /ˈsaɪmənɪ/ *noun* buying or selling of ecclesiastical privileges.

simoom /sɪˈmuːm/ *noun* hot dry dust-laden desert wind.

simper /ˈsɪmpə/ ● *verb* smile in silly affected way; utter with simper. ● *noun* such smile.

simple /ˈsɪmp(ə)l/ *adjective* (**-r**, **-st**) easily understood or done, presenting no difficulty; not complicated or elaborate; plain; not compound or complex; absolute, unqualified, straightforward; foolish, feeble-minded. □ **simple-minded** foolish, feeble-minded. □ **simpleness** *noun*.

simpleton /ˈsɪmpəlt(ə)n/ *noun* stupid or gullible person.

simplicity /sɪmˈplɪsɪtɪ/ *noun* fact or condition of being simple.

simplify /ˈsɪmplɪfaɪ/ *verb* (**-ies**, **-ied**) make simple or simpler. □ **simplification** *noun*.

simplistic /sɪmˈplɪstɪk/ *adjective* excessively or affectedly simple. □ **simplistically** *adverb*.

simply *adverb* in a simple way; absolutely; merely.

simulate /ˈsɪmjʊleɪt/ *verb* (**-ting**) pretend to be, have, or feel; counterfeit; reproduce conditions of (situation etc.), e.g. for training. □ **simulation** *noun*; **simulator** *noun*.

simultaneous /sɪməlˈteɪnɪəs/ *adjective* (often + *with*) occurring or operating at same time. □ **simultaneity** /-təˈneɪɪtɪ/ *noun*; **simultaneously** *adverb*.

sin ● *noun* breaking of divine or moral law; offence against good taste etc. ● *verb* (**-nn-**) commit sin; (+ *against*) offend. □ **sinner** *noun*.

since ● *preposition* throughout or within period after. ● *conjunction* during or in time after; because. ● *adverb* from that time or event until now.

sincere /sɪnˈsɪə/ *adjective* (**-r**, **-st**) free from pretence, genuine, honest, frank. □ **sincerity** /-ˈser-/ *noun*.

sincerely *adverb* in a sincere way. □ **Yours sincerely** *written before signature at end of informal letter.*

sine *noun* ratio of side opposite angle (in right-angled triangle) to hypotenuse.

sinecure /ˈsaɪnɪkjʊə/ *noun* position that requires little or no work but usually yields profit or honour.

sine die /sɪneɪ ˈdiːeɪ/ *adverb formal* indefinitely. [Latin]

sine qua non /sɪneɪ kwɑː ˈnəʊn/ *noun* indispensable condition or qualification. [Latin]

sinew /ˈsɪnjuː/ *noun* tough fibrous tissue joining muscle to bone; tendon; (in *plural*) muscles, strength; framework of thing. □ **sinewy** *adjective*.

sinful *adjective* committing or involving sin. □ **sinfully** *adverb*; **sinfulness** *noun*.

sing *verb* (*past* **sang**; *past participle* **sung**) utter musical sounds, esp. words in set tune; utter (song, tune); (of wind, kettle, etc.) hum, buzz, or whistle; *slang* become informer; (+ *of*) *literary* celebrate in verse. □ **sing out** shout; **singsong** *noun* session of informal singing, *adjective* (of voice) monotonously rising and falling. □ **singer** *noun*.

singe /sɪndʒ/ ● *verb* (**-geing**) burn superficially; burn off tips or edges of (esp. hair). ● *noun* superficial burn.

single /ˈsɪŋg(ə)l/ ● *adjective* one only, not double or multiple; united, undivided; of or for one person or thing; solitary; taken separately; unmarried; (with negative or in questions) even one. ● *noun* single thing, esp. room in hotel; (in full **single ticket**) ticket for one-way journey; pop record with one piece of music on each side; *Cricket* hit for one run; (usually in *plural*) game with one player on each side. ● *verb* (**-ling**) (+ *out*) choose for special attention. □ **single-breasted** (of coat etc.) with only one vertical row of buttons, and overlapping little at the front; **single-decker** bus with only one deck; **single file** line of people one behind another; **single-handed** without help; **single-handedly** *adverb*; **single-minded** intent on only one aim; **single parent** parent bringing up child or children alone. □ **singly** /ˈsɪŋglɪ/ *adverb*.

singlet /ˈsɪŋglɪt/ *noun* sleeveless vest.

Simile

A simile is a figure of speech involving the comparison of one thing with another of a different kind, using *as* or *like*, e.g.

The water was as clear as glass.
Cherry blossom lay like driven snow upon the lawn.

Everyday language is rich in similes:

with *as*:	*as like as two peas*	*as poor as a church mouse*
	as strong as an ox	*as rich as Croesus*
with *like*:	*spread like wildfire*	*run like the wind*
	sell like hot cakes	*like a bull in a china shop*

singleton /ˈsɪŋɡəlt(ə)n/ *noun* player's only card of particular suit.

singular /ˈsɪŋɡjʊlə/ ● *adjective* unique; outstanding; extraordinary, strange; *Grammar* denoting one person or thing. ● *noun Grammar* singular word or form. □ **singularity** /-ˈlær-/ *noun* (*plural* **-ies**); **singularly** *adverb*.

Sinhalese /sɪnhəˈliːz/ ● *noun* (*plural* same) member of a people from N. India now forming majority of population of Sri Lanka; their language. ● *adjective* of this people or language.

sinister /ˈsɪnɪstə/ *adjective* suggestive of evil; wicked, criminal; ominous; *Heraldry* on left side of shield etc. (i.e. to observer's right).

sink ● *verb* (*past* **sank** or **sunk**; *past participle* **sunk** or (as *adjective*) **sunken**) fall or come slowly downwards; disappear below horizon; go or penetrate below surface of liquid; go to bottom of sea etc.; settle down; decline in strength and vitality; descend in pitch or volume; cause or allow to sink or penetrate; cause failure of; dig (well), bore (shaft); engrave (die); invest (money); cause (ball) to enter pocket at billiards or hole at golf etc. ● *noun* plumbed-in basin, esp. in kitchen; place where foul liquid collects; place of vice. □ **sinking fund** money set aside for eventual repayment of debt.

sinker *noun* weight used to sink fishing or sounding line.

Sino- /ˈsaɪnəʊ/ *combining form* Chinese.

sinology /saɪˈnɒlədʒɪ/ *noun* study of China and its language, history, etc. □ **sinologist** *noun*.

sinuous /ˈsɪnjʊəs/ *adjective* with many curves, undulating. □ **sinuosity** /-ˈɒs-/ *noun*.

sinus /ˈsaɪnəs/ *noun* either of cavities in skull communicating with nostrils.

sinusitis /saɪnəˈsaɪtɪs/ *noun* inflammation of sinus.

sip ● *verb* (**-pp-**) drink in small mouthfuls. ● *noun* small mouthful of liquid; act of taking this.

siphon /ˈsaɪf(ə)n/ ● *noun* tube shaped like inverted V or U with unequal legs, used for transferring liquid from one container to another by atmospheric pressure; bottle from which fizzy water is forced by pressure of gas. ● *verb* (often + *off*) conduct or flow through siphon, divert or set aside (funds etc.).

sir /sɜː/ *noun polite form of address or reference to a man*; (**Sir**) *title used before forename of knight or baronet.*

sire ● *noun* male parent of animal, esp. stallion; *archaic form of address to king*; *archaic* father or other male ancestor. ● *verb* (**-ring**) beget.

siren /ˈsaɪərən/ *noun* device for making loud prolonged signal or warning sound; *Greek Mythology* woman or winged creature whose singing lured unwary sailors on to rocks; dangerously fascinating woman.

sirloin /ˈsɜːlɔɪn/ *noun* best part of loin of beef.

sirocco /sɪˈrɒkəʊ/ *noun* (*plural* **-s**) Saharan simoom; hot moist wind in S. Europe.

sisal /ˈsaɪs(ə)l/ *noun* fibre from leaves of agave.

siskin /ˈsɪskɪn/ *noun* small songbird.

sissy /ˈsɪsɪ/ (also **cissy**) *colloquial* ● *noun* (*plural* **-ies**) effeminate or cowardly person. ● *adjective* (**-ier**, **-iest**) effeminate; cowardly.

sister /ˈsɪstə/ *noun* woman or girl in relation to her siblings; female fellow member of trade union, sect, human race, etc.; member of female religious order; senior female nurse. **sister-in-law** (*plural* **sisters-in-law**) husband's or wife's sister, brother's wife. □ **sisterly** *adjective*.

sisterhood *noun* relationship (as) of sisters; society of women bound by monastic vows or devoting themselves to religious or charitable work; community of feeling among women.

sit *verb* (**-tt-**; *past & past participle* **sat**) support body by resting buttocks on ground, seat, etc.; cause to sit; place in sitting position; (of bird) perch or remain on nest to hatch eggs; (of animal) rest with hind legs bent and buttocks on ground; (of parliament, court, etc.) be in session; (usually + *for*) pose (for portrait); (+ *for*) be MP for (constituency); (often + *for*) take (exam). □ **be sitting pretty** be comfortably placed; **sit back** relax one's efforts; **sit down** sit after standing, cause to sit, (+ *under*) suffer tamely (humiliation etc.); **sit in** occupy place as protest; **sit-in** *noun*; **sit in on** be present as guest etc. at (meeting); **sit on** be member of (committee etc.), *colloquial* delay action about, *slang* repress or snub; **sit out** take no part in (dance etc.), stay till end of, sit outdoors; **sit tight** *colloquial* remain firmly in one's place, not yield; **sit up** rise from lying to sitting, sit firmly upright, defer going to bed, *colloquial* become interested, aroused, etc.; **sit-up** physical exercise of sitting up from supine position without using arms or hands.

sitar /ˈsɪtɑː/ *noun* long-necked Indian lute.

sitcom /ˈsɪtkɒm/ *noun colloquial* situation comedy.

site ● *noun* ground chosen or used for town or building; ground set apart for some purpose. ● *verb* (**-ting**) locate, place.

sitter *noun* person who sits for portrait etc.; babysitter.

sitting ● *noun* continuous period spent engaged in an activity; time during which assembly is engaged in business; session in which meal is served. ● *adjective* having sat down; (of animal or bird) still; (of MP etc.) current. □ **sitting-room** room in which to sit and relax.

situ see IN SITU.

situate /ˈsɪtjʊeɪt/ *verb* (**-ting**) (usually in *passive*) place or put in position, situation, etc.

situation *noun* place and its surroundings; circumstances; position; state of affairs; *formal* paid job. □ **situation comedy** broadcast comedy series involving characters dealing with awkward esp. domestic or everyday situations. □ **situational** *adjective*.

six *adjective & noun* one more than five; *Cricket* hit scoring six runs. □ **hit, knock for six** *colloquial* utterly surprise or defeat.

sixpence /ˈsɪkspəns/ *noun* sum of 6 (esp. old) pence; *historical* coin worth this.

sixpenny /ˈsɪkspənɪ/ *adjective* costing or worth 6 (esp. old) pence.

sixteen /sɪksˈtiːn/ *adjective & noun* one more than fifteen. □ **sixteenth** *adjective & noun*.

sixth ● *adjective & noun* next after fifth; any of 6 equal parts of thing. □ **sixth form** form in secondary school for pupils over 16; **sixth-form college** separate college for pupils over 16; **sixth sense** supposed intuitive or extrasensory faculty.

sixty /ˈsɪkstɪ/ *adjective & noun* (*plural* **-ies**) six times ten. □ **sixtieth** *adjective & noun*.

sizable = SIZEABLE.

size[1] ● *noun* relative bigness or extent of a thing; dimensions, magnitude; each of classes into which things are divided by size. ● *verb* (**-zing**) sort in sizes or by size. □ **size up** *colloquial* form judgement of.

size[2] ● *noun* sticky solution used for glazing paper and stiffening textiles etc. ● *verb* (**-zing**) treat with size.

sizeable *adjective* (also **sizable**) fairly large.

sizzle /ˈsɪz(ə)l/ ● *verb* (**-ling**) sputter or hiss, esp. in frying. ● *noun* sizzling sound. □ **sizzling** *adjective & adverb*.

SJ *abbreviation* Society of Jesus.

skate[1] ● *noun* ice-skate; roller-skate. ● *verb* (**-ting**) move, glide, or perform (as) on skates; (+ *over*) refer fleetingly to, disregard. □ **skateboard** *noun* short narrow board on roller-skate wheels for riding on standing up, *verb* ride on skateboard. □ **skater** *noun*.

skate[2] *noun* (*plural* same or **-s**) large edible marine flatfish.

skedaddle /skɪ'dæd(ə)l/ *verb* (**-ling**) *colloquial* run away, retreat hastily.

skein /skeɪn/ *noun* quantity of yarn etc. coiled and usually loosely twisted; flock of wild geese etc. in flight.

skeleton /'skelɪt(ə)n/ ● *noun* hard framework of bones etc. of animal; supporting framework or structure of thing; very thin person or animal; useless or dead remnant; outline sketch. ● *adjective* having only essential or minimum number of people, parts, etc. □ **skeleton key** key fitting many locks. □ **skeletal** *adjective*.

skerry /'skerɪ/ *noun* (*plural* **-ies**) *Scottish* reef, rocky islet.

sketch ● *noun* rough or unfinished drawing or painting; rough draft, general outline; short usually humorous play. ● *verb* make or give sketch of; make sketches.

sketchy *adjective* (**-ier**, **-iest**) giving only a rough outline; *colloquial* insubstantial or imperfect, esp. through haste. □ **sketchily** *adverb*.

skew ● *adjective* oblique, slanting, set askew. ● *noun* slant. ● *verb* make skew; distort; move obliquely.

skewbald /'skju:bɔ:ld/ ● *adjective* (of animal) with irregular patches of white and another colour. ● *noun* skewbald animal, esp. horse.

skewer /'skju:ə/ ● *noun* long pin for holding meat compactly together while cooking. ● *verb* fasten together or pierce (as) with skewer.

ski /ski:/ ● *noun* (*plural* **-s**) each of pair of long narrow pieces of wood etc. fastened under feet for travelling over snow; similar device under vehicle. ● *verb* (**skis**; **ski'd** or **skied** /ski:d/; **skiing**) travel on skis. □ **skier** *noun*.

skid ● *verb* (**-dd-**) (of vehicle etc.) slide esp. sideways or obliquely on slippery road etc.; cause (vehicle) to skid. ● *noun* act of skidding; runner used as part of landing-gear of aircraft. □ **skid-pan** slippery surface for drivers to practise control of skidding; **skid row** *US slang* district frequented by vagrants.

skiff *noun* light boat, esp. for rowing or sculling.

skilful /'skɪlfʊl/ *adjective* (*US* **skillful**) having or showing skill. □ **skilfully** *adverb*.

skill *noun* practised ability, expertness, technique; craft, art, etc. requiring skill.

skilled *adjective* skilful; (of work or worker) requiring or having skill or special training.

skillet /'skɪlɪt/ *noun* long-handled metal cooking pot; *US* frying-pan.

skim *verb* (**-mm-**) take scum or cream etc. from surface of (liquid); barely touch (surface) in passing over; (often + *over*) deal with or treat (matter) superficially; (often + *over*, *along*) glide lightly; read or look over superficially. □ **skim**, **skimmed milk** milk with cream removed.

skimp *verb* (often + *on*) economize; supply meagrely, use too little of.

skimpy *adjective* (**-ier**, **-iest**) meagre, insufficient.

skin ● *noun* flexible covering of body; skin removed from animal, material made from this; complexion; outer layer or covering; film like skin on liquid etc.; container for liquid, made of animal's skin. ● *verb* (**-nn-**) strip skin from; graze (part of body); *slang* swindle. □ **skin-deep** superficial; **skin-diver** person who swims under water without diving suit; **skin-diving** *noun*; **skinflint** miser; **skin-graft** surgical transplanting of skin, skin thus transferred; **skintight** very closefitting.

skinful *noun colloquial* enough alcohol to make one drunk.

skinny *adjective* (**-ier**, **-iest**) thin, emaciated.

skint *adjective slang* having no money.

skip[1] ● *verb* (**-pp-**) move along lightly, esp. by taking two hops with each foot in turn; jump lightly esp. over skipping rope; frisk, gambol; move quickly from one subject etc. to another; omit or make omissions in reading; *colloquial* not attend etc.; *colloquial* leave hurriedly. ● *noun* skipping movement or action. □ **skipping-rope** length of rope turned over head and under feet while jumping it.

skip[2] *noun* large container for refuse etc.; container in which men or materials are lowered or raised in mines etc.

skipjack *noun* (in full **skipjack tuna**) (*plural* same or **-s**) small Pacific tuna.

skipper /'skɪpə/ ● *noun* captain of ship, aircraft, team, etc. ● *verb* be captain of.

skirl ● *noun* shrill sound of bagpipes. ● *verb* make skirl.

skirmish /'skɜ:mɪʃ/ ● *noun* minor battle; short argument etc. ● *verb* engage in skirmish.

skirt ● *noun* woman's garment hanging from waist, or this part of complete dress; part of coat etc. that hangs below waist; hanging part at base of hovercraft; (in *singular* or *plural*) border, outlying part; flank of beef etc. ● *verb* go or be along or round edge of. □ **skirting board** narrow board etc. round bottom of room-wall.

skit *noun* light piece of satire, burlesque.

skittish /'skɪtɪʃ/ *adjective* lively, playful; (of horse etc.) nervous, inclined to shy.

skittle /'skɪt(ə)l/ *noun* pin used in game of skittles, in which number of wooden pins are set up to be bowled or knocked down.

skive *verb* (**-ving**) (often + *off*) *slang* evade work; play truant.

skivvy /'skɪvɪ/ *noun* (*plural* **-ies**) *colloquial derogatory* female domestic servant.

skua /'skju:ə/ *noun* large predatory seabird.

skulduggery /skʌl'dʌgərɪ/ *noun* trickery, unscrupulous behaviour.

skulk *verb* lurk or conceal oneself or move stealthily.

skull *noun* bony case of brain; bony framework of head; head as site of intelligence. □ **skull and crossbones** representation of skull over two crossed thigh-bones, esp. on pirate flag or as emblem of death; **skullcap** close-fitting peakless cap.

skunk *noun* (*plural* same or **-s**) black white-striped bushy-tailed mammal, emitting powerful stench when attacked; *colloquial* contemptible person.

sky /skaɪ/ *noun* (*plural* **skies**) (in *singular* or *plural*) atmosphere and outer space seen from the earth. □ **sky blue** bright clear blue; **skydiving** sport of performing acrobatic manoeuvres under free fall before opening parachute; **skylark** *noun* lark that sings while soaring, *verb* play tricks and practical jokes; **skylight** window in roof; **skyline** outline of hills, buildings, etc. against sky; **sky-rocket** *noun* firework shooting into air and exploding, *verb* rise steeply; **skyscraper** very tall building.

slab *noun* flat thickish esp. rectangular piece of solid material; mortuary table.

slack[1] ● *adjective* (of rope etc.) not taut; inactive, sluggish; negligent, remiss; (of tide etc.) neither ebbing nor flowing. ● *noun* slack part of rope etc.; slack period; (in *plural*) casual trousers. ● *verb* slacken; *colloquial* take a rest, be lazy. □ **slack off** loosen; **slack up** reduce level of activity or speed. □ **slackness** *noun*.

slack[2] *noun* coal dust, coal fragments.

slacken *verb* make or become slack. □ **slacken off** slack off.

slacker *noun* shirker.

slag ● *noun* refuse left after ore has been smelted etc. ● *verb* (**-gg-**) form slag; (often + *off*) *slang* insult, slander. □ **slag-heap** hill of refuse from mine etc.

slain *past participle* of SLAY.

slake *verb* (**-king**) assuage or satisfy (thirst etc.); cause (lime) to heat and crumble by action of water.

slalom /ˈslɑːləm/ *noun* downhill ski-race on zigzag course between artificial obstacles.

slam[1] ● *verb* (**-mm-**) shut, throw, or put down violently or with bang; *slang* criticize severely. ● *noun* sound or action of slamming.

slam[2] *noun* winning of all tricks at cards.

slander /ˈslɑːndə/ ● *noun* false and damaging utterance about person. ● *verb* utter slander about. □ **slanderous** *adjective*.

slang ● *noun* very informal words, phrases, or meanings, not regarded as standard and often peculiar to profession, class, etc. ● *verb* use abusive language (to). □ **slanging match** prolonged exchange of insults. □ **slangy** *adjective*.

slant /slɑːnt/ ● *verb* slope, (cause to) lie or go obliquely; (often as **slanted** *adjective*) present (news etc.) in biased or particular way. ● *noun* slope, oblique position; point of view, esp. biased one. ● *adjective* sloping, oblique.

slantwise *adverb* aslant.

slap ● *verb* (**-pp-**) strike (as) with palm of hand; lay forcefully; put hastily or carelessly. ● *noun* slapping stroke or sound. ● *adverb* suddenly, fully, directly. □ **slapdash** hasty, careless; **slap-happy** *colloquial* cheerfully casual; **slapstick** boisterous comedy; **slap-up** *colloquial* lavish.

slash ● *verb* cut or gash with knife etc.; (often + *at*) deliver or aim cutting blows; reduce (prices etc.) drastically; criticize harshly. ● *noun* slashing cut; *Printing* oblique stroke; *slang* act of urinating.

slat *noun* long narrow strip of wood, plastic, or metal, used in fences, venetian blinds, etc.

slate ● *noun* fine-grained bluish-grey rock easily split into thin smooth plates; piece of this used esp. in roofing or *historical* for writing on; colour of slate; list of nominees for office etc. ● *verb* (**-ting**) roof with slates; *colloquial* criticize severely; *US* make arrangements for (event etc.), nominate for office. ● *adjective* of (colour of) slate. □ **slating** *noun*; **slaty** *adjective*.

slattern /ˈslæt(ə)n/ *noun* slovenly woman. □ **slatternly** *adjective*.

slaughter /ˈslɔːtə/ ● *verb* kill (animals) for food etc.; kill (people) ruthlessly or in large numbers; *colloquial* defeat utterly. ● *noun* act of slaughtering. □ **slaughterhouse** place for slaughter of animals for food. □ **slaughterer** *noun*.

Slav /slɑːv/ ● *noun* member of group of peoples of central and eastern Europe speaking Slavonic languages. ● *adjective* of the Slavs.

slave ● *noun* person who is owned by and has to serve another; drudge, very hard worker; (+ *of*, *to*) obsessive devotee. ● *verb* (**-ving**) work very hard. □ **slave-driver** overseer of slaves, hard taskmaster; **slave trade** dealing in slaves, esp. African blacks.

slaver[1] *noun historical* ship or person engaged in slave trade.

slaver[2] /ˈslævə/ ● *verb* dribble; drool. ● *noun* dribbling saliva; flattery; drivel.

slavery /ˈsleɪvərɪ/ *noun* condition of slave; drudgery; practice of having slaves.

Slavic /ˈslɑːvɪk/ *adjective & noun* Slavonic.

slavish /ˈsleɪvɪʃ/ *adjective* like slaves; without originality. □ **slavishly** *adverb*.

Slavonic /sləˈvɒnɪk/ ● *adjective* of group of languages including Russian, Polish, and Czech. ● *noun* Slavonic group of languages.

slay *verb* (*past* **slew** /sluː/; *past participle* **slain**) kill. □ **slayer** *noun*.

sleaze *noun colloquial* sleaziness.

sleazy /ˈsliːzɪ/ *adjective* (**-ier**, **-iest**) squalid, tawdry. □ **sleazily** *adverb*; **sleaziness** *noun*.

sled *noun & verb* (**-dd-**) *US* sledge.

sledge ● *noun* vehicle on runners for use on snow. ● *verb* (**-ging**) travel or carry on sledge.

sledgehammer /ˈsledʒhæmə/ *noun* large heavy hammer.

sleek ● *adjective* (of hair, skin, etc.) smooth and glossy; looking well-fed and comfortable. ● *verb* make sleek. □ **sleekly** *adverb*; **sleekness** *noun*.

sleep ● *noun* condition in which eyes are closed, muscles and nerves relaxed, and consciousness suspended; period of this; rest, quiet, death. ● *verb* (*past & past participle* **slept**) be or fall asleep; spend the night; provide sleeping accommodation for; (+ *with*, *together*) have sexual intercourse; (+ *on*) defer (decision) until next day; (+ *through*) fail to be woken by; be inactive or dead; (+ *off*) cure by sleeping. □ **sleeping bag** padded bag to sleep in when camping etc.; **sleeping car**, **carriage** railway coach with beds or berths; **sleeping partner** partner not sharing in actual work of a firm; **sleeping pill** pill to induce sleep; **sleeping policeman** ramp etc. in road to slow traffic; **sleepwalk** walk about while asleep; **sleepwalker** *noun* □ **sleepless** *adjective*; **sleeplessness** *noun*.

sleeper *noun* sleeping person or animal; beam supporting railway track; sleeping car; ring worn in pierced ear to keep hole open.

sleepy *adjective* (**-ier**, **-iest**) feeling need of sleep; quiet, inactive. □ **sleepily** *adverb*; **sleepiness** *noun*.

sleet ● *noun* snow and rain together; hail or snow melting as it falls. ● *verb* (after *it*) sleet falls. □ **sleety** *adjective*.

sleeve *noun* part of garment covering arm; cover for gramophone record; tube enclosing rod etc. □ **up one's sleeve** in reserve. □ **sleeved** *adjective*; **sleeveless** *adjective*.

sleigh /sleɪ/ ● *noun* sledge, esp. for riding on. ● *verb* travel on sleigh.

sleight of hand /slaɪt/ *noun* dexterity, esp. in conjuring.

slender /ˈslendə/ *adjective* (**-er**, **-est**) of small girth or breadth; slim; slight, scanty, meagre.

slept *past & past participle* of SLEEP.

sleuth /sluːθ/ *colloquial* ● *noun* detective. ● *verb* investigate crime etc.

slew[1] /sluː/ ● *verb* (often + *round*) turn or swing to new position. ● *noun* such turn.

slew[2] *past* of SLAY.

slice ● *noun* thin flat piece or wedge cut from something; share; kitchen utensil with thin broad blade; stroke sending ball obliquely. ● *verb* (**-cing**) (often + *up*) cut into slices; (+ *off*) cut off; (+ *into*, *through*) cut (as) with knife; strike (ball) with slice.

slick ● *adjective colloquial* skilful, efficient; superficially dexterous, glib; sleek, smooth. ● *noun* patch of oil etc., esp. on sea. ● *verb colloquial* make smooth or sleek. □ **slickly** *adverb*; **slickness** *noun*.

slide ● *verb* (*past & past participle* **slid**) (cause to) move along smooth surface touching it always with same part; move quietly or smoothly; glide over ice without skates; (often + *into*) pass unobtrusively. ● *noun* act of sliding; rapid decline; smooth slope down which people or things slide; track for sliding, esp. on ice; part of machine or instrument that slides; mounted transparency viewed with projector; piece of glass holding object for microscope; hair-slide. □ **let things slide** be negligent, allow deterioration; **slide-rule** ruler with sliding central strip, graduated logarithmically for rapid calculations; **sliding scale** scale of fees, taxes, wages, etc. that varies according to some other factor.

slight /slaɪt/ ● *adjective* small, insignificant; inadequate; slender, frail-looking. ● *verb* treat disrespectfully, ignore. ● *noun* act of slighting. □ **slightly** *adverb*; **slightness** *noun*.

slim ● *adjective* (**-mm-**) not fat, slender; small, insufficient. ● *verb* (**-mm-**) (often + *down*) become slim, esp. by dieting etc.; make slim. □ **slimline** of slender design, not fattening. □ **slimmer** *noun*; **slimming** *noun*.

slime *noun* oozy or sticky substance.

slimy *adjective* (**-ier**, **-iest**) like, covered with, or filled with slime; *colloquial* disgustingly obsequious. □ **sliminess** *noun*.

sling[1] ● *noun* strap etc. used to support or raise thing; bandage supporting injured arm; strap etc. used to throw small missile. ● *verb* (*past & past participle* **slung**) suspend with sling; *colloquial* throw. □ **sling-back** shoe held in place by strap above heel; **sling one's hook** *slang* go away.

sling[2] *noun* sweetened drink of spirits (esp. gin) with water.

slink *verb* (*past & past participle* **slunk**) (often + *off*, *away*, *by*) move stealthily or guiltily.

slinky *adjective* (**-ier**, **-iest**) (of garment) close-fitting and sinuous.

slip[1] ● *verb* (**-pp-**) slide unintentionally or momentarily, lose footing or balance; go with sliding motion; escape or fall because hard to grasp; go unobserved or quietly; make careless or slight mistake; fall below standard; place stealthily or casually; release from restraint or connection; (+ *on*, *off*) pull (garment) easily or hastily on or off; escape from, evade. ● *noun* act of slipping; careless or slight error; pillowcase; petticoat; (in *singular* or *plural*) slipway; *Cricket* fielder behind wicket on off side, (in *singular* or *plural*) this position. □ **give (person) the slip** escape from, evade; **slip-knot** knot that can be undone by pull, running knot; **slip-on** (of shoes or clothes) easily slipped on or off; **slipped disc** displaced disc between vertebrae; **slip-road** road for entering or leaving motorway etc.; **slipstream** current of air or water driven backwards by propeller etc.; **slip up** *colloquial* make mistake; **slip-up** *noun*; **slipway** ramp for shipbuilding or landing boats.

slip[2] *noun* small piece of paper, esp. for making notes; cutting from plant for grafting or planting.

slippage *noun* act or instance of slipping.

slipper *noun* light loose indoor shoe.

slippery /'slɪpərɪ/ *adjective* difficult to grasp, stand on, etc., because smooth or wet; unreliable, unscrupulous. □ **slipperiness** *noun*.

slippy *adjective* (**-ier**, **-iest**) *colloquial* slippery.

slipshod *adjective* careless, slovenly.

slit ● *noun* straight narrow incision or opening. ● *verb* (**-tt-**; *past & past participle* **slit**) make slit in; cut in strips.

slither /'slɪðə/ ● *verb* slide unsteadily. ● *noun* act of slithering. □ **slithery** *adjective*.

sliver /'slɪvə/ ● *noun* long thin slice or piece. ● *verb* cut or split into slivers.

slob *noun colloquial derogatory* lazy, untidy, or fat person.

slobber /'slɒbə/ *verb & noun* slaver. □ **slobbery** *adjective*.

sloe *noun* blackthorn; its small bluish-black fruit.

slog ● *verb* (**-gg-**) hit hard and usually unskilfully; work or walk doggedly. ● *noun* heavy random hit; hard steady work or walk; spell of this.

slogan /'sləʊgən/ *noun* catchy phrase used in advertising etc.; party cry, watchword.

sloop /slu:p/ *noun* small one-masted fore-and-aft rigged vessel.

slop ● *verb* (**-pp-**) (often + *over*) spill over edge of vessel; spill or splash liquid on. ● *noun* liquid spilled or splashed; (in *plural*) dirty waste water, wine, etc.; (in *singular* or *plural*) unappetizing liquid food.

slope ● *noun* inclined position, direction, or state; piece of rising or falling ground; difference in level between two ends or sides of a thing; place for skiing. ● *verb* (**-ping**) have or take slope, slant; cause to slope. □ **slope off** *slang* go away, esp. to evade work etc.

sloppy *adjective* (**-ier**, **-iest**) wet, watery, too liquid; careless, untidy; foolishly sentimental. □ **sloppily** *adverb*; **sloppiness** *noun*.

slosh ● *verb* (often + *about*) splash or flounder; *slang* hit, esp. heavily; *colloquial* pour (liquid) clumsily. ● *noun* slush; act or sound of splashing; *slang* heavy blow.

sloshed *adjective slang* drunk.

slot ● *noun* slit in machine etc. for something (esp. coin) to be inserted; slit, groove, etc. for thing; allotted place in schedule. ● *verb* (**-tt-**) (often + *in*, *into*) place or be placed (as if) into slot; provide with slot(s). □ **slot machine** machine worked by insertion of coin, esp. delivering small items or providing amusement.

sloth /sləʊθ/ *noun* laziness, indolence; slow-moving arboreal S. American mammal.

slothful *adjective* lazy. □ **slothfully** *adverb*.

slouch /slaʊtʃ/ ● *verb* stand, move, or sit in drooping fashion. ● *noun* slouching posture or movement; *slang* incompetent or slovenly worker etc. □ **slouch hat** hat with wide flexible brim.

slough[1] /slaʊ/ *noun* swamp, miry place. □ **Slough of Despond** state of hopeless depression.

slough[2] /slʌf/ ● *noun* part that animal (esp. snake) casts or moults. ● *verb* (often + *off*) cast or drop as slough.

Slovak /'sləʊvæk/ ● *noun* member of Slavonic people inhabiting Slovakia; their language. ● *adjective* of this people or language.

sloven /'slʌv(ə)n/ *noun* untidy or careless person.

Slovene /'sləʊvi:n/ (also **Slovenian** /-'vi:nɪən/) ● *noun* member of Slavonic people in Slovenia; their language. ● *adjective* of Slovenia or its people or language.

slovenly ● *adjective* careless and untidy, unmethodical. ● *adverb* in a slovenly way. □ **slovenliness** *noun*.

slow /sləʊ/ ● *adjective* taking relatively long time to do thing(s); acting, moving, or done without speed; not conducive to speed; (of clock etc.) showing earlier than correct time; dull-witted, stupid; tedious; slack, sluggish; (of fire or oven) not very hot; (of photographic film) needing long exposure; reluctant. ● *adverb* slowly. ● *verb* (usually + *down*, *up*) (cause to) move, act, or work with reduced speed or vigour. □ **slowcoach** *colloquial* slow person; **slow motion** speed of film or videotape in which actions etc. appear much slower than usual, simulation of this in real action; **slow-worm** small European legless lizard. □ **slowly** *adverb*; **slowness** *noun*.

sludge *noun* thick greasy mud or sediment; sewage. □ **sludgy** *adjective*.

slug[1] *noun* slimy shell-less mollusc; bullet, esp. irregularly shaped; missile for airgun; *Printing* metal bar for spacing; mouthful of liquor.

slug[2] *US* ● *verb* (**-gg-**) hit hard. ● *noun* hard blow.
sluggard /'slʌgəd/ *noun* lazy person.
sluggish *adjective* inert, slow-moving. □ **sluggishly** *adverb*; **sluggishness** *noun*.
sluice /slu:s/ ● *noun* (also **sluice-gate**, **-valve**) sliding gate or other contrivance for regulating volume or flow of water; water so regulated; (also **sluice-way**) artificial water-channel; place for or act of rinsing. ● *verb* (**-cing**) provide or wash with sluice(s); rinse; (of water) rush out (as if) from sluice.
slum ● *noun* house unfit for human habitation; (often in *plural*) overcrowded and squalid district in city. ● *verb* (**-mm-**) visit slums, esp. out of curiosity. □ **slum it** *colloquial* put up with conditions less comfortable than usual. □ **slummy** *adjective*.
slumber /'slʌmbə/ *verb & noun poetical* sleep.
slump ● *noun* sudden severe or prolonged fall in prices and trade. ● *verb* undergo slump; sit or fall heavily or limply.
slung *past & past participle* of SLING[1].
slunk *past & past participle* of SLINK.
slur ● *verb* (**-rr-**) sound (words, musical notes, etc.) so that they run into one another; *archaic or US* put slur on (person, character); (usually + *over*) pass over lightly. ● *noun* imputation of wrongdoing; act of slurring; *Music* curved line joining notes to be slurred.
slurp *colloquial* ● *verb* eat or drink noisily. ● *noun* sound of slurping.
slurry /'slʌrɪ/ *noun* thin semi-liquid cement, mud, manure, etc.
slush *noun* thawing snow; silly sentimentality. □ **slush fund** reserve fund, esp. for bribery. □ **slushy** *adjective* (**-ier**, **-iest**).
slut *noun derogatory* slovenly or promiscuous woman. □ **sluttish** *adjective*.
sly *adjective* (**-er**, **-est**) crafty, wily; secretive; knowing, insinuating. □ **on the sly** secretly. □ **slyly** *adverb*; **slyness** *noun*.
smack[1] ● *noun* sharp slap or blow; hard hit; loud kiss; loud sharp sound. ● *verb* slap; part (lips) noisily in anticipation of food; move, hit, etc. with smack. ● *adverb colloquial* with a smack; suddenly, violently; exactly.
smack[2] (+ *of*) ● *verb* taste of, suggest. ● *noun* flavour or suggestion of.
smack[3] *noun* single-masted sailing boat.
smack[4] *noun slang* heroin, other hard drug.
smacker *noun slang* loud kiss; £1, *US* $1.
small /smɔ:l/ ● *adjective* not large or big; not great in importance, amount, number, etc.; not much; insignificant; of small particles; on small scale; poor, humble; mean; young. ● *noun* slenderest part, esp. of back; (in *plural*) *colloquial* underwear, esp. as laundry. ● *adverb* into small pieces. □ **small arms** portable firearms; **small change** coins, not notes; **small fry** unimportant people, children; **smallholding** agricultural holding smaller than farm; **small hours** night-time after midnight; **small-minded** petty, narrow in outlook; **smallpox** *historical* acute contagious disease with fever and pustules usually leaving scars; **small print** matter printed small, esp. limitations in contract; **small talk** trivial social conversation; **small-time** *colloquial* unimportant, petty. □ **smallness** *noun*.
smarmy /'smɑ:mɪ/ *adjective* (**-ier**, **-iest**) *colloquial* ingratiating. □ **smarmily** *adverb*; **smarminess** *noun*.
smart ● *adjective* well-groomed, neat; bright and fresh in appearance; stylish, fashionable; *esp. US* clever, ingenious, quickwitted; quick, brisk; painfully severe, sharp, vigorous. ● *verb* feel or give pain; rankle; (+ *for*) suffer consequences of. ● *noun* sharp bodily or mental pain, stinging sensation. ● *adverb* smartly. □ **smartish** *adjective & adverb*; **smartly** *adverb*; **smartness** *noun*.
smarten *verb* (usually + *up*) make or become smart.
smash ● *verb* (often + *up*) break to pieces; bring or come to destruction, defeat, or disaster; (+ *into*, *through*) move forcefully; (+ *in*) break with crushing blow; hit (ball) hard, esp. downwards. ● *noun* act or sound of smashing; (in full **smash hit**) very successful play, song, etc. ● *adverb* with smash. □ **smash-and-grab** robbery with goods snatched from broken shop window etc.
smashing *adjective colloquial* excellent, wonderful.
smattering /'smætərɪŋ/ *noun* slight knowledge.
smear /smɪə/ ● *verb* daub or mark with grease etc.; smudge; defame. ● *noun* action of smearing; material smeared on microscope slide etc. for examination; specimen of this. □ **smear test** cervical smear. □ **smeary** *adjective*.
smell ● *noun* sense of odour perception; property perceived by this; unpleasant odour; act of inhaling to ascertain smell. ● *verb* (*past & past participle* **smelt** or **smelled**) perceive or examine by smell; stink; seem by smell to be; (+ *of*) emit smell of, suggest; detect; have or use sense of smell. □ **smelling salts** sharp-smelling substances sniffed to relieve faintness.
smelly *adjective* (**-ier**, **-iest**) strong- or evil-smelling.
smelt[1] *verb* melt (ore) to extract metal; obtain (metal) thus. □ **smelter** *noun*.
smelt[2] *past & past participle* of SMELL.
smelt[3] *noun* (*plural* same or **-s**) small edible green and silver fish.
smilax /'smaɪlæks/ *noun* any of several climbing plants.
smile ● *verb* (**-ling**) have or assume facial expression of amusement or pleasure, with ends of lips turned upward; express by smiling; give (smile); (+ *on*, *upon*) favour. ● *noun* act of smiling; smiling expression or aspect.
smirch *verb & noun* stain, smear.
smirk ● *noun* conceited or silly smile. ● *verb* give smirk.
smite *verb* (**-ting**; *past* **smote**; *past participle* **smitten** /'smɪt(ə)n/) *archaic or literary* hit, chastise, defeat; (in *passive*) affect strongly, seize.
smith *noun* blacksmith; worker in metal, craftsman.
smithereens /smɪðə'ri:nz/ *plural noun* small fragments.
smithy /'smɪðɪ/ *noun* (*plural* **-ies**) blacksmith's workshop, forge.
smitten *past participle* of SMITE.
smock ● *noun* loose shirtlike garment, often adorned with smocking. ● *verb* adorn with smocking.
smocking *noun* ornamentation on cloth made by gathering it tightly with stitches.
smog *noun* dense smoky fog. □ **smoggy** *adjective* (**-ier**, **-iest**).
smoke ● *noun* visible vapour from burning substance; act of smoking tobacco etc.; *colloquial* cigarette, cigar. ● *verb* (**-king**) inhale and exhale smoke of (cigarette etc.); do this habitually; emit smoke or visible vapour; darken or preserve with smoke. □ **smoke bomb** bomb emitting dense smoke on bursting; **smoke-free** free from smoke, where smoking is not permitted; **smoke out** drive out by means of smoke, drive out of hiding etc.; **smokescreen** cloud of smoke concealing esp. military operations, ruse for disguising activities; **smokestack** funnel of locomotive or steamship, tall chimney.
smoker *noun* person who habitually smokes tobacco; compartment on train where smoking is permitted.

smoky *adjective* (**-ier**, **-iest**) emitting, filled with, or obscured by, smoke; coloured by or like smoke; having flavour of smoked food.

smolder *US* = SMOULDER.

smooch /smu:tʃ/ ● *verb* kiss and caress. ● *noun* smooching.

smooth /smu:ð/ ● *adjective* having even surface; free from projections and roughness; that can be traversed uninterrupted; (of sea etc.) calm, flat; (of journey etc.) easy; not harsh in sound or taste; conciliatory, slick; not jerky. ● *verb* (often + *out*, *down*) make or become smooth; (often + *out*, *down*, *over*, *away*) get rid of (differences, faults, etc.). ● *noun* smoothing touch or stroke. □ **smooth-tongued** insincerely flattering. □ **smoothly** *adverb*; **smoothness** *noun*.

smorgasbord /'smɔ:gəsbɔ:d/ *noun* Swedish hors d'oeuvres; buffet meal with various esp. savoury dishes.

smote *past* of SMITE.

smother /'smʌðə/ *verb* suffocate, stifle; (+ *in*, *with*) overwhelm or cover with (kisses, gifts, etc.); extinguish (fire) by heaping with ashes etc.; have difficulty breathing; (often + *up*) suppress, conceal.

smoulder /'smaʊldə/ (*US* **smolder**) ● *verb* burn without flame or internally; (of person) show silent emotion. ● *noun* smouldering.

smudge ● *noun* blurred or smeared line, mark, etc. ● *verb* (**-ging**) make smudge on or with; become smeared or blurred. □ **smudgy** *adjective*.

smug *adjective* (**-gg-**) self-satisfied. □ **smugly** *adverb*; **smugness** *noun*.

smuggle /'smʌg(ə)l/ *verb* (**-ling**) import or export illegally, esp. without paying duties; convey secretly. □ **smuggler** *noun*; **smuggling** *noun*.

smut ● *noun* small piece of soot; spot or smudge made by this; obscene talk, pictures, or stories; fungous disease of cereals. ● *verb* (**-tt-**) mark with smut(s). □ **smutty** *adjective* (**-ier**, **-iest**).

snack *noun* light, casual, or hasty meal. □ **snack bar** place where snacks are sold.

snaffle /'snæf(ə)l/ ● *noun* (in full **snaffle-bit**) simple bridle-bit without curb. ● *verb* (**-ling**) *colloquial* steal, seize.

snag ● *noun* unexpected obstacle or drawback; jagged projection; tear in material etc. ● *verb* (**-gg-**) catch or tear on snag.

snail *noun* slow-moving mollusc with spiral shell.

snake ● *noun* long limbless reptile; (also **snake in the grass**) traitor, secret enemy. ● *verb* (**-king**) move or twist like a snake. □ **snakes and ladders** board game with counters moved up 'ladders' and down 'snakes'; **snakeskin** *noun* skin of snake, *adjective* made of snakeskin.

snaky *adjective* of or like a snake; sinuous; treacherous.

snap ● *verb* (**-pp-**) break sharply; (cause to) emit sudden sharp sound; open or close with snapping sound; speak irritably; (often + *at*) make sudden audible bite; move quickly; photograph. ● *noun* act or sound of snapping; crisp biscuit; snapshot; (in full **cold snap**) sudden brief period of cold weather; card game in which players call 'snap' when two similar cards are exposed; vigour. ● *adverb* with snapping sound. ● *adjective* done without forethought. □ **snapdragon** plant with two-lipped flowers; **snap-fastener** press-stud; **snap out of** *slang* get out of (mood etc.) by sudden effort; **snapshot** informal or casual photograph; **snap up** accept (offer etc.) hastily or eagerly.

snapper *noun* any of several edible marine fish.

snappish *adjective* curt, ill-tempered.

snappy *adjective* (**-ier**, **-iest**) *colloquial* brisk, lively; neat and elegant; snappish. □ **snappily** *adverb*.

snare /sneə/ ● *noun* trap, esp. with noose, for birds or animals; trap, trick, temptation; (in *singular* or *plural*) twisted strings of gut, hide, or wire stretched across lower head of side drum to produce rattle; (in full **snare drum**) side drum with snares. ● *verb* (**-ring**) catch in snare, trap.

snarl[1] ● *verb* growl with bared teeth; speak angrily. ● *noun* act or sound of snarling.

snarl[2] ● *verb* (often + *up*) twist, entangle, hamper movement of (traffic etc.), become entangled. ● *noun* tangle.

snatch ● *verb* (often + *away*, *from*) seize quickly, eagerly, or unexpectedly; steal by grabbing; *slang* kidnap; (+ *at*) try to seize, take eagerly. ● *noun* act of snatching; fragment of song, talk, etc.; short spell of activity etc.

snazzy /'snæzɪ/ *adjective* (**-ier**, **-iest**) *slang* smart, stylish, showy.

sneak ● *verb* go or convey furtively; *slang* steal unobserved; *slang* tell tales; (as **sneaking** *adjective*) furtive, persistent and puzzling. ● *noun* mean-spirited, underhand person; *slang* tell-tale. ● *adjective* acting or done without warning, secret. □ **sneak-thief** person who steals without breaking in. □ **sneaky** *adjective* (**-ier**, **-iest**).

sneaker *noun slang* soft-soled shoe.

sneer ● *noun* derisive smile or remark. ● *verb* (often + *at*) make sneer; utter with sneer. □ **sneering** *adjective*; **sneeringly** *adverb*.

sneeze ● *noun* sudden involuntary explosive expulsion of air from irritated nostrils. ● *verb* (**-zing**) make sneeze. □ **not to be sneezed at** *colloquial* worth having or considering.

snick ● *verb* make small notch or cut in; *Cricket* deflect (ball) slightly with bat. ● *noun* such notch or deflection.

snicker /'snɪkə/ *noun & verb* snigger.

snide *adjective* sneering, slyly derogatory.

sniff ● *verb* inhale air audibly through nose; (often + *up*) draw in through nose; smell scent of by sniffing. ● *noun* act or sound of sniffing. □ **sniff at** show contempt for; **sniffer-dog** *colloquial* dog trained to find drugs or explosives by scent.

sniffle /'snɪf(ə)l/ ● *verb* (**-ling**) sniff repeatedly or slightly. ● *noun* act of sniffling; (in *singular* or *plural*) cold in the head causing sniffling.

snifter /'snɪftə/ *noun slang* small alcoholic drink.

snigger /'snɪgə/ ● *noun* half-suppressed laugh. ● *verb* utter snigger.

snip ● *verb* (**-pp-**) cut with scissors etc., esp. in small quick strokes. ● *noun* act of snipping; piece snipped off; *slang* something easily done, bargain.

snipe ● *noun* (*plural* same or **-s**) wading bird with long straight bill. ● *verb* (**-ping**) fire shots from hiding usually at long range; (often + *at*) make sly critical attack. □ **sniper** *noun*.

snippet /'snɪpɪt/ *noun* small piece cut off; (usually in *plural*) scrap of information etc., short extract from book etc.

snitch ● *verb slang* steal; (often + *on*) inform on person. ● *noun* informer.

snivel /'snɪv(ə)l/ ● *verb* (**-ll-**; *US* **-l-**) sniffle; weep with sniffling; show maudlin emotion. ● *noun* act of snivelling.

snob *noun* person who despises people with inferior social position, wealth, intellect, tastes, etc. □ **snobbery** *noun*; **snobbish** *adjective*; **snobby** *adjective* (**-ier**, **-iest**).

snood /snu:d/ *noun* woman's loose hairnet.

snook /snu:k/ *noun slang* contemptuous gesture with thumb to nose and fingers spread. □ **cock a snook** (**at**) make this gesture (at), show contempt (for).

snooker /ˈsnu:kə/ ● *noun* game played on oblong cloth-covered table with 1 white, 15 red, and 6 other coloured balls; position in this game where direct shot would give points to opponent. ● *verb* subject (player) to snooker; (esp. as **snookered** *adjective*) *slang* thwart, defeat.

snoop /snu:p/ *colloquial* ● *verb* pry into another's affairs; (often + *about*, *around*) investigate (often stealthily) transgressions of rules etc. ● *noun* act of snooping. ▫ **snooper** *noun*.

snooty /ˈsnu:tɪ/ *adjective* (**-ier**, **-iest**) *colloquial* supercilious, snobbish. ▫ **snootily** *adverb*.

snooze /snu:z/ *colloquial* ● *noun* short sleep, nap. ● *verb* (**-zing**) take snooze.

snore ● *noun* snorting or grunting sound of breathing during sleep. ● *verb* (**-ring**) make this sound.

snorkel /ˈsnɔ:k(ə)l/ ● *noun* device for supplying air to underwater swimmer or submerged submarine. ● *verb* (**-ll-**; *US* **-l-**) use snorkel.

snort ● *noun* explosive sound made by driving breath violently through nose, esp. by horses, or by humans to show contempt, incredulity, etc.; *colloquial* small drink of liquor; *slang* inhaled dose of powdered cocaine. ● *verb* make snort; *slang* inhale (esp. cocaine); express or utter with snort.

snot *noun slang* nasal mucus.

snotty *adjective* (**-ier**, **-iest**) *slang* running or covered with nasal mucus; snooty; contemptible. ▫ **snottily** *adverb*; **snottiness** *noun*.

snout /snaʊt/ *noun* projecting nose (and mouth) of animal; *derogatory* person's nose; pointed front of thing.

snow /snəʊ/ ● *noun* frozen vapour falling to earth in light white flakes; fall or layer of this; thing resembling snow in whiteness or texture etc.; *slang* cocaine. ● *verb* (after *it*) snow falls; (+ *in*, *over*, *up*, etc.) confine or block with snow. ▫ **snowball** *noun* snow pressed into ball for throwing in play, *verb* throw or pelt with snowballs, increase rapidly; **snow-blind** temporarily blinded by glare from snow; **snowbound** prevented by snow from going out; **snowcap** snow-covered mountain peak; **snowdrift** bank of snow piled up by wind; **snowdrop** spring-flowering plant with white drooping flowers; **snowed under** overwhelmed, esp. with work; **snowflake** each of the flakes in which snow falls; **snow goose** white Arctic goose; **snowline** level above which snow never melts entirely; **snowman** figure made of snow; **snowplough** device for clearing road of snow; **snowshoe** racket-shaped attachment to boot for walking on surface of snow; **snowstorm** heavy fall of snow, esp. with wind; **snow white** pure white. ▫ **snowy** *adjective* (**-ier**, **iest**).

SNP *abbreviation* Scottish National Party.

Snr. *abbreviation* Senior.

snub ● *verb* (**-bb-**) rebuff or humiliate in a sharp or cutting way. ● *noun* snubbing, rebuff. ● *adjective* (of nose) short and turned up.

snuff[1] ● *noun* charred part of candle-wick. ● *verb* trim snuff from (candle). ▫ **snuff it** *slang* die; **snuff out** extinguish (candle), put an end to (hopes etc.).

snuff[2] ● *noun* powdered tobacco or medicine taken by sniffing. ● *verb* take snuff.

snuffle /ˈsnʌf(ə)l/ ● *verb* (**-ling**) make sniffing sounds; speak nasally; breathe noisily, esp. with blocked nose. ● *noun* snuffling sound or speech.

snug ● *adjective* (**-gg-**) cosy, comfortable, sheltered; close-fitting. ● *noun* small room in pub. ▫ **snugly** *adverb*.

snuggle /ˈsnʌg(ə)l/ *verb* (**-ling**) settle or move into warm comfortable position.

so[1] /səʊ/ ● *adverb* to such an extent, in this or that manner or state; also; indeed, actually; very; thus. ● *conjunction* (often + *that*) consequently, in order that; and then; (introducing question) after that. ▫ **so-and-so** particular but unspecified person or thing, *colloquial* objectionable person; **so as to** in order to; **so-called** commonly called but often incorrectly; **so long** *colloquial* goodbye; **so so** *colloquial* only moderately good or well.

so[2] = SOH.

soak ● *verb* make or become thoroughly wet through saturation; (of rain etc.) drench; (+ *in*, *up*) absorb (liquid, knowledge, etc.); (+ *in*, *into*, *through*) penetrate by saturation; *colloquial* extort money from; *colloquial* drink heavily. ● *noun* soaking; *colloquial* hard drinker. ▫ **soakaway** arrangement for disposal of waste water by percolation through soil.

soaking *adjective* (in full **soaking wet**) wet through.

soap ● *noun* cleansing substance yielding lather when rubbed in water; *colloquial* soap opera. ● *verb* apply soap to. ▫ **soapbox** makeshift stand for street orator; **soap opera** domestic broadcast serial; **soap powder** powdered soap usually with additives, for washing clothes etc.; **soapstone** steatite; **soapsuds** suds.

soapy *adjective* (**-ier**, **-iest**) of or like soap; containing or smeared with soap; unctuous, flattering.

soar /sɔ:/ *verb* fly or rise high; reach high level or standard; fly without flapping wings or using motor power.

sob ● *verb* (**-bb-**) inhale convulsively, usually with weeping; utter with sobs. ● *noun* act or sound of sobbing. ▫ **sob story** *colloquial* story or explanation appealing for sympathy.

sober /ˈsəʊbə/ ● *adjective* (**-er**, **-est**) not drunk; not given to drink; moderate, tranquil, serious; (of colour) dull. ● *verb* (often + *down*, *up*) make or become sober. ▫ **soberly** *adverb*.

sobriety /səˈbraɪɪtɪ/ *noun* being sober.

sobriquet /ˈsəʊbrɪkeɪ/ *noun* (also **soubriquet** /ˈsu:-/) nickname.

Soc. *abbreviation* Socialist; Society.

soccer /ˈsɒkə/ *noun* Association football.

sociable /ˈsəʊʃəb(ə)l/ *adjective* liking company, gregarious, friendly. ▫ **sociability** *noun*; **sociably** *adverb*.

social /ˈsəʊʃ(ə)l/ ● *adjective* of society or its organization, esp. of relations of (classes of) people; living in communities; gregarious. ● *noun* social gathering. ▫ **social science** study of society and social relationships; **social security** state assistance to the poor and unemployed; **social services** welfare services provided by the State, esp. education, health care, and housing; **social work** professional or voluntary work with disadvantaged groups; **social worker** *noun*. ▫ **socially** *adverb*.

socialism *noun* political and economic theory advocating state ownership and control of means of production, distribution, and exchange; social system based on this. ▫ **socialist** *noun & adjective*; **socialistic** /-ˈlɪs-/ *adjective*.

socialite /ˈsəʊʃəlaɪt/ *noun* person moving in fashionable society.

socialize /ˈsəʊʃəlaɪz/ *verb* (also **-ise**) (**-zing** or **-sing**) mix socially; make social; organize in a socialistic way.

society /səˈsaɪətɪ/ *noun* (*plural* **-ies**) organized and interdependent community; system and organization of this; (members of) aristocratic part of this; mixing with other people, companionship, company; association, club. ▫ **societal** *adjective*.

sociology /səʊsɪˈɒlədʒɪ/ *noun* study of society and social problems. ▫ **sociological** /-əˈlɒdʒ-/ *adjective*; **sociologist** *noun*.

sock[1] *noun* knitted covering for foot and lower leg; insole.

sock[2] *colloquial* ● *verb* hit hard. ● *noun* hard blow. □ **sock it to** attack or address vigorously.

socket /'sɒkɪt/ *noun* hollow for thing to fit into etc., esp. device receiving electric plug, light bulb, etc.

Socratic /sə'krætɪk/ *adjective* of Socrates or his philosophy.

sod *noun* turf, piece of turf; surface of ground.

soda /'səʊdə/ *noun* any of various compounds of sodium in common use; (in full **soda water**) effervescent water used esp. with spirits etc. as drink. □ **soda fountain** device supplying soda water, shop or counter with this.

sodden /'sɒd(ə)n/ *adjective* saturated, soaked through; stupid, dull, etc. with drunkenness.

sodium /'səʊdɪəm/ *noun* soft silver-white metallic element. □ **sodium bicarbonate** white compound used in baking-powder; **sodium chloride** common salt; **sodium lamp** lamp using sodium vapour and giving yellow light; **sodium nitrate** white powdery compound in fertilizers etc.

sofa /'səʊfə/ *noun* long upholstered seat with raised back and ends. □ **sofa bed** sofa that can be converted into bed.

soffit /'sɒfɪt/ *noun* undersurface of arch, lintel, etc.

soft ● *adjective* not hard, easily cut or dented, malleable; (of cloth etc.) smooth, fine, not rough; mild; (of water) low in mineral salts which prevent lathering; not brilliant or glaring; not strident or loud; sibilant; not sharply defined; gentle, conciliatory; compassionate, sympathetic; feeble, half-witted, silly, sentimental; *colloquial* easy; (of drug) not highly addictive. ● *adverb* softly. □ **have a soft spot for** be fond of; **softball** form of baseball with softer larger ball; **soft-boiled** (of egg) boiled leaving yolk soft; **soft-centred** having soft centre, soft-hearted; **soft drink** non-alcoholic drink; **soft fruit** small stoneless fruit; **soft furnishings** curtains, rugs, etc.; **soft-hearted** tender, compassionate; **soft option** easier alternative; **soft palate** back part of palate; **soft pedal** *noun* pedal on piano softening tone; **soft-pedal** *verb* refrain from emphasizing; **soft sell** restrained salesmanship; **soft soap** *colloquial* persuasive flattery; **soft-spoken** having gentle voice; **soft target** vulnerable person or thing; **soft touch** *colloquial* gullible person, esp. over money; **software** computer programs; **softwood** wood of coniferous tree. □ **softly** *adverb*; **softness** *noun*.

soften /'sɒf(ə)n/ *verb* make or become soft(er); (often + *up*) reduce strength, resistance, etc. of. □ **softener** *noun*.

softie *noun* (also **softy**) (*plural* **-ies**) *colloquial* weak, silly, or soft-hearted person.

soggy /'sɒgɪ/ *adjective* (**-ier**, **-iest**) sodden, waterlogged.

soh *noun* (also **so**) *Music* fifth note of scale in tonic solfa.

soil[1] *noun* upper layer of earth, in which plants grow; ground, territory.

soil[2] ● *verb* make dirty, smear, stain; defile; discredit. ● *noun* dirty mark; filth, refuse. □ **soil pipe** discharge-pipe of lavatory.

soirée /'swɑːreɪ/ *noun* evening party.

sojourn /'sɒdʒ(ə)n/ ● *noun* temporary stay. ● *verb* stay temporarily.

sola /'səʊlə/ *noun* pithy-stemmed E. Indian swamp plant. □ **sola topi** sun-helmet made from pith of this.

solace /'sɒləs/ ● *noun* comfort in distress or disappointment. ● *verb* (**-cing**) give solace to.

solan /'səʊlən/ *noun* (in full **solan goose**) large gooselike gannet.

solar /'səʊlə/ *adjective* of or reckoned by sun. □ **solar battery**, **cell** device converting solar radiation into electricity; **solar panel** panel absorbing sun's rays as energy source; **solar plexus** complex of nerves at pit of stomach; **solar system** sun and the planets etc. whose motion is governed by it.

solarium /sə'leərɪəm/ *noun* (*plural* **-ria**) room with sunlamps, glass roof, etc.

sold *past & past participle* of SELL.

solder /'sɒldə/ ● *noun* fusible alloy used for joining metals, wires, etc. ● *verb* join with solder. □ **soldering iron** tool for melting and applying solder.

soldier /'səʊldʒə/ ● *noun* member of army, esp. (in full **common soldier**) private or NCO; *colloquial* bread finger, esp. for dipping in egg. ● *verb* serve as soldier. □ **soldier on** *colloquial* persevere doggedly. □ **soldierly** *adjective*.

soldiery *noun* soldiers collectively.

sole[1] ● *noun* undersurface of foot; part of shoe, sock, etc. below foot, esp. part other than heel; lower surface or base of plough, golf-club head, etc. ● *verb* (**-ling**) provide with sole.

sole[2] *noun* (*plural* same or **-s**) type of flatfish.

sole[3] *adjective* one and only single; exclusive. □ **solely** *adverb*.

solecism /'sɒlɪsɪz(ə)m/ *noun* mistake of grammar or idiom; offence against etiquette.

solemn /'sɒləm/ *adjective* serious and dignified; formal; awe-inspiring; of cheerless manner; grave. □ **solemness** *noun*; **solemnity** /sə'lem-/ *noun* (*plural* **-ies**); **solemnly** *adverb*.

solemnize /'sɒləmnaɪz/ *verb* (also **-ise**) (**-zing** or **-sing**) duly perform (esp. marriage ceremony); make solemn. □ **solemnization** *noun*.

solenoid /'səʊlənɔɪd/ *noun* cylindrical coil of wire acting as magnet when carrying electric current.

sol-fa /'sɒlfɑː/ *noun* system of syllables representing musical notes.

solicit /sə'lɪsɪt/ *verb* (**-t-**) seek repeatedly or earnestly; (of prostitute) accost (man) concerning sexual activity. □ **solicitation** *noun*.

solicitor /sə'lɪsɪtə/ *noun* lawyer qualified to advise clients and instruct barristers.

solicitous /sə'lɪsɪtəs/ *adjective* showing concern; (+ *to do*) eager, anxious. □ **solicitously** *adverb*.

solicitude /sə'lɪsɪtjuːd/ *noun* being solicitous.

solid /'sɒlɪd/ ● *adjective* (**-er**, **-est**) of firm and stable shape, not liquid or fluid; of such material throughout, not hollow; alike all through; sturdily built, not flimsy; 3-dimensional; of solids; sound, reliable; uninterrupted; unanimous. ● *noun* solid substance or body; (in *plural*) solid food. ● *adverb* solidly. **solid-state** using electronic properties of solids to replace those of valves. □ **solidity** /sə'lɪd-/ *noun*; **solidly** *adverb*; **solidness** *noun*.

solidarity /sɒlɪ'dærɪtɪ/ *noun* unity, esp. political or in industrial dispute; mutual dependence.

solidify /sə'lɪdɪfaɪ/ *verb* (**-ies**, **-ied**) make or become solid.

soliloquy /sə'lɪləkwɪ/ *noun* (*plural* **-quies**) talking without or regardless of hearers; this part of a play. □ **soliloquize** *verb* (also **-ise**) (**-zing** or **-sing**).

solipsism /'sɒlɪpsɪz(ə)m/ *noun* theory that self is all that exists or can be known.

solitaire /'sɒlɪteə/ *noun* jewel set by itself; ring etc. with this; game for one player who removes pegs etc. from board on jumping others over them; *US* card game for one person.

solitary /'sɒlɪtərɪ/ ● *adjective* living or being alone; not gregarious; lonely; secluded; single. ● *noun* (*plural* **-ies**) recluse; *colloquial* solitary confinement.

□ **solitary confinement** isolation in separate prison cell.

solitude /ˈsɒlɪtjuːd/ *noun* being solitary; solitary place.

solo /ˈsəʊləʊ/ ● *noun* (*plural* **-s**) piece of music or dance performed by one person; thing done by one person, esp. unaccompanied flight; (in full **solo whist**) type of whist in which one player may oppose the others. ● *verb* (**-es**, **-ed**) perform a solo. ● *adjective* & *adverb* unaccompanied, alone.

soloist /ˈsəʊləʊɪst/ *noun* performer of solo.

solstice /ˈsɒlstɪs/ *noun* either of two times (**summer**, **winter solstice**) when sun is farthest from equator.

soluble /ˈsɒljʊb(ə)l/ *adjective* that can be dissolved or solved. □ **solubility** *noun*.

solution /səˈluːʃ(ə)n/ *noun* (means of) solving a problem; conversion of solid or gas into liquid by mixture with liquid; state or substance resulting from this; dissolving, being dissolved.

solve *verb* (**-ving**) answer, remove, or deal with (problem). □ **solvable** *adjective*.

solvency /ˈsɒlvənsɪ/ *noun* being financially solvent.

solvent /ˈsɒlv(ə)nt/ ● *adjective* able to pay one's debts; able to dissolve or form solution. ● *noun* solvent liquid etc.

somatic /səˈmætɪk/ *adjective* of the body, not of the mind.

sombre /ˈsɒmbə/ *adjective* (also *US* **somber**) dark, gloomy, dismal. □ **sombrely** *adverb*; **sombreness** *noun*.

sombrero /sɒmˈbreərəʊ/ *noun* (*plural* **-s**) broad-brimmed hat worn esp. in Latin America.

some /sʌm/ ● *adjective* unspecified amount or number of; unknown, unspecified; approximately; considerable; at least a small amount of; such to a certain extent; *colloquial* a remarkable. ● *pronoun* some people or things, some number or amount. ● *adverb colloquial* to some extent. □ **somebody** *pronoun* some person, *noun* important person; **someday** at some time in the future; **somehow** for some reason, in some way, by some means; **someone** somebody; **something** unspecified or unknown thing, unexpressed or intangible quantity or quality, *colloquial* notable person or thing; **sometime** at some time, former(ly); **sometimes** occasionally; **somewhat** to some extent; **somewhere** (in or to) some place.

somersault /ˈsʌməsɒlt/ ● *noun* leap or roll in which one turns head over heels. ● *verb* perform somersault.

somnambulism /sɒmˈnæmbjʊlɪz(ə)m/ *noun* sleepwalking. □ **somnambulant** *adjective*; **somnambulist** *noun*.

somnolent /ˈsɒmnələnt/ *adjective* sleepy, drowsy; inducing drowsiness. □ **somnolence** *noun*.

son /sʌn/ *noun* male in relation to his parent(s); male descendant; (+ *of*) male member of (family etc.); male inheritor of a quality etc.; *form of address, esp. to boy*. □ **son-in-law** (*plural* **sons-in-law**) daughter's husband.

sonar /ˈsəʊnɑː/ *noun* system for detecting objects under water by reflected sound; apparatus for this.

sonata /səˈnɑːtə/ *noun* musical composition for one or two instruments in several related movements.

song *noun* words set to music or for singing; vocal music; composition suggestive of song; cry of some birds. □ **for a song** *colloquial* very cheaply; **songbird** bird with musical call; **song thrush** common thrush; **songwriter** writer of (music for) songs.

songster /ˈsɒŋstə/ *noun* (*feminine* **songstress**) singer; songbird.

sonic /ˈsɒnɪk/ *adjective* of or using sound or sound waves. □ **sonic bang**, **boom** noise made by aircraft flying faster than sound.

sonnet /ˈsɒnɪt/ *noun* poem of 14 lines with fixed rhyme scheme.

sonny /ˈsʌnɪ/ *noun colloquial familiar form of address to young boy*.

sonorous /ˈsɒnərəs/ *adjective* having a loud, full, or deep sound; (of speech etc.) imposing. □ **sonority** /səˈnɒr-/ *noun* (*plural* **-ies**).

soon /suːn/ *adverb* in a short time; relatively early; readily, willingly. □ **sooner or later** at some future time. □ **soonish** *adverb*.

soot /sʊt/ *noun* black powdery deposit from smoke.

soothe /suːð/ *verb* (**-thing**) calm; soften, mitigate.

soothsayer /ˈsuːθseɪə/ *noun* seer, prophet.

sooty *adjective* (**-ier**, **-iest**) covered with soot; black, brownish black.

sop ● *noun* thing given or done to pacify or bribe; piece of bread etc. dipped in gravy etc. ● *verb* (**-pp-**) (+ *up*) soak up.

sophism /ˈsɒfɪz(ə)m/ *noun* false argument, esp. one meant to deceive.

sophist /ˈsɒfɪst/ *noun* captious or clever but fallacious reasoner. □ **sophistic** /səˈfɪs-/ *adjective*.

sophisticate /səˈfɪstɪkət/ *noun* sophisticated person.

sophisticated /səˈfɪstɪkeɪtɪd/ *adjective* worldly-wise, cultured, elegant; highly developed and complex. □ **sophistication** *noun*.

sophistry /ˈsɒfɪstrɪ/ *noun* (*plural* **-ies**) use of sophisms; a sophism.

sophomore /ˈsɒfəmɔː/ *noun US* second-year university or high-school student.

soporific /sɒpəˈrɪfɪk/ ● *adjective* inducing sleep. ● *noun* soporific drug or influence. □ **soporifically** *adverb*.

sopping *adjective* drenched.

soppy *adjective* (**-ier**, **-iest**) *colloquial* mawkishly sentimental, silly.

soprano /səˈprɑːnəʊ/ ● *noun* (*plural* **-s**) highest singing voice; singer with this. ● *adjective* having range of soprano.

sorbet /ˈsɔːbeɪ/ *noun* water-ice; sherbet.

sorcerer /ˈsɔːsərə/ *noun* (*feminine* **sorceress**) magician, wizard. □ **sorcery** *noun* (*plural* **-ies**).

sordid /ˈsɔːdɪd/ *adjective* dirty, squalid; ignoble, mercenary. □ **sordidly** *adverb*; **sordidness** *noun*.

sore ● *adjective* painful; suffering pain; aggrieved, vexed; *archaic* grievous, severe. ● *noun* sore place, subject, etc. ● *adverb archaic* grievously, severely. □ **soreness** *noun*.

sorely *adverb* extremely.

sorghum /ˈsɔːgəm/ *noun* tropical cereal grass.

sorority /səˈrɒrɪtɪ/ *noun* (*plural* **-ies**) *US* female students' society in university or college.

sorrel[1] /ˈsɒr(ə)l/ *noun* sour-leaved herb.

sorrel[2] /ˈsɒr(ə)l/ ● *adjective* of light reddish-brown colour. ● *noun* this colour; sorrel animal, esp. horse.

sorrow /ˈsɒrəʊ/ ● *noun* mental distress caused by loss, disappointment, etc.; cause of sorrow. ● *verb* feel sorrow, mourn. □ **sorrowful** *adjective*.

sorry /ˈsɒrɪ/ *adjective* (**-ier**, **-iest**) pained, regretful, penitent; feeling pity; wretched.

sort ● *noun* class, kind; *colloquial* person of specified kind. ● *verb* (often + *out*, *over*) arrange systematically. □ **of a sort**, **of sorts** *colloquial* barely deserving the name; **out of sorts** slightly unwell, in low spirits; **sort out** separate into sorts, select from miscellaneous group, disentangle, put into order, solve, *colloquial* deal with or punish.

sortie /ˈsɔːtɪ/ ● *noun* sally, esp. from besieged garrison; operational military flight. ● *verb* (**sortieing**) make sortie.

SOS *noun* (*plural* **SOSs**) international code-signal of extreme distress; urgent appeal for help.
sot *noun* habitual drunkard. ◻ **sottish** *adjective*.
sotto voce /sɒtəʊ ˈvəʊtʃɪ/ *adverb* in an undertone. [Italian]
sou /suː/ *noun* (*plural* **-s**) *colloquial* very small amount of money; *historical* former French coin of low value.
soubrette /suːˈbret/ *noun* pert maidservant etc. in comedy; actress taking this part.
soubriquet = SOBRIQUET.
soufflé /ˈsuːfleɪ/ *noun* light spongy dish made with stiffly beaten egg white.
sough /saʊ, sʌf/ ● *noun* moaning or rustling sound, e.g. of wind in trees. ● *verb* make this sound.
sought /sɔːt/ *past & past participle* of SEEK. ◻ **sought-after** much in demand.
souk /suːk/ *noun* market-place in Muslim countries.
soul /səʊl/ *noun* spiritual or immaterial part of person; moral, emotional, or intellectual nature of person; personification, pattern; an individual; animating or essential part; energy, intensity; soul music. ◻ **soul-destroying** tedious, monotonous; **soul mate** person ideally suited to another; **soul music** type of black American music; **soul-searching** introspection.
soulful *adjective* having, expressing, or evoking deep feeling. ◻ **soulfully** *adverb*.
soulless *adjective* lacking sensitivity or noble qualities; undistinguished, uninteresting.
sound[1] /saʊnd/ ● *noun* sensation produced in ear when surrounding air etc. vibrates; vibrations causing this; what is or may be heard; idea or impression give by words. ● *verb* (cause to) emit sound; utter, pronounce; convey specified impression; give audible signal for; test condition of by sound produced. ◻ **sound barrier** high resistance of air to objects moving at speeds near that of sound; **sound effect** sound other than speech or music produced artificially for film, broadcast, etc.; **sounding-board** person etc. used to test or disseminate opinion(s), canopy projecting sound towards audience; **sound off** talk loudly, express one's opinions forcefully; **soundproof** *adjective* impervious to sound, *verb* make soundproof; **sound system** equipment for reproducing sound; **soundtrack** sound element of film or videotape, recording of this available separately; **sound wave** wave of compression and rarefaction by which sound is transmitted in air etc.
sound[2] /saʊnd/ ● *adjective* healthy, not diseased or rotten, uninjured; correct, well-founded; financially secure; undisturbed; thorough. ● *adverb* soundly. ◻ **soundly** *adverb*; **soundness** *noun*.
sound[3] /saʊnd/ *verb* test depth or quality of bottom of (sea, river, etc.); (often + *out*) inquire (esp. discreetly) into views etc. of (person).
sound[4] /saʊnd/ *noun* strait (of water).
sounding *noun* measurement of depth of water; (in *plural*) region near enough to shore for sounding; (in *plural*) cautious investigation.
soup /suːp/ ● *noun* liquid food made by boiling meat, fish, or vegetables. ● *verb* (usually + *up*) *colloquial* increase power of (engine), enliven. ◻ **in the soup** *colloquial* in difficulties; **soup-kitchen** place supplying free soup etc. to the poor; **soup-spoon** large round-bowled spoon. ◻ **soupy** *adjective* (**-ier**, **-iest**).
soupçon /ˈsuːpsɔ̃/ *noun* small quantity, trace.
sour /saʊə/ ● *adjective* having acid taste or smell (as) from unripeness or fermentation; morose, bitter; unpleasant, distasteful; (of soil) dank. ● *verb* make or become sour. ◻ **sour grapes** resentful disparagement of something coveted; **sourpuss** *colloquial* bad-tempered person. ◻ **sourly** *adverb*; **sourness** *noun*.
source /sɔːs/ *noun* place from which river or stream issues; place of origination; person, book, etc. providing information. ◻ **at source** at point of origin or issue.
souse /saʊs/ ● *verb* (**-sing**) immerse in pickle or other liquid; (as **soused** *adjective*) *colloquial* drunk; (usually + *in*) soak (thing). ● *noun* pickle made with salt; *US* food in pickle; a plunge or drenching in water.
soutane /suːˈtɑːn/ *noun* cassock of RC priest.
south /saʊθ/ ● *noun* point of horizon opposite north; corresponding compass point; (usually **the South**) southern part of world, country, town, etc. ● *adjective* towards, at, near, or facing south; (of wind) from south. ● *adverb* towards, at, or near south; (+ *of*) further south than. ◻ **southbound** travelling or leading south; **south-east, -west** point midway between south and east or west; **southpaw** *colloquial* left-handed person, esp. boxer; **south-south-east, south-south-west** point midway between south and south-east or south-west. ◻ **southward** *adjective, adverb, & noun*; **southwards** *adverb*.
southerly /ˈsʌðəlɪ/ *adjective & adverb* in southern position or direction; (of wind) from south.
southern /ˈsʌð(ə)n/ *adjective* of or in south. ◻ **Southern Cross** constellation with stars forming cross; **southern lights** aurora australis. ◻ **southernmost** *adjective*.
southerner *noun* native or inhabitant of south.
souvenir /suːvəˈnɪə/ *noun* memento of place, occasion, etc.
sou'wester /saʊˈwestə/ *noun* waterproof hat with broad flap at back; SW wind.
sovereign /ˈsɒvrɪn/ ● *noun* supreme ruler, esp. monarch; *historical* British gold coin nominally worth £1. ● *adjective* supreme; self-governing; royal; (of remedy etc.) effective. ◻ **sovereignty** *noun* (*plural* **-ies**).
Soviet /ˈsəʊvɪət/ *historical* ● *adjective* of USSR. ● *noun* citizen of USSR; (**soviet**) elected council in USSR.
sow[1] /səʊ/ *verb* (*past* **sowed**; *past participle* **sown** or **sowed**) scatter (seed) on or in earth, (often + *with*) plant with seed; initiate.
sow[2] /saʊ/ *noun* adult female pig.
soy *noun* (in full **soy sauce**) sauce made from pickled soya beans.
soya /ˈsɔɪə/ *noun* (in full **soya bean**) (seed of) leguminous plant yielding edible oil and flour.
sozzled /ˈsɒz(ə)ld/ *adjective colloquial* very drunk.
spa /spɑː/ *noun* curative mineral spring; resort with this.
space ● *noun* continuous expanse in which things exist and move; amount of this taken by thing or available; interval between points or objects; empty area; outdoor urban recreation area; outer space; interval of time; expanse of paper used in writing, available for advertising, etc.; blank between printed, typed, or written words etc.; *Printing* piece of metal separating words etc. ● *verb* (**-cing**) set or arrange at intervals; put spaces between. ◻ **space age** era of space travel; **space-age** very modern; **spacecraft** vehicle for travelling in outer space; **spaceman, spacewoman** astronaut; **space out** spread out (more) widely; **spaceship** spacecraft; **space shuttle** spacecraft for repeated use; **space station** artificial satellite as base for operations in outer space; **spacesuit** sealed pressurized suit for astronaut in space; **space-time** fusion of concepts of space and time as 4-dimensional continuum.
spacious /ˈspeɪʃəs/ *adjective* having ample space, roomy. ◻ **spaciously** *adverb*; **spaciousness** *noun*.
spade[1] *noun* long-handled digging tool with rectangular metal blade. ◻ **spadework** hard preparatory work. ◻ **spadeful** *noun* (*plural* **-s**).

spade² *noun* playing card of suit denoted by black inverted heart-shaped figures with short stems.

spaghetti /spəˈgetɪ/ *noun* pasta in long thin strands. □ **spaghetti western** cowboy film made cheaply in Italy.

span¹ ● *noun* full extent from end to end; each part of bridge between supports; maximum lateral extent of aeroplane or its wing or of bird's wing etc.; distance between outstretched tips of thumb and little finger; 9 inches. ● *verb* (**-nn-**) extend from side to side or end to end of; bridge (river etc.).

span² *past* of SPIN.

spandrel /ˈspændrɪl/ *noun* space between curve of arch and surrounding rectangular moulding, or between curves of adjoining arches and moulding above.

spangle /ˈspæŋg(ə)l/ ● *noun* small piece of glittering material, esp. one of many used to ornament dress etc. ● *verb* (**-ling**) (esp. as **spangled** *adjective*) cover (as) with spangles.

Spaniard /ˈspænjəd/ *noun* native or national of Spain.

spaniel /ˈspænj(ə)l/ *noun* dog of breed with long silky coat and drooping ears.

Spanish /ˈspænɪʃ/ ● *adjective* of Spain. ● *noun* language of Spain.

spank *verb & noun* slap, esp. on buttocks.

spanker *noun Nautical* fore-and-aft sail on mizen-mast.

spanking ● *adjective* brisk; *colloquial* striking, excellent. ● *adverb colloquial* very. ● *noun* slapping on buttocks.

spanner /ˈspænə/ *noun* tool for turning nut on bolt etc. □ **spanner in the works** *colloquial* impediment.

spar¹ *noun* stout pole, esp. as ship's mast etc.

spar² ● *verb* (**-rr-**) make motions of boxing; argue. ● *noun* sparring; boxing match. □ **sparring partner** boxer employed to spar with another as training, person with whom one enjoys arguing.

spar³ *noun* easily split crystalline mineral.

spare /speə/ ● *adjective* not required for ordinary or present use, extra; for emergency or occasional use; lean, thin; frugal. ● *noun* spare part. ● *verb* (**-ring**) afford to give, dispense with; refrain from killing, hurting, etc.; not inflict; be frugal or grudging of. □ **go spare** *colloquial* become very angry; **spare (person's) life** not kill; **spare part** duplicate, esp. as replacement; **spare-rib** closely trimmed rib of esp. pork; **spare time** leisure; **spare tyre** *colloquial* roll of fat round waist; **to spare** left over. □ **sparely** *adverb*; **spareness** *noun*.

sparing *adjective* frugal, economical; restrained. □ **sparingly** *adverb*.

spark ● *noun* fiery particle of burning substance; (often + *of*) small amount; flash of light between electric conductors etc.; this for firing explosive mixture in internal-combustion engine; flash of wit etc.; (also **bright spark**) lively or clever person. ● *verb* emit spark(s); (often + *off*) stir into activity, initiate. □ **spark plug**, **sparking plug** device for making spark in internal-combustion engine. □ **sparky** *adjective*.

sparkle /ˈspɑːk(ə)l/ ● *verb* (**-ling**) (seem to) emit sparks; glitter, scintillate; (of wine etc.) effervesce. ● *noun* glitter; lively quality. □ **sparkly** *adjective*.

sparkler *noun* sparkling firework; *colloquial* diamond.

sparrow /ˈspærəʊ/ *noun* small brownish-grey bird. □ **sparrowhawk** small hawk.

sparse /spɑːs/ *adjective* thinly scattered. □ **sparsely** *adverb*; **sparseness** *noun*; **sparsity** *noun*.

Spartan /ˈspɑːt(ə)n/ ● *adjective* of ancient Sparta; austere, rigorous. ● *noun* native or citizen of Sparta.

spasm /ˈspæz(ə)m/ *noun* sudden involuntary muscular contraction; convulsive movement or emotion etc.; (usually + *of*) *colloquial* brief spell.

spasmodic /spæzˈmɒdɪk/ *adjective* of or in spasms, intermittent. □ **spasmodically** *adverb*.

spastic /ˈspæstɪk/ ● *adjective* of or having cerebral palsy. ● *noun* spastic person.

spat¹ *past & past participle* of SPIT¹.

spat² (usually in *plural*) *historical* short gaiter covering shoe.

spate *noun* river-flood; large amount or number (of similar events etc.).

spathe /speɪð/ *noun* large bract(s) enveloping flower-cluster.

spatial /ˈspeɪʃ(ə)l/ *adjective* of space. □ **spatially** *adverb*.

spatter /ˈspætə/ ● *verb* splash or scatter in drips. ● *noun* splash; pattering.

spatula /ˈspætjʊlə/ *noun* broad-bladed implement used esp. by artists and in cookery.

spawn ● *verb* (of fish, frog, etc.) produce (eggs); be produced as eggs or young; produce or generate in large numbers. ● *noun* eggs of fish, frogs, etc.; white fibrous matter from which fungi grow.

spay *verb* sterilize (female animal) by removing ovaries.

speak *verb* (*past* **spoke**; *past participle* **spoken** /ˈspəʊk(ə)n/) utter words in ordinary way; utter (words, the truth, etc.); converse; (+ *of*, *about*) mention; (+ *for*) act as spokesman for; (+ *to*) speak with reference to or in support of; deliver speech; (be able to) use (specified language) in speaking; convey idea; (usually + *to*) affect. □ **speak for itself** be sufficient evidence; **speaking clock** telephone service announcing correct time; **speak out** give one's opinion courageously; **speak up** speak (more) loudly.

speaker *noun* person who speaks, esp. in public; person who speaks specified language; (**Speaker**) presiding officer of legislative assembly; loudspeaker.

spear ● *noun* thrusting or hurling weapon with long shaft and sharp point; tip and stem of asparagus, broccoli, etc. ● *verb* pierce or strike (as) with spear. □ **spearhead** *noun* point of spear, person(s) leading attack or challenge, *verb* act as spearhead of (attack etc.); **spearmint** common garden mint.

spec¹ *noun colloquial* speculation. □ **on spec** as a gamble.

spec² *noun colloquial* specification.

special /ˈspeʃ(ə)l/ ● *adjective* exceptional; peculiar, specific; for particular purpose; for children with special needs. ● *noun* special constable, train, edition of newspaper, dish on menu, etc. □ **Special Branch** police department dealing with political security; **special constable** person assisting police in routine duties or in emergencies; **special effects** illusions created by props, camera-work, etc.; **special licence** licence allowing immediate marriage without banns; **special pleading** biased reasoning. □ **specially** *adverb*.

specialist *noun* person trained in particular branch of profession, esp. medicine; person specially studying subject or area.

speciality /speʃɪˈælɪtɪ/ *noun* (*plural* **-ies**) special subject, product, activity, etc.; special feature or skill.

specialize *verb* (also **-ise**) (**-zing** of **-sing**) (often + *in*) become or be specialist; devote oneself to an interest, skill, etc.; (esp. in *passive*) adapt for particular purpose; (as **specialized** *adjective*) of a specialist. □ **specialization** *noun*.

specialty /ˈspeʃəltɪ/ *noun* (*plural* **-ies**) *esp. US* speciality.

specie /ˈspiːʃiː/ *noun* coin as opposed to paper money.

species /ˈspiːʃɪz/ *noun* (*plural* same) class of things having common characteristics; group of animals or plants within genus; kind, sort.

specific /spəˈsɪfɪk/ ● *adjective* clearly defined; relating to particular subject, peculiar; exact, giving full details; *archaic* (of medicine etc.) for particular disease. ● *noun archaic* specific medicine; specific aspect. ▫ **specific gravity** relative density. ▫ **specifically** *adverb*; **specificity** /-ˈfɪs-/ *noun*.

specification /spesɪfɪˈkeɪʃ(ə)n/ *noun* specifying; (esp. in *plural*) detailed description of work (to be) done or of invention, patent, etc.

specify /ˈspesɪfaɪ/ *verb* (**-ies**, **-ied**) name or mention expressly or as condition; include in specifications.

specimen /ˈspesɪmɪn/ *noun* individual or sample taken as example of class or whole, esp. in experiments etc.; *colloquial usually derogatory* person of specified sort.

specious /ˈspiːʃəs/ *adjective* plausible but wrong.

speck ● *noun* small spot or stain; particle. ● *verb* (esp. as **specked** *adjective*) mark with specks.

speckle /ˈspek(ə)l/ ● *noun* speck, esp. one of many markings. ● *verb* (**-ling**) (esp. as **speckled** *adjective*) mark with speckles.

specs *plural noun colloquial* spectacles.

spectacle /ˈspektək(ə)l/ *noun* striking, impressive, or ridiculous sight; public show; object of public attention; (in *plural*) pair of lenses in frame supported on nose and ears, to correct defective eyesight.

spectacled *adjective* wearing spectacles.

spectacular /spekˈtækjʊlə/ ● *adjective* striking, impressive, lavish. ● *noun* spectacular performance. ▫ **spectacularly** *adverb*.

spectator /spekˈteɪtə/ *noun* person who watches a show, game, incident, etc. ▫ **spectator sport** sport attracting many spectators. ▫ **spectate** *verb* (**-ting**).

specter *US* = SPECTRE.

spectra *plural* of SPECTRUM.

spectral /ˈspektr(ə)l/ *adjective* of or like spectres or spectra; ghostly.

spectre /ˈspektə/ *noun* (*US* **specter**) ghost; haunting presentiment.

spectroscope /ˈspektrəskəʊp/ *noun* instrument for recording and examining spectra. ▫ **spectroscopic** /-ˈskɒp-/ *adjective*; **spectroscopy** /-ˈtrɒskəpɪ/ *noun*.

spectrum /ˈspektrəm/ *noun* (*plural* **-tra**) band of colours as seen in rainbow etc.; entire or wide range of subject, emotion, etc.; arrangement of electromagnetic radiation by wavelength.

speculate /ˈspekjʊleɪt/ *verb* (**-ting**) (usually + *on*, *upon*, *about*) theorize, conjecture; deal in commodities etc. in expectation of profiting from fluctuating prices. ▫ **speculation** *noun*; **speculative** /-lətɪv/ *adjective*; **speculator** *noun*.

sped *past & past participle* of SPEED.

speech *noun* faculty, act, or manner of speaking; formal public address; language, dialect. ▫ **speech day** annual prize-giving day in school; **speech therapy** treatment for defective speech.

speechify /ˈspiːtʃɪfaɪ/ *verb* (**-ies**, **-ied**) *jocular* make speeches.

speechless *adjective* temporarily silenced by emotion etc.

speed ● *noun* rapidity; rate of progress or motion; gear on bicycle; relative sensitivity of photographic film to light; *slang* amphetamine. ● *verb* (*past & past participle* **sped**) go or send quickly; (*past & past participle* **speeded**) travel at illegal or dangerous speed; *archaic* be or make prosperous or successful. ▫ **speedboat** fast motor boat; **speed limit** maximum permitted speed on road etc.; **speedway** (dirt track for) motorcycle racing, *US* road or track for fast vehicles. ▫ **speeder** *noun*.

speedometer /spiːˈdɒmɪtə/ *noun* instrument on vehicle indicating its speed.

speedwell /ˈspiːdwel/ *noun* small blue-flowered herbaceous plant.

speedy *adjective* (**-ier**, **-iest**) rapid; prompt. ▫ **speedily** *adverb*.

speleology /spiːlɪˈɒlədʒɪ/ *noun* the study of caves etc.

spell[1] *verb* (*past & past participle* **spelt** or **spelled**) write or name correctly the letters of (word etc.); (of letters) form (word etc.); result in. ▫ **spell out** make out letter by letter, explain in detail. ▫ **speller** *noun*.

spell[2] *noun* words used as charm; effect of these; fascination. ▫ **spellbound** held as if by spell, fascinated.

spell[3] *noun* (fairly) short period; period of some activity or work.

spelling *noun* way word is spelt; ability to spell.

spelt[1] *past & past participle* of SPELL[1].

spelt[2] *noun* kind of wheat giving very fine flour.

spend *verb* (*past & past participle* **spent**) pay out (money); use or consume (time or energy); use up; (as **spent** *adjective*) having lost force or strength. ▫ **spendthrift** extravagant person. ▫ **spender** *noun*.

sperm *noun* (*plural* same or **-s**) spermatozoon; semen. ▫ **sperm bank** store of semen for artificial insemination; **sperm whale** large whale hunted for spermaceti.

spermaceti /spɜːməˈsetɪ/ *noun* white waxy substance used for ointments etc.

spermatozoon /spɜːmətəʊˈzəʊən/ *noun* (*plural* **-zoa**) fertilizing cell of male organism.

spermicide /ˈspɜːmɪsaɪd/ *noun* substance that kills spermatozoa. ▫ **spermicidal** /-ˈsaɪd-/ *adjective*.

spew *verb* (often + *up*) vomit; (often + *out*) (cause to) gush.

sphagnum /ˈsfægnəm/ *noun* (*plural* **-na**) (in full **sphagnum moss**) moss growing in bogs, used as packing etc.

sphere /sfɪə/ *noun* solid figure with every point on its surface equidistant from centre; ball, globe; field of action, influence, etc.; place in society; *historical* each of revolving shells in which heavenly bodies were thought to be set.

spherical /ˈsferɪk(ə)l/ *adjective* shaped like sphere; of spheres. ▫ **spherically** *adverb*.

spheroid /ˈsfɪərɔɪd/ *noun* spherelike but not perfectly spherical body. ▫ **spheroidal** /-ˈrɔɪd-/ *adjective*.

sphincter /ˈsfɪŋktə/ *noun* ring of muscle closing and opening orifice.

Sphinx /sfɪŋks/ *noun* ancient Egyptian stone figure with lion's body and human or animal head; (**sphinx**) inscrutable person.

spice ● *noun* aromatic or pungent vegetable substance used as flavouring; spices collectively; piquant quality; slight flavour. ● *verb* (**-cing**) flavour with spice; enhance.

spick and span *adjective* trim and clean; smart, new-looking.

spicy *adjective* (**-ier**, **-iest**) of or flavoured with spice; piquant, improper. ▫ **spiciness** *noun*.

spider /ˈspaɪdə/ *noun* 8-legged arthropod, many species of which spin webs esp. to capture insects as food. ▫ **spider plant** house plant with long narrow leaves.

spidery *adjective* elongated and thin.

spiel /ʃpiːl/ *noun slang* glib speech or story, sales pitch.

spigot /ˈspɪgət/ *noun* small peg or plug; device for controlling flow of liquid in tap.

spike[1] ● *noun* sharp point; pointed piece of metal, esp. forming top of iron railing; metal point on sole of running shoe to prevent slipping; (in *plural*) spiked running shoes; large nail. ● *verb* (**-king**) put spikes on or into; fix on spike; *colloquial* add alcohol to (drink), contaminate. □ **spike (person's) guns** defeat his or her plans.

spike[2] *noun* cluster of flower heads on long stem.

spikenard /'spaɪknɑːd/ *noun* tall sweet-smelling plant; *historical* aromatic ointment formerly made from this.

spiky *adjective* (**-ier**, **-iest**) like a spike; having spikes; *colloquial* irritable.

spill[1] ● *verb* (*past & past participle* **spilt** or **spilled**) allow (liquid etc.) to fall or run out of container, esp. accidentally; (of liquid etc.) fall or run out thus; throw from vehicle, saddle, etc.; (+ *into*, *out*, etc.) leave quickly; *slang* divulge (information etc.); shed (blood). ● *noun* spilling, being spilt; tumble, esp. from horse or vehicle. □ **spill the beans** *colloquial* divulge secret etc. □ **spillage** *noun*.

spill[2] *noun* thin strip of wood, paper, etc. for lighting candle etc.

spillikin /'spɪlɪkɪn/ *noun* splinter of wood etc.; (in *plural*) game in which thin rods are removed one at a time from heap without disturbing others.

spilt *past & past participle* of SPILL[1].

spin ● *verb* (**-nn-**; *past* **spun** or **span**; *past participle* **spun**) (cause to) turn or whirl round rapidly; make (yarn) by drawing out and twisting together fibres of wool etc.; make (web etc.) by extruding fine viscous thread; (of person's head) be in a whirl; tell or compose (story etc.); toss (coin); (as **spun** *adjective*) made into threads. ● *noun* revolving motion, whirl; rotating dive of aircraft; secondary twisting motion e.g. of ball in flight; *colloquial* brief drive, esp. in car. □ **spin bowler** *Cricket* one who imparts spin to ball; **spin-drier**, **-dryer** machine for drying clothes by spinning them in rotating drum; **spin-dry** *verb*; **spinning wheel** household implement for spinning yarn, with spindle driven by wheel with crank or treadle; **spin-off** incidental result, esp. from technology; **spin out** prolong; **spin a yarn** tell story.

spina bifida /spaɪnə 'bɪfɪdə/ *noun* congenital spinal defect, with protruding membranes.

spinach /'spɪnɪdʒ/ *noun* green vegetable with edible leaves.

spinal /'spaɪn(ə)l/ *adjective* of spine. □ **spinal column** spine; **spinal cord** cylindrical nervous structure within spine.

spindle /'spɪnd(ə)l/ *noun* slender rod for twisting and winding thread in spinning; pin or axis on which something revolves; turned piece of wood used as banister etc.

spindly *adjective* (**-ier**, **-iest**) long or tall and thin.

spindrift /'spɪndrɪft/ *noun* spray on surface of sea.

spine *noun* series of vertebrae extending from skull, backbone; needle-like outgrowth of animal or plant; part of book enclosing page-fastening; ridge, sharp projection. □ **spine-chiller** suspense or horror film, story, etc.

spineless *adjective* lacking resoluteness.

spinet /spɪ'net/ *noun historical* small harpsichord with oblique strings.

spinnaker /'spɪnəkə/ *noun* large triangular sail used at bow of yacht.

spinner *noun* spin bowler; person or thing that spins, esp. manufacturer engaged in spinning; spin-drier; revolving bait or lure in fishing.

spinneret /'spɪnəret/ *noun* spinning-organ in spider etc.

spinney /'spɪnɪ/ *noun* (*plural* **-s**) small wood, thicket.

spinster /'spɪnstə/ *noun formal* unmarried woman.

spiny *adjective* (**-ier**, **-iest**) having (many) spines.

spiraea /spaɪ'rɪə/ *noun* (*US* **spirea**) garden plant related to meadowsweet.

spiral /'spaɪər(ə)l/ ● *adjective* coiled in a plane or as round a cylinder or cone; having this shape. ● *noun* spiral curve; progressive rise or fall. ● *verb* (**-ll-**; *US* **-l-**) move in spiral course; (of prices etc.) rise or fall continuously. □ **spiral staircase** circular staircase round central axis.

spirant /'spaɪərənt/ ● *adjective* uttered with continuous expulsion of breath. ● *noun* spirant consonant.

spire *noun* tapering structure, esp. on church tower; any tapering thing.

spirea *US* = SPIRAEA.

spirit /'spɪrɪt/ ● *noun* person's essence or intelligence, soul; rational being without material body; ghost; person's character; attitude; type of person; prevailing tendency; (usually in *plural*) distilled alcoholic liquor; distilled volatile liquid; courage, vivacity; (in *plural*) mood; essential as opposed to formal meaning. ● *verb* (**-t-**) (usually + *away*, *off*, etc.) convey mysteriously. □ **spirit gum** quick-drying gum for attaching false hair; **spirit lamp** lamp burning methylated or other volatile spirit; **spirit level** device used to test horizontality.

spirited *adjective* lively, courageous. □ **-spirited** in specified mood. □ **spiritedly** *adverb*.

spiritual /'spɪrɪtʃʊəl/ ● *adjective* of spirit; religious, divine, inspired; refined, sensitive. ● *noun* (also **Negro spiritual**) religious song originally of American blacks. □ **spirituality** /-'æl-/ *noun*; **spiritually** *adverb*.

spiritualism *noun* belief in, and practice of, communication with the dead, esp. through mediums. □ **spiritualist** *noun*; **spiritualistic** /-'lɪs-/ *adjective*.

spirituous /'spɪrɪtʃʊəs/ *adjective* very alcoholic; distilled as well as fermented.

spit[1] ● *verb* (**-tt-**; *past & past participle* **spat** or **spit**) eject (esp. saliva) from mouth; do this as gesture of contempt; utter vehemently; (of fire etc.) throw out with explosion; (of rain etc.) fall lightly; make spitting noise. ● *noun* spittle; spitting. □ **spitfire** fiery-tempered person; **spitting distance** *colloquial* very short distance; **spitting image** *colloquial* exact counterpart or likeness.

spit[2] ● *noun* rod for skewering meat for roasting over fire etc.; point of land projecting into sea; spade-depth of earth. ● *verb* (**-tt-**) pierce (as) with spit. □ **spit-roast** roast on spit.

spite ● *noun* ill will, malice. ● *verb* (**-ting**) hurt, thwart. □ **in spite of** notwithstanding.

spiteful *adjective* malicious. □ **spitefully** *adverb*.

spittle /'spɪt(ə)l/ *noun* saliva.

spittoon /spɪ'tuːn/ *noun* vessel to spit into.

spiv *noun colloquial* man, esp. flashily-dressed one, living from shady dealings. □ **spivvish** *adjective*; **spivvy** *adjective*.

splash ● *verb* (cause to) scatter in drops; wet or stain by splashing; (usually + *across*, *along*, *about*, etc.) move with splashing; jump or fall into water etc. with splash; display (news) conspicuously; decorate with scattered colour; spend (money) ostentatiously. ● *noun* act or noise of splashing; quantity splashed; mark of splashing; prominent news feature, display, etc.; patch of colour; *colloquial* small quantity of soda water etc. (in drink). □ **splashback** panel behind sink etc. to protect wall from splashes; **splashdown** alighting of spacecraft on sea; **splash down** *verb*; **splash out** *colloquial* spend money freely.

splat *colloquial* ● *noun* sharp splattering sound. ● *adverb* with splat. ● *verb* (**-tt-**) fall or hit with splat.

splatter /'splætə/ *verb & noun* splash, esp. with continuous noisy action, spatter.

splay ● *verb* spread apart; (of opening) have sides diverging; make (opening) with divergent sides.

• *noun* surface at oblique angle to another. • *adjective* splayed.

spleen *noun* abdominal organ regulating quality of blood; moroseness, irritability.

splendid /ˈsplendɪd/ *adjective* magnificent; glorious, dignified; excellent. □ **splendidly** *adverb.*

splendiferous /splenˈdɪfərəs/ *adjective colloquial* splendid.

splendour /ˈsplendə/ *noun* (*US* **splendor**) dazzling brightness; magnificence.

splenetic /splɪˈnetɪk/ *adjective* bad-tempered, peevish.

splenic /ˈsplenɪk/ *adjective* of or in spleen.

splice • *verb* (**-cing**) join (ropes) by interweaving strands; join (pieces of wood, tape, etc.) by overlapping; (esp. as **spliced** *adjective*) *colloquial* join in marriage. • *noun* join made by splicing.

splint • *noun* strip of wood etc. bound to broken limb while it heals. • *verb* secure with splint.

splinter /ˈsplɪntə/ • *noun* small sharp fragment of wood, stone, glass, etc. • *verb* split into splinters, shatter. □ **splinter group** breakaway political group. □ **splintery** *adjective.*

split • *verb* (**-tt-**; *past & past participle* **split**) break, esp. lengthwise or with grain; break forcibly; (often + *up*) divide into parts, esp. equal shares; (often + *off, away*) remove or be removed by breaking or dividing; (usually + *on, over,* etc.) divide into disagreeing or hostile parties; cause fission of (atom); *slang* leave, esp. suddenly; (usually + *on*) *colloquial* inform; (as **splitting** *adjective*) (of headache) severe; (of head) suffer severe headache. • *noun* splitting; disagreement, schism; (in *plural*) feat of leaping or sitting with legs straight and pointing in opposite directions. □ **split hairs** make over-subtle distinctions; **split infinitive** one with adverb etc. inserted between *to* and verb (see note below); **split-level** with more than one level; **split personality** condition of alternating personalities; **split pin** metal cotter with its two ends splayed out after passing through hole; **split second** very short time; **split-second** very rapid, (of timing) very accurate; **split up** separate, end relationship.

■ **Usage** Split infinitives, as in *I want to quickly sum up* and *Your job is to really get to know everybody*, are common in informal English, but many people consider them incorrect and prefer *I want quickly to sum up* or *I want to sum up quickly*. They should therefore be avoided in formal English, but note that just changing the order of words can alter the meaning, e.g. *Your job is really to get to know everybody*.

splodge *colloquial* • *noun* daub, blot, smear. • *verb* (**-ging**) make splodge on. □ **splodgy** *adjective.*

splosh *colloquial* • *verb* move with splashing sound. • *noun* splashing sound; splash of water etc.

splotch *noun & verb* splodge. □ **splotchy** *adjective.*

splurge *colloquial* • *noun* sudden extravagance; ostentatious display or effort. • *verb* (**-ging**) (usually + *on*) make splurge.

splutter /ˈsplʌtə/ • *verb* speak or express in choking manner; emit spitting sounds; speak rapidly or incoherently. • *noun* spluttering speech or sound.

spoil • *verb* (*past & past participle* **spoilt** or **spoiled**) make or become useless or unsatisfactory; reduce enjoyment etc. of; decay, go bad; ruin character of by over-indulgence. • *noun* (usually in *plural*) plunder, stolen goods; profit or advantages accruing from success or position. □ **spoilsport** person who spoils others' enjoyment; **spoilt for choice** having excessive number of choices.

spoiler *noun* device on aircraft to increase drag; device on vehicle to improve road-holding at speed.

spoilt *past & past participle* of SPOIL.

spoke[1] *noun* each of rods running from hub to rim of wheel. □ **put a spoke in (person's) wheel** thwart, hinder.

spoke[2] *past* of SPEAK.

spoken *past participle* of SPEAK.

spokesman /ˈspəʊksmən/ *noun* (*feminine* **spokeswoman**) person who speaks for others, representative.

spokesperson /ˈspəʊkspɜːs(ə)n/ *noun* (*plural* **-s** or **spokespeople**) spokesman or spokeswoman.

spoliation /spəʊlɪˈeɪʃ(ə)n/ *noun* plundering, pillage.

spondee /ˈspɒndiː/ *noun* metrical foot of two long syllables. □ **spondaic** /-ˈdeɪɪk/ *adjective.*

sponge /spʌndʒ/ • *noun* sea animal with porous body wall and tough elastic skeleton; this skeleton or piece of porous rubber etc. used in bathing, cleaning, etc.; thing like sponge in consistency, esp. sponge cake; act of sponging. • *verb* (**-ging**) wipe or clean with sponge; (often + *out, away,* etc.) wipe off or rub out (as) with sponge; (often + *up*) absorb (as) with sponge; (often + *on, off*) live as parasite. □ **sponge bag** waterproof bag for toilet articles; **sponge cake, pudding** one of light spongelike consistency; **sponge rubber** porous rubber.

sponger *noun* parasitic person.

spongy *adjective* (**-ier, -iest**) like a sponge, porous, elastic, absorbent.

sponsor /ˈspɒnsə/ • *noun* person who pledges money to charity in return for specified activity by someone; patron of artistic or sporting activity etc.; company etc. financing broadcast in return for advertising; person introducing legislation; godparent at baptism. • *verb* be sponsor for. □ **sponsorship** *noun.*

spontaneous /spɒnˈteɪnɪəs/ *adjective* acting, done, or occurring without external cause; instinctive, automatic, natural. □ **spontaneity** /-təˈneɪətɪ/ *noun*; **spontaneously** *adverb.*

spoof /spuːf/ *noun & verb colloquial* parody; hoax, swindle.

spook /spuːk/ • *noun colloquial* ghost. • *verb esp. US* frighten, unnerve. □ **spooky** *adjective* (**-ier, -iest**).

spool /spuːl/ • *noun* reel on which something is wound; revolving cylinder of angler's reel. • *verb* wind on spool.

spoon /spuːn/ • *noun* utensil with bowl and handle for putting food in mouth or for stirring etc.; spoonful; spoon-shaped thing, esp. (in full **spoon-bait**) revolving metal fish-lure. • *verb* (often + *up, out*) take (liquid etc.) with spoon; hit (ball) feebly upwards. □ **spoonbill** wading bird with broad flat-tipped bill; **spoonfeed** feed with spoon, give help etc. to (person) without demanding any effort from recipient. □ **spoonful** *noun* (*plural* **-s**).

spoonerism /ˈspuːnərɪz(ə)m/ *noun* (usually accidental) transposition of initial sounds of two or more words.

spoor /spʊə/ *noun* animal's track or scent.

sporadic /spəˈrædɪk/ *adjective* occurring only sparsely or occasionally. □ **sporadically** *adverb.*

spore *noun* reproductive cell of ferns, fungi, protozoa, etc.

sporran /ˈspɒrən/ *noun* pouch worn in front of kilt.

sport • *noun* game or competitive activity usually involving physical exertion; these collectively; (in *plural*) meeting for competition in athletics; amusement, fun; *colloquial* sportsman, good fellow; person with specified attitude to games, rules, etc. • *verb* amuse oneself, play about; wear or exhibit, esp. ostentatiously. □ **sports car** low-built fast car; **sports coat, jacket** man's informal jacket; **sports ground** piece of land used for sport; **sportswear** clothes for sports, informal clothes.

sporting *adjective* of or interested in sport; generous, fair. ▫ **sporting chance** some possibility of success. ▫ **sportingly** *adverb.*

sportive *adjective* playful.

sportsman /ˈspɔːtsmən/ *noun* (*feminine* **sportswoman**) person engaging in sport; fair and generous person. ▫ **sportsmanlike** *adjective*; **sportsmanship** *noun.*

sporty *adjective* (**-ier**, **-iest**) *colloquial* fond of sport; *colloquial* rakish, showy.

spot ● *noun* small mark differing in colour etc. from surface it is on; pimple, blemish; particular place, locality; particular part of one's body or character; *colloquial* one's (regular) position in organization, programme, etc.; *colloquial* small quantity; spotlight. ● *verb* (**-tt-**) *colloquial* pick out, recognize, catch sight of; watch for and take note of (trains, talent, etc.); (as **spotted** *adjective*) marked with spots; make spots, rain slightly. ▫ **in a (tight) spot** *colloquial* in difficulties; **on the spot** at scene of event, *colloquial* in position demanding response or action, without delay, without moving backwards or forwards; **spot cash** money paid immediately after sale; **spot check** sudden or random check; **spotlight** *noun* beam of light directed on small area, lamp projecting this, full publicity, *verb* direct spotlight on; **spot on** *colloquial* precise(ly); **spotted dick** suet pudding containing currants; **spot-weld** join (metal surfaces) by welding at points. ▫ **spotter** *noun.*

spotless *adjective* absolutely clean, unblemished. ▫ **spotlessly** *adverb.*

spotty *adjective* (**-ier**, **-iest**) marked with spots; patchy, irregular.

spouse /spaʊz/ *noun* husband or wife.

spout /spaʊt/ ● *noun* projecting tube or lip for pouring from teapot, kettle, jug, fountain, roof-gutter, etc.; jet of liquid. ● *verb* discharge or issue forcibly in jet; utter at length or pompously. ▫ **up the spout** *slang* useless, ruined, pregnant.

sprain ● *verb* wrench (ankle, wrist, etc.) causing pain or swelling. ● *noun* such injury.

sprang *past* of SPRING.

sprat *noun* small sea fish.

sprawl ● *verb* sit, lie, or fall with limbs spread out untidily; spread untidily, straggle. ● *noun* sprawling movement, position, or mass; straggling urban expansion.

spray[1] ● *noun* water etc. flying in small drops; liquid intended for spraying; device for spraying. ● *verb* throw as spray; sprinkle (as) with spray; (of tomcat) mark environment with urine to attract females. ▫ **spray-gun** device for spraying paint etc. ▫ **sprayer** *noun.*

spray[2] *noun* sprig with flowers or leaves, small branch; ornament in similar form.

spread /spred/ ● *verb* (*past & past participle* **spread**) (often + *out*) open, extend, unfold, cause to cover larger surface, have wide or increasing extent; (cause to) become widely known; cover; lay (table). ● *noun* act, capability, or extent of spreading; diffusion; breadth; increased girth; difference between two rates, prices, etc.; *colloquial* elaborate meal; paste for spreading on bread etc.; bedspread; printed matter spread over more than one column. ▫ **spread eagle** figure of eagle with legs and wings extended as emblem; **spread-eagle** place (person) with arms and legs spread out, defeat utterly; **spreadsheet** computer program for handling tabulated figures etc., esp. in accounting.

spree *noun colloquial* extravagant outing; bout of drinking etc.

sprig ● *noun* small branch or shoot; ornament resembling this, esp. on fabric. ● *verb* (**-gg-**) ornament with sprigs.

sprightly /ˈspraɪtlɪ/ *adjective* (**-ier**, **-iest**) vivacious, lively.

spring ● *verb* (*past* **sprang**; *past participle* **sprung**) rise rapidly or suddenly, leap; move rapidly (as) by action of a spring; (usually + *from*) originate; (cause to) act or appear unexpectedly; *slang* contrive escape of (person from prison etc.); (usually as **sprung** *adjective*) provide with springs. ● *noun* jump, leap; recoil; elasticity; elastic device usually of coiled metal used esp. to drive clockwork or for cushioning in furniture or vehicles; season of year between winter and summer; (often + *of*) early stage of life etc.; place where water, oil, etc. wells up from earth, basin or flow so formed; motive for or origin of action, custom, etc. ▫ **spring balance** device measuring weight by tension of spring; **springboard** flexible board for leaping or diving from, source of impetus; **spring-clean** *noun* thorough cleaning of house, esp. in spring, *verb* clean thus; **spring greens** young cabbage leaves; **spring a leak** develop leak; **spring onion** young onion eaten raw; **spring roll** Chinese fried pancake filled with vegetables etc.; **spring tide** tide with greatest rise and fall; **springtime** season or period of spring.

springbok /ˈsprɪŋbɒk/ *noun* (*plural* same or **-s**) S. African gazelle.

springer *noun* small spaniel.

springy *adjective* (**-ier**, **-iest**) elastic.

sprinkle /ˈsprɪŋk(ə)l/ ● *verb* (**-ling**) scatter in small drops or particles; (often + *with*) subject to sprinkling; (of liquid etc.) fall thus on. ● *noun* (usually + *of*) light shower, sprinkling.

sprinkler *noun* device for sprinkling lawn or extinguishing fires.

sprinkling *noun* small sparse number or amount.

sprint ● *verb* run short distance at top speed. ● *noun* such run; similar short effort in cycling, swimming, etc. ▫ **sprinter** *noun.*

sprit *noun* small diagonal spar from mast to upper outer corner of sail. ▫ **spritsail** /ˈsprɪts(ə)l/ sail extended by sprit.

sprite *noun* elf, fairy.

spritzer /ˈsprɪtsə/ *noun* drink of white wine with soda water.

sprocket /ˈsprɒkɪt/ *noun* projection on rim of wheel engaging with links of chain.

sprout /spraʊt/ ● *verb* put forth (shoots etc.); begin to grow. ● *noun* plant shoot; Brussels sprout.

spruce[1] ● *adjective* of trim appearance, smart. ● *verb* (**-cing**) (usually + *up*) make or become smart. ▫ **sprucely** *adverb*; **spruceness** *noun.*

spruce[2] *noun* conifer with dense conical foliage; its wood.

sprung *past participle* of SPRING.

spry /spraɪ/ *adjective* (**-er**, **-est**) lively, nimble. ▫ **spryly** *adverb.*

spud ● *noun colloquial* potato; small narrow spade for weeding. ● *verb* (**-dd-**) (+ *up*, *out*) remove with spud.

spumante /spuːˈmæntɪ/ *noun* Italian sparkling white wine.

spume /spjuːm/ *noun & verb* (**-ming**) froth, foam. ▫ **spumy** *adjective* (**-ier**, **-iest**).

spun *past & past participle* of SPIN. ▫ **spun silk** cheap material containing waste silk.

spunk *noun colloquial* mettle, spirit. ▫ **spunky** *adjective* (**-ier**, **-iest**).

spur ● *noun* small spike or spiked wheel attached to rider's heel for urging horse forward; stimulus, incentive; spur-shaped thing, esp. projection from mountain (range), branch road or railway, or hard projection on cock's leg. ● *verb* (**-rr-**) prick (horse) with spur; incite, stimulate. □ **on the spur of the moment** on impulse.

spurge *noun* plant with acrid milky juice.

spurious /'spjʊərɪəs/ *adjective* not genuine, fake.

spurn *verb* reject with disdain or contempt.

spurt ● *verb* (cause to) gush out in jet or stream; make sudden effort. ● *noun* sudden gushing out, jet; short burst of speed, growth, etc.

sputnik /'spʊtnɪk/ *noun* Russian artificial earth satellite.

sputter /'spʌtə/ *verb & noun* splutter.

sputum /'spju:təm/ *noun* thick coughed-up mucus.

spy ● *noun* (*plural* **spies**) person secretly collecting and reporting information for a government, company, etc.; person watching others secretly. ● *verb* (**spies, spied**) discern, see; (often + *on*) act as spy. □ **spyglass** small telescope; **spyhole** peep-hole; **spy out** explore or discover, esp. secretly.

sq. *abbreviation* square.

Sqn. Ldr. *abbreviation* Squadron Leader.

squab /skwɒb/ ● *noun* young esp. unfledged pigeon etc.; short fat person; stuffed cushion, esp. as part of car-seat; sofa. ● *adjective* short and fat.

squabble /'skwɒb(ə)l/ ● *noun* petty or noisy quarrel. ● *verb* (**-ling**) engage in squabble.

squad /skwɒd/ *noun* small group sharing task etc., esp. of soldiers or police officers; team. □ **squad car** police car.

squaddie *noun* (also **squaddy**) (*plural* **-ies**) *slang* recruit, private.

squadron /'skwɒdrən/ *noun* unit of RAF with 10–18 aircraft; detachment of warships employed on particular service; organized group etc., esp. cavalry division of two troops. □ **squadron leader** RAF officer commanding squadron, next below wing commander.

squalid /'skwɒlɪd/ *adjective* filthy, dirty; mean in appearance.

squall /skwɔ:l/ ● *noun* sudden or violent gust or storm; discordant cry, scream. ● *verb* utter (with) squall, scream. □ **squally** *adjective*.

squalor /'skwɒlə/ *noun* filthy or squalid state.

squander /'skwɒndə/ *verb* spend wastefully.

square /skweə/ ● *noun* rectangle with 4 equal sides; object of (roughly) this shape; open area enclosed by buildings; product of number multiplied by itself; L- or T-shaped instrument for obtaining or testing right angles; *slang* conventional or old-fashioned person. ● *adjective* square-shaped; having or in form of a right angle; angular, not round; designating unit of measure equal to area of square whose side is one of the unit specified; (usually + *with*) level, parallel; (usually + *to*) perpendicular; sturdy, squat; arranged; (also **all square**) with no money owed, (of scores) equal; fair, honest; direct; *slang* conventional, old-fashioned. ● *adverb* squarely. ● *verb* (**-ring**) make square; multiply (number) by itself; (usually + *to, with*) make or be consistent, reconcile; mark out in squares; settle (bill etc.); place (shoulders etc.) squarely facing forwards; *colloquial* pay, bribe; make scores of (match etc.) equal. □ **square brackets** brackets of the form [ ] (see panel at BRACKET); **square dance** dance with 4 couples facing inwards from 4 sides; **square deal** fair bargain or treatment; **square leg** *Cricket* fielding position on batsman's leg side nearly opposite stumps; **square meal** substantial meal; **square-rigged** having 4-sided sails set across length of ship; **square root** number that multiplied by itself gives specified number. □ **squarely** *adverb*.

squash[1] /skwɒʃ/ ● *verb* crush or squeeze flat or into pulp; (often + *into*) *colloquial* force into small space, crowd; belittle, bully; suppress. ● *noun* crowd, crowded state; drink made of crushed fruit; (in full **squash rackets**) game played with rackets and small ball in closed court. □ **squashy** *adjective* (**-ier, -iest**).

squash[2] /skwɒʃ/ *noun* (*plural* same or **-es**) trailing annual plant; gourd of this.

squat /skwɒt/ ● *verb* (**-tt-**) sit on one's heels, or on ground with knees drawn up; *colloquial* sit down; act as squatter. ● *adjective* (**-tt-**) short and thick, dumpy. ● *noun* squatting posture; place occupied by squatter(s).

squatter *noun* person who inhabits unoccupied premises without permission.

squaw *noun* N. American Indian woman or wife.

squawk ● *noun* harsh cry; complaint. ● *verb* utter squawk.

squeak ● *noun* short high-pitched cry or sound; (also **narrow squeak**) narrow escape. ● *verb* emit squeak; utter shrilly; (+ *by, through*) *colloquial* pass narrowly; *slang* turn informer.

squeaky *adjective* (**-ier, -iest**) making squeaking sound. □ **squeaky clean** *colloquial* completely clean, above criticism. □ **squeakily** *adverb*; **squeakiness** *noun*.

squeal ● *noun* prolonged shrill sound or cry. ● *verb* make, or utter with, squeal; *slang* turn informer; *colloquial* protest vociferously.

squeamish /'skwi:mɪʃ/ *adjective* easily nauseated; fastidious. □ **squeamishly** *adverb*; **squeamishness** *noun*.

squeegee /'skwi:dʒi:/ *noun* rubber-edged implement on handle, for cleaning windows etc.

squeeze ● *verb* (**-zing**) (often + *out*) exert pressure on, esp. to extract moisture; reduce in size or alter in shape by squeezing; force or push into or through small or narrow space; harass, pressure; (usually + *out of*) get by extortion or entreaty; press (person's hand) in sympathy etc. ● *noun* squeezing, being squeezed; close embrace; crowd, crowded state; small quantity produced by squeezing; restriction on borrowing and investment. □ **squeeze-box** *colloquial* accordion, concertina.

squelch ● *verb* make sucking sound as of treading in thick mud; move with squelching sound; disconcert, silence. ● *noun* act or sound of squelching. □ **squelchy** *adjective*.

squib *noun* small hissing firework; satirical essay.

squid *noun* (*plural* same or **-s**) 10-armed marine cephalopod.

squidgy /'skwɪdʒɪ/ *adjective* (**-ier, -iest**) *colloquial* squashy, soggy.

squiffy /'skwɪfɪ/ *adjective* (**-ier, -iest**) *slang* slightly drunk.

squiggle /'skwɪg(ə)l/ *noun* short curling line, esp. in handwriting. □ **squiggly** *adjective*.

squint ● *verb* have eyes turned in different directions; (often + *at*) look sidelong. ● *noun* squinting condition; sidelong glance; *colloquial* glance, look; oblique opening in church wall.

squire ● *noun* country gentleman, esp. chief landowner of district; *historical* knight's attendant. ● *verb* (**-ring**) (of man) escort (woman).

squirearchy /'skwaɪərɑ:kɪ/ *noun* (*plural* **-ies**) landowners collectively.

squirm ● *verb* wriggle, writhe; show or feel embarrassment. ● *noun* squirming movement.

squirrel /'skwɪr(ə)l/ ● *noun* bushy-tailed usually tree-living rodent; its fur; hoarder. ● *verb* (**-ll-**; *US* **-l-**) (often + *away*) hoard.

squirt ● *verb* eject (liquid etc.) in jet; be ejected thus; splash with squirted substance. ● *noun* jet of water etc.; small quantity squirted; syringe; *colloquial* insignificant person.

squish *colloquial* ● *noun* slight squelching sound. ● *verb* move with squish; squash. □ **squishy** *adjective* (**-ier**, **-iest**).

Sr. *abbreviation* Senior.

SRN *abbreviation* State Registered Nurse.

SS *abbreviation* steamship; Saints; *historical* Nazi special police force (*Schutzstaffel*).

SSE *abbreviation* south-south-east.

SSW *abbreviation* south-south-west.

St *abbreviation* Saint.

St. *abbreviation* Street.

st. *abbreviation* stone (weight).

stab ● *verb* (**-bb-**) pierce or wound with knife etc.; (often + *at*) aim blow with such weapon; cause sharp pain to. ● *noun* act or result of stabbing; *colloquial* attempt. □ **stab in the back** *noun* treacherous attack, *verb* betray.

stability /stəˈbɪlɪtɪ/ *noun* being stable.

stabilize /ˈsteɪbɪlaɪz/ *verb* (also **-ise**) (**-zing** or **-sing**) make or become stable. □ **stabilization** *noun*.

stabilizer *noun* (also **-iser**) device to keep aircraft or (in *plural*) child's bicycle steady; food additive for preserving texture.

stable /ˈsteɪb(ə)l/ ● *adjective* (**-r**, **-st**) firmly fixed or established, not fluctuating or changing; not easily upset or disturbed. ● *noun* building for keeping horses; establishment for training racehorses; racehorses of particular stable; people, products, etc. having common origin or affiliation; such origin or affiliation. ● *verb* (**-ling**) put or keep in stable. □ **stably** *adverb*.

stabling *noun* accommodation for horses.

staccato /stəˈkɑːtəʊ/ *esp. Music* ● *adverb & adjective* with each sound sharply distinct. ● *noun* (*plural* **-s**) staccato passage or delivery.

stack ● *noun* (esp. orderly) pile or heap; haystack; *colloquial* large quantity; number of chimneys standing together; smokestack; tall factory chimney; stacked group of aircraft; part of library where books are compactly stored. ● *verb* pile in stack(s); arrange (cards, circumstances, etc.) secretly for cheating; cause (aircraft) to fly in circles while waiting to land.

stadium /ˈsteɪdɪəm/ *noun* (*plural* **-s**) athletic or sports ground with tiered seats for spectators.

staff /stɑːf/ ● *noun* stick or pole for walking, as weapon, or as symbol of office; supporting person or thing; people employed in a business etc.; those in authority in a school etc.; group of army officers assisting officer in high command; (*plural* **-s** or **staves**) *Music* set of usually 5 parallel lines to indicate pitch of notes by position. ● *verb* provide (institution etc.) with staff. □ **staff nurse** one ranking just below a sister.

stag *noun* male deer; person who applies for new shares to sell at once for profit. □ **stag beetle** beetle with antler-like mandibles; **stag-party** *colloquial* party for men only.

stage ● *noun* point or period in process or development; raised platform, esp. for performing plays etc. on; (**the stage**) theatrical profession; scene of action; regular stopping place on route; distance between stopping places; section of space rocket with separate engine. ● *verb* (**-ging**) put (play etc.) on stage; organize and carry out. □ **stagecoach** *historical* coach running on regular route; **stage direction** instruction in a play about actors' movements, sound effects, etc.; **stage door** entrance from street to backstage part of theatre; **stage fright** performer's fear of audience; **stage-manage** arrange and control as or like stage manager; **stage manager** person responsible for lighting and mechanical arrangements on stage; **stage-struck** obsessed with becoming actor; **stage whisper** loud whisper meant to be overheard.

stagger /ˈstægə/ ● *verb* (cause to) walk unsteadily; shock, confuse; arrange (events etc.) so that they do not coincide; arrange (objects) so that they are not in line. ● *noun* staggering movement; (in *plural*) disease, esp. of horses and cattle, causing staggering.

staggering *adjective* astonishing, bewildering. □ **staggeringly** *adverb*.

staging /ˈsteɪdʒɪŋ/ *noun* presentation of play etc.; (temporary) platform; shelves for plants in greenhouse. □ **staging post** regular stopping place, esp. on air route.

stagnant /ˈstægnənt/ *adjective* (of liquid) motionless, without current; dull, sluggish. □ **stagnancy** *noun*.

stagnate /stægˈneɪt/ *verb* (**-ting**) be or become stagnant. □ **stagnation** *noun*.

stagy /ˈsteɪdʒɪ/ *adjective* (also **stagey**) (**-ier**, **-iest**) theatrical, artificial, exaggerated.

staid *adjective* sober, steady, sedate.

stain ● *verb* discolour or be discoloured by action of liquid sinking in; spoil, damage; colour (wood, etc.) with penetrating substance; treat with colouring agent. ● *noun* discoloration, spot, mark; blot, blemish; dye etc. for staining. □ **stained glass** coloured glass in leaded window etc.

stainless *adjective* without stains; not liable to stain. □ **stainless steel** chrome steel resisting rust and tarnish.

stair *noun* each of a set of fixed indoor steps; (usually in *plural*) such a set. □ **staircase** flight of stairs and supporting structure; **stair-rod** rod securing carpet between two steps; **stairway** staircase; **stairwell** shaft for staircase.

stake ● *noun* stout pointed stick driven into ground as support, boundary mark, etc.; *historical* post to which person was tied to be burnt alive; sum of money etc. wagered on event; (often + *in*) interest or concern, esp. financial; (in *plural*) prize-money, esp. in horse race, such race. ● *verb* (**-king**) secure or support with stake(s); (+ *off*, *out*) mark off (area) with stakes; wager; *US colloquial* support, esp. financially. □ **at stake** risked, to be won or lost; **stake out** *colloquial* place under surveillance; **stake-out** *esp. US colloquial* period of surveillance.

stalactite /ˈstæləktaɪt/ *noun* icicle-like deposit of calcium carbonate hanging from roof of cave etc.

stalagmite /ˈstæləgmaɪt/ *noun* icicle-like deposit of calcium carbonate rising from floor of cave etc.

stale ● *adjective* not fresh; musty, insipid, or otherwise the worse for age or use; trite, unoriginal; (of athlete or performer) impaired by excessive training. ● *verb* (**-ling**) make or become stale. □ **staleness** *noun*.

stalemate ● *noun Chess* position counting as draw in which player cannot move except into check; deadlock. ● *verb* (**-ting**) *Chess* bring (player) to stalemate; bring to deadlock.

Stalinism /ˈstɑːlɪnɪz(ə)m/ *noun* centralized authoritarian form of socialism associated with Stalin. □ **Stalinist** *noun & adjective*.

stalk¹ /stɔːk/ ● *noun* main stem of herbaceous plant; slender attachment or support of leaf, flower, fruit, etc.; similar support for organ etc. in animal.

stalk² /stɔːk/ ● *verb* pursue (game, enemy) stealthily; stride, walk in a haughty way; *formal or rhetorical* move silently or threateningly through (place). ● *noun* stalking of game; haughty gait. □ **stalking-horse**

horse concealing hunter, pretext concealing real intentions or actions.

stall[1] /stɔ:l/ ● *noun* trader's booth or table in market etc.; compartment for one animal in stable or cowhouse; fixed, usually partly enclosed, seat in choir or chancel of church; (usually in *plural*) each of seats on ground floor of theatre; stalling of engine or aircraft, condition resulting from this. ● *verb* (of vehicle or its engine) stop because of overload on engine or inadequate supply of fuel to it; (of aircraft or its pilot) lose control because speed is too low; cause to stall. ▫ **stallholder** person in charge of stall in market etc.

stall[2] /stɔ:l/ *verb* play for time when being questioned etc.; delay, obstruct.

stallion /'stæljən/ *noun* uncastrated adult male horse.

stalwart /'stɔ:lwət/ ● *adjective* strong, sturdy; courageous, resolute, reliable. ● *noun* stalwart person, esp. loyal comrade.

stamen /'steɪmən/ *noun* organ producing pollen in flower.

stamina /'stæmɪnə/ *noun* physical or mental endurance.

stammer /'stæmə/ ● *verb* speak haltingly, esp. with pauses or rapid repetitions of same syllable; (often + *out*) utter (words) in this way. ● *noun* tendency to stammer; instance of stammering.

stamp ● *verb* bring down (one's foot) heavily, esp. on ground, (often + *on*) crush or flatten in this way, walk heavily; impress (design, mark, etc.) on surface, impress (surface) with pattern etc.; affix postage or other stamp to; assign specific character to, mark out. ● *noun* instrument for stamping; mark or design made by this; impression of official mark required to be made on deeds, bills of exchange, etc., as evidence of payment of tax; small adhesive piece of paper as evidence of payment, esp. postage stamp; mark, label, etc. on commodity as evidence of quality etc.; act or sound of stamping foot; characteristic mark, quality. ▫ **stamp duty** duty imposed on certain kinds of legal document; **stamping ground** *colloquial* favourite haunt; **stamp on** impress (idea etc.) on (memory etc.); **stamp out** produce by cutting out with die etc., put end to.

stampede /stæm'pi:d/ ● *noun* sudden flight or hurried movement of animals or people; response of many people at once to a common impulse. ● *verb* (**-ding**) (cause to) take part in stampede.

stance /stɑ:ns/ *noun* standpoint, attitude; position of body, esp. when hitting ball etc.

stanch /stɑ:ntʃ, stɔ:ntʃ/ *verb* (also **staunch** /stɔ:ntʃ/) restrain flow of (esp. blood); restrain flow from (esp. wound).

stanchion /'stɑ:nʃ(ə)n/ *noun* upright post or support.

stand ● *verb* (*past & past participle* **stood** /stʊd/) have, take, or maintain upright or stationary position, esp on feet or base; be situated; be of specified height; be in specified state; set in upright or specified position; move to and remain in specified position, take specified attitude; remain valid or unaltered; *Nautical* hold specified course; endure, tolerate; provide at one's own expense; (often + *for*) be candidate (for office etc.); act in specified capacity; undergo (trial). ● *noun* cessation from progress, stoppage; *Military* (esp. in **make a stand**) halt made to repel attack; resistance to attack or compulsion; position taken up, attitude adopted; rack, set of shelves, etc. for storage; open-fronted stall or structure for trader, exhibitor, etc.; standing-place for vehicles; raised structure to sit or stand on; *US* witness-box; each halt made for performance on tour; group of growing plants. ▫ **as it stands** in its present condition, in the present circumstances; **stand by** stand nearby, look on without interfering, uphold, support (person), adhere to (promise etc.), be ready for action; **stand-by** (person or thing) ready if needed in emergency etc., readiness for duty etc.; **stand down** withdraw from position or candidacy; **stand for** represent, signify, imply, *colloquial* endure, tolerate; **stand in** (usually + *for*) deputize for; **stand-in** deputy, substitute; **stand off** move or keep away, temporarily dismiss (employee); **stand-off half** *Rugby* half-back forming link between scrum-half and three-quarters; **standoffish** cold or distant in manner; **stand on** insist on, observe scrupulously; **stand out** be prominent or outstanding, (usually + *against*, *for*), persist in opposition or support; **standpipe** vertical pipe rising from water supply, esp. one connecting temporary tap to mains; **standpoint** point of view; **standstill** stoppage, inability to proceed; **stand to** *Military* stand ready for attack, abide by, be likely or certain to; **stand to reason** be obvious; **stand up** rise to one's feet, come to, remain in, or place in standing position, (of argument etc.) be valid, *colloquial* fail to keep appointment with; **stand-up** (of meal) eaten standing, (of fight) violent, thorough, (of collar) not turned down, (of comedian) telling jokes to audience; **stand up for** support, side with; **stand up to** face (opponent) courageously, be resistant to (wear, use, etc.).

standard /'stændəd/ ● *noun* object, quality, or measure serving as basis, example, or principle to which others conform or should conform or by which others are judged; level of excellence etc. required or specified; ordinary procedure etc.; distinctive flag; upright support or pipe; shrub standing without support, or grafted on upright stem and trained in tree form. ● *adjective* serving or used as standard; of normal or prescribed quality, type, or size. ▫ **standard-bearer** person who carries distinctive flag, prominent leader in cause; **standard English** most widely accepted dialect of English (see panel); **standard lamp** lamp on tall upright with base; **standard of living** degree of material comfort of person or group; **standard time** uniform time established by law or custom in country or region.

standardize *verb* (also **-ise**) (**-zing** or **-sing**) cause to conform to standard. ▫ **standardization** *noun*.

standing ● *noun* esteem, repute, esp. high; duration. ● *adjective* that stands, upright; established, permanent; (of jump, start, etc.) performed with no runup. ▫ **standing order** instruction to banker to make regular payments; **standing orders** rules governing procedure in a parliament, council, etc.; **standing ovation** prolonged applause from audience that has risen to its feet; **standing room** space to stand in.

stank *past* of STINK.

stanza /'stænzə/ *noun* group of lines forming division of poem, etc.

Standard English

Standard English is the dialect of English used by most educated English speakers and is spoken with a variety of accents (see panel at ACCENT). While not *in itself* any better than any other dialect, standard English is the form of English used in all formal written contexts.

staphylococcus /stæfɪlə'kɒkəs/ *noun* (*plural* **-cocci** /-kaɪ/) bacterium sometimes forming pus. □ **staphylococcal** *adjective*.

staple[1] /'steɪp(ə)l/ ● *noun* shaped piece of wire with two points for fastening papers together, fixing netting to post, etc. ● *verb* (**-ling**) fasten with staple(s). □ **stapler** *noun*.

staple[2] /'steɪp(ə)l/ ● *noun* principal or important article of commerce; chief element, main component; fibre of cotton, wool, etc. with regard to its quality. ● *adjective* main, principal; important as product or export.

star ● *noun* celestial body appearing as luminous point in night sky; large luminous gaseous body such as sun; celestial body regarded as influencing fortunes etc.; conventional image of star with radiating lines or points; famous or brilliant person, leading performer. ● *adjective* outstanding. ● *verb* (**-rr-**) appear or present as leading performer(s); mark, set, or adorn with star(s). □ **starfish** (*plural* same or **-es**) sea creature with 5 or more radiating arms; **star-gazer** *colloquial usually derogatory or jocular* astronomer or astrologer; **starlight** light of stars; **starlit** lit by stars, with stars visible; **Stars and Stripes** US national flag; **star turn** main item in entertainment etc. □ **stardom** *noun*.

starboard /'stɑ:bəd/ ● *noun* right-hand side of ship or aircraft looking forward. ● *verb* turn (helm) to starboard.

starch ● *noun* white carbohydrate obtained chiefly from cereals and potatoes; preparation of this for stiffening fabric; stiffness of manner, formality. ● *verb* stiffen (clothing) with starch. □ **starchy** *adjective* (**-ier**, **-iest**).

stare /steə/ ● *verb* (**-ring**) (usually + *at*) look fixedly, esp. in curiosity, surprise, horror, etc. ● *noun* staring gaze. □ **stare (person) in the face** be evident or imminent; **stare out** stare at (person) until he or she looks away.

stark ● *adjective* sharply evident; desolate, bare; absolute. ● *adverb* completely, wholly. □ **starkly** *adverb*.

starkers /'stɑ:kəz/ *adjective slang* stark naked.

starlet /'stɑ:lɪt/ *noun* promising young performer, esp. film actress.

starling /'stɑ:lɪŋ/ *noun* gregarious bird with blackish speckled lustrous plumage.

starry *adjective* (**-ier**, **-iest**) full of stars; starlike. □ **starry-eyed** *colloquial* romantic but impractical, euphoric.

start ● *verb* begin; set in motion or action; set oneself in motion or action; (often + *out*) begin journey etc.; (often + *up*) (cause to) begin operating; (often + *up*) establish; give signal to (competitors) to start in race; (often + *up*, *from*, etc.) jump in surprise, pain, etc.; rouse (game etc.). ● *noun* beginning; starting-place of race etc.; advantage given at beginning of race etc.; advantageous initial position in life, business, etc.; sudden movement of surprise, pain, etc. □ **starting block** shaped block against which runner braces feet at start of race; **starting price** odds ruling at start of horse race.

starter *noun* device for starting vehicle engine etc.; first course of meal; person giving signal to start race; horse or competitor starting in race. □ **for starters** *colloquial* to start with.

startle /'stɑ:t(ə)l/ *verb* (**-ling**) shock, surprise.

starve *verb* (**-ving**) (cause to) die of hunger or suffer from malnourishment; *colloquial* feel very hungry; suffer from mental or spiritual want; (+ *of*) deprive of; compel by starvation. □ **starvation** *noun*.

stash *colloquial* ● *verb* (often + *away*) conceal, put in safe place; hoard. ● *noun* hiding place; thing hidden.

state ● *noun* existing condition or position of person or thing; *colloquial* excited or agitated mental condition, untidy condition; political community under one government, this as part of federal republic; civil government; pomp; (**the States**) USA. ● *adjective* of, for, or concerned with state; reserved for or done on ceremonial occasions. ● *verb* (**-ting**) express in speech or writing; fix, specify. □ **lie in state** be laid in public place of honour before burial; **state of the art** current stage of esp. technological development; **state-of-the-art** absolutely up-to-date; **stateroom** state apartment, large private cabin in passenger ship.

stateless *adjective* having no nationality or citizenship.

stately *adjective* (**-ier**, **-iest**) dignified, imposing. □ **stately home** large historic house, esp. one open to public. □ **stateliness** *noun*.

statement *noun* stating, being stated; thing stated; formal account of facts; record of transactions in bank account etc.; notification of amount due to tradesman etc.

statesman /'steɪtsmən/ *noun* (*feminine* **stateswoman**) distinguished and capable politician or diplomat. □ **statesmanlike** *adjective*; **statesmanship** *noun*.

static /'stætɪk/ ● *adjective* stationary, not acting or changing; *Physics* concerned with bodies at rest or forces in equilibrium. ● *noun* static electricity; atmospherics. □ **static electricity** electricity not flowing as current.

statics *plural noun* (usually treated as *singular*) science of bodies at rest or forces in equilibrium.

station /'steɪʃ(ə)n/ ● *noun* regular stopping place on railway line; person or thing's allotted place, building, etc.; centre for particular service or activity; establishment involved in broadcasting; military or naval base, inhabitants of this; position in life, rank, status; *Australian & NZ* large sheep or cattle farm. ● *verb* assign station to; put in position. □ **stationmaster** official in charge of railway station; **stations of the cross** *RC Church* series of images representing events in Christ's Passion; **station wagon** *esp. US* estate car

stationary *adjective* not moving; not meant to be moved; unchanging.

stationer *noun* dealer in stationery.

stationery *noun* writing materials, office supplies, etc.

statistic /stə'tɪstɪk/ *noun* statistical fact or item.

statistical *adjective* of statistics. □ **statistically** *adverb*.

statistics *plural noun* (usually treated as *singular*) science of collecting and analysing significant numerical data; such data. □ **statistician** /stætɪs'tɪʃ(ə)n/ *noun*.

statuary /'stætʃʊərɪ/ ● *adjective* of or for statues. ● *noun* statues collectively; making statues.

statue /'stætʃu:/ *noun* sculptured figure of person or animal, esp. life-size or larger.

statuesque /stætʃʊ'esk/ *adjective* like statue, esp. in beauty or dignity.

statuette /stætʃʊ'et/ *noun* small statue.

stature /'stætʃə/ *noun* height of (esp. human) body; calibre (esp. moral), eminence.

status /'steɪtəs/ *noun* rank, social position, relative importance; superior social etc. position. □ **status quo** /'kwəʊ/ existing conditions; **status symbol** possession etc. intended to indicate owner's superiority.

statute /'stætʃu:t/ *noun* written law passed by legislative body; rule of corporation, founder, etc., intended to be permanent.

statutory /ˈstætʃʊtərɪ/ *adjective* required or enacted by statute.

staunch¹ /stɔːntʃ/ *adjective* trustworthy, loyal. □ **staunchly** *adverb*.

staunch² = STANCH.

stave ● *noun* each of curved slats forming sides of cask; *Music* staff; stanza, verse. ● *verb* (**-ving**; *past & past participle* **stove** /stəʊv/ or **staved**) (usually + *in*) break hole in, damage, crush by forcing inwards. □ **stave off** (*past & past participle* **staved**) avert or defer (danger etc.).

stay¹ ● *verb* continue in same place or condition, not depart or change; (often + *at, in, with*) reside temporarily; *archaic or literary* stop, check, (esp. in *imperative*) pause; postpone (judgement etc.); assuage (hunger etc.), esp. for short time. ● *noun* act or period of staying; suspension or postponement of sentence, judgement, etc.; prop, support; (in *plural*) *historical* (esp. boned) corset. □ **stay-at-home** (person) rarely going out; **staying power** endurance; **stay the night** remain overnight; **stay put** *colloquial* remain where it is put or where one is; **stay up** not go to bed (until late).

stay² *noun* rope supporting mast, flagstaff, etc.; supporting cable on aircraft. □ **staysail** sail extended on stay.

stayer *noun* person or animal with great endurance.

STD *abbreviation* subscriber trunk dialling.

stead /sted/ *noun* □ **in** (**person's, thing's**) **stead** as substitute; **stand** (**person**) **in good stead** be advantageous or useful to him or her.

steadfast /ˈstedfɑːst/ *adjective* constant, firm, unwavering. □ **steadfastly** *adverb*; **steadfastness** *noun*.

steady /ˈstedɪ/ ● *adjective* (**-ier, -iest**) firmly fixed or supported, unwavering; uniform, regular; constant, persistent; (of person) serious and dependable; regular, established. ● *verb* (**-ies, -ied**) make or become steady. ● *adverb* steadily. ● *noun* (*plural* **-ies**) *colloquial* regular boyfriend or girlfriend. □ **steady state** unvarying condition, esp. in physical process. □ **steadily** *adverb*; **steadiness** *noun*.

steak /steɪk/ *noun* thick slice of meat (esp. beef) or fish, usually grilled or fried. □ **steakhouse** restaurant specializing in beefsteaks.

steal ● *verb* (*past* **stole**; *past participle* **stolen** /ˈstəʊl(ə)n/) take (another's property) illegally or without right or permission, esp. in secret; obtain surreptitiously, insidiously, or artfully; (+ *in, out, away, up*, etc.) move, esp. silently or stealthily. ● *noun US colloquial* act of stealing, theft; *colloquial* easy task, bargain. □ **steal a march on** gain advantage over by surreptitious means; **steal the show** outshine other performers, esp. unexpectedly.

stealth /stelθ/ *noun* secrecy, secret behaviour.

stealthy *adjective* (**-ier, -iest**) done or moving with stealth. □ **stealthily** *adverb*.

steam ● *noun* gas into which water is changed by boiling; condensed vapour formed from this; power obtained from steam; *colloquial* power, energy. ● *verb* cook (food) in steam; give off steam; move under steam power; (+ *ahead, away*, etc.) *colloquial* proceed or travel fast or with vigour. □ **let off steam** relieve pent-up energy or feelings; **steamboat** steam-driven boat; **steam engine** one worked or propelled by steam; **steam iron** electric iron that emits steam; **steamroller** *noun* heavy slow-moving vehicle with roller, used to flatten new-made roads, crushing power or force, *verb* crush or move forcibly or indiscriminately; **steamship** steam-driven ship; **steam train** train pulled by steam engine; **steam up** cover or become covered with condensed steam, (as **steamed up** *adjective*) *colloquial* angry, excited.

steamer *noun* steamboat; vessel for steaming food in.

steamy *adjective* (**-ier, -iest**) like or full of steam; *colloquial* erotic.

steatite /ˈstɪətaɪt/ *noun* impure form of talc, esp. soapstone.

steed *noun archaic or poetical* horse.

steel ● *noun* strong malleable low-carbon iron alloy, used esp. for making tools, weapons, etc.; strength, firmness; steel rod for sharpening knives. ● *adjective* of or like steel. ● *verb* harden, make resolute. □ **steel band** band playing chiefly calypso-style music on instruments made from oil drums; **steel wool** fine steel shavings used as abrasive; **steelworks** factory producing steel; **steelyard** balance with graduated arm along which weight is moved.

steely *adjective* (**-ier, -iest**) of or like steel; severe, resolute.

steep¹ ● *adjective* sloping sharply; (of rise or fall) rapid; *colloquial* exorbitant, unreasonable, exaggerated, incredible. ● *noun* steep slope, precipice. □ **steepen** *verb*; **steeply** *adverb*; **steepness** *noun*.

steep² ● *verb* soak or bathe in liquid. ● *noun* act of steeping; liquid for steeping. □ **steep in** imbue with, make deeply acquainted with (subject etc.).

steeple /ˈstiːp(ə)l/ *noun* tall tower, esp. with spire, above roof of church. □ **steeplechase** horse race with ditches, hedges, etc. to jump, cross-country foot race; **steeplejack** repairer of tall chimneys, steeples, etc.

steer¹ *verb* guide (vehicle, ship, etc.) with wheel, rudder, etc.; direct or guide (one's course, other people, conversation, etc.) in specified direction. □ **steer clear of** avoid; **steering column** column on which steering wheel is mounted; **steering committee** one deciding order of business, course of operations etc.; **steering wheel** wheel by which vehicle etc. is steered; **steersman** person who steers ship.

steer² *noun* bullock.

steerage *noun* act of steering; *archaic* cheapest part of ship's accommodation.

steering *noun* apparatus for steering vehicle etc.

stegosaurus /stegəˈsɔːrəs/ *noun* (*plural* **-ruses**) large dinosaur with two rows of vertical plates along back.

stela /ˈstiːlə/ *noun* (*plural* **stelae** /-liː/) (also **stele** /ˈstiːl/) ancient upright slab or pillar, usually inscribed and sculptured, esp. as gravestone.

stellar /ˈstelə/ *adjective* of star or stars.

stem¹ ● *noun* main body or stalk of plant; stalk of fruit, flower, or leaf; stem-shaped part, e.g. slender part of wineglass; *Grammar* root or main part of noun, verb, etc. to which inflections are added; main upright timber at bow of ship. ● *verb* (**-mm-**) (+ *from*) spring or originate from.

stem² *verb* (**-mm-**) check, stop.

stench *noun* foul smell.

stencil /ˈstensɪl/ ● *noun* thin sheet in which pattern is cut, placed on surface and printed, inked over, etc.; pattern so produced. ● *verb* (**-ll-**; *US* **-l-**) (often + *on*) produce (pattern) with stencil; mark (surface) in this way.

Sten gun *noun* lightweight sub-machine-gun.

stenographer /steˈnɒgrəfə/ *noun esp. US* shorthand typist.

stentorian /stenˈtɔːrɪən/ *adjective* loud and powerful.

step ● *noun* complete movement of leg in walking or running; distance so covered; unit of movement in dancing; measure taken, esp. one of several in course of action; surface of stair, stepladder, etc. tread; short distance; sound or mark made by foot in walking etc; degree in scale of promotion, precedence, etc.; stepping in unison or to music; state of conforming.

● *verb* (**-pp-**) lift and set down foot or alternate feet in walking; come or go in specified direction by stepping; make progress in specified way; (+ *off, out*) measure (distance) by stepping; perform (dance). □ **mind, watch one's step** be careful; **step down** resign; **step in** enter, intervene; **stepladder** short folding ladder not leant against wall etc.; **step on it** *colloquial* hurry; **step out** be active socially, take large steps; **stepping-stone** large stone set in stream etc. to walk over, means of progress; **step up** increase, intensify.

step- *combining form* related by remarriage of parent. □ **stepchild, stepdaughter, stepson** one's husband's or wife's child by previous partner; **stepfather, stepmother, step-parent** mother's or father's spouse who is not one's own parent; **stepbrother, stepsister** child of one's step-parent by previous partner.

stephanotis /stefə'nəʊtɪs/ *noun* fragrant tropical climbing plant.

steppe /step/ *noun* level grassy treeless plain.

stereo /'sterɪəʊ/ ● *noun* (*plural* **-s**) stereophonic sound reproduction or equipment; stereoscope. ● *adjective* stereophonic; stereoscopic.

stereo- *combining form* solid; 3-dimensional.

stereophonic /sterɪəʊ'fɒnɪk/ *adjective* using two or more channels, to give effect of naturally distributed sound.

stereoscope /'sterɪəskəʊp/ *noun* device for producing 3-dimensional effect by viewing two slightly different photographs together. □ **stereoscopic** /-'skɒp-/ *adjective*.

stereotype /'sterɪəʊtaɪp/ ● *noun* person or thing seeming to conform to widely accepted type; such type, idea, or attitude; printing plate cast from mould of composed type. ● *verb* (**-ping**) (esp. as **stereotyped** *adjective*) cause to conform to type, standardize; print from stereotype; make stereotype of.

sterile /'steraɪl/ *adjective* not able to produce crop, fruit, or young, barren; lacking ideas or originality, unproductive; free from micro-organisms etc. □ **sterility** /stə'rɪl-/ *noun*.

sterilize /'sterɪlaɪz/ *verb* (also **-ise**) (**-zing** or **-sing**) make sterile; deprive of reproductive power. □ **sterilization** *noun*.

sterling /'stɜ:lɪŋ/ ● *adjective* of or in British money; (of coin or precious metal) genuine, of standard value or purity; (of person etc.) genuine, reliable. ● *noun* British money. □ **sterling silver** silver of 92½% purity.

stern[1] *adjective* severe, grim; authoritarian. □ **sternly** *adverb*; **sternness** *noun*.

stern[2] *noun* rear part, esp. of ship or boat.

sternum /'stɜ:nəm/ *noun* (*plural* **-na** or **-nums**) breastbone.

steroid /'stɪərɔɪd/ *noun* any of group of organic compounds including many hormones, alkaloids, and vitamins.

sterol /'sterɒl/ *noun* naturally occurring steroid alcohol.

stertorous /'stɜ:tərəs/ *adjective* (of breathing etc.) laboured and noisy.

stet *verb* (**-tt-**) (usually written on proof-sheet etc.) ignore or cancel (alteration), let original stand.

stethoscope /'steθəskəʊp/ *noun* instrument used in listening to heart, lungs, etc.

stetson /'stets(ə)n/ *noun* slouch hat with wide brim and high crown.

stevedore /'sti:vədɔ:/ *noun* person employed in loading and unloading ships.

stew ● *verb* cook by long simmering in closed vessel; *colloquial* swelter; (of tea etc.) become bitter or strong from infusing too long. ● *noun* dish of stewed meat etc.; *colloquial* agitated or angry state.

steward /'stju:əd/ ● *noun* passengers' attendant on ship, aircraft, or train; official managing meeting, show, etc.; person responsible for supplies of food etc. for college, club, etc.; property manager. □ **stewardship** *noun*.

stewardess /stju:ə'des/ *noun* female steward, esp. on ship or aircraft.

stick[1] *noun* short slender length of wood, esp. for use as support or weapon; thin rod of wood etc. for particular purpose; gear lever, joystick; sticklike piece of celery, dynamite, etc.; (often **the stick**) punishment, esp. by beating; *colloquial* adverse criticism; *colloquial* person, esp. when dull or unsociable. □ **stick insect** insect with twiglike body.

stick[2] *verb* (*past & past participle* **stuck**) (+ *in, into, through*) thrust, insert (thing or its point); stab; (+ *in, into, on,* etc.) fix or be fixed (as) by pointed end; fix or be fixed (as) by adhesive etc.; lose or be deprived of movement or action through adhesion, jamming, etc.; *colloquial* put in specified position or place, remain; *colloquial* endure, tolerate; (+ *at*) *colloquial* persevere with. □ **get stuck into** *slang* start in earnest; **stick around** *colloquial* linger; **sticking plaster** adhesive plaster for wounds etc.; **stick-in-the-mud** *colloquial* unprogressive or old-fashioned person; **stick it out** *colloquial* endure to the end; **stick out** (cause to) protrude; **stick out for** persist in demanding; **stick up** be or make erect or protruding upwards, fasten to upright surface, *colloquial* rob or threaten with gun; **stick up for** support, defend; **stuck for** at a loss for, needing; **stuck with** *colloquial* unable to get rid of.

sticker *noun* adhesive label.

stickleback /'stɪk(ə)lbæk/ *noun* small spiny-backed fish.

stickler /'stɪklə/ *noun* (+ *for*) person who insists on something.

sticky *adjective* (**-ier, -iest**) tending or intended to stick or adhere; glutinous, viscous; (of weather) humid; *colloquial* difficult, awkward, unpleasant, painful. □ **sticky wicket** *colloquial* difficult situation. □ **stickiness** *noun*.

stiff ● *adjective* rigid, inflexible; hard to bend, move, turn, etc.; hard to cope with, needing strength or effort; severe, strong; formal, constrained; (of muscle, person, etc.) aching from exertion, injury, etc.; (of esp. alcoholic drink) strong. ● *adverb colloquial* utterly, extremely. ● *noun slang* corpse. □ **stiff-necked** obstinate, haughty; **stiff upper lip** appearance of firmness or fortitude. □ **stiffen** *verb*; **stiffly** *adverb*; **stiffness** *noun*.

stifle /'staɪf(ə)l/ *verb* (**-ling**) suppress; feel or make unable to breathe easily; suffocate. □ **stifling** *adjective*.

stigma /'stɪgmə/ *noun* (*plural* **-s** or **stigmata** /-mətə or -'mɑ:tə/) shame, disgrace; part of pistil that receives pollen in pollination; (**stigmata**) marks like those on Christ's body after the Crucifixion, appearing on bodies of certain saints etc.

stigmatize /'stɪgmətaɪz/ *verb* (also **-ise**) (**-zing** or **-sing**) (often + *as*) brand as unworthy or disgraceful.

stile *noun* set of steps etc. allowing people to climb over fence, wall, etc.

stiletto /stɪ'letəʊ/ *noun* (*plural* **-s**) short dagger; (in full **stiletto heel**) long tapering heel of shoe; pointed implement for making eyelets etc.

still[1] ● *adjective* with little or no movement or sound; calm, tranquil; (of drink) not effervescing. ● *noun* deep silence; static photograph, esp. single shot from cinema film. ● *adverb* without moving; even now, at particular time; nevertheless; (+ *comparative*) even, yet, increasingly. ● *verb* make or become still, quieten. □ **stillbirth** birth of dead child; **stillborn** born dead, abortive; **still life** painting or drawing of inanimate objects. □ **stillness** *noun*.

still[2] *noun* apparatus for distilling spirits etc.

stilt *noun* either of pair of poles with foot supports for walking at a distance above ground; each of set of piles or posts supporting building etc.

stilted *adjective* (of literary style etc.) stiff and unnatural.

Stilton /'stɪlt(ə)n/ *noun proprietary term* strong rich esp. blue-veined cheese.

stimulant /'stɪmjʊlənt/ ● *adjective* stimulating esp. bodily or mental activity. ● *noun* stimulant substance or influence.

stimulate /'stɪmjʊleɪt/ *verb* (**-ting**) act as stimulus to; animate, excite, rouse. □ **stimulation** *noun*; **stimulative** /-lətɪv/ *adjective*; **stimulator** *noun*.

stimulus /'stɪmjʊləs/ *noun* (*plural* **-li** /-laɪ/) thing that rouses to activity.

sting ● *noun* sharp wounding organ of insect, nettle, etc.; inflicting of wound with this; wound itself, pain caused by it; painful quality or effect; pungency, vigour. ● *verb* (*past & past participle* **stung**) wound with sting; be able to sting; feel or cause tingling physical pain or sharp mental pain; (+ *into*) incite, esp. painfully; *slang* swindle, charge heavily. □ **stinging-nettle** nettle with stinging hairs; **stingray** broad flatfish with stinging tail.

stingy /'stɪndʒɪ/ *adjective* (**-ier**, **-iest**) niggardly, mean. □ **stingily** *adverb*; **stinginess** *noun*.

stink ● *verb* (*past* **stank** or **stunk**; *past participle* **stunk**) emit strong offensive smell; (often + *out*) fill (place) with stink; (+ *out* etc.) drive (person) out etc. by stink; *colloquial* be or seem very unpleasant. ● *noun* strong offensive smell; *colloquial* loud complaint, fuss. □ **stink bomb** device emitting stink when opened.

stinker *noun slang* particularly annoying or unpleasant person; very difficult problem etc.

stinking ● *adjective* that stinks; *slang* very objectionable. ● *adverb slang* extremely and usually objectionably.

stint ● *verb* (often + *on*) supply (food, aid, etc.) meanly or grudgingly; (often **stint oneself**) supply (person etc.) in this way. ● *noun* allotted amount or period of work.

stipend /'staɪpend/ *noun* salary, esp. of clergyman.

stipendiary /staɪ'pendjərɪ/ ● *adjective* receiving stipend. ● *noun* (*plural* **-ies**) person receiving stipend. □ **stipendiary magistrate** paid professional magistrate.

stipple /'stɪp(ə)l/ ● *verb* (**-ling**) draw, paint, engrave, etc. with dots instead of lines; roughen surface of (paint, cement, etc.). ● *noun* stippling; effect of stippling.

stipulate /'stɪpjʊleɪt/ *verb* (**-ting**) demand or specify as part of bargain etc. □ **stipulation** *noun*.

stir ● *verb* (**-rr-**) move spoon etc. round and round in (liquid etc.), esp. to mix ingredients; cause to move, esp. slightly; be or begin to be in motion; rise from sleep; arouse, inspire, excite; *colloquial* cause trouble by gossiping etc. ● *noun* act of stirring; commotion, excitement. □ **stir-fry** *verb* fry rapidly while stirring, *noun* stir-fried dish; **stir up** mix thoroughly by stirring, stimulate, incite.

stirrup /'stɪrəp/ *noun* support for horse-rider's foot, suspended by strap from saddle. □ **stirrup-cup** cup of wine etc. offered to departing traveller, originally rider; **stirrup-pump** hand-operated water-pump with footrest, used to extinguish small fires.

stitch ● *noun* single pass of needle, or result of this, in sewing, knitting, or crochet; particular method of sewing etc.; least bit of clothing; sharp pain in side induced by running etc. ● *verb* sew, make stitches (in). □ **in stitches** *colloquial* laughing uncontrollably; **stitch up** join or mend by sewing.

stoat *noun* mammal of weasel family with brown fur turning mainly white in winter.

stock ● *noun* store of goods etc. ready for sale or distribution; supply or quantity of things for use; equipment or raw material for manufacture, trade, etc.; farm animals or equipment; capital of business; shares in this; reputation, popularity; money lent to government at fixed interest; line of ancestry; liquid made by stewing bones, vegetables, etc.; fragrant garden plant; plant into which graft is inserted; main trunk of tree etc.; (in *plural*) *historical* timber frame with holes for feet in which offenders were locked as public punishment; base, support, or handle for implement or machine; butt of rifle etc.; (in *plural*) supports for ship during building or repair; band of cloth worn round neck. ● *adjective* kept regularly in stock for sale or use; commonly used, hackneyed. ● *verb* have (goods) in stock; provide (shop, farm, etc.) with goods, livestock, etc. □ **stockbroker** member of Stock Exchange dealing in stocks and shares; **stock-car** specially strengthened car used in racing where deliberate bumping is allowed; **Stock Exchange** place for dealing in stocks and shares, dealers working there; **stock-in-trade** requisite(s) of trade or profession; **stock market** Stock Exchange, transactions on this; **stockpile** *noun* reserve supply of accumulated stock, *verb* accumulate stockpile (of); **stockpot** pot for making soup stock; **stock-still** motionless; **stocktaking** making inventory of stock; **stock up** (often + *with*) provide with or get stocks or supplies (of); **stockyard** enclosure for sorting or temporary keeping of cattle; **take stock** make inventory of one's stock, (often + *of*) review (situation etc.).

stockade /stɒ'keɪd/ ● *noun* line or enclosure of upright stakes. ● *verb* (**-ding**) fortify with this.

stockinet /stɒkɪ'net/ *noun* (also **stockinette**) elastic knitted fabric.

stocking /'stɒkɪŋ/ *noun* knitted covering for leg and foot, of nylon, wool, silk, etc. □ **stocking stitch** alternate rows of plain and purl.

stockist *noun* dealer in specified types of goods.

stocky *adjective* (**-ier**, **-iest**) short and strongly built. □ **stockily** *adverb*.

stodge *noun colloquial* heavy fattening food.

stodgy *adjective* (**-ier**, **-iest**) (of food) heavy, filling; dull, uninteresting. □ **stodginess** *noun*.

stoic /'stəʊɪk/ *noun* person having great self-control in adversity. □ **stoical** *adjective*; **stoicism** /-ɪsɪz(ə)m/ *noun*.

stoke *verb* (**-king**) (often + *up*) feed and tend (fire, furnace, etc.); *colloquial* fill oneself with food. □ **stokehold** compartment in steamship containing its boilers and furnace; **stokehole** space for stokers in front of furnace.

stoker *noun* person who tends furnace, esp. on steamship.

stole[1] *noun* woman's garment like long wide scarf worn over shoulders; strip of silk etc. worn similarly by priest.

stole[2] *past* of STEAL.

stolen *past participle* of STEAL.

stolid /'stɒlɪd/ *adjective* not easily excited or moved; impassive, unemotional. □ **stolidity** /-'lɪd-/ *noun*; **stolidly** *adverb*.

stomach /'stʌmək/ ● *noun* internal organ in which food is digested; lower front of body; (usually + *for*) appetite, inclination, etc. ● *verb* (usually in negative) endure. □ **stomach-pump** syringe for forcing liquid etc. into or out of stomach.

stomp ● *verb* tread or stamp heavily. ● *noun* lively jazz dance with heavy stamping.

stone ● *noun* solid non-metallic mineral matter, rock; small piece of this; hard case of kernel in some fruits; hard morbid concretion in body; (*plural* same) unit of weight (14 lb, 6.35 kg); precious stone. ● *verb* (**-ning**) pelt with stones; remove stones from (fruit). ▫ **Stone Age** prehistoric period when weapons and tools were made of stone; **stone-cold** completely cold; **stone-cold sober** completely sober; **stonecrop** succulent rock plant; **stone-dead** completely dead; **stone-deaf** completely deaf; **stone fruit** fruit with flesh enclosing stone; **stoneground** (of flour) ground with millstones; **stone's throw** short distance; **stonewall** obstruct with evasive answers etc., *Cricket* bat with excessive caution; **stoneware** impermeable and partly vitrified but opaque ceramic ware; **stonewashed** (esp. of denim) washed with abrasives to give worn or faded look; **stonework** masonry.

stoned *adjective slang* drunk, drugged.

stony *adjective* (**-ier**, **-iest**) full of stones; hard, rigid; unfeeling, unresponsive. ▫ **stony-broke** *slang* entirely without money. ▫ **stonily** *adverb*.

stood *past & past participle* of STAND.

stooge *colloquial* ● *noun* person acting as butt or foil, esp. for comedian; assistant or subordinate, esp. for unpleasant work. ● *verb* (**-ging**) (+ *for*) act as stooge for; (+ *about*, *around*, etc.) move about aimlessly.

stool /stu:l/ *noun* single seat without back or arms; footstool; (usually in *plural*) faeces. ▫ **stool-pigeon** person acting as decoy, police informer.

stoop ● *verb* bend down; stand or walk with shoulders habitually bent forward; (+ *to do*) condescend; (+ *to*) descend to (shameful act). ● *noun* stooping posture.

stop ● *verb* (**-pp-**) put an end to progress, motion, or operation of; effectively hinder or prevent; discontinue; come to an end; cease from motion, speaking, or action; defeat; *colloquial* remain; stay for short time; (often + *up*) block or close up (hole, leak, etc.); not permit or supply as usual; instruct bank to withhold payment on (cheque); fill (tooth); press (violin etc. string) to obtain required pitch. ● *noun* stopping, being stopped; place where bus, train, etc. regularly stops; full stop; device for stopping motion at particular point; change of pitch effected by stopping string; (in organ) row of pipes of one character, knob etc. operating these; (in camera etc.) diaphragm, effective diameter of lens, device for reducing this; plosive sound. ▫ **pull out all the stops** make extreme effort; **stopcock** externally operated valve regulating flow through pipe etc.; **stopgap** temporary substitute; **stop off**, **over** break one's journey; **stop press** late news inserted in newspaper after printing has begun; **stopwatch** watch that can be instantly started and stopped, used in timing of races etc.

stoppage *noun* interruption of work due to strike etc.; (in *plural*) sum deducted from pay, for tax, etc.; condition of being blocked or stopped.

stopper *noun* plug for closing bottle etc.

storage /ˈstɔ:rɪdʒ/ *noun* storing of goods etc.; method of, space for, or cost of storing. ▫ **storage battery**, **cell** one for storing electricity; **storage heater** electric heater releasing heat stored outside peak hours.

store ● *noun* quantity of something kept ready for use; (in *plural*) articles gathered for particular purpose, supply of, or place for keeping, these; department store; *esp. US* shop; (often in *plural*) shop selling basic necessities; warehouse for keeping furniture etc. temporarily; device in computer for keeping retrievable data. ● *verb* (**-ring**) (often + *up*, *away*) accumulate for future use; put (furniture etc.) in a store; stock or provide with something useful; keep (data) for retrieval. ▫ **in store** in reserve, to come, (+ *for*) awaiting; **storehouse** storage place; **storekeeper** person in charge of stores, *US* shopkeeper; **storeroom** storage room.

storey /ˈstɔ:rɪ/ *noun* (*plural* **-s**) rooms etc. on one level of building.

stork *noun* long-legged usually white wading bird.

storm ● *noun* violent disturbance of atmosphere with high winds and usually thunder, rain, or snow; violent disturbance in human affairs; (+ *of*) shower of missiles or blows, outbreak of applause, hisses, etc.; assault on fortified place. ● *verb* attack or capture by storm; rush violently; rage, be violent; bluster. ▫ **storm centre** comparatively calm centre of cyclonic storm, centre round which controversy etc. rages; **storm cloud** heavy rain-cloud; **storm troops** shock troops, *historical* Nazi political militia; **take by storm** capture by direct assault, quickly captivate.

stormy *adjective* (**-ier**, **-iest**) of or affected by storms; (of wind etc.) violent; full of angry feeling or outbursts. ▫ **stormily** *adverb*.

story /ˈstɔ:rɪ/ *noun* (*plural* **-ies**) account of real or imaginary events; tale, anecdote; history of person, institution, etc.; plot of novel, play, etc.; article in newspaper, material for this; *colloquial* fib. ▫ **storyteller** person who tells or writes stories, *colloquial* liar.

stoup /stu:p/ *noun* basin for holy water; *archaic* flagon, beaker.

stout /staʊt/ ● *adjective* rather fat, corpulent; thick, strong; brave, resolute, vigorous. ● *noun* strong dark beer. ▫ **stout-hearted** courageous. ▫ **stoutly** *adverb*; **stoutness** *noun*.

stove[1] /stəʊv/ *noun* closed apparatus burning fuel or using electricity etc. for heating or cooking. ▫ **stove-pipe** pipe carrying smoke and gases from stove to chimney.

stove[2] *past & past participle* of STAVE.

stow /stəʊ/ *verb* pack (goods, cargo, etc.) tidily and compactly. ▫ **stow away** place (thing) out of the way, hide oneself on ship etc. to travel free; **stowaway** person who stows away.

stowage *noun* stowing; place for this.

straddle /ˈstræd(ə)l/ *verb* (**-ling**) sit or stand across (thing) with legs wide apart; be situated on both sides of; spread legs wide apart.

strafe /strɑ:f/ *verb* (**-fing**) bombard; attack with gunfire.

straggle /ˈstræg(ə)l/ ● *verb* (**-ling**) lack compactness or tidiness; be dispersed or sporadic; trail behind in race etc. ● *noun* straggling group. ▫ **straggler** *noun*; **straggly** *adjective*.

straight /streɪt/ ● *adjective* not curved, bent, crooked or curly; successive, uninterrupted; ordered, level, tidy; honest, candid; (of thinking etc.) logical; (of theatre, music, etc.) not popular or comic; unmodified, (of a drink) undiluted; *colloquial* (of person etc.) conventional, respectable, heterosexual. ● *noun* straight part, esp. concluding stretch of racetrack; straight condition; *colloquial* conventional person, heterosexual. ● *adverb* in straight line, direct; in right direction; correctly. ▫ **go straight** (of criminal) become honest; **straight away** immediately; **straight face** intentionally expressionless face; **straight fight** *Politics* contest between two candidates only; **straightforward** honest, frank, (of task etc.) simple; **straight man** comedian's stooge; **straight off** *colloquial* without hesitation. ▫ **straightness** *noun*.

straighten *verb* (often + *out*) make or become straight; (+ *up*) stand erect after bending.

strain[1] ● *verb* stretch tightly; make or become taut or tense; injure by overuse or excessive demands; exercise (oneself, one's senses, thing, etc.) intensely, press to extremes; strive intensely; distort from true intention or meaning; clear (liquid) of solid matter by passing it through sieve etc. ● *noun* act of straining, force exerted in this; injury caused by straining muscle etc.; severe mental or physical demand or exertion; snatch of music or poetry; tone or tendency in speech or writing.

strain[2] *noun* breed or stock of animals, plants, etc.; characteristic tendency.

strained *adjective* constrained, artificial; (of relationship) distrustful, tense.

strainer *noun* device for straining liquids.

strait *noun* (in *singular* or *plural*) narrow channel connecting two large bodies of water; (usually in *plural*) difficulty, distress. □ **strait-jacket** strong garment with long sleeves for confining violent prisoner etc., restrictive measures; **strait-laced** puritanical.

straitened /'streɪt(ə)nd/ *adjective* of or marked by poverty.

strand[1] ● *verb* run aground; (as **stranded** *adjective*) in difficulties, esp. without money or transport. ● *noun* foreshore, beach.

strand[2] *noun* each of twisted threads or wires making rope, cable, etc.; single thread or strip of fibre; lock of hair; element, component.

strange /streɪndʒ/ *adjective* unusual, peculiar, surprising, eccentric; (often + *to*) unfamiliar, foreign; (+ *to*) unaccustomed; not at ease. □ **strangely** *adverb*; **strangeness** *noun*.

stranger *noun* person new to particular place or company; (often + *to*) person one does not know.

strangle /'stræŋg(ə)l/ *verb* (**-ling**) squeeze windpipe or neck of, esp. so as to kill; hamper or suppress (movement, cry, etc.). □ **stranglehold** deadly grip, complete control. □ **strangler** *noun*.

strangulate /'stræŋgjʊleɪt/ *verb* (**-ting**) compress (vein, intestine, etc.), preventing circulation.

strangulation *noun* strangling, being strangled; strangulating.

strap ● *noun* strip of leather etc., often with buckle, for holding things together etc.; narrow strip of fabric forming part of garment; loop for grasping to steady oneself in moving vehicle. ● *verb* (**-pp-**) (often + *down*, *up*, etc.) secure or bind with strap; beat with strap. □ **straphanger** *slang* standing passenger in bus or train; **straphang** *verb* □ **strapless** *adjective*.

strapping *adjective* large and sturdy.

strata *plural* of STRATUM.

■ **Usage** It is a mistake to use the plural form *strata* when only one stratum is meant.

stratagem /'strætədʒəm/ *noun* cunning plan or scheme; trickery.

strategic /strə'ti:dʒɪk/ *adjective* of or promoting strategy; (of materials) essential in war; (of bombing or weapons) done or for use as longer-term military policy. □ **strategically** *adverb*.

strategy /'strætɪdʒɪ/ *noun* (*plural* **-ies**) long-term plan or policy; art of war; art of moving troops, ships, aircraft, etc. into favourable positions. □ **strategist** *noun*.

stratify /'strætɪfaɪ/ *verb* (**-ies**, **-ied**) (esp. as **stratified** *adjective*) arrange in strata, grades, etc. □ **stratification** *noun*.

stratosphere /'strætəsfɪə/ *noun* layer of atmosphere above troposphere, extending to about 50 km from earth's surface.

stratum /'strɑ:təm/ *noun* (*plural* **strata**) layer or set of layers of any deposited substance, esp. of rock; atmospheric layer; social class.

straw *noun* dry cut stalks of grain; single stalk of straw; thin tube for sucking drink through; insignificant thing; pale yellow colour. □ **clutch at straws** try any remedy in desperation; **straw vote, poll** unofficial ballot as test of opinion.

strawberry /'strɔ:bərɪ/ *noun* (*plural* **-ies**) pulpy red fruit having surface studded with yellow seeds; plant bearing this. □ **strawberry mark** reddish birthmark.

stray ● *verb* wander from the right place, from one's companions, etc., go astray; deviate. ● *noun* strayed animal or person. ● *adjective* strayed, lost; isolated, occasional.

streak ● *noun* long thin usually irregular line or band, esp. of colour; strain or trait in person's character. ● *verb* mark with streaks; move very rapidly; *colloquial* run naked in public.

streaky *adjective* (**-ier**, **-iest**) marked with streaks; (of bacon) with streaks of fat.

stream ● *noun* body of running water, esp. small river; current, flow; group of schoolchildren of similar ability taught together. ● *verb* move as stream; run with liquid; be blown in wind; emit stream of (blood etc.); arrange (schoolchildren) in streams. □ **on stream** in operation or production.

streamer *noun* long narrow strip of ribbon or paper; long narrow flag.

streamline *verb* (**-ning**) give (vehicle etc.) form which presents least resistance to motion; make simple or more efficient.

street *noun* road in city, town, or village; this with buildings on each side. □ **on the streets** living by prostitution; **streetcar** *US* tram; **street credibility**, **cred** *slang* acceptability within urban subculture; **streetwalker** prostitute seeking customers in street; **streetwise** knowing how to survive modern urban life.

strength *noun* being strong; degree or manner of this; person or thing giving strength; number of people present or available. □ **on the strength of** on basis of.

strengthen *verb* make or become stronger.

strenuous /'strenjʊəs/ *adjective* using or requiring great effort; energetic. □ **strenuously** *adverb*.

streptococcus /streptə'kɒkəs/ *noun* (*plural* **-cocci** /-kaɪ/) bacterium causing serious infections. □ **streptococcal** *adjective*.

streptomycin /streptəʊ'maɪsɪn/ *noun* antibiotic effective against many disease-producing bacteria.

stress ● *noun* pressure, tension; quantity measuring this; physical or mental strain; emphasis. ● *verb* emphasize; subject to stress.

stressful *adjective* causing stress.

stretch ● *verb* draw, be drawn, or be able to be drawn out in length or size; make or become taut; place or lie at full length or spread out; extend limbs and tighten muscles after being relaxed; have specified length or extension, extend; strain or exert extremely; exaggerate. ● *noun* continuous extent, expanse, or period; stretching, being stretched; *colloquial* period of imprisonment etc. □ **at a stretch** in one period; **stretch one's legs** exercise oneself by walking; **stretch out** extend (limb etc.), last, prolong; **stretch a point** agree to something not normally allowed. □ **stretchy** *adjective* (**-ier**, **-iest**).

stretcher *noun* two poles with canvas etc. between for carrying person in lying position; brick etc. laid along face of wall.

strew /stru:/ *verb* (*past participle* **strewn** or **strewed**) scatter over surface; (usually + *with*) spread (surface) with scattered things.

'strewth = 'STRUTH.

striated /straɪˈeɪtɪd/ *adjective* marked with slight ridges or furrows. □ **striation** *noun*.

stricken /ˈstrɪkən/ *archaic past participle* of STRIKE. ● *adjective* affected or overcome (with illness, misfortune, etc.).

strict *adjective* precisely limited or defined, without deviation; requiring complete obedience or exact performance. □ **strictly** *adverb*; **strictness** *noun*.

stricture /ˈstrɪktʃə/ *noun* (usually in *plural*; often + *on, upon*) critical or censorious remark.

stride ● *verb* (**-ding**; *past* **strode**; *past participle* **stridden** /ˈstrɪd(ə)n/) walk with long firm steps; cross with one step; bestride. ● *noun* single long step; length of this; gait as determined by length of stride; (usually in *plural*) progress. □ **take in one's stride** manage easily.

strident /ˈstraɪd(ə)nt/ *adjective* loud and harsh. □ **stridency** *noun*; **stridently** *adverb*.

strife *noun* conflict, struggle.

strike ● *verb* (**-king**; *past* **struck**; *past participle* **struck** or *archaic* **stricken**) deliver (blow), inflict blow on; come or bring sharply into contact with; propel or divert with blow; (cause to) penetrate; ignite (match) or produce (sparks etc.) by rubbing; make (coin) by stamping; produce (musical note) by striking; (of clock) indicate (time) with chime etc., (of time) be so indicated; attack suddenly; (of disease) afflict; cause to become suddenly; reach, achieve; agree on (bargain); assume (attitude); find (oil etc.) by drilling; come to attention of or appear to; (of employees) engage in strike; lower or take down (flag, tent, etc.); take specified direction. ● *noun* act of striking; employees' organized refusal to work until grievance is remedied; similar refusal to participate; sudden find or success; attack, esp. from air. □ **on strike** taking part in industrial strike; **strikebreaker** person working or employed in place of strikers; **strike home** deal effective blow; **strike off** remove with stroke, delete; **strike out** hit out, act vigorously, delete; **strike up** start (acquaintance, conversation, etc.), esp. casually, begin playing (tune etc.).

striker *noun* employee on strike; *Football* attacking player positioned forward.

striking *adjective* impressive, noticeable. □ **strikingly** *adverb*.

string ● *noun* twine, narrow cord; length of this or similar material used for tying, holding together, pulling, forming head of racket, etc.; piece of catgut, wire, etc. on musical instrument, producing note by vibration; (in *plural*) stringed instruments in orchestra etc.; (in *plural*) condition or complication attached to offer etc.; set of things strung together; tough side of bean-pod etc. ● *verb* (*past & past participle* **strung**) fit with string(s); thread on string; arrange in or as string; remove strings from (bean-pod etc.). □ **string along** *colloquial* deceive, (often + *with*) keep company (with); **string-course** raised horizontal band of bricks etc. on building; **string up** hang up on strings etc., kill by hanging, (usually as **strung up** *adjective*) make tense.

stringed *adjective* (of musical instrument) having strings.

stringent /ˈstrɪndʒ(ə)nt/ *adjective* (of rules etc.) strict, precise. □ **stringency** *noun*; **stringently** *adverb*.

stringer *noun* longitudinal structural member in framework, esp. of ship or aircraft; *colloquial* freelance newspaper correspondent.

stringy *adjective* (**-ier**, **-iest**) like string, fibrous.

strip[1] ● *verb* (**-pp-**) (often + *of*) remove clothes or covering from, undress; deprive (person) of property or titles; leave bare; (often + *down*) remove accessory fittings of or take apart (machine etc.); remove old paint etc. from with solvent; damage thread of (screw) or teeth of (gearwheel). ● *noun* act of stripping, esp. in striptease; *colloquial* distinctive outfit worn by sports team. □ **strip club** club where striptease is performed; **striptease** entertainment in which performer slowly and erotically undresses.

strip[2] *noun* long narrow piece. □ **strip cartoon** comic strip; **strip light** tubular fluorescent lamp; **tear (person) off a strip** *colloquial* rebuke.

stripe *noun* long narrow band or strip differing in colour or texture from surface on either side of it; *Military* chevron etc. denoting military rank. □ **stripy** *adjective* (**-ier**, **-iest**).

striped *adjective* having stripes.

stripling /ˈstrɪplɪŋ/ *noun* youth not yet fully grown.

stripper *noun* device or solvent for removing paint etc.; performer of striptease.

strive *verb* (**-ving**; *past* **strove** /strəʊv/; *past participle* **striven** /ˈstrɪv(ə)n/) try hard; (often + *with, against*) struggle.

strobe *noun colloquial* stroboscope.

stroboscope /ˈstrəʊbəskəʊp/ *noun* lamp producing regular intermittent flashes. □ **stroboscopic** /-ˈskɒp-/ *adjective*.

strode *past* of STRIDE.

stroke ● *noun* act of striking; sudden disabling attack caused esp. by thrombosis; action or movement, esp. as one of series or in game etc.; slightest action; single complete action of moving wing, oar, etc.; whole motion of piston either way; mode of moving limbs in swimming; single mark made by pen, paint brush, etc.; detail contributing to general effect; sound of striking clock; oarsman nearest stern, who sets time of stroke; act or spell of stroking. ● *verb* (**-king**) pass hand gently along surface of (hair, fur, etc.); act as stroke of (boat, crew). □ **at a stroke** by a single action; **on the stroke of** punctually at; **stroke of (good) luck** unexpected fortunate event.

stroll /strəʊl/ ● *verb* walk in leisurely fashion. ● *noun* leisurely walk. □ **strolling players** *historical* actors etc. going from place to place performing.

strong ● *adjective* (**stronger** /ˈstrɒŋgə/, **strongest** /-gɪst/) physically, morally, or mentally powerful; vigorous, robust; performed with muscular strength; difficult to capture, escape from, etc.; (of suspicion, belief, etc.) firmly held; powerfully affecting senses or mind etc.; (of drink, solution, etc.) with large proportion of alcohol etc.; powerful in numbers or equipment etc.; (of verb) forming inflections by vowel change in root syllable. ● *adverb* strongly. □ **come on strong** act forcefully; **going strong** *colloquial* thriving; **strong-arm** using force; **strongbox** strongly made box for valuables; **stronghold** fortress, centre of support for a cause etc.; **strong language** swearing; **strong-minded** determined; **strongroom** strongly built room for valuables; **strong suit** thing in which one excels. □ **strongish** *adjective*; **strongly** *adverb*.

strontium /ˈstrɒntɪəm/ *noun* soft silver-white metallic element. □ **strontium-90** radioactive isotope of this.

strop ● *noun* device, esp. strip of leather, for sharpening razors; *colloquial* bad temper. ● *verb* (**-pp-**) sharpen on or with strop.

stroppy /ˈstrɒpɪ/ *adjective* (**-ier**, **-iest**) *colloquial* bad-tempered, awkward to deal with.

strove *past* of STRIVE.

struck *past & past participle* of STRIKE.

structuralism *noun* doctrine that structure rather than function is important. □ **structuralist** *noun & adjective*.

structure /ˈstrʌktʃə/ ● *noun* constructed unit, esp. building; way in which thing is constructed; framework. ● *verb* (**-ring**) give structure to, organize. ▫ **structural** *adjective*; **structurally** *adverb*.

strudel /ˈstru:d(ə)l/ *noun* thin leaved pastry filled esp. with apple and baked.

struggle /ˈstrʌg(ə)l/ ● *verb* (**-ling**) violently try to get free; (often + *for, to do*) make great efforts under difficulties; (+ *with, against*) fight against; (+ *along, up*, etc.) make one's way with difficulty; (esp. as **struggling** *adjective*) have difficulty in getting recognition or a living. ● *noun* act or period of struggling; hard or confused contest.

strum ● *verb* (**-mm-**) (often + *on*) play on (stringed or keyboard instrument), esp. carelessly or unskilfully. ● *noun* strumming sound.

strumpet /ˈstrʌmpɪt/ *noun archaic* prostitute.

strung *past & past participle of* STRING.

strut ● *noun* bar in framework to resist pressure; strutting gait. ● *verb* (**-tt-**) walk in stiff pompous way; brace with strut(s).

'struth /stru:θ/ *interjection* (also **'strewth**) *colloquial exclamation of surprise*.

strychnine /ˈstrɪkni:n/ *noun* highly poisonous alkaloid.

stub ● *noun* remnant of pencil, cigarette, etc.; counterfoil of cheque, receipt, etc.; stump. ● *verb* (**-bb-**) strike (one's toe) against something; (usually + *out*) extinguish (cigarette etc.) by pressing lighted end against something.

stubble /ˈstʌb(ə)l/ *noun* cut stalks of corn etc. left in ground after harvest; short stiff hair or bristles, esp. on unshaven face. ▫ **stubbly** *adjective*.

stubborn /ˈstʌbən/ *adjective* obstinate, inflexible. ▫ **stubbornly** *adverb*; **stubbornness** *noun*.

stubby *adjective* (**-ier, -iest**) short and thick.

stucco /ˈstʌkəʊ/ ● *noun* (*plural* **-es**) plaster or cement for coating walls or moulding into architectural decorations. ● *verb* (**-es, -ed**) coat with stucco.

stuck *past & past participle of* STICK². ▫ **stuck-up** *colloquial* conceited, snobbish.

stud¹ ● *noun* large projecting nail, knob, etc. as surface ornament; double button, esp. for use in shirtfront. ● *verb* (**-dd-**) set with studs; (as **studded** *adjective*) (+ *with*) thickly set or strewn with.

stud² *noun* number of horses kept for breeding etc.; place where these are kept; stallion. ▫ **at stud** (of stallion) hired out for breeding. **stud-book** book giving pedigrees of horses; **stud-farm** place where horses are bred; **stud poker** poker with betting after dealing of cards face up.

student /ˈstju:d(ə)nt/ *noun* person who is studying, esp. at place of higher or further education. ▫ **studentship** *noun*.

studio /ˈstju:dɪəʊ/ *noun* (*plural* **-s**) workroom of sculptor, painter, photographer, etc.; place for making films, recordings, or broadcasts. ▫ **studio couch** couch that can be converted into a bed; **studio flat** one-roomed flat.

studious /ˈstju:dɪəs/ *adjective* diligent in study or reading; painstaking. ▫ **studiously** *adverb*.

study /ˈstʌdɪ/ ● *noun* (*plural* **-ies**) acquiring knowledge, esp. from books; (in *plural*) pursuit of academic knowledge; private room for reading, writing, etc.; piece of work, esp. in painting, done as exercise or preliminary experiment; portrayal, esp. in literature, of character, behaviour, etc.; *Music* composition designed to develop player's skill; thing worth observing; thing that is or deserves to be investigated. ● *verb* (**-ies, -ied**) make study of; scrutinize; devote time and thought to understanding subject etc. or achieving desired result; (as **studied** *adjective*) deliberate, affected.

stuff ● *noun* material; fabric; substance or things not needing to be specified; particular knowledge or activity; woollen fabric; nonsense; (**the stuff**) *colloquial* supply, esp. of drink or drugs. ● *verb* pack (receptacle) tightly; (+ *in, into*) force or cram (thing); fill out skin to restore original shape of (bird, animal, etc.); fill (bird, piece of meat, etc.) with mixture, esp. before cooking; (also **stuff oneself**) eat greedily; push, esp. hastily or clumsily; (usually in *passive*; + *up*) block up (nose etc.); *slang derogatory* dispose of. ▫ **get stuffed** *slang* go away, get lost; **stuff and nonsense** something ridiculous or incredible.

stuffing *noun* padding for cushions etc.; mixture used to stuff food, esp. before cooking.

stuffy *adjective* (**-ier, -iest**) (of room etc.) lacking fresh air; dull, uninteresting; conventional, narrow-minded; (of nose etc.) stuffed up. ▫ **stuffily** *adverb*; **stuffiness** *noun*.

stultify /ˈstʌltɪfaɪ/ *verb* (**-ies, -ied**) make ineffective or useless, esp. by routine or from frustration. ▫ **stultification** *noun*.

stumble /ˈstʌmb(ə)l/ ● *verb* (**-ling**) accidentally lurch forward or have partial fall; (often + *along*) walk with repeated stumbles; speak clumsily; (+ *on, upon, across*) find by chance. ● *noun* act of stumbling. ▫ **stumbling block** circumstance causing difficulty or hesitation.

stump ● *noun* part of cut or fallen tree still in ground; similar part (of branch, limb, tooth, etc.) cut off or worn down; *Cricket* each of 3 uprights of wicket. ● *verb* (of question etc.) be too difficult for, baffle; (as **stumped** *adjective*) at a loss; *Cricket* put batsman out by touching stumps with ball while he is out of his crease; walk stiffly or clumsily and noisily; *US* traverse (district) making political speeches. ▫ **stump up** *colloquial* produce or pay over (money required).

stumpy *adjective* (**-ier, -iest**) short and thick. ▫ **stumpiness** *noun*.

stun *verb* (**-nn-**) knock senseless; stupefy; bewilder, shock.

stung *past & past participle of* STING.

stunk *past & past participle of* STINK.

stunner *noun colloquial* stunning person or thing.

stunning *adjective colloquial* extremely attractive or impressive. ▫ **stunningly** *adverb*.

stunt¹ *verb* retard growth or development of.

stunt² *noun* something unusual done to attract attention; trick, daring manoeuvre. ▫ **stunt man** man employed to take actor's place in performing dangerous stunts.

stupefy /ˈstju:pɪfaɪ/ *verb* (**-ies, -ied**) make stupid or insensible; astonish. ▫ **stupefaction** *noun*.

stupendous /stju:ˈpendəs/ *adjective* amazing; of vast size or importance. ▫ **stupendously** *adverb*.

stupid /ˈstju:pɪd/ *adjective* (**-er, -est**) unintelligent, slow-witted; typical of stupid person; uninteresting; in state of stupor. ▫ **stupidity** /-ˈpɪd-/ *noun* (*plural* **-ies**); **stupidly** *adverb*.

stupor /ˈstju:pə/ *noun* dazed or torpid state; utter amazement.

sturdy /ˈstɜ:dɪ/ *adjective* (**-ier, -iest**) robust; strongly built; vigorous. ▫ **sturdily** *adverb*; **sturdiness** *noun*.

sturgeon /ˈstɜ:dʒ(ə)n/ *noun* (*plural* same or **-s**) large edible fish yielding caviar.

stutter /ˈstʌtə/ *verb & noun* stammer.

sty¹ /staɪ/ *noun* (*plural* **sties**) enclosure for pigs; filthy room or dwelling.

sty² /staɪ/ *noun* (also **stye**) (*plural* **sties** or **styes**) inflamed swelling on edge of eyelid.

Stygian /ˈstɪdʒɪən/ *adjective literary* murky, gloomy.

style /staɪl/ ● *noun* kind or sort, esp. in regard to appearance and form (of person, house, etc.); manner of writing, speaking, etc.; distinctive manner of person, artistic school, or period; correct way of designating person or thing; superior quality; fashion in dress etc.; implement for scratching or engraving; part of flower supporting stigma. ● *verb* (**-ling**) design or make etc. in particular style; designate in specified way.

stylish *adjective* fashionable, elegant. □ **stylishly** *adverb*; **stylishness** *noun*.

stylist /'staɪlɪst/ *noun* designer of fashionable styles; hairdresser; stylish writer or performer.

stylistic /staɪ'lɪstɪk/ *adjective* of literary or artistic style. □ **stylistically** *adverb*.

stylized /'staɪlaɪzd/ *adjective* (also **-ised**) painted, drawn, etc. in conventional non-realistic style.

stylus /'staɪləs/ *noun* (*plural* **-luses**) needle-like point for producing or following groove in gramophone record; ancient pointed writing implement.

stymie /'staɪmɪ/ (also **stimy**) ● *noun* (*plural* **-ies**) *Golf* situation where opponent's ball lies between one's ball and the hole; difficult situation. ● *verb* (**stymying** or **stymieing**) obstruct, thwart.

styptic /'stɪptɪk/ ● *adjective* serving to check bleeding. ● *noun* styptic substance.

styrene /'staɪəri:n/ *noun* liquid hydrocarbon used in making plastics etc.

suave /swɑ:v/ *adjective* smooth; polite; sophisticated. □ **suavely** *adverb*; **suavity** *noun*.

sub *colloquial* ● *noun* submarine; subscription; substitute; sub-editor. ● *verb* (**-bb-**) (usually + *for*) act as substitute; sub-edit.

sub- *prefix* at, to, or from lower position; secondary or inferior position; nearly; more or less.

subaltern /'sʌbəlt(ə)n/ *noun Military* officer below rank of captain, esp. second lieutenant.

sub-aqua /sʌb'ækwə/ *adjective* (of sport etc.) taking place under water.

subatomic /sʌbə'tɒmɪk/ *adjective* occurring in, or smaller than, an atom.

subcommittee *noun* committee formed from main committee for special purpose.

subconscious /sʌb'kɒnʃəs/ ● *adjective* of part of mind that is not fully conscious but influences actions etc. ● *noun* this part of the mind. □ **subconsciously** *adverb*.

subcontinent /'sʌbkɒntɪnənt/ *noun* large land mass, smaller than continent.

subcontract ● *verb* /sʌbkən'trækt/ employ another contractor to do (work) as part of larger project; make or carry out subcontract. ● *noun* /sʌb'kɒntrækt/ secondary contract. □ **subcontractor** /-'træktə/ *noun*.

subculture /'sʌbkʌltʃə/ *noun* social group or its culture within a larger culture.

subcutaneous /sʌbkju:'teɪnɪəs/ *adjective* under the skin.

subdivide /sʌbdɪ'vaɪd/ *verb* (**-ding**) divide again after first division. □ **subdivision** /'sʌbdɪvɪʒ(ə)n/ *noun*.

subdue /səb'dju:/ *verb* (**-dues**, **-dued**, **-duing**) conquer, suppress; tame; (as **subdued** *adjective*) softened, lacking in intensity.

sub-editor /sʌb'edɪtə/ *noun* assistant editor; person who prepares material for printing. □ **sub-edit** *verb* (**-t-**).

subheading /'sʌbhedɪŋ/ *noun* subordinate heading or title.

subhuman /sʌb'hju:mən/ *adjective* (of behaviour, intelligence, etc.) less than human.

subject ● *noun* /'sʌbdʒɪkt/ theme of discussion, description, or representation; (+ *for*) person, circumstance, etc. giving rise to specified feeling, action, etc.; branch of study; word or phrase representing person or thing carrying out action of verb (see panel); person other than monarch living under government; *Philosophy* thinking or feeling entity, conscious self; *Music* theme, leading motif. ● *adjective* /'sʌbdʒɪkt/ (+ *to*) conditional on, liable or exposed to; owing obedience to government etc. ● *adverb* /'sʌbdʒɪkt/ (+ *to*) conditionally on. ● *verb* /səb'dʒekt/ (+ *to*) make liable or expose to; (usually + *to*) subdue (person, nation, etc.) to superior will. □ **subjection** *noun*.

subjective /səb'dʒektɪv/ *adjective* (of art, written history, opinion, etc.) not impartial or literal; esp. *Philosophy* of individual consciousness or perception; imaginary, partial, distorted; *Grammar* of the subject. □ **subjectively** *adverb*; **subjectivity** /sʌbdʒek'tɪv-/ *noun*.

subjoin /sʌb'dʒɔɪn/ *verb* add (illustration, anecdote, etc.) at the end.

sub judice /sʌb 'dʒu:dɪsɪ/ *adjective Law* under judicial consideration and therefore prohibited from public discussion. [Latin]

subjugate /'sʌbdʒʊgeɪt/ *verb* (**-ting**) conquer, bring into subjection. □ **subjugation** *noun*; **subjugator** *noun*.

subjunctive /səb'dʒʌŋktɪv/ *Grammar* ● *adjective* (of mood) expressing wish, supposition, or possibility. ● *noun* subjunctive mood or form.

sublease ● *noun* /'sʌbli:s/ lease granted by tenant to subtenant. ● *verb* /sʌb'li:s/ (**-sing**) lease to subtenant.

sublet /sʌb'let/ *verb* (**-tt-**; *past & past participle* **-let**) lease to subtenant.

sub-lieutenant /sʌblef'tenənt/ *noun* officer ranking next below lieutenant.

sublimate ● *verb* /'sʌblɪmeɪt/ (**-ting**) divert energy of (primitive impulse etc.) into socially more acceptable activity; sublime (substance); refine, purify. ● *noun* /'sʌblɪmət/ sublimated substance. □ **sublimation** *noun*.

sublime /sə'blaɪm/ ● *adjective* (**-r**, **-st**) of most exalted kind; awe-inspiring; arrogantly undisturbed. ● *verb* (**-ming**) convert (substance) from solid into vapour by heat (and usually allow to solidify again); make sublime; become pure (as if) by sublimation. □ **sublimely** *adverb*; **sublimity** /-'lɪm-/ *noun*.

subliminal /səb'lɪmɪn(ə)l/ *adjective Psychology* below threshold of sensation or consciousness; too faint or rapid to be consciously perceived. □ **subliminally** *adverb*.

sub-machine-gun /sʌbmə'ʃi:ngʌn/ *noun* hand-held lightweight machine-gun.

submarine /sʌbmə'ri:n/ ● *noun* vessel, esp. armed warship, which can be submerged and navigated under water. ● *adjective* existing, occurring, done, or used below surface of sea. □ **submariner** /-'mærɪnə/ *noun*.

submerge /səb'mɜ:dʒ/ *verb* (**-ging**) place, go, or dive beneath water; overwhelm with work, problems, etc. □ **submergence** *noun*; **submersion** *noun*.

submersible /səb'mɜ:sɪb(ə)l/ ● *noun* submarine operating under water for short periods. ● *adjective* capable of submerging.

submicroscopic /sʌbmaɪkrə'skɒpɪk/ *adjective* too small to be seen by ordinary microscope.

submission /səb'mɪʃ(ə)n/ *noun* submitting, being submitted; thing submitted; submissive attitude etc.

submissive /səb'mɪsɪv/ *adjective* humble, obedient. □ **submissively** *adverb*; **submissiveness** *noun*.

submit /səbˈmɪt/ *verb* (**-tt-**) (often + *to*) cease resistance, yield; present for consideration; (+ *to*) subject or be subjected to (process, treatment, etc.); *Law* argue, suggest.

subnormal /sʌbˈnɔːm(ə)l/ *adjective* below or less than normal, esp. in intelligence.

subordinate ● *adjective* /səˈbɔːdɪnət/ (usually + *to*) of inferior importance or rank; secondary, subservient. ● *noun* /səˈbɔːdɪnət/ person working under authority of another. ● *verb* /səˈbɔːdɪneɪt/ (**-ting**) (usually + *to*) make or treat as subordinate. □ **subordinate clause** clause serving as noun, adjective, or adverb within sentence. □ **subordination** *noun*.

suborn /səˈbɔːn/ *verb* induce esp. by bribery to commit perjury or other crime.

subpoena /səˈpiːnə/ ● *noun* writ ordering person's attendance in law court. ● *verb* (*past & past participle* **-naed** or **-na'd**) serve subpoena on.

sub rosa /sʌb ˈrəʊzə/ *adjective & adverb* in confidence or in secret. [Latin]

subscribe /səbˈskraɪb/ *verb* (**-bing**) (usually + *to, for*) pay (specified sum) esp. regularly for membership of organization or receipt of publication etc.; contribute to fund, for cause, etc.; (usually + *to*) agree with (opinion etc.). □ **subscribe to** arrange to receive (periodical etc.) regularly.

subscriber *noun* person who subscribes, esp. person paying regular sum for hire of telephone line. □ **subscriber trunk dialling** making of trunk calls by subscriber without assistance of operator.

subscript /ˈsʌbskrɪpt/ ● *adjective* written or printed below the line. ● *noun* subscript number etc.

subscription /səbˈskrɪpʃ(ə)n/ *noun* act of subscribing; money subscribed; membership fee, esp. paid regularly.

subsequent /ˈsʌbsɪkwənt/ *adjective* (usually + *to*) following specified or implied event. □ **subsequently** *adverb*.

subservient /səbˈsɜːvɪənt/ *adjective* servile; (usually + *to*) instrumental, subordinate. □ **subservience** *noun*.

subside /səbˈsaɪd/ *verb* (**-ding**) become tranquil; diminish; (of water etc.) sink; (of ground) cave in. □ **subsidence** /-ˈsaɪd-, ˈsʌbsɪd-/ *noun*.

subsidiary /səbˈsɪdɪərɪ/ ● *adjective* supplementary; additional; (of company) controlled by another. ● *noun* (*plural* **-ies**) subsidiary company, person, or thing.

subsidize /ˈsʌbsɪdaɪz/ *verb* (also **-ise**) (**-zing** or **-sing**) pay subsidy to; support by subsidies.

subsidy /ˈsʌbsɪdɪ/ *noun* (*plural* **-ies**) money contributed esp. by state to keep prices at desired level; any monetary grant.

subsist /səbˈsɪst/ *verb* (often + *on*) keep oneself alive; be kept alive; remain in being, exist.

subsistence *noun* subsisting; means of supporting life; minimal level of existence, income, etc. □ **subsistence farming** farming in which almost all produce is consumed by farmer's household.

subsoil /ˈsʌbsɔɪl/ *noun* soil just below surface soil.

subsonic /sʌbˈsɒnɪk/ *adjective* of speeds less than that of sound.

substance /ˈsʌbst(ə)ns/ *noun* particular kind of material; reality, solidity; essence of what is spoken or written; wealth and possessions. □ **in substance** generally, essentially.

substandard /sʌbˈstændəd/ *adjective* of lower than desired standard.

substantial /səbˈstænʃ(ə)l/ *adjective* of real importance or value; large in size or amount; of solid structure; commercially successful; wealthy; largely true; real; existing. □ **substantially** *adverb*.

substantiate /səbˈstænʃɪeɪt/ *verb* (**-ting**) support or prove truth of (charge, claim, etc.). □ **substantiation** *noun*.

substantive /ˈsʌbstəntɪv/ ● *adjective* actual, real, permanent; substantial. ● *noun* noun. □ **substantively** *adverb*.

substitute /ˈsʌbstɪtjuːt/ ● *noun* person or thing acting or serving in place of another; artificial alternative to a food etc. ● *verb* (**-ting**) (often + *for*) put in place of another; act as substitute for. ● *adjective* acting as substitute. □ **substitution** *noun*.

substratum /ˈsʌbstrɑːtəm/ *noun* (*plural* **-ta**) underlying layer.

subsume /səbˈsjuːm/ *verb* (**-ming**) (usually + *under*) include under particular rule, class, etc.

subtenant /ˈsʌbtenənt/ *noun* person renting room or house etc. from its tenant. □ **subtenancy** *noun* (*plural* **-ies**).

subtend /sʌbˈtend/ *verb* (of line) be opposite (angle, arc).

subterfuge /ˈsʌbtəfjuːdʒ/ *noun* attempt to avoid blame etc., esp. by lying or deceit.

subterranean /sʌbtəˈreɪnɪən/ *adjective* underground.

subtext *noun* underlying theme.

subtitle /ˈsʌbtaɪt(ə)l/ ● *noun* subordinate or additional title of book etc.; caption of cinema film, esp. translating dialogue. ● *verb* (**-ling**) provide with subtitle(s).

subtle /ˈsʌt(ə)l/ *adjective* (**-r**, **-st**) hard to detect or describe; (of scent, colour, etc.) faint, delicate; ingenious, perceptive. □ **subtlety** *noun* (*plural* **-ies**); **subtly** *adverb*.

subtract /səbˈtrækt/ *verb* (often + *from*) deduct (number etc.) from another. □ **subtraction** *noun*.

subtropical /sʌbˈtrɒpɪk(ə)l/ *adjective* bordering on the tropics; characteristic of such regions.

suburb /ˈsʌbɜːb/ *noun* outlying district of city.

suburban /səˈbɜːbən/ *adjective* of or characteristic of suburbs; *derogatory* provincial in outlook. □ **suburbanite** *noun*.

suburbia /səˈbɜːbɪə/ *noun usually derogatory* suburbs and their inhabitants etc.

Subject

The subject of a sentence is the person or thing that carried out the action of the verb and can be found by asking the question 'who or what?' before the verb, e.g.

The goalkeeper *made a stunning save.*
Hundreds of books *are now available on CD-ROM.*

In a passive construction, the subject of the sentence is in fact the person or thing to which the action of the verb is done, e.g.

I *was hit by a ball.*
Has the programme *been broadcast yet?*

subvention /səb'venʃ(ə)n/ *noun* subsidy.

subversive /səb'vɜ:sɪv/ ● *adjective* seeking to overthrow (esp. government). ● *noun* subversive person. □ **subversion** *noun*; **subversively** *adverb*; **subversiveness** *noun*.

subvert /səb'vɜ:t/ *verb* overthrow or weaken (government etc.).

subway /'sʌbweɪ/ *noun* underground passage, esp. for pedestrians; *US* underground railway.

subzero /sʌb'zɪərəʊ/ *adjective* (esp. of temperature) lower than zero.

succeed /sək'si:d/ *verb* (often + *in*) have success; prosper; follow in order; (often + *to*) come into inheritance, office, title, or property.

success /sək'ses/ *noun* accomplishment of aim; favourable outcome; attainment of wealth, fame, etc.; successful person or thing. □ **successful** *adjective*; **successfully** *adverb*.

succession /sək'seʃ(ə)n/ *noun* following in order; series of things or people following one another; succeeding to inheritance, office, or esp. throne; right to succeed to one of these, set of people with such right. □ **in succession** one after another; **in succession to** as successor of.

successive /sək'sesɪv/ *adjective* following in succession, consecutive. □ **successively** *adverb*.

successor /sək'sesə/ *noun* (often + *to*) person or thing that succeeds another.

succinct /sək'sɪŋkt/ *adjective* brief, concise. □ **succinctly** *adverb*; **succinctness** *noun*.

succour /'sʌkə/ (*US* **succor**) *archaic or formal* ● *noun* help, esp. in time of need. ● *verb* give succour to.

succulent /'sʌkjʊlənt/ ● *adjective* juicy; (of plant) thick and fleshy. ● *noun* succulent plant. □ **succulence** *noun*.

succumb /sə'kʌm/ *verb* (usually + *to*) give way; be overcome; die.

such ● *adjective* (often + *as*) of kind or degree specified or suggested; so great or extreme; unusually, abnormally. ● *pronoun* such person(s) or thing(s). □ **as such** as being what has been specified; **such-and-such** particular but unspecified; **suchlike** *colloquial* of such kind.

suck ● *verb* draw (liquid) into mouth by suction; draw liquid from in this way; roll tongue round (sweet etc.) in mouth; make sucking action or noise; (usually + *down*) engulf or drown in sucking movement. ● *noun* act or period of sucking. □ **suck in** absorb, involve (person); **suck up** (often + *to*) *colloquial* behave in a servile way, absorb.

sucker *noun* person easily duped or cheated; (+ *for*) person susceptible to; rubber etc. cap adhering by suction; similar part of plant or animal; shoot springing from plant's root below ground.

suckle /'sʌk(ə)l/ *verb* (**-ling**) feed (young) from breast or udder.

suckling /'sʌklɪŋ/ *noun* unweaned child or animal.

sucrose /'su:krəʊz/ *noun* kind of sugar obtained from cane, beet, etc.

suction /'sʌkʃ(ə)n/ *noun* sucking; production of partial vacuum so that external atmospheric pressure forces fluid into vacant space or causes adhesion of surfaces.

Sudanese /su:də'ni:z/ ● *adjective* of Sudan. ● *noun* (*plural* same) native or national of Sudan.

sudden /'sʌd(ə)n/ *adjective* done or occurring unexpectedly or abruptly. □ **all of a sudden** suddenly. □ **suddenly** *adverb*; **suddenness** *noun*.

sudorific /su:də'rɪfɪk/ ● *adjective* causing sweating. ● *noun* sudorific drug.

suds *plural noun* froth of soap and water. □ **sudsy** *adjective*.

sue *verb* (**sues**, **sued**, **suing**) begin lawsuit against; (often + *for*) make application to law court for compensation etc.; (often + *to*, *for*) make plea to person for favour.

suede /sweɪd/ *noun* leather with flesh side rubbed into nap.

suet /'su:ɪt/ *noun* hard fat surrounding kidneys of cattle and sheep, used in cooking etc. □ **suety** *adjective*.

suffer /'sʌfə/ *verb* undergo pain, grief, etc.; undergo or be subjected to (pain, loss, punishment, grief, etc.); tolerate. □ **sufferer** *noun*; **suffering** *noun*.

sufferance *noun* tacit permission or toleration. □ **on sufferance** tolerated but not supported.

suffice /sə'faɪs/ *verb* (**-cing**) be enough; meet needs of. □ **suffice it to say** I shall say only this.

sufficiency /sə'fɪʃənsɪ/ *noun* (*plural* **-ies**) (often + *of*) sufficient amount.

sufficient /sə'fɪʃ(ə)nt/ *adjective* sufficing; adequate. □ **sufficiently** *adverb*.

suffix /'sʌfɪks/ ● *noun* letter(s) added to end of word to form derivative. ● *verb* add as suffix.

suffocate /'sʌfəkeɪt/ *verb* (**-ting**) kill, stifle, or choke by stopping breathing, esp. by fumes etc.; be or feel suffocated. □ **suffocating** *adjective*; **suffocation** *noun*.

suffragan /'sʌfrəgən/ *noun* bishop assisting diocesan bishop.

suffrage /'sʌfrɪdʒ/ *noun* right of voting in political elections.

suffragette /sʌfrə'dʒet/ *noun historical* woman who agitated for women's suffrage.

suffuse /sə'fju:z/ *verb* (**-sing**) (of colour, moisture, etc.) spread throughout or over from within. □ **suffusion** /-ʒ(ə)n/ *noun*.

sugar /'ʃʊgə/ ● *noun* sweet crystalline substance obtained from sugar cane and sugar beet, used in cookery, confectionery, etc.; *Chemistry* soluble usually sweet crystalline carbohydrate, e.g. glucose; *esp. US colloquial* darling (as term of address). ● *verb* sweeten or coat with sugar. □ **sugar beet** white beet yielding sugar; **sugar cane** tall stout perennial tropical grass yielding sugar; **sugar-daddy** *slang* elderly man who lavishes gifts on young woman; **sugar loaf** conical moulded mass of hard refined sugar.

sugary *adjective* containing or resembling sugar; cloying, sentimental. □ **sugariness** *noun*.

suggest /sə'dʒest/ *verb* (often + *that*) propose (theory, plan, etc.); hint at; evoke (idea etc.); (**suggest itself**) (of idea etc.) come into person's mind.

suggestible *adjective* capable of being influenced by suggestion. □ **suggestibility** *noun*.

suggestion /sə'dʒestʃ(ə)n/ *noun* suggesting; thing suggested; slight trace, hint; insinuation of belief or impulse into the mind.

suggestive /sə'dʒestɪv/ *adjective* (usually + *of*) conveying a suggestion; (of remark, joke, etc.) suggesting something indecent. □ **suggestively** *adverb*.

suicidal /su:ɪ'saɪd(ə)l/ *adjective* (of person) liable to commit suicide; of or tending to suicide; destructive to one's own interests. □ **suicidally** *adverb*.

suicide /'su:ɪsaɪd/ *noun* intentional self-killing; person who commits suicide; action destructive to one's own interests etc.

sui generis /sju:aɪ'dʒenərɪs/ *adjective* of its own kind, unique. [Latin]

suit /su:t, sju:t/ ● *noun* set of usually matching clothes consisting usually of jacket and trousers or skirt; clothing for particular purpose; any of the 4 sets into which pack of cards is divided; lawsuit. ● *verb* go well with (person's appearance); meet requirements of; (**suit oneself**) do as one chooses; be in harmony with; make fitting; be convenient; adapt;

(as **suited** *adjective*) appropriate, well-fitted. ◻ **suitcase** flat case for carrying clothes, usually with hinged lid.

suitable *adjective* (usually + *to*, *for*) well-fitted for purpose; appropriate to occasion. ◻ **suitability** *noun*; **suitably** *adverb*.

suite /swi:t/ *noun* set of rooms, furniture, etc.; *Music* set of instrumental pieces.

suitor /'su:tə/ *noun* man who woos woman; plaintiff or petitioner in lawsuit.

sulfur etc. *US* = SULPHUR etc.

sulk ● *verb* be sulky. ● *noun* (also **the sulks**) fit of sullen silence.

sulky /'sʌlkɪ/ *adjective* (**-ier**, **-iest**) sullen and unsociable from resentment or ill temper. ◻ **sulkily** *adverb*.

sullen /'sʌlən/ *adjective* sulky, morose. ◻ **sullenly** *adverb*; **sullenness** *noun*.

sully /'sʌlɪ/ *verb* (**-ies**, **-ied**) spoil purity or splendour of (reputation etc.).

sulphate /'sʌlfeɪt/ *noun* (*US* **sulfate**) salt or ester of sulphuric acid.

sulphide /'sʌlfaɪd/ *noun* (*US* **sulfide**) binary compound of sulphur.

sulphite /'sʌlfaɪt/ *noun* (*US* **sulfite**) salt or ester of sulphurous acid.

sulphonamide /sʌl'fɒnəmaɪd/ *noun* (*US* **sulfonamide**) kind of antibiotic drug containing sulphur.

sulphur /'sʌlfə/ *noun* (*US* **sulfur**) pale yellow non-metallic element burning with blue flame and stifling smell. ◻ **sulphur dioxide** colourless pungent gas formed by burning sulphur in air and dissolving it in water.

sulphuric /sʌl'fjʊərɪk/ *adjective* (*US* **sulfuric**) of or containing sulphur with valency of 6. ◻ **sulphuric acid** dense highly corrosive oily acid.

sulphurous /'sʌlfərəs/ *adjective* (*US* **sulfurous**) of or like sulphur; containing sulphur with valency of 4. ◻ **sulphurous acid** unstable weak acid used e.g. as bleaching agent.

sultan /'sʌlt(ə)n/ *noun* Muslim sovereign.

sultana /sʌl'tɑ:nə/ *noun* seedless raisin; sultan's wife, mother, concubine, or daughter.

sultanate /'sʌltəneɪt/ *noun* position of or territory ruled by sultan.

sultry /'sʌltrɪ/ *adjective* (**-ier**, **-iest**) (of weather) oppressively hot; (of person) passionate, sensual.

sum ● *noun* total resulting from addition; amount of money; arithmetical problem; (esp. in *plural*) *colloquial* arithmetic work, esp. elementary. ● *verb* (**-mm-**) find sum of. ◻ **in sum** briefly, to sum up; **summing-up** judge's review of evidence given to jury, recapitulation of main points of argument etc.; **sum up** (esp. of judge) give summing-up, form or express opinion of (person, situation, etc.), summarize.

sumac /'su:mæk/ *noun* (also **sumach**) shrub with reddish fruits used as spice; dried and ground leaves of this for use in tanning and dyeing.

summarize /'sʌməraɪz/ *verb* (also **-ise**) (**-zing** or **-sing**) make or be summary of.

summary /'sʌmərɪ/ ● *noun* (*plural* **-ies**) brief account giving chief points. ● *adjective* brief, without details or formalities. ◻ **summarily** *adverb*.

summation /sə'meɪʃ(ə)n/ *noun* finding of total or sum; summarizing.

summer /'sʌmə/ *noun* warmest season of year; (often + *of*) mature stage of life etc. ◻ **summer house** light building in garden etc. for use in summer; **summer pudding** dessert of soft fruit pressed in bread casing; **summer school** course of lectures etc. held in summer, esp. at university; **summer time** period from March to October when clocks etc. are advanced one hour; **summertime** season or period of summer. ◻ **summery** *adjective*.

summit /'sʌmɪt/ *noun* highest point, top; highest level of achievement or status; (in full **summit conference**, **meeting**, etc.) discussion between heads of governments.

summon /'sʌmən/ *verb* order to come or appear, esp. in lawcourt; (usually + *to do*) call on; call together; (often + *up*) gather (courage, resources, etc.).

summons /'sʌmənz/ ● *noun* (*plural* **summonses**) authoritative call to attend or do something, esp. to appear in court. ● *verb esp. Law* serve with summons.

sumo /'su:məʊ/ *noun* Japanese wrestling in which only soles of feet may touch ground.

sump *noun* casing holding oil in internal-combustion engine; pit, well, etc. for collecting superfluous liquid.

sumptuary /'sʌmptʃʊərɪ/ *adjective Law* regulating (esp. private) expenditure.

sumptuous /'sʌmptʃʊəs/ *adjective* costly, splendid, magnificent. ◻ **sumptuously** *adverb*; **sumptuousness** *noun*.

Sun. *abbreviation* Sunday.

sun ● *noun* the star round which the earth travels and from which it receives light and warmth; this light or warmth; any star. ● *verb* (**-nn-**) (often **sun oneself**) expose to sun. ◻ **sunbathe** bask in sun, esp. to tan one's body; **sunbeam** ray of sunlight; **sunblock** lotion protecting skin from sun; **sunburn** inflammation of skin from exposure to sun; **sunburnt** affected by sunburn; **sundial** instrument showing time by shadow of pointer in sunlight; **sundown** sunset; **sunflower** tall plant with large golden-rayed flowers; **sunglasses** tinted spectacles to protect eyes from glare; **sunlamp** lamp giving ultraviolet rays for therapy or artificial suntan; **sunlight** light from sun; **sunlit** illuminated by sun; **sun lounge** room with large windows etc. to receive much sunlight; **sunrise** (time of) sun's rising; **sunroof** opening panel in car's roof; **sunset** (time of) sun's setting; **sunshade** parasol, awning; **sunshine** sunlight, area illuminated by it, fine weather, cheerfulness; **sunspot** dark patch on sun's surface; **sunstroke** acute prostration from excessive heat of sun; **suntan** brownish skin colour caused by exposure to sun; **suntrap** sunny place, esp. sheltered from wind; **sun-up** *esp. US* sunrise.

sundae /'sʌndeɪ/ *noun* ice cream with fruit, nuts, syrup, etc.

Sunday /'sʌndeɪ/ *noun* day of week following Saturday; Christian day of worship; *colloquial* newspaper published on Sundays. ◻ **month of Sundays** *colloquial* very long period; **Sunday school** religious class held on Sundays for children.

sunder /'sʌndə/ *verb literary* sever, keep apart.

sundry /'sʌndrɪ/ ● *adjective* various, several. ● *noun* (*plural* **-ies**) (in *plural*) oddments, accessories, etc. not mentioned individually. ◻ **all and sundry** everyone.

sung *past participle* of SING.

sunk *past & past participle* of SINK.

sunken *adjective* that has sunk; lying below general surface; (of eyes, cheeks, etc.) shrunken, hollow.

Sunni /'sʌnɪ/ *noun* (*plural* same or **-s**) one of two main branches of Islam; adherent of this.

sunny *adjective* (**-ier**, **-iest**) bright with or warmed by sunlight; cheerful. ◻ **sunnily** *adverb*; **sunniness** *noun*.

sup[1] ● *verb* (**-pp-**) drink by sips or spoonfuls; *esp. Northern English colloquial* drink (alcohol). ● *noun* sip of liquid.

sup[2] *verb* (**-pp-**) *archaic* take supper.

super /'su:pə/ ● *adjective colloquial* excellent, unusually good. ● *noun colloquial* superintendent; supernumerary.

super- *combining form* on top, over, beyond; to extreme degree; extra good or large of its kind; of higher kind.

superannuate /su:pər'ænjʊeɪt/ *verb* (**-ting**) pension (person) off; dismiss or discard as too old; (as **superannuated** *adjective*) too old for work.

superannuation *noun* pension; payment made to obtain pension.

superb /su:'pɜ:b/ *adjective colloquial* excellent; magnificent. □ **superbly** *adverb*.

supercargo /'su:pəkɑ:gəʊ/ *noun* (*plural* **-es**) person in merchant ship managing sales etc. of cargo.

supercharge /'su:pətʃɑ:dʒ/ *verb* (**-ging**) (usually + *with*) charge (atmosphere etc.) with energy, emotion, etc.; use supercharger on.

supercharger *noun* device forcing extra air or fuel into internal-combustion engine.

supercilious /su:pə'sɪlɪəs/ *adjective* haughtily contemptuous. □ **superciliously** *adverb*; **superciliousness** *noun*.

supererogation /su:pərerə'geɪʃ(ə)n/ *noun* doing of more than duty requires.

superficial /su:pə'fɪʃ(ə)l/ *adjective* of or on the surface; lacking depth; swift, cursory; apparent, not real; (esp. of person) of shallow feelings etc. □ **superficiality** /-ʃɪ'æl-/ *noun*; **superficially** *adverb*.

superfluity /su:pə'flu:ɪtɪ/ *noun* (*plural* **-ies**) being superfluous; superfluous amount or thing.

superfluous /su:'pɜ:flʊəs/ *adjective* more than is needed or wanted; useless.

supergrass /'su:pəgrɑ:s/ *noun colloquial* police informer implicating many people.

superhuman /su:pə'hju:mən/ *adjective* exceeding normal human capacity or power.

superimpose /su:pərɪm'pəʊz/ *verb* (**-sing**) (usually + *on*) place (thing) on or above something else. □ **superimposition** /-pə'zɪʃ(ə)n/ *noun*.

superintend /su:pərɪn'tend/ *verb* manage, supervise (work etc.). □ **superintendence** *noun*.

superintendent /su:pərɪn'tend(ə)nt/ *noun* police officer above rank of chief inspector; person who superintends; director of institution etc.

superior /su:'pɪərɪə/ ● *adjective* higher in rank, quality, etc.; high-quality; supercilious; (often + *to*) better or greater in some respect; written or printed above the line. ● *noun* person superior to another, esp. in rank; head of monastery etc. □ **superiority** /-'ɒr-/ *noun*.

superlative /su:'pɜ:lətɪv/ ● *adjective* of highest degree; excellent; *Grammar* (of adjective or adverb) expressing highest or very high degree of quality etc. denoted by simple word. ● *noun Grammar* superlative expression or word; (in *plural*) high praise, exaggerated language.

superman *noun colloquial* man of exceptional powers or achievement.

supermarket /'su:pəmɑ:kɪt/ *noun* large self-service store selling food, household goods, etc.

supernatural /su:pə'nætʃər(ə)l/ ● *adjective* not attributable to, or explicable by, natural or physical laws; magical; mystical. ● *noun* (**the supernatural**) supernatural forces etc. □ **supernaturally** *adverb*.

supernova /su:pə'nəʊvə/ *noun* (*plural* **-vae** /-vi:/ or **-vas**) star that suddenly increases very greatly in brightness.

supernumerary /su:pə'nju:mərərɪ/ ● *adjective* in excess of normal number; engaged for extra work; (of actor) with non-speaking part. ● *noun* (*plural* **-ies**) supernumerary person or thing.

superphosphate /su:pə'fɒsfeɪt/ *noun* fertilizer made from phosphate rock.

superpower /'su:pəpaʊə/ *noun* extremely powerful nation.

superscript /'su:pəskrɪpt/ ● *adjective* written or printed above. ● *noun* superscript number or symbol.

supersede /su:pə'si:d/ *verb* (**-ding**) take place of; put or use another in place of. □ **supersession** /-'seʃ-/ *noun*.

supersonic /su:pə'sɒnɪk/ *adjective* of or having speed greater than that of sound. □ **supersonically** *adverb*.

superstar /'su:pəstɑ:/ *noun* extremely famous or renowned actor, musician, etc.

superstition /su:pə'stɪʃ(ə)n/ *noun* belief in the supernatural; irrational fear of the unknown or mysterious; practice, belief, or religion based on this. □ **superstitious** *adjective*.

superstore /'su:pəstɔ:/ *noun* very large supermarket.

superstructure /'su:pəstrʌktʃə/ *noun* structure built on top of another; upper part of building, ship, etc.

supertanker /'su:pətæŋkə/ *noun* very large tanker.

supertax /'su:pətæks/ *noun* surtax.

supervene /su:pə'vi:n/ *verb* (**-ning**) *formal* occur as interruption in or change from some state. □ **supervention** *noun*.

supervise /'su:pəvaɪz/ *verb* (**-sing**) oversee, superintend. □ **supervision** /-'vɪʒ(ə)n/ *noun*; **supervisor** *noun*; **supervisory** *adjective*.

superwoman *noun colloquial* woman of exceptional ability or power.

supine /'su:paɪn/ ● *adjective* lying face upwards; inactive, indolent. ● *noun* type of Latin verbal noun.

supper /'sʌpə/ *noun* meal taken late in day, esp. evening meal less formal and substantial than dinner.

supplant /sə'plɑ:nt/ *verb* take the place of, esp. by underhand means.

supple /'sʌp(ə)l/ *adjective* (**-r**, **-st**) easily bent, pliant, flexible. □ **suppleness** *noun*.

supplement ● *noun* /'sʌplɪmənt/ thing or part added to improve or provide further information; separate section of newspaper etc. ● *verb* /'sʌplɪment/ provide supplement for. □ **supplemental** /-'ment(ə)l/ *adjective*; **supplementary** /-'mentərɪ/ *adjective*; **supplementation** *noun*.

suppliant /'sʌplɪənt/ ● *adjective* supplicating. ● *noun* humble petitioner.

supplicate /'sʌplɪkeɪt/ *verb* (**-ting**) *literary* make humble petition to or for. □ **supplicant** *noun*; **supplication** *noun*; **supplicatory** /-kətərɪ/ *adjective*.

supply /sə'plaɪ/ ● *verb* (**-ies**, **-ied**) provide (thing needed); (often + *with*) provide (person etc. with something); make up for (deficiency etc.). ● *noun* (*plural* **-ies**) provision of what is needed; stock, store; (in *plural*) provisions, equipment, etc. for army, expedition, etc.; person, esp. teacher, acting as temporary substitute. □ **supply and demand** quantities available and required, as factors regulating price. □ **supplier** *noun*.

support /sə'pɔ:t/ ● *verb* carry all or part of weight of; keep from falling, sinking, or failing; provide for; strengthen, encourage; give help or corroboration to; speak in favour of; take secondary part to (actor etc.); perform secondary act to (main act) at pop concert. ● *noun* supporting, being supported; person or thing that supports. □ **in support of** so as to support. □ **supportive** *adjective*; **supportively** *adverb*; **supportiveness** *noun*.

supporter *noun* person or thing that supports particular cause, team, sport, etc.

suppose /sə'pəʊz/ *verb* **(-sing)** (often + *that*) assume, be inclined to think; take as possibility or hypothesis; require as condition; (as **supposed** *adjective*) presumed. □ **be supposed to** be expected or required to; (in negative) ought not, not be allowed to; **I suppose so** *expression of hesitant agreement.*
supposedly /sə'pəʊzɪdlɪ/ *adverb* as is generally believed.
supposition /sʌpə'zɪʃ(ə)n/ *noun* what is supposed or assumed.
suppositious /sʌpə'zɪʃəs/ *adjective* hypothetical.
suppository /sə'pɒzɪtərɪ/ *noun* (*plural* **-ies**) solid medical preparation put into rectum or vagina to melt.
suppress /sə'pres/ *verb* put an end to; prevent (information, feelings, etc.) from being seen, heard, or known; *Electricity* partially or wholly eliminate (interference etc.), equip (device) to reduce interference due to it. □ **suppressible** *adjective*; **suppression** *noun*; **suppressor** *noun*.
suppurate /'sʌpjʊreɪt/ *verb* **(-ting)** form or secrete pus; fester. □ **suppuration** *noun*.
supra- *prefix* above.
supranational /su:prə'næʃən(ə)l/ *adjective* transcending national limits.
supremacy /su:'preməsɪ/ *noun* (*plural* **-ies**) being supreme; highest authority.
supreme /su:'pri:m/ *adjective* highest in authority or rank; greatest, most important; (of penalty, sacrifice, etc.) involving death. □ **supremely** *adverb*.
supremo /su:'pri:məʊ/ *noun* (*plural* **-s**) supreme leader.
surcharge /'sɜ:tʃɑ:dʒ/ ● *noun* additional charge or payment. ● *verb* **(-ging)** exact surcharge from.
surd ● *adjective* (of number) irrational. ● *noun* surd number.
sure /ʃʊə/ ● *adjective* (often + *of*, *that*) convinced; having or seeming to have adequate reason for belief; (+ *of*) confident in anticipation or knowledge of; reliable, unfailing; (+ *to do*) certain; undoubtedly true or truthful. ● *adverb colloquial* certainly. □ **make sure** make or become certain, ensure; **sure-fire** *colloquial* certain to succeed; **sure-footed** never stumbling; **to be sure** admittedly, indeed, certainly. **sureness** *noun*.
surely *adverb* with certainty or safety; *added to statement to express strong belief in its correctness.*
surety /'ʃu:ərətɪ/ *noun* (*plural* **-ies**) money given as guarantee of performance etc.; person taking responsibility for another's debt, obligation, etc.
surf ● *noun* foam of sea breaking on rock or (esp. shallow) shore. ● *verb* engage in surfing. □ **surfboard** long narrow board used in surfing. □ **surfer** *noun*.
surface /'sɜ:fɪs/ ● *noun* the outside of a thing; any of the limits of a solid; top of liquid, soil, etc.; outward or superficial aspect; *Geometry* thing with length and breadth but no thickness. ● *verb* **(-cing)** give (special) surface to (road, paper, etc.); rise or bring to surface; become visible or known; *colloquial* wake up, get up. □ **surface mail** mail not carried by air; **surface tension** tension of surface of liquid, tending to minimize its surface area.
surfeit /'sɜ:fɪt/ ● *noun* excess, esp. in eating or drinking; resulting fullness. ● *verb* **(-t-)** overfeed; (+ *with*) (cause to) be wearied through excess.
surfing *noun* sport of riding surf on board.
surge ● *noun* sudden rush; heavy forward or upward motion; sudden increase (in price etc.); sudden but brief increase in pressure, voltage, etc.; surging motion of sea, waves, etc. ● *verb* **(-ging)** move suddenly and powerfully forwards; (of sea etc.) swell.
surgeon /'sɜ:dʒ(ə)n/ *noun* medical practitioner qualified to practise surgery; naval or military medical officer.
surgery /'sɜ:dʒərɪ/ *noun* (*plural* **-ies**) manual or instrumental treatment of injuries or disorders of body; place where or time when doctor, dentist, etc. gives advice and treatment to patients, or MP, lawyer, etc. gives advice.
surgical /'sɜ:dʒɪk(ə)l/ *adjective* of or by surgery or surgeons; used for surgery; (of appliance) worn to correct deformity etc.; (esp. of military action) swift and precise. □ **surgical spirit** methylated spirits used for cleansing etc. □ **surgically** *adverb*.
surly /'sɜ:lɪ/ *adjective* **(-ier, -iest)** bad-tempered, unfriendly. □ **surliness** *noun*.
surmise /sə'maɪz/ ● *noun* conjecture. ● *verb* **(-sing)** (often + *that*) infer doubtfully; suppose; guess.
surmount /sə'maʊnt/ *verb* overcome (difficulty, obstacle); (usually in *passive*) cap, crown. □ **surmountable** *adjective*.
surname /'sɜ:neɪm/ *noun* name common to all members of family.
surpass /sə'pɑ:s/ *verb* outdo, be better than; (as **surpassing** *adjective*) greatly exceeding, excelling others.
surplice /'sɜ:plɪs/ *noun* loose full-sleeved white vestment worn by clergy etc.
surplus /'sɜ:pləs/ ● *noun* amount left over when requirements have been met; excess of income over spending. ● *adjective* exceeding what is needed or used.
surprise /sə'praɪz/ ● *noun* unexpected or astonishing thing; emotion caused by this; catching or being caught unawares. ● *adjective* made, done, etc. without warning. ● *verb* **(-sing)** affect with surprise; (usually in *passive*; + *at*) shock, scandalize; capture by surprise; come upon (person) unawares; (+ *into*) startle, betray, etc. (person) into doing something. □ **surprising** *adjective*; **surprisingly** *adverb*.
surreal /sə'rɪəl/ *adjective* unreal; dreamlike; bizarre.
surrealism /sə'rɪəlɪz(ə)m/ *noun* 20th-c. movement in art and literature aiming to express subconscious mind by dream imagery etc. □ **surrealist** *noun & adjective*; **surrealistic** /-'lɪs-/ *adjective*; **surrealistically** /-'lɪs-/ *adverb*.
surrender /sə'rendə/ ● *verb* hand over, relinquish; submit, esp. to enemy; (often **surrender oneself**; + *to*) yield to habit, emotion, influence, etc.; give up rights under (life-insurance policy) in return for smaller sum received immediately. ● *noun* surrendering.
surreptitious /sʌrəp'tɪʃəs/ *adjective* done by stealth; underhand. □ **surreptitiously** *adverb*.
surrogate /'sʌrəgət/ *noun* substitute; deputy, esp. of bishop. □ **surrogate mother** woman who conceives and gives birth to child on behalf of woman unable to do so. □ **surrogacy** *noun*.
surround /sə'raʊnd/ ● *verb* come or be all round; encircle, enclose. ● *noun* border or edging, esp. area between walls and carpet.
surroundings *plural noun* things in neighbourhood of, or conditions affecting, person or thing; environment.
surtax /'sɜ:tæks/ *noun* additional tax, esp. on high incomes.
surtitle /'sɜ:taɪt(ə)l/ *noun* caption translating words of opera, projected on to screen above stage.
surveillance /sə'veɪləns/ *noun* close watch undertaken by police etc., esp. on suspected person.
survey ● *verb* /sə'veɪ/ take or present general view of; examine condition of (building etc.); determine boundaries, extent, ownership, etc. of (district etc.). ● *noun* /'sɜ:veɪ/ general view or consideration; surveying of property; result of this; investigation of public opinion etc.; map or plan made by surveying.
surveyor /sə'veɪə/ *noun* person who surveys land and buildings, esp. professionally.

survival /sə'vaɪv(ə)l/ *noun* surviving; relic.
survive /sə'vaɪv/ *verb* **(-ving)** continue to live or exist; live or exist longer than; come alive through or continue to exist in spite of (danger, accident, etc.). □ **survivor** *noun*.
sus = SUSS.
susceptibility *noun* (*plural* **-ies**) being susceptible; (in *plural*) person's feelings.
susceptible /sə'septəb(ə)l/ *adjective* impressionable, sensitive; easily moved by emotion; (+ *to*) accessible or sensitive to; (+ *of*) allowing, admitting of (proof etc.).
suspect ● *verb* /səs'pekt/ be inclined to think; have impression of the existence or presence of; (often + *of*) mentally accuse; doubt innocence, genuineness, or truth of. ● *noun* /'sʌspekt/ suspected person. ● *adjective* /'sʌspekt/ subject to suspicion or distrust.
suspend /səs'pend/ *verb* hang up; keep inoperative or undecided temporarily; debar temporarily from function, office, etc.; (as **suspended** *adjective*) (of particles or body in fluid) floating between top and bottom. □ **suspended animation** temporary deathlike condition; **suspended sentence** judicial sentence remaining unenforced on condition of good behaviour.
suspender *noun* attachment to hold up stocking or sock by its top; (in *plural*) *US* pair of braces. □ **suspender belt** woman's undergarment with suspenders.
suspense /səs'pens/ *noun* state of anxious uncertainty or expectation.
suspension /səs'penʃ(ə)n/ *noun* suspending, being suspended; means by which vehicle is supported on its axles; substance consisting of particles suspended in fluid. □ **suspension bridge** bridge with roadway suspended from cables supported by towers.
suspicion /səs'pɪʃ(ə)n/ *noun* unconfirmed belief; distrust; suspecting, being suspected; (+ *of*) slight trace of.
suspicious /səs'pɪʃəs/ *adjective* prone to or feeling suspicion; indicating or justifying suspicion. □ **suspiciously** *adverb*.
suss /sʌs/ *verb* (also **sus**) **(-ss-)** *slang* (usually + *out*) investigate, inspect; understand; work out.
sustain /səs'teɪn/ *verb* bear weight of, support, esp. for long period; encourage, support; endure, stand; (of food) nourish; undergo (defeat, injury, loss, etc.); (of court etc.) decide in favour of, uphold; substantiate, corroborate; keep up (effort etc.). □ **sustainable** *adjective*.
sustenance /'sʌstɪnəns/ *noun* nourishment, food; means of support.
suture /'suːtʃə/ ● *noun* joining edges of wound or incision by stitching; stitch or thread etc. used for this. ● *verb* **(-ring)** stitch (wound, incision).
suzerain /'suːzərən/ *noun historical* feudal overlord; *archaic* sovereign or state having some control over another state that is internally self-governing. □ **suzerainty** *noun*.
svelte /svelt/ *adjective* slim, slender, graceful.
SW *abbreviation* south-west(ern).
swab /swɒb/ ● *noun* absorbent pad used in surgery; specimen of secretion etc. taken for examination; mop etc. for cleaning or mopping up. ● *verb* **(-bb-)** clean with swab; (+ *up*) absorb (moisture) with swab; mop clean (ship's deck).
swaddle /'swɒd(ə)l/ *verb* **(-ling)** wrap tightly in bandages, wrappings, etc. □ **swaddling-clothes** narrow bandages formerly wrapped round newborn child to restrain its movements.
swag *noun slang* thief's booty; *Australian & NZ* traveller's bundle; festoon of flowers, foliage, drapery, etc.
swagger /'swægə/ ● *verb* walk or behave arrogantly or self-importantly. ● *noun* swaggering gait or manner.
swain *noun archaic* country youth; *poetical* young lover or suitor.
swallow[1] /'swɒləʊ/ ● *verb* make or let (food etc.) pass down one's throat; accept meekly or gullibly; repress (emotion); engulf; say (words etc.) indistinctly. ● *noun* act of swallowing; amount swallowed.
swallow[2] /'swɒləʊ/ *noun* migratory swift-flying bird with forked tail. □ **swallow-dive** dive with arms spread sideways; **swallow-tail** deeply forked tail, butterfly etc. with this.
swam *past* of SWIM.
swamp /swɒmp/ ● *noun* piece of wet spongy ground. ● *verb* submerge, inundate; cause to fill with water and sink; overwhelm with numbers or quantity. □ **swampy** *adjective* **(-ier, -iest)**.
swan /swɒn/ ● *noun* large web-footed usually white waterfowl with long flexible neck. ● *verb* **(-nn-)** (usually + *about*, *off*, etc.) *colloquial* move about casually or with superior manner. □ **swansong** person's last work or performance before death, retirement, etc.
swank *colloquial* ● *noun* ostentation, swagger. ● *verb* show off. □ **swanky** *adjective* **(-ier, -iest)**.
swap /swɒp/ (also **swop**) ● *verb* **(-pp-)** exchange, barter. ● *noun* act of swapping; thing suitable for swapping.
sward /swɔːd/ *noun literary* expanse of short grass.
swarf /swɔːf/ *noun* fine chips or filings of stone, metal, etc.
swarm[1] /swɔːm/ ● *noun* cluster of bees leaving hive etc. with queen bee to establish new colony; large group of insects, birds, or people; (in *plural*; + *of*) great numbers. ● *verb* move in or form swarm; (+ *with*) be overrun or crowded with.
swarm[2] /swɔːm/ *verb* (+ *up*) climb (rope, tree, etc.) clasping or clinging with arms and legs.
swarthy /'swɔːðɪ/ *adjective* **(-ier, -iest)** dark-complexioned, dark in colour.
swashbuckler /'swɒʃbʌklə/ *noun* swaggering adventurer. □ **swashbuckling** *adjective & noun*.
swastika /'swɒstɪkə/ *noun* ancient symbol formed by equal-armed cross with each arm continued at a right angle; this with clockwise continuations as symbol of Nazi Germany.
swat /swɒt/ ● *verb* **(-tt-)** crush (fly etc.) with blow; hit hard and abruptly. ● *noun* act of swatting.
swatch /swɒtʃ/ *noun* sample, esp. of cloth; collection of samples.
swath /swɔːθ/ *noun* (also **swathe** /sweɪð/) ridge of cut grass, corn, etc.; space left clear by mower, scythe, etc.
swathe /sweɪð/ *verb* **(-thing)** bind or wrap in bandages, garments, etc.
sway ● *verb* (cause to) move unsteadily from side to side; oscillate irregularly; waver; have influence over. ● *noun* rule, government; swaying motion.
swear /sweə/ *verb* (*past* **swore**; *past participle* **sworn**) state or promise on oath; cause to take oath; *colloquial* insist; (often + *at*) use profane or obscene language; (+ *by*) appeal to as witness or guarantee of oath, *colloquial* have great confidence in. □ **swear in** admit to office etc. by administering oath; **swear off** *colloquial* promise to keep off (drink etc.); **swear-word** profane or obscene word.
sweat /swet/ ● *noun* moisture exuded through pores, esp. when one is hot or nervous; state or period of sweating; *colloquial* state of anxiety; *colloquial* effort, drudgery, laborious task or undertaking; condensed

moisture on surface. ● *verb* (*past & past participle* **sweated** or *US* **sweat**) exude sweat; be terrified, suffer, etc.; (of wall etc.) show surface moisture; (cause to) toil or drudge; emit like sweat; make (horse, athlete, etc.) sweat by exercise; (as **sweated** *adjective*) (of goods, labour, etc.) produced by or subjected to exploitation. ▫ **no sweat** *colloquial* no bother, no trouble; **sweat-band** band of absorbent material inside hat or round head, wrist, etc. to soak up sweat; **sweatshirt** sleeved cotton sweater; **sweatshop** workshop where sweated labour is employed. ▫ **sweaty** *adjective* (**-ier**, **-iest**).

sweater *noun* woollen etc. pullover.

Swede *noun* native or national of Sweden; (**swede**) large yellow variety of turnip.

Swedish /ˈswi:dɪʃ/ ● *adjective* of Sweden. ● *noun* language of Sweden.

sweep ● *verb* (*past & past participle* **swept**) clean or clear (room, area, etc.) (as) with a broom; (often + *up*) collect or remove (dirt etc.) by sweeping; (+ *aside*, *away*, etc.) dismiss abruptly; (+ *along*, *down*, etc.) drive or carry along with force; (+ *off*, *away*, etc.) remove or clear forcefully; traverse swiftly or lightly; impart sweeping motion to; glide swiftly; go majestically; (of landscape etc.) be rolling or spacious. ● *noun* act or motion of sweeping; curve in road etc.; range, scope; chimney sweep; sortie by aircraft; *colloquial* sweepstake. ▫ **sweep the board** win all the money in gambling game, win all possible prizes etc.; **sweepstake** form of gambling on horse races etc. in which money staked is divided among those who have drawn numbered tickets for winners.

sweeping *adjective* wide in range or effect; generalized, arbitrary.

sweet ● *adjective* tasting like sugar, honey, etc.; smelling pleasant like perfume, roses, etc., fragrant; melodious; fresh; not sour or bitter; gratifying, attractive; amiable, gentle; *colloquial* pretty; (+ *on*) *colloquial* fond of, in love with. ● *noun* small shaped piece of sugar or chocolate confectionery; sweet dish forming course of meal. ▫ **sweet-and-sour** cooked in sauce with sugar, vinegar, etc.; **sweetbread** pancreas or thymus of animal, as food; **sweet-brier** single-flowered fragrant-leaved wild rose; **sweetcorn** sweet-flavoured maize kernels; **sweetheart** either of pair of lovers; **sweetmeat** a sweet, a small fancy cake; **sweet pea** climbing garden annual with many-coloured scented flowers; **sweet pepper** fruit of capsicum; **sweet potato** tropical plant with edible tuberous roots; **sweet-talk** flatter in order to persuade; **sweet tooth** liking for sweet-tasting things; **sweet william** garden plant with close clusters of sweet-smelling flowers. ▫ **sweetish** *adjective*; **sweetly** *adverb*.

sweeten *verb* make or become sweet(er); make agreeable or less painful. ▫ **sweetening** *noun*.

sweetener *noun* thing that sweetens; *colloquial* bribe.

sweetie *noun colloquial* a sweet; sweetheart.

sweetness *noun* being sweet; fragrance. ▫ **sweetness and light** (esp. uncharacteristic) mildness and reason.

swell ● *verb* (*past participle* **swollen** /ˈswəʊlən/ or **-ed**) (cause to) grow bigger, louder, or more intense; rise or raise up; (+ *out*) bulge out; (of heart etc.) feel full of joy, pride, etc.; (+ *with*) be hardly able to restrain (pride etc.). ● *noun* act or state of swelling; heaving of sea etc. with unbreaking rolling waves; crescendo; mechanism in organ etc. for gradually varying volume; *colloquial* fashionable or stylish person. ● *adjective colloquial esp. US* fine, excellent.

swelling *noun* abnormally swollen place, esp. on body.

swelter /ˈsweltə/ ● *verb* be uncomfortably hot. ● *noun* sweltering condition.

swept *past & past participle* of SWEEP.

swerve ● *verb* (**-ving**) (cause to) change direction, esp. suddenly. ● *noun* swerving motion.

swift ● *adjective* rapid, quick; prompt. ● *noun* swift-flying long-winged migratory bird. ▫ **swiftly** *adverb*; **swiftness** *noun*.

swig ● *verb* (**-gg-**) *colloquial* drink in large draughts. ● *noun* swallow of liquid, esp. of large amount.

swill ● *verb* (often + *out*) rinse, pour water over or through; drink greedily. ● *noun* swilling; mainly liquid refuse as pig-food.

swim ● *verb* (**-mm-**; *past* **swam**; *past participle* **swum**) propel body through water with limbs, fins, etc.; perform (stroke) or cross (river etc.) by swimming; float on liquid; appear to undulate, reel, or whirl; (of head) feel dizzy; (+ *in*, *with*) be flooded. ● *noun* act or spell of swimming. ▫ **in the swim** *colloquial* involved in or aware of what is going on; **swimming bath**, **pool** pool constructed for swimming; **swimming costume** bathing costume; **swimsuit** swimming costume, esp. one-piece for women and girls; **swimwear** clothing for swimming in. ▫ **swimmer** *noun*.

swimmingly *adverb colloquial* smoothly, without obstruction.

swindle /ˈswɪnd(ə)l/ ● *verb* (**-ling**) (often + *out of*) cheat of money etc.; defraud. ● *noun* act of swindling; fraudulent person or thing. ▫ **swindler** *noun*.

swine *noun* (*plural* same) *formal or US* pig; *colloquial* (*plural* same or **-s**) disgusting person, unpleasant or difficult thing. ▫ **swinish** *adjective*.

swing ● *verb* (*past & past participle* **swung**) (cause to) move with to-and-fro or curving motion; sway or hang like pendulum or door etc.; oscillate; move by gripping something and leaping etc.; walk with swinging gait; (+ *round*) move to face opposite direction; (+ *at*) attempt to hit; *colloquial* (of party etc.) be lively; have decisive influence on (voting etc.); *colloquial* be executed by hanging. ● *noun* act, motion, or extent of swinging; swinging or smooth gait, rhythm, or action; seat slung by ropes, chains, etc. for swinging on or in, spell of swinging thus; smooth rhythmic jazz or jazzy dance music; amount by which votes etc. change from one side to another. ▫ **swing-boat** boat-shaped swing at fairs etc.; **swing-bridge** bridge that can be swung aside to let ships etc. pass; **swing-door** door that swings in either direction and closes by itself when released; **swings and roundabouts** situation allowing equal gain and loss; **swing-wing** (aircraft) with wings that can pivot to point sideways or backwards. ▫ **swinger** *noun*.

swingeing /ˈswɪndʒɪŋ/ *adjective* (of blow etc.) forcible; huge, far-reaching.

swipe *colloquial* ● *verb* (**-ping**) (often + *at*) hit hard and recklessly; steal. ● *noun* reckless hard hit or attempt to hit.

swirl ● *verb* move, flow, or carry along with whirling motion. ● *noun* swirling motion; twist, curl. ▫ **swirly** *adjective*.

swish ● *verb* swing (cane, scythe, etc.) audibly through air, grass, etc.; move with or make swishing sound. ● *noun* swishing action or sound. ● *adjective colloquial* smart, fashionable.

Swiss ● *adjective* of Switzerland. ● *noun* (*plural* same) native or national of Switzerland. ▫ **Swiss roll** cylindrical cake, made by rolling up thin flat sponge cake spread with jam etc.

switch ● *noun* device for making and breaking connection in electric circuit; transfer, changeover, deviation; flexible shoot cut from tree; light tapering rod; *US* railway points. ● *verb* (+ *on*, *off*) turn (electrical device) on or off; change or transfer (position, subject, etc.); exchange; whip or flick with switch. □ **switchback** ride at fair etc. with extremely steep ascents and descents, similar railway or road; **switchboard** apparatus for varying connections between electric circuits, esp. in telephony; **switched-on** *colloquial* up to date, aware of what is going on; **switch off** *colloquial* cease to pay attention.

swivel /ˈswɪv(ə)l/ ● *noun* coupling between two parts etc. so that one can turn freely without the other. ● *verb* (**-ll-**; *US* **-l-**) turn (as) on swivel, swing round. □ **swivel chair** chair with revolving seat.

swizz *noun* (also **swiz**) *colloquial* something disappointing; swindle.

swizzle /ˈswɪz(ə)l/ *noun colloquial* frothy mixed alcoholic drink, esp. of rum or gin and bitters; *slang* swizz. □ **swizzle-stick** stick used for frothing or flattening drinks.

swollen *past participle* of SWELL.

swoon /swuːn/ *verb & noun literary* faint.

swoop /swuːp/ ● *verb* (often + *down*) come down with rush like bird of prey; (often + *on*) make sudden attack. ● *noun* act of swooping, sudden pounce.

swop = SWAP.

sword /sɔːd/ *noun* weapon with long blade for cutting or thrusting. □ **put to the sword** kill; **sword dance** dance with brandishing of swords, or steps about swords laid on ground; **swordfish** (*plural* same or **-es**) large sea fish with swordlike upper jaw; **swordplay** fencing, repartee, lively arguing; **swordsman** person of (usually specified) skill with sword; **sword-stick** hollow walking stick containing sword blade.

swore *past* of SWEAR.

sworn ● *past participle* of SWEAR. ● *adjective* bound (as) by oath.

swot *colloquial* ● *verb* (**-tt-**) study hard; (usually + *up*, *up on*) study (subject) hard or hurriedly. ● *noun usually derogatory* person who swots.

swum *past participle* of SWIM.

swung *past & past participle* of SWING.

sybarite /ˈsɪbəraɪt/ *noun* self-indulgent or luxury-loving person. □ **sybaritic** /-ˈrɪt-/ *adjective*.

sycamore /ˈsɪkəmɔː/ *noun* large maple tree, its wood; *US* plane tree, its wood.

sycophant /ˈsɪkəfænt/ *noun* flatterer, toady. □ **sycophancy** *noun*; **sycophantic** /-ˈfæn-/ *adjective*.

syllabic /sɪˈlæbɪk/ *adjective* of or in syllables. □ **syllabically** *adverb*.

syllable /ˈsɪləb(ə)l/ *noun* unit of pronunciation forming whole or part of word, usually consisting of vowel sound with consonant(s) before or after (see panel). □ **in words of one syllable** plainly, bluntly.

syllabub /ˈsɪləbʌb/ *noun* dessert of cream or milk sweetened and whipped with wine etc.

syllabus /ˈsɪləbəs/ *noun* (*plural* **-buses** or **-bi** /-baɪ/) programme or outline of course of study, teaching, etc.

syllogism /ˈsɪlədʒɪz(ə)m/ *noun* form of reasoning in which from two propositions a third is deduced. □ **syllogistic** /-ˈdʒɪs-/ *adjective*.

sylph /sɪlf/ *noun* elemental spirit of air; slender graceful woman. □ **sylphlike** *adjective*.

sylvan /ˈsɪlv(ə)n/ *adjective* (also **silvan**) of the woods, having woods; rural.

symbiosis /sɪmbaɪˈəʊsɪs/ *noun* (*plural* **-bioses** /-siːz/) (usually mutually advantageous) association of two different organisms living attached to one another etc.; mutually advantageous connection between people. □ **symbiotic** /-ˈɒt-/ *adjective*.

symbol /ˈsɪmb(ə)l/ *noun* thing generally regarded as typifying, representing, or recalling something; mark, sign, etc. representing object, idea, process, etc. □ **symbolic** /-ˈbɒl-/ *adjective*; **symbolically** /-ˈbɒl-/ *adverb*.

symbolism *noun* use of symbols; symbols; artistic movement or style using symbols to express ideas, emotions, etc. □ **symbolist** *noun*.

symbolize *verb* (also **-ise**) (**-zing** or **-sing**) be symbol of; represent by symbol(s).

symmetry /ˈsɪmɪtrɪ/ *noun* (*plural* **-ies**) correct proportion of parts; beauty resulting from this; structure allowing object to be divided into parts of equal shape and size; possession of such structure; repetition of exactly similar parts facing each other or a centre. □ **symmetrical** /-ˈmet-/ *adjective*; **symmetrically** /-ˈmet-/ *adverb*.

sympathetic /sɪmpəˈθetɪk/ *adjective* of or expressing sympathy; likeable, pleasant; (+ *to*) favouring (proposal etc.). □ **sympathetically** *adverb*.

sympathize /ˈsɪmpəθaɪz/ *verb* (also **-ise**) (**-zing** or **-sing**) (often + *with*) feel or express sympathy; agree. □ **sympathizer** *noun*.

sympathy /ˈsɪmpəθɪ/ *noun* (*plural* **-ies**) sharing of another's feelings; (often + *with*) sharing or tendency to share emotion, sensation, condition, etc. of another person; (in *singular* or *plural*) compassion, commiseration, condolences; (often + *with*) agreement (with person etc.) in opinion or desire. □ **in sympathy** (often + *with*) having, showing, or resulting from sympathy.

symphony /ˈsɪmfənɪ/ *noun* (*plural* **-ies**) musical composition in several movements for full orchestra. □ **symphony orchestra** large orchestra playing symphonies etc. □ **symphonic** /-ˈfɒn-/ *adjective*.

symposium /sɪmˈpəʊzɪəm/ *noun* (*plural* **-sia**) conference, or collection of essays, on particular subject.

symptom /ˈsɪmptəm/ *noun* physical or mental sign of disease or injury; sign of existence of something. □ **symptomatic** /-ˈmæt-/ *adjective*.

synagogue /ˈsɪnəgɒg/ *noun* building for Jewish religious instruction and worship.

sync /sɪŋk/ (also **synch**) *colloquial* ● *noun* synchronization. ● *verb* synchronize. □ **in** or **out of sync** (often + *with*) according or agreeing well or badly.

synchromesh /ˈsɪŋkrəʊmeʃ/ ● *noun* system of gear-changing, esp. in vehicles, in which gearwheels revolve at same speed during engagement. ● *adjective* of this system.

Syllable

A syllable is the smallest unit of speech that can normally occur alone, such as *a*, *at*, *ta*, or *tat*. A word can be made up of one or more syllables:

cat, *fought*, and *twinge* each have one syllable;
rating, *deny*, and *collapse* each have two syllables;
excitement, *superman*, and *telephoned* each have three syllables;
American and *complicated* each have four syllables;
examination and *uncontrollable* each have five syllables.

synchronize /ˈsɪŋkrənaɪz/ *verb* (also **-ise**) (**-zing** or **-sing**) (often + *with*) make or be synchronous (with); make sound and picture of (film etc.) coincide; cause (clocks etc.) to show same time. □ **synchronization** *noun.*

synchronous /ˈsɪŋkrənəs/ *adjective* (often + *with*) existing or occurring at same time.

syncopate /ˈsɪŋkəpeɪt/ *verb* (**-ting**) displace beats or accents in (music); shorten (word) by omitting syllable or letter(s) in middle. □ **syncopation** *noun.*

syncope /ˈsɪŋkəpɪ/ *noun Grammar* syncopation; *Medicine* fainting through fall in blood pressure.

syncretize /ˈsɪŋkrətaɪz/ *verb* (also **-ise**) (**-zing** or **-sing**) attempt to unify or reconcile differing schools of thought. □ **syncretic** /-ˈkret-/ *adjective*; **syncretism** *noun.*

syndicalism /ˈsɪndɪkəlɪz(ə)m/ *noun historical* movement for transferring industrial control and ownership to workers' unions. □ **syndicalist** *noun.*

syndicate ● *noun* /ˈsɪndɪkət/ combination of people, commercial firms, etc. to promote some common interest; agency supplying material simultaneously to a number of periodicals etc.; group of people who gamble, organize crime, etc. ● *verb* /ˈsɪndɪkeɪt/ (**-ting**) form into syndicate; publish (material) through syndicate. □ **syndication** *noun.*

syndrome /ˈsɪndrəʊm/ *noun* group of concurrent symptoms of disease; characteristic combination of opinions, emotions, etc.

synod /ˈsɪnəd/ *noun* Church council of clergy and lay people.

synonym /ˈsɪnənɪm/ *noun* word or phrase that means the same as another (see panel).

synonymous /sɪˈnɒnɪməs/ *adjective* (often + *with*) having same meaning; suggestive of; associated with.

synopsis /sɪˈnɒpsɪs/ *noun* (*plural* **synopses** /-si:z/) summary; outline.

synoptic /sɪˈnɒptɪk/ *adjective* of or giving synopsis. □ **Synoptic Gospels** those of Matthew, Mark, and Luke.

syntax /ˈsɪntæks/ *noun* grammatical arrangement of words; rules or analysis of this. □ **syntactic** /-ˈtæk-/ *adjective.*

synthesis /ˈsɪnθəsɪs/ *noun* (*plural* **-theses** /-si:z/) putting together of parts or elements to make up complex whole; *Chemistry* artificial production of (esp. organic) substances from simpler ones.

synthesize /ˈsɪnθəsaɪz/ *verb* (also **-ise**) (**-zing** or **-sing**) make synthesis of.

synthesizer *noun* (also **-iser**) electronic, usually keyboard, instrument producing great variety of sounds.

synthetic /sɪnˈθetɪk/ ● *adjective* produced by synthesis, esp. to imitate natural product; affected, insincere. ● *noun* synthetic substance. □ **synthetically** *adverb.*

syphilis /ˈsɪfəlɪs/ *noun* a contagious venereal disease. □ **syphilitic** /-ˈlɪt-/ *adjective.*

Syrian /ˈsɪrɪən/ ● *noun* native or national of Syria. ● *adjective* of Syria.

syringa /sɪˈrɪŋgə/ *noun* shrub with white scented flowers.

syringe /sɪˈrɪndʒ/ ● *noun* device for drawing in quantity of liquid and ejecting it in fine stream. ● *verb* (**-ging**) sluice or spray with syringe.

syrup /ˈsɪrəp/ *noun* (*US* **sirup**) sweet sauce of sugar dissolved in boiling water, often flavoured or medicated; condensed sugar-cane juice; molasses, treacle; excessive sweetness of manner. □ **syrupy** *adjective.*

system /ˈsɪstəm/ *noun* complex whole; set of connected things or parts; organized group of things; set of organs in body with common structure or function; human or animal body as organized whole; method, scheme of action, procedure, or classification; orderliness; (**the system**) prevailing political or social order, esp. seen as oppressive. □ **get (thing) out of one's system** get rid of (anxiety etc.); **systems analysis** analysis of complex process etc. so as to improve its efficiency, esp. by using computer.

systematic /sɪstəˈmætɪk/ *adjective* methodical; according to system; deliberate. □ **systematically** *adverb.*

systematize /ˈsɪstəmətaɪz/ *verb* (also **-ise**) (**-zing** or **-sing**) make systematic. □ **systematization** *noun.*

systemic /sɪˈstemɪk/ *adjective Physiology* of the whole body; (of insecticide etc.) entering plant tissues via roots and shoots. □ **systemically** *adverb.*

Synonym

A synonym is a word that has the same meaning as, or a similar meaning to, another word:

cheerful, happy, merry, and *jolly*

are synonyms that are quite close to each other in meaning, as are

lazy, indolent, and *slothful*

In contrast, the following words all mean 'a person who works with another', but their meanings vary considerably:

colleague — *conspirator*
collaborator — *accomplice*
ally

Tt

T *noun* □ **to a T** exactly, to a nicety; **T-bone** T-shaped bone, esp. in steak from thin end of loin; **T-junction** junction, esp. of two roads, in shape of T; **T-shirt** short-sleeved casual top; **T-square** T-shaped instrument for drawing right angles.

t. *abbreviation* (also **t**) ton(s); tonne(s).

TA *abbreviation* Territorial Army.

ta /tɑː/ *interjection colloquial* thank you.

tab[1] *noun* small piece of material attached to thing for grasping, fastening, identifying, etc.; *US colloquial* bill; distinguishing mark on officer's collar. □ **keep tabs on** *colloquial* have under observation or in check.

tab[2] *noun* tabulator.

tabard /ˈtæbəd/ *noun* herald's official coat emblazoned with arms of sovereign; woman's or girl's sleeveless jerkin; *historical* knight's short emblazoned garment worn over armour.

tabasco /təˈbæskəʊ/ *noun* pungent pepper; (**Tabasco**) *proprietary term* sauce made from this.

tabby /ˈtæbɪ/ *noun* (*plural* **-ies**) grey or brownish cat with dark stripes.

tabernacle /ˈtæbənæk(ə)l/ *noun historical* tent used as sanctuary by Israelites during Exodus; niche or receptacle, esp. for bread and wine of Eucharist; Nonconformist meeting-house.

tabla /ˈtæblə/ *noun* pair of small Indian drums played with hands.

table /ˈteɪb(ə)l/ ● *noun* flat surface on legs used for eating, working at, etc.; food provided at table; group seated for dinner etc.; set of facts or figures arranged esp. in columns; multiplication table. ● *verb* (**-ling**) bring forward for discussion at meeting etc.; *esp. US* postpone consideration of. □ **at table** taking a meal; **tablecloth** cloth spread over table; **tableland** plateau; **tablespoon** large spoon for serving etc., (also **tablespoonful**) amount held by this; **table tennis** game played with small bats on table divided by net; **tableware** dishes etc. for meals; **table wine** wine of ordinary quality; **turn the tables** (often + *on*) reverse circumstances to one's advantage.

tableau /ˈtæbləʊ/ *noun* (*plural* **-x** /-z/) picturesque presentation; group of silent motionless people representing stage scene.

table d'hôte /tɑːb(ə)l ˈdəʊt/ *noun* meal from set menu at fixed price.

tablet /ˈtæblɪt/ *noun* small solid dose of medicine etc.; bar of soap etc.; flat slab of stone etc., esp. inscribed.

tabloid /ˈtæblɔɪd/ *noun* small-sized, often popular or sensational, newspaper.

taboo /təˈbuː/ ● *noun* (*plural* **-s**) ritual isolation of person or thing as sacred or accursed; prohibition. ● *adjective* avoided or prohibited, esp. by social custom. ● *verb* (**-oos**, **-ooed**) put under taboo; exclude or prohibit, esp. socially.

tabor /ˈteɪbə/ *noun historical* small drum.

tabular /ˈtæbjʊlə/ *adjective* of or arranged in tables.

tabulate /ˈtæbjʊleɪt/ *verb* (**-ting**) arrange (figures, facts) in tabular form. □ **tabulation** *noun*.

tabulator *noun* device on typewriter etc. for advancing to sequence of set positions in tabular work.

tachograph /ˈtækəgrɑːf/ *noun* device in vehicle to record speed and travel time.

tachometer /təˈkɒmɪtə/ *noun* instrument measuring velocity or rate of shaft's rotation (esp. in vehicle).

tacit /ˈtæsɪt/ *adjective* implied or understood without being stated. □ **tacitly** *adverb*.

taciturn /ˈtæsɪtɜːn/ *adjective* saying little, uncommunicative. □ **taciturnity** /-ˈtɜːn-/ *noun*.

tack[1] ● *noun* small sharp broad-headed nail; *US* drawing-pin; long stitch for fastening materials lightly or temporarily together; (in sailing) direction, temporary change of direction; course of action or policy. ● *verb* (often + *down* etc.) fasten with tacks; stitch lightly together; (+ *to*, *on*, *on to*) add, append; change ship's course by turning head to wind, make series of such tacks.

tack[2] *noun* horse's saddle, bridle, etc.

tack[3] *noun colloquial* cheap or shoddy material; tat, kitsch.

tackle /ˈtæk(ə)l/ ● *noun* equipment for task or sport; rope(s), pulley(s), etc. used in working sails, hoisting weights, etc.; tackling in football etc. ● *verb* (**-ling**) try to deal with (problem etc.); grapple with (opponent); confront (person) in discussion; intercept or stop (player running with ball etc.). □ **tackle-block** pulley over which rope runs. □ **tackler** *noun*.

tacky[1] /ˈtækɪ/ *adjective* (**-ier**, **-iest**) slightly sticky.

tacky[2] /ˈtækɪ/ *adjective* (**-ier**, **-iest**) *colloquial* in poor taste; cheap, shoddy.

taco /ˈtækəʊ/ *noun* (*plural* **-s**) Mexican dish of meat etc. in crisp folded tortilla.

tact *noun* adroitness in dealing with people or circumstances; intuitive perception of right thing to do or say. □ **tactful** *adjective*; **tactfully** *adverb*; **tactless** *adjective*; **tactlessly** *adverb*.

tactic /ˈtæktɪk/ *noun* piece of tactics.

tactical *adjective* of tactics; (of bombing etc.) done in immediate support of military or naval operation; adroitly planning or planned. □ **tactically** *adverb*.

tactics /ˈtæktɪks/ *plural noun* (also treated as *singular*) disposition of armed forces, esp. in warfare; procedure calculated to gain some end, skilful device(s). □ **tactician** /-ˈtɪʃ-/ *noun*.

tactile /ˈtæktaɪl/ *adjective* of sense of touch; perceived by touch. □ **tactility** /-ˈtɪl-/ *noun*.

tadpole /ˈtædpəʊl/ *noun* larva of frog, toad, etc. at stage of living in water and having gills and tail.

taffeta /ˈtæfɪtə/ *noun* fine lustrous silk or silklike fabric.

taffrail /ˈtæfreɪl/ *noun* rail round ship's stern.

tag ● *noun* label, esp. to show address or price; metal point of shoelace etc.; loop or flap for handling or hanging thing; loose or ragged end; trite quotation, stock phrase. ● *verb* (**-gg-**) furnish with tag(s); (often + *on*, *on to*) join, attach. □ **tag along** (often + *with*) go along, accompany passively.

tagliatelle /tæljəˈtelɪ/ *noun* ribbon-shaped pasta.

tail[1] ● *noun* hindmost part of animal, esp. extending beyond body; thing like tail in form or position, esp. rear part of aeroplane, vehicle, etc., hanging part of back of shirt or coat, end of procession, luminous trail following comet, etc.; inferior, weak, or last part of anything; (in *plural*) *colloquial* tailcoat, evening dress with this; (in *plural*) reverse of coin turning up in toss; *colloquial* person following another. ● *verb* remove stalks of (fruit etc.); *colloquial* follow closely. □ **tailback** long queue of traffic caused by obstruction; **tailboard** hinged or removable back of lorry etc.; **tailcoat** man's coat divided at back and cut away in front; **tailgate** tailboard, rear door of estate car; **tail-light**, **-lamp** *US* rear light on vehicle etc.; **tail off**, **away** gradually diminish and cease; **tailpiece** final part of thing, decoration at end of chapter etc.; **tailplane** horizontal aerofoil at tail of aircraft; **tailspin** aircraft's spinning dive, state of panic; **tail wind** one blowing in direction of travel. ▫ **tailless** *adjective*.

tail² *Law* ● *noun* limitation of ownership, esp. of estate limited to person and his heirs. ● *adjective* so limited.

tailor /ˈteɪlə/ ● *noun* maker of (esp. men's) outer garments to measure. ● *verb* make (clothes) as tailor; make or adapt for special purpose; work as tailor. ▫ **tailor-made** made by tailor, made or suited for particular purpose. ▫ **tailored** *adjective*.

taint ● *noun* spot or trace of decay, corruption, etc.; corrupt condition, infection. ● *verb* affect with taint, become tainted; (+ *with*) affect slightly.

take ● *verb* (**-king**; *past* **took** /tʊk/; *past participle* **taken**) lay hold of; acquire, capture, earn, win; regularly buy (newspaper etc.); occupy; make use of; be effective; consume; use up; carry, accompany; remove, steal; catch, be infected with; be affected by (pleasure etc.); ascertain and record; grasp mentally, understand; accept, submit to; deal with or regard in specified way; teach, be taught or examined in; submit to (exam); make (photograph); have as necessary accompaniment, requirement, or part. ● *noun* amount taken or caught; scene or film sequence photographed continuously. ▫ **take after** resemble (parent etc.); **take against** begin to dislike; **take apart** dismantle, *colloquial* defeat, criticize severely; **take away** remove or carry elsewhere, subtract; **take-away** (cooked meal) bought at restaurant for eating elsewhere, restaurant selling this; **take back** retract (statement), convey to original position, carry in thought to past time, return or accept back (goods); **take down** write down (spoken words), dismantle (structure), lower (garment); **take-home pay** employee's pay after deduction of tax etc.; **take in** receive as lodger etc., undertake (work) at home, make (garment etc.) smaller, understand, cheat, include; **take off** remove (clothing), deduct, mimic, begin a jump, become airborne, (of scheme etc.) become successful; **take-off** act of mimicking or becoming airborne; **take on** undertake, acquire, engage, agree to oppose at game, *colloquial* show strong emotion; **take out** remove, escort on outing, get (licence etc.); **take over** succeed to management or ownership of, assume control; **takeover** *noun*; **take to** begin, have recourse to, form liking for; **take up** adopt as pursuit, accept (offer etc.), occupy (time or space), absorb, (often + *on*) interrupt or correct (speaker), shorten (garment), pursue (matter). ▫ **taker** *noun*.

taking ● *adjective* attractive, captivating. ● *noun* (in *plural*) money taken in business etc.

talc *noun* talcum powder; translucent mineral formed in thin plates.

talcum /ˈtælkəm/ *noun* talc; (in full **talcum powder**) usually perfumed powdered talc for toilet use.

tale *noun* narrative or story, esp. fictitious; allegation or gossip, often malicious.

talent /ˈtælənt/ *noun* special aptitude or gift; high mental ability; people of talent; *colloquial* attractive members of opposite sex; ancient weight and money unit. ▫ **talent-scout**, **-spotter** person seeking new talent, esp. in sport or entertainment. ▫ **talented** *adjective*.

talisman /ˈtælɪzmən/ *noun* (*plural* **-s**) thing believed to bring good luck or protect from harm.

talk /tɔːk/ ● *verb* (often + *to*, *with*) converse or communicate verbally; have power of speech; express, utter, discuss; use (language); gossip. ● *noun* conversation; particular mode of speech; short address or lecture; rumour or gossip, its theme; *colloquial* empty boasting; (often in *plural*) discussions, negotiations. ▫ **talk down** silence by loud or persistent talking, guide (pilot, aircraft) to landing by radio, (+ *to*) speak patronizingly to; **talk into** persuade by talking; **talk of** discuss, express intention of; **talk over** discuss; **talk round** persuade to change opinion etc.; **talk to** rebuke, scold. ▫ **talker** *noun*.

talkative /ˈtɔːkətɪv/ *adjective* fond of talking.

talkie *noun colloquial* early film with soundtrack.

talking ● *adjective* that talks or can talk; expressive. ● *noun* action or process of talking. ▫ **talking of** while we are discussing; **talking point** topic for discussion; **talking-to** *colloquial* scolding.

tall /tɔːl/ ● *adjective* of more than average height; of specified height; higher than surroundings. ● *adverb* as if tall; proudly. ▫ **tallboy** tall chest of drawers; **tall order** unreasonable demand; **tall ship** high-masted sailing ship; **tall story** *colloquial* extravagant tale.

tallow /ˈtæləʊ/ *noun* hard (esp. animal) fat melted down to make candles, soap, etc.

tally /ˈtælɪ/ ● *noun* (*plural* **-ies**) reckoning of debt or score; mark registering number of objects delivered or received; *historical* piece of notched wood for keeping account; identification ticket or label; counterpart, duplicate. ● *verb* (**-ies**, **-ied**) (often + *with*) agree, correspond.

tally-ho /tælɪˈhəʊ/ *interjection huntsman's cry as signal on seeing fox.*

Talmud /ˈtælmʊd/ *noun* body of Jewish civil and ceremonial law. ▫ **Talmudic** /-ˈmʊd-/ *adjective*; **Talmudist** *noun*.

talon /ˈtælən/ *noun* claw, esp. of bird of prey.

talus /ˈteɪləs/ *noun* (*plural* **tali** /-laɪ/) ankle-bone supporting tibia.

tamarind /ˈtæmərɪnd/ *noun* tropical evergreen tree; its fruit pulp used as food and in drinks.

tamarisk /ˈtæmərɪsk/ *noun* seaside shrub usually with small pink or white flowers.

tambour /ˈtæmbʊə/ *noun* drum; circular frame for stretching embroidery-work on.

tambourine /tæmbəˈriːn/ *noun* small shallow drum with jingling discs in rim, shaken or banged as accompaniment.

tame ● *adjective* (of animal) domesticated, not wild or shy; uninteresting, insipid. ● *verb* (**-ming**) make tame, domesticate; subdue. ▫ **tamely** *adverb*; **tameness** *noun*; **tamer** *noun*.

Tamil /ˈtæmɪl/ ● *noun* member of a people inhabiting South India and Sri Lanka; their language. ● *adjective* of this people or language.

tam-o'-shanter /tæməˈʃæntə/ *noun* floppy woollen beret of Scottish origin.

tamp *verb* ram down tightly.

tamper /ˈtæmpə/ *verb* (+ *with*) meddle or interfere with.

tampon /ˈtæmpɒn/ *noun* plug of cotton wool etc. used esp. to absorb menstrual blood.

tan¹ ● *noun* suntan; yellowish-brown colour; bark of oak etc. used for tanning. ● *adjective* yellowish-brown. ● *verb* (**-nn-**) make or become brown by exposure to sun; convert (raw hide) into leather; *slang* thrash.

tan² *abbreviation* tangent.

tandem /ˈtændəm/ ● *noun* bicycle with two or more seats one behind another; vehicle driven tandem. ● *adverb* with two or more horses harnessed one behind another. ▫ **in tandem** one behind the other, alongside each other, together.

tandoor /ˈtændʊə/ *noun* clay oven.

tandoori /tæn'dʊərɪ/ *noun* spiced food cooked in tandoor.

tang *noun* strong taste or smell; characteristic quality; part of tool by which blade is held firm in handle. □ **tangy** *adjective* (**-ier**, **-iest**).

tangent /'tændʒ(ə)nt/ *noun* straight line, curve, or surface touching but not intersecting curve; ratio of sides opposite and adjacent to acute angle in right-angled triangle. □ **at a tangent** diverging from previous course or from what is relevant. □ **tangential** /-'dʒenʃ(ə)l/ *adjective*.

tangerine /tændʒə'riːn/ *noun* small sweet-scented fruit like orange, mandarin; deep orange-yellow colour.

tangible /'tændʒɪb(ə)l/ *adjective* perceptible by touch; definite, clearly intelligible, not elusive. □ **tangibility** *noun*; **tangibly** *adverb*.

tangle /'tæŋg(ə)l/ ● *verb* (**-ling**) intertwine or become twisted or involved in confused mass; entangle; complicate. ● *noun* tangled mass or state. □ **tangly** *adjective*.

tango /'tæŋgəʊ/ ● *noun* (*plural* **-s**) (music for) slow South American ballroom dance. ● *verb* (**-goes**, **-goed**) dance tango.

tank *noun* large receptacle for liquid, gas, etc.; heavy armoured fighting vehicle moving on continuous tracks. □ **tank engine** steam engine with integral fuel and water containers. □ **tankful** *noun* (*plural* **-s**).

tankard /'tæŋkəd/ *noun* (contents of) tall beer mug with handle.

tanker *noun* ship, aircraft, or road vehicle for carrying liquids, esp. oil, in bulk.

tanner *noun* person who tans hides.

tannery *noun* (*plural* **-ies**) place where hides are tanned.

tannic /'tænɪk/ *adjective* of tan. □ **tannic acid** yellowish organic compound used in cleaning, dyeing, etc.

tannin /'tænɪn/ *noun* any of several substances extracted from tree-barks etc. and used in tanning etc.

Tannoy /'tænɔɪ/ *noun proprietary term* type of public address system.

tansy /'tænzɪ/ *noun* (*plural* **-ies**) aromatic herb with yellow flowers.

tantalize /'tæntəlaɪz/ *verb* (also **-ise**) (**-zing** or **-sing**) torment with sight of the unobtainable, raise and then dash the hopes of. □ **tantalization** *noun*.

tantamount /'tæntəmaʊnt/ *adjective* (+ *to*) equivalent to.

tantra /'tæntrə/ *noun* any of a class of Hindu or Buddhist mystical or magical writings.

tantrum /'tæntrəm/ *noun* (esp. child's) outburst of bad temper or petulance.

Taoiseach /'tiːʃəx/ *noun* prime minister of Irish Republic.

tap[1] ● *noun* device by which flow of liquid or gas from pipe or vessel can be controlled; act of tapping telephone; taproom. ● *verb* (**-pp-**) provide (cask) with tap, let out (liquid) thus; draw sap from (tree) by cutting into it; draw supplies or information from; discover and exploit; connect listening device to (telephone etc.). □ **on tap** ready to be drawn off, *colloquial* freely available; **taproom** room in pub serving drinks on tap; **tap root** tapering root growing vertically downwards.

tap[2] ● *verb* (**-pp-**) (+ *at*, *on*, *against*, etc.) strike or cause to strike lightly; (often + *out*) make by taps; tap-dance. ● *noun* light blow or rap; tap-dancing; metal attachment on dancer's shoe. □ **tap-dance** *noun* rhythmic dance performed in shoes with metal taps, *verb* perform this; **tap-dancer** *noun*; **tap-dancing** *noun*.

tapas /'tæpæs/ *plural noun* small savoury esp. Spanish dishes.

tape ● *noun* narrow woven strip of cotton etc. for fastening etc.; this across finishing line of race; (in full **adhesive tape**) strip of adhesive plastic etc. for fastening, masking, insulating, etc.; magnetic tape; tape recording; tape-measure. ● *verb* (**-ping**) tie up or join with tape; apply tape to; (+ *off*) seal off with tape; record on magnetic tape; measure with tape. □ **have** (**person**, **thing**) **taped** *colloquial* understand fully; **tape deck** machine for using audiotape (separate from speakers etc.); **tape machine** device for recording telegraph messages, tape recorder; **tape-measure** strip of tape or thin flexible metal marked for measuring; **tape recorder** apparatus for recording and replaying sounds on magnetic tape; **tape-record** *verb*; **tape recording** *noun*; **tapeworm** tape-like worm parasitic in alimentary canal.

taper /'teɪpə/ ● *noun* wick coated with wax etc. for conveying flame; slender candle. ● *verb* (often + *off*) (cause to) diminish in thickness towards one end, make or become gradually less.

tapestry /'tæpɪstrɪ/ *noun* (*plural* **-ies**) thick fabric in which coloured weft threads are woven to form pictures or designs; (usually wool) embroidery imitating this; piece of this.

tapioca /tæpɪ'əʊkə/ *noun* starchy granular foodstuff prepared from cassava.

tapir /'teɪpə/ *noun* small piglike mammal with short flexible snout.

tappet /'tæpɪt/ *noun* lever etc. in machinery giving intermittent motion.

tar[1] ● *noun* dark thick inflammable liquid distilled from wood, coal, etc.; similar substance formed in combustion of tobacco. ● *verb* (**-rr-**) cover with tar.

tar[2] *noun colloquial* sailor.

taramasalata /tærəməsə'lɑːtə/ *noun* (also **taramosalata**) dip made from roe, olive oil, etc.

tarantella /tærən'telə/ *noun* (music for) whirling Southern Italian dance.

tarantula /tə'ræntjʊlə/ *noun* large hairy tropical spider; large black spider of Southern Europe.

tarboosh /tɑː'buːʃ/ *noun* cap like fez.

tardy /'tɑːdɪ/ *adjective* (**-ier**, **-iest**) slow to act, come, or happen; delaying, delayed. □ **tardily** *adverb*; **tardiness** *noun*.

tare[1] /teə/ *noun* vetch, esp. as cornfield weed or fodder; (in *plural*) *Biblical* injurious cornfield weed.

tare[2] /teə/ *noun* allowance made for weight of packing around goods; weight of vehicle without fuel or load.

target /'tɑːgɪt/ ● *noun* mark fired at, esp. round object marked with concentric circles; person, objective, or result aimed at; butt of criticism etc. ● *verb* (**-t-**) single out as target; aim, direct.

tariff /'tærɪf/ *noun* table of fixed charges; duty on particular class of goods; list of duties or customs due.

tarlatan /'tɑːlət(ə)n/ *noun* thin stiff muslin.

Tarmac /'tɑːmæk/ ● *noun proprietary term* tarmacadam; area surfaced with this. ● *verb* (**tarmac**) (**-ck-**) apply tarmacadam to.

tarmacadam /tɑːmə'kædəm/ *noun* bitumen-bound stones etc. used as paving.

tarn *noun* small mountain lake.

tarnish /'tɑːnɪʃ/ ● *verb* (cause to) lose lustre; impair (reputation etc.). ● *noun* tarnished state; stain, blemish.

taro /'tɑːrəʊ/ *noun* (*plural* **-s**) tropical plant with edible tuberous roots.

tarot /'tærəʊ/ *noun* (in *singular* or *plural*) pack of 78 cards used in fortune-telling.

tarpaulin /tɑːˈpɔːlɪn/ *noun* waterproof cloth, esp. of tarred canvas; sheet or covering of this.
tarragon /ˈtærəgən/ *noun* aromatic herb.
tarry[1] /ˈtɑːrɪ/ *adjective* (**-ier**, **-iest**) of or smeared with tar.
tarry[2] /ˈtærɪ/ *verb* (**-ies**, **-ied**) *archaic* linger; stay, wait.
tarsal /ˈtɑːs(ə)l/ ● *adjective* of the ankle-bones. ● *noun* tarsal bone.
tarsus /ˈtɑːsəs/ *noun* (*plural* **tarsi** /-saɪ/) bones of ankle and upper foot.
tart[1] *noun* pastry case containing fruit, jam, etc. □ **tartlet** *noun*.
tart[2] ● *noun slang* prostitute, promiscuous woman. ● *verb* (+ *up*) *colloquial* smarten or dress up, esp. gaudily. □ **tarty** *adjective* (**-ier**, **-iest**).
tart[3] *adjective* sharp-tasting, acid; (of remark etc.) cutting, biting. □ **tartly** *adverb*; **tartness** *noun*.
tartan /ˈtɑːt(ə)n/ *noun* (woollen cloth woven in) pattern of coloured stripes crossing at right angles, esp. denoting a Scottish Highland clan.
Tartar /ˈtɑːtə/ *noun* member of group of Central Asian people including Mongols and Turks; their Turkic language; (**tartar**) harsh or formidable person. □ **tartar sauce** mayonnaise with chopped gherkins etc.
tartar /ˈtɑːtə/ *noun* hard deposit that forms on teeth; deposit forming hard crust in wine casks.
tartaric /tɑːˈtærɪk/ *adjective* of tartar. □ **tartaric acid** organic acid found esp. in unripe grapes.
tartrazine /ˈtɑːtrəziːn/ *noun* brilliant yellow dye from tartaric acid, used to colour food etc.
task /tɑːsk/ ● *noun* piece of work to be done. ● *verb* make great demands on. □ **take to task** rebuke, scold; **task force** specially organized unit for task; **taskmaster**, **taskmistress** person who makes others work hard.
Tass *noun* official Russian news agency.
tassel /ˈtæs(ə)l/ *noun* tuft of hanging threads etc. as ornament; tassel-like flowerhead of plant. □ **tasselled** *adjective* (*US* **tasseled**).
taste /teɪst/ ● *noun* (faculty of perceiving) sensation caused in mouth by contact with substance; flavour; small sample of food etc.; slight experience; (often + *for*) liking, predilection; aesthetic discernment in art, clothes, conduct, etc. ● *verb* (**-ting**) perceive or sample flavour of; eat small portion of; experience; (often + *of*) have specified flavour. □ **taste bud** organ of taste on surface of tongue.
tasteful *adjective* done in or having good taste. □ **tastefully** *adverb*; **tastefulness** *noun*.
tasteless *adjective* flavourless; having or done in bad taste. □ **tastelessly** *adverb*; **tastelessness** *noun*.
taster *noun* person employed to test food or drink by tasting; small sample.
tasting *noun* gathering at which food or drink is tasted and evaluated.
tasty *adjective* (**-ier**, **-iest**) of pleasing flavour, appetizing; *colloquial* attractive. □ **tastiness** *noun*.
tat[1] *noun colloquial* tatty things; junk.
tat[2] *verb* (**-tt-**) do, or make by, tatting.
ta-ta /tæˈtɑː/ *interjection colloquial* goodbye.
tatter /ˈtætə/ *noun* (usually in *plural*) rag, irregularly torn cloth, paper, etc. □ **in tatters** *colloquial* torn in many places, ruined.
tattered *adjective* in tatters.
tatting /ˈtætɪŋ/ *noun* (process of making) kind of handmade knotted lace.
tattle /ˈtæt(ə)l/ ● *verb* (**-ling**) prattle, chatter, gossip. ● *noun* gossip, idle talk.
tattoo[1] /təˈtuː/ ● *verb* (**-oos**, **-ooed**) mark (skin) by puncturing and inserting pigment; make (design) thus. ● *noun* such design. □ **tattooer** *noun*; **tattooist** *noun*.
tattoo[2] /təˈtuː/ *noun* evening signal recalling soldiers to quarters; elaboration of this with music and marching etc. as entertainment; drumming, rapping; drumbeat.
tatty /ˈtætɪ/ *adjective* (**-ier**, **-iest**) *colloquial* tattered; shabby, inferior, tawdry. □ **tattily** *adverb*; **tattiness** *noun*.
taught *past & past participle of* TEACH.
taunt ● *noun* insult; provocation. ● *verb* insult; provoke contemptuously.
taupe /təʊp/ *noun* grey tinged with esp. brown.
Taurus /ˈtɔːrəs/ *noun* second sign of zodiac.
taut *adjective* (of rope etc.) tight; (of nerves etc.) tense; (of ship etc.) in good condition. □ **tauten** *verb*; **tautly** *adverb*; **tautness** *noun*.
tautology /tɔːˈtɒlədʒɪ/ *noun* (*plural* **-ies**) repetition of same thing in different words. □ **tautological** /-təˈlɒdʒ-/ *adjective*; **tautologous** /-ləgəs/ *adjective*.
tavern /ˈtæv(ə)n/ *noun archaic or literary* inn, pub.
taverna /təˈvɜːnə/ *noun* Greek restaurant.
tawdry /ˈtɔːdrɪ/ *adjective* (**-ier**, **-iest**) showy but worthless; gaudy.
tawny /ˈtɔːnɪ/ *adjective* (**-ier**, **-iest**) of orange-brown colour. □ **tawny owl** reddish-brown European owl.
tax ● *noun* money compulsorily levied by state on person, property, business, etc.; (+ *on*, *upon*) strain, heavy demand. ● *verb* impose tax on; deduct tax from; make demands on; (often + *with*) charge, call to account. □ **tax avoidance** minimizing tax payment by financial manoeuvring; **tax-deductible** (of expenses) legally deductible from income before tax assessment; **tax disc** licence on vehicle certifying payment of road tax; **tax evasion** illegal non-payment of taxes; **tax-free** exempt from tax; **taxman** *colloquial* inspector or collector of taxes; **taxpayer** person who pays taxes; **tax return** declaration of income etc. for taxation purposes.
taxation /tækˈseɪʃ(ə)n/ *noun* imposition or payment of tax.
taxi /ˈtæksɪ/ ● *noun* (*plural* **-s**) (in full **taxi-cab**) car plying for hire and usually fitted with taximeter. ● *verb* (**taxis**, **taxied**, **taxiing** or **taxying**) (of aircraft) go along ground before or after flying; go or carry in taxi. □ **taxi rank** (*US* **taxi stand**) place where taxis wait to be hired.
taxidermy /ˈtæksɪdɜːmɪ/ *noun* art of preparing, stuffing, and mounting skins of animals. □ **taxidermist** *noun*.
taximeter /ˈtæksɪmiːtə/ *noun* automatic fare-indicator in taxi.
taxon /ˈtæks(ə)n/ *noun* (*plural* **taxa**) any taxonomic group.
taxonomy /tækˈsɒnəmɪ/ *noun* classification of living and extinct organisms. □ **taxonomic** /-səˈnɒm-/ *adjective*; **taxonomical** /-səˈnɒm-/ *adjective*; **taxonomist** *noun*.
tayberry /ˈteɪbərɪ/ *noun* (*plural* **-ies**) hybrid fruit between blackberry and raspberry.
TB *abbreviation* tubercle bacillus; tuberculosis.
tbsp. *abbreviation* tablespoonful.
te /tiː/ *noun* (also **ti**) seventh note of scale in tonic sol-fa.
tea *noun* (in full **tea plant**) Asian evergreen shrub or small tree; its dried leaves; infusion of these leaves as drink; infusion made from other leaves etc.; light meal in afternoon or evening. □ **tea bag** small permeable bag of tea for infusion; **tea break** pause in work for drinking tea; **tea caddy** container for tea; **teacake** light usually toasted sweet bun; **tea chest** light metal-lined wooden box for transporting

tea; **tea cloth** tea towel; **tea cosy** cover to keep teapot warm; **teacup** cup from which tea is drunk, amount it holds; **tea leaf** leaf of tea, esp. (in *plural*) after infusion; **teapot** pot with handle and spout, in which tea is made; **tearoom** small unlicensed café; **tea rose** rose with scent like tea; **teaset** set of crockery for serving tea; **teashop** tearoom; **teaspoon** small spoon for stirring tea etc., (also **teaspoonful**) amount held by this; **tea towel** cloth for drying washed crockery etc.; **tea trolley** (*US* **tea wagon**) small trolley from which tea is served.

teach *verb* (*past & past participle* **taught** /tɔ:t/) give systematic information, instruction, or training to (person) or about (subject, skill); practise this as a profession; advocate as moral etc. principle; (+ *to do*) instruct to, *colloquial* discourage from. ▫ **teachable** *adjective*.

teacher *noun* person who teaches, esp. in school.

teaching *noun* teacher's profession; (often in *plural*) what is taught; doctrine.

teak *noun* a hard durable wood.

teal *noun* (*plural* same) small freshwater duck.

team ● *noun* set of players etc. in game or sport; set of people working together; set of draught animals. ● *verb* (usually + *up*) join in team or in common action; (+ *with*) coordinate, match. ▫ **team-mate** fellow member of team; **team spirit** willingness to act for communal good; **teamwork** combined effort, cooperation.

teamster /'ti:mstə/ *noun US* lorry driver; driver of team.

tear¹ /teə/ ● *verb* (*past* **tore**; *past participle* **torn**) (often + *up*) pull (apart) with some force; make (hole, rent) thus; undergo this; (+ *away*, *off*, *at*, etc.) pull violently; violently disrupt; *colloquial* go hurriedly. ● *noun* hole etc. caused by tearing; torn part of cloth etc. ▫ **tear apart** search exhaustively, criticize forcefully, divide utterly, distress greatly; **tearaway** *colloquial* unruly young person; **tearing hurry** *colloquial* great hurry; **tear into** *colloquial* severely reprimand, start (activity) vigorously; **tear to shreds** *colloquial* criticize thoroughly.

tear² /tɪə/ *noun* drop of clear salty liquid secreted from eye and shed esp. in grief. ▫ **in tears** weeping; **teardrop** single tear; **tear duct** drain carrying tears to or from eye; **tear gas** gas causing severe irritation to the eyes.

tearful *adjective* in, given to, or accompanied with tears. ▫ **tearfully** *adverb*.

tease /ti:z/ ● *verb* (**-sing**) make fun of; irritate; entice sexually while refusing to satisfy desire; pick (wool etc.) into separate fibres; raise nap on (cloth) with teasels etc.; (+ *out*) extract or obtain by careful effort. ● *noun colloquial* person fond of teasing; act of teasing.

teasel /'ti:z(ə)l/ *noun* (also **teazel**, **teazle**) plant with prickly flower heads, used dried for raising nap on cloth; other device used for this.

teaser *noun colloquial* hard question or problem.

teat *noun* nipple on breast or udder; rubber etc. nipple for sucking milk from bottle.

teazel (also **teazle**) = TEASEL.

TEC /tek/ *abbreviation* Training and Enterprise Council.

tec *noun colloquial* detective.

tech /tek/ *noun* (also **tec**) *colloquial* technical college.

technic /'teknɪk/ *noun* (usually in *plural*) technology; technical terms, methods, etc.; technique.

technical *adjective* of the mechanical arts and applied sciences; of a particular subject, craft, etc.; using technical language; specialized; due to mechanical failure; in strict legal sense. ▫ **technical knockout** referee's ruling that boxer has lost because he is unfit to continue. ▫ **technically** *adverb*.

technicality /teknɪ'kælɪtɪ/ *noun* (*plural* **-ies**) being technical; technical expression; technical point or detail.

technician /tek'nɪʃ(ə)n/ *noun* person doing practical or maintenance work in laboratory; person skilled in artistic etc. technique; expert in practical science.

Technicolor /'teknɪkʌlə/ *noun proprietary term* process of colour cinematography; (usually **technicolour**) *colloquial* vivid or artificial colour.

technique /tek'ni:k/ *noun* mechanical skill in art; method of achieving purpose, esp. by manipulation; manner of execution in music, painting, etc.

technocracy /tek'nɒkrəsɪ/ *noun* (*plural* **-ies**) (instance of) rule or control by technical experts.

technocrat /'teknəkræt/ *noun* exponent or advocate of technocracy. ▫ **technocratic** /-'kræt-/ *adjective*.

technology /tek'nɒlədʒɪ/ *noun* (*plural* **-ies**) knowledge or use of mechanical arts and applied sciences; these subjects collectively. ▫ **technological** /-nə'lɒdʒ-/ *adjective*; **technologically** /-nə'lɒdʒ-/ *adverb*; **technologist** *noun*.

tectonic /tek'tɒnɪk/ *adjective* of building or construction; of changes in the earth's crust.

tectonics *plural noun* (usually treated as *singular*) study of earth's large-scale structural features.

teddy /'tedɪ/ *noun* (also **Teddy**) (*plural* **-ies**) (in full **teddy bear**) soft toy bear.

Teddy boy /'tedɪ/ *noun colloquial* 1950s youth with Edwardian-style clothing, hair, etc.

tedious /'ti:dɪəs/ *adjective* tiresomely long, wearisome. ▫ **tediously** *adverb*; **tediousness** *noun*.

tedium /'ti:dɪəm/ *noun* tediousness.

tee¹ *noun* letter T.

tee² ● *noun* cleared space from which golf ball is struck at start of play for each hole; small wood or plastic support for golf ball used then; mark aimed at in bowls, quoits, curling, etc. ● *verb* (**tees**, **teed**) (often + *up*) place (ball) on tee. ▫ **tee off** make first stroke in golf, *colloquial* start, begin.

teem¹ *verb* be abundant; (+ *with*) be full of, swarm with.

teem² *verb* (often + *down*) pour (esp. of rain).

teen *adjective* teenage.

teenage /'ti:neɪdʒ/ *adjective* of or characteristic of teenagers. ▫ **teenaged** *adjective*.

teenager /'ti:neɪdʒə/ *noun* person in teens.

teens /ti:nz/ *plural noun* years of one's age from 13 to 19.

teensy /'ti:nzɪ/ *adjective* (**-ier**, **-iest**) *colloquial* teeny.

teeny /'ti:nɪ/ *adjective* (**-ier**, **-iest**) *colloquial* tiny.

teepee = TEPEE.

teeter /'ti:tə/ *verb* totter, stand or move unsteadily.

teeth *plural* of TOOTH.

teethe /ti:ð/ *verb* (**-thing**) grow or cut teeth, esp. milk teeth. ▫ **teething ring** ring for infant to bite on while teething; **teething troubles** initial troubles in an enterprise etc.

teetotal /ti:'təʊt(ə)l/ *adjective* advocating or practising total abstinence from alcohol. ▫ **teetotalism** *noun*; **teetotaller** *noun*.

TEFL /'tef(ə)l/ *abbreviation* teaching of English as a foreign language.

Teflon /'teflɒn/ *noun proprietary term* non-stick coating for kitchen utensils.

Tel. *abbreviation* (also **tel.**) telephone.

tele- *combining form* at or to a distance; television; by telephone.

telecast /'telɪkɑ:st/ ● *noun* television broadcast. ● *verb* transmit by television. ▫ **telecaster** *noun*.

telecommunication /telɪkəmju:nɪ'keɪʃ(ə)n/ *noun* communication over distances by cable, fibre optics, satellites, radio, etc.; (in *plural*) technology of this.

telefax /'telɪfæks/ *noun* fax.

telegram /'telɪgræm/ *noun* message sent by telegraph.

telegraph /'telɪgrɑ:f/ ● *noun* (device or system for) transmitting messages to a distance by making and breaking electrical connection. ● *verb* (often + *to*) send message or communicate by telegraph. □ **telegraphist** /tɪ'legrə-/ *noun*.

telegraphic /telɪ'græfɪk/ *adjective* of or by telegraphs or telegrams; economically worded. □ **telegraphically** *adverb*.

telegraphy /tɪ'legrəfɪ/ *noun* communication by telegraph.

telekinesis /telɪkaɪ'ni:sɪs/ *noun* supposed paranormal force moving objects at a distance. □ **telekinetic** /-'net-/ *adjective*.

telemessage /'telɪmesɪdʒ/ *noun* message sent by telephone or telex and delivered in printed form.

telemetry /tɪ'lemətrɪ/ *noun* process of recording readings of instrument and transmitting them by radio. □ **telemeter** /tɪ'lemɪtə/ *noun*.

teleology /ti:lɪ'ɒlədʒɪ/ *noun* (*plural* **-ies**) *Philosophy* explanation of phenomena by purpose they serve. □ **teleological** /-ə'lɒdʒ-/ *adjective*.

telepathy /tɪ'lepəθɪ/ *noun* supposed paranormal communication of thoughts. □ **telepathic** /telɪ'pæθɪk/ *adjective*; **telepathically** /telɪ'pæθ-/ *adverb*.

telephone /'telɪfəʊn/ ● *noun* apparatus for transmitting sound (esp. speech) to a distance; instrument used in this; system of communication by network of telephones. ● *verb* (**-ning**) send (message) or speak to by telephone; make telephone call. □ **on the telephone** having or using a telephone; **telephone book, directory** book listing telephone subscribers and numbers; **telephone booth, box, kiosk** booth etc. with telephone for public use; **telephone number** number used to call a particular telephone. □ **telephonic** /-'fɒn-/ *adjective*; **telephonically** /-'fɒn-/ *adverb*.

telephonist /tɪ'lefənɪst/ *noun* operator in telephone exchange or at switchboard.

telephony /tɪ'lefənɪ/ *noun* transmission of sound by telephone.

telephoto /telɪ'fəʊtəʊ/ *noun* (*plural* **-s**) (in full **telephoto lens**) lens used in telephotography.

telephotography /telɪfə'tɒgrəfɪ/ *noun* photographing of distant object with combined lenses giving large image. □ **telephotographic** /-fəʊtə'græf-/ *adjective*.

teleprinter /'telɪprɪntə/ *noun* device for sending, receiving, and printing telegraph messages.

teleprompter /'telɪprɒmptə/ *noun* device beside esp. television camera that slowly unrolls script out of sight of audience.

telesales /'telɪseɪlz/ *plural noun* selling by telephone.

telescope /'telɪskəʊp/ ● *noun* optical instrument using lenses or mirrors to magnify distant objects; radio telescope. ● *verb* (**-ping**) press or drive (sections of tube etc.) one into another; close or be capable of closing thus; compress.

telescopic /telɪ'skɒpɪk/ *adjective* of or made with telescope; (esp. of lens) able to magnify distant objects; consisting of sections that telescope. □ **telescopic sight** telescope on rifle etc. used for sighting. □ **telescopically** *adverb*.

teletext /'telɪtekst/ *noun* computerized information service transmitted to subscribers' televisions.

telethon /'telɪθɒn/ *noun* long television programme to raise money for charity.

televise /'telɪvaɪz/ *verb* (**-sing**) transmit by television.

television /'telɪvɪʒ(ə)n/ *noun* system for reproducing on a screen visual images transmitted (with sound) by radio signals or cable; (in full **television set**) device with screen for receiving these signals; television broadcasting. □ **televisual** /-'vɪʒʊəl/ *adjective*.

telex /'teleks/ (also **Telex**) ● *noun* international system of telegraphy using teleprinters and public telecommunication network. ● *verb* send, or communicate with, by telex.

tell *verb* (*past & past participle* **told** /təʊld/) relate in speech or writing; make known, express in words; (often + *of, about*) divulge information, reveal secret etc.; (+ *to do*) direct, order; decide about, distinguish; (often + *on*) produce marked effect or influence. □ **tell apart** distinguish between; **tell off** *colloquial* scold; **tell-tale** *noun* person who tells tales, automatic registering device, *adjective* serving to reveal or betray something; **tell tales** make known person's faults etc.

teller *noun* person employed to receive and pay out money in bank etc.; person who counts votes; person who tells esp. stories.

telling *adjective* having marked effect, striking. □ **tellingly** *adverb*.

telly /'telɪ/ *noun* (*plural* **-ies**) *colloquial* television.

temerity /tɪ'merɪtɪ/ *noun* rashness, audacity.

temp *colloquial* ● *noun* temporary employee, esp. secretary. ● *verb* work as temp.

temper /'tempə/ ● *noun* mental disposition, mood; irritation, anger; tendency to become angry; composure, calmness; metal's hardness or elasticity. ● *verb* bring (clay, metal) to proper consistency or hardness; (+ *with*) moderate, mitigate.

tempera /'tempərə/ *noun* method of painting using emulsion e.g. of pigment with egg.

temperament /'temprəmənt/ *noun* person's or animal's nature and character.

temperamental /temprə'ment(ə)l/ *adjective* regarding temperament; unreliable, moody; *colloquial* unpredictable. □ **temperamentally** *adverb*.

temperance /'tempərəns/ *noun* moderation, esp. in eating and drinking; abstinence, esp. total, from alcohol.

temperate /'tempərət/ *adjective* avoiding excess, moderate; (of region or climate) mild.

temperature /'temprɪtʃə/ *noun* measured or perceived degree of heat or cold of thing, region, etc.; *colloquial* body temperature above normal.

tempest /'tempɪst/ *noun* violent storm.

tempestuous /tem'pestʃʊəs/ *adjective* stormy, turbulent. □ **tempestuously** *adverb*.

tempi *plural* of TEMPO.

template /'templɪt/ *noun* thin board or plate used as guide in drawing, cutting, drilling, etc.

temple[1] /'temp(ə)l/ *noun* building for worship, or treated as dwelling place, of god(s).

temple[2] /'temp(ə)l/ *noun* flat part of side of head between forehead and ear.

tempo /'tempəʊ/ *noun* (*plural* **-pos** or **-pi** /-pi:/) speed at which music is (to be) played; speed, pace.

temporal /'tempər(ə)l/ *adjective* worldly as opposed to spiritual, secular; of time; of the temples of the head.

temporary /'tempərərɪ/ ● *adjective* lasting or meant to last only for limited time. ● *noun* (*plural* **-ies**) person employed temporarily. □ **temporarily** *adverb*.

temporize /'tempəraɪz/ *verb* (also **-ise**) (**-zing** or **-sing**) avoid committing oneself, so as to gain time; procrastinate; comply temporarily.

tempt *verb* entice, incite to what is forbidden; allure, attract; risk provoking. □ **tempter** *noun*; **tempting** *adjective*; **temptingly** *adverb*; **temptress** *noun*.

temptation /temp'teɪʃ(ə)n/ *noun* tempting, being tempted; incitement, esp. to wrongdoing; attractive thing or course of action.

ten *adjective & noun* one more than nine. □ **the Ten Commandments** rules of conduct given by God to Moses. □ **tenth** *adjective & noun*.

tenable /'tenəb(ə)l/ *adjective* maintainable against attack or objection; (+ *for*, *by*) (of office etc.) that can be held for period or by (person etc.). □ **tenability** *noun*.

tenacious /tɪ'neɪʃəs/ *adjective* (often + *of*) keeping firm hold; persistent, resolute; (of memory) retentive. □ **tenaciously** *adverb*; **tenacity** /-'næs-/ *noun*.

tenancy /'tenənsɪ/ *noun* (*plural* **-ies**) (duration of) tenant's status or possession.

tenant /'tenənt/ *noun* person who rents land or property from landlord; (often + *of*) occupant of place.

tenantry *noun* tenants of estate etc.

tench *noun* (*plural* same) freshwater fish of carp family.

tend[1] *verb* (often + *to*) be apt or inclined; be moving; hold a course.

tend[2] *verb* take care of, look after.

tendency /'tendənsɪ/ *noun* (*plural* **-ies**) (often + *to*, *towards*) leaning, inclination.

tendentious /ten'denʃəs/ *adjective derogatory* designed to advance a particular cause; biased; controversial. □ **tendentiously** *adverb*; **tendentiousness** *noun*.

tender[1] /'tendə/ *adjective* (**tenderer**, **tenderest**) not tough or hard; susceptible to pain or grief; compassionate; delicate, fragile; loving, affectionate; requiring tact; immature. □ **tenderfoot** (*plural* **-s** or **-feet**) novice, newcomer; **tender-hearted** easily moved; **tenderloin** middle part of loin of pork; **tender mercies** harsh treatment. □ **tenderly** *adverb*; **tenderness** *noun*.

tender[2] /'tendə/ ● *verb* offer, present (services, resignation, payment, etc.); (often + *for*) make tender. ● *noun* offer to execute work or supply goods at fixed price.

tender[3] /'tendə/ *noun* person who looks after people or things; supply vessel attending larger one; truck attached to steam locomotive and carrying fuel etc.

tenderize *verb* (also **-ise**) (**-zing** or **-sing**) render (meat) tender by beating etc.

tendon /'tend(ə)n/ *noun* tough fibrous tissue connecting muscle to bone etc.

tendril /'tendrɪl/ *noun* slender leafless shoot by which some climbing plants cling.

tenebrous /'tenɪbrəs/ *adjective literary* dark, gloomy.

tenement /'tenɪmənt/ *noun* room or flat within house or block of flats; (also **tenement house**, **block**) house or block so divided.

tenet /'tenɪt/ *noun* doctrine, principle.

tenfold *adjective & adverb* ten times as much or many.

tenner /'tenə/ *noun colloquial* £10 or $10 note.

tennis /'tenɪs/ *noun* ball game played with rackets on court divided by net. □ **tennis elbow** sprain caused by overuse of forearm muscles.

tenon /'tenən/ *noun* wooden projection shaped to fit into mortise of another piece.

tenor /'tenə/ ● *noun* male singing voice between alto and baritone; singer with this; (usually + *of*) general purport, prevailing course of one's life or habits. ● *adjective* having range of tenor.

tenosynovitis /tenəʊsaɪnə'vaɪtɪs/ *noun* repetitive strain injury, esp. of wrist.

tenpin bowling *noun* game in which ten pins or skittles are bowled at in alley.

tense[1] ● *adjective* stretched tight; strained; causing tenseness. ● *verb* (**-sing**) make or become tense. □ **tense up** become tense. □ **tensely** *adverb*; **tenseness** *noun*.

tense[2] *noun* form of verb indicating time of action etc.; set of such forms for various persons and numbers.

tensile /'tensaɪl/ *adjective* of tension; capable of being stretched. □ **tensile strength** resistance to breaking under tension.

tension /'tenʃ(ə)n/ *noun* stretching, being stretched; mental strain or excitement; strained state; stress produced by forces pulling apart; degree of tightness of stitches in knitting and machine sewing; voltage.

tent *noun* portable shelter or dwelling of canvas etc.

tentacle /'tentək(ə)l/ *noun* slender flexible appendage of animal, used for feeling, grasping, or moving.

tentative /'tentətɪv/ *adjective* experimental; hesitant, not definite. □ **tentatively** *adverb*.

tenterhooks /'tentəhʊks/ *plural noun* □ **on tenterhooks** in suspense, distracted by uncertainty.

tenuous /'tenjʊəs/ *adjective* slight, insubstantial; oversubtle; thin, slender. □ **tenuity** /-'ju:ɪtɪ/ *noun*; **tenuously** *adverb*.

tenure /'tenjə/ *noun* (often + *of*) holding of property or office; conditions or period of this; guaranteed permanent employment, esp. as lecturer. □ **tenured** *adjective*.

tepee /'ti:pi:/ *noun* (also **teepee**) N. American Indian's conical tent.

tepid /'tepɪd/ *adjective* lukewarm; unenthusiastic.

tequila /tɪ'ki:lə/ *noun* Mexican liquor made from agave.

tercel /'tɜ:s(ə)l/ *noun* (also **tiercel** /'tɪəs(ə)l/) male hawk.

tercentenary /tɜ:sen'ti:nərɪ/ *noun* (*plural* **-ies**) 300th anniversary; celebration of this.

tergiversate /'tɜ:dʒɪvəseɪt/ *verb* (**-ting**) change one's party or principles; make conflicting or evasive statements. □ **tergiversation** *noun*; **tergiversator** *noun*.

term ● *noun* word for definite concept, esp. specialized; (in *plural*) language used, mode of expression; (in *plural*) relation, footing; (in *plural*) stipulations, charge, price; limited period; period of weeks during which instruction is given or during which law court holds sessions; *Logic* word(s) which may be subject or predicate of proposition; *Mathematics* each quantity in ratio or series, part of algebraic expression; completion of normal length of pregnancy. ● *verb* call, name. □ **come to terms with** reconcile oneself to; **in terms of** with reference to; **terms of reference** scope of inquiry etc., definition of this. □ **termly** *adjective*.

termagant /'tɜ:məgənt/ *noun* overbearing woman, virago.

terminable /'tɜ:mɪnəb(ə)l/ *adjective* able to be terminated.

terminal /'tɜ:mɪn(ə)l/ ● *adjective* (of condition or disease) fatal; (of patient) dying; of or forming limit or terminus. ● *noun* terminating thing, extremity; bus or train terminus; air terminal; point of connection for closing electric circuit; apparatus for transmission of messages to and from computer, communications system, etc. □ **terminally** *adverb*.

terminate /'tɜ:mɪneɪt/ *verb* (**-ting**) bring or come to an end; (+ *in*) end in.

termination *noun* terminating, being terminated; ending, result; induced abortion.

terminology /tɜ:mɪ'nɒlədʒɪ/ *noun* (*plural* **-ies**) system of specialized terms. □ **terminological** /-nə'lɒdʒ-/ *adjective*.

terminus /'tɜ:mɪnəs/ *noun* (*plural* **-ni** /-naɪ/ or **-nuses**) point at end of railway or bus route or of pipeline etc.

termite /'tɜ:maɪt/ *noun* antlike insect destructive to timber.

tern *noun* seabird with long pointed wings and forked tail.

ternary /'tɜ:nərɪ/ *adjective* composed of 3 parts.

terrace /'terəs/ ● *noun* flat area on slope for cultivation; level paved area next to house; row of houses built in one block of uniform style; terrace house; tiered standing accommodation for spectators at sports ground. ● *verb* (**-cing**) form into or provide with terrace(s). ▫ **terrace(d) house** house in terrace.

terracotta /terə'kɒtə/ *noun* unglazed usually brownish-red earthenware; its colour.

terra firma /terə 'fɜ:mə/ *noun* dry land, firm ground.

terrain /tə'reɪn/ *noun* tract of land, esp. in military or geographical contexts.

terra incognita /terə ɪŋ'kɒgnɪtə/ *noun* unexplored region. [Latin]

terrapin /'terəpɪn/ *noun* N. American edible freshwater turtle.

terrarium /tə'reərɪəm/ *noun* (*plural* **-s** or **-ria**) place for keeping small land animals; transparent globe containing growing plants.

terrestrial /tə'restrɪəl/ *adjective* of or on the earth; earthly; of or on dry land.

terrible /'terɪb(ə)l/ *adjective colloquial* very great, bad, or incompetent; causing or likely to cause terror; dreadful.

terribly *adverb colloquial* very, extremely; in terrible manner.

terrier /'terɪə/ *noun* small active hardy dog.

terrific /tə'rɪfɪk/ *adjective colloquial* huge, intense, excellent; causing terror. ▫ **terrifically** *adverb*.

terrify /'terɪfaɪ/ *verb* (**-ies**, **-ied**) fill with terror. ▫ **terrifying** *adjective*; **terrifyingly** *adverb*.

terrine /tə'ri:n/ *noun* (earthenware vessel for) pâté or similar food.

territorial /terɪ'tɔ:rɪəl/ ● *adjective* of territory or district. ● *noun* (**Territorial**) member of Territorial Army. ▫ **Territorial Army** local volunteer reserve force; **territorial waters** waters under state's jurisdiction, esp. part of sea within stated distance of shore. ▫ **territorially** *adverb*.

territory /'terɪtərɪ/ *noun* (*plural* **-ies**) extent of land under jurisdiction of ruler, state, etc.; (**Territory**) organized division of a country, esp. if not yet admitted to full rights of a state; sphere of action etc., province; commercial traveller's sales area; area defended by animal or human, or by team etc. in game.

terror /'terə/ *noun* extreme fear; terrifying person or thing; *colloquial* troublesome or tiresome person, esp. child; terrorism.

terrorist *noun* person using esp. organized violence to secure political ends. ▫ **terrorism** *noun*.

terrorize *verb* (also **-ise**) (**-zing** or **-sing**) fill with terror; use terrorism against.

terry /'terɪ/ *noun* looped pile fabric used for nappies, towels, etc.

terse /tɜ:s/ *adjective* (**-r**, **-st**) concise, brief; curt. ▫ **tersely** *adverb*.

tertiary /'tɜ:ʃərɪ/ *adjective* of third order, rank, etc.

Terylene /'terɪli:n/ *noun proprietary term* synthetic polyester textile fibre.

TESL /'tes(ə)l/ *abbreviation* teaching of English as a second language.

tesla /'tezlə/ *noun* SI unit of magnetic flux density.

tessellated /'tesəleɪtɪd/ *adjective* of or resembling mosaic; finely chequered.

tessellation /tesə'leɪʃ(ə)n/ *noun* close arrangement of polygons, esp. in repeated pattern.

test ● *noun* critical exam or trial of person's or thing's qualities; means, procedure, or standard for so doing; minor exam; *colloquial* test match. ● *verb* put to test; try severely, tax. ▫ **test card** still television picture outside normal programme hours; **test case** *Law* case setting precedent for other similar cases; **test drive** *noun* drive taken to judge vehicle's performance; **test-drive** *verb* take test drive in; **test match** international cricket or Rugby match, usually in series; **test-tube** thin glass tube closed at one end, used for chemical tests etc.; **test-tube baby** *colloquial* baby conceived elsewhere than in a mother's body. ▫ **tester** *noun*.

testaceous /tes'teɪʃəs/ *adjective* having hard continuous shell.

testament /'testəmənt/ *noun* a will; (usually + *to*) evidence, proof; *Biblical* covenant; (**Testament**) division of Bible. ▫ **testamentary** /-'ment-/ *adjective*.

testate /'testeɪt/ ● *adjective* having left valid will at death. ● *noun* testate person. ▫ **testacy** /-təsɪ/ *noun* (*plural* **-ies**).

testator /tes'teɪtə/ *noun* (*feminine* **testatrix** /-trɪks/) (esp. deceased) person who has made a will.

testes *plural* of TESTIS.

testicle /'testɪk(ə)l/ *noun* male organ that secretes spermatozoa, esp. one of pair in scrotum of man and most mammals.

testify /'testɪfaɪ/ *verb* (**-ies**, **-ied**) (often + *to*) bear witness; give evidence; affirm, declare.

testimonial /testɪ'məʊnɪəl/ *noun* certificate of character, conduct, or qualifications; gift presented as mark of esteem.

testimony /'testɪmənɪ/ *noun* (*plural* **-ies**) witness's statement under oath etc.; declaration, statement of fact; evidence.

testis /'testɪs/ *noun* (*plural* **testes** /-ti:z/) testicle.

testosterone /te'stɒstərəʊn/ *noun* male sex hormone.

testy /'testɪ/ *adjective* (**-ier**, **-iest**) irascible, short-tempered. ▫ **testily** *adverb*; **testiness** *noun*.

tetanus /'tetənəs/ *noun* bacterial disease causing painful spasm of voluntary muscles.

tetchy /'tetʃɪ/ *adjective* (**-ier**, **-iest**) peevish, irritable. ▫ **tetchily** *adverb*; **tetchiness** *noun*.

tête-à-tête /teɪtɑ:'teɪt/ ● *noun* private conversation between two people. ● *adverb* privately without third person.

tether /'teðə/ ● *noun* rope etc. confining grazing animal. ● *verb* fasten with tether. ▫ **at the end of one's tether** at the limit of one's patience, resources, etc.

tetra- *combining form* four.

tetragon /'tetrəgɒn/ *noun* plane figure with 4 sides and angles. ▫ **tetragonal** /tɪ'trægən-/ *adjective*.

tetrahedron /tetrə'hi:drən/ *noun* (*plural* **-dra** or **-s**) 4-sided triangular pyramid. ▫ **tetrahedral** *adjective*.

Teutonic /tju:'tɒnɪk/ *adjective* of Germanic peoples or languages; German.

text *noun* main part of book; original document, esp. as distinct from paraphrase etc.; passage of Scripture, esp. as subject of sermon; subject, theme; (in *plural*) books prescribed for study; data in textual form, esp. in word processor. ▫ **textbook** book used in studying, esp. standard book in any subject; **text editor** computing program allowing user to edit text.

textile /'tekstaɪl/ ● *noun* (often in *plural*) fabric, esp. woven. ● *adjective* of weaving or cloth; woven.

textual /'tekstʃʊəl/ *adjective* of, in, or concerning a text.

texture /'tekstʃə/ ● *noun* feel or appearance of surface or substance; arrangement of threads in textile fabric. ● *verb* (**-ring**) (usually as **textured** *adjective*) provide with texture; provide (vegetable protein) with texture like meat. □ **textural** *adjective*.

Thai /taɪ/ ● *noun* (*plural* same or **-s**) native, national, or language of Thailand. ● *adjective* of Thailand.

thalidomide /θə'lɪdəmaɪd/ *noun* sedative drug found in 1961 to cause foetal malformation when taken early in pregnancy.

than /ðən/ *conjunction introducing comparison.*

thane /θeɪn/ *noun historical* holder of land from English king by military service, or from Scottish king and ranking below earl; clan-chief.

thank /θæŋk/ ● *verb* express gratitude to; hold responsible. ● *noun* (in *plural*) *colloquial* gratitude; (as *interjection*) *expression of gratitude.* □ **thanksgiving** expression of gratitude, esp. to God; **Thanksgiving (Day)** US national holiday on fourth Thurs. in Nov.; **thanks to** as result of; **thank you** *polite formula expressing gratitude.*

thankful *adjective* grateful, pleased, expressive of thanks.

thankfully *adverb* in a thankful way; let us be thankful that.

■ **Usage** The use of *thankfully* to mean 'let us be thankful that' is common, but it is considered incorrect by some people.

thankless *adjective* not feeling or expressing gratitude; (of task etc.) unprofitable, unappreciated.

that /ðæt/ ● *adjective* (*plural* **those** /ðəʊz/) *used to describe the person or thing nearby, indicated, just mentioned, or understood; used to specify the further or less immediate of two.* ● *pronoun* (*plural* **those** /ðəʊz/) that one; the one, the person, etc.; /ðət/ (*plural* **that**) who, whom, which *(used to introduce a defining relative clause).* ● *adverb* (+ adjective or adverb) to that degree, so, (with negative) *colloquial* very. ● *conjunction* /ðət/ *used to introduce a subordinate clause expressing esp. a statement, purpose, or result.* □ **at that** moreover, then; **that is (to say)** in other words, more correctly or intelligibly.

thatch /θætʃ/ ● *noun* roofing of straw, reeds, etc. ● *verb* cover with thatch. □ **thatcher** *noun*.

thaw /θɔː/ ● *verb* (often + *out*) pass from frozen into liquid or unfrozen state; (of weather) become warm enough to melt ice etc.; warm into life, animation, cordiality, etc. ● *noun* thawing; warmth of weather that thaws.

the /ðɪ, ðə, ðiː/ ● *adjective* (called the definite article) *denoting person(s) or thing(s) already mentioned or known about*; *describing as unique*; (+ adjective) which is, who are, etc.; (with *the* stressed) best known; *used with noun which represents or symbolizes a group, activity, etc.* ● *adverb* (before comparatives in expressions of proportional variation) in or by that degree, on that account.

theatre /'θɪətə/ *noun* (*US* **theater**) building or outdoor area for dramatic performances; writing, production, acting, etc. of plays; room or hall for lectures etc. with seats in tiers; operating theatre; scene or field of action.

theatrical /θɪ'ætrɪk(ə)l/ ● *adjective* of or for theatre or acting; calculated for effect, showy. ● *noun* (in *plural*) dramatic performances. □ **theatricality** /-'kæl-/ *noun*; **theatrically** *adverb*.

thee /ðiː/ *pronoun archaic* (as object of verb) you (singular).

theft /θeft/ *noun* act of stealing.

their /ðeə/ *adjective* of or belonging to them.

theirs /ðeəz/ *pronoun* the one(s) belonging to them.

theism /'θiːɪz(ə)m/ *noun* belief in gods or a god. □ **theist** *noun*; **theistic** /-'ɪstɪk/ *adjective*.

them /ðem, ð(ə)m/ ● *pronoun* (as object of verb) the people or things in question; people in general; people in authority; *colloquial* they. ● *adjective slang or dialect* those.

theme /θiːm/ *noun* subject or topic of talk etc.; *Music* leading melody in a composition; *US* school exercise on given subject. □ **theme park** amusement park based on unifying idea; **theme song, tune** signature tune. □ **thematic** /θɪ'mætɪk/ *adjective*; **thematically** /θɪ'mæt-/ *adverb*.

themselves /ðəm'selvz/ *pronoun: emphatic form of* THEY *or* THEM; *reflexive form of* THEM.

then /ðen/ ● *adverb* at that time; after that, next; in that case, accordingly. ● *adjective* such at that time. ● *noun* that time. □ **then and there** immediately and on the spot.

thence /ðens/ *adverb* (also **from thence**) *archaic or literary* from that place, for that reason. □ **thenceforth, thenceforward** from that time on.

theo- *combining form* God or god(s).

theocracy /θɪ'ɒkrəsɪ/ *noun* (*plural* **-ies**) form of government by God or a god directly or through a priestly order etc. □ **theocratic** /θɪə'krætɪk/ *adjective*.

theodolite /θɪ'ɒdəlaɪt/ *noun* surveying instrument for measuring angles.

theology /θɪ'ɒlədʒɪ/ *noun* (*plural* **-ies**) study or system of (esp. Christian) religion. □ **theologian** /θɪə'ləʊdʒ-/ *noun*; **theological** /θɪə'lɒdʒ-/ *adjective*.

theorem /'θɪərəm/ *noun esp. Mathematics* general proposition not self-evident but demonstrable by argument; algebraic rule.

theoretical /θɪə'retɪk(ə)l/ *adjective* concerned with knowledge but not with its practical application; based on theory rather than experience. □ **theoretically** *adverb*.

theoretician /θɪərə'tɪʃ(ə)n/ *noun* person concerned with theoretical part of a subject.

theorist /'θɪərɪst/ *noun* holder or inventor of a theory.

theorize /'θɪəraɪz/ *verb* (also **-ise**) (**-zing** or **-sing**) evolve or indulge in theories.

theory /'θɪərɪ/ *noun* (*plural* **-ies**) supposition or system of ideas explaining something, esp. one based on general principles; speculative view; abstract knowledge or speculative thought; exposition of principles of a science etc.; collection of propositions to illustrate principles of a mathematical subject.

theosophy /θɪ'ɒsəfɪ/ *noun* (*plural* **-ies**) philosophy professing to achieve knowledge of God by direct intuition, spiritual ecstasy, etc. □ **theosophical** /θɪə'sɒf-/ *adjective*; **theosophist** *noun*.

therapeutic /θerə'pjuːtɪk/ *adjective* of, for, or contributing to the cure of diseases; soothing, conducive to wellbeing. □ **therapeutically** *adverb*.

therapeutics *plural noun* (usually treated as *singular*) branch of medicine concerned with cures and remedies.

therapy /'θerəpɪ/ *noun* (*plural* **-ies**) non-surgical treatment of disease etc. □ **therapist** *noun*.

there /ðeə/ ● *adverb* in, at, or to that place or position; at that point; in that respect; *used for emphasis in calling attention; used to indicate the fact or existence of something.* ● *noun* that place. ● *interjection expressing confirmation, triumph, etc.; used to soothe a child etc.* □ **thereabout(s)** near that place, amount, or time; **thereafter** *formal* after that; **thereby** by that means or agency; **therefore** for that reason, accordingly, consequently; **therein** *formal* in that place or respect; **thereof** *formal* of that or it; **thereto** *formal* to that or it, in addition; **thereupon** in consequence of that, directly after that.

therm /θɜːm/ *noun* unit of heat, former UK unit of gas supplied.

thermal /ˈθɜːm(ə)l/ ● *adjective* of, for, producing, or retaining heat. ● *noun* rising current of warm air. □ **thermal unit** unit for measuring heat. □ **thermally** *adverb*.

thermionic valve /θɜːmɪˈɒnɪk/ *noun* device giving flow of electrons in one direction from heated substance, used esp. in rectification of current and in radio reception.

thermo- *combining form* heat.

thermodynamics /θɜːməʊdaɪˈnæmɪks/ *plural noun* (usually treated as *singular*) science of relationship between heat and other forms of energy. □ **thermodynamic** *adjective*.

thermoelectric /θɜːməʊɪˈlektrɪk/ *adjective* producing electricity by difference of temperatures.

thermometer /θəˈmɒmɪtə/ *noun* instrument for measuring temperature, esp. graduated glass tube containing mercury or alcohol.

thermonuclear /θɜːməʊˈnjuːklɪə/ *adjective* relating to nuclear reactions that occur only at very high temperatures; (of bomb etc.) using such reactions.

thermoplastic /θɜːməʊˈplæstɪk/ ● *adjective* becoming plastic on heating and hardening on cooling. ● *noun* thermoplastic substance.

Thermos /ˈθɜːməs/ *noun* (in full **Thermos flask**) *proprietary term* vacuum flask.

thermosetting /ˈθɜːməʊsetɪŋ/ *adjective* (of plastics) setting permanently when heated.

thermosphere /ˈθɜːməsfɪə/ *noun* region of atmosphere beyond mesosphere.

thermostat /ˈθɜːməstæt/ *noun* device for automatic regulation of temperature. □ **thermostatic** /-ˈstæt-/ *adjective*; **thermostatically** /-ˈstæt-/ *adverb*.

thesaurus /θɪˈsɔːrəs/ *noun* (*plural* **-ri** /-raɪ/ or **-ruses**) dictionary of synonyms etc.

these *plural* of THIS.

thesis /ˈθiːsɪs/ *noun* (*plural* **theses** /-siːz/) proposition to be maintained or proved; dissertation, esp. by candidate for higher degree.

Thespian /ˈθespɪən/ ● *adjective* of drama. ● *noun* actor or actress.

they /ðeɪ/ *pronoun* (as subject of verb) the people or things in question; people in general; people in authority.

they'd /ðeɪd/ they had; they would.

they'll /ðeɪəl/ they will; they shall.

they're /ðeə/ they are.

they've /ðeɪv/ they have.

thiamine /ˈθaɪəmɪn/ *noun* (also **thiamin**) B vitamin found in unrefined cereals, beans, and liver.

thick /θɪk/ ● *adjective* of great or specified extent between opposite surfaces; (of line etc.) broad, not fine; closely set; crowded; (usually + *with*) densely filled or covered; firm in consistency; made of thick material; muddy, impenetrable; *colloquial* stupid; (of voice) indistinct; (of accent) marked; *colloquial* intimate. ● *noun* thick part of anything. ● *adverb* thickly. □ **a bit thick** *colloquial* unreasonable, intolerable; **in the thick of** in the busiest part of; **thickhead** *colloquial* stupid person; **thickheaded** *adjective*; **thickset** heavily or solidly built, set or growing close together; **thick-skinned** not sensitive to criticism; **through thick and thin** under all conditions, in spite of all difficulties. □ **thickly** *adverb*; **thickness** *noun*.

thicken *verb* make or become thick(er); become more complicated.

thickener *noun* substance used to thicken liquid.

thickening *noun* thickened part; = THICKENER.

thicket /ˈθɪkɪt/ *noun* tangle of shrubs or trees.

thief /θiːf/ *noun* (*plural* **thieves** /θiːvz/) person who steals, esp. secretly.

thieve /θiːv/ *verb* (**-ving**) be a thief; steal. □ **thievery** *noun*.

thievish *adjective* given to stealing.

thigh /θaɪ/ *noun* part of leg between hip and knee. □ **thigh-bone** femur.

thimble /ˈθɪmb(ə)l/ *noun* metal or plastic cap worn to protect finger and push needle in sewing.

thimbleful *noun* (*plural* **-s**) small quantity, esp. of drink.

thin /θɪn/ ● *adjective* (**-nn-**) having opposite surfaces close together, of small thickness or diameter; (of line etc.) narrow, fine; made of thin material; lean, not plump; not dense or copious; of slight consistency; weak, lacking an important ingredient; (of excuse etc.) transparent, flimsy. ● *adverb* thinly. ● *verb* (**-nn-**) make or become thin(ner); (often + *out*) make or become less dense, crowded, or numerous. □ **thin on the ground** few; **thin on top** balding; **thin-skinned** sensitive to criticism. □ **thinly** *adverb*; **thinness** *noun*.

thine /ðaɪn/ *archaic* ● *pronoun* yours (singular). ● *adjective* your (singular).

thing /θɪŋ/ *noun* any possible object of thought or perception including people, material objects, events, qualities, ideas, utterances, and acts; *colloquial* one's special interest; (**the thing**) *colloquial* what is proper, fashionable, needed, important, etc.; (in *plural*) personal belongings, clothing, or equipment; (in *plural*) affairs, circumstances. □ **have a thing about** *colloquial* be obsessed by or prejudiced about.

thingummy /ˈθɪŋəmɪ/ *noun* (*plural* **-ies**) (also **thingumabob** /-məbɒb/, **thingumajig** /-mədʒɪg/) *colloquial* person or thing whose name one forgets or does not know.

think /θɪŋk/ ● *verb* (*past & past participle* **thought** /θɔːt/) be of opinion; (+ *of*, *about*) consider; exercise mind; form ideas, imagine; have half-formed intention. ● *noun colloquial* act of thinking. □ **think better of** change one's mind about (intention) after reconsideration; **think out** consider carefully, devise; **think over** reflect on; **think-tank** *colloquial* group of experts providing advice and ideas on national or commercial problems; **think twice** avoid hasty action etc.; **think up** *colloquial* devise.

thinker *noun* person who thinks in specified way; person with skilled or powerful mind.

thinking ● *adjective* intelligent, rational. ● *noun* opinion, judgement.

thinner *noun* solvent for diluting paint etc.

third /θɜːd/ *adjective & noun* next after second; any of 3 equal parts of thing. □ **third degree** severe and protracted interrogation by police etc.; **third man** *Cricket* fielder near boundary behind slips; **third party** another party besides the two principals; **third-party insurance** insurance against damage or injury suffered by person other than the insured; **third-rate** inferior, very poor; **Third World** developing countries of Africa, Asia, and Latin America. □ **thirdly** *adverb*.

thirst /θɜːst/ ● *noun* (discomfort caused by) need to drink; desire, craving. ● *verb* feel thirst.

thirsty /ˈθɜːstɪ/ *adjective* (**-ier**, **-iest**) feeling thirst; (of land, season, etc.) dry, parched; (often + *for*, *after*) eager; *colloquial* causing thirst. □ **thirstily** *adverb*; **thirstiness** *noun*.

thirteen /θɜːˈtiːn/ *adjective & noun* one more than twelve. □ **thirteenth** *adjective & noun*.

thirty /ˈθɜːtɪ/ *adjective & noun* (*plural* **-ies**) three times ten. □ **thirtieth** *adjective & noun*.

this /ðɪs/ ● *adjective* (*plural* **these** /ði:z/) *used to describe the person or thing nearby, indicated, just mentioned, or understood; used to specify the nearer or more immediate of two;* the present (morning, week, etc.). ● *pronoun* (*plural* **these** /ði:z/) this one. ● *adverb* (+ adjective or adverb) to this degree or extent.

thistle /'θɪs(ə)l/ *noun* prickly plant, usually with globular heads of purple flowers; this as Scottish national emblem. ▫ **thistledown** down containing thistle-seeds. ▫ **thistly** *adjective*.

thither /'ðɪðə/ *adverb archaic or formal* to that place.

tho' = THOUGH.

thole /θəʊl/ *noun* (in full **thole-pin**) pin in gunwale of boat as fulcrum for oar; each of two such pins forming rowlock.

thong /θɒŋ/ *noun* narrow strip of hide or leather.

thorax /'θɔ:ræks/ *noun* (*plural* **-races** /-rəsi:z/ or **-raxes**) part of the body between neck and abdomen. ▫ **thoracic** /-'ræs-/ *adjective*.

thorn /θɔ:n/ *noun* sharp-pointed projection on plant; thorn-bearing shrub or tree. ▫ **thornless** *adjective*.

thorny *adjective* (**-ier**, **-iest**) having many thorns; (of subject) problematic, causing disagreement.

thorough /'θʌrə/ *adjective* complete, unqualified, not superficial; acting or done with great care etc. ▫ **thoroughbred** *adjective* of pure breed, high-spirited, *noun* such animal, esp. horse; **thoroughfare** public way open at both ends, esp. main road; **thoroughgoing** thorough, complete. ▫ **thoroughly** *adverb*; **thoroughness** *noun*.

those *plural* of THAT.

thou[1] /ðaʊ/ *pronoun archaic* (as subject of verb) you (singular).

thou[2] /θaʊ/ *noun* (*plural* same or **-s**) *colloquial* thousand; one thousandth.

though /ðəʊ/ (also **tho'**) ● *conjunction* in spite of the fact that; even if; and yet. ● *adverb colloquial* however, all the same.

thought[1] /θɔ:t/ *noun* process, power, faculty, etc. of thinking; particular way of thinking; sober reflection, consideration; idea, notion; intention, purpose; (usually in *plural*) one's opinion.

thought[2] *past & past participle* of THINK.

thoughtful *adjective* engaged in or given to meditation; giving signs of serious thought; considerate. ▫ **thoughtfully** *adverb*; **thoughtfulness** *noun*.

thoughtless *adjective* careless of consequences or of others' feelings; caused by lack of thought. ▫ **thoughtlessly** *adverb*; **thoughtlessness** *noun*.

thousand /'θaʊz(ə)nd/ *adjective & noun* (*plural* same) ten hundred; (**thousands**) *colloquial* large number. ▫ **thousandth** *adjective & noun*.

thrall /θrɔ:l/ *noun literary* (often + *of*, *to*) slave; slavery.

thrash /θræʃ/ *verb* beat or whip severely; defeat thoroughly; move or fling (esp. limbs) violently. ▫ **thrash out** discuss to conclusion.

thread /θred/ ● *noun* spun-out cotton, silk, glass, etc.; length of this; thin cord of twisted yarns used esp. in sewing and weaving; continuous aspect of thing; spiral ridge of screw. ● *verb* pass thread through (needle); put (beads) on thread; arrange (material in strip form, e.g. film) in proper position on equipment; pick (one's way) through maze, crowded place, etc. ▫ **threadbare** (of cloth) so worn that nap is lost and threads showing, (of person) shabby, (of idea etc.) hackneyed; **threadworm** parasitic threadlike worm.

threat /θret/ *noun* declaration of intention to punish or hurt; indication of something undesirable coming; person or thing regarded as dangerous.

threaten /'θret(ə)n/ *verb* use threats towards; be sign or indication of (something undesirable); (+ *to do*) announce one's intention to do (undesirable thing); give warning of infliction of (harm etc.); (as **threatened** *adjective*) (of species etc.) likely to become extinct.

three /θri:/ *adjective & noun* one more than two. ▫ **three-cornered** triangular, (of contest etc.) between 3 people etc.; **three-dimensional** having or appearing to have length, breadth, and depth; **three-legged race** race for pairs with right leg of one tied to other's left leg; **threepence** /'θrepəns/ sum of 3 pence; **threepenny** /'θrepənɪ/ costing 3 pence; **three-piece** (suit or suite) consisting of 3 items; **three-ply** (wool etc.) having 3 strands, (plywood) having 3 layers; **three-point turn** method of turning vehicle in narrow space by moving forwards, backwards, and forwards again; **three-quarter** *Rugby* any of 3 or 4 players just behind half-backs; **the three Rs** reading, writing, and arithmetic.

threefold *adjective & adverb* three times as much or many.

threesome *noun* group of 3 people.

threnody /'θrenədɪ/ *noun* (*plural* **-ies**) song of lamentation.

thresh *verb* beat out or separate grain from (corn etc.). ▫ **thresher** *noun*.

threshold /'θreʃəʊld/ *noun* plank or stone forming bottom of doorway; point of entry; limit below which stimulus causes no reaction.

threw *past* of THROW.

thrice *adverb archaic or literary* 3 times.

thrift *noun* frugality, economical management. ▫ **thrifty** *adjective* (**-ier**, **-iest**).

thrill ● *noun* wave or nervous tremor of emotion or sensation; throb, pulsation. ● *verb* (cause to) feel thrill; quiver or throb (as) with emotion.

thriller *noun* sensational or exciting play, story, etc.

thrips *noun* (*plural* same) insect harmful to plants.

thrive *verb* (**-ving**; *past* **throve** or **thrived**; *past participle* **thriven** /'θrɪv(ə)n/ or **thrived**) prosper; grow vigorously.

thro' = THROUGH.

throat *noun* gullet, windpipe; front of neck; *literary* narrow passage or entrance.

throaty *adjective* (**-ier**, **-iest**) (of voice) hoarsely resonant.

throb ● *verb* (**-bb-**) pulsate; vibrate with persistent rhythm or with emotion. ● *noun* throbbing, violent beat or pulsation.

throe *noun* (usually in *plural*) violent pang. ▫ **in the throes of** struggling with the task of.

thrombosis /θrɒm'bəʊsɪs/ *noun* (*plural* **-boses** /-si:z/) coagulation of blood in blood vessel or organ.

throne ● *noun* ceremonial chair for sovereign, bishop, etc.; sovereign power. ● *verb* (**-ning**) enthrone.

throng ● *noun* (often + *of*) crowd, esp. of people. ● *verb* come in multitudes; fill (as) with crowd.

throstle /'θrɒs(ə)l/ *noun* song thrush.

throttle /'θrɒt(ə)l/ ● *noun* (lever etc. operating) valve controlling flow of steam or fuel in engine; throat. ● *verb* (**-ling**) choke, strangle; control (engine etc.) with throttle. ▫ **throttle back**, **down** reduce speed of (engine etc.) by throttling.

through /θru:/ (also **thro'**, *US* **thru**) ● *preposition* from end to end or side to side of; between, among; from beginning to end of; by agency, means, or fault of; by reason of; *US* up to and including. ● *adverb* through something; from end to end; to the end. ● *adjective* (of journey etc.) done without change of line, vehicle, etc.; (of traffic) going through a place to its destination; (of road) open at both ends. ▫ **be through** *colloquial* (often + *with*) have finished, cease to have dealings; **through and through** thoroughly, completely; **throughput** amount of material put through a manufacturing etc. process or a computer.

throughout /θruːˈaʊt/ ● *preposition* right through; from end to end of. ● *adverb* in every part or respect.

throve *past of* THRIVE.

throw /θrəʊ/ ● *verb* (*past* **threw** /θruː/; *past participle* **thrown**) propel through space; force violently into specified position or state; turn or move (part of body) quickly or suddenly; project (rays, light, etc.); cast (shadow); bring to the ground; *colloquial* disconcert; (+ *on*, *off*, etc.) put (clothes etc.) carelessly or hastily on, off, etc.; cause (dice) to fall on table etc., obtain (specified number) thus; cause to pass or extend suddenly to another state or position; move (switch, lever); shape (pottery) on wheel; have (fit, tantrum, etc.); give (a party). ● *noun* throwing, being thrown; distance a thing is or may be thrown; (**a throw**) *slang* each, per item. ▫ **throw away** discard as unwanted, waste, fail to make use of; **throwaway** to be thrown away after (one) use, deliberately underemphasized; **throw back** (usually in *passive*; + *on*) compel to rely on; **throwback** (instance of) reversion to ancestral character; **throw in** interpose (word, remark), include at no extra cost, throw (football) from edge of pitch where it has gone out of play; **throw-in** throwing in of football from edge of pitch; **throw off** discard, contrive to get rid of, write or utter in offhand way; **throw open** (often + *to*) cause to be suddenly or widely open, make accessible; **throw out** put out forcibly or suddenly, discard, reject; **throw over** desert, abandon; **throw up** abandon, resign from, vomit, erect hastily, bring to notice.

thrum ● *verb* (**-mm-**) play (stringed instrument) monotonously or unskilfully; (often + *on*) drum idly. ● *noun* such playing; resultant sound.

thrush[1] *noun* kind of songbird.

thrush[2] *noun* fungus infection of throat, esp. in children, or of vagina.

thrust ● *verb* (*past & past participle* **thrust**) push with sudden impulse or with force; (+ *on*) impose (thing) forcibly on; (+ *at*, *through*) pierce, stab, lunge suddenly; make (one's way) forcibly; (as **thrusting** *adjective*) aggressive, ambitious. ● *noun* sudden or forcible push or lunge; forward force exerted by propeller or jet etc.; strong attempt to penetrate enemy's line or territory; remark aimed at person; stress between parts of arch etc.; (often + *of*) theme, gist.

thud /θʌd/ ● *noun* low dull sound as of blow on non-resonant thing. ● *verb* (**-dd-**) make thud; fall with thud.

thug /θʌg/ *noun* vicious or brutal ruffian. ▫ **thuggery** *noun*; **thuggish** *adjective*.

thumb /θʌm/ ● *noun* short thick finger on hand, set apart from other 4; part of glove for thumb. ● *verb* soil or wear with thumb; turn over pages (as) with thumb; request or get (lift) by sticking out thumb. ▫ **thumb index** set of lettered grooves cut down side of book etc. for easy reference; **thumbnail** *noun* nail of thumb, *adjective* concise; **thumbscrew** instrument of torture for squeezing thumbs; **thumbs up**, **down** indication of approval or rejection; **under (person's) thumb** dominated by him or her.

thump /θʌmp/ ● *verb* beat heavily, esp. with fist; throb strongly; (+ *at*, *on*, etc.) knock loudly. ● *noun* (sound of) heavy blow.

thumping *adjective colloquial* huge.

thunder /ˈθʌndə/ ● *noun* loud noise accompanying lightning; resounding loud deep noise; strong censure. ● *verb* sound with or like thunder; move with loud noise; utter loudly; (+ *against* etc.) make violent threats. ▫ **thunderbolt** flash of lightning with crash of thunder, unexpected occurrence or announcement, supposed bolt or shaft as destructive agent; **thunderclap** crash of thunder; **thundercloud** electrically charged cumulus cloud; **thunderstorm** storm with thunder and lightning; **thunderstruck** amazed. ▫ **thunderous** *adjective*; **thundery** *adjective*.

thundering *adjective colloquial* huge.

Thur. *abbreviation* (also **Thurs.**) Thursday.

thurible /ˈθjʊərɪb(ə)l/ *noun* censer.

Thursday /ˈθɜːzdeɪ/ *noun* day of week following Wednesday.

thus /ðʌs/ *adverb formal* in this way, like this; accordingly, as a result or inference; to this extent, so.

thwack ● *verb* hit with heavy blow. ● *noun* heavy blow.

thwart /θwɔːt/ ● *verb* frustrate, foil. ● *noun* rower's seat.

thy /ðaɪ/ *adjective* (also **thine**, esp. before vowel) *archaic* your (singular).

thyme /taɪm/ *noun* herb with aromatic leaves.

thymol /ˈθaɪmɒl/ *noun* antiseptic made from oil of thyme.

thymus /ˈθaɪməs/ *noun* (*plural* **thymi** /-maɪ/) ductless gland near base of neck.

thyroid /ˈθaɪrɔɪd/ *noun* thyroid gland. ▫ **thyroid cartilage** large cartilage of larynx forming Adam's apple; **thyroid gland** large ductless gland near larynx secreting hormone which regulates growth and development, extract of this.

thyself /ðaɪˈself/ *pronoun archaic: emphatic form of* THOU[1] *or* THEE; *reflexive form of* THEE.

ti = TE.

tiara /tɪˈɑːrə/ *noun* jewelled ornamental band worn on front of woman's hair; 3-crowned diadem formerly worn by pope.

tibia /ˈtɪbɪə/ *noun* (*plural* **tibiae** /-bɪiː/) inner of two bones extending from knee to ankle.

tic *noun* (in full **nervous tic**) spasmodic contraction of muscles, esp. of face.

tick[1] ● *noun* slight recurring click, esp. of watch or clock; *colloquial* moment; small mark (✓) to denote correctness etc. ● *verb* make sound of tick; (often + *off*) mark with tick. ▫ **tick off** *colloquial* reprimand; **tick over** (of engine) idle, function at basic level; **tick-tack** kind of manual semaphore used by racecourse bookmakers; **tick-tock** ticking of large clock etc.

tick[2] *noun* parasitic arachnid or insect on animals.

tick[3] *noun colloquial* financial credit.

tick[4] *noun* case of mattress or pillow; ticking.

ticker *noun colloquial* heart; watch, *US* tape machine. ▫ **ticker-tape** paper strip from tape machine, esp. as thrown from windows to greet celebrity.

ticket /ˈtɪkɪt/ ● *noun* piece of paper or card entitling holder to enter place, participate in event, travel by public transport, etc.; notification of traffic offence etc.; certificate of discharge from army or of qualification as ship's master, pilot, etc.; price etc. label; *esp. US* list of candidates put forward by group, esp. political party, principles of party; (**the ticket**) *colloquial* what is needed. ● *verb* (**-t-**) attach ticket to.

ticking *noun* strong usually striped material to cover mattresses etc.

tickle /ˈtɪk(ə)l/ ● *verb* (**-ling**) touch or stroke lightly so as to produce laughter and spasmodic movement; excite agreeably, amuse; catch (trout etc.) by rubbing it so that it moves backwards into hand. ● *noun* act or sensation of tickling.

ticklish /ˈtɪklɪʃ/ *adjective* sensitive to tickling; difficult to handle.

tidal /ˈtaɪd(ə)l/ *adjective* related to, like, or affected by tides. □ **tidal wave** exceptionally large ocean wave, esp. one caused by underwater earthquake, widespread manifestation of feeling etc.

tidbit *US* = TITBIT.

tiddler /ˈtɪdlə/ *noun colloquial* small fish, esp. stickleback or minnow; unusually small thing.

tiddly[1] /ˈtɪdlɪ/ *adjective* (**-ier**, **-iest**) *colloquial* slightly drunk.

tiddly[2] /ˈtɪdlɪ/ *adjective* (**-ier**, **-iest**) *colloquial* little.

tiddly-wink /ˈtɪdlɪwɪŋk/ *noun* counter flicked with another into cup; (in *plural*) this game.

tide ● *noun* regular rise and fall of sea due to attraction of moon and sun; water as moved by this; time, season; trend of opinion, fortune, or events. ● *verb* (**-ding**) (**tide over**) temporarily provide with what is needed. □ **tidemark** mark made by tide at high water, *colloquial* line of dirt round bath, or on person's body between washed and unwashed parts; **tideway** tidal part of river.

tidings /ˈtaɪdɪŋz/ *noun archaic or jocular* (treated as *singular* or *plural*) news.

tidy /ˈtaɪdɪ/ ● *adjective* (**-ier**, **-iest**) neat, orderly; (of person) methodical; *colloquial* considerable. ● *noun* (*plural* **-ies**) receptacle for odds and ends. ● *verb* (**-ies**, **-ied**) (often + *up*) make (oneself, room, etc.) tidy; put in order. □ **tidily** *adverb*; **tidiness** *noun*.

tie ● *verb* (**tying**) attach or fasten with cord etc.; form into knot or bow; (often + *down*) restrict, bind; (often + *with*) make same score as another competitor; bind (rafters etc.) by crosspiece etc.; *Music* unite (notes) by tie. ● *noun* cord etc. used for fastening; strip of material worn round collar and tied in knot at front; thing that unites or restricts people; equality of score, draw, or dead heat among competitors; match between any pair of players or teams; rod or beam holding parts of structure together; *Music* curved line above or below two notes of same pitch that are to be joined as one. □ **tie-break**, **-breaker** means of deciding winner when competitors have tied; **tie-dye** method of producing dyed patterns by tying string etc. to keep dye from parts of fabric; **tie-pin** ornamental pin to hold necktie in place; **tie up** fasten with cord etc., invest (money etc.) so that it is not immediately available for use, fully occupy (person), bring to satisfactory conclusion; **tie-up** connection, association.

tied *adjective* (of dwelling house) occupied subject to tenant's working for house's owner; (of public house etc.) bound to supply only particular brewer's liquor.

tier /tɪə/ *noun* row, rank, or unit of structure, as one of several placed one above another. □ **tiered** *adjective*.

tiercel = TERCEL.

tiff *noun* slight or petty quarrel.

tiger /ˈtaɪgə/ *noun* large Asian animal of cat family, with yellow-brown coat with black stripes; fierce, formidable, or energetic person. □ **tiger-cat** any moderate-sized feline resembling tiger; **tiger lily** tall garden lily with dark-spotted orange flowers.

tight /taɪt/ ● *adjective* closely held, drawn, fastened, fitting, etc.; impermeable, impervious; tense, stretched; *colloquial* drunk; *colloquial* stingy; (of money or materials) not easily obtainable; stringent, demanding; presenting difficulties; produced by or requiring great exertion or pressure. ● *adverb* tightly. □ **tight corner** difficult situation; **tight-fisted** stingy; **tight-lipped** restraining emotion, determinedly reticent; **tightrope** high tightly stretched rope or wire on which acrobats etc. perform. □ **tighten** *verb*; **tightly** *adverb*; **tightness** *noun*.

tights *plural noun* thin close-fitting stretch garment covering legs, feet, and lower torso.

tigress /ˈtaɪgrɪs/ *noun* female tiger.

tilde /ˈtɪldə/ *noun* mark (˜) placed over letter, e.g. Spanish *n* in *señor*.

tile ● *noun* thin slab of concrete, baked clay, etc. for roofing, paving, etc. ● *verb* (**-ling**) cover with tiles. □ **tiler** *noun*.

tiling *noun* process of fixing tiles; area of tiles.

till[1] ● *preposition* up to, as late as. ● *conjunction* up to time when; so long that.

■ **Usage** In all senses, *till* can be replaced by *until*, which is more formal in style.

till[2] *noun* money-drawer in bank, shop, etc., esp. with device recording amount and details of each purchase.

till[3] *verb* cultivate (land).

tillage *noun* preparation of land for growing crops; tilled land.

tiller /ˈtɪlə/ *noun* bar by which boat's rudder is turned.

tilt ● *verb* (cause to) assume sloping position or heel over; (+ *at*) thrust or run at with weapon; (+ *with*) engage in contest. ● *noun* tilting; sloping position; (of medieval knights etc.) charging with lance against opponent or mark. □ **(at) full tilt** at full speed, with full force.

tilth *noun* tillage, cultivation; cultivated soil.

timber /ˈtɪmbə/ *noun* wood for building, carpentry, etc.; piece of wood, beam, esp. as rib of vessel; large standing trees; (as *interjection*) tree is about to fall.

timbered *adjective* made (partly) of timber; (of land) wooded.

timbre /ˈtæmbə/ *noun* distinctive character of musical sound or voice apart from its pitch and volume.

timbrel /ˈtɪmbr(ə)l/ *noun archaic* tambourine.

time ● *noun* indefinite continuous progress of past, present, and future events etc. regarded as a whole; more or less definite portion of this, historical or other period; allotted or available portion of time; definite or fixed point or portion of time; (**a time**) indefinite period; occasion; moment etc. suitable for purpose; (in *plural*) (after numeral etc.) *expressing multiplication*; lifetime; (in *singular* or *plural*) conditions of life or of period; *slang* prison sentence; apprenticeship; date or expected date of childbirth or death; measured amount of time worked; rhythm or measure of musical composition. ● *verb* (**-ming**) choose time for, do at chosen or appropriate time; ascertain time taken by. □ **at the same time** simultaneously, nevertheless; **at times** now and then; **from time to time** occasionally; **in no time** rapidly, in a moment; **in time** not late, early enough, eventually, following time of music etc.; **on time** punctually; **time-and-motion** measuring efficiency of industrial etc. operations; **time bomb** one designed to explode at pre-set time; **time capsule** box etc. containing objects typical of present time, buried for future discovery; **time-honoured** esteemed by tradition or through custom; **timekeeper** person who records time, watch or clock as regards accuracy; **timekeeping** keeping of time, punctuality; **time-lag** interval between cause and effect; **time off** time used for rest or different activity; **timepiece** clock, watch; **time-server** person who adapts his or her opinions to suit prevailing circumstances; **time-share** share in property under time-sharing scheme; **time-sharing** use of holiday home by several joint owners at different times of year, use of computer by several people for different operations at the same time; **time sheet** sheet of paper for recording hours worked; **time-shift** move from one time to another; **time signal** audible indication of exact time of day; **time signature** *Music* indication of rhythm; **time switch** one operating automatically at preset time;

timetable *noun* table showing times of public transport services, scheme of lessons, etc., *verb* include or arrange in such schedule; **time zone** range of longitudes where a common standard time is used.

timeless *adjective* not affected by passage of time. □ **timelessness** *noun*.

timely *adjective* (**-ier**, **-iest**) opportune, coming at right time. □ **timeliness** *noun*.

timer *noun* person or device that measures time taken.

timid /ˈtɪmɪd/ *adjective* (**-er**, **-est**) easily alarmed; shy. □ **timidity** /-ˈmɪd-/ *noun*; **timidly** *adverb*.

timing *noun* way thing is timed; regulation of opening and closing of valves in internal-combustion engine.

timorous /ˈtɪmərəs/ *adjective* timid, frightened. □ **timorously** *adverb*.

timpani /ˈtɪmpənɪ/ *plural noun* (also **tympani**) kettledrums. □ **timpanist** *noun*.

tin ● *noun* silvery-white metal used esp. in alloys and in making tin plate; container of tin or tin plate, esp. for preserving food; tin plate. ● *verb* (**-nn-**) preserve (food) in tin; cover or coat with tin. □ **tin foil** foil of tin, aluminium, or tin alloy, used to wrap food; **tin hat** *colloquial* military steel helmet; **tin-opener** tool for opening tins; **tin-pan alley** world of composers and publishers of popular music; **tin plate** sheet steel coated with tin; **tinpot** cheap, inferior; **tinsnips** clippers for cutting sheet metal; **tin-tack** tack[1] coated with tin.

tincture /ˈtɪŋktʃə/ ● *noun* (often + *of*) slight flavour or tinge; medicinal solution of drug in alcohol. ● *verb* (**-ring**) colour slightly, tinge, flavour; (often + *with*) affect slightly.

tinder /ˈtɪndə/ *noun* dry substance readily taking fire from spark. □ **tinder-box** *historical* box with tinder, flint, and steel for kindling fires.

tine *noun* prong, tooth, or point of fork, comb, antler, etc.

ting ● *noun* tinkling sound as of bell. ● *verb* (cause to) emit this.

tinge /tɪndʒ/ ● *verb* (**-ging**) (often + *with*; often in *passive*) colour slightly. ● *noun* tendency to or trace of some colour; slight admixture of feeling or quality.

tingle /ˈtɪŋg(ə)l/ ● *verb* (**-ling**) feel or cause slight pricking or stinging sensation. ● *noun* tingling sensation.

tinker /ˈtɪŋkə/ ● *noun* itinerant mender of kettles, pans, etc.; *Scottish & Irish* Gypsy; *colloquial* mischievous person or animal. ● *verb* (+ *at*, *with*) work in amateurish or desultory way; work as tinker.

tinkle /ˈtɪŋk(ə)l/ ● *verb* (**-ling**) (cause to) make short light ringing sounds. ● *noun* tinkling sound.

tinnitus /ˈtɪnɪtəs/ *noun Medicine* condition with ringing in ears.

tinny *adjective* (**-ier**, **-iest**) like tin; flimsy; (of sound) thin and metallic.

tinsel /ˈtɪns(ə)l/ *noun* glittering decorative metallic strips, threads, etc.; superficial brilliance or splendour. □ **tinselled** *adjective*.

tint ● *noun* a variety of a colour; tendency towards or admixture of a different colour; faint colour spread over surface. ● *verb* apply tint to, colour.

tintinnabulation /tɪntɪnæbjʊˈleɪʃ(ə)n/ *noun* ringing of bells.

tiny /ˈtaɪnɪ/ *adjective* (**-ier**, **-iest**) very small.

tip[1] ● *noun* extremity, esp. of small or tapering thing; small piece or part attached to end of thing. ● *verb* (**-pp-**) provide with tip. □ **tiptop** *colloquial* first-rate, of highest excellence.

tip[2] ● *verb* (**-pp-**) (often + *over*, *up*) (cause to) lean or slant; (+ *into* etc.) overturn, cause to overbalance, discharge contents of (container etc.) thus. ● *noun* slight push or tilt; place where refuse is tipped.

tip[3] ● *verb* (**-pp-**) give small present of money to, esp. for service; name as likely winner of race or contest; strike or touch lightly. ● *noun* small present of money given esp. for service; piece of private or special information, esp. regarding betting or investment; piece of advice. □ **tip-off** a hint, warning, etc.; **tip off** give warning, hint, or inside information to.

tippet /ˈtɪpɪt/ *noun* cape or collar of fur etc.

tipple /ˈtɪp(ə)l/ ● *verb* (**-ling**) drink intoxicating liquor habitually or repeatedly in small quantities. ● *noun colloquial* alcoholic drink. □ **tippler** *noun*.

tipster /ˈtɪpstə/ *noun* person who gives tips about horse racing etc.

tipsy /ˈtɪpsɪ/ *adjective* (**-ier**, **-iest**) slightly drunk; caused by or showing intoxication.

tiptoe /ˈtɪptəʊ/ ● *noun* the tips of the toes. ● *verb* (**-toes**, **-toed**, **-toeing**) walk on tiptoe or stealthily. ● *adverb* (also **on tiptoe**) with heels off the ground.

TIR *abbreviation* international road transport (*transport international routier*).

tirade /taɪˈreɪd/ *noun* long vehement denunciation or declamation.

tire[1] /taɪə/ *verb* (**-ring**) make or grow weary; exhaust patience or interest of; (in *passive*; + *of*) have had enough of.

tire[2] *US* = TYRE.

tired *adjective* weary, ready for sleep; (of idea) hackneyed. □ **tiredly** *adverb*; **tiredness** *noun*.

tireless *adjective* not tiring easily, energetic. □ **tirelessly** *adverb*; **tirelessness** *noun*.

tiresome *adjective* tedious; *colloquial* annoying. □ **tiresomely** *adverb*.

tiro /ˈtaɪərəʊ/ *noun* (also **tyro**) (*plural* **-s**) beginner, novice.

tissue /ˈtɪʃuː/ *noun* any of the coherent collections of cells of which animals or plants are made; tissue-paper; disposable piece of thin absorbent paper for wiping, drying, etc.; fine woven esp. gauzy fabric; (often + *of*) connected series (of lies etc.). □ **tissue-paper** thin soft paper for wrapping etc.

tit[1] *noun* any of various small birds.

tit[2] *noun* □ **tit for tat** blow for blow, retaliation.

Titan /ˈtaɪt(ə)n/ *noun* (often **titan**) person of superhuman strength, intellect, or importance.

titanic /taɪˈtænɪk/ *adjective* gigantic, colossal.

titanium /taɪˈteɪmɪəm/ *noun* dark grey metallic element.

titbit /ˈtɪtbɪt/ *noun* (*US* **tidbit**) dainty morsel; piquant item of news etc.

titchy /ˈtɪtʃɪ/ *adjective* (**-ier**, **-iest**) *colloquial* very small.

tithe /taɪð/ *historical* ● *noun* one-tenth of annual produce of land or labour taken as tax for Church. ● *verb* (**-thing**) subject to tithes; pay tithes.

Titian /ˈtɪʃ(ə)n/ *adjective* (of hair) bright auburn.

titillate /ˈtɪtɪleɪt/ *verb* (**-ting**) excite, esp. sexually; tickle. □ **titillation** *noun*.

titivate /ˈtɪtɪveɪt/ *verb* (**-ting**) *colloquial* smarten; put finishing touches to. □ **titivation** *noun*.

title /ˈtaɪt(ə)l/ *noun* name of book, work of art, etc.; heading of chapter etc.; title-page; caption or credit in film etc.; name denoting person's status; championship in sport; legal right to ownership of property; (+ *to*) just or recognized claim to. □ **title-deed** legal document constituting evidence of a right; **title-holder** person holding (esp. sporting) title; **title-page** page at beginning of book giving title, author, etc.; **title role** part in play etc. from which its title is taken.

titled *adjective* having title of nobility or rank.

titmouse /ˈtɪtmaʊs/ *noun* (*plural* **titmice**) small active tit.

titrate /taɪ'treɪt/ *verb* (**-ting**) ascertain quantity of constituent in (solution) by adding measured amounts of reagent. ▫ **titration** *noun*.

titter /'tɪtə/ ● *verb* laugh covertly, giggle. ● *noun* covert laugh.

tittle /'tɪt(ə)l/ *noun* particle, whit.

tittle-tattle /'tɪt(ə)ltæt(ə)l/ *noun & verb* (**-ling**) gossip, chatter.

tittup /'tɪtəp/ ● *verb* (**-p-** or **-pp-**) go friskily or jerkily, bob up and down, canter. ● *noun* such gait or movement.

titular /'tɪtjʊlə/ *adjective* of or relating to title; existing or being in name only.

tizzy /'tɪzɪ/ *noun* (*plural* **-ies**) *colloquial* state of nervous agitation.

TNT *abbreviation* trinitrotoluene.

to /tə, before vowel tʊ, when stressed tu:/ ● *preposition* in direction of; as far as, not short of; according to; compared with; involved in, comprising; *used to introduce indirect object of verb etc., to introduce or as substitute for infinitive, or to express purpose, consequence, or cause.* ● *adverb* in normal or required position or condition; (of door) nearly closed. ▫ **to and fro** backwards and forwards, (repeatedly) from place to place; **to-do** fuss, commotion; **toing and froing** constant movement to and fro, great or dispersed activity.

toad *noun* froglike amphibian breeding in water but living chiefly on land; repulsive person. ▫ **toadflax** plant with yellow or purple flowers; **toad-in-the-hole** sausages baked in batter; **toadstool** fungus (usually poisonous) with round top and slender stalk.

toady /'təʊdɪ/ ● *noun* (*plural* **-ies**) sycophant. ● *verb* (**-ies**, **-ied**) (+ *to*) behave servilely to, fawn on. ▫ **toadyism** *noun*.

toast ● *noun* sliced bread browned on both sides by radiant heat; person or thing in whose honour company is requested to drink; call to drink or instance of drinking thus. ● *verb* brown by heat, warm at fire etc.; drink to the health or in honour of. ▫ **toasting-fork** long-handled fork for toasting bread etc.; **toastmaster**, **toastmistress** person announcing toasts at public occasion; **toast rack** rack for holding slices of toast at table.

toaster *noun* electrical device for making toast.

tobacco /tə'bækəʊ/ *noun* (*plural* **-s**) plant of American origin with leaves used for smoking, chewing, or snuff; its leaves, esp. as prepared for smoking.

tobacconist /tə'bækənɪst/ *noun* dealer in tobacco.

toboggan /tə'bɒgən/ ● *noun* long light narrow sledge for sliding downhill, esp. over snow. ● *verb* ride on toboggan.

toby jug /'təʊbɪ/ *noun* jug or mug in shape of stout man in 3-cornered hat.

toccata /tə'kɑ:tə/ *noun Music* composition for keyboard instrument, designed to exhibit performer's touch and technique.

tocsin /'tɒksɪn/ *noun* alarm bell or signal.

today /tə'deɪ/ ● *adverb* on this present day; nowadays. ● *noun* this present day; modern times.

toddle /'tɒd(ə)l/ ● *verb* (**-ling**) walk with young child's short unsteady steps; *colloquial* walk, stroll, (usually + *off*, *along*) depart. ● *noun* toddling walk.

toddler *noun* child just learning to walk.

toddy /'tɒdɪ/ *noun* (*plural* **-ies**) sweetened drink of spirits and hot water.

toe ● *noun* any of terminal projections of foot or paw; part of footwear that covers toes; lower end or tip of implement etc. ● *verb* (**toes**, **toed**, **toeing**) touch with toe(s). ▫ **on one's toes** alert; **toecap** (reinforced) part of boot or shoe covering toes; **toehold** slight foothold, small beginning or advantage; **toe the line** conform, esp. under pressure; **toenail** nail of each toe.

toff *noun slang* upper-class person.

toffee /'tɒfɪ/ *noun* firm or hard sweet made of boiled butter, sugar, etc.; this substance. ▫ **toffee-apple** toffee-coated apple; **toffee-nosed** *slang* snobbish, pretentious.

tofu /'təʊfu:/ *noun* curd of mashed soya beans.

tog[1] *colloquial* ● *noun* (in *plural*) clothes. ● *verb* (**-gg-**) (+ *out*, *up*) dress.

tog[2] *noun* unit of thermal resistance of quilts etc.

toga /'təʊgə/ *noun historical* ancient Roman citizen's loose flowing outer garment.

together /tə'geðə/ ● *adverb* in(to) company or conjunction; simultaneously; one with another; uninterruptedly. ● *adjective colloquial* well-organized, self-assured, emotionally stable. ▫ **togetherness** *noun*.

toggle /'tɒg(ə)l/ *noun* short bar used like button for fastening clothes; *Computing* key or command which alternately switches function on and off.

toil ● *verb* work laboriously or incessantly; make slow painful progress. ● *noun* labour; drudgery. ▫ **toilsome** *adjective*.

toilet /'tɔɪlɪt/ *noun* lavatory; process of washing oneself, dressing, etc. ▫ **toilet paper** paper for cleaning oneself after using lavatory; **toilet roll** roll of toilet paper; **toilet water** dilute perfume used after washing.

toiletries /'tɔɪlɪtri:z/ *plural noun* articles or cosmetics used in washing, dressing, etc.

toilette /twɑ:'let/ *noun* process of washing oneself, dressing, etc.

toils /tɔɪlz/ *plural noun* net, snare.

token /'təʊkən/ ● *noun* symbol, reminder, mark; voucher; thing equivalent to something else, esp. money. ● *adjective* perfunctory, chosen by tokenism to represent a group. ▫ **token strike** brief strike to demonstrate strength of feeling.

tokenism *noun* granting of minimum concessions.

told *past & past participle* of TELL.

tolerable /'tɒlərəb(ə)l/ *adjective* endurable; fairly good. ▫ **tolerably** *adverb*.

tolerance /'tɒlərəns/ *noun* willingness or ability to tolerate; permitted variation in dimension, weight, etc.

tolerant /'tɒlərənt/ *adjective* disposed to tolerate others; (+ *of*) enduring or patient of.

tolerate /'tɒləreɪt/ *verb* (**-ting**) allow the existence or occurrence of without authoritative interference; endure; find or treat as endurable; be able to take or undergo without harm. ▫ **toleration** *noun*.

toll[1] /təʊl/ *noun* charge to use bridge, road, etc.; cost or damage caused by disaster etc. ▫ **toll-gate** barrier preventing passage until toll is paid.

toll[2] /təʊl/ ● *verb* (of bell) ring with slow uniform strokes, ring (bell) thus; announce or mark (death etc.) thus; (of bell) strike (the hour). ● *noun* tolling or stroke of bell.

toluene /'tɒljʊi:n/ *noun* colourless liquid hydrocarbon used in manufacture of explosives etc.

tom *noun* (in full **tom-cat**) male cat.

tomahawk /'tɒməhɔ:k/ *noun* N. American Indian war-axe.

tomato /tə'mɑ:təʊ/ *noun* (*plural* **-es**) glossy red or yellow fleshy edible fruit; plant bearing this.

tomb /tu:m/ *noun* burial-vault; grave; sepulchral monument. ▫ **tombstone** memorial stone over grave.

tombola /tɒm'bəʊlə/ *noun* kind of lottery.

tomboy /'tɒmbɔɪ/ *noun* girl who enjoys rough noisy recreations. ▫ **tomboyish** *adjective*.

tome *noun* large book or volume.

tomfool /tɒm'fu:l/ ● *noun* fool. ● *adjective* foolish. ▫ **tomfoolery** *noun*.

Tommy /'tɒmɪ/ *noun* (*plural* **-ies**) *colloquial* British private soldier.

tommy-gun /'tɒmɪgʌn/ *noun* sub-machine-gun.

tomorrow /tə'mɒrəʊ/ ● *adverb* on day after today; in future. ● *noun* the day after today; the near future.

tomtit *noun* tit, esp. blue tit.

tom-tom /'tɒmtɒm/ *noun* kind of drum usually beaten with hands.

ton /tʌn/ *noun* measure of weight equalling 2,240 lb (**long ton**) or 2,000 lb (**short ton**); metric ton; unit of measurement of ship's tonnage; (usually in *plural*) *colloquial* large number or amount; *slang* speed of 100 m.p.h., score of 100.

tonal /'təʊn(ə)l/ *adjective* of or relating to tone or tonality.

tonality /tə'nælɪtɪ/ *noun* (*plural* **-ies**) relationship between tones of a musical scale; observance of single tonic key as basis of musical composition; colour scheme of picture.

tone ● *noun* sound, esp. with reference to pitch, quality, and strength; (often in *plural*) modulation of voice to express emotion etc.; manner of expression in writing or speaking; musical sound, esp. of definite pitch and character; general effect of colour or of light and shade in picture; tint or shade of colour; prevailing character of morals, sentiments, etc.; proper firmness of body, state of (good) health. ● *verb* (**-ning**) give desired tone to; alter tone of; harmonize. ▫ **tone-deaf** unable to perceive differences in musical pitch; **tone down** make or become softer in tone; **tone up** make or become stronger in tone. ▫ **toneless** *adjective*; **tonelessly** *adverb*; **toner** *noun*.

tongs *plural noun* implement with two arms for grasping coal, sugar, etc.

tongue /tʌŋ/ ● *noun* muscular organ in mouth used in tasting, swallowing, speaking, etc.; tongue of ox etc. as food; faculty or manner of speaking; particular language; thing like tongue in shape. ● *verb* (**-guing**) use tongue to articulate (notes) in playing wind instrument. ▫ **tongue-in-cheek** ironic(ally); **tongue-tied** too shy to speak; **tongue-twister** sequence of words difficult to pronounce quickly and correctly.

tonic /'tɒnɪk/ ● *noun* invigorating medicine; anything serving to invigorate; tonic water; *Music* keynote. ● *adjective* invigorating. ▫ **tonic sol-fa** musical notation used esp. in teaching singing; **tonic water** carbonated drink with quinine.

tonight /tə'naɪt/ ● *adverb* on present or approaching evening or night. ● *noun* the evening or night of today.

tonnage /'tʌnɪdʒ/ *noun* ship's internal cubic capacity or freight-carrying capacity; charge per ton on freight or cargo.

tonne /tʌn/ *noun* 1,000 kg.

tonsil /'tɒns(ə)l/ *noun* either of two small organs on each side of root of tongue.

tonsillectomy /tɒnsə'lektəmɪ/ *noun* (*plural* **-ies**) surgical removal of tonsils.

tonsillitis /tɒnsə'laɪtɪs/ *noun* inflammation of tonsils.

tonsorial /tɒn'sɔ:rɪəl/ *adjective usually jocular* of hairdresser or hairdressing.

tonsure /'tɒnʃə/ ● *noun* shaving of crown or of whole head as clerical or monastic symbol; bare patch so made. ● *verb* (**-ring**) give tonsure to.

too *adverb* to a greater extent than is desirable or permissible; *colloquial* very; in addition; moreover.

took *past* of TAKE.

tool /tu:l/ ● *noun* implement for working on something by hand or by machine; thing used in activity; person merely used by another. ● *verb* dress (stone) with chisel; impress design on (leather); (+ *along*, *around*, etc.) *slang* drive or ride esp. in a casual or leisurely way.

toot /tu:t/ ● *noun* sound (as) of horn etc. ● *verb* sound (horn etc.); give out such sound.

tooth /tu:θ/ *noun* (*plural* **teeth**) each of a set of hard structures in jaws of most vertebrates, used for biting and chewing; toothlike part or projection, e.g. cog of gearwheel, point of saw or comb, etc.; (often + *for*) taste, appetite; (in *plural*) force, effectiveness. ▫ **fight tooth and nail** fight fiercely; **get one's teeth into** devote oneself seriously to; **in the teeth of** in spite of, contrary to, directly against (wind etc.); **toothache** pain in teeth; **toothbrush** brush for cleaning teeth; **toothpaste** paste for cleaning teeth; **toothpick** small sharp stick for removing food lodged between teeth. ▫ **toothed** *adjective*; **toothless** *adjective*.

toothsome *adjective* (of food) delicious.

toothy *adjective* (**-ier**, **-iest**) having large, numerous, or prominent teeth.

tootle /'tu:t(ə)l/ *verb* (**-ling**) toot gently or repeatedly; (usually + *around*, *along*, etc.) *colloquial* move casually.

top[1] ● *noun* highest point or part; highest rank or place, person occupying this; upper end, head; upper surface, upper part; cover or cap of container etc.; garment for upper part of body; utmost degree, height; (in *plural*) *colloquial* person or thing of best quality; (esp. in *plural*) leaves etc. of plant grown chiefly for its root; *Nautical* platform round head of lower mast. ● *adjective* highest in position, degree, or importance. ● *verb* (**-pp-**) furnish with top, cap, etc.; be higher or better than, surpass, be at or reach top of; *slang* kill, hit golf ball above centre. ▫ **on top of** fully in command of, very close to, in addition to; **top brass** *colloquial* high-ranking officers; **topcoat** overcoat, final coat of paint etc.; **top dog** *colloquial* victor, master; **top drawer** *colloquial* high social position or origin; **top dress** apply fertilizer on top of (earth) without ploughing it in; **top-flight** of highest rank of achievement; **top hat** tall silk hat; **top-heavy** overweighted at top; **topknot** knot, tuft, crest, or bow worn or growing on top of head; **topmast** mast on top of lower mast; **top-notch** *colloquial* first-rate; **top secret** of utmost secrecy; **topside** outer side of round of beef, side of ship above waterline; **topsoil** top layer of soil; **top up** complete (amount), fill up (partly empty container); **top-up** addition, amount that completes or quantity that fills something. ▫ **topmost** *adjective*.

top[2] *noun* toy spinning on point when set in motion.

topaz /'təʊpæz/ *noun* semiprecious transparent stone, usually yellow.

tope *verb* (**-ping**) *archaic or literary* drink alcohol to excess, esp. habitually. ▫ **toper** *noun*.

topi /'təʊpɪ/ *noun* (also **topee**) (*plural* **-s**) hat, esp sun-helmet.

topiary /'təʊpɪərɪ/ ● *adjective* of or formed by clipping shrubs, trees, etc. into ornamental shapes. ● *noun* topiary art.

topic /'tɒpɪk/ *noun* subject of discourse, conversation, or argument.

topical *adjective* dealing with current affairs, etc. ▫ **topicality** /-'kæl-/ *noun*.

topless *adjective* without a top; (of garment) leaving breasts bare; (of woman) bare-breasted; (of place) where women go or work bare-breasted.

topography /tə'pɒgrəfi/ *noun* detailed description, representation, etc. of features of a district; such features. □ **topographer** *noun*; **topographical** /tɒpə'græf-/ *adjective*.

topology /tə'pɒlədʒɪ/ *noun* study of geometrical properties unaffected by changes of shape or size. □ **topological** /tBpə'lɒdʒ-/ *adjective*.

topper *noun colloquial* top hat.

topping *noun* thing that tops, esp. sauce on dessert etc.

topple /'tɒp(ə)l/ *verb* (**-ling**) (often + *over*, *down*) (cause to) fall as if top-heavy; overthrow.

topsy-turvy /tɒpsɪ'tɜːvɪ/ *adverb & adjective* upside down; in utter confusion.

toque /təʊk/ *noun* woman's close-fitting brimless hat.

tor *noun* hill, rocky peak.

torch *noun* battery-powered portable lamp; thing lit for illumination; source of heat, light, or enlightenment. □ **carry a torch for** have (esp. unreturned) love for.

tore *past* of TEAR[1].

toreador /'tɒrɪədɔː/ *noun* bullfighter, esp. on horseback.

torment ● *noun* /'tɔːment/ (cause of) severe bodily or mental suffering. ● *verb* /tɔː'ment/ subject to torment, tease or worry excessively. □ **tormentor** /-'men-/ *noun*.

torn *past participle* of TEAR[1].

tornado /tɔː'neɪdəʊ/ *noun* (*plural* **-es**) violent storm over small area, with whirling winds.

torpedo /tɔ'piːdəʊ/ ● *noun* (*plural* **-es**) cigar-shaped self-propelled underwater or aerial missile that explodes on hitting ship. ● *verb* (**-es**, **-ed**) destroy or attack with torpedo(es); make ineffective. □ **torpedo boat** small fast warship armed with torpedoes.

torpid /'tɔːpɪd/ *adjective* sluggish, apathetic; numb; dormant. □ **torpidity** /-'pɪd-/ *noun*.

torpor /'tɔːpə/ *noun* torpid condition.

torque /tɔːk/ *noun* twisting or rotary force, esp. in machine; *historical* twisted metal necklace worn by ancient Gauls and Britons.

torrent /'tɒrənt/ *noun* rushing stream of liquid; downpour of rain; (in *plural*) (usually + *of*) violent flow. □ **torrential** /tə'renʃ(ə)l/ *adjective*.

torrid /'tɒrɪd/ *adjective* intensely hot; scorched, parched; passionate, intense.

torsion /'tɔːʃ(ə)n/ *noun* twisting. □ **torsional** *adjective*.

torso /'tɔːsəʊ/ *noun* (*plural* **-s**) trunk of human body; statue of this.

tort *noun* breach of legal duty (other than under contract) with liability for damages. □ **tortious** /'tɔːʃəs/ *adjective*.

tortilla /tɔː'tiːjə/ *noun* thin flat originally Mexican maize cake eaten hot.

tortoise /'tɔːtəs/ *noun* slow-moving reptile with horny domed shell. □ **tortoiseshell** mottled yellowish-brown turtle-shell, cat or butterfly with markings resembling tortoiseshell.

tortuous /'tɔːtʃʊəs/ *adjective* winding; devious, circuitous. □ **tortuously** *adverb*.

torture /'tɔːtʃə/ ● *noun* infliction of severe bodily pain, esp. as punishment or means of persuasion; severe physical or mental pain. ● *verb* (**-ring**) subject to torture. □ **torturer** *noun*; **torturous** *adjective*.

Tory /'tɔːrɪ/ *colloquial* ● *noun* (*plural* **-ies**) member of Conservative party. ● *adjective* Conservative. □ **Toryism** *noun*.

tosa /'təʊsə/ *noun* dog of a mastiff breed.

tosh *noun colloquial* rubbish, nonsense.

toss ● *verb* throw up, esp. with hand; roll about, throw, or be thrown, restlessly or from side to side; throw lightly or carelessly; throw (coin) into air to decide choice etc. by way it falls, (often + *for*) settle question or dispute with (person) thus; (of bull etc.) fling up with horns; coat (food) with dressing etc. by shaking it. ● *noun* tossing; fall, esp. from horseback. □ **toss one's head** throw it back, esp. in anger, impatience, etc.; **toss off** drink off at a draught, dispatch (work) rapidly or easily; **toss up** *verb* toss coin; **toss-up** *noun* doubtful matter, tossing of coin.

tot[1] *noun* small child; dram of liquor.

tot[2] *verb* (**-tt-**) (usually + *up*) add, mount. □ **tot up to** amount to.

total /'təʊt(ə)l/ ● *adjective* complete, comprising the whole; absolute, unqualified. ● *noun* whole sum or amount. ● *verb* (**-ll-**; *US* **-l-**) (often + *to*, *up to*) amount to; calculate total of. □ **totality** /-'tæl-/ *noun* (*plural* **-ies**); **totally** *adverb*.

totalitarian /təʊtælɪ'teərɪən/ *adjective* of one-party government requiring complete subservience to state. □ **totalitarianism** *noun*.

totalizator /'təʊtəlaɪzeɪtə/ *noun* (also **totalisator**) device showing number and amount of bets staked on race when total will be divided among those betting on winner; this betting system.

totalize /'təʊtəlaɪz/ *verb* (also **-ise**) (**-zing** or **-sing**) combine into a total.

tote[1] *noun slang* totalizator.

tote[2] *verb* (**-ting**) *esp. US colloquial* carry, convey. □ **tote bag** large and capacious bag.

totem /'təʊtəm/ *noun* natural object (esp. animal) adopted esp. among N. American Indians as emblem of clan or individual; image of this. □ **totem-pole** post with carved and painted or hung totem(s).

toto see IN TOTO.

totter /'tɒtə/ ● *verb* stand or walk unsteadily or feebly; shake, be about to fall. ● *noun* unsteady or shaky movement or gait. □ **tottery** *adjective*.

toucan /'tuːkən/ *noun* tropical American bird with large bill.

touch /tʌtʃ/ ● *verb* come into or be in physical contact with; (often + *with*) bring hand etc. into contact with; cause (two things) to meet thus; rouse tender or painful feelings in; strike lightly; (usually in negative) disturb, harm, affect, have dealings with, consume, use; concern; reach as far as; (usually in negative) approach in excellence; modify; (as **touched** *adjective*) *colloquial* slightly mad; (usually + *for*) *slang* request and get money etc. from (person). ● *noun* act of touching; sense of feeling; small amount, trace; (**a touch**) slightly; *Music* manner of playing keys or strings, instrument's response to this; artistic, literary, etc. style or skill; *slang* act of requesting and getting money etc. from person; *Football* part of field outside touchlines. □ **touch-and-go** critical, risky; **touch at** *Nautical* call at (port etc.); **touch down** (of aircraft) alight; **touchdown** *noun*; **touchline** side limit of football etc. pitch; **touch off** explode by touching with match etc., initiate (process) suddenly; **touch on, upon** refer to or mention briefly or casually, verge on; **touch-paper** paper impregnated with nitre for igniting fireworks etc.; **touchstone** dark schist or jasper for testing alloys by marking it with them, criterion; **touch-type** type without looking at keys; **touch-typist** *noun*; **touch up** give finishing touches to, retouch, *slang* molest sexually; **touch wood** touch something wooden to avert ill luck; **touchwood** readily inflammable rotten wood.

touché /tuː'ʃeɪ/ *interjection acknowledging justified accusation or retort, or hit in fencing.* [French]

touching ● *adjective* moving, pathetic. ● *preposition literary* concerning. □ **touchingly** *adverb*.

touchy *adjective* (**-ier**, **-iest**) apt to take offence, oversensitive. □ **touchily** *adverb*; **touchiness** *noun*.

tough /tʌf/ ● *adjective* hard to break, cut, tear, or chew; able to endure hardship, hardy; stubborn, difficult; *colloquial* acting sternly, (of luck etc.) hard; *colloquial* criminal, violent. ● *noun* tough person, esp. ruffian. □ **toughen** *verb*; **toughness** *noun*.

toupee /'tu:peɪ/ *noun* hairpiece to cover bald spot.

tour /tʊə/ ● *noun* holiday journey or excursion including stops at various places; walk round, inspection; spell of military or diplomatic duty; series of performances, matches, etc. at different places. ● *verb* (often + *through*) go on a tour; make a tour of (country etc.). □ **on tour** (esp. of sports team, theatre company, etc.) touring; **tour operator** travel agent specializing in package holidays.

tour de force /tʊə də 'fɔ:s/ *noun* (*plural* ***tours de force*** same pronunciation) outstanding feat or performance. [French]

tourer *noun* car or caravan for touring in.

tourism *noun* commercial organization and operation of holidays.

tourist *noun* holiday traveller; member of touring sports team. □ **tourist class** lowest class of passenger accommodation in ship, aeroplane, etc.

tourmaline /'tʊərməli:n/ *noun* mineral with unusual electric properties and used as gem.

tournament /'tʊənəmənt/ *noun* large contest of many rounds; display of military exercises; *historical* pageant with jousting.

tournedos /'tʊənədəʊ/ *noun* (*plural* same /-dəʊz/) small thick piece of fillet of beef.

tourney /'tʊənɪ/ ● *noun* (*plural* **-s**) tournament. ● *verb* (**-eys**, **-eyed**) take part in tournament.

tourniquet /'tʊənɪkeɪ/ *noun* device for stopping flow of blood through artery by compression.

tousle /'taʊz(ə)l/ *verb* (**-ling**) make (esp. hair) untidy; handle roughly.

tout /taʊt/ ● *verb* (usually + *for*) solicit custom persistently, pester customers; solicit custom of or for; spy on racehorses in training. ● *noun* person who touts.

tow¹ /təʊ/ ● *verb* pull along by rope etc. ● *noun* towing, being towed. □ **in tow** being towed, accompanying or in the charge of a person; **on tow** being towed; **towpath** path beside river or canal originally for horse towing boat.

tow² /təʊ/ *noun* fibres of flax etc. ready for spinning. □ **tow-headed** having very light-coloured or tousled hair.

towards /tə'wɔ:dz/ *preposition* (also **toward**) in direction of; as regards, in relation to; as a contribution to, for; near.

towel /'taʊəl/ ● *noun* absorbent cloth, paper, etc. for drying after washing etc. ● *verb* (**-ll-**; *US* **-l-**) rub or dry with towel.

towelling *noun* thick soft absorbent cloth used esp. for towels.

tower /'taʊə/ ● *noun* tall structure, often part of castle, church, etc.; fortress etc. with tower; tall structure housing machinery etc. ● *verb* (usually + *above*, *up*) reach high, be superior; (as **towering** *adjective*) high, lofty, violent. □ **tower block** tall building of offices or flats; **tower of strength** person who gives strong emotional support.

town /taʊn/ *noun* densely populated area, between city and village in size; London or the chief city or town in area; central business area in neighbourhood. □ **go to town** *colloquial* act or work with energy or enthusiasm; **on the town** *colloquial* enjoying urban night-life; **town clerk** *US & historical* official in charge of records etc. of town; **town gas** manufactured gas for domestic etc. use; **town hall** headquarters of local government, with public meeting rooms etc.; **town house** town residence, esp. one of terrace; **town planning** planning of construction and growth of towns; **township** *South African* urban area for occupation by black people, *US & Canadian* administrative division of county, or district 6 miles square, *Australian & NZ* small town; **townspeople** inhabitants of town.

townie /'taʊnɪ/ *noun* (also **townee** /-'ni:/) *derogatory* inhabitant of town.

toxaemia /tɒk'si:mɪə/ *noun* (*US* **toxemia**) blood poisoning; increased blood pressure in pregnancy.

toxic /'tɒksɪk/ *adjective* poisonous; of poison. □ **toxicity** /-'sɪs-/ *noun*.

toxicology /tɒksɪ'kɒlədʒɪ/ *noun* study of poisons. □ **toxicological** /-kə'lɒdʒ-/ *adjective*; **toxicologist** *noun*.

toxin /'tɒksɪn/ *noun* poison produced by living organism.

toy ● *noun* plaything; thing providing amusement; diminutive breed of dog etc. ● *verb* (usually + *with*) amuse oneself, flirt, move thing idly. □ **toy boy** *colloquial* woman's much younger boyfriend; **toyshop** shop selling toys.

trace¹ ● *verb* (**-cing**) find signs of by investigation; (often + *along*, *through*, *to*, etc.) follow or mark track, position, or path of; (often + *back*) follow to origins; copy (drawing etc.) by marking its lines on superimposed translucent paper; mark out, delineate, or write, esp. laboriously. ● *noun* indication of existence of something, vestige; very small quantity; track, footprint; mark left by instrument's moving pen etc. □ **trace element** chemical element occurring or required, esp. in soil, only in minute amounts. □ **traceable** *adjective*.

trace² *noun* each of two side-straps, chains, or ropes by which horse draws vehicle. □ **kick over the traces** become insubordinate or reckless.

tracer *noun* bullet etc. made visible in flight by flame etc. emitted; artificial radioisotope which can be followed through body by radiation it produces.

tracery /'treɪsərɪ/ *noun* (*plural* **-ies**) decorative stone openwork, esp. in head of Gothic window; lacelike pattern.

trachea /trə'ki:ə/ *noun* (*plural* **-cheae** /-'ki:i:/) windpipe.

tracing *noun* traced copy of drawing etc.; act of tracing. □ **tracing-paper** translucent paper for making tracings.

track ● *noun* mark(s) left by person, animal, vehicle, etc.; (in *plural*) such marks, esp. footprints; rough path; line of travel; continuous railway line; racecourse, circuit, prepared course for runners; groove on gramophone record; single song etc. on gramophone record, CD, or magnetic tape; band round wheels of tank, tractor, etc. ● *verb* follow track of; trace (course, development, etc.) from vestiges. □ **in one's tracks** *colloquial* where one stands, instantly; **make tracks** *colloquial* depart; **make tracks for** *colloquial* go in pursuit of or towards; **track down** reach or capture by tracking; **tracker dog** police dog tracking by scent; **track events** running-races; **track record** person's past achievements; **track shoe** runner's spiked shoe; **track suit** warm outfit worn for exercising etc. □ **tracker** *noun*.

tract¹ *noun* (esp. large) stretch of territory; bodily organ or system.

tract² *noun* pamphlet, esp. containing propaganda.

tractable /'træktəb(ə)l/ *adjective* easily managed; docile. □ **tractability** *noun*.

traction /'trækʃ(ə)n/ *noun* hauling, pulling; therapeutic sustained pull on limb etc. □ **traction-engine** steam or diesel engine for drawing heavy load.

tractor /'træktə/ *noun* vehicle for hauling farm machinery etc.; traction-engine.

trad *colloquial* ● *noun* traditional jazz. ● *adjective* traditional.

trade ● *noun* buying and selling; this between nations etc.; business merely for profit (as distinct from profession); business of specified nature or time; skilled handicraft; (**the trade**) people engaged in specific trade; *US* transaction, esp. swap; (usually in *plural*) trade wind. ● *verb* (**-ding**) (often + *in, with*) engage in trade, buy and sell; exchange; *US* swap; (usually + *with, for*) have transaction. □ **trade in** exchange (esp. used article) in part payment for another; **trade mark** device or name legally registered to represent a company or product, distinctive characteristic; **trade name** name by which a thing is known in a trade, or given by manufacturer to a product, or under which a business trades; **trade off** exchange as compromise; **trade-off** balance, compromise; **trade on** take advantage of; **tradesman, tradeswoman** person engaged in trade, esp. shopkeeper; **trade(s) union** organized association of workers in trade, profession, etc. formed to further their common interests; **trade-unionist** member of trade union; **trade wind** constant wind blowing towards equator from NE or SE. □ **trader** *noun*.

tradescantia /trædɪs'kæntɪə/ *noun* (usually trailing) plant with large blue, white, or pink flowers.

trading *noun* engaging in trade. □ **trading estate** area designed for industrial and commercial firms; **trading post** store etc. in remote region; **trading-stamp** token given to customer and exchangeable in quantity usually for goods.

tradition /trə'dɪʃ(ə)n/ *noun* custom, opinion, or belief handed down to posterity; handing down of these.

traditional *adjective* of, based on, or obtained by tradition; (of jazz) in style of early 20th c. □ **traditionally** *adverb*.

traditionalism *noun* respect or support for tradition. □ **traditionalist** *noun & adjective*.

traduce /trə'dju:s/ *verb* (**-cing**) slander. □ **traducement** *noun*; **traducer** *noun*.

traffic /'træfɪk/ ● *noun* vehicles moving on public highway, in air, or at sea; (usually + *in*) trade, esp. illegal; coming and going of people or goods by road, rail, air, sea, etc.; dealings between people etc.; (volume of) messages transmitted through communications system. ● *verb* (**-ck-**) (often + *in*) deal, esp. illegally; barter. □ **traffic island** raised area in road to divide traffic and provide refuge for pedestrians; **traffic jam** traffic at standstill; **traffic light(s)** signal controlling road traffic by coloured lights; **traffic warden** person employed to control movement and parking of road vehicles. □ **trafficker** *noun*.

tragedian /trə'dʒi:dɪən/ *noun* author of or actor in tragedies.

tragedienne /trədʒi:dɪ'en/ *noun* actress in tragedies.

tragedy /'trædʒɪdɪ/ *noun* (*plural* **-ies**) serious accident, sad event; play with tragic unhappy ending.

tragic /'trædʒɪk/ *adjective* disastrous, distressing, very sad; of tragedy. □ **tragically** *adverb*.

tragicomedy /trædʒɪ'kɒmədɪ/ *noun* (*plural* **-ies**) drama or event combining comedy and tragedy.

trail ● *noun* track or scent left by moving person, thing, etc.; beaten path, esp. through wild region; long line of people or things following behind something; part dragging behind thing or person. ● *verb* draw or be drawn along behind; (often + *behind*) walk wearily; follow trail of, pursue; be losing in contest; (usually + *away, off*) peter out; (of plant etc.) grow or hang over wall, along ground, etc.; hang loosely. □ **trailing edge** rear edge of aircraft's wing.

trailer *noun* set of extracts from film etc. shown in advance to advertise it; vehicle pulled by another; *US* caravan.

train ● *verb* (often + *to do*) teach (person etc.) specified skill, esp. by practice; undergo this process; bring or come to physical efficiency by exercise, diet, etc.; (often + *up, along*) guide growth of (plant); (usually as **trained** *adjective*) make (mind etc.) discerning through practice etc.; (often + *on*) point, aim. ● *noun* series of railway carriages or trucks drawn by engine; thing dragged along behind or forming back part of dress etc.; succession or series of people, things, events, etc.; group of followers, retinue. □ **in train** arranged, in preparation; **train-bearer** person holding up train of another's robe etc.; **train-spotter** person who collects numbers of railway locomotives. □ **trainee** /-'ni:/ *noun*.

trainer *noun* person who trains horses, athletes, etc.; aircraft or simulator used to train pilots; soft running shoe.

training /'treɪnɪŋ/ *noun* process of teaching or learning a skill etc.

traipse *colloquial* ● *verb* (**-sing**) tramp or trudge wearily. ● *noun* tedious journey on foot.

trait /treɪ/ *noun* characteristic.

traitor /'treɪtə/ *noun* (*feminine* **traitress**) person guilty of betrayal or disloyalty. □ **traitorous** *adjective*.

trajectory /trə'dʒektərɪ/ *noun* (*plural* **-ies**) path of object moving under given forces.

tram *noun* (also **tramcar**) electrically powered passenger road vehicle running on rails. □ **tramlines** rails for tram, *colloquial* either pair of parallel lines at edge of tennis etc. court.

trammel /'træm(ə)l/ ● *noun* (usually in *plural*) impediment, restraint; kind of fishing net. ● *verb* (**-ll-**; *US* **-l-**) hamper.

tramp ● *verb* walk heavily and firmly; go on walking expedition; walk laboriously across or along; (often + *down*) tread on, stamp on; live as tramp. ● *noun* itinerant vagrant or beggar; sound of person or people walking or marching; long walk; *slang derogatory* promiscuous woman.

trample /'træmp(ə)l/ *verb* (**-ling**) tread under foot; crush thus. □ **trample on** tread heavily on, treat roughly or with contempt.

trampoline /'træmpəli:n/ ● *noun* canvas sheet connected by springs to horizontal frame, used for acrobatic exercises. ● *verb* (**-ning**) use trampoline.

trance /trɑ:ns/ *noun* sleeplike state; hypnotic or cataleptic state; such state as supposedly entered into by medium; rapture, ecstasy.

tranny /'trænɪ/ *noun* (*plural* **-ies**) *colloquial* transistor radio.

tranquil /'træŋkwɪl/ *adjective* serene, calm, undisturbed. □ **tranquillity** /-'kwɪl-/ *noun*; **tranquilly** *adverb*.

tranquillize *verb* (also **-ise**; *US* also **tranquilize**) (**-zing** or **-sing**) make tranquil, esp. by drug etc.

tranquillizer *noun* (also **-iser**; *US* also **tranquilizer**) drug used to diminish anxiety.

trans- *prefix* across, beyond; on or to other side of; through.

transact /træn'zækt/ *verb* perform or carry through (business etc.).

transaction /træn'zækʃ(ə)n/ *noun* piece of commercial or other dealing; transacting of business; (in *plural*) published reports of discussions and lectures at meetings of learned society.

transatlantic /trænzət'læntɪk/ *adjective* beyond or crossing the Atlantic; American; *US* European.

transceiver /træn'si:və/ *noun* combined radio transmitter and receiver.

transcend /træn'send/ *verb* go beyond or exceed limits of; excel, surpass.

transcendent *adjective* excelling, surpassing; transcending human experience; (esp. of God) existing apart from, or not subject to limitations of, material universe. ▫ **transcendence** *noun*; **transcendency** *noun*.

transcendental /trænsen'dent(ə)l/ *adjective* a priori, not based on experience, intuitively accepted; abstract, vague. ▫ **Transcendental Meditation** meditation seeking to induce detachment from problems, anxiety, etc.

transcontinental /trænzkɒntɪ'nent(ə)l/ *adjective* extending across a continent.

transcribe /træn'skraɪb/ *verb* (**-bing**) copy out; write out (notes etc.) in full; record for subsequent broadcasting; *Music* adapt for different instrument etc. ▫ **transcriber** *noun*; **transcription** /-'skrɪp-/ *noun*.

transcript /'trænskrɪpt/ *noun* written copy.

transducer /trænz'dju:sə/ *noun* device for changing a non-electrical signal (e.g. pressure) into an electrical one (e.g. voltage).

transept /'trænsept/ *noun* part of cross-shaped church at right angles to nave; either arm of this.

transfer ● *verb* /træns'fɜ:/ (**-rr-**) convey, remove, or hand over (thing etc.); make over possession of (thing, right, etc.) to person; move, change, or be moved to another group, club, etc.; change from one station, route, etc. to another to continue journey; convey (design etc.) from one surface to another. ● *noun* /'trænsfɜ:/ transferring, being transferred; design etc. (to be) conveyed from one surface to another; football player etc. who is transferred; document effecting conveyance of property, a right, etc. ▫ **transferable** /-'fɜ:rəb(ə)l/ *adjective*; **transference** /'trænsfərəns/ *noun*.

transfigure /træns'fɪgə/ *verb* (**-ring**) change appearance of, make more elevated or idealized. ▫ **transfiguration** *noun*.

transfix /træns'fɪks/ *verb* paralyse with horror or astonishment; pierce with sharp implement or weapon.

transform /træns'fɔ:m/ *verb* change form, appearance, character, etc. of, esp. considerably; change voltage etc. of (alternating current). ▫ **transformation** /-fə'meɪ-/ *noun*.

transformer *noun* apparatus for reducing or increasing voltage of alternating current.

transfuse /træns'fju:z/ *verb* (**-sing**) transfer (blood or other liquid) into blood vessel to replace that lost; permeate. ▫ **transfusion** *noun*.

transgress /trænz'gres/ *verb* infringe (law etc.); overstep (limit laid down); sin. ▫ **transgression** *noun*; **transgressor** *noun*.

transient /'trænzɪənt/ *adjective* of short duration; passing. ▫ **transience** *noun*.

transistor /træn'zɪstə/ *noun* semiconductor device capable of amplification and rectification; (in full **transistor radio**) portable radio using transistors.

transistorize *verb* (also **-ise**) (**-zing** or **-sing**) equip with transistors rather than valves.

transit /'trænzɪt/ *noun* going; conveying, being conveyed; passage, route; apparent passage of heavenly body across meridian of place or across sun or planet. ▫ **in transit** (while) going or being conveyed.

transition /træn'zɪʃ(ə)n/ *noun* passage or change from one place, state, condition, style, etc. to another. ▫ **transitional** *adjective*; **transitionally** *adverb*.

transitive /'trænsɪtɪv/ *adjective* (of verb) requiring direct object expressed or understood.

transitory /'trænzɪtərɪ/ *adjective* not lasting; brief, fleeting.

translate /træn'sleɪt/ *verb* (**-ting**) (often + *into*) express sense of in another language or in another form; be translatable; interpret; move or change, esp. from one person, place, or condition to another. ▫ **translatable** *adjective*; **translation** *noun*; **translator** *noun*.

transliterate /trænz'lɪtəreɪt/ *verb* (**-ting**) represent (word etc.) in closest corresponding characters of another script. ▫ **transliteration** *noun*.

translucent /træns'lu:s(ə)nt/ *adjective* allowing light to pass through, semi-transparent. ▫ **translucence** *noun*.

transmigrate /trænzmaɪ'greɪt/ *verb* (**-ting**) (of soul) pass into different body. ▫ **transmigration** *noun*.

transmission /trænz'mɪʃ(ə)n/ *noun* transmitting, being transmitted; broadcast programme; device transmitting power from engine to axle in vehicle.

transmit /trænz'mɪt/ *verb* (**-tt-**) pass or hand on, transfer; communicate or be medium for (ideas, emotions, etc.); allow (heat, light, sound, etc.) to pass through. ▫ **transmissible** *adjective*; **transmittable** *adjective*.

transmitter *noun* person or thing that transmits; equipment used to transmit radio etc. signals.

transmogrify /trænz'mɒgrɪfaɪ/ *verb* (**-ies**, **-ied**) *jocular* transform, esp. in magical or surprising way. ▫ **transmogrification** *noun*.

transmute /trænz'mju:t/ *verb* (**-ting**) change form, nature, or substance of; *historical* change (base metals) into gold. ▫ **transmutation** *noun*.

transom /'trænsəm/ *noun* horizontal bar in window or above door; (in full **transom window**) window above this.

transparency /træns'pærənsɪ/ *noun* (*plural* **-ies**) being transparent; picture (esp. photograph) to be viewed by light passing through it.

transparent /træns'pærənt/ *adjective* allowing light to pass through and giving maximum visibility possible; (of disguise, pretext, etc.) easily seen through; (of quality etc.) obvious; easily understood. ▫ **transparently** *adverb*.

transpire /træns'paɪə/ *verb* (**-ring**) (of secret, fact, etc.) come to be known; happen; emit (vapour, moisture) or be emitted through pores of skin etc. ▫ **transpiration** /-spɪ-/ *noun*.

■ **Usage** The use of *transpire* to mean 'happen' is considered incorrect by some people.

transplant ● *verb* /træns'plɑ:nt/ plant elsewhere; transfer (living tissue or organ) to another part of body or to another body. ● *noun* /'trænsplɑ:nt/ transplanting of organ or tissue; thing transplanted. ▫ **transplantation** *noun*.

transport ● *verb* /træns'pɔ:t/ take to another place; *historical* deport (criminal) to penal colony; (as **transported** *adjective*) (usually + *with*) affected with strong emotion. ● *noun* /'trænspɔ:t/ system of transporting, means of conveyance; ship, aircraft, etc. used to carry troops, military stores, etc.; (esp. in *plural*) vehement emotion. ▫ **transportable** /-'pɔ:t-/ *adjective*.

transportation /trænspɔ:'teɪʃ(ə)n/ *noun* (system of) conveying, being conveyed; *US* means of transport; *historical* deporting of criminals.

transporter *noun* vehicle used to transport other vehicles, heavy machinery, etc. ▫ **transporter bridge** bridge carrying vehicles etc. across water on suspended moving platform.

transpose /træns'pəʊz/ *verb* (**-sing**) cause (two or more things) to change places; change position of (thing) in series or (word(s)) in sentence; *Music* write or play in different key. ▫ **transposition** /-pə'zɪʃ(ə)n/ *noun*.

transsexual /træns'sekʃʊəl/ (also **transexual**) ● *adjective* having physical characteristics of one sex and psychological identification with the other. ● *noun* transsexual person; person who has had sex change.

transship /træns'ʃɪp/ *verb* (**-pp-**) transfer from one ship or conveyance to another. □ **transshipment** *noun*.

transubstantiation /trænsəbstænʃɪ'eɪʃ(ə)n/ *noun* conversion of Eucharistic elements wholly into body and blood of Christ.

transuranic /trænzjʊ'rænɪk/ *adjective Chemistry* (of element) having higher atomic number than uranium.

transverse /'trænzvɜːs/ *adjective* situated, arranged, or acting in crosswise direction. □ **transversely** *adverb*.

transvestite /trænz'vestaɪt/ *noun* man deriving pleasure from dressing in women's clothes. □ **transvestism** *noun*.

trap ● *noun* device, often baited, for catching animals; arrangement or trick to catch (out) unsuspecting person; device for releasing clay pigeon to be shot at or greyhound at start of race etc.; curve in drainpipe etc. that fills with liquid and forms seal against return of gas; two-wheeled carriage; trapdoor; *slang* mouth. ● *verb* (**-pp-**) catch (as) in trap; catch (out) using trick etc.; furnish with traps. □ **trapdoor** door in floor, ceiling, or roof.

trapeze /trə'piːz/ *noun* crossbar suspended by ropes as swing for acrobatics etc.

trapezium /trə'piːzɪəm/ *noun* (*plural* **-s** or **-zia**) quadrilateral with only one pair of sides parallel; *US* trapezoid.

trapezoid /'træpɪzɔɪd/ *noun* quadrilateral with no sides parallel; *US* trapezium.

trapper *noun* person who traps wild animals, esp. for their fur.

trappings /'træpɪŋz/ *plural noun* ornamental accessories; (esp. ornamental) harness for horse.

Trappist /'træpɪst/ ● *noun* monk of order vowed to silence. ● *adjective* of this order.

trash ● *noun esp. US* worthless or waste stuff, rubbish; worthless person(s). ● *verb slang* wreck, vandalize. □ **trash can** *US* dustbin. □ **trashy** *adjective* (**-ier**, **-iest**).

trauma /'trɔːmə/ *noun* (*plural* **traumata** /-mətə/ or **-s**) emotional shock; physical injury, resulting shock. □ **traumatic** /-'mæt-/ *adjective*; **traumatize** *verb* (also **-ise**) (**-zing** or **-sing**).

travail /'træveɪl/ *literary* ● *noun* laborious effort; pangs of childbirth. ● *verb* make laborious effort, esp. in childbirth.

travel /'træv(ə)l/ ● *verb* (**-ll-**; *US* **-l-**) go from one place to another; make journey(s), esp. long or abroad; journey along or through, cover (distance); *colloquial* withstand long journey; act as commercial traveller; move or proceed as specified; *colloquial* move quickly; pass from point to point; (of machine or part) move or operate in specified way. ● *noun* travelling, esp. abroad; (often in *plural*) spell of this; range, rate, or mode of motion of part in machinery. □ **travel agency** agency making arrangements for travellers; **travelling salesman** commercial traveller; **travel-sick** nauseous owing to motion in travelling.

travelled *adjective* (*US* **traveled**) experienced in travelling.

traveller *noun* (*US* **traveler**) person who travels or is travelling; commercial traveller. □ **traveller's cheque** cheque for fixed amount, cashed on signature for equivalent in other currencies; **traveller's joy** wild clematis.

travelogue /'trævəlɒg/ *noun* film or illustrated lecture about travel.

traverse ● *verb* /trə'vɜːs/ (**-sing**) travel or lie across; consider or discuss whole extent of. ● *noun* /'trævəs/ sideways movement; traversing; thing that crosses another. □ **traversal** *noun*.

travesty /'trævɪstɪ/ ● *noun* (*plural* **-ies**) grotesque parody, ridiculous imitation. ● *verb* (**-ies**, **-ied**) make or be travesty of.

trawl ● *verb* fish with trawl or seine or in trawler; catch by trawling; (often + *for*, *through*) search thoroughly. ● *noun* trawling; (in full **trawl-net**) large wide-mouthed fishing net dragged by boat along sea bottom.

trawler *noun* boat used for trawling.

tray *noun* flat board with raised rim for carrying dishes etc.; shallow lidless box for papers or small articles, sometimes forming drawer in cabinet etc.

treacherous /'tretʃərəs/ *adjective* guilty of or involving violation of faith or betrayal of trust; not to be relied on, deceptive. □ **treacherously** *adverb*; **treachery** *noun*.

treacle /'triːk(ə)l/ *noun* syrup produced in refining sugar; molasses. □ **treacly** *adjective*.

tread /tred/ ● *verb* (*past* **trod**; *past participle* **trodden** or **trod**) (often + *on*) set one's foot down; walk on; (often + *down*, *in*, *into*) press (down) or crush with feet; perform (steps etc.) by walking. ● *noun* manner or sound of walking; top surface of step or stair; thick moulded part of vehicle tyre for gripping road; part of wheel or sole of shoe etc. that touches ground. □ **treadmill** device for producing motion by treading on steps on revolving cylinder, similar device used for exercise, monotonous routine work; **tread water** maintain upright position in water by moving feet and hands.

treadle /'tred(ə)l/ *noun* lever moved by foot and imparting motion to machine.

treason /'triːz(ə)n/ *noun* violation of allegiance to sovereign (e.g. plotting assassination) or state (e.g. helping enemy).

treasonable *adjective* involving or guilty of treason.

treasure /'treʒə/ ● *noun* precious metals or gems; hoard of them; accumulated wealth; thing valued for rarity, workmanship, associations, etc.; *colloquial* beloved or highly valued person. ● *verb* (**-ring**) value highly; (often + *up*) store up as valuable. □ **treasure hunt** search for treasure, game in which players seek hidden object; **treasure trove** treasure of unknown ownership found hidden.

treasurer *noun* person in charge of funds of society etc.

treasury /'treʒərɪ/ *noun* (*plural* **-ies**) place where treasure is kept; funds or revenue of state, institution, or society; (**Treasury**) (offices and officers of) department managing public revenue of a country. □ **Treasury bench** government front bench in parliament; **treasury bill** bill of exchange issued by government to raise money for temporary needs.

treat ● *verb* act, behave towards, or deal with in specified way; apply process or medical care or attention to; present or handle (subject) in literature or art; (often + *to*) provide with food, drink, or entertainment at one's own expense; (often + *with*) negotiate terms; (often + *of*) give exposition. ● *noun* event or circumstance that gives great pleasure; meal, entertainment, etc. designed to do this; (**a treat**) *colloquial* extremely good or well. □ **treatable** *adjective*.

treatise /'triːtɪz/ *noun* literary composition dealing esp. formally with subject.

treatment *noun* process or manner of behaving towards or dealing with person or thing; medical care or attention.

treaty /ˈtriːtɪ/ *noun* (*plural* **-ies**) formal agreement between states; agreement between people, esp. for purchase of property.

treble /ˈtreb(ə)l/ ● *adjective* threefold, triple; 3 times as much or many; high-pitched. ● *noun* treble quantity or thing; (voice of) boy soprano; high-pitched instrument; high-frequency sound of radio, record player, etc. ● *verb* (**-ling**) multiply or be multiplied by 3. □ **trebly** *adverb*.

tree ● *noun* perennial plant with woody self-supporting main stem and usually unbranched for some distance from ground; shaped piece of wood for various purposes; family tree. ● *verb* (**trees**, **treed**) cause to take refuge in tree. □ **treecreeper** small creeping bird feeding on insects in tree-bark; **tree-fern** large fern with upright woody stem; **tree surgeon** person who treats decayed trees in order to preserve them.

trefoil /ˈtrefɔɪl/ *noun* plant with leaves of 3 leaflets; 3-lobed ornamentation, esp. in tracery windows.

trek ● *verb* (**-kk-**) make arduous journey, esp. (*historical* migrate or journey by ox-wagon. ● *noun* such journey; each stage of it. □ **trekker** *noun*.

trellis /ˈtrelɪs/ *noun* (in full **trellis-work**) lattice of light wooden or metal bars, esp. support for climbing plants.

tremble /ˈtremb(ə)l/ ● *verb* (**-ling**) shake involuntarily with emotion, cold, etc.; be affected with extreme apprehension; quiver. ● *noun* trembling, quiver. □ **trembly** *adjective* (**-ier**, **-iest**).

tremendous /trɪˈmendəs/ *adjective colloquial* remarkable, considerable, excellent; awe-inspiring, overpowering. □ **tremendously** *adverb*.

tremolo /ˈtreməlәʊ/ *noun* (*plural* **-s**) tremulous effect in music.

tremor /ˈtremə/ *noun* shaking, quivering; thrill (of fear, exultation, etc.); (in full **earth tremor**) slight earthquake.

tremulous /ˈtremjʊləs/ *adjective* trembling. □ **tremulously** *adverb*.

trench ● *noun* deep ditch, esp. one dug by troops as shelter from enemy's fire. ● *verb* dig trench(es) in; make series of trenches (in) so as to bring lower soil to surface. □ **trench coat** lined or padded waterproof coat, loose belted raincoat.

trenchant /ˈtrentʃ(ə)nt/ *adjective* incisive, terse, vigorous. □ **trenchancy** *noun*; **trenchantly** *adverb*.

trencher /ˈtrentʃə/ *noun historical* wooden etc. platter for serving food.

trencherman /ˈtrentʃəmən/ *noun* eater.

trend ● *noun* general direction and tendency. ● *verb* turn away in specified direction; have general tendency. □ **trend-setter** person who leads the way in fashion etc.

trendy *colloquial often derogatory* ● *adjective* (**-ier**, **-iest**) fashionable. ● *noun* (*plural* **-ies**) fashionable person. □ **trendily** *adverb*; **trendiness** *noun*.

trepan /trɪˈpæn/ *historical* ● *noun* surgeon's cylindrical saw for making opening in skull. ● *verb* (**-nn-**) perforate (skull) with trepan.

trepidation /trepɪˈdeɪʃ(ə)n/ *noun* fear, anxiety.

trespass /ˈtrespəs/ ● *verb* (usually + *on*, *upon*) enter unlawfully (on another's land, property, etc.); encroach. ● *noun* act of trespassing; *archaic* sin, offence. □ **trespasser** *noun*.

tress *noun* lock of hair; (in *plural*) hair.

trestle /ˈtres(ə)l/ *noun* supporting structure for table etc. consisting of two frames fixed at an angle or hinged or of bar with two divergent pairs of legs; (in full **trestle-table**) table of board(s) laid on trestles; (in full **trestle-work**) open braced framework to support bridge etc.

trews *plural noun* close-fitting usually tartan trousers.

tri- *combining form* three (times).

triad /ˈtraɪæd/ *noun* group of 3 (esp. notes in chord). □ **triadic** /-ˈæd-/ *adjective*.

trial /ˈtraɪəl/ *noun* judicial examination and determination of issues between parties by judge with or without jury; test; trying thing or person; match held to select players for team; contest for horses, dogs, motorcycles, etc. □ **on trial** being tried in court of law, being tested; **trial run** preliminary operational test.

triangle /ˈtraɪæŋg(ə)l/ *noun* plane figure with 3 sides and angles; any 3 things not in straight line, with imaginary lines joining them; implement etc. of this shape; *Music* instrument of steel rod bent into triangle, struck with small steel rod; situation involving 3 people. □ **triangular** /-ˈæŋgjʊlə/ *adjective*.

triangulate /traɪˈæŋgjʊleɪt/ *verb* (**-ting**) divide (area) into triangles for surveying purposes. □ **triangulation** *noun*.

triathlon /traɪˈæθlən/ *noun* athletic contest of 3 events. □ **triathlete** *noun*.

tribe *noun* (in some societies) group of families under recognized leader with blood etc. ties and usually having common culture and dialect; any similar natural or political division; *usually derogatory* set or number of people, esp. of one profession etc. or family. □ **tribesman**, **tribeswoman** member of tribe. □ **tribal** *adjective*.

tribulation /trɪbjʊˈleɪʃ(ə)n/ *noun* great affliction.

tribunal /traɪˈbjuːn(ə)l/ *noun* board appointed to adjudicate on particular question; court of justice.

tribune /ˈtrɪbjuːn/ *noun* popular leader, demagogue; (in full **tribune of the people**) *Roman History* officer chosen by the people to protect their liberties.

tributary /ˈtrɪbjʊtərɪ/ ● *noun* (*plural* **-ies**) stream etc. that flows into larger stream or lake; *historical* person or state paying or subject to tribute. ● *adjective* that is a tributary.

tribute /ˈtrɪbjuːt/ *noun* thing said or done or given as mark of respect or affection etc.; (+ *to*) indication of (some praiseworthy quality); *historical* periodic payment by one state or ruler to another, obligation to pay this.

trice *noun* □ **in a trice** in an instant.

triceps /ˈtraɪseps/ *noun* muscle (esp. in upper arm) with 3 points of attachment.

triceratops /traɪˈserətɒps/ *noun* large dinosaur with 3 horns.

trichinosis /trɪkɪˈnəʊsɪs/ *noun* disease caused by hairlike worms.

trichology /trɪˈkɒlədʒɪ/ *noun* study of hair. □ **trichologist** *noun*.

trichromatic /traɪkrəˈmætɪk/ *adjective* 3-coloured.

trick ● *noun* thing done to deceive or outwit; illusion; knack; feat of skill or dexterity; unusual action learned by animal; foolish or discreditable act; hoax, joke; idiosyncrasy; cards played in one round, point gained in this. ● *verb* deceive by trick; swindle; (+ *into*) cause to do something by trickery; take by surprise.

trickery *noun* deception, use of tricks.

trickle /ˈtrɪk(ə)l/ ● *verb* (**-ling**) (cause to) flow in drops or small stream; come or go slowly or gradually. ● *noun* trickling flow. □ **trickle charger** *Electricity* device for slow continuous charging of battery.

trickster /ˈtrɪkstə/ *noun* deceiver, rogue.

tricky *adjective* (**-ier**, **-iest**) requiring care and adroitness; crafty, deceitful. □ **trickily** *adverb*; **trickiness** *noun*.

tricolour /ˈtrɪkələ/ *noun* (*US* **tricolor**) flag of 3 colours, esp. French national flag.

tricot /ˈtrɪkəʊ/ *noun* knitted fabric.

tricycle /ˈtraɪsɪk(ə)l/ *noun* 3-wheeled pedal-driven vehicle.

trident /ˈtraɪd(ə)nt/ *noun* 3-pronged spear.

Tridentine /traɪˈdentaɪn/ *adjective* of traditional RC orthodoxy.

triennial /traɪˈenɪəl/ *adjective* lasting 3 years; recurring every 3 years.

trifle /ˈtraɪf(ə)l/ ● *noun* thing of slight value or importance; small amount; (**a trifle**) somewhat; dessert of sponge cakes with custard, cream, etc. ● *verb* (**-ling**) talk or act frivolously; (+ *with*) treat frivolously, flirt heartlessly with.

trifling *adjective* unimportant; frivolous.

trigger /ˈtrɪgə/ ● *noun* movable device for releasing spring or catch and so setting off mechanism, esp. of gun; event etc. that sets off chain reaction. ● *verb* (often + *off*) set (action, process) in motion, precipitate. ◻ **trigger-happy** apt to shoot on slight provocation.

trigonometry /trɪgəˈnɒmətrɪ/ *noun* branch of mathematics dealing with relations of sides and angles of triangles, and with certain functions of angles. ◻ **trigonometric** /-nəˈmet-/ *adjective*; **trigonometrical** /-nəˈmet-/ *adjective*.

trike *noun colloquial* tricycle.

trilateral /traɪˈlætər(ə)l/ *adjective* of, on, or with 3 sides; involving 3 parties.

trilby /ˈtrɪlbɪ/ *noun* (*plural* **-ies**) soft felt hat with narrow brim and indented crown.

trilingual /traɪˈlɪŋgw(ə)l/ *adjective* speaking or in 3 languages.

trill ● *noun* quavering sound, esp. quick alternation of notes; bird's warbling; pronunciation of letter *r* with vibrating tongue. ● *verb* produce trill; warble (song); pronounce (*r* etc.) with trill.

trillion /ˈtrɪljən/ *noun* (*plural* same) million million; million million million; (**trillions**) *colloquial* large number. ◻ **trillionth** *adjective & noun*.

trilobite /ˈtraɪləbaɪt/ *noun* kind of fossil crustacean.

trilogy /ˈtrɪlədʒɪ/ *noun* (*plural* **-ies**) set of 3 related novels, plays, operas, etc.

trim ● *verb* (**-mm-**) make neat or tidy or of required size or shape, esp. by cutting away irregular or unwanted parts; (+ *off*, *away*) cut off; ornament; adjust balance of (ship, aircraft) by arranging cargo etc.; arrange (sails) to suit wind. ● *noun* state of readiness or fitness; ornament, decorative material; trimming of hair etc. ● *adjective* (**-mm-**) neat; in good order, well arranged or equipped.

trimaran /ˈtraɪməræn/ *noun* vessel like catamaran, with 3 hulls side by side.

trimming *noun* ornamental addition to dress, hat, etc.; (in *plural*) *colloquial* usual accompaniments.

trinitrotoluene /traɪnaɪtrəˈtɒljʊiːn/ *noun* (also **trinitrotoluol** /-ˈtɒljʊɒl/) a high explosive.

trinity /ˈtrɪnɪtɪ/ *noun* (*plural* **-ies**) being 3; group of 3; (**the Trinity**) the 3 persons of the Christian Godhead. ◻ **Trinity Sunday** Sunday after Whit Sunday.

trinket /ˈtrɪŋkɪt/ *noun* trifling ornament, esp. piece of jewellery.

trio /ˈtriːəʊ/ *noun* (*plural* **-s**) group of 3; musical composition for 3 performers; the performers.

trip ● *verb* (**-pp-**) (often + *up*) (cause to) stumble, esp. by catching foot; (+ *up*) (cause to) commit fault or blunder; run lightly; make excursion to place; operate (mechanism) suddenly by knocking aside catch etc.; *slang* have drug-induced hallucinatory experience. ● *noun* journey or excursion, esp. for pleasure; stumble, blunder, tripping, being tripped up; nimble step; *slang* drug-induced hallucinatory experience; device for tripping mechanism etc. ◻ **tripwire** wire stretched close to ground to operate alarm etc. if disturbed.

tripartite /traɪˈpɑːtaɪt/ *adjective* consisting of 3 parts; shared by or involving 3 parties.

tripe *noun* first or second stomach of ruminant, esp. ox, as food; *colloquial* nonsense, rubbish.

triple /ˈtrɪp(ə)l/ ● *adjective* of 3 parts, threefold; involving 3 parties; 3 times as much or as many. ● *noun* threefold number or amount; set of 3. ● *verb* (**-ling**) multiply by 3. ◻ **triple crown** winning of 3 important sporting events; **triple jump** athletic contest comprising hop, step, and jump. ◻ **triply** *adverb*.

triplet /ˈtrɪplɪt/ *noun* each of 3 children or animals born at one birth; set of 3 things, esp. of notes played in time of two.

triplex /ˈtrɪpleks/ *adjective* triple, threefold.

triplicate ● *adjective* /ˈtrɪplɪkət/ existing in 3 examples or copies; having 3 corresponding parts; tripled. ● *noun* /ˈtrɪplɪkət/ each of 3 copies or corresponding parts. ● *verb* (**-ting**) /ˈtrɪplɪkeɪt/ make in 3 copies; multiply by 3. ◻ **triplication** *noun*.

tripod /ˈtraɪpɒd/ *noun* 3-legged or 3-footed stand, stool, table, or utensil.

tripos /ˈtraɪpɒs/ *noun* honours exam for primary degree at Cambridge University.

tripper *noun* person who goes on pleasure trip.

triptych /ˈtrɪptɪk/ *noun* picture etc. with 3 panels usually hinged vertically together.

trireme /ˈtraɪriːm/ *noun* ancient Greek warship, with 3 files of oarsmen on each side.

trisect /traɪˈsekt/ *verb* divide into 3 (usually equal) parts. ◻ **trisection** *noun*.

trite *adjective* hackneyed. ◻ **tritely** *adverb*; **triteness** *noun*.

tritium /ˈtrɪtɪəm/ *noun* radioactive isotope of hydrogen with mass about 3 times that of ordinary hydrogen.

triumph /ˈtraɪʌmf/ ● *noun* state of victory or success; great success or achievement; supreme example; joy at success. ● *verb* gain victory, be successful; *Roman History* ride in triumph; (often + *over*) exult.

triumphal /traɪˈʌmf(ə)l/ *adjective* of, used in, or celebrating a triumph.

■ **Usage** *Triumphal*, as in *triumphal arch*, should not be confused with *triumphant*.

triumphant /traɪˈʌmf(ə)nt/ *adjective* victorious, successful; exultant. ◻ **triumphantly** *adverb*.

■ **Usage** See note at TRIUMPHAL.

triumvirate /traɪˈʌmvərət/ *noun* ruling group of 3 men.

trivalent /traɪˈveɪlənt/ *adjective Chemistry* having a valency of 3. ◻ **trivalency** *noun*.

trivet /ˈtrɪvɪt/ *noun* iron tripod or bracket for pot or kettle to stand on.

trivia /ˈtrɪvɪə/ *plural noun* trifles, trivialities.

trivial /ˈtrɪvɪəl/ *adjective* of small value or importance; concerned only with trivial things. ◻ **triviality** /-ˈæl-/ *noun* (*plural* **-ies**); **trivially** *adverb*.

trivialize *verb* (also **-ise**) (**-zing** or **-sing**) make or treat as trivial, minimize. ◻ **trivialization** *noun*.

trochee /ˈtrəʊkiː/ *noun* metrical foot of one long followed by one short syllable. ◻ **trochaic** /trəˈkeɪɪk/ *adjective*.

trod *past & past participle* of TREAD.

trodden *past participle* of TREAD.

troglodyte /ˈtrɒglədaɪt/ *noun* cave dweller.

troika /ˈtrɔɪkə/ *noun* Russian vehicle drawn by 3 horses abreast.

Trojan /ˈtrəʊdʒ(ə)n/ ● *adjective* of ancient Troy. ● *noun* native or inhabitant of ancient Troy; person who works, fights, etc. courageously. ▫ **Trojan Horse** person or device planted to bring about enemy's downfall.

troll[1] /trəʊl/ *noun* supernatural cave-dwelling giant or dwarf in Scandinavian mythology.

troll[2] /trəʊl/ *verb* fish by drawing bait along in water.

trolley /ˈtrɒlɪ/ *noun* (*plural* **-s**) table, stand, or basket on wheels or castors for serving food, carrying luggage etc., gathering purchases in supermarket, etc.; low truck running along rails; (in full **trolley-wheel**) wheel attached to pole etc. for collecting current from overhead electric wire to drive vehicle. ▫ **trolley bus** electric bus using trolley-wheel.

trollop /ˈtrɒləp/ *noun* disreputable girl or woman.

trombone /trɒmˈbəʊn/ *noun* brass wind instrument with sliding tube. ▫ **trombonist** *noun*.

troop /tru:p/ ● *noun* assembled company, assemblage of people or animals; (in *plural*) soldiers, armed forces; cavalry unit commanded by captain; artillery unit; group of 3 or more Scout patrols. ● *verb* (+ *in*, *out*, *off*, etc.) come together or move in a troop. ▫ **troop the colour** transfer flag ceremonially at public mounting of garrison guards; **troop-ship** ship for transporting troops.

trooper *noun* private soldier in cavalry or armoured unit; *Australian & US* mounted or State police officer; cavalry horse; troop-ship.

trope *noun* figurative use of word.

trophy /ˈtrəʊfɪ/ *noun* (*plural* **-ies**) cup etc. as prize in contest; memento of any success.

tropic /ˈtrɒpɪk/ *noun* parallel of latitude 23° 27′ N. (**tropic of Cancer**) or S. (**tropic of Capricorn**) of Equator; (**the Tropics**) region lying between these.

tropical *adjective* of or typical of the Tropics.

troposphere /ˈtrɒpəsfɪə/ *noun* layer of atmosphere extending about 8 km upwards from earth's surface.

trot ● *verb* (**-tt-**) (of person) run at moderate pace; (of horse) proceed at steady pace faster than walk; traverse (distance) thus. ● *noun* action or exercise of trotting; (**the trots**) *slang* diarrhoea. ▫ **on the trot** *colloquial* in succession, continually busy; **trot out** *colloquial* introduce (opinion etc.) repeatedly or tediously.

troth /trəʊθ/ *noun archaic* faith, fidelity; truth.

trotter *noun* (usually in *plural*) animal's foot, esp. as food; horse bred or trained for trotting.

troubadour /ˈtru:bədʊə/ *noun* singer, poet; French medieval poet singing of love.

trouble /ˈtrʌb(ə)l/ ● *noun* difficulty, distress, vexation, affliction; inconvenience, unpleasant exertion; cause of this; perceived failing; malfunction; disturbance; (in *plural*) public disturbances. ● *verb* (**-ling**) cause distress to, disturb; be disturbed; afflict, cause pain etc. to; subject or be subjected to inconvenience or unpleasant exertion. ▫ **in trouble** likely to incur censure or punishment, *colloquial* pregnant and unmarried; **troublemaker** person who habitually causes trouble; **troubleshooter** mediator in dispute, person who traces and corrects faults in machinery etc.

troublesome *adjective* causing trouble, annoying.

trough /trɒf/ *noun* long narrow open receptacle for water, animal feed, etc.; channel or hollow like this; elongated region of low barometric pressure.

trounce /traʊns/ *verb* (**-cing**) inflict severe defeat, beating, or punishment on.

troupe /tru:p/ *noun* company of actors, acrobats, etc.

trouper *noun* member of theatrical troupe; staunch colleague.

trousers /ˈtraʊzəz/ *plural noun* two-legged outer garment from waist usually to ankles. ▫ **trouser suit** woman's suit of trousers and jacket.

trousseau /ˈtru:səʊ/ *noun* (*plural* **-s** or **-x** /-z/) bride's collection of clothes etc.

trout /traʊt/ *noun* (*plural* same or **-s**) fish related to salmon.

trove /trəʊv/ *noun* treasure trove.

trowel /ˈtraʊəl/ *noun* flat-bladed tool for spreading mortar etc.; scoop for lifting small plants or earth.

troy *noun* (in full **troy weight**) system of weights used for precious metals etc.

truant /ˈtru:ənt/ ● *noun* child who does not attend school; person who avoids work etc. ● *adjective* idle, wandering. ● *verb* (also **play truant**) be truant. ▫ **truancy** *noun* (*plural* **-ies**).

truce *noun* temporary agreement to cease hostilities.

truck[1] *noun* lorry; open railway wagon for freight.

truck[2] *noun* ▫ **have no truck with** avoid dealing with.

trucker *noun esp. US* long-distance lorry driver.

truckle /ˈtrʌk(ə)l/ ● *noun* (in full **truckle-bed**) low bed on wheels, stored under another. ● *verb* (**-ling**) (+ *to*) submit obsequiously to.

truculent /ˈtrʌkjʊlənt/ *adjective* aggressively defiant. ▫ **truculence** *noun*; **truculently** *adverb*.

trudge ● *verb* (**-ging**) walk laboriously; traverse (distance) thus. ● *noun* trudging walk.

true ● *adjective* (**-r**, **-st**) in accordance with fact or reality; genuine; loyal, faithful; (+ *to*) accurately conforming to (type, standard); correctly positioned or balanced, level; exact, accurate. ● *adverb archaic* truly; accurately; without variation. ▫ **out of true** out of alignment.

truffle /ˈtrʌf(ə)l/ *noun* rich-flavoured underground fungus; sweet made of soft chocolate mixture.

trug *noun* shallow oblong garden-basket.

truism /ˈtru:ɪz(ə)m/ *noun* self-evident or hackneyed truth.

truly /ˈtru:lɪ/ *adverb* sincerely; really; loyally; accurately. ▫ **Yours truly** *written before signature at end of informal letter*; *jocular* I, me.

trump[1] ● *noun* playing card(s) of suit temporarily ranking above others; (in *plural*) this suit; *colloquial* helpful or excellent person. ● *verb* defeat with trump; *colloquial* outdo. ▫ **come** or **turn up trumps** *colloquial* turn out well or successfully, be extremely successful or helpful; **trump card** card belonging to, or turned up to determine, trump suit, *colloquial* valuable resource; **trump up** fabricate, invent (accusation, excuse, etc.).

trump[2] *noun archaic* trumpet-blast.

trumpery /ˈtrʌmpərɪ/ ● *noun* worthless finery; rubbish. ● *adjective* showy but worthless, trashy, shallow.

trumpet /ˈtrʌmpɪt/ ● *noun* brass instrument with flared mouth and bright penetrating tone; trumpet-shaped thing; sound (as) of trumpet. ● *verb* (**-t-**) blow trumpet; (of elephant) make trumpet; proclaim loudly. ▫ **trumpeter** *noun*.

truncate /trʌŋˈkeɪt/ *verb* (**-ting**) cut off top or end of; shorten. ▫ **truncation** *noun*.

truncheon /ˈtrʌntʃ(ə)n/ *noun* short club carried by police officer.

trundle /ˈtrʌnd(ə)l/ *verb* (**-ling**) roll or move, esp. heavily or noisily.

trunk *noun* main stem of tree; body without limbs or head; large luggage-box with hinged lid; *US* boot of car; elephant's elongated prehensile nose; (in *plural*) men's close-fitting shorts worn for swimming etc. ▫ **trunk call** long-distance telephone call; **trunk line** main line of railway, telephone system, etc.; **trunk road** important main road.

truss ● *noun* framework supporting roof, bridge, etc.; supporting surgical appliance for hernia etc. sufferers; bundle of hay or straw; cluster of flowers or fruit. ● *verb* tie up (fowl) for cooking; (often + *up*) tie (person) with arms to sides; support with truss(es).

trust ● *noun* firm belief that a person or thing may be relied on; confident expectation; responsibility; *Law* arrangement involving trustees, property so held, group of trustees; association of companies for reducing competition. ● *verb* place trust in, believe in, rely on; (+ *with*) give (person) charge of; (often + *that*) hope earnestly that a thing will take place; (+ *to*) consign (thing) to (person); (+ *in*) place reliance in; (+ *to*) place (esp. undue) reliance on. □ **in trust** (of property) managed by person(s) on behalf of another; **trustworthy** deserving of trust, reliable. □ **trustful** *adjective*.

trustee /trʌs'ti:/ *noun* person or member of board managing property in trust with legal obligation to administer it solely for purposes specified. □ **trusteeship** *noun*.

trusting *adjective* having trust or confidence. □ **trustingly** *adverb*.

trusty ● *adjective* (**-ier**, **-iest**) *archaic or jocular* trustworthy. ● *noun* (*plural* **-ies**) prisoner given special privileges for good behaviour.

truth /tru:θ/ *noun* (*plural* **truths** /tru:ðz/) quality or state of being true; what is true.

truthful *adjective* habitually speaking the truth; (of story etc.) true. □ **truthfully** *adverb*; **truthfulness** *noun*.

try ● *verb* (**-ies**, **-ied**) attempt, endeavour; test (quality), test by use or experiment test qualities of; make severe demands on; examine effectiveness of for purpose; ascertain state of fastening of (door etc.); investigate and decide (case, issue) judicially, (often + *for*) subject (person) to trial; (+ *for*) apply or compete for, seek to attain. ● *noun* (*plural* **-ies**) attempt; *Rugby* touching-down of ball by player behind opposing goal line, scoring points and entitling player's side to a kick at goal. □ **try one's hand** (often + *at*) have attempt; **try it on** *colloquial* test how much unreasonable behaviour etc. will be tolerated; **try on** put (clothes etc.) on to test fit etc.; **try-on** *colloquial* act of trying it on or trying on clothes etc., attempt to deceive; **try out** put to the test, test thoroughly; **try-out** experimental test.

trying *adjective* annoying, exasperating; hard to bear.

tryst /trɪst/ *noun archaic* meeting, esp. of lovers.

tsar /zɑ:/ *noun* (also **czar**) (*feminine* **tsarina** /-'ri:nə/) *historical* emperor of Russia. □ **tsarist** *noun & adjective*.

tsetse /'tsetsɪ/ *noun* African fly feeding on blood and transmitting disease.

tsp. *abbreviation* (*plural* **tsps.**) teaspoonful.

TT *abbreviation* teetotal(ler); tuberculin-tested; Tourist Trophy.

tub ● *noun* open flat-bottomed usually round vessel; tub-shaped (usually plastic) carton; *colloquial* bath; *colloquial* clumsy slow boat. ● *verb* (**-bb-**) plant, bathe, or wash in tub. □ **tub-thumper** *colloquial* ranting preacher or orator.

tuba /'tju:bə/ *noun* (*plural* **-s**) low-pitched brass wind instrument.

tubby /'tʌbɪ/ *adjective* (**-ier**, **-iest**) short and fat. □ **tubbiness** *noun*.

tube ● *noun* long hollow cylinder; soft metal or plastic cylinder sealed at one end; hollow cylindrical bodily organ; *colloquial* London underground; cathode ray tube, esp. in television; (**the tube**) *esp. US colloquial* television; *US* thermionic valve; inner tube. ● *verb* (**-bing**) equip with tubes; enclose in tube.

tuber /'tju:bə/ *noun* short thick rounded root or underground stem of plant.

tubercle /'tju:bək(ə)l/ *noun* small rounded swelling on part or in organ of body, esp. as characteristic of tuberculosis. □ **tubercle bacillus** bacterium causing tuberculosis. □ **tuberculous** /-'bɜ:kjʊləs/ *adjective*.

tubercular /tjʊ'bɜ:kjʊlə/ *adjective* of or affected with tuberculosis.

tuberculin /tjʊ'bɜ:kjʊlɪn/ *noun* preparation from cultures of tubercle bacillus used in diagnosis and treatment of tuberculosis. □ **tuberculin-tested** (of milk) from cows shown to be free of tuberculosis.

tuberculosis /tjʊbɜ:kjʊ'ləʊsɪs/ *noun* infectious bacterial disease marked by tubercles, esp. in lungs.

tuberose /'tju:bərəʊz/ *noun* plant with creamy-white fragrant flowers.

tuberous /'tju:bərəs/ *adjective* having tubers; of or like a tuber.

tubing *noun* length of tube; quantity of or material for tubes.

tubular /'tju:bjʊlə/ *adjective* tube-shaped; having or consisting of tubes.

TUC *abbreviation* Trades Union Congress.

tuck ● *verb* (often + *in*, *up*) draw, fold, or turn outer or end parts of (cloth, clothes, etc.) close together, push in edges of bedclothes around (person); draw together into small space; stow (thing) away in specified place or way; make stitched fold in (cloth etc.). ● *noun* flattened fold sewn in garment etc.; *colloquial* food, esp. cakes and sweets. □ **tuck in** *colloquial* eat heartily; **tuck shop** shop selling sweets etc. to schoolchildren.

tucker /'tʌkə/ ● *noun Australian & NZ slang* food. ● *verb* (esp. in *passive*; often + *out*) *US & Australian colloquial* tire.

Tudor /'tju:də/ *adjective* of royal family of England from Henry VII to Elizabeth I; of this period (1485–1603); of the architectural style of this period.

Tues. *abbreviation* (also **Tue.**) Tuesday.

Tuesday /'tju:zdeɪ/ *noun* day of week following Monday.

tufa /'tju:fə/ *noun* porous rock formed round mineral springs; tuff.

tuff *noun* rock formed from volcanic ash.

tuft *noun* bunch of threads, grass, feathers, hair, etc. held or growing together at base. □ **tufted** *adjective*; **tufty** *adjective*.

tug ● *verb* (**-gg-**) (often + *at*) pull hard or violently; tow (vessel) by tugboat. ● *noun* hard, violent, or jerky pull; sudden emotion; (also **tugboat**) small powerful boat for towing ships. □ **tug of war** trial of strength between two sides pulling opposite ways on a rope.

tuition /tju:'ɪʃ(ə)n/ *noun* teaching; fee for this.

tulip /'tju:lɪp/ *noun* bulbous spring-flowering plant with showy cup-shaped flowers; its flower. □ **tulip-tree** tree with tulip-like flowers.

tulle /tju:l/ *noun* soft fine silk etc. net for veils and dresses.

tumble /'tʌmb(ə)l/ ● *verb* (**-ling**) (cause to) fall suddenly or headlong; fall rapidly in amount etc.; roll, toss; move or rush in headlong or blundering fashion; (often + *to*) *colloquial* grasp meaning of; fling or push roughly or carelessly; perform acrobatic feats, esp. somersaults; rumple, disarrange. ● *noun* fall; somersault or other acrobatic feat. □ **tumbledown** falling or fallen into ruin, dilapidated; **tumble-drier**, **-dryer** machine for drying washing in heated rotating drum; **tumble-dry** *verb*.

tumbler *noun* drinking glass without handle or foot; acrobat; part of mechanism of lock.

tumbrel /'tʌmbr(ə)l/ *noun* (also **tumbril**) *historical* open cart in which condemned people were carried to guillotine during French Revolution.

tumescent /tjʊ'mes(ə)nt/ *adjective* swelling. □ **tumescence** *noun*.

tumid /'tju:mɪd/ *adjective* swollen, inflated; pompous. □ **tumidity** /-'mɪd-/ *noun*.

tummy /'tʌmɪ/ *noun* (*plural* **-ies**) *colloquial* stomach.

tumour /'tju:mə/ *noun* (*US* **tumor**) abnormal or morbid swelling in the body.

tumult /'tju:mʌlt/ *noun* uproar, din; angry demonstration by mob, riot; conflict of emotions etc. □ **tumultuous** /tjʊ'mʌltʃʊəs/ *adjective*.

tumulus /'tju:mjʊləs/ *noun* (*plural* **-li** /-laɪ/) ancient burial mound.

tun *noun* large cask; brewer's fermenting-vat.

tuna /'tju:nə/ *noun* (*plural* same or **-s**) large edible marine fish; (in full **tuna-fish**) its flesh as food.

tundra /'tʌndrə/ *noun* vast level treeless Arctic region with permafrost.

tune ● *noun* melody; correct pitch or intonation. ● *verb* (**-ning**) put (musical instrument) in tune; (often + *in*) adjust (radio etc.) to desired frequency etc.; adjust (engine etc.) to run smoothly. □ **change one's tune** voice different opinion, become more respectful; **tune up** bring instrument(s) to proper pitch; **tuning-fork** two-pronged steel fork giving particular note when struck.

tuneful *adjective* melodious, musical. □ **tunefully** *adverb*.

tuneless *adjective* unmelodious, unmusical. □ **tunelessly** *adverb*.

tuner *noun* person who tunes pianos etc.; part of radio or television receiver for tuning.

tungsten /'tʌŋst(ə)n/ *noun* heavy steel-grey metallic element.

tunic /'tju:nɪk/ *noun* close-fitting short coat of police or military uniform; loose often sleeveless garment.

tunnel /'tʌn(ə)l/ ● *noun* underground passage dug through hill, or under river, road, etc.; underground passage dug by animal. ● *verb* (**-ll-**; *US* **-l-**) (+ *through*, *into*) make tunnel through (hill etc.); make (one's way) so. □ **tunnel vision** restricted vision, *colloquial* inability to grasp wider implications of situation etc.

tunny /'tʌnɪ/ *noun* (*plural* same or **-ies**) tuna.

tuppence = TWOPENCE.

tuppenny = TWOPENNY.

Tupperware /'tʌpəweə/ *noun proprietary term* range of plastic containers for food.

turban /'tɜ:bən/ *noun* man's headdress of fabric wound round cap or head, worn esp. by Muslims and Sikhs; woman's hat resembling this.

turbid /'tɜ:bɪd/ *adjective* muddy, thick, not clear; confused, disordered. □ **turbidity** /-'bɪd-/ *noun*.

■ **Usage** *Turbid* is sometimes confused with *turgid*.

turbine /'tɜ:baɪn/ *noun* rotary motor driven by flow of water, gas, etc.

turbo- *combining form* turbine.

turbocharger /'tɜ:bəʊtʃɑ:dʒə/ *noun* (also **turbo**) supercharger driven by turbine powered by engine's exhaust gases.

turbojet /'tɜ:bəʊdʒet/ *noun* jet engine in which jet also operates turbine-driven air-compressor; aircraft with this.

turboprop /'tɜ:bəʊprɒp/ *noun* jet engine in which turbine is used as in turbojet and also to drive propeller; aircraft with this.

turbot /'tɜ:bət/ *noun* (*plural* same or **-s**) large flatfish valued as food.

turbulent /'tɜ:bjʊlənt/ *adjective* disturbed, in commotion; (of flow of air etc.) varying irregularly; riotous, restless. □ **turbulence** *noun*; **turbulently** *adverb*.

tureen /tjʊə'ri:n/ *noun* deep covered dish for soup.

turf ● *noun* (*plural* **-s** or **turves**) short grass with surface earth bound together by its roots; piece of this cut from ground; slab of peat for fuel; (**the turf**) horse racing, racecourse. ● *verb* cover (ground) with turf; (+ *out*) *colloquial* expel, eject. □ **turf accountant** bookmaker. □ **turfy** *adjective*.

turgid /'tɜ:dʒɪd/ *adjective* swollen, inflated; (of language) pompous, bombastic. □ **turgidity** /-'dʒɪd-/ *noun*.

■ **Usage** *Turgid* is sometimes confused with *turbid*.

Turk *noun* native or national of Turkey.

turkey /'tɜ:kɪ/ *noun* (*plural* **-s**) large originally American bird bred for food; its flesh. □ **turkeycock** male turkey.

Turkish ● *adjective* of Turkey. ● *noun* language of Turkey. □ **Turkish bath** hot-air or steam bath followed by massage etc., (in *singular* or *plural*) building for this; **Turkish carpet** thick-piled woollen carpet with bold design; **Turkish delight** kind of gelatinous sweet; **Turkish towel** one made of cotton terry.

turmeric /'tɜ:mərɪk/ *noun* E. Indian plant of ginger family; its rhizome powdered as flavouring or dye.

turmoil /'tɜ:mɔɪl/ *noun* violent confusion; din and bustle.

turn ● *verb* move around point or axis, give or receive rotary motion; change from one side to another, invert, reverse; give new direction to, take new direction, aim in certain way; (+ *into*) change in nature, form, or condition to; (+ *to*) set about, have recourse to, consider next; become; (+ *against*) make or become hostile to; (+ *on*, *upon*) face hostilely; change colour; (of milk) become sour; (of stomach) be nauseated; cause (milk) to become sour or (stomach) to be nauseated; (of head) become giddy; translate; move to other side of, go round; pass age or time of; (+ *on*) depend on; send, put, cause to go; remake (sheet, shirt collar, etc.); make (profit); divert (bullet); shape (object) in lathe; give (esp. elegant) form to. ● *noun* turning, rotary motion; changed or change of direction or tendency; point of turning or change; turning of road; change of direction of tide; change in course of events; tendency, formation; opportunity, obligation, etc. that comes successively to each of several people etc.; short walk or ride; short performance on stage, in circus, etc.; service of specified kind; purpose; *colloquial* momentary nervous shock; *Music* ornament of principal note with those above and below it. □ **in turn** in succession; **take (it in) turns** act alternately; **turncoat** person who changes sides; **turn down** reject, reduce volume or strength of (sound, heat, etc.) by turning knob, fold down; **turn in** hand in, achieve, *colloquial* go to bed, incline inwards; **turnkey** *archaic* jailer; **turn off** stop flow or working of by means of tap, switch, etc., enter side road, *colloquial* cause to lose interest; **turn on** start flow or working of by means of tap, switch, etc., *colloquial* arouse, esp. sexually; **turn out** expel, extinguish (light etc.), dress, equip, produce (goods etc.), empty, clean out, (cause to) assemble, prove to be the case, result, (usually + *to be*) be found; **turn-out** number of people who attend meeting etc., equipage; **turn over** reverse position of, cause (engine etc.) to run, (of engine) start running, consider thoroughly, (+ *to*) transfer care or conduct of (person, thing) to (person); **turnover** turning over, gross amount of money taken in business, rate of sale and replacement of goods, rate at which people enter and leave employment etc., small pie with pastry folded over filling; **turnpike** *US & historical* road on which toll is charged; **turnstile** revolving gate with arms; **turntable** circular revolving plate or platform; **turn to** begin work; **turn turtle** capsize; **turn up** increase (volume or strength of) by turning knob etc., discover, reveal, be found, happen, arrive, shorten (garment etc.), fold over or upwards; **turn-up** turned-up end of trouser leg, *colloquial* unexpected happening.

turner *noun* lathe-worker.

turnery *noun* objects made on lathe; work with lathe.

turning *noun* road branching off another, place where this occurs; use of lathe; (in *plural*) chips or shavings from this. ▫ **turning circle** smallest circle in which vehicle can turn; **turning point** point at which decisive change occurs.

turnip /ˈtɜːnɪp/ *noun* plant with globular root; its root as vegetable.

turpentine /ˈtɜːpəntaɪn/ *noun* resin from any of various trees; (in full **oil of turpentine**) volatile inflammable oil distilled from turpentine and used in mixing paints etc.

turpitude /ˈtɜːpɪtjuːd/ *noun formal* depravity, wickedness.

turps *noun colloquial* oil of turpentine.

turquoise /ˈtɜːkwɔɪz/ ● *noun* opaque semiprecious stone, usually greenish-blue; this colour. ● *adjective* of this colour.

turret /ˈtʌrɪt/ *noun* small tower, esp. decorating building; usually revolving armoured structure for gun and gunners on ship, fort, etc.; rotating holder for tools in lathe etc. ▫ **turreted** *adjective*.

turtle /ˈtɜːt(ə)l/ *noun* aquatic reptile with flippers and horny shell. ▫ **turtle-neck** high close-fitting neck on knitted garment.

turtle-dove /ˈtɜːt(ə)ldʌv/ *noun* wild dove noted for soft cooing and affection for its mate.

tusk *noun* long pointed tooth, esp. projecting beyond mouth as in elephant, walrus, or boar. ▫ **tusked** *adjective*.

tussle /ˈtʌs(ə)l/ *noun & verb* (**-ling**) struggle, scuffle.

tussock /ˈtʌsək/ *noun* clump of grass etc.

tut = TUT-TUT.

tutelage /ˈtjuːtɪlɪdʒ/ *noun* guardianship; being under this; tuition.

tutelary /ˈtjuːtɪlərɪ/ *adjective* serving as guardian or protector; of guardian.

tutor /ˈtjuːtə/ ● *noun* private teacher; university teacher supervising studies or welfare of assigned undergraduates. ● *verb* act as tutor (to). ▫ **tutorship** *noun*.

tutorial /tjuːˈtɔːrɪəl/ ● *adjective* of tutor or tuition. ● *noun* period of tuition for single student or small group.

tutti /ˈtʊtɪ/ *Music* ● *adjective & adverb* with all instruments or voices together. ● *noun* (*plural* **-s**) tutti passage.

tut-tut /tʌtˈtʌt/ (also **tut**) ● *interjection expressing rebuke or impatience*. ● *noun* such exclamation. ● *verb* (**-tt-**) exclaim thus.

tutu /ˈtuːtuː/ *noun* (*plural* **-s**) dancer's short skirt of stiffened frills.

tuxedo /tʌkˈsiːdəʊ/ *noun* (*plural* **-s** or **-es**) *US* (suit including) dinner jacket.

TV *abbreviation* television.

twaddle /ˈtwɒd(ə)l/ *noun* silly writing or talk.

twain *adjective & noun archaic* two.

twang ● *noun* sound made by plucked string of musical instrument, bow, etc.; nasal quality of voice. ● *verb* (cause to) emit twang. ▫ **twangy** *adjective*.

tweak ● *verb* pinch and twist; jerk; adjust finely. ● *noun* such action.

twee *adjective* (**tweer** /ˈtwiːə/, **tweest** /ˈtwiːɪst/) *derogatory* affectedly dainty or quaint.

tweed *noun* rough-surfaced woollen cloth usually of mixed colours; (in *plural*) clothes of tweed.

tweedy *adjective* (**-ier**, **-iest**) of or dressed in tweed; heartily informal.

tweet ● *noun* chirp of small bird. ● *verb* make this noise.

tweeter *noun* loudspeaker for high frequencies.

tweezers /ˈtwiːzəz/ *plural noun* small pair of pincers for picking up small objects, plucking out hairs, etc.

twelfth *adjective & noun* next after eleventh; any of twelve equal parts of thing. ▫ **Twelfth Night** evening of 5 Jan.

twelve /twelv/ *adjective & noun* one more than eleven.

twenty /ˈtwentɪ/ *adjective & noun* (*plural* **-ies**) twice ten. ▫ **twentieth** *adjective & noun*.

twerp *noun slang* stupid or objectionable person.

twice *adverb* two times; on two occasions; doubly.

twiddle /ˈtwɪd(ə)l/ ● *verb* (**-ling**) twist or play idly about. ● *noun* act of twiddling. ▫ **twiddle one's thumbs** make them rotate round each other, have nothing to do.

twig[1] *noun* very small branch of tree or shrub.

twig[2] *verb* (**-gg-**) *colloquial* understand, realize.

twilight /ˈtwaɪlaɪt/ *noun* light from sky when sun is below horizon, esp. in evening; period of this; faint light; period of decline. ▫ **twilight zone** decrepit urban area, undefined or intermediate area.

twilit /ˈtwaɪlɪt/ *adjective* dimly illuminated (as) by twilight.

twill *noun* fabric woven with surface of parallel diagonal ridges. ▫ **twilled** *adjective*.

twin ● *noun* each of closely related pair, esp. of children or animals born at a birth; counterpart. ● *adjective* forming, or born as one of, twins. ● *verb* (**-nn-**) join closely, (+ *with*) pair; bear twins; link (town) with one abroad for social and cultural exchange. ▫ **twin bed** each of pair of single beds; **twin set** woman's matching cardigan and jumper; **twin town** town twinned with another.

twine ● *noun* strong coarse string of twisted strands of fibre; coil, twist. ● *verb* (**-ning**) coil, twist; form (string etc.) by twisting strands.

twinge /twɪndʒ/ *noun* sharp momentary local pain.

twinkle /ˈtwɪŋk(ə)l/ ● *verb* (**-ling**) shine with rapidly intermittent light; sparkle; move rapidly. ● *noun* sparkle or gleam of eyes; twinkling light; light rapid movement. ▫ **twinkly** *adjective*.

twirl ● *verb* spin, swing, or twist quickly and lightly round. ● *noun* twirling; flourish made with pen.

twist ● *verb* change the form of by rotating one end and not the other or the two ends opposite ways; undergo such change; wrench or distort by twisting; wind (strands etc.) about each other, form (rope etc.) thus; (cause to) take spiral form; (+ *off*) break off by twisting; misrepresent meaning of (words); take winding course; *colloquial* cheat; (as **twisted** *adjective*) perverted; dance the twist. ● *noun* twisting, being twisted; thing made by twisting; point at which thing twists; *usually derogatory* peculiar tendency of mind, character, etc.; unexpected development; (**the twist**) 1960s dance with twisting hips. ▫ **twisty** *adjective* (**-ier**, **-iest**).

twister *noun colloquial* swindler.

twit[1] *noun slang* foolish person.

twit[2] *verb* (**-tt-**) reproach, taunt, usually good-humouredly.

twitch ● *verb* quiver or jerk spasmodically; pull sharply at. ● *noun* twitching; *colloquial* state of nervousness. ▫ **twitchy** *adjective* (**-ier**, **-iest**).

twitter /ˈtwɪtə/ ● *verb* (esp. of bird) utter succession of light tremulous sounds; utter or express thus. ● *noun* twittering; *colloquial* tremulously excited state.

two /tu:/ *adjective & noun* one more than one. ▫ **two-dimensional** having or appearing to have length and breadth but no depth, superficial; **two-edged** having both good and bad effect, ambiguous; **two-faced** insincere; **two-handed** with 2 hands, used with both hands or by 2 people; **twopence** /'tʌpəns/ sum of 2 pence, (esp. with negative) *colloquial* thing of little value; **twopenny** /'tʌpənɪ/ costing twopence, *colloquial* cheap, worthless; **two-piece** (suit etc.) comprising 2 matching parts; **two-ply** (wool etc.) having 2 strands, (plywood) having 2 layers; **two-step** dance in march or polka time; **two-stroke** (of internal-combustion engine) having power cycle completed in one up-and-down movement of piston; **two-time** *colloquial* be unfaithful to, swindle; **two-tone** having two colours or sounds; **two-way** involving or operating in two directions, (of radio) capable of transmitting and receiving signals.

twofold *adjective & adverb* twice as much or many.

twosome *noun* two people together.

tycoon /taɪ'ku:n/ *noun* business magnate.

tying *present participle* of TIE.

tyke /taɪk/ *noun* (also **tike**) objectionable or coarse man; small child.

tympani = TIMPANI.

tympanum /'tɪmpənəm/ *noun* (*plural* **-s** or **-na**) middle ear; eardrum; vertical space forming centre of pediment; space between lintel and arch above door etc.

type /taɪp/ ● *noun* sort, class, kind; person, thing, or event exemplifying class or group; *colloquial* person, esp. of specified character; object, idea, or work of art serving as model; small block with raised character on upper surface for printing; printing types collectively; typeset or printed text. ● *verb* (**-ping**) write with typewriter; typecast; assign to type, classify. ▫ **-type** made of, resembling, functioning as; **typecast** cast (performer) repeatedly in similar roles; **typeface** inked surface of type, set of characters in one design; **typescript** typewritten document; **typesetter** compositor, composing machine; **typewriter** machine with keys for producing printlike characters; **typewritten** produced thus.

typhoid /'taɪfɔɪd/ *noun* (in full **typhoid fever**) infectious bacterial fever attacking intestines.

typhoon /taɪ'fu:n/ *noun* violent hurricane in E. Asian seas.

typhus /'taɪfəs/ *noun* an acute infectious fever.

typical /'tɪpɪk(ə)l/ *adjective* serving as characteristic example; (often + *of*) characteristic of particular person or thing. ▫ **typicality** /-'kæl-/ *noun*; **typically** *adverb*.

typify /'tɪpɪfaɪ/ *verb* (**-ies**, **-ied**) be typical of; represent by or as type. ▫ **typification** *noun*.

typist /'taɪpɪst/ *noun* (esp. professional) user of typewriter.

typo /'taɪpəʊ/ *noun* (*plural* **-s**) *colloquial* typographical error.

typography /taɪ'pɒgrəfɪ/ *noun* printing as an art; style and appearance of printed matter. ▫ **typographer** *noun*; **typographical** /-pə'græf-/ *adjective*; **typographically** /-pə'græf-/ *adverb*.

tyrannical /tɪ'rænɪk(ə)l/ *adjective* acting like or characteristic of tyrant.

tyrannize /'tɪrənaɪz/ *verb* (also **-ise**) (**-zing** or **-sing**) (often + *over*) treat despotically.

tyrannosaurus /tɪrænə'sɔ:rəs/ *noun* (*plural* **-ruses**) very large carnivorous dinosaur with short front legs and powerful tail.

tyranny /'tɪrənɪ/ *noun* (*plural* **-ies**) cruel and arbitrary use of authority; rule by tyrant; period of this; state thus ruled. ▫ **tyrannous** *adjective*.

tyrant /'taɪərənt/ *noun* oppressive or cruel ruler; person exercising power arbitrarily or cruelly.

tyre /'taɪə/ *noun* (*US* **tire**) rubber covering, usually inflated, placed round vehicle's wheel for cushioning and grip.

tyro = TIRO.

tzatziki /tsæt'si:kɪ/ *noun* Greek dish of yoghurt with cucumber and garlic.

Uu

U[1] ◻ **U-boat** *historical* German submarine; **U-turn** U-shaped turn of vehicle to face in opposite direction, reversal of policy.

U[2] *abbreviation* (of film classified as suitable for all) universal.

UB40 *abbreviation* card for claiming unemployment benefit; *colloquial* unemployed person.

ubiquitous /ju:'bɪkwɪtəs/ *adjective* (seemingly) present everywhere simultaneously; often encountered. ◻ **ubiquity** *noun*.

UCCA /'ʌkə/ *abbreviation* Universities Central Council on Admissions.

UDA *abbreviation* Ulster Defence Association.

udder /'ʌdə/ *noun* baglike milk-producing organ of cow etc.

UDI *abbreviation* unilateral declaration of independence.

UDR *abbreviation* Ulster Defence Regiment.

UEFA /ju:'eɪfə/ *abbreviation* Union of European Football Associations.

UFO /'ju:fəʊ/ *noun* (also **ufo**) (*plural* **-s**) unidentified flying object.

ugh /əx, ʌg/ *interjection expressing disgust etc.*

Ugli /'ʌglɪ/ *noun* (*plural* **-lis** or **-lies**) *proprietary term* mottled green and yellow citrus fruit.

ugly /'ʌglɪ/ *adjective* (**-ier, -iest**) unpleasant to eye, ear, mind, etc.; discreditable; threatening, dangerous; morally repulsive. ◻ **ugly duckling** person lacking early promise but blossoming later. ◻ **uglify** *verb* (**-ies, -ied**); **ugliness** *noun*.

UHF *abbreviation* ultra-high frequency.

uh-huh /'ʌhʌ/ *interjection colloquial* yes.

UHT *abbreviation* ultra heat treated (esp. of milk, for long keeping).

UK *abbreviation* United Kingdom.

Ukrainian /ju:'kreɪnɪən/ ● *noun* native, national, or language of Ukraine. ● *adjective* of Ukraine.

ukulele /ju:kə'leɪlɪ/ *noun* small guitar with 4 strings.

ulcer /'ʌlsə/ *noun* (often pus-forming) open sore on or in body; corrupting influence. ◻ **ulcerous** *adjective*.

ulcerate /'ʌlsəreɪt/ *verb* (**-ting**) form into or affect with ulcer. ◻ **ulceration** *noun*.

ullage /'ʌlɪdʒ/ *noun* amount by which cask etc. falls short of being full; loss by evaporation or leakage.

ulna /'ʌlnə/ *noun* (*plural* **ulnae** /-ni:/) longer bone of forearm, opposite thumb; corresponding bone in animal's foreleg or bird's wing. ◻ **ulnar** *adjective*.

ulster /'ʌlstə/ *noun* long loose overcoat of rough cloth.

Ulsterman /'ʌlstəmən/ *noun* (*feminine* **Ulsterwoman**) native of Ulster.

ult. *abbreviation* ultimo.

ulterior /ʌl'tɪərɪə/ *adjective* not admitted; hidden, secret.

ultimate /'ʌltɪmət/ ● *adjective* last, final; fundamental, basic. ● *noun* (**the ultimate**) best achievable or imaginable; final or fundamental fact or principle. ◻ **ultimately** *adverb*.

ultimatum /ʌltɪ'meɪtəm/ *noun* (*plural* **-s**) final statement of terms, rejection of which could cause hostility etc.

ultimo /'ʌltɪməʊ/ *adjective* of last month.

ultra /'ʌltrə/ ● *adjective* extreme, esp. in religion or politics. ● *noun* extremist.

ultra- *combining form* extreme(ly), excessive(ly); beyond.

ultra-high /ʌltrə'haɪ/ *adjective* (of frequency) between 300 and 3000 megahertz.

ultramarine /ʌltrəmə'ri:n/ ● *noun* (colour of) brilliant deep blue pigment. ● *adjective* of this colour.

ultrasonic /ʌltrə'sɒnɪk/ *adjective* of or using sound waves pitched above range of human hearing. ◻ **ultrasonically** *adverb*.

ultrasound /'ʌltrəsaʊnd/ *noun* ultrasonic waves.

ultraviolet /ʌltrə'vaɪələt/ *adjective* of or using radiation just beyond violet end of spectrum.

ultra vires /ʌltrə 'vaɪəri:z/ *adverb & adjective* beyond one's legal power or authority. [Latin]

ululate /'ju:ljʊleɪt/ *verb* (**-ting**) howl, wail. ◻ **ululation** *noun*.

um *interjection representing hesitation or pause in speech.*

umbel /'ʌmb(ə)l/ *noun* flower-cluster with stalks springing from common centre. ◻ **umbellate** *adjective*.

umbelliferous /ʌmbə'lɪfərəs/ *adjective* (of plant, e.g. parsley or carrot) bearing umbels.

umber /'ʌmbə/ ● *noun* (colour of) dark brown earth used as pigment. ● *adjective* umber-coloured.

umbilical /ʌm'bɪlɪk(ə)l/ *adjective* of navel. ◻ **umbilical cord** cordlike structure attaching foetus to placenta.

umbilicus /ʌm'bɪlɪkəs/ *noun* (*plural* **-ci** /-saɪ/ or **-cuses**) navel.

umbra /'ʌmbrə/ *noun* (*plural* **-s** or **-brae** /-bri:/) shadow cast by moon or earth in eclipse.

umbrage /'ʌmbrɪdʒ/ *noun* offence taken.

umbrella /ʌm'brelə/ *noun* collapsible cloth canopy on central stick for protection against rain, sun, etc.; protection, patronage; coordinating agency.

umlaut /'ʊmlaʊt/ *noun* mark (¨) over vowel, esp. in German, indicating change in pronunciation; such a change.

umpire /'ʌmpaɪə/ ● *noun* person enforcing rules and settling disputes in game, contest, etc. ● *verb* (**-ring**) (often + *for*, *in*, etc.) act as umpire (in).

umpteen /'ʌmpti:n/ *adjective & noun colloquial* very many. ◻ **umpteenth** *adjective & noun*.

UN *abbreviation* United Nations.

un- *prefix added to adjectives, nouns, and adverbs, meaning:* not; non-; reverse of, lack of; *added to verbs, verbal derivatives, etc. to express contrary or reverse action, deprivation of or removal from.* For words starting with *un-* that are not found below, the root-words should be consulted.

unaccountable /ʌnə'kaʊntəb(ə)l/ *adjective* without explanation, strange; not answerable for one's actions. ◻ **unaccountably** *adverb*.

unadopted /ʌnə'dɒptɪd/ *adjective* (of road) not maintained by local authority.

unadulterated /ʌnə'dʌltəreɪtɪd/ *adjective* pure; complete, utter.

unaffected /ʌnə'fektɪd/ *adjective* (usually + *by*) not affected; free from affectation. ◻ **unaffectedly** *adverb*.

unalloyed /ʌnə'lɔɪd/ *adjective* complete, pure.

un-American /ʌnə'merɪkən/ *adjective* uncharacteristic of Americans; contrary to US interests, treasonable.

unanimous /ju:'nænɪməs/ *adjective* all in agreement; (of vote etc.) by all without exception. ◻ **unanimity** /-nə'nɪm-/ *noun*; **unanimously** *adverb*.

unannounced /ʌnəˈnaʊnst/ *adjective* not announced, without warning.

unanswerable /ʌnˈɑːnsərəb(ə)l/ *adjective* that cannot be answered or refuted.

unapproachable /ʌnəˈprəʊtʃəb(ə)l/ *adjective* inaccessible; (of person) unfriendly, aloof.

unassailable /ʌnəˈseɪləb(ə)l/ *adjective* that cannot be attacked or questioned.

unassuming /ʌnəˈsjuːmɪŋ/ *adjective* not pretentious, modest.

unattached /ʌnəˈtætʃt/ *adjective* not engaged, married, etc.; (often + *to*) not attached to particular organization etc.

unaware /ʌnəˈweə/ ● *adjective* (usually + *of, that*) not aware; unperceptive. ● *adverb* unawares.

unawares /ʌnəˈweəz/ *adverb* unexpectedly; inadvertently.

unbalanced /ʌnˈbælənst/ *adjective* emotionally unstable; biased.

unbeknown /ʌnbɪˈnəʊn/ *adjective* (also **unbeknownst** /-ˈnəʊnst/) (+ *to*) without the knowledge of.

unbend /ʌnˈbend/ *verb* (*past & past participle* **unbent**) straighten; relax; become affable.

unbending /ʌnˈbendɪŋ/ *adjective* inflexible; firm, austere.

unblushing /ʌnˈblʌʃɪŋ/ *adjective* shameless; frank.

unbosom /ʌnˈbʊz(ə)m/ *verb* disclose (thoughts etc.); (**unbosom oneself**) disclose one's thoughts etc.

unbounded /ʌnˈbaʊndɪd/ *adjective* infinite.

unbridled /ʌnˈbraɪd(ə)ld/ *adjective* unrestrained, uncontrolled.

uncalled-for /ʌnˈkɔːldfɔː/ *adjective* (of remark etc.) rude and unnecessary.

uncanny /ʌnˈkænɪ/ *adjective* (**-ier**, **-iest**) seemingly supernatural, mysterious. □ **uncannily** *adverb*; **uncanniness** *noun*.

uncapped /ʌnˈkæpt/ *adjective Sport* (of player) not yet awarded his or her cap or never having been selected to represent his or her country.

unceremonious /ʌnserɪˈməʊnɪəs/ *adjective* abrupt, discourteous; informal. □ **unceremoniously** *adverb*.

uncertain /ʌnˈsɜːt(ə)n/ *adjective* not certain; unreliable; changeable. □ **in no uncertain terms** clearly and forcefully. □ **uncertainly** *adverb*; **uncertainty** *noun* (*plural* **-ies**).

uncharted /ʌnˈtʃɑːtɪd/ *adjective* not mapped or surveyed.

uncle /ˈʌŋk(ə)l/ *noun* parent's brother or brother-in-law. □ **Uncle Sam** *colloquial* US government.

unclean /ʌnˈkliːn/ *adjective* not clean; unchaste; religiously impure.

uncomfortable /ʌnˈkʌmftəb(ə)l/ *adjective* not comfortable; uneasy. □ **uncomfortably** *adverb*.

uncommon /ʌnˈkɒmən/ *adjective* unusual, remarkable. □ **uncommonly** *adverb*.

uncompromising /ʌnˈkɒmprəmaɪzɪŋ/ *adjective* stubborn; unyielding. □ **uncompromisingly** *adverb*.

unconcern /ʌnkənˈsɜːn/ *noun* calmness; indifference, apathy. □ **unconcerned** *adjective*.

unconditional /ʌnkənˈdɪʃən(ə)l/ *adjective* not subject to conditions, complete. □ **unconditionally** *adverb*.

unconscionable /ʌnˈkɒnʃənəb(ə)l/ *adjective* without conscience; excessive.

unconscious /ʌnˈkɒnʃəs/ ● *adjective* not conscious. ● *noun* normally inaccessible part of mind affecting emotions etc. □ **unconsciously** *adverb*; **unconsciousness** *noun*.

unconsidered /ʌnkənˈsɪdəd/ *adjective* not considered; disregarded; not premeditated.

unconstitutional /ʌnkɒnstɪˈtjuːʃən(ə)l/ *adjective* in breach of political constitution or procedural rules.

uncooperative /ʌnkəʊˈɒpərətɪv/ *adjective* not cooperative.

uncork /ʌnˈkɔːk/ *verb* draw cork from (bottle); vent (feelings).

uncouple /ʌnˈkʌp(ə)l/ *verb* (**-ling**) release from couples or coupling.

uncouth /ʌnˈkuːθ/ *adjective* uncultured, rough.

uncover /ʌnˈkʌvə/ *verb* remove cover or covering from; disclose.

uncrowned /ʌnˈkraʊnd/ *adjective* having status but not name of.

unction /ˈʌŋkʃ(ə)n/ *noun* anointing with oil etc. as religious rite or medical treatment; oil etc. so used; soothing words or thought; excessive or insincere flattery; (pretence of) deep emotion.

unctuous /ˈʌŋktʃʊəs/ *adjective* unpleasantly flattering; greasy. □ **unctuously** *adverb*.

uncut /ʌnˈkʌt/ *adjective* not cut; (of book) with pages sealed or untrimmed; (of film) not censored; (of diamond) not shaped; (of fabric) with looped pile.

undeniable /ʌndɪˈnaɪəb(ə)l/ *adjective* indisputable; certain. □ **undeniably** *adverb*.

under /ˈʌndə/ ● *preposition* in or to position lower than, below; beneath; inferior to, less than; undergoing, liable to; controlled or bound by; classified or subsumed in. ● *adverb* in or to lower condition or position. ● *adjective* lower.

underachieve /ʌndərəˈtʃiːv/ *verb* (**-ving**) do less well than might be expected, esp. academically. □ **underachiever** *noun*.

underarm *adjective & adverb Cricket etc.* with arm below shoulder level.

underbelly *noun* (*plural* **-ies**) under surface of animal etc., esp. as vulnerable to attack.

underbid /ʌndəˈbɪd/ *verb* (**-dd-**; *past & past participle* **-bid**) make lower bid than; *Bridge etc.* bid too little (on).

undercarriage *noun* wheeled retractable landing structure beneath aircraft; supporting framework of vehicle etc.

undercharge /ʌndəˈtʃɑːdz/ *verb* (**-ging**) charge too little to.

underclothes *plural noun* (also **underclothing**) clothes worn under others, esp. next to skin.

undercoat *noun* layer of paint under another; (in animals) under layer of hair etc.

undercook /ʌndəˈkʊk/ *verb* cook insufficiently.

undercover /ʌndəˈkʌvə/ *adjective* surreptitious; spying incognito.

undercroft *noun* crypt.

undercurrent *noun* current below surface; underlying often contrary feeling, force, etc.

undercut ● *verb* /ʌndəˈkʌt/ (**-tt-**; *past & past participle* **-cut**) sell or work at lower price than; strike (ball) to make it rise high; undermine. ● *noun* /ˈʌndəkʌt/ underside of sirloin.

underdeveloped /ʌndədɪˈveləpt/ *adjective* immature; (of country etc.) with unexploited potential.

underdog *noun* oppressed person; loser in fight etc.

underdone /ʌndəˈdʌn/ *adjective* undercooked.

underemployed /ʌndərɪmˈplɔɪd/ *adjective* not fully occupied.

underestimate ● *verb* /ʌndərˈestɪmeɪt/ (**-ting**) form too low an estimate of. ● *noun* /ʌndərˈestɪmət/ estimate that is too low. □ **underestimation** *noun*.

underexpose /ʌndərɪkˈspəʊz/ *verb* (**-sing**) expose (film) for too short a time. □ **underexposure** *noun*.

underfed /ʌndəˈfed/ *adjective* malnourished.

underfelt *noun* felt laid under carpet.

underfloor /ʌndəˈflɔː/ *adjective* (esp. of heating) beneath floor.

underfoot /ʌndəˈfʊt/ *adverb* (also **under foot**) under one's feet; on the ground.

underfunded /ʌndəˈfʌndɪd/ *adjective* provided with insufficient money.

undergarment *noun* piece of underclothing.

undergo /ʌndəˈgəʊ/ *verb* (*3rd singular present* **-goes**; *past* **-went**; *past participle* **-gone** /-ˈgɒn/) be subjected to, endure.

undergraduate /ʌndəˈgrædjʊət/ *noun* person studying for first degree.

underground ● *adverb* /ʌndəˈgraʊnd/ beneath the ground; in(to) secrecy or hiding. ● *adjective* /ˈʌndəgraʊnd/ situated underground; secret, subversive; unconventional. ● *noun* /ˈʌndəgraʊnd/ underground railway; secret subversive group or activity.

undergrowth *noun* dense shrubs etc., esp. in wood.

underhand *adjective* secret, deceptive; *Cricket etc.* underarm.

underlay[1] ● *verb* /ʌndəˈleɪ/ (*past & past participle* **-laid**) lay thing under (another) to support or raise. ● *noun* /ˈʌndəleɪ/ thing so laid (esp. under carpet).

underlay[2] *past of* UNDERLIE.

underlie /ʌndəˈlaɪ/ *verb* (**-lying**; *past* **-lay**; *past participle* **-lain**) lie under (stratum etc.); (esp. as **underlying** *adjective*) be basis of, exist beneath superficial aspect of.

underline /ʌndəˈlaɪn/ *verb* (**-ning**) draw line under (words etc.); emphasize.

underling /ˈʌndəlɪŋ/ *noun usually derogatory* subordinate.

undermanned /ʌndəˈmænd/ *adjective* having insufficient crew or staff.

undermine /ʌndəˈmaɪn/ *verb* (**-ning**) injure or wear out insidiously or secretly; wear away base of; make excavation under.

underneath /ʌndəˈniːθ/ ● *preposition* at or to lower place than, below; on inside of. ● *adverb* at or to lower place; inside. ● *noun* lower surface or part. ● *adjective* lower.

undernourished /ʌndəˈnʌrɪʃt/ *adjective* insufficiently nourished. □ **undernourishment** *noun*.

underpants *plural noun* undergarment for lower part of torso.

underpass *noun* road etc. passing under another; subway.

underpay /ʌndəˈpeɪ/ *verb* (*past & past participle* **-paid**) pay too little to (person) or for (thing). □ **underpayment** *noun*.

underpin /ʌndəˈpɪn/ *verb* (**-nn-**) support from below with masonry etc.; support, strengthen.

underprivileged /ʌndəˈprɪvɪlɪdʒd/ *adjective* less privileged than others; having below average income, rights, etc.

underrate /ʌndəˈreɪt/ *verb* (**-ting**) have too low an opinion of.

underscore /ʌndəˈskɔː/ *verb* (**-ring**) underline.

undersea *adjective* below sea or its surface.

underseal *verb* seal underpart of (esp. vehicle against rust etc.).

under-secretary /ʌndəˈsekrətərɪ/ *noun* (*plural* **-ies**) subordinate official, esp. junior minister or senior civil servant.

undersell /ʌndəˈsel/ *verb* (*past & past participle* **-sold**) sell at lower price than (another seller).

undershirt *noun esp. US* vest.

undershoot /ʌndəˈʃuːt/ *verb* (*past & past participle* **-shot**) land short of (runway etc.).

undershot *adjective* (of wheel) turned by water flowing under it; (of lower jaw) projecting beyond upper jaw.

underside *noun* lower side or surface.

undersigned /ʌndəˈsaɪnd/ *adjective* whose signature is appended.

undersized /ˈʌndəsaɪzd/ *adjective* smaller than average.

underspend /ʌndəˈspend/ *verb* (*past & past participle* **-spent**) spend less than (expected amount) or too little.

understaffed /ʌndəˈstɑːft/ *adjective* having too few staff.

understand /ʌndəˈstænd/ *verb* (*past & past participle* **-stood**) comprehend, perceive meaning, significance, or cause of; know how to deal with; (often + *that*) infer, take as implied. □ **understandable** *adjective*; **understandably** *adverb*.

understanding ● *noun* intelligence; ability to understand; individual's perception of situation; agreement, esp. informal. ● *adjective* having understanding or insight; sympathetic. □ **understandingly** *adverb*.

understate /ʌndəˈsteɪt/ *verb* (**-ting**) express in restrained terms; represent as being less than it really is. □ **understatement** *noun*.

understudy /ˈʌndəstʌdɪ/ ● *noun* (*plural* **-ies**) person ready to take another's role when required, esp. in theatre. ● *verb* (**-ies**, **-ied**) study (role etc.) for this purpose; act as understudy to.

undersubscribed /ʌndəsəbˈskraɪbd/ *adjective* without sufficient subscribers, participants, etc.

undertake /ʌndəˈteɪk/ *verb* (**-king**; *past* **-took**; *past participle* **-taken**) agree to perform or be responsible for; engage in; (usually + *to do*) promise; guarantee, affirm.

undertaker /ˈʌndəteɪkə/ *noun* professional funeral organizer.

undertaking /ʌndəˈteɪkɪŋ/ *noun* work etc. undertaken; enterprise; promise; /ˈʌn-/ professional funeral management.

undertone *noun* subdued tone; underlying quality or feeling.

undertow *noun* current below sea surface contrary to surface current.

underused /ʌndəˈjuːzd/ *adjective* not used to capacity.

undervalue /ʌndəˈvæljuː/ *verb* (**-ues**, **-ued**, **-uing**) value insufficiently; underestimate.

underwater /ʌndəˈwɔːtə/ ● *adjective* situated or done under water. ● *adverb* under water.

underwear *noun* underclothes.

underweight /ʌndəˈweɪt/ *adjective* below normal weight.

underwent *past of* UNDERGO.

underwhelm /ʌndəˈwelm/ *verb jocular* fail to impress.

underworld *noun* those who live by organized crime; mythical home of the dead.

underwrite /ʌndəˈraɪt/ *verb* (**-ting**; *past* **-wrote**; *past participle* **-written**) sign and accept liability under (insurance policy); accept (liability) thus; undertake to finance or support; engage to buy all unsold stock in (company etc.). □ **underwriter** /ˈʌn-/ *noun*.

undesirable /ʌndɪˈzaɪərəb(ə)l/ ● *adjective* unpleasant, objectionable. ● *noun* undesirable person. □ **undesirability** *noun*.

undies /ˈʌndɪz/ *plural noun colloquial* (esp. women's) underclothes.

undo /ʌnˈduː/ *verb* (*3rd singular present* **-does**; *past* **-did**; *past participle* **-done**; *present participle* **-doing**) unfasten; annul; ruin prospects, reputation, or morals of.

undoing *noun* (cause of) ruin; reversing of action etc.; unfastening.

undone /ʌnˈdʌn/ *adjective* not done; not fastened; *archaic* ruined.

undoubted /ʌnˈdaʊtɪd/ *adjective* certain, not questioned. □ **undoubtedly** *adverb*.

undreamed /ʌn'dri:md, ʌn'dremt/ *adjective* (also **undreamt** /ʌn'dremt/) (often + *of*) not thought of, never imagined.

undress /ʌn'dres/ ● *verb* take off one's clothes; take clothes off (person). ● *noun* ordinary dress, esp. as opposed to (full-dress) uniform; naked or scantily clad state.

undressed /ʌn'drest/ *adjective* no longer dressed; (of food) without dressing; (of leather) untreated.

undue /ʌn'dju:/ *adjective* excessive, disproportionate. □ **unduly** *adverb*.

undulate /'ʌndjʊleɪt/ *verb* (**-ting**) (cause to) have wavy motion or look. □ **undulation** *noun*.

undying /ʌn'daɪɪŋ/ *adjective* immortal; never-ending.

unearth /ʌn'ɜ:θ/ *verb* discover by searching, digging, or rummaging.

unearthly /ʌn'ɜ:θlɪ/ *adjective* supernatural; mysterious; *colloquial* very early.

unease /ʌn'i:z/ *noun* nervousness, anxiety.

uneasy /ʌn'i:zɪ/ *adjective* (**-ier**, **-iest**) disturbed or uncomfortable in body or mind. □ **uneasily** *adverb*; **uneasiness** *noun*.

unemployable /ʌnɪm'plɔɪəb(ə)l/ *adjective* unfit for paid employment.

unemployed /ʌnɪm'plɔɪd/ *adjective* out of work; not used.

unemployment /ʌnɪm'plɔɪmənt/ *noun* lack of employment. □ **unemployment benefit** state payment made to unemployed worker.

unencumbered /ʌnɪn'kʌmbəd/ *adjective* (of estate) having no liabilities; free, not burdened.

unequivocal /ʌnɪ'kwɪvək(ə)l/ *adjective* not ambiguous, plain, unmistakable. □ **unequivocally** *adverb*.

UNESCO /ju:'neskəʊ/ *abbreviation* (also **Unesco**) United Nations Educational, Scientific, and Cultural Organization.

uneven /ʌn'i:v(ə)n/ *adjective* not level; of variable quality; (of contest) unequal. □ **unevenly** *adverb*.

unexceptionable /ʌnɪk'sepʃənəb(ə)l/ *adjective* entirely satisfactory.

■ **Usage** *Unexceptionable* is sometimes confused with *unexceptional*.

unexceptional /ʌnɪk'sepʃən(ə)l/ *adjective* normal, ordinary.

■ **Usage** *Unexceptional* is sometimes confused with *unexceptionable*

unfailing /ʌn'feɪlɪŋ/ *adjective* not failing, constant, reliable. □ **unfailingly** *adverb*.

unfaithful /ʌn'feɪθfʊl/ *adjective* not faithful, esp. adulterous. □ **unfaithfulness** *noun*.

unfeeling /ʌn'fi:lɪŋ/ *adjective* unsympathetic, harsh.

unfit /ʌn'fɪt/ *adjective* (often + *for*, *to do*) not fit, unsuitable; in poor health.

unflagging /ʌn'flægɪŋ/ *adjective* tireless, persistent.

unflappable /ʌn'flæpəb(ə)l/ *adjective colloquial* imperturbable.

unfledged /ʌn'fledʒd/ *adjective* inexperienced; not fledged.

unfold /ʌn'fəʊld/ *verb* open out; reveal; become opened out; develop.

unforgettable /ʌnfə'getəb(ə)l/ *adjective* memorable, wonderful.

unfortunate /ʌn'fɔ:tʃənət/ ● *adjective* unlucky; unhappy; regrettable. ● *noun* unfortunate person. □ **unfortunately** *adverb*.

unfounded /ʌn'faʊndɪd/ *adjective* (of rumour etc.) without foundation.

unfreeze /ʌn'fri:z/ *verb* (**-zing**; *past* **unfroze**; *past participle* **unfrozen**) (cause to) thaw; derestrict (assets etc.).

unfrock /ʌn'frɒk/ *verb* defrock.

unfurl /ʌn'fɜ:l/ *verb* unroll, spread out.

ungainly /ʌn'geɪnlɪ/ *adjective* awkward, clumsy.

unget-at-able /ʌnget'ætəb(ə)l/ *adjective colloquial* inaccessible.

ungodly /ʌn'gɒdlɪ/ *adjective* impious, wicked; *colloquial* outrageous.

ungovernable /ʌn'gʌvənəb(ə)l/ *adjective* uncontrollable, violent.

ungracious /ʌn'greɪʃəs/ *adjective* discourteous, grudging.

ungrateful /ʌn'greɪtfʊl/ *adjective* not feeling or showing gratitude. □ **ungratefully** *adverb*.

ungreen /ʌn'gri:n/ *adjective* harmful to environment; not concerned with protection of environment.

unguarded /ʌn'gɑ:dɪd/ *adjective* incautious, thoughtless; not guarded.

unguent /'ʌŋgwənt/ *noun* ointment, lubricant.

ungulate /'ʌŋgjʊlət/ ● *adjective* hoofed. ● *noun* hoofed mammal.

unhallowed /ʌn'hæləʊd/ *adjective* unconsecrated; not sacred; wicked.

unhand /ʌn'hænd/ *verb rhetorical or jocular* take one's hands off, release (person).

unhappy /ʌn'hæpɪ/ *adjective* (**-ier**, **-iest**) miserable; unfortunate; disastrous. □ **unhappily** *adverb*; **unhappiness** *noun*.

unhealthy /ʌn'helθɪ/ *adjective* (**-ier**, **-iest**) in poor health; harmful to health; unwholesome; *slang* dangerous. □ **unhealthily** *adverb*.

unheard-of /ʌn'hɜ:dɒv/ *adjective* unprecedented.

unhinge /ʌn'hɪndʒ/ *verb* (**-ging**) take (door etc.) off hinges; (esp. as **unhinged** *adjective*) derange, disorder (mind).

unholy /ʌn'həʊlɪ/ *adjective* (**-ier**, **-iest**) profane, wicked; *colloquial* dreadful, outrageous.

unhorse /ʌn'hɔ:s/ *verb* (**-sing**) throw (rider) from horse.

uni /'ju:nɪ/ *noun* (*plural* **-s**) *esp. Australian & NZ colloquial* university.

uni- *combining form* having or composed of one.

Uniate /'ju:nɪət/ ● *adjective* of Church in E. Europe or Near East acknowledging papal supremacy but retaining its own liturgy etc. ● *noun* member of such Church.

unicameral /ju:nɪ'kæmər(ə)l/ *adjective* having one legislative chamber.

UNICEF /'ju:nɪsef/ *abbreviation* United Nations Children's Fund.

unicellular /ju:nɪ'seljʊlə/ *adjective* consisting of a single cell.

unicorn /'ju:nɪkɔ:n/ *noun* mythical horse with single straight horn.

unicycle /'ju:nɪsaɪk(ə)l/ *noun* one-wheeled cycle used by acrobats etc.

unification /ju:nɪfɪ'keɪʃ(ə)n/ *noun* unifying, being unified. □ **Unification Church** religious organization funded by Sun Myung Moon. □ **unificatory** *adjective*.

uniform /'ju:nɪfɔ:m/ ● *adjective* unvarying; conforming to same standard or rule; constant over a period. ● *noun* distinctive clothing worn by members of same organization etc. □ **uniformed** *adjective*; **uniformity** /-'fɔ:m-/ *noun*; **uniformly** *adverb*.

unify /'ju:nɪfaɪ/ *verb* (**-ies**, **-ied**) make or become united or uniform.

unilateral /ju:nɪ'lætər(ə)l/ *adjective* done by or affecting one side only. □ **unilaterally** *adverb*.

unilateralism *noun* unilateral disarmament. □ **unilateralist** *noun & adjective*.

unimpeachable /ʌnɪmˈpiːtʃəb(ə)l/ *adjective* beyond reproach.

uninviting /ʌnɪnˈvaɪtɪŋ/ *adjective* unattractive, repellent.

union /ˈjuːnjən/ *noun* uniting, being united; whole formed from parts or members; trade union; marriage; concord; university social club or debating society. □ **Union flag, Jack** national flag of UK.

unionist *noun* member of trade union, advocate of trade unions; (usually **Unionist**) supporter of continued union between Britain and Northern Ireland. □ **unionism** *noun*.

unionize *verb* (also **-ise**) (**-zing** or **-sing**) organize in or into trade union. □ **unionization** *noun*.

unique /juːˈniːk/ *adjective* being the only one of its kind; having no like, equal, or parallel; remarkable. □ **uniquely** *adverb*.

■ **Usage** The use of *unique* to mean 'remarkable' is considered incorrect by some people.

unisex /ˈjuːnɪseks/ *adjective* (of clothing etc.) designed for both sexes.

unison /ˈjuːnɪs(ə)n/ *noun* concord; coincidence in pitch of sounds or notes.

unit /ˈjuːnɪt/ *noun* individual thing, person, or group, esp. for calculation; smallest component of complex whole; quantity chosen as standard of measurement; smallest share in unit trust; part with specified function in complex mechanism; fitted item of furniture, esp. as part of set; subgroup with special function; group of buildings, wards, etc. in hospital; single-digit number, esp. 'one'. □ **unit cost** cost of producing one item; **unit trust** company investing contributions from many people in various securities.

Unitarian /juːnɪˈteərɪən/ *noun* member of religious body maintaining that God is one person not Trinity. □ **Unitarianism** *noun*.

unitary /ˈjuːnɪtərɪ/ *adjective* of unit(s); marked by unity or uniformity.

unite /jʊˈnaɪt/ *verb* (**-ting**) join together, esp. for common purpose; join in marriage; (cause to) form physical or chemical whole. □ **United Kingdom** Great Britain and Northern Ireland; **United Nations** (treated as *singular* or *plural*) international peace-seeking organization; **United States** = United States of America.

unity /ˈjuːnɪtɪ/ *noun* (*plural* **-ies**) oneness, being one; interconnecting parts making a whole, the whole made; solidarity, harmony between people etc.; the number 'one'.

universal /juːnɪˈvɜːs(ə)l/ ● *adjective* of, belonging to, or done etc. by all; applicable to all cases. ● *noun* term, characteristic, or concept of general application. □ **universal coupling**, **joint** one transmitting rotary power by a shaft at any angle; **universal time** Greenwich Mean Time. □ **universality** /-ˈsæl-/ *noun*; **universally** *adverb*.

universe /ˈjuːnɪvɜːs/ *noun* all existing things; Creation; all humankind.

university /juːnɪˈvɜːsɪtɪ/ *noun* (*plural* **-ies**) educational institution of advanced learning and research, conferring degrees; members of this.

unkempt /ʌnˈkempt/ *adjective* dishevelled, untidy.

unknown /ʌnˈnəʊn/ ● *adjective* (often + *to*) not known, unfamiliar. ● *noun* unknown thing, person, or quantity. □ **unknown quantity** mysterious or obscure person or thing; **Unknown Soldier**, **Warrior** unidentified soldier symbolizing nation's dead in war.

unlawful /ʌnˈlɔːfʊl/ *adjective* illegal, not permissible. □ **unlawfully** *adverb*.

unleaded /ʌnˈledɪd/ *adjective* (of petrol etc.) without added lead.

unleash /ʌnˈliːʃ/ *verb* free from leash or restraint; set free to pursue or attack.

unleavened /ʌnˈlev(ə)nd/ *adjective* made without yeast etc.

unless /ʌnˈles/ *conjunction* if not; except when.

unlettered /ʌnˈletəd/ *adjective* illiterate.

unlike /ʌnˈlaɪk/ ● *adjective* not like, different. ● *preposition* differently from.

unlikely /ʌnˈlaɪklɪ/ *adjective* (**-ier**, **-iest**) improbable; (+ *to do*) not expected; unpromising.

unlisted /ʌnˈlɪstɪd/ *adjective* not included in list, esp. of Stock Exchange prices or telephone numbers.

unload /ʌnˈləʊd/ *verb* remove load from (vehicle etc.); remove (load) from vehicle etc.; remove ammunition from (gun); *colloquial* get rid of.

unlock /ʌnˈlɒk/ *verb* release lock of; release or disclose by unlocking; release feelings etc. from.

unlooked-for /ʌnˈlʊktfɔː/ *adjective* unexpected.

unlucky /ʌnˈlʌkɪ/ *adjective* (**-ier**, **-iest**) not fortunate or successful; wretched; bringing bad luck; ill-judged. □ **unluckily** *adverb*.

unman /ʌnˈmæn/ *verb* (**-nn-**) deprive of courage, self-control, etc.

unmannerly /ʌnˈmænəlɪ/ *adjective* ill-mannered.

unmask /ʌnˈmɑːsk/ *verb* remove mask from; expose true character of; remove one's mask.

unmentionable /ʌnˈmenʃənəb(ə)l/ ● *adjective* unsuitable for polite conversation. ● *noun* (in *plural*) *jocular* undergarments.

unmistakable /ʌnmɪˈsteɪkəb(ə)l/ *adjective* clear, obvious, plain. □ **unmistakably** *adverb*.

unmitigated /ʌnˈmɪtɪgeɪtɪd/ *adjective* not modified; absolute.

unmoved /ʌnˈmuːvd/ *adjective* not moved; constant in purpose; unemotional.

unnatural /ʌnˈnætʃər(ə)l/ *adjective* contrary to nature; not normal; lacking natural feelings; artificial, forced. □ **unnaturally** *adverb*.

unnecessary /ʌnˈnesəsərɪ/ *adjective* not necessary; superfluous. □ **unnecessarily** *adverb*.

unnerve /ʌnˈnɜːv/ *verb* (**-ving**) deprive of confidence etc.

unobjectionable /ʌnəbˈdʒekʃənəb(ə)l/ *adjective* acceptable.

unobtrusive /ʌnəbˈtruːsɪv/ *adjective* not making oneself or itself noticed. □ **unobtrusively** *adverb*.

unofficial /ʌnəˈfɪʃ(ə)l/ *adjective* not officially authorized or confirmed. □ **unofficial strike** strike not ratified by trade union.

unpack /ʌnˈpæk/ *verb* open and empty; take (thing) from package etc.

unpalatable /ʌnˈpælətəb(ə)l/ *adjective* (of food, suggestion, etc.) disagreeable, distasteful.

unparalleled /ʌnˈpærəleld/ *adjective* unequalled.

unparliamentary /ʌnpɑːləˈmentərɪ/ *adjective* contrary to proper parliamentary usage. □ **unparliamentary language** oaths, abuse.

unpick /ʌnˈpɪk/ *verb* undo sewing of.

unplaced /ʌnˈpleɪst/ *adjective* not placed as one of the first 3 in race etc.

unpleasant /ʌnˈplez(ə)nt/ *adjective* disagreeable. □ **unpleasantly** *adverb*; **unpleasantness** *noun*.

unplug /ʌnˈplʌg/ *verb* (**-gg-**) disconnect (electrical device) by removing plug from socket; unstop.

unplumbed /ʌnˈplʌmd/ *adjective* not plumbed; not fully explored or understood.

unpopular /ʌn'pɒpjʊlə/ *adjective* not popular, disliked. ▫ **unpopularity** /-'lær-/ *noun*.

unpractised /ʌn'præktɪst/ *adjective* (*US* **unpracticed**) not experienced or skilled; not put into practice.

unprecedented /ʌn'presɪdentɪd/ *adjective* having no precedent, unparalleled.

unprepossessing /ʌnpri:pə'zesɪŋ/ *adjective* unattractive.

unprincipled /ʌn'prɪnsɪp(ə)ld/ *adjective* lacking or not based on moral principles.

unprintable /ʌn'prɪntəb(ə)l/ *adjective* too offensive or indecent to be printed.

unprofessional /ʌnprə'feʃən(ə)l/ *adjective* contrary to professional standards; unskilled, amateurish.

unprompted /ʌn'prɒmptɪd/ *adjective* spontaneous.

unputdownable /ʌnpʊt'daʊnəb(ə)l/ *adjective colloquial* compulsively readable.

unqualified /ʌn'kwɒlɪfaɪd/ *adjective* not qualified or competent; complete.

unquestionable /ʌn'kwestʃənəb(ə)l/ *adjective* that cannot be disputed or doubted. ▫ **unquestionably** *adverb*.

unquote /ʌn'kwəʊt/ *interjection used in dictation etc. to indicate closing quotation marks.*

unravel /ʌn'ræv(ə)l/ *verb* (**-ll-**; *US* **-l-**) make or become unknitted, unknotted, etc.; solve (mystery etc.); undo (knitted fabric).

unreal /ʌn'rɪəl/ *adjective* not real; imaginary; *slang* incredible.

unreasonable /ʌn'ri:zənəb(ə)l/ *adjective* excessive; not heeding reason. ▫ **unreasonably** *adverb*.

unregenerate /ʌnrɪ'dʒenərət/ *adjective* obstinately wrong or bad.

unrelenting /ʌnrɪ'lentɪŋ/ *adjective* not abating; merciless.

unreliable /ʌnrɪ'laɪəb(ə)l/ *adjective* erratic.

unrelieved /ʌnrɪ'li:vd/ *adjective* monotonously uniform.

unremarked /ʌnrɪ'mɑ:kt/ *adjective* not mentioned or remarked on.

unremitting /ʌnrɪ'mɪtɪŋ/ *adjective* incessant. ▫ **unremittingly** *adverb*.

unremunerative /ʌnrɪ'mju:nərətɪv/ *adjective* unprofitable.

unrequited /ʌnrɪ'kwaɪtɪd/ *adjective* (of love etc.) not returned.

unreserved /ʌnrɪ'zɜ:vd/ *adjective* without reservation. ▫ **unreservedly** /-vɪdlɪ/ *adverb*.

unrest /ʌn'rest/ *noun* disturbance, turmoil, trouble.

unrivalled /ʌn'raɪv(ə)ld/ *adjective* (*US* **unrivaled**) having no equal.

unroll /ʌn'rəʊl/ *verb* open out from rolled-up state; display, be displayed.

unruffled /ʌn'rʌf(ə)ld/ *adjective* calm.

unruly /ʌn'ru:lɪ/ *adjective* (**-ier**, **-iest**) undisciplined, disorderly. ▫ **unruliness** *noun*.

unsatisfactory /ʌnsætɪs'fæktəri/ *adjective* poor, unacceptable.

unsaturated /ʌn'sætʃəreɪtɪd/ *adjective Chemistry* (of fat) containing double or triple molecular bonds and therefore capable of combining with hydrogen.

unsavoury /ʌn'seɪvəri/ *adjective* (*US* **unsavory**) disgusting; (esp. morally) offensive.

unscathed /ʌn'skeɪðd/ *adjective* uninjured, unharmed.

unschooled /ʌn'sku:ld/ *adjective* uneducated, untrained.

unscientific /ʌnsaɪən'tɪfɪk/ *adjective* not scientific in method etc. ▫ **unscientifically** *adverb*.

unscramble /ʌn'skræmb(ə)l/ *verb* (**-ling**) decode, interpret (scrambled transmission etc.).

unscreened /ʌn'skri:nd/ *adjective* (esp. of coal) not passed through screen; not checked, esp. for security or medical problems; not having screen; not shown on screen.

unscrew /ʌn'skru:/ *verb* unfasten by removing screw(s), loosen (screw).

unscripted /ʌn'skrɪptɪd/ *adjective* (of speech etc.) delivered impromptu.

unscrupulous /ʌn'skru:pjʊləs/ *adjective* without scruples; unprincipled. ▫ **unscrupulously** *adverb*; **unscrupulousness** *noun*.

unseasonal /ʌn'si:zən(ə)l/ *adjective* not typical of the time or season.

unseat /ʌn'si:t/ *verb* remove from (esp. parliamentary) seat; dislodge from horseback etc.

unseeing /ʌn'si:ɪŋ/ *adjective* unobservant; blind. ▫ **unseeingly** *adverb*.

unseemly /ʌn'si:mlɪ/ *adjective* (**-ier**, **-iest**) indecent; unbecoming.

unseen /ʌn'si:n/ ● *adjective* not seen; invisible; (of translation) to be done without preparation. ● *noun* unseen translation.

unselfish /ʌn'selfɪʃ/ *adjective* concerned about others; sharing. ▫ **unselfishly** *adverb*; **unselfishness** *noun*.

unsettled /ʌn'set(ə)ld/ *adjective* restless, disturbed; open to further discussion; liable to change; not paid.

unsex /ʌn'seks/ *verb* deprive of qualities of one's (esp. female) sex.

unshakeable /ʌn'ʃeɪkəb(ə)l/ *adjective* firm; obstinate.

unsightly /ʌn'saɪtlɪ/ *adjective* ugly. ▫ **unsightliness** *noun*.

unskilled /ʌn'skɪld/ *adjective* lacking or (of work) not needing special skills.

unsociable /ʌn'səʊʃəb(ə)l/ *adjective* disliking company.

■ **Usage** *Unsociable* is sometimes confused with *unsocial*.

unsocial /ʌn'səʊʃ(ə)l/ *adjective* not social; not suitable for or seeking society; outside normal working day; antisocial.

■ **Usage** *Unsocial* is sometimes confused with *unsociable*.

unsolicited /ʌnsə'lɪsɪtɪd/ *adjective* voluntary.

unsophisticated /ʌnsə'fɪstɪkeɪtɪd/ *adjective* artless, simple, natural.

unsound /ʌn'saʊnd/ *adjective* unhealthy; rotten; weak; unreliable.

unsparing /ʌn'speərɪŋ/ *adjective* lavish; merciless.

unspeakable /ʌn'spi:kəb(ə)l/ *adjective* that words cannot express; indescribably bad. ▫ **unspeakably** *adverb*.

unstable /ʌn'steɪb(ə)l/ *adjective* (**-r**, **-st**) likely to fall; not stable emotionally; changeable.

unsteady /ʌn'stedɪ/ *adjective* (**-ier**, **-iest**) not firm; changeable; not regular. ▫ **unsteadily** *adverb*; **unsteadiness** *noun*.

unstick /ʌn'stɪk/ *verb* (*past & past participle* **unstuck**) separate (thing stuck to another). ▫ **come unstuck** *colloquial* fail.

unstinting /ʌn'stɪntɪŋ/ *adjective* lavish; limitless. ▫ **unstintingly** *adverb*.

unstressed /ʌn'strest/ *adjective* not pronounced with stress.

unstring /ʌn'strɪŋ/ *verb* (*past & past participle* **unstrung**) remove string(s) of (bow, harp, etc.); take (beads etc.) off string; (esp. as **unstrung** *adjective*) unnerve.

unstructured /ʌn'strʌktʃəd/ *adjective* without structure; informal.

unstudied /ʌn'stʌdɪd/ *adjective* easy, natural, spontaneous.
unsung /ʌn'sʌŋ/ *adjective* not celebrated, unrecognized.
unswerving /ʌn'swɜːvɪŋ/ *adjective* constant, steady. ▫ **unswervingly** *adverb*.
unthinkable /ʌn'θɪŋkəb(ə)l/ *adjective* unimaginable, inconceivable; *colloquial* highly unlikely or undesirable.
unthinking /ʌn'θɪŋkɪŋ/ *adjective* thoughtless; unintentional, inadvertent. ▫ **unthinkingly** *adverb*.
untidy /ʌn'taɪdɪ/ *adjective* (**-ier**, **-iest**) not neat or orderly. ▫ **untidily** *adverb*; **untidiness** *noun*.
until /ən'tɪl/ *preposition & conjunction* = TILL[1].

■ **Usage** *Until*, as opposed to *till*, is used especially at the beginning of a sentence and in formal style, as in *Until you told me, I had no idea* or *He resided there until his decease*.

untimely /ʌn'taɪmlɪ/ *adjective* inopportune; premature.
untiring /ʌn'taɪərɪŋ/ *adjective* tireless.
unto /'ʌntʊ/ *preposition archaic* to.
untold /ʌn'təʊld/ *adjective* not told; immeasurable.
untouchable /ʌn'tʌtʃəb(ə)l/ ● *adjective* that may not be touched. ● *noun* Hindu of group believed to defile higher castes on contact.
untoward /ʌntə'wɔːd/ *adjective* inconvenient, unlucky; awkward; refractory; unseemly.
untrammelled /ʌn'træm(ə)ld/ *adjective* not hampered.
untruth /ʌn'truːθ/ *noun* being untrue; lie.
unused *adjective* /ʌn'juːzd/ not in use, never used; /ʌn'juːst/ (+ *to*) not accustomed.
unusual /ʌn'juːʒʊəl/ *adjective* not usual; remarkable. ▫ **unusually** *adverb*.
unutterable /ʌn'ʌtərəb(ə)l/ *adjective* inexpressible; beyond description. ▫ **unutterably** *adverb*.
unvarnished /ʌn'vɑːnɪʃt/ *adjective* not varnished; plain, direct, simple.
unveil /ʌn'veɪl/ *verb* uncover (statue etc.) ceremonially; reveal (secrets etc.).
unversed /ʌn'vɜːst/ *adjective* (usually + *in*) not experienced or skilled.
unwarrantable /ʌn'wɒrəntəb(ə)l/ *adjective* (also **unwarranted**) unjustified.
unwashed /ʌn'wɒʃt/ *adjective* not washed or clean. ▫ **the great unwashed** *colloquial* the rabble.
unwell /ʌn'wel/ *adjective* ill.
unwholesome /ʌn'həʊlsəm/ *adjective* detrimental to moral or physical health; unhealthy-looking.
unwieldy /ʌn'wiːldɪ/ *adjective* (**-ier**, **-iest**) cumbersome or hard to manage owing to size, shape, etc.
unwilling /ʌn'wɪlɪŋ/ *adjective* reluctant. ▫ **unwillingly** *adverb*; **unwillingness** *noun*.
unwind /ʌn'waɪnd/ *verb* (*past & past participle* **unwound**) draw out or become drawn out after having been wound; *colloquial* relax.
unwitting /ʌn'wɪtɪŋ/ *adjective* not knowing, unaware; unintentional. ▫ **unwittingly** *adverb*.
unwonted /ʌn'wəʊntɪd/ *adjective* not customary or usual.
unworldly /ʌn'wɜːldlɪ/ *adjective* spiritual; naïve.
unworthy /ʌn'wɜːðɪ/ *adjective* (**-ier**, **-iest**) (often + *of*) not worthy or befitting; discreditable, unseemly. ▫ **unworthiness** *noun*.
unwritten /ʌn'rɪt(ə)n/ *adjective* not written; (of law etc.) based on tradition or judicial decision, not on statute.
up ● *adverb* towards or in higher place or place regarded as higher, e.g. the north, a capital; to or in erect or required position; in or into active condition; in stronger position; (+ *to*, *till*, etc.) to specified place, person, or time; higher in price; completely; completed; into compact, accumulated, or secure state; having risen; happening, esp. unusually. ● *preposition* upwards and along, through, or into; at higher part of. ● *adjective* directed upwards. ● *noun* spell of good fortune. ● *verb* (**-pp-**) *colloquial* start (abruptly or unexpectedly) to speak or act; raise. ▫ **on the up** (**and up**) *colloquial* steadily improving; **up against** close to, in(to) contact with, *colloquial* confronted with; **up-and-coming** *colloquial* (of person) promising, progressing; **up for** available for or standing for (sale, office, etc.); **upstate** *US* (in, to, or of) provincial, esp. northern, part of a state; **upstream** *adverb* against flow of stream etc., *adjective* moving upstream; **up to** until, below or equal to, incumbent on, capable of, occupied or busy with; **uptown** *US* (in, into, or of) residential part of town or city; **upwind** in the direction from which the wind is blowing.
upbeat ● *noun Music* unaccented beat. ● *adjective colloquial* optimistic, cheerful.
upbraid /ʌp'breɪd/ *verb* (often + *with*, *for*) chide, reproach.
upbringing *noun* child's rearing.
up-country /ʌp'kʌntrɪ/ *adjective & adverb* inland.
update ● *verb* /ʌp'deɪt/ (**-ting**) bring up to date. ● *noun* /'ʌpdeɪt/ updating; updated information etc.
up-end /ʌp'end/ *verb* set or rise up on end.
upfront /ʌp'frʌnt/ *colloquial* ● *adverb* (usually **up front**) at the front; in front; (of payments) in advance. ● *adjective* honest, frank, direct; (of payments) made in advance.
upgrade /ʌp'greɪd/ *verb* (**-ding**) raise in rank etc.; improve (equipment etc.).
upheaval /ʌp'hiːv(ə)l/ *noun* sudden esp. violent change or disturbance.
uphill ● *adverb* /ʌp'hɪl/ up a slope. ● *adjective* /'ʌphɪl/ sloping up; ascending; arduous.
uphold /ʌp'həʊld/ *verb* (*past & past participle* **upheld**) support; maintain, confirm. ▫ **upholder** *noun*.
upholster /ʌp'həʊlstə/ *verb* provide (furniture) with upholstery. ▫ **upholsterer** *noun*.
upholstery *noun* covering, padding, springs, etc. for furniture; upholsterer's work.
upkeep *noun* maintenance in good condition; cost or means of this.
upland /'ʌplənd/ ● *noun* (usually in *plural*) higher parts of country. ● *adjective* of these parts.
uplift ● *verb* /ʌp'lɪft/ raise; (esp as **uplifting** *adjective*) elevate morally or emotionally. ● *noun* /'ʌplɪft/ elevating influence; support for breasts etc.
up-market /ʌp'mɑːkɪt/ *adjective & adverb* of or to more expensive sector of market.
upon /ə'pɒn/ *preposition* on.

■ **Usage** *Upon* is usually more formal than *on*, but it is standard in *once upon a time* and *upon my word*.

upper /'ʌpə/ ● *adjective* higher in place; situated above; superior in rank etc. ● *noun* part of shoe or boot above sole. ▫ **on one's uppers** *colloquial* extremely short of money; **upper case** capital letters; **the upper crust** *colloquial* the aristocracy; **uppercut** hit upwards with arm bent; **the upper hand** dominance, control; **Upper House** higher legislative assembly, esp. House of Lords.
uppermost ● *adjective* highest, predominant. ● *adverb* on or to the top.
uppity /'ʌpɪtɪ/ *adjective* (also **uppish**) *colloquial* self-assertive, arrogant.

upright /ˈʌpraɪt/ ● *adjective* erect, vertical; (of piano) with vertical strings; honourable, honest. ● *noun* upright post or rod, esp. as structural support; upright piano.

uprising *noun* insurrection.

uproar *noun* tumult, violent disturbance.

uproarious /ʌpˈrɔːrɪəs/ *adjective* very noisy; provoking loud laughter; very funny. ▫ **uproariously** *adverb*.

uproot /ʌpˈruːt/ *verb* pull (plant etc.) up from ground; displace (person); eradicate.

upset ● *verb* /ʌpˈset/ (**-tt-**; *past & past participle* **upset**) overturn; disturb temper, digestion, or composure of; disrupt. ● *noun* /ˈʌpset/ disturbance, surprising result. ● *adjective* /ʌpˈset, ˈʌp-/ disturbed.

upshot *noun* outcome, conclusion.

upside down /ʌpsaɪd ˈdaʊn/ *adverb & adjective* with upper and lower parts reversed, inverted; in(to) total disorder.

upstage /ʌpˈsteɪdʒ/ ● *adjective & adverb* nearer back of theatre stage. ● *verb* (**-ging**) move upstage to make (another actor) face away from audience; divert attention from (person) to oneself.

upstairs ● *adverb* /ʌpˈsteəz/ to or on an upper floor. ● *adjective* /ˈʌpsteəz/ situated upstairs. ● *noun* /ʌpˈsteəz/ upper floor.

upstanding /ʌpˈstændɪŋ/ *adjective* standing up; strong and healthy; honest.

upstart ● *noun* newly successful, esp. arrogant, person. ● *adjective* that is an upstart; of upstarts.

upsurge *noun* upward surge.

upswept *adjective* (of hair) combed to top of head.

upswing *noun* upward movement or trend.

uptake *noun colloquial* understanding; taking up (of offer etc.).

uptight /ʌpˈtaɪt/ *adjective colloquial* nervously tense, angry; *US* rigidly conventional.

upturn ● *noun* /ˈʌptɜːn/ upward trend, improvement. ● *verb* /ʌpˈtɜːn/ turn up or upside down.

upward /ˈʌpwəd/ ● *adverb* (also **upwards**) towards what is higher, more important, etc. ● *adjective* moving or extending upwards. ▫ **upwardly** *adverb*.

uranium /jʊˈreɪnɪəm/ *noun* radioactive heavy grey metallic element, capable of nuclear fission and used as source of nuclear energy.

urban /ˈɜːbən/ *adjective* of, living in, or situated in city or town. ▫ **urban guerrilla** terrorist operating in urban area.

urbane /ɜːˈbeɪn/ *adjective* suave; elegant. ▫ **urbanity** /-ˈbæn-/ *noun*.

urbanize /ˈɜːbənaɪz/ *verb* (also **-ise**) (**-zing** or **-sing**) make urban, esp. by destroying rural quality of (district). ▫ **urbanization** *noun*.

urchin /ˈɜːtʃɪn/ *noun* mischievous, esp. ragged, child; sea urchin.

Urdu /ˈʊəduː/ *noun* Persian-influenced language related to Hindi, used esp. in Pakistan.

urea /jʊəˈriːə/ *noun* soluble nitrogenous compound contained esp. in urine.

ureter /jʊəˈriːtə/ *noun* duct carrying urine from kidney to bladder.

urethra /jʊəˈriːθrə/ *noun* (*plural* **-s**) duct carrying urine from bladder.

urge /ɜːdʒ/ ● *verb* (**-ging**) (often + *on*) drive forcibly, hasten; entreat or exhort earnestly or persistently; (often + *on, upon*) advocate (action, argument, etc.) emphatically. ● *noun* urging impulse or tendency; strong desire.

urgent /ˈɜːdʒ(ə)nt/ *adjective* requiring immediate action or attention; importunate. ▫ **urgency** *noun*; **urgently** *adverb*.

uric acid /ˈjʊərɪk/ *noun* constituent of urine.

urinal /jʊəˈraɪn(ə)l/ *noun* place or receptacle for urinating by men.

urinary /ˈjʊərɪnərɪ/ *adjective* of or relating to urine.

urinate /ˈjʊərɪneɪt/ *verb* (**-ting**) discharge urine. ▫ **urination** *noun*.

urine /ˈjʊərɪn/ *noun* waste fluid secreted by kidneys and discharged from bladder.

urn *noun* vase with foot, used esp. for ashes of the dead; large vessel with tap, in which tea etc. is made or kept hot.

urology /jʊəˈrɒlədʒɪ/ *noun* study of the urinary system. ▫ **urological** /-rəˈlɒdʒ-/ *adjective*.

ursine /ˈɜːsaɪn/ *adjective* of or like a bear.

US *abbreviation* United States.

us /ʌs, əs/ *pronoun used by speaker or writer to refer to himself or herself and one or more others as object of verb; used for* ME *by sovereign in formal contexts or by editorial writer in newspaper*; *colloquial* we.

USA *abbreviation* United States of America.

usable /ˈjuːzəb(ə)l/ *adjective* that can be used.

USAF *abbreviation* United States Air Force.

usage /ˈjuːsɪdʒ/ *noun* use, treatment; customary practice, established use (esp. of language).

use ● *verb* /juːz/ (**using**) cause to act or serve for purpose; bring into service; treat in specified way; exploit for one's own ends; (as **used** *adjective*) secondhand. ● *noun* /juːs/ using, being used; right or power of using; benefit, advantage; custom, usage. ▫ **in use** being used; **make use of** use, benefit from; **used to** /juːst/ *adjective* accustomed to, *verb used before other verb to describe habitual action* (e.g. *I used to live here*); **use up** consume, find use for (leftovers etc.).

■ **Usage** The usual negative and question forms of *used to* are, for example, *You didn't use to go there* and *Did you use to go there?* Both are, however, rather informal, so it is better in formal language to use *You used not to go there* and a different expression such as *Were you in the habit of going there?* or *Did you go there when you lived in London?*

useful *adjective* that can be used to advantage; helpful, beneficial; *colloquial* creditable, efficient. ▫ **usefully** *adverb*; **usefulness** *noun*.

useless *adjective* serving no purpose, unavailing; *colloquial* feeble, ineffectual. ▫ **uselessly** *adverb*; **uselessness** *noun*.

user *noun* person who uses a thing. ▫ **user-friendly** (of computer, program, etc.) easy to use.

usher /ˈʌʃə/ ● *noun* person who shows people to their seats in cinema, church, etc.; doorkeeper of court etc. ● *verb* act as usher to; (usually + *in*) announce, show in.

usherette /ʌʃəˈret/ *noun* female usher, esp. in cinema.

USSR *abbreviation historical* Union of Soviet Socialist Republics.

usual /ˈjuːʒʊəl/ *adjective* customary; habitual. ▫ **as usual** as is (or was) usual. ▫ **usually** *adverb*.

usurer /ˈjuːʒərə/ *noun* person who practises usury.

usurp /jʊˈzɜːp/ *verb* seize (throne, power, etc.) wrongfully. ▫ **usurpation** /juːzəˈp-/ *noun*; **usurper** *noun*.

usury /ˈjuːʒərɪ/ *noun* lending of money at interest, esp. at exorbitant or illegal rate; interest at this rate. ▫ **usurious** /juːˈʒʊərɪəs/ *adjective*.

utensil /juːˈtens(ə)l/ *noun* implement or vessel, esp. for kitchen use.

uterus /ˈjuːtərəs/ *noun* (*plural* **uteri** /-raɪ/) womb. ▫ **uterine** /-raɪn/ *adjective*.

utilitarian /juːtɪlɪˈteərɪən/ ● *adjective* designed to be useful rather than attractive; of utilitarianism. ● *noun* adherent of utilitarianism.

utilitarianism *noun* doctrine that actions are justified if they are useful or benefit majority.

utility /juːˈtɪlɪtɪ/ ● *noun* (*plural* **-ies**) usefulness; useful thing, public utility. ● *adjective* basic and standardized. ◻ **utility room** room for domestic appliances, e.g. washing machine, boiler, etc.; **utility vehicle** vehicle serving various functions.

utilize /ˈjuːtɪlaɪz/ *verb* (also **-ise**) (**-zing** or **-sing**) turn to account, use. ◻ **utilization** *noun*.

utmost /ˈʌtməʊst/ ● *adjective* farthest, extreme; greatest. ● *noun* the utmost point, degree, etc. ◻ **do one's utmost** do all that one can.

Utopia /juːˈtəʊpɪə/ *noun* imagined perfect place or state. ◻ **Utopian**, **utopian** *adjective*.

utter[1] /ˈʌtə/ *adjective* complete, absolute. ◻ **utterly** *adverb*; **uttermost** *adjective*.

utter[2] /ˈʌtə/ *verb* emit audibly; express in words; *Law* put (esp. forged money) into circulation.

utterance *noun* uttering; thing spoken; power or manner of speaking.

UV *abbreviation* ultraviolet.

uvula /ˈjuːvjʊlə/ *noun* (*plural* **uvulae** /-liː/) fleshy part of soft palate hanging above throat. ◻ **uvular** *adjective*.

uxorious /ʌkˈsɔːrɪəs/ *adjective* excessively fond of one's wife.

Vv

V¹ *noun* (also **v**) (Roman numeral) 5.
V² *abbreviation* volt(s).
v. *abbreviation* verse; versus; very; verb; *vide*.
vac *noun colloquial* vacation.
vacancy /ˈveɪkənsɪ/ *noun* (*plural* **-ies**) being vacant; unoccupied post, place, etc.
vacant *adjective* not filled or occupied; not mentally active, showing no interest. □ **vacant possession** ownership of unoccupied house etc. □ **vacantly** *adverb*.
vacate /vəˈkeɪt/ *verb* (**-ting**) leave vacant, cease to occupy.
vacation /vəˈkeɪʃ(ə)n/ *noun* fixed holiday period, esp. in law courts and universities; *US* holiday; vacating, being vacated.
vaccinate /ˈvæksɪneɪt/ *verb* (**-ting**) inoculate with vaccine to immunize against disease. □ **vaccination** *noun*.
vaccine /ˈvæksiːn/ *noun* preparation used for inoculation, originally cowpox virus giving immunity to smallpox.
vacillate /ˈvæsɪleɪt/ *verb* (**-ting**) fluctuate in opinion or resolution. □ **vacillation** *noun*; **vacillator** *noun*.
vacuous /ˈvækjʊəs/ *adjective* expressionless; unintelligent. □ **vacuity** /vəˈkjuːɪtɪ/ *noun*; **vacuously** *adverb*.
vacuum /ˈvækjʊəm/ ● *noun* (*plural* **-s** or **vacua**) space entirely devoid of matter; space or vessel from which air has been completely or partly removed by pump etc.; absence of normal or previous content; (*plural* **-s**) *colloquial* vacuum cleaner. ● *verb colloquial* clean with vacuum cleaner. □ **vacuum brake** brake worked by exhaustion of air; **vacuum cleaner** machine for removing dust etc. by suction; **vacuum flask** vessel with double wall enclosing vacuum so that contents remain hot or cold; **vacuum-packed** sealed after partial removal of air; **vacuum tube** tube containing near-vacuum for free passage of electric current.
vagabond /ˈvægəbɒnd/ ● *noun* wanderer, esp. idle one. ● *adjective* wandering, having no settled habitation or home.
vagary /ˈveɪgərɪ/ *noun* (*plural* **-ies**) caprice, eccentric act or idea.
vagina /vəˈdʒaɪnə/ *noun* (*plural* **-s** or **-nae** /-niː/) canal joining womb and vulva of female mammal. □ **vaginal** *adjective*.
vagrant /ˈveɪgrənt/ ● *noun* person without settled home or regular work. ● *adjective* wandering, roving. □ **vagrancy** *noun*.
vague /veɪg/ *adjective* uncertain, ill-defined; not clear-thinking, inexact. □ **vaguely** *adverb*; **vagueness** *noun*.
vain *adjective* conceited; empty, trivial; unavailing, useless. □ **in vain** without result or success, lightly or profanely. □ **vainly** *adverb*.
vainglory /veɪnˈglɔːrɪ/ *noun* extreme vanity, boastfulness. □ **vainglorious** *adjective*.
valance /ˈvæləns/ *noun* short curtain round bedstead, above window, etc.
vale *noun* (*archaic* except in place names) valley.
valediction /vælɪˈdɪkʃ(ə)n/ *noun formal* bidding farewell; words used in this. □ **valedictory** *adjective & noun* (*plural* **-ies**).
valence /ˈveɪləns/ *noun* valency.
valency /ˈveɪlənsɪ/ *noun* (*plural* **-ies**) combining-power of an atom measured by number of hydrogen atoms it can displace or combine with.
valentine /ˈvæləntaɪn/ *noun* (usually anonymous) letter or card sent as mark of love on St Valentine's Day (14 Feb.); sweetheart chosen on that day.
valerian /vəˈlɪərɪən/ *noun* any of various kinds of flowering herb.
valet /ˈvælɪt/ ● *noun* gentleman's personal servant. ● *verb* (**-t-**) act as valet (to).
valetudinarian /vælɪtjuːdɪˈneərɪən/ ● *noun* person of poor health or unduly anxious about health. ● *adjective* of a valetudinarian.
valiant /ˈvæljənt/ *adjective* brave. □ **valiantly** *adverb*.
valid /ˈvælɪd/ *adjective* (of reason, objection, etc.) sound, defensible; legally acceptable, not yet expired. □ **validity** /vəˈlɪd-/ *noun*.
validate /ˈvælɪdeɪt/ *verb* (**-ting**) make valid, ratify. □ **validation** *noun*.
valise /vəˈliːz/ *noun US* small portmanteau.
Valium /ˈvælɪəm/ *noun proprietary term* the tranquillizing drug diazepam.
valley /ˈvælɪ/ *noun* (*plural* **-s**) low area between hills, usually with stream or river.
valour /ˈvælə/ *noun* (*US* **valor**) courage, esp. in battle. □ **valorous** *adjective*.
valuable /ˈvæljʊəb(ə)l/ ● *adjective* of great value, price, or worth. ● *noun* (usually in *plural*) valuable thing.
valuation /væljʊˈeɪʃ(ə)n/ *noun* estimation (esp. by professional valuer) of thing's worth; estimated value.
value /ˈvæljuː/ ● *noun* worth, desirability, or qualities on which these depend; worth as estimated; amount for which thing can be exchanged in open market; equivalent of thing; (in full **value for money**) something well worth money spent; ability of a thing to serve a purpose or cause an effect; (in *plural*) one's principles, priorities, or standards; *Music* duration of note; *Mathematics* amount denoted by algebraic term. ● *verb* (**-ues**, **-ued**, **-uing**) estimate value of; have high or specified opinion of. □ **value added tax** tax levied on rise in value of services and goods at each stage of production; **value judgement** subjective estimate of worth etc. □ **valueless** *adjective*.
valuer *noun* person who estimates or assesses values.
valve *noun* device controlling flow through pipe etc., usually allowing movement in one direction only; structure in organ etc. allowing flow of blood etc. in one direction only; thermionic valve; device to vary length of tube in trumpet etc.; half-shell of oyster, mussel, etc.
valvular /ˈvælvjʊlə/ *adjective* having valve(s); having form or function of valve.
vamoose /vəˈmuːs/ *verb US slang* depart hurriedly.
vamp¹ ● *noun* upper front part of boot or shoe. ● *verb* (often + *up*) repair, furbish, or make by patching or piecing together; improvise musical accompaniment.
vamp² *colloquial* ● *noun* woman who uses sexual attraction to exploit men. ● *verb* allure or exploit (man).
vampire /ˈvæmpaɪə/ *noun* supposed ghost or reanimated corpse sucking blood of sleeping people;

person who preys on others; (in full **vampire bat**) bloodsucking bat.

van[1] *noun* covered vehicle or closed railway truck for transporting goods etc.

van[2] *noun* vanguard, forefront.

vanadium /və'neɪdɪəm/ *noun* hard grey metallic element used to strengthen steel.

vandal /'vænd(ə)l/ *noun* person who wilfully or maliciously damages property. ◻ **vandalism** *noun*.

vandalize /'vændəlaɪz/ *verb* (also **-ise**) (**-zing** or **-sing**) destroy or damage wilfully or maliciously (esp. public property).

vane *noun* weather vane; blade of windmill, ship's propeller, etc.

vanguard /'vængɑːd/ *noun* foremost part of advancing army etc.; leaders of movement etc.

vanilla /və'nɪlə/ *noun* tropical fragrant climbing orchid; extract of its fruit (**vanilla-pod**), or synthetic substitute, used as flavouring.

vanish /'vænɪʃ/ *verb* disappear; cease to exist. ◻ **vanishing point** point at which receding parallel lines appear to meet.

vanity /'vænɪtɪ/ *noun* (*plural* **-ies**) conceit about one's attainments or appearance; futility, unreal thing. ◻ **vanity bag**, **case** woman's make-up bag or case.

vanquish /'væŋkwɪʃ/ *verb literary* conquer, overcome.

vantage /'vɑːntɪdʒ/ *noun* advantage, esp. in tennis; (also **vantage point**) place giving good view.

vapid /'væpɪd/ *adjective* insipid, dull, flat. ◻ **vapidity** /və'pɪd-/ *noun*.

vapor *US* = VAPOUR.

vaporize /'veɪpəraɪz/ *verb* (also **-ise**) (**-zing** or **-sing**) change into vapour. ◻ **vaporization** *noun*.

vaporous /'veɪpərəs/ *adjective* in the form of or consisting of vapour.

vapour /'veɪpə/ *noun* (*US* **vapor**) moisture or other substance diffused or suspended in air, e.g. mist, smoke; gaseous form of substance. ◻ **vapour trail** trail of condensed water from aircraft etc.

variable /'veərɪəb(ə)l/ ● *adjective* changeable, adaptable; apt to vary, not constant; *Mathematics* (of quantity) indeterminate, able to assume different numerical values. ● *noun* variable thing or quantity. ◻ **variability** *noun*.

variance /'veərɪəns/ *noun* (usually after *at*) difference of opinion; dispute; discrepancy.

variant ● *adjective* differing in form or details from standard; having different forms. ● *noun* variant form, spelling, type, etc.

variation /veərɪ'eɪʃ(ə)n/ *noun* varying; departure from normal kind, standard, type, etc.; extent of this; thing that varies from type; *Music* theme in changed or elaborated form.

varicose /'værɪkəʊs/ *adjective* (esp. of vein etc.) permanently and abnormally dilated.

variegated /'veərɪgeɪtɪd/ *adjective* with irregular patches of different colours; having leaves of two or more colours. ◻ **variegation** *noun*.

variety /və'raɪətɪ/ *noun* (*plural* **-ies**) diversity; absence of uniformity; collection of different things; class of things differing from rest in same general class; member of such class; (+ *of*) different form of thing, quality, etc.; *Biology* subdivision of species; series of dances, songs, comedy acts, etc.

various /'veərɪəs/ *adjective* different, diverse; several. ◻ **variously** *adverb*.

■ **Usage** *Various* (unlike *several*) is not a pronoun and therefore cannot be used with *of*, as (wrongly) in *Various of the guests arrived late.*

varnish /'vɑːnɪʃ/ ● *noun* resinous solution used to give hard shiny transparent coating. ● *verb* coat with varnish; conceal with deceptively attractive appearance.

varsity /'vɑːsɪtɪ/ *noun* (*plural* **-ies**) *colloquial* university.

vary /'veərɪ/ *verb* (**-ies**, **-ied**) be or become different; be of different kinds; modify, diversify.

vascular /'væskjʊlə/ *adjective* of or containing vessels for conveying blood, sap, etc.

vas deferens /væs 'defərenz/ *noun* (*plural* **vasa deferentia** /veɪsə defə'renʃɪə/) sperm duct of testicle.

vase /vɑːz/ *noun* vessel used as ornament or container for flowers.

vasectomy /və'sektəmɪ/ *noun* (*plural* **-ies**) removal of part of each vas deferens, esp. for sterilization.

Vaseline /'væsɪliːn/ *noun proprietary term* type of petroleum jelly used as ointment etc.

vassal /'væs(ə)l/ *noun* humble dependant; *historical* holder of land by feudal tenure.

vast /vɑːst/ *adjective* immense, huge. ◻ **vastly** *adverb*; **vastness** *noun*.

VAT *abbreviation* value added tax.

vat *noun* tank, esp. for holding liquids in brewing, dyeing, and tanning.

Vatican /'vætɪkən/ *noun* palace or government of Pope in Rome.

vaudeville /'vɔːdəvɪl/ *noun esp. US* variety entertainment.

vault /vɔːlt/ ● *noun* arched roof; vaultlike covering; underground room as place of storage; underground burial chamber; act of vaulting. ● *verb* leap or spring, esp. using hands or pole; spring over in this way; (esp. as **vaulted** *adjective*) make in form of vault, provide with vault(s).

vaunt /vɔːnt/ *verb & noun literary* boast.

VC *abbreviation* Victoria Cross.

VCR *abbreviation* video cassette recorder.

VD *abbreviation* venereal disease.

VDU *abbreviation* visual display unit.

veal *noun* calf's flesh as food.

vector /'vektə/ *noun Mathematics & Physics* quantity having both magnitude and direction; carrier of disease.

veer /vɪə/ *verb* change direction, esp. (of wind) clockwise; change in opinion, course, etc.

vegan /'viːgən/ ● *noun* person who does not eat animals or animal products. ● *adjective* using or containing no animal products.

vegetable /'vedʒtəb(ə)l/ ● *noun* plant, esp. edible herbaceous plant. ● *adjective* of, derived from, or relating to plant life or vegetables as food.

vegetarian /vedʒɪ'teərɪən/ ● *noun* person who does not eat meat or fish. ● *adjective* excluding animal food, esp. meat. ◻ **vegetarianism** *noun*.

vegetate /'vedʒɪteɪt/ *verb* (**-ting**) lead dull monotonous life; grow as plants do.

vegetation /vedʒɪ'teɪʃ(ə)n/ *noun* plants collectively; plant life.

vegetative /'vedʒɪtətɪv/ *adjective* concerned with growth and development rather than sexual reproduction; of vegetation.

vehement /'viːəmənt/ *adjective* showing or caused by strong feeling, ardent. ◻ **vehemence** *noun*; **vehemently** *adverb*.

vehicle /'viːɪk(ə)l/ *noun* conveyance used on land or in space; thing or person as medium for thought, feeling, or action; liquid etc. as medium for suspending pigments, drugs, etc. ◻ **vehicular** /vɪ'hɪkjʊlə/ *adjective*.

veil /veɪl/ ● *noun* piece of usually transparent material attached to woman's hat or otherwise forming part of headdress, esp. to conceal or protect face; piece of linen etc. as part of nun's headdress; thing that hides or disguises. ● *verb* cover with veil; (esp.

as **veiled** *adjective*) partly conceal. ▫ **beyond the veil** in the unknown state of life after death; **draw a veil over** avoid discussing; **take the veil** become nun.

vein /veɪn/ *noun* any of tubes carrying blood to heart; (in general use) any blood vessel; rib of leaf or insect's wing; streak of different colour in wood, marble, cheese, etc.; fissure in rock filled with ore; specified character or tendency, mood. ▫ **veined** *adjective*.

Velcro /'velkrəʊ/ *noun proprietary term* fastener consisting of two strips of fabric which cling when pressed together.

veld /velt/ *noun* (also **veldt**) *South African* open country.

veleta /və'li:tə/ *noun* ballroom dance in triple time.

vellum /'veləm/ *noun* fine parchment, originally calfskin; manuscript on this; smooth writing paper imitating vellum.

velociraptor /vɪ'lɒsɪræptə/ *noun* small carnivorous dinosaur with short front legs.

velocity /vɪ'lɒsɪtɪ/ *noun* (*plural* **-ies**) speed, esp. of inanimate things.

velour /və'lʊə/ *noun* (also **velours** same pronunciation) plushlike fabric.

velvet /'velvɪt/ ● *noun* soft fabric with thick short pile on one side; furry skin on growing antler. ● *adjective* of, like, or soft as velvet. ▫ **on velvet** in advantageous or prosperous position; **velvet glove** outward gentleness cloaking firmness or inflexibility. ▫ **velvety** *adjective*.

velveteen /velvɪ'ti:n/ *noun* cotton fabric with pile like velvet.

Ven. *abbreviation* Venerable.

venal /'vi:n(ə)l/ *adjective* able to be bribed; involving bribery; corrupt. ▫ **venality** /-'næl-/ *noun*.

■ **Usage** *Venal* is sometimes confused with *venial*.

vend *verb* offer (esp. small wares) for sale. ▫ **vending machine** slot machine selling small items. ▫ **vendor** *noun*.

vendetta /ven'detə/ *noun* blood feud; prolonged bitter quarrel.

veneer /vɪ'nɪə/ ● *noun* thin covering of fine wood; (often + *of*) deceptively pleasing appearance. ● *verb* apply veneer to (wood etc.).

venerable /'venərəb(ə)l/ *adjective* entitled to deep respect on account of age, character, etc.; *title of archdeacon*.

venerate /'venəreɪt/ *verb* (**-ting**) regard with deep respect. ▫ **veneration** *noun*.

venereal /vɪ'nɪərɪəl/ *adjective* of sexual desire or intercourse; of venereal disease. ▫ **venereal disease** disease contracted by sexual intercourse with infected person.

Venetian /vɪ'ni:ʃ(ə)n/ ● *noun* native, citizen, or dialect of Venice. ● *adjective* of Venice. ▫ **venetian blind** window-blind of adjustable horizontal slats.

vengeance /'vendʒ(ə)ns/ *noun* punishment inflicted for wrong to oneself or to one's cause. ▫ **with a vengeance** to extreme degree, thoroughly, violently.

vengeful /'vendʒfʊl/ *adjective* seeking vengeance, vindictive.

venial /'vi:nɪəl/ *adjective* (of sin or fault) pardonable, not mortal. ▫ **veniality** /-'æl-/ *noun*.

■ **Usage** *Venial* is sometimes confused with *venal*.

venison /'venɪs(ə)n/ *noun* deer's flesh as food.

Venn diagram *noun* diagram using overlapping and intersecting circles etc. to show relationships between mathematical sets.

venom /'venəm/ *noun* poisonous fluid of esp. snakes; malignity, virulence of feeling, language, or conduct. ▫ **venomous** *adjective*; **venomously** *adverb*.

venous /'vi:nəs/ *adjective* of, full of, or contained in veins.

vent[1] ● *noun* opening for passage of air etc.; outlet, free expression; anus, esp. of lower animal. ● *verb* give vent or free expression to.

vent[2] *noun* slit in garment, esp. in back of jacket.

ventilate /'ventɪleɪt/ *verb* (**-ting**) cause air to circulate freely in (room etc.); air (question, grievance, etc.). ▫ **ventilation** *noun*.

ventilator *noun* appliance or aperture for ventilating room etc.; apparatus for maintaining artifical respiration.

ventral /'ventr(ə)l/ *adjective* of or on abdomen.

ventricle /'ventrɪk(ə)l/ *noun* cavity in body; hollow part of organ, esp. brain or heart.

ventricular /ven'trɪkjʊlə/ *adjective* of or shaped like ventricle.

ventriloquism /ven'trɪləkwɪz(ə)m/ *noun* skill of speaking without moving the lips. ▫ **ventriloquist** *noun*.

venture /'ventʃə/ ● *noun* risky undertaking; commercial speculation. ● *verb* (**-ring**) dare, not be afraid; dare to go, make, or put forward; take risks, expose to risk, stake. ▫ **Venture Scout** senior Scout.

venturesome *adjective* disposed to take risks.

venue /'venju:/ *noun* appointed place for match, meeting, concert, etc.

Venus fly-trap /'vi:nəs/ *noun* insectivorous plant.

veracious /və'reɪʃəs/ *adjective formal* truthful, true. ▫ **veracity** /-'ræs-/ *noun*.

veranda /və'rændə/ *noun* (sometimes partly covered) platform along side of house.

verb *noun* word used to indicate action, event, state, or change (see panel).

verbal *adjective* of words; oral, not written; of a verb; (of translation) literal. ▫ **verbally** *adverb*.

verbalize *verb* (also **-ise**) (**-zing** or **-sing**) put into words.

verbatim /vɜ:'beɪtɪm/ *adverb & adjective* in exactly the same words.

verbena /vɜ:'bi:nə/ *noun* (*plural* same) plant of genus of herbs and small shrubs with fragrant flowers.

verbiage /'vɜ:bɪɪdʒ/ *noun derogatory* unnecessary number of words.

verbose /vɜ:'bəʊs/ *adjective* using more words than are needed. ▫ **verbosity** /-'bɒs-/ *noun*.

verdant /'vɜ:d(ə)nt/ *adjective* (of grass, field, etc.) green, lush. ▫ **verdancy** *noun*.

verdict /'vɜ:dɪkt/ *noun* decision of jury; decision, judgement.

verdigris /'vɜ:dɪgri:/ *noun* greenish-blue substance that forms on copper or brass.

verdure /'vɜ:djə/ *noun literary* green vegetation or its colour.

verge[1] *noun* edge, border; brink; grass edging of road etc.

verge[2] *verb* (**-ging**) (+ *on*) border on; incline downwards or in specified direction.

verger /'vɜ:dʒə/ *noun* caretaker and attendant in church; officer carrying staff before dignitaries of cathedral etc.

verify /'verɪfaɪ/ *verb* (**-ies, -ied**) establish truth or correctness of by examination etc.; fulfil, bear out. ▫ **verification** *noun*.

verily /'verɪlɪ/ *adverb archaic* truly, really.

verisimilitude /verɪsɪ'mɪlɪtju:d/ *noun* appearance of being true or real.

veritable /'verɪtəb(ə)l/ *adjective* real, rightly so called.

verity /ˈverɪtɪ/ *noun* (*plural* **-ies**) true statement; *archaic* truth.

vermicelli /vɜːmɪˈtʃelɪ/ *noun* pasta in long slender threads.

vermicide /ˈvɜːmɪsaɪd/ *noun* drug used to kill intestinal worms.

vermiform /ˈvɜːmɪfɔːm/ *adjective* worm-shaped. □ **vermiform appendix** small blind tube extending from caecum in man and some other mammals.

vermilion /vəˈmɪljən/ ● *noun* brilliant scarlet pigment made esp. from cinnabar; colour of this. ● *adjective* of this colour.

vermin /ˈvɜːmɪn/ *noun* (usually treated as *plural*) mammals and birds harmful to game, crops, etc.; parasitic worms or insects; vile people.

verminous *adjective* of the nature of or infested with vermin.

vermouth /ˈvɜːməθ/ *noun* wine flavoured with aromatic herbs.

vernacular /vəˈnækjʊlə/ ● *noun* language or dialect of country; language of particular class or group; homely speech. ● *adjective* (of language) of one's own country, not foreign or formal.

vernal /ˈvɜːn(ə)l/ *adjective* of or in spring.

vernier /ˈvɜːnɪə/ *noun* small movable scale for reading fractional parts of subdivisions on fixed scale of measuring instrument.

veronica /vəˈrɒnɪkə/ *noun* speedwell.

verruca /vəˈruːkə/ *noun* (*plural* **verrucae** /-siː/ or **-s**) wart or similar growth, esp. on foot.

versatile /ˈvɜːsətaɪl/ *adjective* turning easily or readily from one subject or occupation to another, skilled in many subjects or occupations; having many uses. □ **versatility** /-ˈtɪl-/ *noun*.

verse *noun* poetry; stanza of poem or song; each of short numbered divisions of Bible.

versed /vɜːst/ *adjective* (+ *in*) experienced or skilled in.

versicle /ˈvɜːsɪk(ə)l/ *noun* short sentence, esp. each of series in liturgy said or sung by minister or priest, answered by congregation.

versify /ˈvɜːsɪfaɪ/ *verb* (**-ies, -ied**) turn into or express in verse; compose verses. □ **versification** *noun*.

version /ˈvɜːʃ(ə)n/ *noun* account of matter from particular point of view; particular edition or translation of book etc.

verso /ˈvɜːsəʊ/ *noun* (*plural* **-s**) left-hand page of open book, back of printed leaf.

versus /ˈvɜːsəs/ *preposition* against.

vertebra /ˈvɜːtɪbrə/ *noun* (*plural* **-brae** /-briː/) each segment of backbone. □ **vertebral** *adjective*.

vertebrate /ˈvɜːtɪbrət/ ● *adjective* having backbone. ● *noun* vertebrate animal.

vertex /ˈvɜːteks/ *noun* (*plural* **-tices** /-tɪsiːz/ or **-texes**) highest point, top, apex; meeting-point of lines that form angle.

vertical /ˈvɜːtɪk(ə)l/ ● *adjective* at right angles to horizontal plane; in direction from top to bottom of picture etc.; of or at vertex. ● *noun* vertical line or plane. □ **vertical take-off** take-off of aircraft directly upwards. □ **vertically** *adverb*.

vertiginous /vɜːˈtɪdʒɪnəs/ *adjective* of or causing vertigo.

vertigo /ˈvɜːtɪgəʊ/ *noun* dizziness.

vervain /ˈvɜːveɪn/ *noun* any of several verbenas, esp. one with small blue, white, or purple flowers.

verve *noun* enthusiasm, energy, vigour.

very /ˈverɪ/ ● *adverb* in high degree; (+ *own* or superlative adjective) in fullest sense. ● *adjective* real, properly so called etc. □ **very good, well** *formula of consent or approval*; **very high frequency** 30–300 megahertz (in radio); **Very Reverend** *title of dean*.

vesicle /ˈvesɪk(ə)l/ *noun* small bladder, blister, or bubble.

vespers /ˈvespəz/ *plural noun* evening church service.

vessel /ˈves(ə)l/ *noun* hollow receptacle, esp. for liquid; ship or boat, esp. large one; duct or canal holding or conveying blood, sap, etc.

vest ● *noun* undergarment worn on upper part of body; *US & Australian* waistcoat. ● *verb* (+ *with*) bestow (powers, authority, etc.) on; (+ *in*) confer (property or power) on (person) with immediate fixed right of future possession. □ **vested interest** personal interest in state of affairs, usually with expectation of gain, *Law* interest (usually in land or money held in trust) recognized as belonging to person.

Verb

A verb says what a person or thing does, and can describe:

an action, e.g. *run, hit*
an event, e.g. *rain, happen*
a state, e.g. *be, have, seem, appear*
a change, e.g. *become, grow*

Verbs occur in different forms, usually in one or other of their tenses. The most common tenses are:

the simple present tense:	*The boy walks down the road.*
the continuous present tense:	*The boy is walking down the road.*
the simple past tense:	*The boy walked down the road.*
the continuous past tense:	*The boy was walking down the road.*
the perfect tense:	*The boy has walked down the road.*
the future tense:	*The boy will walk down the road.*

Each of these forms is a finite verb, which means that it is in a particular tense and that it changes according to the number and person of the subject, as in

I am *you walk*
we are *he walks*

An infinitive is the form of a verb that usually appears with 'to', e.g.
to wander, to look, to sleep.

vestal virgin /'vest(ə)l/ *noun* virgin consecrated to Vesta, Roman goddess of hearth and home, and vowed to chastity.

vestibule /'vestɪbju:l/ *noun* lobby, entrance hall.

vestige /'vestɪdʒ/ *noun* trace, evidence; slight amount, particle; *Biology* part or organ now atrophied that was well-developed in ancestors. □ **vestigial** /-'tɪdʒɪəl/ *adjective*.

vestment /'vestmənt/ *noun* ceremonial garment worn by priest etc.

vestry /'vestrɪ/ *noun* (*plural* **-ies**) room or part of church for keeping vestments etc. in.

vet ● *noun colloquial* veterinary surgeon. ● *verb* (**-tt-**) make careful and critical examination of (scheme, work, candidate, etc.).

vetch *noun* plant of pea family largely used for fodder.

veteran /'vetərən/ *noun* old soldier or long-serving member of any group; *US* ex-serviceman or -woman. □ **veteran car** one made before 1905.

veterinarian /vetərɪ'neərɪən/ *noun formal* veterinary surgeon.

veterinary /'vetərɪnərɪ/ *adjective* of or for diseases and injuries of animals. □ **veterinary surgeon** person qualified to treat animals.

veto /'vi:təʊ/ ● *noun* (*plural* **-es**) right to reject measure etc. unilaterally; rejection, prohibition. ● *verb* (**-oes, -oed**) reject (measure etc.); forbid.

vex *verb* annoy, irritate; *archaic* grieve, afflict.

vexation /vek'seɪʃ(ə)n/ *noun* vexing, being vexed; annoying or distressing thing.

vexatious /vek'seɪʃ(ə)s/ *adjective* causing vexation; *Law* lacking sufficient grounds for action and seeking only to annoy defendant.

vexed *adjective* (of question) much discussed.

VHF *abbreviation* very high frequency.

via /'vaɪə/ *preposition* by way of, through.

viable /'vaɪəb(ə)l/ *adjective* (of plan etc.) feasible, esp. economically; (esp. of foetus) capable of living and surviving independently. □ **viability** *noun*.

viaduct /'vaɪədʌkt/ *noun* long bridge carrying railway or road over valley.

vial /'vaɪəl/ *noun* small glass vessel.

viands /'vaɪəndz/ *plural noun formal* articles of food.

viaticum /vaɪ'ætɪkəm/ *noun* (*plural* **-ca**) Eucharist given to dying person.

vibes /vaɪbz/ *plural noun colloquial* vibrations, esp. feelings communicated; vibraphone.

vibrant /'vaɪbrənt/ *adjective* vibrating; resonant; (often + *with*) thrilling; (of colour) bright and striking. □ **vibrancy** *noun*.

vibraphone /'vaɪbrəfəʊn/ *noun* percussion instrument with motor-driven resonators under metal bars giving vibrato effect.

vibrate /vaɪ'breɪt/ *verb* (**-ting**) move rapidly to and fro; (of sound) throb, resonate; (+ *with*) quiver; swing to and fro, oscillate. □ **vibratory** *adjective*.

vibration *noun* vibrating; (in *plural*) mental (esp. occult) influence, atmosphere or feeling communicated.

vibrato /vɪ'brɑ:təʊ/ *noun* tremulous effect in musical pitch.

vibrator *noun* device that vibrates, esp. instrument used in massage or sexual stimulation.

viburnum /vaɪ'bɜ:nəm/ *noun* shrub with pink or white flowers.

vicar /'vɪkə/ *noun* incumbent of C. of E. parish where in former times incumbent received stipend rather than tithes; *colloquial* any member of the clergy.

vicarage *noun* vicar's house.

vicarious /vɪ'keərɪəs/ *adjective* experienced indirectly; acting or done etc. for another; deputed, delegated. □ **vicariously** *adverb*.

vice[1] *noun* immoral conduct; particular form of this; bad habit. □ **vice ring** group of criminals organizing prostitution; **vice squad** police department concerned with prostitution.

vice[2] *noun* (*US* **vise**) clamp with two jaws for holding an object being worked on.

vice- *combining form* person acting in place of; person next in rank to.

vice-chancellor /vaɪs'tʃɑ:nsələ/ *noun* deputy chancellor (esp. administrator of university).

viceregal /vaɪs'ri:g(ə)l/ *adjective* of viceroy.

vicereine /'vaɪsreɪn/ *noun* viceroy's wife; woman viceroy.

viceroy /'vaɪsrɔɪ/ *noun* ruler on behalf of sovereign in colony, province, etc.

vice versa /vaɪs 'vɜ:sə/ *adjective* with order of terms changed, other way round.

Vichy water /'vi:ʃi:/ *noun* effervescent mineral water from Vichy in France.

vicinity /vɪ'sɪnɪtɪ/ *noun* (*plural* **-ies**) surrounding district; (+ *to*) nearness to. □ **in the vicinity (of)** near (to).

vicious /'vɪʃəs/ *adjective* bad-tempered, spiteful; violent; corrupt. □ **vicious circle** self-perpetuating, harmful sequence of cause and effect. □ **viciously** *adverb*; **viciousness** *noun*.

vicissitude /vɪ'sɪsɪtju:d/ *noun literary* change, esp. of fortune.

victim /'vɪktɪm/ *noun* person or thing destroyed or injured; prey, dupe; creature sacrificed to a god etc.

victimize *verb* (also **-ise**) (**-zing** or **-sing**) single out for punishment or unfair treatment; make (person etc.) a victim. □ **victimization** *noun*.

victor /'vɪktə/ *noun* conqueror, winner of contest.

Victoria Cross /vɪk'tɔ:rɪə/ *noun* highest decoration for conspicuous bravery in armed services.

Victorian /vɪk'tɔ:rɪən/ ● *adjective* of time of Queen Victoria; prudish, strict. ● *noun* person of this time.

Victoriana /vɪktɔ:rɪ'ɑ:nə/ *plural noun* articles, esp. collectors' items, of Victorian period.

victorious /vɪk'tɔ:rɪəs/ *adjective* conquering, triumphant; marked by victory. □ **victoriously** *adverb*.

victory /'vɪktərɪ/ *noun* (*plural* **-ies**) success in battle, war, or contest.

victual /'vɪt(ə)l/ ● *noun* (usually in *plural*) food, provisions. ● *verb* (**-ll-**; *US* **-l-**) supply with victuals; lay in supply of victuals; eat victuals.

victualler /'vɪtlə/ *noun* (*US* **victualer**) person who supplies victuals; (in full **licensed victualler**) publican licensed to sell alcohol.

vicuña /vɪ'kju:nə/ *noun* S. American mammal with fine silky wool; cloth made from its wool; imitation of this.

vide /'vi:deɪ/ *verb* (in *imperative*) see, consult. [Latin]

videlicet /vɪ'delɪset/ *adverb* that is to say; namely.

video /'vɪdɪəʊ/ ● *adjective* relating to recording or reproduction of moving pictures on magnetic tape; of broadcasting of these. ● *noun* (*plural* **-s**) such recording or broadcasting; *colloquial* video recorder; *colloquial* film on videotape. ● *verb* (**-oes, -oed**) record on videotape. □ **video cassette** cassette of videotape; **video game** computer game played on television screen; **video nasty** *colloquial* horrific or pornographic video film; **video (cassette) recorder** apparatus for recording and playing videotapes.

videotape ● *noun* magnetic tape for recording television pictures and sound. ● *verb* (**-ping**) record on this.

vie /vaɪ/ *verb* (**vying**) (often + *with*) contend, compete, strive for superiority.

Vietnamese /vɪetnəˈmiːz/ ● *adjective* of Vietnam. ● *noun* (*plural* same) native, national, or language of Vietnam.

view /vjuː/ ● *noun* range of vision; what is seen, scene, prospect, picture etc. of this; opinion; inspection by eye or mind. ● *verb* look at; survey visually or mentally; form mental impression or opinion of; watch television. ▫ **in view of** considering; **on view** being shown or exhibited; **viewdata** news and information service from computer source, connected to TV screen by telephone link; **viewfinder** part of camera showing field of photograph; **viewpoint** point of view; **with a view to** with hope or intention of.

viewer *noun* television-watcher; device for looking at film transparencies etc.

vigil /ˈvɪdʒɪl/ *noun* keeping awake during night etc., esp. to keep watch or pray; eve of festival or holy day.

vigilance *noun* watchfulness; caution. ▫ **vigilant** *adjective*.

vigilante /vɪdʒɪˈlæntɪ/ *noun* member of self-appointed group for keeping order etc.

vignette /viːˈnjet/ *noun* short description, character sketch; illustration not in definite border; photograph etc. with background shaded off.

vigour /ˈvɪgə/ *noun* (*US* **vigor**) activity and strength of body or mind; healthy growth; animation. ▫ **vigorous** *adjective*; **vigorously** *adverb*.

Viking /ˈvaɪkɪŋ/ *noun* Scandinavian raider and pirate of 8th–11th c.

vile *adjective* disgusting; depraved; *colloquial* abominably bad. ▫ **vilely** *adverb*; **vileness** *noun*.

vilify /ˈvɪlɪfaɪ/ *verb* (**-ies**, **-ied**) speak ill of, defame. ▫ **vilification** *noun*.

villa /ˈvɪlə/ *noun* country house, mansion; rented holiday home, esp. abroad; detached or semi-detached house in residential district.

village /ˈvɪlɪdʒ/ *noun* group of houses etc. in country district, larger than hamlet and smaller than town.

villager *noun* inhabitant of village.

villain /ˈvɪlən/ *noun* wicked person; chief wicked character in play, story, etc.; *colloquial* criminal, rascal.

villainous *adjective* wicked.

villainy *noun* (*plural* **-ies**) wicked behaviour or act.

villein /ˈvɪlɪn/ *noun historical* feudal tenant entirely subject to lord or attached to manor. ▫ **villeinage** *noun*.

vim *noun colloquial* vigour, energy.

vinaigrette /vɪnɪˈgret/ *noun* salad dressing of oil and wine vinegar.

vindicate /ˈvɪndɪkeɪt/ *verb* (**-ting**) clear of suspicion; establish merits, existence, or justice of. ▫ **vindication** *noun*; **vindicator** *noun*; **vindicatory** *adjective*.

vindictive /vɪnˈdɪktɪv/ *adjective* tending to seek revenge. ▫ **vindictively** *adverb*; **vindictiveness** *noun*.

vine *noun* trailing or climbing woody-stemmed plant, esp. bearing grapes.

vinegar /ˈvɪnɪgə/ *noun* sour liquid produced by fermentation of wine, malt, cider, etc. ▫ **vinegary** *adjective*.

vineyard /ˈvɪnjɑːd/ *noun* plantation of grapevines, esp. for wine-making.

vingt-et-un /vætеɪˈœ/ *noun* = PONTOON[1]. [French]

vino /viːnəʊ/ *noun slang* wine, esp. of inferior kind.

vinous /ˈvaɪnəs/ *adjective* of, like, or due to wine.

vintage /ˈvɪntɪdʒ/ ● *noun* season's produce of grapes, wine from this; grape-harvest, season of this; wine of high quality from particular year and district; year etc. when thing was made, thing made etc. in particular year etc. ● *adjective* of high or peak quality; of a past season. ▫ **vintage car** car made 1917–1930.

vintner /ˈvɪntnə/ *noun* wine merchant.

vinyl /ˈvaɪnɪl/ *noun* any of group of plastics made by polymerization.

viol /ˈvaɪəl/ *noun* medieval stringed instrument similar in shape to violin.

viola[1] /vɪˈəʊlə/ *noun* instrument like violin but larger and of lower pitch.

viola[2] /ˈvaɪələ/ *noun* any plant of genus including violet and pansy, esp. cultivated hybrid.

viola da gamba /vɪəʊlə də ˈgæmbə/ *noun* viol held between player's legs.

violate /ˈvaɪəleɪt/ *verb* (**-ting**) disregard, break (oath, law, etc.); treat profanely; break in on, disturb; rape. ▫ **violation** *noun*; **violator** *noun*.

violence /ˈvaɪələns/ *noun* being violent; violent conduct or treatment; unlawful use of force. ▫ **do violence to** act contrary to, outrage.

violent /ˈvaɪələnt/ *adjective* involving great physical force; intense, vehement; (of death) resulting from violence or poison. ▫ **violently** *adverb*.

violet /ˈvaɪələt/ ● *noun* plant with usually purple, blue, or white flowers; bluish-purple colour at opposite end of spectrum from red; paint, clothes, or material of this colour. ● *adjective* of this colour.

violin /vaɪəˈlɪn/ *noun* high-pitched instrument with 4 strings played with bow. ▫ **violinist** *noun*.

violoncello /vaɪələnˈtʃeləʊ/ *noun* (*plural* **-s**) *formal* cello.

VIP *abbreviation* very important person.

viper /ˈvaɪpə/ *noun* small venomous snake; malignant or treacherous person.

virago /vɪˈrɑːgəʊ/ *noun* (*plural* **-s**) fierce or abusive woman.

viral /ˈvaɪər(ə)l/ *adjective* of or caused by virus.

virgin /ˈvɜːdʒɪn/ ● *noun* person who has never had sexual intercourse; (**the Virgin**) Christ's mother Mary. ● *adjective* not yet used etc.; virginal. ▫ **the Virgin birth** doctrine of Christ's birth from virgin mother. ▫ **virginity** /vəˈdʒɪn-/ *noun*.

virginal ● *adjective* of or befitting a virgin. ● *noun* (usually in *plural*) legless spinet in box.

Virginia creeper /vəˈdʒɪnɪə/ *noun* vine cultivated for ornament.

Virgo /ˈvɜːgəʊ/ *noun* sixth sign of zodiac.

virile /ˈvɪraɪl/ *adjective* having masculine vigour or strength; sexually potent; of man as distinct from woman or child. ▫ **virility** /-ˈrɪl-/ *noun*.

virology /vaɪˈrɒlədʒɪ/ *noun* study of viruses.

virtual /ˈvɜːtʃʊəl/ *adjective* being so for practical purposes though not strictly or in name. ▫ **virtual reality** computer-generated images, sounds, etc. that appear real to the senses. ▫ **virtually** *adverb*.

virtue /ˈvɜːtʃuː/ *noun* moral goodness; particular form of this; chastity, esp. of woman; good quality; efficacy. ▫ **by** or **in virtue of** on account of, because of.

virtuoso /vɜːtʃʊˈəʊsəʊ/ *noun* (*plural* **-si** /-siː/ or **-sos**) highly skilled artist, esp. musician. ▫ **virtuosity** /-ˈɒs-/ *noun*.

virtuous /ˈvɜːtʃʊəs/ *adjective* morally good; *archaic* chaste. ▫ **virtuously** *adverb*.

virulent /ˈvɪrʊlənt/ *adjective* poisonous; (of disease) violent; bitterly hostile. ▫ **virulence** *noun*; **virulently** *adverb*.

virus /ˈvaɪərəs/ *noun* microscopic organism able to cause diseases; computer virus.

visa /ˈviːzə/ *noun* endorsement on passport etc., esp. allowing holder to enter or leave country.

visage /ˈvɪzɪdʒ/ *noun literary* face.

vis-à-vis /viːzəˈviː/ ● *preposition* in relation to; in comparison with. ● *adverb* opposite. [French]

viscera /'vɪsərə/ *plural noun* internal organs of body. □ **visceral** *adjective.*
viscid /'vɪsɪd/ *adjective* glutinous, sticky.
viscose /'vɪskəʊz/ *noun* viscous form of cellulose used in making rayon etc.; fabric made from this.
viscount /'vaɪkaʊnt/ *noun* British nobleman ranking between earl and baron.
viscountess /'vaɪkaʊntɪs/ *noun* viscount's wife or widow; woman holding rank of viscount.
viscous /'vɪskəs/ *adjective* glutinous, sticky; semi-fluid; not flowing freely. □ **viscosity** /-kɒs-/ *noun* (*plural* **-ies**).
visibility /vɪzɪ'bɪlɪtɪ/ *noun* being visible; range or possibility of vision as determined by light and weather.
visible /'vɪzɪb(ə)l/ *adjective* able to be seen, perceived, or discovered; in sight; apparent, open, obvious. □ **visibly** *adverb.*
vision /'vɪʒ(ə)n/ *noun* act or faculty of seeing, sight; thing or person seen in dream or trance; thing seen in imagination; imaginative insight; foresight, good judgement in planning; beautiful person etc.; TV or cinema picture, esp. of specified quality.
visionary ● *adjective* given to seeing visions or to fanciful theories; having vision or foresight; not real, imaginary; unpractical. ● *noun* (*plural* **-ies**) visionary person.
visit /'vɪzɪt/ ● *verb* (**-t-**) go or come to see (person, place, etc.); stay temporarily with or at; (of disease, calamity, etc.) attack; (often + *upon*) inflict punishment for (sin). ● *noun* act of visiting, temporary stay with person or at place; (+ *to*) occasion of going to doctor etc.; formal or official call.
visitant /'vɪzɪt(ə)nt/ *noun* visitor, esp. ghost etc.
visitation /vɪzɪ'teɪʃ(ə)n/ *noun* official visit of inspection; trouble etc. seen as divine punishment.
visitor *noun* person who visits; migrant bird.
visor /'vaɪzə/ *noun* movable part of helmet covering face; shield for eyes, esp. one at top of vehicle windscreen.
vista /'vɪstə/ *noun* view, esp. through avenue of trees or other long narrow opening; mental view of long succession of events.
visual /'vɪʒʊəl/ *adjective* of or used in seeing. □ **visual display unit** device displaying data of computer on screen. □ **visually** *adverb.*
visualize *verb* (also **-ise**) (**-zing** or **-sing**) imagine visually. □ **visualization** *noun.*
vital /'vaɪt(ə)l/ ● *adjective* of or essential to organic life; essential to existence, success, etc.; full of life or activity; fatal. ● *noun* (in *plural*) vital organs, e.g. lungs and heart. □ **vital statistics** those relating to number of births, marriages, deaths, etc., *jocular* measurements of woman's bust, waist, and hips. □ **vitally** *adverb.*
vitality /vaɪ'tælɪtɪ/ *noun* animation, liveliness; ability to survive or endure.
vitalize *verb* (also **-ise**) (**-zing** or **-sing**) endow with life; make lively or vigorous. □ **vitalization** *noun.*
vitamin /'vɪtəmɪn/ *noun* any of various substances present in many foods and essential to health and growth.
vitaminize *verb* (also **-ise**) (**-zing** or **-sing**) introduce vitamins into (food).
vitiate /'vɪʃɪeɪt/ *verb* (**-ting**) impair, debase; make invalid or ineffectual.
viticulture /'vɪtɪkʌltʃə/ *noun* cultivation of grapes.
vitreous /'vɪtrɪəs/ *adjective* of or like glass.
vitrify /'vɪtrɪfaɪ/ *verb* (**-ies**, **-ied**) change into glass or glassy substance, esp. by heat. □ **vitrification** *noun.*
vitriol /'vɪtrɪəl/ *noun* sulphuric acid or sulphate; caustic speech or criticism. □ **vitriolic** /-'ɒl-/ *adjective.*
vitro see IN VITRO.
vituperate /vaɪ'tju:pəreɪt/ *verb* (**-ting**) criticize abusively. □ **vituperation** *noun*; **vituperative** /-rətɪv/ *adjective.*
viva[1] /'vaɪvə/ *colloquial* ● *noun* (*plural* **-s**) viva voce. ● *verb* (**vivas**, **vivaed**, **vivaing**) viva-voce.
viva[2] /'vi:və/ ● *interjection* long live. ● *noun* cry of this as salute etc. [Italian]
vivacious /vɪ'veɪʃəs/ *adjective* lively, animated. □ **vivacity** /vɪ'væsɪtɪ/ *noun.*
vivarium /vaɪ'veərɪəm/ *noun* (*plural* **-ria** or **-s**) glass bowl etc. for keeping animals for scientific study; place for keeping animals in (nearly) their natural conditions.
viva voce /vaɪvə 'vəʊtʃɪ/ ● *adjective* oral. ● *adverb* orally. ● *noun* oral exam.
viva-voce *verb* (**-vocees**, **-voceed**, **-voceing**) examine orally.
vivid /'vɪvɪd/ *adjective* (of light or colour) bright, strong, intense; (of memory, description, etc.) lively, incisive, graphic. □ **vividly** *adverb*; **vividness** *noun.*
vivify /'vɪvɪfaɪ/ *verb* (**-ies**, **-ied**) give life to, animate.
viviparous /vɪ'vɪpərəs/ *adjective* bringing forth young alive.
vivisect /'vɪvɪsekt/ *verb* perform vivisection on.
vivisection /vɪvɪ'sekʃ(ə)n/ *noun* surgical experimentation on living animals for scientific research. □ **vivisectionist** *noun.*
vixen /'vɪks(ə)n/ *noun* female fox; spiteful woman.
viz. *abbreviation* videlicet.
vizier /vɪ'zɪə/ *noun historical* high official in some Muslim countries.
V-neck *noun* V-shaped neckline on pullover etc.
vocabulary /və'kæbjʊlərɪ/ *noun* (*plural* **-ies**) words used by language, book, branch of science, or author; list of these; person's range of language.
vocal /'vəʊk(ə)l/ *adjective* of or uttered by voice; speaking one's feelings freely. □ **vocal cords** voice-producing part of larynx. □ **vocally** *adverb.*
vocalist *noun* singer.
vocalize *verb* (also **-ise**) (**-zing** or **-sing**) form (sound) or utter (word) with voice; articulate, express. □ **vocalization** *noun.*
vocation /vəʊ'keɪʃ(ə)n/ *noun* divine call to, or sense of suitability for, career or occupation; employment, trade, profession. □ **vocational** *adjective.*
vocative /'vɒkətɪv/ ● *noun* case of noun used in addressing person or thing. ● *adjective* of or in this case.
vociferate /və'sɪfəreɪt/ *verb* (**-ting**) utter noisily; shout, bawl. □ **vociferation** *noun.*
vociferous /və'sɪfərəs/ *adjective* noisy, clamorous; loud and insistent in speech. □ **vociferously** *adverb.*
vodka /'vɒdkə/ *noun* alcoholic spirit distilled esp. in Russia from rye etc.
vogue /vəʊg/ *noun* (**the vogue**) prevailing fashion; popular use. □ **in vogue** in fashion. □ **voguish** *adjective.*
voice ● *noun* sound formed in larynx and uttered by mouth, esp. in speaking, singing, etc.; ability to produce this; use of voice, spoken or written expression, opinion so expressed, right to express opinion; *Grammar* set of verbal forms showing whether verb is active or passive. ● *verb* (**-cing**) express; (esp. as **voiced** *adjective*) utter with vibration of vocal cords. □ **voice-over** commentary in film by unseen speaker.
void ● *adjective* empty, vacant; not valid or binding. ● *noun* empty space, sense of loss. ● *verb* invalidate; excrete.
voile /vɔɪl/ *noun* thin semi-transparent fabric.
vol. *abbreviation* volume.

volatile /ˈvɒlətaɪl/ *adjective* changeable in mood, flighty; unstable; evaporating rapidly. □ **volatility** /-ˈtɪl-/ *noun*.

vol-au-vent /ˈvɒləʊvɑ̃/ *noun* small round case of puff pastry with savoury filling.

volcanic /vɒlˈkænɪk/ *adjective* of, like, or produced by volcano.

volcano /vɒlˈkeɪnəʊ/ *noun* (*plural* **-es**) mountain or hill from which lava, steam, etc. escape through earth's crust.

vole *noun* small plant-eating rodent.

volition /vəˈlɪʃ(ə)n/ *noun* act or power of willing. □ **of one's own volition** voluntarily.

volley /ˈvɒlɪ/ ● *noun* (*plural* **-s**) simultaneous firing of a number of weapons; bullets etc. so fired; (usually + *of*) torrent (of abuse etc.); *Tennis, Football, etc.* playing of ball before it touches ground. ● *verb* (**-eys, -eyed**) return or send by volley. □ **volleyball** game for two teams of 6 hitting large ball by hand over net.

volt /vəʊlt/ *noun* SI unit of electromotive force. □ **voltmeter** instrument measuring electric potential in volts.

voltage *noun* electromotive force expressed in volts.

volte-face /vɒltˈfɑːs/ *noun* (*plural* **voltes-face** same pronunciation) complete change of position in one's attitude or opinion.

voluble /ˈvɒljʊb(ə)l/ *adjective* speaking or spoken fluently or with continuous flow of words. □ **volubility** *noun*; **volubly** *adverb*.

volume /ˈvɒljuːm/ *noun* single book forming part or all of work; solid content, bulk; space occupied by gas or liquid; (+ *of*) amount or quantity of; quantity or power of sound; (+ *of*) moving mass of (water, smoke, etc.).

voluminous /vəˈluːmɪnəs/ *adjective* (of drapery etc.) loose and ample; written or writing at great length.

voluntary /ˈvɒləntrɪ/ ● *adjective* done, acting, or given willingly; unpaid; (of institution) supported or built by charity; brought about by voluntary action; (of muscle, limb, etc.) controlled by will. ● *noun* (*plural* **-ies**) organ solo played before or after church service. □ **voluntarily** *adverb*.

volunteer /vɒlənˈtɪə/ ● *noun* person who voluntarily undertakes task or enters military etc. service. ● *verb* (often + *to*) undertake or offer voluntarily; (often + *for*) be volunteer.

voluptuary /vəˈlʌptʃʊərɪ/ *noun* (*plural* **-ies**) person who seeks luxury and sensual pleasure.

voluptuous /vəˈlʌptʃʊəs/ *adjective* of, tending to, occupied with, or derived from, sensuous or sensual pleasure; (of woman) curvaceous and sexually desirable. □ **voluptuously** *adverb*.

vomit /ˈvɒmɪt/ ● *verb* (**-t-**) eject (contents of stomach) through mouth, be sick; (of volcano, chimney, etc.) eject violently, belch forth. ● *noun* matter vomited from stomach.

voodoo /ˈvuːduː/ ● *noun* religious witchcraft as practised esp. in W. Indies. ● *verb* (**-doos, -dooed**) affect by voodoo, bewitch.

voracious /vəˈreɪʃəs/ *adjective* greedy in eating, ravenous; very eager. □ **voraciously** *adverb*; **voracity** /-ˈræs-/ *noun*.

vortex /ˈvɔːteks/ *noun* (*plural* **-texes** or **-tices** /-tɪsiːz/) whirlpool, whirlwind; whirling motion or mass; thing viewed as destructive or devouring.

votary /ˈvəʊtərɪ/ *noun* (*plural* **-ies**; *feminine* **votaress**) (usually + *of*) person dedicated to service of god or cult; devotee of a person, occupation etc.

vote ● *noun* formal expression of choice or opinion by ballot, show of hands, etc.; (usually **the vote**) right to vote; opinion expressed by vote; votes given by or for particular group. ● *verb* (**-ting**) (often + *for, against*) give vote; enact etc. by majority of votes; *colloquial* pronounce by general consent; (often + *that*) suggest, urge. □ **vote down** defeat (proposal etc.) by voting; **vote in** elect by voting; **vote with one's feet** *colloquial* indicate opinion by one's presence or absence.

voter *noun* person voting or entitled to vote.

votive /ˈvəʊtɪv/ *adjective* given or consecrated in fulfilment of vow.

vouch /vaʊtʃ/ *verb* (+ *for*) answer or be surety for.

voucher *noun* document exchangeable for goods or services; receipt.

vouchsafe /vaʊtʃˈseɪf/ *verb* (**-fing**) *formal* condescend to grant; (+ *to do*) condescend.

vow /vaʊ/ ● *noun* solemn, esp. religious, promise. ● *verb* promise solemnly; *archaic* declare solemnly.

vowel /ˈvaʊəl/ *noun* speech sound made by vibrations of vocal cords, but without audible friction; letter(s) representing this.

■ **Usage** The (written) vowels of English are customarily said to be *a, e, i, o,* and *u,* but *y* can be either a consonant (as in *yet*) or a vowel (as in *by*), and combinations of these six, such as *ee* in *keep, ie* in *tied, ou* in *pour,* and *ye* in *rye,* are just as much vowels.

---

vox pop *noun colloquial* popular opinion as represented by informal comments.

vox populi /vɒks ˈpɒpjʊlaɪ/ *noun* public opinion, popular belief. [Latin]

voyage /ˈvɔɪɪdʒ/ ● *noun* journey, esp. long one by sea or in space. ● *verb* (**-ging**) make voyage. □ **voyager** *noun*.

voyeur /vwɑːˈjɜː/ *noun* person who derives sexual pleasure from secretly observing others' sexual activity or organs; (esp. covert) spectator. □ **voyeurism** *noun*; **voyeuristic** /-ˈrɪs-/ *adjective*.

vs. *abbreviation* versus.

VSO *abbreviation* Voluntary Service Overseas.

VTOL /ˈviːtɒl/ *abbreviation* vertical take-off and landing.

vulcanite /ˈvʌlkənaɪt/ *noun* hard black vulcanized rubber.

vulcanize /ˈvʌlkənaɪz/ *verb* (also **-ise**) (**-zing** or **-sing**) make (rubber etc.) stronger and more elastic by treating with sulphur at high temperature. □ **vulcanization** *noun*.

vulgar /ˈvʌlgə/ *adjective* coarse; of or characteristic of the common people; in common use, prevalent. □ **vulgar fraction** fraction expressed by numerator and denominator (e.g. ½), not decimally (e.g. 0.5); **the vulgar tongue** native or vernacular language. □ **vulgarity** /-ˈgær-/ *noun* (*plural* **-ies**); **vulgarly** *adverb*.

vulgarian /vʌlˈgeərɪən/ *noun* vulgar (esp. rich) person.

vulgarism *noun* vulgar word or expression.

vulgarize /ˈvʌlgəraɪz/ *verb* (also **-ise**) (**-zing** or **-sing**) make vulgar; spoil by popularizing. □ **vulgarization** *noun*.

Vulgate /ˈvʌlgeɪt/ *noun* 4th-c. Latin version of Bible.

vulnerable /ˈvʌlnərəb(ə)l/ *adjective* easily wounded or harmed; (+ *to*) open to attack, injury, or criticism. □ **vulnerability** *noun*.

vulpine /ˈvʌlpaɪn/ *adjective* of or like fox; crafty, cunning.

vulture /ˈvʌltʃə/ *noun* large carrion-eating bird of prey; rapacious person.

vulva /ˈvʌlvə/ *noun* (*plural* **-s**) external female genitals.

vv. *abbreviation* verses.

vying *present participle* of VIE.

Ww

W *abbreviation* (also **W.**) watt(s); west(ern).

w. *abbreviation* wicket(s); wide(s); with.

wacky /ˈwækɪ/ *adjective* (**-ier**, **-iest**) *slang* crazy.

wad /wɒd/ ● *noun* lump of soft material to keep things apart or in place or to block hole; roll of banknotes. ● *verb* (**-dd-**) stop up or fix with wad; line, stuff, or protect with wadding.

wadding *noun* soft fibrous material for stuffing quilts, packing fragile articles in, etc.

waddle /ˈwɒd(ə)l/ ● *verb* (**-ling**) walk with short steps and swaying motion. ● *noun* such walk.

wade ● *verb* (**-ding**) walk through water, mud, etc., esp. with difficulty; (+ *through*) go through (tedious task, book, etc.); (+ *into*) *colloquial* attack (person, task). ● *noun* spell of wading. □ **wade in** *colloquial* make vigorous attack or intervention.

wader *noun* long-legged waterfowl; (in *plural*) high waterproof boots.

wadi /ˈwɒdɪ/ *noun* (*plural* **-s**) rocky watercourse in N. Africa etc., dry except in rainy season.

wafer /ˈweɪfə/ *noun* very thin light crisp biscuit; disc of unleavened bread used in Eucharist; disc of red paper stuck on legal document instead of seal. □ **wafer-thin** very thin.

waffle[1] /ˈwɒf(ə)l/ *colloquial* ● *noun* aimless verbose talk or writing. ● *verb* (**-ling**) indulge in waffle.

waffle[2] /ˈwɒf(ə)l/ *noun* small crisp batter cake. □ **waffle-iron** utensil for cooking waffles.

waft /wɒft/ ● *verb* convey or be conveyed smoothly (as) through air or over water. ● *noun* whiff.

wag[1] ● *verb* (**-gg-**) shake or wave to and fro. ● *noun* single wagging motion. □ **wagtail** small bird with long tail.

wag[2] *noun* facetious person.

wage ● *noun* (in *singular* or *plural*) employee's regular pay, esp. paid weekly. ● *verb* (**-ging**) carry on (war etc.).

waged *adjective* in regular paid employment.

wager /ˈweɪdʒə/ *noun & verb* bet.

waggish *adjective* playful, facetious. □ **waggishly** *adverb*.

waggle /ˈwæg(ə)l/ *verb* (**-ling**) *colloquial* wag.

wagon /ˈwægən/ *noun* (also **waggon**) 4-wheeled vehicle for heavy loads; open railway truck. □ **on the wagon** *slang* abstaining from alcohol; **wagonload** as much as wagon can carry.

wagoner *noun* (also **waggoner**) driver of wagon.

waif *noun* homeless and helpless person, esp. abandoned child; ownerless object or animal.

wail ● *noun* prolonged plaintive inarticulate cry of pain, grief, etc.; sound resembling this. ● *verb* utter wail; lament or complain persistently.

wain *noun archaic* wagon.

wainscot /ˈweɪnskət/ *noun* (also **wainscoting**) boarding or wooden panelling on room-wall.

waist *noun* part of human body between ribs and hips; narrowness marking this; circumference of waist; narrow middle part of anything; part of garment encircling waist; *US* bodice, blouse; part of ship between forecastle and quarterdeck. □ **waistband** strip of cloth forming waist of garment; **waistcoat** usually sleeveless and collarless waist-length garment; **waistline** outline or size of waist.

wait ● *verb* defer action until expected event occurs; await (turn etc.); (of thing) remain in readiness; (usually as **waiting** *noun*) park briefly; act as waiter or attendant; (+ *on*, *upon*) await convenience of, be attendant to. ● *noun* act or period of waiting; (usually + *for*) watching for enemy; (in *plural*) *archaic* street singers of Christmas carols. □ **waiting-list** list of people waiting for thing not immediately available; **waiting-room** room for people to wait in, esp. at surgery or railway station.

waiter *noun* (*feminine* **waitress**) person who serves at hotel or restaurant tables.

waive *verb* (**-ving**) refrain from insisting on or using.

waiver *noun Law* (document recording) waiving.

wake[1] ● *verb* (**-king**; *past* **woke**; *past participle* **woken** /ˈwəʊk(ə)n/) (often + *up*) (cause to) cease to sleep or become alert; *archaic* (except as **waking** *adjective & noun*) be awake; disturb with noise; evoke. ● *noun* (chiefly in Ireland) vigil beside corpse before burial, attendant lamentations and merrymaking; (usually in *plural*) annual holiday in (industrial) N. England.

wake[2] *noun* track left on water's surface by moving ship etc.; turbulent air left by moving aircraft. □ **in the wake of** following, as result of.

wakeful *adjective* unable to sleep; sleepless; vigilant. □ **wakefully** *adverb*; **wakefulness** *noun*.

waken /ˈweɪkən/ *verb* make or become awake.

walk /wɔːk/ ● *verb* move by lifting and setting down each foot in turn, never having both feet off the ground at once; (of quadruped) go with slowest gait; travel or go on foot, take exercise thus; traverse (distance) in walking; tread floor or surface of; cause to walk with one. ● *noun* act of walking, ordinary human gait; slowest gait of animal; person's manner of walking; distance walkable in specified time; excursion on foot; place or track meant or fit for walking. □ **walkabout** informal stroll by royal person etc., Australian Aboriginal's period of wandering; **walking frame** tubular metal frame to assist elderly or disabled people in walking; **walking stick** stick carried for support when walking; **walk off with** *colloquial* steal, win easily; **walk of life** one's occupation; **walk-on part** short or non-speaking dramatic role; **walk out** depart suddenly or angrily, stop work in protest; **walk-out** *noun*; **walk out on** desert; **walkover** easy victory; **walk the streets** be prostitute; **walkway** passage or path for walking along. □ **walkable** *adjective*.

walker *noun* person etc. that walks; framework in which baby can walk unaided; walking frame.

walkie-talkie /wɔːkɪˈtɔːkɪ/ *noun* portable two-way radio.

Walkman /ˈwɔːkmən/ *noun* (*plural* **-s**) *proprietary term* type of personal stereo.

wall /wɔːl/ ● *noun* continuous narrow upright structure of usually brick or stone, esp. enclosing or dividing a space or supporting a roof; thing like wall in appearance or effect; outermost layer of animal or plant organ, cell, etc. ● *verb* (esp. as **walled** *adjective*) surround with wall; (usually + *up*, *off*) block with wall; (+ *up*) enclose within sealed space. □ **go to the wall** fare badly in competition; **up the wall** *colloquial* crazy, furious; **wallflower** fragrant garden plant, *colloquial* woman not dancing because partnerless; **wall game** Eton form of football; **wallpaper** *noun* paper for covering interior walls of rooms, *verb* decorate with wallpaper; **wall-to-wall** fitted to cover whole floor, *colloquial* ubiquitous.

wallaby /ˈwɒləbɪ/ *noun* (*plural* **-ies**) small kangaroo-like marsupial.

wallah /ˈwɒlə/ *noun slang* person connected with a specified occupation or thing.

wallet /ˈwɒlɪt/ *noun* small flat case for holding banknotes etc.

wall-eye *noun* eye with whitish iris or outward squint. □ **wall-eyed** *adjective*.

wallop /ˈwɒləp/ *colloquial* ● *verb* (**-p-**) thrash, beat. ● *noun* whack; beer.

wallow /ˈwɒləʊ/ ● *verb* roll about in mud etc.; (+ *in*) indulge unrestrainedly in. ● *noun* act of wallowing; place where animals wallow.

wally /ˈwɒlɪ/ *noun* (*plural* **-ies**) *slang* foolish or incompetent person.

walnut /ˈwɔːlnʌt/ *noun* tree with aromatic leaves and drooping catkins; its nut; its timber.

walrus /ˈwɔːlrəs/ *noun* (*plural* same or **walruses**) long-tusked amphibious arctic mammal. □ **walrus moustache** long thick drooping moustache.

waltz /wɔːls/ ● *noun* ballroom dance in triple time; music for this. ● *verb* dance waltz; (often + *in*, *out*, *round*, etc.) *colloquial* move easily, casually, etc.

wampum /ˈwɒmpəm/ *noun* strings of shell-beads formerly used by N. American Indians for money, ornament, etc.

wan /wɒn/ *adjective* (**-nn-**) pale, weary-looking. □ **wanly** *adverb*.

wand /wɒnd/ *noun* fairy's or magician's magic stick; staff as sign of office etc.; *colloquial Music* conductor's baton.

wander /ˈwɒndə/ *verb* (often + *in*, *off*, etc.) go from place to place aimlessly; meander; diverge from path etc.; talk or think incoherently, be inattentive or delirious. □ **wanderlust** eagerness to travel or wander, restlessness. □ **wanderer** *noun*.

wane ● *verb* (**-ning**) (of moon) decrease in apparent size; decrease in power, vigour, importance, size, etc. ● *noun* process of waning. □ **on the wane** declining.

wangle /ˈwæŋg(ə)l/ *colloquial* ● *verb* (**-ling**) contrive to obtain (favour etc.). ● *noun* act of wangling.

wannabe /ˈwɒnəbɪ/ *noun slang* avid fan who apes person admired; anyone wishing to be someone else.

want /wɒnt/ ● *verb* (often + *to do*) desire; wish for possession of; need; (+ *to do*) *colloquial* should; (usually + *for*) lack; be without or fall short by; (as **wanted** *adjective*) (of suspected criminal etc.) sought by police. ● *noun* lack, deficiency; poverty, need.

wanting *adjective* lacking (in quality or quantity), unequal to requirements; absent.

wanton /ˈwɒnt(ə)n/ ● *adjective* licentious; capricious, arbitrary; luxuriant, wild. ● *noun literary* licentious person. □ **wantonly** *adverb*.

wapiti /ˈwɒpɪtɪ/ *noun* (*plural* **-s**) large N. American deer.

war /wɔː/ ● *noun* armed hostility, esp. between nations; specific period of this; hostility between people; (often + *on*) efforts against crime, poverty, etc. ● *verb* (**-rr-**) (as **warring** *adjective*) rival, fighting; make war. □ **at war** engaged in war; **go to war** begin war; **on the warpath** going to war, *colloquial* seeking confrontation; **war crime** crime violating international laws of war; **war cry** phrase or name shouted to rally troops, party slogan; **war dance** dance performed by primitive peoples before battle or after victory; **warhead** explosive head of missile; **warhorse** *historical* trooper's horse, *colloquial* veteran soldier; **war memorial** monument to those killed in (a) war; **warmonger** /-mʌŋgə/ person who promotes war; **warpaint** paint put on body esp. by N. American Indians before battle, *colloquial* make-up; **warship** ship used in war.

warble /ˈwɔːb(ə)l/ ● *verb* (**-ling**) sing in a gentle trilling way. ● *noun* warbling sound.

warbler *noun* bird that warbles.

ward /wɔːd/ *noun* separate division or room of hospital etc.; administrative division, esp. for elections; minor etc. under care of guardian or court; (in *plural*) corresponding notches and projections in key and lock; *archaic* guardianship. □ **ward off** parry (blow), avert (danger etc.); **wardroom** officers' mess in warship.

warden /ˈwɔːd(ə)n/ *noun* supervising official; president or governor of institution; traffic warden.

warder /ˈwɔːdə/ *noun* (*feminine* **wardress**) prison officer.

wardrobe /ˈwɔːdrəʊb/ *noun* large cupboard for storing clothes; stock of clothes; theatre's costume department. □ **wardrobe master**, **mistress** person in charge of theatrical wardrobe.

wardship *noun* tutelage.

ware *noun* things of specified kind made usually for sale; (usually in *plural*) articles for sale.

warehouse ● *noun* building in which goods are stored; wholesale or large retail store. ● *verb* (**-sing**) store in warehouse.

warfare /ˈwɔːfeə/ *noun* waging war, campaigning.

warlike *adjective* hostile; soldierly; military.

warlock /ˈwɔːlɒk/ *noun archaic* sorcerer.

warm /wɔːm/ ● *adjective* of or at fairly high temperature; (of person) with skin at natural or slightly raised temperature; (of clothes) affording warmth; hearty, enthusiastic; sympathetic, friendly, loving; *colloquial* dangerous, hostile; *colloquial* (in game) near object sought, near to guessing; (of colour) reddish or yellowish, suggesting warmth; (of scent in hunting) fresh and strong. ● *verb* make or become warm. ● *noun* act of warming; warmth. □ **warm-blooded** (of animals) having blood temperature well above that of environment; **warm-hearted** kind, friendly; **warming-pan** *historical* flat closed vessel holding hot coals for warming beds; **warm up** make or become warm, prepare for performance etc. by practising, reach temperature for efficient working, reheat (food); **warm-up** *noun*. □ **warmly** *adverb*; **warmth** *noun*.

warn /wɔːn/ *verb* (often + *of*, *that*) inform of impending danger or misfortune; (+ *to do*) advise (person) to take certain action; (often + *against*) inform (person) about specific danger. □ **warn off** tell (person) to keep away (from).

warning *noun* what is said or done or occurs to warn person.

warp /wɔːp/ ● *verb* make or become distorted, esp. through heat, damp, etc.; make or become perverted or strange; haul (ship etc.) by rope attached to fixed point. ● *noun* warped state; mental perversion; lengthwise threads in loom; rope used in warping ship.

warrant /ˈwɒrənt/ ● *noun* thing that authorizes an action; written authorization, money voucher, etc.; written authorization allowing police to carry out search or arrest; certificate of service rank held by warrant officer. ● *verb* serve as warrant for, justify; guarantee. □ **warrant officer** officer ranking between commissioned and non-commissioned officers.

warranty /ˈwɒrəntɪ/ *noun* (*plural* **-ies**) undertaking as to ownership or quality of thing sold etc., often accepting responsibility for repairs needed over specified period; authority, justification.

warren /ˈwɒrən/ *noun* network of rabbit burrows; densely populated or labyrinthine building or district.

warrior /'wɒrɪə/ *noun* person skilled in or famed for fighting.

wart /wɔːt/ *noun* small round dry growth on skin; protuberance on skin of animal, surface of plant, etc. □ **wart-hog** African wild pig. □ **warty** *adjective*.

wary /'weərɪ/ *adjective* (**-ier**, **-iest**) on one's guard, circumspect; cautious. □ **warily** *adverb*; **wariness** *noun*.

was *1st & 3rd singular past of* BE.

wash /wɒʃ/ ● *verb* cleanse with liquid; (+ *out*, *off*, *away*, etc.) remove or be removed by washing; wash oneself or one's hands (and face); wash clothes, dishes, etc.; (of fabric or dye) bear washing without damage; bear scrutiny, be believed or acceptable; (of river etc.) touch; (of liquid) carry along in specified direction; sweep, move, splash; (+ *over*) occur without affecting (person); sift (ore) by action of water; brush watery colour over; *poetical* moisten. ● *noun* washing, being washed; clothes for washing or just washed; motion of agitated water or air, esp. due to passage of vessel or aircraft; kitchen slops given to pigs; thin, weak, inferior, or animals' liquid food; liquid to spread over surface to cleanse, heal, or colour. □ **washbasin** basin for washing one's hands etc.; **washboard** ribbed board for washing clothes, this as percussion instrument; **wash down** wash completely, (usually + *with*) accompany or follow (food); **washed out** faded, pale, *colloquial* exhausted; **washed up** *esp. US slang* defeated, having failed; **wash one's hands of** decline responsibility for; **wash out** clean inside of by washing, *colloquial* cause to be cancelled because of rain; **wash-out** *colloquial* complete failure; **washroom** *esp. US* public toilet; **washstand** piece of furniture for holding washbasin, soap-dish, etc.; **wash up** wash (dishes etc.) after use, *US* wash one's face and hands, (of sea) carry on to shore. □ **washable** *adjective*.

washer *noun* person or thing that washes; flat ring placed between two surfaces or under plunger of tap, nut, etc. to tighten joint or disperse pressure.

washerwoman *noun* laundress.

washing *noun* clothes etc. for washing or just washed. □ **washing machine** machine for washing clothes; **washing powder** soap powder or detergent for washing clothes; **washing-up** washing of dishes etc., dishes etc. for washing.

washy *adjective* (**-ier**, **-iest**) too watery or weak; lacking vigour.

wasn't /'wɒz(ə)nt/ was not.

Wasp /wɒsp/ *noun* (also **WASP**) *US usually derogatory* middle-class white American [Anglo-Saxon] Protestant.

wasp /wɒsp/ *noun* stinging insect with black and yellow stripes. □ **wasp-waist** very slender waist.

waspish *adjective* irritable, snappish.

wassail /'wɒseɪl/ *archaic* ● *noun* festive drinking. ● *verb* make merry.

wastage /'weɪstɪdʒ/ *noun* amount wasted; loss by use, wear, or leakage; (also **natural wastage**) loss of employees other than by redundancy.

waste ● *verb* (**-ting**) use to no purpose or for inadequate result or extravagantly; fail to use; (often + *on*) give (advice etc.) without effect; (in *passive*) fail to be appreciated or used properly; wear away; make or become weak; devastate. ● *adjective* superfluous, no longer needed; uninhabited, not cultivated. ● *noun* act of wasting; waste material; waste region; diminution by wear; waste pipe. □ **go**, **run to waste** be wasted; **wasteland** land not productive or developed, spiritually or intellectually barren place or time; **waste paper** used or valueless paper; **waste pipe** pipe carrying off waste material; **waste product** useless by-product of manufacture or organism.

wasteful *adjective* extravagant; causing or showing waste. □ **wastefully** *adverb*.

waster *noun* wasteful person; *colloquial* wastrel.

wastrel /'weɪstr(ə)l/ *noun* good-for-nothing person.

watch /wɒtʃ/ ● *verb* keep eyes fixed on; keep under observation, follow observantly; (often + *for*) be in alert state, be vigilant; (+ *over*) look after, take care of. ● *noun* small portable timepiece for wrist or pocket; state of alert or constant attention; *Nautical* usually 4-hour spell of duty; *historical* (member of) body of men patrolling streets at night. □ **on the watch for** waiting for (anticipated event); **watchdog** dog guarding property, person etc. monitoring others' rights etc.; **watching brief** brief of barrister who follows case for client not directly concerned; **watchman** man employed to look after empty building etc. at night; **watch out** (often + *for*) be on one's guard; **watch-tower** tower for observing prisoners, attackers, etc.; **watchword** phrase summarizing guiding principle. □ **watcher** *noun* (also *in combination*).

watchful *adjective* accustomed to watching; on the watch. □ **watchfully** *adverb*; **watchfulness** *noun*.

water /'wɔːtə/ ● *noun* transparent colourless liquid found in seas and rivers etc. and in rain etc.; sheet or body of water; (in *plural*) part of sea or river; (often **the waters**) mineral water at spa etc.; state of tide; solution of specified substance in water; transparency and lustre of gem; (usually in *plural*) amniotic fluid. ● *verb* sprinkle or soak with water; supply (plant or animal) with water; secrete water; (as **watered** *adjective*) (of silk etc.) having irregular wavy finish; take in supply of water. □ **make water** urinate; **water-bed** mattress filled with water; **water biscuit** thin unsweetened biscuit; **water buffalo** common domestic Indian buffalo; **water cannon** device giving powerful water-jet to disperse crowd etc.; **water chestnut** corm from a sedge, used in Chinese cookery; **water-closet** lavatory that can be flushed; **water-colour** pigment mixed with water and not oil, picture painted or art of painting with this; **watercourse** stream of water, bed of this; **watercress** pungent cress growing in running water; **water-diviner** dowser; **water down** dilute, make less forceful or horrifying; **waterfall** stream or river falling over precipice or down steep hill; **waterfowl** bird(s) frequenting water; **waterfront** part of town adjoining river etc.; **waterhole** shallow depression in which water collects; **water-ice** flavoured and frozen water and sugar; **watering-can** portable container for watering plants; **watering-place** pool where animals drink, spa or seaside resort; **water jump** jump over water in steeplechase etc.; **water level** surface of water, height of this, water table; **water lily** aquatic plant with floating leaves and flowers; **waterline** line where surface of water touches ship's side; **waterlogged** saturated or filled with water; **water main** main pipe in water supply system; **waterman** boatman plying for hire; **watermark** faint design made in paper by maker; **water-meadow** meadow periodically flooded by stream; **water melon** large dark green melon with red pulp and watery juice; **water-mill** mill worked by waterwheel; **water pistol** toy pistol shooting jet of water; **water polo** game played by swimmers with ball like football; **water-power** mechanical force from weight or motion of water; **waterproof** *adjective* impervious to water, *noun* such garment or material, *verb* make waterproof; **water-rat** water vole; **water rate** charge for use of public water supply; **watershed** line between waters flowing to different river basins, turning point in events; **waterside** edge of sea, lake, or river; **water-ski** ski (esp. one of pair) on which person is towed across water by motor boat; **waterspout** gyrating column of water and spray between sea and cloud; **water table** plane below which ground is saturated with water; **watertight** so closely fastened or fitted that water cannot leak through, (of argument etc.) unassailable; **water tower** tower with elevated tank to give pressure for distributing water; **water vole** aquatic vole; **waterway** navigable channel; **water-wheel** wheel driven by water to drive machinery or to raise water; **water-wings** inflated floats used to support person learning to swim; **waterworks** establishment for managing water supply, *colloquial* shedding of tears, *colloquial* urinary system.

watery *adjective* containing too much water; too thin in consistency; of or consisting of water; vapid, uninteresting; (of colour) pale; (of sun, moon, or sky) rainy-looking; (of eyes) moist.

watt /wɒt/ *noun* SI unit of power.

wattage *noun* amount of electrical power expressed in watts.

wattle[1] /'wɒt(ə)l/ *noun* interlaced rods and sticks used for fences etc.; Australian acacia with fragrant golden yellow flowers. □ **wattle and daub** network of rods and twigs plastered with clay or mud as building material.

wattle[2] /'wɒt(ə)l/ *noun* fleshy appendage hanging from head or neck of turkey etc.

wave ● *verb* (**-ving**) move (hand etc.) to and fro in greeting or as signal; show sinuous or sweeping motion; give such motion to; direct (person) or express (greeting etc.) by waving; give undulating form to, have such form. ● *noun* moving ridge of water between two depressions; long body of water curling into arch and breaking on shore; thing compared to this; gesture of waving; curved shape in hair; temporary occurrence or heightening of condition or influence; disturbance carrying motion, heat, light, sound, etc. through esp. fluid medium; single curve in this. □ **wave aside** dismiss as intrusive or irrelevant; **waveband** radio wavelengths between certain limits; **wave down** wave to (vehicle or driver) to stop; **wavelength** distance between successive crests of wave, this as distinctive feature of radio waves from a transmitter, *colloquial* person's way of thinking.

wavelet *noun* small wave.

waver /'weɪvə/ *verb* be or become unsteady or irresolute, begin to give way.

wavy *adjective* (**-ier**, **-iest**) having waves or alternate contrary curves. □ **waviness** *noun*.

wax[1] ● *noun* sticky pliable yellowish substance secreted by bees as material of honeycomb; this bleached and purified for candles, modelling, etc.; any similar substance. ● *verb* cover or treat with wax; remove hair from (legs etc.) using wax. □ **waxwork** object, esp. lifelike dummy, modelled in wax, (in *plural*) exhibition of wax dummies.

wax[2] *verb* (of moon) increase in apparent size; grow larger or stronger; become.

waxen *adjective* smooth or pale like wax; *archaic* made of wax.

way ● *noun* road, track, path, street; course, route; direction; method, means; style, manner; habitual course of action; normal course of events; distance (to be) travelled; unimpeded opportunity or space to advance; advance, progress; specified condition or state; respect, sense. ● *adverb colloquial* far. □ **by the way** incidentally; **by way of** by means of, as a form of, passing through; **give way** yield under pressure, give precedence; **in the way**, **in** (**person's**) **way** forming obstruction (to); **lead the way** act as guide or leader; **make one's way** go, prosper; **make way for** allow to pass, be superseded by; **out of the way** not forming obstruction, disposed of, unusual, remote; **pay its** or **one's way** cover costs, pay one's expenses as they arise; **under way** in motion or progress; **way back** *colloquial* long ago; **wayfarer** traveller, esp. on foot; **waylay** lie in wait for, stop to accost or rob; **way of life** principles or habits governing one's actions; **way-out** *colloquial* unusual, eccentric; **wayside** (land at) side of road.

wayward /'weɪwəd/ *adjective* childishly self-willed; capricious. □ **waywardness** *noun*.

WC *abbreviation* water-closet; West Central.

W/Cdr. *abbreviation* Wing Commander.

we /wi:/ *pronoun used by speaker or writer to refer to himself or herself and one or more others as subject of verb; used for* I *by sovereign in formal contexts or by editorial writer in newspaper.*

weak *adjective* lacking in strength, power, vigour, resolution, or number; unconvincing; (of verb) forming inflections by suffix. □ **weak-kneed** *colloquial* lacking resolution; **weak-minded** mentally deficient, lacking resolution. □ **weaken** *verb*.

weakling *noun* feeble person or animal.

weakly ● *adverb* in a weak way. ● *adjective* (**-ier**, **-iest**) sickly, not robust.

weakness *noun* being weak; weak point; self-indulgent liking.

weal[1] ● *noun* ridge raised on flesh by stroke of rod or whip. ● *verb* raise weals on.

weal[2] *noun literary* welfare.

wealth /welθ/ *noun* riches; being rich; abundance.

wealthy *adjective* (**-ier**, **-iest**) having abundance, esp. of money.

wean *verb* accustom (infant or other young mammal) to food other than mother's milk; (often + *from*, *away from*) disengage (from habit etc.) by enforced discontinuance.

weapon /'wepən/ *noun* thing designed, used, or usable for inflicting bodily harm; means for gaining advantage in a conflict.

weaponry *noun* weapons collectively.

wear /weə/ ● *verb* (*past* **wore**; *past participle* **worn**) have on one's person as clothing, ornament, etc.; exhibit (expression etc.); *colloquial* (usually in negative) tolerate; (often + *away*, *down*) damage or deteriorate gradually by use or attrition; make (hole etc.) by attrition; (often + *out*) exhaust; (+ *down*) overcome by persistence; (+ *well* etc.) endure continued use or life; (of time) pass, esp. tediously. ● *noun* wearing, being worn; things worn; fashionable or suitable clothing; (in full **wear and tear**) damage from continuous use. □ **wear out** use or be used until useless, tire or be tired out. □ **wearer** *noun*.

wearisome /'wɪərɪsəm/ *adjective* tedious, monotonous.

weary /'wɪərɪ/ ● *adjective* (**-ier**, **-iest**) very tired, intensely fatigued; (+ *of*) tired of; tiring, tedious. ● *verb* (**-ies**, **-ied**) make or become weary. □ **wearily** *adverb*; **weariness** *noun*.

weasel /'wi:z(ə)l/ *noun* small ferocious reddish-brown flesh-eating mammal.

weather /'weðə/ ● *noun* atmospheric conditions at specified place or time as regards heat, cloudiness, humidity, sunshine, wind, and rain etc. ● *verb* expose to or affect by atmospheric changes, season (wood); be discoloured or worn thus; come safely through (storm etc.); get to windward of. □ **make heavy weather of** *colloquial* exaggerate difficulty of; **under the weather** *colloquial* unwell, depressed; **weather-beaten** affected by exposure to weather; **weather-board** board attached at bottom of door to keep out rain, each of series of overlapping horizontal boards on wall; **weathercock** weather vane in form of cock, inconstant person; **weather forecast** prediction of likely weather; **weather vane** revolving pointer on church spire etc. to show direction of wind.

weave[1] ● *verb* (**-ving**; *past* **wove** /wəʊv/; *past participle* **woven**) form (fabric) by interlacing threads, form (threads) into fabric, esp. in loom; (+ *into*) make (facts etc.) into story or connected whole; make (story etc.) thus. ● *noun* style of weaving.

weave[2] *verb* (**-ving**) move repeatedly from side to side; take intricate course.

weaver *noun* person who weaves fabric; (in full **weaver-bird**) tropical bird building elaborately woven nest.

web *noun* woven fabric; amount woven in one piece; complex series; cobweb or similar tissue; membrane connecting toes of aquatic bird or other animal; large roll of paper for printing. □ **web-footed** having toes connected by web. □ **webbed** *adjective*.

webbing *noun* strong narrow closely woven fabric for belts etc.

weber /'veɪbə/ *noun* SI unit of magnetic flux.

Wed. *abbreviation* (also **Weds.**) Wednesday.

wed *verb* (**-dd-**; *past & past participle* **wedded** or **wed**) *usually formal or literary* marry; unite; (as **wedded** *adjective*) of or in marriage, (+ *to*) obstinately attached to (pursuit etc.).

we'd /wi:d/ we had; we should; we would.

wedding /'wedɪŋ/ *noun* marriage ceremony. □ **wedding breakfast** meal etc. between wedding and departure for honeymoon; **wedding cake** rich decorated cake served at wedding reception; **wedding ring** ring worn by married person.

wedge ● *noun* piece of tapering wood, metal, etc., used for forcing things apart or fixing them immovably etc.; wedge-shaped thing. ● *verb* (**-ging**) secure or force open or apart with wedge; (+ *in*, *into*) pack or force (thing, oneself) in or into. □ **thin end of the wedge** *colloquial* small beginning that may lead to something more serious.

wedlock /'wedlɒk/ *noun* married state. □ **born in** or **out of wedlock** born of married or unmarried parents.

Wednesday /'wenzdeɪ/ *noun* day of week following Tuesday.

wee *adjective* (**weer** /'wi:ə/, **weest** /'wi:ɪst/) *esp. Scottish* little; *colloquial* tiny.

weed ● *noun* wild plant growing where it is not wanted; lanky and weakly person or horse; (**the weed**) *slang* marijuana, tobacco. ● *verb* rid of weeds or unwanted parts; (+ *out*) sort out and remove (inferior or unwanted parts etc.), rid of inferior or unwanted parts etc.; remove or destroy weeds.

weeds *plural noun* (in full **widow's weeds**) *archaic* deep mourning worn by widow.

weedy *adjective* (**-ier**, **-iest**) weak, feeble; full of weeds.

week *noun* 7-day period reckoned usually from Saturday midnight; any 7-day period; the 6 days between Sundays; the 5 days Monday to Friday, period of work then done. □ **weekday** day other than (Saturday or) Sunday; **weekend** Saturday and Sunday.

weekly ● *adjective* done, produced, or occurring once a week. ● *adverb* once a week. ● *noun* (*plural* **-ies**) weekly newspaper or periodical.

weeny /'wi:nɪ/ *adjective* (**-ier**, **-iest**) *colloquial* tiny.

weep ● *verb* (*past & past participle* **wept**) shed tears; (often + *for*) lament over; be covered with or send forth drops, exude liquid; come or send forth in drops; (as **weeping** *adjective*) (of tree) have drooping branches. ● *noun* spell of weeping.

weepie *noun colloquial* sentimental or emotional film, play, etc.

weepy *adjective* (**-ier**, **-iest**) *colloquial* inclined to weep, tearful.

weevil /'wi:vɪl/ *noun* destructive beetle feeding esp. on grain.

weft *noun* threads woven across warp to make fabric.

weigh /weɪ/ *verb* find weight of; balance in hand (as if) to guess weight of; (often + *out*) take definite weight of (substance), measure out (specified weight); estimate relative value or importance of; (+ *with*, *against*) compare with; be of specified weight or importance; have influence; (often + *on*) be heavy or burdensome (to); raise (anchor). □ **weighbridge** weighing machine for vehicles; **weigh down** bring down by weight, oppress; **weigh in** (of boxer before contest, or jockey after race) be weighed; **weigh-in** *noun*; **weigh in with** *colloquial* advance (argument etc.) confidently; **weigh up** *colloquial* form estimate of; **weigh one's words** carefully choose words to express something.

weight /weɪt/ ● *noun* force on a body due to earth's gravitation; heaviness of body; quantitative expression of a body's weight, scale of such weights; body of known weight for use in weighing or weight training; heavy body, esp. used in mechanism etc.; load, burden; influence, importance; preponderance (of evidence etc.). ● *verb* attach a weight to, hold down with a weight; impede, burden. □ **pull one's weight** do fair share of work; **weightlifting** sport of lifting heavy objects; **weight training** physical training using weights. □ **weightless** *adjective*.

weighting *noun* extra pay in special cases.

weighty *adjective* (**-ier**, **-iest**) heavy; momentous; deserving attention; influential, authoritative.

weir /wɪə/ *noun* dam across river to retain water and regulate its flow.

weird /wɪəd/ *adjective* uncanny, supernatural; *colloquial* queer, incomprehensible. □ **weirdly** *adverb*; **weirdness** *noun*.

welch = WELSH.

welcome /'welkəm/ ● *noun* kind or glad greeting or reception. ● *interjection expressing such greeting*. ● *verb* (**-ming**) receive with welcome. ● *adjective* gladly received; (+ *to*) cordially allowed or invited to. □ **make welcome** receive hospitably.

weld ● *verb* join (pieces of metal or plastic) using heat, usually from electric arc; fashion into effectual or homogeneous whole. ● *noun* welded joint. □ **welder** *noun*.

welfare /'welfeə/ *noun* well-being, happiness; health and prosperity (of person, community, etc.); (**Welfare**) financial support from state. □ **welfare state** system of social services controlled or financed by government, state operating this; **welfare work** organized effort for welfare of poor, disabled, etc.

welkin /'welkɪn/ *noun poetical* sky.

well[1] ● *adverb* (**better**, **best**) in satisfactory way; with distinction; in kind way; thoroughly, carefully; with heartiness or approval; probably, reasonably; to considerable extent; *slang* extremely. ● *adjective* (**better**, **best**) in good health; in satisfactory state or position, advisable. ● *interjection expressing astonishment, resignation, etc., or introducing speech*. □ **as well** in addition, advisable, desirable, reasonably; **as well as** in addition to; **well-adjusted** mentally and emotionally stable; **well-advised** prudent; **well and truly** decisively, completely; **well-appointed** properly equipped or fitted out; **well away** having made considerable progress, *colloquial* fast asleep or drunk; **well-balanced** sane, sensible; **well-being** hapiness, health, prosperity; **well-born** of noble family; **well-bred** having or showing good breeding or manners; **well-built** big, strong, and shapely; **well-connected** related to good families; **well-disposed** (often + *towards*) friendly, sympathetic; **well-earned** fully deserved; **well-founded** based on good evidence; **well-groomed** with carefully tended hair, clothes, etc.; **well-heeled** *colloquial* wealthy; **well-informed** having much knowledge or information; **well-intentioned** having or showing good intentions; **well-judged** opportunely, skilfully, or discreetly done; **well-known** known to many; **well-meaning**, **-meant** well-intentioned; **well-nigh** almost; **well off** rich, fortunately situated; **well-read** having read (and learnt) much; **well-spoken** articulate or refined in speech; **well-to-do** prosperous; **well-tried** often tested with good result; **well-wisher** person who wishes another well; **well-worn** much used, trite.

well[2] ● *noun* shaft sunk in ground to obtain water, oil, etc.; enclosed space resembling well-shaft, e.g. central space in building for staircase, lift, light, or ventilation; source; (in *plural*) spa; ink-well; railed space in law court. ● *verb* (+ *out*, *up*) rise or flow as water from well. ▫ **well-head**, **-spring** source.

we'll /wiːl/ we shall; we will.

wellington /ˈwelɪŋt(ə)n/ *noun* (in full **wellington boot**) waterproof rubber boot usually reaching knee.

welly /ˈwelɪ/ *noun* (*plural* **-ies**) *colloquial* wellington.

Welsh ● *adjective* of Wales. ● *noun* language of Wales; (**the Welsh**) (treated as *plural*) the Welsh people. ▫ **Welshman**, **Welshwoman** native of Wales; **Welsh rarebit** dish of melted cheese etc. on toast.

welsh *verb* (also **welch** /weltʃ/) (of loser of bet, esp. bookmaker) evade an obligation; (+ *on*) fail to carry out promise to (person), fail to honour (obligation).

welt ● *noun* leather rim sewn to shoe-upper for sole to be attached to; weal; ribbed or reinforced border of garment; heavy blow. ● *verb* provide with welt; raise weals on, thrash.

welter /ˈweltə/ ● *verb* roll, wallow; (+ *in*) be soaked in. ● *noun* general confusion; disorderly mixture.

welterweight /ˈweltəweɪt/ *noun* amateur boxing weight (63.5–67 kg).

wen *noun* benign tumour on skin.

wench *noun jocular* girl, young woman.

wend *verb* ▫ **wend one's way** go.

went *past* of GO[1].

wept *past & past participle* of WEEP.

were *2nd singular past, plural past,* and *past subjunctive* of BE.

we're /wɪə/ we are.

weren't /wɜːnt/ were not.

werewolf /ˈweəwʊlf/ *noun* (*plural* **-wolves**) *Mythology* human being who changes into wolf.

Wesleyan /ˈwezlɪən/ ● *adjective* of Protestant denomination founded by John Wesley. ● *noun* member of this denomination.

west ● *noun* point of horizon where sun sets at equinoxes; corresponding compass point; (usually **the West**) European civilization, western part of world, country, town, etc. ● *adjective* towards, at, near, or facing west; (of wind) from west. ● *adverb* towards, at, or near west; (+ *of*) further west than. ▫ **go west** *slang* be killed or wrecked etc.; **westbound** travelling or leading west; **West End** fashionable part of London; **west-north-west**, **west-south-west** point midway between west and north-west or south-west. ▫ **westward** *adjective, adverb, & noun*; **westwards** *adverb*.

westering /ˈwestərɪŋ/ *adjective* (of sun) nearing the west.

westerly /ˈwestəlɪ/ ● *adjective & adverb* in western position or direction; (of wind) from west. ● *noun* (*plural* **-ies**) wind from west.

western /ˈwest(ə)n/ ● *adjective* of or in west. ● *noun* film or novel about cowboys in western N. America. ▫ **westernize** *verb* (also **-ise**) (**-zing** or **-sing**); **westernmost** *adjective*.

westerner *noun* native or inhabitant of west.

wet ● *adjective* (**-tt-**) soaked or covered with water or other liquid; (of weather) rainy; (of paint) not yet dried; used with water; *colloquial* feeble. ● *verb* (**-tt-**; *past & past participle* **wet** or **wetted**) make wet; urinate in or on. ● *noun* liquid that wets something; rainy weather; *colloquial* feeble or spiritless person; *colloquial* liberal Conservative; *colloquial* drink. ▫ **wet blanket** gloomy person discouraging cheerfulness etc.; **wet-nurse** *noun* woman employed to suckle another's child, *verb* act as wet-nurse to, *colloquial* treat as if helpless.

wether /ˈweðə/ *noun* castrated ram.

we've /wiːv/ we have.

Wg. Cdr. *abbreviation* Wing Commander.

whack *colloquial* ● *verb* hit forcefully; (as **whacked** *adjective*) tired out. ● *noun* sharp or resounding blow; *slang* share.

whacking *colloquial* ● *adjective* large. ● *adverb* very.

whale ● *noun* (*plural* same or **-s**) large fishlike marine mammal. ● *verb* (**-ling**) hunt whales. ▫ **whalebone** elastic horny substance in upper jaw of some whales.

whaler *noun* whaling ship or seaman.

wham *interjection colloquial: expressing forcible impact.*

wharf /wɔːf/ ● *noun* (*plural* **wharves** /wɔːvz/ or **-s**) quayside structure for loading or unloading of moored vessels. ● *verb* moor (ship) at wharf; store (goods) on wharf.

what /wɒt/ ● *interrogative adjective used in asking someone to specify one or more things from an indefinite number.* ● *adjective* (usually in exclamation) how great, how remarkable. ● *relative adjective* the or any ... that. ● *interrogative pronoun* what thing(s); what did you say? ● *relative pronoun* the things which; anything that. ▫ **whatever** anything at all that, no matter what, (with negative or in questions) at all, of any kind; **what for?** *colloquial* for what reason?; **what have you** *colloquial* anything else similar; **whatnot** unspecified thing; **what not** *colloquial* other similar things; **whatsoever** whatever; **know what's what** *colloquial* have common sense, know what is useful or important; **what with** *colloquial* because of.

wheat *noun* cereal plant bearing dense 4-sided seed-spikes; its grain used for flour etc. ▫ **wheat germ** wheat embryo extracted as source of vitamins; **wheatmeal** flour from wheat with some bran and germ removed.

wheatear /ˈwiːtɪə/ *noun* small migratory bird.

wheaten *adjective* made of wheat.

wheedle /ˈwiːd(ə)l/ *verb* (**-ling**) coax by flattery or endearments; (+ *out*) get (thing) from person or cheat (person) of thing by wheedling.

wheel ● *noun* circular frame or disc revolving on axle and used to propel vehicle or other machinery; wheel-like thing; motion as of wheel; movement of line of men etc. with one end as pivot; (in *plural*) *slang* car. ● *verb* turn on axis or pivot; swing round in line with one end as pivot; (often + *about*, *around*) (cause to) change direction or face another way; push or pull (wheeled thing, or its load or occupant); go in circles or curves. ▫ **wheel and deal** engage in political or commercial scheming; **wheelbarrow** small cart with one wheel at front and two handles; **wheelbase** distance between axles of vehicle; **wheelchair** disabled person's chair on wheels; **wheel-spin** rotation of vehicle's wheels without traction; **wheels within wheels** intricate machinery, *colloquial* indirect or secret agencies; **wheelwright** maker or repairer of wheels.

wheelie *noun slang* manoeuvre on bicycle or motorcycle with front wheel off the ground.

wheeze ● *verb* (**-zing**) breathe or utter with audible whistling sound. ● *noun* sound of wheezing; *colloquial* clever scheme. □ **wheezy** *adjective* (**-ier**, **-iest**).

whelk *noun* spiral-shelled marine mollusc.

whelp ● *noun* young dog, puppy; *archaic* cub; ill-mannered child or youth. ● *verb* give birth to puppies.

when ● *interrogative adverb* at what time. ● *relative adverb* (time etc.) at or on which. ● *conjunction* at the or any time that; as soon as; although; after which, and then, but just then. ● *pronoun* what time; which time. □ **whenever**, **whensoever** at whatever time, on whatever occasion, every time that.

whence *archaic or formal* ● *interrogative adverb* from what place. ● *relative adverb* (place etc.) from which. ● *conjunction* to the place from which.

where /weə/ ● *interrogative adverb* in or to what place; in what direction; in what respect. ● *relative adverb* (place etc.) in or to which. ● *conjunction* in or to the or any place, direction, or respect in which; and there. ● *interrogative pronoun* what place. ● *relative pronoun* the place in or to which. □ **whereabouts** *interrogative adverb* approximately where, *noun* person's or thing's location; **whereas** in contrast or comparison with the fact that, taking into consideration the fact that; **whereby** by what or which means; **wherefore** *archaic* for what or which reason; **wherein** *formal* in what or which; **whereof** *formal* of what or which; **whereupon** immediately after which; **wherever** anywhere at all that, no matter where; **wherewithal** /-wɪðɔ:l/ *colloquial* money etc. needed for a purpose.

wherry /'werɪ/ *noun* (*plural* **-ies**) light rowing boat, usually for carrying passengers; large light barge.

whet *verb* (**-tt-**) sharpen; stimulate (appetite etc.). □ **whetstone** stone for sharpening cutting-tools.

whether /'weðə/ *conjunction introducing first or both of alternative possibilities.*

whew /hwju:/ *interjection expressing astonishment, consternation, or relief.*

whey /weɪ/ *noun* watery liquid left when milk forms curds.

which ● *interrogative adjective used in asking someone to specify one or more things from a definite set of alternatives.* ● *relative adjective* being the one just referred to, and this or these. ● *interrogative pronoun* which person(s) or thing(s). ● *relative pronoun* which thing(s). □ **whichever** any which, no matter which.

whiff *noun* puff of air, smoke, etc.; smell; (+ *of*) trace of; small cigar.

Whig *noun historical* member of British political party succeeded by Liberals. □ **Whiggery** *noun*; **Whiggish** *adjective*; **Whiggism** *noun*.

while ● *noun* period of time. ● *conjunction* during the time that, for as long as, at the same time as; although, whereas. ● *verb* (**-ling**) (+ *away*) pass (time etc.) in leisurely or interesting way. ● *relative adverb* (time etc.) during which. □ **for a while** for some time; **in a while** soon; **once in a while** occasionally.

whilst /waɪlst/ *adverb & conjunction* while.

whim *noun* sudden fancy, caprice.

whimper /'wɪmpə/ ● *verb* make feeble, querulous, or frightened sounds. ● *noun* such sound.

whimsical /'wɪmzɪk(ə)l/ *adjective* capricious, fantastic. □ **whimsicality** /-'kæl-/ *noun*; **whimsically** *adverb*.

whimsy /'wɪmzɪ/ *noun* (*plural* **-ies**) whim.

whin *noun* (in *singular* or *plural*) gorse. □ **whinchat** small songbird.

whine ● *noun* long-drawn complaining cry (as) of dog or child; querulous tone or complaint. ● *verb* (**-ning**) emit or utter whine(s); complain.

whinge /wɪndʒ/ *verb* (**-geing** or **-ging**) *colloquial* complain peevishly.

whinny /'wɪnɪ/ ● *noun* (*plural* **-ies**) gentle or joyful neigh. ● *verb* (**-ies**, **-ied**) emit whinny.

whip ● *noun* lash attached to stick, for urging on or for punishing; person appointed by political party to control its discipline and tactics in Parliament; whip's written notice requesting member's attendance; food made with whipped cream etc.; whipper-in. ● *verb* (**-pp-**) beat or urge on with whip; beat (eggs, cream, etc.) into froth; take or move suddenly or quickly; *slang* steal, excel, defeat; bind with spirally wound twine; sew with overcast stitches. □ **whipcord** tightly twisted cord; (**the**) **whip hand** advantage, control; **whiplash** sudden jerk; **whipper-in** huntsman's assistant who manages hounds; **whipping boy** scapegoat; **whip-round** *colloquial* informal collection of money among group of people; **whipstock** handle of whip.

whippersnapper /'wɪpəsnæpə/ *noun* small child; insignificant but presumptuous person.

whippet /'wɪpɪt/ *noun* crossbred dog of greyhound type, used for racing.

whippoorwill /'wɪpʊəwɪl/ *noun* N. American nightjar.

whirl ● *verb* swing round and round, revolve rapidly; (+ *away*) convey or go rapidly in car etc.; send or travel swiftly in orbit or curve; (of brain etc.) seem to spin round. ● *noun* whirling movement; state of intense activity or confusion. □ **give it a whirl** *colloquial* attempt it; **whirlpool** circular eddy in sea, river, etc.; **whirlwind** *noun* whirling mass or column of air, *adjective* very rapid.

whirligig /'wɜ:lɪgɪg/ *noun* spinning or whirling toy; merry-go-round; revolving motion.

whirr ● *noun* continuous buzzing or softly clicking sound. ● *verb* (**-rr-**) make this sound.

whisk ● *verb* (+ *away*, *off*) brush with sweeping movement, take suddenly; whip (cream, eggs, etc.); convey or go lightly or quickly; wave (object). ● *noun* whisking movement; utensil for whipping eggs, cream, etc.; bunch of twigs, bristles, etc. for brushing or dusting.

whisker /'wɪskə/ *noun* (usually in *plural*) hair on cheeks or sides of face of man; each of bristles on face of cat etc.; *colloquial* small distance. □ **whiskered** *adjective*; **whiskery** *adjective*.

whisky /'wɪskɪ/ *noun* (*Irish & US* **whiskey**) (*plural* **-ies** or **-eys**) spirit distilled esp. from malted barley.

whisper /'wɪspə/ ● *verb* speak using breath instead of vocal cords; talk or say in barely audible tone or confidential way; rustle, murmur. ● *noun* whispering speech or sound; thing whispered.

whist *noun* card game, usually for two pairs of opponents. □ **whist drive** whist-party with players moving on from table to table.

whistle /'wɪs(ə)l/ ● *noun* clear shrill sound made by forcing breath through lips contracted to narrow opening; similar sound made by bird, wind, missile, etc.; instrument used to produce such sound. ● *verb* (**-ling**) emit whistle; give signal or express surprise or derision by whistling; (often + *up*) summon or give signal to thus; produce (tune) by whistling; (+ *for*) seek or desire in vain. □ **whistle-stop** *US* small unimportant town on railway, politician's brief pause for electioneering speech on tour.

Whit ● *noun* Whitsuntide. ● *adjective* of Whitsuntide. □ **Whit Sunday** 7th Sunday after Easter, commemorating Pentecost.

whit *noun* particle, least possible amount.

white ● *adjective* of colour produced by reflection or transmission of all light; of colour of snow or milk; pale; of the human racial group having light-coloured skin; albino; (of hair) having lost its colour; (of coffee) with milk or cream. ● *noun* white colour, paint, clothes, etc.; (in *plural*) white garments worn in cricket, tennis, etc.; (player using) lighter-coloured pieces in chess etc.; egg white; whitish part of eyeball round iris; white person. ◻ **white ant** termite; **whitebait** small silvery-white food-fish; **white cell** leucocyte; **white-collar** (of worker or work) non-manual, clerical, professional; **white corpuscle** leucocyte; **white elephant** useless possession; **white feather** symbol of cowardice; **white flag** symbol of surrender; **white goods** large domestic electrical equipment; **white heat** degree of heat making metal glow white, state of intense anger or passion; **white-hot** *adjective*; **white hope** person expected to achieve much; **white horses** white-crested waves; **white lead** mixture containing lead carbonate used as white pigment; **white lie** harmless or trivial untruth; **white magic** magic used for beneficent purposes; **white meat** poultry, veal, rabbit, and pork; **White Paper** government report giving information; **white pepper** pepper made by grinding husked berry; **white sauce** sauce of flour, melted butter, and milk or cream; **white slave** woman entrapped for prostitution; **white spirit** light petroleum as solvent; **white sugar** purified sugar; **white tie** man's white bow tie as part of full evening dress; **whitewash** *noun* solution of chalk or lime for whitening walls etc., means of glossing over faults, *verb* apply whitewash (to), gloss over, clear of blame; **white wedding** wedding where bride wears formal white dress; **whitewood** light-coloured wood, esp. prepared for staining etc. ◻ **whiten** *verb*; **whitener** *noun*; **whiteness** *noun*; **whitish** *adjective*.

whither /ˈwɪðə/ *archaic* ● *interrogative adverb* to what place. ● *relative adverb* (place etc.) to which.

whiting[1] /ˈwaɪtɪŋ/ *noun* (*plural* same) small edible sea fish.

whiting[2] /ˈwaɪtɪŋ/ *noun* ground chalk used in white-washing etc.

whitlow /ˈwɪtləʊ/ *noun* inflammation near fingernail or toenail.

Whitsun /ˈwɪts(ə)n/ ● *noun* Whitsuntide. ● *adjective* of Whitsuntide.

Whitsuntide *noun* weekend or week including Whit Sunday.

whittle /ˈwɪt(ə)l/ *verb* (**-ling**) (often + *at*) pare (wood etc.) by cutting thin slices or shavings from surface; (often + *away*, *down*) reduce by repeated subtractions.

whiz (also **whizz**) ● *noun* sound made by object moving through air at great speed. ● *verb* (**-zz-**) move with or make a whiz. ◻ **whiz-kid** *colloquial* brilliant or highly successful young person.

WHO *abbreviation* World Health Organization.

who /huː/ ● *interrogative pronoun* what or which person(s), what sort of person(s). ● *relative pronoun* (person or persons) that. ◻ **whoever**, **whosoever** the or any person(s) who; no matter who.

whoa /wəʊ/ *interjection used to stop or slow horse etc.*

who'd /huːd/ who had; who would.

whodunit /huːˈdʌnɪt/ *noun* (also **whodunnit**) *colloquial* detective story, play, or film.

whole /həʊl/ ● *adjective* uninjured, unbroken, intact, undiminished; not less than; all, all of. ● *noun* complete thing; all of a thing; (+ *of*) all members etc. of. ◻ **on the whole** all things considered; **wholefood** food not artificially processed or refined; **wholehearted** completely devoted, done with all possible effort or sincerity; **wholeheartedly** *adverb*; **wholemeal** meal or flour made from whole grains of wheat.

wholesale /ˈhəʊlseɪl/ ● *noun* selling in large quantities, esp. for retail by others. ● *adjective & adverb* by wholesale; on a large scale. ● *verb* (**-ling**) sell wholesale. ◻ **wholesaler** *noun*.

wholesome *adjective* promoting physical, mental, or moral health; prudent.

wholly /ˈhəʊllɪ/ *adverb* entirely, without limitation; purely.

whom /huːm/ *pronoun* (as object of verb) who. ◻ **whomever** (as object of verb) whoever; **whomsoever** (as object of verb) whosoever.

whoop /huːp, wuːp/ ● *noun* cry expressing excitement etc.; characteristic drawing-in of breath after cough in whooping cough. ● *verb* utter whoop. ◻ **whooping cough** /ˈhuːpɪŋ/ infectious disease, esp. of children, with violent convulsive cough.

whoopee /wʊˈpiː/ *interjection expressing wild joy.* ◻ **make whoopee** /ˈwʊpɪ/ *colloquial* make merry, make love.

whoops /wʊps/ *interjection colloquial apology for obvious mistake.*

whop *verb* (**-pp-**) *slang* thrash, defeat.

whopper *noun slang* big specimen; great lie.

whopping *adjective colloquial* huge.

whore /hɔː/ *noun* prostitute; *derogatory* promiscuous woman. ◻ **whorehouse** brothel.

whorl /wɜːl/ *noun* ring of leaves etc. round stem; one turn of spiral.

whortleberry /ˈwɜːt(ə)lberɪ/ *noun* (*plural* **-ies**) bilberry.

who's /huːz/ who is; who has.

■ **Usage** Because it has an apostrophe, *who's* is easily confused with *whose*. They are each correctly used in *Who's there?* (= *Who is there?*), *Who's taken my pen?* (= *Who has taken my pen?*), and *Whose book is this?* (= *Who does this book belong to?*).

whose /huːz/ ● *interrogative, pronoun, & adjective* of whom. ● *relative adjective* of whom or which.

why /waɪ/ ● *interrogative adverb* for what reason or purpose. ● *relative adverb* (reason etc.) for which. ● *interjection expressing surprise, impatience, reflection, or protest.* ◻ **whys and wherefores** reasons, explanation.

WI *abbreviation* West Indies; Women's Institute.

wick *noun* strip or thread feeding flame with fuel.

wicked /ˈwɪkɪd/ *adjective* (**-er**, **-est**) sinful, immoral; spiteful; playfully malicious; *colloquial* very bad; *slang* excellent. ◻ **wickedly** *adverb*; **wickedness** *noun*.

wicker /ˈwɪkə/ *noun* plaited osiers etc. as material for chairs, baskets, etc. ◻ **wickerwork** wicker, things made of wicker.

wicket /ˈwɪkɪt/ *noun Cricket* 3 upright stumps with bails in position defended by batsman, ground between the two wickets, state of this, batsman's being got out; (in full **wicket-door**, **-gate**) small door or gate, esp. beside or in larger one. ◻ **wicket-keeper** fielder close behind batsman's wicket.

wide ● *adjective* having sides far apart, broad, not narrow; (following measurement) in width; extending far, not restricted; liberal, not specialized; open to full extent; (+ *of*) not within reasonable distance of, far from. ● *adverb* to full extent; far from target etc. ● *noun* wide ball. ◻ **-wide** extending over whole of; **wide awake** fully awake, *colloquial* wary or knowing; **wide ball** *Cricket* ball judged by umpire to be beyond batsman's reach; **wide-eyed** surprised, naïve; **widespread** widely distributed. ◻ **widen** *verb*.

widely *adverb* far apart; extensively; by many people; considerably.

widgeon /ˈwɪdʒ(ə)n/ *noun* (also **wigeon**) kind of wild duck.

widow /ˈwɪdəʊ/ ● *noun* woman who has lost her husband by death and not married again. ● *verb* make into widow or widower; (as **widowed** *adjective*) bereft by death of spouse. □ **widow's peak** V-shaped growth of hair on forehead. □ **widowhood** *noun*.

widower /ˈwɪdəʊə/ *noun* man who has lost his wife by death and not married again.

width *noun* measurement from side to side; large extent; liberality of views etc.; piece of material of full width. □ **widthways** *adverb*.

wield /wiːld/ *verb* hold and use, control, exert.

wife *noun* (*plural* **wives**) married woman, esp. in relation to her husband. □ **wifely** *adjective*.

wig *noun* artificial head of hair.

wigeon = WIDGEON.

wiggle /ˈwɪg(ə)l/ *colloquial* ● *verb* (**-ling**) move from side to side etc. ● *noun* wiggling movement; kink in line etc. □ **wiggly** *adjective* (**-ier**, **-iest**).

wight /waɪt/ *noun archaic* person.

wigwam /ˈwɪgwæm/ *noun* N. American Indian's hut or tent.

wilco /ˈwɪlkəʊ/ *interjection colloquial: expressing compliance or agreement*.

wild /waɪld/ ● *adjective* in original natural state; not domesticated, cultivated, or civilized; unrestrained, disorderly; tempestuous; intensely eager, frantic; (+ *about*) *colloquial* enthusiastically devoted to; *colloquial* infuriated; random, ill-aimed, rash. ● *adverb* in a wild way. ● *noun* wild place, desert. □ **like wildfire** with extraordinary speed; **run wild** grow or stray unchecked or undisciplined; **wild card** card having any rank chosen by its player, person or thing usable in different ways; **wildcat** *noun* hot-tempered or violent person, *adjective* (of strike) sudden and unofficial, reckless, financially unsound; **wild-goose chase** foolish or hopeless quest; **wildlife** wild animals collectively; **Wild West** western US in lawless times. □ **wildly** *adverb*; **wildness** *noun*.

wildebeest /ˈwɪldəbiːst/ *noun* (*plural* same or **-s**) gnu.

wilderness /ˈwɪldənɪs/ *noun* desert, uncultivated area; confused assemblage.

wile ● *noun* (usually in *plural*) stratagem, trick. ● *verb* (**-ling**) lure.

wilful /ˈwɪlfʊl/ *adjective* (*US* **willful**) intentional, deliberate; obstinate. □ **wilfully** *adverb*.

will[1] *auxiliary verb* (*3rd singular present* **will**) *used to form future tenses; expressing request as question*; be able to; have tendency to; be likely to.

will[2] ● *noun* faculty by which person decides what to do; fixed desire or intention; will-power; legal written directions for disposal of one's property etc. after death; disposition towards others. ● *verb* try to cause by will-power; intend, desire; bequeath by will. □ **at will** whenever one wishes; **will-power** control by purpose over impulse; **with a will** vigorously.

willing /ˈwɪlɪŋ/ *adjective* ready to consent or undertake; given etc. by willing person. □ **willingly** *adverb*; **willingness** *noun*.

will-o'-the-wisp /wɪləðəˈwɪsp/ *noun* phosphorescent light seen on marshy ground; elusive person.

willow /ˈwɪləʊ/ *noun* waterside tree with pliant branches yielding osiers. □ **willowherb** plant with leaves like willow; **willow-pattern** conventional Chinese design of blue on white china etc.

willowy *adjective* lithe and slender; having willows.

willy-nilly /wɪlɪˈnɪlɪ/ *adverb* whether one likes it or not.

wilt ● *verb* wither, droop; lose energy. ● *noun* plant disease causing wilting.

wily /ˈwaɪlɪ/ *adjective* (**-ier**, **-iest**) crafty, cunning.

wimp *noun colloquial* feeble or ineffectual person. □ **wimpish** *adjective*.

wimple /ˈwɪmp(ə)l/ *noun* headdress covering neck and sides of face, worn by some nuns.

win ● *verb* (**-nn-**; *past & past participle* **won** /wʌn/) secure as result of fight, contest, bet, etc.; be victor, be victorious in. ● *noun* victory in game etc. □ **win the day** be victorious in battle, argument, etc.; **win over** gain support of; **win through**, **out** overcome obstacles.

wince ● *noun* start or involuntary shrinking movement of pain etc. ● *verb* (**-cing**) give wince.

winceyette /wɪnsɪˈet/ *noun* lightweight flannelette.

winch ● *noun* crank of wheel or axle; windlass. ● *verb* lift with winch.

wind[1] /wɪnd/ ● *noun* air in natural motion; breath, esp. as needed in exertion or playing wind instrument; power of breathing easily; empty talk; gas generated in bowels etc.; wind instruments of orchestra etc.; scent carried by the wind. ● *verb* exhaust wind of by exertion or blow; make (baby) bring up wind after feeding; detect presence of by scent. □ **get wind of** begin to suspect; **get**, **have the wind up** *colloquial* become, be, frightened; **in the wind** *colloquial* about to happen; **put the wind up** *colloquial* frighten; **take the wind out of (person's) sails** frustrate by anticipation; **windbag** *colloquial* person who talks a lot but says little of value; **windbreak** thing that breaks force of wind; **windcheater** windproof jacket; **windfall** fruit blown down by wind, unexpected good fortune, esp. legacy; **wind instrument** musical instrument sounded by air-current; **wind-jammer** merchant sailing ship; **windmill** mill worked by action of wind on sails, toy with curved vanes revolving on stick; **windpipe** air-passage between throat and lungs; **windscreen** screen of glass at front of car etc.; **windscreen wiper** rubber etc. blade to clear windscreen of rain etc.; **windshield** *US* windscreen; **wind-sock** canvas cylinder or cone on mast to show direction of wind; **wind-swept** exposed to high winds; **wind-tunnel** enclosed chamber for testing (models or parts of) aircraft etc. in winds of known velocities.

wind[2] /waɪnd/ ● *verb* (*past & past participle* **wound** /waʊnd/) go in spiral, crooked, or curved course; make (one's way) thus; wrap closely, coil; provide with coiled thread etc.; surround (as) with coil; wind up (clock etc.). ● *noun* bend or turn in course. □ **wind down** lower by winding, unwind, approach end gradually; **winding-sheet** sheet in which corpse is wrapped for burial; **wind up** *verb* coil whole of, tighten coiling or coiled spring of, *colloquial* increase intensity of, *colloquial* provoke to anger etc., bring to conclusion, arrange affairs of and dissolve (company), cease business and go into liquidation, *colloquial* arrive finally; **wind-up** *noun* conclusion, *colloquial* attempt to provoke.

windlass /ˈwɪndləs/ *noun* machine with horizontal axle for hauling or hoisting.

window /ˈwɪndəʊ/ *noun* opening, usually with glass, in wall etc. to admit light etc.; the glass itself; space for display behind window of shop; window-like opening; transparent part in envelope showing address; opportunity for study or action. □ **window-box** box placed outside window for cultivating plants; **window-dressing** art of arranging display in shop window etc., adroit presentation of facts etc. to give falsely favourable impression; **window-pane** glass pane in window; **window-seat** seat below window, seat next to window in aircraft etc.; **window-shop** look at goods in shop windows without buying anything.

windsurfing *noun* sport of riding on water on sailboard. □ **windsurf** *verb*; **windsurfer** *noun*.

windward /ˈwɪndwəd/ ● *adjective & adverb* on or towards side from which wind is blowing. ● *noun* this direction.

windy *adjective* (**-ier**, **-iest**) stormy with or exposed to wind; generating or characterized by flatulence; *colloquial* wordy; *colloquial* apprehensive, frightened. □ **windiness** *noun*.

wine ● *noun* fermented grape juice as alcoholic drink; fermented drink resembling this made from other fruits etc.; colour of red wine. ● *verb* (**-ning**) drink wine; entertain with wine. □ **wine bar** bar or small restaurant where wine is main drink available; **wine cellar** cellar for storing wine, its contents; **wineglass** glass for wine, usually with stem and foot; **winepress** press in which grape juice is extracted for wine; **wine waiter** waiter responsible for serving wine.

wing ● *noun* each of the limbs or organs by which bird etc. flies; winglike part supporting aircraft; projecting part of building; *Football etc.* forward player at either end of line, side part of playing area; (in *plural*) sides of theatre stage; extreme section of political party; flank of battle array; part of vehicle over wheel; air-force unit of several squadrons. ● *verb* travel or traverse on wings; wound in wing or arm; equip with wings; enable to fly, send in flight. □ **on the wing** flying; **take under one's wing** treat as protégé; **take wing** fly away; **wing-case** horny cover of insect's wing; **wing-chair** chair with side-pieces at top of high back; **wing-collar** man's high stiff collar with turned-down corners; **wing commander** RAF officer next below group captain; **wing-nut** nut with projections to turn it by; **wingspan** measurement right across wings. □ **winged** *adjective*.

winger *noun Football etc.* wing player.

wink ● *verb* (often + *at*) close and open one eye quickly, esp. as signal; close eye(s) momentarily; (of light) twinkle; (of indicator) flash on and off. ● *noun* act of winking; *colloquial* short sleep. □ **wink at** purposely avoid seeing, pretend not to notice.

winkle /ˈwɪŋk(ə)l/ ● *noun* edible sea snail. ● *verb* (**-ling**) (+ *out*) extract with difficulty.

winning ● *adjective* having or bringing victory; attractive. ● *noun* (in *plural*) money won. □ **winning post** post marking end of race. □ **winningly** *adverb*.

winnow /ˈwɪnəʊ/ *verb* blow (grain) free of chaff etc.; (+ *out, away, from,* etc.) rid grain of (chaff etc.); sift, examine.

winsome /ˈwɪnsəm/ *adjective* attractive, engaging. □ **winsomely** *adverb*; **winsomeness** *noun*.

winter /ˈwɪntə/ ● *noun* coldest season of year. ● *verb* (usually + *at, in*) spend the winter. □ **winter garden** garden of plants flourishing in winter; **wintergreen** kind of plant remaining green all winter; **winter sports** sports practised on snow or ice; **wintertime** season or period of winter.

wintry /ˈwɪntrɪ/ *adjective* (**-ier**, **-iest**) characteristic of winter; lacking warmth. □ **wintriness** *noun*.

winy *adjective* (**-ier**, **-iest**) wine-flavoured.

wipe ● *verb* (**-ping**) clean or dry surface of by rubbing; rub (cloth) over surface; spread (liquid etc.) over surface by rubbing; (often + *away, off,* etc.) clear or remove by wiping; erase, eliminate. ● *noun* act of wiping; piece of specially treated cloth for wiping. □ **wipe out** utterly destroy or defeat, clean inside of; **wipe up** dry (dishes etc.), take up (liquid etc.) by wiping.

wiper *noun* windscreen wiper.

wire ● *noun* metal drawn out into thread or slender flexible rod; piece of this; length of this used for fencing or to carry electric current etc.; *colloquial* telegram. ● *verb* (**-ring**) provide, fasten, strengthen, etc. with wire; (often + *up*) install electrical circuits in; *colloquial* telegraph. □ **get one's wires crossed** become confused; **wire-haired** (of dog) having stiff wiry hair; **wire netting** netting made of meshed wire; **wire-tapping** tapping of telephone wires; **wire wool** mass of fine wire for scouring; **wireworm** destructive larva of a kind of beetle.

wireless *noun* radio; radio receiving set.

wiring *noun* system or installation of electrical circuits.

wiry *adjective* (**-ier**, **-iest**) sinewy, untiring; like wire, tough and coarse.

wisdom /ˈwɪzdəm/ *noun* experience, knowledge, and the power of applying them; prudence, common sense; wise sayings. □ **wisdom tooth** hindmost molar usually cut at age of about 20.

wise[1] /waɪz/ *adjective* having, showing, or dictated by wisdom; prudent, sensible; having knowledge; suggestive of wisdom; *US colloquial* alert, crafty. □ **be, get wise to** *colloquial* be, become, aware of; **wisecrack** *colloquial noun* smart remark, *verb* make wisecrack; **wise guy** *colloquial* know-all; **wise man** wizard, esp. one of the Magi; **wise up** *esp. US colloquial* inform, get wise. □ **wisely** *adverb*.

wise[2] /waɪz/ *noun archaic* way, manner, degree.

-wise /waɪz/ *combining form added to nouns to form adjectives and adverbs:* in the manner or direction of (e.g. *clockwise, lengthwise*); with reference to (e.g. *weatherwise*).

wiseacre /ˈwaɪzeɪkə/ *noun* person who affects to be wise.

wish ● *verb* (often + *for*) have or express desire or aspiration; want, demand; express one's hopes for; *colloquial* foist. ● *noun* desire, request, expression of this; thing desired. □ **wishbone** forked bone between neck and breast of fowl; **wish-fulfilment** tendency of unconscious wishes to be satisfied in fantasy; **wishing-well** well at which wishes are made.

wishful *adjective* (often + *to do*) desiring. □ **wishful thinking** belief founded on wishes rather than facts.

wishy-washy /ˈwɪʃɪwɒʃɪ/ *adjective colloquial* feeble or poor in quality or character; weak, watery.

wisp *noun* small bundle or twist of straw etc.; small separate quantity of smoke, hair, etc.; small thin person. □ **wispy** *adjective* (**-ier**, **-iest**).

wisteria /wɪˈstɪərɪə/ *noun* (also **wistaria** /-teər-/) climbing plant with purple, blue, or white hanging flowers.

wistful /ˈwɪstfʊl/ *adjective* yearning, mournfully expectant or wishful. □ **wistfully** *adverb*; **wistfulness** *noun*.

wit *noun* (in *singular* or *plural*) intelligence, understanding; (in *singular*) imaginative and inventive faculty; amusing ingenuity of speech or ideas; person noted for this. □ **at one's wit's** or **wits' end** utterly at a loss or in despair; **have** or **keep one's wits about one** be alert; **out of one's wits** mad; **to wit** that is to say, namely.

witch *noun* woman supposed to have dealings with Devil or evil spirits; old hag; fascinating girl or woman. □ **witchcraft** use of magic, bewitching charm; **witch-doctor** tribal magician of primitive people; **witch**, **wych hazel** N. American shrub, astringent lotion from its bark; **witch-hunt** campaign against people suspected of unpopular or unorthodox views.

witchery /ˈwɪtʃərɪ/ *noun* witchcraft.

with /wɪð/ *preposition expressing instrument or means used, company, parting of company, cause, possession, circumstances, manner, agreement, disagreement, antagonism, understanding, regard.* □ **with it** *colloquial* up to date, alert and comprehending; **with that** thereupon.

withdraw /wɪðˈdrɔː/ *verb* (*past* **-drew**; *past participle* **-drawn**) pull or take aside or back; discontinue, cancel, retract; remove, take away; take (money) out of an account; retire or go apart; (as **withdrawn** *adjective*) unsociable. □ **withdrawal** *noun*.

withe = WITHY.

wither /ˈwɪðə/ *verb* (often + *up*) make or become dry and shrivelled; (often + *away*) deprive of or lose vigour or freshness; (esp. as **withering** *adjective*) blight with scorn etc. □ **witheringly** *adverb*.

withers /ˈwɪðəz/ *plural noun* ridge between horse's shoulder-blades.

withhold /wɪðˈhəʊld/ *verb* (*past & past participle* **-held**) refuse to give, grant, or allow; hold back, restrain.

within /wɪˈðɪn/ ● *adverb* inside; indoors; in spirit. ● *preposition* inside; not beyond or out of; not transgressing or exceeding; not further off than.

without /wɪˈðaʊt/ ● *preposition* not having, feeling, or showing; free from; in absence of; with neglect or avoidance of; *archaic* outside. ● *adverb archaic or literary* outside, out of doors.

withstand /wɪðˈstænd/ *verb* (*past & past participle* **-stood**) oppose, hold out against.

withy /ˈwɪðɪ/ *noun* (*plural* **-ies**) tough flexible shoot, esp. of willow.

witless *adjective* foolish; crazy.

witness /ˈwɪtnɪs/ ● *noun* eyewitness; person giving sworn testimony; person attesting another's signature to document; (+ *to*, *of*) person or thing whose existence etc. attests or proves something. ● *verb* be eyewitness of; be witness to (signature etc.); serve as evidence or indication of; give or be evidence. □ **bear witness to** attest truth of, state one's belief in; **witness-box** (*US* **-stand**) enclosed space in law court from which witness gives evidence.

witter /ˈwɪtə/ *verb* (often + *on*) *colloquial* chatter annoyingly or on trivial matters.

witticism /ˈwɪtɪsɪz(ə)m/ *noun* witty remark.

wittingly /ˈwɪtɪŋlɪ/ *adverb* consciously, intentionally.

witty *adjective* (**-ier**, **-iest**) showing verbal wit. □ **wittily** *adverb*; **wittiness** *noun*.

wives *plural* of WIFE.

wizard /ˈwɪzəd/ ● *noun* sorcerer, magician; person of extraordinary powers. ● *adjective slang* wonderful. □ **wizardry** *noun*.

wizened /ˈwɪz(ə)nd/ *adjective* shrivelledlooking.

WNW *abbreviation* west-north-west.

WO *abbreviation* Warrant Officer.

woad *noun* plant yielding blue dye; this dye.

wobble /ˈwɒb(ə)l/ ● *verb* (**-ling**) sway from side to side; stand or go unsteadily, stagger; waver, vacillate. ● *noun* wobbling motion. □ **wobbly** *adjective* (**-ier**, **-iest**).

woe *noun* affliction, bitter grief; (in *plural*) calamities. □ **woebegone** dismallooking.

woeful *adjective* sorrowful; causing or feeling affliction; very bad. □ **woefully** *adverb*.

wok *noun* bowl-shaped frying-pan used in esp. Chinese cookery.

woke *past* of WAKE[1].

woken *past participle* of WAKE[1].

wold /wəʊld/ *noun* high open uncultivated land or moor.

wolf /wʊlf/ ● *noun* (*plural* **wolves** /wʊlvz/) wild animal related to dog; *slang* man who seduces women. ● *verb* (often + *down*) devour greedily. □ **cry wolf** raise false alarm; **keep the wolf from the door** avert starvation; **wolfhound** dog of kind used originally to hunt wolves; **wolfsbane** an aconite; **wolf-whistle** man's whistle to attractive woman. □ **wolfish** *adjective*.

wolfram /ˈwʊlfrəm/ *noun* tungsten; tungsten ore.

wolverine /ˈwʊlvəriːn/ *noun* N. American animal of weasel family.

wolves *plural* of WOLF.

woman /ˈwʊmən/ *noun* (*plural* **women** /ˈwɪmɪn/) adult human female; the female sex; *colloquial* wife, girlfriend.

womanhood *noun* female maturity; womanliness; womankind.

womanish *adjective derogatory* effeminate, unmanly.

womanize *verb* (also **-ise**) (**-zing** or **-sing**) (of man) be promiscuous. □ **womanizer** *noun*.

womankind *noun* (also **womenkind**) women in general.

womanly *adjective* having or showing qualities associated with women. □ **womanliness** *noun*.

womb /wuːm/ *noun* organ of conception and gestation in female mammals.

wombat /ˈwɒmbæt/ *noun* burrowing plant-eating Australian marsupial.

women /ˈwɪmɪn/ *plural* of WOMAN. □ **women's libber** *colloquial* supporter of women's liberation; **women's liberation**, **lib** *colloquial* movement for release of women from subservient status; **women's rights** human rights of women giving equality with men.

womenfolk *noun* women in general; women in family.

won *past & past participle* of WIN.

wonder /ˈwʌndə/ ● *noun* emotion, esp. admiration, excited by what is unexpected, unfamiliar, or inexplicable; strange or remarkable thing, specimen, event, etc. ● *adjective* having amazing properties etc. ● *verb* be filled with wonder; (+ *that*) be surprised to find that, be curious to know. □ **no** or **small wonder** it is not surprising; **wonderland** fairyland, place of surprises or marvels.

wonderful *adjective* very remarkable or admirable. □ **wonderfully** *adverb*.

wonderment *noun* surprise, awe.

wondrous /ˈwʌndrəs/ *poetical* ● *adjective* wonderful. ● *adverb* wonderfully.

wonky /ˈwɒŋkɪ/ *adjective* (**-ier**, **-iest**) *slang* crooked; unsteady; unreliable.

wont /wəʊnt/ ● *adjective archaic or literary* (+ *to do*) accustomed. ● *noun formal or jocular* custom, habit.

won't /wəʊnt/ will not.

wonted /ˈwəʊntɪd/ *adjective* habitual, usual.

woo *verb* (**woos**, **wooed**) court, seek love of; try to win; seek support of; coax, importune.

wood /wʊd/ *noun* hard fibrous substance of tree; this for timber or fuel; (in *singular* or *plural*) growing trees occupying piece of ground; wooden cask for wine etc.; wooden-headed golf club; ball in game of bowls. □ **out of the wood(s)** clear of danger or difficulty; **wood anemone** wild spring-flowering anemone; **woodbine** honeysuckle; **woodchuck** N. American marmot; **woodcock** game bird related to snipe; **woodcut** relief cut on wood, print made from this; **woodcutter** person who cuts timber; **woodland** wooded country; **woodlouse** small land crustacean with many legs; **woodman** forester; **woodpecker** bird that taps tree trunks to find insects; **wood-pigeon** dove with white patches round neck; **wood pulp** wood fibre prepared for papermaking; **woodwind** wind instrument(s) of orchestra made originally of wood; **woodwork** making of things in wood, things made of wood; **woodworm** beetle larva that bores in wood, resulting condition of wood.

wooded *adjective* having woods.

wooden /ˈwʊd(ə)n/ *adjective* made of wood; like wood; stiff, clumsy; expressionless. □ **woodenly** *adverb*; **woodenness** *noun*.

woody *adjective* (**-ier**, **-iest**) wooded; like or of wood.

woof[1] /wʊf/ ● *noun* gruff bark of dog. ● *verb* give woof.

woof[2] /wuːf/ *noun* weft.

woofer /ˈwuːfə/ *noun* loudspeaker for low frequencies.

wool /wʊl/ *noun* fine soft wavy hair forming fleece of sheep etc.; woollen yarn, cloth, or garments; wool-like substance. □ **wool-gathering** absent-mindedness; **the Woolsack** Lord Chancellor's seat in House of Lords.

woollen /ˈwʊlən/ (*US* **woolen**) ● *adjective* made (partly) of wool. ● *noun* woollen fabric; (in *plural*) woollen garments.

woolly ● *adjective* (**-ier**, **-iest**) bearing or like wool; woollen; indistinct; confused. ● *noun* (*plural* **-ies**) *colloquial* woollen (esp. knitted) garment.

woozy /ˈwuːzɪ/ *adjective* (**-ier**, **-iest**) *colloquial* dizzy; slightly drunk.

word /wɜːd/ ● *noun* meaningful element of speech, usually shown with space on either side of it when written or printed; speech as distinct from action; one's promise or assurance; (in *singular* or *plural*) thing said, remark, conversation; (in *plural*) text of song or actor's part; (in *plural*) angry talk; news, message; command. ● *verb* put into words, select words to express. □ **word-blindness** dyslexia; **word for word** in exactly the same words, literally; **the Word (of God)** the Bible; **word of mouth** speech (only); **word-perfect** having memorized one's part etc. perfectly; **word processor** computer software or hardware for storing text entered from keyboard, incorporating corrections, and producing printout; **word-process** *verb*; **word processing** *noun*.

wording *noun* form of words used.

wordy *adjective* (**-ier**, **-iest**) using or expressed in (too) many words.

wore *past* of WEAR.

work /wɜːk/ ● *noun* application of effort to a purpose, use of energy; task to be undertaken; thing done or made by work, result of action; employment, occupation, etc., esp. as means of earning money; literary or musical composition; actions or experiences of specified kind; (in *plural*) operative part of clock etc.; (**the works**) *colloquial* all that is available or needed, full treatment; (in *plural*) operations of building or repair; (in *plural*; often treated as *singular*) factory; (usually in *plural* or *in combination*) defensive structure. ● *verb* be engaged in activity; be employed in certain work; make efforts; be craftsman in (material); operate or function, esp. effectively; operate, manage, control; put or keep in operation or at work, cause to toil; cultivate (land); produce as result; *colloquial* arrange; knead, hammer, bring to desired shape or consistency; do, or make by, needlework etc.; (cause to) make way or make (way) slowly or with difficulty; gradually become (loose etc.) by motion; artificially excite; purchase with labour instead of money; obtain money for by labour; (+ *on*, *upon*) influence; be in motion or agitated, ferment. □ **get worked up** become angry, excited, or tense; **workaday** ordinary, everyday, practical; **workbasket** basket for sewing materials; **workbench** bench for manual work, esp. carpentry; **workbox** box for tools, needlework, etc.; **workday** day on which work is usually done; **work experience** temporary experience of employment for young people; **workforce** workers engaged or available, number of these; **workhouse** *historical* public institution for the poor; **work in** find place for; **workload** amount of work to be done; **workman** man employed to do manual labour, person who works in specified manner; **workmanlike** showing practised skill; **workmanship** degree of skill in doing task or of finish in product; **workmate** person working alongside another; **work off** get rid of by work or activity; **work out** *verb* solve (sum) or find (amount) by calculation, understand (problem, person, etc.), be calculated, have result, provide for all details of, engage in physical exercise; **workout** *noun* session of physical exercise; **work over** examine thoroughly, *colloquial* treat with violence; **workshop** room or building in which goods are manufactured, place or meeting for concerted activity; **work-shy** disinclined to work; **workstation** location of stage in manufacturing process, computer terminal; **worktop** flat (esp. kitchen) surface for working on; **work to rule** follow official working rules exactly to reduce efficiency as protest; **work-to-rule** *noun*; **work up** bring gradually to efficient or advanced state, advance gradually, elaborate or excite by degrees, mingle (ingredients), learn (subject) by study.

workable *adjective* that can be worked, will work, or is worth working. □ **workability** *noun*.

worker *noun* manual or industrial etc. employee; neuter bee or ant; person who works hard.

working ● *adjective* engaged in work; while so engaged; functioning, able to function. ● *noun* activity of work; functioning; mine, quarry; (usually in *plural*) mechanism. □ **working capital** capital used in conducting a business; **working class** social class employed for wages, esp. in manual or industrial work; **working-class** *adjective*; **working day** workday, part of day devoted to work; **working knowledge** knowledge adequate to work with; **working lunch** lunch at which business is conducted; **working order** condition in which machine works; **working party** committee appointed to study and advise on some question.

world /wɜːld/ ● *noun* the earth, planetary body like it; the universe, all that exists; time, state, or scene of human existence; (**the, this world**) mortal life; secular interests and affairs; human affairs, active life; average, respectable, or fashionable people or their customs or opinions; all that concerns or all who belong to specified class or sphere of activity; vast amount. ● *adjective* of or affecting all nations. □ **out of this world** *colloquial* extremely good etc.; **think the world of** have very high regard for; **world-class** of standard considered high throughout world; **world-famous** known throughout the world; **world music** pop music incorporating ethnic elements; **world war** one involving many important nations; **world-weary** bored with human affairs; **worldwide** *adjective* occurring or known in all parts of the world; *adverb* throughout the world.

worldly *adjective* (**-ier**, **-iest**) temporal, earthly; experienced in life, sophisticated, practical. □ **worldly-wise** prudent in one's dealings with world.

worm /wɜːm/ ● *noun* any of several types of creeping invertebrate animal with long slender body and no limbs; larva of insect; (in *plural*) internal parasites; insignificant or contemptible person; spiral of screw. ● *verb* crawl, wriggle; (**worm oneself**) insinuate oneself (into favour etc.); (+ *out*) obtain (secret etc.) by cunning persistence; rid (dog etc.) of worms. □ **worm-cast** convoluted mass of earth left on surface by burrowing earthworm; **wormeaten** eaten into by worms, decayed, dilapidated.

wormwood /ˈwɜːmwʊd/ *noun* plant with bitter aromatic taste; bitter humiliation, source of this.

wormy *adjective* (**-ier**, **-iest**) full of worms; wormeaten.

worn ● *past participle* of WEAR. ● *adjective* damaged by use or wear; looking tired and exhausted.

worry /ˈwʌrɪ/ ● *verb* (**-ies**, **-ied**) be anxious; harass, importune, be trouble or anxiety to; shake or pull about with teeth; (as **worried** *adjective*) uneasy. ● *noun* (*plural* **-ies**) thing that causes anxiety or disturbs tranquillity; disturbed state of mind, anxiety.

□ **worry beads** string of beads manipulated with fingers to occupy or calm oneself. □ **worrier** *noun*.

worse /wɜːs/ ● *adjective* more bad; in or into worse health or worse condition. ● *adverb* more badly; more ill. ● *noun* worse thing(s); (**the worse**) worse condition. □ **the worse for wear** damaged by use, injured; **worse off** in a worse (esp. financial) position. □ **worsen** *verb*.

worship /ˈwɜːʃɪp/ ● *noun* homage or service to deity; acts, rites, or ceremonies of this; adoration, devotion; (**His**, **Her**, **Your Worship**) *title used of or to mayor, magistrate, etc.* ● *verb* (**-pp-**; *US* **-p-**) adore as divine, honour with religious rites; idolize; attend public worship; be full of adoration. □ **worshipper** *noun*.

worshipful *adjective* (also **Worshipful**) *archaic* honourable, distinguished (esp. in old titles of companies or officers).

worst /wɜːst/ ● *adjective* most bad. ● *adverb* most badly. ● *noun* worst part or possibility. ● *verb* get the better of, defeat. □ **at** (**the**) **worst** in the worst possible case; **do your worst** *expression of defiance*; **get the worst of it** be defeated; **if the worst comes to the worst** if the worst happens.

worsted /ˈwʊstɪd/ *noun* fine woollen yarn; fabric made from this.

wort /wɜːt/ *noun* infusion of malt before it is fermented into beer.

worth /wɜːθ/ ● *adjective* of value equivalent to; such as to justify or repay; possessing property equivalent to. ● *noun* value; equivalent of money etc. in commodity etc. □ **worth it** (*colloquial*), **worth** (**one's**) **while**, **worthwhile** worth the time or effort spent.

worthless *adjective* without value or merit. □ **worthlessness** *noun*.

worthy /ˈwɜːðɪ/ ● *adjective* (**-ier**, **-iest**) deserving respect, estimable; entitled to recognition; (usually + *of*) deserving; (+ *of*) adequate or suitable for the dignity etc. of. ● *noun* (*plural* **-ies**) worthy person; person of some distinction.

would *auxiliary verb* (*3rd singular present* **would**) *used in reported speech or to form conditional mood; expressing habitual past action, request as question, or probability.* □ **would-be** desiring or aspiring to be.

wouldn't /ˈwʊd(ə)nt/ would not.

wound[1] /wuːnd/ ● *noun* injury done by cut or blow to living tissue; pain inflicted on feelings, injury to reputation. ● *verb* inflict wound on.

wound[2] *past & past participle* of WIND[2]. □ **wound up** excited, tense, angry.

wove *past* of WEAVE[1].

woven *past participle* of WEAVE[1].

wow /waʊ/ ● *interjection expressing astonishment or admiration.* ● *noun slang* sensational success. ● *verb slang* impress greatly.

WP *abbreviation* word processor.

WPC *abbreviation* woman police constable.

w.p.m. *abbreviation* words per minute.

WRAC *abbreviation historical* Women's Royal Army Corps.

wrack *noun* seaweed cast up or growing on seashore; destruction.

WRAF *abbreviation historical* Women's Royal Air Force.

wraith /reɪθ/ *noun* ghost; spectral appearance of living person supposed to portend that person's death.

wrangle /ˈræŋg(ə)l/ ● *noun* noisy argument or dispute. ● *verb* (**-ling**) engage in wrangle.

wrap ● *verb* (**-pp-**) (often + *up*) envelop in folded or soft encircling material; (+ *round, about*) arrange or draw (pliant covering) round (person). ● *noun* shawl, scarf, etc.; wrapper; *esp. US* wrapping material. □ **under wraps** in secrecy; **wraparound**, **wrapround** (esp. of clothing) designed to wrap round, curving round at edges; **wrap-over** *adjective* (of garment) overlapping when worn, *noun* such garment; **wrapped up in** engrossed or absorbed in; **wrap up** *colloquial* finish off (matter), put on warm clothes.

wrapper *noun* cover for sweet, book, posted newspaper, etc.; loose enveloping robe or gown.

wrapping *noun* (esp. in *plural*) material used to wrap, wraps, wrappers. □ **wrapping paper** strong or decorative paper for wrapping parcels.

wrasse /ræs/ *noun* (*plural* same or **-s**) brilliant-coloured edible sea fish.

wrath /rɒθ/ *noun literary* extreme anger. □ **wrathful** *adjective*.

wreak *verb* (usually + *upon*) give play to (vengeance etc.); cause (damage etc.).

wreath /riːθ/ *noun* (*plural* **-s** /riːðz/) flowers or leaves wound together into ring, esp. as ornament for head or door or for laying on grave etc.; curl or ring of smoke, cloud, or soft fabric.

wreathe /riːð/ *verb* (**-thing**) encircle (as) with or like wreath; (+ *round*) wind (one's arms etc.) round (person etc.); move in wreaths.

wreck ● *noun* sinking or running aground of ship; ship that has suffered wreck; greatly damaged building, thing, or person. ● *verb* seriously damage (vehicle etc.); ruin (hopes etc.); cause wreck of (ship).

wreckage *noun* wrecked material; remnants of wreck; act of wrecking.

wrecker *noun* person or thing that wrecks or destroys, esp. (*historical*) person who tries from shore to bring about shipwreck for plunder or profit.

Wren *noun* member of WRNS.

wren *noun* small usually brown short-winged songbird.

wrench ● *noun* violent twist or oblique pull or tearing off; tool for gripping and turning nuts etc.; painful uprooting or parting etc. ● *verb* twist or pull violently round or sideways; (often + *off, away*, etc.) pull with wrench.

wrest *verb* wrench away from person's grasp; (+ *from*) obtain by effort or with difficulty.

wrestle /ˈres(ə)l/ ● *noun* contest in which two opponents grapple and try to throw each other to ground; hard struggle. ● *verb* (**-ling**) have wrestling match; (often + *with*) struggle; (+ *with*) do one's utmost to deal with. □ **wrestler** *noun*.

wretch *noun* unfortunate or pitiable person; reprehensible person.

wretched /ˈretʃɪd/ *adjective* (**-er**, **-est**) unhappy, miserable, unwell; of bad quality, contemptible; displeasing. □ **wretchedly** *adverb*; **wretchedness** *noun*.

wriggle /ˈrɪg(ə)l/ ● *verb* (**-ling**) twist or turn body with short writhing movements; make wriggling motions; (+ *along, through*, etc.) go thus; be evasive. ● *noun* wriggling movement. □ **wriggly** *adjective*.

wring ● *verb* (*past & past participle* **wrung**) squeeze tightly; (often + *out*) squeeze and twist, esp. to remove liquid; break by twisting; distress, torture; extract by squeezing; (+ *out, from*) obtain by pressure or importunity. ● *noun* act of wringing. □ **wringing** (**wet**) so wet that water can be wrung out; **wring one's hands** clasp them as gesture of grief; **wring the neck of** kill (chicken etc.) by twisting neck.

wringer *noun* device for wringing water from washed clothes etc.

wrinkle /ˈrɪŋk(ə)l/ ● *noun* crease in skin or other flexible surface; *colloquial* useful hint, clever expedient. ● *verb* (**-ling**) make wrinkles in; form wrinkles. □ **wrinkly** *adjective* (**-ier**, **-iest**).

wrist *noun* joint connecting hand and forearm; part of garment covering wrist. □ **wrist-watch** small watch worn on strap etc. round wrist.

wristlet *noun* band or ring to guard, strengthen, or adorn wrist.

writ *noun* formal written court order to do or not do specified act.

write *verb* (**-ting**; *past* **wrote**; *past participle* **written** /'rɪt(ə)n/) mark paper or other surface with symbols, letters, or words; form or mark (such symbols etc.); form or mark symbols of (word, document, etc.); fill or complete with writing; put (data) into computer store; (esp. in *passive*) indicate (quality or condition) by appearance; compose for reproduction or publication; (usually + *to*) write and send letter; convey (news etc.) by letter; state in book etc.; (+ *into*, *out of*) include or exclude (character, episode) in or from story. □ **write down** record in writing; **write in** send suggestion etc. in writing, esp. to broadcasting station; **write off** *verb* cancel (debt etc.), acknowledge as lost, completely destroy, (+ *for*) order or request by post; **write-off** *noun* thing written off, esp. vehicle etc. so damaged as not to be worth repair; **write up** *verb* write full account of; **write-up** *noun* written or published account, review.

writer *noun* person who writes, esp. author. □ **writer's cramp** muscular spasm due to excessive writing.

writhe /raɪð/ *verb* (**-thing**) twist or roll oneself about (as) in acute pain; suffer mental torture.

writing *noun* written words etc.; handwriting; (usually in *plural*) writer's works. □ **in writing** in written form.

written *past participle* of WRITE.

WRNS *abbreviation historical* Women's Royal Naval Service.

wrong ● *adjective* mistaken, not true, in error; unsuitable, less or least desirable; contrary to law or morality; amiss, out of order. ● *adverb* in wrong manner or direction, with incorrect result. ● *noun* what is morally wrong; unjust action. ● *verb* treat unjustly; mistakenly attribute bad motives to. □ **go wrong** take wrong path, stop functioning properly, depart from virtuous behaviour; **in the wrong** responsible for quarrel, mistake, or offence; **wrongdoer** person who behaves immorally or illegally; **wrongdoing** *noun*; **wrong-foot** *colloquial* catch off balance or unprepared; **wrong-headed** perverse and obstinate; **wrong side** worse or undesirable or unusable side; **wrong way round** in opposite of normal orientation or sequence. □ **wrongly** *adverb*; **wrongness** *noun*.

wrongful *adjective* unwarranted, unjustified. □ **wrongfully** *adverb*.

wrote *past* of WRITE.

wroth /rəʊθ/ *adjective archaic* angry.

wrought /rɔːt/ *archaic past & past participle* of WORK. □ **wrought iron** form of iron suitable for forging or rolling, not cast.

wrung *past & past participle* of WRING.

WRVS *abbreviation* Women's Royal Voluntary Service.

wry /raɪ/ *adjective* (**-er**, **-est**) distorted, turned to one side; contorted in disgust, disappointment, or mockery; (of humour) dry and mocking. □ **wryneck** small woodpecker able to turn head over shoulder. □ **wryly** *adverb*; **wryness** *noun*.

WSW *abbreviation* west-south-west.

wt *abbreviation* weight.

wych hazel /wɪtʃ/ witch hazel.

WYSIWYG /'wɪzɪwɪg/ *adjective indicating that text on computer screen and printout correspond exactly* (*w*hat *y*ou *s*ee *i*s *w*hat *y*ou *g*et).

X[1] *noun* (also **x**) (Roman numeral) 10; first unknown quantity in algebra; unknown or unspecified number, person, etc.; cross-shaped symbol, esp. used to indicate position or incorrectness, to symbolize kiss or vote, or as signature of person who cannot write. □ **X-ray** *noun* electromagnetic radiation of short wavelength able to pass through opaque bodies, photograph made by X-rays, *verb* photograph, examine, or treat with X-rays.

X[2] *adjective* (of film) classified as suitable for adults only.

xenophobia /zenəˈfəʊbɪə/ *noun* hatred or fear of foreigners.

Xerox /ˈzɪərɒks/ ● *noun proprietary term* type of photocopier; copy made by it. ● *verb* (**xerox**) make Xerox of.

Xmas /ˈkrɪsməs, ˈeksməs/ *noun colloquial* Christmas.

xylophone /ˈzaɪləfəʊn/ *noun* musical instrument of graduated wooden or metal bars struck with small wooden hammers.

Yy

Y *noun* (also **y**) second unknown quantity in algebra; Y-shaped thing.

yacht /jɒt/ ● *noun* light sailing vessel for racing or cruising; larger usually power-driven vessel for cruising. ● *verb* race or cruise in yacht. ◻ **yachtsman, yachtswoman** person who yachts.

yah /jɑ:/ *interjection of derision, defiance, etc.*

yahoo /jɑ:ˈhu:/ *noun* bestial person.

Yahweh /ˈjɑ:weɪ/ *noun* Jehovah.

yak *noun* long-haired Tibetan ox.

yam *noun* tropical or subtropical climbing plant; edible starchy tuberous root of this; *US* sweet potato.

yang *noun* (in Chinese philosophy) active male principle of universe (compare YIN).

Yank *noun colloquial often derogatory* American.

yank *verb & noun colloquial* pull with jerk.

Yankee /ˈjæŋkɪ/ *noun colloquial* Yank; *US* inhabitant of New England or of northern States.

yap ● *verb* (**-pp-**) bark shrilly or fussily; *colloquial* talk noisily, foolishly, or complainingly. ● *noun* sound of yapping.

yard[1] *noun* unit of linear measure (3 ft, 0.9144 m.); this length of material; square or cubic yard; spar slung across mast for sail to hang from; (in *plural*; + *of*) *colloquial* a great length. ◻ **yard-arm** either end of ship's yard; **yardstick** standard of comparison, rod a yard long usually divided into inches etc.

yard[2] *noun* piece of enclosed ground, esp. attached to building or used for particular purpose; *US & Australian* garden of house.

yardage *noun* number of yards of material etc.

yarmulke /ˈjɑ:mәlkә/ *noun* (also **yarmulka**) skullcap worn by Jewish men.

yarn ● *noun* spun thread for weaving, knitting, etc.; *colloquial* story, traveller's tale, anecdote. ● *verb colloquial* tell yarns.

yarrow /ˈjærәʊ/ *noun* perennial plant, esp. milfoil.

yashmak /ˈjæʃmæk/ *noun* veil concealing face except eyes, worn by some Muslim women.

yaw ● *verb* (of ship, aircraft, etc.) fail to hold straight course, go unsteadily. ● *noun* yawing of ship etc. from course.

yawl *noun* kind of sailing boat; small fishing boat.

yawn ● *verb* open mouth wide and inhale, esp. when sleepy or bored; gape, be wide open. ● *noun* act of yawning.

yaws /jɔ:z/ *plural noun* (usually treated as *singular*) contagious tropical skin disease.

yd *abbreviation* (*plural* **yds**) yard (measure).

ye /ji:/ *pronoun archaic* (as subject of verb) you (plural).

yea /jeɪ/ *archaic* ● *adverb* yes. ● *noun* 'yes' vote.

yeah /jeә/ *adverb colloquial* yes.

year /jɪә/ *noun* time occupied by one revolution of earth round sun, approx. 365 1/4 days; period from 1 Jan. to 31 Dec. inclusive; period of 12 calendar months; (in *plural*) age, time of life; (usually in *plural*) *colloquial* very long time. ◻ **yearbook** annual publication bringing information on some subject up to date.

yearling *noun* animal between one and two years old.

yearly ● *adjective* done, produced, or occurring once every year; of or lasting a year. ● *adverb* once every year.

yearn /jɜ:n/ *verb* be filled with longing, compassion, or tenderness. ◻ **yearning** *noun & adjective*.

yeast *noun* greyish-yellow fungus, got esp. from fermenting malt liquors and used as fermenting agent, to raise bread, etc.

yeasty *adjective* (**-ier, -iest**) frothy; in ferment; working like yeast.

yell ● *noun* sharp loud cry; shout. ● *verb* cry, shout.

yellow /ˈjelәʊ/ ● *adjective* of the colour of lemons, buttercups, etc.; having yellow skin or complexion; *colloquial* cowardly. ● *noun* yellow colour, paint, clothes, etc. ● *verb* turn yellow. ◻ **yellow-belly** *colloquial* coward; **yellow card** card shown by referee to football-player being cautioned; **yellow fever** tropical virus fever with jaundice etc.; **yellow-hammer** bunting of which male has yellow head, neck, and breast; **Yellow Pages** *proprietary term* telephone directory on yellow paper, listing and classifying business subscribers; **yellow streak** *colloquial* trace of cowardice. ◻ **yellowish** *adjective*; **yellowness** *noun*; **yellowy** *adjective*.

yelp ● *noun* sharp shrill bark or cry as of dog in excitement or pain. ● *verb* utter yelp.

yen[1] *noun* (*plural* same) chief monetary unit of Japan.

yen[2] *colloquial* ● *noun* intense desire or longing. ● *verb* (**-nn-**) feel longing.

yeoman /ˈjәʊmәn/ *noun esp. historical* man holding and farming small estate; member of yeomanry force. ◻ **Yeoman of the Guard** member of bodyguard of English sovereign.

yeomanry *noun* (*plural* **-ies**) group of yeomen; *historical* volunteer cavalry force in British army.

yes ● *adverb indicating affirmative reply to question, statement, request, command, etc.*; (**yes?**) indeed?, is that so?, what do you want? ● *noun* utterance of word yes. ◻ **yes-man** *colloquial* weakly acquiescent person.

yesterday /ˈjestәdeɪ/ ● *adverb* on the day before today. ● *noun* the day before today.

yesteryear /ˈjestәjɪә/ *noun archaic or rhetorical* last year; the recent past.

yet ● *adverb* up to now or then; (with negative or in questions) so soon as, or by, now or then; again, in addition; in the remaining time available; (+ *comparative*) even; nevertheless. ● *conjunction* but nevertheless.

yeti /ˈjetɪ/ *noun* supposed manlike or bearlike Himalayan animal.

yew *noun* dark-leaved evergreen coniferous tree; its wood.

YHA *abbreviation* Youth Hostels Association.

Yiddish /ˈjɪdɪʃ/ ● *noun* language used by Jews in or from Europe. ● *adjective* of this language.

yield /ji:ld/ ● *verb* produce or return as fruit, profit, or result; concede, give up; (often + *to*) surrender, submit, defer; (as **yielding** *adjective*) soft and pliable, submissive; (+ *to*) give right of way to. ● *noun* amount yielded or produced.

yin *noun* (in Chinese philosophy) passive female principle of universe (compare YANG).

yippee /jɪˈpi:/ *interjection expressing delight or excitement.*

YMCA *abbreviation* Young Men's Christian Association.

yob /jɒb/ *noun* (also **yobbo**, *plural* **-s**) *slang* lout, hooligan. ◻ **yobbish** *adjective*.

yodel /ˈjəʊd(ə)l/ ● *verb* (**-ll-**; *US* **-l-**) sing with melodious inarticulate sounds and frequent changes between falsetto and normal voice, in manner of Swiss mountain-dwellers. ● *noun* yodelling cry.

yoga /ˈjəʊgə/ *noun* Hindu system of meditation and asceticism; system of physical exercises and breathing control used in yoga.

yoghurt /ˈjɒgət/ *noun* (also **yogurt**) rather sour semi-solid food made from milk fermented by added bacteria.

yogi /ˈjəʊgɪ/ *noun* (*plural* **-s**) devotee of yoga.

yoke ● *noun* wooden crosspiece fastened over necks of two oxen etc. and attached to plough or wagon to be pulled; (*plural* same or **-s**) pair (of oxen etc.); object like yoke in form or function, e.g. wooden shoulder-piece for carrying pair of pails, top part of garment from which rest hangs; sway, dominion, servitude; bond of union, esp. of marriage. ● *verb* (**-king**) put yoke on; couple or unite (pair); link (one thing) to (another); match or work together.

yokel /ˈjəʊk(ə)l/ *noun* country bumpkin.

yolk /jəʊk/ *noun* yellow inner part of egg.

Yom Kippur /jɒm ˈkɪpə/ *noun* most solemn religious fast day of Jewish year, Day of Atonement.

yon *adjective & adverb literary & dialect* yonder.

yonder /ˈjɒndə/ ● *adverb* over there, at some distance in that direction, in place indicated. ● *adjective* situated yonder.

yore *noun* ▫ **of yore** a long time ago.

york *verb Cricket* bowl out with yorker.

yorker *noun Cricket* ball that pitches immediately under bat.

Yorkist /ˈjɔːkɪst/ ● *noun historical* follower of House of York, esp. in Wars of the Roses. ● *adjective* of House of York.

Yorkshire pudding /ˈjɔːkʃə/ *noun* baked batter usually eaten with roast beef.

Yorkshire terrier /jɔːkʃə/ *noun* small long-haired blue and tan kind of terrier.

you /juː/ *pronoun* the person(s) or thing(s) addressed; one, a person.

you'd /juːd/ you had; you would.

you'll /juːl/ you will; you shall.

young /jʌŋ/ ● *adjective* (**younger** /ˈjʌŋgə/, **youngest** /ˈjʌŋgɪst/) not far advanced in life, development, or existence, not yet old; immature, inexperienced, youthful; of or characteristic of youth. ● *noun* offspring, esp. of animals. ▫ **youngish** *adjective*.

youngster *noun* child, young person.

your /jɔː/ *adjective* of or belonging to you.

you're /jɔː/ you are.

yours /jɔːz/ *pronoun* the one(s) belonging to you.

yourself /jɔːˈself/ *pronoun* (*plural* **yourselves**): *emphatic & reflexive form of* YOU.

youth /juːθ/ *noun* (*plural* **-s** /juːðz/) being young; early part of life, esp. adolescence; quality or condition characteristic of the young; young man; (treated as *plural*) young people collectively. ▫ **youth club** place for young people's leisure activities; **youth hostel** any of chain of cheap lodgings where (esp. young) holiday-makers can stay for the night.

youthful *adjective* young or still having characteristics of youth. ▫ **youthfulness** *noun*.

you've /juːv/ you have.

yowl /jaʊl/ ● *noun* loud wailing cry (as) of cat or dog in distress. ● *verb* utter yowl.

yo-yo /ˈjəʊjəʊ/ *noun* (*plural* **yo-yos**) toy consisting of pair of discs with deep groove between them in which string is attached and wound, and which can be made to fall and rise.

yr. *abbreviation* year(s); younger; your.

yrs. *abbreviation* years; yours.

YTS *abbreviation* Youth Training Scheme.

yuan /juːˈɑːn/ *noun* (*plural* same) chief monetary unit of China.

yucca /ˈjʌkə/ *noun* white-flowered plant with sword-like leaves, often grown as house plant.

yuck /jʌk/ *interjection* (also **yuk**) *slang expression of strong distaste*.

yucky *adjective* (also **yukky**) (**-ier**, **-iest**) *slang* messy, repellent; sickly, sentimental.

Yugoslav /ˈjuːgəslɑːv/ *historical* ● *adjective* of Yugoslavia. ● *noun* native or national of Yugoslavia. ▫ **Yugoslavian** /-ˈslɑːv-/ *adjective & noun*.

yuk = YUCK.

yukky = YUCKY.

yule *noun* (in full **yule-tide**) *archaic* festival of Christmas. ▫ **yule-log** large log burnt at Christmas.

yummy /ˈjʌmɪ/ *adjective* (**-ier**, **-iest**) *colloquial* tasty, delicious.

yuppie /ˈjʌpɪ/ *noun* (also **yuppy**) (*plural* **-ies**) *colloquial usually derogatory* young ambitious professional person working in city.

YWCA *abbreviation* Young Women's Christian Association.

Zz

zabaglione /zæbəˈljəʊnɪ/ *noun* Italian dessert of whipped and heated egg yolks, sugar, and wine.

zany /ˈzeɪnɪ/ *adjective* (**-ier**, **-iest**) comically idiotic; crazily ridiculous.

zap *verb* (**-pp-**) *slang* kill, destroy; attack; hit hard.

zeal *noun* fervour, eagerness; hearty persistent endeavour. □ **zealous** /ˈzeləs/ *adjective*.

zealot /ˈzelət/ *noun* extreme partisan, fanatic.

zebra /ˈzebrə, ˈziː-/ *noun* (*plural* same or **-s**) African black and white striped horselike animal. □ **zebra crossing** striped street-crossing where pedestrians have precedence.

Zeitgeist /ˈtsaɪtgaɪst/ *noun* spirit of times. [German]

Zen *noun* form of Buddhism emphasizing meditation and intuition.

zenith /ˈzenɪθ/ *noun* point of heavens directly overhead; highest point (of power, prosperity, etc.).

zephyr /ˈzefə/ *noun literary* mild gentle breeze.

zero /ˈzɪərəʊ/ ● *noun* (*plural* **-s**) figure 0, nought, nil; point on scale of thermometer etc. from which positive or negative quantity is reckoned; (in full **zero-hour**) hour at which planned, esp. military, operation is timed to begin, crucial moment; lowest or earliest point. ● *adjective* no, not any. ● *verb* (**zeroes**, **zeroed**) adjust (instrument etc.) to zero. □ **zero in on** take aim at, focus attention on; **zero-rated** on which no VAT is charged.

zest *noun* piquancy; keen interest or enjoyment, relish, gusto; outer layer of orange or lemon peel.

zigzag /ˈzɪgzæg/ ● *adjective* with abrupt alternate right and left turns. ● *noun* zigzag line, thing having sharp turns. ● *adverb* with zigzag manner or course. ● *verb* (**-gg-**) move in zigzag course.

zilch *noun esp. US slang* nothing.

zillion /ˈzɪlɪən/ *noun* (*plural* same) *colloquial* indefinite large number; (**zillions**) very large number.

Zimmer frame /ˈzɪmə/ *noun proprietary term* kind of walking frame.

zinc *noun* greyish-white metallic element.

zing *colloquial* ● *noun* vigour, energy. ● *verb* move swiftly, esp. with shrill sound.

zinnia /ˈzɪnɪə/ *noun* garden plant with showy flowers.

zip ● *noun* light sharp sound; energy, vigour; (in full **zip-fastener**) fastening device of two flexible strips with interlocking projections, closed or opened by sliding clip along them. ● *verb* (**-pp-**) (often + *up*) fasten with zip-fastener; move with zip or at high speed.

zipper *noun esp. US* zip-fastener.

zircon /ˈzɜːkən/ *noun* translucent varieties of zirconium silicate cut into gems.

zirconium /zəˈkəʊnɪəm/ *noun* grey metallic element.

zit *noun esp. US slang* pimple.

zither /ˈzɪðə/ *noun* stringed instrument with flat soundbox, placed horizontally and played by plucking.

zloty /ˈzlɒtɪ/ *noun* (*plural* same or **-s**) chief monetary unit of Poland.

zodiac /ˈzəʊdɪæk/ *noun* belt of heavens including all apparent positions of sun, moon, and planets as known to ancient astronomers, and divided into 12 equal parts (**signs of the zodiac**).

zombie /ˈzɒmbɪ/ *noun* corpse said to have been revived by witchcraft; *colloquial* dull or apathetic person.

zone ● *noun* area having particular features, properties, purpose, or use; well-defined region of more or less beltlike form; area between two concentric circles; encircling band of colour etc.; *archaic* girdle, belt. ● *verb* (**-ning**) encircle as or with zone; arrange or distribute by zones; assign as or to specific area. □ **zonal** *adjective*.

zonked /zɒŋkt/ *adjective slang* (often + *out*) exhausted; intoxicated.

zoo *noun* zoological garden.

zoological /zəʊəˈlɒdʒɪk(ə)l, zuːə-/ *adjective* of zoology. □ **zoological garden**(**s**) public garden or park with collection of animals for exhibition and study.

■ **Usage** See note at ZOOLOGY.

zoology /zəʊˈɒlədʒɪ, zuːˈɒl-/ *noun* scientific study of animals. □ **zoologist** *noun*.

■ **Usage** The second pronunciation given for *zoology*, *zoological*, and *zoologist* (with the first syllable pronounced as in *zoo*), although extremely common, is considered incorrect by some people.

zoom ● *verb* move quickly, esp. with buzzing sound; cause aeroplane to mount at high speed and steep angle; (often + *in*, *in on*) (of camera) change rapidly from long shot to close-up (of). ● *noun* aeroplane's steep climb. □ **zoom lens** lens allowing camera to zoom by varying focal length.

zoophyte /ˈzəʊəfaɪt/ *noun* plantlike animal, esp. coral, sea anemone, or sponge.

zucchini /zuːˈkiːnɪ/ *noun* (*plural* same or **-s**) *esp. US & Australian* courgette.

zygote /ˈzaɪgəʊt/ *noun Biology* cell formed by union of two gametes.